THE NEW GROVE®
DICTIONARY OF MUSICAL INSTRUMENTS

Volume Two

The New
GROVE®
Dictionary of
Musical
Instruments

EDITED BY

Stanley Sadie

2

G *to* O

MACMILLAN PRESS LIMITED, LONDON
GROVE'S DICTIONARIES OF MUSIC INC., NEW YORK, NY

Parts of this dictionary were first published in

The New Grove Dictionary of Music and Musicians®
edited by STANLEY SADIE, in twenty volumes, 1980

The New Grove and *The New Grove Dictionary of Music and Musicians*
are registered trademarks of Macmillan Publishers Limited, London

The New Grove® *Dictionary of Musical Instruments,*
edited by STANLEY SADIE, in three volumes, 1984

Reprinted with minor corrections, 1985, 1987, 1989, 1991, 1993

First published 1984 by the Macmillan Press Limited, London. In the United States of America and
Canada, the Macmillan Press has appointed Grove's Dictionaries of Music Inc., New York, NY, as sole
distributor.

Typeset by Edwards Brothers Inc., Ann Arbor, MI, USA

Music examples processed by Halstan & Co. Ltd, Amersham, England

Printed and bound in Hong Kong by China Translation and Printing Services Ltd

**British Library Cataloguing
in Publication Data**
The New Grove® dictionary of musical
instruments.
  1. Musical instruments – Dictionaries
  I. Sadie, Stanley
  781.91'03'21   ML102.15

ISBN 0-333-37878-4

**Library of Congress Cataloging
in Publication Data**
Main entry under title:

The New Grove® dictionary of musical
instruments.
  Includes bibliographies.
  1. Musical instruments – Dictionaries.
  I. Sadie, Stanley
  ML102.15N48 1984 781.91'03'21   84-9062

ISBN 0-943818-05-2

Contents

General Abbreviations

A	alto, contralto [voice]		*c*	circa [about]
a	alto [instrument]		Calif.	California (USA)
AB	see BA		CBC	Canadian Broadcasting Corporation
ABC	American Broadcasting Company; Australian Broadcasting Commission		CBE	Commander of the Order of the British Empire
Abt.	Abteilung [section]		CBS	Columbia Broadcasting System (USA)
AD	anno Domini		CBSO	City of Birmingham Symphony Orchestra
add, addl	additional		CeBeDeM	Centre Belge de Documentation Musicale
add, addn	addition		cel	celesta
ad lib	ad libitum		CEMA	Council for the Encouragement of Music and the Arts [now the Arts Council of Great Britain]
AM	see MA			
a.m.	ante meridiem [before noon]			
AMS	American Musicological Society		cf	confer [compare]
Anh.	Anhang [appendix]		c.f.	cantus firmus
anon.	anonymous(ly)		CH	Companion of Honour
appx	appendix		chap.	chapter
arr.	arrangement, arranged by/for		Chin.	Chinese
ASCAP	American Society of Composers, Authors and Publishers		chit	chitarrone
			Cie	Compagnie
attrib.	attribution, attributed to		cimb	cimbalom
Aug	August		cl	clarinet
aut.	autumn		clvd	clavichord
			cm	centimetre(s)
			CNRS	Centre National de la Recherche Scientifique (F)
B	bass [voice]		Co.	Company; County
B	Brainard catalogue [Tartini]		Cod.	Codex
b	bass [instrument]		col.	column
b	born		coll.	collected by
BA	Bachelor of Arts		collab.	in collaboration with
Bar	baritone [voice]		cond.	conductor, conducted by
bar	baritone [instrument]		Conn.	Connecticut (USA)
BBC	British Broadcasting Corporation		cont	continuo
BC	British Columbia (Canada)		Corp.	Corporation
BC	before Christ		c.p.s.	cycles per second
bc	basso continuo		CSc	Candidate of Historical Sciences
Bd.	Band [volume]		Cz.	Czech
Ben	Benton catalogue [Pleyel]			
Berks.	Berkshire (GB)			
Berwicks.	Berwickshire (GB)			
bk	book		D	Deutsch catalogue [Schubert]; Dounias catalogue [Tartini]
BLitt	Bachelor of Letters/Literature			
BM	British Museum		d.	denarius, denarii [penny, pence]
BMI	Broadcast Music Inc. (USA)		*d*	died
BMus	Bachelor of Music		Dan.	Danish
bn	bassoon		db	double bass
Bros.	Brothers		DBE	Dame Commander of the Order of the British Empire
Bucks.	Buckinghamshire (GB)			
Bulg.	Bulgarian		dbn	double bassoon
BVM	Blessed Virgin Mary		DC	District of Columbia (USA)
BWV	Bach-Werke-Verzeichnis [Schmieder, catalogue of J. S. Bach's works]		Dec	December
			Dept	Department

vii

Derbys.	Derbyshire (GB)		Hon.	Honorary; Honourable
diss.	dissertation		hpd	harpsichord
DLitt	Doctor of Letters/Literature		HRH	His/Her Royal Highness
DMus	Doctor of Music		Hung.	Hungarian
DPhil	Doctor of Philosophy		Hunts.	Huntingdonshire (GB)
DSc	Doctor of Science/Historical Sciences		Hz	Hertz [c.p.s.]

ed.	editor, edited (by)		IAML	International Association of Music Librar-ies
edn.	edition		ibid	ibidem [in the same place]
e.g.	exempli gratia [for example]		i.e.	id est [that is]
elec	electric, electronic		IFMC	International Folk Music Council
EMI	Electrical and Musical Industries		Ill.	Illinois (USA)
Eng.	English		IMS	International Musicological Society
eng hn	english horn		Inc.	Incorporated
ens	ensemble		inc.	incomplete
esp.	especially		incl.	includes, including
etc	et cetera [and so on]		Ind.	Indiana (USA)
ex., exx.	example, examples		inst	instrument, instrumental
			IPEM	Institute for Psycho-acoustics and Electronic Music, Brussels
f, ff	following page, following pages		IRCAM	Institut de Recherche et de Coordination Acoustique/Musique, Paris
f., ff.	folio, folios		ISCM	International Society for Contemporary Music
_f_	forte			
facs.	facsimile		ISM	Incorporated Society of Musicians (GB)
fasc.	fascicle		ISME	International Society of Music Educators
Feb	February		It.	Italian
_ff_	fortissimo			
fff	fortississimo			
fig.	figure [illustration]			
fl	flute		Jan	January
_fl_	floruit [he/she flourished]		Jap.	Japanese
_fp_	fortepiano		_Jb_	Jahrbuch [yearbook]
Fr.	French		Jg.	Jahrgang [year of publication/volume]
frag.	fragment		jr	junior
FRAM	Fellow of the Royal Academy of Music, London			
FRCM	Fellow of the Royal College of Music, London		K	Kirkpatrick catalogue [D. Scarlatti]; Köchel catalogue [Mozart; no. after / is from 6th edn.]
FRCO	Fellow of the Royal College of Organists, London		kbd	keyboard
FRS	Fellow of the Royal Society, London		KBE	Knight Commander of the Order of the British Empire
			KCVO	Knight Commander of the Royal Victorian Order
Gael.	Gaelic		kHz	kilohertz
Ger.	German		km	kilometre(s)
Gk.	Greek		Ky.	Kentucky (USA)
Glam.	Glamorgan (GB)			
glock	glockenspiel			
Glos., Gloucs.	Gloucestershire (GB)		£	libra, librae [pound, pounds sterling]
GmbH	Gesellschaft mit beschränkter Haftung [limited-liability company]		L	Londo catalogue [D. Scarlatti]
			Lancs.	Lancashire (GB)
govt.	government [district in USSR]		Lat.	Latin
GSM	Guildhall School of Music and Drama, London		Leics.	Leicestershire (GB)
			Lincs.	Lincolnshire (GB)
gui	guitar		LittD	Doctor of Letters/Literature
			LlB	Bachelor of Laws
			LlD	Doctor of Laws
H	Hoboken catalogue [Haydn]; Helm catalogue [C. P. E. Bach]		LP	long-playing record
			LPO	London Philharmonic Orchestra
Hants.	Hampshire (GB)		LSO	London Symphony Orchestra
Heb.	Hebrew		Ltd	Limited
Herts.	Hertfordshire (GB)			
HMS	His/Her Majesty's Ship			
HMV	His Master's Voice		M.	Monsieur
hn	horn		MA	Master of Arts

mand	mandolin	perc	percussion
mar	marimba	pf	piano
Mass.	Massachusetts (USA)	PhD	Doctor of Philosophy
MBE	Member of the Order of the British Empire	pic	piccolo
Mez	mezzo-soprano	pl(l).	plate(s); plural
mf	mezzo-forte	p.m.	post meridiem [after noon]
MHz	Megahertz	PO	Philharmonic Orchestra
mic	microphone	Pol.	Polish
Mich.	Michigan (USA)	Port.	Portuguese
Minn.	Minnesota (USA)	posth.	posthumous(ly)
Mlle	Mademoiselle	POW	prisoner of war
mm	millimetre(s)	*pp*	pianissimo
Mme	Madame	*ppp*	pianississimo
MMus	Master of Music	pr.	printed
mod	modulator	PRO	Public Record Office, London
Mon.	Monmouthshire (GB)	PRS	Performing Right Society (GB)
movt	movement	Ps	Psalm
MP	Member of Parliament (GB)	ps	psalm
mp	mezzo-piano	pseud.	pseudonym
MS(S)	manuscript(s)	pt.	part
MSc	Master of Science(s)	ptbk	partbook
Mt	Mount	pubd	published
MusB, MusBac	Bachelor of Music	pubn	publication
MusD, MusDoc	Doctor of Music	qnt	quintet
MusM	Master of Music	qt	quartet
NBC	National Broadcasting Company (USA)	R	[in signature] editorial revision
n.d.	no date of publication	ʀ	Ryom catalogue [Vivaldi]
NJ	New Jersey (USA)	*R*	photographic reprint
no.	number	*r*	recto
Nor.	Norwegian	RAF	Royal Air Force
Northants.	Northamptonshire (GB)	RAI	Radio Audizioni Italiane
Notts.	Nottinghamshire (GB)	RAM	Royal Academy of Music, London
Nov	November	RCA	Radio Corporation of America
n.p.	no place of publication	RCM	Royal College of Music, London
nr.	near	rec	recorder
NSW	New South Wales (Australia)	red.	reduction, reduced for
NY	New York State (USA)	repr.	reprinted
		Rev.	Reverend
		rev.	revision, revised (by/for)
ob	oboe	RIdIM	Répertoire International d'Iconographie Musicale
obbl	obbligato		
OBE	Officer of the Order of the British Empire	RILM	Répertoire International de Littérature Musicale
Oct	October		
OM	Order of Merit	RISM	Répertoire International des Sources Musicales
Ont.	Ontario (Canada)		
op., opp.	opus, opera	RMCM	Royal Manchester College of Music
op cit	opere citato [in the work cited]	RMS	Root mean square
opt.	optional	RNCM	Royal Northern College of Music, Manchester
orch	orchestra, orchestral		
orchd	orchestrated (by)	RO	Radio Orchestra
org	organ	Rom.	Romanian
orig.	original(ly)	RPO	Royal Philharmonic Orchestra (GB)
ORTF	Office de Radiodiffusion-Télévision Française	RSFSR	Russian Soviet Federated Socialist Republic
OUP	Oxford University Press	RSO	Radio Symphony Orchestra
ov.	overture	Rt Hon.	Right Honourable
		RTE	Radio Telefis Eireann (Ireland)
		Russ.	Russian
P	Pincherle catalogue [Vivaldi]	ʀᴠ	Ryom catalogue [Vivaldi]
p., pp.	page, pages		
p	piano		
p.a.	per annum	S	San, Santa, Santo, São [Saint]; soprano [voice]
Penn.	Pennsylvania (USA)		

S.	south, southern	UK	United Kingdom of Great Britain and Northern Ireland
$	dollars	unattrib.	unattributed
s	soprano [instrument]	UNESCO	United Nations Educational, Scientific and Cultural Organization
s.	solidus, solidi [shilling, shillings]		
SACEM	Société d'Auteurs, Compositeurs et Editeurs de Musique (F)	unpubd	unpublished
		US	United States [adjective]
Sask.	Saskatchewan (Canada)	USA	United States of America
sax	saxophone	USSR	Union of Soviet Socialist Republics
Sept	September		
ser.	series		
sf, *sfz*	sforzando, sforzato	v, vv	voice, voices
sig.	signature	*v*	verso
sing.	singular	va	viola
SJ	Societas Jesu (Society of Jesus)	vc	cello
SO	Symphony Orchestra	VEB	Volkseigener Betrieb [people's own industry]
SPNM	Society for the Promotion of New Music (GB)		
		VHF	very high frequency
spr.	spring	vib	vibraphone
SS	Saints	viz	videlicet [namely]
Ss	Santissima, Santissimo	vle	violone
SSR	Soviet Socialist Republic	vn	violin
St	Saint, Sint, Szent	vol.	volume
Staffs.	Staffordshire (GB)		
Ste	Sainte		
str	string(s)		
sum.	summer	W.	West, Western
suppl.	supplement, supplementary	Warwicks.	Warwickshire (GB)
Swed.	Swedish	Wilts.	Wiltshire (GB)
synth	synthesizer	wint.	winter
		Wisc.	Wisconsin (USA)
		WoO, woo	Werke ohne Opuszahl [works without opus number]
T	tenor [voice]		
T	Terry catalogue [J. C. Bach]	Worcs.	Worcestershire (GB)
t	tenor [instrument]	WQ	Wotquenne catalogue [C. P. E. Bach]
Tenn.	Tennessee (USA)	ww	woodwind
timp	timpani		
tpt	trumpet		
Tr	treble [voice]		
tr	tract; treble [instrument]	xyl	xylophone
trans.	translation, translated by		
transcr.	transcription, transcribed by/for		
trbn	trombone		
		Yorks.	Yorkshire (GB)
U.	University		
UHF	ultra-high frequency	z	Zimmerman catalogue [Purcell]

Bibliographical Abbreviations

AcM   *Acta musicologica*   P [Intl 5]
ADB   *Allgemeine deutsche Biographie* (Leipzig, 1875–1912)
AMe (AMeS)   *Algemene muziekencyclopedie* (and suppl.)   D
Ames–King-GHM   D. W. Ames and A. V. King: *Glossary of Hausa Music and its Social Contexts* (Evanston, 1971)
AMf   *Archiv für Musikforschung*   P [D776]
AMI   *L'arte musicale in Italia*   E
AMP   *Antiquitates musicae in Polonia*   E
AMw   *Archiv für Musikwissenschaft*   P [D552]
AMZ   *Allgemeine musikalische Zeitung*   P [D32, 154, 170]
AMz   *Allgemeine Musik-Zeitung*   P [D203]
AnM   *Anuario musical*   P [E91]
AnMc   *Analecta musicologica* (some vols. in series Studien zur italienisch-deutschen Musikgeschichte), Veröffentlichungen der Musikabteilung des Deutschen historischen Instituts in Rom (Cologne, 1963–)
AnnM   *Annales musicologiques*   P [F638]
AntMI   *Antiquae musicae italicae*   E

Baker 5, 6   *Baker's Biographical Dictionary of Musicians* (5/1958 and 1971 suppl., 6/1978)   D
BAMS   *Bulletin of the American Musicological Society*   P [US540]
BeJb   *Beethoven-Jahrbuch* [1953–]   P [D925]
BJb   *Bach-Jahrbuch*   P [D434]
BMB   *Biblioteca musica bononiensis*   E
BMw   *Beiträge zur Musikwissenschaft*   P [D1013]
BNB   *Biographie nationale [belge]* (Brussels, 1866–)
BooneT   O. Boone: *Les tambours du Congo belge et du Ruanda-Urundi* (Tervuren, 1951)
BooneX   O. Boone: *Les xylophones du Congo belge* (Tervuren, 1936)
BordasD   *Dictionnaire de la musique* (Paris: Bordas, 1970–76)   D
Bouwsteenen: JVNM   *Bouwsteenen: jaarboek der Vereeniging voor Nederlandsche muziekgeschiedenis*   P [NL20]
BrownI   H. M. Brown: *Instrumental Music Printed before 1600: a Bibliography* (Cambridge, Mass., 2/1967)
BSIM   *Bulletin français de la S[ociété] I[nternationale de] M[usique]* [previously *Le Mercure musical*; also other titles]   P [F364]
BUCEM   *British Union-catalogue of Early Music*, ed. E. Schnapper (London, 1957)
BurneyH   C. Burney: *A General History of Music from the Earliest Ages to the Present* (London, 1776–89) [p. nos. refer to edn. of 1935/R1957]
BWQ   *Brass and Woodwind Quarterly*   P [US756]

CaM   *Catalogus musicus*   E
CEKM   *Corpus of Early Keyboard Music*   E
CEMF   *Corpus of Early Music in Facsimile*   E
CHM   *Collectanea historiae musicae* (in series Biblioteca historiae musicae cultores) (Florence, 1953–)
CMc   *Current Musicology*   P [US747]
CMI   *I classici musicali italiani*   E
CMM   *Corpus mensurabilis musicae*   E
CMz   *Cercetări de muzicologie*   P [R29]
CS   E. de Coussemaker: *Scriptorum de musica medii aevi nova series* (Paris, 1864–76/R1963)
ČSHS   *Československý hudebni slovnik*   D

DAB   *Dictionary of American Biography* (New York, 1928–)
DAM   *Dansk aarbog for musikforskning*   P [DK88]
DBF   *Dictionnaire de biographie française* (Paris, 1933–)
DBI   *Dizionario biografico degli italiani* (Rome, 1960–)
DBL   *Dansk biografisk leksikon* (Copenhagen, 1887–1905, 2/1933–)
DBP   *Dicionário biográfico de musicos portuguezes*   D
DČHP   *Dějiny české hudby v příkladech*   E
DDT   *Denkmäler deutscher Tonkunst*   E
DHM   *Documenta historicae musicae*   E
DJbM   *Deutsches Jahrbuch der Musikwissenschaft*   P [D980]
DM   *Documenta musicologica*   E
DNB   *Dictionary of National Biography* (London, 1885–1901, suppls.)
DTB   *Denkmäler der Tonkunst in Bayern*   E
DTÖ   *Denkmäler der Tonkunst in Österreich*   E

EDM   *Das Erbe deutscher Musik*   E
EECM   *Early English Church Music*   E
EI   *The Encyclopedia of Islam* (Leiden, 1928–38, rev. 2/1960)
EIT   *Ezhegodnik imperatorskikh teatrov*   P [USSR17]
EitnerQ   R. Eitner: *Biographisch-bibliographisches Quellen-Lexikon*   D
EitnerS   R. Eitner: *Bibliographie der Musik-Sammelwerke des XVI. und XVII. Jahrhunderts* (Berlin, 1877)
EKM   *English (later Early) Keyboard Music*   E
EL   *The English Lute-songs*
EM   *The English Madrigalists*   E
EM   *Ethnomusicology*   P [US664]
EMC   *Encyclopedia of Music in Canada*, ed. H. Kallmann, G. Potvin and K. Winters (Toronto, 1981)
EMDC   *Encyclopédie de la musique et dictionnaire du Conservatoire*
EMN   *Exempla musica neerlandica*   E
EMS   *The English Madrigal School*   E
ES   *Enciclopedia dello spettacolo*   D
ESLS   *The English School of Lutenist-songwriters*   E

FAM   *Fontes artis musicae*   P [Intl 16]
FasquelleE   *Encyclopédie de la musique* (Paris: Fasquelle, 1958–61)   D
FétisB (FétisBS)   F.-J. Fétis: *Biographie universelle des musiciens* (2/1860–65) (and suppl.)   D
FoMRHI Quarterly   *Fellowship of Makers and Restorers of Historical Instruments*   P [GB574]

GerberL   R. Gerber: *Historisch-biographisches Lexikon der Tonkünstler*   D
GerberNL   R. Gerber: *Neues historisch-biographisches Lexikon der Tonkünstler*   D
GfMKB   *Gesellschaft für Musikforschung Kongressbericht* [1950–]
GMB   *Geschichte der Musik in Beispielen*, ed. A. Schering (Leipzig, 1931)   E
Grove 1(–5)   G. Grove, ed.: *A Dictionary of Music and Musicians*, 2nd–5th edns. as *Grove's Dictionary of Music and Musicians*   D
Grove 6   *The New Grove Dictionary of Music and Musicians*   D

GS	M. Gerbert: *Scriptores ecclesiastici de musica sacra* (St Blasien, 1784/*R*1963)
GSJ	*The Galpin Society Journal* P [GB415]
HAM	*Historical Anthology of Music*, ed. A. T. Davison and W. Apel, i (Cambridge, Mass., 1946, rev. 2/1949); ii (Cambridge, Mass., 1950) E
HawkinsH	J. Hawkins: *A General History of the Science and Practice of Music* (London, 1776) [p. nos. refer to edn. of 1853/*R*1963]
HJb	*Händel-Jahrbuch* P [D712, 968]
HM	Hortus musicus E
HMT	*Handwörterbuch der musikalischen Terminologie* D
HMw	Handbuch der Musikwissenschaft, ed. E. Bücken (Potsdam, 1927–) [monograph series]
HMYB	*Hinrichsen's Musical Year Book* P [GB381]
HPM	Harvard Publications in Music E
HR	*Hudební revue* P [CS80]
HRo	*Hudební rozhledy* P [CS176]
HV	*Hudební věda* P [CS204]
IIM	*Izvestiya na Instituta za muzika* P [BG14]
IMa	Instituta et monumenta E
IMi	Istituzioni e monumenti dell'arte musicale italiana E
IMSCR	*International Musicological Society Congress Report* [1930–]
IMusSCR	*International Musical Society Congress Report* [1906–11]
IRASM	*International Review of the Aesthetics and Sociology of Music* P [Intl 32]
IRMO	S. L. Ginzburg: *Istoriya russkoy muzïki v notnïkh obraztsakh* D
IRMAS	*The International Review of Music Aesthetics and Sociology* P [Intl 32]
IZ	*Instrumentenbau-Zeitschrift* P [D806]
Izikowitz-MISAI	K. G. Izikowitz: *Musical and other Sound Instruments of the South American Indians* (Göteborg, 1935)
JAMIS	*Journal of the American Musical Instrument Society*
JAMS	*Journal of the American Musicological Society* P [US613]
JBIOS	*Journal of the British Institute of Organ Studies*
JbMP	*Jahrbuch der Musikbibliothek Peters* P [D336]
JEFDSS	*The Journal of the English Folk Dance and Song Society* P [GB341]
JFSS	*Journal of the Folk-song Society* P [GB183]
JIFMC	*Journal of the International Folk Music Council* P [Intl 10]
JMT	*Journal of Music Theory* P [US683]
JRBM	*Journal of Renaissance and Baroque Music* P [US590]
JRME	*Journal of Research in Music Education* P [US665]
JVdGS	*Chelys: Journal of the Viola da Gamba Society* P [GB537]
JVdGSA	*Journal of the Viola da Gamba Society of America* P [US742]
JVNM	see *Bouwsteenen: JVNM* P [NL20]
KirbyMISA	P. R. Kirby: *The Musical Instruments of the Native Races of South Africa* (London, 1934, 2/1965)
KJb	*Kirchenmusikalisches Jahrbuch* P [D284]
KM	*Kwartalnik muzyczny* P [PL35, 64]
LaborD	*Diccionario de la musica Labor* D
LaMusicaD	*La musica: dizionario* D
LaMusicaE	*La musica: enciclopedia storica* D
LaurentyA	J. S. Laurenty: *Systématique des aerophones de l'Afrique centrale* (Tervuren, 1974)
LaurentyC	J. S. Laurenty: *Les cordophones du Congo belge et du Ruanda Urundi* (Tervuren, 1960)
LaurentyS	J. S. Laurenty: *Les sanza du Congo* (Tervuren, 1962)
LaurentyTF	J. S. Laurenty: *Les tambours à fente de l'Afrique centrale* (Tervuren, 1968)
LM	*Lucrări de muzicologie* P [R27]
LSJ	*The Lute Society Journal* P [GB487]

MA	*The Musical Antiquary* P [GB240]
MAB	Musica antiqua bohemica E
MAM	Musik alter Meister E
MAP	Musica antiqua polonica E
MAS	[publications of the British] Musical Antiquarian Society E
MB	Musica brittanica E
MC	Musica da camera E
MD	*Musica disciplina* P [US590]
ME	*Muzïkal'naya entsiklopediya* D
Mf	*Die Musikforschung* P [D839]
MGG	*Die Musik in Geschichte und Gegenwart* D
MH	Musica hispana E
MJb	*Mozart-Jahrbuch des Zentralinstituts für Mozartforschung* [1950–] P [A254]
ML	*Music and Letters* P [GB280]
MM	*Modern Music* P [US488]
MMA	*Miscellanea musicologica* [Australia] P [AUS19]
MMB	Monumenta musicae byzantinae E
MMBel	Monumenta musicae belgicae E
MMC	*Miscellanea musicologica* [Czechoslovakia] P [CS191]
MME	Monumentos de la música española E
MMFTR	Monuments de la musique française au temps de la renaissance E
MMg	*Monatshefte für Musikgeschichte* P [D188]
MMI	Monumenti di musica italiana E
MMN	Monumenta musicae neerlandicae E
MMP	Monumenta musicae in Polonia E
MMR	*The Monthly Musical Record* P [GB75]
MMRF	Les maîtres musiciens de la renaissance française E
MMS	Monumenta musicae svecicae E
MO	*Musical Opinion* P [GB90]
MQ	*The Musical Quarterly* P [US447]
MR	*The Music Review* P [GB376]
MRM	Monuments of Renaissance Music E
MRS	Musiche rinascimentali siciliane E
MS	*Muzïkal'nïy sovremennik* P [USSR37]
MSD	Musicological Studies and Documents, ed. A. Carapetyan (Rome, 1951–)
MT	*The Musical Times* P [GB33]
MVH	Musica viva historica E
MVSSP	Musiche vocali strumentali sacre e profane E
Mw	Das Musikwerk E
MZ	*Muzikološki zbornik* P [YU37]
NA	*Note d'archivio per la storia musicale* P [I186]
NBJb	*Neues Beethoven-Jahrbuch* P [D636]
NBL	*Norsk biografisk leksikon* (Oslo, 1921–)
NDB	*Neue deutsche Biographie* (Berlin, 1953–)
NM	Nagels Musikarchiv E
NNBW	*Nieuw Nederlandsch biografisch woordenboek* (Leiden, 1911–37)
NÖB	*Neue österreichische Biographie* (Vienna, 1923)
NOHM	*The New Oxford History of Music*, ed. E. Wellesz, J. A. Westrup and G. Abraham (London, 1954–)
NRMI	*Nuova rivista musicale italiana* P [I282]
NZM	*Neue Zeitschrift für Musik* P [D75, 1088]
OHM	*The Oxford History of Music*, ed. W. H. Hadow (Oxford, 1901–5, enlarged 2/1929–38)
OM	*Opus musicum* P [CS222]
ÖMz	*Österreichische Musikzeitschrift* P [A233]
OrtizIMA	F. Ortiz: *Los instrumentos de la música afrocubana* (Havana, 1952–5)
PalMus	Paléographie musicale (Solesmes, 1889–)
PAMS	*Papers of the American Musicological Society* P [US543]
PÄMw	Publikationen älterer praktischer und theoretischer Musikwerke E
PBC	Publicaciones del departamento de música de la Biblioteca de Catalunya E
PGfM	Publikationen der Gesellschaft für Musikforschung E
PIISM	Pubblicazioni dell'Istituto italiano per la storia della musica E
PL	*Patrologiae cursus completus*, i: Series latina, ed. J. P. Migne (Paris, 1844–64)
PM	Portugaliae musica E
PMA	*Proceedings of the Musical Association* P [GB80]

PMFC	Polyphonic Music of the Fourteenth Century E	SMd	Schweizerische Musikdenkmäler E
PNM	*Perspectives of New Music* P [US724]	*SML*	*Schweizer Musiker Lexikon* D
PRM	*Polski rocznik muzykologiczny* P [PL85]	SMM	Summa musicae medii aevi E
PRMA	*Proceedings of the Royal Musical Association* P [GB80]	*SMN*	*Studia musicologica norvegica* P [N45]
		SMP	*Słownik muzyków polskich* D
PSB	*Polskich słownik biograficzny* (Kraków, 1935)	*SMw*	*Studien zur Musikwissenschaft* P [D536]
PSFM	Publications de la Société française de musicologie E	*SMz*	*Schweizerische Musikzeitung/Revue musicale suisse* P [CH4]
		SOB	Süddeutsche Orgelmeister des Barock E
Quaderni della RaM	*Quaderni della Rassegna musicale* P [I272]	*SovM*	*Sovetskaya muzïka* P [USSR66]
		STMf	*Svensk tidskrift för musikforskning* P [S46]
Rad JAZU	*Rad Jugoslavenske akademije znanosti i umjetnosti* (Zagreb, 1867–)	TCM	Tudor Church Music E
		TM	Thesauri musici E
RaM	*La rassegna musicale* P [I197]	*TraceyCSA*	H. Tracey: *Catalogue of the Sound of Africa Series* (Roodepoort, 1973)
RBM	*Revue belge de musicologie* P [B126]		
RdM	*Revue de musicologie* P [F462]	*TVNM*	*Tijdschrift van de Vereniging voor Nederlandse muziekgeschiedenis* P [NL26]
ReM	*La revue musicale* [1920–] P [F475]		
RHCM	*Revue d'histoire et de critique musicales* [1901]; *La revue musicale* [1902–10] P [F320]	UVNM	Uitgaven der Vereniging voor Nederlandse muziekgeschiedenis E
RicordiE	*Enciclopedia della musica* (Milan: Ricordi, 1963–4) D		
RiemannL 12	*Riemann Musik Lexikon* (12/1959–75) D	*VertkovA*	K. Vertkov, G. Blagodatov and E. Yazovitskaya, eds.: *Atlas muzïkal'nïkh instrumentov narodov SSSR* (Moscow, 1963, 2/1975 with 4 discs)
RIM	*Rivista italiana di musicologia* P [I280]		
RISM	*Répertoire international des sources musicales*	VMPH	Veröffentlichungen der Musik-Bibliothek Paul Hirsch E
RMARC	*R[oyal] M[usical] A[ssociation] Research Chronicle* P [GB496]	*VMw*	*Vierteljahrsschrift für Musikwissenschaft* P [D282]
RMFC	*Recherches sur la musique française classique* P [F677]		
RMG	*Russkaya muzïkal'naya gazeta* P [USSR19]	*Wachsmann-TCU*	K. P. Wachsmann and M. Trowell: *Tribal Crafts of Uganda* (London, 1953)
RMI	*Rivista musicale italiana* P [I84]		
RMS	Renaissance Manuscript Studies E	*WaltherML*	J. G. Walther: *Musicalisches Lexicon oder Musicalische Bibliothec* D
RN	*Renaissance News* P [see US590]	WDMP	Wydawnictwo dawnej muzyki polskiej E
RRMBE	Recent Researches in the Music of the Baroque Era E	WE	Wellesley Edition E
		WECIS	Wellesley Edition Cantata Index Series E
RRMR	Recent Researches in the Music of the Renaissance E		
		YIFMC	*Yearbook of the International Folk Music Council* P [Intl 31]
SatoriB	C. Satori: *Bibliografia della musica strumentale italiana stampata in Italia fino al 1700* (Florence, 1952–68)	*YTM*	*Yearbook for Traditional Music* (1981–) [contd from *YIFMC*]
SBL	*Svenska biografiskt leksikon* (Stockholm, 1918–)		
SchmidlD (*SchmidlDS*)	C. Schmidl: *Dizionario dei musicisti* (and suppl.) D	*ZfM*	*Zeitschrift für Musik* P [D75]
SCMA	Smith College Music Archives E	ZHMP	Zrodła do historii muzyki polskiej E
SeegerL	H. Seeger: *Musiklexikon* D	*ZI*	*Zeitschrift für Instrumentenbau* P [D249]
SEM	[University of California] Series of Early Music E	*ZIMG*	*Zeitschrift der Internationalen Musik-Gesellschaft* P [Intl 3]
SH	*Slovenská hudba* P [CS192]		
SIMG	*Sammelbände der Internationalen Musik-Gesellschaft* P [Intl 2]	*ZL*	*Zenei lexikon* D
SM	*Studia musicologica Academiae scientiarum hungaricae* P [H49]	*ZMw*	*Zeitschrift für Musikwissenschaft* P [D556]
SMA	*Studies in Music* [Australia] P [AUS20]		

Fuller bibliographical information on the dictionaries, editions and periodicals listed above are available in *The New Grove Dictionary of Music and Musicians* (D, in the article 'Dictionaries and encyclopedias of music'; E, in 'Editions, historical'; P, in 'Periodicals'). For fuller information on musical Festschriften up to 1967, see W. Gerboth: *An Index to Musical Festschriften and Similar Publications* (New York, 1967); and, on congress reports, J. Tyrrell and R. Wise: *A Guide to International Congress Reports in Music, 1900–1975* (London, 1979). For other items, basic bibliographical information is given above.

Volume Two

G–O

G

Gaasay. Large inverted hemispherical calabash percussion vessel used by the Songhay people of Niger. The calabash is placed in loose sand over a pit and supported by a stick embedded in the earth. It is played in pairs and struck with fan-shaped wooden beaters, each with at least seven rigid spokes (see illustration). The *gaasay* are used with the *goge* (single-string fiddle) in music for the *follay* ritual of the Songhay spirit possession cult.

BIBLIOGRAPHY

B. Surugue: *Contribution à l'étude de la musique sacrée zarma-songhay* (Niamey, 1972)

——: 'Songhay Music', *Grove 6*

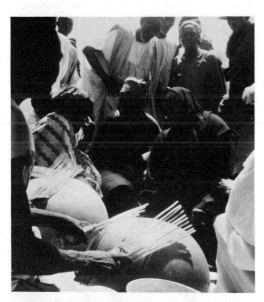

Two gaasay (percussion vessels) used in the follay ritual of the Songhay people, Niger

Găb. Arab term for a pipe or reedpipe. *See* ARGHŪL.

Gaba [gapa]. Name for HOURGLASS DRUM in Motu and several other languages of the Central, Milne Bay and Northern Provinces of Papua New Guinea. *See* KUNDU (i).

Gabamboli [kabamboli, kabambolik]. Idiochord MOUTH BOW of the Jola people of Senegal. It is approximately 80 to 100 cm in length. The player holds the bow under his left arm with the upper end between his lips. He strikes the string with a stick in his right hand, modulating it with the fingers of his left. *See* L.-V. Thomas: 'Les Diola', *Mémoires de l'Institut français d'Afrique noire*, lv (1958–9).

Gabbang. Trough XYLOPHONE of the southern Philippines. The Tausug *gabbang* has about 16 to 19 bamboo keys tuned to a heptatonic scale with equal intervals. The melody is divided between the leading line (*ina*: 'mother') and a following line in the lower register (*anak*: 'child'). As a solo instrument it is used for preludes to songs; it is also an important accompanying instrument for all secular songs and for the *biola* (violin).

Gabbrielli, Giovanni Battista (*fl c*1740–70). Italian violin maker. Gabbrielli, who worked in Florence, is the most significant of the 18th-century Florentine violin makers, and it is generally thought that the other makers in the city may have learnt from him. The work of Stainer seems to have been the main influence in Florence, but Gabbrielli is today regarded as successful because he resisted the temptation to exaggerate Stainer's features, so often a pitfall among his followers. Occasionally a very high-built violin is found attributed to Gabbrielli, but much more often the outline is of Cremonese dimensions and the model well-balanced. His soundholes invariably have a Stainer slant at each end, and the varnish is yellow or yellow-brown. His best instruments are handsome and well-sounding, and he made violas and cellos as well as violins.

BIBLIOGRAPHY

W. L. von Lütgendorff: *Die Geigen- und Lautenmacher vom Mittelalter bis zur Gegenwart* (Frankfurt am Main, 1904, rev. 6/1922/*R*1968)

R. Vannes: *Essai d'un dictionnaire universel des luthiers* (Paris, 1932, 2/1951/*R*1972 as *Dictionnaire universel des luthiers* and *R*1981 incl. suppl. 1959)

CHARLES BEARE

Gabbus [gabbūs]. Lute of Zanzibar, South Yemen and Oman. *See* QANBŪS.

Gabel-Harmon-Pianoforte. A keyboard instrument patented in 1827 by MATTHIAS MÜLLER.

Gabi. Large cog rattle of the Basque region, also called *carracón*. *See* CARRACA, (1).

1

Gabler, Joseph (*b* Ochsenhausen, Upper Swabia, 6 July 1700; *d* Bregenz, 8 Nov 1771). German organ builder. He trained as a carpenter under his father Johann, and from 1719 worked as a journeyman joiner in Mainz for A. Ziegenhorn (*d* 1720), carrying on the business himself after 1726. During these years he also studied organ building, principally, it appears, with G. and J. P. Geissel of Mainz and possibly with other Mainz master organ builders such as J. A. I. Will, J. F. Macrander, J. J. Dahm (known for his mixtureless *piano* manual) and A. and J. Onimus (credited with the Piffaro). Gabler lived in Ochsenhausen (1729–33), then again in Mainz and elsewhere, in Weingarten (until 1750 or later), in Memmingen, and eventually in Bregenz, where he spent his last years. His organs include those for Ochsenhausen Abbey (1729–33; four manuals, 49 stops; extant), Weingarten Abbey (1737–50; four manuals, 63 stops; extant) (*see* ORGAN, fig.45), Zeil Castle (after 1750; two manuals, 15 stops; extant), the Wallfahrtskirche, Steinbach (1755–9; two manuals, 24 stops; extant), and the Stadtkirche, Bregenz (1769–71; case extant). Gabler was a master of foundation stops, and they form a high proportion of his specifications, especially those of narrow scale such as Violone II 16′, Salicional 8′, Piffaro V–VIII 8′ and Viola dolce II 4′. Normally he gave every manual a Principal chorus, including a Cornet consisting of a Tierce mixture. The highest ranks of his mixtures, whose choruses are frequently stronger in the bass than in the treble, lie in the range of *c*750 to *c*4000 Hz and lack the sheen of Brabantine instruments (4000–12,000 Hz). There are few reed stops in Gabler's specifications and almost no mutations. Gabler used to characterize his manuals as: 'scharf und penetrant' (*Hauptwerk*), 'delikat und lieblich' (*Positiv*), 'gravitätisch und gross' (*Brustwerk*) and 'stark und durchdringend' (Pedal), the very words Gottfried Silbermann used in describing his *Positiv, Brustwerk, Hauptwerk* and Pedal respectively. Gabler introduced the detached console to Upper Swabia. His cases demonstrate his skill as a cabinet maker; like those of Michael Engler they are superbly well suited to their buildings, and often sport the hovering 'Crown Positive' that he invented. Gabler's organ at Weingarten is one of the great German Baroque organs; Bédos de Celles' *L'art du facteur d'orgues* (Paris, 1766–78) includes an illustration and the specification of the instrument. The Gabler school includes Joseph Höss (1745–99; his organ at Dischingen survives).

BIBLIOGRAPHY
W. Supper and H. Meyer: *Barockorgeln in Oberschwaben* (Kassel, 1941)
F. Bärnwick: *Die grosse Orgel zu Weingarten* (Kassel, 4/1947)
F. Bösken: 'Der mittelrheinische Orgelbau zur Zeit des Aufenthalts Joseph Gablers in Mainz', *Der Barock, seine Orgeln und seine Musik in Oberschwaben* (Ochsenhausen, 1951), 78
A. Gottron: 'Joseph Gabler in Mainz', ibid, 82
W. Supper: 'Die oberschwäbische Barockorgel', ibid, 89–118
——: 'Gabler', *MGG*
——: 'Die Orgellandschaft Württemberg', *Acta organologica*, i (1967), 127
H. Fischer and T. Wohnhaas: *Historische Orgeln in Schwaben* (Munich, 1982)
HANS KLOTZ

Gabowie. String instrument of the Khoikhoi (Hottentot) people of southern Africa, mentioned in 18th-century writings. Described as a 'rude sort of guitar', it had three to five metal strings. See *KirbyMISA*, 251f.

Gabus [!gabus]. Unbraced MOUTH BOW of the Khoikhoi (Korana Hottentot) people of southern Africa. It is fairly similar, in construction and performing practice, to the Zulu UMQANGALA and related instruments. See *KirbyMISA*, 220, pl.63*a*.

Gabusi [gambusi]. Short-necked lute of the Comoro Islands. *See* QANBŪS.

Gachi. Long metal trumpet of the Mului people of Chad. *See* KAKAKI and GASHI.

Gadigedik [gadik]. LEAF OBOE of Ifalik, Caroline Islands, Micronesia. See H. Fischer: 'Zwei einfache Musikinstrumente aus Blatt in Ozeanien', *Jahrbuch des Museums für Völkerkunde zu Leipzig*, xiv (1955), 67.

Gadulka. Fiddle of Bulgaria; also known as *ganilka*, *kopanka*, *gjola*, *tsigulka*, *kemene* in western Bulgaria, and sometimes, erroneously, *gusla*. It resembles the Greek *lyra* and the Yugoslav *lirica*. Its oval or pear-shaped soundbox is carved from one piece of wood, usually mulberry, manna-ash (*Fraxinus ornus*) or sycamore. Its short, broad neck ends in a circular, triangular or clover-leaf shaped flat peg-disc or head. The soundboard, made of spruce, is glued to the soundbox and has two round or oval soundholes called *ochi* ('eyes'). The strings, which are made of sheep- or cat-gut, are attached to a bone tailpiece and, at the upper end, are wound directly round wooden pegs. They pass over a thin wooden bridge and soundpost, which emerges through one of the soundholes.

The traditional *gadulka* has three strings; in Thrace there are four-string instruments with one or two metal sympathetic strings. The Thracian tuning is the most

Gadulka (fiddle) of Bulgaria

Imperial Palace gagaku ensemble for kangen: (front row, left to right) shōko (gong), tsuridaiko and kakko (barrel drums); (middle rows) two sō (long zithers) and two biwa (lutes); (back rows, left to right) three ryūteki (transverse flutes), three hichiriki (oboes) and three shō (mouth organs); (far back, centre) dadaiko (barrel drum), used only for dance accompaniment (bugaku)

popular: $a' - e' - a$. Other tunings are: the Dobrujan tuning ($a' - a - e'$) and the Gabrovo or Balkan tuning ($a' - e' - d'$). The range on the Thracian tuning is the widest: a to e'', extended to a'' with harmonics. The strings are played with a bow made of cornel wood and horsehair, rubbed with rosin before playing. The first (highest) string is played by sideways pressure of the fingernail, the other strings with pressure from the fingertips. The *gadulka* is held vertically, with the lower end tucked in the player's belt when standing, or held on his hip when seated.

The Thracian *gadulka* is the largest instrument, and has the fullest tone-quality. Dobrujan instruments are smaller. The *kemene* of western Bulgaria has a shallow soundbox and a correspondingly thinner sound; it is always played with a drone note.

The *gadulka* is used as a solo instrument to accompany songs and dances, in different rituals and in small instrumental groups. The Dobrujan *gadulka*, with the accordion and a *gaida* (bagpipe) or *kaval* (flute) forms a typical Dobrujan *troika* (trio).

VERGILIJ ATANASSOV

Gafa. Antelope-horn trumpet of the Galla people of East Africa.

Gaga. Double-headed cylindrical drum of Libya and Algeria. *See* GANGA, (1).

Gagaku. Japanese court music of various genres each performed on a different combination of instruments. It derives from Chinese court music, which the Japanese court adopted together with an amazing variety of instruments during China's Tang period (618–907). About 20 of the early instruments are preserved in the Shōsōin, the Japanese imperial treasure-house. However, many of these instrument types subsequently died out in Japan, or perhaps evolved into new forms, so that despite Japanese claims for the antiquity of gagaku the current performing practice is possibly little more than a century old. The earliest extant gagaku scores indicate that the BIWA (lute) and the *sō* (long zither; *see* GAKU-sō), which now have a subsidiary role, then played a main melody. Today the flutes and *hichiriki* (oboe) provide the basic melody.

The Japanese eventually classified gagaku ('elegant music') according to its supposed origins. Genres of gagaku considered to be Chinese, even though they may have originated in India or Central Asia, were classified as *tōgaku* ('Tang music'). Within this category a further division was made between *kangen* ('wind and string music', i.e. instrumental music) and *bugaku* ('dance music'). *Tōgaku* pieces could usually be performed in either style with a shift in instrumentation. Today the *ryūteki* (transverse flute), *hichiriki*, *shō* (mouth organ), *kakko* (barrel drum) and *shōko* (gong) are included in both orchestras, with the addition for *kangen* of the *biwa*, *sō* and *tsuridaiko* (barrel drum). The *dadaiko* (barrel drum) is added for *bugaku*.

Genres supposedly of Korean lineage were called *komagaku* ('Korean music'). All *komagaku* was dance music. The *komagaku* ensemble today comprises the *komabue* (transverse flute), *hichiriki*, *san-no-tsuzumi* (hourglass drum), *dadaiko* and *shōko*.

There is also a body of gagaku considered to be indigenous and to predate the Tang importations. It is mostly vocal music. The most characteristic feature of these genres, so far as instruments are concerned, is the use for percussion of the *shakubyōshi* (clappers) rather than drums and gongs. Instrumentation of *kagura-uta* (Shintō ritual music), for example, is *kagurabue* (flute), *hichiriki*, *wagon* (zither) and *shakubyōshi*; *azuma-asobi* (Shintō music) has the same instruments except the *komabue* (flute) replaces the *kagurabue*. Of the other major genres the *yamato-uta* (Shintō music) ensemble comprises the *ryūteki*, *hichiriki* and *shakubyōshi*. Although for *rōei* (court songs) just the *ryūteki*, *hichiriki* and *shō* are used, the *saibara* (folksong-based) ensemble includes these three instruments and the *biwa*, *sō* and *shakubyōshi*.

BIBLIOGRAPHY
W. P. Malm: *Japanese Music and Musical Instruments* (Rutland, Vermont, 1959), 77ff
M. Togi: *Gagaku* (New York, 1971)
E. Harich-Schneider: *A History of Japanese Music* (London, 1973)
R. Wolpert and others: '"The Waves of Kokonor": a Dance-tune of the T'ang Dynasty', *Asian Music*, v/1 (1973), 3
R. Garfias: 'Japan', §III, 1, *Grove 6*
L. Picken: *Music from the Tang Court* (London, 1981)
'Gagaku', *Ongaku daijiten* [Encyclopedia of music] (Tokyo, 1981)
DAVID W. HUGHES

Gaganā. Bamboo idioglot JEW'S HARP of the Garo people of Assam, India. A type of MURCANG, it is used by young girls to accompany the *bīhu* songs and dances, together with the *dhol* (drum), *pempā* (double hornpipe) and *tokā* (clappers). See S. Ray: *Music of Eastern India* (Calcutta, 1973).

Gaggara. Metal rattle, in the form of a hollow ring filled with iron pellets, of Mysore, India. It is worn on the finger and used in devotional singing. *See* NŪPUR and GHUṄGRŪ.

Gaggini, Pierre (*b* Nice, 19 July 1903). French violin maker. After studying with his uncle, Albert Louis Blanchi (1871–1942), he set up independently in Nice and succeeded in attracting a strong following, especially in France. He won awards at many exhibitions, including those at Brussels (1935), Paris (1937) and The Hague (1949), and retired in 1980. Gaggini's craftsmanship was of the highest order and his choice of material excellent. His varnish, which varies from golden yellow to orange and orange-red, is of attractive appearance but tends to chip easily. The violins and cellos follow a personal model inspired by Stradivari. The violas, although also patterned after a personal model, are often reminiscent of the familiar Tertis model. However, the soundholes follow a fixed pattern – gracefully curved and slightly inclined – regardless of the instrument or model. In addition to being labelled, his instruments are also branded, P. GAGGINI–NICE, and numbered on the interior back. His bows have the same stamp; these were actually made by various bow makers and only finished off by Gaggini in a personal style.

BIBLIOGRAPHY
R. Vannes: *Essai d'un dictionnaire universel des luthiers* (Paris, 1932, 2/1951/R1972 as *Dictionnaire universel des luthiers* and R1981 incl. suppl. 1959)
JAAK LIIVOJA-LORIUS

Gagliano. Italian family of violin makers who worked in Naples from about 1700 to the middle of the 19th century. They were an industrious family, and produced a large number of violins, many cellos and a few violas. With the exception of Alessandro Gagliano, they usually worked on the Stradivari model. All of the 18th-century Gaglianos could produce a masterpiece if circumstances required it; but as the 19th century approached the demand seems to have been increasingly for hastily made, inexpensive instruments. Except for Alessandro, they all used a similar varnish, harder than that of more classical makers; the most attractive has a distinctive golden orange colour, but there are many that appear stained, with almost a grey-green tinge to the orange. Tonally they all have what is known as the 'Italian' quality, but tend towards brightness, occasionally almost harshness. They are very good all-round instruments, and well liked by all types of players. No work has been published giving the correct dates of each member of the family, and the dates given by most authorities do not always tally with those on the original labels.

Alessandro Gagliano (*fl c*1700–*c*1735) was the first maker in the Gagliano family and the first known Neapolitan maker: it is not known where he learnt his craft. His work differs in almost all respects from that of his descendants, but most of all in the varnish he used. This was of a soft, oily nature, similar to the very best, glowing and transparent and of the deepest red colour. He was only an average workman, but his instruments have great character and are in no sense copies of the work of his great predecessors or contemporaries. He made violins of at least three different sizes, one of them small and another rather too large, with a long string length. The soundholes have an exaggerated swing which can nevertheless be quite charming, but the scrolls are often pinched in design and crudely carved, sometimes with a little extra ornament to the pegbox. His cellos are especially good, but rare.

Nicola Gagliano (i) (*fl c*1740–*c*1780) was a son of Alessandro Gagliano. The majority of his instruments were made between 1750 and 1770, though he is thought to have had a longer working life. They are all much influenced by Stradivari's work, and, with those of his brother Gennaro, are the most sought after of the Gaglianos. The quality of his work is consistently high, but a few of his violins are rather high-built and broad in measurement. Some of the violins with his original label show the collaboration of his son Giuseppe.

Gennaro [Januarius] Gagliano (*fl c*1740–*c*1780) was also a son of Alessandro Gagliano. He is often considered the best maker of his family, though each member was capable of rising above the average productions of the others. Gennaro was a more sensitive craftsman, and his overall concept of violin making was not far behind that of the great Cremonese makers. Although he was most influenced by Stradivari, he often made Amati copies, with strong-grained pine in the front, brown varnish and facsimile Amati labels. Both Gennaro and Nicola (i) made very good cellos on the best Stradivari model, but they also introduced the very narrow design used by most later Neapolitans (see illustration).

Cello by Nicola Gagliano (i),
Naples, 1762 (private collection)

Ferdinando Gagliano (*fl* c1770–c1795) was a son of Nicola Gagliano (i), but is more likely to have been a pupil of his uncle, Gennaro Gagliano. His instruments vary in the quality of their finish, but their outlines have the pleasing flow of typical Gennaro models, with slightly stiffer, more open soundholes. The varnish can be very good looking, but is less striking than that on his father's or uncle's instruments.

Ferdinando Gagliano's three brothers collaborated in their work to a certain extent. Giuseppe [Joseph] Gagliano (*fl* c1770–c1800) was certainly a pupil of his father and his early work suggests he was an excellent maker. His work declined over the years, however, and instruments made in partnership with his brother Antonio are not so good as those he made alone. Antonio Gagliano (i) (*fl* c1780–c1800) was inferior to his brother Giuseppe in his workmanship. Instruments bearing his signature inside often have labels showing them to have been made in partnership with Giuseppe.

Giovanni [Joannes] Gagliano (*fl* c1785–after 1815) began working with Giuseppe and Antonio, but by about 1800 was working by himself. His work, while reflecting that of his uncle Gennaro and his brother Ferdinando, has strong individual features in the slant of the soundholes and the deep cut of the pegbox fluting. He had three sons: Nicola Gagliano (ii) (*fl* c1800–c1825) produced work in the Gagliano tradition, though some workmanship is completely undistinguished and his instruments are now rarely found; Raffaele (*d* 1857) and Antonio Gagliano (ii) (*d* 1860) were responsible for many violins and cellos, usually with their backs left unpurfled, but although the varnish technique remained unchanged the workmanship declined in quality.

BIBLIOGRAPHY

W. L. von Lütgendorff: *Die Geigen- und Lautenmacher vom Mittelalter bis zur Gegenwart* (Frankfurt am Main, 1904, 6/1922/R1968)

R. Vannes: *Essai d'un dictionnaire universel des luthiers* (Paris, 1932, 2/1951/R1972 as *Dictionnaire universel des luthiers* and R1981 inc. suppl. 1959)

J. Roda: *Bows for Musical Instruments of the Violin Family* (Chicago, 1959)

CHARLES BEARE

Gagliano, Carlo (*fl* late 18th century). Italian violin maker who worked in Belluno. There is no evidence to connect him with the GAGLIANO family who worked in Naples.

Gagrī [gagrā]. Metal percussion vessel of north India. It is shaped like a pot and played by striking the body and mouth of the vessel with the hands, which sometimes bear metal rings. *See* GHAṬA, §1.

Gahakan. Heterochord MOUTH BOW of the Jola people of Senegal. It has a wooden bridge between the string and the bow. The instrument is held perpendicularly, one end in the player's left hand, the other between his head and shoulder. The player taps the string with a stick and amplifies the sound using the oral cavity. See L.-V. Thomas: 'Les Diola', *Mémoires de l'Institut français d'Afrique noire*, lv (1958–9).

Gai (Fr.: 'merry', 'cheerful'). A tempo mark. Rousseau (1768) equated it with *allegro*, the fourth of his five main degrees of movement in music; and the frequency of its use from the earliest years of the 18th century suggests that his equation, for once, was a happy one. Couperin used it (with the spelling *gay*), as did Rameau; and they and their contemporaries made much use of the adverbial form *gaiment*, also spelt *gayment*, *gaiement* and *gayement*, as tempo and mood designations. The early history of *gai* as a purely musical instruction is a little difficult to trace because the word appears in musical contexts throughout the 17th century as the title of a dance, the *branle gai*; but its absence from Brossard's *Dictionaire* of 1703 suggests that François Couperin was one of the first to use it. Occasionally Italian composers used the adjective *gajo* or *gaio*, particularly as a qualification to *allegro*.

For bibliography *see* TEMPO AND EXPRESSION MARKS.

DAVID FALLOWS

Gaida. *See* GAJDE.

Gāine sāraṅgī. Small fiddle of the *gāine* singing musicians of Nepal. *See* SĀRAṄGĪ, §3.

Gaita. Term used in Iberia, various parts of south-eastern Europe, the Middle East and Latin America for an aerophone, usually an oboe or a bagpipe. The south-east European GAJDE is a bagpipe; most other instruments to which the term is applied are oboes. For the Middle Eastern instruments, *see* GHAYṬA; for the West African, *see* ALGAITA. This article outlines the etymological background of the term and discusses the instruments of Iberia and the New World.

The term, which is variously spelt (*gaida, gajde, gajdë,*

Gaita de foles (bagpipe) of Portugal

gajdy, ghaida, ghaite, ghayṭa, kaita, aghiyad, algaita), is derived from the Gothic *gait* or *ghaid* ('goat') and originally denoted a bagpipe with a goatskin bag; this is borne out by all surviving specimens of the Portuguese *gaita* (V. de Olivares: *Instrumentos musicais populares portuguesis*, Lisbon, 1982) and the *gajde* of European Turkey (L. Picken: *Folk Musical Instruments of Turkey*, London, 1975). Some Spanish writers have suggested that *ghayṭa* is a Spanish borrowing from Arab Andalusia, meaning 'that which disturbs, is wearisome, is troubling, becomes angry' (alluding to the instrument's sonority); but no such approach can derive from the Arabic language, which does not convey that meaning. It is thus clear that Arab Andalusia borrowed the word from the Visigoths and applied it to the oboe, and if the term shifted from the bagpipe (*gaita*) to the oboe (*ghayṭa*), it was by virtue of similarity of timbre or of social function (the Andalusians would not have thought in terms of instrumental classification).

In Spain, *gaita* can signify the DUCT FLUTE also known as a *pito* in León and Andalusia and *txistu* in the Basque region, where the *gaita navarra* signifies an oboe. In Galicia, Catalonia and parts of the Pyrenees it is the term for a bagpipe (*see* BAGPIPE, §7 (i)). It is also an alternative name for an oboe elsewhere known as *dulzaina, chirimía* or *gralla* (in Catalan). In Castile the *gaita* (*gaita serrana* or *gaita zamorana*) is a capped, single-reed HORNPIPE with a bell of animal horn, now rare. The *gaita gallega* or *gaita de fuelle* is a bagpipe of Galicia, also known in Catalonia (as *sac de gemecs*, 'bag of groans') and in parts of the Pyrenees; the Galician bagpipe ensemble may consist of two bagpipe players and two drummers. In Portugal, the *gaita de foles* is a bagpipe used to accompany dancing in the Alentejo region (with *pifaro* and castanets); in Brazilian usage the term means an accordion (*see* SANFONA (ii)).

In Colombia, the *gaita* is an end-blown duct flute of the Atlantic coastal region, made from long tubes of a cactus-like plant (for illustration *see* TAMBOR MAJOR). A head of beeswax and vegetal carbon is placed on one end with a turkey quill inserted so that the air blown through it breaks on the upper edge of the tube, partly escaping through a hole in the head. The *gaita hembra* ('female flute') has five finger-holes, the *gaita macho* ('male flute') two; one hole in each instrument is stopped with wax. The *gaita hembra* is used for the melody; the player of the *gaita macho* plays a heterophonic part with one hand while shaking a maraca with the other. Both instruments are of Indian origin. The term *gaita* is also used for a Colombian ensemble (including two *gaitas*) which accompanies the *cumbia* folkdance.

CHRISTIAN POCHÉ, JOHN M. SCHECHTER

Gajaḍhakkā. Large cylindrical or barrel-shaped drum mentioned in the 12th-century Kashmiri chronicle *Rājataraṅgiṇī*. *See* ḌHĀK, (1).

Gajde [gaida, gajdë, gajdy, gayda]. Single-reed BAGPIPE of eastern and south-eastern Europe and Asia Minor. The term is related to GAITA, the name used in Spain (where it originated), and GHAYṬA (a Middle Eastern oboe); it derives from the Gothic *gait* or *ghaid* ('goat') and refers to the goatskin used for the bag. In southeast Europe sheepskin may also be used. The instrument is widely played in celebrations (weddings etc), as an accompaniment to dancing, often in small ensembles or in combination with a frame drum.

(a)

1. (a) Gajde (bellows-blown bagpipes) from Pančevo,
Yugoslavia; (b) gayda (mouth-blown bagpipes) from
Bulgaria

(b)

The instrument takes a variety of forms. In Yugoslavia it is usually mouth-blown and may have a single,
double or triple chanter. The single-chanter (or two-part)
instrument is characteristic of Macedonia, the north-east
and south-east parts of Serbia, including Kosovo; it exists
in two sizes. The double-chanter *gajde* is used in other
parts of Serbia, Vojvodina (where bellows may replace
the blowpipe; see fig.1a) and parts of Croatia. The *gajde*
with triple chanter is also known in Slavonia (Croatia);
one of the three chanter pipes serves as a drone, three
octaves above the low drone. The instrument is also
known as the *dude*.

In eastern Albania the *gajdë* is a single-chanter instrument. In Slovakia and Moravia, and the Beskid Śląski
region of Poland, the *gajdy* is bellows-blown; the
single-chanter type prevails in Poland, the double in
Slovakia, where a type with a pair of small supplementary drones is also known. Common tunings, with an
E♭ drone, are *b♭–d(♭)'–e♭'–f'–g'–a♭'–b♭'* and *b♭–e♭'–
f'–g'–a♭'–b♭'–c''*. The Bulgarian *gayda* or *gaida* (see
fig.1b) has a single chanter and is made in three sizes,
of which the Rhodopian *kaba* is the largest and is used
to accompany male voices; a double-chanter instrument
was formerly used in eastern Bulgaria. In Greece, the
gaida is a single-chanter instrument, used in Macedonia
and Thrace.

RADMILA PETROVIĆ, VERGILIJ ATANASSOV

Gajo (It.). *See* GAI.

Gakókwé. Bell of the Ewe people of Togo.

Gakubiwa. Four-string plucked lute of Japan. *See* BIWA,
§2.

Gakudaiko. General term for the large, suspended,
shallow-bodied drums *dadaiko*, *tsuridaiko* and *ninaidaiko* of the Japanese gagaku (court music) (*gaku*:
'music'; *daiko/taiko*: generic term for drums). More
commonly it is used to denote only the *tsuridaiko*, or
the *hiradaiko* of *geza* music when it imitates the *tsuridaiko*.

DAVID W. HUGHES

Gakusō. Scholarly term for the long zither (*see* KOTO,
§1) used in the Japanese gagaku (court music) (*gaku*:
'music'; *sō*: a zither). The *gakusō* was one of the main
melody instruments when it was imported from China
but now has a primarily rhythmic function, mostly playing one of two short patterns (*hayagaki* and *shizugaki*),
each of which ends on a primary melody pitch. These
patterns are frequently used in compositions for popular
koto (*zokusō*) in passages intended to evoke the feeling of court music (for music which closely imitates
shizugaki, *see* KOTO, ex.5, the second koto part). For
illustration *see* ZITHER, fig.1g.

DAVID W. HUGHES

Galdyama [gald'ama]. Five-string arched harp of the
Kotoko people around the Logone river in Chad and
north Cameroon. Its wooden soundbox is completely
covered with cowhide and the end opposite to the neck
is slightly concave. The strings are attached to the neck
by pegs, to which are fixed metal bells called *tyaotyao*

('earrings'). The instrument is placed horizontally on the ground for playing, like the DILLI harp of the Masa people. Three sizes of *galdyama* are played in an ensemble, together forming a pentatonic scale with a range of an 11th. If only two harps are played, the middle-sized harp is left out. The largest harp is the leader and the smallest the *kolo* ('accompanist'); the third is described simply as *direndana* ('in the middle'). These instruments are played only by men. The leader of the musicians is responsible for tuning the three harps, starting from the central string of the largest harp (which he plays himself). They participate in ceremonies associated with spirits and possession, with a *kwashi* (water-drum) played by one woman, and women's singing. They also play for entertainment. The anthropomorphic symbolism of the instrument is evident in the names for parts of the instrument: the neck is called the head, the sound-box the stomach and the soundholes the eyes.

In some Kotoko communities these harps are called *gundi*, in which case the *galdyama* is a three-string lute; *see* GULOM.

MONIQUE BRANDILY

Galizona [gallichone]. *See* COLASCIONE.

Galo. End-blown conical animal-horn flute of the Dongo people of Zaïre (*LaurentyA*, 300).

Galoubet. A three-holed pipe of the PIPE AND TABOR ensemble. It is of Provençal origin, and the name probably derives from an Old Provençal verb, *galaubar*, meaning 'to play magnificently'. It was used to accompany dancing throughout the Middle Ages. Elsewhere it was known as a *flute à trois trous* or *flutet*, but the term 'galoubet' (and its colloquial variant *jombarde*) came into more general use during the 18th century. The *galoubet* was made of wood, usually boxwood, and was about 30 cm long with two front holes and a rear thumb-hole. It had a very narrow cylindrical bore, and was pitched in D. The player held it in the right hand alone, while the left hand played a string drum such as the TAMBOURIN DE BÉARN. There is a *galoubet* in the Victoria and Albert Museum, London.

BIBLIOGRAPHY
A. Jacquot: *Dictionnaire pratique et raisonné des instruments de musique anciens et modernes* (Paris, 1886)
Eighteenth-century Musical Instruments: France and Britain (London, 1973) [Victoria and Albert Museum exhibition catalogue]
D. P. Charlton: *Orchestration and Orchestral Practice in Paris, 1789 to 1810* (diss., U. of Cambridge, 1973)

MARY CYR

Galundhang. Log XYLOPHONE, with five keys, of Madura, Indonesia.

Gamakhas [!gamakha:s]. Unbraced MUSICAL BOW, with separate resonator, of the Bergdama people of south-western Africa. It consists of a simple bow with a string of sinew. One end rests on a hollow wooden block, and the other against the player's chin. The string is plucked with the right forefinger, and a second performer may tap the lower part of the string with a stick. Pitch is changed through altering the tension of the string by bending the stave with the left hand. Similar musical bows of southern Africa are the Tswana *sekokwane* and the Khoikhoi *khas*. See *KirbyMISA*, 214.

DAVID K. RYCROFT

Gamalag. *See* GANBAG.

Gamalan. *See* TABUHAN.

Gamba. (1) *See* VIOL and VIOLA DA GAMBA.
(2) An ORGAN STOP (*Geigen, Viola da Gamba*).

Gambang [gambang kayu]. Wooden or bamboo trough XYLOPHONE used in various types of Indonesian orchestra. In Central Java, it is about 120 cm long and consists of 16 to 21 wooden keys laid stepwise in pitch order on twined rattan or cloth and kept in place by metal pins (fig.1). The range of the instrument varies from two and a half to more than three octaves. It is played with both hands using two disc-shaped padded mallets. The playing style has a high density and elaborate melodic embellishments (*see* IMPROVISATION, §II, 1).

1. Gambang (trough xylophone) of the Central Javanese gamelan (Museum of Wayang, Jakarta)

A complete gamelan (*gamelan seprangkat*) has three *gambang*, tuned to the anhemitonic pentatonic *slendro*, the hemitonic pentatonic *pelog patet bem* (based on tones 1, 2, 3, 5 and 6) and the hemitonic pentatonic *pelog patet barang* (based on tones 2, 3, 5, 6 and 7); *see* GAMELAN, §4. Each *gambang* ranges from pitch 6 of the second octave (6^2) to pitch 5 of the sixth octave of the gamelan (5^6). The *pelog barang gambang* excludes the pitches *pelog* (4) and *bem* (1), while the *pelog bem gambang* excludes the pitches *pelog* (4) and *barang* (7). Some gamelan have only one *pelog gambang* with four 'extra' keys. If the *gambang* contains the pitch *bem* in different octaves, its 'extra' keys are different octaves of the pitch *barang*. If the pitch *barang* predominates in a composition then all the *bem* keys are physically replaced by *barang* keys, and vice versa; this type of *gambang* is called *gambang sorogan*. Because the keys of the *gambang* merely rest on the resonator, key exchanges are easy.

An archaic multi-octave variety, the *gambang gangsa*, has bronze keys (*gangsa*: 'bronze'). It is found in a ritual gamelan at the Surakarta courts but is rarely played; it has been replaced in the gamelan by the single-octave *saron*. A rustic bamboo-key version is found in some areas; in West Java it consists of 20 keys and has a range of four octaves (*see also* XYLOPHONE, §1).

In Bali, a *gambang* with 14 bamboo keys and a range of two octaves is used for sacred music during cremation rites. The keys are not placed in sequential pitch order but arranged to facilitate interlocking (dovetailing) with their partners; they are played with forked hammers (fig.2). A five-key *gambang* is found in the east

2. *Gambang ensemble at Tabanan village, Bali, with (left to right) two saron (metallophones) and four gambang (trough xylophones)*

coast area of North Sumatra. It is played by two women, one being the leader (*pamulu*) and the other the follower (*panirka*), and was formerly used at weddings and by girls calling their fiancés.

BIBLIOGRAPHY
J. Kunst: *De toonkunst van Java* (The Hague, 1934; Eng. trans., rev. 2/1949, enlarged 3/1973)
C. McPhee: *Music in Bali* (New Haven and London, 1966/*R*1976)
M. Kartomi: 'The Angkola People of Sumatra', BM 30L 2568 [disc notes]
HARDJA SUSILO, ERNST HEINS, MARGARET KARTOMI

Gambangan. Leg XYLOPHONE, with three keys, of Central Java. It is a children's instrument.

Gambang calung. Javanese XYLOPHONE. *See* CALUNG.

Gambang gangsa ('bronze xylophone'). (1) Ancient multi-octave METALLOPHONE of Java. *See* GAMBANG.
(2) Metallophone of the northern states of West Malaysia. It consists of a number of iron bars, usually five, held over a boat-shaped wooden resonator, and is played with a wooden beater. This *gambang* is used in the *wayang kulit* (shadow-puppet theatre) ensemble.

Gambang kayu ('wooden xylophone'). *See* GAMBANG.

Gambang kromong. Ensemble used in Jakarta, Indonesia, to accompany *lenong* (folk dramas) and *cokek* (lively dance parties held at Chinese weddings), and formerly *gambang rancak* (impromptu quatrain singing). The ensemble now consists of a *gambang* (xylophone), a *kromong* (high-pitched gong-chime), one or two Chinese spike fiddles, a Chinese transverse flute and Sundanese *gendang* (drum), *kecrek* (metal rattle plates) and gongs. Its music originated in Jakarta among Chinese immigrants who arrived there from the 16th century onwards, but it is now popular among many ethnic groups in the city.

Gambang tali. *See* KERTOK BULU.

Gambare. Plucked lute of the Soninke people of Mali. *See* GURMI.

Gambe (Ger.). VIOL.

Gambili. MUSICAL BOW, with a separate gourd resonator, of the Lobo, Andedeme and Timogia peoples of Zaïre; it is also known as *kambili* and *kumbili* (*LaurentyC*, 113). *See* KITINGBI.

Gambra. Single-string plucked lute of Mauritania. *See also* GUINBRI.

Gambus. Wooden short-necked lute, probably of Middle Eastern origin, found in Muslim areas of Sumatra, Java, Sulawesi and other parts of Indonesia, and in Malaysia. Its pear-shaped body has a decorated soundhole and tapers to form the neck, ending in a receding pegbox. The lowest string of the *gambus* in West Sumatra is tuned approximately to G, and there is a course of two strings tuned to A, a single string tuned to B, and three courses tuned to D, A and E. The instrument is plucked with a feather quill (see illustration) or the fingernails. It is used for solo instrumental music, to accompany a singer, and in the *orkes gambus* (*gambus*

Gambus (short-necked lute) player, Minangkabau, Padang, West Sumatra, 1976

orchestra). It resembles the Middle Eastern '*ūd*; *see* QANBŪS.

In Lampung province, Sumatra, the *gambus Lampung* has a pear-shaped body made from jackfruit wood, with a soundtable of goatskin. It has four pairs of strings called, in descending order of pitch, *kuwin*, *genda*, *goro* and *tala*; they were formerly made of pineapple fibre but now nylon is used. The instrument is about 75 cm long. It is plucked, either solo or to accompany a singer in an ensemble. Sometimes imported *gambus* with six pairs of strings are used.

MARGARET J. KARTOMI

Gambusan. Ensemble, with a *gambus* (plucked lute) as the leading instrument, found in many Muslim areas of Indonesia and Malaysia. On the north coast of Java (e.g. in Pekalongan) the ensemble may consist of a *gambus*, four *biola* (violins), a *seruling* (flute), *klarinet*, *akordion*, a *bas* (double bass), four *tambring* or *marwas* (small frame drums, some with jingles), a *ketipung* (small double-headed drum) and several *nasyidah* (female singers). A smaller, more traditional ensemble consists of four *tambring*, a *seruling* and a *ketipung*. The ensemble plays religious and love songs at weddings and other celebrations.

MARGARET J. KARTOMI

Gambusi. *See* GABUSI.

Gambyong. GONG-CHIME of Central Java used in the *gamelan carabelen*.

GAME [Générateur automatique de musique électronique] (Fr.: 'automatic electronic music generator'). A composition machine developed by the Belgian composer Léo Küpper (*b* Nidrum, 16 April 1935) in Brussels between 1968 and 1978. The first version was completed in 1971. The system is used in concerts and installations and also forms the basis of Küpper's electronic music studio in Brussels, the Studio de Recherches et de Structurations Electroniques Auditives. The GAME consists of 60 separate modules, based on a combination of analogue and digital techniques, which can be freely selected and combined. The modules are programmed in an upright console approximately 4 × 2 metres by making a large number of patchcord interconnections, so that the surface of the console is festooned with cables. Most of the controls operated during a performance are placed in front of the console.

GAME installations, some of which have been set up for as long as a month, are designed primarily to interact with members of the public, who stimulate the operation of the system by means of speech and other sounds; the sounds are analysed digitally and converted into variations in voltage, which elicit responses from the system. Between 100 and 200 loudspeakers are mounted according to a carefully planned pattern on a structure of scaffolding in the shape of half a dome. Two auxiliary constructions may be added: Muvis (*musique visible*, 1978), a series of 20 light-columns that are responsive to frequency, and *Automates sonores*, small programmable boxes that modify sounds fed into them from individual microphones.

BIBLIOGRAPHY

L. Küpper: 'Elaboration de musique électronique à partir d'un ordinateur musical; Tendance à l'automatisation de la composition; Génération d'un monde sonore autonome par interstimulations d'automates sonores', *Faire*, nos.2–3 (1975), 31, 199

HUGH DAVIES

Gamelan. A term used for various ensembles or orchestras in Java, Bali, Madura and other areas where Javanese and Balinese have settled (including parts of Sulawesi, Kalimantan, Sumatra, Surinam and Malaysia); some villages and courts in West Malaysia, especially Kelantan and Trengganu, have an independent gamelan tradition. Instruments are made of bronze, iron, wood or bamboo, and a gamelan may include various combinations of tuned bossed gongs, bossed gong-chimes, keyed metallophones, xylophones, drums, bowed and plucked strings, flute or oboe, small cymbals and solo or choral singers (see fig.1). The present article deals with gamelan as ensembles; for information on individual instruments see separate entries. An alphabetical list of the ensembles mentioned will be found at the end of the article.

1. History. 2. Social functions. 3. Distribution. 4. Tuning systems. 5. Timbre and style. 6. Instrumentation: (i) Central Java (ii) West Java (iii) East Java (iv) Bali. 7. Archaic gamelan in Java and Bali. 8. Related ensembles in South-east Asia.

1. HISTORY. An accurate history of gamelan awaits an adequate accumulation of sources. Bronze kettledrums of the Dongson culture of the 3rd and 2nd centuries BC found in Sumatra, Java, Bali and other parts of Southeast Asia suggest that a high level of workmanship in metal had been reached by that period and that bronze and other metal instruments in the region are very old. However, there is no evidence of a direct line of development between these bronze drums and the bronze instruments of gamelan and related orchestras. Perishable instruments made of wood, leather and bamboo have also presumably existed in South-east Asia since ancient times, but there is no direct evidence of this.

Kunst (1927) accumulated a number of archaeological, iconographical and literary sources proving the existence of prototypes of most Javanese and Balinese gamelan instruments in the latter part of the 1st millenium AD or the early part of the 2nd. For example, xylophones, bamboo flutes and double-headed drums are depicted in reliefs on the 9th-century Borobudur temple in central Java. Other important sources include the Kaḍiri-period carvings in Java (1043–1222), reliefs on the 14th-century Caṇḍi Panataran and a number of Old Javanese literary texts. The *Rāmāyaṇa*, probably dating from the end of the 1st or the early 2nd millennium AD, uses the word 'gong' and other musical terms.

The sources suggest that a distinction has long been made between loud-sounding and soft-sounding gamelan. The former consisted of drums, gongs, oboes and the like and were used for outdoor occasions such as processions and trance ceremonies, as they still are today. The latter included soft metallophones, xylophones and the flute and were reserved largely for indoor occasions. Kunst (1934) postulated that loud and soft ensembles were combined into large gamelan in Java from about the 16th century. Speculations by him and other scholars about some historical implications of archaic Javanese gamelan await the discovery of convincing data, as do theories about which of the two major tuning systems, *pelog* ('seven-note') and *slendro* ('five-note') came first.

Resemblances between gamelan and similar ensembles in West Java, Central Java, East Java, Bali and other parts of the region may be explained by a common Central and East Javanese origin, as has been suggested, but they are more likely to have resulted from con-

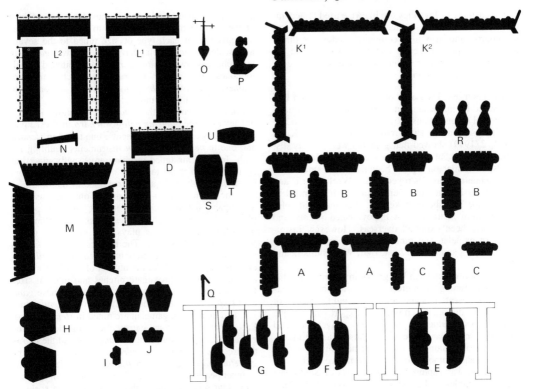

1. Ground plan of a typical Central Javanese gamelan showing positions of instruments arranged in functional groups:

One-octave metallophones
  (A–C = saron)
  A   demung
  B   barung or rincik
  C   panerus or peking
  D   slenṭem
Suspended gongs
  E   gong ageng
  F   gong suwuk or siyem
  G   kempul
Horizontal gongs
  H   kenong
  I   keṭuk
  J   kempyang

Gong-chimes (bonang)
  K^1 barung
  K^2 panerus
Multi-octave metallophones
  (gender)
  L^1 barung
  L^2 panerus
Xylophone
  M   gambang
Zither
  N   siter
Spike fiddle
  O   rebab

Female solo singer
  P   pesinden
End-blown flute
  Q   suling
Choir
  R   gerong
Double-headed drums
  S   kendang gending
  T   kendang ketipung
  U   kendang batangan or ciblon

stant contact over the centuries between the changing centres of power in the southern part of South-east Asia. Some Balinese orchestras appear to be a direct continuation of 15th-century Hindu-Javanese orchestras brought to Bali by refugees from the Majapahit kingdom in the early 16th century. Some Sundanese gamelan in West Java are also direct descendants of orchestras moved there from Central Java after the fall of the Hindu-Sundanese kingdom of Pajajaran in 1579.

The combination in Java of two gamelan, one tuned in *slendro* and the other in *pelog* (see §4), seems to have become widespread during the second half of the 19th century with the development of some forms of musical theatre, mostly in the courts. The proximity of the two sets of instruments facilitates quick changes from pieces in one tonality to pieces in the other. However, separate *slendro* and *pelog* orchestras are still found; *slendro* ensembles only are used in most Central Javanese shadow puppet theatre performances, following a traditional practice over the centuries.

2. SOCIAL FUNCTIONS. Gamelan and related ensembles have traditionally been used to accompany religious rites and dances which have survived from pre-Muslim times (before about the 15th century AD). The instruments are therefore shown respect; no-one may walk over them and special offerings of incense are made before an ensemble is played. In Java a gamelan is often given a revered name of its own. The gamelan's main function is still to accompany religious or ceremonial rituals, held chiefly in the temples in Bali and in village or court environments in Java, Sumatra and elsewhere. Gamelan are played in rain-inducing ceremonies in Central Javanese ricefields, in trance ceremonies such as *reyog* in East Java, and for erotic dances such as the *lengger* in Java and the *ronggeng* in Java and Sumatra. They are also played to welcome guests at weddings and other ceremonies, although cheaper recorded music has often been substituted in recent times.

Gamelan in Bali are used primarily to accompany dance and dance-drama on religious and (in recent times) secular occasions. In Java they are likewise used to accompany dance and dance-dramas in both the villages and the courts, and also to accompany shadow or three-dimensional puppet theatre and to provide music for contemplative listening (*klenengan*), sometimes at concerts or similar gatherings.

3. DISTRIBUTION. Thousands of gamelan in Java and Bali are owned by puppeteers and other private individuals, communal organizations, government offices, radio and television stations, theatres, museums and palaces. Kunst (1934, 2/1949) showed that gamelan were widely distributed throughout the villages and towns of Java in the 1930s; no similar survey has been published since then. Some gamelan were destroyed during World War II and the war for Indonesian independence, which ended in 1949; some have been broken up since then and sold, instrument by instrument, by impoverished owners; and some have been exported overseas. However, instruments of gamelan and other orchestras are still being made in West and Central Java, Bali, West Sumatra and elsewhere.

The export of gamelan has grown in recent years due to the burgeoning of interest in them among overseas educators, researchers and composers and the policy of Indonesian diplomatic missions. Export of antique gamelan is forbidden by law. Many universities and museums in Holland, the USA, Australia, Germany, Japan, Great Britain and elsewhere now own gamelan and teach and promote gamelan performance. Debussy's imagination was captured by the sounds of South-east Asian ensembles at the Exposition Universelle in Paris in 1889, and composers since then have increasingly incorporated musical ideas derived from gamelan and other Asian ensembles into their works. Many Indonesian embassies overseas promote the knowledge of Javanese culture by exposing their visitors to Javanese gamelan, and state universities throughout West Malaysia have purchased gamelan and promote their performance. Advanced performance in Indonesia is taught primarily in the conservatories and academies of music and dance in Denpasar, Bandung, Jakarta, Padang Panjang, Surakarta, Ujung Pandang and Yogyakarta. Some universities in Indonesia also promote traditional orchestras. In the University of North Sumatra, Medan, the first department of ethnomusicology in Indonesia was opened in 1977, and there the performance and theory of various Sumatran ensembles and Javanese gamelan is taught.

4. TUNING SYSTEMS. There are no 'correct' standard tunings for gamelan, and no two gamelan are tuned exactly alike. However, most modern gamelan are tuned in either an anhemitonic five-note system or a hemitonic seven-note system. The former is called *slendro* in Central and East Java, *salendro* in West Java, and *saih gender wayang* in Bali; the latter is called *pelog* in Central and East Java, *pelog* or *pelog degung* in West Java, and *saih pitu* ('row of seven') in Bali. Rarely are all seven notes of the *pelog*-type scale used in a piece, but rather five-note modal scales derived from the seven available. In Central Java both hemitonic and anhemitonic systems are divided into three *patet* (modes). The *slendro* modes (*nem*, *sångå* and *manyurå*) all use the same five basic notes, but one of the *pelog* modes (*barang*) uses a different set (2 3 5 6 7) from the other two (*nem* and *limå*, using notes 1 2 3 5 6). Thus, while gamelan tuned in *slendro* usually include only one of each type or size of

instrument, those tuned in *pelog* must have two of each of the instruments that are tuned to a five-note scale, but only one of each type or size tuned to the seven-note scale. *Pelog* gamelan have therefore two *gambang* (xylophones), two *gender barung* (low-pitched metallophones), two *gender panerus* (high-pitched metallophones) and two *celempung* (zithers) in order to accommodate the two modal tunings.

Complete gamelan (the *gamelan seprangkat* in Central Java and the *gamelan pelog-salendro* in West Java) consist of two sets of instruments, one tuned in *slendro* and one in *pelog,* with a few instruments doubling for both. Instruments tuned in *pelog* are usually placed at right angles to those tuned in *slendro*, so that players can move easily and quickly from one to the other.

Gamelan in *slendro*-type tunings only are used to accompany *wayang purwa* ('ancient' shadow puppet plays) in Central Java and *wayang golek purwa* ('ancient' three-dimensional puppet plays) and *sandiwara* (plays with music) in West Java. The Balinese *wayang kulit* is also accompanied by instruments tuned in the *saih gender wayang* (the scale of the quartet of *gender* for *wayang* theatre; for approximate pitches and interval sizes in cents, see ex.1). The archaic Central Javanese *gamelan kodok ngorek* has a basically two-note *slendro* tuning, and many rural gamelan are tuned in *slendro*. Most East Javanese traditional pieces, including those for the *gamelan asli jawa timur,* the *wayang kulit* and the *ludruk* theatre, are played on *slendro* orchestras, as are the *gamelan angklung* and *gamelan gandrung* pieces of the Osinger people in East Java. *Saih angklung*, an anhemitonic four-note version of the *gender wayang* scale, is used for the *gamelan angklung* in Bali. Some *gamelan arja* in Bali are tuned in anhemitonic four- or five-note scales which resemble those of the *gender* quartet.

Ex.1 *Saih gender wayang* scale

Gamelan in *pelog* tunings only are found in some rural parts of Central and East Java, for example the *gamelan prajuritan* of the mountainous Kopeng area. Pieces played in the almost extinct *wayang gedog* (drama enacting stories of the hero Panji) are almost always in *pelog.* Most archaic gamelan, including the three-note *gamelan munggang,* the four- or six-note *gamelan carabalen* and the seven-note *gamelan sekati,* are in *pelog.* In West Java seven-note *pelog* tunings are rare, but the *gamelan degung* and the *gamelan renteng* use two different types of five-note *pelog* tunings.

Ex.2 *Selisir* scale

Most Balinese gamelan, including the archaic *gamelan luang,* are tuned to the *saih pitu* system, which incorporates many modal scales based on the five main and two auxiliary pitches in the *gamelan gambang* and *gamelan gambuh.* The most popular derivation is a five-note scale called *selisir,* used for such orchestras as the *gamelan gong gede, gamelan gong kebyar* and *gamelan*

2. *Central Javanese gamelan seprangkat, Jakarta, 1977: on the platform (left to right), kenong (horizontal gongs), pairs of gong siyem and gong ageng (large suspended gongs, back), kempul (suspended gongs, centre), ketuk and kempyang (small horizontal gongs, front), four saron (metallophones); centre row (front to back), three celempung (zithers), slentem (metallophone), kendang ciblon, kendang ketipung, kendang gending (double-headed drums); right-hand row (front to back), one gambang (xylophone), four gender (metallophones), bonang (gong-chimes), two rebab (spike fiddles)*

pelegongan, and for some pieces of the *gamelan arja*. The *selisir* scale is derived from the *gamelan gambuh* tuning, but omits the auxiliary pitches; its approximate pitches and interval sizes in cents are shown in ex.2.

Like those of the archaic Central Javanese gamelan, the tunings of the numerous related ensembles in other parts of South-east Asia are extremely varied. Various pentatonic and heptatonic scales are used, together with three- and four-note scales and others with varying intervallic structures. In Sumatra heptatonic scales are the norm in many coastal areas, and pentatonic, four-note, three-note and other scales are often typical of inland areas. As in Java and Bali, the concept of absolute pitch is not relevant, and in some areas the same type of ensemble may vary in tuning from village to village. A complete picture awaits detailed research in all the relevant regions.

It is customary, following the *kepatihan* ('cipher') notation normally used, to represent *pelog* pitches by numbers 1 to 7 and *slendro* pitches by numbers 1, 2, 3, 5 and 6 (the number 4 is not used in *slendro* notation). A dot placed above a number indicates an upper octave, and one below a lower octave. In discussing the compass of instruments superscript numbers are used to indicate the particular octave of the gamelan. Thus, 6^2 indicates pitch 6 in the second (i.e. second-lowest) octave.

5. TIMBRE AND STYLE. The different types of gamelan and related ensembles are numerous and the sounds they produce vary a great deal in character. The sound quality of the large Central Javanese gamelan is dominated by the resonance of its many gongs, gong-chimes and keyed metallophones, most of which need to be damped by the player soon after being beaten. This resonance is contrasted with the soft double-octave or two-part pattering of the xylophones, the sharp and the soft timbres of the drums, and the penetrating melodic lines of the bowed string instrument, flute and vocalists. Pieces normally begin with a short introduction, perhaps on a bowed string instrument or gong-chime, during which the drummer enters and steadies the tempo, preparing for the first gong stroke, upon which most of the other instruments of the orchestra enter and begin the piece proper. The drummer gives rhythmic signals to change tempo. For example, when he wishes to end the piece he gives a rhythmic signal commanding the whole orchestra gradually to slow down, preparatory to the last delayed stroke on the big gong. The gamelan repertory is divided by the Javanese into 'great works', 'middling works' and 'small works'; the last range from bright pieces with short *gongan* (periods between gong strokes), such as might be used to welcome guests at a celebration, to relatively stately, serious pieces with longer *gongan*. The 'great works' have long *gongan* of perhaps 64, 132 or even as many as 1024 slow beats.

The most popular types of Balinese orchestras, the *gamelan gong gede* and *gamelan gong kebyar*, have a much more brilliantly percussive sound than the Javanese gamelan, with frequent metallic clashes on the cymbals, prominent virtuoso drumming, contrasting orchestration of phrases and often frequent changes of tempo and dynamics. Balinese performances, unlike those in Java, are normally carefully rehearsed, as they require precise ensemble. Not all Balinese gamelan are loud and virtuoso, however; some, such as the *gamelan semar pegulingan*, are relatively soft and delicate in sound.

The sound of Sundanese gamelan also ranges from the loud and dynamic to the soft and tranquil. The large orchestras normally comprise fewer instruments than their Central Javanese counterparts and have a thinner ensemble sound and greater clarity of texture; they often specialize in prominent virtuoso drumming. Pieces for *gamelan degung*, on the other hand, are mostly softer and more delicate in sound.

6. INSTRUMENTATION.

(i) Central Java. A 'complete' gamelan, called *gamelan seprangkat* (or *gamelan slendro-pelog*; see fig.2),

comprises two sets of instruments, one tuned in the *slendro* system and the other in the *pelog* system (see §4). Each is complete in itself and has a total range of seven octaves (about 40 to 2200 cycles per second). Normally the two tuning systems have one note in common: *tumbuk* ('to collide').

A complete gamelan includes three sizes of *saron* (one-octave slab metallophone), of which there are usually four of the middle size (*saron barung*) and one or two of the largest size (*saron demung*), three sizes of *bonang* (double-row gong-chimes), a *gambang* (20-key trough xylophone), two sizes of *gender* (2½-octave metallophone with thin keys suspended over resonating tubes) and the deeper-toned *slentem* or *gender panembung* (similar in construction to the *gender* but with a range of one octave only). A set of *kenong* (large single boxed gongs), a *ketuk* (single boxed gong) and the *kempyang* (pair of small boxed gongs) are used only in *pelog* pieces and the *engkuk-kemong* (small suspended gongs) in *slendro* pieces. All the other instruments or instrument sets are used in pairs, one for each scale, except in the case of the *gambang* and the *gender*, where there are three each.

The complete gamelan includes also three sizes of vertically suspended gongs, the *kempul* being the highest-pitched; there may be as many as twelve, tuned in *pelog* and *slendro*. There are three to nine *gong suwukan* (or *gong siyem*, an octave lower than the *kempul*) and two *gong ageng* (large single gongs). The string instruments are the *rebab* (two-string spike fiddle), the *celempung* (zither) and the *siter* (small zither). The only wind instrument is the *suling* (bamboo flute). There are three sizes of *kendang* (double-headed laced drum) and *bedug* (double-headed barrel-shaped drum). Some additional instruments, either obsolete or rarely used, are the *kemanak* (a pair of banana-shaped bronze handbells), the *slento* (a *saron demung* with a boss on each key) and a *gambang gangsa* ('bronze gambang'). A female vocalist (*pesinden*) and choral group (*gerongan*) may be added to the ensemble.

The complete gamelan in Central Java belongs primarily in court and urban contexts, but a number of small village ensembles are also referred to locally as gamelan. One such rural ensemble in the Banyumas area is the *gamelan ebeg*, consisting of *selompret* (oboe), *saron wesi* ('iron *saron*'), gongs and drums; it is used to accompany hobby-horse trance dancing which in other areas is also called *jaran kepang*, *kuda kepang*, *kuda lumping* or *jatilan*. The *gamelan jaran kepang* of Central and East Java is similarly constituted. Another ensemble of the Banyumas area is the *gamelan jemblung*, consisting of tuned bamboo idiophones; the two melody instruments are bamboo xylophones, a bamboo trumpet serves as a gong and another piece of bamboo, open at the ends but closed in the middle by the node, serves as a *kendang*. Also made up mainly of bamboo instruments is the small *gamelan bumbung* ('bamboo gamelan') in the rural areas in and around Kediri and also in Surakarta and Yogyakarta; it usually consists of stick-beaten bamboo zithers, a bamboo xylophone and a *kendang*.

A small ensemble of small bossed gongs and drums (*gamelan prajuritan*) accompanies the *prajuritan* folk drama in eastern parts of Central Java and in East Java; this relates the story of the mythical battle fought between the Majapahit and Blambangan kingdoms in the 15th century. Also from Central and East Java was the gam-

elan ketoprak which accompanied performances of the *ketoprak* dance-drama. It originated in the 1920s in Surakarta and consisted of wooden instruments: three slit-drums, a *lesung* (log-drum) and a *suling*. The instrumentation was later radically altered, gongs and drums replacing the wooden percussion, and the drama is now accompanied in the theatre by a common gamelan. (For the archaic *gamelan carabalen*, *gamelan kodok ngorek* and *gamelan munggang* of Central Java see §7.)

(ii) West Java. In Sundanese-speaking areas of West Java the main orchestras are the *gamelan degung*, the *gamelan renteng*, the *gamelan salendro* and the *gamelan pelog-salendro*. The first of these was formerly associated with courts and the second with villages, but the Kanoman court in Cirebon has a *gamelan renteng*; the associations are clearly not exclusive. The *gamelan salendro* is used for *wayang golek* (puppet theatre), *sandiwara* (plays with music) and dance, and the *gamelan pelog-salendro* for plays and dance. The instrumentarium of each orchestra varies, but a *gamelan degung* may consist of a *bonang*, a *rincik* or *cempres* (three-octave keyed metallophones), one or two single-octave *saron*, a *jengglong* (set of bossed gongs, either suspended or lying in crossed cords in a frame), a *goöng* (large gong), a pair of *gendang* (double-headed drums) and a *suling degung* (small bamboo flute).

The *gamelan renteng* is used for harvest purification rituals, communal gatherings and, in some areas, to accompany *kuda lumping* (hobby-horse trance dancing). In Lebukwangi the ensemble comprises a U-shaped *renteng* (gong-chime), a *rebab*, a *suling*, a *saron* (multi-octave eleven-keyed metallophone), *kecrek* (cymbals), *kempul* or *jengglong* or *kenong*, and one or two *goöng*. In Klayan, Cirebon, a hobby-horse trance ensemble comprises an L-shaped *renteng*, a *selompret*, *kecrek*, a *kenong*, two *ketuk*, three *kebluk* (horizontal bossed gongs in a frame), a pair of *goöng* and a *kendang* and *ketipung* (large and small drums).

While the flute and oboe play the main melodic role in the *degung* and *renteng* orchestras respectively, the *rebab* (spike fiddle) and *pesinden* (female vocalist) are prominent in the *gamelan salendro* and *gamelan pelog-salendro*, together with the *gambang*. A small *gamelan salendro* may in addition include two *saron*, a *bonang*, a *kempul*, a *goöng* and two or three *kendang*, while a large *gamelan salendro* may add two more *saron* (*peking* and *panerus*), a *slentem* and two more gong-chimes (*rincik* and *jengglong*). A *gamelan pelog-salendro* often omits the *kenong* and *ketuk* and has only one *bonang*, but has three *saron*, one *kempul*, one *goöng* and one *kecrek*. The orchestra accompanies dance-dramas and plays concert pieces.

(iii) East Java. The *halus* ('refined') gamelan centring on the cities of Surabaya and Majakerta in the eastern part of East Java is called *gamelan asli jawa timur* (or *gamelan surabaya*). Although its instrumentarium is similar to a large Central Javanese gamelan, its musical style, performing practice, repertory and *patet* (modal) system are different. In the extreme eastern part of East Java, among the Osinger people of Banyuwangi Regency, two styles of *slendro*-tuned *gamelan angklung* are found. The 'old style' ensemble (*gamelan bali-balian*) has one or two pairs of *angklung* (bamboo xylophone), one pair of *slentem*, two pairs of *saron barung*, two

3. Gamelan reyog in Ponorogo, East Java, 1963, with (front, left to right) ketipung (double-headed drum), selom-pret (oboe), kempul (suspended gong), ketuk (small suspended gong); and (back, left to right) kendang (large double-headed drum), two angklung (bamboo rattles)

pairs of *saron panerus*, one *kendang*, one or two *suling* and one *gong agung* ('great gong'). The 'new style' ensemble (*angklung banyuwangi*) is smaller and more intimate, using at least one pair of *angklung*, a *suling*, a *kloncing* (triangle), a *gong agung* and a male or female singer. The Osinger people also play the *gamelan gandrung*, which uses a *slendro* tuning. It comprises two *biola* (violins), a *kendang*, a *ketipung*, two *kenong* (or one *kenong* and one *ketuk*), a *kloncing* and a *gong agung*. It takes its name from the young girl whose dancing and singing it accompanies, and is used at important all-night functions such as wedding receptions.

In the Ponorogo area of East Java the *gamelan reyog* (fig.3) accompanies the popular folk drama, with hobby-horse dancing, called *reyog*. The gamelan may consist of *selompret*, two *angklung*, a *kendang* and *ketipung* (large and small double-headed drums), a *ketuk*, a *kenong* and a *kempul*. The *gamelan saronen* (or *gamelan tetet*) is the most widespread type of *gamelan kasar* ('coarse gamelan') in the eastern part of East Java and the offshore island of Madura (where it is called *gamelan kerapan sapi* because it accompanies the bull races known as *kerapan sapi*). The *saronen* (wooden oboe) is the principal, or only, melodic instrument; the others vary considerably, but may include large and small *ketuk* and *kendang*.

(iv) Bali. Balinese theatrical gamelan include the *gamelan gambuh*, notable for its use of *suling gambuh* (long flutes) and *rebab* rather than melodic percussion instruments; it includes also a pair of *kendang*, several gongs, a pair of *rincik* and a pair of *kangsi* (cymbals), a rack of bells and the *gumanak* (a struck copper or iron

cylinder). It uses the *selisir* scale. Another theatrical ensemble is the *gamelan arja*, using four- and five-note scales of both hemitonic and anhemitonic varieties, and consisting of three *suling*, two *guntang* (tube zithers), *kelenang* (small gong), a pair of *kendang* and a pair of *rincik*.

There exist in Bali various large ensembles more commonly referred to as *gong*. The *gamelan gong* (or *gamelan gong gede*; see fig.4, p.16) may consist of *gender jegogan*, *jublag* and *penyacah* (metallophones), *trompong pengarep* and *trompong barangan* (gong-chimes), *kendang wadon* and *kendang lanang* (double-headed 'female' and 'male' drums), *bende* (suspended gong), two *gong ageng* (*wadon* and *lanang*, suspended gongs), *kempur* (smaller suspended gongs) and *ceng-ceng* (cymbals). Once a court ensemble of about 40 instruments, it is now a village ensemble of some 25 instruments. About half of these are single-octave *gangsa* (*gender-* and *saron-*type metallophones) which play the nuclear melody in unison and octaves. The expanded melody is played on one or two *trompong*, and a four-kettle *reyong* is used for simple figuration. The modern development of the *gamelan gong*, the *gamelan gong kebyar*, is the most vigorously creative musical medium among contemporary Balinese musicians; it uses the *gamelan gong* repertory as well as its own continuously expanding one. Besides many of the instruments of the *gamelan gong*, the *kebyar* ensemble includes a *reyong* (set of 12 gong-chimes) on which musicians play melodic configurations. In North Bali a harder, more brilliant tone is preferred, and *saron* are used as metallophones in the *kebyar* ensemble, suitably adapted to accommodate bamboo resonators.

The *gamelan semar pegulingan* ('gamelan of the god of love') is a delicate-sounding gamelan (tuned to the *selisir* scale) whose instrumentarium resembles that of the *gamelan gong* but has no low-pitched *saron* or large cymbals; as a court gamelan it became rare, but has recently been revived. Even more delicate in timbre is the *gamelan pelegongan*, used to accompany the *legong* dance and other dances and dramas. It replaces the *trompong* with two pairs of 13-key *gender* and includes a pair of smaller drums. An inexpensive version of the *gamelan pelegongan* is the *gamelan pejogedan*, which replaces the metallophones with instruments with split-bamboo keys over bamboo tube resonators and the gong with two bronze slabs of slightly different pitch, struck simultaneously. It is known colloquially as *gamelan joged*. A similar soft-sounding ensemble is the *gamelan pejogedan bungbung*, with its group of flutes and bamboo tube resonators: this dates from about 1950 and is played by teenage boys.

The *gamelan bebonangan* (known also as *bonang* or *bebonang*) is a processional ensemble consisting of a pair of *gong ageng*, a pair of *ceng-ceng* and a pair of *kendang*. The *gamelan gegenggongan*, used for dance and musical performance, consists of *genggong* (bamboo jew's harps), *suling*, *kendang*, *guntang* and *ceng-ceng*. Finally, the *gamelan angklung* is a small Balinese ensemble used for temple festivals, processions and cremations. Besides the *angklung* from which its name derives, its instruments include the *reyong* (dumbbell-shaped gong-chime).

7. ARCHAIC GAMELAN IN JAVA AND BALI. Archaic ceremonial gamelan housed in the Central Javanese courts include the *gamelan carabalen* (tuned to a four- or six-note *pelog* scale) in which there are two gong-chimes called *bonang klenang* and *bonang gambyong*, drums called *kendang gending* and *kendang ketipung*, and a

gong ageng. Another archaic ensemble is the *gamelan kodok ngorek*, tuned to a basically two-note *slendro*-like scale and comprising a *saron demung*, a *rincik*, two *bonang klenang*, a *byong* ('bell tree'), *kempur*, *kenong japan* (gongs), *rojeh* (cymbals), *kendang gending*, *kendang ketipung* and *gong ageng*. The ensemble known as *gamelan munggang* (fig.5), like the *carabalen* and *kodok ngorek*, is thought to have originated in the Majapahit period (late 15th to early 16th centuries). It is tuned to a three-note *pelog* scale and consists of four gong-chimes each with three notes, *kenong japan*, a pair of *penontong* (suspended small gongs), *kendang gending*, *kendang ketipung*, *gong ageng* and a pair of *rojeh*. The instrumentation of the 16th-century *gamelan sekati* (*sekaten*), tuned to a seven-note *pelog* scale, is similar to that of the regular 'loud' gamelan (gongs, metal-keyed instruments, drums and gong-chimes) but with only one *bonang* (*bonang panembung*), a pair of *kempur* and a *bedug*; there is no *kendang* or *kempul*, and the lower octave of the *bonang* is used for *kenong* notes.

Archaic Balinese gamelan include the *gamelan caruk*, consisting of two *saron* and a *caruk* (bamboo xylophone); the *gamelan gambang*, comprising four *gambang* and one or two *saron*; the *gamelan luang*, comprising two *jegogan* (low-pitched metallophones), *caruk*, *trompong*, *kendang*, gong and cymbals; and the *gamelan selundeng*, distinguished by its inclusion of the *selundeng* (metallophone with eight iron keys). These ensembles are used mainly for ceremonies connected with death and cremation, and are so sacred that people are not permitted to see the instruments except on ceremonial occasions.

8. RELATED ENSEMBLES IN SOUTH-EAST ASIA. Gamelan are related in their instruments and musical qualities to most other ensembles throughout the southern part of South-

4. Gamelan gong gede: sacred ensemble at Gianjar, Bali, c1935, with (left and right sides, front to back) gender jegogan, jublag, penyacah (metallophones); centre (front to back), trompong pengarep, trompong barangan (gong-chimes), kendang wadon, kendang lanang (double-headed drums); back row (left to right), bende, gong wadon, gong lanang, kempur (suspended gongs); the musicians at the back are playing ceng-ceng (cymbals)

5. *Gamelan munggang at the Kraton of Yogyakarta, Central Java: back (left to right), kenong japan (horizontal gong), pair of rojeh (cymbals), pair of gong ageng (large suspended gongs), pair of penonţong (smaller suspended gongs); front (left to right), penuntung, kenḍang gending (double-headed drums), four bonang (gong-chimes)*

east Asia. Whether this is due to diffusion from one or from several sources it is not possible to say, although the high level of metal workmanship in Java since ancient times suggests that this island may have been a main source of diffusion of metal instruments. Most ensembles in the area consist of double-headed drums and gongs (or their substitutes), to which gong-chimes, wind and string instruments are often added. Gongs may be vertical (suspended) or horizontal; wind instruments are normally oboes or flutes; and strings are either bowed, as in the case of the *rebab* and *biola*, or plucked, as in the case of the *kacapi* and *celempung*. Less common instruments include xylophones, keyed metallophones and percussion bars. Solo or choral singing may be added to some ensembles, as in the Central Javanese gamelan and in the *alat-alat makyong* ensembles.

Ensembles comprising only drums and gongs include the *gamelan prajuritan* of Central Java, the *gendang bergung* in Riau and the *genrang dan gong* in the Buginese area of Sulawesi. Orchestras consisting essentially of drums, gongs and gong-chimes include the *kulintang* in the southern Philippines, the *gendang* in Pakpak Dairi, the *keromong* and *kelintang* in Jambi, the *kelittang* (*keromong* or *tabuhan*) in Lampung, the *keromongan* in south Sumatra, the *keromong duabelas* in Bengkulu, and the archaic Javanese gamelan (see §7). Drum, gong and wind or string ensembles are exemplified by the *gendang gung* in Serdang, the *nobat* in Riau and West Malaysia (with cymbals in the latter case), the type of *alat-alat makyong* found in East Malaysia, Riau and Kelantan, and the *gamelan reyog* in East Java (to which shaken idiophones are added). Larger examples of this ensemble type are the *genderang* in Pakpak Dairi, to which cymbals and two types of percussion plates are added, and the *gamelan gambuh* in Bali in which wind and string instruments occur with cymbals, a rack of bells, metallophones and a struck metal cylinder.

Ensembles combining drums, gongs, gong-chimes and wind are exemplified by the Mandailing *gondang* and *gordang* ensembles, the Serdang type of *alat-alat mak-*

yong ensemble (to which bamboo clappers are added), the *gendang gung* in Langkat, the *kelintang* in Bengkulu (to which a string instrument is added) and the *orkes lenong* in Jakarta (to which are added fiddle, xylophone, cymbals and metal-bar percussion). The *talempong* in West Sumatra minimally comprises drums and gong-chimes, but a wind instrument or gong may be added in some areas.

Ensembles called 'gamelan' usually include drums, vertical and horizontal gongs, gong-chimes, optional wind and string instruments, xylophones and keyed metallophones, with cymbals or percussion plates sometimes added (see §6) or certain combinations of these. The *gamelan Trengganu*, or JOGET GAMELAN, in West Malaysia comprises drums, gongs, gong-chimes, xylophones and keyed metallophones. In bamboo or wooden ensembles which do not possess drums or metal gongs, other instruments normally take over their functions; for example, in the *kolintang* ensemble of Minahasa the nine xylophones play drum-like, gong-like and melody roles. Drums play an important role in most South-east Asian ensembles, but in exceptional cases they are omitted altogether, as in the *kulintang lunik* in Lampung and the archaic Balinese *caruk* and *gambang* ensembles (see §7). Gongs or gong substitutes also play an important role, except in the *talempong* as it occurs in most areas of West Sumatra, where gongs are traditionally reserved for special royal and theatrical occasions.

References in this article to the following gamelan and related ensembles will be found in the sections indicated: alat-alat ma'yong, 8; angklung, 4, 6(iii and iv); angklung banyuwangi, 6(iii); arja, 4, 6(iv); asli jawa timur, 4, 6(iii); bali-balian, 6(iii); bebonangan [bebonang], 6(iv); bonang, 6(iv), 8; bumbung, 6(i); carabalen, 4, 7; caruk, 7, 8; degung, 4, 5, 6(ii); ebeg, 6(i); gambang, 4, 6(iv), 7, 8; gambuh, 4, 6(iv), 8; gandrung, 4, 6(iii); gegenggongan, 6(iv); gendang, 8; gendang bergung, 8; gendang gung, 8; genderang, 8; genrang dan gong, 8; gong, 6(iv); gondang, 8; gong gede, 4, 5, 6(iv); gong kebyar, 4, 5, 6(iv); gordang, 8; jaran kepang, 6(i); jemblung, 6(i); joged, 6(iv); joget, 8; kasar, 6(iii); kelintang, 8; kelittang, 8; keromong, 8; keromongan, 8; keromong duabelas, 8; kerapan sapi, 6(iii); keţoprak, 6(i); koḍok ngorek, 4, 7; kolintang, 8; kulintang, 8; kulintang lunik, 8; luang, 4, 7; munggang, 4, 7; nobat, 8; orkes lenong, 8; pejodedan bungbung, 6(iv); pejogedan, 6(iv); pejo-

gedan bungbung, 6(iv); pelegongan, 4, 6(iv); pelog-salendro, 4, 6(ii); prajuritan, 4, 6(i), 8; renteng, 4, 6(ii); reog, 6(ii); reyog, 6(iii), 8; salendro, 6(ii); saronen, 6(iii); sekati [sekaten], 4, 7; selundeng, 7; semar pegulingan, 5, 6(iv); seprangkat, 4, 6(i); slendro-pelog, 6(i); surabaya, 6(iii); tabuhan, 8; talempong, 8; tetet, 6(iii).
For the American gamelan, *see* MICROTONAL INSTRUMENTS, §4(iii).

BIBLIOGRAPHY

T. S. Raffles: *The History of Java* (London, 1817)
Gending-gending saking kraton ngajogjakarta [Javanese treatise on the art of music] (MS, Kraton Yogyakarta Library, Java, 1888) [xerox of microfilm copy at *US-LA*, Ethnomusicology Archive]
R. S. Soerawidjaja: *Gandroeng lan gamboeh* [Gandrung and gambuh] (Batavia, 1907)
Djakoeb and Wignjaroemeska: *Over de gamelan* (Batavia, 1913)
Buku piwulang nabuh gamelan [Instructions on gamelan playing] (Surakarta, 1924)
S. Hardasukarta: *Titiasri* (Surakarta, 1925)
J. Kunst: *Hindoe–Javaansche muziekinstrumenten, speciaal die van Oost Java* (Weltevreden, 1927; Eng. trans., 1963, rev. 2/1968)
J. S. Scholte: 'Gandroeng van Banjoewangi', *Djåwå*, vii (1927), 144
J. Kunst: *De toonkunst van Java* (The Hague, 1934; Eng. trans., rev. 2/1949, enlarged 3/1973)
C. McPhee: 'The Five-tone Gamelan Music of Bali', *MQ*, xxxv (1949), 250–81
M. Hood: *The Nuclear Theme as a Determinant of Patet in Javanese Music* (Jakarta and Groningen, 1954/R1977)
——: 'Sléndro and pélog Redefined', *Selected Reports*, i/1 (1966), 28
C. McPhee: *Music in Bali* (New Haven and London, 1966/R1976)
R. Ornstein: 'Gamelan Music of Bali', Lyrichord LLST 7179 [disc notes]
E. Heins: 'The Music of the Serimpi "Anglir Mendung": some Observations on the Music of the Central-Javanese Ceremonial Court Dances', *Indonesia* (Ithaca, NY, 1967), no.3, p.135
H. Susilo: *Drumming in the Context of Javanese Gamelan* (diss., U. of California, Los Angeles, 1967)
R. Ornstein: *Gamelan Gong Kebjar: the Development of a Balinese Musical Tradition* (diss., U. of California, Los Angeles, 1971)
——: 'The Five-tone Gamelan Angklung of North Bali', *EM*, xv (1971), 71
I. M. Bandem: *Pandji Characterization in the Gambuh Dance Drama* (diss., U. of California, Los Angeles, 1972)
R. L. Martopangrawit: *Pengatahuan karawitan* [The science of traditional music] (Surakarta, 1972)
S. Martopangrawit: *Titilaras kendangan* (Surakarta, 1972)
M. J. Kartomi: 'Jaran Kepang and Kuda Lumping', *Hemisphere*, xvii/6 (1973), 20
——: 'Music and Trance in Central Java', *EM*, xvii (1973), 163–208
M. Harrell: *The Music of the Gamelan Degung of West Java* (diss., U. of California, Los Angeles, 1974)
M. J. Kartomi: 'Performance, Music and Meaning of Reyog Ponorogo', *Indonesia* (Ithaca, NY, 1976), no.22, pp.85–130
E. Schlager: *Rituelle Siebenton-Musik auf Bali* (Basle, 1976)
E. Heins: *Goong renteng: Aspects of Orchestral Music in a Sundanese Village* (diss., U. of Amsterdam, 1977)
J. O. Becker: 'Time and Tune in Java', *The Imagination of Reality: Essays in Southeast Asian Coherence Systems*, ed. A. L. Becker and A. Yengoyan (Norwood, NJ, 1979)
——: *Traditional Music in Modern Java: Gamelan in a Changing Society* (Honolulu, 1980)
——: 'A Musical Icon: Power and Meaning in Javanese Gamelan Music', *The Sign in Music and Literature*, ed. W. Steiner (Austin, 1981)
M. Hood, E. Heins, R. Ornstein, I. M. Bandem, H. Susilo, Sudarsono, M. Crawford, M. Harrell and E. Atmadibrata: 'Indonesia', *Grove 6*
B. Hatley: 'The Pleasures of the Stage: Images of Love in Javanese Theatre', *Five Essays on the Indonesian Arts*, ed. M. J. Kartomi (Melbourne, 1981), 17

MARGARET J. KARTOMI

Gammu burui. PANPIPES of the Cuna Indians of the San Blas Islands of Panama. *See* KAMU-PURUI.

Gan. A Brazilian cowbell, with a single bell. *See also* AGOGO.

Gaṅ. Gong of Kampuchea. *See* GAṄ SGAR; GAṄ TŪC; KLAṄ KHAEK.

Ganabir. Lute of the Mali Empire noted in 1352 by the traveller Ibn Baṭṭūta. See H. A. R. Gibb, trans: Ibn Baṭṭūta: *Travels in Asia and Africa, 1325–1354* (London, 1929), 326ff.

Ganang. Pair of double-headed buffalo-skin cylindrical drums of the Cham people of Vietnam. One drum is beaten with the hand, the other with a stick.

Ganbag [gamalag]. DIDJERIDU (aboriginal wooden trumpet) of the Djawan people of south-western Arnhem Land.

Ganbo. STAMPING TUBE of Haiti.

Gand. French family of violin makers. Charles François Gand (*b* Versailles, 5 Aug 1787; *d* Paris, 10 May 1845), known as Gand *père*, was the elder son of Charles Michel Gand, a little-known Mirecourt violin maker who moved to Versailles about 1780. From 1802 to 1810 he was apprenticed to Nicolas Lupot, returning for a few years to his father's workshop. In 1816 he went back to Paris to work at the shop of Köliker, a dealer and restorer in the same street as Lupot. He purchased this business in 1820, but also succeeded Lupot on his death in 1824 by virtue of having married his adopted daughter. His instruments are rare but excellent in every way, though in due course he was overshadowed by the rising fame of J.-B. Vuillaume. Gand *père* was certainly Lupot's finest pupil. His brother Guillaume Charles Louis Gand (*b* Versailles, 22 July 1792; *d* Versailles, 31 May 1858) also worked for Lupot but returned permanently to Versailles, succeeding his father there in 1820. He was an excellent craftsman, whose work closely resembles that of Lupot.

Gand *père* had two sons, Charles Adolphe Gand (*b* Paris, 11 Dec 1812; *d* Paris, 24 Jan 1866) and Charles Nicolas Eugène Gand (*b* Paris, 5 June 1825; *d* Boulogne, 5 Feb 1892). Charles Adolphe inherited his father's shop in 1845. Although an excellent workman he made few instruments, being mostly occupied with the running of the business. Charles Nicolas Eugène learnt his trade in the family shop, and in 1855 became his brother's partner, the firm becoming known as Gand Frères. On his brother's death (1866) the house was merged with that of BERNARDEL, becoming Gand & Bernardel Frères, with Gand as senior partner. He was considered a person of integrity and the firm was held in high repute.

BIBLIOGRAPHY

D. Laurie: *The Reminiscences of a Fiddle Dealer* (London, 1924)
R. Vannes: *Essai d'un dictionnaire universel des luthiers* (Paris, 1932, 2/1951/R1972 as *Dictionnaire universel des luthiers* and R1981 incl. suppl.1959)

CHARLES BEARE

Gan-dama. Small double-headed barrel drum of Burma. It rests on a low horizontal trestle and occasionally is used in the *si-daw* ensemble.

Gandang. (1) FRAME DRUM of West Sumatra and the west coast of North Sumatra. In Sumatra it is played in pairs together with a *biola* (violin) and a singer of melismatic settings of Malay *pantun* or *syair* (four-line rhyming verse forms), and often accompanies local dances. The *gandang indung* ('mother drum') measures about 45 cm in diameter and 10 cm in depth, and the smaller *gandang anak* ('child drum') about 26 cm by 10 cm. The drums are made of goatskin and *lunak* (a softwood). In the Sorkam area sometimes eight, ten or twelve *gandang* are played together. In the Natal area the *gandang* may be replaced by a *gendang bulek* ('round drum'). In Minangkabu the *gandang* is about 35 cm long. It plays in the *talempong* ensemble.

(2) An ensemble of Sumatra, consisting of *biola*, two or more *gandang* drums, an optional male voice and (in the Natal area) an optional guitar. The music was probably developed from music played on European instruments by *cafre* ('heathen') African and Indian slaves brought by Portuguese colonisers to 16th-century Malaccan households. The *biola* plays in an elaborate melismatic style, with double stoppings in 5ths, series of descending 3rds, and melodic phrases that somewhat resemble western Portuguese folksong. After a solo *biola* introduction, the *gandang* enter with a cyclic 16-beat rhythm, followed by the singer, whose part follows the *biola*'s but is much less influenced by functional harmony. Some pieces are played by the instrumental *gandang* ensemble only. For the *gandang lasuang* ensemble of West Sumatra *see* LESUNG.

(3) Double-headed cylindrical drum of the Tausug people in the southern Philippines and of other peoples in Malaysia.

(4) Bamboo percussion pole of the Yakan people of the southern Philippines.

MARGARET J. KARTOMI

Gandang-sarunai Sungai Pagu [bagandang baraguang]. Ensemble consisting of a *gandang* (double-headed drum), *sarunai* (oboe) and *aguang* (gong) in the Sungai Pagu (Solok) area of West Sumatra. It is played at weddings and other festivals to accompany dances and displays of the art of self-defence. Formerly it was played at royal ceremonies.

MARGARET J. KARTOMI

Gandang tigo. Set of three small suspended gongs of the Agam area of West Sumatra. The gongs are made of bronze, about 25 to 30 cm in diameter, and have thin rims. They are played with six *talempong* (very small gongs), one or two *gandang* (double-headed drums) and an optional *rapano* (frame drum) in *randai* theatre interludes and to accompany dancing at ceremonies. See M. J. Kartomi: 'Randai Theatre in West Sumatra: Components, Music, Origins and Recent Change', *Review of Indonesian and Malayan Affairs*, xv (1981), 1–44.

MARGARET J. KARTOMI

Gandar. Double-headed laced drum of Flores, Indonesia. *See* GENDANG, (1).

Gaṅ dham [kong thom]. (1) Kampuchean bronze GONG-CHIME similar to the Thai *khŏng wong yai* and the Laotian *khŏng nyai*. It consists of 16 bossed gongs mounted on a semicircular rattan frame. It is played in the *bin bǎdy* orchestra.

(2) Large metal bossed gong of Kampuchea, played at weddings, religious processions and other festivals.

TRÀN QUANG HAI

Gaṇḍi [gaṇṭi]. Wooden percussion beam of Tibet; a type

of SĒMANTRON. Its origins lie in the oldest traditions of Buddhism in India, and it is still used in Tibetan monasteries. It is a wooden beam, narrowing in the centre, shaped like certain pestles of the Asiatic area. According to canonical treatises, the most common length would be about 1·7 metres. The instrument is held at the centre, placed on the left forearm and struck with a heavy wooden dumbbell-shaped beater. It summons the monks to various communal activities, such as confession, and its use is governed by strict rules which lay down that 108 beats must be sounded in three groups of 36. The shape and use of the *gaṇḍi* invite comparison with the *sēmantron* played in some Greek monasteries, especially on Mount Athos.

BIBLIOGRAPHY
I. Vandor: 'Le gaṇḍi: un instrument de musique de l'Inde bouddhique récemment identifié dans un monastère tibétain', *The World of Music*, xvii/1 (1975), 49
M. Helffer: 'Le gaṇḍi: un simandre tibétain d'origine indienne', *YTM*, xv (1983), 112

MIREILLE HELFFER

Gandingan. Set of four suspended bossed gongs used in the KULINTANG ensemble by the Magindanao people of the southern Philippines. They play an ostinato of four low notes and lend an opaque timbre to the ensemble.

Gandrang. Double-headed drum of the Makassar (Ujung Pandang) area of South Sulawesi. It is played together with a *puwi-puwi* (bamboo clarinet).

Gandu. Footed tuned cylindrical drum of the Digo people of Kenya. *See also* MCHIRIMA.

Ganer, Christopher (*fl* 1774–1809). German piano maker who worked in London. He came to London from Leipzig, settling at 47 Broad Street in 1774 and staying there until the end of 1809 (he also took on the neighbouring premises at 48 in 1782). He started getting in arrears with his rates from 1805 onwards, possibly an indication of financial difficulties.

Ganer mainly made square pianos. His earliest surviving square piano is marked 'Christopher Ganer Londini fecit 1775', and has a compass of nearly five octaves, from G' to f'''. This Latin inscription appears again on a 1778 square piano: until the mid-1780s he used either Latin or English inscriptions. The piano at Fenton House, Hampstead, is marked 'Christopher Ganer Musical Instrument Maker, No. 47 Broad Street Golden Square'; a later instrument is marked 'Christopher Ganer Musical Instrument Maker, Broad Street Golden Square London', while another is labelled 'Christopher Ganer Londini fecit 1784, Broad Street Soho'. A typical nameboard of the late 1780s reads 'C. Ganer, Grand and Small Forte Piano Manufacturer, Broad Street Golden Square, London'. Later models, such as the one at the Russell Cotes Museum in Bournemouth, have a striking Battersea enamel plaque bearing the inscription in capitals.

In outward appearance Ganer's square pianos vary; some are more attractively inlaid than others. The earlier ones tend to be plain with a simple trestle stand whereas later models are Sheraton in style, with brass medallions covering the bolts in the tapered legs of the trestle. Musically, however, the instruments vary little;

a compass of five octaves or slightly less, single action with overdampers, and two or three handstops raising the dampers and engaging a buff stop.

MARGARET CRANMER

Ganga. (1) The most common name for the double-headed cylindrical snare drum used in the music of a number of West and North African cultures, including parts of Niger, Benin, Nigeria, Chad, Cameroon, Upper Volta, Libya, Algeria and Tunisia. The musical prominence of this kind of drum is largely a result of its use with the *kakaki* trumpet and the *algaita* oboe in Hausa ceremonial music, together with the spread of Hausa political influence from the beginning of the 19th century.

The term 'ganga' is applied generically by the Hausa to a number of double-headed cylindrical snare drums, the most common, in ascending order of size, being the *kurya*, a traditional infantry drum about 17 cm long and with a diameter of about 21 cm; the *gangar algaita*, used with the *algaita*, about 33 cm long and about 24 cm in diameter; the *gangar fada* or royal *ganga* (see fig.1), used with the *kakaki*, about 45 cm long and with a diameter of about 33 cm; and the *gangar noma*, beaten for farmers, about 65 cm long and about 45 cm in diameter. Except for the *gangar noma*, which is occasionally laid on the ground, all these drums are suspended from the left shoulder and lie in a near-horizontal position under the performer's left arm. The drum has a wooden body with two goatskin heads lapped over leather hoops and laced together with leather thongs. A piece of cloth is sewn round the body under the lacing, the colour of the cloth indicating the emir to whom the instrument belongs.

The snared skin on the *gangar algaita*, *gangar fada* and *gangar noma* is to the front while on the *kurya* it is to the rear. Apart from the *gangar noma*, which is normally beaten with two sticks, the drums are beaten with a curved stick with a flattened head, held in the right hand, and with the fingers of the left hand. Two techniques, or series of strokes, are used in beating the drum; in *hannun gaba* the left hand beats the front skin and in *hannun baya* or *taushi* the rear. Free or open strokes produced with the flat of the stick-head on the centre of the front skin are the lowest in pitch. Notes of medium, high and extra-high pitch are produced from muted or closed stick strokes: medium notes are made with the flat of the stick-head on the centre of the front skin; high with the edge of the stick-head on the centre of the front skin; and extra-high with the flat or the edge of the stick-head on the centre of the front skin together with pressure from the fingers of the left hand on the top edge of the rear skin. A rising pitch is produced by a free stroke with the flat of the stick-head on the centre of the front skin followed by pressure with the knuckle of the left-hand thumb on the centre of the rear skin.

Performance on the Hausa *ganga* is based primarily on the high and low speech-tones of an unverbalized text and secondarily on its long and short syllabic quantities. Such a text, in praise of the patron of a performance, is called a *take*. The use of strokes of low, medium, high and extra-high pitch to realize the low and high tones of the *take* also allows the musician, if he so wishes, to superimpose certain intonational features on its tonal patterns. A straightforward *take* is shown in KAKAKI, ex.1.

A drum of the name 'ganga' is used by many other

1. Gangar fada (cylindrical drum) of the Hausa people, Nigeria

peoples such as the Nupe, Gunga, Dakakari, Duka, Chawai, Jukun, Tigong, Yeskwa, Bolewa, Tangale, Burum, Ngizim, Tera, Bura, Bata, Zaberma and Kanuri in Nigeria, and in Niger by the Songhay, Djerma and Beri-beri, in Chad by the Salamat Arabs, the Mului, Kanembu and Barma peoples, and in southern Libya by the people of Fiwet, Ghat and Traghan. Other peoples using closely related terms for the instrument are: the nomadic Fulani (*gunguru*), in Nigeria the Janji, Kurama and Piti (*oganga*), Ankwe (*kangak*), Gurka (*gungak*), Kerikeri (*gonga*), Margi (*akangga*), Mumuye, Kam and Pero (*ganggang*), in Benin the Dendi (*gangan*) and the Taneka (*gangangu*), in Chad the Zaghawa (*ganggang*) and in Upper Volta the Mossi (*gangado*); in Libya in the Fezzan region and in Algeria at Batna the drum is known as *gaga*. For illustration of the Fulani drum, *see* KAKAKI, fig.2.

Usage varies according to the degree of social stratification: in highly stratified societies the *ganga* forms part of an ensemble of court musicians, usually with long trumpets or oboes; in others it is used mainly to accompany song and dance. In Nigeria court usage is exemplified among the Kanuri, where the *ganga kura* (big drum) is beaten only for the Shehu of Borno, and among the Nupe at Bida (where it is known locally as *enyabo*), Abuja, Bauchi and Wase. Elsewhere in Nigeria usage is more varied; the Gunga use two or three professional *ganga* players to accompany teams of wrestlers, the Burum play a large *ganga* in drumming for farmers, and the Bura have incorporated the *ganga* into their xylophone ensemble to accompany dancing, a practice common throughout the northern states, where drums of the *ganga* type but with local names are used: for example, *dang* and MBANGAK.

In Benin the Taneka *gangangu* is played with side-blown horns and clapperless bell for masked dancing,

2. Ensemble of Kanembu professional musicians, north-western Chad, with (left to right) algaita (oboe), trembel and ganga (cylindrical drums)

and the Dendi *gangan* with hourglass drums in praise singing for a village chief. In Niger the Songhay *ganga* and the Djerma *ganga* at Dosso are similarly used for praise singing, and the Djerma, like the Beri-beri, use the drum with the *algaita*. In Upper Volta the Mossi *gangado* is used as part of a drum ensemble at the court of Tenkodogo to accompany praise singing and declamation of the history of the rulers.

In Chad the drum is played by professional musicians and is found particularly in the Kanem region. It has a wooden cylindrical body, 60 to 65 cm high and 30 to 35 cm in diameter, cowhide heads and leather lacing in a Y pattern. The upper head, which has two snares, is struck with a hooked stick with a flattened end; this provides the 'masculine' voice. The lower head is struck with the hands and has no snare but in its centre it has a baked disc made from brains, butter and charcoal; its sound is deeper and is the 'female' voice. Sometimes the *ganga* is used alone to convey signals but in a musical context it is always played with another drum, the *trembel*, and very often with the *algaita* (see fig.2). This ensemble also forms part of the orchestras of the sultans of the Kotoko.

The Zaghawa *ganggang* accompanies dancing during rites for a chief and is also used for special rites in case of drought. The Salamat Arabs and Barma are reported to use their *ganga* with other drums and end-blown flutes respectively to accompany dancing or to encourage canoeists, and the Kanembu and Mului with other drums and either long *gachi* trumpets or *algaita* oboes, or both, in the performance of praises and greetings for chiefs.

In Libya in central Fezzan the *ganga* drums are identical with those in Chad, except that sometimes the body is metal, and in performance instead of using the *trembel* two *ganga* drums are paired, one being considered 'male' and the other 'female'. As in Chad these instru-

ments are reserved for professional musicians who, in Fezzan, are usually of slave origin and from regions south of the Sahara. In the large oases in the extreme west of Libya (Ghat, Ghadames) the *ganga* has a comparatively flat body, 10 to 12 cm in height and 30 cm in diameter, although all other features are the same as in Chad. Playing is exclusively by professional musicians who in these oases are generally blacksmiths.

(2) Single-headed drum of the Sara people of southern Chad. It has a wooden body and its head is attached by wooden sticks driven into the body of the drum. The instrument is played upright and the head is struck with the hands.

(3) KETTLEDRUM of Morocco.

BIBLIOGRAPHY

Ames–KingGHM
J. F. J. Fitzpatrick: 'Some Notes on the Kwolla District and its Tribes', *Journal of the African Society*, x (1910–11), 16, 213
C. K. Meek: *Tribal Studies in Northern Nigeria* (London, 1931)
P. G. Harris: 'Notes on Drums and Musical Instruments Seen in Sokoto Province, Nigeria', *Journal of the Royal Anthropological Institute*, lxii (1932), 105
H. E. Hause: 'Terms for Musical Instruments in the Sudanic Languages: a Lexicographical Inquiry', *Journal of the American Oriental Society* (1948), suppl.7
M. F. Smith: *Baba of Karo: a Woman of the Muslim Hausa* (London, 1954)
M.-J. Tubiana: *Survivances pré-Islamiques en pays Zaghawa* (Paris, 1964)
M. Brandily: 'Music of Chad (Kanem)', BM30 L2309 (1967) [disc notes]
K. Krieger: 'Musikinstrumente der Hausa', *Baessler-Archiv*, new ser., xvi (1968), 373–430
M. Huet: *The Dance, Art and Ritual of Africa* (London, 1978)
P. Newman and E. H. Davidson: 'Music from the Villages of Northeastern Nigeria', AHM 4532 [disc notes]
ANTHONY KING/MONIQUE BRANDILY, K. A. GOURLAY

Gangado. Double-headed cylindrical drum of the Mossi people of Upper Volta. *See* GANGA, (1).

Gangan. (1) Double-headed HOURGLASS DRUM of the Yoruba people of Nigeria. *See* DUNDUN.

(2) Double-headed cylindrical drum of the Dendi people of Benin. *See* GANGA, (1).

Gangana. Iron bell of the Dogon people of Mali; it is played at funerals.

Gangangu. Double-headed cylindrical drum of the Taneka people of Benin. *See* GANGA, (1).

Gangar algaita [gangar fada, gangar noma]. Drum of the Hausa people of Africa. *See* GANGA, (1).

Gangária. A Cuban cowbell. *See* CENCERRO.

Gangar yan kama. Open snared HOURGLASS DRUM of fixed pitch used among the Hausa people of northern Nigeria. The *yan kama* comedian-mimes play it either solo or with others to accompany recitations, satirical songs and movements. At times the player inverts the drum and, by humming into the open end, produces a sound like that of the *goge* (single-string fiddle).

BIBLIOGRAPHY

Ames–KingGHM
D. W. Ames: 'Hausa Drums of Zaria', *Ibadan*, xxi (1965), 62
C. G. B. Gidley: 'Yankamanci: the Craft of the Hausa Comedians', *African Language Studies*, viii (1967), 52

Ganggang. Double-headed cylindrical drum of the Mumuye, Kam and Pero peoples of Nigeria and the Zaghawa people of Chad. *See* GANGA, (1).

Gangsa (i). Flat bronze or brass gong of the Kalinga and Bontoc peoples of the northern Philippines. Among the Ifugao they are called *gangha*, and among the Isneg *hansa*. Gangsa have a diameter of approximately 30 cm and their perpendicular rims are about 5 cm high. They produce diffused sounds with or without a focussed pitch. The ways in which they are played increase their timbral variety; they may be played with the hands (slapping, tapping or sliding) and with a beater (hitting the upper or under side of the gong). Various resonating effects are achieved by suspending gongs freely from the left hand, swinging them in the air, resting them partly or fully on the ground, or laying them on the lap (see illustration; *see also* GONG, fig.3a); damping effects are produced with the wrist or forearm, or with pressure from the beater.

Gangsa are played in such ceremonies as peace pacts between two communities, the inauguration of a new house or rice field, life-cycle celebrations given by the rich, or weddings. Gong music is necessary for dancing, for honouring people of the community, for celebrations and for providing the proper ambience for ritual proceedings. A gong's value is measured in different ways: it may be offered as a dowry, sold or exchanged for animals, land or property. During ceremonies, to play the *gangsa* is an honour, for only prominent members of the community are invited to start the performance. *Gangsa* music itself enjoys a certain preference among the Kalinga, and on occasions when *gangsa* playing is not allowed, its music is often played on other instruments.

The Ifugao use the term 'gangha' both for the gong and for an ensemble of three gongs. One of these (*tobob*), higher-pitched with more brilliant overtones, is played with the hands: the left hand taps while the right fist slides on the instrument. The other two gongs (*hebbiat*, *qahot*) are played with sticks beating on their inner (ventral) side. The *gangha* are played during harvest ceremonies or the inauguration of a new house, and accompany line dances (*tayao*). The Isneg have an ensemble consisting of *hansa* (two gongs) and *ludag* (conical drum). The gongs are played by women, the drum by a man. The ensemble accompanies two kinds of dances: *tabok* and *talip*.

See also INILA-UD; ITUNDAK; TOPAYYA; SULIBAO.

JOSÉ MACEDA

Gangsa (ii). A term used for metallophones in the Balinese *gamelan gong gede* and *gamelan gong kebyar* (*see* GAMELAN, §6 (iv)). They are of two types: *saron*, with bronze slabs resting on rattan or cork, which in turn rests on a wooden trough resonator; and *gender*, with bevel-edged keys suspended by cord above tuned bamboo tubes arranged in a wooden frame (see illustration). Each *gangsa* spans one octave. Both types are beaten with a wooden or horn hammer (which is padded in the case of the lowest-pitched *gender*) or with two hammers in each hand in the case of the *gender wayang* and *gamelan pelegongan* ensembles. Each key is damped by the left hand as the next key is struck. *Gangsa* are tuned in pairs, one pitched slightly higher than the other so that when the two instruments are struck simultaneously a beat is produced.

BIBLIOGRAPHY

C. McPhee: *Music in Bali* (New Haven and London, 1966/R1976), 329ff

R. Ornstein: 'Indonesia', §III, 1, *Grove 6*

MARGARET J. KARTOMI

Gangsa (flat gong) ensemble of the Kalinga people, northern Philippines, early 1900s

Gangsa (metallophone) of the gender type, played with a wooden hammer, in a gamelan gong kebyar, Bali, 1968

Gangu (i). Child's single-headed drum of the Kotoko people of Chad and northern Cameroon. The body is usually the neck of a pottery jar which is open at the end opposite the membrane. A closed receptacle is sometimes used, thus making the *gangu* a kettledrum. The membrane, glued on with clay, is a skin from the electric fish (*Malapterurus electricus*) or tetrodon (*Gymnodontes*). The drum is made by young boys who play it by striking the skin with one hand and a stick to accompany girls' dances. The *gangu* is also used to amuse babies and stop them crying.

MONIQUE BRANDILY

Gangu (ii). Side-blown trumpet of the Fali people of Cameroon. It is made from antelope horn and has an oval mouthpiece. The hand is placed over the bell to modify the tone.

Ganilka. Bulgarian fiddle. *See* GADULKA.

Gankogui. Double clapperless bell of the Ewe people of southern Ghana and Togo. The instrument is flanged and is struck with a stick, often in pairs, to accompany dancing. For illustration *see* ATSIMEWU.

Ganrang [genrang]. Double-headed wooden cylindrical drum of the Makassar and Buginese areas of the province of South Sulawesi. It is played in an ensemble with one or two *suling* (flutes) and a *kacapi* (plucked lute) to accompany dancing. *See also* GENDANG, (1).

Ganrang bulo. Idiochord TUBE ZITHER of the province of North Sulawesi. Its two bamboo strings, which are partially prised out of its surface, are raised on bridges at both ends and stretched over a small soundhole. They are beaten with a pair of thin sticks. Instruments vary in size.

Gaṅ sgar [kong skor]. Ancient ensemble of the Khmer people of Kampuchea. It consists of one or two *gaṅ* (suspended gongs), *sraḷai* (oboe) and *sgar dhaṃ* (single-

headed drum; *see* SGAR). This orchestra, considered to be a sacred ensemble, is portrayed on the bas-reliefs of the temples at Angkor Wat. It performs at cremations of important persons. Only a few such ensembles now exist in Kampuchea.

TRÂN QUANG HAI

Ganssu. Single clapperless iron bell of the Mahi people of Benin. *See* GANVIKPAN.

Gaṇṭā [gaṇṭe]. *See* GHAṆṬĀ.

Ganter, Hermann (*b* Munich, 14 Oct 1933). German maker of brass instruments. He learnt his trade from 1948 to 1951 with Anton Schöpf, Munich, founding his own firm in 1959 and becoming a Meister in 1960. In 1969 he was awarded the Bayerischer Staatspreis, a gold medal for outstanding achievements in craftsmanship. The firm produces all the modern brass instruments from trumpets in various pitches to tubas. Ganter's valved instruments are fitted with rotary valves, which he makes himself. His orchestral instruments are highly esteemed and are used internationally.

EDWARD H. TARR

Gaṇṭi. *See* GAṆDI.

Gaṅ tūc [kong touch]. (1) Kampuchean bronze GONG-CHIME similar to the Thai *khǭng wong lek*, the Laotian *khǭng wong* and the Burmese *kyi-waing*. It consists of 17 bossed gongs mounted on a semicircular rattan frame. It is played in the *biṇ bādy* orchestra.
(2) Small metal bossed gong of Kampuchea, played to accompany folkdance.

TRÂN QUANG HAI

Ganu rags (Latvian: 'shepherd's horn'). Clarinet or HORNPIPE of Latvia, analogous to the Lithuanian BIRBYNĖ. The body of the instrument is made of alder, aspen, pine, maple or ash wood and is 50 to 60 cm long, with a cylindrical bore and eight finger-holes. A cow-horn bell is attached to the distal end and a single reed, often fixed to its own mouthpiece, inserted in the upper end. It was particularly popular with herdboys and is still used by many folklore ensembles with the bagpipes, violin or other instruments for dance music. Since the mid-20th century, the *ganu rags* has been made in various sizes as a family of instruments (soprano, alto, tenor, baritone and bass).

Ganvikpan. Double clapperless iron bell of the Mahi people of Benin. It is struck externally and used with the single clapperless bell *ganssu*, horn whistle and calabash percussion vessels for *tchenhukumen* music, played chiefly at funerals.

Ganza. MUSICAL BOW of the Bonda people of Lower Guinea. The string is struck with a stick and stopped with the thumbnail.

Ganzá [canzá]. Type of Brazilian rattle, often resembling a two-headed *chocalho*, usually made of metal. Like other rattles, there is insufficient evidence to trace its origins precisely; it is considered to be of African origin because the Indians had no metal idiophones when the first African slaves were brought to Brazil, but it is strikingly similar to the maraca. The *ganzá* forms part of small ensembles that accompany performances of the *caboclo* (*mestizo*) dramatic dance, *bumba-meu-boi* and the *capoeira angola*, a mock fight.

JOHN M. SCHECHTER

Ganzi. Cylindrical, stopped wooden flute of the Zande people of north-eastern Zaïre (*LaurentyA*, 176).

Gaobian luo. Large Chinese gong. *See* Luo.

Gaodi. Small transverse flute of the Han Chinese. *See* Dɪ (i).

Gaohu. Chinese two-string fiddle. *See* Erhu.

Gapa. *See* Gaba.

Gapachos. Small Maracas of Colombia, used in the Andean Chirimía ensemble. They take their name from the *gapacho* plant, whose seeds are used.

Gapalikwa. End-blown trumpet of central Africa. *See* Nyele.

Gara. Metal bell of the Luo people of Kenya. The bells are attached to the legs of dancers.

Gaṙā. Clay percussion vessel, with a single pellet bell attached, of Kashmir. *See also* Ghata, §1.

Garabato. Afro-Cuban percussion stick, played in pairs. *See* Lungóua.

Garada. A stick rattle of the Ocaina Indians of the Peruvian tropical forest region. The Bora Indians of the same area play both *garada* and seed rattles.

Garamut. Pidgin English term for the wooden Slit-drum of New Guinea. It is characteristic of the coastal and river-dwelling peoples, particularly along the north coast, and is found also throughout most of the Bismarck Archipelago and in the northern Solomon Islands. Its length varies from 40 cm to as much as 4·5 metres; most are between 1·5 and 2 metres. Some are carved or painted with geometrical patterns or with crocodile or snake motifs (see illustration). They are used for signalling, for ceremony and for the accompaniment of song and dance, and are played almost exclusively by men.

MERVYN McLEAN

Garantung. Xylophone of the Batak Toba area of North Sumatra, Indonesia. Its five thick wooden slabs, about 25 to 40 cm long, are tied together by two parallel rows of string, the ends of which are attached to a wooden frame. It is played with two *hasapi* (plucked lutes), a *hesek* (metal idiophone) and a *sordam* (flute).

Garáwung. Single-headed cylindrical drum used by the black Caribs of Central America and reported in the early 20th century. It was 30 to 50 cm in diameter and 50

Garamut (slit-drums) of the Iatmul people, Aibom, Sepik Province, Papua New Guinea, 1956

to 75 cm high, had a mahogany or cedar trunk, and was beaten with one hand. See *IzikowitzMISAI*, 200.

JOHN M. SCHECHTER

Garaya. Two-string plucked lute of the Hausa people of Niger and northern Nigeria. It is about 50 cm in length, with an oval wooden soundbox covered with duiker-hide or goatskin, and strummed with a diamond-shaped pick of stiff cowhide. A long ringed metal jingle is inserted into the handle. The instrument is played by professionals, often with two gourd vessel rattles, in the performance of praise songs or for the *bori* spirit possession cult. *See also* Komo.

BIBLIOGRAPHY

Ames–KingGHM
C. R. Day: 'Music and Musical Instruments', *Up the Niger*, ed. A. F. M. Mockler-Ferryman (London, 1892)
D. W. Ames: 'Hausa Music II', BM30 L2307 [disc notes]
T. Nikiprowetzky: 'Niger: la musique des griots', OCR 20 [disc notes]

K. A. GOURLAY

Garcimartín, Leandro (*b* Villacastín, 11 March 1779; *d* Madrid, 18 Dec 1842). Spanish organ builder. He was the nephew of the organ builder Tomás Ginés Ortega, whose restoration of the two organs in Málaga Cathedral by Julián de la Orden he completed in 1804–5. He succeeded José de Verdalonga as official organ builder to the primatial cathedral of Toledo in 1809, but lost the post in 1823 on account of the liberal opinions he had expressed in 1820. He repaired the organ in the church of S Andrés, Toledo, in 1818. He subsequently moved to Madrid, where he built an organ for the Carmelite monastery in 1831–2. He was made official organ builder to the royal chapel in 1834, succeeding José Marigómez de Echevarría.

BIBLIOGRAPHY

G. Bourligueux: 'Leandro Garcimartín et l'orgue des Carmes Chaussés de Madrid', *Mélanges de la casa de Velázquez*, iv (1968), 349

JOCELYNE AUBÉ

Gardon. Folk cello of Hungary; sometimes actually a converted cello. It is used as a percussion instrument, with a violin performing the melody, by the Székelys, a Hungarian ethnic group in Transylvania (see illustration); its three or four strings, usually tuned to *d* and *D*, are on the same level and are alternately struck with a stick (not a bow), or sounded by plucking a string and letting it snap against the fingerboard, thus providing a rhythmically articulated drone accompaniment.

Gárgara. A Sanskrit term found in the earlier Vedic literature of India. Its general meanings are 'eddy', 'whirlpool' or 'churn', 'waterpot', but in a single early instance (*Ṛgveda*, viii, 69.9) it features together with parts of the archer's bow (including a lizard skin (*godhā*, i.e. the arm-brace) and the bowstring) 'singing' in praise of Indra, god of warriors. If *gárgara* is thus some part of the bow it may not necessarily be an instrument at all, although it has been accepted as a chordophone by Indologists and by Sachs as a harp (*see* VĀṆA and VĪṆĀ, §§1, 2). This may, however, be a reference to a MUSICAL BOW played on a 'pot' (*gárgara*) resonator covered with skin, similar, perhaps, to the KARKARĪ of other Vedic sources, of which it would then be a variant.

BIBLIOGRAPHY

A. A. Macdonnell and A. B. Keith: 'Gárgara', *Vedic Index of Names and Subjects* (London, 1912)

ALASTAIR DICK

Gypsy couple playing the gardon and the violin, Transylvania

Garimberti, Ferdinando (*b* Mammiano, 6 Jan 1894; *d*). Italian violin maker. He initially studied the cello and turned to making instruments while in his teens on the advice of Riccardo and Romeo Antoniazzi. Eventually he set up independently in Milan. Between 1927 and 1939 his instruments won high awards at the exhibitions held in Rome, Padua and Cremona, and consequently developed an enthusiastic following among Italian and Swiss players. In 1963 he was appointed 'specialist teacher' to the International School of Cremona, where he also served as examiner until 1966. Garimberti developed a personal model, inspired by Stradivari, which is outstandingly elegant because of its perfect proportions. The varnish, which varies from a golden yellow-brown to a rich red-brown, is of a good texture. Tonally his instruments have already shown some real promise. In addition to the usual printed labels, he also branded his instruments inside and outside.

BIBLIOGRAPHY

G. Nicolini: *The International School of Cremona* (Cremona, 1978)

JAAK LIIVOJA-LORIUS

Garland (Fr. *couronne*; Ger. *Kranz*; It. *bordo*). The reinforcement of the bell edge of a brass instrument.

Garmonik [garmoshka, garmonya]. Piano accordion of Belorussia. It was introduced from Russia in the second half of the 19th century, at first in Vitebsk province, and by the 1930s it was known throughout the rest of the country, becoming one of the most popular folk instruments. Two types of *garmonik* are particularly popular, the 'khromka' (chromatic model) and the 'Viennese double-rowed' type. It is played either solo or in ensemble with percussion instruments (*buben*, bass drum and triangle), strings (violin and *tsïmbalï*) and wind (clarinet or *truba*), professionally and by amateurs. In peasant society it is made by local artisans, while industrial manufacture is centred on the Molodechnenskii instrument factory.

INNA D. NAZINA

Garras [garris, !garras, !garris]. Stopped conical flute of the San (Bushman) people of south-western Africa. It is made from antelope horn and is used as a decoy whistle when hunting antelope. The Bergdama *nunib* and the Venda *nanga ya ntsa* are similar. See *KirbyMISA*, 92.

Gartner. Bohemian family of organ builders. Anton (*b* Tachau, 28 Jan 1721; *d* ?1771) was an important local organ builder of his day. His work included the organ in the Premonstratensian Monastery at Teplá (1754; three manuals, 34 stops), which still survives, and the organ for St Vitus's Cathedral, Prague (1763; three manuals, 40 stops), of which the case survives. His great-nephew Josef the younger (*b* Tachau, 30 Aug 1796; *d* Prague, 30 May 1863) became well known for his restoration of large Baroque organs: surviving examples include St Mary (1825) and St Nicholas Kleinseite (1835), Prague. Several of his own organs also survive, for example, that at Přeštice, south of Plzeň, built in 1855 (two manuals, 16 stops). As organ builders the Gartner family belong, broadly speaking, to the school of Abraham Stark. Josef the younger made a special study of Silbermann organs in Saxony; his essay, *Kurze Belehrung über die innere Einrichtung der Orgeln*, was published in 1832 (2/1845) and appeared in 1834 in a Czech translation.

BIBLIOGRAPHY

V. Němec: *Pražské varhany* (Prague, 1944)

R. Quoika: *Die altösterreichische Orgel der späten Gotik, der Renaissance und des Barock* (Kassel, 1953)

——: 'Gartner, Familie', *MGG*

HANS KLOTZ

Gasa. Gong of Alor, Indonesia, used in the SARAFEO ensemble.

Gasa-bin. Large SLIT-DRUM of the Gbaya people of the Central African Republic.

Gaṣba. Egyptian term for an oblique rim-blown flute. *See* NĀY.

Gashi. Long metal trumpet, without finger-holes, of several Islamic peoples in Chad and the Kanuri people of Nigeria. The instrument is known as KAKAKI to the Hausa of Nigeria. In Chad, where it is sometimes also known as *kashi* or *gachi*, it is usually made from tin, with one part sometimes of brass. It is over 200 cm long and made up of two sections which are slotted together for performance but separated for ease of transport. The bore contains several joints: the bell (with an external diameter of about 10 cm) is soldered to a narrower cone which in turn is soldered to the central cylindrical part of the bore (15 to 25 mm in diameter). Another conical section with a flange about 7 mm wide completes the tube to form the mouthpiece. The instrument produces two notes approximately a 5th apart.

Among the Kanembu and Kotoko (in Chad and Cameroon) these trumpets are insignia of power belonging to the sultans (see illustration), and are traditionally

Gashi (long metal trumpets) of a sultan of the Kotoko people, central Chad

played with drums. The Kanembu consider the instrument to have originated from Borno (Nigeria).

MONIQUE BRANDILY

Gasparo da Salò [Bertolotti] (*b* Salò, baptized 20 May 1540; *d* 14 April 1609). Italian maker of violins, violas and other bowed instruments. He came from a musical family that had a tradition of instrument making. In 1562 he moved permanently from Salò to nearby Brescia, a centre of viol and keyboard making. He worked initially with Girolamo Virchi, but by 1568 he described himself as 'maestro di violini'. It is likely that he was acquainted with Peregrino di Zanetto, an excellent maker whose work has much in common with Gasparo's. Gasparo was at least 20 years younger than Andrea Amati, and the 19th-century suggestion that he invented the violin is quite false.

Most of Gasparo's output, judging from existing instruments, took the form of tenor violas (*see* VIOLA, fig.1*a*). He also made viols of all sizes, several violins, supposedly at least one cello, at least one cittern, and several double basses. His reputation for crude workmanship is largely a result of the many nondescript 16th- and 17th-century instruments that have been erroneously attributed to him: in fact his designs were always meticulous and his craftsmanship of high quality. Among his characteristics are rather elongated soundholes (foreshadowing Guarneri), noticeable undercutting in the carving of his scrolls, and sometimes two rows of purfling or an inlaid decoration. His violas, many considerably reduced from their original size, are regarded by many players as tonally better than any other. They have a full and reedy tone quality, combined with a stronger response than many Cremonese instruments. The basses have always been eagerly sought after, their most famous champion being Domenico Dragonetti. When Gasparo da Salò died his leading position as a maker in Brescia was taken over by his pupil Giovanni Paolo Maggini, and his trade was also continued by his son Francesco (*b* 1565).

BIBLIOGRAPHY
G. Livi: *I liutai bresciani* (Milan, 1896)
W. L. von Lütgendorff: *Die Geigen- und Lautenmacher vom Mittelalter bis zur Gegenwart* (Frankfurt am Main, 1904, rev. 6/1922/R1968)
A. M. Mucchi: *Gasparo da Salò: la vita e l'opera, 1540–1609* (Milan, 1940)

CHARLES BEARE

Gäta-berē. Double-headed barrel drum of Sri Lanka, so called because of the heavy wooden boss running around the circumference at the widest point (*gäta*: 'knotted'; *berē*: 'drum'). It is the chief drum of the Kandyan school and is used both in Buddhist ritual and for Kandyan dancing.

The *gäta-berē* is carved from a piece of hardwood. *Ähäla* is the preferred wood because of its resonance, but it is also extremely heavy and a lighter variety of *jak* is often substituted. The measurements of a good drum are calculated to suit the performer: the length should be equivalent to three hand-spans and three finger-widths, which usually results in a drum between 66 and 71 cm long. The diameter of the heads should exactly equal a hand-span, this being vital to the complex patterns played on the drum, which demand an accurate reach from one side to the other. The measurement usually results in a diameter of about 22 to 25 cm. When the drum is made for an unknown buyer, or to be used by several players, the maker calculates the length as

Young girl playing a smaller version of the gäta-berē (barrel drum), Sri Lanka

nine times the length of the second joint of his middle finger. The vellum for the heads is chosen with great care, the characteristic of the drum being the contrast in sound between the two heads. The thin and flexible skin of a monkey's stomach is used for the right head, which produces a high-pitched ringing sound. The left head is always of oxhide, producing a heavier muffled tone. Both heads are bound to the drum with a cane hoop, over which a circlet of cowhide is placed, overlapping the vellum by about 2 cm and keeping the vellum taut when a final hoop of plaited creeper is braced against it. Leather braces about 2 cm wide are stretched between the two hoops. A heavy hemp sling is secured to the hoops and passed round the player's waist, so that the weight of the drum is taken by the small of the back. The drum is played standing; traditionally the drummer stands with left knee bent, to tilt the drum into a diagonal position, but it is more often held horizontally.

An elaborate mythology surrounds the construction of the *gäta-berē*, reflecting its importance in the Kandyan tradition. It is said to have been built on the orders of the god Brahma to represent the well-ordered universe. Its two contrasting heads represent the sun and the moon and the boss at the centre of the drum the earth. The tilted playing angle was thought to link the heavens with the lower regions.

One of its main functions is to play the *magul-bera* – the drum signal that inaugurates any important event in the temple or associated with it. This usage is the reason for its being known sometimes as *magul-berē*. It is also the essential drum for any performance of Kandyan dance. The full range of the *gäta-berē*'s repertory is demonstrated in the *Kohombā-Kankāriya*, a three-day dance-drama epic of the Kandyan school. It has a strong ritual significance, often being performed in fulfilment of a vow, but is only rarely staged because of the huge expense involved.

See also BHERĪ.

BIBLIOGRAPHY
L. P. Goonetileke: 'The Drum', *Ceylon Times*, ii/1 (1953), 15
R. Pieris, ed.: *Some Aspects of Traditional Sinhalese Culture* (Peradeniya, 1956), 104ff
B. de Zoete: *Dance and Magic Drama in Ceylon* (London, 1957)
H. Keuneman: 'Sinhalese Drums', *Ceylon Observer Pictorial* (1960)
M. D. Raghavan: *Sinhala Natum: Dances of the Sinhalese* (Colombo, 1967)

NATALIE M. WEBBER

Gatenar, Enrico. *See* CATENARI, ENRICO.

Gatshi [gatci]. Long wooden or metal trumpet of the orchestras of the *lamido*, traditional leaders of the sedentary Fulani people in north Cameroon. *See* KAKAKI.

Gatumbatumba. Single-headed closed GOBLET DRUM of the Luba people of Zaïre. It is played in conjunction with the *ditumba* and *mutumbi* drums.

Gautrot, P. L. *l'aîné* (*fl* Paris, 1835–84). French maker of woodwind and brass instruments. He joined the firm of Guichard about 1835, becoming the owner in 1845. He was the first European manufacturer to use mass production techniques for instruments. At first he specialized in brass instruments, but from 1849 also produced woodwind. Gautrot took over the equipment and trade mark of the oboe maker Triébert on 5 August 1881. He was succeeded by Couesnon in 1884.

Gautrot's early work with brass instruments included the invention of a system of transposition involving cylinders, applicable to the horn and cornet. His attempts at improving the horn are exemplified in an omnitonic horn of 1847 which allowed 12 crook changes with a complicated system of slides and taps; a three-valve omnitonic horn (patented in 1854); and a valved horn of 1858 which anticipated the modern double horn. He devised a *système équitonique*, using valves with dual windways based on the compensator principle. He made numerous ophicleides with 11 or 12 keys, some with rotary-key pitch change, as well as hunting horns, saxhorns with three piston valves, and valve trombones. Gautrot was one of the first makers of the sarrusophone, for which he took out a French patent in 1856. Notable among his woodwind instruments were metal flutes and brass clarinets which were constructed with a double tube, to improve the strength of the instrument and its tuning.

For illustrations of instruments by Gautrot, *see* FLUGELHORN; OPHICLEIDE; SARRUSOPHONE.

BIBLIOGRAPHY

L. A. de Pontécoulant: *Douze jours à Londres* (Paris, 1862)
C. Pierre: *La facture instrumentale à l'Exposition universelle de 1889* (Paris, 1890)
——: *Les facteurs d'instruments de musique* (Paris, 1893/*R*1971)
L. G. Langwill: *An Index of Musical Wind-instrument Makers* (Edinburgh, 1960, rev., enlarged 6/1980)
R. Morley-Pegge: *The French Horn* (London, 1960, 2/1973)
NIALL O'LOUGHLIN

Gaval. FRAME DRUM of Azerbaijan. *See* DIAFF.

Gaval-das. Stone Age LITHOPHONE ('frame drum of stone') from Kobustan, Azerbaijan.

Gaveau. French firm of piano and harpsichord makers. Joseph Gaveau (*b* Paris, 1824; *d* Paris, 1903) founded the firm in 1847, working with his employees in a small shop in the rue des Vinaigriers in Paris; the workshop and the offices were later transferred to the rue Servan. The firm established an excellent reputation for its small upright pianos, and by the 1880s the business was producing about 1000 pianos a year, achieving a degree of success due to commercial acumen rather than intrinsic quality. Joseph was succeeded by his son Etienne Gaveau (*b* Paris, 7 Oct 1872; *d* Paris, 26 May 1943), who organized the construction of a larger new factory at Fontenay-sous-Bois and, following the example of other well-known piano makers, in 1907 opened a new concert hall in the rue la Boétie, Paris. This street also housed the offices of the firm from 1908. Arnold Dolmetsch joined the firm in 1911, and under his direction it produced spinets and small unfretted clavichords along historical principles; this continued after his departure in 1914. The firm undoubtedly hoped to capture part of the new market for plucked keyboard instruments and clavichords from its great rivals, Pleyel. Etienne's sons Marcel and André Gaveau succeeded their father in running the firm. In 1960 Gaveau joined ERARD to form Gaveau-Erard S.A.; the production of Gaveau pianos was taken over by the firm of Schimmel in 1971.

BIBLIOGRAPHY

A. Chenaud: *Les facteurs de pianos et leurs recherches* (?Paris, 1970)
C. Ehrlich: *The Piano: a History* (London, 1976)
MARGARET CRANMER

Gavioli. Italian family of mechanical instrument makers. Giacomo Gavioli began making musical clocks in Modena in 1802; one of his larger municipal clocks is still in use there. His son Ludovico [Louis] Gavioli (i) began making barrel organs for street musicians, but he also made standard 'indoor' barrel organs, one of which was built for Isabella II of Spain. In 1845 he moved to Paris, where his firm at first made a variety of instruments. In 1855 he received a gold medal at the Paris Exposition for a mechanically played flute; that year he also took out an English patent for the clavi-accord, a portable reed organ. The firm's reputation, however, was based on the building of the Stratarmonica, the first true street organ; this was a large barrel organ on wheels with moving figures in its prospect.

Ludovico's son Anselme (*d* 1902) took over the management of the firm in 1863, but suffered a setback when his factory was destroyed during the Franco-Prussian war in 1870. With financial backing from Prosper Yver and Leonce Julaguier, in 1871 he reorganized the company under the name of Gavioli & Cie. In 1876 Anselme patented an improvement in pipe construction called the *frein harmonique*, or harmonic bridge. This consisted of a piece of metal positioned in front of the mouth of a narrow-scaled pipe which enabled it to be blown harder and louder without overblowing, an innovation soon used for church and concert-hall organs as well. Until almost the end of the 19th century all street organs had been operated by pinned barrels (*see* BARREL ORGAN). In 1892, using the principle of the Jacquard loom, Anselme invented the 'keyframe and music book' system, in which a long series of hinged perforated cards (the 'book') is fed through the keyframe mechanism for playing. This system made the playing of longer and more complex pieces of music possible, and, coupled with Anselme's two-pressure system, patented in 1891 (low pressure for the pipes, high pressure for the action), heralded the beginning of a new era for street and fairground organs. Around the turn of the century Anselme's brother Claude invented a book-playing reed organ called the Coelophone Orchestre, but it seems to have had limited production, and none are now known to exist.

The Gavioli firm did not benefit as it should have done from these and other inventions. Financial problems plagued Ludovico Gavioli (ii), Anselme's son and successor, and shortly after his father's death his foreman Charles Marenghi left, with others trained by Gavioli, to start a rival business. Despite this setback, the firm went on to develop what many consider its masterpiece, the large 100-key Gavioliphone, which, after six years of design work, was put on the market in 1906 and seems to have been particularly popular in England. The centre of book-organ building was shifting from Paris to Belgium, where thriving builders such as Mortier were capitalizing on a new interest in organs for dance halls. Nonetheless, the Gavioli firm might have held its lead in the industry, had it not tried to produce an even more ambitious 112-note keyless instrument (using paper rolls) with an experimental action and wind system. Patented in 1907, this new instrument was beset with mechanical problems, and purchasers sued Gavioli for damages under the terms of their guarantee. This, along with the fact that Mortier was infringing Gavioli's patents, is probably what caused the firm's demise just before the outbreak of World War I.

For illustration *see* MECHANICAL INSTRUMENT, fig.6.

BIBLIOGRAPHY
R. de Waard: *From Music Boxes to Street Organs* (New York, 1967)
E. V. Cockayne: *The Fairground Organ* (London, 1970)
A. W. J. G. Ord-Hume: *Barrel Organ* (London, 1978)
                                                BARBARA OWEN

Gawu-khas [!gawu-kha:s]. Mouth-resonated bowed TROUGH ZITHER of the San (Bushman) people of southwestern Africa. It is similar to the Venda TSHIDZHOLO and to the Tswana SEGANKURU (in its simple form).

Gay. *See* GAI.

Gayanda. Single-headed conical drum of the Valley Tonga people of Zambia. It is open-ended and the membrane is pegged on. The side of the drum is tapped with three sticks. It is very similar to the *musuntu* drum of the same people, and accompanies drinking songs. See *TraceyCSA*, ii, 82f.

Gayda. *See* GAJDE.

Gaza. (1) Long drum of the Zande and Barambo peoples of Zaïre (*BooneT*, 25). *See* NABITA, (1).
(2) Cylindro-conical drum of the Zande and Mbanja peoples of Zaïre (*BooneT*, 32). *See* DINDO.

Gazooka [gazoota]. *See* KAZOO.

Gbange. Frame XYLOPHONE of the Tiv people of Nigeria. Up to nine wooden keys rest on pads of rags or of grass and are supported by a wooden frame. The players, facing each other, use wooden beaters. Originally played to scare birds from crops, it has been used more recently to accompany the *gbange* dance, which takes its name from the instrument.

Gbassia. Ceremonial SLIT-DRUM of the Kissi people of Guinea. It is suspended beneath a canopy and used to give orders to young boys during their dance after the first stage of initiation.

Gbea. *See* GE.

Gbedu. Set of three long cylindrical drums of the Yoruba people of Nigeria. It consists of the *afere*, approximately 120 cm tall, with pegged membrane; the smaller, shorter *opere*; and the smallest *obadan*. The drums are kept by the *aworo*, chief priest of the town or village, and the drummers are always from his family. The drums are reserved exclusively for royalty or important dignitaries and played only for death ceremonies of a high official, to announce danger, or to honour the ruler during annual festivals.

Gbegbetele. Seven-string PLURIARC of the Kpelle people of Liberia. The piassava bows, with metal rattles attached to the underside, are attached to a round gourd resonator, and metal or rattan strings are stretched across each bow. The strings are named by kin terminology, for example 'mother', 'mother's child', etc. The player plucks the strings with his right hand and taps the soundbox with a ring on a finger of his left.

BIBLIOGRAPHY
R. M. and V. L. Stone: 'Music of the Kpelle of Liberia', FE 4385 (1970) [disc notes]
R. M. Stone: 'Liberia', *Grove 6*
                                                K. A. GOURLAY

Gbeketele. LAMELLAPHONE of the Mano people of Liberia. It corresponds to the Toma GRUZAVEWONIGI.

Gbele. Small three-footed cylindrical drum of the Guere people of the Ivory Coast. It has laced membranes with tightening pegs in the side. The drum is beaten with two thin sticks and played to accompany singing.

Gbelee. LAMELLAPHONE of the Kpelle people of Liberia. Seven metal tongues are fastened to a board attached to an enamel bowl resonator. The keys are named: (i) *nuu kete* ('great person'); (ii, iii) *nong* ('child'); (iv) *ngulei siye nuu* ('soloist, song-raising person'); (v, vi, vii) *ngulei too muui* ('singers'). In performance the player uses the index, middle and ring fingers. The instrument is used solo or in small groups with others of its kind. See R. M. and V. L. Stone: 'Music of the Kpelle of Liberia', FE 4385 (1970) [disc notes].
                                                K. A. GOURLAY

Gbemgbem. Double-headed cylindrical drum of the Vai people of Liberia. *See* GBUNG-GBUNG.

Gbere. *See* OLIKO.

Gbessi. Small clapper bells in the shape of an elongated cone, used by the Taneka people of Benin. One is held in each hand and played with flutes and cylindrical drum for *margnol* music to encourage farm work. *See also* KETELESSI.

Gbingbe. Log XYLOPHONE of the Mbuja people of Zaïre. *See* PANDINGBWA.

Gblo. Wooden whistle of the Baule people of the Ivory Coast, used with drums and other rhythm-makers to accompany dancing.

Gbo. Log XYLOPHONE of the Guere people of the Ivory Coast. It consists of six to eight wooden keys placed across two banana stems, with wooden pegs between the bars to hold them in place. The instrument is played by two players, squatting face to face, each using two sticks without heads and striking the ends of the bars (for illustration *see* XYLOPHONE, fig.4*b*). It is played by boys watching over the fields in daytime or by young village men when not working. See H. Zemp: 'Musique Guéré, Côte d'Ivoire', Vogue LD 764 [disc notes].

Gbong-kpala. MOUTH BOW of the Kpelle people of Liberia. It is played by one hand striking the string with a stick while the other stops the lower end of the string at various points. The mouth encircles the string at the upper end without touching it so that, by changing the shape of the oral cavity, the player is able to emphasize certain harmonics and thus reproduce tonal speech patterns. The mouth bow is regarded as a young boy's instrument for personal entertainment.

BIBLIOGRAPHY
R. M. and V. L. Stone: 'Music of the Kpelle of Liberia', FE 4385 (1970) [disc notes]
R. M. Stone: 'Liberia', *Grove 6*

K. A. GOURLAY

Gbung-gbung. Double-headed cylindrical drum of the Kpelle people of Liberia. It is slung from the left shoulder and beaten with sticks to provide a steady rhythmic beat in ensembles accompanying singing or dancing. Among the Vai the drum is known as *gbemgbem*. For illustration *see* FELI.

BIBLIOGRAPHY
R. M. and V. L. Stone: 'Music of the Kpelle of Liberia', FE 4385 (1970) [disc notes]
R. M. Stone: 'Liberia', *Grove 6*

Gbwilebo. Log XYLOPHONE of the Sapa people of Liberia. *See* BALO.

Gbwini. Bell of the Mano people of Guinea. Formerly a war bell, it is the shape of a flattened iron cone extended to form a handle. The two sides are cast separately and welded with the clapper hooked inside. The bell is now used in ensemble with drums and vessel rattles. Similar bells for the Gio, Gbunde and Sapa are referred to as *lalo*, *kotigi* and *bwelie* respectively. See G. Schwab: *Tribes of the Liberian Hinterland* (Cambridge, Mass., 1947/*R*1974).

Gcod-dar. Wooden HOURGLASS DRUM of Tibet. *See* DAMARU.

Ge [gbea, gei]. Gourd vessel rattle of the Mano people of Liberia. *See* KPWALE.

Gebunden (Ger.). LEGATO.

Gedackt (Ger.). An ORGAN STOP.

Gede-gede. SLIT-DRUM of the Tiv people of Nigeria. *See* INDIER.

Gedenugbo. Single-string STICK ZITHER of the Fon people of Benin. It is made from a palm frond 100 to 150 cm long, with a split fibre secured at each end and raised over bridges. The centre of the stem is placed on an inverted half-calabash resting on the ground; one player

strikes the string with one or two sticks, while a second stops it with a knife-handle. See C. Béart: 'Jeux et jouets de l'ouest africain', *Mémoires de l'Institut français d'Afrique noire* (Dakar, 1955).

Gedi. Pair of bamboo stilts used as percussion sticks by the tribal peoples of Madhya Pradesh, India. The *gedi* are struck on the ground to emphasize the steps of the *gedi nṛtya* dance.

Gedney, Caleb (*b* ?1728; *d* London, *c*1769). English woodwind instrument maker. He was apprenticed to Thomas Stanesby (ii) from 1743 to 1750. On Stanesby's death (1754) he inherited his tools, materials and unfinished work on condition that he married Stanesby's servant, Catherine Gale. He did so, and continued the business in Stanesby's premises in Fleet Street, London.

While Stanesby is known to have made flutes, recorders and oboes, Gedney made flutes, oboes, clarinets and bassoons. Extant instruments include one- and six-key flutes, a stained boxwood bass flute in G with a square silver key, two-key oboes and bassoons with four (London, Carse Collection no.205) and six keys. Notably advanced for the time is the six-key flute, which included the extra keys (*c'* and *c'♯*) that Quantz had used and Florio had also reintroduced. In 1756 Gedney countered an advertisement by a maker named John Mason for an extended-foot flute by claiming that Thomas Stanesby (ii) had invented this some 20 years previously.

BIBLIOGRAPHY
E. Halfpenny: 'Biographical Notices of the Early English Woodwind-making School, *c*.1650–1750', *GSJ*, xii (1959), 44
L. G. Langwill: *An Index of Musical Wind-instrument Makers* (Edinburgh, 1960, rev., enlarged 6/1980)
M. Byrne: 'Schuchart and the Extended Foot-Joint', *GSJ*, xviii (1965), 7

NIALL O'LOUGHLIN

Gedo. Braced MOUTH BOW of the Bakango pygmies of Zaïre (*LaurentyC*, 113). *See* BOMBO (iv).

Gedombak. *See* GEDUMBAK.

Geduk. Double-headed barrel drum of West Malaysia, usually made of jackfruit wood. The cowhide heads are held in position by up to 30 wooden studs, set 7 cm from the rim. Two wooden bamboo struts are fixed close together near the upper head, diverging to their furthest extent 14·5 cm beyond the lower head. They thus incline the *geduk* towards the player at an angle of about 30°, the upper head facing the player. An iron ring is fixed to the body of the drum so that it can be lifted. The *geduk* is normally played in a pair made up of a *geduk ibu* ('mother *geduk*') and a *geduk anak* ('child *geduk*'), the latter being slightly smaller. A *geduk ibu* may have a diameter of about 27 cm, and its body a length of 40 cm.

The drum is beaten with unpadded wooden drumsticks, held one in each hand, to produce a staccato tattoo; the hands are raised to the level of the player's forehead. It provides a vivid accompaniment to battle scenes and quarrels in the *wayang kulit* (shadow-puppet theatre), and plays an important part in the overture to the play. It is sometimes used in the *makyung* theatre overture, but never in the actual *makyung* performance; neither does it accompany Malay dances.

A prototype of the drum can be seen carved in a bas-relief at Angkor, and it is still used in Kampuchea, where it is called *sgar dham* (*see* SGAR); it is also similar to the Thai *klǭng that* (*see* KLǪNG).

JACK PERCIVAL BAKER DOBBS

Geduk asek. Single-headed barrel drum of West Malaysia. Unlike the GEDUK it has no struts. Its name is derived from its original use in the accompaniment to the *asek* dance.

Gedumbak [gedombak]. HOURGLASS DRUM of northern Malaysia, East Sumatra and Riau islands. It is made from one piece of jackfruit wood. The single head is normally of goatskin and is held firmly in place by rattan; the base of the pedestal is left open. The head, about 23 cm in diameter, is braced with a zigzag lacing of split cane (or cord) to a cane (sometimes metal) ring which passes round the waist of the drum. Two large loops of rattan are often fixed round the waist allowing it to be carried. The *gedumbak* is found in two sizes: *anak* ('child') and *ibu* ('mother'), the height of the *ibu* from base to head being up to 45 cm.

The drum is placed across the player's left thigh, so that the single head can be struck with the right hand. The left hand supports the base of the pedestal and from time to time is used to close it, so changing the quality of the sound. It is used in instrumental ensembles chiefly to accompany *wayang kulit* (shadow-puppet theatre), *menora* theatre and folkdances.

In Riau province and on the east coast of northern Sumatra the drum is called *gedombak* and is used in pairs in the *makyung* theatre ensembles. The player sits cross-legged and holds the drum on his lap; he sometimes covers the lower, open end with his hand to damp the sound. The leather head is stretched by a framework of parallel lengths of bamboo down the upper sides of the bowl. The 'mother drum' is here called *gedombak pengibu* and the 'child drum' *gedombak penganak*.

JACK PERCIVAL BAKER DOBBS, MARGARET J. KARTOMI

Gegedem. Double-headed cylindrical drum of Aceh province, Indonesia. *See* TAMBO (i).

Gehu. Large Chinese four-string fiddle of modern design (*ge*: 'reformed'; *hu*: 'barbarian', now a generic term for fiddles). Like the *erhu* the *gehu* has a round tubular resonating chamber covered at one end with python-skin, but its neck is similar to a cello fingerboard (against which the strings are pressed). The four strings are tuned in 5ths (like those of a cello), and the bridge is mounted on the side of the resonating chamber rather than over the skin; a cello-like bow remains separate from the strings (rather than running between them). The *gehu* was developed in the late 1950s in response to the needs of the modern Chinese orchestra for instruments of greater range and volume. Of the several sizes conceived, the *da gehu* ('large reformed *hu*') and *di gehu* ('bass reformed *hu*') have proved the most enduring.

ALAN R. THRASHER

Gei. *See* GE.

Geib (i). German family of organ builders. Johann Georg Geib (i) (*b* Staudernheim an der Nahe, 9 Sept 1739; *d* Frankenthal, 16 April 1818) was probably apprenticed to the Stumm brothers in Rhaunen-Sulzbach and estab-

lished his own business around 1760 in St Johann, near Saarbrücken, from where he operated over a wide area. In 1790 the business was transferred to Frankenthal, and from about 1786 his son Johann Georg (ii) worked in partnership with him. Geib's work was typical of the Middle Rhine school of organ building, closely related to that of the STUMM brothers but differing quite markedly in particulars. In his large two-manual instruments (up to *c*26 stops) the specifications are well thought out, and the pedals likewise exhibit a solid foundation, although they show more variety. There is a consistent method of construction: the Choir and Great are generally built over one another in the organ loft, and the reed pipes of the manuals are always divided into bass and treble; the pedals consist only of one and a half octaves. Of the 16 instruments that can be attributed to Johann Georg (i), only six survive: the best-preserved is in the Protestant parish church in Lambrecht (it was particularly well restored in 1977 by Johann Klais of Bonn).

Johann Georg Geib (ii) (*b* Saarbrücken, 14 June 1772; *d* Frankenthal, 5 March 1849) ran the family business after his father's death, first on his own and then jointly with Josef Littig. Only about nine of his organs can be traced, and there were several unfinished projects. He worked initially in the style of his father, but made allowances for the prevailing taste, which gradually resulted in changes of specification; his work did not attain the same quality as his father's. The firm ceased after his death.

Two other family members were active as instrument makers. Johann [John] Geib (1744–1818), the brother of Johann Georg Geib (i), emigrated to England and subsequently to the USA (*see* GEIB (ii)). Ludwig [Louis] Geib (*b* Piestorf, 7 Nov 1759; *d* Schiltigheim, nr. Strasbourg, 26 Feb 1827), the nephew of Johann Georg Geib (i), probably learnt the trade from his uncle in Saarbrücken and later worked in Montbéliard in France and in Alsace. He is noted for about eight organs, as well as numerous restorations.

BIBLIOGRAPHY

P. Meyer-Siat: 'Louis Geib, facteur d'orgues', *Pays d'Alsace*, lxv (1969)

O. Ochse: *The History of the Organ in the United States* (Bloomington, Ind., and London, 1975)

B. H. Bonkhoff: 'Die Orgelbauerfamilie Geib und ihr Werk', *Der Turmhahn*, i/2 (1977)

200 Jahre Geib-Orgel Lambrecht: Festschrift zur feierlichen Wiedererindienststellung der restaurierten historischen Geib-Orgel (Lambrecht, 1977) [incl. articles by G. Kaleschke and H. Klotz]

J. Ogasapian: 'New Data on John Geib', *The Tracker*, xxiii/4 (1979), 12

G. KALESCHKE

Geib (ii). German family of piano makers, organ builders and music publishers who worked first in England and later in the USA. John [Johann] Geib (*b* Staudernheim, 27 Feb 1744; *d* Newark, NJ, 30 Oct 1818) migrated to London, where he claimed to be the first to make 'organized pianos'. His factory finished eight to ten pianos every week, and in all he made about 5400 pianos, as well as church and chamber organs. A Geib case (housing a modern organ) survives at St Mary's, Stafford. In 1786 he patented a double action (patent no.1571) for the square piano (which in a modified form eventually superseded the single action in England), with a buff stop along the treble to facilitate tuning (*see* PIANO-FORTE, §I,4, esp. fig.11). His 1792 patent (no.1866) enabled players to combine two keyboard instruments by means of two-manual mechanism.

On 24 July 1797 Geib sailed with his wife and seven children to New York. In the *Argus: Greenleaf's New Daily Advertiser* for 27 December 1798 he advertised his building of an organ for the German Lutheran Church in New York. In this work he had been joined by two of his sons, the twins John (1780–1821) and Adam (1780–1849). By 1800 the firm was known as John Geib & Co. and Geib became the leading figure in American organ building of his time. His instruments were much in demand, both in New York and elsewhere. In the American *Spectator* for 19 March 1800 the firm advertised their work on an organ for Christ Church, New York (at the corner of William and Frankfort streets), and listed their instruments:

Church Organs, to any value above a thousand dols.; Chamber Organs, also; Church and Chamber Organs, to play with barrels and fingers, which will be very convenient and can be used by persons who have no knowledge of music; Organized Piano Fortes; Grand and Patent small Piano Fortes; Common Action ditto [i.e. single action]; Pedal Harps, etc.

From *c*1804 until *c*1814 the firm was known as John Geib & Son (this probably refers to the elder of the twins, John Geib jr) and from 1814 their activities included music publishing – mainly patriotic and religious music. Geib seems to have retired by 1816, but Adam Geib joined his twin in the business: they had a piano warehouse at 23 Maiden Lane, New York, where Adam also taught. In 1818, the year of their father's death, a third brother, William (1763–1860), joined the firm, which then became J. A. & W. Geib. Square pianos with this inscription survive, as do instruments marked A. & W. Geib, presumably dating from 1821, when John died. In 1821 William left the business, and Adam managed it alone until 1829, when he formed a partnership with Daniel Walker. By this time it seems that the firm's activities were devoted to publishing, in which they shared engraved plates with the Ditson firm in Boston. In 1843 Walker left the company, and in 1844 Adam's son, William, joined it. Adam retired in 1847. Between 1849 and 1858 the firm's affairs were increasingly supervised by S. T. Gordon, of Hartford, but William Geib remained with the firm.

BIBLIOGRAPHY
H. Dichter and E. Shapiro: *Early American Sheet Music* (New York, 1941/*R*1977)
A. C. Gildersleeve: *John Geib and his Seven Children* (Far Rockaway, NY, 1945)
R. Wolfe: *Secular Music in America, 1801–1825* (New York, 1964)
J. Ogasapian: 'New Data on John Geib', *The Tracker*, xxiii/4 (1979), 12
MARGARET CRANMER, BARBARA OWEN,
W. THOMAS MARROCCO, MARK JACOBS

Geige (Ger.). Violin or 'fiddle'. In the Middle Ages the term *Geige*, used without qualification, might refer to any bowed string instrument. By the 16th century, however, a distinction was made between the *grosse Geigen* (*viole da gamba*), that is, the viol family, and the *kleine Geigen* (*viole da braccio*), the violin family. In 1619, Praetorius used *Geigen* to mean members of the violin family (he used *Violen* to mean viols); he distinguished the violin as the treble member of the violin family by the term *Discant-Geig* ('treble violin') – or, more exactly, by *rechte Discant-Geig* ('treble violin proper'). The latter term established the meaning precisely in a terminology where *Discant-Geig* might refer not only to the violin proper but also, used loosely, to a small 'violin' (*kleine Discant-Geig*), tuned a 4th higher than the normal violin; it might even be used for a still smaller 'violin' with three strings (rather than four), tuned *g'–d''–a''* – that is, an octave higher than the lower

Geigenwerk: woodcut from Praetorius's 'Syntagma musicum' (2/1619)

three strings of the regular violin. According to Praetorius, the term *Fiddel* was used as the equivalent of *Geige* among the 'common people'.

BIBLIOGRAPHY
M. Praetorius: *Syntagma musicum*, ii (Wolfenbüttel, 1618, 2/1619/*R*1958 and 1980)
DAVID D. BOYDEN

Geigen (Ger.). An ORGAN STOP.

Geigenharz (Ger.). ROSIN.

Geigenwerk. Name (*Geigenwerck*) given by Hans Haiden to an instrument of his own invention, probably the most successful and certainly the most influential of all bowed keyboard instruments. Haiden produced a working example of his instrument by 1575 and an improved version in 1599, for which he received an imperial privilege in 1601. He described this version in two pamphlets, *Commentario de musicali instrumento* (Nuremberg, 1605), and *Musicale instrumentum reformatum* (Nuremberg, n.d., and 1610). His account in the latter was quoted in full by Praetorius (1618), who also provided the only surviving picture of the instrument, which resembled a rather bulky harpsichord (see illustration). At various times Haiden used gut or wire strings, with parchment-covered wire strings in the bass. The bowing action was provided by five parchment-covered wheels against which the individual strings (one for each note) could be drawn by the action of the keyboard. These wheels were turned by means of a treadle. Haiden claimed that the instrument was capable of producing all shades of loudness, of sustaining notes indefinitely, and of producing vibrato. As late as the second decade of the 18th century, there was a *Geigenwerk* in the Medici Collection in Florence, and another at Dresden was examined by J. G. Schröter. An instrument made in Spain in the first half of the 17th century, and apparently based on Haiden's writings, is in the Instruments Museum of the Brussels Conservatory. Several other inventors also modelled bowed keyboard instruments on Haiden's *Geigenwerk* (*see* SOSTENENTE PIANO, §1).

BIBLIOGRAPHY

M. Praetorius: *Syntagma musicum*, ii (Wolfenbüttel, 1618, 2/1619/*R*1964 and 1980), 67ff; iii (Wolfenbüttel, 1620/*R*1964 and 1976), pl.iii

G. Kinsky: 'Hans Haiden: der Erfinder der Nürnbergischen Geigenwerks', *ZMw*, vi (1923–4), 193

F. J. de Hen: 'The Truchado Instrument: a Geigenwerk?', *Keyboard Instruments*, ed. E. M. Ripin (Edinburgh, 1971, 2/1977)

S. Marcuse: *A Survey of Musical Instruments* (London, 1975), 308ff

EDWIN M. RIPIN

Gein, van den. *See* VAN DEN GHEYN family.

Geissenhof, Franz (*b* Vils, 1754; *d* ?Vienna, 2 Jan 1821). Austrian violin maker. Geissenhof holds the same place in the history of Viennese violin making that his contemporary Lupot holds in Paris. Each had comparatively ordinary professional origins, yet raised his art to a very high level, through fine craftsmanship allied to a growing appreciation of the work of Stradivari. Geissenhof went to Vienna to be apprentice and then successor to Johann Georg Thir. By about 1790 he had clearly seen the work of Stradivari, but his own instruments remained predominantly Old Viennese, round in the arching, with Germanic scroll and chocolate-brown varnish. By the turn of the century he had progressed a long way, and a few years later was copying Stradivari wholeheartedly. His varnish became less brittle and lighter in colour as the years advanced. Tonally his results were from the first superior to those of his Viennese predecessors. His violas were of small size, and he made very few cellos. Most of his instruments have a brand 'F.G.' on the button at the top of the back. He used the Latinized form of his name, Franciscus, on his labels.

BIBLIOGRAPHY

W. L. von Lütgendorff: *Die Geigen- und Lautenmacher vom Mittelalter bis zur Gegenwart* (Frankfurt am Main, 1904, rev. 6/1922/*R*1968)

R. Vannes: *Essai d'un dictionnaire universel des luthiers* (Paris, 1932, 2/1951/*R*1972 as *Dictionnaire universel des luthiers* and *R*1981 incl. suppl. 1959)

F. Farga: *Violins and Violinists* (London, 1950)

R. Bletschacher: *Die Lauten- und Geigenmacher des Füssener Landes* (Hofhaim-am-Taunus, 1978)

CHARLES BEARE

Gejjai. *See* KECCAI.

Gejjalu. Metal pellet bells of Andhra Pradesh, south India; the *gejje* are similar instruments of Karnataka State. They are worn round the ankle. *See* GHUṄGRŪ.

Gekkin. Lute of Japan. (1) Japanese equivalent of the Chinese YUEQIN (short-necked lute).

(2) Name in Ming-derived music for the long-necked lute with octagonal body, known also as *genkan* in Japanese and RUAN in Chinese. *See also* MINSHINGAKU.

Geko. XYLOPHONE of Flores, Indonesia. *See* PRESON.

Gelintang. GONG-CHIME of the Kayuagung, Pasemah and some coastal areas of the province of South Sumatra. It consists of four small bossed bronze gongs in a frame, and is played in the *tabuhan* (or *gamelan*) ensemble.

Gemelli (It.: 'twins'). A family of DUPLEX instruments made by GIUSEPPE PELITTI in 1855.

Gemshorn (from Ger. *Gams*, *Gems*: 'chamois') (i). A medieval folk RECORDER (a DUCT FLUTE) made originally from the horn of the chamois. From about 1375 onwards, it was made from the horn of the domestic ox, in sizes from the descant to 8' bass. This sophisticated form was depicted by Virdung (*Musica getutscht*, 1511), Dürer (a prayer book for Maximilian I, 1515) and Agricola (*Musica instrumentalis deudsch*, 1528). The final edition of Agricola's treatise (1548–9) omits it, however, and this deletion is evidence of the instrument's decline. From about 1450, organ builders imitated the characteristic ocarina-like quality of the gemshorn in the flute organ stop which bears its name; indeed, since no specimens of the contemporary gemshorn are known to survive, it is the use of this organ stop which has been chiefly responsible for our knowledge of the instrument's one-time existence.

Sub-types included gemshorns made from the horn of the domestic goat (*capra hircus*) and of certain of the Alpine ibex, notably *capra ibex* and *capra pyrenaica*. Sachs (1918–19) described a specimen then surviving in the Royal Arsenal at Berlin as a definitive gemshorn, but modern zoological opinion is not agreed on whether the example in question was made from the horn of the domestic goat, Pyrenean ibex or even the Caucasian tur. Modern reconstructions based on the description in Sachs's article, and using the horn of the Thomson gazelle (a species first identified in 1884) cannot be regarded as historically authentic.

Reconstructions made from ox horn, based upon 16th-century drawings, have yielded an instrument which fills the gap between the FLAGEOLET and the recorder. Its tone

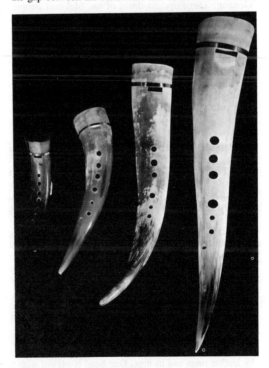

Set of four gemshorns as reconstructed by Horace Fitzpatrick (private collection)

is soft and somewhat husky, with remarkable carrying power; and the gemshorn's ready speech shows the characteristic 'chiff' of its organ stop namesake. In its early use of the thumb-hole the gemshorn is a predecessor of the true recorder: indeed experiments indicate that the gemshorn and cylindrical medieval recorder shared a common voicing. It is not generally appreciated that the pair of transverse lines which appears above the mouth of gemshorn and recorder both in Virdung's work and in that of Agricola represents a movable metal tuning-band. In both instruments this band serves the dual purpose of focussing the tone and counteracting any rise in pitch as the instrument warms up when played. The descant gemshorn has a range of a 6th; the bass and great bass versions encompass a 10th. The most common pitches appear to have been the soprano, the alto and the tenor, each with a range of a 9th. The unique nature of the instrument's bore, a stopped, inverted cone, causes it to overblow to the 14th, producing an erratic short second octave. The gemshorn is appropriate for the performance of medieval and early Renaissance dance music, secular polyphony and religious music of a vernacular character such as carols and sacred madrigals. It blends well with voices. Tenor and bass gemshorns can be used to advantage in a recorder consort since they are louder and respond more quickly than do their counterparts in the recorder family.

BIBLIOGRAPHY
C. Sachs: 'Das Gemshorn', *ZMw*, i (1918–19), 153
H. Fitzpatrick: 'The Gemshorn: a Reconstruction', *PRMA*, xcix (1972–3), 1

HORACE FITZPATRICK

Gemshorn (ii). An ORGAN STOP.

Genang. Large upright drum of the Melanau peoples of Sarawak, Malaysia. It is used at healing ceremonies.

Genbra. Single-string plucked lute of the descendants of black slaves in Mauritania. It is played with a plectrum. The soundbox varies in shape and is made from a calabash, or sometimes a metal container, covered with a skin which supports the handle. The instrument is used solo to accompany singing. See M. Guignard: *Musique, honneur et plaisir au Sahara* (Paris, 1975).

Gendang. (1) A generic Indonesian and Malaysian term for any double-headed laced drum, cylindrical or conical. (For a discussion of such instruments in Java and Bali, *see* KENDANG.) Other cognate terms are *gandang* (in the Dayak areas of Kalimantan and in west and north coastal Sumatra), *gimar* (among the Tanjung Benua people of east Kalimantan), *gondang*, *gordang*, *gonrang* and *genderang* (Batak languages), *geundrang* (Acehnese), *ganrang* (Makassarese and Buginese) and *gandar* (in Flores). The term may also refer to a pair of *gendang* (mostly of unequal size) played in various ensembles as for example in the Pakpak Dairi area of North Sumatra.

The term *gendang panjang* ('long drum') refers to various types of *gendang*. In the Serdang and Langkat areas of North Sumatra it is about 60 to 90 cm long, with goatskin heads about 30 cm and 20 cm in diameter. These are attached to the wooden (coconut-tree) frame by leather rings and lacings. One head is played with a soft wooden stick and the other with the left-hand fingers. In Riau (Tanjung Pinang) the *gendang panjang* is

about 75 cm long and is played in pairs; the slightly larger drum is called the *gendang pengibu* ('mother drum') and the smaller *gendang penganak* ('child drum'). It is used in the *nobat* orchestra. In the *kelintang* ensemble of Bengkulu and Jambi the *gendang panjang* is known also as *redap*. It is also played in the *keromong dua-belas* ensemble in Bengkulu.

The *gendang pelaku* of the coastal region of Bengkulu province, Sumatra, is a pair of different-sized cylindrical drums. They are played in ensemble with a *biola* (violin) or *serunai* (oboe) to accompany traditional dances at weddings and other celebrations.

In the Batak Karo area of the province of North Sumatra the *gendang* is an elongated drum. The player holds it in a vertical position and beats the upper head with a pair of round-ended sticks, about 6 cm long, made of wood from the *jeruk purut* (citrus) tree. The deerskin heads measure about 8 cm in diameter at the top and about 5 cm at the bottom. The body, of jackfruit wood, is about 42 cm long and bulges to a width of about 12 cm near the top. The two heads are laced to the base by thick vertical cords of buffalo- or cowhide. The drum is known also as *gendang indung* ('mother drum') and its player as a *singindungi*. A similar, smaller drum, the *gendang anak* ('child drum') or *gendang singanaki*, may be attached by thick leather cord to the *gendang indung* and used by the same player. The *anak* is about 10 cm long, with one head about 4 cm in diameter and the other 2 cm.

The *gendang bulek* ('round drum') of the Natal area on the west coast of North Sumatra is cylindrical; its goatskin heads are laced with leather or rattan to its wooden frame. It is played with both hands.

A pair of *gendang* is used in the *caklempong* ensemble of Negri Sembilan, Malaysia. The larger is the *gendang betina* ('female drum'), about 65 cm long and with a diameter of about 26 cm at one end and 23 cm at the other; the *gendang jantan* ('male drum') is about 60 cm long, with a diameter of about 23 cm at one end and 21 cm at the other. Skin from a female goat is used for the heads, one of which is played either with a wooden stick or by hand, and the other only by hand. It is also found in the *kulintang* ensemble of the Philippines.

(2) Term used in Sumatra and Malaysia for various instrumental pieces in which the *gendang* (1) is prominent and hence for the ensembles that play them.

In the Pakpak Dairi area of North Sumatra *gendang* refers to the minor ceremonial ensemble. This consists of two *gendang* (one slightly larger than the other), *gerantung* (four suspended flat gongs), a *jujunya* (wind instrument), *cilat-cilat* (pair of small cymbals) and *ogung* (set of four gongs). The ensemble plays at minor festivals such as births, name-givings and agricultural rituals.

The *gendang sarunai* is the main ceremonial instrumental ensemble of the Batak Karo people of North Sumatra. It consists of a *sarunai* (oboe), *gendang indung*, *gendang anak*, *gung* (suspended gong) and *penganak* (large and small bronze or iron gongs). The ensemble accompanies the *tortor adat* (communal ceremonial dancing).

The *gendang bergung* or *gendang silat* ensemble of Riau province, Sumatra, is used to accompany *pencak silat* (a dance genre based on the art of self-defence), and wedding processions. It comprises a pair of *gendang panjang*, *rebano* (frame drum), and *gung*. The *gendang-gung*, an ensemble of the Serdang area of North Sumatra, is used to accompany dances, especially former court dances. It comprises a pair of *gendang panjang*, *gung*, *tawak* (suspended gong), *cilempong* (gong-chime) and a pair of *kobat* (frame drums).

Similar ensembles are found among the Iban people of central Sarawak, Malaysia. The *gendang rayah*, a religious ensemble, includes two *tawak* and three *bandai* (small suspended gongs); the *gendang ajat* and *gendang panjai*, entertainment ensembles, include an *engkromong* (gong-chime), *bandai*, *tawak* and two *dumbak* (small drums).

See also KULINTANG.

MARGARET J. KARTOMI

Gendang-gendang. Leg XYLOPHONE, with three keys, of the Toala people of Sulawesi.

Gender. Multi-octave METALLOPHONE of Java and Bali. In the Central Javanese gamelan it has 12 to 14 thin, bevel-edged bronze keys suspended over individual tube resonators and played with two padded disc-shaped mallets (see illustration). In a complete gamelan there are always three *gender barung* (lower-pitched *gender*, approximately 105 cm long) and three *gender panerus* (higher-pitched, approximately 90 cm long), one for the *slendro* tonality and two for the *pelog* tonality (*see* GAMELAN, §4). The 14-key *gender barung* ranges from pitch 6 of the second octave (6^2) to pitch 3 of the fifth octave (3^5). The 14-key *gender panerus* ranges from 6^3 to 3^6. None of the *pelog gender* has a pitch 4. The *gender* is rare in West Java where it consists of a series of ten rather flat keys suspended over resonating tubes. It is used to accompany the chanting of a puppeteer, and is found in some *slendro*-tuned gamelan.

Gender panerus (multi-octave metallophone) of the Central Javanese gamelan (Museum of Wayang, Jakarta)

In the Balinese *gamelan gong gede* and *gamelan gong kebyar* the *gender* has bevel-edged keys suspended over tuned bamboo tubes set in a wooden case. It is played with a hammer of wood or horn (for illustration *see* GANGSA (ii)) or, in the case of the lowest-pitched *gender*, with a padded mallet. The left thumb and forefinger damp one key as the right hand strikes the next. The *gender* span one, two or three octaves. They are tuned in pairs, one pitched slightly higher than the other, so that when corresponding keys on the two instruments are struck simultaneously the difference in pitch produces an acoustical beat. The three sizes of *gender* are called *jegogan* (the largest), *jublag* and *penyacah*. A pair of ten-key *gender* are called *giying*.

One or two pairs of ten-key *gender*, tuned in *slendro*, are used (under the name *gender wayang* or *gender desa*) to accompany the *wayang kulit* (shadow-puppet play) of Bali. *Gender wayang* requires exceptional co-ordination, not only because the keys are struck and damped by the same hand but also because each player's hands move

independently; a similar technique is used in the *gamelan pelegongan* ensemble (*see* GANGSA (ii)). When one pair of *gender* is used the musicians often play in unison or with figuration divided between their right hands; sometimes there are four separate parts. If a second pair is used, it exactly doubles the first an octave higher.

The term *gender panembung* is used, in Yogyakarta, Java, for a SLENTEM (keyed metallophone).

BIBLIOGRAPHY
C. McPhee: *Music in Bali* (New Haven and London, 1966/*R*1976)
——: 'The Balinese *Wayang Koelit* and its Music', *Djåwå*, xvi (1936), 1–50

MARGARET J. KARTOMI, RUBY ORNSTEIN

Genderang. Single-headed drum of the Pakpak Dairi area of North Sumatra. The name is used also for an ensemble consisting of between five and nine *genderang* of various sizes played by five musicians, two to four *ogung* (gongs), *cilat-cilat* (small cymbals), an optional *gerantung* (flat gongs beaten together) and an optional *sarune* (oboe). It is the main instrumental ensemble for weddings, funerals and other ceremonies of the Pakpak Dairi people.

MARGARET J. KARTOMI

Gending. Ancient term for the *rebab*, a SPIKE FIDDLE of Central Java.

Generalbass (Ger.: 'thoroughbass' or CONTINUO). The term itself was taken by Niedt (*Musicalische Handleitung*, Hamburg, 1700) to reflect the fact that the continuo bass line contains all or nearly all the other parts *generaliter* or *insgemein* ('in common'). Earlier, in 1611, C. Vincentius had called a bass part he added to Schadaeus's *Promptuarium musici* the *basin vulgo generalem dictam*. But *generalis* is not German and cannot be a translation of 'continuo'; rather it was one of the optional names for figured or unfigured bass parts, like *basso principale* (Vecchi, 1598 and 1601), *basso generale* (Fattorini, 1600; Billi, 1601), *sectione gravium partium ad organistarum usum* (Zucchini, 1602), *basso continuo* (Viadana, 1602), *basso continuato* (Calestani, 1603). That Viadana's so-called continuo bass part was, unlike the others, independent of the vocal bass may or may not be significant in this respect. Praetorius (*Syntagma musicum*, iii, Wolfenbüttel, 2/1619) headed his chapter on this subject 'De basso generali seu continuo', and he may have meant to give the two as optional alternative names; later German theorists such as J. Staden (*Kurz und einfältig Bericht*, 1626), H. Albert (prefaces to *Arien*, i–ii, 1638–40) and W. Ebner (*Arte prattica & poëtica*, 1653) either followed Praetorius in using both terms or kept only *bassis generalis*, in which they were followed by all later writers. The term Generalbass became a kind of synecdoche for the science of harmony in general; to learn Generalbass (or, as in France after Rameau, the *basse fondamentale*) meant to learn the science of tonal harmony, made more direct and clear by figured harmony than by the old German keyboard tablatures. Many writers from 1650 to 1850 scarcely mentioned the art of figured bass accompaniment in their treatises on Generalbass.

PETER WILLIAMS

General Development System [GDS]. A polyphonic digital SYNTHESIZER, developed in 1978–80 and manufactured from 1981 by the Digital Keyboards division of Music Technology, the American branch of Crumar,

in Garden City Park, New York. Based on a Z80 micro-computer system with 32 digital oscillators, the General Development System was originally the testbed for the company's SYNERGY. It includes a visual display unit, two disc drives, an alphanumeric keyboard, a five-octave, velocity-sensitive keyboard with 62 controls (32 of which are slide potentiometers) and three foot controls; a printer is also available. Up to eight synchronized tracks can be recorded by the sequencer memory.
See also COMPUTER, §5.

BIBLIOGRAPHY
J. Strawn: 'Report from the 1980 Audio Engineering Society Convention in Los Angeles', *Computer Music Journal*, iv/3 (1980), 66
HUGH DAVIES

Genggo [ego]. JEW'S HARP of eastern Flores, Indonesia, made of palmwood or bamboo. It consists of a long-necked bottle-shaped lath which is split to produce a long vibrating tongue which narrows towards one end. It ranges between 11·5 and 19 cm in length.

Genggong. JEW'S HARP of Indonesia. The bamboo or palmwood varieties consist of a rectangular lath which is split to produce a long vibrating tongue which narrows at one end. Held in the left hand, it is placed in front of the player's half-open mouth while a finger of the right hand vibrates the other end, by either plucking it or rhythmically pulling a small cord attached to it. The metal variety is like the Western jew's harp. The name 'genggong' is found in many parts of Indonesia and in the Malay peninsula, but there are also many local names, such as *duri* or *druri bewe* in Nias, *ego*, *genggo* or *robe* in Flores, *karinding* in West Java, *popo* in the Gayo area of Aceh (Sumatra) and *rinding* and *rinding wesi* in Central Java.

The instrument is usually played privately or for courting. In the Gayo and Alas areas of Aceh province groups of women or girls play several *genggong* in ensemble with up to five *canang kacapi* (tube zithers). In Bali they are played together with flutes, drums, tube zithers and cymbals in the *gamelan gengenggongan*.
MARGARET J. KARTOMI

Genggong sakai. Malaysian instrument combining elements of an idiophone and an aerophone. *See* TAODO.

Genikng. Suspended bossed gong of the Tanjung Benua people of east Kalimantan, Indonesia. *See* KULINTANG.

Genis (It.). TENOR HORN.

Genis corno (It.). TENOR COR.

Genjring. FRAME DRUM with jingles used in parts of West and Central Java. Its goatskin head is pinned or glued to a wooden frame about 30 to 35 cm in diameter. Usually three sets of metal discs are attached around the frame. *Genjring* are mostly played with *terbang* (frame drums without jingles) to accompany religious singing. In Cirebon four *genjring* are used with a set of *dogdog* (single-headed drums) and singers to accompany the *burok* pageant, in which dancers wear animal masks. In the Banyumas area they are used to accompany displays of the art of self-defence, together with gongs and other drums.
MARGARET J. KARTOMI

Genkan. Japanese name for the Chinese long-necked lute now known as RUAN; *see also* MINSHINGAKU. Two 8th- or 9th-century *genkan* are in the Shōsōin Repository in Nara.

Gennaro, Giacomo [Januarius, Jacobus] (*fl* Cremona, *c*1640–55). Italian violin maker. More commonly known by the latinized form of his name which appears on the labels of his instruments, he was a pupil of Nicolo Amati whose small pattern he followed with remarkable fidelity. The choice of wood is good but seldom visually handsome. His instruments have become rare, especially under their original labels; many, if not most, have been attributed to Amati. The varnish is of typical Cremonese quality, usually a golden light brown and of fine transparency. Although the violins are small, their tone is strong and even and of a real Amatese quality. His printed label reads 'Iacobus Ianuarius Cremonensis/Alumnus Nicolai Amati Jaciebat, 16--'.

BIBLIOGRAPHY
R. Vannes: *Essai d'un dictionnaire universel des luthiers* (Paris, 1932, 2/1951/R 1972 as *Dictionnaire universel des luthiers* and R 1981 incl. suppl. 1959)
W. Henley: *Universal Dictionary of Violin and Bow Makers*, i-v (Brighton, 1959–60); vi, ed. C. Woodcock as *Dictionary of Contemporary Violin and Bow Makers* (Brighton, 1965)
JAAK LIIVOJA-LORIUS

Genouillère (Fr.). KNEE-LEVER.

Genrang. *See* GANRANG.

Genrang dan gong. Ensemble of three large double-headed drums and a bronze bossed gong in the Buginese area of South Sulawesi. It is mentioned in the historical chronicle *Lontara bugis* as an ensemble played at the court of a *raja* (chieftain). It is also used in trance ceremonies presided over by a *bissu* (transvestite mystic), through whose mouth the spirit of a *raja* is believed to speak.
MARGARET J. KARTOMI

Gerantung. Idiophone of the Pakpak Dairi area of North Sumatra. It is a set of four, five or six flat metal plates strung together, and beaten by one performer. It is played, together with four gongs (*pongpong, poi, tapudep* and *panggora*) in the *gendang* or *genderang* orchestra, to accompany dancing. The term 'gerantung' is also used for an ensemble consisting of a *gerantung* and three *ogung* (gongs). See L. Moore: 'An Introduction to the Music of the Pakpak Dairi of North Sumatra', *Indonesia Circle* (1981), no.24, p.39.
MARGARET J. KARTOMI

Gerhard. German family of organ builders active in the 18th and 19th centuries. Justinus Ehrenfried Gerhard (*b* 1710 or 1711; *d* Lindig bei Kahla, 16 Jan 1786) probably learnt the art of organ building from the craftsman Tröbs in Weimar. About 1739 he founded a works at Lindig, in which town he married in 1741. He was a great craftsman, whose art is equal to that of Gottfried Silbermann. His instruments are solidly built, with beautiful Baroque façades, good dispositions and fine tone quality. The organ at Ziegenhain (1764; one manual and pedal, nine speaking stops and pedal coupler) is outstanding for its exceptionally powerful, clear sound and excellent voicing.

Christian August Gerhard (*b* Lindig, 1 Sept 1745; *d*

Lindig, 15 Dec 1817), son of Justinus Ehrenfried, continued the business in Lindig. A grandson, Johann Christian Adam Gerhard (*b* Lindig, 17 Aug 1780; *d* Dorndorf an der Saale, 6 May 1837), opened a branch at Dorndorf.

Johann Ernst Gottfried Gerhard (*b* Lindig, 21 April 1786; *d* Merseburg, 23 Oct 1823), another grandson, was an organ builder in Merseburg; his firm survives today under the name of Kühn.

An organ builder with the name Gerhard worked in Boppard in the 19th century.

BIBLIOGRAPHY

A. L. Back: *Chronik der Stadt und des Amtes Eisenberg* (Eisenberg, 1843)

J. and E. Löbe: *Geschichte der Kirchen und Schulen des Herzogthums Sachsen-Altenburg* (Altenburg, 1886–91)

F. Oehme: *Handbuch über ältere und neuere Orgelwerke im Königreiche Sachsen*, ii (Dresden, n.d.), 242f

WALTER HÜTTEL

Gering-gering. Rattle of Aceh province, Sumatra, consisting of jingles in a circular wooden frame; it resembles a frame drum without a skin, and has a diameter of about 28 cm. It is used in the *seurune kaleë* ensemble of West Aceh.

Gerle, Conrad (*d* Nuremberg, 4 Dec 1521). German lute maker. He was active at Nuremberg in 1465 and became well known for his instruments in France as well as in Germany. In 1469 Charles the Bold of Burgundy bought three of his lutes for players at his court. Gerle lived at one time in the Kotgasse in Nuremberg, and moved from there to the Breitengasse in 1516. He was buried at St Rochus, Nuremberg, leaving a widow and several young children, one of whom was probably the instrumentalist and lute maker Hans Gerle (*b* Nuremberg, *c*1500; *d* Nuremberg, 1570), who published three volumes of music, of which the first, *Musica teusch* (1532), includes valuable introductory essays on playing 'Grossgeigen' (violas da gamba), 'Kleingeigen' (rebecs or violins) and lutes, and on notation.

BIBLIOGRAPHY

C. G. von Murr: 'Versuch einer nürnbergischen Handwerksgeschichte vom dreyzehnten Jahrhundert bis zur Mitte des sechszehnten', *Journal zur Kunstgeschichte und zur allgemeinen Literatur*, v (1777), 114

W. L. von Lütgendorff: *Die Geigen- und Lautenmacher vom Mittelalter bis zur Gegenwart* (Frankfurt am Main, 1904, rev. 6/1922/*R*1968)

R. Vannes: *Essai d'un dictionnaire universel des luthiers* (Paris, 1932, 2/1951/*R*1972 as *Dictionnaire universel des luthiers* and *R*1981 incl. suppl. 1959)

M. A. Downie: *The Rebec: an Orthographic and Iconographic Study* (diss., U. of West Virginia, Morgantown, 1981)

Gerle, Georg (*d* Innsbruck, *c*1589). German instrument maker. According to Vannes he came from Immenthal (near St Gall), and in 1548 was made a citizen of Füssen. In 1569 he was employed as organ blower and instrument maker by the Archduke Ferdinand at Innsbruck, and since reference was made in 1572 to his long service it may be supposed that he was previously in the same employ at Prague. An ivory lute by Gerle, made about 1580, is in the Kunsthistorisches Museum, Vienna. It is probably the only surviving six-course lute in apparently original condition and bears the label, 'Georg Gerle, Fürstlicher Durchleuchtig-/kait Chalkandt zu Ynnsprugg'. A 'cembalo del Gherla' is mentioned in the 1598 catalogue of the Este collection at Modena.

Three of Gerle's sons are known. Melchior succeeded

to his father's post at Innsbruck in 1589; after 1596, when the Archduke Ferdinand died and the court was dissolved, he remained at Innsbruck where he had married in 1591 and had a son, Anton, in 1605. Another of Georg Gerle's sons, also called Georg, became organ blower to the Innsbruck court in 1583; at the beginning of the 17th century he was living at Füssen and in 1615 at Immenstadt. A third son, Jacob, his father's pupil and assistant, is known to have been active at Graz in 1585.

BIBLIOGRAPHY

W. L. von Lütgendorff: *Die Geigen- und Lautenmacher vom Mittelalter bis zur Gegenwart* (Frankfurt am Main, 1904, rev. 6/1922/*R*1968)

F. Waldner: 'Verzeichnis der Organisten, Sänger und Instrumentisten am Hofe zu Innsbruck unter Erzherzog Ferdinand 1567–1596', *MMg*, xxxvi (1904), 167

——: *Nachrichten über tirolische Lauten- und Geigenbauer* (Innsbruck, 1911), 51f

R. Vannes: *Essai d'un dictionnaire universel des luthiers* (Paris, 1932, 2/1951/*R*1972 as *Dictionnaire universel des luthiers* and *R*1981 incl. suppl. 1959)

Gerle, Hans. German instrumentalist, lute maker and compiler and arranger of several volumes of instrumental music, probably the son of CONRAD GERLE.

Gerle, Melchior. German instrument maker, son of GEORG GERLE.

German action. A developed form of the *Prellmechanik* piano action credited to Johann Andreas Stein; *see* PIANOFORTE, §I, 3.

German flute. An older name for the transverse FLUTE, used to distinguish it from the RECORDER, also called 'English flute'.

Gernsback, Hugo (*b* Luxembourg, 16 Aug 1884; *d* ?New York, 19 Aug 1967). American writer, publisher and instrument inventor, of Luxembourgeois birth. In 1904 he emigrated to America, where in 1908 he founded the first of a series of radio magazines (including *Radio-Craft*) which he wrote for and edited. He later turned to science fiction magazines (from 1926); the Hugo award for science fiction writing is named after him. He was something of a pioneer in his publishing activities and no less so in the area of electronic instruments; he developed two keyboard instruments, the STACCATONE (1923), which was probably monophonic, and the polyphonic PIANORAD (1926), which was used for some time in broadcasting.

HUGH DAVIES

Gerock, Christopher (*fl* London, 1804–37). English maker of woodwind instruments, music seller and publisher. He worked in London at 76 Bishopsgate Within (*c*1804–21) and at 1 Gracechurch Street (*c*1815–21). Through a partnership with George Astor the firm became known as Gerock, Astor & Co., operating at 76 Bishopsgate (1821–7); from 1821 to 1831 it was also at 79 Cornhill. It was known as Gerock & Wolf during 1831–2, and as C. Gerock & Co. from 1832 to 1837. It then became Robert Wolf & Co. until 1845, when it appears that the business ceased.

Gerock is known to have made flageolets, piccolos, flutes, clarinets, bassoons and serpents. Like other London makers of the time (e.g. George Astor, John Cramer and Thomas Key) he used the unicorn head mark. The flutes and clarinets were normally made in boxwood with ivory rings. A flute (Oxford, Bate Collection) has four silver cupped keys and a tuning slide, and a clarinet in C (Bate Collection) has nine square keys. Gerock & Wolf, the patentees of Boehm's newly invented flute, offered the instrument for sale in 1832, claiming considerable improvements in tone quality, ease of execution and intonation.

BIBLIOGRAPHY

Preceptor for the Improved Octave Flageolet (London, c1806) [published by Gerock]

C. Gerock and R. Wolf: Scale and Description of Boehm's Newly Invented Patent Flute (London, c1832)

R. S. Rockstro: A Treatise on . . . the Flute (London, 1890, 2/1928/R1967)

A. Carse: Musical Wind Instruments (London, 1939/R1965)

C. Humphries and W. C. Smith: Music Publishing in the British Isles (London, 1954, 2/1970)

L. G. Langwill: An Index of Musical Wind-instrument Makers (Edinburgh, 1960, rev., enlarged 6/1980)

A. Baines: The Bate Collection of Historical Wind Instruments (Oxford, 1976)

NIALL O'LOUGHLIN

Gerudeng. JEW'S HARP of the Iban people of central Sarawak, Malaysia. It is used in courting rituals.

Geschwind (Ger.: 'quick'). A word normally used as the German equivalent of the Italian *allegro* (though *presto* would perhaps be a more accurate translation), as in the designation *mässig geschwind*, which means the same as *allegro moderato*. It also appears in the adverbial form *geschwinde*.

See also TEMPO AND EXPRESSION MARKS.

DAVID FALLOWS

Gęśle [gęśl, gusli]. General term used in medieval Poland for various string instruments, originally plucked (*see* ROTTE (ii)), later bowed. The term 'gęśle' is used nowadays by the people of the Tatra mountains for the violin in a string band.

Gęśliki. Small fiddle of Poland. *See* ZŁÓBCOKI.

Gesok-gesok. (1) SPIKE FIDDLE of the Toraja area of central Sulawesi. The resonator may be made from a gourd or half a coconut-shell covered with buffalo or goatskin, or from a wooden box. One or two strings are attached to a wooden rod which passes through the resonator; the strings are raised on a bridge. The thin bamboo bow has hair of rattan fibre. The instrument is used to accompany the singing of epic or historical stories. The player sits cross-legged, holding the instrument upright on its spike.

(2) Single-string fiddle of southern Sulawesi. Its body is made from half a coconut-shell.

BIBLIOGRAPHY

W. Kaudern: Musical Instruments in Celebes (Göteborg, 1927)

MARGARET J. KARTOMI

Gestopft (Ger.: 'stopped'). A term applied to hand-stopping on a horn. It affects the pitch and the tone quality of the instrument. *See* HORN, §2.

Gestossen. *See* ABGESTOSSEN.

Geteilt (Ger.; abbreviated 'get.'). DIVISI.

Getragen (Ger.: 'solemn', 'ceremonious'). A mark of tempo (and mood) found either by itself or as a qualification to some other tempo marks: *langsam getragen* ('slow and solemn').

Getreppte Docke (Ger.). DOGLEG JACK.

Geṭṭuvādyam. Struck lute of south India. The body, of wood, is similar in construction to that of the southern *sarasvatī vīṇā* (*see* VĪṆĀ, §8) and TAMBŪRĀ, but smaller (about 80 cm long). The long wooden neck is attached to a hemispherical resonator, about 25 cm deep, covered with a flat wooden soundtable; there are no frets. Near the top of the neck is a gourd (or mock-gourd) on which the instrument may be rested, face-upwards, on the floor in front of the player. There are two thick wire strings, each in a double course, tuned a 5th apart. They are beaten rhythmically by two small sticks and sometimes also played melodically (neither the stopping operation nor its context has been described). 'Geṭṭuvādyam' should not be confused with 'goṭṭuvādyam' (*see* VĪṆĀ, §9). The 'tambūrā' shown by Sambamoorthy (1962), with octagonal resonators, is probably this instrument.

BIBLIOGRAPHY

P. Sambamoorthy: Catalogue of Musical Instruments Exhibited in the Government Museum, Madras (Madras, 3/1962), pl.3

B. C. Deva: Musical Instruments of India (Calcutta, 1978)

ALASTAIR DICK

Getzen. American firm of brass instrument manufacturers. It was first established in Elkhorn, Wisconsin, as a band instrument repair shop in 1939 by T. J. (Anthony James) Getzen (*b* Grand Rapids, Mich., 25 Sept 1894; *d* Harvard, Ill., 10 March 1968), a former plant supervisor for the Holton Band Instrument Co. Manufacturing began in 1945. Until 1960 the company concentrated on student quality cornets, trumpets, trombones and piston bugles. In June of that year, Getzen bought out the Hoosier Band Instrument Co. of Elkhart, Indiana. The turning-point of the firm's existence came in October 1960 with the merger with a Milwaukee holding company. Harold M. Knowlton, a former attorney, entered as president; a new factory was established on West Centralia Street (destroyed by fire on 13 October 1963 and reopened only 90 days later); and the company emphasis was shifted to include high-quality professional instruments. Carl ('Doc') Severinsen, a popular New York trumpeter, was then engaged as tester for the B♭ trumpets (the first 'Eterna Severinsen' model trumpet was introduced in 1962); Severinsen became vice-president for research and development in 1969, leaving the firm in 1980. William Vacchiano and Knud Hovaldt also joined the firm as consultants for orchestral trumpets. Getzen began to import Meinl-Weston tubas; the line of E. L. DeFord flutes was added in 1972. In that year a second factory, which increased their space by 75%, was purchased from the Yarger Hydraulics Co. in Marengo, Illinois. Getzen's trumpets, upon which much of the firm's success is based, have a notably open response in the high register and have been adopted by many players throughout the world.

In 1965 Donald E(arl) Getzen (*b* Elkhorn, Wisc., 15 May 1928), the son of T. J. Getzen, branched off from the Getzen Co. to found DEG Music Products, Inc., in Lake Geneva, Wisconsin. Their 20 workers (with another 40 in related operations) produce a full line of band instruments, including the 'Caravelle' tuba with detachable bell for easier transportation.

For illustration of an instrument by Getzen, *see* TRUMPET, fig.13*e*.
EDWARD H. TARR

Geudumba. HOURGLASS DRUM of Aceh province, Sumatra. Its body is made of one piece of jackfruit wood and its single head of goatskin. It stands about 30 cm high. In the early part of the 20th century it was often played with a *hareubab* (spike fiddle). Both are now almost obsolete.

Geundrang [geunderang]. Double-headed barrel-shaped drum of Aceh province, Sumatra. There are two sizes. The larger, called *geundrang*, is about 38 cm long and about 30 cm in diameter, and is either suspended by a cord round the player's shoulder or rested on his lap. The right-hand head is made of cowhide and beaten with an inverted L-shaped wooden hammer; the left-hand head is made of goatskin and played by hand. The body is often made of jackfruit wood with one small hole in it, and the heads are laced to it by rattan cord arranged in parallel lines. The smaller variety of *geundrang* (*geundrang ana*, *geundrang peungana* or *tuto*) may be held under the arm and beaten on one end by hand, or held in the lap and played on both ends. Two large and one small *geundrang* are used in the large *seurune kaleë* ensemble. In East Aceh the *geundrang* is played with *rapa'i*, *buloh peurindu* or *bansi* (long and short bamboo flutes), *biola* (violin) and one or two *canang* (small bossed gongs). *See also* GENDANG, (1).
MARGARET J. KARTOMI

Geure. *See* GIEVRE.

Geza [geza-ongaku]. Music played off-stage right to accompany the Japanese kabuki theatre (*ge*: 'lower'; *za*: 'dais'). *Geza* music includes both representational and

Geza (off-stage) musicians (and singers, left) accompanying kabuki theatre, with nōkan (transverse flute) and several percussion instruments, including (top to bottom) hontsurigane (bell), two shimedaiko (shallow barrel drums), hiradaiko (barrel drum, suspended), edaiko (double-headed drum with handle) and dōbatsu (cymbals)

conventional sound-effects as well as various songs and tunes which help to set the mood. This music and its performers are also called *kagebayashi* meaning 'hidden ensemble' (in contrast to *debayashi*, 'on-stage ensemble'; *see also* HAYASHI) or *kuromisu* meaning 'black blind' (through which the musicians watch the action; see illustration). A large number of Buddhist percussion instruments are used, both to evoke temple sounds and moods and for other unrelated effects. The woodblocks *mokugyo* and *mokushō*, for example, are used in comic scenes. Other familiar secular Japanese instruments are used in *geza* music, but several of the other instruments are only rarely heard in another context, for example the *matsumushi* (horizontal gongs), *orugōru* (bells), *mokkin* (xylophone) and *ekiro* (bell).

BIBLIOGRAPHY
W. P. Malm: *Japanese Music and Musical Instruments* (Rutland, Vermont, 1959), 221ff
——: 'Music in the Kabuki Theater', in J. R. Brandon and others, *Studies in Kabuki* (Honolulu, 1978), 133–75
Tōyō ongaku gakkai, ed.: *Kabuki ongaku* [Kabuki music] (Tokyo, 1980)
'Kabuki', *Ongaku daijiten* [Encyclopedia of music] (Tokyo, 1981)
DAVID W. HUGHES

Gezarke. A term occasionally applied to the KISSAR.

Ghadasa (from Sanskrit *gharṣa*: 'rubbing'). A medieval barrel drum of India, played partly by friction. It is described as similar to the HUḌUKKĀ. It was played with much 'booming' (*gomkāra*): the thumb and middle fingertips of the right hand, smeared with beeswax, rubbed the skin; the left-hand fingers struck the skin and the thumb pressed it. The modern *ghasā*, played by the Pāṇa musicians of south Orissa, appears to be directly related in name and construction. It is a barrel drum with raised hoops which is beaten on one side with a cane and rubbed on the other with a crook-stick.

BIBLIOGRAPHY
Śārṅgadeva: *Saṅgītaratnākara* (13th century), ed. S. Subrahmanya Sastri, iii (Madras, 1951)
K. S. Kothari: *Indian Folk Musical Instruments* (New Delhi, 1968)
B. C. Deva: *Musical Instruments of India* (Calcutta, 1978)
ALASTAIR DICK

Ghadiyal. *See* GHAṚIYĀL.

Ghaghar. Spherical terracotta percussion vessel of Sind, Pakistan. *See* DILO.

Ghaita [ghaite]. *See* GHAYṬA.

Ghajir nai. Short open end-blown flute of the Uzbek people of Central Asia. A pastoral instrument, it is made from the wing-bone of a steppe eagle (*ghajir*), and is now found only among the semi-nomadic Uzbeks of the Surkhandarya-Kashkadarya region (an arid steppe and river-valley zone of southern Uzbekistan).

Ghancā. *See* TAIM NĀIM.

Ghanon. Plucked string instrument of medieval Armenia, with 60 silk strings; possibly analogous to the *k'anon* (see QĀNŪN).

Ghaṇṭā [ghaṇṭ, ghaṇṭī, ghaṇṭikā, ghaṇṭo]. A South Asian term found in Sanskrit and the derived north In-

*Pellet bells (muyang, above) and clapper bells (irna)
worn for dancing by the Maria Gond people, Bastar
district, Madhya Pradesh*

dian languages; it is often translated 'bell' but it also
denotes, both historically and in the different modern
regions, other percussion or shaken metallophones.

In many of the modern north Indian languages the
masculine form *ghaṇṭā* denotes the large suspended bell
of the temple, and the feminine *ghaṇṭī* a handbell, either
the medium-sized variety rung by the priests at certain
points of temple ritual or the small bell of domestic worship. The suspended temple bell with interior clapper is
an essential element of the Hindu shrine: hung at the
gateway of small open shrines or, in the large temples,
in the foyer leading to the inner sanctum, it is rung by
each approaching worshipper to invoke the deity. In the
larger temples they can be very large, up to 50 maunds
(roughly 5000 lbs troy) in weight. The metal used in
their casting is in general bell-metal or white copper
(Sanskrit *kāṃsya*, New Indo-Aryan *kåså*), an alloy of
copper and zinc or tin (in a ratio of roughly 3:1), but
a special alloy is known as *saptadhātu* ('the sevenfold
metal').

The *ghaṇṭā* described in the early 13th-century Sanskrit work *Saṅgītaratnākara* is a bell-metal handbell
about 16 cm high and 1 cm thick, said to resemble a
pagoda. A wooden handle, carved in a triangle at the
top, adds to the height; the interior clapper (*jālaka*) is
of iron, 12 cm long and 1 cm thick. The bell is played
face-downwards, and the only usage mentioned is worship of the gods. Modern handbells often have a highly
decorated handle of cast metal, and their use is similarly
restricted to worship. The Tamil term of south India for
a bell is *maṇi*. In Andhra Pradesh the bell is called
gaṇṭā and in Karnataka state *gaṇṭe*; the *hāth ghaṇṭī*
('handbell') is the equivalent in Orissa. *See also* IRNA.

Another use of the term is for round percussion plaques.
These relatively thick bell-metal plates of various sizes
are suspended from the hand by a cord and beaten with
a wooden stick; they are also called *ghaṭī* in Sanskrit.
The medieval *jayaghaṇṭā* ('victory metallophone') of
the *Saṅgītaratnākara* is of this type. It was large, measuring 1 cubit (about 46 cm) in diameter and 1 cm in
thickness, and was beaten by a wooden stick (*koṇa*) suspended by a cord passing through two holes near the
edge. Of the same type, though smaller, is the *ghaṇṭ* of
modern Orissa, east India. These are used in the traditional context of temples and other religious places

but can also appear in drum ensembles for dancing; above
all, they are the traditional Indian clock on which the
hours are beaten (*see* GHAṚĪ and CENNALA).

The term *ghaṇṭā* (and variants) may also denote gongs,
although there is a difficult line of demarcation in South
Asia between gongs (defined by Hornbostel and Sachs
as percussion vessels) and percussion trays, where the
raised edge is often proportionally so small as only
dubiously to constitute a vessel. Both, however, may
be called gongs. The latter (the common Indian eating-
tray used as a metallophone) is known by the generic
term THĀLĪ. The Orissan *ghaṇṭo*, however, is certainly
a gong. It is of bell-metal, about 22 cm in diameter,
with a rear flange, inward-sloping and about 48 mm deep
and 3 mm thick. The front plate, almost imperceptibly
convex, is thicker in the centre; this is emphasized by
filing or scoring, creating a round, thicker central area
about 12·5 cm in diameter, cross-scored in ellipse, and
a thinner outer ring, scored circularly, parallel to the
edge of the gong and about 4·75 cm wide. The outer
half of the flange (but not the edge) and the corner are
coated with dry black resin; a cord passes through two
holes near the edge. The central and outer sections of
the plate have different tones, but the *ghaṇṭo*, when
properly struck in the centre, also produces a deep, slowly
rising note. The KĀSAR of Bengal is of similar construction. Bossed gongs are not typical of the Indian area,
except in the north-east, where the Tibeto-Burman- and
Thai-speaking peoples are South-east Asian in culture
(*see* SENMU). The *ghaṇṭā* of the Santal tribe of Orissa
is a gong about 19·5 cm wide with a slightly outward-
sloping rim 3·75 cm high. It is struck with a stick.

The Sanskrit term *ghaṇṭī*, or the diminutive *ghaṇṭikā*,
can also denote small metal pellet bells, worn cosmeti-
cally or on various parts of the body for dancing. The
kṣudraghaṇṭikā ('little bell-lets') of the *Saṅgītaratnākara* are of this type. The spheres, of bell-metal,
with a slit on one side and interior pellets of *tīkṣṇa*
(probably cast-iron), are threaded on to strings by an
integral ring at the top. They were typical of the
peraṇī dance. Their medieval folk names are given as
gharghara, *ghargharikā* ('gurgling') or *marmara* ('rustling'). Bells of this type worn by dancers are common
throughout the subcontinent (see illustration; *see also*
GHUṄGRŪ); another common type, consisting of hollow
rings with multiple pellets, is the NŪPUR.

BIBLIOGRAPHY

Śārṅgadeva: *Saṅgītaratnākara* (13th century), ed. S. Subrahmanya
  Sastri, iii (Madras, 1951)
C. Sachs: *Die Musikinstrumente Indiens und Indonesiens* (Berlin
  and Leipzig, 1914, 2/1923)
C. Marcel-Dubois: *Les instruments de musique de l'Inde ancienne*
  (Paris, 1941)
K. S. Kothari: *Indian Folk Musical Instruments* (New Delhi, 1968)
B. C. Deva: 'The Santals and their Musical Instruments', *Jb für
  musikalische Volks- und Volkerkunde*, viii (Cologne, 1977)
——: *Musical Instruments of India* (Calcutta, 1978)
                                                ALASTAIR DICK

Gharā. A north Indian term denoting struck pots or
percussion vessels. *See* GHAṬA, §1.

Gharghara [ghargharikā]. A medieval Indian folk name
for small metal pellet bells. *See* GHAṆṬĀ.

Gharī. A common north Indian term for a round percussion plaque made of bell-metal. The Sanskrit term
is GHAṆṬĀ or *ghaṭī*. The *ghaṛī* of northern areas of the

subcontinent is about 20 cm in diameter and 5 mm thick. It is suspended from the left hand by a cord passing through holes near the edge of the plaque and beaten with a wooden stick held in the right hand. The *gharī* can occur in temple music and in drum ensembles for dancing etc; it is also widespread as the traditional Indian clock, on which the hours are beaten, and the term can mean 'watch' or 'clock' in the New Indo-Aryan languages. Local names are also found, such as *ghaṇṭ* (Orissa) and *jhalar* (Rajasthan), and *ghariyāl* (northern areas) often denotes a larger variety (in Bengal it denotes the hereditary player of the *gharī*). (The *gharī* should be distinguished from the struck metallophone with raised edge; *see* THĀLĪ.) Southern equivalents include the *ceṇṇala*, *jaganta*, *jagate* and *sēmakkalam*. *See also* ŚRĪMAṆḌAL.

BIBLIOGRAPHY
C. Sachs: *Die Musikinstrumente Indiens und Indonesiens* (Berlin and Leipzig, 1914, 2/1923)
K. S. Kothari: *Indian Folk Musical Instruments* (New Delhi, 1968)
ALASTAIR DICK

Ghariyāl [ghadiyal]. Large round metal percussion plaque of Rajasthan, India, used to mark the hours of the day. *See* GHARĪ.

Ghasā. A barrel drum of the Pāṇa of south Orissa, eastern India. *See* GHAḌASA.

Ghaṭa [ghaṭam, gharā]. Terms used in South Asia for a waterpot; the Sanskrit *ghaṭa*, the south Indian loanform *ghaṭam* and the modern north Indian derivative *gharā* signify the everyday commodity of South Asian life, usually of terracotta, spherical, with a wide belly and narrow mouth. They occur widely in various musical contexts. The northern and southern terms of modern times denote primarily struck pots, that is, percussion vessels or idiophones, but the historical usage (in addition to other names) may also apply to skin-covered pots, pot-drums or membranophones. The two should be clearly distinguished.

1. Percussion vessels or pots. 2. Pot-drums or membranophones.

1. PERCUSSION VESSELS OR POTS. These, sometimes made of a special sonorous clay, are widely used in various musical contexts, struck with the fingers on belly, neck and mouth. They are sometimes played with drums.

The Sanskrit term *ghaṭa* (or *ghaṭavādya*: 'pot-instrument') occurs in a musical sense from the epics onwards (late centuries BC), but one cannot always know its precise denotation. Pots feature hardly at all in the earlier sculpture, being depicted only from about the 8th century AD, and then as pot-drums (see §2). The same applies to medieval mentions of *ghaṭa*. In modern times the *gharā* is common in the north, though it is sometimes known by other names such as *māṭki* (Rajasthan), *nut* (Kashmir) and *dilo* (Sind). The *gagrī* (*gagrā*) is similar, but is made of metal.

The *ghaṭam* of south India is used in several contexts, including the southern classical music, for which special pots are made at Panruti and Manamadura. The pot is placed on the seated player's lap and its mouth is sometimes pressed against the abdomen to vary the resonance; it is played at the mouth, belly and bottom with hands, wrists, fingertips and nails. It is said that the *ghaṭam* was sometimes thrown in the air to shatter on the ground on the last beat.

2. POT-DRUMS OR MEMBRANOPHONES. The waterpot also provides a natural resonator on which to stretch a skin. Although the term *ghaṭa* and its modern derivatives usually denote percussion vessels, the *ghaṭa* briefly described in the 13th-century *Saṅgītaratnākara* is a pot-drum with a wide belly and a small mouth, thick, smooth and well fired. Its mouth is covered with skin and it is played with both hands in an upright position described as 'half-face' (*ardhavaktra*) in the section on the drum *paṭaha*. Its stroke-syllables are the same as those for the medieval drum *mardala* (*see* MRDAṄGA, §2). This short account seems to have been based purely on written sources.

Pot-drums have a persistent but somewhat shadowy history in the subcontinent, perhaps reflecting their easy availability at every level. The ancient *gárgara* and *karkarí* of the Veda may have been skin-covered pots, though they appear to have acted as resonators for the MUSICAL BOW. The *dardura*, an important member of the classical theatre drum-set *puṣkara*, is described as bell-shaped with a large rim like that of the *ghaṭa*, and it would appear to have been a pot-drum, open at the base. The south Indian Tamil name is *muḷavu*, which survives in the modern form *miḷāvu*, together with a strong tradition of use in temple and dramatic music. It is strange, though, that Marcel-Dubois (1941) was unable to find a representation of pot-drums in earlier sculpture; she records them only from the 8th century, in the form of paired pot-drums sitting in cushion rings on either side of a squatting player, in the eastern Pala-Sena art of Bengal. Similar but more elongated vertical drums, described as like the *dardura*, are seen at 12th-century Bhubanesvar, Orissa, also in the east.

The pot-drums of the subcontinent may be grouped in several classes: whole-pot drums, half-pot or goblet drums and bowl-drums. The skin of a whole-pot drum may cover a wide or narrow mouth, with either a short neck (as in the ancient and southern examples given above, the southern *kudamuḷa* and the very large, five-necked *pañcamukhavādyam*) or a long neck, like the *ghumera* or *gumra* of Orissa. They may have an opening at the bottom of the pot. The long-necked pot-drums occur more often in reversed form as goblet or half-pot drums, with the skin covering the base of the pot's wide belly, which is partly cut away (or moulded in that form). The open mouth at the neck can be covered or partly covered by the hand to manipulate resonance. Long-necked pot-drums include the *ghumaṭ* of Goa and Maharashtra, the *gummaṭi* and the *burra* of Andhra and

Pot-drums (māṭā) played by two bhopā (religious singers) of the god Pabuji, Phalodi region, west Rajasthan

the *tumbaknārī* of Kashmir (related directly to the Persian *dombak* or *zarb*). The *ghumaṭ* is interesting for its construction: the upper side has the thick rim of the short-necked pot, round which the skin is tied, and at the lower side is an open neck or stem of the long-necked type. In the bowl-type pot-drum (such as the *pābūjī ke māṭe* of Rajasthan) the mouth is appreciably wide relative to the overall width (see illustration). A drum possibly of this type is depicted at Pavaya (Gwalior, 4th century), held between the knees of a seated player (it could be a goblet drum, with the stem invisible). Other bowl-shaped drums, such as the *tasa* and *ḍuggī*, with no narrowing at the mouth, are usually related to the kettledrum class, which entered India from the 8th century (*see* NAGĀRĀ).

BIBLIOGRAPHY

Śārṅgadeva: *Saṅgītaratnākara* (13th century), ed. S. Subrahamanya Sastri, iii (Madras, 1951)

C. Marcel-Dubois: *Les instruments de musique de l'Inde ancienne* (Paris, 1941)

P. Sambamoorthy: *Catalogue of Musical Instruments Exhibited in the Government Museum, Madras* (Madras, 3/1962)

B. C. Deva: *Musical Instruments of India* (Calcutta, 1978)

ALASTAIR DICK

Ghaṭī. A Sanskrit term for a round metal percussion plaque. *See* GHARĪ.

Ghaval. FRAME DRUM of Armenia. *See* DAP'.

Ghayṭa [ghaita, ghaite, aghiyad]. Oboe of Morocco, Algeria and Libya, equivalent to the ZŪRNĀ of the Near East. It is known in Egypt as *gheteh*, 'cylindrical pipe terminating in a tinplate bell' (see V. Mahillon: *Catalogue descriptif* (Ghent, 1893)); *ghayṭa* has been taken into use in Tunisia (the Tunisian delegation recorded a '*ghayṭa* dance' at the 1932 Cairo Congress of Arab Music). Only in Morocco and Libya, however, is the word *ghayṭa* exclusively used to denote an oboe (see illustration); in Algeria the name is used alongside *zūrnā*. European writers have used the form *raita* or *rhaita*. The word comes from the Gothic *gait* or *ghaid* ('goat'), for a bagpipe with a goatskin bag, and was transferred in Arab Andalusia to the oboe (for a fuller account of the term, *see* GAITA); it first appears in Arab texts in the 14th century.

The *ghayṭa*, like the *zūrnā*, consists of four parts – reed (called *zummara* in Libya), staple, pirouette and flared body – and conforms to the same organological plan as that instrument, except that the pirouette is placed directly on the body, which is generally carved from olive, walnut, orange wood (in Algeria) or more recently apricot wood. At the beginning of the 20th century some specimens were made of metal, but this type of instrument is now obsolete. The instrument has seven holes (in Libya sometimes six) and a thumb-hole on the anterior surface as well as three sound-holes on the bell and sometimes two more lateral holes. In Morocco, there are different sizes: *ghalīz*, *mudakkar* and *majarī*.

Although the *ghayṭa* is always associated with the double-headed drum, the *ṭabl*, it differs from the homologous *zūrnā* in the way it is integrated into ensembles. Thus there are groups of *ṭbel*, *nafīr* (trumpet) and *ghayṭa* in Morocco, a combination found nowhere else in the Arab world. In the Moroccan Rif area, where the *ghayṭa* reigns supreme, a dozen oboes and drums will be grouped together, another combination not found elsewhere. The players use circular breathing and perform either in unison (two or three

Ghayṭa (oboe) player, Marrakesh, Morocco

ghayṭas together) or with melodic development sustained by the drone. These are the two classic methods, but there is a third, derived from Berber aesthetics, with unison performance tending towards a final drone.

The *ghayṭa* differs from the *zūrnā* in its social functions. The player of the *ghayṭa* (*ghayyāṭ*) is not despised as much as his counterpart elsewhere, and the word conveys no pejorative meaning, except in Algeria where it has the sense of 'good for nothing' (M. Beaussier: *Dictionnaire arabe-français*, 1887/R1968). Apart from being used for its traditional function – enlivening the dancing at festivals – and, in the past, to lead warriors, the *ghayṭa* is played on top of minarets during Ramadan in Morocco and is used in the worship of saints. It accompanies the religious ceremonies of the 'Isawiyya and Hamadsha communities (with a goblet drum, *herrazi*), is used therapeutically (Jajouka) and to lead processions. It is thus an indoor or outdoor instrument.

Although there is a Berber version of the word, *aghiyad* or *ghaita*, the *ghayṭa* is little played by the Berbers. The instrument spread from the Moroccan empire of the 16th and 17th centuries to the cultures of the Sahel, becoming the ALGAITA of Niger, Nigeria, the Cameroons and Chad, and the *kaita* of the Sudan, although with considerable variation in its structure and materials. The instrument as played in the African Sahel was imported into the Gulf States from the Sudan, and there renamed *surnāy* (*see* ṢRNĀJ).

BIBLIOGRAPHY

R. Brunel: *Essai sur la confrérie religieuse des 'Aissâoûa au Maroc* (Paris, 1926)

P. Thornton: *The Voice of Atlas: Search for Music in Morocco* (London, 1936), 76

A. Chottin: *Tableau de la musique marocaine* (Paris, 1938), 166

H. G. Farmer: 'Early References to Music in the Western Sudan', *Journal of the Royal Asiatic Society* (1939), 569 [repr. in *Oriental Studies: Mainly Musical*, 1953]

——:'Ghayta', *EI*

G. Cirot: 'Gaita et rhaita', *Mélanges d'études Luso-Marocaines dédiées à la mémoire de David Lopes et Pierre de Cenival* (Paris, 1945), 41

E. R. Perkhun: *Die Theorien zum arabischen Einfluss auf die europäische Musik des Mittelalters* (Walldorf-Hessen, 1976), 202

P. Schuyler: 'The Music of Islam and Sufism in Morocco', BM30 SL 2027 [disc notes]

CHRISTIAN POCHÉ

Ghazzi. Small oboe of Sind, Pakistan, used in mourning songs during the Shī'ite lamentation of Muharram. *See* SHARNAI.

Ghebomba. Animal-horn trumpet of the Tsogo and related peoples of Gabon, sounded to mark the beginning and end of the Bwete initiation ceremonies.

Ghein [Gheine, Gheyn, Gheyne], **van den.** *See* VAN DEN GHEYN family.

Gherā. Octagonal FRAME DRUM of Rajasthan, India. *See* DAIRE and ḌAPH.

Ghergheranak. Double-headed drum of Afghanistan, with attached beaters on a string.

Gheteh. Egyptian term for the GHAYṬA.

Gheyn, van den. *See* VAN DEN GHEYN family.

Ghichak [gidzhak, gijak]. SPIKE FIDDLE of northern Afghanistan and the Turkmen, Uzbek, Uighur, Tajik and Karakalpak peoples in the USSR. The brightly painted round neck of the *ghichak* projects through the resonator and a large iron nail is hammered into the bottom of the neck to serve as the spike. The top of the neck is grooved to form a pegbox with two lateral tuning-pegs, one each side. The neck is turned on a lathe and the resonator, usually fitted by the player, often consists of a large square tin, for instance a one-gallon oil can. The instrument has two metal strings supported by a nut at the head and by a bridge placed on the resonator. The bow is of horsehair tied to a curved stick; tension is applied by the fingers of the right hand. The strings may be bowed together or singly by rotating the instrument slightly. A modified type of *ghichak* has recently come into use; it has a resonator carved from a square block

Ghichak (spike fiddle) of the Tajik people, USSR

of mulberry wood, with a skin belly and eight sympathetic strings with tuning-pegs along the side of the neck.

The mountain Tajiks in the USSR make the *ghichak* using a tin can as a resonator. Among the other, more westerly, Central Asian peoples the *ghichak* (or *gidzhak*, *gijak*) resembles the Persian KAMĀNCHE; it has a short, fretless neck, a spherical resonator with a skin soundtable and three or four strings (see illustration). The Karakalpaks know it as the *ghirzhak*.

BIBLIOGRAPHY
VertkovA
M. Slobin: *Music in the Culture of Northern Afghanistan* (Tucson, Arizona, 1976), 243
JOHN BAILY

Ghirbāl [girbal, guirbal, kerbal]. Round FRAME DRUM of the 11th-century Islamic world. Literally the word means a sieve. The term was inadvertently introduced into music by the theologian Abū-Ḥamīd al-Ghazālī, in a misquotation of a saying of Mohammed, in which *ghirbāl* was substituted for *duff* (this mistake has assigned the *duff* a circular shape when it may also be angular and double-headed). The anonymous treatise *Kashf al-Ghumūm* notes the smallness of the *ghirbāl*, and a manuscript of the Andalusian author al-Shalaḥī (14th century) gave rise to a definition of the *ghirbāl* by J. B. La Borde (*Essai sur la musique*, 1780) as a Basque drum and to the suggestion of variant spellings, *guirbal*, *girbal*, *kerbal* (Rouanet: 'La musique arabe', *EMDC*, I/v, 1922, p.2745). In the 20th century the *ghirbāl* has been treated by orientalists as part of the pre-Islamic inheritance, though this is unproven. Outside this context the term is not used.

BIBLIOGRAPHY
H. G. Farmer: 'Meccan Musical Instruments', *Journal of the Royal Asiatic Society* (1929), 489 [repr. in *Studies in Oriental Musical Instruments*, 1978]
M. Guettat: *La musique classique du Maghreb* (Paris, 1980), 39
L. I. al Faruqi: *An Annotated Glossary of Arabic Musical Terms* (Westport, Conn., 1981)
CHRISTIAN POCHÉ

Ghironda (It.). HURDY-GURDY.

Ghirzhak. SPIKE FIDDLE of the Karakalpak people of Central Asia. *See* GHICHAK.

Ghisterne (Fr.; Lat. *ghiterna*). GITTERN.

Ghmoh dham [khmuos thon]. Large flat gong of northern Kampuchea. It is played in various ensembles to accompany folkdances, religious ceremonies, weddings and funerals.

Ghodyun [ghodyŭ]. *See* GHORĀLIYAU.

Ghogha. A term used in Maharashtra, west India, for the smaller variety of the TARPO (double clarinet with gourd wind cap).

Ghomma. Small single-headed drum of the Cape Malay people of southern Africa. It is made from a cask and held under the left arm and struck alternately by the right and left palms. Kirby considered that *ghomma* is derived from NGOMA, a term ubiquitous in sub-Saharan Africa, which is applied to many types of drum and to dances accompanied by drumming. See P. R. Kirby: 'Musical

Instruments of the Cape Malays', *South African Journal of Science*, XXXVI (1939), 477.

JAMES MAY

Ghoṛāliyau (jew's harp) played by a Kalbelia woman, Jodhpur, Rajasthan

Ghoṛāliyau [ghoṛaliyo, ghorālio, ghodyū̃, ghodyun]. Idioglot bamboo JEW'S HARP of Rajasthan, north India. Made from a thin plate of bamboo, roughly 8 to 15 cm long, it consists of a vibrating tongue cut out of a narrow rectangular frame. The tongue is set in vibration when a string attached to the tapered end of the frame is pulled; with the other end the musician holds the jew's harp against his mouth, which serves as a resonator.

The *ghoṛāliyau* is played solo or in duet by women among the nomad groups of snake-charmers (the Kalbelia; see illustration) or by young people in certain tribal groups of south-west Rajasthan, notably the Thori who sometimes attach a small pellet bell to the end of the string; the result is an overlying rhythmic sound. Other communities use the heteroglot-iron jew's harp *murcang*, where the end of the tongue is plucked.

The bamboo jew's harp with pulling string is found elsewhere in India and Nepal but is more widespread in South-east Asia and Indonesia.

BIBLIOGRAPHY

G. Dournon-Taurelle and J. Wright: *Les guimbardes du Musée de l'Homme* (Paris, 1978)

GENEVIÈVE DOURNON

Ghugha. Maghrib instrument, possible ancestor of the GOGE single-string fiddle of West Africa.

Ghughrā. Metal pellet bell of Rajasthan and Madhya Pradesh, India. *See* GHUṄGRŪ.

Ghujih [rujih]. Pair of small bronze cymbals with out-turned rims used in the *kelittang* and *kekatak* ensembles in Lampung province, Sumatra.

Ghumaṭ. Indian membranophone made from a pair of earthenware pots with lizard skins tied over the round neck opening; the small base is left open and the diameter of the head is about 20 cm. It is played with the hands and fingers as an accompaniment to folksong and dance in Goa, west India. *See also* GHAṬA, §2.

BIBLIOGRAPHY

K. S. Kothari: *Indian Folk Musical Instruments* (New Delhi, 1968), 37

A. D. Ranade: *Lokasaṅgītaśāstra* (Aurangabad, 1975), 79f

JONATHAN KATZ

Ghumera [gumra]. Pot-drum of Orissa, eastern India. The mouth (about 18 cm in diameter) of a long-necked waterpot is covered with skin, pasted or bound with cords. The base of the spherical pot is open. It is played like the *gummaṭi* of Andhra Pradesh. *See also* GHAṬA, §2.

Ghuṅgrū [ghungar, ghungur, ghuṅur, ghunghrū, ghughrā etc]. Small metal pellet bells of South Asia, usually in the form of a sphere of bell-metal with a slit; inside, a single iron pellet jingles when the bell is shaken. The bells are suspended by a string (or a leather strap) threaded through an integral ring and worn on different parts of the body for dancing; they can also be attached as jingles to drums, clappers, rattles and so on. The name 'ghuṅgrū' is a modern onomatopoeic north Indian form; other northern names and types include *rāmjhol* (Rajasthan), *bhaironjī-ke-ghuṅghrū* (Rajasthan), *painjan* (north India) and *sokocandu* (southern Bihar). Older Sanskrit terms include *nūpura*, *mañjīrā*, *kiṅkinī*, *ghaṇṭī* and *kṣudraghaṇṭikā* (*see* GHAṆṬĀ); all are used nowadays, but sometimes in different senses. Southern terms are *gejjai*, spelt *keccai*, and *salangai* (Tamil Nadu), *gejjalu* (Andhra Pradesh), *gejje* (Karnataka state) and MUYANG among the Gond of Madhya Pradesh (for illustration *see* GHAṆṬĀ). The *ghuṅgrū-gejjai* type is found in folkdance, but also used in classical dance, where they are carefully tuned and are often worshipped by the dancer before being used. In the classical *kathak* style of north India and Pakistan, where rhythmic footwork is of the greatest importance, female dancers traditionally wear 101 bells and male dancers 151, threaded on cords around the lower legs (see illustration). A technique here is to control the shaking of the *ghuṅgrū* so that only one sounds at a time.

Another type of bell, the pellet ring (a hollow metal ring with several pellets of different sizes also worn on different parts of the body), can also be denoted by some of the above terms, typically in folkdances (*see* NŪPUR).

The origins of pellet bells in South Asia lie probably in natural shell rattles, such as the *gilabada* (a belt of

Ghuṅgrū (pellet bells) as used in north Indian Kathak dance

small dried beans worn around the waist by members of the Chenchu tribe of Andhra Pradesh; *see also* ĀGHĀṬĀ). Other South Asian rattles include the *gilki* (calabash rattle of Karnataka state), *jhumjhumī* (rattle toy of Bengal), *jhumrā* (coconut-shell rattle toy of Orissa), *kaniyārī ḍaṇḍā* (stick rattle of the Oraon people of Orissa), *khulkulā* (calabash rattle of Maharashtra) and *khunkhunā* (coconut-shell rattle of Rajasthan).

BIBLIOGRAPHY
R. Singha and R. Massey: *Indian Dances: their History and Growth* (London, 1967)
K. S. Kothari: *Indian Folk Musical Instruments* (New Delhi, 1968)
B. C. Deva: *Musical Instruments of India* (Calcutta, 1978)
ALASTAIR DICK

Ghuṅgrū tarang. Set of tuned pellet bells on strings. It was constructed in an attempt to make melodic use of the Indian pellet bells GHUṄGRŪ.

Gi [≠gi]. Stopped conical flute of the San (Bushman) people of south-western Africa. It is made from the quill of an ostrich feather and is used as a signal whistle.

Giangăraș. Bell of Romania. *See* CLOPOT.

Giangbwa. LAMELLAPHONE of the Zande people of north-eastern Zaïre. It has a box resonator and is carved to represent a human (*LaurentyS*, 193).

Giáo phường. Obsolete Vietnamese folk ensemble comprising a *trường cùng* (slit-drum), a *địch* (transverse flute), a CÁI BÔNG (single-headed hourglass drum), a ĐÀN ĐÁY (long-necked lute) and *địch quản* (double clarinet). It was used in place of court ensembles such as the obsolete *đồng văn* and the NHÃ NHẠC. When performing entertainment music the ensemble had additionally a *trúc sinh* or *đàn gỗ* (slab xylophones), a *đàn cầm* (seven-string zither) and a ĐÀN TRANH (16-string zither).

TRÂN QUANG HẢI

Gibeémba. Wooden cone flute, with one or two finger-holes, of the Pende people of south-western Zaïre (*LaurentyA*, 139).

Gibinji. Wooden-keyed LAMELLAPHONE of Zaïre, with a wooden raft-type base (*LaurentyS*, 191). *See also* KAKOLONDONDO.

Gibson. American company of fretted string instrument makers, founded by Orville H. Gibson (*b* Chateaugay, NY, 1856; *d* Ogdensburg, NY, 19 Aug 1918) in Kalamazoo, Michigan, in the 1870s. The Gibson name was established as a marque in 1894. Mandolins dominated Gibson's output until the mid-1920s; in the 1880s Orville Gibson began to apply violin construction techniques to the production of flat-backed mandolins and he launched his unique 'Florentine' model in the 1890s. Later designs included pear-shaped and f-hole instruments. Before the turn of the century Gibson was making arched-top guitars with oval soundholes, based on the construction techniques he had been using for mandolins.

In 1902 a group of businessmen joined Gibson to form the Gibson Mandolin-Guitar Company Ltd, later renamed the Gibson Mandolin-Guitar Mfg Co. (1904) and the Gibson Mandolin-Guitar Co. (1906). Orville Gibson left in 1909 and negotiated a life-long monthly royalty with the company in 1915. In 1917 the Gibson Co. moved to new premises in Parsons Street, Kalamazoo.

In the 1920s banjos became the most important component of Gibson's production, and they were superseded in turn by guitars. In 1923–4 Gibson marketed the first f-hole guitar, designed by LLOYD LOAR, which was also one of the earliest models to have a neck strengthened with a truss rod – another Gibson innovation. The 1920s also saw the unveiling of a harp-guitar, based on an invention by Orville Gibson, patented in 1908. In an attempt to compete with the Martin Dreadnought guitars, Gibson entered the market for flat-top instruments in 1936–7 with the large SJ200 model. At much the same time it introduced its first electric guitar, the hollow-bodied ES150.

The company became Gibson Inc. in 1924 and in 1944 was taken over by the Chicago Musical Instrument Co.; CMI was later succeeded in this role by Norlin Industries. Until the 1950s the Kalamazoo factory produced mostly acoustic instruments, but in 1952 Gibson introduced the solid-bodied Les Paul electric guitar, and Kalamazoo changed progressively to electric guitar production. Throughout the following decades Gibson created new electric guitars, including the Flying V (1958), Explorer (1958) and Firebird (1963) models, all of which had unorthodox body shapes.

In 1957 Gibson acquired the Epiphone marque and in the 1970s moved production of Epiphone guitars to Japan. A new plant was opened in Elgin, Illinois, in 1973, chiefly to produce pickups and strings (Gibson first marketed its own brand of strings in 1907), and in June 1975 a large factory for the production of guitars was opened in Nashville, Tennessee – primarily because of the inability of the overcrowded Kalamazoo site to cope with the demand for electric guitars. In the early 1980s a reduction in staff was effected, and manufacturing was centralized in Nashville; the Kalamazoo factory was concerned only with custom-built instruments and served as a base for Gibson's small research and development team. The plant closed in 1984.

For more detailed description of Gibson guitars *see* GUITAR, §7, and ELECTRIC GUITAR; for illustration of an instrument by Gibson, *see* BANJO, fig.1a.

BIBLIOGRAPHY
J. Bellson: *The Gibson Story* (Kalamazoo, Mich., 1972)
A. Duchossoir: *Gibson Electrics*, i (Paris, 1981)
T. Wheeler: *American Guitars: an Illustrated History* (New York, 1982)
TONY BACON

Gidayū. Music of the Japanese bunraku (puppet theatre) and some kabuki plays, particularly those derived from puppet plays. It can also be heard as concert music (the only setting which permits female performers), and there are several folk *gidayū* traditions. In standard *gidayū* there is one 'chanter' (*tayū*) and one SHAMISEN (lute) player, both kneeling on a special platform near the 'apron' to the left of the stage. The performers change from time to time during a play, with the best artists doing the most important scenes. There may on occasion be several chanters and instrumentalists, and also, more rarely, a koto (long zither) or *kokyū* (spike lute). There is also *geza* off-stage music, although on a smaller scale than in kabuki and usually called simply *hayashi*. See 'Gidayū-bushi', *Ongaku daijiten* [Encyclopedia of music] (Tokyo, 1981).

DAVID W. HUGHES

Gidigbo. LAMELLAPHONE used by the Fon people in Benin and Togo, and by the Gwari of Nigeria. *See* AGIDIGBO.

Gidirigo. Large box LAMELLAPHONE of the Gonja people of Ghana, equivalent to the Ashanti *prempensua*.

Gidzhak. *See* GHICHAK.

Gievre [geure]. Obsolete FRAME DRUM of the Samish people of Lapland. The membrane was made of reindeer hide and was struck with a small beater of reindeer horn.

Giga. Bowed lyre of Norway. *See* ROTTE (ii).

Gīgas [džingas, džindžas, ġingas, maņihorka]. Bowed monochord of Latvia. It consists of a box resonator, made of birch or pine or other wood, 60 to 115 cm long and 8 to 12 cm wide. Along its upper surface is fixed a fretted fingerboard, and two soundholes are made at one end. A bridge between the soundholes supports a gut or metal string, which is fastened to a button or peg at each end of the box. The *ġīgas* is placed on a table or on the player's knees and bowed with a violin bow. It was popular in the mid and late 19th century, primarily as a teaching aid in schools. It is analogous to the Estonian *mollpill*, the Lithuanian *manikarka* and the Swedish PSALMODIKON, from which the other Baltic instruments may ultimately derive. The term 'ġīgas' (possibly cognate with German 'Geige') has also been used in the past for various musical instruments, particularly the violin. See Ī. Priedīte: *Ko spēlēja sendienās* [What was played in the past] (Riga, 1983).

Gigli, Giulio Cesare (*fl* Rome, *c*1720–62). Italian violin maker. He worked very much in the style of Tecchler; the main differences are that the waists of Gigli's violins are narrower, the edges wider and the scrolls somewhat smaller. His pegboxes match Tecchler's in elegance, and his varnish is usually a transparent golden colour with the occasional reddish or brownish tint. On his labels, his name is latinized to Julius Caesar Gigli Romanus.

BIBLIOGRAPHY
W. L. von Lütgendorff: *Die Geigen- und Lautenmacher vom Mittelalter bis zur Gegenwart* (Frankfurt am Main, 1904, rev. 6/1922/R1968)
R. Vannes: *Essai d'un dictionnaire universel des luthiers* (Paris, 1932, 2/1951/R1972 as *Dictionnaire universel des luthiers* and R1981 incl. suppl. 1959)

JAAK LIIVOJA-LORIUS

Gigue (Fr.). Medieval name for a bowed chordophone; the modern German word, GEIGE, is clearly related to it. Imaginative literature of the late Middle Ages does not make clear whether the word means FIDDLE or REBEC, or simply 'a bowed string instrument' without regard for its specific character. For further information see F. Dick: *Bezeichnungen für Saiten- und Schlaginstrumente in der altfranzösischen Literatur* (Giessen, 1932), and H. Panum: *Middelalderen strengeinstrumenter* (Copenhagen, 1915–31; Eng. trans., London, n.d.).

The word 'gigue', which also denotes a popular Baroque dance (a standard movement of the suite), is derived from the verb 'giguer' (to frolic, leap or gambol) rather than the instrument.

HOWARD MAYER BROWN

Gijak. *See* GHICHAK.

Gil. XYLOPHONE of the Lobi people of Ghana and the Ivory Coast.

Gilabada. Belt of small dried beans, worn around the waist and used as a rattle by the Chenchu tribe of Andhra Pradesh, India. *See also* GHUŃGRŪ.

Gili. Drum of the Bwaka-Mabo people of northwestern Zaïre (*BooneT*, 67).

Gilingwa. BULLROARER of the Zande people of Zaïre. *See* ATUAMBA.

Gilkes, Samuel (*b* Morton Pinkney, 1787; *d* London, 1827). English violin maker. He was a pupil of Charles Harris and subsequently worked for William Forster and possibly for Betts. Although he favoured the Amati model, he also patterned some violins after Stradivari. His late instruments, especially those made after 1820, are particularly fine and are quite Italianate in both workmanship and tone. His varnish, which could be most attractive, was either a rich yellow-brown or a dark red, resembling that of Forster. He was unfortunately not prolific, and had he lived longer, a position as one of England's finest makers would surely have been solidified.

Gilkes's son and successor, William (1811–75), was an assiduous maker but the quality of his work did not match his father's. His double basses, however, have found a considerable following among orchestral players.

BIBLIOGRAPHY
W. M. Morris: *British Violin Makers* (London, 1904, rev. 2/1920)

JAAK LIIVOJA-LORIUS

Gilki. Calabash rattle of Karnataka state, south India. *See also* GHUŃGRŪ.

Gillet, Louis (*b* Nancy, 10 Feb 1891; *d* 1970). French bow maker. He served his apprenticeship in Mirecourt and operated workshops there as well as in Nancy and Chalon-sur-Saône. He worked for Eugène Sartory and later for the Parisian violin maker Georges Dupuy (Sartory's son-in-law), who apparently exported many of Gillet's bows. The Sartory influence is seen mainly in the frog and button work, while the cut of the head is altogether more square and less elegant. Gillet produced many unstamped bows for the trade, apparently reserving his own brand for the best of his bows. These are often made of dense red-brown pernambuco and possess fine playing qualities. His lower grade bows are made of adequate wood and are usually rough and heavy. His brand, L. GILLET, is of medium size and sharp imprint; his work also appears under other brands, most notably DUPUY À PARIS. See E. Vatelot: *Les archets français* (Nancy, 1976).   JAAK LIIVOJA-LORIUS

Gillett & Johnston. English firm of bell founders. It pioneered the extension of the range of the carillon with both higher- and lower-pitched bells. Between World Wars I and II its exports of carillons, with those of JOHN TAYLOR & CO., made the carillon widely known outside Europe for the first time.

The firm was founded by a clockmaker, William Gillett, who had a shop first in the village of Hadlow, Kent, then in Clerkenwell, London, in the early 19th century. In 1844 it moved to Croydon, Surrey, where it began manufacturing tower clocks under the name Gillett & Bland. In 1877, under the name Gillett & Johnston, it began to make bells, first for tower chimes and swinging peals, and from 1921 for carillons. Its carillons include those of Riverside Church, New York (72 bells, *c* to *c''''*), the University of Chicago (72 bells, *c♯* to *c♯''''*), Parliament Buildings of Canada, Ottawa (53 bells, *e* to *a''''*), the National Museum of New Zealand, Wellington (49 bells, *g♯* to *a♯''''*), the University of Louvain, Belgium (48 bells, *f♯* to *g♯''''*) and the West Church of St Nicholas, Aberdeen (37 bells, *g♯*, *d♯'* to *d♯''''*).

PERCIVAL PRICE

Gill Rodríguez, Isidro (*b* Muriel de Zapardiel, Valladolid, *c*1745; *d* ?Cervillego de la Cruz, Valladolid, after 1790). Spanish organ builder. He had a workshop at Cervillego de la Cruz from 1766 to 1790 and built a number of organs in the region of Medina del Campo. He also built instruments in his native town (1768); at S María de Mojados (1770); Santiago el Real de Medina del Campo (1771); Brahojos de Medina (1775); Nueva Villa de las Torres (1777); S Boal de Pozaldez (1779); Bobadilla del Campo (1779); Santiago Apóstol de Alcazarén (1783); Fuente el Sol (1787); and Bocigas (1789). Nicolás Gill Rodríguez, his pupil and partner (and almost certainly his son), carried on the business and built a new organ for the church of Lomoviejo in 1796. See J. A. de La Lama: *El órgano en Valladolid y su provincia: catalogación y estudio* (Valladolid, 1982).

GUY BOURLIGUEUX

Gilo. STAMPING TUBE of the Kwarekwareo people, Malaita, Solomon Islands. *See* KIRO.

Gimar. Double-headed drum of the Tanjung Benua people of east Kalimantan, Indonesia. *See* GENDANG.

Gimbal. Single-headed cylindrical drum of the Mandaya and Palawan peoples of the southern Philippines.

Gimbri. Large plucked lute of North Africa. *See* GUINBRI.

Gingara. *See* GUSLICE.

Gingas. *See* GTGAS.

Ginger. Five-string bowl lyre of the Sudan.

Gingiru [korro]. Small harp-lute (*see* HARP-LUTE (i)) of the Dogon people of Mali, with a canoe-shaped body. The instrument is generally associated with soothsayers or sorcerers.

Gini. Pair of metal cymbals of Orissa and Bengal, east India. *See* KARTĀL, (2).

Gintang. Struck idiochord bamboo TUBE ZITHER of Assam, north-east India. It is made of an internode of thick bamboo, cut beyond the nodes, which are left

Gintang or bādung dungā (tube zither), Goalpara, Assam

whole. The top surface is shaved somewhat flat, leaving two epidermal strings still attached at their ends and raised and tensioned by bamboo slips. A further flatter and wider piece is put under the strings near the middle, eccentrically, giving perhaps four playing areas instead of two. A soundhole is excised near the middle and the instrument is beaten with a light stick (see illustration). The *gintang* is also called *bādung dungā*. A somewhat different instrument is the *kā chap chap*, probably of the Khasis; Sachs (1914) referred to a tube zither of the Lushei-Kuki people.

Although the idiochord tube zithers of the north-eastern areas, together with the raft zither (*see* DENDUNG), display a common South-east Asian cultural pattern, they can also be found in South Asia proper; they chiefly appear among the peoples of the east-central tribal belt, including the *ronza gonṭam* of the Hill Reddi people of Andhra (found in similar form in neighbouring Orissa) and the *bhuyabaja* of the Gonds. In view of the great importance of more sophisticated tube or stick zithers in India since later classical times, it is likely that zithers of the above type used to be more widespread (*see* VĪNĀ, §§1, 4).

BIBLIOGRAPHY

C. Sachs: *Die Musikinstrumente Indiens und Indonesiens* (Berlin and Leipzig, 1914, 2/1923)

C. von Führer-Haimendorf: *The Reddis of the Bison Hills* (London, 1945)

B. C. Deva: *Musical Instruments of India* (Calcutta, 1978)

ALASTAIR DICK

Ginyeli. *See* JINJERAM.

Gio. Double-headed barrel-shaped drum of the Dao people of northern Vietnam. It is made of wood and measures 24 cm in diameter and 22 cm in height. It is covered with buffalo skin, and is beaten with a wooden mallet on the first and fifteenth days of the month.

Giocoso (It.: 'jocular'; adjective from *gioco*, a game). A designation of mood often found qualifying some tempo mark as in *allegro giocoso*. But it also appears alone as a tempo designation in its own right.

Giorgi flute. A keyless cylindrical flute patented by Carlo Tomaso Giorgi of Florence in 1896. It was made of thin-walled ebony and had 11 large finger-holes, one for each semitone, rendering cross-fingering unnecessary. Their wide spacing, however, demanded large hands, especially since the left index finger had two holes to cover; a model with keys and levers was also made for short-fingered players. The mouth-hole was at the end of the instrument in a special head joint. Its lowest note was d' but additional joints allowed it to play $c\#'$, c' or b.

Gipanana. Side-blown ivory trumpet of the Pende people of south-western Zaïre. It has a carved mouthpiece (*LaurentyA*, 424).

Giraffe piano. A type of UPRIGHT PIANOFORTE; *see also* PIANOFORTE, fig.15.

Girard & Cie. French firm of organ builders allied to DAUBLAINE & CALLINET.

Girbal. *See* GHIRBĀL.

Gırnata. *See* KLARNET.

Gisada. *See* LITLIT.

Gitaha. *See* BAYI.

Gitara. A term used for the guitar in the Philippines. Among Westernized groups the guitar is played as an accompaniment to folksongs or as a solo instrument in town feasts, recreations and, more recently, radio programmes. In two centres of manufacture, Cebu in the south and Pampanga in the north, Western guitar music is preferred by young people to Philippine country music. Among isolated non-Westernized groups, such as the Negrito of Zambales in Luzon, a crudely made guitar is used for mimetic dances, and the Hanunoo of Mindoro use guitars (with human hair as strings) for instrumental interludes between stanzas of *urukay* songs.
JOSÉ MACEDA

Gitar bas. XYLOPHONE in the *kolintang* orchestra of Minahasa, North Sulawesi. Its single keyboard consists of 12 keys arranged chromatically in one octave; the longest key is about 35 cm long. It is normally played in virtuoso fashion with a pair of padded hammers about 30 cm long.

Gitarre (Ger.). GUITAR.

Gitgit. Small three-string fiddle of the Hanunoo people of the southern Philippines.

Gittern [gyterne] (Fr. *quitarre, quitaire, quinterne, guitarre, guiterre, guiterne*; Ger. *Quinterne*; It. *chitarra*; Sp. *guitarra*). A short-necked lute of the Middle Ages outwardly similar to the 16th-century MANDORE. Like its relative the lute, it had a rounded back but was much smaller, and it had no clear division between the body and neck. This lute-shaped gittern (or 'guitar'

– the two words were then synonymous) was displaced in the 15th and 16th centuries by the Renaissance GUITAR, which combined the small size of the gittern with the body outline of the much larger vihuela. Thus the medieval gittern bore much the same relationship to the lute as the Renaissance guitar did to the vihuela. It has since become customary to call the medieval instrument 'gittern' and the later one 'guitar', a useful but artificial distinction.

Confusion over the identity of the gittern has existed since the 19th century. It has been referred to, inaccurately, as the mandore, mandora or mandola (an instrument with a different tuning which became common only around 1570); and the name 'gittern' has wrongly been given to the CITOLE, because the latter's outline resembled that of the (vihuela-shaped) guitar (see Wright, 1977). Consequently, many recent works refer to representations of gitterns as mandoras, and to those of citoles as gitterns.

1. Nomenclature. 2. Structure. 3. History.

1. NOMENCLATURE. All the above names for the gittern derive ultimately from the Greek 'kithara' via the Arabic 'qitara'. The Arabic form gave 'chitarra' in Italian and 'guitarra' in Spanish. The French forms include 'quitarre' (from Arabic or Italian), 'gitere' (perhaps from Catalan), and 'quitaire', which became 'qui(n)terne' (by confusion with the unrelated Latin word *quinterna*, meaning 'fivefold'). By analogy, the form 'guiterne' was created, and this was the standard word until the 16th century. 'Guitar(r)e' (probably from Spanish) also occurs, but is rare. The English and German names were borrowed from French.

When the lute shape was displaced by that of the vihuela there was no immediate change of name: 'guiterre' became popular in French alongside 'guiterne' in the 16th century; and both were finally displaced by 'guitare' in the 17th century (probably because of Spanish influence), with the English and German names following suit. The Italian and Spanish names have not changed since the Middle Ages.

2. STRUCTURE. The back, neck and pegbox are usually made of one piece of wood, as in the 15th-century gittern (hitherto called a mandora) in the Wartburg Collection at Eisenach (see Hellwig, 1974). More rarely,

1. Unfretted gittern with four double courses of strings: console figure, north tower of Amiens Cathedral (after 1375)

2. Unfretted three-string gittern: detail of roof sculpture, Northleach Church, Glos.(15th century)

3. Gittern with four double courses of strings: detail from the fresco, 'St Martin Dubbed a Knight' (c1322–6), by Simone Martini, in the lower church of the Basilica di S Francesco, Assisi

the back was built up from separate ribs (as on the lute); these types occur from the late 15th century onwards. In all gitterns the body and neck blend in a smooth curve or straight line: unlike the lute, there is no sharp corner. The pegbox makes an angle with the neck of 30°–90° and is usually curved, sometimes into a semi-circle (the so-called sickle shape) but often into a short, gently curving arc (fig.1). Some pegboxes, especially in English

4. Gittern players: miniature from the 'Cantigas de Santa María', Spanish, late 13th century (E-E b.I.2, f.104r)

representations, are straight, like those of lutes (fig.2). However, most types of pegbox terminate in a human or animal head, a feature foreign to the lute.

There are three or four strings (or more commonly pairs of strings), sometimes five in the later 15th century (as in the Eisenach instrument). On some instruments (particularly French and English) the strings pass over a movable bridge and are attached to endpins, one for each course, or to a single pin or button; on others (notably in Spain and Italy) they terminate at a fixed frontal stringholder, as on the lute. Italian and Spanish instruments also show a predilection for multiple soundholes and decorative inlays on the belly and fingerboard. Frets are shown in some good depictions of gitterns (notably in Italian paintings: fig.3), but they are absent in many good French and English representations. The use of a quill plectrum seems to have been almost universal.

3. HISTORY. The gittern probably entered Europe from Arab countries in the second half of the 13th century, along with other round-backed instruments such as the lute and rebec. Sachs stated that the lute is called 'qitara' in North African countries west of Egypt, and Farmer suggested that the kaitara, used in Muslim Spain from the 10th century, was a type of lute, adding that a diminutive of the same word, 'kuwaitira', is still used for a small lute in the Maghrib. Thus it seems likely that the gittern came from the Arabs of the western Mediterranean rather than from those of the eastern end, among whom the short-necked lute is called 'qupuz'. Tinctoris (*De inventione et usu musicae*, c1487) called the gittern 'the instrument invented by the Catalans'. He may have meant that they modified it in some way to create a 'European' type distinct from the Arab one. This is one possible explanation of a reference to 'guitarra morisca' and 'guitarra latina' ('Moorish' and 'Latin' guitar) by Juan Ruiz (*Libro de buen amor*, c1330), and of references to similarly named instruments in Machaut's writings and in records of the French court of 1350–70. Although the differences between these two types are not known, it can reasonably be assumed that the two gitterns illustrated on f.104r of the *Cantigas de Santa María* (fig.4) are of the 'Latin' variety, since the players' dress implies that they are not Arabs. However,

it has been suggested that another instrument in the same manuscript, with oval belly, long neck and circular (ff.133*r*, 140*v*) or sickle-shaped pegbox (ff.46*v*, 147*r*), is the *guitarra morisca* (*see* CITOLE, fig.3): none of the players is dressed like an Arab, however, and the instrument differs considerably from the gittern in that it has a long neck clearly demarcated from the body and (on ff.46*v* and 140*v*) a raised fingerboard extending on to the belly. There is no more reason to call this instrument a guitar than to call it a plucked fiddle (*vihuela de peñola*).

The earliest datable references to the gittern occur in French literature from around 1270 onwards, but depictions become common only after 1300. Johannes de Grocheo, in his treatise *De musica* (*c*1300), called it 'quitarra sarracenica' ('Saracen guitar'), which suggests it was still a foreign novelty in France. This impression is strengthened by the great variety of its French names, which grew fewer as the instrument became common. In England depictions and references do not become frequent until well after 1300: one looks in vain for gitterns among the instruments appearing in the finely illustrated manuscripts such as the Queen Mary Psalter that were written in the first two decades of the 14th century.

During the 14th century the gittern gained increasing popularity. Whereas there was only one *gitarer* among the 92 musicians named in the accounts for the Feast of Westminster in 1306, the Duke of Brittany is said (in the *Grandes chroniques de France*) to have had in his company 'seven guiterne players, and he himself, so they say, began to play the eighth guiterne' when he left Brest Castle for England in 1348. By then the gittern seems to have ousted its rival, the citole, and to have become enormously popular not only among minstrels but also among the increasing number of amateur musicians of all classes. Small, portable and doubtless easy to play, it seems to have been frequently used in serenading and in visiting taverns, activities that often went hand-in-hand; it is mentioned in this connection in several French and English poems of the period 1350–1410. Machaut (*Prise d'Alexandrie*, *c*1367) mentioned 'guiternes dont on joue par ces tavernes' ('gitterns which are played in taverns'), and Chaucer, in three of the *Canterbury Tales*, referred to the gittern being played by people who frequent taverns. The parish clerk Absalom in *The Miller's Tale* is a typical example:

> In twenty manere coude he trippe and daunce
> After the scole of Oxenforde tho,
> And with his legges casten to and fro,
> And pleyen songes on a small rubible;
> Ther-to he song som-tyme a loud quinible;
> And as wel coude he pleye on his giterne.
> In al the toun nas brewhous ne taverne
> That he ne visited with his solas,
> Ther any gaylard tappestere was.

Accompanying himself on the gittern, he sings a serenade to the carpenter's wife:

> He singeth in his vois gentil and smal,
> 'Now, dere lady, if thy wille be,
> I preye yow that ye wol rewe on me',
> Ful wel acordaunt to his giterninge.

This association with taverns and serenading is also reflected in French legal documents of the same period concerning the brawls and murders which sometimes ensued, making it obvious that gitterns were common household objects. They are also found in inventories of noble households, such as one belonging to the French King Charles V dated 1373 which includes four gitterns, one in ivory and another decorated with silver and enamel. Another example of the gittern's popularity can be seen in the carvings in the nave of Winchester Cathedral (built 1346–1404), where no fewer than seven of the 21 instruments depicted are gitterns.

In the 15th century the gittern was gradually eclipsed by the lute, which appears with increasing frequency in iconography. There is often confusion between them, both in iconography (it is not always possible to distinguish lutes from gitterns in the less accurate representations) and in documentary references to lute players as gitterners (for example, the celebrated Pietrobono, whose lute-playing was praised by Tinctoris, was usually known by the epithet *dal chitarin(o)*).

By around 1487 Tinctoris could remark: 'The *ghiterra* is used most rarely, because of the thinness of its sound. When I heard it in Catalonia, it was being used much more often by women, to accompany love songs, than by men.' He also gave the only information that survives on the gittern's tuning, namely that it was strung like a (four-course) lute, that is, with the intervals 4th–3rd–4th. By this time the vihuela-shaped guitar had begun to appear. It must be this instrument, rather than the vihuela itself, which Tinctoris described, since it is much smaller than the lute:

that [instrument], for example, invented by the Spanish, which both they and the Italians call the *viola*, but the French the *demi-luth*. This viola differs from the lute in that the lute is much larger and tortoise-shaped, while the viola is flat, and in most cases curved inwards on each side.

It is interesting that Tinctoris did not use the name 'guitar' for this new Spanish instrument, but that soon became the practice as the lute-shaped gittern was abandoned in the 16th century.

The gittern and the guitar must have existed side by side for a considerable time, the older instrument steadily losing ground to the newer one. The instruments described as 'quintern' and illustrated in the treatises of Sebastian Virdung (*Musica getutscht*, 1511) and Martin Agricola (*Ein kurtz deudsche Musica*, 1528; *Musica instrumentalis deudsch*, 1529, enlarged 5/1545) are of the old variety. But already in 1530 there was a 'gyterneur suivant le mode espagnole' ('guitarist in the Spanish fashion') in the retinue of Emperor Charles V. Around 1550 a spate of guitar music was published, almost certainly for the new instrument. However, references to the guitar or gittern as a round-backed instrument or small lute are found in the later 16th century, the 17th and even the 18th, suggesting that the lute-shaped guitar was still occasionally used.

BIBLIOGRAPHY

K. Geiringer: 'Der Instrumentenname "Quinterne" und die mittelalterlichen Bezeichnungen der Gitarre, Mandola und des Colascione', *AMw*, vi (1924), 103

C. Sachs: *The History of Musical Instruments* (New York, 1940), 251

V. Denis: *De muziekinstrumenten in de Nederlanden en in Italië* (Antwerp and Utrecht, 1944), 112

A. Baines: 'Fifteenth-century Instruments in Tinctoris's *De inventione et usu musicae*', *GSJ*, ii (1950), 19

F. Lesure: 'La facture instrumentale à Paris au XVIᵉ siècle', *GSJ*, vii (1954), 36

H. G. Farmer: 'The Music of Islam', *NOHM*, i (1957), 421–78

F. V. Grunfeld: *The Art and Times of the Guitar* (London and New York, 1969)

F. Hellwig: 'Lute-making in the Late 15th and the 16th Century', *LSJ*, xvi (1974), 24

H. Turnbull: *The Guitar from the Renaissance to the Present Day* (New York and London, 1974)

L. Lockwood: 'Pietrobono and the Instrumental Tradition at Ferrara in the Fifteenth Century', *RIM*, x (1975), 115

L. Wright: 'The Medieval Gittern and Citole: a Case of Mistaken Identity', *GSJ*, xxx (1977), 8–42

J. M. Ward: 'Sprightly & Cheerful Musick: Notes on the Cittern, Gittern and Guitar in 16th- and 17th-century England', *LSJ*, xxi (1979–81) [whole issue]

LAURENCE WRIGHT

Giusto (It.: 'just', 'exact'). A word found in musical contexts most often within the complicated concept TEMPO GIUSTO. But it has other uses: Liszt and several other composers of his time used *giusto* for a return to the normal tempo after a section marked *a piacere*, and Schubert designated the controlled tempo in the finale of his 'Trout' Quintet with the marking *allegro giusto*. *See also* TEMPO AND EXPRESSION MARKS, §4.

Givelet, (Joseph) Armand (M. V. de P.) (*b* Rheims, 1899). French engineer and physicist. He was one of the pioneers of electronic instruments and especially of the electronic organ in the 1920s and early 1930s; some of his instruments were constructed in collaboration with the organ builder Edouard Eloi Coupleux. In 1917 or 1918, while working in the radio laboratory at the Eiffel Tower in Paris (at the same time as Maurice Martenot and Joseph Béthenod), Givelet first conceived the idea of electronic instruments based on the pitches that could be produced and varied by placing one's hand near or on certain components in a radio receiver. His idea for a dial-operated instrument (similar to the later Dynaphone and Ondium Péchadre) was not followed up until the mid-1920s, when he returned to studying the possibilities of electronic instruments.

Givelet's first completed electronic instrument, the monophonic keyboard *clavier à lampes*, was demonstrated in 1927, and like all his instruments its sounds were generated by electronic oscillators. In 1928 he demonstrated 'silent' recording and broadcasting, a method in which an electronic instrument was connected directly to the recording or transmitting equipment (as in today's 'direct injection'), thus bypassing the microphone. In 1929 the first of Givelet's collaborations with Coupleux, a 'synthesizer', was presented at the Paris Exhibition. Described in a patent as an 'automatically operating musical instrument of the electric oscillation type', it consisted of four oscillators controlled by a roll of punched paper tape, as in the player piano; pitch, loudness, attack, envelope, tremolo and timbre were controlled automatically (some by electropneumatic mechanisms).

Givelet and Coupleux then turned their attention to electronic keyboard instruments, and their pioneering work on the independent control of individual parameters was not taken further until more than 15 years later when the Hanert Electrical Orchestra, the Electronic Music Box and the first model of the RCA Electronic Music Synthesizer were developed.

Later in 1929 Givelet and Coupleux completed their related *piano radioélectrique*, effectively a small electronic organ consisting of a player-piano mechanism that controlled a set of oscillators mounted in a separate cabinet; it could be accompanied on the piano played manually, or, using a second electropneumatic system, by the automatically controlled player piano. Finally, in 1930, the two men demonstrated the COUPLEUX–GIVELET ORGAN at the Académie des Sciences, and in the following five years several of these electronic organs were installed in churches and one at a broadcasting station in Paris. Apart from articles (largely on instruments other than his own) published by Givelet up to 1948, no information is available on the subsequent activities of either man in the field of electronic instruments or elsewhere.

BIBLIOGRAPHY
A. J. Givelet: 'Les instruments de musique à oscillations électriques: le clavier à lampes', *Génie civil*, xciii (1928), 272
E. Weiss: 'Piano et orgue radioélectriques Givelet–Coupleux', *La nature*, lviii (1930), 258
A. J. Givelet: 'Instruments de musique électronique et évolution de l'orgue sans tuyaux', *Bulletin de la Société Française des Electriciens*, x (1940), 447
A. J. Givelet: 'La musique électrique', *Mémorial de la Société des Ingénieurs Civils*, ci (1948), 303
T. Rhea: 'The First Synthesizer (1929)', *Contemporary Keyboard*, v/8 (1979), 70
HUGH DAVIES

Giwga [giwgan]. JEW'S HARP of Wales. *See* STURMANT.

Giwong. JEW'S HARP of the northern Philippines. *See* AFIW.

Giying. A pair of ten-key metallophones of the GENDER type used in the Balinese *gamelan gong kebyar*.

Gjola. Bulgarian fiddle. *See* GADULKA.

Glasschord [glass chord, glassichord]. The name said to have been given by Benjamin Franklin to the *fortepiano à cordes de verre*, a CRYSTALLOPHONE invented by one Beyer of Paris *c*1785. The instrument consisted of a series of glass bars with a three-octave compass, variously given as *c* to *c'''*, *f* to *f'''* and *g* to *g'''*, laid horizontally on a thick cloth strip and struck from above by small wooden cloth-covered hammers controlled by a keyboard. There were no dampers. Similar instruments were produced by other makers well into the following century, for example Chappell's PIANINO (an example of 1815 survives in the Victoria and Albert Museum, London). The musical uses of the glasschord, difficult to specify precisely, probably involved giving the pitch to choirs and perhaps assisting amateurs in tuning pianos in an age when they were less stable and professional tuners less available. The term is occasionally applied to the armonica (*see* MUSICAL GLASSES), invented by Franklin in 1761.

BIBLIOGRAPHY
C. Sachs: *Reallexikon der Musikinstrumente, zugleich ein Polyglossar für das gesamte Instrumentengebiet* (Berlin, 1913/R1962)
S. Marcuse: *Musical Instruments: a Comprehensive Dictionary* (New York, 1964, rev. 2/1975)
——: *A Survey of Musical Instruments* (New York, 1975)
HOWARD SCHOTT

Glass Concert. A composition by ANNEA LOCKWOOD for an environment of glass instruments, which have been referred to by the same name. They include two triple-layered curtains (suspended tubing of thin glass, 1·33 metres long) that are shaken, water gongs consisting of glass sheets which are raised and lowered in water after being struck, bottle trees and a mobile of mirrors and large panes of reinforced glass that are played like gongs.

Glass harmonica. *See* MUSICAL GLASSES.

Glass harp. A type of MUSICAL GLASSES or CRYSTALLOPHONE devised in 1929 by Bruno Hoffmann.

Glass Orchestra. A Canadian ensemble, based in Toronto, which has specialized in constructing and performing on glass instruments. It was founded in 1973 and reached its present form in 1976; its members are V. Eric Cadesky (*b* Toronto, 1956), Miguel Frasconi (*b*

New York, 1956), Marvin Green (*b* Toronto, 1956), Paul Hodge (*b* Toronto, 1955) and John Kuipers. The ensemble's instruments are either made of glass or use glass containers as resonators, and many are closely related to traditional instruments. The instrumentarium includes glass marimbas, 'bow bowls', blown bottles (sopranino to bass), flutes, clarinets, chimes, 'glass icicles', glass loudspeaker (originally constructed for David Tudor's RAINFOREST IV in 1975), 'OBJ raks', glass voice-resonator bowls, 'pookaphone', 'slide pookaphone', 'the box', glass shepherd flute, 'tiltoes', 'silica shakers' and small percussion instruments. The Glass Orchestra performs by candlelight, each member sitting on the floor behind an inverted glass 'aquarium' on which a range of glass bowls and wine glasses (used as musical glasses) are placed; the remaining instruments lie to either side of the player on the floor.

BIBLIOGRAPHY
A. Timar and J. S. Kuipers: 'The Glass Orchestra', Music Gallery Editions, MGE 10 [disc notes]

HUGH DAVIES

Gleichschwebende Temperatur (Ger.). EQUAL TEMPERAMENT.

Glekor. Bamboo flute of Flores, Indonesia. *See* NUREN.

Glen. Scottish family, makers of bagpipes and other musical instruments and publishers of bagpipe music from 1827.

Thomas Macbean Glen (*b* Inverkeithing, Fife, May 1804; *d* Edinburgh, 12 July 1873) established an instrument making firm at 250 Cowgate, Edinburgh, in 1827. Probably the firm at first undertook various kinds of business; it is not listed in the Edinburgh Directory specifically as a 'pipe and flute maker's' until 1833. T. M. Glen claimed to have invented the 'serpentcleide', a form of wooden ophicleide; and a set of his bagpipes was described by Baines. He retired in 1866 and the business was continued as J. & R. Glen by his sons, John Glen (*b* Edinburgh, 1833; *d* Edinburgh, 29 Nov 1904) and Robert Glen (*b* Edinburgh, 1835; *d* Edinburgh, 1911). Both sons were distinguished musical scholars. John Glen formed a collection of old Scottish printed music books which was acquired at his death by Lady Dorothea Ruggles-Brise, and passed in 1927 to the National Library of Scotland. Robert Glen made a unique collection of musical instruments which was exhibited (e.g. at South Kensington in 1872) and was purchased by Glasgow Corporation in 1943.

In 1911 the firm of J. & R. Glen moved to premises at 497 Lawnmarket, Edinburgh, and was thereafter managed by Thomas Glen (*b* Edinburgh, 1867; *d* Edinburgh, 1951), son of John Glen, then by Andrew M. Ross and his son Andrew J. Ross (*b* Edinburgh, 1930; *d* Edinburgh, 1980), descendents of the Glens. The firm passed out of the family's hands in 1978, the premises and name being retained by a commercial concern.

A separate, independent instrument making business was established in 1844 by Alexander Glen (i) (*b* Inverkeithing, 1801; *d* Edinburgh, 1873), elder brother of Thomas Macbean Glen, at 30 West Register Street, Edinburgh. His son David Glen (i) (*b* Edinburgh, 1850) joined the firm in about 1869, and continued it in his own name from 1873. In 1911 Alexander Glen (ii) (1878–1951) and David Glen (ii) (*d* 1958), sons of David Glen

(i), became partners in the firm, which continued as David Glen & Sons until 1949, when it was acquired by J. & R. Glen.

Several members of the family published tutors for the bagpipe and collections of bagpipe tunes.

BIBLIOGRAPHY
Anon.: 'Africa's Part in the Bagpipe', *Edinburgh Evening News* (1 July 1933)
H. G. Farmer: *The Glen Collection of Musical Instruments* (London, c1945)
A. Baines: *Bagpipes* (London, 1960), 128
L. G. Langwill: *An Index of Musical Wind-instrument Makers* (Edinburgh, 1960, rev., enlarged 6/1980) [incl. detailed list of the firms' addresses]

DAVID JOHNSON

Glicibarifono. A bass clarinet. It was invented by Catterino Catterini, a clarinet maker active in Padua (possibly also in Bologna), who first performed on the instrument in Modena on 12 February 1838. Pitched in C and built of boxwood with brass and copper mounts, a surviving specimen (Oxford, Bate Collection) has 24 keys with elaborate mechanisms and an unusual bore. It is constructed with a double parallel bore in a single block of wood of oval section. The mouthpiece is attached by a curved crook and a bell is mounted on the top of the rising tube.

BIBLIOGRAPHY
F. G. Rendall: *The Clarinet* (London, 1954, 3/1971)
A. Baines: *The Bate Collection of Historical Wind Instruments* (Oxford, 1976)

NIALL O'LOUGHLIN

Gling-bu. Bamboo DUCT FLUTE of Tibet. The term is used throughout the areas of Tibetan cultural influence for all aerophones of the flute type. The transverse instruments (*phred-gling*), known in Bhutan as 'zur-lim', usually have six or seven finger-holes; they are used in secular music and are similar to the Indian *vaṃśa*. End-blown duct flutes can be single, double or triple. *See also* LIMBE.

MIREILLE HELFFER

Glissade (Fr.). *See* SLIDE (ii).

Glissando (italianized, from Fr. *glisser*: 'to slide'; It. *strisciando*). A term generally used as an instruction to execute a passage in a rapid, sliding movement. It is, however, susceptible to ambiguity. When applied to playing the piano and the harp, glissando generally refers to the effect obtained not by fingering the key or strings of scales but by sliding over them rapidly with the fingernails or the fingertips. Because of the nature of the piano and the harp, every individual tone or semitone of such glissando scales is clearly heard, no matter how rapid the 'sliding' (*see* HARP, §4 (ix)). On the other hand, in the voice, violin or trombone, a sliding from one pitch to another is more readily effected without distinguishing any of the intervening notes, a method of sliding which is often called PORTAMENTO. Other instruments capable of sliding are the clarinet, the horn and the kettledrum. By their very nature, both types of sliding must be legato and relatively rapid.

In practice, the terms glissando and portamento are often confused and used interchangeably whether the sliding is continuous (as in portamento) or whether it is effected by distinguishing each semitone (as in glissando). However, if, in the interest of clarity (which often entails some degree of arbitrariness), the distinctions made above are kept, it follows that the piano and the harp, which have fixed semitones, can play glissando but not portamento; and the voice, violin and trombone can produce either type of sliding, although glissando is far more difficult for them.

Two examples of sliding on the violin will illustrate the distinctions just made between the two terms. Ex.1 shows a chromatic glissando (Lalo: *Symphonie espagnole*, fourth movement), although no such term is used by Lalo. The passage shows clearly that Lalo wished every semitone to be distinguished in the downward slide from *e''''* to *e''*, even at the speed implied by the demisemiquavers. The slur directs the player to use a single bow stroke for the glissando, and the use of a single finger in sliding is implied (up to the last few notes).

Ex.1

In the second example (ex.2), taken from the second movement of Bartók's Fourth String Quartet, the composer indicated a sliding by a diagonal line – he used no terms. Obviously, at the *prestissimo* tempo of the movement, the slide must be a portamento, there being no time to distinguish any intervening notes. All four instruments of the quartet are directed to slide, as shown. These continuous slides of ex.2 are easier to execute than the chromatically articulated slide of ex.1.

Ex.2

(only notes involving glissando given here)

Flesch proposed that glissando be used to mean a technically essential type of violin shift (the shift to be carried out quickly and unobtrusively) and that portamento be used for a type of shift (carried out either slowly or rapidly) intended to heighten the expression. These distinctions, however, have not been universally accepted. In Galamian's terminology, for instance, Flesch's portamento becomes 'expressive glissando'. Because of the variety and confusion of terms and meanings, Flesch used the term 'chromatic glissando' to describe the passage shown in ex.1 in order to make explicit the articulation of each individual semitone.

BIBLIOGRAPHY
C. Flesch: *Die Kunst des Violin-Spiels* (Berlin, 1923, 2/1928; Eng. trans., 1924, rev. 3/1939)
W. Piston: *Orchestration* (New York, 1955)
I. Galamian: *Principles of Violin Playing and Teaching* (Englewood Cliffs, NJ, 1962)
N. Del Mar: *Anatomy of the Orchestra* (London, 1981)
DAVID D. BOYDEN

Globular flute. VESSEL FLUTE of spherical shape. Many African examples are made from seed shells or small spherical gourds.

Glocke (Ger., pl. *Glocken*). *See* BELL (i) and TUBULAR BELLS.

Glockenspiel (Ger., also *Stahlspiel*; Fr. (*jeu de*) *timbres*, *carillon*; It. *campanelli*, *campanette*). A percussion idiophone, a METALLOPHONE with tuned metal bars (usually of steel) of graduated length, arranged in two rows like the piano keyboard. Modern nomenclature includes the abbreviation 'glock' and the American use of 'bells', a term now universally recognized though frequently confused with TUBULAR BELLS. In Germany 'Glockenspiel' also means CARILLON and is further applied to the smaller diatonic sets of bells known in England as CHIMES. There are two types of orchestral glockenspiel: the open type (see illustration), played with a mallet like a dulcimer (another instrument with which the glockenspiel has been confused); and that with a keyboard mechanism, now seldom used as the mallet-played instrument has a superior tone. Maximum resonance is obtained by the bars being supported on felt (or similar insulation) or otherwise suspended at the nodal points. These positions may be determined by Chladni's method (metal filings or a similar substance strewn on the bar will, when the bar is vibrating, form two ridges transversely where it is to be supported). The 'open' type of glockenspiel has two standard mallet-played patterns with a range of *g''* to *c''''* and *c''* to *c''''*. The instrument with a miniature piano keyboard has a compass of two and a quarter to two and a half octaves and has small metal hammers which strike the bars from below. The mallet-played instrument is struck with small hammers consisting of flexible cane shafts mounted with heads of wood, bone, plastic, rubber or, in rare cases, metal. The beaters are held as timpani sticks. In certain cases the open glockenspiel has tube resonators, as for example the instruments patented in the early 1900s by Messrs J. C. Deagan of Chicago ('Deagan Parsifal Bells'). Movable suspension to adjust the nodal points for decreasing or increasing the resonance, and foot-operated damping mechanism, are now incorporated in certain models, otherwise (where necessary) the performer uses a finger-damping technique.

Metallophones in the form of graduated metal plates struck with beaters have existed in the Far East for over

Modern orchestral glockenspiel by J. C. Deagan Inc., Chicago

1000 years (examples include the Javanese *saron* and *gender*). In Europe, the earliest known reference to a glockenspiel-type metallophone was made by Grassineau (*Musical Dictionary*, 1769), who referred to a 'cymbal' constructed of bars made of bell metal and silver, with a compass of more than three octaves. The bars, which were struck with small hammers, were arranged keyboard-fashion 'in the manner of a spinet'. The earliest use of a glockenspiel dates from this period, in Handel's *Saul* (1739). Handel's instrument, which he called a 'carillon', consisted of a series of metal plates (or possibly small bells) with a compass of two octaves and a 4th, and had a chromatic keyboard. Charles Jennens described this instrument as 'both in the make and tone like a series of hammers striking upon anvils'. Handel scored for this instrument in other works as well, including revivals of *Trionfo del tempo*, *Acis and Galatea*, and in *L'allegro ed il penseroso*. Half a century later Mozart scored for a glockenspiel (*instrumento d'acciaio*) in *Die Zauberflöte* (1791), to represent Papageno's magic bells. This instrument has been described by Berlioz and Gevaert as a series of small bells operated by a mechanism of keys. (Today the celesta, or a combination of celesta and piano-action or normal glockenspiel, is used.)

The mallet-played orchestral glockenspiel, which may have originated from the lyra-glockenspiel (*see* BELL-LYRA) as used in the German military bands, did not make a firm appearance in the orchestra until the middle of the 19th century. An instrument of this type may have been used in Adam's *Si J'étais roi* (1852), and in Wagner's orchestra in place of the then generally used continental keyboard glockenspiel. In England at this period, mention is made of an interesting form of glockenspiel: the 'New Patent Educational Transposing Metallic Harmonicon', an inspiration of Thomas Croger, in which the metal bars were removable for transposition, rendering the instrument – according to its inventor – 'useful in schools where singing is being studied'.

From Wagner onwards writing for the orchestral glockenspiel suggests a frequent employment of the mallet-played instrument, though in circumstances such as Puccini's operas *Turandot* and *Madama Butterfly* (*campanelli tasteria*), Dukas's *L'apprenti sorcier*, Debussy's *La mer*, Respighi's *The Pines of Rome* and Honegger's Fourth Symphony, an instrument with a piano action was obviously intended. The better-known examples of the use of the orchestral glockenspiel include the Dance of the Hours (*La Gioconda*) by Ponchielli, The Bell Song (*Lakmé*) by Delibes, Strauss's *Don Juan*, Tchaikovsky's suite *Nutcracker*, Elgar's *The Dream of Gerontius*, Ravel's *Daphnis et Chloé*, Vaughan Williams's *A London Symphony*, Holst's suite *The Planets*, Kodály's *Dances of Galánta*, Copland's Third Symphony, Britten's *The Prince of the Pagodas*, Orff's *Oedipus der Tyrann* (three glockenspiels, one with keys) and Boulez's *Pli selon pli*. An important part for the glockenspiel is in S. Strohbach's Concerto in G (1959) which is scored for two flutes, glockenspiel and string orchestra.

In the orchestral repertory the glockenspiel is the most freely used of all tuned percussion instruments. Composers often employ its bell-like tone imitatively. The music for the instrument is written in the treble clef, usually two octaves lower than sounding. In *Oceanides* (1914) Sibelius requested *Stahlstäbe* (or *Stahlspiel*). *See also* ORGAN STOP.

BIBLIOGRAPHY

H. Berlioz: *Grand traité d'instrumentation et d'orchestration modernes* (Paris, 1843, 2/1855; Eng. trans., 1855)

F. Gevaert: *Nouveau traité d'instrumentation* (Paris and Brussels, 1885)

W. Ellerhorst: *Das Glockenspiel* (London, 1940)

J. Blades: *Percussion Instruments and their History* (London, 1970, rev. 3/1984)

N. Del Mar: *Anatomy of the Orchestra* (London, 1981)

JAMES BLADES

Glockenspiel, militär (Ger.). BELL-LYRA.

Glockentriangel (Ger.: 'bell triangle'). A triangle made in a V-form out of a metal bar square in section by V. F. Červený of Hradec Králové in 1877. When hit with a normal beater it produced a powerful triangle tone; hit with a wooden hammer it sounded like a bell.

Glosa (Sp.: 'gloss'). A term often used by 16th-century Spanish musicians, in imitation of the glossing technique highly fashionable among poets, to designate variations similar to *diferencias* but generally on a religious theme and less extensive. It is also used to mean musical ornamentation, as for example in Diego Ortiz's *Trattado de glosas* (1553). *See* ORNAMENTS, §IV.

Gloton, Georges (*b* Dijon, 18 Dec 1876; *d* Nantes, 20 March 1955). French organ builder. He was apprenticed to J.-B. Ghys in Dijon and received further training with the firm of Cavaillé-Coll-Mutin in Paris. After World War I (during which he was taken prisoner) he became director of the firm of Louis Debierre at Nantes, a post he held until 1947. He restored and maintained the organs in the cathedrals of Angers, Bordeaux, Lisieux, Moulins, Nantes, Le Puy-en-Velay, La Rochelle, Rouen, St-Malo, Tours and Vannes. He built new instruments at Fougères (St Sulpice, 1919), Batz-sur-Mer (1927), Pontmain (1930), Fresnay-sur-Sarthe (1932), Paray-le-Monial (1933), Beaufort-en-Vallée (1934), St-Jean-de-Monts (1936), Guérande (1939) and les Sables-d'Olonne (1943). He also built more than 130 portative organs, a number of which were exported. See G. Bourligueux: 'Gloton', *DBF*.

GUY BOURLIGUEUX

Glottophone. Term occasionally used for a LAMELLA-PHONE.

Głowiński, Jan (*b* *c*1645; *d* *c*1712). Polish organ builder. He worked in Kraków and south-eastern Poland. In 1679 he built an organ for St Elizabeth's, Stary Sącz, of which the case still exists. Between 1683 and 1690 he finished the three organs begun in 1680 by Stanisław Studziński at the Bernardine monastery in Leżajsk (the cases survive); the largest instrument had 64 stops on four manuals and pedal. In 1712 he was to have built an organ with 30 stops for the parish church of Żywiec, but the work was eventually carried out by Ignacy Ryszak from Opawa. Głowiński seems to have built in the southern Polish style, preferring diapason chorus and foundation stops of various kinds, but using few mutations or reeds. It is not known if he was related to an organ builder of the same name who worked in Kraków in about 1635.

BIBLIOGRAPHY

A. Chybiński: *Słownik muzyków dawnej Polski do r. 1800* [Dictionary of early Polish musicians] (Kraków, 1949)

M. Perz: 'Do historii kunsztu budowy organów w Polsce' [History of the art of organ building in Poland], *Ruch muzyczny*, xxii (1960), 8; xxiii (1961), 6

M. Radojewski: 'Organy xvii-wieczne w kościele Bernadynów w Lżaajsku' [The 17th-century organs in the church of the Bernadines in Leżajsk], *Roczniki humanistyczne*, x (1961), 41–94

J. Gołos: *Zarys historii budowy organów w Polsce* [Outline of the history of Polish organ building] (Bydgoszcz, 1966)

——: 'Polskie organy i muzyka organowa', in J. Gołos and E. Smulikowska: *Prospekty organowe w Polsce jako dzieła sztuki* (Warsaw, 1972)

HANS KLOTZ

Glycleide. A brass baritone instrument in B♭ (with rotary change to A) invented in 1846 by VÁCLAV FRANTIŠEK ČERVENÝ.

Gmbri. Large plucked lute of North Africa. *See* GUINBRI.

Gmebogosse. A portable SYNTHESIZER system designed for groups of children from the age of about five. Conceived by the composer Christian Clozier, it was developed from 1972 by Jean-Claude Le Duc, in collaboration with Pierre Boeswillwald, at the premises of the Groupe de Musique Expérimentale de Bourges (the name consists of the initials GMEB and a phonetic spelling of *aux gosses*, Fr.: 'for kids'); it was first used in 1973 and later versions were constructed in 1978 and planned in 1983. About ten of the systems are in existence: some are in use by members of the GMEB, who have held workshops in many parts of France, and others are permanently installed in French further education centres. The system consists of three independent operating consoles, each with a built-in microphone and variable-speed cassette tape recorder; these are normally linked to one control console, through which voltage-controlled interconnections can be made between them. The same team has also developed an elaborate multi-loudspeaker system, the Gmebaphone (1973; new versions in 1975 and 1979), for diffusing taped electronic music in concerts.

BIBLIOGRAPHY

R. Cochini: 'Le Gmebogosse', *Faire*, nos. 2–3 (1975), 171

Le Gmebogosse (Bourges, 1978)

A. Murat, C. Landy and M. Merra: 'Les 10 ans du Gmebogosse', *Cahiers de l'animation musicale*, no.29 (1983), 22

HUGH DAVIES

Gnagnour. Single-string fiddle of the Tukulor people of Senegal. *See* GOGE.

Gnibra. Plucked lute of North Africa. *See* GUINBRI.

Gnome (i). An electronic keyboard instrument developed by IVAN EREMEEFF in Philadelphia in 1932; it was the smaller and better-known of two instruments based on the same principles which Eremeeff built in that year. Rotating electromagnetic tone-wheels generated the sounds. The keyboard (three and a half octaves) and the bench on which the player sat formed part of an electrical circuit; when one of the stationary, touch-plate keys was fingered, an electrical contact was made through the performer's body with the metal top of the bench. In addition to pedals governing volume and tremolo there was also a decay control. The Gnome was designed for home use, and could be connected to the amplifier and loudspeaker of a domestic radio set. See E. E. Kassel: 'Electromagnetic Music', *Radio-Craft*, iv (1932), 270.

HUGH DAVIES

Gnome (ii). A small SYNTHESIZER manufactured from around 1975 by PAIA Electronics in Oklahoma City.

Go (i). Gourd percussion vessel of the Mahi people of Benin. It is a large jar-shaped gourd whose opening is struck with a flexible piece of leather, causing the air inside to vibrate and produce low muffled sounds. *See also* TOHUN.

Go (ii). Double-headed conical drum of the Sere people of Zaïre. *See* DINDO.

Go (iii). Bossed gongs of Flores, Indonesia. *See* NGGO.

Goala. Five-string lyre of the Hamar people of south Ethiopia. *See* RABABA.

Goasspfeiff (Ger.: 'goat pipe'). Austrian Alpine flute. *See* SCHWEGEL.

Gobato [gong tundu]. Idiochord TUBE ZITHER of Flores, Indonesia. It has between two and five narrow strings and is about 35 to 42 cm long. The strings are prised from the tube's surface and raised on a bridge. A soundhole is often cut beneath the strings and a hole is cut into one or both nodes. These may be closed by the player's hand in rhythmic fashion, not so much to alter the tone as to provide a substitute for a drum. The strings of multi-string instruments are plucked, while those of two- and sometimes three-string instruments are beaten with a small stick. See J. Kunst: *Music in Flores* (Leiden, 1942), 128f.

MARGARET J. KARTOMI

Go beto. Indonesian TUBE ZITHER. *See* BABA (i).

Gobetti, Francesco (*b* Udine, baptized 4 Jan 1675; *d* Venice, 10 July 1723). Italian violin maker. His family moved to Venice in the early 1690s and appears to have been connected with shoemaking. He described himself as a shoemaker when he married (1702) but probably took up violin making within a fairly short time, doubtless as a pupil of Matteo Goffriller, who lived in the same parish. He began to sign his instruments soon after 1710, but because of ill-health was obliged to give up working after 1717.

Though he was active for only a few years and his output was comparatively small, Gobetti ranks as one of the greatest makers of the Venetian school. He was a meticulous workman, yet possessed of considerable verve, showing in his work many of the best qualities of Goffriller and Montagnana. He seems to have made no violas or cellos. His violins are exciting instruments both tonally and visually, sometimes being excellent copies of other makers' work.

BIBLIOGRAPHY

C. Beare: *The Venetian Violin Makers* (in preparation)

CHARLES BEARE

Gobi-gobi. Bamboo zither of southern Nias, Indonesia. *See* TABOLIYA.

Goble, Robert (John) (*b* Thursley, Surrey, 30 Oct 1903). English harpsichord and recorder maker. He began to learn the craft of instrument making in 1925 in the workshop of Arnold Dolmetsch in Haslemere. In 1937 he established his own workshop in Haslemere, producing clavichords, spinets and recorders. Except for a period during World War II he remained in Haslemere until 1947 when he moved to Headington, Oxford. At the new workshop his production expanded to include the larger varieties of harpsichord. The demand for keyboard instruments was so great that in 1950 he was obliged to discontinue making recorders altogether. Until 1971 he continued to build essentially modern instruments in the tradition of Dolmetsch; thereafter he turned increasingly to making instruments on historical lines, modelled on prototypes by Ruckers, Taskin, Dulcken and Hass, while continuing to produce modern instruments as well.

Goble married Elizabeth Brown (b 8 Feb 1907; d Oxford, 23 Dec 1981) who studied early keyboard instruments and viol playing with Arnold Dolmetsch, performing frequently at the Haslemere Festival in both capacities and as a contralto. She toured Europe and North America as a member of the English Consort of Viols and was involved in her husband's workshop in several capacities. Their son Andrea (b 27 June 1931) joined the firm in 1947, and his son Anthony (b 8 July 1957) joined in 1975.

BIBLIOGRAPHY

'A Visit to Robert Goble', English Harpsichord Magazine, i/1 (1973–6), 6

HOWARD SCHOTT

Goblet drum. Goblet-shaped drums have been known since antiquity, in ancient Sumerian and Babylonian cultures (the *lilis* and *lilissu*); they are of particular importance in the Islamic world and its vicinity but most of all in the Arab countries. Goblet drums are single-headed with a membrane head that may be laced, pegged or glued; the body of the drum may be of wood, metal or pottery. (For full details of the classification, *see* MEMBRANOPHONE; for illustration of relative drum shapes, *see* DRUM, figs.2 and 3.)

The following goblet drums are entered in this dictionary: agual; banga (ii); chamutanda; dadabuan; daluka; dap'lika; darabukka; dĕbakan; deplik; derbanka; ditumba; dombak; dümbelek; etumba; feli; gatumbatumba; goma; gomo; gummaṭi; gwangwaragwandi; herrazi; kaamuri; kabitikwila; kadih; kamango; katumbi; khashaba; kingaridi; klŏng; lamba (i); lupondo; lutandu; mbalwe; mitumbwe; mpanje; mtiwiso; mugabe; mujinji; muntundu; ngoma; ntimbo; ò-zi; pati; pere; pininga; pĩpa; sangbai; sgar; tarabuka; tarija; thŏn; timbo; tombak; toumbeleki; tsintsima; tumba (ii); tumbaknārī; turu (iii); zambuna; zarb; zirbaghali.

Gobo (i). Bell of the Shambala people of Tanzania.

Gobo (ii). Brazilian MUSICAL BOW of African origin.

Goč. Large double-headed cylindrical drum of Macedonia, Kosovo and Serbia (Yugoslavia). *See* TAPAN.

Godfroy [Godefroy], Clair, *l'aîné* (*fl* 1814–67; *d* before 1878). French maker of woodwind instruments, especially flutes. Established by 1814, he exhibited instruments in Paris industrial expositions, winning an honourable mention in 1823, bronze medals in 1827, 1834, 1839 and 1844, silver medals in 1849 and 1867, a second class medal at the Universal Exposition in London in 1851 and first class medals at the Universal Expositions of 1855 and 1862. Although he exhibited clarinets, oboes and flageolets it was always his flutes

and piccolos that received the prize. He was the first in Paris to copy Theobald Boehm's conical ring system flute of 1832, announcing the first instrument he had made of this kind in the *Courrier français* of 21 October 1837. Within a year the leading flautists of Paris were said to have adopted the new flute and had instruments made in the Godfroy atelier. Later Godfroy bought the privilege to make Boehm's cylindrical metal flute of 1847. He usually substituted the Dorus G♯ key for Boehm's open G♯, and he seems to have reintroduced perforations into the large padded keys of the 1847 model, thus initiating the 'French model' or 'open-holed' flute. After his death, his widow continued the business for a time, winning a silver medal for her work in 1878. Apparently the only Clair Godfroy instruments now extant are flutes and piccolos, with both Boehm and earlier fingering systems, and flageolets. The richest sources are the Dayton C. Miller and Philip Bate collections.

BIBLIOGRAPHY

A. Farrenc: 'Flute Boehm', *Revue et gazette musicale de Paris*, v (9 Sept 1838), 364f

T. Boehm: *De la fabrication et des derniers perfectionnements des flûtes* (Paris, 1848), 46

A. de Pontécoulant: *Organographie: essai sur la facture instrumentale*, ii (Paris, 1861), 136, 161, 366, 376, 405, 436, 466, 537f

C. von Schafhäutl [C. E. Pellisov]: *Theobald Böhm: Ein merkwürdiges Künstlerleben* (Leipzig, 1882) [Eng. trans. in Welch]

C. Welch: *History of the Boehm Flute with Dr. von Schafhäutl's Life of Boehm* (London, 1883, rev. 3/1896)

R. S. Rockstro: *A Treatise on the Construction, the History and the Practice of the Flute* (London, 1890, rev. 2/1928/R1967), 202, 363, 373ff, 636

C. Pierre: *Les facteurs d'instruments de musique: les luthiers et la facture instrumentale* (Paris, 1893), 296

L. G. Langwill: *An Index of Musical Wind-instrument Makers* (Edinburgh, 1960, rev., enlarged 6/1980)

L. E. Gilliam and W. Lichtenwanger: *The Dayton C. Miller Flute Collection: a Checklist of the Instruments* (Washington, DC, 1961), 1, 30, 46, 69, 72, 74

P. Bate: *The Flute: a Study of its History, Development and Construction* (London, 1969), 121, pl.8

R. J. M. van Acht, C. C. J. von Gleich, and D. M. Klerk: *Historische blaasinstrumenten: de ontwikkeling van de blaasinstrumenten vanaf 1600* (The Hague, 1974), 20f

A. Baines: *The Bate Collection of Historical Wind Instruments: Catalogue of the Instruments* (Oxford, 1976), 5, 10, 13

H. Heyde: *Historische Musikinstrumente im Bachhaus Eisenach* (Eisenach, 1976), 200

——: *Musikinstrumenten-Museum der Karl-Marx-Universität Leipzig: Katalog*, i: *Flöten* (Leipzig, 1978), 99f, 120ff, 139, 143, 147ff, 151, 154ff

N. Toff: *The Development of the Modern Flute* (New York, 1979), 65, 72f, 75, 128, 171

M. Seyfrit: *Musical Instruments in the Dayton C. Miller Flute Collection at the Library of Congress: a Catalog*, i: *Recorders, Fifes, and Simple System Transverse Flutes of One Key* (Washington, DC, 1982), 107, pl.24

JANE M. BOWERS

Godie. Term used by the Yoruba-speaking Nago people of Benin for the GOGE single-string fiddle.

Godje. Ankle rattles of the Tuburi and Kera peoples in southern Chad. They consist of an anklet of forged iron on which are threaded several rings of the same material. Several anklets may be worn on the same leg, separated by a roll of material. Players of the *parwaye* flute wear *godje* on their right ankles to punctuate the melody. In some Sara dialects *godje* are known as *mangla*.

MONIQUE BRANDILY

Godye. MOUTH BOW of the Baule people of the Ivory Coast. It is made from a curved stick and a vegetable fibre string. The string is placed between the lips and is struck with a stick in the right hand, while the vibrating length is varied with a stick held in the left. The player produces harmonics which he amplifies by modifying the shape of his oral cavity. See H. Zemp: 'Baulé Vocal Music', Odeon 3C 064 17842 [disc notes].

Goff, Thomas (Robert Charles) (*b* London, 16 July 1898; *d* London, 13 March 1975). English maker of clavichords, harpsichords and lutes. He was educated at Eton and studied the piano with Irene Scharrer. After service in World War I he read history at Christ Church, Oxford, and was called to the bar. Early in 1932 he received a clavichord as a gift and was so deeply impressed that he determined to build such instruments. In 1933 he formed a partnership with J. C. Cobby, a master cabinet maker, and they established their workshop in Goff's house. The handsome veneering and inlay work of many of their instruments, and the finely chased brass hinges, were the result of this collaboration. A number of instruments with painted cases, including a few decorated by well-known artists such as Rex Whistler, were also produced.

Goff adopted the clavichord design developed by Herbert Lambert, an able craftsman and photographer of Bath, who died soon afterwards and so never joined the partnership. Lambert's model was derived from 18th-century clavichords, but had lighter stringing, a slightly heavier soundboard and a somewhat higher bridge with correspondingly increased down-draft. Goff made four types of clavichord during his career as a builder, but all were based on the Lambert model in their essentials. The smallest, a single-strung instrument (unlike the others, which were classically bichord), was designed to achieve maximum portability and Goff took one with him during his service overseas in World War II.

In 1937 the first Goff harpsichord (in all only 14 were made) appeared, also based on a Lambert model. It was a modern instrument in construction, heavily cased with a metal frame and 4' hitch-pin plate, a 16' stop, registration pedals with half-hitches, and an elaborate and complex jack mechanism. His striving for the maximum variety of timbres and contrast of tonal colour led Goff to use both quill and leather plectra.

In the postwar years he resumed production and played a significant part in bringing about an increased acceptance of the harpsichord in British performances of early music. He also made a small number of lutes and two regals during this period. Although Goff's models lost their position of central importance in later years, as harpsichords modelled more closely on antique instruments came into increasing favour, his small but exquisite output was always admired for the refinement of its craftsmanship.   HOWARD SCHOTT

Goffriller [Gofriller], **Matteo** (*b* Bressanone, *c*1659; *d* Venice, 23 Feb 1742). Italian string instrument maker. He went to Venice in 1685, and is presumed to have learnt his craft there from Martin Kaiser. In the following year he married a daughter of Kaiser and by 1690 had succeeded him in business. From then until about 1710 he was without a serious competitor in Venice, and made many instruments for a wide range of clients, hence the considerable variety in the patterns and quality of his work. He appears to have been less active after about 1720.

Goffriller was the first important maker of the Venetian school and is best known for his cellos, built on

Violin by Matteo Goffriller, Venice, 1698 (private collection)

several patterns but mostly large-size instruments based on those of the Amati family. These larger cellos have almost all been reduced in size to conform with the smaller dimensions in fashion from the second half of the 18th century onwards, and their effectiveness depends on how well this was carried out. Casals used a Goffriller from about 1910 onwards; Janos Starker played another fine example. Many others are in professional use, particularly in chamber music.

Goffriller's violins are also very fine, and his few violas have dimensions ideally suited to modern performance. His instruments seldom carry their maker's label, and many passed unrecognized until recent times. His cellos were often attributed to Carlo Bergonzi; instruments continually appear under more illustrious names.

One of his sons, Francesco Goffriller (*b* Venice, 4 Nov 1692; *d* Udine, *c*1740 or after), followed his father's profession, though with less energy. Some of his instruments are excellent. He went to Udine in 1714 and his labels show that he was active there until at least 1737.

BIBLIOGRAPHY
C. Beare: *The Venetian Violin Makers* (in preparation)
                    CHARLES BEARE

Goge. The most common name for the single-string fiddle of the savanna area of West Africa. The term *goge* (or *goje*) is used by the Hausa and Yoruba peoples of Nigeria, and by the Songhay, Djerma, Mauri and Hausa of Niger, while the Mamprusi-Dagomba peoples of northern Ghana use *gonje* and the Yoruba-speaking Nago of Benin *godie*. The instrument consists of a half-calabash resonator on to which is nailed a monitor-lizard skin. This soundtable has a circular hole on one side. The wooden neck, inserted through the resonator parallel to the soundtable, protrudes a few centimetres at the lower

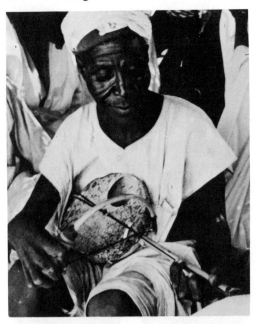

Goge (single-string fiddle) of the Songhay people, Niger

singing. Among the Songhay and Mauri of Niger, at Timbuktu in Mali and among the non-Islamic groups of northern Nigeria, the *goge* is used, with two calabash percussion vessels, in spirit possession cults, the best known of which is *bori*. Contemporary developments among the Hausa of Nigeria include the use of electronic amplification for virtuoso performance. Recent research suggests that the theory that the instrument stemmed from the Maghribi *ghugha* may no longer be correct but that it is rather an indigenous sub-Saharan product, associated primarily with spirit cults, and transported to North Africa by black slaves.

BIBLIOGRAPHY

Ames–KingGHM
P. G. Harris: 'Notes on Drums and Musical Instruments Seen in Sokoto Province, Nigeria', *Journal of the Royal Anthropological Institute*, lxii (1932), 105
H. G. Farmer: 'Early References to Music in Western Sudan', *Journal of the Royal Asiatic Society* (1939), 569
H. Lhoté: *Les Touareg du Hoggar* (Paris, 1955)
M. Bovis and M. Gast: *Touareg Ahaggar* (Paris, 1959)
V. Pâques: *L'arbre cosmique dans la pensée populaire et dans la vie quotidienne du nord-ouest africain* (Paris, 1964)
K. Krieger: 'Musikinstrumente der Hausa', *Baessler-Archiv*, new ser., xvi (1968), 373–430
B. Surugue: *Contribution à l'étude de la musique sacrée zarma-songhay* (Niamey, 1972)
M. Brandily: *Instruments de musique et musiciens instrumentalistes chez les Teda du Tibesti (Tchad)*, Annales sciences humaines (Tervuren, 1974)
——: 'Music of Kanem', BM30 L2309 [disc notes]
K. A. GOURLAY

end so that the horsehair string can be looped round it. After passing across a V- or Y-shaped wooden bridge, the string is fastened to the neck at the upper end with a leather strap. The bow is usually a curved piece of iron with a horsehair string. In performance the instrument is placed in the player's lap so that its body rests against his waist in an almost horizontal position, and the soundtable is tilted so that his right hand, holding the bow perpendicular to the string, moves up and down, while the left hand, holding the neck, stops the string on one side (see illustration).

Elsewhere the corresponding instrument varies in name and construction. In Senegal and the Gambia the Wolof *riti* or *duriti*, Tukulor *gnagnour* and Fula *nyaanyooru* have a hemispherical wooden resonator, made from the silk-cotton tree, with one or two holes in the back but none in the lizard-skin soundtable; the *diarka* of Timbuktu uses snakeskin, the Ahaggar Tuareg *imzad* or *amzad* may use goatskin which is laced round the soundbox, while the Tuareg of Air fix it with acacia spines; in the *kiiki* of the Teda of northern Chad, the resonator may be of wood, a half-calabash, or an enamel bowl, and the wooden neck terminates inside it, the string being tied to the base through a hole in the soundboard; the *duduga* of the Bisa of Upper Volta has a gourd resonator; the Songhay-Djerma *goge* has a long metal jingle with small iron rings round the edges inserted into the handle. Instruments vary in size, those of the Tuareg being the largest with a resonator diameter of 20 to 50 cm, the Songhay of 24 to 28 cm and the Wolof and Tukulor 18 cm.

Tuareg performance is unique in that the players are predominantly women, whose ability is highly respected, and whose playing is regarded as a mark of elegance, especially in their accompaniment of men's love songs. Among the Fula of the Gambia, the Fulani elsewhere and the Hausa communities of Niger and Nigeria, the instrument is associated with professionals who combine displays of technical virtuosity with praise

Gogen [gogenbiwa]. Early BIWA (lute), with five strings, in the 8th-century Shōsōin Repository in Nara, Japan.

Gogeru. Fiddle of the Fulbe people of Cameroon. It has a gourd body and one to three strings.

Gogia bana. A name used erroneously in secondary literature for a bow harp of the Gogia Pardhan people of Madhya Pradesh, central India. See BĪN BĀJĀ (i).

Gogo (i). Metal or bamboo JEW'S HARP of the Gayo area of Aceh province, Sumatra. It is now rare. It may be played in ensemble with one or more *canang kacapi*.

Gogo (ii). SLIT-DRUM of the Mamvu people of northeastern Zaïre. It may be tulip-shaped or zoomorphic (*LaurentyTF*, 139). See GUGU, (1).

Gogogo. Drum of Africa. In Malawi the term refers to a single-headed open-ended conical drum of the Nyanja/Manganja people. The membrane is pegged on and weighted. It is the smallest of the nine tuned drums in their LIKHUBA drum set. In Zambia, the *gogogo* is a single-headed GOBLET DRUM of the Valley Tonga people; see NGOMA.

Gogonjenro. A fretted STICK ZITHER of Orissa, eastern India. See KULLUTAN RĀJAN.

Gogu. Small zoomorphic SLIT-DRUM of the Mangbetu (Day) people of Zaïre (*LaurentyTF*, 140).

Goingoing [!goin!going]. BULLROARER of the San (Bushman) people of south-western Africa.

Goje. Yoruba term for the GOGE single-string fiddle.

Goka. Side-blown animal-horn trumpet of the Logo and Ma peoples of north-eastern Zaïre; it has one stop in the tip (*LaurentyA*, 321, 325).

Goldene Dionys. *See* DENIS D'OR.

Goll, Friedrich. Swiss organ builder who took over the firm of FRIEDRICH HAAS in 1867; it continues as Orgelbau Goll & Cie AG.

Gologod. Folk fiddle of the Kalinga people of the southern Philippines.

Goltukh saza. Small long-necked lute of Azerbaijan. *See* SAZ.

Goma. A central African variant term for NGOMA (drum). In Zaïre it is used for a GOBLET DRUM of the Luba and Songye (*see* DITUMBA), a double-headed conical drum of the Kumu (*see* DINDO) and a cylindro-conical drum of the Fuliru and Vira peoples.

Gombi [nengombi, nengonibi, banzie, ngumbi] **(i).** BOARD ZITHER of the Zande, Makere and other peoples of north-eastern Zaïre. It is 50 cm long and 18 cm wide, with 10 or 11 strings of vegetable fibre and a semi-circular bark resonator attached beneath the board. Among the Bwa, Ngata and Meje five strings are plucked with the left thumb, five with the right. The Zande instrument is played while walking or to accompany singing. Among the Mangbetu and Bwa peoples, zithers of this type are known as *banzu*, among the Sere as *bwanzi*, and among the Mbuja as *ngbandje*. *See also* IKIDI and MALIGBANGA.

BIBLIOGRAPHY
LaurentyC, 116
F. J. de Hen: *Beitrag zur Kenntnis der Musikinstrumente aus Belgisch Kongo und Ruanda-Urundi* (Tervuren, 1960)
K. A. GOURLAY

Gombi (ii). Large cylindrical SLIT-DRUM of the Bati people of northern Zaïre (*LaurentyTF*, 133).

Gombi (iii). Trough XYLOPHONE of the Ngbandi people of Zaïre. *See* MANZA, (3).

Gombos harmonika. Accordion of Hungary, with button keyboard.

Gomboy. Double-headed variable tension HOURGLASS DRUM of the Dogon people of Mali. It is similar to the TAMA. Although not an indigenous instrument, the *gomboy* has now been incorporated into local ensembles. *See also* BOY.

Gombri. *See* GUINBRI.

Gomes, Manoel de São Bento [Gomes de Herrara, Manoel Benito] (*b* Fermedo; *d* Paço de Sousa, 15 March 1747). Portuguese organ builder. A document relating to the construction of a new organ for the chapel of Coimbra University (1732–3) refers to him as 'Padre

Frei Manoel de S Bento, religious, of the same order' (presumably the Benedictine Order of S Bento, Oporto). Another document relating to the final tuning of this organ bears the builder's signature 'Fr. M.[el] de S Bento gs', but he is referred to as 'Manoel de S Bento Gomes' in Arouca and Viseu archives. He appears to have built a new organ for the church of S Bento da Vitória, Oporto (*c*1719), and the archives of Viseu Cathedral record that he was employed in 1721–2 and 1726, presumably to build two large organs for the cathedral. Gomes appears to have repaired the organ in the Benedictine church of S Martinho, Tibães (1729), and contracted to build a *Realejo* organ for the church of the Misericórdia, Oporto (1732). He was involved in work on the organs at Coimbra University (1732–3) and at the convent at Arouca (1738–41). Two organs, which are really large Positivs, built for the chapel of S Clara-a-Nova, Coimbra, date from 1745 and 1749. A document in the university archives relates that Gomes built large organs for Batalha, the Benedictine college of Coimbra, and the towns of Tentugal, Barro and Semide. His work is of great significance, the university organ being especially noteworthy. Though sometimes unconventional, he always worked in the tonal tradition of the Portuguese Baroque. The large organ in the church of S Cruz, Coimbra, was extensively rebuilt between 1719 and 1724 by a Spaniard, Dom Manoel Benito Gomes de Herrara. Documents in the archives of Viseu prove that these builders were the same person, the nomenclative differences being as a result of orthographical error in a secondary source referring to the work of de Herrara.

BIBLIOGRAPHY
W. D. Jordan: 'The Organ of the Capela-Real of S. Miguel: the University of Coimbra, Portugal', *The Organ*, lxi (1982), 4
——: 'Organ Building Traditions in Portugal', *The Organ*, lxii (1983), 51
——: 'Manoel de São Bento Gomes, fabricante de órgãos históricos em Portugal', *Mundo da arte* (in preparation)
W. D. JORDAN

Gom-gom. MOUTH BOW of southern Africa. *See* GORA.

Gomo. A variant term in central Africa for NGOMA (drum). In Zaïre 'gomo' is used (*BooneT*, 11, 41) for a GOBLET DRUM of the Songye people, known also as *lupondo*, and a single-headed drum of the Sengele. The head of the Sengele drum is laced to a tension band which is nailed around the body.

Gondang. (1) Double-headed cylindrical drum of Mandailing, North Sumatra. It is a laced drum with wedge bracing and goatskin membranes, and is held in the lap of the performer who sits cross-legged to play it. He uses a stick in his right hand and the fingers and palm of his left hand. The *gondang* is played in pairs, with the *induk* ('female') drum slightly larger than the *jantan* ('male'); they range in size from about 25 to 27 cm in diameter and from about 43 to 45 cm in length. One drummer 'leads' and the other 'follows' with a more improvisatory and rhythmically freer line. *See also* GENDANG, (1).

(2) The smallest of the three main ceremonial ensembles in Mandailing, North Sumatra. *Gondang* drums are joined by a *sarune* (oboe), an *ogung induk* and *ogung jantan* (suspended gongs), a *doal* (smaller suspended gong), from two to six *momongan* (narrow-rimmed bossed gongs) and a pair of hand cymbals (*talisasayap*).

Gondang (drum-chime) ensemble of the Batak Toba people, Samosir, North Sumatra, with (left to right) ogung (suspended gongs), gordang (single-headed drum), taganing (drum-chime), sarune (oboe) and dancers

The *gondang* ensemble is traditionally played at weddings and funerals of commoners.

(3) The main ceremonial ensemble of the Batak Toba people in the province of North Sumatra (see illustration). It consists of a drum-chime, with five tuned drums (*taganing*), and a large single-headed drum (*gordang*) attached to a wooden frame. Four *ogung* provide a repetitive punctuating melodic pattern. They comprise a pair of muted gongs (*doal* and *panggora*) tuned to match the *taganing* and a pair of unmuted gongs called *oloan* ('leader') and *ihutan* ('follower'). The leading melodic instrument is the *sarune* (oboe) or occasionally the *ole-ole* (clarinet).

BIBLIOGRAPHY
W. Stohr and P. Zoetmulder: *Die Religionen Indonesians* (Stuttgart, 1965)
L. Schreiner: 'Gondang-Musik als Überlieferungsgestalt altvölkischer Lebensordnung', *Bijdragen tot de Taal-, Land- en Volkenkunde*, cxxvi (1970), 400

MARGARET J. KARTOMI

Gondang buluh [nungneng]. Idiochord TUBE ZITHER of the Mandailing area of the province of North Sumatra. Its three strings are prised out of the surface of a bamboo tube about 22 cm in diameter, tautened with pyramidical bridges, and beaten with a pair of sticks. The deepest-pitched string is played like the gong in a *gondang* (drum, gong and oboe) ensemble, and the other strings produce an interlocking melody like the rest of the smaller gongs and the drums. Pieces played have names such as *Gondang katimbung* ('Water-play rhythm piece'). See M. Kartomi: 'The Mandailing People of Sumatra', BM 30SL 2567 [disc, notes].

MARGARET J. KARTOMI

Gondra. Drum of Nias, Indonesia. It consists of a hollowed-out log, up to 1 metre long and 75 cm wide, with goatskin or deerskin stretched across both ends by means of rattan hoops and ropes. It is played by one or two players using rattan sticks with a loop at the head. Several *gondra* may be hung on the rafters of the front room of a traditional house. See J. Kunst: *Music in Nias* (Leiden, 1939), 33.

MARGARET J. KARTOMI

Gondu. Side-blown ivory trumpet of the Mamvu people of north-eastern Zaïre. It has a carved mouthpiece (*LaurentyA*, 384).

Gonfi. Eight-string arched harp of the pygmies of Gabon. *See* NGOMBI (i).

Gong. A percussion instrument of either definite or indefinite pitch, in the form of a circular metal plaque. The vibration is strongest near the vertex and weakest near the rim (the opposite is the case with a bell). Gongs, which are classified by Hornbostel and Sachs as idiophone percussion vessels (*see* IDIOPHONE), are made in various sizes and shapes, being either flat, or with the edge turned over (sometimes called 'kettle gong' or 'metal drum'), or with a turned-down rim and central boss, like the gongs of Java and Burma (see fig.1). The gong's primary importance is in South-east Asia but three types are used in the Western orchestra. In the majority of cases gongs are cast and hammered, the formula of the metal (an alloy) varying from 70% to 80% copper and 30% to 20% tin, or a compound of copper and tin with the addition of lead, iron or zinc. In some special gongs a small portion of silver is added.

The instrument seen most frequently in the Western orchestra is the large flat gong (76 cm or more in diameter) with a shallow lip and of indefinite pitch. Instruments of this type were originally imported only from China and are universally known by the original name 'tam-tam'. Though the Chinese continue to produce fine orchestral tam-tams, there is now a marked employment of the magnificent tam-tams and bossed gongs made in Europe by such famous firms as M. Paiste of Nottwil and Schacht-Audorf, and the Italian firm of Ufip (Unione-Fabbricanti Italiana Piatti Musicali e Tam-Tams).

In the Western orchestra the tam-tam and similarly heavy gongs are suspended in a frame. Unlike the bossed gongs and those with a deep rim, which are invariably struck in the centre (from where the tone issues), the orchestral tam-tam may also be struck off centre (see fig.2). With rare exceptions a heavy beater with felt or wool covering is employed, the tremolo being produced in most cases by rapid strokes with a single beater, the sustaining quality of the instrument 'filling in the gaps'.

The origin of the gong is uncertain. Jaap Kunst (1956) suggested that it came from the west to China at the beginning of the 6th century. Chinese tradition ascribes it to the country Hsi Yu, between Tibet and Burma, where it is mentioned early in the 6th century in the time of Emperor Hsüan Wu (reigned 500–16). The name 'gong' had its origin in Java, where it signifies a bossed, bronze gong. Research has established four principal centres of manufacture: Burma, China, Annam and Java, where there are at least seven different types of gong – gong, kempul, bende, beri, kenong, kempyang and ketuk. To these could be added the bossed gong ageng of the Indonesian gamelan ensemble (fig.3d, p.62), the kăsar, a small flat gong used in India, and many others used in the East and the Far East. Gongs have existed in Java and the other islands of the Malay Archipelago and New Guinea since the 9th century. The making of the best gongs was the speciality of a small number of foundries at Semarang in Java. Only certain families were privileged to be gong makers, the secret craft being handed down from generation to generation. This industry has recently been revived and flourishes in Surakarta (Java). In the East the gong has long been considered a talisman. To be touched by a gong created happiness and strength. The death of a male was announced by strokes on a gong, struck in groups of three. The alarm was also sounded on a gong, and well-known rhythms were used as a language in a manner similar to the style of conveying information by drums.

Gongs may have existed in biblical times: St Paul's 'sounding brass or tinkling cymbal' in the King James Bible is translated in the New English Bible (I Corinthians xiii.1) 'sounding gong or clanging cymbal'. The Romans used gongs and metal discs (discus), which were suspended from a central hole and used as signal instruments. Four bronze discs devised by Hipposos had the same diameters, but differed in thickness, and consequently produced notes of different pitch. A Roman gong discovered during mining operations in Wiltshire is thought to be from the 1st or 2nd century.

The earliest use of the gong in Western orchestral music is attributed to Gossec in his Funeral Music for Mirabeau (1791; see fig.4, p.63). Subsequent composers include Steibelt (Romeo und Juliet, 1793); Le Sueur (Ossian ou Les bardes, 1804); Spontini (La vestale, 1807); Bellini (Norma, 1831); and Meyerbeer (Robert le diable, 1831). Outstanding examples of the use of the large gong (tam-tam) include the solemn stroke in Tchaikovsky's Sixth Symphony, and the impressive stroke to signify the death of Gerontius (The Dream of Gerontius, Elgar). In The Planets (Mars) Holst prescribed a tremolo throughout 39 bars concluding with a fff stroke. Solemn strokes on a descending series of tam-tams are used with great effect in Messiaen's Et

1. Suspended bossed gong, Burma (Horniman Museum, London)

exspecto resurrectionem mortuorum (1964). Two tam-tams (acuto, basso) are required in Stravinsky's Introitus (1965), a player to each. For The Rite of Spring ('The Sacrifice') Stravinsky requested a rapid glissando, to be played on the surface of the tam-tam with a triangle beater. Strauss wrote for a tremolo on four tam-tams (auf dem Theater) in Die Frau ohne Schatten (1919). Puccini scored for a series of 11 tuned gongs (tam-tam giappa) in Madama Butterfly, and a series of Chinese gongs in Turandot. To differentiate between the tuned gongs and the orchestral tam-tam Puccini called the latter tam-tam grave. Classification of this description is

2. Chinese gong (private collection)

3. (a) Ensemble of small flat gongs (gangsa), Philippines; (b) khǫng mǫn (gong-chime, foreground) and bossed gong in a mǫn ensemble, Thailand; (c) reyong (gong-chime), Bali; (d) gong ageng, Bali

welcome as, no doubt because the terms gong and tam-tam are synonymous in Western music, composers frequently prescribe a gong when obviously a tam-tam is intended.

Among the more unusual treatments of the orchestral tam-tam are the following: being kept in vibration by friction on the edge (*The Pleasure Dome of Kubla Khan* (1917), Griffes); vibrated with a bow (*Dimensions of Time and Silence* (1960), Penderecki); laid horizontally, without resonance (*El retablo de Maese Pedro* (1922), Falla). In *Double Music* (1941) by John Cage and Lou Harrison, a water gong is specified, to be lowered and raised in a tub of water after striking. (A vibrating gong

flattens in pitch when lowered into water, as does a bell.) A genuine Chinese tam-tam was used to record the superimposed strokes heard on the J. Arthur Rank film trademark.

The gong and the tam-tam are notated on a space in the staff or on a single line. Tuned gongs are notated in either the treble or the bass clef.

See also GONG-CHIME.

The following gongs are entered in this dictionary: agong; aguang; agung; anungos; araba; aramba; atarigane; babĕndil; balbal; bandai; bandil (ii); bebende-bende; bebondi; bendai; benḍe; beri; betuk; breng; bronze drum; bua; buka; canang; canang kimanis; canh; ceńńala; chaar; chanchiki; changiri; cheng (ii); chiêng; ching (i); chū-sōban; cing; cǒng; daishōko; daluo; dấu; doal; dồng la; dora; douluo; dua-

4. Tam-tam being played during Mirabeau's funeral procession: detail from an engraving (1791) by Laurent Guyot

han; ĕgong; engkuk-kemong; faritia; gaṅ; gaṅ dhaṃ; gandingan; gangsa (i); gaṅ tūc; gaobian luo; gasa; genikng; ghaṇṭā; ghmoḫ dhaṃ; go (iii); gong ageng; gong besar; gong kemoḍong; gongluo; gong suwuk; goong; goŏng; gung; hansa; hebbiat; hibat; hitotsu-gane; hpà-si; huhugan; ihutan; jālar; jiaoluo; jin; jingluo; jingu (ii); kaipucha; kalsa; kane; kapat; kâsar; katanga; katlo; kay; keb-ang; kelenang; kempli; kempul; kempur; kempyang; kenong; kenong japan; kenong penontong; ketawak; kettle gong; ketuk; keṭuk; 'khar-rnga; khǫng; kingkong; kkwaenggwari; klenang; klentong; klǫng khīāt; klǫng mēng; kochnak; kolintang besi; konchiki; kūm (ii); kŭmna; la; lanunu; lebuan; lệnh; lerukan; luo; mahora thụk; māḫ tāḫ; maning gula; mapindil; matsumushi; maùng; meguguning; mkhar-rnga; momong; momongan; mong; mongmongan; mung; na (i); nayi maùng; ninaishōko; nulanting; nyŏ (ii); ogung; oloan; opop; pahuu; palayi; panggora; pa-no; patpat; pattong; pawwok; penganak; pengeguagan; penontong; penuntun; phang hat; phèng la; pinsak; poi; pokpok; pongpong; pulakan; puum; qahot; rujih; ruluo; salbat; saliksik; san-ang; san martín; sapul; saraina; segarun; semagunsun; senmu; setawak; shōko; sōban; soe; sogŭm (ii); solembat; suluo; surigane; taegŭm (ii); taew; taiṃ nāiṃ; talagutok; tale balok; talo balak; talo tang-gung; tam âm la; tambur (ii); tam-tam; tamuk; tapudep; tara (ii); taraai; taslī; tatabug; tawak; tetawak; tetzilácatil; thanh la; thiều canh; tobop; tsurishōko; tumabuk; tumuktuk; tunggalan; ukaya; ulla; unra; waniguchi; weng bai; wenluo; xiaoluo; yosuke; yunluo; zheng (ii); zhengluo.

BIBLIOGRAPHY
E. Jacobson and J.H. van Hasselt: *De Gong-Fabricatie te Semerang* (Leiden, 1907)
H. Simbriger: 'Gong und Gongspiele', *Internationales Archiv für Ethnographie*, xxxvi (1939), 1–172
J. Kunst: 'Gong', *MGG*
J. Montagu: 'What is a Gong?', *Man*, lxv (1965), 18
J. Blades: *Percussion Instruments and their History* (London, 1970, rev. 3/1984)
D. Charlton: *Orchestration and Orchestral Practice in Paris, 1789 to 1810* (diss., U. of Cambridge, 1973)
——: 'New Sounds for Old: Tam-tam, Tuba Curva, Buccin', *Soundings*, iii (1973), 39
F. Harrison: *Time, Place and Music* (Amsterdam, 1973), 86
JAMES BLADES

Gông. TUBE ZITHER, with 13 strings, of the Jörai people of central Vietnam. It has external metal strings raised over bridges and fastened to the tube, and is played by young men, particularly for courting.

Gonga (i). Double clapperless bell of the Benge people of western Zaïre. The term is presumably cognate with the *ngongi* of the Kakongo, the *ngonge* of the Lele, Sundi and Velele, the *kenge* of the Mamvu and the *konga* of the Nkundo. Other double bells in Zaïre include the Boma *malua*, Kusu *elundja*, Luba *lubembo*, Songye and Tetela *ludembo*, Mongo *dibemba*, Makere *kakwumm*, Mbala *malungg*, Mbun *mgung*, Pende *lunga* and Zande *a poro*. All these bells are cup-shaped, made of iron, and are 20 cm to 100 cm high. They are struck with sticks of the umbrella tree or other lightweight wood. In precolonial times small double bells were made by the hundred and used as dowry. The Benge *gonga* is sounded for a birth, a marriage or death; the Songye *ludembo* is used for dance accompaniment; and the Kusu *elundja* is associated with warfare. The term *elundja* is also used by the Onga and Yela for a single bell with a suspension hook; the Jonga refer to bells of this type as *lundja* and the Tetela as *elonga*. Among the Eso the term *elonga* refers to a single bell with a forked handle, a type known to the Bongili as *elondja* and to the Mongo as *elonza*.

BIBLIOGRAPHY
J.-N. Maquet: *Note sur les instruments de musique congolais* (Brussels, 1956)
F.J. de Hen: *Beitrag zur Kenntnis der Musikinstrumente aus Belgisch Kongo und Ruanda-Urundi* (Tervuren, 1960)
G. Knosp: *Enquête sur la vie musicale au Congo belge 1934–1935* (Tervuren, 1968)
A.M. Jones: *Africa and Indonesia* (Leiden, 1971)
K. A. GOURLAY

Gonga (ii). Double-headed cylindrical drum of the Kerikeri people of Nigeria. *See* GANGA, (1).

Gong ageng [gong gede]. The 'great gong' of the large Balinese and Central Javanese gamelan and of some smaller ensembles. It is known in some areas (including East Java) as *gong agung*. It is suspended by a rope from a wooden frame and beaten softly and firmly on its central boss with a padded hammer to produce a low-pitched sound (35 to 45 cycles per second) which may consist of 13 or more musical beats. It is made of bronze and may range from 85 to 100 cm in diameter. It marks the main structural units (*gongan*) in a composition. Two *gong ageng* are used in the *gamelan seprangkat* (complete gamelan); their pitches are so low that they are often used with either tuning system. A *gong agung* is used in the *gamelan angklung* in East Java.

The Balinese *gong ageng* resemble those of Java, where the largest of them are made. They are used in the *gamelan gong*, *gamelan gong kebyar* and *gamelan bebonangan*. They are about 1 metre in diameter and are used in pairs consisting of a *gong wadon* ('female gong') and a slightly higher-pitched *gong lanang* ('male gong'), which are sounded in turn to mark the end of each phrase.

For illustrations *see* GAMELAN, figs.2 and 5, and GONG, fig.3d.

BIBLIOGRAPHY
E. Jacobson and J.H. van Hasselt: 'The Manufacture of Gongs in Semarang', *Indonesia* (Ithaca, NY, 1975), no.19, pp.127–72
C. McPhee: *Music in Bali* (New Haven and London, 1966/R1976)
MARGARET J. KARTOMI, RUBY ORNSTEIN

Gong besar. Suspended gong of Malaysia. *See* TAWAK.

Gong bumbung. Aerophone of Central Java. *See* BOMBERDOM.

Gong-chime. Generic term for a set of small bossed gongs placed upright, usually in a row in pitch order stepwise, on or in a wooden frame, and played by one

TABLE 1

Arrangement of rows		Examples
* (a) single	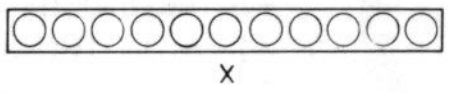	kulintang (S. Philippines, N. Borneo); trompong, reyong (Bali); bonang in gamelan koḍok ngorek, munggang, and carabalen (Java)
(b) two (at right angles)	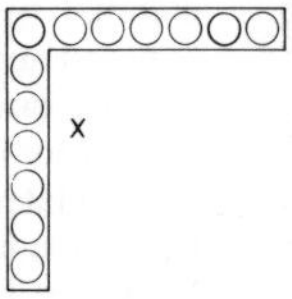	bonang in gamelan degung and gamelan renteng (Sunda)
(c) three (at right angles)	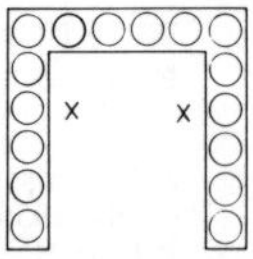	bonang in gamelan renteng (Sunda)
(d) two double (in pairs, at right angles)	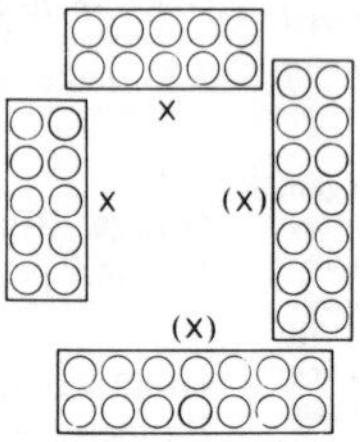	bonang in double gamelan slendro/pelog (Sunda, Central Java)
(e) same (L-position)	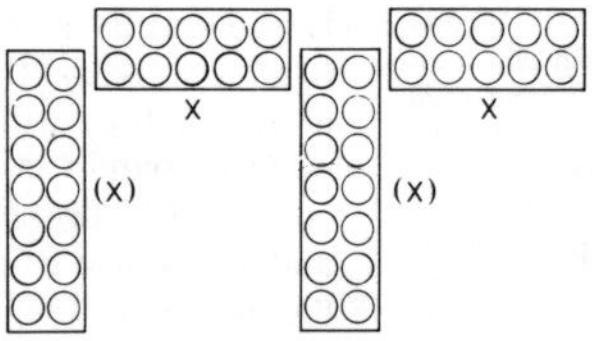	bonang in gamelan slendro/pelog (Central Java) [alternative to (d)]
(f) two double (in pairs, lengthwise)	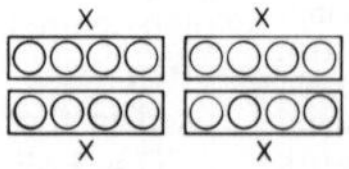	bonang (trompong) in gamelan luang (Bali)
(g) single (circle)	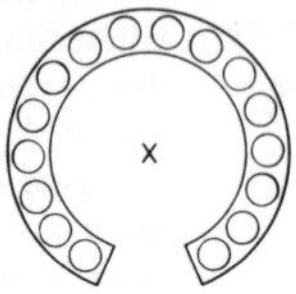	khǭng wong in pī phāt orchestra (Thailand); kyì-waìng in hsaìng-waìng (Burma)
(h) single (semicircle, upright position side view)	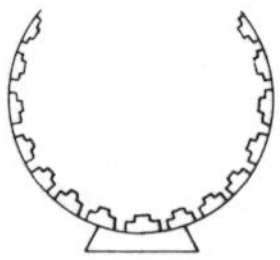	khǭng mǭn in pī phāt (Thailand)

X-position of musicians

*In the single-row arrangement the number of musicians may vary from one to four. The number of gongs in one row may also vary.

to four musicians, each usually with two sticks (see Table 1). Such instruments are common in most orchestras in South-east Asia. Their playing style is almost invariably characterized by a high rhythmic and melodic density. Gong-chimes either have a prominent soloistic role in the ensemble with virtuoso melodic embellishments (generally the smaller, high-pitched gong-chimes), or

they provide rhythm and colour, sometimes having a colotomic role, as with lower-pitched gong-chimes. In Javanese and Balinese gamelan all these playing styles are used.

Other sets of tuned gongs occur in the orchestras of the South-east Asian continent and in the Indonesian and Philippine archipelagos, usually together with gong-

Gongophone played by Hubert Kponton, Lomé, Togo, 1970

chimes. They differ from these in size and pitch and are arranged singly, vertically suspended from a common rack or hand-held by a group of musicians; they do not exceed the octave, and usually have a quite different role in the ensemble. They are the instruments of structural interpunction performed in a low rhythmic and melodic density. However, sets of hand-held tuned gongs played with high rhythmic density (usually in interlocking style) may be included in the term 'gong-chime'. Such are the old type of Balinese *reyong*, the Philippine group of *gangsa*, and the 6- to 16-piece gong orchestras of some of the Vietnamese minorities of the mountainous interior.

The following gong-chimes are entered in this dictionary: bonang; botul; caklempong; calempong; canang; canang situ; celempong; cilempong; engkromong; gambyong; gaṅ dham; gaṅ tũc; gelintang; gulintangan; jengglong; kebluk; kelintang (i); kelittang; keromong; keromongan; keromong duabelas; khǫng; klentangan; kolenang; kolintan; kolintang; kromong; kulintang; kyì-waìng; maùng-zaìng; mong; mong-mong; nggo; nong nôt; pat kôn choh; renteng (i); reyong; rincik (ii); tale; talempong; talempong jao; telempong; thang-rnga; trompong; wong khǫng chai.

ERNST HEINS

Gong drum. A single-headed bass drum; *see* DRUM, §1.

Gong geḍe. *See* GONG AGENG.

Gong kemoḍong. Metallophone used as a substitute for a gong in Central and West Javanese ensembles. Two large iron or bronze keys with bosses and with slightly different pitches are suspended over a soundbox and beaten with a soft hammer.

Gongluo [kung-lo]. Large bronze knobbed or bossed gong of the Han Chinese, found especially in south-east China. In the name, *gong* ('a tribute') is used for its phonetic value, and LUO refers to gong-type idiophones in general. The instrument has a central raised knob (or boss) and sharply turned-back shoulders; it is usually suspended in a standing frame and struck with a padded beater. Construction is similar to that of the GONG AGENG and KEMPUL of the Javanese gamelan and of the KHǪNG of Thailand. Historical and regional names given to this instrument include TONGGU in an 18th-century source, *jingu* ('metal drum') and *ruluo* ('nipple gong'). The knobbed gong is especially prevalent among the Chaozhou and Minnan sub-cultures, and in Taiwan large

instruments are still carried (hung from large beams) and struck in funeral processions.

ALAN R. THRASHER

Gongné. Afro-American term for a struck clapperless bell. *See* AGOGO.

Gongo. Very large cylindrical SLIT-DRUM of the Zande people of north-eastern Zaïre (*LaurentyTF*, 133).

Gongophone. Set of horizontally mounted struck bells invented by Hubert Kponton of Lomé, Togo, in 1966 (see illustration). It employs traditional single bells (*gakókwé*) of the Ewe people, arranged chromatically in piano-key order. The idea came from the Western piano, and from xylophones at the first Festival des Arts Nègres at Dakar in 1966.

GERHARD KUBIK

Gongqin [kung-ch'in]. MOUTH BOW of the tribal peoples of Taiwan. The Chinese name *gongqin* is generic for musical bows. It is known to the Ami people as *fusili*. The instrument is a bow with a curved bamboo frame (*c*45 cm in length) and a string of hemp or other natural fibre (more recently of metal wire) attached at both ends. In performance the upper end of the bow is held in the player's mouth (which acts as a resonator); the left hand holds the lower end and the string is plucked with the fingers of the right hand. The pitch of the string may be changed (using the left hand) by varying either its tension or its vibrating length. The musical bow is traditionally a courting and entertainment instrument. See F. J. Lenherr: 'The Musical Instruments of the Taiwan Aborigines', *Bulletin of the Institute of Ethnology, Academia sinica*, xxiii (Taipei, 1967), 117.

ALAN R. THRASHER

Gong suwuk [gong siyem]. Bronze bossed gong of the Central Javanese gamelan. It is smaller than the GONG AGENG, which it replaces in smaller works. The *suwuk* (or *siyem*) is usually one octave lower than the KEMPUL, and measures about 60 cm in diameter. The number in a gamelan may vary between three and nine. If there are only three they are normally tuned to pitches 1^2 (i.e. pitch 1 in the second lowest octave) and 2^2 of the *slendro* and pitch 7^2 of the *pelog* scale (*see* GAMELAN, §4).

Gong tundu. TUBE ZITHER of Flores, Indonesia. *See* GOBATO.

Gongué. Brazilian cowbell. *See* AGOGO.

Gonje. Single-string fiddle of the Mamprusi-Dagomba peoples of Ghana. *See* GOGE.

Gonongo. Pellet bell of the Shambala people of Tanzania.

Gonrang. Main ceremonial instrumental ensemble of the Simalungun Batak people in North Sumatra. It accompanies the *tortor adat* (communal ceremonial dancing) at funerals and other ceremonies. See A.D. Jansen: *Gonrang Music: its Structure and Functions in Simalungun Batak Society in Sumatra* (diss., U. of Washington, 1980).

Gonrang sipitupitu [gonrang siduadua] ('seven-drum ensemble'). A set of seven tapered single-headed drums of the Batak Simalungun area of North Sumatra. Their bodies are made from hollowed-out wood, such as jackfruit wood, and measure about 61 to 65 cm in length and about 20 to 23 cm in diameter at the top. The buffalo skins are tautened and tuned by means of two twisted strands of rattan or leather lacings placed round the length of the body and wound round six wooden pegs which protrude from the lower end. The drums of the *gonrang siduadua* ('two-drum ensemble') are similarly constructed, with heads of buffalo, cow or goatskin. The larger drum is about 42 to 46 cm long, with a diameter of about 16 to 20 cm at one end and about 13 to 15 cm at the other; the smaller is about 40 to 45 cm long, with a diameter of about 14 to 19 cm at one end and 12 to 14 cm at the other.

The terms 'gonrang sipitupitu' and 'gonrang siduadua' are applied also to ensembles which combine the drums with a pair of *gung* (bronze bossed gongs about 30 to 40 cm in diameter, suspended from a frame or held in the player's left hand by means of cord passing through two holes), a pair of *mongmongan* (similar gongs about 15 to 20 cm in diameter, tuned about 400 cents apart) and a *sarunei* (oboe). The two ensembles are also known respectively as *gonrang bolon* ('great ensemble') and *gonrang dagang* ('incomplete ensemble'). The latter, however, is incomplete in ceremonial, not in musical, terms; it is used on minor occasions, such as house-warmings.

BIBLIOGRAPHY

A. D. Jansen: *Gonrang Music: its Structure and Functions in Simalungun Batak Society in Sumatra* (diss., U. of Washington, 1980)
MARGARET J. KARTOMI

Gonzalez. French firm of organ builders. It was founded in 1921 by Victor Gonzalez (*b* Hacinas, Spain, 2 Dec 1877; *d* Paris, 3 June 1956) and Victor Ephrème, at Châtillon sous Bagneux, near Paris. In 1930, as Etablissements Gonzalez, it was directed by Victor and Fernand Gonzalez; it was then run by Victor Gonzalez's grandson, Georges Danion, at Brunoy (Essonne) with workshops at Rambervillers (Vosges). The firm has built or rebuilt many organs including those at the cathedrals of Meaux (1932), Bayonne (1936), Rheims (1938), Versailles Chapel (1938), Palais de Chaillot, Paris (1939), Rennes Cathedral (1940), St Eustache, Paris (1945), St Merry, Paris (1947), Soissons Cathedral (1956), Auch Cathedral (1959), and also the four-manual, 95-stop organ in Studio 104 at the ORTF, Paris (1967).

GUY OLDHAM

González de Amezua y Noriega, Ramón (*b* Madrid, 27 Oct 1921). Spanish organ builder. While training as an engineer at the Escuela Superior in Madrid, he also studied music at the Madrid Conservatory and later in France. He built organs with Victor Gonzalez, and in 1941 produced his 'Organería Española'. He has built more than 400 instruments in Spain, France, the USA and Asia. In 1965 he was elected vice-president of the International Society of Organ Builders (re-elected several times) and in 1970 to the Real Academia de Bellas Artes de San Fernando, Madrid (president of its advisory council for music, 1974). His publications include *Perspectivas para la historia del órgano español* (Madrid, 1970); he has also been active as a performer, notably of contemporary works, which has resulted in his abandoning organ building for some years. His work in Europe includes the organs at the royal monastery of San Lorenzo at El Escorial (161 stops); the Palacio Nacional de Montjuich, Barcelona (six manuals, 150 stops); San Sebastián Cathedral (five manuals, 126 stops); the basilica of Nuestra Señora del Pilar, Saragossa (four manuals, 80 stops); the monastery at Valle de los Caidos (four manuals, 80 stops); the Teatro Real, Madrid (four manuals, 78 stops); the basilica of St Pie X, Lourdes (three manuals, 53 stops); the basilica Rosaire, Lourdes (four manuals, 50 stops); and the church of the Jesuit Fathers, Madrid (four manuals, 40 stops). He has also restored the instruments in the cathedrals at Toledo (Echevarría and Verdalonga), Salamanca (Echevarría), Málaga (Julián de la Orden), Granada (Fernández Dávila), Segovia (Echevarría) and those at the churches of Santa María, San Sebastián and Nuestra Señora del Juncal, Irún (both Cavaillé-Coll).

BIBLIOGRAPHY

G. Bourligueux: 'Les grandes orgues du Monastère royal de l'Escurial', *L'orgue* (1968), no.127, p.101
GUY BOURLIGUEUX

González Roldán, Gregorio (*b* c1685; *d* ?Valladolid, after 1721). Spanish organ builder. Based at Valladolid, in 1717 he rebuilt the organ at Santiago de Medina de Rioseco which had been so badly constructed by Antonio Pérez that a lawsuit had ensued after its inspection report. Before that he had repaired the instruments at S María and S Salvador de los Escapulados at Peñafiel (1721) and built new organs at the churches of Villalba de los Alcores (1712) and S Miguel de Peñafiel (1715). He was one of the finest masters of the early 18th-century Castilian school. See J. A. de La Lama: *El órgano en Valladolid y su provincia: catalogación y estudio* (Valladolid, 1982).

GUY BOURLIGUEUX

Goodell & Swedien organ. *See* MASTERSONIC.

Goodrich, William Marcellus (*b* Templeton, Mass., 21 July 1777; *d* East Cambridge, Mass., 15 Sept 1833). American organ builder. He is regarded as the founder of the organ building craft in Boston. A member of a gifted family that included two artist sisters, a doctor, and a brother, Ebenezer (1782–1841), who distinguished himself as a music teacher and builder of church and chamber organs, Goodrich was largely self-taught. Both musical and mechanical talents were evident at an early age, and in c1800 he went to Boston, working with a pewterer and an instrument maker, and also studying the various English-made organs in the city. In 1804 he entered into an agreement (now at the Boston Public Library) with BENJAMIN CREHORE to make combination piano-organs. That year he built his first instrument, a chamber organ, and shortly after his first church organ (1805–6). From then on his skill and reputation grew, and by the time of his death his work was found in many major Boston churches and, due to a connection with MACKAY, a Boston merchant family, in certain Southern cities as well. He made instruments for the New South Church (1817) and St Paul's Church (1827) in Boston and the Independent Presbyterian Church, Savannah, Georgia (1821). Goodrich had an original and inquiring mind, and his work displayed much variety of concept. Influenced by Bédos de Celles' *L'art du facteur d'orgues* (1766–78) and his own imagination, he was perhaps the first to begin developing an indigenous American style which broke away from English models. He is credited with several mechanical innovations, including the now common concussion bellows or 'winker'. Nearly all the major Boston builders of the mid-19th century were trained in his workshop, including THOMAS APPLETON, the Hook brothers (*see* HOOK & HASTINGS) and the STEVENS brothers.

See also PANHARMONICON.

BIBLIOGRAPHY

'Biographical Memoir of William M. Goodrich', *New-England Magazine* (Jan 1834)

B. Owen: 'The Goodriches and Thomas Appleton', *The Tracker*, iv/1 (1959), 2

O. Ochse: *The History of the Organ in the United States* (Bloomington, Ind., 1975)

B. Owen: *The Organ in New England* (Raleigh, North Carolina, 1979)

BARBARA OWEN

Goombay. A Jamaican drum made from square boards. It is tuned by means of pegs, hit at the sides, forcing an inner frame against the membrane and thus tightening it and raising the pitch.

Goong. Large bossed gong of the Mnong people of central Vietnam.

Goöng. (1) Large suspended bossed gong found in Sundanese areas of West Java. It is played in the *gamelan degung*, *gamelan renteng*, *gamelan salendro* and *gamelan pelog-salendro*. It is usually made of bronze or iron and is played in pairs, the instruments being struck alternately with a soft hammer. The larger, *goöng gede* (*gong agung*), measures up to 90 cm in diameter, while the smaller, *goöng leutik* (*gong suwukan*), is about 65 cm in diameter.

The *goöng penca*, a smaller suspended gong, is used to punctuate the music of *pencak* (a dance based on *pencak silat*, the art of self-defence). The ensemble includes two *kendang penca* (large drums) and one or two *tarompet* (oboes).

(2) A term meaning 'gamelan' in West Java. *See* GAMELAN, §6(ii).

MARGARET J. KARTOMI

Goöng awi. Aerophone of West Java. *See* BOMBERDOM.

Goöng buyung. Idiophone of Sundanese areas of West Java. It consists of a low-pitched iron bar mounted on a resonator; it is often used to substitute for a gong in the *ketuk tilu* ensemble.

Goong lu. LITHOPHONE of the high plateaus of central Vietnam. The first set, of 11 stones, discovered in 1949, is in the Musée de l'Homme, Paris (see illustration); a second, of 12 stones, and third, of 15 stones, discovered by Vietnamese researchers in 1979–80, are in the Phu Khanh Museum and the Institute of Musicology of Vietnam. (Other stones found in the region have become private property or have not yet been studied as musical instruments.) A fourth set, of 32 stones, mostly broken, was found in southern Vietnam; it is now in Binh Da (southern Vietnam). The recent discovery at Binh Da of stones of metamorphic schist together with pottery artefacts has allowed archaeologists to date the lithophone to c1500 BC.

The stones are hewed, carefully cut and carved in oblong shape; the longest is 103 cm, the heaviest 31 kg. They are made from volcanic rock, metamorphic schist, rhyolite, porphyry and rhyodacite. André Schaeffner considered them the oldest existing lithophones. Their

Goong lu (lithophone) from Ndut Lieng Krak, southern Vietnam (Musée de l'Homme, Paris)

tuning corresponds to no understood system (a drone-cum-melody has been suggested) and it is not known how they were played, though probably they were struck with a large stick or a pebble.

TRÂN VAN KHÊ

Gopīyantra or ektārā (single-string chordophone) player, Bangladesh

Gopīyantra [gopījantra]. Variable tension chordophone ('plucked drum') of Bengal and Orissa (east India and Bangladesh). It is similar to the ṬOKĀRI of neighbouring Assam. The resonator of the instrument resembles that of the ĀNANDALAHARĪ type: a hollow body (here a tapering wood or brass cylinder or a rounded pot or gourd), the lower opening of which is covered by a skin with a double string (here of steel) passing up from its centre. Unlike the arm-tensioned *ānandalaharī*, the *gopīyantra* has a neck (strictly a yoke) of an unusual type for the subcontinent, consisting of a split-bamboo fork whose upper node is left whole and whose lower ends are nailed or bound to the sides of the resonator (see illustration). The string is attached at the top to a tuning-peg inserted laterally through the upper node. When the two sides of the fork are squeezed and released by the fingers and thumb of the holding hand the pitch of the string falls and rises respectively. It is sometimes plucked with the index finger of the right hand while it is holding the instrument, or plucked with the right and held by the left. The *gopīyantra* is played by religious mendicant singers of the Baul and Sadhu type to accompany their own singing or dancing. The name, meaning 'the instrument of [Krishna's loving companions] the milkmaids', appears to be literary; in the countryside it is usually called *ektārā* ('monochord') or *khamak*.

BIBLIOGRAPHY

C. Sachs: *Die Musikinstrumente Indiens und Indonesiens* (Berlin and Leipzig, 1914, 2/1923)
S. Ray: *Music of Eastern India* (Calcutta, 1973)
B. C. Deva: *Musical Instruments of India* (Calcutta, 1978)
A. H. Saaduddin: 'Bangladesh', *Grove 6*
C. J. Adkins, R. C. Williamson, J. V. Flowers and L. E. R. Picken: 'Frequency-doubling Chordophones', *Musica asiatica*, iii (1981), 1
L. E. R. Picken: 'The "Plucked Drums": *Gopīyantra* and *Ānanda laharī*', *Musica asiatica*, iii (1981), 29

ALASTAIR DICK

Gör. Double-headed buffalo-skin barrel drum of the Mnong Rlâm people of central Vietnam.

Gora. MOUTH BOW sounded by the breath, a type of instrument found mainly in southern Africa. The name *gora* is a simplification of the original Korana word *!göra* (in which the initial consonant is a voiced palatal 'click'). Other spellings by various authors include *gorah*, *gorra*, *goura*, *gowra*, *kora*, *t'goerra*, *t'gorrah* and *gomgom*. A similar instrument, the *cora*, has been reported in Argentina. The *gora* was formerly played mainly by the Khoikhoi (Hottentots), although Bushmen and, later, Bantu peoples also adopted it. The instrument resembles a simple mouth-resonated musical bow, but is sounded by blowing on a piece of quill attached to the string (figs.1 and 2). This gives it a distinctive tone quality, somewhat like that from a free reed, as in the harmonica or the concertina.

The *gora* was noted first by Dapper in 1668 and thereafter by many other observers: descriptions by Lichtenstein (1812–15) and Burchell (1822) are particularly notable. Balfour (1902) wrote the first serious historical study, and Kirby (1931) later presented a comprehensive survey. Basing his argument on L. F. Maingard's hypothesis that the Hottentots had acquired the hunting bow from the Bushmen early in the 17th century, Kirby (1934, p.185) postulated that the *gora* and also two simple types of musical bow used by the Hottentots) originated shortly after this as an adaptation of the hunting bow. Balfour (pp.170ff), seeking explanations for the sounding mechanism of the *gora*, noted an analogous means of sound production in the bull-roarer, which is widely used in southern Africa as a toy.

1. Gora (musical bow sounded by the breath) of the Khoikhoi (Hottentot) people, southern Africa

He also cited the existence in north India of miniature aeolian bows strung with a flattened quill and attached to kites. Hornbostel (1933, p.296) mentioned forms of lamina, sounded by blowing, among the Shambala in east Africa. Although no connection with the *gora* had yet been traced, he urged that items such as the *gora* should not be ascribed to caprice or accident, in the hope that they might 'any day be withdrawn from their "splendid isolation" by means of some unexpected discovery, and will then supply the most important evidence for Culture-history'.

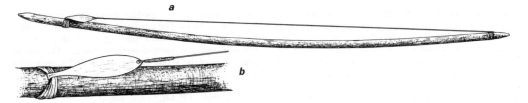

2. *(a) Gora, with (b) detail of quill*

Apparently the *gora* is no longer played among remaining Hottentot-speaking groups, who are mainly found in Namibia, Botswana and southern Angola. It still survives, however, in almost identical form but under different names among several Bantu-speaking peoples who apparently adopted it in the 19th century. It is always played by boys or young men and is strongly associated with cattle herding. The Sotho of Lesotho use it the most extensively and call it the Lesiba. The use of the instrument has mostly died out elsewhere but earlier names given to it among other neighbouring peoples were *ugwala* or *unkwindi* (Zulu), *ugwali* or *igwali* (Xhosa), *makhwindi* (Swazi), *kwadi* (Tswana) and *ugwala* (Venda).

The instrument consists of a slightly curved solid stick or hollow river reed, about 95 to 100 cm long and 1·5 cm in average diameter. The string is made from sinew. One end of the string is secured to a strip of quill from a bird's feather, such as a vulture's or a bustard's. The quill is split and flattened, and the broad end trimmed into a leaf shape (fig.2*b*). The string passes through a tiny hole pierced in the quill and is fastened by splicing or knotting. The quill is secured to the shaft by a narrow strip of hide, which also serves as a nut or bridge, raising the quill and string clear of the shaft: but in later specimens and in the Sotho *lesiba*, attachment is by means of a split peg. The other end of the string is bound to the shaft near its extremity in such a way that it may be tuned by tightening or slackening before performance. The use of a tuning-peg, presumably copied from the violin or the Ramkie, was occasionally noted by observers around Cape Town from 1796.

Ex.1 Mouth-resonated harmonics

In playing the *gora* or the *lesiba*, the quill is placed between slightly parted, though widely stretched, lips. The fingers keep the stave from touching the face, leaving the quill and string free to vibrate. Both inhalation and exhalation are used in agitating the quill, and considerable breath force is necessary. Mouth resonance is employed for the selective amplification of one or other of the upper partials of the harmonic series, as on the mouth bow and jew's harp. The use of harmonic partials 4 to 14 has been noted, although 11 and 13 are seldom heard; the range of partials from 5 to 9 is perhaps the most common, and the tuning of the almost inaudible fundamental, shown as *C* in ex.1, may vary from *F* to *B♭'* among different Sotho players. In such cases the entire series is transposed accordingly. In addition to the

instrumental sound, players often add laryngeal grunts during exhalation; sometimes these are given definite pitch, to add a touch of polyphony to the performance, but some players avoid them altogether.

BIBLIOGRAPHY
KirbyMISA
O. Dapper: *Naukeurige beschrijvinge der Afrikansche gewesten* (Amsterdam, 1668)
M. H. K. Lichtenstein: *Travels in Southern Africa in the Years 1803, 1804, 1805 and 1806*, i–ii (London, 1812–15/*R*1928–30)
W. J. Burchell: *Travels in the Interior of Southern Africa*, i (London, 1822)
H. Balfour: 'The Goura, a Stringed–Wind Musical Instrument of the Bushmen and Hottentots', *Journal of the Royal Anthropological Institute*, xxxii (1902), 156
P. R. Kirby: 'The Gora and its Bantu Successors: a Study in South African Native Music', *Bantu Studies*, v (1931), 89
E. M. von Hornbostel: 'The Ethnology of African Sound Instruments', *Africa*, vi (1933), 129, 277–311
P. R. Kirby: 'A Further Note on the Gora and its Bantu Successors', *Bantu Studies*, ix (1935), 53

DAVID K. RYCROFT

Gordang. Single-headed cylindrical drum of the province of North Sumatra, Indonesia. In the Batak Toba area, the *gordang* is the largest drum in the ceremonial *gondang* ensemble; its single head is approximately 30 cm in diameter and its wooden body about 100 cm in length. The player beats it with a pair of soft wooden sticks. It is tied to a wooden frame, together with a *taganing* (drum-chime). For illustration *see* Gondang.

The drum is also found in the Mandailing area of North Sumatra, where it is known as *gordang lima* or *gordang sembilan* (for ensembles comprising five or nine drums respectively). The skin of the drum, made of buffalo hide, is laced both diagonally downwards and horizontally across the wooden body and is tautened round a number of wooden pegs protruding at the bottom, open end of the drum. The largest pair in a set of nine drums is called *jangat* ('to do something with pleasure'). Their size varies. In Pakantan and other villages the larger of the pair is about 1 to 1·5 metres long and about 40 cm in diameter; in some villages (e.g. Tamiang) the drums are much bigger. The second largest pair is called *undong kudong* ('beginning to sound'); they may be about 90 to 100 cm long and 33 to 36 cm in diameter. The next largest pair is called *padua* ('the second', about 80 to 90 cm long and 28 to 31 cm in diameter), and the smallest pair *patolu* ('the third', 70 to 80 cm long and 24 to 26 cm in diameter). In each pair the *induk* ('female') is slightly larger than the *jantan* ('male'). The set is completed by a single drum (*enek-enek*), which may measure 55 to 60 cm in length and 18 to 20 cm in diameter. The names of some pairs probably derive from the order in which they enter in a *gordang sembilan* piece: this begins with the *undong kudong*, followed in turn by the *padua*, the *patolu*, the *jangat* and the *enek-enek*.

The term 'gordang sembilan' is used also for the largest of three main ceremonial ensembles in the Mandailing area, which uses the drums in combination with an oboe (*sarune*), suspended gongs (*ogung induk* or *ogung dadaboru*, *ogung jantan* or *ogung pangiring*, and *doal*), from two to six narrow-rimmed gongs (*momongan*) and a pair of cymbals (*talisasayap* or *talisasayak*). The *gordang sembilan* ensemble is reserved for important ceremonial occasions, especially funerals and weddings, of a *raja* (chieftain) or his descendant or representative. In its traditional setting the ensemble may be played in an open-walled pavilion (*sopo godang*: 'great house') built specially for ceremonies, with an elaborate gable design symbolizing the Mandailing view of the world and a raised platform on which the *raja* or his descendant sits. The nine drums are attached to the low wall at the other end of the building and beaten by five players, each holding a drumstick in his right hand. They are usually played at a thunderous intensity, but in some areas (e.g. in Tamiang village) the style calls for loud and soft playing.

The *gordang sembilan* existed in the 19th century, but is presumably older. In 1846 Willem reported seeing sets of drums of varying sizes hanging in a chieftain's house, together with a *sarune* and a set of gongs and cymbals, but he did not specify how many drums there were. In 1895 Ris described a Mandailing orchestra consisting of *gordang* with 'nine different tones' and an 'agoeng', a set of *momongan*, a 'talisasajah' (cymbals) and a 'saroenei'. Efforts have been made to promote the modern performance of *gordang sembilan* and other Mandailing music in the city of Medan, mostly in non-ceremonial settings. The *gunung kulabu* group, for example, plays Pakantan-style music in concerts, on television and for ceremonial purposes.

The five drums known as *gordang lima* vary in length from about 35 to 100 cm, and are called (ranging from large to small) *jangat*, *undong kudong*, *padua*, *patolu* and *enek-enek* ('the child'). The term 'gordang lima' is used also for the second largest of three main ceremonial ensembles in the Mandailing area; the drums are used in combination with the same instruments (oboe, gongs and cymbals) as in the *gordang sembilan* ensemble. The *gordang lima* ensemble is normally played only on shamanist ceremonial occasions and was formerly kept in the house of the shaman (*sibaso*). Few villages now possess a set, but the repertory is still performed in Pakantan and by a group of Mandailing musicians (*Gunung Kulabu*) resident at Medan.

See also GENDANG.

BIBLIOGRAPHY
W. Marsden: *The History of Sumatra* (Kuala Lumpur, 1783/*R*1966)
H. Ris: 'De onderafdeeling Klein Mandailing Oeloe en Pahantan en hare bevolking met uitzondering van de Oeloe's', *Bijdragen tot de Taal-Land- en Volkenkunds Nederlandsche Indië*, xlvi (1895), 532
M. J. Kartomi: 'With Bells and Drums', *Hemisphere*, xxi/10 (1977), 21
——: 'Dualism in Unity: the Ceremonial Music of the Mandailing *Raja* Tradition', *Asian Music*, xii/2 (1981), 74–108
——: '"Lovely When Heard from Afar": Mandailing Ideas of Musical Beauty', *Five Essays on the Indonesian Arts*, ed. M. J. Kartomi (Melbourne, 1981), 1

MARGARET J. KARTOMI

Gordună [gurdună]. Cello or small bass of Romania. It is used as an accompanying instrument by *lăutari* (professional folk musicians) in central Transylvania. *See also* BROANCĂ and GARDON.

Gorong. Small KETTLEDRUM of the Wolof people of Senegal and the Gambia. It has cord and peg bracing,

and is placed on the ground during performance and beaten with sticks. The *gorong* is played with the slightly larger *mbalatt* kettledrum and open cylindrical drums for marriage and name-ceremony dances. The *lamba* kettledrum of the Wolof is even larger, and is associated with wrestling. The TABALA is the largest Wolof kettledrum. See D. W. Ames: 'Wolof Music of Senegal and The Gambia', FE 4462 [disc notes].

Gorra. Term occasionally applied to the GORA (mouth bow) of southern Africa.

Gorwe. VESSEL FLUTE of the Ndau people of central Mozambique. It is made of gourd or clay and is played by women, who intersperse blown notes with vocal notes. *See also* SHIWAYA.

Gos. Large drum of medieval Armenia. *See also* DHOL.

Gosha nagara. Medium-sized KETTLEDRUM of Azerbaijan, played in pairs (*gosha*: 'in pairs'). It is made of clay with skin membranes, and played with two wooden sticks; to achieve a clearer and louder timbre the membranes are tightened by heating over a fire. Two drums of different diameter (from 11 to 14 cm and from 24 to 28 cm) are tied together with leather thongs. In the past they were played for women's dances in the women's quarter of the house. Nowadays there still exist women's ensembles of *diaff* (frame drum), *gosha nagara* and accordion. The *gosha nagara* is similar to the Georgian DIPLIPITO, which is played only by men.

JOHANNA SPECTOR

Gosho-dilli-tüidük. DOUBLE CLARINET of the Turkmen people of Central Asia. Similar in construction to the single clarinet (*dilli-tüidük*), it is made of bulrush stems about 15 cm long, with three or four parallel fingerholes in each pipe. It is predominantly a pastoral instrument. *See also* QOSHNAI.

Gottan. Folk version of the Japanese lute SHAMISEN. In place of the shamisen's cat- or dog-skin the *gottan* has a thin cedar soundboard; the neck and body are of softwood, and the body resembles a large cigar-box. It was common in farming villages of the Satsuma region (southwest Kyūshū) until recently.

Gottuvādyam [mahānātaka vīṇā]. Long-necked lute, without frets, of the Karnataka classical music of south India. It is played with a sliding block. *See* VĪṆĀ, §9.

Gough, Hugh (Percival Henry) (*b* Heptonstall, Yorks., 31 Jan 1916). English maker of clavichords, harpsichords and lutes. He was educated in London at Westminster School and University College (BSc in economics, 1937). His interest in early keyboard instruments began in 1932, and he produced his first clavichord in 1935. He had some lessons on the clavichord from Arnold Dolmetsch. After war service in north Africa, Gough set up his own workshop in London in 1946 to produce harpsichords and clavichords based on historical prototypes. He made a great variety of types and sizes of instrument, preferring not to standardize on a few models. In addition to building conventional four- and five-octave clavichords, he made a reconstruction of Silbermann's *cembal d'amour*, of which no specimen had survived. He also built a number of pianos modelled on Viennese instruments of the late 18th century. His harpsichords, relatively few in number, include both Italian and northern European types, and even an exceptionally long instrument with a 16′ set of strings on its own soundboard in the manner of H. A. Hass (*see* HASS).

In 1958 Gough spent six months at the Hubbard & Dowd workshop in Boston, Massachusetts. After a brief return to London he moved his studio to New York in the autumn of 1959. He subsequently added lutemaking to his production and has also been active in promoting concerts of early music and as a dealer in antique instruments in New York.

WRITINGS
'The Classical Grand Pianoforte, 1700–1830', *PRMA*, lxxvii (1950–51), 41

HOWARD SCHOTT

Goukhas [≠goukha:s]. Chordophone of south-western Africa. Among the Damara (Nama) people it denotes a braced MOUTH BOW (*see* OUTA). Among the Bergdama it denotes a five-string PLURIARC. See *KirbyMISA*, 227, 244, pll.64, 70.

Goulding & Co. English firm of music sellers, publishers and instrument makers established in London. The business was founded by George Goulding in about 1786. Early in 1798 he entered into partnership with Thomas D'Almaine (c1784–1866) and a certain Phipps (who in 1810 left to form his own company); they obtained royal patronage, becoming 'music-sellers to the Prince and Princess of Wales', and from 1803 to 1816 operated an agency in Dublin which was first known as Goulding, Knevett & Co. In 1811 premises were acquired in Soho Square, London. Until 1823, when it was known as Goulding & D'Almaine, or Goulding, D'Almaine & Co., the firm existed under various names, and accepted a Potter and Wood into the partnership. Goulding's name was dropped by about 1834, the firm becoming D'Almaine & Co. Soon after 1840 Thomas Mackinlay joined the business. With D'Almaine's death the firm was discontinued.

For illustrations of instruments by Goulding *see* FLUTE, fig.13*a* and OBOE, fig.6*c*.

FRANK KIDSON/R

Goura. MOUTH BOW of southern Africa. See GORA.

Gourd bow [gourd harp]. A MUSICAL BOW with a gourd resonator.

Gouroumi. See GURUMI.

Gowangan. Javanese plucked zither. See KOWONGAN.

Go weto. Indonesian TUBE ZITHER. See BABA (i).

Gowra. MOUTH BOW of southern Africa. See GORA.

Gozoma. Ankle or leg rattles of central and southern Chad. The Banana people make them from leaves of a palmyra tree (*Borassus flabellifer*), plaited and knotted together to trap little seeds. The *gozoma* are attached to the ankles in two or three rows for dancing. They are both made and worn by men. Among the Mului people, *gozoma* are made from a basketwork cone fixed to a

calabash disc, and contain small pebbles (for illustration *see* FANA). Men make them for their wives who wear one on each leg, a little below the knee, for dancing. If men use them, they wear only one at a time. *Gozoma* are worn for ritual dances performed to the sound of groups of *fana* vessel flutes.

MONIQUE BRANDILY

Grace notes. Ornamental notes written or printed smaller than the 'main text' and accorded an unmeasured duration which is not counted as part of the written bar length. Speed of execution depends on the nature of the ornament they represent and to some extent on the tempo of the music but, except in the case of appoggiaturas, grace notes are usually performed lightly and very quickly. The ornament most commonly expressed as a grace note is the simple acciaccatura, but Chopin, Liszt and others often used quite lengthy strings of grace notes for piano figuration that defied precise notation in rhythmic terms or that invited a certain freedom in performance.

Gracieusement [gracieux] (Fr.). See GRAZIOSO.

Graerock. See GRAUROCK.

Graf, Conrad (*b* Riedlingen, Württemberg, 17 Nov 1782; *d* Vienna, 18 March 1851). Austrian piano maker of German birth. He was trained as a cabinet maker, and moved to Vienna in 1799. Following service in the *Jäger Freikorps* he worked for the piano maker Jakob Schelkle. After marrying Schelkle's widow in 1804 he established his own workshop; from 1827 to 1841 the workshop and his distinguished showroom were located in the famous 'Mondscheinhaus' in Vienna. In 1824 he became 'Royal Court Piano and Keyboard Instrument Maker', and at the first Viennese industrial products exhibition (*Gewerbeproduktenausstellung*) in 1835 he won the gold medal for piano.

Graf is recognized as a maker of fine instruments rather than as an innovator. A typical Graf piano has all-wood construction except for the metal gap spacer, a range of six octaves and a 4th or 5th, and three to five pedals. It has a slightly heavier version of the Viennese action in the style of ANTON WALTER, with metal kapsels, long hammer-heads resting directly on the keys, escapement levers tilted forward and a back-check mechanism.

Graf built pianos for Beethoven and for the wedding of Clara and Robert Schumann (*see* PIANOFORTE, fig.17). He also supplied an instrument for Chopin's 1829 concert in Vienna. A painting by J. Danhauser shows Liszt among his admirers, playing a piano by Graf. Examples of his often highly decorated instruments can be found in museums in Vienna, Nuremberg, Stockholm, Trondheim (Norway), Copenhagen, Bonn and Halle.

BIBLIOGRAPHY
F. J. Hirt: *Meisterwerke des Klavierbaues* (Olten, 1955), 444
V. Luithlin: 'Conrad Graf', *NDB*
——: *Kunsthistorisches Museum: Katalog der Sammlung alter Musikinstrumente*, i (Vienna, 1966), 43f
W. S. Newman: 'Beethoven's Pianos Versus His Piano Ideals', *JAMS*, xxiii (1970), 484
D. Wythe: *The Pianos of Conrad Graf* (diss., New York U., in preparation)

MARIBEL MEISEL, PHILIP R. BELT

Gragnani, Antonio (*fl c*1765–95). Italian violin maker. He worked in Livorno, and is one of the most interesting late 18th-century Italian makers, known especially for the neatness of his work. He probably learnt his craft in Florence, but the concept of his violins is different and in many respects better than that of contemporary Florentine makers. Although not a copyist, he was obviously very impressed by Stradivari's work, and strove to obtain the same elegance in his own. His black purfling was of whalebone, almost unique in Italy, and his scrolls were of a curious elongated design, the walls of the pegbox hollowed. Unfortunately his varnish, which was at its best similar to that used in Florence, sometimes has a rather stained appearance. Tonally his violins vary considerably. Most are on a Stradivari pattern, but he made others more feminine in appearance and usually slightly undersized. Violas and cellos are very rare. He branded his initials A.G. on the button, on the sides near the end button, and at the top and bottom of the table. He was aided and succeeded by his son, Onorato Gragnani, who was less skilled as a workman.

BIBLIOGRAPHY
W. L. von Lütgendorff: *Die Geigen- und Lautenmacher vom Mittelalter bis zur Gegenwart* (Frankfurt am Main, 1904, rev. 6/1922/R1968)
R. Vannes: *Essai d'un dictionnaire universel des luthiers* (Paris, 1932, 2/1951/R1972 as *Dictionnaire universel des luthiers* and R1981 incl. suppl. 1959)

CHARLES BEARE

Grainger, (George) Percy (Aldridge) (*b* Brighton, Melbourne, 8 July 1882; *d* White Plains, NY, 20 Feb 1961). American composer, pianist, editor, folksong collector and inventor, of Australian origin.

As a composer and inventor Grainger devoted much time to the attempt to realize his concept of 'free music', a music based on continuous 'gliding' tones, whose melody, rhythm, and texture were liberated from the traditional constraints of scale, beat and harmony. In pursuit of this he considered the use of the siren, the Heliophon, the Electronic Music Box and the RCA Electronic Music Synthesizer, but he made no serious experiments with any of these. In the 1930s he wrote two very short works with graphic scores, *Free Music* no.1 for four theremins (1935; originally scored for string quartet) and no.2 for six theremins (1935–6); both have been realized in electronic music studios (BBC Radiophonic Workshop, *c*1970; Swedish Radio EMS, *c*1972) and on a computer (by Barry Conyngham at the University of Melbourne, 1978). An electronic instrument for playing such scores was planned with Lev Termen in 1937, but the latter's return to the USSR shortly afterwards meant that the project was never carried out. Grainger included other electronic instruments, such as the Una-Fon (probably in the 1930s), in arrangements of his earlier and more conventional compositions, and in 1950 he arranged two works for two Solovoxes, one also with reed organ.

Dissatisfied with the results he obtained by these means, from the mid-1940s Grainger invented and, in collaboration with Burnett Cross and with the help of his wife, Ella Grainger, built a series of mainly electronic composition machines (*see* CROSS–GRAINGER FREE MUSIC MACHINE). His activities never went beyond the development of these pioneering instruments to a full realization of 'free music' and his ideas have not been pursued directly by other composers or inventors.

BIBLIOGRAPHY
P. A. Grainger: 'Free Music', *Recorded Sound*, nos. 45–6 (1972),

16; repr. in *A Musical Genius from Australia: Selected Writings by and about Percy Grainger*, ed. T. Balough (Nedlands, Western Australia, 1981), 143; and in *The Percy Grainger Companion*, ed. L. Foreman (London, 1981), 168

HUGH DAVIES

Gralla. Oboe of Catalonia. It is similar to the *dulzaina* of the Basque region (*see* DULZAINA (i); *see also* SHAWM, §4). Two types, the *tenora* (tenor) and *tiple* (treble), were used in the traditional *cobla* ensemble, together with the FLAVIOL and *tamboret*. At principal feasts in Valls a human tower or pyramid, some six ranks high, is built to the accompaniment of a *toc* (toccata) played on *grallas*.

Granbom, Berndt (*b* Bocholt; *d* in or after 1519). German organ builder, in partnership with Johann GRAUROCK (i).

Gran cassa (It.). Bass drum; *see* DRUM, §2.

Grancino, Giovanni (*fl* c1685–c1726). Italian violin maker. He was the most important Milanese violin maker, at least until the time of Guadagnini and Landolfi. He worked on his own account as early as 1685, but from about 1670 onwards there are instruments labelled by the brothers Francesco and Giovanni 'de Grancinis'. These are rather different in style, though in no way inferior, and the connection has not been established. Nor, for that matter, has the existence of Paolo Grancino, who is sometimes said to have worked in Cremona; the existence of Giovanni Battista Grancino (possibly the same as Giovanni Grancino) is equally uncertain. Giovanni Grancino was a competent workman, influenced by the Amatis yet bringing a strong personal character to the construction of his instruments. He provided for a less wealthy clientèle than that of his nearby Cremonese competitors, often using inexpensive wood for his backs, sides and scrolls. His tables, however, are usually good-looking, with strong, vigorous grain. The varnish in the earlier instruments is dark red-brown or orange, soft and thick, but after 1700 it is normally harder, thinner and light yellow-brown in colour. The soundholes have an individual cut, with broader wings than an Amati. The scrolls are elegantly rounded and deeply and cleanly carved.

Although there are many violins and an occasional viola or viol, Grancino made an unusually large number of cellos. Mostly these were of very large (bassetto) size, and have since been cut down. They are very popular among cellists, being in general good all-round instruments with a powerful A string and clear bass. Grancino had a far-reaching influence on later Milanese makers: Carlo Giuseppe Testore was the best of his pupils, and was very likely followed by Santino Lavazza, Gaetano Pasta and Carlo Rotta.

BIBLIOGRAPHY
W. L. von Lütgendorff: *Die Geigen- und Lautenmacher vom Mittelalter bis zur Gegenwart* (Frankfurt am Main, 1904, rev. 6/1922/R1968)
R. Vannes: *Essai d'un dictionnaire universel des luthiers* (Paris, 1932, 2/1951/R1972 as *Dictionnaire universel des luthiers* and R1981 incl. suppl. 1959)

CHARLES BEARE

Grand-Adam. *See* ADAM family.

Grand bugle (Fr.). FLUGELHORN.

Grand Choeur (Fr.). The Great chorus of a French organ. While GRAND JEU and PLEIN JEU denote the two kinds of major choruses on the Classical French organ (*c*1600–1800), Grand Choeur suggests rather the group of stops added to the FONDS D'ORGUE (16′, 8′ and 4′ ranks) to make FULL ORGAN in music of the post-classical period. It is not a registration as such, nor is it normally used by composers. The term significantly appeared in the stop-lists of Cavaillé-Coll's formative organ at St Sulpice, Paris (completed 1862), to denote the 13 reed and mixture stops played from the Grand Orgue manual but placed on a separate chest from the Diapason chorus ranks of the Grand Orgue proper.

PETER WILLIAMS

Grand jeu (Fr.: 'great registration'). A term found in French organ music (though seldom used by modern composers), denoting one of two registrations: (*a*) the early Diapason chorus, without Flute mutations or reeds, corresponding in smaller organs to the old undivided, stop-less BLOCKWERK (St Etienne, Toulouse, 1531) but as a term soon to be replaced by the better PLEIN JEU (Chartres Cathedral, 1542); and (*b*) a characteristic combination of Bourdons, mutations, Cornet and reeds much used by the composers of the French school *c*1670–1770. Nivers (*Livre d'orgue*, 1665) still included most manual stops in his *grand jeu* but Lebègue (*Les pièces d'orgue*, 1676) gave the classical combination of Bourdon 8′, Prestant 4′, Cornet and Trompette. As such, the *grand jeu* was both used for certain interludes in the Mass (the exuberant finales to the Kyrie, Gloria, Agnus and offertory) and associated with a particular musical style, often contrapuntal or even fugal, sometimes with one hand in a colourful solo against the other on a quieter manual. By 1740, and probably earlier, pedal reeds also took part in the *grand jeu*, like other reeds, Cornets, Tierces and even Tremulants.

PETER WILLIAMS

Grand pianoforte (Fr. *piano à queue*; Ger. *Flügel*, *Hammerflügel*; It. *piano a coda*). A piano in a horizontal wing-shaped case, the form of which is directly derived from that of the harpsichord. Cristofori's original piano, the *gravicembalo col piano e forte*, was constructed in that shape. The earliest recorded use of the term is in a patent granted to Robert STODART in 1777 for a HARPSICHORD-PIANO, which gives a detailed drawing of the grand piano action. Although pianos have been built in many other forms the grand, because of its longer bass strings and less cumbersome action, has always been the type generally accepted as superior for concert use. For a discussion of the history of the instrument, *see* PIANOFORTE, §I.

EDWIN M. RIPIN

Gran tamburo (It.). Bass drum; *see* DRUM, §2.

Grantang. Bamboo XYLOPHONE of Bali, played solo or in groups. It has a two-octave range. Its tuned bamboo tubes are cut on the slant from the top and closed by a node at the bottom. They are fastened to a frame and to each other by a cord running through them. The player uses two long wooden or bamboo sticks with unpadded discs at the end. The *grantang* is used in the gamelan and as a recreational instrument. See C. McPhee: *Music in Bali* (New Haven and London, 1966/*R*1976), 32.

MARGARET J. KARTOMI

Grant, Degens & Bradbeer. English firm of organ builders. It was founded in Hammersmith, London, in 1959 as Degens & Rippin by Maurice Forsyth-Grant on the initiative of E.V. Rippin, John Degens and Eric Atkins, and it pioneered the trend among English builders towards neo-classicism. Under the name Grant, Degens & Rippin, the firm was by 1963 building new organs with such features as independent pedal departments and complete choruses. On the instigation of Grant, the partners toured the Continent to see the work of leading continental builders. They were joined by Frank Bradbeer, a professional architect, and their style moved from 'clarified Romantic' to neo-classical. Their divergence from the English tradition continued with the organ for the Servite Priory, Brompton (1967), which was the first to have mechanical key-action; this led to their building such important instruments as that at New College, Oxford (1969), with its distinctive modern case and innovatory aliquot mutations. The firm now shares a Northampton factory with Alfred Davies & Son, which has exported many organs in traditional style. Although they are stylistically separate, both are managed by Jack Davies. The firm became Grant, Degens & Bradbeer in 1966. See J. P. Rowntree and J. F. Brennan: *The Classical Organ in Britain 1955–1974* (Oxford, 1975).

ANTHONY D. ROLLETT

Gratamüsum. PANPIPES of Italy.

Gratieusement [gratioso]. *See* GRAZIOSO.

Graurock [Grauwrock, Grorockh, Graerock]. German family of organ builders. Johann [Jan, Hans] Graurock (i) (*b* Kalkar; *d* by 1558) was the brother-in-law of the organ builder Berndt Granbom (*b* Bocholt), who had supplied a new *Rückpositiv* for the organ at St Nikolaus, Kalkar, in 1503–4, and a new large organ for St Eusebius, Arnhem, in 1506–9, and had become a citizen of Emmerich on 29 July 1511. Both men set themselves up in Emmerich, probably in partnership. In 1518 they built a large organ for St Jan, Gorinchem, and in 1519 were working in Wesel Cathedral (the last evidence of work by Granbom). Graurock worked at St Nikolaus, Kalkar, in 1530 and settled in Zutphen on 18 April 1534; he may have been the unnamed builder of the large organ at St Walburga completed at this time. In 1535 he was active at St Nikolaus, Kampen, and later the same year supplied a small organ for the Grote Kerk, Breda (he may have built the large one there the previous year). In 1545 he reconstructed the organ of St Nikolaus, Elburg. He sold his house in Zutphen in 1547 and moved back to Emmerich, from where during the same year he worked on both the organs in St Nikolaus, Kampen, and supplied at some point a new organ for Doesburg.

Graurock and Granbom belonged, together with Johann Kavelens from Wesel and Johann Johannsen (Brouckmann) from Münster, to the group of builders active in the Lower Rhine area who separated the *Hauptwerk* into two departments: the Principal chorus, comprising the *plein jeu* stops; and the *Oberwerk*, with the *grand jeu* stops (such as 8′ Hohlpfeife, 4′ Flute, 2′ Gemshorn, Sifflett, Klingende or Rauschende Zimbel, Horns, 8′ Trumpet and 4′ Schalmei). Thus the Pedal coupled to the Principal chorus and embellished with 8′ Trumpet and 2′ Nachthorn was made much more independent, since it could be contrasted with particular stops on the

Oberwerk and *Rückpositiv*. This kind of three-manual organ was to remain standard during the next century for the NIEHOFF, Lampeler and Hocques families of organ builders.

Johann Graurock's sons Johann (ii) and Wilhelm built a new large organ for Cleves parish church in 1567. The 'Johann Graurock, organ builder in Vreden' who supplied a new organ for Bevergern (district of Tecklenburg) in 1562 is possibly Johann (ii). Wilhelm Graurock's sons Johann (iii) and Bernhard 'aus Emmerich' went to Frankfurt am Main in 1598 where Bernhard became a citizen in 1599 (Johann is not mentioned in the civic list until 1606). Johann (iii) built new organs for the Carmelite monastery in Frankfurt (1598) and for the municipal church in Darmstadt (1599). Between 1599 and 1604 Johann and Bernhard worked together in Frankfurt on a large organ for the Franciscan church, the town's main Protestant church. Johann worked at Mainz Cathedral (1605–7) and then seems to have moved back to the Rhineland; his last-known work was in Cologne at St Gereon (1608, 1623) and St Johann Baptist (1632).

BIBLIOGRAPHY

M. A. Vente: *Bouwstoffen tot de geschiedenis van het Nederlandse orgel in de 16de eeuw* (Amsterdam, 1942)

——: *Proeve van een repertorium van de archivalia betrekking hebbende op het Nederlandse orgel en zijn makers tot omstreeks 1630* (Brussels, 1956)

——: *Die Brabanter Orgel* (Amsterdam, 1958, 2/1963)

R. Reuter: *Orgeln in Westfalen* (Kassel, 1965)

HANS KLOTZ

Grave (It., Fr.: 'heavy', 'serious'). A tempo mark and mood designation. In the early 17th century it had no particular musical meaning: Antonio Brunelli's *Ballo grave* (1616) and Biagio Marini's *Symphonia grave* (1617) used it merely as an adjective in the title, and among the Venetian polychoral music of the time the higher and lower choirs were named *acuto* and *grave*. But *grave* appeared as a performance instruction in Cavalli (*Le nozze di Teti e Peleo*, 1639), Marco Uccellini (*Sonate*, 1646) and Marini (op.22, 1655). By 1683 Purcell, in the preface to his *Sonnata's of III Parts*, could describe it as being current in Italy and elsewhere, saying that it and *adagio* 'import nothing but a very slow movement'. Corelli used it for the majority of his slow movements, particularly introductory movements. François Couperin often used *gravement* (the adverbial form in French), which also appears in J.S. Bach. The theorists show no consistency in their opinion as to whether *grave* is faster or slower than *adagio* and *largo*; but its uses suggest interchangeability with *adagio*, though in the 18th century it seems sometimes to have meant the same as *andante*. Koch (*Musikalisches Lexikon*, 1802, article 'Con gravità') said that in *grave* movements overdotting should be used, and referred to the opening sections of operas by Graun and Hasse: the *Messiah* opening should certainly be read in this way; perhaps also the *grave* at the beginning of Beethoven's 'Pathétique' Sonata op.13 (recalling that in Bach's C minor Partita) and of his Piano and Wind Quintet op.16. It seems that *grave* reversed the normal trend in musical tempo and expression marks: not until the middle of the 19th century is there evidence of its being interpreted literally.

For bibliography *see* TEMPO AND EXPRESSION MARKS.

DAVID FALLOWS

Graves, Samuel (*b* New Boston, New Hampshire, 2 July 1794; *d* Wells River, Vermont, 18 Nov 1878). American maker of brass and woodwind instruments. He began making woodwind instruments in West Fairlee, Vermont, in the early 1820s. In 1830 he and three partners opened a large shop in Winchester, New Hampshire. This shop occupied the upper two floors of a four-storey building constructed jointly by Graves & Co. and a clothier, Nathaniel Herrick. The firm turned out large quantities of flutes and clarinets using water-powered machinery and employing several people.

James Keat, third son of the London instrument maker Samuel Keat, went to Winchester about 1837. He evidently introduced brass instrument making to Graves & Co., for a number of keyed bugles and one Stölzel valve cornet have been found in the USA signed 'J. Keat for Graves & Co.'. From that time on through the 1840s Graves & Co. produced both brass and woodwind instruments. By 1842 they had obtained another floor in their building and their products included flutes, clarinets, keyed bugles, ophicleides and several sizes of brasses with Vienna twin-piston valves. Graves called his larger valve brasses trombacellos. The 1844 exhibition of the Massachusetts Charitable Mechanic Association in Boston included the following Graves instruments: 'one trombacello, one tenor valve trombone, one valve trumpet, two valve post horns and one E♭ bugle'.

Graves & Co. rebuilt their premises in 1848 after a fire, but the business in Winchester did not recover. In 1851 the shop was sold and Graves moved to Boston. He and two of his sons continued the business there until the 1870s making brass instruments but no woodwind.

Samuel Graves, with the help of James Keat, was one of the earliest makers of valved brass instruments in the USA. He was well known for his fine E♭ and B♭ keyed bugles, which he produced in large quantities. His eight-key flutes and twelve- or thirteen-key clarinets were also well made and popular. His water-powered factory at Winchester was the largest in the USA for many years. Several examples of his instruments are now in the collections of the Henry Ford Museum, Dearborn, Michigan.

BIBLIOGRAPHY

R. E. Eliason: *Keyed Bugles in the United States* (Washington, DC, 1972)

——: *Samuel Graves, New England Musical Instrument Maker* (Dearborn, Mich., 1974)

——: *Graves & Co., Musical Instrument Makers* (Dearborn, Mich., 1975)

——: 'Letters to Marsh & Chase from Graves & Company'; *JAMIS*, iv (1978), 43

ROBERT E. ELIASON

Gravicembalo. Italian 17th-century name for the HARPSICHORD; the term 'gravicembalo col piano e forte' refers to the early 18th-century PIANOFORTE.

Gravissima (Lat.). An ORGAN STOP.

Gray & Davison. English firm of organ builders. Robert Gray (*d* 1796) was in business at Leigh Street, Red Lion Square, London, in 1774, though the firm may have been founded earlier. By 1787 he had been joined by William Gray (*d* c1820), and a trade card of about 1795 advertises them as 'Robert & William Gray, Organ, Harpsichord & Piano-Forte Makers'. Following Robert's death William carried on business in his own name; he was succeeded by John Gray (*d* 1849) who had, by 1837, taken his son Robert into partnership.

The firm's work was highly regarded in the early 19th century, and several comparatively large organs were built, chiefly in London. Their tonal schemes reflected the growing taste for delicate voices and soft orchestral reeds (the Choir reed was sometimes called 'Violoncello' rather than the more usual 'Cremona') but the Great Organ always contained a complete chorus, with two mixtures in the largest instruments. After about 1805 Pedal pipes made an occasional appearance (e.g. 11 stopped 'doubles' at St Patrick, Soho, 1810), and by the end of the 1820s a Swell 16' double was sometimes provided in large organs (e.g. a Double Dulciana at St Mark, Pentonville, 1830). Important contracts during this period included new organs for St Anne, Soho (1795), St Martin in the Fields (1800) and for the parish churches of St Marylebone (1818), St Pancras (1822) and Blackburn (1828); the firm also rebuilt the organs at St Sepulchre, Holborn (1826, 1834), and Trinity College, Cambridge (1835).

In 1838 Frederick Davison (*b* 1814 or 1815; *d* London, 12 Nov 1889) dissolved his brief partnership with William Hill (*see* HILL (i)), married John Gray's daughter, and entered into a new partnership with his father-in-law. The firm was henceforth known as Gray & Davison. Davison was an able organist (a pupil of Samuel Wesley) and under his direction the firm began to put forward radical schemes for new and rebuilt instruments, incorporating the principles (independent Pedal divisions, fully developed choruses, manuals from *C*) of the 'German system' organ. There was intense rivalry with Hill, though the work of the two firms was significantly different. The specification of Davison's 'Model Organ on the German Plan' (St Paul, Knightsbridge, 1843) illustrates the point. There were none of the novel 'fancy stops' and reeds which contemporary Hill organs possessed; there was a comparatively modest provision of mutations; each manual division was of a similar size. In general, Davison's designs retained a classical balance which Hill and Gauntlett's more daring schemes threw to the winds, though his choruses lacked the brilliance and colour of Hill's because the mixtures tended to break back relatively quickly, and Davison was less insistent on making mixtures with tierces. The firm's chorus reeds were much admired, and contemporaries commented on their resemblance to surviving 18th-century English reeds – again, rather different from Hill's posaunes.

The firm reached its peak during the 1850s, when several large concert instruments were built. The influence of Henry Smart was formative, and he and Davison set about creating a species of concert instrument which could accommodate everything from 'the severest fugue of Sebastian Bach, to the lightest French overture'. Smart was an accomplished engineer as well as player, and was fully conversant with contemporary French organ building; under his influence, Gray & Davison adopted many of the innovations of the modern French school: sub and super octave couplers; French-style reeds (including free reeds), harmonic flutes, and orchestral voices; the application of higher wind pressures in the treble; the tremulant; ventils instead of combination pedals; and a 61-note manual compass. Some or all of these features appeared in the organs for Glasgow City Hall (1853), Birmingham Music Hall (1856), the Handel Festival organ in the Crystal Palace, London (1857), Leeds Town Hall (1857–8) and Newcastle Town Hall (1859); these instruments represent an important stage in the development of the 19th-century English concert organ, setting new standards of orchestral authenticity and offering the player novel console facilities. Other important contracts of this period included the Centenary Chapel, Boston (1850), Magdalen College, Oxford (1855), Sherborne Abbey (1856) and St Mary, Stoke Newington (1858).

Gray & Davison continued to do good but increasingly conservative work until the end of the century, including contracts for Hereford Cathedral (1862), St Lawrence Jewry, City of London (1875), Warrington parish church (1876) and St George's Chapel, Windsor (1883). Characteristic voices, such as the Keraulophon (invented by Gray & Davison, *c*1843), the Clarinet Flute and the Sifflote 2', which had first appeared in the 1840s, were still to be found in new instruments at the end of the century. On Davison's death control of the firm passed to his nephew, Charles Davison, who had previously managed the firm's Liverpool branch (purchased from Bewsher & Fleetwood in 1856), and then to Jess Davison (until 1928). The firm remained active until about 1970.

As with other builders whose best work antedates the arrival of the romantic-symphonic organ, Gray & Davison's instruments have been largely replaced or rebuilt. Some modest, standard instruments survive in country churches. Other notable instruments include the chamber organ by R. & W. Gray at Thornborough, Buckinghamshire (1787), the organ largely by John Gray at Little Bardfield, Essex (1830; case by Renatus Harris from Jesus College, Cambridge); the barrel organ at Raithby Church, Louth (1839); the Exhibition organ at St Anne, Limehouse (1851); and the organs at St Mary, Burnley (1855), St Mary Usk (built for Llandaff Cathedral, 1861), Milton Abbey, Dorset (1867), Clumber Chapel, Nottinghamshire (*c*1890), and St Mary, West Derby, Liverpool (1861 and 1892; later electrified).

BIBLIOGRAPHY
E. J. Hopkins and E. F. Rimbault: *The Organ: its History and Construction* (London, 1855, enlarged 3/1877/*R*1972)
W. Spark: *Life of Henry Smart* (London, 1881)
Obituary [F. Davison], *MO*, xiii (1889), 144
N. J. Thistlethwaite: *A Consideration of the Development of the Organ in England between c.1820 and 1870* (diss., U. of Cambridge, 1980)
NICHOLAS THISTLETHWAITE

Grazioso (It.: 'agreeable', 'graceful', 'dainty'). A mark of expression and, particularly in the 18th century, of tempo. Like many such marks, it was first used for music shortly before 1700 and was cultivated by the French Baroque composers: Couperin and Rameau often used it in its French adverbial form *gratieusement* (or *gracieusement*). *Gratioso* is translated both in Brossard's *Dictionaire* of 1703 and in the anonymous *A Short Explication* of 1724; and in 1768 Rousseau used *gracieux* to translate *andante*, the third of his five main degrees of movement in music. But the extensive use of *gratieusement* by the French composers bred a clearly identifiable tradition of such pieces and somewhat impeded the word's further development even though it also occurred in Italian music of the 18th century. There are numerous appearances of *grazioso* as a tempo designation in later music: for example in the finale of Beethoven's Piano Sonata in A op.2 no.2 or in the seventh of Brahms's Variations on the St Anthony chorale; and Viennese compositions at the end of the 19th century still occasionally had the tempo mark *gracioso*. But by then it appeared most often as an expression mark: Alfredo's first word in the 'Brindisi' from *La traviata* is marked *Con grazia*. Bartók used *grazioso* particularly often, and his close colleague André Gertler ('Souvenirs sur Béla Bartók', *ReM*, 1955, no.224, p.99, on p.103) expressed the opinion that 'entre autres, le mot "*grazioso*" n'a pas le même sens chez Bartók que chez un classique. Le *grazioso* de Bartók est impulsif, souvent tendrement ironique, âpre, etc'.

For bibliography *see* Tempo and expression marks.

DAVID FALLOWS

Great octave. A term still used by some organ builders and once by organ theorists (Hopkins, *The Organ*, 1855; Audsley, *The Art of Organ-building*, 1905) to refer to the (pipes of the) octave *C–c*, in distinction to *C'–C* (the 'contra-octave'), and *c–c'* (the 'small octave'), etc. The term seems to be a translation of *Grossoktave* rather than a reference to the completed Short octave of former periods, as has sometimes been thought.

PETER WILLIAMS

Great organ. Term used in two related but different ways: (i) to denote a large organ as distinct from a smaller chamber organ, in church accounts (York, 1469; Sandwich, 1496; St Andrew's, Holborn, 1553), inventories (1515) and general literature; and (ii) to denote the larger or main manual of a two-manual or double organ of the 17th century (King's College, Cambridge, accounts, 1606), as distinct from the Chair organ. Earlier, it is not always clear which is meant. The contents and function of the Great organ correspond to those of the Grand Orgue, Organo Primo, Hauptwerk (or Oberwerk), *Hoofdwerk*, etc, except that the English main manual has not an unbroken tradition for massive Diapason choruses. Those of the 16th and 17th centuries were usually little more than large-scale chamber organs, often in a place traditionally kept for small organs in the Netherlands, Italy, etc (e.g. on the screen). Larger Great organs were built from *c*1820, particularly under the influence of Dutch organs (especially Haarlem) and German composers (especially J. S. Bach). Following Cavaillé-Coll's example, some English builders gave their Great organ keyboards several chests, including major reed departments often on high wind-pressure. But since the Organ Reform Movement of the 1920s, the Great organ has been recognized as essentially a Diapason chorus, not far removed from the Blockwerk in conception, and in larger examples containing stops along the lines of 16.16.8.8.5⅓.4.2⅔.2.II.V–X.III.16.8.

PETER WILLIAMS

Green, Samuel (*b* Wheatley, nr. Oxford, 1740; *d* Isleworth, Middlesex, 14 Sept 1796). English organ builder. The son of an Oxford distiller, he was apprenticed in 1754 to George Pyke (*c*1725–77), clockmaker and organ builder. In 1768 he entered into partnership with John Byfield (ii). In 1772 he married Sarah, daughter of the clockmaker Eardley Norton, becoming in September of that year a freeman of the Clockmakers' Company. About this time he established himself as an organ builder in Red Lion Street, Holborn. A prolific builder, he worked from Holborn and then Queen's Row, Islington, before settling at Isleworth in 1789. After Snetzler's retirement (1780) Green was patronized by George III. After his death the business was continued

by his widow, Sarah, and his foreman, Benjamin Blyth.

The specifications of Green's instruments are similar to those of other organ builders of the period, such as John and George Pike England. His distinctive style of organ building was to give the organ a more delicate sound, after the more forthright voicing of Snetzler, obtained by large-scale pipes with low mouths, closely 'nicked' and lightly blown (Sumner, 1952). He developed the swell, extending its usual compass downwards and modifying the design of the swell box, frequently adding a Dulciana and Dulciana Principal. The Great on his larger organs also included a second Open Diapason.

Sutton (1847) disparaged Green's style, writing: 'his diapasons, though the quality of tone is sweet, at the same time it is very thin, and his chorus is entirely destitute of either fulness or brilliancy of tone . . . his organs are chamber organs on a large scale.' Green can, however, be seen as one of the finest and most characteristic English organ builders of his time. He built more cathedral organs than any of his contemporaries. Notable organs by Green include: St Botolph, Aldersgate, London (1778, mahogany case remains); St Katherine's Collegiate Church, London (1778, removed to new buildings in Regent's Park in 19th century, where it remains); St Thomas, Ardwick, Manchester (1787 [nameplate, 1788] restored by Hill, Norman & Beard; now at St Paul, Salford); Royal Naval Hospital Chapel, Greenwich (1789, mahogany case and much pipework survive); Salisbury Cathedral (gift of George III, 1792, now at St Thomas, Salisbury; case and much pipework remain). Larger chamber organs survive at Attingham House, Shropshire (1788), and Heaton Park, near Manchester, Lancashire (1790). For a fuller list of Green's instruments see Freeman (1943–5) and Sumner (4/1973).

BIBLIOGRAPHY

J. Sutton: *A Short Account of Organs Built in England from the Reign of King Charles the Second to the Present Time* (London, 1847)
E. J. Hopkins and E. F. Rimbault: *The Organ: its History and Construction* (London, 1855, rev. 3/1877/*R*1972)
A. Freeman: 'Samuel Green', *The Organ*, xxiii (1943–4), 110, 153; xxiv (1944–5), 17, 55
W. L. Sumner: *The Organ* (London, 1952, rev. and enlarged 4/1973)
C. Clutton and A. Niland: *The British Organ* (London, 1963)
D. C. Wickens: 'Studies in Green: the Lichfield Letters', *The Organ*, lx (1981), 153

GUY OLDHAM

Grelots (Fr.). Jingles; *see also* Bell (i).

Gren, Jonas (*b* 13 Jan 1715; *d* 25 March 1765). Swedish organ builder. On gaining his charter in 1748 he went into partnership with Peter Stråhle (1720–65); both men were trained by Peter's uncle, Daniel Stråhle, who was himself a pupil of Johan Niclas Cahman. The Cahman tradition of organ building continued through their own pupils, among whom were Olof Schwan, Matthias Swahlberg and Carl Wåhlström. Gren and Stråhle were Sweden's leading exponents of their craft; they built nearly 30 new organs and rebuilt or enlarged about ten older instruments. The two masters, of whom Gren was the theorist and Stråhle the practitioner, seem to have complemented each other perfectly, and their work was noted for its solid craftsmanship and artistic subtlety in specification. They had their workshop first at Södermalm, then at Kungsholm in Stockholm. Their finest organs, which all had at least 30 stops, were built for Karlsstad Cathedral (1753), Sala City Church (1758), and the churches of St Ulrika Eleonora (1753), St Klara (1761, with 40 stops), and St Hedvig Eleonora (1762) in Stockholm. Smaller organs survive (though with later modifications) at Bunge, Gotland (1750, originally built for the French Reform Church in Stockholm); Järlåsa, Uppsala province (1754, originally built for Västerlövsta, Västmanland); and Överselö, Södermanland.

BIBLIOGRAPHY
SBL
E. Erici: *Inventarium över bevarade äldre kyrkoglar i Sverige* (Stockholm, 1965)
based on *Sohlmans musiklexikon* (iii, 209) by permission of Sohlmans Förlag

BENGT KYHLBERG

Grenié, Gabriel-Joseph (1757–1837). French instrument maker. Originally from Bordeaux, he exhibited his *orgue expressif*, a small organ with free-reed pipes, in Paris in 1810. Activated by air under pressure (as opposed to suction) and blown by foot treadles, it was capable of dynamic variation and was the precursor of the harmonium; *see* REED ORGAN, §1.

Grenser. German family of wind instrument makers.

(1) (Carl) August(in) Grenser (i) (*b* Wiehe, Thuringia, 11 Nov 1720; *d* Dresden, 4 May 1807). Flute and bassoon maker. When he was 13 he apprenticed himself to the well-known instrument maker Johann Poerschmann in Leipzig, and in 1739 he moved to Dresden, establishing his own workshop there in 1744. He became famous throughout Europe as an 'excellente artiste' and in 1753 received the title of 'Kurfürstliche-Sächsischer Hofinstrumentenmacher'. In 1796 he handed over his shop to his nephew (2) Johann Heinrich Wilhelm Grenser, who became his son-in-law. Grenser was not only a careful and ingenious craftsman but also a sensitive musician, and his surviving instruments have exceptionally good tone and intonation as well as superb workmanship. Flutes and bassoons were his speciality, and his instruments were considered the best of the period: he made his flutes with up to seven exchangeable centrepieces and fitted them with one to five keys, and the 'Dresden bassoon' derived its reputation mainly from instruments made in his workshop. He also made oboes, clarinets and basset-horns (full list in Young, 1978; for illustrations *see* FLUTE, fig.11*d* and BASSET-HORN, fig.1*b*). One of his sons, Johann Friedrich Grenser (1758–94), was an oboist and composer at the Swedish court.

(2) (Johann) Heinrich (Wilhelm) Grenser (*b* Lipprechtsroda, 5 March 1764; *d* Dresden, 12 Dec 1813). Instrument maker and inventor, nephew of (1) August Grenser (i). He was apprenticed to his uncle from 1779 to 1786 and continued to increase the fame of the workshop, taking it over in 1796. In 1793 he invented the 'clarinettbass' (not to be confused with the later bass clarinet), and in 1808 he improved the then popular basset-horn by making it straight rather than bent and fitting it with 16 keys.

Grenser wrote several articles for the *Allgemeine musikalische Zeitung* defending his work skilfully and sometimes sharply, as in 1800 against Tromlitz:

To add a key for the improvement of this or that tone is neither difficult nor skilful. Keys are also nothing new, and as a young boy I used these to strengthen the weak notes. It was easy for me to find their correct location. However, since the greatest art is to make flutes without [extra] keys, it is necessary to correct notes with particular weakness in a way that would be comparable to the addition of keys.

He also wrote: 'Not in the number of keys, no, but in the greater simplicity of the flute, without sacrificing its elegance, must we find true perfection of this beautiful instrument'. He had the title Hofinstrumentenmacher, and after Saxony became a kingdom in 1806 his instruments were stamped with a crown above the name. His surviving instruments include flutes, oboes, clarinets, basset-horns, *fagottini* and bassoons (full list in Young, 1978; for illustration *see* BASS CLARINET, fig.1*a*).

The flautist and composer Anton Bernhard Fürstenau published an article (1825) stating a preference for the smaller-bored flutes because of their easier upper register; this change in design made Grenser's flutes old-fashioned. His son Heinrich Otto Grenser (*b* Dresden, 14 Feb 1808) inherited the workshop, but it soon passed to others, continuing under the name Grenser & Wiesner into the mid-19th century.

(3) (Carl) August(in) Grenser (ii) (*b* Dresden, 2 May 1756; *d* Dresden, 8 Jan 1814). Instrument maker, son of (1) August Grenser (i). He had a workshop of his own but was not well known. His three sons were active as musicians in the Leipzig Gewandhaus Orchestra and one of them, (Carl) August(in) Grenser (iii) (*b* Dresden, 14 Dec 1794; *d* Leipzig, 26 May 1864), gained considerable fame as a flautist, teacher, composer, and 'inspector' at the Leipzig Conservatory.

BIBLIOGRAPHY
J. G. A. Kläbe: *Neuestes gelehrtes Dresden* (Leipzig, 1796)
A. B. Fürstenau: 'Etwas über die Flöte und das Flötenspiel', *AMZ*, xxvii (1825), 709
A. Dörffel: *Geschichte der Gewandhausconcerte zu Leipzig* (Leipzig, 1884)
F. A. Dressel: 'Zur Geschichte des Instrumentenbaues in Dresden', *ZI*, xlix (1928), 995
H. Kölbel: *Von der Flöte* (Cologne and Krefeld, 1951)
P. Rubardt: 'Grenser', *MGG*
P. T. Young: 'Inventory of Instruments: J. H. Eichentopf, Poerschman, Sattler, A. and H. Grenser, Grundmann', *GSJ*, xxxi (1978), 100
——: *2500 Historical Woodwind Instruments: an Inventory of the Major Collections* (New York, 1982)

FRIEDRICH VON HUENE

Greo [jreo]. Copper jingles of the Jörai people of central Vietnam.

Griff (Ger.). FRET.

Griffbrett (Ger.). FINGERBOARD, (1). In music for string instruments, the instruction *Am Griffbrett* is usually given in Italian as SUL TASTO.

Griffin, Thomas (*d* c1771). English organ builder or supplier. He was originally a barber (a Thomas Griffin was admitted to the freedom of the Barber Surgeons Company on 3 Dec 1728) and carried on his organ building business from Fenchurch Street. He provided organs for certain City churches, and had agreements with the parishes to arrange for tuning and maintenance of the organs and for the attendance of an organist each Sunday in return for an annuity. He came to these terms, or was a party to agreements, with the churches of St Katherine Coleman (1743), St Mildred, Bread Street (1745), St Helen, Bishopsgate (1744) and St Margaret Pattens (1749); dates recorded are installation dates. He also provided an organ for St Michael Bassishaw (1764), where no annuity arrangements were made.

BIBLIOGRAPHY

D. Dawe: *Organists of the City of London, 1666–1850* (Padstow, 1983)

N. Plumley: *The Organs of the City of London* (Oxford, in preparation)

NICHOLAS PLUMLEY

Grimm, Karl (*b* Berlin, 1794; *d* Berlin, 16 June 1855). German maker of string instruments and a trumpeter. He was an instrument maker to the royal court in Berlin, and had a fine reputation not only for his string instruments, patterned after those of Italian makers, but for his well-built, sonorous harps. His business continued for over 30 years until it was taken over in 1851 by the firm of C. Hellmig. His son Louis Grimm (1821–82) was a distinguished harpist and is considered the founder of the Berlin harp school.

ALICE LAWSON ABER

Grimont, Florentin (*b* Besançon; *d* ? Pamplona, after 1807). French organ builder. He became a Carmelite friar under the name Florentin de Sainte-Cécile at the friary at Tours. In 1789 the Revolution forced him to take refuge in Spain, and he was apparently still living in Pamplona in 1807. His organ building activities were mostly in Brittany, particularly for the Carmelite communities, and he built organs for those of St Anne, Auray (1775), Rennes and Brest. He also built new instruments for the churches of St Sulpice, Fougères (1776–7); St Martin, Morlaix (c1780); and St Louis, Brest (1788). Organs he restored include those at St Peter's Cathedral, Vannes, the churches at Roscoff, Morlaix, Pont-Croix and Sizun, and the monasteries at Vannes, St Pol-de-Léon and Pont-l'Abbé. See G. Bourligueux: 'Grimont', *DBF*.

GUY BOURLIGUEUX

Grinder organ. *See* BARREL ORGAN.

Grneta. Clarinet of Serbia and Macedonia (Yugoslavia). About 70 cm long, it has a cylindrical bore becoming conical at the lower end. In Serbia the instrument is sometimes home-made and is called *klanet*. The *grneta* was used in the *čalgije*, urban instrumental ensembles of Macedonia, particularly for weddings and other celebrations.

Grönlund. Swedish family of organ builders now active in Gammelstad, Norrbotten. Johan William Grönlund (1879–1963), originally a furniture maker, was a self-taught organ builder; he started his own small business at Kåge, Västerbotten, in 1903. His sons, Olof (1910–56) and Gustaf (*b* 1913), were trained at their father's workshop; Olof also studied for several years with Frobenius at Lyngby in Denmark. In 1940 the ownership of the firm was transferred to the sons; they moved the workshop to Notviken in 1944 and to Gammelstad in 1950. After Olof's death, Gustaf continued to direct the firm until his retirement in 1973, when Jan-Olof Grönlund (*b* 1937) took over. The family built organs for St Engelbrekt, Stockholm (1964; 86 stops); St Adolf Fredrik, Stockholm (1966; 46 stops); Nederluleå Church (1971; 55 stops); St Johannes, Norrköping (1972; 50 stops); Teg Church (1973; 50 stops); Holy Trinity, Gävle (1974; 46 stops); St Immanuel, Stockholm (1975; 36 stops); and St Hedvig Eleonora, Stockholm (1976; 58 stops). In general the firm builds instruments with mechanical action, though some have electrical registration; restoration of older instruments is also undertaken, such as the organ at Övertorneå (1970).

based on *Sohlmans musiklexikon* (iii, 237) by permission of Sohlmans Förlag

ANNA KYHLBERG

Groppetto [groppo]. *See* GRUPPETTO.

Grorockh. *See* GRAUROCK.

Gross Cither (Ger.). CETERONE.

Grosse caisse (Fr.; Ger. *Grosse Trommel*). Bass drum; *see* DRUM, §2.

Gross Zittern (Ger.). CETERONE.

Grotrian-Steinweg. German firm of piano makers, historically related to the STEINWAY firm. C(arl) F(riedrich) Theodor Steinweg (*b* Seesen, 6 Nov 1825; *d* Brunswick, 26 March 1889), the eldest son of Heinrich Engelhard Steinweg, continued the family piano-making business in Seesen when his father and the rest of the family emigrated in 1850 to New York where they founded Steinway. In 1855 the German firm moved from Seesen to Wolfenbüttel, where in 1858 Friedrich Grotrian (*b* Brunswick, 13 Jan 1803; *d* 11 Dec 1860), who had sold his Moscow music shop and piano-making business, became Theodor's partner. The firm then moved to Brunswick.

In 1865 Theodor emigrated to New York to assist his father, having sold his share in the business to Wilhelm Grotrian (*b* Moscow, 12 Aug 1843; *d* Brunswick, 21 Feb 1917, the son of Friedrich Grotrian), Adolf Helfferich and H. O. W. Schulz, who continued the business under the name C. F. Th. Steinweg Nachfolger. This trade name was changed to Grotrian, Helfferich, Schulz, Th. Steinweg Nachfolger in 1869.

Wilhelm Grotrian purchased his partners' shares and took control in 1886; in 1890 he began a factory on a different site. His sons, Willi (1868–1931) and Kurt (1870–1929) became partners in 1895; both were later awarded honorary doctorates for their achievements as piano makers. In 1919 the Grotrian family took the name Grotrian Steinweg, adopting the hyphenated form in 1926.

Grotrian-Steinweg pianos have always been famous for their sonority and beauty of tone. Clara Schumann regarded them very highly, and Walter Gieseking described their grand pianos as the most refined in the world. The family tradition has ensured the perfect matching of the pieces of wood in the soundboard through acoustic and physical experiments. The firm has also developed a successful and unique rim construction; the problem of absorbing all the tensions in one rim is met by leading all the braces through one central point.

MARGARET CRANMER

Ground bow. *See* GROUND HARP.

Ground drum. A drum made up of a series of poles stuck in the ground with a membrane stretched across them; the membrane is struck with a stick. The instrument is known in southern Africa. (For full details of the classification, *see* MEMBRANOPHONE.)

Ground harp [earth bow, ground bow] (Fr. *arc-en-terre*; Ger. *Erdbogen*). A simple single-string musical instrument known principally in equatorial Africa (mainly in the Ivory Coast, the Central African Republic, Cameroon, northern Zaïre and Uganda). It comprises a flexible stave planted in the earth with a string stretching from its free end to a soundboard of bark, plantain leaf, or something similar (see illustration). The soundboard is secured above a small pit in the ground, its edges being weighted down by a ring of stones or earth or by a circle of pliable twigs held down by pegs. In Uganda one variant form has the string pegged into the ground under the edge of half a gourd.

Ground harp (tekpede) of the Dan people, Ivory Coast, 1965

Because it resembles a musical bow, this instrument is often referred to as a 'ground bow' or 'earth bow', but in its construction it is really a form of harp. In some varieties a rigid upright stake helps to support the flexible stave near its mid-point. The string may be either plucked or struck with a stick, sometimes by more than one performer. Among pygmies in Zaïre a second player drums on the cover of the pit with two sticks. Pitch variation is usually achieved by stopping the string between the thumb and forefinger of the left hand, but in some areas the string tension is altered.

Ground harps are mainly used as children's toys. Sometimes they are built in groups and played together. Sachs (1940) has suggested the ground harp as ancestor to the monochord *đàn bầu* of Annam, and also to portable instruments such as the *gopīyantra* and *ānandalaharī* of Bangladesh.

The following ground harps are entered in this dictionary: awunene; babakungu; bandingba-ga-sende; bodongo; carángano; ekitulege; itikili; itumbolongonda; jigijigi; kimbumba; korongoe; kungunangu;

malaba; musokolome; nkutu kubidi; omujariko; papakungbu; sekitulege; tambour maringouin; tekpede; tingotalango; tum (ii); tumbandera; zuzu.

BIBLIOGRAPHY

WachsmannTCU, 311–415

B. Ankermann: 'Die africanischen Musikinstrumente', *Ethnologisches Notizblatt*, iii/1 (1901), 1–134

L. Frobenius: 'Die Saiteninstrumente der Naturvölker', *Prometheus*, xii (1901), 625, 648

T. Norlind, ed.: *Systematik der Saiteninstrumente*, i (Stockholm, 1936), 39f

C. Sachs: *The History of Musical Instruments* (New York, 1940), 54

M. Djenda: 'L'arc-en-terre des Gbaya-Bokoto', *African Music*, iv/2 (1968), 44

DAVID K. RYCROFT

Ground zither. In the Hornbostel and Sachs classification, a BOARD ZITHER in which the board is the ground; essentially it is an instrument in which strings are attached to poles stuck into the ground. In practice, the ground beneath the strings is often hollowed out, to form a resonator, and it is usually covered with bark or with leaves. The instrument dates back to Neolithic times and is still used in south-east Asia and parts of Africa. (For full details of the classification, *see* CHORDOPHONE.)

The following ground zithers are entered in this dictionary: dzidzingba; kakalari; kikilo; kudrekene; kuze-gene; tindi de kileru; trống quân.

Grundmann, Jakob Friedrich (*b* 1727 or 1729; *d* Dresden, 1 Feb 1800). German woodwind instrument maker. Like his contemporary, August Grenser (i), he learnt his craft in Leipzig as an apprentice to Johann Poerschman. Soon after Grenser moved to Dresden and opened a workshop in 1744, Grundmann also moved to Dresden and established a workshop of his own. Clearly they competed rather than simply complemented each other. Their workshops continued in competition after their deaths, Grenser's realizing equal or greater acclaim through the skill of Johann Heinrich Wilhelm Grenser (his nephew, apprentice and son-in-law), while Grundmann's was at first continued by a long-time partner, Johann Friedrich Floth (1761–1807), and later by Carl Gottlob Bormann (1770 or 1771–1839). Grundmann seems to have gained particular recognition for his oboes. Most of his instruments are stamped with the year of manufacture, a practice virtually unknown in woodwind history; this affords an opportunity to establish when various new keys and other innovations attributed to Grundmann first appeared. Young has conjectured that all Grundmann woodwind instruments originally carried a date, usually on the bell, since most surviving undated instruments are those on which the present bells are without any stamp, and are therefore likely to be later replacements.

BIBLIOGRAPHY

P. T. Young: 'Inventory of Instruments: J. H. Eichentopf, Poerschman, Sattler, A. and H. Grenser, Grundmann', *GSJ*, xxxi (1978), 100

——: *2500 Historical Woodwind Instruments: an Inventory of the Major Collections* (New York, 1982)

PHILLIP T. YOUNG

Grundstimmen (Ger.). FOUNDATION STOPS.

Grung. Rattle of the Jörai people of central Vietnam. It consists of jingles attached to a round piece of leather, and is used to accompany funerals.

Gruppetto (It.: 'small group'). A term used in the 16th century for a trill, and in succeeding periods for a turn. The terms *groppo*, *groppetto* and *gruppo* were also used. *See* ORNAMENTS, §III, 4, and §IV, 1–4.

Gruzavewonigi. LAMELLAPHONE of the Toma people of Liberia. It has nine raffia-splinted keys varying in length from 9 to 15 cm, mounted on a rectangular or oval piece of split wood. The longest key may be in the centre or at the side. The instrument is sometimes placed against a fence-post to increase the volume of sound. See G. Schwab: *Tribes of the Liberian Hinterland* (Cambridge, Mass., 1947/R1974).

Grzechotka. Polish term signifying different types of rattle, mostly children's toys.

Gshang. Tibetan flat bell, played by the *Bon-po* monks and by certain mediums. It has an internal clapper and widely flared edges, and somewhat resembles a small, thick cymbal to which a clapper has been added. The various types of *gshang* are distinguished by their sizes, which range from about 7 to about 20 cm in diameter. A central hole marks the top of the dome (*pho-brang*); through it passes a leather handle fixed to a wooden clapper which hangs inside the bell. The inside is often decorated with the five syllables of the *Bön-po* mantra: 'am', 'om', 'hum', 'ram' and 'dza'. When used alone the instrument is held in the right hand; when combined with a drum (*rnga* or *ḍamaru*) it is held in the left. In either case it is played with an upward movement. See M. Helffer: 'Note à propos d'une clochette *gshang* (Tibet et régions de culture tibétaine)', *Objets et mondes*, xxi/3 (1981), 129.

MIREILLE HELFFER

Gshang (flat bell) of Tibet, showing wooden clapper and part of handle (British Museum, London)

Gsil-snyan. *See* SIL-SNYAN.

Gu [ku]. A generic name for Chinese drums. In both historical and contemporary practice a prefix is attached to specify the kind of drum. Despite the wide variety in size, shape, beater style and usage, there are several features common to most Chinese-style drums: shell contour in the general shape of a barrel; a drumhead on each end tacked to the shell rather than laced together; and the fact that the instrument is struck on one end with two beaters. That drums of this type were well known in China by the Shang dynasty (1766–1122 BC) is attested by the appearance of drum pictographs of that period and archaeological finds of bronze drums dating to

between the 13th and the 10th century BC. While these bronze drums are entirely constructed of metal (including the heads) the presence of snakeskin designs on the heads and raised imitation tacks in three rows (for each head) suggests the earlier existence of similar wooden-shell drums. Barrel-shaped drums with wooden shells have in fact been found (one dating to the 5th century BC) and they are also mentioned in the classical texts of the period. Their general style and construction have changed very little down to the present day.

For drums associated with state rituals, *see* BOFU, JIANGU, JINGU (i) and TAOGU. For drums associated with the theatre and instrumental ensembles (not all of these are barrel drums), *see* BANGU, MATI GU, SHUGU and TANGGU. For drums used in folk ceremonies and miscellaneous other accompaniments, *see* BAJIAO GU, SHIGU and YAOGU.

BIBLIOGRAPHY
A. C. Moule: 'A List of the Musical and Other Sound-producing Instruments of the Chinese', *Journal of the North-China Branch of the Royal Asiatic Society*, xxxix (Shanghai, 1908), 48
Tong Kin-woon: *Shang Musical Instruments* (diss., Wesleyan U., Middletown, Conn., 1983).

ALAN R. THRASHER

Guáchara [churuca, guacharaca]. SCRAPER of Latin America. The *guáchara* is used in Panamanian *mejorana* or *cumbia* ensembles. Occasionally it is a perforated deer bone or piece of bamboo, but is more frequently a round or oblong notched gourd, scraped with a piece of twisted wire.

The *guacharaca* is found in Maracaibo, Venezuela (*charrasca*), Antioquia, Colombia and Esmeraldas, Ecuador. The notched piece of wood or cane is usually scraped with a stick or nail in a rapid rhythm. A similar type, which may also be made of bone, cow horn, copper or bronze tubing or bamboo, is used in Cuban ensembles. Rasps of bone, stone and wood were known among the Aztecs and other pre-Columbian tribes of North America. *See also* GÜIRO.

Guacho. Tubular rattle of the Colombian Atlantic coast, made of bamboo or tin and filled with dried seeds.

Guadagnini. Italian family of violin makers who worked from before 1740 until the beginning of the 20th century. The first, Lorenzo Guadagnini, worked on his own account for only a very few years, but his son, Giovanni Battista (known as J.B. from the latinized form used on his labels, Joannes Baptista), was prolific, and each produced violins which are now among the most sought after. The later generations of the family are less important.

The original labels on instruments made by Lorenzo Guadagnini (*b* before 1690; *d* 1748) show that his instruments were made in Piacenza, 30 km south-west of Cremona. As his son was born about 1711, and from the first described himself as 'Placentinus' ('of Piacenza'), Lorenzo Guadagnini was presumably born before about 1690, and may himself have lived and worked in Piacenza. He described himself, however, as 'alumnus Antonii Stradivarii', which would imply that he worked in Cremona. If he did work there, he is more likely to have been connected with Giuseppe Guarneri 'filius Andreae', or perhaps Carlo Bergonzi; he may have worked with Stradivari in preparing bows, or cases, but nothing about his violins links them to Stradivari in details

Violin by Giovanni Battista [J.B.] Guadagnini, Milan, 1750 (private collection)

of workmanship. The edgework is deeply grooved, the arch of the back tends to be pointed, the scrolls are magnificent but carved without the slightest attempt at symmetry. All the characteristics of his work are continued, in a feeble way, in that of Gasparo Lorenzini of Piacenza, who must have been a pupil, if not a major collaborator. Another type of violin attributed to Lorenzo Guadagnini, and certainly produced by his workshop, is likely to be the early work of his son.

Giovanni Battista [J.B.] Guadagnini (*b* Piacenza, *c*1711; *d* 18 Sept 1786), the son of Lorenzo Guadagnini, was the most important member of the family. He was a prolific maker, working in five different towns (Piacenza, Milan, Cremona, Parma and Turin) between 1740 and 1786, and his violins are the most highly prized of the mid- to late 18th-century Italian instruments. His cellos are shorter than most, about 4 cm shorter than the best of Stradivari's, but the string length is normal, and their good width and very deep sides make them excellent to play. His violas are in all shapes and sizes, mostly made in the later periods, and usually about 40 cm long.

From 1740 to 1749 Guadagnini worked in Piacenza, and the instruments of that time give the impression of having been made by a neat, young, comparatively unpractised hand; but they are built on his father's pattern and are fine instruments. From the beginning he sometimes used a red varnish of an extremely bright tint, the usual colour being a cooler orange-brown. By the time he left Piacenza the character of his work was already defined, though the basic appearance of his instruments was gradually modified. Their outline was Stradivarian, though with slightly sloping shoulders, soundholes set perpendicularly with notches centrally placed, and scrolls without a trace of classical design,

yet with flowing spirals and cut with great character.

From Piacenza Guadagnini moved to Milan, where he worked until 1758. Those who admire the results of a natural uninhibited Italian flair for the art of violin making tend to prefer his work of this period. A splendid choice of wood was available for the instrument backs, and the violins are often covered with a varnish with the colour and transparency of red wine. The lobes of the soundholes are usually pear-shaped (as are some in instruments made at Piacenza), a feature that was unvaried from 1753 to 1776; the notches of the soundholes are always centrally placed. Guadagnini's instruments give a direct, powerful sound, but without the range of colour or warmth of quality of certain other makes. In 1758 he worked in Cremona, but probably fewer than a dozen of the violins he made there survive. They resemble those of the Milan period, but the shoulders slope a little more from the button of the back, and the varnish has an orange shade a little different from the colours seen in other towns.

Between 1759 and 1771 Guadagnini worked in Parma; the reason for his move, according to his later patron Count Cozio di Salabue, was the patronage of the ducal court there. But after a short time he used neither the fine wood nor the lustrous varnish of his previous work, and a certain meanness is evident in details, particularly the scrolls. The maple he used, a narrow-flamed wood grown in the region, is not handsome but acoustically excellent, and was used by most Cremonese makers at one time or another. The varnish is an unexciting brown-red. In Parma Guadagnini began to place the notches low on the soundholes; this feature, unique in violin making, allowed the soundholes to be placed higher on the instrument without shortening the stop. He described himself as 'Cremonensis', rather than 'Placentinus', on his Parma labels, doubtless for the sake of prestige.

In 1771 Guadagnini moved to Turin, and during his first few years there the less admirable features of his Parma period faded. From 1772 he was well acquainted with Count Cozio di Salabue, one of the most ardent violin lovers of any period, who supported him with orders. In 1775 Cozio acquired from Paolo Stradivari a collection of his father's instruments and effects which had been in his workshop at his death. These perhaps inspired the radical changes Guadagnini introduced to the manufacture of his violins, of which the most important was the adoption of the Stradivari outline and form of soundhole: the pear-shaped lobes were abandoned in favour of round ones, the notches were placed centrally again, and the lower wings of the soundholes were hollowed out in exaggerated Stradivari fashion. Only the scrolls remained independent, though even they had for some years had their chamfers picked out in black. Varnish became important once more, and the red colour increasingly noticeable. The wood, too, was handsome as well as acoustically sound.

Guadagnini's sons are said to have collaborated with their father increasingly in his last years, but, like Stradivari, Giovanni Battista preferred to give his personal stamp to his product. From 1778 his work is that of an old man striving to imitate Stradivari, and with great success: these instruments have a full and loud tone equalled by few others. Guadagnini may have been the most original maker of the mid-18th century, yet at the end of his life he accepted the greatness of Stradivari and tried to copy him. The late Turin labels, in addition to 'Cremonensis', even describe him as 'alumnus Antonii Stradivarii', presumably an indication of respect rather than of historical fact.

It was 100 years before makers began deliberately to copy Guadagnini's work. The lack of recognition for his violins explains the confusion among 19th-century writers about his life. Good copies have been made by some modern Italian makers, and the early 20th-century Berlin school produced some clever fakes, as did the Vollers in London.

Giuseppe Guadagnini, known as 'Il soldato' (*fl* c1770–1805), was the son of Giovanni Battista Guadagnini. His work was independent of his father's during the latter's lifetime, and he also worked in several places, principally Como, Pavia and Milan. Although clearly he was trained by his father, his concept of violin making was much inferior, and the results seldom justify any kind of comparison.

Other descendants of the Guadagnini family, of more or less merit, continued working into the 20th century. Gaetano Guadagnini was a younger brother of Giuseppe, and helped his ageing father; he stayed in Turin after his father's death and died there himself in 1831. The later emergence of d'Espine and Pressenda in Turin was doubtless due to him, but his instruments are very rare. He was followed by Felice, Carlo, a second Gaetano, Antonio and finally Francesco Guadagnini.

BIBLIOGRAPHY
E. N. Doring: *The Guadagnini Family of Violin Makers* (Chicago, 1949)

CHARLES BEARE

Guagua. Afro-Cuban log-drum. It consists of a hollowed trunk, often of the avocado pear tree, which may be longer and narrower than that of the CATÁ, of which it is a reinforced version. Unique to the *guagua* are the two or more pieces of tinplate, nailed to the centre of the instrument, on which the musician strikes his two sticks, producing a distinctive timbre (the wooden surface may also be struck). The *guagua* appears occasionally in Afro-Cuban Congo drum ensembles. See *OrtizIMA*, iii, 135.

JOHN M. SCHECHTER

Guaiá. A rattle used in Afro-Brazilian fetishistic cults and rural sambas in São Paulo state.

Gualambo. MUSICAL BOW used by the Cainguá Indians of South Brazil and Paraguay. The player uses a friction technique, rubbing the string with a stick. In spite of the instrument's use by an Amerindian group, its name suggests an African origin. See *IzikowitzMISAI*, 203, 205; *OrtizIMA*, v, 11, 22.

Guamo. A CONCH-SHELL TRUMPET of Cuba, in use in the 15th century.

Guan [kuan]. Oboe of the Han Chinese. The term *guan*, in addition to identifying this instrument and pipes in general, means 'to control' or 'to manage'. Other names for the instrument include *guanzi* and *bili*. The present-day *guan* is made of a short tube of bamboo or wood, with seven frontal finger-holes, one dorsal thumb-hole and a large double reed (held in shape by a wrapping of copper wire) inserted into the blowing end. Measurements vary with different traditions, but a medium-sized Cantonese *guan* measures about 37 cm in pipe-length and about 5 cm in reed-length. It may also have a small flaring bell, though this appears to be a recent innovation. Unlike the *suona* its bore is cylindrical, and it has a range of only one octave. The *guan* is especially noted for its strident tone quality and its effectiveness in imitating nasal styles of singing.

The application of the name *guan* to this instrument is not very ancient. As mentioned in Zhou dynasty (1122–221 BC) sources, *guan* referred to small single or double end-blown pipes such as the Chinese XIAO and Korean KWAN. The earliest appearance of vibrating reeds in China probably dates from the introduction of the *hujia* reed-pipe from central Asia late in the Han dynasty (206 BC–AD 220). This simple instrument, a short pipe with a double reed and no finger-holes, was used for signalling. Another historical instrument, related to the *hujia* and anticipating the development of the *guan*, is the *bili*, which emerged after the Han period. The *bili* is also relatively short (about 18 cm in length) and is made of bamboo, with a large double reed, seven finger-holes and two thumb-holes, but no bell. During the Tang dynasty (AD 618–907) the *bili* was given an important position in the court orchestras of China, as is the HICHIRIKI in Japanese court music. The instrument continued to be used in Chinese ensemble music and to accompany singing. During the Song dynasty (AD 960–1279) the lower thumb-hole was eliminated. The Korean P'IRI is a survivor from this period, and the Vietnamese PILE, the Thai *pī nai* and the Khmer *pī a* (*see* PĪ) are related instruments. While losing its favour in the later court music the instrument, known as *guan* or *guanzi*, retained great popularity among the people for its use in regional instrumental ensembles (such as *chuida*) and in theatre traditions. The *guan* is still used in these genres, though often in a revised form. During the 1950s metal keys were added to some experimental instruments in an attempt to adjust the tuning to equal temperament and to allow for more chromatic notes. In the Cantonese instrumental and theatre traditions the once-popular *guan* has now largely been replaced by the tenor saxophone.

BIBLIOGRAPHY
A. C. Moule: 'A List of the Musical and Other Sound-producing Instruments of the Chinese', *Journal of the North-China Branch of the Royal Asiatic Society*, xxxix (Shanghai, 1908), 82

ALAN R. THRASHER

Guarneri. Italian family of violin makers.

(1) Andrea Guarneri (*b* Cremona, *c*1626; *d* Cremona, 7 Dec 1698). Son of Bartolomeo Guarneri, he was an apprentice in the house of Nicolo Amati from 1641 to 1646, and thus inherited the Amati principles of violin design and construction. In 1646 he left Amati's household, but in 1650 returned for a further period of four years. In 1652 he married Anna Maria Orcelli, the sister of a fine violinist. In 1654 Andrea and his wife left Amati's house to live in that of his father-in-law, later to be known as the Casa Guarneri. Of their seven children, two of the sons, (2) Pietro Giovanni Guarneri and (3) Giuseppe Giovanni Battista ('filius Andreae') Guarneri, were to become violin makers.

Andrea's distinctive hand is recognizable in a few of Nicolo Amati's violins. His early complete instruments are usually on the 'Grand Amati' pattern, but he never quite attained the elegance of his master's work. In fact the Guarneri character was apparent from the first: here and there a noticeable lack of symmetry, a little extra scoop at the purfling, and a roughness of finish, especially in the scroll. Often the mitres of the purfling point across the corners instead of into them, a unique feature. Once established on his own, working, according to his labels, 'sub titulo Sanctae Teresiae', Andrea Guarneri generally used a compact model of good dimensions. These violins are very highly regarded. Later he relied more and more upon the help of his sons, especially Giuseppe, and the character of the work is variable. Certain violins have a narrow, pinched look and are inadequate for modern performance. Andrea made several splendid smaller violas, well ahead of their time, one of which was played by William Primrose. He was also among the first to make a smaller cello, technically more easily managed than the very large instruments of the Amatis.

(2) Pietro Giovanni Guarneri (*b* Cremona, 18 Feb 1655; *d* Mantua, 26 March 1720). Son of (1) Andrea Guarneri, usually called 'da Mantova' to distinguish him from his nephew (3) Pietro Guarneri. He probably began work in his father's shop in Cremona before 1670, and indeed some of Andrea's productions of the following years show the recognizable imprint of Pietro's hand. In 1677 he married Caterina Sassagni, and soon afterwards left his parents' home. By 1683 he had settled in Mantua, where he made violins and also held an appointment as a court musician. This dual occupation doubtless accounts for the scarcity of his instruments. Compared with his father he was a meticulous workman, yet he retained in all the details of his work that special character which is associated with the Guarneri family. His purfling is set quite close to the edge, which is deeply and delicately worked: his scrolls appear more solid than those of his contemporaries, the ears becoming heavier as time went by (see fig. 1). Most distinctive are his soundholes, designed, placed and cut with great elegance. His varnish, a soft, lustrous, transparent orange-red covering, ranks with the very best. Tonally his violins have a full, rich quality, but sometimes lack edge, perhaps because of the full model: one of the best was played by Szigeti. No violas are known, and only one cello. None of his children succeeded him in his profession, nor is he known to have had pupils, though the later Mantuan makers Camilli and Balestrieri were strongly influenced by his work.

(3) Giuseppe Giovanni Battista Guarneri (*b* Cremona, 25 Nov 1666; *d* Cremona, 1739–40). The younger son of (1) Andrea Guarneri and known as 'filius Andreae', he stayed in Cremona as his father's faithful assistant, inheriting his house and his business in 1698. After about 1680, Giuseppe's had become increasingly the dominant hand in Andrea Guarneri's workshop, borrowing more from the style of his brother Pietro than from his father. In particular, the series of excellent cellos dating from about 1690 onwards would appear to have been made entirely by Giuseppe, possibly with other assistants.

He counts among the greatest violin makers, yet during his lifetime things must have been difficult. To begin with, his were troubled times in Cremona, with Austria taking the city in 1707 and gradually replacing Spain as the dominant power in Italy. Then there was the overwhelming shadow of Antonio Stradivari throughout Giuseppe's working life: just as Andrea Guarneri must have seen the most satisfying orders go to Nicolo Amati, so his son too had to rank as second best. Second he may have been, but going his own way he created some superb violins. He appears to have made no violas after his father's death, but a number of his cellos exist,

1. Violin by Pietro Giovanni Guarneri, 1689 (private collection)

showing by their differing dimensions that he gave extra thought to this instrument.

Not surprisingly, Giuseppe's materials were at times rather ordinary, but just before the turn of the century he learned to make an orange-red varnish, similar to that used by Pietro and quite superior in appearance to that of their father. With this he continued through the next two decades, many of his instruments being first-rate in every respect.

Although he lived for another 20 years, no violins are known with Giuseppe's original label dated after 1720. It is clear that from about 1715 onwards he had substantial help from his two sons, (4) Pietro Guarneri, who later moved to Venice, and (5) Giuseppe Guarneri 'del Gesù'. Alongside them in all probability worked Carlo Bergonzi. These transitional violins are actually better working instruments than the earlier ones, and it is not unusual to find them described as 'early del Gesù'.

(4) Pietro Guarneri (*b* Cremona, 14 April 1695; *d* Venice, 7 April 1762). Son of (3) Giuseppe Giovanni Battista Guarneri. He was known as 'da Venezia' to distinguish him from his uncle. Pietro found life in the Casa Guarneri in some way uncongenial, and about 1718 he left home for good, eventually arriving in Venice. There he found an extensive musical environment, and although restricted at first by the laws of the guilds, there was obviously plenty of room for one with his Cremonese background. It is interesting to observe how Venetian his work became in style in spite of his father's training, literally a blending of the two schools. When he arrived, the chief makers in Venice were Matteo Goffriller, Domenico Montagnana and Carlo Tononi, and Pietro may have obtained work with either of the latter two. In any case, his first original labels from Venice date

2. Violin by Giuseppe Guarneri ('del Gesù'), Cremona, 1737 (private collection)

from around 1730, and no one can be sure how the earlier years there were spent. By 1740 his success rivalled that of Montagnana and Sanctus Seraphin, but after 1750 he slowed down and his inspiration waned.

His instruments are rare, and at least as highly prized as those of his father and uncle. Among the marked characteristics of his work are the broad scroll, with prominent gouge-marks in the volute, and a flamboyant Venetian swing to the soundholes. His cellos are particularly successful, though few survive: Beatrice Harrison used one of them.

(5) (Bartolomeo) Giuseppe Guarneri ('del Gesù') (*b* Cremona, 21 Aug 1698; *d* Cremona, 17 Oct 1744). Younger son of (3) Giuseppe Giovanni Battista Guarneri, this last member of the family was one of the two greatest violin makers of all time. In tone-colour and in response a 'del Gesù' differs quite markedly from a Stradivari, some players preferring one make, some the other. Paganini played on a 'del Gesù' and started the vogue for his instruments. In the 20th century they have been used by Grumiaux, Heifetz, Kogan, Ricci, Stern, Szeryng, Zukerman and many others.

Undoubtedly Giuseppe received his training from his father, but he soon showed that his mind was both original and able to learn from seeing the work of others. He very soon took note of Stradivari's work, which his father had almost completely ignored, and this partly explains the popularity among violinists of the late Giuseppe 'filius Andreae' instruments. In 1722 or 1723 Giuseppe left his father's house to set up on his own, and before the end of the decade was having his own labels printed with the well-known IHS cipher, which later gave rise to his nickname 'del Gesù'. His reason for using the cipher is a matter for speculation; he may have been a Jesuit, and if so this may be significant. By the early 1730s his work was so different in appearance from either his father's or Stradivari's, and so successful tonally, that it is perhaps worth pausing to speculate on what may have been his intentions. There is so much of Brescian influence to be seen throughout his work, the fullness of arching near the edges in the centre part, long, rather pointed soundholes, long waist, that he may well have been trying to make a Cremonese version of the Gasparo da Salò–Maggini instruments. These were probably then, as now, known for their strong sound and ability to withstand strong bow pressure, to go on giving sound however hard the violinist plays. What 'del Gesù' achieved was a combination of this feature with the tonal beauty and ease of response of a Stradivari violin, and it is for this that he is sometimes rated higher than Stradivari himself.

With regard to craftsmanship and design, Giuseppe probably reached his peak around 1735, by which year many of his finest violins had been completed and covered with an unsurpassable varnish of varying tint. By 1737 or 1738 the erratic nature of his genius was beginning to show itself; he continued with the principles developed in the earlier years, but with ever fewer inhibitions, using knife and gouge with increasing abandon. This trend grew, often with magnificent effect, over the next few years. The last two or three years offer some of the most glorious, outrageous fiddles ever seen, yet however wildly Guarneri appears to have lashed out with his tools, that same, inimitable tonal result is still present. Even the unhappiest, most mutilated examples retain something of it, something that died, apparently for ever, in 1744.

BIBLIOGRAPHY

W. L. von Lütgendorff: *Die Geigen- und Lautenmacher vom Mittelalter bis zur Gegenwart* (Frankfurt am Main, 1904, rev. 6/1922/*R*1968)

H. Petherick: *Joseph Guarnerius: his Work and his Master* (London and New York, 1906/*R*1977)

W. H. Hill: *The Violin Makers of the Guarneri Family* (London, 1931)

R. Vannes: *Essai d'un dictionnaire universel des luthiers* (Paris, 1932, 2/1951/*R*1972 as *Dictionnaire universel des luthiers* and *R*1981 incl. suppl. 1959)

CHARLES BEARE

Guarumo. Natural trumpet of the Ecuadorian highlands. *See* HUARUMO.

Guasá. A bamboo rattle of the Pacific coastal region of Colombia. It is filled with seeds, stones or nails, and is similar to the *guacho* of the Atlantic coast, except that many needles of *chonta* (palm wood) are inserted through the wall of the bamboo into its cavity; these modify the timbre produced.

Guat. JEW'S HARP of the Roglai people of Vietnam. *See* ĐAN MÔI.

Guayo. Metal SCRAPER of Cuba and the Dominican Republic. In Cuba it has been largely replaced in many regions by the gourd scraper, also known as *guayo* (or *güiro*). This is usually long, with two holes, one in the back and the other formed by cutting off the neck. The front surface is incised deeply with parallel cuts, across which a wire or other scraping object is drawn. A cow horn incised with marks may also be used as a *guayo*.

In the Dominican Republic the (metal) *guayo* is either cylindrical or open like a grater, and is scraped with a thin metal object or nail. Its sound is metallic and strong, but not very high-pitched.

Gubgubī. Variable tension chordophone ('plucked drum') of Bengal (east India and Bangladesh). *See* ĀNANDALAHARĪ.

Gubo [gubu]. Unbraced gourd-resonated MUSICAL BOW of the Ngoni people of Malawi and Zambia, resembling the Zulu UGUBHU.

Gūdas. Displacement free aerophone of Lithuania (*see* AEROPHONE (411)). It consists of a forked stick with a wire or dried juniper root wound spirally round it. When held by one end and whirled in circles, it produces a continuous sound resembling a siren which was used to frighten brown bears. Analogous instruments are not known in neighbouring countries.

ARVYDAS KARAŠKA

Gudastviri. BAGPIPE of western Georgia (USSR). It consists of a bag (*guda*), a small blowpipe (*chreko*) and a double chanter (*stviri*), one pipe with six finger-holes and the other with three. It has no drone. The instrument is often decorated with metal, coloured glass, small chains and even gems. The *gudastviri* originated in Kartli in eastern Georgia but is now used to accompany recitative-like solo songs of the Rachin people. It is traditionally associated with the *mestvire*, professional musicians who perform heroic, patriotic or satirical songs of social comment as well as *shairis* (popular verses). See *VertkovA*, 125.

Gude (i). Set of flutes of the Boa (Bwa) people of northern Zaïre (*LaurentyA*, 188f). *See* MAPENGO.

Gude (ii). Single-headed laced conical drum of the Mbuti pygmies of Ituri Forest, Zaïre.

Gudok. Ancient three-string fiddle of Russia and Belorussia. It had a pear-shaped body about 80 cm long and was played held on the knee.

Gudugudu. Small zoomorphic SLIT-DRUM of the Zande people of north-eastern Zaïre (*LaurentyTF*, 140). *See* GUGU, (1).

Gudu-gudu [opon]. Small KETTLEDRUM of the Yoruba people of Nigeria. It is suspended against the chest and beaten with a leather strap held in each hand, as part of the DUNDUN hourglass drum ensemble.

Gue. A bowed lyre of Shetland. *See* ROTTE (ii).

Güegüe. Fourth largest single-headed drum in the Cuban ARARÁ ensemble. Because it is small, the drum body is held vertically by a movable iron tripod (it is the only Afro-Cuban drum with such a metal support). The head is made taut by a hoop, cord and spikes, used for all *arará* drums, and it is played with two flexible switches of a plant. It is typically used for rapid rhythms. The term *güegüe* appears to refer to blacks of that name in

Brazil, probably related to the Gangá blacks of Cuba. Thus the drum could be of Gangá origin, inserted in the Arará cult, the two groups having intermingled. See *OrtizIMA*, iii, 345, 352f.

JOHN M. SCHECHTER

Guere. Box-resonated LAMELLAPHONE of the Mfinu people of south-western Zaïre. It has metal keys (*LaurentyS*, 194).

Guero (Fr.). A term for the GÜIRO. The score of Stravinsky's *Rite of Spring* (1921) refers to the instrument as both 'rape guero' and 'guero (rape)'.

Guersan, Louis (*b* c1713; *d* Paris, after 1781). French violin maker. He was a pupil of Claude Pierray in Paris and eventually succeeded to his business. Besides instruments of the violin family he also produced fine viols, quintons and pardessus viols. The quality of his work is by no means consistent, though at its best, the modelling, craftsmanship and varnish are excellent. Although his model is essentially a personal one, there are traces of Pierray's influence. His cellos are almost always small and thus limited in their usefulness. However, his best work has never lacked a following and is exhibited in many European museums.

BIBLIOGRAPHY

R. Vannes: *Essai d'un dictionnaire universel des luthiers* (Paris, 1932, 2/1951/*R*1972 as *Dictionnaire universel des luthiers* and *R*1981 incl. suppl. 1959)

JAAK LIIVOJA-LORIUS

Guerze. Globular pottery VESSEL FLUTE of the Kpelle people of Liberia. They are used in sets of three different sizes. *Guerze* are played with small bells and mirlitons, and are believed to represent the voice of the *poro* spirit.

Guēv. BULLROARER of North Bougainville, Solomon Islands. They were used during initiation to represent the voice of a spirit being, Urar, and were kept secret from women, formerly under pain of death. See B. Blackwood: *Both Sides of Buka Passage* (Oxford, 1935), 215ff.

Gueyoumo. BULLROARER of the Kono people of Guinea. It consists of a lightly hollowed pisciform or triangular spatula 30 cm long which is attached to a cord.

Gugu. SLIT-DRUM of Zaïre. (1) Zoomorphic slit-drum, representing a buffalo or antelope, found in the northern region in the Ubangi-Uele area among the Lobala, Ngbaka, Barambo, Zande, Mamvu, Ngbele (Mangbele), Meje and Mangbetu peoples. These drums are used to transmit messages. The head and legs are carefully carved to express an attitude of impatience. The antelope shape may symbolize the speed of the transmitted message; the buffalo may suggest the sound. De Hen (1960) gives variant names for the Barambo drum as *nerube* or *eguluane*, for the Mamvu as *gogo* or *aligogo*, for the Ngbele as *nerube*, *neguru*, *gulu* or *tchembe*, and for the Zande as *gudugudu*; the Angba call the instrument *lungungu*. Similar zoomorphic drums found in north-western Zaïre, such as the Mbanja *kedengu*, are more likely to be carved in the form of a tortoise or reptile. The Mbole *ongungu*, Bali *mugungu* and Lengola *mungungu*, all of which are large drums, though not zoomorphic in shape would appear to be linguistically cognate with the smaller zoomorphic Angba *lungungu* and Mbanja *kedengu*. Some Pende slit-drums (*kikuvu*) are also made in animal form and used for nocturnal dances of the *mungonge* secret society.

(2) Cylindrical slit-drum of the Zande people of northern Zaïre. See BUGU.

(3) Footed cylindrical slit-drum of the Monga people.

BIBLIOGRAPHY
LaurentyTF, 133f, 139f
J.-N. Maquet: *Note sur les instruments de musique congolais* (Brussels, 1956)
F. J. de Hen: *Beitrag zur Kenntnis der Musikinstrumente aus Belgisch Kongo und Ruanda-Urundi* (Tervuren, 1960)
G. Knosp: *Enquête sur la vie musicale au Congo belge 1934–1935* (Tervuren, 1968)
J. GANSEMANS, K. A. GOURLAY

Gugucu [gūgūchū]. Small pyramid-shaped or conical hollow earthen aerophone of the Uraon tribal group of southern Bihar, India; it was known in the early decades of the 20th century. The narrow end of the instrument, which stood 15 to 22·5 cm high, was covered with a spider's web and the instrument was blown through an opening in the opposite end. The *gugucu* was made by young Uraon boys and played by boys and girls at communal dances. See S. C. Roy: *The Orāons of Chōtā Nāgpur* (Calcutta, 1915), 184.

CAROL M. BABIRACKI

Gugwah. Generic term for the side-blown animal-horn trumpet of the Kagoro people of Nigeria, cognate with the Morwa *gugwe* and the Kaje *agbah*. These and other peoples of southern Zaria have trumpet ensembles of up to seven instruments of different sizes (any of which may be duplicated) played in hocket with double-headed cylindrical drums. Small trumpets (*ajuyo agwah, angurung agwah*) are stopped by placing the free hand over the open end. Medium and large trumpets (*ctswa agwah, ayang agwah*) have a cow-horn bell. In performance the trumpets are controlled by the master drummer. They enter in a set order and, on a given signal from the drums, the players stop blowing their instruments to sing, resuming instrumental performance later. See D. W. Ames and K. A. Gourlay: 'Kimkim: a Women's Musical Pot', *African Arts*, xi/2 (1978), 56.

Guichard, A. G. *l'aîné* (*fl* Paris, 1827–45). French maker of brass instruments. He founded his factory in Paris in 1827, and by 1839 he was able to exhibit his work. He probably died in 1845, when the business passed into the ownership of P. L. Gautrot. Guichard introduced the manufacture of factory-built instruments known as *pacotille*, but also made superior hand-crafted specimens. His firm grew considerably, and by 1844 was employing 210 workmen, using production-line methods which were adopted by Gautrot. Guichard made natural trumpets, normally with numerous crooks, *Inventionshorns* and hunting horns. Even his *cornets à pistons* (derived from earlier posthorns in B♭ and G) had, in addition to B♭ and A shanks, a number of crooks for simplifying playing in various keys. A cornet in B♭ of 1836 had a key to change the pitch instantaneously to C. In 1832 he patented an *ophicleide-à-pistons* in E♭ which was in effect a combination of alto horn and baritone. Guichard was the maker of the clavicor, which had been invented by Danays and patented in 1838. This

had three Stölzel valves, two horizontally mounted for the right hand and the third vertically for the left hand (*see* CLAVICOR for illustration).

BIBLIOGRAPHY
L. A. de Pontécoulant: *Douze jours à Londres* (Paris, 1862)
A. Baines: *Brass Instruments: their History and Development* (London, 1976/R1980)
NIALL O'LOUGHLIN

Gui dounou. *See* DYI DUNU.

Guillami, Juan (*fl* Barcelona, *c*1720–65). Spanish violin maker. Although he was born and worked in Barcelona, he apparently received an Italian training, as evidenced in the tonal quality of his instruments and the fact that his model, largely after Stradivari, is also often reminiscent of the 18th-century Gagliano school. The varnish is an orange-red and quite individual in appearance. Besides using a printed label (with the latinized form of his name, Joannes), he also branded GUILLAMI by the soundpost inside the back of his instruments.

Guillami's son, also named Juan (*d* ? Barcelona, *c*1818–20), probably studied with him but failed to gain any significant recognition as a maker. His earlier instruments are stamped with his father's brand but later this practice was discontinued.

BIBLIOGRAPHY
R. Vannes: *Essai d'un dictionnaire universel des luthiers* (Paris, 1932, 2/1951/R1972 as *Dictionnaire universel des luthiers* and R1981 incl. suppl. 1959)
JAAK LIIVOJA-LORIUS

Guillaume, Edmé. French canon to whom the invention of the SERPENT has been attributed.

Guimbarda (Sp.; Fr. *guimbarde*). JEW'S HARP. *See also* BIRIMBAO.

Guinbri [gimbri, gmbri, gnibra, gombri, gumbri, gunbri, gunibri]. Large plucked lute with one to three strings of North Africa. It is particularly an instrument of the Gnawa brotherhood of Morocco, among whom it has three strings. In construction it is clearly related to the family of plucked lutes found throughout the West African savanna region (*see* KHALAM; KONTING; TIDINIT), although it is somewhat larger than them and the resonator is rectangular in shape. Farmer, in his study of the instrument (1928), traces its ancestry to the ancient Egyptian long-necked lute. The Moroccan *guinbri* usually accompanies singing and rhythmic clapping. A large metal jingle is attached to the end of the neck and extra percussive effect is obtained by the player striking the sound-table with his right-hand fingers. *See also* GURMI.

BIBLIOGRAPHY
M. Park: *Travels in the Interior Districts of Africa* (London, 1799)
H. G. Farmer: 'A North African Folk Instrument', *Journal of the Royal Asiatic Society of Great Britain and Ireland* (1928), 24
P. D. Schuyler: 'The Music of Islam and Sufism in Morocco', BM 30SL2027 [disc notes]
LUCY DURÁN

Guirbal. *See* GHIRBĀL.

Güiro. SCRAPER of the Caribbean, Panama and South America. In Cuba (where it is also known as *guayo* or *rascador*) it is usually made from the gourd of a climbing plant. It is elongated, with raised marks or frets close together on its sides; a switch is rubbed against the frets,

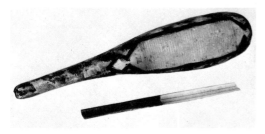

Cuban güiro (private collection)

producing a distinctive sound which gives rhythmic emphasis to the music. It is used in dance ensembles and the name is also applied to the ATCHERÉ, a large rattle with external strikers, used for religious rites of the Afro-Cuban Lucumí cult. In Puerto Rico, the *güiro* is used in most types of folk and popular music, and in certain religious festivals. In Panama, the *güiro* (or *guáchara*) accompanies the *mejorana* and *cumbia* folkdances. In Ecuador, where it is scraped with a small comb, the *güiro* is used by mestizos in Imbabura, by Quechuas in Tungurahua and by Afro-Ecuadorians in Esmeraldas Provinces.

The modern *güiro* has been used in orchestral scores, including Stravinsky's *The Rite of Spring* (Cortège du Sage), where it is called both 'rape guero' and 'guero (rape)'; in Ravel's *L'enfant et les sortilèges* the *güiro* or the *reco-reco* may be used in place of the specified scraped cheese-grater (*râpe à fromage*).

JOHN M. SCHECHTER, JAMES BLADES

Güiro de jobá [güiro de moyubá]. Afro-Cuban water-gourd percussion instrument. *See* JÍCARA DE AGUA and WATER-DRUM.

Guisarke. A term occasionally applied to the KISSAR.

Guitar (Fr. *guitare*; Ger. *Gitarre*; It. *chitarra*; Port. *violão*; Sp. *guitarra*). A string instrument of the lute family, plucked or strummed, and normally with frets along the fingerboard. It is difficult to define precisely what features distinguish guitars from other members of the lute family, because the name 'guitar' has been applied to instruments exhibiting a wide variation in morphology and performing practice. The modern guitar has six strings, a wooden resonating chamber with incurved sidewalls and a flat back. Although its earlier history includes periods of neglect as far as art music is concerned, it has always been an instrument of popular appeal, and has become an internationally established concert instrument endowed with an increasing repertory.

1. Structure of the modern classical guitar. 2. Origins. 3. The four-course guitar. 4. The five-course guitar. 5. The early six-string guitar. 6. The modern classical guitar. 7. Variants of the classical guitar. 8. The diffusion of folk guitars.

1. STRUCTURE OF THE MODERN CLASSICAL GUITAR. Fig.1 (p.88) shows the parts of the modern guitar. In instruments of the highest quality these are made of carefully selected woods: the back and sidewalls of Brazilian rosewood, the neck cedar and the fingerboard ebony; the face or table, acoustically the most important part of the instrument, is of spruce, selected for its resilience, resonance and grain (closeness of grain is considered important, and a good table will have a grain count of between 12 to 16 per inch). The table and back

are each composed of two symmetrical sections, as is the total circumference of the sidewalls. The table is supported by struts of Sitka spruce, which contribute greatly to the quality of sound. The traditional arrangement has the struts radiating from below the soundhole under the lower part of the table, hence the term 'fan-strutting'. Various other patterns, however, have resulted from experiments by different makers, and as high sound quality has been achieved by several of them, it is clear that one cannot speak of a standard strutting pattern; whatever the pattern, the table must be allowed to vibrate adequately. Vibrations of the strings are transmitted to the table by a rosewood bridge, which also acts as lower string fastener. The lower vibrating length of each string is determined by an ivory saddle in the bridge and by an ivory nut at the upper end. The frets (usually 19), giving a total range of three and a half octaves, are of nickel silver. The three upper strings are made of nylon, the three lower of nylon strands overspun with fine metal. Tuning is effected by rear pegs activating a geared mechanism that turns the bone rollers. The standard tuning is $E–A–d–g–b–e'$. Guitar music is notated an octave higher than it sounds.

There are two methods of joining the neck to the body – the 'Spanish method' and the 'dovetail method' (see fig.1). In the former the neck is projected into the body, and the sidewalls are slotted into the heel of the neck, while in the latter the body is completed first and the neck fitted into the top block. The Spanish method is the more difficult to achieve, but it results in a stronger joint between neck and body and is hence preferable as this is an area of great tension. Modern guitar decoration is limited to a mosaic inlay surrounding the soundhole, which may be repeated in the bridge; but the bridge more often has ivory purfling, which is also functional as it protects the wood from the pressure of the strings. Typical measurements for a guitar are: overall length 98 cm; string length 65 or 66 cm; width at the lower bout 37 cm, at the waist 24 cm, and at the upper bout 28 cm; body length 48·5 cm; nut to body 30 cm; depth at the lower bout 10 cm, at the upper bout 9·5 cm.

For a discussion of the acoustics of plucked string instruments, *see* ACOUSTICS, §I, 6. *See also* FRET.

2. ORIGINS. There has been much speculation on the origin of the guitar, and several theories have been proposed to account for its presence in Europe. These include some which regard it as a remote development from the Ancient Greek kithara – as suggested by the etymological relationship of 'kithara' and 'guitar'. Some writers claim to have discovered guitars among the long-necked lutes of early Mesopotamia and Anatolia. From a later period the so-called Coptic lutes found in Egypt, the carved resonators of which sometimes had flat backs and sidewalls, have also been regarded as predecessors of the guitar. One subject of disagreement has been whether the guitar was of indigenous European development or was instead among the instruments introduced into medieval Europe by the Arabs. These speculations often betray a lack of detailed analysis of the instruments considered; clarification will depend on a thorough study of their morphology and performing practice in the light of relevant ethnomusicological information. In the Hornbostel and Sachs classification system the guitar is a 'composite chordophone' of the lute type (*see* LUTE, §1, and CHORDOPHONE). An a priori approach to the problems involved carries little conviction; and the application of the name 'guitar', with its overtones of European musical practice, to oriental lutes

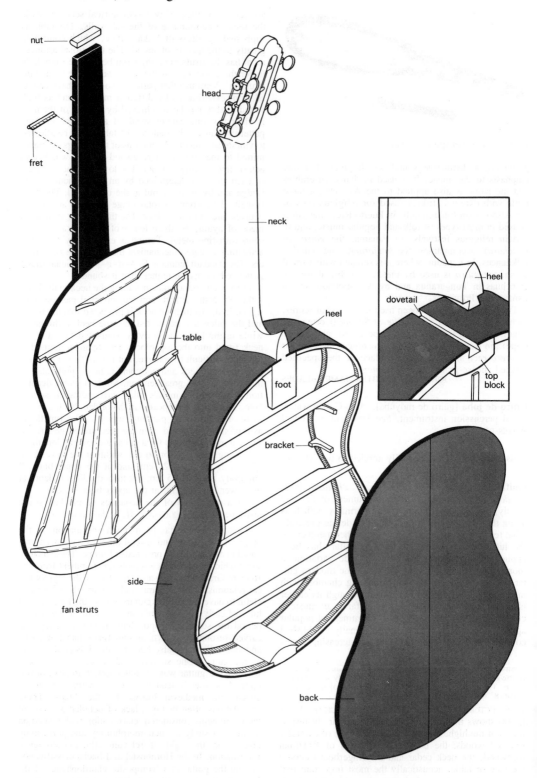

1. Exploded diagram of a modern guitar showing the Spanish and dovetail (see inset) methods of construction; the fan-strutting is in the traditional Torres pattern

betrays a superficial acquaintance with the instruments concerned. Only recently have scholars begun to explore the musical cultures of antiquity in a sufficiently scientific manner, so that there are many difficulties in correlating names and instruments. Further uncertainties arise in establishing the extent to which intercultural connections are a factor in the diffusion of instruments. This is particularly true of lutes in antiquity, which present great variety in their shapes and sizes.

The history of the guitar in Europe, however, can be traced back to the Renaissance with no great difficulty. As guitars from this period were constructed with both curved and flat backs, it would be incorrect, in determining their evolution, to concentrate solely on flat-backed instruments. Morphologically the main identifying feature of the Renaissance guitar is the characteristic outline of its frontal aspect, a shape it shared with the vihuela; this account therefore considers this feature in lutes from antiquity.

The earliest lutes were of the long-necked variety, and only rarely did the body shape deviate from round or pear-shaped. The well-known long-necked lute depicted at the Hittite site of Alaca Höyük does have incurved sides, but the overall shape is not that of the guitar because the incurvations extend almost the full length of the body and the full upper- and lower-bout curvature of the guitar is absent. Guitar-shaped resonators appeared in ancient Egyptian long-necked lutes (it has been suggested that a waisted gourd accounts for the form), but they have not persisted in later long-necked lutes. Short-necked lutes, among which the European guitar is classed, appeared many centuries later than the long-necked type. The earliest occurrence of the guitar shape in a short-necked lute was in central Asia shortly after the beginning of the Christian era (see fig.2). At this time central Asian lutes were of many kinds; the guitar shape is found in examples dating from the 1st to the 4th century. The type is not met again until its appearance (as a bowed instrument) in Byzantine miniatures of the 11th century, and from this time the guitar form was similarly depicted in medieval iconography. But it is notably absent in the many plucked lutes of the Middle Ages.

Instrument names related to 'guitar' occur in medieval literature from the 13th century onwards, but many are now thought to refer to medieval instruments such as the gittern, which differed in several respects from the Renaissance guitar (for a discussion of some of these early names, see GITTERN).

Medieval lutes and descriptions of their construction reveal that the body and neck were carved from one block of wood, and the table then fitted over the resonance cavity. An exception to this was the 'ūd, which had long enjoyed a high status in Arab music; by at least the 10th century it had progressed to a more delicate form, with its domed back fashioned out of a number of thin wooden strips, shaped and bent to form something of a hemisphere. Eventually the construction of the 'ūd and the woodworking techniques that produced it appear to have influenced makers in Europe, where in medieval times woodworking skills were still relatively primitive. Iconographical evidence suggests that the extension of the range of the European lute dates from the beginning of the 15th century (paired strings having been introduced in the 14th). A fifth course was added in the treble, and later in the 15th century a sixth course was added in the bass, resulting – to judge partly by 16th-century musical evidence – in the tuning $G/g-$

2. *Central Asian guitar-shaped lute: detail of a frieze (1st century AD) from Airtam, near Termez, Uzbekistan (Hermitage Museum, Leningrad)*

3. *Woman playing a French four-course guitar: 16th-century engraving*

$c/c'-f/f'-a/a-d'/d'-g'$. This interval pattern, but with all the courses tuned at unison, was shared by the *vihuela de mano*, which replaced the lute in Spain. 'Vihuela' was first qualified by *de mano* (finger-plucked) in the 15th century; earlier related names were *vihuela de peñola* and *vihuela de arco*. It seems clear that the finger-plucked vihuela was an adaptation of the guitar-shaped bowed instrument. The basic form was retained, but features better suited to a plucked instrument were adopted, namely a lute-type bridge and a central rose.

It was also during the 15th century that the Renaissance four-course guitar appeared, an instrument which had much in common with the lute and the vihuela. The strong influence from these two instruments is attributable to their artistic superiority to the guitar; the wider range afforded by their extra strings would have allowed more ambitious music to be played on or composed for them. Depictions of the four-course guitar from various regions have enough in common to indicate that a single type of instrument had been established in general usage; the complete outline of the guitar is apparent in them all, as are the central rose, the lute-type bridge and frets. The guitarist's right hand (in 16th-century depictions) approaches the strings from above (see fig.3); no plectrum is used (as this would not allow polyphonic music to be realized). One of the four-course guitar tunings had doubling at the upper octave in the lowest course. Other features of the lute that appeared in the guitar were the rose, the bridge (fixed to the table) and the rounded, ribbed back. The flat back was shared with the vihuela, as was the waisted frontal outline (for illustrations, *see* Vihuela).

3. The four-course guitar (Fr. *guiterre*, *guiterne*; It. *chitarrino*, *chitarra da sette corde*, *chitarra Napolitana*; Sp. *guitarra de quatro ordines*). 16th-century guitars were much smaller than the modern instrument, and the four-course instrument could be described as a treble guitar. Juan Bermudo (*Declaración de instrumentos musicales . . . libro quarto* (Osuna, 1555/R1957), chap. lxv) described the guitar as smaller (*mas corto*) than the vihuela and this is borne out both by contemporary iconography (fig.4) and by the technical requirements for the left hand in much of the surviving music. Even five-course guitars (as opposed to the five-course vihuelas described by Bermudo) seem to have been small instruments for most of the 16th century. The length of a five-course guitar made by Belchior Dias in 1581 (*GB-Lcm*; see fig.5a) is only 76·5 cm. Other differences from the modern guitar are those features that the 16th-century instrument had in common with other plucked instru-

ments of the period: a rose, often of intricate construction (fig.6, p.92) instead of an open soundhole; gut frets tied round the neck (eight to ten frets seems most usual); and a bridge set low in the table (this allows the Dias guitar to have a vibrating string length of 55·4 cm).

The basic interval pattern of the gut strings was 4th–major 3rd–4th; there was, however, a variety of tunings applied to the courses. Bermudo gave the tunings g/g'–c'/c'–e'/e'–a' (*temple nuevos*) and f/f'–c'/c'–e'/e'–a' (*temple viejos*); the latter is given in contemporary French guitar books as 'à corde avalée' (lowered). Bermudo said that the old tuning (*viejos*) was better for 'old romances and strummed music', and that the new tuning should be preferred for 'modern music'. These tunings have the fourth course in octaves; the lower, and thicker, of the pair of strings is called a 'bordón' by the Spanish and a 'bourdon' by the French. Not all music sources require this lower string. Scipione Cerreto (*Della prattica musica*, 1601) gave a totally re-entrant tuning with no lower octave on the fourth course: g'/g'–d'/d'–f♯'/f♯'–b', that is, Bermudo's *temple viejos* intervals but a tone higher. This tuning is corroborated by an anonymous print of 1645, *Conserto vago*, a suite of pieces for a trio consisting of guitar, lute and theorbo, in which the guitar has to be tuned as above in order to comply with the normal tunings of the other two instruments. Virtually all the evidence of iconography, music sources and tuning instructions indicate that the four-course guitar was a small, treble instrument; however, Michael Praetorius (*Syntagma musicum*, ii, 2/1619) mentioned the tuning c–f–a–d', and the recently discovered fragments of James Rowbotham's *The Breffe and Playne Instruction to Lerne to Play on the Gyttron and also the Cetterne* (London, 1568), give the same pitches as Praetorius. If these pitches were meant to be taken literally and not relatively, there must have been a larger four-course guitar as well, though it would not have been commonly found.

In the performance of polyphonic music guitar technique was similar to that of the lute and vihuela; the right hand was supported by the little finger resting on the bridge or on the table, and the production of sound was generally achieved by the thumb and first two fingers plucking the strings. Such a position was made possible by the low height of the strings over the table, which itself lay flush with the fingerboard. Music was notated in tablature. The various systems used four lines to represent the courses; in music printed in Spain the lowest line represents the highest-sounding course (establishing a physical correspondence between the instrument in playing position and the music), while this is reversed in French sources (establishing an intellectual relationship between the highest line and the higher sounds). The Spanish and Italian systems use numbers to indicate the frets to be stopped (0, open string; 1, first fret etc); the French system uses letters (*a*, open string; *b*, first fret etc). Rhythm is indicated by note values above the 'staff'; these follow the quickest-moving part, so longer-held notes have to be inferred by the performer. Although Bermudo gave advice on locating notes that might not be obtainable in some positions because of ostensibly Pythagorean tuning systems, tablature – and indeed, fretting – is actually based on a temperament with most or all of the semitones equal in size.

The earliest surviving music for the four-course guitar appeared in Alonso Mudarra's *Tres libros de música en*

4. Title-page of Guillaume Morlaye's 'Premier livre de chansons . . . en tablature de guiterne' (1555), showing a typical four-course guitar; note the small size of the guitar in comparison with the book on which it rests

(a)   (b)   (c)   (d)

5. Guitars from the 16th century to the 20th: (a) five-course, by Belchior Dias, Lisbon, 1581; (b) five-course, attributed to Jacob Stadler, Munich, c1625 (rose missing); (c) six-course by José Pagés, Cadiz, 1809; (d) six-course by José Ramirez; (a)–(c) Royal College of Music, London

cifras para vihuela (1546/R1980): four fantasias (one in the *viejos* tuning), a 'pavana' and a setting of *O guardame las vacas*, which uses the romanesca ground. The music is of the same high quality as Mudarra's vihuela music, which comprises the bulk of the collection. The earliest Italian source is Melchiore de Barberiis's lutebook *Opera intitolata contina Intabolatura di lanta . . . libro decimo* (1549[39]) in which are found four 'fantasias' for guitar. These are actually light dance pieces; one of them was reprinted by the Flemish publisher Pierre Phalèse (i) (1570) as a 'branle'.

It was in France that music for the four-course instrument flourished. Beginning with the (lost) first book of Guillaume Morlaye (1550) a series of guitar books was published by the printers Granjon and Fezandat which included music by Morlaye (book 1, *RISM* 1552[32]/R1980, see fig.4; book 2, 1553[34]/R1980; book 4, 1552[33]/R1980) and Simon Gorlier (book 3, 1551[22]/R1980). A concurrent series was published by the printers Le Roy and Ballard with music by Le Roy (book 1, 1551[23]/R1979; book 2, 1555/R1979; book 3, 1552/R1979; book 5, 1554[33]/R1979) and Grégoire Brayssing (book 4, 1553/R1979). The repertory in these publications comprises a wide range of material from simple dance settings and intabulations of chansons to rather fine fantasias. Some of the dance settings have virtuoso divisions and

the fantasias include four by the famous lutenist Alberto da Ripa which compare favourably with his best lute fantasias. Le Roy's second and fifth books are entirely for solo voice and guitar. Among Spanish sources Miguel de Fuenllana's vihuela collection *Orphénicalyra* (1554) also contains guitar music, including Juan Vasquez's *Covarde cavallero* and a *romance*, *Passavase el rey moro*, both for voice and guitar (the vocal line is indicated by red ciphers within the tablatures). There are also six fantasias and a setting of 'Crucifixus est'.

In England, as well, the four-course instrument enjoyed some popularity, to judge by Rowbotham's *The Breffe and Playne Instruction to Lerne to Play on the Gyttron*. Only fragments of the book survive but evidence indicates that it was a translation of one of Le Roy's tutors (also lost). There are also some English lute manuscript sources which contain samples of four-course guitar tablature (*GB-Lbm* Stowe 389; *GB-Lbm* Add.30513; *US-NH* 'Braye lutebook'). Phalèse, who was active in Louvain, printed two collections for the instrument (1570[35]; 1573, lost). Much of the music in the first book was taken from the earlier French publications. A number of Italian manuscript sources from the late 16th and early 17th centuries survive in European libraries. (For an extensive listing of guitar sources see Tyler, 1980, pp.123–52.)

6. *Front and side views (with detail of rose) of a five-course guitar by René Voboam, Paris, 1641 (Ash-molean Museum, Oxford)*

Although the four-course instrument is generally regarded as a Renaissance guitar because of its 16th-century repertory, it continued to be widely used, albeit mainly for playing popular music, throughout the 17th and 18th centuries. Agostino Agazzari (*Del sonare sopra'l basso* (1607) recommended its use in a continuo ensemble; the 1645 *Conserto vago* collection has already been mentioned. Pietro Milioni (*Corona del primo, secondo e terzo libro*, 1627) provided a chord chart for it as well as for the larger, five-course guitar, and thus provided a clue as to its use in the enormous repertory of strummed guitar music. In London John Playford published *A Booke of New Lessons for the Cithern and Gittern* (?2/1652), half of which is devoted to English popular tunes arranged for a small instrument tuned to guitar intervals. It is not clear whether this instrument, the gittern, is wire-strung like the cithern or whether the term 'gittern' was still used at this late date to indicate the guitar.

All known editions of Joan Carlos Amat's *Guitarra española* from 1626 to *c*1819 (1st edn, 1596, lost) contain a chapter on the four-course guitar, indicating perhaps the little instrument's continued, if limited, use through to the 19th century. It is definitely known that in Spanish and Portuguese cultures, both in the Old and New Worlds, small treble guitars have been in use and continue in use to the present day. The modern ukulele tuning $g'-c'-e'-a'$ is the same as Bermudo's tuning (without a *bordón*), and the alternative ukulele tuning $a'-d'-f\sharp'-b'$ is remarkably similar to Cerreto's re-entrant tuning of 1601.

4. THE FIVE-COURSE GUITAR (It. *chitarra spagnuola*; Sp. *guitarra*). Iconographic sources confirm that five-course guitar-like instruments were in use from at least the end of the 15th century, especially in Italy. The Italian term 'viola' was applied to these as well as to instruments with six and seven courses. The terms 'viola' and 'viola da mano' (and their Spanish equivalent, 'vihuela') were often used generically to mean instruments of this general type and shape; sometimes the small four-course instrument was also included. Fuenllana (f.IV), for example, wrote about the 'vihuela de Quatro Ordenes, Que Dizen Guitarra'. He also printed the earliest known music for a five-course instrument ('vihuela de cinco ordenes'), fantasias and vocal intabulations that require an instrument tuned to guitar intervals (starting from the fifth course: 4th–4th–major 3rd–4th), though he made no mention of specific pitches or stringing. Bermudo referred to a 'guitarra de cinco ordenes', saying that one could be made by adding to the four-course guitar a string a 4th above the existing first course (f.xxviii*v*). He also described new and unusual tunings for it as well as for a 'guitarra grande' of six courses and for the four-course instrument. No music survives for any of these tunings. The previously described Dias guitar could be an example of Bermudo's 'guitarra de cinco ordenes' (later Italian sources call this type of small instrument a 'chitarriglia').

A French source, the drawings of Jacques Cellier (*Recherches de plusieurs singularités*, *c*1585; *F-Pn* fonds fr. 9152), shows a four-course instrument (seven strings) with a tuning chart for a five-course instrument: $g-c/c'-e-a-d'$. This re-entrant tuning would be, if the third course were raised a semitone, a typical stringing arrangement (with its bourdon on the fourth course) for the playing of much of the later Italian and French 'art' music written for guitar. The pitch with the first course at *d'* was also fairly common (see, for example, Benedetto Sanseverino, *Intavolatura facile* (1620), though a pitch with the first course at *e'* was to become the standard. Spanish sources often recommended *bordones* on both the fourth and fifth courses, especially if the guitar was to be used only for strumming. The earliest known edition of Amat's booklet on the guitar (1626) gives the following tuning: *A/a–d/d'–g/g–b/b–e'*; one assumes that the lost first edition (1596) gave the same information.

From the 17th century, tuning information frequently indicated no bourdons at all. This produced a totally re-entrant tuning: *a/a–d'/d'–g/g–b/b–e'* with the lowest pitch that of the third course (see Luis de Briçeño: *Método . . . para aprender a tañer la guitara a lo español* (1626); Marin Mersenne: *Harmonie universelle*, ii (1636); Francesco Valdembrini: *Libro primo d'intavolatura di chitarra* (1646), *Libro secondo* (c1647); Antoine Carré: *Livre de guitarre* (1671); Gaspar Sanz: *Instrucción de música sobre la guitarra española* (1674)). One source for this re-entrant tuning offers another variant: *a/a–d'/d'–g/g'–b/b–e'* with an upper octave on the third course (*I-MOe* Campori 612.X.L.10.21). The most common modification to the re-entrant type tuning was *a/a–d/d'–g/g–b/b–e'* which, judging by the musical requirements of their tablatures, was used by the leading composers of guitar solos of the time: Francesco Corbetta, Angelo Michele Bartolotti, Giovanni Battista Granata, Robert de Visée (see ex.1), Ludovico Roncalli, and others.

The reason for these re-entrant tunings becomes clear from the original tablatures: in much of the 'art' music for guitar (as opposed to exclusively strummed music), the high, re-entrant fifth course was used melodically

7. *End view of a five-course guitar by Jacob Stadler, Munich, 1624, later converted into a chitarra battente (private collection)*

in scale passage-work in conjunction with the other treble courses; rarely was the fifth course used as a bass. The fourth course too was used most often in the same fashion as the fifth. A typical idiom was that which Sanz called 'campanellas' (little bells): as many open strings as possible were employed in the notes of scale passages, so that the notes rang on, one melting into the next in the manner of a harp or bells (see ex.2). Even when a bourdon was used on the fourth course the stringing arrangement was technically important, with the upper octave string placed nearest the fifth course and the bourdon nearest the third course; this allowed the player the choice of striking the upper of the pair alone (needed most frequently), or including the bourdon when the music required the lower octave. This stringing was mentioned by Lucas Ruiz de Ribayaz, Antonio Stradivari and Denis Diderot among others and is shown in a number of iconographical sources.

It was up to the player to decide which of the variety of possible tunings was suitable for each source of music; this was not always easy. In general, the sources for exclusively strummed music could be used with any tuning because questions of proper chord inversions and harmonic niceties were rarely touched upon in this repertory. For much of the mixed style of guitar music, which used PUNTEADO technique, some strummed chords (*see* RASGUEADO), and frequent *campanella* passages (found in the most important Italian and French sources), a re-entrant tuning, usually with a bourdon on the fourth course, was suitable. Occasional sources such as Francisco Guerau's *Poemo harmonico* (1694) seem to require bourdons on the fourth and the fifth courses.

With its unique tunings and its emphasis on brighter, higher-ranged music, in an idiom generally quite unlike that of the lute or any other plucked instrument of the time, the five-course guitar was very different from the modern guitar. Only from the middle of the 18th century did the character of the guitar begin to approach that of the instrument we know today in its development of a bass range and its playing technique. Average measurements of the five-course Baroque guitar were: overall length 92 cm; string length 63–70 cm; widths 20 cm–17 cm–24 cm; depth varied according to whether the back was flat or rounded (vaulted). The five-course guitar retained features of the smaller, four-course instrument, but curved pegboxes with laterally inserted pegs no longer appeared.

Although many guitars had rounded backs, this fea-

Ex.1 Robert de Visée: Suite no.9 (*Livre de pièces pour la guittare*, 1686)

Arrows indicate direction of *rasgueado* strokes. Small notes in parentheses are those produced by the upper octave of the fourth course.

Ex.2 Gaspar Sanz: 'Canarios', *Instrucción de música*, i (1674)

The numbers in circles indicate the courses on which the notes are played

8. Front and back views of a five-course guitar (now adapted for six courses) by Joachim Tielke, Hamburg, 1693 (Victoria and Albert Museum, London)

ture alone does not identify the later, special type of guitar known today by its 19th-century name, the *chitarra battente*. Developed in the mid-18th century along the lines of the newly perfected Neapolitan mandolin, the instrument generally had a deeply vaulted back, but metal rather than gut strings and frets. The strings passed over a movable bridge and were fixed at the bottom of the body (fig.7). Like the Neapolitan mandolin, the table of the *chitarra battente* was canted downwards from the bridge instead of being completely flat as on the gut-strung guitar. Although it generally had paired strings, the *chitarra battente* could also have three strings to a course. It seems to have been used primarily for popular music accompaniments, and was probably played with a plectrum. There is no known repertory for it.

Many Baroque guitars have survived, and one of the most noticeable aspects of these instruments is the extent to which they were decorated. This abundance of highly decorated instruments is probably due to the fact that these precious 'objets d'art' were more sought after and preserved by collectors than were their plainer and more unassuming counterparts. A survey of contemporary pictures reveals that instruments made of plain woods and with relatively little decoration were actually more common. In museum collections there are many instruments by makers such as Matteo and Giorgio Sellas, Giovanni Tessler, René and Alexander Voboam, Joachim Tielke (fig.8) and Antonio Stradivari (fig.9). The two surviving instruments by Stradivari are beautifully proportioned with little decoration, though their plainness has been heightened over the years by the removal of decorative details such as the traditional 'moustaches' on either side of the bridge.

The earliest notation specifically for the five-course guitar dates from the latter part of the 16th century. Scholars are not in agreement as to whether an Italian manuscript, supposedly copied *c*1595 by Franco Palumbi (*F-Pn* Español 390), or Amat's booklet of 1596

9. Guitar by Antonio Stradivari, Cremona, 1688 (?1680) (Ashmolean Museum, Oxford)

represents the first appearance of a chord notation system designed for the guitar. In both sources complete five-note chords for the left hand are represented in shorthand by a simple symbol. Palumbi's Italian system used different letters of the alphabet and Amat's Spanish system used numbers. These radically different notations, implying that the performer was to think only in terms of vertical block harmonies, was characteristic of the new Italian trends in the development of monody. Indeed, it is perhaps significant that in the 1589 Florentine *intermedi*, a major landmark in the development of the new monodic style, two guitars were used in Cavalieri's famous *Ballo del Gran Duca*, a piece which remained popular for at least another century. The Italian *alfabeto* system became the standard practical one, while the Spanish system was rarely encountered outside books of musical theory.

Significantly, a Florentine guitar book was the earliest printed collection of music for the new *alfabeto* system, Girolamo Montesardo's *Nuova inventione d'intavolatura per sonare li balletti sopra la chitarra spagnuola, senza numeri e note* (1606). With a few modifications, Montesardo's system was the standard one of the 17th century, during which time an abundance of guitar books appeared in print using only this system for strummed chord solos (many of the pieces could also be considered accompaniment parts for use in ensembles). The important writers of *alfabeto* books were: Foriano Pico (1608), Giovanni Ambrosio Colonna (1620, 1623, 1637), Sanseverino (1620), Carlo Milanuzzi (1622, 1623, 1625), Milioni (1624, 1627), Milioni and Lodovico Monte (1627, 1637, 1644 etc), Giovanni Battista Abatessa (1627, 1635, 1650, 1652), Giovanni Paolo Foscarini (1629), Corbetta (1639), Agostino Trombetti (1639), Antonio Carbonchi (1643), Carlo Calvi (1646), Tomaso Marchetti (1635), Giovanni Bottazzari (1663), Giovanni Pietro Ricci (1677) and Antonio di Michele (1680); for full details of sec-

10. Technique of playing the guitar near the bridge (for punteado playing), and above the rose (for strumming): two sketches of a guitarist by Jean-Antoine Watteau (1684–1721), in the British Museum, London

ond and subsequent editions of many of these collections see Tyler, 1980, pp.123–58. The last known *alfabeto* book was an edition of Milioni and Monte's 1637 book in 1737.

In addition to the *alfabeto* sources of guitar solos, there is an enormous body of publications of Italian arias employing the guitar as the instrument to accompany the voice. In this repertory are found publications by many of the major vocal composers of the time, such as Stefano Landi (1620, 1627) and Sigismondo d'India (1621, 1623), and several books by Andrea Falconieri, Johann Hieronymus Kapsperger, Milanuzzi, Giovanni Battista Vitali, Biagio Marini, Guglielmo Minischalchi, Allessandro Grandi (i), and others. In the collections with contributions by various composers are found five arias by Monteverdi (Milanuzzi, 1624, *RISM* 1634[7]) all unique to these prints, as well as arias by Frescobaldi (*VogelB* 1621[2]), Domenico Mazzochi (*RISM* 1621[16]) and Cavalli (*RISM* 1634[7]). The subject of guitar accompaniment in this important 17th-century aria repertory has not yet been studied, nor has the role of the guitar as a widely used continuo instrument been sufficiently stressed.

In addition to devising accompaniments from the harmonic indications of the *alfabeto*, as the aria books required him to do, the guitarist also learned to read and improvise a CONTINUO accompaniment from the bass line (both with and without figures). Although, because of its tunings, the Baroque guitar was often unable to sound the true bass note, nevertheless an idiomatic continuo accompaniment could be realized for the proper harmonies. The true bass line was played by another, appropriate instrument such as a theorbo or cello. The prefaces of most of the aria books give a chart instructing the guitarist on how to read from the bass, but many of the books of solos give far more detailed instructions. Corbetta's books of 1643 and 1648 give continuo-playing

information, as do Foscarini's of 1640. Sanz devoted an entire section of his book to guitar continuo playing and Santiago de Murcia's *Resumen de acompañar la parte con la guitarra* (1714) was, as its title suggests, in large part devoted to instruction in guitar continuo playing. But the most thorough and extensive instructions of all appeared in Nicola Matteis's *Le false consonanse della musica* (c1680) and the later English edition *The False Consonances of Musick* (1682). This tutor for guitar continuo playing is one of the most useful and detailed of any 17th century continuo treatise for any instrument (including keyboard).

As well as the strummed style of guitar music found in the *alfabeto* sources of the early 17th century, a new style of guitar music began to appear in print from c1630 with Foscarini's second and third books (published together, n.d.). Although one of the chief assets of the guitar was its ability to play block chords in a rhythmic strumming style (this was considered to be the true idiom of the guitar), Foscarini adapted lute tablature and technique in combination with the strummed chords to arrive at a mixed style of solo guitar writing. In his preface he was apologetic about the lute-like elements. It was this new mixed style that was used by the finest guitar composers of the 17th and the early 18th centuries. Although Corbetta included some very fine solos in his 1639 book, it was Angelo Michele Bartolotti who, in 1640, produced the first fully developed, masterful examples of the new idiom, and his second book (c1655) contained some of the finest Baroque guitar music of the 17th century. It was Corbetta, however, who became the best-known Italian guitar composer, with his publications of 1643 and 1648, which contained music of the highest order. Other major Italian writers for the guitar were Granata (1646, c1650, 1651, 1659, 1674, 1680, 1684), Valdambrini (1646, c1647), Domenico Pellegrini (1650), Francesco Asioli (1674, 1676), Matteis (c1680,

1682), and Roncalli (1692). It is ironic that, although the guitar was known as a Spanish instrument, it was in Italy that its repertory was first developed.

In France the five-course guitar was not held in high esteem. Both Mersenne and Pierre Trichet referred to it in disparaging terms, and the general opposition is mentioned in Briçeño's *Método . . . para aprender a tañer la guitara* (1626), which, as the title suggests, is a work advocating the chordal style of performance. Briçeño's book, however, did not succeed in popularizing the instrument, and only later in the century did further publications appear. These reflect an interest in the guitar in court circles, engendered by Corbetta. His *La guitarre royalle* (1674) was dedicated to Louis XIV; although the *rasgueado* style is a strong feature of the pieces in the book, the alphabet has been abandoned and greater freedom achieved by indicating the notes of the chords individually. Corbetta was succeeded by Robert de Visée (c1660–c1720), who became the king's guitar tutor in 1719. His *Livre de guittarre dédié au roy* was published in 1682, and a second work, *Livre de pièces pour la guittare*, appeared in 1686; both contain suites of various length, made up of an introductory prelude followed by dances – allemande, courante, sarabande, gigue, passacaille and others. De Visée also produced a collection of pieces for theorbo and lute, and left a number of works in manuscript. Remy Médard, in his *Pièces de guitare*, acknowledged his debt to Corbetta, who taught him, but like de Visée he cultivated a more delicate style. A concern with melodic and contrapuntal movement is also evident in *Nouvelles découvertes sur la guitare* (op.1, 1705) by François Campion (c1686–1748).

Corbetta's first *La guitarre royalle* (1671; fig.11) was dedicated to Charles II of England, who was an enthusiastic performer. The guitar was extremely fashionable in England; Corbetta, who went to England in 1662, counted many of the nobility among his pupils. However, some distaste for the instrument was expressed, and Pepys, for one, held the guitar in low esteem. (The inclusion in Pepys's library, which survives intact in Cambridge, of a guitar tutor of Cesare Morelli, and the evidence of his own compositions for guitar and voice, suggests, however, that he was eventually won over by the instrument.) The distinction drawn by William Turner in 1697 between the 'brushing way' and the 'pinching way' indicates that, as well as Corbetta's more complex music, there was no lack of strumming in England. Indeed it is likely that a lost work, *Easie Lessons on the Guittar for Young Practitioners*, recorded in 1677 as by Seignior Francisco, was by Corbetta himself. In 18th-century England the guitar went out of fashion. It was replaced by the English guitar which had little in common with the guitar proper, being similar in shape to the cittern and having the tuning c–e–g–c'–e'–g'.

The five-course guitar was first known in Germany as an instrument for strumming. Praetorius so described it, but he also related that 'it can be used to good effect in other graceful *cantiunculae* and delightful songs by a good singer'. Later in the century the guitar appeared in consort with the lute, angel lute and viol, accompanying a collection of songs by Jakob Kremberg, *Musicalische Gemüths-Ergötzung* (1689).

Corbetta's presence in the Netherlands is attested by his *Varii scherzi di sonate per la chitara spagnola*, published in Brussels in 1648. The interest engendered by Corbetta was maintained through the 17th century,

although native sources are lacking until the following century, when François le Cocq's *Recueil de pièces de guitarre* appeared (1729). As well as Le Cocq's compositions, the collection contains works by Corbetta, Sanz, De Visée, Granata and other 17th-century guitarists (added by Jean-Baptiste Castillon, to whom Le Cocq had dedicated the book). A manuscript collection from the Netherlands is *Princes An's Lute Book*, for five-course guitar.

An undated Spanish source by Antonio de Santa Cruz, *Música de vihuela*, is despite its title not to be compared with the 16th-century vihuela books, as its contents consist of 17th-century Spanish dances notated in five-line tablature. It includes the chord alphabet and was obviously intended for the five-course guitar. The most important source of guitar music in 17th-century Spain is the *Instrucción* by Gaspar Sanz, eight editions of which appeared between 1674 and 1697. Sanz, in his preface, states that he went to Italy to study music and became an organist in Naples. He later went to Rome where he studied the guitar with an important composer of the time, Lelio Colista (some of whose guitar music survives in *B-Bc*, littera S no.5615). He also states that he studied the works of Foscarini, Granata and Corbetta. There are many Italian as well as Spanish dance pieces in his publications and he employs a mature and fully integrated style of mixed writing with an equal balance of strummed chords and *punteado* style, especially in his later *passacalles* of 1697.

The *Luz y norte musical* (Madrid, 1677) by Lucas Ruiz de Ribayaz is a work devoted to the guitar and the harp; most of the guitar music was plagiarized from Sanz. Guerau's book of 1694 is notable for containing music in an almost totally *punteado* style, quite different from Sanz and the majority of other guitar composers. Other

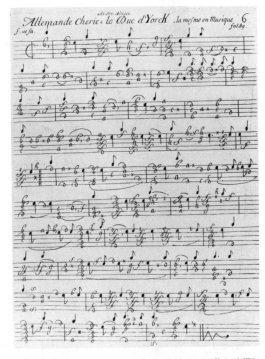

11. A page from Corbetta's 'La guitarre royalle' (1671)

Spanish sources are Santiago de Murcia's *Resumen* (1714) and his manuscript *Passacalles y obras* (1732) which contain music of a very high standard; De Murcia's own *preludios* tend to be both original and masterful, though a study of concordances reveals that the majority of pieces in these two works are actually arrangements of French court music, many of pieces by Lully as well as Le Cocq and Corbetta.

The music for the five-course guitar discussed so far can be regarded as the 'classical' repertory for the late Renaissance and Baroque instrument. On the whole, this music calls for the characteristic re-entrant tunings that were so important to the playing style and idioms employed during these periods and which made the guitar unique. But the nature of the guitar changed noticeably in the middle of the 18th century, along with musical styles in general. The change seems to have occurred first in France, where the guitar began to be used primarily to accompany the voice, using an arpeggiated style similar to that of keyboard instruments. The new style required true bass notes and as early as 1764 (*Journal de musique*, April) instructions for proper accompaniments stressed the use of a bourdon on the fifth course. The appearance of many guitar tutors in France between 1763 and c1800, all for a five-course guitar tuned $A/a–d/d'–g/g–b/b–e'$, as well as the gradual abandonment of tablature in favour of staff notation, leaves little doubt that the guitar was becoming an instrument much closer in character and playing styles to the modern guitar than to the Baroque instrument. Soon, even the double courses in octaves were abandoned in favour of single strings and, as early as 1785, a sixth string was indicated (*Etrennes de Polymnie* (Paris, 1785), p.148).

Historical statements referring to the guitar as an easy instrument should be treated with caution. Such a dismissive attitude is valid only when it is directed towards the guitar at its simplest level. The judgment is certainly not true in the context of art music, where textures more complex than a series of chord patterns demand accu-

12. Front and back views, and view of internal structure of a six-course guitar by Josef Benedid, Cadiz, late 18th century (private collection)

racy of fingering and a high degree of coordination. These
are of particular importance for the Baroque five-course
guitar, which, though first used as a popular instrument,
later gave rise to a literature that presents textures similar to those of the lute. Five-course guitar music has yet
to be heard widely on the instrument for which it was
written. Performance on the modern guitar is only an
approximation of the original sound, as modern tuning
does not allow the music to be realized faithfully.

5. THE EARLY SIX-STRING GUITAR. The transition from the
five-course guitar to the instrument with six single strings
took place during the closing decades of the 18th century in either France or Italy – notwithstanding the claim
by the German maker Jacob Augustus Otto that Nau-
mann, Kapellmeister at Dresden, was responsible for
the added lower E string. During the transitional period
instruments with five single strings and others with six
courses were built; instances of the latter had occurred
earlier in the period of the five-course guitar, but information on tunings suggests that the pattern 4th–4th–4th–
major 3rd–4th (equivalent to a five-course tuning with
an additional 4th) was not employed. Changes in the
basic instrument were many, and the guitar lost much
that it had in common with the lute, establishing during
the early decades of the 19th century the form that was
to develop into the modern guitar. Machine heads were
used instead of wooden pegs, fixed frets (first ivory or
ebony, then metal) instead of gut; an open soundhole
replaced the rose; the bridge was raised to a higher position (and a saddle and pins introduced to fasten the
strings). The flat back became standard, and proportions of the instrument changed to allow the positioning
of the 12th fret at the junction of body and neck. Separate fingerboards were introduced, at first flush with the
table, later raised to lie 2 mm or so above it. The rectangular peghead gave way to heads of various designs,
often a distinguishing mark of the maker. Generally,
lavish decoration disappeared, though some ornate guitars
were made in the 19th century. The most important innovation, however, was the introduction of fan-strutting,
first used in six-course guitars made in Cadiz by José
Pagés and Josef Benedid (figs.5c and 12). As well as
fan-strutting in the lower half of the table, a cross-
strutting system appeared in the part of the table above
the soundhole. Other important makers of this period
were René François Lacote of Paris and Lewis Panormo,
active in London. Instruction books reveal that there
was no standard approach to playing technique. Earlier
traditions persisted; the right hand was still supported
on the table (on some instruments a piece of ebony was
let into the table to prevent wear), although Nicario
Jauralde (A Complete Preceptor for the Spanish Guitar)
warned against resting the little finger on the table as
this prevents the hand moving for 'changes in Piano
and Forte' and inhibits 'the other fingers acting with Agility'. Right-hand finger movement was still confined
mainly to the thumb and first two fingers. The technique
for attacking the strings was normally tirando, with the
fingertips rising after plucking; apoyando, in which the
finger brushes past the string and rests on the string below,
was little mentioned and apparently not generally applied.
Performers were divided over whether or not to employ
the fingernails in the production of sound; Fernando Sor
(1778–1839), the leading Spanish player, dispensed with
nails, while his compatriot, Dionysio Aguado (1784–
1849), employed them. The left-hand thumb was some-

13. Title-page of Alfred Bennett's 'Instructions for the
Spanish Guitar'

times used to stop notes on the lowest (E) string, a
technique made possible by the narrow fingerboard. The
instrument was held in a variety of ways, and was often
supported by a strap round the player's neck; Aguado
even invented a special stand – the tripodion – on which
to rest the instrument. Tablature was abandoned in the
second half of the 18th century, when staff notation
appeared, at first in instruction books. The earliest staff
notation for guitar evolved in France and in Italy, the
notational conventions for violin music being evident in
early solo pieces for 6-string – or, as it is now known,
classic – guitar. The convention of notating guitar music
on one staff headed by the G clef, the actual sounds
being an octave below written pitch, is still in use.

The six-course guitar appeared in Spain some time
before 1780, the date of Obra para guitarra de seis
órdenes by Antonio Ballesteros. Further methods
appeared in 1799: Fernando Ferrandière's Arte de tocar
la guitarra española and Don Federico Moretti's Prin-
cipios para tocar la guitarra de seis órdenes. Both Sor
and Aguado were indebted to Moretti for making them
aware of the possibility of part-writing for the guitar,
and the two became very active outside their native Spain.
Aguado, whose Escuela de guitarra was published in
Madrid in 1825, settled for a while in Paris, but Sor
pursued the career of a travelling recitalist, bringing the
guitar to a much wider audience. Before leaving Spain,
Sor had acquired some reputation as a composer; his
opera Telemaco en la Isla de Calipso was successfully
staged in Barcelona in 1797. In Madrid Sor's patron
was the Duchess of Alba. Also living in Madrid was
Boccherini, who, inspired by the enthusiasm of his
patron, the Marquis of Benavente, made arrangements
of several of his quintets to include the guitar.

14. Six-string Spanish guitar: oval medallion painted on the back of a six-string guitar by Altimira, Barcelona, mid-19th century (Victoria and Albert Museum, London)

Sor left Spain in 1813, a move dictated by the political circumstances, and headed for Paris, where he stayed for two years. He visited London, where he gave several recitals, returning to Paris for a production of his ballet *Cendrillon*. The success of this work enabled him to visit Moscow and St Petersburg, where he played before the court. He then returned to Paris and, except for a further visit to London, resided there until his death in 1839. Paris was one of the main centres of interest in the guitar, and several other virtuoso performers settled there, including Matteo Carcassi (1792–1853) and Ferdinando Carulli (1770–1841). The latter was responsible for *L'harmonie appliquée à la guitare*, the only known theoretical work for the instrument of the early 19th century. It is limited in scope, offering not much more than chordal and arpeggio accompaniment, typical of much guitar music of the period. Paganini abandoned the violin for a while in favour of the guitar, for which he composed several works. A French guitar made by Grobert bears the signatures of Paganini and Berlioz, who included the guitar in his *Grand traité d'instrumentation et d'orchestration modernes* op.10 (1843). The treatment he accorded the guitar is limited, and he commented that 'it is almost impossible to write well for the guitar without being a player on the instrument'.

The most important Italian guitarist was Mauro Giuliani (1781–1829). He first achieved fame in Vienna, where he was established from 1806 to 1819. As well as giving solo recitals, Giuliani appeared with the pianists Hummel and Moscheles and the violinist Mayseder. In 1819 he returned to Italy, settling in Rome and later

Naples, where he continued to give recitals. His daughter Emilia was also a talented guitarist, and they performed together in public. Vienna, like Paris, had many enthusiastic guitarists, and much simple music was published to cater for the demand: Leonhard von Call produced many pieces of this kind, as did Diabelli. Enthusiasm for the guitar was carried to England about 1815, where numerous tutors appeared during the first third of the century. The *Giulianiad*, one of the earliest journals devoted to the guitar, appeared in 1833. Although interest waned in the second half of the century, the publications – into the 1890s – of Mme Sidney Pratten (Catharina Josepha Pelzer), the leading English performer, reveal that there was still a public for the guitar used in a facile way.

The bulk of 19th-century publications was designed to acquaint the public with what was virtually a new instrument; as such many are didactic, and also limited in scope, as it soon became clear that few amateurs were sufficiently dedicated to master the more demanding works of the guitarist-composers. The popularity of the guitar lay in the ease with which one could manage a simple accompaniment to a song, and many of the practical tutors were limited to expounding the fundamental skills needed to achieve this. The simple pieces that take the performer a stage beyond this elementary level contain many clichés, and, as they are the products of guitarists, generally lie easily under the fingers. At a higher level are the studies designed to prepare the performer for recital works; most successful in this context are Sor's studies, which are still of value, but those by Aguado, Carcassi and Napoléon Coste are also notable. It is to the guitarists themselves that one must turn for the best compositions from this period. Although composers of stature were acquainted with the guitar, they wrote nothing for it. Berlioz's criticism of non-playing composers, that they 'give it things to play . . . of small effect', is valid. The achievements of Sor and Giuliani in establishing a repertory of large-scale works is the most notable feature of this period. Their output ranges from easy pieces – always in demand by the publishers – to extended works for the solo instrument and diverse combinations of instruments. Giuliani composed many variation sets, three concertos (opp.30, 36 and 70), two

Ex.3 Fernando Sor: 'Andante largo', *Six petites pièces* op.5 no.5 (?1824)

duos for guitar and violin or flute (opp.84 and 85), a work for guitar, violin and cello (op.19), and one for guitar with string quartet (op.65). Sor's textures are sometimes more complex than Giuliani's, and richer in harmonic variety. In his sonatas (opp.22 and 25) Sor introduced a larger number of themes than is usual in this form, thereby compensating for the restrictions in development imposed by the limitations of the instrument. Although they cannot be classed as works of great stature, the compositions of the early 19th-century guitarists are often charming, elegant and vivacious enough to be heard with pleasure (see ex.3).

6. THE MODERN CLASSICAL GUITAR. The early 19th-century guitar was further developed in the second half of the century by the Spanish maker Antonio de Torres Jurado (1817–92), whose experiments led to instruments that became models for his successors. The guitar thus achieved a standard size and form for the first time in its history (see fig.5 above). Torres increased the overall dimensions of the instrument and established the vibrating length of the strings at 65 cm; he developed the fan-strutting system introduced by his predecessors in Cadiz, using a system of seven struts radiating from below the soundhole, with two further struts lying tangentially below the 'fan'. The modern bridge, with the strings passing over the saddle to be tied to a rectangular block (see fig.15) is also attributable to Torres, and has become standard since his time. It is in the strutting that modern makers have experimented most, varying both the number and the pattern of struts, and even extending the system to include the part of the table above the soundhole. The latest improvement in tone production was the adoption of nylon in place of gut strings in 1946. For a time the improvements brought about by Torres remained confined to Spain, where a number of distinguished makers succeeded him: Vicente Arias, Manuel Ramirez, Enrique García, Marcelo Barbero and – active

16. Andrés Segovia, 1963

15. Modern bridge on a guitar ('La Salvaora') by José Romanillos

in the mid-20th century – José Ramirez, Manuel Contreras, Marcelino Lopez Nieto and others. The revival of interest in the guitar in the 20th century has resulted in the appearance of outstanding makers in other countries: Hermann Hauser (Germany), Robert Bouchet (France), David Rubio (England), and others in Japan, where the instrument has become extremely popular.

Francisco Tárrega (1852–1909), though active in promoting the modern playing technique, did not invent the *apoyando* stroke singlehanded; it is at least as old as Dionysio Aguado. When used on a large instrument,

such as the Torres guitar, this technique and the unsupported *tirando* spurred on the development of a rich repertoire of original etudes and transcriptions for the classical guitar (as it was now called). The larger instrument rested more comfortably on the left thigh than the early 19th-century guitar, and it became standard practice to hold it in this way. Tárrega did not use the fingernails in his right-hand technique, and in this he was followed by his pupil Emilio Pujol (*b* 1886), but Miguel Llobet (1878–1938), also a pupil of his, preferred to use them. Segovia adopted a more relaxed right-hand position than that of Tárrega (see fig.16) and a technique employing the fingernails, in which he has been followed by contemporary recitalists. It is in the right-hand position that one sees most variation among modern performers. The Segovia position entails the strings being sounded by the left side of the nails, whereas the position favoured by the French guitarist Ida Presti (1924–67), adopted by the American recitalist Alice Artzt, brings the right side of the nails into contact with the strings.

It is thus only during the last 100 years that the guitar has been established in its modern form and its technique developed accordingly. At the beginning of this period it lacked a repertory that would have given it a status comparable with that of other instruments. The problem of a meagre literature was first approached by transcribing works from other media, a practice initiated by Tárrega and continued by his successors. Suitable material was obviously to be found in the repertories for instruments closely related to the guitar (i.e. the lute and the vihuela), but works for bowed instruments, and keyboard, were also featured in recitals. Much more important, however, is the extent to which the guitar's repertory has been enlarged in the 20th century by composers who were not guitarists. Segovia, the leading instigator of this departure from the tradition of guitarist-composers, has made it his life-work to raise the guitar's status to that of an internationally respected concert instrument, and his artistry has been a source of inspiration both to players and to composers.

In 1920 Falla wrote *Homenaje pour le tombeau de Claude Debussy* for Llobet, proof of his belief that the guitar 'is coming back again, because it is peculiarly adapted for modern music'. Other Spanish composers have favoured a more nationalist idiom: Joaquin Turina (1882–1949), Federico Moreno Torroba (*b* 1891) and Joaquín Rodrigo (*b* 1901). All produced works for Segovia, and Rodrigo has dedicated compositions to other Spanish recitalists such as Narciso Yepes and Manuel Lopez Ramos; his *Concierto de Aranjuez* (1939) was a tribute to Regino Sainz de la Maza. Several concertos have been written in the 20th century, the first of them by Mario Castelnuovo-Tedesco (1895–1968) in 1939. Castelnuovo-Tedesco's prolific output for guitar includes a quintet (op.143, 1950), and *Platero y yo* (op.190, 1960) for guitar and narrator; and his works are dedicated to many guitarists: the German Siegfried Behrend, the American Christopher Parkening, the Italian Oscar Ghiglia, the Venezuelan Alirio Diaz, the Japanese Jiro Matsuda and others. He also composed several works for guitar duo, including the Concerto for two guitars and orchestra (op.201). The combination of two guitars allows more complex writing than is possible for the solo instrument (see ex.4). The duo genre was firmly established in the 20th century by Ida Presti and Alex-

andre Lagoya, and is being consolidated by the Brazilian brothers Sergio and Eduardo Abreu, the Athenian Guitar Duo (Liza Zoi and Evangelos Assimakopoulos), and the French-Japanese combination of Henri Dorigny and Ako Ito.

Segovia's influence spread to South America, where the Mexican composer Manuel Ponce (1882–1948) composed sonatas, variation sets and the *Concierto del sur*. Villa-Lobos (1887–1959) also wrote a concerto, but he is better known for his *Douze études* (1929) and *Cinq préludes* (1940). The *Etudes* evidence some progress from 19th-century stereotypes, but formulae are still present, as they are in the preludes. A more lightweight work is Villa-Lobos's *Chôro no.1*, with its evocations of folk music. The guitar features prominently in South American folk music, which permeates some of the compositions of Antonio Lauro of Venezuela and Augustín Barrios (1885–1944) of Paraguay. The South American repertory has been augmented by the Brazilian Francisco Mignone (*b* 1897), the Cuban Leo Brouwer (*b* 1939) and Guido Santórsola (*b* 1904) from Uruguay. Performers include Turibio Santos of Brazil and Oscar Caceres of Uruguay.

Although the initial impetus came from Spain, the growth of modern guitar music has been maintained elsewhere in Europe. Works have appeared by Frank Martin, Henze, Krenek, Alexandre Tansman, Malipiero, Petrassi, Milhaud, Daniel-Lesur and Poulenc. The guitar was included in Boulez's *Le marteau sans maître*, though generally the instrument has been little featured in chamber ensembles. In England, where the leading performers are Julian Bream (*b* 1933) and John Williams (*b* 1941), the guitar did not become established in music colleges until 1961. Nonetheless English composers, or composers resident in England, have made a significant contribution to the repertory. Concertos have appeared by Malcolm Arnold, Stephen Dodgson, Richard Rodney Bennett and André Previn, and the solo literature has been enriched by works from Britten (*Nocturnal after John Dowland*), Berkeley (*Sonatina, Theme and Variations*), Dodgson (*Partita, Fantasy-Divisions*), Mellers (*A Blue Epiphany for J. B. Smith*), Stoker (*Sonatina*), Crosse (*Caprices on Bream*) and others. The guitar has also been used effectively as an accompaniment to the voice; settings include *Songs from the Chinese* (Britten), *Cantares* (Gerhard), *Five Love Songs* (Musgrave) and *Anon in Love* (Walton).

The 20th-century repertory exhibits a wide variety of textures and styles, ranging from the predominantly tonal, romantic works inspired by Segovia to avant-garde compositions. Influences from folk music, flamenco and jazz can be found; and experimenters have introduced unexpected sonorities and extended the instrument's percussive and idiophonic resources. In Petrassi's *Suoni notturni* (1959), for example, the performer is instructed to sound notes by pulling the strings so that they slap against the frets; elsewhere he is directed to tap on the table, alternating the sounds thus produced with normally played sounds. Atonal writing and serial techniques have been given expression on the guitar – evidence of its viability in contemporary music. One of the most interesting aspects of the history of the guitar in the 20th century is the extent to which its literature has been vitalized in the transition from music composed by guitarists (or written to the restrictions of a guitarist) to compositions not determined by a conventional conception of the instrument's possibilities (see

Ex.4 Guido Santórsola: Sonata a duo (1967), 2nd movt

Ex.5 Stephen Dodgson: Partita for guitar (1965), 3rd movt

ex.5). This has led to the appearance of works of considerable stature and the growth of an artistic compositional tradition such as has eluded the guitar until the 20th century.

7. VARIANTS OF THE CLASSICAL GUITAR. Instruments departing from the basic form of the guitar first appear in 1690, when Alexander Voboam constructed a double guitar, which had a small guitar attached to the treble side of a normal instrument. However, the 19th century was a more productive period in this respect. A double-necked guitar – *Doppelgitarre* – was made by Staufer in 1807; and J.-F. Salomon constructed a guitar with three necks – the 'Harpolyre' – which, like a number of 19th-century variant guitars, was designed to improve what was felt to be an unsatisfactory instrument. At the beginning of the century the LYRE GUITAR enjoyed a brief vogue. Methods and music were published for this instrument, which had two curved arms (recalling the Ancient Greek lyre) in place of the upper bout. In another group of instruments the number of strings was increased, sometimes in the bass, sometimes in the treble, and one instrument – the 'guitarpa' – had both extra bass and extra treble strings. The 19th century saw the introduction of guitars that varied in size and hence in pitch. These were the *quinte-basse*, *quarte*, *terz* and *octavine* guitars; only the *terz* guitar, tuned *G–c–f–b♭–d′–g′*, has a literature. In the 20th century Narciso Yepes has introduced a ten-string guitar, the added strings lying in the bass, with the tuning *G♭–A♭–B♭–c–E–A–d–g–b–e′*. This tuning permits sympathetic bass-string resonances for every note in the upper range of his guitar, according to Yepes.

Of 20th-century variants, the flamenco guitar is closest to the classical instrument. As the traditional posture of the flamenco guitarist necessitates holding the instrument almost vertically, it is desirable to restrict weight; hence Spanish cypress, a lighter wood than rosewood, is used for the back and sides, and until recently wooden pegs were used instead of machine heads. A plate is positioned on the table to protect the wood from the tapping of the right-hand fingers. Although the basic function of the flamenco guitar is to provide an accompaniment to singing and dancing, it has also been featured as a solo instrument.

In the 20th century many changes have been made to the basic design of the classical guitar, mostly for the purpose of producing greater volume and penetration. These changes have resulted in several distinct types of guitar, each originally designed to meet the specific musical requirements of guitarists playing in popular music forms, principally folk, jazz, blues, dance music and rock and roll.

Some guitarists, especially American country-and-western players and 'crooners', began early in the 20th century to demand more volume from the flat-top acoustic guitar of traditional shape. The company that initially did most to accommodate them was MARTIN of Nazareth, Pennsylvania, which by the end of the 1920s was producing steel-strung guitars, altered structurally to bear the tension of heavier strings, and in some cases larger than the standard instrument. Martin is probably best known for the invention of the so-called 'Dreadnought' flat-top acoustic guitar, apparently named after the British battleship of the period. It was based on instruments made by Martin for the Ditson company of Boston from 1916, though it was not marketed by Martin itself until 1935, when the D18 and D28 models were introduced. The Dreadnought was larger than a normal guitar and had a much broader waist and rather narrower, squarer shoulders. Its resulting 'bassier' tone ideally suited folk, country-and-western, blues and other popular music forms where the guitar's role was to accompany the voice. The design of the Dreadnought has been widely imitated by many guitar makers since its introduction, most notably by companies such as Guild, but also by Gibson in the USA and, later in the century, by Japanese guitar makers.

The large Dreadnought or 'jumbo' is not, however, the only type of steel-strung flat-top acoustic guitar; steel-strung versions of the classical guitar of traditional size and shape, with some internal strengthening, abound. Martin was, again, an innovator in this area of so-called 'folk' steel-strung acoustics, and many guitar makers in the USA, Europe and the Far East now produce similar instruments.

Flat-top, steel-strung acoustic guitars require a stronger and more complex network of internal bracing than does either the classical or the arched-top guitar. The various styles of bracing that have developed are often referred to by descriptive terms, such as 'X'-bracing and 'fan'-bracing. The woods used to construct flat-top guitars vary depending on the degree of excellence required: the top is usually made of spruce (occasionally of cedar), rosewood, mahogany or maple is used for the back, sides and neck, and rosewood or ebony for the fingerboard. Cheaper flat-tops use laminated rather than solid woods. In 1966 the OVATION company in the USA began to produce guitars with a rounded back made of a synthetic material resembling fibreglass, in combination with a wooden top, neck and fingerboard; the aim, once again, was to improve the projectional qualities of an otherwise standard acoustic instrument.

Most flat-top guitars have a fixed bridge, like the classical guitar, to which the lower ends of the strings are secured by pins. The most popular flat-tops are those with six strings, tuned to the standard *E–A–d–g–b′–e′* guitar pitches. But a variant, the 12-string flat-top, is also made, for use chiefly in blues and folk-based music;

the strings are tuned in six courses, some in unison and others an octave apart.

Playing styles and techniques associated with the flat-top acoustic guitar vary widely, depending on musical idiom. Most often, particularly in folk music and other styles where a chordal accompaniment is required, a plectrum is used to strike the strings. In ensembles the instrument is occasionally used to play melody lines, melodic support, or jazz-like solos, though this role is now more usually taken by electric instruments. Sometimes the fingernails, or false nails, are used to play finger-style (or finger-picking) patterns, but the nylon-strung classical guitar is more commonly used for this type of playing.

Some players adapt the standard six-string tunings to suit their own styles and musical requirements, and a number of patterns have evolved, mainly from blues and folk music. The most common adaptations are 'open' tunings, so named because the open strings are tuned to form a single chord (e.g. $D–G–d–g–b–d'$; $D–A–d–f\sharp–a–d'$), which can be played at any pitch by stopping all the strings across the relevant fret. These open tunings probably developed in Hawaiian-style playing and country music, in which a slide, or a bottleneck worn on one of the fingers of the left hand, is pressed down on the strings, stopping them all at the same point; the strings are not separately fingered, the slide or bottleneck being moved up and down so that parallel chords are produced. More conventional players stop the strings in the same way but with the finger, using the 'barré' technique. The other common type of adapted tuning is the 'dropped' tuning, in which the pitch of one or more strings is lowered to allow non-standard fingerings.

The other principal 20th-century acoustic variant of the classical guitar, which differs far more from the original than does the flat-top, is the arched-top (or 'carved-top' or 'cello-bodied') guitar.

It was first developed commercially in the USA in the 1920s as a result of the relatively high volume at which dance bands were playing. Ordinary acoustic guitars could not produce the sound levels needed; the arched-top guitar satisfied this requirement and became increasingly popular in the big-band style which emerged in the 1930s.

Among the earliest such instruments was the GIBSON L5, which was first issued in 1923 and 1924, and which defined the arched-top guitar. Its construction owed more to violin making than traditional methods of guitar building and was strongly influenced by Gibson's experiments with the design of mandolins and guitars in the 1890s. The quest for increased volume was at the root of all the alterations to conventional design introduced in the L5: it had steel strings instead of gut, the extra tension and weight of which necessitated structural strengthening of the body; the top was strong and thick and carved into a characteristic arched shape; in place of a single soundhole there were two f-holes, for greater projection of the sound and enhancement of the sympathetic vibrations of the top; the bridge was not fixed but 'floating' (or adjustable) and the strings passed over it and were secured to a separate metal tailpiece attached to the end of the body.

The first version of the Gibson L5 had an ebony fingerboard on a maple neck, a birch or maple back, a carved spruce top and spruce sides. It was not only the earliest arched-top to feature f-holes, but it was also one of the first guitars to be fitted with a 'truss rod', an

17. 'Duolian' resonator guitar by National, c1930 (Country Music Hall of Fame and Museum, Nashville)

adjustable internal metal rod that counteracts warping and minor movements of the neck.

The L5 heralded the arrival on the market of many other arched-top acoustic guitars. The makers of these have been principally American, and include the Guild company, which was founded in New York in 1952 by Alfred Dronge, moved to New Jersey in 1956 and was later purchased by Avnet Inc.; D'Angelico, set up by John D'Angelico, formerly a violin maker, in New York in 1932, and carried on by his protégé Jimmy D'Aquisto after D'Angelico's death in 1964; and Epiphone, established in New York by Anastasios Stathopoulo in 1873, and purchased by Gibson in 1957 after Stathopoulo's death.

The arched-top acoustic guitar fulfilled a specific role in the heyday of the American big band; although it was designed for plectrum playing and produced the greatest possible volume when a plectrum was used, some guitarists played it with the right-hand fingers. The popularity of the arched-top acoustic waned with the widespread use of the ELECTRIC GUITAR, which easily outclassed it in terms of response and increased volume. Those arched-top guitars that survive, do so primarily as collectors' items.

Other attempts were made in the 1930s to increase the volume projected by the acoustic guitar. Early in the decade MARIO MACCAFERRI designed for the French com-

18. Mexican guitarist

pany Selmer a series of guitars that had distinctive D-shaped soundholes and a unique extra sound chamber inside the body; the resulting clear, piercing tone quality became the hallmark of Django Reinhardt's playing at that period. A similar idea was exploited in the 'ampli-phonic' or 'resophonic' guitar (commonly known by one of its trade names, DOBRO), which had one or more metal resonator discs mounted inside the body under the bridge (fig.17). The dobro was often played across the lap and with a slide, like the HAWAIIAN GUITAR, and both types were used at an early stage in experiments with ampli-fication, which led to the development of the electric guitar.

8. THE DIFFUSION OF FOLK GUITARS. The small guitars of Renaissance Europe were the prototypes of folk instru-ments that have persisted in Spain and Portugal, and which were carried through trade contacts to Central and Southern America and East Asia. The growth in size of the classical instrument also finds its counterpart in the range in size of folk instruments (see figs.18 and 19). Spain has the *bajo de uña*, a very large, short-necked guitar with eight strings, but the *guitarra* is the standard instrument. The *guitarra tenor* has the tuning $G–c–f–bb–d'–g'$; the *guitarra requinto* is tuned $B–e–a–d'–f\sharp'–b'$; and the smallest is the *guitarillo*, with five strings tuned $a'–d''–g'–c''–e''$ (the term *guitarro* also refers to a small instrument, with four or 12 strings, played by strumming). Portugal has the normal guitar, which is called *violão*; the Portuguese *guitarra* is similar to the Spanish *bandurria* (*see* ENGLISH GUITAR), and, in spite of its name, it does not have the waisted outline of the

guitar; the Portuguese *machete* (*cavaco*, diminutive *cavaquinho*), has either six or, more commonly, four strings; and the *rajão*, which sometimes has the body in the form of a fish, has five strings (fig.19).

The *guitarillo* is also known as the *tiple* (treble), and in the Canary Islands, where the name has been trans-formed to *timple*, it has a vaulted back and either four or five strings; these may be tuned to the upper intervals of the standard guitar tuning, but more traditional tun-ings are $c''–f'–a'–d''$ and $f'–c''–e'–a'–d''$, which can be raised a tone for an E tuning. The name *tiple* is also applied to a small *bandurria* in Cuba, which has five pairs of strings. Cuba also has the small guitar *tres*, with three pairs of metal strings. The term *guitarrilla* is found in Bolivia, Guatemala and Peru. In the two last it denotes a small four-string instrument, used to accom-pany song and dance. In Bolivia, where it is the only known instrument of the Chipaya people of the Depart-ment of Oruro, it has five double courses (tuned $d'–a'–f'–c'–g'$) and six frets; it has a guitar-like body with ribs, a flat front and a slightly curved back. *Guitarrillas* are played in pairs for textless *wayñus de cordero* (songs in praise of sheep) or *tonadas del ganado* (songs for cattle) at the *k'illpa* festival. The Chipaya of the village of Ayparavi have three different sizes of *guitarrilla*: *paj*, *taipi* and *qolta*, all with gut strings. The two largest are tuned as above, the smallest a 4th higher (see Baumann, 1981 and 1982). The *jarana* (diminutive *jaranita*) is a small Mexican guitar used in instrumental ensembles and to accompany dances; it is the equivalent of the *char-ango*, which is widely distributed in South America (north-west Argentina, Bolivia, Peru and Chile). The

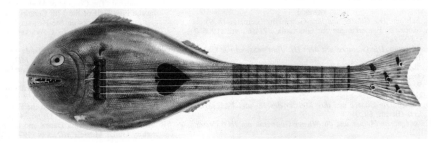

19. Portuguese rajão, 19th century (Horniman Museum, London)

charango has five single or five paired strings, tuned $g'(g')-c''(c'')-e''(e')-a'(a')-e''(e'')$; the body consists of an armadillo shell that has been dried in a mould to produce the waisted guitar shape. The name *violão* has been retained in Brazil for the classical guitar; the Brazilian folk guitar is called *viola* and has a variety of tunings according to place and function; most examples have five double courses (occasionally four or six). In Mexico the term *guitarra de golpe* is used as an alternative to *vihuela* for a small five-course guitar used in folk ensembles. The Mexican *guitarrón* is a large four-string bass guitar, while the Chilean type has 25 strings. Puerto Rico also has a five-course instrument, which has four double strings and one single and is played with a plectrum. The Puerto Rican instrument is known as a *cuatro*, a name more logically identified with the small Venezuelan guitar with four strings; the five-string guitar is called *quinto* in Venezuela. In the hands of a virtuoso performer, the Venezuelan *cuatro*, in spite of its seeming limitations, is capable of more complex textures than those it is obliged to provide in its folk setting, and two *cuatros* can accommodate transcriptions of art music. The *mâchete* was introduced by Portuguese sailors to the Hawaiian islands, where it was developed into the ukulele with its re-entrant tuning $g'-c'-e'-a'$ (for illustrations see UKULELE). Also of Portuguese origin is the small, narrow *kroncong* of West Java, which has five strings. The Montese of Mindanao in the Philippine Islands have a three-string guitar called *tiape*.

The following guitars are entered in this dictionary: arpi-guitare; bissex; bocona; chillador; chitarã; chitarra battente; cinco; cuatro; đàn ghi-ta; dobro; gabowie; gitara; Hawaiian guitar; huapanguera; ikatala; jarana; kroncong; lục huyền cầm; mejoranera; quinto (ii); rajão; requinto; seis; slack-key guitar; socavón; tiape; timple; tiple; tres; udi; viaule; violão; zongorá; Zupfgeige.

BIBLIOGRAPHY

BIBLIOGRAPHIES OF MUSICAL SOURCES
Handbuch der musikalischen Literatur (Leipzig, 1817–) [19th-century printed guitar music]
P. Danner: 'Bibliography of Guitar Tablatures, 1546–1764', *Journal of the Lute Society of America*, v (1972), 40; vi (1973), 33
W. Moser: *Gitarre-Musik: ein internationaler Katalog* (Hamburg, 1973/R1975, 2/1977)
G. Gilmore: *Guitar Music Index: a Cross-indexed and Graded Listing of Music in Print for Classical Guitar and Lute* (Honolulu, 1976–81)
A. Nagytothy-Toth: 'Checklist of Chamber Music for Guitar (Lute) and Keyboard', *Soundboard*, iii/1 (1976), 15
——: 'Checklist of Concerti for Guitar (Lute) and Orchestra', *Soundboard*, iii/3 (1976), 59
W. Boetticher: *Handschriftlich überlieferte Lauten- und Gitarrentabulaturen des 15. bis 18. Jahrhunderts*, RISM, B/VII (1978)
P. Danner: 'Bibliografia delle principali intavolature per chitarra', *Il 'Fronimo'*, vii/29 (1979), 7
J. Tyler: *The Early Guitar: a History and a Handbook* (London, 1980)
T. Heck: *Guitar Music in the Archive of the Guitar Foundation of America and at Cooperating Collections: a Computerized Catalog* (Columbus, 1981)

GENERAL
E. Schroen: *Die Gitarre und ihre Geschichte* (Leipzig, 1879)
A. Koczirz: 'Bemerkungen zur Gitarristik', *ZIMG*, viii (1906–7), 355
E. Biernath: *Die Guitarre seit dem III. Jahrstausend vor Christus* (Berlin, 1907)
A. Koczirz: 'Zur Geschichte der Gitarre in Wien', *Musikbuch aus Oesterreich*, iv (1907), 11
J. Wolf: *Handbuch der Notationskunde*, ii (Leipzig, 1919), 157–218
B. Henze: *Die Gitarre und ihre Meister des 18. und 19. Jahrhunderts* (Berlin, 1920)
J. Zuth: *Simon Molitor und die Wiener Gitarristik um 1800* (Vienna, 1920)

A. Koczirz: 'Die Wiener Gitarristik vor Giuliani', *Die Gitarre*, ii (1920–21), 71, 81, 93
O. Chilesotti: 'Notes sur les tablatures de luth et de guitare', *EMDC*, I/ii (1921), 636–84
A. Koczirz: 'Ueberblick über die Spanische Gitarristik im 16. Jahrhundert', *Zeitschrift für die Gitarre*, i/3 (1922), 2
——: 'Zur Geschichte der Gitarre in Frankreich von 1500 bis 1750', *Zeitschrift für die Gitarre*, i (1922), no.5, p.3; no.6, p.3
E. Schwarz-Reiflingen: 'Beiträge zur Geschichte der Gitarristik nach 1840', *Die Gitarre*, iv (1923), 65, 74, 90; v (1924), 103, 135
K. Prusik: 'Bemerkungen zur Entwicklung der Gitarrenmusik', *Zeitschrift für die Gitarre*, iv/1 (1924), 5
T. Haas: 'Die Verwendung der Lauteninstrumente in der Oper', *Zeitschrift für die Gitarre*, iv (1925), no.9, p.1
M.-R. Brondi: *Il liuto e la chitarra: ricerche storiche sulla loro origine e sul loro sviluppo* (Turin, 1926)
F. Buek: *Die Gitarre und ihre Meister* (Berlin, 1926)
J. Zuth: *Handbuch der Laute und Gitarre* (Vienna, 1926)
S. N. Contreras: *La guitarra, sus antecedentes históricos y biografías de ejecutantes célebres* (Buenos Aires, 1927)
A. Orel: 'Gitarrenmusik in Wien zur Zeit Beethovens', *Oesterreichische Gitarre-Zeitschrift*, i/3 (1927), 46
E. Pujol: 'La guitare', *EMDC*, II/iii (1927), 1997–2035
W. P. Maschkewitsch: 'Zur Geschichte der Gitarre in Russland', *Die Gitarre*, x (1929), 25, 38, 54; xi (1930), 52, 93
O. Gombosi: 'Miscellanea: ad vocem cithara, citharista', *AcM*, ix (1937), 55
G. Chase: *The Music of Spain* (New York, 1941)
F. Lesure: 'La guitare en France au XVIe siècle', *MD*, iv (1950), 187
M. Schulz: 'Francesco Corbetta und das Generalbass-Spielen', *Mf*, iv (1951), 371
J. Duarte: 'Music and the Guitar', *Guitar Review*, nos.13–17 (1952–5); nos.20–21 (1956–7)[series of short articles]
L. Davenport: 'Guitars in Chamber Ensembles', *Guitar Review*, no.16 (1954), 2
A. P. Sharpe: *The Story of the Spanish Guitar* (London, 1954; 2/1959)
W. Boetticher, H. Hickmann and K. Reinhard: 'Gitarre', *MGG*
R. Simoes: 'The Guitar in Brazil', *Guitar Review* (1958), no.22, p.6
V. O. Bickford: 'The Guitar in America', *Guitar Review* (1959), no.23, p.17
J. de Azpiazu: *La guitare et les guitaristes des origines aux temps modernes* (Basle, 1959; Eng. trans., 1960)
D. Heartz: 'Parisian Music Publishing under Henry II: a propos of Four Recently-Discovered Guitar Books', *MQ*, xlvi (1960), 448
B. L. Vol'man: *Gitara v Rossii* (Leningrad, 1961)
R. Keith: 'The Guitar Cult in the Courts of Louis XIV and Charles II', *Guitar Review* (1962), no.26, p.3
D. Heartz: 'An Elizabethan Tutor for the Guitar', *GSJ*, xvi (1963), 3
E. Bowles: 'The Guitar in Medieval Literature', *Guitar Review* (1966), no.29, p.3
C. Carfagna and A. Caprani: *Profilo storico della chitarra* (Ancona, 1966)
S. Garnsey: 'The Use of Hand-plucked Instruments in the Continuo Body: Nicola Matteis', *ML*, xlvii (1966), 135
H. Charnassé: 'Sur l'accord de la guitare', *RMFC*, vii (1967), 25
R. A. Hudson: *The Development of Italian Keyboard Variations on the Passacaglia and Ciaccona from Guitar Music in the 17th Century* (diss., U. of California, Los Angeles, 1967)
B. L. Vol'man: *Gitara i gitaristï* (Leningrad, 1968)
D. George: *The Flamenco Guitar* (Madrid, 1969)
A. Bellow: *The Illustrated History of the Guitar* (New York, 1970)
H. Charnassé and F. Vernillat: 'La guitare', *Les instruments à cordes pincées* (Paris, 1970)
F. V. Grunfeld: *The Art and Times of the Guitar* (New York, 1970)
T. F. Heck: *The Birth of the Classic Guitar and its Cultivation in Vienna, Reflected in the Career and Compositions of Mauro Giuliani (d.1829)* (diss., Yale U., 1970)
R. A. Hudson: 'The Concept of Mode in Italian Guitar Music During the First Half of the 17th Century', *AcM*, xlii (1970), 163
——:'Further Remarks on the Passacaglia and Ciaccona', *JAMS*, xxiii (1970), 302 [reply to T. Walker: 'Ciaccona and Passacaglia', *JAMS*, xxi (1968), 300]
——: 'The Zarabanda and Zarabanda Francese in Italian Guitar Music of the Early 17th Century', *MD*, xxiv (1970), 125
S. Murphy: 'The Tuning of the Five-course Guitar', *GSJ*, xxiii (1970), 49
H. T. David: 'The Six-four Chord without Theory, an Unofficial History', *Bach*, ii (1971), no.3, p.7; no.4, p.3
T. F. Heck: 'The Role of Italy in the Early History of the Classic Guitar', *Guitar Review* (1971), no.34, p.1
R. A. Hudson: 'The Folia Dance and the Folia Formula in 17th-century Guitar Music', *MD*, xxv (1971), 199

——: 'The Music in Italian Tablatures for the Five-course Spanish Guitar', *Journal of the Lute Society of America*, iv (1971), 21

B. Tonazzi: *Liuto, vihuela, chitarra e strumenti similari nelle loro intavolature, con cenni sulle loro letterature* (Ancona, 1971, 3/1980)

R. Chiesa: 'Storia della letteratura del liuto e della chitarra', *Il 'Fronimo': rivista trimestrale di chitarra e liuto* (1972–) [series of articles]

J. Nickel: *Beitrag zur Entwicklung der Gitarre in Europa* (Bad Schussenried, 1972)

M. Sicca: 'La chitarra e gli strumenti a tastiera', *Il 'Fronimo'*, i/1 (1972), 27

R. Strizich: 'Ornamentation in Spanish Baroque Guitar Music', *Journal of the Lute Society of America*, v (1972), 18

E. Fausto Ciurlo: 'Cenni sulle ricerche delle origini etniche della chitarra e del liuto', *Il 'Fronimo'*, i/2 (1973), 16

A. Gilardino: 'Aspetti della musica per chitarra del secolo XX', *Il 'Fronimo'*, i/2 (1973), 7

——: 'La musica contemporanea per chitarra in Gran Bretagna', *Il 'Fronimo'*, i/5 (1973), 8

C. Viglietti: *Origen e historia de la guitarra* (Buenos Aires, 1973/R1976)

R. de Zayas: 'The Vihuela: Swoose, Lute, or Guitar', 'The Music of the Vihuelists and its Interpretation', 'The Vihuelists', *Guitar Review* (1973), no.38, p.2

P. Danner: 'L'adattamento della musica barocca per chitarra all'-esecuzione moderna', *Il 'Fronimo'*, ii/7 (1974), 11

A. Gilardino: 'La musica italiana per chitarra nel secolo XX', *Il 'Fronimo'*, ii/7 (1974), 21

A. Mauerhofer: *Leonhard von Call: Musik des Mittelstandes zur Zeit der Wiener Klassik* (diss., U. of Graz, 1974)

A. Simoes: *A guitarra portuguesa* (Evora, 1974)

H. Turnbull: *The Guitar from the Renaissance to the Present Day* (London and New York, 1974)

T. Wheeler: *The Guitar Book: a Handbook for Electric and Acoustic Guitarists* (New York, 1974, 2/1978)

M. Cano Tamayo: *Un siglo de la guitarra granadina* (Granada, 1975)

M. Sicca: 'Note critiche sul problema delle trascrizioni per chitarra', *Il 'Fronimo'*, iii/11 (1975), 23

L. Witoszynski: 'Vihuela und Gitarre im Spiegel neuer Litteratur', *ÖMz*, xxx (1975), 186

J. Duarte: 'La notazione della musica per chitarra', *Il 'Fronimo'*, iv/14 (1976), 14

M. Ophee: 'Guitar Chamber Music, Why?', *Soundboard*, iii/3 (1976) to iv/2 (1977) [series of 4 articles]

J. W. Tanno: 'Current Discography', *Soundboard*, iii/3 (1976), 56 [first of a series of articles]

L. Witoszynskyi: 'Die Gitarre in der Kammermusik und der Beitrag Wiens', *ÖMz*, xxxi (1976), 640

G. Bakus: *The Spanish Guitar: a Comprehensive Reference to the Classical and Flamenco Guitar* (Los Angeles, 1977)

P. Danner: 'Breve storia della musica per chitarra in America', *Il 'Fronimo'*, v/20 (1977), 18

T. and M. A. Evans: *Guitars: Music, History, Construction and Players from the Renaissance to Rock* (New York, 1977)

M. Ophee: 'Chamber Music for Terz Guitar – a Look at the Options', *Guitar Review* (1977), no.42, p.12

J. Roberts: *Guitar Travels* (Valencia, 1977)

J. Sclar: 'Guitar: Consort to the Voice. Chapter One, Benjamin Britten: Songs from the Chinese', *Guitar Review* (1977), no.42, p.17

P. Camos: *Reportaje a la guitarra* (Buenos Aires, 1978)

D. Gill: 'Bandora, orpharion and guitar', *GSJ*, xxxi (1978), 144

F. Grunfeld: 'L'accord parfait en amour: Incidental Notes to the Graphic Music of Balzac's Paris', *Guitar Review* (1978), no.44, p.1

T. Heck: 'Computerized Guitar Research – a Report', *Soundboard*, v/4 (1978), 104; 'Postscript', vi/1 (1979), 12

D. Lyons: *Lute, Vihuela, Guitar to 1800: a Bibliography* (Detroit, 1978)

K. Ragossnig: *Handbuch der Gitarre und Laute* (Mainz, 1978)

M. Summerfield: *The Jazz Guitar* (Gateshead, 1978)

L. Beck-Neuwirth: 'Die Gitarre im 16. Jahrhundert', *Zupfmusik*, xxxii/4 (1979), 99

M. Giertz: *Den klassika gitarren: instrumentet, musiken, mästerna* (Stockholm, 1979)

H. Haider: 'Die Gitarre im Jazz', *Musica*, xxxiii/1 (1979), 36

J. Libbert: '400 Jahre Gitarre und Gitarristen, Versuch eines historischen Überblicks', *Musica*, xxxiii/1 (1979), 17

M. Materassi: 'Teoria e pratica del "Suonare sopra'l basso" nel primo Seicento', *Il 'Fronimo'*, vii/29 (1979), 24

L. Persson: 'Computer-Aided Instruction for the Guitar', *Soundboard*, vi/3 (1979), 96

F. Pinnell: 'The Theorboed Guitar: its Repertoire in the Guitar Books

of Granata and Gallot', *Early Music*, vii (1979), 323

J. Powroźniak: 'Die Gitarre in Russland', *Gitarre und Laute*, i/6 (1979), 18

G. Radole: *Liuto, chitarra e vihuela: storia e letteratura* (Milan, 1979)

A. Schroth: 'Dem Gesang verschwistert: die Gitarre in der Romantik', *Musica*, xxxiii/1 (1979), 23

J. Sclar: 'Guitar: Consort to the Voice. Chapter Two, Dominick Argento, Letters from Composers', *Guitar Review* (1979), no.45, p.6

G. M. Dausend: 'Die Gitarre im Barockzeitalter: Instrumente, Komponisten, Werke, Notationsformen und Spieltechnik', *Zupfmusik*, xxxiii/5 (1980), 85, 114; xxxiv/5 (1981), 16

A. Gilardino: 'La musica per chitarra nel secolo XX', *Il 'Fronimo'*, viii/31 (1980) [first of a series of articles]

J. I. H. Klier: *Die Gitarre: ein Instrument und seine Geschichte* (Bad Schussenried, 1980)

H. Leeb: 'Die Gitarre', *Gitarre und Laute*, ii (1980), no.2, p.34; no.3, p.32

J. Libbert: 'Musikwissenschaft und Gitarristik: einige Aspekte zu Theorie und Praxis', *Zupfmusik*, xxxiii/2 (1980), 47

J. Schneider: 'The Contemporary Guitar', *Soundboard*, vii/2 (1980), 69 [first of a series of articles]

G. Wade: *Traditions of the Classical Guitar* (London, 1980)

J. Duarte: 'The Guitar in Early Music', *Guitar & Lute*, nos.13–18 (1980–81) [series of articles]

T. Bacon, ed.: *Rock Hardware* (Poole, Dorset, 1981)

M. dell'Ara: 'Iconografia della chitarra', *Il 'Fronimo'*, ix/36 (1981), 28 [first of a series of articles]

D. Gill: 'Vihuelas, Violas and the Spanish Guitar', *Early Music*, ix (1981), 455

G. Gruhn: 'Evolution of the Flat-top Steel-strung Guitar', *Guitar Player*, xv/7 (1981)

R. Jensen and D. Rowe: 'Baroque Guitar for the Modern Performer: a Practical Compromise', *Guitar Review* (1981), no.49, p.22

N. D. Pennington: *The Spanish Baroque Guitar, with a Transcription of De Murcia's Passacalles y Obras* (Ann Arbor, Mich., 1981)

C. S. Smith: 'Aristocratic Patronage and the Spanish Guitar in the 17th Century', *Guitar Review* (1981), no.49, p.2

M. P. Baumann: 'Music, Dance, and Song of the Chipayas (Bolivia)', *Latin American Music Review*, iii (1981), 171–222

R. Strizich: 'L'accompagnamento di basso continuo sulla chitarra barocca', *Il 'Fronimo'*, ix/34–5 (1981) [2-part article]

——: 'The Baroque Guitar – Then and Now', *Soundboard*, viii/3 (1981), 128

M. P. Baumann: 'Music of the Indios in Bolivia's Andean Highlands (Survey)', *The World of Music*, xxv/2 (1982), 80

R. Denyer: *The Guitar Handbook* (London, 1982)

M. Disler: 'Finding Liturgical Music for Classic Guitar', *Soundboard*, ix/1 (1982), 15

J.-A. van Hoeck: *Die Gitarrenmusik im 19. Jahrh.: Geschichte, Technik, Interpretation* (Wilhelmshaven, 1983)

J. M. Ward: 'Sprightly and Cheerful Musick – Notes on the Cittern, Gittern and Guitar in 16th- and 17th-century England', *LSJ*, xxi (1979–81) [whole issue]

THE INSTRUMENT

Arzberger: 'Vorschlag zu einer wesentlichen Verbesserung im Bau der Guitarre', *AMZ*, xi (1809), 481

J. A. Otto: 'Ueber die Guitarre', *Ueber den Bau der Bogeninstrumente* (Weimar, 1828)

F. Bathioli: *Guitarre-Flageolett-Schule mit Bemerkungen über den Gitarrenbau* (Vienna, ?1833)

O. Chilesotti: 'La chitarra francese', *RMI*, xiv (1907), 791

J. Zuth: 'Die englische und deutsche Gitarre des ausgehenden 18. Jahrh.', *Der Gitarrefreund*, xxii (1921), 77, 88, 99

K. Geiringer: 'Der Instrumentenname Quinterne und die mittelalterlichen Bezeichnungen der Gitarre, Mandola und Colascione', *AMw*, vi (1924), 103

A. Koczirz: 'Die alt-Wiener Gitarre um 1800', *Gitarristische Mitteilung aus Oesterreich*, i (1925), no.3, p.1; no.4, p.2; no.5, p.2

E. Schwarz-Reiflingen: 'Die Torresgitarre', *Die Gitarre*, ix (1928), 47

F. Schuster: 'Zur Geschichte des Gitarrenbau in Deutschland', *Die Gitarre*, x (1929), 83

G. Chase: 'Guitar and Vihuela: a Clarification', *BAMS*, vi (1942), 13

M. Ivanov: *Russkaia semistrunnaia gitara* (Moscow, 1948)

F. Lesure: 'Le traité des instruments de musique de Pierre Trichet; des instruments de musique à chordes', *AnnM*, iv (1956), 216

T. Usher: 'The Spanish Guitar in the 19th and 20th Centuries', *GSJ*, ix (1956), 5–36

J. Duarte: 'Variants of the Classic Guitar, an Evaluation', *Guitar Review* (1961), no.25, p.22

F. Jahnel: *Die Gitarre und ihr Bau: Technologie von Gitarre, Laute,*

Sister, Tanbur und Saite (Frankfurt am Main, 1964, 3/1977)

J. C. Tanno: 'A Brief Discussion of the Construction and Assembly of Guitars by Non-Spanish Luthiers', *Guitar Review* (1965), no.28, p.28

I. Sloane: *Classic Guitar Construction: Diagrams, Photographs, and Step-by-Step Instructions* (New York, 1966)

M. Kasha: 'A New Look at the History of the Classic Guitar', *Guitar Review* (1968), no.30, p.3

F. Hellwig: 'Makers' Marks on Plucked Instruments of the 16th and 17th Centuries', *GSJ*, xxiv (1971), 22

D. McLeod: *The Classical Guitar: Design and Construction* (Wood-Ridge, N.J., 1971)

A. Artzt: 'The Guitar: Wet or Dry?', *Guitar Review* (1972), no.37, p.4

M. Kasha: *Complete Guitar Acoustics* (Tallahassee, 1973)

E. F. Ciurlo: 'La chitarra nella liuteria moderna', *Il 'Fronimo'*, ii/6 (1974), 20

J. Godwin: 'Eccentric Forms of the Guitar, 1770–1850', *Journal of the Lute Society of America*, vii (1974), 90

H. Huttig: 'The Tripodison of Dionisio Aguado', *Guitar Review* (1974), no.39, p.23

M. Kasha: 'Adventures in the Physics of String Instruments: from Model Physics to the Modern Instrument', *Britannica Yearbook of Science and the Future* (1974)

J. Meyer: 'Die Abstimmung der Grundresonanzen von Gitarren', *Das Musikinstrument*, xxiii (1974), 179

——: 'Das Resonanzverhalten von Gitarren bei mittleren Frequenzen', *Das Musikinstrument*, xxiii (1974), 1095

D. Teeter: *The Acoustic Guitar: Adjustment, Care, Maintenance, and Repair* (Norman, Oklahoma, 1974)

D. Brosnac: *The Steel String Guitar: its Construction, Origin, and Design* (San Francisco, 2/1975)

——: *The Electric Guitar: its History and Construction* (San Francisco, 1975)

E. F. Ciurlo: 'Chitarra quartitonale', *Il 'Fronimo'*, iii/10 (1975), 25

D. Gill: 'The Stringing of the Five-course Baroque Guitar', *Early Music*, iii (1975), 370

T. F. Heck: 'Stalking the Oldest Six-string Guitar', *Gendai guitar*, (1975), no.98, p.64

M. Longworth: *Martin Guitars: a History* (Cedar Knolls, NJ, 1975)

I. Sloane: *Steel-String Guitar Construction: Acoustic Six-String, Twelve-String, and Arched Top Guitars* (New York, 1975)

J. Tyler: 'The Renaissance Guitar 1500–1650', *Early Music*, iii (1975), 341

D. Young: *The Steel String Guitar: Construction and Repair* (Radnor, Penn., 1975)

M. Hall: 'The "guitarra española"', *Early Music*, iv (1976), 227 [letter]

J. Meyer: 'Die Bestimmung von Qualitätskriterien bei Gitarren: Mitteilung aus der physikalisch-technischen Bundesanstalt', *Das Musikinstrument*, xxv (1976), 1211

D. Poulton: 'Notes on the Guitarra, Laud and Vihuela', *LSJ*, xviii (1976), 46

I. J. Schoenberg: 'On the Location of Frets on the Guitar', *American Mathematical Monthly*, 83/7 (1976), 550

R. Strizich: 'Stringing the Baroque Guitar', *Early Music*, iv (1976), 235

K. Achard: *The Fender Guitar* (London, 1977)

I. Bishop: *The Gibson Guitar from 1950* (London, 1977)

D. Brosnac: *An Introduction to Scientific Guitar Design* (New York, 1978)

C. Elliker: 'On Gasogenes, Penang Lawyers, Echiquiers and Terz Guitars', *Soundboard*, v/4 (1978), 112

J. Meyer: 'Hörtests und akustische Messungen zur Bestimmung der Klangqualität von Gitarren', *Das Musikinstrument*, xxvii (1978), 33

M. Ophee: 'La chitarra terzina', *Il 'Fronimo'*, vi/25 (1978), 8

J. Schneider: 'The Well-Tempered Guitar', *Soundboard*, v/4 (1978), 108

T. Stone: 'A New Tonal Universe for the Guitar – Interchangeable Fingerboards', *Guitar & Lute* (1978), no.6, p.19

M. Weber: 'Gitarrenkorpus geometrisch abgeleitet: Instrumentengeschichte aus Spanien', *IZ*, xxxii (1978), p.774

K. Achard: *The History and Development of the American Guitar* (London, 1979)

D. Denning: 'The Vihuela: Royal Guitar of 16th-century Spain', *Soundboard*, vi/2 (1979), 38

T. Evans *et al.*: *Guitares: chefs d'oeuvre des collections de France* (Paris, 1980)

T. Heck: 'Mysteries in the History of the Guitar', *La guitarra*, nos.37–8, 40–41 (1980) [series of short articles]

M. Sorriso: 'La chitarra battente in Calabria', *Il 'Fronimo'*, viii/31 (1980), 29

D. Gill: 'Vihuelas, Violas and the Spanish Guitar', *Early Music*, ix (1981), 455

T. Heck: 'The Historic Variety in Guitar Sizes', *La guitarra* (1981) no.42, p.2

J. Schneider: 'The Microtonal Guitar', *Guitar & Lute*, nos.16–17, 19–(1981–) [series of 5 articles]

T. Rossing: 'Physics of Guitars: an Introduction', *Journal of Guitar Acoustics*, no.4 (1981), 45

J. Meyer: 'Fundamental Resonance Tuning of Guitars', *Journal of Guitar Acoustics*, no.5 (1982), 19

T. White, ed.: 'Papers from speakers at the guitar session of the meeting of the Acoustical Society of America, Chicago, April 26–30, 1982', *Journal of Guitar Acoustics*, no.6 (1982) [eleven articles]

T. Wheeler: *American Guitars: an Illustrated History* (New York, 1982)

O. Christensen: 'The Response of Played Guitars at Middle Frequencies', *Journal of Guitar Acoustics*, II/3 (1983), 49

GUITAR TECHNIQUE

F. Guthmann: 'Ueber Guitarrenspiel', *AMZ*, viii (1806), 362

O. Seyffert: 'Ueber das Gitarrespiel mit Ring und Nagelanschlag', *Der Guitarrefreund*, viii (1907), 33, 41

E. Just: 'Die Flageolettöne und ihre Notierung', *Der Gitarrefreund* xx (1919), 11, 23, 35

F. Buek: 'Ueber den Nagelanschlag', *Der Gitarrefreund*, xxii (1921) 5

F. Laible: 'Physiologie des Anschlages', *Die Gitarre*, ii (1921), 95

——: 'Physiologie des Greifens', *Die Gitarre*, iv (1923), 45

E. Schwarz-Reiflingen: 'Kuppen- oder Nagelanschlag?', *Die Gitarre*, vi (1925), 65

A. Koczirz: 'Ueber die Fingernageltechnik bei Saiteninstrumenten', *Studien zur Musikgeschichte: Festschrift für Guido Adler* (Vienna, 1930/R1971)

E. Schwarz-Reiflingen: 'Die moderne Gitarrentechnik', *Die Gitarre*, xi (1930), 17, 34, 49, 81

T. Usher: 'The Elements of Technical Proficiency', *Guitar Review* (1953), no.15, p.6

——: 'Tone and Tonal Variety', *Guitar Review* (1954), no.16, p.23

E. Pujol: *El dilema del sonido en la guitarra* (Buenos Aires, 1960)

J. Huber: *Origines et technique de la guitare* (Lausanne, 1968)

S. Murphy: 'Seventeenth-century Guitar Music: Notes on Rasgueado Performance', *GSJ*, xxi (1968), 24

V. Bobri: *The Segovia Technique* (London and New York, 1972)

M. Sicca: 'Il vibrato come arricchimento naturale del suono: suo studio sistematico sulla chitarra e sul liuto', *Il 'Fronimo'*, i/5 (1973), 24

P. Danner: 'Giovanni Paolo Foscarini and his "Nuova inventione"', *Journal of the Lute Society of America*, vii (1974), 4

R. Strizich: 'A Spanish Guitar Tutor: Ruiz de Ribayaz's *Luz y norte musical* (1677)', *Journal of the Lute Society of America*, vii (1974), 51

A. Gilardino: 'Il problema della diteggiatura nelle musiche per chitarra', *Il 'Fronimo'*, iii (1975), no.10, p.5; no.13, p.11

C. Duncan: 'Staccato Articulation in Scales', *Soundboard*, iv/3 (1977), 65

P. Cox: *The Evolution of Playing Techniques of the Six-Stringed Classic Guitar as seen through Teaching Method Books from c.1780–c.1850* (diss., Indiana U., 1978)

C. Duncan: 'About Vibrato', *Soundboard*, v/3 (1978), 69

J. Taylor: *Tone production on the classical guitar* (London, 1978)

F. Cook: 'Die "Batteries" auf der Spanischen Barockgitarre nach Marin Mersenne', *Gitarre und Laute*, i/5 (1979), 34

C. Duncan: 'Articulation and Tone: some Principles and Practices', *Guitar Review* (1979), no.46, p.7

——: 'La tensione funzionale e l'attacco preparato', *Il 'Fronimo'*, vii/28 (1979), 23

M. Sicca: 'Una concezione dinamica di alcuni problemi chitarristici', *Il 'Fronimo'*, vii/29 (1979), 18

P. Danner: 'Lute Technique and the Guitar: a Further Look at the Historical Background', *Soundboard*, vii/2 (1980), 60

C. Duncan: *The Art of Classical Guitar Playing* (Princeton, N.J., 1980)

B. Jeffery: 'La technica di unghia e polpastrello secondo Dionisio Aguado', *Il 'Fronimo'*, viii/33 (1980), 14

E. Lind: 'Haltungsproblematik an der Konzertgitarre', *Gitarre und Laute*, ii/6 (1980), 18

P. Cox: 'Considerazioni sui primi metodi per chitarra', *Il 'Fronimo'*, ix/34 (1981), 5

M. Ophee: 'Il tocco appoggiato: precisazioni e argomenti storici', *Il 'Fronimo'*, xi/43 (1983), 8

GUITARISTS

P. J. Bone: *The Guitar and Mandolin: Biographies of Celebrated Players and Composers* (London, 1914, 2/1954/R1972)

J. Zuth: *Handbuch der Laute und Gitarre* (Vienna, 1926)

S. N. Contreras: *La guitarra, sus antecedentes históricos y biografías de ejecutantes célebres* (Buenos Aires, 1927)

W. P. Maschkewitsch: 'Russische Gitarristen', *Die Gitarre*, xi (1930), 68

D. Prat Marsal: *Diccionario biográfico de guitarras y guitarristas* (Buenos Aires, 1934)

B. Terzi: *Dizionario dei chitarristi e liutai italiani* (Bologna, 1937)

C. Simpson: 'Some Early American Guitarists', *Guitar Review* (1959), no.23, p.16

C. Carfagna and M. Gangi: *Dizionario chitarristico italiano* (Ancona, 1968)

M. J. Summerfield: *The Jazz Guitar: its Evolution and its Players* (Gateshead, 1978)

W. Moser: 'Spanische Gitarristen zwischen Aguado und Tarrega', *Gitarre und Laute*, i/4 (1979), 26

J. Powroźniak: *Leksykon gitary* (Kraków, 1979; enlarged Ger. trans., 1979)

HARVEY TURNBULL/JAMES TYLER (3–4),
with TONY BACON (7) (text),
THOMAS F. HECK (bibliography)

Guitare angloise (Fr.). A term applied to the ENGLISH GUITAR (a type of cittern) about 1770–80.

Guitare d'amour (Fr.). ARPEGGIONE.

Guitare en bateau (Fr.). CHITARRA BATTENTE.

Guitare-harpe. *See* HARP-LUTE (ii).

Guitaret. An electromagnetically amplified lamellaphone manufactured by Hohner in Trossingen in the early 1960s. It consists of a rectangular container about 33 cm long from which protrude the ends of 36 reeds, arranged in three rows and tuned in alternate 4ths and 5ths; this lay-out allows the basic chords in every key to be fingered conveniently. Each reed transmits its vibrations to a smaller second reed, tuned to the same pitch, which is amplified by means of an electromagnetic pickup. The total range of the instrument is a minor 13th.   HUGH DAVIES

Guitarillo (Sp.). Small five-string folk guitar, also known as TIPLE. *See also* GUITAR, §8.

Guitarpa. A DUPLEX (strictly a 'triplex') instrument combining harp, guitar and cello, made by Gallegos and exhibited in London in 1851.

Guitarra (Sp.) (i). GUITAR (see esp. §8).

Guitarra (Port.) (ii). Long-necked lute, related to the Spanish *bandurria* (*see also* ENGLISH GUITAR). A modern folk descendant, known as *guitarra portuguesa*, is used with the *viola* to accompany the *fado*, a vocal genre of Portuguese cafés, cabarets and night clubs; with the *violão* it accompanies the *desafio* (duel song) of Ponta Delgada, Azores.

Guitarre-Violoncell (Ger.). ARPEGGIONE.

Guitarrilla. Term used in Bolivia, Guatemala and Peru for a folk guitar. *See* GUITAR, §8.

Guitarro (Sp.). Small guitar, with four or 12 strings. *See* GUITAR, §8.

Guitarrón. Large guitar of Chile and Mexico. *See* GUITAR, §8.

Guitar violoncello. *See* ARPEGGIONE.

Guiterne (Fr.). GITTERN.

Gujrātan sāraṅgī. Bowed chordophone of the Langa people of Rajasthan, India. *See* SĀRAṄGĪ.

Gujrī. SPIKE FIDDLE of the Gujara people of Rajasthan, north-west India. *See* RĀVAṆHATTHĀ.

Guke. Side-blown animal-horn trumpet of the Lugbara people of Uganda, similar to the OBUTE.

Gulbransen organ. An ELECTRONIC ORGAN, a number of models of which have been manufactured since the mid-1950s by the Gulbransen Company in Melrose Park, near Chicago, and then in nearby Deerfield. The company was set up in 1904 to produce pianos and player pianos; it still manufactures pianos. In 1966 it was taken over by the Seeburg Corp., and it later became a division of CBS Musical Instruments. During the 1960s the Gulbransen organ incorporated elements of the KINSMAN ORGAN and the SEEBURG ORGAN. The models are mostly 'spinet' organs, with two 44-note manuals and a one-octave pedal-board, designed for use in the home. The sounds are generated by an oscillator for each note, or (in the smaller instruments) by 12 oscillators, using frequency division, or in some cases, by a combination of the two systems. Recent models are based on microprocessors. Advances in electronic technology since around 1970 have made possible several new devices that are included in many home organs: rhythm and 'walking bass' units, arpeggiators, small memories and a choice of chord systems; knobs, stop-tabs and other switches have been replaced by a touch panel. Larger models incorporate a LESLIE tremulant loudspeaker.

BIBLIOGRAPHY
H. E. Anderson: *Electronic Organ Handbook* (Indianapolis, 1960), 53

R. H. Dorf: *Electronic Musical Instruments* (New York, 3/1968), 255

N. H. Crowhurst: *Electronic Organs*, iii (Indianapolis, 1975), 42
HUGH DAVIES

Gule. Ceremonial SLIT-DRUM of the Guere people of the Ivory Coast, played with two sticks. In the music of the secret *kwi* ('spirit') society the player holds a mirliton in his mouth and conducts a dialogue with the drum, which is later used for purely rhythmic accompaniment.

Gulimed. MUSICAL BOW of the Ilongot people of the northern Philippines.

Gulintangan. GONG-CHIME of Brunei and Sabah. *See* KULINTANG.

Gullbergson, Pehr Olof (1780–1864). Swedish organ builder. A self-taught man who did not take up his profession until middle age, he became one of the most sought-after organ builders in Uppsala province. He built 24 organs, of which about half are still preserved, among them the organs at Kungs-Husby (1834), Nysätra (1839) and Torsvi (1834). These are characterized by their good workmanship and, in most cases, fine tone. See E.

Erici: *Inventarium över bevarade äldre kyrkorgelar i Sverige* (Stockholm, 1965).

based on *Sohlmans musiklexikon* (iii, 251) by permission of Sohlmans Förlag

BENGT KYHLBERG

Gullum. Three-string plucked lute of the Kilba people of Nigeria. *See* GURMI.

Gulom. Three-string lute of the Kotoko people along the lower Logone river (Chad and north Cameroon). The body of the instrument is a hemispherical calabash covered with a laced cowhide. The strings were traditionally made from horsehair but nowadays are often of nylon. They are attached to the neck by simple ligatures. The longest string of the *gulom* is tuned first; the middle string is tuned to a 4th and the shortest to an octave above the first. The *gulom* is played exclusively by men and is used to hunt spirits and also for entertainment. It is often accompanied by a half-calabash percussion vessel struck with two sticks. The symbolism of the parts of the instrument is similar to that of the *galdyama* (five-string harp): the neck of the instrument is called the head, the soundbox the stomach, the soundhole the mouth and the bridge the nose.

MONIQUE BRANDILY

Gulu (i). Tulip-shaped SLIT-DRUM of the Mamvu people of north-eastern Zaïre. The term also refers to a small zoomorphic slit-drum of the Mamvu, Angba and Ngbele peoples of northern Zaïre (*LaurentyTF*, 139f). *See* GUGU, (1).

Gulu (ii). Term meaning 'large', occasionally used to denote the *chinzumana* xylophone of the Chopi people of Mozambique.

Gulu (iii). Bass drum of the Tonga people of Mozambique. *See* BOMBO (iii).

Gulutindi. MUSICAL BOW with separate gourd resonator of the Logo people of Zaïre; it is also known as *kidrigo* and *kilikingila* (*LaurentyC*, 114). *See* KITINGBI.

Guma [!guma]. Braced MOUTH BOW of the Kung (San) people of south-western Africa.

Gumanak. Antique high-pitched percussion idiophone used singly or in one or two pairs in the *gambuh* theatre ensemble in Bali. It consists of a small rolled cylindrical pipe of copper or iron, the circumference of which does not quite meet. It is held in the hand and tapped with a metal object. See C. McPhee: *Music in Bali* (New Haven and London, 1966/R1976), 121. *See also* KEMANAK.

MARGARET J. KARTOMI

Gumbang. Aerophone of Indonesia. *See* BOMBERDOM.

Gumbé. Type of membranophone of Jamaica and Cuba (where it is unnamed), consisting of a single head stretched (and nailed) over a square wooden form or stool, raised off the ground by four legs. It has been observed in Jamaica since the 19th century and appears to have African provenance, possibly originating in Guinea. See *OrtizIMA*, iii, 415ff.

Gumbeng. Ensemble from the rural Banyumas area o[f] south-west Central Java, consisting entirely of stick beaten bamboo idiochord tube zithers, a hand-beate[n] bamboo idiophone and a bamboo trumpet.

Gumbri [gunbri]. *See* GUINBRI.

Gummaṭi. Clay GOBLET DRUM of Andhra Pradesh, sout[h] India. A long-necked waterpot has an opening about [.] cm wide excised at the base; this is covered by a skin braced on an iron hoop and laced by cotton cords. Th[e] drum is played horizontally, the right hand on the skin and the left closing the mouth of the neck for varie[d] resonance. See P. Sambamoorthy: *Catalogue of Musi[-]cal Instruments Exhibited in the Government Museum[,] Madras* (Madras, 3/1962). *See also* GHUMAṬ an[d] GHAṬA, §2.

ALASTAIR DIC[K]

Gumra. *See* GHUMERA.

Gunda (i). Variable tension HOURGLASS DRUM of th[e] Kanuri people of north-eastern Nigeria. Formerly a roya[l] perquisite, the drum, which can be double-headed o[r] open, is now used in an instrumental ensemble t[o] accompany dancing at marriages and may also be asso[-] ciated with cult usage.

Gunda (ii). Side-blown animal-horn trumpet of th[e] Shambala people of Tanzania.

Gundi (i). Arched harp of the Kotoko people in Cha[d] and Cameroon. *See* GALDYAMA.

Gundi (ii). Side-blown ivory trumpet of the Mamv[u] people of north-eastern Zaïre. It has a carved mouth piece (*LaurentyA*, 384).

Gundu. *See* KUNDU (i).

Gung. Suspended bossed gong of Sumatra. In the Bata[k] Karo area of the province of North Sumatra it is mad[e] of bronze and measures about 65 cm in diameter. It i[s] beaten with a cloth- or rubber-padded stick, usuall[y] without being damped. It is the main punctuating instru[-] ment (usually at 16-, eight- or four-beat intervals) in th[e] *gendang* ensemble. The *gung* in the *nobat* orchestra i[n] Riau province (Tanjung Pinang) is made of iron or bronz[e] and is beaten with a soft hammer. The largest measure[s] about 105 cm in diameter and is called *gung betin[a]* ('female gong'); the second largest (*gung jantan*: 'mal[e] gong') is about 75 cm in diameter, and the smallest abou[t] 60 cm. In the Serdang and Langkat areas of Nort[h] Sumatra the *gung* is about 45 cm in diameter and i[s] deep-rimmed; it forms part of the *gendang-gung* ensem[-] ble. *Gung* in the *gonrang sipitupitu* ensemble of the Bata[k] Simalungun area of North Sumatra are used in pairs an[d] vary between 30 and 40 cm in diameter; they are sus[-] pended from a frame or held in the player's left han[d] by means of cord passing through two holes.

MARGARET J. KARTOMI

Gungak. Double-headed cylindrical drum of the Gurk[a] people of Nigeria. *See* GANGA, (1).

Gunguma. Drum of the Galla people of East Africa.

Gunguru. Double-headed cylindrical drum of the Fulani people of West Africa. *See* GANGA, (1).

Gunibri. *See* GUINBRI.

Gunstar Organ Works. Australian firm of organ builders which amalgamated with DODD (ii) in *c*1940.

Guntang. Idiochord bamboo TUBE ZITHER of Bali. Its single bamboo string, raised on a bridge at each end, is beaten with a light stick (see illustration). The string's vibration is prolonged by a wooden tongue attached to the middle. A hole is cut lengthwise below the string, and the bamboo tube is closed at one end by a node. Normally a larger and a smaller *guntang* are played in the *arja* and *janger* ensembles; the larger is called *kempur* and the smaller *kempli*. See C. McPhee: *Music in Bali* (New Haven and London, 1966/*R*1976), 34 and 294f.

MARGARET J. KARTOMI

Guntang (idiochord tube zither, left) with kendang (double-headed drum) and suling (end-blown flute) in a gamelan arja at Peliatan village, Bali

Gurdună. *See* GORDUNĂ.

Gurmi. A two-string plucked lute (also called *kumbo*) of the Hausa people of northern Nigeria. The instrument has a half-calabash soundbox and is played by men, either solo or to accompany songs, especially those praising wrestlers. In the Sokoto area of Nigeria in the 1930s the instrument had three strings, a long metal ringed jingle, and was associated with hunters.

The term 'gurmi' may be cognate with the north African GUINBRI or *gunibri*. In the 14th century, both Al-Omari and Ibn Baṭṭūṭa referred to *gunibri* as instruments played at the court of the Empire of Mali. Other linguistic links are with the *gambare* of the Soninke of Mali, the *kambre* of Sierra Leone, the *gurumi* (for illustration *see* LUTE, fig.1*g*) of Dosso in Niger and the Mauri people in southern Chad, the *gullum* of the Kilba people of Nigeria, and the *kubru* of Timbuktu. It may be significant that the North African *guinbri* is used mainly in cult activities of the Gnawa sect, who are descendants of black slaves transported across the Sahara and maintain that their ancestors brought the instrument from their country of origin. In Chad the Mauri *gurumi*, a three-string instrument, is used to accompany songs invoking spirits during cult cere-

monies. In Nigeria the Kilba *gullum* also has three strings, a circular calabash soundbox with a side opening, and a hollow bridge containing seeds. Originally the prerogative of the royal clan, it is now played mainly at death ceremonies.

BIBLIOGRAPHY
Ames–KingGHM
G. Demombynes, Fr. trans.: *I. F. A. Al-Omari (Yahya): Masalik el Absar fi Mamalik el Amsar* (Paris, 1927)
H. A. R. Gibb, trans.: *Ibn Baṭṭūṭa: Travels in Asia and Africa, 1325–1354* (London, 1929), 326ff
H. E. Hause: 'Terms for Musical Instruments in the Sudanic Languages: a Lexicographical Inquiry', *Journal of the American Oriental Society*, lxiii (1948), suppl.7
V. Pâques: *L'arbre cosmique dans la pensée populaire et dans la vie quotidienne du nord-ouest africain* (Paris, 1964)
T. Nikiprowetzky: 'Nomades du Niger', OCR 29 (1966) [disc notes]
L. A. Anderson: 'The Interrelation of African and Arab Musics: Some Preliminary Considerations', *Essays on Music and History in Africa*, ed. K. P. Wachsmann (Evanston, Ill., 1971)
K. A. GOURLAY

Guro awal. Friction vessels of the Acholi people of Uganda. Two hemispherical gourds of different sizes are rubbed with their rims on a stone or a wooden board with a grinding movement. The larger is known as *min*, the 'mother', the smaller as *nyig*, 'the little one'. Each gourd is held by a kneeling girl; two different notes are produced. The instrument is reported to be used for funerals. See *WachsmannTCU*.

Guru. Braced MOUTH BOW of the Logo people of Zaïre (*LaurentyC*, 113). *See* BOMBO (iv).

Gurugú. Type of Afro-Cuban single-headed ARARÁ drum, used in Jovellanos, Matanzas, in the Sociedad de S Lázaro. The body, a truncated-cone shape, is some 50 cm tall and roughly the same in diameter, and the head is made taut with spikes. It is struck with two thick thongs about 30 cm long and 2 cm wide, with three other similarly shaped drums. See *OrtizIMA*, iii, 357.
JOHN M. SCHECHTER

Gurugur. Dance sticks of Truk, central Caroline Islands, Micronesia, made from the wood of the wild orange (*gurugur*), which is especially resonant when dry. The rods were cut to lengths of about 1·4 metres and clashed together during men's dances. See F. M. LeBar: *The Material Culture of Truk* (New Haven, 1964).

Guruki. A small variable tension HOURGLASS DRUM of Maharashtra, central India. It has wide heads and is beaten with a stick. It is clearly related in both structure and name to the *huṛuk* (*huṛkī*) of north India. *See* HUḌUKKĀ.

Gurumi [gouroumi]. Three-string lute of the Mauri people of southern Chad and the Dosso of Niger. *See* GURMI.

Gusla. Erroneous term for the Bulgarian GADULKA.

Gusle. Single-string fiddle of Yugoslavia. The root of the term exists in all Slavonic languages denoting various types of string instrument (*see* GĘŚLE; GUDOK; GUSLI). Only in Bulgaria and Yugoslavia does it denote a fiddle with one string, rarely two. The hollow resonator and the neck are carved together from one piece of wood, usually maple. It resembles a large spoon, hence the name for this part of the instrument – *kusalo* ('spoon'); it can be oval, leaf-shaped, round or pear-shaped. The resonator is covered with stretched skin (usually kid); a bridge (*kobilica*) is placed on the lower part of the body, between the soundtable and the horsehair string. The thicker end of the hair is fixed to a protuberance at the base of the resonator, and the other end is wound round a wooden peg inserted in the rear of the neck. In instruments with two strings the second peg is inserted somewhat lower than the first and slanted to the right. The skin soundtable has several small soundholes, arranged in various patterns, and another small soundhole is made at the back or base of the resonator. The length of the horsehair string decrees the length of the instrument (usually between 70 and 80 cm), and the length of the neck (up to the peg) corresponds to the length of the resonator. The bow is made from a thin, strongly curved branch of hardwood and a length of horsehair (generally shorter than the playing string – about 40 cm). Nowadays this type of bow is being replaced by a more elongated form with longer hair, which can be tightened by means of small pegs. The *gusle* is often carved with symbolic figures, for example, a horse's head, a horse and rider or a snake (see illustration).

The *gusle* player (*guslar*) sits holding the instrument upright, inclined to the left, supporting the neck in his left hand and the lower part of the body between his knees. The string is touched with the outstretched fingers (usually the index and middle fingers only) without changing the position of the hand. As the *guslar* sings to his own accompaniment, he tunes the string to suit the tessitura of his own voice.

The *gusle* is used to accompany epic songs; it provides an instrumental prelude and interludes to the song, and a support for the voice. Associations of *gusle* players have been founded in Sarajevo, Belgrade and Titograd, evidence of the instrument's popularity.

CVJETKO RIHTMAN

Gusli (from early Slavonic *gosl*: 'string'). A psaltery (BOX ZITHER) made from thin strips of wood in the form of a rounded-off trapezoid with concave flanks (see illustration). The size varies according to the number of strings (11 to 36): the length of the top ranges from 70 to 100 cm, that of the base from 43 to 77 cm; the width varies between 30 and 55 cm, and the depth between 7 and 12 cm. The gut or metal strings are generally tuned diatonically and are fastened parallel to the base on two inward-curving wooden fillets, and on to one of these with wooden rear pegs. The sides slope inwards, so that the top is substantially wider than the base. The instrument rests on the player's knees, with the narrow, round end normally resting against his chest. When the player is standing or walking, he carries the *gusli* on a sling around his neck, and it rests upright against his chest. The melody strings are plucked with the thumb and index finger of the right hand while the bass strings, tuned in 4ths and 5ths, are plucked with the left hand: they can be damped with the flat of the hand during playing.

The *gusli* may have spread from Byzantium to Russia by AD 1000. The earliest iconographical evidence is on miniatures in the Novgorod style dating from the 14th century. As the instrument was named in the psalms of David, the Greek Orthodox Church did not attempt to prevent its use, as it did with other folk instruments. From the 14th century to the 16th the *gusli* was played primarily by the *skomorokhi*, professional minstrels who toured the towns and villages. It ceased to be used as a popular instrument at the beginning of the 20th century.

In the setting of the imperial court and among the boyars (nobles), landed gentry and city merchants, the *gusli* was inserted into a larger, rectangular box of wood with a front cover, which stood on legs or on a separate frame. The number of strings was increased to between 55 and 66, with a range of two to three octaves. From the second half of the 18th century it was built chromatically with strings on two levels. Its repertory included western European dance music and extracts from operas and ballets as well as folksongs and dances. At the turn of the century the instrument was provided with a one-octave keyboard based on the system of N. P. Fomin, in which each key damped the strings in all octaves. In this modified form the *gusli* is still played in Russian folk music groups.

As a folk instrument the *gusli* is still known by various names to the Tatars (*késlja*) and to the Finno-Ugric peoples of the Volga Basin, such as the Mari (*küsle, kärš*), the Votyaks (*krés, krödž*), the Chuvash (*kesle*) and the Mordvin (*kájga*), who played it sometimes as a solo instrument, sometimes to accompany folksongs or dances, or in ensemble with other instruments such as the bagpipes, drum, fiddle or accordion. At one time, the Mari and Votyaks used the instrument to accompany prayers and dances during sacrificial rites. The design of their instrument corresponded to that of the Russian *gusli*. The Votyaks, however, used to string their instruments with horsehair, and they sometimes fitted metal resonance strings inside the body of the instrument.

In north Russia the word 'gusli' is also used to signify an instrument of the KANTELE type. The term is used for a violin in the western Ukraine and Belorussia, and for

Gusle (single-string fiddle) player from Bosnia and Hercegovina, Yugoslavia

Gusli (psaltery) of the Chuvash people, Russian SFSR

a DUCT FLUTE in some regions of western Russia and Belorussia (*see* DUDKA).
See also ROTTE (ii).

BIBLIOGRAPHY
VertkovA
A. S. Famincin: *Gusli: russkiy narodnïy muzykal'nïy instrument* (St Petersburg, 1890)
A. S. Väisänen: 'Das Zupfinstrument Gusli bei den Wolgavölkern', *Mémoires de la Société finno-ougrienne*, lviii (Helsinki, 1928), 303
V. Vertkov: 'Beiträge zur Geschichte der russischen Guslitypen', *Studia instrumentorum musicae popularis*, i (Stockholm, 1969), 134

ERNST EMSHEIMER

Guslice [gingara]. Idiochord bowed zither of Bosnia and Hercegovina and Serbia (Yugoslavia). It is a children's instrument made from a corn stalk about 20 cm long and is played with another idiochord corn stalk acting as a bow. The *guslice* can also be made with two strings, on the same bridge, in which case the strings are plucked with the fingers and the instrument is called a *tamburica*. *See also* KUKORICAHEGEDŰ.

Gutsib [!gutsib]. Name for the RAMKIE lute of southern Africa.

Guwel. FRAME DRUM of the Gayo people in the Takengon area, Central Aceh, Sumatra. Its goatskin head, about 41 cm in diameter, is attached by rattan lacing to a thick circular wooden frame about 13 cm in depth. About 20 lengths of rattan cord are passed vertically through this lacing around the surface of the wooden frame in order to attach it to a rattan ring placed below ten small wooden blocks which fit between the ring and the frame. The diameter of the base is about 40 cm.

MARGARET J. KARTOMI

Guyrapa-í. Double MUSICAL BOW of the Guaraní people of Paraguay. The smaller or 'female' bow rubs the larger or 'male', which is held in the mouth and moistened by the lips. Different notes are obtained by stopping the string with the four fingers of the left hand.

Guyud. JEW'S HARP of the northern Philippines. *See* AFIW.

Gwabron tambari. KETTLEDRUM of Katsina, Nigeria. *See* TAMBARI.

Gwale. MOUTH BOW of southern Africa. The modern spelling is UGWALA.

Gwanbal. Conical drum of the Mbun people of Zaïre. *See* MUSHITS.

Gwangwaragwandi. Open GOBLET DRUM, with snared membrane and tuning paste, of the Zamfara Hausa people of Nigeria. The drum is slung from the shoulder and beaten with the right hand while the fingers of the left press the skin to produce different tones. It is used to accompany praise songs for the emir of Zamfara. The *gwangwaragwandi* resembles the *turu* or *banga* of the Sokoto Hausa in construction and method of performance. The *turu* was, however, the war drum of the ruling class and was usually played on horseback as the drummer rode in front of the chief.

BIBLIOGRAPHY
P. G. Harris: 'Notes on Drums and Musical Instruments Seen in Sokoto Province, Nigeria', *Journal of the Royal Anthropological Institute*, lxii (1932), 105
K. Krieger: 'Musikinstrumente der Hausa', *Baessler-Archiv*, new ser., xvi (1968), 373–430

K. A. GOURLAY

Gwaningba. MOUTH BOW of the Zande people of Zaïre; it is also known as *ninga* (*LaurentyC*, 113). *See* LUSUBA.

Gwara me akuta. Side-blown trumpet of the Lango people of Uganda. *See* ARUPEPE.

Gwarje. Flanged or unflanged cast-iron clapper bell of the Zamfara Hausa people of Nigeria. It is fastened round the necks of animals, or hung on the inside of woven hut doors as a warning-device against thieves.

Gwasak. SCRAPER of the Birom people of Nigeria. It is made from a cactus stem (*Euphorbia unispina*) into which notches are cut on two sides (or on all four), and is scraped with a piece of wood. It provides rhythmic accompaniment in instrumental ensembles. See L. Bouquiaux: 'Les instruments de musique Birom (Nigeria Septentrional)', *Africa-Tervuren*, viii/4 (1962), 105.

Gwinza. Cylindrical, stopped wooden flute of the Bati people of northern Zaïre (*LaurentyA*, 181).

Gwizdek. Polish whistle, made of willow bark, wood or clay and used by children. It is made in different shapes and sizes. Some kinds of willow-bark *gwizdek* are named after birds (e.g. *żuraw*: 'crane'; *słowik*: 'nightingale') and imitate their calls. Some bird-shaped ceramic whistles are filled with water and produce a warbling sound.

Gworitod. Idioglot transverse clarinet of the Birom people of Nigeria. *See* CLARINET, TRANSVERSE.

Gworogo. End-blown trumpet of the Birom people of Nigeria. It is made from a cow horn with a wooden mouthpiece, and is 67 cm long and 10 cm in diameter at the mouth. The *gworogo* is used solely by men during the *mandieng* harvest rites. It is believed that if the instrument is played during the wet season the harvest will fail. See L. Bouquiaux: 'Les instruments de musique Birom (Nigeria Septentrional)', *Africa-Tervuren*, viii/4 (1962), 105.

Gyamadudu. Large double-headed cylindrical drum of the Ashanti people of Ghana. It measures approximately 80 cm in length and 32 cm in diameter. It is suspended vertically in front of the drummer's legs and beaten with one hand and a heavy, straight stick held in the other hand. It provides a steady rhythmic ostinato, in both popular and state ensembles, against which the DONNO (hourglass drum) players produce more intricate rhythms.

BIBLIOGRAPHY
J. H. K. Nketia: *Drumming in Akan Communities of Ghana* (London, 1963)
——: 'Ashanti Music', *Grove 6*

Gyat. Small wooden CLAPPERS of Burma. They consist of two pieces of wood joined by a hinge, and are used to mark accented beats by the vocalist of an ensemble, who holds the *gyat* in one hand and a pair of *sì* (finger cymbals) in the other (for illustration *see* SAÙNG-GAUK, fig.2).

Gyengreeng ('horse-bell'). Iron, copper or brass clapper bell of the Birom people of Nigeria. It is made from a metal plate rolled into a cylinder with a semicircular or circular suspension ring. The instrument is hung from the neck of a horse by a leather cord, thus enabling the animal to be easily recognized while out grazing. The bell reputedly had apotropaic qualities as, formerly, it was never removed in wartime, the striker being wrapped in grass to muffle the sound. See L. Bouquiaux: 'Les instruments de musique Birom (Nigeria Septentrional)', *Africa-Tervuren*, viii/4 (1962), 105.

Gyilli [dzilli, djil, chohun]. Frame XYLOPHONE of Ghana. The *gyilli* has 12 to 17 wooden keys mounted above gourd resonators, each with a spider-web mirliton. The players use rubber-tipped beaters; when two men play together, they sit opposite each other, one playing the melody and accompaniment while the other provides a rhythmic ostinato by striking only the ends of the keys. In northern Ghana the Dagari people play a similar instrument called the *djil*. It has 14 keys and is played in pairs with kettledrums and small drums for harvest song and dance. The *chohun* is a large version of the *gyilli* and has more keys; it may be cognate with the *cho* of the Bwaba people of Upper Volta.

BIBLIOGRAPHY
S. Jay: 'Africa: Ancient Ceremonies, Dance Music and Songs of Ghana', Nonesuch H-72082 [disc notes]
J. H. Nketia: 'Ghana', *Grove 6*

K. A. GOURLAY

Gyoban. Flat wooden percussion idiophone, in the form of a fish, of Japan. *See* HAN.

Gyterne [gyttrone]. *See* GITTERN.

H

Ha [*//ha*]. MOUTH BOW, sounded by breath, of the Cape Bushmen (San) people of southern Africa. It was similar to the GORA, but is now obsolete.

Haas. German family of brass instrument makers. They were descended from Caspar Haas and his son Lorenz, both tower watchmen who played the trumpet as part of their duties. Lorenz's son, Johann Wilhelm Haas (*b* Nuremberg, 5 Aug 1649; *d* Nuremberg, 2 July 1723), who probably learnt from Hans HAINLEIN, became the most famous of the brass instrument makers in Nuremberg; both his son, Wolf Wilhelm Haas (*b* Nuremberg, 4 March 1681; *d* Nuremberg, 21 Feb 1760), and Wolf Wilhelm's son, Ernst Johann Conrad Haas (*b* Nuremberg, 17 March 1723; *d* Nuremberg, 29 Feb 1792), signed their instruments with his name instead of their own. As late as 1795 Johann Ernst Altenburg (*Versuch*, p.10) praised the trumpets of 'W. Hasen' as being the best for general use.

The products of these three generations of the Haas family were in great demand throughout Europe, as witnessed today by the unusually large number of surviving instruments distributed over a wide area. These instruments exhibit the typical 'late Baroque' bell, with a narrower throat and more rapidly expanding terminal flare than those by earlier makers, notably Schnitzer and Hainlein. Heyde (1980) has shown the existence of at least three types of Haas trumpet, ranging from the simple to the ornate and doubtless corresponding to price categories. Wörthmüller's (1954–5) attribution of any given instrument to Wolf Wilhelm or to Ernst Johann Conrad was mistakenly based on the thought that their maker's marks were identical. The Haas family's mark was a hare running to the left. According to their own registration of their marks (on a brass tablet then in possession of the *Rugamt* and now in the Kunstgewerbemuseum, Berlin) Johann Wilhelm and Ernst Johann Conrad had the hare's head looking forward, but with Wolf Wilhelm it looks back, over its shoulder.

Among the most splendid examples are the 12 solid-silver state trumpets made in 1744 by Wolf Wilhelm for the Elector Palatine Carl Theodor (now in the Bayerisches Nationalmuseum, Munich, no.47/25–36). Despite their magnificent appearance, however, the tone of these 12 instruments is dull – a general property of silver trumpets that was noted by Altenburg (1795). Modern reproductions of trumpets by Wolf Wilhelm Haas were made available by Meinl & Lauber after 1967. The Haas family prospered longer than some other brass instru-

ment makers, but even so Ernst Johann Conrad's son, Johann Adam Haas (*b* Nuremberg, 15 Dec 1769; *d* Nuremberg, 11 Jan 1817), was the last Nuremberg trumpet maker of the 18th century to be approved as a Meister (1796), and one of the last three to practise the trade. None of his instruments has survived.

For illustration of an instrument by Wolf Wilhelm Haas, *see* TROMBONE, fig.5*c*.

BIBLIOGRAPHY

J. E. Altenburg: *Versuch einer Anleitung zur heroisch-musikalischen Trompeter- und Pauker-Kunst* (Halle, 1795/*R*; Eng. trans., 1974)

W. Wörthmüller: 'Die Nürnberger Trompeten- und Posaunenmacher des 17. und 18. Jahrhunderts', *Mitteilungen des Vereins für Geschichte der Stadt Nürnberg*, xlv (1954), 240; xlvi (1955), 425

D. Smithers: 'The Trumpets of J. W. Haas', *GSJ*, xviii (1965), 23

K. Pechstein: 'Die Merkzeichentafel der Nürnberger Trompeten- und Posaunenmacher von 1640', *Mitteilungen des Vereins für Geschichte der Stadt Nürnberg*, lix (1972), 198

H. Heyde: *Trompeten Posaunen Tuben* (Leipzig, 1980)

EDWARD H. TARR

Haas, Friedrich (*b* Laufenburg, Baden, 1811; *d* Lucerne, 1886). Swiss organ builder of German birth. He trained from 1825 to 1829 with the Schaxel family of organ builders of Baden, alternately with the elder Schaxel at Herbolzheim and his sons Matthäus Schaxel at Freiburg and Josef Schaxel at Benfeld (Alsace). He continued his training – particularly in tonal aspects of the craft – with E. F. Walcker at Ludwigsburg, from 1830 to 1835, and is thus customarily regarded as a pupil of Walcker. From 1836 he worked independently. After 1840 he confined his activities exclusively to Switzerland, eventually becoming that country's most important organ builder of the middle of the 19th century. At first Haas, in the traditional way of craftsmen, did not settle in one area, but moved from place to place as his work required. Thus he moved to Lucerne in 1859 to renovate the organ of the Hofkirche. He settled down there, however, and founded the organ-building firm which from 1867 was carried on by his colleague of long standing, Friedrich Goll, and which, as 'Orgelbau Goll & Cie AG', is still in existence. In his retirement he was occasionally employed as a consultant, as during the construction by Johann Nepomuk Kuhn of the organ of the Grossmünster, Zurich (1873–6).

Haas was modern in outlook and played a significant part in the technical and artistic transformation of organ building in the 19th century. At first he built purely mechanical slider-chest organs, but in about 1850 he changed to sliderless wind-chests and made use of Barker's pneumatic lever in order to make the tracker action smoother. In sound, he made the step from the south German late Baroque ideal to the fundamental tone quality of the Romantic organ. He loved wide scaling and double-lipped wooden pipes (Doppelflöte, Doppelbourdon). Many details of scaling and other advice on the technique of organ building were incorporated in the second edition of Töpfer (1888).

New or rebuilt organs by Haas include those at the following places in Switzerland: Grenzach (1837); Neumünster, Zurich (1838–40); Rheinau (1840–41); Temple du Bas, Neuchâtel (1841); Stadtkirche, Winterthur (1841–3); Andelfingen (1842–3); Zofingen (1847); Berne Minster (1849–51); Lenzburg (1851); Fribourg Minster (1852–3); Leuggern (1854); Basle Minster (1852–7); Hofkirche, Lucerne (1859–62); Thalwil (1864).

BIBLIOGRAPHY

J. G. Töpfer: *Lehrbuch der Orgelbaukunst* (Weimar, 1855, rev. 2/ 1888 by M. Allihn as *Die Theorie und Praxis des Orgelbaus*, rev. 3/1936 by P. Smets)
L. Stierlin: *Die Orgel* (Zurich, 1859)
F. J. Breitenbach: *Die grosse Orgel der Hofkirche in Luzern* (Lucerne, 1920)
F. Jakob: *Der Orgelbau im Kanton Zürich* (Berne and Stuttgart, 1969–71)

FRIEDRICH JAKOB

Haavapill. DUCT FLUTE of Estonia. *See* VILEPILL.

Habbān [hibbān]. BAGPIPE of southern Iraq, Kuwait, Bahrain and the Gulf area. *See* QIRBA.

Habiba pudu. Tulip-shaped SLIT-DRUM of the Ngbaka people of north-western Zaïre (*LaurentyTF*, 139).

Hachi. Large Japanese cymbals. *See* DŌBATSU.

Hackbrett (Ger.). DULCIMER.

Hade. MUSICAL BOW of the Xhosa people of southern Africa. The modern spelling is UHADI.

Haegŭm. Two-string SPIKE FIDDLE of Korea (*hae*: name of a Tatar tribe; *gŭm*: 'string instrument'). It is also known as *hyegŭm* (Chin. *xiqin*; *see* ERHU) and (onomatopoeically) *kkangkkangi*. The *haegŭm* is about 70 cm in length and the neck (of bamboo or wood), about 2·5 cm in diameter, curves gently forward at the top and passes at the bottom through a tubular soundbox of large bamboo root or hardwood (about 10 cm in diameter and in length). The soundbox has a paulownia-wood sound-table at the front and is open at the rear. Two strings of twisted silk are attached to a metal clasp at the bottom of the soundbox, pass over a small wooden bridge and are tied to two large pegs skewered into the curved portion of the neck; the pegs (about 11 cm long) have spools on which excess string is wound. The bow, about 65 cm long, is of slender and supple bamboo with loose horsehair; the horsehair passes between the two strings of the fiddle (see illustration). It is said that the *haegŭm*, as it was built in former times, was the only instrument to use all eight sonorous materials of the Chinese classification system (earth, metal, silk, gourd, wood, skin, stone and bamboo).

The performer sits cross-legged, with the *haegŭm* propped up vertically on his left knee, the bow being held horizontally in the right hand. The tension of the

Haegŭm (spike fiddle) of Korea

horsehair is altered by pushing down on it with the fingers of the bowing hand; according to which string is played, both sides of the horsehair are used. The player's left thumb is hooked round the slender neck and the other fingers pull the strings towards the neck, there being no fingerboard. There is a position system for the left-hand fingering, as with the Western violin. The small bridge is slid to the centre of the soundtable when a full sound is required, as in ensembles with loud wind instruments, and closer to the upper edge when a gentler sound is called for, as in ensembles to accompany singing. The strings are tuned a 5th apart, a typical tuning being a♭ and e♭, and the *haegŭm* has an impressive range of three octaves. It has a nasal timbre which, though not especially loud, is distinctive enough to be heard even in large ensembles. It is capable of rich ornamentation and of dynamic contrast.

The *haegŭm* is thought to be of Mongolian (Tatar) origin, and indeed its nasal tone-quality is not dissimilar to certain types of Mongolian singing. It was used in China by the 10th century, and the first known citation of the name in Korea occurs in a poem of the first half of the 13th century. Until at least the end of the 15th century it was used only in Korean *hyangak* ('native music'), but it is now used also in *tangak* ('Chinese music'); this is the reverse of the usual Korean pattern of a foreign instrument used initially for foreign music and only later adapted for native music.

Today the instrument is usually played in mixed ensembles. Like the bowed long zither *ajaeng* it can sustain notes and therefore often appears in so-called 'wind' ensembles. It is a favourite instrument in shaman ensembles (*sinawi*) and folksong accompaniments and it occasionally serves as soloist in the virtuoso genre *sanjo*.

BIBLIOGRAPHY

Sŏng Hyŏn, ed.: *Akhak kwebŏm* [Guide to the study of music] (Seoul, 1493/R1975), 7.8a–9a
L. Picken: 'Early Chinese Friction-chordophones', *GSJ*, xviii (1965), 85
Chang Sa-hun: *Han' guk akki taegwan* [Korean musical instruments] (Seoul, 1969), 61ff

ROBERT C. PROVINE

Haemiol. An ORGAN STOP.

Hagaerts. Flemish family of harpsichord makers. Cornelis Hagaerts (*b* Breda; *d* Antwerp, 17 June 1642) was married in 1613 and is listed as a member of the Guild of St Luke, Antwerp (1626–7); he was also a member of the carpenters' guild. In 1640 he bought a house, 'De clavesimmele', in the Kattenstraat. He had three daughters and two sons, of whom the eldest, Simon Hagaerts (baptized Antwerp, 21 Dec 1613), became a harpsichord maker. Simon appears in the St Luke ledgers for 1641–2. In 1657 he agreed that he would supply instruments for Angela Van den Brant (Joannes Couchet's widow) to sell, probably as Couchet instruments. That year he also agreed to take Couchet's son as an apprentice. He is listed as living at 'Son ende Maan', Lange Klarenstraat, in 1666; he made his will with his wife Catharina Begode at this address.

The inventory of Cornelis Hagaerts's workshop includes 12 bundles (containing 25 pieces each) and 10 separate pieces of wood for soundboards; it also mentions the tools used. Hagaerts instruments were advertised in the 18th-century *Gazet van Antwerpen*. Four of the family's instruments are known to survive: two virginals by Cornelis (1636: Antwerp, formerly in Brussels and sold at Sotheby's, 1980; 1641: Cherbourg, collection Magne) and two harpsichords by Simon (n.d., Brussels Conservatoire; 1632, Paris Conservatoire).

BIBLIOGRAPHY
J. Lambrechts-Douillez: 'Klavicimbelbouwersfamilie Hagaerts', *Mededelingen van het Ruckers-genootschap*, ii (1982)
                                    JEANNINE LAMBRECHTS-DOUILLEZ

Hagēlung. Lute of the southern Philippines. *See* KUDYAPIQ.

Haidi. Chinese oboe. *See* SUONA.

Hail. *See* HAYL family.

Hailuo. Chinese CONCH-SHELL TRUMPET. The same pictograph is used for the (obsolete) Vietnamese *hải loa* (or *hải lo*). *See* FALUO.

Hainlein [Heinlein, Hainla]. German family of brass instrument makers. They were a Nuremberg family, descended from a line of coppersmiths; Sebastian Hainlein the elder (*d* 24 Feb 1631) was the first of the brass instrument makers. His son Sebastian Hainlein the younger (*b* 16 March 1594; *d* 31 Jan 1655) played the trombone; he waited in vain for years to be appointed as a Stadtpfeifer. His instruments were esteemed as far away as Salzburg, from where the Archbishop Paris Lodron ordered a trombone (made in 1622). Another son, Hans [Johannes] Hainlein (*b* 21 April 1598; *d* 26 Oct 1671), was probably the teacher of Johann Wilhelm HAAS and Wolfgang Birckholz. Paul Hainlein (1626–86), a son of Sebastian the younger, was a noted composer and organist, as well as a trombonist and instrument maker. According to Wörthmüller (1954–5), Michael Hainlein (*b* 19 July 1659; *d* before 1725), Paul's son, was the first Nuremberg craftsman to abandon the funnel-shaped bell, characteristic of the late Renaissance and early Baroque, in favour of one with a wider flare (later made famous especially by the Haas family). Michael's daughter Margareta (1687–1732) married the brass instrument maker Daniel Kodisch (*b* 9 Nov 1686; buried 27 Jan 1747), who may have taken over his father-in-law's workshop between 1713 and 1725.

Most of the surviving Hainlein instruments are trombones. Examples include: a tenor trombone made in 1627 by Sebastian the elder, the only surviving instrument by him (Bayerisches Nationalmuseum, Munich); a bass trombone made in 1622 by Sebastian the younger (Museum Carolino-Augusteum, Salzburg); and a trumpet in modern D♭ made in 1632 by Hans (Stadtmuseum, Munich). A trumpet (Carl Claudius Samling, Copenhagen) and trombone (Germanisches Nationalmuseum, Nuremberg) exist as examples of Paul Hainlein's work as an instrument maker.

The dates on at least three instruments presumably made by Sebastian the younger have yet to be explained. Although he died in 1655 (Wörthmüller also gives 1635, 1651 and 1653), there is an instrument by him (Historisches Museum, Basle) bearing the date 1657. A *buisine* attributed to 'Sebastian Hainlein' in the Boston Museum of Fine Arts (Galpin Collection) is dated 1460; a transposition of these numerals would yield the more probable date of 1640, but such a procedure would not explain fully the inscription on the bell of the *buisine* in the Museo degli Strumenti Musicali, Rome (no.452), which reads 'Macht Sebastiano Hainlein Siena, 1461'.

BIBLIOGRAPHY
N. Bessaraboff: *Ancient European Musical Instruments* (New York, 1941, 2/1964), 188
W. Wörthmüller: 'Die Nürnberger Trompeten- und Posaunenmacher des 17. und 18. Jahrhunderts', *Mitteilungen des Vereins für Geschichte der Stadt Nürnberg*, xlv (1954), 208; xlvi (1955), 372
L. G. Langwill: *An Index of Musical Wind-instrument Makers* (Edinburgh, 1960, rev., enlarged 6/1980)
K. Pechstein: 'Die Merkzeichentafel der Nürnberger Trompeten- und Posaunenmacher von 1640', *Mitteilungen des Vereins für Geschichte der Stadt Nürnberg*, lix (1972), 198
                                    EDWARD H. TARR

Hajīr. Cylindrical drum of the Arab world.

Haka, Richard (*b* London, 1645 or 1646; *d* Amsterdam, 1709). English woodwind maker. It is not known when he moved to Amsterdam, but in 1679, when he took his nephew Coenraad Rijkel as apprentice, he lived there on the Spui at 'De Vergulde Bas-Fluit'. Rijkel, who became his partner in about 1696 and succeeded him on his death, issued a trade card (reproduced in *ZI*, lvi, 1936, pp.120–21) showing a three-keyed oboe and a four-keyed bassoon, the fourth key on the latter being placed for a left-handed player. Haka recorders, oboes, shawms, and oboes da caccia survive in continental museums. A shawm made by Haka was formerly in Galpin's collection (sold in 1946) and another was in the Mengelberg Collection (sold in 1952).

BIBLIOGRAPHY
A. C. Carse: *Musical Wind Instruments* (London, 1939)
L. G. Langwill: *An Index of Musical Wind-instrument Makers* (Edinburgh, 1960, rev., enlarged 6/1980)
                                    LYNDESAY G. LANGWILL

Hakenharfe (Ger.). HOOK HARP.

Hak-gediya. CONCH-SHELL TRUMPET of Sri Lanka. *See* SAK.

Hakuhan. CLAPPERS of Japan. *See* MINSHINGAKU.

Halalū (Assyrian). *See* HALIL.

Halam (i). Eight-string idiochord cornstalk or reed RAFT ZITHER of the Serere people of the Gambia. Two sticks are inserted as bridges to raise a sliver of each stalk as a string. The corresponding instrument of the Jola people has been reported as *balambale*.

Halam (ii). Plucked lute of Senegal and the Gambia. *See* KHALAM.

Halan. *See* TUI.

Halary. French firm of wind instrument makers. It was founded in 1768 and was taken over in 1804 from one Engoulevant or Ambouvelant by Jean-Hilaire Asté. He had gone to Paris in 1796 and later adopted the name Halary (i). In 1825 Jean-Louis Antoine (*b* Paris, 14 Jan 1788; *d* Paris, 1861), a former worker with Courtois, joined Halary (i) and succeeded him about 1840; he similarly adopted the name (Halary (ii)) but used the spelling 'Halari' on his instruments. His son Jules-Léon Antoine (*b* Paris, 1 May 1827), i.e. Halary (iii), was a fine horn player; he joined the business and took control on his father's death, selling it in 1873 to Coste & Cie., which was taken over by François Sudre in 1875.

The firm of Halary made a reputation for considerable experiment in the invention and manufacture of brass instruments and of woodwind instruments made of brass or other metals. Halary (i) made three new instruments about 1817 and patented them in 1821: the clavitube, a seven-keyed bugle; the quinticlave, a nine- or ten-keyed alto or bass bugle; and the ophicleide, originally with seven or nine keys, but in an 1822 patent including 12. The KEYED BUGLE may have been copied from Haliday's design of 1810, of which the ophicleide was certainly a modification. In 1818 he made brass flutes, bassoons and clarinets.

Halary (ii) quickly made a reputation for enterprise, gaining a medal in 1827 for brass flutes, clarinets and horns. He devised *plaques tournantes* (disc valves) for brass instruments, possibly after designs by John Shaw, although he also used the more effective Stölzel valve. He later improved the piston mechanism. In 1855 he built a contrabass double-slide trombone. In 1849 Halary (iii) constructed a three-valve horn (as opposed to the then normal two-valve instrument) with an ascending third valve.

See also CORNET (i), §2 and OMNITON; for illustration of a late 19th-century instrument by Halary, *see* TROMBONE, fig.5*d*.

BIBLIOGRAPHY
J. Meifred: 'Notice sur la fabrication des instruments de musique en cuivre', *Annuaire de la Société des anciens élèves des écoles nationales des arts-et-métiers* (Paris, 1851)
C. Pierre: *La facture instrumentale à l'Exposition universelle de 1889* (Paris, 1890)
——: *Les facteurs d'instruments de musique* (Paris, 1893/R1971)
A. Baines: *Brass Instruments: their History and Development* (London, 1976/R1980)

NIALL O'LOUGHLIN

Halbinstrument (Ger.). Term for a trumpet with a bore too narrow to permit the fundamental to be played.

Halbmond. *See* BUGLE (i).

Hale, John (*fl* London, 1785–1804). English wind instrument maker, successor to THOMAS COLLIER; *see also* J. J. SCHUCHART.

Half-tube zither. Term for a zither in which 'the strings are stretched along the convex surface of a gutter' (*see* CHORDOPHONE); the so-called 'long zithers' of East Asia (the *koto* and the *qin*) are of this type.

Halgī. FRAME DRUM of Gujarat and Maharashtra, western India. The rim frame is of iron and the parchment membrane, often painted decoratively, is pasted and laced on. The diameter of the head is about 45 cm. The *raṇahalgī* is a similar instrument. See K. S. Kothari: *Indian Folk Musical Instruments* (New Delhi, 1968), 36.

Haliday [Halliday], Joseph (*b* Yorkshire, *c*1772; *d* Dublin, 1857). Irish musician and poet, inventor of the KEYED BUGLE. He went to Ireland as an infant. As bandmaster of the Cavan Militia, he was noted for his arrangement of an ancient Irish marching song, *O'Donnell Abú*. He was also the author of a musical lampoon, *Secrets Worth Knowing or Rules for Keeping a Music Shop* (1817). But he is best known for his invention of the keyed bugle, which he patented in 1810. A pupil of his was reported to have played a concerto on it in Dublin in 1811. Haliday moved to Wexford the next year, and in his absence, J. B. Logier wrote his *Introduction to the Art of Playing on the Royal Kent Bugle* (1813), dedicated to the Duke of Kent. Logier, leader of the Kilkenny Militia Band and a music shop owner who depended on the sale of instruments to the military, may have encouraged the unauthorized manufacture of keyed bugles in Dublin; it was probably he who had them stamped 'Royal Kent Bugle' to capitalize on the trade in instruments to the military (Haliday's political posture makes it unlikely that he would have done so). The keyed bugle was soon in use by most British regimental bands. Haliday returned to Dublin in 1816, to find Logier and others making keyed bugles (some show the spelling 'Halliday'). To discredit Logier, Haliday published a booklet, *Strictures on Mr. Logier's Pamphlets* (1817), dealing primarily with Logier's 'Chiroplast' and the methods associated with it but also discussing Logier's false claims to the patent rights to the keyed bugle.

BIBLIOGRAPHY
F. W. Saunders: 'O Donnell Abú and the Royal Kent Bugle', *Irish Book Lover*, xxvi (1939), 85
M. I. Hogan: *Anglo-Irish Music* (Cork, 1966)
R. T. Dudgeon: *The Keyed Bugle: its History, Literature and Technique* (diss., U. of California, San Diego, 1980)
——: 'Joseph Haliday, Inventor of the Keyed Bugle', *JAMIS*, ix (1983), 53

RALPH T. DUDGEON

Halikopoulos, Nicolaos. *See* MANTZAROS, NICOLAOS.

Halil (Heb.). A term applied to several types of ancient instrument. It is generally assumed, on various grounds, that the biblical *ḥalil* was the Israelite equivalent of the Greek aulos and the Egyptian *māt*. The etymological derivation suggests that it was a tube and some of the contexts in which it was used (*Isaiah* v.12 and xxx.29, *I Kings* i.40) indicate that it was normally a joyful instrument. Certainly geminate instruments of the aulos type existed in ancient Israel, for they were frequently portrayed (Bayer, group C.V), but other woodwind instruments, including single pipes, were also used. Of the various Hebrew words thought to indicate woodwind instruments, only *ḥalil* appears with any frequency, and it is therefore possible that it meant pipes in general, probably though not certainly those played with a reed. It should be remembered also that the text of the Bible was written over many centuries, quite time enough for words to change their meaning and instruments their type.

BIBLIOGRAPHY
B. Bayer: *The Material Relics of Music in Ancient Palestine and its Environs: an Archaeological Inventory* (Tel-Aviv, 1963, 2/1964)
JEREMY MONTAGU

Halile. Turkish cymbals played in pairs. They are used in religious music, especially in the ensembles of the Mevlevî (whirling dervishes).

Hall, D(avid) C. (*b* Lyme, New Hampshire, 16 May 1822; *d* Boston, 11 Feb 1900). American band-leader and brass instrument manufacturer. He was living in New Haven, Connecticut, in 1845 and 1846, and was by then an accomplished player on the keyed bugle. Shortly after this he became director and E♭ bugle soloist with the Lowell, Massachusetts, brass band. He was presented with an extremely fine E♭ keyed bugle of solid gold on 15 April 1850 by the members of the Lowell band. In 1853 Hall succeeded Patrick Gilmore as leader of the Boston Brass Band and retained this position for many years.

In 1862 after a year of partnership with J. Lathrop Allen, a leading Boston instrument maker, Hall began his own brass instrument manufactory. He was joined by Benjamin F. Quinby, and from 1866 to 1875 Hall & Quinby were leading producers of brass instruments in Boston. These were made in circular and over-shoulder shapes as well as in forms common today, and they were usually equipped with Allen valves. Although most of Hall & Quinby's instruments were pitched alternately in E♭ and B♭ like saxhorns, they also made brass instruments pitched a 3rd apart, like those in the 1872 patent of R. H. Gates. A set of these instruments is in the Janssen Collection, Claremont, California.

After 1880 Hall retired from instrument making but continued his band-leading career until late in the century.
ROBERT E. ELIASON

Hall, Thomas (*b* Philadelphia, 1791; *d* New York, 23 May 1874). American organ builder. He was apprenticed to John Lowe of Philadelphia, where he began his own business in 1811; he moved to New York about 1816, becoming the founder of the New York group of organ builders in the 19th century. One of his first important organs was built in 1818 for the Unitarian Church of Baltimore. In 1824 he formed a partnership with HENRY ERBEN, his brother-in-law and former apprentice, which lasted until 1827 and resulted in several organs for large churches in New York and elsewhere. In 1832 Hall built a substantial organ for St Thomas's, New York. In 1846 he formed a new partnership with John Labagh (1810–92) under the name of Hall & Labagh, and in 1868 James L. Kemp joined the firm, which continued a steady production of quality instruments, including a replacement for their earlier St Thomas's organ in 1870. Hall retired in 1872, and the firm continued under the name of Labagh & Kemp until 1891, when it was sold to the short-lived partnership of Chapman & Symmes.

BIBLIOGRAPHY
P. T. Cameron: 'Business Records of Hall, Labagh & Co.', *The Tracker*, xiv/4 (1969–70), 5; xv (1970–71), no.1, p.1, no.2, p.6, no.3, p.6, no.4, p.14; xvi/1 (1971–2), 11
O. Ochse: *The History of the Organ in the United States* (Bloomington, Ind., 1975)
J. Ogasapian: *Organ Building in New York City, 1700–1900* (Braintree, Mass., 1977)
BARBARA OWEN

Halliday, Joseph. *See* HALIDAY, JOSEPH.

Halmpipe. Idioglot straw pipe of Norway.

Hals (i). Norwegian firm of piano makers. The brothers Karl Hals (*b* Sörum, 27 April 1822; *d* Christiania [now Oslo], 1898) and Petter Hals (1823–71) set up as Hals Brødrene, piano makers, in Christiania in November 1847, having studied piano making abroad. They first made only oblique-strung upright pianos, but later changed to upright vertical and cross-strung instruments, better suited to the harsh Norwegian climate. They manufactured only a small number of instruments, as they also specialized in repair work, but they received medals at exhibitions in 1862, 1866 and 1867.

By 1869 their bichord and trichord upright pianos had three iron bars and metal plates bracing the deepest octaves, the larger trichord upright pianos having five iron bars with metal plates for all the strings. All vertical upright pianos had seven octaves whereas grand and cross-strung upright pianos had seven and a quarter octaves. In cross-strung upright pianos the strings were somewhat longer, giving a rich tone, the metal plate being fastened to an iron frame under the soundboard, and to three iron bars placed over it. The firm made harmoniums from 1886 to 1910.

Karl's sons, Thor and Sigurd, joined the firm in 1888, and in 1900 it became a limited company. In 1925 it was taken over by Grøndahl & Son, of Øvre Slottsgaten, Oslo.

BIBLIOGRAPHY
Hals Brothers, Manufacturers of Piano-fortes (Christiania, 1869)
MARGARET CRANMER

Hals (Ger.) **(ii).** NECK.

Hamburger Cithrinchen (Ger.). *See* CITHRINCHEN.

Hamel, Marie-Pierre (*b* Auneuil, 24 Feb 1786; *d* Beauvais, 25 July 1879). French organ builder and writer. A dedicated advocate of the classical French organ, he deplored the 'mutilations de la mode'. He was a member of the Commission des Arts and founded the Société Philharmonique de Beauvais in 1825. In 1826 he rebuilt the organ in Beauvais Cathedral (five manuals and pedal, 64 stops; destroyed 1940). He wrote a report on the organ at La Madeleine, Paris (1846), and *Nouveau manuel complet du facteur d'orgues* (Paris, 1849, 2/1903), consisting of three volumes of text and one of plates.
GUY OLDHAM

Hamilton, James Baillie. English instrument maker. He began manufacture of the VOCALION in Worcester, Massachusetts, in 1886.

Hammarberg. Swedish family of organ builders active for five generations in Göteborg; in 1898 they began to work under the name 'Olof Hammarberg', which continues to be the name of the family firm. The first member of the family to build organs was Adolf Fredrik Pettersson (1811–72), who was originally a master carpenter; in 1848 he completed the rebuilding and enlargement of the organ in the church of St Karl Johan, Göteborg. His son, Gustaf Adolf Pettersson (1840–98), gained experience in his father's workshop and with the Danish firm of Marcussen at Aabenraa; after his father's death Gustaf registered as an organ builder in Göteborg, where he constructed mainly small-scale pipe organs and harmoniums. His son, Olof Pettersson Hammarberg (1871–1942), was also a pupil at Marcussen's and later trained in Germany and the USA. The 150 organs built during his directorship are all markedly Romantic in character.

Olof's son, Nils Olof Hammarberg (b 23 June 1913), trained at the Chalmers Tekniska Högskola, Göteborg, and obtained practical experience in Denmark and Germany; he took over the management of the family firm in 1935 and obtained the state diploma in 1943. He has always applied classical principles of organ design in his work, though his later output shows some tendency towards a more Romantic style of specification. Among the more than 400 organs built by Nils Olof Hammarberg are those in the churches of St Högalid, Stockholm (1966; 56 stops); St Oscar Fredrik, Göteborg (1969); and St Caroli, Borås (1970). He has also built organs for Finland, the Netherlands and the USA and restored organs at Jonserad, Morlanda and the old church at Nässjö (among others). Since 1972 his son Bo Gunnar Hammarberg (b 10 Sept 1945) has been a partner in the firm.

based on *Sohlmans musiklexikon* (iii, 310–11) by permission of Sohlmans Förlag

BENGT KYHLBERG

Hammer (i). A component of the action of a piano; *see* PIANOFORTE, esp. §I, 2, 6, and figs.19, 32–3, and ACOUSTICS, §II, 4.

Hammer (ii). A term for the mallet with which such instruments as the xylophone, tubular bells and certain types of dulcimer are struck.

Hammer (iii). *See* ANVIL.

Hammerflügel (Ger.). GRAND PIANOFORTE.

Hammerklavier [Hammerclavier] (Ger.). Term for the piano ('hammer-keyboard') favoured in Germany in the second and third decades of the 19th century; it was used by Beethoven and his publisher Steiner for some of his late sonatas. *See* PIANOFORTE, §I, 1.

Hammer-Orgelbau. German firm of organ builders. Its beginnings were in 1830, when Philipp Furtwängler (b Gütenbach, Baden-Württemberg, 6 April 1800; d Elze, Hanover, 5 July 1867), a clockmaker in Elze, took up organ building, teaching himself; he completed his first instrument in 1838. He took his son Wilhelm (b Elze, 5 June 1829; d Elze, 4 Sept 1883) into the firm in 1854, and his son Pius (b Elze, 14 July 1841; d Hanover, 16 Jan 1910) in 1862, when the firm's name was altered to Ph. Furtwängler & Söhne, Elze. Adolf Hammer (b Herzberg im Harz, 6 April 1854; d Hanover, 5 March

1921) entered the firm in 1883, in which year it moved to Hanover and changed its name to P. Furtwängler & Hammer, Hanover. Adolf Hammer's nephew Emil Hammer (b Wesermünde, 22 Feb 1878; d Hanover, 3 Dec 1958) became managing director in 1921 and sole proprietor in 1937. After the war the business had to be rebuilt, and there were several changes of premises in the vicinity of Hanover: Empelde in 1949, Hemmingen-Westerfeld in 1958 and Arnum in 1965. In 1961 Emil Hammer's grandson Christian Eickhoff (b Shanghai, 23 Dec 1935) became managing director; he trained with Emil Hammer, Theodor Kuhn AG (Männedorf), and Axel Starup (Copenhagen), and at the Technical Institute in Ludwigsburg.

Philipp Furtwängler had built slider-chests with tracker action and followed J. G. Töpfer's 'normal scaling'; the firm built its first cone-chests in 1875 and its last slider-chest for many years in 1889; it produced its first organs with tubular pneumatic action in 1893, and its first with electro-pneumatic action in 1901; the first wind-chest with exhaust-pneumatic action was built in 1907. The firm's first organ built in accordance with the principles of the *Orgelbewegung* was that for St Marien in Göttingen, 1925–6 (instigated by Christhard Mahrenholz), and the first instrument for a generation to have a slider-chest and tracker action, in Hamburg-Langenhorn, 1931 (H. H. Jahnn). (These features are characteristic of most modern Hammer organs.) Their largest organ was built in 1914 for the Stadthalle in Hanover (four manuals, 128 stops). Recent instruments include those for the Stadtkirche in Bückeburg, 1966 (three manuals, 52 stops), the Jesus-Christuskirche in Berlin-Dahlem, 1970 (three manuals, 45 stops), St Martini in Stadthagen, 1974 (three manuals, 54 stops), and the monastery church of St Nicolai in Gdańsk, 1976 (two manuals, 33 stops).

BIBLIOGRAPHY
U. Pape: 'Philipp Furtwängler', *ISO Information*, xi (1974), 777

HANS KLOTZ

Hammond organ. An ELECTRONIC ORGAN developed in 1933–4 by the American engineers Laurens Hammond (b Evanston, Ill., 11 Jan 1895; d Cornwall, Conn., 1 July 1973) and John M. Hanert (inventor of the HANERT ELECTRICAL ORCHESTRA). Hammond's early patents included an electric clock (1920), and a small synchronous motor (1922), which achieves great accuracy by being synchronized to the frequency of the electrical supply (60 Hz in North America, 50 Hz in Europe). He founded the Hammond Clock Co. in Chicago in 1928 to manufacture clocks incorporating the synchronous motor, and in 1932 he marketed a bridge table featuring a card-shuffler that used the motor. In 1935 the company began to make the Hammond organ, which Hammond had patented in 1934 and first demonstrated in April 1935. The instrument was an immediate success – Henry Ford and George Gershwin were early purchasers – and Hammond organs have continued to maintain a leading position in the market; since the early 1970s the emphasis has been on home organs. By the end of the 1930s the company (renamed the Hammond Organ Co.) was making about 200 instruments a month, and about 2 million Hammond organs in many different models have been built altogether. In 1936 a Hammond organ was incorporated in a Mortier dance-hall barrel organ by Julius Bax of Antwerp, and in 1938 around 200 Aeolian–Hammond mechanical electronic organs

Part of the upper manual of a Hammond tone-wheel organ, showing the drawbars

were manufactured. Two other instruments, the NOVA-CHORD (1939–*c*1943) and the SOLOVOX (1940 to the late 1960s), were produced, and Hammond engineers took out over 50 US patents up to 1945 alone.

Although its sound quality differed in some respects from that of a pipe organ, the Hammond organ was purchased by some 1750 churches in the first three years of its manufacture (a third of all sales). From 1936 until 1938 the company fought a legal battle with the Federal Trade Commission for the right to call the instrument an organ; somewhat exaggerated claims made in early publicity were also involved. Although the case was decided against the company, Hammond were allowed to continue to call their instrument an 'organ', and soon afterwards a blind test was held in Chicago in which experts failed to distinguish between a Hammond and a pipe organ in a third of the examples played to them.

In models of the Hammond organ built before the mid-1960s the sounds are generated by an electromagnetic system similar to that first used in the Telharmonium at the end of the 19th century, but on a sufficiently small scale for the instrument to be portable by two people. The system consists of a set of 91 rotating tone-wheels (originally of iron, later steel), divided into 12 groups (one for each semitone), which are driven at appropriate speeds by gears attached to a single spindle; the spindle is turned by a stable synchronous motor, which ensures that even if the speed fluctuates all the notes remain in tune with one another. Each tone-wheel is approximately 4·7 cm in diameter and has a wave-shaped or corrugated circumference (*see* ELECTRONIC INSTRUMENTS, fig.2*b*) which produces a regular variation in the magnetic field of a pickup consisting of a bar magnet positioned an average of 0·02 mm away; these variations are converted into audible oscillations. The circumferences of the tone-wheels are shaped to produce 2, 4, 8, 16, 32, 64, 128 or 192 waveforms.

The original Hammond organ Model A has two five-octave manuals and a two-octave pedal-board. The basic waveform produced by the tone-wheels is sinusoidal, but variation and precise control of timbre are effected by a system of drawbars (see illustration) – two for the pedals and two sets of nine each for the manuals. These allow the sound generated by one tone-wheel to have overtones added to it in different combinations and degrees of volume. The overtone series is not the natural one (this is the chief difference between the Hammond and a pipe organ) since all but the octave intervals

are slightly tempered; the seventh harmonic is omitted from the drawbars altogether because the tempering makes it intolerable. Each drawbar has eight notched positions to give successive degrees of loudness. To the left of each manual are 12 reverse-colour keys, ten of which bring into operation preset timbre combinations, while the remaining two select one or other set of drawbars; in most recent models these keys have been replaced with piston buttons. The two pedal drawbars at first provided a rather weak bass; to correct this, more complex profiles were devised for the tone-wheels, producing a richer timbre (supplied by odd-numbered harmonics).

The Hammond Organ Co. pioneered several features of electronic organ design that are still common. In 1949 it produced its first 'spinet' organ, a type that has two staggered manuals (each usually with 44 notes) overlapping by an octave. A one-manual 'chord organ' was first marketed in the early 1950s. Based on the Hammond Solovox, this has a set of buttons like those on an accordion which produce chords to accompany a melody played on the manual; the sounds are generated by 12 oscillators using frequency division. The 'chorus generator' creates a realistic pipe organ sound by means of additional tone-wheels whose frequencies are slightly out of tune with those of the main system and therefore produce the characteristic soft beats. A familiar feature of most Hammond organs is the LESLIE loudspeaker which affects the sound like a tremulant stop on a pipe organ.

In the mid-1960s the electromagnetic tone-wheels were gradually superseded by an electronic sound system. To start with, the pitches of the highest octave were generated by 12 tone-wheels and those of the lower octaves derived from them by frequency division; later in the 1960s, after several years of manufacturing electronic organs for the Everett company, Hammond decided to replace the tone-wheels in this system with 12 oscillators. Since the early 1970s a single VHF crystal oscillator (3·99872 MHz) has been used with two stages of frequency division to produce successively the 12 semitones of the highest octave and of all the lower octaves. During the early 1970s advances in electronic technology made possible new features, which are now incorporated in many home electronic organs: rhythm and 'walking bass' units, arpeggiators, small memories and a choice of chord systems. The Hammond range now includes church, theatre and concert models (the last of which most closely resemble the early instruments), but is largely made up of home organs, the smaller of which have no drawbars. The larger current models (as well as some made by other companies) electronically mimic the 'key-click' that forms a distinctive element of the sound of the original Hammond tone-wheel organ.

Following its initial success the Hammond organ established itself very rapidly and it continues to be the best-known electronic organ. Jazz and popular musicians, including Ethel Smith, 'Fats' Waller, Jimmy Smith and 'Wild Bill' Davis, helped to gain a wide audience for it, and a distinctive Hammond style of 'swinging' staccato playing (due to a lack of control over attack in the early models) soon came into being. After World War II, demand grew for the Hammond organ as an instrument for use at home. In the 1960s it became popular with composers and it features prominently in Kagel's *Tremens* (1963–5) and Stockhausen's *Momente* (1961–4, 1969) and *Mikrophonie II* (1965), as well as in several orchestral works each by Friedrich Cerha, Luis de Pablo, Enrique Raxach and Cristóbal Halffter. At about the same time rock musicians, such as Keith Emerson, also adopted it.

See also ELECTRONIC INSTRUMENTS, §IV, 3. For an illustration of a Hammond organ, see ELECTRONIC ORGAN.

BIBLIOGRAPHY

The Diapason (1935–7) [many short articles]

W. Baggally: 'The Hammond Organ: a New Electro-Acoustic Musical Instrument', *Wireless World*, xli (1937), 134

MT, lxxviii (1937) [3 articles, in February and April issues]

S. Irwin: *Dictionary of Hammond Organ Stops* (New York, 1939, rev. 3/1968)

J. Schillinger: *The Schillinger System of Musical Composition*, ii (New York, 1946), 1549

J. M. Barbour: *Tuning and Temperament: a Historical Survey* (East Lansing, Mich., 1951), 74

R. H. Dorf: *Electronic Musical Instruments* (Mineola, NY, 2/1958), 25, 142

W. H. Barnes: *The Contemporary American Organ: its Evolution, Design and Construction* (Glen Rock, NJ, 7/1959), 348

H. E. Anderson: *Electronic Organ Handbook* (Indianapolis, 1960), 97

A. Douglas: *The Electronic Musical Instrument Manual: a Guide to Theory and Design* (London, 5/1968), 261

T. L. Rhea: *The Evolution of Electronic Musical Instruments in the United States* (diss., George Peabody College, Nashville, Tenn., 1972), 146; section rev. as 'The Hammond Organ, Part I', 'Hammond Organ, Part II: Hammond and the FTC', *Contemporary Keyboard*, iii (1977), no.5, p.47, no.6, p.47

N. H. Crowhurst: *Electronic Organs*, iii (Indianapolis, 1975), 53

O. Ochse: *The History of the Organ in the United States* (Bloomington, Ind., 1975), 375

D. Crombie: 'The Hammond Story', *Sound International*, no.29 (1980), 24; rev. in *Rock Hardware: the Instruments, Equipment and Technology of Rock*, ed. T. Bacon (Poole, Dorset, 1981), 88

HUGH DAVIES

Hampel [Hampl, Hampla], **Anton Joseph** (*b* Prague, *c*1710; *d* Dresden, 30 March 1771). Bohemian horn player, teacher and inventor. He is noted for designing the *Inventionshorn* (*see* INVENTION) and for developing hand-stopping techniques on the horn; his experiments further led to the evolution of the non-transposing mute.

Hamu. SLIT-DRUM of the Polynesian island, Nukumanu. See E. Sarfert and H. Damm: 'Luangiua und Nukumanu: Soziale Verhaltnisse und Geisterkultur', *Ergebnisse der Südsee-Expedition 1908–1910*, IIB, xii (Hamburg, 1931), 461.

Han. The general term for three types of Japanese percussion plaque, each consisting of a 'slab' (*han*) suspended vertically, struck with a mallet and used primarily as a signalling device in Buddhist temples and monasteries. Their names describe them: the *unpan* is a 'cloud-shaped' board of copper or iron; the *moppan* a nearly rectangular 'wooden' slab; and the *gyoban* a 'fish-shaped' slab. They are related to the Chinese BAN. See W. P. Malm: *Japanese Music and Musical Instruments* (Rutland, Vermont, 1959), 70.

DAVID W. HUGHES

Handaeoline (Ger.). A portable instrument of the reed organ family, patented by C. F. L. Buschmann in 1821. *See* ACCORDION.

Handbassel [Handbassl] (Ger.). A bowed string instrument, probably the VIOLA DA SPALLO. According to Leopold Mozart (*Versuch einer gründlichen Violinschule*, Augsburg, 1756), the name was sometimes wrongly used for the VIOLA DI FAGOTTO.

Handbell (Fr. *clochette, sonnette*; Ger. *Tischglocke, Handglocke*; It. *campanello a mano*; Sp. *campanilla, esquila*). A bell with a handle (shaft or loop) enabling it to be held in the hand for ringing. Usually it has a clapper inside and is swung to produce a sound, although it may also be held stationary and tapped with a hammer. Single handbells are used in music to provide an element of pitch, rhythm and tone-colour; from ancient times they have been used frequently in religious music because of the esoteric properties ascribed to bell sound. Handbells are mostly used in sets, which may contain about six to over 60 bells covering a range from a short melodic scale to five chromatic octaves. The largest sets include bells 40 cm to 5 cm in diameter, from 2 kg to 0·2 kg in weight, and sounding c to c''''. There may be a slight increase in loudness towards the upper end of the range (the reverse of the pattern for carillon bells).

Western handbell music is usually performed by a 'team' or 'choir' of four to 15 'ringers' (fig.1). Each ringer either holds one or two handbells in each hand or lifts the appropriate bells from a table as the notes are required. Handbell music contains both harmonic and melodic elements and reflects the fact that handbells are effectively the only bells that can be damped. The

1. *The Sound in Brass handbell team, Chelmsford, Essex; the set of 79 bells, by the Whitechapel Bell Foundry, covers four and a half octaves*

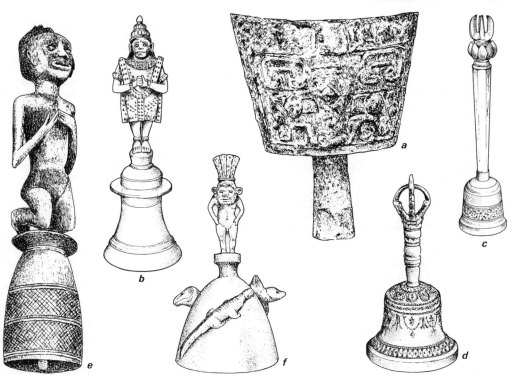

2. Handbells: (a) Chinese, with fish-mouth rim (Shang dynasty, c1766–1028 BC); (b) Hindu, with handle depicting the god Hanuman; (c) rei, used in Japanese goeika music; (d) Tibetan, 19th century; (e) wooden, from Nigeria; (f) Egyptian (c1000 BC), with handle depicting the god Bes

repertory includes both original compositions and arrangements, solo works and combinations with voices and other instruments; there is also music for two handbell choirs. Several systems of scoring handbell music exist, some influenced by the use of numbers in English CHANGE RINGING, others by the letters of tonic sol-fa notation; staff notation is most common, with the notes written an octave below sounding pitch.

The oldest extant handbells are from China, dating from about 1600 BC. Chinese writings refer to still earlier handbells, and ascribe transcendental powers to their sound. Early Chinese handbells are oval in horizontal section and usually have a concave or 'fish-mouth' rim (fig.2a). Around the 6th century BC the Chinese began to tune their handbells and attach them to a frame for striking (see CHIMES).

In ancient India the handbell was venerated for both its sound and its appearance; for the Hindus it symbolized the 'world lotus', out of which issued the hosts of the created world, as sounds issue from a bell. The lotus determined its form, circular in horizontal section with sides flaring towards the rim in vertical profile (fig.2b); this proved also to be the best shape acoustically, and has been adopted for most modern handbells. The oldest extant examples are of the 5th or 6th century BC.

Buddhism inherited this shape of handbell, and spread its use across eastern Asia, and in the 6th century AD introduced it into Japan. In the 9th century handbells came to be used for accompaniment in the singing of Japanese goeika hymns. In goeika performance each singer alternately rings a rei (small handbell) and strikes a small metal disc. Both instruments have a high, indef-

inite pitch and add a sparkle to the vocal tone comparable to that which the Western triangle and cymbals give to Coptic plainchant. The rei is difficult to manipulate; it has a particularly long handle and is only about 5 cm in diameter (fig.2c), whereas the diameter of the average Buddhist handbell is closer to 10 cm (fig.2d). Goeika has always retained its religious nature, in regard both to repertory and to the sanctity of the bell; there are several thousand goeika societies in Japan, which hold annual conventions.

Handbells are indigenous to many parts of Africa as instruments for religious rites, signalling and musical performance. Africans use both cast and forged handbells, the latter having been more prevalent until the 20th century. The bells range in size from 10 cm to 40 cm, handle to rim, and are mostly of a flattened shape, recalling some early Chinese bell forms. In certain areas clusters of two to six or more bells are attached to a handle, and are played by tapping (see BELL (i), fig.10); these are used in ensemble music and to accompany songs and dances.

In ancient Egypt handbells were used in temple rites from the 8th century BC. Egyptian bells are datable chiefly on circumstantial evidence: on early bells the gods are symbolized by animals (fig.2f); then, under new religious influences, animals gave way to flowers, flowers to lines, and eventually, in the case of Coptic altar bells, to the Christian cross. Although small, extant examples show good castings, mostly of an ovoid shape said to be derived from the top of the canopic or funerary urn.

Christian missionaries carried handbells into western Europe on their journeys from Mediterranean Africa,

3. Woman dressed as a hobby-horse and ringing two handbells, accompanied by musician with pipe and tabor: miniature from a French psalter, before 1302 (GB-Ob Douce 118, f.34r)

and made others along the way, although the latter were mostly forged and so lacked resonance. Like orchestral cowbells, they had loop rather than shaft handles and were intended to be joggled rather than swung. Their tone was suitable for funeral processions and wakes, an ancient and universal use based on the belief that the sound of blessed bells protects the souls of the dead. Cast handbells, with their more resonant tone, were made in Italy for church use from the 6th century, but did not become widespread until the 8th century or later. In general the handbell preceded the tower bell as a means of calling to divine services.

In western Europe handbells are first shown in a musical use in manuscripts of the 13th century (fig.3), about the time that small bells were first tuned in diatonic series (*see* CHIMES). Handbells may have been used in some late medieval and early Renaissance music for singers, other instrumentalists, or both, but without notation calling for them. They were apparently played in jubilant processions, where they would have been effective because of their brilliant tone-colour; their almost permanent retention of pitch caused them to be used for retaining standards of pitch and intonation.

In the 17th century handbells were a target for Puritan suppression in England. Subsequently, the bells were given a new use by tower bell ringers as instruments on which to rehearse the new change-ringing sequences then coming into fashion. To improve both the tone of the bell and the control of the clapper in this practice, pegs (of wood and, later, leather) were attached to the ball of the clapper; springs at the top end of the bell kept the clapper from resting against the side. These additions enlarged the instrument's musical resources and opened the way for modern development in handbell music.

By the mid-19th century virtually every village in England had its handbell team. Such groups went through the streets and country lanes playing carols at Christmas, and at other times performed at local entertainments; some travelled and competed. Only a few isolated groups on the Continent took up this type of bell ringing; the term 'Swiss' in relation to it is a misnomer.

There is however a related folk art using herd bells (*see* BELL (i), §4(v), for reference to Balkan and Swiss herd bells). In Great Britain over 100 teams belong to the Handbell Ringers of Great Britain (founded 1967). Among English handbell makers, the Cor brothers were important in the late 17th century; the WHITECHAPEL BELL FOUNDRY, which has been making bells since the late 16th century, is still prominent.

From about 1840 bands of ringers, some of them composed of single immigrant families, began to tour the eastern USA, and for a while many of these continued to flourish in the Chautauqua programmes and in vaudeville circuits. But before the demise of the professional handbell team, the English tradition of amateur home teams had already been established. The first of these was founded in Boston, Massachusetts, in 1895 by Arthur Nichols; a further dozen teams were founded in New England by his daughter, Margaret Shurcliff, in the first half of the 20th century. From these, the popularity of handbell ringing spread across North America. About 1000 teams, representing 10,000 ringers, are members of the American Guild of English Handbell Ringers (founded 1954), which issues periodical publications.

BIBLIOGRAPHY
S. B. Goslin: *The ABC of Musical Handbell Ringing* (Oxford, 1864, rev., enlarged 2/1974)
S. B. Parry: *The Story of Handbells* (Boston, 1957)
N. P. Tufts: *The Art of Handbell Ringing* (New York, 1961, rev. 2/1973)
P. Bedford: *An Introduction to English Handbell Tune Ringing* (Chelmsford, 1974)
——: *Carol Ringing and More* (Chelmsford, 1974)
J. J. Hannon: *50 Popular Tunes* (Oxford, 1974)
A. S. Hudson and N. Bullen: *Music for Handbells* (Chelmsford, 1977)

PERCIVAL PRICE

Handchime. An instrument designed by DAVID SAWYER in Exeter in 1978 and manufactured by the Handchime Company in Exeter and later in nearby Moretonhampstead since 1979. It is one of a series of instruments developed by Sawyer from the early 1970s which consist of a bamboo, aluminium or steel tube, open or closed at the lower end, with one or, more often, two longitudinal slots cut in the upper end (on opposite sides when there are two, so that two tongues, like the arms of a tuning fork, are created); the slot or slots are of such a length that the note produced by striking one of the tongues is identical with that of the resonant cavity or its first overtone. The Handchime itself is a square steel tube, struck at the slotted end with a sprung loop beater which is attached externally. It is played in the same way as, and sounds somewhat like, a handbell (though with a simpler harmonic content), for which it provides a cheaper substitute.

BIBLIOGRAPHY
D. Sawyer: *Vibrations: Making Unorthodox Musical Instruments* (Cambridge, 2/1980), 25

HUGH DAVIES

Handharmonika (Ger.). ACCORDION.

Hand horn. A natural (i.e. valveless) HORN.

Handja. XYLOPHONE of the Fang people of West Africa. It is held between the player's knees, and has a bamboo frame and calabash resonators fitted with mirlitons of spider-egg membrane.

Hand organ. *See* BARREL ORGAN.

Hand piano. *See* LAMELLAPHONE.

Hand-screw drum. A KETTLEDRUM whose tuning screws are operated manually (as opposed to the mechanical devices used in the tuning of 'machine' drums). *See* TIMPANI, §1.

Hanert Electrical Orchestra [Apparatus for Automatic Production of Music]. A graphic composition machine developed in 1944–5 by John Marshall Hanert (*b* 1909), head of research at the Hammond Organ Co. in Chicago, but not manufactured. A scanning unit on wheels is driven by an electric motor along rails above rows of cards (approximately 28 by 30 cm) laid out on a table 18 metres long. On the underside of the unit, brushes make contact with electrically conductive erasable graphite marks on the cards, which control the frequency, intensity, growth, duration, decay, portamento, timbre and vibrato of the tones produced by electronic oscillators. Three keyboards, each with a range of about five and a half octaves, are connected to the machine. Although Hanert's idea was to reverse the procedure used in 'reading' punched paper tape, the programming of his machine may be more accurately related to the principle of DRAWN SOUND. Hanert also assisted in the development of the Hammond organ from 1933, and was responsible for over a dozen of the patents taken out by the company during the 1940s and early 1950s.

BIBLIOGRAPHY
T. L. Rhea: *The Evolution of Electronic Musical Instruments in the United States* (diss., George Peabody College, Nashville, Tenn., 1972), 188; section rev. as 'The Hanert Synthesizer (1945)', *Contemporary Keyboard*, v (1979), no.9 p.78
HUGH DAVIES

Hangar. Bamboo CLAPPERS of the Ifugao people of the northern Philippines. A bamboo tube, about 4 cm in diameter and 35 cm long, is split in half from the top to near the base, where a node prevents further splitting. The middle section of each tube is carved and narrowed, making it flexible enough to bend so that the upper portions of the tube can be flapped against each other.

Hanhye [toba]. Idiochord RAFT ZITHER of the Mahi people of Benin. It has four sets of three strings, which are plucked with the thumbs. The *hanhye* may be played above an empty vessel, such as a bucket, or used with clapperless bells and wicker rattles.

Hanhyego. Gourd vessel rattle of the Fon people of Benin. It has an external network of cowrie shells or snake vertebrae as strikers. The *hanhyego* traditionally was played by women at the palace at Abomey to accompany their songs praising royalty.

Hankin. Single-string long zither of Japan. *See* ICHIGEN-KIN.

Hansa. Flat gong of the northern Philippines. *See* GANGSA (i).

Hanshō. Small clapperless temple bell of Japan. *See* BONSHŌ.

Hansō. Transverse flute of Japan, found in Okinawa. *See* MINTEKI.

Hans von Basel. Alternative name of HANS TUGI.

Haotong. Signal pipe of the Han Chinese. *See* LABA (i).

Hara. Underarm variable tension HOURGLASS DRUM of the Dendi people of Benin. Two are played with cylindrical drums to accompany praise singing.

Hārangī. SPIKE FIDDLE of Rajasthan, north-west India. *See* RĀVAṆHATTHĀ and SĀRAṄGĪ.

Harántfurulya [oldalfuvós furulya]. Transverse flute of Hungary, with six finger-holes. Apart from the absence of a duct, its structure is the same as that of the FURULYA; it is from 30 to 50 cm long, with a diameter of 14 to 18 mm.

Hardanger fiddle [Harding fiddle] (Nor. *hardingfela, hardingfele*). A folk violin of western Norway, generally having four melody strings above the fingerboard, four or five wire sympathetic strings below, and characteristic national decoration. The earliest known example, which has only six strings altogether, is by Ole Jonsen Jaastad of Hardanger and dated 1651 (fig.1*b*, p.126). The next ones known to survive are from *c*1750, by Isak Nielsen Skar (1663–1759) and his son Trond Isaksen (1712–72), who popularized the instrument. These fiddles are narrower than the ordinary violin, often with deeper ribs and more pronounced arching of the belly and back. The neck is short, as the music is normally played in the first position, but the pegbox is long and surmounted by a carved head. The fingerboard is flat and the bridge only slightly curved, to facilitate double stops and droning.

During the 19th century the instrument's shape became nearer to that of the violin, owing mainly to the work of Eric Johsen Helland (1816–68), one of a celebrated fiddle-making family in Telemark. A recent addition is the chin rest (fig.1*a*): the fiddle nowadays is often bowed at the shoulder, whereas before it was held at the chest of the performer.

Over 20 scordatura tunings are known, the most usual being *a–d'–a'–e"* (melody strings) and *d'–e'–f♯'–a'* (sympathetic strings). The repertory consists of folksongs, dances (*slåtter*) such as the *halling*, *gangar* and *springar*, and bridal marches, often embellished. Such tunes were played by Torgeir Augundson (1801–72), a miller's son of Telemark whose playing fired the enthusiasm of the violinist Ole Bull, who used them in his compositions and improvisations; the traditional melodies were later transcribed and were much used by Grieg.

BIBLIOGRAPHY
T. Hannaas: 'Hardingfela', *Bergens museums årbok 1916–17* [with Eng. summary]
S. B. Osa: *Hardingfela* (Oslo, 1952)
E. Groven: 'Om hardingfeleslåttane', *Norsk musikkgranskning årbok 1954–55*
O. Gurvin, ed.: *Hardingfeleslåttar*, Norske folkemusikk, i–v (Oslo, 1958–67)
K. Lange and A. Ostvedt: *Norwegian Music* (London, 1958)
A. Bjørndal and B. Alver: – *og fela ho let* (Oslo, 1966) [with Eng. summary]

(a)   (b)

1. (a) Søren Nomeland in Setesdal costume playing a modern Hardanger fiddle made in Telemark, Norway; (b) Hardanger fiddle by Ole Jonsen Jaastad, 1651 (Historisk Museum, Bergen)

O. Gurvin: 'The Harding Fiddle', *SMN*, i (1968), 10
R. Sevåg: 'The Harding Fiddle', *From Bone Pipe and Cattle Horn to Fiddle and Psaltery*, ed. M. Müller (Copenhagen, 1972), 18
——: 'Geige und Geigenmusik in Norwegen', *Die Geige in der europäischen Volksmusik*, ed. W. Deutsch (Vienna, 1975)
MARY REMNANT

BIBLIOGRAPHY
W. C. Honeyman: *Scottish Violin Makers* (Dundee, 1899, 2/1910/*R*1981)
W. M. Morris: *British Violin Makers* (London, 1904, rev. 2/1920)
JAAK LIIVOJA-LORIUS

Hardie, Matthew (*b* Edinburgh, 1755; *d* Edinburgh, 30 Aug 1826). Scottish violin maker. Although details of his training have not been established, it appears most likely that he was taught by John Blair, who later became his assistant. Hardie's violins are well made but are seldom of handsome wood or exceptionally well finished; they nevertheless show considerable originality in that they were not copies (though inspired by Italian principles), which sets them apart from much of the work of the leading English makers of the time. Nearly all of Hardie's violins are based on either the early Stradivari or later Amati patterns. The fact that these models have many similarities might account for the discrepancies of opinion as to whether he copied Amati or not. Tonally his instruments are clear, strong and even but lack a certain roundness. On his early instruments he often resorted to imitation purfling and a rather inflexible yellow-brown varnish. Both aspects improved in his later instruments but his interest in varnishing was evidently never more than pragmatic.

Hardie's influence on Scottish violin making was important. His students included his cousin Peter Hardie, David Stirrat and his own son, Thomas Hardie (1802–58). Thomas was capable of excellent work but made the grave error of often using 'baked' wood, a practice which virtually guarantees poor tonal results.

Hardingfele [hardingfela] (Nor.). HARDANGER FIDDLE.

Hardy-Goldthwaite organ. An ELECTRONIC ORGAN developed at the Massachusetts Institute of Technology in Cambridge around 1929–30 by Arthur C. Hardy, with Sherwood F. Brown, on the basis of ideas by Du Val R. Goldthwaite of New York. All the pitches in each timbre were produced by a single rotating photoelectric tone-wheel on which the frequencies of 71 notes were photographically recorded as waveforms, arranged concentrically; the waveforms were based on analyses of those produced by conventional instruments, such as a large pipe organ. In most tone-wheel instruments 12 wheels are used, one for each note in all octaves. With only one tone-wheel, those frequencies whose waveforms do not fit on to the wheel an integral number of times will produce clicks; to avoid this, each incomplete waveform was divided into minute sections and spread equally round the wheel between the individual cycles of the waveform concerned.

HUGH DAVIES

Hareubab. Three-string SPIKE FIDDLE of Aceh province, Sumatra. It is about 120 cm long, with gut strings wound round tuning-pegs, two on the player's right and one on his left. The cylindrical wooden spike is about 5 cm long, and the body is bowl-shaped with skin stretched over the top; it is about 23 cm in diameter. The instrument is played with a horsehair bow. It was still widely played in the early 20th century, together with a *geudumba* (hourglass drum), but is now almost obsolete.

MARGARET J. KARTOMI

Harfe (Ger.). (1) HARP.
(2) An ORGAN stop.

Harfenett (Ger.). ARPANETTA.

Ha-rib. Oboe of Ladakh. *See* SUR-NA.

Harmomelo. A cabinet piano invented in 1806 or earlier by WILHELM LEBERECHT PETZOLDT.

Harmonetta. A polyphonic PIANO ATTACHMENT, first manufactured in 1953 by Richard LIPP & Sohn.

Harmonia (i). General term for the accordion used in Poland from the end of the 19th century. Some types, differing in size, scale, construction and system and produced in small workshops, are called *harmonia polska* ('Polish accordion'), *harmonia warszawska* ('War-

saw accordion'), *harmonia chromatyczna* ('chromatic accordion') and so on. In order to facilitate playing, in some regions (e.g. Kurpie) a pedal pump is used for pumping air through a metal pipe to the bellows of the instrument, which is then called *harmonia pedałowa* or simply *pedałówka* ('treadle').

JAN STĘSZEWSKI

Harmonia (ii). An ORGAN STOP.

Harmonica [mouth organ] (Fr. *harmonica à bouche*; Ger. *Mundharmonika*; It. *armonica a bocca*) **(i).** An instrument consisting of a small casing containing a series of free reeds in channels leading to holes on the side of the instrument (*see* REED INSTRUMENTS, fig.1*a*). It is placed between the lips and played by inhalation and exhalation, unwanted holes being masked by the tongue. By moving the instrument to and fro, the varying notes available are brought into play.

There are two main types of harmonica – the diatonic and the chromatic. Basically, the diatonic harmonica is designed to produce the notes of the tonic chord of the key in which it is tuned by exhalation and the other notes of the diatonic scale by inhalation. On this type of instrument only the middle octave of the three-octave range is complete, the lower and upper octaves having a 'gapped' scale (see fig.1*a*). This applies to both the

Fig.1 Tuning chart

Capital letters = 'Blow' notes. Small letters = 'Draw' notes.

(a) *10-hole, 20-reed 'Vamper' or 'Richter' model in C*

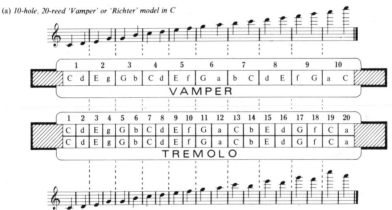

20-double-hole, 40-reed 'Tremolo' or 'Wiener' model in C

(b) *12-hole, 48-reed Chromatic harmonica in C*

2. Modern chromatic harmonica with 12 holes by M. Hohner, Trossingen

'Richter' or 'Vamper' type and the so-called 'Tremolo' or Wiener type which has two reeds for each note, one reed being slightly off-tuned to create a 'voix céleste' or vibrato effect. The chromatic harmonica consists basically of two harmonicas in keys a semitone apart, and originally was based on the 'Vamper' system, two reed plates being fitted, one tuned in C, and the other in C♯ (or D♭), with a slide mechanism operated by a small hand-lever enabling the player to change from one set to the other. This early type of chromatic instrument (10 holes, 40 reeds) was soon superseded by the 12-hole instrument with 48 reeds (see fig.2) in which the tuning of the middle octave of the previously mentioned types was adopted throughout the three-octave range (see fig.1b). This type of instrument is now virtually standard, although a larger model (16 holes, 64 reeds) with a range of four octaves is also available. Many other types of harmonica exist, designed for special purposes, and include bass and chord accompaniment instruments for use in group and band performance.

The introduction of the Chinese *sheng* into Europe in 1777 led to many experiments in the use of the free reed. Christian Friedrich Ludwig Buschmann (1805–64) is credited as the inventor of the harmonica. In 1821 he constructed an instrument with 15 reeds which he called 'aura', designed primarily as a tuning instrument or pitch pipe. He discovered that melodies could be played on it with comparative ease, and that it could be played loud or soft and make crescendos and diminuendos at will. Another early experiment was made in England by Charles Wheatstone (1802–75) who constructed a type of mouth organ using brass reeds controlled by a small button keyboard which he called a 'symphonium' (1829). He did not exploit this instrument and it formed a step towards his bellows-blown 'concertina' or 'aeola' which he patented in 1844. Meanwhile in Germany, Christian Messner, a young clockmaker, brought a sample of Buschmann's aura to his home in Trossingen where he set up a small workshop to construct similar instruments which he sold at country fairs and inns. There was a depression in the clock- and watchmaking industry, and others turned to the manufacture of the little 'mundaeolines' in Trossingen, Christian Weiss starting in 1855 and Matthias Hohner (1833–1902) in 1857. These early instruments were all hand-made, the wooden body-work being carved by hand, the reeds beaten from brass wire and fitted individually into the brass or bell metal reed-plates. Hohner was quick to adopt new methods and techniques of mass-production, and his business grew beyond all expectations. By 1879 his output of harmonicas was over 700,000, of which over 60% were exported to America. He handed over his business to his five sons in 1900. They further developed it and

absorbed the firms of Messner and Weiss by 1928. In the early 1920s the chromatic harmonica was evolved; it was brought into prominence by Larry Adler in the late 1930s.

Apart from its undoubted popularity all over the world as a medium for light entertainment and folk music, the musical stature of the chromatic harmonica has grown considerably in the last 30 years with serious works being written for it by many composers including Darius Milhaud, Vaughan Williams, Gordon Jacob, Adrian Cruft, Hugo Herrmann, Mátyás Seiber, Francis Chagrin, G. Anders-Strehmel, A. von Beckerath and Graham Whettam. Full-scale concertos for harmonica and orchestra have been written by Malcolm Arnold, Arthur Benjamin, Whettam and M. Spivakowsky.

The harmonica has played an essential role in the American blues tradition (where it is usually referred to as a 'blues harp') and hence in much blues-derived popular music; it has entered modern jazz in the work of the Belgian virtuoso Jean 'Toots' Thielemans. It is also being used in music education in schools, and an extensive repertory of educational music has been developed for this purpose.

BIBLIOGRAPHY
J. Zepf: *Die goldene Brücke* (Trossingen, 1956)
Anon.: *Hundert Jahre Hohner 1857–1957* (Trossingen, 1957)
H. Buschmann: *Christian Friedrich Ludwig Buschmann* (Trossingen, 1958)
H. Herrmann: *Einführung in die Satztechnik für Mundharmonika-Instrumente* (Trossingen, 1958)
A. Baines, ed.: *Musical Instruments through the Ages* (Harmondsworth, 1961, 2/1966/R1976)

IVOR BEYNON, G. ROMANI

Harmonica (ii). See MUSICAL GLASSES.

Harmonică. See ARMONICĂ.

Harmonic Canon. The name given by HARRY PARTCH to the members of a group of instruments which are ultimately derived from the Middle Eastern QĀNŪN. Each canon consists of a closed wooden soundbox, with side holes, across which are stretched 44 or 88 strings (usually guitar strings but in some cases piano wire), of total sounding length 64 or 77 cm; movable bridges cut off any desired string proportion so that a great variety of tunings is possible (Partch used the instruments with microtonal and just tunings). The original Harmonic Canon (1945), reconceived as Harmonic Canon I (completed 1959), and the New Harmonic Canon I (1972) each consist of a single canon, and are played with plectra or, occasionally, with the fingers; Harmonic Canons II (Castor and Pollux, 1953) and III (Blue Rainbow, 1965) consist respectively of two and three canons mounted end to end, and are played with plectra or sticks (felted at one end for softer sounds). All the instruments have detachable stands. Harmonic Canon I and New Harmonic Canon I (a near-duplicate, made to obviate the need for time-consuming retuning of a single instrument between pieces using different scales) have two interlocking sets of strings in different planes; one set can be played alone at one end of the instrument and the second set at the other end, or both may be played together at the point of intersection. The intersection point of the lowest 16 strings of each set can be varied by means of a glass rod that moves under the strings up and down a pair of wooden ramps glued to the soundboard. Harmonic Canon II was used with a similar system of ramps and a pair of rods (its normal bridges having been removed) in *Revelation in the Courthouse Park* (1962); the movement of the rods produced powerful gliding tones.

ROSEMARY ROBERTS

Harmonicello. Name given by J. C. Bischoff to a bass string instrument of his construction. Built in 1794, it had five gut strings and ten sympathetic metal ones. It is described in E. S. J. van der Straeten: *History of the Violoncello, the Viol da Gamba, their Precursors and Collateral Instruments* (London, 1915/R1971).

Harmonichord. A friction rod instrument with keyboard, the mechanism of which was related to the KLAVIZYLINDER; *see also* SOSTENENTE PIANO, §3.

Harmonicon. A type of GLOCKENSPIEL.

Harmonics. The individual pure sounds which are normally present and which together constitute what is heard as an ordinary musical note, such as from an organ pipe or vibrating string.

1. General. 2. Air columns. 3. Strings.

1. GENERAL. Harmonics are present because an air column or string can vibrate, not only as a whole, but also as two halves, three thirds, four quarters etc, simultaneously. The nth harmonic therefore has a wavelength of the fundamental (i.e. the note heard) divided by n, and a frequency of n times the frequency of the fundamental.

Many of the harmonics theoretically possible are actually present in a musical note; they blend with the fundamental to give the impression of a single note. The relative strengths of each harmonic give the tone quality or 'colour' to the note as heard. The individual harmonics of a note can sometimes be heard, rather like the notes of a chord, especially in a loud low note on a flute or clarinet, or on a stopped diapason or Quintatön organ stop.

The first 25 harmonics are shown in Table 1, which shows the intervals made with the fundamental and between successive harmonics, and, for example, the notes of the just musical scale which occur in the harmonics of C, the fundamental of the natural trumpet in C. A cent is a hundredth part of a semitone in an equal-tempered scale; thus an octave contains 1200 cents. The decimal places have no practical significance but are given for arithmetical interest. It can be seen how the harmonics become closer as the series ascends, how each octave includes the same intervals as the octave below but with an extra note inserted between each of those in the lower octave, and also how the lower harmonics and several of the upper harmonics coincide with notes of the musical scale (or nearly so).

The continuous tone quality of a musical sound depends on the strength and proportions of its various harmonics. Flutes, recorders and wide-scaled flute stops on organs have a relatively strong fundamental with few upper harmonics, whereas bright-toned instruments (e.g. violins, oboes, harpsichords and narrow-scaled organ pipes) have relatively strong and extensive upper harmonics. Stopped organ pipes and cylindrical reed pipes acting similarly to stopped pipes such as clarinets and crumhorns have a preponderance of odd-numbered harmonics, imparting a 'hollow' sound whose richness depends on the strength of these upper harmonics.

Musical sounds produced by other means than vibrating strings or air columns may lack the normal harmonics. Tuning-forks produce an almost pure fundamental with only faint (and much higher) non-harmonic sounds. Bells normally produce non-harmonic partials.

The term 'harmonics' has been used to signify the study of the physics of music, as in *Harmonics, or The Philosophy of Musical Sounds*, by Robert Smith (Cambridge, 1749, enlarged 2/1759).

2. AIR COLUMNS. On an organ pipe or a wind instrument it is possible to isolate and strengthen individual upper harmonics or 'overtones' where present. Organ pipes may be overblown to sound the 2nd harmonic (or 1st overtone), i.e. the octave, in open pipes, or the 3rd harmonic, i.e. the twelfth in a stopped pipe. A small hole

TABLE 1

Harmonic	Interval from fundamental	Note	Interval between harmonics
1		C	
2	1 octave	c	1200 cents (octave)
3	1 octave + 701·96 cents	g	701·96 cents (perfect 5th)
4	2 octaves	c'	498·04 cents (perfect 4th)
5	2 octaves + 386·31 cents	e'	386·31 cents (major 3rd)
6	2 octaves + 701·96 cents	g'	315·64 cents (minor 3rd)
7	2 octaves + 968·83 cents		266·87 cents (used by Douwes)
8	3 octaves	c''	231·17 cents
9	3 octaves + 203·91 cents	d''	203·91 cents (major tone)
10	3 octaves + 386·31 cents	e''	182·40 cents (minor tone)
11	3 octaves + 551·32 cents		165·00 cents
12	3 octaves + 701·96 cents	g''	150·64 cents
13	3 octaves + 840·53 cents		138·57 cents
14	3 octaves + 968·83 cents		128·30 cents
15	3 octaves + 1088·27 cents	b''	119·44 cents (used by Douwes)
16	4 octaves	c'''	111·73 cents (diatonic semitone)
17	4 octaves + 104·96 cents		104·96 cents (used by J. Wallis)
18	4 octaves + 203·91 cents	d'''	98·95 cents (used by J. Wallis)
19	4 octaves + 297·51 cents		93·60 cents (used by J. Wallis)
20	4 octaves + 386·31 cents	e'''	88·80 cents (used by J. Wallis)
21	4 octaves + 470·78 cents		84·47 cents
22	4 octaves + 551·32 cents		80·64 cents
23	4 octaves + 628·27 cents		76·96 cents
24	4 octaves + 701·96 cents	g'''	73·68 cents (used by Douwes)
25	4 octaves + 772·63 cents	$g\sharp'''$	70·67 cents (chromatic semitone)

at the nodal point, i.e. about halfway along an open pipe, helps this strengthening. This is the principle of the harmonic flute stop which for this reason has pipes of twice the normal length for a given sound. In the flute proper the slit between the lips is narrowed and the breath is made to impinge more sharply on the mouth-hole. In this way, several harmonics may be obtained. Similarly, upper harmonics are obtained on the recorder by allowing the thumb-hole to be partly open and adjusting the breath pressure, and on reed instruments by tightening the lips and by using octave or 'speaker' keys opening small holes near nodal points. Combined with appropriate fingering, these harmonics complete the upper ranges of all the woodwind. In stopped organ pipes and to a large extent in the clarinet, the fundamental is an octave lower than for an open pipe and only the odd-numbered harmonics are present.

On brass instruments, with their longer and narrower tubes, a greater number of harmonics is obtained by tightening the lips; these harmonics provide the only basic notes on the natural (i.e. slideless, keyless and valveless) trumpet and horn. Bach regularly wrote for the trumpet notes between the 3rd and 18th harmonics and once, in Cantata no.31, wrote for the 20th harmonic. Mozart wrote for the horn from the 2nd harmonic to the 24th (12 Duos for two horns K487/496a).

It can be seen from Table 1 that harmonics which are multiples of prime numbers above 5 (e.g. nos.7, 11, 13 and 14) do not correspond to recognized notes in the musical scale. However, on a trumpet nos.7 and 14 can fairly easily be lipped up to a written $b\flat$, and skilled trumpeters can lip no.11 down to f'' or up to $f\sharp''$ and no.13 up to a''; composers regularly wrote these notes. Some trumpeters were more skilled at this than others, as can be seen from the writings of 18th-century music historians. The problem was solved by means of hand-stopping on the horn and the use of a slide on the trumpet, before the invention of valves made it unnecessary to use these particular harmonics. Harmonics nos.17 and 19 are good approximations of $c\sharp'''$ and $d\sharp'''$, but composers do not seem to have used them.

The timbral effects of harmonics have long been used in organ building. Although organ pipes possess a wide harmonic range, the effect can be heightened without forcing by adding further pipes whose fundamentals are the harmonics of the foundation or 'diapason' ranks. Since the 15th century these extra ranks have been made to draw separately, and the organist can synthesize a variety of tone qualities by combining stops corresponding to the 1st to 6th harmonics and compound stops of pre-set combinations of harmonics such as nos.6, 8, 12 and 16 (Mixture), 3, 4, and 5 (Cornet), 3 and 5 (Sesquialtera) or even occasionally 5, 6, 7 and 8 ('harmonics'). Harmonics nos.1, 3 and 5 on flute-toned stops, for example, synthesize quite a good imitation of a clarinet. Some keyboard electronic instruments also use this principle to synthesize various tone-colours. For further discussion of the acoustical basis of harmonics see ACOUSTICS.

3. STRINGS. Upper harmonics are often used for special effects on string instruments and on the harp. In the violin family, the use of harmonics of open strings, 'natural' harmonics ('flageolet notes'), was introduced by Mondonville in *Les sons harmoniques: sonates à violon seul avec la basse continue* op.4 (c1738). In his preface he explained how to obtain harmonics nos.2, 3, 4, 5,

Ex.1(a)   (b)   (c)

6, 8 and above by lightly fingering at a node on any string. The sonatas make considerable use of harmonics nos.2, 3, 4 and 5. For the 2nd harmonic, the note is fingered in its normal position but only lightly. For the 3rd, 4th and 5th harmonics, the player fingers lightly as if to play a perfect 5th, 4th or major 3rd above the open string (or at other nodal points: at any multiple of an nth of the distance along the string for an nth harmonic); harmonics sounding a 12th, two octaves and a 17th above the open string are obtained. In ex.1a the special sign indicates that the player fingers in the positions of the lower notes on the g string and the upper notes (only) are sounded. The passage in ex.1b presumably sounds as in ex.1c. Mondonville also used 2nd (octave) harmonics on the G and d strings of the cello in the same sonatas. In modern notation there is either a small circle over the actual note or a diamond-headed note in the position of the nodal point to be touched (e.g. Ravel: *Ma mère l'oye*).

'Artificial' harmonics are 4th harmonics of the written fingered notes, which sound two octaves above those notes; they are obtained by fingering the written note and lightly touching the string a perfect 4th above, and are notated by writing diamond-headed notes a perfect 4th above the main note.

With a long string strongly bowed as many harmonics may be obtained as on the trumpet. This was the principle of the one-string TRUMPET MARINE, which could play trumpet music with a characteristic out-of-tune effect on the 4th and 6th of the scale.

On the harp 2nd harmonics, sounding one octave above, are obtained by plucking the upper half of the string with the side of the thumb and lightly touching the mid-point of the string with the ball of the thumb. Harp harmonics are designated by a small circle above the written normal note of the string (see HARP, §4 (ix)).

BIBLIOGRAPHY
H. von Helmholtz: *Die Lehre von den Tonempfindungen als physiologische Grundlage für die Theorie der Musik* (Brunswick, 1863; Eng. trans., 1875/R1954 as *On the Sensations of Tone*)
J. Jeans: *Science & Music* (Cambridge, 1937/R1968)
Ll. S. Lloyd: *Music and Sound* (London, 1937, 2/1951)
C. A. Culver: *Musical Acoustics* (Philadelphia, 1941, 4/1956)
H. F. Olson: *Musical Engineering* (New York, 1952/R1967)
R. W. Young: *A Table Relating Frequency Cents* (Bloomington, Ind., 1952)
C. A. Taylor: *The Physics of Musical Sounds* (London, 1965)
GUY OLDHAM

Harmonie (Fr., Ger.). A term applied in its widest sense to music for wind instruments. The French commonly use the term 'harmonie militaire' to refer to a military band (see BAND (i), §II, 2(i), and §III, 2), even the massed wind bands of the Napoleonic era; they distinguish 'harmonie' (wind band) from 'fanfare' (brass and percussion band). Elgar wrote *Harmony Music* for his domestic wind quintet and the Germans refer to the wind quintet as 'Harmonie-Quintett'. The title of Haydn's *Harmoniemesse* (1802) is explained by the prominence of wind instruments, and Mendelssohn's *Ouvertüre für Harmoniemusik* op.24 (1824) is scored for 23 wind instruments and percussion. In its more limited sense the term was fully current only from the mid-18th century until the 1830s, when it was applied to the wind bands (Harmonien) of the European aristocracy; see BAND (i), §II, 2(ii).

Harmonie-Bass. A metal contrabassoon designed and produced in 1839 by Johann Stehle of Vienna. See BASSOON, §8.

Harmonieflûte (Fr.). (1) A type of ACCORDION first built by M. Busson of Paris in 1852. It had a small, three-to four-octave keyboard and could be held either in the lap or set on a stand and operated by a treadle.

(2) A BARREL ORGAN invented by Corvi in 1853.

Harmoniekontrabass. A bass OPHICLEIDE built by the Berlin firm of Griessling and Schlott in 1833. Its range was similar to that of the bass ophicleide in B♭, and according to Sachs (*Real-Lexikon der Musikinstrumente*, Berlin, 1913/R1962) it was renowned for its fullness and strength, resembling organ pedal tone; it also had very precise intonation. No examples have survived.   STEPHEN WESTON

Harmonika. An ORGAN STOP (*Harmonia*).

Harmoniphon. (1) A small free-reed keyboard instrument patented by Paris of Dijon in 1836. It was 38 cm long, 13 cm wide and 8 cm high. The wind was supplied to a reservoir by the player's blowing down a flexible tube; the sound produced resembled that of an oboe.

(2) A harmonica with a built-in mute exhibited by an inventor named Messner in Paris in 1889.

Harmonium. The name given by ALEXANDRE FRANÇOIS DEBAIN to a small REED ORGAN patented in 1842. This original instrument had a three-octave keyboard, one set of reeds and a single blowing pedal. The name was later extensively used in England and on the Continent to refer to all reed organs, of whatever size or construction. Larger instruments in Germany were sometimes called 'Kunstharmonium'.

Such instruments were widely disseminated, especially by the colonial powers, in Africa and India, where they came to play an important role in local traditions. The harmonium was introduced into India by missionaries, probably around the middle of the 19th century (Indian terms for it are *hārmoṇiam*, *härmoṇiā*, *ārmoṇiā*). Though upright models are found, the most common is a small portable instrument set in a box. Models are made in various sizes with a range of stops and couplers. The instrument is usually played while sitting on the floor, the player fingering the keyboard with one hand and pumping a bellows at the back with the other. Its use is widespread in the provision of heterophonic contrapuntal texture for vocal music (where it is often played by the singer himself) in a wide range of classical and urban popular styles. It is less frequently found in village music contexts. It has for a long time been manufactured in India and Pakistan; Palitana, in Gujarat, is regarded as a centre of manufacture of the reeds.

As it is a fixed-pitch instrument, its use in Indian music has been criticized (and banned on Indian radio for some years) on the grounds that it does not conform to the traditional flexible intonation.

BIBLIOGRAPHY
N. A. Jairazbhoy: *The Rags of North Indian Classical Music* (London and Middletown, Conn., 1971)
B. C. Deva: *Musical Instruments of India* (Calcutta, 1978)
                    BARBARA OWEN, ALASTAIR DICK

Harness bells. See JINGLES.

Harp (Fr. *harpe*; Ger. *Harfe*; It., Sp. *arpa*). Generic name for chordophones in which, as defined in the classification system by Hornbostel and Sachs, the plane of the strings is perpendicular to the soundboard.
See also ORGAN STOP.

1. General structure, terminology and performing traditions. 2. Ancient harps. 3. Western distribution. 4. Europe: (i) Medieval and Renaissance (ii) Ireland and Scotland (iii) Other single-rank harps (iv) Harps with two ranks of strings (v) Harps with three ranks of strings (vi) Hook harps and single-action pedal harps (vii) The double-action pedal harp (viii) Technique and repertory, 1750–1820 (ix) Modern technique and repertory (x) Folk usage. 5. Latin America: (i) History and distribution (ii) Structure and performance. 6. African harps: (i) History and distribution (ii) Structure (iii) Performing techniques (iv) Performing practices. 7. Eastern distribution.

1. GENERAL STRUCTURE, TERMINOLOGY AND PERFORMING TRADITIONS. Normally triangular in shape, all harps have three basic structural components: resonator, neck and strings. Hornbostel and Sachs divided them into two categories: 'frame harps' and 'open harps'. Frame harps have a forepillar or column which connects the lower end of the resonator to the neck, adding structural support and helping to bear the strain of string tension. Harps without forepillars are 'open harps'. Only European harps and their descendants are consistently frame harps: most others are open. Hornbostel and Sachs further subdivided open harps into two sub-categories: 'arched' and 'angular' harps. According to Hornbostel and Sachs, the neck of an arched harp curves away from the resonator while the neck of an angular harp makes a sharp angle with it. The term BOW HARP is often applied to arched harps; some organologists have applied the term to a type of MUSICAL BOW with attached resonator. The GROUND HARP (or ground bow) has characteristics of both harps and musical bows.

Resonators of harps may be spoon-shaped, trowel-shaped, boat-shaped, box-shaped (square, trapezoidal or rectangular, often with rounded edges) or hemispherical. Resonators are topped with a wood soundboard or a skin soundtable and a string holder to which one end of a string is usually attached. The other end of a string is attached to the neck either directly with special knots, or indirectly to fixed plugs, movable tuning-pegs, or to tuning-rings or nooses which are themselves attached to the neck. Buzzing mechanisms, attached near one end of the string, either on the neck or the soundboard, and activated by the plucked string, were used on Renaissance European harps and are used on most African harps. Harps have from as few as one string to over 90. Mechanisms for chromatic alteration of the strings range from manually operated hooks to complex pedal-activated systems.

The earliest known use of the word 'harpa' was by Venantius Fortunatus, Bishop of Poitiers, about 600; he wrote, for example: 'Romanusque lyra, plaudat tibi barbarus harpa'. The old Norse word 'harpa' is believed to have been a generic term for string instruments. Around the year 1000, Aelfric glossed *hearpe* as 'lyre'. By this broad definition, even the Sutton Hoo instrument, reconstructed for the second time in 1969 in the form of a long lyre, might have been called a harp. Similarly,

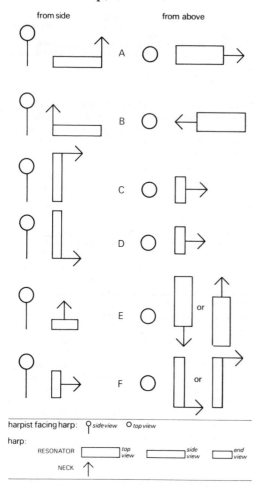

from side   from above

A

B

C

D

E   or

F   or

harpist facing harp: ⚲ side view   ○ top view

harp:

RESONATOR ▭ top view   ▭ side view   ▭ end view

NECK ↑

1. Worldwide distribution of performing positions on harps, regardless of historical period (there are minor variations in the angle of the harp in relation to the human body; information on some performing positions is derived from iconographic sources):

A – Uganda, Zaïre (east), Siberia; formerly Mesopotamia

B – Mauritania; formerly Egypt, Minoa, Mesopotamia

C – Gabon, Cameroon, Chad, Congo, Central African Republic; all Western harps, and Western-influenced harps in the Philippines, Mexico, Peru, Paraguay, Ecuador, Venezuela, Colombia, Argentina, Chile; formerly Egypt

D – Chad (south-west); Chile and Peru (only in processions; the harpist turns the harp upside-down and rests the neck of the harp on his shoulder, enabling him to walk while he plays); formerly Mesopotamia, Middle and Far East, Central Asia, west Asiatic areas; Italo-Greek areas

E – Central African Republic, Zaïre (only Zande and Zande-influenced peoples), Georgia (USSR), Afghanistan, India, Burma; formerly Middle and Far East, Central Asia, Indonesia

F – Chad (south-west), Cameroon (north) [the harp rests entirely on the ground and the performer squats with the resonator close to the body]

the word 'hearpan' in *Beowulf* and other Anglo-Saxon literature is taken to mean playing a string instrument. Early medieval Latin terminology is also ambiguous. 'Cithara' was used for both lyres and harps, while in the 10th and 11th centuries the terms 'lira' and 'lyra' were used for a certain type of bowed instrument. A rare example of a specific use of 'cithara' is in an illustration, said to be from a 12th-century manuscript, which was reproduced in the 18th century by Martin Gerbert in his *De cantu et musica sacra*. It shows a 12-string harp, captioned 'Cythara anglica'. Confusions as to terminology still existed as late as 1511, when Virdung wrote: 'What one man names a harp, another calls a lyre'. Further confusion persists in the application of such terms as 'table harp' to a type of zither, 'mouth harp' to the harmonica, 'jew's harp' to a plucked idiophone (the *guimbarde*) and 'glass harp' to a form of musical glasses. For the harp-lute, see §6 below and HARP-LUTE (i). Hybrid instruments with harp-like features include the HARP-PIANO (or keyed harp) and an English guitar-like instrument of the early 19th century (*see* HARP-LUTE (ii)).

The harp is played in six basic performing positions (see fig.1), of which five were used in ancient civilizations and are still in use today; the sixth (position F) appears only in Africa. Harp tunings are pentatonic, tetratonic, heptatonic (including diatonic) and chromatic. Strings are usually plucked, but they may also be strummed, struck or strummed with a plectrum while strings which are not wanted to sound are damped; occasionally the bass wire strings may be stroked with the palm of the hand. Resonators may be used as percussion instruments and struck with the fingers, hand or hooked rattles. Harpists may use any number of digits from the thumb of one hand with the thumb and forefinger of the other to the thumb and first three fingers of both hands; rarely only a single index finger is used. The fifth finger is seldom used because of its lack of strength and its shortness, which generally causes a claw-like and nearly unusable performing position when all five digits are placed on the strings.

The harp's use ranges from religious ritual to pure entertainment. Harpists are depicted in royal chambers, salons, banquet scenes and processions as soloists or in ensembles. Harpists have accompanied themselves singing ballads, reciting oral history and epic poetry or accompanying rituals of various types. In the ancient world, solo harpists and harpists in large ensembles were usually men while harpists who played in small chamber ensembles were often women. In the Western world until the late 19th century, professional harpists were usually men, while women played the harp as a domestic instrument probably from the 17th century. Today, men and woman play harps throughout the world; but throughout Africa, in India, Georgia (USSR) and Siberia women are rarely professional harpists and, in a few cases, are not even allowed to touch the instrument.

2. ANCIENT HARPS. In ancient times harps were all of the 'open' type, both arched and angular. Many kinds and sizes existed, with different performing positions and playing techniques (see fig.1). For example, ancient arched harps in Mesopotamia were played in position B, in Egypt in positions B and C, in Central Asia and India in position E. While most arched harps were plucked with fingers of both hands, some in ancient India

were played with a plectrum in the right hand while the left hand damped the unrequired notes (see fig.2), a technique first depicted on a plaque (2100–1800 BC) from Eshnunna in Mesopotamia (Musée du Louvre, Paris).

Arched harps are found in many cultures, both simple and highly developed. The earliest known examples of actual instruments are the remains of three sizable and elegant harps found in the so-called Royal Cemetery at Ur in Mesopotamia (c2500 BC). But representations of Sumerian harps go back a further 300 years. These instruments had boat-shaped resonators, were made in various sizes and might have had up to six strings. There is little evidence of arched harps in Mesopotamia after the end of the 3rd millennium BC, but later instruments of this type were depicted in sculpture in India between the 2nd century BC and AD c1000 (see VĪNĀ, §2) and South-east Asia between the 9th and 11th centuries AD. They were probably introduced into India through the Indus Valley civilizations.

The arched harp had a long life in Egypt. It was already familiar in the Old Kingdom and many instruments of the type, with resonator in the shape of a spoon or spade, are represented in tombs round the Giza pyramids. At this time they were usually played by kneeling men (see fig.3) in association perhaps with a singer, flautist and player of double parallel pipes; but in the tomb of Mereruka at Saqqara (Dynasty 6, c2345–2181 BC) the Princess Seshseshat plays to her husband on the harp and accompanies her own song. A scene in the provincial tomb of Ibi at Deir el-Gebrawi containing seven male harpers testifies to the widespread use of the instrument. In the Middle Kingdom, chamber groups tended to be smaller and to contain more women. In the tomb of Amenemḥat at Beni Hasan three singers are accompanied by two harps, a sistrum and a rattle (the group is female except for one of the harpists). The resonator of the harp tended now to be deeper and to develop an oval shape like a ladle. New Kingdom harps show a remarkable variety. Older types persist, and the range now extends from a small portable instrument with boat-shaped resonator, to be played on the shoulder and seen in 18th-dynasty tombs of the Theban necropolis, to the giant harps in 'Bruce's tomb'. These last are played by standing male musicians in the tomb of Ramesses III in the Valley of the Kings. The arched harp was now often in the hands of a blind man, and clearly a class of professional musicians had arisen.

The instruments crudely represented in several small marble figurines of the 3rd millennium from the Cyclades, that also appear schematically on a few later seals and on an incised stone of the 2nd millennium from Megiddo in Palestine, were thought to represent the earliest angular harps. Recent scholarship has suggested they ought rather to be interpreted as asymmetrical lyres, perhaps related to western Semitic lyres of the late 2nd and 1st millennia (see Aign, 1969).

In Mesopotamia, the Old Babylonian period (from c1850 BC) brought changes in many musical instruments. The angular harp now emerged fully along with two new performing positions (see fig.1, A and D). When the strings were vertical, the resonator rested against the player's body, and both hands were used in a plucking action (see fig.1, D); when horizontal, the resonator was held under the left arm, and the strings were strummed, or possibly picked with a plectrum in the right hand, while the left damped the strings the harpist did not wish to sound. These techniques are like those for many hori-

zontally held arched harps of both earlier and later periods. Terracotta plaques of the Old Babylonian period show the vertical angular harp in various sizes: one from Ur (now in the British Museum) has a large resonator; that from Eshnunna (see fig.4, p.134) has seven strings and a resonator apparently covered with skin. This type of instrument established itself quickly and remained in regular use, developing into the elaborate harps depicted as late as the 17th century in Turkey and Persia.

Horizontal angular harps are depicted on Assyrian cylinder seals by the 2nd millennium BC. These were elegant instruments, with long, slim resonators and vertical necks in the form of a human hand. The ends of

2. *Arched harp: Indian terracotta, Gupta period,* AD *c320–500 (British Museum, London)*

3. *The singer Iti and the harpist Hekenu who plays an arched harp with spade-shaped resonator: detail of a relief (5th Dynasty, 2563–2423* BC) *from a tomb at Saqqara (Egyptian Museum, Cairo)*

4. Vertical angular harp: clay plaque (2000–1800 BC) from Eshnunna (Musée du Louvre, Paris)

5. Horizontal angular harps: detail of an Assyrian stone relief from the Palace of Sennacherib at Nineveh, c705–681 BC (British Museum, London)

the strings were continued in the braids which were fastened to them. Each string was wound around the neck until it reached the required pitch, the tasselled ends of the braids falling in a cluster below the resonator (see fig.5).

Pairs of horizontal harps provided music for animal sacrifices and libation rituals, as on Shalmaneser III's bronze gates from Balawat (now in the British Museum), or when Ashurbanipal makes libation over dead lions to the music of two bearded harpists. Vertical harps depicted in the reign of Ashurbanipal had 18 or 20 strings.

The Egyptian angular harp was always vertical. It first appeared in the New Kingdom. The tomb of Paser at Thebes (contemporary with Amenophis II, 1450–1425

BC) depicts it in conjunction with other novelties such as the lute and lyre as well as the traditional arched harp. A statuette in the British Museum shows the instrument in the hands of a woman, naked except for decorations that suggest tattooing; this dates from the 19th dynasty, the period that produced instruments still fragmentarily preserved in the Egyptian Museum, Cairo. Complete instruments of considerable splendour but later date can be found in the museums of Cairo, Berlin, Florence, New York (Metropolitan Museum of Art) and Paris (the Louvre).

There were several types of harp in Greek use: most were angular and usually played by women, and they found little favour in philosophical circles. There were different names for the instrument, the most common of which was TRIGŌNON; the terms MAGADIS, SAMBUCA (i) and PEKTIS usually signified angular harps but were also occasionally applied to other instrument types (for further terminological discussion, *see* PSALTERY, §1). In Rome the angular harp became popular in imperial times; it was played with the *nāy* (flute) during processions, sacrificial ceremonies and mystery rites of the Isis cult. It had previously been used to accompany settings of lyric poems, when the players were always female.

Roman influence is clear in the mosaics at Bishapur in southern Iran. Belonging to the reign of Shapur I (AD 241–72), they depict banqueting scenes and include a woman playing the angular harp. The court orchestra of Husrau II Parvȳz (AD 590–628), as depicted in the caves at Tāq-i Bustān, contained three types of harp: rectangular and oblique-angular vertical harps and also plectrum-struck horizontal angular harps. On another relief court musicians accompany the king at a wild boar hunt: women, perhaps singing, sit in boats playing horizontal and vertical angular harps or clapping their hands (for illustration *see* CHANG (i)).

Although Palestine was between two regions where the harp was widely used – Mesopotamia and Egypt – its music was different, and harps seem to have been unknown there until the 11th century BC (when Israel became a kingdom) or perhaps even until Hellenistic times, about a millennium later. Flavius Josephus (*b* AD 37 or 38) stated that the strings of the NEVEL (or *nebel*, possibly a harp) were thicker and rougher than those of the KINNOR (a lyre, which was probably the instrument played by King David, despite medieval iconography of him as a harpist). The word *nebel*, clearly related to *nabla*, the Phoenician term for a harp, was rendered by St Jerome in his Vulgate translation of the Bible as 'psalterium'. In the King James Bible *nebel* is translated as both 'psaltery' and 'viol', but *kinnor* is translated as 'harp'. Much confusion has been engendered by these translations of the names of Hebrew instruments.

3. WESTERN DISTRIBUTION. The use of both arched and angular harps spread west from ancient Mesopotamia. Presumed to have moved westwards through Egypt in ancient times, and likened to Egyptian harps in structure, the arched (or bow) harp is still part of nearly 50 distinct musical cultures in Africa (see §6 below). The use of the vertically held angular harp spread south-west from Persia (*chang*) to Arabia (*jank*) and west through Turkey to ancient Greece and Rome. That form of harp is found depicted on Greek and Italo-Greek vases from the 5th to 4th centuries BC.

The origin of the harp which developed in Europe into the classic orchestral instrument (see §4(vii)-(ix) below) remains open to debate. The earliest known depictions of the instrument in Europe are in illuminated manuscripts and carvings from the 8th to 10th centuries AD; these suggest a structure and performing position (see fig.1, position C) closely resembling that of the arched harp played today by the Fang of Gabon which in turn resembles one of the ancient Egyptian types. The oldest extant European harps are from 14th-century Ireland and France (see §4(i and ii) below). Descendants of Baroque forms of European harps without pedals are still made and played in Latin America (see §5 below) and the Philippines, where it was introduced by Spaniards in the 16th to 18th centuries. Recent interest in medieval and Renaissance music has engendered many experiments in the reconstruction of some harp types of these periods.

4. EUROPE.

(i) Medieval and Renaissance. Though the oldest extant European harps date from the 14th century AD, the earliest depictions of harps from what is now geographically Europe are those on Greek and Italo-Greek vases of the 5th and 4th centuries BC. These, however, show Asiatic-type harps, mostly derived from Mesopotamian and Persian harps of the previous millennium. No iconographical evidence to suggest the existence of harps in western Europe in the millennium between the Italo-Greek depictions and those of the 8th century AD is known at present. The origins and early development of European harps remain a matter for speculation and debate. Terminology provides little assistance. Anglo-Saxon *hearpe*, from which the word harp is derived, originally denoted a Teutonic lyre. In some early Western depictions, harps are labelled 'cithara', 'lyra' or even 'barbiton', Greek terms for various kinds of lyre.

The primary source of information about medieval European harps is in Christian iconography. Open harps continued to be depicted occasionally up to the 12th century; after that time, frame harps are virtually the only kind shown. Most appear in illustrations of the psalms, in the hands of David himself or one of his attendants.

Dagulf's Psalter, a product of the Court School of Aachen, was presented to Pope Hadrian I by Charlemagne some time before 795. Its carved ivory cover carries two David scenes, one with harp. In the lower scene, soldiers look on as an enthroned David plays the harp accompanied by two musicians: one with clapper cymbals, the other with a plucked three-string lute (see fig.6). This harp is reminiscent of a Greek type, but it has only a vestigial resonator and is held in medieval and not west Asiatic position (see fig.1, positions C and D respectively). There is no trace of such a harp in European use, but similar depictions continue to occur later; for example, in a Greek psalter written and illus-

6. King David playing a harp: detail from the ivory cover of the Dagulf Psalter, Court School of Aachen, late 8th century (Musée du Louvre, Paris)

trated by Theodorus of Caesarea in 1066 and on a 12th-century stone cross at Ardchattan, near Oban, Scotland. In both cases, the harp is played by one of a group of three musicians as it is in Dagulf's Psalter.

Harps in the Byzantine-influenced Utrecht Psalter (816–35) have straight necks, five to eight strings and forepillars either imperfectly delineated or absent. In some cases there is a suggestion of a trefoil or clawed foot at the base of the resonator. Harps are more clearly drawn in the 11th-century Harley Psalter and the Canterbury Psalter (before 1170), both of which derive from the Utrecht Psalter. These harps demonstrate features common to most European harps for several following centuries: the neck is slightly curved inwards towards a trapezoidal box resonator; the neck is joined to the narrower end of the resonator by a narrow shank; and the forepillar is curved outwards, away from the longest string.

Variations on this basic shape (fig.7a), perhaps regional, can be seen. The harp played by the seated figure on the 11th-century Irish Shrine of St Mogue (in the National Museum of Ireland, Dublin) already has the characteristic Irish T-formation strengthening the forepillar (see 4(ii) below). The late 12th-century York and Westminster Psalters depict harps with about 13 strings, zoomorphic, slightly overhanging neck finials, carved or turned forepillars, and resonators whose quatrefoil and oblong markings are probably nonperspective presentations of soundholes. In Beatus initials (e.g. the beginning of Psalm 1) and sometimes

7. Schematic profiles of European harps from the 11th century to the 16th

a   *b*   *c*   *d*   *e*

8. King David tuning a frame harp: miniature from the York (or Hunterian) Psalter, English, c1170 (GB-Gu Hunter 229, f.21v)

elsewhere, David is often tuning his harp, preparing for the performance to come. In the York initial, David is plucking a 5th with his right hand (assuming the forefinger and not the middle finger is used and the harp is tuned diatonically) while turning the peg of the upper string with a tuning-key in his left (see fig.8). This hand position is also often shown in depictions where he is not tuning; it appears to be a thumb and two-finger technique that continued to be the primary technique used in Spain until the mid-18th century.

Another small harp-type instrument was quadrangular. Its string holder was at the top and it had a slim forepillar. Such an instrument is depicted on the cover of a book probably made between 1131 and 1144 for Melissenda, Countess of Anjou, played by one of David's musicians, while another plays a small triangular harp (*see* DULCIMER, fig.10). Other examples are in a Greek psalter and canticles of Eusebius Pamphili, 11th-century Bishop of Caesarea, and on the North and South Crosses at Castledermot in Ireland, probably from the same century.

In the 12th century, harps were often shown in the hands of some of the 24 Elders. Large examples with zoomorphic finial and plain forepillar are found on the Portico de la Gloria of the Cathedral of Santiago de Compostela and the Portail Royal of Chartres Cathedral. A book of Old Testament illustrations of about 1250, with text in an Italian hand and pictures probably by various French artists, shows small, highly decorated 12- or 13-string harps of this type with trefoil foot. Plainer forms were still depicted in the 14th century; one example of 1376 (the Irish Shrine of St Patrick's Tooth, National Museum of Ireland, Dublin) has 22 strings and was made after French models for Thomas de Bramighem, Baron of Athenry. Another with 22 strings, played by one of six attendant angels, was portrayed by the Catalan painter Pere Serra (1375–1404) in his *Virgen de Tortosa* (in the Museum of Catalan Art, Barcelona).

A significant change can be seen in some instruments depicted in the 13th century. While the gentle curve of the neck is retained, the neck extends upwards somewhat at the front, thus giving slightly more length to the lowest strings, and the forepillar is now only gently curved (fig.7*b*). The stained glass in Chartres Cathedral contains a figure of David with this kind of harp, as does the Beatus initial in the English Peterborough Psalter (*c*1300).

By the 14th century, another harp form had developed: its forepillar was still strongly curved, but its neck swept up at the front into a pointed finial balanced by another pointed finial at the neck-to-shank joining point (fig.7*c*). A harp of this type, with nine strings, is depicted being tuned by David in the Tree of Jesse on an orphrey of *Opus anglicanum* made between 1310 and 1340 (see fig.9). Stringing can be deduced from the remains of a late 14th- or early 15th-century ivory harp (now in the Louvre); it has 24 original pegholes and one which seems to be a later addition, bringing the total to the number given by Machaut in his poem *Dit de la harpe* (*Oeuvres de Guillaume de Machaut*, ed. Hoepffner, 1908–21). If modally tuned throughout, it would have a range of a little more than three octaves. With a more probable partly chromatic tuning in at least one octave, it would have slightly less than three octaves overall. The forepillar is 47 cm high on the external curve and is mortised into the neck. Presumably this was the kind of harp used in French 14th-century polyphonic music. The performing instructions of Jacob de Senleches' *La harpe de melodie* (a copy in *US-CN* 54.1 is uniquely notated in the shape of a harp) indicate that its somewhat slow-moving tenor was to be played on the harp and the injunction 'harpe toudis sans espasse

9. King David tuning a harp: detail from an embroidered orphrey of 'Opus anglicanum', 1310–40 (Victoria and Albert Museum, London)

blechier' seems to imply that its long notes should be sustained by reiteration.

While most medieval and Renaissance harps were probably gut-strung, it is likely that some were metal-strung. Irish harps, in which many medieval features were retained, had brass strings which were plucked with long fingernails. This technique is mentioned in the 13th-century *Geste of Kyng Horn*, where the direction 'Teche him to harpe with nayles scharpe' occurs. Extant tuning-pegs from the 12th, 14th and 15th centuries are either perforated or slotted; most are made of bone, which has a higher chance of survival than wood or metal, though the latter materials were also used.

During the early 15th century considerable experiment in harp design took place, resulting in several forms, with some common and some individual features. These changes were contemporary with the downwards extension of bass registers in general and with the development of keyboard instruments. In the late 14th and 15th centuries, the harp and organ were frequently depicted with clerics (as well as in the earlier context with angels), and both instruments must have fulfilled functions which were parallel in some ways.

The methods of achieving a downwards extension of harp compass involved changes in the angles between the rigid parts of the instrument. In one type of harp, neck and curved forepillar were swept upwards to form a high point, accommodating bass strings considerably longer than was possible on earlier harps (fig.7d). The other type showed more fundamental changes. Longer string length was achieved by lowering the bass end of the resonator in relation to the neck. The angle of the forepillar-to-resonator joint thus became more acute at the lower end, while at the upper end it became wider. The forepillar, at first gently curved, was later straight or nearly so, and of T-formation in section. The neck was no longer set directly into the treble end of the resonator but was set on a slim shank. To some extent this improved the line-up of the shortest strings, which had been somewhat splayed and out of plane on earlier harps. Points or scrolls decorated the forepillar finial and the neck-to-shank point (fig.7e).

There was little change in the size of the resonator in either type of harp. It remained slim and fairly shallow, though there was some variation in shape, later examples being generally oval or hexagonal in section and made from two hollowed-out parts put together lengthways. There was one completely new feature common to both types. Each string was fixed into the resonator with a right-angled wooden pin, which later became known as a bray (Fr. *harpion*; Welsh *gwrach*). When a string was plucked, it vibrated against the bray, producing an aesthetically desired buzzing quality (see fig.15, p.141). This was perhaps comparable with that obtainable on certain contemporary wind instruments, though an annotation in a copy of Mersenne's *Harmonie universelle* (1636–7) describes the effect as like 'le doux tremblement d'une orgue'. There are a few instances of brays on much later types of harp, including two-rank chromatic harps (see §4(iv) below) and high-headed single-strung harps with ribbed-back resonators (see §4(iii) below). The new Renaissance harps were gut-strung and seem to have been played with the fingertips rather than with the older nail technique. This Renaissance harp must have been appropriate for the music of the time as it remained in use, from the British Isles to central Europe, until well after the next significant

10. *Renaissance harp with brays, German, maker unknown, 16th century (Germanisches National-museum, Nuremberg)*

redesigning of harps at the end of the 16th century.

Besides a great number of depictions of Renaissance harps, several instruments have survived. The earliest, now in Eisenach, was made in the Tyrol, possibly in the 15th century. It has 26 strings, stands 104 cm high and has delicate inlaid geometrical decoration of a kind found on other 15th-century instruments. Two undecorated 16th-century examples, now in the collection of the Karl-Marx-Universität, Leipzig, and the Germanisches Nationalmuseum, Nuremberg (see fig.10), are 92 cm and 102 cm high, with 25 and 26 strings respectively.

A method of sharpening individual notes by stopping or pinching the string near the neck or close to the soundboard was used to some extent, but sustained change of mode required retuning some strings. Simple tunings of a kind already in use were given in several 16th-century printed treatises: Martin Agricola (*Musica instrumentalis deudsch*, 1529) mentioned a harp with one row of 26 strings (*F* to *c'''*), in which the B strings could be tuned either flat or natural; Venegas de Henestrosa (*Libro de cifra nueva*, 1557) indicated that the fourth string (B) and the seventh (E) could be tuned either natural or flat. Mersenne also mentioned the simple single-strung harp (which had been superseded in France by his time), giving the range of the 24-string harp as *G* to *g''* with natural B in the lowest octave and both flat and natural Bs in the other two. He said the performers of his day tuned by 'putting flats in all sorts of keys', though the tuning of certain strings (known as *modales*) was constant. These tuning methods continued to be used on later single-rank harps of different structure (see §4(iii) below).

A small silver model of a Renaissance harp, made by a Chester silversmith, was one of the awards at the Eisteddfod at Caerwys in Flintshire in 1567. Descriptions in some Welsh poems soliciting the gift of a harp seem to be of a 30- to 34-string Renaissance harp. The use of twisted horsehair for strings, however, appears to have been a carry-over from earlier Welsh harps; there is very little contemporary or definite information about these. Renaissance harps were still used in Wales long after they had been abandoned elsewhere. James Talbot, Regius Professor of Hebrew at Cambridge (1689–1704), made extensive notes on many instruments in use towards the end of the 17th century (Talbot MS; *GB-Och* Music 1187). 'The proper Welsh harp' and 'Welsh or Bray Harp' referred to by some of his informants were in fact large Renaissance harps, with either 31 (*A'* to *c'''*) or 34 (*G'* to *e'''*) strings. Various tunings were codified in Welsh 16th-century harping practice. Though only three were given in a Welsh manuscript of 1676 (*bragod gywair*, mode of A; *gogywair*, mode of C; *braidd gywair*, a pentatonic mode), more had been in use at the time of the ap Huw manuscript, written in tablature about 1613. Though the system of ornamentation in the ap Huw manuscript is not difficult to interpret, there is little agreement on the precise interpretation of its tunings (often not specified) and musical content.

11. Oldest extant Irish harp, known as the 'Brian Boru' harp, 14th century (Trinity College, Dublin)

(ii) Ireland and Scotland. The Irish and Gaelic name for the harp, CLÁIRSEACH (Scottish: CLÀRSACH), is documented from the 15th century onwards; the term 'ceirnin' (now obsolete) is also occasionally found. Harps depicted in medieval Irish shrines (see §4(i) above) show structural features of the type of instrument used in Ireland up to the late 18th century (*see* IRISH HARP).

The oldest extant Irish harp, now at Trinity College, Dublin, had legendary associations with Brian Boroimhe (or Boru, 926–1014), but dates in fact from no earlier than the 14th century (see fig.11). This harp is low-headed, the upper end of its forepillar meeting the neck at a point only slightly higher than the joint between the treble end of the neck and the resonator. Two other harps, known as the Queen Mary and Lamont harps (now in the National Museum of Antiquities, Edinburgh), are also of this type and have been dated to the 15th century. Later, perhaps by the beginning of the 16th century, a larger but still low-headed form emerged.

By the 18th century, however, the typical instrument, as played by itinerant Irish harpers, was much larger. It retained the big one-piece resonator, but the forepillar, now only slightly curved, was very tall (the low-headed Lamont harp has a forepillar height of 59·7 cm, whereas that of the high-headed Sirr harp measures 111·8 cm) and the neck swept upwards to meet it. The bass strings were therefore much longer in relation to the treble strings than on a low-headed harp. Irish harps were strung to the left side of the neck, but tuning was done from the right; the left hand played the treble, the right hand the bass. Irish harpers struck the brass strings of their harps with specially trimmed long fingernails. It seems unlikely that this technique was used by gentleman amateurs in England who took up the Irish harp in the later 17th century. While the sonority of individual notes is not greatly different whether produced by the fleshy fingertips or the fingernails, the use of the latter implies a quite different playing technique and type of attack. It also means that the melodic ornamentation typical of Irish performance on an Irish harp properly 'strung with brass strings and beaten with crooked nails' cannot be reproduced by a harpist playing with the fingertips. Even in Ireland the old technique gradually died out in the 17th and 18th centuries, and of the ten harpists present at the famous meeting in Belfast in 1792 only one, Denis Hempson, then 97 years old, used the traditional fingernail technique. It was very soon to die out altogether – during a period, ironically, of revived interest in Irish music and the Irish harp.

In the early 19th century attempts were made to sustain and revitalize Irish harp playing traditions and repertory. The Belfast Harp Society, founded in 1808, inaugurated the teaching of a number of children by Arthur O'Neill and Bridget O'Reilly, two of the players who had taken part in the 1792 festival. Harps were provided by local makers. Having collapsed in 1813, the society was re-established with similar aims in 1819 but closed in 1839. A Dublin Harp Society, of social rather than pedagogical character, lasted from 1809 to 1812. After 1819 John Egan and, later, his nephew and successor Francis Hewson produced a new design of 'Irish Harp' for amateurs. Although superficially resembling some 18th-century harps, Egan's instruments were much more lightly constructed and closer in conception to the pedal harps of his day, with their thin soundboards and separate, rounded backs (see fig.12). Later, he produced his 'portable harp', the gut strings of which were fixed into the soundboard with pegs. A hand-operated mechanism not unlike that of the *Hakenharfe* ('hook harp', see §4(vi) below) shortened individual strings by a semitone. About 1819, Egan built a harp with seven 'ditals' placed in the forepillar, each of which when pressed down would affect a mechanism in the neck of the harp that shortened all strings of the same note name by a semitone. Like the single-action harp on which it was based, this harp was tuned in E♭; the technique of playing was also derived largely from that of the pedal harp (see §4(vi) below). Egan also made at least one double-action dital harp.

However historically incorrect the terminology, the harp now known as 'Irish' or 'Celtic' is a small instrument of 24 to 34 strings, with a flat soundboard on a round-backed resonator and a hand-operated mechanism (blades or levers) for shortening the strings. Instruments of this kind are still made and played in both Ireland and Scotland. Similar instruments have also been made in England intermittently since the mid-19th century, and since the early part of the 20th century they have also been made in the USA and, more recently, Japan. Their educational possibilities as a cheaper substitute for the pedal harp in the initial stages of harp teaching have been widely recognized since about 1960. Thus Lyon–Healy 'Troubadour' harps have been commercially produced in large numbers since 1961, and both Horngacher and Salvi make a similar instrument, as do many individual professional makers with a smaller production. Recently a few copies of the older Irish harps have also been made.

(iii) Other single-rank harps. Diatonically or partly chromatically tuned harps with one rank of strings continued in use long after the invention of double- and triple-strung fully chromatic harps (see §4(iv) and (v) below) and, later, of pedal harps. In most cases, they were adaptations of earlier types, often structurally influenced in some respects by newer forms. Two chief kinds are traceable. One seems to derive from that regarded by Praetorius in Germany as the 'ordinary' harp (see fig.13). The resonator was generally fairly shallow, four-sided and rectangular in section, though some instruments had a convexly curved soundboard; strings were pegged into a string holder, a wooden strip that ran lengthwise down the middle of the soundboard. Soundholes were sometimes circular, more often clusters of small perforations. Some instruments were plainly made; others had very elaborately carved necks with anthropomorphic or zoomorphic finials (heads of David, Cupids, warriors, lion heads etc). Forepillars were slightly curved in earlier harps, later generally straight. Though low-headed harps of this kind were made even in the 18th century, high-headed forms had already appeared in the 17th century and these were still played by some professional virtuosos at the end of the 18th century. Presumably their repertory (like that in some regions of Latin America) was not more chromatic than could be accommodated by the old system of partly chromatic tuning or different tuning in different octaves. In hooked form, some harps of this type lasted even longer in certain regions (see §4(x) below).

The other main type had a resonator with a ribbed back, a flat soundboard, and a straight forepillar in either low- or high-headed form. Most of the later single-strung Welsh harps are of this type. Although a low-headed form became the predominant type in Latin America (see §5 below) few European examples have been preserved

12. Dital harp by John Egan, Dublin, c1819–31 (Victoria and Albert Museum, London)

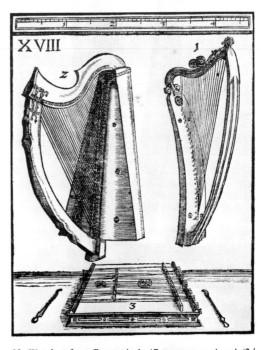

13. Woodcut from Praetorius's 'Syntagma musicum' (2/ 1619): 1 – common harp; 2 – Irish harp with brass strings; 3 – dulcimer

and its early history is difficult to ascertain. It seems to have been derived from Mediterranean (not northern) sources and may have been a byproduct of early triple harps.

A very small harp (forepillar height of 84 cm), bearing the mark 'Stradivarius, Cremona 1681' (in the Naples Conservatory), has a flat pine soundboard (now slightly lifted with string tension) with violin-like double purfling, set on a resonator shaped as if in five ribs, though it is actually made in one piece. The 27 strings are pegged directly into the soundboard, except for the lowest three, which are toggled through large holes; there are four tiny heart-shaped soundholes. In another small Italian instrument (owned by one family since 1860 but pos-

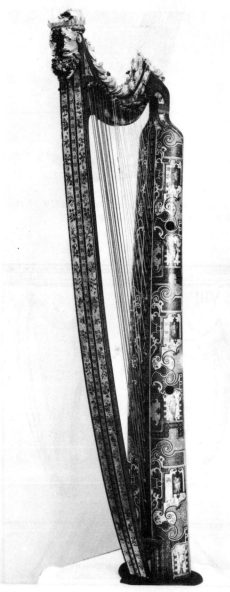

sibly of earlier manufacture), the resonator is five-ribbed: 31 strings are pegged into a central strip on the sound board and there are four soundhole clusters.

A small harp now in the Royal College of Music, London, must have been made for a Welsh player, wh traditionally balanced the harp on his left shoulder, sinc it is strung to the (player's) right of the neck. Its resona tor is five-ribbed; the strings are pegged into the sound board and above each string-hole is the metal strip foun on most 18th-century triple harps. The Richard Hay ward harp (so-called after its last private owner, wh gave it to the National Museum of Ireland, Dublin, i 1947) is similarly strung. It is 150 cm high, with a nine ribbed resonator 109 cm long and 31 strings. Excep that it is single-strung, it is structurally like 18th-centur Welsh-made triple harps. The inscription in Irish ('Ma you never want a string while there are guts in an Eng lishman') and the unlikely date 1657, which are incise on the forepillar, must have been added during its us in Ireland where it is said to have been played in th streets and parks of Belfast about 1780 by the itineran harper Paddy Murphy.

In the 1680s, there were at least six players of a Span ish kind of harp in London. The low-headed, 33-strin instrument measured and described in the Talbot Manu script (GB-Och Music 1187) was a little over 147 cm tall, with a seven-ribbed resonator 137 cm long, wid ening from 12·7 cm at the top to 45·8 cm at the bottom Like several of the cross-strung Spanish chromatic harp that have survived, its soundboard was of pine and th rest of the instrument of walnut. (Talbot mentioned th existence of a double-strung Spanish harp with fiv chromatic strings per octave, but he gave no measure ments and appears not to have encountered one person ally.)

Single-strung Spanish harps from the late 17th cen tury and early 18th, though approximately as tall as tha described by Talbot, had much larger resonators. Where the top-to-bottom resonator-width ratio in the 1692 instrument was 1:3·6 and that prescribed by Nassarre in 1724 (for double-strung harps) was 1:5, it is 1:9 o even 1:11 in some late instruments whose superstruc ture was modelled after that of a pedal harp. In Latin America, very large resonators are found on some instruments which are otherwise still of 17th- or early 18th-century type (see §5 below).

(iv) Harps with two ranks of strings. Two types of harp, both with two ranks (i.e. rows) of strings, were created in an attempt to make the harp a chromatic instrument capable of playing the music of the late Renaissance and later periods. One type had its ranks parallel to one another; in the other, the two ranks crossed each other in the middle, yielding the type often referred to as 'cross-strung'. In his *Declaración de instrumentos musicales* (1555), Juan Bermudo described diatonically tuned single-rank harps (of 24 to 27 strings), but he considered them imperfect compared with the fully chromatic keyboard instruments; he stated that the harp was little played on account of its difficulty and suggested adding five coloured strings to each octave for the required chromatic notes. Alonso Mudarra's *Tres libros de música en cifra para vihuela* (1546) had included one simple item in a tablature usable for organ or harp, where instructions were given as to the method of string-stopping (near the soundboard) for the sharpening of the required chromatic notes, and the fantasía no.10 (for vihuela), in imitation of the harpist Luduvico, who contrived chromatic

14. *The Este harp: two-rank chromatic harp, by Jean le Pot, Amiens, later (c1587) decorated in Ferrara style (Galleria Estense, Modena)*

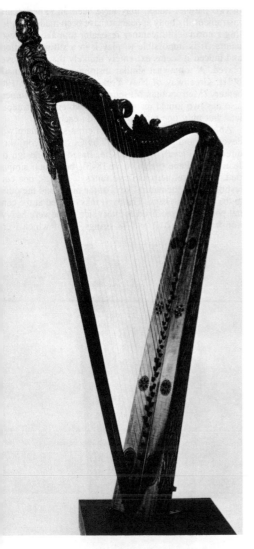

15. *German two-rank chromatic harp, with details of brays and position of brays in the soundboard (Conservatoire Royal de Musique, Brussels)*

notes with good effect on a single-rank harp – perhaps by means of string stopping but more probably by pre-tuning selected strings. Antonio de Cabezón's *Obras de música* (1578) was designated *para tecla, arpa y vihuela*. Cabezón's florid and fairly chromatic pieces could have been played only on a harp with considerable chromatic possibilities.

Completely chromatic tuning was given in schematic form by Galilei (1581); chromatic harps existed before that time and there are surviving instruments of various sizes. They do not exactly match Galilei's 'Temperamento dell' harpa' in every respect but all are based on the same principle. This was that in harps with two parallel ranks, one rank was tuned C–D–E–F–G–A– Bb (i.e. transposed 7th mode), the other C♯–D–Eb– F♯–G♯–A–B. Though present-day harpists might be tempted to regard the main row as being tuned in F major, this was not so in 16th-century terms of musical reference. The total range was about four octaves, divided around middle C into an upper half used by the right hand, where the second or chromatic string rank lay to

the (player's) left of the centrally-set main rank, and a lower half, used by the left hand, where it lay to the right of the main rank; i.e., the chromatic rank changed sides half way up. In each case the player had to reach through the main row in order to pluck the chromatic strings. In several surviving instruments the chromatic rank is set very close to the main rank in the upper register, where florid passages involving chromatic notes were more common than in the lower. In Galilei's chart the compass is from C to d''', the lower chromatic rank starting at D and the upper one ending at c♯'''. In the Este harp (fig.14) whose total compass is D to c''', the lower chromatic rank starts only at F♯ while the upper ends at g♯''; c♯' is duplicated at the cross-over point. This instrument, magnificently decorated in Ferrara style by Giulio Marescotti about 1587, was probably made in France by Jean le Pot several decades earlier. Surviving 16th- and 17th-century examples of this kind of harp are all low-headed. A higher-headed example is shown in a painting attributed to Carlo Francesco Nuvolone (now in the Pinacoteca di Brera, Milan). Cerreto

(*Della prattica musica*, 1601) gave a list of players of 'arpa a due ordini' then living in Naples.

Much confusion has arisen with regard to the term 'arpa doppia', since DOUBLE has been used in several senses in musical terminology (and 'harp' in many more). The *arpa doppia* available to Monteverdi and his contemporaries was 'double' in two senses: as it must have been chromatic, it must have had two ranks; and as its lowest note was *G'*, 'double' implies a downward extension of pitch.

It is ironic that the only depiction of an instrument actually labelled 'Harpa Doppia' came from a region – north Germany – which then had somewhat different musical usages from Italy, and which also used the term 'harp' in several senses. Besides the ordinary and Irish harps, Praetorius described and illustrated what he labelled 'Gross Doppel-Harff – Harpa Doppia'. His description is of a large upright double psaltery, strung with metal strings on both sides of a large soundbox. On the left side, strings were tuned *C* to *g″* and on the right *g* to *c″″*. The use of the term 'harp' in Germany for this kind of instrument was attested to later by James Talbot, who gave a description of a smaller one. Also, J. G. Walther (1732) specified three types of harp in Germany, the first of which was 'the common one, known everywhere, strung with wire and called *harpanetta*'. Praetorius's illustration shows not the instrument referred to in his text but a mechanically unlikely hybrid; evidently the illustrator had never seen an 'Harpa Doppia' of any description. Two later two-rank harps are in the Brussels Conservatory. One, apparently made in Venice in 1675, is an undecorated, workmanlike instrument. There are four soundholes in the soundboard, the back of the resonator is ribbed and the curve of the neck is similar to that of the later pedal harp. The other – of German origin – is an elegant instrument, its forepillar terminating in an anthropomorphic finial (see fig.15). It has 33 strings in its left-hand rank and 26 in its right-hand rank; the five lowest and four highest have no chromatic strings beside them. Both these harps retain the buzzing brays that were a feature of much older Renaissance harps (see §4(i) above).

Attempts to add a second rank on the Irish harp may have been made as early as the beginning of the 17th century. The only remaining fragments of the Dalway harp, made in 1621 (National Museum of Ireland, Dublin), are the complete neck and almost complete forepillar. The neck has 45 pinholes in one row and above them, in its middle part, seven additional pinholes for seven extra strings. It is not known, however, whether these additional strings were chromatically or sympathetically tuned.

Until recently, it was believed that no Spanish chromatic harps had survived, but Arroyo (1979) documented four previously unknown 18th-century Spanish chromatic harps. The two ranks of strings were not parallel, but cross-strung. The Spanish term 'arpa de dos órdenes' is therefore believed to refer to the cross-strung type as opposed to the Italian 'arpa a due ordini' in which the two ranks of strings were parallel. The big 46-string harp which the Moroccan ambassador to Spain noted about 1690 as being played by noble Spanish amateurs may well have been a cross-strung chromatic harp.

A cross-strung chromatic harp, probably from about 1800, is on display in the Victoria and Albert Museum, London. This harp, with its two necks, two crossed forepillars and two resonators each carrying 40 strings

in two parallel ranks, may have been an experimental instrument. Its body appears to have been made by splitting a normal 18th-century resonator to make two resonators. It is impossible to play it in a sitting position and indeed it seems extremely unlikely that it was ever played. A somewhat similar instrument was that made by H. Greenway of New York at the end of the 19th century (Metropolitan Museum of Art). This instrument also has two joined resonators and two crossed forepillars, but only one rank of strings in each half.

An important latterday form of cross-strung harp was developed and patented in 1897 by Gustave Lyon, the director of Pleyel, Wolff & Cie. Based on a design by Jean Henri Pape (patented in 1843), but much simplified, the Pleyel harp had two ranks of strings, one corresponding to the natural keys of the piano and the other to the chromatic keys. The two ranks crossed at the central point and were fixed at either side of the very heavy iron-framed neck. It had 78 strings, 46 of which were

16. *Cross-strung chromatic harp by Pleyel, Paris, early 20th century (Conservatoire Royal de Musique, Brussels)*

fixed on the left-hand side of the soundboard and 32 on the right. Its compass was *D'* to *g'''* and it stood nearly 2 metres high (see fig.16). In order to promote his harp, Pleyel commissioned composers to write for it, and thus Debussy composed his *Danse sacrée et danse profane* (1904). Although classes for chromatic harp were established at conservatories, first at Brussels and later at Paris, the Pleyel harp was never as successful as Gustave Lyon perhaps would have liked, and by the time he died (1936) it had been almost completely abandoned except in Belgium, where classes at the conservatory continued until 1953. Despite its enormous size, its sonority was thin and frail. It was very heavy (60 kg) and demanded an extremely awkward playing technique quite different from that of the pedal harp (see §4(vi) below). The only possible glissandos – by this time a commonplace of harp writing – were the major scale of C and, with difficulty, the pentatonic glissando afforded by the row of strings tuned to the 'black-note' scale. The disappointed Gustave Lyon later attempted to build a *harpe intégrale* combining the cross-strung chromatic stringing of his earlier harp with a pedal-operated mechanism. A similar idea had already been promoted about a century before by the Welsh harpist Oliver Davies, who in 1820 introduced in London and Brecon, Wales, a harp strung with two identically tuned ranks of strings and with a pedal-operated mechanism.

(v) Harps with three ranks of strings. Another form of completely chromatic harp was developed during the 16th century, apparently not much later than the two-rank chromatic harps. This had three ranks of strings, two parallel outer ranks tuned identically and an inner rank of chromatic notes set between them. In practical terms, this allowed mobility with either hand over the whole compass. Whether this consideration or a search for richer sonority and greater volume impelled the development of this kind of harp is not certain. However, all known or depicted three-rank harps from the early 17th century onwards are larger than any known two-rank harps; the duplicated strings certainly produce sympathetic resonance and these harps indeed have a strongly individual tonal character. Their resonators were fundamentally different from those of earlier harps. They consisted of a flat or nearly flat soundboard on a ribbed back, at first fairly small in relation to the harp's overall size but later very large. The use of this new harp in aristocratic Italian circles coincided with the growth of dramatic monody and early opera. So well did it become established in some Italian and French circles that Mersenne (1636–7) referred to it as the 'normal' harp, adding that it was called 'triple'.

The earliest extant triple harp, in the Museo Civico, Bologna, is a large, heavy, low-headed instrument, with a gently curved forepillar 193 cm high. Its resonator (134 cm long) consists of a one-piece soundboard of vertical grain and a nine-ribbed back; there are 96 string-holes. It is triple-strung, the strings running to the (player's) left of the neck; this is stepped so that the three ranks lie separately. The neck lifts clear of the resonator well before the stringing in the upper register starts and it is mortised into the forepillar at an angle. A comparable harp appears in a painting of King David by Domenico Zampieri (1581–1641), an artist of the school of Bologna (see fig.17). Apart from the Bologna harp, no examples of these early low-headed instruments are known to survive, though that illustrated by Mersenne

17. King David playing a triple harp: detail from the painting 'King David' by Domenico Zampieri (1581–1641) (Musée de Versailles)

and described by him as being of Italian origin was low-headed. Even James Talbot, writing in England about 50 years later, mentioned a low-headed triple harp, though he did not give details of it as he did of other triple harps, both English and Welsh. Within the basic concept of duplicated outer ranks and a single inner rank, string plans varied. The Bologna harp, for example, has seven strings per octave in the middle rank. Presumably five of these were tuned to chromatic semitones. The remaining two were either tuned in duplicate with two in the outer ranks (as is the case with Welsh triple harps where, for example, on one tuned in B♭, the inner rank would contain B♮–C♯–D♯–E♮–F♯–G♯–A♯, the D♯s and A♯s being enharmonic doubles of the E♭s and B♭s in the outer ranks) or perhaps to microvariants of two in the inner rank. The harp illustrated by Mersenne also had seven strings per octave in the middle rank, but his text stated that only five per octave were needed to string it 'to perfection'. Several continental triple harps have this kind of stringing. Among them is a very large one made in Vicenza in 1793 by Giovanni Vetorazzo (now in the Instrumenten Museum, Karl-Marx-Universität, Leipzig).

Most triple harps do not have complete duplication of the outer ranks and a full central rank right through the compass. Up to an octave in the lowest register and a 5th in the highest may be strung on one side only; the central rank may be absent in these registers for a few notes or an entire octave. The Barberini harp (*c*1625), with 76 strings and a compass of four octaves and one note, is a rare hybrid; the highest and lowest octaves are strung as in a two-rank chromatic harp while the two middle octaves are triple. Extravagantly carved and decorated, it is still in the Palazzo Barberini in Rome, which also houses a painting in which this instrument is depicted, the *Allegoria della musica* by Giovanni Lanfranco (1582–1647).

The harp compositions of such late Renaissance and early Baroque composers as Rocco Rodio, Ascanio Mayone and Giovanni Maria Trabaci may have been intended for either double or triple harp. Although several kinds of harp were available in London in Handel's time (the title-page used for *Admeto*, for example, shows a two-rank chromatic harp; see fig.18), the B♭ Concerto op.4 no.6 and the harp parts in *Esther*, *Saul* and *Giulio Cesare* were probably played on a triple harp. While it is impossible to be certain that Bach wrote for the triple harp, the suggestion (first made by Hans Neemann in the early 1930s and repeated by Wolfgang Schmieder) that Bach's own transcription of the Violin Partita in E (BWV1006*a*) might have been intended for the harp bears examination. The only harp of the period on which this transcription could have been played successfully is the triple harp. The constantly reiterated notes of the Prelude, in particular, are splendidly stylish on the triple harp.

The triple harp appeared in the British Isles early in the 17th century. William Lawes wrote for it in his

18. *Two-rank chromatic harp: title-page of Handel's opera 'Admeto' (1727)*

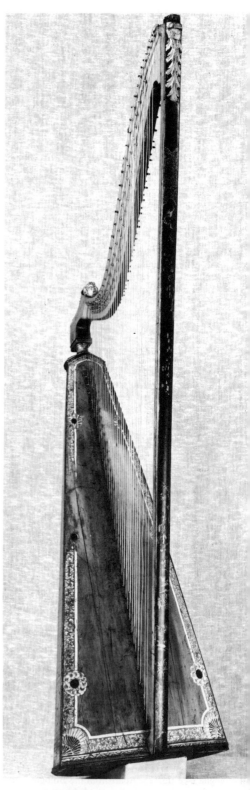

19. *Welsh triple harp by David Evans, London, 1736 (Victoria and Albert Museum, London)*

'Harpe' consorts for violin, theorbo, bass viol and harp, probably composed for the consort of Jean le Flesle, who was harpist at the court of Charles I from 1629 until about 1641 and was mentioned by Mersenne as playing the harp 'perfectly'. Welsh makers were considered the best, including David Evans, who in 1736 made the splendid triple harp now in the Victoria and Albert Museum (fig.19), and his pupil John Richards of Llanrwst, who worked mostly in Wales at the estate of Sackville Gwynne at Glanbrân.

A typical Welsh triple harp (*telyn deires*: 'harp of three rows') is high-headed, the forepillar length of nearly 2 metres allowing for a bottom string of F' or G'. It normally has a range of five octaves and one note, and therefore contains more than 95 strings. Although there are variations, the general rule is that the centre or chromatic rank joins the right-hand rank at F, and the left-hand rank begins at B. The instrument is designed to be played on the left shoulder, the left hand playing the treble and the right hand playing the bass (see fig.20). The strings, fixed into the soundboard by round-headed wooden pegs, pass through slotted tuning-pins placed in three rows in the right-hand side of the stepped neck. The long, slim forepillar is sometimes strengthened along part of its length by an iron insert and is bolted into the base of the resonator. The steeply curved neck is set on a flat-topped shank which forms the upper part of a flut-ed block fixed into the upper part of the resonator. The resonator is strengthened on the inside with six to eleven wooden braces, which help to bear the considerable tension of the strings.

Performers on the triple harp, such as John Parry (c1710–82), the blind Welsh harpist, composed sonatas and variations on Welsh (and other) airs for the harp, and towards the end of the 18th century several important collections of traditional Welsh harp tunes and dances, arranged as themes with variations, were published. Parry's works offer the earliest record of the characteristic 'doubled notes', the fast broken unisons on the two outer string ranks, which are such a brilliant feature of Welsh technique. By the end of the century, the single-action pedal harp superseded the triple harp in England. Edward Jones, whose collection *Musical and Poetical Relicks of the Welsh Bards* appeared in 1784, played both the triple harp and the single-action type.

In addition, the triple harp continued to be played in rural Wales by itinerant gypsy harpers. Augusta Hall (Lady Llanover) (1802–96) encouraged harpists and harp makers to live on her estate in Llanover, Gwent, and many fine triple harps were built there during her lifetime. Many of the Llanover harps are now in museums, the Welsh Folk Museum, St Fagans, having a particularly large collection. Bassett Jones of Cardiff also made good triple harps during the 19th century (see fig.20).

After the early 20th century triple harps were almost completely abandoned in Wales, except among gypsies, in favour of the pedal harp. Were it not for one player, Nansi Richards-Jones (1888–1979), who learnt to play from an elderly relative and from itinerant harpers in the Bala area at the turn of the century, the traditional techniques would have been lost completely. Many details have no doubt perished in transmission; and yet certain elements of Welsh technique seem clearly to reflect Baroque performing practice – the vigorous attack, the big, bright sound, the short articulation of the fingers and the position of the hands near the soundboard. The importance of the triple harp today is that it is a survival

20. Welsh triple harp by Bassett Jones, Cardiff, c1850, played by Nansi Richards-Jones, 1970

into the 20th century of an essentially Baroque instrument.

(vi) Hook harps and single-action pedal harps. Chromatically strung two- and three-rank harps were complicated to make and cumbersome to play if more than a small number of chromatic notes were needed. During the second half of the 17th century a method of obtaining some chromatic notes on a diatonically tuned single-rank harp was developed, apparently in south-east Germany. Strong metal hooks were inserted in the neck below the tuning-pins of the strings most likely, in the musical styles of the time, to need pitch change. At first these were the first, second, fourth and fifth degrees of the scale in which the instrument was tuned. When a hook was turned by the left hand to stop the adjacent string the pitch of that string was raised by a semitone. Earlier examples have hooks only in the middle register, and throughout the period in which hand-turned hooks were used on some harps (i.e. until the mid-18th century) the lowest octave was rarely fitted with hooks. The hook method of chromaticization was applied to instruments of considerably differing structure, ranging from early 17th-century types to imitations of pedal harps. Some had rectangular resonators, some ribbed, some curved. Some had necks and forepillars of austere simplicity (fig.21, p.146), while others were elaborately decorated, occasionally with zoomorphic or anthropomorphic designs such as a lion's head or a representation of David or a satirical regional figure.

Only one string could be sharpened at a time, and the process of turning a hook temporarily prevented the left hand from playing. It was in order to remedy the inconveniences of manually operated hooks that a pedal-operated mechanism for sharpening the strings was developed. This took place in the Tyrol. Although eventually the harp was provided with seven pedals, one for each note of the scale, initially it had five (C, D, F, G and A). These pedals, in the bottom of the resonator, were connected to wire rods that passed up through the resonator to connect with a link mechanism in a hollowed-out recess along the length of the right-hand side of the neck. The link mechanism was connected to the hooks on the outside left of the neck, and when a pedal was depressed the hooks turned and sharpened every string of the same note name in all its octaves. Such harps are still made and played in some villages in the Austrian Tyrol.

Jakob Hochbrucker of Donauwörth, Bavaria, is often credited with the invention of the single-action pedal harp, though it is sometimes attributed to other makers, such as J. P. Vetter of Nuremberg. 1720 is usually given as the approximate date of the invention, but Hochbrucker's son Simon (*b* 1699), in his introduction to an undated collection of *Ariettes*, stated that the pedal harp had

21. Hook harp by Martin Eggert, Wertingen, early 18th century (Metropolitan Museum of Art, New York)

been invented by his father in 1697. It is not known wl had the idea of enlarging the pillar and hollowing it o so that the pedal rods could be accommodated insi (rather than in the resonator), but by the time the sing action harp came to be played regularly in Fren aristocratic circles this placement of the pedal rods w standard.

Simon Hochbrucker introduced his father's harp Vienna in 1729 and to Brussels ten years later. It w not until 1749 that a similar harp was played in Pa by the German harpist Goepfert (Gaiffre), who claim to have invented it. Paris soon took a leading role, ho ever, and with the arrival in 1770 of France's new da phine, Marie-Antoinette – herself a harpist – Paris becan pre-eminent in the harp industry. Harpists and harpis composers converged there, and it is reported that 1784 there were 58 harp teachers in the city. Harp mal ers too were numerous, and it was in Parisian worl shops that all the important developments in ha construction in the second half of the 18th century toc place.

Diderot and D'Alembert's *Encyclopédie* shows a ty ical harp of the period (see fig.22). The resonator w composed of a ribbed back, lidded by a thin flexib soundboard of lateral grain. The curve of the neck va ied slightly according to the number (generally 36 to 4 and pitch of the strings. A box to house the seven peda was added at the base of the harp, and the pedal ro connected to the linkage ran up through the hollow fore pillar, now of necessity absolutely straight. In respons perhaps to the taste of aristocratic patrons, the simp carved forepillars were made highly ornate, sculpture and gilded. Soundboards were painted in the Verni Martin style, and the harp itself became an importar decorative element, indeed a requisite of the most ele gant Parisian salons.

Improvements were made in its mechanism. The cro chets – a French version of the hook mechanism – we right-angled rather than U-shaped. When the pedal wa depressed the *crochet* moved horizontally inwards towar the neck where it squeezed the string against a fixed nu thus shortening it by approximately an 18th of its length The disadvantage of this system – used by all the lead ing harp makers including Louvet, Salomon, Holtz mann, Renault and Chatelain, Naderman, and th Cousineau family – was that strings so sharpened wer pushed out of vertical alignment. Their sonority was the rather dull in comparison with the open strings, and the also tended to buzz against the neck of the harp. T remedy these failings Georges Cousineau and his so Jacques-Georges contrived an improved system (béquilles), in which each string is provided with tw small crutch-ended levers placed to either side of it, on above the other. The downwards movement of the peda causes one lever to turn clockwise and the other anti clockwise, tightening the string in a firmer, more con trolled manner than the *crochets* (see COUSINEAU illustration).

The pedals for D, C and B strings were normally place to the left of the resonator, and those for E, F, G an A to its right. The harp was lightly strung with gut string except for the bottom six, which were wire-covered, an C and F strings were coloured respectively red and blue for ease of identification. The open strings were tune in E♭ to give the widest scope for modulation, eigh major and five minor keys being obtainable by differer pedal combinations. For example, in E♭ all the pedal were in their open position, but in C, the B, E and A pedals were depressed and fixed into the lower notch so that B♭ became B♮, E♭ became E♮, and A♭ became A♮.

In 1792 Sébastien Erard, who by this time had established his firm in London, took out the first British patent ever granted for a harp. This instrument, the fruit of much experiment, represented a radical change in the construction of the single-action harp. The ribbed resonator was abandoned in favour of a body made in two separate parts: a soundboard of Swiss pine and a rounded back reinforced by internal ribs. For strength and stability, the neck was of laminated construction. The mechanism, mounted on two brass plates, was fixed to the neck instead of being housed inside it, and was therefore independent of the frame. Erard also made mechanical improvements to the pedals, but the really revolutionary feature of his harp was its brilliantly simple 'fork' system, which replaced the unsatisfactory *crochets* and *béquilles*. The 'fork' consists of two brass prongs mounted on a small round brass disc. The disc is screwed centrally on to an axis which passes through the brass plates. The string, resting against a bridge-pin which aligns it with the centre of the disc at a distance of approximately 5 mm, passes between the forks. When the pedal is depressed, the axis turns to bring the prongs into firm contact with the string, thus sharpening it by a semitone (figs.23 and 24). The string is held firmly in position by the fork, so that the problem of jarring

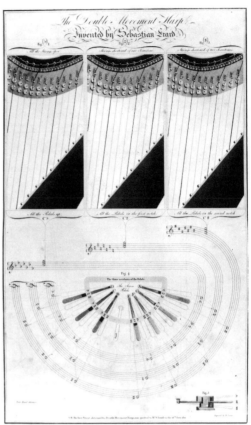

23. *Engraving from Pierre Erard's 'The Harp in its Present improved State' (1821), showing the positions of forks and pedals, and corresponding keys obtainable on the new Erard double-action harp*

strings, common to the *crochets* and *béquilles* systems, is eliminated. The movement of the fork also keeps the affected string perfectly parallel with the others.

(vii) The double-action pedal harp. In spite of mechanical and constructional improvements, musicians and harp makers alike were dissatisfied with the modulatory limitations implicit in the fact that the single-action harp could play in only eight major and five minor keys. In 1782 the Cousineau family built a harp which could play in all keys by means of a complicated apparatus with two sets of pedals placed one above the other, making 14 pedals in all. (The open strings were tuned in C♭.) Around the turn of the century Erard set out to produce a better solution, and, after continuous experiment, in 1810 he patented his double-action harp. Operating on the same fork principle as his earlier single-action harp, Erard's double-action instrument uses C♭ as its open key and has 43 strings (E' to e'''') and seven pedals, each of which can be depressed twice, housed in a box at the base of the harp. Each string passes between two fork-bearing discs, placed one above the other. When the pedal is depressed into its first notch, the upper disc turns so that the forks grip the string and sharpen it by a semitone, while the lower disc turns about 45° but does not touch the string. When the pedal is depressed a second time, and fixed into the bottom notch, the low-

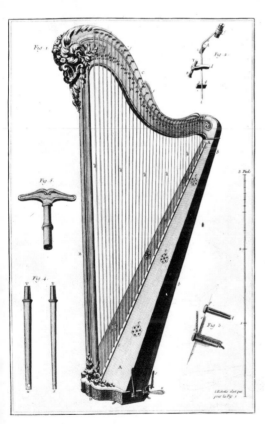

22. *Engraving from Diderot and D'Alembert's 'Encyclopédie', v (1767), plates, showing a single-action pedal harp and structural and mechanical details*

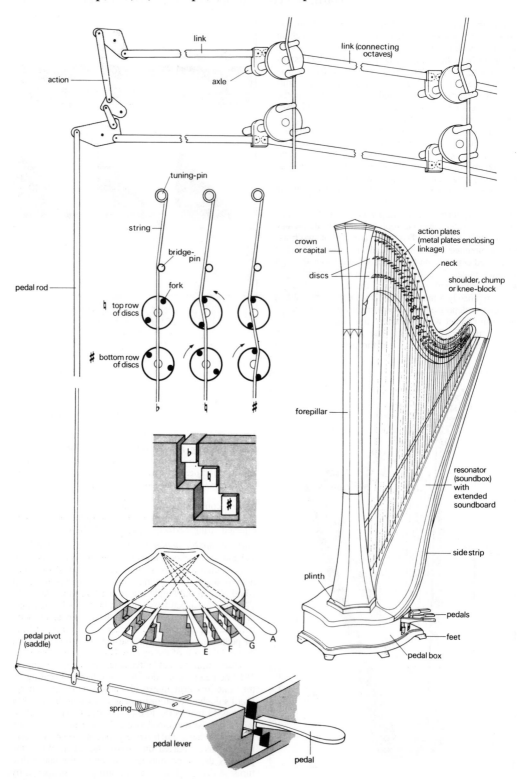

24. *Diagram of a modern double-action harp, showing levers, pedal box, and the positions of forks and pedals for ♭, ♮ and ♯ keys*

er fork turns a further 35° gripping the string and short-ening it by another semitone (see fig.23). Each string can therefore be sharpened two semitones, from flat to natural to sharp, and the harp can be played in any key by the simple expedient of fixing the pedals in the req-uisite notches. This ingenious mechanism has been used, with very few modifications, by most harp makers up to the present day. Between 1811 and 1835 Erard made about 4000 double-action harps, decorated in a 'Gre-cian' style, and many of them are still in use. They are strung with gut from *e''''* (known on the harp as 'First Octave E') to *F* (known as 'Fifth Octave F'), and from *E* to *E'* with wire-covered silk (now often replaced in re-strung Erards with wire-covered nylon).

In 1835 Erard's nephew Pierre, building on the same principles, brought out a larger model (with 'Gothic' decoration) of 46 strings (*C'* to *f'''*), the wire-covered bass strings (*C'* to *F*) having steel cores. Such harps were familiar in most British and French orchestras until the early 1960s, when the age of their mechanism made most of them too unreliable for regular orchestral use and harpists began to import new instruments from Ger-many, Italy and the USA.

When European harps were first imported into the USA in large numbers in the second half of the 19th century, it became obvious that a more robustly constructed instrument was needed to withstand the rigours of the varying climatic conditions. Two rival Chicago-based firms – LYON & HEALY, who made their first harps in 1889, and the Rudolph WURLITZER company, who made harps from 1909 to 1936 – worked to this end. Mechan-ical precision was improved and the mechanism was entirely enclosed between the brass plates of the neck. The pedal rods within the forepillar were enclosed in individual brass tubes, which made their movement eas-ier and less noisy. Soundboards were strengthened by covering the usual single cross grain with a veneer of vertical grain. On bigger harps the soundboard was extended to exceed the width of the body of the instru-ment at its lower end, where the heavier strings needed greater amplification. The average modern concert harp has 46 or 47 strings (*D'* or *C''* to *g''''*), is about 183 cm tall and weighs about 35 kg (see fig.24). The total applied string tension exceeds 730 kg.

(viii) Technique and repertory, 1750–1820. The late 18th-century development and establishment of the single-action pedal harp was paralleled by developments in playing technique and repertory. Stéphanie-Félicité, Countess of Genlis (1746–1830), had been given harp-sichord pieces to play on the harp when she had her first lessons at the age of 13 from Goepfert. It appears to have been her own idea later to adapt keyboard tech-nique to the harp, and to play it using all five fingers of both hands. Her reasons for doing so are admirably expounded in her *Nouvelle méthode pour harpe* (1802), but the only players to adopt her method were her own pupils. The normal method then, as now, was to play with the first four fingers of both hands, the little finger never being used at all on account of its lack of strength.

The three-movement solo for harp in G written by C. P. E. Bach in Berlin in 1762 makes no concessions to either the limitations of the harp of his day or those of the executant; neither does Mozart's Flute and Harp Concerto (K299/297c) of 1778. The Mozart concerto is distinctly easier to play on the lightly-strung harps of the 18th century for which it was intended, however,

than on the larger, heavier-strung instruments now in general use.

Harp writing of the period was normally confined to scale passages, arpeggio figurations and spread chords, embellished by occasional trills and turns. The only spe-cial effects of timbre in common use were single har-monics and *sons étouffés* (damped notes), both executed only by the left hand. Modulation was unadventurous and an enormous number of sonatas, airs with variations and so on were written in Eb, the open key of the single-action harp. Whether such fashionable harpist–composers as Louis Cardon, Simon Hochbrucker, P.-J. Meyer and P. J. Hinner mistrusted the uncertain mechanical func-tioning of their harps or whether they were merely con-tent musically to rely on the available conventional effects is not certain. However, those unafraid of experiment, particularly with the use of the enharmonic 'synonyms' made available by the pedals and by an approximation of equal temperament, were able to compose short pas-sages of a fairly chromatic nature that were well within the harmonic limitations of the instrument. The lovely Adagio opening of Krumpholtz's Sonata no.5 ('dans le style pathétique') is a case in point: the 11 bars of Largo introduction are in Eb minor, with written Gb played by its enharmonic equivalent F♯, Cb by B♮, Fb by E♮, and Db by C♯.

The three composers who made the greatest contri-bution to the literature of the single-action harp – J.-B. Krumpholtz, J. L. Dussek and Louis Spohr – were all married to professional harpists. Krumpholtz, himself a talented harpist, engaged Erard's interest in the tech-nical problems of the instrument, and also made improvements of his own: a short-lived damping mech-anism for the bottom strings, and a more successful 'harpe à renforcements' in which the central back panel of the ribbed body of the harp was replaced by shutters which, when opened by the operation of an eighth pedal (placed centrally between those operated by the left foot and those operated by the right), prolonged and enlarged the sound of the instrument. Krumpholtz wrote several con-certos, some sonatas for flute or violin and harp, duos for two harps and many solos and studies.

Dussek wrote his op.2 harp sonatas (including the well-known one in C minor) in Paris between 1786 and 1789; the op.11 duo for harp and piano, which he dedicated to Mme Krumpholtz, was probably composed after he went to London in 1789, as was the Eb concerto (op.15). Between 1792 (when he married the harpist and singer Sophia Corri) and his departure for Hamburg in 1799, he wrote more duos, solo sonatas and three concertos. The first of these concertos, the two-movement op.30 in C, demands firm, incisive playing and impeccable articulation of the fingers. Without doubt, Dussek's best works for the harp are his late *Trois duos concertants* for harp and piano (op.69 nos.1–3), written for per-formance by himself and F. J. Naderman in Paris in 1810. The problem presented by the inability of the single-action harp to modulate into the remote keys favoured by Dussek is here solved by combining the two instruments in such a way that the remoter modu-lations are accomplished in the piano's solo passages. Although the harp parts are technically extremely demanding, Dussek did not demand of the instrument itself excessive chromaticism or key changes beyond its capabilities.

Spohr's output contains several pieces for solo harp that do not tax to any great extent the modulatory possibilities of the instrument. In the duo sonatas for violin and harp, however, like Krumpholtz he made much use of harmonies rendered possible on the harp by the use of enharmonic equivalents. Dorette Spohr's instrument was a single-action harp made by the elder Naderman, and the unsatisfactory *béquilles* system of these harps (see §4(vi) above) caused the sharpened strings to be dull in sound, to be pulled out of alignment, and, most annoying to the executant, to jar. However, when the harp's pedals were in their open position, none of these problems occurred. It was normal practice when playing in A♭ to tune all the D strings down to D♭. Spohr conceived the idea of tuning all the strings a semitone flat so that pieces in D or G might be played with the pedals in their open position. The manuscript copy of his Concertante for violin, harp and orchestra (*GB-Lcm*) is provided with two harp parts, one in A♭ and one in G. Dorette Spohr eventually gave up the harp around 1820 when, though dissatisfied by the limitations of her own instrument, she found she could not adapt herself to playing one of Erard's splendid new double-action harps tuned in C♭.

Some other works for the single-action harp deserve mention: in Germany the concertos of Eichner (1769) and Albrechtsberger (1773); in France the four concertos and various sonatas, variations and duos of Petrini (1744–1819); and the harp and fortepiano duos of Boieldieu as well as his elegant Concerto in C of 1801. All these works are technically demanding but use only the conventional stock-in-trade of harp writing – trills, arpeggio figuration and scale passages – without any search for musical profundity or attempts to overcome the harmonic limitations of the single-action instrument.

The harp entered the modern orchestra by way of the opera house, where it was at first little used except as an instrument evocative of mythology and romantic legend. Early uses in 18th-century opera include Gluck's *Orfeo ed Euridice* (1762). Haydn used it in his *Orfeo* (1791), and in 1804 Le Sueur called for 12 harps (six to each of two parts) in his *Ossian ou Les bardes*.

(ix) Modern technique and repertory. Elias Parish Alvars (1808–49), a fine composer and outstanding virtuoso, was the first to recognize the numerous effects and harmonic possibilities made available by the double-action harp and had an immeasurable influence on later harp writing. One of his teachers was Théodore Labarre, whose excellent *Méthode complète* (1844) indicates the techniques expected of good performers on the double-action harp. Apart from the usual scales, arpeggios and trills, Labarre particularly stressed harmonics, *glissés* and the use of enharmonic 'synonyms'.

Harmonics are written '°' and in the left hand can be single, doubled or tripled to allow chords in harmonics. Left-hand harmonics are obtained by using the side of the palm as an artificial bridge, placing it at a point halfway down the length of the string and playing only the top half to produce a note one octave higher in pitch. In the right hand only one harmonic at a time can be obtained, as the artificial bridge is formed by the first joint of the index finger, the harmonic being obtained by playing the top half of the string with the thumb. The best range for harmonics is *A* to *g″*.

Another important technique is the sliding movement which Labarre called *glissé*, produced in a downward direction by sliding the thumb from one string to the next, and in an upward direction either with the second finger alone, or with the second and third fingers togeth-

er in parallel 3rds. Yet another important technique was that of producing 'synonyms' – the unisons made possible by the positioning of the pedals. On the double-action harp, every note except D♮, G♮ and A♮ has its synonym, that is, a note of the same pitch obtainable on an adjacent string. For instance, D♭ has C♯ as its synonym, F has E♯, A♭ has G♯. When played at speed, the quickly reiterated notes of the same pitch thus produced give an impression of great virtuosity (*see* BISBIGLIANDO). It was by combining the *glissé* and 'synonym' techniques that Parish Alvars was able to produce the chordal glissando, a device that became essential for any composer writing for the harp. If, for example, the pedals are positioned so that the strings sound B♭–C♭–D♭–E♯–F♮–G♯–A♭, a diminished-7th chord is formed. Many other such combinations are of course possible, and once the pedals are fixed to produce the notes of the chord, a chordal glissando can be obtained by sweeping the fingers across all the strings. Parish Alvars, the first to use this remarkable effect, called it *sdrucciolando* ('slipping'). Berlioz, who heard Parish Alvars in Dresden in 1842, understood its technique though he did not use it in his own works. Parish Alvars was also the first to combine *sdrucciolandi* with harmonics. (The best-known example of this beautiful effect is in the cadenza of Ravel's *Introduction et allegro*.) Another effect pioneered by Parish Alvars was that known as the 'three-handed technique', later adapted for the piano with great success by Sigismund Thalberg.

Almost all the available harp effects, some of them bearing fanciful names (e.g. 'Aeolian flux' for 'glissando'), were detailed by Carlos Salzedo in his *Modern Study of the Harp* (1921). He described, for instance, a 'pedal glissando' (best used on the bass notes of the harp) that is achieved by moving the pedal to flat or sharp and back again within the duration of a note, the 'glissando' effect being produced by the sound of the movement of the fork against the still-vibrating string. The pedal glissando is used to great effect in André Caplet's *Divertissement à l'espagnole* (1924). Salzedo also mentioned the device of weaving a narrow strip of paper between the strings, an effect used by Puccini in *Turandot*. Most of the new effects introduced by Salzedo himself are of a percussive nature: 'esoteric sounds' (in which the pedals are moved without any notes being played), chordal glissandos played with the backs of the nails, plucking the strings with the nails near the soundboard and harmonics at the 12th (produced by playing the top third of the string; Salzedo wrote harmonics at the pitch at which they sound, a departure from the normal practice, both before and since, of writing them at the octave at which they are played). Many of these effects have become a common part of the harpist's technique. From the late 1950s onwards composers such as Berio, Boulez, Holliger, Rands and Miroglio extended this technical vocabulary even further in many experimental works, at the same time establishing the notation and giving instructions for the performance of the required effects.

Much of the solo harp repertory of the 19th century, however, was scarcely more than salon music to be performed by talented amateurs. None of the later virtuosos approached Parish Alvars either as executant or as composer, and with a few exceptions the solos and concertos they wrote for themselves, and the music they wrote for their pupils, have little intrinsic merit, relying for their effect on some of the easier techniques used by Parish Alvars.

The harp continued to be played in opera orchestras – particularly noteworthy are the harmonics in Boieldieu's *La dame blanche* (1825), the use of two harps in Meyerbeer's *Robert le diable* (1831) and the lovely harp solo in Donizetti's *Lucia di Lammermoor* (1835) – but it was Berlioz who pioneered its use in the symphony orchestra (*Symphonie fantastique*, 1830; *Harold en Italie*, 1834). Not until the 1840s, however, did the double-action harp become so widespread that it was available to all Western composers. Liszt's tone poems (particularly *Orpheus*) show the harp to great advantage. Both Schumann (*Drei Gesänge* for tenor and harp op.95) and Brahms (Four Songs op.17) wrote harp parts that are idiomatic and difficult, while those in Wagner's operas are extremely difficult and unidiomatic. Verdi's later ones, on the other hand, are well written and grateful to play. Bruch's *Schottische Fantasie* op.46 (1880) has an important and well-written harp part.

The closing years of the century produced Richard Strauss's *Tod und Verklärung* and *Don Juan* (both 1888–9), Sibelius's *Swan of Tuonela* (1893) and Symphony no.1 in E minor (1898–9), Franck's Symphony in D minor (1886–8) and Debussy's *Prélude à l'après-midi d'un faune* (1892–4), all with parts for harp. The Debussy *Prélude* is scored for two harps, using chords, arpeggios, broken chords, glissandos and harmonics to excellent effect. Also notable are harp cadenzas by Rimsky-Korsakov (*Spanish Capriccio*, 1887) and Tchaikovsky (*Swan Lake*, 1875–6; *Sleeping Beauty*, 1888–9; and *The Nutcracker*, 1891–2).

Early 20th-century works featuring the harp as a solo instrument include Gabriel Pierné's *Concertstück* (1903), Debussy's *Danse sacrée et danse profane* (1904) and Ravel's *Introduction et allegro* (1905). In the opera house, the harp parts of Puccini are idiomatically written and consistently effective. In the concert orchestra, where the inclusion of two harps was now standard, Debussy and Ravel composed effective parts that are models of harp writing, and Stravinsky wrote parts which, though more unconventional, are nevertheless effective. The dominant school of playing was the French, a fact reflected in the repertory, which includes solo works by Fauré, Roussel and Caplet, a concerto by Saint-Saëns (*Morceau de concert* op.154, 1918) and chamber music such as Debussy's Sonata for flute, viola and harp (1915). The impetus derived from such works, allied to the ever-increasing number of good harpists, led to a proliferation of chamber works including harp, particularly in France and later in Great Britain, Germany, the Netherlands, Switzerland and North America. Since the 1950s a considerable number of harp concertos and works for solo harp have been written, most either inspired or commissioned by harp virtuosos.

(x) Folk usage. In what can loosely be called regional, popular and folk practice, harps are now used in only one European area, Wales (but also in Latin America, for which see §5 below). The characteristic instruments are of types that date from no earlier than the 17th century, as was the case in the few parts of continental Europe where harps were formerly played in specific local musicmaking. It should be understood that the concept of 'folk' is a European one and dates only from the late 18th century and its application to music only from the later 19th; its application is dependent on particular kinds of social structure and it is inadvisable to apply it retrospectively or to countries outside Europe.

In Wales, no ancient music or harp technique has survived, though in the 17th century there were still traces of something so different from contemporary practice elsewhere that one European commentator wrote: 'A Welshman misuses the harp as an atheist misuses the Bible'. The old techniques and most of the repertory seem to have disappeared after the adoption of the triple harp (see §4(v) above), and what was considered to be Welsh music (not called Welsh folk music until the later 19th century) was simply transferred to that instrument as it was later still to a pedal harp. Particular Welshness lay in the facts that performance of Welsh music was not confined to one class of society and that the habit of using harps – of whatever kind – has been maintained in Wales for at least nine centuries.

In southern Germany and parts of Austria, harps of 17th-century design, with or without hooks, were still played in the 18th and 19th centuries, and in Bohemia up to the 1940s. Some street performers had up-to-the-minute urban repertory; in 1786 Mozart heard variations on tunes from *Le nozze di Figaro* played by a street harper. A portrait by Severin Pfalz (*b* 1796) of the famous Prague street harpist Josef Häusler shows him playing an instrument with a slightly curved forepillar with high pointed finial, 32 strings and partial hooking. He turns a hook with the forefinger of his left hand while plucking the string which it modified with the right-hand thumb. In Bohemia many players became itinerants because of overpopulation in the east and north; some are known to have travelled as far as Siberia and China. Many of the harpists were young girls who accompanied their own singing. The harps now in museums in Czechoslovakia are from 82 cm to 120 cm high, with 27 to 39 gut strings and slotted pins. Hooks can be on most of the strings or on as few as five. Generally there are two in the lowest and highest octaves and three to five in the others.

In the 18th century, following the overthrow of Turkish domination in parts of Hungary and that country's incorporation into the Austrian Empire, there was an influx of German-speaking people into its north-west regions. This included itinerants, some of them gypsies, who were knife grinders and harpers, occupations which their descendants in a small area near Lake Balaton continued to follow. Their instruments were basically 17th-century-type hooked harps, either purchased or self-assembled from components prepared to specification by local carpenters and smiths. In the 20th century, they have been made up to 160 cm high, with 36 strings giving a range of five octaves. Up to ten of the lowest strings may be metal and toggled inside the resonator; the others are gut and pegged externally. By the 1930s a few younger players rejected the cumbersome hook-turning technique and devised a simple external mechanism for four or five pedals, which was set along the outer right edge of the resonator. Earlier repertory, played almost entirely in German-speaking villages, had been of German songs and such dances as the waltz and polka, but later repertory included also gypsy and Hungarian items.

The use of harps in small ensembles in some Italian regional music seems to derive from Spanish practice and was probably a residue from the long period of Spanish rule. There is now no trace in Spain itself or in southern Italy of the Spanish Baroque combination of harp, violin and guitar. But written and iconographical evidence shows that comparable ensembles once existed in Calabria (where they were known as *Viggianesi*) and the Abruzzi, both of which are still conser-

25. Ensemble of harp, violin, four-keyed clarinet and triangle: engraving, 'I Viggianesi' (mid-19th century), by Francesco Pisante after Filippo Palizzi

vative regions where habits long abandoned in urban areas may persist. A late 18th-century French traveller described and illustrated a group of Calabrians playing beside a shrine of the Madonna near Naples. A man played a violin (or viol) held downwards across the chest and bowed from above, while children played harp and mandolin (or cittern). The last must have provided chordal accompaniment as do the guitars with six or seven double courses in the harp–violin–guitar ensembles of southern Chiapas (see fig.27). Early 19th-century pictures show slight variations – two adult harpists with children playing the cittern and triangle (the last certainly a local addition), and one harp, violin and triangle. Still later there is harp, violin, four-keyed clarinet and triangle (fig.25). 19th-century depictions of musicians from the Abruzzi playing in Rome show two harps, two downward-held violins and large cittern, with two of the players singing also. Some instruments are plain 17th-century types, others show details derived from pedal harp construction. For example, an undated but probably 19th-century harp in the Naples Conservatory has 34 pegs set high in the neck and below them a bridge pin for each string.

Neo-Celtic harps (developed from the kind invented by Egan in the early 19th century for urban domestic use; see 4(ii) above) are used by some singers of Irish traditional songs and they are also featured in some Irish modern folk groups. In pan-Celtic repertories like that of the Breton musician Alan Stivell they are used also for Welsh and Breton items, though rarely in his rock-style arrangements. Kits for simple self-assembled harps are now available.

5. LATIN AMERICA.

(i) History and distribution. The harp was brought to the New World from Spain with the first conquistadors, and later with lay colonists and various missionary orders. With the vihuela, it is said to have prospered more than any other European instrument in New Spain. Just as early 16th-century luthiers of Seville were required by ordinance to be able to make harps, so were Mexico City instrument makers, by an ordinance of 1568. A link remains between 20th-century Latin American diatonic harp traditions – for example those of Paraguay and the Colombian–Venezuelan plains – and Jesuit settlements of the 17th and 18th centuries. The harp and

violin played significant roles in Jesuit evangelistic activities in Paraguay and in the Peruvian–Ecuadorian Oriente; in the mid-18th century, the harp is said to have been the most common instrument among Indians in the Quito area of Ecuador.

In the early colonial period, the harp was also used in cathedrals, for example in the orchestra of that of Mexico City in the late 16th century and throughout the 17th. It was the required instrument for the accompaniment of religious music in 18th-century Montevideo, Uruguay; and the cathedral of Concepción, Chile, boasted an organ and an ensemble of clavichord, two violins, drum, fife and harp in the 18th century. In the Lima Cathedral *capilla de música*, the harp assumed, around 1630, the bass role of the sackbut and continued until 1832 when the position of harpist was abolished.

There is evidence of such a bass role in numerous Mexican and South American archives, which allude to the harp's use as a continuo instrument up to the end of the 18th century. Stevenson's aggregation of colonial manuscripts from different archival sources (1970) gives an idea of the instrument's use as a continuo instrument in Hispanic-American Baroque music (as in Iberian music).

In the 19th century, following the 1767 expulsion of the Jesuits and the widespread replacement of the harp by the organ as a church continuo instrument, descriptions of the harp focus more on folk and salon usage. In the Mexican *son jarocho*, a musical–choreographic genre now centred in the southern coastal plain of Veracruz, the use of the harp dates back at least to 1803. Female harp virtuosos are described in various accounts of 16th-century Spain, and in Chile the tradition of women harpists is documented back to the 18th century; they also performed in 19th-century salons and in outdoor booths set up in towns. The tradition of harp playing in 17th- and 18th-century Córdoba, Argentina, continued in northern Argentina in the following century; in Santiago del Estero, dances at country posts included performances by blind harpists. There are numerous historical references to blind harpists. There is iconographical evidence for the use of harps outside the church in 19th-century Peru; Pancho Fierro (1803–79), the watercolourist, portrayed musicians carrying the instrument on their shoulders, often in procession. It should be noted that the harp was used in processions for Corpus Christi in the 17th and 18th centuries in the Spanish Marañón (as they may have been in 16th-century Spain under Charles V). Illustrations of Peruvian harp usage, including holding the instrument on the shoulder, appear on 19th-century vessel fragments; one portrays the Ayacucho region scissors dance, which is still performed.

The harp was used in 19th-century Venezuela in salons and in shops. By the end of the century it was found throughout the Venezuelan plains, played by men; in Caracas, women performed on European-made harps. Along the Atlantic coast, in Cartagena, Colombia, the harp was a favourite instrument in the early 19th century, played by either sex. In Bogotá, in the 1820s, it was used in the home and in the theatre. In Guayaquil, Ecuador, in the early 19th century, the harp, guitar or violin was often used to accompany dance.

An important early description of Quechua harp playing in highland Ecuador (by F. Hassaurek for San Juan festivities in 1863) details how the harp was carried in a procession of dancers, the instrument being played as

26. *Single-rank harp with ribbed resonator: detail from the painting 'The Adoration of the Shepherds' (1638–9) by Francisco de Zurbarán (Musée de Grenoble)*

27. *Single-rank harp with ribbed resonator, guitar and violin, Zinacantan, Chiapas, Mexico, 1966*

it rested on a boy's back, while a second musician beat it rhythmically. Late 19th-century Ecuadorian Indians also used the harp in a radically different context for a child's wake. In the style of the late 19th-century Quito School, Joaquín Pinto's painting *Velorio de indios* depicts a highland Ecuadorian Indian home, where a harpist plays as one couple dances in the patio and the corpse of a winged figure – probably a child – is visible on a platform within. In the 1980s Quechua communities outside Cotacachi (near Otavalo) still employ a harpist-cum-beater (*golpeador*) for the ritual celebration of the child's wake.

In the 20th century, according to the harpist Alfredo Rolando Ortiz, the harp is particularly used in five countries: Mexico, Paraguay, Argentina, Venezuela and Peru. Although its importance in these cultures is beyond dispute, it should be emphasized that the instruments show unique physical features and possess distinct musical repertories, often representing different cultures, in each country.

Yaqui Indians of Sonora, Mexico, and Arizona, USA, perform the Pascola dance around Holy Week to the music of a harp and a violin; this combination is also used by the Mayo of Sonora for their Pascola dances. Elsewhere in Mexico, in Chiapas, a favoured trio combination among Tzotzil, Chamula and Tzeltal musicians is harp–violin–guitar (see fig.27); it has been suggested that the nature of these instruments, their performing techniques and the structure of their music derive from 16th- and 17th-century Spanish sources (see fig.26). The Veracruz *jarocha* harp shows four principal melodic tendencies: homophonic, with slow rhythmic movement; tremolo arpeggios; arpeggios with 'melodic intent'; and undulating conjunct motion. In Jalisco, some *mariachi* groups include harp, violin and jarana, possibly with other guitars, though the harp is now rare in this context. The harp tradition in Apatzingán, Michoacán, is sufficiently strong to support an annual contest; in that region, rhythmic *sones* and lyric-declamatory *balonas* are sung to harp and vihuela accompaniment.

Paraguay now has the most influential harp tradition in Latin America. The harp is the country's official national instrument and is featured in hundreds of *conjuntos*. Paraguayan folk groups exist in most South American countries and the Paraguayan-style harp (see 5(ii) below) is also used in Chile, Ecuador (see fig.28) and Venezuela. The Paraguayan harp repertory includes the *galopa* and *guarania*, both in sesquialtera rhythm, the latter having frequent arpeggios and great melodic freedom.

According to Isabel Aretz, the harp in Tucumán, northern Argentina, has a tradition that lasted 350 years; it was widely used solo or in dance *conjuntos* both in the countryside and in the city until just after 1900, when the tradition weakened.

In Chile (as in Michoacán-Guerrero, Mexico, Argentina, Peru and highland Ecuador) the practice of *cajoneo* (rhythmic beating of the resonator) is common. The national dance is the *cueca*, in which the harp accompaniment is played by women; *tonadas* and *romances* also are accompanied by the harp.

Throughout Venezuela the harp is closely tied to the performance of the rhythmically complex national dance, *joropo*, but there are two distinct traditions: in the Plains (extending into eastern Colombia) the 'llanera' tradition has a fixed playing style and compositional form, while the 'aragüeña' tradition of Aragua-Miranda has melodic, rhythmic and textual variants. The Aragua harp normally performs with maracas accompaniment (for illustration *see* MARACAS, fig.2), the Plains harp with that of maracas and four-string *cuatro*.

Peruvian harps may be divided into two categories: a longer instrument, found in 20 of the 23 states (covering much of the central and southern coast and the central and southern Sierra), and the *domingacha*, a small harp found principally in the state of Cuzco. Gourd harps, a type observed in 19th-century Colombia (there are examples in the Pedro Traversari Collection of Musical Instruments, Quito, Ecuador), are still played in Piura, north-west Peru. Peruvian harpists perform *waynos*, probably pre-Conquest song-dances in rhythmic duple metre, often with the violin and sometimes other instruments, and lyrical, elegiac *yaravís*, which are frequently solo. In Quechua-speaking areas of Bolivia, harpists attend farras (or fiestas), where they perform *cuecas*, *bailecitos* and *kaluyos* with the *kena* (flute) and occasionally other instruments.

In the Ecuadorian highlands the two major harp traditions are that of primarily mestizo culture, in Tungurahua province, and that of Quechua culture, in Imbabura province (see fig.28). In central highland Tungurahua, harpists of average ability perform national folk musical genres, but there are also superior players with a wider range. Central to the repertory of northern highland Imbabura Quechua harpists, however, is the *vacación*, a cyclical, ametrical non-dance music closely allied to a child's wake, as is the *sanjuán*; the *pareja*, slightly faster than *sanjuán*, is associated with newly-weds, dancing and the dawn.

(ii) Structure and performance. A variety of sources, both written and iconographical, give details of 16th- and 17th-century Spanish harps. Some characteristics are: varnishing; bone or brass pegs; relief work; single-rank (diatonic) or double-rank (chromatic); three parallel sets of soundholes on the soundboard, astride the forepillar, or violin-type f-holes; resonator with seven ribs; a compass of at least two octaves, and up to 46 strings; a C-shape (inverted arch) neck; a long, thin and straight forepillar, turned; a roundish soundboard, large in proportion to the low, slender superstructure of forepillar and neck; a low, walnut head; and gut strings (see fig.26). Many Latin American harps exhibit these features, notably the turned forepillar, inverted arched neck and gut strings. The most important features of Mexican harps are: their straight and turned forepillars; the shape of soundholes in Sonora and Chiapas Indian harps; the neck relief-carving of Chiapas harps (see fig.27); and the gut strings on some Guadalajara harps.

20th-century Paraguayan harps are long and slender (with a resonator of 140 x 40 cm at its widest point). The sound escapes through a large round hole on one side of the resonator (there are no holes in the soundboard). The resonator is traditionally of cedar, surfaced in pine. The strings are secured to the soundboard by a thin external belt of wood (cedar) down its middle, into which bone incrustations are fitted. The tuning-pegs are traditionally of wood, though now aluminium is also used, as are guitar-type, mechanical tuning-pegs. Rural Paraguay harps of about 1940 had a curved neck with a circular finial on top of the forepillar, a feature retained in most recent harps though in an exaggerated form, in effect consisting of two curved segments connected at nearly a right angle. The neck, sometimes painted with an abstract design, consists of two facing halves of

(a)   *(b)*

28. Ecuadorian harps: (a) Paraguayan-style harp of the Tungurahua province, 1980; (b) single-rank harp of Imbabura province, 1968

laminated cedar; the strings emerge from holes in the bottom. The result of this design, apparently peculiar to Latin America, is a truly vertical harp with centralized pressures permitting a very light construction not achieved on other harps. The straight, round forepillar has little or no turning. Up to the mid-20th century the instrument had 32 strings; later examples have 36 or even 40 nylon strings, some of them coloured (e.g. red to mark octaves), with a range of five octaves, often tuned in G. It is played seated for solo music and standing in ensembles.

The mestizos of Tucumán, Argentina, use harps with extensively turned forepillars whose finial is often a small ball or other turned extension; there are seldom holes in the soundboard (when present there is only one or a parallel pair). Other structural features include short, flat-planed legs; a narrow but deep ribbed resonator; and a neck that is uncarved but occasionally painted. The instrument is played seated.

The neck of 20th-century northern highland Ecuadorian harps is uncarved and lightly curved. The forepillar is straight, with rounded edges; it is turned with two concentric incisions, commonly in three places; and occasionally has black painted rings at either end of each incision group. The forepillar is short, creating a low head, and there is usually no forepillar finial. The resonator is slightly arched, wide and deep. Harps in the northern highland Imbabura province (fig.28*b*) have 17 to 27 strings, yielding a range of three octaves and a 5th to four octaves. The general pattern is hexatonic

tuning in the treble, which has steel strings over a range of about a 12th, diatonic but lacking the minor supertonic. Harpists can thus play all pentatonic pieces (the bulk of the repertory) as well as the few but widely played hexatonic pieces.

The harp in the central highland Tungurahua province is made of a combination of several types of wood, usually cedar, walnut and cinnamon. Played seated or standing, it has three soundholes, which are circular or oblong, sometimes flanged and occasionally wood-inlaid; these are present on all Ecuadorian and Venezuelan harps. The neck is elaborately carved, often in a floral pattern; its curvature is substantial, resulting in a near-S shape (similar to the Naderman single-action harp of 1780). The forepillar is tall, straight, squared and unturned, with a carved finial, often in the form of a human or animal head. Master harpists tune the large 34-string harp, with four octaves and a 6th, to play *sanjuanito*, in the 'natural' minor and its relative major; the range in C♯ minor/E major would be $G\sharp'–e'''$. For the slow, expressive *yaraví*, in C minor/E♭ major, the following variant tuning is used: the lowest octave, natural minor; the second, harmonic minor; the third, natural minor; the fourth, Dorian. For the *pasillo*, the alterations from the strict natural minor are, in the second and third octaves, that the subtonic is raised to the leading-note and the submediant is raised a semitone, and in the fourth the subdominant is also raised a semitone (these alterations accommodate frequent recourse to the dominant).

Many central Ecuadorian highland harpists are coming to prefer Paraguayan harps, with their distinctive sharply angled, uncarved necks and their absence of circular soundholes. Some such harps have 'figure S' soundhole patterns on either side of the forepillar, closely resembling those painted by Francisco de Zurbarán for the 17th-century Spanish harp (see fig.26).

6. AFRICAN HARPS. The harp is widely used in Africa; it has a place in the traditions of some 50 African peoples. Harps and harp playing often have rich symbolic meanings: harpists are frequently historians and genealogists as well as the central figures in religious rituals.

For further details of West and central African harps, *see* KUNDI (i); for East African, *see* ENNANGA.

(i) History and distribution. Current forms of African harps have been compared to those of ancient Egypt, and Praetorius (2/1619) suggests that at least one basic type has remained unchanged for 350 years (fig.29*d*). African harps share some basic structural components with harp-lutes (or bridge-harps; *see* HARP-LUTE (i)), pluriarcs and lyres. The relationship between harps and harp-lutes is indicated by the straight neck and hemispheric calabash resonator common to the ARDIN (Mauritanian harp; see fig.29*b*) and the KORA (i) (West African harp-lute). The pluriarc is like a harp-lute except that each string has its own neck rather than sharing a common one. The similarity of the wooden bowl reso-nator and soundtable lacing of the Ganda harp, *ennanga* (fig.29*a*), to those of the Soga lyre indicates a relationship between them. The harp and lyre found at Ur, formerly reconstructed as a single instrument, are now recognized as two different instruments whose resonators had collapsed together over the centuries, and they have been reconstructed accordingly.

Each type of instrument predominates in its own geographic area to the exclusion of the others. Harps are distributed in a belt across Africa from Lake Chad to Uganda, with a western addition in Mauritania, and occur mostly north of the equator. From the eastern border of Mauritania to eastern Nigeria the harp-lute predominates. The lyre occurs east and north-east of harp territory, while the pluriarc appears south of the equator. In the few cases where more than one of these types of instrument exist in the same area the use of the older instrument seems to die out as the newcomer to the area takes over (in parts of Uganda, for example, where the lyre is slowly replacing the harp). Closer relationships between harps and related instruments could probably be established on the basis of a comparative study of bridges and string holders, musical and social customs, geographic distribution and, most important, performing techniques. However, only those instruments considered as harps in the classification system of Hornbostel and Sachs (the plane of whose strings is perpendicular to their soundboards) are discussed here.

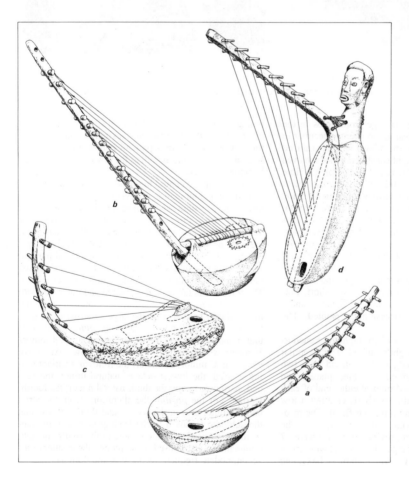

29. African harps: (a) ennanga (Uganda), structural type 1, 'spoon in a cup'; (b) ardin (Mauritania), type 1, 'spoon in a cup'; (c) kinde (Lake Chad area), type 2, 'cork in a bottle'; (d) ngombi (Gabon), type 3, tied to a 'shelf'

ii) Structure. All African harps are classed as 'open' ˈarps, having three main components, neck, resonator ˈnd string holder, but lacking the additional structural ˈupport of a forepillar. Wachsmann (1964) classified them ˈurther into three types, using as a criterion the method ˈy which the neck is connected to the resonator. In type the neck rests in the bottom of the resonator like a spoon in a cup' (fig.29a and b). In type 2 one end of ˈhe neck is shaped to fit into an end of the resonator like ˈ 'cork in a bottle' (fig.29c). In type 3 a 'shelf', someˈimes anthropomorphic in form, projects from the base ˈf the resonator. The neck is usually laced to the 'shelf' ˈvith fibre or a thong (fig.29d).

Necks and string holders are invariably of wood. The ˈlaborate ivory-necked Mangbetu (Zaïre) harps found in ˈnany museums were probably carved for collectors. ˈesonators are hollowed out of wood, with two notable ˈxceptions at geographic extremes: the resonator of the ˈMauritanian *ardin* is a hemispheric calabash (fig.29b), ˈnd the Acholi, Lango and Labwor peoples of Uganda ˈenerally use a tortoise carapace. The soundtables, usuˈlly with soundholes which also provide access for the ˈeplacement of strings, are of mammalian skin stretched ˈver the resonator, and exceptionally of lizard or snake ˈkin. The skin of the soundtable is fastened to the harp ˈn various ways, usually requiring twisted hide or vine ˈhongs. Sometimes the skin is tied to itself, its ends being ˈstretched over the back (fig.29b and d) or sides (fig.29c) ˈf the resonator, or laced through holes in a ledge which ˈncircles and projects from the body of the resonator. ˈr, as on the *ennanga* (fig.29a), a separate smaller piece ˈf skin placed over the bottom of the resonator is decˈratively laced to the soundtable skin. In rare cases the ˈoundtable is nailed to the sides of the resonator. Woodˈn tuning-pegs are fitted into holes along the necks of ˈarps, from which strings are stretched to a stringholder ˈying above (fig.29b) or below (fig.29a and d) the ˈoundtable, or inserted pin-like into it (fig.29c). Strings ˈvere formerly made of animal tendons, twisted hide, ˈvine or raffia, but nylon fishing-line is rapidly replacing ˈraditional materials.

A buzzing sound is integral to the timbre of most ˈAfrican harps, as to many other African instruments. ˈThe objects added to create this effect are usually actiˈvated, directly or indirectly, by plucking the strings, but ˈheir material and position on the harp vary widely. Rings ˈf banana fibres wrapped with the skin of a monitor are ˈplaced on the *ennanga* below each tuning-peg, at a point ˈwhere they can vibrate against the rings (fig.29a). ˈCircular metal plaques attached to the *ardin* soundtable ˈskin are bordered with tiny loose metal jingles (fig.29b). ˈOne soundhole of the *ougdyé* of the Kirdi is covered ˈwith membranes from spider-egg cocoons. There are ˈusually between five and ten strings (though nine-string ˈnarps are exceedingly rare), notable exceptions being ˈhe *ardin* (10 to 16 strings) and the single-string *zamaˈtaba* of Gabon. These two are also the only African harps ˈplayed exclusively by females: the former by profesˈsional musicians of the griot caste, the latter by Fang ˈadolescents. Harps with five or more strings are genˈerally tuned to a pentatonic scale, but not necessarily ˈdiatonically (see tuning key in ex.1). The Gwere of ˈeastern Uganda, however, tune their six-string *tongoli* ˈto a tetratonic scale with nearly equal intervals (soundˈing like a chain of 3rds to Western ears) and the *ardin* ˈplayer frequently changes her tuning to fit the particular ˈmode of the classical poetry she sings.

Ex.1 *Twamusanga ng'azina: twamusanga ng'aloga!* Kiganda song (Kyagambiddwa, 1955)

Vocal line Twa-mu-sa-nga ng'a-zi-na: twa-mu-sa-nga ng'a-lo-ga!

(iii) Performing techniques. In the history of the harp throughout the world, harpists have used only six basic performing positions (see fig.1); only in Africa are all still used, where they depend on local tradition. The position directly affects what can be played on the harp, and harps of the same structural type are often played in different positions. For example: harps of structural type 1 are used in positions A (the *ennanga*) and B (the *ardin*); harps of type 2 are used in positions A (the *kinanga* of the Konjo in western Uganda and eastern Zaïre), C (the *dilli* of the Masa), D (the harp of the Mara of Chad), E (the *kundi* of the Zande of northern Zaïre) and F (the *kinde* of the Barma and others south-east of Lake Chad); harps of type 3 are apparently played only in position C (e.g. the *ngombi* of the Fang and other neighbouring peoples). (For further illustrations *see* ARDIN; DILLI; ENNANGA; NGOMBI (i).)

The African harp is performed most often as a solo instrument in dialogue with the harpist's own voice, and a repertory of songs or sung poetry is performed either for an audience or for the harpist's own pleasure. African harp songs generally have the same basic form. While the harp is usually played throughout a song, predominantly instrumental and vocal sections alternate. It is sometimes impossible to make a rigid distinction between vocal and instrumental sounds; although the preludes and postludes are almost entirely harp solos, during the interludes the harpist often hums or utters syllables which duplicate the pitches of the harp pattern and imitate the sound of the plucking, or uses glottal stops in imitation of a percussion instrument.

African harpists generally play repeated patterns which vary in length from one song to another but remain constant within a song. Patterns range from simple ostinatos to those which closely imitate the vocal melody. Sometimes a tribe uses more than one style, even within the same song. Strings are seldom plucked simultaneously, but when they are the intervals produced are mostly octaves (ex.1) or 4ths, a notable exception being the 5ths of the Teso of Uganda. The vocal melody of a harp song is usually hidden within the harp pattern (see ex.1), but its range is not necessarily limited by the harp pattern, and during the course of a song both the harp pattern and the vocal line may be varied, or, more rarely, changed for another.

Harp patterns are divided between both hands, but the division is most often melodically and rhythmically unequal: however, *ennanga* patterns have equal parts which dovetail; the *ennanga* player uses the thumb and first finger of each hand, the patterns consisting of the isochronal notes of a single melody presented successively by the alternation of hands (ex.1). This form of dovetail interlocking has also been noted as peculiar to Ganda xylophone playing.

(iv) Performing practices. The subject matter of harp song texts is extremely varied. Topical songs, apparently the commonest, are often oblique in meaning and laden with personal allusions. Harp songs frequently record historical events and the deeds of legendary heroes, and are performed in ritual or social contexts. Genealogy and eulogy are sometimes included, as is the performer's name and people. Songs about war, love and incitement to battle are also common. Often the harpist improvises repetitions of important musical and textual phrases or entire verses; the frequency and method of repetition depends on the performer's emotional involvement at the moment, as well as on his sense of timing and responsiveness to his audience.

The harp is sometimes used in ensembles with other harps. Harp duos are frequent among the Nzakara *ba-ya-bia* (poet–musicians) of the Central African Republic who play the harp patterns together but alternate in singing the text. Trios are played on the *dilla* of the Masa. In Kotoko exorcism rituals three harps (*galdyama, direndana, kolo*) form a family with overlapping ranges (for further discussion *see* GALDYAMA). In both these trios one harpist is considered the leader and does all the singing. Among the Barma a women's song and dance encouraging warriors to battle is accompanied by men playing a quartet of *kinde* harps (fig.29*c*) and a calabash rattle. Acholi harpists form a quintet and play the same pattern simultaneously while the leading harpist sings; the others softly sing the refrain with him.

The harp is also played in mixed ensembles. The *ardin* player is usually accompanied by one or more of the following: another *ardin*, a *tbol* (drum), a *tidinit* (four-string lute) or another singer. During a performance she sings in dialogue with another singer, or stops plucking the strings and beats the rhythm on the resonator, or another member of her group taps on the resonator while she continues to play. In Busoga (Uganda) a harpist playing a *kimasa* is sometimes accompanied by three other performers, one playing a single-headed drum (of *engabe* type), another, a small pair of kettledrums, and the third alternately striking the edge of the harp's resonator with a drumstick in his left hand, and the soundtable of the harp with a rattle on a hooked beater held in his right hand; at the same time they all sing together. In a Padhola dance a solo harpist is sometimes accompanied by a percussion trough, single-headed drum, cone flute, side-blown trumpet, the pellet bells on the dancers' ankles and a chorus.

Symbolism is an important aspect of African harps and can lie in the intangible, such as the names given to strings, or in the tangible, in the form of anthropomorphic or zoomorphic designs. For example, the *ngombi* is the most important instrument used in Bwete rituals of the Fang, and represents Nyingwan Mebege, the sister of their god and a benevolent life-giver to whom the Bwete appeal in their songs. The strings of the *ngombi* are considered to be her sinews and tendons; her features are represented in the carved anthropomorphic figure on the resonator; the sound of the harp is her voice.

7. EASTERN DISTRIBUTION. Both the arched and angular harps of the ancient world (see §2 above) were carried eastwards: the arched to South and South-east Asia, where it is still played, and the angular to the Far East.

30. Reconstruction (c1950) of a vertical angular harp (Chinese konghu; Japanese kugo) from early Heian period fragments (before 950 AD) in the Shōsōin Repository at Nara, Japan

Arched harps, first depicted in Mesopotamia in the third millennium BC, appeared in Central Asian and Indian iconography from the 2nd century BC onwards; they were all played in position E (see fig.1, above). Their use apparently spread eastwards through India to Burma. Harps appear in Javanese stone carvings at the Buddhist monument of Borobudor dating from the 9th century AD and at the Cambodian site Angkor Wat (12th century) but it is debatable whether they were ever played in Java. Descendants of these ancient arched harps include the SAŪNG-GAUK (the classical harp of Burma which goes back at least to the 7th century AD) and the WAJI of eastern Afghanistan; a similar instrument survives among the Pardhan of India (*see* BĪN BĀJĀ (i)). The *waji* and the *bīn-bājā* are still played with the same technique as was depicted in the 2nd millennium BC in Mesopotamia and ancient India at least until the Gupta period (*see* VĪNĀ, §2): they are strummed with a plectrum in the right hand while the left damps the unwanted strings (see fig.2). Although a variety of techniques are used on Burmese harps, they are primarily plucked and no plectrum is used.

The earliest depictions of angular harps date from the 2nd millennium BC in Mesopotamia. The vertically held angular harp (see fig.1, position D) spread eastward through Central Asia probably along the Silk Route. Its presence in China is first recorded in the history of the Han Dynasty (200 BC–200 AD). The use of the harp spread from China to Korea and Japan. Its last depiction in Far Eastern iconography was during the late 9th or early 10th century AD, the approximate date of the lone extant specimen, a Chinese harp (*see* KONGHU) now in the Shōsōin Repository at Nara, Japan (see fig.30). This same type of vertically held angular harp probably continued to be played for several more centuries in the Middle East, possibly reaching India during the Muslim period; they were last depicted in Persian and Mughal miniature paintings from the 13th to 17th centuries AD. Occasionally these latter harps were depicted with what appears to be a thin forepillar.

Probably arriving via Central Asia, harps appeared around the 10th century AD among the Georgians of the USSR (*see* CHANGI) and the Ostyaks (often referred to as *torop-jukh*: 'crane'), one of the Finno-Ugric peoples of Siberia. Both survived well into the 20th century. Whether these two different harps are descendants of the same archetype, arched or angular, is debatable. According to the definition of Hornbostel and Sachs, the Georgian harp is angular; however, Georgian harpists use performing position E (see fig.1), known only for arched harps. The Hornbostel–Sachs classification of the Ostyak instrument would be an arched harp, but it usually has a thin forepillar reminiscent of some depictions of angular harps in medieval Persian and Mughal miniatures. In this case, performing position does not help to determine whether the instrument is angular or arched, as Ostyak harpists prefer position A (see fig.1), which is known for horizontally held angular harps as well as arched.

The following harps are entered in this dictionary: adeudeu; adungu (ii); angular harp; arched harp; ardin; awunene; babakungu; bandingba-ga-sende; belly harp; bīṇ bājā (i); bodongo; bolo-bogo; bolombata; bolon; bonguma; bow harp; carángano; ceirnin; chang (i); changi; citrā vīṇā; cláirseach; clàrsach; dilli; direndana; do; domo; ekidongo (ii); ekihako; ekitulege; engkeratong; ennanga; entongoli; frame harp; galdyama; gárgara; gogia bana; gonfi; ground harp; gundi (i); harpinella; harpe intégrale; harp-piano; hook harp; Irish harp; itikili; itumbolongonda; jank; jigijigi; ju-kugo; juru; kesse-kesse; kimasa; kimbumba; kinanga; kinde; kindingding; kolo (ii); komba; kondu; konghou; korro; kudara-goto; kugo; kunda; kundé; kundi (i); kundu (iii); kungunangu; kunnee; kurbi; loma; loterokkuma; magadis; malaba; maringa (i); mi'zafa; mizhar; musokolome; muwannaj; muwattar; na den; nandomo; nango; nedomu; neduna; nevel; ngombi (i); ngonfi (ii); nkundi; nkutu kubidi; ntongoni; ombi; omujariko; open harp; opuk ogoya; ore; orodo; otongoli; ougdyé; para (iii); pēktis; psantria; salan; sambuca; saùng-gauk; sekitulege; seto; shu-konghou; sogonghu; sugonghu; tambour maringouin; tavigh; tekpede; telyn; tinaou; tingotalango; t'na; tongoli; trigōnon; tum (ii); tumbandera; wagonghu; waji; wanj; wo-konghou; wombi; yāḷ; yom biBagirmi; zamataba; zumbul; zuzu.

BIBLIOGRAPHY

ANCIENT HARPS

C. Sachs: *Die Musikinstrumente des alten Aegyptens* (Berlin, 1921)
——: *Die Musikinstrumente Indiens und Indonesiens* (Berlin, 2/1923)
——: 'Eine aegyptische Winkelharfe', *Zeitschrift für ägyptische Sprache und Altertumskunde*, lxix (1933), 68
M. Duchesne-Guillemin: 'La harpe en Asie occidentale ancienne', *Revue d'Assyriologie*, xxxiv (1937), 29
C. Marcel-Dubois: *Instruments de musique de l'Inde ancienne* (Paris, 1941)
H. Hickman: *Catalogue général des antiquités égyptiennes du Musée du Caire* (Cairo, 1949)
——: 'Les harpes de la tombe de Ramses III', *Annales du Service des antiquités de l'Egypte*, 1 (1950), 523
——: 'Das Harfenspiel im alten Aegypten', *Mf*, v (1952), 21
——: 'Le jeu de la harpe dans l'Egypte ancienne', *Archiv orientalni*, xx (1952), 449
——: 'Quelques nouveaux documents concernant le jeu de la harpe

et l'emploi de la chironomie dans l'Egypte pharaonique', *IMSCR, v: Utrecht 1952*, 263
M. Skalska-Zunova: 'Konstruktsiya arfï i igra na arfe v drevnem Yegipet'ye [The construction of the harp and harp playing in ancient Egypt], *Archiv orientalni*, xx (1952), 457
H. Hickmann: 'A New Type of Egyptian Harp', *AcM*, xxvi (1954), 127
——: 'Les harpes de l'Egypte pharaonique (Essai d'une nouvelle classification)', *Bulletin de l'Institut d'Egypte*, xxxv (1954), 309
H. J. Zingel: *König Davids Harfe* (Cologne, 1968)
B. Aign: *Die Geschichte der Musikinstrumente des Ägäischen Raumes bis um 700 vor Christus* (Frankfurt am Main, 1969)
J. Rimmer: *Ancient Musical Instruments of Western Asia in the British Museum* (London, 1969)
H. M. Kümmel: 'Zur Stimmung der babylonischen Harfe', *Orientalia*, xxxix/2 (1970)
S. I. Rudenko: *Frozen Tombs of Siberia* (Berkeley, 1970)
K. Szarvas: 'The Harp in Ancient Israel', *American Harp Journal*, iii/4 (1972), 9
E. Zonis: *Classical Persian Music* (Cambridge, Mass., 1973)
R. D. Anderson: *Catalogue of Egyptian Antiquities in the British Museum*, iii (London, 1976)
C. Ziegler: *Les instruments de musique égyptiens au Musée du Louvre* (Paris, 1979)
M. Duchesne-Guillemin: 'Music in Ancient Mesopotamia and Egypt', *World Archaeology*, xii/3 (1981), 287
B. Lawergren: 'Acoustics and Evolution of Arched Harps', *GSJ*, xxxiv (1981), 110

EUROPE

J. Bermudo: *Declaración de instrumentos musicales* (Osuna, 1555/R1957)
V. Galilei: *Dialogo . . . della musica antica e della moderna* (Florence, 1581/R1968)
M. Mersenne: *Harmonie universelle* (Paris, 1636–7/R1963; Eng. trans., 1957)
E. Jones: *Musical and Poetical Relicks of the Welsh Bards* (London, 1784, 4/1825)
E. Bunting: *A General Collection of Ancient Irish Music* (London and Dublin, 1796–1840/R1969)
S.-F. de Genlis: *Nouvelle méthode pour harpe* (Paris, 1802, 1811/R1974)
P. Erard: *The Harp in its Present Improved State* (London, 1821/R1978)
T. Labarre: *Méthode complète pour la harpe* (Paris, 1844)
R. B. Armstrong: *The Irish and Highland Harps* (Edinburgh, 1904/R1970)
H. Panum: 'Harfe und Lyra im alten Nordeuropa', *SIMG*, vii (1905–6), 1
H. Jónsson: 'Der Harfenspiel des Nordens in der alten Zeit', *SIMG*, ix (1907–8), 530
W. Altmann: *Kammermusik-Katalog* (Leipzig, 1910, 6/1945)
F. W. Galpin: *Old English Instruments of Music* (London, 1910, rev. 4/1965 by T. Dart)
R. Griffith: *Llyfr Cerdd Dannau* (Caernarvon, 1913)
H. Panum: *Middelalderen strengeinstrumenter* (Copenhagen, 1915–31; Eng. trans., 1940)
C. Salzedo: *Modern Study of the Harp* (New York, 1921)
H. J. Zingel: *Harfe und Harfenspiel vom Beginn des 16. bis ins zweite Drittel des 18. Jahrhunderts* (Halle, 1932)
B. Szabolcsi: 'Osztyak es vogul dallamok' [Ostyak and Wogulian melodies], *Ethnographia*, xlviii/4 (1937), 340
A. O. Väisänen: 'Die obugrische harfe', *Finnisch-ugrische Forschungen*, xxiv (1937), 127–153
——: *Untersuchungen über die ob-ugrischen Melodien* (Helsinki, 1939)
G. Chase: *The Music of Spain* (New York, 1941, rev. 2/1959)
H. Hickmann and H. J. Zingel: 'Harfe', *MGG*
H. J. Zingel: *Neue Harfenlehre* (Leipzig, c1961)
A. O. H. Jarman: 'Telyn a Chrwth', *Llên Cymru*, vi (1961)
J. Manga: 'Die Harfner der Plattenseegegend: Varia', *Acta ethnographica*, xi (1962), 191
J. Rimmer: 'James Talbot's Manuscript VI: Harps', *GSJ*, xvi (1963), 63
——: 'Harps in the Baroque Era', *PRMA*, xc (1963–4), 59
F. Harrison and J. Rimmer: *European Musical Instruments* (London, 1964)
S. O. Pratt: *Affairs of the Harp* (New York, 1964)
J. Rimmer: 'The Morphology of the Irish Harp', *GSJ*, xvii (1964), 39
N. Zabaleta: 'The Harp in Spain from the XVI–XVIII Century', *Harp News*, iii/10 (1964), 3
J. Rimmer: 'The Morphology of the Triple Harp', *GSJ*, xviii (1965), 90; xix (1966), 61; repr. in *Studies in Traditional Welsh Music* (Cardiff, in preparation)
H. J. Zingel: *Verzeichnis der Harfenmusik* (Hofheim, 1965)
A. Baines: *European and American Musical Instruments* (London, 1966)

J. Marson: *The Complete Guide to the Harp Glissandi* (New York, 1966)

E. Winternitz: *Die schönsten Musikinstrumente des Abendlandes* (Munich, 1966, Eng. trans., 1967, as *Musical Instruments of the Western World*)

A. Berner, J. H. van der Meer and G. Thibault: *Preservation and Restoration of Musical Instruments* (London, 1967)

A. Griffiths: 'Dussek and the Harp', *MT*, cix (1968), 419

R. Rensch: *The Harp: its History, Technique and Repertoire* (London and New York, 1969)

J. Rimmer: *The Irish Harp* (Cork, 1969, 2/1977)

J. Jenkins, ed.: *Ethnic Musical Instruments* (London, 1970)

G. Lawson: 'Medieval Tuning Pegs from Whitby', *Medieval Archaeology*, xxii (1970), 139

F. Vernillat and H. Charnassé: *Les instruments à cordes pincées* (Paris, 1970)

A. Livermore: *A Short History of Spanish Music* ((London, 1972)

A. Schaefer: *Le Musica neu beroriaeth de Robert ap Huw* (diss., U. of Paris, 1973)

Folk Harp Journal (1973–)

H. J. Zingel: 'Zur Geschichte der Volksharfe', *Musicae scientiae collectanea: Festschrift Karl Gustav Fellerer zum 70. Geburtstag* (Cologne, 1973), 707

L. Kunz: *Die Volksmusikinstrumente der Tschechoslowakei* (Leipzig, 1974), 91ff

H. J. Zingel: *Harfenspiel im Barockzeitalter* (Regensburg, 1974)

A. Griffiths and A. Schaefer: 'Gwilym Puw's "Trefn Cywair Telyn": a Seventeenth Century System for Tuning the Harp', *Welsh Music*, iv/8 (1974–5), 22

H. J. Zingel: *Harfenmusik im 19. Jahrhundert* (Wilhelmshaven, 1976)

——: *Lexikon der Harfe* (Regensburg, 1977)

R. P. Arroyo: 'La arpa de dos órdenes en España', *Revista español de musicología*, ii/1 (1979)

F. Lippmann: 'Volksharfen in Italien', *AnMc*, no.19 (1979), 380

O. Ellis: *The Story of the Harp in Wales* (Cardiff, 1980)

C. E. Patrick: 'The Harp beneath the Ice', *Folk Harp Journal* (1981), no.32, p.4

——: 'The Harp of the North Lands', *Folk Harp Journal* (1981), no.32, p.12

J. Rimmer: 'Telynores Maldwyn: Nansi Richards, a Welsh Harper 1888–1979', *SIMP*, vii (1981), 127; repr. in *Welsh Music*, vi/10 (1982), 18

C. Polin: 'The ap Huw Manuscript', *Musicological Studies*, xxxiv (1982)

B. Durham: 'Archaeological Investigation in St. Aldate's, Oxford', *Oxoniensia*, xlii (1983), 3

A. Griffiths: *The Development of the Non-mechanised Harp from 1546* (diss., U. of Birmingham, 1983)

LATIN AMERICA

J. Byron: *The Narrative of the Honourable John Byron . . . on the Coast of Patagonia* [1740–46] (London, 1768)

B. Recio: *Compendiosa relación de la Cristiandad* [sic] *(en el reino-) de Quito* (Madrid, 1773)

J. P. Hamilton: *Travels through the Interior Provinces of Columbia* [sic] (London, 1827)

M. Soriano Fuertes: *Historia de la música española desde la venida de los Fenicios hasta el año de 1850* (Madrid, 1855–9)

F. Hassaurek: *Four Years among Spanish-Americans* (New York, 1867)

J. Chantre y Herrera: *Historia de la misión de los indios Mainas y de otras muchas naciones . . .* (Madrid, 1901)

B. Frías: *Tradiciones históricas (República Argentina)* (Buenos Aires, 1923–4)

R. and M. d'Harcourt: *La musique des Incas et ses survivances* (Paris, 1925)

P. Grenón: *Nuestra primera música instrumental: datos históricos* (Buenos Aires, 1929)

S. L. Moreno Andrade: 'La música en el Ecuador', *El Ecuador en cien años de independencia: 1830–1930*, ed. J. Gonzalo Orellana (Quito, 1930), ii, 187–276

G. Saldívar: *Historia de la música en México (épocas precortesiana y colonial)* (Mexico City, 1934)

A. Palma: *Pancho Fierro: acuarelista limeño* (Lima, 1935)

R. Gallop: 'The Music of Indian Mexico', *MQ*, xxv (1939), 210

G. Chase: *The Music of Spain* (New York, 1941, rev. 2/1959)

E. Pereira Salas: *Los orígenes del arte musical en Chile* (Santiago, 1941)

G. Furlong: *Músicos argentinos durante la dominación española* (Buenos Aires, 1945)

I. Aretz(-Thiele): *Música tradicional Argentina: Tucumán, historia y folklore* (Buenos Aires, 1946)

A. Jiménez Borja: *Instrumentos musicales del Perú* (Lima, 1951)

L. Ayestarán: *La música en el Uruguay, i* (Montevideo, 1953)

J. M. Boettner: *Música y músicos del Paraguay* (Asunción, 1956)

V. T. Mendoza: *Panorama de la música tradicional de México* (Mexico City, 1956)

I. Aretz: 'Las arpas rústicas de Sudamérica', *El disco Anaranjado* (May–June 1961), 29

F. Domínguez: 'Informe sobre la investigación folklórico-musica realizada en las regiones de los Yaquis, Seris, y Mayos: estado de sonora en abril y mayo de 1933', *Investigación folklórica en México: materiales*, i (Mexico City, 1962), 113–226

J. I. Perdomo Escobar: *Historia de la música en Colombia* (Bogotá 3/1963)

L. Ayestarán: 'El barroco musical hispanoamericano', *Inter-America Institute for Musical Research Yearbook*, i (1965), 55–93

P. Peñaherrera de Costales and A. Costales Samaniego: *El Quishi huar o El Árbol de Dios*, i (Quito, 1966)

I. Aretz: *Instrumentos musicales de Venezuela* (Cumaná, 1967)

F. and J. Harrison: 'Spanish Elements in the Music of Two Maya Groups in Chiapas', *UCLA Selected Reports*, i/2 (1968), 2–44

S. Milligan: 'The Harp in Latin America', *American Harp Journal* i/3 (1968), 16

H. Davidson: *Diccionario folklórico de Colombia: música, instru mentos y danzas*, i (Bogotá, 1970)

R. Stevenson: *Renaissance and Baroque Musical Sources in the Americas* (Washington, DC, 1970)

A. Sas Orchassal: *La música en la catedral de Lima durante e virreinato* (Lima, 1971–2)

A. Livermore: *A Short History of Spanish Music* (London, 1972)

B. Wolfe: 'Folk Harp of Mexico', *American Harp Journal*, iv/1 1973), 3

M. Cárdenas Montes: *Arpa, ave fénix de la música (Historia de arpa)* (Mexico City, 1978)

Mapa de los instrumentos musicales de uso popular en el Perú clasificación y ubicación geográfica (Lima, 1978)

R. Rephann: *A Catalogue of the Pedro Traversari Collection o Musical Instruments* (Washington, DC, 1978)

C. A. G. Coba Andrade: 'Instrumentos musicales ecuatorianos', *Sarance*, vii (Oct 1979), 70

R. Garfias: 'The Venezuelan Harp', *Folk Harp Journal*, (1979) no.24, pp.13

A. R. Ortiz: *Latin American Harp Music and Techniques for Peda and Non-pedal Harpists* (Corona, 1979)

D. E. Sheehy: *The 'Son Jarocho': the History, Style, and Repertory of a Changing Mexican Musical Tradition* (diss., U. of California, Los Angeles, 1979)

J. M. Schechter: *Music in a Northern Ecuadorian Highland Locus. Diatonic Harp, Genres, Harpists, and their Ritual Junction in the Quechua Child's Wake* (diss., U. of Texas, Austin, 1982)

AFRICA

B. Ankermann: *Die afrikanischen Musikinstrumente* (Berlin, ?1919) 3ff, 77ff, 105f, 118ff, 131f

A. Schaeffner: 'Notes sur la musique des populations du Cameroun septentrional', *Minotaure*, ii (1933), 65

G. Balandier and P. Mercier: 'Notes sur les théories musicales maures à propos de chants enregistrés', *IIa conferéncia international dos Africanistas occidentais: Bissau 1947*, 139–92

A. Leriche: 'Poésie et musique maure', *Bulletin de l'Institut français d'Afrique noire*, xii (1950), 710–43

——: 'Instruments de musique et griots', *Bulletin de l'Institut français d'Afrique noire*, xii (1950), 744

K. Wachsmann: 'An Equal-stepped Tuning in a Ganda Harp', *Nature* clxv (1950), 40

G. Rouget: 'Musique maure: par Ali ould Eide et Mneina mint Nana', Institut français d'Afrique noire MH 54–4 [disc notes]

M. Trowell and K. Wachsmann: *Tribal Crafts of Uganda* (London, 1953), 393ff, 412f, pll.112f

J. Kyagambiddwa: *African Music from the Source of the Nile* (New York, 1955), 105ff

K. Wachsmann: 'Folk Musicians in Uganda', *Uganda Museum Occasional Papers*, ii (1956), 1

——: 'Harp Songs from Uganda', *JIFMC*, viii (1956), 23

H. Pepper: 'Anthologie de la vie africaine', Ducretet Thomson 320 C 126–8 [disc notes]

G. P. Murdock: *Africa: its Peoples and their Culture History* (New York, 1959), 93, 227, 231f, 275, 280, 329f, 347f

J. Chaminade and J. Guillard: 'Musique maure', OCR-SOR 7–8 [disc notes]

J. Laurenty: *Les cordophones du Congo belge et du Ruanda-Urundi* (Tervuren, 1960), i, 72ff, 118ff, 146ff, 179ff, 195, 205ff, 215, 219ff; ii, pls.xxiii–xxxvi

H. Tracey: 'The Sound of Africa Series', International Library of African Music TR 1–210 [disc notes]

R. Brandel: *The Music of Central Africa* (The Hague, 1961), 6, 37f, 218, 255

E. de Dampierre, ed.: *Poètes Nzakara* (Paris, 1962), 13ff, 211

T. Nikiprowetzky: 'The Music of Mauritania', *JIFMC*, xiv (1962), 53

G. Kubik: 'Harp Music of the Azande and Related Peoples in the Central African Republic', *African Music*, iii/3 (1964), 37–76

S. Arom and G. Taurelle: 'Musics of the Central African Republic', UNESCO BM L2310 [disc notes]

K. Wachsmann: 'Human Migration and African Harps', *JIFMC*, xvi (1964), 84

F. F. Giorgetti: 'Zande Harp Music', *African Music*, iii/4 (1965), 74

C. Duvelle: 'Musique maure: république islamique de Mauritanie', OCR 28 [disc notes]

W. Conrad: *Buduma (Zentralafrika, Tschadsee) Bau einer Harfe: Encyclopaedia cinematographica*, E573 (Göttingen, 1966) [film notes]

M. Brandily: 'Un exorcisme musical chez les Kotoko', *La musique dans la vie*, ed. T. Nikiprowetzky, i (Paris, 1967), 33–75

L. Anderson: *The Miko Modal System of Kiganda Xylophone Music* (diss., U. of California, Los Angeles, 1968)

C. Duvelle: 'Anthologie de la musique du Tchad', OCR 36–8 [disc notes]

H. Norris: *Shingīṯī Folk Literature and Song* (Oxford, 1968)

R. Barnett: 'New Facts about Musical Instruments from Ur', *Iraq*, xxxi (1969), 96

K. P. Wachsmann: 'Ethnomusicology in Africa', *The African Experience*, ed. J. N. Paden and E. W. Soja (Evanston, 1970), i, 128

S. Swiderski: 'La harpe sacrée dans les cultes syncrétiques au Gabon', *Anthropos*, lxv/5–6 (1970), 833

J. Jenkins, ed.: *Ethnic Musical Instruments* (London, 1970)

R. Knight: 'Toward a Notation and Tablature for the Kora', *African Music*, v/1 (1971), 23

K. Wachsmann: 'Kiganda Musical Instruments', *Essays on Music and History in Africa*, ed. K. Wachsmann (Evanston, 1971), 93–134

W. Fernandez: 'Music from an Equatorial Microcosm: Fang Bwiti Music', FE 4217 [disc notes]

M. Guignard: 'Mauritanie: les maures et leur musique au XIXème siècle', *Musikkulturen Asiens, Afrikas und Ozeaniens im 19. Jahrhundert*, ed. R. Günther (Regensburg, 1973), 241

H. Tracey: *A New Catalogue to the Sound of Africa Series* (Roodepoort, 1973)

A. Ssempeke: 'The Autobiography of an African Musician', *Music Educators' Journal*, lxi/6 (1975), 52

C. Nourrit and W. Pruitt: *Musique traditionelle de l'Afrique noire* (Paris, 1980) [discography]

B. Lawergren: 'Acoustics and Evolution of Arched Harps', *GSJ*, xxxiv (1981), 110

S. C. De Vale: 'Prolegomena to a Study of Harp and Voice Sounds in Africa: a Graphic System for the Notation of Texture', *Selected Reports* (in preparation)

ANN GRIFFITHS, JOAN RIMMER, SUE CAROLE DE VALE (with ROBERT ANDERSON, §2; JOHN M. SCHECHTER, §5)

Harpanetta. A term found in some 18th-century sources to signify the ARPANETTA.

Harpa-phone. Term for a vibraphone without vanes.

Harp bow. (1) *See* HARP ZITHER.
(2) *See* MUSICAL BOW.

Harpe d'Eole [harpe éolienne] (Fr.). AEOLIAN HARP.

Harpégé (Fr.: 'arpeggiated'). A term found in French Baroque music to indicate that a chord or a passage of music is to be played in an arpeggiated manner. *See* ORNAMENTS, §IV, 5–6.

Harpe harmonico-forte. A type of HARP-PIANO built about 1809 by Keyser de l'Isle.

Harpe intégrale (Fr.). A frame harp devised by Gustave Lyon in the late 19th century; *see* HARP, §4 (iv).

Harper, Thomas (*b* Worcester, 3 May 1786; *d* London, 20 Jan 1853). English trumpeter. He is noted for his contributions to the development of the SLIDE TRUMPET (e.g. 'Harper's Improved Model', made by Köhler & Son) at a time when valved instruments were begin-

ning to show their superiority. His famous *Instructions for the Trumpet* (London, *c*1835) is largely devoted to the slide trumpet. His instrument, with its very large mouthpiece, is at the RCM. His son Thomas (John) Harper (1816–98) wrote two methods, *Harper's School for the Cornet à pistons* (London, n.d.) and *Harper's School for the [Slide] Trumpet* (London, *c*1875).

Harp-guitar. *See* HARP-LUTE (ii).

Harpinella. A small harp in the form of a lyre, built by Wilhelm Marstrand of Copenhagen in 1818. It was about 75 cm high and had a width of 35–40 cm; there were two sets of strings, and seven hand-levers instead of pedals to change the tuning. The instrument was pitched in E♭ and had the compass $C–g'''$; contemporary descriptions likened its tone to that of the guitar. It is classified as a frame harp.

Harpion (Fr.). BRAY.

Harp-lute [bridge-harp] **(i).** A family of West African chordophones of which the best known is the 21-string Mandinka *kora* (*see* KORA (i); for full classification details *see* CHORDOPHONE). The neck of the harp-lute pierces the wood or calabash body and protrudes beyond its lower end; the strings are attached at individual points along the neck, pass over a bridge mounted on the soundtable (usually of skin), and are anchored at one point on the lower protrusion of the neck (see fig.1c, p.162). The bridge is tall and has notches up the sides rather than across the top, thus dividing the strings into two planes, both perpendicular (rather than parallel) to the soundtable. The instrument is held upright and plucked with both hands. The kora is associated with Mande culture (Mandinka, Maninka, Malinke) and is much played in the Gambia and also in Senegal, Guinea, Mali and Upper Volta. Other, less common, terms for large harp-lutes in this area are *kasso* and *soron*. Small harp-lutes with only four to six strings, such as the Akan *seperewa* of Ghana, the *sanku* of Togo and the Dogon *gingiru* of Mali are now rare.

Although the harp-lute is best understood organologically as a 'harp-type of lute', it is clearly allied historically not to other lutes but to the distinctive arched harps of West Africa. These instruments (including the *simbing* and the *bolon*) are generally associated with hunting societies among the Mande. They have a curved neck and three to seven strings in one or two planes. As with all harps, they have no bridge, but the string holder, instead of being mounted on or under the soundtable as on a normal arched harp, is mounted at an angle (often perpendicular) to the skin face, with its upper end secured by a cord to the base of the instrument, thus closely resembling the high bridge of the harp-lute.

The following harp-lutes are entered in this dictionary: donsonkoni; dunsukoni; duu; gingiru; kasso; ko; konchuhun; kondene; kora (i); kori; sanku; seperewa; seron; simbing; soron.

BIBLIOGRAPHY

B. Ankermann: 'Die afrikanischen Musikinstrumente', *Ethnologisches Notizblatt*, iii (1901), 1–134

E. M. von Hornbostel: 'The Ethnology of African Sound Instruments', *Africa*, vi (1933), 129–57, 277–311

H. G. Farmer: 'Early References to Music in the Western Sudan', *Journal of the Royal Asiatic Society* (1939), 569

D. Zahan: 'Notes sur un luth Dogon', *Journal de la Société des africanistes*, xx (1950), 193

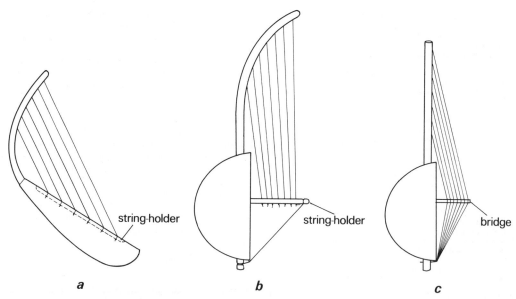

1. Diagram showing structure of (a) arched harp (e.g. ennanga, Ganda people, Uganda); (b) West African arched harp (e.g. bolon and simbing, Maninka people, Guinea); (c) harp-lute (e.g. kora, Mandinka people, Gambia); for further illustrations, see BOLON, ENNANGA, KORA (i) *and* SIMBING

J. H. K. Nketia: *African Music in Ghana* (London, 1962)
R. Knight: *Mandinka Jaliya: Professional Music of the Gambia* (diss., U. of California, Los Angeles, 1973)
K. Wachsmann: 'A "Shiplike" String Instrument from West Africa', *Ethnos*, xxxviii (1973), 44

RODERIC KNIGHT

Harp-lute (ii). A generic term for certain types of guitar that developed in England between 1798 and 1828, all slightly shorter than the conventional guitar and characterized by a soundbox 38–45 cm × 33–40 cm × 8–15 cm with a vaulted back. The earliest, the harp-guitar developed by Edward Light of London in 1798 (see fig.1), had eight gut strings with a vibrating length of about 64 cm, tuned *f–g–c'–e'–g'–c"–e"–g"*. Mordaunt Levien of Paris added three brass stops (*pédales*) on the back of his seven-string *guitare-harpe*, enabling the strings to be raised a semitone. He patented the instrument, including the pedals, in 1825. Edward Light devised a harp-lute-guitar, with a theorbo-like second pegbox and 11 strings tuned *B♭–e♭–f–g–a♭–b♭–c'–d'–e♭'–g'–b♭'* and notated a major 6th higher. The four lowest strings were unfretted.

By 1811 (when music for the instrument was registered at Stationers' Hall) Light had invented the harp-lute (see fig.2b), which had semitone-raising stops like the Levien *guitare-harpe* and a harp-like pillar terminating in a scroll head (later a Corinthian capital), which returned to the soundbox by a sort of 'harmonic curve' on which was fixed a fingerboard. His large flat-backed variant with oval soundbox, the harp-lyre, was referred to in an advertisement in an issue of the *Caledonian Mercury* of 1815. These instruments developed relatively quickly. ANGELO BENEDETTO VENTURA produced a similar, 12-string harp-lyre, the 'Imperial ottavino', and an 'Imperyal' lyre, and in 1813 added a couple of strings to create the 'Imperial' harp-lute. C. Wheatstone added a second fingerboard and called the result a 'Regency'

harp-lute. These instruments were actually tuned a 6th higher than the harp-lute-guitar, and their music was written at pitch. The lower eight strings were open; the upper limits of the range varied with the number of strings, but was at least two octaves above *c'*. Not to be outdone, Light patented in 1816 an improved 'British' lute-harp with up to 13 'ditals' (analogous to harp

1. Harp-guitar: engraving from F. Chabran's 'Instructions' (n.d.)

(a)   *(b)*

*2. (a) Girl playing a dital harp: engraving (1st half of the 19th century) by J. Minasi and J. Stadler after Burney;
(b) harp-lute by Edward Light, London, c1810 (Victoria and Albert Museum, London)*

pedals) for raising open strings one semitone. By 1819 this had become the dital harp (fig.2a), with up to 20 strings, and frets only for the top five or so strings (see ex.1 for its tuning). The use of lever- or piston-operated stops reached its most complex stage of development in Ventura's 'Harp Ventura'.

Ex.1

The intended purchasers of these hybrids were London ladies and, to a lesser extent, their provincial and Parisian counterparts. Inspired by the supposed example of Princess Charlotte of Wales (whose patronage was claimed by both Light and Ventura), ladies were exhorted to accompany their songs with these decorative (albeit increasingly unwieldy) instruments, but this market vanished with the advent of the mass production of pianos.

Tutors for the instruments were published by R. Downes ('Regency' harp-lute), T. Bolton and F. Chabran (harp-guitar and harp-lute-guitar), Light, Parry, Wheatstone and Ventura. Published music consisted of songs and instrumental arrangements and some simple compositions and variations, mostly in 16-, 24- or 32-bar binary form with tonic-dominant harmony.

Michael Praetorius, in his *Theatrum instrumentorum* (1620), had depicted an unnamed precursor to the harp-lute.

BIBLIOGRAPHY
R. B. Armstrong: *Musical Instruments*, ii (Edinburgh, 1908)
J. Godwin: 'Eccentric Forms of the Guitar, 1770–1850', *Journal of the Lute Society of America*, viii (1975), 90
S. Marcuse: *A Survey of Musical Instruments* (London, 1975), 404
                                         STEPHEN BONNER

Harp-lyre. A variant of the HARP-LUTE (ii) developed in the early 19th century.

Harpo-lyre. A hybrid chordophone invented by Jean-François Salomon of Besançon in 1827. It had three necks attached to a guitar-like body, the central one carrying six strings, the others seven and eight. See R. Wright: *Dictionnaire des instruments de musique* (London, 1941).

Harpophone. A percussion idiophone, a METALLO-PHONE of the GLOCKENSPIEL family, introduced in the 1920s by the Leedy Drum Co. (USA). The metal bars, which are individually tube-resonated, are arranged keyboard-fashion. The compass of the standard instrument is two and a half octaves, sounding one octave lower than the orchestral glockenspiel. It is usually played with 'medium-hard' beaters, the tone produced being similar to that of the celesta. That the harpophone (which is no longer manufactured) was little used orchestrally was due to the immediate appeal of the newly introduced VIBRAPHONE.

JAMES BLADES

Harp-piano [keyed harp]. An obsolete instrument in the shape of a harp, fitted with a keyboard action. Ever since Mersenne mentioned an attempt to fit a keyboard action to a harp-type instrument, inventors have experimented repeatedly with mechanisms that pluck or strike the strings. Among the earliest is probably the clavi-arpa, a harp-like instrument controlled from a keyboard, thought to have been invented in the 17th century in Spain by Juan Hidalgo. Adlung and Gerber reported similar 'inventions' in the 18th century. The first such instrument to establish itself seems to have been the claviharpe demonstrated by JOHANN CHRISTIAN DIETZ (i) in Paris in 1814. He founded a firm that continued to produce these until about 1890. The original claviharpe (which developed out of his clavi-lyra, a keyboard instrument with mechanically plucked metal strings) was strung with gut and had three pedals, sustaining, bassoon and buff stop. His son J. C. Dietz (ii) produced a modified version strung in metal with four pedals, bassoon stop, sustaining, soft and 'flageolet' (a kind of buff stop). Both versions were upright models in the typical harp shape, with a column on the left and an S-shaped curved neck on the right. As in the harp proper, the strings were open (i.e. not backed by a soundboard); they were plucked by small brass screws activated by the keyboard mechanism. In its latest form after 1870, the Dietz claviharpe was strung with metal wound with silk and had only two pedals, corresponding to those of the normal piano, a sustaining pedal and the 'flageolet'.

WILLIAM SOUTHWELL is reported to have included among his inventions 'a harp played with keys' produced in 1798, and John Bateman patented one with copper strings plucked by leather-covered tangents under the name Clavi-lyra in 1813. But the leading British instrument of this type was the Euphonicon, patented by John Steward of London in 1841 and later manufactured by F. Beale & Co. This was an upright instrument of over six-octave compass, again with the characteristic harp contour and unbacked strings. Numerous other such hybrids were introduced during the 19th century, notably a modification of the Dietz claviharpe brought out as the Calderarpa by Caldara and Racca of Turin and Bologna in the 1880s; this six-octave instrument had a piano-type action in the bass but the higher octaves were sounded by a sort of *Tangentenflügel* mechanism with cloth-covered tangents. Other examples include the Uranikon (invented in 1805 by Holbein of Breslau), the Harpe harmonico-forte (a harp built *c*1809 by Keyser de l'Isle; its 17 lowest notes, chromatic and bichord strung, were played by a pedal keyboard operating a hammer action), and the Cherubine minor (a combined piano, harp, organ and crystallophone patented in 1859 by Henry Whitaker). By the end of the century interest in the harp-piano had waned.

BIBLIOGRAPHY

GerberL
M. Mersenne: *Harmonie universelle* (Paris, 1636–7/*R*1963; Eng. trans., 1957), iii, 163
J. Adlung: *Anleitung zu der musikalischen Gelahrtheit* (Erfurt, 1758/*R*1953, 2/1783), chap.11, 258
R. E. M. Harding: *The Piano-forte: its History Traced to the Great Exhibition of 1851* (Cambridge, 1933, rev. 2/1978), 244ff
T. Norlind: *Geschichte des Klaviers* (Stockholm and Hanover, 1939), 155ff

HOWARD SCHOTT

Harp-psaltery [psaltery-harp]. A term applied to certain types of triangular psaltery (or box zither); *see* ARPANETTA, PSALTERY, esp. fig.3, and ROTTE (i).

Harpsichord (Dutch *klavecimbel*; Fr. *clavecin*; Ger. *Cembalo, Flügel, Kielflügel*; It. *cembalo, clavicembalo*; Lat. *clavicymbalum*; Port. *cravo*; Sp. *clavicordio*). A stringed keyboard instrument, classified by Hornbostel and Sachs as a BOX ZITHER, and distinguished from the clavichord and the piano by the fact that its strings are plucked rather than struck, and characterized by an elongated wing shape like that of a grand piano. As in the grand piano, this shape results from the fact that the strings, growing progressively longer from treble to bass, run directly away from the player, in contrast to the oblique stringing of a spinet and the transverse stringing of a virginal. The earliest known reference to a harpsichord dates from 1397, when a jurist in Padua wrote that a certain Hermann Poll claimed to have invented an instrument called the 'clavicembalum'; and the earliest known representation of a harpsichord is a sculpture in an altarpiece of 1425 from Minden in north-west Germany. The instrument remained in active use up to and throughout the 18th century, not only for the performance of solo keyboard music but also as an essential participant in chamber music, orchestral music and opera; in fact it retained the last of these functions long after most solo keyboard music and chamber music involving a keyboard was being composed with the piano in mind. The harpsichord had almost completely fallen into disuse by about 1810; its modern revival dates from the 1880s. For a discussion of the repertory *see* KEYBOARD MUSIC, §I; *see also* CONTINUO.

In describing keyboards in this dictionary the following conventions have been followed: an oblique stroke (e.g. *C/E*) indicates a SHORT OCTAVE; a comma indicates a missing accidental (e.g. *G',A'* signifies the absence of *G♯'*).

1. Structure. 2. The Renaissance: (i) Italy (ii) Northern Europe. 3. *c*1590 to *c*1700: (i) Flanders (ii) France (iii) England. 4. 18th century: (i) France (ii) England (iii) Italy (iv) Germany and other European countries. 5. Since 1800: (i) 19th century (ii) 1900 to 1940 (iii) Since 1940.

1. STRUCTURE. The heart of the harpsichord's mechanism is the jack, a slender slip of wood (replaced by plastic in many modern instruments) which stands resting on the back of the key (see fig.1*a*). The top of the jack has a wide vertical slot fitted with a pivoted tongue which in turn carries a plectrum of quill, leather or plastic. When the front of a key is depressed, the jack rises and the plectrum is forced past the string, plucking it (fig.1*b*). When the key is released, the jack falls, the plectrum touches the string (fig.1*c*) and forces the tongue to pivot backwards until the plectrum can pass the string, after which a light spring (formerly made of bristle or thin brass but often now of plastic) returns the tongue forward into its original position. Meanwhile, a piece of soft but stiff cloth held in a slot next to the tongue makes contact with the string, damping its vibrations and silencing it. A padded bar placed overhead – the jackrail – prevents the jack from flying out of the instrument when the key is struck (*see also* ACOUSTICS, §II, 3). In many instruments the jackrail alone limits the vertical motion of the jacks and thereby defines the depth of touch.

This elegant and simple mechanism, though capable

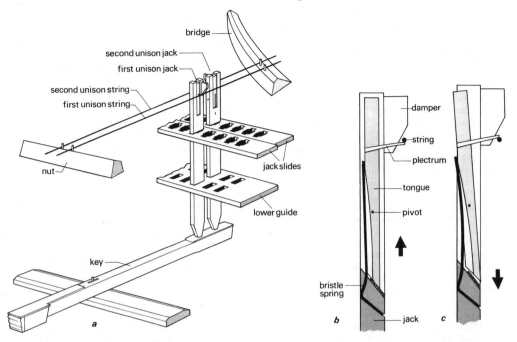

1. Mechanism of the harpsichord

of producing any degree of legato or detachment of notes with great sensitivity, is incapable of producing any appreciable change in loudness in response to a change in the force with which the key is struck, since, regardless of force, the string is displaced virtually the same amount by the plectrum. Accordingly, the player can produce conspicuous changes in loudness only if the harpsichord is equipped with devices that can change the degree to which the plectrum extends beyond the string (thereby changing the amount the string is displaced when it is plucked), or if each key is provided with additional jacks and strings that the player may engage or disengage at will. The second of these options is much the more important; it is greatly facilitated by the harpsichord's longitudinal stringing, since this permits each set of jacks to be placed in a row perpendicular to the strings, with as many rows as desired set one behind another. A set of jacks is engaged by being shifted towards the strings by a lateral movement of the slotted jackslide that supports it; the plectra of the jacks are thus positioned below the strings and will pluck them when the keys are depressed. A set of jacks is disengaged by shifting the jackslide in the opposite direction so that the plectra will pass the strings without plucking them when the keys are depressed. *See also* REGISTRATION, §II.

Although some harpsichords have only a single set of strings and jacks, most have at least two sets with the jacks facing in opposite directions (see fig.1a). (Accordingly, the strings associated with each key tend to be widely spaced to permit the jacks to pass between them, and the closely spaced pairs of strings on such a harpsichord are not tuned to the same pitch but, rather, to adjacent notes.) An arrangement of this kind permits two strings associated with a single key to be placed on a single level; but if there are more than two sets of strings, some must pass the jacks at a different level.

The use of different levels for different sets of strings is especially associated with the fact that ordinarily no more than two of the sets of strings on a harpsichord are tuned to the same pitch. Rather, an additional set of strings is likely to be tuned an octave above normal pitch; a rare, fourth set is tuned an octave below normal pitch; and a still rarer fifth set of strings is tuned two octaves above normal pitch. (As on organs, normal pitch is termed 8′ pitch, a pitch an octave higher is termed 4′ pitch, a pitch an octave lower 16′ pitch, and a pitch two octaves above 8′ pitch is termed 2′ pitch.)

These higher and lower pitches are best sounded by strings proportionally shorter and longer than those which sound 8′ pitch, and it is most convenient to arrange such strings on their own bridges with the shorter ones at a lower level and the longer ones at a higher level. Thus, on a typical 18th-century harpsichord equipped with two sets of 8′ strings and one set of 4′ strings, the 4′ strings would be at a low level, with the wrest plank (pin-block) bridge or nut placed near the jacks and close to the edge of the wrest plank, and the soundboard bridge placed at an appropriate distance away on the soundboard (see fig.8). The two sets of 8′ strings would both pass over a separate, higher nut placed further from the edge of the wrest plank and a separate, higher bridge placed further back on the soundboard. Similarly, in the unusual harpsichords made in Hamburg by the Hass family, for example, the 16′ strings pass over their own nut and bridge, which are higher than the 8′ nut and bridge and placed outside them, while the short 2′ strings pass over a very low bridge and nut placed between those of the 4′ strings. As noted, different levels of strings are required whenever there are more than two sets; accordingly, the relatively rare harpsichords with three sets of 8′ strings must carry them at two different levels where they pass the jacks. This is normally accomplished by using two bridges and two different stringing materials, with two shorter strings of one material (brass) on one bridge, and one longer set of strings (iron) for the other, all tuned to the same pitch. Otherwise either a stepped nut or two separate nuts are used; however, since the separation of levels is required only where the strings pass the jacks, a single bridge without a step may be used on the soundboard. On instruments with a single set of 8′ and a single set of 4′ strings, each set passes over its own bridge and nut, with the 4′ strings on a lower level.

The position of the tuning-pins and the hitch-pins for the 4′ strings raises difficulties, since if they were placed with those of the 8′ strings (in the front part of the wrest plank and in the case lining respectively) the 4′ strings would have to pass through the 8′ nut and bridge and there would, in addition, be an inordinate length of unused 4′ string beyond the 4′ bridge, which would tend to make the 4′ strings go out of tune easily. Accordingly, the tuning-pins for the 4′ strings are usually placed between the 8′ and 4′ nuts, and 4′ hitch-pins are driven into the soundboard between the 4′ and the 8′ bridges. A strengthening bar or 4′ hitch-pin rail is glued to the underside of the soundboard to withstand the tension exerted on the 4′ hitch-pins by the strings. This bar also in effect divides the soundboard into two distinct areas, one of which, lying between the 4′ hitch-pin rail and the curved side of the case, serves the 8′ strings while the other, between the 4′ hitch-pin rail and (usually) an oblique cut-off bar, serves the 4′ strings. The triangular area of the soundboard to the left of the cut-off bar is generally stiffened by the number of transverse ribs. (If 2′ strings are present, they are hitched to pins driven through the soundboard into a second hitch-pin rail, placed between the 2′ and 4′ bridges. If 16′ strings are present, the 8′ strings may pass through holes in the 16′ nut and bridge, or the 16′ strings, instead of having a bridge of their own, may be carried by the 8′ bridge; if the 16′ strings have their own bridge, it may rest on a separate soundboard, and in this event a curving rail separating the two soundboards acts as a hitch-pin rail for the 8′ strings.)

A harpsichord case consists of five basic parts. Clockwise from the left, these are: the spine, the long straight side of the case at the player's left; the tail, a short straight piece set at an acute angle to the spine; the bentside, a curving section that runs more or less parallel to the bridge (occasionally the bentside and tail are combined in a single S-shaped piece, yielding a case with a curved tail rather like that of a modern grand piano); the cheekpiece, a short straight piece at the player's right; and the bottom, which on all harpsichords from the 16th century to the 18th is a piece of wood that closes the instrument and thereby performs both a structural and an acoustical function. The wrest plank is set between the cheekpiece and the spine, with space below it for the keyboard. A space is created for the jackslides between the wrest plank and the belly rail (or header), a transverse member which is sometimes divided into separate upper and lower parts. In this case the lower part is set somewhat behind the upper one in order to leave room for the keys to extend beyond the jacks and reach the slotted rack by which they are usually guided at the back. The upper surface of the belly rail supports the front edge of the soundboard, the other edges of which rest on liners glued to the inside of the spine, tail, bentside and cheekpiece; the 8′ hitch-pins are driven into the liners along the tail and bentside.

The central problem in constructing any stringed key-board instrument is to produce a structure of sufficie strength to withstand the tension exerted by the string yet not unduly massive or so placed as to damp out the sound. In a harpsichord, where there are likely to two or three strings for each note of the instrument compass, this problem can be severe; and the failure with hopelessly warped cases, collapsed soundboar and wrenched-out wrest planks, are to be seen in mar of the world's instrument collections, particularly amo instruments that have suffered at some time from bei strung more heavily than their makers intended.

The methods by which the cases of historical instru ments are braced to withstand the tension of the string are numerous; apart from those remarkable instrumen that have survived with no framing at all, they may t divided into three groups. In the simplest system, a seri of vertical braces running nearly the entire depth of th case somewhat beneath the soundboard are placed trans versely between the bentside and the spine, and/c obliquely between the bentside and the spine and th bentside and the belly rail; these braces may be supple mented by slanting bars (struts) running downwards fro the bentside liner to the bottom. In the second system triangular knees are set between the sides and the bo tom of the case and between the belly rail and the bo tom; again, these knees may be supplemented by slantin bars. In the third and most complicated system, there i more than one set of braces: at the bottom of the cas running transversely from the bentside to the spine, a a higher level running obliquely from the bentside line to the spine liner and the belly rail, and even, in 18th century English instruments, from the upper belly ra to the baseboard (running parallel to the spine).

In any event the function of the bracing is the same namely, to prevent the bentside and the tail from col lapsing inwards owing to the force exerted by the strings A related problem is that the tension of the strings tend to make the wrest plank bend inwards towards the bell rail and twist downwards at its back edge or upward at its front; to some extent the first of these tendencie may be prevented by narrow braces passing from th back edge of the wrest plank to the belly rail (such brace are required only in the middle of the wrest plank, sinc the ends are firmly set into the spine and cheekpiece) The tendency of the wrest plank to rotate is far mor serious. The wrest plank has no support against this excep at its ends; and while the bass end is attached to th spine, which runs the entire length of the instrument making twisting almost impossible in the bass unless th wrest plank tears loose, the treble end is attached to th short cheekpiece, which can be rotated by any twistin of the wrest plank. Such a rotation pushes the uppe corner of the cheekpiece–bentside joint backwards; thi cannot occur unless the curvature of the bentside in th treble increases to some extent at the top and, for thi reason, the bracing of the bentside in this area and th integrity of the bottom of the instrument are crucial, a is the choice of sufficiently stout and high-quality woo for the wrest plank. Without these precautions a harp sichord will develop the 'cocked' appearance seen i many surviving examples.

2. THE RENAISSANCE. 15th-century representations o harpsichords from various parts of western Europe gen erally show short instruments with thick cases. With on exception (which may well have suffered from over painting) none shows a jackrail, indicating that thes

instruments did not work by means of jacks as described above. Instead they appear to have had a variety of far more complex actions, such as those cryptically described and illustrated in the manuscript treatise (c1440) of Henri Arnaut de Zwolle (see fig.2).

(i) Italy. It is believed that no Italian 15th-century harpsichords have survived; thus, any examination of harpsichord making at this time must rely on illustrations and documents, the evidence of music written for keyboard instruments and possibly comparisons with other types of instrument. The fruits of such an approach are necessarily rather speculative. Manuscripts of Italian keyboard music (including organ music) show that a compass of F,G,A to g'',a'' (or c''', or f''') was in use in the second half of the 15th century (see Tagliavini, 1980). An intarsia representation of a harpsichord in the choir stalls in S Lorenzo, Genoa, shows a single-register instrument with a compass of F,G,A to (apparently) g''. In view of the early date of the intarsia (about 1520) and the range of the compass, it seems plausible to assume that the intarsia represents a harpsichord of the late 15th century. Unfortunately, the somewhat crudely made intarsia does not yield much information about constructional details; the case is thick, without mouldings, and the key covers are of boxwood, but most striking is the curious bentside made with two curves, an apparently unique example among harpsichords (illustrated in Winternitz, 1967).

About 40 dated harpsichords have survived from before 1600, so instrument construction in the 16th century can be described in detail. Cases were usually thin (3 to 6 mm) and made of cypress, although maple was occasionally used. The slender shape of the case, which is characteristically Italian, results from the practice of doubling the string length at each octave until the tenor register; the case sides are usually not as deep as in instruments from other countries. Mouldings at the top and bottom edges of the case contribute to an appearance of architectural elegance. Such thin-cased instruments were rarely painted; instead they were provided with a separate, decorated case (this arrangement of an instrument with an outer case is often referred to as an 'inner–outer' instrument). The outer case was supported on stands of a variety of forms; surviving ones range from simple, turned baluster legs to carved stands that were painted and gilded.

Some surviving harpsichords with a single 8' register have no internal bracing; the limited amount of tension of one register made this possible. Internal bracing usually comprised two or three stiffening rails glued to the bottom boards; triangular blocks ('knees') maintained the sides perpendicular to the bottom. Two or three knees on the spine side and five to seven on the bentside was a common arrangement. Diagonal struts from the bentside liner to the bottom were also used, either in cooperation with knees or as the only method of supporting the sides.

The cheeks either side of the keyboard were often cut to a combination of scroll, semicircle and other shapes. Decorative inlaid stripes of contrasting colours in geometrical designs, painted arabesques and patterns, and small ivory knobs were used to embellish some of the finer instruments. The natural keys were usually covered with boxwood, but sometimes with ivory; only rarely were dark woods used. Sharps were commonly made of black-stained wood topped with ebony veneer or some-times with stripes of different types of wood. The nameboard was occasionally panelled with mouldings, and, if signed, often carried the maker's name in small capital letters, though many instruments are without date or signature. The soundboards often had a rose consisting of several layers of parchment and/or thin wood veneer of Gothic or interweaving geometric design. Some instruments had three or four roses, a feature which echoes the illustrations of 15th-century European harpsichords (see chapter by Bowles in Ripin, 1971).

Keyboards were most frequently made of quartered beech, the jack-end of the key-lever being guided by a wooden tongue in a vertical slot on the rack. The keys were arrested by cloth padding on the front key-frame rail, or by the jacks reaching the padded underside of the jackrail, or perhaps a combination of the two. The height of the sharp projecting above the natural keys would indicate in many instruments a fairly shallow depth of touch (about 6 mm).

Italian jacks were normally thicker than those used in other countries, and most often made of pear (or perhaps service wood; in such cases only microscopic analysis can distinguish between closely similar woods). Springs to hold the tongues in their vertical positions were commonly of flat brass strip; the tongue was often centrally placed to enable a damper-slot to be cut on either side. Quill was the usual material employed for the plectra; it cannot be substantiated that leather plectra, which are now found in some jacks, were used originally as many such jacks are either not original or have been altered (see Henkel, *Beiträge*, 1979). A one-piece box-slide about 3 cm deep was used by most Italian makers in preference to the separate upper and lower guides found in other traditions. The jackslides were made either by sawing out the slots and then closing the open side with a thin strip of wood, or by gluing small blocks of wood to a thin strip, with the correct spacing for the thickness of the jacks, and then gluing another strip on the open slide. It seems likely that it was the practice to provide all $1 \times 8'$, $1 \times 4'$ harpsichords with small knobs fixed in the ends of the jackslides and projecting through the cheek, to enable the registers to be engaged and disengaged (see also §3 (i) below). The jackrail was often decorated with mouldings, either cut into the wood or glued to the rail. To hold it in place, slotted blocks were glued to the inside of the case; the rail is slid backwards (i.e. towards the tail) for removal.

A large number of 16th-century harpsichords have cypress (*Cupressus sempervirens*) soundboards, but spruce (of the genus *Picea*), or what in many instances may be fir (*Abies*), was also used. Cypress, walnut and beech were normally used for bridges, which typically had a smaller cross-section than those found in other countries. They were usually made from parallel-sided stock (in contrast to the basically triangular shape often found in other traditions) with a moulding cut on the top edge. A reduction in the height and width of the bridge towards the treble was common; sometimes the ends were finished with a decorative scroll. In other countries the bridge often had a tight curve in the bass, but in Italian harpsichords a small piece was usually mitred at an angle to the main bridge. Nuts were often of the same material, and finished to the same dimensions and with the same decoration as the bridge. They were either fixed on a straight line on the wrest plank or curved with the inside of the curve facing the jacks. (Nuts with the curve in the opposite direction can

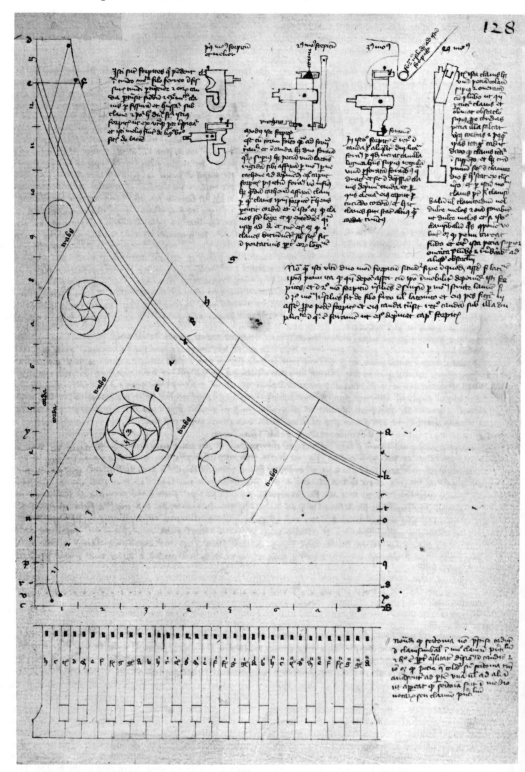

2. *Henri Arnaut de Zwolle's plan drawing of a harpsichord (c1440), with descriptions of three types of mechanism plus one (extreme right) for the dulce melos (F-Pn lat.7295, f.128r)*

usually be shown to be later alterations.)

Ribbing systems have been found with three or four bars ('cross-bars') running at an angle from the spine (towards the front of the instrument) and crossing under the bridge (where they are sometimes undercut to leave the soundboard free), as well as those with a cut-off bar with or without additional cross-bars. The impossibility of access to the inside of many instruments makes it difficult to establish how rigidly makers followed these systems, and, as with instruments of other countries, exceptions to these types of barring can be found. These systems of barring are found in Italian harpsichords from the 16th to the 18th centuries, so that no feature is peculiar to one period of instrument making.

Where a 4' stop was part of the specification, the 4' hitch-pins were often simply driven into the soundboard and secured on the underside with a drop of glue. This practice is only possible with a relatively hard wood such as cypress (and not with spruce or fir), but thin 4' hitch-pin rails glued to cypress soundboards were also used.

The point at which the string is plucked is important in determining the character of the sound of an instrument. When the plucking point is near the nut the sound is nasal; nearer the middle of the string, rounder. It can be seen in Italian harpsichords that the plucking point (in the back register) for an 8' string lay close to a third of the string length in most instances, but sometimes approaching a quarter, at c''. At the extreme treble the plucking point was nearer the middle of the string. In the bass the plucking point was, for obvious practical reasons, quite close to the nut.

A common arrangement of the plucking directions for a $2 \times 8'$ disposition would have one 8' plucked to the left (as seen by the player) and the other, with the jacks nearer the keys, to the right. Some dispositions would appear to have been originally in the reverse order, but repairs and alterations often make it impossible to establish such matters beyond doubt. The difference in sound of the two configurations when both 8' strings are played is small.

In the case of the $1 \times 8'$, $1 \times 4'$ disposition it can be clearly shown from several examples that the registers were arranged with the 8' plucked to the left and the 4' (with the jacks nearer the player) to the right. A comparison between this disposition and that of Ruckers harpsichords is interesting as it reveals a basic difference in the design, and hence in the sound; Ruckers instruments have the 4' plucked to the left and the 8' (jacks nearer the keys) to the right.

The Italian 8' being in the back register gives a rounder tone in the treble than the Flemish instrument (the Italian plucking point is about a third of the string length, at c''; in Ruckers instruments it is a quarter). Given the scales and plucking points that Italian harpsichord makers chose, the two nuts must lie quite close to each other making it impracticable to locate the 4' tuning-pins between the 4' and 8' nuts (which was the Flemish practice). Instead, holes were drilled through the 8' nut so that the 4' strings could reach their tuning-pins at the edge of the wrest plank. One harpsichord which has retained its 4' in use is the Franciscus Patavinus instrument of 1561 in the Deutsches Museum, Munich.

Many Italian harpsichords had the line of jacks running not at 90° to the long side, but at a slight angle so that the jackslides are nearer the front of the instrument at the treble end. This reduces the amount of curve in the bentside, if other factors of scaling and plucking points are unchanged, which may have been the makers' reason for this arrangement.

As many 16th-century instruments have had their dispositions changed and their soundboards repaired, reinforced or differently barred, it is difficult to tell from such surviving examples how they might originally have sounded. A characteristic of most Italian harpsichords is, however, a fairly marked 'attack' and less duration of resonance than in, for example, harpsichords by Ruckers. The type of soundboard and bridge timber, and barring have a distinct influence on the nature of the sound, but the smaller cross-section of Italian bridges (as noted above) is also an important contribution to the type of sound. While certain general characteristics may be defined as 'Italian', it should not be expected that all instruments sounded the same.

One example of an exception to the general characteristics is the Dominicus Pisaurensis harpsichord of 1533 which has a soundboard extending to the wrest plank, so that both the nut and the bridge are on it. The similarity of this arrangement to two other 16th-century harpsichords (those by Hans Müller, Leipzig, 1537, and Lodewijk Theewes, London, 1579; see 2(ii) below), which also have a soundboard under the nut, could be used as evidence to suggest that this type of harpsichord was more widely known in the 16th century than this single example of Dominicus would indicate.

A discussion of 16th-century compasses cannot begin without an appreciation of the extent to which alterations obscure the original condition of many instruments. Barnes (in Ripin, 1971) has drawn attention to many alterations of this kind. Indeed, so often were instruments altered (and sometimes so skilfully as to leave little trace of the work) that it may be true to say there survives no dated Italian harpsichord of the 16th century that has not had its compass, disposition or scale altered. This point can hardly be overstressed as most of the literature about 16th-century harpsichords refers to the altered conditions. The following comments note alterations already reported and draw on the author's own research, but it is too early to present a definitive discussion.

It is often stated that Italian harpsichords typically had two 8' registers, but in many 16th-century instruments a second register has been added to what was originally a $1 \times 8'$ disposition. Hubbard (1965, p.5) introduced the instrument of 1521 by Hieronymus Bononiensis as a typical Italian harpsichord; it has often been cited as the oldest dated harpsichord in existence (the authenticity of some other instruments with earlier dates has not been fully investigated). It now has a $2 \times 8'$ disposition and C/E to d''' compass. In fact it was altered from a $1 \times 8'$ instrument, which, as Debenham (1978) has described, originally had 50 strings. The harpsichord could therefore have been made with a C/E to f''' compass (50 notes).

A number of 16th-century harpsichords with a single 8' register are known (see Hellwig in Ripin, 1971) but it is difficult to make a reliable judgment as to whether the $1 \times 8'$ or $2 \times 8'$ disposition was the more common in the 16th century, since the many undated harpsichords which might belong to this period complicate the issue. There are no reliable criteria for distinguishing 16th- from 17th-century harpsichords. However, on the evidence of dated harpsichords it is clear that it was not

3. Harpsichord by Giovanni Baffo, Venice, 1574 (Victoria and Albert Museum, London)

until the beginning of the 17th century that 2 × 8′ became the more common disposition.

Several instruments which now have a 2 × 8′ disposition were originally 1 × 8′, 1 × 4′ (and in almost all cases these harpsichords were Venetian). The 1574 Baffo (see fig.3) is one such harpsichord which underwent modifications: the disposition was changed to 2 × 8′ and the C/E to f‴ compass changed to G′/B′ to c‴ (see Barnes in Ripin, 1971). Considering the original condition of dated 16th-century harpsichords it seems that the 1 × 8′, 1 × 4′ instruments were more numerous than the 1 × 8′ ones. The two types counted together (i.e. 1 × 8′ and 1 × 8′, 1 × 4′) were clearly in the majority in the 16th century.

Some small harpsichords survive with two unison registers, and although the exact pitch designation is not entirely clear, these are perhaps 4′ instruments, analogous to octave virginals. There are two important examples by Dominicus Pisaurensis (active in Venice): an instrument of 1543 (in the Paris Conservatoire) and the other of 1546 (Gesellschaft der Musikfreunde, Vienna).

The earliest 16th-century harpsichord keyboards possibly had a compass of F, G, A to a″ (probably without g♯″) or c‴ or f‴. Later modifications have obscured the fact that some early keyboards only reached a″, and such keyboards do not appear to have been made in Italy after the 1580s. C/E to f‴ was more common than C/E to c‴ in the 16th century. The 'Arpitarrone' described by Banchieri (*L'organo suonarino*, 2/1611, p.4) had a compass of C, D to c‴. A few instruments have survived to confirm the use of this type of bass octave. It seems unlikely that a compass of G′/B′ to c‴ was ever

made in the 16th century, even though some instruments now have this range. Several have already been shown to be alterations of the 17th or 18th centuries. A compass of G′, A′ to c‴ was common towards the end of the 17th century, and the earliest example is the harpsichord made in 1605 by Ioannis Celestini (in the Gemeente Museum, The Hague), but it is not clear whether such compasses were used in the 16th century. However, the inventory of Medici instruments (reproduced in Gai, 1969, p.9) lists a harpsichord of 1538 made by Dominicus Pisaurensis with a compass of G′ A′ to a″; it seems quite possible that this was the original compass. An instrument with an exceptionally wide range is the 1579 Baffo harpsichord (in the Paris Conservatoire; the date is not 1578 as given in some sources) which originally had a five-octave (57-note), C/E to c‴ compass (or perhaps C′/E′ to c‴, depending on how the pitch of c″ is understood).

About half of the harpsichords attributable to the 16th century were made in Venice. A clear enough pattern emerges of harpsichords with 1 × 8′, 1 × 4′ disposition and cypress soundboards to justify calling this a Venetian tradition. The quality of the best instruments was never improved upon at any time (and rarely equalled) in Italy or abroad. It would seem that Venice was the most important harpsichord-making centre in 16th-century Italy; that the reputation of the Venetian makers was considerable is borne out by the numbers of instruments that found their way to other parts of Italy and elsewhere. Alfonso II of Ferrara had at least six Venetian instruments, and Raimund Fugger in Augsburg had five Venetian harpsichords in his collection.

The question of the pitch of Italian harpsichords is complicated because no agreement has been reached on some of the basic matters of stringing. Italian string lengths covered a range from about 15 cm to 42 cm at c''. It is this wide range of scales (in comparison with other harpsichord-making traditions) which has suggested that instruments were at different pitches. At the shorter end of the range were octave virginals and harpsichords (virginals have usually been included in these analyses as they belong to the same family of instruments); at the longer end were harpsichords of unusually low pitch. It is the scales in the middle and lower end of the range which have engaged the most attention: these varied from about 25 cm to about 36 cm at c''.

Some earlier writers were not convinced that a string length could be identified with a particular pitch (see Russell, 1959, p.32; Hubbard, 1965, p.9). However, later evidence of the scalings used for the different types of string material (i.e. iron, yellow brass and red brass wire) indicates that there was wide agreement among harpsichord makers on certain basic principles. That is, that the strength differences between, for example, iron and brass wire should be reflected in a difference between string lengths (see O'Brien, 1981). Wraight's research has revealed the accuracy with which Italian harpsichord makers worked when laying out the positions of the bridges. Thus it seems clear that the pitch relationships between various instruments were reflected in different string lengths. In principle, an examination of the original string lengths, with due consideration of which scalings were intended for iron wire and which for brass, would yield the scheme of pitches in use in the 16th century.

Such attempts have already been made. After examining 33 Italian harpsichords and virginals, Shortridge (1960) attempted to show that certain scales occurred with such regularity that two groups could be discerned. He gave the averages of these two groups as 26·6 cm and 32·7 cm at c''. It was suggested that the correlation of the shorter scales with keyboards of C/E to c''' range and longer scales with keyboards C/E to f''' indicated that the C/E to f''' instruments were at a pitch a 4th lower. On this interpretation the notes f''' and c''' sounded at the same frequency. What made this seem plausible was the analogy with the Ruckers 'transposing' harpsichords (see §3(i) below) which had keyboards at pitches a 4th apart. Similar arguments were advanced by Barnes (1965) to support the idea that Italian instruments were at two different pitches in order to facilitate transposition.

An essential weakness of these arguments is that there is no exact correlation between the range of the keyboard and whether the scale is long or short, as examination of other Italian instruments has revealed. Furthermore, the difference between the scalings reported is somewhat less than a 4th and cannot confirm the hypothesis. Although Shortridge examined 33 instruments, this is only about a fifth of the total number that have survived from before 1650. Shortridge's list also gives the scales of some altered instruments which further distorts the scheme of original pitches. Thus, the scale averages reported by Shortridge are unreliable as a basis for further study.

Nevertheless, this 'transposition theory' still has a certain immediate appeal, due partly to what is known to have taken place, namely, transpositions of a 4th. It is also due to the fact that notes as high as f''' were practically uncalled for in 16th-century music. This seems to suggest that transposition might be a part of the explanation for the two different keyboards. With the idea of transposition in mind, the difference in pitch of a 4th between the c''' and f''' notes could then appear to be strong circumstantial evidence for a pitch difference of a 4th between the C/E to c''' and C/E to f''' keyboards (see also PITCH, §4).

However, the more the organological evidence is examined, the less plausible it is to assume that there were two basic pitches for instruments, a 4th apart. Indeed, within the range of the examples of the longer scales it seems possible to distinguish several different pitches, so that a statistical average of several string lengths is misleading. The most substantial problem remains that there is too little accurate information of original scalings upon which to base a reliable analysis of the pitches.

Although the first writers on these problems of scalings assumed that all the instruments were strung with the same type of material (see Shortridge, 1960; Barnes, 1965; Hubbard, 1965) an important article by Thomas and Rhodes (1967) argues that the difference between groups of string lengths was simply due to the use of iron and brass scales. While this contribution was important for drawing attention to the use of iron scales in Italian instruments, several difficulties remain in showing which instruments were designed to use iron wire. A contrary view (that all Italian instruments were strung with brass wire, with the pitches proportional to string lengths) was advanced by Barnes (1968; in Ripin, 1971; 1973) and defended against the views of Thomas and Rhodes.

The documentary evidence presently available indicates that some harpsichords and virginals were designed to be strung with iron wire, while others were strung with brass. It is not possible simply to identify the type of stringing material with a type of instrument, even though evidence has been quoted to this end (see Hellwig, 1976). Although it is only one argument among many, there is a good practical reason why most virginals, and harpsichords with a 4' register, to f''' should have had long scales: the longer iron scale permitted the bridges to be placed on a more freely vibrating soundboard instead of being too close to the registers, which would tend to deaden the sound.

Since the original makers' principles of stringing are not completely understood and because of the small amount of accurate information on original scales, an outline of the original pitch schemes must be a tentative one. It does seem that there were indeed several different pitches in use. Some were high: octave and possibly quint pitches; a few were demonstrably low, and would have been a 4th or a 5th lower than some other pitches. Whether this is significant for the idea of 'transposition' is not yet clear. Others in the middle range (about 28 cm at c''; strung with brass wire) would have been close to $a' = 415$ Hz. It seems plausible that most virginals were strung with iron wire and that their range of pitches was substantially the same as the short-scaled harpsichords strung with brass. The arguments concerning the stringing of the long-scaled harpsichords (about 36 cm at c'') are more delicately balanced; it seems presently more plausible to assume that these were strung with iron wire and came to a pitch similar to the virginals and short-scaled harpsichords.

In retrospect, it can be seen that the initial attempts

at making sense of the complexities of Italian string lengths grappled with two problems: the organological evidence of pitches, and the musicological question of 'transposition' practices. Since these first studies were undertaken it has become clearer that there were not simply two groups of instruments with pitches a 4th apart. It is clear though that 'transpositions' a 4th or 5th lower were routine keyboard practices in the 16th century (see Tagliavini, 1974; Meeùs, 1977). As the possibility remains that some harpsichords were at low pitches, questions similar to those posed by Shortridge (1960) and Barnes (1965) must again be asked: whether these harpsichords were 'transposing' instruments depends not simply on a technical explanation of the pitch but on an understanding of their original musical uses. It is no less important to understand the use of the various instruments at other pitches (e.g. at the octave or quint). Such considerations are not isolated from organology, since, as has been seen, they are essential concepts used in organizing evidence into comprehensible schemes.

Theoreticians and inventors were also applying their ideas to produce unusual instruments. In 1548 Dominicus Pisaurensis built a harpsichord for Zarlino with 19 notes to the octave (see Zarlino, 1558). It is not certain whether this was intended to be tuned in equal microtones or to provide sharps not normally available in meantone temperaments (i.e. $c\flat$, $d\sharp$, $g\flat$, $a\flat$, and $a\sharp$; see TEMPERAMENTS, §2). Although it is known that some organs of the 15th century had split sharps, it is not clear how often 16th-century harpsichords were provided with split sharps; most of the surviving instruments have a 17th-century origin.

Nicola Vicentino, in defence of his views of musical theory, published *L'antica musica . . . con l'inventione di uno nuovo stromento* (1555), the 'new instrument' being a harpsichord with 36 keys to the octave so that perfect intervals were always available to the player instead of the imperfect intervals necessary in any temperament (see Tiella, 1975).

References in inventories and other writings give clues to instruments that have not survived. The 'instrumento pian e forte' and instruments with 'two sets of strings forming three different kinds of sound' challenge our ingenuity to find an explanation of their mechanism, but from these scanty descriptions all attempts must remain speculative. Many references can be found to the claviorgan (i.e. a harpsichord coupled to an organ) but it is believed that no original Italian example has survived. A claviorgan in the Brussels Conservatory had its harpsichord part (a 'Bortolotti' of 1585; the name has been changed) altered and coupled with an organ at a later date (see Thomas and Rhodes, 1967). It is not clear whether two-manual harpsichords were made in Italy in the 16th century. Several surviving harpsichords have been shown to be later alterations from one-manual harpsichords. Although it has been suggested (Castellani, 1973, p.19) that the four 'gravicembali doppi' (double harpsichords), used in the *intermedi* for the marriage of Francesco de' Medici and Johanna of Austria (Florence, 1565), were two-manual instruments, it seems more plausible to assume that they were 2 × 8′ harpsichords, 'doppi' distinguishing them from 1 × 8′ harpsichords.

(ii) Northern Europe. The overwhelming majority of the surviving 16th-century instruments are Italian, and knowledge of harpsichord making elsewhere in Europe before about 1590 is derived largely from scanty written sources and the few surviving instruments made during this period. Of the small number of known stringed keyboard instruments made north of the Alps before 1590 one is a clavicytherium and only three are harpsichords, the others being virginals or clavichords. Similarly, no 16th-century representation of a north European harpsichord is known at present. Perhaps the oldest surviving plucked keyboard instrument is the small clavicytherium in the museum of the Royal College of Music, London (for illustration *see* CLAVICYTHERIUM). This instrument was probably built about 1480 and it seems likely that it was made in Ulm. It has a number of features normally associated with Italian instruments, including very thin case sides, but it is clearly not Italian in its origins. It does not use boxslides, but instead the jacks are guided by slots in the soundboard which itself runs under the nut and ends above a very narrow wrestplank into which the tuning-pins are placed. The keyboard has a very wide octave span, making the playing of octaves impossible, and the bridge is a sort of stylized tree trunk with branches emanating from it on either side.

The three surviving north European harpsichords made before 1590 confirm the general impression gained from the slightly more numerous virginals, that shortly after 1500 the Italian thin-cased design became known in Germany, where it was somewhat altered to acquire a group of non-Italian features; these, with further modifications, are found throughout north European instruments of the 17th century.

The most important evidence for this is the harpsichord made by Hans Müller in Leipzig in 1537 and now in the Museo degli Strumenti Musicali in Rome (see fig.4). The general conception of this harpsichord with its thin case and slanting rows of jacks is Italianate, but with its massive mouldings and somewhat chunky outline it could never be mistaken for an Italian specimen. Its most significant non-Italian technical feature is that each of its sets of jacks is held in position by two thin guides rather than by a single thick guide, a feature encountered in all north European harpsichords and virginals (but not bentside spinets) but only rarely seen in Italy. The instrument has other features that may have been relatively common in the 16th century, but the paucity of surviving examples makes this difficult to confirm. It is equipped with two sets of unison strings but has three rows of jacks, one of which is a 'lute stop' (Ger. *Nasalzug*) that plucks close to the nut, producing a penetrating nasal timbre (a mechanism controlled by one of the stops projecting from the cheek probably disengaged this row of jacks when the other row plucking the same string was engaged). In addition, the instrument has a transposing keyboard which can be shifted to permit changing the sounding pitch of the instrument by a whole tone. Finally, the soundboard extends in a single piece across the gaps for the jacks so as to cover the wrest plank, a feature also encountered in other widely scattered instruments of the 16th and 17th centuries, including clavicytheria as well as harpsichords.

The bridge of the Müller harpsichord is not now in its original position (see fig.4). As it stands it was probably designed, in conjunction with a previous keyboard alteration, to give scalings suitable for brass strings at normal pitch. In its original position, and with the original keyboard capable of transposing by a tone, the bridge gives scalings suitable for iron stringing at a pitch an

4. Plan and side views of harpsichord by Hans Müller, Leipzig, 1537 (Museo degli Strumenti Musicali, Rome)

octave or a 9th above normal pitch depending on the position of the movable keyboard. Thus in addition to being the earliest surviving dated north European harpsichord, it is one of the few examples from any period of an octave harpsichord.

The conceptions of instrument design embodied in the Müller harpsichord were soon carried to Flanders and, significantly, the earliest surviving Antwerp virginal was made in 1548 by Joes Karest, an emigrant who brought with him the Germanic tradition from Cologne. Like the Müller harpsichord, Karest's virginal has the look of a weightier version of an Italian design (in this instance the hexagonal virginal): although the case is thin, the mouldings are far heavier and the outline is less graceful than on a typical Italian instrument (*see* VIRGINAL, fig.2). In Flanders, virginals of this type began to be superseded in the late 1560s by instruments with thick cases, and it is possible that thick-cased harpsichords also began to be built then. The only evidence for this is the single-manual harpsichord that forms part of a claviorgan built in London by Lodewijk Theewes, an expatriate Fleming, in 1579. Although this highly important instrument preserves a number of features found in the 1537 Müller harpsichord (most notably the soundboard extending continuously to cover the wrest plank), its case is thicker and its scaling quite long (approximately 35·6 cm for *c″*): both these features correspond to later Flemish practice. The longer scaling produces a relatively shallow inward curve in the bentside and necessitates an appreciable shortening of scaling in the bass. Whereas an Italian harpsichord would be likely to have string lengths that doubled for each octave throughout five sixths of the instrument's range, those of the Theewes

harpsichord double down to only about *c′*, after which the bridge proceeds in a straight line instead of continuing to curve away from the spine. The bass section of the bridge on this instrument is not original, but on later Flemish instruments this section curves towards the spine at the end, instead of having a short section mitred on to it at an angle. The bracing system employed in the Theewes instrument is the first of those discussed earlier: a series of flat rectangular braces set vertically on the bottom of the instrument, and rising to the level of the underside of the case liners, run transversely from the bentside to the spine. This system, with minor variations, is found both in later English harpsichords and in German instruments of the Hamburg school.

The Theewes instrument is unusual for its early date in having three registers, two 8′ and one 4′, where one of the 8′ registers was probably used only as a harpichordium stop with brays, as on a Renaissance harp, on the 8′ bridge producing a buzzing sound on this register. As on most Italian instruments, all the tuning-pins are placed at the front edge of the wrest plank, with the 4′ strings passing through holes drilled in the 8′ nut. Although this important instrument is essentially Flemish, it should be noted that it has a number of features that are probably characteristically English, including the use of oak for the case and the decoration of the inside of the case with embossed paper (both features can be seen in an English depiction of a virginal dating from 1591 and in surviving 17th-century English virginals). Moreover, the chromatic bass octave from *C* may also be a characteristically English feature; it is not normally found on continental instruments at this date (the 1550 Karest virginal and the Müller harpsichord of

1537, both in the Museo degli Strumenti Musicali, Rome, and both with a bass compass from *C* but lacking *C♯* are either exceptions, or a reflection of an earlier practice), but it, too, can be seen in the painting of 1591 cited above. (The low *E♭* appears in English keyboard music of the 16th century; the low *C♯* may have been tuned to *A'*, although this note is not called for before Bull, Gibbons and Tomkins.)

The next surviving harpsichord of north European origin is by Hans Moermans the elder of Antwerp, dated 1584. Much concerning the original state of this instrument must remain conjectural, but it now possesses many of the attributes of the developed Flemish types associated with the Ruckers family: a comparatively thick case made of softwood; a long scaling (35·6 cm for *c''*); soundboard barring consisting of a massive curving 4' hitch-pin rail between the 8' and 4' bridges, with a diagonal cut-off bar to the left of the 4' bridge and a group of transverse ribs stiffening the triangular areas between the cut-off bar and the spine; and bracing provided by deep transverse pieces attached to the bottom, supplemented by flat pieces nailed to the underside of the case liners and running obliquely from the bentside to the spine (the Moermans harpsichord, however, has only two braces of each type in addition to the divided belly rail, whereas later Flemish instruments have three). Unlike the wrest plank of the Theewes instrument, which is hollowed out underneath the nuts so that they stand on a freely vibrating soundboard area, and in which all the tuning-pins are placed near the front, the wrest plank of the Moermans is solid and the 4' tuning-pins are placed between the 8' nut and the 4' nut, so that the 8' nut does not have to be drilled to permit passage of the 4' strings. The single row of 8' jacks is placed in front of the row of 4' jacks and plucks to the right, while the 4' jacks in the back row pluck to the left.

3. *c*1590 TO *c*1700.

(i) Flanders. The developed Flemish harpsichord of the late 16th and 17th century is inevitably associated with the work of the Ruckers family, a dynasty that dominated Antwerp harpsichord building for a century beginning in 1579, and whose instruments continued in use (sometimes radically rebuilt) throughout Europe as long as harpsichords were played. In addition to a wide variety of virginals, the Ruckers workshops produced single-manual harpsichords of several different sizes, double-manual harpsichords and rectangular instruments consisting of a single- or double-manual harpsichord with an octave virginal built into the space beside the tail and played from one side of the rectangular case. Of these, the most common seems to have been a single-manual instrument approximately 183 cm long and 71 cm wide, with one 8' and 4' register and with a buff stop, consisting of leather pads carried on a sliding batten, for the 8'. The range of these instruments was almost invariably four octaves, *C/E* to *c'''*, although a few surviving examples originally had chromatic basses and sometimes extended to *d''''* in the treble. By the mid-17th century the Couchets, heirs of the Ruckers, made instruments of this type with a chromatic bass octave, and even with a keyboard extending chromatically down to *F'* and sometimes with a 2 × 8' disposition. Although no surviving instrument shows evidence of this disposition, documents show that the Couchets also sometimes gave their instruments the more modern 2 × 8',

5. Harpsichord by Andreas Ruckers, Antwerp, 1640 (Yale University Collection of Musical Instruments, New Haven)

1 × 4' disposition. A late instrument, probably by Joseph Joannes Couchet (in the Nydahl Collection, Stockholm) had a compass from *F'* to *e'''*, only one note short of the five-octave compass common by the mid-18th century.

The tone of a two-register Ruckers harpsichord differs appreciably from that of an Italian instrument of the time, in having a more sustained brilliance and a somewhat less pronounced attack. The balanced differentiation in timbre produced by the gradual change in plucking-point from a third of the string length in the extreme treble to about a tenth in the bass is adequate for distinguishing contrapuntal lines but not so pronounced as to prevent projecting a homogeneous sound in homophonic contexts; the 4' register has a pleasant sound in its own right and is usable as a solo stop (as most 4' registers on historic harpsichords are not) and when combined with the 8' lends a marked brilliance and carrying power to the ensemble. A buff stop can be used to damp the higher overtones of the 8' strings, producing a muted pizzicato effect. This buff stop was normally split between *c'* and *c♯'*, enabling either the treble or bass to be damped and contrasted with the sound of the undamped strings of the other half of the register. Registration was changed by reaching round the instrument and pushing or pulling extensions of the jackslides that passed through the treble cheekpiece, thereby moving the jackslide to the left or right to engage or disengage the register. Thus the player could not change registers except during a pause between movements or individual pieces.

The addition of a second 8' register to the basic design (whether by the original maker or at a later date), though increasing the number of possible registers and yielding a louder ensemble when all stops are engaged, seems

spoil the sound of the individual registers, partly as
result of its slightly shifting the plucking-points and
artly by its loading the soundboard with additional
ownward force from the added strings.

The scanty evidence available for harpsichord build-
g before Hans Ruckers's admission to the Guild of St
uke in 1579 suggests that, as with the virginal, the
asic characteristics of the single-manual harpsichord
st described were established by the harpsichord mak-
rs of the preceding generation, one of whom would
ave trained Ruckers. (In this connection it should be
orne in mind that Lodewijk Theewes, who made the
laviorgan of 1579 described in §2(ii) above, had emi-
rated to England at least seven years before he made
at instrument, and had been admitted to the Flemish
uild in 1561). The two-manual harpsichord appears to
ave been invented by a Flemish builder of Hans Ruck-
rs's generation. Presumably the idea was suggested by
e multi-manual organs of the time, with which Hans
uckers would have been familiar in his capacity as an
rgan tuner; but no double-manual harpsichord by him
known.

Like the virginals, the harpsichords of the Ruckers
dynasty were made in a range of standardized sizes, the
smaller instruments having shorter scalings and being
tuned to higher pitches. The harpsichords were also decorated in a similar way, with the outside usually painted
in imitation of marble, or more rarely with strap-work,
and the inside decorated with block-printed papers, of
which four or five different types were usually used on
a single instrument. In instruments in which the inside
of the lid was not decorated with a painting, the printed
paper would have one or more Latin mottoes lettered
on it (see fig.5). The soundboard decorations included
arabesques and flowers and were executed in gouache,
with a cast lead 'rose' – a soundhole ornament that
included the maker's initials (but *see* RUCKERS, fig.3).

Only a few surviving Ruckers and Couchet harpsichords retain their original stands; contemporary paintings showing instruments of this kind reveal two common
designs, either framed structures with thick turned legs
(see fig.6), or complex affairs with heavy pierced fret-
work ends connected by arcades supported by numerous
turned balusters. The natural keys of these harpsichords

. Flemish harpsichord painted in imitation of marble and decorated inside with block-printed paper: painting,
The Music Master' (c1660), by Jan Steen (National Gallery, London)

are covered with bone and the sharps are made of bog oak. The fronts of the natural keys are usually decorated with a punched paper design glued on to a layer of coloured parchment. At the back of the keyboard there is a slotted rack similar to that found in an Italian harpsichord. However, instead of a slip of hardwood to fit into the appropriate slot in the rack, a Flemish keyboard has a metal pin driven into the end of the key, and the rack is topped with a padded overrail that limits the upward motion of the keys. This system is also used in the lower manual of two-manual instruments; however, there is no space for a rack behind the keys of the upper manual of a two-manual instrument, and the backs of the upper-manual keys are therefore guided by vertical wires rising between the keys at the back of the plank of wood on which the upper-manual balance rail is mounted.

Two-manual instruments appear to have been built in the Ruckers workshops perhaps as early as the 1590s. They had only two sets of strings, like the typical single-manual instrument, and only one of the two keyboards could be used at a time. In the most common type of Ruckers double (but see RUCKERS, fig.2) the lower keyboard had 50 keys and a range of C/E to f''', and the upper had 45 keys and the smaller range of C/E to c'''. The c''' key of the upper keyboard was aligned over the f''' key of the lower keyboard, and a wide block filled in the space to the left of its lowest key. Playing a piece on the lower keyboard transposed it down a 4th with respect to the tonality it had when played on the upper manual. As a special refinement, three extra strings were provided; these were played only from the lower manual, so that the E♭ keys would not be obliged to sound D♯ corresponding to the G♯ on the upper manual. Because of these extra strings, the keyboards of such instruments could not use any rows of jacks in common, and instruments so equipped had four rows of jacks for their two sets of strings. Pictorial evidence and a single, much-altered example suggest that occasionally this refinement was omitted, permitting an instrument of this kind to be made with only three rows of jacks, in which the middle row would have had an extension, or dogleg, reaching down to the lower manual so as to be lifted by the keys of either manual. The purpose for which such 'transposing' harpsichords was made remains obscure, and the earliest written description of them (Quirinus van Blankenburg, *Elementa musica*, 1739) dates from nearly a century after they ceased to be made. The purpose may, as Blankenburg stated, have been to facilitate routine transpositions of a 4th, but it may also have been to combine in a single case two instruments tuned to pitch standards a 4th apart. Unfortunately, it is not certain that any Flemish single-manual instrument originally had the very long scaling of the lower manual of a transposing double – a feature that would help to confirm this hypothesis. Because of the addition of strings in the bass to extend the range downwards a 4th from C/E on the upper manual, and the additional space required for the added lower manual, two-manual instruments of this kind are some 7·5 cm wider and 40·5 cm longer than the normal four-octave single-manual harpsichord of just under 2 metres.

The Germanisches Nationalmuseum in Nuremberg possesses a harpsichord, probably made in 1658 by a builder in the Low Countries, though not Ruckers. It originally had two aligned keyboards (i.e. at the same pitch), a four-octave range (C/E to c''') but with only one set of 8′ strings and one set of 4′ strings. However

it had four registers: a close-plucking lute stop played only by the upper manual keyboard, and two 8′ registers both plucking the same string but separated by the 4′ register, all three of which could be played by the lower manual. Such an instrument can be considered as a 'contrasting' double in that the nasal sound of the lute on the upper manual could be contrasted with the more mellow sound of either of the sets of jacks plucking the same string from the lower manual. There would be little dynamic contrast between the combined 1 × 8′, 1 × 4′ on the lower manual and the more aggressive sound of the lute on the upper manual. In any case the sound could not be contrasted without a pause to change registration. The only instantaneous contrast possible would have been between the 4′ played on the lower manual and the 8′ lute played on the upper. Unlike the later aligned two-manual instruments this one must therefore be considered to provide a tonal contrast rather than a dynamic contrast between manuals. Evidence provided by a group of paintings dating from about 1618 to 1626 makes it clear that such instruments existed at least by that date, so that they could well have been known to Sweelinck and Bull in the Low Countries, as well as to their English contemporaries, but musical confirmation of this hypothesis is lacking, since the earliest keyboard works containing *piano* and *forte* indications, Sweelinck's echo fantasias, may well have been intended for a two-manual organ.

The construction of a Flemish harpsichord involved assembling the case sides (including the bentside), wrest plank and internal braces before installing the soundboard or the bottom. It was, therefore, a rather more complex task than the construction of an Italian instrument, which could be assembled by successively adding parts to the bottom, and in which the bentside was thin enough to be simply flexed and glued to the edge of the bottom and triangular supporting knees attached to it. Instead, the parts of the Flemish case were held together by dowels and rabbets (or mortices), which helped to maintain everything in alignment during assembly. With the case and framing completed, the soundboard, already fitted with its bridges and ribs, was installed, and only then was the bottom attached to the lower braces and the lower edge of the case sides.

(ii) France. Notwithstanding the great importance of Flemish harpsichords and the fact that they were shipped all over Europe and even to the Spanish colonies of the New World, harpsichords of a different kind were being made in England, France and Germany, and probably also in the Iberian peninsula. Only a relatively small number of these survive, and they seem more closely related to such instruments as the Müller harpsichord and the Karest virginal than to either Italian instruments or developed Flemish instruments of the Ruckers type.

Much still needs to be learnt about these largely vanished types, especially since so much important harpsichord music was composed for them rather than for the more numerous instruments of the mid- and late 18th century. The single quality that all these instruments seem to share is the tendency to fall between the Italian instruments and the developed Flemish types. Their scalings are usually longer than those of the more common (short-scaled) Italian instruments, but not as long as those of Flemish ones; their cases are usually somewhat thicker – about 6 mm rather than the 3 to 4·5 mm of an Italian instrument or the 14 mm of a Ruckers instrument; and their bridges and nuts, while thicker and less elaborately

. Harpsichord by Jean-Antoine Vaudry, Paris, 1681 (Victoria and Albert Museum, London)

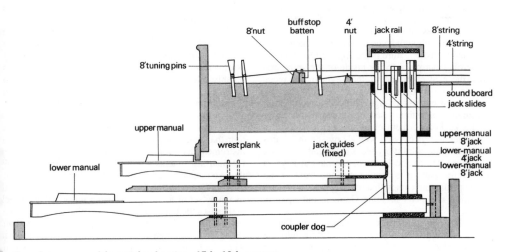

. French two-manual harpsichord action, 17th–18th century

profiled than Italian ones, are usually neither so plain nor so massive as the Flemish. Their sound, at least to judge from the very small number of examples in playable condition, is also intermediate in quality between the Italian and Flemish instruments – punchy and penetrating, yet with more sustaining power in the treble than an Italian instrument, and with an attack sufficiently gentle to permit the performance of graceful ornaments. In sum, they appear to have most of the virtues of both the Italian and Flemish types and to be fully worthy of the wealth of music composed for them. Some of these instruments (including the clavicytherium depicted by Praetorius), though by no means all, have round tails rather than oblique straight ones, so that their bentsides run from the cheekpiece to the spine in a continuous S-shaped curve.

The internal structure of all the surviving instruments of the intermediate type seems to lack the upper level of braces found in the instruments of the Ruckers type, and the sides are assembled around the bottom rather than the bottom being added to an otherwise completed structure. A number have only struts sloping downwards from the bentside liner, others have thin sides supported by triangular knees in the Italian manner, and still others have deep braces running obliquely across the case from the bentside to the spine and belly rail. The types of soundboard barring are at least as variable, with some examples barred exactly as in Ruckers harpsichords except for the use of a less massive 4' hitchpin rail, and others having transverse ribs extending right across the soundboard, occasionally but not invariably cut out under the bridges and occasionally even dividing the 4' hitch-pin rail into separate segments.

Examples of only two representative species survive in any quantity: the well-known English virginals of the mid- and late 17th century, with their characteristically vaulted lids (seen also in pictures of French virginals in the 16th and 17th centuries); and French harpsichords of the second half of the 17th century, almost all of which (in contrast to the majority of Flemish, Italian and English instruments of the period) have two manuals. Whether this latter fact is an accident of preservation is not clear; single-manual instruments are mentioned in inventories of the period and only a single-manual instrument is depicted by Mersenne in his *Harmonie universelle* (1636–7), but it remains true that only doubles survive in any quantity from France. All these are of the contrasting type with aligned keyboards.

The cases of these French harpsichords are generally made of walnut, although some have a spine made from pine. A characteristic feature is the application of a decorative scroll-sawn piece to the inside of the spine and the cheekpiece at each end of the keyboard, a piece resembling those found in the Italian instruments with thick cases and cypress linings intended to counterfeit the appearance of a thin-cased instrument in its outer case. The keyboards themselves are particularly elegant, the natural keys covered with ebony and the sharps usually made from solid ivory blocks. Instead of carved or cut-out arcades on the fronts of the natural keys, a recessed trefoil pattern is formed into the front of the key by deep, slanting cuts with a round gouge, a method of decoration also seen in some German and Spanish keyboards.

As in a Ruckers instrument, the backs of the lower-manual keys are guided by metal pins fitting into the slots of a wooden rack (see fig.8). The keys of the upper manual are, however, guided in a way unique to French instruments, a way that continued in use throughout the 17th and 18th centuries. Instead of pins placed between adjacent keys, each key has its own pin which fits in a narrow longitudinal slot cut through the key-lever near the back. These pins are set in the back rail of a key frame (resembling that which supports the lower manual) rather than in a plank like that of both Flemish and later English instruments.

Originally the range of these keyboards was almost invariably G'/B' to c''', occasionally with one or both of the two lowest sharps divided to permit sounding the missing accidentals. From the 18th century this range was sometimes enlarged by sacrificing the endblocks of the key-frames and the scroll-sawn cheekpiece liners to make room for a chromatic bass (sometimes omitting the $G\sharp'$) and a treble expansion to d'''.

Most 17th-century French harpsichords do not appear to have been painted. Their graceful walnut cases, sometimes decorated with marquetry, were simply varnished, as were their rather elaborate stands with six or more spiral legs and framing or stretchers placed above ball feet.

Information about this highly important part of the history of the harpsichord can be gleaned from written sources, as well as from the French instruments and a handful of English and German examples. Praetorius's illustrations to vol.ii of *Syntagma musicum* (1618; published in 1620 as *Theatrum instrumentorum*) show a harpsichord of this type, which seems to have had two 8' registers and one 4', although Praetorius's text states that four registers, including one tuned a 5th above the 8', were possible. Mersenne also mentioned the possibility of such a quint register, although his illustration shows only a single 8' and 4' with both rows of tuning pins set at the front edge of the wrest plank. Mersenne was concerned with the ways in which the harpsichord can produce changes in loudness and timbre, and stated that the instruments of his time could produce seven or eight different combinations of register. Seven combinations can be achieved on a three-register instrument; eight implies a buff stop used only with one of the registers when it was being played alone, or else a four-register instrument in which one register was tuned to a different pitch from the others in order to provide an equivalent to the Flemish transposing double (perhaps this was the actual function of the quint register); but Mersenne made no explicit statement on this matter.

Mersenne also mentioned instruments with two or even three keyboards. Most information on French two-manual instruments of the first half of the 17th century, however, must be derived from other sources, most notably a letter of 1648 from Pierre de la Barre, harpsichordist to Louis XIV (in the correspondence of Constantijn Huygens, ed. J. A. Worp, The Hague, 1911–17). In this letter La Barre distinguished between French and Flemish harpsichords on the basis of a recent invention that gave each keyboard of a French two-manual instrument its own set of unison strings, whereas on Flemish instruments the unison strings were shared by the two manuals. Although it is possible to interpret this as a reference to the Flemish transposing double with its single set of 8' strings, it may refer to a dogleg jack that causes the upper-manual 8' to sound from the lower manual as well whenever the upper-manual 8' was engaged. If this hypothesis is correct, the invention to which La Barre referred was the manual coupler by means of which the player has the choice of playing the upper-manual 8' register from the lower manual or not.

This simple and elegant device consists of equipping the lower-manual keys with small vertical pieces of wood that rise to the level of the underside of the upper-manual keys, and then allowing one of the two keyboards to be slid in and out of the instrument by rather less than a centimetre while the other is held in position. In one position, the vertical pieces of wood, called 'coupler dogs' (see fig.8), are located directly below the ends of the upper manual, so that when the keys of the lower manual are played the coupler dogs push upwards on the ends of the upper-manual keys, causing the upper-manual register to sound at the same time as the lower-manual registers. Thus, when the keyboards are in this position, the instrument functions much as if it had dogleg jacks. If, however, the upper keyboard is pulled outwards or the lower keyboard is pushed inwards, the coupler dogs are positioned beyond the ends of the upper-manual keys, so that the two keyboards are completely independent and may be used to produce simultaneous differences in timbre between the part played by the right hand and that played by the left, and the same note may even be doubled simultaneously by both hands. (This possibility was exploited in a typically French type of harpsichord piece termed the *pièce croisée*, the earliest extant examples of which were written by Louis Couperin, who died in 1661.)

The exact date when the manual coupler appeared is difficult to establish. La Barre's reference to a recent invention may well have to be taken with some scepticism, since Mersenne in 1636 had described 'little wedges of wood at the backs of the keys by means of which one can effect changes of registration', and it is difficult to imagine what else he might have been thinking of, even though the relevant passage seems concerned otherwise only with single-manual instruments.

In the 17th century it seems that coupling was effected by pulling the lower manual outwards; by the 18th century, however, the lower manual was fixed and the upper manual was pushed inwards. However, some 17th-century French double harpsichords were originally disposed without a coupler, but rather with a dogleg front register and two registers on the lower manual. Most such instruments were later altered by adding a coupler and removing the dogleg from the upper-manual jacks. There is also evidence that the dogleg register or independent upper register was sometimes a 4'. A notable surviving example is the 1693 Nicolas Blanchet double harpsichord in a private collection in Paris (see §4(i) below). It has a coupler and two 8' registers on the lower manual; all the upper-manual jacks are missing but they must have been of a 4' register.

With the creation of the coupler, the resources of the classic harpsichord of the 18th century were all available, at least in theory. An instrument with two independent manuals served by three registers (2 × 8', 1 × 4') can play all of the great harpsichord repertory; and although instruments with greater resources certainly existed before the middle of the 18th century, they must be regarded as somewhat exceptional.

(iii) England. The small group of surviving English harpsichords of the intermediate type include an oak instrument of 1622, which appears to have had three 8' registers of different timbres, and a round-tailed instrument made by Charles Haward in 1683 with two sets of 8' strings and originally with a row of close-plucking lute-stop jacks to produce a different timbre from one of them, much as on the 1537 Müller harpsichord. The earliest known dated two-manual English instrument (apart from an example bearing a somewhat doubtful date of 1623) was made by Joseph Tisseran in 1710 and has three registers – a dogleg 8', a lower-manual 8' and

9. Harpsichord by Thomas Hitchcock, London, c1725 (Victoria and Albert Museum, London)

a 4'; but by about 1725 the disposition that was later to become typical in England is found in an undated walnut instrument made by Thomas Hitchcock (fig.9). It has three sets of strings (2 × 8', 1 × 4') and four rows of jacks: a dogleg 8', the lower-manual 8' and 4' at the main gap at the back of the wrest plank, and a row of close-plucking lute-stop jacks set in a register that runs diagonally across the wrest plank near the 8' nut and plucks the same strings as the dogleg jacks.

Characteristically, the two rows of unison jacks are placed next to one another with the 4' at the back rather than between the 8' rows. This arrangement tends to reduce the contrast between the timbres of the two 8' registers by reducing the difference in the points at which their strings are plucked. This, in turn, improves the blending of the two unison registers when they are both engaged; and since they can never be heard singly in rapid succession owing to the presence of the dogleg, which requires the upper-manual 8' to be disengaged to hear the lower-manual 8' by itself, the lack of contrast in timbre between the two registers cannot be considered a defect. (This may also be the reason why a number of single-manual instruments from countries where the 4' jacks would be found between the 8' rows on a double-manual also have their 8' rows adjacent to one another.) On instruments with a manual coupler, the difference in timbre between the two unison stops may easily be exploited by the performer and is particularly advantageous in distinguishing between the two voices of *pièces croisées*. At the same time a pronounced difference in loudness between the two 8' registers, which might be desirable in voicing either a single-manual instrument or one with a dogleg, cannot be permitted, as the performance of *pièces croisées* requires a similar degree of loudness on each manual.

On instruments like the Hitchcock, the close-plucking lute stop (available only on the upper manual) provides a contrasting unison register that may be used in dialogue with the lower-manual 8', despite the presence of the dogleg unison register, since with the lute stop engaged the upper manual is not silenced when the dogleg register is disengaged. But, because the principal function of the second manual on a two-manual harpsichord was to permit contrasts in loudness, such an independent upper-manual stop was not a necessity on an instrument with dogleg jacks, and it did not appear on Flemish harpsichords until the 18th century (and then only on some of them).

An English development of little influence at the time but of considerable influence on harpsichords of the modern revival was the creation of a foot-operated mechanism for effecting changes of registration. According to Thomas Mace (*Musick's Monument*, 1676), the 'pedal' was a recent invention of John Haward of London. The instrument had four pedal-controlled registers (most probably two 8', a lute stop and a 4'), and the example owned by Mace also had a hand-operated buff stop. Nothing further is heard of pedal-controlled registers until the third quarter of the 18th century, when their primary function was that of producing crescendo effects rather than of changing registration in a framework of terrace dynamics, and Haward's idea was really taken up only when 'modern' harpsichords began to be made in the last years of the 19th century.

4. 18TH CENTURY.

(i) France. The history of harpsichord making from the last decade of the 17th century into the 18th is largely an account of the rather rapid replacement of the relatively thin-cased instruments of the kind described above by a national variant of the thick-cased, long-scale Ruckers design. Although a Louis Denis double of 1658 survives with a thick case and a long scale, the type did not become common until the 1690s. A Nicolas Blanchet double dated 1693, with an original range of G', B' to c''', has a pine case 15 mm thick with the surprisingly long scale of 36·2 cm; however, the case sides overlap the bottom and the moulding on the inside of the top edge of the case is in the 17th-century style. The 8' bridge is of the massive Flemish design (although the slope is on the front rather than the back), while the 4' bridge is Italianate with a moulding. From only 14 years later a large double harpsichord, a 1707 Nicolas Dumont, exists in original condition with a range of F' to e''', having all the characteristics of a mature 18th-century French instrument. The reason for this rather radical shift in building style seems to have been the preference of musicians for the tone of Ruckers instruments. At the turn of the century increasing numbers of Ruckers harpsichords were finding their way to France where they received French keyboards and actions. A normal Ruckers transposing double with the range of C/E to c''' on the upper manual could accommodate the range of G', B' to c''' without altering the string spacing on the bridge or the scale, simply by realigning the keyboards. A second choir of 8' strings would usually be added, and the number of registers would be reduced from four to three, giving the normal French disposition (see fig.8 above). Often an extra note was squeezed into the bass to provide a split Eb and two were added in the treble to extend the range to d'''. A less common type of transposer had chromatic basses, and such an instrument could be altered as above to a range of G' to c''' (see RUCKERS, fig.2). Almost as many Ruckers or Couchet harpsichords with French keyboards and actions, but with unaltered cases and soundboards, survive from the first quarter of the 18th century, as do original French instruments of the period, amply attesting to their popularity. This popularity continued throughout the century, but the demand for an increased range altered the purity of design of these early *ravalements* (see RAVALEMENT).

Three harpsichord makers of this early period who have left important surviving instruments are Dumont and Blanchet, already mentioned, and Pierre Donzelague. Nicolas Dumont was admitted to the Paris guild of instrument makers in 1675. In addition to the 1707 double by Dumont there exist two others dated 1697 (in the Paris Conservatoire collection) and 1704 (privately owned in Paris). The 1704 one was so thoroughly rebuilt in the late 18th century that its original plan is obscure. The earlier one, however, was beautifully rebuilt in 1789 by Pascal Taskin and it is possible to determine its original design: a thick-cased long-scaled instrument with a range of G'/B' to c''', or at most G' to c'''; this shows that the period between the 17th-century small instrument and the large 18th-century model is shorter than has been supposed. Nicolas Blanchet, who was admitted to the guild in 1689, founded the longest and most important dynasty of Parisian harpsichord makers, including his son François Etienne (i), grandson François Etienne (ii) and Taskin. Seven harpsichords, three spinets and at least seven rebuilds of Flemish instruments by the Blanchets are known to survive. Pierre Donzelague went to Lyons from Aix-en-Provence in 1688 and became well known there for his work. There are two large and beautifully made double harpsichords by him: one in a London private collection, dated 1711, the other dated 1716, in the Musée des Arts Décoratifs, Lyons. They are the earliest-known French harpsichords with the full compass of F' to f'''. The majority of 18th-century French harpsichord makers were of the Parisian school, but there was a distinct though similar school in Lyons. 18th-century harpsichords from other parts of France are rare, and most of them are either archaic or are the occasional work of an artisan of another craft such as organ building.

Except for their size, the construction of these early 18th-century harpsichords was very similar to that of Ruckers. The framing was a bit heavier, especially the upper level braces which were more numerous. A horizontal brace was glued to the back edges of the upper belly rail in two Blanchet harpsichords of 1730 and 1733. This brace or 'T' section enormously stiffened the belly rail, and braces were run from it to the treble of the bentside strengthening this critical point. In some instruments the upper braces are set on edge and notched to the liners rather than lying flat under them. The lower braces of the 1707 Dumont have uprights or knees attached to their ends which are notched to the liners. Case sides were sometimes of pine rather than poplar which was invariably used by Ruckers. It should be noted that bentsides were always of poplar, and later lime, pine being difficult to wet-bend. Early in the century, the bentsides assumed a characteristic 18th-century shape with the curve concentrated in the treble and the remainder towards the tail, straight. The 1693 Nicolas Blanchet has a very incurved and parabolic bentside, whereas an undated Nicolas Blanchet of the first quarter of the 18th century (perhaps in the first decade, since its case sides overlap the bottom) has a bentside only slightly so. The bentside of the 1707 Dumont is straight for half its length and those of the 1730 and 1733 Blanchets are straight for almost two thirds of their lengths. This shape continued in use in the Blanchet–Taskin workshop and was also used by Henri Hemsch and others; parabolic bentsides occur only occasionally later in the century.

The soundboard barring, especially in the first half of the century, was not nearly so standardized as Ruckers barring. The 1707 Dumont and 1733 Blanchet lack cut-off bars, and the ribs perpendicular to the spine extend to the 4′ hitch-pin rail. The 1730 Blanchet has a normal cut-off bar but, like the 1707 Dumont, it has two ribs crossing the 8′ section of the soundboard around the mid-section and tenor, and a third approaches the bass of the 8′ bridge from the 4′ hitch-pin rail. Ribs that cross the 8′ bridge or approach it from either the 4′ hitch-pin rail or bentside liner continued in use until mid-century. An Antoine Vater 1738 double and a 1746 François Blanchet have curved cut-off bars following the 4′ bridge; the latter is wide and flat like a smaller 4′ hitch-pin rail. The 1738 Vater and a 1742 Louis Bellot have ribs parallel to the spine crossing both bridges. All 18th-century French ribs observed were cut out where they passed under bridges.

The standard range from early in the century was F' to e''', but G' to e''' was not uncommon. This is strange as the music of the period almost never exceeds the G' to d''' range of the larger Ruckers type. The F' was used in one piece each by Rameau and François Couperin in their solo harpsichord works, but it was not in general use until the 1740s. Neither Couperin nor Rameau

employed e''' in their solo works. Dagincour used it in 1733 (*Pièces de clavecin*), but it was not often found until the F' was commonly written. The e''' seems to have fulfilled a French sense of order: the keyboards were balanced with one natural after a group of sharps at each end. G' to e''' instruments, such as the 1742 Louis Bellot and a 1748 Johannes Goermans, continued to be made almost to mid-century. During the 1720s some of the short-octave Ruckers conversions had chromatic basses to G' (often without $G\sharp'$) crowded into the existing cases.

The keyboards of these instruments continued the design of the previous century with a few stylistic changes. Fruitwood arcades replaced the carved trefoils on the key fronts, and the sharps, instead of being solid ivory or bone, were composed of a thin bone slip glued to a black stained block. In better workshops, such as that of the Blanchets, the sharps were tapered both in height and width, and the key-levers, seldom leaded, were individually carved to balance. The span of an octave remained small, averaging about 15·9 cm. The wooden jackslides and guides were covered with punched leather which became the bearing surface, and the accurately made jacks were slightly tapered in width and thickness, fitting the slide only when at rest. These actions were light, quiet and repeated very quickly. The disposition of an 8′ and 4′ register on the lower manual, coupler, and an 8′ on the upper, with the 4′ between the 8′s and the lower 8′ plucking the longer string, seems to have been absolutely standard until the third quarter of the century.

In the 1740s the Blanchets' relationship with the court began, and shortly after the middle of the century their firm became 'facteur des clavessins du Roi'. During this time, besides their maintenance work for the court, they became increasingly occupied with the rebuilding of Flemish harpsichords into large five-octave French instruments. Two other families should be mentioned: Johannes (Jean) Goermans (1703–77) and his son Jacques Goermans (c1740–89); and the brothers Henri and Guillaume Hemsch. About six harpsichords survive from each family, and five of Henri Hemsch's date from the decade 1751–61, a remarkable survival rate. Mid-century harpsichords continued the style of the earlier ones. Framing became a bit heavier and more sophisticated, the sides were a little heavier and Blanchet began to taper their thickness from the keyboard end towards the tail. Lime and pine were preferred to poplar. Soundboard barring became less experimental and settled into the Ruckers pattern. An f''' was added to the treble but later than musicians asked for it. A 1754 Hemsch ends with e''', and although a 1756 Hemsch has the f''' it may have been added later, as was often done to earlier instruments. 1758 Blanchet keyboards in a 1680 Couchet clearly show the addition of the f''' while the keyboards were being made.

In 1766 Pascal Taskin inherited the Blanchet workshop and from then on dominated Parisian harpsichord making; only a few single examples of other late makers survive. Taskin continued the Blanchet tradition using and refining their plan. The framing, ribbing and 4′ hitch-pin rail were beautifully rounded to save weight without losing strength. He increased the taper of the sides and returned to the curved cut-off bar. The action of his instruments was even more refined than that of his predecessors.

After the mid-century several additions to the standard disposition began to appear. Although common on Ruckers instruments, the buff stop was rare in France in the first half of the 18th century. Neither the 1746 Blanchet nor the 1754 Hemsch originally had one. When it did come into use, it became almost universal, and double buff stops (which can buff either 8′ string) were not unusual.

The three-register disposition sufficed on French instruments until the 1760s, when a fourth register having jacks fitted with plectra of soft buff leather was added behind the other three as a special solo stop. This addition is credited to Taskin in various writings of the period, although it is also ascribed to the organist and composer Claude-Bénigne Balbastre (who is known to have had a harpsichord fitted with *peau de buffle* plectra in 1770) and to a certain 'M. de l'Aine', who in 1769 announced an instrument fitted with leather plectra.

In the late 1750s French harpsichords began to be equipped with a variety of foot- or knee-operated devices for producing crescendo effects and for changing registers without taking the hands from the keyboard. An instrument with a mechanism of this type was offered for sale by one Wittman (or Wetman) in 1758, and several other makers subsequently announced mechanisms of their own. The only examples to survive in any number are made by Taskin and Joachim Swanen, and employ a system (reportedly devised by Taskin in 1768) activated by five or six pommels that can be raised or lowered by the action of the knees. When raised, three of these act to disengage, respectively, the lower-manual 8′, the 4′ and the *peau de buffle* registers; a fourth pommel raises the *peau de buffle* jacks when they are not in use in order to keep the touch as light as possible; a fifth pommel, when gradually raised, disengages first the 4′, then the lower-manual 8′ and then the upper-manual 8′, permitting a gradual decrescendo from the *forte* of all registers sounding at once to the *pianissimo* of the *peau de buffle* alone; an additional sixth pommel, found on a small number of instruments, acts to slide the upper manual inwards, thereby coupling it to the lower manual so that on these harpsichords the only register to be controlled by hand is the buff stop. It should be emphasized that these devices came into being before the piano achieved any popularity in France, and accordingly, they do not represent an attempt to meet the challenge of the piano with its inherent ability to produce dynamic nuance; rather, they appear to have been an independent manifestation of the interest in dynamic expression that had led to the invention of the piano in the closing years of the 17th century.

10. Harpsichord by Pascal Taskin, Paris, 1769 (Russell Collection, University of Edinburgh); see also fig.20

A great portion of the energies of late French harp-sichord makers appears to have gone into the massive rebuilding of older harpsichords, especially those of the Ruckers family. Since a rebuilt Ruckers harpsichord was worth several times as much as a new instrument in 18th-century Paris, such a diversion of the makers' efforts from building new instruments was clearly justified on a financial basis and it led not only to the most elaborate sort of rebuilding, including the conversion of narrow-range single-manual instruments to wide-range doubles and the building of new harpsichords around the sound-boards of old virginals, but also to outright faking of new instruments to make them look like rebuilds (*see* FORGERY, §1). But as the rebuilding was intended to update earlier instruments to current musical require-ments and not to preserve their antique qualities, the sound of a Ruckers harpsichord rebuilt by Taskin repre-sents 18th-century Paris rather than 17th-century Antwerp.

Blanchet and Taskin were famous for their work in this vein, and they applied to it all the ingenuity and craftsmanship found in the instruments they built in their own names, producing neither crude enlargements in which extra notes are crammed into the bass (in effect sliding the keyboard towards the treble, thereby disas-trously shortening the scaling) nor such dubious expe-

dients as the jointing of extensions on to the wrest plank and belly rail. Rather, they used a wide variety of slight-ly differing techniques, determined by the nature of the original instrument. Of these, the most subtle and ingenious involved rebuilding the spine, in addition to the usual extending of the bentside and bridges and replacement of the cheekpiece, wrest plank and belly rail with new ones of appropriate length. The front of the original spine was cut off at the belly rail and the top was cut down to the level of the soundboard. A tapered layer of new wood of the same size would then be added on the outside of the cut-down original spine; then a wholly new spine of the same height as the rest of the case, and long enough to reach the front of the instrument, would be glued on to the outside of the tapered piece. The result was simultaneously to provide more room at the front of the instrument for additional bass keys and to rotate the entire body of the instrument anti-clockwise with respect to the strings. This rotation, in turn, had the effect of lengthening the scaling to com-pensate for the shortening produced by the addition of the new notes in the bass.

The plan of the average 18th-century French harpsi-chord more nearly follows that of the chromatic rather than the short-octave Ruckers transposer. This design had shorter tenor scaling to keep the tailpiece from becoming too wide in a wider instrument of the same length. The French tonal ideal around 1700 was that of Ruckers, but making larger instruments resulted in a grander and smoother tone. Although the 'presence' and immediacy of a small instrument were lost, the sound was no less transparent. As the century passed, the tone grew more complex and less direct; nevertheless even the late Taskins never lost the balance between attack and sustaining power that permits cleanness of articulation. The declamatory style of French keyboard music from the 17th century to the Rococo period required this sensitivity to articulation, and their harpsichords met the demand well.

Whether new or rebuilt, a French 18th-century harpsichord was often a major piece of decorative furniture. The soundboards were painted with flowers in a more sophisticated style than the Flemish, the cases were painted or lacquered in any of a variety of fashionable styles, and the instruments were equipped with elaborate six-, seven- or eight-legged bases often carved and gilded in one of the royal styles. Simpler instruments were painted in one or two colours, panelled with gold bands and mouldings and fitted with less elaborate bases but still in one of the royal styles (see fig.10). Despite the use of walnut and marquetry in 17th-century harpsichords, and the superb quality of veneered furniture in 18th-century France, French harpsichords seem never to have been veneered.

(ii) England. In England the standard 18th-century national type seems to have crystallized in the work of Hermann Tabel (*d* 1738), a builder, trained in Antwerp, who moved to London in about 1700. Both of the makers whose firms dominated English harpsichord building in the 18th century, Burkat Shudi (1702–73) and Jacob Kirckman (1710–92), worked in Tabel's shop and both built instruments strikingly like the sole surviving example of Tabel's work, a double-manual harpsichord dated 1721 (see fig.13).

A typical Shudi or Kirckman double has a 2 × 8', 1 × 4' disposition, with a dogleg jack and a row of lute-stop jacks controlled by the upper manual and a buff stop that on a Shudi acts on the lower-manual 8' strings, and on a Kirckman on the dogleg 8' strings (see fig.12). Their cases are made of oak, and are veneered in walnut with sycamore in early examples and mahogany with satinwood in later ones. The instrument is supported on a trestle stand with four legs, which vary throughout the 18th century from turned George II to square Chippendale; occasional special examples have rather ungraceful cabriole legs curving outwards from the level of the trestle's lower stretchers. The soundboards are not decorated with paintings, and Shudi soundboards do not have a gilded metal rose; the barring and case bracing are rather like those of a Ruckers harpsichord. Like the bottom, all the braces are pine. The lower ones are not as tall as in a Ruckers instrument; there are only two transverse bottom braces in addition to the lower belly rail, but these are supplemented by a diagonal brace running along the bottom from the intersection of the rear brace and the bentside to the centre of the forward brace. In addition, there are two longitudinal braces running upwards from the front bottom brace to the upper belly rail. The upper-level braces are more numerous than on a Ruckers harpsichord, where there are three set nearly parallel to one another and at a slightly oblique angle

to the spine. In a Kirckman or Shudi harpsichord there are four such braces which, however, are set vertically rather than flat, so that they bear on the face of the lining rather than merely being nailed to its underside. These four are supplemented by a fifth, heavier one, that passes from the bentside to the upper belly rail in the crucial treble area. The construction of a single-manual Kirckman or Shudi is identical with that of a double, except that while Shudi's singles often include a lute stop Kirckman's singles seldom have one. Occasional examples of singles by both makers lack the 4' as well.

Except in matters of decoration, these instruments changed little throughout the century, except for a shift in the plucking-points of Shudi harpsichords after 1770 that produces a rounder and less incisive tone in the later instruments (a change in line with the occasional substitution of leather for quill plectra in the lower-manual 8' jacks), and the addition of the pedal-operated mechanisms described below.

Tabel's five-octave *F'* to *f'''* keyboard had lacked the *F♯'* (presumably for reasons of visual symmetry), and Kirckman and Shudi, like other English builders, followed this practice until about 1780, when the *F♯'* was included as a matter of course.

A minor difference between Shudi and Kirckman harpsichords concerns the arrangement of the stop-knobs in two-manual instruments. On Shudi double-manual harpsichords the three stop-knobs at the left side of the nameboard control (from left to right) the lute stop, the 4' and the buff stop, whereas in a Kirckman the order is buff stop, lute stop and 4'; both have 8' stops located at the right side of the nameboard with the dogleg controlled by the left-hand knob and the lower manual 8' controlled by the right-hand knob. As a result of this arrangement, one can rapidly engage whichever of the unison stops may temporarily have been disengaged simply by squeezing the knobs together. Although Kirckman is known only once (1772) to have built an instrument with a range greater than five octaves (a double with a range of *F'* to *c''''*), Shudi regularly made instruments with a range of *C'* to *f'''*, of which 12 dating from 1765 to 1782 have survived.

The tone of a Kirckman or Shudi harpsichord is enormously rich and powerful. As is true of many English and Hamburg harpsichords made in the second half of the 18th century – that is, after the great age of harpsichord composition – the sound of these instruments sometimes tends to call attention to itself rather than merely serving as a vehicle for projecting the music, a quality that may in abstract terms be viewed as a defect despite its splendour.

Beginning no later than the early 1760s, English harpsichords were customarily fitted with crescendo devices. The so-called MACHINE STOP disengages the 4' register and then the front 8' register as a pedal is depressed (on double-manual instruments, since the disengagement of the front 8' register would silence the upper manual, it simultaneously engages the lute stop) thus when the pedal is fully depressed the registration on the upper manual of dogleg 8' is replaced by lute stop, and that on the lower of dogleg 8', lower-manual 8' and 4' by lower-manual 8' alone. In both single- and double-manual instruments, the machine stop can be disengaged when desired to permit normal hand-stop operation. By 1766, the machine stop was supplemented by a second crescendo device, the SWELL, which enabled the performer to open either a section of the

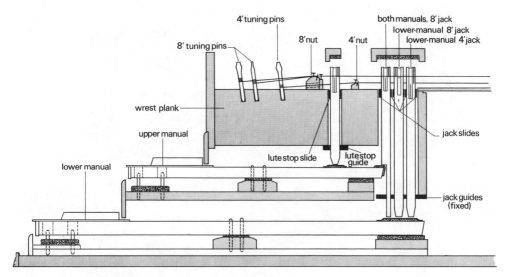

12. *English two-manual harpsichord action, 18th century*

13. *Harpsichord by Hermann Tabel, London, 1721 (Warwickshire Museum, Warwick)*

14. *Harpsichord by Shudi and Broadwood, London, 1775, showing the swell in the open position (Gesellschaft der Musikfreunde, Vienna, on loan to the Kunsthistorisches Museum, Vienna); for a further illustration see* KIRCKMAN, *fig.1*

harpsichord's lid (if not already raised) or a series of louvres covering the soundboard (see fig.14). The two devices used in conjunction with one another produce a surprisingly wide and effective crescendo, beginning with the *pianissimo* of the lower-manual 8' alone with the lid or louvres closed, followed by the successive addition of the front 8' and the 4' and finally the gradual opening of lid or louvres to permit the *fortissimo* of the full harpsichord.

(iii) Italy. To organize the history of instruments into centuries is to risk distorting the view by introducing divisions where perhaps none existed. There is, however, some justification for treating the 16th and 17th centuries separately, as the history of Italian harpsichords is not a 'virtually seamless continuum' (Ripin, 1979, p.34). As Barnes justly noted (in Ripin, 1971, p.9), the impression of uniformity has been conferred by the many alterations of 16th-century instruments to make them conform to the needs of the 17th and 18th centuries.

One detail already noted is the prevalence in the 16th century of the 1 × 8', 1 × 8', 1 × 4' dispositions. These seem to have given way at the beginning of the 17th century to the 2 × 8' disposition, which remained the most common until Italian harpsichords ceased being

made. The latest known Italian harpsichord was made by Sodi of Florence in 1792. Most of the 1 × 8', 1 × 4' harpsichords were made in Venice, yet after the last known instruments by Celestini (1610) there is little sign of harpsichord making in Venice in the 17th century. Such a decline after the achievements of the 16th century is curious but unexplained.

Some harpsichords were made with a 3 × 8' disposition, an arrangement which is possible only with two soundboard bridges. One bridge, nearest the bentside, carried a set of iron strings; the other two sets were of brass wire carried on a second bridge. Inventories from the 1540s onwards include harpsichords with three registers; these might well have been 3 × 8' instruments, but the possibility of 2 × 8', 1 × 4' cannot be ruled out, although it is less likely.

To give detailed descriptions of harpsichord construction in the 17th and 18th centuries would be to repeat much of the information given for the 16th century. It can be noted, however, that many of the later instruments were more simply decorated than the 16th-century harpsichords: soundboards often did not have a rose, keyboards lacked fine embellishments, and elaborate inlay work on cases is hardly to be found.

Towards the middle of the 17th century a *C/E* to *f'''* compass became less common, and a *C/E* to *c'''* com-ass more common. Towards the end of the 17th century a range of *G'*, *A'* to *c'''* was widely used, and in the 18th century a five-octave compass was required as the Cresci of 1778 shows: *F'* to *f'''*, *g'''* (in the Germanisches Nationalmuseum, Nuremberg). However, the view that Italian harpsichords were gradually widened in range to meet the latest demands of music is not entirely acceptable. The increase of the keyboard range from *C/C* down to *G'* (as shown by several 17th-century *G'*, *A'* to *c'''* keyboards) might seem to support this idea. However, a low *G'* was probably required from harpsichords as early as 1538 (as noted above for the Dominicus Pisaurensis harpsichord in the Medici inventory). The increasing frequency of *C/E* to *c'''* compasses in the 17th century in preference to the *C/E* to *f'''* represents a reduction in range. Although the 16th-century musical practices that required the use of keyboards to *f'''* are not well understood, it seems that they changed at some time in the 17th century so that harpsichords with a *C/E* to *c'''* compass were adequate. Paradoxically, the higher notes were required again later, and there are examples of 17th-century harpsichords which were originally *G'*, *A'* to *c'''* having been altered to *C* to *f'''* (see Van der Meer, 1968). It has to be concluded that no single idea is sufficient to explain this variety of keyboard ranges other than the rather uninformatively simple (but nevertheless true) statement that the use made of harpsichords changed.

The *G'/B'* to *c'''* compass which was practically a standard range for French instruments in the 17th century was less well known in Italy. Surviving instruments would indicate that a chromatic bass octave to *C* was never common in Italy. Russell (1959, p.29) reported that an inventory of Cardinal Ottoboni's instruments listed eight harpsichords with a chromatic bass octave, but it seems unlikely that this is correct. The term used to describe the bass octave, *ottava stesa* (literally, 'extended octave'), was used quite generally to judge from the Medici inventory (Gai, 1969, pp.6–14) and probably referred to several types of (unaltered) bass octave.

Whereas 16th-century harpsichords were normally made with thin case sides and light mouldings and kept in separate decorated cases, another style of construction was introduced in the 17th century: a thick-cased, painted harpsichord, possibly with cypress veneer and mouldings around the inside edge above the soundboard, so that it seemed as if an instrument were inside a separate outer case. The view has arisen that in the 16th century harpsichords were taken out of their cases and placed on tables in order to be played, but that by the beginning of the 17th century this was no longer the practice (see Hubbard, 1965, p.19; Henkel, *Beiträge*, 1979, p.91). However, it is quite clear that some of the earliest harpsichords have original outer cases in which the instruments were intended to remain while they were played, since a small door was made in the cheek of the outer case to give access to register knobs (see fig.3 above). Indeed, decorated outer cases were pieces of furniture and intended to be seen as the harpsichords were played; the idea that harpsichords were taken out of their cases to be played has probably been overstated.

Few makers seem to have gone to the trouble to provide means of changing the registers in the 17th and 18th centuries; clearly, contrasts of register or volume were not required. A few harpsichords had a single row of jacks with two tongues (one plucking left, the other right) so that it was physically impossible to disengage one register. On the other hand it seems that the 16th

century 1 × 8', 1 × 4' harpsichords were always equipped with small knobs for engaging or disengaging the registers.

Some two-manual harpsichords were made by Italians. The 1690 harpsichord attributable to Cristofori (in the Paris Conservatoire) and a harpsichord of c1650 (in the Germanisches Nationalmuseum, Nuremberg) each have a 2 × 8', 1 × 4' disposition. The keyboards have no coupler and the 4' is on the upper manual. A few three-manual harpsichords are known, but some are alterations or fakes (*see* FORGERY, §1).

Several harpsichords were made with split sharps in order to provide accidentals not normally available in mean-tone tunings. One such (in the Russell Collection, Edinburgh) had an original compass of *C/E* to *f'''* with a BROKEN OCTAVE (i.e. *F♯* and *G♯* as split sharps in the bass octave) and the extra accidentals *d♯*, *a♭*, *d♯'*, *a♭'* and *d♯"*.

Although many Italian harpsichords survive, the records provided by inventories can fill some of the lacunae. Naples was important as a centre of keyboard composition in the 16th century, yet there are hardly any surviving Neapolitan harpsichords. Florentine archives give evidence that harpsichords were indeed made there, though no exact details are documented. There are several references to instruments with *ottava bassa* but whether this should be identified with a separate register (with its own bridge) at 16' pitch is not clear. However, the length of a Zenti harpsichord described in the Medici inventory (see Gai, 1969, p.6) at about 3·25 metres long leaves little doubt that *ottava bassa* could refer to some arrangement at an octave lower than 8' pitch.

Recent research on harpsichords of all countries has attempted to elucidate the ways in which instruments were strung, that is, not only with which type of wire, but also the sizes of the wire used. Numbers indicating the gauge of wire to be used have been found on several Italian instruments of the late 17th or early 18th century. O'Brien (1981) has argued that the tension of the strings of several harpsichords was closely similar even though they were constructed by different makers. It seems possible, therefore, to assume the existence of a tradition in stringing Italian harpsichords rather than simply ascribing the choice of wire sizes to an individual's preference. Hubbard (1965, p.9) supposed that the apparently light construction of Italian harpsichords required strings having less tension than in other countries. However, the evidence collected of gauge numbers and wire sizes shows that this view is mistaken. Italian string tensions were comparable with harpsichords from other countries (see O'Brien, 1981). They were, however, a little lighter in the treble, resulting mostly from the use of brass scales which are shorter than iron scales. The distinction which Hubbard (1965, p.9) makes between thin-cased harpsichords being more lightly strung than thick-cased ones is not borne out by the evidence of gauge numbers (see Wraight, 1982).

The alteration of harpsichords forms an important part of the history of Italian instruments: without the alterations, the harpsichords would have had a more limited musical use and might therefore have been discarded. A distinction should be made between alterations which kept a harpsichord in use and the fakes resulting from the assembly of various parts, which Franciolini practised at the turn of this century (see Ripin, 1974). A harpsichord made by Dominicus Pisaurensis in 1554 (not

1553; now in the Paris Conservatoire) illustrates several features of alterations carried out in the 17th and 18th centuries. The harpsichord had originally a C/E to c''' compass and a $1 \times 8'$, $1 \times 4'$ disposition. Cristofori can be identified with some confidence as the rebuilder who made new bridges for a $2 \times 8'$ disposition and extended the keyboard to d''''. These alterations illustrate the demise of the use of the 4' register in the 17th century and the need for an increased keyboard range. Although the scale that Cristofori would have inherited from the existing 8' bridges would have been 29 cm at c'' (a scale only 5 mm longer than that which he used in some of his own instruments; the original scale was 27·5 cm at c''), he actually chose a shorter scale of 26 cm. It seems likely that the scales of about 25 cm which occur at the end of the 17th century were intended for brass wire and would sound at about $a' = 440$ Hz.

It would seem that several instruments now in museums were repaired or rebuilt by Cristofori, and the 1554 Dominicus Pisaurensis harpsichord may have been the one referred to in a bill presented by Cristofori dated 10 February 1693 (quoted in Russell, 1959, p.129): 'For rebuilding a *cembalo* by Domenico of Pesaro . . . including remaking the keyboard and bridges'. Cristofori is perhaps best known as the inventor of a piano mechanism; in 1713 he took over the care of Prince Ferdinando de' Medici's instrument collection in Florence. By about this time he had already made several instruments of novel character: a *virginal* of oval shape with $2 \times 8'$, a transverse harpsichord resembling a large wing-shaped spinet, and a harpsichord with 8', 4' and 2'. Examples of all these are in the Musikinstrumenten-Museum, Leipzig.

It has already been suggested that Venetian instrument making was in the forefront in the 16th century. The point has not often been made that the Italian peninsula was divided into different areas of political influence when these harpsichords were made. Thus, the use of the term 'Italian' to refer to all these different areas may be a misleading anachronism, and it remains to be examined how far the instrument-making traditions were different from each other in the various parts of the present geographical entity of Italy.

(iv) Germany and other European countries. Compared to the number of surviving 18th-century harpsichords from Italy, France, England and the Low Countries, there are progressively fewer from Germany, Scandinavia, Portugal and Spain, and hence progressively less information is available concerning the character and development of the instrument in these areas. This is specially regrettable since Germany and Spain in particular produced so much harpsichord music of interest. Moreover, Germany produced at least two distinct schools of harpsichord making in the 18th century, of which only one – the Hamburg school – is represented by an appreciable number of surviving examples (see fig.15).

The Hamburg school included a substantial number of builders, of which the members of the Hass and Fleischer families are the most notable. The earliest surviving Hamburg instrument, a single, built in 1710 by J. C. Fleischer, already has all the basic characteristics of this school, the products of which, among all 18th-century harpsichords, seem most clearly to derive from the intermediate type. Flemish influence is evident only in the use of softwood for the case and in the typical north European 18th-century harpsichord scaling of 34

cm. The instrument has the round tail typical of Hamburg harpsichords, and its case bracing is accomplished by full-depth members crossing the case from the bentside to the spine with no upper-level bracing. Intermediate-type influence is also evident in the coupling system used on Hamburg two-manual instruments, in which the lower manual is moved while the upper one remains fixed. In these instruments, however, coupling is accomplished in an unusual fashion. Short doglegs are provided for the upper-manual 8' jack and, when the lower manual is pushed inwards, small padded blocks on the lower-manual keys are positioned under the doglegs so that the upper-manual jacks are then lifted by the lower-manual keys without the upper-manual keys having to be moved as well.

The harpsichords of the Hass family are noted for their complex dispositions and are the only 18th-century instruments known to include with any regularity a 16' register. Two of the three surviving instruments so provided also have a 2' register in addition to the 16', 4' and two 8' registers. (One, of about 1770, is at Yale University, and the other, dated 1740, is in the Puyana Collection, Paris; there is also a Hass harpsichord of 1723 in the Musikhistorisk Museum, Copenhagen, with three sets of 8' strings plus a 4' set.) No two of the three instruments with a 16' register are exactly alike, but their 16' strings are arranged in the same ingenious fashion. Inside the case a low curving rim is attached to the deep frame members and follows the line that the bentside of a normal instrument would take. This rim serves as hitch-pin rail for the 8' strings. Beyond it and at a slightly higher level there is a completely separate soundboard for the 16' bridge, and the 16' strings are then hitched to the pins driven into the lining of the bentside along the far edge of this separate soundboard. As a result, the 16' bridge does not have to be pierced to permit the 8' strings to be hitched at the bentside, and the layout of the 8' and 4' strings, which still comprise the basic core of the harpsichord, is undisturbed. The addition of this extra soundboard to an already full-size instrument means that such a harpsichord may exceed 275 cm in length.

The surviving instrument with a 16' stop but without a 2' stop, which was made by Hieronymus Albrecht Hass in 1734, is equipped with a close-plucking lute stop (arranged like that on an English harpsichord to pluck the same string as the regular upper-manual 8') as well as buff stops on both the lower-manual 8' and the 16' but the next surviving instrument by this maker, built in 1740, the only unquestionably genuine three-manual harpsichord still in existence, manages to include a 2' stop as well. The upper two manuals of this instrument provide the same resources as an 18th-century English double-manual harpsichord: a lute stop on the upper manual, a dogleg 8' register played by both the upper and the middle manuals, and a 4' and a second 8' playable on the middle manual only. The doglegs in this instance reach down to the middle manual, and there is no coupler between these two keyboards. The 16' and the 2' are confined to the lowest manual, which (like the keyboards of some chamber organs) can be pushed entirely into the case like a drawer for playing on only the 8' and 4' registers, can be pulled forward part of the way so as to play the 16' and 2' by themselves, or further forward to permit all the registers except the lute stop to sound at once from the lowest manual.

This arrangement is certainly the most useful possible way in which to include the 16' and 2' stops if they are

5. Harpsichord by Christian Zell, Hamburg, 1728 (Museum für Kunst und Gewerbe, Hamburg)

be included at all. The problem with the 16' stop, even on an instrument like this (in which the 16' strings have their own bridge permitting them to be of adequate length and preventing their loading down the 8' bridge), is that although the 16' lends enormous solidity and gravity to the bass it tends to produce an undesirable thickening of the texture and a possible effect of downward transposition by an octave when engaged to double all the musical lines at the lower octave. The 2' seems to have been added primarily to brighten an ensemble already made too dark or muddy by the inclusion of a 16' stop; so the two belong together and may properly be isolated on a manual of their own. When this is done, the left hand can play on this lowest keyboard while the right hand plays on the middle manual. With the two manuals coupled, the 16' and 2' can thus strengthen the bass without thickening the texture by unnecessary doubling of the parts played by the right hand. Moreover, by pulling the lower manual only partly out so that it will not be coupled to engage the middle manual, the 16' stop becomes available as a solo register either to be used in contrast to the tutti of two 8' registers and a 4' on the middle manual, or in dialogue with the lute stop on the upper manual or the back 8' on the middle manual.

The remaining Hass instrument equipped with a 16' stop has only two keyboards, but compensates for this by having two rows of 2' jacks (both playing the same strings), one on the upper manual and one on the lower. This instrument bears the signature of H. A. Hass's son Johann Adolph, and a date of 1710, at which time the older Hass was only 21, so that his son could not possibly have made the instrument. Additionally, the fact that the instrument has a fully chromatic F' to f''' keyboard (rather than the G' to d''' of 1734, or the F' to f''' – lacking the low $F\sharp'$ – of the 1740 triple) suggests that it was probably made closer to 1750 than to 1710. As on the 1734 double, buff stops are provided for the lower-manual 8' and the 16', and the lower-manual 2' – like that on the 1740 triple – extends only from F' to c''. This curtailment is necessary because, even with the narrow jackslides used on these instruments, the gap between the wrest plank and the belly rail required for five slides (and thus the minimum distance between the 2' nut and 2' bridge) must be so wide that no string stretched across it could be tuned appreciably higher than the c'''' equivalent to c'' at 2' pitch. This also explains why the sixth slide carrying the jacks of the upper-manual 2' on the (incorrectly dated) 1710 instrument has to be ended even earlier and, in fact, goes only to b.

The ingenuity of these instruments is matched by the care and craftsmanship with which they were made: even the tops of the jacks, for example, are finished with a small 45° bevel on each of the upper corners. The keys are often covered with tortoise-shell, and the painted or lacquered décor is correspondingly elaborate, chinoiserie being the most common style.

In German harpsichords the increase in compass proceeded in a slightly different manner from that of the French. The G'/B' short octave occurs only rarely in German harpsichords (e.g. a single-manual instrument

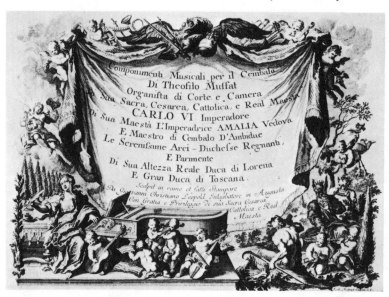

16. Title-page of
'Componimenti musica
(c1739) by Gottlieb
Muffat

by Christian Vater of Hanover, dated 1738); other examples descending below *C* are either fully chromatic from *G'* or *F'*, possibly omitting *G♯'* or *F♯'*, as in the harpsichords by Michael Mietke at Schloss Charlottenburg. The range was expanded downwards to *F'* and upwards to *d'''* almost simultaneously, though at least three surviving instruments with a *C* to *d'''* compass date from the two succeeding decades. The five-octave *F'* to *f'''* compass typical of harpsichords of the second half of the 18th century is found as early as 1722 in a Saxon instrument (by Johann Heinrich Gräbner of Dresden, now at the Villa Bertramka, Prague; a transposing instrument, its keyboard can be shifted down a semitone). But the earliest surviving Hamburg example with such a range is dated 1740 (Puyana Collection, Paris). It is interesting to compare this progression with that found in datable German harpsichord music from before 1750. The 12 suites published by Johann Mattheson in 1714 keep within a *C* to *c'''* compass. Much of J. S. Bach's music also fits within such a range, but a number of his later works ascend to *d'''*, as, for instance, the partitas in C minor (BWV826, published in 1727) and G major (BWV829, published in 1730). Handel's first collection of suites, issued in 1720, requires a *G'* to *c'''* compass, while the second collection of 1733 ascends to *d'''*. Gottlieb Muffat's *Componimenti musicali* (Augsburg, *c*1739) demands the low *F'* but does not rise above *c'''*. Bach's French Overture (BWV831), published in its definitive B minor form in the second part of the *Clavier-Übung* (1734), regularly descends to *G'* but avoids the *F♯'* which would result from the literal transposition of the earlier C minor version of this dance suite. The fourth part of the *Clavier-Übung* (*c*1742), the famous Goldberg Variations (BWV988), also ranges over a *G'* to *d'''* compass. But C. P. E. Bach in his two sets of sonatas *per il cembalo*, the 'Prussian' (WQ48, published in 1742) and the 'Württemberg' (WQ49, published in 1744), wrote for a *G'* to *e'''* compass.

The sound of the Hamburg harpsichords does not usually fulfil the expectations raised by the ingenuity and craftsmanship manifested in their design and construction. Their tone is exceedingly bright and penetrating,

and the upper harmonics seem to sustain rather longe than on other instruments of the 18th century. As a resul the sound lacks some of the transparency of other 18th century instruments, a characteristic that is intensifie in the examples with a 16' stop, where the sub-octav doubling tends to make the musical texture even mor opaque. Similarly, the addition of the 2' stop, whil brightening the tone and increasing pitch definition i the extreme bass, only contributes to the total thicknes when it is used in performance. Both of these stops (an to some extent the entire concept of harpsichord soun apparent in these instruments) reflect an organ-base rather than a harpsichord-based orientation (for a opposing view see Williams, 1971).

The decoration of two surviving harpsichords attrib uted to Michael Mietke of Charlottenburg suggests a dat no later than 1713. The one-manual instrument has tw 8' stops. Its original compass of *G'*, *A'* to *c'''* was late extended to *F'*, *G'* to *e'''*. The two-manual harpsichor has one 4' and two 8' stops with a coupler. Its range o *F'*, *G'*, *A'* to *c'''* was later altered to *F'*, *G'* to *e'''*. Nei ther instrument has a buff stop. It is known that J. S Bach was sent from Cöthen to Berlin in 1719 to tak delivery of a Mietke two-manual harpsichord for the Duk of Anhalt-Cöthen. Both instruments, now at Schlos Charlottenburg, have keyboards with a narrow octav span, even slightly smaller than on most French harp sichords, and keyheads almost as short as the Frenc type. Bach is known to have preferred keyboards of suc dimensions.

No undoubtedly authentic instrument by Gottfrie Silbermann, Bach's friend, survives, but there are number of spinets by his nephew Johann Heinrich Sil bermann. Other extant instruments from outside Ham burg include a small group from Dresden, built by th members of the Gräbner family and their circle; tw highly unusual harpsichords combined with pianos, b J. A. Stein; a Silesian example; and a few anonymou ones. These instruments are all significantly differen from those of the Hamburg school, and they show thei affinities with the intermediate type in rather differen ways. The soundboard barring seems to include trans verse ribs running under the bridges, and the cases are made of hardwood or are veneered rather than being painted, but round tails are rare. With the exception of the harpsichord included in one of the Stein combination instruments, none of these includes a 16' stop, and this register must be considered as something of a Hamburg speciality. The tone of the Gräbner instruments is less brilliant and harsh than that of the Hamburg harpsichords, and has instead a characteristic dark reediness that is unlike the sound of the harpsichords from other countries.

Austrian 18th-century harpsichords are very rare. Boalch (1956) cites just one, signed 'Johann Leydecker, Vienna 1755' (Schloss Eggenberg, Graz). The Mozart household is known to have contained a large two-manual harpsichord by Friederici of Gera in Saxony, rather than one by a native Austrian or Bavarian builder. Evidence as to the extent of harpsichord making in Austria and Bavaria, as in Spain, is too sparse to justify drawing any definite conclusions. The same holds true for the older countries of the Empire, except for those areas of Italy ruled from Vienna. Virtually nothing is known of any 18th-century harpsichord building in what is now Czechoslovakia, Poland and Hungary, although there are indications that the craft had been practised there during the 16th and 17th centuries.

The only catalogued Danish 18th-century instruments of the harpsichord family that survive are a small virginal of 1762 (Rosenborg Castle) by Christian Ferdinand Speer, a Silesian émigré in Copenhagen, and a one-manual harpsichord of 1770 (Musikhistorisk Museum, Copenhagen) by Moritz Georg Moshack, a Copenhagen maker. It is known that there was an active trade in importing harpsichords from Hamburg during the century, and indigenous instruments were probably of similar design.

In Sweden, a number of instruments and some secondary evidence indicate that harpsichord making flourished during the 18th century. A two-manual five-octave harpsichord in the Stockholm Nordiska Museet, dated 1737, is signed by Philipp Jacob Specken, who had learnt his craft in Dresden before moving to Stockholm. Niels (or Nicholas) Brelin, a clergyman, is known to have built an upright harpsichord (clavicytherium) in 1741 with eight registration pedals. A contemporary sketch printed in the proceedings of the Swedish Royal Academy shows that it had a five-octave compass and that its disposition included a 4' stop. Brelin is said to have made two trips abroad to study instrument building, but where and with whom he worked is not known. The harpsichord signed 'Johannes Broman, Stockholm 1756' (Musikmuseet, Stockholm) is a five-octave two-manual instrument, 3·6 metres long and similar in construction to a Hamburg harpsichord (including a double-curve bentside). It has a 4' stop and three unison choirs (and the arrangement of the strings makes it clear that the third 8' was never intended as a 16' stop). The two-manual five-octave instrument signed 'Gottlieb Rosenau, Stockholm 1786' (Musikhistorisk Museum, Copenhagen), while also similar in style to contemporaneous Hamburg instruments, is of relatively normal length, 276 cm.

Few 18th-century harpsichords from the north Netherlands (corresponding approximately to the modern Kingdom of the Netherlands) are recorded as extant: two instruments made in Amsterdam in the 1760s, a 1787 instrument from Leyden, and from Roermond a curious survival of 17th-century style, dated 1734. The Roermond instrument (in the Plantin–Moretus Huis, Antwerp) is an unusual two-manual harpsichord with a virginal filling out the space between the bentside and the extended cheekpiece. The harpsichord portion is reminiscent of an earlier transposing double after alignment. The compass is certainly the normal late 17th-century Flemish range, G'/B' to c'''; the lower manual plays sets of 8' and 4' jacks, and the upper controls a dogleg 8' and a second set of 4' jacks playing on the same strings as do those of the lower-manual 4'. The virginal, with keyboard to the left, is of C to c''' compass and is also archaic in lacking the low $C\sharp$. Johannes Josephus Coenen, as the maker signed himself, was a priest as well as the organist of Roermond Cathedral, and seems to have made instruments in his spare time.

In sharp contrast a modern, large two-manual instrument boasting a 16' stop was advertised for sale in Amsterdam just a year later (1735) by Rutgert Pleunis. This maker's extraordinary career as one of the most inventive keyboard instrument builders of his time was centred from 1741 in London, where he was known as Roger Plenius. Unfortunately no instrument of either his Dutch or English period survives.

A harpsichord now at Leipzig, unsigned but with the initials 'L.V.' in the rose, bears the date 1766 on its top key (f''') and its place of origin, Amsterdam, on its lowest key (G'/B'). This single instrument is in the Flemish tradition, with the ends of the registers that protrude from the cheekpiece serving as stop-knobs for the two 8' and the 4' registers. A one-manual harpsichord of 1768, by C. F. Laeske of Amsterdam (private collection, New York), has two 8' registers and one 4', with a C to f''' compass. A harpsichord of similar disposition and compass, signed 'Dirk van der Lugt, Amsterdam 1700', disappeared from the Staatliches Institut für Musikforschung, Sammlung alter Musikinstrumente (the Berlin Collection), before World War II.

A harpsichord by Abraham Leenhouwer, a musician of Leyden (Gemeentemuseum, The Hague), a quite standard two-manual instrument of five-octave compass, disposed 2 × 8', 1 × 4', is remarkable not only for its very late date, 1787, but also for the archaic stop-knobs – extended register ends protruding through the cheekpiece. This feature, also found in the Coenen, 'L.V.' and Laeske harpsichords, seems to have survived longer in the north Netherlands than anywhere else.

In the south Netherlands (roughly equivalent to modern Belgium) a considerable number of instruments remains to substantiate the written record. In the early 18th century new harpsichords began to be made in the form that was characteristic of earlier instruments of the Ruckers type after they were enlarged in the late 17th century. Two 8' stops rather than a single unison register were the rule. Two-manual instruments had either three sets of jacks (one each for the two 8' and one 4' choirs) or four, as in the former transposing harpsichords. In the latter case, the fourth set would be used either as a second 4' stop playing on the upper manual (as in the Coenen harpsichord of 1734), or for a cut-through lute stop, plucking one of the unison choirs close to the nut. But quite a few simpler instruments continued to be produced, even in the late 18th century: Albert Delin of Tournai, for instance, seems to have done without a second manual or 4' stop, although he was a builder of great skill and refinement, judging from his surviving ten or so instruments, dated 1750–70. In addition to making conventional harpsichords and spinets,

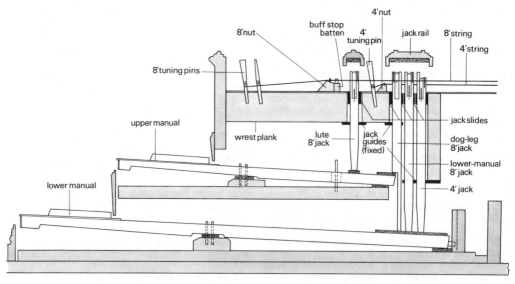

17. *Flemish two-manual harpsichord action, 18th century*

Delin also produced clavicytheria that are outstanding both for their mechanical excellence and their rich sound, which – projected directly at the player – is quite overwhelming at first. Three examples survive (Berlin Collection, Brussels Conservatory and Gemeentemuseum, The Hague).

Jérôme Mahieu of Brussels was probably active before 1732, the earliest date recorded for him, for he died in 1737. He built harpsichords of both one and two manuals, generally with three registers (2 × 8′, 1 × 4′), but occasionally with only two, when he preferred the older 1 × 8′, 1 × 4′ disposition to the more modern 2 × 8′. The compass was either of 58 (*G′* to *e′′′*) or 61 (*F′* to *f′′′*) notes. (The 1732 Mahieu instrument with an apparent compass of *D′* to *d′′′* reported in Paris in 1952 was presumably altered by a 19th-century restoration from the original *F′* to *f′′′* range.)

Also active during the mid-18th century was Jakob van den Elsche of Antwerp. Two instruments from his workshop survive. One, in the Vleeshuis Museum, Antwerp, bears the date 1763 and, save for its exceptionally sturdy construction, is a standard two-manual five-octave instrument of classic 2 × 8′, 1 × 4′ disposition. The other (Berlin), ostensibly dated 1710, seven years before van den Elsche's entry into the Guild of St Luke, is signed to indicate that it was rebuilt in 1790 by Johann Heinemann, a reputedly blind harpsichord and lute maker of Antwerp; how with such a handicap he could have rebuilt the van den Elsche instrument or made any of his own has not been explained. A one-manual harpsichord by Heinemann (Brussels) with a *C/E* to *d′′′* compass, disposed 2 × 8′, is dated 1793; this would make it apparently the latest extant Flemish harpsichord, but the short-octave keyboard is strangely archaic, particularly in view of the date.

Members of the Dulcken family were distinguished harpsichord builders in the region during the 18th century. Anton, a native of Germany, set up his workshop in Brussels early in the century. None of his instruments

seems to have survived, but at least ten harpsichords by his son Johan Daniel Dulcken are known. Born at Maastricht, by 1741 he had settled in Antwerp, where he produced most of his harpsichords. He moved to Brussels in 1764 and died there five years later. Of a somewhat experimental turn of mind, J. D. Dulcken evolved an unusually long model of northern European harpsichord, his two-manual instruments being some 260 cm long. Occasionally he also made use of a singular type of construction with both an inner and an outer bentside. All his mature instruments are of five-octave compass, disposed 2 × 8′, 1 × 4′, often with a cut-through lute stop on the upper manual. Dulcken preferred to use a dogleg jack for the normal upper 8′ rather than a coupler (see fig.17). But since the lute register and the lower 8′ usually pluck the same choir, with the second unison strings sounding only when the dogleg 8′ is engaged, no dialogue of lower 8′ and lute stop is normally possible and the upper manual is limited to providing a softer sound contrasting with the tutti of the lower manual.

Johann Peter Bull, another German who settled in Antwerp, was apprenticed to J. D. Dulcken there. Four of his instruments have survived, dated from 1776 to 1789, all of five-octave compass and disposed 2 × 8′, 1 × 4′. Three are two-manual instruments. One of these, dated 1778, has most ingeniously wrought, very wide upper-manual dogleg jacks, with two tongues facing in opposite directions. These jacks can pluck either 8′ choir and thus a combination of 2 × 8′ is available on each manual, since the dogleg and the lute stop can be combined on the upper keyboard. But the lower 8′ jacks are fitted with *peau de buffle* plectra so that only the dogleg 8′ is available to give a normal quilled 8′ sound on the lower manual. Thus, as with Dulcken, no dialogue of a quilled lower 8′ and a lute stop is possible in the manner of the English double harpsichord. A later two-manual instrument by Bull (1789) lacks the double tongues in the dogleg upper-manual jacks; but it is so arranged that damper interference between the lower 8′ jacks and the

ogleg upper 8' even prevents using the upper keyboard
as an echo manual.

Although in Switzerland some sparse records survive
of harpsichord making as far back as the late 15th century, the only surviving instruments identifiable as Swiss
date from the 18th century and come from the German-
speaking area. There is no firm evidence that the craft
ever took root in the other regions. (A spinettino in the
Schweizerisches Landesmuseum, Zurich, known to have
been decorated in Stupan, Engadin, in 1722, is of
uncertain origin and probably 17th-century.) Swiss
harpsichords of the 18th century were probably similar
in construction to the models produced in Strasbourg,
particularly to those made in the Silbermann workshop.
Peter Friedrich Brosi, a native of Swabia, was apprenticed to Silbermann before moving to Basle where he
set up as an organ and harpsichord builder. A spinet
signed by him (Schweizerisches Landesmuseum) is
somewhat archaic for its date (1755), with a compass
of C to e''', a distinctly 17th-century type of dark walnut
case and a black-stained stand of four heavy turned legs
connected by a stretcher. A spinet of 1775 signed by
his son, Johann Jacob Brosi, is closer in dimensions,
compass (F' to f''') and appearance to the late German
type of instrument. An instrument by the Zurich craftsman Hans Conrad Schmuz, dated 1761, is in the Alstet-
ten Museum. It is a single harpsichord of five-octave
compass with two 8' registers; the rather plain walnut
case and simple turned legs strongly suggest provincial
origins. An ottavino by his elder brother, Leonhard
Schmutz [sic], was sold in Paris in 1924 on the dispersal
of the Savoye Collection.

5. SINCE 1800.

i) 19th century. The Kirckman firm is said to have made
its last harpsichord in 1809; the latest extant example is
dated 1800. 19th-century restorers such as Tomasini,
Danti and Fleury in Paris produced a few new instruments, and the harpsichord still appeared sporadically
as a continuo instrument in oratorio and opera, and even
as a vehicle for virtuoso pianists like Moscheles (1837)
and Pauer (1861–7) to play in 'historical recitals'. But
generally the traditions of harpsichord playing and construction slumbered in the 19th century; scholars, performers and public alike assumed that if Bach and Handel
had known the modern piano in its iron-framed, cross-
strung, double-escapement perfection, they would surely have preferred it to the 'deficient' harpsichords of
their time.

In the mid-1860s the French virtuoso pianist Louis
Diémer began to include in his recitals selections performed on the harpsichord, generally using a 1769
instrument by Pascal Taskin which was owned by the
maker's descendants (but now at the Russell Collection
in Edinburgh; see fig.10 above). In 1882 this harpsichord was restored and subsequently borrowed for study
by the Erard firm of piano and harp makers in Paris,
with a view to resuming production of such instruments.
Shortly thereafter the rival firm Pleyel also examined
the Taskin harpsichord, and at the Paris Exposition of
1889 both firms displayed elaborately decorated harpsichords. Tomasini's more traditional harpsichord, based
on an 18th-century instrument by Hemsch of Paris, was
also shown (all three instruments are now in the Berlin
Collection). Diémer presented with considerable success a series of historical recitals on the harpsichord
during the Exposition.

The early revival Erard and Pleyel harpsichords – two-
manual, five-octave instruments, disposed 2 × 8', 1 ×
4' – are actually constructed more along the lines of
English instruments of the mid- and late 18th century,
such as Kirckman's and Shudi's, than those of Taskin
instruments. Their framing, open at the bottom like that
of the modern grand piano, is much heavier than that
of 18th-century harpsichords, Erard's rather more so than
Pleyel's. (Pleyel had been influenced by the piano to a
greater extent in other respects such as scaling, soundboard ribbing and buttoned-on bridges.) While no metal
bracing was used, the strings and bridges were far heavier than in antique instruments. The jacks were wooden,
with traditional dampers. Erard used quill plectra in the
lower 8', but the other registers were leathered, were as
all of Pleyel's (including the extra English-type cut-
through lute stop which Pleyel added to the Taskin disposition). After initially opting for a combination of knee
levers and pedals, Erard changed to an instrument solely
with pedals, such as Pleyel had made from the start.
The elegant keyboards with ivory naturals and bevelled,
canted ebony sharps are proportioned like those of the
maker's pianos.

In London during the late 1880s Arnold Dolmetsch,
a young French-born violin teacher who had trained at
the Brussels Conservatory (where he had attended historical concerts with early instruments) and the Royal
College of Music, London, began to present concerts of
Renaissance and Baroque music. By 1890 he had acquired
and made serviceable a Kirckman double harpsichord,
an Italian virginal and a large German clavichord as well
as a spinet and a small square piano. His concerts attracted
a growing and influential circle of artists, writers and
critics. In 1894 he constructed his first clavichord, and
in 1896 at the suggestion of William Morris his first
harpsichord, for display at the Arts and Crafts Exhibition in London. This was a one-manual instrument of
G' to f''' compass, disposed 2 × 8' with buff stop, and
it so impressed the conductor Hans Richter that he
engaged Dolmetsch, with the instrument, to accompany
the recitatives in the 1897 Covent Garden production of
Mozart's Don Giovanni. It was also used in Purcell performances in Birmingham. While antique instruments
had served on rare occasions during the 19th century
for continuo playing, this was apparently the first such
use of a modern harpsichord. The revival in Britain owed
much also to the efforts of A. J. Hipkins, a concert pianist, associate of the Broadwood firm and historian of
keyboard instruments. In the 1880s and 1890s Hipkins
gave lecture-demonstrations on 18th-century English
harpsichords, using both his personal Kirckman and
Shudi-Broadwoods from his firm's collection, and later
the new Pleyel and Erard revival instruments.

In Germany and central Europe the harpsichord revival took hold more slowly. Almost from the first, moreover, a baleful influence made itself felt – the acceptance,
as a model specimen, of a much-altered instrument that
was falsely associated with Bach (harpsichord no.316
in the Berlin Collection) which had in fact been rebuilt
earlier in the 19th century to replace a third 8' register
with a 16' stop and to remove the 4' register to the upper
manual from its normal place on the lower keyboard.
As early as 1899 a modern instrument based on no.316
was built by Wilhelm Hirl of Berlin for the Dutch collector D. F. Scheurleer, of The Hague. Other early German revival makers, such as Karl A. Pfeiffer (Stuttgart),
Johannes Rehbock (Duisburg) and Georg Steingräber

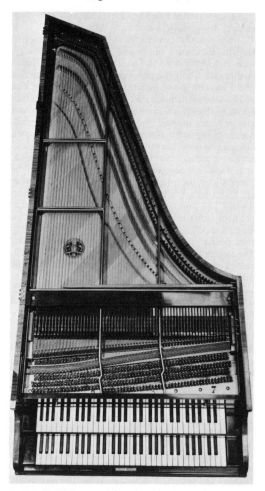

18. Harpsichord by Pleyel, Paris ('Landowska' model, first made in 1912)

(Bayreuth), soon followed with their own versions of the spurious 'Bach' harpsichord. Even more elaborate and curious instruments were occasionally attempted in central Europe at this time, for instance a three-manual one by Seyffarth of Leipzig (1909; now in the Musikinstrumenten-Museum der Karl-Marx-Universität, Leipzig). The director of the Berlin Collection, Oskar Fleischer, published an article in 1899 summing up the aesthetics of the early harpsichord revival. He reported that the new Erard harpsichord had been seen and heard at the Vienna Music and Theatre Exposition of 1892 along with historical instruments from such collections as those of Moritz Steinert (New Haven). He found the sound of the Erard 'hard, brittle and unsatisfying, quite apart from the lack of tonal combinations', and went on to praise Hirl's copy, allegedly faithful (save for a few small improvements) to the 'Bach' harpsichord which Fleischer had had acquired by the collection. He stressed, as a principle, variety of timbres and ease of changing registrations. The perfected modern harpsichord, with its pedals with half-hitches or special hand stops for dynamic variation, variety of plectra material and historically rare registers (16' and cut-through lute), in addition to the basic 2 × 8', 1 × 4' disposition of the classic instrument, embodies the fulfilment of this ideal. In extolling such features, Fleischer particularly emphasized 18th-century music and the works of Bach and his contemporaries. (Apart from the Fitzwilliam Virginal Book, published in 1894–9, earlier keyboard music was largely unedited and little known). The practicality and desirability of the 'Bach' disposition (lower manual: 16', 8'; upper manual: 8', 4'; plus buff stop and coupler) were assumed without question. Fleischer also raised some of the practical questions that continue to plague those concerned with presenting early music in the concert hall: whether the harpsichord can or should be capable of the level of loudness required to fill large auditoriums and balance modern string and wind instruments; and the best specification for an all-purpose harpsichord. At the time, when the shift from piano back to harpsichord was getting under way, there was as yet no concept of specialized instruments being specially suited to performing particular music.

(ii) 1900 to 1940. The Erard firm built harpsichords for only a limited period, but Pleyel continued their production. In 1912, at the urging of Wanda Landowska, the first modern harpsichord virtuoso of international renown, a new Pleyel model was introduced at the Breslau Bach Festival, and it was on this type of instrument that she performed, recorded and taught until her death in 1959. After 1923 the new Pleyel (see fig. 18) also had an iron frame holding thick strings at high tension. The barring was almost identical to that of the modern grand piano, and the finely veneered case correspondingly heavily constructed. The touch depth and the dimensions of the five-octave keyboard were those of the modern piano. The cheekpiece and the spine were cut away in a delicately curved line to reveal the harpsichordist's hands playing on the keyboards. An extra set of overhead dampers was provided for the 16' strings, and a highly sophisticated fine-tuning system was also fitted. The registers were controlled by seven pedals (but without half-hitches), disposed as follows – lower manual: 16', 8', 4'; upper manual: 8', lute (*Nasat*) and buff; and coupler. The pedal action was largely negative (i.e. a pedal was raised to engage the register), a system that may have derived from the English 18th-century machine-stop pedal.

The arrival of this new Pleyel, first demonstrated in Germany, had a marked effect on harpsichord making in that country. Some makers now favoured the Pleyel disposition over that of the 'Bach' model, and the iron frame and generally heavier construction were taken up by such firms as Maendler-Schramm, a Munich workshop set up in 1906, and Neupert of Bamberg, a piano manufacturer (established 1868) that began harpsichord making at about the same time. The preference for the Pleyel disposition owed much to Landowska's influence as professor of harpsichord at the Berlin Hochschule für Musik, where she taught from 1913 to 1919, training an entire generation of harpsichordists. (In Germany, as elsewhere, very few harpsichords were made during World War I.)

From about 1930 most German harpsichord makers reverted to the 'Bach' disposition, and abandoned metal framing. Organist-harpsichordists, especially, had complained that an upper manual with only a single 8' stop could not balance the mass of registers on the lower manual of the Pleyel-type instrument. Compromises of considerable mechanical ingenuity were offered by German makers, and later by some English builders as well: 4' stop normally played on the lower manual which could be coupled up to the second keyboard; 4' strings playable by two sets of jacks, one for each manual; and two sets of 4' strings, one for each keyboard.

From 1902, while the German revival was beginning, Arnold Dolmetsch had toured the USA extensively, presenting concerts of early music. In 1905 he was invited by the Chickering firm of piano makers in Boston to establish a department for the production of harpsichords, clavichords, lutes and viols. He accepted, and headed this department until 1910, when the firm's financial difficulties forced them to discontinue it. About 15 instruments of all types, including 13 harpsichords, were produced. These were two-manual instruments freely derived from a French 18th-century harpsichord used in Dolmetsch's concerts (the so-called 'Couchet-Taskin', actually by Goermans, dated 1764 and rebuilt in 1783–4 by Taskin; now in Edinburgh). The keyboards were back-pinned in the Taskin manner. While heavily cased, the Dolmetsch-Chickering harpsichords were lighter in construction than most other contemporaneous examples. The scaling was authentically 18th-century French but the ribbing of the soundboard, while light, was distinctly modern, crossing under the bridge. The tone, somewhat lacking in brightness, was none-

theless closer to the sound of antique instruments than any modern harpsichord had been. The lower 8' was leathered and was provided with two sets of jacks, rather than half-hitches, to offer two dynamic levels. The upper 8' was quilled, which rendered a combination with the lower 8' less homogeneous, as in the case of the Erard model of 1889. The 4' and the 16', the latter added in 1908 to the last three harpsichords, were leathered, and the 16' was stacked on top of the 8' bridge by using overspun strings. The instrument case was not extended to accommodate the deep register; in fact, it was made (like that of earlier Dolmetsch instruments) shorter than the Taskin prototype, with an incongruously Germanic or piano-like double-curved bentside, and, for good measure, with a heavy timber under the soundboard which actually rendered its last 23 cm ineffectual.

From Boston, Dolmetsch moved to Paris, where he continued his work at the piano manufacturers Gaveau, who had not previously made early keyboard instruments. The models produced were essentially similar to the Chickering instruments. The heavy timber member under the soundboard was abandoned, but the case was shortened still further. The 16' register was now a standard feature of the larger Dolmetsch harpsichords. In the spring of 1914, Dolmetsch returned to England, and by 1918 he had established his workshop in Haslemere, Surrey, where his successors have maintained their fac-

9. Harpsichord by J. C. Neupert, Bamberg ('Bach' model, first made in 1931)

tory. Gaveau continued to build harpsichords and related instruments (from Dolmetsch's plans) until the economic crisis of the 1930s.

The Pleyel firm introduced a smaller version of its 'Landowska' model concert harpsichord in 1927, still iron-framed but without a 16′ stop and descending only to A′ instead of F′; the pedal action was negative as in the large model. In 1925 Dolmetsch implemented a new conception in harpsichord actions, a mechanism intended to avoid the accessory noises and jangle that can mark the passage of the plectrum past the string on the jack's return to its original position. Regulation of the new action, however, was difficult to attain and maintain; and though the action did afford the possibility of fitting a damper pedal, this was insufficient to redeem it and it was eventually discarded. A device fitted to the upper manual allowing for a kind of clavichord-like *Bebung* was a feature of Dolmetsch harpsichords for some years afterwards. A compound metal frame of wrought iron and steel welded together was introduced by Dolmetsch in 1930 but given up a few years later as it did not bring about the desired increase in stability of tuning. Modernization of the instrument was attempted by other makers as well. Karl Maendler in Munich, for instance, worked for years to develop a harpsichord with an action that would admit touch dynamics. The resulting instrument, dubbed the 'Bachklavier', was introduced with some success by the German harpsichordist Julia Menz, but it failed to survive (see Wörsching, 1946, pp.36f). Maendler's addition of a damper pedal, which raised the dampers of the lower-manual jacks only, was longer-lived. About 1933, again in response to the wishes of organists, Ammer Brothers (Eisenberg) began producing pedal keyboards with independent sets of strings and jacks which could be placed under a conventional harpsichord. Other builders, such as Neupert and Maendler-Schramm in Germany, and Alec Hodsdon in England, began a similar production shortly after.

Despite unfavourable economic conditions, professional harpsichord building in the USA, which had been suspended since the departure of Dolmetsch for Paris in 1910, was resumed in 1931 when John Challis returned to his homeland after four years at Haslemere as the first Dolmetsch Foundation scholar-craftsman. In the earliest Challis harpsichords framing was wholly of wood and no adjusting screws were added to the traditional wooden jacks. But subsequent instruments reflected Challis's ingenuity in adapting the latest synthetic materials and technological advances. In his last years he achieved his aim of creating a harpsichord that would be at least as stable in the rigorous North American climate as were indigenous pianos. His late instruments were constructed wholly of metal, including the soundboard, with wood veneers used only as a decorative covering on keyboards and casework. While the tonal quality of Challis instruments – very little influenced by the sound of the early harpsichord – was not to everyone's taste, his craftsmanship was universally admired. Two pedal harpsichords built for organist clients represent the summit of his achievement. The disposition of the more elaborate of the pair set a record for sheer complexity – Pedals: 16′, 8′, 4′, 2′; lower manual: 16′, 8′, 4′; upper manual: 8′, 4′; plus the usual buff stops and manual coupler.

In 1935 Thomas Goff, a London barrister, set up a workshop to build instruments to the designs of Herbert Lambert, which were influenced by both the later Dol-metsch and the modern German harpsichords. Only 1 Goff harpsichords were produced, disposed like the larg Pleyel model, with metal frame and heavy case as wel as heavy stringing and plectra (on later instruments bot of leather and quill). They were widely used as concer instruments in the years immediately after World Wa II. Robert Goble, after 12 years in the Dolmetsch work shop, set up on his own in 1937, but undertook larg two-manual instruments only a decade later. These stur dy wood-framed harpsichords in the modern tradition offered the resources of the Pleyel disposition but wit greater volume of sound and stability of tuning an regulation.

(iii) Since 1940. Harpsichord making suffered exten sively from the havoc wrought by World War II. Tal ented younger builders died, including Rudolp Dolmetsch, the elder son of Arnold. Maendler's work shop and others were destroyed by bombing and neve regained the momentum of their pre-war years. Afte 1945 such surviving shops as Neupert and Pleyel resume production much as it had been in 1939. Many renowne modern makers began learning their craft as apprentice during the postwar years: Konrad Sassmann, Kurt Witt mayer and John Feldberg at the Neupert workshop, Fran Hubbard at the Dolmetsch shop, and William Dowd an Frank Rutkowski at Challis's. Hubbard also worke briefly in London with Hugh Gough, who was influ enced by Dolmetsch and who had built early keyboar instruments from 1946. Gough made relatively fev harpsichords, but these were remarkable at the time fo their closer resemblance to historical instruments tha any modern ones since the Dolmetsch-Chickering models After moving to the USA in 1959, however, Goug devoted himself exclusively to other types of instru ment.

In 1949 Hubbard and Dowd established their join workshop in Boston, Massachusetts, the first in moder times dedicated to the construction of harpsichord according to historical principles. Their collaboratio continued until 1958, and, in the words of Ralp Kirkpatrick, 'accomplished the major revolution o this century in harpsichord building . . . a return t seventeenth- and eighteenth-century traditions and prin ciples of construction that had hitherto been practice only in isolated instances'. From this point on players were faced with a fundamental choice betwee the modern harpsichord as it had evolved since th beginning of the revival, and reconstructions of histor ical instruments.

Working independently, Martin Skowroneck of Bre men completed his first harpsichord built on historica lines in 1953. But in Germany it was specially difficu for the traditional type of instrument to gain a foothold In no other country had the modern type of harpsichor become so firmly established. Every concert hall an radio station had acquired or had ready access to a mod ern instrument, invariably a large two-manual harpsi chord with the spurious 'Bach' disposition. Conservator teaching was based on this standard concert model. Per formers and public alike had grown used to it, and eve its appearance – because this instrument was exporte round the world to an extent unparalleled by harpsi chords of any other country – was a part of musical life Though Skowroneck's work was followed in a few year by that of other historically orientated makers, such a Ranier Schütze and Klaus Ahrend, the modern instru

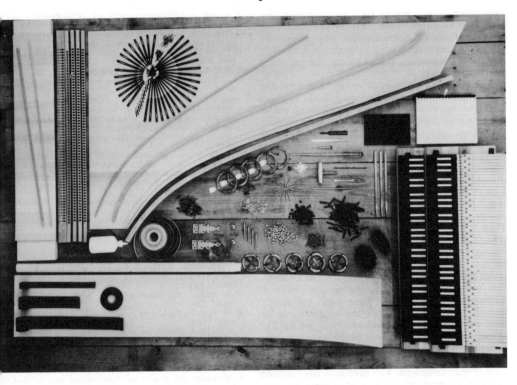

20. Complete harpsichord kit by Frank Hubbard, Boston; a replica of the harpsichord by Pascal Taskin (1769) shown in fig.10

ment continued to dominate the concert stage in Germany into the 1970s. In the USA, on the other hand, the use of traditional harpsichords became widespread, the modern instrument being used almost exclusively for 20th-century music, at least by the younger generation of performers.

With the shift away from the modern harpsichord to the historical instrument, performing style has also been greatly reformed, with far less emphasis being placed on registration changes than formerly. Earlier types of harpsichord, such as models after Ruckers and the older Italian school, are coming into wider use for specialized purposes, although the large 18th-century double harpsichord has tended to assume the central role formerly occupied by the modern concert instrument. The influence of builders active in the RESTORATION of antique harpsichords has contributed to a greater awareness of the special qualities of the best historical instruments. The new generation of harpsichord makers, without significant exception, are concentrating on the historical instrument. A certain share of the credit for the growing interest in harpsichord making and playing in recent years is due to the introduction of instruments in kit form. This was pioneered by W. J. Zuckermann in 1960 with a simplified, modern type of instrument, and shortly thereafter reproductions of historical instruments in kit form were introduced by Frank Hubbard (see fig.20). In recent times the higher-quality kits have come to offer potentially excellent harpsichords of quite authentic construction and materials. It remains to be seen whether contemporary composers, who have generally favoured the modern instrument (and most often prescribed specific registration changes possible only on the pedal harpsichord with all its resources), will now accept the limitations of the classic instrument in this respect. A few composers have accepted commissions to write works for the hand-stop instrument with a classic disposition. But whatever contemporary composers may prefer, it is clear that most performers of early music have now opted for the harpsichord in its traditional form.

Walther ML

BIBLIOGRAPHY

S. Virdung: *Musica getutscht* (Basle, 1511/R1931); ed. E. K. Niemöller, DM, 1st ser., xxxi (1970)
G. Zarlino: *Le istitutioni harmoniche* (Venice, 1558/R1965, rev. 3/1573/R1966)
A. Banchieri: *L'organo suonarino* (Venice, 2/1611/R)
M. Praetorius: *Syntagma musicum*, ii (Wolfenbüttel, 1618, 2/1619/R1958 and 1980)
B. Jobernadi: *Tratado de la musica*, 1634 (*E-Mn* 8931); extracts in *AnM*, viii (1953), 193
M. Mersenne: *Harmonie universelle* (Paris, 1636–7/R1963; Eng. trans., 1957)
C. Douwes: *Grondig ondersoek van de toonen der musijk* (Franeker, 1699/R1970)
J. Adlung: *Musica mechanica organoedi* (Berlin, 1768/R1961)
C. Burney: *The Present State of Music in France and Italy* (London, 1771, 2/1773); ed. P. Scholes as *Dr. Burney's Musical Tours*, i (London, 1959)
D. Diderot: 'Clavecin', *Encyclopédie*, iii (Geneva, 1772), 509
C. Burney: *The Present State of Music in Germany, The Netherlands, and the United Provinces* (London, 1773, 2/1775); ed. P. Scholes as *Dr. Burney's Musical Tours*, ii (London, 1959)
L. de Burbure: *Recherches sur les facteurs de clavecins et les luthiers d'Anvers, depuis le XVIe jusqu'au XIXe siècle* (Brussels, 1869)
G. Correr: *Elenco degli strumenti musicali antichi da arco, fiato, pizzico e tasto* (Venice, 1872)
V. Mahillon: *Catalogue descriptif et analytique du Musée instrumental du Conservatoire royal de musique de Bruxelles* (Ghent, 1880–1922/R; i, 2/1893; ii, 2/1909)
C. Krebs: 'Die besaiteten Klavierinstrumente bis zu Anfang des 17. Jahrhunderts', *VMw*, vii (1892), 92, 288; ix (1893), 245
M. Steinert: *Catalogue of the M. Steinert Collection of Keyed and Stringed Instruments* (New Haven, 1893)
A. J. Hipkins: *A Description and History of the Pianoforte and the Older Keyboard Instruments* (London, 1896, 3/1929/R197
G. Donaldson: *Catalogue of the Musical Instruments and Objec forming the Donaldson Museum* (London, 1899)
O. Fleischer: 'Das Bach'sche Clavicymbel und seine Neukonstru tion', *ZIMG*, i (1899–1900), 161
K. Nef: 'Clavicymbel und Clavichord', *JbMP 1903*, 15
——: *Katalog der Musikinstrumente im Historischen Museum Basel* (Basle, 1906)
——: 'Zur Cembalofrage', *ZIMG*, x (1908–9), 236
J. Schlosser: *Die Sammlung alter Musikinstrumente* (Vienna, 192(
C. Sachs: *Sammlung alter Musikinstrumente bei der Staatliche Hochschule für Musik zu Berlin* (Berlin, 1922)
P. Macquoid and R. Edwards: *The Dictionary of English Furnitu* (New York, 1924–7, 2/1954)
E. U. Kropp: *Das Zupfklavier* (diss., U. of Berlin, 1925)
P. James: *Early Keyboard Instruments* (London, 1930/R1970)
G. Le Cerf and E.-R. Labande: *Instruments de musique du XV siècle: les traités d'Henri-Arnaut de Zwolle et de divers anonym* (Paris, 1932)
K. Matthaei: 'Über Cembalo-Neukonstruktionen', *Zeitschrift f Hausmusik*, ii (1933)
H. Neupert: *Das Cembalo* (Kassel, 1933, 4/1969; Eng. trans., 196 as *Harpsichord Manual*)
W. Skinner: *The Belle Skinner Collection of Musical Instrumen* (Holyoke, 1933)
E. Harich-Schneider: *Die Kunst des Cembalospiels* (Kassel, 193!
F. Trendelenburg, E. Thienhaus and E. Franz: 'Zur Klangwirku von Klavichord, Cembalo and Flügel', *Akustische Zeitschrift*, (1940), 309
H.-H. Dräger: 'Anschlagsmöglichkeiten beim Cambalo', *AMf*, (1941), 223
A. M. Pols: *De Ruckers en de klavierbouw en Vlaanderen* (An werp, 1942)
J. A. Stellfeld: *Bronnen tot de geschiedenis der Antwerpsche cl vecimbel- en orgelbouwers in de XVI en XVII eeuwen* (Antwer 1942)
E. Halfpenny: 'Shudi and the "Venetian Swell"', *ML*, xxvii (1946 180
J. Wörsching: *Die historischen Saitenklaviere und der modern Klavichord- und Cembalobau* (Mainz, 1946)
W. Landowska: *Commentaries for the 'Treasury of the Harpsicho Music'* (New York, 1947)
N. Dufourcq: *Le clavecin* (Paris, 1949, 2/1967)
F. Hubbard: 'Two Early English Harpsichords', *GSJ*, iii (1950), 1
A. Berner: *Die Berliner Musikinstrumentensammlung: Einführun mit historischen und technischen Erläuterungen* (Berlin, 1952)
E. Harich-Schneider: *Kleine Schule des Cembalospiels* (Kassel, 195 Eng. trans., 1954, as *The Harpsichord*)
R. Kirkpatrick: *Domenico Scarlatti* (Princeton, 1953, 5/1966)
J. Boston: 'An Early Virginal-maker in Chester, and his Tools *GSJ*, vii (1954), 3
F. Ernst: *Der Flügel Johann Sebastian Bachs* (Frankfurt am Mair 1955)
F. J. Hirt: *Meisterwerke des Klavierbaues* (Olten, 1955; Eng. trans 1968, 2/1981, as *Stringed Keyboard Instruments 1440–1880*)
R. Russell: 'The Harpsichord since 1800', *PRMA*, lxxxii (1955–6 61
D. H. Boalch: *Makers of the Harpsichord and Clavichord 1440 1840* (London, 1956, 2/1974)
F. Hubbard: 'The *Encyclopédie* and the French Harpsichord', *GSJ ix (1956), 37
P. J. Hardouin and F. Hubbard: 'Harpsichord Making in Paris *GSJ*, x (1957), 10; xii (1959), 73; xiii (1960), 52
R. Russell: *Catalogue of the Benton Fletcher Collection of Earl Keyboard Instruments* (London, 1957, rev. 2/1969 by H. Schott
——: *The Harpsichord and Clavichord* (London, 1959, rev. 2/1973
A. Curtis: 'Dutch Harpsichord Makers', *TVNM*, xix/1–2 (1960) 44
S. Marcuse: *Musical Instruments at Yale: a Selection of Wester Instruments from the 15th to 20th Centuries* (New Haven, 1960
J. D. Shortridge: 'Italian Harpsichord Building in the 16th and 17t Centuries', *Smithsonian Institution Bulletin* (1960, 2/1970), no.22
E. Winternitz: *Keyboard Instruments in the Metropolitan Museur of Art* (New York, 1961)
J. Lade: 'Modern Composers and the Harpsichord', *Consort*, xi. (1962), 128
F. Hubbard: *Harpsichord Regulating and Repairing* (Boston, Mass. 1963)
J. Barnes: 'Pitch Variations in Italian Keyboard Instruments', *GSJ xviii (1965), 110
F. Hubbard: *Three Centuries of Harpsichord Making* (Cambridge Mass., 1965, 4/1972)
J. Barnes: 'Two Rival Harpsichord Specifications', *GSJ*, xix (1966 49

V. Luithlen and K. Wegerer: *Katalog der Sammlung alter Musik-instrumente*, i: *Saitenklaviere* (Vienna, 1966)

J. H. van der Meer: *Beiträge zum Cembalobau im deutschen Sprachgebiet bis 1700* (Nuremberg, 1966)

L. Cervelli and J. H. van der Meer: *Conservato a Roma il più antico clavicembalo* (Rome, 1967)

E. M. Ripin: 'The Early Clavichord', *MQ*, liii (1967), 518

——: 'The French Harpsichord before 1650', *GSJ*, xx (1967), 43

W. R. Thomas and J. J. K. Rhodes: 'The String Scales of Italian Keyboard Instruments', *GSJ*, xx (1967), 48

E. Winternitz: *Musical Instruments and their Symbolism in Western Art* (New York, 1967, 2/1979)

J. Barnes: 'Italian String Scales', *GSJ* xxi (1968), 179

C. Mould: 'James Talbot's Manuscript (Christ Church Library Music Manuscript 1187), vii: Harpsichord', *GSJ*, xxi (1968), 40

S. Newman and P. Williams: *The Russell Collection and other Early Keyboard Instruments in St Cecilia's Hall, Edinburgh* (Edinburgh, 1968)

I. Otto: *Das Musikinstrumenten-Museum Berlin* (Berlin, 1968)

E. M. Ripin: 'The Two-manual Harpsichord in Flanders before 1650', *GSJ*, xxi (1968), 33

R. Russell: *Victoria and Albert Museum: Catalogue of Musical Instruments*, i: *Keyboard Instruments* (London, 1968, rev. edn. by H. Schott in preparation)

J. H. van der Meer: 'Harpsichord Making and Metallurgy: a Rejoinder', *GSJ*, xxi (1968), 175

V. Gai: *Gli instrumenti musicali della corta medicea* (Florence, 1969)

C. Hoover: *Harpsichords and Clavichords* (Washington, DC, 1969)

R. de Maeyer: *Exposition des instruments de musique des XVIème et XVIIème siècles* (Brussels, 1969)

J. H. van der Meer: 'Die klavierhistorische Sammlung Neupert', *Anzeiger des Germanischen Nationalmuseums* (Nuremberg, 1969)

E. M. Ripin: 'The Couchet Harpsichord in the Crosby Brown Collection', *Metropolitan Museum Journal*, ii (1969), 169

W. J. Zuckermann: *The Modern Harpsichord* (New York, 1969)

J.-L. Val: 'Une détermination de la taille des cordes de clavecin employées en France au XVIIIᵉ siècle', *ReM*, lvi (1970), 208

Restauratieproblemen van Antwerpse klavecimbels (Antwerp, 1970)

K. and M. Kaufmann: 'Le clavecin d'Arnaut de Zwolle', *GAM: Bulletin du Groupe d'acoustique musicale*, liv (1971), Feb, p.i

J. H. van der Meer: *Wegweiser durch die Sammlung historischer Musikinstrumente* (Nuremberg, 1971)

N. Meeùs: 'Le clavecin de Johannes Couchet, Anvers, 1646: un moment important de l'histoire du double clavecin en Flandres', *Brussels Museum of Musical Instruments Bulletin*, i (1971), 15

W. D. Neupert: 'Physikalische Aspekte des Cembaloklanges', *Das Musikinstrument*, xx (1971), 857

E. M. Ripin, ed.: *Keyboard Instruments: Studies in Keyboard Organology 1500–1800* (Edinburgh, 1971, 2/1977) [articles by J. Barnes, E. A. Bowles, F. Hellwig, J. Lambrechts-Douillez, G. Leonhardt, J. H. van der Meer and others]

M. Thomas: 'String Gauges of Old Italian Harpsichords', *GSJ*, xxiv (1971), 69

P. Williams: 'Some Developments in Early Keyboard Studies', *ML*, lii (1971), 272

O. Rindlisbacher: *Das Klavier in der Schweiz* (Berne and Munich, 1972)

J. Barnes: 'The Stringing of Italian Harpsichords', *Der klangliche Aspekt beim Restaurieren von Saitenklavieren*, ed. V. Schwarz (Graz, 1973), 35

M. Castellani: 'A 1593 Veronese Inventory', *GSJ*, xxvi (1973), 15

L. Cervelli: 'Arpicordo: mito di un nome e realtà di uno strumento', *Quadrivium*, xiv (1973), 187

E. M. Ripin: 'A "Five-foot" Flemish Harpsichord', *GSJ*, xxvi (1973), 135

——: 'The Surviving Oeuvre of Girolamo Zenti', *Metropolitan Museum Journal*, vii (1973), 71

K. Bakeman: 'Stringing Techniques of Harpsichord Builders', *GSJ*, xxvii (1974), 95

H. Bedard and J. Lambrechts-Douillez: 'Rapports de restauration', *Brussels Museum of Musical Instruments Bulletin*, iv (1974), 17

G. G. O'Brien: 'The Numbering System of Ruckers Instruments', *Brussels Museum of Musical Instruments Bulletin*, iv (1974), 75

——: 'The 1764/83 Taskin Harpsichord', *Organ Yearbook*, v (1974), 91

E. M. Ripin: *The Instrument Catalogues of Leopoldo Franciolini* (New York, 1974)

H. Schott: 'The Harpsichord Revival', *Early Music*, ii (1974), 85

J. H. van der Meer: 'Studien zum Cembalobau in Italien', *Festschrift für Ernst Emsheimer* (Stockholm, 1974), 131

L. F. Tagliavini: 'Considerazioni sulle vicende storiche del corista', *L'organo*, xii (1974), 119

M. Campbell: *Dolmetsch: the Man and his Work* (London, 1975)

P. Dumoulin: 'La découverte de bobines de cordes de clavecin du XVIIIᵉ siècle', *RdM*, lxi (1975), 8

F. Hammond: 'Musical Instruments at the Medici Court in the Mid-seventeenth Century', *AnMc*, no.15 (1975), 202

L. Libin: 'A Dutch Harpsichord in the United States', *GSJ*, xxviii (1975), 43

M. Tiella: 'The Archicembalo of Nicola Vicentino', *English Harpsichord Magazine* (1975), Oct, 134

La facture de clavecin du XVᵉ au XVIIIᵉ siècle: Louvain-la-Neuve 1976 [articles by J. Bosquet, M. K. Kauffmann, J. Lambrechts-Douillez, H. Legros, N. Meeùs, P. Mercier and J. Tournay]

F. Hellwig: 'Strings and Stringing: Contemporary Documents', *GSJ*, xxix (1976), 91

J. Lambrechts-Douillez, ed.: *Ruckers klavecimbels en copieën* (Antwerp, 1977)

M. Lindley: 'Instructions for the Clavier Diversely Tempered', *Early Music*, v (1977), 18

N. Meeùs: 'Renaissance Transposing Keyboards', *FoMRHI Quarterly* (1977), nos.45, 57

W. Debenham: *A Description of the Alterations to the 1521 Hieronymus Harpsichord* (London, 1978)

W. R. Dowd: 'A Classification System for Ruckers and Couchet Double Harpsichords', *JAMIS*, iv (1978), 106

S. Germann: 'Regional Schools of Harpsichord Decoration', *JAMIS*, iv (1978), 54

J. H. van der Meer: 'A Contribution to the History of the Clavicytherium', *Early Music*, vi (1978), 247

F. Hammond: 'Girolamo Frescobaldi and a Decade of Music in Casa Barbarini: 1634–1643', *AnMc*, no.19 (1979), 94–124

H. Henkel: *Beiträge zum historischen Cembalobau*, Beiträge zur musikwissenschaftlichen Forschung in der DDR, xi (Leipzig, 1979)

——: *Kielinstrumente*, Musikinstrumenten-Museum der Karl-Marx-Universität Leipzig Katalog, ii (Leipzig, 1979)

J. Koster: 'The Importance of the Early English Harpsichord', *GSJ*, xxxii (1979), 45

G. G. O'Brien: 'Ioannes and Andreas Ruckers: a Quatercentenary Celebration', *Early Music*, vii (1979), 453

D. Alton Smith: 'The Musical Instrument Inventory of Raymund Fugger', *GSJ*, xxxiii (1980), 36

J. Koster: 'The Importance of the Early English Harpsichord', *GSJ*, xxxiii (1980), 45

L. F. Tagliavini: 'Appunti sugli ambiti delle tastiere in Italia dal rinascimento al primo barocco', *Arte nell'Aretino* (Florence, 1980), 26

W. R. Thomas and J. J. K. Rhodes: 'Harpsichords and the Art of Wiredrawing', *Organ Year Book*, x (1980), 126

E. Nordenfelt-Åberg: 'The Harpsichord in 18th-century Sweden', *Early Music*, ix (1981), 47

G. G. O'Brien: 'Some Principles of 18th-century Harpsichord Stringing and their Application', *Organ Year Book*, xii (1981), 160

M. Spencer: 'Harpsichord Physics', *GSJ*, xxxiv (1981), 2

J. Koster: 'A Remarkable Early Flemish Transposing Harpsichord', *GSJ*, xxxv (1982), 45

D. Wraight: 'Considerations on the Categorisation of Italian Harpsichords', *Congress: Premeno 1982*

H. Schott, ed.: *The Historical Harpsichord: Essays in Honor of Frank Hubbard*, i (1984) [articles by W. R. Dowd, F. Hubbard, G. Leonhardt, C. Page and H. Schott]

EDWIN M. RIPIN/HOWARD SCHOTT (with JOHN BARNES, G. GRANT O'BRIEN, WILLIAM DOWD) (1, 2(ii), 3, 4(ii)), DENZIL WRAIGHT (2(i), 4(iii)), WILLIAM DOWD (4(i)), HOWARD SCHOTT (5)

Harpsichord-piano. An instrument combining the hammer action of the piano with the plucking jacks of the harpsichord. Secondary evidence of the existence of such hybrid instruments in the 18th century abounds, but surviving specimens are rare. The earliest experiments on record must predate 1716, when Jean Marius submitted models of four different 'hammer harpsichords' (*clavecins à maillets*) to the Académie Royale des Sciences in Paris, one of which was indeed a combined piano and harpsichord with both hammers and jacks. In the combination instrument demonstrated by Weltman before the same institution in 1759, however, the sounds generated by the plucking action were contrasted with piano-like tones produced by a mechanism anticipating that of the TANGENT PIANO (*Tangentenflügel*) rather than by the normal hammer action invariably used by other makers of the harpsichord-piano.

Combination instruments were produced by some of the most distinguished early piano makers, notably Johann Andreas Stein of Augsburg, Sébastien Erard of Paris and Robert Stodart of London. Stein in particular was captivated by the notion of the harpsichord-piano and persisted in building a variety of models over a number of years. In 1769 he brought out his *polytoniclavichordium*, which despite its name was a combination of a two-manual harpsichord (disposed 1 × 16′, 3 × 8′) and a piano, each with its own set of strings to permit string scaling and striking-points appropriate to each type of instrument. By 1777 he had followed this with a *vis-à-vis* harpsichord-piano. The two surviving examples of this instrument, in Verona and Naples, have three keyboards at one end (a two-manual harpsichord plus piano) and a single keyboard for a second piano at the other end. The earlier (Verona) instrument includes in its harpsichord portion a 16′ stop in addition to the normal two unisons and 4′. The slightly less elaborate instrument in Naples was considered a worthy gift from Emperor Joseph II of Austria to King Ferdinand when presented in 1784 in appreciation of the king's hospitality. For those in more modest circumstances Stein created the *Saitenharmonika* in 1788, described as a 'bichord pianoforte' with a special 'spinet stop' allowing the instrument to be played as either a piano or spinet. It is not known whether this simpler device was a true harpsichord-piano or merely a piano fitted with one of the then prevalent special-effect stops. At least one of Stein's disciples, Ignaz Joseph Senft of Koblenz, is known to have constructed a *vis-à-vis* harpsichord-piano in 1793.

No example of Erard's *clavecin mécanique* of the 1770s is known, but the instrument is said to have been a combined harpsichord and piano with separate keyboards that could be coupled. Robert Stodart's 1777 patent for a combination instrument (including a harpsichord disposed 1 × 8′, 1 × 4′) gives the first detailed drawing of the English grand piano action. (The harpsichord-piano in Washington signed 'Robertus Stodard et Co.' is now thought probably to be the work of a later English maker, James Davis, who obtained a similar patent in 1792.)

Joseph Merlin of London was an instrument maker whose inventiveness ran to such extremes as the 'Barrel Harpsichord', the 'Patent Piano Forte Harpsichord with Kettle Drums' and the 'Patent Double Bass Piano Forte Harpsichord', in addition to such non-musical inventions as the roller-skate and the wheel-chair. He patented a compound harpsichord in 1774. An instrument of his dated 1780 in Munich is remarkable as the only surviving English harpsichord that includes a 16′ stop as well as the normal 8′ and 4′. The downstriking piano hammer action sounds both the strings of the 8′ harpsichord register and a second set. In addition the instrument is fitted with a device for recording improvisations by mechanically inscribing pencil lines on a moving strip of paper. While many harpsichords in the late 18th century were subsequently converted to pianos Merlin is the only maker known to have transformed them into combination instruments.

The harpsichord-piano seems never to have gained wide currency. No music demanding its special capabilities is known, and by the 1790s the instrument was seemingly extinct. Yet in 1861 a British patent was issued for an invention by Robert Thomas Worton, the 'lyro-pianoforte', which combines both jack and hammer actions for plucking and striking the strings.

HOWARD SCHOTT

Harp stop. See BUFF STOP; *see also* ORGAN STOP (*Harfe*).

Harp Ventura. A HARP-LUTE (ii) patented in 1828 by ANGELO BENEDETTO VENTURA.

Harp way. A tuning name which, together with others such as 'viol way', 'lute way', 'plain way', 'Allfonso way', 'lyra way', and 'high harp way', is found in 17th-century tablatures for the LYRA VIOL. These terms refer to certain lyra viol tunings (*see* TUNING), which, because of their wide use, were recognizable by name alone without the need for an elaborate chart. 'Harp way' includes a triad among six open-string viol pitches.

This tuning appears in two forms, one calling for a major triad ('harp way sharp', that is, $D–G–d–g–b–d'$), and one for a minor triad ('harp way flat', that is, $D–G–d–g–b♭–d'$). Tablature itself does not indicate pitch. There is some evidence, however, which links the pitch names given here with these two tunings. The term *sette* was sometimes used as a synonym for way as in *harp sette sharpe*, *French sette* and *sette of eights*.

BIBLIOGRAPHY
F. Traficante: 'Lyra Viol Tunings: "All Ways have been Tried to do It"', *AcM*, xlii (1970), 183

FRANK TRAFICANTE

Harp zither [harp bow]. A ZITHER in which a board serves as string bearer; there are several strings and a bridge.

Harraz. See HERRAZI.

Harris. English family of organ builders.

(1) **Thomas Harris** (*d* ?London, *c*1684). He was middle-aged when, with the DALLAM family (whose servant he is said to have been), he left for Brittany in 1642. He married Katherine Dallam (daughter of Robert) by whom he had six children, including Renatus. He built three organs while in Brittany (Roscoff, 1649–50), Brélevenez (1654–6) and Morlaix, Notre Dame du Mûr (1656–61), and may have helped his father-in-law on others. He returned to England with his family about 1662, after the Restoration. An agreement here made in 1666 with the Dean and Chapter of Worcester described him as living in New Sarum, where he was engaged on the restoration and installation of the pre-Commonwealth organ in the cathedral. This work was followed in the same year by a new organ for Gloucester Cathedral (embodying the old Chair organ Thomas Dallam made for the cathedral in 1641) and by new cathedral organs for Carlisle (1667), Salisbury (1668–9) and Chichester (1677–8). He built instruments for All Hallows, Barking (1675–7), St Sepulchre without Newgate (1676), Winchester College (1664) and St Nicholas, Newcastle (1676), among many others, and was possibly assisted by his son Renatus in the later works. Little survives of his pipework except at Gloucester and Chichester, though the cases remain from four of the above-mentioned organs. Such specifications as are known are conservative in style. His reputation is overshadowed by that of his more famous son (2) Renatus Harris who described him in his letter of 30 August 1683 to the Dean and Chapter of Durham as his 'poore aged father'; by then Renatus seems to have taken over the business.

(2) **Renatus** [René] **Harris** (*b* ?Quimper, *c*1652; *d* ?Bristol, 1724). Son of (1) Thomas Harris. His approximate date of birth derives from a lawsuit of 1703 in

hich he was said to be about 51 years old. He went) England with his father after the Restoration and radually took over the business in the years preceding is father's death. In 1677 he married Joan Hiett, by hom he had a son, (3) John Harris, and a daughter ho married the organ builder John BYFIELD (i). He was Roman Catholic and enjoyed the support of Catherine f Braganza; he built an organ for the Popish Chapel at Vhitehall in 1686–8. G. B. Draghi, the queen's organ- t, demonstrated the instrument Harris built for the emple Church in the conflict with 'FATHER' SMITH which arted in 1683. Towards the end of his life he moved) Bristol.

Renatus Harris was the most flamboyant English organ uilder of his time – not above sharp practice to gain dvantage over his hated rival, Smith, in the famous battle of the organs' contest in the Temple Church (he ; alleged to have sabotaged Smith's bellows, but lost ne contract), or to procure more work for himself. He ell foul of several city vestries and in particular of the iovernors of Christ's Hospital, Horsham, who must have onsidered themselves well rid of him in 1711 (he put neir organ out of order as money was owed to him, and as even alleged to have stolen 23 pipes from the hall rgan). He had a flair for publicity, and never shrank rom the opportunity to recommend himself for work, s for example to the Dean and Chapter at Durham in 683. In 1698 he advertised himself in the *Post Boy* as eing able to divide a note into 100 parts, and he invited all Masters and others of curious and Nice Ears' to visit is house in Wyne Office Court, Fleet Street, to witness is demonstration of such a feat. A sore point with Har- is had been the choice of his rival to build the St Paul's Cathedral organ (finished in 1697), and in about 1712 e produced a pamphlet describing an organ he wished) build at the west end of the cathedral: it would com- rise 'six entire sets of keys for the hands, besides pedals or the feet', and the sixth manual was 'to be adapted or the emitting of sounds to express passion by swell- ng any note, as if inspired by human breath; which is ne greatest improvement an organ is capable of except : had articulation'. At Salisbury Cathedral he built a our-manual organ, borrowing 14 stops of the Great organ by communication' as a second Great, as well as pro- iding a Chair organ of eight stops and an Echo of 11. here was full mutation work on both the Great and cho organs, and eight reeds. He had an engraving pub- ished, with a flattering description of the organ's mer- s, which can claim to be the earliest picture of an English rgan case in its own right.

Harris soon outgrew his father's conservatism and ettled into a mature style apparently much influenced y French practice. This may have been as much the esult of his court connections as of his upbringing. His arger specifications usually have mutation work on the ireat, reeds and metal Chimney Flutes in the French tyle (though he did produce wooden Stopped Diapa- ons: an example may still be heard at All Hallows, wickenham), and diapasons more foundational in sound nan Smith's. Some of the larger schemes have mutation vork on the Choir (e.g. St Bride's, Fleet Street, 1696). Ie handed down to John Harris and John Byfield (i), vho succeeded him in the business, a tradition of reed oicing in the French manner which was noted even by 9th-century writers on the organ. His action work was enerally considered superior to Smith's, and the judg- nent of history may well be that he was the better uilder.

Harris made about 30 new organs after 1684, over half of them for London churches, and rebuilt or exten- sively repaired some 30 others. 12 of his cases survive, and ten organs contain pipework by him. Organs and cases which are typical of his work may be seen at St Andrew Undershaft, London (1696; some pipework and case survives with typical shouldered outline, good carving and varied pipe-mouths); Bristol Cathedral (1685; the two cases, with good carving – moved to stand side by side – survive, as does some pipework); All Hal- lows, Twickenham (formerly All Hallows, Lombard Street, 1700; a case and much pipework survive); and St James, Piccadilly, London (1686–8; Great case from the Popish Chapel, Whitehall, carved by Grinling Gib- bons and with fine figure sculpture). Other organs were built for St Lawrence Jewry (1684–5); St Michael, Cornhill (1684 and 1704); Temple Church (1684); Hereford Cathedral (1686); King's College, Cambridge (1686); Jesus College, Cambridge (1688); Christ Church, Newgate Street (1690); St Bride, Fleet Street (1694); Winchester Cathedral (1694); St Clement, Eastcheap (1696); St Patrick's Cathedral, Dublin (1696–7); Christ Church Cathedral, Dublin (1697); St Andrew, Holborn (1700); Bedford Road Chapel (1700); All Hallows, Lombard Street (1700); St Mary, Lambeth (1701); St Giles, Cripplegate (1705); St Peter Mancroft, Norwich (1707); Salisbury Cathedral (1710); Cork Cathedral (1710); St James, Bristol (1718–19); and St Dionis, Backchurch (1722–4).

(3) **John Harris** (*b* ?London, probably after 1677; *d* ?London, 1743). Son of (2) Renatus Harris. He seems to have worked for his father in London after about 1715, and later apparently settled in Bristol. He took out let- ters of administration to his father's estate in 1725 in partnership with his brother-in-law John Byfield (i), with whom in 1726 he built an important organ for St Mary Redcliffe, Bristol. The builders gave an account of this instrument, with an engraving of the case and gallery, in an advertisement published in 1728–9, by which date they were in Red Lion Street, Holborn, London. The organ had three manuals, 'Pedals to the lower Octave of this great Organ' and '1928 valuable speaking pipes, which are considerably more than either the organ in St Paul's Cathedral or that in St Martin's Church in Lon- don'. The Great organ had 63 keys, complete from *C'*; there was a coupler (the first recorded in England); and of the 26 speaking stops, eight were reeds, including a Bassoon, a 'Vox Humane' and a 'Cromhorn'.

Fine instruments built by the partnership were those of St George, Doncaster (1740; the agreement dated 1738 is quoted in Hopkins and Rimbault, p.131), and St Mary, Shrewsbury (1729, where the case and one rank of pipes remain). The organ now at St Vedast, Foster Lane, Lon- don, was built by them for St Bartholomew-by-the- Exchange in 1732 (it retains its case and much original pipework). Other organs by Harris and Byfield were made for St Alban, Wood Street, London (1728; destroyed in World War II), St Thomas, Bristol (1728–9), Grantham parish church (1736), St Mary, Haverfordwest (1737), St Lawrence, Reading (1741), and the New Music Hall, Fishamble Street, Dublin (1742).

After John Harris's death Byfield carried on the busi- ness in the French-inspired style inherited from Renatus Harris.

BIBLIOGRAPHY
E. J. Hopkins and E. F. Rimbault: *The Organ: its History and Con- struction* (London, 1855, 3/1877/R1972)

A. Freeman: 'John Harris and the Byfields', *The Organ*, xxv (1945–6), 112, 145

——: 'An Organ by Renatus Harris', *The Organ*, xxvi (1946–7), 178

W. L. Sumner: *The Organ; its Evolution, Principles of Construction and Use* (London, 1952, rev. 4/1973)

N. M. Plumley: *The Organs of the City of London* (Oxford, in preparation)

MICHAEL GILLINGHAM/NICHOLAS PLUMLEY

Harris, John (i) (*fl* 1716–30). English trumpet maker. He may have been the successor to the best-known English trumpet maker of the period, William Bull. Herald trumpets of his are known to have been bought in 1716. An extant natural trumpet in F (Oxford, Bate Collection), marked 'Iohn Harris Londini fecit' (*c*1720), has been expertly rebuilt as a slide trumpet. Later it apparently became the model for John Köhler's slide trumpets. Pierre (1890) reported a typical old natural trumpet by Harris, dating from 1730, which had brass fittings and elaborate decorations.

BIBLIOGRAPHY

A. J. Hipkins and W. Gibb: *Musical Instruments, Historic, Rare and Unique* (Edinburgh, 1888/R1945), pl.36

C. Pierre: *La facture instrumentale à l'Exposition universelle de 1889* (Paris, 1890), 284

C. R. Day: *A Descriptive Catalogue of the Musical Instruments Recently Exhibited at the Royal Military Exhibition, London, 1890* (London, 1891/R1971)

W. F. H. Blandford: 'The French Horn in England', *MT*, lxiii (1922), 544

L. G. Langwill: *An Index of Musical Wind-instrument Makers* (Edinburgh, 1960, rev., enlarged 6/1980)

D. L. Smithers: *The Music and History of the Baroque Trumpet before 1721* (London, 1973), 61

A. Baines: *The Bate Collection of Historical Wind Instruments* (Oxford, 1976)

NIALL O'LOUGHLIN

Harris, John (ii) (*fl* London and Boston, *c*1730–69). English spinet and harpsichord maker. The son of Joseph Harris, also a spinet and harpsichord maker, by 1730 he was working in Red Lion Street, London. That year he was granted a patent for 'a new (!) invented harpsichord', whose description implies a type of instrument with only unison stringing but fitted with some octave coupler device. Harris emigrated to Boston in 1768 and the *Boston Gazette* (18 Sept 1768) contains the following notice:

It is with pleasure that we inform the Public, that a few days since was shipped for Newport, a very curious Spinnet, being the first ever made in America, the performance of the ingenious Mr. John Harris, of Boston, (Son of the late Mr. Joseph Harris of London, Harpsichord and Spinnet Maker), and in every respect does Honour to that Artist, who now carries on Business at his House, a few Doors Northward of Dr. Clark's, North End of Boston.

A spinet by John Harris of Boston, dated 1769, is in the Metropolitan Museum of Art, New York.

BIBLIOGRAPHY

D. H. Boalch: *Makers of the Harpsichord and Clavichord* (London, 1956, rev. 2/1974)

R. Russell: *The Harpsichord and Clavichord* (London, 1959, rev. 2/1973), 89

HOWARD SCHOTT

Harrison, G. Donald (*b* Huddersfield, 21 April 1889; *d* New York, 14 June 1956). English organ builder. He joined the AEOLIAN-SKINNER ORGAN CO. in 1927, ultimately becoming president.

Harrison, Lou (*b* Portland, Oregon, 14 May 1917). American composer and instrument builder. He studied with Cowell and Schoenberg, and during the war collaborated with Cage in organizing recitals of percussion music. Among his earliest instruments was the 'tac piano' (1941), an upright piano with thumb tacks or drawing pins driven into the hammers to create a metallic, percussive quality (other musicians, probably working independently, have treated the piano in a similar way, *see* MODIFICATIONS AND NEW TECHNIQUES); the 'tac piano' is used in several of Harrison's scores, and two are called for in *Concerto in slendro* (1961). Everyday and found objects have appeared as percussion in many of his compositions: packing cases and six muted iron pipes in *Canticle no.3* (1941), flowerpots and washtub in *Koncherto* for violin and percussion (1959), and metal pails or cans in *Concerto in slendro* and several other works. Harrison has also experimented with the manual registration of sound on gramophone discs (*Photophonograph*, 1944).

His interest in pitch relations, in particular just intonation, and the music of other cultures, has led Harrison to include non-Western or folk instruments in a number of his works: during the 1960s he wrote three pieces for psaltery and one for Korean court orchestra; he has often used hybrid Eastern and Western instrumentations, adding such instruments as the *changgo*, *p'iri*, *jaltarang* and *xiao* to Western ensembles. An intriguing insight into his musical and compositional approach is given by the booklet *Lou Harrison's Music Primer* (New York, 1971).

Harrison has also constructed a wide range of instruments, often tuned in just intonation. These include some instruments based on historical models, such as the clavichord and the Phrygian aulos, and others made from found objects and materials. Following a tour in the Far East in 1961–2 he collaborated with William Colvig in building the first of two Western gamelans tuned in just intonation, for which he has composed several works; this led to the construction in the USA of many other such Western or American gamelans (*see also* MICROTONAL INSTRUMENTS, §4(iii)). Harrison has also built jade flutes and developed complete families based on individual oriental wind and string instruments.

BIBLIOGRAPHY

W. Colvig: 'A Western Gamelan', *Sound Sculpture: a Collection of Essays by Artists*, ed. J. Grayson (Vancouver, 1975), 162

C. Crawford: 'Interview with Lou Harrison', *Musicworks*, no. (1979), 3

HUGH DAVIES

Harrison & Harrison. English firm of organ builders. It was founded in Rochdale in 1861 by Thomas Hugh Harrison (*b* London, 27 Dec 1839; *d* Spring Grove, 2 March 1912), the son of a London maker of organ parts, following his apprenticeship with Henry Willis. It moved to Durham in 1870; in 1872 Harrison was joined by his brother James Harrison – who had also been apprenticed with Willis – and the firm became Harrison & Harrison. About 1895 Thomas retired and his son Arthur Harrison assumed effective control. Arthur's brother Henry Shaw (Harry) Harrison joined the firm in 1897, but the two brothers did not take complete control until their father's death. In 1904 they built a very large three-manual instrument designed by George Dixon for St Nicholas, Whitehaven. Among its many striking features was the Great tonal structure, which was complete from 32′ to 1′ but without reeds. (Dixon's writings and practice in tonal design have had a significant influence on organ building, as is evident in all the firm's important

ant work.) The Whitehaven instrument attracted much attention and led to the firm's rebuilding the Willis organ in Durham Cathedral in 1905, and to their reconstructing and enlarging another Willis organ at Carlisle Cathedral in 1907.

Like Willis, Harrison & Harrison built or rebuilt a large number of cathedral organs, including those at Belfast (1907), Ely (1908), Glasgow (St Mary's, 1909), Wells (1910), Newcastle upon Tyne (1911), Ripon (1913), Downpatrick (1914), York (1915), Manchester (1916), Gloucester (1920), Oxford (1922), Worcester (1924), Shanghai (1925), Leicester (1929), Edinburgh (St Mary's, 1931) and Exeter (1933). Arthur Harrison died while he was finishing the instrument in Westminster Abbey. The firm also built or rebuilt a number of instruments in college chapels and parish churches, including Magdalen College, Oxford; King's, Trinity and St John's colleges, Cambridge; and St Mary Redcliffe, Bristol, which Arthur regarded as his best work. The firm's most ambitious work was the reconstruction and enlargement of the Willis instrument in the Royal Albert Hall, London (1924 and 1934), while its most important contribution to the art of organ building was the revival of chorus and mixture work, which, partly owing to the influence of the Hope-Jones school, had fallen into almost total disuse. All its large organs are well supplied with compound stops, and even small organ schemes provide for a chorus. The most notable feature of all Harrison & Harrison instruments, whether designed for a large cathedral or a tiny village church, is the beauty and regularity of their finish, and this is attributable to Arthur Harrison.

Following Arthur's death, Harry Harrison maintained the firm with the same high standards. Cuthbert T. L. Harrison (b 1905), Harry's son, who had been apprenticed to the firm in the early 1930s, joined his father in partnership in 1937, and in 1945 took full control. Cuthbert has been one of the leaders of the organ reform movement in England, his most notable contribution being the Royal Festival Hall organ (1954; see ORGAN, fig.48), designed by Ralph Downes. Other important organs built by the firm after World War II include those at the Fairfield Halls, Croydon, and the cathedrals of Wells, Ely, Coventry and St Albans.

BIBLIOGRAPHY
W. L. Sumner: *The Organ: its Evolution, Principles of Construction and Use* (London, 1952, rev. 4/1973)
C. Clutton and A. Niland: *The British Organ* (London, 1963)
L. Elvin: *The Harrison Story* (Lincoln, 1973)
REGINALD WHITWORTH/WILLIAM J. CONNER

Hart. English family of violin makers and dealers. John Thomas Hart (b 17 Dec 1805; d 1 Jan 1874) was first a pupil of Samuel Gilkes, and opened his own business in Princes Street, London, about 1825. He was primarily known as a connoisseur of early Italian instruments, and his dealing activities included the formation of such well-known collections as those of Goding, Plowden, Gillott and Adam. George Hart (i) (b London, 23 March 1839; d nr. Newhaven, 25 April 1891) continued his father's business, which became Hart & Son. His interest extended to the historical and literary side of the violin, and he is chiefly known for his excellent book *The Violin: its Famous Makers and their Imitators*, published in 1875 with several later editions. It was followed by *The Violin and its Music* in 1881. He was succeeded at 28 Wardour Street by his sons George Hart

(ii) (b nr. Warwick, 4 Jan 1860; d c1931–2) and Herbert Hart (b London, 1883; d 20 Oct 1953). In the early 1890s the Harts expanded to include trade in new instruments. Some of these were made for them in France, but others were the work of the Voller brothers, who made some excellent copies of celebrated violins that passed through the Hart shop. Bows were also imported from abroad and branded with the firm's name. Although overshadowed by the Hills, the good reputation of the firm continued and it handled many fine instruments and bows. It closed down with the retirement of Herbert Hart in the autumn of 1939.

BIBLIOGRAPHY
W. M. Morris: *British Violin Makers* (London, 1904)
R. Vannes: *Essai d'un dictionnaire universel des luthiers* (Paris, 1932, 2/1951/R1972 as *Dictionnaire universel des luthiers* and R1981 incl. suppl. 1959)
CHARLES BEARE

Hartung. German family of organ builders. They originally came from Thuringia, but worked until about 1703 in the Worms and Darmstadt region, then in Dürkheim (Leiningen) and subsequently in a wider area. Augustinus Hartung (1677–1739) established a thriving workshop, working initially in the mid-German and later in the south German tradition. About ten of his organs survive. His son Johann Michael Hartung (1703–1763) was the most important member of the family and was widely acknowledged and respected as an organ builder and surveyor; under his direction the firm attained great importance. Only some 13 single- and two-manual organs can be attributed to him but he may have built many more. They have a distinctive, mellow tone with a broad range of timbres; the keyboards are full, and the pedals follow the south German tradition and have a genuine bass function. His reed pipes are insignificant in comparison with those of other builders. His organ cases (even the small ones) are characteristically splendid, with noteworthy wood-carving. An example of his work survives in the Stadtkirche at Edenkoben, but only the case is preserved.

Johann Michael's son Johann Philipp Hartung (1750–1806) carried on the business after the death of his father, with Johann Peter Kampff. After learning the trade with his father, he was also probably apprenticed to J. G. Geib in Saarbrücken. In 1780 the business was transferred to Kallstadt, but the effects of the French Revolution in the Palatinate prevented its further development, and only three organs survive.

BIBLIOGRAPHY
G. Kaleschke: 'Zur Geschichte der Orgelwerke in der protestantische Kirche Lachen', *Protestantische Kirche Lachen: Orgelweihe am 28. März 1976* (Lachen, 1976)
A. Tröscher: 'Die Orgelbauerwerkstatt Hartung', *Mitteilungen der Arbeitsgemeinschaft für mittelrheinische Musikgeschichte*, xxxvii (1978)
G. KALESCHKE

Hartung, Michael [Harton, Michielle] (fl Padua, early 17th century). German lute maker. He came from Tieffenbruck in the Bavarian Alps and apparently served his apprenticeship with Leonardo Tieffenbrucker in Venice, adopting there the more Italianate version of his name. It seems from the labels in his instruments that he was active in Padua at least until 1640. Few of his instruments have survived; among them are a lute and a theorbo in the Nuremberg museum and another theorbo at Copenhagen. These are typical of their period, with a rounded profile and a back made from a large number of narrow ribs, mostly of yew, often exploiting the light and dark colours of its heart and sapwood. One of Hartung's lutes appears in a still-life by the Italian painter Evaristo Baschenis, where it can be identified by the maker's mark on the capping-strip.

For a bass lute by Hartung, *see* LUTE, fig.9*g*.

BIBLIOGRAPHY

W. L. von Lütgendorff: *Die Geigen- und Lautenmacher vom Mittelalter bis zur Gegenwart* (Frankfurt am Main, 1904, rev. 6/1922/R1968)
R. Vannes: *Essai d'un dictionnaire universel des luthiers* (Paris, 1932, 2/1951/R1972 as *Dictionnaire universel des luthiers* and R1981 incl. suppl. 1959)

Harwood, Ian (*b* Petersfield, 29 Aug 1931). English maker of lutes and viols, lutenist and singer. He received his early musical training as a chorister at Winchester Cathedral, and was later an alto at St Albans Cathedral, New College, Oxford, and Ely Cathedral. He also studied aircraft design (graduate of the Royal Aeronautical Society, 1953). His interest in early music led him to make a lute in 1956 and to begin lessons with Diana Poulton; in 1958 he set up as an instrument maker in Oxford, then moved in 1960 to Ely, where he was soon joined by John Isaacs, his partner until 1972. His début as a professional lutenist dates from 1960, when he demonstrated as a performer the musical effect of the lighter construction and low-tension stringing which he advocated as a maker. In 1964 he received the Tovey Prize for his research into the sources of English lute music. He founded the Campian Consort (1967) and has performed and recorded much 16th- and 17th-century music with it and other ensembles. An active teacher of lute playing and construction, he is a founder-member of the Lute Society and edited its journal (1965–70). In 1972–3 he was curator of the Benton Fletcher Collection of early keyboard instruments at Fenton House, Hampstead, and in 1974 he began making 16th-century-type viols. His extensive influence on British lute making and playing has determined younger lutenists' rejection of the elements of construction and playing technique based on the guitar that some noted earlier modern builders and performers cultivated. His pioneer work in the revival of the Renaissance viol has had a similar degree of influence on an entire school of younger British makers.

WRITINGS

'A Fifteenth-century Lute Design', *LSJ*, ii (1960), 3
'John Maynard and "The Twelve Wonders of the World"', *LSJ*, iv (1962), 7
'The Origins of the Cambridge Lute Manuscripts', *LSJ*, v (1963), 32
'Rosseter's *Lessons for Consort* of 1609', *LSJ*, vii (1965), 15
'An Introduction to Renaissance Viols', *Early Music*, ii (1974), 234

HOWARD SCHOTT

Hasapi. Boat-shaped lute of the Batak Toba area of the province of North Sumatra, varying in length between about 50 and 65 cm. Its soundbox is about 8 to 10 cm at its maximum width and it has a large hole at the rear. Its two metal strings are stretched from tuning-pegs on each side of the neck and pinned to a piece of wood near the base of the instrument. At the top of the neck there may be a carving, usually of a human face or body, and some rare antique models feature eyes of silver. Two *hasapi* are used in an ensemble to play *uning-uningan* (instrumental music). The *hasapi ina* ('mother lute') plays the main melody, along with a *sordam* (flute) and a *gar-*

antung (five-key xylophone), both playing an octave lower, and the *hasapi anak* ('child lute') plays melodic figurations, while the *hesek* (metal idiophone) marks the quadruple metric pulse. The ensemble is played when young people mix socially and at Opera Batak performances.

MARGARET J. KARTOMI

Haseneier [Haseneir], **Heinrich J.** (1798–1890). German wind instrument maker, principally known for his invention of the contrabassophon in 1847 (*see* BASSOON, §8) and the BASS-EUPHONIUM about 1850.

Haskell, Charles S. (*b* Massachusetts, 1840; *d* ?Philadelphia, 1903). American organ builder. He was esteemed as a furniture maker before entering the organ-building trade around 1880. He worked for his cousin Hilborne Roosevelt in Philadelphia and opened his own shop at 1521 Kasler Street in 1893. The business was continued after his death by his son Charles E. Haskell (*b* Massachusetts, 1878; *d* Philadelphia, *c*1928), who installed an average of six to eight organs each year until 1928. Charles's elder son, William (*b* Chicago, 29 Nov 1865; *d* Brattleboro, Vermont, 8 May 1927), became the guiding genius of the ESTEY Organ Company in Brattleboro, Vermont. Haskell organs are of solid construction though tonally conservative; they are similar to English church organs of the period, largely because of a personal tie between the Haskells and the younger Henry Willis in London. Charles S. Haskell shared inventor's rights for an important pneumatic ventil windchest and pneumatic action and also for a membrane (diaphragm) valve wind-chest and a small chamber organ. Later innovations included organ consoles with stop controls conveniently located on an auxiliary keyboard and a luminous console with lights to identify stops drawn. While a superintendent at Estey, William became the most prolific inventor of organ devices. These included an open pipe with a sounding length double the external length, a reedless reed voice and pneumatic chimes; he was also responsible for the technology of Estey's parlour automatic player organ.

BIBLIOGRAPHY

G. A. Audsley: *The Art of Organ-building* (New York, 1905/R1965), ii, 314, 322
The Philosophy of an Organ Builder (Brattleboro, 1923) [published by the Estey Organ Co.]
R. M. Strippy: letters to the editor, *The Tracker*, xxi/4 (1977), 24; xxviii/2 (1982), 4

LLOYD P. FARRAR

Hass. German family of wind and string instrument makers. Hieronymus Albrecht Hass was born in Hamburg, and baptized on 1 December 1689; he died between 1746 and 1761. Johann Adolph Hass, his son, received Hamburg citizenship on 28 October 1746 and had died by 1776. Dietrich Christopher Hass (*b* Hamburg, 1731) was only remotely related, if at all, to these makers.

An assessment of the work of the Hass family can be based on Russell's view (2/1973) that the 'extent and quality of their surviving work must place them first in German instrument making' and Hubbard's comment (1965) that of all their instruments 'only one has what could be regarded as a normal disposition'. Although little is known of their other activities, Gerber (*Lexicon*, 1790–92) reported that they also made organs, and Russell's idea that all their harpsichords may have been made to special order is not unlikely. Certainly Hamburg was more a harpsichord centre than most German cities; Mattheson preferred harpsichords in church to regals (*Das neu-eröffnete Orchester*, 1713). H. A. Hass was baptized in the Jacobikirche, one of the several Hamburg churches to have large Schnitger organs; but it is a gross oversimplification to see his harpsichords, as Hubbard did, as 'the grotesque result of the barbarous imposition of tonal concepts appropriate to the organ'. Still more harm has been done to the cause of harpsichord playing by the old idea that the much altered Hass-like instrument with 16', 8', 4' stops in Berlin was a true 'Bach harpsichord'.

As a harpsichord made by Christian Zell in 1728 shows, Hamburg builders had established their own style of decoration, construction and (probably) sound by the 1720s. Several Hass instruments show an attempt to develop the potential of the harpsichord. That of 1721 (Göteborg) is 2·55 metres long, that of 1723 (Copenhagen) has four sets of strings (8', 8', 8', 4', *F'* to *c'''*) and a sliding lower manual for coupling, several have a 16' row (including one made in 1734) and even a 2' for the lower half or so of the lower manual. Their scale is similar to that of English harpsichords (though the bass of the 4' is normally longer), their plucking points to French instruments. Stop levers are usually placed on the wrest plank, so that the player has to reach over the nameboard; decoration usually incorporates many techniques, e.g. lacquered casework, tempera-painted soundboard, olive wood, ivory, mother-of-pearl and tortoise-shell veneers or plates for various details, the latter more especially on clavichords. The largest harpsichord known to have been made before the 20th century was built by H. A. Hass in 1740, with three manuals, five sets of strings (16', 8', 8', 4', 2'), six rows of jacks (including a lute stop), harp for the 16' row, and coupling devices. What it was built to play is uncertain.

Apart from a harpsichord, J. A. Hass's known instruments are clavichords, rarely fretted, often long, large, brass-strung instruments, with a continuous compass of *F'* to *f'''*; some have a second soundboard below the keys, with 4' strings in the bass (which were not admired by C. P. E. Bach; *see* FRIEDERICI), and at least one with strings of 8', 8', 8', in the treble, 8', 8', 4', in the bass to *c'*. It was large instruments such as these that so many later 18th-century German composers had in mind, with their good *Bebung* effects, discreet volume and a fairly bright tone. For details of surviving Hass instruments see Boalch (2/1974).

See also CLAVICHORD, §4, esp. fig.8.

BIBLIOGRAPHY
D. H. Boalch: *Makers of the Harpsichord and Clavichord, 1440–1840* (London, 1956, rev. 2/1974)
R. Russell: *The Harpsichord and Clavichord* (London, 1959, rev. 2/1973)
F. Hubbard: *Three Centuries of Harpsichord Making* (Cambridge, Mass., 1965)
DONALD HOWARD BOALCH, PETER WILLIAMS

Hát cải lương [hát chèo, hát tuồng, hát bội]. Music theatre genre of Vietnam. The *hát cải lương* is the modernized genre, created in 1918. In the 1930s the instrumental ensemble used to accompany it consisted of five instruments: a *đàn kìm* (moon-shaped lute; *see* ĐÀN NGUYỆT), a *đàn cò* (two-string fiddle), a *đàn tranh* (16-string zither), an *ống sáo* (transverse flute) and a *song lang* (woodblock). Nowadays an electric guitar and a Western violin, with a special tuning, are used togeth-

er with the *đàn kìm* and *đàn tranh*. In certain troupes an electric organ and saxophones are also used.

The *hát chèo* is the folk genre. Before 1945 the accompanying instrumental ensemble comprised two groups, percussion and melody instruments: a *trống dê* (small double-headed cylindrical drum beaten with two sticks), a *trống cơm* (barrel-shaped 'rice drum'), a *mõ* (slit-drum), a *thanh la* (small gong), a *sáo* (transverse flute) and a *đàn nhị* (two-string fiddle). Since 1945 additional instruments have been used: a *tiêu* (end-blown flute), a *dai hô* (two-string fiddle larger than the *đàn nhị*), a *đàn nguyệt* (moon-shaped lute), a *đàn bầu* (single-string box zither), a *đàn tranh* (16-string zither) and a *đàn tam thập lục* (many-stringed zither).

The *hát tuồng* or *hát bội* is the traditional genre. In the accompanying instrumental ensemble percussion instruments play an important part. They feature a *trống chiến* (double-headed barrel drum) together with a *đầu đường* (flat gong), a *trống cơm*, a *trống bát cấu* (single-headed barrel drum), a *song lang* and *chập choã* (cymbals); the main wind instrument is the *kèn* (oboe, similar to the *suona*), and the leading string instrument the *đàn cò* or *đàn nhị*, sometimes together with a *đàn gáo* (two-string fiddle) and a *đàn kìm*.

TRÂN VAN KHÊ

Hāth ghaṇṭī. Brass bell of Orissa, India. *See* GHAṆṬĀ.

Ḥatzotzerah (Heb.; pl. *ḥatzotzeroth*). The trumpet of the Bible. The specification of the construction and use of *ḥatzotzeroth* in the Bible (*Numbers* x.2ff) and, many centuries later, Josephus's description of them (*Antiquities*, iii, §291 = chap.12, §6) makes it clear that these trumpets were similar to those found in Tutankhamun's tomb (see illustration). Moses was commanded to make two trumpets of silver, of beaten work (i.e. of sheet metal raised by the hammer, and not cast like most ancient trumpets apart from the Egyptian) and to use them as signal instruments, both for war and for normal movement of the encampment in the desert. They were to be blown by the priests and they remained exclusively a Temple instrument, often used in considerable

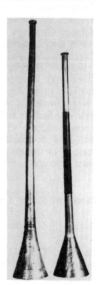

Trumpets found in Tutankhamun's tomb, 1361–1352 BC (Egyptian Museum, Cairo)

numbers (*II Chronicles* v.12), until the Temple was destroyed by the Romans (AD 70). All references to trumpeting in the Bible by persons other than priests are translations of SHOFAR and it is only because the shofar was not exclusively a priestly instrument that it could continue in use after the destruction of the Temple. Experiment with copies of Tutankhamun's trumpets shows that each could produce one good note, with two other possible pitches, and it is likely therefore that the *hatzotzeroth* produced only rhythmic blasts on a single pitch.

See also BIBLICAL INSTRUMENTS and TRUMPET, §3.

BIBLIOGRAPHY

H. Hickmann: 'La trompette dans l'Egypte ancienne', *Annales du Service des antiquités de l'Egypte*, suppl.i (Cairo, 1946), 1–75
J. Montagu: 'One of Tutankhamon's Trumpets', *GSJ*, xxix (1976), 115

JEREMY MONTAGU

Haui. CONCH-SHELL TRUMPET of Puluwat. *See* SAUI.

Haulteterre. *See* HOTTETERRE family.

Haupa. Long thin bamboo flute of the Marindanim people of Irian Jaya (West New Guinea). Its lower end is stopped with a plug. The bamboo tube is split along its entire length and wrapped tightly with bark strips. The instrument produces a 'cracked' tone; it is played with the *sosom* (bullroarer). See J. Kunst: *Music in New Guinea* (The Hague, 1967).

MARGARET J. KARTOMI

Hauptwerk (Ger.: 'chief department'; Dutch *Hoofdwerk*). Like GREAT ORGAN, Grand Orgue and Organo Primo in some of their usages, *Hauptwerk* today denotes the main manual of an organ. *Werk* itself is an equivalent of *opus* used in church documents (Utrecht, *c*1400) or theoretical manuscripts (Arnaut de Zwolle, *F-Pn* lat.7295; *c*1450), and was first used to refer to the organ in general (Schlick, *Spiegel der Orgelmacher und Organisten*, 1511). It soon meant by implication the main manual, i.e. the first to be planned, that with the main chorus – as distinct from (*a*) the CHAIR ORGAN, (*b*) the POSITIVE below or above the main chest, and (*c*) the pedals (*see* PEDAL). Praetorius (*Syntagma musicum*, 2/1619) still used OBERWERK to refer to this main manual, since it was placed above the player; other terms found in church archives and contemporary treatises had been *Principael* (referring to its purpose of supplying the Blockwerk), *Werk* (Gorinchem St Jan, 1518), *Manual* (Schlick, 1511), *der vulle Orgel* (Hamburg Petrikirche, 1548), *Prinzipall-Lade* (Münster Cathedral, 1610). Terminology became stable early in the 17th century, but it was some time before *Hauptwerck* (Würzburg Cathedral, 1614) became the most usually accepted term. The contents of the *Hauptwerk* and its relationship to the other departments are the history of the organ itself.

PETER WILLIAMS

Hausorgel (Ger.). CHAMBER ORGAN.

Hausse (Fr.). FROG.

Hautbois (Fr.). (1) OBOE; for further terminological discussion, *see* SHAWM.
(2) An ORGAN STOP.

Hautbois baryton (Fr.). BARITONE OBOE.

Hautbois d'amour (Fr.). OBOE D'AMORE.

Hautbois de Poitou (Fr.: 'Poitou oboe'). A straigh wind-cap shawm (*see* WIND-CAP INSTRUMENTS) described by Mersenne (1635–6), who illustrated three sizes with ranges of about a 9th upwards from *d'*, *f* and *E*; the bass had a bore which doubled back on itself like a bassoon These three instruments and a small bagpipe with one drone called a 'cornemuse' (not to be confused with the wind-cap CORNAMUSA), which doubled the descant *haut bois de Poitou*, formed a regular consort in the Grande Ecurie of the kings of France until well into the 17th century. Indeed this consort survived at least in name throughout the *ancien régime*, though it probably no longer functioned as a musical unit in the 18th century In both his treatises Mersenne included a composition for this combination of instruments by Henry le Jeune. one of the French royal composers. The *hautbois de Poitou* survived in France as a folk instrument into the 19th century.

BIBLIOGRAPHY

M. Mersenne: *Harmonicorum instrumentorum libri IV* (Paris, 1636) pubd with *Harmonicorum libri* (Paris, 1635–6) as *Harmonicorum libri XII* (Paris, 1648, 2/1652/R1972)
——: *Harmonie universelle* (Paris, 1636–7/R1963; Eng. trans. of the book on instruments, 1957)
B. R. Boydell: *The Crumhorn and Other Renaissance Windcap Instruments* (Buren, 1982), 342ff

HOWARD MAYER BROWN

Hautboy. (1) *See* OBOE.
(2) An ORGAN STOP.

Haut-dessus (Fr.: 'high treble'). The uppermost part in a vocal or instrumental ensemble. The term is mostly used where there is a divided treble, the second part being called the 'bas-dessus'; *see also* DESSUS.

Haute-contre (Fr.). A term for the member of an instrumental family corresponding to the high tenor voice (the voice known by this name was cultivated in France until about the end of the 18th century). The term originated in the late 15th century or early 16th as a French form of 'contratenor altus', a line in polyphony lying just above the tenor. Philibert Jambe de Fer, in his *Epitome musical* (1556), used the early version 'contre-haute' as well as the more common 'hautecontre'. Subsequently, and until the early 19th century, *haute-contre* (with the hyphen) was the standard French word for an 'alto' part in instrumental music, but 'alto' and 'tenor' parts frequently overlapped and were often played either on the same instrument or on instruments only slightly different in size and tuned alike. Jean Rousseau described in his *Traité de la viole* (1687) a viol 'a little smaller than the Taille to serve as *Haute-contre*', but he explained that the two instruments were tuned to the same pitch (*see also* TAILLE).

OWEN JANDER/R

Hauteterre [Hauterre]. *See* HOTTETERRE family.

Hauyani. Term used in Zambia, Zimbabwe, Malawi and parts of Mozambique for a type of triadic tuning and a specific guitar-playing technique. In the 1940s and

'50s the Hawaiian guitar attained popularity in south-
n Africa. This led to a revitalization of an old instru-
ental technique: playing on one string by means of a
ider' (usually a piece of calabash, a knife or a small
ttle). This technique is used in sub-Saharan Africa,
r example on single-string idiochord zithers. It was
ployed in southern Africa to reproduce the glissando
fects of Hawaiian guitar music, a style akin to the
ottleneck' guitar style of the southern USA. The term
awaiian has been adapted into the local Bantu lan-
ages, hence 'hauyani'. See G. Kubik: 'Neo-traditional
pular Music in East Africa since 1945', *Popular Music*,
1981), 83.

GERHARD KUBIK

avirare. Reed PANPIPES documented in the late 19th
ntury among the Camayurá Indians of the upper Xingú
ver of Amazonian Brazil. See *IzikowitzMISAI*, 408.

awaiian guitar [steel guitar]. A variant of the GUI-
R, developed in Hawaii in the second half of the 19th
ntury. Around 1830 Mexican cattle herders intro-
ced the guitar into Hawaii. The Hawaiians took up
e instrument and incorporated it into their own music
ith appropriate 'slack key' or open tuning in which the
rings are all tuned to the notes of a major triad. Joseph
ekuku is said to have been the first person to place
e guitar across his knees and to slide a comb (later a
nknife) along the strings to produce the glissandos for
hich Hawaiian music has become known. In the early
th century this music became popular in the USA,
here guitar companies began to market Hawaiian gui-
rs with a raised nut, which held the strings higher above
e fingerboard than on a normal guitar, and a steel bar
an accessory for slide playing (hence the name 'steel
itar'); the use of other objects, such as a bottleneck,
r a similar sort of slide playing developed in blues at
uch the same time, and later became common in coun-
y music. Many musicians who played in Hawaiian style
opted the DOBRO during the early 1930s, while others
ok up the earliest manufactured ELECTRIC GUITAR, the
ckenbacker 'Frying Pan' (1931), a small steel guitar
at was designed to be played across the lap. Leg-
ounted electric steel guitars were introduced by the
ibson company during the 1930s. By the 1950s some
odels had as many as four necks. Others, known as
edal steel guitars', incorporated knee-levers and sev-

Tawaiian guitar (model De Luxe 6) by Fender, 1957–
0

eral pedals for rapid alterations in tuning. On instruments with multiple necks (which are often differently
tuned) one is often reserved for special effects, such as
animal and bird sounds in Hawaiian music and train
noises in American country music.
See also HAUYANI.

BIBLIOGRAPHY
M. Brisenden: 'In a Hula Heaven: the Story of the Hawaiian Gui-
  tar', *Collusion*, no.4 (1983), 10
M. Hood: 'Musical Ornamentation as History: the Hawaiian Steel
  Guitar', *YTM*, xv (1983), 141

HUGH DAVIES

Haward. English family of spinet and harpsichord
makers, three of whom were active in London in the
17th century. Charles Haward worked in Aldgate Street,
and Queen Anne had a virginal made by him. John
Haward made a harpsichord fitted with registration pedals
(which Mace described in *Musick's Monument*, 1676/
R, p.235). A harpsichord now at Knole and dated 1622
is the only surviving instrument made by John Haward.
Thomas Haward was living in Bishopsgate in 1656 and
in the parish of St Giles, Cripplegate, in 1663.

'Possibly the most important English harpsichord-
making dynasty of the 17th century' (Hubbard, 1950),
the Hawards left two particularly important harpsichords. John Haward's instrument at Knole combines
elements of English, Italian and Flemish styles, though
the general concept is Italian; similar points could be
made about English organs from c1620. For instance,
the 'counter-soundboard' or second internal soundboard
of this instrument could be a Flemish feature, but it is
also known from an Italian harpsichord of 1533. It may
also have been designed to provide two pitches (8', 8'
at one pitch; a further 8' at a 4th or 5th below). In either
case, the 1622 harpsichord is the oldest English domestic keyboard instrument extant except for the claviorgan made by THEEWES in 1579 (now in the Victoria and Albert
Museum). Similarly, Charles Haward's 1683 harpsichord (now at Hovingham Hall) is the only firmly
recorded English harpsichord from the second half of
the century. While the special instrument constructed
for Thomas Mace had a buff stop, the 1683 harpsichord
has a lute stop, a more remarkable feature. It also has
a rounded tail, and stops piercing the cheekpiece; its
scale is short, its bridge and specification (8', 8')
Italianate, its case-members somewhat heavier than the
1622 instrument, that is, more Flemish; its four roses
suggest rather the influence of English virginals. Such
commixtures were not uncommon in English, French
and German harpsichord making before c1725, and the
end results often make it difficult to discern dominant
trends.

Charles Haward left at least 11 'bentside' spinets, that
is, small, single-strung, obliquely planned harpsichords, with what were considered advantages over the
common rectangular virginals. In his diary for 4 April
1668 Pepys noted that he 'called upon one Hayward,
that makes virginalls, and did there like of a little espinette . . . I had a mind to a small harpsichon, but this
takes up less room' (see also his entries for 10, 13 and
15 July). Scale was often rather short in the treble and
the soundboard of small dimensions in the bass. The
rack keyboards and other details of jacks and keys
remained standard for all spinets well into the 18th century. But how much can be credited to Charles Haward
and how much to his contemporaries, such as Player
and Keene, is not clear. Nor is it known how far Mace's

foot-operated stop-changing, or his specification of 8′, 8′, lute, 4′ and buff, were applied in the standard models produced by either John or Charles Haward. For details of surviving Haward harpsichords see Boalch (2/1974).

BIBLIOGRAPHY
F. Hubbard: 'Two Early English Harpsichords', *GSJ*, iii (1950), 12
D. H. Boalch: *Makers of the Harpsichord and Clavichord 1440–1840* (London, 1956, rev. 2/1974)
R. Russell: *The Harpsichord and Clavichord* (London, 1959, rev. 2/1973)
F. Hubbard: *Three Centuries of Harpsichord Making* (Cambridge, Mass., 1965)
T. McGeary: 'Early English Harpsichord Building', *Harpsichord Magazine*, i/1 (1973), 7
                    DONALD HOWARD BOALCH, PETER WILLIAMS

Hawkins, John Isaac (*fl* 1799–1845). English engineer, inventor and piano maker. He spent part of his life in the USA and is best known for his invention of the upright piano. (Matthias Müller invented the upright piano independently in Vienna about the same time.) Previously upright pianos were either grands or squares turned on end and placed on a stand, but Hawkins's achievement was to use the space below the keyboard down to the floor. He called his piano a 'portable grand' and patented it in 1800 in Philadelphia and London, his father, Isaac Hawkins, acting as his agent in England. The patent contains a wide range of additional inventions including a soundboard suspended within a metal frame and braced from behind with metal rods, and mechanical wrest pins that worked in a metal-covered wrest plank (*see* PIANOFORTE, §I, 6). This was the first use of metal to stabilize the frame in an upright piano, and the frame was later adopted by a number of makers. Hawkins also used an outer covering of cloth on top of layers of leather on the hammers. Hawkins's two surviving pianos (one formerly in the Broadwood collection and the other in the Smithsonian Institution, Washington, DC) are fine examples of cabinet work, incorporating a keyboard that folds up and handles on either side for easy transport. Hawkins advertised that his pianos could be purchased 'at little more than half the price of imported grand or square pianofortes', but his instruments were never popular. The 1885 International Inventions Exhibition catalogue states that Hawkins brought his upright piano to London, and that daily performances were given on it, but with no success: 'the ingenuity and even genius displayed in its invention being unsupported by that first desideratum of a Pianoforte, good tone'.

Hawkins also invented the Claviola (*see* CLAVIOLA (i)), a bowed keyboard instrument in the shape of an upright piano. It was first demonstrated in Philadelphia in 1802 and again in London in 1813. Hawkins is last recorded in London in 1845.

BIBLIOGRAPHY
International Inventions Exhibition: John Broadwood & Sons (London, 1885)
R. E. M. Harding: *The Piano-forte: its History Traced to the Great Exhibition of 1851* (Cambridge, 1933, rev. 2/1978)
H. R. Hollis: *The Piano: a Pictorial Account of its Ancestry and Development* (Newton Abbot and London, 1975)
                                    MARGARET CRANMER

Haxby, Thomas (*b* York, baptized 25 Jan 1729; *d* York, 31 Oct 1796). English musical instrument maker. He was the son of Robert Haxby, a joiner, from whom he presumably learnt his woodworking skills. In 1750 he became parish clerk of St Michael-le-Belfry, York, and at about the same time he was appointed a singing man

of York Minster; he held both posts until his death. F opened a music and instrument shop 'at the Organ Blake Street' in York on 15 June 1756. No mention made of his making instruments until he became a fre man of York in 1758, but from 1754 he received a annual salary for tuning and repairing the organ in Yo Minster. He made harpsichords, spinets, pianos, organ citterns and violins; he also published music. He repair the organ of Leeds Parish Church in 1760 and built new organ for St Mary's Church, Scarborough, in 176 His largest instrument was the organ for Louth Pari Church (1768; two manuals, 15 stops); this was replace by Gray & Davison in 1857, but survived until 1868 the church of St Thomas, Agar Town, in north-we London. On 28 December 1770 he was granted a pate (no.977) for a 'single harpsichord' (two 8′ stops, 4 lute and harp), which produced ten registrations by t use of one pedal.

In the *York Courant* of 14 October 1788 Hax announced the disposal of his printed music business Samuel Knapton, who succeeded him at a new shop Blake Street. Haxby's brother-in-law and nephew, w had both worked for him for some years, particularly finishing his instruments, took over his instrument bus ness on his death, renaming it Tomlinson & Son (*Yo Herald*, 5 November 1796).

Haxby's surviving square pianos are carefully mad and attractive with tasteful nameboard decoration. H annual production increased to 24 instruments from 178 and reached 36 in 1790. They were numbered and date on the bottom key-lever, and were based on the earlie English models (up to five octaves, single action wi overdampers). Haxby sometimes replaced the hand stop with pedals, one of which operated a lid swell. He wa a finer craftsman than many of his contemporaries i London.

BIBLIOGRAPHY
D. Haxby and J. Malden: 'Thomas Haxby of York (1729–179 – an Extraordinary Musician and Musical Instrument Maker', *Yo Historian*, ii (1978), 43
                                    MARGARET CRANME

Hayashi. A term for a wide range of types of Japanes instrumental ensemble, the main instruments of whic are generally transverse flutes (*see* FUE), drums (*se* TAIKO) and gongs or cymbals (*see* CHAPPA and KANE) The term may designate the instruments themselves, th performers or occasionally (used as a suffix, *-bayash* the genre of music itself. The word is a nominaliz form of a verb meaning 'to encourage' or 'spur on', an indeed the *hayashi* usually provide impetus for singer dancers or an entire festival. Because of its broad bási meaning the term has many other applications, such to the chorus which supports the solo singer in folkson

The exciting *gigaku* masked dances, imported fro the Asian mainland no later than the 7th century, a the ancestors of many local public ritual performanc of today; they were accompanied by transverse flute drums and cymbals and gongs, and this remains th standard ensemble for such folkdances.

There are also several specialized subtypes of *h yashi*. The Nō *hayashi* comprises three rhythm instr ments and a flute. In the kabuki musical theatre the ter appears as *debayashi* ('on-stage *hayashi*') and *kageb yashi* ('hidden *hayashi*'), the latter being another term f the GEZA music and the former most commonly refe ring to the NAGAUTA ensemble when it appears on stag

Iayashi' alone usually denotes just the *nagauta* drums
d flutes, omitting the shamisen (lute) and singers. On-
age musicians other than the *nagauta* ensemble – for
ample *kiyomoto* or *tokiwazu* singers and shamisen
ayers – are called *degatari* ('on-stage recitation').
atsuri-bayashi ('festival *hayashi*') can encompass the
tyashi music of any large festival (hence *gion-bayashi*,
ama-bayashi etc), but it has come to refer more spe-
fically to a genre of Shintō shrine music played in and
ound Tokyo. Once played by parishioners and called
y the name of the shrine (e.g. *kanda-bayashi*), it is
bw often performed by semi-professional guilds.

BIBLIOGRAPHY
. P. Malm: '*Shōden*: a Study in Tokyo Festival Music', *YIFMC*,
vii (1975), 44

DAVID W. HUGHES

ayir. Bass drum played by Arab men in the Malindi
strict of Kenya. Other Arabic drums of the area are
e *marwas* and *tasa*.

ayl [Hail, Heyl]. German family of organ builders.
f Swabian origin, they worked from about 1590 to 1640
the northern foothills of the Alps from Lake Con-
ance to Salzburg, as well as in the Tyrol. Active fam-
y members included Daniel Hayl the elder and his
other, the Cistercian monk Abraham, and Daniel's sons
aniel the younger (*b* *c*1590; *d* after 1640) and Simon
*c*1590; *d* after 1642). Around 1600 the family lived
Irsee; subsequently Daniel the younger moved to the
alzburg area and Simon to Upper Bavaria. There is
vidence of Daniel the elder's work, from before 1592
after 1612, in the following places: Ravensburg;
onstanz Minster; Langnau Monastery; Rheinau Abbey;
chsenhausen Imperial Abbey; Trinity Church, Kauf-
euren; Church of Our Blessed Lady, Landsberg; the
istercian monastery at Stams (with his brother); St Ste-
en's, Lindau; Stiftskirche, Schloss Zeil; and the
enedictine abbey, Irsee. Daniel the younger can be
aced in Salzburg from 1618 to 1638, and Simon in
ozen, Polling and Wessobrunn from 1618 to 1624. For
s work in Konstanz, Daniel the elder won particular
spect and praise. The Hayl family adhered to the aus-
re style of the south-west German master organ build-
s of the 16th century (*see* STURM, KASPAR).

BIBLIOGRAPHY
Quoika: 'Über die österreichische und oberschwäbische Barock-
orgel', *Der Barock, seine Orgeln und seine Musik in Ober-
schwaben: Ochsenhausen 1951*, 59
—: 'Dispositionen von Orgeln', ibid, 126
, Forer: *Orgeln in Österreich* (Vienna and Munich, 1973)

HANS KLOTZ

aynes, William S. (*b* Providence, Rhode Island, 27
ly 1864; *d* Boston, Mass., 28 Jan 1939). American
oehm flute maker. He was trained in the Gorham fac-
ries in Providence as a silver craftsman. In 1888 he
ompleted his first flute, and for the next six years worked
conjunction with his brother, George W. Haynes. He
vered this connection early in 1894, and later that year
was engaged by John C. Haynes & Co. to start a
ranch for this firm until 1900, after which he started
s own company at 180–86 Washington Street in Bos-
n, Massachusetts.

Haynes first made Boehm flutes in wood, but in 1913
nished his first instrument in silver, and made his last
ooden flute in 1917. In 1919 he made his first gold
ute and piccolo, and in 1930 his first platinum flute.

Besides flutes and piccolos, he manufactured 'alto' flutes
in G and even double-walled silver clarinets. Haynes's
son William worked for some time with his father, but
later joined John Schwelm. Haynes's wife, Lola Allison, continued his business after his death until 1967.
Wm. S. Haynes Co. is still at 12 Piedmont Street, Boston.

Haynes, with his foreman Verne Q. Powell, was
responsible for introducing the manufacture of French-
type silver flutes, alto flutes and piccolos to the USA;
he achieved wide acclaim internationally and set standards for many other makers in the same field.

BIBLIOGRAPHY
C. M. Ayars: *Contributions to the Art of Music* (New York, 1937)

FRIEDRICH VON HUENE

He. Prototype of the Chinese mouth organ SHENG.

Hearpe. A medieval term for the lyre, often interpreted as
harp (*see* HARP, §1). The Anglo-Saxon verb 'hearpan'
is generally taken to mean to play a string instrument.

Hebbiat. Flat gong of the Ifugao people of the northern
Philippines. *See* GANGSA (i).

Hebenstreit [Hebestreitt], **Pantaleon** (*b* Eisleben, 1667;
d Dresden, 15 Nov 1750). Inventor of the PANTALEON.
In 1737 he also made a glockenspiel of porcelain.

Heckel. German family of woodwind instrument makers. It was through them that the German bassoon, based
on the research of CARL ALMENRAEDER, reached its present degree of perfection. Many of the reforms carried
out by successive members of the Heckel family are of
so fundamental a nature that today the German-style
instrument is frequently known as the 'Heckel' bassoon
regardless of its actual maker. A collateral branch of the
family has long been established as brass instrument
makers. The first member to specialize in woodwind
instruments was Johann Adam Heckel (*b* Adorf, Saxony,
14 July 1812; *d* Biebrich, 13 April 1877). Having learnt
his craft in his native town, he was for a time employed
by Schott of Mainz, who was carrying out experimental
work for Almenraeder. In 1831 Heckel, encouraged by
Almenraeder, opened his own business at Biebrich near
Wiesbaden, where the firm has remained ever since. Until
1843 Heckel-Almenraeder bassoons were produced there
for Schott and were stamped with his name. J. A. Heckel was followed in business by his son Wilhelm (*b* Biebrich, 6 July 1856; *d* Biebrich, 13 January 1909) and
Wilhelm's two sons: Wilhelm Hermann (*b* Biebrich, 6
July 1879; *d* Biebrich, 12 Jan 1952) and August (*b* Biebrich, 4 Oct 1880; *d* 19 Sept 1914). After the death of
Wilhelm Hermann the ownership and direction of the
firm passed to his son-in-law Franz Groffy (*b* Boppard,
5 March 1896; *d* Biebrich, 13 Oct 1972).

While the name of Heckel is associated particularly
with the bassoon and double bassoon, in its most
advanced form, the firm produces all kinds of woodwind instruments. It has also introduced several entirely
new wind instruments of which the most important is
the HECKELPHONE. Other innovations have included the
heckel-clarina (1890), virtually a saxophone with the
traditional German oboe fingering and designed to meet
the needs of German players of the period. This instrument was not itself patented, but protection was obtained
for its automatic octave mechanism which the maker

claimed to have invented. Less important novelties included the kalophone (c1900), a flute based on the Boehm system, and the heckelphone-clarinet (1907). The latter was somewhat similar to Schunda's redesigned TÁROGATÓ but with a larger bore and a slightly bulbous bell. Intended to reinforce the lower clarinets in military music, it is now all but forgotten. The TRISTAN SCHALMEI was designed by Wilhelm Heckel.

The brass instrument activities of the Heckel family began with the work of Karl Heckel (b Adorf, 1808; d Dresden, 1866). He was the elder brother of Johann Adam, but does not seem to have had any interest in woodwind instruments. He seems to have moved early in his career to Dresden, where he founded his own business. His successors were his son Friedrich Alwin (b Dresden, 18 July 1845) and Friedrich's son Theodor (b Dresden, 1885). Certain brass instruments from c1835 exist bearing the mark 'J. A. Heckel, Dresden', and the Zeitschrift für Instrumentenbau for 1 September 1929 states that Theodor Heckel was then heir to that firm. But the precise connection between the two branches of the family at that time is obscure.

For illustrations of modern instruments by Heckel, see BASS CLARI-NET, fig.1d and BASSOON, figs.1a, 10.

PHILIP BATE

Heckel-clarina. A single-reed aerophone invented by the HECKEL family. (The name 'Heckelclarind' is incorrect, and arose from a misprint in an early account of the instrument.)

Heckelphone. A baritone double-reed woodwind instrument generically allied to the oboe, but with a conical bore of markedly different proportions. The idea of such an instrument was conceived by Wilhelm HECK-EL after an interview with Wagner in 1879, in which the composer complained of the lack of a baritone voice among the orchestral double reeds of sufficient power in a large orchestral ensemble. After much experiment Heckel, assisted latterly by his sons, produced his first model in 1904. In designing deeper-toned oboes it is usual to enlarge the mean cross-sectional area of the bore approximately in proportion to the increased length, but in his quest for a powerful tone Heckel enlarged the mean diameter of the contemporary German oboe. The resulting large air column called for a powerful reed, so one of bassoon type, carried on a curved crook, was adopted. The instrument was built in three sections, with a globular bell vented by a large hole. A later form, illustrated here, had three smaller vents and a muting cap.

In 1905 Richard Strauss wrote an important part for the heckelphone in Salome, and since then it has been used freely, either for its characteristic tone, or as a substitute for the true bass oboe. The success of the heckelphone in C (A to g″) led to the production of a terz-heckelphone in E♭ and a piccolo-heckelphone in F. Their written compass is b to e‴, sounding respectively a minor 3rd and a 4th higher. Heckelphones are now built to any accepted system of fingering.

PHILIP BATE

Heckelphone-clarinet. An instrument invented by the HECKEL family.

Hedlund, Olof (d 20 April 1749). Swedish organ builder. He was a pupil of Johan Niclas Cahman and

Heckelphone in C by Wilhelm Heckel, Biebrich, first quarter of the 20th century

took over the latter's workshop during his final illness after Cahman's death he completed the organ for the church of St Maria in Stockholm. He obtained his charter as an organ builder in 1742. His masterpiece was the 30-stop organ built for St Jacob's Church in Stockholm (1741–6); only the façade of this organ is still preserved, as are those of the smaller-scale organs at Björskog, Västmanland (1737); Delsbo, Gävleborg (1739–46); and Tierp, Uppsala province (1747). Organs are preserved complete in the Elim Chapel, Sandviken (1739; eight stops; originally at Sorunda); Björklinge, Uppsala province (1742; eight stops); and Utö, Stockholm province (1745; eight stops; originally in the Dutch Reform Church, Stockholm).

BIBLIOGRAPHY
B. Wester: 'Studier i svensk orgelkonst under 1600- och 1700-talen', STMf, xiii (1931), 45
E. Erici: Inventarium över bevarade äldre kyrkorglar i Sverige (Stockholm, 1965)
based on Sohlmans musiklexikon (iii, 386) by permission of Sohlmans Förlag

BENGT KYHLBERG

Heel. (1) See FROG.

(2) On a guitar, the broad bottom end of the neck (often shield-shaped in cross-section), by means of which

he neck is attached to the body. The heel is as long as the instrument is deep and curves into the neck; it may be of one piece with the neck, or it may be a separate lock glued to the neck, or it may be built up from several layers glued to one another and to the neck. *See* GUITAR, fig.1.

Meerpauke (Ger.: 'army drum'). An obsolete term for the KETTLEDRUM; *see also* TIMPANI.

Megit [egit, eğit]. SPIKE FIDDLE of Turkey. It has a gourd resonator with a skin soundtable, and three strings. It is found only among certain Türkmen tribes of the Taurus mountains.

Hehéi. Reed PANPIPES reported in the early 20th century among the Kobéua, or Cubeo, Indians of the Uaupés-Caquetá region of the western Amazon basin. *See zikowitzMISAI*, 407.

Heikebiwa. Japanese four-string lute. *See* BIWA, §4.

Heilman, Matthäus (*b* Hofheim-am-Taunus, 10 May 1744; *d* Mainz, 1799 or 1817). German piano maker. It is possible that he learnt his trade in the workshop of Johann Andreas Stein in Augsburg. By 1777 he had become a freeman of the city of Mainz, a member of the Goldsmiths' Guild and married. In 1788 he was appointed court tuner. Heilman's few surviving instruments are certainly in Stein's tradition although he wrote disparagingly of the older maker's instruments and claimed that his own were in far less need of frequent repair, as he well knew from his work as a technician keeping Stein pianos in playable condition.

BIBLIOGRAPHY
C. F. Colt and A. Miall: *The Early Piano* (London, 1981)
HOWARD SCHOTT

Heinlein. *See* HAINLEIN family.

Hel, (Pierre) Joseph (*b* Mazirot, 8 Feb 1842; *d* Lille, 14 March 1902). French violin maker. He served his apprenticeship at the Salzard atelier in Mirecourt and subsequently worked for Sébastien Vuillaume in Paris and Nicolas Darche at Aix-la-Chapelle. He established himself independently in Lille in 1865, becoming one of the leading 19th-century French luthiers. He patterned most of his instruments after Stradivari, Guarneri, Amati and Maggini, and the details of craft are scrupulously carried out. Personal touches are slightly over-prominent edges and rather flat archings. The varnish is generally a rich red brown and can be unusually becoming. Tonally, his instruments rank with the best of the French school.

Pierre Jean Henri Hel (*b* Lille, 5 March 1884; *d* Lille, 13 July 1937), son and successor of Joseph, took over the shop in 1902. Before working with his father he served his apprenticeship at the Bazin atelier in Mirecourt. His work is quite similar to his father's although a little harder in appearance. He won several awards at competitions, including those at St Louis, Missouri (1904), Milan (1906), Roubaix (1911) and Geneva (1927). He also gained an enviable reputation as an expert restorer. After his death the business was continued for a few years by his widow and their long-time assistant, Marcel Demey.

BIBLIOGRAPHY
R. Vannes: *Essai d'un dictionnaire universel des luthiers* (Paris, 1932, 2/1951/R1972 as *Dictionnaire universel des luthiers* and R1981 incl. suppl. 1959)
JAAK LIIVOJA-LORIUS

Helicon (Gk. *helikōn*: 'the mountain of the Muses', but apparently confused with *helix*, 'a coil'; Ger. *Helikon*). A valved brass instrument made in the same pitches as the military band brass basses in F, E♭ and B♭ but in circular form. It encircles the player's head, passing beneath the right arm and resting on the left shoulder, and may thus be comfortably carried for long periods by a player on foot or mounted; the usually narrow bell points forwards. The helicon was produced by Ignaz Stowasser, Vienna, in 1845, by some accounts following a suggestion of Wieprecht. An early example by Stowasser, in B♭, is in the Nuremberg Collection (*D-Ngm*). The instrument has since been made in every European country (rarely in Britain) and is a favourite form of bass in southern and eastern Europe. The SOUSAPHONE is similarly constructed except for the form of its bell.

ANTHONY C. BAINES

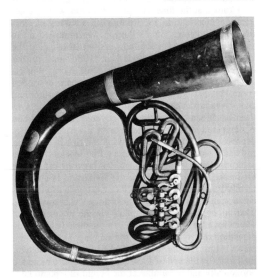

Helicon in B♭ by Ignaz Stowasser, Vienna, 1850 (Germanisches Nationalmuseum, Nuremberg)

Helicon trombone. TROMBONE DA TRACOLLA.

Heliophon. An electronic keyboard instrument developed by Bruno Helberger (*b* Frankfurt am Main, 1884; *d* Vienna, 1951) from the HELLERTION, the result of an earlier collaboration with Peter Lertes. The first version of the Heliophon was completed in Berlin in 1936, but it was destroyed during World War II; a second version was built in Vienna in 1947 (one of the two models is now in the musical instrument museum of the Staatliches Institut für Musikforschung, Berlin). Helberger continued to develop and improve the instrument until his death, after which the work was continued in Vienna by Wolfgang Wehrmann. The sounds of the Heliophon are generated by electronic oscillators. Its total range is seven octaves and it has two 58-note, touch-sensitive manuals (staggered as in a 'spinet' organ), on each of which up to three pitches (with different timbres) can be played simultaneously; six pedals control individual volume levels and two knee-levers produce vibrato. In front of each manual is a fingerboard, which is used to create glissandos and timbre changes.

During the late 1940s and early 1950s Helberger used the Heliophon in many dramatic contexts, including music for several films, and it replaced the ondes martenot in performances of Honegger's *Jeanne d'Arc au bûcher* in Vienna and Graz. In addition to realistic imitations of several orchestral instruments, it could imitate the human voice and produce a wide range of new sounds.

BIBLIOGRAPHY
J. Marx: 'Heliophon, ein neues Musikinstrument', *ÖMz*, ii (1947), 314
    HUGH DAVIES

Hellertion. A monophonic electronic instrument developed in 1928–9 by Bruno Helberger (*b* Frankfurt am Main, 1884; *d* Vienna, 1951) and Peter Lertes of Leipzig (from whose names that of the instrument was derived), several variants of which were constructed with the assistance of Schneider-Opel in Frankfurt. Helberger, who had studied the piano with Artur Schnabel, was well known at the time as a pianist; Lertes was an electrical engineer and in 1933 published a survey of electronic instruments. The Hellertion was modified up to the mid-1930s, and a second version, also called the HELIOPHON, was demonstrated in 1936 and further developed by Helberger in Vienna after World War II.

The Hellertion introduced the fingerboard or ribbon controller that became better known in the trautonium and was reintroduced in the mid-1960s in the Moog synthesizer. When the flat, leather-covered metallic ribbon is depressed it makes contact with a resistance strip; depression at different points along the ribbon alters the resistance and produces different frequencies from an audio oscillator, while the degree of pressure affects the loudness. The pitch range of the Hellertion is approximately five octaves, and special markings aid pitch orientation and alignment. The instrument was sometimes used in conjunction with a piano (in the manner of the somewhat later PIANO ATTACHMENT), the melody line being played on the Hellertion and the accompaniment on the piano. More ribbons were added to make at first two, then four (by the end of 1930) and six; they are mounted horizontally and in parallel at the height of a piano keyboard. Both the four- and six-ribbon versions provide four polyphonic voices, the two ribbons nearest to the performer being linked to the two principal ribbons and played by the thumbs for greater ease of execution. Around 1931 a version tuned to ten subdivisions of the octave was demonstrated.

The 'Mellertion' described by Percy Scholes in the *Oxford Companion to Music* resulted from a misprint in a review (*MT*, lxxii (1931), 1037) of a demonstration of the Hellertion.

BIBLIOGRAPHY
P. Lertes: 'Hellertion, ein neues elektro-akustisches Musikinstrument', *Die Umschau*, xxxv (1931), 13
——: *Elektrische Musik: ein gemeinverständliche Darstellung ihrer Grundlagen, des heutigen Standes der Technik und ihre Zukunftsmöglichkeiten* (Dresden and Leipzig, 1933)
T. L. Rhea: *The Evolution of Electronic Musical Instruments in the United States* (diss., George Peabody College, Nashville, Tenn., 1972), 69; section rev. as 'The Hellertion', *Contemporary Keyboard*, v/3 (1979), 76   HUGH DAVIES

Hellhorn. A valved brass instrument, akin to th EUPHONIUM, patented by Ferdinand Hell of Brno an exhibited at the London Great Exhibition (1851).

Hembra. FRAME DRUM of Colombia. *See* BOMBO (ii).

Hémbu. Wooden cone flute, with one or two finge holes, of the Lele people of south-western Zaï (*LaurentyA*, 145).

Hémen. *See* DE HÉMAN family.

Hemiol. An ORGAN STOP (*Haemiol*).

Hemony. Netherlands family of bronze casters. Th family originated in Lorraine and were outstandin makers of carillons. The brothers François Hemony (Levécourt, *c*1609; *d* Amsterdam, May 1667) and Piete Hemony (*b* Levécourt, Jan 1619; *d* Amsterdam, 17 Fe 1680) may have been the sons of the church bell caste Peter Hemony from Lorraine or of his brother Blais Hemony. In 1634 François and Pieter left their hom because of disturbances caused by war. In 1636 Françoi in collaboration with Josephus Michelin, cast a churc bell for Repelen (Rhineland); in 1638 François ca another for the same place. In 1640 he and his brothe delivered several bells for Wankum and in 1641 a se of three for Goor. Shortly before, François had marrie Marie Michelin.

In 1642 the Hemony brothers were commissioned b the town of Zutphen to build and deliver a carillon which produced after several years' detailed study, was of beauty and purity previously unknown. This immedi ately brought the Hemonys to the fore among carillo makers in the Netherlands. Later the brothers settled i Zutphen until 1657. Between 1657 and 1664 Françoi was the inspector of bells and guns in Amsterdam, whil Pieter had his own workshop in Ghent. From 1664 t 1667 the brothers once more worked together i Amsterdam, where Pieter managed the workshop alon from 1667 to 1680 after François' death. The craft o the Hemonys was maintained in the work of their bes pupil, Claes Noorden (1633–1716).

The number of church bells produced by the Hem onys was probably between 300 and 400, and about 10 are extant, most of them in the Netherlands. They als produced cannon, mortars and statues, for instance those made by François (to designs by Quellinus) for Amster dam Town Hall. Of the 53 carillons produced by the Hemonys (catalogued in Lehr, 1959, pp.102–16), 3 are in more or less good condition. Among the mos beautiful are those in Nieuwe Kerk, Delft (1659–60); Onze-Lieve-Vrouw, Amersfoort (1659–63); Utrech Cathedral (1663–4); Gasthuistoren, Zaltbommel (1654) St Hippolyt, Middelstum (1661–2); and Drommedaris, Enkhuizen (1671).

The lighter Hemony carillons usually had 23 or 28 bells, the heavier ones 32, 35 or 37. The largest bells of the lighter instruments might weigh 570 kgs (*g♯* '), 345 kgs (*b'*) or 250 kgs (*c♯* "): in heavier instruments the largest bells might weigh 4600 kgs (*g♯*), 2750 kgs (*b*) or 1900 kgs (*c♯*). The largest Hemony bell weighed 5600 kgs (*g*); the smallest by François was about 8·5 kgs (*c♯* ''''), that by Pieter about 7 kgs (*f♯* ''''). The keyboards of the heavy instruments usually reached from

' to a''', c'''' or d'''' (there were occasionally one to three
dditional notes, such as g, a, a and b♭, or g, a and b).
The keyboards of the light instruments usually had a
ompass from c' to c'''' or f'''' (with occasional additional
notes such as f', a', or g', a', b♭' and b'). The keys
or c♯', e♭', c♯'' and e♭'' are regularly lacking; otherwise
the succession is generally chromatic. The Hemonys used
mean-tone temperament of the scale, with the semi-
ones tuned to C♯, E♭, F♯, G♯ and B♭. The pitch level
s usually a major 3rd lower or a semitone lower or higher
than modern pitch.

The minimum requirement of 18% tin for good bell
metal was always exceeded by the Hemonys. Pieter
Hemony declared that he added 28 to 30 units of tin to
00 units of copper according to its quality. At the Wes-
erkerk in Amsterdam there is 21·26% tin (as well as
2·25% zinc, 2·23% lead and 0.48% antimony), at St
Laurens in Rotterdam 18·9% (3·4% zinc, 1·8% lead and
0·3% nickel), and at Darmstadt Castle 21·5% (2% lead,
2·5% nickel and traces of iron and arsenic).

The so-called 'rib' section of Hemony bells is fairly
constant: the octave below each note has twice the
diameter and eight times the weight, except among the
highest bells, where the difference is less. Thus, for
example, their bell in Gouda (1675) sounding c♯'''' has
a diameter of 221 mm (instead of 185, as one would
expect from the size of the lower bells) and a weight of
about 7·8 kgs (instead of 3·9). (A similar procedure was
then in use for the measuring of organ pipes.) In its
absolute strength the Hemony rib oscillates slightly
between the light and the normal strength of a middle-
weight rib from a modern bell foundry. This fluctuation
may have been intentional, as an analogous practice can
be discerned in organ pipe measurements of the same era.

Of particular significance is the way in which the
Hemonys tuned a bell after it was cast. To achieve the
proper relation among the main partial tones within the
bell timbre and also among melodic intervals between
bells, each bell is tuned by removing part of its mass
from the inside (see BELL (i)). Previous makers had done
this by chipping off appropriate amounts, an inherently
inaccurate process resulting in a lack of symmetry in
the shape of the bell and consequently disadvantages for
the tone. The Hemonys ground the bell on a lathe, thus
achieving both a symmetrical structure and a previously
unattainable degree of accuracy to about 1/20 of a
semitone. They compared the pitches obtained with those
of a metallophone (perhaps from Indonesia) made up of
a series of metal rods. They also singled out partial tones
and zones of resonance by observing the sound made
by grains of sand falling on various parts of the bell.
The Hemonys made the rib for the casting thicker than
necessary, so that they could take an adequate amount
from the mass when tuning. In their tuning and in the
casting itself they were extremely careful, and would
often redo the casting, sometimes more than once.

To a significant extent the superiority of the Hemonys' art was due to the pioneering investigations of
Jacob van Eyck, municipal carillonist of Utrecht and the
leading campanologist of the day. After he established
the best pattern of partial tones and ascertained from
which parts of the bell these partials were produced, the
Hemonys appropriated his findings and developed a
corresponding method of tuning. Thus they learnt to
produce musically euphonious bells whereas their predecessors (and most of their successors) produced bells
more or less impure in tone. The Hemonys were also
the first to make chromatic carillons and to extend the
compass to three or more octaves. They thereby developed the carillon into a musically viable instrument.

BIBLIOGRAPHY

P. Hemony: De on-noodsakelijkheid en ondienstigheid van Cis en
    Dis in de bassen der klokken (Delft, 1678/R1964)
P. T. A. Swillens: 'Jonkheer Jacob van Eyck', Jaarboekje van Oud-
    Utrecht 1928, 88–131
E. W. van Heuven: Acoustical Measurements on Church-bells and
    Carillons (The Hague, 1949)
A. Lehr: 'The System of the Hemony-carillon Tuning', Acustica,
    i (1951), 101
——: 'A General Bell-formula', Acustica, ii (1952), 35
——: De klokkengieters François en Pieter Hemony (Asten, 1959)
——: Historische en muziekale aspekten van Hemony-beiaarden
    (Amsterdam, 1960)
K.-F. Waack: 'Von der Kunst des Glockenspiels', Ars organi, xxxiv
    (1969), 1270
A. Lehr: Van paardebel tot speelklok: de geschiedenis van de klok-
    gietkunst in de Lage Landen (Zaltbommel, 1971)

HANS KLOTZ

Hencke [Henke], Johann (baptized Geseke, 3 Dec 1697;
d Vienna, 24 Sept 1766). Austrian organ builder. He
was of Westphalian descent and training; after his years
of travel as a journeyman, he settled in Vienna where
he became a freeman in 1725 and founded his own business. Extant examples of his work include the organs
at Maria Kirchbüchl in the district of Neunkirchen and
St Anna, Vienna: the choir organs at Bruck an der
Leitha and Herzogenburg; and the organ cases at
Herzogenburg and Maria Taferl. Hencke, who was
closely associated with Andreas Silbermann among
others, is regarded as the outstanding Viennese organ
builder of his day. In conformity with the style in south-
east central Europe of that time, his instruments contained finely articulated, richly assorted diapason choruses
and a wealth of foundation flue stops, but only a few
flute and wide-scale mutation stops, in this respect
resembling the organs of his contemporaries Michael
Engler (ii) and T. J. Schwarz. His business was carried
on after his death by his son-in-law.

BIBLIOGRAPHY

O. Eberstaller: 'Die Orgel der Stiftskirche zu Herzogenburg und ihr
    Meister Johann Henke', Musica divina, xxvi (1938), 59, 77
R. Quoika: 'Dispositionen von Orgeln', Der Barock, seine Orgeln
    und seine Musik in Oberschwaben: Ochsenhausen 1951, 126
——: Die altösterreichische Orgel der späten Gotik, der Renais-
    sance und des Barock (Kassel, 1953)
K. R. Kasling: 'Master Builder Johann Henke & his Place in Aus-
    trian Organ History', The Diapason, lix/11 (1968), 30
K. Schütz: Der Wiener Orgelbau in der zweiten Hälfte des 18. Jahr-
    hunderts (Vienna, 1969)
O. Biba: 'Die Orgelakten des Stiftes Herzogenburg', Unsere Hei-
    mat, Zeitschrift des Vereins für Landeskunde von Nieder-
    österreich, xli (1970), 9
H. Haselböck: Barocker Orgelschatz in Niederösterreich (Vienna,
    1972)
O. Biba: 'Hencke', MGG

HANS KLOTZ

Hengdi [hengchui]. Transverse flute of the Han Chinese.
See DI (i).

Henke, Johann. See HENCKE, JOHANN.

Henry, Joseph (b Mirecourt, 10 Dec 1823; d Paris,
1870). French bow maker. He went to Paris in 1837
and became a pupil of Dominique Peccatte, with whose
work his own is often confused. His bows were sometimes made for dealers, including Georges Chanot and
the brothers Gand, and he had a brief partnership with
Simon. In 1851 he established his own business at 8 rue

des Vieux Augustins, later moving to the rue Pagevin. Henry's bows are frequently regarded by players as equal to those of Peccatte, and are much sought after. They are sometimes branded HENRY A PARIS on the handle, and should not be confused with bows branded E. HENRY which were not made by him but for a dealer of that name, and are comparatively ordinary.

BIBLIOGRAPHY
R. Vannes: *Essai d'un dictionnaire universel des luthiers* (Paris, 1932, 2/1951/R1972 as *Dictionnaire universel des luthiers* and R1981 incl. suppl. 1959)
J. Roda: *Bows for Musical Instruments of the Violin Family* (Chicago, 1959)

CHARLES BEARE

Hentshi. Percussion sticks of the Kaka people of the Central African Republic. They consist of two planks and a thick branch 150 to 180 cm long. Each of three players holds his piece of wood vertically in the left hand and alternately raises and lowers it on to the ground, at the same time striking it with a stick held in his right hand. These instruments are played as part of a rhythm ensemble which also includes a wicker rattle, *kama*, filled with husks, and a clapperless iron bell, *bongo*, which is struck with a wooden stick. The resulting polyrhythm is used as accompaniment to singing (for example, songs in honour of the birth of twins). See P. Collaer: 'Musics of the Central African Republic', BM 30 L 2310 [disc notes].

K. A. GOURLAY

Hera [madhebe, matepe]. Large LAMELLAPHONE of the Sena-Tonga, Nyungwe, Tavara, Korekore and Budya peoples of the Zambezi basin of south-eastern Africa. It has 24 to 30 keys, and is placed inside a large shell-decorated half-calabash and played with the thumbs and index fingers. It is used primarily for religious purposes.

ANDREW TRACEY

Herculesophone [Herkulesphone]. Name given to a group of brass band instruments made by Šediva of Odessa in 1888. They were a complete family, from contrabass to soprano, and of wide bore.

Herdenglocken (Ger.). COWBELLS.

Herebyme. An early English term for a military horn or bugle. *See* BEME.

Hermans, Willem [Guglielmo] (*b* Thorn, nr. Roermond, 6 March 1601; *d* Rome, 14 Feb 1683). Netherlands organ builder active mainly in Italy. In October 1631 he entered the Jesuit novitiate at Mechelen as an organ builder and lay brother. His early organs were for the Jesuit establishments at Breda (1632), Mechelen (1633), Ghent (1634), Louvain (1637), Ieper (1644) and Genoa (1648, where the fine case survives in the west gallery). From 1648 to 1663 he was based at the Jesuit house in Genoa. He built the organ at Como Cathedral (1649–50: *C* short octave to *c'''*, 57 notes), which had the following specification: Organo grande, Principale (16'), Ottava, Superottava, Decimanona, Vigesimaseconda, Vigesimasesta II, Vigesimanona II, Principale (wood), Flauto in ottava, Flauto in duodecima, Cornetto (mounted), Sesquialtera, Tromboni, Tromba; Organo

piccolo (divided chests either side of the console), Principale (8'), Ottava, Superottava, Quinta, Ripieno IV Cornetto in eco, Terza, Voce umana (reed); Tamburo Usignuolo, Tremulo, manual coupler and pedal pull downs.

Shortly after the organ was finished, and again in 1718 a booklet was published listing recommended combinations of stops, including: all three Principali; all three reeds; 8' and Sesquialtera; 8' and 2'; 8 and 1½'; 8' and flutes 4' and 2⅔'; flutes 4' and 2⅔' alone; and flute 2⅔ alone with the drum. Only the case survives.

From 1657 to 1660 he built the organ at S Maria Assunta di Carignano, Genoa, assisted by Johann Heinrich and Hans Dietrich. Only the case (by Georges Heigenmann) in the west gallery survives. The small organ which he built for S Spirito, Pistoia, survives but is altered beyond recognition. Hermans also worked at Palermo (1672), La Flèche and Trent and in Sicily, and built about 80 organs. His work in Italy may be seen as an early example of the interesting fusion of central European organ tone colours with the traditional Italian organ. Casparini and Chrismann were his natural successors.

BIBLIOGRAPHY
A. G. Hill: *The Organ-cases and Organs of the Middle Ages and Renaissance*, ii (London, 1891/R1975), 83ff
W. Shewring: 'Notes on the Organ in Italy', *The Organ*, xxx (1950–51), 131
R. Lunelli: 'Descrizione dell'organo del Duomo di Como e l'attività italiana di Guglielmo Hermans', *CHM*, ii (1956), 259, 272
——: *Der Orgelbau in Italien in seinen Meisterwerken* (Mainz, 1956), 32
P. Williams: *The European Organ 1450–1850* (London, 1966, R1978), 222f

GUY OLDHAM

Herrara, Manoel Benito Gomes de. *See* GOMES, MANOEL DE SÃO BENTO.

Herrazi [harraz]. GOBLET DRUM of Morocco. *See* TARIJA.

Hervortretend (Ger.: 'coming forward'). A direction to bring out a part that might otherwise be buried in the texture. Various qualifications appear: for instance Bruckner used *immer deutlich hervortretend, sanft hervortretend* and *zart hervortretend* ('always coming out clearly', 'coming out gently', 'coming out sweetly').

Herz, Daniel (*b* Munich, 4 June 1618; *d* Wilten, 28 May or 5 June 1678). Tyrolean organ builder. He settled in Brixen [Bressanone] in 1646, became court organ builder in Innsbruck in 1656 at the latest and established his workshop in Wilten, near Innsbruck, in 1671. His first known work was the reconstruction of the organ at Klausen (1641–3). Among his new organs are: Silliar (1644); the Church of Our Lady of the Cloisters, Brixen (1648–9; only parts survive); an organ for the Brotherhood of Corpus Christi, in the parish church of Brixen (1650); Brixen Cathedral (positive, 1651–2); Stilfes (1656); Trens (1656); Tschengls (contract 1657); Latsch (1659); Maria Waldrast (1660); St Martin in Passeier (1660–61); Niederdorf (contract 1664); Belluno Cathedral (1665); Partenkirchen (before 1671); Meran [Merano] parish church (1671–2); Virgen (contract 1675) Strigno (undated); Jerusalem (undated); and perhaps the Collegiate Church, Wilten (a positive after the extensions system with nine stops out of three ranks). Herz was the most important Tyrolean organ builder of the 17th century; his reputation spread widely outside the ountry. The traditions of the Herz workshop were arried on in Brixen by Jacob Köck (1630–73) and in Nilten by Johann Hackhofer (1645–88).

BIBLIOGRAPHY
V. Senn: 'Herz', *MGG*
A. Reichling: *Orgellandschaft Südtirol* (Bozen [Bolzano], 1982)
                                ALFRED REICHLING

Herz, Henri [Heinrich] (*b* Vienna, 6 Jan 1803; *d* Paris, 5 Jan 1888). German pianist, composer, teacher and piano maker. He studied at the Paris Conservatoire (from 1816), where he was piano professor from 1842 to 1874. He toured extensively in Europe, South America and he USA, becoming one of the most celebrated virtuosos of his time. His compositions, mostly salon pieces and variations for the piano, include the composite *Hexameron* (1837), written with Liszt, Thalberg, Pixis, Czerny and Chopin.

As a piano maker, Herz is noted for his simplification of the Erard double escapement action; the Herz–Erard (rather than the original Erard) model remains the prototype of all modern grand piano repetition actions. Herz established a piano factory with one Klepfer in Paris in 1825; after financial vicissitudes, in 1851 he founded an independent factory, his firm soon acquiring a reputation in Europe that ranked with those of such leading French makers as Erard and Pleyel. Herz instruments were awarded first prize at the Paris exhibition of 1855. The business was continued after his death until the early 20th century by Amadée Thibout & Cie.

BIBLIOGRAPHY
E. Pauer: *A Pianist's Dictionary* (London, 1895)
F. J. Hirt: *Meisterwerke des Klavierbaus* (Olten, 1955; Eng. trans., 1968)
H. Leuchtmann: 'Herz, Henri', *Grove 6*
                                HOWARD SCHOTT

Hesek. Metal idiophone of the Batak Toba area of the province of North Sumatra. It consists of a small metal sheet (about 15 sq cm) and is beaten with a metal rod. It is used primarily in an *uning uningan* (instrumental music) ensemble and is also played in a *gondang* ensemble for ceremonial purposes. A *ting-ting* (tapped bottle) is sometimes substituted for the *hesek*.
                                MARGARET J. KARTOMI

Hevehe. Common name for the bullroarer among the Orokolo people, Gulf Province, Papua New Guinea. For illustration *see* BULLROARER, fig.2*g*. See F. E. Williams: *Bullroarers in the Papuan Gulf* (Port Moresby, 1936), 5.

Hēvisi. Term used for Buddhist ritual music of Sri Lanka and the ensemble used to play it, which consists of a *horanāva* (oboe) and two drums, the *daula* and the *tammätta* (see illustration). The ensemble developed from an earlier group, the PANCATŪRYA NĀDA, and is now highly developed, complex and essential to Buddhist ritual, both in and out of the temple. The correct but rarely used name for the *hēvisi* ensemble is *sinhārakkāra*.

Traditionally, and particularly in the hill country, the

Hēvisi ensemble accompanying a Buddhist initiation dance, Sri Lanka, with daula (double-headed cylindrical drums), tammätta (paired kettledrums) and horanāva (oboes)

players wear a special costume, generally only for important occasions or at prestigious temples like the Temple of the Tooth, Kandy. Nearly every temple has its *hēvisi* group, whose responsibility it is to mark the three important stages of the day, sunrise, noon and sunset (*yāma-hēvisi*); to announce the times of services and pujas (*tēvā-hēvisi* and *pūjā-hēvisi*); and to accompany the temple relics in procession (*gaman-hēvisi*). Strictly speaking, each occasion, each time of day and some centres of worship possess characteristic and exclusive drum rhythms, played on the *daula* and elaborated on the *tammäṭṭa*. The pattern used at the Temple of the Tooth, for example, occurs nowhere else on the island. In traditional *hēvisi* music, the *horanāva* has only a secondary function, its presence in the ensemble being largely symbolic. It echoes the *daula* rhythm in a very simple and restricted melodic pattern. Today's *horanāva* players, however, seem discontented with this role, and secular melodies, such as those of the Sinhalese *vannam* (wedding music), are commonplace, even in the Temple of the Tooth.

In addition to their daily duties players are responsible for much longer sessions on *pōya* (full-moon days), while privileged groups are entitled to participate in the various *perahära* (processions) which take place during the year. There is a clear hierarchy of *hēvisi* ensembles, the least dignified being those responsible for *minī-bera* (funeral drumming). The ensemble walks ahead of the procession, and the drumheads, and sometimes the whole drum, are swathed in a white cloth. At the other end of the scale stand the four *panikkiyā* of the Tooth Temple – members of the *näkati* caste, whose families are granted land in the area in return for their services. Apart from their daily duties in the temple these musicians take pride of place in the annual *Äsala perahära*, flanking the temple entrance as the Buddha relics are carried out and playing the exclusive rhythm of *ambara hēvisi-pūjā*.

BIBLIOGRAPHY

A. M. Hocart: *The Temple of the Tooth at Kandy* (London, 1931), 15ff, 18ff
J. E. de Jonville: 'Sinhalese Music', *Sinhale and the Patriot*, ed. P. E. Pieris (Colombo, 1950), 625f
M. D. Raghavan: *Sinhala Natum: Dances of the Sinhalese* (Colombo, 1967), 76, 178
C. de S. Kulatillake and Ranjan Abeysinghe: *Background to Sinhalese Music* (Colombo, 1976), 9f
Sarath Amunugama: 'The Kandy Perahera', *Notes on Sinhala Culture* (Colombo, 1980), 24ff

NATALIE M. WEBBER

Hewa. Cylindrical stopped wooden flute of the Ma people of Zaïre (*LaurentyA*, 173).

Hexenscheit. A type of Alpine zither. *See* ZITHER, §2.

Heyl. *See* HAYL family.

Hibat. Flat gong of the northern Philippines. *See* GANGSA (i).

Hibbān. *See* HABBĀN.

Hibernicon. A contrabass wind instrument of the BASS-HORN class. It was invented by Joseph Rogerson Cotter, vicar of Castlemagner, Co. Cork, and patented by him in 1823. The patent, in which the name hibernicon does not occur, covers two varieties of the instrument, a bass (contrabass) and a tenor.

Hibernicon by Thomas Key, London, 1823 (Bate Collection, University of Oxford)

Until recently it was thought that no specimen had survived, but in about 1970 an instrument, in poor condition, was found in Antrim (Northern Ireland). It is now repaired and in the Bate Collection at Oxford. It is marked 'Royal Patent Basso Hibernicon. Cotter Inventor. Manufactured by T. Key, 20 Charing Cross' (see illustration). The crook, which was missing, has been reproduced in accordance with the measurements given in the patent specification. The instrument's overall dimensions are a length of 5 metres, with a bore that increases steadily from 13 mm at the mouthpipe to 60 mm at the root of the bell, whence it flares to 240 mm. It has eight keys, of which six take the place of the usual finger-holes, and two are downward extension keys. The fundamental is *D'*, and the inventor claimed that it was the sole instrument 'with only six holes capable of giving the whole chromatic scale for two octaves or more'.

The only known instance of its use in a major festival orchestra was at the 1835 York Festival. Reporting the festival for the *Allgemeine musikalische Zeitung*, Pellisov wrote:

. . . and another contrabass trumpet called 'Hibernicon' which, like a Goliath, towered heavenwards above the rest of the ophicleides: it was supported on a folding tripod and played by a seated performer. Such is the power of this Hibernicon that the walls of Jericho, nay the last trump itself would be as child's play to it.

REGINALD MORLEY-PEGGE

Hichiriki. Japanese oboe. It is used in gagaku (court music), where it shares the main melody with the *ryūteki* flute. The bamboo body has a reverse conical bore tapering from roughly 15 mm to 10 mm in diameter and is about 18 cm long; the reed adds another 4 cm to the length. There are seven finger-holes on the front and two thumb-holes on the back; the thumb-holes are between the first and second and the fourth and fifth finger-holes from the top. The body is wrapped with bark and string and then lacquered inside and out, like the *ryūteki*. To form the broad reed, which is played using the lips to control the sound, one end of a length of reed stalk is flattened and shaved to a bevel (as for the European oboe); a cane regulating-ring is fitted over the reed to adjust tone colour and volume. 'Hichiriki' is the Japanized pronunciation of the ideograms for the Chinese *bili*, the immediate ancestor of the modern instrument, which would have entered Japan by the 8th century. The *hichiriki* is used not only in imported music but also in native court vocal genres. A softer reed is used for *kagura* songs, so as not to overwhelm the singers. The *hichiriki* is considered very difficult to play. The melody is embroidered with a continuous stream of subtle ornamentation and pitch gliding, effected both by fingering techniques and by embouchure and collectively called *embai*. Furthermore, whereas flutes of three different pitch levels are used in gagaku, the *hichiriki* player must make do with a single instrument with a narrow range ($g'-a''$). The flexibility of pitches, made available by the large reed, makes it difficult to describe the instrument's 'basic scale', and the narrow range does result in some surprising melodic leaps, in contrast to the *ryūteki*.

An earlier *dai-hichiriki* ('large *hichiriki*'), known from manuscripts, was reconstructed in 1878 and briefly used in the court orchestra, tuned a 4th lower than the *hichiriki* itself. The *hichiriki* is similar to the Chinese GUAN and the Korean P'IRI.

Hichiriki (oboe) used in gagaku (court music), Japan

BIBLIOGRAPHY

W. P. Malm: *Japanese Music and Musical Instruments* (Rutland, Vermont, 1959), 95ff

K. Masumoto: *Gagaku* (Tokyo, 1968)

'Hichiriki', *Ongaku daijiten* [Encyclopedia of music] (Tokyo, 1981)

DAVID W. HUGHES

Hicks, George (*b* England, *c*1818; *d* Brooklyn, NY, 21 Feb 1863). Anglo-American maker and seller of cylinder pianos and barrel organs. Probably related to the Hicks family of street organ and piano makers of Bristol, England, he arrived in the USA after 1845 and first appears in Brooklyn street directories in 1849. By 1856 he maintained a retail outlet or manufactory in Manhattan, but in 1860 he is listed again only in Brooklyn, where his family resided after his death. Although he advertised as a 'maker', it is uncertain whether he manufactured all the parts of his instruments, including the laboriously pinned cylinders, or assembled parts imported from England; the latter seems more likely. His products, of standard design and quality, were intended mainly for sale or rental to itinerant street musicians who carried them on their backs. Some examples are equipped with percussion devices and with articulated, costumed figures that move in time to the music. Examples at the Metropolitan Museum of Art (New York), the Smithsonian Institution (Washington, DC) and the Henry Ford Museum (Dearborn, Michigan) share a popular repertory that includes American patriotic tunes as well as various ethnic pieces suitable for different neighbourhoods. Their approximately two-octave compass is chiefly diatonic, with occasional chromatic notes.

BIBLIOGRAPHY

L. Libin: *American Musical Instruments in the Metropolitan Museum of Art* (New York, 1981) [unpubd catalogue]

N. Groce: *Musical Instrument Making in New York City during the Eighteenth and Nineteenth Centuries* (diss., U. of Michigan, 1982)

LAURENCE LIBIN

Hiefhorn (Ger.). Term for a bugle or hunting horn.

Hieronimus de Zentis Viterbiensis. *See* ZENTI, GIROLAMO.

Hieronymus Bononiensis [? Jerome of Bologna]. Italian harpsichord maker working in Rome in 1521. An instrument of this date now at the Victoria and Albert Museum, London, is the earliest surviving dated harpsichord. One dated 1503, by an anonymous builder, is in the Museo Civico, Milan, but this has been converted into a clavichord.

Recent work has established that the instrument was originally single-strung, of short C to c''' or F to f''' compass, low pitch; only later was it given two sets of 8' strings, 47 keys, its present outer case and its (rebalanced) keyboard, as well as its set of 14 pull-down pedal keys attached to the bass manual keys, which have since disappeared. The earlier opinion that 'this 1521 harpsichord . . . can scarcely be distinguished from Italian harpsichords made 150 years later' (Hubbard) must therefore be reconsidered, despite the important original parts (including the thin cypress walls) that do indeed appear to have become standard. Little is known of the maker.

A 'Jerome of Bologna' was referred to by Michel Corrette in *Le maître de clavecin* (Paris, 1753).

BIBLIOGRAPHY
F. Hubbard: *Three Centuries of Harpsichord Making* (Cambridge, Mass., 1965)
R. Russell: *Victoria and Albert Museum: Catalogue of Musical Instruments*, i: *Keyboard Instruments* (London, 1968, rev. edn. by H. Schott in preparation)
J. Barnes: 'The Specious Uniformity of Italian Harpsichords', *Keyboard Instruments*, ed. E. M. Ripin (Edinburgh, 1971), 1ff
F. Hellwig: 'The Single-strung Italian Harpsichord', ibid, 27ff

DONALD HOWARD BOALCH, PETER WILLIAMS

Hierrillo (Sp.: 'little iron'). Triangle of Spain and the New World. In Galicia it is known under the names *binco* and *ferriño*; in Mallorca the term *ferreguins* is used. It appears also in certain mestizo dance ensembles in north-west Argentina. In Venezuela it is rare, but is reportedly in use among descendants of Antillan blacks in El Callao, Bolívar state. The triangle was widely reported in other parts of South America during the 19th century, and is included in ensembles on Taquile Island, Lake Titicaca, Peru.

BIBLIOGRAPHY
I. Aretz: *El folklore musical argentino* (Buenos Aires, 1952)
——: *Instrumentos musicales de Venezuela* (Cumaná, 1967)
H. C. Davidson: *Diccionario folklórico de Colombia: musica, instrumentos y danzas* (Bogotá, 1970)
A. Valencia Ch.: 'Los sikuris de la Isla de Taquile', *Boletín de Lima*, nos.8–9 (1980)

JOHN M. SCHECHTER

Hifthorn (Ger.). Term for a bugle or hunting horn.

Higham, Joseph (*b* Manchester, 1818; *d* Manchester, 1883). English maker of brass instruments. In 1842 he established J. Higham at 127 Strangeways, Manchester. He was the first maker to give instruments as prizes at contests, and in 1860 founded the band of the 1st Manchester Volunteer Battalion. Higham was succeeded by his son-in-law Peter Robinson who in 1895 had more than 90 employees, producing all the components of their instruments in the factory. (At the time parts were often imported from the Continent.) The 60,000th instrument was manufactured in 1892, and Robert Cubitt became London representative at 84 Oxford Street. In 1930 the firm was taken over by Mayers & Harrison. Higham patented a rotary valve in 1857 (British Patent no.123). He pioneered the 'clear-bore' system, in which the windways through the valves were always in a straight line. At the London International Exhibition of 1862 he was awarded a medal for 'improved tubular arrangements in cornets to supersede the piston in common use'. He also received a medal at Dublin in 1865. A contrabass tuba in B♭, known as 'Jumbo' and claimed to be the largest in the world, was exhibited in 1873 in Chicago; its bell diameter was about 56 cm, and it is said to have produced *G″* with ease. The Highamphone was a combined euphonium and valve trombone (*see* DUPLEX). Many Higham brass band instruments are still in use; there are numerous other examples, including ophicleides, keyed bugles and metal clarinets, in museums and private collections.

BIBLIOGRAPHY
L. A. de Pontécoulant: *Douze jours à Londres* (Paris, 1862)
A. S. Rose: *Talks with Bandsmen* (London, 1895)
L. G. Langwill: *An Index of Musical Wind-instrument Makers* (Edinburgh, 1960, rev., enlarged 6/1980)
C. Bevan: *The Tuba Family* (London, 1978)

CLIFFORD BEVAN

Hi-hat cymbals. *See* CHOKE CYMBALS and DRUM SET.

Hiiukannel ('*kannel* of Hiiu Island'). Bowed lyre of Estonia, also known as the *rootsikannel* ('Swedish *kannel*'), or *tallharpa* by Swedish settlers in Estonia. It was found in the coastal region and islands of western Estonia and survived until the first decades of the 20th century. The term KANNEL refers to a psaltery. *See also* STRÅKHARPA (with illustration).

Hildebrandt [Hildebrand]. Surname of two German organ builders and instrument makers, Zacharias (*b* Münsterberg, Silesia, 1688; *d* Dresden, 11 Oct 1757) and his son, Johann Gottfried (*b* Freiberg, 1724 or 1725; *d* Sorau, 7 Nov 1775). Zacharias first trained as a joiner, but apparently became interested in organ building at an early age. He apprenticed himself in 1713 to Gottfried Silbermann for three years, and continued to work for him thereafter; as 'Orgel Macher', that is as master craftsman, he was a co-signatory of the contract for the Silbermann organ in St Georg, Rötha. He left Silbermann in 1722; a legal dispute between them was settled in 1724. J. S. Bach performed his own Cantata no.194 at the consecration of Hildebrandt's organ at Störmthal in 1723. From 1727 to 1731, Hildebrandt lived in Sangerhausen; he was appointed court organ builder to the Prince of Saxe-Weissenfels in 1730. He moved to Leipzig in 1734, or perhaps earlier. In *c*1739 he built a 'lute-harpsichord' for Bach, to the composer's specifications, with two rows of 8′ gut strings and one row of 4′ brass strings. In 1748 he succeeded Johann Scheibe as overseer of the Leipzig organs. From 1750 to 1754 he supervised the work on Silbermann's organ for the Catholic Hofkirche in Dresden, which Silbermann did not live to see completed. Zacharias Hildebrandt's largest organs were those in St Jakobi, Hettstedt (southern Harz Mountains) (1741–9; two manuals, 31 stops; the case survives), St Wenzel, Naumburg an der Saale (1743–6; three manuals, 53 stops; extant), and the Dreikönigskirche in Dresden-Neustadt (1754–7; two manuals, 38 stops; completed after his death by his son). Other organs survive at Störmthal (from 1722; one manual, 14 stops), Hilbersdorf (from 1723; one manual, five stops), St Jacobi, Sangerhausen (from 1727; two manuals, 27 stops), and St Georg, Sotterhausen (1730; one manual, nine stops). Organs in the following places survive in rebuilt condition: Langhennersdorf (1717–22; two manuals, 21 stops), Lengefeld (from 1725; two manuals, 22 stops) and Goldbach (from 1755; one manual, ten stops).

The effects of Hildebrandt's training under Silbermann are seen mainly in technical and structural aspects; in matters of tone he went his own way, and may well have had advice from Bach. Hildebrandt normally added to Silbermann's complement of stops elements of the Hamburg Baroque organ (Rauschpfeife, Sesquialtera, Tertian, Scharf, Weitpfeife 8′, Blockflöte 4′, Waldflöte 2′, Dulzian 16′, Hautbois 8′, Schalmei 4′ in the manual, Nachthorn 2′, Posaune 32′ and Kornett 2′ in the pedal), as well as the string-tone stops favoured by Bach (Viola da gamba 8′, Fugara 4′, Violone 16′ and 8′ and Gemshorn 8′ and 4′). He also used richer mixture stops with their top pitches higher than Silbermann's, and he did not adopt Silbermann's characteristically broad mouth-to-circumference ratio of 2:7. Dähnert considered his organ in St Wenzel, Naumburg, 'one of the outstanding examples of late Baroque organ building'.

Between 1754 and 1757 Zacharias's son Johann Gottfried assisted his father in Dresden-Neustadt and Goldach; his own most important organ was that of St Michaelis, Hamburg (1762–7 and 1769; three manuals, 0 stops) (*see* ORGAN, Table 24), described by Burney s 'the largest and most complete in Europe'.

BIBLIOGRAPHY

, Adlung: *Musica mechanica organoedi*, ed. J. L. Albrecht (Berlin, 1768/R1961)
. Flade: *Der Orgelbauer Gottfried Silbermann* (Leipzig, 1926, 2/1953)
. Cortum: *Die Orgelwerke der evangelisch-lutherischen Kirche im Freistaate Hamburg* (Kassel, 1928)
V. Nichterlein: *Die Hildebrandtorgel in der St Wenzelskirche zu Naumburg (Saale) und ihr Erbauer* (Ludwigsburg, 1933)
. Rubardt: *Alte Orgeln erklingen wieder* (Kassel, 1936)
. Schering: *Musikgeschichte Leipzigs*, iii (Leipzig, 1941)
W. David: *Johann Sebastian Bachs Orgeln* (Berlin, 1951)
. Flade: 'Hildebrandt', *MGG*
J. Dähnert: 'Zacharias Hildebrandt', *Ars organi*, xi (1957), 189
——: *Der Orgel- und Instrumentenbauer Zacharias Hildebrandt* (Leipzig, 1962)

HANS KLOTZ

Hill (i). English family of organ builders.

(1) William Hill (*b* Spilsby, Lincs., 1789; *d* London, 19 Dec 1870). In 1815 he went to work with THOMAS ELLIOT, making his mark with the laying out of an organ for a difficult site in the Earl of Bridgewater's chapel at Ashridge House, Hertfordshire (1816–18). He married Mary, Elliot's daughter, and in 1825 became his partner, the firm being known as Elliot & Hill until the former's death in 1832. Thereafter Hill carried on the business under his own name (except in 1837–8, when he was in partnership with Frederick Davison, the firm being known as Hill & Davison until Davison left to form the rival firm of GRAY & DAVISON); in the mid-1840s the firm was renamed Hill & Co. Some ten years later Hill took his son (2) Thomas Hill into partnership, and the firm became Hill & Son.

William Hill's work falls into three main periods, the first of which extends from 1815 to 1838. Little distinguished the organs built during the first decade of this period from other contemporary English organs with their long manual compasses and circumscribed specifications. Towards the end of the 1820s Hill began to experiment with ways of increasing the size and scope of the English organ: manual compasses were extended below G'; large-scale double (16′) or unison (8′) pedal pipes became more common; duplication and larger scales were tried; and he attempted to increase the power of the reeds. The most important essays were the huge organs for York Minster (1829–33; with extensive duplication and a seven-stop Pedal Organ including three of 32′) and Birmingham Town Hall (1832–4; with fluework of enormous scale and such novel reeds as Posaune, Horn, and Octave Clarion); in 1840 the world's first high-pressure solo reed, an Ophicleide on 30 cm of wind, was added to the latter. The construction of these instruments stimulated further invention: the Box Pallet to wind large pipes (*c*1828) and a machine to roll zinc for the first metal pipes of 32′ (*c*1830).

The mature work of Hill's second period (1838–*c*1858) is associated with a radical redesigning of the English organ, stimulated by a growing awareness of historic European schools of organ building, and a desire to provide an instrument suitable for the performance of Bach and the repertory of orchestral and choral transcriptions (*see* ORGAN, §vi, 3). The composer and organist Henry Gauntlett was Hill's most influential collaborator in the crucial years 1838–46. The result was the 'German sys-

tem' organ (also termed by Gauntlett the 'Anglo-Lutheran or Protestant Organ', and, in its concert-hall version, the 'Concerto Organ') in building which Hill claimed that he was acting 'in the spirit of the old and most celebrated builders of Holland and Germany'. The manual choruses were extended to include 16′ tone, the $5\frac{1}{3}$′ Quint, and additional mixture work; a Pedal chorus of 16.16.8.4.III.16 or 16.8.16 was provided wherever possible with a compass of C to d' or e' ('required in the execution of the music of Sebastian Bach'); the Swell was redesigned as a full-compass division rather on the lines of a German *Oberwerk*; and manual compasses were standardized as C to f'''. There was usually a wide provision of novelty registers, for example the Wald Flute, Suabe Flute, Oboe Flute and Corno Flute; the Hohl Flute (paradoxically, a string), Salcional, Cone Gamba, Gemshorn, Violone and Echo Dulciana Cornet V are characteristic Hill registers which William Hill either adapted or introduced, and he was among the first English builders to use harmonic flutes and undulating ranks. There were more conservative features. The temperament was still, normally, unequal; the construction and scaling of the diapasons showed no radical departure from prevailing English practice; the Choir Organ remained a collection of mild accompanimental and solo voices; and tierce mixtures continued to be standard. Hill's organs almost invariably employed tracker action, though the size of some of the organs he was called upon to build provoked an interest in non-mechanical agencies: he is said to have suggested the introduction of an exhaust valve in one of C. S. Barker's early models of a pneumatic lever, and he himself added pneumatic levers to the Great Organ action at Birmingham Town Hall in 1849 (he may have used them previously to strike the carillons in that instrument). Hill was the first English builder to dispense with manual blowing and substitute steam power (Royal Panopticon, 1854). Among Hill's most important 'German system' instruments were: Christ Church, Newgate Street (1838); St Luke, Cheetham Hill, Manchester (1840); St Peter, Cornhill (1840); Great George Street Chapel, Liverpool (1841); Worcester Cathedral (1842); Edinburgh Music Hall (1843); Ashton-under-Lyne Parish Church (1845); Ely Cathedral (1850); and the Royal Panopticon, Leicester Square (1854).

By the late 1850s the character of Hill's organs was changing (possibly under the influence of his son, (2) Thomas Hill). Pipe metal was more substantial and of better quality, with the occasional use of spotted metal. Large scales, generous flues, regular nicking, and pressures which (as in the previous period) seldom exceeded 7·5 cm made for bright, strong-toned flue choruses. Reeds were still, usually, on the same pressure as the flues, and this, together with their large scales, ensured a colourful, rather free tone. Equal temperament was now always employed in new organs. Organ cases became less common, though the row of front pipes would usually be richly decorated, and panelling would complete the sides of the organ. Mixtures and mutations were not as lavishly provided as in the 1840s, the Swell would sometimes have more stops than the Great, and upper-work was seldom found in the Pedal divisions of all but the largest instruments. Yet Hill's organs of this period remained remarkably bright in tone and rich in character, and individual registers blend with one another superbly. Important instruments during this third period (*c*1858–70) included: St Albans Abbey (now Cathedral,

1860); Ulster Hall, Belfast (1861); York Minster (1863; nave organ); St Andrew's Cathedral, Sydney (1866); and Melbourne Town Hall (1870).

It is difficult to form an adequate impression of William Hill's best work because so many of his organs have been destroyed or altered beyond recognition, but the instruments in Ashridge House, Hertfordshire (1816–18), Christ's Hospital, Horsham (1830), St Mary-at-Hill, City of London (1848), Kidderminster Town Hall (1855), Ulster Hall, Belfast (1861), St John, Hyde Park Crescent (1865), and the Church of the Annunciation, Dublin (1869; formerly in Holy Trinity, Sydenham) may be regarded as representative.

(2) **Thomas Hill** (b 1822 or 1823; d 1893). Son of (1) William Hill. Hill & Son's work continued with little change in character following William Hill's death. The firm enjoyed considerable prestige, built many major organs (including the vast Sydney Town Hall organ – in many ways a culmination of the developments of the 1840s) and became perhaps slightly old-fashioned in outlook. Some modest progress was made along the lines laid down in William Hill's last years. A low pressure was still customary for the fluework (7·5 cm at Sydney Town Hall) but it became usual to place chorus reeds on a higher pressure in the largest instruments (normally, 12·5 cm) and even to provide a single large open diapason on the same pressure. There was a slow extension of the use of strings, undulating registers and orchestral voices, and, as a result, Choir and Solo divisions became larger and were occasionally enclosed in a Swell box. Large organs more commonly had mixed actions – tracker, pneumatic lever and tubular pneumatic – though tracker remained the norm, and Thomas Hill seldom built an organ solely on pneumatics. The console became more elegant, with angled jambs and over-hanging keys; it was not until Thomas Hill's last years that pneumatic pistons became usual for even the largest instruments.

Significant organs included Manchester Cathedral (1871), Adelaide Town Hall (1872), Worcester Cathedral (1874; transept organ), Cambridge Guildhall (1882), Lichfield Cathedral (1884), Westminster Abbey (1884), Sydney Town Hall (1886–90), King's College Chapel, Cambridge (1889), Birmingham Town Hall (1890), Queen's Hall, London (1893), and Peterborough Cathedral (1893). Apart from Sydney Town Hall, most of Thomas Hill's larger instruments have been either destroyed or rebuilt beyond recognition. Smaller organs survive in many churches, for example St Philip, Battersea (1870), and Dinton Parish Church, Buckinghamshire (1886).

(3) **Arthur George Hill** (b London, 12 Nov 1857; d London, 16 June 1923). Son of (2) Thomas Hill. He was educated at Westminster School and Cambridge, and took the degree of docteur ès lettres at the University of Lille with a dissertation on Christian art in Spain. He was an accomplished draughtsman, as evidenced in his two-volume The Organ-Cases and Organs of the Middle Ages and Renaissance (London, 1883–91/R1975) and in the many cases which he designed for organs built by the Hill firm. Among his designs should be mentioned the case for Sydney Town Hall with its 32' front (1886), Chichester Cathedral (1888), Peterborough Cathedral (1904) and Beverley Minster (1916).

Hill was in partnership with his father and in 1893 became senior partner. During the next few years there was a marked development in the tonal character of the firm's organs, which now entered an 'Edwardian' phase. The former vigour and colourfulness diminished; flue choruses became more refined, reeds smoother, flutes a little bland; mixture work was less brilliant and pressures were slightly increased all round. Solo and Swell divisions became larger and Pedal registers were seldom of higher pitch than 8'. The firm's consoles, with solid ivory stop-knobs, ivory tell-tales, moulded key slips, and highly polished woodwork suggested a degree of opulence which earlier work had lacked. Yet by comparison with the work of many contemporary organ builders (e.g. Willis or Harrison) the balance and proportion of A. G. Hill's organs faithfully reflected the classical origins of the firm's tradition. The increasing use of tubular pneumatic action and the provision of pneumatic accessories marked a significant change, but as late as around 1905 Hill maintained that tracker action was best for smaller instruments.

Among the firm's most important instruments built during A. G. Hill's direction are Middlesbrough Town Hall (1898), Eton College Chapel (1902), All Saints' Hove (c1905), Selby Abbey (1909), Chester Cathedral (1910) and Beverley Minster (1916). All these survive though only those at Middlesbrough and Hove without significant alteration.

In 1916 the Hill firm was amalgamated with Norman & Beard (see HILL, NORMAN & BEARD).

BIBLIOGRAPHY
Obituaries, Musical Standard, xiv (1871), 4; MO, xvii (1893–4) 147; The Organ, iii (1923–4), 118
C. Clutton: 'Eton College Chapel Revisited', The Organ, xxiv (1944–5), 145
C. Clutton and A. Niland: The British Organ (London, 1963 2/1982)
N. J. Thistlethwaite: '"E pur si muove": English Organ Building 1820–1851', Organ Yearbook, vii (1976), 101
B. B. Edmonds and N. J. Thistlethwaite: 'An Effect Probably Never Before Obtained', The Organ, lv (1976–7), 74
N. J. Thistlethwaite: A Consideration of the Development of the Organ in England between c.1820 and 1870 (diss., U. of Cambridge, 1980)

NICHOLAS THISTLETHWAITE

Hill (ii). English firm of violin and bow makers, restorers and valuers. Joseph Hill (1715–84) was a pupil of Peter Wamsley in Piccadilly, London, before he established himself at the sign of the 'Violin' in Angel Court, Westminster, and in 1762 at the 'Harp and Flute' in Haymarket. At the latter address he made many violins, violas and especially cellos. His instruments were of all qualities; he was capable of refined and elegant workmanship, though more often there are signs of haste. The cellos are made on a good pattern with ample air-space, and have been praised. Of Joseph Hill's five sons the elder two were quite well known as violin makers. William Hill (1745–90), no doubt after assisting his father, opened his own shop in Poland Street and largely followed his father's patterns. By contrast, the first Lockey Hill (1756–1810) was a prolific maker mostly of inferior instruments, all rather scooped towards the edges and the cellos a little undersized.

Henry Lockey Hill (1774–1835), the son of Lockey Hill, is usually known as 'the second Lockey Hill'. Until about 1810 he worked for John Betts; as Betts was London's leading dealer at the time Hill would have seen many fine Italian instruments, learnt to appreciate the superiority of Stradivari, and certainly become well

:cquainted with Vincenzo Panormo. Hill's shop was in Brandon Road, Newington Causeway, Southwark, as is often recorded in pencil on the interior of his instruments. He made many violins and a fair number of cellos; the best of them show a high standard of workmanship and are among the finest of all English instruments, with superior tonal qualities and varnish similar to Panormo's. He was assisted by his elder son Joseph (c1805–1837), a talented craftsman.

William Ebsworth Hill (b 20 Oct 1817; d 2 April 1895), son of the second Lockey Hill, was a highly respected craftsman and authority on old instruments. He made a few violins but was much more a specialist in restoration, in which his work was a turning-point. Before him in England all was butchery; after him, and especially under the supervision of his sons, came an era when thousands of the finest string instruments were saved by a combination of ingenuity and meticulous workmanship. At his shop in Wardour Street, Hill pioneered the techniques of restoration with a unique expertise.

The legacy of William Ebsworth Hill's experience and authority was developed by his four sons, William Henry (b 3 June 1857; d 1927), Arthur Frederick (b 25 Jan 1860; d 5 Feb 1939), Alfred Ebsworth (b Feb 1862; d 21 April 1940) and Walter Edgar (b 4 Nov 1871; d 27 April 1905). The firm moved from Wardour Street to 38 New Bond Street, and then in 1895 to a new building at number 140 almost opposite. In addition, workshops were established at Hanwell in west London. No praise can be too high for the contribution of this unique firm to the history of the violin and its accessories. Their repair workshop, at first staffed by French craftsmen from Mirecourt and closely supervised by the brothers, repaired thousands of the finest instruments that now exist. The Hills's connoisseurship was unrivalled and was reflected in several publications which form the basis of knowledge of old string instruments. Short monographs on the 'Messiah' and 'Tuscan' Stradivari violins (1891) were followed in 1892 by a more substantial volume, a biography of Maggini. The first edition of the invaluable *Antonio Stradivari: his Life and Work* appeared in 1902 (2/1909/R1963; Fr. trans., 1907) and *The Violin Makers of the Guarneri Family* in 1931. Alfred Ebsworth Hill was the world's leading expert on old violins. His memory for instruments was legendary, and his judgment concerning authenticity was unchallenged. His musical interests were extremely broad and included much research and documentation.

In addition to restoration work the Hill workshops produced fine new instruments, partly in the French tradition and perhaps never reflecting their intimate knowledge of the great Italians. Materials and workmanship were invariably the finest, and the firm also manufactured cases. Between 1939 and 1948 the firm fulfilled a long-standing wish of the Hill brothers to make a bequest to the British nation, presenting to the Ashmolean Museum in Oxford a number of exquisite violins, viols, bows, guitars and citterns, including the celebrated 'Messiah' Stradivari violin of 1716.

The Hill bow workshop occupies a significant place in the history of craftsmanship. Although bows stamped with their brand had been sold since the mid-19th century, a workshop producing bows exclusively for the firm appears not to have been established until the 1890s. Among the early makers who supplied bows to the firm, James TUBBS and Samuel Allen stand out. Using the work of Allen as a point of departure, a team of bow makers

(William C. Retford, William Napier and his son Frank, William Johnston, Sidney Yeoman and Charles Leggatt) developed a bow which combined exceptional craftsmanship with grace of line. The Hill bow not only set new standards for workshop-produced bows but also established a style, uniquely English, which has not been surpassed in consistency of quality. Most of the bows produced between 1920 and 1970 have a letter and two-digit number stamped on the lower facet of the butt under the frog. These marks have often wrongly been thought to indicate the maker; the digits designate the year of manufacture, with the letter serving as a bench mark to coordinate the frog and stick. After 1900 the heads are invariably fitted with silver or gold facings. The frogs of many bows were set into a recessed track in the butt, a practice which has been adopted by many contemporary makers. The grading of the bows was largely determined by the quality of pernambuco used in each stick and reflected by the style and extent of the mountings. Production of the lower-grade bows seems to have been discontinued around 1950. Bows stamped in the 19th century usually carry the brand 'W. E. HILL', while the series of brands 'HILL, H. & S', 'W. E. H. & S' and 'W. E. HILL & SONS' was inaugurated in the 20th century.

The Hill traditions have been maintained under the direction of (Albert) Phillips Hill (b 30 Sept 1883; d 25 March 1981) and his son Desmond (d'Artrey) Hill (b 5 Dec 1916) as well as Desmond Hill's sons Andrew Philip Hill (b 3 July 1942) and David Roderick Hill (b 28 Feb 1952). Phillips Hill continued to make instruments well into his 90s. The workshops have been modernized, and in 1974 the firm moved its headquarters from London to Havenfields, an 18th-century house at Great Missenden, Buckinghamshire.

Other members of the Hill family were distinguished in the same or related fields, but they were apparently unconnected with the firm. HENRY HILL (1781–1839), a grandson of Joseph Hill, was an instrument maker, music seller and publisher. Another Henry Hill (b London, 2 July 1808; d London, 11 June 1856), a son of Henry Lockey Hill, was the leading viola player of his time in opera and at provincial festivals and principal oratorio concerts; he made a name for himself particularly in chamber music. A cultivated musician and scholar, he was a member of the Queen's Private Band, Ella's Musical Union and the Queen's Square Select Society; in association with Alsager he was a founder of the Beethoven Quartet Society, for which he wrote the analytical programmes. He made the acquaintance of Berlioz and played the solo part in *Harold en Italie* for its first London performance, 7 February 1848. Berlioz, in *Les soirées de l'orchestre*, wrote of him and his incomparable instrument, which was by the English maker Barak Norman.

A Frederick Hill (fl ?1830–40; d ?Paris), who may have been related to this family, was a celebrated flautist associated with the Philharmonic Society.

BIBLIOGRAPHY

W. L. von Lütgendorff: *Die Geigen- und Lautenmacher vom Mittelalter bis zur Gegenwart* (Frankfurt, 1904, 6/1922/R1968)

W. M. Morris: *British Violin Makers* (London, 1904)

R. Vannes: *Essai d'un dictionnaire universel des luthiers* (Paris, 1932, 2/1951/R1972 as *Dictionnaire universel des luthiers* and R1981 incl. suppl. 1959)

W. C. Retford: *Bows and Bow Makers* (London, 1964)

M. R. Sadler: *The Retford Centenary Exhibition* (London, 1975)

M. A. Alburger: *The Violin Makers: Portrait of a Living Craft* (London, 1978)

CHARLES BEARE, ARTHUR F. HILL, JAAK LIIVOJA-LORIUS

Hill, Henry (*b* 14 Oct 1781; *d* London, 23 Jan 1839). English instrument maker, music seller and publisher. A grandson of the string instrument maker Joseph Hill (*see* HILL (ii)), he became a partner of TEBALDO MONZANI in 1808 at 3 Old Bond Street and 100 Cheapside, London. By 1814 the firm also operated from 24 Dover Street. Monzani & Hill continued at 28 Regent Street from 1820 to 1829, when the partnership was terminated and Hill continued in sole charge, the firm being renamed Hill, late Monzani & Co. Hill continued to make flutes and clarinets to Monzani's designs and to the same specifications, with liberal use of silver and the fitting of small finger-holes. A number of superbly finished ivory flutes with silver rings and keys survive and testify to his excellent craftsmanship. On Hill's death his widow took over until 1845, when the business ceased, with the stock being sold at auction.

BIBLIOGRAPHY
R. S. Rockstro: *A Treatise on . . . the Flute* (London, 1890, 2/ 1928/*R*1967)
L. G. Langwill: *An Index of Musical Wind-instrument Makers* (Edinburgh, 1960, rev., enlarged 6/1980)
NIALL O'LOUGHLIN

Hill, Norman & Beard. English firm of organ builders. It was founded in 1916 with the amalgamation of Hill & Son (*see* HILL (i)) and NORMAN & BEARD of Norwich. The firm was directed by A. G. Hill and G. W. Beard from 1916 to 1923 when John Christie assumed direction. In 1930 Herbert la French Norman took over the firm, remaining until his retirement in 1974. His son Herbert John la French Norman joined the firm in 1960 and retired from the managing directorship in 1974, at which time Francis Norman Fowler took over.

The firm's instruments have been typical of 20th-century English organs. During Christie's directorship a number of theatre organs were built including those at The Dome, Brighton, the Regal Cinema, Marble Arch, London, and the Gaumont Theatre, Paris. After World War II the firm became one of the principal supporters of the organ reform movement in England and has restored several historic instruments. Among its most important organs are those at Norwich Cathedral; Bath Abbey; St John's College, Cambridge; Exeter College, Oxford; Ellesmere College, Shropshire; the Guard's Chapel, Wellington Barracks, London; and the Royal College of Organists, Kensington Gore, London.

BIBLIOGRAPHY
C. Clutton and A. Niland: *The British Organ* (London, 1963, 2/1982)
WILLIAM J. CONNER

Hillebille [Hellebylle]. Percussion plaque of northern Germany. It is a board 80 cm long and 20 cm wide, struck with two mallets. It was used as a signalling instrument but nowadays is played only during Carnival.

Hillyard, William (*b* Athlone, 1821; *d* ?Philadelphia). Irish maker of military instruments. He was apprenticed at the age of 11 to his uncle, the Dublin instrument maker John McNeill. He emigrated to England in 1852. After working with Joseph Higham for 10 years (playing solo baritone in Higham's Manchester Volunteers Band), and a short time with Henry Distin, he established his own business in Rochester Row, Westminster, in 1862. He also played the baritone in the band of the Victorias and later in St George's Rifles. In 1894, after many changes of address, he sold the business to

Arthur Chappell, emigrating to Philadelphia to manage an instrument factory there in the following year. In 188_ Hillyard made a five-valve F tuba to the order of Han_ Richter for J. H. Guilmartin, ophicleidist in Richter' London concerts. Brass instruments by Hillyard are t_ be found in a number of collections, notably an author in the Historisches Museum, Basle (formerly Bernouil_ Collection, Greifensee), and a ballad horn in the Fin_ Arts Museum, Boston, Massachusetts.

BIBLIOGRAPHY
A. S. Rose: *Talks with Bandsmen* (London, 1895)
L. G. Langwill: *An Index of Musical Wind-instrument Maker* (Edinburgh, 1960, rev., enlarged 6/1980)
C. Bevan: *The Tuba Family* (London, 1978)
CLIFFORD BEVA_

Hindewhu. Single-note whistle of the Ba-Benzele pyg_ mies of the Central African Republic and adjoining areas It is 7 to 8 cm long, and made of pawpaw stem. Th_ whistle, which may be played by a woman, is blown i_ alternation with sung notes, for example to announc_ the result of a successful hunt.

Hinen nimbwilei. The largest SLIT-DRUM in the slit-drum ensemble of the Seniang people of Malekula, Vanuatu It is known as the 'mother' drum. Others, in descendin_ order of size, are *nerumbwen*, *simbesimb* and *bewelep* Except for the *bewelep*, which is portable, the drum_ stand vertically in the ground and are similar to thos_ of other Malekulan standing ensembles (*see* NAKI an_ NA-MBWE). They surround the dancing-ground and ar_ used for secular and ceremonial signalling and fo_ accompanying dances. See A. B. Deacon: *Malekula a Vanishing People in the New Hebrides* (London 1934/*R*1970), chap.17.

MERVYN McLEA_

Hinners. American firm of organ builders. It wa_ founded in Pekin, Illinois, in 1879 by John L. Hinner_ (1846–1906) for the manufacture of reed organs. J. J Fink became his partner for a short time in 1881, an_ in 1886 he was joined by U. J. Albertsen, the nam_ changing to Hinners & Albertsen. Around 1890 the_ began making pipe organs, the first recorded instrumen_ being installed in 1892 in the German Evangelical Churc_ of Huntingburg, Indiana. In 1902 the firm incorporate_ under the name of Hinners Organ Co., with John Hin_ ners, his son Arthur, Jacob A. Roelf and Heilo J. Ru_ as principals. Although the company's output was con_ siderable, and 97 employees are recorded for 1921 Hinners was content to build small organs for smal_ churches. Tracker-action organs continued to be pro_ duced in quantity long after other firms had abandone_ this type of mechanism; the largest organ was a 25-sto_ instrument in St Paul's, Pekin. Damaged by the Dep_ ression, Hinners ceased building pipe organs in 1936_ but continued to make reed organs until the firm wa_ dissolved in 1942.

BIBLIOGRAPHY
R. E. Coleberd: 'The Hinners Organ Story', *American Organist*, _ (1960), 20
O. Ochse: *The History of the Organ in the United States* (Bloom_ ington, Ind., 1975)
BARBARA OWE_

Hintersatz (Ger.). The ranks of pipes placed behin_ the case pipes in the late medieval organ; *see* ORGA_ STOP.

Hiohkat (scraper) of the Papago Indians, southern Arizona

Hiohkat. Notched-stick rasp, or SCRAPER, of the Papago Indians of Arizona. The rasp consists of a curved stick 45 to 60 cm long, notched along its length, and a shorter, smooth stick. One end of the curved stick is held in the left hand and the other is placed on an inverted basket which functions as a resonator (see illustration). The smooth stick, held in the right hand, is scraped over the notches, producing a rasping or rattling effect. It is used by the Papago to accompany songs begging for rain, and during the *viikita*, an important harvest festival. *See also* KANÓ'OSKAE'.

MARY RIEMER-WELLER

Hiradaiko. A term for certain shallow-bodied Japanese barrel drums (*hira*: 'flat'; *daiko/taiko*: generic term for drums). They have two membranes tacked to the body; for further details of construction *see* TAIKO. The drum used in *geza* (off-stage) music of the kabuki theatre is about 40 cm in diameter (for illustration *see* GEZA); it is called *hiramarudaiko* when suspended nearly horizontally, *hiratsuridaiko* if suspended vertically, and *gakudaiko* when it is used to imitate the *tsuridaiko* of court music. A slightly larger drum, suspended flat, is used in modern performances of Japanese folksong as a substitute for the ŌDAIKO of traditional folk music. In Okinawan music a vertical version is played in tandem with the *shimedaiko*.

DAVID W. HUGHES

Hirîitoare. Cog rattle of Romania. *See* DURUITOARE.

Hirri. Globular terracotta VESSEL FLUTE of the Bisa people of Upper Volta. It has three finger-holes, and is used for producing hunting calls.

Hitchcock. An English family of spinet and harpsichord makers. Thomas Hitchcock (i) died before 1700. His son, Thomas Hitchcock (ii) (*b* c1685; *d* after 1733), was made free of the Haberdashers' Company in 1715. John Hitchcock (*d* 1774) was almost certainly a son of Thomas Hitchcock (ii), and was made free of the Haberdashers' Company in 1750. All worked in London.

There were certainly two and may even have been three Thomas Hitchcocks engaged in harpsichord making, but the instrument bearing this name in the Victoria and Albert Museum collection may well be the oldest surviving two-manual English harpsichord, and the earliest with the standard specification of 8', 8', lute, 4' (for illustration *see* HARPSICHORD, fig.9). As in the case of the spinets for which the firm became famous, the fine veneering of some of the inner facings of the harpsichord became the normal kind of decoration on English instruments. There are also other characteristics suggesting an experienced spinet maker: a compass of G' to g''', the oblique-grained soundboard, the double curved bentside (rounded tail), case-wood of solid walnut. Whatever its precise date – 1690–1720, c1720, c1725, c1720–30 have all been suggested – the instrument would have to vie for its historical position with such early doubles as that by F. Coston, now in a private collection. Although 'copies' have been made of the Hitchcock instrument, its natural tone is not yet established nor, by any documentary evidence, its purpose and registration. However, it can be guessed that its upper manual was meant to be voiced like 'an Eccho, very soft', in the words of a letter of 1712 concerning a contemporary harpsichord made by Player (quoted by Russell, p.73). Like a few other keyboards of this and the following two decades, the sharps have the old-fashioned striped appearance produced by a slip of ivory inset in the ebony key-top and familiar on Mercier's portrait of Handel. In scaling, the instrument is more Italianate than Kirckman's and Shudi's, that is, somewhat shorter.

Judging by extant instruments, the Hitchcocks concentrated on spinet making, producing some of the best examples of this genre. The walnut case, inside harewood stringing, engraved strap-hinges, ebony-ivory sharps ('skunktail') and general style became typical of the hundreds of spinets made, though the rounded tail did not. It is possible that Thomas Hitchcock (i) made the earliest English bentside spinets, but although it is noticeable that the harpsichord in the Victoria and Albert Museum resembles the 1683 HAWARD instrument, it belongs more to the 18th-century style in the details and cross-section of the bridges. For details of surviving Hitchcock instruments see Boalch (1956).

BIBLIOGRAPHY
D. H. Boalch: *Makers of the Harpsichord and Clavichord, 1440–1840* (London, 1956, rev. 2/1974)
R. Russell: *The Harpsichord and Clavichord* (London, 1959, rev. 2/1973)
F. Hubbard: *Three Centuries of Harpsichord Making* (Cambridge, Mass., 1965)
DONALD HOWARD BOALCH, PETER WILLIAMS

Hitiribo. Idioglot transverse clarinet of the Gunga people of Nigeria. *See* CLARINET, TRANSVERSE.

Hitotsugane. Japanese thick-walled horizontal gong, used in *geza*, off-stage music of the kabuki theatre. It is also called *chū-sōban* ('middle-size *sōban*'). It measures 20 cm or more in diameter and is struck with a hardwood mallet to accompany scenes set in graveyards or similarly eerie settings. *See also* KANE and SŌBAN.

Hitoyogiri [hitoyogiri-shakuhachi]. The form of the Japanese SHAKUHACHI (end-blown NOTCHED FLUTE) which was used in popular urban music of the early Edo period

(1603–1868) (*hito*: 'one'; *yo*: 'node'; *giri*: 'cutting'). Performance on the *fuke-shakuhachi*, the direct ancestor of today's instrument, was restricted by law to members of the Fuke sect of Zen, and so it was the *hitoyogiri* which was used in the early SANKYOKU (chamber music) ensembles; both instruments were, however, usually just called *shakuhachi*.

The *hitoyogiri* was made from the same type of bamboo as the Fuke instrument but from a higher section of the stalk; the end nearest the root became the blowing-end. There was only one bamboo node in the length of the instrument (hence its name). It was both straighter than the Fuke instrument and more nearly round in cross-section, with a cylindrical bore; usually it did not have an inlaid blowing-edge. The *hitoyogiri* was once made in several sizes, but gradually the length became standardized at 34 cm. The range was limited to an 11th, far less than the modern instrument but equal to that of the end-blown flute *tempuku* (with which, however, no historical connection has been shown).

The basic interval structure of the *hitoyogiri* is close to that of the *shakuhachi*, in that there are no semitones, but the narrower bore and smaller finger-holes of the former meant that there could be less alteration of the basic pitches by embouchure and half-holing than there is on the modern *shakuhachi*. It has been suggested that the semitones characteristic of the *in* scale which dominates modern music for koto, shamisen and *shakuhachi* would have been too difficult for the *hitoyogiri*, a point cited as evidence for the persistence of the anhemitonic *yō* scale well into the early Edo period.

References to the *shakuhachi* in the 15th and 16th centuries are thought to concern the *hitoyogiri*. The earliest surviving notation, accompanied by detailed playing instructions, dates from 1664. By the late 18th century the instrument's popularity had waned, and a brief revival around 1820 had no lasting effect. Other names for the *hitoyogiri* include *tanteki*, *kotake* and *dōshō* (from Chin. *dongxiao*). *Tanteki* ('short flute') is written with the same Chinese pictograph as that used as an alternative designation for the *chiba* (see XIAO), the ancestor of the *shakuhachi*.

BIBLIOGRAPHY
W. P. Malm: *Japanese Music and Musical Instruments* (Rutland, Vermont, 1959), 151
S. Kishibe: *The Traditional Music of Japan* (Tokyo, 1966, 2/1981), pl.52
'Shakuhachi', *Ongaku daijiten* [Encyclopedia of music] (Tokyo, 1981)
DAVID W. HUGHES

Hitsu [hitsu-no-koto]. Obsolete Japanese zither. *See* KOTO.

Hjulgiga. Swedish hurdy-gurdy. *See* VEVLIRA.

Hkalauk. Wooden cowbell of Burma.

Hkaya [hkara]. Burmese term for any kind of trumpet, bugle, cornet or whistle (such as a police or referee's whistle).

Hkayú. CONCH-SHELL TRUMPET of Burma; it is used for religious ceremonies.

Hkwet-hkwìn. *See* YAGWÌN.

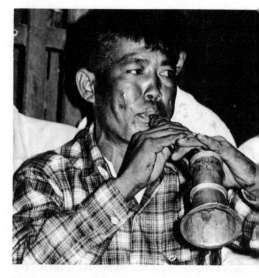

Hnè (oboe) player, Burma

Hnè. Burmese oboe with a conical bore and a composite double reed. It is made in two sizes pitched a 5th apart. The small *hnè-galeì* is about 26 cm long and the larger *hnè-gyì* is about 40 cm long. Both instruments have a compass of two octaves, the lowest note of the large *hnè* being about *c'*, and that of the small *hnè*, *g'*. Both have seven equidistant finger-holes at the front and a thumb-hole at the back, which is positioned half-way between the first and second finger-holes. The conical metal staple, *thabut*, continues the taper of the body.

The reed, *hnè-gin*, is made from young leaves of the toddy palm which are soaked and smoked for several months before being folded and cut into shape; about six to eight fan-shaped layers of the palm leaf are bound together with a thick cord. *Hnè* players often soak the reed in green tea before playing and use small pointed ivory picks to widen and shape the aperture.

The *hnè* often has a flared metal bell, *hnè-gyì*, although it is not essential. It is attached by a cord, usually red, which is tied at the top of the instrument. There are two ridges at the top of the pipe which prevent the bell cord from slipping; it is thought that these ridges might be vestigal pirouettes. The bell, which hangs at an angle, is so loosely attached that it does not affect the pitch, although *hnè* players feel that it improves the tone. The bell of the large *hnè* is often covered with gold leaf and decorated with pieces of glass.

The *hnè* is only used for outdoor performances. It is played both in small amateur ensembles which accompany village events such as rice planting or reaping and processions which form part of religious celebrations. It is also used in larger professional orchestras hired to play for festive occasions, spirit-worshipping ceremonies and stage performances. As the penetrating sound of the *hnè* is not suitable for quiet passages or for indoor performances, its part in those circumstances is played on a bamboo flute (*palwei*).

BIBLIOGRAPHY
J. Okell: 'The Burmese Double-Reed "Nhai"', *Asian Music*, ii/1 (1971), 25

Hnyìn. Small MOUTH ORGAN of Burma. It consists of

bamboo pipes with free reeds mounted in a gourd wind-chest.

Hobday, Arthur. New Zealand organ builder, partner in the Australian firm of Fincham & Hobday; *see* FINCHAM & SONS.

Hoboe (Ger.). OBOE.

Hoboy. Early English spelling of 'hautbois' (OBOE); for further terminological discussion, *see* SHAWM (introduction).

Hochbrucker [Hochprugger], **Jakob** (*b* Augsburg, *c*1673; *d* Donauwörth). German maker of lutes, violas and harps. Son of Georg Hochbrucker, a violin maker in Augsburg around 1670, he lived in Donauwörth from at least 1699. He is chiefly remembered as the inventor of the single-action pedal harp around 1720 (or earlier), though this has also been attributed to other makers (*see* HARP, §4(vi)). His son, the harpist Simon Hochbrucker (1699–*c*1750), introduced this instrument to a wide public in recital tours of Germany and elsewhere, notably in Paris. See R. Rensch: *The Harp: its History, Technique and Repertoire* (London, 1969).

Hochet (Fr.). RATTLE.

Hochquintfagott (Ger.). A tenoroon pitched a 5th above the normal bassoon; *see* BASSOON, §9.

Hoddu [hodu]. Plucked lute of the Fula (Fulani) and Tukulor peoples of the West African savanna region. It resembles the Mandinka KONTING in having a boat-shaped

Hoddu (three-string lute) played by a Fulani musician, Pouytenga, Upper Volta, 1970

soundbox, strings attached to the neck by leather thongs, and no frets. In Guinea and Upper Volta the *hoddu* usually has three strings (see illustration), in Mali and Niger four, and in Senegal, the Gambia and Mauritania five. The strings are made from goat-leather, nylon or wire. The *hoddu* is used by professional musicians to accompany epic and praise poems. The *hoddu* of the Tukulor of north-eastern Senegal is related to the Mauritanian TIDINIT.

BIBLIOGRAPHY
S. Chauvet: *Musique nègre* (Paris, 1929)
C. Duvelle: 'Rhythmes et chants du Niger', SOR 4 [disc notes]

Hodsdon, (Wilfred) Alec (*b* Sidcup, Kent, 27 Dec 1900). English instrument maker. He established a workshop at Lavenham, Suffolk, for the restoration and production of early types of instruments, including stringed keyboards, lutes, cornetts, regals and positive organs. Of an experimental turn of mind, Hodsdon produced a wide range of instruments of each type, including a number of highly complex harpsichords, among them instruments with pedal-boards sounding their own sets of strings. Later he more often based his instruments on simpler and more historical lines.

HOWARD SCHOTT

Hodŭgi. Idioglot cylindrical oboe of Korea. It is also called *pŏdŭl p'iri* ('willow oboe'). The body of the instrument is made by stripping a tube of willow or poplar bark away from the wood of a slender branch. The integral double reed is made by shaving down the upper layers of bark on two sides of one end of the tube. There is no standard size and finger-holes may or may not be added.

For playing, the entire reed is placed in the mouth, and the sound from the open end may be modified with the open or cupped hands. The *hodŭgi* is both a toy for children and an amusement for adults. It is used in rural competitions between adult males during the period of rice-seedling transplanting; more practically it is used as a bird-lure. It is rarely called upon to play a melody as such.

There may be a historical connection between the present *hodŭgi* and the extinct CH'OJŎK ('grass flute') described in the treatise *Akhak kwebŏm* (1493) as consisting of a rolled-up tree leaf or piece of birch bark.

BIBLIOGRAPHY
Sŏng Hyŏn, ed.: *Akhak kwebŏm* [Guide to the study of music] (Seoul, 1493/R1975), 7.31*a, b*
L. Picken: 'The Korean *hodŭgi* – a Double-reed, Cylindrical Pipe of Stripped Bark, with or without Fingerholes – and its Pan-Eurasiatic Parallels', *Articles on Asian Music: Festschrift for Dr Chang Sa-hun* (Seoul, 1977), 297
ROBERT C. PROVINE

Hoen toong. JEW'S HARP of Vietnam. See ĐÀN MÔI.

Hoffmann, Gerhard (*b* Rastenberg, Thuringia, 11 Nov 1690; *d* Rastenberg, *c*1756). German composer and wind player. According to Gerber, Hoffmann was a man outstanding in both arts and sciences. At Jena he studied mathematics and architecture, and in 1719, as architect or surveyor, he entered the service of the Duke of Weimar. Under instruction from the Weimar Kapellmeister J. W. Drese, Hoffmann then studied musical theory and later turned to the composition of cantatas and other church music, of which he left a considerable amount (presumably unpublished). As a player Hoffmann was irked by the defects of contemporary wind instruments; he is reputed to have made improvements to both the flute and the oboe. Some manuscript notes added by Walther to the first edition of his *Lexicon* refer to this work. These, however, are somewhat ambiguous and hardly justify the assumption of some scholars that Hoffmann added $g\sharp''$ and $b\flat''$ keys to the oboe in about 1727. No instruments so equipped of so early a date are known. In addition Hoffmann is said to have invented a device whereby all four strings of the violin could be adjusted simultaneously to accord with the different pitch standards then in use (*Cammer-Ton*, *Chor-Ton*, *Cornett-Ton*, etc) and to have experimented with different scale temperaments. In 1736 Hoffmann was elected Bürgermeister of his native town.

BIBLIOGRAPHY
GerberL; *WaltherML*
L. Bechler and B. Rahm: *Die Oboe* (Leipzig, 1914), 35f
PHILIP BATE

Hoffmann, Johann (*b* Lauda, *c*1660; *d* Würzburg, 12 Aug 1725). German organ builder. He went to Würzburg before 1695, becoming a freeman and 'court organ maker' in 1697 and 'cathedral organ maker' in 1707. His art was based on that of his probable teacher, Johann Jost Schleich (*c*1645–*c*1707), who introduced into Franconia the richness of the foundation stops of south-east central European organs, thereby providing the basis for the Frankish high-Baroque organ. Hoffmann's instruments were the prime examples of this tradition, along with those of such masters as J. J. Dahm, J. S. Will and J. P. Seuffert, his most important pupils. Their organs contained a large, complete diapason chorus in the *Hauptwerk*, whereas those of the *Postiv* and Pedal were quite often incomplete. There were a number of foundation flue stops in the *Hauptwerk* and *Positiv*, but few reeds and wide-scale mutation stops; the Pedal organ had only a few stops.

Hoffmann's biggest organ was built for Neustadt (am Main) Abbey (2 manuals, 25 stops; now in the parish church, Amorbach). Other instruments survive in Geusfeld and Reupelsdorf (originally Unterzell and Wiesentheid), and the cases are preserved of the organs at Stiftskirche, Grosskomburg, Carmelite Church, Würzburg (now in Arnstein); Oberzell monastery; Fulda Cathedral (choir organ); and Theres Abbey (now in Treysa).

BIBLIOGRAPHY
E. F. Schmid: *Die Orgeln der Abtei Amorbach* (Mainz, 1938, 2/1963)
H. Fischer: 'Der mainfränkische Orgelbau bis zur Säkularisation', *Acta organologica*, ii (1968), 101–204
H. Fischer and T. Wohnhaas: *Historische Orgeln in Unterfranken* (Munich, 1981)
HANS KLOTZ

Hoffmann, Johann Christian (*b* Leipzig, baptized 2 May 1683; *d* Leipzig, 1 Feb 1750). German maker of string instruments. He was the most famous member of a family of instrument makers active in Leipzig between 1650 and 1750. Like his father, Martin Hoffmann (1654–1719), he made mainly bowed instruments. From 1712, or earlier, he made instruments for the Dresden court, and he became a close friend of J. S. Bach, at whose request he is said to have designed and made the first viola pomposa about 1724. In 1734 he relieved Bach of the responsibility of looking after the string instruments in the two main Leipzig churches, and in his will (1748) he left Bach a share in his own instruments. Hoffmann's

work was much sought after both inside and outside Germany, and over 40 instruments are extant. They include lutes and theorbos, viols and all the standard members of the violin family, as well as violoncelli piccoli and viole pompose; many are in the Musikinstrumenten-Museum der Karl-Marx Universität, Leipzig. They are distinguished by the quality of their wood, their golden-yellow varnish and their careful craftsmanship, which avoids excessive ornamentation. Their tone is light and even.

Hoffmann married twice, in 1710 and 1736, but had no children. His younger brother Christian Gottlieb (1691–1735) also made violins and viols, and some wind instruments. A violino piccolo by him was listed in an inventory at the Cöthen court in 1773, alongside several instruments by his more famous brother.

BIBLIOGRAPHY
W. L. von Lütgendorff: *Die Geigen- und Lautenmacher vom Mittelalter bis zur Gegenwart* (Frankfurt am Main, 1904, rev. 6/1922/R1968)
G. Kinsky: 'Die Leipziger Geigen- und Lautenmacherfamilie Hoffmann', *ZI*, lv (1934–5), 124
P. Rubardt: 'Hoffmann', *MGG* [with extensive bibliography]

Hoffmann, Johann Wilhelm. German keyboard instrument maker, successor of CHRISTIAN GOTTLOB HUBERT.

Hofmans, Mathijs (*fl* Antwerp, *c*1670–*c*1700). Belgian violin maker. Influenced by the work of the Amatis, and probably a pupil of Hendrik Willems of Ghent, he achieved a rare elegance in the appearance of his instruments. His outlines, especially the central curves, are unusually rounded; in contrast, the soundholes are set stiffly perpendicular. An orange varnish of Italian quality completes the finish. The tonal excellence of his violins has at times allowed them to pass under the best Italian names. He is considered the greatest of the Belgian makers; his followers included Johannes Baptista van der Slaghmeulen in Antwerp and several members of the Snoeck family in Brussels, none of whom was quite his equal as a craftsman.

BIBLIOGRAPHY
W. L. von Lütgendorff: *Die Geigen- und Lautenmacher vom Mittelalter bis zur Gegenwart* (Frankfurt am Main, 1904, rev. 6/1922/R1968)
R. Vannes: *Essai d'un dictionnaire universel des luthiers* (Paris, 1932, 2/1951/R1972 as *Dictionnaire universel des luthiers* and R1981 incl. suppl. 1959)
M. Möller: *Violin Makers of the Low Countries* (Amsterdam, 1955)
CHARLES BEARE

Högor. Double-headed buffalo-skin barrel drum of the Jörai people of central Vietnam.

Hohlflöte [Hohlpfeife] (Ger.). An ORGAN STOP.

Hohner, M(atthias). German manufacturer of harmonicas, accordions and keyboard instruments. Founded by Matthias Hohner in 1857, its factory in Trossingen now employs hundreds of people. It has become the world's best-known maker of harmonicas (*see* HARMONICA (i), esp. fig.2) and accordions and has contributed greatly to their technical and musical advancement; it is also the largest publisher of original works for these instruments.

After World War II, the company branched out into the manufacture of a wide range of keyboard instruments, most of which are electroacoustic (often using amplified free reeds) or electronic. They include the Melodica (a keyboard harmonica), electronic and hybrid accordions such as the Electronium, Elektravox, Hohnerola, Hohnervox and Multimonica and the Bassophon bass unit (1950s and early 1960s; all except the Electronium, Hohnervox and Melodica are now discontinued) and string synthesizers such as the Stringthing. The Symphonic range of one- and two-manual electronic organs (about 30 church, entertainment and home models, several of them portable) use electronic oscillators – one for each note in the larger instruments, a set of 12 using frequency division in the smaller ones. Other electronic organs and pianos have also been produced. Three portable five-octave keyboards, related to the electric piano, were marketed in the early 1960s: the Cembalet, Clavinet and Pianet; in the same period the company also produced the Organet and the unusual Guitaret. Hohner's designers of electronic instruments have included René Seybold (who also devised accordion mechanisms), Siegfried Mager, Richard Bierl, Ernst Zacharias, Paul Dorner and K. E. Kretschmer.

BIBLIOGRAPHY
R. Bierl: *Elementare technische Akustik der elektronischen Musikinstrumente* (Frankfurt am Main, 1965)
E. Zacharias: *Elektronische Musikinstrumente* (Trossingen, 1968)
IVOR BEYNON/HUGH DAVIES

Hohnervox. An electronic keyboard instrument developed in the 1950s and manufactured by Hohner of Trossingen. It is a combination of the company's Electronium (*see* ELECTRONIUM (i)) and an accordion, and is similar in conception to Hohner's MULTIMONICA. In recent models the monophonic electronic section has been replaced by an electronic organ of up to six voices, with rhythm, bass and chord units housed in a separate cabinet.
HUGH DAVIES

Hoho. Rudimentary PANPIPES of Lifu, Loyalty Islands. They consist of pieces of cane, closed at one end and partly filled with water to produce the desired pitch. In Lai they are called *utköwi*. See S. H. Ray: 'The People and Language of Lifu, Loyalty Islands', *Journal of the Royal Anthropological Institute of Great Britain and Ireland*, xlvii (1917), 273; E. Hadfield: *Among the Natives of the Loyalty Group* (London, 1920), 134.

Hoja de capulí. A cherry leaf used in Ecuador as an aerophone by highland Quechua and Afro-Ecuadorians. See C. A. Coba Andrade: 'Instrumentos musicales ecuatorianos', *Sarance*, vii (1979), 70.

Hojŏk. Korean conical oboe. *See* T'AEP'YŎNGSO.

Hōkiokio. *See* IPU HŌKIOKIO.

Hokku. Japanese barrel drum used in Buddhist music. *See* ŌDAIKO.

Holbeck, Severin (*b* Friedericia, Denmark, *c*1647; *d* Mehlis, Thüringer Wald, 3 March 1700). German organ builder of Danish birth. Holbeck established his workshop in Zwickau but worked also in Hamburg, Lübeck, Copenhagen and Stockholm. From 1690 he also held office at the court of the Prince of Gotha-Altenburg. The parochial register of Zwickau describes him as a greatly respected figure and a most distinguished citizen; the account for his organ at Waldenburg refers to

him as a famous organ maker. Holbeck's daughter, Maria Margarethe, married in 1701 the organ builder and clavichord maker Johannes Jacobus Donati, who took over the court appointment and business of his father-in-law.

In the last quarter of the 17th century Holbeck supplied instruments to churches in Saxony, Thuringia and Bavaria, including the Michaeliskirche in Hof (1679) and St Moritz in Zwickau (1700). In Delitzsch his work was opposed by the examining church musicians, but in general there was no lack of praise and recognition for his achievement as a master craftsman. The comparatively large organ at Schneeberg (St Wolfgang, 1695; 39 speaking stops) was especially admired, by F.-J. Fétis among others.

BIBLIOGRAPHY
FétisB
H. Mendel: *Musikalisches Conversations-Lexikon*, v (Berlin, 1875)
R. Vollhardt: *Geschichte der Cantoren und Organisten von den Städten im Königreich Sachsen* (Berlin, 1899)
A. Werner: 'Zur Musikgeschichte von Delitzsch', *AMw*, i (1918–19), 535
K. Halbauer: 'Hinweis auf einen Zwickauer Orgelbaumeister', *Alt-Zwickau*, no.2 (1931)
P. Smets, ed.: *Orgeldispositionen* (Kassel, 1931)
WALTER HÜTTEL

Holdich, George Maydwell (*b* Maydwell, Northants., 1816; *d* Forest Hill, 1896). English organ builder. He established himself in London in 1837 at 12 Greek Street, Soho, moving in 1854 to 4 Judd Place East, King's Cross, and in the 1860s to Liverpool Road, Islington. The business was sold in 1894 to Eustace Ingram. Holdich is chiefly remembered as a builder of distinguished small church organs. A number survive in country churches, especially in Northamptonshire and in the neighbouring counties. The earlier examples have neat Gothic or Classical cases, and the tonal schemes of all but the smallest instruments have properly developed choruses, frequently capped with a two-rank mixture, and including an independent tierce. The Great Stopped Diapason usually has a Clarabella treble, and Holdich often included an octave of bourdons (16′) which could be played either by hand, or on the permanently coupled pedal pull-downs. More ambitious instruments have a short-compass Swell, sometimes with the characteristic Double Dulciana. To extend the scope of the small organ, in 1843 Holdich adapted the 'Diaocton', an octave coupler with an extra octave of pipes at the top of the compass.

Holdich's larger organs were not as successful as the smaller ones. Among them were instruments for the parish church at Henley on Thames (1854) and St Margaret's, Westminster (1859). His most important work, the Lichfield Cathedral organ (1861), had a 10-stop pedal organ with two mixtures, a complete 32′ flue chorus and two reeds, but in other respects (stops drawing in halves, no 16′ manual reed, a choir organ which could have been designed 50 years before) it underlined his essential conservatism. Surviving instruments include those at Redenhall, Norfolk (1843), and, in Northamptonshire, Southwick (*c*1845), Easton-on-the-Hill (1850), and Old (1853); a larger (though altered) organ survives at St Neots (1855). As an example of his sensitivity with old material, Holdich's rebuilding (1852 and 1872) of the 1717 Shrider organ at Finedon is worth examination.

BIBLIOGRAPHY
B. B. Edmonds: 'Once upon a time', *Organ Club Handbook*, vi (1960)
NICHOLAS THISTLETHWAITE

Hollis, Douglas (*b* Ann Arbor, 21 April 1948). American sculptor. He has used sound elements in several outdoor installations constructed in Berkeley, California, since the mid-1970s. These include large aeolian harps, and (from 1980) a series of 'singing bridges' in which wind and water are involved. In Waterwalker (1981), for example, a jetty 30 metres long, floating on large empty oil drums, is built out into a lake; it functions as a resonator for a wind harp constructed from some 60 polypropylene strings which are anchored in the water on each side and cross a metal pipe, supported on five upright poles 6 metres high, so as to form a roof-shaped triangular structure above the jetty.

HUGH DAVIES

Hollister. Irish family of organists and keyboard instrument makers.

(1) Robert Hollister. He was appointed organist at St John's Church in Fishamble Street, Dublin, in 1688, someone else being appointed to this position in 1715. It has been suggested that he may have been the father or a brother of (2) Thomas Hollister.

(2) Thomas Hollister (*fl* Cork and Dublin, 1695–1720). He may have been the son or brother of (1) Robert Hollister. He was appointed assistant organist at St Finn Barre's Cathedral, Cork, in 1695, with the added duty to 'tune and keep clean the organ at an agreed stipend'; someone else was appointed to this position in 1703. He was presumably the Thomas Hollister who moved from Cork and built an organ for St Werburgh's Church in Dublin in 1719, having been appointed organist at that church in the same year. About a year later an inspection committee, consisting of Daniel and Ralph Roseingrave, Robert Woffington and the organ builder Cuvillie, declared the instrument to be unsatisfactory. It was not replaced until 1767, but Hollister received only a portion of his fee and was replaced as organist in 1720 by John Woffington.

(3) Philip Hollister (*d* Dublin, May 1760). Son of (2) Thomas Hollister. He was an organ builder who worked in York Street, opposite the Charter School Nursery. In April 1733 he was appointed in the place of John Byfield to maintain the organs at both the Dublin cathedrals at an annual fee of £10 from each cathedral; he also tuned the organ at St Mary's (1732–60) and in 1744 repaired the organ in Limerick Cathedral. In September 1749 he was reported as having completed an organ for Londonderry Cathedral. He married Deborah Mundy in 1736, and had two daughters, Elizabeth and Charlotte. The latter married Alexander Castels in 1757.

(4) William Castels [Castles] **Hollister** (*b* ?Dublin; *d* Dublin, 1802). He may have been the son or nephew of (3) Philip Hollister. He was an organ builder, harpsichord maker and impresario, and succeeded Philip Hollister at York Street either in 1760 or late in 1759. The reason for his assumption of 'Castels' as a second name (also used by another member of the family, born in 1760) is not clear, though it is presumably connected with the marriage into the family of Alexander Castels. He was admitted to the Guild of St Luke as a joiner by service at Michaelmas 1751, and carried on the business in York Street until shortly before April 1764, when he moved to Parliament Street. He is listed in the Dublin Directories as an organ builder and harpsichord maker at six widely separated addresses up to 1802. The main-

tenance of the organs in the cathedrals seems to have passed into the hands of Ferdinand Weber not long after 1760, and by August 1768 Hollister had branched out into concert promotion, opening 'a new place for the Entertainment and Amusement of the Citizens in imitation of Ranelagh Gardens near London'. Although he erected lamps at his own expense to light the way out of the city on concert nights, the popularity of this venture was no serious rival to that of the more centrally situated Rotunda Gardens, and Ranelagh was closed by Hollister in 1777.

(5) Frederick Hollister (*b* Dublin, Sept 1761). The son of (4) William Castels Hollister. He is listed in the Dublin Directory of 1803 as a piano maker and tuner at 10 St Anne Street – the same address as his father's business between 1794 and 1802.

BRIAN BOYDELL

Holpijp (Dutch). An ORGAN STOP (*Hohlflöte*).

Holtkamp Organ Co. American firm of organ builders. It was founded in 1855 in Cleveland, Ohio, by Gottlieb Ferdinand Votteler (*b* Germany, 1817), who had previously worked in New York and Baltimore. On Gottlieb's death in 1894, his son Henry B. Votteler (*b* 1849) formed a partnership with J. H. Hettche, and from 1903 the firm was known as the Votteler–Hettche Organ Co. In 1900 Henry H. Holtkamp (1858–1931) joined the company, becoming sole manager upon the retirement of the partners in 1905. Allen G. Sparling, a Canadian, arrived in 1911, and in 1914 the firm became the Votteler–Holtkamp–Sparling Co. On Henry Holtkamp's death, his son Walter Henry (*b* St Mary's, Ohio, 1894; *d* Cleveland, 1962) assumed leadership, and under him the firm rose to prominence. Walter H. Holtkamp jr (*b* 1929) joined the firm in 1956 and became president on his father's death.

W. H. Holtkamp shared with G. Donald Harrison the distinction of having been among the first to recognize and return to classical tonal principles, but his unique contribution (soon widely copied) lay in the successful efforts he made to bring organ pipework out of chambers and into the open. This began with the *Rückpositiv* of the organ for the Cleveland Museum of Art (1933), which was followed by a totally uncased three-manual organ for St John's Catholic Church, Covington, Kentucky (1934). Although the company's earliest organs had mechanical action, electro-pneumatic action (often with slider chests) had been used since early in the 20th century. Since 1969, however, Holtkamp has been building organs both with electro-pneumatic and with mechanical actions. Later Holtkamp organs are in the Crouse Auditorium, Syracuse, New York (1950), the Massachusetts Institute of Technology (1957), the Church of the Ascension, New York (1967), and Union Theological Seminary, New York (1980).

For illustration *see* ORGAN, fig.47.

BIBLIOGRAPHY
E. M. Nye: 'Walter Holtkamp: a Master Organ Builder', *The Organ*, li (1971–2), 66
O. Ochse: *The History of the Organ in the United States* (Bloomington, Ind., 1975)
J. A. Ferguson: *Walter Holtkamp: American Organ Builder* (Kent, Ohio, 1979)

BARBARA OWEN

Holz (Ger.: 'wood'). *Holzblasinstrumente*, or simply *Holz*, are woodwind instruments. The terms *Holzblock* and *Holzblocktrommel* designate the WOODBLOCK. *Holzfiedel, Holzharmonika, Holz- und Strohinstrument* and *Holzstabspiel* (also the obsolete South German and Austrian term *Hölzernes Gelächter*) all signify XYLOPHONE.

Holzhay, Johann Nepomuk (*b* Rappen, Upper Swabia, 26 Feb 1741; *d* Ottobeuren, 17 Sept 1809). German organ builder. He was probably apprenticed first to his uncle Alexander Holzhay of Anglberg; he went to KARL JOSEPH RIEPP at the time when Riepp was building the two organs in Ottobeuren Abbey (1757–66), and from then Ottobeuren was Holzhay's permanent home. He completed his most important organ in 1798, at Neresheim (three manuals, 47 stops; the case is still extant). There are surviving instruments by him at Ursberg (1755; two manuals, 26 stops), Obermarchthal (1782–4; three manuals, 41 stops) and Rot an der Rot (1785–93; three manuals, 36 stops). Holzhay's specifications follow those of his teacher Riepp in some points, and those of JOSEPH GABLER in others. Like Riepp, Holzhay built complete Principal choruses for the *Hauptwerk* and the *Positiv* (though not for the *Echowerk*) with Trumpets and Cornet V in the *Hauptwerk*; but instead of Riepp's mutations supplemented with a few foundation-stop variants, Holzhay, like Gabler, specified groups of various kinds of foundation stops (including a few mutations). For the *Echowerk* a group of this kind would include a discreet 8′ reed stop and a Cornet IV. The Pedals are economical, but adequate to provide a firm bass. At the highest pitches Holzhay's Zimbals are not substantially different from his mixtures. Holzhay, along with Gabler and Riepp, was one of the leading 18th-century organ builders of Upper Swabia.

BIBLIOGRAPHY
W. Supper and H. Meyer: *Barockorgeln in Oberschwaben* (Kassel, 1941)
W. Supper: 'Die oberschwäbische Barockorgel', *Der Barock, seine Orgeln und seine Musik in Oberschwaben: Ochsenhausen 1951*, 89
——: 'Holzhay', *MGG*

HANS KLOTZ

Holzklapper (Ger.). WHIP; *see also* CLAPPERS.

Holztrompete (Ger.). (1) A wooden trumpet in general, and, more specifically, an ALPHORN or alpenhorn, a Swiss folk instrument of the horn hamily with a cup-shaped mouthpiece, made of wood, which plays simple tunes (for example, *ranz des vaches*) using only harmonics. Similar folk instruments are known in other countries.

(2) A wooden instrument with the bell of an english horn, one valve and a cup mouthpiece, invented to play the shepherd's melody in the third act of Wagner's *Tristan und Isolde*. The music is more often played on the english horn.

Hommel [hummel, humle]. An onomatopoeic name (probably derived from *hommelen* (Dutch), 'to hum' or 'buzz') for a partly fretted BOX ZITHER used in the Low Countries and adjacent parts of Germany, and in Scandinavia. The hommel may have been developed in the Netherlands from the smaller and less dynamically powerful SCHEITHOLT and EPINETTE DE VOSGES, which examples from the early 17th century greatly resemble; in later instruments shape and stringing were not standardized. Hommels have been trapeziform, rectangular, and in the shape of a fiddle, viol or half bottle. Some have a superimposed fretboard or fretbox (the latter, sometimes called a second soundbox in the Low Countries, is also found in Appalachian dulcimers) and up to 12 bourdons arranged in double or triple courses and attached to metal wrest pins instead of wooden pegs. The fretted strings are stopped and all the strings sounded by the same methods as on the *épinette de Vosges*; there is evidence, however, of hommels having sometimes been bowed in Friesland and the province of Holland. Some forms, with local names such as *vlier*, *blokviool, krabber* and *pinet*, are still played in Belgium and reproductions of earlier hommels are often used in modern folk groups in the Netherlands.

BIBLIOGRAPHY
K. Douwes: *Grondig ondersoek van toonen der. musijk* (Franeker, 1699/*R*1971)
S. Walin: *Die schwedische Hummel* (Stockholm, 1953)
F. J. de Hen: 'Folk Instruments of Belgium, Part One', *GSJ*, xxv (1972), 112
H. Boone: 'De hommel in de Lage Landen', *Brussels Museum of Musical Instruments Bulletin*, v (1975) [special issue, incl. Eng. and Fr. summaries]

JOAN RIMMER

Homolka, Ferdinand (August Vincenč) (*b* Velvary, 19 Jan 1828; *d* Prague, 22 April 1890). Bohemian violin maker. The leading member of an undeservedly neglected family of violin makers, he received his initial

Hommel, Swedish, 19th century (Musikmuseet, Stockholm)

training from his father, Emanuel Adam Homolka (1796–1849), a much respected maker whose best instruments, usually those with double purfling, are still much sought after. Before opening his own workshop in Prague in 1857, Ferdinand worked with an unusually large number of makers, including Josef Kratschmann in Znojmo, Franz Schmidt and (later) Anton Fischer in Vienna, Johann Fritsch in Linz, and Franz Lehner, Jan Stoss and Jan Baptist Dvořák in Prague, as well as with other members of his family in Kutna Hora (Kuttenberg) and Prague. Dubbed the 'Prager Stradivarius', he was unquestionably the family's most successful copyist of the Stradivari model, although he also copied other Italian and Tyrolean masters; the labels of his Tyrolean instruments usually note the name of the original maker. His instruments are very well made with obvious care having been spent on all details of craft.

Other notable members of the Homolka family (relationships are to F. A. V. Homolka) were Ferdinand Josef (uncle, 1810–62), Vincenč Emanuel (brother, 1826–61), Eduard Emanuel Karel (son, 1860–1933) and Eduard Ferdinand (grandson, 1896–1915). Their violins follow various patterns, with an apparent preference for the Stradivari model; the greatest diversity in their instruments is shown in the archings. Much of their work is covered with dark varnish, varying from chocolate brown to red-brown; however, lighter shades are also occasionally seen. Tonally, their best instruments have a fine, rounded fullness.

BIBLIOGRAPHY

K. Jalovec: Cešti houslaři [Violin makers of Bohemia] (Prague, 1959; Eng. trans., 1959)

JAAK LIIVOJA-LORIVS

Hontsurigane [hontsuri]. Small indoor version of the Japanese temple bell BONSHŌ. It is used in *geza* music to represent the temple bell or the *hanshō* fire-bell, as well as to deepen the loneliness of a night scene (for illustration, *see* GEZA). It may be around 60 cm tall and it is struck with a padded mallet.

DAVID W. HUGHES

Hoofdwerk. *See* HAUPTWERK.

Hooghuys. Belgian family of organ builders. The most important member of the family is Louis Hooghuys (*b* Bruges, 21 March 1822; *d* Bruges, 1885), son of the organ builder Simon-Gerardus Hooghuys; his work includes a large instrument for the National Music Festival held at Bruges in 1878 and a number of church organs in Belgium. In 1880 the family firm began making street organs and fairground organs; this branch of the work was continued into the 1920s in Grammont by R. Charles Hooghuys, a son of Louis. Aimé Hooghuys, another son of Louis, was also active in the firm.

BIBLIOGRAPHY

G. Moortgat: Oude orgels in Vlaanderen, ii (Brussels, 1965)
E. V. Cockayne: The Fairground Organ (London, 1970)

BARBARA OWEN

Hook & Hastings. American firm of organ builders. It was founded in 1827 by Elias Hook (1805–81) and George Greenleaf Hook (1807–80), both sons of a Salem, Massachusetts, cabinet maker and former apprentices of William Goodrich. In 1831 they moved from Salem to Boston, and in 1833 built their first three-manual organ for the First Baptist Church of Providence, Rhode Island. In 1845 they built what was considered the first concert organ in Boston, for Tremont Temple, and by the middle of the 19th century the firm of E. & G. G. Hook was acknowledged the leading builder in New England. Their reputation during the following decades was solidly based on their outstanding reed and chorus voicing and the sound engineering of their actions. In 1855 Frank H. Hastings (1836–1916) came to the Hook firm, soon becoming prominent in the design department. In 1871 he became a full partner, and the name was changed to E. & G. G. Hook and Hastings. He became president after the death of both founders, and in 1889 built a large new factory in Weston, Massachusetts. During the 1870s and 1880s a series of 'stock' organs was introduced, and the success of these helped increase production to the point where by 1893 the firm, now known as Hook & Hastings, was producing more than one organ a week. As early as the 1860s Barker levers had been used in constructing the actions of large organs, and by the turn of the century pneumatic and electro-pneumatic actions as well as tracker were being built. Competition from younger firms was keen, however, and a decline began even before the death of Hastings, when Arthur L. Coburn (*d* 1931) became president. After the Depression, the firm went into liquidation in 1936. Hook & Hastings built many notable organs during the second half of the nineteenth century, including those for Immaculate Conception Church and Holy Cross Cathedral, Boston (1863; 1876), the Mechanics Hall, Worcester, Mass. (1864), Cincinnati Music Hall (1877) and St Francis Xavier Church, New York (1881).

BIBLIOGRAPHY

W. J. Conner: 'Pipe Scaling in Hook Organs, 1849–1895', *The Diapason*, lxii/10 (1971), 18
T. Murray: 'The Hook & Hastings Organ in Holy Cross Cathedral, Boston', *The Diapason*, lxiii/11 (1972), 4
B. Owen: 'A Salem Chamber Organ', *Essex Institute Quarterly*, cx/2 (1974), 111
O. Ochse: *The History of the Organ in the United States* (Bloomington, Ind., 1975)
B. Owen: 'Organs at the Centennial', *The Bicentennial Tracker* (Wilmington, Ohio, 1976)
——: *The Organ in New England* (Raleigh, North Carolina, 1979)

BARBARA OWEN

Hook harp (Ger. *Hakenharfe*). A diatonic frame harp, fitted with a row of hooks set in the neck to permit the player to raise the pitch of each string by a semitone (*see* HARP, §4(vi), esp. fig.21). This device was apparently developed in Austria in the second half of the 17th century. By the early 18th century a further refinement had been introduced, a mechanism to enable the player to operate the hooks by means of a foot pedal. Some later 17th- and 18th-century harps are supplied with hooks only for the F and C strings. For further information, see R. Rensch: *The Harp* (New York, 1969).

Hoop drum. A term occasionally applied to a FRAME DRUM.

Hope-Jones, Robert (*b* Cheshire, 9 Feb 1859; *d* Rochester, NY, 13 Sept 1914). English organ builder. He was apprenticed as an engineer at the Laird shipyard, Birkenhead, and later became chief electrician of the Lancashire and Cheshire Telephone Co. In 1887 he used his skills to rebuild and electrify the organ of St John's,

Birkenhead, introducing several revolutionary features. He first established himself as an organ builder in 1889 in Birkenhead, experimenting with electric mechanisms and pipe-voicing. All his organ building was subcontracted to various firms, including Norman & Beard, to whom he supplied the electric-action mechanisms until he founded his own firm, the Hope-Jones Organ Co., in 1894. In 1898 he moved to Norwich but bankruptcy followed and Norman & Beard purchased the assets in 1899. By 1901 Hope-Jones was in partnership with Eustace Ingram of London and Hereford as a designer but in 1903 he went to the USA to work briefly for Austin, L. C. Harrison and Skinner. In 1907 he founded the Hope-Jones Electric Organ Co. in Elmira, New York, and from this factory came the first 'unit orchestras' (*see* CINEMA ORGAN). In 1910, again in financial difficulty, he sold his interests to the Rudolph Wurlitzer Co., staying on merely as a figurehead. This arrangement seriously restricted Hope-Jones's opportunities for invention, and in 1914, despondent over the failure of an attempt to break his contract with the firm, he committed suicide.

To Hope-Jones must be credited the first extensive use of the 'unit' principle, whereby single ranks of pipes are made to serve in several divisions at different pitches. His belief that traditional organ choruses had evolved through inadequate wind supply from hand-blowing led to his use of electric blowing machinery providing unlimited volume and high wind pressure. The Hope-Jones chorus consisted of powerful unison and octave ranks alone, with narrow-scaled unison pipes adding a brilliance to the tone quality. However, his concepts in this area have not stood the test of time. No Hope-Jones organ has survived unaltered in England, although there is a good example of his work at St Paul's, Burton-on-Trent (1894); his organ at Worcester Cathedral (1895) survived until the 1920s. In the USA important instruments included Park Church, Elmira, New York (1906), and The Auditorium, Ocean Grove, New Jersey (1908). *See also* ORGAN, §VI, 4.

BIBLIOGRAPHY
G. L. Miller: *The Recent Revolution in Organ Building* (New York, 1913)
R. Whitworth: *The Electric Organ* (London, 1948)
M. Sayer: 'New Light on Hope-Jones', *The Organ*, lx (1981), 20
BARBARA OWEN, MICHAEL SAYER

Hopkins, Asa (*b* Litchfield, Conn., 1779; *d* New Haven, 27 Oct 1838). American maker of woodwind instruments in a section of Litchfield, Connecticut, later known as Fluteville. A clockmaker from before 1810 until 1825, Hopkins began making musical instruments in 1829 in a new shop on the Naugatuck River. In 1832 Hopkins encouraged Jabez McCall Camp (*b* 1811) to become one of four partners. In June 1837 Camp became the general partner, and for two years all instruments bore his stamp. The Camp firm sold the majority of its stock in 1839 to Firth & Hall of New York, which by 1846 (then as Firth, Hall & Pond) owned all shares. The firm was sold once again by 1867 to Frederick Porter, probably their plant superintendent, who sold it, in about 1875, to John Hall. Not long after, the factory went over to the manufacture of cutlery.

Hopkins is principally noted for producing finely crafted instruments that met the needs of the provincial American musical community. Although he filed a patent for wooden clock wheels in 1814, no musical instrument patents are known. Some of his flutes and clarinets are at the Library of Congress (Dayton Miller Flute Collection), Smithsonian Institution, Yale University and in various other American collections. The instruments, usually made of boxwood with ivory rings, have conservative key systems: the clarinets often have five flat brass keys; the flutes four to six flat brass or cupped silver keys. As musical taste changed, Hopkins's successors, Firth, Hall & Pond, began the manufacture of guitars, castanets, bones and drumsticks.

BIBLIOGRAPHY
P. T. Young: *Asa Hopkins of Fluteville* (diss., Yale U., 1962)
CYNTHIA ADAMS HOOVER

Hopkinson. English firm of piano makers. In 1837 John Hopkinson (*b* Chatham, 5 Dec 1811; *d* Criccieth, 4 April 1886) became a music professor in Leeds; his brother James joined him in new premises at 6 Commercial Street by 1841. The 1842 directory also lists them as music sellers and publishers; by 1845 they were advertising their own microchordon, cottage, semi-cabinet and cabinet pianos. Piano making became their sole activity by 1900.

In 1846 John opened a factory in London, James staying in Leeds until 1856, when another brother took over. Business flourished, and in 1851 they advertised in London (at 6 and 7 Store Street), claiming that their pianos were 30–40% cheaper than most other first-class instruments. In 1851 Hopkinson patented a grand piano action, whereby a 'tremolo' like that on a violin could be produced (patent no.13,652); such an instrument with $6\frac{7}{8}$ octaves 'in a neat plain mahogany case' cost 110 guineas.

John retired in 1869, having established a reputable firm and won prizes at various exhibitions. The firm moved many times in London in the area of New Bond Street. In Leeds (*c*1860–70), the firm changed to Hopkinson Bros., and to Hopkinson Bros. & Co. (*c*1870). James Hopkinson retired in 1883, and in 1940 the family lost control over the firm when Hopkinsons' Successors Ltd took over at the same premises (5 and 6 Commercial Street). In London, the Hopkinson firm amalgamated with Rogers into the Vincent Piano Co. Ltd shortly after World War I. In 1963 H. B. Lowry and I. D. Zender took over the manufacture of pianos under both names at George Rogers & Sons (Tottenham) Ltd.

BIBLIOGRAPHY
International Exhibition, 1862, Jurors' Reports, xvi: *Musical Instruments* (London, 1862)
E. Pauer: *A Dictionary of Pianists and Composers for the Pianoforte with an Appendix of Manufacturers* (London, 1895)
R. E. M. Harding: *The Piano-forte: its History traced to the Great Exhibition of 1851* (Cambridge, 1933, rev. 2/1978)
MARGARET CRANMER

Hopper. A component of the action of the piano; *see* PIANOFORTE, §I, esp. figs.11–12, 16, 21–2.

Hoqa. GOBLET DRUM of Egypt. *See* DARABUKKA.

Hōragai. Japanese CONCH-SHELL TRUMPET (*hōragai*: 'conch shell'). It has been used since at least the 7th century in Buddhist music, especially *shugendō*, and its sound, likened to a lion's roar, is said to drive out evil spirits. It has also been used for signalling troops in battle. A wooden (now often metal) mouthpiece is usually attached at the narrow end, but the point of the shell may simply be snipped off and the resulting orifice polished smooth. The Korean NAGAK and the Chinese FALUO are related instruments.

DAVID W. HUGHES

Horanāva. Small oboe, with cylindrical bore, of Sri Lanka. It is closely related to the Indian ŚAHNĀĪ. It is usually made of ebony or other hardwood, the barrel being carved in an externally conical shape. The bell and mouthpiece are of brass, the latter having a small circular pirouette near the top. Its total length varies from 28 cm to 33 cm. The player fashions the broad, blunt reed by binding together two or four thicknesses of dried *talipot* palm. The instrument has seven finger-holes and a range of about two octaves. The lowest obtainable note is nearly always near *a'*, though the lowest three finger-holes are rarely used.

The *horanāva* has a unique position in Sinhalese music in that it is the only genuine melody instrument; instruments such as the *sak* and *kombu* produce pitched sound but are used monotonally. The *horanāva* is essential to the HĒVISI ensemble of Buddhist ritual.

The *horanāva* is also the melody instrument used in *kōlam*, a low-country dance-drama where masked dancers enact social satires, thinly disguised as legends and Buddhist folk-tales. The combination of *horanāva* and *yak-berē* (drum) found in this genre is unique in Sinhalese music. It is also sometimes used, with the *uḍäkki* and *gāṭa-berē* (drums), to accompany *sokari*, an up-country folk play.

See also MAHVARĪ; for illustration *see* HĒVISI.

BIBLIOGRAPHY
O. Pertold: *Ceremonial Dances of the Sinhalese* (Prague, 1930), 63ff
A. M. Hocart: *The Temple of the Tooth at Kandy* (London, 1931)
M. H. Goonatilleka: *Sokari of Sri Lanka* (Colombo, 1976)
NATALIE M. WEBBER

Horde. The most common percussion instrument of the Fula (Fulani) people of the West African savanna. It is made from a half-calabash with a metal rattling plaque attached inside. The player holds the open side towards his chest and beats the outside with his palms and with finger-rings as rhythmic accompaniment to singing. See D. W. Arnott: 'Fulani Music', *Grove 6*.

Horil, Jakob (*fl* Vienna and Rome, *c*1720–60). Violin maker of Bohemian descent. He worked in Vienna between 1720 and 1740 and in Rome until about 1760. Indeed, Rome seems to have been the one centre in Italy that allowed expatriate German and Austrian violin makers to flourish. The nature of his instruments indicates that his training was largely in the Tyrol, though his later, Roman instruments also show a slight Italian influence, for instance in the cut of the soundholes. His model recalls Stainer but the positioning of the soundholes varies from being almost upright to strongly slanting. The varnish, which varies from yellow-brown to red-brown, tends to lack lustre. The best of his instruments are strong and even in tone and certainly far superior to most similarly modelled violins being produced in Germany and Austria at the time.

BIBLIOGRAPHY
W. L. von Lütgendorff: *Die Geigen- und Lautenmacher vom Mittelalter bis zur Gegenwart* (Frankfurt am Main, 1904, rev. 6/1922/*R*1968)
JAAK LIIVOJA-LORIUS

Horn (Fr. *cor, cor d'harmonie*; *cor à pistons* [valve horn]; *cor simple, cor à main* [hand horn]; *cor de chasse, huchet, trompe de chasse* [hunting horn]. Ger. *Horn*; *Ventilhorn* [valve horn]; *Naturhorn* [hand horn]; *Hiefhorn, Hifthorn, Jagdhorn, Waldhorn* [hunting horn]. It. *corno; corno a macchina* [valve horn]; *corno naturale* [hand horn]; *corno da caccia* [hunting horn]. Sp. *trompa*). A term that refers, in its broadest sense, to a variety of wind instruments usually of the lip-reed class. An inessential distinction often drawn between horns and trumpets is that the bore of a trumpet is mainly cylindrical, that of a horn mainly conical. In the Hornbostel–Sachs classification system, however, horns are considered to be within the family of trumpets (*see* AEROPHONE). Horns used for signalling (and sounding perhaps only one note) have been fashioned from conches, animal horns etc, as well as metal. Horns capable of playing many notes usually consist of a conical brass (or other metal) tube in a curved, coiled or folded shape. This article is concerned with the European orchestral horn, often referred to as the french horn. For a discussion of non-European horns and further details relating to horns as members of the trumpet family *see* TRUMPET.

See also ORGAN STOP.

1. General. 2. Technique. 3. History to *c*1800. 4. History from *c*1800. 5. Solo repertory.

1. GENERAL. In its simplest form the horn is a slender, gradually tapered tube between approximately 2 metres and 5·5 metres in length, coiled in one, two or three circles and expanding into a widely flared bell. It is played with a relatively small, funnel-shaped mouthpiece that produces a softer and more mellow tone than the shallow, cup-shaped trumpet mouthpiece, which favours a brilliant tone. The *trompe de chasse* still used in France is just such a simple horn: pitched in D, it is about 4·5 metres long, coiled in three complete circles and tapered throughout its entire length. On the other hand the modern orchestral horn carries a considerable amount of cylindrical (i.e. untapered) tubing, partly because of the valves with which it is equipped. By virtue of its length and slender proportions the horn can be made to sound a larger number of notes in its natural harmonic series than can other brass instruments.

The natural horn, as used in 18th- and 19th-century orchestras, was equipped with a number of crooks – lengths of tubing that when fitted into the horn served to add to its basic length, enabling it to play a different harmonic series. The crooks most often used were those that pitched the horn in the keys of B♭ alto, A, G, F, E, E♭, D, C and B♭ bass. On natural horns a diatonic scale was possible only in the top octave or by hand-stopping (see §2). Modern horns generally have four or three, sometimes five, or occasionally six valves, which act to extend or shorten the basic length of tubing. Table 1 shows how a complete chromatic scale can be played by using the valves singly and in combination. The valve layout shown in Table 1 is that of the major-

'Single' horns are pitched in B♭ or F; in 'double' horns the fourth valve transforms the instrument from one pitch to another. Most of the notes within the compass of the double horn are common to several series, which gives the performer a liberal choice of alternative fingerings. The valve layout shown in Table 1 is that of the major-

TABLE 1: Harmonic series chart

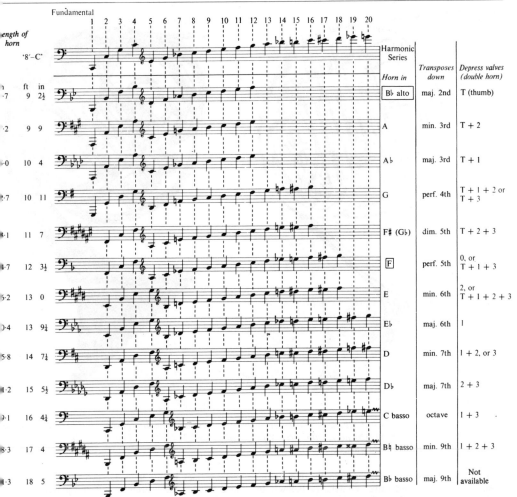

Tube lengths calculated for diapason normal: *a'* = 435

Valve 1 lowers pitch by 2 semitones, valve 2 by 1 semitone, valve 3 by 3 semitones; T (thumb valve) raises pitch by 5 semitones.

(i) The top stave shows the natural harmonic series. The remainder show the actual sound of each harmonic with any given crook.
(ii) Harmonics 7, 11, 13 and 14 are out of tune with the tempered scale and are not used in modern horn technique.
(iii) The extreme notes shown are possible for most good professional players, at least when practising. Some have greater natural facility for one end of the register, but they are likely to have more trouble with the other. In the days of the hand horn players specialized in the higher or lower register, according to natural aptitude, but modern technique and instruments have greatly extended the range of the average player.

TABLE 2

As written for horn in F	Actual sounding pitch	Harmonic number	Horn in	Alternative valve combinations
		5	A	T + 2
		6	F♯ (G♭)	T + 2 + 3
		8	D♭	2 + 3
		9	B♭ basso	1 + 2 + 3
		6	B♭ alto	T
		8	F	T + 1 + 3 or 0
		9	E♭	1
		10	D♭	2 + 3
		8	B♭ alto	T
		9	A♭	T + 1
		10	G♭	T + 2 + 3
		12	E♭	1
		15	B♭ basso	1 + 2 + 3

1 = 1st valve; 2 = 2nd; 3 = 3rd; T = thumb

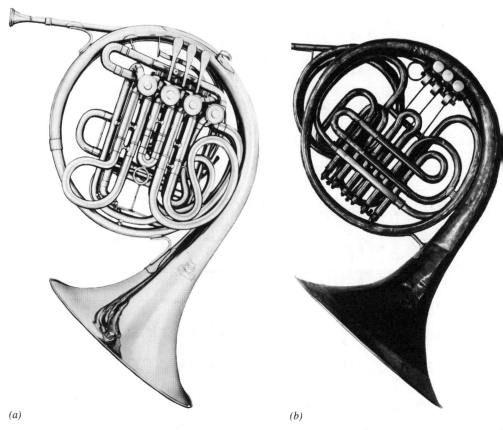

(a)   *(b)*

1. (a) Modern double horn in F/B♭ with four rotary valves by Paxman, London (modern form of the instrume designed by Kruspe, c1898); (b) horn with three Vienna valves and F crook by Leopold Uhlmann (i), Vienn c1850 (Boosey & Hawkes Museum, London)

ity of modern horns, both single and double (but not the French 'ascending third-valve' model; see below). In the three examples in Table 2 the alternatives given are those available on the standard double horn. If a single horn is used, the combinations that include a 'T' (i.e. thumb valve of the double horn) are those of the B♭ horn, and the remainder those of the F horn.

The range of the horn is basically from the 2nd partial to the 16th. On shorter horns (above F) notes above the 12th partial sound with difficulty, but the fundamental (1st partial) is more easily obtainable than on the longer horns.

Traditionally horn parts were written in the key of C and the actual pitch of the horn specified as 'horn in F', 'horn in D' etc, but it has become customary to write everything for horn in F. The practice of re-editing Classical symphonies with all the horn parts transposed into F offers no advantage except to beginners, and may easily cause an experienced player who is familiar with the original to make an error.

Of the several varieties of valve horn in use, the most common is the double horn in F/B♭ with four valves (see fig.1a). In the standard model one of these valves, controlled by the thumb, cuts out approximately 1 metre of tubing, thereby instantly transforming the medium-length F horn into a short horn in B♭ alto. Each of the three normal valves is provided with a double set of

tuning-slides so that the valve notes may always be tune whether the instrument is being played in F or B♭. The single horn in B♭ alto (tube length 2·73 metre occurs in a four-valve version in which the thumb val lowers the pitch by a semitone or up to three quarte of a tone (for hand-stopping) or else by a 4th to F. The is also a five-valve version (sometimes known as th Sansone model after its designer, the American ho player Lorenzo Sansone) with both a semitone thum valve and a valve to lower the pitch of the instrume by a 4th; this downward extension gives the instrume a range equal to that of a double horn, but the lowe semitones are difficult to play in tune. Players som times make supplementary use of a 'descant' horn, i. a single horn in F alto (or rarely in B♭ altissimo, usual referred to as soprano). Single descant horns are n general-purpose instruments because of their incomple scale and their relatively poor tone quality in the low register, and are commonly used only for very hig passages in Baroque and Classical music. The doub horn in B♭/F alto is rapidly gaining popularity. Le usual, but nonetheless played by leading professional are double horns in F/F alto, B♭/B♭ soprano, triple hor in F/B♭/F alto or F/B♭/B♭ soprano, and a 'doub model in F/F alto of which the F section can be change to B♭ or A by means of a set of slides. The single ho in F, previously the standard orchestral instrument, h en almost totally superseded by the F/B♭ horn, though ginners sometimes use it. In Vienna the unique Vienhorn in F (with a detachable crook and three twin-ston valves, see fig.1b) is still used, but this practice mostly confined to 19th-century Romantic music. The cline of the single F horn has unquestionably been stened by the heavy demands of composers who expect rns to play parts as complex as those for the cello, d by the economics of the recording studio and the sistence of conductors on power and accuracy at all sts (whereby they consider a 'split' note a worse crime an poor tone or even indifferent style). The shorter rns are less prone to cracked notes than the longer F rn, but this advantage was at first often offset by the ss of that poetic tone quality justifiably claimed as the rn's chief asset. Later, however, many outstanding ayers used the very short horns without such loss, particularly after the introduction in the 1960s of improved signs by Merewether (London) using tapered tubes in e valve system and thereby permitting the combina-n of instruments as widely differing as 1·3 metres and 75 metres in length (B♭ soprano and F, respectively) to double or triple horns. At present almost all players e a German model horn with a relatively large bore, 31-cm bell and rotary valves; the older French model d a smaller bore, a bell of 28 cm and piston valves. The French 'ascending third-valve' horn differs from e more usual horn in that depressing the third valve ises the pitch by a tone instead of lowering it by three mitones. The instrument is built in G, but the air-normally passes through the third-valve tubing, hich is sufficient in length to lower the horn by one ne, giving the equivalent of a two-valve horn in F. hen the third valve is depressed and its dependent tub-g thereby cut out of the circuit, it becomes a two-valve rn in G. The system allows simplified fingering for ssages involving many sharps and flats and offers ternative fingering for certain notes liable to be treach-ous on the ordinary F horn. As against seven effective lve combinations available with the ordinary (or scending) system, the French system (in its single-rn version) has only five (see Table 3). As D♭, C and basso tube-lengths are unavailable with this system, w E♭ (sounding A♭) and pedal A♭, G and F♯ (sound-g D♭, C and B♭') cannot be played as valve notes; it as it is a system intended primarily for those who ibitually play either first or third horn, this is a sec-idary consideration. A double horn in F/B♭ in the rench system gives a complete range of tonalities from in alt down to D. The pedal A♭ (sounding D♭) is still iobtainable with the valves, as there is no D♭ tube-igth (an extra valve can be fitted for this and other ses), but pedal G and F♯ (sounding C and B♭') can be ayed as fundamentals of the C alto and B alto horns.

TABLE 3

Valve combination	Transposes down	Gives horn in
1	a tone lower	E♭
2	a semitone lower	E♮
1 + 2	three semitones lower	D
3	a tone higher	G
3 + 2	a semitone higher	G♭ (F♯)
3 + 1	cancel each other out	F

There have existed two 'omnitonic' valve horns, a haussier four-valve model (developed in the 1880s by ie French hand-horn player Henri Chaussier) and a

Prager (Zurich) six-valve model; neither has survived in use. A full discussion of the Chaussier horn is found in Constant Pierre's *La facture instrumentale à l'Exposition universelle de 1889* (Paris, 1890). The Prager horn had an elaborate combination of descending and ascending valves. Neither had a practical advantage over the double horn; in addition, the Chaussier horn presented difficulties with intonation and had an unorthodox fingering system, while the Prager horn's extra valves and tubing made the instrument very heavy.

Horns are now almost always made of brass (copper and zinc in varying proportions) or nickel silver (brass with a small amount of nickel added). In the past they were also sometimes made of copper or, very occasionally, of silver. The mouthpiece, formerly made of sheet metal in the form of a deep cone, is now always turned and bored either from a casting or from a solid cylinder of brass, German silver or silver. Modern mouthpieces generally have some degree of 'throat' restriction and are often slightly cupped inside as well.

2. TECHNIQUE. As it was considered difficult for one man to master both the extreme high and the extreme low notes of the horn's very large compass, players used to be divided into two categories: 'first' horn or *cor alto* and 'second' horn or *cor basse*. According to his natural abilities a player adopted one category at the outset of his career and restricted himself to it until he retired. With the E♭ crook, then considered the best for solo playing, the approximate ranges were from the 4th harmonic to the 24th for the *cor alto*, and from five semitones below the 2nd harmonic up to the 16th for the *cor basse*. The best part of the horn's compass for solos, between the 6th and 12th harmonics (where the tonal inequalities between open and stopped notes can be effectively disguised), was common to both categories; nevertheless most of the greatest soloists were *cor basse* players.

At the beginning of the 19th century a third category known as the *cor mixte* came into being. The player confined himself to about two octaves in the best part of the instrument, making up for his neglect of the low and extremely high notes by great dexterity in the execution of chromatic passages. A number of celebrated soloists (such as F. N. Duvernoy, Giovanni Puzzi and J. F. Gallay) belonged in this category, as do most present-day players.

The physical effort required to produce a given sound on the horn depends solely on its actual pitch: the higher the note, the greater the effort required, with notes above the staff being particularly tiring for the player. In the early 18th century composers wrote long passages in the highest register, but they used horns and trumpets rather as though they were organ stops (i.e. to strengthen the melody line in a tutti) or purely as a solo voice. Even for the *cor alto* players who specialized in the high range this sort of playing was a strain, but the performer could then generally count on a good rest before he had to play again, whereas today a first horn seldom has more than a few bars' rest here and there. At the low end of the range, the fundamental tones can be played on horns in B♭ alto or A, but they are rarely written for horns pitched lower than this because they are very difficult to produce. Sometimes, however, a player meets with a pedal G for E♭ horn, as in the well-known solo for fourth horn in Beethoven's Ninth Symphony. In Beethoven's era this was played as a 'factitious' note obtained from the 2nd harmonic by relaxing the lip. The pedal C in the opening bars of Beethoven's Fourth Symphony was intended for horn in B♭ basso. Today either note would be played as a fundamental tone of the B♭ alto horn.

As soon as partial occlusion of the bell with the hand had become an accepted method of obtaining notes outside the harmonic series germane to the tube length in use, much study was devoted to the elaboration of technique. Apart from its use for the production of notes, the normal slightly cupped position of the hand gave the sound a certain mysterious quality that was previously quite unknown, transforming the naturally coarse, brassy tone of the instrument into one of the most refined voices at the composer's disposal. A correct position of the hand in the bell is still essential to fine tone production. The importance of this is often overlooked through lack of awareness of the hand's precise function there. Held in the bell-throat as described below, it slightly flattens the general pitch and modifies the instrument's response so as to add many secure notes to its upper register, as well as to bring a further octave of frequencies known as 'formant partials' to enrich its timbre over the whole range. The open hand – fingers and thumb close together in one plane – is placed in the bell so that the backs of the fingers, turned away from the player, are in contact with the metal, and the thumb is just under the bell stay or in alignment with it; the knuckles and wrist are then flexed so as to leave an opening of about 40 mm. The only subsequent movements are the flexing or extension of knuckles and wrist necessary to give the correct opening for any particular note. Part of the chart in Gallay's *Méthode complète pour le cor* (c1845), the last important tutor to be published for hand horn alone, is given as ex.1.

Ex.1 Explanation of signs used:
    o = open note (i.e. with c40 mm between the palm of the hand and the inner wall of the bell)
    ● = completely stopped note
Fractions indicate to what extent the 40 mm opening is to be further reduced

Enharmonic Scale

† To play these notes in tune the bell must be opened more than for other notes.
∗ This note has a tendency to be sharp with the F, G and A crooks, and the bell must be very slightly closed.

'Stopped notes' (Fr. *sons bouchés*; Ger. *gestopft*; It. *chiuso*; often shown also by the sign '+') for valve horns should denote sounds produced with the bell tightly closed and an appropriately transposed fingering. The difficulty many people find in adequately stopping the bell has resulted in some erroneous accounts of this effect. Closing the bell always lowers pitch – grossly in lower notes but ever less so in ascending the range, with high notes barely flattened at all. By gradually closing the bell, any note may be flattened by stages to its particular

limit at maximum possible occlusion – that is the ve basis of hand-horn technique. In fact this yields a pa doxical but useful phenomenon: horns of pitches ad cent to E♮ (i.e. about 4 metres long) when fully stopp may be reckoned to rise by exactly a semitone – a fa recognized by the Classical composers of hand-ho music, and governing their choice of keys for it. Th discernible rise in pitch is greater for shorter tube leng and less in longer horns; thus modern single B♭ hor need an extra valve descending either a semitone or t to three quarters of a tone for use in hand-stopping. On rarely do composers specify less than full closure as d Dukas in the introduction to *L'apprenti sorcier* (see ex.2 where a fingering instruction demands this necessar muffled sound. A fully stopped bell gives a tone qual pungent, penetrating and rather sinister in *forte* (see ex.3 or distant and echo-like in *piano* (ex.3b). The ter 'cuivré' is sometimes taken to mean 'stopped and play *fortissimo*', but as it only means 'brassy' it should app also to open notes.

Ex.2 Dukas: *L'apprenti sorcier* (1897)

Ex.3

(a) Franck: *Le chasseur maudit* (1884)

(b) Glazunov: *Rêverie* for horn and piano, op.24 (1890)

As an alternative to hand-stopping small mutes a made; for many players these are more efficient tha the hand for stopped notes played *forte* in the lower re ister, which become increasingly difficult to produ below the 4th harmonic. Their great disadvantage is th the composer often does not allow time for their inse tion into the bell (e.g. in the Polovtsian Dances fro Borodin's *Prince Igor*, ex.4).

Ex.4 Borodin: from the Polovtsian Dances (*Prince Igor*, 1889)

The mute (Fr. *sourdine*; Ger. *Dämpfer*; It. *sordin* was known and used for the trumpet at least as early the first half of the 17th century, and a drawing of on was given by Mersenne (*Harmonie universelle*, 1636 Mutes may be made of wood, cardboard, papier-mâch plastic, various metals and even of suitably shape gourds; they can be pear-shaped, truncated cones or hav an outline similar to that of the instrument's bell, an are liable to vary enormously in construction detai Although there is no standard mute for the horn, th most usual form is a truncated cone made of thin woo and cardboard or similar synthetic composition. The sma

l is left open and the large end closed; three or four
n strips of cork fixed longitudinally to the outside
sure sufficient space for the appropriate amount of air
escape from the bell. The mute should be propor-
ned so that it fits just far enough into the bell to pro-
ce accurate, well-centred pedal notes. The influence
design and material on the tone quality of a mute is
great that it is advisable that each member of a horn
artet use the same type. Apart from the special pitch-
sing mute mentioned in connection with stopped notes,
e aim is to select mutes that are properly in tune over
e whole compass of the horn.

One of the first horn players to experiment with mutes
as A. J. Hampel in the mid-18th century, and his hand
hnique was probably the direct outcome of these
periments. The Bohemian virtuoso Carl Türrschmidt,
other early experimenter, is said to have invented a
echanical mute so constructed that chromatic passages
uld be played with it, the *con sordino* effect being
eserved throughout. In some such contrivance as this
ist lie the explanation of a passage such as ex.5, from
ethoven's Rondino for eight wind instruments. Wag-
r was the first to write extensively for muted horns,
t it was the French impressionist school, headed by
bussy, that brought them into regular use.

.5 Beethoven: Rondino for wind octet, WoO25 (1830)

It is possible to produce chords of two, three or even
ur notes on the horn by playing one note and hum-
ing another. If the intervals played and sung are suit-
ole, difference and summation tones are generated and
chord becomes audible. The horn may play either the
oper or the lower note; the timbre of the voice has
uch to do with effective performance. The artistic value
horn chords is questionable, but in the hands of the
onsummate practical joker Eugène Vivier they mysti-
ed such musical pundits as Castil-Blaze, Adolphe Adam,
uber and Halévy. Adam even published a long article
a the subject in *Le charivari* (29 May 1843): 'La chose
apossible'. L. F. Dauprat considered chord production
aworthy of the attention of serious artists, and Duver-
ay once advised a pupil not to waste his time on such
tilities that might adversely affect his intonation. (For
arther discussion of chord production see Blandford,
'T, 1926; Coar, 1947, pp.92–7; Kirby, 1925; Kling,
)11; and Martin, 1843.)

, HISTORY TO *c*1800. By the end of the 16th century
ere were two types of horn, both of which influenced
ie hoop-like horn of the following century. The first
as the so-called *trompe Dufouilloux*, a slender, one-
ote hunting horn made in a crescent shape with a small
oil in the middle. The second, which is far more

*2. Arcuate hunting horn: miniature from the Manes-
sische Liederhandschrift, German, early 14th century
(D-HEu pal.germ.848, f.202r)*

important in the history of the horn, was considerably
longer and was close-coiled in helical form; it was
sometimes known as the *trompe Maricourt*. By the early years of the 17th century it had already attained a
length of as much as 2 metres, which gave it the same
pitch as the contemporary trumpet; in skilled hands it
was capable of reaching the 16th harmonic, or even
higher. These helical horns were certainly not much used
in the actual hunting-field, but this is scarcely surprising
when it is remembered that hunting-signals were still
purely rhythmical, and that the instruments themselves
were comparatively heavy as well as difficult to sound.
In the 16th and early 17th centuries the most usual types
for hunting were the *trompe Dufouilloux* in France, a
large arcuate horn in Germany, and in England a straight
horn similar to but rather longer than that used nowadays for fox hunting. Such simple horns were, of course,
far better suited to the 'antient hunting noats' than the
more sophisticated helical horn, as the contemporary
works on venery show. In *La vénerie* by Jacques du
Fouilloux only one note is used, indicated as in ex.6*a*.
Different episodes of the chase are signalled by vari-

Ex.6
(a) Tran   (b) Stag at bay.

(c) To call hounds to their reward.

ations of rhythm, as in ex.6*b* and *c*. Turberville's *The Noble Art of Venerie* (London, 1575) gives examples of calls in one to four 'winds', or sections, alerting the hunters to the progress of the game. In *La vénerie royalle* by de Salnove (1655) very little is said about the horn, but the following passage occurs on p.147: 'et sonnez, si vous voulez, le premier ton du gresle, et les autres entrecoupez du gros ton, en cette sorte: Ton hon, Ton hon, Ton hon'. In *The Gentlemans Recreation* by Nicolas Cox (4/1697/*R*1928) occur the names and signs

Ex.7

The antient Hunting Noats with Marsh's additions.

Names of the Noats

H tone, ⌢ ton, ó tavern, ŏ ton-tavern,

ℬ ton-ton-tavern. etc

given in ex.7. These names appear to indicate respectively a long note, a note half that length, a short note and two or more short notes of which the first only is tongued, the others being 'jirked' – the self-explanatory term used in an early English tutor for the french horn (*c*1745). Various combinations of these 'noats' told the hunters what was afield. Two examples are given in ex.8.

Ex.8

When the Hounds hunt a game unknown,

ŏ *H* ó ó o ó ó ó, ó ŏ ó ó

To draw the Company out of the Field,

H ó ó ó ŏ ŏ *H*

These Noats are Taught and Sould by Michaell Marsh at the Huntsman at Holbourne Bridge.

All these calls obviously postulate a one-note horn, the simpler the better, and it is not unreasonable to suppose that the longer horns were left to specialists whose chief if not only duty was, in the words of Ned Ward, 'to accommodate sportsmen with the delightful harmony of hunting', before and after but not during the progress of the chase.

The importance of the helical type of horn in the evolution of the instrument has not been given the notice it merits, for although of coarser proportions than the later hoop-like *trompe*, it nevertheless represents the first stage in the development of the musical horn. Although the earliest known true orchestral use of the horn is in Keiser's opera *Octavia* (Hamburg, 1705), in which two *cornes de chasse* are specified, it had made sporadic appearances in the theatre during the preceding 60 years or so. The helical type of horn may have been used, for example, in Cavalli's *Le nozze di Teti e di Peleo* (Venice, 1639; Paris, 1654) and Lully's *La princesse d'Elide* (May 1664). The horn parts in both these works have been much discussed, because if the original scores have been correctly transcribed, use has been made of low notes theoretically playable only on instruments 4·8 metres and 5·4 metres long. If the instrument that Cavalli required was indeed a horn (the part is not labelled) the note he wanted was *e* at the pitch of the 5th harmonic of the shorter horn; and Lully required a *d* and a B♭', equivalent to the 5th and 2nd harmonics of the longer instrument. On the assumption that the gap between the 2nd and 3rd harmonics is unbridgeable and that the fundamental is not practicable, it has been argued that such long horns must have been available to the composers. There is no proof that they were not, but it is highly improbable; moreover, there is an alternative solution. It is not generally realized that the fundamental of a 2·4

metre or 2·7 metre horn 'speaks' more readily than the 2nd harmonic of a 4·8 metre or 5·4 metre horn, and is also far more resonant. This accounts for Lully's B♭'; the notes *d* and *e* offer a rather more difficult but not insoluble problem. By slackening the lip tension a note can be lowered to an extent dependent on the interval between it and the harmonic immediately below it – the greater the interval the more the note can be lowered. Thus the 2nd harmonic, an octave above the fundamental, can be lowered by as much as five semitones, and Beethoven actually used these so-called 'factitious' notes in his Sextet for two horns and strings (op.81*b*). Between the 2nd and 3rd harmonics the interval is only a 5th, so the latter can be lowered only by three semitones, and that with difficulty; it is, however, possible, and that just brings Cavalli's *e* and Lully's *d* within range on the shorter horns. It is admittedly a very difficult note to attack, so much so, in fact, that in the days of the hand horn it was generally played completely stopped. But the note is there as an open note, and in his *Méthode pour cor alto et cor basse* (1824) Dauprat devoted the second part of 'Leçon 14' entirely to its production without the aid of the hand in the bell. This explanation does not in itself rule out the existence of the longer horns in the first half of the 17th century, but it does show that they were not essential to the performance of these works.

Specimens of the early helical horns have not found their way into the most important collections of musical instruments; it was therefore of particular interest when in 1934 W. F. H. Blandford noticed two very early examples in the *Jagdzimmer* of the Dresden Staatliches Historisches Museum. The smaller of these, shown in fig.3*a*, is dated *c*1572; it has a maximum diameter across the coils of 16·5 cm, a bell diameter of 10 cm, a tube length of about 167 cm, and is pitched at approximately A♭ alto. The larger horn, from the early 17th century, is 21 cm across the coils, 11 cm across the bell, has a tube length of about 216 cm, and is pitched in D (the pitch of the old natural trumpet in D). The mouthpiece of both instruments are of normal horn pattern, but somewhat constricted at the apex of the cone. That of the smaller horn, being of a piece with the mouthpipe, is unquestionably original. Mersenne gave a very rough drawing of a six-coil helical horn ('le cor à plusieurs tours'), which, he remarked, was less widely used than other types of hunting horn. He wrote, however, that some huntsmen could cover a range as great as that of the trumpet: to do so they must obviously have used helical horns.

Although it cannot yet be proved that the hoop-like *trompe* actually originated in France, the available evidence seems to point in that direction. There is no indication that any such horn existed in France or elsewhere before the middle of the 17th century. The large-bore circular horn figured on the choir stalls in Worcester Cathedral, said to date from the 14th century, can have no bearing on the development of the *trompe*. Nor do we learn anything conclusive from the curious horn, or bass trumpet, played helicon-wise in one of Sebastian Brant's illustrations in the Grüninger (Strasbourg, 1502) and Sacon (Lyons, 1517) editions of Virgil (and reproduced in the 11th edition of the *Encyclopaedia Britannica*, see 'Horn'), in the absence of evidence that such an instrument ever existed outside the artist's imagination.

It is of little significance that the French contribute

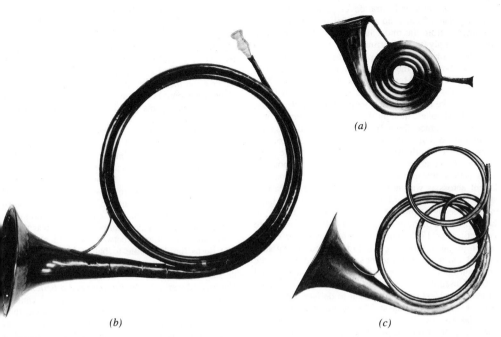

(a) Helical horn, c1572 (Staatliches Historisches Museum, Dresden); (b) triple-coil horn in F by William Bull, ndon, 1699 (Horniman Museum, London); (c) horn by George Henry Rodenbostel, London, late 18th century ty Museum, Gloucester), shown with master crook and two couplers (mouthpiece missing)

Large circular French trompe: painting, 'Hunt in the forest of Compiègne', by Jean Baptiste Oudry (1686– 5), in the Château de Fontainebleau; this is one of the cartoons for the tapestry 'The Hunts of Louis XV'

nothing to the early orchestral development of the horn, as they made virtually no orchestral use of any brass instrument before the mid-18th century. They regarded the horn simply as an instrument of the chase, but as such they carried its development to a very advanced stage, as shown by the elaborate fanfares, still in use, written for it by the Marquis de Dampierre (1676–1756) when he was Gentilhomme des Chasses et Plaisirs to Louis XV. The French authority on the *trompe de chasse*, Gaston de Marolles, thought that the circular *trompe* was first used in France about 1660. He described it as having two and a half coils, a diameter across the coils of 20 cm, a tube length of about 2·27 metres and the same pitch as the contemporary cavalry trumpet. About 20 years later a new model appeared; with only one coil 45 cm across it was now large enough to be carried round the body. According to de Marolles the large *trompe* (see fig.4) pitched an octave lower – that is, at the pitch of the orchestral horn in D – did not come into use until after 1705. Further indirect evidence of the French origin of the *trompe* is to be found in England. In 1661 the Royal Buckhounds, suppressed during the Commonwealth, were brought into service again, and in the Household Accounts of Charles II an entry dated 20 February 1662 reads: 'Warrant to deliver to Gervice Price, Esquire, His Majesty's sergeant trumpeter, two silver hornes after the same manner as he shall inform you'. To judge from the wording, the horns were of an unfamiliar type. Charles was in very close touch with France in 1661, when the Royal Buckhounds were in the process of reorganization. And, indeed, to sound a *trompe* of 2 metres properly would, in the first instance, require the skill of a trained trumpeter. In 1668 the king made a present to Price of a silver hunting horn, weighing about 934 grams, which was about 120 grams heavier than the contemporary silver ceremonial trumpet; we may therefore assume that the horn was of the same length and pitch as the trumpet and capable of reaching at least the 16th harmonic. These two entries in the Household Accounts are, of course, no more than pointers, but that they point in the direction of France is suggested by the following advertisement in *The Loyal Protestant and Domestick Intelligence* for 7 March 1682:

William Bull, one of His Majestie's Trumpeters-in-Ordinary, and trumpet maker, is remov'd from the Trumpet and Horn in Salisbury street near the Strand, to the Trumpet and Horn at the lower e of the Haymarket near the Pall-Mall-end; where any Gentleman m be furnished with Trumpets, French Horns, Speaking Trumpets a Flasks of all sorts both Silver and Brass.

Clearly the french horn was quite familiar in Engla by this time, and that the instrument should have be thus designated at so early a date greatly strengthens t supposition that it did, in fact, originate in France. T Bohemian Count Franz Anton Sporck (1662–1738), wh in France during his grand tour (1680–82), heard t *trompe*, hitherto completely unknown to him. He w so delighted by it that he had two of his retainers taug to sound the *trompe* and took some instruments hor with him. From this beginning grew a school of Boh mian horn players who became internationally famo in the second half of the following century. Sporck connection with the horn was mentioned by Gerb (*Lexikon*, 1792), but although it is not stated outrig that the hoop-like horn was a French invention, mo subsequent writers have assumed that this was the cas

Failure to distinguish between the helical and hoo like horns has led some to believe that the hoop-li horn did not originate in France at all, but in Germa or Italy, and that it was introduced to the French l Cardinal Mazarin. In the *Encyclopaedia Britannica* it even suggested that the term 'french horn' came in use only after the publication of Gerber's work, thou in fact it was current in England more than a centu before. It has never been suggested that the helical ho originated in France, but it was certainly known a used there long before Mazarin introduced his *chanteu italiens*. Nor is there reason to think that the horn pa of Cavalli and Lully must have been played on the hoo like *trompe* when, as has been said, they could ha been satisfactorily played on the helical horns. On t other hand, there is no reason for surprise if the *tromp* a more elegant and slender form of the helical hor designed purely for use in the hunting-field, did aft all make its first appearance in France, whose court the 17th century far outshone those of contempora monarchs in refinement and pageantry. Had the *trom* been known in Germany or Italy it is very unlikely th it would have been a novelty to Sporck when he fir heard it in Paris. So, until more firm evidence to t contrary is forthcoming, France must be accepted as t birthplace of the french horn.

5. Natural horns (held 'pavillons en l'air') in an 18th-century Italian orchestra pit: detail of a painting (1740) by Pietro Domenico Olivero showing the interior of the Teatro Regio, Turin, during a performance of Feo's opera 'Arsace' (Museo Civico d'Arte Antica, Turin)

*Horn (hand-stopped),
cello, violin and oboe
played by Rodolphe,
Dupont, Vachon and
Vernier: watercolour by
Louis Carrogis de
Carmontelle (1717–
1806), in the Musée
Condé, Chantilly*

The instruments that Sporck took home with him were copied by the Nuremberg and other German makers. Probably the oldest dated *trompe* in existence is an anonymous one described in Kinsky's catalogue of the Heyer collection as 'no.1661 – Grosses Jagdhorn in B mit der eingestanzten 1689'. This is a single-coil instrument in B♭ alto, as is another by the Ehe family of Nuremberg dated 1698, in the Pfälzisches Gewerbe-Museum, Kaiserslautern. At the Horniman Museum, London (no.307 in the Carse collection), is a three-and-a-half-coil horn by William Bull dated 1699 (fig.3*b* above). It is in F, though nearly a semitone flat by modern standards, and is of a much more advanced design than the German examples. The James Talbot MS (*GB-Och* Mus.1187), extracts from which were published with comments by A. C. Baines (*GSJ*, i, 1948, p.9), shows that french horns of 2·4 metres to 4·8 metres long were being made in England at least as early as 1700. We do not, however, hear of the instrument's being used in the English orchestra until Handel included it in his score of the *Water Music* (*c*1717). The french horn in the English hunting-field was mainly confined to buck hunting, although at least one pack of foxhounds, the Old Charlton, employed it on occasion. During the 18th century fashionable parties visiting the London pleasure gardens, such as Ranelagh or Vauxhall, sometimes hired horns to play to them while they supped. In France it remained simply the hunting horn, in spite of an occasional performance of a 'symphonie avec cors de chasse', until about 1748, when the wealthy *fermier général*, La Riche de La Pouplinière, imported the horn in its orchestral form from Germany and introduced it into his own private orchestra, where it became known as 'le nouveau cor de chasse allemand'. The Concert Spirituel in Paris had two regular horn players from 1751, but it

was not until 1759 that two horns were added to the permanent personnel of the Opéra orchestra.

The earliest orchestral horns were complete units, which meant that a different instrument had to be used for each change of key. About 1700, however, developments in design by the Leichnamschneider brothers of Vienna led to the horn's being made shorter and to the replacement of its fixed mouthpiece by a socket into which could be fitted a series of 'crooks' – rings of tubing of assorted lengths. A set of crooks consisted normally of six: two 'master' crooks into which the mouthpiece fitted and four couplers for insertion between the 'master' and the instrument. By using one of the master crooks either alone or in conjunction with one or more of the couplers, the horn could be put into any required key, the final tuning being effected by the insertion below the mouthpiece of a short shank called a 'tuning bit'. Until recently the earliest known reference to horn crooks was in an article by J. Rühlmann (*NZM*, 1870), which mentioned a pair of Viennese concert horns with six crooks apiece bought in Dresden in 1718 for 50 thalers each. Fitzpatrick discovered a bill in Michael Leichnamschneider's handwriting, dating from 1703 and made out to the Abbot of Kremsmünster, that includes 'four new double crooks' (*Krumbögen*; see Fitzpatrick, 1971, p.33). Crooks appear to have been unknown in England before the 1740s, and Frederick Messing was probably the first to use them in a public performance. (Fig.3*c* above shows an English horn with crooks dating from the late 18th century.)

Notwithstanding the obvious limitations of such instruments, Bach, Handel and other composers of their time did not hesitate to write high, florid horn parts similar to those for contemporary trumpet players. Such parts now try even the best players to the limit of their capacity, but to players of Bach's day – most if not all of them trained trumpeters who only took over the horn when required – the technique was that of the clarino, whose range was confined to the two upper octaves and was never carried below the 4th harmonic.

During this time Bohemian players were cultivating the lower and middle registers, which led to the realization that some of the gaps in the harmonic series could be satisfactorily bridged by partial occlusion of the bell with the hand (see fig.6). This technique also induced a marked refinement of tone quality, resulting in the rather veiled, mysterious timbre that makes the horn indispensable in the orchestra. In the mid-18th century the Dresden horn player A. J. Hampel became the first to codify a simple form of hand technique when he and his colleague Carl Haudek trained a large number of pupils, among them the celebrated Giovanni Punto. Punto and other contemporary concert soloists greatly extended this technique, but it remained strictly within the province of the virtuoso. With the exception of the fourth-horn solo in Beethoven's Ninth Symphony there are very few stopped notes in the orchestral works of the later Classical composers, though both Mozart and Beethoven made liberal use of them in their chamber music. Haydn, on the other hand, ignored stopped notes almost entirely, writing the high parts as if for clarino (trumpet) and frequently carrying a part down to the 2nd harmonic.

Horns with crooks that fitted one into another (the only kind known in the early 18th century) were far from ideal for hand-work in the bell. Hampel therefore devised a new layout that left the mouthpipe fixed while the crooks fitted into the body of the horn. This involved cutting out a short section of the inner coil from the standard two-and-a-half-coil orchestral horn; the cut ends were then bent at right angles towards the centre of the hoop and crooks fitted on to them. The new model,

7. The horn player Frédéric Nicolas Duvernoy with a cor solo: portrait by an unknown 19th-century artist (Bibliothèque de l'Opéra, Paris)

known as the *Inventionshorn*, is said to have been first made by Johann Werner, a Dresden brass-instrument maker, probably about 1750. Bierdimpfl (in a Munich catalogue) mentioned that a pair of the newly invented Waldhorns was supplied to the Munich electoral orchestra by the electoral Waldhorn-maker Philipp Schöller in Munich in 1753. Both Domnich and L. A. de Pontécoulant attributed the invention of the tuning-slide to Haltenhof, as did Fétis (see 'Haltenhoff' in *FétisB*) who gave a wrong date (1781) in which he was followed by Sachs (*Reallexikon*, 1913). A very fine *Inventionshorn* by Haltenhof, dated 1776, in the Paris Conservatoire museum (no.1183 in the Catalogue, suppl.i) proves that the tuning-slide existed earlier than 1781. This horn has eight crooks, from Bb alto to Bb basso, each with long branches graduated for tuning purposes (see fig.8a). About the same time Joseph Raoux and his son Lucien-Joseph, of Paris, brought out an improved *Inventionshorn* based (according to W. Schneider) on suggestions made by the Bohemian virtuoso Carl Türrschmidt, then living in Paris. The new model, as its name *cor solo* implies, was intended for the concert soloist and had only five crooks, G, F, E, Eb and D, which were sufficient for concerto playing and chamber music. The *cor solo* differed from the German *Inventionshorn* in that the branches to which the crooks fitted were made to cross one another, which made the instrument more rigid (see figs.7 and 8b).

The use of terminal crooks diminished after the appearance of the *Inventionshorn*, but about 1800 they were reintroduced, this time in the form of a separate crook for each key. The standard French set of terminal crooks consisted of those for Bb alto, A, G, F, E, Eb, D and C. An Ab crook was added in about 1828, and a Bb basso crook was occasionally provided; ordinarily for Bb and Bb basso, as well as for Db, a combination of crook and coupler sufficed, while Ab and Gb could be obtained by using an A or G crook and pulling out the tuning-slide. For some unknown reason, in the days when the tuning-slide was still a novelty terminally crooked horns provided with slide (see fig.8c) were known in France as 'cors à l'anglaise'. A possible explanation could be that the English, who did not cultivate hand-stopping to any great extent until well after 1800, saw no reason to adopt the *Inventionshorn*; but realizing the advantage of being able to tune the instrument with a slide, they adapted the latter to the old Viennese model with which they were familiar before the improved continental horn with slide and separate crook for each key came into use.

Although the horn did not really become a chromatic instrument until after the application of valves to brass instruments (*c*1815), several abortive attempts were made during the 18th century to solve the problem of filling the gaps in the natural harmonic series. Apart from the mysterious *corno da tirarsi* called for now and again in J. S. Bach's cantatas, an instrument whose exact nature is still unknown, the earliest known attempt to render the horn chromatic by mechanical means was Kölbel's *Amor Schall*. This is believed to have been a horn with two keys placed near the bell, the bell itself being covered with a perforated lid, evidently in order to minimize the difference in tone quality between the bell notes and those obtained by opening one or other of the keys. Assuming that the keys were normally closed, and were so placed that when one was opened the air column was shortened by either a semitone or a tone, a complete

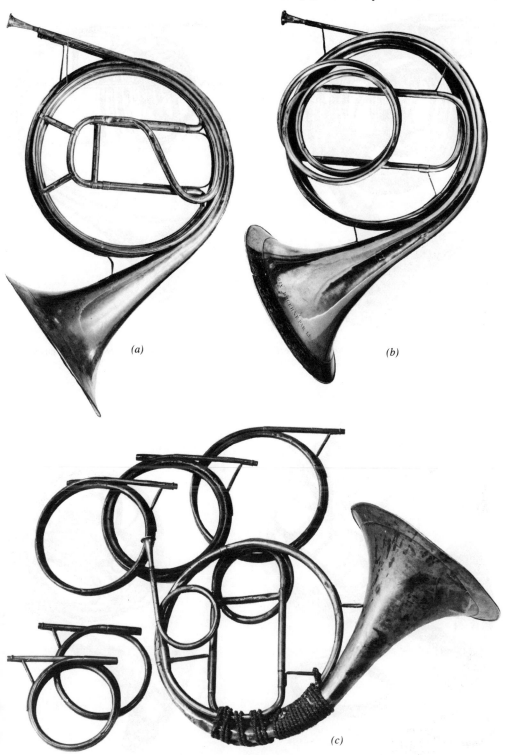

8. (a) Inventionshorn by J. G. Haltenhof, Hanau-am-Main, 1776, shown with crook for G; (b) cor solo by Lucien-Joseph Raoux, Paris, late 18th century, shown with crook for E♭ (both Conservatoire de Musique, Paris); (c) horn with tuning-slide and six terminal crooks by Carl Gottlieb Schuster, Markneukirchen, c1840 (Germanisches Nationalmuseum, Nuremberg)

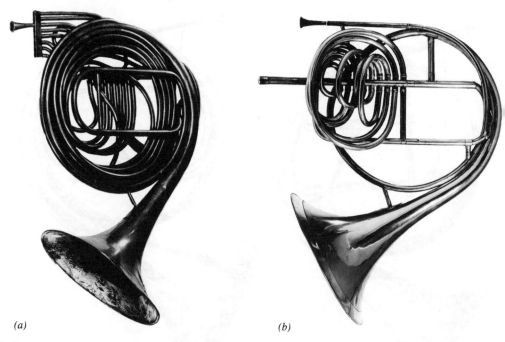

(a)   (b)

9. Omnitonic horns: (a) by J.-B. Dupont, Paris, c1815; (b) by Charles Sax, Brussels, c1824 (both Conservatoire de Musique, Paris)

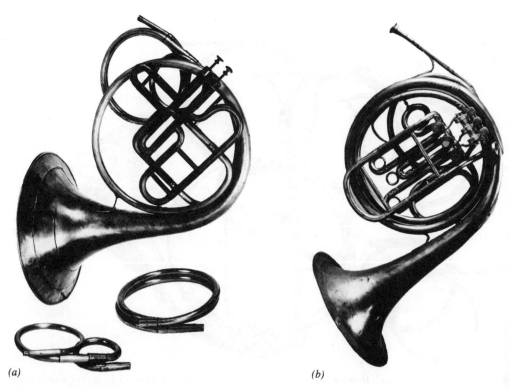

(a)   (b)

10. (a) Horn with two detachable valves by Thomas Key, London, c1840, shown crooked in F (G master crook and F coupler), with D coupler (below right) and B♭ master crook and A coupler (below left); (b) horn with three rotary valves and F crook by W. Glier, Warsaw, 1835 (both Bate Collection, University of Oxford)

hromatic scale would be possible from the 5th harmonic upwards. The instrument is said to have had some success in Russia, where it was produced in the mid-18th century. In 1788 Charles Clagget of London took out a patent for improvements to musical instruments, one of which consisted in 'uniting together two French horns or trumpets in such a manner that the same mouthpiece may be applied to either of them instantaneously during the time of performance as the music may require'. The two mouthpipes were brought together in a curious kind of box into whose cover the mouthpiece was fixed; a small, projecting pin, operated by the finger, brought the point of the mouthpiece to the opening of either horn 'by means of a piece of elastic, gum or leather', while another piece of the same material stopped up the horn not in use. Public performances on these fearsome instruments were actually given in London and Bath. It is unfortunate that no surviving specimen of Clagget's invention has come to light, for it may be said in a way to embody the underlying principle of the valve. Another stillborn curiosity was an attempt by Christian Dickhuth, a member of the Mannheim electoral orchestra in 1812, to apply to the horn the principle of the trombone slide.

4. HISTORY FROM *c*1800. A more successful method of enabling the horn to play a chromatic scale was embodied in the 'omnitonic' horn, in which sufficient tubing was included to put the instrument into any desired key without having recourse to loose crooks. Various mechanical devices (sliding shutters, plungers, rotary taps and valvelets) were used to bring the required tube-length into operation. The earliest known example, by J.-B. Dupont, is in the Paris Conservatoire museum (Catalogue, suppl.i. no.1184). This curious instrument (fig.9a) is probably an experimental model, for it has eight separate mouthpieces and complete tube-lengths, and is the only omnitonic horn not built on a compensating principle. It was probably made in about 1815, for in 1818 Dupont patented a much improved model which J. C. Labbaye marketed under his own name in 1819. Probably the most successful was that patented in 1824 by Charles Sax of Brussels (see fig.9b) – the French patent was taken out in 1827 in the name of Stuckens. Various other models appeared from time to time in France and elsewhere, including an ingenious English one by Callcott (shown at the Great Exhibition, 1851), though by that time the valve was too well established for it to have any chance of success. These instruments all owed any favour they may have enjoyed to the relative inefficiency of the valve in its early days. The omnitonic horn never threatened the ordinary hand horn, in spite of the drawbacks of loose crooks.

The earliest valve horns were developed by Heinrich Stölzel and Friedrich Blühmel, both of Silesia. It is thought likely that Stölzel's first valves were of tubular form, but in the joint patent with Blühmel taken out in 1818 the valves were rectangular; valves of this pattern were made and marketed by the Karlsruhe maker Schuster. The various types of valves are considered elsewhere (*see* VALVE (i)); almost every kind of valve has been applied to the horn at some time or other. The early valves had many defects, not the least of which was that the additional tubing they controlled was not provided with slides, so that it was impossible to make any tuning adjustment, as well as extremely difficult to get rid of the moisture that inevitably collects in the tub-

ing during performance (the 1824 Sax patent (fig.9b) includes the prototype of the modern water key designed to cope with this problem).

The valve horn first reached France in the mid-1820s through Spontini, then director of the Court Opera in Berlin, who sent valve horns and trumpets to Paris. These instruments, of the square valve type, had various structural disadvantages. They were built in F and no alternative crook could be used; the valve tubing had no slides and general tuning had to be done by shifting the whole valve mechanism forward, which altered the balance of the instrument as well as the position of the left hand. In 1827, however, P.-J. Meifred and the maker Labbaye together produced a more satisfactory model eliminating these defects, and at the Paris Industrial Exhibition of 1827 Labbaye was awarded a silver medal. Jules Léon Antoine (Halary) also produced an improved model for which he gained a bronze medal at the same exhibition. On 9 March 1828 Meifred played a valve-horn solo at the first concert ever given by the Société des Concerts du Conservatoire.

In England the new instrument made little headway before the middle of the century, although 'I. P.' in *The Harmonicon* (1830) wrote that the hand-horn scale 'has been improved by means of two valves or tubes, which Pace of Westminster and Percival of St James's Street have added to the horn'. Hogarth, however, in his paper on the horn (*Musical World*, iv, 1837, p.81) made no mention of valves, though deploring the inequalities of tone characteristic of the hand horn. A correspondent replying to Hogarth stated that he had heard 'a fantasia by Mr Perry at a concert of the Mary-le-bone Literary and Scientific Institution, upon a horn with valves or plugs . . . with a perfect equality of tone in every note', but the writer concluded that the invention could not be widely known since Hogarth had not noticed it in his article. The valve horn made its orchestral début in Halévy's *La juive* (Paris, 1835). The score calls for two natural and two valve horns; Wagner used the same combination in his early works. It was then considered desirable to retain hand-horn technique as far as was consistent with equality of tone; both Meifred and J. R. Lewy claimed that only by this method could the true character of the french horn be retained. Wagner, who probably consulted Lewy at Dresden, evidently shared this view to a considerable extent. One of the first composers, if not the first, to break entirely away from the hand-horn tradition was Schumann, who in 1849 wrote his Adagio and Allegro for horn in F and piano; it is pure valve-horn music throughout, as is his *Konzertstück* for four horns and orchestra of the same year.

In France, notwithstanding its auspicious beginnings, the valve horn had a particularly hard struggle, especially in official circles. A class for it was inaugurated at the Paris Conservatoire under Meifred in 1833, but was discontinued in 1864, when the professor retired. Thereafter, the valve horn was banned from the Conservatoire until 1896, when François Brémond, then professor of the horn, reintroduced it; in 1903 it finally became the officially recognized instrument. The system favoured by both Meifred and Brémond was the ascending third-valve horn, devised by Antoine (Halary) and first made in the late 1840s.

Another system used in both England and France during the latter part of the 19th century was a set of detachable valves that could be replaced when desired by a plain tuning-slide, thus converting the instrument

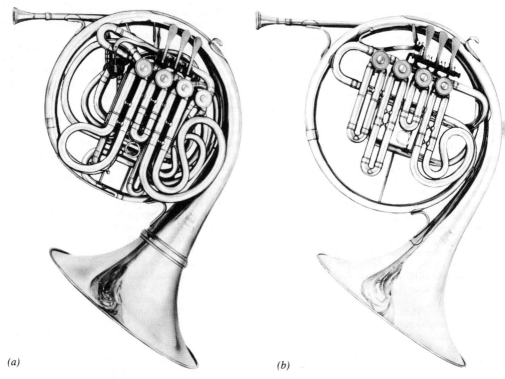

11.   (a) Triple horn in F/Bb/F alto (with 5 rotary valves; first manufactured 1965); (b) single horn in Bb(A) (wit
4 rotary valves; modern form of the instrument first produced in the late 19th century); both by Paxman, Londo

into a simple hand horn (see fig.10*a*). Instruments so constructed were very fragile, however, and when the hand horn was finally abandoned the valves were generally fixed permanently to the horn by a couple of extra stays. For a long time the addition of a third valve was held to be not only unnecessary but even detrimental, on account of the extra weight involved, and as late as the early years of the 20th century two-valve horns figured regularly in the price lists of leading makers.

In Germany at the end of the 19th century the Erfurt maker Fritz Kruspe, in conjunction with a nephew of the Gewandhaus horn player Friedrich Gumbert, produced the first F/Bb double horn, soon followed by similar models from the workshops of Alexander Brothers (Mainz), Schmidt (Berlin), Knopf (Markneukirchen) and others. Although the F/Bb concept was altogether new, the principle of the double horn already existed in Gautrot's 'système équitonique' patented in 1865. Originally conceived as a compensating system, of which it was one of the earliest, Gautrot's scheme consisted of three valves, each with a double set of additional tubing – a primary set tuned normally and a shorter auxiliary set whose length was added to that of the primary set by depressing a fourth valve. Although intended chiefly to correct the intonation of the lowest notes of the euphonium and bombardon, the system was also applied to the horn, where it made possible the use of an Eb or an F crook without having to reset the valve-slides after changing from one crook to the other. The object attained was not in this case worth the extra weight and cost, but the instrument was in essence a double horn. In 1912 D. J. Blaikley patented a piston-valve double horn in

F/Bb almost identical with the Gautrot 1865 layout, bu it met with little favour among players. It nevertheles served in a measure as inspiration for the double horn in F/Bb built on the ascending third-valve principle originally designed by Louis Vuillermoz, the son of former horn professor at the Conservatoire and himsel an able horn player. The instrument was first made an marketed by the Parisian instrument maker Jérôm Thibouville-Lamy and, like Blaikley's 1912 design had piston valves. It has since been improved by othe makers and is used, generally with the addition o rotary valves, by many leading French players.

By the mid-20th century piston valves in horns ha been virtually superseded by rotary valves, which were more suitable for the double instruments then in wide demand. After World War II serious attempts – not a first completely successful – were made in Germany t build double horns combining a Bb horn with a 'des cant' in F alto. By 1960 a 'dual-bore' system had bee developed by a London player, Richard Merewether and adopted by the firm of Paxman. This design intro duced tapered lengths into the circuits carrying the valve and enabled such combinations as Bb(A)/F alto, F/I alto and even Bb(A)/Bb soprano to be built, with bot horns in each combination of a quality that bears com parison with good single instruments ('Bb(A)' denote that the horn is equipped with an additional valve tha allows the instrument to be put into A). Triple horns i F/Bb/F alto and F/Bb/Bb soprano have also been buil (see fig.11*a*), wherein the same system adds a descan horn to the regular F/Bb double horn without harmfu acoustic compromise. The ascending third valve, stil opular in France, may be employed in the longer parts f these horns, with the F alto carrying the usual three-emitone descent remaining the more useful device. All ese models, with a wider or narrower bell-taper ccording to the player's choice, are increasingly used many countries, along with double horns in F/B♭ ig.1a above) and single horns in B♭(A) (see fig.11b). ince the mid-20th century there has been a tendency due partly to the wide availability of recordings and e frequent international exchange of orchestras – for cal or national schools of style to merge into a more eneral, international approach.

. SOLO REPERTORY. The worthwhile repertory for the orn as a solo instrument is not extensive, but it includes ome first-rate works. Vivaldi wrote two concertos for wo horns and strings, and also included the horn in the olo groups of other concertos. The best-known Baroque oncerto with horns, however, is Bach's First Branden-urg Concerto. Haydn's two solo concertos in D (a third, lso in D, is of doubtful authenticity) have been eclipsed y Mozart's three concertos in E♭; Mozart's other con-erto (no.1 in D) brings together two isolated move-nents composed at different times. Beethoven composed is Horn Sonata in F op.17 for the Bohemian player ʒiovanni Punto. Weber was perhaps the first to explore he Romantic potential of the instrument (e.g. in the vertures to *Oberon* and *Der Freischütz*), and he also vrote for it the genial Concertino in E minor op.45.

These works were all written for natural (valveless) orn, and Brahms also had this instrument in mind as ate as 1865, when he wrote his Trio op.40 for violin, orn and piano. The first significant solo work for the ewer valve instrument was probably Schumann's Ada-ʒio and Allegro for horn and piano op.70 (1849); the omposer's equally interesting *Konzertstück* for four horns nd orchestra dates from the same year. The Romantic oncerto, which demanded more strenuous, non-stop laying of the soloist, was a less likely vehicle for the orn; thus solo horn concertos are rare in the 19th cen-ury, the only one to enter the standard repertory after Veber's being the First Concerto (1882–3) of Richard Strauss, whose Second Horn Concerto is a much later vork (1942). The instrument has been quite well served y 20th-century composers. Hindemith wrote a sonata or horn and piano, and both he and Michael Tippett ave written sonatas for four horns. The playing of Den-is Brain inspired several fine works, including a con-erto by Hindemith and two vocal works by Britten with orn obbligato, *Canticle III* ('Still falls the rain') and he Serenade op.31. Among younger composers Thea Musgrave has made striking solo use of the horn in her *Vight Music* (1969) and Horn Concerto (1971).

Fuller surveys of the horn repertory appear in Gre-ʒory (1961) and Schuller (1962).

BIBLIOGRAPHY

H. Domnich: *Méthode de premier et de second cor* (Paris, 1807)
L. F. Dauprat: *Méthode pour cor alto et cor basse* (Paris, 1824)
F. J. Fétis: 'Cors à pistons', *Revue musicale* (1828), no.2
F. J. Gossec: 'Notes concernant l'introduction des cors dans les orchestres', *Revue musicale* (1829), no.5
P. J. Meifred: *De l'étendue, de l'emploi et des ressources du cor* (Paris, 1829)
W. Schneider: *Historisches-technische Beschreibung der musikal-ischen Instrumente* (Leipzig, 1834)
P. J. Meifred: *Méthode de cor chromatique ou à pistons* (Paris, 1840, rev. 2/1849)
A. Martin: 'Le cor de M. Vivier mis à la portée de tout le monde' [letter], *France musicale* (18 June 1843)
J. F. Gallay: *Méthode complète pour le cor* (Paris, c1845)
P. J. Meifred: 'Notice sur la fabrication des instruments de musique en cuivre', *Annuaire de la Société des anciens élèves des écoles nationales des arts-et-métiers, année 1851* (Paris, 1851)
H. Eichborn: *Die Dämpfung beim Horn* (Leipzig, 1897)
G. de Marolles: *Essai de monographie de la trompe de chasse* (?Paris, n.d.)
——: *Trois questions relatives à l'historique de la trompe de chasse* (?Paris, n.d.)
——: *Monographie abrégée de la trompe de chasse* (n.p., n.d.)
V. C. Mahillon: *Le cor: son histoire, sa théorie, sa construction* (Brussels, 1907)
H. Kling: 'Giovanni Punto, célèbre corniste', *BSIM*, iv (1908), 1066
D. J. Blaikley: 'The French Horn', *PMA*, xxxv (1908–9), 123
H. Kling: 'Le cor de chasse', *RIM*, xviii (1911), 95–136
W. F. H. Blandford: 'The French Horn in England'; 'Wagner and the Horn Parts of "Lohengrin"', *MT*, lxiii (1922), 544, 622, 693
——: 'The Fourth Horn in the Choral Symphony', *MT*, lxv (1925), 29, 124, 221
P. R. Kirby: 'Horn Chords: an Acoustical Problem', *MT*, lxvi (1925), 811 [see also reply by Blandford, *MT*, lxvii (1926), 128]
F. Piersig: *Die Einführung des Hornes in die Kunstmusik* (Halle, 1927)
G. de Saint-Foix: 'Les concertos pour cor de Mozart', *RdM*, x (1929), 16
W. F. H. Blandford: 'Bach's Horn Parts', *MT*, lxxvii (1936), 748
——: 'Handel's Horn and Trombone Parts', *MT*, lxxx (1939), 697, 746, 794
R. Morley-Pegge: 'The Evolution of the Modern French Horn from 1750 to the Present Day', *PMA*, lxix (1942–3), 35
A. H. King: 'Haydn's Trio for Horn, Violin and 'Cello', *MT*, lxxxvi (1945), 367
B. Coar: *The French Horn* (Ann Arbor, 1947)
J. Marx: Introduction to *Mozart: Twelve Duos for Two French Horns* (New York, 1947)
M. K. Ward: 'Mozart and the Horn', *ML*, xxxi (1950), 318
B. Coar: *A Critical Study of the Nineteenth-century Horn Virtuosi in France* (De Kalb, Ill., 1952)
R. Gregory: 'The Horn in Beethoven's Symphonies', *ML*, xxxiii (1952), 303
P. Farkas: *The Art of French Horn Playing* (Chicago, 1956)
R. Morley-Pegge: *The French Horn* (London, 1960, 2/1973)
H. Fitzpatrick: 'Notes on the Vienna Horn', *GSJ*, xiv (1961), 49
R. Gregory: *The Horn* (London, 1961, 2/1969)
M. Rasmussen: 'The Manuscript Kat. Wenster Litt. I/1–17b (Uni-versitetsbiblioteket, Lund): a Contribution to the History of the Baroque Horn Concerto', *Brass Quarterly*, v (1961–2), 135
G. Schuller: *Horn Technique* (Oxford, 1962)
H. Fitzpatrick: 'Some Historical Notes on the Horn in Germany and Austria', *GSJ*, xvi (1963), 33
——: 'The Valveless Horn in Performances of Eighteenth-century Music', *PRMA*, xci (1964–5), 45
B. Brüchle: *Horn Bibliographie* (Wilhelmshaven, 1970)
P. Farkas: *A Photographic Study of 40 Virtuoso Horn Players' Embouchures* (Bloomington, Ind., 1970)
H. Fitzpatrick: *The Horn and Horn-playing and the Austro-Bohemian Tradition 1680–1830* (Oxford, 1971)
R. Merewether: 'The Question of Hand Stopping', *Horn Call*, v/2 (1975), 45
B. Brüchle and K. Janetzky: *Kulturgeschichte des Horns: ein Bild-sachbuch/A Pictorial History of the Horn* (Tutzing, 1976)
K. Janetzky and B. Brüchle: *Das Horn: eine kleine Chronik seines Werdens und Wirkens* (Berne and Stuttgart, 1977)
R. Merewether: *The Horn, the Horn* (London, 1978)
E. Schmid: *'Überlegungen zur Qualität eines Waldhorns', Das Orchester*, xxix (1981), 867
F. Cousins: *On Playing the Horn* (London, 1983)
B. Tuckwell: *The Horn* (London, 1983)
                                REGINALD MORLEY-PEGGE/
                        FRANK HAWKINS, RICHARD MEREWETHER

Horn band. In 1751 (by some accounts 1754) J. A. Maresch, a horn player of Bohemian birth attached to the court of Empress Elizabeth of Russia, conceived the idea of forming a band composed entirely of hunting horns. The instruments, later described as Russian horns, had a wide conical bore and ranged in length from 30 cm to 2 metres. The 37 different sizes gave a compass of four octaves, each player being required to sound only one note; the number was later increased to 60, giving five octaves. The difficulty of playing with precision

A Russian horn band: detail from an early 19th-century engraving

must have been enormous; nevertheless, the first concert in Moscow in 1755 was a huge success. Horn bands were popular among the Russian nobility, who often sold them to one another, players as well as horns. In 1817 one such band visited Germany and performed in a *Te Deum* at Mannheim. Another visited France and England in 1833, in the latter case with 22 performers led by a clarinettist. Smaller bands of about 13 horns came into use in Bohemia and Saxony; each player could sound the fundamental note, its octave and (by placing one hand over the bell) the octave's leading note; A. F. Anacker was among those who composed for such a band.

Horn bands are common throughout much of Africa, from Uganda and West Africa southwards. The horns may be made of ivory, antelope horn, wood or gourd; each performer can sound one or two notes. *See also* AMAKONDERE.

BIBLIOGRAPHY

J. C. Hinrichs: *Entstehung, Fortgang und jetzige Beschaffenheit der russischen Jagdmusik* (St Petersburg, 1796)

J. G. Dalyell: *Musical Memoirs of Scotland with Historical Annotations* (Edinburgh, 1849), 170

H. C. COLLES/ANTHONY C. BAINES

Horngacher, Maximilian (*b* Scheffau, Kufstein, Austria, 10 June 1926). Austrian harp maker. Initially trained as a cabinet maker, in 1952 Horngacher joined the harp making firm of JOSEPH OBERMAYER.

Hörnli (Ger.). An ORGAN STOP (*Horn*).

Hornpipe. A single-reed AEROPHONE incorporating animal horn, either around the reed, or forming a bell, or both; some are played with a bag. The word appears in Chaucer's *Romaunt of the Rose* as 'hornpipes of Cornewaile' (*see* ESTIVE), and in two 15th-century vocabularies and an inventory of an Oxford scholar (see Langwill, 1950). As a rustic instrument it is cited both by Spenser in *Shepheards Calender* and by Ben Jonson in *The Sad Shepherd*. A 'Lancashire hornpipe' is mentioned with other wind instruments in the report of a lady's concert in *The Tatler* of 11 April 1710. Hawkins

wrote that 'we have no such instrument as the hornpip but referred to its common use in Wales, where it w called PIBGORN (or pibcorn). He cited Daines Barrin ton's paper of 1779 (in *Archaeologia*) where this a other wind instruments of Welsh shepherds are describe Subsequent references to 'hornpipe' as an instrument a antiquarian, as in Stainer's and Barrett's *Dictionary Musical Terms* (London, 1876), until in 1890 Hen Balfour revived the word as a generic term for nume ous folk instruments resembling the Welsh pibgorn st to be found in Europe and North Africa.

The general characteristics of these are a simple pip of elder, cane or bone, sounded by a beating reed cane or elder; in the majority of species two such pip are joined parallel together (double pipe). Over the di

1. Double and single hornpipes in the Beauchamp win dow designed by John Prudde (1447) at St Mary' Church, Warwick

tal end of the pipes is fixed a bell of cowhorn or in certain instances two bells. Instruments of this description are depicted in medieval art from the 10th century, and in English art and sculpture of the 14th and 15th centuries, and to such as these the contemporary name 'hornpipe' is reasonably presumed to refer. Examples are in the Beauchamp Psalter (in which it is held by a shepherd) and in the glass of St Mary's Church, Warwick (see fig.1). In these as in the pibgorn (of which 18th-century specimens survive) the reed(s) are covered by a second cowhorn forming a cup which is held to the player's mouth – an arrangement which is retained in the Basque hornpipe, the *alboka*. In some Russian and Albanian species the reeds are taken directly in the mouth, as they were in older Scottish forms of the instrument ('stock-and-horn') of which late 18th-century accounts are by Alexander Pennecuik and Robert Burns (see Langwill): these were single pipes of sheep's thighbone or bower-tree with cowhorn bell and oaten reed, made by shepherds. Later Scottish examples have a turned wooden reed-cap like that of a bagpipe practice-chanter. The majority of hornpipes are, however, double pipes played with an inflated bag of goatskin, cow's stomach, etc. Such 'bag-hornpipes' occur iconographically in the West from the 14th century and today exist as folk instruments from the Caucasus and the Volga regions in Russia to the Greek islands and North Africa (*see*

BAGPIPE, §8). A summary of the astonishing variety of musical techniques accruing from different arrangements of finger-holes on these and on bagless hornpipes also has been attempted by Baines (1960). The melodic compass, however, reaches a 9th at very most. Fig.2 shows a Moroccan bagless hornpipe.

The earliest reed instrument carrying a horn bell is that which became known in Rome as the Phrygian AULOS, described briefly by Pollux and others. The two pipes, one longer than the other, were held one in each hand and the longer ended with a cowhorn bell, as first depicted on a Minoan sarcophagus of *c*1400 BC in the Iráklion Museum (Crete). A likeness to the mouth-blown double hornpipe as now known occurs in a figurine of the 8th century BC from Asia Minor (see Rimmer, 1969). Several pairs of bird-bone pipes found in Avar graves of the 5th and 6th centuries AD are considered to be parts of hornpipes, and likewise some wooden pipes of the 9th century or earlier in the Fries Museum, Leeuwarden (see Crane, 1972).

The following hornpipes are entered in this dictionary: alboka; bebeulen; bryolka; cornicyll; gaita; ganu rags; mizmäh; pempä; pibgorn; stock-and-horn; swegel-horn; zhaleyka.

BIBLIOGRAPHY
HawkinsH
H. Balfour: 'The Old British "Pibcorn" or "Hornpipe" and its Affinities', *Journal of the Anthropological Institute*, xx (1890), 142
L. G. Langwill: 'The Stock-and-Horn', *Proceedings of the Society of Antiquaries of Scotland*, lxxxiv (1950), 175
A. Baines: *Bagpipes* (Oxford, 1960)
J. Rimmer: *Ancient Musical Instruments of Western Asia in the British Museum* (London, 1969), pl.viii
G. S. Emmerson: 'The Hornpipe', *Folk Music Journal*, ii (1970), 12
F. Crane: *Extant Medieval Musical Instruments: a Provisional Catalogue by Types* (Iowa City, 1972), 46
ANTHONY C. BAINES

Hornwerk. A name given to certain 16th- and 17th-century tower organs of central Germany and Austria. At first such outdoor organs could play only a few chords, and were used for signalling in the same manner as bells. Later they were enlarged and fitted with self-playing mechanism of the pinned barrel type (*see* BARREL ORGAN), enabling them to play melodies in the manner of a carillon. Two examples still exist in operable condition in Austria. One, dating from 1502, is known as the 'Salzburg Stier', and is in the tower of the bishop's castle in Salzburg. It plays three times daily; most of the tunes presently pinned on its barrels are by 18th-century composers, including Haydn and Mozart. Its popular name (Ger. *Stier*: 'bull') is apparently derived from the fact that at the end of each tune all the pipes sound at once. The other extant Hornwerk is in Heilbrunn.

BIBLIOGRAPHY
R. Quoika: *Altösterreichische Hornwerke; ein Beitrag zur Frühgeschichte der Orgelbaukunst* (Berlin, 1959)
BARBARA OWEN

Hosho. Rattle of the Shona people of Zimbabwe. Traditionally it was made of gourd, but modern instruments are often made from tin cans. They are usually played in pairs and accompany most Shona ensembles.

Hosszú furulya. DUCT FLUTE played by shepherds of south-western Hungary. It is 90 cm long, 16 to 18 mm in diameter and has five finger-holes. These are near the bottom of the flute (see illustration, p.250), so it can only be played with the head held high. Overtones

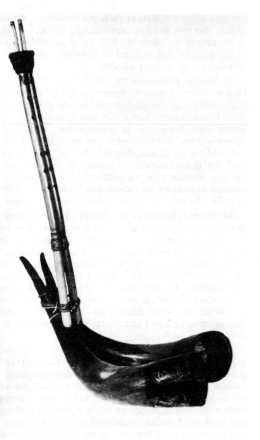

2. Bagless hornpipe from Morocco (Pitt Rivers Museum, Oxford)

Hosszú furulya (duct flute) player, south-western Hungary, 1962

are used more than the basic scale, which is f–g–a (or $a\flat$)–$b\flat$–b–c'.

Hotteterre [Haulteterre, Hauterre, Hauteterre, Hoteterre, Hoterre, Obterre, etc]. French family of woodwind instrument makers, instrumentalists at the French court, and composers (see family tree, p.252). During the 17th century various members of the family emigrated from the district of La Couture-Boussey in Normandy to Paris where they gained fame as instrument makers and players. They are sometimes credited with initiating important changes that took place in the construction of woodwind instruments during the second half of the 17th century – the development of the oboe from the shawm, the bassoon from the curtal, the conical one-keyed transverse flute from the cylindrical flute, and the three-jointed recorder from that of one piece (*see* FLUTE, §4). Though their leadership in this area cannot be proved, the importance of their work was acknowledged by their contemporaries. The principal instrument makers in the family are discussed below (for fuller details of their compositions and writings, see *Grove 6*). Others, about whom little is known, are the eldest Nicolas (*d* 1693); Louis [*le jeune*] (*d* 1692), son of the eldest Louis; Philippe (1681–1736), the son of Louis [*le jeune*]; and Philippe (1714–73) and Louis (1717–1801), both sons of the elder Philippe.

(1) **Jean Hotteterre (i)** (*b* ?La Couture-Boussey; *d* ? between 1690 and 1692). Son of Loys de Haulteterre,

a wood turner in the town of La Couture, and Jehanne Gabriel. Jean was already a 'master turner in wood' at the time of his marriage in 1628. By 1636 he had settled in Paris where he played and made woodwind instruments. Between about 1650 and 1667 he played in the Hautbois et Musettes de Poitou and for ballets performed at court. He is probably the 'Osteterre' cited in 1656 by Michel de Marolles for his ravishing flageolet playing as well as the Hotteterre to whom Borjon's *Traité de la musette* of 1672 referred as 'unique for the construction of all kinds of instruments of wood, of ivory and of ebony, such as musettes, *flûtes*, flageolets, oboes and *cromornes*, and even for making complete families of all these instruments'. It is certain that he made some improvements in the drones of the musette, and he may also have been the leading figure behind the developments the other woodwind instruments underwent at about the same time. His last signature is dated 20 June 1689.

(2) **Jean Hotteterre (ii)** (*b* La Couture-Boussey, *c*1648; *d* Paris, buried 20 Feb 1732). Son of the eldest Louis Hotteterre and the grandson of Loys de Haulteterre. Jean was another of the outstanding instrument makers of his family. Emigrating to Paris as a young man, he played for various entertainments at court after 1676 and in 1683 took over his deceased cousin Jean Hotteterre's post in the Grands Hautbois. In 1692 Du Pradel listed him as one of the 'masters for the playing and fabrication of wind instruments', and in 1701 Joseph Sauveur named him and Jean-Jacques Rippert as 'among the most capable makers of Paris' for woodwind instruments. Jean may still have been making instruments up to the time of his death in 1732; the possessions catalogued after he died included tools for turning, several 'old flutes' and an ivory musette.

(3) **Martin Hotteterre** (*d* 1712). Son of (1) Jean Hotteterre (i). Like his father he made important improvements in the musette, adding the *petit chalumeau* (small chanter) with its six keys to the instrument before 1672. From 1657 he seems to have played for numerous court entertainments, and about 1665–7 was a member of the Grands Hautbois. In 1667 he replaced his father in the Hautbois et Musettes de Poitou, retaining that position until his death in 1712 although he obtained its reversion for his son Jean Hotteterre (*d* 1720) in 1699. Martin is also known to have been a composer

(4) **Nicolas Hotteterre (i)** [*l'aîné*] (*b* ?La Couture-Boussey, *c*1637; *d* Versailles, 10 May 1694). Son of the eldest Nicolas Hotteterre. By 1657 he was living in Paris, where he established himself as an instrument maker, player and teacher. By 1660 he had sent for his father and for a time they worked together in instrument building. By 1666 Nicolas had become a member of the Grands Hautbois and in 1668 he became a bassoonist for the royal chapel. He continued to make instruments on his own and to play in the Grands Hautbois until his death.

(5) **Louis Hotteterre** (*d* Ivry, Aug 1716). Son of the eldest Nicolas Hotteterre. He entered the Grands Hautbois in 1665 and played for numerous dramatic performances at court. After his elder brother struck out on his own, Louis worked with his father and younger brother (6) Nicolas Hotteterre (ii) in instrument making and teaching. Later he established his own workshop and Du Pradel cited him 'for all the woodwind instruments' in 1692. He may have made an alto recorder now in the Dayton C. Miller Collection, Washington.

C, and the lower two joints of a recorder in the eutsches Museum, Munich, which are marked with a ur-de-lis and the name 'L. HOTTETERRE'. A two-key oboe th the same name that has sometimes been attributed him is of too late a design to have come from his orkshop. In 1714 he gave the reversion of his place the Grands Hautbois to his great-nephew Pierre iédeville. He died at Ivry in August 1716; later pearances of his name on wage lists are erroneous.

(6) Nicolas [Colin] **Hotteterre (ii)** [*le jeune, le cadet*] La Couture-Boussey, baptized 19 Feb 1653; d Paris, Dec 1727). Son of the eldest Nicolas Hotteterre. He so worked with his father and brother (5) Louis Hotte- rre in instrument making and teaching. The sons clear- surpassed their father in craftsmanship: a statement their mother shortly after their father's death in 1693 id that the sons perfected all the instruments they made nce the father could not render them in tune. Probably 1666 Nicolas entered the Grands Hautbois, retaining is position until his death. Around 1704 and 1713 he so played in the opera orchestra. Du Pradel cited him ong with his cousin (2) Jean Hotteterre (ii) in 1692 for celling in playing and making woodwind instruments. nce he had by far the longest working period of the ree Nicolas Hotteterres and seems to have run by far e largest operation (if the tools, materials and instru- ents inventoried after his wife's death in 1708 and aft- his own in 1727 fairly represent its size and scope), may deserve the credit for the three instruments marked ith a six-pointed star and the name 'N HOTTETERRE' an alto recorder in the Rosenbaum Collection of Musical struments, a three-key oboe in the Brussels Instrument useum and a tenor recorder which formerly belonged M. Petit of Blois.

(7) Jacques(-Martin) Hotteterre ['Le Romain'] (b aris, 29 Sept 1674; d Paris, 16 July 1763). Son of (3) [artin Hotteterre. Jacques was the most illustrious of l the Hotteterres in composition and teaching; he was so skilled as an instrumentalist and instrument maker. ne reason for his adoption of the appellation 'le Romain' unknown; the generally accepted assumption that he ay have travelled to Italy during his youth is without ocumentation. According to the Etat Civil Reconstitué the Archives of the Seine, Jacques was born on 29 ptember 1674. As early as 1689 he was listed as 'basse hautbois et basse de violon' in the Grands Hautbois, it only in 1692 does he seem to have officially suc- eeded to that post. (The elusive Jacques-Jean Hotte- rre to whom Thoinan assigned this post probably never xisted.) By 1708, according to the title-page of his first ok of flute works, Jacques had become a 'flute of the amber of the king', but it was not until 26 August 717 that he received the reversion of René Pignon Des- oteaux's post with a similar title.

From the dedications of his works it appears that cques was highly sought after as a teacher of the ama- urs of the fashionable world. From the diary of J. F. . von Uffenbach we learn of his remarkable musette aying and of his flute- and musette-making activities. ossibly the three magnificent transverse flutes marked ily 'HOTTETERRE' with an anchor, now in the Staatlich- Institut für Musikforschung, Berlin, the Institute of heatre, Music and Cinematography, Leningrad, and e Landesmuseum Joanneum, Graz, originated in his orkshop. Not all eight instruments with this mark point Jacques's period of activity, however. In 1746–8

Jacques gave the reversion of his posts in the Grands Hautbois and chamber music to his sons, although his name continued to figure in royal accounts until 1761. The date of his death is recorded in the Archives Nation- ales.

Jacques Hotteterre's first published work, *Principes de la flûte traversière* (1707), was the first treatise on flute playing to appear in any country. His first book of suites for transverse flute and bass (1708), apparently modelled on a similar book by Michel de la Barre that had come out in 1702, was the second such set to reach publication in France and also contained unprecedented pieces for one and two unaccompanied flutes. His sec- ond book of suites which appeared in 1715 contained the first French multi-movement works for flute and bass described as sonatas (literally as 'suite sonatas'), although these works differed little from the suites in the same book except for their inclusion of 3/2 Grave move- ments. Jacques Hotteterre's other important works include two further treatises – one on improvising preludes on the flute, recorder and oboe, and the other an instruction manual for the musette; three duet suites for two unac- companied flutes or other instruments; six trio sonatas for two flutes, recorders, oboes or violins and bass; and arrangements for two flutes of sonatas by Robert Val- entine and Francesco Torelio. The *Tendresses ba- chiques* and other works listed by Fétis are erroneous.

The *Principes de la flûte traversière*, which includes instructions for playing the recorder and oboe as well as the flute, was a tremendous success in France and in other countries and was reprinted numerous times. It is a significant source of information about early wood- wind practice, particularly tonguing and ornamentation. Jacques Hotteterre's second treatise, *L'art de préluder sur la flûte traversière* (1719), is the only important work about the improvisation of preludes on the transverse flute ever to appear in France; moreover, it contains an informative discussion of metres and rhythmic alteration as well as preludes and *traits* (practice studies) which stand as rare examples of this art in the literature of the 18th-century French flute school. His third treatise, *Méthode pour la musette* (1737), contains preludes and airs for that instrument and is the best method for the musette written during the 18th century.

See also FLUTE, fig.10.

BIBLIOGRAPHY

FétisB

[C.-E. Borjon]: *Traité de la musette* (Lyons, 1672), 25, 27, 38

[J.] Sauveur: 'Principes d'acoustique et de musique, ou systême gén- éral des intervalles des sons', *Histoire de l'Academie royale des sciences, année 1701, avec les memoires de mathematique & de physique pour la même année, tirés de registres de cette Academie* (Paris, 1704), 197–364 in *Memoires*

M. de Marolles: 'De l'excellence de la ville de Paris', *Mémoires* (Paris, 2/1755); repr. in *Paris ou description de cette ville*, ed. V. Dufour (Paris, 1879), 319

A. du Pradel [pseud. of N. de Blegny]: *Le livre commode des adresses de Paris pour 1692*, ed. E. Fournier (Paris, 1878), i, 212; ii, 72

Anon.: description of an oboe by L. Hotteterre, *Revue et gazette musicale de Paris* (3 Aug 1879), 253

E. Thoinan: *Les Hotteterre et les Chédeville: célèbres joueurs et facteurs de flûtes, hautbois, bassons et musettes des XVIIᵉ et XVIIIᵉ siècles* (Paris, 1894)

N. Mauger: *Les Hotteterre: célèbres joueurs et facteurs de flûtes, hautbois, bassons et musettes des XVIIᵉ & XVIIIᵉ siècles: nouvelles recherches* (Paris, 1912)

J.-G. Prod'homme, ed.: 'Mémoire de M. de la Barre: sur les musettes et hautbois &c.', *Ecrits de musiciens (XVᵉ–XVIIIᵉ siècles)* (Paris, 1912), 241

E. Preussner: *Die musikalischen Reisen des Herrn von Uffenbach* (Kassel, 1949), 128f

J. Marx: 'The Tone of the Baroque Oboe', *GSJ*, iv (1951), 3

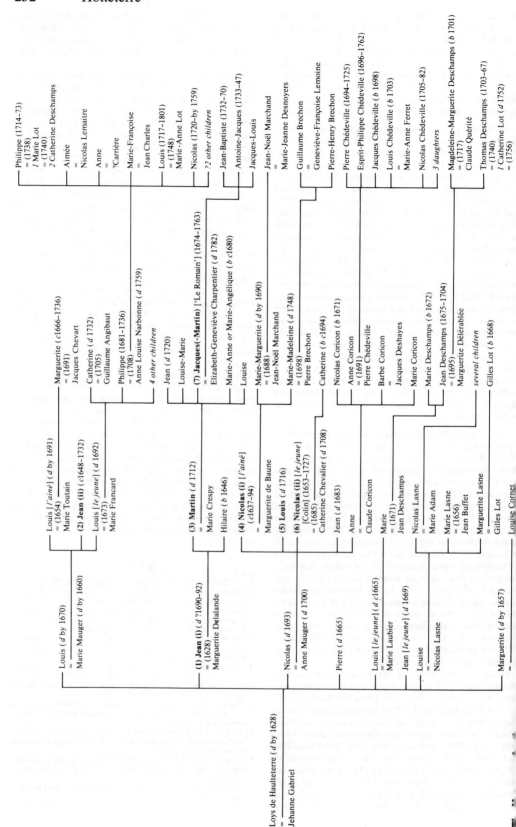

P. Schmitz: *Querflöte und Querflötenspiel in Deutschland während es Barockzeitalters* (Kassel, 1951, 2/1958)
Baines: *Woodwind Instruments and their History* (London, 1957, /1967), 273ff, 286, 290f
Cotte: 'Hotteterre', *MGG*
G. Langwill: *An Index of Musical Wind-instrument Makers* Edinburgh, 1960, rev. 6/1980)
Dufourcq and M. Benoit: 'Les musiciens de Versailles à travers es minutes notariales de Lamy versées aux Archives épartementales de Seine-et-Oise', *RMFC*, iii (1963), 193
E. Warner: *Indications of Performance Practice in Woodwind nstruction Books of the Seventeenth and Eighteenth Centuries* diss., New York U., 1964)
E. S. J. de Laborde: *Musiciens de Paris, 1535–1792*, ed. Y. de Brossard (Paris, 1965), 50, 151
Baines: *European and American Musical Instruments* (New York, 966), 81, 83, 86, 93, 103ff, pll. 430, 466, 550
E. Warner: *An Annotated Bibliography of Woodwind Instruction ooks, 1600–1830* (Detroit, 1967), 9, 11, 13, 16
Lasocki: Introduction to J. Hotteterre le Romain: *Principles of he Flute, Recorder and Oboe* (New York, 1968)
Bate: *The Flute: a Study of its History, Development and Con-truction* (London, 1969), 78ff
Benoit and N. Dufourcq: 'Documents du Minutier central: musi-iens français du XVIII⁵ siècle', *RMFC*, ix (1969), 217ff; x (1970), 02ff
Krickeberg: 'Studien zu Stimmung und Klang der Querflöte wischen 1500 und 1850', *Jb des Staatlichen Instituts für Musik-rschung Preussischer Kulturbesitz 1968* (Berlin, 1969), 99
Benoit: *Musiques de cour: chapelle, chambre, écurie, 1661–733* (Paris, 1971)
Machard: 'Les musiciens de France au temps de Jean-Philippe Rameau, d'après les actes du secrétariat de la maison du roi', RMFC, xi (1971), 30f, 85, 93f
Marvin: 'Recorders and English Flutes in European Collections', GSJ, xxv (1972), 39f
Thibault, J. Jenkins and J. Bran-Ricci: *Eighteenth Century Musi-al Instruments: France and Britain* (London, 1973), 120f, 124, 26
von Huene: 'Makers' Marks from Renaissance and Baroque Woodwinds', *GSJ*, xxvii (1974), 42
Bowers: 'New Light on the Development of the Transverse Flute etween about 1650 and about 1770', *JAMIS*, iii (1977), 12ff, 8, 22f
—: 'A Catalogue of French Works for the Transverse Flute, 1692–761', *RMFC*, xviii (1978), 100, 108, 115, 124f
Abondance: 'Les Hotteterre – artisans de La Couture et enovateurs de l'art de la flûte aux XVIIème et XVIIIème siècles', *ourneurs sur bois et manufactures d'instruments à vent en Haute-Normandie* (Rouen, 1980), 16ff
Bran-Ricci, F. Abondance, C. Massip and F. Lesure: *Musiques anciennes: instruments et partitions (XVIᵉ-XVIIIᵉ siècles)* (Paris, 1980), 65ff, 79, 98
T. Young: *The Look of Music: Rare Musical Instruments, 1500–1900* (Vancouver, 1980), 24, 71ff
e *Recorder Collection of Frans Brüggen: Drawings by Frederick Morgan* (Tokyo, 1981), 6
Seyfrit: *Musical Instruments in the Dayton C. Miller Flute Col-ection at the Library of Congress: a Catalog*, i: *Recorders, Fifes, and Simple System Transverse Flutes of One Key* (Washington, DC, 1982), 20, pl. 4
T. Young: *2500 Historical Woodwind Instruments: an Inventory of the Major Collections* (New York, 1982), 66, pl.8
Bowers: 'The Hotteterre Family of Woodwind Instrument Mak-ers', *Pythagoras at the Forge: an Annotated Catalogue of the Rosenbaum Collection of Western European Musical Instruments*, ed. R. M. Rosenbaum (in preparation)

JANE M. BOWERS

ottinger Collection. The best-known mid-20th-entury collection of rare violins, formed by Henry Hot-nger in New York. Hottinger was born in New York n 4 February 1885, and was a founder-member of ertheim & Co., investment bankers and members of e New York Stock Exchange. He had an early interest the violin, and bought his first Stradivari in 1935. is ambition after the war was to acquire one outstand-g example of each of the old Cremonese masters, and the case of Stradivari and Guarneri 'del Gesù', one xample from each significant period of their produc-on. An illustrated catalogue of the collection was pub-shed at the time of its sale to Rembert Wurlitzer Inc.

in 1966. The finest instruments in the collection (about 30 violins in all) were the Stradivaris known as the 'Hellier' (1679, an inlaid instrument), the 'Earl of Plymouth' (1711), the 'Dolphin' (1714), the 'Comte de Cessole' (1716), and the 'Salabue' (1742), made by his son Francesco; the 'Joachim' (1737) and 'Ysaÿe' (1740) violins by Guarneri 'del Gesù'; and also exceptional examples of the work of Pietro Guarneri of Venice and Alexander Gagliano. The collection was dispersed all over the world, the violins by Andrea and Nicolo Amati being purchased by the city of Cremona, where they are exhibited in the town hall.

BIBLIOGRAPHY
The Hottinger Collection (New York, 1966)

CHARLES BEARE

Hourglass drum. Hourglass-shaped drums are found in a wide area stretching from about 40° north of the equator to 15° south, from Africa in the west to Japan and the Pacific islands in the east. They are perhaps the most distinctively shaped of all the tubular drums: the body of each instrument has a constricted waist and open cup ends (for illustration of drum shapes, *see* DRUM, figs.2 and 3). The length of these drums varies from about 30 cm, as with the Yoruba *kanango*, to 90 cm or more in the case of the Korean *changgo*, the largest of the family. The body may be made of wood, wood cased in metal, metal, earthenware or bone, as on the Tibetan *thod-rnga* made from two skullcaps. The drum may be single- or double-headed, and the skins may be glued, nailed, laced or lapped to the body. (For details of the classification, *see* MEMBRANOPHONE.)

The most complicated type is the hourglass pressure drum, also known as the variable tension drum. It is distinguished from the general family of hourglass-shaped drums by the lacing which attaches the skins to the body and at the same time controls the tension of the drum-heads. This type has two forms: a double-headed drum with leather hoops at either end and a continuous ten-sioning thong laced back and forth between the two skins

Hourglass drum (hutamba) player, Sierra Leone

at equal intervals around their circumference (see illustration); and a single-headed drum, similarly laced, with the tensioning thong threaded between the leather hoop and the skin at one end, and through holes drilled around the open cup of the body at the other. The hourglass pressure drum is a portative instrument; other hourglass-shaped drums may be portative or nonportative.

The hourglass pressure drum is characteristically hung from the left shoulder so that it lies in an almost horizontal position under the left arm. The player is able to alter the skin tension, and thus the pitch of individual drumstrokes, by the pressure of his arm or hand on the central lengths of the tensioning thong. If only a single pitch is required, the drum may be tuned by tying a belt around the lengths of the tensioning thong at the instrument's waist. It may be beaten by hand, with a stick, or by hand and stick: if a stick is used, it is often a hooked beater with a flattened head at right angles to the main shaft; if it is beaten by hand, a snare or a central ring of tuning-paste, or both, may be added to the skin.

The West African hourglass pressure drum is often used as a 'talking' drum, and has been inaccurately described as the principal talking drum in an area where almost every instrument, including rattles, can be made to 'talk'. Its tonal flexibility and its range of about an octave have made it increasingly popular since its first appearance from the north in the late 16th century. In many areas its use has superseded that of older more traditional instruments which survive in some cases as rural curiosities. The hourglass pressure drum is used as a solo instrument, or in a variety of combination with such instruments as cylindrical dums, frame drums kettledrums, bells, castanets, rattles, bowed and plucke lutes and wind instruments.

Strokes on the pressure drum lead to notes either leve in pitch or gliding. A level note results from striking th skin without subsequently altering arm or hand pressu on the tensioning thong, while a gliding note results from striking the skin and increasing or decreasing pressur on the tensioning thong to produce a rising or fallin glissando, or both. These tonal capabilities have mad the hourglass pressure drum an ideal 'talking' instru ment for tonal languages in which syllables are not onl placed on individual pitch levels, but may also rise o fall from these levels. The use of the drum in this wa to perform a Yoruba *oriki* (traditional praise text) is show in ex.1, in which high-tone syllables are marked wit an acute accent, low-tone syllables with a grave; mid tone syllables are unmarked.

In Oceania, the hourglass drum is the characteristi membranophone of New Guinea and northern Islan Melanesia (*see* KUNDU (i)) and has spread from ther into the eastern Micronesian islands of the Marshall (*see* AJE), Ponape and Mokil (*see* AIP), Kosrae (*see* ASIS and Nomoi. Within eastern Micronesia it occurs also in the Polynesian outlier of Nukuoro (*see* AISI). In wester Micronesia and in the rest of Melanesia drums are absent In Polynesia they take a distinctively different cylindri cal form (*see* PAHU).

For bibliography *see* DRUM.

The following hourglass drums are entered in this dictionary: ābzem adja; adscha; agyesowa; aip; aisi; aiva; aje; āmantirikai; asi; asis atabule; āži; bala (ii); bandǫ; bara karanku; batá; budbudaka; budu gu; cái bồng; cang-te'u; changgo; dabudabu; dai; ḍakkā; dama ḍamaru; damba; dang fokku; daning; dan karbi; danko; daunde dawura; davaṇḍai; ḍeru; ḍhāk; donno; doodo; dundun; elemú; eḷu parey; emele isaju; fimkhang'u; gaba; gangan; gangar yan kama gcod-dar; gedumbak; geudumba; gomboy; gunda (i); guruki; hara huḍko; huḍukkā; huṛuk; hutamba; ichi-no-tsuzumi; ida; iḍaisu rangu parai; iḍakka; idi; ikko; imi; isaju ikanhin; jauje; kalali; kalan gu; kalgo; kanango; kandara; kanjau; kāntāṃdabadaba; kazagi; ker ikeri; khishba; kodam; kolo (i); kootso; koso; kotso; kotsuzumi; kuba kuli (i); kundu (i); kuretsuzumi; kurkutu; kuru; longa (i); luinsse lunga (i); lunsi; maṇḍiḍakkā; mukupiela; munugi; ndamula; nduntsu ngoma; ni-no-tsuzumi; nnonka; ntum; nyanyúlua; odi (ii); ōkawa ōtsuzumi; paṇava; pandareta; para (i); phong yêu cổ; san-no-tsuzumi seyogo; shi-no-tsuzumi; shō (iii); sōlchanggo; ta'impe; tama; thod rnga; timila; tomba; trikulyā; trivalī; tsuzumi; tudi; uḍākki uḍukku; urumi; uṭukkai; yaogu; zakka; zanbūr; zhanggu.

ANTHONY KING (with MERVYN McLEAN

Ex.1 from an *oriki*, performed on Yoruba *dundun* pressure drums

Howard, Emmons (*b* Brimfield, Mass., 1 Oct 1845; *c* Westfield, Mass., 18 March 1931). American orga builder. He received his early training from William A Johnson, later working for John W. Steere, and estab lished his own business in Westfield in 1883. For some time his firm remained small, providing modest tracker action instruments for small churches in New Englan and New York state. In 1901 he received a contract fo a substantial organ for the Pan-American Exposition ir Buffalo, New York, temporarily moving his workshop to that city to complete it. This did not result in the hoped-for large contracts, however, and he returned t Springfield, Massachusetts, where he continued build ing on the same small scale as before until his retiremen in 1929.

BIBLIOGRAPHY

O. Ochse: *The History of the Organ in the United States* (Bloom ington, Ind., 1975)

B. Owen: *The Organ in New England* (Raleigh, North Carolina 1979)

BARBARA OWEN

Howarth. English family of woodwind instrument makers and repairers. George Howarth (*b* London, 1860; *d* London, 1933), son of Henry Howarth (a pastry cook originally from Rochdale), was apprenticed to Liddle, a London woodwind maker, in 1874. On the termination of Liddle's business in 1879, Howarth went to Boosey & Co., and was principally employed in making flutes. He was chosen as 'trade artisan' to report on the woodwind instruments at the Paris Exhibition of 1889. He set up his own business in 1894, later with his two sons as apprentices, the firm becoming known as G. Howarth & Sons. The elder son, James Daniel Howarth (*b* 1901), had begun work at the age of 14 and from 1924 was employed by Hawkes & Sons, becoming foreman of the repair shop. His brother Thomas William Howarth (1904–77) went to Canada in the 1920s; after his return to London (? *c*1925) he was employed for some years in assembling imported saxophones for the American firm of Lewin Bros. About 1935 he set up a repair business on his own. After war work he established, with three partners, a firm of oboe makers, T. W. Howarth & Co., from which he withdrew in 1949. Meanwhile James Howarth, after war work in Boosey & Hawkes's factory, had set up a repair business and was joined by Thomas in 1956 and by his younger son Paul in 1961. In 1965 James and Paul Howarth became established as J. & P. Howarth Ltd, continuing the repair business and importing high-class foreign instruments until 1975, when James Howarth retired to work privately; Paul moved to Yorkshire, then to Sussex, where he repairs both woodwind and string instruments.

PHILIP BATE

Howe. English family of organ builders. The business operated by John Howe (i) (*b* ?York; *d* London, 1519) and John Howe (ii) (*b* ?London; *d* London, 1571) was the first of its kind of any importance in England. The guild of organ builders became extinct in 1531, and that year John Howe (ii) received permission to become a member of the Skinners Company.

The first mention of the family comes from York, where repairs were made to the minster organs in 1485, and it is possible that the family came from there. The Howes's workshops were at Walbrook, 'at the sign of the Organe Pype'. During their lives there were over 100 churches in the City of London alone; records for about a quarter of these survive, and only two of them fail to mention the Howes, who carried out minor repairs and tuning under a covenant which seems to have been at the rate of one shilling a year per organ.

They are known to have built or repaired at least 26 organs, including 19 in the cities of London and Westminster and others in the London areas of Lambeth and Wandsworth, as well as at Eton, Bletchingley, York, Coventry and Sheffield.

BIBLIOGRAPHY

A. Freeman: 'Records of British Organ Builders', *The Dictionary of Organs and Organists* (London, 1919, rev. 2/1921)

W. L. Sumner: *The Organ: its Evolution, Principles of Construction and Use* (London, 1952, rev. 4/1973), 109ff

C. Clutton and A. Niland: *The British Organ* (London, 1963, 2/1982)

HUGH BAILLIE/R

Hpà-si. Bronze idiophone of Burma, sometimes called 'frog drum' after the small carved frogs which decorate four points of the drum head. The head is struck with a padded stick and sometimes also on the side with a thin stick. When not being played, *hpà-si* are sometimes turned upside down and used as containers for rice.

See also BRONZE DRUM and MAHŌRA THŲK.

Hradetzky, Gerhard G(regor) (*b* Weilheim, nr. Munich, 8 Feb 1944). Austrian organ builder. His grandfather, Gregor Hradetzky (i), founded an organ-building firm in Krems in 1912; after World War II, under the control of Gregor Hradetzky (ii), Gerhard's father, the workshop achieved international renown. Gerhard Hradetzky received his early training from his father and then worked with Rudolf von Beckerath in Hamburg (1962–5) before attending the Fachschule für Instrumentenbau in Ludwigsburg (1972). In 1974 he resigned from his father's business and set up his own firm in Oberbergern near Krems.

Hradetzky has specialized in building smaller organs using old construction techniques; his instruments mostly have two manuals, slider-chests and mechanical action, and some use historical tunings. He has built organs of this sort for the Immanuel Presbyterian Church, Los Angeles (two manuals, 15 stops; 1978), St Paul's, Döbling, Vienna (two manuals, 21 stops; 1978), St Paul's, Riverside, Connecticut (two manuals, 31 stops; 1980) and the Servitenkirche, Rossau, Vienna (two manuals, 25 stops; 1981). Hradetzky's workshop has also carried out a number of stylistically authentic restorations of old organs, including those of the parish church at Imbach (1600, one manual, seven stops; 1977), the parish church at Purgstall (1750, two manuals, 21 stops) and the Stiftskirche, Zwettl (1732, three manuals, 36 stops; 1982–3).

HANS HASELBÖCK

Hsaìng-waìng. Burmese percussion ensemble. The term also refers to the DRUM-CHIME (also called PAT-WAÌNG) played in the ensemble. The *hsaìng-waìng* ensemble is used to accompany theatre performances such as the *zat-pwè* (all-night drama), the *bala-zaìng* (concert performance) and the now rare puppet shows, as well as other festive, ritual and religious occasions. The instrumentation varies with the availability of the instruments, but a full ensemble includes the *hsaìng-waìng* (drum-chime), the KYÌ-WAÌNG (gong-chime), the MAÙNG-ZAÌNG (gong-chime), the HNÈ (oboe), the CHAUK-LÒN-BAT (set of six drums), WALET-HKOK (bamboo clappers), YAGWÌN (cymbals), a BYAUK (slit-drum) and SÌ (hand cymbals).

JUDITH BECKER

Hsiao. See XIAO.

Hsing. See XING.

Hsin-ti. See XINDI.

Hsün. See XUN.

Huagu. Small barrel drum of the Han Chinese. *See* YAOGU.

Hu'a-hu'a. Bamboo clarinet of Flores, Indonesia. *See* ORUPI.

Huaigu. Double-headed FRAME DRUM of the Han Chinese. *See* SHUGU.

Huân. Vietnamese globular VESSEL FLUTE derived from the Chinese XUN. It comprises a small bulging clay receptacle with a blow-hole at the top and three finger-holes on the front and two behind. It was traditionally played in Confucian temple music.

Huang. JEW'S HARP of China. See KOQIN.

Huapanguera. A large five-course guitar of Mexico, with eight or ten strings. It is used in an ensemble to accompany the *huapango*, a type of *son* (rural music) of the mestizos.

Huapen gu. Large drum of the Han Chinese. See TANGGU.

Huarumo [guarumo]. End-blown natural trumpet of the Ecuadorian highlands, sometimes called BOCINA. The *huarumo* is a straight bamboo trumpet, 2 metres or more in length; it is sometimes played in an ensemble with flute and *bombo* (large double-headed drum).

Hubbard, Frank (Twombly) (*b* New York, 15 May 1920; *d* Newton, Mass., 25 Feb 1976). American harpsichord maker. He studied English literature at Harvard (AB 1942, MA 1947) where his growing interest in early music led him and his friend William Dowd to construct a clavichord. Its success encouraged them to abandon academic pursuits and to prepare for careers as builders of early keyboard instruments constructed on historical principles. In 1947 Hubbard went to England to learn the craft and worked briefly at the Dolmetsch workshop before joining Hugh Gough at his London premises. He also studied early keyboard instruments in British and continental collections. On his return to the USA in 1949 he and Dowd founded a workshop to build harpsichords on historical principles rather than in the modern fashion then practised by virtually all professional makers. Their firm produced models based on the surviving instruments made by the leading historical makers of Italy, Flanders, France and England. Numerous restorations of many such harpsichords from important public and private collections helped them evolve their own designs and refine their methods of construction. The partnership with Dowd continued until 1958, after which each continued to make instruments independently.

Meanwhile Hubbard had been doing the research that led to the publication in 1965 of his authoritative historical study of harpsichord making from the 16th century to the 18th. During 1955–7, partly supported by grants, he had been able to examine many more instruments in Europe and to establish close contacts with museums there. As a result he was asked in 1967 to set up the restoration workshop for the Musée Instrumental at the Paris Conservatoire, where he worked in 1967–8 and taught the restoration of historical instruments and the construction of harpsichords on historical principles.

Hubbard's own production of finished instruments was necessarily limited, but he also developed a harpsichord, based on a Taskin instrument of 1769, which could be produced in kit or semi-finished form (*see* HARPSICHORD, fig.20). By the end of 1975 about 1000 of these kit instruments had been produced. As a dedicated amateur violinist and chamber musician Hubbard

also restored a number of early violins to their pre-19th century state and made bows of a pre-Tourte type for instruments of the viol and violin families.

WRITINGS
'Two Early English Harpsichords', *GSJ*, iii (1950), 12
'The *Encyclopédie* and the French Harpsichord', *GSJ*, ix (1956) 37
Harpsichord Regulating and Repairing (Boston, Mass., 1963)
Three Centuries of Harpsichord Making (Cambridge, Mass., 1965

BIBLIOGRAPHY
H. Haney: 'Portrait of a Builder: Frank Hubbard', *The Harpsi chord*, v/1 (1972), 5, 14
T. McGeary: 'Frank Hubbard', *English Harpsichord Magazine*, (1973–6), 98
H. Schott: 'Tribute to Frank Hubbard', *Early Music*, iv (1976), 25.
M. Steinberg: 'Frank Hubbard 1920–1976', *Boston Sunday Glob* (7 March 1976)

                                                    HOWARD SCHOT

Hubert, Christian Gottlob (*b* Fraustadt [Wschowa], . May 1714; *d* Ansbach, 16 Feb 1793). German make of clavichords, organs, harpsichords and pianos, of Polis origin. He left Poland to work at Bayreuth in 1740 and in 1769 moved to Ansbach, where he became cour instrument maker. Early in his life he built a number o organs; Meusel stated that his pianos were exported t France, England and the Netherlands, reckoning tha while they were cheaper than English ones, they wer equally good. His clavichords and pianos were deeme to be durable as well as beautiful in tone.

Hubert became one of the best-known clavichor makers of his time, and surviving instruments justify th praise of his contemporaries; most of these are clavi chords (see Strack, 1979), including a number of frette ones dating from as late as 1787. The Germanische Nationalmuseum, Nuremberg, contains a small repre sentative collection of Hubert's work including severa clavichords and a transverse grand. The latter's com pass is four octaves and a fourth and the action has n escapement (see Hirt, 1955). The compass of Hubert': clavichords varied from four octaves to five and a thir octaves. Johann Wilhelm Hoffmann (1764–1809) Hubert's assistant from 1789, took over the business o Hubert's death.

BIBLIOGRAPHY
J. G. Meusel: *Miscellaneen artistischen Inhalts*, xxvii (Erfurt, 1786) 137
F. Krautwurst: 'Hubert, Christian Gottlob', *MGG*
F. J. Hirt: *Meisterwerke des Klavierbaus* (Olten, 1955; Eng. trans. 1968)
D. H. Boalch: *Makers of the Harpsichord and Clavichord 1400– 1840* (London, 1956, rev. 2/1974)
Katalog zu den Sammlungen des Händel-Hauses in Halle, v Musikinstrumentensammlung besaitete Tasteninstrumente (Hall an der Saale, 1966)
W. Strack: 'Christian Gottlob Hubert and his Instruments', *GSJ* xxxii (1979), 38

                                                    MARGARET CRANMER

Huchet (Fr.). Hunting horn; *see* HORN.

Hu-ch'in. See HUQIN.

Hudie qin. Struck BOX ZITHER of the Han Chinese. Se YANGQIN.

Hudko. HOURGLASS DRUM from the Himalayan area of west Nepal, Kumaon and Garhwal. The body is of turned wood or metal and not more than 30 cm high. The waisted section of the drum is pierced by a small hole which is

Huḍko (hourglass drum), with metal body, played by a ḍholi, Nepal

described as allowing the instrument to breathe. The two heads are closed with circular frames covered with a membrane and laced together. The tension of the heads is regulated by a little cord or strip of fabric around the lacing, fixed to a shoulder strap bearing several small bells.

Musicians who play the *huḍko* are usually members of an 'untouchable' caste. They place the strap over the left shoulder and slip the left hand under the lacing to grip the narrow section of the drum and pull it forwards so that they can strike its upper skin with the right-hand fingers. The instrument's playing style is characterized not only by the use of fixed rhythmic structures but also by variations in timbre and pitch obtained through regulation of the tension of the heads.

The *huḍko* is used in western Nepal to accompany sung and danced ballads; in Kumaon, sometimes supported by a little gong, it takes a place in the *jāgar* ceremonies, during which mediums are said to be possessed by the deities whose stories the musician is relating and singing.

See also Huḍukkā and Ḍhāk.

BIBLIOGRAPHY
M. Helffer and M. Gaborieau: 'A propos d'un tambour du Kumaon et de l'ouest du Népal: remarques sur l'utilisation des tambourssabliers dans le monde indien, le Népal et le Tibet', *Festschrift to Ernst Emsheimer* (Stockholm, 1974), 75, 268
A. Chandola: *Folk Drumming in the Himalayas: a Linguistic Approach to Music* (New York, 1977)

MIREILLE HELFFER

Huḍukkā [huruk, hurkī, hurko, uṭukkai, uḍukkai, uḍukku]. Variable tension drum, principally an HOUR-GLASS DRUM, of India. The names date from medieval times and are doubtless onomatopoeic. *Huḍukkā* is Sanskrit, *huruk* (and its variants) Hindi and modern north Indian and *uṭukkai* (and its variants) the modern south-

ern form of the name. The older term for an hourglass drum in Sanskrit (*panava*) occurs in epic and classical texts. The three main medieval terms for variable-tension drums are *huḍukkā* (raised barrel drum), *ḍakkā* (hourglass drum), and *ḍamaru*, (hourglass-shaped rattle drum). There is some interchange of names and types in modern drums.

The body of the medieval *huḍukkā* (described by Śārṅgadeva in the 13th century) was a barrel about 48 cm long, with a diameter of 18 cm in the middle and 14 cm at the ends; the shell was about 2 cm thick. The instrument was converted into a raised barrel drum (functionally equivalent to an hourglass drum) by the much wider (about 22 cm) hoops and skins of the heads; the lacing, which runs well above the wall of the drum, can be tightened by central cross-cords. The hoops, about 2 cm wide, are of creeper and bound to the skins with thin animal membrane; each one has six holes for the lacing. Over the central cross-lacing is a decorative 'waist-cloth' about 6 cm wide. A cotton rope is attached tightly to both heads and then to a shoulder strap. The drum is played only with the right hand; the left varies the pitch by pressing on the waist-cloth against the shoulder-strap. There are small pins with cup-shaped jingles (*kalaśa*) at either end. A similar drum (without jingles) is the *kuḍukkā*, played with a stick.

The later northern *huruk* and southern *uṭukkai* also have the wide heads of the *huḍukkā* but they are true hourglass drums. The *huruk* was described as resembling 'two falconers' drums (small kettledrums) attached together and bound with strings of silk' (Abu'l Fazl, c1590). Men of the *Hurukīyā* musician class used it to accompany their singing of *karkā* (martial ballads associated especially with the Panjab and Rajasthan), then of *dhrupad*. In the north the names *huruk, hurkī* etc alternate with the names *ḍāk*, Gujarati *ḍāklu* and the *ḍhāk* or *ḍeru* of Rajasthan denoting similar drums. The *hurkī* of Garhwal, northern Uttar Pradesh, is an hourglass drum about 25 cm long. Its two heads, of goatskin attached to bamboo or figwood hoops, are about 15 cm in diameter and wider than the drum-faces; they are braced by cotton Y-lacing through six holes and by a central cross-lacing attached to the shoulder-strap. The left hand grips the waist of the drum under the lacing to vary the tension; only the right face is played. The instrument is used to accompany dancing girls. The *guruki*, a similar folk drum of Maharashtra, is clearly related in name.

The *uṭukkai* of Tamil Nadu and the *uḍukku* of Kerala are also hourglass drums. They are of similar size and construction to the northern *huruk* but their bodies are sometimes of brass or clay and they have a snare of two crossed hairs or wires under the left-hand skin. They are also called *tudi* or *iḍaisurangu parai* and are mostly played with the right-hand fingers. A larger size is the *davandai*, with thicker skins and lacing, played with a stick. These drums are played mostly in temples and are also used by professional fortune-tellers.

For the instrument played in west Nepal and Kumaon, see Huḍko.

BIBLIOGRAPHY
Śārṅgadeva: *Saṅgītaratnākara* (13th century), ed. S. Subrahmanya Sastri, iii (Madras, 1951)
Abu'l Fazl: *Ā'īn-i-akbarī* (c1590), trans. H. Blochmann in *The Imperial Musicians* (Calcutta, 1873, 2/1927), 680ff; trans. H. S. Jarrett, rev. J. Sarkar in *Saṅgīt*, Bibliotheca Indica, cclxx (Calcutta, 1948), 260ff

C. Marcel-Dubois: *Les instruments de musique de l'Inde ancienne* (Paris, 1941)
P. Sambamoorthy: *Catalogue of Musical Instruments Exhibited in the Government Museum, Madras* (Madras, 3/1962)
K. S. Kothari: *Indian Folk Musical Instruments* (New Delhi, 1968)
A. Chandola: *Folk Drumming in the Himalayas* (New York, 1977)
B. C. Deva: *Musical Instruments of India* (Calcutta, 1978)

ALASTAIR DICK

Hueco. Generic term used in Oriente Province, Cuba, for Afro-Cuban drums. Sometimes it is a synonym for CATÁ, a horizontal log-drum. In earlier times it was a single-headed drum, with the head made taut with spikes (as with the *arará* drums); it was used for the *tajona*, an obsolete Afro-Cuban dance of Santiago de Cuba, accompanied by an ensemble of drums of the *arará*, or *tumba francesa*, variety. See *OrtizIMA*, iii, 119, 419; iv, 109.

JOHN M. SCHECHTER

Huehuetl. A three-footed cylindrical drum of the Aztecs of pre-Conquest America. It had a single head of jaguar skin or deerskin, beaten with bare hands, and was open at the bottom. Along with the *teponaztli* (wooden slit-drum), it was one of the most important instruments of Aztec culture. The *huehuetl* (and such related drums as the *panhuehuetl* and *tlalpanhuehuetl*) incorporated the name of the tree *ahuehuete*, which supplied the wood from which the instrument was made. It was tuned by

Aztec huehuetl (cylindrical drum) from Malinalco (Museo de Arqueología, Toluca)

heating the interior with live coals which dried and taut-ened the head. The Aztecs frequently inscribed their musical instruments with symbolic carvings. A *hue-huetl*, about 90 cm tall, in the Toluca Museum shows a group of captured warriors being forced to dance to music of their own making before having their hearts torn out and waved aloft as offerings to the war god Huitzilopochtli (see illustration). Like the *teponaztli*, the *huehuetl* was held to be a god temporarily forced to endure earthly exile. Both drums were therefore treated as idols as well as musical instruments. The Mayan form of the *huehuetl* was the *zacatán*.

Huele [m'bono]. STOPPED FLUTE ENSEMBLE of the Fali people of Cameroon. The set comprises seven instruments of different sizes classified according to kin terminology which determines the relationship between pitches. See J.-G. Gauthier: *Les Fali (Hon et Tsalo)* (Oosterhut, 1969).

Huene, Friedrich (Alexander) von (Hoyningen-) (Breslau, 20 Feb 1929). American maker of recorde and flutes. He grew up on a farm in Mecklenburg, an emigrated to the USA in 1948 at the age of 19. Aft three years in a US Air Force band he attended Bowdo College in Brunswick, Maine, and received his BA music there in 1956. From 1956 to 1960 he worked the shop of Verne Q. Powell, flute maker, in Bostor and spent his spare time experimenting with the co struction of recorders, a problem that had occupied hi for some time. Since 1960 he has been building recorde and Baroque and Renaissance flutes in his own sho first in Waltham, Massachusetts, and later in Brooklin Massachusetts. In 1966–7 he held a Guggenheim fe lowship to study the instruments built in the 16th, 17 and 18th centuries, preserved in various museums. Vo Huene was one of the first modern makers of recorde to model his exceptionally fine instruments directly o the designs of the old craftsmen. He has made more less exact copies of particularly good Baroque instru ments – both flutes and recorders – by the Hotteterre Denner and others, and has designed recorders for mas production, including a model based on the work of Jear Hyacinth Rottenburgh (1672–1756), manufactured an distributed by Moeck Verlag in Celle, and a model base on the work of Bressan, manufactured and distribute by Zen-On in Japan. Von Huene has trained such mak ers as Thomas Prescott, Richard Palm and Robert Ma vin. He is also a performer (particularly on the recorde and flute) and teacher of early music.

BIBLIOGRAPHY
M. Lewis: 'How Recorders are made at the Workshop of Friedric von Huene', *American Recorder*, i/4 (1960), 4
C. E. Merger: 'Friedrich von Huene, the Man, his Work and hi Family', *American Recorder*, xi (1970), 3

HOWARD MAYER BROW

Huene, Stephan von (*b* Los Angeles, 1932). America sculptor. Since 1965 (working at first in Los Angeles then, from around 1982, in Hamburg) he has construct ed a range of automated sculptures involving sound. The are all powered by a pneumatic system similar to tha of a player piano and have lively and often humorou movement and sound relationships.

The Kaleidophonic Dog (1965–7) consists of the fron half of a dog lying on its back above a small xylophon on a plinth; five loops of punched tape inside the plint control the movement of the dog's legs and the playing not only of the xylophone but also of eight hidden orga pipes and a wooden drum. Tapdancer (1969) is a pai of men's legs from the knees downwards, clad in trou sers and shoes, mounted on a plinth; a tape-operate system strikes hidden woodblocks and moves the hinge toe-caps in synchronization, so that they appear to tap Rosebud Annunciator (1968), which has a number o separate units, is programmed by a pinned cylinder. A drum, a 24-note xylophone (played 'virtuosically') cymbals and a diatonic octave of organ pipes (mounte internally) are sounded automatically, while a whit leather rose contained in a frame, and other forms or top of two side columns, inflate and deflate.

Huene has built five Totem Tones (1969–70), each consisting of two or three large wooden organ pipe powered by a vacuum-cleaner motor and controlled by punched tape; the sounds of the pipes are varied by automatic opening and closing of the upper or lower en or of a vent in the middle. Washboard Band (1969) programmed by two loops of punched tape of differ ent lengths, consists of a washboard struck by four small beaters and scraped by a skeletal hand, a cymbal, saucepan lids and a box containing tuned reeds. More recently (in APT, 1979–80, for example) Huene has incorporated glass tubing and electronic circuitry into his work to create percussive sounds from noises picked up by a microphone. He also collaborated with the composer James Tenney on Drum (1975), in which specially composed pieces by Tenney are played on a drum surrounded by a circle of sticks.

BIBLIOGRAPHY
D. Newmark: 'An Interview with Stephan von Huene on his Audio-Kinetic Sculptures', *Leonardo*, v (1972), 69; repr. in *Kinetic Art: Theory and Practice*, ed. F. Malina (New York, 1974), 99
J. Grayson, ed.: *Sound Sculpture: a Collection of Essays by Artists* (Vancouver, 1975), 24
The Sounds of Sound Sculpture', ARC Records, ST 1001 [disc notes]
R. Block: 'Die Summe aller Klänge ist grau', *Für Augen und Ohren* (Berlin, 1980), 141 [exhibition catalogue]
Stephan von Huene: Klangskulpturen (Baden Baden, 1983) [exhibition catalogue]

HUGH DAVIES

Huesitos. SCRAPER of Spain, made of bones tied parallel to each other and hung around the neck. It is sounded by scraping the bones with a conch-shell. In Catalonia, where it is known as a *bandurria d'ossos*, the bones are from birds' feet and are scraped with a castanet.

Hugán. Afro-Cuban drum. *See* HUN (ii).

Hugoniot, Charles-Emile (*d* France, 1927). French researcher into electronic sound systems and inventor of an early ELECTRONIC ORGAN, the photoelectric Hugoniot organ. From the end of World War I Hugoniot systematically explored and improved on all the electronic sound-generating and -recording methods known at the time, starting in 1919 with the rotating electromagnetic tone-wheels pioneered in the Telharmonium and known in France from Cahill's patents, and continuing with electromagnetic steel discs. He also tried out audio and beat-frequency oscillators. The only instrument that he appears to have completed was a photoelectric organ (1921), in which rotating tone-wheels with concentric rings of radial slits interrupted beams of light (there were presumably 12 discs, each producing all the octave registers of a single note); behind the wheels were shaped timbre masks that modified the light-beams before they reached photoelectric cells.

Through his patents Hugoniot influenced the design of several electronic instruments developed in France in the late 1920s, including the ondes martenot (1928). In many cases the systems with which he experimented – for example magnetic recording and oscillators using electronic valves – were not sufficiently technically reliable to support his ideas. He died shortly before the great proliferation at the end of the 1920s of electronic instruments based on more sophisticated technology.

BIBLIOGRAPHY
Lt.-Col. Jullien: 'Applications du courant électrique, des oscillations radioélectriques et des phénomènes photoélectriques à la réalisation d'instruments de musique', *Conférences d'actualités scientifiques et industrielles* (Paris, 1929; repr. 1930), 142, 171, 176, 181, 189

HUGH DAVIES

Huhe [foi duri udi]. Bamboo flute of the Nage and Ngada area of Flores, Indonesia. The player blows into a hole in the centre of the open tube, which is about 14 to 17 cm long, and the pitch is altered by opening and closing both ends of the tube. Some Ngada flutes (*foi duri udi*) have one or two small finger-holes in the top of the tube. The instrument is played by young girls. See J. Kunst: *Music in Flores* (Leiden, 1942), 150f.

MARGARET J. KARTOMI

Huhugan. Gong of the southern Philippines. *See* DUAHAN and KULINTANG.

Huhupal. Hittite instrument, probably a form of CLAPPERS; *see also* SCABELLUM.

Huibe. Bass fiddle of northern Belgium. It is composed of a wooden board, about 115 cm long, 20 cm wide and 1·5 cm deep, sawn in the shape of a stylized cello. It has four or five strings of gut, cord or brass. There is no specific tuning as the *huibe* is used only to produce a rhythmic noise. It was traditionally accompanied by triangle and *rommelpot* (friction drum) at dances and songs at Epiphany or Mid-Lent.

F. J. DE HEN

Huilacapitztli. An aerophone, probably an end-blown flute, of the Aztecs. In modern times the term has been used for a VESSEL FLUTE. See T. Stanford: 'A Linguistic Analysis of Music and Dance Terms from Three Sixteenth-Century Dictionaries of Mexican Indian Languages', *Inter-American Institute for Musical Research Yearbook*, ii (1966), 101–59; and R. Stevenson: *Music in Aztec and Inca Territory* (Berkeley, 1968).

JOHN M. SCHECHTER

Huisorgel (Dutch). CHAMBER ORGAN.

Hujia. Central Asian precursor of the Chinese oboe GUAN.

Hültze glechter. An obsolete German term for the XYLOPHONE.

Hulu sheng. Mouth organ of the Yi people of southwest China. *See* SHENG.

Humle. *See* HOMMEL.

Hümmelchen (Ger.). A term used by Praetorius (*Syntagma musicum*, 2/1619) for a bagpipe with one chanter and two drones; *see* BAGPIPE, §7 (ii), esp. fig.12.

Hummer. Old English term for a FRICTION DRUM with whirling stick (*see* MEMBRANOPHONE for the Hornbostel–Sachs definition of the type).

Humming top [whistling top] (Fr. *toupie bourdonnante*; Ger. *Brummkreisel*). A rotating AEROPHONE. Humming tops, which embody reeds that are set in vibration when the top spins, although usually toys for children, are widely used as musical instruments.

Humstrum. An English folk fiddle, now extinct, that resembled a REBEC. The hollowed-out soundbox of the rebec was replaced by a tin canister and the four strings were of wire. Apparently it was last in use in Dorset – see William Barnes's *Poems in the Dorset Dialect*, 1862 – and a specimen exists in the County Museum, Dorchester. Ritson, in 'Observations on the Ancient English Minstrels', *Ancient Songs and Ballads* (1829), wrote of a man playing the humstrum in the streets of London about 1800.

The humstrum is not the same as the 'bladder and string' or BUMBASS, a drone instrument.

FRANCIS W. GALPIN/HOWARD MAYER BROWN

Hun (i). Globular VESSEL FLUTE of Korea, related to the Chinese XUN. It is made of clay and shaped like two-thirds of a large egg, with a blowing-hole at the apex, three finger-holes at the front and two thumb-holes at the back. There is no fixed size but the instrument is small enough to fit easily into cupped hands. It is required to produce the 12 chromatic notes of a single octave; partial holing is necessary for five of the notes. Since the *hun* is made of baked clay, it is difficult to predict how the tuning of any particular example might turn out. The treatise *Akhak kwebŏm* (1493) suggests that a great many *hun* should be made and the correctly tuned ones selected.

Flutes of the hŏn'ga (courtyard ensemble) at the twice-yearly Sacrifice to Confucius, Seoul, Korea: hun (globular flute; back), yak (notched flute; middle) and chŏk (notched flute; front)

Among the instruments given to Korea by the Chinese emperor in 1114 and 1116 were 72 *hun*, and the Korean performing tradition appears to date from that time. *Hun* were first constructed in Korea in the 15th century and used in the ritual music (*aak*). Today the instrument is considered purely Chinese and used only in the musical ensembles at the twice-yearly Sacrifice to Confucius in Seoul (see illustration). At the end of each note of the very slow melody the performer executes an upwards glissando.

BIBLIOGRAPHY
Sŏng Hyŏn, ed.: *Akhak kwebŏm* [Guide to the study of music] (Seoul, 1493/*R*1975), 6.18*b*–19*a*
Chang Sa-hun: *Han'guk akki taegwan* [Korean musical instruments] (Seoul, 1969), 53f

ROBERT C. PROVINE

Hun (ii). Collective name for four different sizes of drum in the ensemble of the Afro-Cuban Arará cult. Museum specimens are elaborately carved or painted, and range from approximately cylindrical drums, slightly tapered at the base, to instruments with wide bodies ending in a base with a small opening. Their names, in descending order of size, are *hugán*, *xumpé*, *hun-hogúlo* and *huní*. A mallet-shaped or hooked stick is used for the largest drum; it is occasionally struck on the body of the drum above the pegs. See H. Courlander: 'Musical Instruments of Cuba', *MQ*, xxviii (1942), 227.

JOHN M. SCHECHTER

Hūn. Idioglot bamboo JEW'S HARP of Laos and north-eastern Thailand.

Hungo. Braced gourd-resonated MUSICAL BOW of the Lenge people of Mozambique. See H. Balfour: *The Natural History of the Musical Bow* (Oxford, 1899), fig.15.

Hun-hogúlo [huní]. Afro-Cuban drums. *See* HUN (ii).

Hunt, Richard (*d* ?London, 1683). English instrument maker, music dealer and publisher. He worked in London at the Sign of the Lute in St Paul's Churchyard, where his customers included the diarist Samuel Pepys. References to Hunt are found in Pepys's diary between October 1661, when he converted Pepys's lute to a theorbo with double strings, and August 1664, when he sold Pepys a lute for his servant to learn on. After he retired from making instruments Hunt turned to publishing (see C. Humphries and W. C. Smith: *Music Publishing in the British Isles* (London, 1954, rev. 2/1970), and *Grove 6*).

Hunting horn (Fr. *cor de chasse, huchet, trompe de chasse*; Ger. *Jagdhorn, Waldhorn*; It. *corno da caccia*). *see* HORN.

Hupep. Idioglot bamboo clarinet of the Ifugao people of the northern Philippines. It is about 7 mm in diameter and 24 cm long. Near the blowing end a narrow strip of the outer shell is carefully thinned to act as a reed.

Hupfeld. German firm of instrument makers. Active in Leipzig, it is noted for having introduced various types of PLAYER PIANO in the early 20th century. For illustration of the firm's 'Phono-Liszt-Violina', a mechanical violin, *see* MECHANICAL INSTRUMENT, fig.9.

Huqin [hu-ch'in]. General term for Chinese chordophones. *See* ERHU and JINGHU.

Hurdy-gurdy [organistrum] (Fr. *vielle à roue, chifonie, symphonie*; Ger. *Leier, Drehleier, Bauernleier, Bettlerleier, Radleier*; It. *lyra tedesca, ghironda, sambuca, rotata, sinfonia*; Lat. *symphonia*). A mechanically bowed chordophone with three basic elements: a set of melody and drone (or bourdon) strings, a resin-coated wooden wheel which when made to rotate by a crank acts as a bow, and a keyboard with tangents that bear on the melody string or strings when depressed. Its origin remains unclear: source material provides no specific proof that the instrument was used in the East before its appearance in Europe. With its ability to sound two or more notes simultaneously while producing a continuous drone, it became widespread during the Middle Ages in many social contexts, both religious and secular.

During the Gothic period a large hurdy-gurdy (*organistrum*) was used in many cloisters and monastic schools to teach music, perform religious polyphony and provide correct intonation for singers. Indeed, the name 'organistrum' was probably derived from 'organum', meaning in its broadest sense an instrument on which several parts could be rendered simultaneously. It was not represented in art before the 12th century, when the *organistrum* was depicted, among other places, in sculpture over the portico of the cathedral of Santiago de Compostela (see fig.1) and on a capital at St Georges-de-Bocherville; it was shown as fiddle-shaped, between 1·5 and 2 metres long, and set horizontally across the two players' laps. One man operated the tangents while the other turned the crank, making the three strings sound simultaneously. The first undisputed description of an *organistrum* is in a 13th-century treatise, *Quomodo organistrum construatur* ('How an organistrum should be constructed'), previously attributed to Odo (9th or 10th century), where it is characterized as having its eight tangents positioned according to Pythagorean principles, providing a diatonic octave (with B♭ as well as B) from C. The outer drone or bourdon strings were tuned an octave apart, and the centre melody string a 4th or 5th below the highest drone.

The most important role of the hurdy-gurdy was its function in secular music. During the 13th century the instrument was completely altered into a much smaller, portable device known as a *chifonie* (Fr.) or *symphonia* (Lat.), played by a single musician (see fig.2). The term 'symphonia' probably came from contemporary music theory, having been used originally to describe consonance or simultaneity of sounds. As with all instruments during the Middle Ages, the hurdy-gurdy was classified by its sonority and was grouped with the soft, or *bas* instruments. Many literary references from this period show that it was found among the other string instruments, usually paired with the plucked varieties. Sometimes it was associated with bourdon instruments such as the vielle (a medieval fiddle).

The hurdy-gurdy was used to accompany *chansons de geste* with instrumental preludes and interludes and, when appropriate, to double the vocal line at the unison or octave. However, another 200 years elapsed before it left the cloister altogether and became firmly established as a minstrel instrument. Its spread was facilitated by the wandering players who found employment in increasing numbers as court and town life flourished and the church began to accept their participation in religious processions and similar events. In this way the hurdy-gurdy insinuated itself into every level of Western society from palace to village green. It was used as a melodic instrument in dance music, especially during festivities and church holidays; it was found in the 'orchestra' at mystery plays; it was played by pilgrims and above all by itinerant minstrels, peasants, beggars and blind musicians.

The hurdy-gurdy's fortunes have fluctuated not only

1. Organistrum (hurdy-gurdy) in fiddle shape, with two players: detail of relief (12th century) on the portico of the 'Puerta de la Gloria' of the cathedral of Santiago de Compostela, Spain

2. Chifonie or symphonia (hurdy-gurdy): miniature from the Luttrell Psalter, English, 14th century (GB-Lbm Add.42130, f.176r)

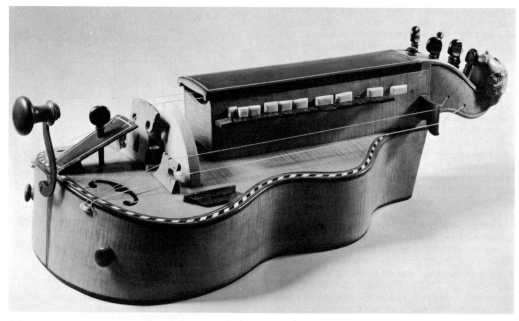

(a)

(b)

3. (a) Hurdy-gurdy by Henry Thouvenel, Mirecourt, France, 18th century (Metropolitan Museum of Art, New York); (b) with tangent box open

the French aristocracy during the 18th century, when rusticity and the pastoral idea were in vogue. Disguised as shepherds and shepherdesses, they played the instrument at the *fêtes champêtres* at Versailles (see fig.5, p.264). In 1731–3 the hurdy-gurdy was featured with orchestral accompaniment at the Concert Spirituel in Paris. (Numerous ladies and gentlemen at court played not only this instrument but the small bagpipes, or musette, as well.) Contemporary writers struggled valiantly to find a classical and 'respectable' origin for the instrument, or else wrapped it up in mythology. This renewed interest led to the production of a musical repertory of sorts. For example, Haydn wrote concertos for two 'lire organizzate', strings and horns (HVII*h*:1–5), and Mozart included the hurdy-gurdy in a set of minuets (K601) and four German dances (K602). (The LIRA ORGANIZZATA, a hurdy-gurdy with one or two ranks of organ pipes and bellows housed in its body, enjoyed a brief vogue during the late 18th century, particularly in France.) In addition, many transcriptions and arrangements were made from music for other instruments, usually unidentified operas and ballets. One particularly active composer was Nicolas Chédeville, who adapted (among other works) Vivaldi's 'Four Seasons' for hurdy-gurdy, violin, flute and basso continuo. Donizetti used the hurdy-gurdy to accompany two arias in his opera *Linda di Chamounix* (1842).

Usually the hurdy-gurdy was shaped rather like a viol, and its strings passed through the box that housed the tangents (see fig.3). Instruments with strings arranged in that way continued to be made in Portugal until the 18th century, furnished with three rows of tangents that indicated there were three melody strings and one drone. It became more common for the drone strings to be

with partiality or distaste for its rather rasping sound, but also with attitudes towards dance-type instruments generally and the player's social position. For example, Mersenne in his *Harmonie universelle* (1636–7) referred to the ignoble nature of the instrument in the hands of beggars and blind musicians. Paintings by Brueghel and Bosch also reflect the negative symbolic value imputed to the hurdy-gurdy. However, the tenacity of the hurdy-gurdy as a folk instrument made it ripe for adoption by

deflected to either side of the bridge, however, and the instrument was found throughout most of Europe in this form. In the 17th century the French increased the number of strings to six (two melody, four drones) and the compass to two chromatic octaves. Some of these instruments possessed a remarkable beauty, inlaid with pearl and surmounted by a carved head. Those by Pierre and Jean Louvet (c1750) were particularly fine examples, shaped like either a lute or a guitar. Such performers as HENRI BÂTON and his son CHARLES BÂTON also made notable modifications to the construction of the instrument in the early to mid-18th century.

The hurdy-gurdy is hung around the neck or strapped to the body at such an angle as to allow the keys to fall back under their own weight. The bridges and tailpiece are usually glued in position. The tangents can be swivelled around for tuning purposes. The wheel is usually of pearwood, continually shaved to keep it true, and coated with resin. Cotton wool is spun around the strings where they contact the wheel in order to soften the sound and encourage the drone strings to speak. The French hurdy-gurdy plays in either the key of C or G, but the two melody strings are always tuned to g'. The four drone strings (*gros bourdon*, *bourdon*, *mouche* and *trompette*) pass over small subsidiary bridges to the right

and left of the main bridge (see fig.3*b*). The two larger drones are overspun; the *gros bourdon* sounds G an octave below the *mouche* and is used only when playing in that key, whereas the *bourdon* sounds the intermediate c and is employed when playing in the key of C. The *trompette*, tuned either to c' or d' according to key, causes its bridge to tremble like that of a trumpet marine: by fine adjustment from a peg in the tailpiece a leg extending down to the instrument's belly is encouraged to rattle continually against it. By minute interruptions of the wheel's rotation a clearly articulated rhythm can be produced without disturbing the melody. The left hand, at the keyboard, can play staccato, as well as performing all manner of grace notes.

Variants of the hurdy-gurdy include the *Schlüsselfiedel*, which is played with an ordinary bow in place of the revolving wheel and has survived in Sweden under the name *Nyckelfidl* or NYCKELHARPA. In another form the hurdy-gurdy was fingered like a violin (i.e. having no tangent keyboard); such an instrument (called a *Bauern Lyren*) and the *Schlüsselfiedel* were illustrated in Praetorius's *Syntagma musicum* (2/1619). Some instruments were based on a more conventional keyboard: Leonardo da Vinci's *viola organista* was designed as a keyboard instrument the strings of which would be set

4. Hurdy-gurdy player: painting by Georges de La Tour (1593–1652) in the Musée des Beaux-Arts, Nantes

5. Hurdy-gurdy accompanying dancers: detail from 'The Country Dancing Lesson' by Nicolas Lancret (1690–1743)

in vibration by an endless friction band; Hans Haiden's GEIGENWERK (also illustrated by Praetorius) had many parchment-covered wheels turning at once and metal strings pulled down onto the wheels by means of a keyboard. 20th-century applications of the hurdy-gurdy principle include Luigi Russolo's INTONARUMORI, in which a wheel rotated against a string whose tension was controlled by a pitch lever; the RADIOTONE, a monophonic keyboard instrument using a movable wheel on a single string to give a three-octave range; and several large keyboard instruments with one or two strings bowed by treadle-operated rosined wheels, constructed by BOB BATES.

The following hurdy-gurdies are entered in this dictionary: hjulgiga; lira organizzata; lirepilk; perwg; ratukinė lyra; sanfona (i); tererő; vevlira; vierelète.

BIBLIOGRAPHY
E. de Bricqueville: *Notice sur la vielle* (Paris, 1911)
H. Panum: *Middelalderen Strengeinstrumenter* (Copenhagen, 1915–31; Eng. trans., 1941)
C. Sachs: *Handbuch der Musikinstrumentenkunde* (Leipzig, 2/1930)
F. W. Galpin: *A Textbook of European Musical Instruments* (London, 1937)
W. Bachmann: *Die Anfänge des Streichinstrumentenspiels* (Leipzig, 1964; Eng. trans., 1969 as *The Origins of Bowing and the Development of Bowed Instruments up to the 13th Century*)
F. Ll. Harrison and J. Rimmer: *European Musical Instruments* (London, 1964)
F. W. Galpin: *Old English Instruments of Music* (London, rev. 4/1965 by T. Dart)
E. Veiga de Oliveira: *Instrumentos musicais populares portugueses* (Lisbon, 1966)
B. Sarosi: *Die Volksmusikinstrumente Ungarns* (Leipzig, 1967)
A. Buchner: *Folkmusic Instruments of the World* (London, 1971)
M. Bröcker: *Die Drehleier: ihr Bau und ihre Geschichte* (Düsseldorf 1973, enlarged 2/1977)
H. Zeraschi: *Drehorgeln* (Leipzig, 1976)
FRANCIS BAINES, EDMUND A. BOWLES

Huruk [hurkī, hurko]. Variable tension HOURGLASS DRUM of northern India. *See* HUDUKKĀ.

Husla [husle]. A bowed instrument played by the Wends or Sorbs of eastern Germany and Slavonic countries. In general outline it resembles a medieval fiddle (from which type it is derived), the bouts being less pronounced than on the violin. The back is flat, the belly curved and the ribs of uneven depth. The soundholes consist of a rose by the fingerboard, and two narrow rectangular holes near the curved bridge. The short neck ends in a flat pegholder into which the pegs are set from behind. The tailpiece is long. The instrument is held across the chest and supported by a strap, as were certain fiddles in that part of Europe during the Middle Ages. The traditional tuning is $d'–a'–e''$.

By the early 20th century the greater potentialities of the violin had made the *husla* almost extinct, and in 1923 there remained only one master of the old tradition, Jan Kusík (whose portrait, by Ludvík Kuba, is in the National Museum at Prague). Through his efforts, and those of the clockmaker J. Mencl (Menzel), the instrument managed to survive, and since 1950 it has

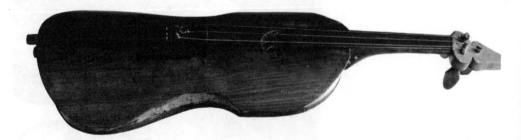

Husla, 19th century (Musikhistorisk Museum, Copenhagen)

:quired a new lease of life, as a result of the revival ' interest in folk culture of eastern Europe.

BIBLIOGRAPHY

Kinsky: *Katalog, Musikhistorisches Museums von Wilhelm Hey-er in Cöln*, i–ii, iv (Cologne, 1910–16)

Hammerich: *Das Musikhistorische Museum zu Kopenhagen: Beschreibender Katalog* (Copenhagen, 1911), 102f

. Sachs: *Real-Lexikon der Musikinstrumente* (Berlin, 1913, rev. 2/1964), 193

. Bessaraboff: *Ancient European Musical Instruments* (New York, 1941, 2/1964), 254

. Buchner: *Hudební nástroje od pravěku k dnešku* [Musical Instruments through the Ages] (Prague, 1956; Eng. trans., 1956, 4/1962), pl.315 [portrait by Ludvík Kuba of Jan Kusík playing the *husla*]

Kunz: 'Die Bauernfiedeln', *Zwischen Kunstgeschichte und Volkskunde: Festschrift für Wilhelm Fraenger* (Berlin, 1960), 145

Raupp: *Sorbische Volksmusikanten und Musikinstrumente*, Schriftenreihe des Instituts für sorbische Volksforschung in Bautzen bei der Deutschen Akademie der Wissenschaften zu Berlin, xvii (Bautzen, 1963), 191ff

. Bachmann: *Die Anfänge des Streichinstrumentenspiels* (Leipzig, 1964), 104; Eng. trans. (1969), 89

. D. Boyden: *The History of Violin Playing* (London, 1965), 9

Raupp: *Sorbische Musik* (Bautzen, 1966)

MARY REMNANT

usson. The name of several French bow makers. A laude-Charles Husson (1811–93) was one of the unding members of the firm Jérôme Thibouville-Lamy : Cie; he should not be confused with Charles Claude usson (i), a mid-19th-century maker whose precise dates nd early background remain obscure. Noted as the acher of Alfred Lamy and J. A. Vigneron, Charles laude Husson (i) made bows that foreshadow the Lamy yle but possess an elasticity which is reminiscent of ie early Parisian makers. They are characterized by ncircled mother-of-pearl dots inlaid in the sides of the ogs and by banded buttons.

His son and pupil Charles Claude Husson (ii) (1847–915) continued his apprenticeship with J.-B. Vuil-ume and A. J. Lamy. In 1878 he joined the workshop f Gand & Bernardel in Paris and some years later set p in Paris independently. His bows resemble his father's ut are not as finely made and are generally heavier in uild; distinguishing features include silver-capped but-ms and circled mother-of-pearl dots on the frogs. Fath-r and son have virtually identical brands, CH. HUSSON À ARIS.

August Husson (1870–1930), no relation of the above, orked for Vuillaume, Bazin, Thomassin and Vigneron efore setting up independently in Paris. His bows, of ood material and well executed, are patterned along ie lines of Vigneron's, as evidenced particularly in the ello bows. His bows are stamped A. HUSSON-PARIS.

BIBLIOGRAPHY

. Vannes: *Essai d'un dictionnaire universel des luthiers* (Paris, 1932, 2/1951/R1972 as *Dictionnaire universel des luthiers*, and R1981 incl. suppl. 1959)

. Roda: *Bows for Musical Instruments of the Violin Family* (Chicago, 1959)

. Vatelot: *Les archets français* (Nancy, 1976)

JAAK LIIVOJA-LORIUS

lutamba. HOURGLASS DRUM of the Limba people of Sierra Leone. *See* TAMA.

lutchings, George Sherburn (*b* Salem, Mass., 9 Dec 835; *d* Cambridge, Mass., 1 June 1913). American rgan builder. Trained as a carpenter, Hutchings entered ne Hook firm of Boston in 1857 as a case maker, and vas soon appointed foreman of his department. In 1861

he took a two-year leave of absence to serve in the Union Army, and shortly after his return was appointed factory superintendent. In 1869, with fellow employees from Hook (Mark Plaisted, G. V. Nordstrom and C. H. Preston), he formed the J. H. Willcox Co., named after its chief financial backer, a prominent organist and design consultant. A reorganization in 1872 resulted in a change of name to Hutchings, Plaisted & Co., and with Plaisted's withdrawal in 1883 Hutchings carried on under his own name. He was an astute businessman, a good mechanic and a leader in the growing trend towards the Romantic style in organ building, with the result that by the 1890s the volume of his firm's work vied with that of the older Hook & Hastings Co. In 1901 the firm reorganized under the name of the Hutchings–Votey Organ Co., and a large new factory was built. Following this, various business difficulties caused a gradual decline, and the company failed entirely in 1919. Some of their large and important instruments include those in the Mission Church, Boston (1898), and Woolsey Hall, New Haven (1903).

BIBLIOGRAPHY

O. Ochse: *The History of the Organ in the United States* (Bloomington, Ind., 1975)

B. Owen: *The Organ in New England* (Raleigh, North Carolina, 1979)

BARBARA OWEN

Hüttenrauch, Karl August (*b* Lichtenstein, nr. Zwickau, 21 March 1794; *d* Glauchau, 26 Feb 1848). German organ builder. He came from a family of Kantors and scholars in Waldenburg (Saxony) of which five members were enrolled at Leipzig University between the years 1716 and 1779. He lived in Oberlungwitz from about 1800, when his father became pastor there. He learnt organ building in Lichtenwalde from Johann Christian Günther, who in 1803–4 had built the new organ for St Martin in Oberlungwitz. He also studied mechanics and mathematics at the academy in Budapest and worked abroad for several years. From 1816 he again lived in Oberlungwitz, then moved to Glauchau, where he obtained citizenship on 24 November 1823. Hüttenrauch was a master organ builder, conscientious and skilled, who constructed excellent register combinations and tasteful façades. In the specification for his 1821–2 organ at Oberwiera an inclination towards a newer concept of tone is evident, in that the Hauptmanual, of solemn, rather broad scaling, was contrasted with an Oberwerk of rather narrower string-like scaling. The organ at Waldenburg (Lutherkirche, 1822–4; two manuals and pedal, 22 speaking stops, manual and pedal couplers), a valuable specimen of its type, has a light, silvery and yet strong and clear tone, with a suggestion of a pleasantly warmer timbre. Hüttenrauch also built pianofortes.

BIBLIOGRAPHY

C. G. Dietmann: *Kirchen- und Schulen-Geschichte der Hochreichsgräflich Schönburgschen Länder in Meissen* (Breslau, Brieg and Leipzig, 1787)

F. Krummacher: 'Zur Sammlung Jacobi der ehemaligen Fürstenschule Grimma', *Mf*, xvi (1963), 324

WALTER HÜTTEL

Hwa. Obsolete 13-pipe mouth organ of Korea. *See* SAENGHWANG.

Hyangbal. Historical name for small cymbals of Korea. *See* CHABARA.

Hyang-pip'a. Obsolete plucked lute of Korea. *See* PIPA (i), §2.

Hyang-p'iri. Cylindrical oboe of Korea. *See* P'IRI.

Hydraulic organ. *See* WATER ORGAN.

Hydraulis (from Gk. *hydōr*: 'water' and *aulos*: 'pipe'). The ancient pneumatic organ, in which water was used to control the wind pressure; it is an important musical instrument of later classical antiquity and the direct ancestor of the modern pipe organ. (It should not be confused with the WATER ORGAN, or hydraulic organ, an automatic organ without bellows, blown by air that is compressed by water.)

1. Invention. 2. Description. 3. History.

1. INVENTION. Ancient Greek writers on music, for example Athenaeus, Pseudo-Plutarch and Pseudo-Aristotle, very often named the inventors of musical instruments; these inventors, however, are generally mythical figures or men who long postdate the instrument's first appearance. The inventor of the hydraulis is a significant exception. All the evidence suggests that the instrument was invented by Ctesibius, a famous Alexandrian engineer who lived in the 3rd century BC and who was less remarkable for his theoretical ability than for his highly ingenious solutions to practical problems. He was the first to use air pressure to operate mechanical devices, in particular the pump with plunger and valve, the water clock, the pneumatic catapult and the hydraulis. He described his work in the *Commentaries*, a book frequently cited in classical times (for example by Vitruvius and Pliny the Elder) but not now extant.

The invention of the hydraulis was first attributed to Ctesibius by Philo of Byzantium, an engineer of the late 3rd century BC, who if not actually his pupil was much under his influence. He described the hydraulis as a 'syrinx played by the hands'. Vitruvius, the famous technical writer of the 1st century AD, also attributed the hydraulis to him and gave one of the two extant descriptions of the instrument. The other is by Hero of Alexandria, a mathematician and engineer of the later 1st century AD; although Hero did not explicitly mention Ctesibius, he is generally believed by both ancient and modern authors to have been dependent upon him when he described pneumatic devices.

Taking into account these facts and the absence of any references to the hydraulis pre-dating Ctesibius, there is strong evidence for supposing him to be the instrument's originator. Moreover, it is particularly plausible that the hydraulis should have been the invention of a single individual and should have originated in Alexandria at that time. It was not, as Curt Sachs has suggested, simply the union of a panpipe with a new wind mechanism, since it also included a highly sophisticated wind chest and keyboard. It did not, then, have the elemental evolutionary origin of most ancient musical instruments. It is a complex machine involving more new elements than old, and therefore precisely the kind of invention one might expect from the 3rd-century Alexandria of Euclid, Eratosthenes, Archimedes and Ctesibius. Accordingly it was first looked upon more as a mechanical marvel than a musical instrument.

2. DESCRIPTION. Approximately 40 representations of the hydraulis survive, in rough outline, in mosaics (see fig.1), vases, coins and sculptures. Its height from base to the top of its pipes was about 165 cm. The base itself, often octagonal in shape, was about 30 cm high and 90 cm in diameter; on this was a brass cistern which appears to have been covered with decorated wood. The cistern might be cylindrical, octagonal or rectangular in shape and was from 60 cm to 90 cm in height with a diameter somewhat less than that of the pedestal; usually it was flanked by a pair of cylindrical pumps. Resting on it was the rectangular wind chest approximating to the base in size. Finally there were the pipes whose overall height represented from a third to half the total height of the instrument. The number of pipes appearing in a rank ranged from four or five to 18, approximately eight being the average. There were no more than four ranks. Normally only the front of the instrument was shown, with the organist looking out over the pipes. On the exceptional three dimensional views such as that on the Carthaginian lamp, he is seen seated at a keyboard which extends from the wind chest (*see* ORGAN, fig.24).

There are two complementary descriptions of the precise functioning of the organ, that of Vitruvius (*De architectura*, x, chap.8, §§3–6) and that of Hero of Alexandria (*Pneumatica*, i, chap.42). Vitruvius, writing in the early 1st century AD, included developments such as the use of two pumps rather than one and of a wind chest allowing ranks of pipes to be played separately. Hero, although writing later in the same century described the original somewhat simpler instrument of Ctesibius. The description that follows is a composite of the two; it deals first with the wind-producing mechanism and then with the keyboard and wind chest.

It is from the wind-producing mechanism that the instrument derives its name 'hydraulis', since Ctesibius used the tendency of water to seek its own level to supply a steady flow of air as opposed to the ebb and flow produced by bellows. Fig.2 shows a pump-handle A

1. Hydraulis and cornu players; from a Roman mosaic (AD 230–240) at Nennig bei Trier

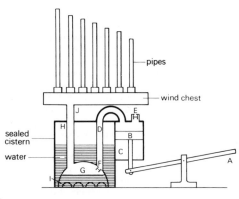

2. The wind-producing mechanism of the hydraulis

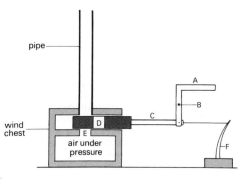

3. The key mechanism of the hydraulis

of Jean Perrot, indicate that the difficulties become insuperable with more than four ranks, a conclusion confirmed by ancient iconographic and archaeological evidence. Vitruvius, using the terms tetrachordal, hexachordal and octochordal, was evidently indulging in a kind of theoretical symmetry.

Vitruvius and Hero were technical writers who limited their descriptions to the mechanical aspects of the instrument; they thus force speculation on the most basic musical considerations. Two in particular demand attention: timbre and pitch.

The central question concerning timbre is whether the hydraulis had not only flue pipes but also reeds (as several organologists have maintained). On the positive side is the name of the instrument, from the two Greek words 'hydōr' ('water') and 'aulos' ('pipe'). There are also literary references to the instrument's widely differing tone quality, at one time sweet and at another thunderous. Organologists have tended to associate the latter quality with reed pipes.

On the other hand, surviving representations do not at all suggest reed pipes. The absence of anything resembling the bulbous *holmos* of the aulos which houses the reeds is particularly noteworthy. Also very much to the point is Walcker-Mayer's reconstruction of the Aquincum organ's pipes with the same kinds of metal as were used in the original pipes. The organ has four ranks, all of flue pipes, three being closed and one open. He found both open and closed to be entirely unlike any modern pipes in timbre, the open being particularly harsh and shrill and the closed being only somewhat less harsh with a kind of throaty rattle. In summary, the case for reed pipes has yet to be proven, and it is seriously anachronistic to assume that the variety of tone suggested by the literary sources takes the form of a contrast between, for example, a sweet flue Gedackt and a thunderous reed Cornopean.

The question of pitch and its corollary, tonality, is even more difficult than that of timbre. Archaeological remains might be expected to lead to firm conclusions. Nevertheless the two modern scholars, Walcker-Mayer and Perrot, who have studied the pipes of the Aquincum organ, differ radically, the former maintaining that the instrument was diatonic, the latter that it was chromatic.

The study of pictorial evidence is similarly inconclusive. The method normally employed is to measure the longest pipe and the shortest, thus determining the instrument's range, and then after counting the number of pipes, to fill in the intermediate pitches and establish the tonality. Behind this method lies the fallacious assumption that each representation was a precisely scaled depiction of a particular instrument rather than a conventional schematization. Possibly the most serious specific problem is created by the angle of the slanting line described by the tops of the pipes. It is always a straight line; if the artists had been attempting realistic depictions, the line, while not describing the parabolic curve of the equal-tempered scale, would necessarily have described something other than a straight line. Moreover, it requires only a minor variation in the angle, in the length of the pipes or in the number of pipes to change the presumed tonality from one genus to another. This is particularly true if the organologist grants himself the liberty of deciding whether conjunct or disjunct tetrachords are involved.

Possibly the least valuable evidence for determining pitch is that of the theoretical sources: a wide gap sepa-

operating the plunger B within the cylinder C and forcing air into the conduit D. The valve E allows air to enter the cylinder when the plunger is depressed and prevents it from escaping when the plunger is raised; the valve F prevents air from returning to the cylinder when the plunger is depressed. The air then entering the *pigneus* G forces the water level in the cistern H upward, since the water has access to the *pigneus* by apertures at its base. While the plunger is being depressed in preparation for the next stroke the weight of the receding water maintains air pressure in the *pigneus* and consequently a steady flow through the conduit J to the wind chest.

Fig.3 shows how the air once reaching the wind chest is distributed to the pipes. The finger depresses key A which, pivoting on point B, pushes slider C along a track in the chest until hole D is in alignment with the bottom of the pipe and hole E, thus allowing the compressed air within the wind chest to enter the pipe. When the player lifts his finger from the key, spring F returns the slider to its original position.

Vitruvius described the chest with four, six or eight channels, each running beneath a separate rank of pipes, and being opened or closed by a stopcock fitted with an iron handle. This stop action is very simple in conception, being nothing more than a division of the wind chest into separate compartments. However, it creates serious practical difficulties, particularly for the slider, which is subject to an increase in both friction and the leakage of air. Modern experiments, particularly those

rates the theory of late antiquity (with its mathematical bias) from musical practice. But even ignoring this gap and taking the sources literally, as several historians of the organ have done, leads to unsatisfactory conclusions. The conventional starting point is the assertion of the Bellermann Anonymous that the hydraulis plays in no tropes but the Hyperlydian, Hyperastian, Lydian, Phrygian, Hypolydian and Hypophrygian. Theorists such as Alypius indicate that the precise meaning of these tropes results in a hydraulis capable of playing more than 30 notes. In attempting to reconcile this with the relatively simple instrument of pictorial evidence organologists have tended to opt for either of two unsatisfactory alternatives. According to one of them, each organ was tuned in only one trope; thus there were Hyperlydian organs, Hyperastian organs, etc. According to the other, each rank represented a different trope; in this case an instrument must have been confined to four of the six desired tropes, resulting in an uneconomical duplication of pitch and the preclusion of the mixture or register principle.

It seems, in summary, that the state of the evidence allows only the most general conclusions. Pictorial evidence indicates a relatively high tessitura for the pipes and a relatively small compass for each rank; literary sources indicate substantial versatility in dynamics if not timbre. A similar situation of uncertainty, therefore, prevails as with other ancient instruments, the one difference being the remarkably precise knowledge gained from Vitruvius and Hero of the hydraulis's mechanical functioning.

It is not certain whether the hydraulis could play polyphonic music; on the negative side is the generally nonpolyphonic character of Greco-Roman music, but on the positive side is the instrument's technical capacity. All literary, pictorial and archaeological evidence indicates that the keys were depressed by the fingers, and with relative facility, thus creating obvious polyphonic possibilities for the two hands of the organist. Yet to what extent such possibilities were exploited or in what musical direction they tended (for example, drones, parallelisms) is not known.

3. HISTORY. Although the hydraulis was at first viewed as a marvel of mechanical ingenuity, its musical potential was realized in a relatively short time. The claim of Athenaeus that Ctesibius's wife Thais was the first organist has an apocryphal air about it, but there is no reason to doubt a Delphic inscription which describes the success of the hydraulis player Antipatros in the *agones* of 90 BC.

Texts mentioning the hydraulis, particularly at Rome, multiplied during the following centuries. Suetonius wrote of Nero's infatuation with the instrument; the *Aetna* poem placed it in the theatre and Petronius referred to its accompanying of chariot fights in the arena.

There are approximately 50 known literary references to the instrument and rather fewer pictorial representations of it. The impression they create is of an instrument in fairly general usage, if not so common as the smaller and presumably less expensive kithara and tibia. Both at Rome and in the provinces it was found in the homes of the wealthy, the theatre and the arena, this last setting being the most characteristic, particularly in pictures, where it is shown sometimes alone but more often playing with brass instruments like the CORNU and TUBA (ii); *see* ORGAN, fig.21.

Another type of hydraulis, replacing Ctesibius' hydraulic pump with bellows, was at first less prominent than the hydraulis proper. Bellows had been in use long before the invention of the hydraulis, but were not practical for musical purposes because they could supply only intermittent air pressure. However, it seems to have been simple to adapt Ctesibius's principles by replacing the cistern with a flexible leather reservoir weighted on top, fitted with valves to prevent the escape of air and fed by one or more bellows. This device had the advantages of being lighter in weight, cheaper and less liable to corrosion.

The earliest extant reference to the instrument is from Pollux, the rhetorician of the 2nd century AD, who described it as smaller and less powerful than the hydraulis. The Aquincum organ, with its dedicatory plate from 228 AD, was probably of this type, since there is no trace of a bronze cistern and *pigneus* associated with the substantially preserved pipes and wind chest (*see* ORGAN, fig.23). Julian the Apostate (332–63) seems to be describing it when in his poetic description of an organ he mentioned a bag of bull-hide feeding the pipes as is the case with the 5th-century bishop Theodoret of Cyrrhus, who compared the bellows of the organ to the human lungs.

These texts suggest that the more practical pneumatic organ, which could be readily portable, came to replace the hydraulis in the Eastern Empire during late classical times. Meanwhile the hydraulis disappeared in the West with the collapse of the Western Empire in the 5th and 6th centuries. The pneumatic organ maintained a place of some prominence in the court at Byzantium and found its way into the West when Emperor Constantine Copronymus in 757 presented a small organ to Pepin the Short.

From that time there began the dramatic development of the Western pipe organ. Pictorial and documentary evidence overwhelmingly demonstrates that it was a pneumatic organ; the hydraulis was mentioned only in confused invocations of the classical past. For example, the 11th-century Berne Anonymous, after a careful description of the bellows organ, stated that the pipes can be made hydraulic by simply placing beneath them a cistern of water, which the air sucks through the pipes causing them to sound. Even after the *De architectura* of Vitruvius was popularized in the Renaissance, an expert like Bédos de Celles was able to believe that the hydraulis was powered by a waterfall and marvelled at the alleged construction by the 10th-century monk Gerbert of a hydraulis in a church in an area where rivers and streams are rare.

The first author to give an accurate description of the instrument may have been the architect Claude Perrault in his *Abregé des dix livres d'architecture de Vitruve* (1673, 2/1684). The general confusion, however, was not dispelled until early in the 20th century by projects such as Galpin's reconstruction (c1900) and Degering's excellent monograph (1905). Jean Perrot and Werner Walcker-Mayer have produced reconstructions of great accuracy.

BIBLIOGRAPHY

H. Degering: *Die Orgel, ihre Erfindung und ihre Geschichte bis zur Karolingerzeit* (Münster, 1905)

F. W. Galpin: *A Textbook of European Musical Instruments* (London, 1937)

W. Apel: 'The Early History of the Organ', *Speculum*, xxiii (1948), 191

H. G. Farmer: 'Hydraulis', *Grove 5*

Perrot: *L'orgue de ses origines hellénistiques* (Paris, 1965; Eng. trans., 1971)

Walcker-Mayer: *Die römische Orgel von Aquincum* (Stuttgart, 1970)

Kaba: *Die römische Orgel von Aquincum* (Budapest, 1976)

JAMES W. Mc KINNON

yegŭm. Two-string SPIKE FIDDLE of Korea. *See* HAE-ᴜM.

ymnerophon (from Gk. *hymnos*: 'song'). A type of ᴏsᴛᴇɴᴇɴᴛᴇ ᴘɪᴀɴᴏ invented by Pierre Riffelsen of ᴏpenhagen in 1814. Lead forks were moved by the ᴇys and brought into contact with a rotating cylinder ᴛed with brass discs. It was praised for its ability to produce flute-, trumpet- or bell-like sounds, depending on how the player applied his fingers to the keys; a special device could also imitate a roll of thunder. *See also* KLAVIZYLINDER.

Hyōboshi. Wooden concussion sticks of Japan. *See* CLAPPERS.

Hyŏn'gŭm. Literary name for the Korean long zither KŎMUN'GO, an abbreviation of the ancient term *hyŏnhakkŭm* ('black crane zither').

Hyōshigi. Wooden percussion idiophone of Japan. *See* KI (i).

I

Iamba malebe. Tin-can rattle of the Kamba people of Machakos district, Kenya.

Ibach. German firm of piano and organ makers. In 1794 Johannes Adolph Ibach (*b* Kluse, nr. Beyenburg [now Barmen], 1766; *d* 1848) founded the firm in Beyenburg and built his first square piano. At about the same time he restored the organ of the monastery at Beyenburg.

In the *Westphälischen Anzeiger* of 14 October 1800 Ibach advertised 'all kinds of fortepianos, including grand pianos of the highest quality and in the finest taste, as well as large and small pipe-organs'. The firm grew and by 1816 he had a workshop in the Alleestrasse, Unterbarmen, producing 40 to 50 instruments annually. Ibach's sons, Carl Rudolph Ibach (1804–63) and Richard Ibach (1813–89), joined the firm in 1834 and 1839 respectively; it subsequently became known as 'Adolph Ibach und Söhne, Orgelbauanstalt und Pianofortefabrik'. Richard took over the organ building part of the firm in 1869, and Carl's son P. A. Rudolf Ibach (1843–92) was left to run the piano department as 'Rud. Ibach Sohn', the title under which the firm has continued. In 1885, after ten years of study abroad, the founder's grandson, Walter Ibach, opened a factory solely for the production of modern uprights. Output was rapidly increased, averaging about 2000 instruments a year by 1900.

The firm developed a reputation for building both high-quality and good medium-class instruments. Tributes to the Ibach piano have come from such composers as Bartók, Schoenberg, Webern and Richard Strauss; the grand played by Wagner right up to the evening before his death is in the Richard-Wagner-Museum, Bayreuth. More than 136,600 pianos had been made by 1980.

BIBLIOGRAPHY
H. Neupert: 'Ibach', *MGG*
J. A. Ibach: '175 Jahre Firma Ibach', *Beiträge zur Heimatkunde der Stadt Schwelm und ihrer Umgebung*, xix (1969)
G. Beer: *Orgelbau Ibach Barmen, 1794–1904* (Cologne, 1975)
C. Ehrlich: *The Piano: a History* (London, 1976)
MARGARET CRANMER

Ibeka. LAMELLAPHONE of the Kalai (Bakelle) people of Gabon.

Ibi. A generic term for drum in Sudanic languages. *See* BI.

Ibid. Generic term for open conical drums of the Ibibio people of Nigeria. The drums are laced with tuning wedges, the lacing being fastened to a central ligature, not to the base. *Ibid* are distinguished according to size: *eka ibid* (large) and *etok ibid* (small). See S. E. Akpa bot: *Ibibio Music in Nigerian Culture* (East Lansing Mich., 1975).

Ibin. Double-headed cylindrical drum of Nigeria. *See* BI.

Ibiturani. Percussion bells of the Kuria people of Kenya. *See* LITUNGU.

Ibuma [iboma]. Large clapperless bell of the Igbo people of Nigeria. *See* ALO.

Icangca. Rattle used by members of the Zionist sect among the Mpondo (Xhosa) people of southern Africa. It is made from metal bottle-tops mounted on wire.

Ichaka [achaka]. (1) Generic term for the gourd vessel rattle of the Igbo people of Nigeria. They may have either internal strikers (seeds, stones, pieces of iron) or a net of external strikers. *See also* OYO.

(2) Conical wicker vessel rattle of the Idoma people of Nigeria. It has a gourd base, and is used in pairs in dance societies, mainly by men.

Ichaoró. *See* CHAGUORÓ.

Ichicha. Large gourd vessel rattle of the Idoma people of Nigeria. It is used by women who have passed the age of child-bearing as the principal instrument in *ichicha* music sung at night before a funeral.

Ichigen-kin. Single-string long zither of Japan (*ichigen*: 'one-string'; *kin*: a zither). It is occasionally called *hankin*. It is about 110 cm long and 10 cm wide. It was modelled on the Chinese QIN but has a large vertical tuning-peg at the (player's) left end. The player touches the silk string lightly with a diagonally truncated bamboo or ivory tube worn on the left middle finger, and plucks the string with a shorter, similarly truncated tube worn on the right index finger. The left-hand cylinder makes possible the delicate portamento found frequently in the music of the *ichigen-kin*. Under the string are inlaid 12 position markers (unlike the *qin*, however, harmonics are not used). The instrument is set on a low stand, about 25 cm from the ground.

The body of the earliest version consisted of a single

270

oard, slightly convex around its longitudinal axis, whose ides were indented as on the *qin*. Later, the construcion followed the *qin* much more closely, with a ollowed-out body and a flat backboard. A distinctive eature is that the backboard extends further than the ace of the instrument to the player's left; the tuning-eg rests on this platform. The string passes over a ounded bridge at the player's right but is attached directly o the tuning-peg without passing over a nut. There may e seven or more decorative tassels hanging from the nstrument and its stand.

In spite of various legends concerning possible ancient rigins (one resulting in the alternative name *suma-*goto*), the instrument seems to have been invented during the late 17th century. It enjoyed a limited popularity rom about 1750 to 1920 but is rarely heard today. The *chigen-kin*'s repertory consists of self-accompanied songs pecific to the instrument as well as some pieces bor-owed from the koto and shamisen.

ee also NIGEN-KIN.

BIBLIOGRAPHY
. Piggott: *The Music and Musical Instruments of Japan* (London, 1893, 2/1909/R1971), 115
'Ichigen-kin', *Ongaku daijiten* [Encyclopedia of music] (Tokyo, 1981), 92

DAVID W. HUGHES

chi-no-tsuzumi. HOURGLASS DRUM of Japan. *See* IKKO.

cilongo [ixilongo]. End-blown trumpet of the Zulu eople of southern Africa. It consists of a bamboo tube, 0 to 120 cm long, with an ox-horn bell. Use of har-monic partials 3, 4 and 5 is reported. It is played by erdboys and by young men on courting expeditions or when going to a wedding. The name is also applied by he Zulu to any European brass instrument. See KirbyMISA, 81f, pl.30*a*.

cirin. Iron pellet-bells of the Teso people of Uganda, trung together with a rope of waterbuck skin and fas-ened round the ankles or calves of dancers.

combi. End-blown trumpet found in the Buluceke area of Gishu, Uganda. *See* OLWET.

Iconography of music. Panofsky (1939) defined conography simply as 'that branch of the history of art which concerns itself with the subject matter or meaning of works of art, as opposed to their form'. The icon-ography of music, then, is that branch of the history of music which concerns itself with the analysis and interpretation of musical subject matter in works of art. The term 'musical iconography' does not describe the discipline that deals with the meaning or subject matter of music itself, even though studies like those dealing with 18th-century *Affektenlehre*, Schweitzer's interpre-tation of Bach's symbolism, Smend's analysis of Bach's alleged numerological manipulations, Lowinsky's hypothesis concerning a secret chromatic art in the Netherlands motet and Elder's exposition of symbolism in the Flemish music of the Renaissance all deal with music in much the same way that iconographers exam-ine works of art.

1. Scope and history of the study. 2. History of instruments. 3. History of performance. 4. Iconography of composers. 5. Intellec-tual and cultural history.

1. SCOPE AND HISTORY OF THE STUDY. Panofsky isolated three stages in the process of studying a work of art: pre-iconographical description, the process of identify-ing the objects, the events and the expressive qualities in the work, that is, their primary or natural meanings which constitute artistic motifs; iconographical analysis in the narrower sense, the process of connecting motifs and combinations of motifs with stories and allegories, that is, the secondary or conventional subject matter of the work of art; and iconographical interpretation in a deeper sense, the process whereby 'those underlying principles which reveal the basic attitude of a nation, a period, a class, a religious or philosophical persuasion' are revealed, that is, the intrinsic meaning or content of the work of art. A similar series of stages is necessary for a proper evaluation of art as musicological evidence. The musical iconographer cannot be content merely to identify the instruments in a painting, sculpture, minia-ture, print or whatever, nor can he be satisfied merely to describe the performers, the conditions of perfor-mance, or the musical symbols. Only after analysing the subject matter of the work of art, and hence evaluating it as evidence, can he begin to understand what the work of art can reveal about the history of instruments, musi-cal style or performing practice, or about cultural or intellectual history.

Works of art supplement and help to make vivid our knowledge about composers' lives and the milieus in which they worked; they offer concrete evidence about physical details – playing positions, acoustical environ-ments and minutiae of instrumental construction, for example – that other kinds of source seldom reveal; and they help us to understand the role of music in a society, and hence are valuable documents of cultural history. For earlier periods, pictures furnish basic information that cannot be acquired in any other way, since the instruments themselves do not survive, and the written records fail to supply necessary details. Similarly, pic-tures are essential records of performing practice and other aspects of music in oral traditions. Thus for the study of non-Western and folk music, and for many problems in the history of music before 1700, iconog-raphy is a central discipline. And even for the study of 18th-, 19th- and 20th-century music pictures are some-times the only means to answer important questions – about stage settings and concert rooms, operatic cos-tumes and various facets of instrumental performance, for example – and they often help the student to recon-struct imaginatively the milieu in which music was con-ceived. Knowing what composers and their teachers, friends, families, homes and favourite haunts, for instance, actually looked like may not be essential for an understanding of music, but such pictures are useful auxiliary aids in attempting to grasp intuitively the social and intellectual atmosphere in which composers worked.

The value of pictures as musicological evidence has been recognized for some time; there is even a small body of scholarly work that demonstrates exemplary mastery of the discipline, by Valentin Denis, Reinhold Hammerstein, Emanuel Winternitz and various others. In the early part of this century (1905–6), Hugo Leich-tentritt pointed the way in a pioneering article, 'Was lehren uns die Bildwerke des 14.–17. Jahrhunderts über die Instrumentalmusik ihrer Zeit?' In 1930 Eric Blom wrote in the introduction to Georg Kinsky's *History of Music in Pictures* that 'it should one day become pos-sible to see portraits of any musicians, pictures of any instrument and pictorial representations of all sorts of musico-historical events at a moment's notice', and since then scholars and performers have repeatedly pointed out their dependence on pictorial as well as on literary and other non-musical sources in solving problems of performing practice. Gustave Reese, for example, wrote in *Music in the Middle Ages* (1940): 'concerning the manner in which all this music was performed, we have some information, but it is unfortunately scanty. . . . However chary of information the [musical] MSS may be, literary references and artistic representations give numerous hints concerning the instruments upon which a musician might draw'. And Frank Harrison (in *Aspects of Medieval and Renaissance Music*, 1966) stated that:

of the kinds of evidence that exist for our period [1100–1450] – written music, archives and chronicles, iconography and imaginative writing – only the first has as yet been investigated systematically in depth. . . . The written music of any time represents only the top of the iceberg that stands for musical events as a whole. . . . For the centuries under discussion, it is particularly instrumental practice outside the church that belongs to the invisible part of the iceberg. Evidence about it cannot be direct, but indirect evidence may be drawn from comparable practices of the unwritten traditions where they still exist, as well as from documents and depictions properly evaluated.

Musical iconography, then, is as yet a relatively undeveloped field, and one in which most of the major problems remain to be solved. Scholars have agreed that an important preliminary step in encouraging iconographical studies would be to collect and catalogue art works of all kinds that include representations of musical instruments, performances, notation and so on, since conclusions about the common practices of an era must be based on as large a sampling of the sources as possible. This and related topics were discussed, for example, at the congresses of the International Musicological Society in Basle in 1906, at Paris in 1914, and at New York in 1961, and at various meetings of the American Musicological Society since then. At the meeting of the International Association of Music Libraries in St Gall (Switzerland) in August 1971, an organization for the encouragement of iconographical studies, the Répertoire International d'Iconographie Musicale (RIdIM), was established under the sponsorship of the International Musicological Society, the International Association of Music Libraries and the International Council of Museums, with Geneviève Thibault, Harald Heckman and Barry S. Brook as co-presidents. The initial goals of RIdIM are to establish a method of cataloguing and collecting information on iconographical materials, and the setting up of national or regional working committees to explore, collect and catalogue the resources of each participating country.

2. HISTORY OF INSTRUMENTS. Instruments may not be correctly drawn in pictures, and even the most accurate pictures cannot tell certain details of construction, such as the material from which an instrument is made, the size and shape of the bore, the thickness of a soundboard or the tension of a string. Yet despite these inherent deficiencies, works of art are often the best source of information on the history, construction and playing techniques of early instruments. And they often reveal details about later instruments that are difficult to discover in any other way. Conclusions drawn from pictorial evidence can sometimes be corroborated from literary or archival sources; but written records alone often tell us little, because we may not know to which sort of instrument one of the many literary terms applies.

The written sources are ambiguous, instruments from the Middle Ages and the Renaissance are scarce, and those from later times have often been restored in a way that obscures their original form. Thus art works are a major source of information about the musical instruments that were actually in common use at a given place and time, and can show us how the instruments actually looked and how they were played. Paintings have furnished Edwin M. Ripin (1968), for example, with crucial evidence about the history of double-manual harpsichords in early 17th-century Flanders. Without pictorial evidence, Ripin could not have argued that non-transposing double-manual harpsichords existed in the first quarter of the 17th century. And David Boyden (1965) has drawn extensively on iconographical evidence in documenting the early history of the violin and its techniques of performance. In short, works of art can furnish strong evidence that specific instruments were used at a particular time and place, even when that conclusion cannot be corroborated from literary, archival and musical documents.

There are, however, factors which may prevent the evidence offered by art works about the history and construction of instruments from being trusted to represent reality in the artist's own time. On the one hand, an artist's lack of skill or his ignorance of instruments may

1. King David playing the harp: from an 11th-century MS (GB-Ccc 391, p.24)

ve prevented him from depicting them accurately; on
e other, skill and knowledge notwithstanding, he may
ve had no intention of depicting an actual instrument
' his own time. Artists sometimes depicted instruments
ey had in all probability never really seen, because
ey were copying some earlier source or artistic tration, because they were painting a historical scene and
ished to include 'ancient' instruments, or because they
ished to modify or invent instruments for some intel-
ctual or symbolic reason.

As might be expected, medieval artists normally
picted instruments more schematically than later art-
ts. And yet it is not true, as is often assumed, that
edieval art is necessarily less valuable as organolog-
al evidence than that produced later, when art had
come more 'realistic'. By realistic art most of us mean
otographic art – that is, objects drawn in correct per-
ective and modelled in light and shade to look three-
mensional. By valuable organological evidence, we
ean pictures of instruments drawn with accurate pro-
ortion and detail. Three-dimensionality is no more
cessary to their accuracy than it is to an architect's
awing. There are, of course, many medieval pictures
instruments that are schematic and inaccurate. But
ere are also many later examples that are 'realistic'
d inaccurate, one of the best-known examples being
rünewald's 16th-century Isenheim Altar: the three-
mensional angels play recognizable three-dimensional
struments, but both the instruments and the playing
chnique are distorted. Conversely, while modern
strument makers have based reconstructions of instru-
ents on 15th-century paintings by Memling and van
yck, they could also reconstruct instruments from well-
osen earlier pictures such as the harp in an 11th-century
S from Corpus Christi College, Cambridge (fig.1;
own in F. W. Galpin, 1910). The artist's skill, medi-
n, scale and goal have more to do with making a pic-
re organologically valuable than the picture's date.

Even the most schematic representations can tell us
gnificant facts: the kinds of instrument in common use,
r instance, and information on their construction and
e, such as their approximate shapes and how they were
ld and played. Such conclusions must of course be
ased on as broad as possible a sampling of the sources,
d even then accepted with some caution. But there is
least some hope that the histories of most instruments
an eventually be written with the help of iconograph-
al evidence. Emanuel Winternitz's essays (1967) on
e *lira da braccio* and on the survival of the kithara
nd the evolution of the English cittern can serve as
odels of what such research incorporating iconograph-
al evidence can accomplish.

In using pictorial evidence, the musical scholar must
ke care to investigate the possibility that the artist has
epicted an instrument copied from an earlier artistic
urce and not from real life. The 9th-century Utrecht
salter, for instance, itself perhaps based on an earlier
riginal, was copied several times in the 11th and 12th
enturies. Some of the representations of musical instru-
ents were taken over with only minor changes into the
ewer versions, but others show more significant dif-
rences. Thus the value of the pictures as organological
vidence increases greatly when we know that they are
opied, and from what. Similarly, details of many other
rt works are merely copies from earlier works: indis-
riminate reliance on them as evidence of contemporary
ality is unjustified.

2. *King David with a harp or psaltery: miniature from
Alexander Straub's edition (1901) of the 12th-century
MS 'Hortus deliciarum' by Herrad of Landsberg (the
original was destroyed by fire in 1877)*

In the Renaissance some artists painted scenes of
classical antiquity and included in them pseudo-ancient
instruments. The works of both Filippino Lippi and Piero
di Cosimo, for example, abound in examples of musical
instruments which cannot have been in common use in
the 16th century, instruments invariably associated with
neo-classical scenes. Some of them may well be more
or less accurate representations of instruments actually
in use during ancient times, perhaps copied from older
artefacts. Yet often the artists simply invented instruments in neo-classical shapes; many of them could never
have existed for they are absurdly non-functional. And
sometimes painters depicted those imaginatively designed
mock pseudo-ancient instruments that were carried by
actors in theatrical productions of the Renaissance and
that often contained functioning 'modern' instruments
or were playable themselves. Emanuel Winternitz (1967)
discussed the problem of ancient instruments and those
intended for theatrical performances in his essays on
musical archaeology of the Renaissance in Raphael's
Parnassus, and on musical instruments for the stage in
paintings by Filippino Lippi, Piero di Cosimo and Lorenzo Costa.

Some artists may have modified the details of an
instrument's construction for purely intellectual, artistic
or symbolic reasons. For example, the anonymous illu-
minator of Herrad of Landsberg's 12th-century encyclopedia, *Hortus deliciarum*, showed King David carrying
a triangular harp or psaltery with ten courses (fig.2).

Both its shape and the number of its strings may have been determined by the artist's desire to associate David with sacred symbols, the triangle suggesting the Trinity and the number of strings the Ten Commandments, although triangular instruments are not uncommon and medieval psalters refer to ten-stringed instruments. In short, even for the musical scholar who is interested solely in organological evidence, pictorial sources must be used with some caution; each picture must be studied in its artistic and historical context before it can be accepted as an illustration of contemporary reality.

3. HISTORY OF PERFORMANCE. In addition to increasing our knowledge about the history and construction of musical instruments, pictorial sources can also help us to learn how music was performed during earlier times. Pictures can tell us which groupings of instruments and voices were customary for various kinds of music at a given place and time, and about the social context of performances and the sorts of musical 'accessory' (like music stands) that were normally used.

Composers in the Middle Ages and the Renaissance scarcely ever indicated that their music was written for specific groupings of instruments and/or voices. In some cases, perhaps, the performing forces were so conventional that no such indications were necessary: every musician would have known which instruments and voices the composer intended from the nature of the music. For example, Notre Dame organa in the 12th a[nd] 13th centuries may normally have been performed by [a] more or less fixed ensemble of musicians. In most case[s], however, the composer seems not to have had in mi[nd] any one specific sonority. He left to the performer [the] task of adapting the written notes to the acoustical en[vi]ronment, the social context, the forces available, and [so] on. On the one hand, then, modern scholars must red[is]cover lost conventions; on the other, they must establi[sh] the limits within which earlier performers were free [to] interpret the music given them by the composer. Sin[ce] the musical MSS themselves do not supply answers [to] the sorts of question about performing practice that lat[er] sources do, works of art, along with literary and arch[i]val documents (difficult as these are to interpret), mu[st] perforce constitute the principal sources of informati[on] about the ensembles customarily employed to perfor[m] earlier music.

Once composers began regularly to write music f[or] specific combinations of voices or instruments, that [is] from the 17th century onwards, pictures no longer fulfi[l] as important a function as a source of information abo[ut] performing practice. Nevertheless, iconographical ev[i]dence can sometimes reveal facts about the performi[ng] conventions of music after 1600 that are not easy to di[s]cover in any other way, for example the constitution [of] orchestras (how many players were used for each par[t] and the sorts of instrument in the continuo group, f[or]

3. The chorus and orchestra for the Handel commemoration ceremonies of 1784 in Westminster Abbey: engravin[g] from Charles Burney's 'An Account of the Musical Performances . . . in Commemoration of Handel' (1785)

nstance), the size and seating arrangements of choirs, the size and specifications of organs, harpsichords, pianos and other instruments used for various sorts of performance, and so on (see, for example, fig.3, showing the orchestra and chorus in Westminster Abbey for the commemoration of Handel in 1784). And pictorial evidence is as important for the study of music without a written tradition – ancient, non-Western and folk music – as for western European art music of the Middle Ages and the Renaissance.

Pictures can also tell us many things about the social context of musical performances that would otherwise be difficult or impossible to discover. Works of art that depict real scenes show not only the number and kinds of performers, and whether or not a conductor leads the group, but also the locations and occasions for musical performances (whether indoors or out), where the musicians sat or stood, whether or not an audience was present (and, if so, where they sat), what the scenery for theatrical productions looked like, what sorts of music were appropriate for weddings, funerals, civic and religious processions, and so on. Works of art reveal the sorts of occasion for which town bands played, for example, what musical forces were available to princes, and even the extent to which professional musicians were joined by well-born amateurs in concerts at court. In short, works of art are an invaluable aid in discovering the role that music played in the social life of a culture. And pictures are virtually the only evidence we shall ever have for knowing which musical 'accessories' were used, when musicians played from written or printed music, when they used music stands, instrument cases, cheek bands and so on.

If the student of organology needs to exercise caution in using pictorial evidence, anyone wishing to learn how music was actually performed during earlier times must be even more prudent in his use of works of art as evidence, for the questions he can answer using pictorial material depend entirely on the notion that artists depict contemporary reality. The extent to which an individual art work reflects true and common practice must be assessed before its testimony can be accepted as literal fact. The principal check on a picture's realism must come about through an evaluation of its subject matter. The precept that only scenes depicting real life can be said to illustrate reality may seem tautological, but it is the basic assumption which underlies the work of the careful musical iconographer, for the truth of that statement will be his principal assurance that his evidence is trustworthy.

The musical scholar must, in other words, concern himself with the intention of the artist, who often set out to bring new life to a traditional iconographical programme in which many elements were fixed, or to illustrate a text which specified many of the details, including the number and kinds of musical instruments. The illumination in Herrad of Landsberg's 12th-century *Hortus deliciarum* which shows three Sirens, one of them singing while the other two play a transverse flute and a harp-psaltery, may illustrate a sermon by the theologian Honorius of Autun, who developed the allegory of the tempted Christian using the image of Ulysses and the Sirens. Honorius equated the singing Siren with *avaricia* (covetousness), the flute or 'tybia' with *jactantia* (boastfulness) and the harp-psaltery or 'lira' with *luxuria* (lust). Thus the picture may illustrate a specific text and furnish no information about the normal chamber

ensembles of the 12th century. Similarly the traditional association of musical angels with the Virgin Mary very likely tells us little about musical practices in the Middle Ages and the Renaissance, even though some scholars have based conclusions about 15th-century instrumentation on such angel consorts. In short, the first task of the musical iconographer is to attempt to identify the text on which each picture is based, or the traditional iconography of the subject illustrated.

Many manuscript illuminations, sculptures and paintings, especially those created during the Middle Ages, are based on theatrical productions: that is, artists depicted scenes, especially ones derived from the Bible or from saints' lives, by showing contemporary theatrical representations of them, using as their model mystery and miracle plays (see, for example, fig.4 (p.276), showing Jean Fouquet's version of *Le mystère de Sainte Apolline*, *c*1450). Needless to say, this practice aids the musical scholar, for even when an artist illustrates a biblical scene, if he copies a stage production he is in some sense depicting reality, and his picture may then reveal normal musical practices. But the cautious musical iconographer must first take some pains to establish the connection of the work of art with theatrical convention, lest his conclusions be based more on fancy than on fact.

Some artists illustrate traditional scenes by portraying mythical, biblical or historical figures in modern dress, and they too may therefore be depicting contemporary reality. 16th-century paintings of the Prodigal Son, for example, often show him at the banquet table surrounded by his high-living companions. In such cases, there seems to be little reason to doubt that the artist was painting a situation that he himself might have seen in his own time. Similarly, 15th-century Netherlands painters transposed biblical events to their own time and place, so that their works can often be accepted as evidence of reality, although Netherlands artists included disguised symbolism well into the 18th century.

The musical scholar, then, must assure himself that the artist's choice of musical instruments does not depend entirely on a textual source, some form of symbolism, or on a traditional iconographical programme only distantly related, if at all, to contemporary reality. The most solid iconographical evidence, of course, comes from paintings which illustrate contemporary events, and which thus have almost the force of photographic reality. The many works of art, for example, which show specific rulers in military activities, at courtly entertainments, weddings and so on, can presumably be accepted at face value as musicological evidence. Even one such painting may be enormously useful in revealing performing practice.

Similar historical scenes can sometimes be found even in the Middle Ages: MS illuminations are a particular rich source for them. Indeed, the margins of the MSS illuminated from the 13th century onwards are an especially fertile field of investigation for the musical iconographer, for along with a host of grotesque creatures, beasts and birds, and angels and devils, some of whom spill over from the main miniatures, a number of quite ordinary people seem to be engaged in everyday activities: hunting, weaving, fighting, playing games and making music. The relationship of these marginal ornaments to the main miniatures, which usually embody a more traditional iconographic programme or at least more clearly illustrate the accompanying text, is often prob-

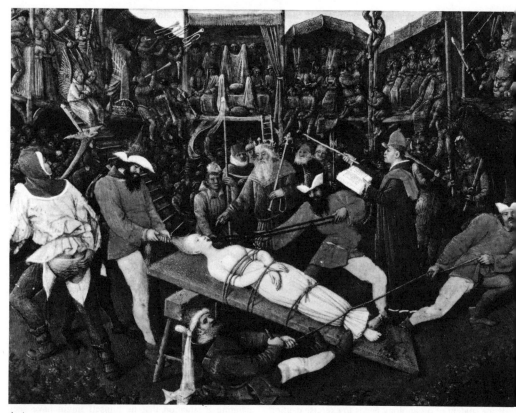

4. *A representation of 'Le mystère de Sainte Apolline'. detail of a painting (c1450) by Jean Fouquet (Musée Condé, Chantilly)*

lematical; art historians attempt, whenever they can, to show how the marginalia are linked with the total plan of the page. Nevertheless, many of these everyday scenes can probably be accepted as straightforward musicological evidence, even though their connection with the real world must always remain in question and may one day be convincingly denied.

On the one hand, then, works of art show historical events and scenes from everyday life, which seem to be factually true. It would be difficult to argue, for example, that the portraits of the Minnesinger in the 14th-century Manessische MS, many of whom are shown engaging in typical musical activities, or the minstrels in the 13th-century *Cantigas de Santa María*, do not represent at least some degree of reality, although the extent to which conclusions based on these miniatures alone can be applied beyond a very limited place and time remains an open question. On the other hand, pictures of angel concerts and mythological figures can scarcely ever constitute the major part of the evidence in any convincing argument about performing conventions, for such images are always derived from literary sources or from tradition rather than from reality. A musical scholar who wishes to argue that in certain cases such scenes are based on contemporary theatrical productions would be well advised to consider that the burden of proof for demonstrating that hypothesis lies with him. Unfortunately the intent of many art works is not clear; they may well reveal actual performing practice, or they may merely illustrate some unknown text. The musical scholar must often make difficult decisions about

the reliability of a work of art as musicological evidence, knowing full well that further research might reverse his decision. But such difficulties are an inherent part of the problem of dealing with pictorial sources, and the musical scholar must simply accustom himself to dealing with working hypotheses as much as with established fact.

4. ICONOGRAPHY OF COMPOSERS. Assembling iconographical material to illustrate the life and times of a composer poses methodological problems quite different from those encountered in using art works as raw material for a history of instruments or of performing practice. The aim of pictorial biography is general rather than particular: to build up an impression of a style of life rather than to answer specific questions of style or convention. Like other sorts of biographical studies, those using pictorial evidence hope to reveal the life and personality of a composer in an effort to make him seem more human and more comprehensible to us, and to explain the special qualities of mind and personality that distinguish him from his contemporaries and from other great musicians.

5. INTELLECTUAL AND CULTURAL HISTORY. Along with data about musical instruments and about performing practice and composers, works of art also furnish information about the role of music in culture at large. Pictures not only help to explain the place of actual sounding music in society, but they also reveal the characteristic ways in which musical subjects were used symbolically

r allegorically, and how music was used to illuminate ɪe mythical, philosophical, theological or educational octrines of an age. This aspect of iconography brings ɪusic into the sphere of cultural history, and indeed raises uestions which relate more closely to the latter disci- ʟine than to music history as it has been most narrowly onceived. Perhaps for that reason there are few models mong published works for the musical cultural his- ɔrian to follow. Hammerstein's *Die Musik der Engel* 1962) and some of the essays by Emanuel Winternitz ɪre the most distinguished examples of this approach to late.

Analysing the sorts of scene with which musical per- ɔrmances are traditionally associated will reveal the role ɪat actual musical sounds played in a society. This ategory of pictures is virtually synonymous with that ɪecessary to answer questions about the social context ɔf performances. The evidence is the same, but the cul- ʊral historian will put his material to slightly different ɪse. One facet of music as a part of cultural history, for ʒxample, will surely involve the frequent appearance in ʋorks of art of musical compositions accurately notat- ʒd. Study of these images of musical notation can some- imes prove surprisingly revealing, as when Lowinsky lemonstrated by means of such evidence that the St erome in the Scuola di S Giorgio degli Schiavoni in Jenice was in fact probably St Augustine. Reese (1968) ɪas studied a number of such examples in Renaissance *ɪntarsia*.

The ways in which artists reveal the characteristic nythical, philosophical, theological and educational ɔeliefs of their age by means of musical subjects become ːlear from studies of scenes which are traditionally lepicted with musical motifs. Representations of music ɪs a liberal art, allegories of hearing as one of the five senses, and music as one attribute of the various planets, nonths and zodiacal signs, for example, all furnish the cultural historian with rich material for research, as do the many personifications of music, or of church modes, and the representations of figures like Tubalcain, King David, Apollo (with and without Marsyas), the Muses and Orpheus, each with his own musical iconography.

Sometimes musical instruments have symbolic mean- ings when they appear in paintings. Wind instruments, for example, may have an erotic significance quite aside from their more literal relevance to a scene. Patricia Egan (1959) has stressed the contrast between the 'Apollon- ian' lute and the 'Dionysiac' recorder in Giorgione's *Fête champêtre* in the Louvre. Hieronymous Bosch's paint- ings furnish abundant examples of instruments assumed to be included because they are symbolic rather than realistic. On occasion instruments merely identify the role of an individual more precisely: shepherds are traditionally shown with reed pipes, recorders or bag- pipes, fools with bagpipes and so on. And some artists painted allegories of music that attempt a more or less systematic survey of all instruments, or all classes of music.

In short, the musical scholar wishing to use works of art must face the fact that the success of his research depends on a careful assessment of the artistic evidence, and that the questions he must ask are as much the pro- vince of art as of music history. The information fur- nished by a work of art can be believed unreservedly only if the artist's original intentions can be clearly understood, and a means established of comparing it with other works in the same tradition. Then a picture is truly worth a thousand words.

BIBLIOGRAPHY

F. Crane: *Bibliography of the Iconography of Music* (in preparation) will contain a complete list of exhibition catalogues, calendars, collections of prints and reproductions, illustrated histories and pictorial biographies, as well as more specialized studies. The bibliography below is restricted to works dealing with the aims and methods of musical iconography, a selective list of histories of music in pictures, and studies specifically referred to in the preceding text.

E. Buhle: *Die musikalischen Instrumente in des Miniaturen des frühen Mittelalters* (Leipzig, 1903)

H. Leichtentritt: 'Was lehren uns die Bildwerke des 14.–17. Jahr- hunderts über die Instrumentalmusik ihrer Zeit?', *SIMG*, vii (1905– 6), 315–64

K. Andorfer and R. Epstein: *Musica in nummis* (Vienna, 1907)

F. W. Galpin: *Old English Instruments of Music* (London, 1910, rev. 4/1965 by T. Dart)

D. F. Scheurleer: 'Iconography of Musical Instruments', *ZIMG*, xii (1910–11), 305

G. Kanth: *Bilder-Atlas zur Musikgeschichte von Bach bis Strauss* (Berlin, 1912)

H. H. Ewers and J. E. Poritzky: *Musik im Bild* (Munich and Leipzig, 1913)

D. F. Scheurleer: *Iconographie des instruments de musique* (The Hague, 1914)

M. Seiffert: 'Bildzeugnisse des 16. Jahrhunderts für die instrumen- tale Begleitung des Gesanges und den Ursprung des Musik- kupferstiches', *AMw*, i (1918–19), 49

——: *Wat leeren ons de schilderijen en prenten der zestiende eeuw over de instrumentale begleiding van den zang en den orsprong van de muziekgravure?* (Leipzig, 1920)

W. B. Squire: 'L'iconographie musicale', *Congrès d'histoire de l'art: Paris 1921*, 731

W. zur Westen: *Musiktitel aus vier Jahrhunderten* (Leipzig, 1921)

M. Sauerlandt: *Die Musik in fünf Jahrhunderten der europäischen Malerei etwa 1450 bis 1850* (Königstein im Taunus and Leipzig, 1922)

W. B. Squire: 'Musical Iconography', *Bulletin de la Société 'Union musicologique'*, ii (1922), 33

C. Moreck: *Die Musik in der Malerei* (Munich, 1924)

G. Kinsky: *Geschichte der Musik in Bildern* (Leipzig, 1929; Eng. trans., 1930)

E. Panofsky: *Studies in Iconology* (New York, 1939, 2/1950)

L. Parigi: *Musiche in pittura* (Signa, 1939)

M. F. Schneider: *Alte Musik in der bildenden Kunst Basels* (Basle, 1941)

H. Nannen: *Kleines Musikbrevier: ein Buch der Bilder aus 8 Jahr- hunderten abendländischer Kunst* (Munich, 1943)

V. Denis: *De muziekinstrumenten in de Nederlanden en in Italië naar hun afbeelding in de 15ᵉ-eeuwsche kunst* (Utrecht, 1944)

M. F. Schneider: *Musik der Neuzeit in der bildenden Kunst Basels* (Basle, 1944)

A. della Corte: *Satire e grotteschi di musiche e di musicisti d'ogni tempo* (Turin, 1946)

K. Pahlen: *Musikgeschichte der Welt* (Zurich, 1947)

L. B. Meyer: *A History of Musical Instruments in Slides* (Chicago, c1951)

M. Bernardi and A. della Corte: *Gli strumenti musicali nei dipinti Galleria degli Uffizzi* (Turin, 1952)

A. G. Hess: 'The Cataloguing of Music in the Visual Arts', *Notes*, xi (1954–5), 527, 542

——: *Italian Renaissance Paintings with Musical Subjects: a Cor- pus of such Works in American Collections*, i [no more issued] (New York, 1955)

J. Banach: *Tematy muzyczne w plastyce polskiej* (Kraków, 1956– 62)

A. Buchner: *Hudební nástroje od pravěku k dnešku* [Musical instru- ments through the ages] (Prague, 1956; Eng. trans., 1956, 4/ 1962)

P. Egan: 'Poesia and the Fête champêtre', *Art Bulletin*, xli (1959), 305

E. E. Lowinsky: 'The Music in St. Jerome's Study', *Art Bulletin*, xli (1959), 298

M. Pincherle: *Histoire illustrée de la musique* (Paris, 1959)

P. Collaer and A. van der Linden: *Atlas historique de la musique* (Brussels, 1960)

O. E. Deutsch: 'Was heisst und zu welchem Ende studiert man Ikonographie?', *SMz*, c (1960), 230

D. Keresztury, J. Vécsey and Z. Falvy: *A Magyar zenetörténet képeskönyve* (Budapest, 1960)

P. H. Lang and O. Bettmann: *A Pictorial History of Music* (New York, 1960)

H. Besseler and M. Schneider, eds.: *Musikgeschichte in Bildern* (Leipzig, 1961–)

K. M. Komma: *Musikgeschichte in Bildern* (Stuttgart, 1961)

A. Ott: *Tausend Jahre Musikleben, 800–1800* (Munich, 1961)

R. Hammerstein: *Die Musik der Engel* (Berne and Munich, 1962)

F. Ll. Harrison and J. Rimmer: *European Musical Instruments* (London, 1964)

D. Boyden: *The History of Violin Playing from its Origins to 1761* (London, 1965)

S. Beck and E. E. Roth: *Music in Prints* (New York, 1965)

E. Höhne: *Musik in der Kunst* (Hanau am Main and Leipzig, 1965; Eng. trans., n.d.)

R. Wangermée: *La musique flamande dans la société des XVe et XVIe siècles* (Brussels, 1965)

R. Goldron: *Histoire de la musique* (Lausanne, 1965–6)

Aspects of Medieval and Renaissance Music: a Birthday Offering to Gustave Reese (New York, 1966, 2/1978)

R. Bragard and F. J. De Hen: *Les instruments de musique dans l'art et l'histoire* (Rhode-St-Genèse, Belgium, 1967)

E. Winternitz: *Musical Instruments and their Symbolism in Western Art* (New York, 1967, 2/1979)

G. S. Fraenkel: *Decorative Music Title Pages* (New York, 1968)

F. Lesure: *Music and Art in Society* (University Park and London, 1968)

G. Reese: 'Musical Compositions in Renaissance Intarsia', *Medieval and Renaissance Studies*, ii (Durham, North Carolina, 1968), 74

E. Ripin: 'The Two-manual Harpsichord in Flanders before 1650', *GSJ*, xxi (1968), 33

H. M. Brown and J. Lascelle: *Musical Iconography: a Manual for Cataloguing Musical Subjects in Western Art before 1800* (Cambridge, Mass., 1971)

H. Steger: *Philologia musica* (Munich, 1971)

E. Winternitz: 'The Iconology of Music: Potentials and Pitfalls', *Perspectives in Musicology*, ed. B. S. Brook, E. O. D. Downes and S. van Solkema (New York, 1972)

T. Seebass: *Musikdarstellung und Psalterillustration im frühen Mittelalter* (Berne, 1973)

V. Scherliess: 'Notizen zur musikalischen Ikonographie', *AnMc*, no.14 (1974), 1; no.15 (1975), 21

L. Vorreiter: 'Musikikonographie im Schrifttum 1850–1949 und 1950–1974', *AcM*, xlvi (1974), 1–41

E. A. Bowles: 'Iconography as a Tool for Examining the Loud Consort in the Fifteenth Century', *JAMIS*, iii (1977), 100

R. D. Leppert: *The Theme of Music in Flemish Paintings of the Seventeenth Century* (Munich, 1977)

H. M. Brown: 'Trecento Angels and the Instruments they Play', *Modern Musical Scholarship: Studies in Musical History: Oxford 1977*, 112

B. Disertori: *La musica nei quadri antichi* (Calliano, 1978)

R. D. Leppert: *Arcadia at Versailles* (Amsterdam and Lisse, 1978)

W. Salmen: *Bilder zur Geschichte der Musik in Österreich* (Innsbruck, 1979)

H. C. Slim: 'Mary Magdalene, Musician and Dancer', *Early Music*, viii (1980), 460

J. Braun: 'Musical Instruments in Byzantine Illuminated Manuscripts', *Early Music*, viii (1980), 312

H. M. Brown: 'The Trecento Harp', *Performance Practice: New York 1981*

E. A. Bowles: 'A Preliminary Checklist of Fifteenth-century Representations of Organs in Paintings and Manuscript Illuminations', *Organ Yearbook*, xiii (1982)

J. McKinnon: 'Iconography', *Musicology in the 1980s*, ed. D. K. Holoman and C. V. Palisca (New York, 1982), 79

M. Rasmussen and F. von Huene: 'Some Recorders in 17th-century Dutch Paintings', *Early Music*, x (1982), 30

HOWARD MAYER BROWN

Icough. Cylindrical tin vessel rattle of the Tiv people of Nigeria. It has a wooden handle, and is used by women in the popular *icough* dance.

Ida. Variable tension HOURGLASS DRUM of the Edo/Bini people of Nigeria. It is associated with royalty.

Idaisurangu parai. A name applied to the south Indian variable tension HOURGLASS DRUM *utukkai. See* HUDUKKĀ.

Idakka [itekka, edakkya]. A variable tension HOURGLASS DRUM of Kerala, south-west India. The body, from 21 to 26 cm long and about 1 cm thick, is of acacia or red sandalwood; it is slightly waisted in the middle (see illustration). The shell-faces are about 11 cm wide, the drumheads about double that. The skins, made of the

Idakka (drum) and kombu (trumpet), Kerala, south Indi

internal stomach-wall of a cow, are pasted to thick jack wood hoops (about 2 cm in diameter) with six hole drilled in each for the V-lacings which are tightened by a central cross-lacing. Four large decoratively turned wooden dowels hung with 64 multi-coloured tassels are inserted as tuning-sticks between the lacing. The head are simply held over the faces by the lacing, usually of centre. Beneath them is a snare of two crossed palmyra fibres held on four copper nails. The drum is suspended from a strap on the left shoulder. The right hand beat the front face with a thin wooden or horn stick, slightly curved at the tip; the player varies the timbre and pitch over a range of up to two octaves by squeezing the lacing and pushing against the shoulder-strap with the left hand. The construction of the *idakka* is similar to that of the medieval DAKKĀ.

The *idakka* is a temple drum used by the hereditary temple musician caste, the Mārār, and by the Poduvā in north Kerala; it is played in temple worship, processions, the ceremonial ensemble *pañcavādyam*, the devotional music *sopānā sangīta*, performed on temple steps, and the Sanskrit drama *kutiyattam*. Its pitch range is so large that it is sometimes played melodically. There is a tradition that it must never be placed on the ground.

BIBLIOGRAPHY

K. S. Kothari: *Indian Folk Musical Instruments* (New Delhi, 1968)

L. S. Rajagopalan: 'Idakka', *Journal of the Music Academy Madras*, xlviii (1977), 164

B. C. Deva: *Musical Instruments of India* (Calcutta, 1978)

ALASTAIR DICK

'Īdān (Arabic). Plural of 'ŪD.

Idara. Double-headed cylindrical drum of Nigeria. *See* DANG.

Idedjai [idzdjai]. Double-headed conical drum of the Hima people of Rwanda and eastern Zaïre (*BooneT*, 70). *See* DINDO.

Ideteta. Drum of the Teso people of Uganda. *See* ATENESU and EMIDIRI.

di [odi]. Double-headed HOURGLASS DRUM of the Igbo people of Nigeria.

dioglot reed. A REED that is cut out of (but remains attached to) the body of an aerophone. Often a hair, a thread or a piece of string is inserted at the inner end of the cut to prevent the reed from sealing completely when played. The Egyptian *arghūl*, the Turkish *çifte*, the Nigerian *veng-kung* and the Sardinian *launeddas* are examples of idioglot clarinets.

idiophone. General term for musical instruments that produce their sound from the substance of the instrument itself, being solid or elastic enough not to require stretched membranes or strings. Idiophones form one of the four main classes of instruments (along with membranophones, chordophones and aerophones – to which a fifth, electronophones, has recently been added) in the system of CLASSIFICATION devised by E. M. von Hornbostel and C. Sachs and published by them in *Zeitschrift für Ethnologie* in 1914 (Eng. trans. in *GSJ*, xiv, 1961, p.3). Their system, the one most commonly used today, is based on Victor Mahillon's division of instruments according to the nature of their vibrating bodies, which he devised for his catalogue of the instruments in the Royal Conservatory in Brussels. Idiophones are subdivided according to whether they are struck, plucked, blown or caused to vibrate by friction. Struck idiophones can be struck either directly (as with clappers, castanets, cymbals, gongs and bells) or indirectly (as with rattles and various scraped sticks and tubes). Plucked idiophones are generally constructed so that lamellae, that is elastic plaques, fixed at one end, that can be flexed and then released, vibrate either within a frame or hoop (as with the jew's harp and the various guimbardes) or in board- or comb-form (as with musical boxes and African *mbilas*). Friction idiophones can take the form of sticks (nail violin, nail piano), plaques (the *livika* of New Ireland) or vessels (glass harmonica); and blown idiophones take the form of sticks (*Äolsklavier*) or plaques. Each category may be further subdivided according to the more detailed characteristics of an instrument. To each category Hornbostel and Sachs gave a number derived from the Dewey decimal library classification system. Their classification (from the *GSJ* trans., with minor alterations) follows as an appendix to this article.

HOWARD MAYER BROWN

APPENDIX

Idiophones: the substance of the instrument itself, owing to its solidity and elasticity, yields the sounds, without requiring stretched membranes or strings
1   *Struck idiophones*: the instrument is made to vibrate by being struck upon
11   *Idiophones struck directly*: the player himself executes the movement of striking; whether by mechanical intermediate devices, beaters, keyboards, or by pulling ropes, etc, is immaterial; it is definitive that the player can apply clearly defined individual strokes and that the instrument itself is equipped for this kind of percussion
11.1   *Concussion idiophones or clappers*: two or more complementary sonorous parts are struck against each other
11.11   *Concussion sticks or stick clappers* – found in Vietnam, India and the Marshall Islands
11.12   *Concussion plaques or plaque clappers* – found in China and India
11.13   *Concussion troughs or trough clappers* – found in Burma
11.14   *Concussion vessels or vessel clappers*: even a slight hollow in the surface of a board counts as a vessel
11.141   *Castanets*: vessel clappers, either natural, or artificially hollowed out

11.142   *Cymbals*: vessel clappers with everted rim
111.2   *Percussion idiophones*: the instrument is struck either with a non-sonorous object (hand, stick, striker) or against a non-sonorous object (human body, the ground)
111.21   *Percussion sticks*
111.211   *(Individual) percussion sticks* – found in Japan, Vietnam and the Balkans; (also the triangle)
111.212   *Sets of percussion sticks*: several percussion sticks of different pitch are combined to form a single instrument (all xylophones, as long as their sounding components are not in two different planes)
111.22   *Percussion plaques*
111.221   *(Individual) percussion plaques* – found in the oriental Christian Church
111.222   *Sets of percussion plaques* (lithophone [China], and most metallophones)
111.23   *Percussion tubes*
111.231   *(Individual) percussion tubes* (slit-drum, tubular bell)
111.232   *Sets of percussion tubes* (tubaphone, tubular xylophone)
111.24   *Percussion vessels*
111.241   *Gongs*: the vibration is strongest near the vertex
111.241.1   *(Individual) gongs* – found in South and East Asia; (including the so-called metal drums, or rather kettle-gongs)
111.241.2   *Sets of gongs* (gong-chimes) – found in South-east Asia
111.242   *Bells*: the vibration is weakest near the vertex
111.242.1   *(Individual) bells*
111.242.11   *Resting bells*: the cup is placed on the palm of the hand or on a cushion; its mouth faces upwards – found in China, Indochina [now Vietnam] and Japan
111.242.12   *Suspended bells*: the bell is suspended from the apex
111.242.121   *Suspended bells struck from the outside*: no striker is attached inside the bell, there being a separate beater
111.242.122   *Clapper bells*: a striker (clapper) is attached inside the bell
111.242.2   *Sets of bells* [chimes] (subdivided as 111.242.1)
112   *Indirectly struck idiophones*: the player himself does not go through the movement of striking; percussion results indirectly through some other movement by the player. The intention of the instrument is to yield clusters of sounds or noises, and not to let individual strokes be perceived
112.1   *Shaken idiophones or rattles*: the player executes a shaking motion
112.11   *Suspension rattles*: perforated idiophones are mounted together, and shaken to strike against each other
112.111   *Strung rattles*: rattling objects are strung in rows on a cord (necklaces with rows of shells)
112.112   *Stick rattles*: rattling objects are strung on a bar (or ring) (sistrum with rings)
112.12   *Frame rattles*: rattling objects are attached to a carrier against which they strike
112.121   *Pendant rattles*: rattling objects are hung from a frame (dancing shield with rattling rings)
112.122   *Sliding rattles*: non-sonorous objects slide to and fro in the slots of the sonorous object so that the latter is made to vibrate; or sonorous objects slide to and fro in the slots of a non-sonorous object, to be set in vibration by the impacts (*angklung*, sistrum with rods [recent])
112.13   *Vessel rattles*: rattling objects enclosed in a vessel strike against each other or against the walls of the vessel, or usually against both. NB The Benue gourd rattles with handle, in which the rattling objects, instead of being enclosed, are knotted into a net slipped over the outer surface, count as a variety of vessel rattle (fruit shells with seeds, 'pellet bells' enclosing loose percussion pellets)
112.2   *Scraped idiophones*: the player causes a scraping movement directly or indirectly: a non-sonorous object moves along the notched surface of a sonorous object, to be alternately lifted off the teeth and flicked against them; or an elastic sonorous object moves along the surface of a notched non-sonorous object to cause a series of impacts. This group must not be confused with that of friction idiophones
112.21   *Scraped sticks*: a notched stick is scraped with a little stick
112.211   *Scraped sticks without resonator* – found in South America, India (notched musical bow) and Congo
112.212   *Scraped sticks with resonator* – found in East Asia (δ)
112.22   *Scraped tubes* – found in south India
112.23   *Scraped vessels*: the corrugated surface of a vessel is scraped – found in South America and the Congo region
112.24   *Scraped wheels or cog rattles*: a cog wheel, whose axle serves as the handle, and a tongue fixed in a frame which is free to turn on the handle; when whirled, the tongue strikes the teeth of the wheel one after another – found in Europe and India
112.3   *Split idiophones*: instruments in the shape of two springy arms connected at one end and touching at the other: the arms are forced apart by a little stick, to jingle or vibrate on recoil – found

in China, Malacca [now West Malaysia], Iran and the Balkans
12 *Plucked idiophones*: lamellae, i.e. elastic plaques, fixed at one end, are flexed and then released to return to their position of rest
121 *In the form of a frame*: the lamella vibrates within a frame or hoop
121.1 *Clack idiophones* (cricri): the lamella is carved in the surface of a fruit shell, which serves as a resonator – found in Melanesia
121.2 *Guimbardes* (jew's harps): the lamella is mounted in a rod or plaque-shaped frame and depends on the player's mouth cavity for resonance
121.21 *Idioglot guimbardes*: the lamella is carved in the frame itself, its base remaining joined to the frame – found in India, Indonesia and Melanesia
121.22 *Heteroglot guimbardes*: a lamella is attached to a frame
121.221 *(Single) heteroglot guimbardes* – found in Europe, India and China
121.222 *Sets of heteroglot guimbardes*: several heteroglot guimbardes of different pitches are combined to form a single instrument – found in Aura
122 *In board or comb-form*: the lamellae are tied to a board or cut out from a board like the teeth of a comb
122.1 *With laced-on lamellae*
122.11 *Without resonator* (all lamellaphones on a plain board)
122.12 *With resonator* (all lamellaphones with a box or bowl below the board)
122.2 *With cut-out lamellae* (musical boxes): pins on a cylinder pluck the lamellae – found in Europe
13 *Friction idiophones*: the instrument is made to vibrate by friction
131 *Friction sticks*
131.1 *(Individual) friction sticks* (unknown)
131.2 *Sets of friction sticks*
131.21 *With direct friction*: the sticks themselves are rubbed (nail violin, nail piano, Stockspiele)
131.22 *With indirect friction*: the sticks are connected with others which are rubbed and, by transmitting their longitudinal vibration, stimulate transverse vibration in the former (Chladni's euphon)
132 *Friction plaques*
132.1 *(Individual) friction plaques* (unknown)
132.2 *Sets of friction plaques* [livika] – found in New Ireland
133 *Friction vessels*
133.1 *(Individual) friction vessels* – found in Brazil (tortoise shell)
133.2 *Sets of friction vessels* (verillon [glass harmonica])
14 *Blown idiophones*: the instrument is made to vibrate by being blown upon
141 *Blown sticks*
141.1 *(Individual) blown sticks* (unknown)
141.2 *Sets of blown sticks* (Åolsklavier)
142 *Blown plaques*
142.1 *(Individual) blown plaques* (unknown)
142.2 *Sets of blown plaques* (piano chanteur)

Suffixes for use with any division of this class:
8 with keyboard
9 mechanically driven

Appendix reprinted from Hornbostel and Sachs, 1914 (by permission of Limbag Verlag, Berlin); Eng. trans., 1961

Idje. Drum of the Lendu people of north-eastern Zaïre (*BooneT*, 72).

Idjendje [isusu]. STICK ZITHER of the Konda people of western Zaïre (*LaurentyC*, 115). *See* ZEZE (i).

Idonongo. Single-string TUBE FIDDLE of Burundi corresponding to the ENDINGIDI of Uganda and the *taratibu* of Rwanda and Zaïre. The soundbox is made from a section of ox horn, one end of which is covered with a pegged skin; the vibrating string and bow string are made from ox tendon. The *idonongo* is used to accompany laments and other songs. See M. Vuylstèke: 'Musique du Burundi', OCR 40 [disc notes].

Idzdjai [idedjai]. Double-headed conical drum of the Hima people of Rwanda and eastern Zaïre (*BooneT*, 70). *See* DINDO.

Idzibile. Drum of the Lendu people of north-eastern Zaïre (*BooneT*, 72).

Ifata [ikole]. STICK ZITHER of the Eso people of Zaïre. *See* ZEZE (i).

Ifohlwane. Zulu ankle rattle. *See* AMAFOHLWANE.

Ifondo [ifonde]. VESSEL FLUTE of the Ikongo, Saka, Kutu, Yaka and Eso peoples of Zaïre. *See* DIPULU.

Ifonge na ndzulu. NOSE FLUTE of the Mongo people of Zaïre. *See* BOLUKULUKU.

Igba (i). A general term for the open conical drum of the Igbo people of Nigeria. The skin may be nailed, glued or pegged. The drum is played with a stick, the hands, or both, and is used either singly or in sets for dancing, entertainment or wrestling. The Northern Igbo (Onitsha) version of the drum has a laced head with tuning wedges and is beaten with the fingers. Similar Nigerian drums are known in Owerri as *nkwa*, in western Igboland as *egede* and in Brass as *okuma*. A small, high-pitched Igbo drum of the same type is known as *ikpirikpe*; it is played with stick or hand, the open end being at times inserted into a bucket of water.

BIBLIOGRAPHY
W. W. C. Echezona: 'Ibo Music', *Nigeria Magazine*, lxxxiv (1965), 45
——: 'Igbo Music', *Grove 6*
A. King: 'Nigeria', *Grove 6*

K. A. GOURLAY

Igba (ii). A half-calabash percussion vessel of the Nago people of Benin. It is struck with metal finger-rings in rapid succession as part of the rhythmic accompaniment in the instrumental ensemble for the popular *sakara* music.

Igbin. A set of thick, squat cylindrical drums of the Yoruba people of Nigeria. Each has three feet and a single membrane fixed by a securing ring and large wooden pegs. Names of individual drums vary according to locality, for example, in descending order of size *ita igbin*, *jagba*, *apele* (or *iya nla*), *iya gan*, *keke* and *afere*. The largest drum is played with a stick by the right hand and the palm, fist or fingers of the left; the other drums are played with two unfashioned sticks. The drums are sacred to the god Orishanla (also known as Obatala, 'king of the white cloth') and drummers are specialists from a particular family responsible for his worship. Linked with *igbin* is *ipese* music, the two names being alternatives for the same large drum according to context and instrumental group. The *ipese* set comprises, in decreasing order of size, *ipese*, *afere* and *aran*, all three of which have pegged membranes, though only *afere* need be footed. Used with the *agogo* clapperless bell, the drums are specially made for *ifa* priests of divination, and the music is restricted to ceremonial and social occasions connected with the cult and its members. See W. Bascom: 'Drums of the Yoruba of Nigeria', FE 4441 [disc notes].

K. A. GOURLAY

Igemfe [igekle, igenkle, igenxe, igerre, igexhle] (pl amagemfe). (1) End-blown NOTCHED FLUTE of the Zulu people of southern Africa. Its length varies between about 30 and 50 cm. It has no finger-holes, and usually consists of two sections: an upper short tube of reed, and a thinner one inserted into the end of this (see illustra-

Two pairs of amagemfe (end-blown flutes) of the Zulu people of southern Africa

tion). The mouthpiece is wedge-shaped: the upper end of the thicker reed is cut aslant from both sides at an angle of about 45 degrees, one cut being larger than the other; this larger edge rests against the player's lower lip. With the lower end alternately left open and stopped by the right forefinger, two notes about a 4th apart are produced. The *igemfe* is used for duets, by boys, two flutes being tuned about a semitone apart and referred to as 'male' and 'female'. Formerly their use was taboo until celebration of the annual first fruits ceremony.

(2) A small transverse flute of the Zulu. It is a rare instrument among the Zulu, made of reed with two to four finger-holes, stopped at both ends, resembling the Venda Tshitiringo. See *KirbyMISA*, 120ff, pll.42–3.

DAVID K. RYCROFT

Igihumulizo (i). Cylindro-conical drum of the Ngoma ensemble of Rwanda.

Igihumulizo (ii). Flute of the *insengo* ensemble of the Tutsi people of Rwanda. *See* Insengo (i).

Igil. Two-string fiddle of the Tuva people of Siberia.

Igo. Log Xylophone of the Igbo people of Nigeria. *See* Ngedegwu.

Igogo. Slit-drum of the Buudu people of north-eastern Zaïre. The *igogo deja* is the large slit-drum. Carved from a single log, it is shaped like an antelope, about 3 metres long from tip to tail. Yielding a different note from each flank, it is used for message transmission and also, with the small *igogo tade* slit-drums, for dance accompaniment. See *TraceyCSA*, ii, 284.

Igonga [bogonga]. Mouth bow of the Ngombe people of Zaïre (*LaurentyC*, 113).

Igubu. Double-headed drum used by diviners among the Xhosa people of southern Africa. *See also* Isigubhu.

Iguí-egún. One of several African names for a long Afro-Cuban Stamping tube (more than a metre in length) used in funeral rites. The term in Yoruba refers to 'the stick of Egún', the mythical entity of the dead. *See* Ayíguí.

Igwali. Unbraced Mouth bow of the Xhosa people of southern Africa. *See* Ugwali.

Ihara. Obsolete percussion tube of Tahiti, made from a single joint of bamboo cut a short distance beyond the nodes. In the centre a long aperture was cut between the nodes, or else several slits were cut and a stick inserted through two of them to hold them open. It was placed horizontally on the ground and beaten for amusement with two light sticks.

BIBLIOGRAPHY
W. Ellis: *Polynesian Researches* (New York, 1833), 158
T. Henry: *Ancient Tahiti* (Honolulu, 1928), 275

MERVYN McLEAN

Ihawu. Dancing-shield of the Zulu people of southern Africa. *See* Ikhawu.

Ihembe. Side-blown trumpet of Rwanda. It is made from antelope horn, and is used as a signalling instrument for hunting and communal work.

Ihutan [pangalusi]. Suspended bossed gong in the *gondang* ensemble from the Batak Toba area of North Sumatra. *See* Gondang, (3).

Iikh. Two-string fiddle of the Khakass people of Siberia.

Ii'tostha' kastaweh'shae'. Vessel rattle of the Iroquois Indians of north-eastern North America. *See* Onyohsa' kastaweh'shae'.

Ijachi. An iron rod (or bell-staff) of the Igede people of Nigeria. It has eight small clapper bells, a group of four near the head and a second group near the base. The staff may originally have been a spear with bells attached. In current usage the *ijachi* is either held in the hand and shaken while dancing or set up in the ground as an emblem of the dance association owning it.

K. A. GOURLAY

Ikatala. Term of the Xhosa people of southern Africa for both the Ramkie lute and the European guitar.

Ikawu. *See* Ikhawu.

Ikelekele. Wooden-keyed Lamellaphone of the Kwango and Kasai regions of Zaïre. It has a wooden raft-type base (*LaurentyS*, 191).

Ikembe [ikimbe]. Small box-resonated lamellaphone which has spread from Zaïre to southern Rwanda, Burundi and Tanzania; see LAMELLAPHONE, §2(iii). As *ikembe*, it is played, for example, by the Kuma and Kunda peoples in Zaïre and the Rundi/Hangaza people of Tanzania.

Ikengere. Metal percussion rod of the Bukusu people of Kenya. *See* SIIRIRI.

Ikhawu [ikawu]. Dancing-shield of the Xhosa people of southern Africa, used as an idiophone. It is a piece of ox-hide shaped like a war shield but smaller; it is struck with a knob-stick to accompany dances. The Zulu *ihawu* and Swazi *lihawu* are similar. See *KirbyMISA*, 23ff, pl.7c.

Ikidi [akidi, akimbi, ekidi]. BOARD ZITHER of the Mamvu and Budu peoples of Zaïre. It measures 35 cm by 5 cm, and has five to eight strings of vegetable fibre. In performance the zither is placed on top of a calabash resonator and plucked with a palm-leaf plectrum, while the thumb plays arpeggios on the strings. The instrument is traditionally used by the *siba* sect for their dances and also reputedly has magic powers which enable young men to steal members of the opposite sex. Among similar instruments in Zaïre the Luba seven-string *ngyela* is placed over a calabash on the ground; it is a man's instrument associated with the hunting rites of the *buyanga* sect, and is also used to accompany singing, especially lamentations. The player depresses certain strings with his fingers, while playing arpeggios on the remaining strings. The *ngyela* appears to have reached the Luba from present-day Zambia, and is reputedly related to the Bemba and Shila *kalimba*. The *kalimba*, however, measures 40 cm by 14 cm and has nine strings. Other zithers with few strings are the Mamvu and Balese *kpai* (five strings), which is placed between the knees and plucked with a plectrum (5 cm long), the Mangutu *dingba* (six or seven strings) and the Lega *kungu* (five strings).

See also MALIGBANGA and GOMBI (i).

BIBLIOGRAPHY
LaurentyC
F. J. de Hen: *Beitrag zur Kenntnis der Musikinstrumente aus Belgisch Kongo und Ruanda-Urundi* (Tervuren, 1960)
G. Knosp: *Enquête sur la vie musicale au Congo belge 1934–1935* (Tervuren, 1968)
J. Gansemans: *Les instruments de musique Luba* (Tervuren, 1980)
K. A. GOURLAY

Ikil. Mongolian fiddle. *See* KHUUR.

Ikili. Two-string fiddle of the Altai people of Siberia, related to the Khakass *ïïkh* and the Tuva *igil*. It has horsehair strings. *See also* KHUUR.

Ikimbe. *See* IKEMBE.

Ikinyuguri. Gourd rattle of the Lyangombe cult of Rwanda.

Ikivuvu. TROUGH ZITHER of the Rundi people of Zaïre and Burundi (*LaurentyC*, 116). *See* INANGA.

Ikko. Japanese HOURGLASS DRUM. It is also called *ichino-tsuzumi* ('number one drum'). The *ikko* is about 36 cm long and has a head diameter of 24 cm. It is the smallest of a set of four drums once used in gagaku (court music); *see* TSUZUMI. The drum is placed horizontally in front of the player and its right head only is struck with a stick held in the right hand. It has long been replaced by the *kakko* in all but a couple of special contexts.

DAVID W. HUGHES

Ikobott [ikobót]. Wooden or ivory VESSEL FLUTE of the Kuba (Ngend) people of south-western Zaïre (*LaurentyA*, 88, 95f, 253).

Ikofe. Set of conical stopped flutes threaded on cord or wire played by the Topoke people of Zaïre (*LaurentyA*, 201).

Ikoka. MOUTH BOW of the Lokalo people of Zaïre (*LaurentyC*, 113). *See* LUSUBA.

Ikoko (i). Single-headed pot drum of the Yoruba people of Nigeria. The drum stands on a raffia ring or in soft sandy soil and accompanies dancing for the triennial *epa* festival and the *ipa ode* hunters' dance.

Ikoko (ii). LAMELLAPHONE of the Ngando, Saka and Yasayama peoples of Zaïre.

Ikokole [y'embambo]. Small SLIT-DRUM of the Nkundo and Boyela peoples of Zaïre (*LaurentyTF*, 135).

Ikokolo. Percussion trough of the Gishu people of Uganda. It is made from a short, broad beam about 90 cm long, hollowed on one side. The trough is placed on the ground with the opening downwards, and is beaten with two drumsticks. The term *ikokolo* is also used to refer to the Gishu percussion pot, which is beaten on the mouth with the palm of the hand. See *WachsmannTCU*, 314, 321.

Ikole [ifata]. STICK ZITHER of the Eso people of Zaïre. *See* ZEZE (i).

Ikolo. *See* IKORO.

Ikombe. Trapezoidal SLIT-DRUM of the Mbole and Opala peoples of Zaïre (*LaurentyTF*, 137).

Ikon eto. Log XYLOPHONE of the Ibibio people of Nigeria. It consists of up to 15 (but usually eight) keys resting on two banana stems and separated by thin isolating wands. The instrument may have one or two players, each using two sticks; it is used to accompany *uta* dancing. See S. E. Akpabot: *Ibibio Music in Nigerian Culture* (East Lansing, Mich., 1975).

Ikónkolo [okónkole, amelé]. Drum of the Afro-Cuban Lucumí cult. *See* BATÁ.

Ikookole. SLIT-DRUM of the Konda people of western Zaïre. It is used for dancing (*LaurentyTF*, 135).

Ikoro [ikolo]. SLIT-DRUM of the Igbo people of Nigeria. It is up to 180 cm long and 120 cm high, with a 'double'

ikoro (slit-drum) of the Igbo people, Nigeria

lit, that is a narrow slit widened at each end into an elongated rectangle (see illustration). Like the double-lit EKWE it is able to imitate the tonal patterns of Igbo speech and is used to summon assemblies and sound proclamations. It is also beaten at times of emergency, for instance on the outbreak of war, and at the funeral ceremonies of eminent members of the community, which include dancing and recitation of the heroic qualities of the deceased. If available *ikoro* slit-drum ensembles are

Ex.1 Rhythms used on an *ikoro* slit-drum ensemble

used as accompaniment, and the music is characterized by its tempo and polyrhythmic character, shown in ex.1. The *ikoro-ute*, another Igbo slit-drum, is 210 cm long and has a double slit.

Ikórrokót. Carved wooden VESSEL FLUTE of the Kuba people of south-western Zaïre (*LaurentyA*, 92).

Ikouli. Wooden cone flute with one or two finger-holes of the Boma people of Zaïre (*LaurentyA*, 141).

Ikpa. LAMELLAPHONE of the Igbo people of Nigeria. *See* UBO.

Ikpa mboto. LAMELLAPHONE of the Ibibio people of Nigeria. It consists of tuned metal keys mounted on a board which fits into a hollow half-calabash resonator. The instrument is supported by the fingers of both hands and plucked with the thumbs. It produces a melodic rhythm over which the player tells a story. See S. E. Akpabot: *Ibibio Music in Nigerian Culture* (East Lansing, Mich., 1975).

Ikpirikpe. Small open conical drum of the Igbo people of Nigeria. *See* IGBA (i).

Ikpo. Set of iron bells with clappers of the Igbo people of Nigeria. About 12 bells are mounted on a square palm frame and worn by various dancers.

Ikú-achán [pachán]. Afro-Cuban idiophone. It is actually a liturgical staff consisting of a bundle of nine sticks of the type normally used to dry tobacco leaves; about a metre long, it is generally tied in three places with ribbons and is struck on the ground by the cult leader in rites of Oyá, deity of the graveyard. See *OrtizIMA*, i, 166.

Ikwankwa [ikwata]. Wooden CLAPPERS of Nigeria. *Ikwankwa* is attributed to the Igbo; *ikwata* to the Edo-speaking peoples.

Ikwemgbo. Log XYLOPHONE of the Igbo people of Nigeria. *See* NGEDEGWU.

Ikwirikwe. SLIT-DRUM of the Igbo people of Nigeria. It is 60 cm long and has a double slit. *See also* EKWE, (1).

Ilatālam [elathalam]. Flat cymbals of Kerala, south India. The brass discs, flat and with quite prominent bosses, measure 12 to 15 cm in diameter and 5 mm in thickness. There are two methods of playing them: they are either held horizontally by the two short cords passing through their centre and, after clashing them together, the edge of one is slipped against the rim of the other to obtain a prolonged, ringing sound; or they are held vertically in the hollow of the hand and clashed by contracting the fingers towards the palm. They are used in temple music (for illustration *see* CENDA), in *kathakali* and *krishnattam* dance-dramas and in the shadow play *Tōlpavakoothu*. The *jālra* and *tālam* are other types of south Indian cymbals. For generic discussion of South Asian cymbals, *see* TĀL.

BIBLIOGRAPHY
L. S. Rajagopalan: 'Thayambaka', *Journal of the Music Academy Madras*, xxxviii (1967), 83
P. Sambamoorthy: *A Dictionary of South Indian Music and Musicians* (Madras, 1952–71), ii, p.229
                                                    PRIBISLAV PITOËFF

Ilenga. STOPPED FLUTE ENSEMBLE of the Konjo people of Toro district, Uganda. There are ten flutes: *malenge*, *bakanangabo*, *njanju*, *sepira*, *ekitanda*, *nzakubela*, *wawawa*, *sekiza*, *chikekuru* and *kabyabo* (in descending order of pitch). They are played by men dancing in a circle, accompanied by three conical drums. See *TraceyCSA*, ii, 296f.

'Ili'ili ('pebbles'). Hawaiian CLAPPERS. Two matched pairs of water-worn, dense (usually basaltic lava), flat, round or oval pebbles are selected both for quality of sound (lava from recent flows gives a brighter sound) and for comfortable fit in the seated dancer's hands.

Ilimba. A term for LAMELLAPHONE and XYLOPHONE in south-eastern Africa. Among the Gogo and Nkonde peoples of Tanzania it denotes a lamellaphone with a box-type body and pentatonic tuning. Among peoples of Zambia *ilimba* can be a one-bar xylophone; *see* IMBILA, (1).

Ilonge. End-blown flute of the Nyakyusa people of Tukuyu district, Tanzania. It is open-ended and has four finger-holes. The player partly closes the mouth-hole with his tongue and blows from the side of his mouth. It is frequently used for lamenting the dead. See *TraceyCSA*, ii, 356.

Ilongo. Drum of Zaïre. (1) Pot drum of the Konda, Yembe, Lia-Ibeke and Nkundo peoples. Most drums are 20 to 26 cm high and very broad; the base may be narrower than the overall diameter and curve gently towards the sides. The head, made from antelope skin, is fastened by cord bracing, which may cover the greater part of the pot. Among the Konda the drum is beaten by women to accompany the dancing of other women. The Loi refer to a pot drum of this type as *bonkenge*, the Mbwanja and Eso as *bongemba* and the Ngando as *ebondza*.

(2) Long cylindro-conical drum of the Nkundo people. See KIMBANDU.

BIBLIOGRAPHY
BooneT, 7, 37, 62
F. J. de Hen: *Beitrag zur Kenntnis der Musikinstrumente aus Belgisch Kongo und Ruanda-Urundi* (Tervuren, 1960)
G. Knosp: *Enquête sur la vie musicale au Congo belge 1934–1935* (Tervuren, 1968)

K. A. GOURLAY

Ilpirra. See ULBURA.

Ilu. Cylindrical single-headed drum, of African origin, of the north-eastern provinces of Brazil, especially Pernambuco and Ceará; the term was formerly used for a double-headed barrel-shaped drum. See also TAMBU.

Ilyu. SLIT-DRUM of the Tiv people of Nigeria. See INDIER.

Imana. Mouth-resonated chordophone of the Ngonda and Ngando peoples of central Zaïre (*LaurentyC*, 110). See EMANA.

Imangu. Large double-headed drum of Zambia. It is made from petrol drums and laced cowhide, and is played with beaters while suspended from a pole.

Imbalanyi. Percussion beam of the Gishu people of Uganda. It is approximately 175 to 200 cm long. The beam is placed on the ground and beaten by two young men, each with a short, thick stick in either hand, to induce edible ants to leave the soil.

Imbande. NOTCHED FLUTE of the Zulu and Xhosa peoples of southern Africa. It is made from a portion of the legbone of a bird, about 13 cm long, and is covered with skin. The lower end is stopped, and there are no finger-holes. The mouth-hole is notched from both sides (as with the IGEMFE) and is held against the player's lower lip. It was used by medicine men in a ceremony for making warriors immune against defeat. See *KirbyMISA*, 107f, pll.34, 36.

DAVID K. RYCROFT

Imbembb. Wooden-keyed LAMELLAPHONE of the Lele people of south-western Zaïre. It has wooden keys and a wooden raft-type base (*LaurentyS*, 191).

Imbila. (1) One-bar XYLOPHONE of Zambia. It is known as *imbila* by the Ngumbo people of the Luapula province and *ilimba* by the Lala and Nsenga of the Central and Eastern provinces (for illustration *see* XYLOPHONE fig.5). It consists of a wooden key mounted over a calabash resonator, and is held between the thighs with the left arm and played singly or in pairs with beaters. The pair is tuned a 3rd apart by the Ngumbo (who sing in parallel 3rds) and a 4th apart by those groups who harmonize in 4ths.

(2) XYLOPHONE of the Karanga people of south-eastern Africa. See also AMBIRA and MBILA.

Imbilta. See EMBILTA.

Imboccatura (It.). EMBOUCHURE.

Imborivungu. Traditional cult pipe of the Tiv people of Nigeria, named after the night birds. The instrument may have consisted originally of a hollow human leg bone, one end of which was covered with membrane from a bat wing or frog skin. In later versions the bone was surmounted by a pottery or brass human head.

BIBLIOGRAPHY
R. East: *Akiga's Story* (London, 1939/R1965)
H. Balfour: 'Ritual and Secular Uses of Vibrating Membranes as Voice-Disguisers', *Journal of the Royal Anthropological Institute*, lxxxviii (1948), 45

K. A. GOURLAY

Imele. PLURIARC of the Oli people of Zaïre (*LaurentyC*, 117). See LUKOMBE (i).

Imfengwane [impempe, indweba]. Whistle of the Zulu people of southern Africa. The name is applied to the European police whistle and to imitations of this, made from reed. Police whistles are often used by Zulu girls to accentuate the rhythm in recreational dance-songs, as also among the Swazi to whom the whistle is known as *impembe*. See *KirbyMISA*, 88ff, 130, pl.34.

Imi [ta'impe]. HOURGLASS DRUM of the Mimilea area of West New Guinea (Irian Jaya). The skin is glued to the drumhead. See J. Kunst: *Music in New Guinea* (The Hague, 1967), 16.

Imiguza. Dancing-rattles of the Xhosa people of southern Africa, consisting of a number of dry gourds fastened round the waist.

Imillutaq [imiglutaq, imilguptak]. BULLROARER made as a toy by the Inuit of Canada. A piece of bone or ivory is carved so that the edge is notched, and a sinew cord is attached.

Imitungu. STAMPING TUBE of the Bemba people of Zambia. It is played in sets of three or four which function like drum ensembles.

Impalampala [mpalampala]. Side-blown trumpet of the Zulu people of southern Africa. It was made from the horn of a kudu and used for signalling but is rarely found today. Similar trumpets of southern Africa are the *imphalamphala*, *lepapata*, *phalaphala*, *shipalapala* and *uphondo*.

npembe. Whistle of the Swazi people of southern frica. *See* IMFENGWANE.

npempe. End-blown flute of the Xhosa and Zulu peoles of southern Africa. It is a short stopped pipe of ed, bone or porcupine quill, blown by laying the open id on the player's hollowed tongue. It is used by boys id by medicine men. Among the Zulu the name also pplies to the European police whistle and to imitations f this, made from reed; *see* IMFENGWANE. The Xhosa se the term for a flute (also known as *ixilongo*) resembling the Zulu UMTSHINGO. See *KirbyMISA*, 88ff, 112, 30 and pll.34*b* and 46*a*.

DAVID K. RYCROFT

nperial euphonium. KAISERBARYTON.

nphalamphala. Side-blown trumpet of the Swazi eople of southern Africa, cognate with the IMPALAMLA. It is made from the horn of a sable antelope and erves as a royal instrument at important ceremonies and unts.

mprovisation. The creation of a musical work, or the nal form of a musical work, as it is being performed. : may involve the work's immediate composition by its erformers, or the elaboration or adjustment of an existg framework, or anything in between. Well-known xamples of improvisation in Western art music include ie supplying of a part not fully notated; the ornamention of a given part or parts; the addition of a cadenza; r the creation of a piece in some standard form (e.g. igue or variations) from given material. To some extent very performance involves elements of improvisation, ough its degree varies according to period and place, nd to some extent every improvisation rests upon a series f conventions or implicit rules. The term 'extemporiation' is used more or less interchangeably with mprovisation'. By its very nature – in that improvisaon is essentially evanescent – it is one of the subjects ast amenable to historical research.

The present article deals with the traditions of nprovisation, as far as they can be ascertained, in Vestern art music and in the art musics of certain parts f Asia. For information about particular aspects of nprovisation *see* CADENZA; CONTINUO; DIVISION; ORNAENTS; PERFORMING PRACTICE.

Western art music. II. Asian art music.

I. Western art music

. Up to 1600: (i) Ensemble improvisation (ii) Ornamentation (iii) nprovisation on 'perfect instruments'. 2. The Baroque period: (i) arly 17th-century Italian practice (ii) English divisions and florid ong (iii) France (iv) Later Italianate embellishments (v) Varied prises (vi) Cadenzas (vii) Continuo realization (viii) Bach and andel (ix) Complete pieces. 3. The Classical period: (i) Attitudes) Hiller's rules (iii) The Viennese Classics. 4. After 1800: (i) rnamentation (ii) Cadenzas (iii) Preludes (iv) Free improvisation.

. UP TO 1600. After the breakdown of Greco-Roman ivilization, music in western Europe was preserved by ote memory, and new music was presumably worked ut in performance or created spontaneously in improviation. Since our knowledge of this music is limited to aditional liturgical chants written down in imprecise otation long after they were created, it is difficult to raw concrete conclusions about any improvisatory

techniques used in their creation. The most reliable extant evidence relates to the spontaneous improvisation of the *jubilus*, a melismatic flourish found on the last syllable of certain alleluias preserved in the early Christian liturgy. Clear references to this type of improvisation appear in the writings of the early Christian Fathers. St Augustine (354–430) described this *jubilus* as the musical outpouring of 'a certain sense of joy without words . . . the expression of a mind poured forth in joy'. In its melismatic, virtuoso style it is not unlike the vocal cadenza added centuries later at the cadence of a Baroque aria.

A second, more controlled, improvisatory technique is hinted at in the structure of a number of surviving chant melodies. The chants in a particular mode, such as Dorian, often use the same, or a similar, vocabulary of melodic motifs. This is taken as indicating an improvisatory practice in which the modes, like the ragas of India, included thematic materials as well as a roster of notes in their identities.

(i) Ensemble improvisation. Although melodic improvisation remained a factor in Western culture, it is indicative of its later development that the earliest substantial information about improvisation appears in treatises instructing the singer how to add another line to a liturgical chant as it was being performed. This is no doubt due to the fact that, although this early organum may have been derived from folk practice, the problem of improvising a melody to fit with a given chant required a technical knowledge of vertical consonance and dissonance and of the melodic materials available in the diatonic system. Furthermore, while at first the improvising singer may have relied on his memory of the chant to which he was adding a counter-melody, the improvisers eventually saw this chant in some sort of visual notation so that they could anticipate its notes. Thus the first manuals on improvisation are those concerned with the beginning of contrapuntal theory and practice and with the development of mensural staff notation.

Starting in the 9th century with the anonymous *Musica enchiriadis* and *Scholia enchiriadis*, which tell how to double a chant at the perfect intervals and to make oblique motion at the beginning and end of the chant, there was a steady growth and refining of the technique of organum. By the 11th century, when Guido of Arezzo described in his *Micrologus* the use of contrary motion and of rudimentary cadence formulae, there are also, in one of the Winchester tropers, a number of two-voice organa written down in staffless neumes that apparently use these same devices. From this time on, many writtendown organa are found outside theoretical treatises, but the precise relation of these to improvised style is not defined. Two- and three-voice organa which introduce the use of several notes against one in the cantus firmus, such as those found in 12th-century manuscripts at St Martial, Limoges, and Santiago de Compostela, have the appearance of written-down improvisations, and it is unlikely that a composition was yet worked out by writing it down. Musical forms of the 13th century – discant, organum, motet, etc – were created by adding one line at a time to a previously worked-out melody, each of the added lines agreeing with this melody but not necessarily with each other. The interrelation of the parts was the same as when two singers improvised on a cantus firmus. By the 14th century, when a precise visual notation for music was established, complex structures, such as the isorhythmic motet, that could be worked out only by being written down, had also developed. Thenceforward the dependence on notation for composing music as well as for preserving it became one of the distinguishing features of Western musical culture, and in due course composed music, precisely notated, became the primary basis for performance.

Improvised music, however, remained an important element in art music for several centuries, and the interaction of the two types was fruitful. A well-known instance of the influence of improvised style on composed music is the introduction of the fauxbourdon style into the music of Burgundian composers, such as Dufay and Binchois, in the 15th century. In Britain in the late 14th and early 15th centuries, the practice of improvising above a 'sighted' chant took the forms of parallel 3rds (gymel) and parallel 3rds and 6ths together (English discant). Although scholars still differ as to the exact historical process and the meanings of certain terms, the musical effect of these techniques on styles of composition is clear. In Britain this resulted in compositions that were structurally based on a series of 3rds or 6-3 chords that were freely ornamented and sometimes interspersed with other combinations of intervals. In Burgundian music, sections of parallel 6-3 chords (fauxbourdon) are inserted into the common styles and are found frequently at cadence points.

It was also in the 15th century that theorists of counterpoint first made a distinction between improvised and written-down styles. In 1412 Prosdocimus de Beldemandis simply mentioned the existence of two types of counterpoint – the 'sung' or 'performed' and the written – but in 1477 Tinctoris clearly spelt out the difference between the two in his *Liber de arte contrapuncti*. Because each improviser could make his line agree with the cantus firmus alone, dissonances and awkward part-writing could not be avoided. Moreover, an improvised piece was looser in construction, whereas the composer could order such features as cadences and rhythmic motion, thus producing a finished work (*res facta*) with a distinctive character.

The difference between the two styles became even greater in the 16th century, when the practice of writing all the parts simultaneously, rather than adding them one at a time to a cantus firmus, became the rule in composition. Composed works appeared in a number of new styles and forms, while singers still improvised over a cantus firmus in long notes, often repeating a single figure as long as it fitted. At this period, improvisation was widely practised in Italian churches, where it was normally used over the chants of the introits in the Proper of the Mass, as well as over the hymns, antiphons and graduals. Since motets and the Ordinary of the Mass were set as artfully worked-out compositions, listeners will have apprehended two distinct usages.

It was not until 1553, when Vicente Lusitano's *Introdutione facilissima* was published, that a methodical procedure for learning to improvise on a cantus firmus was made available. His 'secrets' seem very simple, as he was presenting a basic method by which the technique could be learnt; it may well have been based on his own way of improvising. He first gave a number of mechanical patterns in long notes that fit over the different intervals found in plainchant, such as those in ex.1a, where the syncopated line makes a series of 3rds, 5ths and 6ths over a succession of horizontal 3rds in the cantus firmus. Once the basic pattern was learnt, the singer could fill in the long notes with florid passages.

Ex.1 Lusitano
(a)
(b)

Lusitano also included a number of single melodies in florid counterpoint above a cantus firmus (ex.1b). This exemplifies another of his suggestions: if a passage will fit more than once, the singer should continue to use it. Although more than one part above the cantus firmus is known to have been used in this practice, Lusitano gave no examples. He did, however, give a number of florid examples above the same cantus firmus, and when two of these are combined, as they would be in performance, a number of dissonances and parallel 5ths appear between them.

Two years after Lusitano's treatise appeared, Nicola Vicentino, in *L'antica musica ridotta alla moderna prattica*, condemned these devices as old-fashioned and recommended more modern ways, such as having the imitating voices imitate each other rather than the cantus firmus. Zarlino, in the second edition of his *Institutioni harmoniche* (1573), gave, for the first time, instructions for more sophisticated devices, such as the improvisation of strict two-voice canons on a cantus firmus and two- and three-part canons without a cantus firmus. These techniques signalled a great change in improvised counterpoint. Both require more technical skill on the part of the performers. The leading singer must know all the possible combinations at specific times over precise pitches, and those following him must have good ears and memories. But this kind of planning also makes correct part-writing and dissonance treatment possible in improvisation. Zarlino also introduced rules for creating invertible counterpoint and for adding a third part in the performance of an already composed duet. During the last quarter of the 16th century his successors expanded the possibilities inherent in these new devices and also continued with the old. The art of improvised vocal counterpoint came to a final climax among the theorists and practitioners of counterpoint in the *prima prattica* style.

Although there are many early visual and literary references to instrumental ensemble music, no direct discussion of improvisation by instrumental groups has been found. We can only surmise that when contrapuntal – as opposed to heterophonic – improvisation took place in instrumental performance it was by players who had been trained in the vocal practice of improvising on a cantus firmus. The first sure evidence of such a practice is in the improvisation of the music for the bassadanza and saltarello danced in 15th-century Italy. Surviving collections of bassadanza tenors in long notes, along with pictures showing two high instruments presumably improvising on a tenor played by a sackbut, show that the music accompanying these dances may well have been produced by just such an improvising group. Later compositions on one of these bassadanza tenors, La Spagna, in which the tenor in long, even notes is accompanied by florid melodies in the upper parts, add weight to this conclusion.

Ex.2 Diego Ortiz
a) Ricercada 1 (on La Spagna tenor)

b) Ricercada 1 (on Italian dance tenor)

It is significant too that the only book in this period giving examples of ensemble improvisation (for violone and harpsichord), Diego Ortiz's *Trattado de glosas* (1553), still used the old *La Spagna* tenor when illustrating the technique of improvising on a cantus firmus. The beginning of one such improvisation (ex.2a), when contrasted with another (ex.2b) from the same book, shows the archaic nature of this improvisation. The one shown in ex.2b has a 16th-century Italian dance bass, which acts as a series of roots for triads, and the improvised melody is shaped by the notes of each chord and is organized motivically. The bass also gives the rhythm of the dance and is organized in phrases that are multiples of four bars. It is also short and is repeated several times, showing a series of improvised variations – a form and style that were to be used in improvisation for several centuries to come.

(ii) *Ornamentation*. A less difficult type of ensemble improvisation occurred in the 16th century when florid passages were added to a single line of a composed work while it was being performed. These ornaments were called diminutions, since they reduced the longer notes of a piece into a number of shorter notes; this practice was also referred to as the 'breaking' of a melodic line. Skill in diminutions belonged to the performer rather than to the improvising composer, and it required little theoretical knowledge, since the performer needed only to fit florid patterns into the longer notes of an already composed piece. More care had to be taken by the singer or instrumentalist who embellished the single line of a polyphonic work of which he saw only his own part than by the organist who had a complete work under his control, but the procedures taught by the various published manuals on diminution were designed to help him avoid these difficulties. There were lists of the numerous melodic patterns that fitted into each melodic interval and note length commonly found in music of the

time, and these patterns could be transferred directly to the melodic line that the soloist wished to ornament.

Three general procedures were followed in creating these embellishments. The simplest was to have the substitute passage begin and end on the pitch of the notes being ornamented and then move immediately to the next note in the melody, a procedure shown in ex.3a. This was considered the safest, for it preserved the original contrapuntal movement of the work. The second way, shown in ex.3b, was to start on the original note but, instead of ending on it, to move on and arrive at the next note by stepwise motion. Although this way might produce contrapuntal errors such as unauthorized dissonances or parallel 5ths, it was assumed that they would not be noticed by the listener because the notes were so short. The third manner was simply to be freer, perhaps encompassing a longer segment of the original line in the embellishment or replacing one of the main melodic notes with a pattern not touching on it. While it was not approved, this technique can be seen in the ornamented works that are given in the diminution manuals; it often involved motivic or sequential patterns, as seen in ex.3c. It could be successful, however, only if the performer knew what was going on in the other parts.

Ex.3
simple line

embellished versions
(a)

(b)   etc

(c)

This type of improvised ornamentation was usually applied to only one voice of a polyphonic work, but when a madrigal or motet was performed by soloists, each improvising diminutions on his part, care was taken to agree in advance the order in which they would add ornaments, to avoid contrapuntal confusion and dissonant clashes that might result from simultaneous ornamentation. Care was also taken by the performer of the bass part not to let his ornaments go above the tenor part and to limit his embellishments, so that the overall structure of the supporting bass line was retained throughout.

The first manual teaching the art of improvising diminutions for a solo singer or wind or string player in ensemble performances of polyphonic works was the *Fontegara* of Silvestro Ganassi, published in Venice in 1535. It is believed, however, that this practice must have appeared early in the development of polyphonic music, since the earliest known keyboard tablature, the Robertsbridge Fragment (c1320), contains elaborately ornamented versions of contemporary motets, and it is generally considered that the published manuals of the 16th century were a late attempt to codify and make available to all musicians the 'secrets' of this technique.

Improvised diminutions had a definite influence on composed music, for they introduced elements into the performance of Renaissance music that became an integral part of Baroque style. The ornamentation of a single line of a polyphonic work by a solo instrument while the entire work was played on a keyboard instrument, as seen in the second book of Ortiz's *Trattado de glosas*, anticipated the solo instrumental writing of the early Baroque period. In the same manner, the ornamented cantus parts of frottolas such as the anonymous *Aime sospiri* printed in Petrucci's sixth book of frottolas (1505), and the embellished top voices of selected four-part madrigals by Rore included in Girolamo dalla Casa's *Il vero modo di diminuir* (1584), which were sung while the other parts were played on the lute, were forerunners of early 17th-century monody.

(iii) Improvisation on 'perfect instruments'. For the Renaissance musician, the 'perfect instrument' was one such as the organ or lute, on which a single performer could play all the parts of a polyphonic composition. Starting with the Robertsbridge Fragment and the Faenza Codex (early 15th century), elaborately ornamented versions of polyphonic motets and secular works appeared as a constant part of the repertory and can doubtless be seen as written-down examples of a common improvisatory procedure. Highly embellished intabulations of polyphonic vocal works continued to appear in keyboard manuscripts into the 16th century, when, with the development of music printing, a great many such arrangements for lute and vihuela, as well as for keyboard, were published. From the 14th century on, keyboard tablatures also included sacred chants and secular songs used as cantus firmi with florid counter-melodies. The fact that a number of 15th-century manuscripts, such as the *Fundamentum organisandi* (1452) of Conrad Paumann, give practical instructions for adding keyboard-style counter-melodies to fit with the intervals commonly found in such pre-existing melodies tends to confirm that contrapuntal improvisation on a chant in church or on a popular song in secular music-making was a common practice with the professional keyboard virtuoso. While these techniques were still important in 16th-century keyboard improvisation, the gradual abandonment of the central cantus firmus and the use of free forms based on fugal imitation in vocal music are reflected in the inclusion of canonic and fugal devices in Hans Buchner's *Fundamentum* (c1520) and the *Arte de tañer fantasia* (1565) of Tomás de Santa María.

A new form, the set of variations on a popular tune or dance bass already familiar to the listener, also became a major element in improvisatory practice in the 16th century. These variations used both the older technique of cantus firmus and the new one mentioned above (see ex.2*b*), which has a set of chords as the 'theme'. In some cases both the melody and the harmony of a popular song form the basis of a set of variations. This practice is paralleled in vocal music, where poet–composers, and less sophisticated figures too, improvised both words in fixed forms such as *terza rima* and ottavas, and vocal embellishments, over standard melodies, such as the romanesca and Ruggiero, and their attendant harmonies.

A special genre associated with the keyboard was the prelude or intonation, a free improvisation meant to establish the mode for a vocal or instrumental piece that followed it. The earliest written-out examples of this type are found in the keyboard tablature of Adam Ileborgh (1448). This genre was characterized from th beginning by idiomatic virtuosity, rhythmic freedom an loose thematic construction – features that listeners hav always considered the true hallmarks of extemporane ous improvisation.

The line between improvising and composing was les clearly drawn in solo improvising because here the play er normally had his own repertory, playing from mem ory, improvising and often changing his composition and re-using materials from earlier improvisations. Th fact that there were so many famous keyboard compos ers was no doubt due to this practice. The great man collections of printed works for keyboard, lute and sim ilar instruments in the 16th century, bringing music from the repertory and inventions of the professional per former into the hands of the amateur, led to a grea change. The works of the professional virtuoso, whethe devised through his own improvisations, worked out o his instrument in playing or first created in written nota tion, became in published form the repertory for th amateur, and improvisation became associated with th professional virtuoso.

2. THE BAROQUE PERIOD.

(i) Early 17th-century Italian practice. The 16th century practice of improvised embellishment by voca and instrumental virtuosos, described above, continued to flourish after 1600, but important modifications were now introduced. The written-out embellishments in 'Possente spirto', the great aria in Act 3 of Monteverdi's *Orfeo* – the words of which are, significantly, in *terza rima* – represent an extreme example, now in early Baroque style, of the type of embellishment earlier improvised by poet–musicians and referred to in §1 (iii) above. Stylistic modifications of the old, melodically orientated embellishment occurred about 1600 through the establishment of a true basso continuo and as a consequence too of the new emphasis on emotional qualities in singing. The basso continuo, with its firm bass line and improvised chords, emphasized vertical rather than linear aspects, and embellishment gradually attained more harmonic implications, adding the spice of dissonance to the written notes. The new emotional style in vocal music caused two modifications in the melodic lines: the smoothly flowing notes of 16th-century *passaggi* were alternately dotted to form either trochaic or iambic figures that might emphasize sobbing or sighing qualities; and a new vocabulary of short embellishments was invented for use on notes sung to the accented syllables of emotive words in the text. The new style of embellishment is first seen in G. B. Bovicelli's *Regole, passaggi di musica* (1594), but the aforementioned modifications came about largely through the influence of the Florentine Camerata and their insistence on correct and emotive declamation of the text. *Passaggi* were for the most part relegated to penultimate syllables of verses, where they did not obscure the meaning of the words; they can thus be seen as early forerunners of the later cadenza.

The preface to Caccini's *Le nuove musiche* (1601/2), the most celebrated expression of the passionate attitude of the men who invented the new style, contains much discussion of vocal embellishments; some of these are illustrated in ex.4. His description of the *esclamazione* makes clear that it is to be performed as indicated by the dynamics added to ex.4*a*. His cadential *trillo* and

Ex.4 Caccini

(a) Esclamazione languida   Esclamazione più viva

cor___ mio, deh   non lan-gui - - - re

(b) trillo

gruppo

(c)

Performed thus:

trillo

gruppo are seen in ex.4*b*. The early Baroque preference for dotted figures is seen in his illustrations of the desirable way of performing the phrases shown in ex.4*c*. That the embellishment of penultimate (and sometimes other) syllables often reached cadenza-like proportions can be seen in several songs in *Le nuove musiche*, notably *Fortunato augellino*, and in those of other Italian monodists of the period. The new kinds of embellishment became known in due course in Germany, where descriptions are found in such works as *Syntagma musicum* (1614–18) by Michael Praetorius and *Musica moderna prattica* (1653) by J. A. Herbst. Praetorius provided some of the best examples of Italian devices. Ex.5 shows four of them: (*a*) *accento*, (*b*) *anticipatione della nota*, (*c*) *anticipatione della sillaba* and (*d*) *cercar della nota*.

Ex.5 Praetorius

(a)   (b)   (c)   (d)

can - tar.   can - tar.   can - tar.   can-tar.___   can - tar.___

The embellishments so far discussed belong to the new style of monody, not to the *stile rappresentativo* – the strict recitative of theatre music – where the written notes were adhered to except for an occasional cadential *trillo* or flourish. The keyboard, lute or theorbo realization of the continuo was likewise very simple at this early stage, as is shown by the written-out lute realizations of Caccini's *Amarilli mia bella* and *Dovrò dunque morire* in Robert Dowland's *A Musicall Banquet* (1610). Three- or four-note chords suffice, with passing notes to keep the music moving when the singer has a sustained note or rest. The accompaniment should not double the

melodic line, a stricture enunciated in Agazzari's *Del sonare sopra 'l basso* (1607). A probable exception to this rule can be seen in the stanzas in *stile recitativo* beginning with the word 'Notte' in Monteverdi's *Il combattimento di Tancredi e Clorinda*, which is also the only place in the work where the composer allowed the singers freedom to improvise embellishments; a richer, broken-chord style with occasional passage-work seems a more appropriate accompaniment here. Such a style would be in line with the advice of Viadana (the supposed inventor of the basso continuo) in his *Cento concerti ecclesiastici* (1602).

The organist should accompany quite simply, especially in the bass; if he wishes occasionally to ornament a cadence or introduce runs in the right hand, he should do so in such a way that the singers will not be covered or confused by too much movement.

Agazzari also discussed the role of instruments in the improvised embellishment of vocal music. He counselled restraint, decorum and the judicious enhancement of the written notes and he outlined the roles appropriate to the various instruments (translation from Strunk, 1950):

He who plays the lute . . . must play it nobly, with much invention and variety, not as is done by those who, because they have a ready hand, do nothing but play runs and make divisions from beginning to end, especially when playing with other instruments which do the same, in all of which nothing is heard but babel and confusion, displeasing and disagreeable to the listener. Sometimes, therefore, he must use gentle strokes and repercussions, sometimes slow passages, sometimes rapid and repeated ones, sometimes something played on the bass strings, sometimes beautiful vyings and conceits, repeating and bringing out these figures at different pitches and in different places; he must, in short, so weave the voices together with long groups, trills, and accents, each in its turn, that he gives grace to the consort and enjoyment and delight to the listeners, judiciously preventing these embellishments from conflicting with one another and allowing time to each, especially when there are other similar instruments, a thing to be avoided, in my opinion, unless they play at a great distance or are differently tuned or of different sizes. . . . The violin requires beautiful passages, distinct and long, with playful figures and little echoes and imitations repeated in several places, passionate accents, mute strokes of the bow, groups, trills, etc. The *violone*, as lowest part, proceeds with gravity, supporting the harmony of the other parts with soft resonance, dwelling as much as possible on the heavier strings, frequently touching the lowest ones. The theorbo, with its full and gentle consonances, reinforces the melody greatly, restriking and lightly passing over the bass strings, its special excellence, with trills and mute accents played with the left hand. The *arpa doppia*, which is everywhere useful, as much so in the soprano as in the bass, explores its entire range with gentle plucked notes, echoes of the two hands, trills, etc.; in short, it aims at good counterpoint. The cithern, whether the common cither or the *ceterone*, is used with the other instruments in a playful way, making counterpoints upon the part. But all this must be done prudently; if the instruments are alone in the consort, they must lead it and do everything; if they play in company, each must regard the other, giving it room and not conflicting with it; if there are many, they must each await their turn and not, chirping all at once like sparrows, try to shout one another down.

(ii) *English divisions and florid song*. In just the manner described by Agazzari, there was a flourishing school of instrumental improvisation in England in the 17th century. Variation was a process inherited from the virginalists, and English instrumentalists were fond of improvising diminutions or variations on popular songs such as *Greensleeves*, itself based on the *passamezzo antico*. From this practice it was only a simple step to composing an original ground and repeating it ad libitum while another instrumentalist or two improvised divisions on it. A valuable source for this practice is Christopher Simpson's *Division Violist* (1659); ex.6 shows excerpts from a set of divisions from it for solo bass viol. The vocal lines of English continuo songs were also subjected to extensive embellishments of various kinds, and several manuscript sources are largely devoted to such florid songs (see Till, 1975).

Ex.6 Christopher Simpson

ground

Var. 9

Var. 11

Var. 17

Var. 18

(iii) France. The *air de cour* of the 17th century was to some extent influenced by the new style of Caccini, who visited the French court with his family in the winter and spring of 1604–5. Pierre Guédron, an almost exact contemporary of Caccini, introduced Italianate accompanied monody to France. Another prominent composer of *airs de cour* was Antoine Boësset. Ex.7 shows an *air* by him with diminutions by Henri de Bailly and Antoine Moulinié (taken from Mersenne) in the form in which they would have been improvised; the Moulinié version illustrates the French penchant for the Italian *anticipatione della sillaba* (*avantson* or *port de voix*).

The *airs* of the 1620s and 1630s adopted the ornamented style of Italian monody without much of its inner spirit, and were criticized by the following generation for their lack of correct declamation and the placing of roulades on syllables regardless of their importance or length. The leader of the new generation, Pierre de Nyert, was in Rome from 1633 to 1635, but perhaps the most famous and influential of the court singers in 17th-century France was Michel Lambert, a pupil of Nyert, whose

Ex.7

Bailly

2. Les   pleurs   n'ont plus___   de ___   lieu   Dans

Moulinié

N'e - spe - rez plus,___ mes___ yeux,   De

Boësset

1. N'e - spe - rez plus,   mes   yeux,   De

___ le coeur ___ de ___   ce _ dieu   Dont le feu ___ me

re - voir ___   en   ces _   lieux ___   la beau - té

re - voir   en   ces   lieux   la beau - té

___ de - vo - - re. ___

que ___ j'a - do - - re.

que ___ j'a - do - - re.

ower at court in musical matters was second only to hat of Lully (who became his son-in-law). Lambert's tyle and teaching are reflected in the *Remarques curieuses sur l'art de bien chanter* (1668) of Bénigne de Bacilly, another pupil of Nyert. This treatise, certainly he most important one on the art of singing in the later 7th century, is concerned primarily with improvised ornaments (*port de voix, cadence, tremblement, accent, aspiration*, etc) and with diminutions and their proper placing on vowels and syllables. Bacilly's numerous examples include second couplets of *airs* published by himself and Lambert. Ex.8 illustrates some alternative final cadences for *Je voy des amans*, an *air* presumably by Bacilly himself. That such vocal improvisations were practised even in the provinces can be seen from *C'en est fait a ce coup*, an *air* from *La belle méthode, ou L'art de bien chanter* (1666) by the Besançon musician Jean Millet.

Ex.8 ?Bacilly

Two important treatises by the viol player Jean Rousseau provide much information about improvised ornamentation. His *Méthode claire, certaine et facile pour apprendre à chanter la musique* (1678), dedicated to Lambert, reflects the latter's practice, and in his *Traité de la viole* (1687) he made an attempt, which may be unique, to transfer this vocal practice to the viol. The *Traité* contains the illustrations seen in ex.9, together

Ex.9 Rousseau

(a) Ports de voix

(b) tremblements

with elaborate rules for the placing of the *port de voix* and *tremblement* in performance. The practice of anticipating the beat by dividing the note preceding the ornament reflects a vocal practice, already on the wane, that Etienne Loulié (1696) and Michel L'Affilard (1705) were the last to advocate. It has been demonstrated that the performer sustains the upper or lower note on to the strong beat before beginning the beating of the *tremblement* or the mordent of the *port de voix*. For the most part, anticipatory ornaments were not used in keyboard music, though there are rare examples in the *récit* of Nivers' *Suite du 1er ton* from his third *Livre d'orgue* (1675).

There was another important change of French style in the early 18th century. The harmonic orientation of the *agréments* was now complete. In his *L'art de toucher le clavecin* (1716), Couperin began all his ornaments on the beat. Montéclair, in his *Principes de musique* (1736, p.86), poured scorn on the sort of embellishments (*passages*) taught by Lambert and Bacilly and praised 'the incomparable Lully' for preferring 'melody, beautiful modulation, agreeable harmony, exactness of expression, naturalness and finally noble simplicity to the ridiculousness of *doubles*'. This does not mean, of course, that Montéclair, or Lully for that matter, was opposed to the use of real *agréments*, since he explained in detail the placing and performance of such ornaments as the *pincé*, *port de voix* and *tremblement*. Like those of Couperin, they are all harmonically orientated on the beat. Indeed, as early as 1687, in his *Traité de la viole* (p.72), Rousseau anticipated Montéclair in condemning 'a profusion of ornamental *passages*, which only confuse the melody and obscure its beauty', while advocating, as has been seen above, the proper treatment of more restrained ornaments such as the *port de voix* and *tremblement*. The most widely used French keyboard ornaments begin squarely on the beat. The improvisation of a large number of *agréments* is necessary in the music of some French composers, especially in that of Louis Couperin, who was very sparing in his use of ornament signs.

Another form of French improvisatory practice involves rhythm, since such practices as over-dotting and *notes inégales* were never notated in the music. The performer was in fact expected to improvise the entire rhythmic fabric of many preludes, which were printed only in skeletal form in long notes and with very few ornament signs. (*See also* DOTTED RHYTHMS and NOTES INÉGALES.)

(iv) Later Italianate embellishments. While French performers were becoming more cautious about introducing *passages*, Italian ones were reaching unprecedented heights of improvisatory embellishment for the solo violin and the opera aria. Quantz recognized this basic difference between the French and Italian approaches (see his *Versuch einer Anweisung, die Flöte traversiere zu spielen*, 1752; chap.10, §115), and Burney remarked later of Italian practice that 'an adagio in a song or solo is generally little more than an outline left to the performer's abilities to colour'. The practice of ornamenting Italian adagios indeed continued throughout the Baroque period. Examples of improvisation in Italian adagio movements have fortunately survived, foremost among them, perhaps, those found in Corelli's op.5 sonatas in Roger's Amsterdam edition of about 1715. According to Roger, these were 'composez par Mr A. Corelli comme il le joue'; ex.10 presents the

opening bars of no.3. From other extant examples it can be inferred that even the faster movements of Corelli's sonatas were embellished.

In his *Compendium musicae signatoriae et modulatoriae vocalis* (1689, chap.5, §19) W. C. Printz described some Italian ornaments – *figure corte, messanze* and *salti* (see ex.11) – that are somewhat less florid than those encountered in adagios. Even Montéclair, who was against *passages* (see §2(iii) above), admitted this type, which he called *diminutions*. The best way to see how they can be improvised is to strip the *figure corte* from a written-out piece, for which the aria 'Singet dem Herrn' from Buxtehude's cantata of the same title (BUXWV98) has been selected (see ex.12). Bach's cantatas are replete with examples of written-out *figure corte*.

Ex.11 W. C. Printz

(a) figure corte

(b) messanze

(c) salti

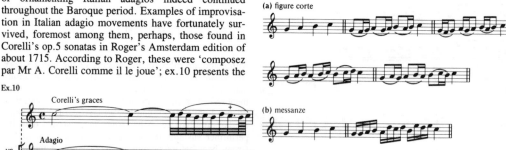

(v) Varied reprises. The varying of a reprise with improvised embellishment is a basic principle in music of the Baroque period. Quantz wrote about it as follows (op cit, from the translation *Easy and Fundamental Instructions*, *c*1790):

It is a principal Rule with regard to Variations that they must have a just reference to the plain Air, the variation is made upon . . . the first Note of the Variation must for the most part be same with the original or plain Note . . . or any other Note may be chosen instead of it from the Harmony of the Bass, provided the Principal or plain Note be heard immediately after it . . .

Ex.10

Corelli's graces

Adagio

vn solo

bc

6
5   4   3

Ex.12 Buxtehude

sin - get, sin - get   sin - get, sin - get, sin-get dem Herrn ein neues Lied

Brisk and lively Variations must not be introduced in an Air that is soft, tender and mournful, unless the Performer knows how to render them more suitable and agreeable in the manner of executing them.

Variations are only to be introduced after the simple Air has been heard first, otherwise it will be impossible for the Hearer to distinguish the latter from the former; nor does an Air, compos'd in a pleasing and graceful Stile, require any such additions, unless one was sure to improve still more upon it, they being used for no other end, than to render an Air in the cantabile Stile more melodious, and Divisions in general more brilliant.

Those that consist in a continual series of swift Notes or quick Passages, though ever so much admired by some, in general are not so pleasing as those of the more simple kind, the latter being more capable of touching the Heart, a Point that certainly is most to be aim'd at, and indeed at the same time the most difficult Part in Music, for which reason a young Beginner is advis'd to be cautious and moderate in the use of Embellishments and Graces.

Practical consideration occasionally led a composer to write out varied reprises, as C. P. E. Bach did in his *Sechs Sonaten für Clavier mit veränderten Reprisen* (1760). He wrote in the foreword (translation, 1961, from Ferand, 1956):

Variation upon repetition is indispensable today. It is expected of every performer. The public demands that practically every idea be repeatedly altered, sometimes without investigating whether the structure of the piece or the skill of the performer permits such alteration. It is this embellishing alone, especially if it is coupled with a long and sometimes bizarrely ornamented cadenza, that often squeezes the bravos out of most listeners. How lamentably are these two adornments of performance misused. One no longer has the patience to play the written notes the first time; the too long absence of bravos is unbearable. Often these untimely variations, contrary to the setting, contrary to the *Affect*, and contrary to the relationship between the ideas, are a disagreeable matter for many composers. Granted, however, that a performer has all the qualities necessary to vary a piece in the proper way; is he always ready to do so? Are not new difficulties raised thereby in unfamiliar pieces? However, aside from these difficulties and from misuse, good variations always retain their value. . . . In writing these sonatas I have had in mind mainly beginners and such amateurs as . . . no longer have enough time and patience to practise especially assiduously. I have wanted to give them . . . the satisfaction of being heard playing variations without having either to invent them themselves or to have others write them down and then themselves learn them by heart with much effort, I am happy to be the first, so far as I know, to work in this manner for the use and the pleasure of his patrons and friends.

Ex.13 shows the beginning of no.1, with the embellished reprise below (the right-hand part is shown; there are only minor differences in the left).

The varied reprise is mandatory in da capo arias. P. F. Tosi gave good advice to singers on this matter in his *Opinioni de' cantori antichi e moderni* (1723), here cited in J. E. Galliard's translation of 1742 (chap.7, §4):

In the first [part] they require nothing but the simplest Ornaments, of a good Taste and few, that the Composition may remain simple, plain, and pure; in the second they expect, that to this purity some artful Graces be added, by which the Judicious may hear, that the Ability of the Singer is greater; and, in repeating the Air, he that does not vary it for the better, is no great Master.

Because the principle of embellishment in arias did not change radically during the 18th century, except perhaps in the 'reform' operas of Gluck, the rules given by J. A. Hiller in his *Anweisung zum musikalisch-zierlichen Gesange* (1780; see §3(ii) below) are equally applicable to Baroque music. He stated that an aria must first be performed as the composer wrote it, though the singer could add one or two small graces. The varied da capo must appear easy and pleasant, but should actually be difficult in order to give the singer an opportunity to demonstrate his skill. In slow arias it is best to introduce legato ornaments, in *allegro*, staccato ones. *Passaggi* and similar ornaments should never be sung twice in the same way, and generally speaking the same graces should not be used too close to one another or too often in succession.

Ex.13 C. P. E. Bach

Ex.14 Heinichen

(vi) Cadenzas. A special instance of free improvisation is the cadenza (for a fuller account *see* CADENZA). In his section on cadences Quantz defined them as

those Embellishments commonly introduced on the last Note but one, mostly on the Fifth of the Key . . . the Productions of the momentary Invention of the Performer. Regular Time is seldom to be observ'd in Cadences . . . Those for Voice or Wind Instruments ought to be short and so manag'd that they may be perform'd in one Breath, but those for String Instruments are not limited, but the Performer has so much Latitude given him, as his own skill and fruitfulness of Invention will permit, but notwithstanding will gain more Applause from the Judicious by a moderate length than otherwise.

C. P. E. Bach, in his *Versuch über die wahre Art das Clavier zu spielen* (1753; end of chap.2), also discussed cadenzas in terms of fermatas appearing at cadences as well as other places (trans. W. J. Mitchell, 1949):

Fermate are often employed with good effect . . . there are three places at which the *fermata* appears: over the next to the last, the last, or the rest after the last bass note . . . *Fermate* over rests appear most frequently in allegro movements and are not embellished. The two other kinds are usually found in slow, affettuoso movements and must be embellished if only to avoid artlessness. In any event elaborate decoration is more necessary here than in other parts of movements.

The cadenzas improvised in da capo arias by singers such as the famous castrato Farinelli often ran to inordinate length, notwithstanding the stricture that they should be sung in one breath. Tosi (op cit, 128f) criticized such cadenzas thus:

Every *Air* has (at least) three *Cadences*, that are all three final. Generally speaking, the Study of the Singers of the present Times consists in terminating the *Cadence* of the first Part with an overflowing of *Passagges* and *Divisions* at Pleasure, and the *Orchestre* waits; in that of the second the Dose is encreased, and the *Orchestre* grows tired; but on the last *Cadence*, the Throat is set a going, like a Weather-cock in a Whirlwind, and the *Orchestre* yawns.

The gigantic written-out cadenza for harpsichord in the first movement of Bach's Fifth Brandenburg Concerto is an excellent example of its type, though it may be considered too extensive for the usual extemporization and even to constitute an example of the soloist's abuse of privilege. When the two outer movements of a Baroque concerto – or indeed any two movements in any other type of work – are separated only by two chords, usually constituting a Phrygian cadence, the first of them should be elaborated into an improvised

Ex.15

cadenza; a familiar instance occurs in Bach's Third Brandenburg Concerto.

(vii) Continuo realization. Developments in the realization of the thoroughbass kept pace with the elaboration of the melodic line in the late Baroque period (for a fuller account *see* CONTINUO). The most exhaustive treatment of this subject is by Heinichen in *Der General-Bass in der Composition* (1728). He declared that the simple three-part realizations of the 17th century were old-fashioned and advocated the doubling of chords in both hands and the introduction of improvised ornamentation. He provided (i, chap.6) three realizations of a single bass line (see ex.14), first in a simple manner (*a*), which can be avoided by introducing ornamentation and a true melodic line in the right hand (*b*); or, to give even more freedom to the melodic line, the chords may be played entirely by the left hand (*c*).

Early 18th-century Italian continuo practice went far beyond Heinichen, especially in the accompaniment of recitatives. Gasparini's *L'armonico pratico al cimbalo* (1708), Joseph de Torres y Martinez Bravo's *Reglas generales de acompañar, en organo, clavicordio y harpa* (enlarged 2/1736), which cites Gasparini with clearer musical examples, and Alessandro Scarlatti's *Per sonare il cembalo* (*GB-Lbm* Add.14244) give rules for the addition to triads of handfuls of acciaccaturas, to be played 'quasi arpeggiando'. But other examples, now and later in the century – for instance in Niccolo Pasquali's *Thorough-bass made Easy* (1757) – are more subdued.

There are two first-hand accounts of Bach's continuo improvisation. The first is L. C. Mizler's (1738) of his accompanying 'every thorough-bass to a solo so that one thinks it is a piece of concerted music and as if the melody he plays in the right hand were written beforehand' (translation from Aldrich, 1949). The second is from Bach's pupil J. C. Kittel, who described (*Der angehende praktische Organist*, iii, 1808, p.33) how Bach would become impatient with the inadequate accompaniment of a pupil and how 'one had to be prepared to find Bach's hands and fingers mingling with the hands and fingers of the player and, without further troubling the latter, adorning the accompaniment with masses of harmony, which were even more impressive than the unexpected proximity of the strict teacher'. Two of Bach's accompaniments are thought to be examples of his own realizations in written-out form, since they are marked 'cembalo obligato' and are not in the same style as his usual composed harpsichord parts: they are those of the second aria in the solo cantata *Amore traditore* BWV207 and of the second movement of the Sonata in B minor for flute and harpsichord BWV10.

(vii) Bach and Handel. High Baroque improvised ornamentation at its best may be seen in Bach's transcriptions of the works of other composers as well as his own (though they were adversely criticized by J. A. Scheibe). His transcription of the Adagio from an oboe concerto of Alessandro Marcello in his own Concerto in D minor BWV974 for harpsichord alone, is a familiar example. The less familiar transcription of Vivaldi that appears in his Concerto in G BWV973 for harpsichord alone offers a judicious fusion of French stereotyped graces and Italian florid embellishment (see ex.15). An invaluable guide to performers is furnished by 'Les agréments de la même sarabande' that Bach provided for the English Suites nos.2 in A minor and 3 in G minor

BWV807–8 which should be adopted for the reprise of each section. The *double* of the rather Handelian Sarabande in the English Suite no.4 in D minor BWV809 represents yet another type of embellishment worthy of study. Performers might attempt to reduce the flowing semiquavers of the Sarabande from the C minor Partita BWV826 to solid chords with French ornaments for the

Ex.16 J. S. Bach

first time through each section, using Bach's written version as a *double*, as was reportedly done by Wanda Landowska: ex.16 shows how the first few bars might go.

Handel's rich manner of improvised embellishment may be represented by the Air from his Suite no.3 in D minor (*Suites de pièces*, 1720), which in its plain form is known from a manuscript, now lost, called by Chrysander 'Klavierbuch aus der Jugendzeit' (Händel-Gesellschaft edn., xlviii, 156). A passage (xlviii, 206ff) he is said to have improvised on the harpsichord in accompanying the opera *Rinaldo* (1711) was published by Walsh, and other keyboard versions of arias from the opera, arranged by William Babell, may owe something to his example (xlviii, 210ff); such material may well be of a similar kind to that he provided at the sections marked 'ad libitum' in his organ concertos. Examples of Handel's vocal embellishment are to be found in a manuscript containing versions of three arias from the opera *Ottone* (1723; *GB-Ob* Don.c.69; see also Dean, 1970).

(ix) Complete pieces. Improvisation of complete pieces of music was not new to the Baroque period, but some of the great composer–performers of the era achieved new heights of virtuosity. In the 17th century the organ improvisations of Sweelinck, Frescobaldi and Buxtehude won the admiration of crowds who were attracted from far and wide. Bach is known to have improvised a prelude and fugue, an organ trio in three obbligato parts, a chorale prelude and a final fugue, all on a single hymn tune. Forkel (*Über Johann Sebastian Bachs Leben, Kunst und Kunstwerke*, 1802) remarked on Wilhelm Friedemann's impressions of his father's improvisations at the organ, saying that his organ compositions were indeed

full of the expression of devotion, solemnity and dignity; but his unpremeditated organ playing, in which nothing was lost in the process of writing down but everything came directly to life out of his imagination, is said to have been still more devout, solemn, dignified and sublime.

A famous story that hardly needs repeating tells how in 1747, while visiting Frederick the Great, Bach extemporized a fugue on a 'royal theme' given him by the king that he later worked out in his *Musical Offering*. Two of the rare places in his music where Bach allowed the performer some freedom to improvise are seen in the bars of minim chords in the Chromatic Fantasia BWV903 and the semibreve chords that constitute the entire prelude of the keyboard fugue in A minor BWV895.

Handel was equally famous for his improvising, as is attested by Hawkins's description of his playing of his own organ concertos:

His amazing command of the instrument, the grandeur and dignity of his style, the copiousness of his imagination, and the fertility of his invention were qualities that absorbed every inferior attainment. When he gave a concerto, his method in general was to introduce it with a voluntary movement on the diapasons, which stole on the ear in a slow and solemn progression; the harmony close wrought, and as full as could possibly be expressed, the passages concatenated with stupendous art, the whole at the same time being perfectly intelligible, and carrying the appearance of great simplicity. This kind of prelude was succeeded by the concerto itself, which he executed with a degree of spirit and firmness that no one ever pretended to equal.

A new type of improvisatory piece called a *partimento* arose in the Baroque period with the inception of the thoroughbass. In thoroughbass practice both the bass line and the melody are given, while in the *partimento* only the bass line with figures is given, over which it was the performer's responsibility to improvise self-

contained pieces, character-pieces often called toccatas and even fugues. Practised mostly in Italy, the *partimento* is closely related to the English practice of making divisions on a ground (see §2(ii) above). *Partimento* improvisations were cultivated extensively as pedagogical exercises in the later Baroque period, when numerous collections were published by Gaetano Greco, Francesco Durante, Carlo Contumacci, Gaetano Franzaroli and Giuseppe Saratelli.

The art of improvisation flourished to the very end of the Baroque era in the free fantasia. J. S. Petri, in his *Anleitung zur practischen Musik* (1767), claimed that the fantasia was 'the highest degree of composition . . . where meditation and execution are directly bound up with one another'. The whole final chapter of C. P. E. Bach's *Versuch* (1753) is devoted to the improvisation of fantasias. A free fantasia is given at the end both in written-out form and as a *partimento*. The absence of bar-lines emphasizes the freedom of such a composition.

3. THE CLASSICAL PERIOD. There were two seemingly contradictory trends in the second half of the 18th century. On the one hand, singers and instrumentalists tended towards an increased display of virtuoso and improvisatory skills; on the other, 'classical simplicity' became increasingly important. Great composers, with specific requirements for the realization of their music, restricted the traditional freedom of performance, and promoted this by notating more than had previously been usual, or possible, in order to secure unspoilt performances. This applies equally to Haydn and Mozart and, of course, Gluck.

Essentially, improvisation in this period comes into two categories: the embellishment of an existing original, and the creation of entire pieces. Between these falls the addition of improvised sections within existing works (*see* CADENZA). Most of the discussion that follows is concerned with improvised embellishment or ornamentation.

(i) Attitudes. In his autobiography Dittersdorf (1801) told how, in 1751, when he was about 12, he was playing the violin in the orchestra of the Vienna Schottenkirche. The leader, Karl Huber, asked him to take over his 'solo'. The boy agreed: 'At the beginning, I played the solo not without a beating heart; however, when I had an encouraging feeling that I was playing better than expected, I took courage in the repeat and varied the passages and modulations. I did this entirely in Huber's own manner'. Huber's admirers, he added, were surprised afterwards to learn that he had not played the solo himself. This makes clear that the average listener expected a good violinist to vary the repeats; that it took courage for a beginner to do so; that it was regularly done, not only in theatre and chamber music but also in church music (at least in the Catholic south of central Europe and wherever Italian music prevailed); and, finally, that not only every famous singer but also every well-known instrumentalist had his own specific manner of embellishment.

Many contemporary reports refer to this individual manner of great performers, and it doubtless concerned ornamentation in the broadest sense – 'style', 'gusto', 'manner', 'taste' or 'goût'. Thus musicians such as Lolli, Nardini and Ferrari each had his own performance style, and Hiller (1780, chap.19), paraphrasing Mancini, spoke of Bernacchi's pupils Amadori, Guarducci and Raaff: 'these three have earned general applause, each of them in his diverse, peculiar and personal manner'. Not all violinists reckoned to be as versatile as Tartini, whose *L'arte del arco* contains a chart (printed in the French edition of *c*1788) with suggestions for 17 different ways of playing an Adagio (for extract, see illustration), or as Luigi Marchesi, who in 1784 offered 14 different embellished versions of a Cherubini subject (see Haas, 1931, pp.225ff). Other important examples of authentic violin embellishments from early in the second half of the 18th century are to be found in sonatas by Nardini and Franz Benda.

According to another report on Dittersdorf, in the 1760s he varied the finale of a violin concerto only after the audience had asked for an encore (a request on which he had counted); he produced brilliant 'improvised' virtuosity which, he later admitted, he had prepared in advance. This confirms what Dittersdorf wrote elsewhere: that not every 'capriccio' (as final cadenzas were often still called) or improvised embellishment was a matter of extempore invention, and that the best performers prepared their variations and cadenzas carefully. In the last decades of the 18th century free and spontaneously invented embellishments and cadenzas became increasingly unusual. Too many musicians spoilt the otherwise good impression they had made when playing, at the end of a concerto, a capriccio of their own invention, according to Dittersdorf, who added:

Part of chart showing 17 different ways of playing an Adagio, from J. B. Cartier's reprint (Paris, late 18th century) of Tartini's 'L'arte del arco'

However, a new custom developed which I liked only with persons like Mozart, Clementi and other creative geniuses. To show their improvisatory creativity they start fantasias in which they play a simple subject which they then very artfully vary several times according to the best rules of composition. Soon after, a lot of small-minded men tried to imitate this all like apes, and now the mania for varying and playing fantasias is so general that everywhere where one hears the sound of a piano at a concert one can be sure of being regaled with every sort of twist and twirl and turn. How angry I was when, a couple of years ago, I heard Dulon with his flute in a fantasy in which he dared to botch and bundle fripperies and finally play variations without any accompaniment.

Of course, spontaneous embellishment and variation was easier for the trained musician than for the amateur. During the 18th century amateurs increasingly came to take part in the music-making, and needed instruction; accordingly, many treatises of the middle of the century started to teach ornamentation. The didactic master-pieces of the time – notably those of Quantz, Tartini, C. P. E. Bach, Leopold Mozart, Mancini, Manfredini and Hiller, and the Galliard and Agricola annotated translations of Tosi's earlier work – are repeatedly at pains to warn that nobody should dare to embellish unless he has fully grasped the art of composition and has sufficient taste and talent to invent melodic lines more beautiful than the composer's. A late English translation of Quantz (*Easy and Fundamental Instructions*, c1790) says:

The Graces and Embellishments to be treated of in this Place, are the production of a momentary Invention or Fancy of the Performer, and in this respect are different from the common Graces that are distinguish'd by particular marks, such as Shakes and Beat etc.

Few, and perhaps no one that professes Music, content themselves with those common Graces, but the greatest part discover an Affection for Embellishments of their own Invention, which, however commendable in itself, yet if introduced by Persons entirely ignorant of the Principles of Harmony are seldom proper, but rather apt to destroy the Intention and original Beauties of the composition, than to improve it; such Performers would always do better to play the Notes simply as they are written, and to prefer the Invention of the Composer to their own.

Leopold Mozart warned similarly (*Violinschule*, p.27):

Many imagine themselves to have brought something wonderfully beautiful into the world if they befrill the notes of an Adagio cantabile thoroughly, and make out of one note at least a dozen. Such note-murderers expose thereby their bad judgment to the light, and tremble when they have to sustain a long note or play only a few notes singingly, without inserting their usual preposterous and laughable frippery.

C. P. E. Bach's remarks, in the preface to his *Sechs Sonaten mit veränderten Reprisen* (1760), are quoted above; see §2(v) and ex.13.

Although there were many complaints from these masters that interpreters of their time went too far in embellishing, they would all have been equally horrified at the notion of performers' reproducing nearly bare skeletons of music. 18th-century composers sometimes voluntarily left their work incomplete and sketched. Padre Martini wrote: 'notated music is but a skeleton' and 'vocal music is written down . . . but only as a simple cantilena, a simple melodic line, in order to allow a good performer full freedom to embellish a composition according to his ability'. J. A. Hiller compared graces to spices, which were necessary ingredients but could spoil a dish if taken in too great a quantity or without proper taste; in his opinion da capo parts in arias and repeats in instrumental works, if left unaltered by the composer, should be varied.

In French music ornaments were usually indicated by signs, but it seems that some Italian embellishment customs had been introduced during the first half of the 18th century, mainly by violinists. Vocal training methods, however, continued to differ considerably from Italian ones. Lacassagne (1766) spoke of ornamenta-

tion, calling it 'goût', and cited several rules that h claimed should not be violated. Rousseau (1768) ga⋅ the following explanation of 'goût du chant':

A French term for the art of singing . . . with appropriate orn mentation partly in order to conceal the insipidity of French so . . . 'Goût du chant' also often denotes a singer's artificial add tion, for better or worse, of a popular artist's tone quality. Som times it involves nasal intonation, sometimes it gives rise to a bre in the voice, sometimes to bleating, sometimes to screeching: these ornaments, however, are purely ephemeral and continual change with their inventors.

Though Rousseau's well-known sarcasm about Frenc singing and his preference for Italian singers we⋅ responsible for his choice of terms, it is interesting t note that he referred to 'breaking the voice', 'bleatin; and 'screeching' as ornaments. That ornamentation mea not only the division of long notes into short ones an the application of standard unwritten graces such appoggiaturas, trills and turns, but also all kinds of mear of heightening the expression, tallies with the broa understanding of the term in other countries during th century, when dynamic and articulation shades as we as tempo rubato or Lombardic rhythms were regarde as ornaments. All ornaments were applied to enhanc the affect, to avoid literal repetition (for example in d capo sections and recapitulations), and to arouse a interest in the qualities of a performer.

(ii) Hiller's rules. The clearest rules for free ornamen tation ('Willkürliche Veränderungen') during the Clas sical period were probably those given by Hiller, wh devoted the entire eighth chapter of his *Anweisung zur musikalisch-zierlichen Gesange* (1780) to improvise embellishments. The contents of this chapter are repro duced here in a condensed form:

§1 A singer should be respected for his skill in ornamentatio because he can prove his knowledge (of composition) and his abi ities with his embellishments more than in any other way.

§2 There are three kinds of ornamentation: divisions, in whic longer notes are subdivided into several notes of smaller value; man notes are changed into fewer (longer) ones; and a certain numbe of notes are exchanged for others of different pitch or value (in th last category tempo rubato should be included).

§3 Means for embellishment, apart from appoggiaturas and trill are certain figures which form *passaggi* if put together. Staccatc legato, tempo rubato and also everything else that enhances the effe of the voice can be used for ornamentation; often these latter embel lishments give a better effect than the division of notes which make everything so variegated that sense and expression may vanish.

§4 Does the freedom to alter hold throughout an aria, or are the⋅ only certain points for ornamentation? Strictly, this freedom is lim ited, and embellishments should be applied only to passages need ing more vitality and glamour or those that would have little effec if performed a second time exactly as they were the first time. Thes short melismatic passages should occur not at the beginning bu towards the middle of an aria. Not only adagios but also allegro can be ornamented. [According to Leopold Mozart, Türk and oth ers, this was less usual.]

§5 Only arias with repeated sections should be varied. It is prope to present such an aria first in the way it was written, otherwise th audience will not know what comes from the composer and wha from the performer.

§6 It is always essential to keep in time, especially where a clear distinct and expressive representation of the composer's cantilen is preferable to an altered version.

§7 The singer must understand harmony and have knowledge an taste. If he does not have taste, he will mix appropriate with inap propriate, old with new, in his variations and may add legato an rubato ornaments to a cheerful piece with nonsensical results.

§8 The knowledge of harmony is necessary because the orna ments might not fit the accompaniment. It is not sufficient for th singer to see the figured bass, he must try to read the whole score

§9 Rules for improvised embellishments, therefore, are: (*i*) orna mentation must sound easy even when it is difficult to sing; (*ii*) is necessary that the embellishments do not interfere with the sing er's declamation and his proper expression; (*iii*) slow and patheti arias favour legato and rubato ornaments and *allegro* movement allow staccato; (*iv*) dynamic gradations must be carefully observe and must give proper light and shade; (*v*) ornamental notes in

elody should be close together, not far-flung; (*vi*) only where the
mpo and harmony allow it should the singer combine different
gures in a *passaggio*: the best opportunities are in long accented
/llables – a singer who wants to be more than a student should
ever sing such *passaggi* alike if they recur; (*vii*) the same kinds of
rnament should not recur too often close together because they
ound objectionable and show a singer's poverty of invention; (*viii*)
e feeling and not the 'throat' should dictate ornamentation; (*ix*)
ne should never do much on the difficult vowels 'i' and 'u'; (*x*)
 everything he does the singer must try not to obscure the com-
oser's intentions but to beautify and clarify them.
  §10 Generally speaking it is most important that a composer's
atentions must remain clear and unspoilt; they should never be
oscured.

ii) The Viennese Classics. Of the Viennese Classical
omposers, both Haydn and Mozart left examples of
ritten-out ornamentation. Haydn's best-known vocal
nes occur in his oratorio *Il ritorno di Tobia* (1775),
robably for a performance in 1784. Ex.17 shows the
ria 'Quando mi dona un cenno', with the unembel-
shed version, the embellished version, and the version
t the da capo. The most florid section is naturally towards
e end of the aria; it is scarcely altered in the second
ersion. Other examples of Haydn's ornamentation
chnique are rather less a matter of improvisation than
f his desire to retain control over the elaboration of his
usic.
  Mozart also provided examples of those embellish-
ents which traditionally were not notated but were
nprovised or prepared in advance. In 1778 he asked
is father to send him some arias from his opera *Lucio*

Silla (1772), and wrote (14 February 1778), 'please
remember [to send] these arias I mentioned in my last
letter. If I am not mistaken, there are also some cadenzas which I once jotted down, and at least one aria cantabile with coloratura indications'. Mozart also
embellished the 'Ah se a morir me chiama' from *Lucio
Silla*, first sung by the castrato Rauzzini: the difference
between the plain and the embellished version repays
study (ex.18). So, for the treatment of an expressive
cantabile, does his embellished version of the aria 'Non
sò d'onde viene' by J. C. Bach (ex.19). Gluck was the
first outspoken enemy of ornamentation among composers of Italian opera. In his famous preface to *Alceste*
(1767) he also indirectly confirmed the freedom that
interpreters took for themselves in everyday operatic life.
  With the abandonment of figured bass in favour of a
more carefully worked-out treatment of the middle voices,
notably in Haydn's string quartets from the late 1760s
onwards, the freedom of performers was increasingly
restricted. This emphasized the diverse trends of the time:
towards virtuoso display on the one hand, classical simplicity on the other. This new tendency may be attributed to composers' awareness of the uniqueness of what
they wanted their music to express, but may also be
connected with their unhappy experience with inadequate performers or their concern to help less skilled
amateur musicians who would be grateful for more precise performance instructions (articulation marks,
dynamics, ornaments). It may be generally observed that
the better and more self-critical composers were, the more
interested in protecting their artistic output they became,

x.17 Haydn

Ex.18 Mozart

Ex.19 J. C. Bach

Non sò___ d'on-de vie - ne quel te - ne-ro af-
fet - to, quel te - ne - ro af-fet-to, quel
mo - to,___ che i-gno-to mi nas-ce_____ nel
pet-to quel gel, che___ le___ ve - ne scor-
- ren - do mi va.

and the more they tended to notate every detail. Thus it is not surprising that the great composers of the Viennese Classical period – after having reached a state of maturity where they were demanding the utmost of themselves – notated nearly everything with unusual care and finality. One of the most beautiful examples of fully written-out ornamentation of the 18th century is Mozart's Rondo in A minor K511. The ultimate stage of this development is reflected in Beethoven's reported anger upon hearing that Czerny had dared to add some notes in the piano part during a performance of the Quintet op.16. It is however related that in a performance of this very work Beethoven himself improvised an exceptionally long cadenza.

It may accordingly be noted that an aria by Mozart or Haydn looks entirely different on paper from one by an Anfossi or a Zingarelli, for the number of notes in each bar of the Viennese masters is considerably larger. Thus the greatest caution is needed in considering any addition or alteration: otherwise an already ornamented version may be further ornamented. To avoid this, many composers (according to Leopold Mozart) wrote small grace notes when they wanted an appoggiatura, thus indicating that no additional grace note could be added. Only in their youth, or in exceptional cases, did Haydn or Mozart sketch passages the way Italian composers did, and only rarely did Mozart write 'skeletons'. In Mozart's mature operas practically no opportunity is given to singers for displaying good or bad taste in embellishing melodies. There exist a number of contemporary embellishments to several arias from *Le nozze di Figaro*, *Don Giovanni* and *Die Zauberflöte* (in D-DO, GB-

Lbm), some tasteless, others more sensible or even good but none is necessary because none beyond doubt beau tifies Mozart's score. Only two kinds of embellishme. in Mozart's operas are indispensable. One is the embe lishment of the fermatas at cadential points or betwee sections of, for example, a rondo, where the ear requir a linking passage: examples are Figaro's 'Non più andra and the Countess's 'Dove sono' from *Figaro* and Ott vio's 'Il mio tesoro' from *Don Giovanni*. Their corre mode of performance may possibly be inferred fro Mozart's own surviving 'lead-ins' (*Eingänge*) at ana ogous points in his piano concertos, like that in th Andante from K414/385p. Full vocal cadenzas follow ing a 6-4 chord and comparable to the cadenzas instrumental concertos were to be taken in one breat an example being Idamante's 'Non ho colpa' (*Idome neo*).

The other points where performers are not only allowe to alter notes but are sometimes obliged to do so if the wish to avoid violating 18th-century convention are thos where appoggiaturas have to be applied. The voc appoggiatura was an expressive device that helped stress a strong syllable; it was part of the musical la guage of opera for more than 200 years. Especially i recitatives, but also in arias and ariosos, until the tim of Schubert and Rossini certain notes were written di ferently from how they were supposed to be sung. (Th convention derived from the theories of strict *stile ant co* counterpoint, according to which a dissonance shoul if possible not appear on a strong beat, and accente syllables were usually placed on strong beats.) All th orists of the Baroque and Classical periods agreed th certain appoggiaturas were indispensable. Mancini wrot (1774):

All the excellence of the recitative depends on the knowledge the proper use of the appoggiatura, or the musical accent, as it generally called. This precious accent, in which is contained all th grace of a cantilena, consists, in short, of a note at a pitch or higher than that written; and this is practised especially when a wo of several syllables is written with notes of the same pitch.

Some vocal appoggiaturas are compulsory, others no Manfredini (*Regole armoniche*, 1775) explained:

Whereas an instrumentalist is not strictly required to perform appog giaturas not indicated by the composer, this is not the same for th singer, who (especially in recitatives) whenever he sees two note of the same value and pitch, must consider the first of these as a appoggiatura from above; that is, particularly on a strong beat, h must perform it a tone or a semitone higher, according to the ke in which the notes are written.

Other theorists are less strict in the application of appog giatura rules for repeated notes, demanding them onl for the ends of phrases (sentences). Manfredini went o to discuss the treatment of such Italian words as 'mai or 'dei':

Poets sometimes treat these as monosyllables and therefore com posers set them as one single note. The singer must nevertheles always treat them as disyllables and sing them with an appoggiatu from above, as already described.

It is often helpful to study the instrumental parts of a aria because there – as the instrumental tradition wa less specific over ornamentation than the vocal on – composers wrote down the notes the way they want ed them to sound. Ex.20, from the Act 1 trio of *Cos fan tutte*, may serve to demonstrate the point. That th tradition continued into Beethoven's time is demon strated by the recitative at the beginning of the final of the Ninth Symphony, where the repeated *f* on th singer's word 'Töne' is earlier paralleled by the instru ments' *g–f*.

Apart from vocal appoggiaturas, fermatas requirin

20 Mozart

ob
n 8va
RANDO
LIELMO
O fuo - ri la spa-da, o fuo - ri la spa-da.

ıbellishment, and final cadenzas, no ornamentations alterations are commendable in Haydn's or Mozart's ›rks or permitted in Beethoven's. Only those few pasges in Mozart's piano concertos that he left in outline ɾm must, or can legitimately, be filled out. Such a eleton passage is found in the finale of the Piano Conɾto in E♭ K482 (bars 164–72), where Mozart supplied erely one note to each bar in the right-hand part; such ɔassage as bars 334–42 of the finale of the Piano Conɾto in B♭ K595 may serve as a model for its comple›n (ex.21). Similar passages in the concertos K491 and 8 (here more disputably, for the unembellished verɔn sounds convincingly beautiful) call for elaboration. ıat Mozart himself embellished the slow movements his concertos is known from a contemporary report; d his apparent dislike of allowing anyone else the ɛedom to embellish his melodies is attested by his havg sent his father and sister an ornamented version of passage from the Andante of the concerto K451 (letter 9–12 June 1784). It is equally significant that three his piano sonatas (K284/205*b*, 332/300*k*, 457) show npler readings in Mozart's autographs than in the verɔns he published, suggesting that at least in some of s slow movements he wanted and expected embelhment in recapitulation sections but preferred to supy it himself.

The topic of entire improvised movements in the assical period is difficult to discuss, because imprososed movements by their nature cannot exist in written form. It is known that Mozart, for example, often improvised sets of variations or fugues, and at least once he played an entire sonata impromptu (see his letter of 23 October 1777). Others, including such keyboard players as C. P. E. Bach, Hässler, Beecke, Clementi and Hummel, did likewise, and so did Beethoven. Inferences about the nature of such improvisations have to be based on surviving material, and it is clear that works like the fantasias of C. P. E. Bach and Mozart bear some relation to what they may have played spontaneously. Similarly, many sets of variations by Mozart and the young Beethoven may be seen as written-down versions of the kinds of piece they expected to improvise at musical soirées or concerts.

.21 Mozart

a) K482
165
170
) K595
335
340
tr

4. After 1800. In the 18th century there existed, in ideal terms, a personal relationship between composer and solo performer. There were few classic works; most music was new and, in the solo genres, usually written for a specific performer or for the composer to play himself. This did not mean that the composer, knowing a performer's temperament and capabilities, necessarily tailored his part to them to the last detail; rather, he left much of the ornamental detail to be added or adjusted in the act of performance. The realization of a score in a specific performance was thus intended to be the result of the coming together of the reflective creativity of the composer, who provided the structure and general lines of the composition, and the spontaneous creativity of the performer, who gave it much of its specific colouring, which might to some extent be varied from one performance to another (the analogy with painting was a favourite 18th-century one). When this procedure worked as it was meant to, performances must have had an immediacy and personal effect of a sort for which today one must look to other branches of music to find in like degree. By the 20th century the situation had changed radically: performers are now mostly engaged in the relentless replaying of a smaller body of familiar classic works, with a personal stamp imparted to their performances almost entirely through nuances in the interpretation of the written notes; free ornamental elements play virtually no part. The 19th century was the period of transition between these two approaches and so presents a considerable change of attitude towards ornamentation and improvisational practices.

(i) Ornamentation. Ornamentation in this period consisted, first, of conventionalized diminutions of single notes that could be indicated by symbols; second, of free diminution and variation of melodic lines; and, third, of insertions interrupting the written continuity of a piece, such as cadenzas, and additions to it, such as improvised preludes. The tendency in the 19th century was towards the writing out of all these by the composer and towards compositional styles in which they had less importance than before.

Both these trends can be seen in Italian opera, perhaps the genre in which, in the 18th century, the performer's prerogatives and obligations in regard to ornamentation had been most completely recognized by composers and audiences. In most Italian opera houses the fashionable part of the audience attended an opera throughout an often lengthy run. To hold such an audience's attention a singer was expected to vary the way he sang his arias from night to night. Several arias are extant with varied vocal parts supposed to have been sung by Luigi Marchesi, the greatest castrato of the end of the century. When just one such version is provided for an aria, it consists mostly of diminutions of the composer's original melody, but when there are several alternatives (as in the aria partly printed by Haas, 1931) they often consist for long stretches of entirely new lines in which the original is not to be found beneath the ornamentation. Such examples suggest that as the run of an opera drew on and the arias became ever more familiar to the audience, a great virtuoso like Marchesi might play a subtle game with the audience, by means of ornamentation and variation teasingly departing from and returning to the original melody.

By the first decades of the 19th century ornamentation had, by 18th-century standards, become excessive in Italian opera. Marchesi's diminutions had already reached an elaboration almost incredible today (he is also said to have been one of the first to add ornamental passages to recitative, a practice that became widespread in the early 19th century). Critics still praised the dramatic side of his work, but there was considerable complaint about some of the most famous singers of the next generation. Symptomatic of the trend was the celebrated soprano Angelica Catalani, who turned a phenomenal technique to the end of superficial display. In her concerts she sang Rode's famous violin variations as a vocal solo, and she perpetrated similar enormities in her opera performances, in which the dramatic element was almost totally and deliberately obscured. The regulation of ornamentation had always depended largely on the nebulous concept of 'good taste', and in the early 19th century, a period of artistic and social upheaval, this concept was particularly difficult to define and enforce.

Early in his career (probably about 1813) Rossini began to write out the ornamentation of his operas. This should probably be understood mainly as a gesture against the existing situation. Italian singers continued to ornament in their own way: for example, Meyerbeer, touring Italy in 1834, compared three famous Normas: 'Ronzi de Begnis . . . for the most part sings the role very beautifully, but far less simply than Pasta, in fact with even more ornamentation than Malibran, and this is largely contrary to the character of the role'. Italian singing methods still printed models for deriving diminutions of the melody. Antonio Calegari's *Modi generali del canto* (1836), one of the most elaborate works of this sort, purported to be based on the method of the old castrato Pacchiarotti, but still had practical value.

Italian opera after Rossini tended increasingly towards a style in which exuberant ornamentation (and the grand solo aria) was ever less important as a primary means of dramatic expression. This tendency, coming to fulfilment in Verdi's operas, was accompanied by a change in singing itself, in which 'bel canto' gave way to a more 'dramatic' style, not only with ornamentation less appropriate but also with singers trained in the new style less able to perform it. Lamperti's *Guida teorico-pratica-elementare per lo studio del canto* (1865) provides one of many negative comments by admirers of the old school: 'Vocal music, in order to assume a more dramatic character, has almost entirely stripped itself of all agility, to such a degree that soon, if it continues in this way, it will be no more than a musical declamation'.

In the German tradition the balance had always been weighted more strongly in favour of the composer, the performer being treated with considerable mistrust in regard to ornamentation. In Beethoven this tradition produced a figure of such forcefulness and individuality that a creative collaboration in which the performer added something of his own to the composer's conception became increasingly unthinkable, and the performer was made to feel that his highest calling – going beyond the traditional good taste to an almost spiritual mission – was to subject himself to the composer's will as the means by which his masterpieces were communicated to the world. In compensation, Beethoven in many of his most characteristic works embodied a quasi-improvisational 'fantasy' element in the conception of the work itself.

With the widening influence of the German tradition throughout Europe during the 19th century, this attitude towards the performer's role became ever more widespread. One result was that, much more than in the 18th century, a distinction was made between the high and low in musical styles and genres, with the performer standing in different relation to each of them. For example, Beethoven's pupil Czerny, in his *Systematisch Anleitung zum Fantasieren auf dem Pianoforte* (written c1829), source of the most detailed information on improvisation in this period, was always careful to distinguish between what was allowable in the higher regions dominated by Beethoven and more ephemeral music intended for the salon (Czerny himself is said to have been reprimanded by Beethoven for having introduced a cadenza into a performance of the Septet). Thus the singer Luigi Lablache, in his *Méthode de chant* (1829) stated the traditional attitude towards ornamentation and good taste as it still existed in the milieu of opera (Eng trans., 1840):

An injudicious selection, or a superabundance of ornament, betrays bad taste – good taste . . . is revealed by moderation and elegance . . . Real taste . . . consists in the perfect knowledge and adaptation of our resources – in the power of completely imbibing the character of a composition – of increasing its force by analogous colouring, and of placing the Singer's own feelings in such close relation with those of the Author, that a perfect whole is formed as if the conception and execution were alike the result of one effort of thought.

By contrast Liszt, writing some ten years later, stated the negative view of free ornamentation in the performance of 'serious' works (see Chantavoine, 1912):

I then frequently performed . . . the works of Beethoven, Weber and Hummel, and I confess to my shame that in order to compel the bravos of an audience always slow to grasp beautiful things in their august simplicity, I had no scruples against changing their tempos and intentions; I even went so far as insolently to add to them a host of passages and cadenzas. . . . You wouldn't believe, my friend, how much I deplore these concessions to bad taste, these sacrilegious violations of the SPIRIT and the LETTER, because in me the most absolute respect for the masterpieces of the great masters has replaced the need for novelty and individuality.

With the increase of amateur music-making in the 18th and 19th centuries there arose a large class of performers who could not be expected to have the knowledge or sensitivity necessary to provide their own ornamentation. This formed a further stimulus to writing it out. One who recognized this need was the publisher and composer Domenico Corri, who from about 1780 published vocal collections complete with typical ornamentations of familiar songs and arias (many of them from the favourite song collections of the London operas, still bearing the singers' names; this has led some modern scholars to assume, probably incorrectly, that Corri's ornamentation is that of the singers themselves).

The 19th century was a great age of vocal and instrumental instruction manuals, another reflection of the rowing body of amateur students. Nearly all of them have sections on ornamentation. No systematic study of them has been made, but even a superficial survey reveals that the instructions given for the performance of many ornaments vary greatly from writer to writer. This fact, combined with the increasing complexity of much music in this period, as well as the increasing idiosyncrasy of many composers' styles, also explains why many composers began to indicate the exact value of appoggiaturas and to write out other ornaments instead of using symbols. Wagner, for example, used the symbol for his favourite ornament, the turn, in his early works, but wrote it out in various forms in his later ones. In recitative a similar situation obtained: in the straightforward melodic formulae of simple recitative it had been relatively easy to substitute the unwritten appoggiaturas required by textual accent, but as recitatives became more elaborate, composers found it safer to indicate exactly the notes that were meant to be sung. This practice was fairly general by the middle of the century (although published scores do not always seem completely consistent in this).

(ii) Cadenzas. The cadenza (or *point d'orgue*) continued in use in both vocal and instrumental music of the first half of the 19th century and continued to be of two sorts: the fermata (or *comune*) and the cadenza properly so called. The fermata was an elaboration of the final chord of the cadence, usually a dominant half-cadence, preceding an important formal change within a piece. It was thus a feature particularly of highly sectional forms, where, according to Czerny's *Systematische Anleitung*, it was 'useful and often indispensable to decorate a passage that would otherwise seem too bare and too tedious', but not to be used in works 'of profound content and serious character'.

The fermata was supposed not to depart harmonically from the chord being decorated, but to draw it out in a manner appropriate to the work's character and length. The Calegari–Pacchiarotti *Modi generali* contains 41 models of increasing length and elaboration for singers, and Czerny gave several keyboard examples, some of which are quite long. The fermata was often written out by the composer in this period, but in all but the most serious works it was permissible for a performer to replace the composer's with one of his own.

Cadenzas of the second type (the distinction of terminology seems to have been maintained by the Italians more strictly than by others) were decorations of the dominant chord in a full cadence at or near the end of a piece, most often arias or concerto movements. Beethoven characteristically provided an influential example by composing the cadenza in Piano Concerto no.5 (1809) as an integral part of the work. By the 1820s this seems to have been normal practice in concertos.

The classical vocal cadenza of the 18th century was to be taken in one breath, begin with a *messa di voce* and end with a trill on the supertonic, with intervening passage-work usual but not required. By the 1820s, when one often finds them written out by composers, cadenzas usually display none of the three classic constituents, frequently even containing bits of text. In practice, singers freely replaced composers' cadenzas with their own. Many of these were printed in singing methods of the time. For example, Gilbert Duprez's *L'art du chant* (1845) includes 18 cadenzas by 12 celebrated singers, without, however, identifying the arias to which

they belong. The vocal cadenza survived into music of the second half of the century, but was increasingly optional and out of place. Verdi had occasionally ordered its suppression as early as the first version of *Macbeth*.

(iii) Preludes. The improvisation of preludes, mostly by keyboard players, before the performance of a written composition continued to flourish in the early 19th century. To begin with the work itself, especially in the informal atmosphere of the salon, was considered poor taste. Samuel Webbe wrote in introducing his *Preludes* (*c*1825):

It is desirable . . . to avoid the abruptness of entering upon a Sonata or other exercise without any previous sound of the instrument: but as it is unreasonable to expect from VERY beginners a PROPER prelude, the Author takes the liberty to recommend that, in order to avoid such abruptness, they strike simply the chord of the key in which they are about to play . . . or with the addition perhaps of one or two other chords in close affinity to that key in preference to the absurd formality of playing up and down the scale or two or three measured Arpeggios which has the PRETENCE of being a prelude without possessing the least resemblance to its genuine characteristic spontaneity.

In his *Traité d'harmonie du pianiste: principes rationnels de la modulation pour apprendre à préluder et à improviser* op.185 (1849) Kalkbrenner wrote: 'How many among our best pianists can make a prelude, however unsatisfactory? And as for students, there is not one in a thousand who in his improvisations tries to do more than a full cadence'. For the incapable several collections of written-out preludes were published by such well-known figures as Hummel, Cramer, Ries, Czerny, Moscheles and Kalkbrenner and in England by a number of local composers: Cipolla (1799), Jansen, Crotch, Neate, Burrowes (in 1827 there also appeared in London a collection of 47 preludes by 22, mostly local, composers). Instructions for making one's own preludes are found in Grétry's *Méthode simple pour apprendre à préluder en peu de temps avec toutes les ressources de l'harmonie* (1802), Czerny's *Systematische Anleitung* and Kalkbrenner's *Traité*. Grétry's and Kalkbrenner's works were primarily introductions to keyboard harmony for the musically illiterate. Grétry's 'three ways of using chord progressions in playing *de tête*' include, first, striking the chords or playing them as arpeggios; second, sometimes introducing fast passages, with or without bass, between two chords; and third, using a fragment of bass or melody as the subject of 'a more or less rigorous fugue'. Kalkbrenner taught a series of harmonic formulae and how to elaborate them in various keyboard styles. He then showed how short passages could be joined together or expanded to form longer improvisations. Both these works are as applicable to free improvisation as to strict preluding.

Czerny's much more detailed discussion distinguished two sorts of preludes or 'short fantasias'. The first ends on the tonic chord of the following piece, which may be preceded by its dominant alone or by a short cadential progression (stated in simple chords or elaborated in brilliant passages). However, the prelude can also begin in a foreign key and proceed to its goal by 'bold and strange modulations'. The second is longer and more developed in the manner of an introduction, using motifs from the piece in alternation with brilliant passage-work and ending on the dominant 7th. Such an introduction can also begin in a foreign key and continue with bold modulations. Czerny forbade the use of such preludes with compositions in a strict style, such as Beethoven's Piano Sonata op.57.

Preluding seems to have largely died out in the later

19th century, probably coming to seem out of place in the increasingly formal atmosphere of public recitals (Wangermée, 1950, mentioned as a later instance that Emil Sauer extemporized brief transitions between the keys of successive pieces in his recitals). The practice left an important artistic legacy in the Chopin Preludes (1839), for several aspects of which it provides an illuminating context, most obviously in the epigrammatic ones: the second, for example, by beginning at a tonal point different from its end, reflects one of the possibilities mentioned by Czerny.

(iv) Free improvisation. Free improvisation remained a significant aspect of solo performances in the first part of the 19th century, in both the salon and the concert hall, and the suggestion of a subject by one of the audience continued to be a favourite device. Such subjects consisted usually not of lengthy themes but of short, plastic motifs adaptable to a variety of treatments. Czerny distinguished six types of independent improvisations: on a single subject, on several subjects, the potpourri, variations, the chordal and fugued style, and the capriccio. Any subject, according to Czerny, could be used as the basis for an improvisation in any style or form: sonata, adagio, rondo, variations, fugue, etc. Alternatively, a subject or a series of them could be treated in a succession of sections in the style of several genres, without any of them being fully worked out in form. The potpourri and capriccio made use of more extreme contrasts between sections than the improvisation on several subjects. The potpourri, based on 'anything in vogue', was the most suitable for performance in large halls for audiences of mixed musical attainment.

Improvisation was mainly a keyboard phenomenon, although players of other instruments improvised too, sometimes in pairs: Hummel and the violinist Clement, Brahms and Remenyi. Chopin and Liszt improvised on two pianos. With the decline of the salon as a centre of musical performance, in which improvisation was more at home than in the increasingly formal atmosphere of the concert hall, and of the composer–performer, in whom the art had usually reached its peaks, improvisation gradually died out. The Romantic myth that the great composer created his masterpieces in a kind of inspired improvisation also tended to diminish interest in concert improvisations, which had always been seen more as a skill than as an act of genius. Although kept up for a while by such late composer–performers as D'Albert and Busoni, it eventually preserved a tenuous existence in certain artistic limbos: the dance class, the organ loft, etc. In the latter it filled a continuing need in the church service and remained a required part of the church organist's training, reflected in numerous instructional manuals, such as Marcel Dupré's *Traité d'improvisation à l'orgue* (1925); the tradition is particularly strong in France, where the ability to improvise a dramatic piece in fugal style has continued to be valued, in recitals as well as ecclesiastical contexts. But until very recent times, when improvisational elements began to reappear in art music, usually in an ensemble setting, one had to look to other genres of music, most notably jazz, to find improvisation in vigorous creative use.

BIBLIOGRAPHY

BurneyH; HawkinsH

G. Caccini: *Le nuove musiche* (Florence, 1601/2/R1973); ed. in RRMBE, ix (1970)

A. Agazzari: *Del sonare sopra 'l basso* (Siena, 1607/R1969; Eng. trans. in Strunk, 1950, pp.424ff)

M. Mersenne: *Harmonie universelle* (Paris, 1636–7/R1963; Er trans., 1957)

B. de Bacilly: *Remarques curieuses sur l'art de bien chanter* (Par 1668, 3/1671/R1971; Eng. trans., 1968)

J. Rousseau: *Traité de la viole* (Paris, 1687/R1965)

P. F. Tosi: *Opinioni de' cantori antichi e moderni* (Bologna, 172 Eng. trans. by J. E. Galliard, 1742, 2/1743/R1969, as *Obse vations on the Florid Song*; Ger. trans. by J. F. Agrico 1757/R1966, as *Anleitung zur Singekunst*)

J. D. Heinichen: *Der General-Bass in der Composition, oder: Ne und gründliche Anweisung* (Dresden, 1728)

F. Geminiani: *The Art of Playing on the Violin* (Londc 1751/R1952)

J. J. Quantz: *Versuch einer Anweisung die Flöte traversiere zu sp len* (Berlin, 1752, 3/1789/R1952; Eng. trans., 1966)

C. P. E. Bach: *Versuch über die wahre Art das Clavier zu spiele i* (Berlin, 1753/R1957, rev. 2/1787); ii (Berlin, 1762/R195 rev. 2/1797); Eng. trans. of both by W. J. Mitchell (New Yo 1949)

F. W. Marpurg: *Anleitung zum Clavierspielen* (Berlin, 1755, 1765/R1970)

L. Mozart: *Versuch einer gründlichen Violinschule* (Augsburg, 175 4/1800; Eng. trans., 1951)

J. Adlung: *Anleitung zu der musikalischen Gelahrtheit* (Erfu 1758/R1953, 2/1783)

J. Lacassagne: *Traité général des élémens du chant* (Paris, 176€

J. S. Petri: *Anleitung zur practischen Musik* (Lauban, 1767, enlarg 2/1789/R1969)

J.-J. Rousseau: *Dictionnaire de musique* (Paris, 1768/R1969; En trans., 1771, 2/1779/R1975)

C. Burney: *The Present State of Music in France and Italy* (Londc 1771, 2/1773); ed. P. Scholes as *Dr. Burney's Musical Tours Europe* (Oxford, 1959)

G. Tartini: *Regole per arrivare a saper ben suonar il violino* (M *I-Vc*); facs. edn. of 1771 version by E. R. Jacobi (Celle, 196 [with Eng. and Ger. trans.]

C. Burney: *The Present State of Music in Germany, the Netherlan and the United Provinces* (London, 1773, 2/1775); ed. P. Scho as *Dr. Burney's Musical Tours in Europe* (Oxford, 1959)

J. A. Hiller: *Anweisung zum musikalisch-richtigen Gesange* (Leipzi 1774, enlarged 2/1798)

——: *Exempelbuch der Anweisung zum Singen* (Leipzig, 1774)

G. Mancini: *Pensieri e riflessioni pratiche sopra il canto figura* (Vienna, 1774, 2/1777; Eng. trans., 1967, comparing 2 edns

J. A. Hiller: *Anweisung zum musikalisch-zierlichen Gesange* (Leipz 1780)

H. C. Koch: *Versuch einer Anleitung zur Composition* (Rudolsta and Leipzig, 1782–93/R1969)

D. G. Türk: *Clavierschule* (Leipzig and Halle, 1789, enlarged 1802; Eng. trans., abridged, 1802/R1967)

J. A. Hiller: *Anweisung zum Violinspielen für Schulen und zu Selbstunterrichte* (Leipzig, 1792)

K. von Dittersdorf: *Lebensbeschreibung* (Leipzig, 1801; Eng. tran 1896/R1970); ed. N. Miller (Munich, 1967)

A. E. M. Grétry: *Méthode simple pour apprendre à préluder peu de temps avec toutes les ressources de l'harmonie* (Paris, 180 H. C. Koch: *Musikalisches Lexikon* (Frankfurt am Main, 1802/R196 2/1817)

A. M. Peliegrini-Celoni: *Grammatica o Regole di ben cantare* (Rom 1810, 2/1817)

C. Czerny: *Systematische Anleitung zum Fantasieren auf de Pianoforte*, op.200 (Vienna, c1829)

L. Lablache: *Méthode de chant* (Paris, 1829; Eng. trans., 1840)

A. Calegari: *Modi generali del canto* (Milan, 1836)

G. L. Duprez: *L'art du chant* (Paris, 1845)

F. Kalkbrenner: *Traité d'harmonie du pianiste: principes rationne de la modulation pour apprendre à préluder et à improviser*, op.1 (Paris and Leipzig, 1849)

F. Lamperti: *Guida teorico-pratica-elementare per lo studio del can* (Milan and Naples, 1865)

E. D. Wagner: *Musikalische Ornamentik* (Berlin, 1869)

E. Dannreuther: *Musical Ornamentation* (London, 1893–5)

M. Kuhn: *Die Verzierungs-Kunst in der Gesangs-Musik des 16 17. Jahrhunderts, 1535–1650* (Leipzig, 1902/R1969)

A. Schering: 'Zur instrumentalen Verzierungskunst im 18. Jah hundert', *SIMG*, vii (1905–6), 365

H. Goldschmidt: *Die Lehre von der vokalen Ornamentik*, i: *Das 17. und 18. Jahrhundert bis in die Zeit Glucks* (Charlottenbur 1907)

A. Beyschlag: *Die Ornamentik der Musik* (Leipzig, 1908/R195 J. Chantavoine, ed.: *F. Liszt: Pages romantiques* (Paris and Leipzi 1912)

J. P. Dunn: *Ornamentation in the Works of Frederick Chopin* (Lo don, 1921)

A. M. Richardson: *Extempore Playing* (New York, 1922)

E. Bücken: *Die Musik des Rokoko und der Klassik* (Potsdam, 192

T. Arnold: *The Art of Accompaniment from a Thorough-bass as Practised in the 17th and 18th Centuries* (Oxford, 1931/R1965)

Haas: *Aufführungspraxis der Musik* (Potsdam, 1931)

Della Corte: *Canto e bel canto* (Turin, 1934)

T. Ferand: *Die Improvisation in der Musik* (Zurich, 1938)

Reese: *Music in the Middle Ages* (New York, 1940)

Stubington: *Practical Extemporization* (London, 1940)

Aldrich: *The Principal 'Agréments' of the Seventeenth and Eighteenth Centuries: a Study in Musical Ornamentation* (diss., Harvard U., 1942)

—: 'Bach's Technique of Transcription and Improvised Ornamentation', *MQ*, xxxv (1949), 26

Fasano: *Storia degli abbellimenti musicale dal canto gregoriano a Verdi* (Rome, 1949)

Aldrich: *Ornamentation in J. S. Bach's Organ Works* (New York, 1950, 2/1969)

Strunk: *Source Readings in Music History* (New York, 1950, 2/1965)

Wangermée: 'L'improvisation pianistique au début du XIXe siècle', *Miscellanea musicologica Floris van der Mueren* (Ghent, 1950), 227

Horsley: 'Improvised Embellishment in the Performance of Renaissance Music', *JAMS*, iv (1951), 3

Kreutz: 'Ornamentation in J. S. Bach's Keyboard Works', *HMYB*, vii (1952), 358

Emery: *Bach's Ornaments* (London, 1953)

-P. Schmitz: *Die Kunst der Verzierung im 18. Jahrhundert* (Kassel and Basle, 1955, 3/1973)

T. Ferand: *Die Improvisation in Beispielen aus neun Jahrhunderten abendländischer Musik*, Mw, xi (1956, rev. 2/1961; Eng. trans., 1961)

—: 'Improvised Vocal Counterpoint in the Late Renaissance and Early Baroque', *AnnM*, iv (1956), 129–74

Heriot: *The Castrati in Opera* (London, 1956)

Badura-Skoda: 'Über die Anbringung von Auszierungen in den Klavierwerken Mozarts', *MJb 1957*, 186

and P. Badura-Skoda: *Mozart-Interpretation* (Vienna and Stuttgart, 1957; Eng. trans., 1962, as *Interpreting Mozart on the Keyboard*)

Duckles: 'Florid Embellishment in English Song of the Late 16th and Early 17th Centuries', *AnnM*, v (1957), 329

T. Ferand: 'What is "Res facta"?', *JAMS*, x (1957), 141

Georgh: *Die Verzierungen in der Musik: Theorie und Praxis* (Zurich and Freiburg, 1957)

Tappolet: 'Einige prinzipielle Bemerkungen zur Frage der Improvisation', *IMSCR*, vii *Cologne 1958*, 287

F. Schmid: 'Joseph Haydn und die vokale Zierpraxis seiner Zeit, dargestellt an einer Arie seines Tobias-Oratoriums', *Internationale Konferenz zum Andenken Joseph Haydns: Budapest 1959*, 117

Bartha and L. Somfai, eds.: *Haydn als Opernkapellmeister: die Haydn-Dokumente der Esterhazy-Opernsammlung* (Budapest, 1960)

Horsley: 'The Sixteenth-century Variation and Baroque Counterpoint', *MD*, xiv (1960), 159

-H. Neumann: *Die Ästhetik des Rezitativs: zur Theorie des Rezitativs im 17. und 18. Jahrhundert* (Strasbourg, 1962)

Aldrich: 'On the Interpretation of Bach's Trills', *MQ*, xlix (1963), 289

Donington: *The Interpretation of Early Music* (London, 1963, rev. 3/1974)

Mackerras: 'Sense about the Appoggiatura', *Opera*, xiv (1963), 669

B. Caswell: *The Development of Seventeenth-century French Vocal Ornamentation and its Influence upon the Late Baroque Ornamentation Practice* (diss., U. of Minnesota, 1964)

Geoffroy-Dechaume: *Les secrets de la musique ancienne* (Paris, 1964)

Neumann: 'A New Look at Bach's Ornamentation', *ML*, xl (1965), 4, 126

Rose: 'Agazzari and the Improvising Orchestra', *JAMS*, xviii (1965), 382

T. Ferand: 'Didactic Embellishment Literature in the Late Renaissance: a Survey of Sources', *Aspects of Medieval and Renaissance Music: a Birthday Offering to Gustave Reese* (New York, 1966), 154

Wichmann: *Der Ziergesang und die Ausführung der Appoggiatura* (Leipzig, 1966)

Apel: *Geschichte der Orgel- und Klaviermusik bis 1700* (Kassel, 1967; Eng. trans., rev., 1972)

Jeans: 'English Ornamentation of the 16th to 18th Centuries (Keyboard Music)', *Musica antiqua: Brno II 1967*, 128

Polk: *Flemish Wind Bands in the Late Middle Ages: a Study of Improvisatory Instrumental Practices* (diss., U. of California, Berkeley, 1968)

Melkus: 'Zur Auszierung der Da-capo-Arien in Mozarts Werken', *MJb 1968–70*, 159

W. Dean: 'Vocal Embellishment in a Handel Aria', *Studies in Eighteenth-century Music: a Tribute to Karl Geiringer* (New York and London, 1970), 151

E. Melkus: 'Die Entwicklung der freien Auszierung im 18. Jahrhundert', *Der junge Haydn Internationale Arbeitstagung des Instituts für Aufführungspraxis: Graz 1970*, 147

T. Borgir: *The Performance of the Basso Continuo in Seventeenth-century Italian Music* (diss., U. of California, Berkeley, 1971)

M. Cyr: 'A Seventeenth-century Source of Ornamentation for Voice and Viol: British Museum MS, Egerton 2971', *RMARC*, ix (1971), 53

M. Vinquist and N. Zaslaw, eds.: *Performance Practice, a Bibliography* (New York, 1971) [orig. in *CMc*, no.8 (1969), 5–96; no.10 (1970), 144–72], suppls., *CMc*, no.12 (1971), 129–49; no.15 (1973), 126–40

H. C. Wolff: *Die Oper*, ii, Mw, xxxix (1971; Eng. trans., 1971)

—: *Originale Gesangsimprovisationen des 16. bis 18. Jahrhunderts*, Mw, xli (1972)

M. Collins: 'In Defense of the French Trill', *JAMS*, xxvi (1973), 405–39

B. B. Mather: *Interpretation of French Music from 1675 to 1775 for Woodwinds and other Instruments* (New York, 1973)

A. Caswell: 'Mme Cinti-Damoreau and the Embellishment of Italian Opera in Paris: 1820–1845', *JAMS*, xxviii (1975), 459–93

H. J. Marx: 'Some Unknown Embellishments of Corelli's Violin Sonatas', *MQ*, lxi (1975), 65

D. H. Till: *English Vocal Ornamentation, 1600–1660* (diss., U. of Oxford, 1975)

H. M. Brown: *Embellishing Sixteenth-century Music* (London, 1976)

D. A. Lee: 'The Embellished Versions of Sonatas by Franz Benda', *MQ*, lxii (1976), 58

B. B. Mather and D. R. G. Lasocki: *Free Ornamentation in Woodwind Music, 1700–1775* (New York, 1976)

C. A. Monson: 'Consort Song and Verse Anthem: a Few Performance Problems', *JVdGSA*, xiii (1976), 4

E. Thom: *Studien zur Aufführungspraxis und Interpretation von Instrumentalmusik des 18. Jahrhunderts* (Leipzig, 1976)

W. Dean: 'The Performance of Recitative in Late Baroque Opera', *ML*, lviii (1977), 389

E. Derr: 'Zur Zierpraxis im späten 18. Jahrhundert', *ÖMz*, xxxii (1977), 8

P. Holman: 'Continuo Realizations in a Playford Songbook', *Early Music*, vi (1978), 268

M. Morrow: 'Musical Performance and Authenticity', *Early Music*, vi (1978), 233

F. Neumann: *Ornamentation in Baroque and Post-Baroque Music* (Princeton, 1978)

A. Ransome: 'Towards an Authentic Vocal Style and Technique in Late Baroque Performance', *Early Music*, vi (1978), 417

J. E. Smiles: 'Directions for Improvised Ornamentation in Italian Method Books of the Late Eighteenth Century', *JAMS*, xxxi (1978), 495

T. Mulhern: 'Improvisational Avant-garde Guitar, its History, its Proponents, its Future', *Guitar Player*, xiii (1979), 36

Music Educators' Journal, lxvi (1980)

G. Sadler: 'The Role of the Keyboard Continuo in French Opera 1673–1776', *Early Music*, viii (1980), 148

II. Asian art music. Improvisation is important in several Asian musical traditions. The extent of its practice and the techniques used vary with each tradition; but certain implications of this Western term do not apply in Asian music, for example the absence of advanced preparation. An Asian musician usually spends many years memorizing and absorbing traditional models before he improvises, and his final rendering may well include fragments composed earlier. Improvisation may also imply the giving way to natural impulse, without premeditation; but this impulse is highly schooled and usually guided by an underlying scheme of development.

In general, improvisation in Asian music requires imagination within the constraints of a framework in which particular musical elements are either obligatory, optional or forbidden. It is largely the manipulation of the optional elements that marks the excellence of a musician. All forms of traditional improvised music have obligatory features which must be referred to in order to preserve the model; the frequency of these features may be described in terms of 'density'. A form with a high density of obligatory features generally leaves less scope for improvisation than a low-density form; this does not imply that a musician performing in a dense medium is necessarily less imaginative than one performing in a sparse medium.

1. East and South-east Asia. 2. South Asia. 3. The Middle East.

1. EAST AND SOUTH-EAST ASIA. Most art music of East Asia has a maximum of obligatory features and permits little or no improvisation. Although the main traditions of China, Japan and Korea emphasize composed forms, some improvisation is perhaps practised in China. In Korea an instrumental form, sanjo, often played on the kayagŭm (12-string zither) with changgo (hourglass drum) accompaniment, is evidently derived from improvisation. In Japanese music occasional instances of improvisation occur, as for example in nagauta (a genre used in the kabuki theatre) in which sanju (partly improvised instrumental interludes) are played on the shamisen while the actor changes costume.

South-east Asian ensemble music generally includes some improvisation but the degree varies with each tradition; in general, the density of obligatory features is high. In Bali the gamelan gong, the traditional cere-

monial ensemble used at all festive and formal occasions, has as many as 40 musicians. Most of these play one-octave metallophones (saron, penyacah, jublag an jegogan) whose sole function is to play a nuclear or fixe melody (gending pokok) or certain important notes of the melody: they are not allowed to improvise. The ensemble also includes a soloist who plays the trompong (set of gong-chimes) which introduces each orchestral composition with a partly improvised solo; the trompong also fills in the nuclear melody and provides the linking sections between the movements of the composition (see ex.22: it should be noted that the following examples convey only an approximation of the intonation used in the different systems). The obligatory features are the notes of the mode to which the gongs are tuned and the notes of the nuclear melody. The relationship of these notes to the improvisation is often complex: 6ths or 5ths, for example, are sometimes resolved to unisons or octaves. The trompong player uses devices such as playing off the beat to produce syncopated counter-rhythms, and avoiding, anticipating or following the notes of the nuclear melody. The nuclear melody is contained within an octave and is generally characterized by disjunct motion. The trompong improvisations are, however, spread over two octaves and are primarily in conjunct motion, providing a more fluid realization of the nuclear melody (ex.22).

In the Balinese gamelan gong some improvisation also occurs in the performance of the two reyong players (see ex.23). A reyong consists of four gongs mounted horizontally, tuned to four of the notes of the mode, as follows: first player, g♯ (left hand), a' (right hand); second player, d' (left hand), e' (right hand). The musicians produce interlocking rhythms and a continuous stream of figuration while preserving a relationship with the nuclear melody. Improvisation on the reyong is complicated because the obligatory notes of the nuclear melody might alternate within the range of the two players.

Ex.22 *Trompong realization of pokok tones; gending silir* (McPhee, 1966)

TROMPONG

POKOK

Ex.23 *Reyong* figuration (McPhee, 1966)

REYONG

POKOK

While improvisation is limited to very few instruments in Bali, group improvisation is characteristic of the Javanese gamelan. A Javanese gamelan may consist of more than 30 instrumentalists with a dozen male singers and three female singers. Together they have a range of six octaves and can produce as many as 25 different rhythmic–melodic lines, more than half involving improvisation. The main (nuclear) melody, played in slow notes on the saron (bronze metallophone), is the basis for improvisation. Instruments such as the gongs mark the periods, the drums regulate the

mpos and the dynamics, while some of the melody
astruments play in smaller note values, filling in the
uclear melody. The main improvising role is allotted
» the *rebab* (two-string spike fiddle), traditionally played
y the leader of the gamelan, and the *gender barung*
pronze metallophone); a number of other instruments,
or instance the *gambang* (wooden xylophone), the *gen-
er panerus* (bronze metallophone), the *celempung*
zither) and the *suling* (end-blown flute) also have sig-
ificant improvising roles. Most of these improvising
astruments have a high density of obligatory musical
eatures. In addition to the constraints of the nuclear
nelody and the *patet* (mode) each instrumentalist is
ssigned a specific pace for his improvisations in a par-
cular piece. The *gender barung*, for instance, may play
our notes to each note of the melody in one piece, and
s many as 32 in another. Only slight variations of pulse
nd rhythm are generally practised and are usually com-
ensated for almost immediately. Ex.24 shows three
ossible ways in which a *gambang* player might approach
n important structural note of the nuclear melody through
mprovisation (in bar 3).

x.24 Three possible *gambang* improvisations

Ensemble music is also characteristic of mainland
South-east Asia. The *pī phāt* and *mahōrī* ensembles in
Thailand, Kampuchea and Laos, as well as the *hsaing-
waìng* ensemble in Burma, practise forms of stratified
polyphony similar to that in Java and Bali. Improvisation around a nuclear melody prevails in varying degrees.
The music of Vietnam is more an extension of Chinese
music and, as far as is known, includes little improvisation. On mainland South-east Asia small ensembles that
generally play a reduced version of the music of the
larger ensembles are also common. In Burma, for
instance, traditional songs may be accompanied only by
a solo melody instrument such as the *saùng-gauk* (arched
harp) and time-keeping instruments such as *gyat* (clappers) and *sì* (finger cymbals). The harpist improvises
much of his accompaniment, roughly following the contours of the melody, but he sometimes deviates from
the song melody enough to create counterpoint. The
constraints are the song, the mode and the metre. Since
Burmese songs are usually through-composed with no
repeats the accompanist is expected to preserve unity by
referring to motifs stated earlier; a good accompanist
also introduces new motifs to differentiate each verse.

2. SOUTH ASIA. Improvisation is one of the most prominent aspects of South Asian art music. While polyphony is characteristic of South-east Asian music, South
Asian music often features a single melodic line – vocal
or instrumental – accompanied by a drone and percussion. Heterophony is also characteristic, as the soloist
may often be accompanied by one or more instrumentalists. While the soloist is performing a composed section the accompanists play more or less in unison, but
when he improvises they imitate his phrases as closely
as possible. The density of obligatory features is generally considerably lower than in the music of South-
east Asia. Some of the obligatory features, however, are
subtle and require extensive training before they are
absorbed. The primary constraint is imposed by the Indian
modal form, the raga (Sanskrit *rāga*), a conceptual
framework for both composition and improvisation. A
raga is identified by such features as its characteristic
phrases, ascending and descending lines, the accidentals
permitted, the tessitura and obligatory ornaments. Traditional teaching methods do not emphasize these
abstractions, but require students to memorize lengthy
compositions in each raga so that the features of the
ragas embodied in them will be absorbed.

In two main art music traditions of South Asia (that
of north India, Pakistan and Bangladesh, and that of
south India) the density of obligatory features is lowest
in the opening improvised section called *ālāpa* or *ālāpana*
(the northern form being *ālāp*). The rhythm and metre
of the improvised phrases of the *ālāpa* must be irregular. In addition to modal considerations of the raga the
musician is expected to follow certain guidelines. He
should begin his improvisation in the lower middle register and gradually expand the tonal range to the acceptable limits of the raga. Phrases should begin slowly and
simply, gradually developing in pace and complexity.
The musician is permitted some freedom to deviate but
must, on the whole, abide by the accepted models.

The raga comprises several nuclear subjects that can
be expanded, and in an *ālāpa* the musician is generally
expected to elaborate on them. Their precise form is by
no means standardized and it is debatable whether such
a simplified form even exists in the mind of the performing musician. The nuclear form becomes apparent,
however, when a musician teaches a simplified version
of a raga to his students, and in the notations found in
Indian music texts. The teacher's version may vary from
one musician to another and from one occasion to the
next. While the precise delineation of a nuclear subject
might be quite subjective, it appears that much Indian
improvisation involves the elaboration, expansion and
variation of some such nuclear scheme, as illustrated in
ex.25, which is in the north Indian raga *darbārī*. The
first line gives one possible nuclear version and the succeeding lines show examples of *ālāpa* improvisations on
this subject; note that the concluding notes of the nuclear phrase (*bb*, *g*) are withheld until the series of improvisations is completed.

The *ālāpa* may be followed by a rhythmic but non-
metrical improvised section called *tānam* in south India,
jor or *jhālā* in north Indian instrumental music and *nom-
tom* in north Indian vocal music. This section is characterized by a more or less regular pulse, which on string
instruments is produced on the drone strings and in vocal
music by using nonsense syllables (such as *tā, nā, re,
ne, nom* and *tom*) with a degree of regularity. While the
ālāpa is largely melismatic, the *tānam* and *jor* tend to

Ex.25 Improvisations on a nuclear subject in *darbārī* raga

〰️ a wide, slow vibrato

be more syllabic. These sections customarily begin in the middle register and gradually expand their range while increasing the tempo and complexity of the improvised phrases. The final section of a classical performance is set in a *tāla* (time measure, time cycle). This section is always introduced by a composition and is accompanied by a percussionist. Compositions, which may begin at any point in the *tāla*, vary considerably in length, those in south India generally being longer and more prominent. In the *baṛā khayāl* form of north Indian classical song, for instance, not even one full verse of the composition need be sung in its entirety. Both the *tāla* and the composition influence the nature and the length of the improvisations although the soloist need not follow the stress pattern of the *tāla*. The improvisations may begin at any point in the time cycle and conclude with

a return to the composition, theoretically at any point provided the relationship of the composition to the *tāla* is maintained. Some improvisations may be much longer, extending over several cycles of the *tāla*. In practice the improvisations frequently conclude by returning to the composition either on the *sam* (first beat) of the *tāla* or just before the beat on which the composition begins. This is illustrated by the north India sitar improvisations, also in the raga *darbārī*, shown in ex.26. The type of composition, called *masītkhānī gat*, is played primarily on plucked string instruments. It is generally performed in *tīntāl* (a time cycle of 16 beats) in a slow or medium tempo. In ex.26 the slide from *f'* to *eb'* occurs on the first beat in the *gat* and in the second improvisation concludes with a *tīhāī* (a thrice-repeated cadence pattern) with the same slide on the first beat, so that the return to the composition is accomplished smoothly. In other compositions in the same raga some other note may appear on the first beat, in which case the improviser would need to shape his phrases accordingly.

In vocal music the same pattern is followed: composition, improvisation, return to composition. Two main types of improvisation are used: in one (called *nirava* in south India and *bol-tān* in north India) the words of the composed song are set to improvised melodic lines; in the second (called *kalpana svara* in south India and *sargam tān* in north India) the notes *sā*, *ri*, *ga*, *ma*, *pa*, *dha* and *ni* are named as they are sung. In the north Indian *khayāl* song form it is customary to include *ākār tān* (rapid improvised vocalizations on the vowel *ā*).

In South Asian music percussion improvisation is common. The most frequently used drums are the *mṛdaṅgam* (in south India) and the pair of drums generally referred to as *tablā* (in north India). Both produce a variety of sounds which are represented by mnemonic syllables. Improvisations on the *mṛdaṅgam* and *tablā* are restricted by the *tāla*. To preserve continuity a single series of improvisations may use only certain syllables or strokes, rhythmic patterns and configurations. Beginning with a starting pattern the musician may change the order of the syllables, repeat some and omit others, introduce pauses, vary tempo, etc. He may not, however, introduce syllables which do not occur in that particular starting pattern.

Ex.26 *Masītkhānī gat* and improvisations in *darbārī* raga; *tīntāl*

3. The Middle East. The art music of the Middle East includes several related Islamic musical traditions of which the Arabic, Persian and Turkish are best known. The music of this area somewhat resembles that of South Asia. Small ensembles performing homophonically or heterophonically with drum accompaniment are characteristic of most of this region. Occasionally larger ensembles perform *nawba* (suites) which consist of composed orchestral sections interspersed with instrumental solos and vocal recitatives of classical poetry. Analogous to the South Asian raga are modal forms such as the Arabic and Turkish *maqām* and the Persian *dastgāh* which are the basis for composition and improvisation. A further similarity lies in the division of the music into two sections: an unmeasured section (similar to the *ālāp* of South Asia), called *taqsīm* in Arabic music and *āvāz* in Persian music, and metric sections (similar to *gat*, *khayāl*, etc) such as *tasnif*, *reng*, *beste* and *bashraf*, which are often accompanied by drums. The development of the *taqsīm* and *āvāz*, like the *ālāp*, is based on gradual expansion of the tonal range. This expansion is more formalized in some Islamic traditions: the Persian *dastgāh*, for instance, is composed of a number of clear *gusheh-hā* (developmental stages) each of which focus on a particular note or notes of the *dastgāh*. A special feature of this system is that the traditional repertory of these stages may involve modulations of the parent *dastgāh* scale. In the performance of a *dastgāh* a musician will elaborate the various *gusheh-hā* in succession. A full rendering of a *gusheh* might include a *darāmad* (introductory improvisation in free time), one or more metric pieces such as *kereshmeh*, *chahārmezrāb*, *zarbi*, *reng*, *tasnif* often with drum accompaniment, a *tahrir* (vocal melismatic section), and a characteristic *forūd* (cadence).

The metric pieces in Middle Eastern music are largely composed and it is in the unmeasured *āvāz* and *tasnif* that most of the improvisation occurs. The *āvāz* is primarily a vocal style for the rendering of Persian classical poetry. Although the *āvāz* is not measured, there is nevertheless a clear relationship between the long and short syllables of the verse and the duration of the notes of the improvised melodic line. Ex.27 is an extract of a *ghazal* (poem) by Sa'di sung by Gholamhoseyn Banan. The metre of each line of the couplet is short–long–long–long, short–long–long–long, short–long–long. The short syllables are generally confined to semiquavers while the long syllables, especially the final long syllable of each section, are greatly extended, illustrating the vocal melisma called *tahrir*. Instrumental renderings of these poems also tend to complement the underlying metric structure. Thus the *āvāz* adds a further constraint to that imposed by mode (*dastgāh*) and stage of development (*gusheh*).

Ex.27 *Tahrir* (vocal melisma) in *ghazal* by Sa'di

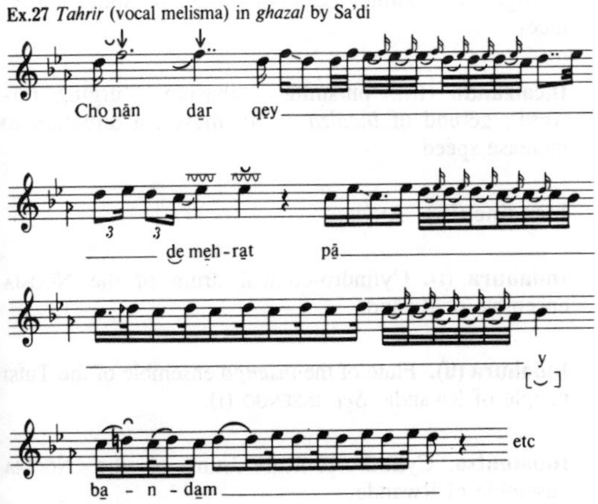

◡ slightly shorter than notated
⌢ slightly longer than notated
↓ slightly lower than notated
∿∿ a wide vibrato below the note

As in the music of South Asia the techniques of improvisation are not taught directly. Each teacher has his own teaching version of a *gusheh* or stage of *taqsīm*. In Persian music this teaching version is called *radif*. A student is expected to memorize these teaching versions more or less exactly. Sometimes the student may be taught more than one version of a *gusheh*. This, supplemented by exposure to improvised variations performed by his teacher and others, gradually reveals new possibilities for paraphrasing the traditional materials.

Viewing improvisation largely in terms of the obligatory musical features of each system is an ethnomusicologist's approach. A student of an Asian music, however, first absorbs the traditional models in their composed forms. After this his greatest problem is to use his imagination to break away from the constraints of the composition. In a tradition in which the density of obligatory events is variable the student generally begins to learn improvisation with the most dense elements. In South Asian music he begins with the metric sections where he is taught not only the composed song or tune but composed versions of improvisations. Improvisation within the unmeasured *ālāpa* is generally learnt much later. In Javanese music improvisation is first learnt on the simple colotomic instruments, the various types of gong, progressing then to the *saron* family of instruments which carries the nuclear melody. The student may then learn some of the basic drum patterns, and later the instruments of the *bonang* family which are used to elaborate the nuclear melody and perform simple improvisations. He may also learn the male chorus parts before he begins to study the more complicated improvising instruments such as the *gambang*, the *gender* family and the *rebab*. In this way the obligatory features are thoroughly absorbed before the student considers improvisation.

BIBLIOGRAPHY

M. Hood: 'Improvisation as a Discipline in Javanese Music', *Music Educators' Journal*, li (1964), 34
C. McPhee: *Music in Bali* (New Haven and London, 1966)
M. Hood and H. Susilo: *Music of the Venerable Dark Cloud* (Los Angeles, 1967) [with disc]
W. P. Malm: *Music Cultures of the Pacific, the Near East, and Asia* (Englewood Cliffs, NJ, 1967)
J. Becker: 'The Anatomy of a Mode', *EM*, xiii (1969), 267
G. Tsuge: 'Rhythmic Aspects of the Āvāz in Persian Music', *EM*, xiv (1970), 205
N. A. Jairazbhoy: *The Rāgs of North Indian Music* (London and Middletown, Conn., 1971)
H. H. Touma: 'The Maqam Phenomenon: an Improvisation Technique in the Music', *EM*, xv (1971), 38
B. Nettl and B. Fontin jr: *Daramad of Chahargah: a Study in the Performance Practice of Persian Music* (Detroit, 1972)
E. Zonis: *Classical Persian Music* (Cambridge, Mass., 1973)
B. Nettl: 'Thoughts on Improvisation: a Comparative Approach', *MQ*, lx (1974), 1

I: IMOGENE HORSLEY (1), MICHAEL COLLINS (2), EVA BADURA-SKODA (3), DENNIS LIBBY (4)
II: NAZIR A. JAIRAZBHOY

Imvingo. *See* Umakhweyana.

Imzad (single-string fiddle) of the Tuareg people, North Africa

Inanga (trough zither) of Rwanda

Imzad [amzad, inzad]. Single-string fiddle of the Tuareg people of North Africa. It has a resonator made from half a gourd covered with goatskin; its horsehair string is stretched over a bridge made of two small pieces of wood which form a cross. The bow stick is curved, with a ribbon of horsehair knotted to its two ends (see illustration). The *imzad* is usually used to accompany men's songs. *See also* GOGE.

Inanga. Eight-string TROUGH ZITHER of Rwanda, Burundi and the Kivu area of Zaïre. It is carved from a single piece of wood 65 to 95 cm long and 20 to 30 cm wide. The interior is slightly concave; the ends and sides are steeply concave. The ends, slightly rounded, have a number of deep triangular notches corresponding to the number of strings. In practice only one length of string is used; it is threaded via the notches from one side to the other. A wooden stick may be inserted beneath the strings at each end to reinforce tension and assist tuning. In performance the strings are normally plucked with the fingers (see illustration; *see also* ZITHER, fig.1*c*), though an early account of the Rundi zither suggests that they are also struck with the nails of the middle and index fingers supported by the thumb. This zither is pre-eminently the instrument of skilful musicians and poets, who accompany their own compositions in praise of heroes or of martial exploits. In Rwanda, Yuki III Mazimpaka, who reigned in the first half of the 18th century, was a remarkable poet–composer of *inanga* songs depicting the rise of the Tutsi kingdom and his own heroic deeds. Most of the *inanga* repertory has been transmitted orally, with little variation, and is thus an important source of information about the Rwandan kingdom. Among the Rundi and Twa the *inanga* is also used to accompany other songs and dances; in the north and north-east of Kivu it is traditionally associated with magic practices and the cult of Biheko, the renowned

king's daughter who miraculously escaped death during the slaughter of her family. Among the Bembe people the variant term *nanga* is used for a seven-string zither of this type; the Shi call this instrument *langa* and the Hutu and Fuliru *lulanga*. *Ikivuvu* and *indimbagazo* are alternative names for the Rundi zither.

BIBLIOGRAPHY
LaurentyC
F. J. de Hen: *Beitrag zur Kenntnis der Musikinstrumente aus Belgisch Kongo und Ruanda-Urundi* (Tervuren, 1960)
G. Knosp: *Enquête sur la vie musicale au Congo belge 1934–1935* (Tervuren, 1968)
J. Gansemans: 'Rwanda', *Grove 6*

K. A. GOURLAY

Inano. BULLROARER of the Mbole people of Zaïre. *See* ATUAMBA.

Inca bells. Idiophone of Bolivia, known also as *zacapa*. Of pre-Hispanic origin, they were originally made of large brown kidney-bean pods found in Andean provinces.

Incalzando (It.: 'pursuing', 'chasing', 'urging forward'; gerund of *incalzare*). In music, a direction to increase speed.

Incudine (It.). ANVIL.

Indahura (i). Cylindro-conical drum of the NGOMA ensemble of Rwanda.

Indahura (ii). Flute of the *insengo* ensemble of the Tutsi people of Rwanda. *See* INSENGO (i).

Indamutsa. Cylindro-conical drum of the NGOMA ensemble of Rwanda.

Indang. FRAME DRUM of Minangkabau, West Sumatra. Its goatskin head is about 20 to 25 cm in diameter. The ame is used also for an ensemble of drums played by men or boys (recently also by girls in separate groups), who sit cross-legged in a long row and accompany dancing and singing with a variety of rhythms. In the Pariaman area *indang* are known as RAPA'I. See M. J. Kartomi: 'Minangkabau Musical Culture: The Contemporary Scene and Recent Attempts at its Modernisation', *What is Modern Indonesian Culture?*, ed. G. Davies (Athens, Ohio, 1979), 19ff.

MARGARET J. KARTOMI

Indier. Largest of the three ceremonial slit-drums (*see* SLIT-DRUM) of the Tiv people of Nigeria, the others being the *ilyu* and the *gede-gede*. According to legend the body of a living man was used to determine the size of the interior; he was later killed and his blood poured into the drum. The drum is beaten with two wooden strikers and used for signalling on important occasions in the Tiv life cycle. The *ilyu* drum was formerly used in litigation contests during which rival performers sang satirical songs against each other.

BIBLIOGRAPHY

R. C. Abraham: *The Tiv People* (Lagos, 1933/R1968)
R. East: *Akiga's Story* (London, 1939/R1965)
R. M. Downes: *Tiv Religion* (Ibadan, 1971)

K. A. GOURLAY

Indimba. LAMELLAPHONE of the Plateau Tonga people of Zambia. It has a board-type body and 14 keys, with heptatonic tuning.

Indimbagazo. TROUGH ZITHER of the Rundi people of Burundi (*LaurentyC*, 116). *See* INANGA.

Indingidi [iningiti, izeze]. TUBE FIDDLE of the Rundi people of Burundi (*LaurentyC*, 122). *See* TARATIBU.

Indip. Single-headed cylindrical drum of the Dzing people of Zaïre (*BooneT*, 51).

Indongoli. Short eight-string lyre of the Wanga people of northern Nyanza district, Kenya.

Indono. Braced MUSICAL BOW, with a gourd resonator, of the Rundi people of the Muhinga region of Zaïre (*LaurentyC*, 113). *See* KAKULUMBUMBA.

Indonyi. Small, slightly barrel-shaped drum of the Marach people of Kenya. It has a single laced head and wooden body. The drum is placed on the thigh of a seated player, who beats it with a single wooden stick. It is used as part of a set which includes the *izidonyi* and the *ngoma* (*ing'oma*). The *izidonyi* is a small double-headed cylindrical drum; the body is often made of metal and the two skins are laced together. It is placed in the lap of a seated player and beaten with two sticks. The *ngoma* is a long tapering cylindrical drum with nailed membrane; it is placed across the lap and beaten with the hands. See G. Hyslop: *Musical Instruments of East Africa*, i: *Kenya* (Nairobi, 1975).

K. A. GOURLAY

Induk. Javanese FRAME DRUM. *See* TERBANG.

Indweba. *See* IMFENGWANE.

Ingabe. Dynastic drums of the Tutsi people of Rwanda. The four types are called *kalinga*, *cyimumugizi*, *mpatsibihugu* and *kiragutse*.

Ingaraba. Single-headed cylindrical drum of the Twa people of Rwanda, usually played as part of an ensemble.

Ingolongolo. SLIT-DRUM of the Nkundo people of Zaïre, used for dancing. A similar drum is named *bongoo* by the Impolo (*LaurentyTF*, 134).

Ingoma [iñgoma, ing'oma]. *See* NGOMA.

Ingonbin. Double-headed drum of Nigeria. *See* BI.

Ingonga. MOUTH BOW of the Nkundo people of Zaïre; it is also known as *itumbolongonda*, *inkoko* and *lonkoko* (*LaurentyC*, 112). *See* LUSUBA.

Ingqongqo. Skin idiophone the Xhosa people of southern Africa. It comprises the hide of a bull, fastened to poles stuck in the ground, or hand-held at the corners, and beaten with sticks. It is used mainly at male initiation dances. See *KirbyMISA*, 20ff.

Ingqongqo (skin idiophone) played by Xhosa women, southern Africa

Ingulube. FRICTION DRUM of the Xhosa people of southern Africa. It resembles the Zulu *ingungu*.

Ingungu. FRICTION DRUM of the Zulu people of southern Africa. It is made by lacing a piece of goatskin to a large clay pot (*imbiza*) or some other receptacle, and is used to accompany obscene songs at girls' puberty ceremonies. A stick or reed is placed vertically on the drumhead and the player's wetted hands are drawn alternately down it, as when milking a cow, producing a roaring or booming sound. See *KirbyMISA*, 26ff, pl.9.

DAVID K. RYCROFT

Inguvo. *See* TSHINGUFU.

Inila-ud. Ensemble of the Kalinga and Tinggian peoples of the northern Philippines, consisting of three gongs (*see* GANGSA (i)) and a cylindrical drum. The first gong is called *patpat*, the second *keb-ang*, the third *sapul* and the drum *tambul*. Each gong is laid on the lap of a performer, who strikes it with the left hand using a stick, while tapping it with the palm of the right hand.

Iningiti. TUBE FIDDLE of the Rundi people of Burundi (*LaurentyC*, 122). *See* TARATIBU.

Inkanka. Side-blown bamboo trumpet of the Twa people of Rwanda, used in the *amakondera* ensemble (*see* AMAKONDERE).

Inkin. Small Japanese bell, used in Buddhist processions. It is clapperless and bowl-shaped, about 6 to 8 cm long and is attached to a wooden handle; its rim is struck with a tiny stick. (For illustration *see* MOKUGYO.) *See also* KANE.

Inkinge. Unbraced MOUTH BOW of the Xhosa people of southern Africa, resembling the Zulu UMQANGALA. It is made from reed, has a string of twisted hair, and is played with a plectrum. Players are mainly women and girls. See *KirbyMISA*, 220ff, pl.62.

Inkohlisa. Braced or unbraced MUSICAL BOW of the Zulu people of southern Africa. *See* UGUBHU and UMAKHWEYANA.

Inkoko (i). LAMELLAPHONE of the Saka, Ngando and Yala peoples of Zaïre. It has wooden keys and a hollowed-out box resonator (*LaurentyS*, 193).

Inkoko (ii). MOUTH BOW of the Nkundo people of Zaïre; it is also known as *itumbolongonda*, *ingonga* and *lonkoko* (*LaurentyC*, 112). *See* LUSUBA.

Inkota. LAMELLAPHONE of the Ngombe, Kotu and Mbole peoples of Zaïre.

Inse. Ring flute of the Maranao people of the southern Philippines.

Insengo (i). Flute ensemble of the Tutsi people of Rwanda. The instruments are tubular, made from wood, and covered with the hide from a bull's throat. The best-known flutes have the same names as those of some NGOMA drums, for example *igihumulizo*, *indahura*, *ishakwe*. See J. Gansemans: 'Rwanda', *Grove 6*.

Insengo (ii). Side-blown bamboo trumpet of the Twa people of Rwanda, used in the *amakondera* ensemble (*see* AMAKONDERE).

Inshingili. Double-headed drum played by royal musicians among the Bemba people of Zambia. It is struck by hand while hanging from the player's shoulder or neck.

Inshuragane. Side-blown trumpet of the Twa people of Rwanda, used in the *amakondera* ensemble (*see* AMAKONDERE).

Instrumentenkunde (Ger.). ORGANOLOGY.

Intambula. Drum of the Swazi people of southern Africa. It consists of a clay beer pot with a goatskin held across the top (by an assistant) and beaten with a single stick. It was used for exorcism. *See also* MOROPA.

Interpretation. Term used in music in two principal, though overlapping, senses. First, it stands for those minor divagations from a mechanical representation of the notation of a piece of music as may represent a personal contribution, or a personal view of the piece, on the part of the performer or performers; second, as dealt with in such books as Arnold Dolmetsch's *Interpretation* (1915) and Thurston Dart's *The Interpretation of Music* (1954), it stands for those departures from an exact representation of notation that seem to be justified by the performing practices of the period, the region and the style from which the music concerned originated.

In the former sense, the term is not susceptible of discussion within the confines of a reference work (though individual elements of it are, for example ARTICULATION, DYNAMICS, RUBATO and TEMPO); for the second, *see* PERFORMING PRACTICE.

Intona. A trade name used by Schmidt & Co. of Leipzig for a small model BARREL ORGAN; *see also* MECHANICAL INSTRUMENT.

Intonarumori (It.: 'noise intoners'). A family of ten types of instrument mostly based on the principle of the HURDY-GURDY, invented by LUIGI RUSSOLO and constructed in Milan between 1913 and 1921 with the assistance of his fellow futurist Ugo Piatti (?1880–1953). Each instrument was built inside a rectangular, brightly painted box, from the front of which protruded a large horn; the largest box was around 120 cm high. At the back of the box the player turned a crank (or in some cases pressed an electric button) with the right hand to produce the sound, the pitch of which was controlled by a lever operated by the left hand; quartertone steps were sometimes used. The internal mechanism consisted of a wheel 15 to 20 cm in diameter and made either of wood, with a rosined or notched rim, or of steel, toothed like the blade of a saw, which rotated against a metal or gut string. The tension of the string was varied by the pitch lever, which in most of the instruments also operated a movable bridge that slid along the string. One end of the string terminated in a diaphragm consisting of a small single-headed drum whose skin had been treated with various chemical preparations (depending on the timbre required), which in turn was attached to the projecting horn. In the *crepitatore* there was no bridge and the bowed string was attached at right angles to a second, tunable string which was fixed to the diaphragm. In the *ronzatore* and *gorgogliatore* there was neither bridge nor wheel: in the former an electrically operated beater struck the diaphragm from close to, to produce a reiterated sound; in the latter the same type of beater struck the string from somewhat further off, to create what Russolo described as 'a curious rhythm'. At least three types of *intonarumori* had a second lever for changing the timbre; these included the *gorgogliatore*, which when the second lever was in operation was transformed into the *scrosciatore* (Russolo also seems originally to have used the two names interchangeably, regardless of which timbre was referred to). The *sibilatore* had two timbre levers.

By spring 1914 Russolo and Piatti had built 17 or 18 instruments of eight types, with ranges of one to two octaves; where two or three of a single type were made, each had a different range. The basic principle was patented as 'intonatore di rumori' early in 1914. During World War I Russolo added little to his inventions, apart from expanding the ranges of four existing types, but spent time preparing his book *L'arte dei rumori* (1916). By 1921 two further types had been produced, the *gracidatore* and the *frusciatore*, making a probable total of 29 instruments. They were used in works by Russolo, his brother Antonio, Francisco Balilla Pratella and other futurists. Since the mid-1970s at least one instrument of each of the ten types has been reconstructed in Europe and North America. Throughout the 1920s Russolo worked on four successive versions of his RUMORARMONIO, which united the individual features of the *intonarumori*. He explored other approaches to bowed strings in the ARCO ENARMONICO (1925) and the PIANO ENARMONICO (1931).

BIBLIOGRAPHY
L. Russolo: 'Gl'intonarumori futuristi', *Lacerba*, i/13 (1913); Eng. trans. as 'The Futurist *Intonarumori*', *Futurist Performance*, ed. M. Kirby (New York, 1971), 175
S. Prokof'yev: 'Muzykal'nye instrumenty futuristov', *Muzyka*, no.219 (1915); It. trans. in C. G. De Michelis: *Il futurismo italiano in Russia 1909–1929* (Bari, 1973), 153
L. Russolo: *L'arte dei rumori* (Milan, 1916); repr. in Maffina (1978); Fr. trans., ed. G. Lista, as *L'art des bruits* (Lausanne, 1975)
G. F. Maffina, ed.: *Russolo: L'arte dei rumori 1913–1931* (Venice, 1977) [exhibition catalogue]
G. F. Maffina: *Luigi Russolo e l'arte dei rumori* (Turin, 1978), 26, 72, 178
F. K. Prieberg: 'Probleme der Vergegenwärtigung', *Für Augen und Ohren* (Berlin, 1980), 106 [festival programme book]
B. Brown: 'The Noise Instruments of Luigi Russolo', *PNM*, xx/1–2 (1981–2), 31
HUGH DAVIES

Intonation. (1) In singing, or playing instruments without notes of fixed pitch, 'intonation' is used to describe the accuracy of pitch of a performer's individual notes as judged by a critical hearer. Although theoretically the fundamental problem of temperament is relevant, in practice the performer's musicianship and technique are usually overriding factors. Since the middle of the 18th century, mechanical developments in wind instruments have been largely concerned with easing problems of intonation.

(2) The German term for the 'voicing' of organ pipes, i.e. the final skilful and artistic shaping of the mouth and languid to give a beautiful tone quality and attack. *See* VOICING, §1.

GUY OLDHAM

Inuit [Eskimo] **fiddle.** *See* TAUTIRUT.

Invention (Ger.). As applied to valveless brass instruments, a curved sliding CROOK which can be inserted into the body of the horn (*Inventionshorn*) or trumpet (*Inventionstrompete*) without disturbing the mouthpiece. The *Inventionshorn* was probably designed by the horn player Anton Joseph Hampel and built by Johann Werner in Dresden in the early 1750s. The insertion of *Inventions* into the horn enabled the mouthpipe to remain fixed, avoiding removal with every change of crook; this enabled the player to keep the instrument close to the body, making hand-stopping possible. Modifications were introduced about 1776 by Johann Gottfried Haltenhof at Hanau-am-Main: in particular, shorter crooks with an independent mouthpipe were fitted to improve intonation. In 1781 Carl Türrschmidt improved the blowing response of the instrument by realigning the tubing; his design became known as the *cor-solo* and was manufactured by the firm of Raoux. The shape and general design of the *Inventionshorn* proved ideal when valves came to be fitted to the horn about 30 years later and was almost universally adopted.

Built on the same principle as the *Inventionshorn*, the *Inventionstrompete* also allowed the player to change crooks without adversely affecting embouchure. Examples of *Inventionstrompete* include those by A. F. Krause (1793), J. A. Heckel (1836–7) and many anonymous ones in the Karl-Marx-Universität, Leipzig.

See also HORN, §3 and fig.8a; RAOUX; TRUMPET, §4 and fig.7e.

BIBLIOGRAPHY
R. Morley-Pegge: *The French Horn* (London, 1960, 2/1973)
H. Fitzpatrick: 'Some Historical Notes on the Horn', *GSJ*, xvi (1963), 33
H. Fitzpatrick: *The Horn and Horn-playing and the Austro-Bohemian Tradition 1680–1830* (London, 1970)
H. Heyde: *Trompeten Posaunen Tuben* (Leipzig, 1980)
NIALL O'LOUGHLIN

Inzad. *See* IMZAD.

Inzhe. RAFT ZITHER with 18 strings of the Irigwe people of Nigeria. It is constructed and played like the Birom YOMKWO. It has a metal jingle on the back and traditionally was used to accompany death music for a former head of a compound.

Inzogera. Ankle rattles of Rwanda, worn by *intore* and *imbyino* dancers.

Ionga. SLIT-DRUM of the Nkundo, Boyela and Ngando peoples of Zaïre (*LaurentyTF*, 135).

Ipaánda. Side-blown gourd trumpet of the Salampasu people of south-western Zaïre (*LaurentyA*, 310).

Ipese. Set of cylindrical footed drums of the Yoruba people of Nigeria. *See* IGBIN.

Ipiano. Obsolete MOUTH BOW of the Swazi people of southern Africa. *See* UTIYANE.

Ipu. Obsolete coconut-shell CLAPPERS of Samoa and Tokelau. Two half shells, one held in each hand, were struck together to accompany song and dance. See R. Moyle: 'Samoan Musical Instruments', *EM*, xviii (1974), 64.

Ipu hōkiokio. Globular NOSE FLUTE of Hawaii. It was made from a gourd and generally had three finger-holes. It is said to have been used by lovers to entertain each other. See P. Buck: *Arts and Crafts of Hawaii* (Honolulu, 1957), 391.

Ipu hula (gourd drum) played by a Hawaiian ho'opa'a (chanter-drummer)

Ipu hula. Stamping vessel or gourd drum of Hawaii. It is made from two gourds (*Lagenaria siceraria*), the lower being large, long and globular, and the upper short and squat. Both are selected for the quality of sound produced by striking the dried, hard rind. The stem ends are cut off, inner seeds removed, and the two gourds are joined, forming a neck. A hole is centered above the resonance chamber. The player secures the instrument in one hand through a wrist loop, raises it, thumps it down on a mat, raises it again and gives it quick flexible slaps with the fingers of the other hand.

ZANETA HO'OŪLU CAMBRA

Iqliq. Obsolete SPIKE FIDDLE of Arabia and Central Asia. *See also* KHUUR.

Ira (i). A term used in the Peruvian and Bolivian Alti Plano for one of a pair of hocketing PANPIPES, each played by a different male musician. The *ira* is considered masculine and typically leads the 'feminine' panpipes, the *arca*. In certain areas other terms are used; among the Chipaya of the Department of Oruro, Bolivia, for example, the *ira* is also called *lutaqa* and the *arca mataqa* ('man' and 'woman' respectively). The *ira* panpipe-rank usually has one pipe more or less than the *arca*. *See also* JULA-JULA, esp. ex.1.

Ira (ii). End-blown gourd trumpet of the Logo people of north-eastern Zaïre. It is in three sections, glued together (*LaurentyA*, 309).

Irana. Beaked end-blown flute in a *pinkillo* ensemble of Bolivia. *See* ASU.

Irili [irli]. Side-blown animal-horn trumpet of the Logo people of north-eastern Zaïre. It has a globular bell made from gourd (*LaurentyA*, 329). *See* MOTUTU.

Irimba. LAMELLAPHONE of the Makua people of Mozambique. It has a box-type body and seven keys.

Irish harp. A term applied to the type of harp used in Ireland up to the late 18th century. It is also now used for small gut-strung harps with hand-operated apparatus for producing semitone changes to individual strings. (These have little in common with the historic Irish harp. The Irish name for the harp, CLÁIRSEACH (cognate with the Gaelic CLÀRSACH), is documented from the 15th century onwards; for a discussion of the history of harps in Ireland, *see* HARP, §4 (ii).

The constant structural features of the Irish harp were (1) a resonator hollowed from a single block of willow to a thickness of about 1·3 cm on the belly (more elsewhere), with a separate back; (2) a curved forepillar most of which was T-shaped in section; (3) diatonically tuned brass strings set in the left side of the neck. Other characteristic features were its heavy neck and strings (30–36) fixed with toggles inside the resonator. In order to prevent the strings from cutting into the wood, horseshoe-shaped metal loops (called 'shoes') were riveted into the surface of the belly around the upper part of the string-holes. The instrument was held on the left shoulder, the left hand playing in the upper register and the right hand in the lower; the strings were plucked with fingernails kept long for the purpose. The 1· instruments and remains of instruments which have survived provide ample evidence about the development of Irish harps. In the 14th and 15th centuries they were small and low-headed; in the 16th and 17th centuries but larger; in the 18th century larger still and high-headed; by the early 19th century they were no longer made or played.

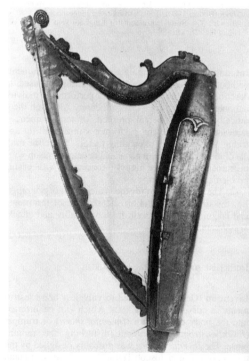

Irish harp: Fitzgerald-Kildare harp, early 17th century (National Museum of Ireland, Dublin)

BIBLIOGRAPHY
. B. Armstrong: *The Irish and Highland Harps* (Edinburgh, 1904/R1970)
Rimmer: 'James Talbot's Manuscript: VI. Harps', *GSJ*, xvi (1963), 63
—: 'The Morphology of the Irish Harp', *GSJ*, xvii (1964), 39
—: *The Irish Harp* (Cork, 1969, rev. 2/1977)
. Larchet Cuthbert: *The Irish Harp Book* (Dublin, 1975)
JOAN RIMMER

rish organ. A term occasionally applied to the UNION IPE; *see also* BAGPIPE, §4.

rızva. Turkish long-necked lute of the *saz* type. It has 3 frets and is played with the fingertips. It is made in wo sizes: small (*cura*) and large (*baz*). The *ırızva*, ometimes known as the *karaduzen*, is found among the ürkmen of the Taurus mountains.

rna. Dance bells of Madhya Pradesh (Bastar district), entral India. The term is Gondi, denoting conical bells vith a clapper. They are made of bronze and are about 3 cm high. About ten bells are attached, together with MUYANG pellet bells, to a wide belt worn by boys of the Muria and Maria tribes; placed on the small of their backs, he bells and pellets jingle with the rhythm of the dan-ers' movements. *See also* GHANȚĀ (with illustration).

BIBLIOGRAPHY
. Dournon: 'India: Tribal Music of Bastar', LDX 74736 [disc notes]
GENEVIÈVE DOURNON

sagogo. Rattle of the Edo-speaking peoples of Nige-ia.

saju ikanhin. Small HOURGLASS DRUM of the Yoruba eople of Nigeria. *See* DUNDUN, (2).

saka [ishaka]. Conical wickerwork rattle of the Igbo eople of Nigeria.

Ísal dádestl'ooni (Apache: 'bucket bound around'; '*ísal*, pot' or 'bucket'). WATER-DRUM of the White Mountain Apache of Arizona. It is made from a large iron pot. The buckskin head is held tightly in place with buckskin hongs or strips of inner tubing.

sambu. Side-blown trumpet made of gourd or animal horn of the Ziba (Haya) people of Tanzania.

sangi. LAMELLAPHONE of the Ndengese people of cen-ral Zaïre. It has wooden keys mounted on a raft-type base (*LaurentyS*, 191). *See* KISAANJ.

sanj. Flat-board LAMELLAPHONE of the Akwa-Sonjo eople of Zaïre. It has metal keys (*LaurentyS*, 195). *See also* KISAANJ and KAKOLONDONDO.

sankuni. *See* ISIGANKURI.

sanzi. LAMELLAPHONE of the Teke and other peoples of West Africa. *See* KISAANJ.

sa ura. DUCT FLUTE of the Ende area of Flores, Indo-nesia. Its bamboo tube is about 15 cm long and has a

node at the bottom. A small flat piece of wood plugs the top opening of the tube, except for a tiny duct. See J. Kunst: *Music in Flores* (Leiden, 1942), 150.

Isa'vaota'p. Drum beater made of arrow-weed stalks; it was used with the basket drum (KWÉNXO') of the Yuman Indians of the south-western USA. It was also used as a rattle.

Ise. Gourd vessel rattle, with a network of external strikers, of the Edo-speaking peoples of Nigeria.

Iseka [iseke]. Side-blown animal-horn trumpet of Zaïre; it has one stop in the tip. It is called *iseka* by the Oshwe people of north-western Zaïre and *iseke* by the Bolia people of western Zaïre (*LaurentyA*, 317f).

Iselwa. Hand-held vessel rattle of the northern Zulu people of southern Africa, resembling the Tsonga NDJELE.

Isese. Bar zither of the Northern and Luapula provinces of Zambia. There are two types (both rare): one variety has a single string and the other two strings, one for the melody and the other mounted on the side for a drone. Both have a calabash resonator fitted with a collar attached at one end, and three frets positioned to pro-duce a scale of four notes with a semitone between the 2nd and 3rd notes. When present the drone is tuned a 3rd below the open melody string.

Ishaka. *See* ISAKA.

Ishakwe [ishaakwe, ishako] **(i).** Leading drum of a drum ensemble of Rwanda. *See* NGOMA and CHIHUMURIZO.

Ishakwe (ii). Flute of the Tutsi *insengo* ensemble of Rwanda. *See* INSENGO (i).

Ishek. Side-blown ivory trumpet of the Ngend people of western Zaïre (*LaurentyA*, 377, 390).

Ishémbb. Wooden cone flute with one or two finger-holes of the Kuba people of south-western Zaïre (*LaurentyA*, 121).

Ishiriri. Two-string fiddle of western Kenya. *See* SIIRIRI.

Ishwaadyé [ishwar]. Wooden cone flute with one or two finger-holes, of the Kuba and Lele peoples of south-western Zaïre (*LaurentyA*, 145f, 148).

Isigankuri [isankuni]. Single-string fiddle of the Mpondo (Xhosa) people of southern Africa. It consists of a curved wooden bow stave inserted into the open end of an emp-ty one-gallon paraffin can. A wire string is secured to the bottom of the can and to the tip of the stave. In performance the instrument is held with the resonator downwards, with the top of the stave resting against the player's left shoulder or projecting above it. The string may be stopped with the left thumb or a finger, near its attachment to the bottom of the resonator. Harmonics are elicited through selective bowing technique in the same way as with the Tswana *segankuru* and Venda *tshidzholo*, to which this instrument is probably related, despite being held the other way up. It is played by males only, either for solo performance, or to accompany the player's singing.

BIBLIOGRAPHY
KirbyMISA, 242 and pl.65*b*
D. K. Rycroft: 'Friction Chordophones in South-eastern Africa', *GSJ*, xix (1966), 94

DAVID K. RYCROFT

Isigodlo [isigodhlo]. Side-blown ox-horn trumpet of the Xhosa people of southern Africa, used for signalling.

Isigubhu. Double-headed cylindrical drum of the Zulu people of southern Africa. The body may be carved from wood or be made from a tin can. The heads are laced together with thongs. The drum is usually slung horizontally in front of the player's chest and beaten at both ends with a padded stick held in each hand. Like the *ongoma* of the Herero people of south-western Africa, it is possibly copied from the European military drum; it is used to accompany young men's neo-traditional recreational dancing. See *KirbyMISA*, 44ff, and pl.15.

DAVID K. RYCROFT

Isigubu. Double-headed cylindrical drum used in southern Africa, based on European models. (1) Drum of the Bhaca and Xesibe (Xhosa) peoples with the head laced to a biscuit tin or wooden body.

(2) Drum of the Zulu people. *See* ISIGUBHU.

Isikehlekehle. *See* SIKHELEKEHLE.

Isikunjane. Vessel rattle of the Xhosa people of southern Africa. It consists of a small tin can containing pebbles. Such rattles are attached to the legs of male dancers.

Isiqomqomana. *See* ISITHONTOLO.

Isiqwemqwemana. Zulu MUSICAL BOW. *See* UMAKHWEYANA.

Isitholotholo [isithwelethwele]. Term of the Zulu people of southern Africa for a commercially produced JEW'S HARP (not to be confused with the mouth bows, *isithontolo* and *setolotolo*).

Isithontolo [isitontolo, isiqomqomana]. Braced composite single-string MOUTH BOW of the Zulu people of southern Africa. It has a tripartite stave, with a thick middle section and thinner, curved ends (*see* MOUTH BOW, fig.1). Cognate instruments among neighbouring peoples are the Sotho *setolotolo*, Venda *tshihwana* and Shona CHIPENDANI (with illustration), and the Northern Sotho *lekope* (which also denotes a simpler form of mouth bow). Players are generally male. See *KirbyMISA*, 228, 234, 245, pl.64.

DAVID K. RYCROFT

Isithwelethwele. *See* ISITHOLOTHOLO.

Isitontolo. *See* ISITHONTOLO.

Isnard. French family of organ builders. Jean-Espr (baptized Bédarrides, Vaucluse, 22 Jan 1707; burie Tarascon, 16 March 1781) was one of the geniuses c French organ building. Among his instruments are thos for Ste Marthe, Tarascon (1742; restoration); church c the Frères Prêcheurs, Tarascon (1743); St Cannat, Mar seilles, and Aix-en-Provence Cathedral (1744–6); Bas ilique St Maximin-en-Var (1773). This last is Isnard" masterpiece and survives in its entirety. The 16′ *Gran orgue* contains a Gross nazard 5⅓′, a Grosse tierce 3⅕" three chorus mixtures and a second treble Trompette *e chamade*; the *Positif* contains three 8′ flue stops, bot the full separate mutations including a Quart de nasar and a Larigot and also a five-rank Cornet, and thre reeds; a three-stop *Récit* of 32 notes constitutes the fourt manual while the third manual, called *La résonance* consists of a 27-note *Echo* of Flûte à cheminée 8′, Cor net V and another Trompette *en chamade*, and a full compass Bombarde consisting of Flûtes 16′, 8′ and 4 and reeds 16′, 8′, 8′ and 4′ which serves both as a peda division and as an extra manual with *grand jeu* effects The organ is still tuned in an unequal temperament, an its pitch is still about two semitones below present pitch It remains one of the most remarkable, beautiful-tone organs ever built in France.

Jean-Baptiste Isnard (*b* Bédarrides, 24 June 172€ *d* Orléans, 18 Aug 1800), nephew and pupil of Jean Esprit, settled in Orléans in 1756. He built the orga at Pithiviers parish church (1784–9) and restored that a Puy-en-Velay. Joseph (*b* Bédarrides, 5 April 1740; ‹ Bordeaux, 9 April 1828), Jean-Baptiste's brother, wa a pupil and colleague of Jean-Esprit. He built the organ at Frères Minimes, Marseilles (1778), and Notre-Dame Lambesc (1788). He settled in Bordeaux and repaire organs in the area that had been damaged during th Revolution.

BIBLIOGRAPHY
F. Raugel: *Recherches sur quelques maîtres de l'ancienne factur française d'orgues* (Paris, 1925)
——: 'Les Isnard', *Cahiers d'art sacré* (Paris, 1946)
M.-R. Arbus: *Une merveille d'art provençal* (Aix-en-Provence, 1955
P. Williams: *The European Organ* (London, 1966/R1978)
F. Douglass: *The Language of the Classical French Organ* (Ne Haven, 1969)

GUY OLDHAN

Issanje. *See* TXISSANJE.

Issheembu. Wooden cone flute, with one or two finger holes, of the Wongo people of Zaïre (*LaurentyA*, 121)

Issimba. Open single-headed tubular drum of the Bak wiri people of Cameroon. *See* LITEMBE.

Istesso tempo, l' (It.: 'the same pace'). A direction t maintain the tempo in spite of apparent disturbances particularly changes of time signature or note value. Thu in a change from 2/4 to 6/8 time the beat would remai constant: the crotchet of the former would equal the do ted crotchet of the latter. *Medesimo tempo* was also used By the later 19th century these directions were increas ingly replaced by equivalence equations.

DAVID FALLOW

Isuguti. Cylindro-conical drum of the Manyisi peopl of Kenya. It is made in different sizes, two of whic are used in a set with the *mutiiti* drum. The large *isugu* measures about 70 cm in length with large and small diameters of about 20 and 13 cm respectively. The small *uguti* has diameters of 15 and 12 cm. The *mutiiti* is similarly shaped, but is only 45 cm long with large and small diameters of 13 and 10 cm. All drums have wooden bodies and are slung from the left shoulder so that they can be beaten with the hands. The *mutiiti* serves as lead drum. See G. Hyslop: *Musical Instruments of East Africa*, i: *Kenya* (Nairobi, 1975).

Isusu. STICK ZITHER of the Konda people of western Zaïre; is also known as *idjendje* (*LaurentyC*, 115). *See* ZEZE (i).

Ita igbin. Drum of the Yoruba people of Nigeria. *See* IGBIN.

Itanda. Frame XYLOPHONE of the Yaka people of Zaïre. *See* MANZA, (2).

Itanki. Whistle of the Xhosa people of southern Africa. The name is applied to the European police whistle, which is commonly used by dance leaders to signal changes in the routine. *See also* IMFENGWANE.

Itekka. *See* IDAKKA.

Itelele. Small drum of the Teso people of Uganda. *See* ETIDA.

Itikili. GROUND HARP of the Lugbara people of Uganda. *See* SEKITULEGE.

Itótele. Drum of the Afro-Cuban Lucumí cult. *See* BATÁ.

Itotsi. VESSEL FLUTE of the Mbole people of Zaïre. *See* DIPULU.

Itsim. Long cylindro-conical drum of the Kutu people of Zaïre. *See* KIMBANDU.

Itsina. Footed cylindrical drum of the Kutu people of Zaïre. *See* MOKITA.

Itūlasi. Obsolete shark-skin drum of Samoa. See R. Moyle: 'Samoan Musical Instruments', *EM*, xviii (1974), 9.

Itumba. Single-headed drum of the Aushi people of Zaïre. *See* DITUMBA.

Itumbolongonda. (1) MOUTH BOW of the Nkundo people of Zaïre, also known as *ingonga*, *inkoko* and *lonoko* (*LaurentyC*, 112). *See* LUSUBA.
   (2) Simple chordophone of the Nkundo people of Zaïre (*LaurentyC*, 110 and 113). *See* EMANA.
   (3) GROUND HARP of the Beloko and Bokote peoples of Zaïre (*LaurentyC*, 111). *See* BABAKUNGU.

Itundak [tinebtebak]. Ensemble of the northern Philippines, consisting of seven flat gongs (*see* GANGSA (i)). It accompanies dances of the Karao people, the players beating the centres of the gongs with sticks. Each *gang-sa* has a V-shaped wooden handle from which the gong is suspended by a string. The left hand holds the handle while the right strikes the gong with a cloth-headed stick. Among the Karao the inner (ventral) side of the gong is struck, while among the Kalinga the dorsal side is struck. Gongs are played during large feasts, especially in the *babeng*, traditionally given by rich men in the community. The Karao's ensemble has seven performers, each playing a different rhythm on a gong with a distinctive timbre. The *tinebtebak* is identical with the *itundak*, but uses different rhythmic patterns.

JOSÉ MACEDA

Iula. An ORGAN STOP (*Jula*).

Iuolouolo. *See* TXIUOLOUOLO.

Ivare. End-blown flute of Irian Jaya, Indonesia. *See* YOKUË.

Ivenge. *See* UMTSHINGO.

Ivom. Clapperless bell of the Igbo people of Nigeria. *See* ALO.

Ivuur. SCRAPER of the Tiv people of Nigeria. It is traditionally used with the *abume* bullroarer and *imborivungu* pipe in the *agbande* rite for a pregnant woman. The instrument is either a hollow, notched wooden stick across which another stick or a cow's jawbone is drawn, or a series of notched rods fixed to a box resonator and scraped in the same manner. See R. East: *Akiga's Story* (London, 1939/*R*1965); R. M. Downes: *Tiv Religion* (Ibadan, 1971).

Ixilongo (i). Trumpet of the Zulu people of southern Africa. *See* ICILONGO.

Ixilongo (ii). Flute of the Xhosa people of southern Africa. *See* IMPEMPE.

Iyá. A drum of the Afro-Cuban Lucumí cult. *See* BATÁ.

Iya ilu [iya gan, iya nla]. Drums of the Yoruba people of Nigeria, used in particular ensembles. *See* BATA; DUNDUN; IGBIN.

Ïya-kovïzh. Two-string fiddle of the Mari people of the Volga-Ural region (USSR).

Iyash. Carved wooden VESSEL FLUTE of the Kuba (Bashi-Biyeng) people of south-western Zaïre (*LaurentyA*, 100).

Iyashina. Single-headed conical drum of the Luvale/Chokwe people of Vila Luzo district, Angola. It is open-ended and the membrane is weighted with beeswax. It is the deepest of a set of three drums (the others are the *mukundu* and *yasongo*) and plays syncopated rhythms. See *TraceyCSA*, ii, 67f.

Iyup-iyup. Idioglot clarinet of the Alas districts of Aceh province, Sumatra. It is made of fresh rice stalks. The instrument is placed in the player's mouth while blowing so that its tongue, which is cut into the stalk, vibrates. It has several finger-holes. The same instrument is known in the Batak Toba areas of North Sumatra as an *ole-ole*, in the Gayo districts of Aceh province as a *pepeon*, and in other parts of Aceh as a *wa*; in the S'adan and north-west Toraja areas of central Sulawesi it is an *om-om*, in the Manggarai area of Flores a *ra'us woga*, and in Nias a *lai waghe*.

MARGARET J. KARTOMI

Izaduma. Obsolete war-drum of the Edo/Bini people of Nigeria.

Izeze (pl. *amazeze*). *See* INDINGIDI.

Izidonyi. Small cylindrical drum of the Marach people of Kenya. *See* INDONYI.

Izikloko. Ankle bells of southern Africa. *See* AMAGI DEMSI.

Izumo-goto. Two-string long zither of Japan. *See* NIGEN KIN.

J

abisen. *See* JAMISEN.

ach'a. PANPIPES of the Bolivian Alti Plano. *See* LAK-rA.

ach'a much'a. DUCT FLUTE of the Bolivian Alti Plano. *See* PINCULLO.

ack (Fr. *sautereau*; Ger. *Docke, Springer*; It. *salter-llo*). (1) The essential part of a harpsichord action that arries the plectrum past the string, plucking it and mak-ng it sound (*see* HARPSICHORD, fig.1).

(2) The pivoted vertical lever in a piano action that orces the hammer upward when the key is depressed *see* PIANOFORTE, esp. figs.32–3).

ackdaw. *See* STRING DRUM.

acobs, David (*b* Niagara Falls, NY, 1 March 932). American sculptor. Since 1957 his work has ncluded some sound elements: his main period of activ-ty in this area (1967–73) resulted in two groups of pieces, Wah Wahs' and 'Wah-Wah: Hanging Pieces'. The first roup – about ten works (1967–70), including Breather, Champ and Horn – features reeds operated pneumati-ally by vacuum-cleaner motors and programmed by lectromechanical timers; the reeds are usually con-ained in inflatable rubber sacks positioned on plinths r metal pillars (though one is a large floor piece). When he motor is switched on the sack slowly takes shape nd the reeds begin to vibrate – the sound resembles an normous bagpipe; the fully inflated shape is held for a eriod determined by the timer, then the motor is switched ff and the container slowly collapses. The works in the econd group – about seven (1970–73) – consist of one r two organ flue pipes fixed into the bottom ends of uspended columns of bulbous rubber 4 to 5 metres high; hey are operated and programmed in the same way as he earlier works and produce sustained drones with var-ed overtones.

BIBLIOGRAPHY

). Jacobs: 'Notebook', *Sound Sculpture: a Collection of Essays by Artists*, ed. J. Grayson (Vancouver, 1975), 34

The Sounds of Sound Sculpture', A.R.C. Records, ST1001 [disc notes]

HUGH DAVIES

acobsz [Jacobs], **Hendrik** (*b* Amsterdam, 1629 or 1630; *d* Amsterdam, 1699). Netherlands violin maker. He is reputed by some to have been a pupil of Nicolo Amati, but this seems unlikely; he probably became familiar with good Italian instruments that had been taken to Amsterdam, perhaps also those of the Austrian maker Jacob Stainer. Jacobsz was the most celebrated of the Netherlands makers, but instruments made entirely by him are quite rare. His copies of the Amati 'grand pat-tern' achieve the ultimate in visual elegance, the sweep-ing outlines highlighted by the use of jet-black whalebone for the dark strips of purfling. The varnish is of Italian quality. He spelt his name either Jacobsz or Jacobs on his labels. Through his marriage in 1676 he acquired a stepson, PIETER ROMBOUTS, who eventually took over from him; Rombouts's work is increasingly evident in Jacobsz's later instruments, especially in the broad pur-fling.

BIBLIOGRAPHY

W. L. von Lütgendorff: *Die Geigen- und Lautenmacher vom Mittelalter bis zur Gegenwart* (Frankfurt am Main, 1904, 6/1922/R1968)

R. Vannes: *Essai d'un dictionnaire universel des luthiers* (Paris, 1932, 2/1951/R1972 as *Dictionnaire universel des luthiers* and R1981 incl. suppl. 1959)

M. Möller: *Violin Makers of the Low Countries* (Amsterdam, 1955)

CHARLES BEARE

Jacquet. French family of instrument makers and musicians. Four of Jehan Jacquet's brothers or cousins were master builders and the family was related to or had close ties with the Lorillart (Lorillac) family of instrument makers, the Duchesne family of painters, the painter Philippe de Champaigne, the lutenist René Mes-angeau, and the organists Claude de la Barre and Louis-Claude Daquin. Fig.1 summarizes what is known about the genealogical connections among the more important members of the family.

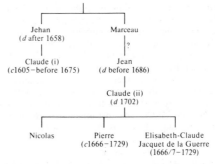

Fig.1

319

Jehan Jacquet (d Paris, after 1658), a 'maître espinetier', was highly regarded as an instrument maker. In *Harmonie universelle* (1636–7) Mersenne referred to him as one of the best harpsichord makers of his time. His son, Claude Jacquet (i) (b Paris, baptized 28 Jan 1605; d Paris, before 1675), 'm[aîtr]e faiseur d'instrumens' and 'joueur d'instrumens de musique' worked in a style so similar to his father's that only a few instruments can be positively identified as being made by him. A 1652 two-manual harpsichord by Claude Jacquet (i) (now in the Ringling Art Museum, Sarasota, Florida) exhibits in several respects (scaling, case construction, placement of 8′ bridge) characteristics intermediate between contemporary Flemish and Italian models and significantly different from mid-18th-century French instruments. As late as 1784, in the edition of *Affiches, annonces et avis divers* for 9 July, a 'clavecin fait en 1646 par Jacquet' was offered for sale.

Claude Jacquet (ii) (b Paris; d Paris, 6 Nov 1702) was the son of the master builder Jean Jacquet (d before 1686; he may have been a son of Marceau Jacquet, also a master builder and a brother of Jehan Jacquet) and was *maître de clavecin* and organist of the church of St Louis-en-l'Ile, Paris. Pierre Jacquet (b Paris, c1666; d Paris, 28 June 1729), a son of Claude Jacquet (ii), was active in Paris in 1695 as an organist and *maître de clavecin*. The other son of Claude Jacquet (ii), Nicolas Jacquet, was organist of St Pierre, Bordeaux. The daughter of Claude Jacquet (ii), Elisabeth-Claude Jacquet de la Guerre, is the most distinguished member of the Jacquet family, highly regarded as a harpsichord player and organist, and especially as a composer.

BIBLIOGRAPHY
J.-B. de La Borde: *Essai sur la musique ancienne et moderne*, iii (Paris, 1780/*R*1972)
F. Lesure: 'La facture instrumentale à Paris au XVIe siècle', *GSJ*, vii (1954), 15

HANS KLOTZ

Jagate [jaganta]. Flat, round, metal percussion plaque of Karnataka and Andhra Pradesh, south India. It is struck with a wooden stick and used by mendicants. It also provides an important rhythmic accompaniment for the *yakṣagāna* dance-drama of the Karnataka region. *See* GHAṚĪ.

Jagba. Drum of the Yoruba people of Nigeria. *See* IGBIN.

Jagd-Hautbois. *See* OBOE DA CACCIA.

Jagdhorn (Ger.). Hunting horn; *see* HORN.

Jāhele. Idiophone of Kuwait, Bahrain and the Gulf region. It is an empty, glazed earthenware pot, 50 to 100 cm in height, without a membrane, played by striking *dum* (dull or heavy) beats with the palm of the right hand across the opening and the *tik* (clear or light) beats with the left hand on the rim. Usually several *jāhele* are played together with other percussion instruments to create intricate polyrhythms. They are used, with several MIRWĀS, by pearl-divers to accompany their songs (*fijirī* and *ḥaddādī*). The instrument has recently reappeared in Iraq, where it is known as a *bastūga*.

BIBLIOGRAPHY
P. Rovsing Olsen: 'Arabian Gulf', *Grove 6*
S. Qassim Hassan: *Les instruments de musique en Irak et leur rôle dans la société traditionelle* (Paris, 1980)

T. Kerbage: *The Rhythms of Pearl Diver Music in Qatar* (Doh Qatar, 1982)

SCHEHERAZADE QASSIM HASSA

Jahn, D. (*fl* Paris, 1820–59). Maker of brass instruments. He worked in Paris at 10 rue Mandar (1820 26), at 7 rue Meslay (1827–32), 21 rue Bond (1835–7) and 74 rue Bondy (1853–9). In 1834 h made various modifications to the valve trombon which he patented. In 1835 he produced a very careful made three-piston bugle. In 1836 he extensively re designed the layout of the valve trombone, adding a thir piston at the same time as his contemporary Labbay did so. In 1839 he produced a prize-winning alto trom bone and a horn with three pistons. An extant early cir cular trumpet in F (Oxford, Bate Collection), probabl originally equipped with seven crooks and a tuning slide has elaborate decoration in red and gilt. A surviving *cc d'harmonie* has nine crooks.

BIBLIOGRAPHY
H. Lavoix: *Histoire de l'instrumentation depuis le 16e siècle* (Paris 1878)
C. Pierre: *Les facteurs d'instruments de musique* (Paris, 1893/*R*1971

NIALL O'LOUGHLI

Jahnn, Hans Henny (b Stellingen, nr. Hamburg, 1 Dec 1894; d Hamburg, 29 Nov 1959). German writer publisher and authority on organ building. In 1923 h rebuilt the Schnitger organ in the Jakobikirche, Ham burg, thereby providing one of the most important ini tiatives in the *Orgelbewegung*. From 1931 to 1933 h was head of the experimental division of the Germa Council of Organists, and Hamburg's official authorit on all matters relating to organs. During his exile i Bornholm (1934–45) he was adviser to the Copenhage firm of Frobenius. Jahn built and restored more tha 100 organs, including the Klopstock organ in Altona Ottensen, the organ of the Pädagogische Akademie i Kiel, the Maximilian organ in Düsseldorf, the Cavaillé Coll organ in Metz Cathedral, and those of St Petri Malmö, and the German broadcasting service in Berlin In 1921 he and Gottlieb Harms founded the Glaubens gemeinde Ugrino in Hamburg, from which the publish ing house of Ugrino later developed. Jahnn's publication on music include *Die Orgel und die Mixtur ihres Klange* (1922) and *Der Einfluss der Schleifenwindlade auf di Tonbildung der Orgel* (1931) as well as several article in journals and congress reports on the technical prob lems of organ building. He also wrote a number o important expressionist plays and novels; his first pub lished drama, *Pastor Ephraim Magnus*, earned him th Kleist Prize in 1920.

BIBLIOGRAPHY
J. Meyer: *Verzeichnis der Schriften von und über Hans Henny Jahr* (Neuwied and Berlin, 1967)
R. Wagner: *Der Orgelreformer Hans Henny Jahnn* (Stuttgart, 197([incl. list of writings]
based on *MGG* (xvi, 858–9) by permission of Bärenreiter

DIETRICH KILIA

Jaja. *See* AJA (ii).

Jak. Bell-shaped wicker rattle of the Birom people o Nigeria. It has a gourd base and a holding ring at th top. It is played by men, women or children for th *mandieng* rites.

Jakhē. *See* ČHAKHĒ.

kob, Friedrich. Swiss organ builder, associated with e firm of THEODOR KUHN.

lājil. Arabic term for jingles. See also FLABELLUM.

ilaka. A Sanskrit term in medieval Indian texts :noting the clapper of a bell. See GHAṆṬĀ.

ilar. Thin circular metal gong, with raised edges, of ʲujarat, India. See THĀLĪ.

ilousieschweller (Ger.). VENETIAN SWELL.

ilra [jalar, jalara, kaimaṇi]. Thin, flat cymbals of south ɪdia. They are made of copper or bell-metal and mea- ʉre 10 cm in diameter, and are connected by a string assing through their centres. They are used to mark me in devotional song meetings and sometimes as a ₂condary rhythm instrument in concerts of classical ɪusic. In Kerala they are called kaimaṇi, and the equi- alent instrument in north and west India and Pakistan ₅ the manjīrā. For generic discussion of South Asian ymbals, see TĀL.

BIBLIOGRAPHY
ˈ. R. Day: The Music and Musical Instruments of Southern India and the Deccan (Delhi, 1891/R1974)
ˈ. Sambamoorthy: 'Catalogue of the Musical Instruments Exhibited in the Government Museum, Madras', Bulletin of the Madras Government Museum, ii/3 (1931), 22
——: A Dictionary of South Indian Music and Musicians (Madras, 1952–71), ii, p.242
ˈ. Krishnaswami: Musical Instruments of India (Delhi, 2/1967), 143
PRIBISLAV PITOËFF

¹altarang [jalataraṅga]. Indian set of percussion bowls ʲilled with water. The bowls vary in size and can be uned by adjusting the water level. They are arranged ɪ a semicircle and the musician, who sits at the centre, ʲtrikes them with two thin bamboo sticks. The tones ₚroduced are staccato, and the instrument may some- ːimes be used to play ragas.

Jamaku. See JAMUKU.

Jamiḍikā. See JHAMALIKĀ.

Jamisen [jabisen]. Term in mainland Japan for the ʲOkinawan SANSHIN (long-necked lute); it was also used in the late 19th century to denote the Chinese sanxian (long-necked lute) of minshingaku music. The Okina- wan and Chinese instruments both have snakeskin soundtables, and the term 'jamisen' seems to have derived from the substitution of 'ja' ('snake') for 'sha-' in 'shamisen'. See also TSUGARU-JAMISEN.
DAVID W. HUGHES

Jamuku [jamaku]. Variable tension chordophone ('plucked drum') of Andhra, India (for discussion of the type, see ĀNANDALAHARĪ). The body is a slightly taper- ing metal cylinder, open at both ends; the lower opening is covered with a skin and a gut string passes from the centre of the skin up to a wooden handle. The instru- ment is held under the left arm, and the string, tensioned variably by the left hand, is plucked by the right. The jamuku accompanies ballad singing, particularly in the

Godavari area. The jhamalikā of Maharashtra and the Deccan is a similar instrument. See K. S. Kothari: Ind- ian Folk Musical Instruments (New Delhi, 1968).
ALASTAIR DICK

Janājil. Arabic term for jingles. See also FLABELLUM.

Jangat. Pair of cylindrical drums in the gordang sem- bilan ensemble of North Sumatra. They may also be played separately to announce a death, in which case the drumming has sometimes been intensified by gun- shots. The drum rhythms differ between a chieftain and a commoner. See GORDANG.

Jangu. Chinese barrel drum. See TANGGU.

Janil. NOSE FLUTE of Satowal, central Caroline Islands, Micronesia, usually made of bamboo. Its primary use was by men to call women to rendezvous. See H. Damm and E. Sarfert: 'Inseln um Truk: Polowat, Hok und Satowal', Ergebnisse der Südsee-Expedition 1908–1910, IIB, vi (Hamburg, 1935), 263.

Janissary music [Turkish music] (Ger. Janitscharen Musik, türkische Musik; It. banda turca). The Turkish percussion ensemble (also called mehter) introduced into European military music (see BAND (i), §II, 2(i)) and later adopted by the orchestra.

Jank. Angular harp of the Arab world; the term is derived from the Persian chang (see CHANG (i); for ter- minological discussion see WANJ). It was introduced in pre-Islamic times into Arabia, later into Turkey and Egypt, and used up to the 17th century.

Janko, Paul von (b Totis [now Tata], 2 June 1856; d Constantinople, 17 March 1919). Hungarian musician and engineer. A mathematician by training, he made a study of the question of temperament ('Über mehr als zwölfstufige gleichschwebende Temperaturen', Bei- träge zur Akustik und Musikwissenschaft, iii, 1901, p.6). Possibly as a result of this, in 1882 he patented a radical attempt to systematize the piano keyboard (retaining 12- note equal temperament, however). Based on the prem- ise that the hand can barely stretch more than a 9th on the piano, and that all scales are fingered differently, Janko's new keyboard had two interlocking 'manuals', with three touch-points for each key lever, so that it appears to have six tiers of short, narrow, keys (see illustration, p.322). These six tiers constitute one key- board operating on the same set of strings; odd-numbered tiers produce a whole-tone scale from C, even-numbered ones a whole-tone scale from C♯. Accidentals are marked with a black stripe. The advantage of this system is that all major scales are fingered alike, as are all minor, and an octave span is only 13 cm instead of the standard 18·5 cm. Huge arpeggios can be negotiated with barely any arm movement, by moving the hand up or down the tiers. The system is unique in that it compensates for the unequal lengths of the fingers (see also KEY- BOARD, §3).

The invention met with some enthusiasm, notably from the American Alfred Dolge. A short-lived Paul von Jan- ko Conservatory was established in New York about 1891, and a Janko Society was founded in Vienna in

Upright piano (with Janko keyboard) by Decker Brothers, New York, c1890 (Smithsonian Institution, Washington, DC); for a detail of the keyboard, see KEYBOARD, *fig.3*

1905. A number of piano makers in Austria, Germany and the USA made Janko keyboards and Paul Perzina even produced a reversible double keyboard – 'standard' on one side, 'Janko' on the other. E. K. Winkler in the *Musical Courier* (1891) blandly declared that 'On the old keyboard . . . the hand is forced to defy its anatomical construction. We hear of a great many instruments and devices to train and shape the fingers and wrists in opposition to what nature has intended. . . . It seems to be somewhat wiser trying to overcome the difficulties in a different way – namely, by changing the keyboard to suit the hands'. The Janko keyboard never caught on, because few were prepared to relearn their repertory on a strange keyboard with totally new fingering. It was a far more radical change for the pianist than, for example, for the clarinettist to change to the Boehm system.

BIBLIOGRAPHY
P. von Janko: *Eine neue Klaviatur* (Vienna, 1886)
A. Dolge: *Pianos and their Makers* (Covina, Calif., 1911/R1972)
H. H. Dräger: 'Janko, Paul von', *MGG*
C. Ehrlich: *The Piano: a History* (London, 1976)
                                    MARGARET CRANMER

Jann, Georg (*b* Kalkberge, 17 Jan 1934). German organ builder. The son of an organist, he was trained by the firm of Alexander Schuke in Potsdam and at the Meisterschule in Ludwigsburg, where he passed his examinations with distinction. He worked with the firm of Karl Schuke in Berlin, with the Austrian firm of Rieger in Schwarzach and with Sandtner in Dillingen (Donau). In 1974 he took over the firm of Hirnschrodt in Regensburg, but transferred it in 1977 to Allkofen (in Lower Bavaria) under the name Georg Jann, Orgelbau Meisterbetrieb. Jann works according to the traditional art of organ building, using solid timber (no plastic), slider-chests and mechanical action; his speciality is the reconstruction of historic organs. He has written, with Richard Rensch, the article 'Versuche mit Zungenstimmen-Mensuren' (*ISO-Information*, ix, 1973). Among the organs built by his firm are those in Etzelwang parish church (1975; one manual, seven stops); München-Forstenried (1978; two manuals, 17 stops); St

Moritz, Augsburg (1979; choir organ with two manua[l] 14 stops); Scheyern Abbey (1979; three manuals, stops); St Quirin, Tegernsee (1980; three manuals, stops); St Josef, Memmingen (1980; four manuals, stops); Bad Tölz parish church (1981; choir organ w[ith] one manual, seven stops); St Thomas Morus, Neusä[ss] (1981; two manuals, 20 stops); Reisach (1981; t[wo] manuals, 24 stops); St Sebastian, Würzburg-Heuchel[heim] (1981; two manuals, 26 stops); St Peter, Straubing (198[2]; two manuals, 19 stops); and St Walburga, Nürnber[g-] Eibach (1982; two manuals, 29 stops).

                                          HANS KLO[TZ]

Janszoon, Peter. *See* SWART, PETER JANSZOON DE.

Jantar. Fretted STICK ZITHER, with resonators, of Raja[s]than, north India. The bamboo body of the instrume[nt] (104 cm long) is extended by an upward-bent piece [of] wood which serves as both string holder and lower bridg[e]. In the central section 14 (or 13) frets of coconut-she[ll] or tortoise-shell are fixed with wax. Two bulky sphe[r]ical gourds are fixed underneath, serving as resonato[rs] (see illustration). There are four metal strings. Two ma[in] strings pass over the frets and are attached at the en[d] of the bamboo to two wooden pegs. They are tuned [a] a 5th: the melody is played on the first one (*pa*) whi[le] the other (tuned to a lower *sā*) is a drone, in additio[n] to the two lateral strings (on an upper octave of *sā*) whic[h] provide rhythmic accompaniment. The musician hol[ds] the instrument obliquely across his chest, one resonato[r] resting on his shoulder; the strings are plucked from belo[w] with the right-hand fingers, the drones with the thum[b] and the main strings by the middle and ring fingers.

The *jantar* is peculiar to the *bhopā* (religious singers[)] for accompanying the epic-pastoral ballads *Bagravat* an[d] *Neo-Narayan* in the regions of Ajmer, Kota and Jodh[pur]. (For *jantar* as a Mughal court instrument, *see* VĪNĀ, §§4, 6 and 7.)

BIBLIOGRAPHY
K. S. Kothari: *Indian Folk Musical Instruments* (New Delhi, 1968[)]
K. Kothari: *Folk Musical Instruments of Rajasthan* (Borunda, 1977[)]
                                    GENEVIÈVE DOURNO[N]

Januarius, Jacobus. *See* GENNARO, GIACOMO.

Jarana. A five-course guitar of Mexico, slightly large[r] than the vihuela but smaller than the normal guitar. I[t] appears in various *son* (folk music) ensembles in urba[n] centres and elsewhere. Its name may have resulted fro[m] its association with the *son* type, *jarana*, from the Yuca[-]

Jantar (stick zither) played by a bhopā (religious singer), Ajmer district, Rajasthan

tán Peninsula, a genre today performed mostly by folk-dance groups. The instrument is used also in the *mariachi* ensemble and in private music making.

Jaran kepang. Hobby-horse trance-dance ensemble of Central and East Java, also known as *ebeg* in the Banyumas area of Central Java, and *kuda lumping* in West Java (*see also* GAMELAN, §6 (i)). The ensemble consists of the *selompret* (oboe), *kendang* (double-headed drum), *gong campur* (set of small iron gongs) and *saron wesi* (metallophone with iron keys). See M. J. Kartomi: 'Music and Trance in Central Java', *EM*, xxxvii (1973), 163–208.

Jardine, Frederick Wincott (*b* London, 1822; *d* London, 1907). English organ builder, nephew of George Jardine. He was apprenticed to J. C. Bishop in 1836 and in 1837 went with his uncle to New York; he returned to London in 1842, completing his apprenticeship with Bishop. After the death of SAMUEL RENN (1845) Jardine joined his widow as co-manager of the firm in Manchester in 1846. Sarah Renn died in 1850 and was replaced by James Kirtland (Renn's nephew and ex-apprentice) until his retirement in 1866; the business continued as Kirtland & Jardine until 1867, when it became known as Jardine & Co. Jardine retired in 1874, when he sold the business and returned to London. The firm remained active until 1976; its records are in the English Organ Archive, Keele University.

Jardine introduced innovations learnt in the USA and was the first in England to use Vogler's SIMPLIFICATION SYSTEM; there were no pipes standing off the soundboard and a simplified mechanism without rollerboards was evolved. Pedal choruses were developed using a simple mechanism to derive two stops (16′ and 8′, 8′ and 4′, etc) from each rank of pipes. The Kirtland & Jardine coupler is illustrated in Hopkins and Rimbault. Serious case design was abandoned for Gothic frets, cut by machine to simple geometrical patterns. The firm made only simple mechanical actions but, influenced by the organist Benjamin Joule, developed a Romantic style. Jardine's largest organ was that in St Peter's, Manchester (1856–72), built for Joule; it had four manuals and 61 speaking stops, foreshadowing the Cavaillé-Coll organ of 1877 in the neighbouring Town Hall.

BIBLIOGRAPHY
E. J. Hopkins and E. F. Rimbault: *The Organ: its History and Construction* (London, 1855, rev. 3/1877/*R* 1972)
M. Sayer: 'Kirtland & Jardine of Manchester', *The Organ*, liv (1975–6), 169
——: 'Frederick Wincott Jardine', *The Organ*, lxi (1982), 78
MICHAEL SAYER

Jardine, George (*b* ?Dartford, England, 1801; *d* New York, 1883). American organ builder. He was apprenticed to Flight & Robson in England, emigrating to New York in 1837. He immediately began building small church organs and church barrel organs, the latter having been common in England during the period but never popular in America. One of these unique instruments, which plays from both a keyboard and barrels, dates from 1842, and is still in existence in Zion Church, Pierrepont Manor, New York. Only a year after Jardine's arrival in New York, he received a gold medal from the American Institute for a church organ and a self-playing organ. In 1860 his son Edward G. Jardine (*d* 1896) joined the firm, which then became known as Jardine & Son. The son travelled widely,

making several trips to study the work of Cavaillé-Coll and others. The result of these trips is evident in the transition of the firm's work during the latter part of the 19th century from a style of design and voicing reminiscent of late 18th-century English work to one representing the fully-fledged European Romantic idiom. Like other New York builders, Jardine's work was widely distributed in New York and the Southern states. He built organs for the Fifth Avenue Presbyterian Church (1856), St George's (1870) and St Michael's (1893) (all in New York City).

BIBLIOGRAPHY
B. Owen: 'Hymn Tunes from an American Barrell-Organ of 1842', *The Hymn*, xi (1960), 69
O. Ochse: *The History of the Organ in the United States* (Bloomington, Ind., 1975)
J. Ogasapian: *Organ Building in New York City, 1700–1900* (Braintree, Mass., 1977)
BARBARA OWEN

Jarmusiewicz, Jan. Polish musician and theorist, inventor of the KLAWIOLIN.

Jarumbi Mandar. Bamboo idiophone of North Sulawesi. It resembles the RERE, but exists in two sizes: one about 90 cm long and the other about 60 cm.

Jaspuria mãdar. Drum of southern Bihar, India. *See* MÃDAR.

Jata. BULLROARER of the central Ende region of Flores, Indonesia. It consists of a flat piece of bamboo about 12 cm long and 2 cm wide, into one end of which a hole is pierced and a length of cord inserted. The player swings the instrument round, producing a buzzing sound. The name is used also for a whizzing bow, consisting of a double strip of young coconut-palm leaf, about 15 cm by 3 cm, which holds the extremities of a bent leaf nerve in a bow shape, with the folded leaf taking the place of a bowstring. It is swung round on the end of a long leaf nerve, producing a rattling sound.

Similar instruments are known in the Batak Toba districts of North Sumatra as *dengeng-dengeng*, in Sundanese districts of West Java as *kekinciran*, in Nias as *riwi-riwi löcö*, and in Central Java as *wer-wer* (*ower-ower*, or *ereg-ereg*).

MARGARET J. KARTOMI

Jatanga [katango]. Bambassi term for a single-headed drum of African origin used by black musicians in southern Iraq and the Gulf area. (Bambassi is an African-derived language.) It is similar to the MSÕNDO, but larger.

Jatun aymara. Transverse flute of the Bolivian Alti Plano. *See* MOHOCEÑO.

Jatung utang. XYLOPHONE of the Kenyah people of eastern Kalimantan, Indonesia.

Jatun k'ewa. DUCT FLUTE in a Christmas ensemble of the Bolivian Alti Plano. *See* PINCULLO.

Jatun tukana. Transverse flute of the Bolivian Alti Plano. *See* MOHOCEÑO.

Jauje. Double-headed variable tension HOURGLASS DRUM of the Hausa people of Nigeria. Measuring about 50 cm in length, 16 cm in diameter at each end and 10 cm at the waist, it is the largest Hausa drum of this type. It is played under the arm with a hooked stick. Although formerly used as a war drum to accompany praise songs for warriors, it is now a status symbol for emirs, high officials or district heads. Its main use is in sets with *kolo* hourglass drums in the instrumental performance of praise epithets (*take*) or to accompany songs praising the performers' patron. The instrument is probably the same as the *jojo* sighted by the German traveller, Heinrich Barth, near Katsina in 1851.

BIBLIOGRAPHY
Ames–KingGHM
D. W. Ames: 'Hausa Drums of Zaria', *Ibadan*, xxi (1965), 62
F. E. Besmer: *Kidan Daran Salla: Music for the Eve of the Muslim Festivals of Id-al-Fitr and Id-al-Kabir in Kano, Nigeria* (Bloomington, Ind., 1974)
A. King: 'Nigeria', *Grove 6*

K. A. GOURLAY

Javata. Side-blown animal-horn trumpet of the Shambala people of Tanzania.

Jāwan [mihbash, najr]. Wooden pestle and mortar used as an idiophone by beduin tribes. The pestle is about 50 cm long and the mortar between 30 and 50 cm high. A specialist from the black population (associated with a specific sheikh) pounds coffee beans to a rhythm (*dagga*) which identifies the chief and the tribe. This serves as an open invitation to the tribesmen to come and take coffee and discuss the problems of the day. See S. Qassim Hassan: *Les instruments de musique en Irak et leur rôle dans la société traditionelle* (Paris, 1980).

SCHEHERAZADE QASSIM HASSAN

Jāwan (pestle and mortar) of the Shamar beduin

Jawbone. A term applied to various types of RATTLE. See QUIJADA.

Jaw's harp [jaw's trump]. See JEW'S HARP.

Jayaḍhakkā. Large cylindrical or barrel-shaped drum documented in the Kashmiri chronicle *Rājataraṅgiṇī*. See ḌHĀK.

Jayaghaṇṭā. Large round metal percussion plaque of medieval India. See GHAṆṬĀ.

Jaye, Henry (*fl* c1610–67). English maker of string instruments. He was one of the earliest and best English makers and the first of several generations of makers by that name. He had his workshop in Southwark, London, where he made treble, tenor and bass viols and also lutes and pochettes. Jaye is mentioned in Thomas Mace's *Musick's Monument* (1676) as being one of the best of the older generation of viola da gamba makers, and in the list of instruments left by the small-coal merchant Thomas Britton one of the viols is described as 'the neatest that Jay ever made'. Jaye's instruments are finely cut, light in construction and of small dimensions (*see* VIOL, figs.11*a* and *b*). Beautifully executed heads and open scrolls are usual, the varnish is often a dark cherry, and an ornamental oval rose hole is sometimes carved in the belly. The tone is soft and velvety. The earliest extant example of Jaye's work known, a bass viol that formerly belonged to Galpin, is in the Gemeentemuseum in The Hague. Its label reads 'Henrie Jaye in Southwarke.1611' (photograph in Galpin, 1910). Galpin also reported having seen one that was made in 1610. The latest example known, a tenor viol, dates from 1667 and is in the Victoria and Albert Museum, London. Other Jaye instruments are in the Paris Conservatoire museum (no.106, dated 1624) and privately owned. Examples of his labels are shown in Vannes (1932, no.1004) and Lütgendorff (1904, no.385).

BIBLIOGRAPHY
C. Stainer: *A Dictionary of Violin Makers* (London, 1896/*R*1973)
W. L. von Lütgendorff: *Die Geigen- und Lautenmacher vom Mittelalter bis zur Gegenwart* (Frankfurt am Main, 1904, 6/1922/*R*1968)
F. Galpin: *Old English Instruments of Music: their History and Character* (London, 1910, rev. 4/1965 by T. Dart)
R. Vannes: *Essai d'un dictionnaire universel des luthiers* (Paris, 1932, 2/1951/*R*1972 as *Dictionnaire universel des luthiers* and *R*1981 incl. suppl. 1959)

MURRAY LEFKOWITZ

Jazz flute (Fr. *jazzo-flûte*). See SWANEE WHISTLE.

Jazz-horn. A term applied to a KAZOO amplified by fitting a trumpet or trombone bell to its end.

Jedinka [jednojka]. Terms for particular types of DUCT FLUTE of Yugoslavia. See SVIRALA.

Jegogan. Balinese METALLOPHONE. See GENDER.

Jehmlich. German family of organ builders. Gotthelf Friedrich Jehmlich (*b* Neuwernsdorf, 1775; *d* Dresden, 30 April 1827) learnt his trade with Hamann in Meissen from 1799 to 1802 and worked, together with his brother Johann Gotthold (*b* Neuwernsdorf, 16 Nov 1781; *d* Dresden, 1862) as an apprentice to Johann Christian Kayser in Dresden. Johann Gotthold and a third brother, Carl Gottlieb (*b* Neuwernsdorf, 1786; *d* Zwickau, 1867), were master carpenters before becoming organ builders. These three had a workshop initially in Cämmerswalde, but in 1824 Johann Gotthold went to Dresden, where he became court organ builder (1 Dec 1836), and Carl Gottlieb moved to Zwickau in 1839. They were representatives of the Silbermann tradition, which they adapted slightly to suit the prevailing taste: they supplied small rgans with a 16' Bourdon, which introduced a more sombre tone, and they made a limited number of string-tone stops. An organ by Gotthelf Friedrich survives in Lauenstein (1817–18; two manuals, 19 stops), and one by Johann Gotthold, with Carl Gottlieb, in Freital-Somsdorf, near Tharandt (1826; two manuals, 16 stops).

Carl Gottlieb had four sons. Anton (1817–56), who built a 22-stop organ in Lugau in 1844, eventually went to America. Wilhelm Friedrich (1826–74) was director of the Zwickau workshop from 1867 and built organs in Pfaffroda, near Altenburg (1861; 21 stops), Lengenfeld (1864; 33 stops), Oelsnitz (1865; 23 stops) and Gersdorf, near Hohenstein-Ernstthal (1866–8; 31 stops). Ernst (1828–78) worked from 1867 with his brother Carl Eduard (b Cämmerswalde or Dresden, 1824; d Dresden, 7 Jan 1889), who was the most important member of the family artistically and prominent as a voicer. Assisted by his brothers and later by his sons, Carl Eduard built organs exclusively with slider-chests and mechanical action. On 14 December 1858 he became assistant to the court organ builder in Dresden, and was promoted court organ builder on 1 February 1861. His organs include one at Weinböhla (1852; two manuals, 20 stops), and those at Prausitz (1863; two manuals, 31 stops), the city church, Dahlen (1865–7; two manuals, 30 stops) and Neuhausen (1868–9; two manuals, 28 stops), all of which survive. A large organ in St Paul, Chemnitz (now Karl-Marx-Stadt) (1880; three manuals, 46 stops), rebuilt by the family firm in 1904, and again in 1929, when it was enlarged to 85 stops, was destroyed in 1945.

Carl Eduard's sons Emil (1854–1940) and Bruno (1856–1940, court organ builder at Dresden), who directed the Dresden firm from 1888, manufactured organs with cone-chests and pneumatic and electro-pneumatic action. Their surviving instruments include those at Lössnitz (1899; three manuals, 55 stops) and St John, Meissen (1898; two manuals, 31 stops), and they also built organs at the Kreuzkirche, Dresden (1900–01; 91 stops, rebuilt & enlarged to 113 stops in 1940), and Zwickau Cathedral (1929; 108 stops), neither of which survives. Carl Eduard had other sons who worked for the family firm, Hans (1863–1943) and Georg (1866–1928), who worked as a voicer.

Emil's sons Otto (b 13 Dec 1903; d 27 Jan 1980) and Rudolf (b 28 June 1908; d 18 Jan 1970) took over the firm in 1936. In about 1955 they reverted to the slider-chest, taking contemporary requirements into account in their specifications. Their organs include those at the Kreuzkirche, Dresden (1959–63; four manuals, 76 stops); the Town Hall, Karl-Marx-Stadt (1976; four manuals, 67 stops); St Peter, Stavanger, Norway (1977; three manuals, 40 stops); the Church of the Brotherhood, Prague (1980; two manuals, 21 stops); and a former theatre in Berlin (begun 1974 and still in progress; four manuals, 74 stops). In 1972 the company was transferred to public ownership under the direction of Horst Jehmlich, and it now operates from no.32 Grossenhainer Strasse, Dresden.

BIBLIOGRAPHY

F. Oehme: Handbuch über ältere, neuere und neueste Orgelwerke im Königreich Sachsen, i–iii (Dresden, 1889–97, R with suppl., 1978)
E. Flade: Der Orgelbauer Gottfried Silbermann (Leipzig, 1926, 2/1953), 209ff
U. Dähnert: Historische Orgeln in Sachsen (Leipzig, 1980)

ULRICH DÄHNERT

Jehring, Julius (b ?Adorf, 1824; d 1905). German maker of woodwind instruments. His father, Johann Georg Jehring, was a bassoon maker. Sachs (1913) credited him with the invention of the OCTAVIN (i) in 1894; German and British patents taken out by Oskar Adler and Hermann Jordan in the previous year would contradict this, though he may have originally designed the instrument. He certainly made a wide variety of bassoons, with extant specimens having five keys (Oxford, Bate Collection), eight keys (Hamburg, Museum für Hamburgische Geschichte), 15 keys (Markneukirchen) and 18 keys (Halle, Händelshaus). An oboe of c1850 (Vienna, Kunsthistorisches Museum) in stained boxwood is a finely crafted specimen with 11 silver keys.

BIBLIOGRAPHY

C. Sachs: 'Octavin', Reallexikon der Musikinstrumente (Berlin, 1913/R1962)
L. Bechler and B. Rahm: Die Oboe und die ihr verwandten Instrumente (Leipzig, 1914/R1972)
J. Schlosser: Die Sammlung alter Musikinstrumente (Vienna, 1920)
L. G. Langwill: An Index of Musical Wind-instrument Makers (Edinburgh, 1960, rev., enlarged 6/1980)
H. Heyde: 'Die Blasinstrumentenbauer Jehring (Adorf) und Heckel (Adorf, Dresden, Biebrich)', BMw, xix (1977), 121

NIALL O'LOUGHLIN

Jejeneng. Bell of Siberut island, Mentawei, Indonesia. It is made of buffalo horn.

Jejo [jejy]. A Malagasy term used in compound forms to denote a MUSICAL BOW or STICK ZITHER. The qualifier indicates the type of instrument by size, material or area.

Jejo (*jejy*) *lava* ('long' *jejo*) is a musical bow with a gourd resonator and a tuning noose. It may be up to two metres long. (In northern Madagascar a shorter instrument is called *jejy fohy* or 'short' *jejy*.) The upper end may be tapered or cut into a tenon or a fork-tip. The string, traditionally of vegetable fibre but now made of metal, is either plucked or struck. The pitch is varied by stopping the string with one finger. *Jejo lava* is played at funerals and is also used as a secular instrument. Boys who worked in the rice-fields as bird-scarers would play the instrument at the same time as a rattle used to frighten the birds.

Jejo voatavo ('calabash' *jejo*) is the accepted term for the stick zither, except among the Bara, who call it *jejo bory*. (*Bory* refers to the Betsileo, who migrated to central Madagascar and brought the instrument with them.) The stick is carved at one end to form a fingerboard, and on modern instruments there are one to ten pegs at the same end. A calabash soundbox, open at the bottom, is hung from the other end, which may be curved or forked. There may also be a feather as a bridge at the curved end. The sound is produced mainly by plucking.

The Betsileo and the Merina still use the *jejo voatavo*. Until the end of the 19th century it was also found among the Antandroy, Sakalava, Tanala, Antaisaka and Antemoro peoples, and in the first half of the 20th among the Bezanozano and the Sihanaka. It was formerly played at home or while on watch during rice harvests, but is now generally used to entertain at fairs, bull-fights and other popular events.

BIBLIOGRAPHY

R. Blench: 'The Morphology and Distribution of Sub-Saharan Musical Instruments of North African, Middle Eastern, and Asian, Origin', Musica asiatica, iv (1984), 168

MICHEL DOMENICHINI-RAMIARAMANANA

Jengglong [jengglong degung]. GONG-CHIME in a Sundanese gamelan, especially the *gamelan degung*, in West

Java. Its six small bossed gongs, ranging over an octave, are about 30 to 45 cm in diameter, and are suspended from one or two frames. The highest note is duplicated an octave lower. See M. Harrell: *The Music of the Gamelan Degung of West Java* (diss., U. of California, Los Angeles, 1974), 19.

MARGARET J. KARTOMI

Jenje. Single-headed cylindrical drum of the Sena/Tonga people of Mtoko district, Zimbabwe. It is open-ended and has three legs. A single player beats it by hand, together with the *mutumba* drum (*see* MUTUMBA (ii)), using his right heel to raise or lower its pitch. These and two other drums accompany a flute ensemble for *gororambe* dances. See *TraceyCSA*, ii, 175f.

DAVID K. RYCROFT

Jerome of Bologna. *See* HIERONYMUS BONONIENSIS.

Jeté (Fr.: 'thrown'). In string playing, a bowstroke that bounces or ricochets off the string. The number of rebounds specified by composers generally varies between two and six. *See* BOW, §II, 3 (x).

DAVID D. BOYDEN

Jeu barré. *See* BARRÉ.

Jeu de timbres (Fr.). GLOCKENSPIEL.

Jeux (Fr.). Free reeds, as in a REED ORGAN; *see also* ORGAN, §III, 3.

Jew's [jaw's] **harp** [trump] (Fr. *guimbarde, trompe de Béarn*; Ger. *Brummeisen, Maultrommel*; It. *ribeba*). A generic term for a type of mouth-resonated instrument consisting of a flexible tongue, or lamella, fixed at one end to a surrounding frame; it is classified as a plucked idiophone (for details of classification *see* IDIOPHONE). It is known by many vernacular names, including variants of 'trump' and 'trompa'. The origin of the name remains obscure. Carrington Bolton (1906) cited the 16th-century terms 'jewes harp' and 'jewes trump' and, although there is no evidence that the instrument was ever associated with the Jewish people, the attempt to explain away the problem with the term 'jaw's harp' seems unfounded. In north-east England the name 'gewgaw' is used, which may be related to the Swedish *munngiga* ('mouth fiddle') and the German (Saar region) *Maulgeige*.

The player places the free end of the lamella in front of his mouth cavity and sets it in vibration manually; the resulting oscillation produces a sound of constant pitch, rich in overtones which correspond closely to a harmonic series. By various movements of the tongue and larynx the player is able to regulate the frequency of the air in the mouth cavity and, using the mouth cavity in the manner of a Helmholtz resonator, amplify selected overtones to produce a wide variety of sonorous and musical effects. There are several ways of making the lamella vibrate, including the use of a string. The instrument is grasped by the player in two basic ways: with the lamella pointing inwards towards the palm or outwards away from it (see figs.1 and 2); also many ingenious systems exist for enhancing acoustic and mechanical performance, factors which lead to a remarkable variety of forms. Jew's harps may be idio-

glot (i.e. lamella and frame made from the same piece of material) or heteroglot (i.e. with a separately made lamella). Materials used include bamboo, palm wood, bone, ivory, brass, iron, steel and various combinations of these.

The design of the part of the lamella and frame placed before the mouth cavity is important. Here the clearances between the two must be very small (Ledang, 1972, suggested that the optimum gap is in the region of 0·01 to 0·02 mm, but the possible tolerance may be greater than that, and instruments exist with air gaps ranging from probably as little as 0·005 mm to as much as 0·04 mm) and their alignment must be perfect. Under such conditions the vibration of the lamella through the restricted air-space creates a turbulence heard as a rich spectrum of partials, many of which the player can select and, by breathing, further modify in terms of tone-colour and rhythm.

Because the physical limitations of the mouth cavity prevent one from tuning in to frequencies lower than about 450 Hz, the melodic scope of any jew's harp depends on the lamella's vibrating frequency. The first usable overtone (i.e. higher than 450 Hz) of a low-pitched instrument will be high in the harmonic series and the musical scale available will be correspondingly more complete. However, a jew's harp that is too low in pitch loses in sonority and flexibility, so it is generally made as high-pitched as possible, depending on the particular melodic requirements. The problem is sometimes bypassed by coupling instruments tuned, for example, a 4th apart. The Bunun people of Taiwan make multi-lamella instruments (see Li Hwei, 1956); Scheibler's AURA of 1816 was a device enabling three to five jew's harps to be mounted radially on an axis.

Geographic distribution is wide but by no means universal. Commercially manufactured European instruments were widely exported as barter goods and sometimes imitated by local makers, but the jew's harp is indigenous to much of the Eurasian land mass as well as South and South-east Asia, Indonesia and Oceania. Several bronze specimens in the Museum of Antiquities at Rouen suggest that the instrument has been known to western Europe at least since Gallo-Roman times. Emigrants took them to North America, where they are still made and played.

In Oceania, idioglot bamboo jew's harps are distributed throughout New Guinea, the Bismarck Archipelago and the northern and central Solomon Islands. They also appear in parts of Vanuatu and in New Caledonia and Fiji. Throughout most of Melanesia they take the same cutaway tapered form as in New Guinea (*see* SUSAP). In Micronesia, the instrument seems to have been confined to the Chamorro of Guam (*belembaupachot*) and to the Caroline Islands where it was present in Palau (*tumtum ra lild*), Yap, Truk and Ponape. As in Melanesia, it was made of bamboo and seems to have been of idioglot construction. Judging by the Chamorro and Palau instruments, the bamboo was fully rounded and untapered. In Polynesia the jew's harp took two forms. Bamboo instruments were formerly used in Tonga (*mokena*), but are characteristic rather of eastern Polynesia where they are reported for Aitutaki (*pokaka-kaka*), Mangaia (*tangi ko'e*) and Rarotonga (*see* TITAPU) in the Cook Islands, the Marquesas Islands (*see* TITA'A KOHE) and possibly Hawaii. The original form in Hawaii (*nī 'au kani*) and the preferred form in Western Polynesia is made from the midrib of the coconut leaf. Both

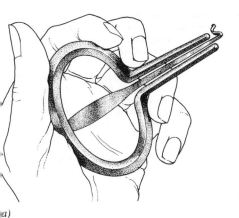

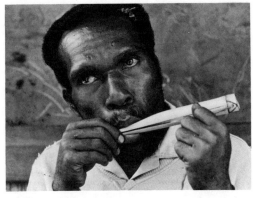

(a)

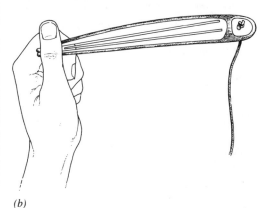

(b)

1. Metal jew's harps (finger activated): (a) holding position, with lamella pointing away from the palm of the hand; (b) playing position

2. Bamboo jew's harps (string activated) from Papua New Guinea: (a) playing position; (b) holding position, with lamella pointing towards the palm of the hand

dioglot and heteroglot forms are made (*see* UTETE). In New Zealand, where bamboo did not grow, the jew's harp was made from supplejack (*see* ROORIA). Throughout the Pacific, European jew's harps were a popular 19th-century article of trade and in many places they supplanted the indigenous instrument.

The jew's harp has a variety of uses. In South-east Asia in particular it serves as an artificial voice or voice-mask for spoken communication between courting couples. It is also used for rhythmic purposes; in India it sometimes supplements the sound of a tuned drum. In Indonesia and South-east Asia rich, rhythmic, gong-like music is produced by alternately holding the breath and breathing strongly through the restricted air-space. In Indo-European traditions, however (including those of western Europe), melodic styles predominate and the instrument is frequently used to provide dance music. Angus Lawrie of Oban (*d* 1973), a notable Scottish exponent, played Highland bagpipe tunes with rich and rhythmic gracing.

The following jew's harps are entered in this dictionary: abafiw; afiw; alibaw; aman khuur; ankuoc; ata; aura; bambaro; bamboro; bandūrélis; belembaupachot; binaiyo; biqqung; birimbao; biwba; bombom; bungkau; cang (ii); changko'uz; đàn môi; doromb; drîmbă; drombulja; druri bewe; drymba; duri; ego; gaganā; genggo; genggong; gerudeng; ghoŕăliyau; giwga; giwong; gogo (i); guat; guimbarda; guyud; hoen toong; huang; hūn; isitholotholo; junggotan; juring; juring rangguin; kā-mien; karinding; karombi; kaur; kha-rnga; kha-wang; khulsan khuur; ko-ding; koma; koqin; kovïzh; kubing; kukau;

kulibao (i); kunka; kwadili; lokanga; mabu; machinga; macunga; mapuíp; mokena; muhonyu; mukkuri; murcang; murjanga; muxu-kitarra; nggoec; nī 'au kani; olat; oli; onat; oribao; pang teu ing; parmupill; pingoru; pokakakaka; popo; pumbune; qobiz; quongon; rab ncas; rangoyd; rangun; ribeba; rinding; robe; röding; rooria; sagasaga; scacciapensieri; sekebeku; setjoli; songer; sturmant; susap; suupill; tangi ko'e; temir komuz; temür khuur; tendor; then; tita'a kohe; titapu; tivtiv; tõi; tömör khuur; toung; trompa (ii); tumtum ra lild; tungge; turiding; ulibao; utete; vanniyayar; vargan; vivo (i); zagada.

BIBLIOGRAPHY

VertkovA

H. Scheibler: 'Die Aura', *AMZ*, xviii (1816), col.505

H. Carrington Bolton: 'The Jewsharp', *Popular Science Monthly*, lxviii (1906), 239

F. W. Galpin: *Old English Instruments of Music* (London, 1910, rev. 4/1965 by T. Dart)

J. F. Rock: 'The Romance of K'a-mä-gyu-mi-gkyi: a Na-khi Tribal Love Story', *Bulletin de l'Ecole française d'extrême-orient*, xxxix (1910), 1–152

C. Sachs: 'Die Maultrommel: eine typologische Vorstüdie', *Zeitschrift für Ethnologie*, xlix (1917), 185

W. A. Kaudern: *Musical Instruments in Celebes* (Göteborg, 1927)

P. A. Scholes: *The Puritans and Music in England and New England: a Contribution to the Cultural History of Two Nations* (London, 1934)

J. Kunst: *Music in Nias* (Leiden, 1939), 27

——: *Music in Flores* (Leiden, 1942), 119

——: *Music in Java* (The Hague, 1949), i, 199, 360; ii, 430, 443

K. M. Klier: 'Die Maultrommel', *Volkstümliche Musikinstrumente in den Alpen* (Kassel and Basle, 1956), 71

Li Hwei: 'A Comparative Study of the Jew's Harps among the Aborigines of Formosa and East Asia', *Bulletin of the Institute of Ethnology, Academia Sinica*, i (1956), 85–140

L. Picken: 'The Music of Far Eastern Asia: 2. Other Countries', *NOHM*, i (1957), 152, 154, 170, 179, 185

E. Emsheimer: 'Maultrommeln in Sibirien und Zentralasien', *Studia ethnomusicologica eurasiatica* (Stockholm, 1964), 13

P. Collaer: *Ozeanien*, Musikgeschichte in Bildern, i/1 (Leipzig, 1965)

E. Leipp: 'La guimbarde', *Bulletin du Groupe d'acoustique musicale*, xxiii (1967)

F. Crane: 'The Jew's Harp as an Aerophone', *GSJ*, xxi (1968), 66

R. Sevag: 'Munnharpa', *Norsk musikktidsskrift*, vii (1970), 111

H. Boone: 'Bijdrage tot de geschiedenis van de mondtrom, voornamelijk in de Nederland', *Brussels Museum of Musical Instruments Bulletin*, ii (1972), 5–49

O. K. Ledang: 'On the Acoustics and the Systematic Classification of the Jaw's Harp', *YIFMC*, iv (1972), 94

W. Meyer and H. Oesch: 'Maultrommelfunde in der Schweiz', *Festschrift Arnold Geering* (Stuttgart, 1972)

J. Wright: 'Another Look into the Organology of the Jew's Harp', *Brussels Museum of Musical Instruments Bulletin*, ii (1972), 51

C. J. Adkins: 'Investigation of the Sound-producing Mechanism of the Jew's Harp', *Journal of the Acoustical Society of America*, lv (1974), 667

G. Dournon-Taurelle: *La guimbarde* (diss., U. of Paris, 1975)

C. Reimers: *Medelitda mungigor i Sverige* (Stockholm, 1977)

G. Dournon-Taurelle and J. Wright: *Les guimbardes du Musée de l'homme* (Paris, 1978)

JOHN WRIGHT (with MERVYN McLEAN)

Jew's trump. *See* JEW'S HARP.

Jhalar. Round metal percussion plaque of Rajasthan, north-west India. *See* GHARĪ.

Jhālda. Double-headed drum of the Muṇḍā people of east India. *See* MĀDAR.

Jhallarī. Drum of ancient and medieval India. Mentioned in the *Nāṭyaśāstra* as a minor type, it is described in the 13th-century *Saṅgītaratnākara* as small (about 24 cm long and 10 cm in diameter) and cylindrical, probably with one skin head and metal ring-jingles. The *bhāṇa* is a smaller version.

Jhamalikā [jamiḍikā]. Variable tension chordophone ('plucked drum') of Maharashtra and the Deccan, central India (for discussion of the type, *see* ĀNANDALAHARĪ). A hollow brass cylinder, roughly 22·5 cm in diameter and 25 cm long, is covered at the lower end by a skin, through the centre of which a gut string passes up to a wooden handle. The instrument is held under the left arm and the string, tensioned variably by the left hand, is plucked by the right. It is played by beggars. The *jamuku* of Andhra is a similar instrument. See P. Sambamoorthy: *Catalogue of Musical Instruments Exhibited in the Government Museum, Madras* (Madras, 3/1962).

ALASTAIR DICK

Jhānjh [jhāni, jhānj, jhān-jhān]. Terms for various large cymbals of India. For a generic discussion of South Asian cymbals, *see* TĀL.

Jhāṅkri bājā. Double-headed FRAME DRUM of the Newari people of Nepal. *See* DHYĀṄGRO.

Jhiṅ [ching]. Small cup-shaped cymbals of Kampuchea. They are made of brass or iron and are used to keep time for the *pī phāt*, *mahōrī* and *khr͏̣ang sāi* orchestras.

Jhumrā. Coconut-shell rattle of Orissa, east India. A hollow coconut shell is filled with pellets and attached to a handle and shaken. It is used as a toy. Similar instruments are found throughout India, for example *jhumjhumī* (or *jhunjhunī*, in Bengal), *khunkhunā* and *khulkhulā*. *See also* GHUṄGRŪ.

Jhyālī. Cymbals with a central boss, used by the *damāi* tailor–musicians of Nepal. In the Kathmandu valley similar cymbals are called by a variety of names in the Newari language. *Jhyālī* are used in the *damāi bājā* (instrumental ensemble) and are akin to the *babu* of the Newari people.

Jiagban. Single-headed drum of the Edo/Bini people of Nigeria. *See* SAMBA (i).

Jiangdi. Historic end-blown flute of western China. *See* XIAO.

Jiangu [chien-ku]. Medium-sized barrel drum of the Han Chinese, used in state rituals (*jian*: 'to mount'; *Gu* generic term for 'drum'). The drum has two heads (as large as 70 to 80 cm in diameter) and is mounted horizontally on a post which passes through its shell. Historically it was covered with an elaborate canopy, with tassels hanging from its four corners (a feature retained in the Korean KŎN'GO). It is struck with two wooden beaters. A related drum is the *yinggu* ('responding drum'), which survives in Korea as the ŬNGGO. The *jiangu* is mentioned in connection with ritual in Shang (1766–1122 BC) bone-inscriptions, and both drums are discussed in the classical texts of the Zhou dynasty (1122–221 BC). While their appearance and specific rhythmic patterns have changed in detail over the centuries, their usage in punctuating the ritual music has continued in China until recent times. As at the Taipei Confucian Shrine, both drums are played in percussion interludes between sections of the hymns.

BIBLIOGRAPHY
Tong Kin-woon: *Shang Musical Instruments* (diss., Wesleyan U., Middletown, Conn., 1983)

ALAN R. THRASHER

Jiao [chiao] (i). End-blown animal-horn trumpet of the Han Chinese. *Jiao* refers to a 'horn' of an animal, such as a water buffalo, but it may also be applied to instruments made of other materials (such as wood and leather). Among many local names, *niojiao hao* ('cow-horn signal') is common in south-east China and Taiwan. The instrument assumes the natural shape and size of the hollow animal horn, with a small cup mouthpiece of the same material set in the end. There are no finger-holes. The animal horn with a free-beating reed mounted on its side, known as *kub twg* and found among the hill tribes of south-west China, may also be related to this instrument. It can be assumed that animal-horn instruments were in use in China by the Han dynasty (206 BC–AD 220) because stone rubbings of this period show long curved horns (sometimes of metal, but nonetheless imitating animal horns; *see* LABA (i)) as military instruments. In recent times natural horns have been used more frequently in the context of religious practice. In Taiwan the *niojiao hao* is still played in outdoor Taoist funeral processions.

ALAN R. THRASHER

Jiao [chiao] (ii). SLIT-DRUM of the Han Chinese. *See* BAN.

iaoluo. Gong of the Minnan sub-culture of south-east China and Taiwan. *See* LUO.

icara de agua [jícara de jobá, jícara de moyubá, güiro e jobá, güiro de moyubá]. Terms denoting various types f water-gourd (*see* WATER-DRUM, (2)). The Afro-Cuban *icara de jobá* is used to mark rhythms in funeral and ecret liturgical rites (*OrtizIMA*, iii, 160).

icarita (Sp., diminutive of *jicara*: 'gourd'). Cuban diophone. It consists of two small half-gourds, about 5 m in diameter and split lengthwise; the musician holds ne in each hand, at its narrow end, and strikes the centre f the convex surface on a table-top or on the ground. he gourd-spoons are not struck against each other like astanets. *See OrtizIMA*, i, 203f.

JOHN M. SCHECHTER

icotea (Sp.: 'tortoise'). Afro-Cuban SCRAPER and rat-le. On certain Caribbean–Atlantic shores, the edible turtle s offered as a meal to the deity Changó; in these rites he turtle shell, closed and with small stones and a han-lle inserted, becomes a rattle. It is also used in Cuba s a scraped or struck idiophone. The Mexican ÁYOTL vas also made of turtle shell. *See OrtizIMA*, ii, 188f.

JOHN M. SCHECHTER

idiga. LAMELLAPHONE of the Songhay people of Mali nd Niger. It is played by children and adult men as a olo instrument.

idur. Double-headed barrel-shaped drum, about 60 cm ong, used in the *orkes Abdul Muluk* ensemble on the outh Sumatra and Jambi coasts.

iegu. Chinese term for the Japanese KALGO.

ifti. Small DOUBLE CLARINET of the Arabian Gulf. *See lso* MIZMĀR.

igijigi. GROUND HARP of the Alur people of Uganda. *See* SEKITULEGE.

ilawiri [kilawiri]. PANPIPES in the CHIRIHUANO ensem-le of Bolivia.

ilel [djillil, dschilil]. CONCH-SHELL TRUMPET of the Marshall Islands of Micronesia. It was used primarily s a signalling instrument. There are numerous accounts f its being carried and blown in battle, being played y the highest ranking man in a canoe, and used to sound he alarm and to call people together. It was also blown during dance, with the *aje* (hourglass drum) to accom-any a vocal duet, and was blown at the water's edge during a chant intended to calm high waves.

BIBLIOGRAPHY
O. Finsch: 'Marshall-Archipel', *Ethnologische Erfahrungen und Belegstücke aus der Südsee*, iii (Vienna, 1888), 133
A. Kramer and H. Nevermann: 'Ralik-Ratak (Marshall-Inseln)', *Ergebnisse der Südsee-Expedition 1908–1910*, IIB, xi (Hamburg, 1938), 210

BARBARA B. SMITH

Jimba. Calabash-resonated XYLOPHONE of the Lunda people of Zaïre. *See* MADIMBA (i).

Jimökmök [dimuggemuck]. Dance sticks of the Marshall Islands of Micronesia. They are short wooden sticks beaten in pairs during women's sitting dances. See O. Finsch: 'Marshall-Archipel', *Ethnologische Erfahrungen und Belegstücke aus der Südsee*, iii (Vienna, 1888), 132.

Jin. Historic Chinese military gong. *See* LUO.

Jina. Name formerly applied to the Chinese oboe *hai-di*. *See* SUONA.

Jindaiko. Japanese barrel drum. *See* ŌDAIKO.

Jingainga. End-blown trumpet of central Africa. *See* NYELE.

Jingbo. Chinese cymbals used in Peking opera. *See* BO (i).

Jinghu [ching-hu]. Two-string fiddle of the Han Chinese, found especially in the north (*jing*: the capital city, Beijing; *hu*: 'barbarian', used in reference to fiddles). The instrument is sometimes called *huqin* ('barbarian string instrument'), though this term more properly refers to string instruments in general. Constructed in a manner similar to the *erhu*, the *jinghu* is considerably smaller (about 50 cm in length), with a slender bamboo neck, tubular bamboo resonating chamber and two silk strings tuned $a'-e''$ or higher (see illustration). The holding position is slightly different from that of the *erhu* and the bowing style more animated. The *jinghu* may have appeared in north China as late as the 19th century. Its high pitch and bright, nasal tone-colour are considered ideal for the accompaniment of Peking opera, in which this is the most important melody instrument.

ALAN R. THRASHER

Jingles (Fr. *grelots*; Ger. *Schellen*; It. *sonagli*). The name given to a cluster of small bells, such as sleigh bells (*see* BELL (i)), arranged either on a strap or a loop

Jinghu (fiddle) of China

of wire, or on a wooden handle. Those attached to frame drums are often small metal discs. Jingles (with isolated exceptions) are indefinite in pitch, since the unit is made up of bells of varying size and sound. They are shaken to produce a tremolo, or such rhythmic patterns as may be prescribed. For an extremely delicate sound the player may tap the bells on the palm of the hand.

Small bells and tinkling pieces were known in ancient times. In Sumer, Babylonia, Assyria and Egypt they were commonly suspended from the trappings of horses, mules and camels, as for instance the bells on horses mentioned in the Old Testament book of Zechariah xiv. 20.

In the Western orchestra, jingles are used imitatively; to punctuate rhythmic sequences; and as tone-colour. Only on the rarest occasions (except for their former use in vaudeville) are specific pitches prescribed, the most notable example being Mozart's use of Schlittenschellen (c″–e″–f″–g″–a″) in the third of his Three German Dances K605. As grelots they occur in A. Adam's Le postillon de Longjumeau (1836). 20th-century composers to score for jingles in various forms include Elgar in Cockaigne (1901; harness bells), Ireland (A London Overture, 1936), Vaughan Williams (A London Symphony, 1913, rev. 1933) and Respighi (Feste romane, 1928).

See also Ling and Nūpur.

JAMES BLADES

Jingling Johnny. See Turkish crescent.

Jingluo. Small gong of the Han Chinese. See Luo.

Jingu [chin-ku] (i). Large barrel drum of the Han Chinese, used in state rituals (jin: a dynasty of the 3rd and 4th centuries AD; Gu: generic term for 'drum'). It is the largest drum in the Chinese instrumentarium (over 130 cm in both length and diameter), and rests either vertically or horizontally in a large frame; it is struck with two wooden beaters. The jingu is mentioned in sources of the Zhou dynasty (1122–221 BC) as a military instrument, used in issuing orders. Its function (as a signalling instrument) in opening and closing the state rituals is maintained at the Confucian Shrine in Taipei. The Korean chin'go is a related instrument.

ALAN R. THRASHER

Jingu (ii). Historical name for the Chinese gong Gong-Luo.

Jinjeram [ginyeli]. Musical bow, with gourd resonator, of the Dagomba people of northern Ghana.

Jinjimba. Two-key Xylophone of the Luvale people of north-eastern Angola. See also Marimba.

Jinkojiao. Historical name for the Chinese oboe Suona.

Jirba. Bagpipe of Iraq and the Arabian Gulf. See Qirba.

Jisk'a k'ewa. Duct flute of the Bolivian Alti Plano. See Pincullo.

Jode [jodī]. See Jore.

Joget gamelan [gamelan Trengganu]. Instrumental ensemble of Trengganu, West Malaysia. It comprises gambang kayu (trough xylophone), a keromong (gong chime), three kenong (horizontal gongs), two saro (metallophones), a gendang (cylindrical drum) and two gong (suspended bossed gongs). The ensemble accompanies the joget gamelan style of dancing, and the current name for it is gamelan Trengganu. Central Javanese court musicians and dancers probably developed the joget gamelan style at the mid-18th-century Malay court in the Riau-Lingga archipelago, where it flourished for about 150 years. When the last Sultan of Riau and Lingga abdicated in 1912 it ceased to be performed there, but it had reached the fief territory of Pahang in the early 19th century, and Frank H. Swettenham heard it there in 1875. When the Sultan of Pahang died in 1914 the practice of the gamelan also died out in Pahang. His daughter, however, borrowed the Pahang gamelan and brought it to the palace of her husband, the Sultan of Trengganu, where it became popular in the 1920s and 1930s. Performance ceased in 1942, following the Japanese invasion and the death of the Sultan, but in 1966 it was rediscovered by Mubin Sheppard, and revived by elderly musicians. Ensembles using similar sets of instruments bought in Java were formed in other parts of Malaysia. Although the instruments are almost identical in construction to the Javanese slendro tonality, they are tuned quite differently, to pitches 7 1 2 4 5 (see Gamelan, §4).

BIBLIOGRAPHY
F. Swettenham: British Malaya (London, 1907)
G. Mills: 'Joget Gamelan Music', Australian-Indonesian Association Journal (1981), 26

MARGARET J. KARTOMI

Jogiyā sāraṅgī. See Sāraṅgī.

Johannsen [Brouckmann], **Jasper** (d ?Münster 1558). German organ builder, an associate of Heinrich Niehoff.

Johannus organ. An Electronic organ, about 20 models of which have been developed by the Dutch designer and organist Johannus Versteegt and manufactured by Johannus Orgelbouw in Ede, near Arnhem, since 1967. Versteegt had previously designed the original models of the electronic home organ manufactured by Eminent, Riha and Viscount. Intended primarily for church use, the Johannus organ combines elements of 18th-century and modern tone qualities; the range of two- and three-manual models includes a couple of two-manual 'positive' organs.

Since the early 1970s the Johannus organ has used between one and seven master oscillators (c2 MHz) to generate sounds; each oscillator, using two stages of frequency division, successively produces the 12 semitones of the highest octave and all the lower octaves. Other features introduced recently include digital reverberation and electronic simulation of the 'chiff' transient attack found in flute stops on pipe organs. The multiple loudspeaker systems have different frequency characteristics, and are mounted in cabinets whose appearance is modelled on a rank of organ pipes.

BIBLIOGRAPHY
B. Hesford: 'The Johannus Organ', MO, ciii (1979–80), 345

HUGH DAVIES

hnson, John (*fl* London, *c*1745–62). English violin
aker. Details of his life remain obscure, though his
riod of activity (previously listed as 1750–60) has been
tended on the basis of recently discovered examples
his work. His violins are loosely based on the Stainer
odel but differ in their higher ribs and broader arching
ich give rise to an unusually tubby appearance. The
ality of his work varies considerably: the purfling is
ten merely simulated and the dry yellow-brown var-
sh borders on extreme thinness, though these aspects
ow considerable improvement on his best instru-
ents, as does the cut of the scroll. Unlike most of his
ntemporaries, Johnson seems to have made fairly
nsistent use of nicely figured maple. The soundholes
e perhaps the weakest aspects of his craft, being rather
en and stiff.

BIBLIOGRAPHY
M. Morris: *British Violin Makers* (London, 1904, rev. 2/1920)
Vannes: *Essai d'un dictionnaire universel des luthiers* (Paris, 1932,
2/1951/R1972 as *Dictionnaire universel des luthiers* and R1981
ncl. suppl. 1959)

JAAK LIIVOJA-LORIUS

hnson, William Allen (*b* Nassau, NY, 27 Oct 1816;
Westfield, Mass., Jan 1901). American organ build-
The son of a contractor, he was trained as a mason
Westfield; his interest in the organ was kindled when
helped in the installation of a Hook organ in a church
had worked on. The following winter, in 1844, he
empted the construction of a chamber organ. It was
ccessful, and he spent subsequent winters in this way
til 1851, when he abandoned masonry for full-time
gan building and opened a small shop. In 1854 his
st three-manual organ was built for the South Church
Hartford, Connecticut, and by the following year he
s employing up to 20 men. In 1871 his son William
Johnson (1840–1921) joined the firm, and in the same
ar the factory was destroyed by fire. The name of the
m was changed to Johnson & Son in 1875, and in
85, owing to increasing popularity in the Western
serve states, a larger factory was built. William A.
hnson retired in 1890, and his son closed the company
1898, possibly because of his unwillingness to con-
rt their operations to the increasingly popular pneu-
atic or electric types of action, although the Barker
ver had been used in large installations since the 1870s.
hnson's work was noted for its agreeable voicing, and
s important instruments include those in St Mary of
e Sacred Heart Church, Boston (1877), the First
ethodist Church, Westfield (1876), and the Central
usic Hall, Chicago (1880). He also built two studio
gans for the organist and composer Dudley Buck.

BIBLIOGRAPHY
V. V. Elsworth: 'Five Johnson Organs in Westfield', *American
Organist*, xxvi (1943), 33
Murray: 'The 1877 Johnson Organ in St. Mary's Church, Bos-
on', *The Diapason*, lxv/11 (1974), 1
Ochse: *The History of the Organ in the United States* (Blooming-
on, Ind., 1975)
Owen: *The Organ in New England* (Raleigh, North Carolina,
1979)

BARBARA OWEN

hnston, Thomas (*b* Boston, 1708; *d* Boston, 8 May
67). American organ builder, musician and engrav-
. A man of many skills, Johnston was the first regular
ilder of organs in New England. He is known to have
ned and repaired the few existing English organs in
ston, doubtless studying their construction at the same
time. He began by building chamber organs, one of which
he kept in his own home. In 1754 he built an organ for
St Peter's Church, Salem, and in 1759 another for Christ
Church, Boston. About the same time he also built one
for the Concert Hall of Lewis and Gilbert Deblois in
Boston. He made an organ for St John's Church, Portsmouth, New Hampshire, in 1760, and was working on
a chamber organ at the time of his death. His musical
activities included leading the singing in the Brattle
Square Church in 1739, and singing in King's Chapel
(1754–6). In 1758 he published his *Rules to Learn to
Sing, and Hymns*. The 68 hymns are largely set in
three parts, and the publication is usually found bound
into psalm books of the period.

BIBLIOGRAPHY
J. Fesperman: 'Music and Organs at "The Old North"', *Organ
Institute Quarterly*, x/3 (1963), 15
S. Hitchings: 'Thomas Johnston', *Boston Prints and Printmakers*
(Boston, 1973)

BARBARA OWEN

Joint. The detachable sections which form the tubes of
modern woodwind instruments are generally termed
'joints'. They are connected by matched tenons and
sockets turned from the mating pieces, the union being
made firm and airtight with greased thread or thin cork
sheet. Occasionally telescopic sections of thin metal
tubing are also used for this purpose.

Towards the end of the 17th century, and in the early
years of the 18th, transverse flutes, recorders and various double-reed types underwent a great transformation, mainly in the hands of distinguished instrument
maker-players attached to the French court. The prototypes of our modern instruments emerged and among
their characteristic features was a jointed construction.
Hitherto virtually all woodwind instruments had been
turned and bored from a single billet except perhaps where
the available material was of limited size. The new construction permitted more accurate boring as well as a
finer internal adjustment; it made possible the provision
of alternative sections of slightly different length and
hole spacing (*corps* or *pièces de rechange*) as an aid to
adjustment to varying pitch standards.

PHILIP BATE

Jojo. Drum reported in Nigeria in the mid-19th century. *See* JAUJE.

Jombarde (Fr.). A colloquial term found in the 18th
century for the GALOUBET.

Jones, Joe (*b* New York, 19 June 1934). American
instrument inventor and composer. Since 1962 (working
at first in New York, then, from around 1973, in Asolo,
near Vicenza) he has constructed many instruments,
influenced particularly by his involvement from 1963
with the Fluxus group in New York. He has concentrated on self-playing instruments operated by small
electric motors, to which beaters or lengths of leather
bootlace that rotate like propellers are attached; many
of them incorporate existing string and percussion
instruments (often toys, and including zithers and normal and toy violins and guitars). Both motors and
instruments are suspended on long strings or wires; their
operation causes them to move around so that the sound
varies continuously. Despite the simplicity of the basic

idea of nearly all Jones's instruments, in most of which sustained sounds are derived from sources that are normally percussive, they produce a surprisingly wide range of delicate and subtle sounds.

Four works, all from the mid-1960s, that illustrate the principle are Black Hat (a toy drummer and dancer, who perform on top of a hat); a 'sound helmet'; a large koto-like instrument with movable bridges, above the strings of which are suspended motor-controlled bootlaces that can be switched on and off individually and raised or lowered to alter the degree of contact with the strings; and a 'double bass', square in section and resembling a newel post, which rests at the normal playing angle against a stand and is played mechanically by a hand, to the accompaniment of chimes, rattles and other small suspended objects (the instrument was stolen in 1964). Other instruments made by Jones at this time, some of which incorporate digital electronic elements, photo-electric cells and other sensing devices, are Jazz Set, Music Bike (a construction mounted on a homemade tricycle), Windchimes and Bird Cage.

From 1963 Jones's mechanical orchestra was presented in Fluxus concerts; beginning with drums, gongs, violin and wind chime, it attained 24 self-playing instruments (operated by motors or pneumatically), including whistles, reeds, horns, violins, bells and gongs, by 1966. A group of more sculptural constructions, the 'Erector-Set' series (c1968–9, rebuilt 1978), involves motor-powered toy violins and guitars, fixed on stands. Five of Jones's simpler instruments were sold in limited quantities by Fluxus during the late 1960s; they included Fluxmusic, a set of ten or 12 spring-wound noise-makers mounted inside an attaché case with only their winders protruding above a wooden partition, and two of the 'Erector-Set' instruments – a violin and an 'aerophone or bell'. More recently several works have been issued in limited editions in West Germany and Italy, including Music Kit (Do-it-yourself Joe Jones).

For two years (1969–70) Jones maintained his 'Music Store' at his home in shop premises near Canal Street in New York. Seven doorbell push-buttons were mounted beside the street door, each of which operated a motor that played one of the instruments hanging in the shop window; they could be operated by visitors or passers-by at any time, and the instruments were heard over a loudspeaker through an open fanlight window above the door. In 1971 Jones and his Tone Deaf Music Co. (an updated mechanical orchestra) contributed to Yoko Ono's double record album Fly.

Jones's recent work, which continues to use the same techniques, has included a motor-operated harpsichord (c1975) and piano (1977); Flux-Toy-Pianos (c1975); five modified decrepit upright pianos, the central one of which controls motors inside the other four by means of switches mounted on its keys (Five Player Pianos for Berlin, 1979–80); and Violin in a Bird Cage (1981).

BIBLIOGRAPHY

H. Sohm, ed.: *Happening & Fluxus* (Cologne, 1970) [exhibition catalogue]

R. Block: 'Die Summe aller Klänge ist grau', *Für Augen und Ohren* (Berlin, 1980), 107 [exhibition catalogue]

HUGH DAVIES

Jonkamentótzi. A transverse flute of the Campa (or Ashaninka) people of Peru. It is made from a reed about 70 cm long. It has no finger-holes; the pitch is modified instead by plugging and unplugging the lower end with the forefinger.

Jonkari. PANPIPES of the Campa (or Ashaninka) peop of Peru.

Jōra. Small long-necked lute of Iraq. *See* ṬANBŪR.

Jordan. English organ builders. Hawkins said that t elder Abraham Jordan (*b* ?Maidstone; *d* ?London, *c*171 was a distiller who started making organs in about 17 and, being an ingenious man, 'succeeded beyo expectation'. He taught his son, the younger Abraha Jordan (*d* ?London, 1755 or 1756), and they built organ for the chapel of the Duke of Chandos and 'ma organs for parish churches'. Their most famous instr ment was that built in 1712 for St Magnus the Marty London Bridge, probably in collaboration with Chr topher Schrider, which incorporated the first Swell b in an English organ (the case remains). It was advertis in *The Spectator* (8 Feb 1712) as 'a very large org . . . consisting of four sets of keys, one of which adapted to the art of emitting sounds by swelling note which never was in any organ before'. Another org by the Jordans, referred to in the *London Journal* (7 F 1730), had a reversed console so that 'the master wh he plays sits with his face to the audience and, the ke being but three foot high, sees the whole company'. 1726 the younger Jordan was organist of St Giles, Cr plegate, London. After his death his foreman, Jo Sedgwick, succeeded to the business.

It may be inferred from Burney that partnershi between John Byfield (i), Richard Bridge and the young Jordan were at least occasionally formed for the buil ing of individual organs. Hawkins wrote that this w 'to prevent their underworking each other', and Hopki and Rimbault attributed the arrangement to a fear shoddy work by untrained builders, as a result of t demand for organs in the newly built churches of t early 18th century. Although no evidence survives any formal connections, the younger Jordan's organs St Luke's, Old Street, London (1733; case and son pipework survive at St Giles, Cripplegate), and Exe Cathedral (1742–4) were built in collaboration wi Bridge, and that for Westminster Abbey (1730) has be ascribed to Christopher Schrider and Jordan togeth Jordan, Byfield and Bridge are said to have work together at St Nicholas's, Great Yarmouth (1732) a St George's Chapel, Great Yarmouth (1733; case no at St John's, Smith Square). The Jordans' trade ca depicts a case in the later style of 'Father' Smith, whi resembles that built by the Jordans for St Saviour's (no the cathedral), Southwark, in 1705. Their later cases a similar to those of Bridge, with one favourite mode an example of which survives at St Thomas's (now t cathedral), Portsmouth (1718). This has a large oval f in the centre, and derives from Renatus Harris (e.g. A Hallows, Lombard Street, London, now at All Hallow Twickenham; and St Clement's, Eastcheap).

Other notable organs associated with the Jordans a St George's, Botolph Lane, London (1723; now Southall; case and some pipework survive) and Helen's, Abingdon (1725; case survives). The organ Trinity Church, Boston, USA (1744; case survives) w built according to Jordan's detailed written instructio in an extant letter dated 3 July 1744; the same sour mentions organs built for Lord Brook, Lord Gurns and the church at St Michael's Mount, Cornwall.

BIBLIOGRAPHY
rneyH; *HawkinsH*
J. Hopkins and E. F. Rimbault: *The Organ: its History and Construction* (London, 1855, rev. 3/1877/*R*1972)
. L. Sumner: *The Organ* (London, 1952, rev. and enlarged 4/
1973)
Clutton and A. Niland: *The British Organ* (London, 1963, 2/
1982)

MICHAEL GILLINGHAM, GUY OLDHAM,
NICHOLAS PLUMLEY

rdan, Hermann (*fl* Markneukirchen, late 19th cen-
·y). German maker of woodwind instruments. In 1893
and Oskar Adler took out German and British patents
r the OCTAVIN (i), though its invention is usually
ributed to JULIUS JEHRING.

·re [jode, joḍī, jorī]. North Indian terms meaning
air', applied to such instruments as paired drums (*see*
JKKAŘ) and double duct flutes (*see* PĀVA).

·rnagārā. A term used by the Newari people of Nepal
r the NAGĀRĀ (KETTLEDRUM).

·ruri. A general term for certain Japanese narrative
nres accompanied by the SHAMISEN (lute). It often refers
gidayū (music of the Japanese puppet theatre), but in
e kabuki theatre it designates the *kiyomoto* or *tokiwazu*
usicians.

·ucoujou. Rattle of Haiti, used during the Rara sea-
n, a seven-week period of festivities starting on Ash
ednesday. It consists of three gourd rattles carried on
wooden cross, one of which is attached to the end of
long, thin stick, while the other two are placed at the
ids of a short transverse bar. *See also* TCHANCY.

·uhikko [jouhikannel, jouhikantele]. Bowed lyre of
nland. It originated in Scandinavia and is related, *inter
ia*, to the Welsh CRWTH. It has two to four strings and
body hollowed out from the front and fitted with a
undboard (see illustration). There is a hole for the hand
one end to enable the melody string to be stopped
ith the knuckles. The instrument is played while sit-
ng. The strings are usually tuned in 4ths (though some-
nes in 5ths) and one string is usually left to vibrate
eely, producing a drone. Folk mastery of the *jouhikko*
as last noted in parts of Savo and Karelia at the begin-
ng of the 20th century. *Jouhikko* melodies suggest that
e instrument was used chiefly to play dance music;
any are the same as those played on the KANTELE (zith-
).

ILKKA KOLEHMAINEN

·yeuse, Jean de (*b* ?Paris, *c*1635; *d* Carcassonne,
598). French organ builder. He was trained in Paris,
it his organ-building career was largely in the south
France. Several of his contracts survive; these testify
his having introduced to the region such recent Pari-
an developments as a new type of bellows and the use
the Grosse Tierce in the chorus of 16' organs. He
so served as organist of St Nazaire, Carcassonne.
mong his more notable instruments were those in St
azaire, Beziers (1697), St Michel, Carcassonne (1664),
d Auch Cathedral (1688).

BIBLIOGRAPHY
. Dufourcq: *Jean de Joyeuse* (Paris, 1958)
. Douglass: *The Language of the Classical French Organ* (New
Haven, 1969)
BARBARA OWEN

Joze. Four-string SPIKE FIDDLE of Iraq, formerly also
known as *al kamāna al-baghdādiyya*. It is between 60
and 75 cm long, with a small resonator made from a
hollowed-out coconut, cut off at both ends. One opening is covered by the skin of a still-born lamb or a fish;
the other remains open. The shape and size of the
instrument depend on those of the coconut; on average
the diameter of the membrane is from 5 to 7 cm, that
of the opposite opening between 10 and 13 cm. The
neck, between 50 and 60 cm long, is of apricot or bitter
orange wood; there are four pegs (*mafātīḥ*), two on each
side. A metal spike at the other end passes through the
coconut. Steel strings of different gauges are attached
to the spike and pass over a grooved wooden bridge
(*ghazāla*) on the membrane. The bow is made of pliable
wood – bitter orange, oak or white beech – and is slightly curved; lengths of horsehair are attached to each end
and drawn tight.

The *joze* is traditionally tuned in perfect 4ths, usually
$a–d'–g'–c''$, but sometimes $g–d'–g'–c''$. A tuning in 5ths,
akin to that of the Western violin family, is also found.
The exact pitch is chosen to suit the voice it accompanies, and transposition is often effected by a *capo tasto* made of thread. The compass is about two octaves.
This is increased, and a more brilliant technique made
possible, if a Western tuning is employed, but the traditional sonority associated with the instrument is sacrificed as a result. The instrument rests at an angle on
the knee of the player, who grasps the neck in his left

*Jouhikko (bowed lyre) player from Ladoga Karelia,
Finland*

Joze (spike fiddle) player, Iraq

hand (see illustration). To reach certain positions, the player must swivel the neck while playing.

The *joze* is used to accompany urban classical music. With the *santūr*, *daff* and *dumbuk*, it is part of the local traditional ensemble, *chālghī baghdādī*. Recently the instrument has been played solo and, more rarely, in newly created ensembles. Its technique was formerly transmitted orally; more recently it has been taught in music schools where Western methods have had increasing influence.

See also KAMĀNCHE.

BIBLIOGRAPHY
S. Qassim Hassan: *Les instruments de musique en Irak et leur rôle dans la société traditionelle* (Paris, 1980)
SCHEHERAZADE QASSIM HASSAN

Jreo [greo]. Copper jingles of the Jörai people of central Vietnam.

Ju [juh]. Stopped bamboo pipe of the Birom people of Nigeria. It is played in a set of eight instruments (*be-ju*) of different sizes, using hocket technique, for social song and dance (*see* STOPPED FLUTE ENSEMBLE). Traditionally playing was forbidden during the wet season as it was believed that this would cause a shortage of rainfall.

Juan. Long-necked lute of the Han Chinese. *See* RUAN.

Juba [martinique]. Drum of Haiti and Jamaica. The instrument is laid on its side and one drummer sits astride it, pressing his heel against the drumhead to modulate pitch and timbre, while another, standing behind, strikes the body of the instrument with two sticks.

Jublag. Balinese METALLOPHONE. *See* GENDER.

Juch'uy k'ewa. DUCT FLUTE in a Christmas ensemble of the Bolivian Alti Plano. *See* PINCULLO.

Juco. BULLROARER of Nicaragua.

Jufti-saz. *See* SAZ.

Juftnai. DOUBLE CLARINET of the plains and river-valley Tajik people of Central Asia. It has six or seven parallel finger-holes in each pipe. The Uzbeks know this instrument as the *qoshnai*, the Turkmen as the *gosho-dili tüidük*.

Jug. XYLOPHONE of Sulawesi. *See* YUK.

Jug band. An instrumental ensemble developed among black Americans in the 1920s and 1930s. The jug itself is frequently an earthenware demi-john; the player purses his lips over the narrow opening and exhales short plosive bursts that are amplified by the jug, which acts as a resonator. Generally only one jug is used in the band; the rest of the group comprises strings and a melody instrument such as a harmonica or kazoo. However, one of the earliest such groups to record, the Dixieland Jug Blowers from Louisville, Kentucky, occasionally used two jugs, as in *Skip Skat Doodle Do* (1926), and as many as three horns, as in *Southern Shout* (1927). The jazz clarinettist Johnny Dodds performed with them on some recordings and the jazz pianist Clarence Williams also favoured the jug, playing it himself in *Chizzlin' Sam* (1933) among others. The jug is mainly associated with folk blues groups. Will Shade's Memphis Jug Band and Gus Cannon's Jug Stompers, both based in Memphis, Tennessee, were pre-eminent among early jug bands; the former's *K. C. Moan* (1929) and Cannon's *Goin' to Germany* (1929) feature an interplay of harmonica and kazoo against strings and jug, making these pieces masterpieces of the genre. The style of Jack Kelly's South Memphis Jug Band was more primitive (witness *Highway No. 61 Blues*, 1933), but members of this loosely formed group were still performing in the 1960s. Similar jug bands existed in other states, including the Birmingham Jug Band from Alabama, who recorded a fine *Gettin' Ready for Trial* (1930), and the Cincinnati Jug Band led by the guitarist Bob Coleman in *Newport Blues* (1929). Other domestic items could be used instead of a jug; Gus Cannon frequently used a kerosene can, Hammie Nix a whiskey bottle, and Sam Jones recorded several items on a stovepipe (e.g. *Court Street Blues*, 1927). In rural districts the jug continued to be used as a folk instrument, though it lost its popularity on record later in the 1930s. During the folk revival of the 1960s jug bands were briefly reintroduced by white performers in the blues idiom.

BIBLIOGRAPHY
S. B. Charters: *The Country Blues* (New York, 1959), chap.8
P. Oliver: 'The Tub, Jug and Washboard Bands 1924–1932', RL 8802 [disc notes]
B. Olsson: *Memphis Blues and Jug Bands* (London, 1970)
——: 'South Memphis Jug Band', FLY LP 113 [disc notes]
PAUL OLIVER

Juh. *See* JU.

uk. Plucked lute of southern Timor, Indonesia. *See* ₊EKO.

u-kugo. Vertical harp of Japan. *See* KUGO.

ula. An ORGAN STOP.

ula-jula [julu-julu]. PANPIPES of Bolivia. The term *jula-*
ula refers to those of the Alti Plano and *julu-julu* to
ꭓose of the Andes. The panpipes of the Alti Plano are
 played in pairs, each with three or four pipes made from
ꭓe *caña-hueca* reed. In some instances the four pitches
₊f the 'masculine' rank in the pair (*see* IRA (i)) join with
ꭓe three pitches of the 'feminine' *arca* rank to form a
₊entatonic gamut (see ex.1). For the *chukarubailes*

Ex.1

arca

ira

ances, and on other occasions, too, there can be 12
ula-julas of different sizes, each tuned an octave above
ꭓe next larger type; the two ranks of each pair are *guía*
₊our tubes) and *arca* (three tubes), and the full range
₊f the ensemble is four octaves. The panpipes groups
ꭓe, in decreasing order of size, one pair of *macho*, one
₊f *mali*, two of *likus*, one of *tijli* and one of *ch'ili*. The
₊ngest pipe (*macho guía*) measures 1·2 metres, the
ꭓallest (*ch'ili arca*) 3 cm. *Guía*, representing the male,
ꭓd *arca*, the female, play alternate pitches in hocket,
ꭓus achieving a pentatonic gamut over an octave range;
ꭓelody is predominantly in descending contours.

In Canton Viluyo, Pantaleón Dalence Province, Oru-
₊ Department, panpipes ensembles may incorporate five
₊fferent sizes called (in descending order of size) *machu*
₊ne pair), *mala* (one pair), *likus* (two pairs), *urbanistas*
ꭓwo pairs) and *ch'ilis* (three pairs). The ensemble per-
₊rms on various saints' days; at the fiesta of St Antho-
₊y (21 September) it plays before a *tinku* (ritual battle)
₊ enacted. These *jula-julas* are grouped in pairs termed
₊nja (four tubes) and *arca* (three tubes), each pair pro-
₊ucing a pentatonic gamut over the range of a major
₊h. Hocket technique is again employed.

The panpipes of the Andes (*julu-julu*) are made from
₊k'osa reed (*caña-hueca*) but with four pipes in the *arca*
ꭓnk and three in the *ira*. One ensemble, in Irpuma-Irpa
₊rande Canton, Ingavi Province, La Paz Department,
₊mprised (in descending order of size) *akarapi* (or
₊cosa; one *arca* and two *ira* ranks), a group of *likus*
₊ne *arca* and two *ira*), a second group of *likus* (one
ꭓca and three *ira*) and a pair of *ch'ilis* (one *arca* and
ꭓe *ira*). Hocket technique, typical for Bolivian Alti Plano
ꭓnpipes, is used.

Before 1952 *julu-julu* players assisted at the annual
₊remonies marking the installation of a new *alcalde de
₊mpo* ('mayor of the countryside'), and they were heard
₊so during the first days of the potato harvest. The *julu-*
₊lu is also a dance drama, dating back at least to 1809
₊d representing the hunt for creatures that threaten
₊omestic animals; it is performed on 3 May at the Fiesta
₊ la Cruz. In it the players of the panpipes carry a
₊unter's lance or arrow.

BIBLIOGRAPHY
₊. P. Baumann: 'Musica andina de Bolivia', LPLI/S-062 [disc notes]

H. C. Buechler: *The Masked Media: Aymara Fiestas and Social
Interaction in the Bolivian Highlands* (The Hague, 1980)
JOHN M. SCHECHTER

Jumbush. Long-necked lute of Turkish origin (*see*
CÜMBÜŞ), used by the Turkmen, Kurds and Yazīdī of
Iraq. It has a circular metal resonator, a skin soundtable
and three to five double courses of strings.

Junggotan. JEW'S HARP of the Bedayuh people of
southern Sarawak, Malaysia. Its range is usually less
than a 4th and no fixed series of notes can be measured.
It is used both for entertainment and for courtship rituals.

Juno. A SYNTHESIZER manufactured in several models
by ROLAND.

Jupiter. A SYNTHESIZER manufactured in several models
by ROLAND.

Jurī. A term of Bengal and Orissa, eastern India and
Bangladesh, used to denote a pair of small cymbals. *See*
KARTĀL, (2).

Juring. Bamboo JEW'S HARP of the Krui area of Lampung province, Sumatra.

Juring rangguin. Idioglot JEW'S HARP of the Temiar
people of West Malaysia. It is about 12 cm long and is
cut from the midrib of a palm leaf. Great care is needed
to fashion the vibrating tongue of the instrument so that
it will produce a satisfying tone. The player holds the
jew's harp in front of his half-open lips and pulls regularly and audibly with a string of rattan, one end of which
is tied to the tongue.

TRÂN QUANG HAI

Juru. Arched harp of the Baule people of the Ivory
Coast. Six strings are stretched across an arc-shaped stick
attached to a half-calabash resonator. In performance
the resonator is held against the stomach (see illustra-

Juru (arched harp) of the Baule people, Ivory Coast

tion). The *juru* is used to accompany men's drinking and humorous songs.

Jūshichigen-kin. Japanese 17-string bass zither. *See* KOTO.

Just [pure] intonation. When pitch can be intoned with a modicum of flexibility, the term 'just intonation' refers to the consistent use of harmonic intervals tuned so pure that they do not beat, and of melodic intervals derived from such an arrangement, including more than one size of whole tone. On normal keyboard instruments, however, the term refers to a system of tuning in which some 5ths (often including D–A or else G–D) are left distastefully smaller than pure in order that the other 5ths and most of the 3rds will not beat (it being impossible for all the concords on a normal keyboard instrument to be tuned pure; *see* TEMPERAMENTS, §1). The defect of such an arrangement can be mitigated by the use of an elaborate keyboard.

1. General theory. 2. Instruments.

1. GENERAL THEORY. In theory, each justly intoned interval is represented by a numerical ratio. The larger number in the ratio represents the greater string length on the traditional MONOCHORD and hence the lower pitch; in terms of wave frequencies it represents the higher pitch. The ratio for the octave is 2:1; for the 5th 3:2; for the 4th 4:3. Pythagorean intonation shares these pure intervals with just intonation, but excludes from its ratios any multiples of 5 or any higher prime number, whereas just-intonation theory admits multiples of 5 in order to provide for pure 3rds and 6ths.

To find the ratio for the sum of two intervals their ratios are multiplied; the ratio for the difference between two intervals is found by dividing their ratios. In Pythagorean intonation the whole tone normally has the ratio 9:8 (obtained by dividing the ratio of the 5th by that of the 4th), and so the major 3rd has the ratio 81:64 (obtained by squaring 9:8). But a pure major 3rd has the ratio 5:4, which is the same as 80:64 and thus smaller than 81:64. (The discrepancy between the two (81:80) is called the syntonic comma and amounts to about one ninth of a whole tone.) Since 5:4 divided by 9:8 equals 40:36, or rather 10:9 (a comma less than 9:8), just intonation has two different sizes of whole tone – a feature that tends to go against the grain of musical common sense and gives rise to various practical as well as theoretical complications. Some 18th-century advocates of just intonation and others since have admitted ratios with multiples of 7 (such as 7:5 for the diminished 5th in a dominant 7th chord).

Two medieval British theorists, Theinred of Dover and Walter Odington, suggested that the proper ratio for a major 3rd might be 5:4 rather than 81:64, and some 15th-century manuscript treatises on clavichord making include quintal and, in one instance, septimal ratios (see Lindley, 1980). Quintal ratios were introduced into the mainstream of Renaissance musical thought by Ramos de Pareia, whose famous theoretical monochord (1482) provided just intonation for the notes of traditional plainchant, but with G–D, B♭–G and D–B implicitly left a comma impure (see fig.1a). Thence Ramos derived the 12-note scale by adding two 5ths on the flat side (A♭ and E♭) and two on the sharp (F♯ and C♯); in this scheme (see fig.1b), C♯–A♭ would make a good 5th, hardly 2 cents smaller than pure. Ramos did not intend

1. (a) Ramos's monochord scheme for students [of] plainchant; (b) his extension to form the chromatic sc[ale]

or expect this tuning to be used in any musical perfo[r]mances, however, for in his last chapter (giving advi[ce] to 'cantors' and describing what he called 'instrumen[ta] perfecta') he said that G–D was a good 5th but C♯–A[?] must be avoided (*see* TEMPERAMENTS, §2).

Gioseffo Zarlino (1558) argued that although voic[es] accompanied by artificial instruments would match the[?] tempered intonation, good singers when unaccompani[ed] would adhere to the pure intervals of the 'diatonic sy[n]tonic' tetrachord which he had selected (following t[he] example of Ramos's disciple, Giovanni Spataro) fro[m] Ptolemy's various models of the tetrachord (see fig.2[a]). Zarlino eventually became aware that this would ent[ail] a sour 5th in any diatonic scale consisting of seven rigid[ly] fixed pitch classes (see fig.2b, where D–A is labell[ed] 'dissonant'); but he held that the singers' capacity [to] intone in a flexible manner would enable them to avo[id] such problems without recourse to a tempered sca[le] – and that they must do so because otherwise the 'na[t]ural' intervals (those with simple ratios) 'would nev[er] be put into action', and 'sonorous number . . . wou[ld] be altogether vain and superfluous in Nature'. Th[is] metaphysically inspired nonsense was to prove a stim[?]ulating irritant in the early development of experiment[al] physics, and during the next three centuries a numb[er] of distinguished scientists paid a remarkable amount [of] attention to the conundrum of just intonation (as well [as] to various attempts to explain the nature of consonan[ce] by something more real than sonorous numbers).

In the 1650s Giovanni Battista Benedetti, a math[e]matician and physicist, pointed out in two letters to t[he] distinguished composer Cipriano de Rore (who had be[en] Zarlino's predecessor as *maestro* at St Mark's, Venic[e]) that if progressions such as that shown in ex.1 were sun[g]

Ex.1 One of Benedetti's demonstrations that just intonation, if us[ed] consistently, will disturb the pitch

$$\tfrac{4}{3} \times \tfrac{2}{3} \times \tfrac{5}{3} \times \tfrac{2}{3} = \tfrac{80}{81}$$

repeatedly in just intonation, the pitch level would chan[ge] quite appreciably, going up or down a comma each tim[e]. In 1581 Vincenzo Galilei, a former pupil of Zarlin[o] denied that just intonation was used in vocal music, a[nd] asserted that the singers' major 3rd 'is contained in [an] irrational proportion rather close to 5:4' and that the whole tones made 'two equal parts of the said 3rd'. [In] the ensuing quarrels, Vincenzo Galilei's search for ev[i]dence against Zarlino's mystical doctrine of the 'sen[a]rio' (the doctrine that the numbers 1–6 are the essen[ce] of music) led him to discover by experiment that f[or] any interval the ratio of thicknesses between two strin[gs] of equal length is the square root of the ratio of length[s] between two strings of equal thickness. This unde[r]

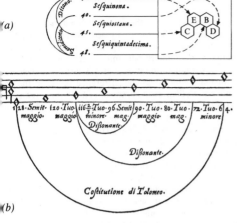

. *Models by Zarlino (after Ptolemy): (a) of the tetra-*
hord ('sesquinona', 'sesquiottava' and 'sesquiquinta-
ecima' mean 10:9, 9:8 and 16:15 respectively); (b)
f the octave [boxed material, upper right, is an edi-
orial clarification]

Lite-rals.	Ratios.	New Notation. Σ+f+m			Numerals.	recip. Logar.
C	1÷2	612	12	53	VIII, or Octave.	·3010299,96
B	8÷15	555	11	48	VII	·2730012,72
B♭	9÷16	508	10	44	7	·2498774,73
A	3÷5	451	9	39	VI	·2218487,50
G♯	16÷25	394	8	34	Ext. ♯V	·1938200,26
G	2÷3	358	7	31	V	·1760912,59
F♯	32÷45	301	6	26	IV	·1480625,35
F	3÷4	254	5	22	4	·1249387,37
E	4÷5	197	4	17	III	·0969100,13
E♭	5÷6	161	3	14	3	·0791812,46
D	8÷9	104	2	9	II (or T)	·0511525,22
C♯	128÷135	47	1	4	I	·0231237,99
C	1÷1	0	0	0	1	·0000000,00
A♭	5÷8	415	8	36	6	·2041199,83
D♭	9÷10	93	2	8	II (or t)	·0457574,91
D♭	15÷16	57	1	5	2 (or S)	·0280287,24
C	80÷81	11	0	1	c	·0053950,32
32768÷32805		1	0	0	Σ	·0004901,07
4502·3905 &c		0	1	0	f	·0000733,50
292·297733 &c 292·300327 &c		0	0	1	m	·0000038,53
1	2	3			4	5

3. Farey's 'New Notation' for justly intoned intervals, from 'On Different Modes', 'American Journal of Science', ii (1820)

ined the theoretical status of the traditional ratios of
st intonation as far as the eminent Dutch scientist Simon
tevin was concerned; it might have had further con-
quences had not Galilei retracted in 1589 his 1581
ccount of vocal intonation, and had not his son Gali-
o's generation devised the 'pulse' theory of conso-
ance, according to which the eardrum is struck
multaneously by the wave pulses of the notes in any
onsonant interval or chord (thus mistakenly assuming
at the waves are always in phase with one another).
uch a theory tended rather to undermine the concept
f tempered consonances, where the wave frequencies
re theoretically incommensurate.

Descartes found Stevin's dismissal of simple ratios
so absurd that I hardly know any more how to reply',
ut Marin Mersenne advanced the real argument that the
uperiority of justly intoned intervals is shown by the
act that they do not beat (1636–7). (He probably gained
nis argument from Isaac Beeckman, who seems to have
nvented the 'pulse' theory of consonance.) 50 years lat-
r, however, Wolfgang Caspar Printz said that a 5th
empered by ¼-comma remains concordant because
Nature . . . transforms the confusion into a pleasant
eating [which] should be taken not as a defect but
ather as a perfection and gracing of the 5th'. Andreas
Verckmeister agreed (*Musicalische Temperatur*, 1691).

About this time Christiaan Huygens developed Bene-
letti's point (although he did not associate it with Bene-
letti) in his assertion that if one sings the notes shown
n ex.2 slowly, the pitch will fall (just as in ex.1); 'but

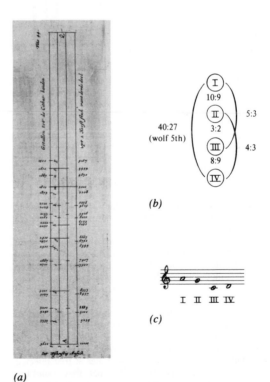

(a)

(b)

40:27
(wolf 5th)

I — 10:9 — II — 3:2 — III — 8:9 — IV
5:3
4:3

(c)

I II III IV

4. Nierop's design for a justly intoned cittern: (a) the fretting scheme; (b) the intervals between the open strings; (c) note names given to the open strings in the transcription shown in ex.4

x.2 *Huygens's example of a succession of notes for which the use of just intonation which make the pitch fall*

f one sings quickly, I find that the memory of the first
keeps the voice on pitch, and thus makes it state the
onsonant intervals a little falsely'. Rameau said
Génération harmonique, 1737) that an accompanied

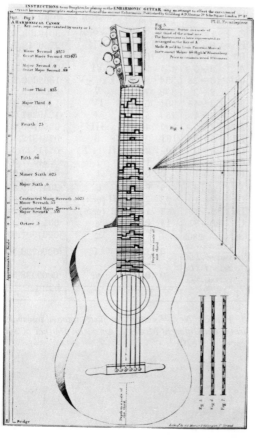

5. *Guitar with frets placed for just intonation, from Thomas Perronet Thompson's 'Instructions to my Daughter for Playing on the Enharmonic Guitar' (1829)*

singer is guided by the 'temperament of the instruments' only for the 'fundamental sounds' (the roots of the triads), and automatically modifies, in the course of singing the less fundamental notes, 'everything contrary to the just rapport of the fundamental sounds'. While this represents a musicianly departure from the common error that there is something natural about the scheme shown in fig.2b, it does rather overlook the fact that the tuning of the 'fundamental sounds' was normally tempered on keyboard instruments and lutes.

The most eminent scientist among 18th-century music theorists, Leonhard Euler, developed an elaborate and remarkably broad mathematical theory of tonal structure (scales, modulations, chord progressions and gradations of consonance and dissonance) based exclusively upon just-intonation ratios. He failed to observe that a 5th tuned a comma smaller than pure sounds sour, and so allowed himself to be misled by an inept passage in Johann Mattheson's *Grosse General-Bass-Schule* into supposing that keyboard instruments of his day were actually tuned in just intonation. Euler at first rejected septimal intervals, saying in 1739 that 'they sound too harsh and disturb the harmony', but declared in 1760 that if they were introduced, 'music would be carried to a higher degree' (an idea previously voiced by Mersenne and Christiaan Huygens). He published two articles in 1764 to demonstrate that 'music has now learnt

to count to seven' (Leibnitz had said that music cou only 'count to five').

Another extreme of theoretical elaboration was reach in the early 19th century by John Farey, a geologis who reckoned intervals by a combination of thre mutually incommensurate units of measurement deriv from just-intonation ratios. Farey's largest unit was t 'schisma', which was the difference between the sy tonic and Pythagorean commas. (The Pythagorean com ma is the amount by which six Pythagorean whole ton exceed an octave; the schisma is some 1·95 cents ar has the ratio 32805:32768.) His smallest unit was t amount by which the syntonic comma theoretical exceeds 11 schismas (or by which 11 octaves theoret cally exceed the sum of 42 Pythagorean whole tones ar 12 pure major 3rds; this is some $\frac{1}{65}$-cent, and its rat would require 49 digits to write out). His intermedia unit (some 0·3 cent) was the amount by which each the three most common types of just-intonation sem tone (16:15, 25:24 and 135:128) theoretically excee some combination of the other two units (see fig.3) the amount by which 21 octaves theoretically exceed th difference between 37 5ths and two major 3rds.

2. INSTRUMENTS. Rameau reported (1737) that som masters of the violin and *basse de viol* tempered the open-string intervals – an idea also found in the writing of Werckmeister (1691) and Quantz (*Versuch eine Anweisung die Flöte traversiere zu spielen*, 1752). B Boyden has shown (1951) that evidence from the wri ings of 18th-century violinists, particularly Geminian and Tartini, points to a kind of just intonation flexibl applied to successive intervals with adjustments whe necessary both melodically and harmonically on each the four strings, tuned in pure fifths, as points of ref erence. In the 1760s Michele Stratico, a former pup of Tartini, worked out a fairly efficient system of nota tion for this kind of just intonation, including septima intervals (see ex.3).

To model a fretted instrument upon just intonatio entails the use of zig-zag frets. Dyrck Rembrantz va Nierop, a mathematician who favoured just intonatio for all sorts of instruments as well as voices, worke out (1659) an exact fretting scheme for a cittern (se

Ex.3 Stratico's pragmatic notation for just intonation: *(a)* the bas signs; *(b)* the harmonic series and its inversion; *(c)* some chor progressions

(a)

(b)

(c)

.4a), according to which, if the open-string intervals ∴re tuned as in fig.4b, then each position on the high-t course could be supplied with one or more justly :oned chords as shown in ex.4. Some other devotees

.4 Pure chords available on Nierop's justly intoned cittern (the fourth fret, 'e' in the tablature notation, is a whole tone above the third fret, 'd'; the others are a semitone apart)

just intonation who designed fretted instruments were ∂iovanni Battista Doni, Thomas Salmon and Thomas ∋rronet Thompson (see fig.5).

The simplest way to provide all possible pure con-∂rds among the naturals of a keyboard instrument with ×ed intonation is to have two Ds, one pure with F and and the other, a comma higher, pure with G and B ∋ee fig.6a). (The concept of a diatonic scale in just

(a)   (b)

. (a) The set of naturals upon which Mersenne's ℩ιvoured just-intonation scheme (b) is based

∴tonation with two Ds a comma apart goes back to ∂odovico Fogliani's *Musica theorica*, 1529.) If this group ∫ eight notes is then provided with a complement of ∋n chromatic notes as indicated in fig.6b, each natural ∕ill have available all six of its possible triadic con-∂rds. This scheme was described by Mersenne and ∋mployed by Joan Albert Ban for a harpsichord built in ⌡aarlem in 1639 (see fig.7). Mersenne said that on a ∋eyboard instrument of this type the 'perfection of the ∩armony' would abundantly repay the difficulty of play-⌐g, 'which organists will be able to surmount in the ∖pace of one week'.

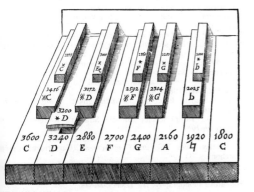

⁊. Ban's harpsichord after Mersenne: diagram from Zangh-bloemzel van Ioan Albert Ban' (1642)

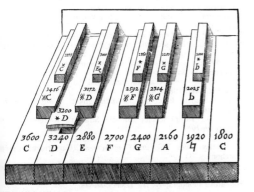

8. The scheme of Helmholtz's 'justly intoned harmonium'

The 'justly intoned harmonium' of Helmholtz (in mathematical terms not exactly embodying just inton-ation, but deviating from it insignificantly from a prac-tical and acoustical point of view) combined two normal keyboards for the scheme shown in fig.8. The 12 pitch classes shown to the left are on the upper manual, the 12 to the right on the lower manual. No justly intoned triadic note is present beyond the lines along the top and bottom of the diagram, but the three notes at the right end (A, C♯ or D♭, and E) make justly intoned triads with the three at the left (E, G♯ or A♭, and C). Thus the major and minor triads on F, A, and D♭ or C♯ require the use of both manuals at once. The 12 pitch classes shown in the upper half of the diagram are each a comma lower in intonation than their equivalents in the lower half of the diagram. Every 5th except C♯– G♯ or D♭–A♭ is available at two different pitch levels a comma apart, and the same is true of six triads: the major ones on E, B and F♯, and the minor ones on G♯, D♯ or E♭, and B♭. In the case of triads on C, D, F, G and A, however, the major triad is always intoned a comma higher than its parallel minor triad.

Various other elaborate keyboard instruments capable of playing in just or virtually just intonation have been built by G. Sabbatini, Doni, H. Poole, H. Liston, R. H. M. Bosanquet, S. Tanaka, Eitz, Partch, the Moto-rola Scalatron Corporation and others (*see* MICROTONAL INSTRUMENTS). Playing such an instrument involves choosing which form of each note to use at which moment. If the proper choice is consistently made, impure vertical intervals will be avoided and the occurrence of impure melodic ones minimized. The criteria for choos-ing, which differ in detail with each kind of elaborate keyboard pattern, are intricate but capable of being incorporated in a pattern of electric circuits amounting to a simple computer programme. In 1936 Eivind Gro-ven, a Norwegian composer and musicologist, built a harmonium with 36 pitches per octave tuned to form an extension of Helmholtz's quasi-just-intonation scheme, but with a normal keyboard, the choice of pitch inflec-tions being made automatically while the performer plays as on a conventional instrument. He later (1954) devised a single-stop pipe organ of the same type, now at the Fagerberg Church in Oslo, a complete electronic organ with 43 pitches per octave (1965), now at the Valer-encen Church in Oslo, and a complete pipe organ incor-porating his invention (c1970, built by Walcker & Cie.). Groven's work has made just intonation practicable on keyboard instruments that are no more difficult to play than ordinary ones.

While the distinctive quality of justly intoned inter-vals is unmistakable, their aesthetic value is bound to depend upon the stylistic context. In 1955 Kok report-ed, on the basis of experiments with an electronic organ capable of performing in various tuning systems, that musicians, unlike other listeners, heard the difference between equal and mean-tone temperaments, giving preference to the latter, 'and *a fortiori* the just intonation, but only in broad terminating chords and for choral-like music. However, they . . . do not like the pitch fluctuations caused by instantaneously corrected thirds'. According to McClure ('Studies in Keyboard Temperaments', *GSJ*, i (1948), 28), George Bernard Shaw recalled that in the 1870s the progressions of pure concords on Bosanquet's harmonium (with 53 pitches in each octave) had sounded to him 'unpleasantly slimy'. E. H. Pierce (1924), describing the 1906 model of the Telharmonium, which was capable of being played in just intonation with 36 pitches in each octave, reported:

The younger players whom I taught . . . at first followed out my instructions, but as time went on they began to realize (as in fact I did myself) that there is a spirit in modern music which not only does not demand just intonation, but actually would suffer from its use, consequently they relapsed more and more into the modern tempered scale.

The composer and theorist J. D. Heinichen remarked (*Der Generalbass in der Komposition*, 1728, p.85) that because keys with two or three sharps or flats in their signature were so beautiful and expressive in well-tempered tunings, especially in the theatrical style, he would not favour the invention of the 'long-sought pure-diatonic' keyboard even if it were to become practicable. These remarks suggest that the recently achieved technological feasibility of just intonation on keyboard instruments is but a step towards its musical emancipation and that further steps are likely to depend on the resourcefulness of composers who may be inclined in the future to discover and exploit its virtues.

BIBLIOGRAPHY

TO 1800

B. Ramos de Pareia: *Musica practica* (Bologna, 1482, 2/1482/*R*1969)
G. Spataro: *Errori di Franchino Gafurio da Lodi* (Bologna, 1521)
G. Zarlino: *Le istitutioni harmoniche* (Venice, 1558/*R*1965, rev. 3/1573/*R*1966)
——: *Dimostrationi harmoniche* (Venice, 1571/*R*1966, 2/1573, rev. 1588)
F. de Salinas: *De musica libri septem* (Salamanca, 1577, 2/1592)
V. Galilei: *Dialogo della musica antica et della moderna* (Florence, 1581/*R*1968)
G. B. Benedetti: *Diversarum speculationum mathematicarum, & physicarum liber* (Turin, 1585), 282
G. Zarlino: *Sopplimenti musicali* (Venice, 1588/*R*1966)
V. Galilei: *Discorso intorno all'opere di Messer Gioseffo Zarlino da Chioggia* (Florence, 1589, repr. 1933)
S. Stevin: *Van de spiegeling der singconst*, c1600, ed. D. Bierens de Haan (Amsterdam, 1884); ed. A. Fokker in *The Principal Works of Simon Stevin*, v (Amsterdam, 1966)
G. M. Artusi: *Considerationi musicali* (Venice, 1603) [bound with his *Seconda parte dell'Artusi*]
G. B. Doni: *Compendio del trattato de' generi e de' modi della musica* (Rome, 1635)
M. Mersenne: *Harmonicorum libri, in quibus agitur de sonorum natura* (Paris, 1635–6)
——: *Harmonie universelle* (Paris, 1636–7/*R*1963; Eng. trans., 1957)
G. B. Doni: *Annotazioni sopra il Compendio de' generi e de' modi della musica* (Rome, 1640)
D. R. van Nierop: *Wis-konstige musyka* (Amsterdam, 1659) [bound with his *Mathematische calculatie*]
I. Newton: unpubd MSS on music, 1665 (*GB–Cu* Add.4000)
C. Huygens: writings on music, ed. in *Oeuvres complètes*, xx (The Hague, 1940)
W. C. Printz: *Exercitationum musicarum theoretico-practicarum curiosarum tertia di Quinta* (Frankfurt and Leipzig, 1687)
T. Salmon: *A Proposal to Perform Musick in Perfect and Mathematical Proportions* (London, 1688)
——: 'The Theory of Musick Reduced to Arithmetical and Geometrical Proportion', *Philosophical Transactions of the Royal Society*, xxiv (1705), 2077
J. Mattheson: *Grosse General-Bass-Schule* (Hamburg, 1731/*R*1968; Eng. trans., 1981)
P. Prelleur: *The Modern Musick-master*, v: *The Art of Playing on the Violin* (London, 1731/*R*1965)
L. Euler: *Tentamen novae theoriae musicae* (St Petersburg, 1739; Eng. trans., 1960)
F. Geminiani: *The Art of Playing the Violin* (London, 1751)
G. Tartini: *Trattato di musica secondo la vera scienza dell'armor* (Padua, 1754/*R*1966)
G. B. Doni: *Lyra Barberina amphieordos: accedunt eiusdem ope* i–ii, ed. A. F. Gori and G. B. Passeri (Florence, 1763/*R*197*)
L. Euler: 'Conjecture sur la raison de quelques dissonanc généralement reçues dans la musique'; 'Du véritable caractère la musique moderne', *Mémoires de l'Académie des sciences* Berlin, xx (1764), 165, 174; repr. in *Opera omnia*, iii/1, 5C 516
——: *Lettres à une princesse d'Allemagne* (Mietan and Leipz* 1770)
M. Stratico: MS treatises on music (*I–Vnm* it. iv 341–3)

SINCE 1800

H. Liston: *An Essay on Perfect Intonation* (Edinburgh, 1812)
J. Farey: 'On Different Modes of Expressing the Magnitudes a Relations of Musical Intervals', *American Journal of Science*, (1820), 74
T. P. Thompson: *Instructions to my Daughter for Playing on t Enharmonic Guitar* (London, 1829)
H. W. Poole: 'An Essay on Perfect Intonation in the Organ', *Ame ican Journal of Science and the Arts*, 2nd ser., ix (1850), 68, 19
M. Hauptmann: *Die Natur der Harmonik und der Metrik* (Leipzi 1853, 2/1873; Eng. trans., 1888)
C. F. L. Delèzenne: *Table de logarithmes acoustique* (Lille, 185
T. P. Thompson: *On the Principles and Practice of Just Intonatic with a View to the Abolition of Temperament* (London, 1860)
H. von Helmholtz: *Die Lehre von den Tonempfindungen, als ph siologische Grundlage für die Theorie der Musik* (Brunswick, 186 4/1877; Eng. trans. by A. J. Ellis as *On the Sensations of Ton* rev. 2/1885/*R*1954)
G. Engel: *Das mathematische Harmonium* (Berlin, 1881)
S. Tanaka: 'Studien im Gebiete der reinen Stimmung', *VMw*, (1890), 1–90
C. A. Eitz: *Das mathematisch-reine Tonsystem* (Leipzig, 1891)
M. Planck: 'Die natürliche Stimmung in der modernen Vokalm* sik', *VMw*, ix (1893), 418
E. P. L. Atkins: 'Ear-training and the Standardization of Equ Temperament', *PMA*, xli (1914–15), 91
E. H. Pierce: 'A Colossal Experiment in "Just Intonation"', *MC* x (1924), 326
C. de Waard, ed.: *Correspondance du P. Marin Mersenne* (Pari 1932)
N. L. Norton: 'A New Theory of Untempered Music', *MQ*, x (193* 217
J. M. Barbour: 'Just Intonation Confuted', *ML*, xix (1938), 48
E. Groven: *Temperering og renstemning* (Oslo, 1948; Eng. trans 1970)
J. M. Barbour: *Tuning and Temperament: a Historical Survey* (Ea Lansing, Mich., 1951/*R*1972, 2/1953)
D. Boyden: 'Prelleur, Geminiani, and Just Intonation', *JAMS*, i (1951), 202
E. Groven: 'My Untempered Organ', *Organ Institute Quarterly* v/3 (1955), 34
H. Stephani: *Zur Psychologie des musikalischen Hörens; hören w naturrein, quintengestimmt, temperirt?* (Regensburg, 1956)
C. V. Palisca: *Girolamo Mei, Letters on Ancient and Modern Mus* (Rome, 1960)
——: 'Scientific Empiricism in Musical Thought', *Seventeen* *Century Science and the Arts*, ed. H. H. Rhys (Princeton, 1961 91–137
Ll. S. Lloyd and H. Boyle: *Intervals, Scales and Temperamen* (London, 1963, 2/1978)
C. Dahlhaus: 'Die "Reine Stimmung" als musikalisches Problem *Festschrift til Olav Gurvin* (Oslo, 1968), 49
R. Damann: 'Die musica mathematica von Bartolus', *AMw*, xx* (1969), 140
E. Groven: *Equal Temperament and Pure Tuning* (Oslo, 1969)
M. Dickreiter: *Der Musiktheoretiker Johannes Kepler* (Berne an Munich, 1973)
D. P. Walker: *Studies in Musical Science in the Late Renaissanc* (London, 1978)
M. Lindley: 'Pythagorean Intonation and the Rise of the Triad' *RMARC*, xvi (1980), 4–61
——: 'Leonhard Euler als Musiktheoretiker', *Kongressberich* *Bayreuth 1981*
——: 'Der Tartini-Schüler Michele Stratico', *Kongressberich* *Bayreuth 1981*
R. Rasch: 'Ban's Intonation', *TVNM*, xxxiii (1983), 75
M. Lindley: *Lutes, Viols and Temperaments* (Cambridge, in pre* aration)
——: 'Stimmung und Temperatur', *Geschichte der Musiktheorie* vi, ed. F. Zaminer (Berlin, in preparation)
For further bibliography, *see* TEMPERAMENTS.

MARK LINDLE*

Juwāk. North African term for an oblique rim-blow* flute. *See* NĀY.

K

a (i). Five-string plucked zither of the Ainu people of orth Japan. *See* TONKORI.

a (ii). Cuban drum with a single, nailed head; its body made of an ordinary commercial barrel or keg and it as an open bottom. Drums of this type are common in uba, but the term *ka* is particularly prevalent in Oriente Province, facing Haiti. The type has also been bserved in Haiti, the French Antilles, the Virgin Islands nd New Orleans. *See Ortiz/MA*, iii, 420f.

JOHN M. SCHECHTER

aamuri. Single-headed open-ended GOBLET DRUM of he Nika/Giryama people of Malindi district, Kenya. he membrane is pegged on, and it is played with the ands.

a'ara. (1) Large SLIT-DRUM of Mangaia, Cook Islands, lso found in Rarotonga and Aitutaki. It is of rotund orm with a characteristic figure-of-eight soundhole, wide t the extremities and connected by a narrow medial slit. ll extant specimens are elaborately carved, even on the laying surface (see illustration). Their average length s 90 cm, and their circumference only slightly less. The nstrument was struck in the centre, on either side of the nedial slit, producing two fundamental notes. A third click) note could be produced by tapping the ends. Descriptions of the two fundamental notes as produced rom opposite ends rather than from opposite sides are rroneous.) Two mallets were used, making possible rapid olls on either of the two fundamental notes. By the late

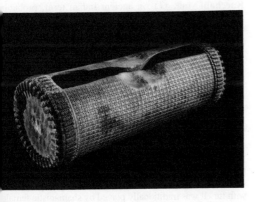

Ka'ara (slit-drum) of Mangaia, Cook Islands, first half of the 19th century (Peabody Museum, Harvard University, Cambridge, Massachusetts)

1960s the *ka'ara* had become obsolete. It was revived as a high-pitched *to'ere*, similar to the *tini-tokere*, by the Cook Islands National Arts Theatre dance company, but without the older instrument's two-pitch capacity. See W. Laird: *Drums and Drumming in the Cook Islands* (diss., U. of Auckland, 1982).

(2) Term sometimes applied to the TINI-TOKERE slit-drum of Aitutaki.

MERVYN McLEAN

Kabak. Turkish SPIKE LUTE. The bowl resonator is made of a water gourd with a skin soundtable. The neck is made of wood. The *kabak* has three metal strings played with a short horsehair bow. It is played by men and used for entertainment music, particularly indoors. It is popular in western and southern Anatolia. *See* L. Picken: *Folk Musical Instruments of Turkey* (London, 1975).

Kabamboli [kabambolik]. *See* GABAMBOLI.

Kabanj. Yemeni name for the *'ūd* (lute). *See* QANBŪS.

Kabara. BULLROARER of the Achipawa people of Nigeria. In traditional usage it represented the people's ancestors at the annual *okiso* festival and was so sacred that only the priest could see and use it. Women and children were banned from its presence and men could only see it represented on the ground.

Kabaro. Cylindrical or tapered KETTLEDRUM of Ethiopia, 40 to 80 cm high. It is used to accompany services in the Ethiopian church.

Kabarome. Term applied both to a braced MOUTH BOW and LAMELLAPHONE of the Mbuti pygmies of the Amba District of Uganda. (1) In the mouth bow, the bow measures 87 cm and the brace, which is used for tuning, is slightly left of centre. The string is placed between the teeth quite close to the brace and both sections of the string are plucked with a plectrum made from a short piece of grass; a finger of the left hand stops the string.

(2) The lamellaphone has nine or ten keys made from rattan cane; the keys are mounted on a piece of bark and pass over a straight bridge.

Kåbdes. FRAME DRUM of Lapland with a membrane of reindeer skin. It is played with a small beater of reindeer horn. Unlike other shaman drums, it is used not only as an instrument but also for fortune-telling, by placing small objects on the vibrating membrane.

Kabile. Tubular MIRLITON of the Mbae people of Zaïre. Used in connection with initiation rituals, its sound is said to be the voice of the spirit Kabile (*LaurentyA*, 35).

Kabili. NOSE FLUTE of the Kuma and Lega peoples of Zaïre. *See* BOLUKULUKU.

Kabiry. Oboe of Madagascar. It is larger than the ANJOMARA, and is probably of Comorian origin.

Kabisa. Large ceremonial SLIT-DRUM of the Jola people of the Casamance region of Senegal. The drum is 150 to 180 cm long and 80 to 120 cm in diameter; it is often placed underneath a canopy and is beaten by hand or with sticks. It is manufactured in secret and used only to announce important events in the life of the community. See L. -V. Thomas: 'Les Diola', *Mémoires de l'Institut français d'Afrique noire*, lv (1958–9); M. Huet: *The Dance, Art and Ritual of Africa* (London, 1978).

Kabitikwila. GOBLET DRUM of the Tumbwe people of Zaïre. *See* DITUMBA.

Kabosa. Lute of Madagascar. *See* QANBŪS.

Kabuki. Genre of traditional Japanese musical theatre, including both dance numbers and purely dramatic plays. It developed during the 17th century as a popular theatre in intimate connection with the evolving bourgeoisie. All kabuki is accompanied by GEZA off-stage music. Dance numbers are accompanied by NAGAUTA music or by other shamisen-based musics, and scenes derived from or in the style of the bunraku puppet theatre use GIDAYŪ music. In contrast to the nō (musical dance-drama), there is no singing by the actors.

DAVID W. HUGHES

Kaburu. Large three-string plucked lute of the Gwari people of Nigeria. It can measure up to 100 cm in length, excluding the long metal jingle fitted into the handle. Originally found mainly in the Kuta area, it has now been adopted by the Gwari of Diko. Its original function was performing ritual music; it is now used in impressive displays with up to eight instruments in an ensemble.

Kabwaye. LAMELLAPHONE of the Luba people of Kalémié, Zaïre (*LaurentyS*, 196).

Kabyabo. End-blown single-note flute of the Konjo people of Toro district, Uganda, used in the ILENGA flute ensemble.

Kacakaura. *See* KACIKAURA.

Kacapi (i). Plucked BOX ZITHER used in Sundanese areas of West Java. The name is derived from the Sanskrit *kacchapī vīṇā*. The *kacapi* has a boat-shaped wooden frame, with metal strings stretched lengthwise over the soundboard, which is the upper part of the box body and tapers towards its base (for illustration *see* TARAWANGSA). A hole is cut in the base of the instrument. The strings are fixed at one end to metal or wooden pins and attached at the other to tuning-pegs; fine tuning is achieved by adjusting the movable wooden pyramids over which each string passes. The strings are plucked with the nails of thumb and index finger. There are two sizes. The *kacapi indung* ('mother zither'), known also as *kacapi parahu* or *kacapi gelung*, has 12 to 18 strings; the ends of the box are about 31 cm deep and the middle about 20·5 cm deep, while the top surface is about 14 cm long and the bottom about 77 cm. The *kacapi anc* ('child zither'), or *kacapi rincik*, has 15 strings; its body is about 18·5 cm deep at one end and 15·5 cm at the other, while its top surface is about 88·5 cm long and its base about 37 cm. The two *kacapi* (*indung* and *rincik*) are used with the *suling* (bamboo flute) in the *kacapi suling* ensemble. Pieces of both the *gamelan salendr* and the *gamelan degung* repertories may be played on it, and it also serves to accompany court songs of Ciamjur and Bandung. Another type of *kacapi* ensemble comprises *kacapi indung*, *suling* and *tarawangsa* (fiddle).

The KUCAPI, (1) in Minangkabau is a similar instrument.

BIBLIOGRAPHY
C. Sachs: *Die Musikinstrumente Indiens und Indonesiens* (Berlin and Leipzig, 1914, 2/1923)
Z. Afiff: *About the Sundanese Suling and Katjapi* (diss., Monash U., 1970)

MARGARET J. KARTOMI

Kacapi [kacaping] **(ii).** Boat-shaped plucked lute used in the Buginese and Makassar (*kacaping*) areas of the province of South Sulawesi and on the island of Sumba, Indonesia. The handle, soundboard, foot and bridge are all cut from one piece of wood, and the back of the resonator is closed by a lid which is perforated with several holes. It is elegantly shaped and often elaborately carved. It has two strings. Men or women play it, either solo or in an ensemble together with a *lea-lea* (bamboo zither), *ganrang* (double-headed drum) and gong. Although it is a popular instrument it is not mentioned in the historical *Lontara* (chronicles), which suggests that it has not been used as a court instrument.

Similar instruments include the HASAPI in Batak Toba North Sumatra, the KULCAPI in Batak Karo and the KUCAPI, (2) in Minangkabau.

BIBLIOGRAPHY
C. Sachs: *Die Musikinstrumente Indiens und Indonesiens* (Berlin and Leipzig, 1914, 2/1923)
W. Kaudern: *Musical Instruments in Celebes* (Göteborg, 1927)

MARGARET J. KARTOMI

Kacaura. *See* KACIKAURA.

Kacchapī vīṇā. (1) An ancient Indian term, probably denoting a short-necked pear-shaped lute. *See* VĪṆĀ, §3
(2) A 19th-century literary term for the *kachvā sitār*, a sitar with a flat-backed soundbox. *See* SITAR, §2 (iii) and VĪṆĀ, §10.

Kā chap chap. Struck TUBE ZITHER of north-east India, probably of the Khasi people. *See* GINTANG.

Kachisi. Single-headed open-ended conical drum of the Nyanja/Chewa people of Malawi.

Kacho. Single-headed circular or oval FRAME DRUM of the Ainu people of north Japan. The skin is of reindeer, seal etc, and is struck with a short stick partly covered with fur. It was traditionally played by shamanistic female mediums or their male assistants. Various coloured strings or pieces of cloth would be attached to the drum for ritual purposes. See Nihon Hōsō Kyōkai [Japan Broadcasting Corporation], ed.: *Ainu dentō ongaku* [Traditional Ainu music] (Tokyo, 1965).

DAVID W. HUGHES

Kachvā sitār. Type of flat-backed sitar. *See* SITAR, §2 (iii).

Kacikaura [kacakaura, kacaura, cakaura, lalajo]. Stick rattle of the Hausa people of Nigeria. It consists of pieces of calabash strung on a thin straight stick. Both ends of the stick are held in the hands and the rattle is shaken from side to side to provide rhythmic support for songs of entertainment. *See Ames–KingGHM.*

Kadia m'buji. Double-headed drum of the Luluwa people of Zaïre. *See* MUKUPIELA.

Kadih. Open GOBLET DRUM of the Angas people of Nigeria. It has a lapped and pegged membrane and is 22 to 25 cm in diameter at the head and approximately 45 cm in length. The drum is played under the arm and beaten with the hands. Its usage is essentially religious, and women and children are forbidden to play it.

Kadimba [kadimba-tu]. LAMELLAPHONE of the Bena people of Zaïre (*LaurentyS*, 195). *See* KAKOLONDONO and KALIMBA (i).

Kadimbwa. *See* DIMBWA.

Kading. Small metal bell of the Muong people of Vietnam and Laos, used for the ceremony of the buffalo sacrifice.

Kadongo. LAMELLAPHONE of Uganda. *See* BUDONGO.

Kā duitārā. Long-necked fretless lute of the Khasi people of Meghalay state, India. *See* DOTĀRĀ.

Kā'eke'eke. Hawaiian STAMPING TUBE, played in pairs. Each tube is made of hard, thin-walled native Hawaiian bamboo (*Schizo-stachyum*) open at the top and with the closed node end near the bottom. The pairs are of unequal length and are stamped vertically on a hard surface.

Kaen. *See* KHAēN.

Kāēng. Free-reed mouth organ of the Hmong or Miao people in southern China, Vietnam, Laos and Thailand. It has six pipes and is used to accompany sacred and secular dances. It is related to the *raj qeej* (*see* RAJ).

Kafo. Side-blown animal-horn trumpet of the Sokoto and Zamfara areas of northern Nigeria. *See* KAHO.

Kagan. Barrel drum of the Anlo-Ewe people of Ghana. It is about 55 cm high but otherwise resembles the ATSI-MEWU.

Kagebayashi. A term for Japanese GEZA music.

Kagel, Mauricio [Maurizio] (**Raúl**) (*b* Buenos Aires, 24 Dec 1931). Argentine composer, performer, film maker, dramatist and instrument inventor. In 1957 he went to live in Cologne. He has constructed 'experimental sound-producers' for about a dozen compositions (from 1965), most of them theatrical works. Many of his instruments are small, often hand-held percussion, but they also include the RAHMENHARFE, which is 6 metres long, props for dramatic works including MUSICAL COSTUMES, and simple toy-like instruments. Substantial verbal and visual documentation on all of Kagel's work has been published, including the introductions to scores and gramophone record sleeve notes.

The first 'instrument' devised by Kagel was for his composition *Pas de cinq – Wandelszene* (1965), in which five performers, each equipped with a walking stick, walk at different speeds across and along the edges of a pentagonal platform with slopes and steps, constructed from a variety of different materials. The sounds, notated rhythmically in the score, are produced entirely from the tapping of the sticks. In 1968 Kagel wrote *Der Schall*, the first of several compositions in which each member of a small ensemble (normally three to five musicians – the works were first performed by Kagel's Kölner Ensemble für Neue Musik) plays a large and varied array of instruments of all families. In *Der Schall* five performers play 54 early, exotic, folk, toy and invented instruments; the last include a Gummiphon, which consists of rubber bands looped round two or more hooks inserted in a sheet of hardboard with regularly spaced holes, and several lengths of plastic tubing. (The Gummiphon is also known as the Saitensprung or Escapade of Strings, under which name it was manufactured in 1970 by VICE-Versand in Remscheid.) The next such work, *Unter Strom* (1969), includes the Rahmenharfe and three guitars (all activated by ventilator propellers and other rotating devices), sirens, buzzers and motor horns; another invented instrument is a wooden rod (1 metre long) with a contact microphone attached to one end, which is held in the performer's mouth and bowed on the side away from the microphone. The much longer *Acustica* (1968–70) employs an enormous range of

1. 'Drum-man' from the 'Spielplan' section of Kagel's 'Staatstheater' (Staatsoper, Hamburg, 1971)

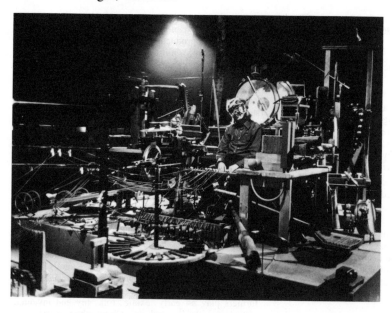

2. *One of the performers in Kagel's 'Zwei-Mann-Orchester' (1973)*

special instruments and objects, from comb-and-paper and nail violins with wooden and metal rods, to a 12-note castanet 'keyboard', a wooden pole with eight bicycle bells attached (a modern version of the jingling Johnny), a 'whistle tree' (a mixture of small organ pipes and penny whistles) powered by compressed air, and a selection of objects held in the hand, mouth and ear with which to play gramophone records; a hand-operated conveyor belt transfers instruments from one player to another.

A similarly large instrumentarium occurs in sections of Kagel's *Staatstheater* (1967–70), commissioned by the Hamburg State Opera. Around 75 instruments were specially constructed, adapted or modified for the work, including over a dozen shoe attachments that rattle, clatter, clank, clash, clap, scrape and hoot. In the section *Spielplan* some of the more memorable images are two giant güiros (each *c*6 metres long); a contrabass, double-ended string drum on wheels (*c*2·5 metres long, 1·6 metres in diameter); and the 'drum-man' whose body is encased in up to ten single-headed frame drums, which are played by other musicians (fig.1). The first of the nine sections of the work, *Repertoire*, is often performed separately since its staging requirements are comparatively simple: several screens divide the stage into sections in which the performers, often singly, carry out a total of 100 short, sometimes humorous, playing activities, of which about a third use simple invented instruments. These include a sheet of thick polystyrene from which six long springs hang down to the floor, which is first 'worn' by a performer on his bent back as he moves across the stage and is then drawn across on stage wires; and a thin flexible strip of flat steel, 4 metres long, each end of which is attached to one of the performer's shoes and which is struck with a beater. A number of invented or adapted instruments, including most of the shoe attachments, are used in the section *Saison* (an operatic parody).

A simpler set-up is found in *Tactil* (1970), which includes the Schwinger ('vibrator'), a lamellaphone consisting of a selection of everyday metal blades clamped to a small table. The larger instrumentarium returns in

Zwei-Mann-Orchester (1971–3), mostly constructed by Klaus Schaefer, where two seated performers on separate large stages each operate a collection of mainly traditional instruments in various states of repair, many by means of pedals, wires, chains, rods, electrical connections and other methods of remote control (fig.2). The score for this orchestral 'machine' includes precise indications for the movements of 19 parts of the body (up to four simultaneously), so that the performers are integrated with their instruments. Invented instruments are also incorporated into some of Kagel's radio plays, especially *Die Umkehrung Amerikas* (1975–8), and his second major work for an opera house, *Die Erschöpfung der Welt* (1974–7). The latter relates the origins of music to the creation of the world, and uses a 27-piece 'prehistoric orchestra' and a group of fantastic animals such as a giraffe with springs for its neck and front legs, a frog with panpipes round its lower jaw and a hippopotamus with castanet toes and two guitar bodies for its jaws.

Kagel's explorations have encompassed instruments from other cultures and periods, as well as less common sound-sources: 43 early instruments are used in *Musik für Renaissance-Instrumente* (1965–6), and 200 non-Western ones in *Exotica* (1971–2); 70 caged birds produce the sounds of *Ornithologica multiplicata* (1968) and a wide range of birdcalls are required in *Bestiarium* (1974–5). Kagel's curiosity has also led him to explore recording methods, such as the use of unconventional 'pickups' for playing a gramophone record in *Acustica* (1968–70) and the related project *Der Umweg zur Höheren SubFidelität* (1970), and the manipulation of records in *Tremens* (1963–5) and tape in *Antithese* (1962). During the Kölner Kurse für Neue Musik in 1971 Kagel directed a group that developed 34 instruments for young children, ranging from variants of familiar instruments (many percussive) via acoustical demonstrations, toys and games, to interpretations of existing principles using unusual materials or objects.

BIBLIOGRAPHY

M. Kagel: 'Saitensprung', *Pages*, no.1 (1970), 22

D. Schnebel: *Mauricio Kagel: Musik Theater Film* (Cologne, 1970)

. Kagel: 'Der Umweg zur Höheren SubFidelität', *Interfunktionen*, no.4 (1970), 104; rev. Fr. trans. as 'Détour vers une plus haute sous-fidélité', *VH101*, no.4 (1971), 56
 Hansberger: 'Mauricio Kagel regt zur Erfindung von Kinderinstrumente an – Kölner Kurse für Neue Musik 1971', *Musik und Bildung*, iv (1972), 378
1. Kagel, ed.]: *Kinderinstrumente* (Cologne, 1972)
-H. Zarius: 'Das Instrument als Symptom', *Mauricio Kagel: Theatrum Instrumentorum* (Cologne, 1975), 8 [exhibition catalogue]
Karger: 'Mauricio Kagel's Repertoire', *Melos/NZfM*, ii (1976), 375
auricio Kagel: Instrumentales Theater (Bonn, 1976) [programme book]
 Clasen: 'Mauricio Kagel und seine Bedeutung für ein sich wandelndes Berufsbild des Schulmusikers', *Musik und Bildung*, ix (1977), 614
. Gruhn: 'Die instrumentale Inszenierung des Klanges bei Mauricio Kagel', *Musik und Bildung*, ix (1977), 606
Klangerzeuger, Instrumenten-Tiere, Tier-Monster, Kostüme', *Die Erschöpfung der Welt*, ii (Stuttgart, 1980) [programme book]
. Klüppelholz: *Mauricio Kagel 1970–80* (Cologne, 1981)
. Schöning, ed.: *Mauricio Kagel: Das Buch der Hörspiele* (Frankfurt, 1982)

HUGH DAVIES

.agul. Suspended percussion beam of the Tiruray people of the southern Philippines. Five beams, graded in ze, are used to play a 'melody', while a drone is beat-n on a sixth beam.

.agura. Any of the various genres of Japanese reli-ious music and dance which are in principle related to hintō rather than to Buddhism. Scholars generally dis-nguish court Shintō music from the myriad folk *kagura* y calling the former *mikagura* ('most honourable *gura*') and the latter *satokagura* ('village *kagura*'), ut terminology varies. In the court tradition the actual usical repertory (as opposed to the ceremony as a whole) called *kagura-uta* ('*kagura* songs'). The instruments sed in *mikagura* are the *kagurabue* (transverse flute), *ichiriki* (oboe), *wagon* (long zither) and two pairs of *akubyōshi* (clappers). The folk forms, performed at cal Shintō shrines, are quite diverse but are generally ccompanied by some kind of *hayashi* (ensemble) of *fue* lutes), *taiko* (drums) and *kane* (gongs) or *chappa* ymbals); certain shrines influenced by the court may so use *mikagura* instruments, sometimes substituting e koto for the *wagon*.

BIBLIOGRAPHY
 B. Waterhouse: 'Japan', §II, *Grove 6*
agura', *Ongaku daijiten* [Encyclopedia of music] (Tokyo, 1981)
DAVID W. HUGHES

.agurabue. Japanese transverse flute, with six finger-oles, used in Shintō court music and in some local Shintō rine music. It is also called *yamatobue* ('Japanese ute'). It is similar to the RYŪTEKI, but longer (about 5 cm) and thinner, tuned a whole tone lower, has only x finger-holes and has red and green embroidered cloth nbedded in its left end. Like the *ryūteki* it shares the ain melody with the *hichiriki* (oboe) in gagaku (court usic).

DAVID W. HUGHES

ähäh. Long copper trumpet of Nepal. It is similar to e *pomgah* of the Newari people. *Kähäh* are played in irs of unequal length: the longer one is tuned to *sa* d the shorter to *pa*, that is a 5th apart. Other related struments include the DUNG-CHEN, the KARNĀL and the \YMTĀH.

BIBLIOGRAPHY
 O. Ballinger and P. H. Bajracharya: 'Nepalese Musical Instruments', *Southwestern Journal of Anthropology*, xvi/4 (1960), 398

F. Hoerburger: *Studien zur Musik in Nepal* (Regensburg, 1975)
S. Wiehler-Schneider and H. Wiehler: 'A Classification of the Traditional Musical Instruments of the Nevars', *Journal of the Nepal Research Centre*, iv (1980), 67–132

MIREILLE HELFFER

Kāhalā. Straight metal trumpet of medieval India. *See* ŚRṄGA.

Kahamaxé tahpeno. COURTING FLUTE of the Cheyenne Indians of the USA.

Ka'hnyá' [ka'wásta'] (Seneca: 'stick'). Stamping sticks of the Iroquois Indians of north-eastern North America. The sticks, used in pairs, are long wooden poles from 1·5 to 1·8 metres long and about 5 cm in diameter. They are held vertically by two women of the *towisas* (society of women planters) and are used to beat time to the songs of the women's rite, performed at the Green Corn and Midwinter ceremonies. According to Seneca belief, the stamping is said to represent thunder, wind and rain.

MARY RIEMER-WELLER

Kaho. Side-blown trumpet of the Hausa people of northern Nigeria. It is made from the horn of a cow, kob or roan antelope. The instrument is held to the mouth in a near horizontal position so that the forefinger of the right hand is able to stop the open tip, while the fingers of the left hand are placed over the bell. In the Zaria, Kano and Katsina areas the horn, played alone or with the *kakaki* (long metal trumpet), *farai* (short wooden trumpet) and *gangar fada* (royal drum: *see* GANGA, (1)), is used by musicians of an emir to perform praises in his honour. In the Sokoto and Zamfara regions, where the instrument is known as *kafo*, it is also used by hunters for signalling and, with the *gangar noma* (cylindrical drum), to encourage farm work.

BIBLIOGRAPHY
Ames–KingGHM
P. G. Harris: 'Notes on Drums and Musical Instruments seen in Sokoto Province, Nigeria', *Journal of the Royal Anthropological Institute*, lxii (1932), 105
K. Krieger: 'Musikinstrumente der Hausa', *Baessler-Archiv*, new ser., xvi (1968), 373–430
F. E. Besmer: *Kidan Daran Salla: Music for the Eve of the Muslim Festivals of Id-al-Fitr and Id-al-Kabir in Kano, Nigeria* (Bloomington, Ind., 1974)

K. A. GOURLAY

Kaiccilampu [kaichilambu]. Pair of 'rattling rings' (or jingles) of south India. The rings are elliptical and contain metal pellets; they are worn on the wrists or around the fingers of each hand (*kai*) and are shaken to produce a rhythmic accompaniment to devotional singing and the dance *kaiccilampu paṭṭu*. They are similar to the *silampu* of Tamil Nadu. *See also* NŪPUR.

Kaimaṇi. *See* JĀLRA.

Kaipucha. Small bronze gong of Bhaktapur, India. *See* TAIM NĀIM.

Kairak. *See* QAIRAQ.

Kaiserbaryton (Ger.: 'imperial euphonium'). A wide-bore completely conical baritone invented by V. F. Červený of Hradec Králové in 1882. It was oval or tuba-

1. Kakaki (trumpet) of the Hausa people, Nigeria

shaped, pitched in either B♭ or C and had four rotary valves; its compass was *D–d″* and its tone softer and fuller than that of the normal baritone. Červený also produced a Kaiserbass (1883, a bombardon in F, E♭, C or B♭) and a Kaisertenor (1885, a tenor horn in C or B♭).

Káistatkos kastaweh'shae' (Seneca: 'tin rattle'). Vessel rattle of the Iroquois Indians of north-eastern North America. It consists of a baking powder tin or large condensed milk tin filled with pebbles or corn kernels, mounted on a wooden handle; it may be from 20 to 38 cm long. It is used as a temporary substitute for the large turtle rattle, KANYÁHTE' KÁ'NOWA'.

MARY RIEMER-WELLER

Kaita. Variant spelling of GAITA.

Kaithros. One of the BIBLICAL INSTRUMENTS. It is mentioned as one of the instruments heard at Nebuchadnezzar's court (*Daniel* iii). It would seem likely that the word is an Aramaic approximation to the Greek kithara, and the *kaithros* may therefore have been a lyre.

Kajakiri. Single-headed open-ended conical drum of the Valley Tonga people of Gwembe district, Zambia. It is one of the three MILUPA drums. A similar drum of the same name is played by the neighbouring Lozi and Mbunda peoples.

Kajamba. Rattle of the Bondei people of Tanzania.

Kajeomak. Single-headed cylindrical drum of th Mentawei Islands, Indonesia. *See* KATEOBAK.

Kájga [kayga]. BOX ZITHER of the Mordvin people o the Volga-Ural region (USSR). *See* GUSLI.

Kajimba. LAMELLAPHONE of the Luvale people o southern Africa. *See* KALIMBA (i).

Kajumba. Royal drum of the Nyoro and Toro people of Uganda. *See* UGANDA DRUM.

Kakaki. The most common name for the exceptionall long metal trumpet found in West Africa (see fig.1). is used in the ceremonial music of certain tradition states in the east and south of the Republic of Nige the central and northern zones of Nigeria, central Cam eroon, and parts of Chad and the Central Africa Republic. It is normally associated with Islam.

The earliest known reference to the instrument is b the 16th-century historian Mahmoud Kâti in an accou of the conquest of Aïr (now in Niger) by the army o the Songhay emperor Askia Mohammed I. During th 15th and 16th centuries the expansion of the Songha empire (with its capital at Gao on the Niger) led to th spread of the instrument eastwards via the Hausa state and Borno to beyond Lake Chad and south-eastwar down the Niger valley via the former Nupe state beyond the river's confluence with the Benue. Its ado tion by the Hausa states of the 17th and 18th centuri as part of the regalia of kingship established it as a roy instrument throughout the areas of their influence. Aft the jihad of Usuman Dan Fodiyo (early 19th century) Fulani emirs who had control of the Hausa kingdoms adopted not only the traditional Hausa administrative organization, but also the associated regalia including the *kakaki*. It either replaced or was used in conjunction with long trumpets of wood or cane, such as those seen in the 1820s by the explorers Denham and Clapperton at the courts of Kukawa, Mandara and Logone.

The status of the instrument was reinforced in the following period and its use spread in neighbouring areas, including those which in many respects remained hostile to the growing cultural and political influence of the Hausa emirates. The exclusive association of the *kakaki* with kingship (or an equivalent degree of authority) is reflected in two traditional Hausa *kirari*, identifying praise epithets: *kakaki busan mutum 'daya* ('*kakaki*, blown for one man alone'); and *barawon kakaki ba shi da iko ya busa shi* ('he who steals a *kakaki* nonetheless has no authority to blow it').

In both form and usage the Hausa *kakaki* has become a model for practices over a considerable area of West Africa. In Nigeria the Nupe people refer to the instrument as *kakati* and Edo-speakers as *kaki*, while to peoples around Lake Chad (including the Kanuri of Nigeria, the Mului of Chad and the sedentary Fulani of northern Cameroon), it is known variously as *kashi*, *gashi*, *gachi*, *gatshi* or *gatci*. Although the etymology of *kakaki* remains a mystery, *gashi* etc would appear to be connected with the Hausa praise-words 'ga shi' meaning 'see him', which are frequently 'blown' on the instrument to announce the appearance of a high official; this usage was first recorded of the Sultan of Borno in the 1850s by the German traveller, Heinrich Barth (1857).

The *kakaki* is usually made from kerosene tins, more rarely from large brass measuring pans. Gold and silver trumpets are mentioned in legends which should, perhaps, not be taken too literally. Normally made in two detachable sections of approximately equal length, the whole instrument is between 2 and 4 metres long. A typical example from the emirate of Katsina in Nigeria consists of a mouthpiece section formed from three tubes soldered together (total length about 1·25 metres) with a fairly uniform bore of about 25 mm; and a bell section formed from two tubes (total length about 1·25 metres) and a bore which increases from 25 mm at the junction with the mouthpiece section to 70 mm at the start of the actual bell and 100 mm at the end of the instrument. An unusual instrument from Niger has two bells branching from the narrow stem. The trumpet's 2nd and 3rd partials, forming an interval of between a perfect and an augmented 5th (approximately 750 cents), are the two principal notes blown. The 2nd partial of a *kakaki* such as that described is around *c*, with a frequency of about 130 Hz. A third note, rarely used, is produced from the 2nd partial but is pitched about a semitone below it.

In performance the player is either standing or on horseback, with the trumpet held to his mouth in a near horizontal position by one hand and supported part way down the stem by the extended other hand. The *kakaki* may at times be blown as a solo instrument (e.g. for the Emir of Zaria, Nigeria, or at Kano Airport to herald the arrival or departure of high officials) but is normally used in groups of four or more with matching groups of the double-headed cylindrical GANGA drums. Their performance is based on the linguistic tones and syllabic quantities of an unverbalized text, the *take*, in praise of an official patron. This is frequently divided into a solo

2. Kakaki (trumpet), algaita (oboes) and ganga (drum) of the Fulani people, Tungo, Cameroon, 1963

statement and a chorus response; the solo trumpet is pitched about a semitone below the chorus trumpets, as in ex.1. This *take* was formerly performed for the installation of the head of Kusada District in Katsina Emirate, Nigeria. Acute and grave accents mark high- and low-tone syllables in the text, the sequence of long and short syllables is shown in the scansion, and the small note heads on the top staff represent secondary strokes used either to fill in long syllables or to complete a phrase before its repetition.

Ex.1 Drum and trumpet *take* for the head of Kusada District, Katsina Emirate.

Often included with the *kakaki* and *ganga* is the *algaita* (oboe; see fig.2). Other instruments in the ensemble vary according to locality and may include the *kuge* (clapperless bell), *farai* (wooden trumpet) and *kaho* (side-blown trumpet). As the *kakaki* itself is generally associated with kingship and its blaring timbre and deep tone are immediately recognized as symbolic of status, it is blown only on ceremonial occasions, such as the Thursday evening salutation to the ruler, the procession to the mosque the following day, and the great parades accompanying the major Islamic festivals. Former uses include signalling in warfare; for example, among the Nupe of Nigeria it would signal the order to charge. Although today the *kakaki* is almost entirely associated with Islamic functions, this has not always been so: at the end of the 19th century the Chief of Illo at Girris (now on the Nigeria-Benin border) ordered a blast from twelve trumpeters to drive away evil spirits.

The instrument itself is probably much older and considerably more widespread in distribution than its documented history would indicate. A depiction of a Roman *tuba* on Trajan's Column, Rome (AD 113; for illustration see TUBA (ii)), bears a remarkable resemblance to the *kakaki*, as do trumpets shown in an Egyptian military band of the 14th century, in China in the later Middle Ages, and in the mouths of Giotto's angels in the painting *The Crowning of the Virgin* (c1317). It can be assumed that the long metal trumpet, if not its name, reached West Africa from the north.

There may be a relationship between the West African *kakaki* and the Maghribi *nfīr*, which Chottin (1927) suggested was devised by the Moors in Spain and introduced in the mid-14th century into Fez, from where it spread throughout the Maghrib. He also suggested that

it was initially used as a military instrument but later acquired a religious role, being blown from the tops of minarets during the nights of Ramadan. However, he described the *nfīr* as producing only a single note, unlike the *kakaki*, whether blown singly or in pairs.

BIBLIOGRAPHY

Ames–KingGHM

H. Barth: *Travels and Discoveries in North and Central Africa* (London, 1857/R1967)

O. Houdas and M. Delafosse, eds.: *Mahmoud Kâti: Tarikh el-fettach* (Paris, 1913/R1964), 135f

A. Chottin: 'Note sur le "Nfîr" (trompette du Ramadan)', *Hespéris*, vii (1927), 376

P. G. Harris: 'Notes on Drums and Musical Instruments Seen in Sokoto Province, Nigeria', *Journal of the Royal Anthropological Institute*, lxii (1932), 105

S. F. Nadel: *A Black Byzantium* (London, 1942)

A. Schaeffner: 'Timbales et longues trompettes', *Bulletin de l'Institut français d'Afrique noire*, xiv (1952), 1466

K. Krieger: 'Musikinstrumente der Hausa', *Baessler-Archiv*, new ser., xvi (1968), 373–430

F. E. Besmer: *Kidan Daran Salla: Music for the Eve of the Muslim Festivals of Id-al-Fitr and Id-al-Kabir in Kano, Nigeria* (Bloomington, Ind., 1974)

C. Duvelle and M. Vuylstèke: 'Anthologie de la musique du Tchad', OCR 36–8 [disc notes]

ANTHONY KING/R

Kakalari. GROUND ZITHER of the Logo people of Zaïre (*LaurentyC*, 110). See KUDREKENE.

Kakati. Long metal trumpet of the Nupe people of Nigeria. See KAKAKI.

Ká'keeta' (Seneca: 'flute' or 'whistle'). Whistle of the Iroquois Indians of north-eastern North America. It is made of cane, about 45 cm long, and it has an external duct, like the COURTING FLUTE, but no finger-holes. Only two notes are produced, the fundamental and its overblown octave. It is used only during the ceremony of the Little Water Medicine Society and in the Eagle Dance, a curing ritual.

MARY RIEMER-WELLER

Kakel-kultrún. Double-headed drum of the Chilean Araucanian Indians. See CAQUEL-KULTRÚN.

Kaki. Long metal trumpet of the Edo/Bini peoples of Nigeria. See KAKAKI.

Kakko. Japanese cylindrical or barrel-shaped drum. It is used in the *tōgaku* genre of gagaku (court music). The heads are lapped on to iron rings before being laced to the body (see TAIKO). The body of the drum is about 15 cm in diameter and 30 cm long; the head diameter is 23 cm. Since its introduction from China (by the 8th century), the *kakko* has gradually become the leading rhythm instrument of *tōgaku*. It is set horizontally on a low stand in front of the player, who strikes the heads with two thin sticks (see illustration). When substituting for the IKKO hourglass drum, it adopts the playing method of that drum, and only the right-hand stick is used. The *kakko* plays only three named patterns, but these serve to set the rhythm for the entire ensemble. It is occasionally used in *geza* (off-stage music of the kabuki theatre), to set the mood in scenes at the imperial court, and smaller versions are used as dance properties in nō, kabuki and some folk traditions.

The name *kakko* is written with the same Chinese characters as the Korean *kalgo*, but there seems to be

Kakko (barrel drum) used in gagaku (court music), Japan

...o historical connection; pronounced *jiegu* in Chinese, ...ne characters have historically referred to a variety of ...ypes of drum.

DAVID W. HUGHES

Kakolondondo [kakolondondd, kakolondond, kako-...ondd]. Board-type LAMELLAPHONE of the Chokwe, ...unda, Pende, Sandoa and Akwa-Songo peoples of Zaïre. ...he base is usually rectangular and decorated with panels ...f incised patterns. Instruments are usually played over ...calabash or similar vessel serving as a resonator. Other ...ames reported by Laurenty for this type of instrument ...re *minungu, isanj, kadimba, kibinjj, lungandu, mujem-...a, muyembba, lusukia, lukangu* and *buka-...anga* (*LaurentyS*, 195).

PETER COOKE

Kakonti. Bamboo instrument, combining elements of ...n idiophone and aerophone, of the Sula Islands, Indo-...esia. *See* RERE.

Kakosh. Fiddle of the Holo people of Zaïre (*LaurentyC*, ...22). *See* KALEMBETE.

Kakoxa. Two-string fiddle of Angola.

Kakubi. Side-blown ivory trumpet of the Hunde peo-...le of eastern Zaïre. It has a carved mouthpiece and ...ointed tip (*LaurentyA*, 422).

Kakulumbumba. Braced MUSICAL BOW of the Lunda ...eople of Zaïre. It has an attached half-calabash resona-...or. The instrument is held vertically near the lower end ...n the left hand in such a way that the middle finger can ...e extended to touch the string lightly. The calabash is ...laced on the chest of the player and raised from time

to time to modulate the tone. The bow is essentially a solo instrument for the accompaniment of singing. Other names reported are: *lungungu, lukungu, ngwosto, dik-upu, akaheto* and *indono.*

BIBLIOGRAPHY
LaurentyC, 113
F. J. de Hen: *Beitrag zur Kenntnis der Musikinstrumente aus Bel-gisch Kongo und Ruanda-Urundi* (Tervuren, 1960)

Kakwumm. Double clapperless bell of the Makere people of Zaïre. *See* GONGA (i).

Kal. Name given to the *ŏ*, a Korean wooden SCRAPER in the form of a sitting tiger, only when it is used in the *tŭngga* ('terrace ensemble') at performances of ritual music (*aak*) for sacrificial rites. *See* Ŏ.

Kala. Ankle rattles of the Kanem and Ouaddai areas of northern Chad. Each anklet is made of three or four large palmyra nuts with seeds or date stones inside. The rat-tles are used exclusively by men of prisoner descent for dancing accompanied by *dangala* (drums). For illustra-tion *see* DANGALI.

Kālā'au. Concussion sticks of Hawaii. They are made from two rods of hard, resonant wood; although tradi-tionally *kauila* (*Alphitonia ponderosa*) was used, now rosewood and coffee are also used. The older form of the instrument requires one rod about a metre long, and another about a third as long, both slightly thicker in the middle and tapered at each end. Using the left-hand fingers, the player holds the long rod loosely at the centre, balancing it over the left forearm, and beats a simple rhythm on the rod's extended portion with the short rod held in the right hand. A newer form dating from the 1870s is a matched pair of rods the size and shape of the smaller of the older rods. For illustration *see* PAPA HEHI.

ZANETA HO'OŪLU CAMBRA

Kalaka. A Basque cog rattle. Placed on a support about 2 metres high, it is sounded by the motion of the wind and serves to frighten birds from planted fields.

Kalaki. Side-blown trumpet of Chad. *See* BETENE.

Kalali. Single-headed HOURGLASS DRUM of the Kotoko people of central Chad. The body is of wood and is about 45 cm long and 15 cm in diameter. The mem-brane is made from the skin of a monitor lizard (*Var-anus niloticus*), an animal sacred to the Kotoko; it is tightened by a ring of cowhide and attached by lacing of hippopotamus skin. The *kalali* is slung from the shoulder and held under the left arm of the drummer, who beats it with bare hands (see illustration, p.350). The drummer is always male. These drums are played in pairs on important occasions concerning the Kotoko community. For more private entertainment, *ganga* and *bandil* drums are played; if the *kalali* is played for a private festival, only one is used. The *kalali* are public property; they are combined with a pair of *betene* trum-pets and accompany men's choruses, especially for war songs (for illustration *see* BETENE). In some Kotoko dia-lects these drums are called *buli* or *kodam* and the trum-pets *mongom* or *kalaki*. The *kalali* are described

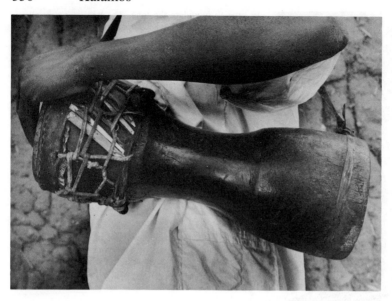

Kalali (hourglass drum of the Kotoko people, central Chad

anthropomorphically: the narrow section is the waist, the lower section the rump, the upper section the head, and the skin is the mouth.

MONIQUE BRANDILY

Kalamos (Gk.; pl. *kalamoi*; Lat. *calamus*). A term used in antiquity for various aerophones; *see* AULOS, §2. Theocritus and Virgil use the word for reference to the individual pipes of the syrinx or fistula, the panpipes. The plural *kalamoi* (or *calami*) is an alternative word for the instrument itself. Apuleius noted an *oblicus* (*obliquus*) *calamus* which 'reached to the right ear of the piper' (*Metamorphoses*, xi, chap.9) and was used in the worship of Isis. This was probably the *monaulos*, which had a reed mouthpiece set into the single tube at an angle and a recurved bell.

ROBERT ANDERSON

Kalangba. XYLOPHONE of central Africa. (1) Calabash-resonated xylophone of the Togbo and Mono peoples of Zaïre. The Mono also call this instrument *karangba*; the Ngbandi call it *kalangwa* or *menza gwe* and the Gobu *baza*. These xylophones are similar to the *madimba* (*see* MADIMBA (i)) but each key has its own isolating cushion, instead of a strip of fibre, to separate it from the wooden frame. Some Ngbandi and Togbo instruments have nine or ten keys; smaller Ngbandi and the Yakpa instruments have five.

(2) Ten-key xylophone of the Linda people of the Central African Republic. The keys are strung together by a raffia suspension rope and are mounted on a frame containing calabash resonators. The keys are struck with two beaters, one held in each hand. The instrument is used to accompany dancing.

(3) Small five-key portable xylophone of the Ndokpa people of the Central African Republic. It is used for playing dance rhythms, sometimes with another xylophone, the *lingassio*.

BIBLIOGRAPHY

BooneX
F. J. de Hen: *Beitrag zur Kenntnis der Musikinstrumente aus Belgisch Kongo und Ruanda-Urundi* (Tervuren, 1960)
C. Duvelle: 'République Centrafricaine', OCR 11 [disc notes]
K. A. GOURLAY

Kalangu [kalanggual, kalungu, danko]. Double-headed HOURGLASS DRUM of West Africa, known principally among the Hausa people of Nigeria, who call the drum *kalangu* or *kalungu*. It is a variable tension drum, held under the arm and beaten with a hooked stick. The drum is of medium size for an hourglass drum, being about 35 cm long, 17 cm in diameter at each end and 8 cm in diameter at the waist. The past and present patrons of Hausa *kalangu* drumming are butchers. Originally the drum was associated exclusively with them, but today it is used for drumming not only their praise epithets but also those of boxers and of young people, and is used to accompany young girls' dancing and by popular freelance professional musicians such as Alhaji Muhamman Shata. The main additional occasions of performance are at name and marriage ceremonies and during co-operative farm work; in the Sokoto and Zamfara areas the drum is used with single-string GOGE fiddles and calabash or metal percussion vessels in music and dance of the *bori* spirit possession cult.

In the performance of praise epithets the Hausa drum may be used solo but is more often played with a fixed-pitch hourglass drum, *dan karbi*, and the small *kuntuku* kettledrum. The *dan karbi* is strapped to the thigh of the *kalangu* player, who beats both drums. A smaller version of the *kalangu*, the *karamar kalangu*, is played in the market both by amateur freelance musicians, sometimes to promote trade for butchers, and by professional satirists (*yan gambara*). Other Nigerian peoples use the *kalangu* (or *kalangu*-type) drums to accompany dancing, including the Bolewa, Batonobu (Borgawa), Kambari, Gwari and Fulani (who refer to the drum as *kalanggual*). The Busa and Kenga peoples employ the drum for *bori* dancing at the conclusion of a lengthy funeral feast. The Dakakar *kalangu* is used traditionally for drumming on the death of noted warriors and their immediate kin, and the Nupe version of the instrument, the *danko*, is used together with a very small *kalangu*-type drum, the *munugi*, by royal musicians on Muslim festivals, Fridays and other important occasions.

See also JAUJE; KAZAGI; KOLO (i); KOTSO; KURKUTU; TAMA.

BIBLIOGRAPHY
nes–KingGHM
C. Duff and W. Hamilton-Browne: *Gazetteer of the Kontagora Province* (London, 1920)
G. Harris: 'Notes on Drums and Musical Instruments seen in Sokoto Province, Nigeria', *Journal of the Royal Anthropological Institute*, lxii (1932), 105
W. Ames: 'Hausa Drums of Zaria', *Ibadan*, xxi (1965), 62
Krieger: 'Musikinstrumente der Hausa', *Baessler-Archiv*, new ser., xvi (1968), 373–430
Harper: 'A Festival of Nigerian Dances', *African Arts*, iii/2 (1970), 48
King: 'Hausa Music', *Grove 6*
—: 'Nigeria', *Grove 6*
Newman and E. H. Davidson: 'Music from the Villages of North-eastern Nigeria', AHM 4532 [disc notes]

K. A. GOURLAY

alangwa. *See* MENZA GWE.

alapácsos kereplő. Hammer-clapper of Hungary. It onsists of a wooden hammer swinging on a shaft and inging on a wooden board (see illustration). It is used Catholic church services as a substitute for bells.

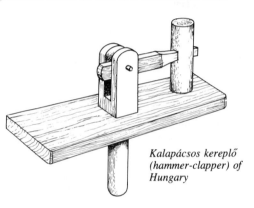

Kalapácsos kereplő (hammer-clapper) of Hungary

alaśa. Jingles attached to the HUḌUKKĀ (variable ten-ion drum) of India.

aleidophon [Kaleidosphon] **(i).** A monophonic elec-onic keyboard instrument invented by JÖRG MAGER.

aleidophon (ii). A SYNTHESIZER controller developed y the British musician David Vorhaus (*b* Los Angeles, 4 Sept 1943) in London between 1972 and 1974. It :sembles the neck and fingerboard of a fretless bass uitar, and is held almost vertically in front of the play-r, supported by a strap. Instead of strings there are four uch-sensitive flat plastic strips which are fingered with ie left hand. The range and compass of each strip is djustable, and it is possible to create the equivalent of ets and half-frets electronically. Unlike the guitar, owever, the spacing of the intervals is linear, remain-ig identical throughout the range, and only one strip t a time can trigger a signal. The right hand operates nobs, switches and a joystick at the lower end of the istrument. Up to three oscillators can be connected to ie fingerboard to produce three-note chords moving in arallel with the notes fingered on one strip; the inter-als making up the chords are determined by the posi-on of the joystick within the two interlocked dimensions which it can move. The joystick can also control any vo of several other aspects besides interval (timbre,

volume, attack etc). The Kaleidophon can be linked either to the small synthesizer specially built for it or to other synthesizers. Vorhaus has also achieved considerable success with three record albums produced under the title *White Noise* in his own electronic music studio.

BIBLIOGRAPHY
S. Steward: 'Shozygs, Springboards, Squeakboxes and Other Musi-cal Instruments', *Sound International*, no.29 (1980), 43
D. Ellis: 'David Vorhaus and Kaleidophon Studios', *Electronics & Music Maker*, i/3 (1981), 74

HUGH DAVIES

Kaleleng (i). *See* RERE.

Kaleleng (ii). NOSE FLUTE of the Bontok people of the northern Philippines.

Kalembete. Two-string fiddle of the Holo and Suku peoples of north-western Zaïre. The resonator is carved from a cylindrical piece of wood, the upper face of which is replaced by a soundtable of thin, pliable wood. The short, thick neck terminates in a carved head. Two tuning-pegs pierce the head laterally and a string from each passes over a wooden bridge on the soundtable and is fastened to a knob projecting from the other end of the cylinder. The instrument's total length is 50 cm and the resonator is 30 cm long and 10 cm in diameter. The strings are made from vegetable fibre, as is the bow-string, which is about 35 cm long and attached to each end of a curved stick. In performance the instrument is placed on the ground or held horizontally against the player's chest. It is played for entertainment. Among some groups of the Holo the instrument is known as *kakosh*. Similar anthropomorphic instruments known as *kalyakalya* or *kalyalya* were formerly reported from the Lunda and Chokwe peoples but, apparently, are no longer found.

See also TARATIBU.

BIBLIOGRAPHY
LaurentyC, 122
F. J. de Hen: *Beitrag zur Kenntnis der Musikinstrumente aus Bel-gisch Kongo und Ruanda-Urundi* (Tervuren, 1960)
G. Knosp: *Enquête sur la vie musicale au Congo belge 1934–1935* (Tervuren, 1968)

K. A. GOURLAY

Kalgo. Obsolete double-headed HOURGLASS DRUM of Korea (*kal*: 'deerskin'; *go*: 'drum'). In construction it closely resembled the CHANGGO, though it had twice as many leather sleeves for adjusting head-tension and thin skins for both heads. The player struck both heads with thin bamboo sticks.

The name *kalgo* appears in official writings as early as 1505, when the king ordered that a large number of the instruments should be constructed. The earliest depictions appear in early 19th-century illustrated books of rubrics for performance at court banquets. The *kalgo* has not been used since the end of the 19th century.

The Japanese KAKKO has the same pictographs as the Chinese *kalgo*, but it is much smaller and perhaps unre-lated in evolution. The Chinese *jiegu* (also written with the same pictographs) appears to be a completely dif-ferent instrument, at least as represented in Wang Chi's *Sancai tuhui* ('Collected illustrations of the three powers of nature') of 1607.

BIBLIOGRAPHY
Hayashi Kenzō: *Dongya yueqi kao* [Investigations of East Asian musical instruments] (Beijing, 1962), 92ff
Chang Sa-hun: *Han'guk akki taegwan* [Korean musical instruments] (Seoul, 1969), 131

L. Picken: 'T'ang Music and Musical Instruments', *T'oung Pao*, lv (1969), 103

ROBERT C. PROVINE

Kaligo [mngoli]. Single-string fiddle of south-eastern Africa.

Kalimba (i). LAMELLAPHONE of eastern, central and south-western Africa. Its wide occurrence and its relationship with many other types of lamellaphone indicate that it may be an early progenitor of the lamellaphone family of these regions. A smaller type, with 8 to 14 or more keys, played with the thumbs and held over a small gourd, is played to the north of the Zambezi; a larger type, with 14 to 25 keys, held inside a large calabash and played with the thumbs and index finger, is played to the south of the Zambezi. Among the peoples using it are the Kunda (Chikunda), Nyanja/Chewa, Tumbuka/Henga, Ngoni, Shona, Aushi, Bisa, Lala, Swaka, Nsenga, Sena/Tonga and Nyungwe. Variants of the term include *kadimba*, *kajimba* and *karimba* (*see also* KAKOLONDONDO).

BIBLIOGRAPHY
H. Tracey: 'A Case for the Name Mbira', *African Music*, ii/4 (1961), 17

ANDREW TRACEY, DAVID K. RYCROFT

Kalimba (ii). BOARD ZITHER of the Bemba and Shila peoples of Zaïre. *See* IKIDI.

Kalinga. (1) Royal drum of the chief of the Havu people of eastern Zaïre (*BooneT*, 66).
(2) Drum of the Tutsi people of Rwanda. *See* INGABE.

Kalkant (Ger.). An accessory stop-lever on German organs; *see* ORGAN STOP.

Kalluraq. *See* KALUKHAQ.

Kalondang. XYLOPHONE of Pakpak Dairi, North Sumatra. It has between six and twelve tuned wooden keys (nine are required for a complete set), either suspended or placed in a wooden frame. It is played by two or four performers, either as a solo instrument for shamanistic practices (for example to cure a sick person) or together with a *sordam* (oboe), a *pelobat* or *lobat* (flutes) or a small gong. See L. Moore: 'An Introduction to the Music of the Pakpak Dairi of North Sumatra', *Indonesia Circle* (1981), no.24, pp.41f.

MARGARET J. KARTOMI

Kalophone. An improved flute, using the Boehm system, built by WILHELM HECKEL around 1900.

Kalove. MOUTH BOW of Florida Islands, near Guadalcanal, Solomon Islands, made from a hollow reed about 40 cm long. Two strings were tuned in unison and kept from touching the bowstick by small bridges of reed. One string was permanently stopped and the other alternately stopped and released with the fingers of the left hand to produce three notes. The curved back of the bow was held in the teeth and the strings sounded by plucking them with a plectrum held in the right hand. See R. H. Codrington: *The Melanesians* (New Haven, 1957), 339.

MERVYN McLEAN

Kalsa. Flat gong in a SULIBAO ensemble of the norther Philippines.

Kaltsang. BOARD ZITHER of the Ibaloi people of th northern Philippines. It has four wire strings which a plucked.

Kalukhaq [kalluraq, kaylukuk, kotlookuk]. Ceremoni box drum associated with the Messenger Feast of th Inupiaq-speaking people of Alaska. It consists of a re tangular wooden case, which may be from 45 to 90 c deep, with a decorative zigzag top edge and eagle feath ers. A fur-padded rail along one side is struck with short stick. The drum is suspended from the roof an played by a seated drummer.
In the myth which explains the origin of the feast th drum is said to represent an eagle's heartbeat.

BEVERLEY CAVANAG

Kalumbu. Braced gourd MUSICAL BOW of the Tong people of Zambia.

Kalumpemba. Cuban FRICTION DRUM with a flexibl stick, used by the Musundi Congos; of African prove nance, it appears in mortuary rituals or with magic rite (*OrtizIMA*, v, 202f).

Kalungu. *See* KALANGU.

Kalur. Gourd cone whistle of the Copi people c Uganda. *See* KILUKA.

Kalutang. Concussion sticks of the Hanunoo people o the southern Philippines. They are played in pairs t produce harmonics of 2nds, 3rds or 4ths.

Kalyakalya [kalyalya]. Fiddle of the Lunda and Chokw peoples of Zaïre (*LaurentyC*, 122). *See* KALEMBETE.

Kama. Wicker vessel rattle of the Kaka people of th Central African Republic. *See also* HENTSHI.

Kamāc [kamāci]. Smaller version of the long-necke lute DANBŪRO of the Sind and Baluchistan regions c Pakistan.

Kamāicā [kamāic, kumāic, kamāyachā]. Heavy, shor necked fiddle of Rajasthan, north-west India (see illus tration). The body, about 75 cm long, is carved from single piece of wood, and the resonator, with a goatski soundtable pasted over it, is hemispherical and over 3 cm wide. It is surmounted by a wooden ridge projectin around the back of the lower neck; the broad neck, rath er short, tapers towards an open pegbox, in which th main pegs are inserted laterally, in a carved rounde back-projection, crowned with a crest. There are two t four main playing strings, of gut and steel, which ar stopped by the fingernails on the side (as on th *sārangī*); there is also a variable number of steel sym pathetic strings, also bowed. All the strings are attache to a wooden bar held by an inferior integral hooked strin holder. The wooden bow is long and lightly curved.
The *kamāicā* is played by the Manghaniyar, a cast

Manghaniyar musicians playing kamāicā (short-necked fiddle) and khaŕtāl (wooden clappers), Jaisalmer region, west Rajasthan

both Hindu and Muslim) of musicians and reciters of western Rajasthan (they are also found in Sind, Pakistan), to accompany their own singing of bardic and devotional songs. The name *kumāic* is mentioned in a list of Rajasthani instruments in the early 18th-century epic poem *Hammīrarāso* of Jodhraj; it appears to be a variant of the Persian bow and fiddle name *kamānche* of the lute name *kamāc* of Sind; see DANBŪRO). Although it has clearly been influenced by the *sārangī*, and its neck made shorter, the *kamāicā* is almost identical with the long-necked plucked lute *rabāb*, an important court instrument of India until the 19th century (*see* RABĀB).

BIBLIOGRAPHY
K. S. Kothari: *Indian Folk Musical Instruments* (New Delhi, 1968)
K. Kothari: *Folk Musical Instruments of Rajasthan* (Borunda, 1977)
J. Dournon: 'Inde, Rajasthan: musiciens professionels populaires', Ocora OCR 81 [disc notes]
ALASTAIR DICK, NEIL SORRELL

K'aman. Fiddle of Armenia. It has a narrow rectangular body with a wooden belly and fingerboard, and is played held vertically on the knee. The three (sometimes four) metal strings do not have a fixed tuning, but are often tuned in 4ths. A special characteristic of the *k'aman* is the presence of sympathetic strings under the fingerboard, which are tuned either in unison with the main strings or an octave above them. The *k'aman* was one of the favourite instruments of the Armenian *ashughner* (folk poet-singers), but is now rarely encountered. It is also found in other countries of the Near East; *see* KEMENÇE and LYRA, §2.

ROBERT AT'AYAN

Kamāna al-baghdādiyya [al kamāna al-baghdādiyya]. Former name for the JOZE (spike fiddle).

Kamānche (Persian: 'little bow'). SPIKE FIDDLE of Iran and the Caucasus – Armenia (*k'amancha*), Azerbaijan and Georgia (*kemanche*) – also known in Turkey and Egypt as the RABĀB, in Iraq as the JOZE and in northern Afghanistan and parts of Central Asia as GHICHAK. The word is documented from the 10th century; the instrument reached Byzantium via Anatolia in the 11th or 12th century, and a 15th-century manuscript states that gut strings had been replaced by horsehair ones tuned a 5th

apart. Other early forms of the term are *kamānja agūz* ('old fiddle'), an obsolete Egyptian name, and *kamānja rūmī* ('Byzantine' or 'Anatolian fiddle'), which denotes the Greek *lyra* (*see* LYRA, §2), and in Turkey survives as *fasıl kemençesi* (*see* KEMENÇE).

The classical Caucasian and Iranian *kamānche* has a spherical body built of tapering wooden sections or carved in one piece; the type used in popular music may have a cone-shaped body open at the back, or be made of a spherical gourd. It is often decorated with mother-of-pearl and bone. The bridge rests on a circular sound-table which is made of animal membrane, bladder or fish-skin. The rounded neck is fixed to a spike which passes through the body and acts as a support for the instrument; the total length is usually 65 to 90 cm. Formerly the *kamānche* had three silk strings, while the modern classical instrument has four metal strings attached to wooden pegs (see fig.1). Originally they were tuned in 4ths; contemporary tuning is in 4ths and 5ths: *a–e'–a'–e''*. This tuning was standardized in Armenia by the virtuoso *k'amancha* player Sasha Oganezashvili (Aleksandr Oganyan) at the beginning of the 20th century. During performance the player rests the instrument vertically on the knee, and turns the instrument to meet the bow rather than guiding the bow across the strings, as in Western practice. The bow hair is tightened by inserting the fingers between the horsehair and the wood.

The classical *kamānche* in Iran dates from the 15th century or earlier (see fig.2, p.354), and was mentioned in Azerbaijan by Nezāmī Ganjavī (1141–1203). The Turkmen regard it as their principal instrument alongside the *dutār*, as do the Lors in south-west Iran, and it is also found among the Kurds in the north, and in Khorāsān. The *kamānche* is more widespread in the classical and folk traditions of the Caucasus and Central Asia than in Persian music. It is used for light music (*motrebi*), and is the only bowed string instrument in the classical tradition of Iran.

Because of its soft, beautiful timbre and technical possibilities, the *kamānche* is used equally as a solo or

1. Kamānche (spike fiddle) of Iran

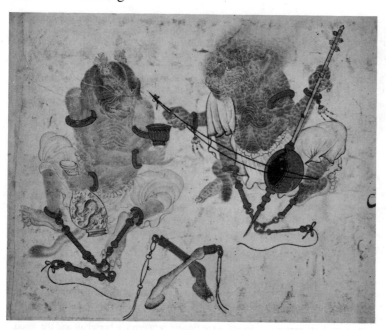

2. Kamānche played b a fettered demon: Persian painting, Turkmen or Timurid period, 15th century (Freer Gallery of Art, Washington, DC)

an ensemble instrument. At the end of the 1920s, the Armenian master Vardan Buni (Buniatyan) created a *k'amancha* family (soprano, alto, bass and double bass) which he used in the Erevan Oriental Symphony Orchestra. A well-known ensemble of *k'amancha* players using five instruments of varying sizes toured the USSR widely in the 1930s, led by the virtuoso Levon Karakhanyan.

The 18th-century *ashugh*-poet Sayat-Nova celebrated the *k'amancha* in a poem called *K'amancha*.

BIBLIOGRAPHY
VertkovA
N. Caron and D. Safvate: *Iran: les traditions musicales* (Paris, 1966)
J. Spector: 'Musical Tradition and Innovation', *Central Asia: a Century of Russian Rule*, ed. E. Allworth (New York, 1967), 434–84
J. During: *La musique iranienne: tradition et evolution* (in preparation)
JEAN DURING, ROBERT AT'AYAN, JOHANNA SPECTOR

Kamango. Single-headed GOBLET DRUM of the Nyanja/ Manganja people of southern Malawi. It is used exclusively for rituals connected with the chief.

Kamāyachā. See KAMĀICĀ.

Kambili. MUSICAL BOW with separate gourd resonator of the Lobo, Andedeme and Timogia peoples of Zaïre; it is also known as *gambili* and *kumbili* (*LaurentyC*, 113). See KITINGBI.

Kambre. Plucked lute of Sierra Leone. See GURMI.

Kā-mien. Flat bamboo JEW'S HARP, with idioglot tongue, of the Khasi people of Assam and Meghalay states, northeast India. See also MURCANG.

Kammerorgel (Ger.). CHAMBER ORGAN.

Kammerton (Ger.: 'chamber pitch'). The pitch at which chamber music was performed in Germany in the 18th century. See CAMMER-TON and PITCH.

Kampeko. End-blown trumpet of central Africa. See NYELE.

Kamrā [kamrikā]. Paired wooden or bamboo CLAPPERS described in Sanskrit texts of medieval India. They are of acacia wood or thick bamboo, about 24 cm long and 4 cm wide, and taper slightly at the end. They are played either with a pair in each hand, held loosely by the root of the thumb and middle finger and clapped by shaking the wrists, or with one pair held between the thumb and ring finger of the right hand and struck against the left thumb and fist. The diminutive *kamrikā* can also denote a wooden rod used to stop the medieval stick zither *ekatantrī vīṇā* (*see* VĪṆĀ, §4). See Śārṅgadeva: *Saṅgītaratnākara* (13th century), ed. S. Subrahmanya Sastri, iii (Madras, 1951).

ALASTAIR DICK

Kāṃsyatāla. Large cymbals of India described in the medieval *Saṅgītaratnākara*. See TĀL.

Kamu. Pot drum of the Kabre people of northern Togo. Two *kamu* are used with flutes and wooden drums in the rain dance.

Kamu-purui [gammu burui]. PANPIPES of the Cuna Indians of the San Blas Islands of Panama. The *kamu-purui* has seven bamboo tubes bound into groups of three and four tubes. The tuning of the tubes is distinctive, as is the manner in which they are played. The group of four tubes is tuned in ascending perfect 5ths and the group of three in descending perfect 5ths, with the higher notes of each group separated by an interval of a minor or major 2nd, or a major or minor 3rd. The musician holds the group of four tubes in his left hand and the group of three in his right, with the smallest tube of each group touching in the centre to form one solid row of tubes (see illustration). A single player can sound two notes simultaneously by blowing between the tubes, most often producing the interval of a perfect 5th.

The *kamu-purui* are constructed in pairs, as are nearly

ll Cuna flutes. They are designated male and female,
or man and wife, with the female tuned a major or minor
nd higher than the male. The male and female instru-
nents are played in hocket, the male leading and the
emale following, producing a composite melodic line
n parallel 5ths. Three or more pairs of musician-dancers
usually men, but sometimes mixed pairs) play the *kamu-
urui* while dancing. The instruments are not perfectly
uned to each other, so that unusual sonorities are pro-
uced. The *kamu-purui* is the only flute of the Cuna in
vhich the female instrument has as many notes as the
nale.

ROQUE CORDERO

Kanango [kannango]. Double-headed HOURGLASS DRUM
f the Yoruba people of Nigeria. *See* DUNDUN.

Kanásztülök. *See* TÜLÖK.

Kanbiwa. Japanese term for the Chinese *pipa* of the
Han dynasty. *See* BIWA, §1.

Kañcam [kancatālam, kanjam]. Small metal cymbals
of south India. They are also called *tālam*, and have
een equated with the ancient cymbals *pāṇṭil*. For generic
discussion of South Asian cymbals, *see* TĀL.

Kanci. Pair of iron or brass cup-cymbals of the Bug-
nese and Makassar areas of the province of South
Sulawesi. They are played with *genrang* (drums) and
a *lea-lea* (tube zither) to accompany dancing at weddings and other festivities.

Kandara. HOURGLASS DRUM of the Marindanim people
n Irian Jaya (West New Guinea). Its narrow cylindrical
waist widens towards each end, and a handle forming
a rectangle is attached to the middle. The drums vary
n size from 10 cm to over 1·5 metres. A glue consisting
of mixed lime, blood and urine fixes the skin to the
body. Iguana or kangaroo skin is used. The sound is
mproved by placing tiny spider secretion balls on the
drumhead, which is tautened by warming it over a fire.
See J. Kunst: *Music in New Guinea* (The Hague, 1967),
167f.

MARGARET J. KARTOMI

Kāṇḍavīṇā. A STICK ZITHER or TUBE ZITHER of ancient
ndia. *See* VĪṆĀ, §1.

*Kamu-purui (panpipes) played by Cuna Indians, Pan-
ama*

Kandiri kandiri. Braced MOUTH BOW of the Balese
people of Zaïre, also known as *undemoü* (*LaurentyC*,
113). *See* BOMBO (iv).

Kane. A generic term for various types of Japanese
METALLOPHONE; compound forms take the suffix *-gane*
('metal'). It has two main sub-meanings, distinguished
in writing – 'gong' and 'bell'; in practice, however, these
categories are not so distinct. *Kane* is also used in some
areas to refer to cymbals (*see* CHAPPA). The pitch of the
instruments is not musically significant: they are never
tuned to other instruments, nor do they play melodies.
(An unimportant exception is the *unra* (Chin. *yunluo*),
which was rarely used in Japan.) On instruments using
multiple *kane* (e.g. *orugōru*, *matsumushi*) is important only that their pitches differ.

Most Japanese gongs and bells are comparatively thick-
walled for their size. Most are closely associated with
Buddhism, whether in present practice or in origin, and
a large number are also used in *geza* (music of the kabuki theatre) for sound-effects – particularly to evoke a
Buddhist setting or mood. Although *kane* are also frequently encountered in folk music, they are less common in secular urban music than in China. The name
for a single type of *kane* frequently varies between different sects of Buddhism or in different regions, and the
same term may also designate different *kane*. Despite
this, and the questionable distinction between 'gong' and
'bell' mentioned above, it will still be useful to give an
idea of the basic forms of *kane*.

(1) The most common gong is thick-walled and somewhat resembles a shallow flat-top hat with a narrow brim.
They are usually of brass or bronze (occasionally iron)
and have a short reverberation time. They may vary in
diameter from about 8 cm to 60 cm. The upper surface
is slightly convex in most cases. Such gongs either rest
horizontally on three tiny feet on the rim (e.g. *hitotsu-
gane*, *matsumushi*) or are suspended vertically by a cord
or cords attached to two or more small 'ears' on the side
walls (e.g. *shōko*, *sōban*). The latter variety may be struck
either on the convex surface or from the inside. The
most highly developed gong music is that of the SURI-
GANE of *matsuri-bayashi*.

(2) Less common is the thin-walled, very shallow,
hanging gong called DORA, or sometimes *nyō*. These
come in various sizes and proportions, and many have
a central boss. They are always struck on the outside
face or occasionally on the rim.

(3) The thick-walled 'temple bell' category includes
clapperless deep-bowl bells suspended mouth-downward;
they are struck on the outside with the end of a horizontally suspended swinging log (*see* BELL (i), fig.9).
Sometimes called collectively *shō* (Chin. *zhong*), these
bronze bells range from about 30 cm to 150 cm in depth.
They are often highly decorated on the exterior with lines
and rows of knobs. They have a characteristic profile
and do not flare at the mouth. Examples are the BONSHŌ
and the *hontsurigane*.

(4) The spherical slit-bell type, resembling a Western
'jingle-bell' or crotal, is generally called SUZU. These
may have a pellet inside, or they may be empty and ring
only when several are rattled together. Some types, like
the *nyō* slit-bell, may have a handle. They can range in
size from about 2 cm to 30 cm.

(5) The large Buddhist bowl-bell, the *kin* (*see* KIN
(ii)), sits mouth-upward on a cushion and is struck on
the rim with a wrapped stick, giving a gentle and lin-

gering sound. It comes in a small size for home use and also in a form with a handle (*inkin*).

(6) The REI, a small Buddhist handbell, is the only common bell with a clapper of traditional Japan.

Among the various other types of *kane* are the WANI-GUCHI, a circular slit-gong, the KEI, a Buddhist percussion plaque, and the DŌTAKU, an ancient bronze bell.

BIBLIOGRAPHY

W. P. Malm: *Japanese Music and Musical Instruments* (Rutland, Vermont, 1959)
S. Kishibe: *The Traditional Music of Japan* (Tokyo, 1966/R1982)
E. Harich-Schneider: *A History of Japanese Music* (London, 1973)
F. Koizumi, Y. Tokumaru and O. Yamaguchi, eds.: *Asian Musics in an Asian Perspective* (Tokyo, 1977), 177
Tōyō Ongaku Gakkai [Society for Asian Music]: *Kabuki ongaku* [Kabuki music] (Tokyo, 1980)
'Kane', *Ongaku daijiten* [Encyclopedia of music] (Tokyo, 1981)
DAVID W. HUGHES

Kanengu. Large side-blown animal-horn trumpet of the Taneka people of Benin. Small trumpets of this type are called *kanenengu*. In performance, the hand is placed over the open end of the horn to modulate the pitch. The instruments are used with a clapperless bell and cylindrical drums to accompany masked ritual harvest dances and other ceremonies.

Kang. Name given to the CH'UK, a Korean percussion idiophone, only when it is used in the *tŭngga* ('terrace ensemble') at performances of ritual music (*aak*) for sacrificial rites.

Kanga (i). End-blown gourd trumpet of the Logo people of north-eastern Zaïre (*LaurentyA*, 309).

Kanga (ii). MIRLITON of the Alur people of Uganda. It resembles a side-blown trumpet but is fitted with a nasalising membrane. The instrument is also known in neighbouring areas of the Congo, where it is used by medicine men and at investiture rituals (*LaurentyA*, 35).

Kangak. Double-headed cylindrical drum of the Ankwe people of Nigeria. See GANGA, (1).

Kangamva. End-blown gourd trumpet of the Logo people of north-eastern Zaïre, also known as *oriwa* (*LaurentyA*, 308).

Kangan ['kan'gan]. Braced MOUTH BOW of southern Africa, reputedly borrowed from the San (Bushman) people and resembling the OUTA. See *KirbyMISA*, 228.

Kangombio. LAMELLAPHONE of the Kalanga and Lozi peoples of Zambia. It has a box-type body. See NDIMBA.

Kangsi. Pair of small cymbals used in the *gambuh* theatre ensemble in Bali. The cymbals are mounted between forked rods and struck against the ground. A pair is held in each hand of the player. See C. McPhee: *Music in Bali* (New Haven and London, 1966/R1976), 121.

Kanhang. Metal jingles of the Muong people of Vietnam and Laos, used for the ceremony of the buffalo sacrifice.

Kani (i). Frame zither of the Sapa people of Liberia. See KONIGI.

Kani (ii). BULLROARER of the Tami islanders, Huon Gulf, Morobe Province, Papua New Guinea. See A. C. Haddon: 'Migration of Cultures in British New Guinea', *Journal of the Anthropological Institute of Great Britain and Ireland*, 1 (1920), 253.

Kani (iii). Obliquely held, end-blown flute of Sind, Pakistan, a smaller version of the NAŘ.

Kanini. LEAF OBOE of Sorol, western Caroline Islands, Micronesia. See H. Fischer: 'Zwei einfache Musikinstrumente aus Blatt in Ozeanien', *Jahrbuch des Museums für Völkerkunde zu Leipzig*, xiv (1955), 67.

Kaniyārī ḍanḍā. Stick rattle of the Oraon people of Orissa, India. Hundreds of dried *champa* or *kaniyār* fruit are tied to a long bamboo pole, held vertically and struck on the ground to accompany dancing. See also GHUŃGRŪ.

Kanjam. See KAŃCAM.

Kanjau. Double-headed variable tension HOURGLASS DRUM of the Tera and associated peoples of north-eastern Nigeria. The drum is held between the knees and pressure is exerted on the tensioning chords to change the pitch. Its main use is as part of an ensemble which includes other drums and the xylophone to accompany dancing. See P. Newman and E. H. Davidson: 'Music from the Villages of North-eastern Nigeria', AHM 453. [disc notes].

Kanjhyun. Pair of metal cup-cymbals of Sind, Pakistan. They measure about 50 to 75 mm in diameter and are tied together by string to be played by concussion in the accompaniment of vocal and instrumental music, especially in eastern Sind. They are also called *tālyun* (for generic discussion of South Asian cymbals, *see* TĀL). See N. A. Baloch: *Musical Instruments of the Lower Indus Valley of Sind* (Hyderabad, 1966).
ALASTAIR DICK

Kañjīrā [kanjeera]. A FRAME DRUM of south India. It consists of a skin (usually iguana) stretched and pasted on a circular wooden frame. There are three or four slits in the side of the frame, in which bell-metal jingle-discs are suspended from metal cross-bars. The width of the drum is from 21 to 25 cm and the depth from 7 to 10 cm. The name *kañjīrā* probably relates to the *khanjar* and *khanjani* of north and east India, but the construction of the instrument is closer to that of the DAPH. The *kañjīrā* is tuned to various pitches by wetting the skin. It is held at the bottom of the frame by the left hand which also varies the tension of the skin, and is beaten with the fingers of the right hand. It is used by mendicants in devotional music (*bhajana*) but also often to accompany south Indian classical vocal music along with the barrel-drum *mṛdaṅgam* and the percussion vessel *ghaṭam*. These three instruments also feature (along with the jew's harp *mursing*) in the southern percussion ensemble *tālavādyakacceri*.

BIBLIOGRAPHY
Sambamoorthy: *Catalogue of Musical Instruments Exhibited in the Government Museum, Madras* (Madras, 3/1962)
C. Wade: *Music in India: the Classical Traditions* (Englewood Cliffs, NJ, 1979)

ALASTAIR DICK

ankarma. MOUTH BOW of the Gan people of Upper Volta. The string passes between the player's lips, is struck with a wooden stick in one hand and modulated by a second stick in the other. Harmonics are produced by varying the size of the mouth cavity. See C. Duvelle: 'Musique du pays Lobi', OCR 51 [disc notes].

Kanklės. BOX ZITHER (psaltery) of Lithuania, analogous to the Karelo-Finnish KANTELE, the Latvian *kokle* and the Estonian *kannel*. A variety of shapes and sizes is known but the most common type is trapezoidal. The body is usually made of ash, maple, linden, alder, fir or birch, the soundboard of fir, ash, linden or aspen. The tuning-pegs were made of oak, hornbeam, ash or maple, and more recently of iron. In older examples, the strings are gut; iron, copper or steel are now used. The soundholes are usually ornamented with segmented stars or other geometric designs.

The player rests the *kanklės* on his knees, with the higher strings towards him; it can also be placed on a table (the listeners sometimes putting their ears to the table), on an empty upturned barrel, or sometimes on the left hand (the instrument is then played with only one hand); or the player can lie down and place the instrument on his chest or stomach thus forming a natural resonator. The strings are plucked with the fingers of the right or of both hands, or with a plectrum. The tuning is diatonic and the timbre of the *kanklės* is soft.

Four types of *kanklės* in Lithuania can be distinguished. Early types have a resonator hollowed from one piece of wood and four to seven strings (usually five). They were used solo for playing polyphonic songs (*sutartinės*), and were known in north-east Lithuania ('Aukštaitija'). Also in Aukštaitija and Žemaitija a larger form (the 'simple' *kanklės*) with nine to 12 strings was known. This also had a hollowed-out body. The more 'complex' *kanklės* of Suvalkija (south-west Lithuania) has 11 to 13 strings, and the body is constructed from several wooden boards. The narrow end is shaped in an extended semicircle and the wider end in a scroll. Modern modified *kanklės* are built in several sizes (soprano, bass and double bass) and have up to 29 strings. The three later types of *kanklės* are used to play folksongs, dances and instrumental music. The *kanklės* was known throughout Lithuania, except in Dzūkija (south Lithuania) and was very popular, fulfilling several functions (magic, ritual and purely aesthetic).

ARVYDAS KARAŠKA

Kankobela [kankobele, kankowela]. LAMELLAPHONE of Zambia. It has a fan-shaped soundboard and from eight to 12 keys. It is played by the Bisa, Lala, Lenje and Valley Tonga peoples.

Kannel. Estonian BOX ZITHER (psaltery). Early instruments, with five to seven strings, had a trapeziform body made from a hollowed-out tree trunk covered with a soundboard. This type of *kannel* could be played by plucking individual strings for the melody or by strumming chords (found only in Setu). In the latter case, all unnecessary strings were damped with the fingers. This early type of *kannel* survived longest in Setu and on the islands. Analogous instruments are widespread among neighbouring peoples (*see* KANTELE).

A new type of *kannel* (sometimes called *simmel*) came to be used in the 19th century, at first with 15 or more melody strings, later with the addition of three bass strings and, in the 20th century, with special accompanying strings tuned in chords. This instrument can be played in one of two ways (with some variations): one hand strums chords while the other damps the unnecessary strings (the highest notes of the chords form the melody, usually complemented by additional plucked notes); or the melody is plucked with one hand and the accompaniment with the other. The latter 'harp technique' is the more recent.

In south Estonia a *kannel* producing chords, the *akordkannel*, was introduced at the beginning of the 20th century, as an accompanying instrument in folk ensembles. The newer types of *kannel* are still encountered in the folk tradition.

INGRID RÜÜTEL

Ka'nohko'wah (Seneca: 'covered keg'). Small WATER-DRUM of the Iroquois Indians of north-eastern North America. It is their only traditional drum type and it is used to accompany the majority of social dances and many rituals. The drum is a small wooden vessel covered with a soft-tanned hide which is held taut by a cloth-wound wooden hoop. Water is kept in it at all times and before being played it is inverted to soak the skin, which is then tightened until a characteristic high 'pinging' tone is heard when it is tapped lightly with a beater. The body may be carved from a solid block of wood, in which case a binding ring is wrapped round it to prevent it from splitting, or it may be made from a cut-down wooden keg with staved walls. The drums are usually 13 to 15 cm in diameter and 11 to 13 cm deep. A bung-hole about halfway up the side allows water to be added without removing the head: if allowed to dry out, solid-bodied drums tend to split and stave-walled drums loosen and may collapse. The carved drumstick is about 21 cm long and has a small unpadded knobbed head.

The drum is held either in the palm of the hand or by a bunched corner of the hide that projects from under the hoop. It rests lightly on the player's left thigh and is tilted to the right. The stick is held between the thumb and index finger of the right hand and the striking action is produced by an oscillating movement of the wrist. Drummers play with light strokes and frequently execute rapid tremolo passages that cue changes in the dance. The instrument is played in the Longhouse, by men, and in people's homes, where women also sing and play in an informal setting. Social dances and rituals are accompanied by one drum, played by the song leader, and one or more cow-horn rattles (*see* ONÓ'KAH KASTA-WEH'SHAE').

The Iroquois also use a larger water-drum, the OHGIWE KA'NOHKO'WAH.

BIBLIOGRAPHY
H. C. Conklin and W. C. Sturtevant: 'Seneca Indian Singing Tools at Coldspring Longhouse: Musical Instruments of the Modern Iroquois', *Proceedings of the American Philosophical Society*, xcvii (1953), 262

MARY RIEMER-WELLER

Kanon (Ger.). CANON.

K'anon [kanonaki]. *See* QĀNŪN.

Kanó'oskae'. Notched-stick rasp, or SCRAPER, of the Iroquois Indians of north-eastern North America. It consists of a pair of flat sticks, each about 25 cm long, 1·5 cm wide, and 5 mm thick. One stick is notched along two-thirds of its length and the other is smooth with slightly rounded edges. The notched stick is held by its smooth end and the notched end rests on the left leg. The smooth stick, held in the right hand, is scraped over the notches with a downward motion. The sticks produce a rasping sound and are played in the same rhythm as the water-drum KA'NOHKO'WAH that leads the singing.

Rasping sticks are used only at wakes, held in people's homes, and even here their use is quite rare. They are either buried with the person for whom the wake is held or are broken and burned with the drum-beater used during the singing.

BIBLIOGRAPHY
H. C. Conklin and W. C. Sturtevant: 'Seneca Indian Singing Tools at Coldspring Longhouse: Musical Instruments of the Modern Iroquois', *Proceedings of the American Philosophical Society*, xcvii (1953), 262

MARY RIEMER-WELLER

Kanowar. End-blown flute of western New Guinea. *See* FOH PETE.

Kānsalā. *See* KĀSALĀ.

Kānsale. *See* KĀSALE.

Kansar [kansi]. *See* KĀSAR.

Kansia jodi. *See* KĀSIĀ JOŘĪ.

Kāntāṃdabadaba. A Newari term for a small HOUR-GLASS DRUM beaten with attached pellets. *See* DABUDABU.

laba   kolju

1. (a) Latvian kokle; (b) Estonian kannel; (c) Finnish kantele

Kantele. Psaltery (BOARD ZITHER or BOX ZITHER) of Finland, analogous to the *kannel* (Estonia), *kokle* (Latvia), *kanklés* (Lithuania) and *gusli* (north-western Russia), particularly in the areas bordering the Baltic province of Novgorod, Pskov and Smolensk). Its body was originally fashioned from a single narrow, smooth piece of wood in an atypical trapezoidal shape, hollowed out the side, the bottom or the top (see fig.1). It is 45 to 80 cm long, 3 to 8 cm deep, and its greatest width 10 to 40 cm. In some instruments a thin wooden soundboard is nailed or glued to the body. The soundhole (one or more) cut into the soundboard vary greatly in size, shape and position. Most surviving specimens have a U-shaped raised section, the *ponsi* (Finnish) or *kolju* (Estonian), at the narrow end of the body; its sides are drilled to take a wooden or metal dowel which serves as a tailpiece (often the tailpiece is a simple iron clamp). There are usually five strings (up to 13 on modern instruments) of copper, brass or steel wire; they are tuned by wooden pegs mounted from below at the wide end of the body. Here the top corner ends in a small whorl with a hole for the carrying strap. In some areas in the Baltic provinces, in north-western Russia and in the territory of the Veps (a Finno-Ugric people of the Novgorod area), the body is extended to give an armrest for the performer's left arm (known as the *laba* in Estonia). These instruments differ from the *kantele* discussed above in having considerably broader bodies. The tuning of the strings varies according to the musical style and region. For example, in Finland the five strings were traditionally tuned to form a major, minor or neutral pentachord. In Russia, Lithuania and Latvia, however, the lowest strings traditionally provided a drone bass tuned a 4th or a 5th apart, while the upper strings had various tetrachord tunings. The player rests the instrument in his lap or props it on his knees and leans it against his body; indoors it can be placed on a table. The shortest string is usually nearest to the player. The playing technique varies as much as the tuning; when playing monophonic music the player plucks the open strings with the right hand fingertips, and damps the others with the fingers of his left hand. Very occasionally a small plectrum of bone, wood or metal is used. In multipart music the fingers of both hands pluck the strings.

Almost nothing is known of the early repertory. The small number of strings suggests that the range of the melodies was narrow, seldom more than a 4th or a 5th. According to early sources musicians accompanied their singing of runes by unison playing on the instrument; presumably it was used similarly for accompanying any singing. It was and still is used to accompany dance. Lithuanian dancers danced barefoot or in *nagines* (bark shoes) so that the weak sound of the instrument could still be heard. It is impossible to say when the simple melodic style began to accommodate simple harmonic intervals and, in the case of 19th-century instruments, chords. After the end of the 19th century instruments carved from a single piece of wood gradually gave way to box types consisting of several wooden strips and cross bridges (see fig.2). Between 12 and 46 strings are fastened to wood or iron wrest pins. Generally they are tuned diatonically in the major or the minor with a range of three to four octaves. Since the 1940s various chromatic types have been built in the Baltic countries. Their strings can be seen on two planes and even arranged chordally.

The modern instrument is built in different sizes and its repertory in both the Baltic states and Finland con-

E. Nieminen: 'Finnisch *kantele* und die damit verbundenen Namen baltischer Musikinstrumente', *Studia fennica*, x/2 (1963), 1–43

E. Emsheimer: 'Die Streichleier von Danczk', *Studia ethnomusicologica eurasiatica* (Stockholm, 1964), 99

K. Jażdżewski: 'Ueber das Problem der polnischen Saiteninstrumente des frühen Mittelalters', *Travaux et matériaux du Musée archéologique et ethnographique de Łódź*, xii (1966), 25

K. Vertkov: 'Beiträge zur Geschichte der russischen Guslitypen', *Studia instrumentorum musicae popularis*, i, ed. E. Stockmann (Stockholm, 1969), 134

J. Braun: 'Die Anfänge des Musikinstrumentenspiels in Lettland', *Musik des Ostens*, vi (1971), 88–125

F. Crane: *Extant Medieval Musical Instruments: a Provisional Catalogue by Types* (Iowa City, 1972)

S. Reynolds: 'The Baltic Psaltery: Bibliographical Problems and Desiderata', *2nd Conference on Baltic Studies in Scandinavia: Stockholm 1973*, ii, 7

I. Tōnurist: 'Kannel vepsamaast setumaani', *Soome-ugri rahvaste muusikapärandist* (Tallinn, 1977), 149–82 [with Ger. and Russ. summary]

C. J. Niles: *The Baltic Folk Zithers: an Ethnological and Structural Analysis* (diss., U. of California, Los Angeles, 1980)

ERNST EMSHEIMER

Kantung. Bar zither of North Sulawesi. *See* DUNDE.

Kanun. *See* QĀNŪN.

Kanyáhte' ká'nowa' (Seneca: 'snapping turtle'). Large vessel rattle of the Iroquois Indians of north-eastern North America. It is made from the shell, head and neck of the common snapping turtle (*Chelydra serpentina*; *see* RATTLE, fig.1*i*). Its construction is a skilled and lengthy process: the legs, tail and viscera are removed and the shell is cleaned; chokecherry pips are placed inside the shell and all openings are sewn. The head and neck are stretched out to form a handle, which is supported by a wooden rod and splints and wrapped with a rawhide thong, friction tape, or strips of inner bark (hickory or slippery elm are preferred). After the rattle has dried, it may be coated with varnish and painted with red, black or brown dots, bands or crosses, but these markings have no ritual significance. The dimensions of rattles vary according to the size of the turtle and the total length may be from 25 to 50 cm. Instruments of about 30 cm are considered best for playing.

The large turtle rattle is the most prominent and significant of Iroquois instruments: according to Iroquoian mythology, the earth rests on the turtle's back. The rattle is used without other instruments and only by singers for the Great Feather Dance and by the False Face Company. The Great Feather Dance, an important and recurring dance of the ceremonial calendar, requires two singers, each with a rattle. The singers face each other astride a wooden bench in the centre of the Longhouse. Holding the rattle in both hands, they forcefully beat out the rhythms of the dance, striking the edge of the carapace on the bench. Members of the False Face Company appear during the Midwinter ceremony carrying rattles which they shake, scrape, and rub on the door frame and floor of the Longhouse as part of their ritual behaviour.

The snapping turtle rattle is unique to the Iroquois. A similar rattle found among close neighbours of the Iroquois, the Delaware and the Munsee, was probably derived from the Iroquoian rattle.

BIBLIOGRAPHY

H. C. Conklin and W. C. Sturtevant: 'Seneca Indian Singing Tools at Coldspring Longhouse: Musical Instruments of the Modern Iroquois', *Proceedings of the American Philosophical Society*, xcvii (1953), 262

F. Speck: *The Iroquois: a Study in Cultural Evolution* (Bloomfield Hills, Mich., 1955)

MARY RIEMER-WELLER

2. Kantele player from the Karelian Isthmus, Finland, 1938

sists mainly of folksongs, dances and marches, as well as pieces composed for the instrument. It is played with both hands, melodic playing alternating with harmonic. The melody is mostly played simply or in 3rds, plucked by the fingertips of the right hand, and the accompaniment is played with the left hand. In Finland, where the *kantele* has been a national symbol since the 19th century, *kantele* playing is taught in music academies in Helsinki and Tampere.

In spite of extensive research the etymology of the terms for the instrument and its ethnic origins, diffusion and chronology remain obscure. The various related names in the individual countries doubtless derive from a common word, which seems to be the old Baltic *kantlis* or *kantli*. In many places its association with supernatural folklore suggests a long history. For example the Finnish Kalevala epic tells how Väinämoinen, the mythical national hero of the Finns, conquered his foes and, like Orpheus, made nature subject to him by playing on his *kantele*, made from the jawbone of a gigantic fish and strung with a young maiden's hair. Archaeological research shows that an instrument with three to nine strings has been used since the 11th century in the medieval towns of Opole (Oppeln) and Gdańsk (Danzig) and since the 13th and 14th centuries in the vicinity of Novgorod. Some of these specimens have a large opening in the body at the peg end. Whether or not this suggests that the instrument was played as a bowed lyre must, however, remain an open question.

BIBLIOGRAPHY

VertkovA

A. O. Väisänen: *Kantele- ja jouhikko- sävelmiä* [*Kantele* and bowed lyre melodies] (Helsinki, 1928) [with Ger. summary]

E. Arro: 'Zum Problem der Kannel', *Sitzungsberichte der Gelehrten Estnischen Gesellschaft* (1929), 158–90

J. Žilevičius: 'Native Lithuanian Musical Instruments', *MQ*, xxi (1935), 99

Z. Slaviūnas: 'Lietuviu kanklės', *Tautosakos darbai*, iii (1937), 244–318 [with Eng. summary]

A. O. Väisänen: 'Wirklichkeitsgrund der finnisch-estnischen Kantelerunen', *Acta ethnologica*, iii (1938), 31

F. V. Sokolov: *Gusli zvonchatye* [The ringing *gusli*] (Moscow, 1959)

Kapakala. Single-headed drum of the Mbagani people of Zaïre. *See* DITUMBA.

Kapat. Flat gong in a TOPAYYA ensemble of the Kalinga people of the northern Philippines.

Kapelle (Ger.). Band; *see* BAND (i).

Kapsel (Ger.). A wooden or metal block or fork serving as a pivot in the action of the piano; *see* PIANOFORTE, §I, 3.

Kapudi. Carved wooden VESSEL FLUTE of the Songye people of Zaïre (*LaurentyA*, 47).

Kapulu. VESSEL FLUTE of the Luba people of Zaïre. *See* DIPULU.

Kaṙa [kārā]. *See* KARAH.

Kārā. Large clay or wooden KETTLEDRUM of Bengal (eastern India and Bangladesh). Its head is braced with rope or leather straps, and it is hung around the neck and struck with wooden sticks at festival or martial occasions. It is similar to the *ṭikārā* of Bengal and Orissa, but larger. See B. K. Roy Choudhury: *Bhāratīya saṅgīt-koś* (Calcutta, 1965). ALASTAIR DICK

Karadeniz kemençesi. *See* KEMENÇE.

Karaduzen. Long-necked lute of Yugoslavia. In Bosnia and Hercegovina it is about 40 cm long and has two or three strings tuned in unison, 2nds or 4ths. It is used to accompany dances. The Macedonian *karaduzen* has four strings and wire frets on the neck. *See* ŠARGIJA.

The name is probably derived from the Turkish *karadüzen* (long-necked lute). This term is now sometimes used among the Türkmen of the southern Taurus mountains to denote the IRIZVA.

Karah [kaṙa, kārā, kaṙha, khaṙa]. Name given to double-headed drums such as the *tāpar*, *rabaga* and *ḍholkī* played by tribal and non-tribal musicians in southern Bihar, India. A drum functions as *karah* when only the larger of its heads is played with two small sticks to provide a rapid and regular pulse for other drummers. In a traditional ensemble of *karah*, *ḍholkī* and *mādar* (double-headed drums), *nagaṙa* (kettledrum) and cymbals, the *karah* drummer's fast, even strokes, four or eight per beat, alternating with rapid rolls, also fill in the more complicated syncopated patterns of the other drummers.

In West Bengal, *kārā* refers to a specific double-headed drum with a truncated-conical wooden body and laced-on skin heads, resembling the *tāpar* and *rabaga* of southern Bihar. CAROL M. BABIRACKI

Karakaraka. A Malagasy rattle. *See* KOTRA.

Karamouza. Greek oboe played in central and southern mainland Greece. It is somewhat smaller than the northern Greek ZOURNAS.

Karanay. *See* KARNĀ (i).

Karangba. Calabash-resonated XYLOPHONE of the Mono people of Zaïre. *See* KALANGBA, (1).

Karaṭā. A medieval double-headed drum of India probably cylindrical in shape. It is described as about 42 to 48 cm long, 24 to 28 cm in diameter and 5 mm thick in the shell, which was made of citrus wood. The close-fitting heads were attached with thread and skin to iron hoops which had 14 holes; the threads passed through every second hole to form a net lacing (*vignikā*, said to resemble a fish. The drum was carried on a shoulder- or hip-strap and played with two crooked sticks (*kuḍupa*).

BIBLIOGRAPHY
Śārṅgadeva: *Saṅgītaratnākara* (13th century), ed. S. Subrahmanya Sastri, iii (Madras, 1951)
ALASTAIR DICK

Karcilampu [karchilambu]. Pellet-bell ring of south India. It is worn around the ankle unlike the *kaiccilampu*, which are worn on the hands. The *karcilampu* is similar to the *silampu* of Tamil Nadu. *See also* GHUṄGRŪ and NŪPUR.

Kargach. Bamboo SCRAPER of Rajasthan, north India. It consists of a piece of bamboo, 65 cm long, split lengthwise; the edges, cut in notches, are scraped with the split end of a stick (for illustration *see* ŚUKTIVĀDYA, fig.1*b*). Used among the Bhil groups of the Aravalli Hills region, it is the ritual instrument of the healer to accompany his chanting during healing sessions (sickness, snake-bite, possession etc). GENEVIÈVE DOURNON

Kaṙha. *See* KARAH.

Karigo. Single-string fiddle of the Nyanja/Manganja people of Malawi. The string is made from twisted bark. The goatskin soundtable is pinned to a carved wooden bowl, which has a soundhole cut into its side. The bow, made from reed, is called *uta*. See *TraceyCSA*, ii, 434f.

Karimba. LAMELLAPHONE of the Lenge people of Zaïre. *See* KALIMBA (i).

Karinding. JEW'S HARP of rural Sundanese areas of West Java. It is made of sugar-palm wood with a small resonator consisting of a loose open bamboo tube. It may be played solo or in pairs.

Karjapasun. Trumpet of Estonia. It is an outdoor instrument made of wood or bark, usually played during cattle herding or night watches by the camp fire.

Kärjennoukka. Idioglot clarinet of Finland. It is made of two pieces of wood, with the upper end of the upper part shaped to form a reed. It has finger-holes and at the lower end a bell made from strips of birch. It was common in south Pohjanmaa.

Karkarí [karkariká]. A Sanskrit term which appears in the earlier Vedic literature of India (*Ṛg-* and *Atharva-*

eda, c1000 BC). It has been translated by Indologists ⸢s 'lute', but without justification; it may have been a ⸢usical bow (*see also* GÁRGARA), played by 'scratching' ⸢nd resonated by a bottle-gourd or a pot (a later avail-⸢ble meaning of *karkarí* etc, as well as of *gárgara*) with ⸢ skin, probably of lizard, stretched over it and embed-⸢ed in the earth, 'lest the wind stir it up'. It may well ⸢us be a transitional stage between an earth-bow (cf the *⸢hūmidundubhi*; *see* DUNDUBHI) and the bow harp (*see* ⸢ĪNĀ, §§1–2). Its half-buried pot is compared with a ⸢est, and the deep sound to the flying up (from the nest) ⸢f the sacrifice-bird. It was played in association with ⸢e ĀGHĀTĀ by the Apsaras nymphs in the *Atharvaveda*, ⸢nd in later texts (*Śrautasūtra*, called *ghātakarkari*) by ⸢e wives of the participants in the winter-solstice ⸢Mahāvrata ritual (the men playing the probably newer ⸢arp *vīṇā* and the earth-drum). *See also* PINĀK; VILLĀ-⸢VĀDYAM; VĪNĀ, §§1, 5.

BIBLIOGRAPHY

⸢ A. Macdonnell and A. B. Keith: *Vedic Index of Names and Subjects* (London, 1912)

ALASTAIR DICK

⸢armo. Idiophone of the Kanuri people of Nigeria. It ⸢ a pestle; four or five of them are placed on the ground ⸢nd struck with sticks by a group of elderly women for *⸢oskori* music which is performed on the eve of mar-⸢age ceremonies, or to accompany songs requesting rain.

⸢arn. Canadian firm of reed organ, piano and organ ⸢manufacturers. Dennis W. Karn (*b* North Oxford Co., ⸢anada West, 6 Feb 1843; *d* Toronto, 19 Sept 1916), ⸢n amateur musician, joined the reed organ firm of John ⸢l. Miller around 1867, buying out his employer in 1870 ⸢nd continuing under the name of Karn & Miller in ⸢Voodstock, Ontario. The firm was also known at var-⸢ous times as the Woodstock Organ Factory and the ⸢Voodstock Church Organ Co. In the late 1880s the firm ⸢egan making pianos, and after a merger in 1896 with ⸢e firm of WARREN continued the latter's pipe organ ⸢usiness in Toronto under the name of Karn & Warren. ⸢he first Karn player piano was made in 1901, and by ⸢e first decade of the 20th century the firm had branches ⸢ several major Canadian cities as well as London and ⸢amburg. Karn retired in 1909, and the business was ⸢erged with the Morris piano firm as Karn Morris Piano ⸢ Organ Co. Ltd; both companies retained their original ⸢ctories and produced their own lines of instruments. ⸢his partnership was dissolved in 1920, and the ⸢iano operation was purchased by John E. Hoare (Cecil-⸢n Piano Co.) and A. A. Barthelmes (Sterling Action ⸢ Keys). The firm was again sold in 1924 to Sherlock-⸢Manning, which continued to make the Karn piano until ⸢957.

BIBLIOGRAPHY

⸢MC

⸢ Kallman: *A History of Music in Canada 1534–1914* (Toronto, 1960)

BARBARA OWEN

⸢arnā [karanay, karnai, karnay, karranay, karranāy] ⸢). Long brass trumpet of Persia dating from the Sas-⸢nid era (AD 224–651) and mentioned by Firdausī (934–⸢020 or 1026). It is sometimes identified with the NAFĪR ⸢f the Islamic world. It had a conical brass bore, some-⸢mes curved in an S-shape, up to two metres long and ⸢roducing a single pitch. It was taken to India with the

Karnā (trumpets) with zūrnā (oboes) and kettledrums, ? early 20th century

spread of Islam, where it was played in ceremonial *naubat* ensembles. In Iran it was used until the early 20th century in military ensembles and NAQQĀRAKHĀNA bands, and was part of the military and state music of the kingdom of Bukhara. Now obsolescent in Iran, it is still played at weddings in Uzbekistan and by the Uighurs and plains and river-valley Tajiks of Central Asia.

Karnā (ii). Large folk oboe of the ZŪRNĀ type, played by the Bakhtyari and Qashqai nomads of Iran. About 90 cm long, it is constructed from the bell of a long trumpet (*karnā*) fastened to a conical oboe, hence its name. See J. Jenkins and P. Rovsing Olsen: *Music and Musical Instruments in the World of Islam* (London, 1976).

Karnāl [karnal]. Long brass trumpet, with a flared bell, of Nepal. It is played by the *damāi* tailor–musicians and is usually included in the DAMĀI BĀJĀ (instrumental ensemble). See M. Helffer: 'Fanfares villageoises au Népal', *Objets et mondes*, ix/1 (1969), 51.

Karnyx. *See* CARNYX.

Karombi. Small JEW'S HARP of the Sa'dan Toraja area of South Sulawesi. Its total length is usually 8 cm or less.

Karra [katta]. Pair of concussion sticks of Andhra, south India. *See also* ḌAṆḌĀ.

Karraka. Cog rattle of the Basque region. *See* CARRACA, (1).

Karranay [karranāy]. *See* KARNĀ (i).

Kärš [karsh]. BOX ZITHER of the Mari people of the Volga-Ural region (USSR). *See* GUSLI.

Kartāl [karatāla, kartāḷa, kartār]. A South Asian term denoting primarily pairs of wooden CLAPPERS, but in east India small cymbals. Although it is widespread in the subcontinent, the name does not appear to be very ancient and its meaning in Sanskrit and the derivative north Indian languages – 'hand percussion' (*see* TĀL) – is obvious enough to make any attempt at connection with the ancient Akkadian *katral* or the Greek *krotala* unnecessary.

(1) In the Indian subcontinent generally the term mostly denotes wooden clappers, with or without jingles (either inserted bronze discs, or pellet bells, or both). Wooden or bamboo clappers, held two in each hand, are described in medieval Sanskrit works as KAMRĀ. In Tamil Nadu *kartāḷa* denotes flat, round or oblong, wooden bats, with handles held between the fingers of one hand, which are struck together; these are called *cekkai* (Tamil) for the oblong type or *cekkalu* (Telegu) for the circular type with handles found in Andhra. Other simple wooden clappers include the *catkulā* of Madhya Pradesh, the *kāthi* of Orissa, the *rāigidgidī* of Rajasthan and the *daṇḍā* of Bihar; the *cimṭā* of South Asia and the *ṭokā* of Assam are analogous, sprung clappers (tongs).

In north and central areas *kartāl* denotes pairs of thick wooden clappers, about 15 to 30 cm long, with flat inner surfaces; attached to the outer sides, which may be convex or concave, are metal rings, leather straps or incised wooden handles by which the clappers are held with thumb and fingers. They are clashed together in performance. Some have no jingles (*see also* KHARTĀL) but most have thin bronze discs held vertically in slits at each end by metal pins; sometimes also bronze pellet bells are attached to the ends. These are used primarily in religious music. In the south this type is known as *ciplā*, in Maharashtra *ciplyā* and in Sind *caprun*, names which are clearly related.

(2) The *kartāl* of Bengal and Orissa is a pair of medium-size bell-metal cymbals with a central depression and a flattish outer rim. They are connected by a piece of string, and are 8 cm to 10 cm in diameter and about 2 mm thick. They are similar to the *tāl* of north India and may also be called *gini*. They are widely used in religious music. In this area wooden clappers are called *kāṭh kartāl*.

BIBLIOGRAPHY

C. R. Day: *The Music and Musical Instruments of Southern India and the Deccan* (Delhi, 1891/R1974)

C. Sachs: *Die Musikinstrumente Indiens und Indonesiens* (Berlin and Leipzig, 1914, 2/1923)

P. Sambamoorthy: *A Dictionary of South Indian Music and Musicians* (Madras, 1952–71)

——: *Catalogue of the Musical Instruments Exhibited in the Government Museum, Madras* (Madras, 3/1962)

N. A. Baloch: *Musical Instruments of the Lower Indus Valley of Sind* (Hyderabad, 1966)

K. S. Kothari: *Indian Folk Musical Instruments* (New Delhi, 1968)

B. C. Deva: *Musical Instruments of India* (Calcutta, 1978)

ALASTAIR DICK

Karwasi. A rattle of Surinam. It is a small closed basket without a handle, containing dry seeds, and is used to accompany women's songs among the Carib Indians.

Kāš [kasch]. Obsolete bamboo NOSE FLUTE of the Micronesian island of Ponape. It had a thumb-hole and two finger-holes. See P. Hambruch and A. Eilers: 'Ponape', *Ergebnisse der Südsee-Expedition 1908–1910*, IIB, vii (Hamburg, 1936), 224.

Kāsāka. LITHOPHONE of Kosrae, eastern Caroline Islands, Micronesia. It is made of thin basalt plates which are struck together. See E. Sarfert: 'Kusae', *Ergebnisse der Südsee-Expedition 1908–1910*, IIB, iv (Hamburg, 1920), 488.

Kāsalā [kānsalā]. Large metal cymbals of Orissa, eastern India. They are similar in shape to the BARTĀL of Assam and are used in devotional singing and dancing, for example in *pālā kīrtan* and *bhajan*. For generic discussion of cymbals in South Asia, *see* TĀL.

Kāsale [kānsale]. Two-piece cymbals of Karnataka state, south India. Their distinguishing feature is that the two pieces are not identical: one is a deep cup, the other a metal disc. The *kāsale* is used as a percussion instrument for *kāsale pada* (songs). For generic discussion of cymbals in South Asia, *see* TĀL.

Kasandji [kasambi, kasansi, ka-sanzi]. Variant form of the term KISAANJ denoting a LAMELLAPHONE in central Africa. The *kasambi* is attributed to the Warega people of Shabunda, Zaïre (*LaurentyS*, 197). The *kasandji* is the lamellaphone of the Teke and other peoples of south and south-eastern Gabon; the instruments have metal keys with beads threaded on them to make a continuous buzzing and, in Teke music, ensembles of two or three lamellaphones with a common tuning are used as vocal accompaniment (P. Sallée: 'Gabon', *Grove 6*). The *ka-sanzi* is a flat-board instrument, of the Luba people of south-eastern Zaïre, with metal keys (*LaurentyS*, 195). *Kasansi*, *sansi* or *nsansi*, is found as a general term for lamellaphone in the Zambezi basin; it has been noted, for example, among the Chikunda of Mozambique.

Kāsar [kansar, kansi, kāsī, kāsya]. Brass gong of Bengal (east India and Bangladesh). Beaten with a stick, it has a flange and is generally thicker at the centre than at the rim. It is played together with the large drums *dhāk* and *dhol* in festivals, processions, folkdances, etc. The name derives from the Sanskrit *kāṃsya* ('brass') and the instrument is similar to the north Indian THĀLI. See S. Ray: *Music of Eastern India* (Calcutta, 1973).

ALASTAIR DICK

Kāsāt. Cymbals used in Arab religious processions and other ritual contests, often with a cylindrical drum.

Kasch. See KĀŠ.

Kaschendorff [Caschindorff, Castendorfer, Kasterdörffer], **Stephan** (*b* Breslau, *c*1425; *d* ?Schweidnitz, Silesia, after 4 Feb 1499). German organ builder. He was apprenticed to a carpenter called Nickel in Breslau whom he later instructed in the art of organ building and pipe making. On 14 May 1460, when he concluded an agreement to build the large organ in St Elisabeth, Breslau, he was already considered an 'egregius magister in ista arte', who had proved his ability in Nuremberg and other cities. In the 1460s Kaschendorff was again working in Nuremberg as well as in Nördlingen and in Grossenhain, Saxony. His sons Kaspar, Melchior and Michael helped him in his work on the cathedral organ in Erfurt and at that time Kaschendorff owned houses in Schweidnitz and Dresden. In 1483 he laid the lead for the towers of St Sebald, Nuremberg, and in 1490 he worked on some organs in Augsburg. He is recorded as being in Schweidnitz in 1496 and 1499. He seems to have ended his life in poverty and solitude.

Although not gifted with the outstanding artistic ingenuity and enterprise of his contemporary Leonhard Mertz, Kaschendorff ranks with Burkhart Dinstlinger, Friedrich Krebs, Heinrich Traxdorff and Hans Tugi as one of the leading organ builders of south and central Germany in the second half of the 15th century. The exact dispositions of his organs are not preserved but surviving examples indicate that he built independent divisions and stops; his organ for St Elisabeth, Breslau, was constructed with twin projections and towers; the organ in Erfurt Cathedral had two manuals (*Hauptwerk* and *Brustwerk*) and an independent Pedal with over 20 stops. A later illustration of the 'swallow's nest' organ in the Frauenkirche, Nuremberg, shows that Kaschendorff was already building *Rückpositive* in 1465. His far-reaching work in Silesia, Saxony, Thuringia, Swabia and Franconia reflects the freedom of the organ builder at the end of the Middle Ages. Lütgendorff's erroneous assertion that Kaschendorff was probably also a lute and violin maker is explained by an incorrect reading of the Nördlingen records.

BIBLIOGRAPHY

W. L. von Lütgendorff: *Die Geigen- und Lautenmacher vom Mittelalter bis zur Gegenwart* (Frankfurt am Main, 1904, rev. 6/1922/*R*1968)

.. Burgemeister: *Der Orgelbau in Schlesien* (Strasbourg, 1925, rev. 2/1973)

. Rücker: *Die deutsche Orgel am Oberrhein um 1500* (Freiburg, 1940)

*. Krautwurst: 'Konrad Paumann in Nördlingen', *Festschrift Heinrich Besseler* (Leipzig, 1961), 203

——: 'Die erste Orgel der St. Jakobskirche in Rothenburg o. T., ein Werk des Frankfurter Barfüssers Leonhard Mertz', *Jb für fränkische Landesforschung*, xxiii (1963), 155

——: 'Das Wirken des Breslauer Orgelbauers Stephan Kaschendorff in Nördlingen (1464) 1466–1483 (1496)', *Jb für fränkische Landesforschung*, xxiv (1964), 145

. Bösken: *Quellen und Forschungen zur Orgelgeschichte des Mittelrheins*, i (Mainz, 1967)

. Orth: 'Das Wirken des Breslauer Orgelbauers Stephan Kaschendorff in Erfurt 1480–1484', *AMw*, xxv (1968), 148

ased on *MGG* (xvi, 921–2) by permission of Bärenreiter

FRANZ KRAUTWURST

Kasengosengo [kasénggsêng, kasengu]. Wooden cone lute of the Lunda, Akwa-Songo, Lwena, Chokwe, Holo and Tabi peoples of Zaïre. The term *kasengosengo* also refers to a VESSEL FLUTE of the Kete, Lunda, Mwanzwa and Akwa-Songo peoples of Zaïre (*LaurentyA*, passim).

Kashane. Braced composite MOUTH BOW of the Lovedu (Northern Sotho) people of southern Africa, resembling the Zulu ISITHONTOLO.

Kashéweh'ta'. Strung rattle of the Iroquois Indians of north-eastern North America. It consists of small bells attached to a leather strap. The rattle may be worn by men during costumed dances at the Longhouse, either tied round the leg just below the knee or round the ankle, or hung vertically from the waist down the outside seams of the leggings. These commercially purchased metal bells are recognized by some of the older Seneca as substitutes for the traditional deer-hoof rattles.

BIBLIOGRAPHY

H. C. Conklin and W. C. Sturtevant: 'Seneca Indian Singing Tools at Coldspring Longhouse: Musical Instruments of the Modern Iroquois', *Proceedings of the American Philosophical Society*, xcvii (1953), 262

MARY RIEMER-WELLER

Kashi. Long metal trumpet of Chad. *See* GASHI.

Kashiba. Term for a VESSEL FLUTE or cylindrical wooden flute among the Luntu, Kete and neighbouring peoples of south-central Zaïre. The vessel flutes may be carved into various shapes including stylised animal forms. Among the Kanyok people a similar ivory flute in anthropomorphic form is known as *kashib*. The name is related to the LUSHIBA, a term for similar types of flute among the Chokwe and other peoples of south-western Zaïre (*LaurentyA*, passim).

Kashila. Double-headed drum played by royal musicians of the Bemba people of Zambia. It is struck by hand while suspended from the player's shoulder or neck.

Kāsī. *See* KĀSAR.

Kāsiā jorī [kansia jodi]. Medium-size metal cymbals of Gujarat, west India. For generic discussion of South Asian cymbals, *see* TĀL.

Kaşık [kašike, žlice]. Spoons of Turkey (*kaşık*, pl. *kaşıklar*) and Bosnia, Yugoslavia (*kašike*, *žlice*). The Turkish spoons are wooden and struck together in pairs. They are played in all parts of western Anatolia, usually by dancers who hold a pair in each hand. They may provide the sole accompaniment for dancing or be played with wind or string instruments. They are particularly associated with certain *zeybek* dances (martial dances) and *kaşık oyunları* ('spoon dances').

The Bosnian spoons are metal, with small jingles attached to the bowls. The player holds one spoon in each hand and strikes the convex parts together. The *kašike* also used as accompaniment for dance.

BIBLIOGRAPHY

L. Picken: *Folk Musical Instruments of Turkey* (London, 1975)

R. CONWAY MORRIS, CVJETKO RIHTMAN

Kasinaku. Side-blown cow-horn trumpet of the Jola people of Senegal and the Gambia. It is played to accompany men's wrestling songs.

Kasra [kassar]. Variant forms of KISSAR.

Kasso. Harp-lute of the Gambia. *See* HARP-LUTE (i).

Kastagnetten (Ger.). CASTANETS.

Kastendörffer, Stephan. *See* KASCHENDORFF, STEPHAN.

Kastens, Lambert Daniel (*d* Viborg, 30 Oct 1744). Danish organ builder of German origin. He was the leading figure in Danish organ building during the high Baroque period. He was a pupil of Arp Schnitger in Neuenfelde, near Hamburg, and eventually became one of his most trusted workmen. After Schnitger's death, Kastens took over his organ-building licence in Schleswig, Holstein, Oldenburg and Delmenhorst in 1721; he also established a workshop in Copenhagen in 1724. He built new organs in most of the big churches in the city after they had been destroyed in a great fire in 1728; a few façades survive. His instruments are similar in style to those of Schnitger, whose traditions were carried on by Kastens's pupils Johann Daniel Busch and Hartvig Jochum Müller.

BIBLIOGRAPHY
N. Friis: *Orgelbygning i Danmark* (Copenhagen, 1949, 2/1971)
W. Bauer: 'Eine Orgelbauwerkstatt in Itzehoe, 1721–1787', *Festschrift zum 100-jährigen Bestehen des Kaiser-Karl-Gymnasiums in Itzehoe* (Itzehoe, 1967)
O. Schumann: *Quellen und Forschungen zur Geschichte des Orgelbaus im Herzogtum Schleswig vor 1800* (Munich, 1973)
G. Fock: *Arp Schnitger und seine Schule* (Kassel, 1974)
OLE OLESEN

Kastner, Georges Frédéric Eugène. French physicist, inventor of the PYROPHONE.

Kasuto. SCRAPER of Angola. *See* CASSUTO.

Kãsya. *See* KÃSAR.

Kata batang. Bamboo trumpet of the Murut area of central Sabah, Malaysia. It varies in length from about 35 cm to about 65 cm and is often played in groups. See E. M. Frame: 'The Musical Instruments of Sabah, Malaysia', *EM*, xxvi (1982), 247.

Katako. Wooden rectangular concussion CLAPPERS of the Yergum people of Nigeria. They are still used in modern ensembles with raft zithers, arched harps and a struck bottle.

Katanga (pl. *tutanga*). Secret wooden gong used in circumcision ceremonies in eastern Angola.

Kã tang-muri. Reed aerophone, possibly an oboe, of the Khasi people of Meghalay state (formerly Assam), north-east India. See B. C. Deva: *Musical Instruments of India* (Calcutta, 1978).

Katango. Drum of southern Iraq and the Arabian Gulf region. *See* JATANGA.

Katchel. *See* QUATCHEL.

Kateobak [kajeomak]. Single-headed cylindrical drum of the Mentawei Islands, Indonesia. The body is a hollowed-out piece of coconut tree trunk, varying between about 75 and 100 cm in length. It is about 14 to 18 cm in diameter at one end, tapering to about 10 to 14 cm at the other. The larger end is covered with snake- or lizard-skin. This is laced to the body with thin rattan string sewn round the circumference and linked by vertical lacing to a thickly woven band of rattan a few centimetres lower down. This band is tautened by about ten wooden wedges placed around the circumference of the drum, and the skin is further tightened before playing by heating it near a naked flame. The player holds the head of the drum between his knees and beats it with both hands (see illustration).

The name 'kateobak' is used also for an ensemble of three, sometimes four, drums and *sinna* (concussion bars). In south Siberut island the largest *kateobak* is called *inania* ('the mother') and the others *katalaga* ('the middle one') and *kateitei* ('the back one'). The *kateitei* usually plays syncopated rhythms, while the *inania* plays on the downbeats and the *katalaga* on the upbeats. The ensemble accompanies dances at ceremonies and festivities.

MARGARET J. KARTOMI

Katera. End-blown flute of the Vira, Fuliru and Rundi peoples of eastern Zaïre and Burundi. It is made from a hollow stalk about 65 cm long and 2 cm in diameter at the mouthpiece, narrowing to 1 cm at the extremity. The flute has two or three finger-holes and is used by herdsmen for entertainment.

Katero. Set of three stopped end-blown flutes of the Sena/Tonga people of Mtoko district, Zimbabwe. The *katero* forms one of four complementary sets in a form of STOPPED FLUTE ENSEMBLE, the others being named *dendera*, *madobi* and *shauriro*. The flutes in each set are made from reeds, tied together like panpipes. The ensemble accompanies *gororambe* dances, with drum and rattles (*see* MUTUMBA (ii)). See *TraceyCSA*, ii, 175.

DAVID K. RYCROFT

Kathandi. LAMELLAPHONE of the Mbunda people of Zambia. *See* NDIMBA.

Kãthi. CLAPPERS of Orissa, eastern India, consisting of two strips of wood, with pellet-bell jingles. Also called *dãskãthi* ('devotee's stick'), they accompany the religious narrative songs *dãskãthia*. In Bengal and Orissa the term *kãth kartãl* denotes a pair of wooden clappers usually with inset pairs of small cymbals. For generic discussion of such instruments, *see* KARTÃL, (1).

Katiboky. A Malagasy free-key xylophone. *See* ATRANATRA.

Katimbok. Bamboo TUBE ZITHER, with two parallel or paired strings, of the Tagakaolo people of the southern Philippines. *See also* DUNGADUNG.

Katlo. Flat gong in a TOPAYYA ensemble of the Kalinga people of the northern Philippines.

Katõlã. Portable bell-shaped SLIT-DRUM of Madhya Pradesh, central India. *See also* KOTURKA.

Katongoa kayu. Log XYLOPHONE of Sumbawa, Indonesia.

Katral. Akkadian and Assyrian term for small cymbal of the 1st millennium BC.

Kateobak (single-headed cylindrical drum) player Malilimok village, Siberut, Mentawei Islands, Indonesia, 1980

Katta. See KARRA.

Katu-katu. SLIT-DRUM of southern Nias, Indonesia. See 'ABOLIYA.

Katumbi [katumba ka vidye]. GOBLET DRUM of the Luba, Luba-Shankadi, Luluwa and Bena peoples of Zaïre. (BooneT, 9f). See DITUMBA.

Ká'tyaaskwa' kastaweh'shae' (Seneca: ká'tyaaskwa', 'box turtle'; kastaweh'shae', 'rattle'). Small vessel rattle of the Iroquois Indians of north-eastern North America. It is made from the shell of a box turtle (Terrapene carolina), cleaned and filled with pellets or small pebbles. The shell is 11 to 13 cm long, 9 to 10 cm wide and 6 to 7 cm deep, and small enough to be held in the palm of the hand. The rattle is used only to accompany the songs of the women planters (towisas) sung at two longhouse ceremonies, the Green Corn and Midwinter. It is owned and played by women, but made by men. It is fairly scarce, since Terrapene carolina is not found in the north-east.

According to tradition, the towisas ceremony was introduced by two Seneca women who had been captured by the Cherokee, of the south-eastern United States, and the Iroquois may have originally obtained the rattle from a southern tribe. (For a related instrument, see CAXKO'XKC.)

MARY RIEMER-WELLER

Kauaha [kawaha]. Rattle of Easter Island made from the dried-out jawbone of a horse. The teeth are loose in their sockets and rattle when the jawbone is beaten on the ground or on the palm of the player's hand. The instrument was probably introduced from South America, where it is known as quijada. See R. Campbell: La herencia musical de Rapanui (Santiago, 1971).

Kaueya. Flat-board LAMELLAPHONE of the Mbala people of northern Zaïre. It has metal keys over a bowl-shaped resonator (LaurentyS, 195).

Kaufmann. German family of makers of automatic instruments. Its most influential members were Johann Gottfried Kaufmann (b Siegmar, Saxony, 1752; d Dresden, 1818) and his son Friedrich (1785–1866). They developed an instrument called the BELLONION, which included free reeds with resonators and kettledrums. Shortly afterwards they built an automaton in the form of a Spanish trumpeter which played at predetermined times by clockwork, and was praised by Weber. Friedrich Kaufmann's Salpingion, consisting of free reeds, trumpets and kettledrums, could produce such works as the Hallelujah Chorus from Handel's Messiah. Other instruments built by the family included the CHORD-AULODION, Symphonium and Orchestrion (all self-playing free-reed instruments) and the Harmonichord, a keyboard instrument whose strings were played by rosined wheels, and upon which Friedrich became a proficient performer. The founder's grandson, Friedrich Theodor (1823–72), joined the firm in the 1840s. The Kaufmanns toured Europe with their instruments, taking part in the Great Exhibition at the Crystal Palace, London (1851). All their instruments were subsequently exhibited at the Acoustic Cabinet, Dresden.

BIBLIOGRAPHY
A. Buchner: Hudebni automaty (Prague, 1959; Eng. trans., 1959)
A. W. J. G. Ord-Hume: Barrel Organ (New York, 1978)
BARBARA OWEN

Kaulo švilpynė. Bone DUCT FLUTE of Lithuania. Several have been found by archaeologists in castle mounds from the Bronze and Early Iron Age (i.e. the 1st millenium BC). They are made from tubular bones of birds, with both ends open. Fragments of kaulo švilpynė found in the mound at Norkūnai are 54 mm long and 9 to 13 mm in diameter. Two finger-holes through the tube can be seen in the top and bottom sections, and traces of a third can be seen at the fracture point. Most examples have three or four finger-holes. The instrument is thought to have had a magic function and was used as a signalling instrument by hunters. Similar bone whistles can be found in neighbouring countries.

ARVYDAS KARAŠKA

Kaur ('bamboo'). (1) A term applied in the Gazelle Peninsula, New Britain, to the bamboo NOTCHED FLUTE, bamboo PANPIPES, bamboo JEW'S HARP and even harmonicas.
(2) Bamboo panpipes of New Ireland.
(3) Bamboo SLIT-DRUM of the Duke of York Islands.
(4) Bamboo panpipes (ka'ur) of Buka, Solomon Islands, played at dances in association with either slit-drums or wooden trumpets (see MABU, (1)) and discarded after each performance. They may not be played by women.

BIBLIOGRAPHY
O. Finsch: Ethnologische Erfahrungen und Belegstücke aus der Südsee (Vienna, 1888–93), 27f
E. M. von Hornbostel: 'Notiz über die Musik der Bewohner von Süd-Neu-Mecklenburg', Sammelbände für vergleichende Musikwissenschaft, i (1922), 351
B. Blackwood: Both Sides of Buka Passage (Oxford, 1935), 412
MERVYN McLEAN

Kaval [kavali, kavall]. Wooden rim-blown flute of south-eastern Europe and Turkey, similar to the NĀY of the Arab world. It is generally made of boxwood, with seven finger-holes and one thumb-hole, and is primarily a pastoral instrument.

The Bulgarian kaval, once made of a single piece of wood, is now constructed of three separate sections (of cornel, plum or boxwood), with a total length of 60 to 90 cm (see illustration, p.366). Bone rings cover the joints, to prevent the wood from cracking. Metal decoration is also found. The finger-holes are located in the central section, while the lower (shorter) section has four additional holes called dushnitsi or dyavolski dupki ('devil's holes'); these are not covered in performance. The kaval can be made in various tunings, D being the most common. Its range is almost three octaves, mostly chromatic.

In the south-west Rhodope mountains, two kavals in the same tuning (called chifte kavali) are played together, one performing the melody, the other a drone. This type of kaval is made from one piece of wood. A similar use of the kaval is also known in Macedonia and Kosovo (Yugoslavia), where one kaval of the pair is 'male', the other 'female'. The Albanian kavall is better known as the FYELL.

In Turkey the term 'kaval' is used generally to refer to all shepherd's pipes and more particularly (though not invariably) to ductless flutes. The presence or absence of a duct is sometimes specified by the addition of a

Kaval (rim-blown flute) player, Bulgaria

qualification: *dilsiz kaval* ('*kaval* without a tongue'), *dilli kaval* ('*kaval* with a tongue'). Other qualifications may be added to describe materials, size or constructional features: *kamış kavalı* ('reed *kaval*'), *çam kavalı* ('pine *kaval*'), *madenı kavalı* ('metal *kaval*'); *cura kavalı* ('small *kaval*'), *çoban kavalı* ('shepherd's *kaval*', i.e. long *kaval*); *üç parçalı kavalı* ('*kaval* with three parts'). The *kaval* can be made of wood, cane, bone or metal (usually brass) and has five or more finger-holes, one thumb-hole, and sometimes additional unfingered holes like the Bulgarian instrument. It is primarily associated with shepherds and nomads; among the southern Türkmen, it is used for instrumental laments. Outside the pastoral context, the *kaval* is used to accompany dancing (sometimes with other instruments); in Yugoslavia this is a recent development.

In Thrace and some of the Aegean islands the term 'kavali' refers to an end-blown flute of the FLOYERA family. It has seven finger-holes and sometimes an additional thumb-hole. In northern Greece the term *kavali* is also used to denote the SOURAVLI.

See also CAVAL DOBROGEAN.

VERGILIJ ATANASSOV, R. CONWAY MORRIS,
RADMILA PETROVIĆ

Kavikāra maḍuva. Buddhist ritual ensemble of singers and instrumentalists, found in Sri Lanka. It was originally an 18th-century courtly institution, employed to chant and accompany traditional praise-songs to the monarch. When the monarchy fell to the British in 1815 the tradition was transferred to the most important centre of Buddhist worship in Sri Lanka, the Temple of the Tooth, Kandy. Membership in the group is hereditary and the families concerned hold temple land for their services. On Wednesday mornings, when the relic is ritually cleansed, four *kavikāra* instrumentalists gather in the drumming-hall of the temple, a little apart from the HĒVISI ensemble and partly hidden from the worshippers. Two players hold *uḍäkki* (drums), one *pantēruva* (jingles) and one a pair of small cymbals known as *tālampota*. They begin their panegyrics only when the *hēvisi* ensemble starts to play, and the sound of their chanting and playing is almost drowned by the much bigger sound of the *hēvisi*. Close listening reveals the faint sound of their instruments but the performers deliberately distort the pronunciation and insert nonsense words to prevent comprehension of the poems.

The ensemble is thus a unique example of 'secret' music in Sri Lanka.

BIBLIOGRAPHY

A. M. Hocart: *The Temple of the Tooth at Kandy* (London, 1931) 13ff

C. de S. Kulatillake and R. Abeysinghe: *A Background to Sinhala Music of Sri Lanka* (Colombo, 1976), 6

NATALIE M. WEBBE[R]

Kawaha. *See* KAUAHA.

Kawai. Japanese firm of piano makers. Established on a small scale in 1925, it was incorporated in 1930, eventually becoming Japan's second largest piano manufacturing firm. Annual production rose from approximately 2000 instruments during the early 1950s to about 90,000 by the late 1970s; 10% of these were exported. The firm based in Tokyo, trades under the name of Kawai Musical Instrument Manufacturing Co. Less familiar than Yamaha in Europe, the firm's pianos have established a considerable reputation in the USA. Designs include a concert grand (about 2·8 metres), several excellent grands over 1·5 metres, all fitted with a third sostenuto pedal, and an upright about 1·3 metres tall (model K 48), which is one of the best instruments of its kind currently available. Kawai also makes percussion instruments, electric pianos (upright and baby grand) electronic organs (including a demonstration model with eight manuals) and synthesizers, which were for a time marketed under the name Teisco (the company's original name).

See also PIANOFORTE, §I, 9.

CYRIL EHRLICH

Ka'wásta'. *See* KA'HNYÁ'.

Kawayawaya. Scraped unbraced MOUTH BOW of the Mbwela and neighbouring peoples of south-eastern Angola. It is similar to the XIZAMBI of the Tsonga, but is sounded by rubbing a plain stick, not a rattle stick, across the notches in the stave. See G. Kubik: *Music traditional e aculturada dos !Kung de Angola* (Lisbon, 1970), 33, pll.14, 15.

Kaw law [bong lang]. Vertical XYLOPHONE with 12 logs found principally in Kalasin Province, north-eastern Thailand. Though related to ancient instruments of the Vietnamese highlands, the *kaw law* attained its present form during the 20th century. *See also* TLING TLÖOR and TRÜNG.

Kaw law (vertical xylophone), near Kalasin, Thailand

sanjo kayagŭm (long zither) of Korea

awnadron. A small double-headed cylindrical drum ~~~ed by the rural blacks of Surinam.

awombo. MOUTH BOW of the Chokwe and Lunda peo~~~es of Zaïre (*LaurentyC*, 112). *See* LUSUBA.

ay [kaypuimcā]. Small bronze gong of Bhaktapur, ~~~epal. *See* TAIM NĀIM.

ayab. Percussion idiophone of Mexico. *See* ÁYOTL.

ayagŭm. Korean 12-string plucked long zither (*Kaya*: ~~ame of an ancient Korean tribal league; *gŭm*: 'string ~~strument'). It is often called *kayago*. The *kayagŭm* ~~w occurs in two basic sizes: a large instrument (var-~~usly called *pŏpkŭm*, *chŏngak kayagŭm* or *p'ungnyu ~~yagŭm*) for court and aristocratic music, about 160 ~~m long by 30 cm wide; and a smaller instrument ~~ometimes called *sanjo kayagŭm*, see illustration) for ~~lk and virtuoso music, about 142 cm long by 23 cm ~~ide.

The larger instrument is fashioned from a single piece ~~f paulownia wood, with a gently curving front and par-~~ally hollowed out from the rear. At the lower end styl-~~ed ram's horns are carved out of the board. The 12 ~~rings, of twisted silk, run from pegs under the top end, ~~rough small holes, over a curved, fixed bridge, across ~~2 individual movable bridges ('wild-goose feet', 6 to ~~ cm high), and across another fixed bridge to looped ~~oorings where reserve string is kept in coils.

The smaller and more recent instrument resembles its ~~redecessor in most ways but is fashioned like the six-~~ring KŎMUN'GO, the top from paulownia wood and the ~~ar from chestnut. The ram's horns are only hinted at ~~d the lower fixed bridge is eliminated. The curvature ~~f the face of the instrument is also more pronounced. ~~he smaller size and greater curvature permit more rap-~~ and virtuoso performance.

The *kayagŭm* is usually tuned pentatonically, and there ~~e various tunings in each repertory. A typical tuning ~~ court music is $E\flat-F-A\flat-B\flat-e\flat-f-a\flat-b\flat-c'-$ ~~'-f'-a\flat'$, with $e\flat$ as tonic; a common tuning for folk music is $F-B\flat-c-f-g-b\flat-c'-d'-f'-g'-b\flat'-c''$, with f as tonic. Retuning is possible during performance by sliding the movable bridges. The treatise *Akhak kwebŏm* (1493) demonstrates a number of tunings and modes for the *kayagŭm*, as well as giving some information on a tablature notation system.

The instrument is played with the lower end pointing somewhat away from the performer's left, so that it passes in front of the left knee; the top end is supported on the right knee. The strings are plucked with the fleshy part of the fingers of the right hand (thumb and first three fingers), as well as by an outward flick using the finger-nails. Two or three fingers of the left hand press down on the strings a few centimetres to the left of the mov-able bridges, thereby making intermediate pitches avail-able and producing various ornaments, including the wide vibrato characteristic of Korean music. The tone of the *kayagŭm* is more delicate than that of the *kŏmun'go* and is considered more feminine.

The history of the *kayagŭm* can be traced back to the Silla dynasty (57 BC–AD 935). A legend, recounted in the *Samguk sagi* ('History of the Three Kingdoms', 1145), explains that King Kasil of the tribal league Kaya (6th century AD) built the *kayagŭm* based on instruments from China and commanded the music master U Rŭk to compose 12 pieces for the new instrument; U Rŭk, because of turbulent times in Kaya, went over to King Chinhŭng of Silla (ruled 540–76) and was well received, his music and the instrument being perpetuated.

A few pottery figures survive from the Silla period which clearly depict a *kayagŭm*-like instrument, com-plete with ram's horns, but the best evidence comes from four early 9th-century examples in excellent condition in the Shōsōin Repository in Nara, Japan (where they are referred to as *shiragi-goto*: 'KOTO from Silla'). These instruments reveal that the modern *kayagŭm* is striking-ly similar to its ancient ancestors.

Today the *kayagŭm* is perhaps the best-known and favourite of traditional Korean musical instruments. Many court and aristocratic pieces (such as the suite *Yŏngsan hoesang*) call for it and there are numerous schools of virtuoso solo performance (*sanjo*). Modern composers also write for the *kayagŭm* in a variety of styles, one leading composer being Hwang Byungki (*b* 1936). In recent years there have been experiments with new versions of the instrument, including one pitched an octave lower and (in north Korea) one with 13 strings. The *kayagŭm* has been adopted in Mongolia as a native instrument (*see* YATGA).

BIBLIOGRAPHY
Sŏng Hyŏn, ed.: *Akhak kwebŏm* [Guide to the study of music] (Seoul, 1493/*R*1975), 7.24*a*–28*a*
Hayashi Kenzō: *Dongya yueqi kao* [Investigations of East Asian musical instruments] (Beijing, 1962), 158ff
K. Hayashi and others: *Shōsōin no gakki* [Musical instruments in the Shōsōin] (Tokyo, 1967) [with Eng. summary]
Chang Sa-hun: *Han'guk akki taegwan* [Korean musical instruments] (Seoul, 1969), 75ff
Yi Chae-suk: *Kayagŭm sanjo* [Sanjo for the *kayagŭm*] (Seoul, 1971)
Kim Chŏng-ja: *Chŏngak kayagŭm po* [Aristocratic music for *kayagŭm*] (Seoul, 1979)
ROBERT C. PROVINE

Kayamba. Raft rattle of Kenya. It consists of a tray-shaped box made from reeds with seeds inside, measuring up to about 40 cm in length and 20 cm in width. A stick projecting from each side enables the rattle to be held between the middle and ring fingers of each hand. On some instruments a strip of coconut palm is fastened down the centre and beaten rhythmically with the thumbs. The rattle is used to accompany singing or instrumental performance. A similar rattle in Tanzania has been reported as *kiyamba*. See G. Hyslop: *Musical Instruments of East Africa*, i: *Kenya* (Nairobi, 1975). For illustration, *see* CHIVOTI.
K. A. GOURLAY

Kayambi. Tin-can rattle of the Swahili/Nguja people of Tanzania.

Kayanda. Single-headed open-ended conical drum of the Luba/Sanga people of Zaïre. The membrane is pegged on, and weighted. It is beaten by hand and is used for dance music, with the *ditumba* and *mitumbwe* drums. See *BooneT*, 59f; *TraceyCSA*, ii, 414.

Kayga. *See* KÁJGA.

Kaylukuk. *See* KALUKHAQ.

Kayoma [alungu]. Seven-string BOARD ZITHER of the Amba people of Uganda. A single rattan cane string is laced through holes at each end of the board and passes over wooden bridges at each end. The individual sections are tuned with auxiliary bridges. The instrument is held in both hands; the thumb of the player's left hand plucks the three left-hand strings, while his right hand plucks the remainder with a plectrum (6 cm long) made from a piece of grass. See *WachsmannTCU*.

Kayum. Upright single-headed cylindrical drum or KETTLEDRUM of the pre-Conquest Maya Indians. It was made from fired clay, had a decorated sound opening and was played with the hands. It appears in Mayan codices and wall paintings and is still used by the Lacandón Indians of the forest regions of Chiapas, Mexico; it is rested on a wheel plaited from lianas or on a three-legged stand.
JOHN M. SCHECHTER

Kazagi [kazage]. Open HOURGLASS DRUM of fixed pitch of the Hausa people of Nigeria, found also among the Bolewa. A small snared drum, approximately 22 cm lon 14 cm in diameter at the ends and 9 cm in diameter the waist, it is either suspended from the player's ne and beaten with wire thongs or plaited leather strips, hung from his left shoulder and beaten with a hook stick. Its main function is as supporting instrument cylindrical drums such as the *ganga*, *gangar noma dundufa* in accompanying girls' dancing, the perfo mance of praise songs for farmers, and among tl Maguzawa (non-Muslim Hausa) at marriages, feasts a other ceremonies.

BIBLIOGRAPHY
Ames–KingGHM
P. G. Harris: 'Notes on Drums and Musical Instruments Seen Sokoto Province, Nigeria', *Journal of the Royal Anthropologic Institute*, lxii (1932), 105
K. A. GOURLA

Kazoo [bazooka, gazooka, gazoota]. An instrume which amplifies the human voice while also impartir a buzzing, rasping quality to it. It is classified by Hor bostel and Sachs as a 'singing membrane'. Probably Afro-American origin and first manufactured in the US around 1850, it has been produced since the 1890s many countries and in a variety of forms. It now co sists of a cigar-shaped tube of plated metal or plast with a flattened opening at one end and a smaller, ci cular opening at the other. Over a large hole on the t a circular disc of animal membrane or equivalent mat rial is held in place by a screw-on metal cup. As tl performer sings or hums into the flattened end the men brane vibrates (strongly if the cup is uncovered but le so if partly covered by the hand) and many kinds wavering and loud, quacking effects are possible. Tl sound of the kazoo could be amplified by fitting a trun pet or trombone bell to the end. In this form it was ofte known as a 'jazz-horn'. It originally had an importa role in black American music, especially in country strir bands and early jazz ensembles, but is now often regarde as a toy. In England the kazoo was known as bazook gazoota, gazooka or hooter and was popularly used the 1920s and 1930s in working men's bands. In tl West Riding of Yorkshire, where the kazoo was know as a 'Tommy Talker', there were many 'Tommy Talk bands' and 'Waffen Fuffen bands' which played at ca nivals and galas. In these the kazoo was the princip instrument, augmented by a variety of others which, fc the purposes of competition, had to be made of tin (se R. Wharton and A. Clarke: 'The Tommy Talker Ban of the West Riding', *Musical Traditions*, i (1983), 16 It is also used in some professional popular musi ensembles.

See also CANTOPHONE; EUNUCH-FLUTE; MIRLITON.
ANTHONY C. BAINES, PAUL OLIVE

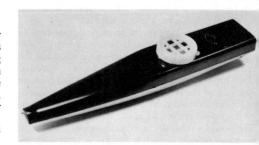

Modern kazoo, made in Germany (Horniman Museum London)

āzu puķe ('wedding flower'). Rattle of Latvia. *See* RIDEKSNIS.

bandu. In Jamaica, one of a pair of twinned drums; e other is called 'playing cast'.

bili [kibili]. Conical drum of the Hima people of wanda and eastern Zaïre (*BooneT*, 70). *See* DINDO.

'cindo. Idioglot transverse clarinet of the Dakakari eople of Nigeria. *See* CLARINET, TRANSVERSE.

(raft) d(urch) F(reude)-Grosston-Orgel. An ELEC-RONIC ORGAN designed by OSKAR VIERLING in 1935–6 at e Heinrich-Hertz-Institut für Schwingungsforschung . the Technische Hochschule, Berlin. Based on a pro-type two-manual electronic organ built in 1934, and riginally intended for research, it was completed at great eed when, at only two months' notice, it was com-issioned for use at the Olympic Games in Berlin in 936 by the National Socialist association Kraft durch reude (the KdF car was the famous Volkswagen 'Bee-e'). Only two models were constructed. In open-air vents the instrument was used with a 200-watt ampli-cation system for accompanying 20,000 singers. It had ree 56-note manuals, a 27-note pedal-board and 44 ops. The sounds were generated by 96 oscillators (one r each note), which produced sawtooth waves. The scillators were housed in removable drawers in a cabi-et that was separate from the console but connected to by an umbilical cable; this arrangement permitted the rgan to be transported in two sections. A separate eadphone amplifier enabled tuning adjustments to be ade, when necessary even during performances. A low-equency oscillator provided an amplitude-modulated ibrato of between 6 and 10 Hz.

BIBLIOGRAPHY
. Barkow: 'Die elektroakustische Orgel: Erfolge deutscher Inge-nieurarbeit', *ZI*, lv (1934), 35
. Gradenwitz: 'Problème de l'orgue électro-acoustique: ses solu-tions', *La nature*, lxv (1937), 260
. Vierling: 'Praktischer Einsatz der elektrischen Orgel auf der Dietrich-Eckart-Bühne und auf der Rundfunk-Ausstellung', *Elek-trotechnische Zeitschrift*, lviii (1937), 90
——: 'Eine neue elektrische Orgel', *Deutscher Musikkultur*, iii/1 (1938), 16
HUGH DAVIES

Keat, James (*b* London, 7 May 1813; *d* Winchester, New Hampshire, 17 March 1845). English maker of rass instruments, active in the USA. The third son of he London instrument maker Samuel Keat, he worked ith SAMUEL GRAVES & Co. in Winchester, New Hamp-hire, from 1837 to about 1842. He probably assisted ne firm in introducing keyed and valved brass instru-ments to its production; several keyed bugles and an F rumpet with two Stölzel valves are known signed 'J. Keat for Graves & Co., Winchester, New Hampshire'.

The exact date of Keat's arrival in Winchester is not nown, but Henry Keat, a younger brother, is known o have toured the USA in 1836 and 1837 with the Cov-nt Garden Opera orchestra. Although James may have rrived earlier, it seems likely that he went with his rother. In March 1837 he purchased one half of the econd floor and water rights in the building where Graves & Co. occupied the upper two floors. In December 1841 e purchased another piece of land with water power ights nearby. Soon afterwards he was taken ill and was nable to continue working. In May 1842 he sold his shop to Graves & Co. and in June also his recently pur-chased land. Whether he was able to work again before his death is not known.

BIBLIOGRAPHY
L. G. Langwill: *An Index of Musical Wind-instrument Makers* (Edinburgh, 1960, rev., enlarged 6/1980)
R. E. Eliason: *Graves & Co., Musical Instrument Makers* (Dear-born, Mich., 1975)
ROBERT E. ELIASON

Keb-ang. Flat gong in the INILA-UD ensemble of the northern Philippines.

Kebele. Stick rattle of the Dogon people of Mali, con-sisting of pieces of gourd threaded on to a forked stick. Boys shake the *kebele* during the retreat following cir-cumcision, always using the same rhythm.

Kebluk. Set of three bossed gongs used in the *gamelan renteng* of West Java. They rest on crossed cords in a wooden frame and are beaten with padded hammers by one performer.

Keccai [gejjai]. Metal pellet bells of Tamil Nadu, India, worn around the ankle. *See* GHUŇGRŪ.

Kecer. METALLOPHONE used in the gamelan of Bali and Central Java. It consists of bronze plates in a wooden frame which are struck with loose bronze plates. It is rarely used in Java.

Kecrek. Central Javanese idiophone. It consists of metal plates of indefinite pitch suspended from a box of pup-pets and clashed together by the puppeteer's (*dalang*) foot. They accompany dance movements in the Central Javanese shadow puppet play or dance-drama. Alter-natively, they are placed on the floor and beaten with a wooden mallet. *See also* CEMPALA.

Kedenggene. Single-headed drum of the Masa Mului people of central Chad. The body is a large pottery jar with the bottom open and the neck covered; the mem-brane is goatskin, stuck to the clay and encircled by a string. The *kedenggene* is beaten by hand by the men to accompany women's dances in which the women imitate men with the help of accessories such as clothes, weapons and *gozoma* rattles. The *kedenggene* is also struck to accompany funeral songs connected with sac-rifice three days after the death of an important person. According to tradition, it has taken the place and func-tion of a wooden drum of the past called *teni*.
MONIQUE BRANDILY

Kedengu [kedengo]. SLIT-DRUM of the Mbanja and Ngbaka peoples of Zaïre (*LaurentyTF*, 133, 140). *See* GUGU, (1).

Kediding. *See* TELENG.

Kedondolo. Braced composite MOUTH BOW of the Kwe-bo (Northern Sotho) people of southern Africa. It resembles the Zulu ISITHONTOLO.

Kee. Gourd vessel rattle of the Kpelle people of Liber-ia, with net and external strung beads. It is used to pro-vide rhythmic accompaniment to singing.

Keer [kitiar]. Lute of the Shuar people in the Oriente region of Ecuador. See C. A. Coba Andrade: 'Instrumentos musicales ecuatorianos', *Sarance*, vii (1979), 70.

Kegbier. Plucked lute of the Konkomba people of northern Togo. *See* KIBEWE.

Kegürge. *See* KÖGÜRGE.

Keho. Idiophone of Easter Island. It consisted of a stone plate over a gourd resonator in a pit in the ground. The plate was stamped rhythmically to accompany singing and dancing.

Kei [kin]. Japanese LITHOPHONE or METALLOPHONE. It is a percussion plaque, vertically suspended, of stone or, more commonly today, metal. It is derived from the Chinese *qing* (the Japanese term 'kei' uses the same pictograph; *see* QING (i)), and is related also to the Korean T'ŬKKYŎNG. It is used now in Buddhist services and rites: the single metal slab some 2 cm thick and 25 cm wide is suspended in a wooden frame and struck with a round-headed wooden stick. Although the shape of early specimens was quite variable the modern *kei* is fairly consistent. For generic discussion of Japanese metallophones, *see* KANE.

BIBLIOGRAPHY
W. P. Malm: *Japanese Music and Musical Instruments* (Rutland, Vermont, 1959), 68
S. Kishibe: *The Traditional Music of Japan* (Tokyo, 1966, 2/1981), pl.44

DAVID W. HUGHES

Keirōko. Japanese term for a barrel drum imported from China in the 8th century for use in GAGAKU (court music). It measures about 18 × 18 cm, has two tacked heads and has always been paired with the FURITSUZUMI. The *furitsuzumi* was held in the left hand and the *keirōko* suspended either from the same hand or from the neck and struck with a stick held in the right hand. It has survived only as a dancer's prop in the court dance *Ikkyoku*. See 'Keirōko', *Ongaku daijiten* [Encyclopedia of music] (Tokyo, 1981).

DAVID W. HUGHES

Keisu. Japanese bell, used in Buddhist music. *See* KIN (ii).

Keka. Tortoise-shell percussion vessel of the Sapa people of Liberia. *See* KONO (i), (2).

Kekatak. 12-keyed XYLOPHONE of Kotaagung in Lampung province, Sumatra. It is about 1 metre in length. It plays the same repertory as the *kulintang*, in an ensemble with a *terbang* (drum), a *ghujih* (cymbals) and a *penuntun* (suspended gong).

Keke (i). Drum of the Yoruba people of Nigeria. *See* IGBIN.

Keke (ii). STICK ZITHER of the Ngbandi people of northern Zaïre (*LaurentyC*, 115). *See* ZEZE (i).

Kekese. Basket rattle of the Yogo people of northe[rn] Zaïre.

Kekinciran. BULLROARER of the Sundanese districts [of] West Java. *See* JATA.

Kelangen. KETTLEDRUM of the Jola people of the Cas[a]mance area of Senegal, now obsolete. The drum had [a] goatskin membrane, and its use was restricted to c[ir]cumcision ceremonies, the installation of the chief or [a] high official, and announcing the death of the ruler. I[ts] function was primarily as a signalling instrument. S[ee] L.-V. Thomas: 'Les Diola', *Mémoires de l'Insti[tut] français d'Afrique noire*, lv (1958–9).

Kele. *See* KELEI.

Kele'a. Side-blown Triton CONCH-SHELL TRUMPET [of] Tonga. Formerly blown at funeral ceremonies, it is no[w] used both as a signalling device and, in ensembles [of] up to nine players, to sustain excitement during inte[r-] village football matches. Each ensemble instrument pla[ys] one note only, tuned by thrusting a hand up the bell [of] the conch. See R. Moyle: 'Tongan Musical Instr[u]ments', *GSJ*, xxix (1976), 77.

Keledi [keladi, kledi]. Bamboo mouth organ of sever[al] peoples of East Malaysia and Kalimantan, including th[e] Kayan, Kenyah, Iban and Orang Ulu. It is related to th[e] mainland South-east Asian KHAĒN. Four to six bambo[o] tubes about 75 to 105 cm long are fitted vertically in[to] holes cut in a hollow gourd about 8 to 15 cm wide, [to] which a blowpipe about 20 cm long is attached. B[y] opening and closing the finger-holes near the base [of] each tube and using circular breathing, the player ca[n] produce various polychordal effects. An instrument [of] this type is depicted on the bas-reliefs of the 8th-centu[ry] temple at Borobudur, Central Java.

MARGARET J. KARTO[MI]

Mouth organ of the keledi type of the Iba[n] people, Indonesia: fro[m] 'Indonesische Siermotieven' (Batavi[a] [now Jakarta], 1949)

Kelei [kele]. SLIT-DRUM of the Mende and other people[s] of Sierra Leone. It is made from a hollow log or can[e] with one to four slits. The instrument, measurin[g] approximately 55 cm in length and 15 cm in diamete[r], has holes bored through the ends which are sometime[s]

rge and small kelei (slit-drums) of the Gola people,
erra Leone

vered with metal discs. The drum is suspended from
e neck and beaten with two sticks. Different pitches
e obtained by striking the instrument between or on
her side of the slits, near the ends of the log or cane,
near the middle. The instrument is used as a 'talking
um', and is sometimes played in sets of two or three,
which case a large version made from wood is slung
om rafters beneath an awning (see illustration).

BIBLIOGRAPHY

van Oven: 'Sierra Leone', *Grove 6*
Schulze: 'Music of the Mende of Sierra Leone', FE 4322 [disc
notes]

eleli. Plucked lute of the Teda people of Tibesti,
orthern Chad. It has a hemispherical soundbox about
cm in diameter made from gourd, wood or an enamel
wl. According to the type of music played it has two
three strings. The neck is inserted through a slot in
e laced camel-skin soundboard, its lower end reap-
aring under a circular hole in the skin. The strings are
w often nylon instead of animal sinew but they are
ill fastened to the neck by the traditional method with
ather thongs, and attached to the lower end of the neck
rough the hole. It is similar to the *chegeni*.

MONIQUE BRANDILY

elenang [klenang]. Small high-pitched bossed gong
Bali. It is played in the *gamelan gong, gamelan gong
byar* and *gamelan bebonangan* (*see* GAMELAN, §6 (iv)).
smaller ensembles the *kelenang* is struck on every
f-beat. See C. McPhee: *Music in Bali* (New Haven
d London, 1966/*R*1976), 119f.

eleng. Large wooden SLIT-DRUM of the Kpelle people
Liberia.

elenongan. Ensemble in the Menggala area of Lam-
ung province, Sumatra. It comprises a *kelittang* (gong-
nime), a pair of *talo balak* (large suspended gongs),
ende (small suspended gong), *ghujih* (pair of cym-
als), *ketipung* (cylindrical drum), *terbang* (frame drum),
etuk (gong) and a pair of *canang* (small gongs).

MARGARET J. KARTOMI

Keli. DUCT FLUTE of Sri Lanka. It is from 30·5 cm to
33 cm long, with six finger-holes, producing the first
seven notes of a diatonic major scale from c'. The *keli*
is nearly always lacquered in characteristic Sinhalese
style.

Kelintang (i). GONG-CHIME of Kerinci, Rejang-Lebong,
and neighbouring areas in the Bengkulu and Jambi
provinces of Sumatra. Its four, five, six, seven or (in
northern Rejang-Lebong only) nine small bronze or iron
bossed gongs are arranged in a single row in a horizontal wooden frame and beaten with a pair of soft hammers. On the coast of Bengkulu province it accompanies
the 'candle' dance.

The name 'kelintang' is used also for an ensemble
consisting in Rejang-Lebong of a *kelintang* (with six
gongs), a *gendang panjang* (cylindrical drum), *redap* or
deb (frame drums) and a suspended bronze bossed gong
about 38 to 45 cm in diameter. The instruments are
periodically cleaned with oil at a mystical ceremony.
Sometimes a *serunai* (oboe) or *biola* (violin) substitutes
for the *kelintang*. In Kerinci and Bangko-Tabo (Jambi
province) the ensemble comprises four *kelintang* (with
four gongs), a *gendang panjang* and two suspended
gongs.

MARGARET J. KARTOMI

Kelintang (ii). XYLOPHONE of West Jambi province,
Sumatra, consisting of six wooden keys tuned to a pentatonic scale. These are held together on a long scarf
tied round the player's waist and rest on the player's
legs and feet; they are beaten with a pair of soft hammers.

MARGARET J. KARTOMI

Kelittang [kelittangan]. GONG-CHIME in the Pepadon
(Menggala and east coast) area of Lampung province,
Sumatra. In Menggala it has 12 small bossed gongs and
on the east coast nine gongs in a wooden frame. The
name is used also for an ensemble consisting of a *kelittang, talo balak* and *talo tanggung* (pair of large suspended gongs), *bende* (small suspended gong), *ghujih*
(pair of cymbals), *ketipung* (cylindrical drum) and *terbang* (frame drum). The ensemble exists also in coastal
areas under the names of *kulitang, kulintang, keromong*
and *tabuhan*, the last being a general term for ensembles
in the area.

MARGARET J. KARTOMI

Kelmas ('stump'). Single-headed drum of Lithuania,
known mostly in Samogitia (west and north-west Lithuania). The body of the *kelmas* is hollowed out of the
stump of a willow, lime or birch tree, leaving the walls
2 to 3 cm thick. A goat- or dog-skin is attached to one
end with X or Y lacing. The *kelmas* is 30 to 40 cm high,
and has a diameter of 25 to 40 cm. It is usually placed
on the ground and struck with one or two wooden sticks
or padded felt beaters. Until the beginning of the 20th
century the *kelmas* was used as a rhythm instrument in
village bands. Nowadays a modified type of *kelmas* is
combined with *skrabalai* (cowbells). This type is 45 cm
deep and 55 cm in diameter, and is struck by means of
a foot pedal.

ARVYDAS KARAŠKA

Kelo. Set of small tuned kettledrums (*see* KETTLEDRUM)
of the Kanuri people of north-eastern Nigeria. They are

used with the *gunda* (hourglass drum) at marriages in the Maiduguri, Monguno and Benisheik areas.

Kelutviaq. A single-string fiddle used by the Inuit people of south-west Alaska and Nelson Island. In T. Johnston: *Eskimo Music by Region: a Circum-polar Study* (Ottawa, 1976, p.107) it is described as follows:

It is made from a Prince Albert tobacco can, wooden fingerboard, and small stone bridge. The string is struck with a quill made from a swan's feather which has been shaved in the middle to allow it to be flexible enough to bounce on the string.

Kemae. Turtle-shell SCRAPER, played by the Bora Indians of the Peruvian tropical forest region.

Keman. Turkish term for the European violin. The *keman* is increasingly being used to replace the traditional KEMENÇE (fiddle) in both folk ensembles and classical *fasıl* (Turkish art music). *See also* VIOLIN, §IV, 2.

Kemanak [kenawak]. Idiophone of the Sundanese areas of West Java. It consists of a pair of metal tubes in the shape of bananas with a split in the concave surface and the stalk still attached. They are played by striking the bottom of one against the rim of the other. The instrument is found in court gamelan and, in the Cirebon area, in village *slendro*-tuned ensembles. It accompanies certain ritual *bedaya* court dances. The GUMANAK of Bali is a similar instrument. See J. Kunst: *De toonkunst van Java* (The Hague, 1934; Eng. trans., rev. 2/1949, enlarged 3/1973), 180.

MARGARET J. KARTOMI

Kemanche. SPIKE FIDDLE of Georgia and Azerbaijan (USSR). *See* KAMĀNCHE.

Kembe. 12-key LAMELLAPHONE of the Mpiemo people of the Central African Republic and south-eastern Cameroon and the Mpopo of south-eastern Cameroon. The keys pass over two transverse bridges and are plucked with the thumbs, while the fingers of both hands support a small wooden trapezoidal box resonator. This box is placed in a half-calabash, suspended from the player's neck by a cord so that he can play either sitting or standing. The instrument is used for self-accompaniment in song. See P. Collaer: 'Musics of the Central African Republic', BM 30 L 2310 [disc notes].

Kemençe. Short-necked fiddle of Turkey. The *kemençe* of the eastern Black Sea coastal region is sometimes called the *karadeniz kemençesi* ('Black Sea fiddle'; Gk. *kementses*). Its box resonator is carved in the shape of a trough with rounded ends and covered with a coniferous wood sound-table. The short neck, with or without fingerboard, tapers to a flat pear-shaped pegbox. There are three strings of gut or metal which are played underhand with a short horsehair bow. The strings are tuned in 4ths and played in two-part polyphony. The *kemençe* is played either sitting, with the lower part of the body resting on the knee, or standing (see illustration). Sometimes the player leads a dance while playing. The instrument is used solo and to accompany song as well as dance.

In western Turkey the *kemençe* is similar to the Greek *lyra* of the eastern Aegean type, and is sometimes called the *fasıl kemençesi* ('classical *kemençe*') or *kemençe rumi* ('Greek *kemençe*'). It has a pear-shaped body and three

Kemençe (short-necked fiddle) player, Sürmene, Turkey, 1963

metal or gut strings which are stopped from the side with the fingernails. It is rested on the player's knee or held against the chest and played with underhand bowing. This type of *kemençe* is used mainly in classical *fasıl* (Turkish art music) and is becoming rarer as the *keman* (European violin) gains in popularity. See L. Picken: *Folk Musical Instruments of Turkey* (London, 1975). *See also* K'AMAN.

R. CONWAY MORRIS

Kemene. Bulgarian fiddle. *See* GADULKA.

Kementses. The KEMENÇE (short-necked fiddle) played by Greek refugees from the Turkish Black Sea coast. It is sometimes called the *Pondiaki lyra* ('Pontic *lyra*').

Kemper. German firm of organ builders. Adolf Kemper (1811–80) became a citizen of Lübeck in 1839. His son Emanuel (1844–1933) took over the workshop of Theodor Voigt in 1868 and founded the present firm, which has remained under the control of the original family, from Kempringen, Westphalia. Emanuel's son Karl Reinhold (1880–1957), well known for his collaboration with H. H. Jahnn, took over the firm in 1910. Karl's son Emanuel Magnus (*b* Apenrade, 30 Sept 1906) entered the firm in 1944, and greatly broadened its interests to include clavichords, spinets and harpsichords. On 1 January 1974 Emanuel Reinhold (*b* Lübeck 8 Jan 1947), son of Emanuel Magnus, became head of the firm, which was renamed Orgelbau Lübeck, Emanuel und Ella Kemper in 1981. It is uncertain whether Peter Kemper (*b* Menden, baptized 18 April 1734; *d* Bonn, 24 Oct 1820) was a member of this family. He was an organ builder in the tradition of Johann Balthasar König, and his work included the organs in Bonn Minster and Aachen Cathedral.

The firm builds organs of all types: it played a leading

rt in the *Orgelbewegung*. Major contracts have included gans for the monastery of St John, Berlin-Spandau; Marien, Gdańsk; Frauenburg Cathedral; the south-st organ, Jakobikirche, Hamburg; the west organ, kobikirche, Lübeck; the north and west organs, St arien, Lübeck; the Bonnewegkirche, Luxembourg; St kolai, Siegen, Westphalia. The firm has carried out number of important restorations: at St Nikolai, Brieg rgan by Engler), the Jakobikirche, Hamburg (Schnit-r), and elsewhere.

BIBLIOGRAPHY

Stahl: *Geschichte der Kirchenmusik in Lübeck* (Kassel, 1931)
K. Rössler: 'Kemper', *MGG*
Lottermoser: 'Orgelneubau auf akustischer Grundlage: Haupt-orgel St. Nikolai in Siegen/Westfalen', *Gravesaner Blätter*, iv (1958), 131 [with Eng. trans.]

HANS KLOTZ

empli. (1) Small bossed gong of Bali, used in the *gam-an gong*, *gamelan gong kebyar* and *gamelan bebonan-an* (*see* GAMELAN, §6 (iv)). In smaller ensembles the *mpli* is struck on every beat. See C. McPhee: *Music Bali* (New Haven and London, 1966/*R*1976), 191ff. (2) TUBE ZITHER of Bali. *See* GUNTANG. (3) Javanese FRAME DRUM. *See* TERBANG.

empul. Suspended bronze gongs used in the West, entral and East Javanese gamelan. They are approxi-ately 38 cm in diameter and are beaten with a padded allet. In the Central Javanese gamelan the *kempul* are sually struck alternately with the *kenong* (boxed gong) equal time intervals; the gong beat marking the end f each phrase always coincides with one of the *kenong* eats. *Kempul* are sometimes used in groups of five to even (or even as many as eleven), tuned to notes of he *slendro* or *pelog* scales (*see* GAMELAN, §4), some-mes doubling for both a *slendro* and a *pelog* pitch (of ifferent scale levels); but in the 19th century only one r two *kempul* were normally used in a gamelan. *Kem-ul* are tuned one octave lower than the KENONG, and sually have the same number of pitches. In the Sun-anese ensembles of West Java only one *kempul* is used; is about 50 cm in diameter, with a rim of 12 cm.

MARGARET J. KARTOMI

empur. (1) Balinese gong used in the *gamelan gong*, amelan gong kebyar* and *gamelan bebonangan* (*see* GAMELAN, §6 (iv)). It is beaten with a heavily padded allet. In smaller ensembles the *kempur* provides the ain punctuation, sounding at the end of each main hrase. See C. McPhee: *Music in Bali* (New Haven and ondon, 1966/*R*1976), 234ff. (2) TUBE ZITHER of Bali. *See* GUNTANG.

MARGARET J. KARTOMI

empur komodong. Balinese idiophone, consisting of large bamboo key suspended over an earthen jar. It ay be played in the *gamelan pejogedan*.

empyang. (1) Term used for one or two small high-itched unmuted bossed gongs in the Central Javanese amelan. They rest on crossed cords in a wooden box nd are struck simultaneously with a padded mallet, lternating with other gongs in cyclic rhythms. The *empyang* belong to the *pelog* set in a complete *gamelan eprangkat* and may be tuned to pitches 6^5 (i.e. pitch 6 n the fifth lowest octave) and 7^5 (*see* GAMELAN, §§4 nd 6(i)).

(2) Javanese FRAME DRUM. *See* TERBANG.

MARGARET J. KARTOMI

Kèn. Generic term for the wooden oboe of Vietnam. It is similar to the Chinese SUONA, with seven finger-holes at the front and one at the back and a bell made of brass or wood. For the various types of Vietnamese oboe *see* KÈN BÀU.

Kena [kena-kena, quena, quena-quena]. An Andean open NOTCHED FLUTE, dating from the Chavin era (900–200 BC) in Peru. The early *kena* was made from animal, bird or human bone, or of gold, silver, clay or gourd. The modern *kena* is longer (25 to 50 cm) and is com-monly made of cane, although bone, clay, gourd, stone and metal *kenas* have been used. The instrument has five or six equidistant finger-holes in the lower half of the tube and one thumb-hole in the centre at the rear; occasionally there are as many as eight finger-holes. Capable of producing a two-octave chromatic scale, the *kena* is used both for pentatonic melodies among high-land Quechua and Aymara and for mestizo songs displaying a wider gamut. While often played unaccompanied, traditionally by males, it is frequently combined in parallel 3rds with another *kena* and with a *bombo* or *caja* (drums) to perform *waynos*, *bailecitos*, *carnavalitos*, *cacharparis*, *cuecas*, *taquiraris* and other regional dances. The *kena* is also played by Andean shepherds, as an instrument to inspire love, and in processions celebrating major festivals in Cuzco, for-merly the Inca capital. The *kena* is found principally in the Peruvian and Bolivian sierra and plateau; it is found also in northern Chile, in northern and north-western Argentina, and less frequently in Ecuador, Colombia, Venezuela and the Guianas.

The *kena-kena* has been known since at least the 16th century among the Aymara people in the Lake Titicaca

Kena (notched flute) played by an Aymara Indian, Lake Titicaca, Bolivia

region of the Bolivian Alti Plano. It is between 50 and 70 cm long and 25 mm in diameter, and has six finger-holes at the front and another hole at the rear. *Pusiphiá kenas* can be as long as 72 cm and are often played in groups of three: the largest (*taikapusiphia*) plays the melody, the *malta* sounds a 5th above, and the smallest (*liku*) an octave above. These ensembles are sometimes called *mucululos*. According to one source, the *kena-kena* melody is accompanied a perfect 5th above by the *kena mala* (*kena mediana* in Aymara), two-thirds the length of the *kena-kena*. The *kena-kena* is popular in Bolivian patronal and agrarian festivals. In Compi, on the shores of Lake Titicaca, it is reserved for the period between Easter and the end of the dry season, when the *kollko*, a six-holed beaked flute, is played until All Saints' Day. In Irpa Chico, 30 km south of La Paz, the *kena-kena* is played during harvest-time.

BIBLIOGRAPHY
A. González Bravo: 'Kenas, pincollos y tarkas', *Boletín latino-americano de música*, iii/3 (1937), 25
R. Stevenson: *Music in Aztec and Inca Territory* (Berkeley, 1968)
H. C. Buechler: *The Masked Media: Aymara Fiestas and Social Interaction in the Bolivian Highlands* (The Hague, 1980)
JOHN M. SCHECHTER

Kenawak. *See* KEMANAK.

Kèn bầu. Vietnamese oboe akin to the Chinese SUONA. It consists of a double reed, a brass pirouette, a cedar-wood body with seven finger-holes and a thumb-hole and a copper bell. It is played in the ĐAI NHAC court ensemble, in ensembles for funerals and for traditional theatre. In various regions of Vietnam it is also called *kèn bóp*, *kèn bát* and *kèn giả nam*. The size and pitch of these Vietnamese oboes varies enormously: high-pitched ones include the *kèn vặt*, *kèn củn* and *kèn tiểu*; medium-pitched the *kèn nam*, *kèn trung pha* and *kèn trung đục*; and low-pitched the *kèn đại*, *kèn đại trường* and *kèn quá khổ*. Among the ethnic minorities oboes include the *phẩn ty* (Dao people), *sona* (Nung) and the *sarunai* or *sarinai* (Cham).

TRÂN QUANG HAI

Kencane. FRAME DRUM used in pairs in the *nobat* orchestra of Riau province (Tanjung Pinang), Indonesia. Its skin measures about 45 cm in diameter.

Kencek. Medium-sized pair of cymbals of Bali, used in the *gamelan kebyar*.

Kendang [kendang]. A generic term for any double-headed laced drum, cylindrical or conical, of the islands of Java and Bali. For a discussion of related instruments of other Indonesian and Malaysian regions and the ensembles associated with them, *see* GENDANG. All ordinary gamelan include one or more *kendang* played by the orchestral leader, who gives cues to the other musicians regarding formal structure, speed, number of repetitions, beginnings and endings, etc. This is done through an elaborate standardized system of fixed rhythmical patterns composed of the various sounds each drum may produce.

In Central Java the *kendang* has a double-conical, or 'bellied' body, to which the heads are laced with leather. It is played by hand. In the Central Javanese gamelan there are three sizes. The smallest, the *kendang ketipung*, is about 40 cm long. It is played also in rural gamelan such as the *gamelan reyog* in Ponorogo, East Java, where its name is abbreviated to *tipung* (for illustration *see* GAMELAN, fig.3). The *kendang batangan* (*kendang ciblon*) is about 65 cm long and is usually made of jackfruit wood or coconut trunk. It formerly accompanied only a few pieces, but it now has a large repertory and is used in the *wayang* (puppet) theatre and in dance music. It is played in a relatively elaborate style. The *kendang gending* (or *kendang gede*) is the large drum in the Central Javanese gamelan. It is about 77 cm long and is played either alone or (by the same player) with the *ketipung*. Only conically shaped *kendang* are used in the archaic gamelan of the Central Javanese courts (*see* GAMELAN, fig.5).

In Sundanese areas of West Java the *kendang* has the shape of a truncated cone. Its heads are laced with cord of buffalo hide and tautened by sliding rings. In ensembles a pair of *kendang* are often used. The larger is the *kendang ageung* ('big drum'), about 65 cm long, its heads measuring about 30 cm and 26 cm in diameter. It rests slanting downwards on a low wooden trestle. The player beats the larger head with his right hand, sometimes with a drumstick, and his left hand plays the smaller head. The heel of the right foot is used continuously in Sundanese *kendang* playing to modify the pitch of the larger drum head. This *kendang* is always played in combination with one or two smaller drums, *kulanter*. The *kulanter* is about 36 to 38 cm long, with heads measuring about 18 and 16 cm in diameter. It is played in an upright position to the left of the performer. The *kendang penca* are one or two pairs of drums used for the Sundanese *penca* (a dance based on *penca silat*, the art of self-defence). These drums are similar to but larger than Sundanese *kendang*, and have tighter skins; they therefore sound much louder. They accompany *penca* performances together with a *tarompet* (oboe) and a gong.

The *kendang* of Balinese orchestras is made of jackfruit wood and its heads of water-buffalo skin or cowhide. Its outside is cylindrical, tapering slightly at one end, and inside it is shaped like an hourglass (*see* DRUM, figs.1*d* and 3*a*). Their average length (in the large gamelan) is 60 to 65 cm. *Kendang* are tuned and played in pairs, the *kendang wadon* ('female drum') leading and the *kendang lanang* ('male drum') following. For ceremonial music they are played with the hand and a drumstick, and for most dance and theatre music with the hands alone. They give a variety of open and muted sounds which are combined into conventional interlocking patterns determined by the musical form.

BIBLIOGRAPHY
C. McPhee: *Music in Bali* (New Haven and London, 1966/*R*1976)
H. Susilo: *Drumming in the Context of Javanese Gamelan* (diss. U. of California, Los Angeles, 1967)
MARGARET J. KARTOMI, ERNST HEINS, RUBY ORNSTEIN

Kende (i). Arched harp of southern Chad. The Sara-Gor instrument has eight strings, while that of the Sara-Madjingaye has seven. The *kende* is held vertically and the player accompanies his own singing.

Kende (ii). XYLOPHONE of some Sara groups of southern Chad. *See* KUNDU (ii).

Kende (iii). Metal percussion idiophone of the Kissi people of Guinea. In shape, it resembles a 'split banana', it is tapped rhythmically with a metal rod.

Kendo. An iron clapper bell with a bent handle of the

Kota people of Gabon. It is used during masked ceremonies associated with Mungala, mythical protector of fecundity and redresser of ills. It is dangerous to speak to Mungala without the magic protection of the *kendo*, which an 'interpreter' continuously shakes. See P. Sallée: 'Gabon', *Grove 6*.

Kèn đôi. DOUBLE CLARINET of Vietnam, now obsolete.

Kendrā [kendera, kendra, kenra]. A name for various chordophones of South Asia. It is a variant of the term *kingrā* (*see also* KING (i) and VĪNĀ, §§4, 6, 7).

1. Rajasthan. 2. Central India.

1. RAJASTHAN. In Rajasthan *kendra* denotes a bamboo STICK ZITHER with resonators. The body is made from a 60 cm length of bamboo, below which are attached two spherical gourd resonators. It is fitted with two metal strings, raised by a vertical bridge and tensioned by two lateral pegs, which the player plucks with a plectrum. The instrument provides a drone accompaniment to the ballads and epic songs of the Jogi, a caste of itinerant professional singers of the region of Banswara and Dungarpur in the hills of the south-west. The *kendra* is similar to the JANTAR, but differs in its smaller size and in having only two strings and no frets.

2. CENTRAL INDIA. In east-central India *kendra* denotes the plucked or bowed chordophones of tribal groups, particularly in the states of Bihar and Orissa. It appears often in traditional song texts of the Muṇḍā people of southern Bihar, where it is usually paired with the *ṭuila* (single-string plucked stick zither). The exact nature of the *kendrā*, however, appears to be unclear or unknown to most of the Muṇḍā people, and it is possible that for them it is a generic term for all plucked chordophones. Since at least the early decades of the 20th century the term has been applied to a wide variety of string instruments, many of them similar in form to the chordophones of non-tribal folk musicians in north India.

(i) Lute kendrā. The instrument known as *kendrā* among some Muṇḍāri Christian converts in southern Bihar, and also among some non-converts, is a single-string plucked lute with a gourd soundbox resembling the *ektāra* of the area's non-tribal folk musicians (*see* EKTĀR, §2). The gourd tends to have a deeper, more rounded back than that of the *ektāra*, and the area of its skin belly tends to be smaller in relation to the diameter of the gourd. The lute-type *kendrā* is played by men as a drone to accompany solo or small-group singing or while they dance in the village dancing-ground. It is associated more with walking and sitting than with dancing. The *kendrā* is played rarely, but while it seems of little musical significance to the Muṇḍā people, whether converts or non-converts, it nevertheless remains an important cultural symbol.

(ii) Gopīyantra kendrā. This version of the *kendrā* is a single-string plucked chordophone with a gourd body and resonating skin membrane. It apparently resembles the *gopīyantra* or *ānandalaharī*, widely known in north India and particularly associated with Bengali folk music. A *kendrā* of this type may have been known to recent generations of the Muṇḍā people, but appears now to be unknown to most. The body of this *kendrā* is formed from half an oval-shaped hollowed gourd, cut crosswise from the whole. A mouth cut in the gourd's narrow lower end is covered with a nailed goatskin membrane. The wider mouth of the gourd is held between the two halves

of a bamboo stick which has been split down half its length. A brass wire, attached to the skin membrane, passes through the hollow gourd, between the two bamboo arms and is tied at the instrument's upper end, directly to the unsplit portion of the bamboo or to a lateral wooden peg. The instrument is held by the gourd and, as it is played, the tension of the plucked string can be varied by pressure on the bamboo arms.

(iii) Stick-zither kendrā. A two-string fretted and plucked STICK ZITHER with two gourd resonators called *kendrā* appears to have been played by the Muṇḍā people in southern Bihar earlier this century in areas in which they had close contact with Hindus. It is now extremely rare, perhaps even non-existent, in Muṇḍāri villages. As described by Hoffmann (1938–50), this *kendrā* appears to resemble the *kullutan rājan* of the relatively isolated Sora (Savara, Saora) people of Orissa, apart from having two gourd resonators instead of one. It also appears to be related in general form to both the south Indian *kinnarī vīṇa* and the present-day *rudra vīṇā* of north India.

According to Hoffman, the instrument's body is a bamboo tube roughly 84 cm long and 2 cm in diameter, with a carved wooden handle fitted over one end. The handle curves out at right-angles to the tube to a distance of about 15 cm from the tube. Two brass wires wrapped around the handle pass over the length of the tube, each secured at the opposite end to its own ebony peg. These two square pegs, each topped with rounded knobs, fit into the bamboo tube at right-angles to each other. Nine small ridges of beeswax, each topped with a small piece of bamboo, are positioned as frets on the tube towards its peg end.

The two gourd resonators, each about 10 cm high and 15 cm in diameter, are fixed to the underside of the bamboo tube, one at each end. Each gourd has a hole in its lower end and is joined to the tube by a neck of hollowed, turned wood.

(iv) Fiddle kendrā. According to Deva (1978), in Orissa the word *kendrā* refers to a fretless fiddle with a tortoiseshell soundbox and skin belly. Kothari (1968) also applied the term to several varieties of fiddle, with membrane belly, of both Orissa and Bihar.

The *jogi kendrā* is a fiddle about 42 cm long, with a bamboo-tube fingerboard and a coconut-shell soundbox covered with laced 'parchment'. A single-'hair' playing string is hooked on the lower end of the soundbox by a cotton loop. On the upper end of the fingerboard the string is either tied to a peg or fixed directly to the fingerboard by wrapped cotton cord. Small bells may be attached to the small triangular-shaped bow. Thumb pressure adjusts the tension of the bow hair.

The *majhi kendrā* is a fiddle popular in tribal areas of the Mayurbhanj district of Orissa. This *kendrā* is like the *jogi kendrā* in form and material, but it is larger, about 64 cm long. The hollow soundbox may be of coconut shell, horn or wood and is covered with a nailed 'parchment' belly. The single-hair playing string is hooked at the lower end by cotton cord, passes over a wooden bridge and is tied directly to the instrument's body at the upper end. String tension is regulated by a movable piece of wrapped cotton cord on the fingerboard.

In southern Bihar, the above instruments would most commonly be called BANAM, and it should be noted that no sources originating in southern Bihar mention a *kendrā* of this type.

BIBLIOGRAPHY
J. Hoffmann and A. van Emelen: *Encyclopaedia mundarica*, v/1–13 (Patna, 1938–50), 2286f
K. S. Kothari: *Indian Folk Musical Instruments* (New Delhi, 1968), 69
O. Prasad: *Munda: Music and Dance* (diss., Ranchi U., 1971), 68
K. Kothari: *Folk Musical Instruments of Rajasthan* (Borunda, 1977)
B. C. Deva: *Musical Instruments of India: their History and Development* (Calcutta, 1978), 159, 169
GENEVIÈVE DOURNON (1), CAROL M. BABIRACKI (2)

Kenge. Double clapperless bell of the Mamvu people of Zaïre. *See* GONGA (i).

Kengele. Metal bell of the Gishu people of Mbale district, Uganda. The bells are attached to the leg of a player of the *litungu* lyre and sound when he beats his heel on the ground. See *TraceyCSA*, ii, 295.

Kengere (i). Tall, open single-headed cylindrical drum of the Madi people of Uganda. It resembles the Jopadhola *fumbo* and forms part of a battery with three different-sized Uganda drums. It is always beaten by a woman using her bare hands. The *kengere* of the Alur formed part of the sultan's regalia and was goblet-shaped with a very long stem and a buckskin head. It was beaten with two Uganda drums and two *ntimbo*, which had lizard-skin heads. See *WachsmannTCU*.

Kengere (ii). Iron idiophone of Kenya. *See* BERU.

Kenggerge. *See* KHENGEREG.

Kenite [santo, surondopi]. Idiochord TUBE ZITHER of Flores, Indonesia. It is made from a stout piece of bamboo about 70 cm long, but its body (about 10 to 12 cm wide) consists of only about one-fifth of its circumference. It has three, six, seven or nine bamboo strings. See J. Kunst: *Music in Flores* (Leiden, 1942), 129f.

Kèn một. Clarinet of Vietnam.

Kennedy, Thomas (*b* London, 24 Jan 1784; *d* 1870). English violin maker. He was the son and pupil of John Kennedy (*c*1730–1816); the family, originally Scottish, included several other violin makers who worked anonymously. Before setting up his own workshop in London, he worked for Thomas Powell and William Forster. Kennedy was a prolific maker whose output varied considerably in quality. Indeed some of his more hastily produced violins are of only peripheral interest. His reputation rests on his cellos, of which the best follow a broad and flat model; they are mostly varnished a rich red-brown. However, his usual varnish was a yellow or yellow-brown and seems to be of a more durable, sturdier texture. Kennedy frequently signed the lower rib around the end-pin in ink, virtually duplicating the wording of the printed label inside the back of the instrument.

BIBLIOGRAPHY
W. M. Morris: *British Violin Makers* (London, 1904, rev. 2/1920)
W. Henley: *Universal Dictionary of Violin and Bow Makers*, i–v (Brighton, 1959–60); vi, ed. C. Woodcock as *Dictionary of Contemporary Violin and Bow Makers* (Brighton, 1959)
JAAK LIIVOJA-LORIUS

Kennu. Leg XYLOPHONE of the Bariba people of Benin. Four solid, rounded pieces of wood are placed across the thighs of a seated player. He beats these keys with two stones to scare birds and monkeys from the crops

Kenong. High-rimmed bossed gong used in sets in Central Javanese gamelan. It is about 38 cm wide and 27 cm high, and rests on crossed cords in a wooden box. The *kenong* has a higher pitch than the KEMPUL with which it usually alternates at equal time intervals There are usually five gongs for the *slendro* tuning system (*see* GAMELAN, §4), the Yogyakarta set ranging from pitch 3^4 (i.e. pitch 3 in the fourth lowest octave) to 2^5 and the Solo set from 2^4 to 1^5. The number of gongs for the *pelog* system varies from five to seven; if there are only five the two omitted pitches are usually pitch 4 and the *tumbuk* ('colliding note'). The range is 3^4 to 2^5 in the Yogyakarta set, and 2^4 to 1^5 in the Solo set In addition the Yogyakarta *kenong* may include one or two KENONG JAPAN.

A *kenong* is used in rural ensembles, such as the *reyog* ensemble in Panaraga, East Java, and the *gamelan gandrung* of the Osinger people of Banyuwangi Regency Five *kenong* are used in large Sundanese gamelan, and three in the *joget gamelan* of West Malaysia.
For illustration, *see* GAMELAN, figs.2 and 5.

Kenong japan. High-rimmed bossed gong of Central Java. It rests on crossed cords in a wooden box and is tuned to pitch 5^3 (i.e. pitch 5 in the third lowest octave) of the *pelog* and *slendro* tonalities (*see* GAMELAN, §4). It is used only in Yogyakarta gamelan, including the *gamelan munggang*, and in areas under Yogyakarta influence. It is regarded as being 'female' in contrast to the ordinary 'male' KENONG. See J. Kunst: *De toonkunst van Java* (The Hague, 1934; Eng. trans., rev. 2/1949, enlarged 3/1973), 161.

MARGARET J. KARTOMI

Kenong penontong. Bossed gong of central Java. *See* PENONTONG.

Kent bugle [Kent horn]. *See* KEYED BUGLE.

Kentucky dulcimer. *See* APPALACHIAN DULCIMER.

Kenyir. Small antique METALLOPHONE used in the *gambuh* theatre ensemble in Bali. Its three keys are all of the same pitch and are struck with a three-headed hammer. See C. McPhee: *Music in Bali* (New Haven and London, 1966/*R*1976), 119f.

Keo. Cylindrical stopped wooden flute of the Angba people of northern Zaïre (*LaurentyA*, 182).

Keprak. Small wooden SLIT-DRUM of Central Java, beaten with a wooden mallet (*cempala*). It is used by the puppeteer (*dalang*) in the *wayang kulit* (shadow-puppet play) as a means of signalling messages to the gamelan players, emphasising the movements of the puppets, and also for providing sound effects.
MARGARET L. SARKISSIAN

Keranting [kerantung, kerantegn, kereb, kerim, kreb]. TUBE ZITHER, idiochord or heterochord, of the various Orang Asli peoples of West Malaysia. It is constructed of a stout piece of bamboo, which may vary in length from about 33 to 170 cm, with nodes at each end, from the surface of which narrow, parallel strips of bark are prised lengthwise, attached at both ends, to serve as strings. Over each end of the tube a strong rattan ring is placed, to prevent the instrument from splitting and to stop the strings from breaking away. Wedges are inserted under the strings to act as bridges and the instrument may be tuned by moving the wedges. In some cases, holes are made in the bamboo to increase resonance and small pieces of wood may be stuck on to it to serve as frets. The number of strings varies.

The *keranting* of the Semog Beri people is about 170 cm long. It has two metal strings sounding a semitone apart which are plucked simultaneously. A shorter instrument, about 75 cm long and with three bamboo strings, is used in Pahang state; the strings are normally of bamboo but can also be of metal, and are beaten with a pair of sticks.

The *kerantung* of the Temiar people has seven strings, of which three are plucked by the first finger of the left hand and the remaining four are made to vibrate in other ways. This instrument is particularly used by shamans. Holding the instrument in his left hand, the player simultaneously plucks the open strings and strikes the upper end of the bamboo with the hollow of the right hand in rapid succession; he thus sets up vibration not only in the body of the instrument and the strings, but also in the air column inside it. This instrument is about 84 cm long.

The Temiar *kereb* (or *kreb*) is about 40 cm long and has two strings of rattan. It is held against the breast and the strings are plucked with the right hand, using two basic rhythmic motifs. It produces a sound akin to that made by walking in ground covered with leaves, branches and creepers.

The *kerantegn* of the Jahai people also has three strings, of bamboo or rattan. It is not a melody instrument but is used to indicate the rhythm. As the strings are not wrapped or reinforced they usually shred after a short time, when the instrument must be discarded.

The *kerim* of the Semai Senoi may have from one to seven strings of bamboo or of rattan or resam; they are usually plucked but may be beaten with bone or hard wood. In modern versions of these instruments the string may be of wire, attached at one end to tuning-pegs and at the base passing through small holes and tied to wood.

BIBLIOGRAPHY
. A. R. Blacking: 'Musical Instruments of the Malayan Aborigines', *Federation Museums Journal*, new ser., i–ii (1954–5), 35

JACK PERCIVAL BAKER DOBBS, TRÂN QUANG HAI

Kerâr. *See* KRAR.

Keraulophon. An ORGAN STOP.

Kerbal. *See* GHIRBĀL.

Kercek. Idiophone of the Sundanese areas of West Java. It consists of a set of four small cymbals, two of which are loosely mounted on a wooden stand and struck by the other two cymbals held in the player's hands. Alternatively a pair of metal sticks may be used. It is played in the *gamelan renteng*.

Kereb. *See* KERANTING.

Kereteta. Obsolete SLIT-DRUM of Mangareva (Gambier Islands), made from a thick branch of the *miro* tree. See P. Buck: *Ethnology of Mangareva* (Honolulu, 1938), 399.

Kerikeri. Double-headed variable tension HOURGLASS DRUM of the Yoruba people of Nigeria. *See* DUNDUN.

Kerilu. Bamboo ring flute of the coastal regions of Bengkulu province and Minangkabau, West Sumatra. It is about 40 cm long and has four finger-holes in front and one thumb-hole.

Kerim. *See* KERANTING.

Keriten [/keriten]. Ankle rattles of the San (Bushman) people of south-western Africa, worn by male dancers. They are made from springbok ears or from cocoons, containing pieces of ostrich eggshell, threaded on a cord or thong.

Keromong [kromong]. GONG-CHIME of Sumatra and Malaysia. In northern Jambi province (Kuala Tungkal), Sumatra, it consists of nine small, thin-rimmed, bossed gongs in a single-row frame. The name is used also for an ensemble comprising a *keromong*, a pair of *gendang panjang* (cylindrical drums) and a pair of gongs. It is used to accompany ceremonial dances, and is said to have originated in South Sumatra, where the name is also used (*see* KELITTANG).

In the *joget gamelan* of Malaysia the *keromong* has ten gongs in two rows in a wooden frame.

MARGARET J. KARTOMI

Keromongan. GONG-CHIME of South Sumatra consisting of 16 small horizontal gongs arranged in a wooden frame. The name is used also for an ensemble comprising a *keromongan*, a *gendang* (double-headed drum), a *tawak-tawak* (suspended medium-sized bossed gong), a *canang* (small bossed gong), a *gong* (large suspended gong) and a *rujih* (small high-pitched gong).

MARGARET J. KARTOMI

Keromong duabelas. GONG-CHIME of Bengkulu province, Sumatra. Its 12 small, bronze bossed gongs are arranged in two horizontal rows in a wooden frame, and beaten with a pair of soft hammers. The term is used also to accompany traditional dances at ceremonies, including the 'betel-nut offering' dance. It comprises a *keromong duabelas*, a *gendang panjang* (cylindrical drum) and a suspended *gong* about 45 cm in diameter. The instruments are periodically cleaned with oil in a mystical ceremony.

MARGARET J. KARTOMI

Keronaru. Name given by the Fula people of Sierra Leone to the KONTING lute.

Kertok buluh [gambang tali]. Chime of six bamboo slit-drums of West Malaysia (*see* SLIT-DRUM). Each instrument is about 60 cm long and is suspended horizontally in a rectangular wooden frame by rattan strings; another slit-drum is suspended perpendicularly from a side-wing of the frame. The drums are played with a small, thick wooden beater and are used for public proclamations as well as for purely musical purposes in Malay ensembles.

Kertok kelapa. Bar XYLOPHONE of West Malaysia. The single resonator consists of a large dried-out coconut (*kelapa*: 'coconut') with the top sawn off. A soundboard of *nibong* wood is placed across the open top of the

Kertok kelapa (single-bar xylophone) played by two musicians, Kelantan, Malaysia

resonator. A piece of softwood serves as a pad between the soundboard and the coconut. The soundboard is struck with a short wooden beater padded with rubber or raw cotton. It is held in position by three long wooden pegs: one passes through the board while the others grip its sides and act as wedges. A tall ornamental wing is sometimes added. Occasionally four additional projections are used, two on each side of the soundboard. A well-made *kertok kelapa* may last four or five seasons.

Originally a form of *kertok kelapa* was used in mosques and prayer houses to call worshippers to prayer, and in the villages as a signal drum. It was also beaten for public proclamations and for visiting rulers. It is now chiefly used by Malays in competitions in Kelantan, Kedah and Trengganu. Groups of ten or more players sometimes accompany folkdances. The *kertok kelapa* is regarded by Malays as indigenous to their northern states, but similar instruments are found elsewhere. McPhee (1966) wrote that in a few remote Balinese villages coconut shells sawn open at the top have been found serving as resonators for xylophone keys.

BIBLIOGRAPHY
C. McPhee: *Music in Bali* (New Haven and London, 1966/*R*1976)
J. Kunst and R. Goris: *Hindoe-Javaansche muziekinstrumenten* (Batavia, 1927; rev. 2/1968 as *Hindu-Javanese Musical Instruments*)
M. Sheppard: *Taman Indera* (Kuala Lumpur, 1972)
JACK PERCIVAL BAKER DOBBS

Keru. End-blown flute of Irian Jaya, Indonesia. *See* YOKUË.

Keruncong. Bamboo idiophone of the Bedayuh people of southern Sarawak, Malaysia. *See* PERUNCONG.

Kesangi. Flat board LAMELLAPHONE with metal keys, of the Tetela people of Zaïre (*LaurentyS*, 195). *See* KISAANJ.

Kesi. Pair of small cymbals of Malaysia and the Serdang area of North Sumatra. Their diameter is about 11 cm and they have a central boss and a flat brim. Usually made of brass, they are joined with a string. When played, one or two pairs are laid on the ground horizontally, with the open end of their bosses facing upwards. These are struck by another pair with their open ends facing downwards. In West Malaysia *kesi* are used in ensembles

to accompany folkdances, *manora* theatre and *wayang kulit* (shadow puppet theatre), for which performances they have a secret name, *set gersek*. In North Sumatra they accompany the *makyong* theatre ensemble.
JACK PERCIVAL BAKER DOBBS, MARGARET J. KARTOMI

Kesle. BOX ZITHER of the Chuvash people of the Volga-Ural region (USSR). *See* GUSLI.

Késlja [keslya]. BOX ZITHER of the Tatar people of the Volga-Ural region (USSR). *See* GUSLI.

Kessa. Side-blown ivory trumpet of the Mamvu people of north-eastern Zaïre. It has a carved mouthpiece and one stop in the tip (*LaurentyA*, 360, 371).

Kesse-kesse. Angular harp of the Kissi people of Guinea. It is similar to the Toma KONIGI but is played with the calabash resonator placed on the knees. The players are always the last-born of families and have no other occupation.

Kessler, Dietrich M(artin) (*b* Zurich, 21 July 1929). English string instrument maker and viol player, of Swiss origin. He was trained as a violin maker at the Schweizerische Geigenbauschule in Brienz under Adolph König, from 1946 to 1950, passing his examinations with distinction, having built a perfectly matched set of instruments. In Switzerland he made violins, violas, cellos, double basses, viols, quintons and guitars. He also studied the cello as a performer. In 1950 he moved to Haslemere, England, where he worked for the firm of Arnold Dolmetsch, making and repairing viols and studying the bass viol with Nathalie Dolmetsch. In 1952 he joined the firm of Albert Arnold Ltd and worked under C. W. Jacklin in string instrument repairing, meanwhile continuing to make viols in his spare time. Kessler began his own workshop in Welling, Kent, in September 1955, and in 1959 moved to London. During this time his instruments, particularly his viols, became increasingly popular, and he was also active as a performer, touring and recording throughout Europe and the USA at various times with the Elizabethan Consort, the English Consort of Viols and the Jaye Consort of Viols. In October 1969 he took over the London firm of Edward Withers Ltd, and continued to make and repair viols and violins. He has also contributed valuable research into the methods of early English viol making (see *Early Music*, x, 1982, p.340).

Kessler's viols are built to the pattern of the English masters. His workmanship is very clean and the instruments are light in weight, with varnish of orange-brown or reddish hue, double purfling, closed or open or carved scrolls, and beautifully inlaid designs in the manner of Barak Norman and Maggini on the back or belly or both. The sound is clear, penetrating and rich. Kessler is one of the best modern makers of viols; his instruments bear the label 'D. M. Kessler, London 19 . . .', though some earlier ones have 'Dietrich M. Kessler of Zurich, No. . . . London 19 . . .' and others are not labelled in his own name.
MURRAY LEFKOWITZ

Kesuling. Flute of the Iban people of central Sarawak, Malaysia. It is used in courting rituals, and varies in length from about 45 cm to 75 cm. *See also* SULING.

Ketadu mara. Boat-shaped plucked lute of the Kupang area of Timor, Indonesia. It is made from a single piece of wood, with a head about 6 cm long, carved like the head of a bird, a neck about 10 cm long and a body about 45 cm long. It has two metal strings.

MARGARET J. KARTOMI

Ketawak. Suspended gong of Malaysia. *See* TAWAK.

Kete. Drum ensemble of the Akan people of southern Ghana.

Ketelessi. Small clapper bell in the shape of an elongated cone, used by the Dompago people of Benin. Two are sounded with side-blown flutes as encouragement before circumcision. *See also* GBESSI.

Keteng-keteng. Bamboo idiochord TUBE ZITHER of the Batak Karo area of the province of North Sumatra. It is between 60 and 80 cm long and usually about 10 to 15 cm in diameter. The tube is cut so that there is a node at each end. A hole is cut in one node and at the front and back of the tube. Two (or occasionally three) bamboo strings are prised lengthwise from the tube's surface, raised over bridges and beaten by one performer with a pair of wooden sticks. The higher string is tautened by a bridge at each end and in the middle, producing two different pitches. The lower string has a bridge at each end and a bamboo or wooden tongue attached to it over the front hole. It thus vibrates when the string is beaten and produces a low-pitched resonant sound resembling that of a gong. The part played on this string resembles the punctuating part of a *gung* (gong) in the main Batak Karo ceremonial orchestra, the *gendang sarunai*; it is played mostly at four-, eight- or 16-beat intervals. The other string, producing two pitches, contributes to the stock melodic patterns; rhythmically its part resembles the drumming in the main ceremonial orchestra. The *keteng-keteng* is part of the *gendang keteng-keteng* or *perketeng-keteng* orchestra which is played at minor Batak Karo ceremonies, together with the *baluat* and *surdam* (flutes), *kulcapi* (plucked lute) and *mangkuk* (bowl used as a small gong).

MARGARET J. KARTOMI

Ketipung. Name used for various drums of Sumatra and Java. In southern Lampung province, Sumatra, it is a double-headed cylindrical drum made of *jilaton* wood with a body about 60 cm long and goatskin heads measuring about 37 cm and 20 cm in diameter. The skins are laced to the body with leather in vertical, horizontal and diagonal patterns. The name 'ketipung' is used also in Lampung for a short double-headed drum known in Riau as a MARWAS (i), and for a FRAME DRUM, sometimes with jingles.

The term is used also for a small drum in Central Java (*kendang*) and West Java (*kulinter*): *see* KENDANG. In Ponorogo, East Java, where it is used in the *gamelan reyog*, the name is abbreviated to *tipung*.

MARGARET J. KARTOMI

Ketoff, Paolo (*b* Rome, 8 April 1921). Italian recording engineer and designer of synthesizers. Working independently of American inventors with similar ideas, he constructed in 1964 one of the earliest modular synthesizers, the SYNKET.

Kettledrum (Fr. *timbale*; Ger. *Pauke*; It. *timpano*). A membranophone with an egg-shaped or hemispherical body acting as resonator (for comparative illustration of drum shapes *see* DRUM, figs.2 and 3; for details of the classification *see* MEMBRANOPHONE). The single head is tensioned over the open end of the body by various means. Material for the body ranges from tortoiseshells and kettle-shaped hollow tree-trunks to clay or metal bowls.

There is no evidence of the kettledrum in ancient Egypt, but a plaque in the British Museum (from Larsa, early 2nd millennium BC) attests the instrument in Mesopotamia and shows two men engaged in boxing or wrestling while to one side are players of the cymbals and kettledrum (*see* TIMPANI, fig.7). A Babylonian plaque (*c*700 BC) shows a kettledrum, considered to be of metal, in the form of a deep drum shaped like a goblet. Akkadian texts of the Seleucid period (*c*300 BC) from tablets found at Uruk (now in the British Museum) deal with priestly instructions for furnishing the *lilis* (plural *lilis-su*), a bronze kettledrum, with a skin head of bull's hide. The Chinese history *Shiji* (1st century BC) reports the use of kettledrums and trumpets by the Huns in the 3rd and 2nd centuries BC; and there is further evidence of their ancient use in the military music of the Parthians, who used the drum to strike fear into the Roman army.

The military orchestra of the Sassanid Husrau II Parviz (AD 590–628), as represented in the Ṭaq-i Bustān rock reliefs, included the kettledrum with a wide selection of other drums. A pair of kettledrums, one giving a higher note than the other, was used in the Middle East in early Islamic times and this usage was adopted in Europe for martial music during the time of the Crusades (13th century). These drums, termed 'timpan' in various medieval sources, were small and their heads were secured by lacing. This type of drum and the method of thong-tensioning are still used by various peoples in the Middle East, and they have an important place in Ethiopian liturgical music where they are used to emphasize the rhythm of the chanting. Kettledrums with shells fashioned from tree-trunks and with laced or pegged heads are used in Africa. In India a small thong-tensioned kettledrum constitutes the lower drum of the TABLĀ. The first type of kettledrum to reach Europe was the Arabic NAQQĀRA. These small kettledrums were known to the French as *nacaires* and to the English as NAKERS or nakeres. The English word 'kettledrum' (possibly from Latin *catinus*) is not found before the 16th century. The German *Heerpauke* ('army drum') is found in some 16th-century sources and occasionally thereafter.

Owing to the shape of the body and the consequent strengthening of certain overtones in the harmonic series a kettledrum produces a note of definite musical pitch: thus orchestral kettledrums (*see* TIMPANI) function in the harmonic structure of the orchestra.

The following kettledrums are entered in this dictionary: ajigo; angúarai; banga (ii); bāyā; bāz; bher; bheri; bowl drum; bugnas katilas; chindaul; damāhā; damāmā; da-man; damaū; damua; deger; dhamsā; ḍhankī; dinger; diplipito; doolbas; ḍuggi; ettebel; ganga; gangu (i); gorong; gosha nagara; gudu-gudu; gwabron tambari; Heerpauke; jornagārā; kabaro; kārā; kayum; kelangen; kelo; khurḍak; kögürge; kollo; kuenda; kultrún; kundi (iii); kuntuku; kuntukun tambura; kurkutu; kus; kuttuku; kuvargah; kyos; lamba (ii); ldumbol; lengkara; lilis; lingarai; mbalatt; naas; nagārā; nagarit; naghārā; nakers; naqqāra; negara; nihass; niḥsāna; nissān; nuqairat; opon; pedal drum; rebana; salo-salo; spilendz-churi; tabala; tablā; tablak; tabshi; talambas; tamāk; tamal; tambal; tambari; tammätta; tamukku; ṭāsa; taushi; tevelbas; ṭikārā; timki; timpani; tobol; tulumbas; tumbakī; tumbal; tungda; turam; turuburi; ṭyāmko; vara bungas; 'yan dai-dai; zakka; zambuna.

JAMES BLADES, ROBERT ANDERSON

Kettle gong. Gong with a deep rim and a flat surface (*see* GONG), known particularly in South-east Asia; the type has been called 'metal drum'. *See also* IDIOPHONE.

Kettős furulya. Double DUCT FLUTE of Hungary, now rarely encountered. It consists of two pipes, one like that of the *furulya*, the second of the same size and structure but without finger-holes. The pipes can be bored in the same piece of wood, or attached together.

Ketuba. Eight-string bowl lyre of the Kipsigis people of Kenya. It has the same order of notes as the *thum* of the Luo people near Lake Victoria. See *TraceyCSA*, ii, 375.

Ketuk. (1) Horizontal bossed gong of West Java. It rests on crossed cords in a wooden box and is beaten with a wooden mallet in a few Sundanese gamelan. The name is used also for small flat gongs on a wooden frame, played by two musicians in the *ketuk tilu* ensemble.

(2) SLIT-DRUM of Riau province, Sumatra. It is about 120 cm long, with a slit about 60 cm long. It is used in the *celempung kayu* ensemble.

(3) Bamboo idiophone of the Pakpak Dairi area of North Sumatra. A slit approximately 3 cm wide is cut along most of the top end of a bamboo tube, and two bamboo sticks of unequal length protrude at one end. One player rests this end on his ankle and beats between and on the two protrusions, while another plays across the lower part of the slit at the other end. They beat the instrument in interlocking fashion, each with a pair of wooden sticks about 25 cm long. The *ketuk* varies in size, but the tube is often about 32 by 10 cm and the protruding sticks about 20 and 23 cm long. It is played to ward off pests from the fields.

MARGARET J. KARTOMI, LYN MOORE

Ketuk. One or a pair of small, low-pitched, muted bossed gongs in the Central Javanese gamelan, tuned to pitch 2^4, i.e. pitch 2 in the fourth lowest octave, or 6^3, or both (*see* GAMELAN, §4). A *ketuk* rests on crossed cords in a wooden box and is beaten with a wooden mallet, alternating with the other gongs in cyclic rhythms. It is about 24 cm in diameter.

MARGARET J. KARTOMI

Ketuk tilu ('three gongs'). Small ensemble of the Sundanese area of West Java, used to accompany dance in both rural and urban areas. It takes its name from its main instrument and consists of three KETUK (small flat gongs), played in interlocking fashion by two musicians, a *rebab* (fiddle) or *tarompet* (oboe), gongs, drums and voice.

MARGARET J. KARTOMI

K'ewa. DUCT FLUTE of the Bolivian Alti Plano. *See* PINCULLO.

Key. As applied to such instruments as the organ, accordion, piano or harpsichord a key is a balanced lever which when depressed by the finger either operates a valve to admit air to a pipe or reed, or mechanically energizes (strikes or plucks) a tuned string.

In mouth-blown instruments it is a mechanical device which governs a tone-hole that is out of reach of, or too large for, the unaided finger. It has three elements, a padded plate or cup to close the hole, a pivoted lever, or shank, and a touchpiece for the finger. This touchpiece may be a ring surrounding a directly fingered hole. Keys when at rest may be either open or closed, and two or more simple levers may be combined to form one key. *See* KEYWORK.

PHILIP BATE

Key, Thomas (*fl* London, *c*1800–1853). English wind instrument maker and publisher. He apparently established his business in London about 1800, although its whereabouts are not known. He operated at 2 Pall Mall with JOHN CRAMER as Cramer & Key (1804–8) and, having dissolved the partnership, as Key & Co. (1808–13). He then seems to have worked at 20 Charing Cross for the rest of his life. In 1853, possibly on the death of Thomas Key, his son Frederick took over the firm, becoming associated in 1854 with George Rudall as Key, Rudall & Co. Soon afterwards Rudall's partner, the flute maker J. M. Rose of Edinburgh, had his name added to the firm's title (Key, Rudall & Rose) and in 1857 the name of Richard Carte, who had joined the firm in 1850, was also added (Key, Rudall, Rose, Carte & Co.); Key's name was dropped in 1858, though the reason for this is not known.

Extant instruments by Key are very numerous, including the four main woodwinds, horns, trumpets and serpents, as well as unusual examples such as the basso hibernicon. His most famous woodwind instruments are the clarinets, of which Luke (1969) located 33 specimens. Generally constructed of boxwood with ivory rings and fitted with six to 13 brass keys, they set a standard of excellence among English instruments in the first half of the 19th century. The virtuoso Lazarus was one of many players to use Key clarinets. The extant bassoons, which produce a distinctive sweetness in the tenor register and show Key's awareness of the value of extra keys and trill mechanisms, date from late in his career.

Key's horns are notably ingenious: one in London (Carse Collection), with two Stölzel valves and ten crooks, plays the full range of pitches from B♭ basso to B♭ alto; another in Oxford (Bate Collection) also has two Stölzel valves as well as two master crooks (single and double coil) and seven cylindrical couplers to play at every pitch from G basso to C alto; the 'Radius french horn' of 1851, designed by JOHN CALCOTT (Bate Collection), was probably built by Key. Interesting among his serpents is one with 13 keys (seven open) in the Carse Collection. He also made a pure copper serpentcleide (designed to replace the OPHICLEIDE), which does not survive, and a brass basso HIBERNICON, now in the Bate Collection.

For illustration of instruments by Key, *see* HIBERNICON; HORN, fig.10*a*; SERPENT, fig.1*c* and *d*.

BIBLIOGRAPHY

A. Carse: *Catalogue of the Adam Carse Collection of Old Musical Wind Instruments* (London, 1951)
F. G. Rendall: *The Clarinet* (London, 1954, 3/1971)
A. Baines: *Woodwind Instruments and their History* (London, 1957, 3/1967)
R. Morley-Pegge: *The French Horn* (London, 1960, 2/1973)
G. Melville-Mason, ed.: *An Exhibition of European Musical Instruments* (Edinburgh, 1968)
J. W. Luke: *The Clarinets of Thomas Key of London* (diss., U. of Missouri, Kansas City, 1969)
A. Baines: *The Bate Collection of Historical Wind Instruments* (Oxford, 1976)
J. Montagu: *Romantic and Modern Musical Instruments* (Newton Abbot and London, 1981)

NIALL O'LOUGHLIN

Keyboard (Fr. *clavier*; Ger. *Klaviatur, Tastatur*; It. *tastiera, tastatura*). A set of levers (keys) actuating the mechanism of a musical instrument such as the organ, harpsichord, clavichord, piano etc. The keyboard probably originated in the Greek hydraulis, but its role in antiquity and in non-European civilizations appears to have remained so limited that it may be considered as characteristic of Western music. Its influence on the development of the musical system can scarcely be overrated. The primacy of the C major scale in tonal music, for instance, is partly due to its being played on the white keys, and the 12-semitone chromatic scale, which is fundamental to Western music even in some of its recent developments, could be derived from the design of the keyboard. The arrangement of the keys in two rows, the sharps and flats being grouped by two and three in the upper row, already existed in the early 15th century.

1. History. 2. Layout. 3. Experimental keyboards.

1. HISTORY. The earliest European keyboards were simple contrivances, played with the hands rather than the fingers. Praetorius (2/1619) and others after him stated that some primitive organs were played with the fists, the wrists or even the knees, but there is little confirmation of this in medieval documents. The spacing between the organ keys remained that which separated the pipes, sometimes over 10 cm, until an abridgment mechanism was invented. Up to the 13th century the keyboards were usually diatonic except for the inclusion of B♭. They often showed a C as first key. This seems surprising, considering that the musical system was then based on Guido's gamut, the lowest note of which was G (*Gamma ut*). But the solmization system represented no more than a series of intervals, the theoretical compass of which had to be reduced, by transposition of some of the melodies, when played on an instrument of fixed sounds as an accompaniment to voices. The addition of the B♭ to the early diatonic keyboard was not intended merely for the playing of melodies including that note, but also permitted transpositions by which the *Gamma ut*, for instance, could be played on the apparent c key. These transpositions compressed the total compass of plainsong to less than two octaves, and, so long as keyboards were used only for the playing of plainsong melodies, no wider range was needed, nor any chromatic degree other than the B♭. The medieval practice of transposition must have caused some difficulties in using the same notation for both vocal and keyboard music, since a given note on the staff may have been played at different places on the keyboard; and in fact it seems that the medieval keyboard repertory usually remained unnotated. For theoretical discussions, a special alphabetical notation was often preferred to the Guidonian terminology; the notation, which has since been dubbed 'organ notation', consisted in attributing the letters A to G to the modern C major scale.

By the beginning of the 14th century, however, the development of polyphony had caused a widening of keyboard compass and the progressive addition of chromatic keys. Jehan des Murs (first half of the 14th century) mentioned keys for f♯ and g♯, and Jacques de Liège (c1330) wrote that on the organ 'the tone is almost everywhere divided into two semitones'. The late 14th-century organ of Norrlanda in the National Historical Museum in Stockholm still possesses its manual keyboard covering one octave and a 6th, from c to a', fully

1. Manual keyboard of the late 14th-century positive organ from Norrlanda (Musikmuseet, Stockholm); for an illustration of the complete instrument, see ORGAN, *fig.30*

chromatic, and a pedal keyboard of eight keys, probably from C to B with B♭. The chromatic keys are placed at a higher level, except for the b♭ and B♭, which are ranged among the diatonic ones, as shown in fig.1. The Robertsbridge Codex (c1320), the earliest surviving keyboard music, attests to the advanced level of keyboard playing sometimes reached in the 14th century; the rapid and flexible melodies, together with a few three-part chords, imply a highly developed finger technique. The range covered is two octaves and a 3rd, from c to e″ (fully chromatic above f). The addition of chromatic keys to the late medieval keyboards may not at first have been intended to permit transpositions other than those involving only one flat in the key signature; it seems that the added chromatic degrees may have been used primarily to gain a certain number of perfect or virtually perfect 3rds in polyphony, and that this function was underlined by their being placed at a different level. The chromatic degrees were in fact sometimes tuned as pure or nearly pure 3rds to some of the diatonic ones, thus foreshadowing the mean-tone temperaments of the Renaissance (*see* TEMPERAMENTS and PYTHAGOREAN INTONATION).

Before the second half of the 15th century the lowest part of keyboard compositions was often based on plainsong, or written in plainsong style. Owing to the limited number of transpositions then performed, there was no need for chromatic degrees other than the B♭ in the bass of the keyboard. This explains why pedal or bass manual keyboards remained diatonic up to a late date. As late as the 17th century, even manual keyboards sometimes lacked the first chromatic degrees when they were provided with a SHORT OCTAVE. In the first half of the 15th century keyboards often began at F or B. The B keyboard was only a slight extension of the medieval c one. The significance of the F keyboard is more complex. The following hypothesis provides a possible explanation: the apparent c key had sometimes been used to play the *Gamma ut*; when solmization names were given to the keys, it may have seemed more convenient to call *Gamma ut* the c key (this was feasible at a time when the pattern of raised keys was not yet complete). One note, F fa ut, was then added below the *Gamma ut*. The F keyboard would thus have been, in effect, a variant of the B one, producing virtually the same pitches. Later in the 15th century, however, some B keyboards were enlarged down to F, so that two types of F keyboards may then have been in existence, about a 4th apart in pitch. This difference of pitch, the origin of which could be traced in the medieval practice of transposition, survived for almost two centuries. As late as the 17th century keyboards a 4th apart were sometimes combined in a single instrument, a practice exemplified by the Ruckers transposing harpsichord (*see* HARPSICHORD, §3 (i) and TRANSPOSING KEYBOARD).

The most common keyboard compass in the second half of the 15th century and the first half of the 16th century was from F to a″, often without F♯ or G♯. In Italy, upper limits of c‴ or even f‴ were common. The instruments reaching f‴ were perhaps made at a lower pitch standard. The low limit was extended to C, often with short octave, in the second half of the 16th century. From then, the compass of the stringed keyboard instruments increased more rapidly than that of the organ, as the latter had a pedal and octave stops that made a wide compass less necessary. Harpsichords reached five octaves, usually from F′ to f‴, about 1700. Pianos attained six octaves, often from F′ to f⁗, by 1800 and seven octaves, from A″ to a⁗, by 1900. Pianos now usually cover seven octaves and a 3rd from A″ to c⁗‴ and some reach eight octaves. Modern organ keyboards rarely cover more than five octaves.

In the 18th and 19th centuries keyboard instruments gained a leading position in European musical practice. This led to attempts to provide all types of instrument with a keyboard mechanism. The most successful of these attempts were the harmonium and the celesta; but keyboard harps, keyboard guitars or the numerous bowed keyboard instruments have remained mere curiosities. The keys of the hurdy-gurdy often have been given an arrangement similar to that of the ordinary keyboard. The treble keyboard of the accordion is often fitted with piano-style keys; the bass usually has a button keyboard. Carillons often are equipped with a 'baton' keyboard (*see* CARILLON, §1 and fig.1). Attempts to give certain wind instruments a keyboard fingering through a rearrangement of the keys or valves generally met with little success.

Das I. vnd II. Difcant-clavier.

Das III. Clavier.

Das IV. Pedal-Clavier.

2. *Manual and pedal keyboards for the Halberstadt organ of 1361: woodcut from Praetorius's 'Syntagma musicum' (2/1619)*

Very many of the electric and electronic instruments produced in enormous numbers since the 1930s are controlled by means of a keyboard (*see* ELECTRONIC INSTRUMENTS, esp. §IV). The advent of electronic technology has made common many adaptations of the conventional keyboard. The split and staggered manuals of the 'spinet' organ (usually with two 44-note manuals staggered by an octave) were introduced in the late 1940s for purposes of economy, but the design found favour for other reasons and electronic organs and synthesizers now frequently have keyboards that are arranged in the normal way but can be split (at a fixed point, or in some cases at various points) by means of switches. In instruments with 'transposable' keyboards the range controlled by a three-octave keyboard can be fixed within six or seven octaves. The keyboards of electronic instruments may be touch-sensitive, pressure-sensitive or velocity-sensitive (*see* TOUCH-SENSITIVE DEVICE). Although the conventional design predominates, instruments have been made in which the 'keyboard' is a continuous touch- or pressure-sensitive strip, on which the outlines of keys are traced to aid the player's orientation.

2. LAYOUT. Both for playing comfort and aesthetic appearance, it is desirable to have all natural key heads of equal width; each head should thus have one seventh of the octave span. At the same time, it would seem desirable that the natural key tails (i.e. the parts of the natural keys between the sharps) and the sharps all be of equal width, but this is incompatible with the first requirement. Each octave may be considered as divided into two sections separated by straight lines between B and C and between E and F. The section from C to E, which includes three heads and five tails and sharps, should thus also ideally comprise three-sevenths and five-twelfths of an octave; and the section from F to B, which includes four heads and seven tails and sharps, should comprise four-sevenths and, at the same time, seven-twelfths of an octave. Modern keyboards offer a sophisticated solution: the keys look equal in width, but actually present minute discrepancies. In former times the discrepancies were more visible. Arnaut de Zwolle (c1440) avoided the problem by making a step in the line between the E and F keys (*see* HARPSICHORD, fig.2). Italian keyboards often showed a relatively wide key tail for D, while the instruments belonging to the Flemish tradition had wider tails for E and F and for B and C.

Wide keys, as in the early keyboards, suit simple and slow melodies, but make the playing of more than one part in each hand difficult. Narrow keys permit more velocity and an easier playing of chords, but require more precision on the part of the player. In order to account for possible discrepancies in the key widths, it is usual to measure keyboards in terms of the octave span (seven naturals) or the three-octave span (21 naturals). The main source of information on the measurement of medieval keyboards is Praetorius's *Syntagma musicum* (2/1619), which is perhaps less reliable than is often thought. Praetorius mentioned keys about 8 cm wide for the Halberstadt organ of 1361 (see fig.2). 15th-century octave spans, however, seem closer to about 18 cm. In the 16th and 17th centuries an octave span of about 16·7 cm was common, which is surprisingly close to the modern span of 16·5 cm. Narrower keys were often made in the 18th century, with octave spans of about 16 cm or sometimes even 15·5 cm. The shape of the keys varied during the Middle Ages. Some were spade-shaped, as in the Hal-

3. Detail of the Janko keyboard of an upright piano by Decker, New York, c1890 (Smithsonian Institution, Washington, DC)

perstadt keyboards depicted by Praetorius. Others, particularly in portative organs, were T-shaped, somewhat like the keys of the hurdy-gurdy. These forms were superseded by rectangular plates in the 15th century, when the keys were often so stubby as to be almost square, and the surface slightly convex (for illustration, *see* PORTATIVE). The natural heads remained quite short, about 3·5 cm, up to the 18th century. Modern piano key heads are 5 cm, the tails and sharps 10 cm long. Short keys are particularly needed in instruments with more than one keyboard, where they facilitate shifting from one keyboard to the other. Longer keys seem preferable for playing music with many sharps or flats. The depth of touch, the height of the sharps above the naturals and, to some extent, all key measurements, depend heavily on the hand position and the finger technique used, which in turn are dependent on the type of mechanism actuated by the keys. Pianos, which call for more muscular force than harpsichords or organs, have a deeper touch. The colour of the keys is a matter of taste and usage, the only requirement being that the pattern of lower and raised keys be underlined by contrasting colours. In the past the naturals were often white and the sharps black, as they are now, but in the 17th and 18th centuries these colours were often reversed. Italian makers generally used brown boxwood naturals with black sharps; tortoiseshell, mother-of-pearl, or rare precious woods of various colours have also been employed.

3. EXPERIMENTAL KEYBOARDS. The 'sequential keyboard', invented by William A. B. Lunn under the name of Arthur Wallbridge in 1843, aimed at reducing the supremacy of the C major scale. Each octave included six lower keys, for C♯, D♯, F, G, A and B, and six raised ones, for C, D, E, F♯, G♯ and A♯. A similar arrangement was advocated by the Chroma-Verein des Gleichstufigen Tonsystems in 1875–7. Paul von Janko's keyboard (1887–8) is a later application of the same principle. As shown in fig.3, the two rows of keys are triplicated, providing a total of six rows, each slightly higher than the other and each including six keys in the octave. This arrangement permitted the same fingering in all tonalities. Jozef Wieniawski designed a piano with reversed keyboards, patented by E. J. Mangeot in 1876, which was actually made of two superposed pianos, one with the treble at the right as usual and the other with the treble at the left. The purpose was to permit the same fingering for the same passages in both hands. This arrangement is reminiscent of some medieval representations of keyboard instruments where, for reasons that remain unclear, the treble is shown at the left. In 1907 F. Clutsam patented a keyboard with keys arranged in the shape of a fan according to a principle already conceived by Staufer and Heidinger in 1824 and supposed to facilitate playing in the extreme bass and treble. Another important group of experiments concerns the ENHARMONIC KEYBOARD. The fact that the majority of the keyboard repertory has been written for the standard keyboard militates against the success of experiments with its design.

BIBLIOGRAPHY

M. Praetorius: *Syntagma musicum*, ii (Wolfenbüttel, 1618, 2/1619/*R*1958 and 1980)

G. Le Cerf and E.-R. Labande: *Instruments de musique du XVe siècle: les traités d'Henri-Arnaut de Zwolle et de divers anonymes (Ms. B. N. latin 7295)* (Paris, 1932)

F. Ernst: *Der Flügel Johann Sebastian Bachs: ein Beitrag zur Geschichte des Instrumentenbaues im 18. Jahrhundert* (Frankfurt, 1955)

F. W. Riedel: 'Klavier', *MGG*

K. Bormann: *Die gotische Orgel zu Halberstadt: eine Studie über mittelalterlichen Orgelbau* (Berlin, 1966)

J. C. Schuman: ' "Reversed" Portatives and Positives in Early Art', *GSJ*, xxiv (1971), 16

E. M. Ripin: 'The Norrlanda Organ and the Ghent Altarpiece', *Festschrift to Ernst Emsheimer* (Stockholm, 1974), 193, 286

N. Meeùs: 'Some Hypotheses for the History of Organ-pitch Before Schlick', *Organ Yearbook*, vi (1975), 42

C. Page: 'The Earliest English Keyboard: New Evidence from Boethius' *De musica*', *Early Music*, vii (1979), 308

For further bibliography *see* CLAVICHORD; HARPSICHORD; ORGAN; PIANOFORTE.

NICOLAS MEEÙS

Keyboard music. Before the mid-17th century composers made little stylistic distinction between one keyboard instrument and another, and players used whichever happened to be available or was best suited to the occasion. Liturgically based works and those containing either long-sustained notes or pedal parts would be heard most often on the organ, and dances and settings of popular tunes on the harpsichord; nevertheless, much of the repertory could be shared. While a number of high Baroque composers exploited the individual characteristics of the organ, harpsichord or clavichord, it was not until the latter half of the 18th century that a distinctive style for the piano, which had been invented about 1700, began to appear: hence the main divisions of this article.

I. Keyboard music to *c*1750. II. Organ music from *c*1750. III. Piano music from *c*1750.

I. Keyboard music to c1750. The term 'keyboard' is here understood to include not only the early string keyboard instruments (the clavichord, harpsichord, virginals etc), but also the various types of organ (the positive, regal, church organ with and without pedals etc).

1. 14th and 15th centuries. 2. 16th century. 3. 17th century. 4. The period of J. S. Bach.

1. 14TH AND 15TH CENTURIES. Although the surviving sources of keyboard music go back no further than the early 14th century, players and instruments are known to have existed long before. It therefore seems likely that the lack of an earlier repertory is due partly to the wholesale loss of the manuscripts concerned, and partly to the fact that players during the earliest period relied largely on vocal originals and improvisation.

The earliest known keyboard source by almost a century is the Robertsbridge Codex of about 1320 (*GB-Lbm* Add.28550). This incomplete two-leaf manuscript from the former priory of Robertsbridge, Sussex, is a curious hybrid, for though it may have been copied in England, it is written in a form of Old German keyboard tablature, and the music it contains is probably either French or Italian in origin. It consists of two and a half dances in the form of *estampies* and two and a half arrangements of vocal motets, two of which are found in the 14th-century *Roman de Fauvel*. Thus the two main categories of early keyboard music are already represented: namely, purely instrumental works, and works that are derived in some way from a vocal original. In the *estampies* the writing is mostly in two parts, though at cadences the texture tends to become fuller, as often happens in keyboard music. In the motet arrangements the top part of the three-voice original is decorated, or 'coloured', mainly in conjunct motion and in relatively short note values. The remaining parts are generally left unchanged, though occasionally one is omitted or an extra part added. There is no indication of the instrument for which the pieces were intended.

The bulk of the Reina Manuscript (*F-Pn* nouv.acq.fr.6771) and the musical sections of the Faenza Manuscript (*I-FZc* 117) belong respectively to the late 14th century and the early 15th. Only a keyboard setting of Francesco Landini's ballata *Questa fanciulla* and an unidentified keyboard piece are included among Reina's otherwise exclusively vocal repertory; but the oldest part of Faenza consists entirely of keyboard pieces, though at one time it was thought they might have been intended for two non-keyboard instruments. There are arrangements of secular vocal works by Italian and French composers of the 14th and early 15th centuries (such as Landini, Jacopo da Bologna, Machaut and Pierre des Molins) and settings of liturgical chants including two Kyrie–Gloria pairs based on the plainsong Mass IV, *Cunctipotens genitor Deus* (see ex.1, the conclusion of a Kyrie verse). The Kyrie–Gloria settings are the first of countless plainsong settings designed for *alternatim* performance during the liturgy, in which only the alternate verses are set for organ, while the remainder are sung in unison by the unaccompanied choir. Except for a few three-part cadential chords in Faenza, the pieces in both manuscripts are all in two parts, though many of the secular vocal originals are in three.

The remaining 15th-century sources are all German, three of the most significant being Adam Ileborgh's tablature of 1448 (formerly in *US-PHci*; now privately owned), Conrad Paumann's *Fundamentum organisandi* of 1452 (*D-Bds* mus.40613), and the Buxheim Organ-

Ex.1 Faenza ms: Conclusion of a Kyrie verse (. . . .eleison)

book of about 1460–70. Ileborgh's tablature is notable for its five short preludes which are the earliest known keyboard pieces (other than dances) that do not rely in any way on a vocal original. In one of them pedals are indicated; and a double pedal part seems to be required in two others, where a florid upper line crosses a pair of lower lines as they move slowly from a 5th to a 3rd and back again. Paumann's *Fundamentum* is one of several treatises that illustrate techniques used in extemporization and composition. It provides examples of a florid part added above various patterns of bass; of decorated clausulas; of two free parts; and of two parts above a static bass. In addition, it includes a number of preludes, and of two- and three-part pieces based on both sacred and secular tenors, by Georg de Putenheim, Guillaume Legrant, Paumgartner and (presumably) Paumann himself. The Buxheim Organbook, which may also be associated with Paumann or his disciples, is the most comprehensive of all 15th-century keyboard sources. It contains over 250 pieces, of which more than half are based on either chansons or motets by German, French, Italian and English composers. They are of two main types. In the first, the whole of the original texture is used, one part being embellished while the rest are left more or less untouched, as in the Robertsbridge motets. In the second, the tenor alone is borrowed, to provide the foundation for what is otherwise a new composition. The rest of the manuscript includes liturgical plainsong pieces, preludes, and pieces based on basse-danse melodies. In the liturgical pieces the plainsong generally appears in long equal notes in one part, while the remaining parts have counterpoints in more varied rhythms. But occasionally the plainsong itself is ornamented or even paraphrased. The preludes are mostly regularly barred (unlike Ileborgh's), and often alternate chordal and florid passages in a way that foreshadows the later toccata. Most of the pieces are in three parts, although sometimes in two and occasionally in four (an innovation for keyboard music). The tenor and countertenor lines – the two lowest in the three-part pieces – have roughly the same compass; and as the countertenor was always added last, as in earlier vocal music, it constantly and often awkwardly has to cross and recross the tenor in order to find a vacant space for itself. Pedals are sometimes indicated by the sign *P* or *Pe*; apparently

ey could also be used elsewhere, for a note at the end
· the volume explains that they should always play
hichever tenor or countertenor note happens to be the
·wer.

16TH CENTURY. Printed keyboard music began to
·ppear during the 16th century. Liturgical plainsong
·ieces remained of paramount importance; but they were
·ined by settings of Lutheran chorales (hymn tunes)
·nd an increasing number of secular works such as
·ances, settings of popular tunes, variations, preludes
·nd toccatas. Of great significance, too, were the sec-
·onal contrapuntal forms of keyboard music derived from
·6th-century vocal forms, including the contrapuntal
·eyboard ricercare as well as the canzona, capriccio and
·antasy.

The earliest known printed volume devoted at least
·n part to keyboard music is Arnolt Schlick's *Tabula-
·uren etlicher Lobgesang und Lidlein uff die Orgel und
·auten* (Mainz, 1512). Besides lute solos and songs with
·ute accompaniment, it contains 14 pieces for organ with
··edals. They are in either three or four parts and are
·lmost all based on plainsong, an exception being a set-
·ing of the vernacular sacred song *Maria zart*, which
·oreshadows a later type of chorale prelude by echoing
·he phrases of the melody in the accompaniment. In
·chlick's unique ten-part manuscript setting of the chant
·Ascendo ad Patrem* (*I-TRa* tedesca 105) no fewer than
·our of the parts are assigned to the pedals.

The remaining German sources contain dances and
·rrangements of both sacred and secular vocal music,
·ome being anthologies while others appear to be the
·vork of a single composer. Although most of them are
·lescribed as being for either 'Orgel', or 'Orgel oder
·nstrument', they are generally equally well (or even
·etter) suited to harpsichord or spinet. The two earliest
·re a pair of manuscripts (*CH-Bu* F.IX.22 and F.IX.58)
·vritten by Hans Kotter between 1513 and 1532 for the
·ise of the Swiss humanist Bonifacius Amerbach. In
·ddition to embellished arrangements of vocal works by
·Paul Hofhaimer, Heinrich Isaac, Josquin Desprez and
·others, they include preludes and dances, some of which
·are by Kotter himself. Typical of the latter is a *Spani-
·oler* in which the basse danse melody *Il re di Spagna*
·is given to the tenor, each note being played twice in
·long–short rhythm, while treble and bass have more lively
·counterpoints. Later tablatures, some printed and others
·manuscript, are those of Elias Nikolaus Ammerbach
·(1571, 1583), Bernhard Schmid the elder (1577), Jacob
·Paix (1583), Christhoff Leoffelholz von Colberg (1585)
·and August Nörmiger (1598). A new trend is shown by
·the inclusion of 20 Lutheran chorales in Ammerbach's
·volume and over 70 in Nörmiger's. The plain melody
·is generally, though not invariably, given to the top part,
·while the remaining three parts provide simple harmony
·with an occasional suggestion of flowing counterpoint.
·A *Fundamentum* of about 1520 by Hans Buchner, simi-
·lar to Paumann's but dealing with a later style of three-
·part counterpoint, contains the earliest known example
·of keyboard fingering.

The dances in the tablatures and other sources are often
·grouped in slow–quick pairs, such as a passamezzo and
·saltarello, or a pavan and galliard, in which the second
·dance (in triple time) may or may not be a variation of
·the first (in duple). Not infrequently they are based on
·one or other of the standard harmonic patterns known
·throughout western Europe, of which the *passamezzo*

antico and the *passamezzo moderno* or quadran were the
most common.

In Italy the printing of keyboard music began in 1517
with a book of anonymous arrangements entitled *Frottole intabulate da sonare organi*. The mainly homophonic textures of the four-part vocal originals (mostly
by Bartolomeo Trromboncino) are lightly embellished to
give a more flowing effect; but, as is characteristic of
keyboard music, the number of parts employed at any
moment depends more on the capacity of a player's
hands, and the demands of colour and accent, than on
the rules of strict part-writing. Similar freedom was
exercised, as illustrated in ex.2, by Marco Antonio Cavazzoni, whose *Recerchari, motetti, canzoni* (1523) was
the earliest keyboard publication by a named Italian
composer. His brilliant son Girolamo Cavazzoni, perhaps working under the influence of the Spaniard Antonio de Cabezón (see below), developed from his father's
rambling ricercares a clearly defined form in dovetailed
imitative sections that became the standard pattern of
such works. His two books of *intavolature* (1542) contain hymn and plainsong settings for organ and two canzonas with French titles. At least one of the latter, the
lively *Il est bel et bon*, is virtually an original composition, for it uses no more than the first bar and a half
of the chanson by Passereau on which it is allegedly
based.

Ex.2 M. A. Cavazzoni: Intabulation of *Plus de regres*

During the second half of the century the most important centre for Italian keyboard music was Venice, where
Andrea Gabrieli, his nephew Giovanni Gabrieli and
Claudio Merulo were numbered among the organists of
St Mark's Cathedral. Andrea's keyboard works were
issued posthumously between 1593 and 1605 by Giovanni, who added several of his own compositions to
his uncle's. Each contributed a set of *intonazioni* in all
the 'tones' or modes – short pieces used during the liturgy either as interludes, or to give the choir the pitch
and mode of the music they were about to sing. Like
earlier preludes, they often include some brilliant passage-
work; this led by extension to the toccata, essentially a
keyboard piece in several contrasted sections designed
to display the varied capabilities of a player and his
instrument. The toccatas of Andrea and Giovanni Gabrieli

rely mainly on the contrast between sustained writing and brilliant passage-work; but Merulo enlarged the form by introducing one or more sections of imitative counterpoint. In addition to toccatas all three composers wrote ricercares, ornate chanson arrangements and original canzonas. The ricercares follow the sectional pattern established by Girolamo Cavazzoni; but those of Andrea and Giovanni Gabrieli have fewer themes (sometimes only one) and achieve variety by the use of inversion, augmentation, diminution and stretto, and by the importance given to secondary material such as a countersubject or a new thematic tag. Canzonas tend to be lighter in feeling than ricercares, and often begin with a rhythmic formula of three repeated notes, for instance minim–crotchet–crotchet. None of the works requires pedals, and many of them are as well suited to the harpsichord as to the organ.

The earliest Italian keyboard dances are found in a small anonymous manuscript of about 1520 (*I-Vnm* Ital.IV.1227). Both here and in the anonymous *Intabolatura nova di varie sorte di balli* (1551), the melody is confined to the right hand, while the left has little more than a rhythmical chordal accompaniment. More sophisticated textures appear in the dance publications of Marco Facoli (1588) and Giovanni Maria Radino (1592), proving that the addition of simple counterpoint and right-hand embellishments can make such pieces sufficiently interesting to be played and heard for their own sake, and not merely as an accompaniment for dancing.

Although England lagged far behind the Continent in printing keyboard music, British composers led the way in developing keyboard techniques. The broken-chord basses characteristic of later string keyboard writing appear in a manuscript of about 1520–40 (*GB-Lbm* Roy.App.58), which contains an adventurous 'Hornpype' by Hugh Aston and two anonymous pieces, *My Lady Careys Dompe* and *The Short Mesure of My Lady Wynkfylds Rownde*, which may also be by him. All three have ostinato left-hand parts. The repertory for organ (manuals only) from about the same period consists of almost 100 liturgical plainsong pieces (*GB-Lbm* Roy.App.56, Add.15233, Add.29996; and *Och* Mus.371; see *Early Tudor Organ Music*, i, ed. J. Caldwell, and ii, ed. D. Stevens, London, 1966–9). The plainsong is used in various ways. It may be given to a single part in long equal notes, decorated rhythmically and/or melodically, or paraphrased so freely as to be almost unrecognizable; or again, either a single section or several sections of the melody may form the basis of an otherwise free composition. At first the most favoured plainsongs were the offertory *Felix namque* and the antiphon *Miserere mihi Domine*; but later these gave place to the antiphon *Gloria tibi Trinitas*, which, under the title *In nomine*, remained immensely popular with English composers for more than a century. The only known English setting of the Ordinary of the Mass is by Philip ap Rhys 'of St Paul's in London'. Among the remaining named composers, the two whose works are outstanding in both quality and quantity are John Redford (*d* 1547) and Thomas Preston. At first glance much of their music may seem vocal in style; but a genuine understanding of the keyboard is shown by the widely ranging parts, the skilful deployment of the hands, and the idiomatic figuration. Virtually no ornament signs are used, but written-out shakes and turns are occasionally incorporated in the text.

More of Redford's works are found in the antholog known as the Mulliner Book (*c*1550–75; *GB-Lbm* Add.30593), to which the other principal contributo were Thomas Tallis and William Blitheman. In additio to many plainsong pieces the manuscript contains sin ple transcriptions of Latin and English motets, secula partsongs and consort music. Most of the music wa probably intended primarily, though not exclusively, fc organ; but three anonymous pieces at the beginning c the manuscript, and a later pavan by Newman (no.116 have the chordal basses that distinguish string keyboar music. Similar basses are found in the Dublin Virgina Manuscript (*c*1570; *EIRE-Dtc* D.3.30), which consist almost entirely of anonymous dances. These contain sprinkling of the double- and single-stroke ornament and many of the varied repeats or 'divisions' that late became ubiquitous features of the virginals style.

The only surviving French sources of the 16th centur are seven small books of anonymous pieces publishe by Pierre Attaingnant of Paris in 1530–31. Three ar devoted to chanson arrangements (some of them als known in lute versions); two to *alternatim* plainsong settings of the Mass, *Magnificat*, and *Te Deum*; one t motet arrangements; and one to dances (galliards, pavans branles and basse danses). All are described as being 'en la tablature des orgues, espinettes et manicordions' but the dances and chanson arrangements are best suitee to string keyboard instruments, and the remainder to the organ.

The most outstanding keyboard composer of the firs half of the century was Antonio de Cabezón, organis to Charles V and Philip II of Spain. A number of hi works (ascribed simply to 'Antonio') were included ir Venegas de Henestrosa's anthology, *Libro de cifra nueva* (1557); but the principal source is the volume of Cabezón's own *Obras de música* published posthumously in 1578 by his son Hernando. Although both collections are described as being for 'tecla, arpa y vihuela' (keyboard, harp and lute), they were intended primarily for keyboard – the plainsong settings for organ, the *diferencias* (variations) for harpsichord, and the *tientos* (ricercares) for either instrument. Cabezón's style is severe, with textures that are generally contrapuntal and always in a definite number of parts. The tientos presen a number of themes in succession, each section beginning with strict imitation and culminating in free counterpoint, often in relatively small note values. No ornament signs are used, but a favourite embellishment is a written-out shake with turn. Moreover, it seems likely that contemporary players would have added extempore *redobles* (turns), *quiebros* (shakes, and upper or lower mordents), and *glosas* (diminutions), as recommended in Tomás de Santa María's treatise, *Libro llamado Arte de tañer fantasía* (1565). The diferencias are lighter in mood, though still strictly contrapuntal. In one of the finest, *El canto llano del caballero*, the melody is at first plainly harmonized, then given successively to soprano, tenor, alto, and again tenor, with flowing counterpoint in the remaining voices. As a member of Philip's private chapel, Cabezón visited Italy, Germany and the Netherlands in 1548–51, and the Netherlands and England in 1554–6; yet he appears to have had surprisingly little influence on the many composers he must have met in his travels.

Keyboard music from Poland survives in several manuscripts, of which the most comprehensive is the so-called Lublin Tablature, copied by Jan z Lublina during the years 1537–48 (*PL-Kp* 1716). It contains some 250 works, mostly anonymous, and includes liturgical plainsong pieces, preludes, dances (often in slow–quick pairs), and arrangements of vocal works with Latin, German, French, Italian and Polish titles. The influence of the German school is apparent throughout and extends even to the notation used.

3. 17TH CENTURY. Among the principal forms and types of keyboard music introduced during the 17th century were suites, genre or character-pieces, paired preludes and fugues, chorale preludes, and (from about 1680) sonatas. Superb organs in northern and central Germany encouraged the use of the newly independent pedal registers, thus underlining the difference between organ and string keyboard idioms. But the earlier more 'generalized' style of keyboard writing tended to persist wherever organs were less highly developed.

During the early part of the century the main advances in technique still took place in England, where the printing of keyboard music began at long last with *Parthenia or the Maydenhead of the First Musicke that Ever was Printed for the Virginalls* (1612–13). Its three contributors, Byrd, Bull and Orlando Gibbons, represented successive generations of the great school of virginalists that spanned the late 16th and early 17th centuries. The remaining sources of solo virginals music are manuscripts, however, for the apparent sequel, *Parthenia In-violata* (*c*1624), is for virginals and bass viol. The most comprehensive manuscript source is the Fitzwilliam Virginal Book (*c*1609–19), which provides a cross-section of the whole repertory from Tallis (*c*1505–1585) to Tomkins (1572–1656). Besides containing many unique texts, this remarkable anthology shows the ever-growing popularity of secular works such as dances, settings of song-tunes, variations, fantasias and genre pieces.

Typical of the virginals idiom, as developed by Byrd, are textures that range from contrapuntal imitation to plain harmony in either broken or block chords; a constantly varying number of parts; short figurative motifs; and florid decoration – particularly in the 'divisions', or varied repeats, that are often included in the text. Profuse ornamentation is a constant feature of the style, though oddly enough there is no contemporary explanation of the two signs commonly used to designate ornaments – the double and single stroke. Organ music is distinguished mainly by its liturgical function, but also by an absence of broken-chord basses and a preference for contrapuntal textures in a definite number of parts.

Keyboard techniques were enormously extended by Bull, who was the greatest virtuoso of the day, and by Farnaby, a minor master of rare charm. Brilliant effects were achieved by figuration based on broken octaves, 6ths, 3rds and common chords, by the use of quick repeated notes and wide leaps, and even (in Bull's 'Walsingham' variations, MB, xix, no.85; see ex.3) by the crossing of hands. Farnaby's tiny piece 'For Two Virginals' (MB, xxiv, no.25), one of the earliest works of its kind, consists of no more than a plain and a decorated version of the same music played simultaneously. A clearer grasp of the true principles of duet writing is shown, however, in Tomkins's single-keyboard 'Fancy: for Two to Play' (MB, v, no.32); for though based on choral procedures, its mixture of antiphonal and contrapuntal textures neatly displays the essential individuality-cum-unity of two performers.

Ex.3 Bull: 'Walsingham' variations

By the time the aged Tomkins died in 1656 younger composers were already turning towards a new style, French-influenced, in which the main thematic interest lay in the top line. The change can be seen clearly in the short, tuneful pieces of *Musicks Hand-maide* (1663), a collection of 'new and pleasant lessons for the virginals or harpsycon'. One of the few composers named in it is Matthew Locke, whose more ambitious anthology, *Melothesia* (1673), is prefaced significantly by 'certain rules for playing upon a continued-bass'. It includes seven of his own pieces (voluntaries) for organ and 'for double [i.e. two-manual] organ', and a number of suites (not so named) by himself and others, consisting generally of an almain, corant, saraband and one or more additional movements. Similar suites were written later by Blow and his pupil Purcell, the principal contributors to *The Second Part of Musick's Hand-maid* (1689); Purcell's were issued posthumously as *A Choice Collection of Lessons for the Harpsichord and Spinnet* (1696) and four of Blow's appeared two years later with the same title. All these publications were aimed at the amateur. But Purcell's harpsichord music, though small in scale, is no less masterly than his more ambitious works for theatre, court and the church; and at times it achieves a depth and poignancy – particularly in the ground basses of which he was so fond – that is quite disproportionate to its size. Blow was the more significant organ composer of the two. His 30-odd voluntaries and verses (Purcell wrote only half a dozen) are sectional contrapuntal pieces based on either one or two subjects. Two of them (nos.2 and 29 in Watkins Shaw's edition) unaccountably quote sizeable passages from Frescobaldi's *Toccate e partite d'intavolatura di cimbalo* (1615) and another (no.5) is similarly indebted to one of Michelangelo Rossi's published toccatas.

More orthodox musical exchanges between the Continent and England had already taken place during the early years of the century. Arrangements of madrigals by Marenzio and Lassus and original works by Sweelinck, organist of the Oude Kerk in Amsterdam, were included in the Fitzwilliam Virginal Book; and even more significantly, Bull, Peter Philips and other Catholic recusants found refuge in the Netherlands and elsewhere, and thus spread abroad the advanced English keyboard techniques. Sweelinck himself was much influenced by the innovations, as can be seen not only from his harpsichord works, but also from his organ variations on Lutheran chorales and his echo-fantasias that exploit the dynamic contrast between one manual and another. Although none of his keyboard works appeared in print, Sweelinck's fame as the foremost teacher in northern Europe brought him numerous pupils, particularly from the neighbouring parts of Germany. The latest techniques were thus passed on to a younger generation of composers, who in their turn carried them still farther afield.

German composers of the period may conveniently be divided into two groups: those who worked in the Protestant north and centre; and those of the Catholic south, including Austria. To the former group belong Sweelinck's pupils, Scheidt and Scheidemann. Scheidt's keyboard works were issued in two collections, the *Tabulatura nova* (1624) and the *Tabulatur-Buch hundert geistlicher Lieder und Psalmen* (1650). (In the first of these the description 'new' refers to the use of open score in place of letter notation.) The organ pieces cover a wide range, for in addition to the forms used by Sweelinck they include fugues and canons as well as plainsong settings for use during the Catholic liturgy. The later volume consists of simple four-part settings of Lutheran chorales for accompanying unison singing. One of the sets of variations for harpsichord is based on the English song *Fortune my Foe*, which was also set by Sweelinck, Byrd and Tomkins. Scheidemann's works, like those of most northerners, remained unpublished. The majority are organ settings of chorales in which the borrowed melody is either left plain, ornamented, treated in motet style, or (more rarely) used as a theme for variations. The most outstanding of all the northerners was, however, Buxtehude, who left his native Denmark in 1668 to become organist of the Marienkirche in Lübeck. His organ preludes and fugues are not unlike toccatas, for they often contain two quite distinct fugal sections in addition to brilliant flourishes and sustained passages. He also wrote numerous chorale settings of various kinds, even including a set of variations on *Auf meinen lieben Gott* in the form of a dance suite. Some of the works are for manuals only, but the majority make full use of the pedals. Although Buxtehude was primarily an organ composer, the publication in 1941 of the Ryge Manuscript (*DK-Kk* C.11.49.4°) made available his suites and variations for clavichord or harpsichord; these are so similar in style to those of Nicolas-Antoine Lebègue that the editor did not notice the inclusion of one of Lebègue's suites in the Buxtehude manuscript.

The earliest and most significant German composer of the south was Froberger, who, though born in Stuttgart, held the post of court organist in Vienna for 20 years. His ricercares, canzonas and fantasias are strongly influenced by his master, Frescobaldi, but his toccatas are less Italian in style. Although they begin with the usual sustained chords and brilliant flourishes (see ex.4), they generally include two fugal sections in rhythmic variants of a single subject, each section being rounded off with further flourishes. His suites are in an expressive, romantic vein better suited to the clavichord than to the harpsichord. They are French in style, and are said to have been the first to establish the basic suite pattern of four contrasted national dances: i.e. an allemande (German), courante (French) or corrente (Italian), sarabande (Spanish) and gigue or jig (English). In Froberger's autographs the gigue either precedes the saraband or is omitted altogether; but when the works were published posthumously (Amsterdam, 1693) the order was changed ('mis en meilleur ordre') and the gigue placed at the end. During the last ten years of his life Froberger travelled widely in Germany, France, the Netherlands and England, meeting Chambonnières and

Ex.4 Froberger: Toccata no.9 (*Diverse . . . curiose partite*, Mainz, 1693)

Louis Couperin in Paris and Christopher Gibbons (son of Orlando) in London; thus he too played a significant part in the cross-fertilization of national styles.

Among the lesser southerners were Alessandro Poglietti, Georg Muffat and J. C. F. Fischer. Although Poglietti was probably an Italian, he became court organist in Vienna shortly after Froberger, and in 1677 presented Leopold I and his empress with an autograph collection of his harpsichord pieces entitled *Rossignolo*. Besides a ricercare, a capriccio and an *Aria bizarra*, all based on the *Rossignolo* theme, it includes a virtuoso 'imitation of the same bird', and an *Aria allemagna* with 20 variations. Each of the latter has an illustrative title ('Bohemian Bagpipes', 'Dutch Flute', 'Old Woman's Funeral', 'Hungarian Fiddles' etc), and in number they match the age of the empress, to whom they were dedicated. Muffat's *Apparatus musico-organisticus* (1690) contains 12 organ toccatas with elementary pedal parts, and four harpsichord pieces of which the large-scale Passacaglia in G minor and the shorter Ciacona in G have a power and breadth more typical of the north than of the south. In contrast to these, the four collections by Fischer are wholly southern in their delicacy of feeling. *Les pièces de clavessin* (1696) and the *Musicalischer Parnassus* (1738) are devoted to harpsichord suites, each of which begins with a prelude of some sort and continues with a group of dances or other pieces, not always including the usual allemande, courante, sarabande and gigue. The other two volumes, *Ariadne musica* (1702) and *Blumen Strauss* (1733), contain miniature preludes and fugues for organ. The *Ariadne* group interestingly foreshadows Bach's *Das wohltemperirte Clavier* in the wide range of its key scheme, and even in some of its themes (Fischer's eighth fugue in E obviously inspired Bach's ninth from book 2).

In Italy the main centre for keyboard music moved from Venice to Naples and then to Rome. From Ascanio Mayone's *Diversi capricci* (1603 and 1609) and Giovanni Maria Trabaci's *Ricercare* (1603 and 1615) it can be seen that although the Neapolitans retained the strict contrapuntal style of the Gabrielis in their ricercares, they broke new ground in toccatas by shortening the sections, increasing their number and heightening the contrast between one section and the next. The same distinction was made by Frescobaldi, who, as organist of St Peter's in Rome, was the most widely acclaimed player and keyboard composer of the day. Although he visited the Netherlands in 1607, when the 45-year-old Sweelinck was at the height of his powers, he was little influenced by the techniques of the north. His works

vere published during the next 35 years in a series of
en volumes of which some are revised and enlarged
editions of others. The three definitive collections are
l primo libro di capricci, canzon francese e recercari
1626) and the *Toccate d'intavolatura di cimbalo et
organo* with its sequel *Il secondo libro di toccate* (both
637). (The first two contain important prefaces by the
composer concerning interpretation.) Most of the toc-
atas, capriccios and canzonas in these collections are
-qually suited to harpsichord and organ, for though some
have a primitive pedal part, it generally consists of no
more than long-held notes that are already present in the
eft hand. The works intended primarily for harpsichord
nclude dances (sometimes grouped in threes, with the
opening balletto serving as theme for the following cor-
-ente and passacaglia), and sets of variations or partitas,
a number of which are based on harmonic patterns such
as the romanesca and the Ruggiero. The ricercares and
plainsong pieces are essentially organ music, as in the
liturgical *Fiori musicali* (1635), of which Bach possessed a manuscript copy.

One of the few 17th-century Italian publications
devoted wholly to dances was Giovanni Picchi's *Intavolatura di balli d'arpicordo* (1621). Besides the customary passamezzo, saltarello and padoana (pavan), it
includes imitations of alien idioms such as a 'Ballo alla
polacha', a 'Ballo ongaro' and a 'Todesca'. The cor-
antos in Michelangelo Rossi's *Toccate e correnti d'intavolatura d'organo e cimbalo* (c1640) are in a lighter,
more tuneful style, though his toccatas are still closely
related to Frescobaldi's. This new style can be seen even
more clearly in the works of Bernardo Pasquini, who
was among the first to apply the title 'sonata' to solo
keyboard music. Originally it denoted no more than a
'sound piece' as opposed to a 'sung piece' or 'cantata',
for it was applied indiscriminately to toccatas, fugues,
airs, dances and suites. But Pasquini, following the
example of Corelli's ensemble sonatas, also gave the
title to solos in more than a single movement. Among
his other works are 15 sonatas for two harpsichords, in
which each part consists rather oddly of no more than
a figured bass (*GB-Lbm* Add.31501). The 40-odd toccatas of Alessandro Scarlatti are of interest mainly
because each contains at least one *moto perpetuo* section, thus anticipating the much later *moto perpetuo* type
of toccata.

Much French keyboard music of the 17th century
appeared in print while the composers were still alive;
and as the title-pages generally specified either organ or
harpsichord, but not both, there is rarely any doubt about
the instrument intended. A manuscript dated 1618
(*GB-Lbm* Add.29486), however, contains over 100 short
pieces in the church modes, all anonymous apart from
G. Gabrieli's 12 *intonazioni*. They include preludes, *fugae*
and *alternatim* settings of the Mass, *Magnificat* and *Te
Deum*, all simple enough technically for parochial use.
More sophisticated are Titelouze's *Hymnes de l'église
pour toucher sur l'orgue* (1623) and *Le Magnificat . . .
suivant les huits tons de l'église* (1626), the first French
keyboard publications devoted to the works of a single
composer. The earlier volume contains settings of 12
plainsong hymns, each consisting of three or four versets for which the plainsong provides either a cantus firmus or several short themes for treatment in contrapuntal
motet style. The eight *Magnificat* settings of the second
volume, though also in motet style, are more adventurous harmonically. Titelouze was essentially conserva-

tive, however, and his strict polyphonic idiom attracted
no immediate disciples. More typically French are the
many *Livres d'orgue* issued during the second half of
the century by composers such as Guillaume Nivers,
Nicolas-Antoine Lebègue, Nicolas Gigault, André Raison and Jacques Boyvin. They mostly contain short pieces
which, though still in the church modes and intended
for use during the liturgy, are fairly simple in style and
often unabashedly tuneful. As was customary in France,
though not elsewhere, the registration is often indicated
in the title, for instance 'Récit de nazard' or 'Basse de
cromorne'. Also typical is the frequent use of contrasted
manuals heard either simultaneously or in alternation.
Lebègue was the first Frenchman to exploit the pedals
fully, for generally they were either optional or omitted
altogether.

The mid-century saw the emergence of the distinctive
French harpsichord idiom that exercised a potent influence throughout Europe. In essence it was based on the
richly ornamented and arpeggiated textures of lute music.
The founder of the school was Chambonnières, who late
in life published two books of *Pièces de clavessin* (1670)
containing 60 dances grouped according to key. The
commonest types are allemandes, courantes (often in sets
of three) and sarabandes; occasionally a gigue or some
other dance is added. More of his pieces survive in the
Bauyn Manuscript (*F-Pn* Res.Vm^7.674–5), which also
contains almost all the compositions of his pupil Louis
Couperin, the one outstanding French keyboard composer who never saw any of his own works in print. In
addition to the forms used by his master, Couperin wrote
a number of 'unmeasured preludes' of a type peculiar
to France. Another pupil of Chambonnières was Jean-
Henri d'Anglebert, whose *Pièces de clavecin* were published in 1689. The volume is unusual in two respects,
for it includes five fugues for organ, and 15 of its 60
harpsichord pieces are arrangements of movements from
operas by Lully. D'Anglebert's magnificent *Tombeau de
Mr. de Chambonnières* is a good example for keyboard
of a type of memorial composition of which French
composers have always been specially fond.

4. THE PERIOD OF J. S. BACH. All the forms employed
during the 17th century remained in use during the first
half of the 18th; but sonatas (of other than the classical
type) acquired increasing importance, and ritornello form
(derived from the Neapolitan operatic aria) provided the
foundation on which every concerto and many extended
solo movements were built.

French keyboard composers were untouched by these
developments, however, and continued to confine themselves to dances and genre pieces for harpsichord, and
to short liturgical and secular works for the organ. The
two outstanding figures among them were Louis Couperin's nephew François Couperin the younger and Jean-
Philippe Rameau, a near-contemporary of Bach. François
Couperin's four books of *Pièces de clavecin* (1713–30)
are the crowning achievement of the French clavecin
school. The 220 pieces range from elegant trifles to the
majestic Passacaille in B minor (*ordre* no.8) and the
sombre allemande *La ténébreuse* (*ordre* no.3), which is
almost too intense in mood for the dance form in which
it is embodied. Two organ masses, written at the age
of 21, are sufficiently unlike the mature works to have
been attributed at one time to his father, François the
elder. Couperin's views on teaching, interpretation,
ornamentation and fingering are set forth in his *L'art de*

toucher le clavecin (1716, rev.2/1717), a fascinating treatise which nevertheless often fails to answer questions that remain puzzling. Rameau's instructions to the player are contained in two of the prefaces to his four books of harpsichord pieces issued between 1706 and 1741 (he wrote nothing for organ). The works are generally simpler in texture and less richly ornamented than Couperin's, but more adventurous harmonically and in their use of the keyboard. The composer himself noted that it would take time and application to appreciate the (harmonic) beauty of parts of the piece entitled *L'enharmonique*; and he provided fingering for the widely spaced left-hand figure in *Les cyclopes* because of its unusual difficulty. Rameau's final keyboard publication, *Pièces de clavecin en concerts* (1741), is primarily a collection of five suites for violin, bass viol and harpsichord, but it also includes a solo harpsichord version of four of the movements. This practical plan was anticipated, though in reverse, in Gaspard le Roux's *Pièces de clavecin* (1705). There the main works are suites for harpsichord solo, while the arrangements consist of selected movements for trio (instruments unspecified), and several for two harpsichords, the latter being the earliest known French works for that medium. Composers other than Couperin who wrote for both harpsichord and organ include Marchand, Clérambault, Dandrieu, Dagincour and Daquin. Most of their works are in the customary forms; but the organ volumes by Dandrieu (1715) and Daquin (1757) are devoted to sets of variations on popular Christmas melodies, entitled noëls, a type which first appeared in Lebègue's *Troisième livre d'orgue* (c1685).

One of the greatest of all harpsichord composers was the Italian Domenico Scarlatti, son of Alessandro and exact contemporary of Bach and Handel. The last 35 years of his life were spent in the service of Maria Barbara of Braganza, at first in Portugal and later in Spain; during that period he appears to have written almost all his 555 single-movement sonatas. Apart from a volume of 30 *Essercizi per gravicembalo* (1738), published under his own supervision, the main sources of his works are two contemporary manuscript collections (*I-Vnm* It.iv.199–213; and *I-PAc* AG 31406–20), the first of which was copied for his royal patron. Their contents are similar but not identical, and it has been suggested by Ralph Kirkpatrick (*Domenico Scarlatti*, Princeton, 1953) that the order of their contents is to a large extent chronological, and that more than two-thirds of the sonatas were, as the manuscripts indicate, originally grouped in pairs, or sometimes in threes, according to key (this order is retained in Kirkpatrick's facsimile edition, New York and London, 1972, and in Kenneth Gilbert's excellent complete edition, Paris, 1971–). Although Scarlatti rarely used any structure other than binary form, and seldom aimed at emotional extremes, he achieved an astonishing variety within those self-imposed limits. Moreover he exploited the keyboard in ways never imagined by any of his contemporaries. In the later works he virtually abandoned his wilder flights of hand-crossing; but he never lost his command of both sparkling brilliance and an unexpected vein of reflective melancholy, his delight in technical and harmonic experiment, and his love for the sounds and rhythms of the popular music of Spain. Five of the sonatas (K254–5, 287–8 and 328) are for two-manual chamber organ without pedals, and some others are not unsuited to a single-manual organ; but by far the greater number are essentially harpsichord

works. (Among the harpsichords possessed by his royal patron, however, none of those with more than two registers appear to have had the full five-octave compass required by some of the sonatas.)

Scarlatti's followers in Portugal and Spain, among whom were Seixas and Soler, wrote numerous single-movement sonatas similar in style to his own; but as an expatriate he exercised little influence on Italian composers, whose sonatas are of several different types. Those by Della Ciaia (1727) are not unlike sectional toccatas; Durante's (c1732) each contain a *studio* in imitative counterpoint followed by a brilliant *divertimento*; Marcello's (MS) are in either three or four movements; and Zipoli's (1716) include liturgical and secular pieces for organ as well as suites and variations for harpsichord. Also intended for either instrument are Martini's two volumes of sonatas (1742, 1747), the first devoted to two- and three-movement works, and the second to five-movement works that combine features of both the *sonata da camera* and the *sonata da chiesa*.

English keyboard composers during the post-Purcell period rarely rose above a level of honest competence. Tuneful airs and lessons, sometimes grouped into suites, appeared in serial anthologies such as *The Harpsichord Master* (1697–1734) and *The Ladys Banquet* (1704–35), among whose contributors were Jeremiah Clarke, William Croft and Maurice Greene. In addition, separate volumes were devoted to works by Philip Hart, Clarke, Thomas Roseingrave and Greene. Although Croft was not accorded that distinction, he was the most accomplished composer of the group and the only one to come within hailing distance of Purcell. Indeed, the Ground from his Suite no.3 in C minor is actually ascribed to Purcell in one source. Collections of fugues and/or voluntaries were issued by Hart, Roseingrave, Greene, Boyce and Stanley. Although described as being 'for the organ or harpsichord', these are best suited to the organ. The early voluntaries consist of a single movement, generally contrapuntal in texture, while the later tend to be in two movements (slow–fast), of which the second is often a fugue. Outstanding among them are the three volumes containing Stanley's 30 voluntaries, in some of which the number of movements is increased to three or four.

A Scarlatti cult was at one time fostered in England, first by Roseingrave's edition of *XLII suites de pièces pour le clavecin* (1739), which added 12 more Scarlatti sonatas to the 30 published a year earlier in the *Essercizi*; and secondly by Charles Avison's arrangement of a number of the sonatas as Twelve Concertos (1744) for strings and continuo.

Of far greater significance to English musical life, however, was the arrival of Handel, who settled in London in 1712 after a successful visit two years earlier. Although at first occupied mainly with Italian opera and later with oratorio, he was obliged to publish his [8] *Suites de pièces de clavecin* (1720) in order to counteract the many 'surrepticious and incorrect copies' that were circulating in manuscript. Other collections of his pieces, all unauthorized, appeared later in London and Amsterdam. Some of the suites follow the normal pattern of allemande–courante–sarabande–gigue; but more often they include Italianate allegros, andantes etc, or consist of nothing else. His keyboard works combine relaxed informality with masterly rhetoric in a way that doubtless reflects the improvisations for which he was famous; this is particularly noticeable in the 14 or 15 oncertos for organ, a medium he invented for use during the intervals at his oratorio performances. In many of them the soloist is expected to improvise long sections (even whole movements) where his part is marked ad lib'. This would have been a perfectly simple matter for Handel himself, but it does pose problems for other players. Most of the works require an orchestra of no more than strings and oboes, and as all but one are for organ without pedals, the title-pages describe them as being 'for organ or harpsichord'. It seems likely that the appearance of the first set of six in 1738 encouraged Stanley to issue a keyboard version of the concertino parts of his Six String Concertos op.2, thus helping to acclimatize the keyboard concerto in England.

Meanwhile in Germany the way had been prepared for the greatest of all pre-classical keyboard composers, J. S. Bach. Among his many musical ancestors, other than relatives, the most significant was Buxtehude (see above), whose organ toccatas and chorale fantasias, and highly developed pedal technique, provided foundations on which Bach could build. So great was Bach's reverence for Buxtehude that in 1705 he walked the distance from Arnstadt to Lübeck in order to hear his Abendmusiken – the yearly choral and instrumental performances given on the five Sundays before Christmas. Somewhat less influential were Pachelbel, Kuhnau and Georg Böhm. Nevertheless, Pachelbel's chorale preludes, published in 1683 and 1693, were the forerunners of one important type used by Bach. In this, each successive phrase of the borrowed melody is treated in diminution to provide the theme for a short fughetta, towards whose conclusion the phrase itself appears as a cantus firmus. The keyboard works of Kuhnau, Bach's predecessor at the Thomaskirche in Leipzig, include two notable volumes: firstly, the *Frische Clavier Früchte, oder sieben Suonaten* (1696), the earliest publication in which the title 'sonata' is given to a solo as distinct from an ensemble work; and secondly, [6] *Musicalische Vorstellungen einiger biblischen Historien* (1700), the 'musical representations of biblical stories' that provided the model for Bach's early *Capriccio sopra la lontananza del suo fratello dilettissimo* BWV992. The influence of Böhm, though conjectural, would have been earlier and more direct, for he was organist of the Johanniskirche in Lüneburg when Bach was a choirboy at the nearby Michaeliskirche. Böhm's organ partitas (variations on chorales) and sensitive suites in the French style for clavichord or harpsichord were unpublished, but the evidence of Bach's own works suggests that he must have been familiar with them as a boy.

A near-contemporary of Bach and Handel, and a friend of both, was the prolific Telemann. The admiration of the two slightly younger men for his music can best be understood by reference to works such as the *XX kleine Fugen* (1731). Although these miniature keyboard fugues are based on the church modes (which were then virtually obsolete), and though they are quite small in scale, each one establishes unerringly a mood as precise as its structure.

Comparatively few of Bach's own keyboard works were published during his lifetime. The most comprehensive collection, the *Clavier-Übung*, was issued in four parts between 1731 and 1742, of which the first, second and fourth contain compositions for both single- and double-manual harpsichord, while the third is mainly devoted to the organ.

Of Bach's total output of over 250 organ works, more than two-thirds are based on chorales. They range from the early sets of *Partite diverse* BWV766–8, in the style of Böhm, to mature chorale preludes of every type. From the Weimar period come the 46 preludes of the *Orgelbüchlein*, 'wherein the beginner may learn to perform chorales of every kind and also acquire skill in the use of the pedals'. In most of them a single, continuous statement of the melody, either plain or ornamented, is supported by an accompaniment whose figuration either symbolizes the words or intensifies the mood of the hymn concerned. They are generally small in scale; yet some of the settings, such as the richly embellished *O Mensch, bewein' dein' Sünde gross* BWV622, can be numbered among Bach's profoundest utterances. The third part of the *Clavier-Übung*, from the Leipzig period, contains 21 preludes based on catechism and other hymns, of which the six that illustrate the catechism are set twice – elaborately for two manuals and pedals, and more simply for manuals only. Four quite unconnected keyboard Duettos BWV802–5 are also included in part 3; and the whole volume is framed by the magnificent Prelude and Fugue in E♭ BWV552, known in England as the 'St Anne'. During the same period Bach published the recondite [5] *Canonische Veränderungen über das Weynacht Lied 'Vom Himmel hoch'* BWV769, which, as Schweitzer wrote, 'pack into a single chorale the whole art of canon'. He also virtually completed the revision of 18 large-scale chorale preludes, mostly written originally in Weimar; but failing health and eyesight forced him to abandon dictating the last of them, *Vor deinen Thron tret' ich hiermit* BWV668, whose ending luckily is known from other sources. Earlier chorale preludes include 24 copied by his pupil Kirnberger, 28 from various other manuscripts, and a set of six published by Schübler (c1746), five of which are arrangements of movements from cantatas.

In almost all of Bach's secular organ music, none of which was published, fugue is an essential element. From the beginning of the Weimar period, or even earlier, come four immature and fairly small-scale preludes and fugues BWV531–3 and 535 and two much finer toccatas in C and D minor BWV564–5, all written under Buxtehude's influence. Increasing mastery and individuality is apparent in four later Weimar works – the preludes and fugues in F minor and A BWV534 and 536, the Fantasia and Fugue in C minor BWV537 and the Toccata and Fugue in F BWV540, with its tremendous pedal solos. The finest of all the fugal works are, however, the ten written either during or just before the Leipzig period. They include the Fantasia and Fugue in G minor BWV542, the Prelude (or Toccata) and Fugue in D minor BWV538, known as the 'Dorian', and the six magnificent preludes and fugues BWV543–8, which are Bach's crowning achievements in this form.

The great Passacaglia and Fugue in C minor BWV582 and the six trio sonatas BWV525–30 far transcend their original purpose as instructional works for Bach's eldest son, Wilhelm Friedemann. They are described merely as being 'for two manuals and pedals', so it remains uncertain whether they were intended primarily for organ or for a harpsichord fitted with a pedal-board (such as used by some organists for home practice).

Much of Bach's music for normal harpsichord and/or clavichord was also didactic in aim. The 15 two-part inventions and 15 three-part sinfonias BWV772–801 were first included in a manuscript collection of keyboard pieces for Wilhelm Friedemann dated 1720, and were described in a revision of 1723 as showing not only how 'to play clearly in two voices but also, after further progress, to deal correctly and well with three obbligato parts . . . and above all to achieve a singing style in playing'. Friedemann's book also contained early versions of 11 of the preludes from the first book of *Das wohltemperirte Clavier* (1722), a more advanced collection of 24 preludes and fugues in all the major and minor keys 'for the use and profit of young musicians desiring to learn, as well as for the pastime of those already skilled in this study'. The second book, containing a further 24 preludes and fugues, was not completed until 1744. Two other manuscripts, dated respectively 1722 and 1725, were compiled for the use of Bach's second wife, Anna Magdalena. The first contains five of the six French suites BWV812–17, each consisting of the usual allemande, courante, sarabande and gigue, with one or more additional dances (*Galanterien*) following the sarabande. The six so-called 'English' suites BWV806–11 and six partitas BWV825–30 are on a larger scale, for each begins with a prelude of some sort. Those of the English suites (with the exception of no.1) are ritornello-type movements, while those of the partitas are in various forms. The partitas were published singly between 1726 and 1730, and complete in 1731 as part 1 of the *Clavier-Übung*, of which part 2 (1735) consists of the Italian Concerto BWV971 and the French Overture BWV831 (sometimes known as the Partita in B minor), both for two-manual harpsichord. Part 4 (1742), also for two-manual harpsichord, is devoted to a single work: the monumental Aria with 30 Variations BWV988, usually known as the Goldberg Variations, which Tovey described as 'not only thirty miracles of variation-form, but . . . a single miracle of consummate art as a whole composition'.

Slightly later in date is the *Musikalisches Opfer* BWV1079, a collection of fugues, canons etc for various instruments on a theme provided by Frederick the Great. It includes two ricercares for solo keyboard, of which the second, in six parts, was originally printed in open score. This was not an unusual method of presenting keyboard music when its aim was partly didactic. It was used again for Bach's posthumous treatise *Die Kunst der Fuge* BWV1080, in which the majority of the fugues are clearly intended for solo keyboard, though they have frequently been arranged for various ensembles in the 20th century.

During the Weimar period Bach made solo keyboard versions, some for organ and others for harpsichord, of 22 concertos by various composers, including Vivaldi, Marcello and Telemann. These paved the way for his later concertos for solo harpsichord and strings BWV1052–8, which were the first of their kind (and roughly contemporary with Handel's organ concertos). All seven are arrangements of earlier concertos of his own – mostly for solo violin and strings – several of which have not survived. The only original keyboard work in this form appears to be the Concerto in C for two harpsichords and strings BWV1061; the remaining two for the same medium, and those for three and four harpsichords and strings, are also arrangements of concertos originally by either Bach himself or other composers such as Vivaldi.

In its depth and range of emotion, contrapuntal skill and perfection of design, Bach's keyboard music far surpasses that of any of his contemporaries or predecessors; yet by the time of his death it was generally regarded as old-fashioned. The Baroque era had ended; the contrapuntal style was outmoded; and the harpsichord and clavichord were beginning to make way for the fortepiano, which combined the power of the one with the sensitivity of the other. The gradual change can be seen in the works of three of Bach's sons. The eldest, Wilhelm Friedemann, still wrote some fugues; but, like his polonaises and three-movement sonatas, they were in the new *empfindsamer Stil*, of which his brother Carl Philipp Emanuel was the chief exponent. Philipp Emanuel's numerous sonatas, fantasias, rondos etc, embodying the violent dynamic contrasts typical of the style, were immensely influential; and his book, *Versuch über die wahre Art das Clavier zu spielen* (1753–62), was the most important treatise of its day. The youngest brother, Johann Christian, was a less original composer; nevertheless, his Italianate sonatas and concertos in the *galant* style gained great popularity in England, where he settled in 1761. And there it was that he met and befriended the eight-year-old Mozart, when that astonishing boy visited London in 1764–5.

BIBLIOGRAPHY

LISTS OF COMPOSITIONS

B. Weigl: *Handbuch der Orgelliteratur* (Leipzig, 1931)
E. Hutchinson: *The Literature of the Piano* (New York, 1938, rev. 3/1964)
W. S. Newman: 'A Checklist of the Earliest Keyboard "Sonatas"', *Notes*, xi (1953–4), 201
J. Friskin and I. Freundlich: *Music for the Piano . . . from 1580 to 1952* (New York, 1954/R1973)
H. Alker: *Literatur für alte Tasteninstrumente: Wiener Abhandlungen zur Musikwissenschaft und Instrumentalkunde* (Vienna, 1962)
K. Wolters: *Handbuch der Klavierliteratur* (Zurich, 1967)
C. R. Arnold: *Organ Literature: a Comprehensive Survey* (Metuchen, NJ, 1973)
M. Hinson: *Guide to the Pianist's Repertoire*, ed. I. Freundlich (Bloomington, Ind., 1973) [comprehensive bibliography]
H. Ferguson: *Keyboard Interpretation* (London, 1975)

GENERAL SURVEYS

A. G. Ritter: *Zur Geschichte des Orgelspiels* (Leipzig, 1884/R1969)
M. Seiffert: *Geschichte der Klaviermusik* (Leipzig, 1899/R1966)
J. Wolf: 'Zur Geschichte der Orgelmusik im 14. Jahrhundert', *KJb*, xiv (1899),14
O. Kinkeldey: *Orgel und Klavier in der Musik des 16. Jahrhunderts* (Leipzig, 1910/R1968)
A. Pirro: 'L'art des organistes', *EMDC*, II/ii (1926), 1181–359
K. G. Fellerer: *Orgel und Orgelmusik: ihre Geschichte* (Augsburg, 1929)
G. Frotscher: *Geschichte des Orgel-Spiels und der Orgel-Komposition* (Berlin, 1935–6, enlarged 3/1966)
G. Schünemann: *Geschichte der Klaviermusik* (Berlin, 1940)
W. Georgii: *Klaviermusik* (Zurich and Freiburg, 1941, 4/1965)
M. F. Bukofzer: *Music in the Baroque Era* (New York, 1947)
G. S. Bedbrook: *Keyboard Music from the Middle Ages to the Beginnings of the Baroque* (London, 1949/R1973)
M. Kenyon: *Harpsichord Music* (London, 1949)
L. Hoffmann-Erbrecht: *Deutsche und italienische Klavier-Musik zur Bach-Zeit* (Leipzig, 1954)
G. Reese: *Music in the Renaissance* (New York, 1954, rev. 2/1959)
A. E. F. Dickinson: 'A Forgotten Collection' [*D-Bds* Ly.A1 and A2], *MR*, xvii (1956), 97
W. Apel and K. von Fischer: 'Klaviermusik', *MGG*
F. W. Riedel: *Quellenkundliche Beiträge zur Geschichte der Musik für Tasteninstrumente in der zweiten Hälfte des 17. Jahrhunderts* (Kassel, 1960)
Y. Rokseth: 'The Instrumental Music of the Middle Ages and Early 16th Century', *NOHM*, iii (1960), 406–65
F. W. Riedel and T.-M. Laquer: 'Orgelmusik', *MGG*
W. Young: 'Keyboard Music to 1600', *MD*, xvi (1962), 115–50; xvii (1963), 163–93
A. E. F. Dickinson: 'The Lübbenau Keyboard Books' [*D-Bds* Ly.A1 and A2], *MR*, xxvii (1966), 270
F. E. Kirby: *A Short History of Keyboard Music* (New York, 1966)
W. Apel: *Geschichte der Orgel- und Klaviermusik bis 1700* (Kassel, 1967; Eng. trans., rev. 1972)
——: 'Solo Instrumental Music', *NOHM*, iv (1968), 602–708

ENGLAND

E. Walker: *A History of Music in England* (Oxford, 1907, rev. 3/1952 by J. A. Westrup)

C. van den Borren: *Les origines de la musique de clavier en Angleterre à l'époque de la Renaissance* (Brussels, 1913; Eng. trans., 1913)

W. Niemann: *Die Virginalmusik* (Leipzig, 1919)

M. Glyn: *About Elizabethan Virginal Music and its Composers* (London, 1924, enlarged 2/1934)

M.-L. Pereyra: 'Les livres de virginal de la bibliothèque du Conservatoire de Paris', *RdM*, vii (1926), 204; viii (1927), 36, 205; ix (1928), 235; x (1929), 32; xii (1931), 22; xiii (1932), 86; xiv (1933), 24

L. Neudenberger: *Die Variationstechnik der Virginalisten im Fitzwilliam Virginal Book* (Berlin, 1937)

H. M. Miller: 'Sixteenth-century English Faburden Compositions for Keyboard', *MQ*, xxvi (1940), 50

——: *English Plainsong Composition for Keyboard in the Sixteenth Century* (diss., Harvard U., 1943)

——: 'The Earliest Keyboard Duets', *MQ*, xxix (1943), 438

R. Donington and T. Dart: 'The Origin of the English In Nomine', *ML*, xxx (1949), 101

G. Reese: 'The Origin of the English "In Nomine"', *JAMS*, ii (1949), 7

D. Stevens: 'Pre-Reformation Organ Music in England', *PRMA*, lxxvii (1951–2), 1

——: 'A Unique Tudor Organ Mass', *MD*, vi (1952), 167

——: *The Mulliner Book: a Commentary* (London, 1952)

E. E. Lowinsky: 'English Organ Music of the Renaissance', *MQ*, xxxix (1953), 373, 528

T. Dart: 'New Sources of Virginal Music', *ML*, xxxv (1954), 93

J. Ward: 'Les sources de la musique pour le clavier en Angleterre', *La musique instrumentale de la Renaissance: CNRS Paris 1954*, 225

J. L. Boston: 'Priscilla Bunbury's Virginal Book', *ML*, xxxvi (1955), 365

H. J. Steele: *English Organs and Organ Music from 1500–1650* (diss., U. of Cambridge, 1958)

R. L. Adams: *The Development of Keyboard Music in England during the English Renaissance* (diss., U. of Washington, 1960)

J. A. Caldwell: *British Museum Add.MS 29996* (diss., U. of Oxford, 1965)

——: 'Keyboard Plainsong Settings in England, 1500–1660', *MD*, xix (1965), 129

R. D. Johnstone: 'An Unknown Book of Organ Voluntaries', *MT*, cviii (1967), 1003

J. Beechey: 'A New Source of 17th Century Keyboard Music', *ML*, i (1969), 278

A. Curtis: *Sweelinck's Keyboard Works: a Study of English Elements in Seventeenth-century Dutch Composition* (London and Leiden, 1969, 2/1972)

M. C. Maas: *Seventeenth-century English Keyboard Music: a Study of Manuscripts Rés. 1185, 1186 and 1186bis of the Paris Conservatory Library* (diss., Yale U., 1969)

T. Dart: 'An Early Seventeenth-century Book of English Organ Music for the Roman Rite', *ML*, lii (1971), 27

B. A. R. Cooper: 'The Keyboard Suite in England before the Restoration', *ML*, liii (1972), 309

M. Boyd: 'Music MSS in the Mackworth Collection at Cardiff', *ML*, liv (1973), 133

J. Caldwell: *English Keyboard Music before the Nineteenth Century* (Oxford, 1973)

M. Tilmouth: 'York Minster MS M.16(s) and Captain Prendcourt', *ML*, liv (1973), 302

B. A. R. Cooper: *English Solo Keyboard Music of the Middle and Late Baroque* (diss., U. of Oxford, 1974)

R. Petrie: 'A New Piece by Henry Purcell', *Early Music*, vi (1978), 374

GERMANY, AUSTRIA AND POLAND

F. Arnold and H. Bellermann: *Das Locheimer Liederbuch nebst der Ars organisandi von Conrad Paumann* (Wiesbaden, 1864, rev. 3/1926/R1969)

R. Eitner: 'Das Buxheimer Orgelbuch', *MMg*, xix–xx (1887–8), suppl.

A. Seiffert: 'J. P. Sweelinck und seine direkten deutschen Schüler', *VMw*, vii (1891), 145–260

A. Chybiński: 'Polnische Musik und Musikkultur des XVI. Jahrhunderts', *SIMG*, xiii (1911–12), 463–505

Z. Jachimecki: 'Eine polnische Orgeltabulatur aus dem Jahre 1548', *ZMw*, ii (1919–20), 206

P. Nettl: 'Die Wiener Tanzkompositionen in der zweiten Hälfte des 17. Jahrhunderts', *SMw*, viii (1921), 45–175

H. Schnoor: 'Das Buxheimer Orgelbuch', *ZMw*, iv (1921–2), 1

K. Scheide: *Zur Geschichte des Choralvorspiels* (Hildinghausen, 1926)

W. Merian: *Der Tanz in den deutschen Tabulaturbüchern* (Leipzig, 1927/R1968)

G. Kittler: *Geschichte des protestantischen Orgelchorals* (Ueckermünde, 1931)

W. Apel: 'Die Tabulatur des Adam Ileborgh', *ZMw*, xvi (1933–4), 193

O. A. Baumann: *Das deutsche Lied und seine Bearbeitungen in den frühen Orgeltabulaturen* (Kassel, 1934)

A. Booth: *German Keyboard Music in the 15th Century* (diss., U. of Birmingham, 1954–5)

L. Schierning: *Die Überlieferung der deutschen Orgel- und Klaviermusik aus der 1. Hälfte des 17. Jahrhunderts* (Kassel, 1961)

E. Southern: *The Buxheim Organ Book* (Brooklyn, 1963)

O. Mischiati: 'L'intavolatura d'organo tedesca della Biblioteca nazionale di Torino', *L'organo*, iv (1963), 1–154

J. R. White: 'The Tablature of Johannes of Lublin', *MD*, xvii (1963), 137

H. R. Zöbeley: *Die Musik des Buxheimer Orgelbuchs* (Tutzing, 1964)

G. T. M. Gillen: *The Chorale in North German Organ Music from Sweelinck to Buxtehude* (diss., U. of Oxford, 1970)

S. Wollenberg: *Viennese Keyboard Music in the Reign of Karl VI (1712–40): Gottlieb Muffat and his Contemporaries* (diss., U. of Oxford, 1975)

ITALY, SPAIN AND PORTUGAL

A. Sandberger: 'Zur älteren italienischen Klaviermusik', *JbMP 1918*, 17

H. Anglès: 'Orgelmusik der Schola Hispanica vom XV. bis XVII. Jahrhundert', *Festschrift Peter Wagner* (Leipzig, 1926/R1969), 11

K. G. Fellerer: 'Zur italienischen Orgelmusik des 17./18. Jahrhunderts', *JbMP 1937*, 70

K. Jeppesen, ed.: *Die italienische Orgelmusik am Anfang des Cinquecento* (Copenhagen, 1943, rev., enlarged 2/1960)

D. Plamenac: 'Keyboard Music of the 14th Century in Codex Faenza 117', *JAMS*, iv (1951), 179

——: 'New Light on Codex Faenza 117', *IMSCR*, v Utrecht 1952, 310

N. Pirrotta: 'Note su un codice di antiche musiche per tastiera' [*I-FZc* 117], *RMI*, lvi (1954), 333

R. Lunelli: *L'arte organaria del Rinascimento in Roma* (Florence, 1958)

J. F. Monroe: *Italian Keyboard Music in the Interim between Frescobaldi and Pasquini* (diss., U. of North Carolina, 1959)

B. Hudson: *A Portuguese Source of Seventeenth-century Iberian Organ Music* (diss., Indiana U., 1961)

H. Anglès: 'Die Instrumentalmusik bis zum 16. Jahrhundert in Spanien', *Natalicia musicologica Knud Jeppesen* (Copenhagen, 1962), 143

K. Jeppesen: 'Ein altvenetianisches Tanzbuch' [*I-Vnm* Ital.IV.1227], *Festschrift Karl Gustav Fellerer* (Regensburg, 1962), 245

R. Hudson: *The Development of Italian Keyboard Variations on the Passacaglio and Ciaccona from Guitar Music in the Seventeenth Century* (diss., U. of California, Los Angeles, 1967)

M. Kugler: *Die Tastenmusik im Codex Faenza* (Tutzing, 1972)

THE NETHERLANDS, BELGIUM AND FRANCE

A. Méreaux: *Les clavecinistes de 1637 à 1790* (Paris, 1867)

C. van den Borren: *Les origines de la musique de clavier dans les Pays-Bas (nord et sud) jusque vers 1630* (Brussels, 1914)

A. Pirro: *Les clavecinistes* (Paris, 1925)

Y. Rokseth: *La musique d'orgue au XVe siècle et au début du XVIe* (Paris, 1930)

S. Clercx: 'Les clavecinistes belges', *ReM* (1939), no.192, p.11

N. Dufourcq: *La musique d'orgue française de Jean Titelouze à Jehan Alain* (Paris, 1941, 2/1949)

A. Curtis: Introduction to *Nederlandse klaviermuziek uit de 16e en 17e eeuw*, MMN, iii (1961)

T. Dart: 'Elisabeth Eysbock's Keyboard Book', *STMf*, xliv (1962), 5

E. Southern: 'Some Keyboard Basse Dances of the Fifteenth Century', *AcM*, xxxv (1963), 114

D. Fuller: *18th-century French Harpsichord Music* (diss., U. of Harvard, 1965)

A. Curtis: *Sweelinck's Keyboard Works: a Study of English Elements in Seventeenth-century Dutch Composition* (London and Leiden, 1969, 2/1972)

B. Gustavson: *French Harpsichord Music of the 17th Century*, i–iii (Ann Arbor, 1979)

J. P. Kitchen: *Harpsichord Music of 17th-century France, with Particular Emphasis on the Work of Louis Couperin* (diss., U. of Cambridge, 1979)

FORMS

R. Eitner: 'Tänze des 15. bis 17. Jahrhunderts', *MMg*, vii (1875), suppl.

T. Norlind: 'Zur Geschichte der Suite', *SIMG*, vii (1905–6), 172–203

I. Faisst: 'Beiträge zur Geschichte der Claviersonate von ihrem ersten Auftreten an bis auf C. Ph. Bach', *NBJb*, i (1924), 7–85

O. Deffner: *Über die Entwicklung der Fantasie für Tasteninstrumente bis J. P. Sweelinck* (diss., U. of Kiel, 1927)

L. Schrade: *Die ältesten Denkmäler der Orgelmusik als Beitrag zu einer Geschichte der Toccata* (Münster, 1928)

R. Gress: *Die Entwicklung der Klavier-Variation von Andrea Gabrieli bis zu Johann Sebastian Bach* (Augsburg, 1929)

E. Valentin: *Die Entwicklung der Tokkata im 17. und 18. Jahrhundert bis J. S. Bach* (Munich, 1930)

A. Schering: 'Zur Alternatim-Orgelmesse', *ZMw*, xvii (1935), 19

E. Epstein: *Der französische Einfluss auf die deutsche Klavier-Suite im 17. Jahrhundert* (Würzburg, 1940)

J. L. Hibberd: *The Early Keyboard Prelude* (diss., Harvard U., 1940)

M. Reimann: *Untersuchungen zur Formgeschichte der französischen Klavier-Suite* (Regensburg, 1941)

L. Schrade: 'The Organ in the Mass of the 15th Century', *MQ*, xxviii (1942), 329, 467

R. Murphy: *Fantasia and Ricercare in the Sixteenth Century* (diss., Yale U., 1954)

S. Podolsky: *The Variation Canzona for Keyboard Instruments in Italy, Austria and Southern Germany in the Seventeenth Century* (diss., Boston U., 1954)

I. Horsley: 'The 16th-century Variation', *JAMS*, xii (1959), 118

W. S. Newman: *The Sonata in the Baroque Era* (Chapel Hill, 1959, rev. 4/1983)

F. M. Siebert: *Fifteenth-century Organ Settings of the Ordinarium Missae* (diss., Columbia U., 1961)

R. S. Douglass: *The Keyboard Ricercar in the Baroque Era* (diss., U. of North Texas, 1963)

M. C. Bradshaw: *The Origin of the Toccata*, MSD, xxviii (1972)

N. Bergenfeld: *The Keyboard Fantasy of the Elizabethan Renaissance* (diss., U. of New York, 1978)

II. Organ music from c1750. Notable influences on the development of organ music since the mid-18th century include changes in the liturgy, a profound respect for the music of J. S. Bach, innovations in the mechanism of the organ and a growing tendency to write for the instrument in symphonic terms. In the following account, the major schools of organ composition will be considered in this context, with particular attention to those parts of the repertory less familiar today.

1. The Bach tradition: 1750–1850. 2. The 'symphonic' organ: 1850–1920. 3. Trends in 20th-century organ music.

1. THE BACH TRADITION: 1750–1850. The period between the death of J. S. Bach in 1750 and the publication of Mendelssohn's organ works nearly a century later is regarded as one of the least productive ones in the history of organ music. Except for a small number of miscellaneous preludes by Bach's followers and the famous fantasias for mechanical organ by Mozart, few works from this period are played today. The secularizing influence of the Enlightenment, with its reaction against organized religion and its emphasis on the natural and rational, effectively removed the organ from the mainstream of musical activity. That it was not completely neglected is evident from the innumerable articles on organ building, organ playing and organ music which appeared in contemporary journals.

During the second half of the 18th century church musicians did not enjoy a high social status, and were forced by their inadequate remuneration to enter other fields of musical activity. Many became renowned as theoreticians and teachers, while others applied their abilities to secular music. In England the decline in the influence of the Chapel Royal and the cathedrals, and the growing importance of the parish church, allowed organists sufficient freedom to perform in theatres and concert rooms. The element of showmanship which naturally resulted was the first stage in the secularization of the art. In Germany a tendency to reject the established contrapuntal and fugal forms as too complicated for ordinary listeners resulted in a similar emphasis on superficial display. In the preface to his *Vierstimmige Choräle mit Vorspielen* (1803), J. C. Kittel stressed that it was the duty of the organist to play 'for the people'. In this respect, the learned manner of J. S. Bach was considered inappropriate for liturgical purposes, and was soon superseded by a more directly appealing style. This prejudice against elaborate structures persisted for many years; in *Der musikalische Kirchendienst* (1832), F. Kessler barred performances in church services of the large-scale works of Bach, Handel, J. G. Albrechtsberger, Mozart, Krebs and Johann Schneider (1702–88), on the grounds that they provided 'intellectual pleasure for the initiated listener rather than for the ordinary man'.

While the prelude and voluntary continued to play a significant part in the service, increasing importance was attached to congregational singing, and the role of the organ became more and more that of providing simple accompaniment. The extent of this development is evident in the assertion made by the Rostock organ builder Paul Schmidt, in 1789, that 'a church organ is not meant for playing all kinds of pretty pieces, but for keeping the congregation in tune'. Owing to the slow pace at which hymns, metrical psalms and chorales were sung, organists were required to improvise short interludes in the breathing-spaces between individual lines and verses. Both in England and on the Continent, innumerable anthologies were published comprising cadenzas and interludes for the purpose, and these gained particular popularity among a growing number of untrained and comparatively inexpert organists unable to improvise service music or perform technically difficult pieces. This orientation towards the amateur undoubtedly deterred the great composers of the period, many of whom were renowned for their improvisations, from publishing music for the organ.

Contemporary accounts indicate that the general standard of organ playing was affected. In Germany, Burney's high expectations were continually thwarted. After a visit to Augsburg he explained that 'the rage for crude, equivocal and affected modulation which now prevails . . . renders voluntary playing so unnatural that it is a perpetual disappointment and torture to the ear' (*The Present State of Music in Germany, the Netherlands and the United Provinces*, 1773). Composers of the period, however, did not disregard the achievements of their predecessors, nor did the music of Bach lie forgotten until its rediscovery nearly a century later. In his history (1789), Burney stated that the organ music of Handel and Bach 'established a style for that instrument which is still respected and imitated by the greatest organists in Germany'.

That tradition continued to flourish in the northern provinces of Germany. In Berlin, J. F. Agricola, J. P. Kirnberger, F. W. Marpurg and their followers were strongly influenced by the contrapuntal style of Bach's later works. While their interest in the more technical aspects of this style often resulted in a dry and academic manner, their most successful compositions, inspired by chorale melodies, are equal to the best German organ music. J. L. Krebs and J. P. Kellner reveal in their large-scale works a close adherence to the traditional forms and a profound understanding of Bach's techniques. Their treatment of the organ trio deserves particular attention. While their lesser contemporaries cultivated a purely melodic style in which the thematic interest lay primarily in the upper part, Krebs, Kellner, and the latter's pupil J. E. Rembt retained the kind of motivic development and true independence of part-writing exploited by Bach in his six trio sonatas. It is curious that the trio should have retained its popularity in this period, for as the contrapuntal style gave way to the simpler and more expressive textures of the *galant*, composers began to use the pedals less systematically, and publications of organ music increasingly bore the sub-title 'für Orgel und Klavier' to provide for optional performance. G. A. Sorge's *XI Sonaten* (*c*1745–9) are typical of this. At first German composers were reluctant to dispense entirely with the traditional contrapuntal style, but the gradual infiltration of elements from the Italian keyboard sonata produced a tendency to use the organ simply as an expressive instrument. This weakness is apparent in C. P. E. Bach's *Preludio e sei sonate per organo*, published posthumously by Rellstab in 1790. The most original and stylistic organ compositions of the period are undoubtedly the *Grosse Präludien* of J. C. Kittel, one of J. S. Bach's most gifted pupils. As the author of the treatise *Der angehende praktische Organist* (1801–9), and as the teacher of J. C. H. Rinck and M. G. Fischer, Kittel must be regarded as the most important link between Bach and the Romantic school.

Until the mid-19th century, organs in central Europe were rarely provided with full pedal-boards. For this reason, the organ music of southern Germany, Austria and Czechoslovakia does not exhibit a breadth and complexity equal to that of the north German school. The eclectic style of Georg Muffat and his son, Gottlieb, was continued by J. E. Eberlin in his *IX toccate e fughe per l'organo*, and reached its highest point of development in the works of J. G. Albrechtsberger and his pupils Ambros Rieder and Simon Sechter. Albrechtsberger, described by a contemporary critic as 'Vienna's Johann Sebastian Bach', wrote prolifically for the organ; his independently conceived preludes and fugues are particularly diverse in style, technique and thematic material.

Most of the organ music published in England after 1750 was secular in character and, stylistically, almost indistinguishable from other English keyboard music of the time. The voluntary, a purely indigenous form, had existed during the early part of the century as a single movement in fugal style. The English preference for colourful sonorities, however, produced a type of composition in which the newly incorporated Trumpet and Cornet stops of the organ were used as solo instruments. The early experiments in this style were consolidated by the mid-18th-century composers Maurice Greene, William Boyce, William Walond and John Stanley. Their voluntaries consist for the most part of slow introductions followed by brisk movements in solo concerto style, with occasionally an additional movement. Lesser composers of the period soon deprived the form of its true vitality and used increasingly orchestral sonorities provided by the new Cremona, Bassoon and Hautboy stops. The subsequent reaction against this manner from such composers as John Keeble received great stimulus from the importation of German organ music, and resulted in a renewed ascendance of the fugue over other forms. At first, the fugal compositions of Handel and his English imitators provided the basic pattern, but the growing interest in the music of Bach, initiated by Samuel Wesley, produced a more flexible and imaginative approach to the form. Thomas Adams wrote some particularly fine voluntaries in this traditional manner, but it was the orchestral and pianistic style of his more secular organ pieces that, to the detriment of the English school, prevailed during the remainder of the 19th century. The stagnation of the school may also be attributed to the comparatively late recognition of the pedal organ, which in many instruments consisted merely of a pull-down attachment for the lowest octave of the manual compass. Even in 1884, the organ of Canterbury Cathedral had only one octave of short pedals.

While the general standard of early Romantic organ music in Germany is disappointing, the true art of organ playing was not wholly forgotten. Under the guidance of Rinck and Fischer, the Bach tradition remained a vital force and provided the basis for the organ tutors written by their pupils K. C. Kegel (1830), L. E. Gebhardi (1837), A. G. Ritter (1844) and W. Wedemann (1847). The appearance of Bach's trio sonatas as a *Praktische Orgelschule* in 1832 supports this argument. It is nonetheless surprising that of the many original compositions for organ published at that time, only a small number require a highly developed technique. Most composers did no more than publish numerous anthologies of short, simple pieces suitable for liturgical use and for the limited abilities of amateurs. The works of such composers as J. G. Schneider (1789–1864), however, belong to a different class. H. F. Chorley's impressions of Schneider's performance on a Silbermann organ in the Sophienkirche, Dresden, recounted in his *Music and Manners in France and Germany* (1841), highlights this organist's purely classical training. His published compositions, such as the fine Fantasia and Fugue in D minor op.3, were conceived entirely in terms of the classical organ with its clear sonorities, balanced manual choruses and independent pedal division. In originality and breadth of conception, compositions of this calibre clearly anticipated the organ music of Mendelssohn.

Whereas Schneider adhered to the established German tradition, G. J. Vogler and J. H. Knecht represent an entirely new school of thought in which the organ is seen as an expressive symphonic instrument. Vogler, whom Mozart described as a 'loathsome musical buffoon', toured extensively throughout Europe playing programmatic improvisations on his 900-pipe Orchestrion. His influence was considerable. Knecht not only sanctioned and strongly advocated Vogler's descriptive effects in his *Vollständige Orgelschule* (1795–8), but also published a musical representation for organ entitled *Die durch ein Donnerwetter unterbrochene Hirtenwonne*.

In France, the secularization of organ music was carried to even greater limits. While the instrument retained its close relationship with the church, the vitality and originality of invention which had characterized classical organ literature were replaced by an empty formalism in which virtuosity was exploited for its own sake. Burney's impressions, recorded in *The Present State of Music in France and Italy* (1771), reveal the extent of this transformation: the interludes played between verses of the *Te Deum* by A.-L. Couperin at St Gervais, Paris, allowed 'great latitude' to the performer; nothing was considered 'too light or too grave' and 'all styles were admitted'. A similar lapse of musical integrity beset the music at St Roque, where C. B. Balbastre improvised 'minuets, fugues, imitations and every species of music, even to hunting pieces and jigs, without surprising or offending the congregation'. The growing popularity of these interludes, together with the vogue for mediocre noëls and meretricious storm representations, contributed to the century-long decline of the French school. The translation of Knecht's *Orgelschule* by J. P. A. Martini, and the use of the organ during the French Revolution as a means of awakening 'a holy love of the fatherland in the mind of the hearers', served merely to accentuate these tendencies. In the marches and transcriptions of L. J. A. Lefébure-Wély and A. E. Batiste, the most renowned virtuosos of the 19th century, the art of organ composition reached its lowest ebb.

The foundation of the first organ class at the Paris Conservatoire in 1819 established a more salutary trend in French organ music. A. P. F. Boëly and François Benoist (the first *titulaire*) advocated a return to the principles of classical tradition, and learnt much from their acquaintance with the music of the German school. Furthermore, relations were close with the Brussels Conservatory, where J. N. Lemmens (a pupil of A. F. Hesse) had a high regard for the music of Bach. The growing concern for the Bach tradition together with new developments in organ building provided the basis for the Romantic school of composition, whose full possibilities were first recognized by Franck in his *Six pièces pour orgue* (1860–63).

2. THE 'SYMPHONIC' ORGAN: 1850–1920. Liszt's Prelude and Fugue on B–A–C–H, dedicated to Alexander Winterberger, was originally conceived for the inauguration of the rebuilt organ at Merseburg Cathedral in 1855. Ladegast's renovation of this instrument represents a turning-point in the history of organ music, for it clearly inspired in Liszt a new approach to composition. In the same way that Ladegast incorporated the tonal concepts of the Romantic organ within a purely classical framework, Liszt reconciled Bach's formal procedures and sonorous polyphony with his own highly expressive idiom. But Liszt's most profound innovation was his application to the organ of the artistic virtuosity which he had developed in the realm of piano music. Hans von Bülow (1856) rather graphically ascribed Winterberger's abilities to the perfection he had achieved as a pianist under Liszt's direction: 'The facility which he acquired in pedal playing surpasses the feats of the organists of the old school in quietness and certainty, in energy and fluency, to the same degree that his finger execution is superior to theirs. He represents the Liszt school with both hand and foot'.

The importance of this school in the development of organ music has to a large extent overshadowed many earlier attempts to compose for the instrument in true concert style. The diverse elements which Liszt combined in his organ works had been tentatively employed by many of his predecessors. In his Six Sonatas (1845), Mendelssohn made frequent use of pianistic techniques to produce new textures and sonorities. As the first major 19th-century composer to turn to the organ, his influence was considerable, but his formal approach to organ composition belonged to a very different tradition from that of Liszt. Since the beginning of the century, a firm distinction had been drawn in Germany between organ music for recital and liturgical purposes. During the 1830s, such organists as F. K. Kühmstedt, M. Brosig, A. G. Ritter, A. F. Hesse, A. Freyer and F. G. Klauer concentrated on recital work. While their compositions rarely achieve a consistently high level of inspiration, their free rhythms, extreme dynamic contrasts, frequent

manual changes and shattering pedal passages are often highly original and effective. In his *Fantasia eroica* op.29, Kühmstedt avoided the sentimentality and indiscriminate use of chromaticism which marred much of the music of the period. Though lacking in formal cohesion, this fantasia has at its climactic points a relentless drive and energy which make it a worthy precursor of Liszt's best efforts in the medium.

Liszt's influence was surprisingly short-lived; with the exception of the brilliant and colourful *Sonata on the 94th Psalm* by his pupil Julius Reubke, few works followed in this tradition. The revival of interest in early organ music during the first half of the century had in many cases produced a more conservative approach to organ composition. Ritter (a composer as well as the author of a valuable textbook on the history of organ playing and composition, *Zur Geschichte des Orgelspiels*, 1884) used his understanding of Baroque techniques to produce an entirely original cyclic sonata form, incorporating within a purely Romantic context formal elements from Buxtehude's toccatas. Less capable musicians, however, succumbed to mere pastiche. The organ music of G. A. Merkel, for example, though technically accomplished, is devoid of freshness and vitality. J. G. Rheinberger's rigorous academic training also produced a certain dryness and lack of flexibility in his early works; but as his own personality came to the fore he was able to inject new life into the traditional contrapuntal forms, and in many of his slow movements achieved a Brahmsian warmth and breadth.

Several important 19th-century composers came to the organ through the music of earlier masters, which they realized could be a living force in their own works. Schumann's Six Fugues on B–A–C–H op.60 (1845) reveal a profound respect for the music of Bach, while Brahms's 11 Chorale Preludes op.122, most of which were composed during the last year of his life, undoubtedly owed their existence to the work he did in connection with the Denkmäler Deutscher Tonkunst. To Reger, Bach's organ works were 'the beginning and end of all music'. They provided the basis for his entire output from the early Suite in E minor op.16, 'den Manen Joh. Seb. Bach's gewidmet', to the great Fantasia and Fugue in D minor op.135b. Reger's organ music stands at the crossroads as the culmination of 19th-century attempts to clothe the old contrapuntal forms in a truly Romantic idiom and as a profound influence on the composers of both the new Viennese school and the school of Hindemith.

The reform in organ building brought about by the work of Aristide Cavaillé-Coll had a far-reaching influence on organ composition in France. 'The modern organ is essentially symphonic', wrote Widor. 'A new language is required for the new instrument, something very different from scholastic polyphony'. The truly symphonic tradition initiated in the works of Saint-Saëns and Franck cannot be equated, however, with the orchestral style of playing fostered in England by such organists as W. T. Best during the latter part of the century. French composers never lost sight of the organ as an instrument in its own right with its own peculiar expressive qualities. In his *Technique de l'orchestre moderne* (1904), Widor stressed that 'we must employ this expression with conscientious reserve and artistic feeling; otherwise we shall ignore the essential characteristics of the instrument and convert it into a pseudo-orchestra'.

Franck's importance in the history of organ music

derived from the *Six pièces* (1860–63), the *Trois pièces* (1878) and the *Trois chorals* written shortly before his death in 1890. These few pieces foreshadowed the most significant features of modern French organ music: while the *chorals* (described by Flor Peeters as 'three monuments of unforgettable beauty') inspired the liturgical approach to composition advocated by Franck's pupil and successor at Ste Clothilde, Charles Tournemire, the *Grande pièce symphonique* (from the *Six pièces*) was the first organ symphony ever written. It illustrated the brilliant concert style of organ composition and also established the trend towards large cyclic structures as featured in the works of C.-M. Widor and Louis Vierne.

The strength of the French school arose from the highly disciplined training provided at the official institutions in Paris. As direct heirs of the Lemmens tradition, Widor and F. A. Guilmant subjected their pupils to detailed studies of form, technique and improvisation. The benefit of this approach is apparent in such substantial works as Marcel Dupré's Three Preludes and Fugues op.7. Many early compositions, however, had a scholarly rather than musical appeal. In the eight sonatas of Guilmant, for instance, where the basic material lacks originality, the interest lies completely in the elaborate thematic development and infallible formal control. This consummate mastery of technique is also evident in the ten symphonies of Widor, but here the freedom from classical tradition produces music of greater character and individuality. The pure concert style of composition which Widor developed in his early symphonies were crystallized in the works of his pupil, Vierne. While Vierne's influence on the succeeding generation of organists was considerable, his persistent use of excessive chromaticism soon rendered his music unfashionable. Nevertheless, the Second Symphony was hailed by Debussy in *Gil Blas* (25 February 1903) as a remarkable composition in which 'the most generous musical qualities are combined with ingenious innovations in the particular sonorities of the organ.'

3. TRENDS IN 20TH-CENTURY ORGAN MUSIC. During the first part of the 20th century, interest in early organ music intensified and the many limitations of the symphonic organ became evident. Because the works of the great classical composers could be fully appreciated only on appropriate instruments, there was incentive for a return to the true principles of classical organ design. The foundation of the Société des Amis de l'Orgue in Paris in 1926, and the numerous organ conferences which took place in Germany around that time, served to formulate the basic precepts of the new movement, which was to have great influence on the future development of organ music. German composers were immediately impressed by the clarity of the newly refined instrument and developed an appropriate style of composition based mainly on Baroque forms and techniques. In France, where the symphonic school remained a more vital force in contemporary music, the desire to compromise between classical and Romantic traditions of organ building produced the highly versatile instrument which inspired the music of Tournemire, Alain and Messiaen.

In England, where the new movement progressed more slowly, the Romantic tradition of organ composition persisted longer. The aesthetic which guided most composers was clearly expounded by C. H. Parry (1911): 'This capacity of holding indefinitely any number and any combination of notes is the source of the organ's being the mightiest of all means for tremendous effects of harmony, and this quality is essentially the most important element in organ style'. Parry's own compositions and those of his contemporary C. V. Stanford are frequently marred by this predilection for heavy and overcrowded textures, but nonetheless they are conceived for the organ in particular and thus represent a significant stylistic advance over the orchestrally conceived organ music of the previous century. In the works of their followers the musical possibilities of the traditional, texturally more sophisticated idiom were fully exploited, promoting a new approach to the instrument. In his first set of Psalm Preludes op.32, Herbert Howells cultivated a relatively polyphonic style, yielding greater lightness and transparency in texture. It is these qualities, clearly achieved in the works of Britten, P. R. Fricker, John McCabe and Kenneth Leighton, that distinguish the most successful of the contemporary school. Composers working in England have also been receptive to influences from abroad. Malcolm Williamson turned to the organ as a direct result of his encounter with the music of Messiaen; his indebtedness to the French school is evident in both *Fons amoris* and *The Vision of Christ-Phoenix*. Serial techniques of composition have also produced some highly original organ music, including Humphrey Searle's *Toccata alla passacaglia* op.31 and Nicholas Maw's *Essay*, a substantial and colourful work of five sections derived from one series of notes.

The linear contrapuntal style of Reger's later works provided the basis for the music of Hugo Distler, the central figure of the new German school, and his followers J. N. David, Heinrich Kaminski, Ernst Pepping, Helmut Bornefeld and Siegfried Reda. Motivated by the organ reform movement, these composers reacted against the excesses of late Romantic music and established a more objective approach to structure and technique. They conceived their organ music within a purely liturgical context and revived the chorale to assume its former importance as a source of musical inspiration. The contrapuntal textures of Hindemith's three organ sonatas (1937–40) are an aspect of these same principles and are therefore more effective when registered in terms of the classical organ. But it is interesting to note that in the original edition of the second sonata the composer sanctioned the use of the general crescendo and swell pedals 'to give richer colours and more dynamic expression than is suggested in the text'. This inclination away from Baroque terrace registration is more apparent in two significant works dating from 1941, Schoenberg's *Variations on a Recitative* op.40 and Ernst Krenek's Sonata (neither of which adheres to strict serial techniques). Like Frank Martin's Passacaglia, written three years later, these were conceived according to the Romantic ideal of continuous and progressive development, and in many passages the organ is forced to serve ends that it cannot meet. Significantly Martin later arranged his Passacaglia for string orchestra. In its adherence to classical formal procedures and its successful incorporation of Baroque textures into a 20th-century idiom, Carl Nielsen's *Commotio* avoids these disadvantages and poses fewer problems to the organist.

The development of the modern French school has been profoundly influenced by the importance that composers have increasingly attached to the spiritual and liturgical aspects of their work. This can be traced to the revival of interest in plainsong during the latter part of the 19th century, when Guilmant, Gigout and Widor (notably in his last two symphonies) used the ecclesiastical modes as a source of inspiration. But it was after World War I that the liturgical movement, led by Tournemire, rose to true prominence. His *L'orgue mystique* (1927–32) is a collection of 51 suites, each consisting of five movements based on the plainsong theme appropriate to the Office for which the suite was intended. Tournemire's preoccupation with the mystical qualities of plainsong inspired him to original means of expression for his highly evocative musical style and his unconventional exploitation of the organ's tonal resources. The freedom which he achieved within the limitations of his thematic material provided a point of departure for many similar compositions by his followers, including Jean Langlais' *Trois paraphrases grégoriennes*, Maurice Duruflé's *Prélude, adagio et choral varié sur le thème du Veni Creator* and the *Toccata, fugue et hymne sur Ave maris stella* by the Belgian organist Flor Peeters. Plainsong extended an influence far beyond those compositions which it directly inspired; its supple melodic contours have pervaded the language of contemporary French organ music.

The symphonic style fostered by Widor and Vierne culminated in the purely concert compositions of André Fleury, Gaston Litaize, Duruflé and Dupré, in which unprecedented demands are made on both the player's virtuosity and the capabilities of the instrument. While the more recent French school has continued to emphasize these features, virtuosity is no longer regarded as an end in itself. It has become the means to a more subjective and expressive art, the style of writing being conditioned in many cases by the composer's reactions to a chosen text or idea. The earliest manifestations of this in a purely secular form were during the first quarter of the century when such composers as Georges Jacob, Ermend Bonnal and the Belgian Joseph Jongen incorporated impressionistic techniques into their compositions. In his *Symphonie-passion* (1925), Dupré reconciled this approach with the aims of the liturgical school and established a concept of religious programme music which gave a new impetus to composers for the organ. The significant developments in form, style and rhythm exemplified in the programmatic works of Langlais, Tournemire, Jacques Charpentier, Daniel-Lesur and Grunewald have been consummated in the organ cycles of Messiaen: *L'Ascension, La nativité du Seigneur, Les corps glorieux* and *Méditations sur le mystère de la Sainte Trinité*. To Messiaen, music is an integral part of philosophy and religion; his highly disciplined approach to composition is a response to the divine order he perceives in the universe, though in the most recent cycle this preoccupation has perhaps resulted in a less communicative musical language. The rhythmic complexity which characterized Messiaen's early works and which he has subsequently enriched through his acquaintance with plainsong and Hindu music was also a feature of the works of Jehan Alain. In their originality and freedom, Alain's three dances *Joies, Deuils* and *Luttes* (1939) may be ranked among the most remarkable contributions to the 20th-century organ repertory.

The concept of the organ as purely a church instrument has to a large extent discouraged its use as a vehicle for extreme experimentation. Since the mid-20th century, however, several composers have begun to overcome this inhibition. György Ligeti's *Volumina* (1961–2) is an interesting experiment in changing and stationary note-clusters and derives many new effects from the unconventional use of traditional organ registers. Like Mauricio Kagel's *Improvisation ajoutée* (1961–2), this work ideally employs three performers, two of whom merely assist with the registration. Kagel also composed a *Phantasie für Orgel mit Obbligati* (1967), in which traditional sonorities are combined with tape-recorded sounds, a technique which has gained particular favour in the USA among such composers as William Bolcom, Alden Ashforth and Richard Felciano. Within a more conventional framework, some noted performers are using their experience of the classical repertory and their profound understanding of the organ's resources as a basis for some highly original music; Anton Heiller's *Tanz Toccata* is a fine example. But the most satisfying trends are furnished by the many non-organist composers who are writing for the instrument without compromising their styles. Such diverse compositions as Patrick Gowers's *Toccata* and Charles Camilleri's *Missa mundi* reveal an imaginative approach which has benefited from recent developments in organ building as well as from a growing discrimination among performers and audiences.

BIBLIOGRAPHY

GENERAL REFERENCE

Musica Sacra: Vollständiges Verzeichnis aller seit dem Jahre 1750–1867 gedruckt erschienenen Compositionen für die Orgel, Lehrbücher für die Orgel . . . usw (Erfurt, 1867)

D. Buck: *The Influence of the Organ in History* (London, 1882, 2/1911)

T. Forchhammer and B. Kothe: *Führer durch die Orgel-Literatur* (Leipzig, 1890, rev. 3/1931)

L. Hartmann: *Die Orgel: gemeinverständliche Darstellung des Orgelbaus und Orgelspiels* (Leipzig, 1904, 3/1921)

C. F. A. Williams: *The Story of Organ Music* (London, 1905/*R*1968, 2/1916)

A. Schweitzer: *Deutsche und französische Orgelbaukunst und Orgelkunst* (Leipzig, 1906/*R*1962, 2/1927)

C. W. Pearce: *The Organist's Directory . . . with a Full List of Voluntaries* (London, 1908)

H. C. Lahee: *The Organ and its Masters* (London, 1909)

H. H. Statham: *The Organ and its Position in Musical Art* (London, 1909)

H. Grace: *The Complete Organist* (London, 1920)

F. Sauer: *Handbuch der Orgel-Literatur: ein Wegweiser für Organisten* (Vienna, 1924)

D. E. Berg: *The Organ: Composers and Literature* (New York, 1927)

H. Westerby: *The Complete Organ Recitalist: British and American* (London, 1927)

C. M. Widor: *L'orgue moderne* (Paris, 1928)

K. G. Fellerer: *Orgel und Orgelmusik: ihre Geschichte* (Augsburg, 1929)

C. F. Waters: *The Growth of Organ Music* (London, 1931, enlarged 2/1957)

H. Westerby: *The Complete Organ Recitalist: International Repertoire Guide to Foreign, British, and American Works* (London, 1933)

A. C. D. de Brisay: *The Organ and its Music* (London, 1934)

G. Frotscher: *Geschichte des Orgel-Spiels und der Orgel-Komposition* (Berlin, 1935–6, enlarged 3/1966)

H. Klotz: *Das Buch von der Orgel* (Kassel, 1938; Eng. trans., 7/1969)

G. D. Cunningham: 'The History and Development of Organ Music', *MT*, lxxix (1938), 685, 769, 848, 924; lxxx (1939), 50, 205, 282, 366 [series of articles]

F. Münger: *Choralbearbeitungen für Orgel* (Kassel, 1952)

G. A. C. de Graaf: *Literatur over het orgel* (Amsterdam, 1957)

F. W. Riedel, W. Apel and T.-M. Langner: 'Orgelmusik', *MGG*

V. Lukas: *Orgelmusikführer* (Stuttgart, 1963)

C. Probst: *Literatur für Kleinorgel* (Zurich, 1964)

W. Gurlitt: *Musikgeschichte und Gegenwart*, i–ii, ed. H. H. Eggebrecht (Wiesbaden, 1966)

L. F. Tagliavini: 'Organo', *LaMusicaE*

A. Reichling, ed.: *Acta organologica*, i–ii (Berlin, 1967–8)

F. Jakob: *Die Orgel: Orgelbau und Orgelspiel von der Antike bis zur Gegenwart* (Berne, 1969)

E. Kraus: *Orgeln und Orgelmusik: das Bild der Orgellandschaften* (Regensburg, 1972)

G. S. Rowley: *A Bibliographic Syllabus of the History of Organ Literature: the Nineteenth Century* (Iowa City, 1972)

W. M. Liebenow: *Rank on Rank: a Bibliography* (Minneapolis, 1973)

C. R. Arnold: *Organ Literature: a Comprehensive Survey* (Metuchen, NJ, 1973)

H. Lohmann: *Handbuch der Orgelliteratur* (Wiesbaden, 1975)

T. R. Nardone: *Organ Music in Print* (Philadelphia, 1975)

SPECIFIC STUDIES

H. F. Chorley: *Music and Manners in France and Germany* (London, 1841)

H. von Bülow: 'Alexander Winterberger und das moderne Orgelspiel', *NZM*, xlv (1856), 1; Eng. trans. in *Dwight's Journal of Music*, x (1856), 65

R. J. Voigtmann: 'Der Einfluss der neudeutschen Schule auf das Orgelspiel', *NZM*, lxv (1869), 30

H. H. Statham: 'Wanted: a Composer for the Organ', *MT*, xx (1879), 633

A. G. Ritter: *Zur Geschichte des Orgelspiels, vornehmlich des deutschen, im 14. bis zum Anfange des 18. Jahrhunderts* (Leipzig, 1884/R1969)

K.-E. von Schafhäutl: *Vogler: sein Leben, Charakter und musikalisches System: seine Werke, seine Schule* (Augsburg, 1888)

O. Dienel: *Die moderne Orgel: ihre Einrichtung, ihre Bedeutung für die Kirche und ihre Stellung zu J. S. Bachs Orgelmusik* (Berlin, 1891)

C. H. H. Parry: *Style in Musical Art* (London, 1911)

H. Keller: *Reger und die Orgel* (Munich, 1923)

Freiburger Tagung für deutsche Orgelkunst: Freiburg 1926

Tagung für deutsche Orgelkunst: Freiberg in Sachsen 1927

W. W. Donat: *Christian Heinrich Rinck und die Orgelmusik seiner Zeit* (diss., U. of Heidelberg, 1931)

N. Dufourcq: 'La pénétration en France de l'oeuvre d'orgue de J. S. Bach', *ReM* (1932), no.131, p.27

A. Dreetz: *Johann Christian Kittel: der letzte Bach-Schüler* (Berlin, 1932)

K. G. Fellerer: *Studien zur Orgelmusik des ausgehenden 18. und frühen 19. Jahrhunderts* (Kassel, 1932)

H. Kelletat: *Zur Geschichte der deutschen Orgelmusik in der Frühklassik* (Kassel, 1933)

F. J. Wagner: *Die Orgelmusik in Thüringen in der Zeit von 1830–1860* (diss., U. of Heidelberg, 1937)

N. Dufourcq: 'Panorama de la musique d'orgue française au XXe siècle', *ReM* (1938), no.184, p.369; no.185, p.35; no.186, p.120; (1939), no.189, p.103 [series of articles]

H. Schweiger: *Abbé G. J. Voglers Orgellehre* (diss., U. of Freiburg, 1938)

N. Dufourcq: *La musique d'orgue française de Jean Titelouze à Jehan Alain: les instruments, les artistes et les oeuvres, les formes et les styles* (Paris, 1941, 2/1949)

M. Schneider: *Die Orgelspieltechnik des frühen 19. Jahrhunderts in Deutschland, dargestellt an den Orgelschulen der Zeit* (Regensburg, 1941, 3/1973)

H. Distler: 'Die Orgel unserer Zeit', *Musica*, i (1947), 147

C. E. Vogan: *The French Organ School of the Seventeenth and Eighteenth Centuries* (diss., U. of Michigan, 1949)

P. Peters: 'The Belgian Organ School', *HMYB*, vi (1949–50), 270

W. Sumner: 'The French Organ School', *HMYB*, vi (1949–50), 281

H. Kalkoff: *Das Orgelschaffen Max Regers im Lichte der deutschen Orgelerneuerungsbewegung* (Kassel, 1950)

H. Bornefeld: *Orgelbau und neue Orgelmusik* (Kassel, 1952)

R. Walter: 'Die zeitgenossische deutsche Orgelmusik', *Melos*, xx (1953), 37

H. J. Moser: 'Orgel und Orgelspiel', *Die evangelische Kirchenmusik in Deutschland* (Berlin, 1954), 418–54

R. Quoika: *Albert Schweitzers Begegnung mit der Orgel* (Berlin, 1954)

W. Kolneder: 'Johann Nepomuk David und das Orgelschaffen in Österreich', *ÖMz*, xiii (1958), 262

W. Stockmeier: *Die deutsche Orgelsonate der Gegenwart* (diss., U. of Cologne, 1958)

Various authors: 'Organ Music of our Century', *MT*, cii (1961), 44, 175, 331, 723; ciii (1962), 184; civ (1963), 54, 208; cv (1964), 134, 924; cvi (1965), 374

P. Williams: *English Organ Music and the English Organ under the First Four Georges* (diss., U of Cambridge, 1962)

R. Kremer: *The Organ Sonata since 1845* (diss., Washington U., St Louis, Missouri, 1963)

P. Williams: 'J. S. Bach and English Organ Music, 1800–35', *ML*, xliv (1963), 140

R. Vendrey: *Die Orgelwerke von Felix Mendelssohn-Bartholdy* (diss., U. of Vienna, 1964)

H. J. Seyfried: *Adolph Friedrich Hesse als Orgelvirtuose und Orgelkomponist* (diss., U. of Saarbrücken, 1965)

R. Quoika: *Die Orgelwelt um Anton Bruckner: Blicke in die Orgelgeschichte Alt-Österreichs* (Ludwigsburg, 1966)

P. Williams: *The European Organ, 1450–1850* (London, 1966/R1978)

H. H. Eggebrecht: *Die Orgelbewegung* (Stuttgart, 1967)

A. Haupt: 'Orgelkunst in Italien', *Der Kirchenmusiker*, vi (1967), 241

D. C. Johns, P. Gehring and P. M. Young: 'A Survey of Contemporary Organ Music', *Church Music*, ii (River Forest, Ill., 1967), 25

M. Rudd: *Stylistic Trends in Contemporary Organ Music: a Formal and Stylistic Analysis of post World War II Works, 1945–1965* (diss., U. of Louisiana, 1967)

H. H. Eggebrecht: *Orgel und Orgelmusik heute* (Stuttgart, 1968)

F. Högner: 'Max Reger und die deutsche Orgelbewegung', *Ars organi*, xvi (1968), 1153

E. Routley: *The Musical Wesleys* (London, 1968)

G. E. Watkins: 'Schoenberg and the Organ', *Perspectives on Schoenberg and Stravinsky* (Princeton, 1968, 2/1972)

S. Waumsley: *The Organ Music of Oliver Messiaen* (Paris, 1968/R1975)

F. Douglass: *The Language of the Classical French Organ: a Musical Tradition before 1800* (New Haven, 1969)

M. Weyer: *Die deutsche Orgelsonate von Mendelssohn bis Reger* (Regensburg, 1969)

G. Beechey: 'Charles Tournemire, 1870–1939', *MT*, cxi (1970), 543

A. J. G. Jones: *A Survey of Organ Works Based on the Motive B–A–C–H* (diss., U. of Texas, 1970)

S. Walsh: 'Schumann and the Organ', *MT*, cxi (1970), 741

O. Biba: 'The Unknown Organ Music of Austria', *The Diapason*, lxii (1971), 10

A. Bond: 'Brahms' Chorale Preludes, Op. 122', *MT*, cxii (1971), 898

F. Peeters and M. Vente: *The Organ and its Music in the Netherlands* (New York, 1971)

H. Searle: 'Liszt's Organ Music', *MT*, cxii (1971), 597

W. Sutton: 'The Organ Music of Herbert Howells', *MT*, cxii (1971), 177

M. L. Jacquet: 'Jean Langlais: un indépendant. Essai sur son oeuvre d'orgue', *L'orgue*, cxliv (1972), 1

F. Peters: 'César Franck's Organ Music', *MT*, cxiii (1972), 395, 499

H. Busch: 'Max Reger und die Orgel seiner Zeit', *Musik und Kirche*, xliii (1973), 63

D. L. Butler: *The Organ Works of Felix Mendelssohn-Bartholdy* (diss., U. of Oregon, 1973)

J. Caldwell: *English Keyboard Music before the Nineteenth Century* (Oxford, 1973)

F. Routh: *Early English Organ Music from the Middle Ages to 1837* (London, 1973)

P. Prince: 'Reger and the Organ', *Diapason*, lxiv/4 (1973), 1

H. P. Reiners and W. Syré: 'Max Reger und die Orgel', *Max Reger in seiner Zeit*, ed. S. Kross (Koblenz, 1973)

P. Schwarz: *Studien zur Orgelmusik Franz Liszts: ein Beitrag zur Geschichte der Orgelkomposition im 19. Jahrhundert* (Munich, 1973)

H. Wunderlich: 'Zur Bedeutung und Interpretation von Regers Orgelwerken: ein Beitrag zum Regerjahr 1973', *Musik und Kirche*, xliii (1973), 7

B. D. Wye: 'Gregorian Influences in French Organ Music before the Motu Proprio', *JAMS*, xxvii (1974), 1

G. Beechey: 'The Organ Music of Jehan Alain', *MT*, cxv (1974), 422, 507

W. Blankenburg: 'Max Reger und das evangelische Kirchenlied', *Max Reger 1873–1973: ein Symposion*, ed. K. Röhring (Wiesbaden, 1974)

M. Boyd: 'John Stanley's Voluntaries', *MT*, cxv (1974), 598

R. A. Kotek: *The French Organ Mass in the 20th Century* (diss., U. of Illinois, 1974)

E. Kraus: 'Anton Bruckner in der Orgelliteratur', *Musica sacra*, xciv (1974), 215

C. Palmer: 'The Music of Karg-Elert', *MT*, cxv (1974), 247

S. Vendrey: 'Stilprobleme in Mendelssohns Orgelsonaten op.65', *Das Problem Mendelssohn*, ed. C. Dahlhaus (Regensburg, 1974)

H. Haupt: 'Max Regers Orgelmusik: Ausdruck unserer Zeit', *Reger Festschrift 1973* (Meiningen, 1975)

C. Johnson: *20th-century Solo Organ Music which is Indeterminate with Respect to Performance* (diss., Northwestern U., 1975)

H. Mayer: 'Avant-garde Organ Music in the Netherlands', *Key Notes*, ii (1975), 37

E. Rieke: *The Organ Chorale Preludes of Leo Sowerby* (diss., Eastman School of Music, Rochester, NY, 1975)

M.-L. Jacquet: 'La musique d'orgue après Jehan Alain', *ReM* (1978), no.316, p.135

R. Gower: 'John Ireland's Organ Music', *MT*, cxx (1979), 682

G. de la Salle: 'L'Orgue Symphonique', *ReM* (1979), no.326, p.173
P. Hardwick: 'Healey Willan's Organ Miniatures', *MT*, cxxi (1980), 651
A. Plender: 'Henri Mulet, 1878–1967', *MT*, cxxii (1981), 697
J. O. Thomas: 'Ligeti's Organ Music', *MT*, cxxiv (1983), 319
J. S. Whiteley: 'Jongen's Organ Music', *MT*, cxxiv (1983), 189

THE ORGAN AND THE LITURGY

W. Riley: *Parochial Music Corrected: Containing Remarks on . . . the Use of Organs and the Performance of Organists* (London, 1762)
F. W. T. Linke: *Der rechte Gebrauch der Orgeln beym öffentlichen Gottesdienste* (Altenburg, 1766)
D. G. Türk: *Von den wichtigsten Pflichten eines Organisten* (Halle, 1787/R1966, rev. 2/1838)
F. Kessler: *Der musikalische Kirchendienst* (Iserlohn, 1832)
J. H. Göroldt: *Die Orgel und deren zweckmässiger Gebrauch bei dem öffentlichen Gottesdienst* (Quedlinburg, 1835)
R. S. Candlish: *The Organ Question: For and Against the Use of the Organ in Public Worship* (Edinburgh, 1856)
R. J. Voigtmann: *Das neuere kirchliche Orgelspiel* (Leipzig, 1870)
F. Zimmer: *Die Kirchenorgel und das kirchliche Orgelspiel* (Gotha, 1891)
G. Rietschel: *Die Aufgabe der Orgel im Gottesdienst bis in das 18. Jahrhundert* (Leipzig, 1893)
W. Baumann: *Das Orgelspiel im evangelische Gottesdienst* (Karlsruhe, 1915)
F. Blume: *Die evangelische Kirchenmusik*, HMw, x (1931, rev. 2/1965 as *Geschichte der evangelischen Kirchenmusik*; Eng. trans., enlarged, 1974, as *Protestant Church Music: a History*)
K. G. Fellerer: *Beiträge zur Choralbegleitung und Choralverarbeitung in der Orgelmusik des ausgehenden 18. und frühen 19. Jahrhunderts* (Strasbourg, 1932)
J. Petzold: *Die gedruckten vierstimmigen Choralbücher für die Orgel der deutschen evangelischen Kirche, 1785–1933* (diss., U. of Halle, 1935)
R. Lachmann: 'Das moderne Choralvorspiel als gottesdienstliche Gebrauchsmusik', *Zeitschrift für Kirchenmusiker*, xx (1938), 60
J. G. Mehl: *Die Aufgabe der Orgel im Gottesdienst der lutherischen Kirche* (Munich, 1938)
R. Haupt: *Die Orgel im evangelischen Kultraum in Geschichte und Gegenwart* (Northeim, 1954)
H. J. Moser: *Die evangelische Kirchenmusik in Deutschland* (Berlin, 1954)
M. Blindow: *Die Choralbegleitung des 18. Jahrhunderts in der evangelischen Kirche Deutschlands* (Regensburg, 1957)
H. Klotz: 'Die kirchliche Orgelkunst', *Leiturgia*, iv (1961), 759–804

III. Piano music from c1750. The century after the death of Johann Sebastian Bach saw a dramatic rise in the popularity and prestige of the piano, both as a household instrument and as the vehicle for some of Western music's most enduring masterpieces. Although the principal contributions were made by relatively few composers, virtually all those active before World War I wrote music for or with piano.

1. The advent of the piano. 2. The classical sonata. 3. Romanticism and the miniature. 4. The age of virtuosity. 5. 19th-century national trends. 6. The growth of pianism, 1900–1940. 7. After World War II.

1. THE ADVENT OF THE PIANO. The dominance of the harpsichord was not broken overnight; indeed, not until the dawn of the 19th century did the newer instrument altogether vanquish its plectra-activated rival. As late as 1802, Beethoven's three keyboard sonatas of op.31, though clearly designated for the 'pianoforte' by their composer, were published in Nägeli's series *Repertoire des clavecinistes*. Conversely, in 1732 Lodovico Giustini had published sonatas designated specifically for the 'cimbalo di piano e forte'. Although it became evident shortly after J. S. Bach had played on Silbermann's improved models in 1747 that the future belonged ultimately to the piano, the two designs coexisted peacefully throughout the second half of the 18th century. In January 1777 Mozart composed the Concerto in E♭, K271, on commission for a French *claveciniste* (i.e. harpsichordist). He performed it himself on a 'wretched' for-tepiano in Munich in October 1777; the following January his sister played it on a harpsichord in Salzburg. The differences between performances on these two opposed instruments were narrower than they might seem today. The early piano was housed in a frame largely identical to that of the harpsichord, with equally light stringing. The fortepiano offered new possibilities for gradations in volume, but its tone was still characterized by the rapid decay of the harpsichord's. In terms of sheer sound, a triple-strung French double from this period produced as much, if not more, volume than its double-strung rival.

Conservative French composers such as Armand-Louis Couperin (1727–89) and Jacques Duphly (1715–89) continued to cultivate a lavishly intricate style perfectly suited to the opulent double harpsichords made by the Flemish builder Taskin. In Italy, the birthplace of the piano, Platti, Galuppi and others wrote music equally suited to either harpsichord or piano. The same interchangeability – doubtless designed to encourage sales – prevailed among the Iberians (Soler, Seixas, Blasco de Nebra), the Germans and Bohemians (some in Germany or Austria, such as Neefe in Bonn or Kozeluch in Vienna; others abroad, such as Schober and Eckhardt in Paris or Hässler in Russia), and the English (Nares, Hook). Carl Philipp Emanuel Bach, arguably the greatest keyboard player and composer in the generation after his father's, expressed a preference in his *Versuch* of 1753 for the subtle gradations and *Bebung* of the clavichord over any of its more extrovert relatives. In spite of their general designation as 'Clavier-Sonaten', the series from the 1760s and 1770s (often characterized as 'leichte' or 'pour l'usage des dames') were probably intended primarily for this most private of instruments. Along with the sonatas of Scarlatti, whose distribution turns out to have been far wider than was once believed, they exercised a considerable influence on the early sonatas of Haydn, who admitted: 'Anyone who knows me very well must realize that I owe a great deal to Emanuel, that I understood and studied him diligently'. Beginning in 1780 with C. P. E. Bach's second collection of *Sonaten nebst einigen Rondos . . . für Kenner und Liebhaber*, the 'fortepiano' is specified, a designation that carried through to his sixth and final set in 1787. Their composer revelled most in the kinds of dramatic contrasts of range and register that the new instrument made possible. Simple dynamic contrasts, though not as concentrated, are already called for in the six 'cembalo' sonatas dedicated to the Duke of Württemberg and published in 1744; these, achieved by discreet changes in registration, are fully realizable only on a two-manual instrument. The more complex range of effects that saturates the 'Kenner und Liebhaber' series – encompassing *pp* to *ff* and numerous shades in between – was scarcely equalled before late Beethoven. They are best understood as a natural extension of the registration shifts from three decades earlier. Nevertheless, as late as 1788 C. P. E. Bach was able to compose a Double Concerto for harpsichord and fortepiano, WQ47, in which the writing for the solo instruments is essentially identical; the chief delight lies simply in the tonal contrasts between them.

The rapid, experiment-orientated evolution of keyboard instruments during this period was reflected in the musical styles that flourished. The inevitable breakdown in High Baroque continuity was not to be fully replaced by Classical phrase structure until the 1780s; hence composers embracing *Empfindsamkeit* had to ontent themselves with a series of small-scale dramatic ffects whose overall impact was often less than the sum of its parts. A great many movements in C. P. E. Bach's utput fulfilling the minimum requirements of sonata orm are diluted by the remoteness of secondary mod-lations and a surfeit of thematic material; indeed, only a composer of his extraordinary inventiveness could maintain interest amid such stylistic upheaval. His older brother Wilhelm Friedemann, in some respects even more gifted than Emanuel, never took final leave of his father's tyle. In an eclectic production that included sonatas, ugues and polonaises (these last enjoyed a vogue in the 9th century), nowhere was the dilemma of composers fter the mid-century portrayed more clearly. Their younger half-brother Johann Christian shunned the com-lexities of the north for the relaxed *galant* style acquired during his formative years in Italy. His two sets of key-oard sonatas, opp.5 and 17, are model specimens of music created for domestic consumption: facile (though ot without occasional technical challenges), diatonic to a fault, and highly polished. Between J. C. and C. P. E. Bach, virtually all the ingredients necessary for Vien-ese Classicism were present. Mozart seems to have acknowledged this when, although it was scarcely noticed in London, he mourned the death of J. C. Bach in 1782. About C. P. E. he is alleged to have said: 'He is the ather, we are the children'. As late as 1809 Beethoven could write to Breitkopf & Härtel that 'I have only a few items from Emanuel Bach's keyboard works, yet ome of them not only provide the real artist with great pleasure, but also serve as objects to be studied'.

2. THE CLASSICAL SONATA. Although the music of the sons of Bach is among the earliest to benefit from sym-pathetic performance on the fortepiano, it is doubtful that any of them ever enjoyed the opportunity of per-forming on instruments as reliable as those praised by Mozart when he visited Stein's workshop in 1777. Even more than the singing tone, the composer was impressed by the regularity and evenness of the action, with its deceptively simple escapement. Though eventually ren-dered obsolete by the steadily increasing size of concert halls throughout the 19th century, Stein's design was both perfectly engineered on its own terms and perfectly suited to the world that Mozart was about to enter. After exclaiming that K284/205b (with its surprisingly lengthy set of variations as a finale) 'sounds exquisite' on Stein's instrument, Mozart – further stimulated by the Mann-heim style with its emphasis on contrast – set down in the next several weeks two sonatas (K309/284b and 311/284c) more dramatically expansive and brilliant than any of the half-dozen surviving examples composed previ-ously. These were succeeded the following summer by the first of his two sonatas in the minor mode, K310/300d, a work of remarkable intensity and tautness. In the space of a few years, and in direct response to devel-opments in instrument design, Mozart had succeeded in transforming the easy-going three-movement form inherited from J. C. Bach (whose sonatas he had arranged as keyboard concertos at the age of nine) into a vehicle for considerable display and elaborate working-out.

With his final break from the archbishop in May 1781 and the decision to take up permanent residence in Vienna, Mozart inaugurated a series of masterpieces for keyboard dominated by 17 remarkable concertos, in which virtuosity is blended with a superb sense of oper-atic pacing. Though fewer in number, the ten solo sona-

tas now known to have been created after the move to Vienna (portions of K330–32/300h, i, k may have been composed a few months earlier) afford a unified view of the composer's development. A few, such as the 'lit-tle keyboard sonata for beginners', K545, were designed to fulfil pedagogic needs, but the remainder encompass a broad spectrum of mature styles. The group of four sonatas K330–33/300h, i, k, 315c (traditionally ascribed to Mozart's Paris sojourn of 1778, but now known to date from between 1781 and 1784) demonstrate his sure handling of practically every Classical form: sonata, both with coda (K332 finale) and without (K333 first move-ment); theme and variations (K331 opening movement); binary (K331 Menuetto and Trio); ternary (K330 Andante); rondo-type (K331 finale) and sonata-rondo (K333 fina-le). The last-named of these, with its tutti–solo oppo-sition and elaborate cadenzas, offers a prime example of cross-fertilization with the concertos Mozart was composing during the same period. His treatment of all these forms is rarely perfunctory; the coda to the finale of K332 incorporates a *buffa* theme presented in the exposition but slyly omitted from the recapitulation. The 'Alla turca' of K331 adopts the thematic virtues of the straight rondo while employing an ingenious *ABCBAB* scheme to skirt its inherent structural squareness. The highly decorated version of the Adagio of K332 pub-lished by Artaria in 1784 (and presumably originating with Mozart) shows that improvised embellishment remained an integral component of his style; present-day performers might do well to contemplate the gulf between their abilities and Mozart's before undertaking their own decorations. The two-piano sonata, K448/375a, composed less than ten months after his arrival in Vien-na on a commission from his talented pupil Josepha von Auernhammer, gravitates towards virtuoso display while displaying Mozart's intuitive understanding of the 'orchestral' capabilities of two fortepianos; the synco-pated chordal responses in the opening Allegro's closing group are particularly striking. The composer's contact with the music of J. S. Bach and Handel at the concerts of Baron Gottfried van Swieten in 1782–3 resulted in a modest burst of contrapuntal works, including the underrated Prelude and Fugue in C, K394/383a, written at the urging of Constanze Weber.

Although Mozart soon tired of aping an archaic Baroque style, the effects on his own music of his expe-riences with Bach and Handel were profound and long-lasting. The unique single-voiced opening of K533 invokes the atmosphere of fugue, realized more fully in the second group, as well as in the minor-mode episode of the Rondo (published in 1788 with the two move-ments of K533 though composed in 1786). The opening movement of the Sonata in D K576, perhaps Mozart's masterpiece in this genre, bristles with lean, athletic counterpoint; it maintains the composer's predilection for the open-ended half-cadence that moves to the domi-nant in the exposition, while remaining in the tonic for the recapitulation (nearly half of the 35 major-mode sonata movements in the keyboard sonatas use this 'bifocal close'). Baron van Swieten's advocacy of C. P. E. Bach immediately stimulated two fantasias, K396/385f and 397/385g, both remaining fragments, although the second in D minor, is still a favourite. The Fantasia in C minor K475, a work of great emotional scope, was published at the head of the sonata in the same key, completed five months earlier. Its impact on Beethoven's obsessive bouts with C minor can scarcely be exaggerated. A late Fantasia in F minor K608, composed in March 1791 for a mechanical organ but published as early as 1799 for piano four-hands, deserves more frequent hearings. Yet by far the most important development during this period was Mozart's deepening relationship with Haydn, whom he probably first met in 1781. Although Haydn's musical influence is most readily traceable in Mozart's mature chamber music, it is still felt in movements like the monothematic opening Allegro of K570, or in the bold choice of the lowered submediant as the secondary key of the Adagio of K576. The remarkable two-year period framed by the composition of *Le nozze di Figaro* and of *Don Giovanni* saw Mozart add four jewels to the crown of his works for keyboard, including the four-hand sonata K497, an unqualified masterpiece; an inspired set of four-hand variations K501; the chromatically rich A minor Rondo K511 and an outstandingly expressive Adagio in B minor K540. All this music was written for a five-octave instrument about which Mozart is not known to have voiced reservations. When the recapitulation of a sonata movement threatened to exceed its compass, his imagination was fired by the limitation, resulting in some of his most adroit touches, as in the opening movements of K333/315c (ex.5) or the concerto K449. The concert

Ex.5. Mozart: K333/315c

(a)

(b)

instrument used by Mozart and built by Anton Walter around 1780 included only two tone-modifying devices: a pair of knee-levers that raised either all the dampers or only the treble ones (the presence of hand-stops as well for the dampers on the original suggests Mozart may have requested the addition of knee-levers, perhaps taking his cue from Stein's instruments); and a hand-stop over the middle of the keyboard that placed a thin strip of cloth between the hammer and the strings, acting as a mute. In passages such as the middle section of the Andante of K330/300h, this *sourdine* imparts an ethereal effect fundamentally different from that achieved with the shift on a modern instrument. Both the mute and the raising of the dampers were regarded in Mozart's time as special effects; his celebrated remark that phrases should 'flow like oil' has often been construed as an unqualified endorsement of legato, inviting indiscriminate application of the modern damper pedal. In practice, both the rapid tonal decay on the fortepiano and the articulative richness of Mozart's scores preclude any uniform solutions. It is no condemnation of present-day instruments that the carefully marked phrasing at the opening of K332/300k (ex.6) is almost impossible to achieve naturally except on a fortepiano.

Haydn's reputation rested far less than Mozart's on

Ex.6 Mozart: K332/300k

his abilities as a keyboard performer. His longstanding positions as composer-in-residence to aristocratic patrons, including three decades of service to the Esterházy family, filled his days with the closely monitored composition of sacred, operatic, orchestral and chamber music, as well as with supervising performances. It is all the more surprising that Haydn found the time to compose over 60 multi-movement works for solo keyboard. Fewer than 50 of these can be proved authentic, and about a dozen more early harpsichord works were attributed to Haydn during his lifetime. As fewer than a dozen autographs (some only fragments) of Haydn's solo sonatas survive, the severe problems of chronology and authenticity among works circulating in the 1750s and 1760s are likely to remain unresolved unless new evidence is discovered. Most of these early pieces appear to have been teaching aids intended for the amateur, perhaps the children of Haydn's aristocratic patrons. It is unlikely that all, or even most, of them have survived. Entitled 'divertimento' or 'partita', they typically consisted of three movements, most often two fast outer ones encasing a minuet, though not infrequently with the latter as a finale. Apart from a few simple binary forms in works of questionable authenticity (HXVI:7–9), virtually all the non-minuet movements present rudimentary sonata forms with modest transitions and well-demarcated secondary groups. Clearly designated for harpsichord, they exude the easy-going *galant* manner of Wagenseil without obsessive reliance on the broken-chord basses purportedly popularized by Alberti. Significant increases in technical demands, perhaps stimulated by Scarlatti, are registered in the group of sonatas that includes HXVI:45, 19 and 46, composed in the late 1760s. The last movement of the Sonata in A♭ (no.46) foreshadows the irresistible *buffa* finales that Haydn was to perfect in the sonatas, quartets and symphonies of the 1780s and 1790s. Beginning around 1771 with the first works called 'sonate' (HXVI:18, 20 and 44), Haydn's unpretentious style is blended with increasingly complex emotional moods, easily traceable to the influence of C. P. E. Bach. The single dynamic marking in the autograph fragment of the Sonata in C minor (no.20) can still be rendered on a two-manual harpsichord, but by the time Artaria published this landmark in 1780 it included a wealth of additional dynamics (including a *crescendo* in the finale) that demanded the new flexibility of the fortepiano.

he five other sonatas that appeared simultaneously
(XVI:35–9) are the last Haydn approved 'per il clavi-
embalo, o forte piano'. It may have been more than
coincidence that the trio of sonatas published in 1784
y Bossler (HXVI:40–42), and calling specifically for
ortepiano, were the first that Haydn composed after the
tart of his friendship with Mozart. In 1788 Haydn wrote
o his publisher Artaria that he had been compelled to
urchase a new fortepiano in order to do justice to the
ree piano trios HXV:11–13.

Haydn's long life allowed him to continue to absorb
nd recast the most important advances of Viennese
lassicism. The sonatas of Haydn's maturity are all the
more remarkable for the stylistic distance that their
omposer had traversed to create them. The obligatory
a capo minuet of previous decades disappears almost
ntirely; when required to supply one around 1789, the
omposer responded in the Sonata in Eb (HXVI:49) with
large-scale 'Tempo di minuet' containing an elabo-
ately rewritten repeat. A standard three-movement, fast–
low–fast scheme avoids tedium by incorporating at least
ne movement not in regular sonata form: the alternat-
ng major–minor variations (a favourite technique) that
pen HXVI:39 and close no.34; the spacious binary form
vith rondo elements that concludes HXVI:50; or the
nexpected sonata-rondo that opens HXVI:51. But Haydn
roved equally drawn in this period to a two-movement
rouping, providing Beethoven with a point of depar-
ure for his subsequent experiments. Two of the three
wo-movement sonatas that appeared together in 1784
in G and D) go so far as to abandon any references to
onata style. In the finale of no.40 Haydn took special
lelight in punctuating cadences with abrupt leaps of three
octaves (ex.7); the fortepiano, with its clearly delin-

Ex.7 Haydn: HXVI:40

eated registers, conveys the humour of these gestures
with particular effectiveness. The pervasive imitation
throughout the finale of the Sonata in D may reflect
Haydn's encounters with J. S. Bach at Baron van Swieten's. Equally important is the surge of cantabile writing
found in the slow movement of the Sonata in Eb written
about 1789 for Marianne von Genzinger, to whom Haydn
extolled the virtues of a fortepiano by Wenzel Schantz.
In the freewheeling Fantasia in C (HXVII:4), published
around the same time, Haydn instructs the performer at
two points to hold the cadential octave until the tone
dies away; on a well-regulated modern grand the sound
lingers for almost a minute. Between his first and second London sojourns, the composer penned an elaborate
keyboard farewell to the double variation (HXVII:7), built
on a pair of utterly non-symmetrical themes that erupt
during only the third variation into a rhapsodic coda.
Three highly individual sonatas (nos.50–52) composed
during the next year in London provide a fitting climax
to Haydn's output in this medium. The 'open pedal'
demanded in the first movement of no.50 marks the
migration of the Viennese knee-levers to a location on
the forward supporting legs of English models where

they could be depressed with the foot. The finale of the
same work exploits the 5½-octave range of the newest
English models; their fuller, weightier sound may be
partly responsible for the symphonic grandeur that permeates the opening movement of no.52. Throughout his
career Haydn's approach to sonata form was punctuated
by surprise and experiment, continually nourished by
his longstanding fascination with monothematicism. Even
more than in the music of Mozart, Haydn's frequent
changes of texture and spiky rhythms depend upon
the quick response and rapid tonal decay of the early
piano.

The most remarkable aspect of Beethoven's monumental 32 keyboard sonatas (including three teaching
pieces in the spirit of Mozart's K545) is that they continue to expand and refine a genre that seemed to have
reached perfection in the music of Haydn and Mozart.
Three early sonatas (WoO 47) published before the
composer was 13 present rather stiff imitations of
C. P. E. Bach's 'Sturm und Drang' style. By the time
he brought out his three op.2 sonatas in Vienna in 1796,
Beethoven had obviously made a thorough study of
Mozart and Haydn, in spite of his exaggerated claim to
have learnt nothing from his most celebrated teacher.
The older man's influence is easily traceable in the con-
ciseness and wit of the Sonata in F op.10 no.2 or in the
humorous scherzos of op.2 nos.2 and 3, borrowed from
Haydn's quartets. But the most persistent strand up to
op.22 is the loose, additive post-Classical language
already discernible in Mozart's late piano concertos.
Virtually every gambit in the opening movement of
Mozart's K467 – the *piano* opening and subsequent tutti
explosion, the bifocal close preceding a dramatic inter-
jection of the minor dominant, the wealth of closing ideas
that confirm the major – appear in the first movement
of op.2 no.3, in the same key. The *con gran espressione*
of op.7 and the Largo e mesto of op.10 no.3 invest
Beethoven's slow movements with new dignity and
pathos. Blatant sectionalism pervades the 'Rondo' finales of opp.7 and 22; here, as elsewhere, what separates
Beethoven from the transitional generation of Clementi,
Dussek, Hummel and Weber is his unflagging reliance
on the sonata principle. By the 1790s the pressures on
composers to abandon the symmetrical resolution of
sonata form were considerable. Muzio Clementi, essentially a contemporary of Mozart who lived well into the
new century, played an important role in these developments. His nearly six dozen keyboard sonatas published between 1779 and 1821 take Mozart as their point
of departure (opp.7, 9 and 10 were published in Vienna), with greater emphasis on virtuoso techniques (such
as the rapid parallel 3rds and octaves of op.2 no.4) and
Italianate melody, especially in slow movements. After
their contest before Joseph II on Christmas Eve 1781,
Mozart characterized Clementi as a 'mere mechanicus'.
The substantial increase over the next decade in the scale
of his works is not matched by a corresponding increase
in the capacity of thematic material to support the larger
structures. Clementi's recapitulations frequently exhibit
only a casual relationship to his expositions, with minimal attention paid to resolving long-range harmonic tension. The virtues of his last and best-known sonata, op.50
no.3, sub-titled 'Didone abbandonata', remain those of
lean, athletic textures and dramatic changes of mood
familiar from his earliest works. Curiously, although he
was closely tied to piano manufacture from the 1790s,
little of the increased capacity of the new six-octave

instruments is reflected in Clementi's keyboard music, probably because most of it was composed by 1805.

Between 1817 and 1826 Clementi brought out a series of volumes under the title *Gradus ad Parnassum*, devoted to the attainment of a fluent technique. Debussy paid an affectionate tribute to the popularity of these exercises in his 'Doctor Gradus ad Parnassum' from *Children's Corner*. Clementi was joined in these endeavours by two other distinguished men, Carl Czerny and Johann Baptist Cramer. Czerny had studied as a youngster with Beethoven before becoming a private instructor from the age of 15, numbering among his pupils Kullak, Thalberg, Heller and the young Liszt. Although Liszt frequently played Czerny's Sonata no.1 in A♭ op.7, it was as an indefatigable pedagogue that Czerny chose to make his mark. In more than 800 works devoted largely to technical studies (the best known being the *Complete Theoretical and Practical Pianoforte School* op.500), Czerny compiled and codified the technical advances of the piano during a period of extremely rapid development. If Czerny's methods were already beginning to show signs of age before his death, he continued to command the respect and admiration of his peers. Cramer, although an essentially conservative force like Czerny, was (according to Ries) considered by Beethoven to be the finest pianist of his day. He is remembered chiefly today for two fine sets each of 42 studies, published in 1804 and 1810 and endorsed by Beethoven, Schumann and Chopin.

Foreshadowings of at least a dozen composers from Beethoven and Schubert to Liszt and Brahms have been detected by proponents of the music of Dussek. In terms of pianistic figuration, there is no doubt that Dussek was a pioneer; formally he was much less so, relying heavily on the rondo and other sectional schemes. No hard evidence remains to show that Beethoven was familiar with his music, as can be demonstrated in the case of Clementi. Nearly 30 sonatas (several bearing programmatic titles) composed between 1788 and 1812 bear witness to a highly eclectic style stimulated by Dussek's peripatetic career as a travelling virtuoso. His association with the firm of Broadwood contributed to an expansion of the piano's range to six octaves ($C'-c''''$) as early as 1794. Hummel's ties to Viennese Classicism were considerably stronger, for he had studied with Mozart as a child and returned frequently to Vienna. Until the 1820s Hummel's fame nearly rivalled Beethoven's. Apart from an early sonata issued in London, his five remaining works in this genre were published in Vienna between 1805 and 1825, including a near-masterpiece, the Sonata in F♯ minor op.81, which appeared just after Beethoven's op.106. The exposition of its opening movement arrives in A major after a generous interlude in C major, pointing up Hummel's continued loosening of high Classical structures, as well as his anticipation of Schumann's harmonic palette (ex.8). Like Clementi's and Dussek's, Weber's career was marked by extensive travels; unlike either, his principal field of activity was opera. When, on examining the score of *Der Freischütz* in 1823, Beethoven remarked that its composer 'must write operas, nothing but operas', he displayed a keen appreciation of Weber's special gifts. Throughout his four sonatas (all but the third in four movements) the pacing is consistently operatic, aided by directives such as *con duolo*, *mormorando* and *consolante* in no.4. Running passage-work over simple chordal accompaniments, as in the first movement of the Sonata in A♭,

Ex.8 Hummel: op.81

ook forward to such patterns in the works of Chopin. For his own part, Weber remarked in 1810 that Beethoven's compositions after 1800 were 'a confused chaos, an unintelligible struggle after novelty'.

Weber was almost certainly referring to Beethoven's resolve not to settle into the structurally less demanding language of the proto-Romantics. In the highly experimental sonatas of opp.26–8 it looked as if Beethoven might indeed pursue this path. The A♭ Sonata dispenses altogether with straight sonata form. Both of the op.27 sonatas exhibit novel structures, and op.28 is noteworthy for its off-tonic beginning and third-related modulatory scheme. The conflicts in Beethoven's style around 1800 are drawn cleanly in op.27 no.2 (the 'Moonlight'), whose famous opening demands the intimacy of the drawing-room, while its stormy and very public finale pushes the five-octave instrument inherited from Mozart right to (though not beyond) its limits. Op.31 no.3 was the last four-movement sonata until the inaptly labelled 'Hammerklavier' (the generic term for the Viennese piano after 1815) of 15 years later. In the autumn of 1802 Beethoven wrote to the publisher Breitkopf & Härtel concerning the 'new manner' of his two sets of variations, opp.34 and 35. Continuing with the 'Waldstein', and even more emphatically with the 'Appassionata', Beethoven re-created the taut, integrated aesthetic of the high Classical period, though on a greatly intensified scale. It scarcely seems an accident that this dramatic turnabout in Beethoven's style paralleled equally dramatic developments in the Viennese piano. Within six years the instrument nearly doubled its weight and more than trebled its string tension. The menacing opening of op.57, plumbing the lowest note on the keyboard, is unthinkable without the powerful yet clear bass of the new six-octave models. The lush sweetness of these instruments is reflected in the two movements of op.78, Beethoven's only work in F♯ and a particular favourite of the composer's. 'Les Adieux', op.81a, composed in the same year and key as the 'Emperor' Concerto, provided a fitting close for the solo sonata to the 'heroic decade'. Both opp.90 and 101 show a closer affinity with the later styles of Schubert and Mendelssohn respectively, revealing a composer once again at the crossroads. Much like op.57 of a dozen years earlier, the monumental Sonata in B♭ op.106 marked Beethoven's final return to an expanded vision of the high Classical style, spurred by another burst in the size and weight of Viennese pianos. The frequent choice of non-dominant secondary areas in sonata movements after 1817 is overshadowed by continually deepening levels of thematic integration, such as the relentless chains of descending 3rds that saturate the first movement of op.106 (ex.9). The Adagio of this remarkable work, placed after the Scherzo and in the remote key of F♯ minor, is both the longest and the most deeply felt among Beethoven's slow movements. But it was the composer's renewed interest in fugue, first seen in the finales of opp.101 and the 102 no.2 cello sonata, that dominated the late style. The equally fugal yet diametrically opposed finales of both opp.106 and 110 demonstrate the extent to which Beethoven could impose his will upon the intractable rules of counterpoint. Closely allied with this absorption was the practice of variation, culminating in the Arietta of op.111, whose transcendant blend of variation and sonata inspired Kretschmar's impassioned homage in Thomas Mann's *Dr Faustus*. When invited to contribute a variation on the publisher Diabelli's 'Schusterfleck'

of a waltz, Beethoven responded over a period extending from 1818 to 1823 with a series of 33 variations that constitute a final compendium of Classical techniques. He took his leave from the piano with his third cycle of (as Beethoven referred to them) Bagatelles op.126, which not only served as an experimental laboratory for the late quartets but also anticipated the character-pieces of the Romantics.

Ex.9 Beethoven: op.106

Although Schubert never billed himself as a pianist, he produced a prodigious quantity of keyboard music over scarcely more than a decade, including 11 solo sonatas, substantial fragments of nine others, three sets of Impromptus and *Moments musicaux*, and more than 400 dances for occasional use. During his lifetime the 16-bar *Trauerwalzer* D365 no.2 became so popular that its citation did not require the identification of Schubert as the composer. He began half a dozen sonatas before completing D537, the first of three impassioned works in A minor. Two of these, along with the 'little' A major (a perennial favourite) are in only three movements; otherwise Schubert – unlike Beethoven after 1802 – preferred the spaciousness of a four-movement plan. Among the dance movements scherzos are most re-presented, but a work as late as the Fantasia in G D894 (1826) presents an old-fashioned Menuetto. In certain respects Schubert was formally less experimental than Beethoven. All of his opening movements are in sonata form; after 1819 all but one of his finales is a sonata-rondo or an even simpler straight rondo. His slow movements are slightly more adventurous, favouring the two- and three-part forms whose simple contrasts proved so appealing to the next generation. But it is the relationship in Schubert's music between theme and tonality that differentiates him from his great contemporary and that so profoundly influenced Brahms and Mahler. The 'heavenly length' praised by Schumann points up the leisurely unfolding of long, arching themes rooted in song. Rather than struggling to create dynamic transitions along Beethovenian lines, Schubert viewed the obligatory modulation in expositions as an opportunity for a series of bold, common-tone key changes that minimize the structural significance of the secondary tonality. In movements like the finale of the C minor Sonata D958 this process is carried to almost bizarre lengths; in others, such as the deeply moving Molto moderato that opens the last of the late sonatas, D960, the motion through the flattened submediant (both major and minor) is achieved effortlessly through what amounts to thematic transformation. Schubert's models in these sonatas, which compare in importance with those of late Beethoven, are clearly the mature sonatas of Hummel (to whom he planned to dedicate his final three). Although lacking the technical challenges routinely confronted in Beethoven's music, their figuration is rarely perfunctory; a compelling performance demands an outstanding sensitivity to proportion and pacing. The two exceptions to these moderate technical demands are the Sonata in D D850, composed during the same summer, that of 1825, which saw the composition of the 'Great' C major Symphony, and, emphatically, the *Wanderer* Fantasy, a work of unabashed virtuosity whose continuous structure inspired the cyclic forms of Liszt. The song that provides the starting-point for its slow section, and from which the work derives its name, provides perhaps the most splendid example in Schubert of the poignant contrast between major and minor.

Schubert's interest in smaller forms ran considerably deeper than Beethoven's, and resulted in some of his finest efforts. The two sets of four impromptus and the six *Moments musicaux* (a title invented by the publisher Leidesdorf) were created largely in the last two years of the composer's life, at least partly in response to exhortations from publishers for less demanding music. It is a tribute to Schubert's greatness that he was able to produce masterpiece after masterpiece among works directed solely at the domestic market. Only the first of the op.142 impromptus uses sonata form, inspiring some writers to interpret its other three members as the remainder of a four-movement sonata. At least half of the 14 pieces in these works are straightforward ternary forms with verbatim repeats of their opening sections. Others, such as op.94 no.2, introduce the double varia-

tion (*ABA'B'A"*) inherited from Haydn and later exploited by Mahler. The care lavished by Schubert on the countless sets of *ländler*, German dances, waltzes and ecossaises (the first three of these stylistically indistinguishable) far exceeded the demands of the form; many invite enrichment by the discreet addition of the pedal-activated buff or Janissary stops in vogue during the first quarter of the 19th century. Their application was mandatory in the fashionable battle pieces first popularized by Koczwara's *The Battle of Prague* (c1788). Although Schubert rarely exploited the available range of the Viennese pianos (none of the last three sonatas uses the extra 4th added in the bass around 1816), his relationship to these instruments is considerably more sensual than that of Beethoven. The idiosyncratic wide spacing of chords, so frequently featuring the 3rd in the soprano and the placement of tunes in the clear, singing tenor register reflect the special virtues of the pianos on which Schubert composed and performed.

Schubert's achievements in smaller forms were not without precedent in works by two Bohemian composers, Jan Tomášek and Jan Voříšek. With a series of evocatively titled eclogues, rhapsodies or dithyrambs published between 1807 and 1818, Tomášek laid good claim to being the originator of the short character-piece that proved so appealing to Romantic composers. His pupil Voříšek took up residence in Vienna, where he enjoyed fruitful relationships with Beethoven, Hummel and Schubert. Although documentation is lacking, it seems likely that Voříšek's impromptus influenced Schubert's compositions of the same name.

3. ROMANTICISM AND THE MINIATURE. After the deaths of Beethoven (1827) and Schubert (1828) the decline of the sonata was swift and precipitous. Although its prestige remained enormous, largely because of the achievement of Beethoven, stylistic developments turned rapidly in other directions. The sonatas of Schumann, Chopin and Brahms, however imaginative in certain respects, project a sense of imitation rather than continued evolution. In Germany the chief architect of this aesthetic shift was Robert Schumann, who used his editorship of the *Neue Zeitschrift für Musik* as a forum for proclaiming both Chopin and the young Brahms. Composed during the 1830s, Schumann's first 23 opus numbers were all for solo keyboard, including several of his best-known works. From his op.1 (the 'Abegg' Variations) on, the voice is clear and assured, characterized by an extraordinarily poetic harmonic imagination, strong root movements, frequent doublings and a preference for the middle range of the piano. Although Robert and Clara did not receive the grand manufactured by Conrad Graf until their marriage in 1840 (the instrument was later bequeathed to Brahms), the music composed by both demonstrates the warmth and intimacy of the Viennese instruments. Many of his most successful works, including *Papillons* op.2, the *Davidsbündlertänze* op.6, *Carnaval* op.9 and *Kreisleriana* op.16, consist of cycles of miniatures whose interdependency is analogous to that found in the later song cycles like *Dichterliebe*. In *Carnaval* a series of epigrammatic mottos provides a modicum of musical connection, but the deeper unity is more elusive, based on harmonically open beginnings or closes and a keen sensitivity to contrasts in mood. Along with figures from the *commedia dell'arte*, Schumann presents sympathetic portraits of Clara Wieck, Chopin and Paganini, as well as of Eusebius and Florestan, the

ntrovert and extrovert sides of his own musical personality. It is surprising to find the density of short internal repeats – betraying binary origins – in movements of wide-ranging harmonic freedom like those in *Kreisleriana* (inspired by E. T. A. Hoffmann's character and dedicated to Chopin). Often accompanying these repetitive forms are the kinds of motoric rhythm familiar from the Baroque (Schumann acknowledged that his music was closer in spirit to Bach than to Mozart). The predilection for building on short, symmetrical harmonic sequences can lead to a marked squareness, often rescued by highly original figuration. Apart from the opening movements of the three sonatas, sonata form surfaces only rarely in Schumann's works. An effective example is the finale of the *Faschingsschwank aus Wien* op.26, whose opening rondo remains one of the composer's freshest inspirations.

In such works as the *Studien nach Capricen von Paganini* op.3, the Toccata op.7, the *Symphonische Etüden* op.13 and the *Phantasie* op.17, Schumann made important contributions to an expansion of the piano's range and sonority, keeping pace with the new iron-framed instruments being built in the 1830s. The *Phantasie*, dedicated to Liszt and whose proceeds Schumann contributed to the fund for the Beethoven monument in Bonn, is considered by many to be his masterpiece. With its pointed references to the last of Beethoven's songs from *An die ferne Geliebte*, it offers an eloquent farewell to Classicism. In spite of a reliance on structures of the da capo type and strong subdominant leanings, it is one of Schumann's most successful large-scale works, concluding with a serene slow movement in C that evokes the spirit of the Arietta finale of Beethoven's op.111. Schumann's considerable reliance on the metronome has been attacked on numerous occasions, but used with care (and sometimes modified by Clara's own editorial suggestions) his markings provide a very useful guide. He was also one of the first composers to designate long passages as simply 'mit Pedal', confirming the shift of the dampers' function from that of a special effect to a continuous ingredient in the texture. Finally, Schumann's commitment to high-quality pieces in his studies for children resulted in such welcome additions to this repertory as the *Kinderszenen* op.15 and most especially the *Album für die Jugend* op.68.

Although Schumann's innovations appeared less radical by the end of the century, they remained more far-reaching than those of his contemporary Mendelssohn. After leading a revival of the *St Matthew Passion* in 1829, Mendelssohn issued a series of keyboard works that included preludes and fugues (a set of six appeared in 1837), capriccios and fantasias, evoking a Baroque atmosphere overlaid with post-Classical phrase structure. A favourite arrangement was the slow introductory opening succeeded by a fleet Allegro or even Presto, most familiar from the *Rondo capriccioso* op.14, composed when Mendelssohn was only 15. A quarter of his output consists of eight books of *Lieder ohne Worte*, shorter lyric pieces predominantly in simple ternary form, whose moderate technical demands offered sustenance to the amateur player in danger of being swamped in a sea of virtuosity.

The designation 'revolutionary' is properly reserved in the 19th century for a figure like Chopin. In spite of precedents to be found in the music of Hummel and Field, even Chopin's earliest works are stamped with an originality that could scarcely have been expected.

All of his more than 200 works involve the piano (the vast majority are for piano solo), and in this respect he typifies the increasing specialization of the Romantics. Only a handful of concertos, sonatas and chamber works employed what were by now academic forms. Otherwise Chopin preferred generic titles that readily conjured up poetic images (ballade, barcarolle), though he stopped short of overt programmaticism, maintaining the tradition of absolute music in the two composers he most revered, Bach and Mozart. His discomfort with large, multi-movement forms is betrayed in the two youthful concertos, whose opening movements reverse the customary sequence of modulations in exposition and recapitulation. Visits to Vienna in 1829 and 1831 saw the première, on an instrument placed at Chopin's disposal by Conrad Graf, of the variations on 'Là ci darem la mano' (the work to be greeted by Schumann's prophetic review: 'Hats off, gentlemen, a genius!'). The Waltz in E♭ op.18, the first of the large concert waltzes, was also set down in Vienna. But Chopin's decision in the autumn of 1831 to take up at least temporary residence in Paris sealed the decline of the imperial capital and marked the ascendancy of the French metropolis to its position as the centre of new musical fashion for the next 90 years. Most importantly for the evolution of the piano, developments now shifted to the French–English design. Both the more conservative English action retained by Pleyel and the double escapement patented by Erard in the 1820s (the model for virtually all modern grand actions) provided more leverage with less effort than the increasingly cumbersome Viennese action, whose mechanical disadvantage multiplied as the instruments grew in size and weight. Many of Chopin's effects depend upon the increased sustaining power, particularly in the treble, of the newest French instruments. At the same time, both Pleyel and Erard's flat-strung pianos retained a clarity and transparency, even in the bass, that was aided by a more lightweight and efficient damping system. Gone for good were the exotic multiple pedal stops of the Viennese instruments; Romantic pianists made do with the damper and shift pedals now standard on English models. Chopin's preference for the more intimate sound of the Pleyel (whose action was slightly shallower than that of the Erard and had virtually no after-touch) shows that he resisted over-simplified notions of 'progress'.

On his arrival in Paris, Chopin began the regular and systematic cultivation of almost ten different genres. Dominant among the smaller forms were the mazurkas and nocturnes, which collectively reveal an astonishingly varied approach to ternary form. The modal colouring of the Mazurka in C♯ minor op.41 no.4 (caused by the use of the lowered 2nd and 7th degrees) sets up the return to the opening A section via the augmented 6th rather than the dominant, a technique that was to become a Romantic cliché. While still a youth in Warsaw Chopin had access to an intriguing new genre of composition by the Irishman John Field: the nocturne. The first four examples bearing this atmospheric title appeared in St Petersburg and Moscow in 1812, and doubtless made their way to Warsaw soon after. To Field goes the credit for evolving the arpeggiated accompaniment over which an expressive melody is free to spin out. Traces of the nocturne as it was inherited from Field are evident in op.9 no.2 (a perennial favourite of amateurs) but Chopin soon transformed the species to accommodate a much wider emotional range.

The extreme contrasts of op.15 no.1 provide a memorable early example; 15 years later the highly ornamented return in the Nocturne in B op.62 no.1 raises subtlety to new heights while assimilating Chopin's love of Italian *bel canto*. Although performers frequently present them in different groups, many of these sets were arranged by Chopin as collections unified in sequence of mood and tonal plan. The almost 20 waltzes are more openly sectional, as befits their dance origins, and prompted some of the composer's most spontaneous melodies, reinforced in the larger concert waltzes by ingenious repetition schemes. His most direct homage to Bach, the 24 Preludes, encompasses an array of formal schemes far richer than their aphoristic character might suggest. A large number are built upon a single phrase that requires only a single repetition rather than contrasting material to attain completeness. An even more virtuoso treatment of repetition underlies the Berceuse op.57, where a simple alternating pattern of tonic and dominant harmonies repeated 54 consecutive times supports a remarkably free and florid set of seamless melodic variations. A similar union of circumscribed harmonies and operatic display (frequently in duet textures) informs the equally remarkable Barcarolle op.60, which captures perfectly the gentle undulations of a Venetian gondola without the sentimentality so often attached to the genre.

Apart from his one youthful sonata, Chopin's experiments in this form produced two highly individual works, both in the old-fashioned four movements though with the scherzo placed second. In both opening allegros the focus on thematic rather than tonal processes leads to a marked sectionalization between vigorous first and lyrical second groups. The finale of the B♭ Sonata is one of the most original movements Chopin ever wrote, subjugating all the traditional elements to a single bare, fleeting texture. His ten or so remaining large-scale works (all in one movement) evince two opposed approaches. The polonaises, the first three of the scherzos and the second of the ballades employ large-scale ternary or rondo structures built around highly contrasted material. However, the three remaining ballades (in G minor, A♭ and F minor), as well as the Scherzo in E op.54, the Fantasie op.49 and the Polonaise-fantaisie op.61, each offer highly individual solutions to the special formal problems posed by thematic transformation and seamless transitions. The influence of sonata procedures is obvious in the first and last ballades and in the Fantasie, though with a minimum of emphasis on resolving material from secondary keys in the tonic. By establishing A♭ major as emphatically at the close as it does F minor in its opening, the Fantasie promotes the interchangeability of relative major and minor; the conclusion in A minor of the F major Ballade, which made such an impression upon Schumann, provides an even stronger example of Chopin's undermining of a single, central tonality. Although the Fantaisie-impromptu, published posthumously, has always been the most popular of Chopin's compositions in this vein, his 'fantasy' masterpiece is doubtless the Polonaise-fantaisie, in which the most heroic and extrovert characteristics of the genres cultivated by Chopin are blended with the most intimate flights of fancy. Performances that ignore the single basic tempo marking of Allegro maestoso obscure the underlying unity.

4. THE AGE OF VIRTUOSITY. Keyboard virtuosos had tra-

velled across Europe since the mid-18th century, but the bulk of published music was aimed at the amateur market. Beginning with Beethoven, the situation was rapidly transformed; Czerny reported to the composer in a conversation book that a woman in Vienna could still not play the opening of the 'Hammerklavier' even though she had been practising it for months. The 84 studies of Cramer, published in 1804 and 1810, were considered by Beethoven to be the 'best preparation for his own works', receiving praise in the next generation from Schumann. Czerny's *Complete Theoretical and Practical Pianoforte School* op.500, although not published until 1839, codified earlier practices. The era of the Romantic virtuoso was properly launched with the publication of Chopin's two sets of études in 1833 and 1837 (though the earliest were composed in 1829). He combined the solution to a single technical problem (including rapid parallel 3rds, 6ths, or octaves in the same hand; black keys, large jumps) with works of intrinsic artistic merit, worthy of placement alongside any others in the concert repertory. Schumann's description of op.25 no.1 as 'a lovely picture in a dream' acknowledges Chopin's highly original figuration, in which 'it would be a mistake to suppose that he allowed us to hear every one of its small notes' (ex.10). He was equally adroit in studies that develop touch rather than bravura, especially evident in the three composed in 1839 for inclusion in Moscheles's *Méthode des méthodes*.

Ex.10 Chopin: op.25 no.1

The only 19th-century performer capable of doing justice to the expansive arpeggios of Chopin's op.10 no.1 was said to have been Franz Liszt, and it was he who carried the evolution of the Romantic pianist to its fever pitch. Beginning at the astonishingly early age of 15, and inspired by the example of Paganini, Liszt published between 1826 and 1849 (he retired from concert touring in 1848) almost three dozen studies encompassing a dazzling spectrum of keyboard effects, an achievement not supplemented until the publication of Debussy's 12 Etudes during World War I. The orchestral basis of these efforts is illustrated by the well-known *Mazeppa*, which demands three staves for the opening tune. A similar orchestral effect is imparted by the superhuman leaps in Liszt's transcription of Paganini's *La campanella*. Unlike Chopin's, Liszt's studies are peppered with improvisatory cadenzas and flourishes remarkable for their constant inventiveness. More than any other 19th-century figure, Liszt kept the tradition of improvisation alive, and there is no doubt that the printed version of the studies represent the distillation of years – perhaps even decades – of performance experience. The title 'transcendental' given to the best-known set (final version, 1852) proved an apt description of Liszt's technique, for only one that transcended the capabilities of virtually all his contemporaries could do justice to his own music.

Apart from a rash of studies, Liszt produced a bewildering array of works for solo piano, many of which underwent continuous revision during his lifetime, and many of which remain unavailable in any reliable modern edition. The proportion of 'salon music' among his output is far less than that found among such contemporaries as Thalberg and Henselt. Outstanding among the larger collections are the three volumes of *Années de pèlerinage*, aural mementos of Liszt's sojourn in Switzerland and Italy. His sources of inspiration were frequently literary (the three Petrarch sonnets) or scenic ('Au bord d'une source', 'Les cloches de Genève'), but are programmatic in only the most evocative sense. The 'fantasia quasi sonata' (the 'Dante' Sonata) that closes the second year is a large-scale work of tremendous intensity, in which the symbolic interval of the tritone serves as a unifying motto. The series of four 'Mephisto' waltzes presents a comprehensive catalogue of the demonic' devices that proved so attractive to Liszt. The work reckoned his most impressive in the 20th century has been the B minor Sonata (1852–3), which succeeds in harnessing technical brilliance to the architectural demands of four-movements-in-one. The sonata is perhaps Liszt's most impressive display of thematic transformation, built upon an edifice of five mostly cryptic and open-ended motifs. It would be a serious error, however, to overlook the tremendous investment made by Liszt in arrangements, transcriptions and works based on previous material. Most important among the latter are the 21 Hungarian Rhapsodies based on processed folk material, planting the seeds for the nationalistic movements at the end of the century. Liszt's high opinion of Schubert is reflected in the more than 60 song transcriptions, including the complete *Schwanengesang* and *Winterreise*. His many operatic transcriptions and paraphrases are now rarely heard, but in his own day they not only provided opportunity for technical display but served many of the functions of the gramophone. Liszt lavished considerable care upon such arrangements, and in his 'Reminiscences from Mozart's Don Juan' he left behind a graphic representation of technique as sexual conquest.

Although much has been made of Liszt's enthusiastic endorsement of Steinway's new overstrung models in the 1870s, the vast majority of his music for piano was composed during the period in which he endorsed the flat-strung Erards with equal enthusiasm. He even found time to provide testimonials for Chickering, and for the Bösendorfer with its old-style Viennese action. In any event, all the instruments used by Liszt were equipped with softer wire and more elastic accretions of felt and leather hammer coverings than 20th-century concert instruments. His long career spanned a phenomenal period in the piano's development, and he never tired of dreaming up new and seemingly unattainable effects, such as the 'vibrato assai' in his transcription of Schumann's *Widmung* (ex.11).

Ex.11 Liszt: Transcription of Schumann's *Widmung*

Liszt's achievements inspired both competitors and imitators. His sharpest competition in the late 1830s was from Thalberg, who dazzled audiences with his novel device of placing the melody in the thumbs while surrounding it with a sea of arpeggios, giving the impression that more than one piano was being played. Thalberg specialized in operatic paraphrases (that on Rossini's *Moïse* enjoyed particular popularity) and variations such as those on *God Save the King*; none of his extensive output remains in the active repertory today. A similar fate has befallen the transcriptions and salon pieces of two other celebrated virtuosos, Herz and Henselt. The most interesting and original pianistic figure next to Liszt in the mid-century was Alkan, who spent much of his life in obscurity. Novel (and sometimes epic) notions of structure and harmony have served to rekindle interest in Alkan's music, whose variety rivals that of his better known contemporaries. His virtuosity was uncompromising, at times requiring an almost superhuman stamina.

Brahms's virtuosity took Beethoven's 'Hammerklavier' as its starting-point, evidenced in the rhythms and proportions of his C major Sonata, published when he was scarcely 20. After the three early sonatas, however,

Brahms turned his attentions elsewhere. The chief focus during the late 1850s and 1860s was variation form. The 25 Variations and Fugue on a Theme of Handel op.24 injected new life into a genre virtually moribund since Beethoven's set for Diabelli four decades earlier. Brahms summarized his technique – more severe and less effect-orientated than that of Liszt – in two striking sets of variations on Paganini's Caprice no.24. Typical among the uncompromising problems aired are the 'blind' octaves in no.11 of the second book (ex.12). Beginning with the Eight Piano Pieces of op.76, published when he was in his mid-40s, Brahms focussed almost exclusively for the next 15 years on six groups of smaller pieces described variously as Capriccio, Intermezzo, Rhapsody, Ballade or Romanze. Although he occasionally included literary inscriptions (from Sternau over the Andante of the F minor Sonata, from Herder at the beginning of op.117), Brahms's fundamental allegiance remained with the absolute music tradition of the Viennese Classicists. Strife between him and the avant-garde advocates of Liszt and Wagner proved inevitable. A few of these shorter works fulfil the dramatic demands of sonata form (the B minor Capriccio and the B♭ Intermezzo from op.76), but Brahms relied most heavily, as had Chopin and Schumann before him, on the simple ternary scaffolding. If he rarely infused it with the endless flexibility of Chopin, Brahms's resourcefulness, particularly in matters of rhythm and phrase, rarely faltered. Regardless of mood, he gravitated towards the middle and lower registers of the piano, preferring chains of closely spaced, poignant dissonance to clearly articulated textures. In spite of opportunities to experiment with the newer, high-leverage actions, Brahms remained loyal until the very end to the Viennese models that soon after his death were to pass into obscurity. He remains one of the few composers in the Western tradition for whom nostalgia for a bygone era provided a fresh and original impulse.

Ex.12 Brahms: op.35

non legato e scherzando

5. 19TH-CENTURY NATIONAL TRENDS. By the 1870s the piano and its literature had attained a pre-eminence unrivalled both in the salons of the upwardly mobile middle class and on the concert stage. It claimed a repertory from Bach to Brahms that was, and remains, beyond comparison in its scope and its extent. To expect the flood of masterpieces that had issued forth for almost a century to continue indefinitely would have been unrealistic even had it not been that the piano's popularity reached a peak, to be followed by a shift of focus back to the orchestra. The piano continued to inspire composers and performers alike, but much of the activity now took place beyond the main arenas of Germany, Austria and France.

In Mozart's time there had been relatively little distinction between teaching or domestic pieces (sonatas, variations) and those intended for public consumption (primarily concertos and chamber music). After Beethoven's death the emphasis among professionals on the development of a 'superhuman' technique (assisted by mechanical aids such as finger stretchers and dumb keyboards) led to a bifurcation of the solo repertory. A few major composers like Schumann attempted to fill the void with instructional cycles of high quality (*Album für die Jugend*); others such as Stephen Heller, who also composed large quantities of ambitious music, are remembered primarily for a steady stream of undemanding pieces aimed at the amateur market.

As in opera and orchestral music, nationalist piano music betrayed considerable western European influences, particularly that of Liszt. Almost all the Russians wrote for piano. The salon pieces of Glinka, Borodin and Rimsky-Korsakov are surpassed in interest by those of Tchaikovsky, but it was two other Russians who made the major contributions. Perhaps the most original of these was Musorgsky's *Pictures at an Exhibition* (1874), a series of tableaux inspired by paintings of Victor Hartmann and linked by a recurring promenade theme in 5/4 metre. The writing, both stark and colourful, captures the folk flavour more effectively than Ravel's opulent orchestration. Balakirev's *Islamey* (two versions, 1869 and 1902) has acquired a certain status as the technically most demanding work in the virtuoso repertory – too difficult for even its composer, an accomplished pianist – but it is also skilfully written and dramatically effective.

The English-speaking world boasted its most successful 19th-century keyboard composer in Sterndale Bennett, most of whose music is unknown today. Admired by Schumann and Mendelssohn, and himself a great admirer of Beethoven, Bennett developed a piano style that avoided empty display but made considerable demands upon the performer, and maintained most interest in shorter forms. The American MacDowell, like most of his countrymen, received a thoroughly European training that included the encouragement of Liszt and Raff. Though remembered primarily for the *Woodland Sketches* (1896), an amiable series of portraits in the spirit of Schumann, he composed a substantial amount of ambitious music including four sonatas and more than two dozen concert études; the best of this repertory is receiving more frequent hearings today, especially in the USA.

The greater publicity accorded to the French impressionists has served to obscure the unique achievements of Spanish composers at the end of the century. It is easily forgotten that Albéniz's style was already well-formed before Debussy wrote his most important piano works. He enjoyed good relations with both Debussy and Ravel; the influences among the three composers were mutual. Albéniz's major keyboard works, beginning with *La vega* (1897) and culminating in the four books of his *Suite Iberia* (1905–9), were contemporary with important keyboard works of Debussy. Though not as subtle structurally, these pieces are marked by spontaneity and novel figurations, including skilful evocations of both guitar and castanet. Albéniz's countryman Granados excelled in the best tradition of salon music, as in the seven *Valses poeticos*, but his most important publication was the series of *Goyescas* (1911) stimulated by his favourite painter. The best work of Falla and Turina builds upon the achievements of Albéniz and Granados.

Ex.13 Franck: *Prélude, choral et fugue*

Born in the year that Beethoven completed his *Missa solemnis*, the Belgian César Franck did not complete his two most important piano works, the *Prélude, choral et fugue* (1884) and the *Prélude, Aria et Final* (1887), until Romanticism was about to enter its twilight. In the former especially, he succeeded in tempering a Lisztian technique and cyclic procedures to solemn purpose, often recalling (and almost demanding) an organ pedal board. Though greatly influenced by Wagner, Chabrier is often most characteristic in his piano pieces, which contributed in France to the emancipation of dissonance and the interest in modal melodies. Neither Saint-Saëns, Dukas nor D'Indy invested their solo piano music with anything like the interest of their orchestral compositions (and, in Saint-Saëns' case, of his keyboard concertos).

The most important French composer for solo piano in the generation before Debussy was Fauré. Although he cultivated the by now celebrated genres of Chopin (especially the nocturne, impromptu and barcarolle), he brought to each a highly idiosyncratic figuration based upon equal importance of the hands and free polyphony within an arpeggiated background. Unlike much late Romantic keyboard music, Fauré's character-pieces sound less difficult than they are but repay careful study. While Debussy was still writing in a post-Romantic style his contemporary Erik Satie was setting down the three *Gymnopédies* (1888) that, in their sardonic simplicity, helped stake out the composer's iconoclastic position in French musical life. These were succeeded by more than a dozen sets of humorous piano pieces with provocative titles like *Sonatine bureaucratique*; more than his actual music, Satie's acerbic unpretentiousness has exercised considerable influence on 20th-century composers like John Cage.

6. THE GROWTH OF PIANISM, 1900–1940. If the 20th century has so far produced less music for the piano than did the 19th or 18th, the range of its achievement, in terms of widening the expressive potential of the instrument, is notable. With the single exception of Bartók, no composer has contributed to the repertory to anything like the same extent as did Haydn, Mozart, Beethoven or Schubert. Nevertheless, there has been more written for the piano since 1900 than for any other solo instrument, and it is possible to chart the main lines of 20th-century musical thinking from a study of the piano music alone, particularly since a number of composers (including Debussy, Bartók, Schoenberg, Boulez and Stockhausen) have made some of their most important stylistic discoveries through their keyboard works.

Although it may appear that Bartók was the most radical of the early 20th-century composers in attitude to keyboard technique, Debussy, barely a generation his senior, represents an even more fundamental secession from the 19th-century Austro-German pianistic tradition. His imaginative disregard of the essentially percussive qualities of the instrument enabled him to develop a new pianism, dependent on sonority rather than attack, on subtle dynamic shading rather than sustained cantabile. His own playing was evidently notable for its range of colour within a *pianissimo* dynamic (aided by the use of both pedals) and this is reflected in a Chopinesque notation that details every nuance of touch, as well as of dynamics and phrasing. Although precise indications of pedalling are rare, Debussy's use of sustained bass notes reveals a new awareness of the possibilities of the sustaining pedal and of the minute differences that can obtain between the total clarity of legato pedalling and the total blurring of undamped strings (see ex.14).

Ex.14 Debussy: *La terrasse des audiences du clair de lune*

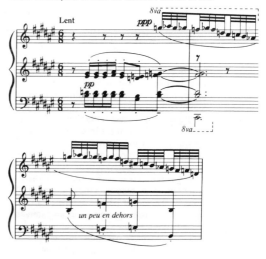

Ravel's more traditional virtuosity, however, marries this new impressionism to a bravura inherited from Liszt, developing a characteristic brilliance of keyboard usage that was, in turn, to have as great an influence on Bartók as were Debussy's more far-reaching experiments in keyboard sonority. As early as 1911, Bartók was stressing the percussive aspect of the instrument through the use of ostinato rhythms; this 'xylophonic' approach was later extended to embrace the more vibraphone-like qualities of a *laissez vibrer* that made expressive use of the suspension and decline of a sound as well as of its initial attack. He was also to continue a Beethovenian investigation of the sharply defined contrasts possible within the instrument's wide dynamic range, and of the contrasts in sound quality suggested by its high, middle and low registers. He continued Debussy's exploration of the resonances obtainable from overlapping harmonies coloured by the sustaining pedal, which later proved equally important in the light of the instrumental techniques proposed by such composers as Messiaen, Boulez and Stockhausen.

Debussy's most important contribution to contemporary pianism resulted from his refusal to acknowledge the essentially mechanical limitations of the instrument, but Ives was to make his contribution through a disregard for the limitations of the ten fingers of the pianist, some of his chords necessitating the assistance of a third hand or of the pianist's arms. If Ives was a prophet ahead of his time, his almost exact contemporary, Rakhmaninov, while making a sizable contribution to piano literature, proved much less significant in relation to the future of both musical thought and keyboard technique. Similarly, Prokofiev's nine sonatas and numerous smaller pieces are characteristic of his own stylistic scope and Lisztian virtuosity rather than indicative of future developments. The same is true of the works of other important composers of piano music during the first three decades of the century, including those of Valen, Pijper, Dohnányi, Martinů, Casella, Skalkottas, Shostakovich and, most notably, Hindemith.

Although he was not a pianist, Schoenberg made his two most important musical discoveries, that of atonality and, later, of 12-note composition, through the medium of the piano. The last of the Three Pieces op.11 (his first work for solo piano) was confidently cast in a language that owed little either to the impressionistic colouring of contemporary French music or to the more Romantic, large-scale gestures of the late 19th-century Austro-German keyboard composers. The massive stretch of its atonal counterpoint, combined with the extreme contrasts of its fleeting textures and eruptive dynamics (in addition to the exploration of keyboard harmonics in the first piece) remained unique for almost 40 years, until overtaken by still more demanding techniques after World War II. Equally significant in the trend away from Romantic rhetoric, his Six Little Pieces op.19 explore the expressive qualities of the instrument (mostly at the lowest end of the dynamic range) with a restraint more typical of his friend and pupil, Webern, whose single mature work for the piano was such a major landmark. Webern's Variations op.27 renounce the grandiose technical obsessions of the recent past to return to a much earlier conception of instrumental music as an extension of, and almost indistinguishable from, vocal music. The essential simplicity of the piece becomes complex through the continual overlap of wide-ranging contrapuntal lines (and thus of the pianist's hands), demanding a new technical approach to extended part-writing, as well as to the delicate balance between harmonic and rhythmic phrasing (see ex.15). Webern's piece, with its structural finesse and 'abstracted' *espressivo*, has cast its benevolent shadow on all subsequent composers of piano music.

Stravinsky's pianistic influence extends well beyond the few works he originally wrote for keyboard; not least

Ex.15 Webern: Variations, op.27

because he was one of the first composers to establish the piano as an orchestral instrument (Symphony in Three Movements, *Petrushka*, *The Wedding*). His piano (or piano duet) versions of many of his orchestral works are, in effect, original pianistic conceptions, such was his instinctive feeling for the characteristic spacing of keyboard sonorities.

During the 1920s the American composer Henry Cowell, then regarded merely as an interesting eccentric, began to experiment with hand and arm clusters as a means of colouring and outlining his melodic shapes and of creating harmonic 'areas' rather than defined chords. In addition to these keyboard effects he explored the production of sounds directly from the strings themselves, either as pizzicatos; as glissandos on single strings or across the strings (as in *The Banshee*) or in conjunction with silently depressed keys (in order to produce glissando chords, as in *Aeolian Harp*); or as harmonics, produced by the simultaneous 'stopping' of relevant strings.

7. AFTER WORLD WAR II. The possibilities explored by Cowell were woven by John Cage into the aleatory fabric of his most substantial work for piano, *Music of Changes*. Cage also undertook a more radical examination of the piano as a resonating body: the accompaniment to his song, *The Wonderful Widow of Eighteen Springs*, is rendered entirely on various parts of the frame, which is made to resonate in sympathy with the strings by depressing the sustaining pedal. Moreover, he transformed the basic sound quality of the instrument by a 'prepared' extension of its timbral possibilities: by forcing certain strings to vibrate against wedges made of various materials (metal, wood, rubber etc), Cage opened up a range of keyboard sonorities limited only by the possible damage to the instrument. This, in turn, led to as many variations in the basically harp-like sound of the strings themselves. Robert Sherlaw Johnson has used timpani sticks to stunning effect (in his second sonata), as well as other types of beater; plectra of differing weights and materials have also been used (the eerie sound of a nail-file glissando in Gerhard's *Gemini* is a good example), as have wooden blocks of varying widths (used by David Bedford to produce string clusters in *Piece for Mo*). Bedford has also made weirdly fascinating use of rotating glass milk bottles (at the end of his song *Come in here, child*). The palette of available pianistic colour has continued to be expanded and refined, notably in the chamber works of the American George Crumb, whose (gadgetless) effects are completely viable, often beautiful and never gimmicky.

It seems unlikely, however, that such methods of sound production can become established ingredients of instrumental technique unless manufacturers standardize the shape of the piano's mechanical structure. Because strings freely available on one make of instrument may be hidden or separated by crossbars on another, it is often impossible to carry out the composer's instructions to the letter. In any case, a whole new range of 'string' techniques would need to be developed and practised by the pianist. It is perhaps indicative of the lack of sophistication with regard to these techniques that the two postwar composers to have written the most substantial number of piano works, Boulez and Stockhausen, have so far ignored these more peripheral possibilities, as indeed have the majority of other important contributors to the mid-20th-century repertory, including Barber, Sessions, Copland, Feldman, Tippett, Maxwell Davies and Messiaen.

Even the most opulent of Messiaen's recent scores have a muscular background related to the kind of rhythmic counterpoint first developed in his *Modes de valeurs et d'intensités* (1949), in which the basic idea of a rhythmic ostinato was widened into an 'ostinato system' of serial control over the separate elements of duration, dynamics and attack as well as of pitch. This made almost insuperable demands on the performer (as, later, did Boulez's *Structures* for two pianos and Stockhausen's early piano pieces) since such minute degrees of expressive and rhythmic definition, within lines 'broken' by extremes of pitch, are scarcely realizable except by electronic means (see ex.16). The intellectual strictures of Messiaen's early works eventually merged with a freer, unmistakable pianism in his *Cantéyodjayâ* and later in the vast *Catalogue d'oiseaux*, creating a range of keyboard colour as pervasive in its influence on the works of younger composers as was that of Bartók or Stravinsky on the music of an earlier generation.

Boulez's three sonatas and Stockhausen's *Klavierstücke* (all dating from the late 1940s and 1950s) stand as models of contemporary keyboard writing, as yet

Ex.16 Messiaen: *Mode de valeurs et d'intensités*

unsurpassed in the variety of their neo-virtuosity or in the range of their textural contrasts and expressive sonorities. Musically they display a sharp-edged violence whose stinging contrasts require a comparably 'honed' performing technique – so that these pieces (which had at first seemed unplayable) have had the effect of enlarging the scope and the standards of virtuoso pianism. They have demanded an increase in pianistic speed and agility in order to encompass complex counterpoint (whether of lines or chords) often involving hand-crossing to an extent that even Webern would not have regarded as possible. They also require an ability to define each degree of a dynamic palette that extends from *ppp* to *fff* and beyond, in combination with as many varieties of touch or attack. In the case of Stockhausen, these controls must additionally be linked to an ability to play

Ex.17 Stockhausen: *Klavierstück X*

Clusterglissandi schnell und leicht ohne Rücksicht auf nicht ansprechende Tasten

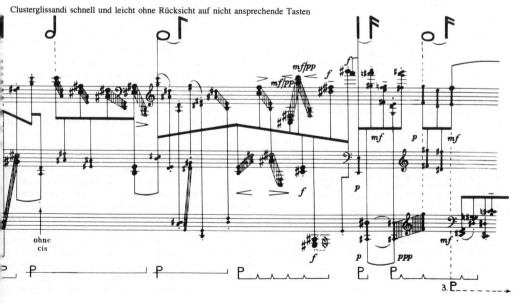

cluster chords of precisely defined exterior limits, whether these take the form of single attacks, arpeggiated decorations or multiple glissandos (see ex.17). Moreover, all these new technical requirements involve asymmetrical shapes that need to be mastered as thoroughly as symmetrical scales and arpeggios.

In such works, and in pieces by such stylistically diverse composers as Barraqué, Dallapiccola, Berio, Pousseur, Xenakis, Carter and Cage, pedal technique is no longer left to the good taste of the performer but must comply with the specific demands of the score. The use of the sustaining pedal has become as integral to musical expression as dynamics or phrasing: techniques such as half-pedalling, 'after'-pedalling (catching the resonance of a chord after releasing the attack) and 'flutter'-pedalling (effecting the gradual release of an attack) have become commonplace. An increasing number of works (Boulez's Sonata no.3, Stockhausen's *Klavierstücke V–XI* and Berio's *Sequenza IV*, for instance) also require the use of the sostenuto (centre) pedal on concert instruments to free selected strings from the damping mechanism, so allowing them to vibrate in sympathy with any other notes which may be sounded. Berio's *Sequenza IV*, built on the ground bass effect of such sustained notes or chords continually reinforced by the movement of the decorations superimposed on them, provides an ideal study in the use and management of the centre pedal.

BIBLIOGRAPHY

GENERAL REFERENCE

W. Niemann: *Das Klavierbuch: Geschichte der Klaviermusik und ihre Meister* (Leipzig, 1922)

E. Blom: *The Romance of the Piano* (London, 1928)

D. F. Tovey: *Essays in Musical Analysis* (London, 1935–9)

A. Lockwood: *Notes on the Literature of the Piano* (Ann Arbor and London, 1940)

A. Loesser: *Men, Women and Pianos* (London, 1940)

W. Georgii: *Klaviermusik* (Zurich and Freiburg, 1941, 4/1965)

D. Brook: *Masters of the Keyboard* (London, 1946)

E. Hutcheson: *The Literature of the Piano* (New York, 1948, rev. 2/1964/R1973)

J. Friskin and I. Freundlich: *Music for the Piano . . . from 1580 to 1952* (New York, 1954/R1973)

J. Gillespie: *Five Centuries of Keyboard Music* (Belmont, Calif., 1965/R1972)

F. E. Kirby: *A Short History of Keyboard Music* (New York, 1966)

K. Wolters: *Handbuch der Klavierliteratur*, i (Zurich and Freiburg, 1967)

M. Hinson: *Keyboard Bibliography* (Cincinnati, 1968)

D. Matthews, ed.: *Keyboard Music* (London, 1972)

M. Hinson: *Guide to the Pianist's Repertoire*, ed. I. Freundlich (Bloomington, Ind., 1973) [comprehensive bibliography]

D. Gill, ed.: *The Piano* (London, 1981)

SPECIFIC STUDIES

E. J. Dent: 'The Pianoforte and its Influence on Modern Music', *MQ*, ii (1916), 271

A. Cortot: *La musique française de piano* (Paris, 1930–48; i–ii, Eng. trans., 1932)

C. Parrish: *The Early Piano and its Influence on Keyboard Technique and Composition in the Eighteenth Century* (diss., Harvard U., 1939)

J. F. Russell: 'Mozart and the Pianoforte', *MR*, i (1940), 226

N. Broder: 'Mozart and the Clavier', *MQ*, xxvii (1941), 422

E. Reeser: *De zonen van Bach* (Amsterdam, 1941; Eng. trans., 1946)

C. Parrish: 'Haydn and the Piano', *JAMS*, i/1 (1948), 27

J. Kirkpatrick: 'American Piano Music: 1900–1950', *MTNA Proceedings*, xliv (1950), 35

F. H. Garvin: *The Beginning of the Romantic Piano Concerto* (New York, 1952)

D. Stone: *The Italian Sonata for Harpsichord and Pianoforte in the Eighteenth Century (1730–90)* (diss., Harvard U., 1952)

A. G. Hess: 'The Transition from Harpsichord to Piano', *GSJ*, vi (1953), 75

K. Dale: *Nineteenth Century Piano Music* (London, 1954) [foreword by Myra Hess]

H. F. Wolf: *The 20th Century Piano Sonata* (diss., Boston U., 1957)

E. Blom: 'The Prophesies of Dussek', *Classics Major and Minor* (London, 1958), 88

N. Demuth: *French Piano Music* (London, 1958)

T. L. Fritz: *The Development of Russian Piano Music as Seen in the Literature of Mussorgsky, Rachmaninoff, Scriabin, and Prokofiev* (diss., U. of Southern California, 1959)

P. F. Ganz: *The Development of the Etude for Pianoforte* (diss., Northwestern U., 1960)

J. Lade: 'Modern Composers and the Harpsichord', *The Consort*, xix (1962), 128

W. S. Newman: *The Sonata in the Classic Era* (Chapel Hill, 1963, rev. 3/1983)

E. Badura-Skoda: 'Textural Problems in Masterpieces of the Eighteenth and Nineteenth Centuries', *MQ*, li (1965), 301

T. A. Brown: *The Aesthetics of Robert Schumann in Relation to his Piano Music 1830–1840* (diss., U. of Wisconsin, 1965)

L. D. Stein: *The Performance of Twelve-tone and Serial Music for the Piano* (diss., U. of Southern California, 1965)

M. J. E. Brown: 'Towards an Edition of the Pianoforte Sonatas', *Essays on Schubert* (New York, 1966), 197

K. Heuschneider: *The Piano Sonata in the 18th Century in Italy* (Cape Town, 1966)

D. L. Arlton: *American Piano Sonatas of the Twentieth Century: Selective Analysis and Annotated Index* (diss., Columbia U., 1968)

M. K. Ellis: *The French Piano Character Piece of the Nineteenth and Early Twentieth Centuries* (diss., Indiana U., 1969)

E. Glusman: *The Early Nineteenth-century Lyric Piano Piece* (diss., Columbia U., 1969)

W. S. Newman: *The Sonata since Beethoven* (Chapel Hill, 1969, rev. 3/1983)

K. Michałowski: *Bibliografia chopinowska 1849–1969* (Kraków, 1970)

W. S. Newman: 'Beethoven's Pianos Versus his Piano Ideals', *JAMS*, xxiii (1970), 484

H. Truscott: 'The Piano Music – I', *The Beethoven Companion*, ed. D. Arnold and N. Fortune (London, 1971)

K. Michałowski: 'Bibliografia chopinowska 1970–1973', *Rocznik chopinowski*, ix (1975), 121–75

E. Badura-Skoda: 'Prolegomena to a History of the Viennese Fortepiano', *Israel Studies in Musicology*, ii (1980), 77

HOWARD FERGUSON (I), GLYN JENKINS (II)
ROBERT WINTER (III, 1–5), SUSAN BRADSHAW (III, 6–7)

Keyed bugle [key bugle, Kent bugle, Royal Kent bugle, Kent horn, etc] (Fr. *bugle à clefs, trompette à clefs, cor à clefs*; Ger. *Klappenhorn, Klappenflügelhorn*; It. *cornetta a chiavi*; Dutch *Klephoorn*). A conical, wide-bore, soprano brass instrument, with side-holes controlled by keys similar to those found on woodwind instruments. It is classified as a trumpet, and is the precursor of the modern flugelhorn.

Keyed bugles are important in the brass band movement on both sides of the Atlantic. Early examples had only five keys, but keyed bugles with up to 12 keys are found. The key closest to the bell of the instrument is the only one that remains open when the instrument is at rest. Some later instruments have a whole-tone valve in place of the E and F key. Short, double-wound models are found. Most early keyed bugles were pitched in C with a crook to B♭; later, others appeared in high E♭.

Most keyed bugles were made of copper with brass or German silver keys and fittings; instruments made of solid silver, gold and tortoiseshell also exist. Most of the fingering systems are extensions of the original concept, but the instruments made by Kersten of Dresden are notable exceptions: here an attempt was made to divide the arrangement of six keys equally between the hands. Keyed bugle mouthpieces are similar to those used on modern flugelhorns and 19th-century cornets in that they have a deep and conical cup. The mouthpieces are made of brass or ivory and are sometimes silver-plated. The rims tend to be flatter and sharper in shape than modern ones. As a result of the wide conical bore and the deep conical mouthpiece, a very mellow and woolly sound is produced, similar to but not identical

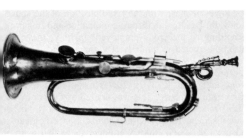

*. Keyed bugle by Metzler & Co., London, c1820–40
(Horniman Museum, London)*

with the sound of the modern flugelhorn. Because of
the sonic phenomena associated with venting, the keyed
bugle has a unique timbre.

The bandmaster of the Cavin Militia, JOSEPH HALIDAY,
added five keys to the common military bugle in Dublin
in 1810. Haliday's patent (British patent no.3334) is dated
5 May 1810. Shortly after the instrument's invention,
Haliday is believed to have sold the patent rights to the
Dublin maker Matthew Pace for £50. It must have been
about this time that a sixth key was added. While Haliday was stationed in Wexford with his band, J. B. Logier
wrote his *Introduction to the Art of Playing on the Royal
Kent Bugle* (1813), dedicating it to the Duke of Kent.
It is probable that Logier made Haliday's 'bugle horn'
commercially successful by stamping 'Royal Kent Bugle'
on instruments sold to military bandsmen (which Haliday, as a nationalist Irishman, was unlikely to have
done). Haliday attempted to discredit Logier, but he no
longer had control of his invention.

One of the most famous English keyed bugle players
was John Distin, whose playing may have inspired keyed
bugle obbligato parts in some English operas of the period. Many English orchestral trumpeters also played the
keyed bugle. Thomas Wallis of the Covent Garden
orchestra of 1818 was paid 9s. 2d. per night with an
extra 5s. when required to play the keyed bugle. John
Hyde, who was the first trumpet in the King's Theatre
orchestra, was a fine keyed bugle player and wrote a
method book for it.

Keyed bugles were commonplace in most British bands
by the time of the Allied occupation of Paris in 1815.
After Grand Duke Konstantin of Russia heard Distin
playing with the Grenadier Guards Band, he asked the
Parisian instrument maker Halary (Jean Hilaire Asté) to
duplicate the English instruments. Halary's instrument
French patent no.1849, 1821) extended the idea of the
keyed bugle to a whole consort of instruments, the tenor
and bass members of which he called ophicleides. In
1822 a rider was attached to the original patent allowing
for an even greater range of instruments, some of which
were apparently never produced. Halary's instruments
were approved by the Académie des Beaux-Arts, and
the Athénée des Arts awarded him a medal for his
achievement. This provoked a surge of keyed bugle
making in London and the main European musical centres
as well as in the USA. The American names of Graves
and E. G. Wright and the British firms of Percival, Pace
and Köhler represent a high standard of craftsmanship;
many beautiful instruments survive in museums and private collections.

In Germany, catalogues mention *Klappenhorn* or
Klappenflügelhorn quite frequently among listings of

military and wind music, but it appears that the keyed
bugle was not considered seriously as an orchestral or
solo instrument. However, the keyed bugle met with
great success in the USA where famous soloists like
Richard Willis (the first director of the West Point Military Academy Band), Frank Johnson (a black bandmaster in Philadelphia) and Edward ('Ned') Kendall (the
last of the legendary keyed bugle soloists) performed
solos and band pieces that were to establish an important band music tradition. The earliest documented use
of the keyed bugle in the USA occurred in 1815. Many
performers received ornate gift or presentation bugles:
Frank Johnson was given a handsome silver bugle by
Queen Victoria; some performers are known only through
the inscriptions on the bugles they were given.

Kendall's famous duel with the great cornet player
Patrick Gilmore in 1856 has been thought to signal the
demise of the popularity of the keyed bugle in the USA.
Before then, however, both valved and keyed instruments co-existed in many bands. By the 1840s most bands
were supplied with valved instruments. Keyed bugles
were, however, still used on both sides of the Atlantic
up to the mid-1860s.

Most method books for the keyed bugle contain a brief
section on the instrument's technique, a fingering chart
and possibly a few basic exercises followed by a selection of operatic airs and popular tunes of the day (in
solo and duet form). Band arrangements with parts for
keyed bugle are common in catalogues of the period.
Contemporary programmes indicate that vocal solos with
keyed bugle obbligato were quite popular, but few

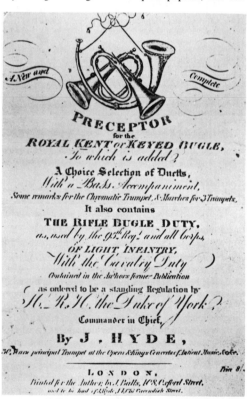

*2. Title-page of J. Hyde's 'A New and Complete Pre-
ceptor for the Royal Kent or Keyed Bugle' (c1818)*

selections were actually published in this format. An example of this type of parlour literature is a ballad by T. Phillips, entitled *The Last Bugle* (Philadelphia, 1822). The keyed bugle was assigned important parts in a number of operas including Bishop's *The Miller and his Men* (1813) and *Guy Mannering* (1816), Phillips's *The Opera of the Russian Imposter* (1822), Rossini's *Semiramide* (1823) and Kreutzer's *Ipsiboé* (1824). The parts for *trompettes à clefs* in the Paris score of Rossini's *Guillaume Tell* and in Meyerbeer's *Robert le diable* were, according to Dauverné, played on valved instruments and not the keyed bugles that the score indicated. At least two substantial works for solo bugle and orchestra are known, A. P. Heinrich's *Concerto for Kent Bugle or Klappenflügel* (1834) and Joseph Küffner's *Polonaise pour le cor de signal-à-clef obligée* (1823).

See also REGENT'S BUGLE.

BIBLIOGRAPHY

J. B. Logier: *Introduction to the Art of Playing on the Royal Kent Bugle* (Dublin, 1813, rev. 2/c1820–23)
J. Hyde: *A New and Complete Preceptor for the Royal Kent or Keyed Bugle* (London, c1818)
E. Goodale: *The Instrumental Director* (Hallowell, 3/1829) [only this edn. has keyed bugle instructions]
Noblet: *Nouvelle méthode de bugle* (Paris, 1831)
Z. T. Purday, ed.: *Tutor for the Royal Kent Bugle* (London, c1835)
Tully: *Tutor for the Kent Bugle* (London, c1838)
Scherer: *Méthode de bugle* (Paris, 1845)
B. A. Burditt: *The Complete Preceptor for the Bugle* (Boston, c1850)
H. B. Dodworth: *Dodworth's Brass Band School* (New York, 1853)
A. Carse: *Musical Wind Instruments* (London, 1939/R1965)
——: *The Orchestra from Beethoven to Berlioz* (Cambridge, 1948)
R. Morley-Pegge: 'Key Bugle', *Grove 5*
——: 'The Horn and Later Brass', *Musical Instruments through the Ages*, ed. A. Baines (Harmondsworth, 1961, 2/1966/R1976)
A. Baines: *European and American Musical Instruments* (London, 1966)
J. Wheeler: 'New Light on the Regent's Bugle, with some Notes on the Keyed-Bugle', *GSJ*, xix (1966), 65
R. E. Eliason: *Keyed Bugles in the United States* (Washington, DC, 1972)
——: *Graves & Company, Musical Instrument Makers* (Dearborn, Mich., 1975)
A. Baines: *Brass Instruments: their History and Development* (London, 1976/R1980)
R. E. Eliason: 'The Dresden Key Bugle', *JAMIS*, iii (1977)
R. T. Dudgeon: *The Keyed Bugle: its History, Literature and Technique* (diss., U. of California, San Diego, 1980)
——: 'Joseph Haliday, Inventor of the Keyed Bugle', *JAMIS*, ix (1983)

RALPH T. DUDGEON

Keyed harp. *See* HARP-PIANO.

Keyed monochord. *See* MONOCORDE À CLAVIER.

Keyed trumpet (Fr. *trompette à clefs*; Ger. *Klappentrompete*; It. *tromba a chiavi*). A trumpet, generally with two double bends held in a horizontal plane. In the type developed by the Austrian trumpeter Anton Weidinger (1766–1852), the keys are brought together on one side of the instrument so as to be operated by one hand only; the other hand merely holds the instrument. Austrian specimens are usually fingered with the left hand, Italian ones with the right. The keys cover soundholes, and when opened raise the pitch: the key nearest the bell by a semitone, the next by a tone, etc. Some trumpets have four, and some six keys, but five is the most common number (for illustration, *see* TRUMPET, fig.7*d*).

The first keyed trumpets were pitched in D and E♭. Later (c1820) they were made in G, A or A♭, with crooks for lower pitches; with the fixed position of the soundholes, this resulted in differing intonation and fingering, according to the crook employed. In Italy, they were also constructed in families of various sizes.

The first keyed trumpet was made in Dresden in c1770 (according to information in Schubart's *Ästhetik der Tonkunst*), and in 1791–2 Nessmann built a keyed trumpet in Hamburg. This was praised by Gerber (*Neues historisch-biographisches Lexikon*, 1812–14). In an advertisement for his 'Grand Public Concert' given in Vienna (28 March 1800) Weidinger stated that work on his 'organisirte Trompete', which had taken seven years, was finally accomplished. He also claimed the concert to be the first public performance on the instrument, which was equipped with several keys. However, in 1798 Weidinger had played in Kozeluch's *Symphonie concertante* for mandolin, trumpet, double bass, keyboard and orchestra at a public concert; the instrument used was called 'organisirte Trompete', so that the 'first performance' of 1800 must have been on a perfected model. The concert also included Haydn's Trumpet Concerto in E♭, written for Weidinger as early as 1796; the Kozeluch work is less demanding and less chromatic.

With Weidinger the keyed trumpet gained considerable success as a solo instrument. It was also used in military music from about 1820, especially in Austria and Italy, but towards 1840 it was superseded by the valve trumpet. Reconstructions of keyed trumpets have been made since 1971 by Adolf Egger of Basle and distributed by Meinl & Lauber.

The tone of the keyed trumpet is softer and less penetrating than that of the previously employed natural trumpet, frequently being compared with a sonorous oboe or clarinet.

The keyed trumpet is not to be confused with the KEYED BUGLE, a member of the flugelhorn family, although it, too, was often called *trompette à clefs*.

BIBLIOGRAPHY

A. Carse: *Musical Wind Instruments* (London, 1939/R1965)
P. Bate: *The Trumpet and Trombone* (London, 1966)
R. Dahlqvist: *The Keyed Trumpet and its Greatest Virtuoso, Anton Weidinger* (Nashville, Tenn., 1975)
——: *Bidrag till trumpeten och trumpetspelets historia från 1500-talet till mitten av 1800-talet* (diss., U. of Göteborg, 1984) [with Eng. summary]

REINE DAHLQVIST

Keylowtik [qilaun]. *See* KILAUT.

Keywork. The term used to denote collectively the various mechanical contrivances which have been devised to supplement the fingers in controlling the tone-holes of wind instruments. The function of a key is to enable finger pressure applied at a convenient point to open or close a hole of any required size in any required position. Without the prior existence of established principles of keywork, some modern instruments designed along rational acoustic lines, for example the saxophone or heckelphone, could not have been realized.

1. History. 2. Key structure. 3. Covers, pads and seatings. 4. Key body and touchpiece. 5. Mountings and springs.

1. HISTORY. From very early days the need has been felt to provide wind instruments with a more extensive and musically useful scale than the mere harmonic series proper to a tube of fixed length. The process of varying the 'effective length' of a tube by means of side-holes opened and closed by the fingers has been used empiri-

ally since the time of neolithic man, as shown for example by bone pipes preserved in his burial places, but the systematic disposition of such holes seems to belong to a much later cultural stage. The oldest surviving examples of organized side-hole arrays known at present are of Sumerian origin, and date from about 2800 BC. Thereafter deliberately positioned side-holes are found in instruments of successive cultures up to the eclipse of the Roman Empire and the coming of the Dark Ages but there is no sure evidence among them of any device in the nature of a key to supplement the fingers, unless the movable rings used on some Greek *auloi* to close off unwanted holes when playing in specific modes are accepted as such.

From the 12th century onwards there is some evidence of both reed pipes and flutes with six holes giving a diatonic scale of seven degrees, the octave being sounded by overblowing the lowest note. This organization also provided certain more or less satisfactory intermediate tones by the process of 'fork fingering'. In addition, the overall compass was sometimes extended by lengthening the tube and boring a further hole which could be stopped by the lowermost little finger. By the early 16th century such pipes were being made in various sizes paralleling the different ranges of the human voice and it was at this stage that practical difficulties began. The acoustic laws relating the size and position of side holes made possible the placing of the six primary holes in two fairly close-set groups of three, but this device could be carried only so far. By simple proportion the longer the tube the wider the spacing between holes necessary for reasonable intonation, which soon exceeds the stretch of the normal hand. On some instruments the player can adjust the pitch of certain notes by blowing; when the limit of this ability is reached mechanical assistance becomes essential.

The first primitive keys were most likely designed to assist the little finger; the oldest surviving authoritative illustrations, by Virdung (1511) and Hans Burgkmair (before 1531), show no other arrangement. Accounts of the Duke of Burgundy for 1423 and 1439 recording the purchase of 'bombardes à clef' and 'teneurs à clef' for the court, show that keys were in fact used nearly a century earlier. Teseo Ambrosio's account of the PHAGOTUS offers some proof that a more advanced application of simple keys existed by 1539 and Praetorius in *Theatrum instrumentorum* (1619) shows keys for the thumbs on both large shawms and bassoon types. From this period on there is growing evidence of an increasing use of simple mechanism, though at the end of the 18th century it remained somewhat crude and often inefficient. As late as 1815 Gustave Vogt, professor of oboe at the Paris Conservatoire, questioned the efficiency of keys and advocated using as few as possible. At that time instrument makers in Germany and Austria were already quite generous in providing them.

At least three centuries seem to have elapsed between the invention of keys for wind instruments and their application to improve the layout of the primary holes. Borjon de Scellery, in a celebrated plate published with his *Traité de la musette* (1672), did show a sort of bass oboe which appears to have something of the sort and a few similar instruments are preserved in continental museums as 'basses de musette', but these are thought to have been exceptional and their history is obscure. A bass transverse flute by J. Beuker in the Paris Conservatoire collection has two jointed open keys which

much improve the primary layout; the instrument has been somewhat questionably dated as late 17th century. Similar instruments employing simple second-order levers were illustrated by Diderot and d'Alembert in 1747 and were being made by Delusse of Paris in about 1760. In 1810 the London maker McGregor patented an instrument of this type and the principle was revived again by Siccama of London in 1847. These apparently unrelated recurrences of a single idea prove the difficulty of tracing clear and unbroken lines of development (if indeed such exist) with keywork as with many other features of musical instruments. There is unfortunately no authoritative instrumental historian between Agricola (published 1528 and later) and Praetorius (1619), a period rich in important developments. It is well to keep in mind that through natural conservatism or prejudice new devices were often slow to replace older, less efficient ones, and to avoid reading into slender evidence more than is warranted.

The use of keys to create a chromatic scale probably began about the last quarter of the 18th century, first with the transverse flute. Before that time fork fingering had furnished all the primary semitones except the lowest and with reed instruments, where this technique was quite satisfactory, it continued to do so for many more years; even today this process is of much service. Modern research has explained why the acoustic properties of the one-keyed flute make it more difficult to 'pull' into tune when fork fingered than was, for example, the 18th-century oboe, and no doubt this deficiency stimulated experiment with chromatic keys.

With the dawn of the 19th century a tremendous change began, and the period 1800–1850 saw rapid and brilliant progress. The ingenuity of such men as the Triéberts and Louis-Auguste Buffet in Paris, and Almenraeder, J. A. Heckel and Boehm in Germany, together with the skill of their workmen, had by mid-century established the principles of a keywork which today is completely reliable and little less responsive than the finger itself (for illustration *see* OBOE, fig. 10). With modern mechanism there seems at first sight to be no reason why the tone-holes of all wind instruments should not be placed exactly as theory demands. This apparent ideal is, however, seldom realized, for the following reason. Most of the tone-holes on the shawms, for example, and on their modified successors the true oboes, were made relatively small to compensate for the inevitable displacement imposed by the limited span of man's fingers. This applied even more to the bassoons and in turn gave rise to tonal qualities which became esteemed characteristics of these instruments and which it was found desirable to preserve. From time to time attempts have been made to design both oboes and bassoons with advanced keywork and tone-holes both disposed and sized according to geometrical ideals, but the resulting departure from traditional tone quality has made these instruments unacceptable to the great majority of players. The traditional timbre of instruments can nonetheless be preserved while by the aid of suitable mechanism some of the traditional fingering problems are smoothed out. Within the last few years a movement has been started in England to introduce oboes modified in this way for school music, but the outcome is still uncertain. The greatest benefit conferred on side-hole instruments by modern keywork is that each genre now has a complete family at different pitches, all consistent as to finger technique.

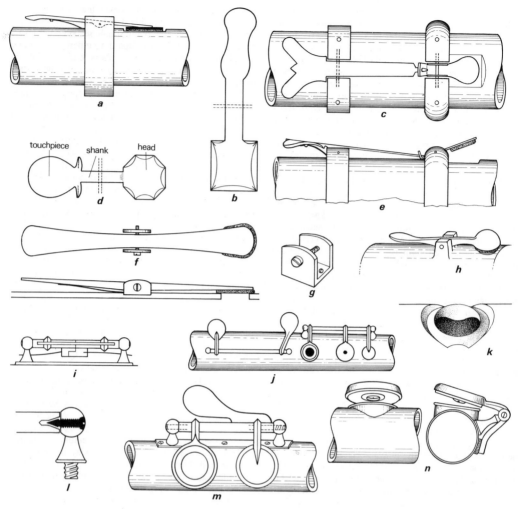

1. Examples of keywork from the 17th century to the 20th

2. KEY STRUCTURE. The function of a single key requires only a very simple mechanism; the highly complex equipment of many modern instruments is in fact only a combination of a number of such elements. In general a key consists of three essential parts: a plate or touchpiece for the finger; a second plate or cover for the hole, faced with some resilient material to ensure airtight closure; and a bar or shank uniting the other two parts. The shank may be in one piece or two, with an intermediate hinge, according to the action required. The whole is carried by one or two transverse pivots and is maintained in the position of rest by a spring. The mechanical principle is that of the simple lever of first, second or third order, depending on the relative disposition of the touchpiece, pivot and cover. There is practically no limit to the size, shape or arrangement of the three parts of a key but most commonly the touchpiece and the cover are attached to the body in line with each other, with the axis of the pivot set transversely. This layout is, however, not essential and about 1830 a most useful variant appeared in which the cover and the touchpiece are attached to the two ends of a long rod or tube carried

between point screws or threaded on a fixed axle. Keys of this sort are a great improvement on long levers where wide stretches have to be bridged, since they can be made more positive in action and are free from backlash; this type of key is still mechanically a simple lever. Keys are termed 'open' (fig.1e) or 'closed' (fig.1a) according to whether they open or stop the associated hole when at rest, and in identifying them it is customary to name them by the note sounded when the finger is applied, except in certain modern instruments where even the six primary holes are controlled by keys. Although it is not possible to trace unbroken lines of development in keywork generally or to assign firm dates in the earlier stages, the individual components of the simple key do show clear sequences of progress. As these changes appear to have been largely independent they will be considered separately.

3. COVERS, PADS AND SEATINGS. The cover of the earliest known key was simply a flat piece of metal, round or racquet-shaped, derived from the body of the key itself and faced with leather either sewn or cemented on. This

rangement persisted on lower-grade instruments even after improved forms had become general. The airtightness of such a key-cover depended entirely on the resilience of the facing material and little could be done to improve matters, except to flatten the tube surface around the hole (fig.1*a*). With the advent of the true oboes, musettes and jointed flutes which appeared in France at the end of the 17th century a considerable advance is seen. The key-heads were now either round or rectangular (fig.1*b*), still faced with plain leather but with the associated seatings much more strongly developed. By the end of the 18th century octagonal keys were fitted by many oboe makers who used characteristic ornament, datable by association (fig.1*d*). Occasionally seatings were omitted and the key itself curved to match the surface of the tube. Some makers of the early 19th century attached key-heads to the shank by a loose rivet or screw, thus allowing freer accommodation to the seating. The major objection to all plain key-leathers is their tendency to harden in use and lose their resilience. Richard Potter of London patented an ingenious solution in 1785 by which flute keys were made with conical plugs of soft pewter which fitted the holes closely, bearing either directly on the wood or on inserted metal bushes. The scheme had some success and survived on the foot keys of even superior flutes till the 1890s. The ideal solution, a resilient stopper analogous to the natural finger tip, was achieved before the middle of the 19th century with the first stuffed pads, or 'elastic plugs' as some makers called them. These were 'purses' of fine kid, filled with a ball of lamb's wool and drawn together with a thread. Such pads could accommodate themselves to any hole and even better results were obtained by providing a countersunk seating. As the pads could not easily be attached to flat cover-plates by shellac, the cement in common use, the key-heads were themselves modified to a hemispherical cup form, which also helped preserve the roundness of the pad (fig.1*h*). Stuffed pads themselves proved to have a defect: in use, they tended to bulge and 'shade' the tone-hole. The modern pad meets all requirements: it comprises a disc of card, a layer of felt and a covering of fine kid, animal membrane or waterproof plastic film, supported in a much shallower cup, closing on a raised collar in the wall of metal instruments (fig.1*n*); and on a conically recessed seating in non-metal instruments (fig.1*k*). It is either cemented into place or retained by a tiny screw and washer and its basic construction can be modified to provide ring-pads for instruments with perforated finger-plates.

4. KEY BODY AND TOUCHPIECE. In its first form the key body was simply cut out of sheet metal as were the cover-plate and the touchpiece; the pivot was a wire passing through bent-up and perforated lugs (*see* SHAWM, fig.4). This arrangement was somewhat delicate and was provided with protecting covers of wood or metal in almost all the earliest examples. The chief disadvantage of sheet construction, its lack of stiffness when of any considerable length, was soon countered by forming the metal into a channel or flattened tubular section (fig.1*f*). Cast or forged bar metal was used on the earliest clarinets (mid-18th century) for the long keys, sheet construction only for the smaller ones. Brass remained the usual metal for keywork through the early 19th century, with silver at times for superior instruments, but the advent of the white bronzes – generically known as German silver or nickel silver – in about 1830 brought many changes. These alloys, which can in different degree be cast, forged or pressed, and hard soldered, serve admirably for keywork: they polish well and can be silver- or even chrome-plated. In the later 19th century the hand production of standard-pattern keys in quantity flourished as a home industry in France, and this source of supply contributed much to the ability of French makers to sell instruments of decent quality at highly competitive prices. Exceptionally, keys have been made of hardwood and occasionally, in fairly recent times, of ivory.

The form of the touchpiece sometimes helps to date old woodwind instruments. The 'fishtail' shape may well indicate an origin before the firm adoption of 'left hand above right' in playing (fig.1*c*), though on oboes it survived as an ornament perhaps as late as 1830. The *d*♯′ keys on early flutes are also sometimes indicative of date. Of all the forms of touchpiece, the ring surrounding an open finger-hole (fig.1*j*) has had the most influence on modern keywork. First conceived by F. Nolan in 1808, it was most fully exploited by Boehm in his flute design of 1832 and was applied to the clarinet by Sax about 1840 as the well-known 'spectacle' or *brille*; it is now used on most woodwind instruments. A device which has proved a great boon to players on the simple-system clarinet and several types of bassoon is a small ebonite or ivory roller set into the adjacent edges of a pair of touchpieces, whereby sliding the finger from one to the other is greatly facilitated.

5. MOUNTINGS AND SPRINGS. However well designed a key may be, it will soon become a nuisance if its mounting is inefficient. The wire pivots of the first sheet-metal keys were held in place merely by a staple at each end driven into the tube wall. This somewhat precarious arrangement yielded in the later 17th century to a device by which the key shank lay in a slot cut in a ring (fig.1*a* and *c*), later reduced to a block (fig.1*h*), left standing above the surface of the body tube. A small hole bored tangentially through both ring and shank carried a close-fitting pivot pin. This arrangement is in fact efficient, if inelegant, and remained in use until the early 1900s. Ring or block mountings were easily formed as part of the basic wood-turning in the smaller instruments, but apparently not on the large, irregularly shaped joints of the bassoons, where they were abandoned, together with turned ornamentation, in the early 18th century; metal saddles of channel section, screwed or pinned to the joint, took their place (fig.1*g*). Saddles of this sort are often found with block mountings on oboes and clarinets and their presence has been taken to indicate additions or repairs to the original keywork. This may sometimes be so, but in many cases they were contemporary with the instrument and were adopted as a convenience in manufacture. On the other hand, wooden rings and blocks are known on oboes with as many as 12 keys, some of them interlocking and with alternative touches of modern form.

A device now fundamental to all keywork made its first appearance about 1800, on instruments of high quality. A pair of turned metal pillars is attached to a fitted metal footplate or screwed directly into the tube wall (fig.1*i*). The pivots associated with these pillars may be simple pins or more commonly, accurately made steel axles which screw into place and are capable of fine adjustment (fig.1*l*). In complicated keywork such as that of the Boehm flute several key bodies in the form of tubes can be carried on a single axle (fig.1*j*); in other cases, a solid rod is supported between point screws, one in each of the paired pillars (fig.1*m*).

The final element in efficient keywork is the return spring, which requires great accuracy of manufacture. It originally consisted of a leaf of hard brass fixed to the surface of the instrument body and pressing upwards or downwards as required against the key body. Later, springs of brass, then steel, were screwed or riveted to the key itself and, to reduce friction and wear, bore on slips of metal set into the tube. Leaf springs were effective only with lever-type keys, and were not easily applicable to those with tubular bodies; soon after these came into use the needle spring was invented, most probably by Buffet in Paris: a tempered wire of gold or steel is anchored in one of the pillars, while its free end bears on a tiny hook soldered to the key tube (fig.1*i*). The bias of such springs is very easily adjusted and they are widely used today on instruments of all sizes.

PHILIP BATE

Khabulubulu [kgabudubudu, kgabududu]. BULL-ROARER of southern Africa. *Khabulubulu* is attributed to the Southern Sotho people, the other terms to the Pedi (Northern Sotho). *See* SEVUVU.

Khāēn [kaen, khène, khen]. Bamboo mouth organ of Laos and north-east Thailand. It consists of a set of bamboo pipes grouped together in two rows and graduated from longest to shortest. The free reeds of copper and silver are mounted in the pipe walls inside a carved wooden windchest called *dao* ('gourd'). Any small openings around the windchest are caulked with a kind of beeswax called *kiroot*. Finger-holes are cut at convenient distances above the windchest so that all the fingers may be used to open and close the holes. *Khāēn* are made in four sizes: *khāēn hok* ('six'), a child's toy with six pipes; *khāēn jet* ('seven') with 14 pipes; *khāēn paet* ('eight') with 16 pipes; and *khāēn kao* ('nine') with 18 pipes. By the 1970s *khāēn paet* were nearly universal, measuring approximately one metre in length, although instruments measuring two to three metres were common in the 1920s. Although found throughout northeast Thailand, *khāēn* making is centred in Roi Et province and especially in the sub-district town of Sī kaeo. Most makers in Laos came from Thailand. *Khāēn* are properly held tilted to the left or right with the hands cupped over the windchest. The 16 pipes of the *khāēn paet* play 15 pitches (one doubled at the unison) within a range of two octaves consisting of semitones and whole tones averaging 100 and 200 cents respectively. Although there is certainly no Western influence, the pitches parallel the piano's naturals from *a* to *a''*, but their physical arrangement follows no recognizable pattern. Instead the pipes have been arranged to facilitate fingering and to avoid the technical problem of playing three consecutive pipes. Inhaling and exhaling produce identical pitches, but pipes sound only when finger-holes are covered.

The *khāēn* is related to other free-reed aerophones distributed in Asia from Japan to Thailand and from Bangladesh to Borneo. Best known is the Chinese SHENG (Japanese SHŌ (i)) whose metal or wooden bowl was formerly a gourd and whose circular form superseded the earlier raft form. The Hmong in Laos and southern China use a mouth organ with six tubes, each with a metal reed set into a carved wooden windchest (*see* LU

Khāēn paet (mouth organ with 16 pipes) player near Roi Et, Thailand

SHENG), while both Tibeto-Burman and Mon-Khmer upland groups on the mainland and certain tribes in Borneo use similar instruments with gourd windchests (*see* SUMPOTAN). Buffalo horns with a metal free reed on the concave side are found chiefly among the Karen of Burma, but they are also known to the Lao and Khmer. Lastly, side-blown free-reed pipes with and without gourd windchests are widespread, the latter found chiefly in Burma, the former in northern Thailand, among the Hmong, Phūthai and Khmer (*see* PĪ SŌ).

Whether playing solo or accompanying a singer, *khāēn* players, who are always male, have at their disposal five mode positions called *lai*, each an anhemitonic pentatonic scale. They are called *sutsanaen* (G–A–C–D–E), *bo sai* (C–D–F–G–A), *sọi* (D–E–G–A–B), *yai* (A–C–D–E–G) and *nọi* (D–F–G–A–C). Each *lai* requires certain drones produced by closing the finger-holes with either a finger or a piece of beeswax. Notes are played singly, in octaves, or in combination with other notes, usually as 4ths or 5ths (see ex.1). *Khāēn* players may accompany the *lam* scale with *sutsanaen*, *bo sai* or *sọi* and the *yao* scale with *yai* or *nọi* depending on the singer's range. Besides the five basic improvisations in each *lai*, there are others known to all competent players, for example *Māēng phū dọm dọk* ('Bees around the flowers'), *Lom phat sāi khao* ('The wind through the hills'), and *Lai rot fai* (an imitation of a steam engine). Modern players also imitate the many styles of Lao singing and invent new pieces, but all remain within the five *lai*. While *khāēn* players in Laos

.1 *Khāēn piece in bo sai*; rec. and transcr. T. Miller (Miller, 1977)

...se the same *lai*, they are not known as systematically ...s in Thailand. The *khāēn wong* ('ensemble') of six or ...more instruments commonly encountered in schools is ...f recent origin and plays only the classical songs of ...entral Thailand.

BIBLIOGRAPHY
R. de Berval, ed.: 'Présence du royaume Lao', *France-Asie*, xii (1956), 703–1153; Eng. trans., 1959 as *Kingdom of Laos* [incl. Souvanna-Phouma: 'La musique', 777; T. Kene: 'Le fabricant de *khène*', 897]
).. Yupho: *Khrūang dontri Thai* [Thai musical instruments] (Bang-kok, 1957, 2/1967; Eng. trans., 1960, 2/1971)
)obalee-koonoo-bamajan: *Rūang kaen* [The story of the *kaen*] (Bangkok, 1964)
A. M. Gagneux: 'Le khene et la musique Lao', *Bulletin des Amis du royaume Lao*, vi (1971), 175
Jarernchai Chonpairot: *Kaen Wong* [The *kaen* ensemble] (Maha-sarakam, Thailand, 1972)
K. Ratanavong: *Learn to Play the Khene* (Vientiane, 1973)
D. Morton: *The Traditional Music of Thailand* (Berkeley, 1976)
T. Miller: *Kaen Playing and Mawlum Singing in Northeastern Thai-land* (diss., Indiana U., 1977)

TERRY E. MILLER

Khais (pot drum) played by a Khoikhoi (Hottentot) woman: drawing (1834) by Charles Bell (Africana Museum, Johannesburg)

Khais [/khais, rommelpot, seckoa]. Pot drum of the Khoikhoi (Hottentot) people of southern Africa, men-tioned in 18th- and 19th-century writings. It was made of a wooden or clay milk pot (*bambus*) over which was tied a piece of deerskin or sheepskin. It was used by women to accompany singing and dancing (see illustra-tion), being played with the wetted fingers of the right hand. One report says pitch was regulated by pressure on the membrane with the left thumb and forefinger. See *KirbyMISA*, 14ff, pl.6.

DAVID K. RYCROFT

Khalam [halam, xalam]. Five-string plucked lute of the Wolof people of Senegal and the Gambia. It has a nar-row boat-shaped soundbox with a cowhide soundtable and an unfretted cylindrical neck. The neck emerges at the lower end of the soundtable and acts as the string bearer. The five strings, formerly made of horsehair but now made of nylon, are attached to the neck with leath-er tuning thongs. They are arranged in re-entrant tuning, with the string nearest the player's face being the high-est in pitch. The *khalam* belongs to a family of West African plucked lutes which is probably of ancient Egyptian origin. It is believed to be the ancestor of the banjo. In construction it is identical with the Mandinka *konting* and the Fula *hoddu*.

The *khalam* probably derives from the Mandinka *konting*, but its exact origins are obscure. Oral evidence suggests that it was introduced to the Wolof by profes-sional Mandinka musicians in the 19th century. Like the *konting* it is played exclusively by men from the profes-sional musician's caste (Wolof: *gewel*) as accompani-ment to praise song and historical narrative. It may also be played in instrumental duets. The strings are plucked with the thumb and forefinger, and the other fingers are used for strumming the strings or striking the sound-table. Only two of the strings are stopped against the neck; the others are played open. The *khalam* shares much of the repertory of the *konting*, and some of the choruses of the songs are in Mandinka. This may con-firm the theory that it is of Mandinka origin, but it could also be the result of Wolof musicians playing to both Wolof and Mandinka patrons. As the main melody instrument of the Wolof it enjoys great popularity today throughout Senegal. The majority of players come from the Sine-Saloum region on the north bank of the Gambia river. Other similar Wolof lutes are the *bappe*, *diassare* and *ndere*; other related lutes are the *kuntigi*, *nkoni*, *tidinit*.

BIBLIOGRAPHY
L. Durán: 'A Preliminary Study of the Wolof Xalam', *Recorded Sound*, lxxix (1981), 29
D. W. Ames: 'Wolof Music of Senegal and The Gambia', FE 4462 [disc notes]
T. Nikiprowetzky: 'La musique des griots du Sénégal', OCR 15 [disc notes]

LUCY DURÁN

Khamak. A term for two variable tension chordo-phones ('plucked drums') of Bengal (east India and Bangladesh). *See* ĀNANDALAHARĪ and GOPĪYANTRA.

Khánh. LITHOPHONE played in Vietnamese ritual music.

Khañjan [khañjanī]. A name of eastern India (Bengal and Orissa) and Bangladesh denoting either a pair of small cymbals (*see* MANDĪRĀ and KARTĀL, (2)) or a small

FRAME DRUM, with inset jingles, the same as the conical *khanjari* of north India and the *kañjīrā* of the south. It is used mostly in the accompaniments to religious songs, such as the Baul song of Bengal; in northern Orissa a class of song, *khañjanīgīt* ('tambourine songs'), relating to the local cults of Alekh and Mahimadharma, is named after it.

BIBLIOGRAPHY
B. K. Roy Choudhury: *Bhāratiya saṅgīt-koś* (Calcutta, 1965)
S. Ray: *Music of Eastern India* (Calcutta, 1973)
A. H. Saaduddin: 'Bangladesh', *Grove 6*
ALASTAIR DICK

Khanjari [khanjani, khañjarī]. Small FRAME DRUM or tambourine of the Indian subcontinent. In northern India, Pakistan and Nepal it is usually called *khanjari*, and in eastern India (Bengal, Orissa) and Bangladesh *khanjani* (for southern India, *see* KAÑJĪRĀ). Though similar to the ḌAPH frame-drum type, with glued or nailed skin on a circular wooden frame, the *khanjari* type is distinguished by its small size (13 to 25 cm in diameter) and proportionally deep and heavy frame; in many areas the frame flares or tapers, and some have inset metal disc jingles. In Rajasthan the term *khañjarī* denotes two different instruments: a circular frame drum (22 cm in diameter, 5 cm high) of wood in which are fixed small brass cymbals and whose head of sheepskin or cowhide is nailed on; and a drum on a slightly truncated conical frame of heavy wood over which is glued a snakeskin. Both drums are beaten with the hand. The first is used by mendicants to accompany songs and dances. The second is played, together with the *pūngī* (double clarinet), by nomadic snake-charmers called Kalbelia.

The *khanjani* of Bengal and Orissa is approximately 13 cm across and 8 cm deep and has a heavy wooden frame, usually outward-sloping and often inset with small cymbals; it is covered with iguana skin. The *khanjani* is especially prominent in Orissa, where it accompanies a class of religious song, the *khanjani bhajan* (relating to the cult of Alekh or Mahimadharma), which is named after the drum.

BIBLIOGRAPHY
C. Sachs: *Die Musikinstrumente Indiens und Indonesiens* (Berlin and Leipzig, 1914, 2/1923), 66
K. S. Kothari: *Indian Folk Musical Instruments* (New Delhi, 1968), 34f
S. Ray: *Music of Eastern India* (Calcutta, 1973)
K. Kothari: *Folk Musical Instruments of Rajasthan* (Borunda, 1977)
B. C. Deva: *Musical Instruments of India: their History and Development* (Calcutta, 1978), 73ff
ALASTAIR DICK, GENEVIÈVE DOURNON

Khap mai. Early ensemble of Thailand, now obsolete, consisting of *sǭ sām sāi* (spike fiddle), a *bandǫ* (hourglass drum) and a singer.

Khara. *See* KARAH.

Kharan dizau. Cylindrical drum of the Dimacha Kachari people of Nagaland, north-east India. It is played with the *mauri dizau* (oboe) to accompany folkdances.

Kha-rnga ('mouth drum'). JEW'S HARP of Tibetan origin, made from bamboo. It is used by young girls in the Tukucha region of Nepal. See G. Dournon-Taurelle and J. Wright: *Les guimbardes du Musée de l'Homme* (Paris, 1978).

'Khar-rnga. Tibetan gong. *See also* RNGA.

Khartāl. Wooden CLAPPERS of Rajasthan, north India. They consist of four separate rectangular wooden block 15 cm long and 5 cm wide. The player holds them i pairs across the palm of each hand and claps them together. The musicians of the Manganiyar caste, livin, in the desert regions of the west, use the *khartāl* with great virtuosity to add rhythmic patterns to a repertor of songs accompanied also by the *kamāicā* (fiddle; fc illustration *see* KAMĀICĀ). *See also* KARTĀL, (1).

BIBLIOGRAPHY
C. Sachs: *Die Musikinstrumente Indiens und Indonesiens* (Berli and Leipzig, 1914, 2/1923), 14f
K. S. Kothari: *Indian Folk Musical Instruments* (New Delhi, 1968; 23
K. Kothari: *Folk Musical Instruments of Rajasthan* (Borunda, 1977
B. C. Deva: *Musical Instruments of India: their History and Deve opment* (Calcutta, 1978), 55, 59
G. Dournon-Taurelle and J. Schwarz: 'Musiques du monde: le instruments de musique traditionnels', *LDX* 74675 [disc notes]
GENEVIÈVE DOURNON

Khas [kha:s, kxab]. Unbraced MUSICAL BOW with sep arate resonator, played by the Korana Hottentot (Khoi khoi) people of southern Africa. It consists of a simple bow with a string of twisted sinew. It is played by women. The player, being seated, rests one end of the stave on a dry skin bag or on some vessel, steadying it with the right foot. The upper end rests against her right shoulder. The string is struck with a stick. A second stopped fundamental can be obtained by pressing the chin against the string, and the second partials can be elicited by touching the string at mid-point. A second performer may strike the string lower down. The instrument is used for vocal accompaniment. See *KirbyMISA*, 211ff, pl.57a. *See also* SEKOKWANE and GAMAKHAS.
DAVID K. RYCROFT

Khashaba. Wooden GOBLET DRUM of Iraq.

Kha-wang. Metal JEW'S HARP of the Thakali people o Nepal. *See* MURCANG.

Khel. Double-headed drum of the Uraon tribe of eastern India. *See* MĀDAR.

Khen [khène]. *See* KHAĒN.

Khengereg [kenggerge]. Term used generally for drums in Mongolia, and especially for a suspended drum struck with a hooked beater (*dokhiur*) in Buddhist monasteries. *See also* BŌMBŌR; KHETS; KÖGÜRGE; RNGA.

Khets. Mongolian FRAME DRUM, known also as *dünger* and *khengereg*. It has a single deerskin head and is held by an interior wooden handle and struck with a wooden beater tipped with metal (*tsokhiur, orow*). The drum is made up of metal and wooden parts symbolizing the various organs of a deer. There are regional varieties of drum and stick, and some drums have a horse's head carved at the top of the handle. The drum is thought of as the mount that carries the invoked spirit to the shaman, or that carries the shaman to the spirit when he enters a trance. Among the Tsaatan people of northern Mongolia the frame and handle of the drum must be made of larch that has been struck by lightning.

BIBLIOGRAPHY
S. Badamkhatan: *Khövsgöliin tsaatan ardyn aj baidlyn toim* [A sketch of the life style of the Tsaatan (reindeer) people of Khubsugul] (Ulan Bator, 1962)

V. Diószegi: 'Ethnogenic Aspects of Darkhat Shamanism', *Acta orientalia hungarica*, xvi (1963), 55
S. Badamkhatan: *Khövsgöliin Darkhad Yastan* [The Darkhat tribe of Khubsugul] (Ulan Bator, 1965)   ANDREA NIXON

Khiil. Mongolian fiddle. *See* KHUUR and DÖRVÖN CHIKHTEI KHUUR.

Khim. (1) BOX ZITHER of Kampuchea, Laos and Thailand, with a trapezium-shaped soundbox. It has 14 sets of triple strings which are struck with two sticks. The *khim* derives from the Chinese *yangqin*; related instruments include the Burmese *don-mìn*, the Korean *yang-gŭm*, the Vietnamese *dương cầm* and the Mongolian *yoochin*.
(2) Mouth organ of the Samrê people of Kampuchea. *See* BLAY.

Khīm. Double-headed barrel drum of the Newari people of Nepal. In Newari the word designates a barrel drum with two laced heads struck directly with the hands, but it is also a generic term used compositely in the names of many membranophones with one or two heads, for example *komcākhīm*, *komkhīṃcā* (small drum); *dāpā khīm mākhīm* (for *dāpā* music); *desīkhīm* (drum from the *des* area, i.e. India); *dyokhīm* (drum used in the cult of Nasadiyo); *magakhīm*, *mādal* (barrel drum); *paymtakhīm* (drum used with the *paymtāḥ* trumpet); *nāykhīm* (drum used by butchers); and *yakakhīm* (drum with buffalo horns).

BIBLIOGRAPHY
T. O. Ballinger and P. H. Bajracharya: 'Nepalese Musical Instruments', *Southwestern Journal of Anthropology*, xvi/4 (1960), 398
F. Hoerburger: *Studien zur Musik in Nepal* (Regensburg, 1975)
S. Wiehler-Schneider and H. Wiehler: 'A Classification of the Traditional Musical Instruments of the Nevars', *Journal of the Nepal Research Centre*, iv (1980), 67–132   MIREILLE HELFFER

Khimilele. Plural of KHUMULELE.

Khirki [khirkiri]. Wood or bamboo cog rattle of the tribal peoples of the Mandla district of Madhya Pradesh, central India. The toy form of this rattle is common in many parts of India.

Khishba [zanbūr]. Single-headed narrow HOURGLASS DRUM used by gypsies in Iraq. It is made from mulberry, lemon, pomegranate or apricot wood, about 30 to 35 cm in length. A sheepskin membrane between 6 and 11 cm in diameter is stretched and glued over a narrow cylinder fitted at the top of the body, which is often worked or decorated with motifs or with gilt and silver studs. If seated, the player holds the instrument on his thighs; it may also be played standing, in which case it hangs by a shoulder strap. The gypsies seem to have introduced the instrument into the rural regions and marshlands for use in festivals and marriage-feasts. They use it solo or with other drums and the *rabāb* (single-string fiddle) to accompany songs and dances. During the second half of the 20th century the *khishba* and its players moved into urban centres, where the influence of radio and television has led to its adoption by several non-traditional ensembles. The term 'khishba' has taken on a generic meaning and is also used in the south of Iraq to denote drums made from baked clay. See S. Qassim Hassan: *Les instruments de musique en Irak et leur rôle dans la société traditionelle* (Paris, 1980).
SCHEHERAZADE QASSIM HASSAN

Khlang khêk [khlań khaek]. *See* KLAṄ KHAEK.

Khloi. *See* KHLUY.

Khlui. Bamboo DUCT FLUTE of Thailand. It has seven finger-holes (six on the *khlui ū*) and a thumb-hole at the back; the duct is also on the back. As on many Chinese flutes, there are also two pairs of holes cut at right-angles at the lower end of the flute; the transverse pair is laced with a cord for ease of carrying or decoration, and the other pair remains empty. The characteristic buzzing sound of the *khlui* is produced by means of an extra hole which is covered with bamboo fibre or, more commonly nowadays, tissue paper. This hole is located on the right side of the instrument (as it is held in the playing position), just above the thumb-hole. All *khlui* are tuned to approximate an equidistant heptatonic scale.
The three main sizes of *khlui* are the *khlui līp* (36 cm long and 2 cm wide with the lowest pitch around e''), the *khlui phīang ǭ* (45 cm long and 4 cm wide with the lowest pitch around a'), and the *khlui ū* (60 cm long and 4·5 cm wide). The *khlui phīang ǭ* is the instrument in general use today. As well as being a solo instrument, the *khlui* is played in some Thai ensembles, such as the *khrǔang sāi* (strings), the *mahōrī* (mixed strings and percussion) and the *pī phāt* (percussion).
A fourth type of *khlui*, the *khlui krūat*, has a tonal range one note higher than the *khlui phīang ǭ*, and is played in the *khrǔang sāi* ensemble when Western instruments, such as the violin and organ, are added.
In north-eastern Thailand, the term *khlui* also refers to an idioglot clarinet. It consists of a piece of cane or reed, closed by a node at the proximal end, with a down-cut reed (the beating end of which is nearest the player) and seven approximately equidistant finger-holes.

BIBLIOGRAPHY
D. Yupho: *Khrǔang dontri Thai* [Thai musical instruments] (Bangkok, 1957, 2/1967; Eng. trans., 1960, 2/1971)
D. Morton: *The Traditional Music of Thailand* (Berkeley, 1976)
L. E. R. Picken: 'The Sound-producing Instrumentarium of a Village in North-East Thailand', *Musica asiatica*, iv (1984), 237
DAVID MORTON

Khluy [khloi]. A term for the flute of Kampuchea. It may be notched or transverse, is generally made of bamboo and has seven finger-holes. *Khluy* are played solo or in the *mahōrī* orchestra, and are similar to the Laotian *khui* and the Thai *khlui*.

Khmuos thom. *See* GHMOḤ DHAM.

Khoko. SLIT-DRUM of Zaïre. *See* NKOKO, (1).

Khol. Double-headed drum of eastern India and Bangladesh (Bengal, Orissa and Assam). It is made of clay (the almost identical *pung* of neighbouring Manipur is of wood). The body is about 75 cm long; it has an asymmetrical barrel shape, with a longer right side tapering to a small face (about 15 cm in diameter) and a lesser taper to the left (about 25 cm). The two heads are braced by narrow V-lacings which almost cover the whole body, protecting the clay (for illustration *see* MRDAṄGA, fig.1c). Like all the classical drums of India (of which this is the eastern representative), the heads are composite. Each is a double skin laced together by plaited leather hoops, over which the bracing straps are looped; about three-quarters of the upper skin on each face is cut away in the centre, and on the exposed lower skin of the right head is a permanent round of black tuning paste (of cooked rice, soot etc), applied in several layers, while on the left is a paste of dough freshly applied at each performance. There are no tuning blocks.

The *khol* is played with the fingers, palms and whole hand on both sides and different areas of the heads, singly and together. The right head, comparatively small for Indian drums of the *mṛdaṅga* type, has a high, tinny sound and the bass, though less definite in pitch, and variable by pressure, is perhaps about an 11th lower. As for other drums, each stroke has an oral notation of *bol*-syllables, here including *jhā, jhī, nāk, jhīnī, thete, khīkhi*, and the fast roll *guruguruguruguru*, which the drummer often calls out while playing.

Although it can be found in other music and in dance the *khol* is pre-eminently the main accompaniment of *kīrtan*, the sacred Vaiṣṇava devotional music of Bengal and east India and northern pilgrimage cities settled by Bengalis (hence its other names: *śrīkhol* ('venerable *khol*') and *kīrtankhol*); it is worshipped, together with the cymbals *kartāl*, at the beginning of a performance. In *padāvali* or *pālākīrtan* ('episodic *kīrtan*'), in which a *kīrtanya* (cantor) threads together *tālgān* (metric songs drawn from poems of medieval saints and illustrating, dramatically, episodes from the life of Krishna), the players of *khol* and *kartāl* show great skill in following the improvised changes of tempo and leading the chorus. This music is an east Indian version of the ancient Hindu high-art tradition of raga and tala. Some of the many *tāl* are long and complex, such as *baṙa daśkuśī* of 28 (or 56) beats. The performance begins with a prelude on *khol* and *kartāl*, followed by the *gauracandrikā*, an invocation of the saint Caitanyadeva (*fl* 1486–1533), who revitalized eastern Vaishnavism and whose disciple Narottam Das is credited with the development of this music.

BIBLIOGRAPHY
S. M. Tagore: *Yantra-kośǎ* (Calcutta, 1875/R1977)
K. S. Kothari: *Indian Folk Musical Instruments* (New Delhi, 1968)
S. Ray: *Music of Eastern India* (Calcutta, 1973)
B. C. Deva: *Musical Instruments of India: their History and Development* (Calcutta, 1978)

ALASTAIR DICK

Khōng. In Thailand and Laos, a generic name for a gong or kettle gong.

Gongs in Thailand are found in a variety of sizes and grouped into several different types of GONG-CHIME. A single *khōng* is made of thick metal and is a bossed gong with a deep lip-flange, similar to the kettle gongs of Java and Bali. The boss is struck with a padded beater. Individual *khōng* may be hung on a tripod or stand, or suspended manually. When used in sets as gong-chimes the gongs are tied to a curved rack which stands on the floor, so that when the player sits in the middle the kettle gongs are within easy reach. Gongs and gong-chimes are used in many of the instrumental ensembles of Thailand.

Six types of *khōng* are used as rhythm instruments. The *khōng mōng* has a diameter ranging from 30 cm to 45 cm and a lip-flange 5 cm deep. It is not tuned to a definite pitch. It is usually hung on a tripod or metal stand and played with a padded beater, and is found in the *pī phāt* ensembles, the double *khrǔang sai* ensemble and the large *mahōrī* ensemble. The *khōng chai* is a large gong, up to 80 cm in diameter. It is decorated with gold-painted designs and used in important ceremonies. It is also known as *khōng mui*. The *khōng mēng* is a

small gong, 19 cm in diameter. Held suspended from the hand rather than a stand it is used singly in the *buǎ lǒi* and *pī chawā klǒng khāēk* ensembles. The smaller *khōng kratāē* is made from thin metal; it was used to call the watches at night or to attract the attention of a crowd before important public proclamations.

The *khōng khū* is a pair of small gongs, similar in size to the *khōng kratāē* but made of thick metal. The gongs are suspended together in a wooden box with the boss upward. One gong has a high tone and the other a low tone. They are used only in the *pī phāt* ensembles which accompany certain types of stage performance (*lakhōn chātrī* and the *nōrā*). The *khōng rǎo* (also called *khōng hui* or *khōng rabēng*) consists of three gongs, small, medium and large, suspended from a stand; their sizes range from about 30 to 50 cm. Now virtually obsolete, it was formerly used chiefly in royal ceremonies.

To play melodies, *khōng* are grouped together on a rack. An ancient and obsolete Thai gong-chime, which had eight kettle gongs, was the *khōng rāng*. This was a further development of the set of three gongs described earlier. It was a straight-rack version of the arc-shaped gong-chimes in use in Thailand today. These 'circles of gongs' are known as *khōng wong*, and they vary in the number of kettle gongs they employ. The *khōng* are arranged in ascending order of pitch from left to right and tied on to a rattan frame about 25 cm high. The frame is placed on the floor and forms nearly a complete circle around the player. This shape distinguishes the Thai gong-chimes from those of Bali and Java, such as the *trompong*, *reyong* and *bonang*, which all have straight racks. Fine tuning is effected by melting a mixture of beeswax and lead shavings on to the underside of the bosses.

The *khōng wong yai* ('large circle of gongs') has 16 kettle gongs, 12 to 17 cm in diameter, which cover a range of two octaves; it is usually used alone in small percussion ensembles such as the *khrǔang yai*. In larger ensembles it is played with its smaller equivalent, the *khōng wong lek*, which has 18 kettle gongs of 9·5 to 13 cm in diameter (the two outermost being redundant). The *khōng wong lek* is pitched one octave higher than the *khōng wong yai*. A medium-sized set of kettle gongs, called the *khōng (wong) klāng*, is usually used in string ensembles.

An unusual variation on the horizontal, arc-shaped rack is the ornate framework which holds the kettle gongs of the *khōng mōn* (for illustration *see* GONG, fig.3b). This instrument is in the form of a crescent with each end extending upwards rather than lying parallel with the floor. The stand is of heavy wood, beautifully carved and decorated with gold paint. The carvings at each end represent the head and tail of a mythical creature, half bird, half human. The instrument usually has about 15 kettle gongs and is made in two sizes to match the two common sizes of the floor-standing models (*khōng wong yai* and *khōng wong lek*). The range, pitch and sound of the *mōn*-type gong-chimes is identical to that of the regular Thai models, but they are differentiated by function: the *mōn* instruments traditionally replace the *khōng wong* chimes in ensembles which play funeral music.

In Laos the *khōng wong* and the *khōng nyai* are semicircular gong-chimes; the *khōng wong* has 17 bossed gongs and the *khōng nyai* has 16 bossed gongs. They are both played in the *seb nyai* royal orchestra and the *seb nǒi* folk ensemble.

BIBLIOGRAPHY
D. Yupho: *Khrǔang dontri Thai* [Thai musical instruments] (Bangkok, 1957, 2/1967; Eng. trans., 1960, 2/1971)

D. Morton: *The Traditional Music of Thailand* (Berkeley, 1976)
DAVID MORTON

Khongada. A name used in Maharashtra, western India, for the larger variety of the TARPO (double clarinet with gourd wind cap).

Khorototo [sakhviri, sanker]. Natural brass trumpet of Georgia (USSR), from 130 to 200 cm long. The mouthpiece is soldered on one end of the mainly cylindrical tube which broadens into a spherical bulge before forming a conical bell. The *khorototo* could also be made of wood or birch bark. It produced a powerful sound (*khoro* means 'thunder' in Georgian) and was used as a military signalling instrument and to call people to public gatherings. It began to fall out of use at the turn of the 19th century. See *VertkovA*, 126.

Khrab. See KRAP.

Khrims-dung. Trumpet of Tibet. See DUNG.

Khrŭang khŭ. Medium-sized or double PĪ PHĀT ensemble of Thailand. The terms for a small and large *pī phāt* ensemble are *khrŭang hā* and *khrŭang yai* respectively.

Khrŭang sāi. Indoor instrumental ensemble of Thailand, comprising string instruments, percussion and a flute. There are three sizes: a small ensemble consisting of a *sŏ duang* and a *sŏ ū* (bowed string instruments), a *čhakhē* (plucked tube zither), a *khlui phīang ŏ* (duct flute), a *thōn* (goblet drum), a *rammanā* (frame drum) and a pair of *ching* (cymbals); a medium-sized or double ensemble consisting of two *sŏ duang*, two *sŏ ū*, two *čhakhē*, two *khlui* (*khlui līp* and *khlui phīang ŏ*), a *thōn*, a *rammanā*, a pair of *ching*, a pair of *chāp* and a *mōng* (bossed gong); and a large ensemble for which there is no standard instrumentation but which may include additional instruments such as the low-pitched *khlui ū*, the *sŏ sām sāi* and occasionally the *khāēn*.
TRÂN QUANG HAI

Khuchir. Two- or four-string SPIKE FIDDLE of the Buryat people of Siberia. The resonator is cylindrical, hexagonal or octagonal and made of wood, more rarely of metal. The front is covered with a skin soundtable, the back is left open. The rounded neck has no frets. The silk or metal strings are tuned in 5ths; in the case of the four-string instrument, the first and third, and second and fourth strings are tuned in unison. The bow hair is threaded between the strings. On four-string types, the bow hair is divided into two strands, one fixed between the first and second strings, the other between the third and fourth. The *khuchir* is related to the Nanai *ducheke*, the Nivkhi *tïgrïk* and the Mongolian KHUUCHIR.
See also DÖRVÖN CHIKHTEI KHUUR.

Khudra ghaṇṭikā. Alternative term for *kṣudra-ghaṇṭikā* (metal pellet bells of India). See GHAṆṬĀ.

Khui. Bamboo DUCT FLUTE of Laos, with six fingerholes. See also KHLUI.

Khulkhulā. Calabash rattle of Maharashtra, western India, similar to the JHUMRĀ of Orissa, east India. See *also* GHUṄGRŪ.

Khulsan khuur. Bamboo JEW'S HARP of Mongolia. *See* AMAN KHUUR.

Khumbgwe. End-blown flute with spherical mouthpiece played by the Venda people of southern Africa. It is similar to the Karanga OMBGWE, but has three fingerholes.

Khumulele [kumurere, khumurere] (pl. *khimilele*). NOTCHED FLUTE of the Masaba (Gisu) people of eastern Uganda. It is 20 to 28 cm long and has two finger-holes, a rectangular notch at the mouthpiece and a wide bore for its length. It is always played in pairs, notably at weddings where the *musezza* (male instrument) and the *mukassi* (or *mukazzi*, female) are combined with the singing of the leading flautist, using a brilliantly rhythmic hocket technique.
PETER COOKE

Khung. A free-reed mouth organ of Manipur, northeast India. It is related to the *khāēn*, *sheng* and *shō* of South-east and East Asia. A cane blowpipe is fixed into a protruding spout on a small round gourd, from whose top six pipes, tied in two bundles of three, issue vertically; each of these contains a free-beating brass reed and is capped by a spherical fruit-shell mute. The pipes are sounded by closing a hole at their base. The instrument is used to accompany dance.

BIBLIOGRAPHY
K. S. Kothari: *Indian Folk Musical Instruments* (New Delhi, 1968)
ALASTAIR DICK

Khunkhunā [runjhunia]. Coconut-shell rattle of Rajasthan, India. *See also* GHUṄGRŪ.

Khunto. Single-headed cylindrical drum of the Yao people of Malawi. It is open-ended, and the membrane is pinned on and weighted.

Khurḍāk. KETTLEDRUM of central India similar to the DUGGI.

Khuuchir. Mongolian two-string SPIKE FIDDLE. The Mongolian name is derived from the Chinese *huqin*, at present used to describe a two-string instrument similar to the Mongolian one, but which has also been applied to plucked and bowed lutes of different types. The modern *khuuchir* consists of a wooden rod spiked through a cylindrical or polygonal resonator of wood or tin, with two gut strings strung over a bridge on the soundtable of sheepskin or snakeskin to two posterior pegs. A small metal ring attached to a loop of string tied to the shaft pulls the strings towards the shaft and can be adjusted to alter the pitch of the open strings, which are usually tuned to a 5th. The instrument is used mostly in ensembles. The *Yueshu* of the 12th century describes a two-string fiddle *xiqin*, bowed with a piece of bamboo between the strings and used by a Mongolian tribe. Later, in the Manchu dynasty, a similar instrument with two strings bowed with a horsehair bow threaded between the strings was used in Mongolian music. *See also* DÖRVÖN CHIKHTEI KHUUR and KHUUR.

BIBLIOGRAPHY
J. Badraa: 'Mongol ardyn khögjmiin zebseg' [Mongolian folk musical instruments], *Orchin üeiin mongol uls*, iii (1963), 16
ANDREA NIXON

Khuur. Mongolian term for a chordophone. It may

Morin khuur (fiddle) played by a Mongolian street musician

denote plucked or bowed string instruments or jew's harps. Some of these have decorative carvings at the top of the neck in the shape of animal or bird heads, real or mythological. The *morin khuur* (or *moriny tolgoit khuur*: 'khuur with a horse's head') is a two-string fiddle with a horse's head carved at the top of the neck (see illustration), often with a dragon's head directly underneath the horse's. Heads of dragons, sea monsters, birds and horses are also found on Tibetan lutes and in Mongolian and Tibetan iconography of lutes held by Buddhist gods.

In the modern standard *morin khuur* a wooden handle pierces a trapeziform wooden frame. The back is made of wood with a soundhole cut out and the front is covered with sheepskin or goatskin; in recent instruments the front, too, is wooden. Two horsehair strings run from the end of the spike at the base over a bridge on the body, and then over a smaller bridge on the neck to the two tuning-pegs. The strings are called *nariin* ('thin') and *büdüün* ('thick'), but they have also been known as 'female' and 'male'. The thinner string should have about 105 hairs from a mare's tail, the thicker string about 130 hairs from a horse's tail. The strings used to be tuned a 5th apart, but are now usually tuned a 4th apart, giving a compass of three octaves.

Playing techniques vary from region to region, but usually the index and middle fingers of the left hand stop the strings from underneath (i.e. with the flat surface of the nails), while the annular and little fingers stop them from above. The instrument is bowed underhand, the player adjusting the tension of the loosely strung horsehair bow.

Other forms of bowed two-string *khuur* include the

shanagan (ladle) *khuur*, which is carved out of a single piece of wood, and spike fiddles with a bowl-shaped body (*ikil*). The *shanagan khuur* often has at the top of the neck a carving of the head of a dragon or a sea monster. In western Mongolia the two-string bowed *khuur* is known as *ikil* or *ekil*, a name related to the Tuva *igil* and the Turkish *iqliq*, and possibly to the Mongolian name sometimes used for two- and four-string fiddles, *khiil* (*kigili*). The *ikil* is trapeziform or bowl-bodied, often lacking a horse-head carving and having instead a jewel symbol. Sagittal pegs are sometimes found.

The *khuur* is used to accompany both the singing of tales and legends and the singer of long song (*urtyn duu*). In the west, the *ikil* is used to play melodies (*tatlaga*) which may be named after animals or birds and provide a repeatable tune with a regular rhythm for dancing (*bielgee*). It is used for playing a particular melody to camel cows to persuade them to suckle calves they have rejected (a function fulfilled by many Mongolian instruments and practised at least since the 18th century, when a source described the use of a bowed *khur* with horsehair strings to imitate the melancholy tones of a baby camel; see Pallas). The *shanagan khuur* type of instrument has been bowed by Mongolians since the 14th century, when the *Yuan shi* described a two-string dragon-headed instrument bowed with a horsehair bow.

The word *khuur*, cognate with Turkic *qobuz*, was also used to refer to plucked instruments. It is notable that all types of Mongolian chordophone bowed with a separate bow are found in Mongolia in plucked forms; *see* TOBSHUUR and SHUDRAGA.

See also AMAN KHUUR and DÖRVÖN CHIKHTEI KHUUR.

BIBLIOGRAPHY

P. S. Pallas: *Sammlungen historischer Nachrichten über die mongolischen Völkerschaften*, i (Frankfurt and Leipzig, 1776)

E. Emsheimer: 'Preliminary Remarks on Mongolian Music and Instruments', *The Music of the Mongols*, i: *Eastern Mongolia* (Stockholm, 1943), 69–100

G. Badrakh: *Mongolyn khögjmiin tüükhees* [From the history of Mongolian music], *Studia ethnographica*, i/3 (Ulan Bator, 1960)

D. Tserensodnom: 'Khuuryn tatlaga tuul'tai kholbogdokh n' ' [The relationship between *khuur* melodies (*tatlaga*) and epic], *Studia linguae et litterarum*, xii (Ulan Bator, 1976), 209

B. Ravdan, ed.: *Soyol, urlag, khevlel, nomyn khudaldaa, kinony turshlaga* [Experiences in culture, art, printing, bookselling and cinema] (Ulan Bator, 1979)

B. Katuu: 'Khuuryn tatlagyn tukhai' [About *khuur* melodies (*tatlaga*)], *Soyol*, iv (1981), 50

ANDREA NIXON

Khyalgasan khuur. SPIKE FIDDLE of Mongolia. *See* DÖRVÖN CHIKTEI KHUUR.

Khyrda saza. Small long-necked lute of Azerbaijan. *See* SAZ.

Ki (i). Japanese concussion or percussion idiophones consisting of two heavy rectangular hardwood bars. They were originally Buddhist instruments and are still used as such in some temples. There are two varieties, either of which may simply be called *ki*.

(1) *Hyōshigi* ('rhythm wood') are about 25 cm long and slightly curved on one surface; the rounded surfaces are struck together to mark the opening or closing of the curtain and other scene shifts in kabuki and bunraku theatre. Because of their penetrating sound they are also traditionally used by town criers to attract attention.

(2) *Tsuke* are somewhat shorter and are struck (on a flat side) against a board placed stage-left in kabuki to heighten the excitement in certain scenes.

The Chinese BAN is a related instrument.

BIBLIOGRAPHY
W. P. Malm: *Japanese Music and Musical Instruments* (Rutland, Vermont, 1959), 227

DAVID W. HUGHES

Ki (ii). *See* VIVO (i).

Kiak [kiyak]. Two-string fiddle of the Kirghiz people of Central Asia. Its body is shaped like a ladle and the strings are of horsehair. It is related to the Kazakh *qobuz*, and perhaps also to the analogous Mongol *khiil* (*see* KHUUR).

Kiaman. Rattle of Azerbaijan. It consists of a bow, tensed with a bowstring, from which rings, discs and other small objects are suspended. It is used in men's dances: the dancer holds the instrument in both hands at the centre of the bow and shakes it while dancing.

Kiana. LAMELLAPHONE of the Luba people of Mwanza, south-eastern Zaïre (*LaurentyS*, 196).

Kibalamba. PANPIPES of the Mbala people of Zaïre. *See* MISHIBA.

Kibeémbá. Wooden cone flute with one or two finger-holes of the Pende people of south-western Zaïre (*LaurentyA*, 139).

Kibewe [kegbier]. Plucked lute of the Konkomba people of northern Togo. It has a hemispherical calabash soundbox and metal strings. It is used by young men to accompany satirical or love-songs to dance rhythms.

Kibi. A name for the CONCH-SHELL TRUMPET in Motu and other languages of the Central Province, Papua New Guinea.

Kibili. *See* KBILI.

Kibinjj. LAMELLAPHONE of the Pende and Lunda peoples of south-western Zaïre. It has wooden keys and a raft-type base. It is also known as *kakolondd* by the Chokwe people. Another Pende type, known more specifically as *kibinjj kia masaamba*, is box-resonated and has metal keys (*LaurentyS*, 191, 193, 195). *See also* KAKOLONDONDO.

Kibitiko. Drum of the hunting guilds of the Sanga people of south-eastern Zaïre (*BooneT*, 60).

Kibudikidi. Large crescent-shaped SLIT-DRUM of the Bas-Congo region of Zaïre (*LaurentyTF*, 139).

Kibugandet. Five-string wishbone-shaped frame lyre of the Kipsigis people of Kenya. It is held against an external resonator (which may be an empty fuel can). See *TraceyCSA*, ii, 371.

Kicak. Small cymbals of Bali, used in some *angklung* ensembles in Karangasem.

Kichik nagara. Small double-headed drum of Azerbaijan. *See* NAGARA.

Kidebe. LAMELLAPHONE of the Nguja people of Zanzibar. It has a board-type body and six keys.

Kidi. (1) Double-headed drum of the Teda people of Tibesti, northern Chad. It is cylindrical in shape tapering to a truncated cone, with a maximum diameter of about 20 cm. It is carved from a lightweight wood and its membranes are laced. Played only by professional musicians of the blacksmiths' group, the *kidi* is suspended from the player's neck, and beaten with both hands, the player also singing, to accompany recreational dances. The *egidi* is a similar drum of the Zaghawa people of north-eastern Chad. See M. Brandily: *Instruments de musique et musiciens instrumentistes chez les Teda du Tibesti (Tchad)*, Annales sciences humaines (Tervuren, 1974).

(2) Barrel drum of the Anlo-Ewe people of the south-eastern coast of Ghana. It is played with two sticks, and is part of an ensemble which includes the *atsimewu* and *sogo* drums (for illustration *see* ATSIMEWU).

MONIQUE BRANDILY (1)

Kidimbadimba. Single-key XYLOPHONE of the Luba people of Zaïre. *See* DIDIMBADIMBA.

Kidiyo. A term applied in the Amba area of Uganda both to a rare end-blown trumpet made from a cow horn and to a side-blown ivory trumpet. The ivory horn has a rhomboid block which forms a prominent mouthpiece, and the tip of the tusk is pierced to provide a stop. Variation in pitch is achieved by opening and closing this stop and by placing the palm of the hand over the wide opening. Side-blown cow horns are also used for signalling or personal enjoyment. In eastern Africa horns are never played in sets as in West Africa. See *WachsmannTCU*.

Kidrigo. MUSICAL BOW, with separate gourd resonator, of the Logo people of Zaïre; it is also known as *gulutindi* and *kilikingila* (*LaurentyC*, 114). *See* KITINGBI.

Kiel (Ger.). PLECTRUM.

Kielflügel (Ger.). HARPSICHORD.

Kigili. Mongolian fiddle. *See* KHUUR and DÖRVÖN CHIKTEI KHUUR.

Kigogolwa. Log XYLOPHONE of the Vira, Fuliru and Rundi peoples of Burundi. *See* PANDINGBWA.

Kigoma. Large conical laced drum of the Soga people of Kamodi district, Uganda.

Kigware. VESSEL FLUTE of the Gishu people of Uganda. It is made from a dry oncoba fruit, or the tip of a gourd, with a blow-hole at the top and a finger-hole to the left and the right. Similar instruments are known among the Nyole people as *ebundi* and among the Gwere as *kigwara*.

Kiigamba. Leg rattle of the Kikuyu people of Kiambu district, Kenya. It comprises a small tin can containing stones.

Kiiki. Single-string fiddle of the Teda and Daza peoples of Tibesti and Ouaddai, northern Chad. In construction it is identical with the KELELI lute except that it has one horsehair string. This string, which is attached to the neck at the top by leather straps, passes over a small wooden bridge placed on the skin soundtable, and goes down through the soundhole to tie at the base of the neck. The bow is of horsehair, fixed to a supple rod which is strongly arched. The same fiddle is known as *finini* by the Zaghawa people of north-eastern Chad and western Sudan and by the Kanembu and other peoples of north-western Chad. *See also* GOGE and KUU.

MONIQUE BRANDILY

Kijibiwa. Japanese term for a lute of the ancient kingdom of Kucha, Central Asia. *See* BIWA, §1.

Kikakamba. Medium-sized cylindrical SLIT-DRUM of the Luwa people of south-western Zaïre. The narrow slit is widened at each end to make square or circular openings (*LaurentyTF*, 133).

Kikasa. Drum of Zaïre. *See* TSHIKASA.

Kikilo. GROUND ZITHER of the Dongo people of Zaïre (*LaurentyC*, 110). *See* KUDREKENE.

Kikir. Three-string fiddle of Madhya Pradesh (Bastar district), central India. It resembles the BANA fiddle of the Pardhan in the Mandla region, but is less sophisticated. It is 86 cm long and the wooden soundbox is covered with a snakeskin. The *kikir* is found sporadically among the Maria people around Dantewada, and they also call it *kingiri*, or *kingri*. A similar instrument is the *kinkrī* or *kinjrī* of the Raj Gonds of Adilabad, Andhra Pradesh. *See also* KENDRĀ and RĀVAṆHATTHĀ.

BIBLIOGRAPHY
E. K. Jain: 'Wooden Musical Instruments of the Gonds of Central India', *EM*, ix (1965), 39

GENEVIÈVE DOURNON

Ki kohe puru. *See* PU IHU.

Kikongwe. Wide-bore flute, made of plant stalk, of the Shambala people of Tanzania.

Kikoya. Side-blown trumpet of the Dagomba people of northern Ghana. It is made from the horn of a bushcow, and is used in an ensemble with a clapperless bell and hourglass and other drums to accompany singing.

Kikuvu. Large trapezoidal SLIT-DRUM of the Pende, Chokwe and Lunda peoples of southern Zaïre (*LaurentyTF*, 139). *See* GUGU, (1).

Kikwara. SCRAPER of the Luchazi people of Zaïre. *See* BOYEKE.

Kilangay. A Malagasy free-key xylophone. *See* ATRANATRA.

Kilarnet. *See* KLARNET.

Kilaut [kilaun, qilain, qilaun, keylowtik, qilaut]. Single-headed FRAME DRUM used by the Inuit of Canada and the Inupiaq-speaking people of Alaska; it is closely related to the Greenlandic *qilaat* (*qidat*) and the Alaskan Yupik *tchauyuk* (*cauyuk*). Constructional details and playing techniques are regionally variable.

The circular frame is made of wood in all areas although bone may have been used during an earlier period. The diameter ranges from about 37·5 cm in Greenland to over 90 cm in central Canada. Alaskan drums have narrow frames (2·5 cm), permitting a more varied repertory of playing techniques. In central Canada the frame is much heavier. A wooden, bone or ivory handle is notched to fit over the frame and tied in place. Greenlandic drum handles are often carved to represent a human head.

A great variety of materials has been used to cover the frame. In central Canada, caribou skin is traditional but sail-cloth and plastic or other synthetics have been introduced. Alaskan drums are covered with a whale peritoneum or stomach lining, or heavy plastic, while in eastern Greenland, the stomach of a bear, shark skin, seal or dog skin, seal stomach or intestine, the stomach lining of a walrus, and the placenta of a seal have been reported. The membrane is tied over the frame with sinew or cord which fits into a groove in the frame. In preparation for playing, the membrane is made wet and stretched tight.

The physical characteristics of the drumstick help to determine playing techniques. In Greenland, the rib-bone of a seal is favoured by the northern Polar Eskimos, while in the east, a drift-wood stick is preferred. The drum is hit on the underside of the frame (see illustration). Victor (1973) described the performing technique as follows:

The drum handle is held in the left hand; the left elbow is kept close to the body with the left forearm forward and slightly raised. The frame is supported in the bend of the right elbow. The drumhead faces the singer, inclined up and out. The stick is held in the palm of the right hand with the finger-nails on the outside; the right elbow is kept close to the body and a wrist movement is used to strike the frame. The drum is held flexibly and when it is hit it oscillates around an axis formed by the stick. Certain very rapid beats give the impression that the frame bounces on the handle.

Qilain (single-headed frame drum) players, Angmagssalik, Greenland, 1906

Various combinations of accented beats, slightly accented beats, and unaccented rebounds are played in short, repeated groups.

Alaskan drums are played with a thin, slightly curved stick which is longer than the diameter of the drum. In the north-west the drum is struck from below, on either one or both rims, or rim plus membrane. In the south-west the drum is struck from above, making a different range of rim and membrane strokes possible. In both areas, the instruments are played in groups by a chorus which sits to the side of the dance area. A variety of rhythmic patterns, played in unison, either coordinate with the song rhythms or form a rhythmic counterpoint. Dances, some of them mimetic, may have fixed or variable motions.

In Canada, west of Hudson Bay, the large, heavy drum is played by a solo drum-dancer who holds the instrument in one hand and rotates it along an axis formed by the handle. Using a short, padded wooden club, the drummer strikes the sides of the frame alternately, producing a steady beat which gradually accelerates. He faces the hub of an imaginary circle and moves around the perimeter, bending forward from the waist and interjecting shouts to intensify his performance. A chorus accompanies his dance with narrative songs.

By the 1970s, in both Alaska and Canada, the frame drum was used primarily as an accompaniment to social dances or inter-community dance competitions. Earlier references to its use in drum duels or shamanic ritual are ambiguous. In Greenland, Gessain's work in Ammassalik (1934–5) produced documentation for a wide variety of functions. Secular usage was in association with long poems, theatrical representations, or satirical drum duels between two adversaries. Religious usage was by the shaman or *angakok*. Drum duels and shamanic rituals have also been studied in the Polar Eskimo area.

See also SHAMAN DRUM.

BIBLIOGRAPHY

R. Gessain and P.-E. Victor: 'Le tambour chez les Ammassalimiut', *Objets et mondes*, xiii/3 (1973)

BEVERLEY CAVANAGH

Kilawiri. PANPIPES of the CHIRIHUANO ensemble of Bolivia.

Kilemi. An idiophone, the 'foot drum', of the Maidu Indians of California, also known among other north and central Californian tribes. The foot drum, so-called because it was stamped upon with the feet, was made from a log (usually sycamore) about 1·5 to 1·8 metres long and about 60 cm in diameter. The log was split lengthwise and one half was hollowed out by charring and scraping to form a half cylinder open at both ends. The log was placed, hollowed side down, over a shallow trench dug into the ground which functioned as a resonating chamber. It was played by two or three men who either stood on the log and stamped their feet in time with the singing, or stood beside the drum and pounded it with heavy sticks or clubs. The clubs, over one metre long, were held vertically like pestles.

Considerable care was taken during the manufacture of a drum and the finished instrument was treated as a revered object. It was used to accompany many kinds of musical activity, particularly religious and ceremonial.

MARY RIEMER-WELLER

Kilgen. American firm of organ builders. It was founded in New York in 1851 by George Kilgen (*d* 1902), a native of Durlach, Germany, who had been apprenticed there to an organ builder named Voijt and who went to the USA with a group of political refugees in 1848, finding employment with the Jardine firm. In 1873 Kilgen moved his company to St Louis, where it prospered. In 1886 his son, Charles Christian Kilgen (1859–1932), joined as a partner, the firm becoming known as George Kilgen & Son; during his presidency one of the most noted Kilgen organs, that of St Patrick's Cathedral, New York, was built in 1928. After Charles Kilgen's death the firm was reorganized under the name Kilgen Organ Co. but, although it continued to produce many small instruments, its fortunes declined until the business was dissolved in 1960.

BIBLIOGRAPHY

W. H. Barnes: *The Contemporary American Organ* (Glen Rock, NJ, 8/1964)

O. Ochse: *The History of the Organ in the United States* (Bloomington, Ind., 1975)

BARBARA OWEN

Kilibongo. MOUTH BOW of the Azo and Andemaderi peoples of Zaïre (*LaurentyC*, 113). See LUSUBA.

Kilikingila. MUSICAL BOW with separate gourd resonator of the Logo people of Zaïre; it is also known as *gulutindi* and *kidrigo* (*LaurentyC*, 114). See KITINGBI.

Kilimba. LAMELLAPHONE of the Sampwe people of Zaïre.

Kilingbindiri. MUSICAL BOW with separate gourd resonator of the Dongo people of the Sirinka region of Zaïre (*LaurentyC*, 114). See KITINGBI.

Kilu. Globular VESSEL FLUTE of the Dzing people of Zaïre; it is made from a seed shell (*LaurentyA*, 222).

Kiluka [kilu, kalur]. Cone whistle of Uganda. It is made from a gourd with the tip blocked and a single fingerhole. The instrument is 9 cm long, has a cupped mouthpiece, and is capable of producing several notes through a combination of stopping the hole and changing the angle of the player's lips. This whistle is called *kiluka* by the Alur people, *kalur* by the Copi and *kilu* by the Acholi. See *WachsmannTCU*.

Kimama. Antelope-horn trumpet of the Luba people of Zaïre. See KIMPUNGIDI, (2).

Kimasa. Arched harp of the Soga people of Uganda. See ENNANGA.

Kimbal. Conical drum in the SULIBAO ensemble of the Ibaloi people of the northern Philippines.

Kimball. American firm of reed organ, piano and organ makers. It was founded in Chicago in 1857 by William Wallace Kimball (*b* Rumford, Maine, 22 March 1828; *d* Chicago, 16 Dec 1904), the firm becoming known as the W. W. Kimball Co. He had previously been involved in insurance and as an estate agent in Decorah, Iowa. Sensing the growing commercial importance of Chicago, he moved there in 1857; a chance purchase of a consignment of pianos at an auction shortly afterwards launched his career as a piano dealer. A few years later he added reed organs to his stock, but for over 20 years he purchased his instruments from east coast manufacturers. In 1865 Kimball married Evalyne M. Cone, whose brother Albert (*d* 1900) soon entered the firm, eventually becoming treasurer. The fire in Chicago (1871) destroyed the Kimball store but this was only a temporary setback, and in 1880 Kimball opened his first factory, for the manufacture of reed organs. In 1882 the firm was incorporated with Kimball, Cone and Edwin S. Conway as principals, and in 1887 piano manufacturing was begun. Kimball's business credo stressed volume, reasonable price and quality of construction; he encouraged his technicians to develop improvements, and many patents were granted for reed organ designs and improvements in piano plates. These factors doubtless helped Kimball to secure the highest awards for organs, reed organs and pianos at the World's Columbian Exposition (1893). Among the technicians were a number of skilled immigrants, including Peter Tapper and one Guricke, both trained in Bechstein's piano factory in Berlin, and Frederic W. Hedgeland, who trained in his family's organ works in England and in 1890 superintended a new pipe organ-building department for Kimball. Beginning with an ingenious small 'portable' organ of two manuals and pedals which employed free reeds for its pedal stops, the firm soon began building larger organs, and during the first half of the 20th century produced many notable instruments, including several for large churches in Chicago, a reconstruction of the organ in the Mormon Tabernacle, Salt Lake City (1901), and the organ in the Municipal Auditorium of Pretoria, South Africa (1935). In 1883 Kimball's nephew Wallace W. Lufkin (*d* 1945) joined the firm, eventually becoming its president, as did another nephew, Curtis N. Kimball (*d* 1936). In 1896 Kimball began making self-playing organs, followed by player pianos in 1901. From 1915 to 1925 Kimball also manufactured a gramophone invented by Albert A. Huseby, a Norwegian who was superintendent of the piano works. The reed organ branch of the firm closed in 1922, having produced 403,390 instruments, while the organ building branch continued until 1942, with a total of 7326. C. N. Kimball became president of the firm on his uncle's death, and was in turn succeeded by W. W. Lufkin. W. W. Kimball, a grand-nephew of the founder, became president in 1945, and many other family members remained in the firm's hierarchy. After World War II the Kimball firm concentrated chiefly on pianos; in 1955 a new factory was built for that purpose in Melrose Park, Illinois. In 1959 Kimball became part of the Jasper Corporation of Jasper, Indiana, which has wide interests in timber and furniture making, and it moved to Indiana in 1961. The company took over Bösendorfer of Vienna in 1966, since when some Bösendorfer features have been incorporated into Kimball pianos.

In 1961 the company began to manufacture electronic organs designed for home use, a number of models of which have been produced. The company subsequently became known as the Kimball Piano and Organ Co., and in the mid-1970s the parent corporation became Kimball International. The sound of the Kimball electronic organ is normally generated by 12 oscillators using frequency division, and an electronic rhythm section and automatic bass are included. The majority of current models are two-manual 'spinet' organs with 37 or 44 notes on each manual and a one-octave pedal-board. *See* ELECTRONIC ORGAN.

BIBLIOGRAPHY
A. Dolge: *Pianos and their Makers* (Covina, Calif., 1911/*R*1972)
V. A. Bradley: *Music for the Millions* (Chicago, 1957)
N. H. Crowhurst: *Electronic Organs*, iii (Indianapolis, 1975), 67
O. Ochse: *The History of the Organ in the United States* (Bloomington, Ind., 1975)
BARBARA OWEN

Kimbalom. *See* CIMBALOM.

Kimbandu. Long cylindro-conical drum of the Yaka people of Zaïre. It is supported on a pedestal and the head is secured by nails. The drum was traditionally used for initiation ceremonies, when it was placed between the legs, secured with a strap and beaten with the hands. Other drums of this type found in Zaïre include the Bembe *kolongwa* and *mwimbi*, the Kutu *itsim*, the Nkundo *ilongo* and those of the Aushi, Bakwa Nkate, Boma, Mbala, Nkundo, Hungana, Yans and Yaka peoples, reported under the ubiquitous name of *ngoma* (*ngomm*).

BIBLIOGRAPHY
BooneT
F. J. de Hen: *Beitrag zur Kenntnis der Musikinstrumente aus Belgisch Kongo und Ruanda-Urundi* (Tervuren, 1960)
K. A. GOURLAY

Kimbi. Box-resonated LAMELLAPHONE of the Ngbandi people of north-western Zaïre. It has metal keys, and the soundtable projects past the box (*LaurentyS*, 194).

Kimbumba [tingotalango, tumbandera]. Caribbean GROUND HARP (ground bow), called *tumbandera* in rural eastern Cuba, and *tingotalango* in the Trinidad region. A thin section or leaf of royal palm, some 40 cm in diameter, is stretched over an open pit and held at the edges by forked sticks hammered into the ground. At some distance from the covered hole, a flexible stick is thrust into the ground. To its tip is attached a cord or fibre, the opposite end of which is secured beneath the centre of the stretched covering; the string is then played. Although not common, the instrument is not extinct. See *OrtizIMA*, iii, 183f.

JOHN M. SCHECHTER

Kimene. Ivory or cow-horn trumpet of the Vira, Fuliru and Rundi peoples of Burundi and eastern Zaïre. The term refers to both side- and end-blown instruments. The former was used to announce a chief's arrival, the latter a notable's. *See also* KIMPUNGIDI, (2).

Kimkim. Plosive aerophone of the Kagoro, Ataka and adjoining peoples of the southern Zaria region of Nigeria. (1) An instrument of dumb-bell shape made from hollow unfired clay. Played by women as rhythmic accompaniment to song and dance, it is gripped round the narrow waist by one hand and produces plopping sounds when the lower end is bounced off the bare thigh; the free hand cups the upper opening. Traditionally it is used to accompany women's songs such as *kuku*, giving pre-nuptial advice. More recently it has acquired considerable popularity through its introduction into instrumental ensembles for accompanying women's church choirs, where it is used with the gourd vessel rattle and the *kimkim* fired pot.

(2) An ordinary water pot of fired clay with a hole in the side. It is placed in the player's lap with the side

hole uppermost, and both openings are cupped alternately by the player's hands. This instrument would appear to be the *udu* pot drum of the Igbo people, introduced into the area. As the *kimkim* it is, however, played only in the position described; in Igboland it may be placed on the ground and the mouth tapped with a beater made from palm fronds. It should be noted that the instrument is neither a 'pot drum' nor a 'percussion vessel' as it has often been described; the sound is produced, not by causing the material to vibrate, but through compression and release of the air inside it.

BIBLIOGRAPHY
D. W. Ames and K. A. Gourlay: 'Kimkim: a Women's Musical Pot', *African Arts*, xi/2 (1978), 56

K. A. GOURLAY

Kiṃnarī vīṇā. *See* KINNARĪ VĪṆĀ.

Kimpungidi [kimama]. Antelope-horn trumpet of the Luba people of Zaïre. (1) End-blown trumpet made from a long horn cut off about 5 to 10 cm from the tip to leave a 2 cm blow-hole.

(2) Side-blown trumpet with a rectangular blow-hole about 5 cm from the tip. Another hole in the tip is covered or uncovered by the thumb when the horn is blown. The resultant two notes, at an interval of an approximate minor 3rd, enable the player to send messages while hunting or to summon people to work. Knosp gives *kimpungili* and the root term *pungi* for a side-blown Luba trumpet. Other words reported for the same or similar instruments of other peoples of Zaïre are *m'pugni* (Luluwa), *mponge* and *pongi* (Lia) and *ponge* (Mbole). The alternative Luba term *kimama* resembles *kimene*, an instrument which was attributed by Knosp to the Vira, Fuliru and Rundi (of Burundi).

See also MOMPATE and MOTUTU.

BIBLIOGRAPHY
LaurentyA
G. Knosp: *Enquête sur la vie musicale au Congo belge 1934–1935* (Tervuren, 1968)
F. J. de Hen: *Beitrag zur Kenntnis der Musikinstrumente aus Belgisch Kongo und Ruanda-Urundi* (Tervuren, 1960)
J. Gansemans: *Les instruments de musique Luba* (Tervuren, 1980)

K. A. GOURLAY

Kimpungili. Tubular MIRLITON of the Luba people of south-eastern Zaïre (*LaurentyA*, 34). The term has also been used for a side-blown trumpet (*see* KIMPUNGIDI, (2)).

Kimsa ppía. End-blown NOTCHED FLUTE of the Bolivian Alti Plano, with three finger-holes.

Kin [shichigen-kin: 'seven-string zither'] (**i**). Japanese term, using the same pictograph as the Chinese QIN (seven-string zither), which had entered Japan by the 8th century. Written evidence shows that at first the *kin* was played both solo and with other instruments. It faded into obscurity after the 12th century, but was revived in the 17th as a result of renewed cultural influences from China and flourished well into the 20th century among the literati, who aspired to the lifestyle of the early *qin*-playing Chinese sages. The Japanese performers both adopted Chinese tunes and composed their own. The Korean *kŭm* (*see* KŬM (i)) is the result of a different borrowing of the *qin*. See R. H. van Gulik: *The Lore of the Chinese Lute: an Essay in Ch'in Ideology* (Tokyo, 1940).

DAVID W. HUGHES

Kin (ii). Japanese Buddhist bell of copper or bronze; it is used also in *geza* (off-stage music of the kabuki theatre) in temple scenes. The *kin* is bowl-shaped and is set upwards on a cloth ring; its rim is struck with a padded stick to help punctuate the progress of a service (for illustration *see* MOKUGYO). The name and size of the bell vary among different Buddhist sects. It may also be called *keisu*, *kinsu*, *rin*, *sahari* or *uchinarashi*, among other names, and the tiny variety (sometimes only 5 cm across) found on Buddhist household altars is called *namarin*. Larger *kin* may exceed 30 cm, and are sometimes called *daikin* ('large *kin*'). The *kin* is related to the Chinese QING (ii).

Kin may also refer to the percussion plaque KEI, depending on the sect. Such profusion and confusion of terminology is common in Buddhist instruments. For generic discussion of Japanese metallophones, *see* KANE.

BIBLIOGRAPHY
S. Kishibe: *The Traditional Music of Japan* (Tokyo, 1966, 2/1981), pl.40

DAVID W. HUGHES

Kina. Side-blown animal-horn trumpet of the Shi people of eastern Zaïre (*LaurentyA*, 324).

Kinanda (i). STICK ZITHER of the Bene Bukwamadi and Luba peoples of Zaïre (*LaurentyC*, 115). *See* ZEZE (i).

Kinanda (ii). BOARD ZITHER of the Komo people of eastern Zaïre (*LaurentyC*, 116).

Kinanga [ekihako]. Arched harp of the Konjo people of Uganda. *See* ENNANGA.

Kinde. Five-string arched harp of the Barma people of southern Chad. It has tuning-pegs and small clapper bells attached to the bridge and soundbox. In performance the *kinde* is laid sideways on the ground so that the strings are horizontal. A group of four are used to accompany a song to encourage warriors before battle. *See also* HARP, §6, esp. fig.29*c*.

BIBLIOGRAPHY
C. Duvelle and M. Vuylstèke: 'Anthologie de la Musique du Tchad', OCR 36, 37, 38 [disc notes]

Kindet. End-blown wooden trumpet, conical in shape, used in the upper Digul area of Irian Jaya (West New Guinea). It is known as *buge* by the Wani-anim people. See J. Kunst: *Music in New Guinea* (The Hague, 1967), 171.

Kindingding. Five-string arched harp of the Fali people of northern Cameroon. It has a boat-shaped wooden resonator and tuning-pegs. The resonator skin has two holes covered with a mirliton membrane. The sheepskin strings are knotted at their lower end under a convex crosspiece. Tuning is designated by kin terms and all parts of the instrument have strong sexual symbolism. For a woman to touch the instrument in public would be an obscenity, in private an invitation. The harp is used to accompany both satirical and sacred songs.

BIBLIOGRAPHY
J.-G. Gauthier: *Les Fali (Hon et Tsalo)* (Oosterhut, 1969)

K. A. GOURLAY

Kindri. Drum of the Logo people of Zaïre. *See* DINDO.

Kinfuíti [manfúla]. Cuban single-headed FRICTION DRUM. Its wooden body measures 60 to 80 cm in height by some 40 cm in diameter and it always has an internal friction stick or cord. The term *kinfuíti* refers not only to the instrument but also to its characteristic rhythm and to a specific dance performed to its music. See *OrtizIMA*, v, 150, 155.

JOHN M. SCHECHTER

King (i). A fretted STICK ZITHER of the Panjab and Jammu, north-western India. The stick is about 80 cm long; a deep flat bridge of Indian type sits on a vertical projection at the lower end. Two large whole gourd resonators are tied into small wooden sockets at about one-quarter distance from the ends. There are seven upright brass-capped wooden frets and a nut; the single wire string is attached to a lateral tuning-peg. The *king* is held diagonally across the body with the left gourd resting on the shoulder and is plucked with the fingers. It is of the *kinnarī vīṇā* type, whence its name (*see* VĪṆĀ, §§4, 6).

BIBLIOGRAPHY
C. Sachs: *Die Musikinstrumente Indiens und Indonesiens* (Berlin and Leipzig, 1914, 2/1923)
K. S. Kothari: *Indian Folk Musical Instruments* (New Delhi, 1968)
ALASTAIR DICK

King (ii). A SLIT-DRUM of Pororan Island, Buka, Solomon Islands. See TUI.

Kingaridi. Single-headed GOBLET DRUM of the Valley Tonga people of Zambia. See NGOMA.

Kingiri [kingri]. Three-string fiddle of Madhya Pradesh, central India. See KIKIR.

Kingkong. Small bronze gong of Alor, Indonesia, used in the SARAFEO ensemble.

King Musical Instruments. American firm of wind instrument makers. One of the earliest manufacturers of distinguished brass instruments in the USA, it was founded in Cleveland, Ohio, in 1893 by Henderson N. White (1873–1940), an instrument repairman, amateur musician and businessman. With Thomas King (a professional trombonist whose name was subsequently used as the company's trademark), White produced first a tenor trombone, improving the instrument's slide mechanism, bell taper and bore size; later the firm expanded and manufactured the silver cornet, tuba, baritone and trumpet.

In 1909 White moved from his original shop on 9th Street, in Cleveland's old music printing district, to a factory on Superior Avenue. Expansion after World War I included the production of metal clarinets (later discontinued) and saxophones; many of the latter are still produced by the King Co.

Family ownership was relinquished in 1965 with the sale of the firm to Nathan Dolan Associates. It was renamed King Musical Instruments, and within the same year became a subsidiary of the Seeburg Co. In 1965 King also purchased the Strasser-Marigaux-Lemaire Woodwind Co., France, which markets a complete line of wind instruments. Later acquisitions included Benge trumpets and DeFord flutes. In 1966 its offices and manufacturing plant were moved to expanded new facilities at Eastlake, Ohio. In 1983 the firm was bought by

Daniel J. Henkin, who also owns the firm of Conn. For illustration *see* TUBA (i), fig.1c.

MARTIN KRIVIN

Kingr̄ā. Fretted STICK ZITHER of India. The *Ā'īn-i-akbar* (*c*1590) describes it as having two gut strings and small gourds. It is of the *kinnarī vīṇā* type, whence its name (*see* VĪṆĀ, §§4, 6).

Kingri. See KINGIRI.

Kingwéde. Wooden cone flute, with one or two fingerholes, of the Mbala people of northern Zaïre (*LaurentyA* 141).

Kiṅkiṇī jāla. Decorative waistband garlanded with pellet bells (*see* GHUṄGRŪ) of India. It is also known as *kṣudraghaṇṭikā. See also* NŪPUR.

Kiṅkrī [kinjrī]. Three-string fiddle of the Raj Gonds of Adilabad, Andhra Pradesh, India. *See* KIKIR.

Kinku. Side-blown trumpet of the Bembe people of the Republic of the Congo. *See* MAMPONGUI-NGUEMBO.

Kinnārāt. Arabian lyre of the early Islamic era. The name, used for a lyre (*kinnāru*) in all Semitic languages, dates back to the 18th century BC in the correspondence of Mari of Syria. It is also found in other Asiatic cultures: in the Hittite *kinirtalla* and the Dravidian *kinnārī*. The term is of fundamental importance and may come from a single root, 'k-n' or 'q-n', from which the Arabic *qayna* ('slave-girl musician'), among other words, is derived. In Arabic the term is always used in the feminine plural, a tradition also found in Hebrew, where *kinnor* ('lyre') has two plurals, the masculine *kinnōrim* and the feminine *kinnōrōt*; the singular form, *kinnara*, appeared relatively late, in the 9th century. The lyre was usually associated in performance with a wind instrument (MIZMĀR) or a frame drum (DUFF), as mentioned in a passage in *Genesis* xxxi.27.

See also MI'ZAF; QINĪN; 'ŪD.

BIBLIOGRAPHY
H. G. Farmer: *A History of Arabian Music to the XIIIth Century* (London, 1929/*R*1973)
——: 'A Maghribi Work on Musical Instruments', *Journal of the Royal Asiatic Society* (1935), 339
J. Robson: 'Kitāb al-malāhī of Abū Ṭālib al-Muffaḍḍal Ibn Salama', *Journal of the Royal Asiatic Society* (1938), 231
A. J. Wensick and J. P. Mensing: 'Barbat', *Concordances et indice de la tradition musulmane* (Leiden, 1943)
CHRISTIAN POCHÉ

Kinnarī vīṇā [kiṃnarī vīṇā]. A medieval and later Indian term for a fretted STICK ZITHER. *See* VĪṆĀ, §§4, 6.

Kinnhalter (Ger.). CHIN REST.

Kinnin. A variant spelling of QINĪN.

Kin-no-koto. Japanese zither. *See* KOTO.

Kinnor. Modern Hebrew name for the violin. The *kinnor* is mentioned in *Genesis* (iv.21) and is the archetypal string instrument of the Bible (*see* BIBLICAL INSTRUMENTS). It is usually assumed to have been a LYRE

Kinnor played before a king: ivory plaque (1350–1150 BC) from Megiddo (Archaeological Museum, Jerusalem)

probably asymmetric and similar to those shown on a pot found at Megiddo (Bayer, 214; Loud, pll.76,142) and elsewhere. While the references to David playing the instrument stressed that he played 'with his hand', there is evidence, particularly from later periods, that as in other areas a plectrum was also used. The number of strings and the shape of the instrument clearly varied from one period to another and the only definite descriptions that we have, in the Mishna and Josephus, are both very late and contradictory; the iconography, also mostly late (Bayer, group D.III), is normally schematic at best. Biblical references make it clear that the *kinnor* was a general purpose instrument: David played it for Saul (*I Samuel* xvi.23); it was used on many joyous occasions; it was played by harlots (*Isaiah* xxiii.16); it was a Temple instrument used to praise the Lord (Psalm xliii.4 and elsewhere). The number of references to it in the Bible are evidence enough that it was the most important of all the melodic instruments used in ancient Israel.

See also HARP, §2 and KINNĀRĀT.

BIBLIOGRAPHY
G. Loud: *Megiddo II* (Chicago, 1948)
B. Bayer: *The Material Relics of Music in Ancient Palestine and its Environs: an Archaeological Inventory* (Tel-Aviv, 1963, 2/1964)
JEREMY MONTAGU

Kinsman organ. An ELECTRONIC ORGAN developed by a team consisting chiefly of former employees of the Minshall Organ Co., with RICHARD H. DORF; it was made in several models by the Kinsman Manufacturing Co. (founded by Earle V. Kinsman) in Laconia, New Hampshire, from 1957 to the early 1960s, when the company was taken over by the Seeburg Corp. The instruments are 'spinet' organs, with two staggered 44-note manuals, intended for home use. The sounds are generated by 12 neon-lamp oscillators using frequency division (the Kinsman was the first electronic organ to make commercial use of this type of oscillator).

BIBLIOGRAPHY
H. E. Anderson: *Electronic Organ Handbook* (Indianapolis, 1960), 153
HUGH DAVIES

Kinsu. Japanese Buddhist bell. *See* KIN (ii).

Kinura. An ORGAN STOP.

Kio. LEAF OBOE of Tanga Island, Bismarck Archipelago, made from a short length of green lily stem and a piece of areca-nut leaf. Its principal use is to make a variety of named noises collectively called *pongor kinit* ('cries of the ghost') which herald the approach of Soka-pana, a man-devouring ghost.

BIBLIOGRAPHY
F. L. S. Bell: 'Report on Field Work in Tanga', *Oceania*, iv (1934), 306
——: 'Sokapana: a Melanesian Secret Society', *Journal of the Royal Anthropological Institute of Great Britain and Ireland*, lxiii (1935), 317ff
MERVYN McLEAN

Kiondo. SLIT-DRUM of the Holoholo, Sampwe, Luba and Mwanza peoples of Zaïre (*LaurentyTF*, 134, 141). *See* KYONDO.

Kipango. Six-string BOARD ZITHER of the Hehe people of Iringa district, Tanzania.

Kipelevelegu. Log XYLOPHONE of the Gbande people of Liberia. *See* BALO.

Kipenga. MIRLITON of the Nyakyusa people of Tanzania. It resembles the MALIPENGA.

Kipkurkur [kipkurguroik]. Bell of the Nandi people of western Kenya. The *kipkurguroik* is reported as a metal bell worn on the legs of dancers.

Kipokan [kipukandet]. Lyre of the Nandi people of western Kenya. The *kipukandet* is described as a six-string bowl lyre used for song accompaniment. It is strummed with the right hand, the left hand stopping the strings, as on the *bangwe* zither of Malawi. See *TraceyCSA*, ii, 370.

Kiragutsi. Drum of the Tutsi people of Rwanda. *See* INGABE.

Kirān. Arabian lyre. The name is found in pre-Islamic poetry and is probably derived by metathesis from KINNOR or KINNĀRĀT. Its earliest use is in a line by the 6th-century writer Imru' al-Qays, where it is preceded by 'safīḥ', an adjective used for the flat and wide surface of an object; this suggests a lyre rather than a lute. During succeeding centuries the poetic terminology changed (as in the case of other pre-Islamic instruments) and the word 'kirān' became a literary metaphor for the 'ŪD (lute). But, unlike the MUWATTAR or the MIZHAR, the *kirān* was not entirely assimilated, and preserved a double connotation, 'lute' and 'lyre'. Modern scholars have seen the *kirān* as a precursor of the *'ūd*, like the *muwattar* and the *mizhar*, even describing it as having three or four strings and a body covered with skin (*see* QANBŪS). This results from a misreading of a line by the 9th-century writer Ibn al-Rūmī ('Each child called by various names – *'ūd*, *mizhar*, and *kirān*'), from which it has been conjectured that the last (*kirān*) was part of an evolutionary line culminating in the '*ūd*.

BIBLIOGRAPHY

H. G. Farmer: '''Ūd', *EI*

——: 'A Maghribi Work on Musical Instruments', *Journal of the Royal Asiatic Society* (1935), 339

——: *Music: the Priceless Jewel* (Bearsden, 1942)

Nāṣir al-Dīn Asad: *al-Qiyān wal ghinā' fī al-'aṣr al-jāhilī* [Singing-girls and music in pre-Islamic Arabia] (Beirut, 1960/*R*1968)

M. al-'Aqīlī: *Al-Samā' 'ind al-'Arab* [The Music of the Arabs] (Damascus, 1966–79), ii, p.46 and iv, p.18

A. Shiloah: *The Theory of Music in Arab Writings (c.900–1600): Descriptive Catalogue of Manuscripts*, RISM, B/X (1979)

M. Guettat: *La musique classique du Maghreb* (Paris, 1980), 41

CHRISTIAN POCHÉ

Kirckman [Kirchmann, Kirkman]. English family of harpsichord and piano makers, of Alsatian origin. Jacob Kirckman (*b* Bischweiler, 1710; *d* Greenwich, buried 9 June 1792) came to England in the early 1730s, and worked for HERMANN TABEL, whose widow he married in 1738. He took British citizenship on 25 April 1755, and in about 1770 went into partnership with his nephew, Abraham Kirckman (*b* Bischweiler, 1737; *d* Hammersmith, buried 16 April 1794). (The Jacob Kirckman who was organist of St George's, Hanover Square, at this time is probably to be identified with another of Jacob Kirckman's nephews, who died in 1812.) Abraham Kirckman in turn took into partnership his son, Joseph Kirckman (i) (dates of birth and death unknown), whose son, Joseph Kirckman (ii) (*c*1790–1877), worked with his father on their last harpsichord in 1809. The firm continued as piano makers until absorbed by Collard in 1896.

'The first harpsichord maker of the times' was Fanny Burney's description of Jacob Kirckman; but by then Shudi was dead and her father had become increasingly associated with Kirckman, judging by the correspondence with Thomas Jefferson (1786; quoted in Russell, 1959), the entries in *Rees's Cyclopaedia* and other sources. Clearly Kirckman and Shudi had a near monopoly of the English harpsichord at its apogee and various estimates have been made of how many they produced. In the event, over twice as many Kirckmans of one period or another have survived, and Hubbard' phrase 'almost mass produced', though an exaggera tion, is an understandable one. It is not known how man men worked for Kirckman in any one year, nor are th details of his organization and working methods entirel clear. Burney related several anecdotes about Kirckma – about his becoming a money-lender, his wooing o Tabel's widow and his way of dealing with the com petition of the 'keyed guitar' – that clung to his repu tation; more pertinent to his development as a harpsichor maker are his willingness to make experimental harp sichords (such as the enharmonic instrument for Rober Smith of Trinity College, Cambridge, *c*1757), his real istic approach to new-fangled inventions (such as Walk er's quasi-*Geigenwerk*, the CELESTINA, popular in th 1780s), his experience in related keyboard instrument (spinets, claviorgans, pianos *c*1770, square pianos *c*1775 and even his membership of the German Reforme Church of the Savoy, with which were associated bot a musical repertory and an organ tradition much mor cosmopolitan than even the most exceptional Londo parish churches. The fact that he sued his former worke R. Faulkner in 1771 for putting up for sale as by Kirck man a harpsichord made by somebody else (probably Faulkner, like those now in the University of Glasgo and the Russell Collection, with Kirckman nameboards does not suggest vindictiveness; no doubt his complain was justified and accords with other masters suing for mer apprentices at this period (e.g. Gottfried Silber mann and Hildebrandt).

The detailed differences and similarities of construc tion between a Kirckman and Shudi harpsichord are stil being studied, and comparisons of their tone (based usu ally on restored instruments of highly questionable tona authenticity) will remain conjectural for some years to come. What can be said is that there were three main Kirckman–Shudi harpsichord types: singles of 8', 8' singles of 8', 8', 4' and doubles of 8', 8', 4', lute. More often than not there is a buff batten (normally, but not always, for the lower 8') after *c*1760, but lutes were not included on Kirckman singles; sometimes on singles,

1. Harpsichord by Jacob and Abraham Kirckman, London, 1776 (Victoria and Albert Museum, London)

the buff was activated by a foot-lever (or 'pedal'). The machine stop, which is unlikely to date before 1765 (and then only at first for special instruments), was a registration aid whereby on being 'cocked' by a hand stop the foot could operate machinery attached to the register ends in such a way that stops could be changed without the hands needing to be removed from the keys. The standard system – though there were others – was that on, for example, the Shudi harpsichord now in the Vienna Kunsthistorisches Museum (said to have been Haydn's): on depression, the pedal changed the tutti (I 8′, I 4′ + II 8′) to a softer and different colour (I 8′ only, not coupled to II lute). On such English harpsichords, there was no coupler as such, the common 8′ row of strings being a 'dogleg' stop, that is the jacks were so shaped that they rested on the ends of each manual's key-levers. This is today commonly regarded as a weakness of design, that the upper 8′ cannot be contrasted with the lower 8′ in two-manual play since the lower manual automatically plays it; but virtually no literature known to an English harpsichord player in the 18th century required such 'manual contrast and equality'. Either way it is unlikely that the upper manual was voiced other than as an echo. No English organ builder of 1750 was aware of the possibilities of two well-matched manuals; much the same could be said of the harpsichord makers.

The inner construction of a Kirckman was noticeably more complex, and might be thought more clumsy, than a French harpsichord of the same period, but both had developed fairly directly and clearly from the 17th-century Flemish harpsichord. Why English makers by the 1720s were so firmly committed to an idiosyncratic outward appearance to their harpsichords – veneered inside, then outside, with inlay and marquetry – is less clear; of more importance to the player, Kirckman devised an unusual keyboard and key-bed construction, whereby the keys of both manuals were placed on a three-rail frame with front rail pins, so that the key-fall is limited by a rail at the finger end of the keys, a very unpleasant system for fingers used to a French keyboard. Judging by the music written for French harpsichords in 1750, the manual coupling system, whereby the upper manual slid into and out of play with the lower manual and thus did without dogleg jacks, was not at the time understood to have the subtle advantage over the English dogleg system for which recent authors have given it credit. By 1750, French upper manuals also were required for echoes.

Kirckman harpsichords made from c1766 may be found to have two pedals: one for the machine stop, one for the lid swell (see fig.1). The latter was the name given to the device whose mechanism, operated through various types of lever by a pedal, opened a segment of the top lid along the bentside. Some kind of lid swell was incorporated in Plenius's *lyrichord* or *lyrachord* (a version of the gut-strung *Geigenwerk*), of which a description was published in 1755; in 1769 SHUDI patented his Venetian Swell, later adopted by Kirckman. Jefferson (in a letter dated 25 May 1786) called the device a 'machine on the top resembling a Venetian blind for giving a swell' and requested one for his commissioned Kirckman harpsichord. This was some years after Burney reported (in his travels in Italy) that the two Kirckmans he saw in Venice, and the Shudi in Naples, were 'regarded by the Italians as so many phenomena', although it is significant that the known exported Shudis (to Berlin, Vienna and Russia) had all the paraphernalia of the mature English harpsichord: machine stop, Venetian swell, four registers and a compass extended to *C′*.

2. Portrait of a member of the Kirckman family, believed to be Abraham: pen and ink drawing, with wash (c1785), by John Nixon (private collection)

Why Kirckman should have extended at least one of his harpsichords to *c″″* is not known; perhaps in rivalry to Shudi (Kirckman's *c″″* of 1772; Shudi's *C′* for Maria Theresia, 1773) or in inspired anticipation of piano compass (Merlin, 1777, *C′* to *c″″*).

It is possible that circumspect experience would suggest Shudi's harpsichords to have a more 'round' tone than Kirckman's; if so, such an opinion may be based on the more distant plucking-points reputedly given to Shudi's basic design by John Broadwood after c1770, or on the leather (or hard cowhide) plectra that details of jack design suggest to be authentic for at least some spinets and harpsichords from about 1785 or earlier. It seems to be true that Kirckman's lute registers pluck nearer the nut than Shudi's, thus pointing to a more incisive, nasal sound. So subjective is this area of study that Hubbard's considered view that such English harpsichords 'are too good. The tone . . . almost interferes with the music' could be precisely denied by others who found the tone suitably neutral for music in a very wide stylistic spectrum. All things being equal, the Venetian swells must have dulled the tone, both by interfering with its passage (even when open) and by increasing the weight of the whole structure; but there is no evidence that all things were equal, e.g. that builders did not compensate by voicing more brilliantly. Precise details of voicing and stringing, and of the materials used for both, are still imperfectly understood; the question of pitch is also difficult, since low *ton de chambre* of *a′* equal to about 415–20 Hz appears to be correct for many Shudi and Kirckman harpsichords, but perhaps not for all. At least one harpsichord from the 1770s has an apparently contemporary machine stop system whereby two foot-levers depressed in a particular order produce the 4′ alone on the lower manual, thus suggesting that the voicing was meant to give the register more character of one sort or another than is usually the case today. The buff, or so-called harp, effect, produced by a batten studded with small pieces of *peau de buffle* (not felt) brought into contact with the ends of the 8′ strings at the nut, is called 'guitar or harp' by Shudi in the directions on an instrument sent to Frederick the Great; but its purpose can only be conjectured, although special effects in continuo work are the most likely (e.g. in the slow movement of a flute sonata). Machine stops can produce a simulated crescendo–diminuendo effect when applied gradually, while the lid and Venetian swells change the timbre of the sound being produced as much as they do its volume. It has been suggested that, especially as the century neared its end, Kirckman and Shudi harpsichords were intended to be voiced very strongly, and Burney may well have written comparatively when he made his cryptic and unexpected remark about 'quilling, which in France is always weak'. As for the musical repertory of such harpsichords, it is probably fair to regard an enlightened English harpsichord player of c1770, with his interest in Scarlatti and Rameau, Handel and Corelli, J. C. Bach and Mozart, Arne and Purcell, Kirnberger and Hasse, C. P. E. Bach and Sammartini, as requiring a particularly, even uniquely, versatile instrument.

For illustration of a Kirckman–Snetzler instrument, *see* CLAVIORGAN.

BIBLIOGRAPHY
D. H. Boalch: *Makers of the Harpsichord and Clavichord, 1440–1840* (London, 1956, rev. 2/1973) [with details of surviving Kirckman instruments]
R. Russell: *The Harpsichord and Clavichord* (London, 1959, rev. 2/1973)
F. Hubbard: *Three Centuries of Harpsichord Making* (Cambridge, Mass., 1965, 4/1972)
J. Barnes: 'Two Rival Harpsichord Specifications', *GSJ*, xix (1966), 49
P. Williams: 'The Earl of Wemyss' Claviorgan and its Context in Eighteenth-century England', *Keyboard Instruments*, ed. E. M. Ripin (Edinburgh, 1971), 75
DONALD HOWARD BOALCH/PETER WILLIAMS

Kirgicha. Metal SCRAPER of the Dhurwa people, Bastar, central India. *See* CĀRĀ and ŚUKTIVĀDYA, esp. fig.1a.

Kirikiṭṭā. Folk name for the ŚUKTIVĀDYA, a Sanskrit term for a metal SCRAPER.

Kirimba. LAMELLAPHONE of the Bisa people of Zambia.

Kiringi. SLIT-DRUM of the Susu people of Guinea, made from a hollowed log and beaten with two rubber-headed sticks.

Kirisu. Single-headed open-ended drum of the Tonga people of Inhambane region, Mozambique. Two drums are played, with beaters, in conjunction with the *shikulu* bass drum and other percussion to accompany dancing.

Kirki [kirkinchu]. Name used in Peru and Bolivia for the CHARANGO (small fretted lute).

Kirkland, Alfred. English organ builder. *See* BOOTH, JOSEPH and BRYCESON.

Kirkman. *See* KIRCKMAN family.

Kiro. STAMPING TUBE of the 'Are'are people of Malaita, Solomon Islands. Among the neighbouring Kwarekwareo the instrument is called *gilo*. Each tube is made from bamboo 5 to 10 cm in diameter and 45 to 140 cm long, with one end closed and the other open. The longest are stamped on the ground and the shortest on the palm of the hand. They are used in ensemble to provide a rhythmic accompaniment to two-part men's singing at ceremonial feasts. The different lengths are not used for melodic purposes. See H. Zemp: 'Instruments de musique de Malaita', *Journal de la Société des Océanistes*, xxvii/

30 (1971), 39. *See also* 'AU NI MAKO.
MERVYN McLEAN

Kirst, Friedrich Gabriel August (*b* ?Dresden, 1750; *d* Potsdam, 29 April 1806). German woodwind instrument maker. He served his apprenticeship with August Grenser (i) in Dresden and about 1770 entered the employ of one Freyer of Potsdam. On Freyer's death in 1772, Kirst married the widow and took over the business, thereafter producing a wide range of extremely handsome woodwind instruments stamped F.G.A. KIRST/POTSDAM surmounted by the Prussian eagle. He eventually received *privilegium privatum* to supply instruments to the Prussian army and by 1779 had become the salaried flute maker to Frederick the Great. Kirst retired in 1804, and the workshop was taken over by his stepson, Johann Gottlob Freyer, in short-lived partnership with one Martin, after which the two worked independently. Freyer sold out soon thereafter to Griessling & Schlott, Berlin. Kirst's flutes, often of ebony with ivory mounts and silver keys, are very similar in design to those of Quantz but for additional, beautifully designed and executed keys. His bassoons (including one of 1801, his only dated instrument), however, are distinctly in the earlier style of Grenser, with broad, decorated key shanks and ornamented swallowtail touches; several specimens have decorative brass bands around the bell openings.

For illustration of an instrument by Kirst, *see* BASSOON, fig.7c.

BIBLIOGRAPHY
J. Zimmermann: 'Die Flötenmacher Friedrichs des Grossen', *ZI*, lx (1940), nos.14–19
P. T. Young: *2500 Historical Woodwind Instruments* (New York, 1982)
PHILLIP T. YOUNG

Kīrtankhol. Double-headed drum of east India and Bangladesh, used in the accompaniment of *kīrtan* (sacred Vaiṣṇava devotional music). *See* KHOL.

Kirtland & Jardine. English firm of organ builders. James Kirtland, nephew of SAMUEL RENN, continued Renn's business in partnership with FREDERICK WINCOTT JARDINE from 1850 until his retirement in 1866.

Kisaanj. A term which in its many linguistic variant forms denotes a number of types of LAMELLAPHONE found mainly in western and southern Zaïre and bordering countries. Three main types have been reported by Laurenty: the flat-board and raft types, with or without separate resonators, and the box-resonated type. Instruments of this name were collectively labelled 'sanzas' by Montandon and later European scholars. The following variants have been reported from Zaïre by Laurenty, de Hen and Knosp (the names of the peoples using the term are given in parentheses); in many cases the minor variations indicate no more than the lack of a standard orthography for the many dialects at the time when the instruments were listed or collected. They are: *bisanji* (Luluwa); *esandji* (Ngbaka); *esandjo* (Mbole and Bodua); *esandju* (Konda, Mongo, Kota, Ngombe, Bwende and Inganda); *esanjo* (Oli and Ngombe); *esanyo* (Oli); *esanzo* or *ezanza* (Bonkoso Mongo); *isangi* (Ndengese); *isanj* (Akwa-Sonjo); *isanzi* (Teke); *kasambi* (Warega); *kasandji* (Teke); *ka-sanzi* (Luba); *kesangi* (Tetela); *kisaaji* or *kisazhi* (Chokwe); *kisaanda* (Mbagani); *kisaanj*, *kisaandj*, *kisaandji*, *kisaanji*, *kisanjj* (Suku, Sonde, Lunda and Holo); *kisachi* (Sankuru); *kisaji ia Londe* (Lunda); *kisanchi* or *kisanshi* (Sampwe); *kisanji kia mulope* (Luba of Kabongo); *kisanzi* (Luba of Mwanza); *ndjanga* (Yans); *nkisansi* (Bwalayulu); *quisangi*

(Kuba); *risandji* (Holo); *sanzi* (Solongo); *sanzu* (Luluwa region); *tshanji* (Koshi); *tshisaanji* (Luluwa-Bakwa); *tshisaji* (Chokwe and Lunda); *tshisanji* (Bakwa-Luntu); *tshisanshi* (Luba of Dibaya); *tshisazi tsha mudidi* (Binji); and *udjanga* (Ngbaka). Other variants, reported principally for southern Zaïre, Angola and Zambia, are: *chisandzi*; *chisandzi cha likembe*; *chisanje*; *chisanji*; *chisanzhi*; *chisanzi*; and *txissanje*. For further information on the above instruments, where it has been possible to provide it, see their respective entries.

BIBLIOGRAPHY
LaurentyS, 192ff
F. J. de Hen: *Beitrag zur Kenntnis der Musikinstrumente aus Belgisch Kongo und Ruanda-Urundi* (Tervuren, 1960)
G. Knosp: *Enquête sur la vie musicale au Congo belge 1934–1935* (Tervuren, 1968)

PETER COOKE

Kisarka. A term occasionally applied to the KISSAR.

Kisengele. Metal bell of the Chaga/Meru people of Arusha district, Tanzania. The bells are worn on the legs of singers and dancers.

Kisfejes citera. BOX ZITHER of Hungary with carved horse heads. *See* CITERA, esp. illustration.

Kishyaata. Box-resonated LAMELLAPHONE of the Mbagani people of Zaïre. It has metal keys, and the soundtable projects past the box (*LaurentyS*, 194).

Kissar. Five-string bowl lyre of Egypt and the Sudan. The term is a corruption of the Coptic, from the Greek. The phrase 'gegen atkithara' appears frequently in the Coptic psalter but is of no help to organological understanding since the reference is to a harp or a lute. Travellers in the 18th and 19th centuries, however, noted a link between the *kissar* and the lyre: 'I saw, among the . . . Barbari from Dongola, a sort of harp . . . [five-string] that in their language they call *kussir*, and the Arabs *tambura*' (C. Niebuhr: *Voyage in Arabia* (Amsterdam, 1776), i, 145); 'The sounding body of the *kissar* or Ethiopian lyre is made from a roughly worked small bowl of maple wood that the Nubians call *goussa*' (Villoteau: *Description . . . des instruments de musique* [Egypt], ii (Paris, 1817), 920). Nowadays in northern Sudan, the bowl is called *koos*. These observations have been taken as basic references by Westerners. However, a number of distortions have been noted: *gezarke, guisarke, kisarka, qitara barbariya, qitar* (C. Sachs: *Real-Lexikon der Musikinstrumente*, 1913); *kassar, kasra* (H. G. Farmer: 'The Music of Ancient Mesopotamia', *NOHM*, i (1957/R1975), 244). The term *kissar* has prevailed, coming into use in the West in the 19th century. Although oriental writers have never mentioned it, it has been used to describe all the lyres in the Nile valley and even those of Uganda, although in that area the word *kissar* is scarcely known. The preference for the term *kissar* over such equivalents as *rababa* or *ṭanbūra* was designed to establish a link between the Nile valley and Ancient Greece and to prove that the tuning of the *kissar* explained that of Apollo's lyre, which had survived in Egypt: 'the *kissar* or Ethiopian lyre stems from the Greek *kithara*' (V. Mahillon: *Catalogue descriptif* (Brussels, 1893), no. 153); that view is still held (see A. Kebede, in *EM*, xxi (1977), 385). The term *kissar* exists in Upper Egypt and the Sudan, where it is called *kisir* in the northern area of Sukkot, but it is necessary to circumscribe its application. It is one of the variations in terminology that has affected the understanding of the history of musical instruments. Tunings of the *kissar* put forward by Niebuhr and Villoteau may be compared with the more recent ones of Maḥmud Sāmi Ḥāfiẓ (1954, p.146) and Simon (1980) which must be those of the *ṭanbūra*. Niebuhr gave *eb″–f′–a′–b′–c″–d″* (*kussir*), Villoteau *d″–g′–a′–b′–e″* (*kissar*), Ḥāfiẓ *f′–a′–b′–d″–e″* and *e″–a′–b′–c″* (*qissar*), and A. Simon *d′–c′–a–g–e″* (*kisir*).

The 19th-century description of the five-string *kissar* conforms to that of the *ṭanbūra*, though it is smaller (about 70 cm long) and the soundholes are replaced by tiny holes. Some archaic examples from central Africa, at the Metropolitan Museum of Art, New York, show the use of animal horns, with monkey skulls forming the soundbox. Saint-Saëns, during his journey in Egypt, reported on the way of playing: the left hand, far from reinforcing the action of the right-hand plectrum, pulled the string that was struck, or else dampened it ('Lyres et cithares', *EMDC*, I/v (1922), 538).

BIBLIOGRAPHY
J.-B. de La Borde: *Essai sur la musique ancienne et moderne* (Paris, 1780/R1972), i, 382
C. Engel: *Descriptive Catalogue of the Musical Instruments in the South Kensington Museum* (London, 1874)
G. Chouquet: *Le Musée du Conservatoire national de musique* (Paris, 1884), 207
F. Clément: *Histoire de la musique* (Paris, 1885), 72
E. Bailly: *Le pittoresque musical à l'Exposition* (Paris, 1900), 14ff
J. Stainer: *The Music of the Bible* (London, n.d.), 18ff
K. Schlesinger: *Instruments of the Modern Orchestra and Early Records of the Precursors of the Violin Family* (London, 1910/R1969)
H. G. Farmer: 'Mi'zaf', *EI*
M. M. S. Ḥāfiẓ: *La connaissance de la musique égyptienne en France avant 1800* (diss., U. of Paris, 1954)
A. Baines: 'Lyre', *Grove 5*
B. W. Dietz and M. B. Olatunji: *Musical Instruments of Africa* (New York, 1965), 76ff
T. Alexandru: 'De la kissar la semsemiya, traditie si inovatie in muzica populara din Egypt', *CMz*, iii (1971), 403; repr. in *Folclorista organologie muzicologie studii* (Bucharest, 1980)
J. Hill: *The Harold E. Cook Collection of Musical Instruments* (London, 1975)
G. A. Plumley: *El Tanbur: the Sudanese Lyre or the Nubian Kissar* (Cambridge, 1976)
A. Simon: 'Nordsudan: Musik der Nubier', Museum für Völkerkunde, Berlin Staatliche Museen, MC 9 (1980) [disc notes]

CHRISTIAN POCHÉ

Kit [kytte] (Fr. *poche, pochette, sourdine*; Ger. *Posch, Tanzmeistergeige, Taschengeige*; It. *canino, pochetto, sordina, sordino*; Lat. *linterculus*). A small, unfretted fiddle, generally with four strings, made in a great variety of shapes and played from the 16th century to the 19th. Kits can be divided into two general types: a member of the rebec family, either pear-shaped or resembling a narrow boat, with a distinctly vaulted back; or a miniature viol, violin or guitar, with a slightly arched back and a long neck. Not all have a soundpost or bassbar; their presence depends on the size and shape of each instrument. The tuning is generally in 5ths, sometimes at the pitch of the violin, but more often a 4th or a 5th and occasionally an octave higher if there are only three strings. Surviving kits range from simple rustic instruments to the products of such makers as Joachim Tielke and Stradivari (who left working patterns for different types of kit, including the boat shape labelled 'canino' and elongated violin shapes of which the last is dated 1733).

1. Terminology. 2. History. 3. Repertory.

1. TERMINOLOGY. It has been suggested that the word 'kit' derives from *kithara* (itself a plucked instrument), but unless real evidence is found this theory cannot be

held with conviction. Perhaps more likely is the idea that it was the 'kitten' to the larger bowed instruments such as those of the violin family, which were said, however erroneously, to be strung with catgut. The term 'poche' was said by Trichet (*c*1630) to describe the leather case in which the instrument was kept; Mersenne (1636–7) said that it was kept in the pockets (*poches*) of violinists who taught dancing. 'Taschengeige' also relates the instrument to a pocket, and 'Tanzmeistergeige' indicates its use by a dancing-master. 'Sordino' and 'sourdine' are descriptive of its small sound, and 'canino' compares it with a canine tooth. 'Linterculus' points to its resemblance to a small boat. There was considerable overlapping between the use of these names and the instruments to which they were applied; for the sake of consistency 'kit' will be used here to cover all types, except when an actual source is being quoted.

2. HISTORY. Some kits could be regarded simply as rebecs, but it is to the rebec that the name 'kit' seems first to have been applied. When this happened is uncertain, but the term was in use in England in the first quarter of the 16th century. In the *Interlude of the Four Elements* (*c*1517) Humanity says: 'This dance would do mich better yet/If we had a kit or taberet'. There is no evidence that this meant anything other than the pear-shaped rebec, an instrument which is often seen in English artistic sources of the time, and is known to have been used frequently at the court of Henry VIII. In the late 17th century Randle Holme III drew a picture of a rebec and wrote by it 'A Kit with foure bowed strings' (*GB-Lbm* Harl.2027, f.272). The French term *poche* also included instruments of the rebec shape, as indicated by several references to its similarity to the mandora. For instance, on 7 January 1625 an inventory was made of the instruments belonging to François Richomme, 'violinist in ordinary to the king, and king of the minstrels of the kingdom of France', and among its items was 'une . . . poche façon de mandore'. One of Praetorius's three pictures (*Syntagma musicum*, 2/1619) of

Poschen is identical with a three-string rebec.

During the 16th century some members of the rebec family became narrower in proportion to their length than had hitherto been usual. One of these, now in the Museo Civico at Bologna, has the inscription 'Baptista Bressano'. It is in the form of a fish, and was perhaps used for an *intermedio* or some other dramatic production. A similar instrument, though less exotic, can be seen in the woodcut 'Youth', from *The Ages of Women* by Tobias Stimmer (1539–84). By the end of the 16th century this type was firmly established in the shape of a narrow boat, still with a vaulted back, but sometimes with a clear demarcation between the body and neck, even when they were made from one piece of wood. Perhaps to compensate for its relatively simple shape, it was often lavishly decorated with inlaid wood, ivory, ebony or jewels, such as was another 'poche' from the collection of François Richomme. 'Enriched by rubies, mother-of-pearl and seed pearls', its case was furnished with a lock and key, an indication of the instrument's value. Mersenne, however, remarked that such ornamentation would not improve an instrument's musical qualities. Other kits had carved backs, a notable example being one now in the Musikhistorisk Museum, Copenhagen. Its inscription reads 'Conradus Muller 1520', but this is now held to be false and the instrument thought to date from the 17th century. A somewhat later German or Swiss kit in the Victoria and Albert Museum, London, has its back carved with animals, birds, isolated musical instruments (including a jew's harp) and cherubic dancers and instrumentalists (fig.2*a*). Although it was still being made in the early 19th century, the boat-shaped kit flourished most during the 17th, when it was described in Cotgrave's *Dictionarie of the French and English Tongues* (1611):

Poche: f. . . . also, the little narrow, and long Violin (having the backe of one peece) which French dauncers, or dauncing Maisters, carrie about with them in a case, when they goe to teach their Schollers.

Late in the 17th century new shapes appeared. The body and neck became quite separate, the former resem-

1. Dancing-master with a kit: engraving (1745) by Le Bas after Philippe Canot

2. Kits: (a) German or Swiss, first half of the 18th century; (b) Italian, c1700; (c) pochette d'amour by Giovanni Battista Genova, Turin, c1765; (d) by Dimanche Drouyn, Paris, late 17th century; (a), (d) Victoria and Albert Museum, London; (b), (c) Royal College of Music, London

bling a viol, violin or guitar, but sometimes being a festooned hybrid (fig.2b). The viol form, however, was different from its prototype in that it had no frets, and also that the back was often slightly arched like that of a violin. Unlike the boat-shaped kit, this type was rarely decorated, its visual beauty being in the outer design, the wood, and the varnish. In the late 18th century Hawkins, having referred to the narrow 'poches' described by Mersenne, added 'In England this instrument is called a Kit, it is now made in the form of a violin'. By this time the influence of the viola d'amore had caused the occasional addition of sympathetic strings, resulting in the *pochette d'amour* (an example by Giovanni Battista Genova of Turin (c1765) is in the Royal College of Music, London; fig.2c).

The kit was played at all social levels. The writer of *The Christian State of Matrimony* (1543) condemned those people who came to church with 'a great noise of harpes, lutes, kyttes, basens and drommes, wherwyth they trouble the whole church, and hyndre them in matters pertayninge to God'. Drayton in his *Poly-Olbion* (London, 1613) described the kit as being a favourite instrument of wandering fiddlers. In Cesare Negri's masque *Le gratie d'amore*, performed before Don John of Austria on 26 June 1574, the allegorical figure 'La Perseveranza' was followed on to the stage by a shepherd carrying a 'sordina'. Shepherds are also associated with kits in Monteverdi's *Orfeo* (1607), but here the

instruments are described as 'violini piccoli alla Francese'. In the painting *Peasant Children* by Antoine le Nain, now in the Glasgow Art Gallery, one child plays a kit and another a pipe. His *Young Musicians* (in the private collection of Lord Aldenham) depicts a kit played in consort with a singer and guitarist. Lully's violin-shaped kit is now in the Paris Conservatoire, and at the top of the social scale the grand dauphin, eldest son of Louis XIV, had a boat-shaped kit made by Dimanche Drouyn of Paris (fig.2d). This ivory-backed instrument, together with its bow and leather case, is now in the Victoria and Albert Museum. Leopold Mozart wrote in his *Violinschule* (1756) that the kit was then 'almost obsolete'. However, Robert Bremner in London published among his list of wares (c1765):

Little Violins and Kits
Bows for small Violins & Kits
Bridges for Kits, Violins, Tenors, Viol de Gambo's and Basses
Pegs or Pins for ditto
Tail Pieces for ditto.

One of his customers may have been Francis Pemberton, described by Hawkins as

a dancing master of London, lately deceased, who was so excellent a master of the Kit, that he was able to play solos on it, exhibiting in his performance all the graces and elegancies of the violin, which is all the more to be wondered at as he was a very corpulent man.

3. REPERTORY. Very little music was composed specifically for the kit so the performer generally played vio-

3. Kit by Antonio Stradivari, Cremona, 1717 (Conservatoire de Musique, Paris)

lin pieces or popular tunes. Hawkins wrote that the powers of the kit were 'co-extensive with those of the violin', but whether or not the performer played above the first position depended on the instrument and the manner in which it was held. A kit by James Aird of Glasgow made in about 1780, complete with a book of tunes written out by a former owner, John Hall of Ayr (1788–1862), is now in the Glasgow Museum. No instrument is specified for the music, but the dance, songs and marches in the book are playable on the violin and some are accompanied. Many of them are suitable for the kit. In 1858, when performance on the instrument was rare, Louis Clapisson acquired a kit by Stradivari, and composed a gavotte for it in his opera *Les trois Nicolas*. This instrument, violin-shaped and dated 1717 (fig.3), was originally brought to France by Luigi Tarisio, and is now in the Museum of the Paris Conservatoire (Clapisson was its first curator).

BIBLIOGRAPHY

HawkinsH

M. Praetorius: *Syntagma musicum*, ii (Wolfenbüttel, 2/1619/*R*1958 and 1980)
M. Mersenne: *Harmonie universelle* (Paris, 1636–7/*R*1963; Eng. trans., 1957)
P. Trichet: *Traité des instruments de musique* (*F-Psg* 1070, *c*1640); ed. F. Lesure (Neuilly-sur-Seine, 1957)
A. Kircher: *Musurgia universalis* (Rome, 1650/*R*1970)
F. W. Galpin: *Old English Instruments of Music* (London, 1910, rev. 4/1965 by T. Dart)
G. Kinsky: *Musikhistorisches Museum von Wilhelm Heyer in Cöln* (Cologne, 1910–16)
C. Sachs: *Sammlung alter Musikinstrumente bei der Staatlichen Hochschule für Musik zu Berlin: beschreibender Katalog* (Berlin, 1913)
D. Fryklund: *Studien über die Pochette* (Sundsvall, 1917)
L. Greilsamer: 'La facture des instruments à archet', *EMDC*, II/iii (1927), 1708
N. Bessaraboff: *Ancient European Musical Instruments* (New York, 1941)
F. Lesure: 'La facture instrumentale à Paris au seizième siècle', *GSJ*, vii (1954), 11; x (1957), 87
D. D. Boyden: 'Monteverdi's *Violini Piccoli alla Francese* and *Viole da Brazzo*', *AnnM*, vi (1958–63), 387
N. and F. Gallini: *Comune di Milano: Museo degli strumenti musicali* (Milan, 1963)
L. Cervelli: *Mostra di antichi strumenti musicali* (Modena, 1963)
E. Halfpenny: 'An Eighteenth-century Trade List of Musical Instruments', *GSJ*, xvii (1964), 99
S. Marcuse: *Musical Instruments: a Comprehensive Dictionary* (New York, 1964)
D. D. Boyden: *The History of Violin Playing from its Origins to 1761* (London, 1965)
A. Baines: *European and American Musical Instruments* (London, 1966)
E. Winternitz: *Musical Instruments of the Western World* (London, 1966)
A. Baines: *Non-Keyboard Instruments*, Victoria and Albert Museum: Catalogue of Musical Instruments, ii (London, 1968)
I. Otto: *Das Musikinstrumenten-Museum Berlin* (Berlin, 1968)
C. van Leeuwen Boomkamp and J. H. van der Meer: *The Carel van Leeuwen Boomkamp Collection of Musical Instruments* (Amsterdam, 1971)
P. Frisoli: 'The *Museo Stradivariano* in Cremona', *GSJ*, xxiv (1971), 33
S. F. Sacconi: *I 'segreti' di Stradivari* (Cremona, 1972)
W. Stauder: *Alte Musikinstrumente* (Brunswick, 1973)
A. Pushman: 'A 16th-century Pochette', *The Strad*, lxxxiv (1973–4), 646
M. Remnant: *Musical Instruments of the West* (London, 1978)
A. Buchner: *Colour Encyclopedia of Musical Instruments* (Prague and London, 1980)

MARY REMNANT

Kit, The. An ELECTRONIC PERCUSSION instrument developed by Clive Button in 1980 and manufactured by MPC Electronics in Willingham, Cambridgeshire, from 1982. It consists of a small console, 26·5 by 24 cm, incorporating four large and three small drum-pads (played with the fingers) which trigger a range of electronically generated percussion sounds; a rhythm unit (hi-hat only) is included. Three additional consoles, which can be triggered from The Kit, provide timpani, hand-clap and non-imitative percussion sounds. In 1983 the company produced the much larger Music Percussion Computer (also designed by Clive Button), with eight drum-pads, which can be interfaced with a small home computer, the Sinclair ZX 81, to expand its capabilities.

For illustration *see* ELECTRONIC PERCUSSION, fig.1.

HUGH DAVIES

Kitaj. A fiddle played by the Aguaruna people of the Peruvian tropical forest region south of the Marañón River. It is made of balsa wood and has two strings of plant fibre.

Kiteba. PANPIPES played in the MISHIBA panpipes ensemble of the Luba/Songe people of southern Zaïre.

Kithara [cithara]. (1) The most important string instrument of Greco-Roman antiquity. Like the LYRE it was distinguished from most string instruments by the absence of a neck. Instead it had two arms rising vertically from its sound-chest which were crossed by a yoke near their upper extremities. Strings of equal length were stretched between the yoke and the soundbox and were tuned by varying their tension and possibly thickness. The kithara differed from the lyre in Greco-Roman nomenclature in that its sound-chest was constructed from wood, while that of the lyre was originally a tortoise-shell. The vertical arms are also of wood and are often hollow; this was a means of extending the sound-chest. Two shapes of sound-chest can be distinguished, the more common rectangular (illustrated here) and a somewhat smaller one with a rounded bottom referred to by historians as the 'cradle kithara'. (For illustration, *see* LYRE, fig.5.)

Early Greek iconography pictured the kithara, called at first the PHORMINX, with from three to five strings. Even before the classical period seven strings had become standard, a development often attributed to the shadowy 7th-century figure Terpander, while after the 5th century there is evidence, particularly from literary sources, that the number was often increased. Iconographic sources nevertheless continued to represent the standard number of seven strings; this is probably due to iconographic convention in dealing with mythological scenes. The kithara, larger and heavier than the lyre, was usually played while the performer was standing; it pressed against the left side of the body and was strapped to the left wrist. The lighter 'cradle kithara' was sometimes played with the performer sitting; it then rested in the lap of the player. The player's hands were held in precisely the same manner as with the lyre, that is, the left hand behind the strings, either plucking, strumming or dampening them while the right plucked them with a plectrum.

Kithara player: detail from a Greek amphora (c480 BC), Attic red-figure style, attributed to the 'Brygos painter' (Museum of Fine Arts, Boston)

The kithara is fairly common throughout North Africa and the Near East, where it would normally be referred to as a lyre. Though known in Mesopotamia from early times (in the 'royal' cemetery of Ur, for instance), this type of instrument did not attain popularity in Egypt until the 18th dynasty. Asia Minor seems to be the source of the Greco-Roman type as well as the Etruscan kithara, the most frequently depicted of Etruscan string instruments. In spite of its foreign origins, the kithara became so thoroughly naturalized in Greece that it gained a privileged position, retaining few if any foreign or barbarous connotations. As early as in the Homeric epics it had become the indispensable accompaniment to the singing of the praises of Hellenic heroes. It was used also in choral performances of all types. Together with the lyre, it was the instrument which served to symbolize that which is most Hellenic in Greek musical mythology. Apollo played it in his contest with the satyr Marsyas and Orpheus played it to charm wild beasts and mollify the guardians of the underworld.

The kithara and lyre were broadly similar in function: differences, if any, resulted from the larger instrument's adaptability to concert usage and virtuoso display. For example, the kithara was considerably more prominent in the musical *agones* (competitions) at civic festivals, and during the 5th and 4th centuries BC virtuoso and professional kithara playing was associated with the new musical trends criticized by Plato and Aristotle. The new style particularly affected the *nomos kitharōdikos*, a solo song usually with epic text accompanied on the kithara, introducing greater freedom in rhythm and modulation. Among leading innovators were Phrynis and Timotheus (c450–360 BC), who are supposed to have added more strings (up to 12) to the kithara. In post-classical Greece and in Rome the lyre increasingly gave way to the kithara; the latter was correspondingly used in new ways. At Rome in particular, after the conquest of Greece, it appeared in virtually every area of musical life including the theatre, the *convivium*, and cult music, where at one time the tibia had been used exclusively. 'Dionysiac artists', often from Greece, used the kithara among other instruments for public festivals; settings were made of such Latin poets as Catullus and Horace to be accompanied by the lyre or kithara; and the kithara featured in the dramatic performances of the *pantomimi*. There were eventually a sufficient number of kithara players employed in cult music to warrant their being organized in the *collegium fidicinum Romanum*, the Roman society of string players. Perhaps because of such religious associations, the kithara eluded the ban in the early Church against instrumental music: it was used to accompany the psalms.

See also GUITAR, §2; HARP, §1; ROTTE (ii).

(2) The name given by HARRY PARTCH to the members of a group of instruments resembling the ancient Greek kithara. Kithara I was built in 1938 but did not reach its final form until 1959. It has the Greek kithara's hollow arms, linked at the top by a cross-piece that carries the tuning-pegs, and there is an additional soundboard in the form of a slender central pillar. The soundbox at the base of the arms has an open top; there is no external bridge, the strings passing into the soundbox and fastening below bridges mounted on internal soundboards. The instrument is bolted to a large trapeziform resonator and the whole assemblage stands 180 cm high. All the upright kitharas have 72 strings, grouped in 12 sets of six; they are plucked with the fingers or a plectrum. Glass rods, held against the vertical soundboards by the

sets of strings adjacent to them, act as movable bridges and allow retuning and sliding sounds (when moved as the strings are plucked); the eight sets of strings without rods are played 'open'. Kithara I has an alto range (the highest note is around bb').

The other members of the kithara family were all built to supplement or modify the first instrument. Some of the parts that Partch wrote for Kithara I, especially that in *Castor and Pollux* (1952), were too demanding for a single player, so he built the Surrogate Kithara (1953; second version, 1966) to share them. The Surrogate Kithara bears little resemblance to the rest of the family. It consists of a large horizontal triangular stand ($c36$ cm high), at the apex of which the player sits; in front of him are two horizontal 'canons' (multiple monochords) mounted on closed soundboxes with side holes, the further one higher than the nearer one. Each canon carries eight strings which hold movable glass rods against the soundboard; the range of the canons (they are tuned differently) is approximately D to e'. Kithara II (1954) was designed as a bass version of the first instrument; its lowest note is C. In place of the original soundbox and resonator, it has six vertical resonators about 1·5 metres tall; the whole instrument is 206 cm high and an integral riser (a hollow box that gives additional resonance) is provided, on which the player stands. Kithara II lacks the central pillar of the earlier instrument but carries two of its sets of strings on the outside of the arms, allowing glass rods to be used with sets 1, 2, 11 and 12. New Kithara I (1972) is an improved version of Kithara I, giving greater resonance.

BIBLIOGRAPHY

I. Henderson: 'Ancient Greek Music', *NOHM*, i (1957), 336–40?
E. Winternitz: 'The Survival of the Kithara and the Evolution o the Cittern: a Study in Morphology', *Music, Libraries and Instru ments*, ed. U. Sherrington and G. Oldham (London, 1961), 20?
M. Wegner: *Griechenland*, Musikgeschichte in Bildern, ii/4 (Leipzig 1963)
G. Fleischhauer: *Etrurien und Rom*, Musikgeschichte in Bildern ii/5 (Leipzig, 1964)
J. F. Mountford and R. P. Winnington-Ingram: 'Music', *Oxford Classical Dictionary* (Oxford, 2/1970), 705

JAMES W. Mc KINNON, ROBERT ANDERSON (1 ROSEMARY ROBERTS (2

Kithembe. Single-headed open-ended conical drum o the Kamba people of Machakos district, Kenya.

Kitiar. Lute of Ecuador. *See* KEER.

Kitingbi. Braced MUSICAL BOW of the Mamvu, Balese Mangutu, Ndo and Dongo peoples of Zaïre. In performance the bow is placed against an inverted half-calabash on the ground or, among the Mamvu, against an earthenware pot. The instrument is plucked (or struck with the middle finger of the right hand and stopped by gripping the string with the index and thumb of the left. Mangutu women reputedly stop the instrument by placing their chins on the string. The *kitingbi* is generally played by women, traditionally in connection with rites associated with first menstruation, but also with women's dances; among the Ndo the instrument was traditionally also played by young boys. Other names reported are: *bendukuku, bikife, elingingile, gambili, gulutindi*

(a)   *(b)*

1. Kízh kízh díhí (fiddle) of the Apache: (a) photograph, c1882–6; (b) painted fiddle of the White Mountain Apache, Arizona (Museum of the American Indian, New York)

kambili, kidrigo, kilikingila, kilingbindiri, kumbili and *kwendibe*.

BIBLIOGRAPHY

LaurentyC, 114

F. J. de Hen: *Beitrag zur Kenntnis der Musikinstrumente aus Belgisch Kongo und Ruanda-Urundi* (Tervuren, 1960)

K. A. GOURLAY

Kito. Animal-horn hunting whistle of the Luba people of Zaïre. It measures 8 to 10 cm in length. Ingredients believed to be magical are placed inside the horn to protect or assist the hunter. On discovering the tracks of an antelope, the hunter blows his whistle, imitating the sound of the fawn.

Kitutu. LAMELLAPHONE of the Holo people of south-western Zaïre. It has metal keys and a box resonator hollowed out at the end nearest the player (*LaurentyS*, 195).

Kiumvi [kiumvu]. SLIT-DRUM of the Luba, Ankoro, Kabongo and Sampwe peoples of Zaïre (*LaurentyTF*, 138). *See* NKUMVI.

Kiyak. *See* KIAK.

Kiyamba. Rattle of Tanzania. *See* KAYAMBA.

Kiyangall. Carved wooden VESSEL FLUTE of the Yaka people of south-western Zaïre (*LaurentyA*, 82).

Kízh kízh díhí (Apache: 'buzz buzz sound') [Navajo violin]. Single- or two-string fiddle of the White Mountain and San Carlos Apache of Arizona and the Diegueno Indians of California. It is also called *tsii' edo' áli* ('wood singing'). It is made from a sturdy mescal stalk 40 to 45 cm long and 5 to 13 cm in diameter. The stalk is hollowed out either by splitting it lengthwise or by cutting a large triangular, round, or rhomboid soundhole and gouging out the pith. 5 to 8 cm of pith are left at each end to give structural support to the string holder and the tuning-peg; the ends are also wound with sinew. The horsehair strings are stretched over small rectangular bridges, one at each end of the instrument. The bow is made from a twig 35 to 45 cm long, with a length of horsehair tied to it at both ends; the hair is fastened under enough tension to cause the twig to arch. A lump of pinyon pine pitch may be fixed to one end of the fiddle to provide rosin for the bow.

The fiddle is held horizontally, in the left hand, with its end resting on the player's chest or abdomen (fig.1*a*). The instrument has a faint, dry, squeaky tone (hence its name) and is played as a solo instrument, usually for self-entertainment at home or with a small group of friends. It is not known whether the Apache fiddle is of aboriginal design or related to European models.

BIBLIOGRAPHY

D. McAllester: 'An Apache Fiddle', *EM*, viii (1956), 1

MARY RIEMER-WELLER

Kizugo. Wooden hourglass-shaped double bell of the Shambala people of Tanzania with pellet bells around the waist.

K'jom [tamborón]. A term used among the Maya people of Guatemala for a cylindrical double-headed drum of the European type. It has replaced older Maya types. *See also* ATABAL.

Kkangkkangi. Folk term for the HAEGŬM, a Korean fiddle.

Kkwaenggwari. Small, lipped, flat bronze gong of Korea. It is known by another onomatopoeic name, *kkaengmaegi*, as well as *sogŭm* ('small gong') and *soe* ('metal'). Its dimensions are not fixed, but a typical

Kkwaenggwari (small gong) of Korea

instrument would be about 20 cm in diameter, with a lip of about 5 cm. The player supports the instrument by putting his left thumb and fingers under the upper lip (see illustration), allowing both an open sound (*kkaeng*) and, by touching the left fingers against the resonating surface, a damped sound (*maek*); the instrument is struck with a small wood or bamboo mallet with a wooden ball at the end. The sound of the *kkwaenggwari* is remarkably loud, penetrating and clangorous.

The treatise *Akhak kwebŏm* (1493) describes the small gong in connection with dance at the Sacrifice to Royal Ancestors (*Chongmyo*) and indicates that it was also used to announce the beginning of the ritual performance. At present the instrument is used chiefly in *nongak* ('farmers' music'), played by the band leader. Patterns played on the *kkwaenggwari* are very rapid and complex, being reinforced on strong beats by the *ching* (large gong).

A similar Chinese gong is the LUO.

BIBLIOGRAPHY

Sŏng Hyŏn, ed.: *Akhak kwebŏm* [Guide to the study of music] (Seoul, 1493/*R*1975), 8.9*b*

Chang Sa-hun: *Han'guk akki taegwan* [Korean musical instruments] (Seoul, 1969), 123

ROBERT C. PROVINE

Klabatas [klabačas, klabanas, klabeklis]. Percussion plaque of Latvia. It was a wooden board hung by the gatepost or on its own post and cross-beam. When beaten with one or two hardwood hammers, it produced a penetrating sound to call farm workers home from the fields. In some areas it was sounded only to warn of fire or some other calamity, hence its local name *briesmu dēlis* ('danger board'). Unlike otherwise analogous instruments of eastern Europe (*klepalo*, *sēmantron* etc) it was not used for religious purposes. The term 'klabatas' was also used for a wooden bell (*see* KLABEKLIS). See Ī. Priedīte: *Ko spēlēja sendienās* [What was played in the past] (Riga, 1983).

Klabeklis [klabatas, skrabeklis]. Wooden bell of Latvia. It was generally trough-shaped with one or two clappers, and was hung round the necks of farm animals while grazing. At the end of the 19th century, a series of such wooden bells without the clappers were set in a wooden frame and used as a rhythm instrument in village bands. They were then sometimes called *koka zvans* ('wooden bell'), and are analogous to the Lithuanian *skrabalas*.

Klagend (Ger.: 'plaintive', 'complaining', 'lamenting'). An expression mark used most famously by Beethoven in the finale of his op.110 Piano Sonata.

Klais, Johannes. German firm of organ builders. Johannes Klais (1852–1925) founded the company in Bonn in 1882, having broken with his family's farming tradition in becoming an organ builder. Some of his pupils later set up their own firms: Anton Feith, Wilhelm Furtwängler (son of the organ builder of the same name; *see* HAMMER-ORGELBAU) and Hans Steinmeyer. He was succeeded by his son Hans (Johannes Caspar Wilhelm Maria Klais, 1890–1965), whose own son Hans Gerd (*b* Bonn, 2 Dec 1930) directs the firm in Bonn.

The majority of Klais organs are in the Rhineland, Hesse and Westphalia, but they are also found elsewhere in Germany, Europe, and overseas; the firm's largest instrument was built for the Messehalle in Cologne in 1924 (five manuals, 130 stops). Klais initially built organs with slider-chests and tracker action; they made their first mechanical sliderless chests in 1895, their first using pneumatic action in 1897 and their first with electric action in 1906; in 1928 they built a slider windchest with mechanical action again, and this has been their usual type since 1948. Among the firm's restorations are those of J. M. Stumm's organ (1742) at Oberlahnstein and Geib's (1777) at the Evangelical Church, Lambrecht (1977; two manuals, 26 stops). New instruments include those at the Musikakademie, Detmold (1968; four manuals, 53 stops), Würzburg Cathedral (1969; five manuals, 86 stops), the Liebfrauenkirche, Oberursel, Hesse (1970; four manuals, 52 stops), the University of Arts, Nagoya, Japan (1971; three manuals, 37 stops), Trier Cathedral (1974; four manuals, 67 stops), St Hedwig's Cathedral, Berlin (1976; three manuals, 67 stops), the minster in Ingolstadt (1977; four manuals, 69 stops), Limburg Cathedral (1978; four manuals, 60 stops), Graz Cathedral (1978; four manuals, 70 stops), Altenberg Cathedral (1980; four manuals, 82 stops), and Elisabeth University, Hiroshima (1981; three manuals, 38 stops).

BIBLIOGRAPHY

H. Klotz: 'Klais', *MGG*
J. Klais: 'Klais, Johannes d. Ältere', *Rheinische Musiker*, ii, ed. K. G. Fellerer (Cologne, 1962), 41
——: 'Klais, Johannes Caspar Wilhelm Maria', *Rheinische Musiker*, ii, ed. K. G. Fellerer (Cologne, 1962), 43
H. G. Klais: 'Gedanken über die Neuplanung von Orgeln', *Acta organologica*, iii (1969), 133
H. Hulverscheidt: 'Die Bonner Orgelbauanstalt Johannes Klais', *Bonner Kirchenmusik* (1970)
H. G. Klais: 'Who's Who?', *ISO Information*, iii (1970), 218
——: *Die Würzburger Domorgeln* (Frankfurt am Main, 1970)
——: *Überlegungen zur Orgeldisposition* (Frankfurt am Main, 1973; Eng. trans., 1975)
H. Steinhaus: *Aus der Geschichte des Hauses Klais* (Bonn, 1976)
HANS KLOTZ

Klanet. Clarinet of Serbia. *See* GRNETA.

Klangumwandler (Ger.). A device used in electronic music to change the frequency of a signal; *see* RING MODULATOR.

Klań khaek [khlań khaek, khlang khêk]. Orchestra of the Khmer people of Kampuchea. It includes the *sralai klań khaek* (oboe), two *sgar klań khaek* (double-headed drums) and the *gań chaiÿāṃ* (small bossed gong). This ensemble traditionally played during battle; in modern times it performs at boxing matches.
TRÂN QUANG HAI

Klappenhorn [Klappenflügelhorn] (Ger.). KEYED BUGLE.

Klappentrompete (Ger.). KEYED TRUMPET.

Klapperbretter. Wooden percussion plaques of Switzerland.

Klarino. Greek keyed clarinet, introduced into Greece from Turkey in the early 19th century. The Albert-system clarinet in C is now the most common. The *klarino* usually forms part of an instrumental ensemble consisting of *laouto* (long-necked lute) or guitar, violin, which doubles the *klarino* in unison or at the octave in heterophonic style, and sometimes the *defi* (frame drum). These ensembles accompany both dance and song.
R. CONWAY MORRIS

Klarnet [kılarnet, gırnata]. Turkish term for the European clarinet. Formerly the low G clarinet was popular, but this has been superseded by the B♭ clarinet. The *klarnet* is increasingly used as a substitute for the *zurna*, particularly in urban settings.

Klavecimbel (Dutch). HARPSICHORD.

Klaviatur (Ger.). KEYBOARD.

Klaviatur-Kontrafagott (Ger.). A double bassoon with a piano-accordion-type keyboard designed in 1845 and patented in 1856 by C. W. MORITZ.

Klaviatursphärophon. A version of the SPHÄROPHON with a monophonic two-manual keyboard (1928), designed by JÖRG MAGER.

Klavier (Ger.: 'manual', 'keyboard', 'keyboard instrument'). (1) As 'clavier', used to denote 'manual keyboard' at Rouen as early as 1386; *see* CLAVIER (i).

(2) Occasionally used for CLAVICHORD in later 18th-century central Germany (but usually 'Clavier'). Very often it is uncertain which instrument is being referred to in a source, even when a distinction is intended; Kittel (*Der angehende praktische Organist*, 1801–8) used *Flügel* to mean harpsichord when referring to J. S. Bach's music, pianoforte when referring to his own and *Klavier* to mean clavichord.

(3) Piano or Hammerklavier, especially in southern Germany and Austria.

(4) As a modern reference term or generic name, 'Klavier' usually denotes stringed keyboard instruments only; in popular usage, it normally stands for piano (*Klavierkonzert*, *Klavierspiel* etc).

PETER WILLIAMS

Klaviergamba (Ger.: 'clavier-gambe'). The name given by several 18th-century writers and inventors to bowed keyboard instruments. Around 1725 Johann Georg Gleichmann of Ilmenau, inspired by his acquaintance with an example of Hans Haiden's *Geigenwerk*, built a keyboard instrument with an oval body, the strings of which were bowed by several small wheels driven by a single large wheel under the body. A similar instrument was invented by Nils Söderström about 40 years later. Walther (*Musikalisches Lexikon*, 1732) and Majer *Museum musicum*, 1732) used the term generically of gut-strung, bowed keyboard instruments. *See also* SOSTENENTE PIANO, §1.

Klavier-Harmonika (Ger.). ACCORDION.

Klavierzusatzgerät (Ger.). PIANO ATTACHMENT.

Klaviziterium (Ger.). CLAVICYTHERIUM.

Klavizylinder (Ger.: 'clavicylinder'). A friction rod instrument with a keyboard developed in Halle in 1799 by Ernst Friedrich Chladni from his earlier EUPHON. It was the size and shape of a square piano. The compass of the first version was C to f'''; in the second and final version, built in 1814, this was increased at both ends to cover the range G' to a'''. A series of C-shaped metal rods of different lengths were attached horizontally to the rear of the keys. Inside the instrument a wet glass cylinder was constantly rotated by means of a treadle operated by the right foot. When a key was depressed the attached rod was brought into contact with the cylinder and a ringing sound was produced. Several inventors imitated Chladni's idea: Pierre Riffelsen of Copenhagen made two such instruments, the Melodikon (1800) and the Hymnerophon (1814), both of which used tuning-forks; in Emmerich in 1805 JOHANN CHRISTIAN DIETZ (i) constructed the mélodion which had metal instead of glass rods; (in 1812) Louis Klatte of Erfurt gave the name Euphonia to an instrument in which brass bars were made to vibrate by being rotated against a brass cylinder. Other versions of the same principle were used in Franz Leppich's Panmelodikon (1810) and Vanderburg's Odéophone (1818).

Klawiolin (Pol.). A mechanical instrument combining the attributes of keyboard and strings, invented by Jan Jarmusiewicz (1781–1844). It was made in the form of a hump-backed piano with gut strings which were equipped with small bows activated by an internal mechanism; the instrument was intended to produce the effect of a string quartet.

Kledi. *See* KELEDI.

Kleine Flöte (Ger.). PICCOLO; *see* FLUTE, §3.

Kleine Trommel (Ger.). Side drum; *see* DRUM, §3.

Klekor. Bamboo ring flute of Flores, Indonesia. *See* NUREN.

Klekotka. Polish CLAPPERS. *See* KOŁATKA.

Klemm [Clemm, Clem], **Johann Gottlob** (*b* nr. Dresden, 12 May 1690; *d* nr. Bethlehem, Penn., 5 May 1762). American Moravian organ builder. Klemm learnt his trade in Dresden, possibly from Gottfried Silbermann. Later he became attracted to the Moravian religious movement and moved to Count Zinzendorf's settlement at Herrnhut. In 1733 he emigrated to America, settling in Philadelphia. There in 1741 he built a three-manual organ for Trinity Church in New York, and is known also to have made smaller organs and harpsichords. In 1745 or 1746 he moved to New York, and in 1757 settled in Bethlehem. Here, assisted by DAVID TANNENBERG, then a young apprentice, he continued to build small organs until his death.

BIBLIOGRAPHY
W. H. Armstrong: *Organs for America* (Philadelphia, 1967)
O. Ochse: *The History of the Organ in the United States* (Bloomington, Ind., 1975)

BARBARA OWEN

Klemm & Brother(s). German importers of musical instruments and music publishers active in Philadelphia. John G. Klemm (*b* Neukirchen, 18 June 1795) emigrated from Saxony in 1819 to join Frederick August Klemm (*b* Neukirchen, *c*1795; *d* Philadelphia, 6 July 1876) in Philadelphia; together they formed the firm of Klemm & Brothers. From 1819 until 1879, the Klemms supplied the American musical public with wind instruments, strings and, for a time, pianos and music. Although city directories and advertisements occasionally list them as both manufacturers and importers, it appears that most of the instruments were supplied by the German firm of George and August Klemm in Markneukirchen.

From 1819 until 1822 the firm sold imported instruments at 1 North 4th Street. From 1823 until 1832 only John G. Klemm was active. During that period he sold instruments imported from G. and A. Klemm, published music from plates purchased in 1823 from Bacon & Hart, Philadelphia publishers, and established (at 287½ High Street) a piano warehouse at which Alpheus Babcock (who came from Boston) built pianos from about 1830 to 1832. Klemm began to sell pianos in 1825; the same year he deposited a Babcock piano at the second annual exhibition of the Franklin Institute. In 1833 Frederick August Klemm returned and the firm of Klemm & Brother was established from 1833 until 1838 as a piano and musical warehouse, and from 1839 until 1879 as importers and dealers in musical instruments. Apparently F. A. Klemm ran the firm alone until the 1860s when his sons John George and Edward Meinel joined him in 1864 and 1868, respectively. The firm of Klemm & Brother does not seem to have functioned after 1879 although Frederick's two sons remained in Philadelphia for nearly two more decades.

The Klemm firm in Markneukirchen was founded in about 1795, and by about 1802 was run by Michael Schuster, a brother-in-law of the Klemms. It was not a manufacturing firm, but bought instruments from Markneukirchen craftsmen to sell to the world market. An ornamented violin with a Klemm label won an honourable mention at the Great Exhibition, London, 1851. The Philadelphia Klemms supplied instruments to many military bands, especially during the Civil War. Their wind instruments can be found in major American collections; a piano made by Babcock for Klemm is at the Smithsonian Institution.

CYNTHIA ADAMS HOOVER

Klenang. Balinese bossed gong. *See* KELENANG.

Klentangan. GONG-CHIME of east Kalimantan, Indonesia. *See* KULINTANG.

Klentong. Small bossed gong in the Balinese *gamelan gong gede*, *gamelan gong kebyar* and *gamelan bebonangan* (*see* GAMELAN, §6 (iv)). In smaller ensembles the *klentong* provides secondary punctuation, dividing the musical phrase in half.

Klepalo. Large wooden percussion beam of eastern Yugoslavia (Serbia, Macedonia and Bosnia and Hercegovina). It consists of a large wooden board hung on a chain and struck with a mallet. The *klepalo* is used in orthodox monasteries during Holy Week instead of bells. The *klepalo* and similar instruments are equivalent to the Greek SĒMANTRON.

CVJETKO RIHTMAN

Klephoorn (Dutch). KEYED BUGLE.

Klokkenspel (Dutch). CARILLON.

Klokló. Smallest single-headed drum in the Cuban ARARÁ ensemble. Although it shares with the other sizes the feature of a head made taut by a hoop secured by cord woven about spikes, the *klokló* is cylindrical without the distinctive 'foot' that marks the bottom of the larger *arará* drums. The *klokló* is played seated, with two sticks. See *OrtizIMA*, iii, 345f.

JOHN M. SCHECHTER

Klompviool. Clog fiddle of the Low Countries. For illustration of this type of instrument, *see* TRÄSKOFIOL.

Kloncing. Triangle used in the *gamelan gandrung* by the Osinger people of the Banyuwangi Regency, East Java.

Klǫng. In Thailand, the generic name for drum. Several major types are used in modern Thai classical and folk music. The *klǫng khāēk* is a long double-headed cylindrical drum made of hardwood. The two goatskin or calfskin heads are laced down with leather thongs. The drum is played with the hands and used in pairs, the two drums in any one pair differing in pitch. The *klǫng khāēk* is played in percussion and string ensembles where the occasion is informal, the *taphon* (barrel drum) being substituted for specific, formal functions. It is also played with the *pī chawā* (oboe) to accompany Thai fencing and boxing. The *klǫng khāēk* ensemble formerly consisted of two *klǫng khāēk* drums, the *pī chawā* and a *khǫng mēng* (gong); it was probably used for sad ceremonies, such as funerals. The *klǫng khāēk* is sometimes known as *klǫng chawā* ('Javanese drum').

The *klǫng malāyū* ('Malayan drum') is a cylindrical drum similar to the *klǫng khāēk*, but shorter and with larger heads, which are laced down with leather thongs strung between them. The larger of the heads is played with a curved stick, and the smaller with the palm of the hand. The drum was formerly used in groups of four, but it is now played in pairs in the *bua lǫi* ensemble and the *pī phāt nāng hong* ensemble (used for funeral ceremonies).

Similar to the *klǫng malāyū*, but shorter and fatter, is the *klǫng chana*, which was played in the 16th century for army processions and to accompany the training of army recruits. Later it was used, sometimes in large numbers, in royal ceremonies.

The *klǫng that* is a large barrel drum made from a solid block of hardwood 50 cm high. The inside is hollow, the outside smoothed and polished. The heads are attached to the body with pegs. The drum is tilted at an angle to the player by means of two poles which are crossed through a metal ring attached to the side of the body furthest from the player. The lower head is tuned with tuning paste (a mixture of rice and ashes). The top head is beaten with two bamboo beaters, which are sometimes padded. This drum appears to have been in use since ancient times and is traditionally found in the *pī phāt* (percussion) ensemble. Originally only one *klǫng that* was used, but since the early 19th century another has been added, and nowadays the drum is always played in pairs.

Similar in shape and construction to the *klǫng that* are the *klǫng khōn*, used in the *khōn* masked drama; the *klǫng nāng*, used in the accompaniment of shadow plays; and the *klǫng chātrī*, which is much smaller than the *klǫng that*, with a body length of about 25 cm, and which is used in pairs in the *pī phāt* ensemble to accompany the *lakhǫn chātrī* (a form of itinerant theatrical performance, formerly widespread in southern Thailand). The *klǫng chātrī* is also known as the *klǫng tuk*. The *klǫng seng* of north-eastern Thailand is a pair of long barrel drums, used in contests.

Another form of barrel drum is the *klǫng taphōn*, a pair of TAPHŌN drums. They are placed on a single slanting stand and played in the manner of the *klǫng that* drums (with padded sticks). Originally conceived for use during performances of the theatrical drama *lakhǫn dǫk dam ban* in the last half of the 19th century, this instrument is also used in the *pī phāt mai nuam* ensemble. The *klǫng jeen* is a small double-headed drum also played in theatrical performances, used when Chinese characters appear.

The *klǫng yāo* is a single-headed GOBLET DRUM found in several sizes; the hardwood body, which averages 75 cm in length, is customarily decorated with pieces of cloth which hang loosely from the edge of the head. The instrument is slung from the shoulders by a cord and played mainly with the hands, but also sometimes with other parts of the player's body, such as elbows and knees. It can be found throughout Thailand and is used in ceremonial processional ensembles.

A much larger version of the *klǫng yāo* is the *klǫng āe*, which can average 3 metres in length. It has a large resonance chamber covered by thongs of leather and twisted cane which stretch the head and attach it to the body (as on the *taphōn*). It is used mainly in Buddhist temples in the northern provinces of Thailand, usually to signal the start of daily activities for the monks. It also accompanies folksinging, dancing and processions.

BIBLIOGRAPHY
D. Yupho: *Khrūang dontri Thai* [Thai musical instruments] (Bangkok, 1957, 2/1967; Eng. trans., 1960, 2/1971)
D. Morton: *The Traditional Music of Thailand* (Berkeley, 1976)
DAVID MORTON

Klŏng khīāt [klong kop]. BRONZE DRUM of Northern Thailand. *See* MAHŌRA THŲK.

Klŏng mēng. Gong of Thailand, used in the *bua lǭi* ensemble.

Klong put. Aerophone of the Sedang and Bahnar peoples of the high plateau of central Vietnam. It comprises a set of seven bamboo tubes of uniform section but different length placed side by side, horizontally, on a bamboo frame. By clapping the hands before one end of each tube air is pushed through the tube; the pitch of each sound varies with the length of the tube.
TRÂN VAN KHÊ

Klöpping, Helmut (*b* Schwelm, 14 June 1936). German organ builder, in partnership with WILLI PETER.

Klosé, Hyacinthe Eléonore (*b* Corfu, 11 Oct 1808; *d* Paris, 29 Aug 1880). French clarinettist notable for his collaboration with the instrument maker Louis-Auguste Buffet in the production of a clarinet incorporating the ring-key mechanism applied to the flute by Theobald Boehm. The clarinet was exhibited in 1839 and patented in 1844 as a 'clarinet with moving rings'. In the 1860s it was given the name of Boehm clarinet. It became increasingly popular and is the system most generally in use today (*see* CLARINET, §4(iii)). Klosé also wrote an admirable tutor for the Boehm clarinet which is still used extensively.

BIBLIOGRAPHY
F. G. Rendall: *The Clarinet* (London, 1954, 3/1971)
O. Kroll: *Die Klarinette* (Kassel, 1965; Eng. trans., enlarged, 1968)
P. Weston: *Clarinet Virtuosi of the Past* (London, 1971)
——: *More Clarinet Virtuosi of the Past* (London, 1977)
PAMELA WESTON

Klotz [Kloz]. German family of violin makers active in Mittenwald, Bavaria. Although members of the family have continued intermittently in the trade, the famous Klotz instruments date from the 18th century.

Mathias Klotz (*b* Mittenwald, 11 June 1653; *d* Mittenwald, 16 Aug 1743) was the originator of violin making in Mittenwald, and is commemorated by a statue in the centre of the town. So little is known of his life and work that much has had to be invented: visitors to Mittenwald are sometimes told that he studied violin making in Cremona, first with Amati, then with Guarneri, and finally with Stradivari himself. What is certain is that he was an apprentice with Giovanni Railich, a Paduan maker of lutes and kindred instruments, but almost certainly not of violins, and left the Railich workshop in 1678. He returned to Mittenwald and married, but his violins (now extremely rare) date from much later, and it seems that for 20 years or so he only used what he had learnt with Railich. A violin dated 1714 shows very good workmanship, more in the Italian style than after Stainer. Another from 1727 appears much more Germanic, though recognizably by the same hand. The varnish on both is excellent by Tyrolean standards.

Georg Klotz (*b* 31 March 1687; *d* 31 Aug 1737), Sebastian Klotz (*b* 18 Jan 1696; *d* c1760) and Johann Carl Klotz (*b* 29 Jan 1709; *d* c1770) were sons of Mathias Klotz; all were born and died in Mittenwald. Sebastian was undoubtedly the best of these, as well as the most prolific. His instruments are made with delicacy and good taste, the best of them covered with a soft, glowing varnish, and have a quality of sound to match.

Aegidius Klotz (*b* Mittenwald, 1733; *d* Mittenwald, 1805) and Joseph Klotz (*b* Mittenwald, 1743; *d* Mittenwald, late 18th century) were sons of Sebastian Klotz. Each had a pleasing, individual style. By the last quarter of the 18th century violin making had become an industry in Mittenwald, employing many craftsmen whose names are for the most part little known. The term 'Klotz School' is often used to describe their instruments.

BIBLIOGRAPHY
W. L. von Lütgendorff: *Die Geigen- und Lautenmacher vom Mittelalter bis zur Gegenwart* (Frankfurt am Main, 1904, rev. 6/1922/R1968)
R. Vannes: *Essai d'un dictionnaire universel des luthiers* (Paris, 1932, 2/1951/R1972 as *Dictionnaire universel des luthiers* and R1981 incl. suppl. 1959)
CHARLES BEARE

Knabe. American firm of piano makers. In 1837 William Knabe (*b* Kreuzburg, Berlin, 1803; *d* Baltimore, Maryland, 1864) established the firm in Baltimore in partnership with Henry Gaehle after training as a piano maker in Germany and emigrating to Baltimore in 1833. The firm Knabe & Gaehle advertised 'pianos of quality for genteel people of means'. When Gaehle died in 1855, Knabe continued the business under the title Knabe and Co. Knabe controlled the piano market in the majority of the southern states by 1860, but the Civil War had a disastrous effect on the firm because its market was so dependent on the South.

Knabe's sons Ernest Knabe (1827–94) and William Knabe (1841–89) were brought up in the business, and when their father died they re-established the firm's position as one of the leading piano makers in the USA. Ernest toured to arrange new agencies for the sale of Knabe pianos in the northern and western states, and a direct agency was founded in New York in 1864. He also designed new string scales for their concert grands and upright pianos. The firm became one of the most important American piano makers, and by the turn of the century they were building about 2000 pianos annually. The Japanese government selected Knabe in 1879 to supply pianos for use in Japanese schools. The firm continued to prosper as a family concern until Ernest and William died, when it became a public company. Like other well-known American piano manufacturers (e.g. Chickering), Knabe was purchased by the American Piano Company in 1908. (William's two grandsons left the American Piano Company in 1911 to establish their own firm, Knabe Brothers Company, which lasted until 1914.) The firm continued to flourish, and in 1926 its pianos were officially chosen to be used at the Metropolitan Opera, New York, an association which has continued. In 1929 the firm moved to East Rochester, and since 1932 it has formed part of the Aeolian American Corporation there. In the early 1970s the firm continued to manufacture a range of grand pianos for domestic and concert use, in addition to 'console pianos', upright instruments about one metre high.

BIBLIOGRAPHY
D. Spillane: *History of the American Pianoforte* (New York, 1890/R1969)
A. Dolge: *Pianos and their Makers* (Covina, Calif., 1911/R1972)
MARGARET CRANMER

K'nar. 10-string zither of medieval Armenia.

Knari. Ancient string instrument of Georgia (USSR). The earliest information concerning the *knari* dates from the 7th century, and it disappeared from use around the

13th century. It apparently had a wooden frame and five strings. At first a religious instrument, it then became popular at the courts of feudal lords and in military circles. See *VertkovA*, 129.

Knarre (Ger.). RATCHET.

Knee-lever (Fr. *genouillère*; Ger. *Kniehebel*). Any of a variety of devices moving either horizontally or vertically, operated by the knee, and used for the production of expressive effects on a number of different types of keyboard instruments. A knee-lever was occasionally provided on reed organs to permit control of loudness, since the feet were already occupied with the pedal-operated bellows. Knee-levers preceded pedals for operating damper-lifting, muting and action-shifting mechanisms on continental pianos, and they were also used to activate the elaborate register-changing devices found on late 18th-century French harpsichords. *See also* PEDAL.

EDWIN M. RIPIN

Kney, Gabriel (*b* Speyer, 1929). Canadian organ builder of German birth. He was apprenticed to Paul Sattel in Speyer, where he also studied at the Institute of Church Music. In 1951 he emigrated to London, Ontario, to work for the Keates Organ Co.; when Keates moved to Toronto in 1955 Kney entered into partnership with John Bright, establishing the firm of Kney & Bright. On the dissolution of the partnership in 1963 the firm was renamed Gabriel Kney & Co. Kney built 30 instruments with electric action before specializing in mechanical action. Among his most important instruments are those in the Cathedral of SS Luke and Paul, Charleston, South Carolina (1976), Massey Hall, Toronto (contract 1979), and Pease Auditorium, Eastern Michigan University (1982).

BIBLIOGRAPHY
U. Pape: *The Tracker Organ Revival in America* (Berlin, 1978)
BARBARA OWEN

Knicky-knackers. A term occasionally used for BONES or CLAPPERS.

Kniehebel (Ger.). KNEE-LEVER.

Knopf. German family of horn makers. The firm was founded by (Heinrich) August Knopf (*b* 14 June 1865; *d* 31 May 1947), whose two sons, Herbert (Fritz) Knopf (*b* 17 March 1894; *d* 26 June 1969) and (August) Kurt Knopf (*b* 4 Nov 1900; *d* 1945), worked together with their father until 1919, when Herbert set up in business under his own name. Both businesses are now carried on respectively by Kurt's son Edgar (*b* 27 Oct 1928) and Herbert's son Johannes (Fritz) (*b* 11 Dec 1929). In 1918 August Knopf and his sons began working jointly on the Prager horn (*see* HORN, §1), a project undertaken by the firm which eventually proved abortive but which was continued even after the separation of 1919. Herbert Knopf's principal contribution to horn development, a double horn (1920–21), was extensively copied by various other manufacturers and was until recently one of the three basic models of double horn available. He also pioneered the hand-stopping valve on B♭ horns (which lowers the pitch by three-quarters of a tone), the ball and socket linkage for rotary valves and the double Wagner tuba in F and B♭.

BIBLIOGRAPHY
R. Morley-Pegge: *The French Horn* (London, 1960, 2/1972)
FRANK HAWKINS

Knoth. German firm of brass instrument manufacturers. It was founded in Markneukirchen in 1900 by (Gustav) Emil Knoth (1870–1936), succeeded in turn by his son (Emil) Kurt Knoth (1891–1970) and grandson Walter (1910–57). Walter Knoth inaugurated the 'Rino' model of brass instruments which have been continued by Johannes Scherzer (*see* SCHERZER (ii)) and are much admired by orchestral players.

Ko. HARP-LUTE (i) of the Dan people of the Ivory Coast. The *ko* has six or seven strings arranged in two parallel rows, and a skin-covered calabash resonator. The instrument is used by hunters to accompany singing and dancing before and after a hunt. See H. Zemp: *Musique Dan: la musique dans la pensée et la vie sociale d'une société africaine* (Paris and The Hague, 1971); 'Music of the Dan', BM30 L2301 [disc notes].

Koa. SACRED FLUTES of the Kuman people, Chimbu Province, Papua New Guinea. As elsewhere in New Guinea they are side-blown bamboo flutes lacking finger-holes and played in pairs. The notes are obtained both by lipping and by alternately opening and shutting the open end of the flute with the index finger of the right hand. Boys are shown the flutes and taught to play them for the first time at initiations. They represent for them a benevolent tutelary spirit. See J. Nilles: 'The Kuman of the Chimbu Region, Central Highlands, New Guinea', *Oceania*, xxi (1950), 37, 48.

MERVYN McLEAN

Koala [koali]. Unbraced MOUTH BOW, sounded by breath, of the Northern Sotho people of southern Africa. It resembles the Tswana *kwadi* and Southern Sotho LESIBA.

Kōauau. See KOOAUAU.

Kobat. FRAME DRUM of the Langkat area of North Sumatra. The wooden frame is about 15 cm deep and about 60 cm in diameter, and a goatskin head is fastened to it with rattan lacing. It is played in pairs and forms part of the *gendang-gung* ensemble.

Kobuz. See QOBUZ.

Kobza. Plucked lute of the Ukraine, now obsolete. There are no accurate descriptions of the instrument, but from iconographical evidence of the 16th to the 18th centuries, there were two types. One was short-necked and resembled the Romanian and Moldavian COBZA; the other was long-necked and resembled the ṬANBŪR. Subsequently melody strings stretched over the right-hand side of the body were added to the latter type of *kobza*. This may have influenced the evolution of the BANDURA, although the exact relationship is unclear. See *VertkovA*, 52.

Koch. German family of organists and organ builders. Paul Koch the elder (*d* Zwickau, 1546), from St Joachimsthal (Bohemia), went to Zwickau in 1543 and there renovated the organs in the Marienkirche and the atharinenkirche. Paul Koch the younger (buried Zwickau, 28 Sept 1580) worked as organist in Zwickau, from 1544 at St Katharinen, and from 1552 at St Marien. He renovated the organ in Weiden. Hans Koch was organist from 1563 to 1568 at the Petrikirche in Freiberg, Saxony. Stephan Koch (d Zwickau, 29 Dec 1590) was organist at St Dorotheen in Vienna in 1564, and later in Annaberg (Erzgebirge), where he married in 1570. From 21 July 1575 he lived as a wealthy citizen and organist and highly esteemed instrument maker in Zwickau. He completed an organ begun by Jakob Weinlebe in Bischofswerda (Christuskirche, 1571) and built instruments in Olomouc (St Mauritius, 1585), Kulmbach (1587) and Jihlava (1590). Three positive organs are ascribed to him by M. Fürstenau in the Dresden instrument inventory.

Georg Koch the elder was no doubt closely related to the Zwickau branch of the family. He built an organ in Glauchau (Georgenkirche, 1580) and from 1582 until 1585 was in Glauchau, where he owned a house and garden (though he later suffered a period of financial hardship). In 1585 he was living in Zwickau, where he remained until at least 1590. He renovated organs in Zeitz (cathedral) and Leipzig (St Nicolai) and built organs at Taus (large organ, 1572–3), Schmölln (Stadtpfarrkirche, 1583) and Brno (St Jakob, 1590). He was assisted by his son Georg in building an organ at Waldenburg, Saxony (St Bartholomäus, 1598–9); in 1602 Georg Koch the younger made some improvements to the instrument, which had in the meantime been damaged by stormy weather. A son born to Georg Koch (the younger) and his wife Martha was baptized in Altwaldenburg on 27 October 1616.

The capable organ builders of this well-known family combined carefully planned register combinations with solid workmanship, and they are of considerable importance in the art of 16th-century organ building. Their instruments are found chiefly in Saxony, Bohemia, Moravia, Silesia and Bavaria.

BIBLIOGRAPHY

E. Herzog: Chronik der Kreisstadt Zwickau, ii (Zwickau, 1845)
E. Eckardt: Chronik von Glauchau (Glauchau, 1882)
P. Smets, ed.: Orgeldispositionen (Kassel, 1931)
E. Müller: 'Musikgeschichte von Freiberg', Altertumsverein, lxviii (1939), 80
W. Haacke: 'Orgelbauten im Zeitzer und Naumburger Dom', AMf, vii (1942)
R. Quoika: Der Orgelbau in Böhmen und Mähren (Mainz, 1966)
                                        WALTER HÜTTEL

Koch, Stephan (b Vesprin, Hungary, 1772; d 1828). Austro-Hungarian wind instrument maker. He established himself in Vienna about 1809. His products included flutes, clarinets and basset horns of fine quality as well as extremely elegant oboes. In 1828 he made the first oboes on the Sellner system (see OBOE, fig.11a); these may be regarded as the parents of the modern German type of instrument. Many examples survive in various instrument collections. Koch was also notable for his flutes with an extension down to a, or sometimes to g, in which case the long foot joint was reflected on itself near the B♮ hole; these were similar to the large flutes made by the Austrian flute maker Trexler.
                                        PHILIP BATE

K'o-ch'in. See KOQIN.

Kochnak. Hand-held gong of Armenia, now obsolete. It was used to signal the hours of prayer.

Köcsögduda. FRICTION DRUM of Hungary, consisting of a pot covered with a membrane of pig's bladder. The membrane is excited by means of a wooden stick which does not pierce it, but is bound into it from beneath. The instrument was used in rituals of New Year greeting, but nowadays is also used to accompany the citera.

Kodaiko. Small Japanese barrel drum. See SHIMEDAIKO.

Kodam. Single-headed HOURGLASS DRUM of the Kotoko people of Chad. See KALALI.

Kode. BULLROARER of the Maninka people of Guinea, played in pairs. The 'male' produces a lower sound, the 'female' (or 'child') a higher pitch.

Kod girkutu. Double-headed conical drum of the Sara-Madjingaye people of Chad. The instrument is placed horizontally on the ground and the seated player strikes one head with each hand. It is used in an ensemble which includes 12 nal flutes and a long cylindrical drum. Among the Sara-Gor people the corresponding drum, known as dala, is wedged between the drummer's thighs and beaten with both hands to accompany dancing. See C. Duvelle and M. Vuylstèke: 'Anthologie de la musique du Tchad', OCR 36-8 [disc notes].
                                        K. A. GOURLAY

Kodia. Snail-shell vessel rattle, containing small pebbles, of the Ladi people of the Republic of the Congo. The rattle is held in the right hand and shaken to and fro between the shoulder and the left wrist with the left arm bent. At the same time the inner side of the right wrist taps the inner side of the left wrist and the left shoulder alternately, producing muffled sounds which mingle with the rattling. See C. Duvelle: 'Musique Kongo', OCR 35 [disc notes].
                                        K. A. GOURLAY

Ko-ding. JEW'S HARP of the northern Philippines. See AFIW.

Kodisch. German family of brass instrument makers, active in Nuremberg. Johann Carl Kodisch (b 14 or 15 April 1654; buried 8 May 1721) became a Meister in 1681 (not 1680, as given in Wörthmüller). His maker's mark was a jumping horse. The similarity of his highly developed engraving to that of Johann Wilhelm Haas suggests an association between the two or, more likely, a training with the same master; other details of his ornamentation show that he must have studied with a member of the Hainlein family. His trombone bells are more or less funnel-shaped, but his trumpet bells have a narrow throat and a rapid, steep flare, a characteristic first developed by Michael Hainlein and later made famous by members of the Haas family; the bell throats of J. C. Kodisch's trumpets, however, are much narrower than those of the Haas family. A dozen of his instruments survive.

Daniel Kodisch (b 9 Nov 1686; buried 27 Jan 1747), son of Johann Carl, became a Meister on 8 April 1710, the day after his marriage to Margareta Hainlein (1687–1732), the daughter of his presumed teacher, Michael Hainlein. He is thought to have taken over his father-in-law's shop (between 1713 and 1725), since his later address is the same. Furthermore, his maker's mark, a rooster lying down, is almost identical with that of Hainlein. Only one of his instruments survives, a horn in the Germanisches National-Museum, Nuremberg (MIR 76).

Johann Reichard Kodisch was also an instrument maker; he took his master's examination on 17 Feb 1739. In the Nuremberg register of makers' marks, there is only a cross by his name, signifying that he probably died before registering his mark.

BIBLIOGRAPHY
W. Wörthmüller: 'Die Nürnberger Trompeten- und Posaunen-macher des 17. und 18. Jahrhunderts', *Mitteilungen des Vereins für Geschichte der Stadt Nürnberg*, xlv (1954), 208; xlvi (1955), 372
K. Pechstein: 'Die Merkzeichentafel der Nürnberger Trompeten- und Posaunenmacher von 1640', *Mitteilungen des Vereins für Geschichte der Stadt Nürnberg*, lix (1972), 198
EDWARD H. TARR

Kodol. Wooden percussion trough of the Maninka people of Guinea. It is boat-shaped with a projecting handle, and is struck with a stick to accompany singing.

Kōdōn (Gk.) (1) Greek term for bell, attestable from the 5th century BC (Aeschylus, *Seven against Thebes*, ll.386, 399; ?Euripides, *Rhesus*, l.308; Aristophanes, *Frogs*, l.963). The oldest known Greek depiction of a bell, on a silver coin of Euaenetus from the Sicilian city of Catana (now Catania), has also been dated from the last third of the 5th century. Small bronze bells, termed kōdōnion, 6·2 and 8 cm long, have been excavated on Delos and in the shrine of Hera at Argos. Like other instruments in Greece bells originally served a religious (mostly apotropaic) function: a wall-painting in a Delos house shows a small bell suspended round the neck of a sacrificial pig; this was also done with other animals, particularly horses in battle. According to Aeschylus small bells were hung at the edges of soldiers' shields to avert evil and inspire fear in the enemy; Euripides compared them with the face of the Gorgon as an apotropaic symbol.

(2) An ancient Greek synonym for SALPINX; the term was occasionally used in this sense when denoting a signalling instrument.

BIBLIOGRAPHY
C. Waldstein and others: *The Argive Heraeum*, ii (Boston and New York, 1905), 299, no.2257, pl.126
G. Herzog-Hauser: 'Tintinnabulum', *Paulys Real-Encyclopädie der classischen Altertumswissenschaft*, 2nd ser., vi (Stuttgart, 1937), 1406
W. Déonna: *Le mobilier délien*, Exploration archéologique de Délos, xviii (Paris, 1938), 325, pl.92, 816
J. Liegle: 'Euainetos', *Programm zum Winckelmannsfest der archäologischen Gesellschaft zu Berlin*, ci (1941), 44, pl.12
reprinted from *MGG* (vii, 1311) by permission of Bärenreiter
MAX WEGNER

Ko'e. In Polynesia the term for 'bamboo', also signifying two types of aerophone.

(1) Bamboo flute of the southern Cook Islands. In Rarotonga and Mangaia it is said formerly to have had two finger-holes and to have been nose-blown; later instruments of Aitutaki and Mangaia are said to have had six holes and to have been mouth-blown.

(2) Bamboo MOUTH BOW of Mangaia. Post-contact instruments had a wire string tightened by a wooden bridge. The player held one end of the bamboo clenched tightly between the teeth and tapped the stretched wire

with a piece of hardwood the size of a pencil. See R. W. Robson and J. Tudor, ed.: *Where the Trade Winds Blow* (Sydney, 1946), 160.

See also AKATANGI KO'E; KOFE; 'OFE; PU IHU; PU KO'E.
MERVYN McLEAN

Koenig. French organ builders. Joseph (*b* Luxeuil-les-Bains, 22 Feb 1846; *d* Caen, 30 July 1926) was the pupil of his brother-in-law Charles Mutin. In 1896 Mutin became the manager of the firm of Cavaillé-Coll, whereupon Joseph Koenig set up on his own in Caen. He restored a number of instruments in accordance with the Romantic trend in French organ building, including those at St Etienne, Caen (three manuals, 50 stops), Bayeux Cathedral (three manuals, 41 stops), Beuron Abbey (three manuals, 60 stops) and St Joseph, Gerleve (Westphalia). Joseph's son Paul-Marie (*b* Paris, 19 July 1887; *d* Draveil, 14 Oct 1977) began work in Caen, but moved to Paris in 1929. Whereas the Cavaillé-Coll organ favoured Bombardons, Trumpets and Clairons at the expense of Mixtures and Cymbales, P.-M. Koenig strove to create an even balance between all these groups of stops, in the tradition of the classical French organ. But he departed from that tradition in the matters of resonance and volume, there following the model of Cavaillé-Coll. The organs he built on these principles include those in Beirut Cathedral (two manuals, 25 stops), St Joseph's, Beirut (two manuals, 27 stops), St Sauveur, Caen (four manuals, 58 stops), Gap Cathedral (three manuals, 62 stops), and the Basilica, Mézières (three manuals, 43 stops). He also restored a number of older organs along the same lines.

HANS KLOTZ

Kofe. (1) Bamboo NOSE FLUTE of Niue, reportedly played by women. There were two finger-holes. Some instruments were made from hollow branches of the *pao* tree with one end plugged. See E. Loeb: *History and Traditions of Niue* (Honolulu, 1926), 94.

(2) Bamboo STAMPING TUBE of Tonga. Graduated tubes up to 180 cm long, closed at one end, were stamped on the ground by a seated circle of men to accompany dancing and singing. See J. Cook and J. King: *A Voyage to the Pacific Ocean* (London, 1784), 540; R. Moyle: 'Tongan Musical Instruments (concluded)', *GSJ*, xxx (1977), 95.

See also KO'E and 'OFE.
MERVYN McLEAN

Kögürge [kegürge]. Large Mongolian KETTLEDRUM, formerly used in battle. It was described in the 13th century as being covered with black bull's hide and having a deep sound. See I. de Rachewiltz: *Index to the Secret History of the Mongols* (Bloomington, 1972).

Kogut. Single-string fiddle of the Manobo people of the southern Philippines. *See also* DAYUDAY.

Köhler. English family of military wind instrument makers, of Hessian origin. John [Johannes, Hans] Köhler (*b* Volkenroda, nr. Kassel, *c*1735; *d* London, *c*1805) went with a regiment of Hessian mercenaries to London in about 1775, and there became bandmaster to the Lancaster Volunteers. In 1780 he set up as an instrument maker at 87 St James Street. He had no children, but sent to Germany for his nephew, John Köhler (*b* ?Volkenroda, c1770; d London, ?c1870), who succeeded to the family business in 1801. The younger John Köhler was appointed musical instrument maker to the Duke of York, and later to the Prince of Wales. His son and successor, John Augustus Köhler (b London, c1810; d London, 20 June 1878), in 1838 acquired the rights to Shaw's swivelling disc valves, which derived from Halary's invention in Paris of 1835 (see VALVE (i)). Soon after, he moved the business to Henrietta Street and introduced an improved version of the device called the New Patent Lever. On this he based the two-valve 'New Patent Lever French Horn', for the Great Exhibition of 1851. This and other inventions by him won medals at the 1851 and 1862 exhibitions, and enjoyed some favour among military instrumentalists as late as 1890; Day's catalogue for the Royal Military Exhibition of that year gives a detailed description of Köhler's device. The disc valve, even with Köhler's improvements, proved impossible to keep airtight, and despite its initial success did not survive into the 20th century.

For instruments by the Köhler family, see ALTHORN; CORNET (i), fig.3; FLUTE, fig.4a; POST HORN, fig.4b.

HORACE FITZPATRICK

Kohorn. Swedish cow-horn trumpet. See BOCKHORN.

Kōjinbiwa. Japanese lute. See BIWA.

Kokā. SPIKE FIDDLE of Maharashtra, west India. The resonator is a coconut shell with parchment membrane pasted over a flat opening and the neck is a wooden stick which passes through the resonator. Two metal strings are fastened below the resonator and pass along the neck and through holes in a nut to be tied to tuning-pegs. The bow is of curved wood and, like that of the rāvanhatthā, has small bells attached which give an added 'percussive' effect to the bowing.

BIBLIOGRAPHY
K. S. Kothari: *Indian Folk Musical Instruments* (New Delhi, 1968), 75
A. D. Ranade: *Lokasaṅgītaśāstra* (Aurangabad, 1975), 74f
JONATHAN KATZ

Koka taure. Wooden trumpet of Latvia. See TAURE.

Koka zvans ('wooden bell'). Set of wooden bells of Latvia. A number (8 to 13) of trough-shaped wooden bells without clappers (individually known as *klabeklis*) were set in a wooden frame and used as a rhythmic instrument in village bands.

Kokin. Fiddle of Japan, derived from the Chinese *huqin* (see JINGHU). See also MINSHINGAKU.

Kokiriko. Japanese concussion sticks consisting of two thin bamboo stems, about 20 to 30 cm long, which are struck across each other rhythmically, often by dancers (*ko*: 'little'; *kiri*: 'cut short').

Kokk. SLIT-DRUM of the Holo people of south-western Zaïre (*LaurentyTF*, 136). See MUKOKO.

Kokkara. Metal SCRAPER of Kerala, south India. It is constructed from a sheet of iron rolled into a tube about 60 cm long and 5 cm in diameter. The edges are left slightly apart and then raised and serrated; when they are scraped with an iron bar the instrument produces a rasping sound. The *kokkara* is used by the Pulaya and Kanikar peoples for ceremonials of sorcery and witchcraft. See also ŚUKTIVĀDYA.

Kokle. BOX ZITHER or psaltery of Latvia, analogous to the Lithuanian KANKLĖS, Estonian *kannel* and Karelo-Finnish KANTELE. The body of the *kokle*, shaped like an irregular trapezium narrower at one end (see illustration), is hollowed out from a single piece of wood and fitted with a soundboard which is usually ornamented with geometrically-shaped soundholes. The earliest instruments have five to nine gut strings; in the late 19th and early 20th century the number was increased to between 17 and 23 and the strings were often made of metal. They are fastened to a metal rod at the narrow end and wound round wooden or metal pegs, inserted from the underside, at the wider end. The tuning is diatonic. Traditional *kokles* were made in two forms. The *kokle* from Kurzeme was narrower, smaller and slightly curved in shape; those from Latgale were larger and heavier, and had an extension to the resonator at the wider end.

Kokle (box zither) player, Latvia

In performance the *kokle* is placed on the player's knees or on a table; the strings can be plucked with the fingers of both hands, or strummed with a plectrum in the right hand to produce chords, the unnecessary strings being damped with the left hand. In the 1950s the instrument was modified considerably by the addition of more strings, levers which made completely chromatic tuning possible, and dampers. The modern *kokle* is now made in six sizes and played in homogeneous ensembles. See *VertkovA*, 96; Ī. Priedīte: *Ko spēlēja sendienās* [What was played in the past] (Riga, 1983).

Koko (i). Wooden concussion CLAPPERS of the Mbuti pygmies of Zaïre.

Koko (ii). Whistle of central Africa.

Koko (iii). Term for a cylindrical SLIT-DRUM of the Suku, Kongo and Mayombe peoples of western and south-western Zaïre. Amongst the Kongo people the drum is of medium size, its narrow slit widened at each end to make square or circular openings. Amongst the Mayombe the term denotes a large cylindrical slit-drum, while amongst the Suku it denotes a drum of this type with a carved anthropomorphic extension (*LaurentyTF*, 133, 135). *See also* MUKOKO.

Kokpworo [okporo]. Drum of the Mono people of north-western Zaïre. *See* DINDO.

Kokyū. SPIKE FIDDLE of Japan (*ko*: 'foreign', 'barbarian'; *kyū*: 'bow'). It is about 69 cm long, with a sound-box measuring 14 × 12 × 7·5 cm; the bow is about 95 to 120 cm long. This is Japan's only indigenously evolved fiddle (although several others were used in *minshingaku* music). It is smaller than the SHAMISEN, but otherwise nearly identical in shape and construction, differing mainly in its long spike, the shape and position of the bridge and the lack of any device to generate the buzzing sound called *sawari*. The *kokyū* is held vertically, its spike inserted between the knees of the kneeling performer or (especially for women) resting on the floor in front of the knees (see illustration). As with the Javanese *rebab* the instrument itself, not the bow, is rotated to select the appropriate string; the bow always follows the same path. There are usually three strings, but certain schools double the highest string (a practice introduced in the mid-18th century).

Kokyū (spike fiddle) player, Japan

The *kokyū* had appeared at least by the early 17th century; in early depictions its body is smaller and rounder than that of the modern instrument. It may have developed from a marriage of the shamisen not with a *jinghu*-type Chinese lute but with the European rebec, a hypothesis suggested by organological evidence, by Japan's ties with Europe around the time that the *kokyū* appeared, and by the apparent occurrence of *raheika* (the Japanese word for rebec is *rabeika*) as an early alternative name for the instrument. The *kokyū* was quickly adopted both by low-caste itinerants and by the guild of blind shamisen and koto players. The blind musicians developed a small repertory of 'basic pieces' (*honkyoku*), a few of which survive. By the mid-17th century the *kokyū* alternated with the *hitoyogiri* as the third member of the SANKYOKU (chamber music) trio. In the bunraku puppet theatre (*see* GIDAYŪ) it joined the shamisen in scenes of extreme pathos. It also came to be used in certain regional folk music. By the late 19th century the role of the *kokyū* in *sankyoku* had been usurped by the *shakuhachi* except in accompaniments to the stately *jiuta-mai* dances. Today it survives mainly as an instrument of worship in the Tenri-Kyō religion. The *kokyū* is usually tuned a 5th above the shamisen, in *san-sagari* tuning. It does not change tuning in mid-piece, unlike the shamisen and koto.

The *kokyū* is similar to the Okinawan *kūchō*, although the relationship has not yet been clarified.

BIBLIOGRAPHY
S. Kishibe: *The Traditional Music of Japan* (Tokyo, 1966, 2/1981), pl.53
D. Waterhouse: 'An Early Illustration of the 4-stringed Kokyū', *Oriental Art*, xvi/2 (1970), 1
F. Koizumi, Y. Tokumaru and O. Yamaguchi, eds.: *Asian Musics in an Asian Perspective* (Tokyo, 1977), 187
                                    DAVID W. HUGHES

Kōl [koul]. Oboe of the Kota people of the Nilgiri Hills, south India. Locally made, it is about 30 cm to 35 cm long and is composed of four parts telescoped into one another, to which is added the reed: the bell, of conical bore, is of neemwood, its outer rim reinforced by a brass flange; the cylindrical body has six finger-holes and is of fig- or rosewood, its two ends bound by brass bands; a brass tube or staple, of much smaller diameter, carries a large metal disc against which the player rests his lips; and the mouthpiece, made of the quill of a bird-feather, carries a double reed fixed by binding. A simpler type has the bell and body made from a single piece of wood. It is played in pairs, together with other Kota instruments – *tābeteke* (drums) and *kombu* (semicircular trumpets) – to accompany songs, dances and processions. The Kota play music also for the mourning ceremonies of the Toda and certain Badaga clans, the latter sometimes call the Kota *Hāre–kōl* ('drums and oboes').

BIBLIOGRAPHY
E. Thurston: *Castes and Tribes of Southern India*, iv (Madras, 1909), 14ff
                                    PRIBISLAV PITOËFF

Kola [kula]. Cylindrical stopped wooden flute of the Zande people of north-eastern Zaïre (*LaurentyA*, 173, 174ff).

Kolalu [kolavi]. Kannarese terms of south India denoting a transverse flute.

Kolatka [klekotka]. Wooden CLAPPERS of Poland, with one, two, four or eight small hammers. The instrument is often used by children as a toy, and also replaces bells in church on Good Friday.

Kōlaṭṭam karra. Pair of short concussion sticks of Andhra Pradesh, India. The sticks are lathe-finished and painted with lacquer; they are used in the *kōlaṭṭam* stick-dance. *See also* DAṆḌĀ.

Kolavi. *See* KOLALU.

Kolenang. GONG-CHIME of West Java. *See* BONANG.

Kolesing. Polychordal TUBE ZITHER of the Ilongot people of the northern Philippines. *See* KOLITONG.

Kolilo. Large SLIT-DRUM of Pukapuka, northern Cook Islands. It is similar to the *koriro* of Manihiki. See E. and P. Beaglehole: *Ethnology of Pukapuka* (Honolulu, 1938), 216.

Kolintan. GONG-CHIME of the Philippines. *See* KULINTANG.

Kolintang. (1) Orchestra of xylophones in Minahasa, North Sulawesi. It consists of two *yuk*, one *bas*, one *selo*, two *gitar bas*, two *terkwin* and one *melodi*. The *melodi* is played with two short headless sticks and the others with two or three hammers (two in the player's right hand and one in the left). They are tuned in semitones. All instruments are made entirely of *cempaka* wood (frangipani). National, religious and local folksongs are played in harmony by adult and school groups. Generally, the higher the pitch the more notes the instrument plays. According to a local theory, *kolintang* derives from 'kulit kayu yang berbunyi' ('sounding tree bark'); *tang* means 'to sound' in Minahasan.

(2) GONG-CHIME of the Philippines. *See* KULINTANG.

MARGARET J. KARTOMI

Kolintang besi. Gong of Minahasa, North Sulawesi. *See* MOMONGAN.

Kolitong [kulibit]. Polychordal TUBE ZITHER of the Kalinga people of the northern Philippines. Similar instruments are played by the Ilongot (*kolesing*), the Isneg (*kuritao*, *uritang*), the Ata (*saluray*), the Bilaan (*sloray*, *sluday*), the Mansaka (*takol*), the Mangguangan (*tangko*), the Bukidnon (*tangkol*) and the Tiruray (*togoq*). They have from five to 11 strings which are plucked by the fingers of both hands. For illustration *see* ZITHER, fig.1*d*.

Kollko. DUCT FLUTE of Compi in the Bolivian Alti Plano. *See* KENA.

Kollo. KETTLEDRUM, played as a pair by professional musicians in the sultan's orchestra of the Kotoko people of Chad. The drum's hemispherical body, about 20 cm in diameter, is made either from wood, calabash or, in present times, enamelled iron. The laced cowhide head is hit with two straight sticks. The *kollo* drums are insignia of power, like the long *gashi* trumpets.

MONIQUE BRANDILY

Kollu. Single-headed pot drum played by professional musicians of north-western Chad. It is made from unbaked dried clay with a goatskin head under which are stretched two snares made from cow sinews. The head is struck with two thick plaits of leaves from the doom palm. *Kollu* players are always associated with *bala* drummers; *see* BALA (ii).

MONIQUE BRANDILY

Kolo (i). Double-headed underarm HOURGLASS DRUM of the Hausa people of northern Nigeria. It has fixed pitch. The *kolo* resembles the slightly larger *jauje* drum but has the tension cords bound in. For its use, *see* JAUJE.

Kolo (ii). One of a trio of harps of the Kotoko people of West Africa. *See* GALDYAMA.

Kologo. Plucked lute of Ghana.

Kolokocho. Obsolete ankle rattle of the Shambala people of Tanzania.

Kolongwa. Long cylindro-conical drum of the Bembe people of Zaïre. *See* KIMBANDU.

Kolongwe. Double-headed drum of the Bena Kalundwe people of Zaïre (*BooneT*, 57).

Kolophonium (Ger.). ROSIN.

Koloratur (Ger.). COLORATURA.

Kolorieren (Ger.). To introduce COLORATION. The term is often used with special reference to German organists of the late Renaissance who made extensive use (though in fact no more than others in their period) of that technique of written or improvised variation; hence *Koloristen*, composers to whom such reference is made.

Kōlu. Concussion sticks of south India, used in the stick dance *kōlaṭṭam*. *See also* DAṆḌĀ.

Kölwök. Free-reed aerophone of the Köho people of central Vietnam. It consists of a metal free reed mounted in the wall of a water-buffalo horn. *See* PĪ SANAI.

Koma. JEW'S HARP of the Shambala people of Tanzania.

Komabue. Japanese transverse flute, with six fingerholes, used in the *komagaku* and *azuma-asobi* genres of gagaku (court music). It is similar to the RYŪTEKI, except that it is shorter (about 36 cm) and much thinner, tuned a whole tone higher, has only six holes and usually has blue or green embroidery embedded in its left end. It shares the main melody heterophonically with the *hichiriki* (oboe).

DAVID W. HUGHES

Komba. Arched harp of the Budu people of Zaïre (*LaurentyC*, 119). *See* KUNDI (i).

Komboat. Mouth organ of Vietnam; it has six pipes and a gourd windchest. *See also* MBUAT.

Kombu [kompu]. Semicircular trumpet of south India. This Tamil name is equivalent to the Sanskrit *śṛṅga*. The *kombu* has a conical bore and consists of from three to five brass tubes telescoped into one another. The whole is reinforced by a cord tied to the two ends. It is often played in pairs (or several pairs) tuned to a 4th (the pitches *pa* and *sā*). It features in various temple music ensembles (*kombu pāṭṭu*, *ceṇḍa melam*, *pañcavādyam* etc), in military band music, and for village signals.

Both name and instrument were imported to Sri Lanka from Tamil Nadu. It is still found there in various shapes and sizes, always made of brass. The crescent-shaped and coiled varieties are used to replace the *sak* (conch) in Buddhist and Hindu temple worship, and the double crescent-shaped instrument, believed to have been a later importation, is now used in most school and college *hēvisi* bands, to blow a single repeated note at the beginning of a performance.

For illustrations *see* IḌAKKA and PAÑCAVĀDYAM.

BIBLIOGRAPHY
C. R. Day: *The Music and Musical Instruments of Southern India and the Deccan* (Delhi, 1891/*R*1977)
P. Sambamoorthy: 'Catalogue of Musical Instruments Exhibited in the Government Museum, Madras', *Bulletin of the Madras Government Museum*, ii/3 (1931)
——: *A Dictionary of South Indian Music and Musicians* (Madras, 1952–71), ii, p.323
S. Krishnaswami: *Musical Instruments of India* (New Delhi, 1965/*R*1967)
PRIBISLAV PITOËFF

Komcākhīm [komkhīmcā]. Small single-headed vertical drum, with a bulging wooden body, of Nepal. The head is struck directly with the hands. It is carried on the left shoulder, supported by a strap, and is played by the Newari people of the Jyāpu caste in an ensemble with a *bāmsurī* or *bay* (flutes), a *tāḥ* (frame drum) and *babu* (small cymbals).

BIBLIOGRAPHY
T. O. Ballinger and P. H. Bajracharya: 'Nepalese Musical Instruments', *Southwestern Journal of Anthropology*, xvi/4 (1960), 398
F. Hoerburger: *Studien zur Musik in Nepal* (Regensburg, 1975)
S. Wiehler-Schneider and H. Wiehler: 'A Classification of the Traditional Musical Instruments of the Nevars', *Journal of the Nepal Research Centre*, iv (1980), 67–132
MIREILLE HELFFER

Komïs. Two-string lute of the Khakass people of Siberia. *See also* TOPSHUR.

Komo [babbar garaya]. Two-string plucked lute of the Hausa people of Nigeria. The alternative term 'babbar garaya' means 'large *garaya*' and the instrument is similar in construction to the GARAYA, except that the soundbox is made from gourd not wood. The *komo* is 75 cm long, to which is added a further 22 cm by a ringed metal jingle, and it is plucked with a pick of cow- or hippopotamus-hide. It is played either solo or with gourd vessel rattles to accompany song and dance both for entertainment and for the *bori* spirit possession cult. These uses have largely replaced the *komo*'s original function of praising hunters.

BIBLIOGRAPHY
Ames–KingGHM
K. Krieger: 'Musikinstrumente der Hausa', *Baessler-Archiv*, new ser., xvi (1968), 373–430
D. W. Ames: 'Hausa Music I', BM30 L2306 [disc notes]
K. A. GOURLAY

Kompang. *See* KUMPANG.

Komponium (Ger.). COMPONIUM.

Kompu. *See* KOMBU.

Kŏmun'go. Korean six-string, fretted, plucked long zither (*kŏmun*: 'black'; *go*: 'zither'). In Chinese-character texts it is referred to as *hyŏn'gŭm*. The *kŏmun'go* is about 150 cm long and its slightly tapering width is 20 cm at the widest point. The body is made of two main pieces, the slightly curved front of paulownia wood and the back of chestnut; the interior is hollow. Six strings of twisted silk run from a broad, curved bridge on the performer's right to moorings looped through holes at the far end; reserve string is kept in coils near the moorings. Glued

1. Kŏmun'go (long zither) of Korea

perpendicularly to the body are 16 thin wooden frets, nearly rectangular in shape and ranging in height from 5·7 cm to 6 mm. The frets are only wide enough to lie under the second, third and fourth strings, the tallest fret acting as a bridge which suspends these three strings just above the remaining frets. The first, fifth and sixth strings are held up with small movable wooden bridges ('wild-goose feet'). The strings are plucked with a pencil-shaped wooden plectrum (*sultae*) and the face of the instrument is protected in the plucking area by a leather cover.

The *kŏmun'go* has several tunings, a typical one for court music being *Eb–Ab–Db–Bb–Bb–Bb'*. Its compass is quite wide, from the open *Bb'* up to *bb'* on the 16th fret. The instrument is played propped slightly up on edge and angled away from the performer so that the bottom lies against his left knee and the outer edge of the right end is supported above his right knee; as a result, only a single corner rests on the floor (see fig.1). The performer plucks the string, both downwards and upwards, with a plectrum held in the right hand between forefinger and middle finger, being secured by thumb and forefinger. The left hand is positioned by keeping the ring finger pressed on the second string (normally on the fourth or seventh fret) and the middle finger on the third; the forefinger and thumb move about freely, the melody normally being played on the second and third strings. Shading and vibrato are obtained by pressing the strings laterally along the top of the frets.

The sound of the *kŏmun'go* is rather weak, partly as a result of low string tension, and there are intrusive sounds from the performing techniques, such as the plectrum striking the leather guard or the rubbing of wound strings against the frets. But the *kŏmun'go* is considered a noble and masculine instrument, as distinct from the more feminine *kayagŭm*, and its player is normally the most influential member of an ensemble.

Fretted long zithers, apparently forerunners of the *kŏmun'go*, appear in a number of tomb paintings of the Koguryŏ period (37 BC–AD 668; see fig.2). Indeed, the richness of the tomb iconography, which extends westward into China, has led to some controversy as to whether the drawings depict proto-*kŏmun'go* or ancient Chinese *wo-konghou* ('horizontal harps'); see KONGHOU.

The *kŏmun'go* was one of the three main string instruments, together with the *kayagŭm* and *pip'a*, during the Three Kingdoms period (57 BC–AD 935). A legend in the *Samguk sagi* ('History of the Three Kingdoms', 1145) recounts how a man named Wang San-ak of Koguryŏ modified a Chinese *qin* and made a new instrument; when he played it black cranes flew in and danced, so he named the instrument *hyŏnhakkŭm* ('black crane zither'), the name later being shortened to *hyŏn'gŭm* ('black zither') or, in pure Korean, *kŏmun'go*.

The *kŏmun'go* has a continuous performing tradition. The important treatise *Akhak kwebŏm* (1493) devotes to it the longest single instrumental entry, with detailed modal and technical information, and the descriptions apply to the modern instrument in nearly every detail. At about the turn of the 16th century an efficient and precise tablature notation system (*hapchabo*) was devised, based in part on Chinese *qin* tablature, and numerous volumes in this notation survive from 1572 onwards, providing a prime source of insight into the historical development of Korean music.

Today the *kŏmun'go* is used in many court and folk ensembles, as well as in the solo virtuoso genre *sanjo*, in which it is particularly effective.

2. *Kŏmun'go (long zither) of Korea: detail from a tomb painting (c6th century AD) at Tonggou (formerly in Manchuria), Jilin province, China*

BIBLIOGRAPHY

Sŏng Hyŏn, ed.: *Akhak kwebŏm* [Guide to the study of music] (Seoul, 1493/*R*1975), 7.13b–21a

Chang Sa-hun: *Han'guk akki taegwan* [Korean musical instruments] (Seoul, 1969), 64ff

Song Bang-song: *Kŏmun'go sanjo: an Analytical Study of a Style of Korean Folk Instrumental Music* (diss., Wesleyan U., Middletown, Conn., 1975)

Yi Hye-gu: *Han'guk ŭmak nonch'ong* [Essays on Korean music] (Seoul, 1976), 147ff

ROBERT C. PROVINE

Komus. Two-string plucked lute of the Siberian Shor people, related to the Altai *topshur*. It is used to accompany epics, tales and songs.

Komuz. Unfretted three-string lute of the Kirghiz people of Central Asia. In the most common tunings, the middle string is the highest in pitch. It is the only three-string lute among the Central Asian long-necked lutes, and one of the few that have no frets.

Konchiki. Gong of Japan. See SURIGANE.

Konchuhun. Seven-string HARP-LUTE (i) of the Gwin people of Upper Volta. It has a large calabash resonator and resembles the *kora* in construction.

Koncovka. DUCT FLUTE of Slovakia. It has no fingerholes; closing and opening of the distal end and overblowing are used to change the pitch, as on the TILINCĂ.

Kondale. Double-headed barrel drum of the Sara-Kaba people of Chad. It rests on the ground in front of a crouching player who beats one membrane with each hand. The drum is used with others to provide rhythmic accompaniment to xylophone music for social song and dance. See C. Duvelle and M. Vuylstèke: 'Anthologie de la musique du Tchad', OCR 36–8 [disc notes].

Konde. Two-string plucked lute of the Bisa people of Upper Volta. It is played by non-professionals to accompany singing, or as a 'talking' instrument simulating tonal speech patterns.

Kondene. HARP-LUTE (i) of the Yalunka people of Guinea and Sierra Leone. It is used to accompany hunting songs.

Kondi. LAMELLAPHONE of the Temne, Limba and Loko peoples of northern Sierra Leone. Up to seven slender lamellae, with the longest in the centre and the shortest at the sides, are mounted on a rectangular box resonator, which is held against the stomach. The lamellae are plucked with the thumbs at the ends furthest from the body. The instrument provides the melody to which the larger KONGOMA lamellaphone adds a rhythmic ostinato accompaniment.

Kondingi. Three-string PLURIARC of the Susu and Temne peoples of Sierra Leone. The flexible string-bearers are held by tension at almost a right-angle to the curved wooden soundboard (see illustration).

Kondingi (three-string pluriarc) of the Susu people, Sierra Leone

Kondo. Small SLIT-DRUM of the Luba people of Zaïre. *See* KYONDO.

Kondu. Arched harp of the Zande people of Zaïre (*LaurentyC*, 119). *See* KUNDI (i).

Kone. LAMELLAPHONE of the Bisa people of Upper Volta. It comprises a small tin soundbox, containing rattling seeds, on which are mounted five or six adjustable metal tongues. The box is held between the player's thighs, slanting slightly towards him, with the open ends of the keys, which are plucked with the fingers, away from his body. The *kone* may be played either solo or with another of its kind to accompany dancing. See C. Duvelle: 'Musique Bisa du Haute-Volta', OCR 58 [disc notes].

Konene. MIRLITON of the Madi people of Uganda. *See* EGGWARA (ii).

Kong. Double-headed barrel drum of the Muong people of Vietnam and Laos. Its heads are of buffalo-skin. The drum is struck with two wooden mallets, and is used in a gong ensemble for the ceremony of the buffalo sacrifice.

Konga (i). Double clapperless bell of the Nkundo people of Zaïre. *See* GONGA (i).

Konga (ii). Drum owned by chiefs of the Lia people of Zaïre (*BooneT*, 61).

Kong dae. Double-headed barrel drum of the Karen people of Thailand and Burma.

Kǫng düng. Large single-headed FRAME DRUM of the Lao people of Laos, also called *rammanā lam tat*.

Konggoma. LAMELLAPHONE of Liberia and Sierra Leone. *See* KONGOMA.

Kongguli. Large double-headed drum of the Kotoko people of central Chad. *See* NGULO.

Konghou [k'ung-hou]. Generic term for various historical Chinese string instruments, usually translated as 'harp'. The related term *konghu* refers to obsolete harps of Korea.

1. The Chinese konghou. 2. The Korean konghu.

1. THE CHINESE KONGHOU. The word *konghou* appears in the official history of the Han dynasty (*Qian Han shu*) with reference to the date 111 BC, but as yet there is no iconographical evidence that any type of harp was known in Han China. A significant use of the term was for describing musical instruments in the non-Chinese musical ensembles which performed at the courts of the Sui (AD 581–618) and Tang (AD 618–907) dynasties. As *konghou* is used to describe string instruments from numerous cultures as disparate as India and Korea, it is almost certainly not the name of a particular form of instrument and perhaps not even a term for a distinct sub-class of string instrument. The word was modified in three chief ways: *wo-konghou* ('horizontal *konghou*'), *shu-konghou* ('vertical *konghou*') and *fengshou konghou* ('phoenix-head *konghou*'). Various scholars have attempted to match these names to particular instruments, using historical and iconographical means. Hayashi Kenzō (1962), for example, has concluded that the *wo-konghou* was the fretted long zither found in 5th- and 6th-century mural paintings and considered to be a forerunner of the Korean KŌMUN'GO. He also related the *fengshou konghou* to early forms of the Indian *vīṇā*.

Drawings of *konghou* in illustrated sources after the Tang period are quite various: Chen Yang, in the treatise *Yueshu* of AD 1104, for example, gives a drawing for each of the three types of *konghou*, but the *wo-konghou* is simply the *shu-konghou* (a small angular harp) turned on its side; and the encyclopedia *Sancai tuhui* (1607) shows the *konghou* as a long zither placed on a four-legged stand. More study is required before the use of the term *konghou* can be fully explained.

2. THE KOREAN KONGHU. The existence of harps in Korea in former times is attested by Chinese descriptions of Korean ensembles, by depictions in bell-reliefs of the Unified Silla period (668–935) and by a suggestion of Korean provenance in the labelling of two instruments in the Japanese Shōsōin repository (*see* HARP, fig.30). There is no evidence that harps have been played in Korea since Silla times.

A basic source of information is the description of various musical ensembles recorded in the Chinese *Sui*

Sogonghu (small harp) and saeng (mouth organ): detail of a relief on a bronze bell (AD 725) at Sangwŏn temple, Korea

shu ('History of the Sui dynasty'), which covers the period 581–618. This work asserts that the Korean ensemble included *sugonghu* (Chin. *shu-konghou*: 'vertical harps') and *wagonghu* (Chin. *wo-konghou*: 'horizontal harps'). Since the same source applies the same terms to instruments from several countries disparate in both culture and location, a sensible interpretation is that the terms are simply descriptions, rather than specific names of particular instruments. In short, little is known from this source about the nature of the Korean 'harps' at the Sui court.

The instrument which appears in relief on the bronze bell dated AD 725 at Sangwŏn temple in Korea (see illustration) is a small angular harp with 13 vertical strings, tucked into the belt and played with both hands. The Koreans now call this small hand-held harp *sogonghu* ('small harp'). There are two very similar instruments of the 8th century or earlier in the Shōsōin repository in Nara, Japan; they were labelled *kudaragoto* (string instruments from the Korean Kingdom Kudara, or Paekche, 18 BC–AD 663; see KUGO). Japanese scholars have referred to them as *ju-kugo* ('vertical harps'), using the same pictographs as Korean *sugonghu* and Chinese *shu-konghou*. Depictions of a nearly identical harp from ancient Assyria reveal the origins of this instrument in the Middle East.

The *wagonghu* has been the subject of some investigations by Japanese scholars (Kishibe Shigeo and Hayashi Kenzō) and a Korean scholar (Yi Hye-gu). The point at issue is whether the 5th- or 6th-century tomb paintings of fretted long zithers in Manchuria and northern Korea may be identified with either the *wagonghu* or the zither *kŏmun'go*, or both.

The instrument that the Koreans currently refer to as *wagonghu* is essentially the Burmese arched harp *saùnggauk*. The examples of harps now in Korea, at the National Classical Music Institute in Seoul, were all brought from Beijing in 1937.

BIBLIOGRAPHY

Gujin tushu jicheng [The imperial encyclopedia] (1725), music section, chap.115
Kishibe Shigeo: 'The Origin of the *K'unghou* (Chinese harp)', *Tōyō ongaku kenkyu*, xiv–xv (1958), 1–51
Hayashi Kenzō: *Dongya yueqi kao* [Investigations of East Asian musical instruments] (Beijing, 1962), 196, 213
Chang Sa-hun: *Han'guk akki taegwan* [Korean musical instruments] (Seoul, 1969), 98ff
L. Picken: 'T'ang Music and Musical Instruments', *T'oung Pao*, lv (1969), 115
Yi Hye-gu: *Han'guk ŭmak nonch'ong* [Essays on Korean music] (Seoul, 1976), 147ff
Niu Longfei: *Jiayuguan Wei-Jin muzhuan bihua yueqi kao* [Studies on musical instruments in Wei and Jin tomb paintings at Jiayuguan] (Gansu, 1981), 15–65

ROBERT C. PROVINE

Kong kai. XYLOPHONE of the Kupang area of Timor, Indonesia. Its nine redwood (*kai nalla*) keys range from about 30 to 52 cm in length and 2 to 5 cm in width. They rest on a frame of kapok wood which measures about 74 cm by 30 cm, with a height of 23 cm. The keys are beaten with a padded stick. It is now almost obsolete. Four *kong kai* are traditionally played in ensemble with a *tambur* (drum).

MARGARET J. KARTOMI

Kongo. A term used for the LAMELLAPHONE in northern Uganda. *See* LUKEME.

Kŏn'go. Obsolete large barrel drum of Korea. The two tacked cowhide heads were about 110 cm in diameter and the slatted wooden body about 150 cm long. The drum was mounted on and penetrated by a single large pillar rising from a four-part base fashioned as four sitting tigers (see illustration). On top of the drum was a

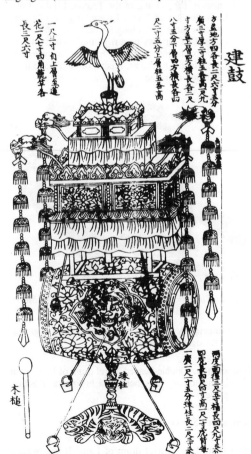

Kŏn'go (large barrel drum) of Korea, as depicted in 'Akhak kwebŏm' (1493)

highly decorated pagoda-like structure with two storeys; four wooden dragon heads, each with long silk tassels hanging from its mouth, protruded from the four corners of the first storey, while on top of the smaller second storey was a white crane with spread wings.

The *kŏn'go* was built in Korea in the 15th century (modelled on descriptions in Chinese sources) and used in ensembles for court ceremonies and banquets in conjunction with the drums *sakko* and *ŭnggo*. It appears in late 19th-century screen paintings depicting similar ceremonies, but has not been in use since. The only surviving historical instrument was destroyed during the Korean War (1950–53) and current ones are smaller reconstructions. A related instrument, the JIANGU, survives in China.

BIBLIOGRAPHY
Sŏng Hyŏn, ed.: *Akhak kwebŏm* [Guide to the study of music] (Seoul, 1493/R1975), 6.5b–6b
Chang Sa-hun: *Han'guk akki taegwan* [Korean musical instruments] (Seoul, 1969), 136ff

ROBERT C. PROVINE

Kongolongo nkueko. Drum or small FRICTION DRUM with stick formerly used in Cuba; its body was made of a coconut shell (see *Ortiz*IMA, v, 203).

Kongoma [konggoma]. LAMELLAPHONE of the Kpelle and Vai peoples of Liberia and of the Temne, Limba, Loko and Mende peoples of Sierra Leone. It generally consists of two or three metal tongues on a large box resonator and is used for playing a rhythmic ostinato during song accompaniment, often with other instruments. Among the Mende, however, it is reported to have three or four bamboo lamellae.

Kongoma (lamellaphone) of the Limba people, Sierra Leone

Kongo-maria. A term for a lamellaphone of Uganda. See LAMELLAPHONE, §2 (iii).

Kǒng saphōn. Double-headed barrel drum of Laos, with calfhide membrane. It is held in a horizontal position when played.

Kong skor. *See* GAṄ SGAR.

Kǒng that. Large barrel drum of Laos. It has pegged heads, is used in pairs, and is beaten with sticks; it can be used in the folk orchestra *seb nǫi*.

Kong thom. *See* GAṄ DHAM.

Kong touch. *See* GAṄ TŪC.

Koni (i). Four-string plucked lute of the Maninka people of Guinea. *See* NKONI.

Koni (ii). Transverse flute, without finger-holes, of the Tsonga people of southern Africa. It is played by boys.

Kŏni. Single-string fiddle of the Jörai people of central Vietnam. It is composed of a section of bamboo 50 cm long with a wooden base carved in the shape of a crook (see illustration). The single metal string is fixed at the base, raised over a bridge and tightened with a peg, stretching lengthwise over the four wax frets. The bow is a simple bamboo stick. A piece of thread as long as the section of bamboo is fastened at one end to the metal string and at the other to a round plastic piece which is held inside the player's mouth. The string is made to vibrate in two ways: by the bow moving to and fro and by the voice, which is transmitted from the mouth to the string through the thread. This instrument is played at home or in the field for domestic entertainment.

TRÂN QUANG HAI

König. German family of organ builders. They were active for three generations in the region of the Eifel, the old electorate of Cologne, and in the northern Rhineland. Balthasar König (*b* c1685; *d* c1760), founder of the family firm, was resident in Münstereifel from 1711 and moved to Cologne in 1735. He established his own type of organ, and this was taken up and continued by his sons and grandsons without any significant modifications; this 'König type' remained a standard model in the German part of the Rhineland up to the second half of the 19th century. It gave prominence to the *Hauptwerk*, which was often the only manual. The second manual was a *Positiv*, and wherever possible a *Rückpositiv*. The third manual served as the 'Echo', and was equipped with flute stops. Free as well as coupled pedals frequently reached only as far as *f*, though larger instruments would extend to *c'* or *d'*. Balthasar König also showed a liking for mixture stops featuring the interval of a 3rd; the solo stops were generally distributed between the bass and the treble.

Christian Ludwig König (1717–89), son of Balthasar, studied with his father but subsequently also with Christian Müller (1690–1773) and was resident in Cologne from 1744. He frequently added to his organs characteristic stops in imitation of orchestral instruments (e.g. Viola da gamba, Flûte traversière and Hautbois).

Johann Kaspar Joseph König (1726–63), another son of Balthasar, worked mostly with his father and is on record as an independent organ builder in only five places. Johann Nicolaus König (1729–75), also a son of Balthasar, is similarly seldom mentioned as an independent organ builder. He studied with his father, and as they shared the same house in Cologne it may be assumed that he eventually took over the business from him.

Balthasar Franz Joseph König (1744–66), a son of Johann Kaspar, was considered his father's successor; he died young, however. Carl Philipp Joseph König (1750–95), a son of Christian Ludwig, worked at first with his father and later independently. Adolph Daniel

Köni (single-string fiddle) of the Jörai people, central Vietnam

König (*b* 1768), a son of Johann Nicolaus, was the last organ builder of the König family, and is last known to have been active in 1803.

BIBLIOGRAPHY

van Heurn: *De orgelmaker* (Dordrecht, 1804–5)
H. Boeckeler: *Die neue Orgel im Kurhaussaal zu Aachen* (Aachen, 1876)
J. Merlo: *Kölnische Künstler* (Düsseldorf, 1895)
FRIEDRICH JAKOB

Könighorn. An instrument combining characteristics of an althorn and a french horn. It was named after the man who devised it in 1855 and was built by Antoine Courtois. It was pitched in F and had three piston valves.

Konigi [koning, kani]. Triangular frame zither of Liberia. The strings are wound round the arms, and the point of the 'V' inserted into a half-calabash. The *konigi* of the Toma people has six to nine strings, the Gbunde instrument of the same name five to seven, and the *konng* of the Kpelle people eight to nine strings. In performance the open end of the calabash rests on the player's chest and the strings, held horizontally, are plucked with the thumb of the left hand and four fingers of the right. Among the Kpelle melodic motifs sometimes imply a text. Among the Sapa the instrument is known as *kani*.

BIBLIOGRAPHY

G. Schwab: *Tribes of the Liberian Hinterland* (Cambridge, Mass., 1947/R1974)
R. M. and V. L. Stone: 'Music of the Kpelle of Liberia', FE 4385 (1970) [disc notes]
R. M. Stone: 'Liberia', *Grove 6*
K. A. GOURLAY

Konimesin. Plucked lute of upper Guinea, related to the NKONI. Its soundbox is either hemispherical (when made from a half-calabash) or boat-shaped. It has two long and two short strings and a metal jingle. It is used by professional musicians and played with a panther's claw plectrum.

Koning. *See* KONIGI.

Koningei. MUSICAL BOW of the Mende people of Sierra Leone. It has several strings.

Konkenam. Whistle of the Jola people of Senegal. It was made from wood, horn or bone and formerly was blown at war-dances and funerals.

Konko. Cylindrical wooden SLIT-DRUM of the Bas-Congo region of south-western Zaïre. It has a carved anthropomorphic extension (*LaurentyTF*, 136).

Kon-kón. MUSICAL BOW of the Mari people (USSR).

Kono (i). Percussion instrument of Liberia. (1) Small bamboo or wooden SLIT-DRUM of the Kpelle people. It is held vertically in the hand for performance. Two may be used for bush-clearing activities, and several *kono* of different sizes are played in ensembles. In an ensemble of three, for example, the largest and therefore lowest pitched is *kono-lee* ('mother'), the medium-sized *kono-sama* ('middle') and the smallest *kono-long* ('child').

(2) Struck tortoise-shell percussion vessel. It is used by Kpelle women in rites of the *sande* (women's) society. The same instrument, from the forest tortoise *Cynixis*, is used similarly by the Mano, Gio and Sapa women who refer to it as *kwai kuo*, *baka* and *keka* respectively. The Sapa also use it to accompany a harp in honouring a successful hunter.

BIBLIOGRAPHY

R. M. and V. L. Stone: 'Music of the Kpelle of Liberia', FE 4385 (1970) [disc notes]
R. M. Stone: 'Liberia', *Grove 6*

Kono (ii). Lute of northern Ghana.

Konsonanzpianino. A miniature piano with sympathetic strings on the back of the soundboard, invented by Friedrich Hölling of Zeitz in 1877.

Kontigui. *See* KUNTIGI.

Konting [kontingo, koonting]. Five-string plucked lute of the Mandinka and Jola peoples of Senegal and the Gambia. In construction it is identical with the KHALAM of the Wolof people and much of the two instruments' repertory and playing technique is similar. The *konting* probably derives from the NKONI of Mali which was mentioned by the Arab traveller Ibn Baṭṭūṭa who visited Mali in 1353. It was already then an instrument of the court. Mungo Park (1799) described a three-string lute called 'koonting'. The plucked lute remained one of the main instruments of the professional court musicians (Mandinka: *jali*) until the early 20th century when it was overshadowed by the KORA (i). Today the *konting* has almost disappeared as a Mandinka instrument and is found mainly in eastern Senegal, but the Jola of southern Senegal occasionally use it. *Konting* tunings and certain stylistic features of the playing technique have been borrowed by the *kora*. *See also* HODDU and KURANG.

BIBLIOGRAPHY
M. Park: *Travels in the Interior Districts of Africa* (London, 1799)
H. A. R. Gibb, trans.: *Ibn Baṭṭūṭa: Travels in Asia and Africa, 1325–1354* (London, 1929)
                                                    LUCY DURÁN

Kontrabasharpa. A keyed fiddle; *see* NYCKELHARPA.

Kontrabass (Ger.). CONTRABASS.

Kontrafagott (Ger.). DOUBLE BASSOON.

Kontrastbombardon. Contrabass OPHICLEIDE in F, constructed in 1840 by Andreas Barth of Munich. C. Sachs (*Real-Lexikon der Musikinstrumente*, 1913) noted no patent application and was unable to describe the instrument. A. Baines's *Brass Instruments* (London, 1976), however, mentions an 11-key instrument in F, 140 cm tall (in the Deutsches Museum, Munich), which is possibly a *Kontrastbombardon*; he suggests that '*Kontrast*' should read '*Kontra*'.
                                                    STEPHEN WESTON

Konzerthorn. *See* PRIMHORN.

Konzertina (Ger.). CONCERTINA.

Kooauau [kōauau]. Open-tube flute of the Maori people of New Zealand, 12 to 15 cm long with a bore of 1 to 2 cm and three finger-holes. Some were made of wood, others of bone (see illustration), and many were beautifully carved. When not in use they were often worn around the neck as an ornament. Contrary to popular belief, the *kooauau* was not a nose flute, but was played with the mouth. The traditional blowing technique, which is diagonal or oblique rather than vertical or horizontal, can still be found. There were three or four standard scales, identical to those of many present-day songs (*waiata*). This provides support for statements by informants that the instrument played *waiata* melodies and was used principally for unison accompaniment of group singing.
                                                    MERVYN McLEAN

Kooauau (flute) of the Maori people, New Zealand, made from human thighbone, c1870 (Auckland Institute and Museum)

Kóombo. Carved wooden VESSEL FLUTE of the Luw people of south-western Zaïre (*LaurentyA*, 94).

Koondé. Carved wooden VESSEL FLUTE of the Penc people of south-western Zaïre (*LaurentyA*, 81).

Koonting. *See* KONTING.

Koororohuu [kōrorohū]. BUZZER of the Maori peopl of New Zealand. It was a children's toy made from small piece of thin flat wood or pumpkin rind pointe at both ends. Two holes were pierced near the centr through which the two ends of a piece of string wer threaded and then tied. One thumb was inserted in th tied end and the other in the loop end; the disc was nex swung towards the operator to twist the string and whe it was sufficiently wound up an outward pull on the strin caused it first to unwind rapidly and then, by its ow momentum, to wind up again in the opposite direction By timing the outward pull on the strings, the playe could keep the instrument revolving rapidly in alternat directions, producing a whizzing noise during th unwinding parts of the cycle. Songs in *pao* style wer sung to the accompaniment of the sound.
                                                    MERVYN McLEAN

Kootso. Small HOURGLASS DRUM of Nigeria. *See* KOTSO

Kopanka. Bulgarian fiddle. *See* GADULKA.

Kopfstück (Ger.). BELL (ii).

Kopiak. *See* KOPRAK.

Kopo ['kopo]. Chordophone of the San (Bushman people of southern Africa. It was possibly an imitation of the Zulu UGUBHU (musical bow).

Kopok-kopok. Pair of silver cymbals of Malaysia, foun only in the NOBAT ensemble of Trengganu.

Koppel (Ger.). An ORGAN stop (*Coppel*).

Koprak [kopiak]. SLIT-DRUM of Bali. It has severa lengths of bamboo, each of which is played by a sep arate performer. It is mounted horizontally in a scaffol and played at festival time. See C. McPhee: *Music i Bali* (New Haven and London, 1966/R1976), pp. 3! and 363.
                                                    MARGARET J. KARTOM

Kopuz [qopuz, qupuz]. Long-necked lute, dating fron the 11th century, of the Oğuz Turkish tribes of soutl Central Asia. *See* BAĞLAMA.

Koqin [k'o-ch'in]. JEW'S HARP of China. Its historica name is *huang*. *Koqin* (*ko*: 'mouth'; *qin*: 'string instru ment') is a generic term for all plucked idiophones o this type. There are two varieties.
    The instrument native to the Taiwan sub-cultures i: known to the Ami (dominant sub-culture) as *tivtiv*. The body of the instrument is a half-tube rectangular frame of bamboo (55 to 110 mm in length), with single, dou-

le or multiple tongues of bamboo (more recently of
rass or iron) bound to the frame with twine. In per-
ormance the frame is held between the teeth; the left
and holds the left end of the frame to steady the instrument, while the right hand pulls a thin hemp cord
attached to the right side) with regular jerks which causes
he tongue(s) to vibrate. The mouth cavity acts as a
esonator, reinforcing selected overtones. Its traditional
unction includes use in courtship, personal entertain-
nent and some ceremonies.

The second variety of *koqin* is the Western-style jew's
arp of north China. The body is in the shape of a
orseshoe, with a single tongue of metal. In perform-
nce the extending prongs of the frame are held between
he teeth and the bent tongue plucked by a finger.

BIBLIOGRAPHY

ü Ping-chuan: 'Instruments of the Taiwan Tribes', *Tunghai Eth-
    nomusicological Journal*, i (Taichung, 1974), 85–203 [Chin. and
    Eng.].

ALAN R. THRASHER

1. Mandinka kora (harp-lute)

Kora (i). A 21-string plucked harp-lute (fig.1). It is used
y professional male musicians of the Manding linguistic and cultural family (in particular the Mandinka
of the Gambia and Senegal), and is found in an area of
West Africa that includes the Gambia, Senegal, Guinea-
Bissau, the Republic of Guinea, Mali, Upper Volta and
northern Ivory Coast. The musicians are known as *jal-
lu* (sing.: *jali*). While the instrument is widely distributed, the Gambia River valley is one of the main centres
of *kora* playing and merits consideration as the homeland of the instrument. Its origins are obscure. *Kora*
players ascribe its introduction in the distant past to an
unknown musician associated with the Nyencho
warrior-princes of Kabu, in what has become Guinea-
Bissau. Its popularization is ascribed to Koriyang Musa,
a pupil of the legendary Jali Madi Wuleng who, with his
pupil, served the mid-19th-century Mandinka hero Kelefa
Sane. Knight ('Mandinka kora') suggested that the *kora*
developed from similar but smaller instruments not more
than 300 years ago. This hypothesis is apparently supported by the fact that the *balo*, the Mandinka–Maninka
xylophone, was noted by travellers at a considerably
earlier date than the first account of the *kora* (as the 18-
string 'korro') by Mungo Park in 1799.

While the *kora* is classified as a harp-lute (*see* HARP-
LUTE (i)), and Knight ('Mandinka kora') has proposed
the alternative designation 'bridge-harp', it is similar in
certain of its general features to a number of large plucked
and bowed lutes found throughout West Africa. Its fairly
long neck passes diametrically through a large hemispherical gourd resonator which is covered with a leather soundtable. The strings are attached to the upper end
of the neck with tuning collars and to the base of the
neck by anchor strings tied to an iron anchor ring set in
the neck. Distinctively, however, the *kora* has 21 strings
arranged in two parallel ranks at right angles to the soundtable on either side of a vertical notched bridge, 11 strings
on the left and 10 on the right. Notched bridges are
found on a number of other instruments used on or near
the African coast from Senegal in the north to Angola
in the south (*see* MVET). The strings of the *kora* were
traditionally made from leather, but more recently nylon
fishing line, of different gauges to suit the different registers of the instrument, is preferred because it is stronger
and more easily available and because of its brighter and

*2. Playing technique of the kora at Kankan, Guinea,
1952*

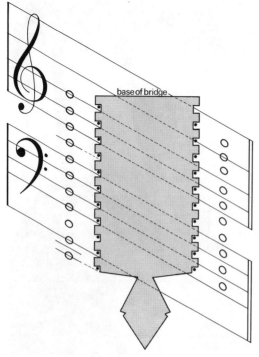

3. Approximate pitches of strings (tuned to tomora ba) in relation to their position on the bridge

string with the index finger, or with the index finge and thumb, is widely used; the index fingers may als be drawn across two or more adjacent strings in a strum ming action. In certain pieces a rhythmic interruptio of the melody is achieved by flicking the nail or th knuckle of the right index finger against the right har dle. A rhythmic accompaniment to the *kora* is ofte supplied by a second musician who strikes the back c the resonator with the *loyo* repair needle. In additior if women singers are present, they may supply a rhythm accompaniment by striking their slit iron percussion tube: known as *ne*, or by clicking their thumbs and middl fingers.

The *kora* is used principally to accompany narration: recitations and songs in honour of a patron. The son; texts are largely improvised; many lament the death o great patrons. It may, however, be used for purel; instrumental performances which often consist of highl; virtuoso elaborations of pieces in the accompanimen repertory. The *kora jali* may himself be the vocalist, o he may simply accompany one or more singers, mal. or female; in either case a chorus may sometimes pro vide a refrain. The *kora* is frequently used in urban danc bands, especially in Guinea and Mali, where the tra ditional *kora* repertory forms the basis of much popula music. There are four predominant regional styles (i; Guinea, Mali, Gambia and the Casamance region o Senegal), which differ in repertory, language and tex type, tuning preference and instrumental technique.

Each accompaniment is performed in a specific tun

more resonant sound. The two handles, the neck and the bridge are preferably of African rosewood, mahogany serving as a substitute for the handles and the neck, but not for the bridge. The leather soundtable was traditionally made from the skin of a male antelope (*Tragelophus scriptus*) but since such game is increasingly scarce, cowhide is more commonly used. The soundtable is nailed to the back of the resonator, and the leather on the back of the resonator may be embellished with metal studs. A soundhole, usually circular or square, is cut in the top of the resonator behind the right-hand handle, allowing the *jali* to use the body of the *kora* as a receptacle for spare strings, the large iron repair needle known as *loyo*, amulets and gifts of money from his audiences. An ornamental cloth is almost always attached to the neck at the back of the instrument. A flattish metal jingle (*nyenyemo*) with small wire loops attached to its edges may be fastened to the bridge for outdoor performances.

In Casamance (southern Senegal), an extra bass string is sometimes added to the left-hand side for use in the characteristic strumming styles of the region. Another modification whereby lateral tuning-pegs are used instead of rings was devised by the inhabitants of the Keur Monastery in Senegal, where the *kora* is used to accompany mass, but this has not been widely adopted.

In performance the *jali* sits, holding the *kora* nearly vertical, as in fig.1, so that the base of the neck rests on the ground and the bass resonances of the instrument are amplified. Playing technique consists essentially of plucking the strings towards the player with the curved index fingers and away again with the thumbs (see fig.2). The index fingers usually play the melody while the thumbs provide the accompaniment. A staccato effect (*dettero*), obtained by immediately stopping a vibrating

TABLE 1: An interpretation of the relationships between the three main tunings of the kora

Hardino	Tomora ba	Tomora mesenge
C	C	C
	16:15	
	B	
	10:9	
	A	
	9:8	
G	G	G
	9:8	
F	F	F
	16:15	
	E	
	10:9	
	D	
	9:8	
C	C	C

(arrows indicate balanced sharpening or flattening of the central tomora ba tuning)

ng or, more rarely, in one of two tunings. There are four tunings, known as *tomora ba* (the great *tomora*) or *sila ba* (the great road), *hardino*, *sauta*, and the *tomora nesengo* (the lesser *tomora*). The range of the *kora* is just over three octaves, and the approximate pitches of the strings are dictated by the range, and particularly the upper limits, of the voice or voices the instrument accompanies. Thus, in practice, the pitch of the *kora* may vary by almost an octave on different instruments and between different players. The *hardino* and *tomora nesengo* tunings possibly originated in pieces borrowed from two older instruments of the Manding peoples, the BALO and the KONTING. Each piece is based on a short recurring theme (*kumbengo*) and involves improvised ornamentation and variation (*birimintingo*). There are two vocal styles: the *donkilo* (for song and choral refrain), and the *sataaro* (for recitation or narration), which is either sung or spoken. Ex.1 shows the accompaniment

Ex.1 *Kelefa ba* (in *tomara ba* tuning)

to *Kelefa ba*, a praise song to Kelefa Sane; it is reputed to be the earliest piece composed specifically for the *kora* and is the first piece learnt by a beginner on the instrument.

BIBLIOGRAPHY
M. Park: *Travels in the Interior Districts of Africa* (London, 1799), 278f
C. A. Moloney: 'On the Melodies of the Volof, Mandingo, Ewe, Yoruba, and Houssa People of West Africa', *Journal of the Manchester Geographical Society*, v (1899), 277
J. Tiersot: 'Un instrument soudanais, la kora', *EMDC*, I/v (1922), 3224
D. Coly: 'Chant mandingue de Casamance', *Notes africaines*, xxxviii (1948), 22
R. Knight: 'Towards a Notation and Tablature for the *Kora*', *African Music*, v/1 (1971), 23
——: 'Mandinka kora: Gambie', OCR 70 [disc notes]
A. King: 'The Construction and Tuning of the *Kora*', *African Language Studies*, xiii (1972), 113
R. Knight: *Mandinka Jaliya: Professional Music of the Gambia* (diss., U. of California, Los Angeles, 1973)
A. King: 'Music: the Performance Modes', in G. Innes: *Sunjata: Three Mandinka Versions* (London, 1974), 17
L. Durán: 'Theme and Variation in Kora Music: a Preliminary Study of Tutu Jara', *Music and Tradition*, ed. D. R. Widdess and R. F. Wolpert (Cambridge, 1981), 183
ANTHONY KING, LUCY DURÁN

Kora (ii). Term occasionally applied to the GORA (mouth bow) of southern Africa.

Kora (iii). Fiddle of Flores, Indonesia. *See* REMBA.

Kôrac-kôrang. Pair of copper cymbals of the Jörai people of central Vietnam. They are played with the *cing arap* gong ensemble.

Körber, Günter (*b* 9 Jan 1922). German wind instrument maker. He is noted for his reconstructions of Renaissance and Baroque woodwind instruments. Educated in Berlin, he served as an army musician during World War II, afterwards continuing as a professional woodwind player. In 1958 he met Otto Steinkopf, and worked with him from 1959, setting up his own workshop in Berlin in 1964 when Steinkopf moved to West Germany. Körber has always aimed to improve the possibilities for performing early music, and his considerable output includes reconstructions of most varieties of early woodwind instruments, copied mainly from originals in Brussels, Berlin and Vienna. His reputation is most firmly based on wind-cap instruments, and in particular the crumhorn, which he and Steinkopf restored to active musical use.

CHRISTOPHER MONK

Korg. A range of electronic instruments, chiefly synthesizers, manufactured by Keio Electronic Laboratory Corp. in Tokyo from 1968. Keio began by constructing rhythm units for Yamaha's Electone electronic organs, and went on to become one of the most successful Japanese manufacturers of electronic instruments. The Korg ('Keio organ') synthesizer (1968) was the first to be produced in Japan. The company now makes about 20 types of instrument, ranging from monophonic synthesizers (including the pre-set Sigma) to programmable polyphonic synthesizers (such as the Polysix), as well as electronic organs and pianos, string synthesizers (including the Delta, Lambda and the programmable Trident), electronic percussion units, guitar synthesizers and a vocoder. Different organs and synthesizers include front panel controls and other features (drawbars, adjustable key-click control, joystick, pitch-bend and modulation wheels, and electronic simulation of rotary loudspeaker effects) that are more familiar from electronic instruments produced earlier by other companies; but Korg instruments are notable for the ingenious design of their electronic circuitry, particularly in the basic devices common to most instruments of a similar type. *See also* SYNTHESIZER.

HUGH DAVIES

Kori. Six-string HARP-LUTE (i) of the Senufo people of the Ivory Coast.

Koriro. SLIT-DRUM of Manihiki, northern Cook Islands, similar to the PĀTĒ of Rarotonga. The term is cognate with *kolilo* and *riro*, related idiophones of the Cook Islands. See P. Buck: *Ethnology of Manihiki and Rakahanga* (Honolulu, 1932), 203.

Kornett (Ger.). (1) CORNET (i).
(2) An ORGAN STOP (*Cornett*).

Koro. Percussion plaque of the Dogon people of Mali.

Korongoe. Ground bow of the Gbaya-Bokoto people of the Central African Republic. A small round hole approximately 20 cm deep and 25 to 30 cm in diameter is made in the ground, and a pliant stick, over a metre long, is fixed in the ground about 1 metre away from it. A strong string about 80 cm long is attached to the free end of the stick, which is bent over so that the string descends perpendicularly to the hole. The string passes through a small hole in the base of an open preserve tin and is knotted inside. The tin is placed open-end downwards in the hole in the ground and kept in position by the flat of the player's feet as he sits on the ground with the string in front of him. The string is struck with the index finger of the right hand and stopped at the upper end by gripping it between the thumb and index finger of the left. See M. Djenda: 'L'arc-en-terre des Gbaya-Bokoto', *African Music*, iv/5 (1968), 44.

K. A. GOURLAY

Kororai. A term used by the Kanuri people of north-eastern Nigeria for small bells which are wound in a chain round the hips of young girl dancers.

Kōrorohū. *See* KOOROROHUU.

Koroso. Iron ankle rattle of the Hausa people of Nigeria. *See* AKAYAU.

Korotil [liita]. Small transverse clarinet of the Kanembu people of north-western Chad. The idioglot reed is cut into the side of the tube and is completely covered by the player's mouth. The tube, made from reed, is about 20 cm long and has a single finger-hole. By stopping the hole and the ends of the tube the player can produce a range of a tetrachord. *See* CLARINET, TRANSVERSE.

MONIQUE BRANDILY

Korough. Side-blown trumpet of the Tiv people of Nigeria. Originally it was used as a war horn but today it is blown to announce a death or, more commonly, as part of an ensemble to accompany dancing.

Korro. 18th-century term for the *kora*. *See* KORA (i).

Korro. (1) Wooden SLIT-DRUM of the Dogon people of Mali. It is unusual in having both lips of equal thickness, thus sounding one pitch only. The drum plays an important role in dance and ceremonial activities of the village.

(2) Small harp of the Dogon people of Mali. *See* GINGIRU.

Kortholt [Kort Instrument; Kurz Pfeiff] (from Ger. *kurzes Holz*: 'short woodwind'). A generic term, referring to double-reed instruments from the 16th and 17th centuries with bores that double back on themselves (as in bassoons). The pitch of such instruments is thus deeper than their length would suggest. Specifically the word 'Kortholt' was applied to four kinds of instrument: a dulzian or early BASSOON (especially in England, according to Praetorius (2/1619), where the word 'curtal', a corruption of Kortholt, was used); a RACKET, according to various late 16th- and early 17th-century inventories cited by Kinsky (1925) and Boydell (1982); a SORDUN, or 'courtaut' as Mersenne (1636–7) called a similar instrument; and a wind-cap sordun.

The instrument Praetorius illustrates as a Kortholt is of the last type; he depicts an instrument with a wind cap over a double reed and an apparently cylindrical bore, doubled back on itself within a single wooden column (see illustration). The bore issues through a small lateral hole at the back below the wind cap. The instrument has 16 soundholes in all: the tips of all the fingers and the thumbs cover ten holes and the joints of the index fingers cover two more; the latter and the little-finger holes are duplicated to allow for left- and right-handed playing (the four holes not in use are presumably stopped with wax). There are two closed keys which extend the range upwards. The range is shown in the illustration as C–b♭, though elsewhere Praetorius writes that it is a full two octaves, B♭'–b♭. In dealing with most wind instruments Praetorius both illustrated them and described them in the text; this is not the case with the Kortholt, which is only mentioned in passing

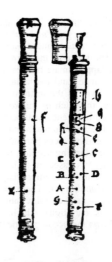

Kortholt as illustrated by Praetorius; woodcut from 'Syntagma musicum' (2/ 1619–20)

(sometimes by the name 'Kort Instrument'), though its range is given with those of the sorduns.

Describing the 'courtaut', which Mersenne characterized as an open-reed sordun, Trichet (see Lesure, 1955) wrote that 'one covers the reed with a cap, and [the instrument] is used as a bass in consort with musettes'; according to Trichet, therefore, the *courtaut* is effectively the same as Praetorius's 'Kortholt'.

BIBLIOGRAPHY

M. Praetorius: *Syntagma musicum* (Wolfenbüttel, 1618, 2/ 1619/*R*1958 and 1980)

M. Mersenne: *Harmonie universelle* (Paris, 1636–7/*R*1963; Eng. trans. of the book on instruments, 1957)

G. Kinsky: 'Doppelrohrblatt-Instrumente mit Windkapsel', *AMw*, vii (1925), 253

F. Lesure: 'Le Traité des instruments de musique de Pierre Trichet', *AnnM*, iii (1955), 368; edn pubd separately (Neuilly-sur-Seine, 1957)

B. R. Boydell: *The Crumhorn and other Renaissance Windcap Instruments* (Buren, 1982)

HOWARD MAYER BROWN, BARRA R. BOYDELL

Kös. Large Turkish KETTLEDRUM, now obsolete. An instrument of the Ottoman *mehter* (military or Janissary band), it was made of metal with a skin membrane, and played with wooden beaters. Pairs of *kös* were sometimes slung on horse- or camelback, on either side of the rider (for illustration, *see* BAND, fig.4). For similar instruments, *see* KUS and KYOS.

Koshnai. *See* QOSHNAI.

Koso. Snared open HOURGLASS DRUM of Nigeria. *See* KOTSO.

Kota. LAMELLAPHONE of the Dan people of the Ivory Coast. It derives from the word 'ko' meaning calabash and 'ta' meaning on. The instrument comprises seven to nine metal keys on a board fixed to a half-calabash resonator. Attached to a protruding portion of the board is a vibrator consisting of a piece of tin with metal rings pierced through holes round the edges. The player sounds the keys with his thumbs and occasionally strikes the board rhythmically. The instrument is played for self-entertainment during leisure hours, either with or without the addition of singing. Among the Baule a similar seven-keyed instrument is reported as *kote*.

BIBLIOGRAPHY
. Zemp: 'Music òf the Dan', BM30 L2301 [disc notes]
—: *Musique Dan: la musique dans la pensée et la vie sociale d'une société africaine* (Paris and The Hague, 1971)
K. A. GOURLAY

Kotāh [kwotaa]. Double barrel drum of the Newari people of Nepal. It results from the juxtaposition of two barrel drums: a *khĩm* lying horizontally with a *nāy-hĩm* placed vertically in front of it. Thus the player has t his disposal both heads of the horizontal drum and ne of the vertical one, the three heads being struck with ne hands. The *kotāh*, placed iconographically in the ands of the god Nasadiyo, is played solely by the members of the highest Buddhist castes (Gubhāju, Sākya, ulādhar) during the singing of certain religious hymns; *aymtāh* (long trumpets) and *tāh* and *babu* (cymbals) re used with it.

BIBLIOGRAPHY
. O. Ballinger and P. H. Bajracharya: 'Nepalese Musical Instruments', *Southwestern Journal of Anthropology*, xvi/4 (1960), 398
. Hoerburger: *Studien zur Musik in Nepal* (Regensburg, 1975)
. Wiehler-Schneider and H. Wiehler: 'A Classification of the Traditional Musical Instruments of the Nevars', *Journal of the Nepal Research Centre*, iv (1980), 67–132
MIREILLE HELFFER

Kotake. End-blown NOTCHED FLUTE of Japan. *See* HITOYOGIRI.

Kote. LAMELLAPHONE of the Baule people of the Ivory Coast. *See* KOTA.

Kotigi. Clapper bell of the Gbande people of Liberia. *See* GBWINI.

Kotin. Plucked lute attributed to the Jola people of the Gambia. Today their lute is known as KONTING.

Kotlookuk. *See* KALUKHAQ.

Koto. Long zither, with movable frets, of Japan. It is the most important Japanese member of the family of East Asian long zithers, the best-known members of which are the *zheng* and the *se* in China, the *kayagŭm* and *kŏmun'go* in Korea, the *đàn tranh* in Vietnam and the *wagon* and the koto in Japan. All these instruments probably originated in China with the possible exception of the *wagon*, which has been claimed to be indigenously Japanese. The exact date of the introduction of the koto into Japan is unknown, but is generally assumed to have been at the beginning of the Nara period (710–84) or shortly before.

During the Nara and Heian (794–1185) periods the word 'koto', the original meaning of which is obscure, was applied to several types of string instrument, like the Sanskrit word 'vīnā' in India. Examples were the *kin-no-koto* (the *shichigen-kin*, *kin* or Chinese *qin*); the *sō-no-koto* (the *sō* or koto); the *hitsu-no-koto* (the *hitsu*, or Chinese *se*); the *biwa-no-koto* (or *biwa*); the *yamato-goto* (or *wagon*); the *kudara-goto* (the harp, *kugo*); and the *shiragi-goto* (the modern Korean *kayagŭm*). Later the term came to be applied exclusively to the *sō-no-koto*. The *hitsu-no-koto*, *kudara-goto* and *shiragi-goto* were no longer used in Japan, while the names of two of the other instruments lost the suffix *-no-koto* to become simply *kin* and *biwa*, and the *yamato-koto* became *wagon*.

1. Construction and performing practice. 2. Repertory and social context. 3. Schools of koto music. 4. Innovations since the Meiji era (1868–1912).

1. CONSTRUCTION AND PERFORMING PRACTICE. Although the koto has not undergone any essential changes since its introduction into Japan, several types can now be distinguished, depending on the musical genre or school in which they are used. The various types may be classified into four groups: GAKUSŌ, used in gagaku (court music); *tsukushisō*, the instruments of tsukushi-goto (the older tradition of koto music); *zokusō*, used in *zokusō* (the later tradition of koto music); and *shinsō*, the group of new koto types, many of which were invented by Miyagi Michio (1894–1956) and which are used in specially composed music. *Shinsō* include the *jūshichigen-kin* (17-string bass koto) and the *tansō* (a small koto, whose strings are tightened by pegs; the performer places

1. Koto (long zither) player, Japan

(a)

(b)

2. Techniques of koto playing: (a) basic stroke, using the right-hand thumb; (b) ko (or oshide) technique, in which the string is depressed with the left hand to raise its pitch

it on a table and plays it sitting in a chair rather than kneeling on the floor).

The koto has a long (about 180 to 190 cm), slender (about 24 cm at the midpoint), rectangular body of *kiri* wood (*Paulownia imperialis*) with a slight convex longitudinal curve and sharper lateral curve. There are 13 silk strings of equal length and thickness, stretched under equal tension over fixed bridges placed about 10 cm from the right end (as viewed by the player) and about 20 cm from the left end; nowadays stronger materials such as nylon and tetron are also used, although principally for practice. The length of the vibrating part of the strings is determined by the placement of movable bridges (*ji*), each string having one bridge (for illustration *see* BRIDGE, fig.1*e*). The *ji* are made of wood or ivory (plastic is used on cheap modern instruments). Different placements of the *ji* produce different tunings. Depending on the player's school, the strings are plucked with bamboo, bone or ivory plectra (*tsume*) of varying shape.

In all schools the player is behind the instrument, its right end slightly to his right. The player sits on the floor, cross-legged (in gagaku and Kyōgoku: see §4 below), kneeling (Ikuta and Yamada schools: see §3 below), or with one knee raised (traditionally in *tsukushi-goto*, although female players have now changed this unfeminine position to a kneeling one). The Ikuta player kneels at an oblique angle, facing slightly to the left; in all other schools the player is positioned at a right angle

to the instrument. The *tsume* are worn on thumb, index finger and middle finger of the right hand, and pluck towards the palmar side of the hand. The main playing digit is the thumb, which usually plucks the strings in a movement directed away from the player (fig.2*a*). The main function of the left hand is to provide pitches not available on the open strings by pressing down on a string to the left of the movable bridge, raising the tension of the string and thereby the pitch (fig.2*b*). The left hand is additionally used to produce ornamental pitch inflections. Direct plucking of the strings with the left hand, although used today, occurred only rarely before the late 19th century.

The tuning of the koto depends on the scale system of the musical genre or composition for which the instrument is used. All traditional tunings consist of five pitches to an octave, representing the five most important notes of the mode. Additional pitches may be obtained by left-hand pressure to the left of the movable bridges. The tunings of the koto in gagaku, *tsukushi-goto* and in Okinawan koto music approximate to the requirements of the Pythagorean system; in *zokusō* this is true for the first, fourth and fifth degrees; the second and sixth degrees are somewhat lower. The exact 'lowness' of these latter pitches is not standardized: the 'minor 2nds' in the tuning produced by the more traditional musician vary, averaging about 75 cents, whereas more modern musicians tend to equate this interval with the Western tempered semitone of 100 cents. The relation between scale and tuning in gagaku and *tsukushi-goto*

Ex.1 Relationship between scale and tuning, transcr. W. Adriaansz
(a) The scale *ichikotsuchō*

(b) The tuning *ichikotsuchō* in gagaku

(c) The tuning *ichikotsuchō* in *tsukushi-goto*

is shown in ex.1 (*see also* BIWA, §2); *zokusō* is represented by its typical scale (the *in* scale) and its three most common tunings (ex.2). The location of the first

Ex.2 Tunings in *zokusō*, transcr. W. Adriaansz
(a) The *in* scale of *zokusō*

(b) The tuning *hira-jōshi*

(c) The tuning *hon-kumoi-jōshi*

(d) The tuning *nakazora-chōshi*

egree of the scale is shown in the tuning patterns, which shows that the *zokusō* tunings are transpositions of the same scale, not (as is often thought) different modes.

2. REPERTORY AND SOCIAL CONTEXT. Although modern *sōkyoku* ('koto music', i.e. music in which the koto has a solo role) has developed in an unbroken line from gagaku-based traditions in the Heian period, the existing non-court repertory can be traced back no further than the last decades of the 16th century. Throughout the Edo period (1603–1868) *sōkyoku* was one of the most common genres, and it was only during the last years of the 19th century that increasing Westernization began gradually to transform the tradition. Two main subdivisions may be distinguished: *tsukushi-goto*, the older tradition, once the privilege of high social classes, with characteristics still close to those of older forms of 'elegant music'; and the more recent *zokusō* ('popular koto music'), limited to low-class professional musicians and the bourgeoisie. Because *tsukushi-goto* is almost extinct, *sōkyoku*, for all practical purposes, may be identified with *zokusō*.

The development of *zokusō* through several schools, as a typical product of the Edo period, reflects the social situation of the time, which, because of the country's almost complete seclusion from the outside world, is considered to be one of the most specifically 'Japanese'. The feudal system with its four-class structure is reflected in the direction of *sōkyoku* towards one specific social group, the bourgeoisie (mainly belonging to the merchant class, officially the lowest of the four classes); in the organization of players of koto and certain types of shamisen music into a guild of professional blind musicians, the *shokuyashiki*, which had a strictly organized system of professional ranks; and in the teacher–student relationship, which mirrored that of the lord–vassal. The combination of these factors resulted in an authoritarian system, characterized by strong reciprocal obligations, that discouraged the development of individual initiative in younger musicians. This suppression of initiative, combined with the exclusion of a good deal of available talent by the practical limitation of professional koto musicians to blind men, is undoubtedly largely responsible for the striking homogeneity of the repertory of the various schools; to a lesser degree aesthetic considerations have also been responsible. Homogeneity eventually led to stagnation, which could be broken only by the emergence of a musician of exceptional talent who might initiate a new style of composition and thereby a new school. This inevitable sequence (creation of a school–stagnation–eventual revolt and creation of a new school) was repeated several times during the Edo period. Disregarding sub-schools, three main *ryū* (schools) of *zokusō* were created and maintained in the Edo period: the Yatsuhashi-ryū, the Ikuta-ryū and the Yamada-ryū. Beginning in the Meiji period (1868–1912), gradual Westernization of *sōkyoku* led to innovations within the Ikuta- and Yamada-ryū, as well as to the formation of new schools.

The limitation of *sōkyoku* to the lower social strata was responsible for the almost total absence of contemporary scholarly writing on this subject. Because scholarly pursuit during the Edo period was primarily the concern of the higher classes (especially samurai), *zokusō* was rarely considered worthy of the attention of scholars. Contemporary publication in the field of *sōkyoku* was limited almost entirely to collections of song texts and, rather exceptionally, collections of tablatures. Among the latter, the most outstanding is the *Sōkyoku taiishō* (1799) by Yamada Shōkoku: this collection of *kumiuta* and *danmono* of the Ikuta school is preceded by the (relatively) most scholarly introduction to the subject in the Edo period.

3. SCHOOLS OF KOTO MUSIC.

(i) Tsukushi-goto. During the last decades of the 16th century *tsukushi-goto* (named after a province in northwestern Kyūshū) was created by a Buddhist priest, Kenjun (1547–1636), who established a new tradition, partly by selecting and arranging existing music and partly by composing new songs with koto accompaniment. Solo koto music of aristocratic origin had been played in northern Kyūshū since the end of the Heian period, and the growing political insecurity in Kyoto during the Kamakura (1185–1338) and Muromachi (1338–1573) periods led to increased cultural intercourse between the capital and south-western Honshū and northern Kyūshū, which were relatively safe. A popular pastime of the nobility during these periods was the improvisation of *imayō* ('contemporary songs'). Such 'noble *imayō*' (distinct from 'common *imayō*' – popular religious songs sung by the common people) often used the melody *Etenraku* as a vehicle for their poetry. Then, as now, *Etenraku* was one of the most popular compositions of gagaku. Such *etenraku-imayō* are the prototypes of the song cycles with koto accompaniment (*kumiuta*) of *tsukushi-goto*. *Fuki*, the oldest and most influential *kumiuta*, has been shown to be a direct descendant of such poetic improvisation on a section of the music of *Etenraku*. Besides aristocratic traditions, *zokkyoku* ('popular music') is said to be another source from which Kenjun drew. Its influence, however, was considerably less, and in the new arrangements the original character was lost. A third influence on *tsukushi-goto*, that of Chinese *qin* music, is often mentioned; so far, however, research has not established any relationship between them.

The most important part of the *tsukushi-goto* repertory consists of ten *kumiuta* by Kenjun. Normally the texts of these cycles were taken from old sources of high literary quality. It is typical of *kumiuta* that the poems of the individual songs (*uta*) were not related to one another. The musical structure of each *uta* tends to be strictly quadratic: eight phrases, each containing four bars in duple metre, already found in *tsukushi-goto*, later became standard in *zokusō kumiuta*.

Throughout the Edo period *tsukushi-goto* remained primarily the privilege of Buddhist priests and Confucian scholars, who respectfully preserved the aristocratic, ceremonial character of the music as originally established by Kenjun. Especially after the time of Genjo (*d* 1662), the second head of the school, restrictions were severe. Blind men – the professional musicians – and women were banned from instruction. Stylistic development within the school was minimal and this, combined with the general aloofness of *tsukushi-goto*, caused stagnation. A serious decline began in the late 19th century with the rapid modernization of Japan. Today the school is almost extinct, and it is no longer possible to acquire sufficiently reliable information for scholarly research because the scores are incomplete and no performers of professional standard are still alive.

(ii) The Yatsuhashi-ryū. Towards the middle of the 17th century, it is said that Hōsui, a musician of *tsukushi-*

goto, settled in Edo where he taught a blind shamisen virtuoso, Jōhide (1614–85). Later known as Yatsuhashi and given the title Kengyō, this blind musician became the founder of *zokusō*, a step considered of such importance that he is commonly regarded as the father of modern koto music. Yatsuhashi Kengyō was responsible for the formation of a small repertory of 13 *kumiuta* and, possibly, two *danmono* or *shirabemono* (compositions for koto solo, consisting of several *dan* – parts – each of which contains 104 beats). The *kumiuta* and the *danmono* are in part arrangements of compositions of *tsukushi-goto* and in part newly composed. In the process Yatsuhashi made a revolutionary innovation by using the popular *in* scale rather than the scales of *tsukushi-goto*. This modal change was of great importance: with it the music began to move away from older aristocratic traditions, including *tsukushi-goto*, towards more modern, popular idioms represented, for example, by shamisen music. This again caused a shift in social milieu and, beginning with the activities of Yatsuhashi Kengyō, koto music became the concern of professional musicians and of a bourgeoisie well-educated in artistic matters. The use of the rather unflattering term 'zokusō' is justified by this shift in social milieu and to a lesser degree by a shift in function (from spiritually inclined ceremony to secular entertainment); it is not justified by the quality of the music, which, though it was adapted to professional technical standards, did not lose its restrained aristocratic character.

The repertory of the Yatsuhashi-ryū contains 13 *kumiuta* traditionally ascribed to Yatsuhashi Kengyō, one *kumiuta* by Yatsuhashi's student Kitajima Kengyō (*d* 1690) and prototypes of two *danmono*. Ten of Yatsuhashi's *kumiuta* and the one by Kitajima follow the standard form in the construction of the individual *uta*: eight phrases of four bars in duple metre. The remaining three (the most venerated ones, collectively called *Yatsuhashi no sankyoku*, 'Yatsuhashi's three pieces') show freer construction. The two *danmono*, *Kudan* and *Rinzetsu*, are prototypes of compositions which, in slightly altered form, later became two of the most famous pieces of koto music: *Rokudan* and *Midare*.

The first *dan* of the most typical *kumiuta*, *Fuki*, demonstrates the characteristic features of *kumiuta* (see ex.3). Form and content are directly related to the first part of the gagaku composition *Etenraku*. In this *uta* the beginning of each four-bar phrase is marked by an ornamented octave pattern (the octave is on the third beat of the first and the first beat of the second bar of each phrase); in addition, equally standardized figures occur at the conclusion of several phrases (bars 4, 8, 12 and 16). The third and fourth phrases are slightly varied repetitions of the first and second. The eight phrases of the first 32 bars can be divided into three groups: phrases 1–4 (bars 1–16: ex.3), phrases 5 and 6 (bars 17–24) and phrases 7 and 8 (bars 25–32). The first group is characterized by the use of a high register and great stability (all phrases end on E, the first degree of the mode); the second group moves in a middle register and is less stable (phrases end on 5th and 1st degrees); the third group uses the lowest register and is relaxed in quality, reaching a conclusion on the first degree in bar 31. The last bar and a half of the koto part, ending on the 5th, is a characteristic short interlude between *uta*; it never occurs at the conclusion of the final *uta*, which normally ends on the 1st degree in both voice and koto parts. The three parts reflect the *jo-ha-kyū* concept. This regular quad-

Ex.3 First *dan* of *Fuki*, Yatsuhashi-ryū style, transcr. W. Adriaansz (*The Kumiuta and Danmoro Traditions of Japanese Koto Music*, 1973)

ratic structure, the grouping of the phrases into three groups following the *jo-ha-kyū* order and the descending tendency throughout the *uta* can be seen throughout the *kumiuta* repertory. Because voice and koto simultaneously realize an individual, idiomatic version of the same underlying melody, their parts are closely related; occasional dissonances are the result of melodic activity and have no harmonic function. The temporal relationship between voice and koto is rather complex: whereas the koto tends to play on the beats, the voice frequently falls between the beats, often resulting in a characteristic lagging effect. The tempo of the first *uta* of a *kumiuta* is always slow (MM crotchet = *c*42). Virtuosity has no place in this form.

As with *tsukushi-goto*, the repertory of the Yatsuhashi-ryū remained stagnant. The school flourished throughout the Edo period, after which it gradually declined. Through the activities of Shin Sanada (1883–1975), for a time the sole carrier of the tradition, there was a minor renaissance in the 1960s. The tradition has been preserved in a sufficiently reliable state to make responsible scholarly study possible.

iii) Koto music in Okinawa. A small repertory of koto music of Japanese origin has survived in Okinawa (see RYŪKŌ). It consists of three songs in popular style, which are obviously derived from Japanese folk music of around 1600, and seven prototypes of *danmono*. Of the *danmono* prototypes five are compositions in one movement and therefore not *danmono* in the literal sense; musical material and structure, however, justify their classification as *danmono* in a wider sense. The remaining two *danmono* are compositions in six and seven movements respectively. They are closely related to their Japanese counterparts in *zokusō*, with which they also share their names: *Rokudan* and *Shichidan*. Compared with similar compositions in Japan, the Okinawan *danmono* show archaic qualities. Their tuning, as well as that of the three songs, is similar to that of *tsukushigoto*. The repertory, which must have reached Okinawa at various times during the 17th century, has been well preserved in print as well as in oral tradition.

iv) The Ikuta-ryū. The music of the Yatsuhashi-ryū and of *tsukushi-goto* was so firmly rooted in aristocratic musical traditions that it soon lost contact with the developing bourgeois culture of the 17th century. By the Genroku period (1688–1704), when the new culture was fully developed, *kumiuta* offered little more than historical interest. In contrast to the somewhat formal koto, with its highly respected tradition acting as a brake on stylistic development, the more popular shamisen, unburdened by such venerable traditions, had succeeded in keeping abreast of the changing times. In 1695 Ikuta Kengyō (1656–1715) founded a new school in Kyoto which established close collaboration between the koto and the shamisen in the performance of *jiuta*. In doing so, he opened the door to new developments in koto music. In this context the term *jiuta* ('regional songs', i.e. songs from the Kyoto–Osaka area) refers to predominantly lyrical songs composed to contemporary texts in a flexible musical form. *Jiuta* were originally sung with shamisen accompaniment. In the Ikuta-ryū the shamisen could be replaced by the koto, although the combination of koto and shamisen was more common. It is typical of the Ikuta-ryū that in such ensembles the leading musician plays the shamisen, not the koto.

Jiuta composers were greatly interested in instrumental techniques. This interest eventually led to new forms as the musical interludes (*ai-no-te*) were gradually extended until they were frequently longer than the sung parts. These long *ai-no-te* were called *tegoto* and the form in which they occurred was *tegotomono*. This development assumed its definitive shape in Osaka around the Kansei period (1789–1801) in the works of Minezaki Kōtō. Basically, the *tegoto* form, which occurs in many variants, consists of three parts: *mae-uta* ('foresong'), *tegoto* and *ato-uta* ('after-song').

The relationship between the shamisen and the koto gradually changed from the almost complete dependence of the koto on the shamisen in the earlier *jiuta* to an increasing independence of the two instruments. When koto and shamisen play equally important, although interdependent, parts, one speaks of *kaeteshiki sōkyoku*. *Kaete* refers to an ornamental version, added to the original part, called *honte*. This development, although begun in Osaka during the Bunka period (1804–18) in the compositions of Ichiura Kengyō, reached the peak of its development in Kyoto, especially in the works of Yaezaki Kengyō (*d* 1848), where such compositions were called *kyōmono*. Yaezaki's strength lay in his virtuoso

arrangements as *kaeteshiki sōkyoku* of shamisen compositions by other composers, especially Matsuura Kengyō (*d* 1822) and Kikuoka Kengyō (*d* 1847). The development of instrumental virtuosity can be seen in the beginning of the fifth *dan* of *Godan ginuta* (ex.4),

Ex.4 Beginning of the fifth *dan*, *Godan ginuta* by Mitsuzaki Kengyō; transcr. W. Adriaansz

a composition for two koto by Mitsuzaki Kengyō (*d* 1853). As in most traditional Japanese music, its two parts are closely related. A characteristic feature of 19th-century combinations of a koto pair (or koto and shamisen) is the occasional rapid alternation of short motifs between the two instruments, as in the fourth bar.

In the middle of the 19th century a reaction against the strongly shamisen-dominated *sōkyoku* resulted in a neo-classical movement, which attempted to revive pure koto music. Inspiration was sought in the old *kumiuta*. The most important composers in this movement were Mitsuzaki Kengyō in Kyoto, best known in this connection for *Akikaze no kyoku* (a *danmono* followed by a *kumiuta*, both conforming strictly to the old forms); and Yoshizawa Kengyō (1800–72) in Nagoya, the composer of *Chidori* and the *Kokingumi*, in which *kumiuta* have been used as stylistic examples without their structures being followed.

The repertory of the Ikuta-ryū was not limited to new types of composition, but also incorporated the *kumiuta* and *danmono* from the Yatsuhashi-ryū. For this purpose *kumiuta* and *danmono* were subjected to a final polishing process, in the course of which all compositions were made to adhere to strict structural schemes. As the structure of three of Yatsuhashi's *kumiuta* deviated too markedly from the norm, they were replaced by new compositions, but retained the old texts. They continued to be referred to as *Yatsuhashi no sankyoku*, however, and remained the object of the same veneration as the original compositions. The musician responsible for this final adaptation was Kitajima Kengyō. Later *kumiuta* composed within the Ikuta-ryū, mainly by Mitsuhashi Kengyō (*d* 1760), usually follow the standard form.

(v) The Yamada-ryū. The Ikuta-ryū remained chiefly confined to the Kansai (Kyoto–Osaka) area. Attempts during the 18th century to export the school to Edo met with little success, partly because the repertory of that city still consisted largely of the, by then, thoroughly old-fashioned *kumiuta* and partly because the modern *jiuta* were so typical of the Kansai area that they did not appeal to the taste of Edo. Only at the end of the 18th century did Edo acquire its own school of koto music, the Yamada-ryū, named after its creator, Yamada Kengyō (1757–1817). A remarkable parallel between the creation of the Ikuta-ryū in Kyoto in the late 17th century and the Yamada-ryū in Edo a century later is that both schools adopted modern styles by absorbing features of certain shamisen styles. A significant difference, however, is that in this process the Ikuta-ryū sought inspiration in lyrical, the Yamada-ryū in narrative and dramatic, shamisen (and other) styles (*katōbushi*, *itchūbushi*, *tomimotobushi* among the shamisen styles; *yōkyoku* of the nō theatre; and *heikyoku*, epic poetry with *biwa* accompaniment). Another typical difference between the two schools is the relative importance of the performing instruments. In the Ikuta-ryū the shamisen is the main instrument, played by the leading musician of the group; in the Yamada-ryū, which also combines the koto and the shamisen, the main function is assigned to the koto, the shamisen having no more than an obbligato part.

The Yamada-ryū repertory contains a selection of *kumiuta* and *danmono*; *saku-uta*, including Yamada Kengyō's own compositions; *shin saku-uta*, which contains all works other than *kumiuta*, *saku-uta*, *tegotomono* and *shin sōkyoku* ('new koto music'); *tegotomono*, a small group containing a few compositions adapted from the Ikuta-ryū, as well as some composed within the Yamada-ryū; and *jōrurimono*, arrangements from narrative shamisen literature, such as *katōbushi* and *tomimotobushi*.

The beginning of the section *gaku* from *Kogō no kyoku* by Yamada Kengyō (ex.5) illustrates the combination of tradition and original elements, a typical technique of this composer. *Gaku* refers to reminiscences of gagaku, which are prompted by the text. Because such allusions are not made by mere imitation, the result is an interesting combination of gagaku and *zokusō* styles. The gagaku element is strongest in the second koto part, which consistently plays four-bar phrases consisting of gagaku-based octave patterns (e.g. bars 504–5) and single notes (e.g. bar 506). This may be compared with similar gagaku-inspired phrases in *kumiuta* (ex.3). In spite of the four-bar phrases in the second koto part, however, the actual structure of the *gaku* section does not produce the effect of a similarly predictable, regular quadratic structure. The gagaku element in the second koto part requires a tuning providing major 2nds and minor 3rds. Thus the notes used in bars 503–26 are e', $f\sharp'$, a', b' and d''; after the instrument is retuned in bar 527 (retuning never occurs during a true gagaku composition), these become e', g', a', b' and d''. The voice is ambiguous in its allegiances: it joins the second koto in using anhemitonic pentatonic material; structurally, however, it aligns itself with the first koto and the shamisen, which remain completely in the *zokusō* sphere, as shown by the frequent occurrence of minor 2nds and major 3rds. The simultaneous use of gagaku and *zokusō* elements results in different key signatures, which here indicate the simultaneous use of two different modes, built on the same tonic, E.

The Yamada-ryū is as typical of the Kantō area (Edo and surroundings) as the Ikuta-ryū is of Kansai. The most significant composers in the Yamada-ryū were Yamada Kengyō and three of his pupils: Yamato Kengyō, Yamaki Kengyō and Yamase Kengyō.

Ex.5 Beginning of the *gaku* section of *Kogō no kyoku* by Yamada Kengyō; transcr. W. Adriaansz

4. INNOVATIONS SINCE THE MEIJI ERA (1868–1912). During the last decade of the 19th century *sankyoku* ('music for three') became especially popular: this was a special performing practice in which a third instrument was added to the usual ensemble of koto and shamisen. Earlier this third instrument had often been the *kokyū* (spike fiddle) but it was gradually replaced by the *shakuhachi* (end-blown flute); it plays another variant of the existing melody.

In the confrontation between Japanese and Western music the koto proved to be a favoured instrument for experimentation with combinations of traditional Japanese and Western music. Within *sōkyoku* the initial changes were slight and involved modest experimentation with different modes and an increased use of left-hand plucking, which created harmony-like effects. Contrasting with this *meiji shinkyoku* ('new music of the Meiji period'), which flourished mainly in Osaka, was the response to Western music of Suzuki Koson (1875–1931) in Kyoto around 1900; he attempted in his works to combine modern poetry and romantic feeling with classic practices of the Heian period. His school, called Kyōgoku, commanded attention for a short time, but declined rapidly. More drastic Westernization was accomplished by the koto musician Miyagi Michio: this included the composition of chamber music for Japanese instruments, the orchestral use of Japanese instruments, the combination of Japanese and Western instruments and also the invention of new instruments, notably the 17-string bass koto (*jūshichigen-kin*). Miyagi's influence was, and still is, very strong and, although the lasting value of his innovations cannot yet be assessed, his historical importance cannot be denied. The Yamada and Ikuta schools continue to flourish, and since 1945 there has been a notable growth in the performance of koto music, both solo and in ensemble. There are also strong indications that Western-trained Japanese composers may contribute greatly to the development of new types of koto music.

BIBLIOGRAPHY
S. Yamada: *Sōkyoku taiishō* [Compendium of koto music], i–vi (Edo, 1779), vii (1903)
F. T. Piggott: *The Music and Musical Instruments of Japan* (London, 1893, 2/1909/R1971)
T. Takano: 'Shichiku shoshinshū' [Comprehensive collection of Japanese songs and ballads], *Nihon kayō shūsei*, vi (Tokyo, 1928)
T. Fujita: *Sōkyoku to jiuta no ajiwaikata* [Introduction to koto music and jiuta] (Osaka, 1930)
K. Takano: 'Theorie der Japanischen Musik, 1: Untersuchungen über die Form der Koto Musick "Danmono"', *Tōhoku psychologica folia*, iii (1935), 69–169
K. Hirano and S. Kishibe: *Tsukushi-goto kenkyū shiryō* [Materials for the study of tsukushi-goto] (Tokyo, 1955)
H. Eckardt: 'Koto', *MGG*
E. Kikkawa: 'Sōkyoku to jiuta no rekishi' [History of sōkyoku and jiuta], SLR 510–13 [disc notes]
K. Hayashi: *Shōsōin gakki no kenkyū* [A study of early Japanese music based on the instruments in the Shōsōin] (Tokyo, 1964)
Y. Nakazato: *Ryūkyū sōkyoku kun kun shi* [History of Ryūkū koto music] (Naha, 1965)
W. Adriaansz: 'Research into the Chronology of Danmono', *EM*, xi (1967), 25
Tōyō Ongaku Gakkai, ed.: *Sōkyoku to jiuta*, *Tōyō ongaku sensho*, iii (Tokyo, 1967)
W. Adriaansz: 'A Japanese Procrustean Bed: a Study of the Development of Danmono', *JAMS*, xxiii (1970), 16–60
——: 'The Yatsuhashi-Ryū: a Seventeenth Century School of Koto Music', *AcM*, xliii (1971), 55–93
——: 'Midare', *Nihon no ongaku to sone shūhen* (Tokyo, 1973), 9–54
——: *The Kumiuta and Danmono Traditions of Japanese Koto Music* (Berkeley, 1973)
C. Read: *A Study of Yamada-ryū Sōkyoku and its Repertoire* (Ann Arbor, 1975)
D. Loeb: 'An Analytic Study of Japanese Koto Music', *Music Forum*, iv (1976), 335–94
B. C. Wade: *Tegotomono: Music for the Japanese Koto* (Westport, Conn., 1976)
F. Koizumi, Y. Tokumaru and O. Yamaguchi, eds.: *Asian Musics in an Asian Perspective* (Tokyo, 1977), 190
L. Picken and Y. Mitani: 'Finger-techniques for the Zithers *sō-no-koto* and *kin* in Heian Times', *Musica asiatica*, ii (1979), 89
'Jiuta', 'Sō', 'Sōkyoku', 'Zokusō', *Ongaku daijiten* [Encyclopedia of music] (Tokyo, 1981)

W. ADRIAANSZ

Kotor. SLIT-DRUM of Madhya Pradesh, central India. See KOTURKA.

Kotra. Modern Malagasy term for the bamboo rattle which was an import from South-east Asia (*see* ANGKLUNG). The rattle is also known as *karakaraka*, *lonjo* and *enjoenjo*. It is not found in southern Madagascar.

Kotso [kootso, koso]. Snared open HOURGLASS DRUM of variable pitch of northern and western Nigeria. The drum is held under the arm and beaten with the fingers. The *kotso* of the Hausa people measures approximately 40 cm in length with a diameter of 15 cm at each end and about 7 cm at the waist. It is associated closely with the ruling group and its main contemporary function is in the performance of praise epithets (*take*) and the accompaniment of praise songs for the ruler. At one time it was associated with warfare. In the Zamfara area it has been replaced by the TABSHI kettledrum. The Yoruba *koso* is similar, although its former restriction to royalty has now been extended to include performance in *sekere* music with gourd rattles and other drums. Among the Nupe people the *kotso* is included in the musical entourage of the head official, the Etsu Nupe.

BIBLIOGRAPHY
Ames–KingGHM
C. A. Moloney: 'On the Melodies of the Volof, Mandingo, Ewe, Yoruba and Houssa People of West Africa', *Journal of the Manchester Geographical Society*, v (1889), 277
P. G. Harris: 'Notes on Drums and Musical Instruments seen in Sokoto Province, Nigeria', *Journal of the Royal Anthropological Institute*, lxii (1932), 105
K. Krieger: 'Musikinstrumente der Hausa', *Baessler-Archiv*, new ser., xvi (1968), 373–430
F. E. Besmer: *Kidan Daran Salla: Music for the Eve of the Muslim Festivals of Id-al-Fitr and Id-al-Kabir in Kano, Nigeria* (Bloomington, 1974)
A. Euba: 'Yoruba Music', *Grove 6*
A. King: 'Nigeria', *Grove 6*

K. A. GOURLAY

Kotsuzumi. Japanese HOURGLASS DRUM (*ko*: 'small'; TSUZUMI: generic term for hourglass drums). It is used in nō (dance-drama), *nagauta* (dance music), *geza* (off-stage music of the kabuki theatre) and many local folk musics, and is by far the most widely used Japanese hourglass drum, so much so that the generic term *tsuzumi* alone may be taken to refer to the *kotsuzumi*. (It is called *kotsuzumi* – or *shō*: 'small' – by comparison with its frequent companion, the *ōtsuzumi*, and the two are often called by the broader term *daishō*: 'large–small'.) The ornately lacquered cherrywood body is about 10 cm in diameter and 25 or 26 cm long; the horsehide heads, which are lapped on to iron rings before being laced around the body, are about 20 cm in diameter. The front head is slightly thicker than the rear one, as on the *ōtsuzumi* and *shimedaiko*, the other two nō drums.

The *kotsuzumi* is by far the subtlest of Japanese drums, the only one on which the performer must adjust the tension of the heads while playing. The left hand holds

Kotsuzumi (hourglass drum) being played in the nō theatre, Japan

the drum on the right shoulder and squeezes the rope with precise timing while the right hand strikes the front head in various ways. (The heads are laced much more loosely than on the *ōtsuzumi*.) The notes produced are not intended to have any particular pitch. New heads will not respond readily to the subtle tension changes, and even well-seasoned heads need constant attention before the distinctive liquid *pon* sound will be satisfactorily produced. The player must adjust timbre by applying deerskin patches to the backs of the heads and tiny squares of paper to the surface of the rear head. During performance, to adjust to temperature, humidity or the acoustics of the hall, moisture is applied by breathing on the rear head or applying saliva with the fingertips.

In nō, the *kotsuzumi* plays more than 200 named patterns, consisting of combinations of a handful of stroke-types with anticipatory off-beat cries from the player. In *nagauta* these are supplemented by much faster interlocking patterns for *kotsuzumi* and *ōtsuzumi*, known onomatopoeically as *chirikara* rhythms. Folk usage is much less complex, and the drums are less carefully adjusted.

BIBLIOGRAPHY
W. P. Malm: *Japanese Music and Musical Instruments* (Rutland, Vermont, 1959), 122ff
R. Emmert and Y. Minegishi, eds.: *Musical Voices of Asia* (Tokyo, 1980), 229
A. Tamba: *The Musical Structure of Nō* (Tokyo, 1981), 159
DAVID W. HUGHES

Koturka. Wooden SLIT-DRUM of Madhya Pradesh (Bastar district), central India. The instrument is known by the Gondi words *kotor*, or *koturka* (the more common), or by the Halbi *durdera*. It is a hollow block of wood,

either trapeziform or semicircular, or occasionally crescent shaped. The drum is hollowed from a slit cut on the longer base. Its width varies from 37 cm to 70 cm, its height from 13 cm to 35 cm, and its thickness is about 10 cm. The *koturka* is found in most of the Maria *ghotul* (a socio-religious institution), used either for calling or as a percussion instrument, to accompany dancing, in which case the player carries the instrument hung around his neck by a strap, with the slit positioned towards the bottom; he beats the lower part of the instrument with two sticks (see illustration).

Wooden slit-drums are very rare in India, found only among a few tribal groups, such as the Muria and Bastar Muria, and the Naga of Assam, whose instruments are very large.

BIBLIOGRAPHY
W. Grigson: *The Maria Gonds of Bastar* (London, 1938, 2/1949)
V. Elwin: *The Muria and their Ghotul* (Bombay, 1947)
W. Kaufmann: 'The Songs of the Hill Maria, Jhoria Muria and Bastar Muria Gond Tribes', *EM*, iv (1960), 115
——: 'The Musical Instruments of the Hill Maria, Jhoria and Bastar Muria Gond Tribes', *EM*, v (1961), 1
S. K. Jain: 'Wooden Musical Instruments of the Gonds of Central India', *EM*, ix (1965), 39
GENEVIÈVE DOURNON

Koul. *See* KŌL.

Koutalia. Wooden or metal spoons of Greece, struck together in pairs. They are used almost exclusively in the Aegean islands and by Greek refugees from Asia Minor. The players (usually women) hold a pair in each hand while dancing.

Kovïzh. JEW'S HARP of the Mari people, USSR.

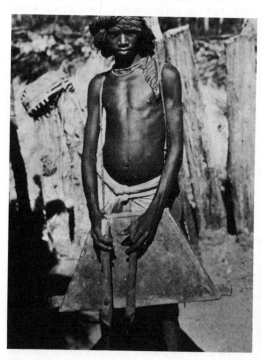

Koturka (slit-drum) played by a young Muria Gond of the Jatpuri 'ghotul', Bastar district, Madhya Pradesh

Ko voro. Six-string PLURIARC of the Maninka people of Guinea. Each separate string-bearer passes through an inverted calabash. The instrument is played by young men to accompany song-stories.

Köwao. Bamboo clarinet, with five finger-holes, of the Koho people of central Vietnam.

Kowongan [gowangan, celempungan]. Plucked zither used in the mountainous areas of Central and East Java, including the Dieng plateau. A trellis-work bamboo frame shaped like a hood is covered with bamboo leaves strung together with aren fibres. Six or seven strings are stretched horizontally across the inside of the frame and plucked with the fingernails. The hood serves both as a sounding board and an umbrella for field workers and herders. See J. Kunst: *De toonkunst van Java* (The Hague, 1934; Eng. trans., rev. 2/1949, enlarged 3/1973), 200f.

MARGARET J. KARTOMI

Koza [kozioł] (Pol.: 'goat'). BAGPIPE of Poland and the Ukraine. The *koza*, found in the Ukraine (where it is also called *duda*) and the Tatra Highlands of Poland (*dudy podhalańskie*), has single reeds. It differs considerably from other types of Polish bagpipe (*see* DUDY) in that it has two drones, one in the separate straight drone-pipe, and one in the chanter; this has three channels, one without finger-holes, the second with one finger-hole, the third with five. An example of its tuning is $b\flat'-c''-d''-e\flat''-f''-g''$ with $B\flat$ and f' drones. It has no bell and is mouth-blown. The *koza* is usually played solo.

The *kozioł*, found in western Wielkopolska, Poland, is similar to the *dudy wielkopolskie* (*see* DUDY), but its larger size and chanter with eight finger-holes result in a deeper and wider range (e.g. $b\flat-c'-d'-e\flat'-f'-g'-a\flat'-b\flat'-c''-d''-e\flat''$; drone $E\flat$); the two highest notes are produced by overblowing. The bag is made from a white goatskin with the hair on the outside. The *kozioł* is bellows-blown; its drone pipe is bent back on itself twice, and all the pipes have a curved bell. In regions where the instrument is known as *kozioł biały* ('white buck'), a smaller variant is also known, called *kozioł czarny* ('black buck'), *doślubny kozioł* or *dudki doślubne* ('wedding bagpipe'), with a straight drone-pipe and of higher pitch. The *kozioł biały* is played with the violin, sometimes a clarinet, the *kozioł czarny* with a *mazanki* (fiddle).

JAN STĘSZEWSKI

Kpai. BOARD ZITHER of the Mamvu and Balese peoples of Zaïre (*LaurentyC*, 116). *See* IKIDI.

Kpaliga. Double metal clapperless bell of the Fon people of Benin. It is struck with a wooden stick and is used with pot drums at Porto Novo by the royal wives in the performance of *ajogan* music. It is also used for *vodun* ceremonial processions.

Kpandu. Iron percussion instrument of the Baule people of the Ivory Coast. It consists of a hollow cylinder split lengthwise which is fixed to a handle and struck with a metal rod.

Kpedimbe [kpendimbe, kpenigba, kpeningba]. Log XYLOPHONE of the Zande people of Zaïre. *See* PANDINGBWA.

Kpen 'n'ok. Double-headed horizontal barrel drum of the Mon people of Burma and Thailand.

Kpingbi. XYLOPHONE of the Benge people of Zaïre. It comprises six loose slabs, lying across two banana stalks.

Kpokpolo. Struck percussion vessel of the Baule people of the Ivory Coast. It comprises an antelope horn struck with a stick, used in an ensemble with other rhythm instruments for masked dancing.

Kpolo. Double iron clapperless bell of the Ngbaka people of the Central African Republic. It is struck with a wooden stick, and played together with the *ngombi* (arched harp) as accompaniment to singing.

Kponimbo [kponingbo, kpweningba, kpweningwa]. XYLOPHONE of the Zande people of the Central African Republic and Zaïre. *See* PANDINGBWA and AKPANINGBO.

Kpwale. Gourd vessel rattle of the Gbande people of Liberia. It has external strikers, consisting of a network of beads or seeds. The players draw and release the base of the net so that the strikers snap against the gourd in a steady rhythmic pattern. In the past the *kpwale* was reserved for cult ceremonial dances. The instrument is known by different names among associated peoples: Toma *alizabai*, Mano *gei, ge* or *gbea*, and Sapa *sambli*. See G. Schwab: *Tribes of the Liberian Hinterland* (Cambridge, Mass., 1947/R1974).

Kpweningba [kpweningwa]. *See* KPONIMBO.

Kpwokolo. MOUTH-BOW of the Balese people of Zaïre (*LaurentyC*, 112). *See* LUSUBA.

Kpwokpwo. SLIT-DRUM of the Mamvu and Mangutu peoples of northern Zaïre (*LaurentyTF*, 140). *See* NKUMVI.

Kpworo. Drum of the Mbanja people of Zaïre. *See* DINDO.

Kraakdoos (Dutch: 'cracklebox'). A tactile SYNTHE-SIZER devised by MICHEL WAISVISZ and developed since 1969. The original model was produced in The Hague with the help of the technician Geert Hamelberg, and was followed by a series of improved versions built in collaboration with the Belgian technician and composer Peter Beyls, who had been working independently along similar lines. The early models were designed primarily for operation by visitors to exhibitions. Beginning in 1973 the Studio voor Electro-instrumentale Muziek (STEIM) in Amsterdam has sponsored a Kraakdoos project in which its technicians Johan den Biggelaar and Nico Bes are collaborating. STEIM has manufactured a pocket-sized toy, the Kraakdoosje (from 1973) and limited numbers of the Kraaksynthesizer (from 1977). The smaller crackleboxes have been used for educational and therapeutic purposes, as well as by several improvisers.

All crackleboxes are battery powered and have a solid 'keyboard' of soldered square touch-plates (a square of 16 plates in the exhibition version, two rows of three in the toy model, and 20 controlling three oscillators in the synthesizer). By touching two or more plates with his fingertips the performer makes connections through his body to certain parts of an oscillator circuit; the degree of finger contact with the plates and the amount of the body separating the fingers have a substantial effect on the sound that results. Each plate controls a different aspect of the sound in rather the same way as do the knobs on the modules of a synthesizer, but because of the special circuit design and the complexity of the sounds produced the plates cannot be labelled in terms of individual functions. Even the toy model, which contains only an oscillator and no signal-processing devices, can produce sounds that resemble those obtainable by filtering, ring modulation and triggering features. On the synthesizer, each of the three oscillators has six plates and an adjustable range control, and each oscillator can be used to provide voltage control for one of the others; two additional plates are used for overall controls. Any combination of oscillators can be connected to a 12-note monophonic keyboard, on which each key can be independently tuned; when more than one key is depressed a 'pitch average' results: for example two keys tuned a tone apart produce a single pitch exactly between them.

In 1977 Waisvisz devised a four-octave Kraakorgel on which each note has touch-plate controls; a spin-off from this, proposed by the Dutch composer Misja Mengelberg in 1978, is based on the organ's central bank of oscillators and has a seven-octave 'keyboard' of small circular plates arranged in a block of 7 by 12 rows. Since 1982 Waisvisz has developed the 'Waiscrack', which combines the crackle principle with the type of programmable microprocessor on which small digital electronic keyboard instruments are based.

BIBLIOGRAPHY
M. Waisvisz: De Kraakdozententoonstelling (Amsterdam, 1975) [exhibition catalogue]; excerpt trans. as 'The Cracklebox Project', Musics, no.7 (1976), 7
——: 'The Crackle Project: the Need for New Instruments in Music and Theatre', Key Notes, no. 8 (1978), 24
HUGH DAVIES

Krabber. Variant term for the Flemish VLIER (box zither).

Kräftig (Ger.: 'powerful', 'vigorous'). As a tempo direction it is particularly frequent in the work of Schumann and later German composers.

Krajappī [kračhappī]. Plucked lute of Thailand. It has a resonating box shaped somewhat like a tortoise-shell (from which the instrument derives its name), 44 cm long, 40 cm wide and 7 cm deep; a narrow, fretted neck up to 138 cm long tapering backwards at the end; and four strings in two courses. It is played with a plectrum. The krajappī was formerly used in ensembles but is now a solo instrument.

Krämer, Michael. See MERCATOR, MICHAEL.

Kranz (Ger.). GARLAND.

Krap [krāp', khrab]. CLAPPERS of Thailand and Kampuchea. They are made of various materials, including bamboo, wood and metal; some take the form of concussion sticks. They are generally used to beat the rhythm for dancing and singing. The Thai krap khū (concussion sticks) are made from a section of bamboo 40 cm long, cut in half and then smoothed and polished, and played

by striking the two cut sides together. Wooden krap khū are also made in the same shape as the bamboo variety. Krap phuang (clappers) are made of several thin pieces of wood (or ivory), alternating with sheets of brass and placed between two heavier pieces of wood with curving ends. A hole is made at the lower end of each piece and a cord is threaded through and tied, fastening the pieces together. The krap phuang are played by holding the lower ends with one hand and striking the wood and metal strips against the palm of the other hand. A pair of wooden concussion sticks known as krap sēphā are used in the sēphā (a type of chant) in Thailand. They are 21 cm long, 3 to 4 cm wide and square in cross-section. One side is convex and the reverse side shorter and flat, so that the other two sides bevel in slightly towards the short, flat side. The ends of the sticks are cut at a 45° angle, and the wood is smoothed and polished. In north-eastern Thailand a pair of clappers known as kringkrap is made from a section of bamboo about 14 cm long, cut in half and then smoothed and polished. In performance a pair is held in each hand and is played by striking together the two convex surfaces.

BIBLIOGRAPHY
D. Yupho: Khrǔang dontri Thai [Thai musical instruments] (Bangkok, 1957, 2/1967; Eng. trans., 1960, 2/1971)
D. Morton: The Traditional Music of Thailand (Berkeley, 1976)
L. E. R. Picken: 'The Sound-producing Instrumentarium of a Village in North-east Thailand', Musica asiatica, iv (1984), 214
DAVID MORTON

Krapeu (Khmer: 'crocodile'). Three-string fretted zither of Kampuchea. Its soundboard is carved in the shape of a crocodile; it is similar to the Burmese MÍ-GYAÙNG and the Thai ČHAKHĒ. It may be played solo or in the mahōri orchestra.

Krar [kerâr]. Bowl lyre of Ethiopia. The krar typically has six strings and is smaller than the other main type of Ethiopian lyre, the BEGANNA. Unlike the beganna, which is played only by men, the krar may also be played by women. It is used to accompany popular secular ballads and love-songs. Whereas the strings of the beganna (and most other east African lyres) vibrate against the soundtable, producing a buzzing timbre cultivated in other African string instruments, the krar usually has a bridge and produces clearer sounds. The krar and other bowl lyres are usually played by rhythmic strumming (usually with a plectrum) and by damping all but the strings that are required to ring out. Strumming is sometimes interspersed with arpeggiated plucking. For illustration see MASENQO.

RONALD LAH

Krause, August Friedrich (b Leipzig, 1757; d Berlin, 23 April 1806). German brass instrument maker. He served in the Regiment of Prince Heinrich in the Prussian Army, later becoming established as an instrument maker (like his father) in Potsdam. On 17 March 1787 he petitioned King Friedrich Wilhelm II of Prussia to bestow on him the title of Hofinstrumentenmacher, which was granted, and later made other petitions to increase his business. He made horns and trombones, but is particularly notable for his trumpets. Krause is known to have made Inventionstrompete with various slide crooks from F to A; there is a good specimen of 1793, with a beautifully ornamented bell, at the Karl-Marx-Universität, Leipzig. Two long natural trumpets in D (also Leipzig) date from 1792.

BIBLIOGRAPHY
H. Heyde: *Trompeten Posaunen Tuben* (Leipzig, 1980)
NIALL O'LOUGHLIN

Kreb. See KERANTING.

Krebs [Krebser, Kress], **Friedrich** (*b* Schalkhausen, nr. Ansbach; *d* Strasbourg, 1493). German organ builder. He was active in Franconia from 1471 until his death. New organs or restorations are known for the churches of St Sebald, Nuremberg (small organ 1471; large organ 1481), St Martin, Amberg (1476), St Moritz, Coburg (Meister Friedrich 1487), and Strasbourg Cathedral (small organ 1478; large organ 1491); his work at St George's, Hagenau (1493), was completed by his nephew Michael Dürr. Krebs was a significant organ builder in the line of development from the Gothic *Blockwerk* organ to the slider-chest organ with divided *Blockwerk*, as reflected in his specification of Fleiten (Principal), Zymmel (Zimbel) and Werck (Hintersatz or Mixture). The organ was divided into Diskant (*Hauptwerk*), *Rückpositiv* and Tenor (pedal). Krebs extended the range of the manuals (*F* to *a"*, previously *B* to *f"'*) and that of the pedals (*F* to *c'*, previously *A* to *a*), but he did not achieve the state of development prescribed by Arnold Schlick (1510). The organ screen of the Gothic 'swallow's nest' organ in Strasbourg Cathedral survives, though altered.

BIBLIOGRAPHY
M. Praetorius: *Syntagma musicum*, ii (Wolfenbüttel, 1618, 2/ 1619/*R*1958 and 1980)
M. Vogeleis: 'Ein Orgelvertrag aus dem Jahre 1491', *MMg*, xxxii (1900), 155
I. Rücker: *Die deutsche Orgel am Oberrhein um 1500* (Freiburg, 1940)
M. Barth: 'Elsass, das Land der Orgeln', *Archives de l'église d'Alsace* (Hagenau, 1966)
H. Fischer: 'Der mainfränkische Orgelbau bis zur Säkularisation', *Acta organologica*, ii (1968), 105, 109
HERMANN FISCHER

Krés. BOX ZITHER of the Votyak people, USSR. *See* GUSLI.

Kress horn. A toy instrument marketed by the American firm of Kress (a chain of stores) in the early 20th century. It consisted of a cardboard cone fitted with a wooden mouthpiece. A pentatonic scale can be played on a trumpet mouthpiece, while a clarinet mouthpiece and reed can be played as an instrument. A trumpet or clarinet mouthpiece could replace that of the Kress horn, thus increasing the volume. In this form it was used in New Orleans by improvising 'spasm' bands, by aspiring jazz musicians and by street vendors. For a survey of instruments used as toys, *see* TOY INSTRUMENTS.
PAUL OLIVER

Kreutzbach. Danish–German family of organ builders and instrument makers. Urban Kreutzbach (*b* Copenhagen, 24 Aug 1796; *d* Borna, nr. Leipzig, 20 Aug 1868), the son of a merchant, learnt cabinet making and travelled to Germany in about 1820. In 1830 he established himself as an organ builder in Borna. His instruments, splendid examples of the Saxon Silbermann tradition, are outstanding for their thoughtful specifications, fine voicing and strong, metallic tone. Notable ones include those at Ortmannsdorf (1856), Callenberg (1859), Glauchau-Jerisau (1860) and Dresden-Hosterwitz (1863). He invented a playing valve loop, and used a fairly high wind pressure in his instruments.
Richard Kreutzbach (*b* Borna, 27 July 1839, *d* Borna,

21 June 1903), Urban's son, continued throughout his lifetime in his father's business; he adopted pneumatic action, and built good organs without, however, ever equalling his father's mastery. He built instruments in the Stadtkirche, Johanngeorgenstadt, Erzgebirge (1872) and in Waldenburg, Saxony (1878–9). Emil Bernhard Hermann Kreutzbach (*b* Borna, 5 Dec 1843), another son, also worked in his father's business, leaving it in 1875. Other employees of the firm, which produced approximately 300 instruments, included J. G. Bärmig, H. Beygang, W. Grisard, C. Ladegast, E. Müller and H. Walcker.

Julius Urban Kreutzbach (*b* Döbeln, 29 Nov 1845; *d* Leipzig, 22 Sept 1913), another relative, founded the famous Leipzig firm of piano makers that bears his name. Emil Müller (*b* Borna, 11 Oct 1857; *d* Pillnitz bei Dresden, 4 Oct 1928), a grandson of Urban Kreutzbach, who accomplished nothing of significance in organ building, took over J. G. Bärmig's works at Werdau in 1887 and made it the largest harmonium factory in Europe.

BIBLIOGRAPHY
F. Oehme: *Handbuch über ältere und neuere Orgelwerke im Königreiche Sachsen*, iii (Dresden, 1897)
R. Fritzsche: *Werdau und seine Industrie* (Werdau, 1936)
WALTER HÜTTEL

Kriegelstein. French firm of piano makers. It was founded in 1831 by Jean-Georges Kriegelstein (*b* Riquewihr, Alsace, 1801; *d* Paris, 20 Nov 1865). In addition to making many improvements in square pianos, in 1842 he introduced and subsequently developed a highly successful small upright model (108 cm high), the 'Mignon Pianino', remarkable for its rich tone and even registers; he also produced grands with improved damping and tuning systems. In 1844 the firm introduced a new repetition grand piano action that was claimed to be more durable and less complex than the Erard double escapement mechanism. The firm was carried on by later generations after Jean-Georges retired in 1858 and continued to make high-quality instruments (*c*300–400 a year) until it ceased operations during the 1930s.

BIBLIOGRAPHY
E. Pauer: *The Pianist's Dictionary* (London, 1895), 146
A. Dolge: *Pianos and their Makers* (Covina, Calif., 1911/*R*1972)
R. E. M. Harding: *The Piano-forte: its History traced to the Great Exhibition of 1851* (Cambridge, 1933, rev. 2/1978), 162, 175
C. Ehrlich: *The Piano: a History* (London, 1976)
HOWARD SCHOTT

Krindie. Stick rattle of the Baule people of the Ivory Coast. Gourd rings are threaded on a piece of wood with a forked end and the rattle is jerked sideways. It is part of an ensemble, used originally for initiation rituals, now for entertainment during festivities.

Kringkrap. CLAPPERS of north-eastern Thailand. *See* KRAP.

Krismann, Franz Xaver. See CHRISMANN, FRANZ XAVER.

Kristadin. An ELECTRONIC ORGAN constructed around 1960 at the Sound Recording Institute in Moscow by Saul Korsunsky, who had worked at the acoustics laboratory of the Moscow Conservatory during the 1930s. The portable transistorized instrument has one five-octave keyboard. See S. G. Korsunsky and I. D. Simonov:

Elektromuzïkal'nïye instrumentï (Moscow and Leningrad, 1957).

HUGH DAVIES

Kriyāṅgapañcavādyam. Ceremonial instrumental ensemble of Kerala, south India. *See* PAÑCAVĀDYAM.

Križman, Frančišek Ksaver. *See* CHRISMANN, FRANZ XAVER.

Krǫ. Small SLIT-DRUM of Thailand. It is made from a section of bamboo, cut with nodes at each end, with a small slit running the length of the tube between the nodes. The drum is held in one hand and struck with a small bamboo or wooden beater held in the other. In this way it was originally used for signalling the time. Larger versions are also played, sometimes carried horizontally by a leather thong attached to each end. The larger the *krǫ*, the greater the distance at which it can be heard. The drum is nowadays used in theatrical performances, whereas formerly it was used mainly as a signalling instrument, to call meetings or warn of danger, but never for musical performances.

DAVID MORTON

Krȍdž. BOX ZITHER of the Votyak people, USSR. *See* GUSLI.

Kromong. GONG-CHIME in the *gamelan Trengganu* in West Malaysia. It comprises two rows of five gongs each, which are beaten with a pair of padded hammers. In Java the instrument is called a BONANG. *See also* KEROMONG.

Kroncong. Hand-made guitar of Indonesia and Malaysia. The name is used also for traditional ensembles which may consist of ukulele (*cuk*), banjo (*cak*), melodic guitar, cello (played pizzicato), double bass, violin, transverse flute and singer. Other instruments, such as bongo drums, may be added, and when playing *langgam Jawa* songs certain gamelan instruments such as the *siter* may also be used. The ensemble is apparently of Portuguese-Indonesian origin and several centuries old.

BIBLIOGRAPHY
A. T. Manusama: *Krontjong als muziekinstrument, als melodie en als gezang* (Batavia, 1919)
J. Becker: 'Kroncong, Indonesian Popular Music', *Asian Music*, vii/3 (1975), 14
E. Heins: 'Kroncong and Tanjidor: Two Cases of Urban Folk Music in Jakarta', *Asian Music*, vii/3 (1975), 20
B. Kornhauser: 'In Defence of Kroncong', *Studies in Indonesian Music*, ed. M. J. Kartomi (Melbourne, 1978), 104f
MARGARET J. KARTOMI

Krȍng. Large bamboo SLIT-DRUM of Thailand, up to 2 metres in length. Slits may be made in a variety of places along the bamboo: along the sections only, omitting the nodes; along alternating sections between nodes; or one long slit the length of the bamboo. As an aid to resonance, the instrument is placed horizontally, resting on wooden supports, a few inches above the ground. It is played with bamboo or wooden beaters 30 to 40 cm long. Several players may beat the *krȍng* in unison or it may be played by a single player. Nowadays it is used outdoors only, but formerly it was used to accompany singing, particularly at New Year's celebrations, and, in the *pī phāt* ensemble, to accompany shadow plays.

DAVID MORTON

Krotalon [krotala]. *See* CROTALUM.

Krotong. Log XYLOPHONE with six keys of the Iban people of Sarawak, Malaysia.

Kroupalon [kroupezion]. *See* SCABELLUM.

Krummbogen [Krummbügel] (Ger.). CROOK.

Krummhorn [Krumbhorn] (Ger.). (1) CRUMHORN. (2) An ORGAN stop (*Cromorne*).

Krupezion. *See* SCABELLUM.

Kruspe. German firm of horn makers. It was founded in Erfurt on 2 January 1864 when Eduard Kruspe, an instrument maker since 1829, purchased a brass instrument-making business from Carl Zielsdorf; the firm still trades under the name of Ed. Kruspe. On 1 April 1893 the firm was taken over by Fritz Kruspe, who together with a nephew of the distinguished horn player Friedrich Gumbert, produced the first double horn in F/Bb about 1898. The association between player and craftsman is particularly strong in the history of this firm; Georg Wendler, at one time principal horn of the Boston SO, married Fritz Kruspe's daughter and took over the business in 1928. On his retirement in 1955 the affairs of the firm were managed by Rudi Schneider, an apprentice who became the owner in 1961. The Kruspe double horn is one of the three basic models until recently available to players, as well as original instruments and copies. All Kruspe horns have a characteristic tone, rather less brilliant than some other makes but very popular with some players.

BIBLIOGRAPHY
R. Morley-Pegge: *The French Horn* (London, 1960, 2/1972)
FRANK HAWKINS

K'shots. FLABELLUM of medieval Armenia. It consists of a metal disc on a long handle, fitted with small bells. It is still used during the Mass and has a ritual significance.

Kṣudraghaṇṭikā. A medieval and modern Sanskrit term for small metal pellet bells of India. *See* GHAṆṬĀ.

Ku. *See* GU.

Kū. Putative MOUTH BOW of the New Zealand Maori, said to have been about 25 cm long with one string sounded by tapping it with a rod. See E. Best: *Games and Pastimes of the Maori* (Wellington, 1925), 175.

Kuan. *See* GUAN.

Kūba. Single-headed HOURGLASS DRUM of the Arab world. It is documented from the 9th century or earlier.

Kubing. JEW'S HARP of the southern Philippines. It is made from various kinds of bamboo in many sizes and shapes, producing various sounds and dynamics. Some are barely audible, with quick sound-decay; others twang loudly and vibrate for a long time. Pitch and timbre vary according to the tongue placement of the performer. Plucking the jew's harp with the tongue placed near the alveolar ridge produces vibrations similar to the vowel 'i'; other vowels can be suggested as well, using other tongue placements. The jew's harp can thus simulate words, phrases, simple conversations and speeches. Using the *kubing*, young boys and girls 'converse' in front of their elders without being understood by them.

JOSÉ MACEDA

Kubru. Three-string plucked lute of Timbuktu, Mali. It has a boat-shaped soundbox and metal-ringed jingle. The instrument symbolizes the primordial blacksmith and its 'wife' is the *diarka* single-string fiddle. *See* GURMI.

Kub twg. Side-blown free-reed aerophone of the Hmong people of Laos, northern Vietnam, north-east Thailand and southern China. It consists of a buffalo horn, or sometimes a bamboo tube closed at one end; the reed is fixed in the middle of the horn and two notes a 5th apart can be produced. The *kub twg* is played at funerals.

Kubu. Gourd-resonated MUSICAL BOW of the Nyanja/ Chewa people of northern Malawi. The string is braced near the lower end.

Kucapi. (1) Plucked zither of the Minangkabau area of West Sumatra. It is laid across the player's knee, and the steel strings are stopped by keys played with the left hand and plucked with a plectrum held in the right. The instrument accompanies the singer of *sijobang* narrative stories. See N. Phillips: *Sijobang Sung Narrative Poetry of West Sumatra* (Cambridge, 1981), 41, 236.

(2) Boat-shaped plucked lute of the Pakpak Dairi area of North Sumatra. Its two strings are traditionally made of *ejuk* (sugar-palm fibre) but plastic guitar strings are now commonly used. The soundbox and neck are carved from one piece of wood and the belly and bridge constructed separately. A large diamond-shaped hole is carved in the back of the soundbox and at the top of the neck is a carved wooden figure, usually of an anthropomorphic shape. This is believed to guard the *kucapi* and to sound its voice when the instrument is played. It is usually played solo for courting and for private entertainment. It also accompanies dancing, in which case it is joined by a *pongpong* (gong) and *kalondang* (xylophone).

MARGARET J. KARTOMI, LYN MOORE

Ku-ch'in. Chinese zither. *See* QIN.

Kūchō. Three-string SPIKE FIDDLE of Okinawa, Japan. It is about 70 cm long, 10 cm in body diameter and has a bow length of 60 cm. The *kūchō* is strung and played in the same way as the KOKYŪ, but the historical relationship of the two is not clear. It has a snakeskin soundtable on a body made from half a coconut-shell; the neck resembles that of the SANSHIN (long-necked lute). It is used in the classical song and theatre ensemble with the *sanshin* and other instruments. See F. Koizumi, Y. Tokumaru and O. Yamaguchi, eds.: *Asian Musics in an Asian Perspective* (Tokyo, 1977), 195.

DAVID W. HUGHES

Kuckuck (Ger.). ORGAN STOP (*Vogelgesang*).

Kuda lumping. Ensemble of West Java. *See* JARAN KEPANG.

Kuḍamuḷā [kuḍamuzhā]. Small copper pot-drum of Tamil Nadu, south India. The over-sized skin is braced on the narrow mouth by an iron ring and cord V-lacing to another ring at the base. It is played in pairs with the pot-drum *pañcamukhavādya* in Hindu temples.

Kudara-goto (Jap.). Ancient harp, possibly of Korean origin. *See* KUGO.

Kudēku. Barrel drum of Okinawa, Japan. *See* TĒKU.

Kudlung. (1) Bamboo TUBE ZITHER, with two parallel or paired strings, of the Hanunoo people in the southern Philippines. *See also* DUNGADUNG.

(2) Two-string lute of the southern Philippines. *See* KUDYAPIQ.

Kudre. Drum of the Mangutu and Mamvu peoples of Zaïre. *See* DINDO.

Kudrekene [kudrenene]. GROUND ZITHER of the Daka people of Zaïre. A pit about 25 to 30 cm deep and 20 cm in diameter is dug in the ground and covered with a piece of bark which is pegged to the ground. From the centre of the bark rises a vertical stick across which passes a single string that is also pegged to the ground at each end in such a way that the two parts of the string are of different lengths, thus producing two different notes when made to vibrate. The instrument is played by two boys, each with two sticks. One strikes the left section of the string, the other the right. Other names reported are: *kuze-gene*, *kakalari*, *tindi de kileru*, *kudrugu* (Kilima and Andemanza peoples), *kikilo*, and *dzidzingba* (*LaurentyC*, 110).

K. A. GOURLAY

Kudu [rapapa, baku] **(i).** Bowl lyre of north-eastern Zaïre. The term *kudu* is used by the Mundo people and *rapapa* by the Bari; elsewhere in this area the instrument is called *baku*. In Zaïre the bowl lyre is restricted in distribution to a small part of the country adjoining Uganda. As the instrument resembles the Ugandan bowl lyre in almost all respects, it may be considered part of the same complex (*see* NDONGO). The roughly oval, concave soundbox may be of wood; among the Bari, a tortoise-shell is used. The Bari soundtable is made from antelope skin, that of the Logo from elephant. Instruments have five to seven cowhide strings and are 40 to 50 cm long.

BIBLIOGRAPHY
LaurentyC, 121
F. J. de Hen: *Beitrag zur Kenntnis der Musikinstrumente aus Belgisch Kongo und Ruanda-Urundi* (Tervuren, 1960)

K. A. GOURLAY

Kudu (ii). *See* KUNDU (i).

Kuḍukkā. Variable tension drum of India, similar to the HUḌUKKĀ.

Kudüm [kudum]. Small KETTLEDRUM of Turkey, played in pairs. They are made of copper with skin membranes, and are played with wooden sticks. *Kudüm* are used to provide the rhythmic element in the ensembles of the Mevlevî (whirling dervishes) and in classical *fasıl* (Turkish art music).

Kudungba. Braced MOUTH BOW of the Amaza, Adoï, Amanga, Andebogo, Andekudju and Atalo peoples of Zaïre (*LaurentyC*, 113). *See* BOMBO (iv) and LUSUBA.

Kudyapiq. Two-string lute of the Bilaan, Bukidnon, Magindanao, Maranao, Tiboli and other peoples of the southern Philippines. One string provides a rhythmic drone; the other has movable frets allowing melodies to be played in hemitonic and anhemitonic scales. Melodic patterns of the Magindanao *kudyapiq* resemble some *kulintang* melodies. A *kudyapiq* may be played alone or with a *saluray* (polychordal bamboo tube zither), *kutet* (single-string fiddle) or *tumpung* (duct flute). A four-part ensemble consists of the *kudyapiq*, jew's harp, fiddle and flute.

Similar instruments to the *kudyapiq* in Mindanao and Palawan are the *kusyapiq*, *kudlung*, *faglung* and *hagĕlung*.

Kuenda. A Bambassi term for a KETTLEDRUM used by black musicians in Basra, Iraq; it is known also as a *ṭabl*. (The Bambassi language is of African origin.) The earthenware body of the instrument is 17 to 20 cm high and 19 to 33 cm wide. The *kuenda* is made to order, and its form and size vary. The most common shape now is the truncated cone. A cowhide head is attached by leather thongs threaded through eyelets round the edge. The drum is placed on the ground in front of a seated (usually cross-legged) player who strikes it with both hands. Sometimes instead he uses a palm stick in the right hand.

Four *kuenda* make up part of the *nūbān* ensemble, which also includes the *ṭanbūra* (lyre) and the *manjūr* (belt with rattling goat hooves). The ensemble plays during ceremonies associated with marriage, circumcision, thanksgiving, healing, invocation of spirits, the anniversary of a death and eclipses. See S. Qassim Hassan: *Les instruments de musique en Irak et leur rôle dans la société traditionelle* (Paris, 1980).

SCHEHERAZADE QASSIM HASSAN

Kuge. Double clapperless bell, made of iron, bronze or silver, of the Hausa people of Nigeria and Niger. It is beaten with an iron rod in the Zamfara area and with the pointed end of a duiker horn in the Zaria and Katsina regions (for illustration *see* BELL (i), fig.10). The instrument is used either solo for official proclamations, or with the long *kakaki* trumpet and *ganga* palace drum in the instrumental performance of praise epithets for an emir; in Niger the *algaita* oboe may also be included. The *kuge* is now used for the same purposes by peoples who have come under Hausa cultural influence, such as the Kambari, Kebbi and Jarawa. The Jarawa considered their *kuge* a sacred emblem, as well as a means of summoning the people to war, and many of their instruments were confiscated by the Fulani during the jihad (religious war) at the beginning of the 19th century. The *kuge* would appear to be associated with the Nupe *kule*, a single or double clapperless bell, and with the Gwari *kulle*. Both these instruments originally had ceremonial functions and are beaten with an iron rod.

BIBLIOGRAPHY

Ames–KingGHM

K. Krieger: 'Musikinstrumente der Hausa', *Baessler-Archiv*, new ser., xvi (1968), 373–430

T. Nikiprowetzky: 'Niger: la musique des griots', OCR 20 [disc notes]

K. A. GOURLAY

Kugiklï. Russian PANPIPES. *See* KUVIKLÏ.

Kugo. Japanese term for the angular harp known in modern Korea as *sogonghu* and formerly known in China as *shu-konghou* (*see* KONGHOU). Fragments of two such instruments of before AD 950 are in the 8th-century Shōsōin imperial repository (*see* HARP, fig.30); they were labelled *kudara-goto*, suggesting that the Japanese of that period associated the harp with the Kudara (Paekche) kingdom in the Korean peninsula. The Shōsōin fragments both had attachments for 23 strings. See 'Kugo', *Ongaku daijiten* [Encyclopedia of music] (Tokyo, 1981).

DAVID W. HUGHES

Kuhglocken (Ger.). COWBELLS.

Kuhn, Franz. German trombone maker who worked under contract with HERBERT LÄTZSCH from 1953.

Kuhn, Theodor. Swiss firm of organ builders. The firm was founded in Männedorf, near Zurich, by Johann Nepomuk Kuhn (1827–88). He was succeeded by his son, Carl Theodor Kuhn, after whose death in 1925 ownership of the company passed to family friends, who with their successors control the company. By 1876 it had built organs for such important cathedrals as St Gall and the Zurich Grossmünster, and by 1900 had exported widely, especially to France.

The company has always been noted for its progressiveness, and has patented several major technical innovations, such as the 'System Kuhn', developed in 1891 for the firm's first tubular pneumatic organ. It responded quickly to the *Orgelbewegung*, and in 1937 built its first large 'reformed' instrument with slider chests and mechanical key and stop action. In 1964 it built its last electric action organ, and since then, under the guidance of Friedrich Jakob, who became associated with Kuhn in 1963 and director in 1968, the firm has specialized in the development of modern mechanical action organs. Kuhn is noted for responsive key actions, imaginative case design, excellent reed stops and superior craftsmanship and tonal finishing. The tonal design of Kuhn organs is generally more cosmopolitan than that of other European organs, fitting them for a wide range of organ literature. Modern playing aids are utilized. Some of their notable modern organs are in St Gall Cathedral (1968), the Prediger-Kirche, Zurich (1970), Alice Tully Hall, Lincoln Center, New York (1974, designed in collaboration with Lawrence Phelps), and in the Symphony Hall of Asahi Broadcasting Corporation, Osaka (1982). Through Jakob's scholarly expertise the firm has restored important historic instruments, such as the 1735 Bommer organ in St Katharinenthal (1965–9) and the Gabler-Organ of 1736–50 at Weingarten (1982); it has also constructed new organs in a specific historical style, such as the organ after Andreas Silbermann for St Leonhard, Basle (1969), created within the old Silbermann cases.

GILLIAN WEIR

Kuhschellen (Ger.). COWBELLS.

Kui. Side-blown free-reed aerophone, made from a buffalo horn, of the Karen people of Burma and Thailand.

Kui lopu [lopu]. Bamboo STAMPING TUBE of the Polynesian outlier Ontong Java, played in sets. In Nukumanu they are called *tuki lopu*. They are beaten by a seated chorus as an accompaniment to a men's dance called *lopu*. See E. Sarfert and H. Damm: 'Luangiua und Nukumanu: soziale Verhaltnisse und Geisterkultur', *Ergebnisse der Südsee-Expedition 1908–1910*, IIB, xii (Hamburg, 1931), 461.

Kuizi. A term used for paired flutes, probably a double DUCT FLUTE, among the Kogi (Cágaba) of the Sierra Nevada de Santa Marta on the Atlantic coast of Colombia. The instrument is similar to the GAITA of the same region.

Kujamba. Rattle used in Tanzania. *See* KAYAMBI.

Kukau. Obsolete JEW'S HARP of the Maori people of New Zealand. *See* ROORIA.

Kukoricahegedű [cirokhegedű]. 'Corn fiddle' or idiochord bowed zither of Hungary. It is about a span long, with one to three strings, made of sorghum stalk or corn stalk, serving as a children's toy. Two are used together, one as the 'fiddle', the other acting as a bow. *See also* GUSLICE.

Kukuma. Single-string fiddle used in modern popular music of the Hausa people of Nigeria.

Kula [kola]. Cylindrical stopped wooden flute of the Zande people of north-eastern Zaïre (*LaurentyA*, 173ff).

Kulak. Stick rattle of the Tangale people of Nigeria. It consists of a long, thick pole, 90 cm long, on which a number of wooden discs slide freely backwards and forwards.

Kuḻal [kuzhal, kuṟal]. An ancient Tamil name for the transverse flute, found in the literature of south India in the 1st millennium AD. Another name was *vankiyam*. Descriptions suggest the flute was about 38 cm long and 9 cm in circumference; it was generally made of bamboo, but bronze, sandalwood and rosewood are also mentioned. The left end was closed and ringed with thin bronze. The blowing-hole was about 4 cm from the left end and there were seven finger-holes, with an eighth hole (*muttirai*) left open. Other *kuḻal* are mentioned, such as the *mullaikuḻal* with five holes. The flute was a leading instrument of the dance orchestra. It is nowadays usually called *veṇu* (*see* VAMŚA). The same name is found in modern times for a reed or bamboo panpipe played by shepherds in south India.

BIBLIOGRAPHY
H. A. Popley: *The Music of India* (Calcutta, 1921, 3/1966)
S. Ramanathan: *Music in Cilapatikaaram* (diss., Wesleyan U., Middletown, Conn., 1974)
ALASTAIR DICK

Kulanter. Double-headed drum of the Sundanese areas of West Java. *See* KENDANG.

Kulasing. DUCT FLUTE of the northern Philippines. *See* ONGIYONG.

Kulcapi. Short-necked plucked lute of the Batak Karo area of North Sumatra. Its two metal strings are stretched through a bridge near the base of the soundbox to the end of the carved scroll neck, where they may each be tautened by a tuning-peg. There are four frets at the top of the neck. The soundbox is diamond-shaped, often with elaborate carving below and at its base. The *kulcapi* forms part of the ensemble called *gendang ketengketeng* or *perketeng-keteng*.

MARGARET J. KARTOMI

Kule. Clapperless bell of the Nupe people of Nigeria. *See* KUGE.

Kulema. *See* KWABIRA.

Kuli (i). Long open HOURGLASS DRUM of the Salamat Arabs of Chad. It resembles the Barma BUDUGU and is used with other drums and flutes to accompany dancing for entertainment.

Kuli (ii). SLIT-DRUM of southern Cameroon and the Central African Republic.

Kulī. CONCH-SHELL TRUMPET of Nissan, Solomon Islands. See F. Krause: 'Zur Ethnographie der Insel Nissan', *Jahrbuch des Stadtischen Museums für Völkerkunde zu Leipzig*, i (1906), 146.

Kulibao (i). JEW'S HARP of the northern Philippines. *See* AFIW.

Kulibao (ii). Three-string fiddle of the northern Philippines. *See* LITLIT.

Kulibit. *See* KOLITONG.

Kulik, Jan (*b* Domasin, 14 Jan 1800; *d* Prague, 5 May 1872). Bohemian violin maker. Of humble origin, he rose to become one of the most accomplished Bohemian violin makers of the 19th century. He was apprenticed to K. Sembera in Prague and completed his training under Martin Stoss in Vienna. The craftsmanship and varnishing of his mature work is excellent, though (apart from his cellos) the tonal quality of his instruments is surprisingly inferior. The cellos are patterned after two widely differing models, one rather small, with high ribs and designed by an engineer named Leopold Savoi, and the other a standard Stradivari copy. His earlier violins are patterned after various Italian models, including those of Stradivari, Guarneri 'filius Andreae', Pietro Guarneri 'da Mantova' and Maggini; after 1850 he became interested in the instruments of Andrea Guarneri, and most of his violins dating from this time are patterned after this maker's model. Instruments which were actual copies of originals usually bear Kulik's printed label attesting to this fact.

BIBLIOGRAPHY
K. Jalovec: *Cešti houslaři* [Violin makers of Bohemia] (Prague, 1959; Eng. trans., 1959)
JAAK LIIVOJA-LORIUS

Kulimbet. Ensemble of the Ibaloi people of the northern Philippines, used for a dance of the same name. It consists of a flat gong (*see* GANGSA (i)) and two long, narrow conical drums, one high-pitched and one low-pitched.

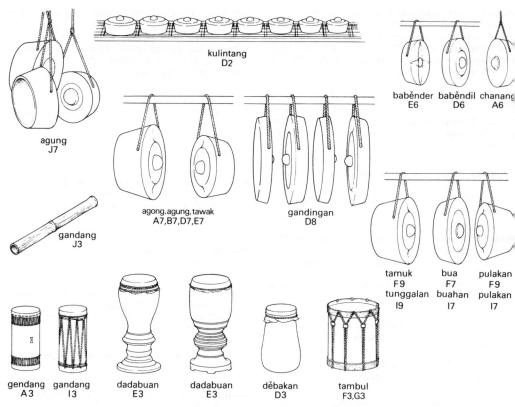

1. Some instruments of the kulintang ensemble of South-east Asia; letters and numbers refer to Table 1

Kulintang [gulintangan, klentangan, kolintang, kwin-tangan etc]. GONG-CHIME of the Philippines, Indonesia and other parts of South-east Asia. The term is used also for an ensemble of gongs, drums and other percussion instruments in which the *kulintang* gong-chime is the main constituent. The origins of the *kulintang* are obscure, but its distribution and musical techniques link it with other ensembles in the area; the *engkromong* of Sara-wak, for example, employs the same instruments and performance technique. *See also* TALEMPONG.

1. The *kulintang* gong-chime. 2. The *kulintang* ensemble. 3. Tuning and performing styles.

1. THE KULINTANG GONG-CHIME. The gong-chime con-sists of a number of bossed bronze gongs laid horizon-tally in a row in front of the performer, with the largest on the left and the smallest on the right. The number of gongs varies: there are from seven to nine in Sabah and Brunei, usually eight in the Philippines, six in Sumatra and up to 12 among some ethnic groups. The larger gongs measure about 22 cm in diameter, with turned-in rims 7 cm wide and bosses 3 cm high; the smaller gongs are approximately 18 cm in diameter, with rims 7 cm wide and bosses 2·5 cm high. They are manufactured by the lost-wax process. Some gongs are plain, with no designs, but the faces of others are etched with geometrical figures.

The gongs are laid on two parallel strings stretched out in a wooden frame. Some frames are very elaborate, especially among the Maranao people, where motifs with arabesque contours and rich colours (shades of blue, yellow and purple) display traditional craftsmanship in wood and brass sculptures. Simpler frames have no paintings or carvings. Among poorer families, who may not possess a frame, the gongs are sometimes placed on mats, clothes, leaves, sacks or some other surface which does not completely damp the sound. The gongs are played with two soft wooden mallets.

2. THE KULINTANG ENSEMBLE. The *kulintang* gong-chime is the melody instrument of the *kulintang* ensemble, the other instruments consisting of suspended gongs, drums and other percussion (see figs.1 and 2). The suspended gongs vary in size, thickness and profile, with faces between about 30 and 60 cm in diameter and turned-in rims from about 10 to 20 cm wide. The gongs may weigh five kilogrammes or more. Outside the *kulintang* ensemble they are widely distributed in South-east Asia and used in various ensembles. The bigger instruments are more valuable than the *kulintang* itself, and are important as heirlooms, bridal gifts and a means of exchange. In performance they are suspended from the beam of a house or the branch of a tree and struck on their bosses with a rubber- or cloth-padded mallet to produce either long vibrations or short sounds damped by the player's left hand or right knee.

Table 1 shows the instrumentation of some *kulintang* ensembles as they exist among various cultural groups in insular South-east Asia. The melody instrument (Table 1, col. 2) is supported by a drum (3) which provides a rhythm and the basic metre on which all *kulintang* mel-odies depend. The other percussion timbres (4, 5) col-our the rhythm and melody. The special timbres of one gong of the *kulintang* gong-chime (5) may supply a dis-creet metallic or rim sound, which in the case of groups

) and *F* may be assisted by special ostinato techniques of the player. The suspended gongs are very varied in type and musical function. Gongs with a plane face (6), usually played on the rim, provide the metallic sound which in some cases is produced by a gong of the *kulintang* (5). Other suspended gongs (7) produce muted sounds in counterpoint to each other, and may be played together with a long-sounding gong (9), as among the Sama (*F*) and the Tausug (*I*). The *gandingan* of the Magindanao (*D8*) is a special group of four gongs, graded in pitch and played by one musician; their long resonances overlay each other and lend a homogeneity to the whole orchestra.

The ensemble of suspended gongs and varied percussion serves to accompany the *kulintang* melody, but it also has its own internal structure, different from that found in the Javanese GAMELAN. In the *gendang ajat*, an ensemble of the Iban (*B7, 9*), the *bendai* sounds a basic beat to which the *tawak* adds its syncopations. Among the Maranao *agung* players (*E7*) collaborate to produce rhythms which can be highly complex. A similar musical dialogue takes place among the Sama of Sitangkai, where the *bua* and *pulakan* (*F7*) adjust to each other to fit in with the regular beats of the *tamuk* (*F9*). In the case of the Magindanao the two *agung* (*D7*) are played by one person, and so the contrapuntal play is between him and the *děbakan* player (*D3*). (*See also* AGUNG.)

3. TUNING AND PERFORMING STYLES. There is no standard tuning for *kulintang*, and almost as many scales exist as there are ensembles. There is a general tendency for an eight-gong *kulintang* to be tuned in narrow and wide steps similar to those of *pelog* and anhemitonic scales (*see* GAMELAN, §4). However, these gaps have a wide range of measurements; in some old gong-chimes intervals measure less than 20 or even 10 cents, and are accepted by local performers only because there are no other gongs available. Moreover, the distribution of narrow and wide steps within the eight-gong row varies, thus changing the measurements of 5ths and octaves. The scale structure of several *kulintang* produced by a rural gong factory in Cotabato, Mindanao, is approximately C–D–F–F♯–G–A♯–B–C.

TABLE 1: Instrumentation of some kulintang ensembles of insular South-east Asia

CULTURAL GROUP	MELODY INSTRUMENT		PERCUSSION TIMBRES			SUSPENDED GONGS		
	Gong-chime	Drum	Bamboo pole or castanets	One gong of the kulintang	Plane-face gong	Gong, or pair of gongs, with turned-in rim and high boss	Gongs with narrow rim and shallow boss	Heavy gong
1	2	3	4	5	6	7	8	9
A Groups in Brunei	gulintangan (7, 9 to 12 gongs)	1- or 2-headed gendang (cylindrical)			2 or 3 canang	1 or 2 agong		1 or more tawak-tawak
B Iban of Sarawak	engkromong (5 to 7 gongs)	2 gendang or dumbak (cylindrical)				tawak (vary in numbers)		bendai
C Kadazan of Sabah	gulintangan (7, 9 to 12 gongs)	2-headed gendang (cylindrical)			sanang			tawak
D Magindanao of Mindanao	kulintang (8, and up to 12 gongs)	děbakan (conical, 2 sticks)		replaces babĕndil	babĕndil (1 or 2 sticks)	1 or 2 agung (damped, 1 player)	4 gandingan	
E Maranao of Mindanao	kulintang (usually 8 gongs)	dadabuan (goblet, 2 sticks)		replaces babĕnder	babĕnder (2 sticks)	1 or 2 agung (damped, 1 or 2 players)		
F Sama of Sitangkai	kulintangan (7 to 9 gongs)	tambul (cylindrical, 2 sticks)	bolaq bolaq (clappers)	solembat		bua (narrow rim) and pulakan (wide rim) (1 player)		tamuk (wide rim)
G Sama of Sulu	kulintang	tambul (cylindrical)	tuntungan			huhugan and pulakan		tunggalan
H Tanjung Benua of east Kalimantan	klentangan (6 gongs)	gendang or gimar (2-headed)					taraai and genikng (small and large)	
I Tausug of Sulu	kulintang (8 to 11 gongs)	gandang (cylindrical, 2 sticks)	tuntung	(one gong used)		buahan (narrow rim) and pulakan (1 player)		tunggalan (wide rim, damped and undamped)
J Yakan of Basilan	kwintangan (5 to 7 gongs)	gandang		nulanting or mapindil		3 agung (damped), lebuan, pengeguagan, lerukan (2 players)		

2. *Kulintang ensemble of the Magindanao people, Mindanao, Philippines, with (left to right) gandingan and babĕndil (suspended gongs), dĕbakan (conical drum), agung (suspended gong) and (front) kulintang (gong-chime)*

Kulintang ensembles are used for feasts, weddings, celebrations and entertainments. Whenever *kulintang* music is heard an audience usually gathers, listens and participates. Among the Iban people gong ensembles have specific social uses: the *gendang panjai* for feasts, the *gendang ajat* for dances and weddings and the *gendang rayah* for feasts other than weddings. In many cultural groups the *kulintang* players are women, but among the Iban they are usually men. Among the Magindanao of Dulawan young men have developed a virtuoso style initiated in the 1950s by Amĕl Lĕmuntod, a performer of considerable repute. Pieces take on the character of an informal contest between young players who try to outlast each other in rapid and muscularly tense performances.

Two fundamental elements of *kulintang* music, as of other ensembles in South-east Asia, are the melody and the drone, or ostinato. In the *kulintang* ensemble the *kulintang* gong-chime provides the melody, and each of the punctuating instruments (Table 1, cols. *3–9*) contributes its own drone or ostinato. A drum, bamboo pole, pair of castanets, *kulintang* gong or heavy gong repeats its sound and thereby becomes a drone. The *babĕndil* (*6*), *agung* (*7*) and *gandingan* (*8*) play repetitive rhythmic patterns. These are all drone patterns producing a rich variety of colours which characterize the unique quality of *kulintang* music and set it apart from that of other gong families.

Among the Yakan people *kulintang* melodies tend to be stationary; patterns played on a limited number of gongs are repeated at high speed with few note changes. Among the Sama people of Sulu melodic lines may be developmental, using many notes, as in the *titik to-ongan*, an independent instrumental piece or the *tariray*, which accompanies a dance performed, especially by elderly women, in ceremonies of possession. Some melodies are cellular, with short phrases repeated many times before changing to another melodic cell; an example is the *titik tabawan*, used at marriage ceremonies.

A characteristic Magindanao melodic form from the town of Datu Piang, Cotabato, consists of cells played by two, three or four gongs which change in number and pitch as they move up and down the eight-gong register. The musical interest lies in the permutation of the cells, the performer deciding on the combination of gongs, the length of time he will repeat it, when to add some and to suppress others, and when to transfer to another register or to a cell above or below. A closing pattern is a melodic rise and fall, ending on a middle note.

As far as is known, the Magindanao is the only cultural group to use rhythmic modes as the basis of all their *kulintang* melodies. There are three such modes (ex.1), which are announced first by the drum and taken

Ex.1

duyug

sinulug

tidtu

up by the other instruments. Two pieces of music are played in each mode to complete one musical rendition.

BIBLIOGRAPHY

H. Simbriger: 'Gong und Gongspiele', *Internationale Archiv für Ethnographie*, xxxvi (1939), 1–80
H. C. Conklin and J. Maceda: 'Hanunoo Music from the Philippines', FE 4466 [disc notes]
I. Polunin: 'Murut Music of North Borneo', FE 4459 [disc notes]
J. Maceda: 'The Music of the Magindanao', FE 4536 [disc notes]
——: 'Field Recording Sea Dayak Music', *Sarawak Museum Journal*, x (1963), 486
——: *The Music of the Magindanao in the Philippines* (diss., U. of California, Los Angeles, 1964)
T. Kiefer: 'Music from the Tausug of Sulu', EST 8000–1 [disc notes]
U. Cadar: *The Maranao Kulintang Music: an Analysis of the Instruments, Musical Organization, Ethnologies, and Historical Documents* (diss., U. of Washington, 1971)
P. Ivanoff: 'Musique dayak; Borneo, Kalimantan', Vogue, LDM 30108 [disc notes]
'A Short Survey of the Brunei Gulintangan Orchestra', *Traditional Drama and Music of Southeast Asia*, ed. M. T. Osman (Kuala Lumpur, 1974), 298

. Garfias and U. Cadar: 'Some Principles of Formal Variation in the Kolintang Music of the Maranao', *EM*, xviii (1974), 43
  Maceda: 'Drone and Melody in Philippine Musical Instruments', *Traditional Drama and Music of Southeast Asia*, ed. M. T. Osman (Kuala Lumpur, 1974), 246
. P. Ongkili: 'The Traditional Musical Instruments of Sabah', *Traditional Drama and Music of Southeast Asia*, ed. M. T. Osman (Kuala Lumpur, 1974), 327
  Takacs: 'A Dictionary of Philippine Musical Instruments', *Archiv für Volkerkunde*, xxix (1975), 121–217
. Revel-Macdonald: 'Les épopées palawan (Philippines): fonction sociale et contenu culturel', *Bulletin du Centre de Documentation et de Recherche sur l'Asie du Sud-est et le Monde Insulindien*, viii (1977), 45
. Maceda: 'A Report of a Music Workshop in East Kalimantan', *Borneo Research Bulletin*, x (1978), 82
. Otto and U. Cadar: 'Maranao Kakolintang: Philippine Gong Music from Lanao', Lyrichord, LLST 7322 and 7326 [disc notes]
. Maceda: 'A Search for an Old and New Music in Southeast Asia', *AcM*, li (1979), 160
. Becker: 'A Southeast Asian Musical Process: the Thai *Thaw* and Javanese *Irama*', *EM*, xxiv (1980), 453
. Franklin: *Kelenang: a Musical Genre from Lombok Timur* (diss., U. of New England, 1981)
. Maceda: *A Manual of a Field Music Research with Special Reference to Southeast Asia* (Quezon City, 1981)
. Dioquino: 'Musicology in the Philippines', *AcM*, liv (1982), 124
. Frame: 'The Musical Instruments of Sabah, Malaysia', *EM*, xxvi (1982), 247

JOSÉ MACEDA

Kulintang lunik. Small ensemble of Lampung province, Sumatra, consisting of a KELITTANG (gong-chime with three small gongs), a *gong* (large suspended gong), a *bende* (small gong), and a *ghujih* (pair of cymbals).

Kulinter [ketipung]. Double-headed laced drum of West Java. *See* KENDANG.

Kulittālam. Bronze cymbals of south India. *See* TĀLAM.

Kulkul. Wooden or bamboo SLIT-DRUM used for signalling in Bali. The wooden instrument is a hollowed tree trunk closed at both ends, with a longitudinal slit. Suspended in a high tower, it is struck near the edge of the slit with a stick or hammer. *Kulkul* are played singly, but most commonly in differently-pitched pairs, and sometimes in groups of three or four. Some are very large and may be heard over long distances. The small bamboo slit-drum consists of a joint of bamboo, closed at each end by a node, with a longitudinal slit. It is hung in a tree and used for signalling to family members and for sounding alarms. See C. McPhee: *Music in Bali* (New Haven and London, 1966/*R*1976), 34f.

MARGARET J. KARTOMI

Kulle. Clapperless bell of the Gwari people of Nigeria. *See* KUGE.

Küllküll. A cow-horn trumpet used by the Mapuche (Araucanian) people of southern-central Chile. An oval mouthpiece is made on one side near the pointed end. The strident sound of the *küllküll* is used for communications between *rukas* (Mapuche homes), and the instrument is combined with the *trutruka* (bamboo trumpet) to accompany certain *machi* (shaman) dances.

JOHN M. SCHECHTER

Kullutan rājan. A fretted STICK ZITHER of the Saora (or Savara) people of east-central India. It consists of a small or medium-sized stick with a gourd attached near the upper end and capped with another pointed gourd segment. About five frets (sticks embedded in a waxy glue)

are fitted above the gourd. Two sticks or pegs are inserted, one vertically, one diagonally, on either side of the upper end of the stick, to which a drone string is attached. A similar instrument of the neighbouring Khondh people of Orissa has two gourds and eight frets; Sachs illustrates it but does not give a name. The *gogonjenro* of Orissa is also similar. These instruments are often played with the gourd pressed against the chest; the pressure is varied to alter the resonance. They are of the medieval and later *kinnarī vīṇā* type (*see* VĪṆĀ, §§4, 6).

BIBLIOGRAPHY
C. Sachs: *Die Musikinstrumente Indiens und Indonesiens* (Berlin and Leipzig, 1914, 2/1923)
N. A. Jairazbhoy: 'Folk Music of India (Orissa)', Lyrichord LLST 7183 [disc notes]
B. C. Deva: *Musical Instruments of India* (Calcutta, 1978)
ALASTAIR DICK

Kulongbe. Box resonated LAMELLAPHONE of the Budu people of north-eastern Zaïre (*LaurentyS*, 192). *See* AGBOMBOYA.

Kulongkoing. MOUTH BOW of the Jola people of Senegal and the Gambia. It is tapped with a stick and the left hand alters the pitch by up to a minor 3rd.

Kultrún [cultrun]. A small conical KETTLEDRUM, 35 to 45 cm in diameter, used by the Mapuche (Araucanian) people of southern Chile and Neuquén, Argentina. The shell is made of laurel or from a large calabash and is covered with a hide of goat, calf, sheep or horse. The hollow basin contains several small stones, seeds or coins, which rattle when the instrument is struck with a drumstick or shaken. Wooden mallets covered in wool are used as drumsticks. In Argentina the *kultrún* was played by a female shaman who stood holding the drum on her left arm and struck it with a drumstick, or sat with the drum on the ground before her, in which case she used two drumsticks. Less commonly the instrument was shaken as an idiophone. In Chile the distribution of the *kultrún* encompasses four southern provinces: Bío-Bío, Malleco, Valdivia and especially Cautín (see illustration, p.484). Among the Chilean Mapuche the *kultrún* is a principal instrument of the *machi* (shamans), frequently but not always female. They use it primarily in connection with healing rituals and also for other shamanic ceremonies. The head of the instrument is painted in various forms and colours. See M. E. Grebe: 'El kultrún mapuche: un microcosmo simbólico', *Revista musical chilena*, nos.123–4 (1973), 3–42.

JOHN M. SCHECHTER

Kulu. Horn whistle of the Mahi people of Benin. It is used with clapperless bells, rattles and percussion instruments in the performance of funeral music.

Kulukulu. Ivory VESSEL FLUTE of the Samba people of Zaïre (*LaurentyA*, 233).

Kulukwoo. Globular VESSEL FLUTE of the Teke people of Zaïre; it is made from a seed shell (*LaurentyA*, 222).

Kŭm (i). Korean name for the QIN, a Chinese seven-string long zither. The present Korean use of the instrument is much more restricted than the Chinese: it appears only in the ritual music (*aak*) ensembles, in one cere-

Kultrún (kettledrums) and gourd rattles played by an Araucanian shaman (centre) and his two assistants, Cautí province, Chile

mony (the twice-yearly Sacrifice to Confucius in Seoul) and with one tuning (*C–D–E–G–A–c–d*).

In 1116 73 *qin* were given to Korea by the Song Chinese emperor as part of a huge gift of musical instruments. The *qin* were in one-, three-, five-, seven- and nine-string versions (a single-string instrument is the Japanese ICHIGEN-KIN). They were used only in ritual music for sacrificial rites and other ceremonies requiring the utmost decorum. Since the reform of ritual music in the early 15th century only the standard seven-string instrument has been used. *See also* KIN (i).

BIBLIOGRAPHY
Sŏng Hyŏn, ed.: *Akhak kwebŏm* [Guide to the study of music] (Seoul, 1493/*R*1975), 6.21*b–22b*
Yi Hye-gu: *Han'guk ŭmak yŏn'gu* [Studies in Korean music] (Seoul, 1957), 374ff
Chang Sa-hun: *Han'guk akki taegwan* [Korean musical instruments] (Seoul, 1969), 87ff
ROBERT C. PROVINE

Kŭm (ii). Large flat bronze gong of Korea. *See* CHING (i).

Kumāic. *See* KAMĀICĀ.

Kumbili. MUSICAL BOW, with separate gourd resonator, of the Lobo, Andedeme and Timogia peoples of Zaïre; it is also known as *gambili* and *kambili* (*LaurentyC*, 114). *See* KITINGBI.

Kumbo. Two-string plucked lute of the Hausa people of Nigeria. *See* GURMI.

Kumgulumi. Single-headed open-ended conical drum of the Lala people of Zambia. *See also* CHIRARIRA.

Kŭmna. Large flat bronze gong of Korea. *See* CHING (i).

Kumpang [kompang]. (1) FRAME DRUM, with goatskin head, of the southern states of West Malaysia. Its diameter is about 33 cm and the body of the drum, which is about 7 cm deep, is made of jackfruit wood. The head is nailed to the body with brass tacks. The player holds the drum in the curve of the left arm, with the left hand gripping the rim; it is beaten with the fingers of the right hand.

(2) An ensemble of seven frame drums of West Malaysia, each with a different timbre, played in wedding processions by friends of the bridegroom to accompany Arabic choruses. It is also played in religious processions. In Kelantan and Trengganu the *kumpang* is called *rebana*, and when fitted with brass discs just below the rim it is called *rebana kerceng* (*see also* TAR).
JACK PERCIVAL BAKER DOBBS

Kumurere. NOTCHED FLUTE of Uganda. *See* KHUMULELE.

Kumvi. Trapezoidal SLIT-DRUM of the Luba people of Ankoro, south-eastern Zaïre; it is also known as KYONDO (*LaurentyTF*, 138).

Kunce. Double-headed cylindrical drum of the Songhay people of Niger. It is used in sets of three to accompany dancing, and at wrestling matches.

Kunda. Arched harp of the Mombati (Bati) people of Zaïre (*LaurentyC*, 119). *See* KUNDI (i).

Kundé. Six-string arched harp of the Sara-Gambaye people of southern Chad. Its body is of wood, enveloped in stitched cowhide, and its neck has tuning-pegs. The instrument, which is played exclusively by men, is held vertically against the player's body with the soundbox at the bottom. Among neighbouring peoples *kundé* and *kundi* refer to arched harps with seven or sometimes eight strings, and there are also instruments with four strings among the Masa groups. Among the Sara the arched harp accompanies singing but it can also be used instead of the human voice to transmit messages.

MONIQUE BRANDILY

Kundi [nkundi, kunda, kundu, kondu, komba] **(i).** Arched harp of north-eastern and north-western Zaïre and associated peoples of the Central African Republic, including the Nzakara and Sabanga. It is akin to the *ngombi* (*see* NGOMBI (i)) of Gabon. The instrument has a carved wooden soundbox, soundtable of snakeskin or of antelope, buffalo or elephant skin, and a wooden stick handle inserted into one end of the soundbox. The shape of the handle may be either angular or gently arched. Most instruments have five strings, traditionally made from vegetable fibre, though the versions played by Bale, Bajanje and Hima peoples have seven. Each string is attached to a tuning-peg in the handle at the upper end and passes through a hole in the soundtable to be secured by fastening it to a small piece of wood beneath the table. Although organologists may differentiate instruments according to the shape of the soundbox, this distinction is not reflected in local terminology. The term *kundi* is used for the Zande harp, in which the most conspicuous feature is the curved indentation in each side, for other harps in which the soundbox is approximately oval, and, with the Gunda, for a harp in which the soundbox is rectangular with a rounded end. Conversely, the name *domo* is used by the Bari people, *domu* by the Ngbele, *maringa* by the Babjande and *neduma* by the Meje for a five-string harp with a soundbox either indented or rounded. A number of harps are anthropomorphic, the soundbox representing the torso: carved legs extend at one end and a head is carved at the end of the handle. The Ngbaka people refer to a harp of this type as *seto*, the name of the mythical figure represented; the Budu, however, use the name *komba*, which is cognate with *kundi*, and the Mangbetu *nandomo* and *nedomu* cognate with the Meje term, *neduma*. In performance the harp is held between the thighs with the handle pointing away from the player. The lower strings are plucked with the thumbs and the higher with the index fingers. The harp is used by singers to accompany themselves; many of these musicians are highly respected specialists in the art of composing praise songs, particularly of important people, or narratives of heroic prowess. *See also* KUNDÉ.

BIBLIOGRAPHY

LaurentyC, 119

J.-N. Maquet: *Note sur les instruments de musique congolais* (Brussels, 1956)

F. J. de Hen: *Beitrag zur Kenntnis der Musikinstrumente aus Belgisch Kongo und Ruanda-Urundi* (Tervuren, 1960)

S. Arom: 'Centre Afrique: danses de la forêt', HM 733 [disc notes]

P. Collaer: 'Musics of the Central African Republic', BM 30 L 2310 [disc notes]

J. H. K. Nketia: *The Music of Africa* (New York, 1974)

K. A. GOURLAY

Kundi (ii). Transverse flute of China, used in the *kun* opera. *See* DI (i).

Kundi [kundiri] **(iii).** KETTLEDRUM of tribal India. *See* TIMKI.

Kundrukundru. BULLROARER of the Adoi, Amanga, Andebogo and Andowi peoples of Zaïre. *See* ATUAMBA.

Kundu [gundu, kudu] **(i).** Pidgin English name for the HOURGLASS DRUM of New Guinea. Its distribution extends from West Irian through every district of Papua New Guinea, including the Bismarck Archipelago, as far south as Buka and Bougainville in the Solomon Islands. One end is covered by the skin and the other left open. It is usually 75 to 100 cm long and 15 to 25 cm in diameter at each end, with a narrow waist to which a carrying handle is often attached. Some drums are almost cylindrical and in others the open end is cut away to resemble the mouth of a fish or the jaws of a crocodile. The wood is hollowed out with great care over a long period to avoid its cracking through drying too quickly. The drum is then polished and decorated, and a drumhead made from lizard, snake or opossum skin is fixed with adhesive made from tree-gum or from lime mixed with blood. The skin is tightened by warming it over a fire, and finally small pellets of beeswax are affixed to tune the drum. The heating process is repeated if the head slackens during performance. The main use of the drum is to provide a rhythmic accompaniment at 'sing-sing' dances, each player carrying his own instrument.

MERVYN McLEAN

Kundu [kende] **(ii).** XYLOPHONE of central Africa. (1) Xylophone with 13 to 15 keys of the Sara, Barma and neighbouring peoples of southern Chad. The keys are strung together each above a gourd resonator, which can be either curved or straight and is fitted with a mirliton made of fish bladder, bat's wing or spider's web. Gen-

Kundu (hourglass drums) at Goroka, Eastern Highlands Province, Papua New Guinea

erally one of the keys is mute. The frame has an arched wooden bar, which rests against the player's thighs when the instrument is suspended on a strap from the player's neck. The *kundu* is also played on the ground, notably by the Sara Kaba and the Barma, and then the position of the keys can be horizontal or almost vertical. For all instruments the player has four sticks, two in each hand, whose ends are covered with balls made of plaited leather thongs. This enables him to sound up to four keys at once. A roll of rubber or wax placed around the hole of the gourd resonators allows the quality of the sound to be changed.

(2) Portable XYLOPHONE of the Lito people of the Central African Republic. It is suspended by a cord round the player's neck and beaten with latex-tipped beaters. The xylophone has been recorded with two drums and handclapping as accompaniment to seasonal dancing in honour of ancestors.

MONIQUE BRANDILY (1), K. A. GOURLAY (2)

Kundu (iii). Arched harp of northern Zaïre. *See* KUNDI (i).

Kundung. Portable XYLOPHONE with 14 or 15 keys of the Birom people of Nigeria. It derives its name from and resembles the portable *kundu* xylophone of the Sara people of southern Chad. However, it can have cow-horn resonators or hollow wooden cones of cow-horn shape or gourd resonators. It uses a spider's web membrane for the mirliton. It is tuned pentatonically and the keys are arranged 5 + 5 + 4 (or 5, according to the total number). Two performers may play side by side, using a rubber-tipped beater in each hand (see illustration). The instrument is played mainly for entertain-

Kundung (xylophone) of the Birom people, Nigeria

ment, either alone or as part of an ensemble, and skille players have developed considerable virtuosity in per formance.

BIBLIOGRAPHY

L. Bouquiaux: 'Les instruments de musique Birom (Nigeria Sep tentrional)', *Africa-Tervuren*, viii/4 (1962), 105

C. Duvelle and M. Vuylstèke: 'Anthologie de la musique du Tchad' OCR 36–8 [disc notes]

Kundye. Single-string fiddle of the Susu people o Guinea.

Kung. Short squat open cylindrical drum of the Anga people of Nigeria. It is made of mahogany and has pegged membrane and four feet. The purpose of the fee is unclear as, in contemporary performance, the drum is laid on its side resting on the pegs. It is beaten by one man, using a straight stick in each hand, as part o a set that includes three smaller, upright versions, each on a single pedestal. The bodies of all four drums are carved with curved parallel lines. During manufacture sacrifices are made to tree and animal spirits, and the maker avoids all contact with women. The drum is usually owned by a religious group and housed in a special room; it is taken out only for performance during death celebrations (*nep*) and festivals in the religious calendar.

Kungagiwa. Idioglot transverse clarinet of the Kambari people of Nigeria. *See* CLARINET, TRANSVERSE.

Kung-ch'in. *See* GONGQIN.

K'ung-hou. *See* KONGHOU.

Kungkurak. Idioglot oboe of the Dusan rice-growing area of Sabah, Malaysia. It is a rice stem with holes cut in the side and is played by reapers and children.

Kung-lo. *See* GONGLUO.

Kungu. Board ZITHER of the Lega people of Zaïre. *See* IKIDI.

Kungunangu. GROUND HARP of the Mondo people of Zaïre (*LaurentyC*, 111). *See* BABAKUNGU.

Kunka. JEW'S HARP of the Nanay people of Siberia. It is played mainly by women, often to imitate natural sounds such as animal cries or the sound of wind or rain, or as a courting instrument.

Künkülkawe. MUSICAL BOW of the Mapuche (Araucanian) people of southern-central Chile, now obsolete. It was made from wood and horsehair and consisted of two interlocked bows.

Kunnee. Five-string arched harp of the Gula people of southern Chad. Its wooden body is covered with the skin of a warthog (*Phacochoerus aethiopicus*). The end of the soundbox opposite the neck is flat; with this as base the instrument is placed vertically on the ground with the neck upwards. The strings are made from antelope sinews and are attached by pegs.

MONIQUE BRANDILY

Kunri. Large wooden SLIT-DRUM of the Luba people of Zaïre.

Kunstharmonium (Ger.). A name applied to larger examples of the HARMONIUM.

Kuntigi [kuntiji, kontigui]. Single-string plucked lute of the Songhay and Hausa peoples of Niger and the Hausa peoples of northern Nigeria. Formerly it had a half-calabash soundbox, but recent instruments have a metal one. In Niger the *kuntigi* is used in solo performance by men and children. In Nigeria it was used by professional musicians for accompanying praise songs in disreputable surroundings but now has gained respectability largely through use by the distinguished praise singer, Dan Maraya, who refined its tone by using the quill of a vulture's feather as plectrum. *See also* KHALAM.

BIBLIOGRAPHY
Ames–KingGHM
P. G. Harris: 'Notes on Drums and Musical Instruments seen in Sokoto Province, Nigeria', *Journal of the Royal Anthropological Institute*, lxii (1932), 105
K. Krieger: 'Musikinstrumente der Hausa', *Baessler-Archiv*, new ser., xvi (1968), 373–430
B. Surugue: 'Songhay Music', *Grove 6*
C. Duvelle: 'Rhythmes et Chants du Niger', SOR 4 [disc notes]
K. A. GOURLAY

Kuntuku [kurkutu, kuttuku, kuntukuru, zakka]. Small KETTLEDRUM of the Hausa people of Nigeria. It is approximately 18 cm in height and slightly less in diameter. In the Zamfara area (where the term 'kurkutu' refers exclusively to an hourglass drum) the drum is known as *zakka*. The drum is either slung from the player's neck to lie vertical at waist level, or placed on a grass ring on the ground in front of the player. It is beaten with two straight or slightly curved wooden sticks. Essentially an ensemble instrument, it provides a rapid staccato rhythm and is used, together with hourglass drums *kalangu* and *dan karbi*, in the performance of praise songs for butchers, or in Zaria with the cylindrical drum *dundufa* in praise songs for blacksmiths. In the Zamfara area it was previously played with the *dundufa*. The drum is often a beginner's instrument, played by boy apprentices before they graduate to the *kalangu*.

BIBLIOGRAPHY
Ames–KingGHM
K. Krieger: 'Musikinstrumente der Hausa', *Baessler-Archiv*, new ser., xvi (1968), 373–430
D. W. Ames: 'Hausa Music I', BM30L 2306 [disc notes]
K. A. GOURLAY

Kuntukun tambura. Small kettledrums of the Hausa people of Nigeria. *See* TAMBARI.

Kunu [kunyu]. Drum of the Dogon people of Mali. Its body is made from the fruit of the baobab tree covered with the skin of a goat or rat and it is struck with wooden or cornstalk beaters. *See also* BARBA.

Kunz, Thomas Anton (*b* Prague, 21 Dec 1756; *d* Prague, *c*1830). Czech inventor, composer and pianist. He studied law and philosophy at Prague University and music with the Prague organist Joseph Prokop. After constructing a combined piano and positive organ, in 1791 he built an improved orchestrion; in 1796–8 he designed and constructed another such instrument with the Prague piano makers Johann and Thomas Still. This latter instrument was built in the form of an upright piano in a mahogany case with sides of blue taffeta stretched in ornamentally carved frames; it had two manuals (65 keys each, *F* to *a'''*) and a pedal (25 keys, *C* to *c''*). On the left side above the pedal was a mechanism for the foot operation of the bellows. 230 strings and 360 pipes, together with 21 registers, made possible 105 tonal combinations. Kunz also perfected the mechanism of Meyer's *violin piano*; he introduced extended notes and removed the unpleasant cacophony of the bow mechanism.

BIBLIOGRAPHY
Beckers National-Zeitung der Teutschen (1796), 434
T. A. Kunz: 'Beschreibung des Orchestrions', *AMZ*, i, (1798), 88
J. U. von Rittersberg: 'Die Tonkunst in Böhmen von den ältesten bis auf die gegenwärtigen Zeiten', *Archiv für Geschichte, Statistik, Literatur und Kunst*, xvi (1825), 51
R. Haas: 'Thomas Anton Kunz und sein Orchestrion', *Der Auftakt*, xi (1931), 43
ALEXANDR BUCHNER/R

Kunzukunzu. BULLROARER of the Aimeri people of Zaïre. *See* ATUAMBA.

Kūpe'e niho 'īlio. Hawaiian ankle rattle. It is made from multiple rows of canine teeth strung on a net backing. *See also* 'ULĪʻULĪ.

Kupkup [dupdup]. LEAF OBOE of Möwehafen, Southwest New Britain. It is used to represent spirit voices and to frighten women into submission in cases of dispute. See J. A. Todd: 'Redress of Wrongs in South-West New Britain', *Oceania*, vi (1936), 428ff.

Kuppers, Johannes Theodorus. *See* CUYPERS, JOHANNES THEODORUS.

Kur. Small clapperless bell of the Birifor people of Upper Volta. It is struck externally to provide rhythmic accompaniment with drums to singing.

Kurach'ŏlsa küm. Trapeziform wire-strung zither of Korea. *See* YANGGÜM.

Kurai [kuray]. Long end-blown flute of the Bashkir and Tatar peoples, USSR. It usually has four finger-holes. The player maintains a strong fundamental hum under the flute melody, a style found among widely separated peoples such as the Baluchi in Iran and Afghanistan and certain east Europeans (for instance, the Romanians). The *kurai* player seems to be accorded the importance associated with lute-players among the Kazakhs and Kirghiz. Among the Bashkirs, the *kurai* is one of the few surviving folk instruments.

Kural. *See* KUḼAL.

Kurang [kurango]. Rare three-string plucked lute of the Mandinka people of Senegal and the Gambia. It is related to the smaller five-string Mandinka lute, the KONTING.

Kurbelsphärophon. A monophonic electronic instrument invented by JÖRG MAGER and made in two versions; it was one of the group of instruments known generically as the SPHÄROPHON.

Kurbi. Harp of Sudan. It was originally used by the Nubians in the north, but is no longer known in that area. The *kurbi* has five strings which the player plucks with the fingers of both hands. At the same time he uses his right hand to drum a rhythmic accompaniment on the leather cover of the resonator.

Kuretsuzumi. HOURGLASS DRUM of Japan. *See* TSU-ZUMI.

Kuritao. Polychordal TUBE ZITHER of the Isneg people of the northern Philippines. *See* KOLITONG.

Kurkutu [kurkuttu]. Drum of the Hausa people of Nigeria. (1) Open snared HOURGLASS DRUM of fixed pitch of the Sokoto and Zamfara regions. The drum is suspended from the player's neck, or attached to his thigh if he is seated, and is beaten with flexible leather thongs. In Sokoto its uses are the same as those of the KAZAGI; in Zamfara, where it is often referred to as *zakka*, it is at times used in ceremonies of the *bori* spirit possession cult.

(2) Small KETTLEDRUM. *See* KUNTUKU.

BIBLIOGRAPHY
P. G. Harris: 'Notes on Drums and Musical Instruments Seen in Sokoto Province, Nigeria', *Journal of the Royal Anthropological Institute*, lxii (1932), 105
K. Krieger: 'Musikinstrumente der Hausa', *Baessler-Archiv*, new ser., xvi (1968), 373–430

K. A. GOURLAY

Kuromisu. Term for the Japanese GEZA ensemble.

Kuru. Open snared HOURGLASS DRUM of fixed pitch used by the Hausa people of northern Nigeria. The drum is suspended from the player's neck and tapped by the fingers on a wax layer at the centre of the membrane as accompaniment to song and dance, particularly during co-operative farmwork. *See Ames–KingGHM*.

Kurua. A SLIT-DRUM in the PARA NI 'O'O ensemble of the 'Are'are people, Malaita, Solomon Islands.

Kurudutu [kurududu]. An S-shaped copper trumpet of the Muṇḍā and related tribal peoples in southern Bihar, India. It is also known as NARSĪGĀ, and is played by folk musicians of the Ghāsi caste at weddings. See S. C. Roy: 'The Mundas: their Country, their Character and their Poetry', *Indian World*, vii (1908), 308.

Kurugu. Gourd vessel rattle of the Barma people of Chad, with internal strikers. It is held in the right hand and slapped against the palm of the left as rhythmic accompaniment to singing.

Kurya. Double-headed drum of the Hausa people of Nigeria. *See* GANGA, (1).

Kurze Oktave (Ger.). SHORT OCTAVE.

Kurz Pfeiff. *See* KORTHOLT.

Kus. Large bronze KETTLEDRUM of Persian origin, used in military music from antiquity until the 19th century.

It is still played in Armenia and Azerbaijan, where it is called KYOS or *kuus*. The Turkish KÖS is now obsolete.

Kusder. English flute maker. Described by Langwill as a shadowy figure, he is credited in various reference books with making improvements to the flute; Lavoix even ascribed the invention of the conoidal bore to him, a claim firmly demolished by Rockstro (article 415). A considerable number of Kusder's instruments survive in various collections but only one positive date has been established. He appears as 'Henry Kusder, Elask Row, Chelsea' in Holden's London Directory for 1799, and one of his instruments bears a silver ring with the date 1782.

BIBLIOGRAPHY
H. Lavoix: *Histoire de l'instrumentation depuis le seizième siècle* (Paris, 1878)
R. S. Rockstro: *A Treatise on . . . the Flute* (London, 1890, rev. 2/1928/R1967)
L. G. Langwill: *An Index of Musical Wind-instrument Makers* (Edinburgh, 1960, rev., enlarged 6/1980)

PHILIP BATE

Kushney. DOUBLE CLARINET of Central Asia. *See* DOZĀLE and QOSHNAI.

Küsle. Trapezoidal BOX ZITHER (psaltery) of the Mari and Chuvash peoples of the Volga-Ural region (USSR). It is probably related to the Russian GUSLI and the Finnish KANTELE. It has 17 to 22 strings, plucked with the fingers, and is one of the most widespread traditional instruments.

Küss, Wolfgang (*b* Sandau, 1779; *d* Vienna, 1834). Austrian woodwind instrument maker of Bohemian birth. He worked at various addresses in Vienna between 1811 and his death. He was succeeded by Johann Stehle. He was particularly noted for his numerous oboes and bassoons, made at a time when there was considerable experimentation with new keys. Surviving instruments of his show a wide variety of keywork. Existing oboes have between three and 15 keys, english horns normally 12, and bassoons between nine and 15; they are of high quality materials and excellent workmanship.

BIBLIOGRAPHY
L. G. Langwill: *An Index of Musical Wind-instrument Makers* (Edinburgh, 1960, rev., enlarged 6/1980)
O. Oromszegi: 'Bassoons at the Narodni Museum, Prague', *GSJ*, xxiv (1971), 96

NIALL O'LOUGHLIN

Kussir. *See* KISSAR.

Kusyapiq. Lute of the southern Philippines. *See* KUDYAPIQ.

Kutet. Single-string fiddle of the southern Philippines.

Kutiriba [kutirindingo]. Conical drum of the Mandinka people of the Gambia. *See* SABARO.

Kutti. Wooden whistle of the Gunga, Kenga and Shanga peoples of north-west Nigeria. It is blown in a vertical position and played by young men at harvest time during wrestling matches.

Kuttuku. Small KETTLEDRUM of the Hausa people of Nigeria. *See* KUNTUKU.

Kutū. The Japanese KOTO (long zither) as adopted in Okinawa. It is basically identical with the mainland versions (indeed, most are imported from mainland Japan) and is played with plectra of a shape which is a compromise between those of the Ikuta and Yamada schools of Japan. The most common tuning is *g–c–d–e–g–a–c'–d'–e'–g'–a'–c"–d"* (relative pitches), namely a Japanese *hirajōshi* with the semitones eliminated (*see* KOTO, ex.2). The tunings and certain musical elements seem to link the Okinawan *kutū* tradition with the *tsukushi-goto* tradition of Japanese koto music, but the history of the instrument and its repertory in Okinawa remain unclear. The *kutū* repertory proper consists of three songs and seven instrumental pieces called *danmono* (*see* KOTO, §3). Since the early 19th century the *kutū* has also been part of the court ensemble built around the *sanshin* (long-necked lute).

BIBLIOGRAPHY
E. Higa: *Okinawan Classical Music: Analysis of Vocal Performance* (diss., U. of Hawaii, 1976)
F. Koizumi, Y. Tokumaru and O. Yamaguchi, eds.: *Asian Musics in an Asian Perspective* (Tokyo, 1977), 199
DAVID W. HUGHES

Kützialflöte (Ger.). An ORGAN STOP.

Kuu. Single-string SPIKE FIDDLE of north-western Chad. The soundbox is half a calabash, about 30 cm in diameter; the soundtable is of varan skin, glued on, and has one soundhole. The neck, which has no pegs, is almost straight. The string, of horsehair, is tied on and raised from the neck and resonator by a little bridge placed on the soundtable. The bowstick, made from hard thickish wood, is strongly arched; the bowstring is horsehair. The *kuu* is believed to originate from Borno in present-day Nigeria. It is distinguished from other Saharan fiddles like the IMZAD of the Tuareg or the *kiiki* of the Teda-Daza by being part of a sultan's orchestra and being played by musicians of the professional caste.
MONIQUE BRANDILY

Kuu (spike fiddle) played by a professional musician of northwestern Chad

Kuus. *See* KYOS.

Kuvargah [kuwargāh]. A term in Mughal Indian texts for various types of large KETTLEDRUM. *See* NAGĀRĀ, §1 and NAQQĀRAKHĀNA.

Kuviklï [kugiklï]. PANPIPES of south-western Russia. The instrument consists of two to five stopped reedpipes of equal diameter but of various lengths (10 to 16 cm). Dance-tunes are usually played on *kuviklï* with five pipes, while those with three or four are played in ensemble as accompanying instruments. The usual ensemble of performers (*kugikal'nitsï*) consists of three or four women. One or two play the pipes, at the same time producing vocal sounds similar to those of the pipes, a technique known as *fifkan'ye*. The other two women accompany the basic tune with harmony notes in syncopation. Each set of pipes played by one performer is known as a 'pair', regardless of the actual number of pipes; the commonest number is five. They are usually tuned to a pentachord containing a neutral 3rd.

Kuwaitara [kūwayṭara, kuwīthra, kuwīṭra]. *See* QUWAYṬARA.

Kuypers, Johannes Theodorus. *See* CUYPERS, JOHANNES THEODORUS.

Kuze-gene. GROUND ZITHER of the Balese people of Zaïre (*LaurentyC*, 110). *See* KUDREKENE.

Kuzhal. *See* KUḶAL.

Kuzhittālam [kuḷittālam]. Bronze cymbals of Kerala, India. They are about 12 cm in diameter and have a deep boss. *See* TĀḶAM.

Kvickhorn. Swedish animal horn. *See* BOCKHORN.

Kvieslė. Idiophone of Lithuania. It consists of a forked stick 150 to 170 cm long, adorned with sashes and ribbons; a small clapper bell is fastened to the top. Until the beginning of the 20th century the *kvieslė* was widely used as a ceremonial instrument by the *kvieslys* ('caller') at weddings in Lithuania and East Prussia. Nowadays a modified version of the *kvieslė*, called the *džingulis*, is used in folk music groups. This is a stick 170 cm long and 3 cm thick, covered with metal plates, bells and other tinkling objects.
ARVYDAS KARAŠKA

Kwa [!kwa]. Pot drum of the San (Bushman) people of southern Africa. It resembled the KHAIS of the Khoikhoi and was possibly an imitation of it.

Kwabira [kwagira, kulema]. Globular VESSEL FLUTE, with two finger-holes, of the Zamfara Hausa of Nigeria. It is made from baked clay and used by boys for entertainment or for signalling while guarding the crops. The term also applies to a gazelle-horn cone whistle of the Hausa, formerly used by porters as a marching whistle.

Kwacha. *See* CHARA.

Kwadi [lesiba, losiba]. Unbraced MOUTH BOW, sounded

by breath, of the Tswana people of southern Africa. It apparently derives from the GORA of the Khoikhoi, which it closely resembles. It is played by inhaling and exhaling strongly over a piece of quill which connects the string to the stave. The instrument is played by men and boys, and is often carried by herdsmen and travellers. Neighbouring peoples have other names for it: the Sotho, for example, call it LESIBA. See *KirbyMISA*, 180ff, pl.50*a*.

FELICIA M. MUNDELL, DAVID K. RYCROFT

Kwadili. (1) MOUTH BOW of northern Malaita, Solomon Islands.

(2) Term applied to the European JEW'S HARP by the To'abaita people of Malaita, Solomon Islands.

Kwagira. Globular VESSEL FLUTE of the Hausa people of Nigeria. *See* KWABIRA.

Kwai kuo. Tortoise-shell percussion vessel of the Mano people of Liberia. *See* KONO (i).

Kwakwa. A small wooden bench, beaten with two sticks, used by Bush negroes and other blacks in Surinam at religious feasts and rituals.

Kwan. Obsolete double DUCT FLUTE of Korea. According to the treatise *Akhak kwebŏm* (1493) it was 36·6 cm long and had five finger-holes on each of the two identical pipes. The instrument was constructed by shaving each of two bamboo pipes down one side and then binding the tubes together along the flattened sides with silk string. A whistle mechanism was notched into the back of the pipes at the first node from the top. The performer blew both pipes equally and simultaneously, closing pairs of corresponding holes in the two pipes with single fingers. The *kwan* was required to produce the range of a minor 10th, overblowing for the notes in the higher octave. It was considered a Chinese instrument and was used primarily in ritual music (*aak*) ensembles.

The pictograph used to write *kwan* also means simply 'tube', and various musical instruments have apparently shared this name. The modern Chinese GUAN, written the same way, is an oboe.

BIBLIOGRAPHY
Sŏng Hyŏn, ed.: *Akhak kwebŏm* [Guide to the study of music] (Seoul, 1493/*R*1975), 6.12*b*–13*a*

ROBERT C. PROVINE

Kwarya. Inverted half-calabash percussion vessel of the Hausa people of Nigeria. It varies in size and usage. It can be a small half-calabash held against the player's chest and beaten with the fingers of both hands, both with and without rings; this is played by men or women, either singly or with others, to accompany singing. It can also be a larger half-calabash placed on the ground and beaten either with the fingers of both hands or with sticks; this is played either singly or with others to accompany singing, or as rhythmic accompaniment to the single-string *goge* fiddle and the smaller *kukuma* fiddle. The term also denotes any one of three inverted half-calabashes, each known more specifically as *kwaryar kidan ruwa* (calabash for water drumming). The set

comprises a large calabash on a cushion, beaten with the fingers; a small calabash placed on the ground and beaten with a pair of sticks; and a small calabash (*tulluwa*) floating in a bowl of water, beaten with a small stick. See *Ames–KingGHM*.

K. A. GOURLAY

Kwashi. WATER-DRUM of the Kotoko people of Chad. *See* TEMBOL.

Kwatha. Alternative term for the PHALAPHALA side-blown trumpet of the Venda people of southern Africa.

Kwele. Steatite cone whistle of the Kono people of the Ivory Coast. It is used with pot vessels for producing 'spirit voices' of the *poro* cult.

Kwelli. Double-headed drum of the Teda and Daza peoples of Tibesti, Chad. *See* NANGARA.

Kwen. Double metal clapperless bell of the Tiv people of Nigeria. It is used rhythmically in almost every type of music from praise singing and traditional dancing to modern *swange* dance music.

Kwendibe. MUSICAL BOW, with separate gourd resonator, of the Aimeri people of Zaïre (*LaurentyC*, 113). *See* KITINGBI.

Kwengwe. Log XYLOPHONE of the Ngbandi people of Zaïre. *See* PANDINGBWA.

Kwěnxo' (Yuman: 'basket drum'). A household basket used as a drum by the Yuman Indians of the south-western USA. Baskets 35 to 50 cm in diameter and 10 to 15 cm deep, acquired from the neighbouring Papago, were inverted on the ground and struck either with the hands or with beaters made of willow sticks or arrowweed stalks. The willow beater (*nyima' lwakwĭt*), about 38 cm long, consisted of two sticks which were held in the right hand. The arrowweed beater (*isa'vaota'p*) was about 60 cm long and consisted of a bundle of thin stalks tied at one end to form a handle. The beaters were also rattles and were similar to the split-stick rattles of the Indians of California (*see* PAK'PAPA).

The drums were used to accompany singing and dancing. The number of drums depended upon the size of the dance circle. For a small circle, from two to four men would play on one basket; for a larger ceremonial dance, three baskets with four singers at each basket were normally used.
See also TAMOA.

MARY RIEMER-WELLER

Kwese. BULLROARER of the Dakakari people of Nigeria. It is used to represent the voice of Maigiro in the cult of that name.

Kwidi. Bamboo MIRLITON of the Tsangi people of Bas-Zaïre (*LaurentyA*, 35).

Kwigirize. End-blown single-note flute of the Nyoro (Toro) people of Uganda, used in the LUMA stopped flute ensemble.

Kwintangan. *See* KULINTANG.

Kwita. A term used by various peoples of central Africa, including the Chokwe and Pende of Zaïre, for a FRICTION DRUM. The Mbala of Zaïre call this instrument *pwita*, the Suku *pwitta* (or *pwitt*) and the Mbun *nkwit*. In Angola this drum is also known as *tambwe* or *ngoma-nkwita*. A recently recorded Chokwe drum consists of a metal cylinder with a membrane and a wooden bar across the base. The Suku and Mbala use antelope skin for the membrane. Pende drums were formerly used in ritual and warfare.

With the deportation of black slaves to the New World, the friction drum was introduced to Cuba, Brazil, and other parts of Latin America where it is known as *cuíca*, *puíta*, *boi* and *onça*.

BIBLIOGRAPHY
TraceyCSA, ii, 417
F. J. de Hen: *Beitrag zur Kenntnis der Musikinstrumente aus Belgisch Kongo und Ruanda-Urundi* (Tervuren, 1960)
B. Schmidt-Wrenger: *Muziek van de Tshokwe uit Zaïre* (Tervuren, 1975)
K. A. GOURLAY

Kwītra [kwitra]. *See* QUWAYṬARA.

Kwororo. *See* PAKWULO.

Kworria. Calabash drum of the Duka people of Nigeria. *See* BATTA.

Kwotaa. *See* KOTĀH.

Kwur. CONCH-SHELL TRUMPET of Biak island, Irian Jaya, Indonesia. See J. Kunst: *Music in New Guinea* (The Hague, 1967), 134.

Kxab. *See* KHAS.

Kyaa. STAMPING TUBE of the Kamba people of Machakos district, Kenya. It is a hollowed tube of euphorbia wood with a hide cap on the lower end and an attached circlet of metal rattles. It is struck vertically on the ground. See *TraceyCSA*, ii, 361.

Kyanya. Board LAMELLAPHONE of the Luba, Lunda and Chokwe peoples of Zaïre. It has 18 keys arranged in three rows. The board is placed inside a cut-away gourd that serves as resonator. The rows of keys are tuned in octaves; the left thumb plays keys 1 to 8 and the right thumb 9 to 18.

BIBLIOGRAPHY
G. Knosp: *Enquête sur la vie musicale au Congo belge 1934–1935* (Tervuren, 1968)
J. Gansemans: *Les instruments de musique Luba* (Tervuren, 1980)
J. GANSEMANS

Kyegira [kyenuma, kyigira kike]. End-blown single-note flute of the Nyoro (Toro) people of Uganda, used in the LUMA stopped flute ensemble. The three terms denote flutes of different pitch.

Kyì-waìng. Burmese GONG-CHIME of the HSAÌNG-WAÌNG ensemble. It consists of 21 small knobbed gongs strung horizontally on a circular wooden frame (see illustration); they are struck with two buffalo-hide beaters. The

Kyì-waìng (gong-chime) player, Burma

tuning of the gongs can be altered by the application of a mixture of beeswax and lead filings. This is one of the instruments common to South-east Asian percussion ensembles. The circular wooden frame, found in Burma, Thailand, Kampuchea and Laos, contrasts with the straight row found in insular South-east Asia (Indonesia, Kalimantan and the Philippines). Among the Mon people of lower Burma the instrument occurs in another form, with the small knobbed gongs suspended from a U-shaped, upright circular frame.

JUDITH BECKER

Kyì-zi. Percussion plaque of Burma. It consists of a suspended, ornate triangular slab of metal which is struck during religious ceremonies.

Kymbalon (Gk.). CYMBALUM.

Kymbos (Gk.). CYMBALS.

Kyobanggo. Large barrel drum of Korea. It has two large tacked cowhide heads and the depth of the wooden body is only about half the diameter of the heads. The drum is suspended skin-upwards in a four-pole stand by means of four metal rings attached to both drum body and poles. The top head is decorated with a yin–yang symbol in the centre and a multi-coloured pattern around the edge; the body is brightly painted with a dragon motif.

The *kyobanggo* is cited both in the official history of the Koryŏ dynasty (918–1392) and in the treatise *Akhak kwebŏm* (1493); these sources refer to the drum's being used in *tangak* ('Chinese music'). Use of the instrument is now very restricted: it appears only in a court dance called *mugo* ('dance drum'), in which it is struck by the dancers themselves. Strokes on the *kyobanggo* usually reinforce the main left-hand beats on the hourglass drum, CHANGGO.

BIBLIOGRAPHY
Sŏng Hyŏn, ed.: *Akhak kwebŏm* [Guide to the study of music] (Seoul, 1493/*R*1975), 7.2*b* and 8.12*a*, *b*
Chang Sa-hun: *Han'guk akki taegwan* [Korean musical instruments] (Seoul, 1969), 133f

ROBERT C. PROVINE

Kyondo [kiondo]. Cylindrical SLIT-DRUM of Zaïre. The drum of the Luba people is made from a hollowed tree trunk and measures 50 to 60 cm in length by 15 to 20 cm in diameter. Other names reported for slit-drums of this size in Zaïre are *yondo*, *tshondo*, *tshiondo* (*ekole*), and *eshiondo*. Two square holes linked by a slit are cut in the upper part and the sides are so carved that each has a different thickness, producing two tones at an interval of a 2nd or a 3rd. The side giving the highest pitch is called *didimba dilume* ('male side'), the other *didimba dikasi* ('female side'). Two beaters are used in playing the drum. The instrument has three functions: to transmit messages in and around the village; to attract the attention of spirits and bring luck to the players of the men's game *kisolo*, a form of draughts; and to accompany songs and dances as a rhythm instrument. The *kyondo* belongs to the village chief and the best player is at his disposal. Nevertheless, anyone can call upon the player's services provided payment is made. A smaller version of the Luba *kyondo* is known as *kondo* and a larger as *londo*. The Ngbandi MAKILINGU also comes in three sizes.

The *kyondo* is also a cylindrical slit-drum of the Bangubangu, Kamfwa, Holoholo, Mwanza, and Sampwe peoples. The Bangubangu drum is 110 cm long and 53 cm in diameter. The Holoholo *kiondo* is smaller and has square holes at each end of the slit, like the Kondo *yeye*.

The term *kyondo* or *kumvi* is used by the Luba of Ankoro of south-eastern Zaïre for a trapezoidal slit-drum.

BIBLIOGRAPHY
LaurentyTF, 133, 134, 141
J.-N. Maquet: *Note sur les instruments de musique congolais* (Brussels, 1951)
F. J. de Hen: *Beitrag zur Kenntnis der Musikinstrumente aus Belgisch Kongo und Ruanda-Urundi* (Tervuren, 1960)
G. Knosp: *Enquête sur la vie musicale au Congo belge 1934–1935* (Tervuren, 1968)
J. Gansemans: *La musique et son rôle dans la vie sociale et rituelle Luba* (Tervuren, 1978)
——: *Les instruments de musique Luba* (Tervuren, 1980)

J. GANSEMANS, K. A. GOURLAY

Kyos [kuus]. Military KETTLEDRUM of copper or bronze, mentioned in the ancient literature of Azerbaijan. It was so large it had to be transported on the backs of animals; it was played with leather- or fabric-covered mallets, leather thongs or a whip and was used for military signalling and to frighten the enemy in battle – its sound was compared to the rolling of thunder. The term *kyos* is now used for a large NAGARA (double-headed drum). *See also* KÖS and KUS.

Ky pa. Free-reed side-blown aerophone of the highlanders of Vietnam.

Kytte. *See* KIT.

Kyuijibiwa. Japanese term for a lute of the ancient kingdom of Kucha, Central Asia. *See* BIWA.

L

L. Abbreviation occasionally used for LARGAMENTE.

La. Flat gong of Vietnam.

Laala. *See* LALA.

Laba [la-pa] (i). End-blown metal trumpet of the Han Chinese (*la*: a reference to Lamaism; *ba*: used for phonetic value); it is related to the Korean NABAL. Names of related trumpets include *haotong* ('signal pipe'), *tongjiao* ('copper trumpet') and *da tongjiao* ('large copper trumpet'). *Laba* is also popularly used to identify the *suona* oboe. The instruments are usually constructed of copper or an alloy, and may be either straight or with a curved-back flaring bell; they usually have two or three separate sections of tubing which collapse into each other for storage. (The total sounding length of the trumpet is not changed by sliding these sections during performance as it is with the Western trombone.) A hemispherical cup mouthpiece at the blowing end has a characteristic wide flattened rim and a very small cup. Dimensions are not fixed, but for trumpets with curved-back bells the extended length may reach about 110 cm. Introduced from India or Persia into west China, long curved metal trumpets were pictured in Han dynasty (206 BC–AD 220) stone-rubbings as military instruments. Metal trumpets, known as *tongjiao*, were known in the 8th and 9th centuries, and similar instruments under a variety of names (such as those given above) have been described and pictured down to the present day. *Laba*-type horns have served a number of functions: formerly they were military instruments, but more recently they have been used either as outdoor religious (especially funeral) instruments or as backstage opera instruments. In all cases they have been used to celebrate auspicious occasions. *See also* JIAO (i).

BIBLIOGRAPHY

A. C. Moule: 'A List of the Musical and Other Sound-producing Instruments of the Chinese', *Journal of the North-China Branch of the Royal Asiatic Society*, xxxix (Shanghai, 1908), 98

Hayashi Kenzō: *Dongya yueqi kao* [Investigations of East Asian musical instruments] (Beijing, 1962), 352

ALAN R. THRASHER

Laba (ii). Cylindrical single-headed drum of Flores, Indonesia, played with gongs on solemn and festive occasions in the *nggo laba* ensemble. There are two varieties. The *laba dera* is about 40 to 50 cm long and 25 to 30 cm wide. It is made of coconut palm, *tuak* or other wood, and one head is covered with dried horsehide, which is laced to the body with rattan. The other variety, *laba bhegu*, is much narrower, with a body made from bamboo. It is about 75 to 80 cm in height and of variable width (often 15 to 20 cm) depending on the variety of bamboo tube used. Its horsehide head is laced to the body with rattan, and it stands on three legs. It is beaten with two wooden sticks by a standing player.

MARGARET J. KARTOMI

Laba bu [laba buu]. Ensemble of three or four animal-horn trumpets (BU) and two drums (*laba bhegu*) used in the Ngada area of Flores, Indonesia.

Labagh & Kemp. American firm of organ builders, formed in 1872 on the retirement of THOMAS HALL from his partnership with John Labagh.

Laba hu. Modern two-string fiddle of the Han Chinese, found especially in Taiwan (*laba*: end-blown metal trumpet; *hu*: generic term for fiddles). Other names also occur. In this recent invention the normal lower resonator and neck (*see* ERHU) are replaced by a conical metal trumpet with a flaring bell at the top for projection of the tone. The *laba hu* is sometimes used instead of the *erhu* in local instrumental traditions and theatre ensembles of Taiwan.

ALAN R. THRASHER

Laba wai [waning, wani, laba toda]. Cylindrical or slightly barrel-shaped drum of Flores, Indonesia. Its slender wooden or bamboo body stands vertically, on short legs, and is played with two sticks. Its total height is about 60 cm. The skin is tautened by one or two rattan hoops and wooden wedges. It is used to accompany dance, and may be accompanied by gongs, flutes and singing, or xylophone. The *laba toda* is usually played in pairs in the *todagu* ensemble. See J. Kunst: *Music in Flores* (Leiden, 1942), 123f.

MARGARET J. KARTOMI

Labbaye. French family of brass instrument makers. The most important members are Jacques Charles Labbaye (*fl* 1818–30) and his son Jacques Christoph Labbaye (*b* Paris, 15 Oct 1814; *d* after 1878). The older Labbaye was a pupil of Courtois, coming into prominence in 1819 with an exhibition of 'mechanical' horns. His son also entered the business, receiving early recognition at the 1834 Paris exhibition for his ophicleides. After succeeding his father, the younger Labbaye studied the valve horn at the Paris Conservatoire, an experience which considerably helped his manufacturing work. In 1857 he acquired the firm of M. A. Raoux, selling the whole business to François Millereau on 20 August 1878. He continued to work for the firm until his death.

Labbaye senior was one of the leading Parisian makers to champion the use of fully chromatic brass instruments in the first quarter of the 19th century. He constructed a nine-tonality horn after Dupont's patent (1818), which used a slide to operate any of the nine built-in crooks (extant in the Paris Conservatoire). By 1827 he had produced a horn with two improved Stölzel-type valves which won a silver medal at the Paris Industrial Exhibition of 1827. That year he patented a *trompette à ventilateur* with three valves of improved quality, and a bass trumpet (*trompette d'harmonie*). In 1820 he attempted to perfect the ophicleide, giving it 'a strange sound somewhere between the horn, the bassoon and the serpent' (Lavoix, 1878). Labbaye junior exhibited ophicleides in 1834, 1839 and 1844, and produced numerous trombones and trumpets.

BIBLIOGRAPHY
L. A. de Pontécoulant: *Organographie* (Paris, 1861/R1973)
——: *Douze jours à Londres* (Paris, 1862)
H. Lavoix: *Histoire de l'instrumentation depuis le 16e siècle* (Paris, 1878)
C. Pierre: *Le facture instrumentale à l'Exposition universelle de 1889* (Paris, 1890)
——: *Les facteurs d'instruments de musique* (Paris, 1893)
R. Morley-Pegge: *The French Horn* (London, 1960, 2/1973)
A. Baines: *Brass Instruments: their History and Development* (London, 1976/R1980)
NIALL O'LOUGHLIN

La Borde, Jean-Baptiste (Thillaie) de (*b* Nevers, 9 June 1730; *d* Colancelle, late Jan 1777). French physical scientist and mathematician, inventor of the CLAVECIN ÉLECTRIQUE, the first musical instrument to use static electricity as an essential part of the action.

Laddī shāh. Stick rattle of Jammu and Kashmir. *See* ḌAHĀRĀ.

Ladegast, Friedrich (*b* Hochhermsdorf, 30 Aug 1818; *d* Weissenfels, 1 July 1905). German organ builder. He trained under his brother Christlieb in Geringswalde and with Urban Kreutzbach in Borna, Mende in Leipzig and Zuberbier in Dessau; his years as a journeyman gave him first-hand knowledge of instruments by the Silbermann family and by Cavaillé-Coll, with whom he later held a regular exchange of ideas. He set up in business on his own in Weissenfels in 1846. The excellence of his organ at Hohenmölsen (two manuals, 25 stops; extant) led to a contract to repair and enlarge the organ in Merseburg Cathedral. When completed in 1855, this was the largest organ in Germany (four manuals, 81 stops); among those who played it was Liszt, whom it inspired to compose his Prelude and Fugue on *B–A–C–H*. Other major works by Ladegast include the organs of St Nikolai, Leipzig (1858–62; four manuals, 86 stops), Schwerin Cathedral (1866–71; four manuals, 84 stops; extant, unaltered), and the Gesellschaft der Musikfreunde in Vienna (1872; three manuals, 55 stops; the case and pipes standing in the front survive). Ladegast was in the forefront of German organ builders of the 19th century. Unlike such master craftsmen as Walcker and Steinmeyer, he built slider-chests, but went over to the *Kegellade* chest as early as *c*1875, much earlier than Ibach, Klais and Stahlhuth, for instance. He introduced pneumatic action in 1890. Ladegast followed the trends of German Romantic organ building (*see* SCHULZE) both in tone and in the relatively small proportion (by com-

parison with Cavaillé-Coll, for instance) of reeds in the specification. In the scale of his pipes he followed older methods in his early instruments, employing a basic ratio of 1:2 for the diameters of pipes an octave apart (also used by Bédos de Celles), but he later adopted J. G. Töpfer's ratio (*see* ORGAN, §III, 1), at first for the Principal chorus only, eventually for all stops. Ladegast was known in professional circles as the 'Nestor of German organ building'.

BIBLIOGRAPHY
R. Rupp: *Die Entwicklungsgeschichte der Orgelbaukunst* (Einsiedeln, 1929)
W. Ellerhorst: *Handbuch der Orgelkunde* (Einsiedeln, 1936)
H.-G. Wauer: 'Friedrich Ladegast, ein bedeutender Orgelbauer des 19. Jahrhunderts', *Musik und Kirche*, xxv (1955), 293
E. K. Rössler: 'Ladegast', *MGG*
G. Beer: *Orgelbau Ibach Barmen (1794–1904)* (Cologne, 1975)
HANS KLOTZ

Lafleur, Jacques (*b* Nancy, 28 March 1757; *d* Paris, 1832). French violin and bow maker. He served an apprenticeship in both violin and bow making in Mirecourt and went to Paris in 1783. There are a substantial number of violins bearing his label, while his bows, resembling those of the early Adam school, are comparatively rare. His brand, LAFLEUR, was occasionally used by Maire and Pajeot *fils*.

BIBLIOGRAPHY
J. Roda: *Bows for Musical Instruments of the Violin Family* (Chicago, 1959)
E. Vatelot: *Les archets français* (Nancy, 1976)
J. Liivoja: 'The Bows of Lafleur, Maire and Pajeot', *The Strad*, xcii (1981–2), 646
JAAK LIIVOJA-LORIUS

Lafleur, Joseph René (*b* Paris, 9 June 1812; *d* Maisons-Laffitte, nr. Paris, 18 Feb 1874). French bow maker, son of Jacques Lafleur. He appears to have worked initially as a violinist. Details concerning his apprenticeship as a maker do not survive, though he did not learn from his father, whose work he far surpassed. It is reasonable to assume that his earlier career as a violinist afforded him many opportunities to examine and consider a wide range of transitional and post-transitional bows. This would explain his early tendencies towards experimentation with shaft resistance and flexibility and the use of a 'pikes-head' tip. His later association with Nicolas Maire, who had assumed management of Jacques Lafleur's workshop after his death, probably resulted in a further apprenticeship of sorts. Following this period the 'pikes-head' tips are modified, although a certain elongation remains. His mature work possesses playing qualities of the highest order. His bows are occasionally branded LAFLEUR; it is also possible that a certain amount of his work bears the brand of Nicolas Maire.

BIBLIOGRAPHY
J. Roda: *Bows for Musical Instruments of the Violin Family* (Chicago, 1959)
E. Vatelot: *Les archets français* (Nancy, 1976)
J. Liivoja: 'The Bows of Lafleur, Maire and Pajeot', *The Strad*, xcii (1981–2), 646
JAAK LIIVOJA-LORIUS

Lagalogo. Clapperless bell of the Edo/Bini people of Nigeria. *See* AGOGO.

Lage (Ger.). In string playing, position playing or position fingering. The equivalent term in the 18th century was *Applicatur*. *See* APPLICATION.

Laghouto. *See* LAOUTO.

Lagoncinha, Manoel de Sá Couto. *See* SÁ COUTO, MANOEL DE.

Lag-rnga. FRAME DRUM of Tibet. *See* RNGA.

Lagwìn. *See* YAGWÌN.

Lahutë. Single-string fiddle of north Albania, used by epic singers for accompanying heroic songs and epics. It is made from one piece of wood and has a skin sound-table. The string is stopped from the side by the fingers or nails because there is no fingerboard on the neck; it is bowed with a strong curved horsehair bow. The *lahutë* is held vertically on the knees and is normally made by the singer himself, who is often a semi-professional musician. It is analogous to the Yugoslav *gusle*.

Laisser vibrer (Fr.: 'let vibrate'). A performing direction instructing that the sound should not be damped. It is found in music for the harp, certain percussion instruments (notably cymbals), the piano (indicating that the sustaining pedal should remain depressed) and occasionally string instruments.

Lai waghe. Clarinet of Nias, Indonesia. *See* IYUP-IYUP.

Laka (i). MIRLITON of the Baule people of the Ivory Coast. It is used to produce a spirit voice in conjunction with the *sro*, an earthenware vessel filled with water into which the musician blows through a reed. The spirit is invoked by the striking of a clapperless bell and its 'voice' is accompanied by a second bell, two gourd rattles and two empty calabashes struck against the hand. See H. Zemp: 'Baule Vocal Music', Odeon 3C 064 17842 [disc notes].

Laka (ii). Chilean PANPIPES of pre-Columbian origin. They are found in ensembles in the Andean region of Tarapacá, the northernmost province of Chile.

Lakita [laquita]. PANPIPES of the Bolivian Alti Plano. They are usually played in pairs at certain religious and community feasts. At the feast of the Virgen de la Concepción (8 December) four musicians play *lakitas* with the left hand while beating with the right a drum known as a *wankara*. *Lakitas* may have a single rank of seven or eight tubes, or two ranks, the second serving as resonating tubes and as physical support for the played rank. There are two ensemble groupings. The first comprises (in descending order of size) two pairs of *sanjas*, three pairs of *likus* and one pair of *ch'ilis*; the second comprises one pair of *sanjas* (or *jach'as*), one pair of *malas*, two pairs of *likus* and one pair of *ch'ilis*. They are played *ira* and *arca* (*see* IRA (i)), using hocket technique. See M. P. Baumann: 'Música andina de Bolivia', LPLI/S-062 [disc notes]. *See also* LLAKITA.

Lal. End-blown stopped pipe of the Sara-Kaba people of Chad. *See* NAL.

Lala [laala]. A pair of L-shaped stick rattles of the Fulani (Fula or Fulbe) people of West Africa. Each rattle is a type of sistrum with discs of calabash loosely threaded on one arm, while the other arm forms a handle. With variations short rhythmic patterns are repeated indefinitely. The name derives from *laalawal* or *laalagal* ('piece of broken gourd'); other related names include *lalajo*, a stick rattle of the Hausa people of Nigeria (*see* KACIKAURA).

Lalango. Unbraced MUSICAL BOW of the Apagibiti people of Zaïre (*LaurentyC*, 113).

Lali. SLIT-DRUM of Fiji and Western Polynesia. It is believed to have originated in Fiji, where it is the only

A pair of lali (slit-drums) from Bau Island, Tailevu, Fiji, 1959

form of slit-drum, and to have spread from there as part of the normal equipment of the sea-going double canoe. In Fiji large instruments of hardwood up to 1·8 or even 2·7 metres are used. They have a characteristic trough or canoe shape and are beaten with two sticks for signalling. Formerly they were played to signal events of social significance such as wars, victories, births and deaths. Nowadays they are used to call people together for church services or other meetings. Generally a pair of instruments is used, one larger than the other, and they are played either by two players or by one person standing between them. The sound can be heard for up to 8 km or even further. A smaller type, the *lali ni meke*, is played singly to accompany chants and dances; the best sound is thought to be produced by cradling it in the arms at chest level while another person beats it, the chest cavity adding to the resonance.

In Tonga large *lali* (1·6 to 2 metres long) are used to call meetings and to announce church services. They are played in pairs of unequal size and pitch, one drummer to an instrument, each with two sticks (*kautā*). Smaller *lali faiva* (equivalent to the Fijian *lali ni meke*) are used to accompany dance. In Uvea and Futuna the *lali* is 1·2 to 1·8 metres long and is played in pairs with a single beater to announce meetings. In Samoa it is the middle-sized of the several slit-drums used there, with an average length of 1 metre (*see also* LOGO, NAFA, (1) and PĀTĒ). It is used to call villagers together and is played in pairs (called *tatasi* and *talua*), each with its own player using two sticks ('*autā*). The Samoan *lali* has a narrower and shallower slit than those of Fiji and Tonga. Tokelau instruments are similar to those of Samoa but are beaten with one stick, or by two people, each with a single beater. Here also they are used for calling people to meetings.

BIBLIOGRAPHY

W. Deane: *Fijian Society* (London, 1921), 196ff
E. G. Burrows: *Ethnology of Futuna* (Honolulu, 1936), 211
——: *Ethnology of Uvea* (Honolulu, 1937), 145
G. MacGregor: *Ethnology of Tokelau Islands* (Honolulu, 1937), 74
G. K. Roth: *Fijian Way of Life* (Melbourne, 1953), 29ff
R. Moyle: 'Samoan Musical Instruments', *EM*, xviii (1974), 59
——: 'Tongan Musical Instruments', *GSJ*, xxx (1977), 87ff

CHRIS THOMPSON SAUMAIWAI, MERVYN McLEAN

Lalo. Clapper bell of the Gio people of Liberia. *See* GBWINI.

Lamba [bedug] **(i).** GOBLET DRUM of Flores, Indonesia. It rests vertically on a horizontal base. The larger variety is called *lamba ria* and the smaller, and most commonly used, is called *lamba loo*. The latter is played on festive and solemn occasions in the *nggo lamba* ensemble, with six gongs. Its body, about 71 cm in height, is made from coconut palm or other wood. The head, about 22 cm in diameter, is made of goatskin and laced with rattan on to the lower part of the body cup. The stem, about 7 cm high, is attached to a wooden base about 18 cm by 2 cm, to which another wooden base, about 18 cm by 5 cm, is attached underneath, with a short wooden neck between the two bases. It is played with two wooden sticks.

MARGARET J. KARTOMI

Lamba (ii). KETTLEDRUM of the Wolof people of Senegal and the Gambia. *See* GORONG.

Lambda. A STRING SYNTHESIZER manufactured by Keio of Tokyo as part of the KORG range.

Lambeg drum. A large double-headed drum associated with the Ulster Orange Order of Northern Ireland. Approximately 90 cm in diameter, 75 cm in depth and weighing about 20 kg, it traditionally accompanies fife tunes in Orange processions. Among the many myths about its origin is one that it was introduced by Duke Schomberg's troops at the time of the Battle of the Boyne (1690). However, its name probably derives from the first use of such a drum at a demonstration about 1894 in the village of Lambeg near Belfast. The 'Lambeg', as it is colloquially known, is beaten with bamboo canes: earlier drums were smaller and beaten with boxwood drumsticks.

Although the fife-and-drum bands, playing reel, jig or hornpipe tunes in march time, have largely been replaced by brass bands in the towns, the drum and its playing art have survived, mainly as a sport or hobby, and the Lambeg still accompanies certain processions in country districts and in Ballymena. Regularly in the summer there are Lambeg drumming contests in which solo drummers display the good tone or 'ring' of their drums and their skill in maintaining and ornamenting traditional rhythms. Each district of Ulster has its own march-rhythm dialects based on traditional dance rhythms. Some are based on popular songs. Ex.1 illustrates the relationship between a Lambeg rhythm and its fife tune.

Ex.1 *Boyne Water*, transcr. F. Scullion

Two families, Johnson and Hewitt, have traditionally been responsible for the manufacture and maintenance of Lambeg drums, though the hard-wearing oak shells need little attention; many drummers have learnt to recover their own shells with the traditional goatskin. Before World War II occasional 'stick-ins' were held in which champion drummers, often representing rival families, faced each other in a test of endurance and strength, playing for up to nine hours at a time as the one attempted to outlast the other or to confuse his rhythm.

FIONNUAGHLA SCULLION

Lambert, Herbert. English clavichord maker, active in Bath in the early 20th century; his instruments served as models for those built by THOMAS GOFF.

Lambertini. Portuguese firm of piano makers. Luigi Gioacchino Lambertini (*b* Bologna, 17 March 1790; *d* Lisbon, 13 Nov 1864) was a fellow student of Rossini at the Liceo Musical Giambattista Martini, Bologna. He emigrated to Lisbon for political reasons in 1836, and started his piano-making business, receiving a prize for his instruments in 1838. In 1860, under the direction of his sons Evaristo and Ermete Lambertini, the firm became Lambertini Filhos & Ca., selling and publishing music as well as making pianos. The firm later became Lambertini & Irmão. Evaristo's son, Michel' Angelo Lambertini, was a fine pianist and founded the Grande Orchestra Portuguesa in 1906. The firm closed in 1922. See *DPB*.

MARGARET CRANMER

Lambi. A Jamaican CONCH-SHELL TRUMPET. It is used to summon workers to a 'digging match' (cooperative work session).

Lamellaphone. A term for an instrument whose sound is produced essentially by the vibration of thin lamellae (Lat. *lamella*, from *lamina*: 'a thin plate or layer') or tongues (hence the term 'linguaphone') of metal, wood or other material. It is classified by Hornbostel and Sachs as a plucked idiophone (for details, *see* IDIOPHONE; but see §1 below), along with the jew's harp and the European musical box; 'lamellaphone' is not however applied to free-reed aerophones like the accordion or the mouth organ.

Various European terms have been applied to this essentially African instrument, for example thumb piano, hand piano, linguaphone ('glottophone' might also be appropriate) and 'sanza'. Some common African names are *mbira*, *kalimba*, *likembe* and *sansi* or *kisaanj*.

1. General. 2. Central, southern and eastern Africa: (i) Marimba types (ii) Mbira types (iii) Likembe types. 3. West Africa. 4. Latin America.

1. GENERAL. Though construction details vary greatly, the African lamellaphone consists basically of a set of tuned tongues, made of metal, bamboo or other vegetable, fitted to a box or calabash resonator or a plain board so that one end of each tongue can vibrate freely. Most board types are usually further resonated during play by holding or propping them inside or on top of a section of a gourd or a bowl of some kind. The timbre of most lamellaphones is frequently modified by means of shell or metal rattling devices attached to the board or the resonator, or both, or by means of small metal sleeves which vibrate freely at the base of the tongues. Sometimes the desired buzzing sound is produced by a mirliton fitted over a small hole in the instrument.

The term 'plucked idiophone', though frequently used, is not strictly accurate, for the lamellae are not plucked; their free ends are depressed and released by the player, who may use his thumbs and fingers, or, more rarely, just one or two of his fingers. The tuning arrangement of the keys is important in distinguishing between some instrumental types, but generally the keyboard is arranged to facilitate the production of the desired sound pattern when its notes are divided between the two hands. The lamellaphone is commonly used to accompany song; it is often played solo by a singer, or in small groups to accompany a singer who again is usually one of the players. In some cases, however, it appears that the music is purely instrumental, as in the case of the Nsenga *kalimba*, the sound patterns of different melodies being produced by similar motor patterns. These patterns are often based on separate rhythms common to the music of the particular society.

In several parts of Africa, xylophones and lamellaphones are linked by terminology, and it has been suggested by Nurse (1970) that this results from the similar shape of the sounding agents. Jones (1964) suggested that lamellaphones are the portative equivalents of xylophones, and, in those societies where one name is used for both types of instrument, lamellaphones are often distinguished by the use of a diminutive prefix, or by adding an adjective. Thus, in Tanzania xylophones are called *marimba*, and lamellaphones are called *marimba madogo* ('small marimba'). *See also* MARIMBA.

2. CENTRAL, SOUTHERN AND EASTERN AFRICA. Three sets of names for lamellaphones are notable for their frequent appearance and wide distribution, though a survey of 467 instruments collected in Zaïre (*LaurentyS*) shows a far greater variety of types and terminology for that country alone. The first set of names, found in an extensive area of eastern and south-east Africa, uses the stem *rimba* or *limba* ('r' and 'l' are one phoneme in many Bantu dialects) with a variety of prefixes, as, for instance, in *cilimba*, *kalimba* and *marimba*. The form *marimba* is preferred in this article for referring to instruments of this group. A second set of names is found in the Zimbabwe or lower Zambezi culture area, where the instrument is commonly termed *mbira* or *mbila*, a term to which extensions of various kinds may be added, as in *mbira dza vadzimu*, *mbira dza vaNdau* and *mbila deza*, to indicate the specific instrument. However, the word *mbira* (*mbila*) also occurs with various plural prefixes to indicate xylophones, as in *timbila*, *dimbila* and *mambira*, as well as with reduplication as in *mambirira*. Nevertheless, the word 'mbira' is used in this article for referring to the Zimbabwe and lower Zambezi group of lamellaphones. A third set of names comprises those based on the stem *kembe*, as in *dikembe*, *ikembe*, *likembe* and *lukeme*. The members of this group are small, box-resonated instruments that are generally of Zaïrean origin. In this article the term 'likembe' is preferred for referring to the members of this group. Laurenty includes another large category of calabash-resonated board instruments most often called *kakolondondo*, as well as a wide range of lamellaphones whose names are derived from the Bantu root 'sanj-' or 'sanz-'. This root was the inspiration for Montandon's designation 'sanza' (1919), since used by many scholars as a general term for lamellaphones; *see* KISAANJ for a fuller list of names with this root.

(i) Marimba types. The term 'marimba', with a variety of prefixes, is used by many Bantu societies in wide areas of eastern and south-east Africa and in parts of the Angola–Zaïre region to denote both xylophones and lamellaphones. The singular form usually denotes a one-note xylophone. In such languages in Malawi as Chewa and Yao the term 'limba' conveys the notion of a flattish object sticking out (Nurse, 1970). In the wide inland region of Tanzania the term 'marimba' or 'malimba' is used exclusively for lamellaphones.

The largest instruments occur among the Gogo of the Central Province of Tanzania: their *ilimba* consists of a rectangular soundbox which is made not from one piece of hollowed-out wood (as are the box-resonated lamellaphones in central Africa) but of top and side parts nailed or glued together. The box has two soundholes, one at the back for the left middle finger to generate vibrato effects, the other in the centre of the soundboard, which is covered with a membrane from a spider's web that produces a humming or droning effect, particularly when deep notes are sounded. Gogo instruments vary in size and have 19 to 36 lamellae. They are usually decorated with brass nails, beads and pieces of animal skin and are played either solo or in groups of two or three, sometimes in combination with other instruments. Large lamellaphones called *malimba* also occur in southern Malawi and central Mozambique, particularly in the lower Shire–Zambezi valley. They are played by Sena, Zimba and Podzo musicians (see fig.1). These instruments have a bell-shaped body and usually 26 notes arranged in two ranks. The body is propped inside a large calabash with two sticks or pieces of river reed. Pieces of shell are attached to the gourd resonator to give a buzzing sound quality. The playing technique entails using both thumbs and the right index finger, the latter sounding certain notes in upward movement. In playing techniques and organology the Shire–Zambezi lamellaphones are related to the *mbira* types.

Among the Pangwa, Kinga, Bena, Kisi and Nyakyusa of south-western Tanzania the name 'malimba' is given to a small box-resonated instrument with eight lamellae made of umbrella ribs. This instrument is similar to the *likembe* types but lacks the characteristically cut-out section of the top of the *likembe* and the metal sleeves. Instead a chain of beads or metal links lies across the keyboard to give the desired buzzing sound. Furthermore, the Pangwa *malimba* is made not from one piece of wood but from two; a trough-shaped resonator is covered with a separate board nailed or glued to it. At the back of the body is a soundhole which the left middle finger alternately covers and opens to produce 'timbre-melodies'. This technique is highly developed among Pangwa and Kisi musicians. This instrument (see fig.2) is often used during long walks in the Livingstone mountains and on the Njombe plateau.

Virtually the same instrument is called *kalimba* by the Tumbuka of Malawi, the diminutive prefix *ka-* referring to the smallness of the instrument. The *kalimba* of the Nsenga of Zambia is, however, quite different. It is also very small, but has a shovel-shaped soundboard which is played over a small gourd. Its 14 notes are laid out

2. Malimba of the Kisi people of south-western Tanzania

in two ranks and a hole made in the middle of the soundboard is covered by a spider's-web mirliton. Blacking (1961) reported the Nsenga *kalimba* as an instrument for youths who would often play it when walking alone or with friends; he found certain recurrent patterns of 'fingering'.

(ii) Mbira types. In the singular the term 'mbira' is used for several types of large gourd-resonated lamellaphone found in the Zimbabwe and lower Zambezi culture region of south-east Africa. In north-eastern Zambia and southern Zaïre the same term denotes single-note xylophones. When used for lamellaphones the word has a plural significance meaning 'the notes' of a single instrument or, as in the case of the Podzo *malimba*, a certain section of the keyboard only.

The name 'mbira' was first reported in João dos Santos's *Ethiopia oriental* (1609). Dos Santos was a Dominican priest who arrived on the Mozambique coast in 1586 and travelled up the Zambezi river to the trading posts of Sena and Tete. He wrote extensively about music in Mozambique and described instruments called *ambira*, referring to gourd-resonated xylophones and to lamellaphones 'all made of irons about a palm in length, tempered in the fire so that each has a different sound'.

The *mbira dza vadzimu* is considered to be an ancient form of lamellaphone played by the Shona-speaking peoples in southern Africa. It is used mainly for religious ceremonies for ancestors; the terms 'mbira dza vadzimu' (in the Zezuru dialect) and 'mbira dze midzimu' (Karanga) mean 'notes of the ancestral spirits'. It is closely related to the HERA or *matepe*, another type of large lamellaphone which is also played for the *vadzimu* by Korekore, by Sena–Tonga musicians of Zimbabwe and by the Tavara and Nyungwe of Mozambique. The instrument is large, usually with 22 or 23 metal lamellae. Two distinguishing features of this type are its tray-shaped body and the hole in the lower right-hand corner of the soundboard; the hole enables the player to hold his instrument by hooking the little finger of his right hand into it (see fig.3). The instrument is wedged inside

1. Malimba of the Zimba people of southern Malawi

a calabash with two pieces of river reed or stick which are placed on the lamellae just above the straining bar and wedged tightly under the lip of the calabash. The calabash is called *deze*, a name which is also often used for the instrument itself. Another distinctive characteristic is the arrangement of the keys; all the treble notes are on the right-hand side and all the bass notes on the left (A. Tracey, 1963). On the left-hand side the notes are arranged in two ranks. The tuning plan is also distinctive, the keys being tuned to a nearly equidistant heptatonic scale. Tracey suggested a close relationship in the tuning pattern between the *mbira dza vadzimu* and the eight-note *kalimba* which occurs north of the Zambezi; he wrote, 'at the centre of the *mbira dza vadzimu* there is a *kalimba*'. This would account for a certain irregularity in the tuning pattern of the former. On the *mbira dza vadzimu* (see fig.4) the *kalimba* layout is, however, reversed left to right.

The *mbira dza vadzimu* is played with the two thumbs and the right-hand index finger. The playing action is described by Zezuru musicians as *kukwenya* ('to scratch', 'to strike'). The thumbs play in the normal manner while the right index finger 'scratches' the six reeds of its playing area (outer right) in an upward movement. Zezuru songs for the *mbira dza vadzimu* are all the same length with 48 elementary pulses making up the total pattern for this form. The music is based on chord sequences, the most important regulative feature in Shona *mbira* music (A. Tracey, 1963). The *mbira dza vadzimu* is often a duet instrument. Two or more players form a group, and rattles known to the Zezuru as *hosho* are played with the *mbira* ensemble in ancestor-cult rituals, in which rattles stress the three-pulse rhythm. A full performance includes various voices, used in three or four different styles and pitches, including *kuhongera* ('singing the bass'), humming and *kunguridzira* ('yodelling'). The first part of the music is called *kushaura* ('to start', 'to lead') and is usually played by the junior musician. Any following part is called *kutsinhira* ('to sing a refrain', 'to exchange notes').

In 1872 Carl Mauch, a German traveller and geologist, saw a *mbira dze midzimu* of a Karanga musician at Pika's village near Zimbabwe (Bernhard, 1969). In a diary note of 13 March he described the instrument and its music, gave a sketch of its tuning (see fig.5) and notated some melodies. This tuning is identical with a tuning observed 88 years later by A. Tracey in the area surrounding Salisbury (now Harare; Tracey, 1963; Kubik, 1971).

In the 1930s there were few players of the *mbira dze midzimu*, and in the Karanga-speaking area it has been replaced by the *njari*, another type of large lamellaphone, imported from the Sena–Nyungwe group of peoples at Tete, Mozambique. However, the *mbira dze midzimu* survived among the Zezuru, who live in the area around Harare, and there are now a great number of players, some of them organized into *mbira* clubs.

The *mbila dza madeza* of the Venda in northern Transvaal, South Africa, is similar to the Zezuru *mbira dza vadzimu*. It also occurs among the Lemba and was probably imported into Vendaland. This large calabash-resonated instrument is heptatonic and has 27 notes. It is often used to accompany songs at beer parties and is also played by men other than Lemba. Three instruments are often played together. Another Venda type is called the *mbila tshipai*. It has 11 to 18 lamellae and a pentatonic tuning. According to some oral traditions, both

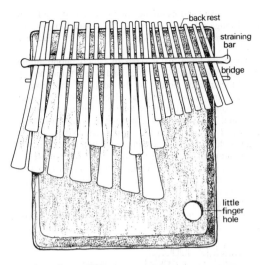

3. *Mbira dza vadzimu*

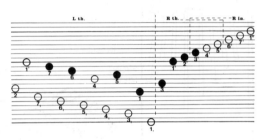

4. *Tuning pattern of the mbira dza vadzimu (the kalimba core is shown in black)*

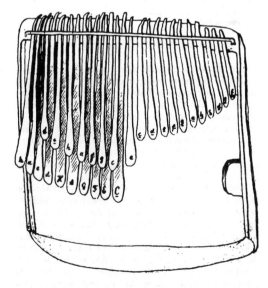

5. *Carl Mauch's sketch (1872) of the mbira dze midzimu of a Karanga musician, Zimbabwe*

the instrument and its tuning pattern were borrowed from the Tsonga who live to the south of the Venda. This small *mbila* is usually played by boys (see Blacking, 1965).

There are three major types of lamellaphone among the Ndau: the *tomboji* or 'highland type', found around the Mozambique border to the south of the town of Umtali, and played mostly by older people; the *danda*, a development of the older *tomboji*, the most common type and played by young people; and the *utee*, characterized by soft, flexible, deep notes. Ndau lamellaphones differ from the Shona types both in tuning and in layout of the notes; furthermore, they are not used in religious contexts. The tuning pattern shows two very small and four very large intervals within a hexatonic division of the octave.

Other closely related kinds of lamellaphone in southeastern Africa include the *njari huru* of the Kunda, the *hera* of the Korekore, the *malimba* of the Zimba and

likembe a specific term in these languages.

The *likembe* is a distinct kind of lamellaphone; the origin and etymology of the word are uncertain. 162 specimens of this type form the most important group out of Laurenty's total of 467 lamellaphones, collected in 1904–58 for the Musée Royal de l'Afrique Central in Tervuren, Belgium. They indicate how popular *makembe* may have been during the first half of the 20th century in the vast Congo region. In the 1970s the *likembe* was known all over Zaïre, in the Republic of the Congo, various parts of the Central African Republic, the southeast corner of Cameroon, north-western Zambia, eastern and south-eastern Angola, the southern Sudan, most parts of Uganda, parts of Rwanda and Burundi and in border areas of western Tanzania.

The *likembe* (see fig.6) has a distinctive cut-out section projecting from one end of the hollowed-out box. Instrument makers usually begin by cutting out this top section from a log of hard, dry wood (in southern Zaïre,

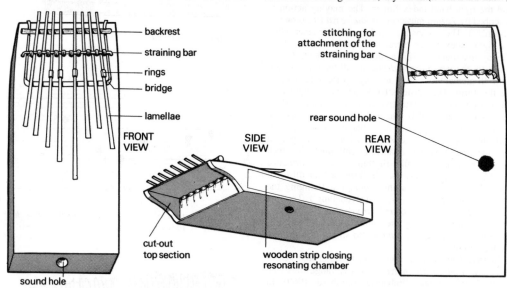

backrest
straining bar
rings
bridge
lamellae

FRONT VIEW   SIDE VIEW   REAR VIEW

stitching for attachment of the straining bar

rear sound hole

cut-out top section   wooden strip closing resonating chamber

sound hole

6. *Front, side and rear views of a likembe*

Podzo, the *mana embudzi* (also called the *mbira dza vaTonga*) and the *nyonganyonga*. Tracey believes that the ten or more types of lamellaphone that occur in this region are, like the *mbira dza vadzimu*, all descended from one instrument, the eight-note *kalimba*.

(iii) Likembe types. Likembe (plural *makembe*) is the most common form of a name given to a distinctive type of box-resonated lamellaphone of Zaïrean (Congolese) origin. Members of some language groups give other prefixes to the stem, for example *dikembe* and *ikembe*, or omit the prefix, as in the *kembe* played by the Mpiemo of the Central African Republic. Speakers of Sudanic or Nilotic languages deformed even the word stem when they adopted the instrument, e.g. *lukeme* in Acholi (northern Uganda); others have given it an entirely different name. This instrument is also often referred to by the generic term '-sanji' (*esanji*, *chisanji*, *kisaanj* etc). Among Ngangela, Luchazi, Mbwela and Mbunda speakers of south-eastern Angola and north-western Zambia the full term 'chisandzi cha likembe' is often used. This establishes that *chisandzi* is the generic and

Zambia and Angola the wood most frequently used is *Pterocarpus angolensis*); the box is then hollowed out, usually from the left side, but in some areas from both. Before closing the resonating chamber with a thin strip of wood the maker usually inserts a few small pieces of glass, one or two bottle-tops or small stones to create additional vibration when the instrument is played. The wooden strip, sometimes made from eucalyptus, is glued in place with wax. Two soundholes are burnt into the body of the *likembe*, one in the end closest to the player's body, the other in the back. By alternately opening and closing the back hole with the middle finger of the left hand the musician produces timbre modifications, vibrato and 'wow' effects. This is regarded as the most difficult part of the playing technique, as the middle finger often moves in a counter-rhythm to the motor patterns of the thumbs. The lamellae, straining bar and bridge of the *likembe* are of forged iron. Eight to 12 lamellae are commonly used and, in contrast to some other types of lamellaphone, the width of each does not vary throughout its length. The ends are filed smooth in order not to hurt the player's thumbs. A strong straining bar is stitched to the projecting section of the soundboard and holds the lamellae down between bridge and backrest. The latter, a piece of hard wood, is held in place solely by the pressure of the lamellae. Layout of the lamellae and tuning plan vary from region to region but one arrangement seems to be particularly widespread: the lower-pitched, longer lamellae are in the centre, but a further bass note with a long lamella is added at the extreme right (see fig.6). Buzzing metal rings, which are usually threaded on to the lower-pitched keys, are another important feature. Musicians often aim at obtaining an accentuation of certain notes and note patterns by their careful distribution of such buzzing devices.

Montandon (1919) called the *likembe* 'type Bangala et du Bas-Congo', associating it with Lingala-speaking peoples of the Lower Congo. Maes (1921) called this 'sanza' the 'type fluvial' and confirmed that it was already in existence among the Ngala before the arrival of the Belgians, though he could not say whether it originated there or in the Lower Congo. Coquilhat, the first Belgian agent in this territory, described the *likembe* in his writings about the Upper Congo (1888). According to LaurentyS the Kongo and the Ngala probably carried this instrument across the Congo. In the decade before World War I the *likembe* was well established along the Congo River (among the Kongo, Mfinu and Teke peoples) and as far up as Kisangani (formerly Stanleyville). It was known among the Loi and Mbuja and had also already spread along the Ubangi River, where it was collected several times from Ngbaka musicians in the years 1911–13, and from the Ngbandi. In the south it was known in the Kasai region at that time.

Evidence suggests that the *likembe* is a relatively recent offshoot of the lamellaphone family, and has become widespread in many territories only since the late 19th century. In Zaïre it was played mainly for personal diversions during long journeys on foot; its melodic motor patterns combined with the rhythm of walking to sustain the traveller for long distances. Being thus favoured by porters, workers and servants it quickly spread across the continent during the period of European exploration and colonization. The process quickened with the onset of vast labour migrations, as men travelled to the mines and the new industrial and agricultural centres. There were two processes: in the first, workers who came from *likembe*-playing societies introduced the instrument into a new region; in the second, workers from societies not playing the *likembe* adopted the instrument at their place of work and later introduced it to their home areas.

A chronology of the recent spread of the *likembe* can be reconstructed from the still abundant oral traditions of central and east Africa. For example, one independent Ganda informant, Ephraim Bisase (*b* 1912; see Kubik, 1976), related that the instrument was played in his youth by the Alur, a Nilotic people settled in northwestern Uganda, who had adopted it from the Congo. The Alur went to Buganda as porters and agricultural workers, playing and singing to their lamellaphones in the Luganda tongue, 'Maria, jangu, tugende Kongo' ('Maria, come, let us go to Congo'). Consequently people in Buganda named the new instrument *kongo-maria*. Bisase first heard this expression in Mengo (Buganda) as a schoolboy in 1924. The Alur lamellaphones were small, and when the Soga, a Bantu-speaking people living to the east of the Ganda, adopted these instruments from the Alur, they called them *budongo* (plural of

kadongo). This term derives from the word 'ndongo', the name the Ganda and Soga use for the bowl lyre, an instrument well established in this area, and the diminutive prefix 'ka'. In Busoga it is used as a group instrument: a *kadongo* ensemble often comprises three to five lamellaphones of different sizes and a flat container rattle. In 1929 Tucker found the *likembe* firmly established among the Zande of southern Sudan; again, it was associated with porters. Later it spread further north to the town of Wau and north-east to the Ethiopian border. After 1945 the *likembe* lost much of its popularity in Zaïre when the guitar appeared and began to assume a similar social role, being often used on journeys. In Kinshasa in the 1950s the *likembe* was sometimes combined with the guitar in small dance bands playing rumba music but it disappeared from modern Congolese bands with the introduction of electrically amplified instruments.

The spread of the *likembe* has not halted everywhere. In the remote south-eastern parts of Angola it is still advancing and has been played by Mbwela and Luchazi musicians only since the 1950s. Young workers who travelled north to work on Portuguese plantations adopted it from the Chokwe and Lwena, hence many of their songs are in one of these languages.

3. WEST AFRICA. Although both box- and gourd-resonated lamellaphones are found in West Africa, the distribution of the instrument is not as widespread as in Bantu-speaking Africa. Lamellaphones in this part of Africa include the Tikar *mbo nggo* and the Vute *timbrh* in Cameroon; the Yoruba *agidigbo*, the Edo/Bini *akpata* and the Igbo *ubo* in Nigeria; the Songhay *jidiga* in Niger; the Ashanti *prempensua* in Ghana; the Kpelle *gbelee* and *kongoma* and the Gola *bonduma* in Liberia; and the *kondi* and *kongoma* in Sierra Leone. These instruments may have spread into the West African coastal zone via Cameroon. With a few exceptions, like the Edo *akpata* and some of the larger instruments such as the *kongoma* of Sierra Leone and Liberia, used in ensembles, the lamellaphone is used for personal music-making, and is sometimes considered merely a child's instrument. On the whole, it is overshadowed by the historical, social and religious significance of other instruments.

4. LATIN AMERICA. During the 19th century lamellaphones were taken by African slaves to various parts of the New World. Ewbank reported its great popularity among Africans in Rio de Janeiro in 1856 and described a calabash-resonated instrument similar to that in fig.1. The instrument has also been reported in Louisiana and as far south as Montevideo, Uruguay, where in the 1950s it was still known as *quisanche*, which is the Zaïrean 'chisanji' (*see* KISAANJI). Variants of the name 'marimba', reported by Ewbank as in common use in Brazil by Africans of Mozambique origin, have been reported in the Caribbean; there the instrument is still very popular, whereas in South America it appears to be obsolescent.

A survey (1952–5) of Afro-Cuban instruments mentions the small type, commonly held in the lap of seated performers (*OrtizIMA*). But by the 1970s the large box-resonated instrument, the size and shape of a small suitcase, was apparently much more popular. Thompson (1971) described its manufacture and use in the Caribbean area in some detail. He reported that in Haiti and Dominica the instruments usually have three or four steel tongues, whereas in Cuba and Puerto Rico they have ten or more. They are usually made from lengths of discarded gramophone spring, but clock springs and saw- or knife-blades have also been used. The player sits on the instrument, reaching down to sound the keys with the fingers of one hand while beating out sometimes complex rhythms on the sides and front of the box with the other hand. The MARÍMBULA (a common name-variant in this area) serves as a rhythmic and harmonic bass instrument in folk and commercial popular dance ensembles, the keyboard being divided from the centre so that two sets of notes (each sounding, for example, the tonic, supertonic and dominant degrees of a scale) provide tolerable bass harmony for two or more different tonalities, keeping the need for extreme changes of hand position to a minimum. Used in this manner the instrument serves as a robust and portable 'poor man's string bass' (Thompson, 1971).

In Jamaica, where it is known as the 'rumba-box', the instrument is also used in the ensembles of religious groups such as the Rastafarians. Like the *prempensua* in Ghana it serves to replace drums.

The following lamellaphones are entered in this dictionary: abele; abengu; abole; abongwa; agbomboya; agidigbo; ahyewa adaka; akadongo k'abaluru; akpata; ambira; bandakwi; bass box; bene; bisanji; bonduma; bolo; budongo; bukongo; chikelekele; chilimba; chirimba; chisanji; chitengane; cilimba; danda; deza; dikadi; dikembe; djigbwangi; djikembi; djimba; dongo; ebim; ebongei; ebumba; eenya; egbongu; ekembi; ekumba; ekwongolia; elenge; esamo; esanjo; ezanza; gbeketele; gbelee; giangbwa; gibinji; gidigbo; gidirigo; gruzavewonigi; guere; hera; ibeka; ikelekele; ikembe; ikoko (ii); ikpa; ikpa mboto; ilimba; imbembb; indimba; inkoko (i); inkota; irimba; isangi; isanj; isanzi; jidiga; kabarome; kabwaye; kadimba; kadongo; kajimba; kakolondondo; kalimba (i); kangombio; kankobela; karimba; kasandji; kathandi; kaueya; kembe; kesangi; kiana; kibinjj; kidebe; kilimba; kimbi; kirimba; kisaanji; kishyaata; kitutu; kondi; kone; konggoma; kongo; kongoma; kongo-maria; kota; kote; kulongbe; kyanya; lekemba; libeke; libelenge; likembe; likimbi; likwengu; lkimbi; lobiko; longombe (i); losokio; losukia; lugungu; lukangu; lukeme; lulimba; lungandu; lusukia; madaku; madedoku; madimba (ii); madoku; magbomboyo; magbua; malimba; malobia; mambamboli; mana embudzi; mandoku; mangele; manimba; marimba; marimbe; marímbula; maringa (ii); marombe; mbila; mbira; mbo ngo; minungu; modeku; mudoku; mujemba; mumamba; musical box; mutshahats; mutshapata; muyembba; namombwele; ndandi; ndimba; ndjanga; ndoko; ngato; ngombi (ii); njari; nkisansi; nkola; nsansi; nyonganyonga; nzenze; ogumh; ogumogu; opanda; paulugledi; pokido; prempensua; quisanche; quisangi; risandji; rumba-box; sandji; sangu (i); sansi; sanzi; sanzu (i); sasi; shitata; sikbi; sipi; sithandi; tamatama; timbrh; tomboji; tsambi (ii); tshanji; tshisaji; tsimbi; tudimba; txissanje; ubo; udjanga; utee; valdímbula.

BIBLIOGRAPHY

KirbyMISA; LaurentyS; OrtizIMA; WachsmannTCU
J. dos Santos: *Ethiopia oriental e varia historia de cousas notaveis do Oriente* (Evora, 1609, 2/1891)
T. Ewbank: *Life in Brazil* (London, 1856), 111f
D. and C. Livingstone: *Narrative of an Expedition to the Zambesi and its Tributaries: 1858–64* (London, 1865)
C. Coquilhat: *Sur le Haut-Congo* (Paris, 1888), 364
G. Montandon: 'La généalogie des instruments de musique et les cycles de civilisation', *Archives suisses d'anthropologie générales*, iii/1 (1919), 1–95
J. Maes: 'La sanza du Congo belge', *Congo*, ii (1921), 542–72
H. P. Junod: 'The Mbila or Native Piano of the Tshopi Tribe', *Bantu Studies*, iii (1929), 275
J. Kunst: 'A Musicological Argument for Cultural Relationship between Indonesia – Probably the Isle of Java – and Central Africa', *PMA*, lxii (1935–6), 57
F. J. de Hen: *Beitrag zur Kenntnis der Musikinstrumente aus Belgisch Kongo und Ruanda-Urundi* (Tervuren, 1960)
J. Blacking: 'Patterns of Nsenga Kalimba Music', *African Music*, ii/4 (1961), 26
H. Tracey: 'A Case for the Name Mbira', *African Music*, ii/4 (1961), 17
G. Kubik: 'The Phenomenon of Inherent Rhythms in East and Central African Instrumental Music', *African Music*, iii/1 (1962), 33 [see also corrigenda, *African Music*, iv/4 (1970), 136]
A. Tracey: 'Three Tunes for "Mbira dza vadzimu"', *African Music*, iii/2 (1963), 23
A. M. Jones: *Africa and Indonesia: the Evidence of the Xylophone and other Musical and Cultural Factors* (Leiden, 1964, 2/1970)
G. Kubik: 'Generic Names for the Mbira', *African Music*, iii/3 (1964), 25; iii/4 (1965), 72 [see also corrigenda, *African Music*, iv/4 (1970), 136]
J. Blacking: 'The Role of Music in the Culture of the Venda of Northern Transvaal', *Studies in Ethnomusicology*, ii (1965), 20–53
M. Dias: 'Os instrumentos musicais de Moçambique', *Geográphica: revista da Sociedade de geografia de Lisboa*, ii/6 (1966), 2
G. Kubik: 'Ethno-musicological Research in Southern Parts of Malawi', *Society of Malawi Journal*, xxi/1 (1968), 20
F. O. Bernhard, trans.: *The Journals of Carl Mauch: his Travels in the Transvaal and Rhodesia* (Salisbury, 1969)
H. Tracey: 'The Mbira Class of African Instruments in Rhodesia (1932)', *African Music*, iv/3 (1969), 78
G. Kubik: *Natureza e estrutura de escalas musicais africanas* (Lisbon, 1970)
G. T. Nurse: 'Cewa Concepts of Musical Instruments', *African Music*, iv/4 (1970), 32
R. Garfias and D. A. Maraire: 'The African Mbira: Music of the Shona People of Rhodesia', H 72043 [disc notes]
P. Kazadi: 'Congo Music: Africa's Favorite Beat', *Africa Report*, xvi/4 (1971), 25
G. Kubik: 'Carl Mauch's Mbira Musical Transcriptions of 1872', *Review of Ethnology*, iii/10 (1971), 73
D. Thompson: 'The *Marimbula*, an Afro-Caribbean Sanza', *Yearbook for Inter-American Musical Research*, vii (1971), 103
A. Tracey: 'The Original African Mbira?', *African Music*, v/2 (1972), 85
J. Blacking: *How Musical is Man?* (Seattle and London, 1973)
C. van Oven: 'The Kondi of Sierra Leone', *African Music*, v/3 (1973–4), 77
G. Kubik: 'Uganda Music of the Past: an Interview with Ephraim Bisase', *African Musicology*, no.1 (1976)
——: *Angolan Traits in Black Music, Games and Dances of Brazil* (Lisbon, 1979)
——: *Ostafrika, Musikgeschichte in Bildern*, i/10 (Leipzig, 1982)
A. Simon, ed.: *Musik in Afrika* (Berlin, 1983)
        ROBERT A. KAUFFMAN (1), GERHARD KUBIK (2),
                ANTHONY KING (3), PETER COOKE (4)

Lame musicale (Fr.). SAW, MUSICAL.

Lamy, Alfred Joseph (*b* Mirecourt, 8 Sept 1850; *d* Paris, 1919). French bow maker. He learnt his craft in Mirecourt with Charles Claude Husson (i) from 1862 to 1868. He then took up a position with the firm of Gautrot at Château-Thierry, but his career was firmly established when he went to Paris to be assistant to F. N. Voirin. With exceptional gifts of hand and eye he copied every detail of his master's work, and it is difficult to tell their bows apart. He may have made certain of Voirin's bows unaided, but on Voirin's death in 1885 Lamy was employed by his widow for some years, and Voirin's brand continued in use. By 1889, when he won a gold medal at the Paris exhibition, Lamy was working on his own account, at premises at 24 rue Poissonnière. His brand-mark was A. LAMY À PARIS. He never varied from his teacher's style, with the characteristic small, elegant head and mostly round sticks, though they tend to be more yielding. The heads and frogs also follow Voirin's model but are slightly fuller. Most of his bows are ebony and silver mounted, the buttons being banded with two rings. Occasionally ivory or tortoise-shell is used for the frogs, with gold mountings and mother-of-pearl dots, which are either circled or plain. Generally Lamy's bows have a little more weight than Voirin's, a feature particularly appreciated by cellists, but their overall lightness has diminished their viability for the modern violinist. His output was quite large. His bows are highly regarded, and the value of well-preserved examples has risen constantly.

On his death, Lamy was succeeded by his son Alfred Lamy (*b* after 1875; *d* 1944). As they worked together for over two decades it is not surprising that their bows are remarkably similar; identification is further complicated by the fact that both used the same stamp, though there are a few distinguishing details: the mother-of-pearl slide in the frogs of Lamy the elder tend to be narrower than the son's; the buttons of Lamy the younger are not only slightly larger but also often silver-capped; and the ferrules on the son's bows can be narrower than those on the father's.

BIBLIOGRAPHY
R. Vannes: *Essai d'un dictionnaire universel des luthiers* (Paris, 1932, 2/1951/R1972 as *Dictionnaire universel des luthiers* and *R*1981 incl. suppl. 1959)
J. Roda: *Bows for Musical Instruments of the Violin Family* (Chicago, 1959)
E. Vatelot: *Les archets français* (Nancy, 1976)
CHARLES BEARE, JAAK LIIVOJA-LORIUS

Lamzdelis [lumzdelis]. DUCT FLUTE of Lithuania. It is made from various woods (ash, maple, linden, apple, pear or cherry wood) or, in spring, from the bark of willow, aspen, alder or sometimes pine. It can be from 15 to 40 cm long, 2 to 4 cm in diameter, and often ornamented. The upper end can be straight or obliquely-cut, and the bore is cylindrical or slightly flared at the lower end. The *lamzdelis* has from three to eight finger-holes producing a diatonic scale; it can be overblown. The lower notes are soft, the higher notes gradually becoming stronger. The *lamzdelis* was common throughout Lithuania, especially in the extreme northeast, and it was used mostly for various genres of improvisatory pastoral music. It was also used by shepherd-boys and adults for folkdance and song-tunes or vocal *sutartinės* (a polyphonic genre based on the 2nd as a consonant interval), solo or in groups of two or three. The *lamzdelis* was used to play dances in village bands with the violin, accordion, *birbynė* (folk clarinet), *ožragis* (goat horn) and *dūdmaišis* (bagpipe). A double *lamzdelis* is also known; a musician could on occasion play two separate instruments together. The traditional *lamzdelis* is still made by some village musicians. Folk music groups use the traditional and modified instrument (made of ebony, with ten finger-holes and a chromatic range from *c'* to *g'''*).

ARVYDAS KARAŠKA

Landolfi, Carlo Ferdinando (*fl* c1750–c1775). Italian violin maker. He worked in Milan, where he may have started as an assistant to one of the Testores (perhaps Paolo Antonio) but was more likely associated with G. B. Guadagnini, who went there in 1749. His instruments draw much more from the Guadagnini workshop than from the earlier Milanese makers. By the mid-1750s he was producing his best violins, elegant in design and neat in workmanship, though with strong personal character. The varnish is rich in appearance, sometimes the deep red of the Venetians but more often a lighter orange-brown. His violins are desirable tonally, but mostly not in the same class as those of Guadagnini. Equally interesting are his violas, varying in size from a minute 38·1 cm body length, to a good 38·9 cm model and an occasional splendid pattern just over 40·6 cm. Landolfi cellos are invariably small, though good instruments.

Landolfi's main pupils were Pietro Giovanni Mantegazza, who was independent before 1760, and his son Pietro Antonio Landolfi (*fl* c1760–c1785). Some of Pietro's instruments were spoilt by their rather high build and a harder varnish than that used by his father. His

influence is increasingly noticeable in the Landolfi instruments after 1760, but his enthusiasm for the craft seems to have waned from 1770.

BIBLIOGRAPHY
W. L. von Lütgendorff: *Die Geigen- und Lautenmacher vom Mittelalter bis zur Gegenwart* (Frankfurt am Main, 1904, 6/1922/R1968)
O. Möckel: *Die Kunst des Geigenbaues* (Leipzig, 1930, rev. 2/1954)
R. Vannes: *Essai d'un dictionnaire universel des luthiers* (Paris, 1932, 2/1951/R1972 as *Dictionnaire universel des luthiers* and *R*1981 incl. suppl. 1959)
H. Hamma: *Meisterwerke italienischer Geigenbaukunst* (Stuttgart, 1933)
CHARLES BEARE

Lang [Lange], **Johann** [Hans, Hanss] (*b* Wesselburen, 1543; *d* Kamenz, buried 19 Nov 1616). German organ builder. He learnt his trade in Hamburg, perhaps from Jakob Scherer, and possibly also from Hans Scherer the elder. He spent some time in Leipzig, and became a freeman of Kamenz in 1578. His son Johann Lang was also an organ builder, and Joachim Zschugk and probably Gottfried Fritzsche were among his pupils. He built organs for the Nikolaikirche, Leipzig (1575–6, 1597–8; two manuals, 27 stops); St Matthäi, Leisnig (1584; 29 stops); Dresden (1584; *Altarpositiv*); Bischofstwerda (1590, 1602); the Church of Our Lady, Torgau (1592; two manuals, 26 stops); St Kunigund, Rochlitz (1593–4, 1605–7; two manuals, 23 stops); the Thomaskirche, Leipzig (1598–9; two manuals, 25 stops); and the Nikolaikirche, Döbeln (1603–4), a new organ built in the tower with only the *Rückpositiv* in the church. His instruments were characterized by a well-finished principal chorus and *Brustwerk* with 8' and 4' regals; none of them survives.

BIBLIOGRAPHY
K. F. Zinck: *Geschichte und Beschreibung der Kunigundenkirche in Rochlitz* (Rochlitz, 1864), 25ff
P. Stöbe: 'Geschichte des Orgelbaues in Sachsen', *Der Kirchenchor*, xiii (1902), 37
P. Rubardt: *Kamenzer Orgelbuch* (Kamenz, 1953), 13f
U. Dähnert: *Historische Orgeln in Sachsen* (Leipzig, 1980)
ULRICH DÄHNERT

Langa. TROUGH ZITHER of the Shi people of Zaïre. *See* INANGA.

Langadron. A single-headed cylindrical drum of the rural and urban blacks of Surinam. It is used in religious rituals.

Langeleik. Fretted Norwegian BOX ZITHER. It resembles the *Scheitholt* depicted by Praetorius (*Syntagma musicum*, 2/1619), having only one melody string and three to seven drone strings. It was apparently well established around 1600 and was the most common instrument for domestic rural entertainment until the mid-19th century. Thereafter it rapidly became obsolete except in the Valdres district, where an unbroken playing tradition persists that has enabled thorough documentation of *langeleik* music. Its playing technique differs considerably from that of similar instruments outside Norway: the middle three fingers of the left hand stop the melody string and also rapidly strike (on ascending) and pluck (on descending) the notes between the rhythmic plectrum strokes of the right hand. The melodic idiosyncrasies of *langeleik* music may be related to this technique (see Ledang, 1974). Modern instruments have the frets placed to produce a major scale; on early spec-

Langeleik (box zither) played in an old Valdres house at the Norsk Folkemuseum, Oslo

imens, however, the spacing of the frets shows no pattern of large and small intervals. In the 1920s, when the problem of scale, mode and neutral tones was the focus of much Norwegian research and discussion, Eggen (1923) attempted an evaluation of *langeleik* scales. Sevåg (1974), using a greater number of early instruments, concluded that a heptatonic scale structure with a relatively fixed framework of tonic, 5th and octave can be abstracted. Other intervals vary as much as 60 cents, but no interval is smaller than a somewhat short $\frac{3}{4}$-tone. This suggests an early idiom of scale and mode, which Sevåg termed 'anhemitonic heptatonism'.

See also ZITHER, §3.

BIBLIOGRAPHY

E. Eggen: *Skalastudier* [Studies in scales] (Christiania [now Oslo], 1923)

O. K. Ledang: 'Instrument – Player – Music: on the Norwegian *Langeleik*', *Festschrift to Ernst Emsheimer* (Stockholm, 1974), 107

R. Sevåg: 'Neutral Tones and the Problems of Mode in Norwegian Folk Music', *Festschrift to Ernst Emsheimer* (Stockholm, 1974), 207

REIDAR SEVÅG

Långharpa. An obsolete instrument of Sweden, probably a fretted zither, known in the 17th century; *see* ZITHER, §3.

Langhedul. Flemish family of organ builders. Active about 1475 to 1635 in Ieper, the family was particularly significant in the early development of the French Baroque organ.

Victor (*d* ?1513) was one of the great organ builders at the turn of the 16th century, as can be concluded from the importance of the churches for which he worked (Courtrai, St Omer and Lille). After his death his work was taken over by Matthijs de Wulf [Matthieu le Leup] (*fl* 1515–22), husband of one of his four daughters.

Michiel the elder, Victor's son, went to England in his youth, probably to allow Matthijs de Wulf to work unhindered; while there he improved and enlarged the organ at Trinity Chapel, Salisbury Cathedral (1530–31). Apparently Michiel returned to Ieper after the early death of his brother-in-law and continued the family business from 1534 to *c*1570. His name is linked with a great number of organs, including many which he built new, though all are within the narrow geographical range of south-west Flanders and surroundings: Ieper, Courtrai (1534, 1546, 1570), Bruges (1535), Veurne (1536, 1557), St Omer (1546), Bergues (1548, 1557), Nieuwpoort (1553, 1557), Dunkirk (1555, 1559), Poperinghe (1569). And as very many village churches in the 16th century had organs, a large number in west Flanders must naturally be ascribed to Michiel. Towards the end of his life he was particularly occupied with the restoring of organs destroyed during the religious troubles of 1566.

Jan (*d* Ghent, 6 Feb 1592), son of Michiel the elder, was active at first in the same area (Courtrai, Ieper), but war, the temporary regime of the Calvinists and economic confusion forced him to move, in 1583 to Lille, and in 1585 to Paris. His Paris organ restorations (St Benoît, the Sainte-Chapelle, Couvent des Augustines,

St Eustache) and the new instrument he built in St Jacques-de-la-Boucherie show several important innovations: a balanced *plein jeu*, a progressive Cornet of four, five and six ranks, and a rich complement of reed stops. He received the title 'Organ Builder to the King of France' for his work in the Sainte-Chapelle, part of the royal palace. Jan left Paris some time after 15 October 1590 and returned to Ieper; his last works are found especially in Ghent and were produced in partnership with Guillames [Guillaume] (*fl* Ghent, 1590–95), probably his son. Jan is buried in the Dominican Church, the only church in Ghent whose organ survived the religious uprisings.

Guillames' methods are especially known from a pair of plans for a new organ in St Baaf Cathedral, Ghent (*c*1590), which he submitted but which were not realized. They closely resemble the instruments constructed by his father in Paris.

Matthijs [Mattheus, Matthieu, Mateo] (*b* Ieper; *d* Brussels, 1635–6), son of Jan, was perhaps the most important organ builder of the family. It is likely that he was with his father during the latter's Paris years; when Jan decided to return to Flanders, Matthijs went to Spain. From 1592 to 1599 he was the organ tuner (*templador*) for the Spanish court. From mid-1599 to mid-1605 he was again in Paris, where his family's reputation brought him immediate work: restoration of organs in St Jean-en-Grève, Saints-Innocents, Hôpital de St Esprit-en-Grève, St Benoît, Chapelle St Leu and St Jacques-de-la-Boucherie, and provision of a new *Rückpositiv* organ and a modernized great organ for St Eustache (1604–5). Matthijs's most important organ was the new one he built for St Gervais (1601–2), which provided the basis for the later instrument of the Couperin family. This organ still contains an amount of important pipework by Matthijs, including some with his signature.

It was Jan and Matthijs, together with CRESPIN CARLIER, who laid the groundwork for the classic French organ of the 17th and 18th centuries. In 1605 Matthijs returned to Ieper, from where he built the organ in Hondschoote (1611), the *Rückpositiv* of which is still preserved. About 1613 he settled in Brussels and became court organ builder to the Archduke Albertus and Archduchess Isabella. While there, he built organs over a wide radius including St Omer, Antwerp and Tongeren, as well as one for the Spanish court at Madrid.

Other family members are: Michiel the younger, son of Michiel the elder, resident of Ieper, organ builder and organist, mentioned in 1610 as organist at Hazebrouck; and two other Jans. One was choirmaster of the Church of Our Lady at Antwerp about 1570. Another was city magistrate at Ieper, and though himself a Calvinist was able to save the new organ of the main church there (built 1573 by Gillis Brebos) from destruction during the Calvinist interregnum of 1578. He was a signatory of the Union of Utrecht (1579); after the restoration of Catholicism in 1584, he fled to England, where he died in Norwich.

BIBLIOGRAPHY

E. Grégoir: *Historique de la facture et des facteurs d'orgues* (Antwerp, 1865)

E. vander Straeten: *La musique aux Pays-Bas avant le XIXe siècle* (Brussels, 1867–88/R1969), i, 160f; ii, 9, 309f; viii, 400ff

M. A. Vente: 'Figuren uit Vlaanderens orgelhistorie: het geslacht Langhedul', *De schalmei*, i (1946), July, 2; Sept, 2

B. de Keyzer: 'Charles Blanquaert en Guillames Langhedul in de St. Baafs-kathedraal te Gent', *De schalmei*, iii (1948), 2

A. Deschrevel: 'Het orgel in de St. Maartenskathedraal te Ieper', *De schalmei*, iii (1948), 68

M. A. Vente: *Proeve van een repertorium van de archivalia betrekking hebbende op het Nederlandse orgel en zijn makers tot omstreeks 1630* (Brussels, 1956)

N. Dufourcq: 'Recent Researches into French Organ-building from the Fifteenth to the Seventeenth Century', *GSJ*, x (1957), 66

A. Deschrevel: 'Historische terugblik op het orgel in West-Vlaanderen, Ieper, international centrum van orgelbouw en orgelcultuur', *West-Vlaanderen*, xi (1962), 23

M. Vanmackelberg: *Les orgues d'Arras* (Arras, 1963), 20

G. Moortgat: *Oude orgels in Vlaanderen*, ii (1965), 11f

M. Jurgens: *Documents du minutier central concernant l'histoire de la musique, 1600–1650* (Paris, 1967), 787ff

N. Dufourcq and J. Krug-Basse: 'A propos de l'orgue dit "Des Couperin"', *Mélanges François Couperin* (Paris, 1968), 72

F. Douglass: *The Language of the Classical French Organ* (New Haven and London, 1969), 60f

N. Dufourcq: *Les sources*, i: *Le livre de l'orgue français 1589–1789* (Paris, 1969)

P. Hardouin: 'A propos de l'orgue dit des Couperin', *Renaissance de l'orgue* (1969), no.4, p.27

——: 'Facteurs d'orgues flamands en France sous Henri IV', *Renaissance de l'orgue* (1970), no.8, p.8; *Connaissance de l'orgue* (1973), no.4, p.18

G. Persoons: 'De orgels en organisten van de Onze Lieve Vrouwkerk te Antwerpen van 1500 tot 1650', *Verhandelingen van de Koninklijke Academie voor Wetenschappen, letteren en schone kunsten van België*, xliii (1981), 54

MAARTEN ALBERT VENTE

Länglur. Wooden trumpet of Scandinavia. *See* LUR, (2).

Langorony. A Malagasy term for several types of drum. It most commonly designates 'military' drums, which are found sparsely throughout Madagascar. Their special use is in ensembles basically made up of flutes (*see* SODINA).

Langsam (Ger.: 'slow'). A tempo mark, the German equivalent of *adagio*, *lento* or *largo*; it was used as early as the 17th century by Schütz in his madrigal *Itzt blicken durch des Himmels Saal*. Wagner's *Tristan* opens with the direction *langsam und schmachtend*.

Langsflöte (Ger.). RECORDER.

Langspil (Swed. *långspel*). Bowed BOX ZITHER of Iceland related to the Norwegian *langeleik*. It has one to six strings and a fretted fingerboard giving a diatonic scale; some instruments have additional semitones for the melody string and occasional or constant drones. Frets are of brass or wood; some are fixed and others movable. The soundboard, which may be ornamented, has soundholes of differing shape. The instrument is placed on a table (or on a board held on the lap) with the broad, thicker end to the right (see illustration, p.506). The horsehair bow is held with the right hand. Although the instrument became obsolescent in the latter part of the 19th century, it was reintroduced into music education by teachers and folklorists in the mid-20th century and has been used orchestrally by at least one composer.

BIBLIOGRAPHY

M. Müller, ed: *From Bone Pipe and Cattle Horn to Fiddle and Psaltery* (Copenhagen, 1972)

AMANDA M. BURT

Langueur (Fr.). A type of ornament; *see* ORNAMENTS, §III, 2.

Langspil (box zither) player, Iceland

Languid (Fr. *biseau, languette*; Ger. *Kern, Pfeifenkern*). In an organ flue pipe, an adjustable metal plate fixed inside the pipe-foot; *see* ORGAN, §III, 1, fig.15, and VOICING, §1.

Lansaran. Idiophone of the Murut people of Sabah, Malaysia. This unusual instrument is a dance floor which springs vertically about 30 cm or more when activated by dancers (who also sing) and produces regular crashes as it hits its base supports. The rhythm of the crashes and the tempo of the song sometimes move gradually out of phase despite the physical difficulty of breathing and dancing in different rhythms.

Lantoy [lantuy]. External DUCT FLUTE of the Manobo people of the southern Philippines.

Lanunu. Small bronze gong of Alor, Indonesia, used in the SARAFEO ensemble.

Lanzas. Thick cane STAMPING TUBE of northern Ecuador.

Laouto [laghouto]. Greek long-necked lute, the chief accompanying instrument of traditional ensembles. The bowl resonator is carvel-built, and the soundtable has a single soundhole. The neck has 11 movable gut or nylon frets and an additional eight or more wooden ones are glued to the soundtable. The four double courses of metal strings are tuned in 5ths ($c – g – d' – a'$). Although the *laouto* is traditionally played with a goose quill, plastic plectra are also used. The prime role of the *laouto* is to provide a rhythmic and chordal accompaniment except in Crete, where it is used to play a simplified version of the melody in heterophony with the *lyra* (see illustration).

In some areas the *laouto* has been replaced by the *laoutokithara*, a long-necked lute strung, fretted, tuned and played like a *laouto* but constructed with the resonator of a guitar.

R. CONWAY MORRIS

La-pa. *See* LABA (i).

Lapinka [pinka]. CONCH-SHELL TRUMPET used by black musicians of Iraq and the Arabian Gulf. (The name derives from the Bambassi language, of African origin.) The last spiral of the conch is cut off to form a mouthpiece. Elderly men play the *lapinka* to summon people to participate in the *wāya* ceremony.

Lap organ [rocking melodeon, elbow organ]. A portable instrument of the reed organ family. It was probably invented by James A. Bazin and was made in the eastern USA (particularly New Hampshire) in the first half of the 19th century. *See* REED ORGAN, §1.

Laqin. Bowed long zither of China. *See* YAZHENG.

Laquita. Bolivian PANPIPES. *See* LAKITA.

Larchemi. PANPIPES of Megrelia, western Georgia (USSR). In Guria the instrument is known as *soinari*. It consists of six cane pipes of varying length fastened in a row (see illustration). These are tuned in 3rds outwards from the two lowest pipes, which are in the centre and are tuned a 2nd apart. The tuning varies according to the piece being performed. The *larchemi* is usually larger than the *soinari*: the pipes of the former are from 9 to 14 cm long; those of the latter are 6·5 to 10·5 cm

Laouto (long-necked lute) and lyra (fiddle) players leading a Cretan wedding procession

Larchemi (panpipes) player, Georgia, USSR

long. Sometimes pieces are performed by two players who can divide the instrument in two, taking three pipes each. The *larchemi* is generally considered a shepherds' instrument but is also used during hunting, although its use is now dying out. *See VertkovA, 124.*

Largamente (It.: 'broadly', 'generously'). Though strictly the adverb from LARGO, this word is rather different in its uses. It is used as an expression mark to denote a more stately manner of playing; or it can be an instruction to slow down the tempo. In this second sense it was a particular favourite of Elgar who found it so indispensable that in some of his works he even abbreviated it to *L* (together with *A* for *accelerando* and *R* for *ritardando*); see especially the scores of the Second Symphony and *The Kingdom*.
See also TEMPO AND EXPRESSION MARKS.

DAVID FALLOWS

Larghetto (It.: 'rather wide'; diminutive of *largo*). A tempo mark indicating a rather more lighthearted *largo*. 'Handel's Largo' ('Ombra mai fù' from *Serse*) is marked *larghetto*, as are many other movements in the same opera; 'Comfort ye' from *Messiah* is marked *larghetto e piano*. The word seems to have come into use early in the 18th century: Brossard (1703) did not mention it; but Rousseau (1768, article 'Mouvement') gave it as one of the main adjustments of tempo (though not of mood) and described it (article 'Largo') as being 'a little less slow than *largo*'. Koch (1802) said it was 'normally the same as *andante*'.
For bibliography *see* TEMPO AND EXPRESSION MARKS.

DAVID FALLOWS

Largo (It.: 'large', 'broad'). A tempo mark, considered by many theorists of the 18th century, particularly in France, to be the slowest of all: Rousseau (1768) listed it as the slowest of his five main degrees of movement in music, and many other writers agreed with him; but there is no overall consistency of opinion among earlier writers about its relation to such designations as *adagio*, *lento* and *grave*. Early Italian writers and 19th-century usage seem to have been more consistent in placing it somewhere between *adagio* and *andante*: it was surely in this sense that Bach had used it for the opening fugue of his B minor Mass and the final fugue in book 1 of the '48'; and Vivaldi had used the direction *largo ma più tosto andante* (P211/RV227).

Largo appeared relatively often in music from the beginning of the 17th century, though normally to indicate a contrast in tempo within a faster movement. Caccini (*Le nuove musiche*, 1601/2) included an instruction 'escla con misura più larga'; Frescobaldi (*Partite e toccate*, 1615) recommended a *tempo largo* for runs and embellishments; and a similar usage in Giovanni Scipione (1650) endorses the conclusion that for them, at least, *largo* was already more a tempo than a tempo. Praetorius (*Syntagma musicum*, iii, 2/1619) gave the equation *adagio: largo: lento: langsam*. In the late 17th and early 18th centuries the term was commonly applied to third movements, in 3/2 time and saraband rhythm, of *sonate da chiesa*.

In England *largo* may have had a firmer position similar to that of *andante* in later centuries. Purcell, in the preface to his *Sonnata's of III Parts* (1683), gave *largo*, along with *presto largo* and *poco largo*, as the moderate tempo between *adagio* and *allegro*; and the anonymous *A Short Explication* (London, 1724) gave the progression *adagio, grave, largo, vivace, allegro, presto*. Brossard's *Dictionaire* (1703), followed by J. G. Walther's *Musicalisches Lexicon* (1732), gave an interesting description of *largo*:

Very slowly as though expanding the beat, and often marking the major accents unusually, etc. This happens above all in the *Recitative* of the Italians, in which one often does not make the beats equal because it is a kind of declamation in which the actor must follow the movement of the passion which affects him and which he wishes to express instead of following that of an equal and regulated beat.

For bibliography *see* TEMPO AND EXPRESSION MARKS.

DAVID FALLOWS

Lari. (1) Long drum of the Mangbetu people of northeastern Zaïre. *See* NABITA, (1).

(2) Drum of the Logo and Bari peoples of Zaïre, also known as *larimva*. *See* DINDO.

Larigot (Fr.). An ORGAN STOP.

Lasuang. Idiophone of West Sumatra, Indonesia. *See* LESUNG.

Låthorn. Swedish animal-horn trumpet with fingerholes. *See* BOCKHORN.

Latīf-jo-tanbūro. Long-necked plucked lute of Sind, Pakistan. *See* TANBŪRO.

Lätzsch, Herbert (*b* Störmthal, nr. Leipzig, 23 Dec 1917). German maker of brass instruments. He learnt to play the trumpet as a youth, and studied with Schopper, a master craftsman of metal wind instruments, in Leipzig (1933–6). After his qualifying examination (1936) he served in the navy. At the end of World War II he and the violin maker Fritz Riedel rebuilt the firm of Riedel in Bremen, and in 1949 he founded his own firm (taking his master's examination in Hamburg in 1954). His work has been considerably influenced by the distinguished trombone maker Franz Kuhn of Langenberg, who began working under contract with Lätzsch in February 1953 after he lost his own workshop and sold the remainder of his tools to the firm of Monke (Cologne). Lätzsch was able to continue making the 'Alschausky–Kuhn' trombone as the 'Lätzsch–Kuhn' model, and developed the 'Kuhn' trombone, which has won worldwide esteem for its good, delicate tone, particularly well suited to interpreting German Classical and Romantic compositions.

Lätzsch has built trombones in five sizes and thus continues the German tradition, which is also distinguished from English and American practice in that the instruments have longer slides and shorter bodies. A particular feature of his instruments is that the normal rounded tube at the upper end of the body may be replaced by a tube that lowers the horn by a 4th when its valve is opened, thus making it a Bb/F instrument. (When C. F. Sattler first developed this concept in 1839, the additional tubing was a permanent fixture; *see* TROMBONE.) The firm also makes trumpets and flugelhorns.

ARMIN ROSIN

Laúd. Spanish term (from the Arabic 'ŪD) for the lute, which was introduced to Spain by Arabs during the 13th century. Together with bandurria and guitars, it appears in folk ensembles known as *rondallas*. The back of the resonator is flat, not pear-shaped as in the *'ūd*. In Spain the instrument is played with a *púa* (plectrum). The *laúd español* appears also in Puerto Rican folk music. In Cuba a *laúd* with seven courses of double strings may substitute for a guitar in the accompanimental ensemble for the dance *punto guajiro*. *See also* LUTE, esp. §4.

JOHN M. SCHECHTER

Lau lau. A leg xylophone of the Pacific. *See* XYLOPHONE, §5.

Launeddas. Triple idioglot clarinet of southern Sardinia. Its name may be derived from *Lionasci* ('oleander', the tree from which it is said originally to have been made); or, more likely, from a union of *lau* (the laurel from which the ancient aulos was constructed) with *cannas* ('reed'), producing *canneddas* ('little reed'). It has reed pipes of different lengths: the *tumbu* (longest) is the bass drone; the *mancosa* (medium-sized reed) gives the middle register (and is bound to the *tumbu* with a

short cord); the *mancosedda* (smallest) plays the highest notes (see illustration). The player holds the *tumbu* and the *mancosa* in his left hand and the *mancosedda* in the right. Each of the three reeds has a small piece of wax fixed to its lower free end which is extremely flexible and can produce quarter-tones. The player holds all three reeds in his mouth at once and produces a continuous stream of sound by using circular breathing.

BIBLIOGRAPHY
A. F. W. Bentzon: 'Is launeddas', Dischi del Sole DS 529-31 [disc notes]
——: *The Launeddas; a Sardinian Folk-music Instrument* (Copenhagen, 1969)

ROBERTO LEYDI

Launut [livika, lounuat, nunut]. Wooden friction idiophone or 'rubbing block' of New Ireland. There are numerous other local names. It is shaped rather like an upside-down pig and has been likened also to an upside-down bird with tucked-in head, legs and twisted tail (see illustration). *Launut* are, on average, about 40 cm long, 15 to 30 cm high and 15 to 20 cm wide. Three (or, rarely, four or five) cavities cut transversely through the instrument communicate with thin surface slits. These divide the surface into tongues which almost close the cavities. The player sits or crouches with the instrument held lengthwise between his knees and strokes it into resonance with hands covered with resin or the sap of the breadfruit tree. The cavities are usually tuned to provide triadic 'fanfare' scales similar to the vocal scales of the area. Traditionally the instrument was used during ceremonies for the dead.

BIBLIOGRAPHY
O. Finsch: *Ethnologische Erfahrungen und Belegstücke aus der Südsee* (Vienna, 1888–93), 58
A. Krämer: *Die Malanggane von Tombara* (Munich, 1925), 56f
A. W. Ligtvoet: 'An Interesting Musical Instrument from New-Ireland', *Antiquity and Survival* (1955), 299
S. Wolf: 'Bemerkungen zu den Neuirländischen Reibhölzern der Völkerkundemuseen Dresden und Leipzig', *Jb des Museums für Völkerkunde zu Leipzig*, xvii (1958), 52

Friction idiophone (launut) from New Ireland, carved in the form of an upside-down bird, before 1924 (Auckland Institute and Museum)

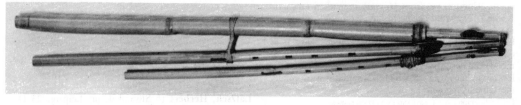

Launeddas (triple clarinet) from Sardinia (Horniman Museum, London)

P. H. Lewis: 'Notes on a Friction Drum Collected at Amba, New Ireland, in 1970', *Staatlichen Museums für Völkerkunde, Dresden, Abhandlungen und Berichte*, xxxiv (1975), 581

MERVYN McLEAN

Laurent, Claude (*fl* 1806–57). French flute maker. Although it is clear that he was active in the first half of the 19th century, few biographical details are available. Throughout his working life he produced flutes made of crystal or cut glass (*see* FLUTE, fig.13c). As early as 1806 he produced and patented a crystal flute. It is sometimes (wrongly) stated that he invented pillar-mounting for keys at the same time: as he was forced to use this method on his crystal flutes, he was responsible for the technique becoming well known. In 1834 he made a flute that descended to *g*, and was said by Pierre (1893) to be making flutes in 1835 with from one to 12 keys. According to Pierre he ceased production after 1848, but Pontécoulant (1861) referred to a new patent of 1857.

Many Laurent flutes survive, Miller (1925) listing 25 and Langwill (1960) over 40. These are all clearly luxury instruments, with silver mountings and keys normally fitted, though sometimes parts were made of gold. Laurent also made early use of forged steel springs. The tone of these instruments, sometimes said to be lifeless, is nothing of the kind; while limited in upper partials, it has an unearthly and ethereal character quite unlike the vibrant sound of the wooden models.

BIBLIOGRAPHY
L. A. de Pontécoulant: *Organographie* (Paris, 1861/*R*1973)
R. S. Rockstro: *A Treatise on . . . the Flute* (London, 1890, 2/1928/*R*1967)
C. Pierre: *Les facteurs d'instruments de musique* (Paris, 1893/*R*1971)
D. C. Miller: 'Flutes of Glass', *The Flutist*, iv (1925)
L. G. Langwill: *An Index of Musical Wind-instrument Makers* (Edinburgh, 1960, rev., enlarged 6/1980)
P. Bate: *The Flute* (London, 1969, 2/1979)
H. Heyde: *Flöten* (Leipzig, 1978)

NIALL O'LOUGHLIN

Lausmann. Austrian family of woodwind and brass instrument makers, active between 1789 and 1867. Johann Anton Lausmann made brass instruments in Graslitz in the late 18th and early 19th centuries. Two natural horns dated 1791 and two long natural brass trumpets (in Eb and D) both dating from 1803 are in the Karl-Marx-Universität, Leipzig. One M. Lausmann, also of Graslitz, repaired a 1770 horn by Carl Stärzer of Vienna; in 1878 he apparently took over the Viennese firm of Ziegler. The woodwind maker I. A. Lausmann had instruments at the Paris exhibitions of 1855 and 1867 and in London in 1862; his flutes at the 1855 exhibition descended to *b*, *bb* and *a*; according to Fétis (1868), in 1867 he produced a fine display of oboes, clarinets, trumpets and saxhorns. Joseph W. Lausmann also had woodwind instruments at the Paris exhibitions.

BIBLIOGRAPHY
F. J. Fétis: *Exposition universelle de 1867 . . . rapports*, ii: *Instruments de musique* (Paris, 1868)
H. Lavoix: *Histoire de l'instrumentation depuis le 16e siècle* (Paris, 1878)
L. G. Langwill: *An Index of Musical Wind-instrument Makers* (Edinburgh, 1960, rev., enlarged 6/1980)
H. A. Fitzpatrick: *The Horn and Horn-playing and the Austro-Bohemian Tradition 1680–1830* (London, 1970)
H. Heyde: *Trompeten Posaunen Tuben* (Leipzig, 1980)

NIALL O'LOUGHLIN

Lauta. Plucked fretted lute of Macedonia. It is played as an accompanying instrument in ČALGIJE ensembles.

Làută [lǎùtǎ]. Old Romanian term for the lute. In the Banat, neighbouring areas of Transylvania, Muntenia and southern Moldavia, it signifies the violin; in writings from the 16th century onwards the term (or *alǎutǎ*) probably also referred to a short-necked lute, now known in Romania as the COBZĂ. The word 'lǎutǎ' has given rise to the term 'lǎutar' (or *lǎutaş*, pl. *lǎutari*). *Lǎutari* are professional folk musicians, usually gypsies, also known in the 16th and 17th centuries as *alǎutari*. For the folk fiddle *làută cu tolcer*, *see* VIOLIN, §IV, 1.

TIBERIU ALEXANDRU

Laute (Ger.). LUTE.

Lautenklavier [Lautenklavecimbel, Lautenwerk] (Ger.). LUTE-HARPSICHORD.

Lautenzug (Ger.). BUFF STOP.

Lauto (It.). LUTE.

Lavazza, Antonio Maria (*fl* Milan, *c*1703–32). Italian violin maker. His background and training remain obscure, though as he was a contemporary of the Grancinos and lived in the same vicinity of Milan, it is not unreasonable to assume that he could have received at least some of his training from them. His few surviving instruments are based on a modified Stradivari pattern and are covered with an attractive pale red or golden-brown varnish; it is possible that some of his work has been relabelled.

The life of Santino Lavazza, son of Antonio Maria, is similarly undocumented, though more of his instruments have survived. His earliest surviving label is dated 1718. The style of his work is similar to that of his father, though the influence of Stradivari and Giovanni Grancino is rather more evident. The scrolls are particularly well cut and show a joining of the Stradivari and Grancino models.

JAAK LIIVOJA-LORIUS

Lawle [dawle]. Clapperless bell of the Baule people of the Ivory Coast. It is thin, flat and slightly cup-shaped, and attached by a cord to an ornately carved padded wooden hammer. Differing pitches are obtained by 'stopping' parts of the bell. The *lawle* provides the rhythm for ritual chanting in the male cults and is also used with a group of drums for the festival of chiefs.

BIBLIOGRAPHY
S. Chauvet: *Musique nègre* (Paris, 1929)
B. Holas: *Craft and Culture in the Ivory Coast* (Abidjan, 1968)

Lda-man. *See* DA-MAN.

Ldumbol. KETTLEDRUM of the Kilba people of north-eastern Nigeria. It is approximately 60 cm high and 45 cm in diameter. The membrane is lapped over the sides of the wooden body-shell and kept in position by solid wooden pegs driven into holes at right angles to the shell. The drum is beaten with hands or fists, according to the rhythm required, after being placed slantwise on the ground and anchored with three or four large pieces of stone. Drums are owned by lineages, each lineage being expected to possess one; the instrument is kept by the eldest male and used for death ceremonies of his kindred.

It is also played for a ritual dance on the birth of twins and for recreational dancing by young men and women. The drum is never played alone but most commonly with a *dang birni* (cylindrical drum) or *dang fokku* (hourglass drum) and *algaita* (oboe).

K. A. GOURLAY

Lê. Conical drum of Bahia, Brazil. *See* ATABAQUE.

Leaf oboe. Aerophone made from a leaf and blown like an oboe. It can be made simply by doubling a leaf, though a more elaborate form has the leaf wrapped in a cone shape with the narrow end pressed flat; sometimes a leaf (serving as a reed) or piece of tubing (mouthpiece) is inserted into the narrow end. It is known to be widely distributed in Oceania. In mainland New Guinea the instrument is generally a toy and blown only for entertainment. In island Melanesia it tends to be associated with initiations and men's secret or graded societies to represent spirit voices (*see* KIO, KUPKUP) or the sound of women crying for their novitiate sons. In Micronesia it is found in Nauru and in the Caroline Islands from Puluwat and Satowal westwards as far as Yap. In island Polynesia it occurs nearly everywhere and is exclusively a child's plaything; it is made from banana, coconut, pandanus or *ti* leaves. In New Zealand (*see* TEETERE) it also served adults as a makeshift trumpet.

The following leaf oboes are entered in this dictionary: agididik; atigetix; dupdup; fa'aili; fakatangi lau futsi; gadigedik; kanini; kio; kupkup; me'a ifi lbu niu; pepet wuno nio; pia'u; pī bai maphrāo; pu ko'e rauti; pū lā 'ī; pu launiu; pu rau nikau; puwi-puwi; raj; teetere; uchif.

BIBLIOGRAPHY

H. Fischer: 'Zwei einfache Musikinstrumente aus Blatt in Ozeanien', *Jb des Museums für Völkerkunde zu Leipzig*, xiv (1956), 67

K. A. Gourlay: *An Approach to the Traditional Music of Papua New Guinea* (Goroka, 1979), 52f

MERVYN McLEAN

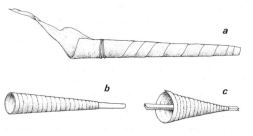

Types of leaf oboe: (a) simple form (Hawaii); (b) with mouthpiece (Ulithi, Caroline Islands); (c) with reed (Trans-Fly, New Guinea)

Leaf whizzer. Free aerophone made from a strip of leaf bent into an oval with a leaf rib standing over it as a sort of saddle; it is whirled in the air on a short stick or on a cord like a BULLROARER. It is known to be widely distributed in Oceania, especially in the Solomon Islands and Micronesia but also in New Guinea, the Bismarck Archipelago and Santo, Vanuatu. In Polynesia it appears to be present only in Tonga and the Cook Islands. It is used everywhere as a children's toy.

The following leaf whizzers are entered in this dictionary: aburiburi; epốp; papuanga; patangitangi; wakatangitangi.

BIBLIOGRAPHY

H. Fischer: 'Zwei einfache Musikinstrumente aus Blatt in Ozeanien', *Jb des Museums für Völkerkunde zu Leipzig*, xiv (1956), 67

MERVYN McLEAN

Lea-lea. Idiochord bamboo zither of various sizes used in the Makassarese and Buginese areas of the province of South Sulawesi. The strings, which are partially prised out of its surface, are raised on bridges at both ends, stretched over a small soundhole, and beaten with a pair of thin sticks. The instrument is usually played in ensemble with the *kacapi* (plucked lute), *ganrang* (double-headed drum) and gong.

MARGARET J. KARTOMI

Lebendig (Ger.: 'lively'). *See* VIVACE.

Lebhaft (Ger.: 'lively', 'sprightly', 'brisk'). A tempo mark. In the second movement of his Piano Sonata in A op.101 Beethoven translated *lebhaft, marschmässig* as *vivace alla marcia*; but in the first movement *etwas lebhaft und mit der innigsten Empfindung* becomes *allegretto ma non troppo*. The introduction to Act 3 of *Lohengrin* is headed *sehr lebhaft*.

Leblanc. French firm of woodwind instrument makers. It was formed in 1904, when Georges Leblanc acquired the business of NOBLET. This has been continued by his son, Léon Leblanc (*b* La Couture Boussey, 24 Nov 1900), who is the principal stockholder of the firm. Subsidiary distribution companies have been formed abroad: in 1965 G. L. Leblanc (London) Ltd was established in partnership with William [Bill] Lewington, while in the USA, G. Leblanc Corporation is based in Kenosha, Wisconsin.

Although Leblanc does produce some flutes and oboes, it is especially notable for its range of clarinets: piccolo instruments in Ab, Eb and D, soprano instruments in C, Bb and A, basset-horns, alto, bass, contra-alto and contrabass clarinets (*see* CLARINET, fig.1a, *c–h*). There is also the unusual sub-contrabass clarinet made for Leblanc by M. Houvenaghel. The reputation of the soprano instruments is based on their clear, bright tone. These use a normal cylindrical bore and a standard Boehm system. However, the firm also produces instruments with tapered bore, others with a large bore to produce a more penetrating sound richer in overtones, and models with additions to and deviations from the standard keywork. With the exception of the contra-alto, contrabass and sub-contrabass instruments, which are made of nickel-plated metal, Leblanc clarinets are normally built of African blackwood, with nickel-silver mounts and keys.

NIALL O'LOUGHLIN

Lebuan. Suspended bossed gong of the Yakan people of the Southern Philippines. *See* KULINTANG.

Leaf whizzer (Kosrae, Micronesia)

Le Caine, Hugh (*b* Port Arthur [now Thunder Bay], Ont., 27 May 1914; *d* Ottawa, 3 July 1977). Canadian electronics engineer, musician and inventor of electronic instruments. Following a brief period at the Toronto Conservatory, Le Caine studied engineering and then physics at Queen's University in Kingston (1934–9); after the war he carried out doctoral work at the University of Birmingham in Britain (1948–52). Soon after returning to Canada he set up the Elmus Labs in the Radio and Electrical Engineering Division of the National Research Council (NRC) of Canada in Ottawa in 1954; there he pursued the work on electronic instruments that he had begun while still at high school and continued privately afterwards. Le Caine was closely involved in setting up the University of Toronto Electronic Music Studio in 1959. He retired in 1974. His electronic instruments and devices, mostly built for use in the electronic music studios of universities in Toronto, Montreal and Kingston, are characterized by their inventiveness, practicality, ergonomic design and pioneering character. Since 1979 the Hugh Le Caine Project has documented his work and is assembling a collection of his instruments.

In 1937 Le Caine constructed an electrostatically amplified reed organ (now lost), the principle of which was later adopted in his 'vibrating reed electrometer'. Between 1945 and 1948 he developed at his home in Ottawa what may be regarded as the first synthesizer – the ELECTRONIC SACKBUT – which included elements of voltage control. It was subsequently modified at the NRC in the late 1950s and again between 1969 and 1973; four models were built. The first instrument constructed at the Elmus Labs was Le Caine's 'touch-sensitive organ' (1953–5) which incorporated a cheap and simple system for a frictionless, touch-sensitive keyboard. Two or three examples of this electronic organ were built: one was similar to a small commercial instrument, having 12 oscillators and using frequency division; another had 99 oscillators and a glide pedal, and is featured in Le Caine's tape composition *Ninety-Nine Generators* (1956). None of the instruments is known to survive: they were either lost or 'cannibalized' for later projects. The Baldwin company bought the organ's patent, but apart from making use of its 'clickless' key mechanism did not pursue the matter. In 1955 Le Caine developed his 'special purpose tape recorder' (usually known as the 'Multi-Track') based on research from the late 1940s; this is a multi-track, voltage-controlled, variable-speed machine, operated from one or two three-octave keyboards (tunable to any scale or temperament) and a ribbon controller. It resembles the Mellotron but is more flexible, since it can play back up to 10 stereo tapes or long tape loops, either in synchronization or independently at different speeds. Le Caine's best-known tape composition, *Dripsody* (1955), was created in a few hours with this tape recorder, of which five models still exist.

In 1957 the 12-note 'sinebank and keyboard' was produced, and a similar 13-note 'tone mixture generator' was developed some time afterwards. A later model (late 1950s) had 100 oscillators, controlled by means of either a photoelectric system or a touch-sensitive 'keyboard' consisting of 'printed circuit keys' (devised in 1962 and also used as the basis of a multichannel sound distribution system). This formed the prototype for the two models of the Sonde (1968), whose resources consist of 200 sine waves derived by means of difference tones from 20 fixed-frequency oscillators and ten converter-oscillators; one model also used 'printed circuit keys'. Around 1967 a modular sequencer, the 'serial sound structure generator', was devised, of which five models exist. Le Caine's last important instrument, the Polyphone (1970), is an early voltage-controlled polyphonic synthesizer with an oscillator for each note on the three-octave touch-sensitive keyboard and pedals for controlling several parameters; only one was built and Le Caine used it to produce his tape composition *Paulution* (1971). A hybrid computer-controlled analogue synthesizer, the Paramus (1972), was developed by John Chong under Le Caine's supervision.

For illustration of the 'electronic sackbut', *see* ELECTRONIC INSTRUMENTS, fig.7.

BIBLIOGRAPHY

H. Le Caine: 'Touch-sensitive Organ Based on an Electrostatic Coupling Device', *Journal of the Acoustical Society of America*, xxvii (1955), 781
——: 'Electronic Music', *Proceedings of the Institute of Radio Engineers*, xliv (1956), 457
——: 'A Touch-sensitive Keyboard for the Organ', *Canadian Music Journal*, iii/3 (1959), 26
——: 'A Tape Recorder for Use in Electronic Music Studios and Related Equipment', *JMT*, vii (1963), 83
——: 'Electronic Music', *New Scientist* (16 Dec 1965), 814
H. Le Caine and G. Ciamaga: 'A Preliminary Report on the Serial Sound Structure Generator', *PNM*, vi/1 (1967), 114
H. Le Caine: 'Some Applications of Electrical Level Controls', *Electronic Music Review* (1967), no.4, p.25
——: 'Apparatus for Generating Serial Sound Structures', *Journal of the Audio Engineering Society*, xvii (1969), 258
H. Le Caine and G. Ciamaga: 'The Sonde: a New Approach to Multiple Sinewave Generation', *Journal of the Audio Engineering Society*, xviii (1970), 536
Hugh Le Caine Project Newsletter (1979–)

HUGH DAVIES

Lechaka [lichaka]. End-blown flute of the Tswana people of southern Africa. The modern spelling is LETLHAKA.

Lecompte, Arsène-Zoé (*b* Ferrière-Haut-Clocher, 3 June 1818; *d* Paris, April 1892). French wind instrument maker. After being an employee of Gautrot, he set up his own business in Paris in 1859. He specialized in the production of brass instruments for export. In 1874 he designed a DUPLEX clairon/trumpet which had two supplementary pistons fitted, and in 1885 a cornet with instant transposition facility. In 1888 he was the first maker to apply part of the mechanism of the Boehm system to the saxophone. His metal bassoon of 1889 was reported by Pierre to have 'sonorité extraordinaire et justesse absolue', light mechanism, beautiful low notes, and upper notes with a metallic sound not unlike those on the saxophone. Lecompte also produced ophicleides, natural trumpets, tenor saxhorns, helicons, cornets, bugles, oboes and clarinets. He gained bronze (1867) and silver (1878) medals in Paris, a diploma of honour in Philadelphia (1876), a first prize in Melbourne (1881) and a Croix de la Légion d'honneur (1881).

BIBLIOGRAPHY

F. J. Fétis: *Exposition universelle de 1867 . . . rapports*, ii: *Instruments de musique* (Paris, 1868)
C. Pierre: *La facture instrumentale à l'Exposition universelle de 1889* (Paris, 1890)
L. G. Langwill: *An Index of Musical Wind-instrument Makers* (Edinburgh, 1960, rev., enlarged 6/1980)

NIALL O'LOUGHLIN

Ledabul. Long single-headed cylindrical drum of the Konkomba people of northern Togo. It has cord and belt bracing.

Ledor. XYLOPHONE of Flores, Indonesia. *See* PRESON.

Leedy Manufacturing Co. American firm of drum makers. It was established in Indianapolis in 1900 by Ulysses G. Leedy and Samuel L. Cooley as Leedy & Cooley, and made 'everything for the band and orchestra drummer'. Leedy (1867–1931), a professional musician and amateur drum maker, became sole owner in 1903 and expanded the firm's production to include over 900 items, among them orchestral bells, vibraphones and numerous sound-effect instruments to accompany silent movies. Most important were the timpani designed by the factory superintendent Cecil Strupe and patented in 1923. These used a foot pedal with a ratchet-and-pawl system clutch, linked to cables connected to the tensioning screws; the copper bowls were formed in a specially designed hydraulic press rather than hammered over wooden moulds. This design served as the model for the first English pedal timpani manufactured by the Premier Drum Co. Leedy drums were exported to England during the 1920s, but owing to heavy import duties, eventually only the parts were shipped and the drums themselves assembled by the Hawkes firm. Leedy was purchased by C. G. Conn in 1927 and its production combined with that of Ludwig & Ludwig, which was acquired by Conn in 1930 (*see* LUDWIG). The Leedy–Ludwig division continued to operate until its sale to Slingerland Drum Co. in 1955; production of Leedy instruments ceased in 1958.

EDMUND A. BOWLES

Leero [leerow] **viol.** *See* LYRA VIOL.

Lefèvre [Lefebvre, Fêvre, Lefeure, Lefébure]. French 16th- to 19th-century organ builders. The name belonged to at least 23 builders, mostly members of the same family.

Some of the early Lefèvres include: Antoine (*fl* Paris, 1524–51), who built an organ for Les Mathurins, Paris, in 1524 and made his will at Sens in 1528; Guillaume (*fl* 1572–81), his son, an organ builder of Rouen, who worked at Le Mans in 1572 and at Chartres from 1574 to 1581; Charles (i) (*fl* Rouen, 1573), another son of Antoine, who cleaned and repaired the organ at St Maclou, Rouen, in 1573; Léonard (*d* Angoulême, *c*1659), son of Guillaume, a native of Fresnay-sur-Sarthe who worked at Le Mans from 1603 to 1613, Angoulême in 1615, Mitry-Mory and the St Ausone Abbey; Nicolas (i) (*fl* 1606–10), son of Charles (i), both an organist and organ builder, who worked at Angoulême (1606–8), Rouen (1609), Mantes and then Chevreuse (St Martin, 1610); Nicolas (ii) (*fl* 1629–*c*1635), a grandson of Charles (i), who is known to have worked in Rouen about 1635.

Clément (*b* Rouen, *c*1630; *d* Rouen, 29 Sept 1709), son of Nicolas (ii), was organist of Notre-Dame-la-Ronde in 1663. He rebuilt the organ of St Nicaise, Rouen, in 1684. From 1681, he worked with his son Germain (baptized Rouen, 6 Oct 1656; *d* Rouen, 1694) until the latter's death; together they built a four-manual and pedal organ at St Herbland, Rouen (1685–8), and an almost identical organ at St Denis, Rouen (1688–97) (*Grand orgue*: Montre 8′, Bourdon 16′, Bourdon 8′, Prestant, Flûte 4′, Nazard, Doublette, Tierce, Fourniture IV, Cymbale III, Cornet V, Trompette, Clairon, Voix humaine; *Positif*: Montre 4′, Bourdon 8′, Flûte 4′, Nazard, Doublette, Quarte de nazard, Tierce, Fourniture III, Cymbale II, Larigot, Cromhorne; *Récit*: Cornet V, Trompette; *Echo*: Bourdon, Prestant, Nazard, Doublette, Tierce, Fourniture III, Cromhorne, Voix humaine; *Pédale*: Bourdon (open) 8′, Flûte (open) 4′, Trompette). The St Herbland organ is now at Bolbec. On the completion of this organ Germain became organist at St Herbland, remaining there until his death. Another son of Clément, Claude (baptized Rouen, 29 Dec 1667), crossed the Atlantic in 1707. His letters from Cartagenas, where he built three organs, and Caracas, where he built one or two others, are printed in Dufourcq (1934–5, p.394). Charles (ii) (baptized Rouen, 22 May 1670; *d* 8 Sept 1737), a third son of Clément, worked as an organ builder with his father after his brother Germain's death. He restored the organ of St Maclou (1696–1707) and built that at St Vivien (1710–12, enlarged 1719). His last organ was for St Nicolas, Rouen. He was organist of St Vivien from 1698 to 1735.

Jean-Baptiste Nicolas (baptized Rouen, 6 Feb 1705; *d* Rouen, 26 March 1784), son of Charles (ii), was the most famous of the Lefèvres, of comparable importance to F.-H. Clicquot and Riepp. Characteristics of his style were an extension of the manual compass up to *e‴* but a curtailment of the upper range of the pedal from the old *e′* to *c′* only; an extension of some of the cornets from *c′* down to *f*; an increase in the number of ranks of the Fournitures and Cymbales, often up to five each; the addition of 8′ flutes to both *Grand orgue* and *Positif* of narrow-scale leaded metal from *c*; the addition of extra trumpets (frequently in large numbers), his normal arrangement being two on the *Grand orgue* and one each on the *Positif* and *Récit*, besides those on the *Pédale* and *Bombarde* (on organs having one); the use of a Bombarde 16′; up to five cornets, one on each manual; and the addition on the *Pédale* of a Nazard and a 16′ Trompette.

A list of the principal organs of Jean-Baptiste Nicolas Lefèvre is given in Dufourcq (1934–5, p.305f). Chief among these were the instruments at Notre Dame, Caudebec-en-Caux (1738–40; including a new Flûte allemande dessus); St Etienne, Caen (1743–7); Abbaye de Montivilliers (1746); St Maclou, Rouen (1761); St Martin, Tours (1761; the largest French classical organ, it has the following specification: *Grand orgue*: 32, 32, 16, 16, 8, 8, two 8′ flutes, 4, 2, VI, V, IV, Gros nazard, Grosse tierce, Nazard, Quarte de nazard, Tierce, Larigot, Cornet, two Trompettes, two Clairons; *Positif*: 8, 16, 8, two 8′ flutes, 4, 2, V, IV, Nazard, Quarte, Tierce, Larigot, Cornet, Trompette, Cromorne, Voix humaine, Clairon; *Bombarde*: 8, 4, Cornet, Bombarde, two Trompettes, Clairon; *Récit*: Cornet, Trompette; *Echo*: Cornet; *Pédale*, 36 notes: 16, 8, 8, 4, 4, Gros nazard, Grosse tierce, Nazard, Quarte, Tierce, Bombarde (24′), two Trompettes, two Clairons); Evreux Cathedral (1774); St Pierre, Caen (1753, 1778; including a new Bombarde on the *Grand orgue*, a new Flûte of three octaves, Quarte and Hautbois on the *Positif* and a new Bombarde on the *Pédale*); Verneuil (1779; including a Flûte allemande on the *Grand orgue* and Quarte, Cornet, Voix humaine and Hautbois de deux octaves on the *Positif*; recently restored). Jean-Baptiste Nicolas was also organist of St Nicaise, Rouen, in 1737, at which time he appears to have succeeded his father at St Vivien, Rouen, where he was organist until 1782.

Another son of Charles (ii), Louis (baptized 23 May 1708; buried Rouen, 23 Dec 1754), worked sometimes alone and sometimes with his brother Jean-Baptiste Nicolas. In 1739 he restored the organ of St Vivien, Rouen, and together with his brother he restored and reconstructed the organ of Notre Dame, Caudebec-en-Caux, Normandy (1738–40; four manuals and pedal, the keyboards with bone naturals and ebony accidentals). The inventory of his possessions made on 17 January 1755 is printed in Dufourcq (1934–5, pp.390–92).

Other Lefèvre organ builders were apparently not related to the main Lefèvre family. Jacques Liévin (*b* Hesdin, 1621; *d* ?Rouen, after 1665), son of a half-brother of the De Héman nephews, was their pupil in Paris and later their colleague. He married a sister of Pierre Desenclos, with whom he worked at Mitry and at St Médard, Paris. He later went to Rennes, where he built the organ of St Georges in 1654 (now in St Sauveur), and to Dôle (1657), and built the organ at the Église du Voeu, Cherbourg (1661). Jean (*fl* 1650–66) was an organist and Carmelite priest; as an organ builder he restored the instrument at St Vivien, Rouen. Pierre (*b* Troyes, *c*1670; *d* Paris, 1737) worked as an organ builder in Paris from 1692. Charles (iii) (*fl* Abbeville, mid-19th century) built the organ at St Sépulcre, Abbeville.

BIBLIOGRAPHY
N. Dufourcq: *Documents inédits relatifs à l'orgue français* (Paris, 1934–5)
——: *Esquisse d'une histoire de l'orgue en France* (Paris, 1935)
M. Vanmackelberg: 'Les orgues d'Abbeville', *Mémoires de la Société d'Emulation d'Abbeville* (Abbeville, 1967)
F. Douglass: *The Language of the Classical French Organ* (New Haven, 1969)
GUY OLDHAM

LeForestier [LeForrestier, LeForester], **Alexandre** (*b c*1835). French brass instrument maker. He began his apprenticeship with Besson in Paris about 1850 and was with Joseph Higham in Manchester for 11 years. Later, as bell and tube maker for Auguste Courtois, he was honoured at exhibitions. He lived in Philadelphia from 1888 to 1895, where he was foreman of the bell and tubing department of J. W. Pepper's factory. He developed the designs and technology for Pepper's brass instruments, and his efforts to perfect the passage of air through a smoothly tapering bore extended the accomplishments of Gustave Besson in France and anticipated the work of Ernst A. Couturier in the USA. He also invented in 1888 a quick-action piston valve with helical grooves, which added rotary motion to the normal vertical passage of a valve.

LLOYD P. FARRAR

Legato [ligato] (It.: 'bound'; Fr. *lié*; Ger. *gebunden*). Of successive notes in performance, connected without any intervening silence of articulation. In practice, the connection or separation of notes is relative, and achieved through the presence or absence of emphasis, ACCENT and attack, as much as silences of articulation; degrees of connection and separation vary from legatissimo (representing the closest degree of connection), tenuto, portamento, legato (more or less synonymous with the string player's *detaché*), portato, non legato, mezzo-staccato, STACCATO (the natural antonym of legato), to staccatissimo, and some of these terms have connotations going beyond simple degrees of connection or separation.

In 20th-century notation, legato is generally indicated by means of the SLUR across a succession of notes; the beginnings and ends of slurs are now generally marked by articulations (of bowing or tonguing in string and wind instruments, and of phrasing in keyboard instruments). The slur often, however, had a vaguer general meaning of 'legato' in the 18th and early 19th centuries. Successions of notes in modern notation are seldom left without any indication of articulation, but if they are, the performer will normally presume that a legato style of playing is called for.

This notion, that legato playing represents an 'ordinary' style of performance rather than a special effect, perhaps originated in the cavatina style of early 19th-century Italian opera and its imitation in Romantic instrumental music, or before that in the cantabile slow-movement styles of the 18th century. In earlier centuries, both legato and staccato styles of playing were normally available as special effects, the normal style of playing and singing often being something between the two: in medieval and Renaissance music, the ligature seems sometimes to have been a prescription of a special legato effect. The degree of legato to be used also depended on repertory and instrument: for example, Diruta (*Il transilvano*, 1597) distinguished between a legato organ style and a detached harpsichord style for dance music. For Baroque and early Classical fast movements, a non-legato style was regarded as usual, whereas the legato was normally reserved for long notes and slow movements (C. P. E. Bach, *Versuch*, 1753; Quantz, *Versuch*, 1752, etc; this style of performance is still called for by Türk, *Klavierschule*, 1804). In some 18th-century music, slurs over arpeggiated chords imply a kind of legatissimo, where all notes are to be held down until the chord changes.

For translations from relevant early authorities, see Donington, 3/1974, pp.473–81; for useful general advice on legato and staccato in early music, see Badura-Skoda, Ferguson and Keller.

See also ARTICULATION.

BIBLIOGRAPHY
H. Keller: *Phrasierung und Artikulation* (Kassel, 1955; Eng. trans., 1965, 2/1973)
E. and P. Badura-Skoda: *Mozart-Interpretation* (Vienna and Stuttgart, 1957; Eng. trans., 1962 as *Interpreting Mozart on the Keyboard*)
R. Donington: *The Interpretation of Early Music* (London, 1963, rev. 3/1974)
H. Ferguson: *Keyboard Interpretation* (London, 1975)
GEOFFREY CHEW

Léger (Fr.: 'light'). As a tempo designation, particularly in its adverbial form *légèrement* (or *légérement*), a term widely used in the early 18th century by French composers. J. G. Walther (1732) defined it as a mark of expression to indicate a light performing style, but there can be little doubt that François Couperin, who used it along with *tres légérement, d'une légéreté modérée, d'une légéreté gracieuse* and *d'une légéreté tendre*, regarded it as a fairly precise indication of tempo as well as of mood. So did Rousseau (1768), who placed it between *gai* and *vite* as the equivalent of the Italian *vivace*.

For bibliography *see* TEMPO AND EXPRESSION MARKS.

DAVID FALLOWS

Leggermente. *See* LEGGERO.

Leggero [leggiero] (It.: 'light'). A performance direction which belongs characteristically to the 19th century and is also found in the adverbial forms *leggermente* and *leggiermente*, occasionally misspelt by Beethoven *leg-*

geramente (op.120) and *leggieramente* (opp.47, 74 and 95). Normally it called for a light, detached style of playing in rapid passages. But it can be interpreted more loosely: *legato* passages are marked *leggeramente* in the 25th of Beethoven's Diabelli Variations; the *forte* opening of the scherzo in Beethoven's Eb Quartet op.74 is marked *leggieramente*; and Mendelssohn has *leggero* simultaneously with *forte* and *legato* in the finale of his G minor Piano Concerto. Verdi used the superlative form *leggerissimo*, e.g. for Alfredo in the 'Brindisi' from *La traviata* and for Preziosilla in Act 2 of *La forza del destino*; Elgar used the form *leggierissimo* in the second movement of his Cello Concerto.

See also TEMPO AND EXPRESSION MARKS.

DAVID FALLOWS

Leggiadro (It.: 'pretty', 'graceful'). A performance instruction found as early as the 18th century. J. G. Walther (*Musicalisches Lexicon*, 1732) gave for *leggiodro* (presumably a misprint) and *leggiadramente* (the adverbial form) the entry: 'sehr schön, über die Massen annehmlich, mit einer artigen Manier' ('very beautiful, exceptionally charming, with a pleasing manner').

Leggiero [leggiermente]. See LEGGERO.

Legno (It.: 'wood'). *Strumenti di legno*, or simply *legni*, are WOODWIND INSTRUMENTS. In string-instrument playing COL LEGNO means setting the strings in motion with the wood of the bow. In some orchestral scores 'legno' denotes a WOODBLOCK.

Legnofono. A XYLOPHONE made by Lasina of Rome in 1882.

Le Héman. See DE HÉMAN family.

Lehmänsarvi. Animal-horn trumpet of Finland, similar to the *pukinsarvi* but made of cowhorn.

Lehnert, Henry G. (*b* Freiberg, Saxony, 3 Feb 1838; *d* Philadelphia, 14 Oct 1916). American brass instrument maker of German origin. He established a business at 68 Albany Street, Boston, Massachusetts, in 1865. The following year he took out an American patent for a tapering lead-pipe in bugles and cornets, which was one of the earliest to be issued in its class. A Carl Lehnert remained in Boston as an associate of the instrument maker and dealer Benjamin F. Richardson until after 1900. Henry, however, had moved by 1867 to 753 Race Street, Philadelphia, then worked for five years at 911 Vine Street before finding a permanent shop at 927 North 9th Street in 1873. He won prizes at fairs in Boston (1865), Philadelphia (1876) and Baltimore (1878). Although his instruments show some technical affinities with those of William Seefeldt, Lehnert alone of the Philadelphia makers worked frequently in German silver; he and J. L. Allen of Boston were the only makers to use rotary valves with narrow rotors and flattened ports, which allowed quicker key strokes. Lehnert produced many varieties of brass instruments with upright and forward-facing bells, including circular ones. A baritone, known as the Centennial, rested on the player's shoulders and offered improved drainage from horizontally arranged tubing. In later years Lehnert manufac-tured American Standard cornets. George Fredericks, whose name appears on some Philadelphia cornets, apparently worked with Lehnert during the years 1906–16.

LLOYD P. FARRAR

Lehofu. Term for a variety of vocal amplifiers, megaphones or trumpet-like instruments used among the Sotho people of Lesotho, southern Africa, for the sounding of alarms.

Leichnamschneider [Leichamschneider, Leichnambschneider, Leicham Schneider]. Austrian family of brass instrument makers, of Swabian origin. Working mainly in Vienna, they evolved the first specifically orchestral model of horn with crooks in 1700. Michael Leichnamschneider (*b* Osterberg, nr. Memmingen, 26 Aug 1676; *d* Vienna, after 1746) appears to have been the head of the firm. He took his oath as a citizen of Vienna in 1700 and married in 1701. In 1700 and 1703 he furnished horns with crooks and tuning-bits – the earliest of their kind – to the abbey of Kremsmünster, signing himself as a maker of horns before his brother on the bill of 1703. His brother Johannes (*b* Osterberg, 26 June 1679; *d* Vienna, after 1725) was also a maker of brass instruments, though Michael was the more prolific.

To the list of Michael's instruments given in Langwill (1960) may be added two horns with crooks of 1700 and a pair with crooks of 1703 (both for Kremsmünster); a pair of horns with crooks (Göttweig Abbey, 1709); and an orchestral horn with crooks, presumably one of a pair, from 1721 (surviving in the Oettingen-Wallerstein collection, Harburg; only the bell-branch is authenticated, however). The pair of silver parforce horns with gold mounts made by Johannes Leichnamschneider in 1725 for Lord Tredegar, whose family still owns them, lend support to the theory that the brothers worked with Count Sporck, the first patron of artistic horn playing: Michael Heinrich Rentz, a copper engraver to the courts of Vienna and Prague and a protégé of Sporck, engraved the hunting scenes on the gold garlands of these horns.

The name of Franz Leichnamschneider, presumably the son of Michael, appears on a gold-mounted silver trumpet that Maria Theresia presented to the Viennese court orchestra in 1746. The instrument is associated with, but not part of, a set of five silver trumpets by Michael Leichnamschneider dated 1741, and is in the Kunsthistorisches Museum, Vienna. Johann Leichnamschneider, a copper engraver, appears in the parish records of St Stephen's Cathedral in 1747. The rarity of the name points to a relationship with the family of instrument makers; he probably worked as an associate, engraving garlands and collars.

BIBLIOGRAPHY

L. G. Langwill: *An Index of Musical Wind-instrument Makers* (Edinburgh, 1960, rev., enlarged 6/1980)
H. A. Fitzpatrick: *The Horn and Horn-playing, and the Austro-Bohemian Tradition from 1680 to 1830* (London, 1970)

HORACE FITZPATRICK

Leier (Ger.). (1) LYRE.

(2) HURDY-GURDY, as in *Drehleier*, *Radleier* and *Bettlerleier*. A *Leierkasten*, on the other hand, is a BARREL ORGAN.

Lekemba. LAMELLAPHONE of the Dilolo district of the Zaïre–Angola border.

Lekhitlane. (1) A conical flute of the Southern Sotho people of southern Africa, made from the horn of a female blesbok, open at the wider end. When sounded, it was placed on the player's hollowed tongue. A small hole near the tip of the horn could be closed by a finger, making two notes possible. This instrument is rare today, but was formerly used at midnight in the *lebollo* male initiation dance. See *KirbyMISA*, 108, pl.39*a*. *See also* LUVEVE; NAKA; PALA; UVEVE.

(2) A megaphone (vocal resonator) of the Southern Sotho people of southern Africa. It is made from goat or sheep horn and is used as a signalling device.

DAVID K. RYCROFT, CHARLES R. ADAMS

Lekhorn. Swedish animal-horn trumpet with finger-holes. *See* BOCKHORN.

Leko [leok, juk]. Plucked lute of southern Timor, Indonesia. It has a pear-shaped body made from an old dried gourd about 20 cm in diameter. The rounded wooden neck is about 30 to 40 cm long and 3 to 4 cm wide; the pegs protrude from the sides of a backward-slanting piece of wood at the top. Four strings, made of dried goatskin, intestines or thin wire, are stretched from near the base, over a round soundhole, to the pegs at the top. It is usually played with a *biola* (violin) in the *leko-biola* ensemble.

MARGARET J. KARTOMI

Lekoko. Idiophone of the Southern Sotho people of Lesotho, southern Africa, comprising a hard rolled cow-hide beaten with sticks and used to accompany dancing. The names MOROPA or SEKUPU (normally applying to drums) are also sometimes used for it. The term *lekoko* basically means 'a hide'.

Lekolilo [lekolilwe, lekolulo]. End-blown flute of the Southern Sotho people of southern Africa. One type, without finger-holes, resembles the Zulu UMTSHINGO and the *mokoreie* of the Tswana. A second type (possibly more recent) has three or four finger-holes. Both extensively exploit harmonic partials.

Lekope. MOUTH BOW of the Sotho peoples of southern Africa. Among the Southern Sotho of Lesotho alternative names for it are *lekotje* or *moqakana*, and two types occur: one resembles the Zulu UMQANGALA but usually has a small twig bridge; the other type is braced, having a tuning loop. They are plucked with a short grass plectrum, and finger-stopped. Both the bridge and the loop are used to store spare plectra. The *lekope* is usually played by women, sometimes to accompany the player's dancing. Among the Northern Sotho, besides denoting the unbraced type noted above, the name has also been applied to a composite braced mouth bow resembling the Southern Sotho SETOLOTOLO or Zulu ISI-THONTOLO. See *KirbyMISA*, 220ff and pll.62, 64 and 65*a*.

DAVID K. RYCROFT, CHARLES R. ADAMS

Lėkštės. Cymbals of Lithuania, consisting of two iron discs of the same size. The *lėkštės* appeared in Lithuania in the 17th and 18th centuries, in court orchestras and opera and ballet companies, finding their way into folk music groups in the late 19th and early 20th centuries, when brass band instruments became popular in small towns and villages. The *lėkštės* can be used in a variety of ways but are mostly played with the double-headed drum. One cymbal is suspended horizontally over the drum and struck with the other, held by a loop. Both cymbals can also be fixed on to the drum and clashed by means of a foot pedal. Even nowadays the instrument is often made by blacksmiths or musicians themselves, from various kinds of metal.

ARVYDAS KARAŠKA

Lelega. Indonesian XYLOPHONE. *See* TUDDUGLAG.

Le Maire, Jean (*b* Chaumont-en-Bassigny, Haute-Marne, *c*1581; *d c*1650). French polymath. Among his musical activities was the invention of the ALMÉRIE (an anagram of his name).

Lemana. Bamboo flute of the Galla people of East Africa.

Lembe-nsoni. Wooden trumpet of the Bembe people of the Republic of the Congo. *See* MAMPONGUI-NGUEMBO.

Lembõck, Gabriel (*b* Ofen, Budapest, 16 Oct 1814; *d* ?Vienna, 27 March 1892). Austrian violin maker of Hungarian birth. He was apprenticed in Budapest to Peter Teufelsdorfer. He subsequently worked for Anton Fischer (later becoming his son-in-law and successor) and Bernard Stoss in Vienna, where he opened his own shop, 'Zum Weissen Engel', in the Mariahilferstrasse in 1840. His instruments are of bold modelling and are very well made. By and large, he followed three models: Stradivari, Guarneri 'del Gesù' and Maggini. The Guarneri model was actually a copy of Paganini's concert violin, known as the 'Canon', an instrument which Lembõck had repaired and adjusted on several occasions. The Maggini copies are always double-purfled and can be regarded, along with his copies of the 'Canon', as his best work. Lembõck's best varnish, somewhat heavily applied, is usually a golden red-brown; on lesser instruments it is less thickly applied and of lighter colour. He used a variety of printed labels, some in germanic type, and he usually branded his initials on the button of the neck.

BIBLIOGRAPHY

W. L. von Lütgendorff: *Die Geigen- und Lautenmacher von Mittelalter bis zur Gegenwart* (Frankfurt am Main, 1904, rev. 6/1922/*R*1968)

JAAK LIIVOJA-LORIUS

Lenga. SLIT-DRUM of the Banda-Linda people of the Central African Republic.

Lenge. *See* ELENGE.

Lengkara. KETTLEDRUM of Selangor, West Malaysia, used in the NOBAT ensemble.

Lengope. Unbraced MOUTH BOW of the Tswana people of southern Africa. The stave is made from a piece of river reed 50 to 60 cm long; the string is of plant fibre or sinew and is sounded with a plectrum. Players are girls or young married women. Playing technique resembles that for the Venda *lugube* and the Zulu UMQANGALA. See *KirbyMISA*, 220ff and pl.62.

Lengwane. NOTCHED FLUTE of the Pedi (Northern Sotho) people of southern Africa. It is made from the leg-bone of a goat or sheep, covered with skin, and the end is plugged with wax. It is played only by boys.

Lênh. Large flat gong of Vietnam, struck with a wooden beater.

Lent. See LENTO.

Lentando (It.: 'becoming slower'). See RALLENTANDO and TEMPO AND EXPRESSION MARKS.

Lentement. See LENTO.

Lento (It.: 'slow'). One of the earliest tempo marks to be used in music. Mentioned in passing by Zarlino ('movimenti tardi e lenti'), it was used by Praetorius (*Polyhymnia caduceatrix*, 1619; *Puericinium*, 1621), Thomas Selle (1636) and Schütz. Praetorius (1619) gave the equation *lento vel adagio: tardè: mit langsamen Tact*, and in *Syntagma musicum*, iii (2/1619) equated *adagio: largo: lento: langsam*. The word never achieved the same popularity as *adagio*, *largo* and *grave*; but in French music from Lully onwards it became one of the major tempo marks in its adverbial French form *lentement. Sans lenteur* was a particular favourite of François Couperin. Rousseau (1768) gave the French adjective *lent* and its adverb *lentement* as being the same as the Italian *largo*, which he considered the slowest of all tempos; but there is no evidence that his opinion was generally held and he may well simply have been avoiding the dangers of translation by cognate. In the Polonaise of his B minor orchestral suite J. S. Bach marked *lentement* in the violin part but *moderato e staccato* in the flute part: even if this is an oversight it strongly suggests that he thought of *lentement* and *moderato* in the same way.

For bibliography see TEMPO AND EXPRESSION MARKS.

DAVID FALLOWS

Leok. See LEKO.

Leonardo da Vinci (*b* Vinci, nr. Empoli, 1452; *d* château of Cloux, nr. Amboise, 2 May 1519). Italian artist and scientist who was profoundly occupied with music. He performed and taught it, he was deeply interested in acoustics, he wrestled with the concept of musical time, and he had some highly original ideas about the philosophy of music. His universal command of technology enabled him to construct novel musical instruments, and to improve existing ones radically. In his notebooks there are numerous drawings of such instruments from rapid sketches, often not easily decipherable, to exact blueprints for their execution in the workshop. They reveal his systematic efforts to realize some basic aims: automation of certain instruments (see MECHANICAL INSTRUMENT, §2) and the wider use of various types of keyboard to facilitate playing technique; increasing the speed of playing; extension of tonal range to play, for instance, melodies on drums; and overcoming the quickly fading sound of plucked strings. Among other instruments, he constructed glissando flutes, flutes with key systems anticipating Boehm's invention of more than three centuries later, bells with variable pitch, drums of which the pitch could be changed during performance or which

could produce chords, and, above all, the 'viola organista' (see illustration), a keyboard instrument the strings of which were set into vibration by an endless friction band, and which permitted polyphonic playing with dynamic gradation – a virtual string orchestra under the control of ten fingers. Here, as in other cases, Leonardo tried to obtain from one instrument what could normally be produced only by several or by a whole set of instruments.

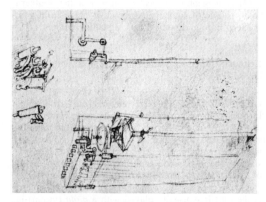

Sketch by Leonardo da Vinci for his 'viola organista' with its endless bow (F-Pi MS H, f.45v)

The sensational reappearance in 1967 at the National Library, Madrid, of two of Leonardo's notebooks, comprising 700 pages, substantially enriched our information about his novel ideas for the construction of musical instruments. The notebooks include drawings of new types of bellows for *organetti* and chamber organs, another drawing for the *viola organista*, and one for the *viola a tasti*, a keyed string instrument operated by segments of cogwheels.

BIBLIOGRAPHY

J. P. Richter: *The Literary Works of Leonardo da Vinci* (London, 1883)

G. Panconcelli-Calzia: *Leonardo als Phonetiker* (Hamburg, 1943)

A. Marinoni: *I rebus di Leonardo da Vinci* (Florence, 1954)

E. Magni-Dufflocq: 'Da Vinci's Music', *Leonardo da Vinci* (London, 1957), 227

E. Winternitz: 'Lira da braccio', *MGG*

——: 'Keyboards for Wind Instruments Invented by Leonardo da Vinci', *Raccolta Vinciana*, xx (Milan, 1964), 69

——: 'Leonardo's Invention of the Viola Organista', *Raccolta Vinciana*, xx (Milan, 1964), 1

——: 'Melodic, Chordal and other Drums Invented by Leonardo da Vinci', *Raccolta Vinciana*, xx (Milan, 1964), 49

——: 'Anatomy the Teacher – on the Impact of Leonardo's Anatomical Research on his Musical and other Machines', *Proceedings of the American Philosophical Society*, iii/4 (1967), 234

——: 'Strange Musical Instruments in the Madrid Notebooks of Leonardo da Vinci', *Metropolitan Museum Journal*, ii (New York, 1969), 115

——: 'La musica nel "Paragone" di Leonardo da Vinci', *Studi musicali*, i (1972), 79

——: 'Leonardo and Music', *The Unknown Leonardo* (New York, 1974), 110

——: *Leonardo da Vinci as a Musician* (New Haven and London, 1982)

EMANUEL WINTERNITZ

Lepakala [lipakala]. Side-blown ivory or animal-horn trumpet of the Bali people of north-eastern Zaïre. It sometimes has a carved mouthpiece (*LaurentyA*, 351).

Lepapata. Animal-horn trumpet of the Tswana people of southern Africa. It is side-blown, like the Venda and

Northern Sotho PHALAPHALA, and is made from the horn of a sable antelope or a kudu. It is essentially a ceremonial instrument, blown only for war, or during initiation, or when a lion or leopard is killed. See *KirbyMISA*, 78, pll.26*a* and 27*b*.

Le Picard. Northern French and Belgian family of organ builders. Philippe (i) (*fl* Amiens, 1667; *d* early 1702) built a new organ at Montdidier in 1667 and restored that in Amiens Cathedral in 1671. With his sons Antoine (*fl* 1685–1716) and Joseph he enlarged the organ at Liessies in 1693–5 and restored that in Noyon Cathedral in 1698. Antoine constructed a new organ with three manuals and 36 stops at St Hubert's Basilica in 1685 (case survives) and repaired that at Amiens Cathedral early in the 18th century. Philippe (ii) (*b* Noyon; *d* ? Liège, *c*1730), another son, married Marie-Anne Delaplace before 1701. A fine builder, he worked on the organs at St Pierre, Liège (1702); the Cathedral of St Lambert, Liège (1705; with French pedals); St Alexandre and St Hermes, Theux (1710 and 1716); and St Croix, Liège (1716).

Jean-Baptiste (baptized Liège, 23 May 1706; *d c*1760), son of Philippe (ii), spent his whole life in Liège where in 1755 he was known to be a priest, probably at St Pierre. Also a fine builder in the French style, he made organs with short compass divisions (*Récit, c'*, and *Echo, c*), and pedal pull-downs. His instruments include those at: St Jean-Baptiste, Namur (1731; restoration); Abbaye de Beaufais, Liège (1741–2; one manual, 13 stops, with pull-downs; still extant); Nunhem, near Roermond (1742; two manuals, with pull-downs; the *Positif* survives as the choir organ in the Martinikerk at Groningen); Houtain-l'Evêque (*c*1745; one manual, with pull-downs; extant); Roermond (*c*1745; now in the Gereformeerde Oosterkerk, Utrecht); Roermond, Groot-Seminarie (1745; case and seven stops survive); Abbaye St Michel, Torn (1745); Hodimont (1747); Roermond Cathedral (1750–52; three manuals, with pull-downs); Notre-Dame-aux-Fonts, Liège; St Loup, Namen; St Pierre, Liège (1739–41; four manuals, 39 stops, with pull-downs); the Abbaye, Herkenrode (1744–6); Onze-Lieve-Vrouwen, Tongeren (1750–52; case survives); Benedictine Abbey, St Truiden (1753–6).

BIBLIOGRAPHY
N. Dufourcq: *Esquisse d'une histoire de l'orgue en France* (Paris, 1935), 311
G. L. J. Alexis: 'Un facteur français établi à Liège', *Bulletin trimestriel des Amis de l'orgue*, x/34 (1938), 21
A. Bouman: *De orgels in de Groote of Martinikerk te Groningen* (Amsterdam, 1941), 98ff
M. Waltmans and M. Smeets: *Kerkorgels te Roermond* (Heythuysen, 1957)

GUY OLDHAM

L'Epine [Lépine, Lespine]. French family of organ builders. Adrian L'Epine (*fl* Bordeaux, 1711–31) worked on the organs of Bordeaux Cathedral (1711), St Jean-de-Luz (1724) and St Michel, Bordeaux (1731). Jean-François L'Epine (i) (*b* Abbeville, *c*1682; *d* Toulouse, 1762), brother of Adrian, settled in Toulouse about 1725 and worked at Albi, Rodez and Lodève. His son Jean-François L'Epine (ii) *l'aîné* (*b* Toulouse, 1732; *d* Pézenas, 1817) was a pupil and colleague of Bédos de Celles. He built the organs at Pézenas (1755–6; with an early example of a Hautboy on the *Récit*) and Montpellier Cathedral (in collaboration with Dominique Cavaillé-Coll). He worked for a long time with Isnard at Béziers

and at Narbonne (1776–80). Another son of Jean-François L'Epine (i), Adrien (*b* Toulouse, 1735; *d* Paris), married F.-H. Clicquot's sister. He worked at Nantes (1767), Nogent-sur-Seine, Brie-Comte-Robert, the chapel of the Ecole Militaire, Paris (1772; three manuals, 31 stops including two Dessus de flûte), Montargis (1778) and St Médard, Paris (1778). He also built harpsichords and presented a combined piano and organ at the Académie des Sciences in 1772.

BIBLIOGRAPHY
F. Raugel: 'Autour de Jean-François l'Epine', *L'orgue*, nos.40–43 (1946–7)
F. Douglass: *The Language of the Classical French Organ* (New Haven and London, 1969)

GUY OLDHAM

Lera. LIRA of Belorussia.

Leriyo. Drum set of the Kakwa people of Uganda. *See* UGANDA DRUM.

Leru. Idioglot transverse clarinet of the Dogon people of Mali. *See* CLARINET, TRANSVERSE.

Lerukan. Suspended bossed gong of the Yakan people of the southern Philippines. *See* KULINTANG.

Leshoao. Rattle of the Southern Sotho people of southern Africa. *See* MORUTLHOANA.

Lesiba. A MUSICAL BOW sounded by the breath, of the Southern Sotho people of southern Africa. It is similar to and historically related to the GORA of the Khoikhoi. It is made of a stick of willow, poplar, or parsnip tree wood (about 1 metre long and 2·5 cm wide) which is slightly tapered and curved. A slender foliate quill, split and flattened, is affixed to the larger end with a split peg inserted through a hole in the stick. The quill is attached to a string of sinew, gut or wire running to the thinner end of the stick where it is secured with a knot made of braided horsehair; the knot serves both as a tuning loop and as a small bridge. The *lesiba* is played

1. Lesiba (musical bow) of southern Africa

2. Lesiba: detail showing placement on the lips

by inhaling and exhaling across the edges of the quill, setting the string in motion; a vocalized melodic line is often produced at the same time. Harmonic partials (8th to 14th) of the string fundamental are selectively mouth-resonated. Songs played on the *lesiba* are known as *linong* and employ four formal elements, played in any order and combination: parallel patterns of voice and string harmonics at high, mid, and low levels, and contrary motions of voice and string harmonics. Song endings are indicated by a rapid, short, forceful inhalation on the quill. The *lesiba* is played by men in three contexts: while herding cattle, ostensibly to convey directions and security to cattle while feeding, watering and travelling; in periodic competitions between expert performers from different areas, which serve to display technical facility and share musical understanding; by older men for younger men and boys as instruction in both musical and herding techniques. The term *lesiba* is also used by the Tswana people as an alternative for *kwadi*.

BIBLIOGRAPHY
KirbyMISA, 171
H. Balfour: 'The Goura, a String-Wind Instrument of the Bushmen and Hottentots', *Journal of the Royal Anthropological Institute*, xxxii (1902), 156
P. R. Kirby: 'The Gora and its Bantu Successors: a Study in South African Native Music', *Bantu Studies*, v (1931), 89
——: 'A Further Note on the Gora and its Bantu Successors', *Bantu Studies*, ix (1935), 53
CHARLES R. ADAMS

Leslie. A tremulant loudspeaker for use with electronic organs, designed by Donald J. Leslie around 1940 and manufactured from the early 1940s by the Electro-Music Co. in Pasadena, California. Besides producing a range of different models, the company has licensed the manufacturers of several electronic organs – the Hammond and later the Baldwin, Conn, Gulbransen, Kawai, Kimball, Lowrey, Thomas and Wurlitzer organs – to use the loudspeaker in their instruments; sometimes it is built into the organ console and sometimes the console carries controls for operating an external Leslie loudspeaker in a separate cabinet. The tremulant effect is produced by a two-speed rotating curved reflector, placed below a downward-facing loudspeaker; its speeds of rotation are seven times a second or once in every 1·3 seconds. The cabinet is normally placed several metres away from the instrument, and may be used instead of or in combination with the instrument's normal loudspeaker.

BIBLIOGRAPHY
H. E. Anderson: *Electronic Organ Handbook* (Indianapolis, 1960), 22, 251
HUGH DAVIES

Lespine. *See* L'EPINE family.

Lesung. Javanese and Sundanese term for a long rice-stamping trough beaten with heavy poles of coconut palm or other wood by women who make music while stamping the husks off rice grain. In Minangkabau, West Sumatra, it is called a *lasuang* and in Burai, South Sumatra, a *cintuk*. The trough is usually made of wood, such as jackfruit wood, which produces a clear tone when beaten. By striking the edges and bottom of oblong or round holes cut in the trough, sounds of varying pitch and timbre are produced in complex interlocking rhythms. The pieces are given picturesque and evocative titles. The *lesung* was formerly used in Java in the *gamelan ketoprak*. Since World War II rice-husking machines have increasingly replaced traditional methods, and round-the-clock rice-stamping parties at harvest-time have died out. In Minangkabau *lasuang* troughs often had seven holes, and seven women used to play *lasuang* music, but the only remnant of this tradition is the *gandang lasuang* ensemble, which comprises a *lasuang*, *talempong jao* and drum (e.g. a *dol*). In Aceh province, a small round trough resembling those of mainland southeast Asia is used by each rice-stamper. In Burai, South Sumatra, *cintuk* have two holes played by four women; low-pitched sounds are produced inside the holes and high-pitched ones on top of the trough.

BIBLIOGRAPHY
J. Kunst: *De toonkunst van Java* (The Hague, 1934; Eng. trans., rev. 2/1943, enlarged 3/1973)
M. J. Kartomi: 'Music and Trance in Central Java', *EM*, xvii (1973), 201
MARGARET J. KARTOMI

Letlhaka [lethlaka, lechaka, lichaka]. End-blown flute of the Tswana people of Botswana. A set of these is called DITLHAKA. The name *letlhaka noka* applies to a boy's flute resembling the end-blown *naka ya lehlaka* of the Pedi people.

Letor. XYLOPHONE of the Sikka area of Flores, Indonesia. It has six wooden keys (about 50 by 10 cm) which rest on two perpendicular banana stems about 1 metre long. It is played with two sticks in the right hand, while the left damps the keys and keeps them in position. *See also* PRESON.
MARGARET J. KARTOMI

Leuto (It.). LUTE.

Lewis, Edward (*fl* London, *c*1687–*c*1745). English violin maker. His background and training remain obscure, though it is possible that he worked for the Jaye family in London. His few surviving instruments show great care in the choice of wood, the cutting of graceful and symmetrical scrolls, the quality of varnish and even the internal work, indicating that he must have been one of the best craftsmen of his time. His outline is essentially a personal one, although the archings are somewhat reminiscent of the early Brescian school. The soundholes are nicely cut but a little stiff and out of keeping with the curves of the outline. The varnish is of unusually good quality and ranges in colour from golden brown to red over a lighter ground. Lewis's earliest known instrument (in the Paris Conservatoire museum) is a bass viol whose printed label reads 'Edward Lewis/in St. Paul Allay [sic] in London, 1687'. A late violin of his is recorded as being branded E. LEWIS 1742 on the table where the chin-rest would now be fitted.

BIBLIOGRAPHY
W. L. von Lütgendorff: *Die Geigen- und Lautenmacher vom Mittelalter bis zur Gegenwart* (Frankfurt am Main, 1904, rev. 6/1922/R1968)
Anon: 'Edward Lewis', *The Strad*, lxvii (1966–7), 46
JAAK LIIVOJA-LORIUS

Lewis, Thomas Christopher (*fl c*1861–*c*1900). English organ builder and bellfounder. Lewis was an architect before setting up as an organ builder in London in about 1861. His style of organ building, modelled on that of Edmund Schulze and Aristide Cavaillé-Coll, is characterized by a bold and powerful chorus on the Great organ, the blend being attributable to the mixture (15, 19, 22 and sometimes 26). The manual double is normally a bourdon, the quieter flutes are of particularly good voicing, and there is usually a good mixture (15, 19, 22) on the Swell. His custom was to use spotted metal in his pipework. His instruments suffer from a certain lack of blend between individual chorus stops on the Great, very poorly developed Choir organs, uneven and nasal manual reeds (too loud in the bass because of an exaggerated scale) and badly designed specifications. They are well built and impressive in their big effects, with some beautiful soft tones, but are unsuitable for the performance of much of the organ repertory.

Lewis organs survive at St Mary the Virgin, Beddington, Surrey (1869; original); All Saints, Hatcham Park, Surrey (1871); St Matthew's, Croydon (1882); All Saints, Ilkley, Yorkshire (1882; rebuilt); St George's, Jesmond, Newcastle upon Tyne (1886; rebuilt); Holy Trinity, Bramley, Surrey (1894); Southwark Cathedral (1896); Hatfield House Chapel, Hertfordshire; St Anne's, Brondesbury, Middlesex (originally at Hanover Square (London) Rooms); St Matthias, Richmond, Surrey.

BIBLIOGRAPHY
G. Benham: 'Interesting London Organs XXXII: Southwark Cathedral', *The Organ*, xii (1932–3), 90
——: 'Interesting London Organs XXXIII: St Mary's, Kennington Park Road, S.E.', *The Organ*, xii (1932–3), 172
——: 'Interesting London Organs XXXIV: St John-the-Evangelist, Wilton Road, Victoria', *The Organ*, xii (1932–3), 218
H. Snow: 'A Lewis Residence Organ at Frodsham, Cheshire', *The Organ*, xiv (1934–5), 116
A. Niland: 'The Lewis Organ at St Peter's Church, Eaton Square, Revisited', *The Organ*, xxvii (1947–8), 155
GUY OLDHAM

Lezim. Strung rattle of Maharashtra, western India. It consists of pairs of small iron plates threaded on to a cord, the ends of which are tied to either end of a wooden rod. The player holds the rod in one hand and jerks the cord with the other, producing a jingling sound. This rattle is used in dances, processions and mass drills.

Lha. SPIKE FIDDLE of the Kabui Naga people of Manipur valley, north-east India. It is similar to the Manipuri PENA, but smaller (about 31 cm long).

Lhambilbilg. DIDJERIDU (aboriginal wooden trumpet) of the Nunggubuyu people of eastern Arnhem Land, Australia.

Lhokan'. COURTING FLUTE of the Yuchi Indians of the south-eastern USA.

Liahan. BULLROARER of the island of Pororan, Buka, Solomon Islands, used during initiation ceremonies. See G. Thomas: 'Customs and Beliefs of the Natives of Buka', *Oceania*, ii (1931), 228.

Liba. *See* MOFONGO.

Libeke. LAMELLAPHONE of the Samba people of Zaïre. It has wooden keys and a rectangular box resonator (*LaurentyS*, 192).

Libelenge. Term for LAMELLAPHONE among the Topoke people of Isingi, Zaïre (*LaurentyS*, 196).

Libitshi [limbitji]. Drum of the Ngando and Mbesa peoples of Zaïre. It is used by women to accompany dancing (*BooneT*, 63).

Lichaka. End-blown flute of southern Africa. *See* LETLHAKA.

Lichiwayu. NOTCHED FLUTE, a large KENA, of the Bolivian Alti Plano, also found in Tarapacá province, Chile. It is made from *tokoró* wood, with six finger-holes and another hole at the back (called *pheta* by the Chipaya people). The instruments accompany dancing, particularly at the feast of St Santiago (July 25) among the Chipaya of the Department of Oruro. In the *lichiwayu* ensemble of Ayparavi village there are three sizes of flute: the *qolta* (about 31 cm long), the *taipi* (41 cm) and the *paqi* (58 cm, with an inside diameter of 3·5 cm).

BIBLIOGRAPHY
M. P. Baumann: 'Music, Dance, and Song of the Chipayas (Bolivia)', *Latin American Music Review*, ii (1981), 171–222
——: 'Musica Andina de Bolivia', LPLI/S-062 [disc notes]
JOHN M. SCHECHTER

Lichtelektrisches Klavier (Ger.: 'photo-electric piano'). *See* SUPERPIANO.

Lichtenthal, Herman (*fl c*1830–51). Keyboard instrument maker, active in Brussels. In 1830 he was granted a patent for a 'piano viole', presumably some variety of sostenente or bowed keyboard instrument. He seems to have specialized in upright pianos, especially a small (103 cm) type of unusual design known as his 'doghouse' model, so called because of the ogive-shaped opening in the lower part of the case. Lichtenthal's enduring reputation is based on his invention, patented in 1832, of an upright piano action; its use of a leather thong anticipated the tape-check mechanism that is still in use, and is often incorrectly credited to Robert Wornum, who patented it in 1842. In 1851 Lichtenthal left Brussels for St Petersburg.

BIBLIOGRAPHY
R. E. M. Harding: *The Piano-forte: its History Traced to the Great Exhibition of 1851* (Cambridge, 1933, rev. 2/1978), 98, 245
C. F. Colt and A. Miall: *The Early Piano* (London, 1981), 120
HOWARD SCHOTT

Lichtton-Orgel (Ger.: 'light–sound organ') [Welte Lichtton-Orgel]. An ELECTRONIC ORGAN developed from around 1933 in Freiburg by Edwin Welte (1876–1957), with W. Faass; it was constructed in three increasingly substantial versions by the organ builders Th. Mannborg in Leipzig between 1934 and 1936. Welte had been the co-designer with Karl Bockisch of the Welte–Mignon 'reproducing' player piano around 1901–4. The Lichtton-Orgel had two five-octave manuals and a pedal-board. The sound was generated by 12 rotating photoelectric tone-wheels in the form of glass discs (40 cm in diameter) on which the frequencies of all the pitches were photographically recorded as waveforms, arranged concentrically (this method of reproduction was partly based on patents from the mid-1920s by R. Michel); the waveforms were mostly derived from the timbres of well-known European pipe organs. 18 waveforms were reproduced on each disc, which gave three timbres for all the octave registers (including the pedals) of a single note (for illustration see ELECTRONIC INSTRUMENTS, fig.2c); other timbres were obtained by means of filters. Additional discs, offering alternative timbres, could be used instead of the basic set. The original Lichtton-Orgel was destroyed during World War II in an air-raid on Leipzig, where it was on exhibition. Welte worked for a while on a new model in the late 1940s. Some English-language sources call the instrument 'Phototone' or 'Photophone'.

BIBLIOGRAPHY

K. Mannborg: 'Werdegang der Lichttonorgel', ZI, lvii (1936), 42
A. Gradenwitz: 'Problème de l'orgue électro-acoustique: ses solutions', La nature, lxv (1937), 258
O. Laass: 'Die Lichtton-Orgel, ein neues elektrisches Musikinstrument', Wissen und Fortschritt, x (1937), 396

HUGH DAVIES

Licu. See LIKU.

Lídl. Czech instrument makers. Joseph Lídl (b Manětin, 1 July 1864; d Brno, 11 Jan 1946) founded the first Moravian music instrument factory. He was apprenticed to a wind instrument maker in Brno, where in 1892 he was an agent for piano and harmonium factories. Later he started making his own instruments, and in 1909 he opened a factory manufacturing brass and string instruments and accordions. Because these instruments were of a very high quality the firm was given the title 'Supplier to the Imperial and Royal Household', together with the right 'to use the Imperial eagle in the sign of the firm'. Joseph's son Václav (b Brno, 31 Oct 1894) took over the management of the firm in 1918, having served his apprenticeship in his father's factory, and later worked in Vienna. His instruments were popular, and Václav established a second factory in Olomouc, and in 1921, together with his partner Velík, he founded a piano and harmonium factory in the town of Moravský Krumlov. Lídl's instruments, particularly the brass instruments, were of very high standard and quality, and had a number of improvements in their construction and design. His double horn was widely used and appreciated, at home and abroad. This was the result of cooperation with the acoustician and mathematician Čupr. In 1948 the factory was nationalized, but Lídl continued to manage it until 1957.

BIBLIOGRAPHY

ČSHS
Bericht der Handels- und Gewerbekammer in Brünn (1900–01)
'Erste Mährische Musikinstrumenten-Fabrik Josef Lidl, k. und k. Hofund Heeres-Lieferant Brünn', Musikalische Anzeiger (1912–13)

ALEXANDR BUCHNER

Liduku [litungu]. Idiochord RAFT ZITHER of the Gishu people of Uganda. The instrument is also played in the Samia, Gwe, Gwere, Soga and Kiga districts of Uganda. The raft comprises seven, nine or 11 millet stalks and measures 30 cm by 12 cm. A strip of epidermis is loosened from each stalk; this idiochord 'string' is raised over two pieces of twig, one at each end, which serve as bridges. The strings are bound round at the ends to prevent breakage. Different pitches are obtained by using strings of different thicknesses and by adjusting the position of the bridge. The instrument is held between the open palms of the hands and plucked with the forefingers in an upward movement away from the raft. The instruments are generally regarded as toys and made for the amusement of young girls. See WachsmannTCU.

Lidungu. Seven-string lyre of the Gishu people of Mbale district, Uganda. See also LITUNGU.

Lié (Fr.). LEGATO.

Liebesfuss (Ger.). In a woodwind instrument, a globular or pear-shaped bell (see BELL (ii)) with a narrow opening, a distinguishing feature of such instruments as the CLARINETTE D'AMOUR and OBOE D'AMORE (see also OBOE, §§1–3).

Liebesgeige (Ger.). VIOLA D'AMORE.

Liebes-Oboe (Ger.). OBOE D'AMORE.

Lieblich Gedackt (Ger.). An ORGAN STOP.

Liera viol. See LYRA VIOL.

Lifaha. Decorative bells of the Southern Sotho people of southern Africa. See MANGENENGENE.

Lifogo. Long cylindrical drum of the Eso and Topoke peoples of Zaïre (BooneT, 4). See LILENGA.

Liga-liga. Idioglot transverse clarinet of the Kilba (Huba) people of Nigeria. See CLARINET, TRANSVERSE.

Ligature. The metal band with two screws by which the reed of a clarinet or saxophone is secured to the mouthpiece. It replaces the earlier method of binding the reed with a wool or silk cord, still regarded as the correct method in Germany.

Ligawka [ligawa]. Wooden trumpet of the Mazowsze region of Poland. It is about 1·5 metres long and has a slightly conical wooden tube which is either straight or slightly curved. The ligawka is played with a funnel-shaped mouthpiece. The instrument can produce only four to eight harmonics. It is used by shepherds, and is also played in the evenings during Advent. Similar instruments of Poland include the bazuna and trombita.

Ligazi. Basket rattle of the Luba/Lulua people of southern Zaïre.

Light, Edward (c1747–c1832). English composer and inventor. He created seven plucked, fretted chordophones compounded from lute, lyre and harp structures. In 1798 he invented the harp-guitar, later also a harp-lute-guitar and diplo-kithara (c1800). Between 1810 and 1813 he invented a harp-lute, which was patented in 1818, and at some time he invented an apollo lyre with 12 strings. In 1815 a harp-lyre was advertised in the *Caledonian Mercury*, and in 1816 he patented a British lute-harp and a dital harp. Extant examples of his work are sometimes labelled as being made for him by A. Barry (18 Frith Street, Soho) and Wheatstone & Co. The title-page of his undated *Collection of Psalms &c.* indicates that he was organist of Trinity Chapel, St George's, Hanover Square, and 'Lyrist to H. R. H. The Princess [Charlotte] of Wales'. His teaching activity required his presence in London; and instrument labels and title-pages show that at various times he lived at 16 Harley Street; 34 Queen Ann Street, Portland Chapel; 3 and 8 Foley Place; 43 Portland Place (where his partner Angelo Ventura also lived); and 38 Berners Street.

He arranged, composed and published much of his own teaching material. Three of the vocal collections, published between c1805 and c1814, include parts for harp-lute, and he published three solo collections for that instrument (c1810–c1817). His instrumental tutors include one for guitar (c1785), *A Tutor, with a Tablature, for the Harp-lute-guitar* (c1810), *New and Compleat Instructions for Playing on the Harp-lute* (?1812) and *A New and Complete Directory to the Art of Playing on the Patent British Lute-harp* (c1816).

For an instrument by Light *see* HARP-LUTE (ii), fig.2b.

BIBLIOGRAPHY
T. Busby: *Concert Room Anecdotes*, ii (London, 1825), 275f
R. B. Armstrong: *Musical Instruments*, ii (Edinburgh, 1908)
L. Fryklund: *Förteckning över Edward Lights musikaliska verk* (Hälsingborg, 1931)
A. Baines: *Non-keyboard Instruments*, Victoria and Albert Museum Catalogue of Musical Instruments, ii (London, 1968)
STEPHEN BONNER

Ligo. Trapezoidal SLIT-DRUM of the Aimeri people of Zaïre (*LaurentyTF*, 138).

Ligombo. Six-string TROUGH ZITHER of the Hehe people of Iringa district, Tanzania.

Ligoshu. Hand-held vessel rattle of the Swazi people of southern Africa, resembling the Tsonga NDJELE. Now it is often made from a tin can instead of a calabash.

Ligubhu [ligubo]. Unbraced gourd-resonated MUSICAL BOW of southern Africa. *Ligubhu* denotes the instrument of the Swazi people; it is similar in construction and performing practice to the Zulu UGUBHU, but the two fundamentals are often a whole tone apart (as with the Xhosa UHADI) rather than a semitone, and a wire string is used (*see* MUSICAL BOW, §4, esp. ex.3a, fig.2a). The *ligubo*, or *gubo*, is a similar bow of the Ngoni people of eastern Zambia.

Lihawu. Dancing-shield of the Swazi people of southern Africa. *See* IKHAWU.

Liita. Small transverse clarinet of the Kanembu people of Chad. *See* KOROTIL.

Lijerica. *See* LIRICA.

Lī-keli. Cylindrical hardwood concussion sticks of Sri Lanka; also the dance associated with them. They vary from 30·5 cm to 38 cm in length and are sometimes tasselled at both ends, when the dance is known as *lī-keli savaran*. Both forms are traditionally danced by women, who perform a simple step-dance, beating the sticks together, to the accompaniment of the drum (the *yak-berē* or the *gäta-berē*). The dance lacks the speed and excitement of many Indian stick-dances.

NATALIE M. WEBBER

Likembe [likemba, likembi, lipunga, dikembe, dikembi]. LAMELLAPHONE of eastern, central and south-western Africa. It has a box-type body and from eight to 12 keys, sometimes of metal; *see* LAMELLAPHONE §2 (iii). Peoples to whom it is attributed include the Nyoro, Amba and Toro of Uganda, the Chokwe and Luvale of Angola and Zambia, and several Zaïre groups including the Ngala, Lunda, Chokwe, Topoke, Luba of Bukama, Lese, Shi, Kibudu, Kusu, Ngombe and Luba of Albertville (*LaurentyS*, 194).

Lik haanga. Long side-blown trumpet, made of cowhorn and a wooden tube, of the Luhya people of Kenya.

Likhuba [ntanda]. DRUM-CHIME of the Manganja and Sena peoples of south-eastern Africa. It consists of up to ten long, cylindrical open-ended drums tuned to a pentatonic scale by means of heating and tuning-paste. The leader plays five or six of these with his hands, accompanied by three or four other drummers, rattles, singing and solo exhibition dancing. See *TraceyCSA*, ii, 187.

ANDREW TRACEY

Likimbi. LAMELLAPHONE of the Bangobango people of Zaïre (*LaurentyS*, 197).

Liku [licu]. (1) Bolivian end-blown NOTCHED FLUTE. *See* KENA.

(2) PANPIPES in the CHIRIHUANO, JULA-JULA, LAKITA, SIKU and ZAMPOÑA ensembles of Bolivia. *See also* SIKURI.

Likwengu. LAMELLAPHONE of the Bango people of Zaïre (*LaurentyS*, 193). *See* EKEMBI.

Lilemo. Drum of the Topoke people of Zaïre (*BooneT*, 63).

Lilenga. Long, open cylindrical drum of the Lalia Ngolu people of Zaïre, 152 cm in height. The distinguishing feature of the drum is that the casing has a cut-away 'step' at each end so that the ends are slightly narrower in diameter than the remainder of the body. The membrane is fixed by wooden or iron nails. Other drums conforming to this pattern of construction are the Kumu *mongungu* (93 cm), Binja *lukombe* (105 cm) and Eso *lifogo* (94 cm). The *lilenga* is the largest Lalia drum and is traditionally used to accompany dances of the *Liloa* sect.

BIBLIOGRAPHY
BooneT, 4, 63
F. J. de Hen: *Beitrag zur Kenntnis der Musikinstrumente aus Belgisch Kongo und Ruanda-Urundi* (Tervuren, 1960)

G. Knosp: *Enquête sur la vie musicale au Congo belge 1934–1935* (Tervuren, 1968)

K. A. GOURLAY

Lileten. Ensemble of the western Kupang area of Timor, Indonesia. Five musicians play four *kong kai* (xylophones) and a *tambur* (drum).

Liletsa [liletsoa] (sing. *seletsa*). A generic term for musical instruments among the Southern Sotho people of southern Africa. *Liletsa tsa masoho* designates all instruments sounded by the hand, and *liletsa tsa malomo* denotes those sounded by the mouth (or by hand and mouth, e.g. the *lekope*, *lesiba* and *setolotolo*). Songs played on instruments (except those played on the *lesiba*) are called *pina tsa liletsa*.

CHARLES R. ADAMS

Lili. See FIFI.

Lilis. An ancient bronze KETTLEDRUM of the Akkadian Seleucid period (*c*300 BC).

Lilt-pipe. Term used by Richard de Holand (*Buke of the Howlat*, 1450) in a list of musical instruments; it is probably a cognate of the Dutch *lullepijp*, a bagpipe or shepherd's pipe.

Limba. Side-blown wooden trumpet of the Madi people of Uganda, approximately 60 cm long. The instrument resembles the YUGE of the Kakwa, but is carved in the shape of a human figure.

Limbe. Mongolian transverse flute made from bamboo or plastic, with six finger-holes. The term, derived (through classical Mongolian, *lingbu*) from the Tibetan, *gling-bu*, has been used also to denote end-blown flutes of metal or reed. An older regional name for end-blown and transverse flutes is *bishgüür* (classical Mongolian, *biskigür* or *bisigür*), a word probably related, as Sachs suggested, to the Persian *bīsha*, or *pīsha*, a shepherd's reed flute. The transverse *limbe* was used to encourage mother camels to accept their calves and, together with the *morin khuur* (spike fiddle), it accompanied *urtyn duu* ('long songs'). It is also used in ensembles. Circular breathing is often employed in playing it.

BIBLIOGRAPHY
J. van Oost: 'La musique chez les mongols des Urdus', *Anthropos*, x–xi (1915–16), 358–96
C. Sachs: *The History of Musical Instruments* (New York, 1940)

ANDREA NIXON

Limbitji. See LIBITSHI.

Limbombe. Cylindrical drum of the Bango and Soko peoples of central Zaïre (*BooneT*, 69).

Limele. PLURIARC of the Nkundo and Saka peoples of Zaïre (*LaurentyC*, 117). See LUKOMBE (i).

Linceo. See COLONNA, FABIO.

Lincoln, Henry Cephas (*b* ?1789; *d* ?1864). English organ builder. His father, John Lincoln, started the firm about 1789. Chamber organs survive from 1805 and 1807 specifically ascribed to H. C. Lincoln; this is hard to reconcile both with his putative date of birth (Sumner,

1952) and with the tradition that he was apprenticed to Flight & Robson, whose partnership began around 1806. For much of his career H. C. Lincoln's 'manufactory' was at 196 High Holborn, London; the business seems to have ended about 1850.

Lincoln's published lists (*c*1824 and 1843) indicate a considerable output of new organs throughout Britain and abroad. He held the royal warrant from about 1819 and as a result built organs for the Chapel Royal and the Pavilion, Brighton, and for a number of fashionable Brighton churches. During the early 1840s he made his contribution to the new 'German system', working with Gauntlett on at least four organs including the vast instrument for St Olave, Tooley Street, Southwark (1844), with its 27-stop Great based on a 32' bourdon. It proved to be beyond Lincoln's resources, and the organ was completed by Hill in 1846.

Lincoln's best work probably dates from the last phase of the English long-compass organ without Pedal which (by the 1820s) had mild imitative reeds, clear-toned flutes, broad unison diapasons and silvery mixtures. A remarkable three-manual organ by Lincoln, built originally for St John's Chapel, Bedford Row, London (*c*1820), survives at Thaxted, Essex, and remains virtually unaltered. The magnificent Regency case contains an instrument which (despite its dilapidated condition) is one of a handful of large early English organs to have survived the Victorians.

BIBLIOGRAPHY
W. L. Sumner: *The Organ* (London, 1952, rev. 4/1973)
M. Wilson: *The English Chamber Organ* (London, 1968)
J. Boeringer: 'The Organs of the Lincolns', *JBIOS*, i (1977), 11

NICHOLAS THISTLETHWAITE

Lindanda. In Zaïre, a Lingala term for the accordion and the guitar.

Lindegrens Orgelbyggeri. Swedish firm of organ builders. Mårten Bernhard Söderling (1786–1836) set up a workshop in Göteborg in 1812 for building small-scale organs. An example of his work is preserved at Lundby Old Church, Göteborg (1818, later modified). About 1830 the business was taken over by his sons: Johan Nikolaus Söderling (1802–90) became the director and was joined by Emanuel (1806–53), who had studied with Pehr Zacharias Strand, and Carl Fredrik (1813–72). The Söderling brothers built more than 150 organs, mainly in the west and south of Sweden; most of them retain a classical tone quality and about 20 are preserved, including those at Övre Karup (1842), Voxtorp, Jönköping province (1852), and Väse (1858).

Salomon Molander (1833–1905) was a pupil of the Söderling brothers and obtained the organ builder's diploma by 1870. In 1874 he took over the firm with his colleague E. G. Eriksson; it was called Molander & Eriksson until 1877, when Molander continued alone under his own name. His firm built about 120 organs, mostly with slider-chests; he never used pneumatic action. Eskil Ragnar Lundén (1881–1945) became a pupil of Molander in 1897, obtained his diploma in 1898, and after a brief period of study in Germany, took over the firm in 1903. He completely rebuilt the organ of Göteborg Cathedral and provided a 40-stop organ for Vasa Church (1909); all his instruments had pneumatic action. Lundén left the firm in 1918 and it was continued by Harald Lindegren (1887–1956), who had been a member of the firm since 1907. He built more than 80 organs including those at Nor, Värmland (1926), Gislaved and Björketorp

(1935), Fröjel (1938), Dillnäs (1940), Brunflo (1941), Lekåsa (1944) and Los (1946). In 1956 Lindegren's son Tore (*b* 1927) took over the firm, which became a limited company in 1963. His work includes the organs at Uddevalla (1958; 60 stops); Ljungby (1965; 29 stops); Brämaregården, Göteborg (1966; 24 stops); Vänersborg (1970; 39 stops); Herrestad (1971; 17 stops); and the Pater Noster Church, Göteborg (1976; 14 stops). Tore's son Leif (*b* 1952) has been a member of the firm since 1971.

BIBLIOGRAPHY
E. Erici: *Inventarium över bevarade äldre kyrkoglar i Sverige* (Stockholm, 1965)
based on *Sohlmans musiklexikon* (iv, 327–8) by permission of Sohlmans Förlag

BENGT KYHLBERG/ANNA KYHLBERG

Lindeman, Charles A. (*b* Chicago, *c*1881). American harp maker. He worked as a toolmaker for Lang & Heckenlauer in Chicago, where he learnt to repair pedal harps under the direction of Cyrus Heckenlauer, a former employee of Erard in Europe. At the age of 24, Lindeman set up his own business as C. A. Lindeman Harp Manufacturer (6224 Peterson Avenue, Chicago), and later as the Lindeman Harp Company. Originally he did all the work himself, and took two to three months to complete one harp. He was joined in the late 1930s by his son Carl who continued the business after his father's death until the 1960s. Lindeman harps were made in several different styles; before World War II they were sold in Europe and South America as well as in the USA. Charles Lindeman was a traditional rather than an innovative harp maker and his instruments were carefully crafted and reliable; he also had a reputation for good harp repair work.

ROSLYN RENSCH

Lindner, Leonhard Georg. *See* LINTNER, LEONHARD GEORG.

Ling. Small bell with internal clapper of the Han Chinese. *Ling* is a generic name for several different types of small bells. The instrument is usually hemispheric, of bronze or brass, with a small semi-circular loop of the same material for suspension and an internal clapper. Among the more common varieties are the *maling* ('horse bell'), hung from the neck of a horse; the *fengling* ('wind bell'), hung from the outer eaves of a Buddhist temple or pagoda, with a broad clapper extending below the mouth of the bell and blown freely by the wind; and the PENGLING ('colliding bells'), a pair of clapperless bells which are struck together. *Ling* bells were known in China by the Shang dynasty (1766–1122 BC); the character graph appears in early bone-inscriptions and a number of bronze bells have been found in burial-sites at Anyang. Such bells have been used over the centuries more in the context of signalling and religious practice (especially Buddhist and Taoist) than they have in ensemble music. Other Chinese bell types include the *duo*, *zhong*, *xing* and *pailing*; the *sun*, *t'ak* and *yo* are related Korean preservations. The *rei* is the only common Japanese bell with a clapper.

BIBLIOGRAPHY
A. C. Moule: 'A List of the Musical and other Sound-producing Instruments of the Chinese', *Journal of the North-China Branch of the Royal Asiatic Society*, xxxix (Shanghai, 1908), 42
Tong Kin-woon: *Shang Musical Instruments* (diss., Wesleyan U., Middletown, Conn., 1983)

ALAN R. THRASHER

Lingarai. Small KETTLEDRUM, played in pairs, of Abuja, Nigeria. *See* TAMBARI.

Lingassio. Four-key XYLOPHONE of the Ndokpa people of the Central African Republic. Its large solid wooden keys rest on straw supports and are struck with two rubber-tipped beaters. The *lingassio* is generally used as a talking instrument, three of the keys representing high, medium and low language tones. It is played with the KALANGBA xylophone and may continue 'speaking' while supporting the *kalangba* dance rhythm.

A similar instrument is attributed as *linga sho* to the Dakpa people of the Central African Republic. It consists of four pieces of wood placed on two bundles of straw at the bottom of a pit dug in the earth. It is played by two musicians, using wooden beaters; one plays the basic rhythm while the other improvises. The rhythms are used in ceremonies connected with mourning or for dances of the circumcision and excision rites, e.g. on the emergence of the newly-circumcised from seclusion.

BIBLIOGRAPHY
S. Arom and G. Dournon-Taurelle: 'République Centre-Africaine: musiques d'initiation', HM 934 [disc notes]
C. Duvelle: 'République Centrafricaine', OCR 11 [disc notes]

Lingbo. Pair of small clapperless bells of the Han Chinese. *See* PENGLING.

Lingele. Rectangular SLIT-DRUM of the Mbuja people of western Zaïre (*LaurentyTF*, 137).

Lingita. Cylindro-conical drum, with laced membranes, of the Ngombe people of north-western Zaïre (*BooneT*, 31, 64).

Lingongo. MOUTH BOW of the Ngando people of Zaïre (*LaurentyC*, 113). *See* LUSUBA.

Lingualpfeife (Ger.). REEDPIPE.

Linguaphone. A term sometimes applied to a plucked idiophone whose primary sounding agents consist of tongues or slats of metal or vegetable material attached at one end. *See* LAMELLAPHONE.

Linn Drum [LinnDrum]. An ELECTRONIC PERCUSSION instrument developed by Roger Linn (originally with Roger Moffatt) and manufactured by Linn Electronics first in Hollywood and then Tarzana, California, from 1980. In 1982 the original LM-1 Linn Drum Computer was superseded by the LinnDrum. Both are polyphonic devices using digitally stored recordings of 15 percussion instruments and hand-claps, and can produce 'shuffled' syncopations. The LinnDrum can be triggered from external drum-pads or any other acoustic sound source.

BIBLIOGRAPHY
R. Hammond: *The Musician and the Micro* (Poole, Dorset, 1983), 75

HUGH DAVIES

Linterculus (Lat.). KIT.

Lintner [Lindner], **Leonhard Georg** (*b* Augsburg, 31 Jan 1794; *d* Augsburg, 18 March 1859). German maker of woodwind instruments and horns. Son of the Augsburg maker Johann Georg Lintner (1766–1840), he received a licence to manufacture musical instruments in Augsburg on 29 July 1819, remaining there until his death. His widow carried on the business until 1864. Lintner was well known in his time for the craftsmanship of his instruments. Extant flutes have various numbers of keys, usually between six and eight; an interesting one in the Karl-Marx-Universität, Leipzig, has an elaborate eight-key layout. His prize-winning clarinet of 1820 was fitted with silver keys. A number of oboes, a bassoon and a watchman's horn also survive.

BIBLIOGRAPHY
D. Degen: *Zur Geschichte der Blockflöte* (Kassel, 1950)
L. G. Langwill: *An Index of Musical Wind-instrument Makers* (Edinburgh, 1960, rev., enlarged 6/1980)
H. Heyde: *Flöten* (Leipzig, 1978)
P. T. Young: *2500 Historical Woodwind Instruments: an Inventory of the Major Collections* (New York, 1982)
NIALL O'LOUGHLIN

Linz [linzi]. Log XYLOPHONE of the Bale and Hima peoples of eastern Zaïre and Rwanda. *See* PANDINGBWA.

Lion's roar. *See* STRING DRUM.

Lipakala. *See* LEPAKALA.

Lipenga. *See* MALIPENGA.

Liphala. A generic term for wind instruments among the Southern Sotho people of southern Africa. *See* PHALA.

Lipombo. MOUTH BOW of the Bwa people of Zaïre (*LaurentyC*, 113). *See* LUSUBA.

Lipp. German firm of keyboard instrument makers. The company, founded by Richard Lipp in Stuttgart in about 1875, moved to nearby Heimerdingen around 1950, and is now known as Richard Lipp & Sohn. It has been principally concerned with the manufacture of pianos, which constituted a large part of its business from 1895 to 1965, but in the 1950s Lipp introduced a series of electronic instruments. Between 1950 and 1955 they produced several devices of the piano attachment type – the monophonic Pianoline (1950), derived from Georges Jenny's Ondioline, and Pianetta (1951), and the polyphonic Harmonetta (1953) and Artista (1955); some of their piano attachments were manufactured by Ahlborn-Orgel and Apparatewerk Bayern (respectively makers of the Ahlborn organ and the AWB organ).

The Lipp organ, an ELECTRONIC ORGAN designed by Otto Riegg for use in churches, has been manufactured since 1955 (constructed by Ahlborn) in several models. In the earlier models the sound is generated either by an individual oscillator for each note (up to 360 oscillators) or by 12 oscillators using frequency division. In organs made since about 1972 these have been replaced by a single very-high-frequency master oscillator, which uses two stages of frequency division to produce successively the 12 semitones of the highest octave and all the lower octaves. In 1978 an electronic simulation of the 'chiff' attack found in flute stops on pipe organs was introduced in the Cantate model. In the 1960s at least one hybrid organ was produced, in which one manual controlled organ pipes and the other (plus the pedals)

electronic oscillators. Riegg also designed some models of the AHLBORN ORGAN and manufactured electronic organs under his own name (as Riegg & Co.) between 1958 and 1961.

HUGH DAVIES

Lipunga. *See* LIKEMBE.

Lira [lyra]. A term used to refer to various string instruments. For lyre- and fiddle-type instruments *see* LYRA and LIRONE. The present article is concerned with instruments of the HURDY-GURDY type.

The term 'lira' was applied to the hurdy-gurdy by Virdung (*Musica getutscht*, 1511). It is still used for a folk hurdy-gurdy, particularly in northern and eastern Europe. For the Swedish instrument, *see* VEVLIRA. In the Ukraine and Belorussia, *lira* (or *lera, relya, rïlya*) signifies a hurdy-gurdy with three or four strings, with a wooden resonator that can be rectangular with rounded corners, oval and slightly waisted, or shaped like a fiddle. It may have from four to 13 keys. It has been regarded as the instrument played by mendicants and blind itinerant musicians. A modified chromatic *lira* with a two-octave range is used by state folk orchestras and ensembles in Belorussia. The instrument (under the name *lira korbowa*, 'handle lyra') is also known in southern Poland.

For the so-called 'organized lira', used in 18th-century art music in western Europe, *see* LIRA ORGANIZZATA.

Lira da braccio. One of the most important bowed string instruments of the Renaissance, used especially by courtly Italian poet-musicians of the 15th and 16th centuries to accompany their improvised recitations of lyric and narrative poetry. In its fully developed form, not documented before the late 15th century, the *lira da braccio* had a body shaped like a violin, but with a wide fingerboard, a relatively flat bridge and a leaf-shaped pegbox with frontal pegs (fig.1). It normally had seven strings, five on the fingerboard and two off-board drones. In 16th-century sources it is often called simply 'lira', or even 'viola'; it was undoubtedly the principal instrument of Francesco di Viola, Alfonso dalla Viola and the

1. Lira da braccio and bow, with a shawm: detail from the 'Allegory of Hearing' (1617) by Jan Brueghel the Elder (Museo del Prado, Madrid)

other Italian composer-performers similarly named. Sometimes writers (for example, Ganassi in *Regola rubertina*, 1542) called it 'lira di sette corde' or 'lira moderna', to differentiate it from the antique lyre from which it was supposed (erroneously) to derive.

1. The instrument and its playing technique. 2. History.

1. THE INSTRUMENT AND ITS PLAYING TECHNIQUE. Lanfranco (in *Scintille di musica*, 1533) and writers after him gave the tuning for the seven-string *lira da braccio* as *d*/*d'*–*g*/*g'*–*d'*–*a'*–*e"*, that is, like a violin with a low *d* string and with the bottom two pairs of strings in octaves. Although Lanfranco called the two G strings 'bordoni', the Pesaro manuscript cited below makes clear that the D strings were in fact the off-board drones. Praetorius (2/1619) was the only theorist to depict the instrument with frets, and he gave the pitch of the top string as *d"* not *e"*, a 4th and not a 5th above the second string.

The instrument was designed for chordal playing. The bows, therefore, were either very long or, if short, designed so that the hair and the stick were as far apart as possible, as pictorial sources attest. The many pictures reproduced by Winternitz show, too, that the instrument was supported against the left shoulder, but held with the pegbox considerably lower than the body of the instrument, although in some pictures smaller instruments are held horizontally or even with the pegbox slightly raised.

Disertori (1941) was the first to attempt to reconstruct the playing technique of the *lira da braccio*, by examining the possibility that the instrument was used to play late 15th- and early 16th-century frottolas; and he drew attention to the fact that some pictures show players apparently stopping the off-board drones by means of a metal ring attached to their left thumb. An idea of the chordal character of *lira* accompaniments can be gained from studying the fragments of 'recitative' (only the vocal part survives) sung as an invocation to Pan by Andrea dalla Viola accompanying himself on a *lira da braccio* at the first performance of Agostino Beccari's *Il sacrificio* in 1554 (the music is in Einstein, 1949/R1971, and Solerti, 1905/R1968).

The most tangible evidence, though, of the way the *lira da braccio* was actually played comes from a late 16th-century manuscript in Pesaro's Biblioteca Oliveriana (1144, olim 1193), first studied by Walter Rubsamen (*JAMS*, xxi, 1968, pp.286–99). The short section of the manuscript devoted to the *lira* includes several charts showing standard chord positions on the instrument, one complete setting of the romanesca for solo *lira* and a fragment of a passamezzo. The manuscript

shows that the *lira* normally played triple and quadruple stops, but there are certain limitations to the chord positions available on the instrument. The notes of a chord always have to lie on adjacent strings, for example, since the bow cannot skip over middle strings. And the player can stop strings below an open one only occasionally because of the difficulty of the left-hand technique. Indeed, the Pesaro manuscript often indicates that one finger is required to stop all three middle strings (*jeu barré*). Thus the instrument could not play all chords in all inversions; the C major triad, for example, lies most conveniently under the fingers in 6-4 position. The romanesca, the beginning of which appears in ex.1, consists largely of a melody accompanied by multiple-stopped triads, a feature that suggests that the top two or three strings were reserved for melodic writing or passage-work, and the lower ones for chords.

The range of the instrument and its playing technique indicate, too, that performers must customarily have sung in a range below that of their accompaniment. Ganassi (*Lettione seconda*, 1543) said as much when describing the technique as the 'prattica del dire i bassi accompagnado con il suon della Lyra' ('the practice of singing basses accompanied by the lira'). And Mersenne (1636–7), in writing about the *lira da gamba*, explained that 'the bass voice is more suitable than the others for joining to this instrument so as to offset the roughness of the fourth, which ofttimes is met without the fifth below. But it produces a very good effect when the voice produces the fifth'. That is, the singer can supply the root of a 6-4 chord. And a sung bass line offsets nicely the soprano passage-work and the chords that can go below *g* only when the drones are called into play.

Only a few museums possess *lire da braccio* in a state approaching their original condition. The most beautiful by far is one by Giovanni d'Andrea da Verona, dated 1511, now in the instrument collection of the Kunsthistorisches Museum in Vienna (fig.2). The belly is shaped like a male torso and the front of the pegbox shows a grotesque male face; the back, on the other hand, is carved in the form of a female torso with a mask and acanthus leaves superimposed and with a female face on the back of the pegbox. The length of its body is 51·5 cm, thus longer than either of the other two most notable surviving instruments, the undated one by Joan Maria in the Ashmolean Museum, Oxford (with a body length of 38·7 cm), and the undated anonymous one in the Brussels Royal Conservatory (with a body length of 44 cm).

2. HISTORY. Although its tuning by 5ths resembles that of the REBEC, the *lira da braccio* is more closely related to the medieval FIDDLE, and, indeed, it might best be regarded as a member of the fiddle family with especially well-defined characteristics. By the second half of the 13th century, Jerome of Moravia described some fiddles with drone strings, and fiddles are often to be seen in 14th-century pictures of fiddles with two to five strings. The characteristic violin-like shape of the *lira*, on the other hand, seems not to have evolved until the late 15th century. Winternitz (*MGG*) described three principal stages in the development of the instrument's shape: a relatively long, thin body with a gently incurved waist without corners, and with either C-shaped, round, square or rhomboid soundholes (fig.3); a body divided into two parts, a relatively narrow upper and a shorter, broader lower section, almost invariably with C-holes

Ex.1 Romanesca for solo *lira da braccio*
I-PESo 1144, p.174

[etc]

(fig.4); and the fully developed violin-like shape with three bouts, corners and f-holes.

These three shapes appear in innumerable pictorial sources (many of them reproduced in the various studies by Winternitz) and especially Italian pictures, for the instrument was developed and cultivated chiefly in Italy during the 15th and 16th centuries, and appeared in other European countries only to the extent that Italian culture had an influence. In line with the instrument's supposed ancient lineage it is most often shown in the hands of mythological or allegorical characters, or sometimes as a member of angel consorts. Above all, the *lira da braccio* was associated with Orpheus (taming the animals, subduing the infernal spirits or leading Euridice out of hell) and Apollo (winning the contest with Marsyas or Pan, or leading the Muses), to judge from the quantity of pictorial evidence. But the instru-

ment is also shown being played by Homer, King David, Musica, angels and various others.

The relationship of the instrument to ancient culture explains why it was taken up by those 15th-century Italian poet-improvisers, the Brandolini brothers, Leonardo Giustiniani in Venice, Pietrobono in Ferrara, Atalante, Benedetto Gareth in Naples, Serafino all' Aquila in the service of Ascanio Sforza in Rome, the philosopher Marsilio Ficino, the painters Raphael and Leonardo da Vinci and so on, who often sang their epic and narrative verses, their *strambotti* in *ottava rima*, their *capitoli* and other narratives in *terza rima*, odes, sonnets, ballate and other poetic forms, to the accompaniment of the *lira da braccio*. It is not surprising, then, that Baccio Ugolino played the instrument as Orpheus in the Mantuan performance of Angelo Poliziano's *Orfeo* in 1471, and that it was associated with ancient gods and heroes in dramatic and quasidramatic entertainments in Italy throughout the 16th century. Among the greatest virtuosos of the 16th century was the composer Alessandro Striggio (i), whom Cosimo Bartoli (*Ragionamenti*, 1567) described as being able to play on the instrument four parts at once with such lightness and so musically that the listeners were astounded ('eccellentissimo nel sonar la viola e far sentir in essa quattro parti a un tratto con tanta leggiadria et con tanta musica che fa stupire gli ascoltanti').

The instrument played some part in 16th-century ensembles, as well as accompanying solo singing, its chief role. Italian *intermedio* orchestras sometimes called for *lire*. As an ensemble instrument it may sometimes have played a single line in the soprano register, and it may sometimes have served as a protocontinuo instrument, taking advantage of its special qualities by adding chords beneath the given melodic line. The LIRONE or *lira da gamba*, a bass counterpart to the *lira da braccio*, played between the knees like a viol, was developed in the 16th century, and seems to have gained more and more prominence as the century wore on. But both instruments disappeared from use early in the 17th century, and have never been revived.

BIBLIOGRAPHY

A. Hajdecki: *Die italienische Lira da Braccio* (Mostar, 1892/*R*1965)
A. Solerti: *Musica, ballo e drammatica alla corte medicea dal 1600 al 1637* (Florence, 1905/*R*1968)
G. R. Hayes: *The Viols and other Bowed Instruments* (London, 1930/*R*1969)
B. Disertori: 'L'arciviolatalira in un quadro del seicento', *RMI*, xliv (1940), 199
——: 'Practica e tecnica della lira da braccio', *RMI*, xlv (1941), 150–75
A. Einstein: *The Italian Madrigal* (Princeton, 1949/*R*1971)
E. Winternitz: 'Lira da braccio', *MGG*
E. Haraszti: 'La technique des improvisateurs de langue vulgaire et de latin au quattrocento', *RBM*, ix (1955), 12
E. Winternitz: *Musical Instruments and their Symbolism in Western Art* (New York, 1967)
H. M. Brown: *Sixteenth-century Instrumentation: the Music for the Florentine Intermedii*, MSD, xxx (1973)
L. C. Witten: 'Apollo, Orpheus, and David', *JAMIS*, i (1975), 5–55

HOWARD MAYER BROWN

Lira da gamba [lira doppio, lira grande]. *See* LIRONE.

Liraki. Short-necked fiddle of Greece. *See* LYRA, (2).

Lira organizzata (It.; Fr. *vielle organisée*; Ger. *Orgelleier*). A HURDY-GURDY with one or two ranks of organ pipes and bellows housed in its body. It is occasionally

2. Lira da braccio by Giovanni d'Andrea, Verona, 1511 (Kunsthistorisches Museum, Vienna)

4. *Lira da braccio: detail from 'The Presentation at the Temple' (1510) by Vittore Carpaccio (Gallerie dell'Accademia, Venice)*

3. *Poet with a lira da braccio: woodcut from 'Epithome Plutarchi' (1501)*

5. *Recitation with lira da braccio accompaniment: woodcut from the epic 'Morgante maggiore' by Luigi Pulci, printed in Florence, c1500 (A-Wn Sign.Ink.5.G.9)*

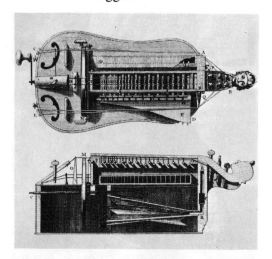

Lira organizzata (shown from above, and in cross-section) from Bédos de Celles' 'L'art du facteur d'orgues', iv (1778): AG is the wind-chest, F the organ pipes, P the stop-knob to disengage the pipes from the strings, and Q the knob for the tremulant stop (the remaining letters refer to the HURDY-GURDY*)*

referred to as an 'organized hurdy-gurdy'. A crank operates both the wheel that activates the strings and the bellows that make the pipes sound. On most instruments a mechanism permitted the player to engage either the strings or the pipes, or both together. The instrument seems already to have existed in the middle of the 18th century. It reached a peak of popularity about 1780, notably in France, but its vogue did not last long. A number of composers wrote for the instrument, including Adalbert Gyrowetz, Ignace Pleyel, Johann Sterkel and Haydn, who composed five concertos for two *lire organizzate* and orchestra (HVIIh: 1–5), commissioned by Ferdinand IV, King of Naples. See H. R. Edwall: 'Ferdinand IV and Haydn's Concertos for the Lira Organizzata', *MQ*, xlviii (1962), pp.190ff.

HOWARD MAYER BROWN

Lireggiare (It.). A term used in F. Rognoni Taeggio's *Selva de varii passaggi secondo l'uso moderno* (Milan, 1620), to mean slurring several notes in one bowstroke on the violin. It is still defined in the same way in J. G. Walther's *Musicalisches Lexicon* (Leipzig, 1732). For a discussion of the term, see D. D. Boyden: *The History of Violin Playing from its Origins to 1761* (London, 1965), pp.164ff.

Lirepilk. Swedish hurdy-gurdy. *See* VEVLIRA.

Lirica [lijerica]. Three-string fiddle of Croatia. It is related to the Greek *lyra,* and is made of a single block of wood, with a short neck (see illustration). The body is covered with a thin wooden soundboard. The melody is performed on the highest string, the second string is tuned a perfect 5th below, and the third a major 2nd below the first. The open second string is used for the accompaniment, the open third string occasionally for the melody. The *lirica* chiefly accompanied dances and is found mostly in the area around Dubrovnik.

Lirone [lira da gamba, arciviolatalira, lira grande, lirone perfetto, lyra perfecta, lira doppia, lyrone, lyra, lira] (It.). A bass counterpart to the LIRA DA BRACCIO. As its name implies, the 'lirone' is a larger version of the *lira da braccio,* necessarily played between the knees rather than under the chin because of its size. This expanded member of the *lira* family could accommodate as many as nine to 14 strings on the fingerboard and two to four drone strings; its ingenious tuning system and remarkable sound were admired by a number of 16th- and 17th-century writers. The *lirone* was designed for chordal playing, its chief use being to accompany the voice. Its impressive repertory (mainly Italian) extended from the mid-16th to the late 17th century.

1. Structure, tunings and playing techniques. 2. History in Venice, Florence and Rome: *c*1530–*c*1690. 3. Other Italian and European centres. 4. Surviving instruments.

1. STRUCTURE, TUNINGS AND PLAYING TECHNIQUES. From iconographical sources and from the few surviving instruments, it can be concluded that the *lirone* was usually fretted and that its ribs were usually shallow, often half the depth that might be expected for its body size. Most examples show frontal pegs, although a few are lateral. There was little uniformity in shape or design from one example to the next; some were based on the principles of violin construction, others on those of the viol. A few were highly decorated to increase their visual effectiveness in theatrical settings.

The *lirone* could provide both sustained chords and the ethereal effect of freely ringing strings, with the added dimension of dynamic nuance like that of the viol, or better, a consort of viols. This was achieved by a system

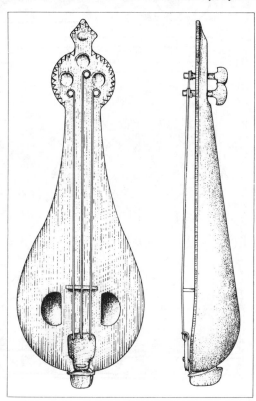

Lirica (three-string fiddle) of Croatia, Yugoslavia

of RE-ENTRANT TUNING, the strings on the fingerboard being tuned in a series of ascending 5ths and descending 4ths, and the drones adapted to the tonality of the particular piece of music being played.

Cerreto (1601) described an 11-string instrument tuned *G–g* [the two drones]–*c–c'–g–d'–a–e'–b–f♯'–c♯'*. Praetorius (2/1619) gave the tuning of his 14-string *lirone* as *G♭–d♭* [the two drones]–*A♭–e♭–B♭–f–c–g–d–a–e–b–f♯–c♯*. Mersenne (1636–7, in the fourth book of string instruments) mentioned an 11-string instrument described to him by a Roman friend (the composer Stefano Landi), which Mersenne thought (probably mistakenly) to be a *lira da braccio*, tuned *e♭–e♭'* [the two drones]–*b♭–f–c'–g–d'–a–e'–b–f♯'*. And he gave two tunings for the 15-string instrument (which he called simply 'lyre'): *c–c'* [the two drones]–*d–d'–g–g'–d'–a–e'–b–f♯'–c♯'–g♯'–d♯'–a♯'* which he said was the most common tuning; and *c–c'* [the two drones]–*d–d'–g–g'–d'–a'–e'–b'–f♯'–c♯''–g♯'–d♯'–a♯'*, a tuning he associated with Le Baillif of the Académie de la Poésie et de la Musique.

The tunings make it possible to play a series of four- and five-note chords using the same fingering pattern across the entire fingerboard. For example, with Praetorius's tuning, beginning on the bass side of the instrument, all major chords from *A♭* to *e*, following the circle of 5ths, are playable with one basic two-finger position. A slightly different fingering pattern is required for minor chords. Also at the player's disposal are all the common suspensions required for 17th-century figured basses, 4-3, 7-6 and so on. Cerreto's tablature examples show that normally only the top members of a given chord should be stopped, the lower members being allowed to ring freely. This technique is important for achieving freely ringing harp-like sonority. Although the technique of *jeu barré* (using the index finger of the left hand as a temporary nut by placing it across a block of strings) is an important one, particularly for rapid bass lines, excessive string-stopping should be avoided.

The number of possible chord positions on the *lirone* is limited because the notes of the chords must lie on adjacent strings owing to the nearly flat bridge (see fig.1)

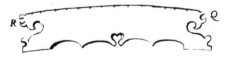

1. Lirone bridge: detail of woodcut from Mersenne's 'Harmonie universelle' (1636–7)

and the inability of the bow to skip over strings. Alternate chords emerge in the second inversion, creating problems of part-writing and an incomplete bass line, a feature common to the early guitar and cittern. However, the sustained string sound of the *lirone* creates an unusually eerie effect. In the late 16th century both Giulio Caccini and Alessandro Striggio (i) were known to have played the *lirone* without a supporting bass instrument, but with the later repertory (for example the oratorios of Luigi Rossi) the *lirone* was often paired with the violone, the lute or the harpsichord.

The most common way of notating a *lirone* part was by means of a figured or unfigured bass. Mersenne and Cerreto gave tablature examples, though tablature is impractical for such a consistent and simple fingering system on an instrument with so many strings.

There is abundant evidence that the *lirone* was not an arpeggiating instrument, but that its purpose was to provide sustained chords. Mersenne compared its sound to that of the organ, and Agazzari (1607) recommended that 'the player of the lirone must bow with long, clear, sonorous strokes', and Cerreto agreed. Nearly all the known repertory for the instrument exploited the feature of sustained string sound. Composers created variety and interest by varying the speed of harmonic movement, and particularly in the 17th century, by exploring distant tonalities and unusual harmonic shifts. Sustained string sound was also appropriate for the accompaniment of recitatives, for it provided nuanced and unobtrusive yet firm support for the singer's declamation of the text. The concept of sustained string sound was carried on long after the *lirone* went out of use, in the accompanied recitatives of 18th-century Passion music.

2. HISTORY IN VENICE, FLORENCE AND ROME: *c*1530– *c*1690. The earliest known reference to the *lirone* is in a document of 1536 (*I-Vas*) of the Venetian religious confraternity, the Scuola di S Giovanni Evangelista. Further references appear in connection with another important confraternity, the Scuola di S Rocco, and these references continue to appear until 1631 (the year of the Great Plague). The Venetians preferred using several *lironi*; there were as many as six at S Rocco. No Venetian music specifying the *lirone* has yet been discovered, but presumably in the 16th century simple chordal settings of psalms and hymns would have been appropriate, particularly for processions in which *lirone* players were known to have participated. In the early decades of the 17th century, the much admired Giovanni Priuli and Giovanni Picchi worked at S Rocco. The continuo body available there in 1618 would have been most effective for their concerted motets: three larger organs, two small organs, two *lironi*, three theorboes and a violone.

As early as 1560 the *lira* was used to accompany singing for the services of the Florentine Compagnia dell'Arcangelo Raffaelo. It is difficult to determine which instrument was being referred to here, the *lira da braccio* or the *lirone*, but it is known that the latter, referred to as the *arciviolatalira*, was called upon to accompany a lament in the *intermedi* for Francesco d'Ambra's comedy *La cofanaria* performed in Florence in 1565. This association with dolorous subject matter was retained throughout the instrument's history. In addition to its role in Italian *intermedio* orchestras and in religious services, the *lirone* had an important role in two early Florentine operas, namely Jacopo Peri's *Euridice* (1601) and Francesca Caccini's *La liberazione di Ruggiero* (1625). The last known reference to the playing of the instrument is dated 1669, but presumably the Medici court *lirone* player Piero Salvetti continued to play it to the end of his life in 1697. Well past the heyday of the instrument, two *lironi* were listed in the Medici court inventory of 1716.

Undoubtedly some of the finest repertory for the *lirone* came from Rome in the 17th century. In the preface to Emilio de' Cavalieri's *Rappresentatione di Anima, et di Corpo* (1600) Alessandro Guidotti recommended the use of the *lira doppia*, and it may have been during Cavalieri's professional work at the Florentine court in the 1580s that he first heard the instrument. Landi included the *lira* in the continuo body of his sacred opera *Il San Alessio* (1634). In 1639 the French viol player André Maugars reported performances which took place at a

2. *Pier Francesco Mola's 'Homer' (Gemäldegalerie Alte Meister, Dresden), showing a lirone that probably belonged to the Medici court collection in the 17th century*

private home and in an oratory. The strong association of the *lirone* with religious music continued in Rome until the end of the 17th century and a number of fine composers called for it in sacred operas, oratorios, concerted motets and related forms. Six oratorios attributed to Luigi Rossi (*d* 1653) include *lira* parts; one attributed both to Rossi and to Marco Marazzoli (*d* 1662) is particularly notable. In the *Oratorio di Santa Caterina* (*I-Rvat* Barb.lat.4209) the *lira* accompanies a soldier's lament for the saint before her death, and the music is correspondingly rich in harmonic intensity. Other Roman composers who used the special colours and effects of the *lirone* were Bernardo Pasquini (*d* 1710) in his oratorio *Cain e Abel* and Domenico Mazzocchi (*d* 1665) whose printed collection *Sacrae concertationes* (1664) specifies the *lira* in three works, all written most effectively for the instrument.

3. OTHER ITALIAN AND EUROPEAN CENTRES. Although it would appear that Venice, Florence and Rome were the major centres for the cultivation of the *lirone*, there is a smattering of information about activities elsewhere. A *lirone* in the National Conservatory, Lisbon (formerly in the Keil Collection), by L. Morella bears a label whose place and date have been deciphered as Mentone (?Mantua), 1530s or 1550s. Alessandro Striggio (i) was known to have visited Ferrara in 1584 with his *arciviolatalira*; Jerome Cardan's *De musica* (*I-Rvat* 5850), completed in 1574, gives a detailed description of Striggio's instrument. The printed inventory (1666) of the Milanese nobleman Manfredo Settala included an 11-string *arciviola* and another with fewer strings made in Naples. The Graz inventory of 1580 listed a *lira in camba* on which the Bavarian coat-of-arms was embossed. In France the *lirone* was used in connection with Le Bailiff, and a *grande lire* was included in the 1589 inventory of the luthier Robert Denis *le jeune*.

4. SURVIVING INSTRUMENTS. A small number of original instruments has survived, perhaps the most attractive being a *lirone* in the Kunsthistorisches Museum in Vienna (an instrument made by Wendelin Tieffenbrucker of Padua, *c*1590). Other examples are in the Royal Conservatory in Brussels (an anonymous instrument), the

Musikinstrumenten-Museum, Karl-Marx-Universität, Leipzig (an instrument made by Francesco da Salò, *c*1612), and the instrument by Morella in Lisbon (see §3). A mid-17th-century *lirone* of Florentine provenance, formerly in the Heyer collection but destroyed in World War II, was illustrated in numerous 17th-century paintings including Pier Francesco Mola's *Homer* (Gemäldegalerie Alte Meister, Dresden; fig.2), Ferdinand Bol's *Woman with Lira da Gamba* (Kunsthistorisches Museum, Vienna) and A. D. Gabbiani's *Il Principe Ferdinando de Medici e i suoi musici* (Pitti Palace, Florence), the last of which portrays the Florentine player Salvetti.

BIBLIOGRAPHY

S. Ganassi: *Regola rubertina* (Venice, 1542/*R*1970)

L. Zacconi: *Prattica di musica*, i (Venice, 1592/*R*1967)

S. Cerreto: *Della prattica musica vocale, et strumentale* (Naples, 1601, 2/1611)

A. Agazzari: *Del sonare sopra 'l basso'* (Siena, 1607)

A. Banchieri: *Conclusioni nel suono dell'organo* (Bologna, 1609, 2/1626)

P. Cerone: *El melopeo* (Naples, 1613/*R*)

M. Praetorius: *Syntagma musicum*, ii (Wolfenbüttel, 2/1619/*R*1958 and 1980)

F. Rognoni: *Selva di varii passaggi* (Milan, 1620/*R*1970)

M. Mersenne: *Harmonie universelle* (Paris, 1636–7/*R*1963; Eng. trans., 1957)

A. Maugars: *Response faite à un curieux sur le sentiment de la musique d'Italie* (Paris, 1639)

A. Kircher: *Musurgia universalis* (Rome, 1650/*R*1970)

B. Disertori: 'L'arciviolatalira in un quadro del seicento', *RMI*, xliv (1940), 199

D. Arnold: 'Music at the Scuola di San Rocco', *ML*, xl (1959), 229

——: 'Music at a Venetian Confraternity in the Renaissance', *AcM*, xxxvii (1965), 62

H. M. Brown: 'Psyche's Lament: some Music for the Medici Wedding in 1565', *Words and Music: the Scholar's View . . . in Honor of A. Tillman Merritt* (Cambridge, Mass., 1972), 1

——: *Sixteenth-century Instrumentation: the Music for the Florentine Intermedii*, MSD, xxx (1973)

H. E. Smither: *A History of the Oratorio*, i (Chapel Hill, 1977)

J. Hill: 'Oratory Music in Florence, I: *Recitar cantando*, 1583–1655', *AcM*, li (1979), 108

——: 'Oratory Music in Florence, II: at San Firenze in the Seventeenth and Eighteenth Centuries', *AcM*, li (1979), 246

ERIN HEADLEY

Liru. Clarinet of Karelia. It is made of wood wrapped in birch bark and has a conical bore 40 to 50 cm long.

A single reed is attached to the upper end and the bore has four or five finger-holes producing a diatonic scale. A larger version of the *liru*, about 60 to 65 cm long and with a long, wide bell, is known as the *luddu*; it has four to six finger-holes. Both instruments were soaked in water before being played; used mostly as pastoral instruments, they are now rare. See *VertkovA*, 84.

L'isstesso tempo. *See* ISTESSO TEMPO, L'.

Litembe. Large single-headed tubular drum of the Bakwiri people of Cameroon. The membrane is made from the skin of a giant lizard; the drum is held between the legs and beaten with the hands. The *litembe* is played with the *mulumba musseli* (a smaller drum of the same type, which is placed on the ground with the membrane facing to one side so that the player sits on the body to beat it) and the *issimba* (a single-headed open cylindrical drum with four feet carved out of the base, which is beaten with sticks). The drums are used in the *male* funeral dance with a mixed chorus. See T. Nikiprowetzky: 'Musiques du Cameroun', OCR 25 [disc notes].

Litenda. Cylindrical drum of the Bango and Soko peoples of central Zaïre (*BooneT*, 69).

Lithophone (from Gk. *lithos*: 'stone'; Fr. *lithophone*; Ger. *Lithophon*, *Steinspiel*; It. *litofono*). A series of resonant stone slabs or plaques (for the Hornbostel–Sachs classification *see* IDIOPHONE). Lithophones occur in several forms: oblong bars suspended horizontally; vertically suspended plaques; or (as has been introduced in the 20th century) circular stone discs arranged chromatically.

In Asia ringing stones are found in Annam, China, Korea, Samoa, and in southern India. Prehistoric lithophones found in Indo-China (Annam) include three stone slabs (discovered actually in use in 1958) in which the surfaces show the typical flaking technique of Stone Age man, the edges apparently fashioned for tuning pur-

poses. A lithophone discovered in 1949 is now in the Musée de l'Homme, Paris (for illustration *see* GOONG LU). This instrument has ten slabs 65 to 100 cm in length, and yields two sonorous pentatonic octaves. Lithophones dating back to Neolithic times, also from Indo-China, are preserved in the Horniman Museum, London.

Stone chimes are among the most ancient and valued instruments of the Chinese (*see* QING (i)). The foremost of these is the *bianqing*, said to have existed as far back as 2300 BC. The *bianqing* consists of 16 calcareous L-shaped stone slabs (*teqing*) which are suspended vertically in two rows of eight in a rectangular frame (see fig.1). The stones are tuned to the 12 notes of the *lü* octave and its four additional notes. They are struck on

1. Chinese bianqing (Conservatoire Royal de Musique, Brussels)

2. Rock harmonica by Richardson & Sons: 19th-century engraving

the long side with wooden mallets or padded sticks. A remarkable specimen of *bianqing* consisting of 16 exquisitely ornamented tuned slabs is in the Brussels Conservatory.

Sonorous stones occur in many and widely scattered regions. In Ethiopia, stone chimes are used as church bells in certain Christian places of worship. Resonant stones have been found in Venezuela and in Europe on the islands of Chios and Sardinia. Ringing rocks used for the production of musical notes have been discovered in Nigeria and in southern Africa. Hammered depressions provide evidence of their having been used as percussion instruments. Rock gongs are used currently, their purposes varying from use in religious services to providing accompaniment to singing and dancing.

Some of the most remarkable lithophones in existence are to be found in the English Lake District. A set of 16 musical stones embracing two diatonic octaves and one note is in the Fitz Park Museum, Keswick. These stones were discovered in 1785: eight in the bed of the river Greta and eight on the nearby mountain of Skiddaw. There is also in the same museum the Richardson rock harmonica comprising five chromatic octaves of stone slabs measuring 15 to 93 cm in length. The slabs lie over a soundbox and are insulated at the nodal points on ropes of straw (see fig.2). The instrument (which was completed in 1840) was 'invented and manufactured by Messrs Richardson and Sons after 13 years' incessant labour and application from rocks dug out of the mighty Skiddaw'. The Richardson family became expert performers on this unique construction which is reputed to have at times embraced a compass of seven octaves and various bell effects. They toured extensively, performing on two occasions at command performances before Queen Victoria. A rock harmonica of similar proportions, also from Skiddaw, was completed in 1886; it was housed in Keswick for many years and remains privately owned. An instrument contemporary with the Richardson rock harmonica was the *lithokymbalom*, of alabaster slabs, built by Franz Weber and displayed in Vienna in 1837.

Modern composers have (to date) made sparing use of the lithophone. It occurs as *Steinspiel* in Carl Orff's *Die Kluge*, *Die Bernauerin*, *Astutuli*, *Trionfi*, *Antigonae* and *Oedipus*.

The following lithophones are entered in this dictionary: bianqing; biên khánh; gaval-das; goong lu; käsäka; kei; khánh; picancala; p'yŏn'gyŏng; qing (i); teqing; tetzilácatl; t'ŭkkyŏng.

BIBLIOGRAPHY
C. Sachs: *The History of Musical Instruments* (New York, 1940)
K. Wachsmann: 'The Primitive Musical Instruments', *Musical Instruments Through the Ages*, ed. A. Baines (Harmondsworth, 1961, 2/1966/R1976)
J. Blades: *Percussion Instruments and their History* (London, 1970, rev. 3/1984)
                                        JAMES BLADES

Litlit [gisada, kulibao]. Three-string fiddle of the Ilonggot people of the northern Philippines.

Litofono (It.). LITHOPHONE.

Litswakaie. Basket rattle of the Lunda people of southern Zaïre.

Litterae significativae (Lat.). SIGNIFICATIVE LETTERS.

Litungu. (1) Seven-string bowl lyre of the Kusu, Logoli and Tachoni peoples of Kenya and the Kusu, Gishu and

Wanga peoples of Uganda. In Kenya it measures about 90 cm overall, the wooden resonating bowl, which is covered with monitor lizard skin, being about 35 cm by 25 cm with a depth of about 15 cm. The strings are held in position by knobbles of string on the crossbar, which also facilitate tuning. The strings go over a fretted wooden bridge on the membrane, through which they pass to emerge at the wooden base where they are anchored to a small metal rod. In performance the player is seated and the instrument is either held vertically or placed across the lap. Often more than one lyre is used to accompany singing. The rhythmic accompaniment is provided by the *luhengere*, a wooden percussion plaque in the shape of a flattened arch; it is placed on the ground and beaten with sticks.

(2) Eight-string bowl lyre of the Kuria people of Kenya, similar to the Luo *thum*. It traditionally had a wooden resonating bowl, but a large circular metal bowl (about

Bowl lyre (thum) of the litungu type of the Luo people, Kenya; the instrument is secured in an upright position by a spike at one end of the crossbar and is accompanied by ibiturani (percussion bells)

40 cm in diameter) may now be substituted. Zebra skin is used for the soundtable. The frame is about 40 cm long and the crossbar carrying the strings 60 cm. Otherwise the lyre resembles that of the Kusu. In performance it is accompanied by the *ibiturani*, a percussion instrument made from three large, pea-pod shaped bells which are tied on to the end of a long stick and held between the player's toes. From this position he is able to strike the lower frame of the instrument with the stick (see illustration). See G. Hyslop: *Musical Instruments of East Africa*, i: *Kenya* (Nairobi, 1975).

(3) RAFT ZITHER of the Gishu people of Uganda. *See* LIDUKU.

(4) Long seven-string box lyre of the Luyia/Ragoli people of Uganda. See *TraceyCSA*, ii, 295f, 364ff.
                                        K. A. GOURLAY

Lituus. A Roman brass instrument consisting of a long tube turning in upon itself at the end and thus producing the shape of the letter J. Pictorial representations indicate that it had a large detachable mouthpiece. Sachs's contention that it derived from the Celtic CARNYX, a similarly shaped instrument, is not widely accepted: it was known to the Etruscans long before the Romans had any significant contact with the Celts. The instrument is now looked upon as being distinctly Etruscan–Roman since it is unusual among ancient instruments in having no counterpart among instruments used by the Greeks, Egyptians or other Near Eastern peoples (most ancient instruments follow a general progress from east to west in the Mediterranean basin).

The earliest extant picture of a lituus occurs in a mural from the Tomba della Scimmia in Chiusi (dating from the early 5th century BC). A number of instruments survive, including one found in 1827 in a grave at Caere and now in the Museo Etrusco-Gregoriano at the Vatican. It is approximately 1·5 metres long and sounds six notes of a natural scale based on G.

Etruscan and early Roman representations of the lituus show it in processions, especially funeral processions, the *pompae funebres* (see illustration; *see also* TIBIA and TRUMPET, fig.3). Players in these processions were described as *siticines*, a generic term embracing the players of various instruments: *liticines* (lituus players), *tubicines* (trumpet players) and *cornicines* (horn players). Etruscan sarcophagi from Caere also depict the lituus in marriage ceremonies, along with players on double pipes, string instruments, and the cornu, all wearing ceremonial robes. In Roman literature, however, the lituus had mainly military associations, like most brass instruments. This presents something of a problem: other instruments are well represented in military scenes and on inscriptions, but the lituus is rarely seen. Behn (1954) suggested that the lituus was used at cohort rather than at legionary level. Thus, one presumes, it would not have appeared in column reliefs and other monumental sources where only higher military orders were more likely to have been celebrated. Another possibility, raised by Wille (1967), is that the term 'lituus' may often have been used loosely as a substitute for 'tuba'. The evidence supporting this includes the remark in *Noctes atticae* (Aulius Gellius, c130–180) that 'Virgil uses this word in place of tuba' (v, chap.8, 11). Both views are quite plausible: the many literary references certainly indicate that the lituus had at least some military associations, but it seems not to have been as important as the tuba (*see* TUBA (ii) and CORNU).

In post-classical times the term 'lituus' has been applied to other wind instruments, notably 18th-century brass.

An inventory of 1706 formerly in Ossig monastery, Bohemia, mentions 'Litui vulgo Waldhorner duo ex Tono G'; Bach's Cantata no.118, a one-movement funeral motet, calls for two litui in B♭ which play in the range of the tenor trumpet.

BIBLIOGRAPHY

C. Sachs: *Real-Lexikon der Musikinstrumente* (Berlin, 1913/R1962)
F. Behn: *Musikleben im Altertum und frühen Mittelalter* (Stuttgart, 1954)
G. Fleischhauer: *Etrurien und Rom*, Musikgeschichte in Bildern, ii/5 (Leipzig, 1964)
G. Wille: *Musica romana* (Amsterdam, 1967)
S. Marcuse: *A Survey of Musical Instruments* (Newton Abbot and London, 1975), 789

JAMES W. McKINNON

Liuqin. Abbreviated name for the Chinese lute LIUYE QIN.

Liutaio (It.). LUTHIER.

Liuto (It.). (1) LUTE.
    (2) BUFF STOP.

Liuto attiorbato (It.). A term that suggests a lute rebuilt into a theorbo-like instrument, but was stated by Alessandro Piccinini (1623) to be merely a synonym for *arciliuto* (*see* ARCHLUTE; in any event the top two courses of a theorbo are tuned an octave lower than those of a *liuto attiorbato*). The English term 'theorbo lute' referred, in many instances, to the theorbo and not to the *liuto attiorbato*. Thomas Mace (*Musick's Monument*, 1676) used the terms 'theorbo' and 'theorbo lute' interchangeably, and called the two-headed lute merely a 'French lute with two heads' (not 'theorbo lute').

BIBLIOGRAPHY

R. Spencer: 'Chitarrone, Theorbo and Archlute', *Early Music*, iv (1976), 407
——: 'English Nomenclature of Extended Lutes', *FoMRHI Quarterly* (1981), no.23

ROBERT SPENCER

Liuto romano. A large, wire-strung mandolin; *see* MANDOLIN, §4.

Liuye qin. Small lute of the Han Chinese (*liuye*: 'willow leaf'; *qin*: 'string instrument'). *Liuye qin* is some-

Double pipes, lyre and lituus (right) in a wedding procession: detail of a relief on a sarcophagus (mid-5th century BC) from Caere (Museo Etrusco-Gregoriano, Rome)

times abbreviated to *liuqin*. In shape the instrument has the appearance of a small *pipa* (*see* PIPA (i)). It came into common use within the last century or two in the music of north-east China, and during the late 1950s, in an effort to give it a position in the modern Chinese orchestra, its strings were increased from two to three (tuned in a similar manner to the SANXIAN, an octave higher), and the frets from 7 to as many as 24 (in half-step intervals). Four-string instruments may also be found. Today it plays an important part as one of the higher-pitched instruments of the Chinese orchestra.

ALAN R. THRASHER

Livenge [umntjingozi]. Flute of the Swazi people of southern Africa, resembling the Zulu UMTSHINGO.

Livi. Earthenware pot or gourd used as a musical instrument in Benin. It can be either empty or filled with water and is tapped on the open mouth with a leather or basketry fan. At Porto Novo it is played in the palace by the king's wives under the leadership of an elder. At Abomey a similar instrument, known as *zenli* and found only in the palace, is used also by the ruler's wives. See G. Rouget: 'Court Songs and Traditional History in the Ancient Kingdoms of Porto-Novo and Abomey', *Essays on Music and History in Africa*, ed. K. P. Wachsmann (Evanston, Ill., 1971), 27.

Livika. *See* LAUNUT.

Lkimbi. LAMELLAPHONE of the Attundewanianga people of Kivu, Zaïre (*LaurentyS*, 197).

Llakita [llaquita]. Eleven- and twelve-pipe PANPIPES of Irpa Chico, a community 30 km south of La Paz in the Bolivian Alti Plano. They appear two weeks before Candlemas (February 2) and are not heard after Palm Sunday. They are associated with the grain and potato harvest, and accompany the *imillani* dance of adolescent girls. See H. C. Buechler: *The Masked Media: Aymara Fiestas and Social Interaction in the Bolivian Highlands* (The Hague, 1980). *See also* LAKITA.

Llamador. Single-headed drum of the Atlantic coastal region of Colombia. It is held on one knee and played with one hand. See G. List: *Music and Poetry in a Colombian Village* (Bloomington, 1983).

Llamasenca. Quechua term (literally 'llama nose') for the FLAUTILLA of northern Jujuy, Argentina.

Llano. Bolivian PANPIPES. The instrument is used at the feast of St Peter (June 29) in Irpa Chico, 30 km south of La Paz, to accompany ceremonies aimed at protecting the potato harvest.

Llaquita. Bolivian PANPIPES. *See* LLAKITA.

Llaute [bozuk, ut]. Albanian term for the Arab short lute, occasionally used by urban Tosks in south Albania to accompany songs. It is also used in instrumental ensembles consisting of *llaute*, *dajre* (frame drum with jingles), clarinet, accordion and sometimes the violin.

Lleno (Sp.). An ORGAN STOP (*Compuestas*).

Llugorn. Early horn of Wales. For illustration of a similar instrument, *see* CORN.

Lo. BRONZE DRUM (also described as a metal drum, a kettle gong or a drum gong) of the Dao people of northern Vietnam. The drum, 22 cm high, is suspended during performance and beaten with a padded mallet; it consists of a flat gong set horizontally on a deep circular base with concave sides. The surface of the gong is usually ornamented with geometric patterns and small frogs along the rim. It is played during funerals. Similar drums are used by the Shan people of Burma and the Muong people of Vietnam (*trông đông*). 'Lo' is also used as a generic name for gongs among the Han Chinese (*see* LUO).

TRÂN QUANG HAI

Loar, Lloyd A(llayre) (*b* Cropsey, Ill., 9 Jan 1886; *d* Rogers Park, Ill., 14 Sept 1943). American pioneer in the development of the electric guitar. Having failed to convince his employers at the Gibson Mandolin-Guitar Co. (where he was chief engineer from 1919) of the potential success of an electric guitar based on an electrostatic pickup that he had developed in 1923, Loar left in 1924 and in 1934, with Lewis A. Williams, set up the Acousti-Lectric Co. in Kalamazoo, Michigan. They manufactured a range of 'Vivi-Tone' instruments, including acoustic guitars, mandolins, mandolas (mando-violas) with ten strings, and mando-cellos, as well as some of the first magnetic pickups for guitars; they also marketed an electric violin, viola and double bass, electric guitars and bass guitars. It was probably the first company to manufacture (albeit on a limited scale) a solid-bodied electric guitar. In 1934 Loar developed an electric piano, the Vivi-Tone Clavier (*see* CLAVIER (ii)). An unusual hybrid (acoustic-electric) guitar, produced around 1934, had as its back a 'secondary soundboard' with f-holes and an extended rim that prevented its being damped by the player's body. The instrument had two bridges which could be independently adjusted; one was connected through the instrument to the back, while the other was attached to a magnetized plate that terminated inside the body, close to a magnetic pickup fitted inside a removable drawer. In the 1930s Loar was granted 15 patents for acoustic piano mechanisms and electric bowed and plucked string instruments, all but one of which were assigned to the Gulbransen Co. in Chicago or the Acousti-Lectric Co. in Kalamazoo. The latter survived until 1936 and was briefly continued as the Vivi-Tone Co. in Detroit.

BIBLIOGRAPHY
R. H. Siminoff: 'Lloyd Loar: a Genius ahead of his Time', *Frets*, i/5 (1979), 38
T. Wheeler: *American Guitars: an Illustrated History* (New York, 1982), 100, 356

HUGH DAVIES

Lobat. Small open DUCT FLUTE of the Pakpak Dairi area of North Sumatra, Indonesia. It is made from bamboo, with a fitted mouthpiece and five finger-holes. As a solo instrument it is played for ceremonies involving love and magic and for lullabies; it may also accompany dances together with a *kalondang* (xylophone). *See also* BALUAT and PELOBAT.

LYN MOORE/MARGARET J. KARTOMI

Lobiko. Term for the calabash-resonated LAMELLAPHONE among the Warega people of Shabunda, Zaïre (*LaurentyS*, 197).

Lobo, Heitor (*fl* 1537–62). Portuguese organ builder. The style of his surviving work suggests Italian origin. His identified work includes two organs for Oporto Cathedral (1537–8), which were probably removed in the 18th century to make way for the present Baroque instruments; an organ for the convent of Villar de Frades (1551); and either installation or at least major reconstruction of the organ at the church of S Cruz, Coimbra (1559), parts of which survive in the façade of the present Baroque instrument. There is some evidence to suggest that Lobo may have built an organ for Évora Cathedral as early as 1544; nevertheless, little doubt remains that the present Renaissance-style organ in the cathedral was Lobo's work, and dates from about 1560. Another case in the cathedral, identical to that of the surviving organ, was lost about 1940; it is not known if the instrument itself was ever completed. The Évora organ is unquestionably one of the most important in Portugal, being virtually the sole survivor of a large number of 16th-century Portuguese organs. An instrument for the Colegiada of Nossa Senhora da Oliveira, Guimarães, was built in 1562.

W. D. JORDAN

Lockwood, Annea [Anna] (*b* Christchurch, 29 July 1939). New Zealand composer and instrument maker. She studied at the University of Canterbury, New Zealand, and then went to London, where she enrolled in courses given at the Royal College of Music by Peter Racine Fricker; she later attended courses at the Staatliche Hochschüle für Musik, Cologne, and the Electronic Music Centre, Bilthoven. Her work as an instrument builder began in London in 1967–8 with her stage work *Glass Concert* for two performers and a range of glass objects: chemical rods, thin tubes, fluorescent tubes, micro-glass sheets, panes, wine glasses and bottles, jars and marbles, as well as waste products from a glass factory such as chunks of cullet, glass threads and other fragments. These form both 'scenery' and 'instruments' and the performers move among them striking, rubbing, shaking and even snapping the various pieces. Later, at Ingatestone in Essex, she turned her attention increasingly to environmental installations and various applications of taped sound. In 1969 she produced a 'sound hat' and a 'sound umbrella', which incorporated hanging sound elements such as bamboo chimes and table tennis balls. Her other work around 1970 was on a larger scale and included sound environments and a variety of treatments of old, mainly upright, pianos under the collective title 'Piano Transplants'. They were prepared, burnt, 'drowned' in a shallow lake or installed in an outdoor 'piano garden'; the instruments were subjected in these ways to the activity of three of the four elements to create conditions of rapid decay and transformation, and careful documentation on tape was made regularly of those in the water and air environments. Since 1973 Lockwood has lived and worked in and near New York; she has ceased to be active as an instrument maker.

BIBLIOGRAPHY
A. Lockwood: 'Glass Concert 2', *Source*, no.5 (1969), 3
——: 'Sound-hat', *OU*, nos.36–7 (1970) [loose sheet in a folder]
——: 'Piano Burning', *Source*, no.9 (1971), 48
——: 'Piano Transplants', *Womens Work*, ed. A. Knowles and A. Lockwood (New York, n.d., [c1976])
HUGH DAVIES

Loco (Lat.: 'in its place'). A term used to countermand a previous instruction such as *8va bassa*, ALL'OTTAVA

or *sul ponticello* (*see also* TEMPO AND EXPRESSION MARKS, §3).

Lodrë. Cylindrical double-headed drum of Albania, beaten with two sticks. With the *surle* (conical oboe), it forms the traditional instrumental ensemble for dance music of the Gegs in northern and central Albania; it is also customarily used for wedding ceremonies. The *lodrë* is played mostly by gypsy musicians.

Lofolenge [lofonde, lofonono, loforongo]. VESSEL FLUTE of Zaïre. *See* DIPULU.

Logical bassoon. An electrically operated version of the bassoon, invented in 1967 by Giles Brindley (*b* 1926), a British neurophysiologist, acoustician and amateur musician. Brindley describes the instrument as evolutionary rather than revolutionary, having a bore that is square in section, folded twice for compactness, and with 17 tone-holes and 11 'speaker' holes evenly spaced along its length; the pads are opened and closed electrically by means of a logical circuit operated from tabs under the player's fingers. A heating wire running through the bore regulates tuning and controls condensation. This invention facilitates fingering technique and increases evenness of response, if at the cost of some loss of character. Brindley has also applied his principle to the double bassoon and the bass clarinet.

BIBLIOGRAPHY
G. Brindley: 'The Logical Bassoon', *GSJ*, xxi (1968), 152
——: 'Logical Wind Instruments', *Proceedings of the Royal Institution of Great Britain*, xlviii (1975), 207
WILLIAM WATERHOUSE

Logier, Johann Bernhard (*b* Kassel, 9 Feb 1777; *d* Dublin, 27 July 1846). German pianist, inventor, teacher, author and composer. After emigrating to England in 1791 he became leader of the Marquis of Abercorn's regimental band, and settled in Dublin on his discharge in 1807, setting up a music shop in 1810. His business ventures extended to the commercial exploitation of Haliday's 'bugle horn' (*see* KEYED BUGLE), for which he wrote a tutor (1813, rev. 2/1823). He taught piano and became interested in developing new training methods. In 1814 he patented the 'Chiroplast' or 'hand director' mechanism, which he used in group tuition of up to 20 pupils. His methods were highly controversial but became fashionable and were widely taken up in Germany (he taught in Berlin, 1822–6), the USA and elsewhere. Logier returned to Dublin in 1829.

Logier's importance lay in amalgamating techniques that had previously been adopted separately. The Chiroplast consisted of a wooden framework fixed over the piano keyboard. Parallel rails prevented the wrist from moving vertically. Along a brass rail above the piano keys slid two 'finger guides', or sets of vertical plates, preventing the fingers from moving horizontally. A 'gamut board', extending the length of the keyboard, labelled the notation of each note. Logier's system prevented the thumb crossing under the other fingers; Kalkbrenner improved it by removing the finger guides but keeping the lower wrist rail and using a sliding wooden mould over the palms, to which the back of the hand was strapped. This device was sold in England as late as 1877. Logier published *An Explanation and Description of the Royal Patent Chiroplast, or Hand-director* (?1814, 2/1816) and *A Companion to the Royal Patent Chiroplast* (c1815, with a sequel) as well as many other

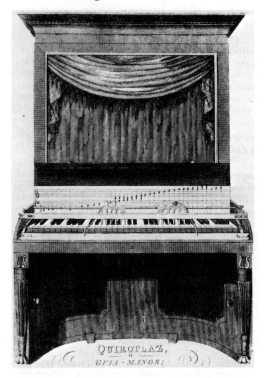

Logier's 'hand-director' mechanism, or chiroplast: engraving from 'The First Companion to the Royal Patent Chiroplast' (9/1819)

theoretical works. Critiques published around 1818 pointed to faults in Logier's harmony teaching, the great discordance of class pianos, the hampering of individual technique and the production of excessive arm force.

BIBLIOGRAPHY

[G. Smart and others]: *An Exposition of the Musical System of Mr Logier with Strictures on his Chiroplast* (London, 1818)

C. Cummins: *Logierian Sensibility, or Marsayas in the Chiroplast* (Bath, 1819)

F. Taylor: 'Chiroplast', *Grove 1*; rev. in 'Gymnastics', *Grove 2*

DAVID CHARLTON

Logo [longo]. SLIT-DRUM of Samoa, Niue and Tokelau. In Samoa it is the largest of the slit-drums (about 2 metres long) and is sounded with a single heavy beater (*'auta*). It is thought to have originated in Samoa as a redesigned LALI made for 19th-century missionaries to use as a church 'bell', and it was probably carried to Niue and Tokelau by Samoan missionaries. In Tokelau it is a medium-sized slit-drum, smaller than a *lali* and bigger than a PĀTĒ, used with two sticks for calling meetings.

BIBLIOGRAPHY

E. Loeb: *History and Traditions of Niue* (Honolulu, 1926), 94

R. Moyle: 'Samoan Musical Instruments', *EM*, xviii (1974), 61f

MERVYN McLEAN

Lohenga. War drum of the Tetela people of Zaïre, struck with the fingers (*BooneT*, 52).

Lokando. Small SLIT-DRUM of the Bangwedo region of Zaïre. It is made from a sculpted piece of wood (*LaurentyTF*, 136).

Lokanga. Malagasy generic term for several instruments which are unrelated or not closely related.

Lokanga antandroy, a FIDDLE, is usually found in the extreme south of Madagascar, among the Antandroy. It has a wooden body with an arched lower end; the belly is nailed on. It has three or four strings, made now of metal, but formerly of nylon and originally of animal or vegetable fibres. It is used to accompany songs, including laments, lullabies and ceremonial songs invoking the dead. The songs may be performed by a mixed duo.

Lokanga hisatra ('bark zither') is a fragile STICK ZITHER made by children from a reed (*Cyperus acqualis*). One or more strings are raised from the outer layer of the reed. It is found among the many peoples in the highlands, and elsewhere in Madagascar, but its exact distribution is not known.

Lokanga bara, a viol, is similar to the European instrument, which was introduced to the island by European sailors during the 16th and 17th centuries. However, different materials are used in its construction; for example, the strings are of goat gut or vegetable fibres. As its name indicates, it has been used mainly by the Bara, but neighbouring peoples have also used it from time to time. It is used in Bara ceremonies of exorcism and possession, such as *bilo*, *sabo* and *sandratse*.

Lokanga bazaha ('foreign' *lokanga*) is the name usually given to the violin, which was introduced in the 17th century; the Sakalava name for it is *lokanga bemola*. The widespread use of the violin throughout Madagascar led some to believe that it had become a folk instrument. (European missionaries considered it to be an instrument of the devil and urged people to burn their violins.) It is now little used, except in Imerina, where it has had an important role in the traditional troupes (*mpilalao*) since the early 19th century. String quartets and trios appeared regularly at court, especially during the reign of Ranavalona II (1868–83) and of the last queen, Ranavalona III (1883–97).

Lokanga vava ('mouth' *lokanga*) was a children's toy similar to the European JEW'S HARP. It had a brief existence in Imerina and then among the Betsileo. It may have been named with the chordophone group because its lamella was regarded as a 'string'.

Lokanga voatavo, a STICK ZITHER, was made by the Merina and played by male slaves. It is now made only to sell to tourists, and the shape of its gourd resonator rarely resembles that of the traditional instrument. A similar instrument in use in other parts of Madagascar is the *jejo voatavo* (see JEJO).

MICHEL DOMENICHINI-RAMIARAMANANA

Logo (slit-drum) of Upolu, Samoa, struck with a single beater

Lokilo [lokiru, lokiro]. Cylindro-conical drum of the Sengele and Lia peoples of Zaïre. The conical lower part is elongated into a single foot, and the head is laced in a complex manner to a tiny patch of hide covering the foot. The drum was originally used in times of crisis such as the death of a chief or during battle (*BooneT*, 34ff, 61). *See also* BOKENZA.

Lökkelje. NYCKELHARPA of Norway.

Lokole. General term for SLIT-DRUM among the Mongo, Doko, Nkundo, Kota, Mbole and Yela peoples of Zaïre and the Bas-Congo. The word 'lokole' denotes slit or hollow. Amongst the northern and north-western peoples the term denotes a trapezoidal slit-drum (*LaurentyTF*, 133). *See* NKUMVI.

Lokombe [lokumbe]. A term used generically to signify a musical instrument, especially a PLURIARC or SLIT-DRUM, among many peoples of Zaïre. It denotes the pluriarc of the Ngando and the trapezoidal slit-drums of the Mbole, Yela and Lengola peoples. Pluriarcs of very similar name are the *lokombele* of the Nkundo, *lokombi* of the Oli, Mongo, Lia, Yela and Bai, and the *lukombe*; similarly named trapezoidal slit-drums include the *lokombee* of the Kutu, Ngombe and Mbole, *lokomele* of the Nkundo, *lukombe* and *lukombi* of the Kusu, Nkutu and Tetela. See *LaurentyC*, 117; *LaurentyTF*, 137ff. *See also* LUKOMBE (i) (ii) (iii) and LUKUMBI (i).

Lokporo (i). SLIT-DRUM of the Hima and Bale peoples of Zaïre (*LaurentyTF*, 141).

Lokporo (ii). Conical drum of the Hima people of Rwanda. *See* DINDO.

Lokulu. Cylindrical SLIT-DRUM of the Mongo and Yembe peoples of north-western Zaïre. Amongst the Yembe the narrow slit is widened at each end to make square or circular openings (*LaurentyTF*, 133).

Lolkiñ. Straight cylindrical trumpet of the Mapuche (Araucanians) of southern-central Chile. It is made of dried thistle sprout, about 1·5 metres long, and has a mouthpiece of two or three notched reed portions. The sound is produced by strong inhalations and resembles that of a muted trumpet. It is used, along with the *trutruka* (a longer trumpet of similar shape) in the initiation rites of the *machi* (shamans).

JOHN M. SCHECHTER

Lololglag. Bamboo SLIT-DRUM set of Siberut, Mentawei Islands, Indonesia. Its three or four large internodal bamboo tubes are suspended from a cross-beam and beaten by one or two players. There is no standard size or tuning. See R. Schefold: 'Schlitztrommeln und Trommelsprache in Mentawei', *Zeitschrift für Ethnologie*, xcviii (1973), 44.

MARGARET J. KARTOMI

Lolongo papa. Makeshift SOUNDING BOARD of Futuna: an upside-down canoe underbody pounded with two sticks. A similar instrument in Tikopia is called a *ta*. See E. G. Burrows: *Ethnology of Futuna* (Honolulu, 1936), 211.

Loma. Angular harp of Liberia.

Lomana. Mouth-resonated chordophone of the Saka people of central Zaïre (*LaurentyC*, 110). *See* EMANA.

Lombardic rhythm. Reversed dotting. It is difficult to trace any rational origin for this name, which is found in the treatises of both Quantz (1752) and J. F. Agricola (1757). *See* SCOTCH SNAP.

Lomeka. Carved wooden VESSEL FLUTE of the Ngombe people of north-western Zaïre (*LaurentyA*, 102).

Londo. Largest SLIT-DRUM of the Luba people of Zaïre. *See* KYONDO.

Longa (i). Double clapperless bell of southern and central Africa. It was reported in Angola by Merolla (*Breve e succinta relatione del viaggio nel regno di Congo*, Naples, 1692).

Longa [longga] **(ii).** HOURGLASS DRUM of the Ivory Coast. *See* LUNGA (i).

Longdi. Chinese transverse flute (*long*: 'dragon'; *di*: 'flute'), now very rare. A flute by this name is mentioned many times in sources of the Tang dynasty (AD 618–907), a notable citation being in a poem of the famous Li Po (701–62). The flute was exported to Japan, where its modern descendant is the *ryūteki* (written with the same Chinese graphs). An instrument called *longdi* (not necessarily descended from the Tang instrument) was in use in Chinese court ensembles in the 12th century, and Chen Yang's *Yueshu* ('Treatise on music') of 1104 shows a drawing of a transverse 'dragon-neck flute' (*longjing di*) with seven finger-holes and a dragon's head and neck fitted on to the opposite end from the blow-hole. The later *Yuan shi* ('History of the Yuan dynasty'), covering the years 1206–1368, describes a *longdi* quite similar to that illustrated by Chen Yang. A similar *longdi* was used during the Ming period (1368–1644), but few details are known. The *longdi*'s subsequent history in China is obscure.

BIBLIOGRAPHY
Chen Yang: *Yueshu* [Treatise on music] (1104, repr. Guangzhou, 1876), 130.12*ab*
Song Lian: *Yuan shi* [History of the Yuan dynasty] (1370/*R* Beijing, 1977)

Long drum. Term for the bass drum, in use in England in the 18th century and the early 19th.

Longjing di. Chinese transverse flute with seven finger-holes. *See* LONGDI.

Longman & Broderip. English firm of music publishers and instrument makers, established in London. The business was founded in or before 1767 by James Longman and others, and was first known as J. Longman & Co. Its Harp & Crown sign, though not its premises, was apparently acquired from the widow of John Johnson (ii). From 1769 to 1775 the firm was known as Longman, Lukey & Co., becoming Longman, Lukey & Broderip when Francis Broderip entered the business in September 1775. Lukey withdrew from the business in

1776 and the firm remained as Longman & Broderip until its bankruptcy in 1798. From December 1782 it had a circulating music library and in 1789 it advertised that it was opening branches at Margate and Brighthelmstone (now Brighton) 'during the watering season'.

The harpsichords made for Longman & Broderip and sold with their nameboards were of the standard Kirckman–Shudi type, the biggest examples including machine and swell stops. A full list of makers working for the firm and the exact form of their agreement have not yet been established, although it is known that the firm would produce a specific marquetry design to order. An instrument with its label numbered 735 is at Mount Vernon, having been acquired by George Washington in 1773; others, such as that in the Cambridge Music School, suggest that the firm's standards of workmanship were not very high. Unusually in English instrument making, the firm did much advertising, and in addition to its harpsichords, pianos and more usual instruments it offered such curious items as 'Glove horns', 'Sticcado pastorales', 'upright harpsichords with a curious new invented swell' (1786), 'piano-fortes in commodes, sideboards & dressing-tables' (1786), and, from Paris, 'portable clavecins . . . agreeable for travelling with, as they may be conveyed and even performed on in a coach' (1789). Among the violin makers to have made instruments for Longman, Lukey & Co. are Joseph and Lockey Hill.

After Longman & Broderip's bankruptcy, John Longman, who had succeeded James, went into partnership with Muzio CLEMENTI until 1801, and then set up for himself; Giles Longman, John's successor, was in partnership with James Herron as Longman & Herron until 1822. The other partner, Francis Broderip, entered into partnership with C. Wilkinson. Broderip died in 1807, and the firm became Wilkinson & Co. until 1810, when it ceased business.

For details of the firm's publishing activities, see Grove 6.

BIBLIOGRAPHY

T. Busby: Concert Room and Orchestra Anecdotes (London, 1825), i, 126f

R. Russell: The Harpsichord and Clavichord (London, 1959, rev. 2/1973)

PETER WILLIAMS

Longo. See LOGO.

Longombe (i). LAMELLAPHONE of the Eso people of central Zaïre. It has wooden keys and a hollowed-out box resonator (LaurentyS, 193).

Longombe [longombi] (ii). PLURIARC of the Nkundo, Ngata, Mongo, Yaelima, Ibeke, Lia, Bokatola, Ngongo, Mbole and Eso peoples of Zaïre (LaurentyC, 117). See LUKOMBE (i).

Long zither. A term applied particularly to the half-tube zithers of East Asia, such as the Japanese KOTO and the Chinese QIN. See also CHORDOPHONE.

Lonjo. A Malagasy rattle. See KOTRA.

Lonkoko. MOUTH BOW of the Nkundo people of Zaïre; also known as itumbolongonda, inkoko and ingonga (LaurentyC, 112). See LUSUBA.

Lontore. Transverse flute of the Bisa people of Upper Volta. It has four finger-holes and is usually played solo with great virtuosity by amateur musicians.

Loops console. A multiple percussion instrument invented and constructed by the American percussionist Ron(ald M.) George (b 1937) at the Center for Music Experiment of the University of California at San Diego, in collaboration with the composer Robert Erickson; it was originally developed for Erickson's composition Percussion Loops (1973) and was designed to bring a large number of instruments within easy reach of the performer. Originally constructed in 1973, it has been modified several times since and can be adapted for performances of other works. Since 1971 George has developed other percussion consoles and instruments, such as extended and two-manual vibraphones.

The 'loops console' consists of 36 conventional percussion instruments suspended from a frame or mounted on adjustable stands assembled from heavy metal tubing; within this 'keyboard' the instruments are arranged horizontally in seven families and vertically by pitch in five columns. There is a 'pedal-board' of three larger instruments – two gongs and a tam-tam – which are played by beaters attached to large levers operated by a hydraulic pedal system; a lever mechanism is also used to strike some of the smaller instruments, shake maracas and scrape a güiro. A pedal controls the speed at which the score, notated on a scroll, moves across a horizontal track in front of the performer. The specially designed notation uses colour-coded note-heads, differently shaped for each of the seven families of instruments; the staff has five spaces, one for each of the five pitch groups.

BIBLIOGRAPHY

R. George: 'Research into New Areas of Multiple-percussion Performance and Composition', Percussionist, xii/3 (1975), 110

HUGH DAVIES

Loosemore, John (b ?Bishops Nympton, Devon, 1613 or 1614; d Exeter, 18 April 1681). English organ builder and virginal maker. He was the son of Samuel Loosemore, also an organ builder, and may be related to the brothers George and Henry Loosemore, both organists and composers. The earliest references to John Loosemore are in connection with the organ at Hartland Church, Devon, where he carried out work between 1635 and 1638. A house organ built for Sir George Trevelyan survives in the minstrels' gallery at Nettlecombe Court, Somerset (c1665). His most important organ was built in about 1665 for Exeter Cathedral; the case remains. This instrument was heard by Francis North, 1st Lord Guilford, in 1675, during his circuits as Lord Chief Justice. His verdict suggests that in some respects it was more pleasing to the eye than to the ear. A chamber organ of six stops formerly in the Exeter Cathedral Choir School was destroyed about 1935. A virginal built by Loosemore and dated 1655 is in the Victoria and Albert Museum, London (see Grove 5, ix, frontispiece; for plan view see VIRGINAL, fig.8). Loosemore is buried in Exeter Cathedral, where his tomb can still be seen.

BIBLIOGRAPHY

C. Clutton and A. Niland: The British Organ (London, 1963, rev. 2/1982)

M. Wilson: The English Chamber Organ: History and Development, 1650–1850 (Oxford, 1968)

B. B. Edmonds: 'John Loosemore', JBIOS, v (1981), 23

JOHN MOREHEN, STEPHEN BICKNELL

Lõõtspill. Accordion of Estonia, introduced at the end of the 19th century. It became the most popular folk instrument in Estonia, often used in folk ensembles. Alongside manufactured instruments hand-made ones were popular, especially those made by August Teppo from south-east Estonia. The instrument survives in the folk tradition.

Lopu. Bamboo STAMPING TUBE of the Polynesian outlier, Tikopia. See N. McLeod: *The Social Context of Music in a Polynesian Community* (diss., London School of Economics, 1957), 115. *See also* KUI LOPU.

Lorée. French firm of oboe makers. François Lorée (*d* 1902), who had worked for Triébert as his *chef d'atelier* from 1867, set up his own firm in 1881 when the Triébert trademark was bought by the firm of Gautrot. Lorée secured Triébert's contracts with the Conservatoire and the national music schools and continued to develop the 'Système 6' oboe of Triébert. At the Paris Exposition of 1889 an oboe d'amore and a baryton by Lorée received silver medals. He also exhibited an oboe with the key-work adapted to Boehm fingering, a design taken up by other makers. What may be considered the perfected form of the Lorée oboe was produced in 1906 by François' son, Adolphe Lucien Lorée (1867–1942), who carried on the business after his father's death; this oboe is generally termed the 'Gillet model', after the oboist Georges Gillet, who influenced the Lorées' work. A. L. Lorée sold the firm to Raymond Dubois in 1925 but continued to work for him until 1942. On Dubois' death in 1957 the company was taken over by Robert de Gourdon.

CAROLYN BRYANT

Lorentz, Johann [Johan] (*b* c1580; *d* Elsinore, buried 18 June 1650). Danish organ builder of German origin. He learnt organ building under Nicolaus Maas in Stralsund (now in Rostock, East Germany) before settling down as a master builder in Flensburg in 1608. In 1616 or 1617 he was brought to Copenhagen by Christian IV and received the royal privilege as builder of organs in Denmark and Norway in 1639. He built and repaired many notable organs, for example those at Kristianstad (now in Sweden); St Mary's, Elsinore; St Nicholas' and St Peter's, Copenhagen; and those at Nakskov, Odense and Sorø. The instrument in Kristianstad is the best surviving example of his work.

BIBLIOGRAPHY
N. Schiørring: 'Lorentz, Johan (i)', *DBL*
B. Lundgren: 'Nikolaj-organisten Johan Lorentz i Kopenhamn', *STMf*, xl (1961), 249

JOHN BERGSAGEL

Lorenzini, Gasparo (*fl* Piacenza, 1743–1804). Italian violin maker. According to some of his labels, he was a pupil of G. B. Guadagnini; his violins bear strong similarities to those made by Guadagnini during his Parma period. It has not been determined whether Lorenzini also studied in Piacenza, the only city where he is known to have been established. While the outline of his violins shows Guadagnini's influence, his scrolls and soundholes bear little if any resemblance. The scrolls in particular are more deeply carved and have considerably smaller turns. His varnish is of very good texture and is generally a warm golden brown. As his surviving instruments are boldly made and good tonally, it is unfortunate that examples of his work are so scarce.

JAAK LIIVOJA-LORIUS

Losca. Wooden flute with slender conical bore of the Mbwanja people of Zaïre (*LaurentyA*, 157).

Losiba. *See* KWADI.

Losokio. LAMELLAPHONE of the Mongo Bwende people of western Zaïre (*LaurentyS*, 196).

Losukia. Board LAMELLAPHONE of the Jong and Mbuja peoples of Zaïre, with six to seven keys. A half-calabash is linked to the soundtable by means of a stick. This resonator is pressed against the chest of the player to modulate the timbre of the instrument (*LaurentyS*, 195).

Lot. French family of woodwind instrument makers. The name occurs with some frequency on French woodwind instruments of the 18th and 19th centuries, though the relationships of its different bearers are somewhat obscure; in several cases dates of birth and death have not been determined and working periods only approximately deduced from directories and other documents. Thomas Lot is recorded in Paris between c1740 and 1785. His cousin Gilles had by 1752 taken over the business of his deceased father-in-law Jean Nicholas Leclercq, and continued to run it until at least 1772. He is credited with having introduced in that year his *bassetube*, the earliest bass clarinet so far recorded. Martin Lot of St Germain (c1775–?1783) does not figure in the directories but was probably one of two Lots listed in the *Tablettes de renommée* in 1785. He appears to have been successor to Gilles, possibly his son.

Louis Lot (*d* Paris, 1890) was established in Paris by 1855; it is not known if he was directly descended from any of the above-mentioned. He was said to be the son-in-law of the flute maker Clair Godefroy *l'aîné*; his products won high awards in various mid-19th-century exhibitions. The Louis Lot mark, though passing into other ownership in 1875, has continued to the present day and now belongs to the combine of Strasser, Marigaux & Lemoine.

The name of Isidore Lot of La Couture appeared in exhibition catalogues between 1867 and 1886, but his family connections are again uncertain. His instruments were imported into England by Beare & Son of London. For an oboe by Thomas Lot *see* OBOE, fig.6a.

BIBLIOGRAPHY
C. Pierre: *Les facteurs d'instruments de musique* (Paris, 1893)
L. G. Langwill: *An Index of Musical Wind-instrument Makers* (Edinburgh, 1960, rev., enlarged 6/1980)

PHILIP BATE

Loterokuma. Arched harp of the Acholi people of Uganda. *See* ENNANGA.

Loti. NOTCHED FLUTE of the Mombutu people of Zaïre (*LaurentyA*, 280).

Lotong. Bamboo idiochord TUBE ZITHER of the Kayan and Kenyah peoples of Sarawak, Malaysia. The six bamboo strings are tuned by bridges placed along the cylinder.

Lotongo ngoma. Single-headed closed conical drum of the Genya people of Zaïre. *See also* UKE.

Lotosflöte (Ger.). SWANEE WHISTLE.

Lototsi [lototsi na litofe, lototsi na nsaw, lototsi na yomba, lototi]. Terms for VESSEL FLUTE used by the Mongo, Konda, Kota, Ngombe, Bwende and other peoples of Zaïre (*LaurentyA*, 223). *See* DIPULU.

Lott, John [Jack] **Frederick** (*b* London, early 1800s; *d* 1871). English violin maker. He was the finest 19th-century English maker, and as an imitator of Guarneri del Gesù and Stradivari was unequalled in his own country. His father, John Frederick Lott (1775–1853), went to London from Germany about 1795, and is said to have become in 1798 an employee of Thomas Dodd, for whom he made many fine cellos and basses. According to *Jack of All Trades*, a novel by Charles Reade which was based on his life, Lott was among other things an organizer of firework displays and an elephant handler before returning to the profession in which he had originally been apprenticed. It can be deduced that he began serious violin making before 1843, as Sandys and Forster (1864) noted that he worked for the firm of Davis, who sold out to Edward Withers in that year. By that time Bernard Simon Fendt had explored with considerable success the idea of making new instruments appear old and used, the most difficult aspect being the imitation of worn Italian varnish. In this Lott was probably Fendt's pupil.

Whereas Vuillaume and Fendt, among others, took pains to reproduce precisely the features that they saw on the early Cremonese instruments, Lott's appeal is that he tried more to capture their mood. His aim was to generate in the beholder the excitement which connoisseurs feel when they contemplate the real thing. He seems to have made few exact replicas of individual instruments, but perhaps saw himself as continuing where the masters that he admired, in particular Guarneri, had left off. Lott had nearly equal success tonally, the quality of sound of his instruments sometimes being deceptively Italian. Ida Haendel used one of his instruments early in her career, and one can regard his work with uninhibited admiration, unlike the Victorian writer who said of him that 'all the talent and skill a craftsman of this sort has will not atone for a life of fraud'.

BIBLIOGRAPHY
W. Sandys and S. A. Forster: *The History of the Violin* (London, 1864)
W. M. Morris: *British Violin Makers* (London, 1904, rev. 2/1920)
CHARLES BEARE

Lotus flute. *See* SWANEE WHISTLE.

Loud. Anglo-American family of piano makers. Thomas Loud (i) (*b* c1762; *d* New York, 2 Jan 1833) was active in London in the early 19th century. His exact relationship to the firm of Loud & Brothers of Philadelphia (renamed Loud & Co. in 1835) remains unclear.

In 1802 Thomas Loud (i) was granted a British patent for an upright piano just under two metres high, with diagonal stringing. He stated that, by using diagonal stringing, 'an instrument standing only five feet high and four feet wide in front will admit of the bass strings their full length which is five feet two inches'. This was not the first time that oblique stringing had been used,

as Friederici had strung his pyramid piano of 1745 obliquely, in order to accommodate the exceptionally long bass strings. Loud emigrated to New York about 1816, and was building overstrung 'piccolo' upright pianos by 1830.

In 1812 the Philadelphia *Aurora* announced the dissolution of a partnership between Thomas Loud Evenden sr (Thomas Loud (ii)) and the cabinet maker Joshua Baker. A square piano of about 1810 (now owned by Jörg Demus), marked 'New Patent. Thomas Loud from Clementi & Compy', may be the work of Thomas Loud (i) or (ii), if indeed they are distinct. Thomas Loud (i) was survived by a widow, Harriet; from 1814 a Harriet Evenden is listed in Philadelphia directories with a Thomas Loud Evenden jr. A piano of about 1815 marked 'Tho. L. Evenden & Son, from London' (in the Metropolitan Museum of Art, New York) is the only known instrument bearing the Evenden name, which was dropped in 1817 when Thomas Loud (ii) went into business with his brother John. Their piano of about 1818–22 marked 'Thomas & John Loud' is in the Smithsonian Institution, Washington, DC. Around 1825 Philologus Loud joined the partnership, now known as Loud & Brothers; Joseph Edward Loud entered in 1828, when the firm expanded to new quarters on Chesnut Street. By this time the family firm was among the most prolific in the USA, producing about 600 pianos annually at retail prices of $180 to $1200 and exporting instruments to the West Indies and South America. In 1832 the firm exhibited two distinctive square pianos at the Franklin Institute, Philadelphia, one of them triple strung for greater brilliance, the other better suited to vocal accompaniment – evidence that musical function was considered in tonal design. In 1830 the Louds advertised a metal frame, which they did not patent until 1835. Their other six patents between 1827 and 1865 include a transposing action (1842) and swell device (1865); their upright piano dated as early as 1831 (in the Metropolitan Museum) is equipped with pedal-operated swell shutters and a curiously shifted action. Other family members in the piano business included Thomas C., William H. and Joseph R. Loud. Joseph R.'s career paralleled the firm's decline: in 1855 he was listed as a piano maker, in 1860 as a tuner, and in 1862 as a plumber.

BIBLIOGRAPHY
D. Spillane: *History of the American Pianoforte* (New York, 1890/*R*1969)
R. E. M. Harding: *The Piano-forte: its History Traced to the Great Exhibition of 1851* (Cambridge, 1933, rev. 2/1978)
K. G. Grafing: *Alpheus Babcock: American Pianoforte Maker* (diss., U. of Missouri, 1972)
W. E. Mann: *Piano Making in Philadelphia before 1825* (diss., U. of Iowa, 1977)
L. Libin: *American Musical Instruments in The Metropolitan Museum of Art* (New York, 1981) [unpubd catalogue]
MARGARET CRANMER, LAURENCE LIBIN

Loud pedal. Colloquial term for the SUSTAINING PEDAL.

Loulié, Etienne (*b* ?Paris, c1655; *d* Paris, c1707). French musician, theorist and inventor. His musical inventions include the *chronomètre* (a metronomic pendulum device used to fix tempo), discussed in his *Eléments ou principes de musique* (Paris, 1696/*R*1977, 2/1698; Eng. trans. with suppl., 1965/*R*1971), and the *sonomètre* (an instrument intended to facilitate the tuning of keyboards), described in *Nouveau système de musique ou nouvelle division du monocorde . . . avec* *la description et l'usage du sonomètre* (Paris, 1698). Both instruments were approved by the Académie des Sciences (in 1701 and 1699 respectively). *See also* MET-RONOME, esp. fig.1.

Lounuat. *See* LAUNUT.

Loure [lourette, louvre, louvrette] (Fr.). A term for a type of bagpipe known in Normandy during the 16th and 17th centuries. It is not known whether the word is related to the dance and instrumental *air* of the same name that was popular in France during the late 17th and early 18th centuries (as the small bagpipe known as MUSETTE is to the dance of that name).

Louré (Fr.). A type of bowstroke; *see* BOW, §II, 2 (v).

Lourenço de Souza. *See* CONCEIÇÃO, MANOEL LOUR-ENÇO DA.

Lourer (Fr.). A term for a species of NOTES INÉGALES. Etienne Loulié (*Eléments*, 1696) wrote: 'In any time signature, but especially in triple metre, the quavers are performed in two different ways although they are written the same . . . sometimes they are performed equally' – called 'detaching' (*detacher*), for foreign music and music containing leaps – '[and] sometimes one makes the first quavers a little longer; this is called "lourer", and is used in melodies of conjunct motion'. Loulié did not say explicitly whether the lengthening applies to the first quavers of each beat or the first of each bar, but he presumably meant the former.

   Lourer should not be confused with the loure, a French dance and instrumental *air* popular in the late 17th and early 18th centuries, or with the term 'Louré', a type of bowstroke.

DAVID D. BOYDEN

Löwengebrull (Ger.). STRING DRUM.

Lowrey organ. An ELECTRONIC ORGAN, a large number of models of which have been manufactured by the Lowrey Organ Co. in Lincolnwood, near Chicago (later in nearby Deerfield), from around 1949. In 1918 the F. C. Lowrey Co. (founded by Frederick C. Lowrey) purchased the CHORALCELO, and from the 1920s the company experimented with many types of sound-generating systems in pursuit of a fully electronic organ. The first electronic instrument marketed by Lowrey was the ORGANO (1949), a small electronic organ controlled from the keyboard of a piano. Since the early 1950s a wide range of organs has been produced, including church, theatre and home organs. In 1977 Lowrey became a division of Norlin Industries.

   In the first instruments the sounds were generated by 12 oscillators, using frequency division; during the early 1970s this system was replaced by a single very-high-frequency master oscillator which uses two stages of frequency division to produce successively the 12 semi-tones of the highest octave and of all the lower octaves. The instruments usually have two manuals and a pedal-board. The current range consists primarily of home organs, especially 'spinet' organs in which two manuals (usually each with 44 notes) are staggered by one octave; in the late 1950s and 1960s the interval was normally

a minor 6th, which is the only interval at which the two halves of a standard 88-note keyboard, sawn in half to produce two 44-note manuals (A–E, F–C), can be staggered. Since 1956 Lowrey organs have incorporated an upward semitone glide. Many of the earlier models included an additional LESLIE tremulant loudspeaker; in the 1970s Lowrey replaced this with an electronic equivalent. Advances in electronic technology since the late 1960s have made possible several new devices that are now included in many home organs; rhythm and 'walking bass' units, arpeggiators, a choice of chord systems, memories for pre-set registrations, and (since 1980) a selection of different accompaniments, for which microprocessors are used. An uncommon recent feature is the provision of synthetic vocal sounds. Around 1970 some models had a built-in cassette tape recorder.

BIBLIOGRAPHY
H. E. Anderson: *Electronic Organ Handbook* (Indianapolis, 1960), 189
R. H. Dorf: *Electronic Musical Instruments* (New York, 3/1968), 225
N. H. Crowhurst: *Electronic Organs*, iii (Indianapolis, 1975), 81
HUGH DAVIES

Lozhky (Russ.: 'spoons'). A Russian instrument of the janissary-music class which produced an effect similar to the Turkish crescent. According to Mahillon (2/1909), it was adopted by the Russians from the Turks when janissary music became the rage in the early 18th century. The Turks called it *kaşıklar* ('spoons'), and when the Russians borrowed the device they merely translated its name. It consisted of a round hollow case of brass to which were fixed, at an angle of 60°, two brass tubes adorned with jingles (see illustration). These tubes were joined at the extremity of the angle by a solid brass arm, by which the instrument was held. The overall shape was that of a lyre. It was used in pairs and played by clashing the two round hollow cases together. The *lozhky* were much favoured by the Russian cavalry and often used to accompany the soldiers' songs. They

One of a pair of lozhky (Conservatoire Royal de Musique, Brussels)

became a special feature particularly in the bands of the Uhlans, which usually comprised a clarinet, oboe, tambourine, Turkish crescent, a pair of cymbals and the *lozhky*. Specimens are in the Instrument Museum of the Brussels Conservatory (nos.883–4).

BIBLIOGRAPHY
V.-C. Mahillon: *Catalogue descriptif et analytique du Musée instrumental du Conservatoire royal de musique de Bruxelles*, ii (Ghent, 2/1909), 182f
C. Sachs: *Real-Lexikon der Musikinstrumente* (Berlin, 1913/R1962)
H. G. FARMER/R

Ƚppumin [chelshpumin] (Flathead; *chelsh*: 'hand'; *Ƚppumin*: 'drum'). Single-headed FRAME DRUM of the Flathead Indians of Montana. Traditionally the frame was made from thin strips of wood, preferably fir, soaked and bent into a circle, or from part of a hollowed-out tree stump, but it may now be made from a circular cheese crate or a metal wheel rim. The frame may be from 33 to 50 cm in diameter and 5 to 13 cm in depth. The head is of untanned deer-hide that has been soaked and allowed to dry in place over the frame. It may be fastened to the frame with drawing-pins and a buckskin thong around the perimeter, or by buckskin thongs extending from the four corners of the hide and crossed on the reverse side of the drum to form a hand-hold. The head is now rarely decorated, but formerly could be painted according to directions given by a guardian spirit or in keeping with standard decorations for dances that the drum would accompany.

The drum is held in the left hand by cross-ties on the underside, with the face tilted towards the right, and it is struck with a cloth-padded wooden beater, about 40 cm long. It is tuned by exposing the head to heat, causing the hide to tighten; a resonant, fairly high-pitched tone is considered ideal. The drum is used mostly for the scalp dance and to accompany personal songs.

BIBLIOGRAPHY
A. P. Merriam: *Ethnomusicology of the Flathead Indians* (New York, 1967)
MARY RIEMER-WELLER

Lribab. A flat-bellied, single-string fiddle of the Berbers of North Africa (*see* RABĀB); it is used, with drums, for the accompaniment of song.

Luba. Side-blown animal-horn trumpet of the Ngbandi people of northern Zaïre. It has a globular gourd bell and one stop in the tip (*LaurentyA*, 330).

Lubembo. Double clapperless bell of the Luba people of Zaïre. Playing the *lubembo* was the prerogative of a designated notable when the chief wished to assemble his counsellors and notables or when he desired to communicate a message to the village people. The instrument is used for signalling, the two bells having different tones at an interval of a minor 3rd. Usually, the *lubembo* belongs to chiefs as a sign of power, wealth and status. *See also* GONGA (i).

BIBLIOGRAPHY
J. Gansemans: *La musique et son rôle dans la vie sociale et rituelle Luba* (Tervuren, 1978)
——: *Les instruments de musique Luba* (Tervuren, 1980)
J. GANSEMANS

Lubongo. Side-blown animal-horn trumpet of the Pende people of south-western Zaïre. It has one stop in the tip (*LaurentyA*, 325).

Lục huyền cầm [đàn ghi-ta]. Vietnamese version of the Spanish guitar. The number of strings varies from four to six, and the instrument is strung less tightly than its model. There are two brass frets with space between hollowed deeply enough to enable the player to pull the strings while performing and to use the playing techniques of the ĐÀN NGUYỆT (moon-shaped lute). One of the tunings found is $c'-f'-c''-g''-c'''$. The instrument was introduced into southern Vietnam in the *hát cải lương* (renovated theatre genre) during the 1930s and remains very popular.

TRẦN QUANG HẢI

Ludag. Long conical drum of the Isneg people of the northern Philippines. *See* GANGSA (i).

Frame drums of the Ƚppumin type played by Crow Indians at a tobacco-planting ceremony in Montana, 1915–25

Lục huyền cầm: Vietnamese version of the Spanish guitar

Ludaya. Transverse flute played by Gishu herdboys in Uganda. It is made from the stalk of a lobelia with a rectangular mouthpiece cut near the end. The smaller end of the pipe may be used as a stop.

Luddu. Large clarinet of Karelia; *see* LIRU.

Ludembo. Double clapperless bell of the Songye and Tetela peoples of Zaïre. *See* GONGA (i).

Lúdjasaúga (Creek: 'turtle rattle'). Vessel rattle of the Creek Indians of the south-eastern USA; it is also used by the Yuchi, Cherokee and Seminole tribes. The rattle is made from six to ten dried terrapin shells. Holes are bored in the shells, which are filled with pebbles and attached to a piece of rawhide. Dancers wear one set on the outside of each leg, tied just below the knee. The rattle is worn only by women, in the corn and stomp dances of the Cherokee and Seminole, and in the ribbon dance which is part of the Green Corn ceremonial of the Muskogee Creek.

MARY RIEMER-WELLER

Ludwig. American firm of percussion instrument makers. William F. Ludwig (i) (*b* Nenderoth, 15 July 1879; *d* Chicago, 14 June 1973) left Germany for Chicago as a boy, and in 1909 founded Ludwig & Ludwig with his brother Theobald (1888–1917). Their first product was a foot-pedal for trap drums. Having played hand-tuned kettledrums in the Pittsburgh SO, Ludwig decided to build his own pedal timpani. With his brother-in-law, the engineer Robert C. Danly, he designed a model, patented in 1913, with a hydraulic pump and an expandable rubber tube which pressed a hoop against the membrane from inside the kettle. An improved model with tuning cables operated by a foot-pedal with self-locking device was patented in 1920. The 'Natural Way Balanced Action' timpani (patented 1923) made use of a compression spring for tension balance to hold the pedal in place. The firm expanded and made quantities of trap-drum sets and sound-effect instruments for the flourishing silent movie theatres. However, the arrival of talking pictures and the Depression resulted in declining sales, and in 1930 the company merged with C. G. Conn. Its production was combined with that of the Leedy drum division (*see* LEEDY MANUFACTURING CO.) and moved to Elkhart, Indiana, with Ludwig as manager. During this period he introduced the first lightweight, chromatic bell-lyra for marching bands (for illustration *see* BELL-LYRA). In 1936 Ludwig resigned to set up the W. F. L. Drum Co. in Chicago, and over the next 20 years produced several new models of timpani and a variety of percussion instruments. (For illustration of Ludwig machine

timpani, *see* TIMPANI, figs.2 and 3.) In 1955 he purchased the Ludwig portion of Conn's percussion business, which became the Ludwig Drum Co. The Musser Marimba Co. (a manufacturer of vibraphones, marimbas, xylophones, bells and chimes) and its two subsidiaries was acquired in 1966; a parent company, Ludwig Industries, was subsequently organized over all the divisions. William F. Ludwig (ii) became president in 1972 and in 1982 the firm was acquired by Selmer, a North American Philips subsidiary.

EDMUND A. BOWLES

Luff, William (*b* London, 7 Sept 1904). English violin maker. At the age of 16 he joined the staff of Dykes & Sons of New Bond Street, London, where he was trained by Max Millant. In 1932 he began working independently and started to make some new violins, patterned after Guarneri 'del Gesù'. During World War II he worked on radar for the RAF. In 1945 he joined the staff of J. & A. Beare, where he was mainly occupied with repairing, and in 1955 opened his own workshop in Shepherd's Bush, London. His output of new instruments increased, but much of his time was still taken up by repairs. Although officially retired in 1970, he has continued to make new violins. He was made an MBE in 1979 and has gained a reputation as one of the finest 20th-century English makers.

Luff's output numbers around 300 instruments, all copies of specific instruments and mostly violins patterned after Guarneri 'del Gesù'. He has made about 45 violas (several of which are copies of two G. B. Guadagnini instruments, one previously owned by Watson Forbes) and one cello (a Montagnana copy). After his retirement he made several copies of the 'Alard' Stradivari (formerly in private ownership in Scotland and sold privately in 1981 for over a million dollars).

BIBLIOGRAPHY

M. A. Alburger: *The Violin Makers: Portrait of a Living Craft* (London, 1978)

JAAK LIIVOJA-LORIUS

Luftpause (Ger.: 'air-break'). A momentary interruption of the metre by silence, often indicated by a comma or 'V' above the staff. Though strictly an opportunity for a singer or wind player to take a breath, this device was used by Mahler and others at moments of such musical tension as to make the actual intake of breath almost impracticable. Within the Viennese tradition the word *Cäsur* or *Zäsur* ('caesura') seems to have been preferred: Mahler used it in his scores, and it remains the standard word for the interruptions that have come to be considered traditional in the Viennese waltz repertory. In the same tradition, *Atempause* ('breath-break') has occasionally been used to designate a slight hesitation before the third beat of the bar in a waltz, but there is some disagreement as to whether a waltz should be performed in this way; the word is more often used to describe a breathing-pause indicated by a superscript comma. In some cases *Luftpause* designates such a break taken by the whole ensemble, whereas *Atempause* applies within a solo line.

DAVID FALLOWS

Lugaya. Single-headed closed conical drum of the Nyamwezi people of Tabora district, Tanzania. Three of these large drums are slung from a crossbar and played with sticks by three performers. Like the NDANDALE, they have ritual functions connected with the chief. See *TraceyCSA*, ii, 336.

Lugube. Unbraced MOUTH BOW of the Venda people of southern Africa. The stave comprises a piece of river reed 50 to 60 cm long; the string is of plant fibre or sinew and is sounded with a plectrum. Players are girls or young married women. Playing technique resembles that for the cognate Zulu instrument, the UMQANGALA. See *KirbyMISA*, 220ff and pls.62, 63*b*.

Lugungu. LAMELLAPHONE of the Angba people of northern Zaïre. It has metal keys and a boat-shaped wooden resonator (*LaurentyS*, 192, 196).

Luhengere [luhingele]. Percussion vessel of the Kusu and Tachoni peoples of Kenya. It consists of a long bowl or platter, inverted and beaten with two pairs of double sticks. It is used to accompany music on the *litungu* lyre. See *TraceyCSA*, ii, 365f.

Luikku. Bark trumpet of Finland. A shepherd's instrument, it has a hollowed wooden interior and is covered with strips of birch or other tree bark. It is long and narrow, and resembles the Scandinavian lur (*see* LUR, (2)).

Luinsse. HOURGLASS DRUM of the Mossi people of Tenkodogo, Upper Volta. The court orchestra has two *luinsse*, four cylindrical and six large calabash drums. *See also* LUNGA (i).

Lujiba. Carved wooden VESSEL FLUTE of the Luluwa people of south-western Zaïre (*LaurentyA*, 99, 109ff).

Lukangu [bukalanga]. LAMELLAPHONE of the Chokwe and Lunda peoples of Zaïre (*LaurentyS*, 196). See KAKOLONDONDO.

Lukeme. LAMELLAPHONE of the Acholi people of Uganda. The term is cognate with the Amba *likembe*, and derived from the Alur *lukembe*. The instrument appears to have reached Uganda through the Alur, its source being indicated by use of the name *kongo* (i.e. from the former Belgian Congo) in many places throughout the north. Among the Ganda of the south the instrument is known as *akadongo k'abaluru*, 'the little instrument of the Alur'. All instruments have iron lamellae which pass over a U-shaped bridge; some are provided with metal rings which jingle when the keys are plucked. The wooden soundbox to which they are attached is often

trapezoidal, often with a hole in the base or end, which can be stopped with the player's finger. Keys are usually arranged with the longest in the centre and the shorter at the sides. Most types are small, but three different sizes are found in Acholi, the largest being up to 40 cm long. They are used either solo or in sets to accompany singing. See *WachsmannTCU*.

K. A. GOURLAY

Lukombe (i). PLURIARC of the Titu, Yaelima, Ipanga, Nkutu, Ntomba, Sakata, Shongo and adjoining peoples of Zaïre and the Republic of the Congo. The term is either cognate with or a variant of others which resemble it closely: *lokombe* (Ngando), *lukomb'* (Lele), *lokombi* (Oli, Mongo, Lia, Yela), *longombe* (Nkundo, Ngata, Mongo, Yaelima, Ibeke, Mbole, Eso, Lia, Bokatola, Ngongo), *longombi* (Mongo) and *lokombele* (Nkundo). All the instruments have a wooden soundbox, generally rectangular in shape, approximately 30 to 50 cm long by 15 to 20 cm wide; in some the base retains the semi-circular form of the tree from which it is carved. There are usually five strings, though Sakata, Mongo, Nkundo and Ngando pluriarcs may have six and some Mongo seven. Each string is attached to a separate bow which rises from the base of the soundbox; in some cases bows may be fixed in the end. The string passes through a hole in the soundtable, either with or without a small 'bridge', and is secured beneath it. Tuning is effected by winding the string round the bow to increase tension or vice versa.

Although limited to western and central Zaïre in distribution, different terminologies are used either in different places or for different versions of the same instrument within one area. Thus the Nkundo *limele* (Oli *imele*) is a smaller version of the *longombe*; the term may be cognate with the *bolima* of the Ngando and Yasayama. Another linguistic grouping is that of the Soyo *ngomi*, Hum *ngwim*, Teke *ngwomi* and Yans *ngwen*, while *sambi* (or *saambi*) is used by the Sango, Nkutu, Tsam, Songo, Saamba and Mbala, *esandju* by the Ngando and *ntsambi* by the Sundi. In performance larger instruments such as the *longombe* are placed across the thighs and plucked with the thumb around which has been woven a liana stem as plectrum; the index finger is at times also used. In contrast the smaller *limele* is placed on the knees and plucked with bare thumb and index finger; unlike the *longombe*, which is always used to accompany singing, often providing only a rhythmic accompaniment, the *limele* may be played as a solo instrument. Occasions for performance vary according to area. Laurenty gives the following summary: in the Equatorial and coastal regions to accompany singing; among the Saka, Oli, Ikongo and Bongongo peoples in connection with hunting, and among the Yela with hunting rituals; among the Nkundo, Lia and Dikidiki to accompany dancing; among the Hum and Hungana in the coastal area as a ritual instrument; and among the Bakanda Moma in connection with warfare. He also states that Oli pluriarcs are an appendage of the chief and played at his installation and death.

BIBLIOGRAPHY

LaurentyC, 117

F. J. de Hen: *Beitrag zur Kenntnis der Musikinstrumente aus Belgisch Kongo und Ruanda-Urundi* (Tervuren, 1960)

G. Knosp: *Enquête sur la vie musicale au Congo belge 1934–1935* (Tervuren, 1968)

K. A. GOURLAY

Lukombe (ii). Single-headed cylindrical drum of the Songola and Binja people of central Zaïre (*BooneT*, 4). *See also* LILENGA.

Lukombe [lukombi] (iii). Trapezoidal SLIT-DRUM of the Kusu, Nkutu and Tetela peoples of Zaïre (*LaurentyTF*, 137). *See* NKUMVI.

Lūk pī khāēn. Free-reed aerophone of Laos and north-eastern Thailand.

Lukulu. Large cylindrical SLIT-DRUM of the Nkundo people of Zaïre (*LaurentyTF*, 133).

Lukumbi (i). SLIT-DRUM of Zaïre. (1) Trapezoidal slit-drum of the Ombo, Bangubangu, Songola, Lega and Kusu peoples (*LaurentyTF*, 137f). *See* NKUMVI.
(2) Tulip-shaped slit-drum of the Lega people (*LaurentyTF*, 139).

Lukumbi [alindi] (ii). Drum of the Kumu people of Zaïre (*BooneT*, 64).

Lukungu. A very old type of MOUTH BOW of the Luba people of Zaïre. The wooden bow is held horizontally between the lips of the musician while he plucks the string with the right thumb, using the fingers of the right hand to touch the string lightly to obtain harmonics. According to Knosp (1968) this was a woman's instrument, usually played in private for the entertainment of her husband. De Hen (1960) attributed the term *lukungu* to the braced MUSICAL BOW of the Mwanza and Pende peoples of western Zaïre. Laurenty attributed the term to the Lwala people of Luisa region, also of western Zaïre. *See also* KAKULUMBUMBA.

BIBLIOGRAPHY
LaurentyC, 113
F. J. de Hen: *Beitrag zur Kenntnis der Musikinstrumente aus Belgisch Kongo und Ruanda-Urundi* (Tervuren, 1960)
G. Knosp: *Enquête sur la vie musicale au Congo belge 1934–1935* (Tervuren, 1968)
J. Gansemans: *Les instruments de musique Luba* (Tervuren, 1980)
J. GANSEMANS, K. A. GOURLAY

Lulanga. TROUGH ZITHER of the Hutu and Fuliru peoples of Rwanda and eastern Zaïre (*LaurentyC*, 116). *See* INANGA.

Lulat. Copper percussion plaque of Siberut, Mentawei Islands, Indonesia. It resembles the SALAWEK DULANG of West Sumatra.

Lulimba. A LAMELLAPHONE of the marimba type, played in northern Mozambique.

Luma. STOPPED FLUTE ENSEMBLE of eastern-central Africa. (1) Ensemble of the Mbuti pygmy people of Ituri Forest, Zaïre. The set consists of ten end-blown flutes; they are made by the neighbouring Nande people, who keep them for the use of the Mbuti. The flutes are accompanied by rattles and two laced drums.
(2) Ensemble of the Nyoro (Toro) people of Toro district, Uganda. There are seven flutes named (from high to low pitch) *kyenuma*, *kyegira*, *sikuse*, *pee*, *kwigirize*, *kyigira kike*, and *chahomya*. They are played, together with a conical drum, for recreational dances. See *TraceyCSA*, ii, 281, 360.

Lumzdelis. *See* LAMZDELIS.

Lund, Carsten (*b* Copenhagen, 12 May 1940). Danish organ builder. He was an apprentice of Troels Krohn in Hillerød from 1957 to 1961, and worked for Poul-Gerhard Andersen in Copenhagen from 1962 to 1966; he founded his own workshop in Copenhagen in 1966. He is the organ builder who has followed and developed the ideas of the Danish Organ Reform Movement with the greatest consistency; he does not make reproduction instruments, although his own designs are rooted in classical European organ-building traditions. He has pioneered the use in Denmark of flexible winding, suspended action, soldered caps, hammered pipe metal and classical keyboard design, and has developed his key action to a high degree of perfection. Examples of his work are in Hedeager Church, Herning (1975); Husum Church, Copenhagen (1977); Tagensbo Church, Copenhagen (1979); and St Stefan, Copenhagen (1983).

BIBLIOGRAPHY
O. Olesen: 'The New Organ Revival in Denmark', *JBIOS*, iii (1979), 46
F. Brouwer: *Orgelbewegung und Orgelgegenbewegung* (Utrecht, 1981)
OLE OLESEN

Lundberg, Robert (*b* Berkeley, Calif., 25 June 1948). American lute maker. Having developed craft skills through working as a model maker and racing car designer, he began to make musical instruments as a hobby. In 1971 he began an apprenticeship with Paul Schuback, a violin maker trained in Mirecourt, and in 1973 became journeyman in the workshop of the Swiss lute maker Jacob van de Geest at Vevey. During these years Lundberg photographed, measured and studied the lutes and viols in major European collections. By the mid-1970s he had established his own workshop in Portland, Oregon, and gained a reputation as an important maker of lutes and related instruments on historical models. Lundberg is also active as a restorer of historical instruments for museums and collectors. He lectures frequently on lute construction, in particular at Erlangen where he has taught regularly since 1978.
HOWARD SCHOTT

Lundja. Bell of Zaïre. *See* GONGA (i).

Lunengele. Percussion vessel of the Wanga people of northern Nyanza district, Kenya. It is a struck inverted bowl, used to accompany singing, together with clapping.

Lunetta, Stanley (*b* Sacramento, Calif., 5 June 1937). American composer, percussionist and sound sculptor. He studied at Sacramento State College and the University of California at Davis, where he was taught composition by Larry Austin, Jerome Rosen and Richard Swift. He was one of the founders of the New Music Ensemble in 1963. Around 1967 he began to construct electronic devices for his compositions. In 1970 he built Moosack Machine, the first of a series of self-playing sound sculptures, all based on electronic sound-sources with digital sequencers and memories, which have increasingly occupied his creative energies. Their appearance emphasizes the everyday and scrap materials used, and they are often festooned with electronic circuitry and wiring. In De Daddle Dee a circuit replaces the bell of a telephone, and the 'sound hat' contains a similar circuit which is activated when the wearer removes a top hat. Most of the other machines are affected by the random environmental elements of light, temperature, wind and the proximity of people. Cosmic Cube is a self-playing synthesizer that can also be operated by a performer.

BIBLIOGRAPHY
S. Lunetta: 'Moosack Machine', Source, no.8 (1970), 46 [incl. disc]
——: 'Moosack Machines: Sound Hat, De Daddle Dee', Source, no.11 (1972), 40

HUGH DAVIES

Lunga [longa, longga] **(i).** Underarm HOURGLASS DRUM of the Ivory Coast. It is a variable tension drum identical to the TAMA. The Baule people play it with a hooked stick and use it with other drums and percussion instruments at masked dances or for entertainment. Etymologically the Baule term 'lunga' appears to derive from *kalangu*, a similar drum in northern Nigeria, and the term was believed to be used by other peoples, for example the Dagomba of northern Ghana, the Jola of the Gambia and the Mossi of Upper Volta. But it is now known that the Mossi at Tenkodogo refer to their hourglass drums as *luinsse* and the Dagomba to theirs as *lunsi*. The Agni people prefer the term 'longga'.

BIBLIOGRAPHY
H. E. Hause: 'Terms for Musical Instruments in the Sudanic Languages: a Lexicographical Inquiry', Journal of the American Oriental Society, lxxiii (1948), suppl.7
J. H. K. Nketia: 'History and the Organisation of Music in West Africa', Essays on Music and History in Africa, ed. K. P. Wachsmann (Evanston, Ill., 1971), 3
——: 'Ghana', Grove 6
C. Duvelle: 'Haute-Volta', SOR 10 [disc notes]

K. A. GOURLAY

Lunga (ii). Double clapperless bell of the Pende people of Zaïre. *See* GONGA (i).

Lunga (It.: 'long') **(iii).** A word often placed above a note or, particularly, a fermata to indicate a longer wait than might be expected. The words 'lunga pausa' or 'pausa lunga' also appear to indicate that a pause is to be made at the performer's discretion, not according to rests showing the precise length.

DAVID FALLOWS

Lungandu. LAMELLAPHONE of the Dilolo region of Zaïre (*LaurentyS*, 195). *See* KAKOLONDONDO.

Lungóua [garabato]. Afro-Cuban percussion stick, played by the Congo people and their descendants in Cuba. The sticks are struck on the ground, in pairs; they have a fork, or 'hook', at the end. See *OrtizIMA*, i, 196f, 199.

Lungungu (i). Braced MUSICAL BOW of the Sonde people of Zaïre. It has a gourd resonator (*LaurentyC*, 113). *See* KAKULUMBUMBA.

Lungungu (ii). Small zoomorphic SLIT-DRUM of the Angba people of northern Zaïre (*LaurentyTF*, 139). *See* GUGU, (1).

Lunsi. HOURGLASS DRUM of the Dagomba people of northern Ghana. An ensemble of *lunsi* provides drumming for dancing and household and community ceremonies. *See also* LUNGA (i).

Lunzeze. STICK ZITHER of Zaïre. *See* ZEZE (i).

Luo [lo]. Generic name for gongs among the Han Chinese. The name is usually preceded by a prefix to specify each different kind of gong. Chinese gongs are made of an alloy of copper, zinc and tin, hammered into a dish-shaped structure with shoulders turned back at about 90 degrees. The central resonating area is either flat or convex (*see* GONGLUO). They range in size from about 10 cm to over 60 cm in diameter. Larger gongs are generally struck with padded beaters, and smaller gongs with either padded beaters or unpadded slips of wood. Unlike the cymbals (*see* BO (i)), gongs are tuned instruments.

Gongs known as *zhenggu* and *tonggu* were in use in China by the period of the Tang dynasty (AD 618–907). Although named *gu* ('drum'), they were in fact gong types, and both have been preserved in similar forms to the present day. In function gongs are used primarily in theatre ensembles to underline dramatic moments, in outdoor religious processions and, occasionally, in instrumental ensemble music.

Among the varieties commonly found are the *zhengluo, douluo, wenluo, daluo* and *xiaoluo*.

(i) *Zhengluo* [chengluo]. This gong is commonly known as *zheng* (pronounced 'jeng': used here for its phonetic value). The Minnan sub-culture of south-east China and Taiwan have a variant called *jiaoluo* ('call gong'). The *zhenggu* mentioned in the Tang dynasty, and preserved in the *shōko* of the Japanese *gagaku*, appears to be the historical predecessor of the *zhengluo*. In construction gongs of this type tend to be basin-shaped (with a narrow rim extending out from the shoulder), are relatively small (about 10 cm in diameter, or larger) and have a flat striking-surface. They are either suspended in individual frames, tied with cords through holes in the rims, or hand-held, and are struck with small unpadded beaters. As instruments of definite pitch and soft tonal qualities *zhengluo* are very often used in indoor ensemble music. The *yunluo* is a set of similar instruments.

(ii) *Douluo*. This is a Chaozhou name (*dou*: 'container') for a large gong with a flat striking-surface and wide shoulders, suspended in a standing frame and struck with an unpadded beater. The Cantonese *gaobian luo* ('high-rim gong') is similarly constructed. The *douluo* is used both in the local theatre ensemble to accompany fighting scenes and in *luogu* ('gong-drum') music. Related to the *douluo* is an instrument known in 18th-century sources as *jin* ('metal'), a military gong suspended by cords from a handle and struck with a padded beater akin to the Korean *ching*.

(iii) *Wenluo*. This is a Cantonese name (*wen*: 'civilian', suggesting a non-military function) for a large gong with a slightly convex striking-surface and narrow shoulders, suspended in a standing frame. It is used among the percussion instruments in Cantonese opera.

(iv) *Daluo* [suluo]. The *daluo* (*da*: 'large') is about 30 cm in diameter, with narrow shoulders and a convex surface with a flattened central striking-area. The instrument is hand-held by a cord which is attached through holes in its shoulders, and is struck in the centre with a padded beater. Its characteristic acoustical feature is a sudden descent in pitch after being struck. The *daluo* is most commonly used in theatre ensembles, especially in the percussion section accompanying the Peking opera.

(v) *Xiaoluo* [jingluo]. Although similar in construction to the *daluo*, the *xiaoluo* (*xiao*: 'small') measures only about 22 cm in diameter; it is held by the fingertips (under the shoulder of the instrument) and struck in the centre with an unpadded slip of wood. Its characteristic acoustical feature is a sudden ascent in pitch after being struck. It is most often used today with the *daluo* and *bo* (cymbals) in theatre ensembles, especially in the accompaniment of Peking opera.

BIBLIOGRAPHY
A. C. Moule: 'A List of the Musical and Other Sound-producing Instruments of the Chinese', *Journal of the North-China Branch of the Royal Asiatic Society*, xxxix (Shanghai, 1908), 25
ALAN R. THRASHER

Luojiao. CONCH-SHELL TRUMPET of the Han Chinese and many Chinese sub-cultures. *See* FALUO.

Lupa. Side-blown animal-horn trumpet of the Sere people of northern Zaïre. It has a globular gourd bell and one stop in the tip (*LaurentyA*, 330).

Lupakala. Side-blown ivory trumpet of the Bali people of north-eastern Zaïre. It has a carved mouthpiece. The term may also refer to a side-blown conical wooden trumpet of the Bali people (*LaurentyA*, 335, 352).

Lupe, de. Spanish family of organ builders of French (probably Gascon) origin.

(1) **Guillaume de Lupe** (*b* c1540; *d* Daroca, 7 July 1607). He was active in Tarazona, and built new organs at Paracuellos de Jiloca (1564), El Castellar, S Miguel, Daroca (1565–7), S María de Palacio, Logroño (1577), and S María, Tafalla (1581). He also constructed organs at Saragossa: at S Cruz (1567) and the Franciscan convent (1598). He repaired the instruments at the collegiate church, Daroca (1569 and from 1597), S Pedro de los Francos, Calatayud (1600), and three at Saragossa: the Metropolitan Cathedral (1577 and 1591), S Pablo (1584), and the basilica of Nuestra Señora del Pilar (1595 and 1602; also enlarged).

(2) **Marco de Lupe** (*b* Tarazona, baptized 5 Feb 1566; *d* Saragossa, 20 Dec 1617). Son and pupil of (1) Guillaume de Lupe. He worked with his father and his brother (3) Gaudioso de Lupe.

(3) **Gaudioso de Lupe** (*b* Tarazona, 8 Nov 1575; *d* Saragossa, after 1622). Son and pupil of (1) Guillaume de Lupe. He worked with his father, notably at the collegiate church, Daroca, from 1597. At Saragossa he built organs at the basilica of Nuestra Señora del Pilar (1610), S Felipe (1613) and the convent of Santa Fe (1614); he enlarged an organ for the Dominicans at Saragossa (1612) and worked on those at the Metropolitan Cathedral (1610 and 1622) and at Huesca Cathedral (1613), where he was official organ builder.

BIBLIOGRAPHY
P. Calahorra Martínez: *La música en Zaragoza en los siglos XVI y XVII*, i (Saragossa, 1977)
GUY BOURLIGUEUX

Lupondo [gomo]. GOBLET DRUM of the Luba, Songye and Tetela peoples of Zaïre (*BooneT*, 11, 41). *See* DITUMBA.

Lupot, Nicolas (*b* Stuttgart, 4 Dec 1758; *d* Paris, 14 Aug 1824). French violin maker of German birth. He is considered the greatest of the French makers, and is often referred to as the French Stradivari. His father, François Lupot (i), an undistinguished maker of the Vosgien (Mirecourt) school, lived and worked in several places, finally settling at Orleans in 1769. For a time father and son worked together, but Nicolas's superiority quickly came to the fore in every department of violin making. From the beginning he determined to learn from Stradivari's work and had made considerable progress by the time he moved to Paris in 1794. The move was due principally to the encouragement of François-Louis Pique, himself a fine maker, born in the same year as Lupot but established in Paris since about 1777. The two were in close contact during the last years at Orleans, and Pique was probably Lupot's agent. Once in Paris, working together with Pique, Lupot quickly perfected his models and the style of his workmanship, doubtless inspired by an abundance of Stradivari instruments in the city. In 1798 he opened his own workshop in the rue de Grammont, but moved again in 1806 to the rue Croix des Petits Champs. Like that of Stradivari, Lupot's career had so far been one of constant, steady improvement. He reached the highest level of his achievement towards 1810, and generally sustained it to the end of his life.

Although the work of Stradivari was Lupot's guide, he was anything but a slavish copyist. What he did grasp as well as any Stradivari follower was incomparable good taste in workmanship; within this discipline he gave expression to his own admirable ideas. His rich orange-red varnish, perfectly transparent, gave the final touch. Occasionally he copied Guarneri 'del Gesù', whose violins were rapidly achieving fame in the first two decades of the 19th century. Lupot's production was almost entirely of violins; violas and cellos are a rarity. The aristocratic tonal qualities of his instruments have always been well appreciated by players. Lupot's most important pupil was Charles François Gand, who also became his successor through having married his adopted daughter. Another was Auguste Sébastien Philippe Bernardel. Lupot's influence was strongly felt in Paris throughout the 19th century; above all, he created the standard by which the rest of the great French school is judged.

François Lupot (ii) (*b* Orleans, 1774; *d* Paris, 4 Feb 1837) was a younger brother of Nicolas and is said to have made violins but was celebrated principally as a bow maker; he at times rivalled François Tourte. Of the many bows branded LUPOT on the handle, a considerable number are the work of other contemporaries, but thousands of cheap bows were thus branded in Germany at the end of the 19th century.

BIBLIOGRAPHY
W. H., A. F. and A. E. Hill: *Antonio Stradivari: his Life and Work (1644–1737)* (London, 1902/R1963)
R. Vannes: *Essai d'un dictionnaire universel des luthiers* (Paris, 1932, 2/1951/R1972 as *Dictionnaire universel des luthiers* and R1981 incl. suppl. 1959)
J. Roda: *Bows for Musical Instruments of the Violin Family* (Chicago, 1959)
W. C. Retford: *Bows and Bow Makers* (London, 1964)
CHARLES BEARE

Lur. (1) Trumpet dating from the late Nordic Bronze Age. It consists of a conical tube, some 2 to 3 metres in length, made of several sections joined by bands and twisted into the shape of a contorted 'S'. At the speaking end in place of a bell is a bronze disc ornamented with geometric figures. Some examples of the instrument have small metal plates hanging from rings near the mouthpiece; these swing against each other to create a rattle effect. A large number of lurs have been excavated from peat bogs in the vicinity of the Baltic Sea, particularly in Denmark (see illustration) and southern Sweden.

Its remarkable record of preservation and the striking appearance of the instrument, together with a certain measure of ethnic motivation, have led to enthusiastic claims for its musical importance which appear in some respects to be exaggerated. The fact that they are usually found in pairs inspired the claim that they played part-music, and that in their survival we have the source

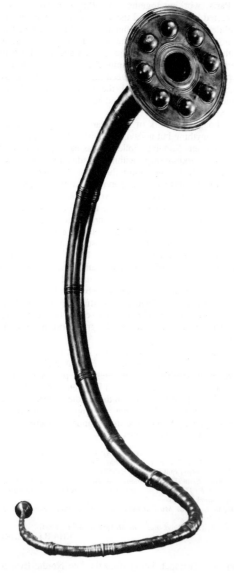

Lur: one of a pair found at Tellerup, Fyn (National-museet, Copenhagen)

of Western polyphony. This is not convincing, particularly since the phenomenon of ancient brass instruments appearing in pairs is widespread (for example, the Jewish Temple trumpets, the *ḥatzotzeroth*). Somewhat more plausible are the claims for its musical versatility. These stem from experiments in which modern players using modern mouthpieces have produced all the notes of the chromatic scale. Sachs (1940) argued against these claims on the grounds that it is fallacious to equate an ancient instrument's potential with what was actually played on it. He cited the ability of modern string players to play medieval instruments in several positions whereas they were in fact played only in the 1st.

A further area of dispute is the timbre of the instrument, its protagonists attributing a noble, somewhat mellow, character to it. However, there is virtually unanimous testimony to the raucous character of other ancient trumpets. There is also the question of whether the lur was primarily a cult or a military instrument, a mellow quality being supposed more appropriate for religion and a strident tone more appropriate for war. Perhaps the instrument was used for both, as was the case with brass instruments of the Mediterranean cultures. There, the raucous quality of trumpets served to strike fear into the enemy and likewise performed an apotropaic function in cult, that is, they warded off unwanted evil spirits during sacrifice. The SISTRUM, a kind of metal rattle, performed the same function on a smaller scale and one cannot but compare it with the rattle-like attachments of the lur.

(2) The term 'lur' was used in Scandinavia for bark and wooden trumpets played by herdsmen, until late in the 19th century, to frighten away wild animals and to round up cattle.

The simpler and more perishable bark trumpet (*bark-horn* or *barklur*) was made from a spiral bark shaving stripped from alder, ash, willow or spruce when the sap was rising. This was bound firmly into a cone-shape and fastened at the wider end. The instrument was also known as *arderlur* (made from alder), *straut, stroit* or *strait* ('cornet') and *stacklur* ('short trumpet').

The wooden trumpet (*raklur, långlur* or *basu*) was usually made from two halves of a long piece of wood, hollowed out; sometimes the air duct was simply bored. To hold the halves together and stop air leakages, the edges were tarred or glued, and the trumpet strengthened with bands of osier or metal or, in some cases (as in the *näverlur*), with a complete covering of birch-bark. Most wooden trumpets were straight but curved varieties were known, as were ones shaped like modern trumpets or trombones. The bore was cylindro-conical, with a flared bell at the end. Some instruments had a thickening at the blowing end as a support for the lips. The average length was from 60 to 150 cm, although examples up to 2 metres long were known. The wooden trumpet was also a means of communication and, like the so-called *åldermanslur* or *bylur* ('alderman's trumpet' or 'village trumpet'; an animal horn or a straight trumpet made of copper plate), it played a part in village administration.

BIBLIOGRAPHY

C. Sachs: *The History of Musical Instruments* (New York, 1940)

H. C. Broholm, W. P. Larsen and G. Skjerne: *The Lurs of the Bronze Age* (Copenhagen, 1949)

F. Behn: *Musikleben im Altertum und frühen Mittelalter* (Stuttgart, 1954)

C.-A. Moberg: 'Om vallåtar: en studie i de svenska fäbodarnas musikaliska organisation', *STMf*, xxxvii (1955), 7–95

E. Emsheimer: 'Zur Typologie der schwedischen Holztrompeten', *Studia instrumentorum musicae popularis*, i, ed. E. Stockmann (Stockholm, 1969), 87
JAMES W. McKINNON (1), BIRGIT KJELLSTRÖM (2)

Lure. *See* FEKO.

Luru. End-blown trumpet of the Lugbara people of Uganda. It is made from a bottle gourd, and is sometimes used instead of the *guke*, a side-blown animal-horn trumpet.

Lusese. STICK ZITHER of the Luntu people of central Zaïre (*LaurentyC*, 115). *See* ZEZE (i).

Lu sheng. Mouth organ of the tribal sub-cultures of south-west China (*lu*: 'reed'; *sheng*: a generic term for mouth organs). It is also inaccurately referred to as *liu sheng* (*liu*: 'six', the usual number of pipes); the Lao name is *kāēng*. In construction the *lu sheng* resembles the Chinese *sheng*, in that its six pipes of varying lengths are fitted with free-beating metal reeds and inserted into a common wind chamber; the two instruments sound very similar. The pipes are tuned pentatonically. It differs from the *sheng* in that the wind chamber is relatively narrow, with a long straight blowpipe extending outwards, while its six sounding pipes pass through the wind chamber and protrude at the bottom (similar to the Thai *khāēn*). As traditionally used among the Miao (Hmong) and other minority peoples of south-west China (and across the border in south-east Asia) the *lu sheng* is played as a dance accompaniment by the dancers themselves. During the 1950s, owing to revisions encouraged by the Chinese government, additional pipes were added to increase the playing range and individual metal tubes fitted over the top of each pipe to increase the resonance. This revised *lu sheng* has now become a concert-hall instrument, in both solo and ensemble music.

ALAN R. THRASHER

Lushiba. Common name for a carved wooden VESSEL FLUTE, cone flute (whistle) or ocarina among various peoples of the Kasai Occidental province of Zaïre. Among the Luba it is used as a signalling instrument during hunting and is frequently of a roughly cruciform shape and approximately 10 to 12 cm long. Here it is held upright between the thumb and index finger and placed against the lower lip; the thumb covers and uncovers a small hole in the side, thus enabling the production of two notes. Through one 'arm' is a second hole for the attachment of a suspension cord. Before use, the interior of the whistle is moistened with several drops of palm oil. The whistle may also be used as a rhythmic accompaniment for dancing.

According to Knosp, the Luluwa *lushiba* is also a type of ocarina with up to four finger-holes, and Laurenty, who describes 34 specimens of *lushiba*, also includes one Luba ocarina made of clay but with no finger-holes. Among the Luluwa the *lushiba* was traditionally blown by a father of twins so that others could either meet him and share his good fortune or avoid him entirely, according to the disparate beliefs held by different clans. *See also* KASHIBA and SCHIBA.

BIBLIOGRAPHY
LaurentyA
G. Knosp: *Enquête sur la vie musicale au Congo belge 1934–1935* (Tervuren, 1968)

J. Gansemans: *Les instruments de musique Luba* (Tervuren, 1980)
J. GANSEMANS, K. A. GOURLAY

Lusingando (It.: 'coaxing', 'wheedling', 'caressing'; gerund of *lusingare*, to flatter). An expression mark also found in the adjectival form *lusinghiero* ('seductive', 'flattering').

Lusse, Christophe de. *See* DELUSSE family.

Lusse, Jacques. *See* DELUSSE family.

Lusuba. MOUTH BOW, about 45 cm in length, of the Luba people of Zaïre. It is played by girls to accompany narrative songs. The bow rests on the left shoulder with the string held between the lips of the musician, who hits the string with a thin stick held in her right hand, while stopping the string with another stick held in the left hand. This produces two tones; timbre is changed by closing or opening the lips. Simple mouth bows of this type are not confined to any particular area of Zaïre and are known by different local names: *ingonga, inkoko, lonkoko, itumbolongonda, kawombo, bombo, kpwoko-lo, ninga (gwaningba), bongoga (bongombo, bongenda), bongengee, bongogo, ikoka, bogonga (igonga), lingongo, dingba, kudungba, kilibongo, bawa, bandingba* and *lipombo*.

BIBLIOGRAPHY
LaurentyC, 112
F. J. de Hen: *Beitrag zur Kenntnis der Musikinstrumente aus Belgisch Kongo und Ruanda-Urundi* (Tervuren, 1960)
G. Knosp: *Enquête sur la vie musicale au Congo belge 1934–1935* (Tervuren, 1968)
J. Gansemans: *La musique et son rôle dans la vie sociale et rituelle Luba* (Tervuren, 1978)
——: *Les instruments de musique Luba* (Tervuren, 1980)
J. GANSEMANS, K. A. GOURLAY

Lusukia. LAMELLAPHONE of the Ombo-binja and Songola Kindu peoples of Zaïre. It is of the type described for KAKOLONDONDO, but has a projecting gourd resonator attached to the box (*LaurentyS*, 195).

Lutandu. GOBLET DRUM of the Bena Nkongolo people of Zaïre. *See* DITUMBA.

Lutao. Chinese pair of drums. *See* TAOGU.

Lutaqa. PANPIPES of the MAIZU ensemble, Bolivia.

Lutar. Lute of the Berber people of North Africa.

Lute (Arabic *'ūd*; Fr. *luth*; Ger. *Laute*; It. *lauto, liuto, leuto*; Sp. *laúd*). A plucked chordophone, made of wood, of Arab origin (*see* 'ŪD) which flourished throughout Europe from medieval times to the 18th century. Broader, generic uses of the term are discussed in §1.

1. The generic term. 2. Ancient lutes. 3. Structure of the Western lute. 4. History. 5. Technique. 6. Ornamentation. 7. Repertory.

1. THE GENERIC TERM. In the Hornbostel and Sachs classification system (*Zeitschrift für Ethnologie*, xlvi, 1914, 553–90; Eng. trans. in *GSJ*, xiv, 1961, 3) the term 'lute' covers those 'composite chordophones' – string instruments in which a string bearer and a resonator are 'organically united' and cannot be separated without destroying the instrument – in which the plane of the

1. *Examples of plucked lutes: (a) sitar (India); (b) yueqin (China); (c) shamisen (Japan); (d) 'ūd (Syria); (e) ukulele; (f) gurmi (Niger)*

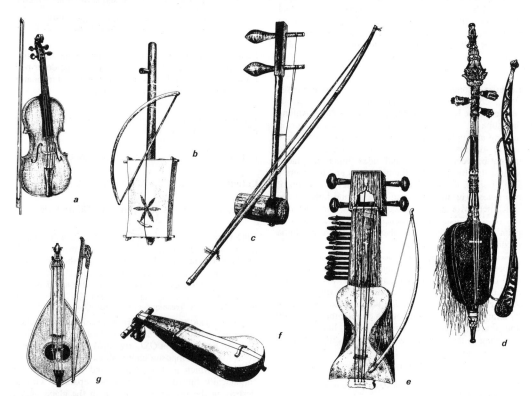

2. *Examples of bowed lutes: (a) violin; (b) rabāba (Syria); (c) jinghu (China); (d) rebab tiga tali (West Malaysia); (e) sāraṅgī (India); (f) rebab (North Africa); (g) lyra (Crete)*

string runs parallel with the soundtable (see figs.1 and 2). This definition excludes harps and zithers but includes pluriarcs (or bow lutes), lyres of various sorts and 'handle lutes' proper. The following excerpt from Hornbostel and Sachs (from the *GSJ* translation, with minor alterations) shows the classification of handle lutes; for their complete classification of lute types, *see* CHORDOPHONE.

321.3   *Handle lutes*: the string bearer is a plain handle; subsidiary necks are disregarded, as are also lutes with strings distributed over several necks, like the *harp-lyre*, and those like the lyre-guitars, in which the yoke is merely ornamental

321.31   *Spike lutes*: the handle passes diametrically through the resonator

321.311   *Spike bowl lutes*: the resonator consists of a natural or carved-out bowl – found in Persia [now Iran], India, Indonesia

321.312   *Spike box lutes or spike guitars*: the resonator is built up from wood – found in Egypt

321.313   *Spike tube lutes*: the handle passes diametrically through the walls of a tube – found in China, Indochina [now Vietnam]

321.32   *Necked lutes*: the handle is attached to or carved from the resonator, like a neck

321.321   *Necked bowl lutes* (mandolin, theorbo, balalaika)

321.322   *Necked box lutes or necked guitars* (violin, viol, guitar); NB a lute whose body is built up in the shape of a bowl is classified as a bowl lute

321.33   *Tanged lutes*: the handle ends within the body resonator

Common usage also excludes bowed instruments (such as the violin). However, the Hornbostel and Sachs classification provides suffixes for use with any division of the class of chordophones to indicate the method of sounding; thus, for example, a violin if played with a bow is classified as a bowed lute.

Spike lutes and necked lutes differ from each other by the manner in which neck and resonator are assembled. Fig.3 illustrates possibilities of assembly as found in a series of instruments of the lute family (played with a bow) from the Indonesian island of Sulawesi. If the neck clearly passes through the resonator, as it does in the first four examples, the label 'spiked lute' applies. But in six cases the handle is 'attached', and in this sense the instruments are 'necked lutes'. However, the examples show that there are several transitional forms to which neither label applies well; hence a third category has been added to the Hornbostel and Sachs classification above, under the code 321.33, for instruments in which, as Hornbostel himself described it, 'the handle ends within the body'.

Sachs ascribed the earliest types to a period from the 4th to the 2nd millennium BC, basing his conclusion on cultural geography. Seen in the perspective of human development, lutes are in any event a comparatively late invention. Because the use of a bow to play string instruments is even more recent – the earliest documentation dates from around the end of the 1st millennium AD – the following discussion of ancient lutes deals exclusively with plucked instruments.

2. ANCIENT LUTES. Two types of ancient lute are clearly distinguishable: the earlier long-necked lute and the short-necked lute. There is a wide range of difference within each type, but the most common features of the long-necked lute are an unfretted, rod-like neck and a small oval or almond-shaped body, which before the advent of wood construction was fashioned from a gourd or tortoise-shell. In many early examples where the table is of hide, the neck or spike is attached to it by piercing it a number of times in the manner of stitching. The strings, usually two, are attached at the lower end of the spike in varying ways and are bound at the top by ligatures from which hang decorative tassels. Pegs were not used until comparatively late in the instrument's history.

The long-necked lute is now thought (by Turnbull and Picken, for example) to have originated among the West Semites of Syria. Turnbull (1972) has argued convincingly for its earliest appearance being that on two cylinder seals (see fig.4a) of the Akkadian period (*c*2370–2110 BC); on one the lute is in the hands of a crouching male who plays while a birdman is brought before a seated god. In contrast to the draped female harpists, the lutenists of early Mesopotamia are men, sometimes shown naked or with animals. None of these instruments has survived, but its popularity is attested by many objects of the Babylonian period. The Louvre possesses a Babylonian boundary stone, found at Susa, which shows bearded men with bows on their backs playing the lute in the company of such animals as the lion, panther, antelope, horse, sheep, ox, and an ostrich. In the early 2nd millennium BC the lute is also attested for the Hittite Old Kingdom: a sherd from Alishar Höyük has preserved the end of a neck with two strings hanging from it.

The lute first appeared in Egypt as a result of Hyksos influence, which opened the country to Western Asiatic ideas. In the New Kingdom (1567–1085 BC) the long-necked lute was often represented in banquet scenes,

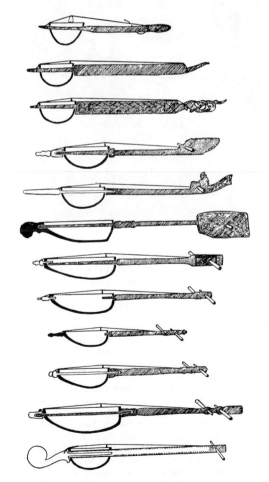

3. *Bowed lutes from the Indonesian island of Sulawesi, in cross-section, showing the varying ways in which neck and resonator are assembled*

4. *(a) Long-necked lute on a Mesopotamian cylinder seal, Akkadian period, c2370–2110 BC (British Museum, London); (b) long-necked lute and arched harp: detail from a painting in the tomb of Djeserkare'sonb, Thebes, from the time of Tuthmosis IV (reigned 1425–17 BC); (c) short-necked lute: terracotta figurine (3rd century BC) from Tanagra (Musée du Louvre, Paris)*

(a)

(c)

(b)

played either by men or women. The two main types of instrument, with round (usually tortoise-shell) or oval soundbox, appear in a scene now at the British Museum showing details of the frets and soundholes as well as the plectrum. The earliest Egyptian evidence of the lute to survive is a soundbox now in the Metropolitan Museum, New York, and a well-preserved instrument in the Cairo Museum was found in the Theban tomb of the singer Harmose. The lute had a function in ritual processions such as those depicted in the Luxor temple at the festival of Opet, when a number of players performed together. It appeared most often, though, in the chamber groups that featured at court functions and official banquets. The end of the neck is sometimes carved with the head of a goose or falcon. This probably had religious significance, as is clearly the case when a Hathor head is carved. The dwarf-god Bes, himself probably of Asiatic origin, is an adept at the lute, and satirical scenes show it in the hands of a crocodile.

Greco-Roman lutes (*see* PANDOURA), which are depicted in a number of Hellenistic sculptures and on late Roman

sarcophagi, are comparatively rare. They appear to have at least three strings, plucked with the fingers, and a thick unfretted neck. (The evidence indicating this last feature, however, may be influenced by the sculpture medium.) One depiction, a terracotta in the Louvre (see fig.4c), shows the body tapering to form the neck in the manner of the short-necked lute. The surviving representations from Byzantium, most notably a 5th-century mosaic from the former imperial palace of Istanbul and a 6th-century mosaic from a church near Shahhat, Libya, show lutes of the pandoura type.

The short-necked lute, which is characterized by a wooden body tapering off to form the neck and fingerboard, probably also originated in Asia. There are only rare representations of it until the first centuries AD. A number of statuettes and reliefs (see Geiringer, 1927–8, plates 1–3) are preserved from the Gandhara culture of the time, named from an area in north-west India under the influence of Greek civilization; these show short-necked lutes with a pear-shaped body, a frontal string-holder, lateral pegs and four or five strings plucked with a plectrum. The Sassanid lute or *barbaṭ*, as shown on a 6th-century silver cup from Kalar Dasht, was of this type. Apparently these instruments are related to those lutes which spread eastward to China and Japan, as well as to the Arabian '*ūd*, the immediate ancestor of the European classical lute.

3. STRUCTURE OF THE WESTERN LUTE. The typical features of the Western lute are: a vaulted body constructed from a number of separate ribs shaped, bent and glued together; a flat soundboard or belly in which is carved an ornate soundhole or 'rose'; a distinct neck and fingerboard tied with gut frets; a pegbox, usually at nearly a right angle to the neck, with tuning-pegs inserted laterally; a bridge, to which the strings are attached, glued near the lower end of the soundboard; and strings of gut, arranged in paired courses, with the frequent exception of a single treble string (see fig.5).

The longitudinal strips of wood (often sycamore or maple) of which the body is constructed are cut to shape and bent over a mould to form a symmetrical shell. At the lower end, where these 'ribs' taper together, they are reinforced internally and externally with short strips of the same kind of wood. At the other end is a block, usually of softwood, to which the neck is attached. In historical lutes the standard method was to use a simple butt joint, secured with one or more nails driven through the block into the end-grain of the neck, which was often made of beech. The mortice-and-tenon joint, used on most modern string instruments, was evidently not applied to this purpose until towards the end of the 18th century.

On the oldest surviving lutes and in early illustrations the neck is considerably thicker than in later examples, which are thinned down almost to the limit, especially towards the pegbox end. On these later lutes the neck is often veneered with ebony. The front was at first flat, and itself formed the fingerboard, though later this was made separately from a thin plate of hardwood. Later still, the top surface of the fingerboard was given a slight curve, helping the lie of the frets and making the fingering easier. At the top end of the neck is a straight-sided pegbox, tapering slightly in both width and depth, set back at an angle of something like 80° to the plane of the fingerboard. The neck is cut away to form a housing for the end of the pegbox, which is usually secured

by glue alone, though sometimes reinforced with a nail. Slender hardwood tuning-pegs are inserted from the sides; fruitwood such as plum seems to have been a preferred material.

There is some controversy about the soundboard material, mainly as a result of confusion about the exact historical distinction between fir, pine and spruce. At all events, it is a flat straight-grained softwood plate, into which is carved an ornamental rose soundhole, whose pattern usually shows decidedly Arabic influence (see Wells, 1981). The soundboard is often made from two halves joined along the centre line, but on larger instruments several pieces may be used. The soundboard usually overlaps the neck slightly, and two narrow 'points' descend from the sides of the fingerboard to terminate over the neck-block position (see fig.5). Old lute soundboards are quite thin, normally of the order of about 1·5 mm; the bridge, drilled with a row of holes through which the strings are fastened, is glued to the surface. The tension of the strings tends to cause the soundboard to distort; this is resisted by a number of transverse bars, of the same wood as the soundboard, set on edge across its underside with their ends glued to the adjacent ribs of the back. On lutes of the 17th and 18th centuries, the whole length of the joint between soundboard and back is often covered on the outside with a narrow strip of parchment or cloth, known as the 'lace'.

The bars, besides supporting the table, have an important effect on the sound quality. By dividing the soundboard into a number of sections, each with a relatively high natural resonant frequency, they cause it to reinforce the upper harmonics produced by a string rather than its fundamental tone. This is matched by the strings themselves, which are quite thin compared with those of a modern guitar; a thin string tuned to a certain note produces many more high harmonics than a thicker string tuned to the same note. Thus the whole acoustical system of the lute is designed to give a characteristically clear, almost nasal, sound. The total volume as such is not great, but because of this distinctive edginess, which can be modified by subtle variations of thickness and by the player's technique, the lute can be heard perfectly well in appropriate circumstances. Another curious feature of the tone of the lute is that its volume does not seem to the ear to decrease with distance to the same

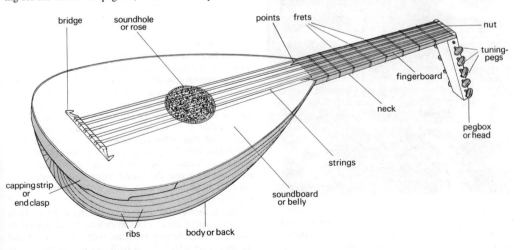

5. Features of the Western lute

6. *Lute ('ūd) with nine strings, and rabāb: miniature from the 'Cantigas de Santa María', late 13th century (E-E b.I.2, f.162r)*

extent as that of more 'rounded' sounds (*see also* ACOUSTICS, §I, 6).

4. HISTORY. The European lute derives from the Arab instrument known as the 'ŪD (which means literally 'wood'). There are two possible reasons why this word might have been applied to this particular instrument: either because it had a soundboard of wood as distinct from a parchment skin stretched over the body, or because the body itself was built up from wooden strips rather than made from a hollow gourd. The Arab lute was

7. *Lute with four courses, and harp: detail from the painting 'The Last Judgment' by Stefan Lochner, fl 1442–51 (Wallraf-Richartz-Museum, Cologne); note the plectrum between the first and second fingers of the right hand, which is parallel to the strings*

introduced into Europe by the Moors during their conquest and occupation of Spain (711–1492). Pictorial evidence shows Moorish lutenists, and 9th- and 10th-century accounts tell of visits of famous players such as Ziryāb to the court of the Andalusian emir 'Abd al Rahman II (822–52). The lute was not confined to Muslims, however, as is shown by illustrations to the *Cantigas de Santa María* of Alfonso el Sabio (1221–84; fig.6) which include players in distinctive Christian costume. The date at which the lute was introduced into other parts of medieval Europe is less well defined, though possibly the Moors brought it with them when they invaded Sicily in the 8th century. From the end of the 10th century the Crusades would have provided another means of bringing the instrument into Europe; moreover, greatly increased trading activities with the Near East, particularly through Venice, followed these campaigns. The 'ūd is still in use (although, unlike its ancestor, it no longer has frets) and is still remarkably similar to the lutes in early medieval European paintings.

As no lutes from before the 16th century have survived, information must be gathered from pictures, sculpture and written descriptions. These indicate that the lute has always had its strings in courses, and that at first there were only four such 'courses' (fig.7). There is no contemporary evidence for the tuning, but the 16th-century four-course guitar was supposedly tuned like the earlier lute, and its intervals were 4th, major 3rd, 4th. (As absolute pitch is virtually impossible to establish, tunings will normally be given in terms of intervals, reading from bass to treble, thus: 4–3–4. The figure 3 without qualification means a major 3rd; later tunings require distinction between major and minor (3'). Note names will occasionally be given to clarify a particular point.)

From the start, the instruments were of widely different sizes, which must imply different pitches, for reasons which are explained below. During the 15th century a fifth course was added, and the first direct indications of tuning date from this time. The most familiar is that of Johannes Tinctoris (*c*1487). After describing the ancient lyra as having seven diatonic strings, he continues:

But since seven strings differing by tones and semitones do not suffice for every composition, an arrangement of five, sometimes six, principal courses [*ordinationes*] was later adopted, first, I think, by the Germans. According to this, the two middle ones are tuned to a major third [*ditonum*] and the rest in fourths [*diatessaron*], that the lute may be perfect.

With a five-course instrument it is impossible to know which are 'the middle ones', although it has been assumed that the intervals intended were 4–3–4–4; in other words that the fifth course was added in the treble. However, in an important article drawing attention to some lesser-known sources of the late 15th century, Page (1981) showed that 4–4–3–4 was also considered 'most common', and that other variations were known as well. These last may have been 'drone' tunings, which are sometimes found in the early 16th century. When actual pitches were given, the lowest string was considered as either *G* (gamma ut) or *c*, though this cannot be certainly established in modern terms.

The earliest extant account of structural details is in a manuscript of about 1440 written by Henri Arnaut de Zwolle (fig.8). Arnaut described both the lute itself and the mould on which it was built, combining the two in the same diagrams. The whole design was worked out

n terms of geometrical proportion, including the positions of bridge, soundhole and three transverse bars.
Almost 200 years later, Mersenne (1636) explained the
construction of a lute by remarkably similar methods.
By this time the number of soundboard bars had doubled, but the placing of three of them, as well as that
of the soundhole and bridge, corresponds with that giv-
en by Arnaut. There can be no doubt that there was a
well-established tradition of instrument design by geometrical methods, going back to the Arab lute at least
as far as the 9th and 10th centuries (see Bouterse, 1979).

The oriental lute was, and still is, played with a plectrum, and at first the same method was used in Europe
(figs.6 and 7). With this technique the lute must have
been mainly a melodic instrument, playing basically a
single line of music, however highly ornate, with perhaps strummed chords at cadences and other important
points. During the second half of the 15th century, there
was a change to playing with the fingertips, though, as
Page (1981) pointed out, the two methods continued for
some time side by side. Tinctoris wrote of holding the
lute 'while the strings are struck by the right hand either
with the fingers or with a plectrum', but did not imply
that the use of the fingers was a novelty. However, the
change was very significant for the lute's future development, for it allowed the playing of several parts at
once, leading to the invention of special systems of
notation known as tablature. There were three main kinds
of tablature for the lute, developed in Germany, France
and Italy, of which examples are known that may date
from this very period (see Tischler, 1974; Brown, 1973–
4; Fallows, 1977). A fourth system, 'intavolatura alla
Napolitana', appears at this early date and is used from
time to time. Of the four types the French may have
been the earliest, one example from the 14th century
having recently been discovered (see Page, 1980). The
German one was probably written during the lifetime of
Conrad Paumann (d 1473), the supposed inventor of the
system. Although Tinctoris had hinted at a six-course
lute, these first tablatures, and indeed the very names
by which the strings of the instrument were known, suggest five courses as the most usual number (fig.13). Such
lutes probably persisted longer than has sometimes been
supposed (see Gill, 1981).

Nevertheless, some time around 1500 improvements
in string-making techniques made it possible to extend
the range of the open strings by another 4th, by the
addition of a sixth course (fig.11). Thus the symmetrical tuning of the old four-course lute was restored (4–
4–3–4–4), giving a total open-string range of two
octaves. Lutes of various sizes were still widely used,
but the top string of the most usual type was regarded
as either g' (giving a tuning of G–c–f–a–d'–g') or a'.
Gut was used for all the strings and it was usual on at
least the three lowest courses to set one of the pair with
a thin string tuned an octave higher, to lend some brilliance to the tone of its thick neighbour.

Arnaut's 15th-century construction produces a very
'round' instrument, but this is by no means the most
common shape to be seen in paintings. In the early years
of the next century the first of the surviving 'classic'
forms of the lute appeared. A centre of lute making had
developed in Bologna, where a colony of German
craftsmen was established under the leadership of Laux
MALER and his son Sigismond, and which included HANS
FREI and Nicola Sconvelt. The main characteristic of their
lutes is a long narrow body with rather straight shoul-

ders and fairly round at the base. This form is remarkably close to that proposed by Bouterse (1979) in his
interpretation of Persian and Arabic manuscripts of the
14th century. The chief difference is that these Middle
Eastern descriptions, which agree with Arnaut, indicate
a semicircular cross-section, whereas the instruments of
Maler and Frei are somewhat flatter. Their lutes usually
have nine or 11 broad ribs, often made from sycamore.
They remained highly prized as long as the lute was in
use, but became increasingly rare as time went on. No
unaltered example is known to have survived, for their
prestige was such that they were adapted (sometimes
more than once) to keep abreast of new fashions. They

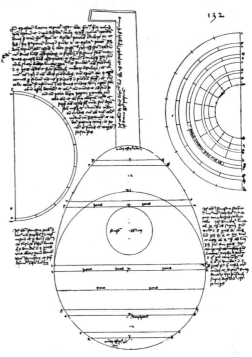

8. Henri Arnaut de Zwolle's diagrams (c1440) for the
construction of a lute (F-Pn lat.7295, f.132r)

have all been fitted with replacement necks to carry more
strings (fig.9b); sometimes, indeed, the vaulted back is
the only original part remaining.

It is remarkable that virtually every lute maker working in Italy in the 16th century, and many in the 17th,
came from a very small area of Germany, situated around
Füssen on the river Lech not far from Augsburg (see
Bletschacher, 1978, and Layer, 1978). In the second
half of the 16th century another family of German
instrument makers from the same region began working
in Italy. Their name was TIEFFENBRUCKER, from their
original village of Tieffenbruck, but regional spellings
produced variants such as Duiffoprugcar and even Dub-
rocard. With them is associated the rather shadowy figure of Vendelio Venere, who may have been a relation
(perhaps identical with Wendelin Tieffenbrucker) or
pupil, and also MICHAEL HARTUNG. These craftsmen
worked chiefly in Venice and Padua. The typical body
shape of their lutes was less elongated than that of Maler
and Frei, with more curved shoulders (fig.9a, c-f). The

first examples had 11 or 13 ribs, but later the number was increased, a feature associated with the use of yew, which has a brown heartwood and a narrow white sapwood; for purposes of decoration, each rib was cut half light, half dark, which restricted the available width and required a large number of ribs, often totalling up to 50 or more.

The use of geometrical methods of lute design has already been mentioned, and it has been found by several writers (Edwards, 1973; Abbott and Segerman, 1976; Söhne, 1980; Samson, 1981) that the shape of these instruments can readily be reproduced by such means; this may account for the similarity in basic form between instruments of different sizes and by different makers.

By comparison with the modern guitar, these early lutes, whether of the Bolognese or Paduan type, are distinguished by the lightness of their construction. The egg-like shape of the lute body is inherently strong and does not need to be built of very thick materials. Also, the total tension of six courses of thin gut strings was far less than is now considered normal on other instruments, so the soundboard could be made thin as well. When the modern revival of interest in early music began in earnest, there was a great demand for instruments, and it was natural for makers and players of the modern guitar to turn their attention to the lute. This resulted in some extremely heavily built and unauthentic instruments being produced. In reaction against these, some makers have gone to the opposite extreme and produced instruments even lighter than the original models. Clearly, what is required is a happy medium that can be achieved only by careful study of surviving examples, though it is not necessarily wise simply to make blind copies of particular museum instruments. It is arguable that a more

thoughtful approach to the methods and intentions of the early makers might produce better results.

The instruction to tune the top string as high as it will stand without breaking, repeated in many early lute tutors, may raise a smile of amusement today, but is really a matter of practical necessity. Wire-wound bass strings were unknown until after 1650; before then lutes were strung in gut throughout. This allows very little leeway, for if the highest string is lowered for safety's sake beneath its breaking point, the thickest basses will be too slack to produce an acceptable sound. Rather surprisingly, the breaking pitch of a string depends on its length but not on its thickness, so the working level of a given instrument is fixed within quite narrow limits.

In the second half of the 16th century there was a tendency to build instruments in families of sizes, roughly corresponding with the different types of human voice, and the lute was no exception. With typical thoroughness, Praetorius (2/1619) listed no fewer than seven sizes, whose highest strings were tuned as follows: *Kleinen Octavlaut – d''* or *c''*; *Klein Discantlaut – b'*; *Discant Laut – a'*; *Recht Chorist- oder Alt Laute – g'*; *Tenor Laute – e'*; *Der Bass gennant – d'*; *Die Gross Octav Bass Laut – g*. German inventories of the 16th century, such as that of Raymund Fugger in 1566 (see Smith, 1980), already indicate as many sizes as this, but Italian, French and English sources generally mention only three: small, medium and large. Musical considerations of course determine the nominal or relative pitches required for duet or ensemble playing. Where pitch is given in relation to another instrument or a voice, it is clear that the *g'* lute is the most usual, as Praetorius suggested, although a nominal pitch a tone higher is also quite frequent.

9. (a) Large 'mean' lute by Magno Tieffenbrucker, Venice, 1609; (b) large 'mean' lute by Hans Frei, Bologna, 1550; (c)–(f) descant and two treble lutes (1600) and a 'mean' lute (1582) by Wendelin Tieffenbrucker, Padua; (g) great bass lute by Michael Hartung, Padua, 1602; (a) Museo Bardini, Florence; (b) and (c)–(f) Kunsthistorisches Museum, Vienna; (g) Germanisches Nationalmuseum, Nuremberg (all are reproduced to the same scale)

(a)   (b)

In England the *g'* lute was known as the 'mean', and was normally the size intended, as in most of the books of ayres, unless otherwise specified. The only other names used in English musical sources are 'bass' (nominally at *d'*) and 'treble', which is specified for the Morley and Rosseter *Consort Lessons*. Curiously enough, the nominal pitch for the treble lute implied by the other parts is also *g'*, but there is a distinct possibility (see Harwood, 1981) that this music was to be played at a pitch level a 4th higher than that of the mean lute. The treble lute could thus be regarded as tuned either in *g'* at 'high pitch' or in *c"* at 'low pitch'.

Lutes of many different sizes are extant, but the picture is complicated by the fact that so few of them are now in their original state. Fine examples are a number of instruments by Wendelin Tieffenbrucker in the Vienna Kunsthistorisches Museum (fig.9*c-f*) and a magnificent great bass by Michael Hartung in the Germanisches Nationalmuseum, Nuremberg (fig.9*g*). Strictly speaking, the smallest of these (fig.9*c*) should be called a mandore (*see* MANDOLIN, §2).

String makers were constantly trying to improve their products to increase the total range available, either by increasing the tensile strength of the trebles or by making the thick basses more elastic and flexible. An early method of extending the range of the lute was to tune the sixth string one note lower than usual. Francesco Spinacino called this device 'bordon discordato' (*Intabulatura de lauto*, 1507), and from then on it was used occasionally; in Germany it was known as 'Abzug' and in France 'corde avallée'. In 1511, however, Virdung mentioned a seventh course, and in the 15th-century pieces written into Pietro Borghi's *Chi de arte matematiche ha piachere* (1484) a staff of seven lines is used (see Rubsamen, 1968). Subsequent authorities also referred to the device, including Gerle (1532) and the anonymous author of the *Discours non plus mélancholique* (1557), but it was only in the 1580s that the seventh course became at all common, tuned sometimes a tone, sometimes a 4th, below the sixth. The improved strings provided not only a greater range, but also a better tone in the existing bass courses. Thus it became possible to abandon the octave stringing and to tune each pair in unison, giving a more satisfactory result

(c)   *(d)*   *(e)*   *(f)*   *(g)*

at least in theory. The situation was summed up by John Dowland in his additions to his son Robert's *Varietie of Lute Lessons* (1610):

these basses must be both of one bignes, yet it hath beene a generall custome (although not so much used any where as here in England) to set a small and great string together, but amongst learned musicians that custome is left, as irregular to the rules of Musicke.

The same book reflects the growing tendency to increase the number of bass strings, including English and continental music for lutes with six, seven, eight and nine courses. The extra basses were tuned in various ways, descending to a low *C* in some pieces. The process culminated in the ten-course lute, with the additional strings tuned to a scale of *C–D–E–F* below the sixth course. These strings were known as 'diapasons', and the *E* could be flattened to suit the music being played. They were presumably introduced to eliminate the awkward fingerings resulting from having to stop the seventh course. Despite Dowland's strictures, the diapasons were usually doubled at the upper octave.

Yet another innovation reported by Dowland in *Varietie* was the lengthening of the neck of the instrument. Hitherto, he wrote, 'all the Lutes which I can remember used eight frets'. Sometimes extra wooden frets were glued on to the soundboard, which he attributed to the English player Mathias Mason, but 'some few yeeres after, by the French Nation, the neckes of the Lutes were lengthned, and thereby increased two frets more, so as all those Lutes, which are most received and disired, are of tenne frets'. Initially this may have been done to improve the tone of the low basses, but unless stronger treble strings became available at the same time, the pitch level of these longer lutes must have been lower than the older eight-fret instruments.

The French were also the first to introduce departures from the *vieux ton* or old Renaissance tuning. In Anthoine Francisque's *Le trésor d'Orphée* (1600) there is a section for a nine-course lute with 'cordes avallées', where the inner strings are retuned, not the sixth course as previously. The fingered strings are tuned 3′–5–4–3–4, spanning two octaves as before, but with different distribution. Three years later, Besardus followed a similar procedure in his *Thesaurus harmonicus*, but his tuning, for an eight-course instrument, is 4–5–4–3–4 for the six fingered strings. (It is worth noting in passing that both these tunings, and a somewhat similar one used by John Daniel in England in 1606, have the major 3rd in the same place as the second 'most common' tuning of the 15th-century five-course lute.)

Once the strait-jacket of the *vieux ton* was broken,

10. Man playing a two-headed 'French' lute: detail of a painting by Hendrik Martensz Sorgh (1611–70) in the Rijksmuseum, Amsterdam

there was a spate of 'accords nouveaux ou extraordinaires', as Mersenne (1636) called them. These were often known by the names of the composers who first used them, which are sometimes given in the manuscripts. Thus pieces may be marked 'Ton Mésangeau' or 'Ton Mercure', which has led to their being catalogued as 'affectionately signed by the composer'. These tunings have been listed by D. and E. Segerman (1979), from which some of the most widely used are given below, with the names by which they were commonly known. As before, only the six fingered courses are shown; the diapasons could be tuned as the music required, and even small changes such as *E* to *E♭* could be enough to give rise to a new name.

4–4–3′–3–4	Harpway flat
4–4–3–3′–4	Harpway (sharp)
4–4–3–3′–3	Sharp Tune
4–4–3–3′–3′	Mésangeau
4–4–3′–3–3′	Flat French
3–3′–4–3–3′	Trumpet; Jenkins
4–3–3′–4–3	B sharp (modern name D major)
4–3′–3–4–3′	B flat; Goat; Mercure; New Tuning (modern name D minor)

The confusion in the naming of the last two arises from different notional pitch levels. They are normally transcribed as *A–d–f♯–a–d′–f♯′* and *A–d–f–a–d′–f′* respectively, but they were sometimes thought of as being a 4th higher, *d–g–b–d′–g′–b′* and *d–g–b♭–d′–g′–b♭′*; hence the names B sharp and B flat. Most of these tunings were introduced in the 1630s; the last one, probably due to Ennemond Gautier, was printed for the first time in Pierre Ballard's *Tablature de luth de différents autheurs sur les accords nouveaux* (Paris, 1638) and became the most widely used of all. Indeed, many modern commentators have called it simply 'the Baroque lute tuning'.

All the ten-course lutes shown in contemporary illustrations are constructed like their predecessors, with the strings running over a single nut to the pegbox, which of course has to be considerably longer to accommodate the additional pegs (fig.14). About the time of the appearance of the new tunings, yet another course was added, giving rise to the 11-course lute. At first this, too, was built in the usual way, but soon the idea of taking the lowest strings to a second head (see fig.10) to increase their length was borrowed from the THEORBO. However, whereas on the theorbo all the diapasons passed over one extra nut to the pegbox at the end of the extension, these new lutes had four separate nuts in steps, each carrying a single pair of strings. In this way the string lengths increased gradually, avoiding the sudden jump, and consequent change of tone colour, of the theorbo proper. Once the two-headed principle was adopted, it enabled still further extension to be made in the bass, resulting in the 12-course lute.

The two-headed 'French' lute was enthusiastically adopted in England, where it was played throughout the 17th century, despite criticisms that the extra-long bass strings were too strong for the rest of the instrument. As the author of the Burwell lute tutor (*c*1670) wrote: 'All England hath accepted that Augmentation and ffraunce at first but soone after that alteration hath beene condemned by all the french Masters who are returned to theire old fashion'. Perhaps the best-known English book on the two-headed lute is Thomas Mace's *Musick's Monument* (1676), though he, too, pointed out the dangers of over-long bass strings. In his music he used mostly the 'flat French' tuning and also the 'new tuning'. It is

11. Mary Magdalen playing a six-course lute: painting (first quarter of the 16th century) by the 'Master of the Female Halflengths' (Kunsthalle, Hamburg); the music is a two-part intabulation of the French chanson 'Si j'ayme mon amy' (see Heartz, 1972); the right arm and hand are still in the old 'plectrum' position, despite the use of the fingertips

interesting that when Talbot (*c*1690) gave details and measurements of a 12-course instrument of this type, he called it the 'English two headed lute'; for him the 'French lute' had 11 courses, with all the strings on a single head.

One of the chief factors that led the French to return to a single head and pegbox was the invention of wire-wound or overspun strings, first advertised in England by Playford in 1664, though not mentioned by either Mace or the Burwell tutor. The extra weight of the new strings enabled lower notes to be obtained with good resonance on a comparatively short string length; on the extension neck of the two-headed lute they would be overpowering, despite their appeal to some modern players. There are now only two or three examples of the double-headed 11- or 12-course lute, but the single-headed 11-course instrument is relatively common in collections. The most obvious feature not found on earlier lutes is the small 'rider' or bracket, mounted on the side of the pegbox, to take the treble string or 'chanterelle'. Other differences are the wider fingerboard and the longer pegbox needed for the 20 or so strings. Another characteristic of these lutes is that the lowest course often runs beyond the fingerboard over an extension of the nut, and is fastened to the outside of the pegs.

Towards the end of the 17th century, the centre of activity in lute music shifted from France to Germany. Following the tendency already established, the German makers and composers extended the range of the instrument still further, writing for 13 courses. The so-called D minor tuning was still employed, but now the octave diapasons ran down to *A′A*. A single pegbox was still used, with the two lowest courses accommodated on a second saddle or 'rider' on the bass side of the pegbox,

12. Detail of pegbox showing treble and bass riders on a 13-course lute, originally by Hanns Burkholtzer, Füssen, 1596; string arrangement by Thomas Edlinger, Prague, 1705 (Kunsthistorisches Museum, Vienna)

complete with its own nut and the four pegs (fig.12). This device was peculiar to the 18th-century German lute, and is not found on any earlier instruments. The bass rider gives something like 5 cm more length on the example shown, on which the main strings are 68 cm long, though many other lutes of this period are between 70 and 75 cm. Considerably greater length was given to the five lowest courses on another variant that appeared in Germany at this time. Although it is described as a THEORBO, its 13 courses were tuned exactly as just described, and it may well have been used as a solo lute. Lowe (1976) pointed out that there are no surviving historical 14-course instruments, however desirable they may seem to modern players wanting a low G' for Bach's lute suite in G minor. Besides the tuning already mentioned, yet more variants are found in the works of Reusner (3–3'–3–4–3'; 4–3'–3–3'–3) and of Bach (6'–3'–3–4–3').

German Baroque lutes, particularly those of J. C. Hoffmann, have a body outline close to that of the early 16th-century models of Frei and Maler; this resemblance may well have been deliberate, for the old instruments continued to be highly prized. It was about this time (1727) that the first systematic history of the lute was written, by E. G. Baron. Referring to the lutes of Laux Maler, he wrote:

But it is a source of wonder that he already built them after the modern fashion, namely with the body long in proportion, flat and broad-ribbed, and which, provided that no fraud has been introduced, and they are original, are esteemed above all others. They are highly valued because they are rare and have a splendid tone.

But, as Lowe has shown, 100 years earlier the French were already buying up and converting early 16th-century Bologna lutes, because of their suitability for the music of that time. The makers then were no doubt producing new instruments of the same form, so the later German makers were following a well-established tradition.

The development of the lute in 17th-century Italy followed a very different path from that in the countries already discussed, and has been less well studied up to

the time of writing (1982). As might be expected in the region where the CHITARRONE was invented, the principle of an extended neck for the bass strings was fully developed, but there was far less experimentation with tunings than further north. Indeed, the old 'Renaissance' tuning was continued into the 18th century. (For a detailed account of the lute in Italy, *see* ARCHLUTE and LIUTO ATTIORBATO.)

The number of frets on the neck of the lute varied from country to country and from time to time. Page (1981) published a mid-15th-century description of a lute from Prague, in which nine are mentioned. In the Italian painting of about the same time by Lorenzo Costa (fig.13), a five-course lute is shown with a total of 11 frets, including one at the join of the neck and body and three on the soundboard itself, presumably made of wood and glued in position. Virdung (1511) said that lutes had seven frets; a diagram in Judenkünig's *Ain schone kunstliche Underweisung* (1523) shows eight, and the same number appears in the diagrams in Hans Neusidler's books. Gerle (*Tabulatur auff die Laudten*, 1533) showed seven frets, but John Dowland (see above) did not remember ever having noticed fewer than eight, although mentioning the recent addition of three extras glued to the soundboard. In France there seems little evidence for more than eight frets until the lengthening of the neck of the lute at the beginning of the 17th century (*see* FRET).

The placing of the frets on the neck of the lute has always been a problem to both theoreticians and players, and many attempts have been made to find a system that will give the nearest approach to true intonation on as wide a range of intervals and in as many positions as possible. A number of writers, including Gerle (1532), Bermudo (1555), the anonymous author of *Discours non plus mélancholique* (1557), Vincenzo Galilei (*Il Fronimo*, 1568) and John Dowland put forward various systems, many of which were based on Pythagorean intervals. Late 16th-century theorists in Italy, as well as 17th-century writers such as Praetorius and Mersenne, habitually assumed that the intonation of the lute (and other fretted instruments) represented equal temperament, whereas keyboard instruments were tuned to some form of mean-tone temperament (*see* TEMPERAMENTS).

5. TECHNIQUE. Several writers of instruction books for the lute have remarked that many masters of the art were, as Mace put it, 'extreme *Shie* in revealing the *Occult* and *Hidden Secrets* of the *Lute*'. Bermudo had lamented the same characteristic in teachers: 'What a pity it is (and those who have Christian understanding must weep for it) that the great secrets of music die in a moment with the person of the musician, for lack of having communicated them to others'. The training of professional players was almost certainly carried on through some system of apprenticeship, and this may well be one of the reasons why comparatively few books give really informative instructions on all aspects of playing technique. Nevertheless, details have been left by the more conscientious authors that are sufficiently clear to establish the main characteristics of lute technique in each period.

Although little was written about left-hand techniques, certain basic rules were mentioned from the Capirola Lutebook (c1517; ed. O. Gombosi, 1955) onwards. The lute must be held in such a way that no weight is taken by the left hand. The thumb should be placed lightly on the underside of the neck, opposite the first and second fingers. The tips of the fingers should always stay as close as possible to the strings so that each one is ready to take its position without undue movement. Fingers must be kept in position on the strings until they are required to stop another string, or until the harmony changes. Judenkünig went so far as to say they must never be lifted until needed elsewhere.

In Capirola's lutebook the player was advised to keep the fingers in readiness and not to avoid using the little finger; the first finger could be laid across several strings to form a *barré* chord. Sometimes a finger was placed on one string only of a course in order to create an extra voice (a device also described by Bálint Bakfark and the vihuelist Miguel de Fuenllana); the right hand would then strike through the whole course as usual.

It was, however, the German masters who first codified a system of fingering. Judenkünig gave a series of diagrams of left-hand positions. In the first of these the hand spans the first three frets and the fourth fret on the sixth course; the first finger is marked with the six characters of the first fret in German tablature; the second finger is marked with the next series; the third finger takes the lower three courses on the third fret; and the little finger takes the upper three courses as well as the fourth fret on the sixth course. Each diagram shows the fingers rigidly aligned on the appropriate fret. A small cross placed above a letter indicates that the finger must be held and the following note played with the next finger, whatever fret it may be on. Judenkünig did not describe the fingering of chords, or cross-fingering where the counterpoint makes it necessary to depart from the prescribed alignment. Neusidler (*Ein newgeordnet künstlich Lautenbuch*, 1536) indicated by means of dots the fingering of a number of simple compositions. In general he followed the rules laid down by Judenkünig,

but he also showed how chords constantly demand the use of fingers on frets other than those allotted to them in a strict diagrammatic scheme.

In England and France little attention was given to left-hand technique until the publication of Adrian Le Roy's tutor *Tres breve et tres familière instruction* (now known only in its English translations, see §7, v), which described the *barré* chord as 'couching' the first finger 'along overthwart the stoppe'. Robinson described how to finger certain chord passages and also how to finger ascending and descending melodic lines. He also added fingering marks to the first five compositions in his books. Besard described in considerable detail the use of the *barré* and half *barré*, and also gave advice on how to choose the correct finger for holding notes, particularly in the bass. Later in the 17th century more complete markings were given by Nicolas Vallet (*Secretum musarum*, 1615), and, for a 12-course French lute, Mace.

Until about the second half of the 15th century most representations of lute players (where the details are visible) show the strings being struck with a quill or plectrum. The hand approaches the strings from below the bridge and lies nearly parallel with them. The plectrum or quill is held either between the thumb and first finger, or the first and second, or even the second and third. Gradually the fingers replaced the plectrum. In pictures of about 1480 it is common to see players with the hand in a slightly more transverse position. For any composition involving chords the advantage of this change is obvious. Tinctoris observed that players were becoming so skilful that they could play four voices together on the lute perfectly.

The earliest printed books gave little information about right-hand techniques. A dot placed under a note signified that it was to be played upwards, and the absence of a dot downwards; all passages of single notes were

13. Five-course lute with 11 frets, the top three glued to the soundboard: painting 'The Concert' (c1490) by Lorenzo Costa (National Gallery, London); the player's right arm and hand are again nearly parallel to the strings, in the old 'plectrum' position, although he is playing with the fingertips

played accordingly. Later sources specified that the downward stroke was always taken by the thumb on the accented beat, while the unaccented beat was taken upwards, usually with the first finger. This type of fingering was to remain standard practice until about 1600. It was still mentioned by Alessandro Piccinini (*Intavolatura di liuto, et di chitarrone*, 1623) and by Mersenne (1636–7), and it survived for runs of single notes across the lute from bottom to top and for certain other passages until 1660–70.

According to the instructions in the Capirola manuscript (the first to give any real insight into the playing position of the right hand), the thumb was held under the second finger, that is, inside the hand. Adrian Le Roy was the first to mention that the little finger is placed on the belly of the lute, although many representations of players before 1568 show the hand with the little finger in this position. Le Roy wrote: 'the little finger serveth but to keep the hande from [firm] upon the bealie of the Lute'. From then onwards it was frequently mentioned. Robinson, for example, said: 'leane upon the bellie of the Lute with your little finger onelie, & that neither to far from the *Treble* strings, neither to neere'. Mace wrote: 'The 2d. thing to be gain'd is, setting down your *Little Finger* upon the *Belly*, as aforesaid, *close under the Bridge*, about the *first*, 2d, 3d, or 4th. *Strings*; for thereabout, is its *constant station*. It *steadies the Hand*, and gives a *Certainty* to the *Grasp*'. From this time onwards, portraits of performing lute players always show the little finger placed either on the soundboard, in front of or behind the bridge, or on the bridge itself (as in fig.14).

During the Renaissance chords were usually played with the thumb on the bass, playing downwards, and the first and second, or the first, second and third fingers, playing upwards. For chords of more than four

14. Ten-course lute with all the strings on one head: painting 'The Singing Lute Player' (1624) by Hendrick Terbruggen (National Gallery, London); note the right-hand little finger on the bridge, and the thicker octave strings of the bass courses; the right hand is now almost at right angles to the strings; note also the overhanging nut, carrying the lowest course outside the neck

notes the following procedure was given by Le Roy and Besard; for five-note chords the thumb plays the bass downwards, the third and fourth courses are raked upwards by the first finger, and the first and second courses are played respectively by the third and second fingers; six-note chords are played in a similar way with the thumb playing downwards across both the sixth and fifth courses. The upper note of two-part chords was generally taken by the second finger, although Robinson preferred the third.

A single dot under a chord of two or three notes generally means that it is played upwards with the usual fingers, but without the thumb. Gerle, however, used a dot under a chord to show that all the notes were to be played upwards with the first finger, while Judenkünig said that in dance music chords may be stroked or strummed with the thumb throughout. Neusidler also mentioned the 'thumb-stroke'. Robinson, however, made use of the fingers in a more natural way. He advocated the third finger for notes farthest from the thumb, the second for the next note, and the first for those nearest. Besard was the first writer to describe a new position for the thumb; his directions are translated as follows in Dowland's book of 1610:

stretch out your Thombe with all the force you can, especially if thy Thombe be short, so that the other fingers may be carryed in the manner of a fist, and let the Thombe be held higher than them, this in the beginning will be hard. Yet they which have a short Thombe may imitate those which strike the strings with the Thombe under the other fingers, which though it be nothing so elegant, yet to them it will be more easie.

The length of stretch is greatly increased by the extended position of the thumb, which was introduced perhaps in connection with the addition of a ninth course. The increase in the number of courses was probably also responsible for a general shift in the position and movement of the hand. Besard suggested:

the first two fingers may be used in Diminutions very well insteed of the Thombe and the fore-finger, if they be placed with some Bases, so that the middle finger be in place of the Thombe, which Thombe whilst it is occupied in striking at least the Bases, both the hands will be graced and that unmanly motion of the Arme (which many cannot well avoide) shall be shunned. But if with the said Diminutions there be not set Bases which are to be stopped, I will not counsell you to use the two first fingers, but rather the Thombe and the forefinger: neither will I wish you to use the two fore-fingers if you be to proceede (that is to runne) into the fourth, fift or sixt string with Diminutions set also with some parts.

Markings for the use of the second finger occur in many manuscripts from the early 17th century. Vallet used a special sign for the second finger consisting of two small strokes under the note. With the increasing number of bass strings more attention was paid to the thumb. Piccinini described an *apoyando* stroke:

The thumb, on which I do not approve of a very long nail, must be employed in this manner, that every time you sound a string you must direct it towards the soundboard, so that it is crushed onto the string below, and it must be kept there until it has to be used again.

This type of stroke was mentioned by other writers and appears to have become standard practice during the Baroque period. In fact, such a technique is almost essential when the thumb has to make rapid jumps among a number of diapasons. If the thumb is held free, no point of reference is provided from which each movement can be judged accurately.

In the second decade of the 17th century many new technical devices began to appear. Bataille's *Airs de différents autheurs* (iv, 1613) used a dot for a quasi-*rasgueado* device (see ex.1) that is described by Mersenne: the dot at the top of the chord stands for an upward stroke with the first finger, while the dot at the bottom stands for a downward stroke with the back of the same finger. For this device Jacques Gallot (*Pièces de luth*, after 1670) placed dots before each of the notes of the chord for the upward stroke and dots behind for the downward.

Ex.1

Italy was apparently the first country in which the slur was developed as part of normal technique instead of being confined to the execution of graces. Pietro Paoli Melii (*Intavolatura di liuto attiorbato libro secondo*, 1614) described the action of the left hand, and placed a ligature under pairs of notes to be slurred, a marking which was always used to indicate the slur. There seems to be no evidence that the slur was used in France, England or Germany at this early date, but Mersenne described it in 1636.

Piccinini introduced some individualistic traits into his playing: although the use of the nails was deprecated by nearly all writers, Piccinini said that they should be 'a little long, in front of the flesh, but not much, and oval in shape'. He played the rapid '*groppo* that is made at the cadence' with the first finger alone, striking upwards and downwards with the tip of the nail. (This is similar to the vihuela's 'dedillo', which was usually played with short nails.) He also advocated a change of tone colour by moving the right hand nearer or farther from the bridge. In France an increasing number of different right-hand strokes were used. Mersenne gave the traditional fingerings both for chords and single-note passages, and some new strokes which had evidently become popular by then. He described several ways of playing chords, and a system of marking by which each method could be distinguished. Some chords were played downwards with the thumb; others with all the notes played by the thumb except the top one which was played by the first finger; others with the thumb playing the single bass note while the first finger raked the rest of the notes upwards. Many of these devices became part of the French Baroque style, and in volumes such as Denis Gaultier's *Pièces de luth* (1670), Denis and Ennemond Gaultier's *Livre de tablature des pièces de luth* (1672) and Jacques Gallot's *Pièces de luth*, markings are given for arpeggiating or 'breaking' chords. Some writers described the 'slipping' of the first finger across two notes on adjacent strings; this was shown by two different markings (ex.2).

Ex.2

Many of these techniques were carefully described in English lute books such as the Mary Burwell Lute Tutor (*c*1660–67) and in Mace's *Musick's Monument*. Similar techniques were passed on to the German school; the same variety of strokes is described by Baron who also mentioned a change of right-hand position for tone colour. As in other countries, German sources vary greatly in the extent to which technique marks were added to the tablature.

The development of playing technique was thus closely related to the continual process of extending the resources of the instrument. Moreover, each technique produces particular qualities suited to its own time, and the modern lutenist must know this in order to do justice to the music.

6. ORNAMENTATION. The use of what in modern terms would be called trills, mordents, appoggiaturas and vibrato has evidently always been an integral part of the performance of lute music. The fact that ornament signs are frequently not included in printed books or manuscripts and are written about comparatively rarely in early tutors may be due to several causes; probably the most important was that there was a living tradition that was considered unnecessary to mention or notate. Another reason may have been that cited by Mersenne, namely that printers lacked the requisite signs in their equipment. These ornaments never acquired a standardized nomenclature or system of signs, although some degree of conformity developed towards the end of the Baroque period.

In the Capirola Lutebook (*c*1517), the earliest known source of information, two signs are used: one shows figures notated with red dots; the other consists of two red dots placed over the figure. Of the first sign it is said only that the finger on the lower fret is held firm and another finger is used to 'tremolize' on or from the fret above. The second sign is said to indicate that the note is 'tremolized' with a single finger; it probably represents a mordent.

More precise information was given by Pietro Paolo Borrono in the second printing (Milan, 1548) of the *Intavolatura di lauto*. Ex.3 shows how the ornaments are indicated; Borrono described their execution as follows:

Where a circle is found (O), two fingers must be placed on the string and the finger on the lesser number must be held firm. Pull down the string with the finger which is on the higher number as if the voice were notated on the lesser of the two frets. This is done because the lute will sound sweeter. But the said circle is one stroke only.

Ex.3

In 1550 R. Wyssenbach of Zurich printed a transcription in German tablature of part of the contents of the Francesco–Borrono book of 1546; the half circles are said to indicate *mordanten*, but no further explanation is given. The word *mordanten* appears to have been used in German as a general term for ornaments rather than as a specific term for any one type of ornament. It occurs in Martin Agricola's *Musica instrumentalis deudsch* (1528) and was still used by Matthäus Waissel in his *Lautenbuch darinn von der Tabulatur und Application der Lauten* (1592). Waissel's remark that the fingers are put 'a little later on the letters and moved up and down two or three times' indicates (as was also suggested by Borrono's description) that the ornament came on or after the beat and not before.

No information appears to have survived concerning ornamentation of French lute music before Besard, who made the following remark:

You should have some rules for the sweet relishes and shakes if they could be expressed here, as they are on the LUTE: but seeing they cannot by speech or writing be expressed, thou wert best to imitate some cunning player.

Vallet used two signs: a comma, signifying a fall from above the main note (upper appoggiatura), and a single cross, signifying the same thing repeated several times, i.e. a trill. In his *Regia pietas* (1620) Vallet described what is in effect a vibrato and used a double cross to indicate its position.

Mersenne gave the most complete exposition of the art of ornamentation of the period. Excluding minor variants (such as whether a tone or semitone is involved), seven ornaments may be tallied: the *tremblement* (trill); the *accent plaintif* (appoggiatura from below, equal in duration to half the value of the main note); the *martelement* or *soupir* (mordent); the *verre cassé* (vibrato, which Mersenne said was not much used in his time, although it was very popular in the past; in his opinion, however, it would be as bad a fault to omit it altogether as to use it to excess); the *battement* (long trill, more suitable to the violin, he said, than to the lute); a combination (for which no name is given) of appoggiatura from below with trill from above; and a mordent ending with *verre cassé*. He gave a sign to indicate each of the seven types, but remarked that in French music the small comma was generally used to 'express all sorts'.

In Italy, Kapsberger (*Libro primo d'intavolatura di chitarrone*, 1604) placed two dots above many notes to indicate the *trillo*, and also added a sign (an oblique stroke with a dot on either side) below certain chords to show that they were to be arpeggiated. Melii marked the notes on which a 'tremolo' should be performed, but gave no explanation of the meaning of the word, though he described a method of performing an appoggiatura from below by sliding the auxiliary to the main note with a single finger. This is indicated by a ligature above the two notes and appears to be unique in this period. Piccinini, however, gave detailed descriptions of the trill, the mordent and the vibrato, which he called the first, second and third tremolo, but he did not include signs for them in the tablature.

Early English manuscript sources show no ornament signs, but all the books copied by Matthew Holmes contain ornaments, although his placing of the signs is often curious. At least 17 other manuscripts also have signs, and William Barley's *A Newe Booke of Tabliture* (1596) includes the double cross, but with no explanation of its meaning. The only English book of this period containing information on the subject is Robinson's *The Schoole of Musicke* (1603). He gave no signs nor any indication of where the graces should be placed, but he described three that could be used: the relish (perhaps an appoggiatura from above, or a trill); the fall (an appoggiatura from below); and a fall with a relish (possibly the same as Mersenne's combination of lower appoggiatura and upper trill). Robinson said of the relish:

The longer the time of a single stroke . . . the more need it hath of a relish, for a relish will help, both to grace it, and also it helps to continue the sound of the note his full time: but in a quicke time a little touch or jerke will serve, and that only with the most strongest finger.

The variety of graces in use around 1625 is indicated in Table 1, taken from the Margaret Board Lutebook (f.32). Generally, however, the lack of standardization in signs and the absence of any indication of their meaning as used by different scribes poses a formidable problem in interpretation, and it is possible only to offer suggestions based on a study of their context in all the available material. Table 2 shows the signs most generally found in English manuscript sources. Sign (*a*) is often the only sign in a manuscript, and, like the French comma, can be taken 'to express all sorts'. If it appears

TABLE 1

,	a pull back
.	a fall forward
χ	to beat down the finger with a shake
:	three pricks to be struck upward with one finger
#	for a long shake
c	for a slide

in company with other signs it seems to signify an ornament from above the main note, perhaps an appoggiatura or trill. Sign (*b*) indicates an appoggiatura from below, a mordent, or a slide (the ornament that comes up to the main note from a minor or major 3rd below). Sign (*c*) appears in the Sampson Lutebook; its possible interpretation as a slide on a major 3rd is discussed below. Sign (*d*) indicates an appoggiatura from below, in the Sampson Lutebook; this is suggested by the fact that the sign appears before a note which is followed by (*a*), presumably indicating Robinson's 'fall with a relish'. Sign (*e*) is used similarly (*US-Ws* 1610.1). Signs (*f*) and (*g*) (the latter from *GB-Lbm* Add.38539) indicate a mordent, appoggiatura from below or a slide. Sign (*h*) occurs in a limited number of pieces in *GB-Lbm* Add.38539, always on a note immediately preceded by the note above, and often in fairly fast runs. This may

TABLE 2

(a) #	(b) •	(c) +	(d) ׀	(e) :	(f) ⊦
(g) ×	(h) ⸍	(i) ⒫#	(j) :#	(k) •#	

be the 'little touch or jerke' mentioned by Robinson, or possibly an inverted mordent. Although this ornament was clearly described in Spain from the time of Tomás de Santa Maria (in *Arte de tañer fantasia assi para tecla como para vihuela*, 1565) to Pablo Nassare (*Escuela musica*, 1724), in Italy by Girolamo Diruta (*Il Transilvano*, 1593) and in Germany by Praetorius (*Syntagma musicum*, iii, 2/1619), there is no mention of it in any English source. It would, however, fit into the passages in which the sign is used. Signs (*i*), (*j*) and (*k*) indicate a fall with a relish. In compositions in John Dowland's hand, (*c*), which appears on both open and stopped notes, presumably indicates an upper appoggiatura or trill; (*f*), which appears on stopped notes only, may indicate an appoggiatura from below; and (*b*), which appears on open notes only, may indicate a trill.

A curious feature of the appoggiatura in England is the fact that it remained short, consisting of only a quarter of the value of the main note, right up to the time of the printing of Purcell's *The Harpsichord Master* (1697), where it is given in the 'Rules for Graces' as a semiquaver followed by a dotted quaver. On the Continent, meanwhile, it had gradually lengthened. Praetorius (*Syntagma musicum*, iii, 2/1619) showed the appoggiatura as taking one third of the length of the main note, and Mersenne (*Harmonie universelle*, 1636–7) described it as half the length of the main note.

Evidently, then, Renaissance ornaments were of a simple character and the frequency of their use was to a certain extent a matter of personal choice. Fashion may have varied from country to country; English players of the first two decades of the 17th century graced their music perhaps to a greater extent than those in any other part of Europe. A Fantasie by Dowland (*GB-Lbm* Add. 38539, f.14*v*; see ex.4), with nine ornaments in the space of five bars, is typical of English practice.

Ex.4 Dowland: Fantasie, *GB-Lbm* Add.38539, f.14*v*

No exact line of demarcation can be drawn between Renaissance and Baroque ornamentation. Most graces used in the earlier period continued in favour, but a few more elaborate combinations appeared. From Mersenne's time onwards, French manuscripts have a large variety of signs: the comma, 'x' and 'v' for *martelements*, something like an ordinary mordent sign placed under a note, and, to indicate the appoggiatura from below, a bow-like sign placed beneath the tablature letter, identical with Mace's sign for a slur (see Table 3). Double shakes or appoggiaturas began to appear. In many cases, however, the interpretation is uncertain and each case has to be judged according to context. The *étouffement* (Mace's 'tut') is also mentioned in some sources, and the sign 'x' is used. Mace's *Musick's Monument*, in many ways the most thorough study of the French lute ever written, includes (pp.101ff) a complete list of the ornaments he customarily used. The information given by Mace appears in Table 3. He also wrote of loud and soft play and the use of the pause as additional graces to be observed.

In Denis Gaultier's *Pièces de luth* (1670) less elaboration is found. The two ornaments given are indicated by the comma and the slur and are equivalent to Mace's back-fall and fore-fall. In *Livre de tablature des pièces de luth* by Denis and Ennemond Gaultier (1672) the explanation of the comma shows that the number of falls should be increased according to the length of the note. Three ornament signs are listed by Gallot: *tremblement*, or trill, indicated by a small comma after the tablature letter; *martelement*, or mordent, indicated by 'v'; *choutte*, or *tombé*, an appoggiatura from below, indicated by an inverted 'v' before the letter. Both Gallot's and Gaultier's books show the typical oblique line through chords to denote the 'breaking'.

German Baroque lutenists used many of the French signs. Esaias Reusner (ii), several of whose books appeared in the last quarter of the 17th century, used a cross and a comma but did not explain their meaning. The context in each case suggests that the comma indicates a trill and the cross a vibrato. He indicated the appoggiatura by the bow under a letter. Le Sage de Richée gave, together with other information about performing practice, three ornaments: the trill indicated by a comma; the appoggiatura from above, which he called *Abzug*; and the appoggiatura from below, which he called *Fall*. Both appoggiaturas are indicated by the bow under the letters. Wenzel Ludwig von Radolt, in his *Die aller treueste, verschwigneste und nach sowohl fröhlichen als traurigen humor* (1701), provided an exhaustive list, extracts from which are shown in Table 4. Baron (1727) used the same signs as Radolt for the appoggiaturas from above and below and for the trill, but in addition described two forms of vibrato: one (on the higher strings) performed with the thumb released from the back of the neck, the other with the thumb held firm. He called these *Mordanten* and *Bebungen* and indicated them with a double and single slanted cross. He also described the

use of ornamental *toni intermedii* to connect two distant notes, as in ex.5 (p.566). Baron added that the ornaments he mentioned were not the only ones that could be used; as many more could be added with the use of skill and taste.

Adam Falckenhagen, Rudolf Straube, the Weiss

TABLE 3

shake		a trill. According to the instructions this would begin on the main note. Two forms are given, the 'Tearing-Shake', executed by 'scratching' the string with the appropriate finger of the left hand 'with the Tip (near the Nail)'; and the 'Soft-Shake' which is executed by 'Beating the String' only.
beate		a mordent
back-fall		an appoggiatura from above
half-fall		an appoggiatura from below
whole-fall		a slide, through a major or minor 3rd.
elevation		to be made on the middle note of three:

ascending — the explanation

descending — the explanation

∴ **single relish**

ascending — the explanation

descending — the explanation

⁘ **double relish** — Strictly speaking this is not an ornament in the sense in which the word is used here. It is a combination of fingered notes analogous to the fingered trills often found at a cadence in Renaissance lute music.

the plain notes

the explanation

⌣ **slur and slide** — Upward and downward legato; a technical device rather than an ornament.

/ **spinger** — After the main note has been struck, just before the following note is played, a finger of the left hand is 'dabbed' lightly on the string, one or two frets below, so that 'only a small tincture of a New Note' is heard.

⨭ **sting** — Vibrato. Mace describes it as 'not *Modish* in *These Days*', but he goes on to explain how it is performed.

: **tut** — This consists of stopping the sound of a note with a finger of the right hand immediately after it has been played.

TABLE 4

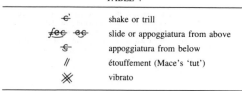

$\text{\textcent}$	shake or trill
$\text{\textcent}\text{\textcent}$ $\text{\textcent}\text{\textcent}$	slide or appoggiatura from above
$\text{\textcent}$	appoggiatura from below
//	étouffement (Mace's 'tut')
※	vibrato

brothers, Johan Kropffganss, David Kellner and others of the period all used a set of signs codified in Johann Christian Beyer's *Herrn Prof. Gellerts Oden* (1760), as shown in Table 5. Occasionally a composer might adopt an individualistic use of a sign, such as in ex.6 where the comma obviously indicates a long trill. A source of particular interest is the manuscript tablature copy of Bach's Lute Suite in G minor written out by the lutenist J. C. Weyrauch either during Bach's life or very soon after his death, containing many of the same signs.

Ex.5

Ex.6

However, the one which resembles Radolt's sign for the *étouffement* almost certainly stands for the *semi-trillo*. A noticeable feature is the frequent use of ornaments in the slower movements and their scarcity in the faster ones: this conforms with other music of the period.

From the early years of the 16th century to the end of the 18th, the use of graces was an integral part of performing practice on the lute. Because of its lack of sustaining power (compared with bowed instruments)

these devices were essential, and tablatures in which the signs appear suggest that probably more graces were added than in music for any other instrument. Finally the necessity promoted the fashion and composers expected graces to be added, whether or not they were actually indicated.

During the 17th and 18th centuries the art of ornamentation received careful attention in numerous treatises on singing and on playing various instruments, and also in composers' prefaces to their works; this valuable information is often applicable to the lute as well as to the particular subject under consideration (*see* ORNAMENTS).

7. REPERTORY. From the 1270s, when Jehan de Meung in *Le roman de la rose* mentioned 'quitarres e leüz', the presence of the lute in western Europe is evident in literary sources, court records and inventories. The Duke of Orleans is said to have had in his service in 1396 'un joueur de vièle et de luc' called Henri de Ganière. The names of a few players from other parts of Europe have also survived, such as a certain Obrecht in Basle in 1363, and the brothers Drayer, minstrels at Mechlin from 1371 to 1374. During the 14th century, representations of the lute in drawings, paintings and sculpture became common, often in combination with other instruments, sometimes accompanying one or more voices.

Extant 15th-century records mention sums of money paid to lute players in service at the French court. In 1491 for example, Antoine Her, a lute player of the chamber royal, received a monthly stipend of 10 livres and 10 sols. The great esteem in which virtuosos were held is evident in the case of Pietrobono, who served the Este family at the court of Ferrara from about 1440 until his death in 1497. Other courts competed for his services; he was widely travelled, became a rich man and was celebrated by poets and writers of the time (including Tinctoris). Surviving documents imply that he accompanied himself in singing and that he was associated with another player who was listed as a 'tenorista' – possibly another lute player or a viol player who, in either case, would have supplied a 'tenor' against which

TABLE 5

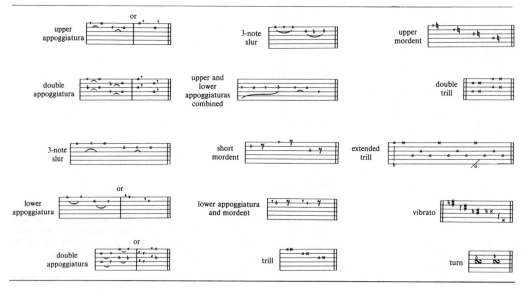

Pietrobono would have improvised. He seems to exemplify an age in which Italian lute players were passing from a style that had been mainly improvisatory to one in which, as Tinctoris suggested, a full training in the technique of contrapuntal writing or playing was essential.

This development was associated with the change from playing the lute with a plectrum to using the right-hand fingers. Whereas previously the lute had been a melodic instrument, it could now be used for polyphony. This in turn soon led to the invention of special forms of notation to overcome the particular problems involved in transmitting the music to the written or printed page. Recently examples of German and Italian tablatures from the end of the 15th century have come to light, but these fragments reveal little about the early repertory. In addition, there are in the Segovia Cathedral manuscript some instrumental duos with elaborate divisions by Tinctoris, Agricola and Roelling that well suit the lute and clearly reflect the improvisational demands on players of the time; some of the compositions in the earliest printed sources show a similar style. In the Baroque period the lute and similar plucked string instruments were widely used as CONTINUO instruments.

(i) Italy. The Venetian printing press of Petrucci distributed music by the early composers of the great Italian school, whose influence was felt throughout Europe for the entire 16th century. Petrucci published six volumes of lute tablature between 1507 and 1511. The first two books, entitled *Intabulatura de lauto* (1507), contain works by Spinacino, mainly for solo lute but there are also a few duets. There are 25 pieces called 'recercare' but most of the pieces are intabulations of Flemish chansons (from the 1490s) originally for voices. The *Intabulatura de lauto, libro tertio* (1508) is now lost; the *Libro quarto* by Dalza (1508; ed. H. Mönkemeyer, 1967) contains dances and a few intabulations of frottolas by contemporary Italians such as Tromboncino. These books include rudimentary instructions for tablature reading and right-hand technique. Songs for solo voice and lute appeared in the *Tenori e contrabassi intabulati col sopran in canto figurato per cantar e sonar col lauto* (*Libro primo*, 1509; *Libro secundo*, 1511), in which the lutenist Franciscus Bossinensis intabulated the lower parts of frottolas whose vocal originals had already been printed by Petrucci. The first book contains 70 such compositions, the second 56; each contains 20 or more ricercares as well. The six Petrucci volumes form a substantial collection of first-rate music in what must have been a well-established tradition of lute writing. The types of composition they contain evidently reflect the unwritten procedures of late 15th-century lute playing. The 'first phase' of Italian printed books for lute included one more collection of frottolas with voice part and tablature, by Tromboncino and Marchetto Cara. The sole extant copy is undated, but it certainly appeared in the 1520s.

The earliest example of Italian lute music probably consists of the two pieces found in Bologna by Hans T. Davis and described in his paper 'An Italian Tablature Lesson of the Renaissance' (American Musicological Society, Boston, 1958; unpublished). They are written out in a copy of Pietro Borgi's *Chi de arte matematiche ha piacere* (Venice, 1484), whose first page gives an explanation of the tablature headed 'La mano ala viola'. There has been some discussion about the meaning of

'viola' in this instance but, since the discovery of Francesco Canova da Milano's *Intavolatura de viola o vero lauto* (Naples, 1536/R1977), it is clear that it refers to the flat-backed, waisted instrument which closely resembles the Spanish vihuela and which was considered suitable for playing lute music. The form of tablature used in this case is the rare 'Intavolatura alla Napolitana' in which the second volume of Francesco's book is printed and which is explained in Michele Carrara's *Regola ferma e vera* (Rome, 1585). In appearance it resembles Italian tablature but it is the reverse way up, with the figures for the lowest course lying on the bottom line of the staff. The figure 1 is used throughout for the open course. Here, surprisingly, a seven-line staff is shown.

Two manuscripts survive from the first two decades of the 16th century; the earliest (c1505; *F-Pn* Rés.Vmd.ms.27) contains 25 pieces for solo lute and 89 accompaniments to vocal pieces. Although the cantus part is not given many of these can be identified and are listed in the facsimile *Tablature de luth italienne* (1981). The other manuscript, the Capirola Lutebook (c1517), is beautifully written and includes instructions for playing and the use of ornamentation (see §6 above); the composer, Vincenzo Capirola, was clearly a great master.

Capirola is the outstanding figure of the earliest period of written lute music; the acknowledged leader of the 'second phase' was Francesco Canova da Milano. He was already famous for his remarkable skill at improvisation (his contemporaries often referred to him as 'Il divino') when his first works were published: *Intabolatura di liuto* (Venice, 1536), and the abovementioned *Intavolatura de viola o vero lauto*. Some 120 to 150 of his compositions are known today; many continued to appear in print until late in the century and also appeared in manuscript collections in several countries besides Italy. Francesco's lute music consists chiefly of pieces entitled ricercare or fantasia. He expanded the scope of the quasi-improvisatory ricercare of the older generation of composers often making greater use of sequence, imitation and repetition, and sometimes writing in the strictly contrapuntal style that became characteristic of the ricercare during and after the latter part of the 16th century. There are also intabulations of chansons and other vocal works. Most of these were published after Francesco's death; they seem to be corrupt versions and may well represent the attempts of other musicians to write down from memory performances they had heard him improvise. (For a modern edition of Francesco's lute works see *The Lute Music of Francesco Canova da Milano (1497–1543)*, ed. A. J. Ness, 1970.)

Borrono published several collections of his own works and those of Francesco from 1546 onwards. He wrote both fantasias and dances for the lute and was one of the first to use printed ornament signs. Also in 1546 a large number of publications appeared containing works by minor composers such as Giulio Abondante, Melchiore de Barberiis, Giovanni Maria da Crema, Marc'Antonio Pifaro, Antonio Rotta and Francesco Vindella.

Among the great number of Italian composers for the lute working in the second half of the 16th century, none reached the stature of Francesco Canova da Milano, although Giacomo Gorzanis (from 1561 to 1579) and Simone Molinaro (1599) published some excellent works.

All the current types of composition are represented in their works: ricercares and fantasias in the contrapuntal style developed by Francesco; intabulations of vocal originals; settings of dances, including the various popular grounds such as the *passamezzo antico*, the *passamezzo moderno* and the romanesca, as well as other famous tunes of the time. Much of this music was for solo lute, but a collection of dances for three lutes by Giovanni Pacoloni, long thought to have been lost, survives in an edition printed by Pierre Phalèse in Antwerp in 1564. Until the middle of the 16th century, lute music was generally within the prevailing modal ideas of the time, although some composers occasionally departed from strict modal structure. In 1567, however, Gorzanis produced a remarkable manuscript of 24 passamezzos, each with its accompanying saltarello, in all the major and minor keys, rising in chromatic succession.

Vincenzo Galilei was another important figure of the period, though less as a composer than as a writer; his theoretical and practical studies are contained in books printed between 1568 and 1584. Diomedes Cato and Lorenzini were outstanding composers, each with a very personal style. The latter was known as 'equitus romanus' and may have been 'the Knight of the Lute' mentioned by Robert Dowland. The distinguished composer Giovanni Terzi published two books of fine music (1593 and 1599) – fantasias, vocal intabulations and dances – mainly for solo lute but including music for two and four lutes as well as lute parts to be played with other instruments.

(ii) Germany, Bohemia and Austria. The largest German songbook of the 15th century is the Königstein Liederbuch (*D-Bds* germ.qu.719; ed. P. Sappler, *Münchner Texte und Untersuchungen zur deutschen Literatur des Mittelalters*, xx, 1970). The melodies for the songs are written in normal German tablature for a five-course lute, the numbers 1 to 5 representing the open courses, from the lowest upwards. The letters *a* to *e* represent the first frets, *f* to *k* the second and so on, no staff being needed. It was probably written not later than 1473 and thus appears to be the earliest surviving lute tablature (see Tischler, 1974). Outside Italy the first printed lute music appeared in the Germanic states of the Holy Roman Empire. Virdung included instructions for the lute and one piece as a pedagogical illustration. Schlick's *Tabulaturen etlicher Lobgesang und Liedlein* (1512) contains 14 songs for voice and lute and three solo pieces. Judenkünig's *Utilis et compendiaria introductio* (c1515–19) and *Ain schone kunstliche Underweisung* (1523) both include instructions for playing as well as music. The first contains solo lute intabulations of settings of Horace's odes by Peter Tritonius published for voices in 1507, together with other similar pieces and dance music; the second is a mixture of dances, lute versions of vocal originals, and five pieces called 'Priamel', corresponding to the Italian ricercare. Gerle (1532) gave instructions and music for viol and rebec as well as for lute; his book was reprinted in 1537, and in 1546 a revised and enlarged edition was published. His *Tabulatur auff die Laudten* (1533) comprises music for solo lute, including intabulations and pieces entitled 'Preambel'.

The publications of Hans Neusidler began with his book of 1536. He was the first writer of instruction books to show real pedagogic talent; not only did he give clear instructions for both right and left hands, but his pieces are carefully graduated, leading the beginner by gentle degrees through the initial difficulties. Two modified tunings are found in his work: one, known as 'Abzug', consisted in lowering the sixth course by a tone, and the other was used in the famous Judentanz. (The scordatura notation of this piece has been misread by some scholars, who thereby mistook it for an early example of polytonality.)

Collections of music in German tablature continued to be printed until 1592, some under the name of the publisher, such as those of Rudolf Wyssenbach (1550) and Bernhard Jobin (1572), others by composer, collector or arranger, such as Sebastian Ochsenkun (1558), Matthäus Waissel (1573, 1591, 1592) and Wolff Heckel (including music for two lutes, 1556, 1562). A total of about 20 or 30 volumes appear to have been printed. Most of these show considerable influence from Italian, French and even Spanish music of the time.

After 1592, German publications for the lute used either Italian or French tablature, although German tablature continued in manuscript sources until about 1620. Important printed collections were those of Adrian Denss (*Florilegium*, 1594), Matthius Reymann (*Noctes musicae*, 1598) and Johann Rude (*Flores musicae*, 1600); these are extensive collections of pieces from the international repertory, and similar compilations continued to appear in the 17th century. An important anthology published in Cologne was Besard's *Thesaurus harmonicus*. Others were those of Georg Leopold Fuhrmann (*Testudo Gallo-Germanica*, Nuremberg, 1615), Elias Mertel (*Hortus musicalis*, Strasbourg, 1615), and Johann Daniel Mylius (*Thesaurus gratiarum*, Frankfurt am Main, 1622). Another important publication was Michelangelo Galilei's *Il primo libro d'intavolatura di lauto* (Munich, 1620), which, unlike most other publications of the time, was devoted to works by one composer.

After a period of comparative inactivity in 17th-century Germany, there was a revival of interest in the lute among Baroque composers, which continued until late in the 18th century. Among these musicians were Le Sage de Richée (*fl* c1695), French by birth but living in Breslau; Ernst Gottlieb Baron (1696–1760), already mentioned as an early historian of the lute; Jacques Bittner (possibly the same as Jacob Büttner) (works of 1682 and 1683); Adam Falckenhagen (published works, c1742, and manuscript works, 1756); and Sylvius Leopold Weiss (1686–1750), the most prolific composer of his day for the lute and a great master of his instrument; there is some very fine music among his numerous compositions, mostly manuscript; he worked at Dresden and was acquainted with Bach.

Bach's solo works for the lute still provoke discussion: some may have been written for the gut strung harpsichord (known as the 'Lautenclavicymbel' or 'Lautenwerk'), but there can be no doubt that the lute was intended in the *St John Passion* and the *Trauerode*. The Leipzig manuscript of the Suite in G minor, in French tablature and fully marked with ornament signs and indications of right-hand technique, provides a valuable guide to the style in which Bach's contemporaries would have played his music on the lute.

Compositions for the lute at this time often took the form of suites, generally beginning with a prelude and continuing with an arrangement of various dance forms selected from among those fashionable at the time, such as the minuet, courante, allemande, polonaise, bourrée and gigue. Some composers went outside these conventional forms and introduced freer types of movement with titles descriptive only of the tempo, such as Largo, Andante, Allegretto or Presto. The fantasia was by now very different from its Renaissance ancestor. Often unbarred, it was composed in an extremely free manner and generally showed no trace of the contrapuntal structure so typical of the 16th- and early 17th-century fancy. A fine example of this type of work is E. G. Baron's lute fantasia (in E. G. Baron and F. Seidel: *Fantasia für die Laute*; *12 Menuetten für die Laute*, Leipzig, 1757).

Works for combinations of instruments such as two lutes, lute and violin, and lute and flute became popular, as did music for small chamber ensembles consisting of various wind and string instruments together with the lute. Concertos, sonatas and partitas were composed by Joachim Bernhard Hagen (*fl* 1766), Adam Falckenhagen, August Kühnel (*b* 1645), Wolff Lauffensteiner (1676–1754) and many others.

In Bohemia Aureus Dix (1669–1719) wrote some sonatas and suites, and Iwan Jelinek wrote a 'Lautenpartie' for lute, horn, violin and bass. Karl Kohaut (1726–84), the best-known lutenist of his time in Austria, composed a number of works for small chamber ensemble. Haydn arranged two of his string quartets to include an obbligato lute. The last work written for any member of the lute family before the entire family disappeared into temporary obscurity was a set of 12 variations for the 13-course theorbo by Christian Gottlieb Scheidler (*d* 1815) on a theme by Mozart, inspired by the first performance of *Don Giovanni* in Prague in 1787.

(iii) France. The earliest French tablature appears in a manuscript (*I-PESo* 1144 (*olmi*)). When opened it is heart-shaped. Folios 25–87, the oldest part of the book, contain a number of pieces in French tablature on a six-line staff. The manuscript is considered to date from between 1490 and 1500 (see Rubsamen, 1968). The first printed French tablature, using a five-line staff, appeared in Guillaume Vorsterman's *Livre plaisant et tres utile* (Antwerp, 1529), a translation of Virdung's book of 1511. Virdung's musical example was replaced with the Flemish chanson *Een vrolic wesen* (in organ tablature and staff notation as well as for lute). Also in 1529 Pierre Attaingnant at Paris printed his *Tres breve et familière introduction*; his *Dixhuit basses dances* of 1530 contained some 66 lute pieces (for a modern edition of some of Attaingnant's music, see *Preludes Chansons and Dances for the Lute*, ed. D. Heartz, 1964).

Between 1551 and 1596 Adrian Le Roy printed books of music for guitar and cittern as well as for lute. His surviving lutebooks extend from *Premier livre de tablature de luth* (1551) to *Livre d'airs de cour* (1571) for voice and lute. His instructions for playing the lute survive in English translation, and give an exceptionally clear description of the technique used in France at the time.

Guillaume Morlaye was associated with the printer Michel Fezandat, also of Paris, who brought out not only Morlaye's own works (1552–8) but also those of the Italian, Alberto da Ripa (1552–62). Julien Belin's *Premier livre* (1556) was printed by Nicolas du Chemin, and Jean Paul Paladin's (1560) at Lyons by Simon Gorlier.

In the latter part of the 16th century French music publishing declined somewhat, and few lutebooks were issued except for some reprints of earlier works. With the increase of diapason strings, the use of a five-line

tablature staff gave way to six lines, and around the end of the century further changes began to appear. Somewhat earlier, the term 'à cordes avallées' had been used in one of Gorlier's guitar books to denote the lowering of certain strings. The application of this term to the lute in Anthoine Francisque's *Le trésor d'Orphée* (1600) signified a departure from the basic Renaissance tuning and foreshadowed a period of disintegration in which many composers evolved systems of their own, though the old set of intervals continued in use for some time. The most notable collection of this period was Besard's *Thesaurus harmonicus* (1603). The ten-course lute figured largely in the books of Robert Ballard (ii) (1611, 1614) and of Vallet (1615, 1619, 1620), whose pieces for a quartet of lutes ranging from 'superius' to 'bassus' are of exceptional interest. Other distinguished composers of this period include Victor de Montbuisson, René Mesangeau and Mercure de Lyons. Jacques Gautier and Charles Bocquet were the first representatives of two families destined to play a prominent role in French music for some 50 years.

Together with the increase in the number of diapason strings a marked change of style became apparent. Preludes, courantes, voltes and sarabandes became the favourite forms, and polyphonic structure gave place to a polarization between melody and bass with simple chordal structure – a kind of texture to which the lutesong was particularly amenable. The eight volumes of *Airs de différents autheurs* (1608–18), the first six of which were arranged by Gabriel Bataille, include works by all the finest French songwriters of the time and show the influence of *musique mesurée à l'antique*. Although the exact setting of long and short syllables was not always strict, the verbal rhythms and poetic structure became of prime importance, and the restriction of the bar-line almost entirely disappeared. Many songs of great beauty were written in this style, notably by Pierre Guédron.

Dufaut, Chancy, Belleville, Vincent and several lesser composers were active in the 1630s, a period during which a number of individualistic tunings were in use. Eventually the 'D minor' arrangement and 11 courses of strings predominated (see §4 above). From the 1640s onwards Ennemond Gaultier of Lyons (known as 'le vieux'), Pierre Gautier of Orleans, Denis Gaultier of Paris, Jacques Gallot and Charles Mouton all produced fine music intended for a more flexible type of performance than before (see *La rhétorique des dieux et autres pièces de luth de Denis Gaultier*, ed. A. Tessier, 1932). More rubato was introduced, and playing became more 'expressive'; a variety of strokes and fairly extensive ornamentation were expected even when not specifically indicated in the notation, and the use of *notes inégales* was also left to the taste and discretion of the player. The unbarred prelude, demanding a freedom of interpretation previously unknown, reached a high point of development at this time. Only a small amount of important music was written after about 1680, although Robert de Visée was still writing for the lute, as well as for the guitar, well into the 18th century. In two books printed in 1680 (*Livre de musique pour le luth*, and *Pieces de luth en musique*), Perrine made a determined effort to convert lutenists to the use of staff notation in place of tablature, but with little success. By now the centre of activity had shifted to Germany. (See also *Chansons au luth et airs de cour français du XVIe siècle*, ed. L. de La Laurencie, A. Mairy and G. Thibault, 1934; and

15. *The lutenist Charles Mouton: portrait by Jean François de Troy (1679–1752) in the Musée du Louvre, Paris*

Corpus des luthistes français, a series produced by the CNRS, 1957–.)

An integral characteristic of the music of the French Baroque school was a convention of performance that came to be known as *style brisé*; in many passages the notes of the treble and bass (or other voices) were sounded one after another instead of simultaneously as was the more general practice in polyphonic music. This style exerted a considerable influence over the writing of some French *clavecin* composers and that of Froberger. A related feature was the breaking or arpeggiating of chords that were written plain. This was often indicated by oblique lines placed between the component notes; ex.7 shows the interpretation of these signs given by Perrine in his *Pieces de luth* (1680).

Ex.7

(a) ♪ = ♫ (b) ♪: = ♩ ♪ (c) ♩ = ♩. ♪

(d) ♪: = ♫♪ (e) ♩ = ♫♪ (f) ♪: = ♩ ♫

(iv) The Netherlands, Spain and eastern Europe. In Antwerp Guillaume Vostermann, who had published the French translation of Virdung's *Musica getutscht*, brought out a Flemish translation, *Dit is een zeer schoon boecxken . . . opt clavecordium luyte ende fluyte* (1554, 2/1568). Of greater scope were the activities of Pierre Phalèse, whose first lutebook, *Des chansons reduictz en tabulature de lut* (Louvain, 1545), contained works by many composers. Phalèse, something of a pirate among publishers, specialized in large anthologies of music from all over Europe, collecting vocal as well as instrumental music of many kinds. The only surviving edition of Giovanni Pacoloni's book, with music for three lutes, was published by Phalèse at Louvain in 1564. He later moved his press to Antwerp, where he joined Jean Bellère. Emanuel Adriaensen's books *Pratum musicum*, 1584, and *Novum pratum musicum*, 1592, with other editions up to 1600, were printed by Phalèse at Antwerp, and contain work by other composers besides Adriaensen himself, in arrangements for one to four lutes with and without voices. These books adopted the addition of the sixth line to French tablature.

Joachim van den Hove produced two large collections of works by internationally famous composers: *Florida* (1601) and *Delitiae musicae* (1612). A number of his own compositions appear in the Schele manuscript (*D-Hs*). In 1626 Adriaen Valerius published an unusual collection of music for voice, lute and cittern with or without other instruments called *Nederlandtsche Gedenckclanck*. This was a thinly disguised book of patriotic songs directed against the occupying Spanish forces, using many popular tunes, some of them English.

After the expulsion of the Moors in 1492 the history of the lute in Spain becomes obscure. It was referred to by Bermudo as 'vihuela de Flandes', implying a degree of unfamiliarity. The only extant books of tablature printed in Spain are for the vihuela, which, though tuned to the same intervals as the lute, is a quite distinct instrument. Nevertheless there is much evidence to suggest that the lute was more commonly used than has been generally recognized. The most famous 16th-century east European lutenist was Bálint Bakfark, born in 1507 in Transylvania. He wrote some fine fantasias in the Italian manner, and his great renown as a player took him to various courts and the houses of nobles and magnates all over the Continent. His books testify to his cosmopolitan reputation: *Intabulatura liber primus* (1553) was printed in Italian tablature in Lyons and was partially reprinted as *Premier livre de tabelature de luth* (1564) in French tablature, by Le Roy & Ballard in Paris. His *Harmoniarum musicarum in usum testudinis factarum tomus primus* (1565) was printed in Kraków and reprinted in Antwerp (1569), both editions in Italian tablature. Wojciech Długoraj, born in Poland about 1557, published no books of his own, but his works are found in several collections. Jacob Reys ('Polonois') was also born in Poland, but went to France when quite young and was appointed lutenist to Henri III; his works are mostly found in French anthologies.

(v) England. Little is known about the use of the lute in England before the 14th century. Social development was hardly ripe for the general spread of art music outside the church, the court and a few great houses. Under the Tudors, however (following the Wars of the Roses which ended with the seizure of the English throne by Henry VII), a wealthy middle class began to appear, and the few urban centres of population grew at an unprecedented rate. From the time of Henry VIII onwards, manuscripts containing lute tablature began to appear, though none extant dates from before 1540. Most of the professional lutenists at Henry's court were Flemish or Italian. The three royal children were taught to play, and evidence suggests that in general some amateur performers were beginning to become quite proficient.

The growth of the 'leisured classes' by about the middle of the 16th century led to a demand for instructions for playing the lute, which was best satisfied by printed books. The register of the Stationers' Company records licences to John Alde for *The Sceyence of Lutynge* (1565) and to Robert Ballard for *An Exortation to All Kynde of Men How they shulde Learn to Play of the Lute* (1567), but neither of these is now extant. The first three surviving instruction books in English are all derived from a single French source, Le Roy's *Tres breve et tres familière instruction*, now lost. *A Briefe and easye Instru[c]tion* (1568) 'englished by J. Alford Londenor' contains instructions in the form of rules with music examples, followed by a collection of fantasias and dances. The rules, with certain minor variants, are reprinted as the second part of *A Briefe and Plaine Instruction* (1574), which also teaches 'to set all music of eight divers tunes in Tableture for the Lute' (almost all the examples being chansons by Lassus). The third part comprises a collection of music, quite different from that of 1568, 'conteinynge diverse Psalmes, and manie fine excellente Tunes'; the latter are versions of French chansons that Le Roy had set for voice and lute in his *Livre d'airs de cour* (1571). English Protestant taste (the book is dedicated to Edward Seymore, Earl of Hertford) is catered for by the inclusion of metrical psalm tunes.

Le Roy's instructions were again translated, but without acknowledgment, by William Barley in *A New Booke of Tabliture* (1596), which also contains sections for the orpharion and bandora. This work is the first printed collection for lute by English composers, and includes, in the bandora section of the book, the earliest English solo songs with tablature accompaniment. Robinson's *The Schoole of Musicke* is a thorough lute method, written in the form of a dialogue 'between a Knight, having children to be taught, and Timotheus, who should teach them'. The music that follows is all by Robinson himself, and includes some pieces for two lutes as well as fantasias, dances and settings of popular tunes for solo lute.

The last English instruction book for the Renaissance lute was Robert Dowland's *Varietie of Lute-lessons* (1610), comprising a translation of the instructions from Besard's *Thesaurus harmonicus* (1603) and other observations on lute playing, by John Dowland. These are the only words on the subject that John Dowland left, despite references to 'my father's greater work' in Robert Dowland's other publication of the same year, the songbook *A Musicall Banquet*. The *Varietie* contains a selection of fantasias, pavans, galliards, almains, currants and voltes (by English and continental composers) which must surely have been collected originally by John Dowland on his European travels.

These books, together with a considerably larger body of manuscript collections dating from about 1580 to about 1625, reveal music of the highest quality by composers such as John Johnson, Francis Cutting, Richard Allison, Daniel Bacheler, Philip Rosseter, Robert Johnson (ii), Alfonso Ferrabosco (i) (who spent most of his time in England between about 1562 and 1578), and above all John Dowland whose international fame at this time was unique among lutenists.

Solo lute music circulated mainly in manuscript, but starting with Dowland's *First Booke of Songes* (1597) a series of songbooks for voice and lute was published in England – some 30 volumes averaging about 20 songs apiece. The duration of this vogue was only 25 years (the last collection was John Attey's *First Booke of Ayres* of 1622) but it was responsible for some of the finest English songs of any period. A few of the composers also wrote in the madrigal style, and a few also composed solo lute music; but in general the writers of lute-songs in England kept almost entirely to that genre. Its appeal lay in a direction other than that of madrigals or solo lute music, for it entailed a much more concise setting of the text than the former, and had a less abstract emotional effect than the latter.

Many books of ayres were arranged so that they could be performed either as solo songs with lute and usually bass viol accompaniment, or as partsongs for four voices with lute. The favouring of a sustained bass line to balance the melody in the voice reflects the tendency to think in terms of a polarization of harmonic interest between those two parts. Many collections include lute parts as contrapuntal as the texture of a madrigal, but eventually accompaniments showed a tendency towards simplification, with less imitative part-writing and more straightforward chordal structure. Ultimately this led to the 'continuo song', where only the melody and bass were written down and the lutenist or theorbo player was expected to fill out the harmonies according to certain conventions known as the 'rule of the octave'. The partsong alternative, started by Dowland in his *First Booke* and originally intended to appeal to a public eagerly immersed in madrigal singing, lent a characteristic stamp to the English ayre that makes it quite distinct from anything produced on the Continent. (For a modern edition of some of Dowland's music, see *Collected Lute Music*, ed. D. Poulton and B. Lam, London, 1974.)

Another English use of the lute was in the mixed consort of three melody instruments (treble viol, flute, bass viol) and three plucked (lute, cittern, bandora), a grouping almost certainly conceived originally as an accompaniment to a solo voice somewhat in the manner of the older songs with viols (*see* CONSORT, §2). The treble viol, flute and bass viol played in three-part harmony which, often incomplete on its own, was filled in by the three plucked instruments. The cittern and bandora (both wire-strung) formed the alto, tenor and deep bass, while the lute had a dual role. Much of the music was in dance forms, with repeated sections, in the first of which the lute played chords; but in the repeats the lute played elaborate and rapid 'divisions', giving a silvery, shimmering quality to the music. This technique was known as 'breaking the ground in division'; hence the expression 'broken music'. The light texture of the three melody instruments allowed the lute prominence, while the cittern and the deep bandora provided fullness and body.

Printed collections of music for such a combination include the *First Booke of Consort Lessons* edited by Morley in 1599 and reissued with additional pieces in 1611 (ed. S. Beck, 1959) and Philip Rosseter's 1609 edition of *Lessons for Consort*. No complete set of partbooks has survived for any of the editions. There are, however, two manuscript collections (the Matthew Holmes manuscripts in *GB-Cu* and the Walsingham consort books in *GB-BEV* and *US-OAm*), both also incomplete but whose contents overlap to some extent with those of the printed books. Part of William Leighton's *The Teares or Lamentacions of a Sorrowfull Soule* (1612) is devoted to 'consort songs' set for four voices with the same six instruments.

With the development of the Jacobean and Caroline masque, larger groups of instruments began to appear. In Ben Jonson's *Oberon* (1611) '20 lutes for the Prince's dance' were required, and the description of *Love freed from Ignorance* (1611) tells of the entrance of '12 Musitions that were preestes that songe and played' and '12 other lutes'. The theorbo, said to have been introduced into England by Inigo Jones in 1605, soon found its way into favour in these entertainments. In James Shirley's masque, *The Triumph of Peace* (1633–4), as many as seven lutes and ten theorbos were used.

Soon after the death of John Dowland in 1626, however, the English school of lutenist-composers declined. For some time the popularity of the lute had been overshadowed by that of the lyra viol, which was now cultivated by those amateurs who were avid players of ensemble music for viols. With the coming of Charles I's wife, Queen Henrietta Maria, and her entourage from France, a fashion grew up at court for all things French. The famous lutenist Jacques Gautier arrived from Paris with the Duke of Buckingham in 1617, was appointed to the court in 1619 and soon became popular in London, where he entered the literary circles of writers such as John Donne.

An interesting English manuscript spanning the change from the 'old' lute music of the Elizabethan and Jacobean composers to that of the new French style was compiled by Lord Herbert of Cherbury. It includes music by Dowland, Rosseter, Holborne and other such composers, along with that of Gautier and some compositions of Cherbury himself, the latest dated 1640. Also represented in this manuscript is Cuthbert Hely, who is otherwise virtually unknown. His music is of astonishing intensity: firmly grounded in the earlier English tradition, it nonetheless explores previously untried harmonic territory. Cherbury retained the 'old' tuning of the main six courses despite his interest in the new music and the French lute, but the new tunings are in evidence in other manuscripts, such as the latter part of Jane Pickering's Lutebook where compositions by John Lawrence (*d* c1635) and Gautier demonstrate the 'Harpe way', 'flat way' and 'tuning Gautier'.

With a few exceptions, such as the solos and duos by William Lawes, little music of any great value was written for the lute by English composers up to the time of the Civil War; but Lawes, using the theorbo as thoroughbass in his 'Royal' and 'Harpe' consorts, produced some of the most distinguished instrumental music of his time. During the Commonwealth and at the Restoration, trio sonatas continued to appear for viols or violins with the theorbo specified as a suitable continuo. A set of unnamed pieces for solo theorbo by John Wilson (1595–1674) is of outstanding interest. In his exploration of key structure he followed Gorzanis and anticipated Bach.

Meanwhile, the French lute and music by French composers began to enjoy considerable popularity, although the contents of Richard Mathew's *The Lute's Apology for Her Excellency* (which he claimed was the first printed book for the French lute to appear in England) fall well below the standard of excellence maintained in such manuscript collections as the Hender Robarts Lutebook, the Mary Burwell Lute Tutor and the Panmure Lutebook. These collections show that the works of the Gaultiers, Vincent, Pinel and other distinguished French composers were familiar to English and Scottish players of the second half of the 17th century. An 18th-century repertory for the French lute in Scotland is found in the Balcarres Lutebook, whose approximately 200 pieces consist of dance-tunes and intabulations of Scottish melodies and well-known English songs such as 'Lillibulero' and 'The King Enjoys his Own Again'.

The last great figure in the history of the lute in England was Mace, whose *Musick's Monument* contains the most thorough extant set of instructions for the French lute,

as well as some appealing music. He discussed technique, ornamentation, playing style, stringing, tuning, care of the instrument and many aspects of its history. The section on the theorbo is also valuable.

As a continuo instrument, particularly in accompanying the voice, the theorbo was important throughout the 17th century and well into the first half of the 18th. The theorbo or theorbo-lute is mentioned on the title-pages of many volumes ranging from Angelo Notari's *Prime musiche nuove* (London, c1613) through most of Playford's songbooks to Purcell's *Orpheus Britannicus* (1698–1702), John Blow's *Amphion Anglicus* (1700) and John Eccles's *Songs for One, Two and Three Voices* (1704). Walter Porter included both lutes and theorbos among the accompanying instruments of the consort in his *Madrigales and Ayres* (1632).

The lute and theorbo were used by Handel in a number of his operas, both as continuo and as obbligato in certain arias. There is a particularly beautiful piece of writing for lute in the aria 'The soft complaining flute' in his *Ode for St Cecilia's Day* (1739). According to Burney, the final appearance of the lute in an opera orchestra in England was in the aria 'Due bell'aline' in Handel's *Deidamia* (1741).

Little more is heard of the lute in England in the 18th century, although a few distinguished foreign players are known to have visited London. Among these were Jacob Kremberg and Rudolf Straube, from whom Thomas Gainsborough requested lessons in 1759. The English court had an official lutenist until 1752; the post was abolished in 1846. The latest appearance of any genuine lute music before the modern revival is a manuscript (*GB-Lbm* Add.31698) where some pieces, though written in staff notation, are described as being for the 'Theorboe-Lute' and bear the caption 'Copied in 1813'.

In 1800 a curious anticipation of the modern revival took place, when three publications, allegedly for the lute, appeared in London: Broderip and Wilkinson's *New and Complete Instructions for the Lute*, Mrs. M. A. Bryan's *The Lute of Lisette: an Elegiac Canzonet for the Pianoforte, Harp or Lute* and an arrangement by Joseph Buckinger of Dorothea Jordan's amazingly popular 'The Blue Bells of Scotland' with an 'accompaniment for the pianoforte, harp, guittar or lute'. None of the music itself, however, shows any discernible relationship with the real lute. (For other modern editions of English lute music see the series *English Lute Songs*, London, 1967–71, and *Music for the Lute*, ed. D. Lumsden, 1966–.)

The following lutes are entered in this dictionary: adigidi; akanyembe; alābu sāraṅgī; almérie; amṛtī; amzad; angel lute; arababu; araltu khuur; arbab; arbajo; archlute; arcimandola; arpeggione; arpiguitare; 'arṭaba; bāḍī sāraṅgī; bağlama; bajlama; bajo sexto; balalaika; bambir (ii); bana; banam; banderinha; bandola; bandolim; bandolín; bandora; bandurria; banghu; banhu; banjeaurine; banjo; banjolin; banjo-mandolin; banjo zither; banjú; banjulele; bappe; barbat; baryton (i); bas (ii); basedla; basetla; basetlya; basolya; bassecontre; basse de violon; bassett; bass viol; basy; behalā; bela; belikan; berda; biola; bisaanz; bisernica; bissex; biwa; bjonla; Black Sea fiddle; bocona; bouzouki; bozuk; brač; braga; broancă; bugarija; bulgari; bulgariya; buzuq; çaǧur; cak; campuran; cāpī; cāpī tūc; ca trù cầm; cautara; cavaco; cavaquinho; cellone; ćemane; ceterà; ceterone; cetra; charango; chartar; cheche; chegeni; chianuri; chikuzenbiwa; chikwesa; chillador; chitarȧ; chitarra battente; chitarrone; chizeze; chogur; chongur; chonguri; chör; chungur; chuniri; çifteli; cikka vīṇā; cinco; ćitelija; cithrinchen; citole; citra (i); cittern; cobzȧ; cococello; çöğür; cȯke; colascione; contrȧ; contrabass; contraviolin; crwth trithant; cúʼa; cuatro; cuk; cümbüş; cura; dahu; dai hô; dala-fandīr; dambiro; dambura; danbūro; đàn cò; đàn đáy; đàn đoản; đàn gáo; đàn ghi-ta; đàn nguyệt; đàn nhật; đàn nhi; đàn tam; đàn tầu; đàn tính; đàn tỳ bà; đàn xến; dayuday; đến sin; diabélskie skrzypce; diarka; diassare; di gehu; dihu; dilrubā; divan sazı; dīwān

sāz; djut'ak; dobro; đói căm; dombor; dömbra; dörvön chikhtei
khuur; dotārā; double bass; dra; drunka; ducheke; duduga; dumbra;
dumbrak; durunga; dutār; duwagey; eingeng; ekanāda; ekil; ektār;
endingidi; endingindo; engkerabab; english guitar; english violet;
epske gusle; erhu; erxian; esrāj; faglung; fiddle; finini; fombe; gabbus; gabowie; gabusi; gadulka; gāine sāraṅgī; gakubiwa; gambare;
gambra; gambus; ganabir; ganilka; gaohu; garaya; gardon; gehu;
Geige; gekkin; genbra; genḍing; genkan; geśle; geśliki; gesok-
gesok; geṭṭuvādyam; ghichak; ghirzhak; ghugha; gigue; gimbri; gitara;
git-git; gittern; gjola; gmbri; gnagnour; gnibra; goge; gogen; gogeru;
gologod; goltukh saza; gonje; gordunā; gottan; goṭṭuvādyam; gudok;
guinbri; guitar; guitarillo; guitarra (ii); gujrī; gullum; gulom; gunibri; gurmi; gurumi; gusle; gusli; gutsib; haegŭm; hagēlung; halam
(ii); handbassel; hārangī; Hardanger fiddle; hareubab; harmonicello;
hasapi; Hawaiian guitar; hegit; heikebiwa; hoddu; huapanguera; huibe;
humstrum; hyang-pip'a; hyegŭm; idonongo; igil; ïïkh; ikatala; ikil;
ikili; imzad; indingidi; iningiti; ınzva; ishiriri; isigankuri; ïya-kovïzh;
jamisen; jarana; jinghu; jōra; joze; juan; juk; jumbush; kabak; kabanj;
kabosa; kaburu; kacapi; kacchapī vīṇā; kā duitārā; kakosh; kakoxa;
kalembete; kaligo; kalyakalya; kamāc; kamāicā; k'aman; kamānche;
kambre; karaduzen; karigo; keer; kegbier; keleli; kelutviaq; keman;
kemanche; kemençe; kemene; kementses; kendrā; keronaru; ketadu
mara; khalam; khiil; khuchir; khuuchir; khuur; khyalgasan khuur;
khyrda saza; kiak; kibewe; kigili; kiiki; kijibiwa; kikir; kingiri; kirki; kit; kitaj; kitiar; kízh kízh díhí; kkangkkangi; klompviool; kobza;
kogut; kōjinbiwa; kokā; kokin; kokyū; kologo; komïs; komo; komus;
komuz; konde; koni (i); köni; konimesin; kono (ii); konting; kontrabasharpa; kopanka; kopuz; kora (iii); kotin; krajappī; kroncong;
kubru; kucapi; kūchō; kudlung; kudyapiq; kukuma; kulcapi; kulibao
(ii); kumbo; kundye; kuntigi; kurang; kusyapiq; kutet; kuu; kyuijibiwa; laba hu; lahutē; lasum; laqin; latīf-jo-tanbūro; laúd; lauta; leko;
lha; lira da braccio; liraki; lirica; lirone; litlit; liuqin; liuto romano;
liuye qin; llaute; lokanga; lribab; lục huyền căm; luṭar; lute-guitar;
lyra bastarda; lyra viol; lyra-harpe; machete; mandalone; mandar
bahār; mandolin; mandolin-lute; mandore; marbab; maryna; masenqo;
matou qin; mayūrī; mazanki; mbebe; mbeka; mbike; mejoranera;
métallicorde à archet; meydan sazı; mizhar; mngoli; mogolo; molo;
moolo; morin khuur; mōsōbiwa; mugole; muwattar; muzika-barškalas;
nanduni; nanhu; nārelī; ndere (ii); ngenge; ngime; ngonfi (i); ngulang; nhị huyền; nini; n'jarka; nkoni; nsambi (i); nyaanyooru;
nyckelharpa; nzeze (ii); ohyōn; oktávka; orpharion; orutu; òn-mok-
tayàw; outi; pandoura; panduri; panjtar; pena; penorcon; phīn; pipa
(i); pi shi gong; pivačka tambura; pi-wang; pīzanchī; poliphant; pomsa;
pondiaki lyra; pulluvan vīṇā; punya pratāp vīṇā; pūšļa vijole; pyong;
qanbūs; qeychak; qin-hanzi; qin pipa; qinqin; qobuz; qolta (ii);
Quartgeige; quinterne; quinto (ii); quinton; quwaytara; rabāb; rabe-
ca; rabeka; rabékin; rabel; rabouquin; rajāo; ra'king; ramgyib; ramkie;
rāmsāgar; ravāj; rāvaṇhatthā; rāvaṇa vīṇā; rbab; rebec; regency harp-
lute; remba; requinto; riti; robeka; ruan; sa lõ; samica; samsien;
sananta; sangen; sanshin; sanxian; sapeh; sarān; sarang; sāraṅgī;
sarasvatī vīṇā; sarejā; šargija; sārindā; şarkı; sarod; saroz; sasa-
biwa; sason; sasong; sato (i); sato (ii); satsumabiwa; saz; sāz-ī-
kāshmīr; seis; setār; sgra-snyan; shamisen; shanagan khuur; shandz;
shanza; sharki; shashtar; shidurgu; shlopcoky; shudraga; sihu; siilili;
siiriri; silverbasharpa; siribo; sitar; skripka; skrzypce; slack-key
guitar; smuikas; sǫ; socavón; sǫ ĩ; sǫ pīp; sorud; sǫ ū; souravli;
spike fiddle; spike lute; string bass; stroh violin; stump; subaga-
nkoni; subu; suka; sultana; sundatang; sụng; surando; sūrbahār;
surindā; sursŕṅgār; svarāj; syron; takare; tamboer; tambur (iii); tambura (i); tambūrā; tamburica; tam huyền; ṭanbūr; tanbūrah; tanbūro;
tandūrā; tang-pip'a; tār; taratibu; tarawangsa; tar śahnāī; tatu; tā'ūs;
tayàw; tchambar; tembir; tenkaya burra; tenor violin; terzina;
thangara; theorbo; tidinit; tigrïk; timple; tính tàu; tiple; tiqin; tobshuur; toe-yoe; tondu; tonkur; topshur; toshpulur; träskofiol; tres;
tro so; trostrune gusle; tro u; trumpet marine; tsigulka; tsii' edo'áłí;
tsugaru-jamisen; tube fiddle; ṭunbūr; tỳ bà; tympanocorde; tzouras;
'ūd; udi; ukulele; umkiki; ut; velviool; vena; venava; viaule; vicitrā
vīṇā; vihuela; viol; viola; viola alta; viola bastarda; viola da braccio;
viola da gamba; viola da mano; viola d'amore; viola da spalla;
viola di fagotto; violalin; violão; viola pomposa; violetta; violetta
marina; violetta piccola; violin; violino piccolo; viololira; violon-
alto; violoncello; violoncello piccolo; violone; violɐ̄ cu goarnă; vô
đề căm; vrondolira; wandindi; wanham; wǒlgŭm; wuxian; xalam;
xguthe; xianzi; xiao sanxian; xiqin; xirribita (ii); yakta; yaktāro;
yehu; yüeh-ch'in; yueqin; zhonghu; zither-banjo; złobcoki; zogo-
zogo; zongoră; Zupfgeige.

BIBLIOGRAPHY

ANCIENT AND NON-EUROPEAN LUTES

C. Sachs and E. M. von Hornbostel: 'Systematik der Musikinstrumente', *Zeitschrift für Ethnologie*, xlvi (1914), 553–90 [Eng. trans.
in *GSJ*, xiv (1961), 3]
F. Behn: 'Die Laute im Altertum und frühen Mittelalter', *ZMw*, i
(1918–19), 89
K. Geiringer: 'Vorgeschichte und Geschichte der europäischen Laute
bis zum Beginn der Neuzeit', *ZMw*, x (1927–8), 560–603
L. Picken: 'The Origin of the Short Lute', *GSJ*, viii (1955), 32

H. Hickmann: *Ägypten*, Musikgeschichte in Bildern, ii/1 (Leipzig,
1961)
W. Stauder: 'Zur Frühgeschichte der Laute', *Festschrift Helmuth
Osthoff* (Tutzing, 1961), 15
G. Fleischhauer: *Etrurien und Rom*, Musikgeschichte in Bildern,
ii/5 (Leipzig, 1964)
R. A. Higgins and R. P. Winnington-Ingram: 'Lute-players in Greek
Art', *Journal of Hellenic Studies*, lxxxv (1965), 62
H. Turnbull: 'The Origin of the Long-necked Lute', *GSJ*, xxv (1972),
58
S. Marcuse: *A Survey of Musical Instruments* (London, 1975), 406ff
L. Picken: *Folk Musical Instruments of Turkey* (London, 1975), 261ff,
583
C. Ziegler: *Les instruments de musique égyptiens au musée du Lou-
vre* (Paris, 1979)

WESTERN LUTE

H. Arnaut de Zwolle: MS treatise (c1440; *F-Pn* lat.7295); facs., Fr.
trans. and commentary in G. le Cerf and E.-R. Labande: *Instru-
ments de musique du XVe siècle* (Paris, 1932) [see Harwood (1960)]
J. Tinctoris: *De inventione et usu musicae* (Naples, c1487); ed. K.
Weinmann (Regensburg, 1917, 2/1961) [see Baines (1950)]
S. Virdung: *Musica getutscht* (Basle, 1511/R1970)
H. Gerle: *Musica teusch* (Nuremberg, 1532; rev., enlarged 3/1546)
J. Bermudo: *Declaración de instrumentos musicales* (Osuna, 1555/
R1957)
J.-B. Besard: *Thesaurus harmonicus* (Cologne, 1603[15]; Eng. trans.
of appx in R. Dowland: *Varietie of Lute-lessons*, 1610)
T. Robinson: *The Schoole of Musicke* (London, 1603); ed. in CM
(1971)
R. Dowland: *Varietie of Lute-lessons* (London, 1610[23]/R1958) [incl.
section by J. Dowland, and Eng. trans. of appx to J.-B. Besard:
Thesaurus harmonicus, 1603]
M. Praetorius: *Syntagma musicum*, ii (Wolfenbüttel, 1618,
2/1619/R1958 and 1980) [see Morrow and Graubart (1960)]
M. Mersenne: *Harmonie universelle* (Paris, 1636–7/R1963; Eng.
trans., 1957)
T. Mace: *Musick's Monument* (London, 1676/R1966) [see Gill
(1950)]
E. G. Baron: *Historisch-theoretische und practische Untersuchung
des Instruments der Lauten* (Nuremberg, 1727/R1965; Eng. trans.,
1976)
H. Nirrnheim: 'Hamburgische Instrumentenbauer insbesondere Gei-
gen und Lautenmacher', *Mitteilungen des Vereins für Hambur-
gischer Geschichte*, xix (1898–9), 129
O. Körte: *Laute und Lautenmusik bis zur Mitte des 16. Jahrhun-
derts* (Leipzig, 1901/R1974, 2/1968)
E. Duncan: 'Of the Lute or Theorbo', *MMR*, xxxii (1902), 65
W. L. von Lütgendorff: *Die Geigen- und Lautenmacher vom
Mittelalter bis zur Gegenwart* (Frankfurt am Main, 1904,
6/1922/R1968)
T. Wortmann: *Philipp Franz Le Sage de Richée und sein Cabinet
der Lauten* (diss., U. of Vienna, 1919)
J. Zuth: *Handbuch der Laute und Gitarre* (Vienna, 1926–8/R1972)
L. de La Laurencie: *Les luthistes* (Paris, 1928)
R. Vannes: *Essai d'un dictionnaire universel des luthiers* (Paris, 1932,
2/1951/R1972 as *Dictionnaire universel des luthiers* and *R*1981
incl. suppl. 1959)
R. Donington: 'VI: Plucked Strings: IB, 1: The Family of Lutes',
The Instruments of Music (London, 1949, 2/1951)
M. W. Prynne: 'An Unrecorded Lute by Hans Frei', *GSJ*, ii (1949),
47; iv (1951), 46
A. Baines: 'Fifteenth-century Instruments in Tinctoris's *De inven-
tione et usu musicae*', *GSJ*, iii (1950), 19
D. Gill: 'The Lute and *Musick's Monument*', *GSJ*, iii (1950), 9
B. Disertori: 'Remarques sur l'évolution du luth en Italie au XVe
siècle et au XVIe', *Le luth et sa musique: CNRS Neuilly-sur-Seine
1957*, 19
G. Guegmos: 'Die Tieffenbrucher von Tieffenbruck in Alt-Füssen',
Füssner Blatt, x/1, 3, 8 (1958)
J. Jacquot: 'Le luth et sa musique: vers une organisation interna-
tionale des recherches', *AcM*, xxx (1958), 89
D. Gill: 'The Elizabethan Lute', *GSJ*, xii (1959), 60
LSJ (1959–)
I. Harwood: 'A Fifteenth-century Lute Design', *LSJ*, ii (1960), 3
G. Hayes: 'Musical Instruments: Mandora and Lute', *NOHM*, iii
(1960), 487f
M. Morrow and M. Graubart: 'Lutes and Theorboes: their Use as
Continuo Instruments described by Michael Praetorius in his *Syn-
tagma musicum*', *LSJ*, ii (1960), 26
D. Gill: 'Brief Notes on the Bass Lute', *LSJ*, iii (1961), 27
M. Prynne: 'James Talbot's Manuscript: IV: Plucked Strings – the
Lute Family', *GSJ*, xiv (1961), 52
——: 'Some Remarks on Lute Forgeries', *LSJ*, iii (1961), 17
——: 'The Fretted Instruments: I: the Lute', *Musical Instruments
through the Ages*, ed. A. Baines (Harmondsworth, 1961, 2/
1966/R1970)

——: 'The Old Bologna Lute-makers', *LSJ*, v (1963), 18

G. Hellwig: 'Joachim Tielke', *GSJ*, xvii (1964), 28

M. Prynne: 'Lute Bellies and Barring', *LSJ*, vi (1964), 7

L. Cervelli: 'Brevi noti sui liutai tedeschi attivi in Italia dal secolo XVI° al XVIII°', *AnMc*, no.5 (1968), 299–337

G. Hayes: 'Instruments and Instrumental Notation: the Lute', *NOHM*, iv (1968), 721ff

F. Hellwig: 'On the Construction of the Lute Belly', *GSJ*, xxi (1968), 129

E. Pohlmann: *Laute, Theorbe, Chitarrone: Die Instrumente, ihre Musik und Literatur von 1500 bis zur Gegenwart* (Bremen, 1968, rev. 4/1975) [incl. bibliography]

Journal of the Lute Society of America (1968–)

F. Hellwig: 'An Example of Lute Restoration', *GSJ*, xxiii (1970), 64

——: 'Makers' Marks on Plucked Instruments of the 16th and 17th Centuries', *GSJ*, xxiv (1971), 22

S. Bonner: 'Two Renaissance Lute Carvings', *LSJ*, xiii (1971), 36

P. Danner: 'Before Petrucci: the Lute in the 15th Century', *Journal of the Lute Society of America*, v (1972), 4

D. Edwards: 'A Geometrical Construction for a Lute Profile', *LSJ*, xv (1973), 48

D. Abbott and E. Segerman: 'Strings in the 16th and 17th Centuries', *GSJ*, xxvii (1974), 48

F. Hellwig: 'Lute Construction in the Renaissance and the Baroque', *GSJ*, xxvii (1974), 21

——: 'Lute-making in the late 15th and the 16th Century', *LSJ*, xvi (1974), 24

FoMRHI Quarterly (1975–)

D. Abbott and E. Segerman: 'The Geometric Description and Analysis of Instrument Shapes', *FoMRHI Quarterly*, no.2 (1976), 7

M. Lowe: 'The Historical Development of the Lute in the 17th Century', *GSJ*, xxix (1976), 11

R. Spencer: 'Chitarrone, Theorbo and Archlute', *Early Music*, iv (1976), 407

I. Firth: 'Acoustical Experiments on the Lute Belly', *GSJ*, xxx (1977), 56

W. B. Samson: 'The Twelve-course English Lute', *LSJ*, xix (1977), 50

A. Layer: *Die Allgäuer Lauten- und Geigenmacher* (Augsburg, 1978)

R. Bletschacher: *Die Lauten- und Geigenmacher des Füssener Landes* (Hofheim am Taunus, 1978)

C. Bouterse: 'Reconstructing the Medieval Arabic Lute', *GSJ*, xxxii (1979), 2

G. Hellwig: *Joachim Tielke, ein Hamburger Lauten- und Violenmacher der Barockzeit* (Frankfurt am Main, 1979)

D. and E. Segerman: 'On Baroque Lute Stringing and Tunings', *FoMRHI Quarterly*, no.16 (1979), 215

D. A. Smith: 'The Musical Instrument Inventory of Raymund Fugger', *GSJ*, xxxiii (1980), 36

G. Söhne: 'Zur Geometrie der Laute', *Gitarre & Laute*, iv (1980), 14

D. Gill: 'Mandores and Colachons', *GSJ*, xxxiv (1981), 130

I. Harwood: 'A Case of Double Standards?: Instrumental Pitch in England c1600', *Early Music*, ix (1981), 470

F. Hellwig: 'The Morphology of Lutes with Extended Bass Strings', *Early Music*, ix (1981), 447

C. Page: 'The 15th-century Lute: New and Neglected Sources', *Early Music*, ix (1981), 11

W. Samson: 'Lute Outlines: a Pragmatic Approach to Geometrical Description', *FoMRHI Quarterly*, no.25 (1981), 35

R. Spencer: 'Lute and Guitar', *How Music Works*, ed. K. Spence and G. Swayne (New York and London, 1981), 79

R. H. Wells: 'Number Symbolism in the Renaissance Lute Rose', *Early Music*, ix (1981), 32

REPERTORY

M. Praetorius: *Syntagma musicum*, ii (Wolfenbüttel, 1618, 2/1619/R1958 and 1980)

W. Tappert: 'Philip Hainhofer's Lautenbücher', *MMg*, xvii (1885), 29

M. Brenet: 'Notes sur l'histoire du luth en France', *RMI*, v (1898), 637–76; vi (1899), 1–44; publ separately (Turin, 1899/R1973)

A. Wotquenne-Plattel: 'Etude sur l'Hortus Musarum de Pierre Phalèse', *Revue des bibliothèques et archives de Belgique* (1903), 65

O. Chilesotti: 'Il primo libro di liuto di Vincenzo Galilei', *RMI*, xv (1908), 753

——: 'Jacomo Gorzanis, liutista del cinquecento', *RMI*, xxi (1914), 86

A. Koczirz: 'Österreichische Lautenmusik zwischen 1650 und 1720', DTÖ, l, Jg. xxv/2 (1918)

A. Pirro: 'Les "frottole" et la musique instrumentale', *RdM*, iii/3 (1922), 3

H. Sommer: *Lautentraktate des 16. und 17. Jahrhunderts in Rahmen der deutschen und französischen Lautentabulaturen* (diss., Free U. of Berlin, 1922)

A. Koczirz: 'Böhmische Lautenkunst um 1720', *Alt-Prager Almanach* (1926), 88

H. Osthoff: *Der Lautenist Santino Garsi da Parma* (Leipzig, 1926, rev. 2/1973)

P. Warlock: *The English Ayre* (London, 1926)

K. Koletschka: 'Esaias Reussner der Jüngere und seine Bedeutung für die deutsche Lautenmusik des XVII. Jahrhunderts', *SMw*, xv (1928), 3–45

L. de La Laurencie: *Les luthistes* (Paris, 1928)

H. Halbig: 'Eine handschriftliche Lautentabulatur des Giacomo Gorzanis', *Theodor Kroyer: Festschrift zum sechzigsten Geburtstage* (Regensburg, 1933), 102

H.-P. Kosack: *Geschichte der Laute und Lautenmusik in Preussen* (Würzburg, 1935)

R. Newton: 'English Lute Music of the Golden Age', *PMA*, lxv (1938–9), 63

H. Neemann: 'Die Lautenistenfamilie Weiss', *AMf*, iv (1939), 157

——: 'Esjas Reusner und Sylvius Leopold Weiss', *EDM*, 1st ser., xii (1939)

W. Apel: *The Notation of Polyphonic Music, 900–1600* (Cambridge, Mass., 1942, 4/1953)

W. Boetticher: *Studien zur solistischen Lautenpraxis des 16. und 17. Jahrhunderts* (Berlin, 1943)

A. Verchaly: 'Gabriel Bataille et son oeuvre personelle pour chant et luth', *RdM*, xxvi/1 (1947), 1, 24

E. A. Wienandt: *Musical Style in the Lute Compositions of Francesco da Milano* (diss., U. of Iowa, 1951)

K. J. Levy: '"Suzanne un jour": the History of a 16th Century Chanson', *AnnM*, i (1953), 375

A. Verchaly: 'Poésie et air de cour en France jusqu'à 1620', *Musique et poésie au XVIe siècle: CNRS Paris 1953*, 211

J. M. Ward: *The Vihuela da mano and its Music (1536–1576)* (diss., New York U., 1953)

J. Jacquot, ed.: *La musique instrumentale de la Renaissance: CNRS Paris 1954*

M. Rollin: 'Le "tombeau" chez les luthistes D. Gautier, J. Gallot, Ch. Mouton', *Bulletin de la Société d'Etudes du xviie siècle*, xxi–xxii (1954), 463

F. Lesure and G. Thibault: *Bibliographie des éditions d'Adrian Le Roy et Robert Ballard (1551–1598)* (Paris, 1955)

D. Lumsden: *The Sources of English Lute Music, 1540–1620* (diss., U. of Cambridge, 1955) [thematic index in vol.ii]

J. Pohanka: 'Loutnové tabulatury z rajhradského kláštera' [Lute tablature from Rajhradsko Monastery], *Časopis moravského musea*, xl/2 (1955), 193

E. A. Wienandt: 'Perino Fiorentino and his Lute Pieces', *JAMS*, viii (1955), 2

R. Buggert: *Alberto da Ripa: Lutenist and Composer* (diss., U. of Michigan, 1956)

L. H. Moe: *Dance Music in Printed Italian Lute Tablatures from 1507 to 1611* (diss., Harvard U., 1956)

J. Jacquot, ed.: *Le luth et sa musique: CNRS Neuilly-sur-Seine 1957*

P. Pidoux: 'Les psaumes d'Antoine de Mornable, Guilleaume Morlaye et Pierre Certon (1546, 1554, 1555): étude comparative', *AnnM*, v (1957), 179

E. A. Wienandt: 'David Kellner's *Lautenstücke*', *JAMS*, x (1957), 29

D. Heartz: *Sources and Forms of the French Instrumental Dance in the Sixteenth Century* (diss., Harvard U., 1958)

J. Jacquot and A. Souris, eds.: *Thomas Mace: Musick's Monument, vol.II: commentaire et transcriptions* (Paris, 1958/R1966)

LSJ (1959–)

W. S. Casey: *Printed English Lute Instruction Books, 1568–1610* (diss., U. of Michigan, 1960)

B. Hambraeus: *Codex carminum gallicorum* (Uppsala, 1961)

W. Rubsamen: 'Scottish and English Music of the Renaissance in a Newly-discovered Manuscript', *Festschrift Heinrich Besseler* (Leipzig, 1961), 259

F. J. Giesbert: *Schule für die Barock-Laute* (Mainz, 1962)

H. Radke: 'Beiträge zur Erforschung der Lautentabulaturen des 16. bis 18. Jahrhunderts', *Mf*, xvi (1963), 34

——: 'War Johann Sebastian Bach Lautenspieler?', *Festschrift Hans Engel* (Kassel, 1964)

E. Vogl: 'Aureus Dix und Antoni Eckstein, zwei Prager Lautenisten', *Mf*, xvii (1964), 41

H. Radke: 'Wodurch unterscheiden sich Laute und Theorbe', *AcM*, xxxvii (1965), 73

J. Sutton: 'The Lute Instructions of Jean-Baptiste Besard', *MQ*, li (1965), 345

E. Vogl: 'Lautenisten der böhmischen Spätrenaissance', *Mf*, xviii (1965), 281

H. J. Schulze: 'Wer intavolierte Johann Sebastian Bachs Lautenkompositionen?', *Mf*, xix (1966), 32

C. M. Simpson: *The British Broadside Ballad and its Music* (New Brunswick, NJ, 1966)

K. Dorfmüller: *Studien zur Lautenmusik in der ersten Hälfte des 16. Jahrhunderts* (Tutzing, 1967)

O. Gombosi: *Der Lautenist Valentin Bakfark Leben und Werke 1507–1576* (Budapest, 1967)

Journal of the Lute Society of America (1968–)

E. Pohlmann: *Laute, Theorbe, Chitarrone: Die Instrumente, ihre Musik und Literatur von 1500 bis zur Gegenwart* (Bremen, 1968, rev.4/1975) [incl. bibliography]

W. Rubsamen: 'The Earliest French Lute Tablature', *JAMS*, xxi (1968), 286

D. Lumsden, ed.: *T. Robinson: The Schoole of Musicke* (Paris, 1971)

H. Radke: 'Zum Problem der Lautentabulatur-Übertragung', *AcM*, xliii (1971), 94

D. Heartz: 'Mary Magdalen, Lutenist', *Journal of the Lute Society of America*, v (1972), 52

E. Maier: *Die handschriftlich überlieferten Tabulaturen für Lauteninstrumente des 17. und 18. Jahrhunderts aus dem Bestand der Oesterreichischen Nationalbibliothek mit dem Wiener Lautenbuch des Jacques de Saint Luc* (diss., U. of Vienna, 1972) [thematic index in vol.ii]

D. Poulton: *John Dowland* (London, 1972)

W. Rave: *Some Manuscripts of French Lute Music, 1630–1700* (diss., U. of Illinois, Urbana, 1972)

J. Tichota: 'Francouzská loutnová hudba v Čechách' [French lute music in Bohemia], *MMC*, nos.25–6 (1973), 7–77

H. M. Brown: 'Embellishment in Early Sixteenth-century Italian Intabulations', *PRMA*, c (1973–4), 49

H. Tischler: 'The Earliest Lute Tablature?', *JAMS*, xxvii (1974), 100

C. N. Amos: *Lute Practice and Lutenists in Germany between 1500 and 1750* (diss., U. of Iowa, 1975)

D. Poulton: 'Graces of Play in Renaissance Lute Music', *Early Music*, iii (1975), 107

G. Ungerer: 'The French Lutenist Charles Tessier and the Essex Circle', *Renaissance Quarterly*, xxviii (1975), 190

D. Fallows: '15th-century Tablatures for Plucked Instruments: a Summary, a Revision and a Suggestion', *LSJ*, xix (1977), 3

D. Poulton: 'The Lute in Christian Spain', *LSJ*, xix (1977), 34

J. Jacquot: 'Le luth et sa musique: from the Neuilly Colloquium to the *Corpus* of French Lutenists', *LSJ*, xx (1978), 7

I. Harwood: 'Thomas Robinson's "Generall Rules"', *LSJ*, xx (1978), 18

F. Dobbins: 'The Lute Airs of Charles Tessier', *LSJ*, xx (1978), 23

P. Holman: 'New Sources of Music by Robert Johnson', *LSJ*, xx (1978), 43

C. Page: 'French Lute Tablature in the 14th Century?', *Early Music*, viii (1980), 488

H. Radke: 'Zur Spieltechnik der deutschen Lautenisten des 16 Jahrhunderts', *AcM*, lii (1980), 134

J.-M. Vaccaro: *La musique de luth en France au XVIe siècle* (Paris, 1981)

KLAUS WACHSMANN (1), JAMES W. Mc KINNON,
ROBERT ANDERSON (2), IAN HARWOOD (3–4),
DIANA POULTON (3–7)

Lute-guitar (Fr. *guitare-luth*; Ger. *Lautengitarre*). A guitar with a lute-shaped body invented by G. Gelmini and G. Sbordoni of Brescia about 1850.

Lute-harpsichord (Fr. *clavecin-luth*; Ger. *Lautenklavecimbel, Lautenklavier, Lautenwerck*). A variety of harpsichord strung with gut (occasionally supplemented with a choir of metal strings) and intended to imitate the sound of a lute. The lute-harpsichord, thus, should properly be considered as an instrument differing from the *arpicordo* mentioned in various Italian writings and the *Harfentive* mentioned by Virdung (*Musica getutscht*, 1511), which also were strung in gut but which seem to have been intended to imitate the harp. Although some pre-18th-century references to the lute-harpsichord may be cited, including an *arpicordo leutato* and *arpitarrone* mentioned by Adriano Banchieri (*L'organo suonarino*, 1605, rev. 2/1611), the lute-harpsichord appears to have been particularly interesting to German makers in the first half of the 18th century, and a number of different types were made by such builders as Johann Christoph Fleischer, Zacharias Hildebrandt and Johann Nicolaus Bach.

The form and layout of lute-harpsichords was highly variable. Some were rectangular, some oval, some wing-shaped like a harpsichord; some had a hemispherical resonator below the soundboard; some had individual bridges for each string and others had continuous bridges like those in a conventional harpsichord; some had a buff stop and two or even three keyboards activating jacks plucking at different points in order to produce sounds of different timbre and loudness from a single set of strings. Of all these instruments, Fleischer's *Theorbenflügel* was probably the most elaborate, having three sets of strings; the one at unison pitch and the one tuned an octave lower were made of gut and the one tuned an octave higher was of metal.

The inventory of J. S. Bach's instruments taken at the time of his death included two lute-harpsichords. In a note by J. F. Agricola in Adlung's *Musica mechanica organoedi* it is claimed that one of them was designed by Bach himself and made by Hildebrandt, and it is possible that certain of Bach's keyboard works were conceived for instruments of this kind.

BIBLIOGRAPHY

J. Adlung: *Musica mechanica organoedi*, ii (Berlin, 1768/*R*1961), 133ff

H. Ferguson: 'Bach's "Lautenwerck"', *ML*, xlviii (1967), 259

U. Henning: 'The Most Beautiful among the Claviers', *Early Music*, x (1982), 477

EDWIN M. RIPIN

Lute stop (Fr. *nasale, registre d'hautbois*; Ger. *Nasal-Register, Nasalzug, Oboezug*). A row of jacks plucking one of the unison registers of a harpsichord very close to the nut, producing a characteristically penetrating sound. There is considerable confusion as to the proper use of the term, since such apparently equivalent foreign terms as 'jeu de luth', 'Lautenzug' and 'liuto' actually refer to the BUFF STOP.

EDWIN M. RIPIN

Luth (Fr.). LUTE.

Luthéal (Fr.). A type of PREPARED PIANO, called for by Ravel in two works of the 1920s, *L'enfant et les sortilèges* and *Tzigane*; *see* MODIFICATIONS AND NEW TECHNIQUES.

Luthier (Fr.; It. *liutaio*). Originally the word for a lute maker, it has become a general term for a maker of violins or other string instruments. Though French, the word has gained currency in English and German. Similarly, and to an even greater extent, the derivative 'lutherie' (lute making) has acquired the meaning of instrument making in general.

Luveve. End-blown flute of the Swazi people of southern Africa. It is made from the horn of an antelope, open at the wider end, and when sounded is placed against the player's hollowed tongue. Substitutes may be carved from wood, to this shape, and covered with tail skin from an ox. It is used by diviners, and as a signal whistle by hunters and warriors. See *KirbyMISA*, 110f and pl.38*b*.

See also LEKHITLANE; PALA; UVEVE.

DAVID K. RYCROFT

Luvugamahame. Single-headed closed conical drum of the Rwanda people of Rwanda. It is the second largest in a set of 15 drums; largest is the *chihumurizo*.

Luvuvu [tshihwilili, tshivhilivhi]. BULLROARER of the Venda people of southern Africa.

Luwanzo. Percussion sticks of the Gishu people of Mbale district, Uganda. They comprise two split poles balanced on bunches of banana fibre. These are struck rhythmically, near ant hills, to encourage the emergence of flying ants, which are caught and eaten. See *Tracey CSA*, ii, 296.

Luzenzu. STICK ZITHER of the Luluwa and Luba peoples of Zaïre (*LaurentyC*, 115). *See* ZEZE (i).

Lyon, Gustave. French instrument maker, director of the PLEYEL firm from 1887. He is particularly noted for his development of the chromatic harp (*see* HARP, §4 (vi, vii)).

Lyon & Healy. American instrument manufacturers and music dealers. Founded in 1864 in Chicago by George Washburn Lyon and Patrick Joseph Healy as a Midwest outlet for the publications of the Boston company of Oliver Ditson, the firm rapidly expanded to include retail distribution of music from all publishers and musical instruments of all types, some of which were manufactured by the firm itself. Under Healy's direction (Lyon retired in 1889) the store became widely known in Chicago and throughout the USA for its broad range of merchandise and advanced advertising and selling methods. Healy died in 1905. In 1979 the company closed all its retail music stores, and the name of the firm was changed to Lyon & Healy Harps.

As an instrument manufacturer, the firm is best known for the Lyon & Healy harp, first placed on the market in 1889. Healy was interested in developing a harp which would be better suited to the rigours of the American climate than the available European models, and his engineers, basing their instrument on Erard's pedal harp, succeeded in producing a harp notable for its strength, reliability of pitch, and freedom from unwanted vibra-

Lyra (short-necked fiddle) player, Crete

tion. When Wurlitzer, the firm's major competitor, stopped producing harps before World War II, Lyon & Healy remained the sole large-scale harp builder in the USA. Other contributions to American harp manufacture made by Lyon & Healy include innovations in the style of the instrument, notably the modern, ungilded 'Salzedo' model of 1935, and the development of a small, pedal-less instrument after medieval models (the 'Troubador', 1962) intended, according to the firm, for 'beginners and hobbyists'.

ANNETTE FERN

Lyra [lira]. (1) A term used for various instruments, most often string instruments. In army bands and the like a lyra is a portable glockenspiel, used since the disappearance of the Turkish crescent (or Jingling Johnny) and consisting of a lyre-shaped metal frame to which are attached tuned metal bars in the conventional two rows for diatonic and chromatic notes (*see* BELL-LYRA).

In medieval and Renaissance writings, the terms 'lyra' and 'lira' designated various string instruments of the time (for instance LIRA DA BRACCIO, LIRONE and LYRA VIOL) as well as the ancient Greek lyre, but seldom members of the zither family (which were more likely to derive their names from other ancient terms, such as 'kithara' or 'psalter'). Martin Gerbert (*De cantu*, ii, 1774, pl. 5), on the basis of medieval manuscript sources since destroyed, illustrated a rebec-like instrument as 'lira', and a similar instrument is called 'lyra' in modern Greece (see §(2) below). Tinctoris (*De inventione et usu musicae*, c1487) referred to the lute as 'lyra', and Virdung (*Musica getutscht*, 1511) used the term for the hurdy-gurdy (for instruments related to the latter and occasionally referred to as 'lyra', *see* LIRA).

(2) Short-necked fiddle of Greece. In contemporary usage, the name 'lyra' is applied to two structurally distinct instruments: a pyriform instrument, found principally on the Greek islands (particularly the Dodecanese and Crete) and in the northern mainland areas of Thrace and Macedonia; and a rectangular, bottle-shaped, three-string instrument called the Pontic lyra (*kementses*), found primarily near the mainland Greek-Turkish border, a Turkish instrument brought to Greece by refugees from the Turkish Black Sea coast in the early 20th century (*see also* KEMENÇE).

The pear-shaped lyra is bipartite, with a back (*kafki*: 'skull'), integral neck (*lemos*) and pegdisc (*kephali*: 'head') carved out of a block of hardwood and a belly, made of a separate piece of coniferous wood, which is typically flat or very slightly vaulted and in which are carved two D-shaped soundholes (*mathia*: 'eyes'). Usually made by the player in whatever size desired, lyras in Crete have been produced in four sizes and styles, including the small *liraki*, the large *vrondolira*, the common, medium-size *lyra* (c40 to 63 cm long, 11 to 23 cm wide, 3 to 6 cm deep) and the *viololira*, a waisted instrument similar in shape to the violin.

Three strings of gut or wire are commonly used (Dodecanese lyras sometimes have four). According to Anoyanakis (1979), some lyra players added as many as three sympathetic strings; these are rare on modern instruments. The strings are fastened at the upper end to sagittal posterior pegs (*striftalia*: 'turners') and at the lower to a projection of the soundbox (*oura*: 'tail'), to a tailpiece or to a string-holder (*kteni*: 'comb'). Traditionally, lyras have no nut, but some contemporary instruments have one to equalize string lengths. The middle string, attached to the uppermost of the three pegs, has a longer vibrating length than the two outer strings, but many lyras have a small wooden string support (*pano kavalaris*: 'rider') which functions as a nut for the middle string, thereby equalizing string lengths. Tuning is in perfect 5ths (at relative, not absolute pitches); *alla turca* tuning, in perfect 4ths and 5ths, is sometimes used.

A unique feature of the pear-shaped lyra is the use of a soundpost (*stylos*: 'pillar', or *psychi*: 'soul') placed through the soundhole directly beneath the side of the bridge and wedged between the bridge and the back, which supports and lifts the left side of the bridge slightly off the belly. The Greek and Dalmatian pyriform lyras and the Bulgarian *gadulka* appear to be the only bowed string instruments that use this specific bridge/soundpost arrangement. A second unusual feature is the presence of one or more small holes (1·5 to 2 mm in diameter) near the centre of the back 'for the voice' of the lyra. Formerly, lyra makers and players felt that this would improve the sound, but modern makers have abandoned it, noting that it serves no crucial acoustic purpose.

Until about World War II, the bow of the lyra had a convex camber, a rudimentary tightening mechanism and several small pellet-bells (*yerakokoudhouna*) attached for rhythmic accompaniment. Contemporary players commonly use violin bows.

When seated, lyra players may hold the instrument vertically upon the left thigh (see illustration) or between the legs; if standing, they support it against the chest or belt (for illustration *see* LAOUTO). The bow is held palm-up and the strings are stopped from the side with the fingernails.

Used primarily as a melody instrument to perform dance-tunes, the lyra is played with rapid, separate bow-strokes, near the tip of the bow. The highest-sounding string is used for the melody, as is the middle string, which occasionally, along with the lowest-sounding string, is used to produce a polyphonic drone accompaniment. Customarily played by men only, the lyra may be played alone, in combination with modern Western instruments, or with the *daouli* (drum), the *laouto* (lute) or the *dachares* (tambourine). In many areas of Greece, the lyra has been replaced by the violin.

Portions of four pyriform lyra-like instruments, dating from between c1055 and 1382, have been unearthed in archaeological excavations in Novgorod, Russia. Bachmann (1964) noted that pear-shaped instruments exist in 10th-century Byzantine iconographic sources, and that the term 'lyra' refers to fiddle-like instruments in literature as early as the 9th century.

BIBLIOGRAPHY

N. Mavris and E. Papadopoulos: *Dōdekanēsiaka Lyra* (Port Said, 1928)
M. Gavazzi: 'Jadranska "lira" – "lirica"', *Narodna starina*, xxii (Zagreb, 1930), 103
A. Koczirz: 'Über die Fingernageltechnik bei Saiteninstrumenten', *Studien zur Musikgeschichte: Festschrift für Guido Adler* (Vienna, 1930), 164
W. Bachmann: *Die Anfänge des Streichinstrumentenspiels* (Leipzig, 1964, 2/1966; Eng. trans., 1969)
F. Anoyanakis: *He morphologikè elélixe tês lýras stèn Kréte* (Athens, 1964)
——: *Instruments de musique populaires grecs: Ellinika laida mousika organa* (Athens, 1965)
B. Rusić: 'Dalmatinska "lira" i "gusla" makedonska', *Etnološki pregled*, vi–vii (Belgrade, 1965)
A. Stojanović: 'Jadranska lira', *Narodna umjetnost*, iv (1966), 59
B. A. Kolchin: *Novgorodskie drevnosti: derevyanneïe izdeliya* (Moscow, 1968), 86f, 94, 178ff
M. Downie: *The Modern Greek Lyra: an Organological Study of the Lyra Collection of San Chianis, Binghamton, New York* (diss., State U. of New York, Binghamton, 1974)
F. Anoyanakis: 'Lira', 'Kementzés', *Greek Popular Musical Instruments* (Athens, 1979), 259, 275
M. Downie: 'The Modern Greek Lyra', *JAMIS*, v–vi (1979–80), 144

HOWARD MAYER BROWN (1), MARGARET DOWNIE (2)

Lyra Barberina. Lyre invented by GIOVANNI BATTISTA DONI after the ancient Greek *tripous*.

Lyra bastarda. A term used for a LYRA VIOL with sympathetic strings. It is occasionally, though incorrectly, applied to the baryton (*see* BARYTON (i)).

Lyrachord. Name for a piano built by the Rev. J. R. Cotter, of Donoughmore, Co. Cork, in 1840–65, with the striking point halfway along the vibrating length of the strings; the intention was to adjust the overtone balance and obtain the effect of a CEMBAL D'AMOUR. The name was later used for an electric keyboard instrument by a firm in New York.

Lyraflügel (Ger.: 'lyre piano'). A type of UPRIGHT PIANOFORTE.

Lyra-Glockenspiel. See BELL-LYRA.

Lyra perfecta. See LIRONE.

Lyra tedesca (It.). HURDY-GURDY.

Lyra [leero, leerow, liera, lyro] **viol.** A small bass VIOL popular in England during the 17th century. As an instrument it differed little from the standard bass viol. Its importance rests on the large, specialized and musically valuable repertory which was written for it.

1. Structural characteristics. 2. Sources and nature of the repertory. 3. Notation. 4. Tuning. 5. Ornament signs.

1. STRUCTURAL CHARACTERISTICS. Structurally, differences between the lyra viol and other members of the viol family are neither distinct nor decisive as identifying factors. There were some attempts, particularly during the 17th century in England, to provide the lyra viol with sympathetic strings, but with no lasting influence. John Playford (*A Brief Introduction*, 1667) described the lyra viol as the smallest of three kinds of bass viol – consort bass, DIVISION VIOL, lyra viol. From Christopher Simpson (*The Division-Violist*, 1659) we learn that the strings of a lyra viol were lighter and the bridge less rounded than those of the consort bass and division viol. The strings of the lyra viol were fitted more closely to the fingerboard than were those of the consort bass.

It seems clear that although an instrument called lyra viol did exist it was nothing more than a bass viol of small dimensions with some quite minor peculiarities of adjustment. One also finds that a performer in the 17th century, such as Pepys, would not have hesitated to play lyra viol music on any bass viol which happened to be ready at hand. It is, therefore, more to the point to speak of a tradition of playing the viol 'lyra-way' rather than one of playing the lyra viol.

2. SOURCES AND NATURE OF THE REPERTORY. There are 18 English sources of printed music for lyra viol, issued

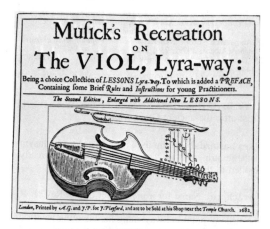

1. Title-page of 'Musick's Recreation on the Viol, Lyra-way', published by John Playford (4/1682)

2. Lyra viol (supposed) by John Rose, London, 1598 (Ashmolean Museum, Oxford)

from 1601 to 1682. More than 75 MS sources of music in tablature for viol from various countries also exist, some mere fragments, others large anthologies. Included in this impressive heritage are works by such notable composers as Coprario, Jenkins, Simpson, Colman and William Lawes. Fancies and sectional dance types of the period are found. The sources include pieces for one lyra viol, ensemble music for two or three lyra viols, for lyra viol with one or more other instruments, and lyra viol accompaniments for songs. Although some parts are melodic and others chordal the most characteristic texture of lyra viol music is polyphonic. It is similar to lute music with regard to the free appearance and disappearance of voice parts (*Freistimmigkeit*).

The development of a polyphonic style of music capable of being performed on a bowed viol having a rounded bridge can be traced through extant music back to Ganassi in mid-16th-century Italy. A literary description of the performance of such music, however, goes back as far as Tinctoris's treatise *De inventione et usu musicae* in the late 15th century. The term lyra viol seems to have been adopted in England around the beginning of the 17th century as a result of the notion (expressed by Ganassi) that this way of playing the viola da gamba was similar to the technique of the lira da gamba.

3. Notation. With the exception of one set of MSS (*GB-Ob* Mus.Sch.D.233 and D.236) all lyra viol music is in tablature. The notational symbols are in the style of French lute tablatures, which use a series of letters in alphabetical order to indicate the fret at which any given string is to be stopped.

Some non-English viol tablatures, on the other hand, are based on systems other than the French. Ganassi (*Regola rubertina*, Venice, 1542–3), for example, used Italian tablature, with numbers instead of letters, the lowest line of the staff representing the highest string. And Gerle (*Musica teusch*, Nuremberg, 1532) combined letters and numbers in his German tablature.

Since the lyra viol is played with a bow there are certain characteristic differences between its music and that intended for plucked instruments such as the lute. Chords, for instance, in lyra viol tablature always call for adjacent strings only, since it is impossible for the bow to leave out intervening strings. The peculiarities of the bow as sound generator may also be responsible for the more or less frequent appearance in lyra viol music of unison double stops. Sometimes this seems to result from the necessarily close harmonic formations which cause contrapuntal lines to come together at the unison when they might otherwise form an octave. It is also possible that the motivation for unison double stops might have sprung in part from a desire to imitate on a viol the 'unison quality' produced by the lute due to its double courses of strings.

4. Tuning. Perhaps the most curious aspect of the lyra viol tradition is the degree to which variability of tuning was extended. A preliminary investigation of the sources has uncovered nearly 60 tunings in use during the 17th century. This figure includes eight which have turned up so far only in non-English sources. With the exception of one seven- and three four-string tunings these all represent variations on the tuning of the standard six strings. With the printed sources of lyra viol music as a guide we can see that only three or four tuning variants had achieved popularity during the first 15 years or so of the 17th century. By the third quarter of the cen-

tury, however, variant tunings had proliferated to such an extent that Thomas Mace could write in 1676, 'The Wit of Man shall never Invent Better Tunings . . . for questionless, All ways have been Tryed to do It' (*Musick's Monument*).

5. ORNAMENT SIGNS. A number of MS sources of lyra viol music are important repositories for signs of ornamentation. Three of them (*GB-Lbm* Eg.2971, *Mp* 832 Vu51, and the Mansell tablature, *US-LAuc*) contain valuable tables of ornament signs. Unfortunately, their meaning is often ambiguous and changeable not only from source to source but even within a given source. One ornament or 'grace' which came to be almost a trade mark of lyra viol playing was the 'thump'. This refers to the practice of plucking open strings with the fingers of the left hand. This technique was usually used in conjunction with certain tunings such as those which provided triads among the open-string pitches. In some cases the player is instructed to pluck the strings with the fingers of the right hand, thus allowing for the use of stopped as well as open notes. For some passages the performer is to keep the bow in his hand while plucking and for other (more extended) passages he is instructed to put it aside. There is also evidence that the viol was sometimes held on the lap and the strings plucked as though it were a lute. The earliest printed source calling for plucking dates from 1605 (Tobias Hume, *The First Part of Ayres*). This is some years before Monteverdi's *Combattimento di Tancredi e Clorinda* (1624), frequently cited as the earliest source of pizzicato. Hume's book also contains the earliest of a number of examples in the lyra viol literature of *col legno* playing.

Of great historical significance is the position which the lyra viol holds as the connecting link between two aesthetic ideals of instrumental sound and function. It could approximate to the polyphonic textures and self-accompaniment capabilities which helped to raise continuo instruments such as the harpsichord and lute to a high level of esteem during the late 16th and early 17th centuries. On the other hand, it could also produce a rich singing line, the growing taste for which led to the predominance of the violin and the solo voice by the beginning of the 18th century. During its period of popularity the lyra viol successfully performed both roles. At the beginning of the 17th century Hume wrote (to the chagrin of Dowland) that the viol could produce equally well the musical excellencies of the lute. By the turn of the century Roger North was writing that 'all the sublimitys of the violin' were to be found in the music of the viol.

BIBLIOGRAPHY

T. Hume: *The First Part of Ayres* (London, 1605/R1969)
——: *Captaine Humes Poeticall Musicke* (London, 1607/R1969)
J. Playford: *Musick's Recreation on the Viol, Lyra-way* (London, 1652, 1661, 1669, 1682/R (partly) 1960)
E. Cowling: 'A Manuscript Collection of Viola da Gamba Music', *JVdGSA*, i (1964), 16
F. Traficante: *The Mansell Lyra Viol Tablature* (diss., U. of Pittsburgh, 1965)
——: 'The Manchester Lyra Viol Tablature: Further Information', *JVdGSA*, iii (1966), 52
——: 'Music for the Lyra Viol: the Printed Sources', *LSJ*, viii (1966), 7
W. V. Sullivan: 'Tobias Hume's *First Part of Ayres* (1605)', *JVdGSA*, v (1968), 5; vi (1969), 13; vii (1970), 92; viii (1971), 64–93; ix (1972), 16
K. Neumann: 'Captain Hume's "Invention for Two to Play Upon One Viole"', *JAMS*, xxii (1969), 101
F. Traficante: 'Lyra Viol Tunings: "All Ways have been Tryed to do It"', *AcM*, xlii (1970), 183
A. Woodford: 'Music for Viol in Tablature: Manuscript Sources in the British Museum', *Chelys*, ii (1970), 23
C. Coxon: 'Some Notes on English Graces for the Viol', *Chelys*, ii (1970), 18
J. Sawyer: 'Music for 2 and 3 Lyra Viols', *Journal of the Canadian Association of University Schools of Music*, i (1971), 71
M. Cyr: 'A Seventeenth-Century Source of Ornamentation for Voice and Viol: British Museum MS. Egerton 2971', *RMARC*, ix (1971), 53
——: 'Song Accompaniments for Lyra Viol and Lute', *Journal of the Lute Society of America*, iv (1971), 43
C. Harris: 'Tobias Hume: a Short Biography', *Chelys*, iii (1971), 16
——: 'The Viol Lyra-way', *Chelys*, iv (1972), 17
J. Sawyer: *An Anthology of Lyra Viol Music in Oxford, Bodleian Library, Manuscripts Music School d245–7* (diss., U. of Toronto, 1972)
A. Erhard: 'Zur Lyra-Viol-Musik', *Mf*, xxvii (1974), 80
P. Walls: 'Lyra Viol Song', *Chelys*, v (1973–4), 68
J. Lejeune: 'The Lyra-viol: an Instrument or a Technique?', *The Consort*, xxxi (1975), 125
T. Crawford: 'An Unusual Consort Revealed in an Oxford Manuscript', *Chelys*, vi (1975–6), 61
P. Furnas: *The Manchester Gamba Book: a Primary Source of Ornaments for the Lyra Viol* (diss., Stanford U., 1978)
F. Traficante: 'Music for Lyra Viol: Manuscript Sources', *Chelys*, viii (1978–9), 4
G. Dodd: 'Matters Arising from Examination of Lyra-viol Manuscripts', *Chelys*, ix (1980), 23
I. H. Stoltzfus: 'The Lyra Viol in Consort: an Example from Uppsala, Universitetsbiblioteket IMhs 4:3', *JVdGSA*, xiii (1980), 47
——: *The Lyra Viol in Consort with other Instruments* (diss., Louisiana State U., 1982)

FRANK TRAFICANTE

Lyre (from Gk.; Lat. *lyra*). A chordophone whose strings are attached to a yoke which lies in the same plane as the soundtable and consists of two arms and a crossbar. It is this characteristic by which Hornbostel and Sachs in their classification system of 1914 distinguished lyres from other types of string instrument (for details, *see* CHORDOPHONE; for a discussion of the ambiguity of medieval terminology, *see* HARP, §§1–2). The earliest known examples, from the 3rd millennium BC, have been recovered from sites in Mesopotamia. Lyres appeared in several Mediterranean lands in antiquity and subsequently spread throughout medieval Europe; in modern times lyres are played in Ethiopia and neighbouring countries. From its Hellenic associations the lyre has often symbolized music in general (and lyric music in particular) in Western art and literature since the Renaissance. Most lyres are plucked; for medieval bowed lyres, *see* ROTTE (ii).

1. General. 2. Ancient Greece.

1. GENERAL. Hornbostel and Sachs distinguished between bowl lyres and box lyres, according to the shape of the resonator. Two further distinctions should also be made because of their importance in regard to the position of the player's hands during performance: between a symmetrical and an asymmetrical arrangement of the arms and strings, and between strings that run parallel to each other and strings that fan out from their holder at the lower rim of the resonator (see fig.1). The number of strings and certain aspects of the tuning pattern are also germane to playing technique. Some lyres have a bridge, almost in the manner of a violin bridge, that lifts the strings clear of a soundtable; but on many modern east African lyres there are no bridges and the plucked strings buzz against the soundtable (made of lizard skin). In the course of reconstructing an ancient lyre at the British Museum impressions have been found, fanning out on the silver surface of the soundtable. This indicates that the plane of the strings must have risen away

from the soundtable at an angle of only a few degrees so that their vibrations could have caused the scarring. The bridge might have been extremely shallow, no more than a few millimetres high; or the yoke might have leaned forward slightly. It seems that the strings were low in pitch and that the player struck them with great force. Any one or any combination of these factors would account for the impressions on the soundtable.

The lyre has been adapted to many local traditions and its various playing styles range from extremely soft to extremely vigorous. In ancient Greece a plectrum was

(a)

(b)

used, as it is today in Sudan, and in Ethiopia for playing the BEGANNA. Some instruments have a strap across the arms, halfway between the yoke and the resonator, which supports the left hand, leaving some of the fingers free to damp strings that are not required to sound (see Plumley, 1976). Generally east African lyre players pluck the open strings with the fingertips without arpeggiation. In Buganda the near arm of the instrument is grasped between the thumb and index finger of the left hand, and from this firmly anchored position the index and middle finger may then pluck the three nearest strings; the playing motion of the right hand is free (though occasionally the elbow may rest on the seated performer's thigh) and is often characterized by sweeping and vigorous circular gestures. To accommodate this playing technique, the three highest notes (thin strings, the highest around f' or g') are crowded towards the near arm of the instrument while the other strings are spread wider apart; their tuning zigzags instead of descending consistently to the right. This kind of tuning arrangement is characteristic also of lyres in Ethiopia; and the ancient Greek writer Nicomachus also gave a tuning of four strings in a partly irregular layout.

Generally the strings are attached to the yoke by being wrapped in strips of leather, cloth or malleable bark to form bulges against which the string is held in tension by friction. Ancient Sumerian depictions show clearly how the string was wound in criss-cross fashion round the bulge wrapped upon the yoke. This might seem an

(c)

1. Lyres from the north-east shore of Lake Victoria: (a) asymmetrical, strings and arms fan out, strings are crowded towards left arm, Soga type; (b) symmetrical, strings run parallel between parallel arms, Gwe type; (c) asymmetrical, strings and arms fan out, strings placed equidistant between arms, Luo type (in playing, this lyre is placed on its side with the knob at one end of the yoke resting on the ground)

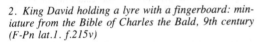

2. King David holding a lyre with a fingerboard: miniature from the Bible of Charles the Bald, 9th century
(F-Pn lat.1. f.215v)

3. Orpheus with a lyre: detail of a fresco (250–400) in
the catacomb of Petrus and Marcellinus, Rome

4. Lyre with parallel strings between asymmetrical arms,
and a resonator decorated with a bull's head: detail of
a banquet scene on the 'Mosaic Standard' from Ur, c2600
BC (British Museum, London)

inefficient device, but anyone who has observed an
African musician tuning knows that it is effective. In
modern Ethiopia, however, levers are often tied to the
bulges to make tuning easier; and in those lyres recovered
from tombs in Mesopotamia, levers about 10 cm long
were attached to the tuning bulges.

There is no evidence of precursors of the bowl lyre:
it seems to have been devised in its complete form in
Mesopotamia during the 3rd millennium BC (fig.4). (Much
speculation has followed the discovery on Mesopotamian cuneographs of the 2nd millennium of texts referring to the strings of a harp or, more likely, a lyre; the
tuning was heptatonic. Other finds have provided song
texts and attempts have been made to hypothesize and
reconstruct the music.) During the Hyksos migration the
lyre appeared in ancient Egypt (where its name was a
hieroglyphic transcription of the Hebrew word kinnor);
it was the chief kind of musical instrument in ancient
Greece (see Winternitz, 1961; see also §2 below). In a
9th-century (European) illustration King David is shown
holding a lyre with an added fingerboard (fig.2; see also
ROTTE (ii)). The 10th-century Arab theoretician and
musican al-Fārābī reported that in Baghdad the lyre was
laughed at – as a rat trap – but al-Fārābī himself evidently acknowledged it as a proper instrument (see
Farmer, 1957). In modern times lyre players along the

littoral of the Red Sea and the coast of Arabia are often
from the Sudan or Eritrea. James Bruce (in a letter to
Burney, see BurneyH) described and discussed the
instrument as used in Ethiopia, where it still survives
both as a bowl lyre and as a box lyre. From Ethiopia it
evidently spread south-west of the Amharic area into
what is now Kenya and Uganda, the Sudan and Zaïre.
Its progress along the south-western fringe of this area
may have occurred as recently as the second half of the
19th century. An instrument of about 1910 found at Tagul
in north-east Zaïre (and now at the Royal Central African Museum at Tervuren) is unmistakably of east Nile
origin (Busoga district, Uganda) and was no doubt
brought in by a migrating labourer (see LaurentyC).

Lyres are used today mainly as solo instruments, by
a player accompanying his own singing. In east Africa
his role and way of life are often comparable with that
of the medieval minstrel. Plumley (1976) estimated that
in the Sudan 90% of the repertory is love-songs.
According to Anyumba (1970), among some Luo families in western Kenya 'the lyre itself is a ritual object
with healing powers. For this reason playing at a wedding ceremony serves both as entertainment and as a
blessing'. Lyres also appear in certain ensembles: in
Buganda, for instance, in consort with a flute, a drum
and perhaps one or two tube fiddles. Used mostly at

secular events such as wedding parties, a lyre is a common adjunct to the entertainments, and the player sometimes refers to members of the audience in his songs.

This use as an entertainer's tool goes back to the earliest times. On the 'peace' face of the Ur standard (c2600 BC) a man plays a large 11-string lyre at a princely banquet (see fig.4). The instrument is ornamented with a bull's head, a characteristic of the Sumerian lyre which certainly links the instrument with the divine power and creativity thought to reside in the animal. From c2800 BC the lyre is often illustrated on cylinder seals, and sometimes the strings seem to emerge out of a bull-body, expressive of the divine voice itself. From the 'royal' cemetery at Ur nine lyres have been identified, of wood decorated with gold or silver and inlaid with semi-precious stones. The Sumerians had small portable lyres and larger ones that rested on the ground, played with the fingers and in an upright position. Small tuning-sticks were placed through the knots where the strings were attached to the cross-bar; a slight movement of them could alter the tuning and tension of the strings. A lyre with bull-shaped soundbox appears on an early 2nd millennium seal from Kültepe in Anatolia, evidence of a type similar to the Mesopotamian instrument, which hardly survives the Sumerian period. From c1850 BC the Babylonian lyre was held tilted and even horizontal and was now played with a plectrum.

The first representation of a lyre in ancient Egyptian iconography is in the Tomb of Khnumhotep (Dynasty 12, c1911–1786 BC) at Beni Hasan, where it appears with a group of Asiatic beduin bringing eye-paint to the nomarch. It later takes its part in New Kingdom banquet scenes and actual instruments survive from the 16th century BC. The god Thoth was supposed to have invented it, making the strings from the guts of Seth; divine associations may be reinforced by the frequent presence of a goose (or duck) head as decoration, which might link the instrument with Amun. It was frequently played by the household god Bes, and in satirical scenes it was the instrument of the lion. The Egyptian lyre was either symmetrical or asymmetrical in appearance, depending on the length of the two arms protruding from the soundbox. A giant instrument, resting on the ground and needing two players, was introduced in the reign of Akhenaten (1379–1362 BC). Of this there is no further

5. *Three Muses playing lyre (right), kithara (centre) and harp: detail of a volute cup (end of the 5th century BC), by the Sisyphos painter, from southern Italy (Staatliche Antikensammlungen und Glyptothek, Munich)*

evidence till the Roman period, when it reappears in the temple of Philae with only one player. The lyre was called *kinnor* in ancient Egypt, the name by which it was also known to the Hebrews.

The *kinnor* had an important part to play in the Temple at Jerusalem. Use was made of a plectrum, and the instrument had seven strings, though Josephus says there could be as many as ten. The *kinnor*, essentially a male instrument and particularly associated with King David, expressed joy and was avoided at times of mourning. It was played in company of other instruments when the ark was brought on a new cart from Kirjath-jearim, but it was hung 'upon the willows' by the rivers of Babylon. Occasional denunciations by the prophets stigmatize the abuse of what was essentially a sacred instrument. Such it remained even in the writings of the Dead Sea Scrolls.

In the ancient world the religious associations of the lyre were strong, as is suggested by its wealth of zoomorphic ornamentation. Occasionally there is a similar hint in the modern world. Perhaps the string holder in the form of an animal in a Nubian lyre at the Pitt Rivers Museum in Oxford also belongs to this category. In modern east Africa decorative tassels of goat's hair are often attached to the end of the yokes. Additional evidence for the use of the lyre outside entertainment comes from ancient Greece (see §2); and the possibility that its association with Orpheus might have been extended in early Christian days to Christ as well as to David is suggested by the presence, in the catacomb of Petrus and Marcellinus at Rome, of a fresco depicting Orpheus with a lyre (see fig.3).

2. ANCIENT GREECE. The lyre and the generally similar kithara (*see* KITHARA, (1)) were the most important string instruments of ancient Greece and Rome. The specific characteristics of the lyre as distinct from those of the kithara were clearly set out in the myth of Hermes' invention of the lyre, narrated in the Homeric *Hymn to Hermes*. According to the myth the clever young Hermes caught a large tortoise, cleaned the shell, stretched cowhide over the opening and thus produced a soundchest. For the vertical frame he used gracefully curving antelope horns to which he attached a yoke of wood. Sheep gut was used for the strings. This description corresponds precisely with pictorial representations of the lyre (see fig.5) and probably defines an early period in its development when its principal parts were directly derived from natural materials. When other materials came to be used in its construction, it retained its original appearance, particularly with regard to the tortoise-shell. There is extant a bronze soundchest evidently moulded from a tortoise-shell. Because of this striking feature ancient writers, particularly poets, frequently referred to the lyre as 'tortoise' (Gk. *chelys*; Lat. *testudo*).

The kithara, on the other hand, was larger and more powerful than the lyre, with a stoutly constructed wooden soundchest and sturdy wooden arms (for further illustration, *see* KITHARA, (1)). Some organologists see the two as different stages in the development of the same instrument, but most regard them as distinct in view of their substantially differing construction and the fact that the Greeks attributed a northern provenance to the lyre and various localities in Asia Minor to the kithara.

There is no evidence of the lyre in Homeric times; the PHORMINX, frequently mentioned, was a type of kithara. The lyre appeared first in late 7th-century iconography and became increasingly common during the following two centuries. The number of strings increased from three or four to a standard seven. It was normally depicted with the player sitting, his left hand against the strings and his right with a plectrum, either plucking the strings or at rest. This has led to considerable speculation concerning the musical function of each hand: for example, that the left, in addition to damping the strings, played an accompaniment to the singer, while the right with its plectrum played preludes and postludes to the song.

Much has been made in modern literature of the radical ethical antithesis between the lyre, instrument of Apollonian measure and restraint, and the AULOS, instrument of Dionysian ecstasy and excess. The sources, however, present a more complex picture. For example, Apollo plays the kithara as much as, if not more than, the lyre; yet Aristotle would have excluded the kithara from his ideal state because, like the aulos, it was difficult to play. At the same time the aulos seems to have occupied an honourable position in the actual musical life of Greece, being the primary instrument of the classical drama and of the officially sanctioned cults. Indeed in ancient literature virtually every instrument is at one time treated with respect and at another with disapprobation.

Nevertheless there remains a long-standing ethical antithesis between the lyre and the aulos, even if it seldom appeared explicitly and consciously. It finds its best expression in the myth of Apollo, the player of the kithara or lyre who defeated the aulos-playing Marsyas in a musical contest. Apollo represented the civilized world of the Greeks as opposed to the satyr Marsyas, half-man and half-animal, who symbolized foreign barbarism. In a related legend the goddess Athena, female counterpart of Apollo as the representative of Athenian civility, discovered that blowing the aulos distorted her features and so she threw it away; it was subsequently found by Marsyas. Certain historical phenomena lie at the basis of such myths. Among them there is the absence of the aulos from the aristocratic Hellenic society celebrated in the Homeric epics. Achilles sang and accompanied himself on the phorminx, and Odysseus relaxed at royal banquets listening to a phorminx player singing the praises of other heroes. The aulos, on the other hand, had an insignificant role in the countryside. There was also the association of the aulos with the orgiastic cults of Dionysus and the Magna Mater. There were periods in which Greco-Roman society was prepared to compromise with such cults and even to absorb them, yet a fundamental antipathy to them never disappeared entirely. And, finally, the lyre and kithara had numerous specifically mathematical, learned associations; they were better suited to precise tuning, and more demonstrative of it, than the fluttery-toned aulos.

This broad dualism found its most explicit expression in the political writings of Plato and Aristotle, who presented, however, an isolated and indeed exaggerated picture as a result of the circumstances of their writings. They described Greek life not as it was but as they conceived it in a utopia with a strong intellectual bias. At the same time both (especially Plato) wrote with a reactionary tendency, invoking the values of aristocratic Athens before the disillusionment following the Peloponnesian War.

Relevant to this aspect is Aristotle's alignment of the kithara with the aulos rather than with the lyre, as mentioned above. Aristotle's position is surprising since the lyre and the kithara were so generally similar in function and ethical connotation. Indeed, many ancient authors, particularly Roman poets in recounting the Greek myths, tended to use the terms interchangeably. In fact there was only one functional difference between the two instruments. The larger kithara was played by virtuosos on public occasions such as the musical *agones* (festival competitions sponsored by various Greek and Roman cities), whereas the less powerful lyre was more suited to private use. Thus Aristotle's attitude is explained by the fact that for him, as for Plato, the lyre was the instrument associated with the education of the free Athenian citizen. This was a part of the aristocratic Greek educational tradition, evolved from Homeric times, with its concept of the ideal citizen brave in battle, athletic and yet cultivated – skill at arms and a degree of musical accomplishment being the mark of the complete male in many societies. The kithara, on the other hand, became associated towards the end of the 5th century BC with a new virtuosity represented by professionals such as Timotheus and Philoxenus, whose exciting playing appealed to the less cultivated members of Athenian society. Musically this involved a breakdown of the traditional distinctions between melodic types such as the Dorian and Phrygian and genres such as the kitharodic nome and the dithyramb. Innovations generally appeared first on the aulos and were copied on the kithara. This breaking down of musical traditions coincided with the change from the proud optimism of the Periclean age to bitterness and humiliation after the Peloponnesian debacle. Thus for a brief period the kithara assumed vulgar, demagogic and dissolute connotations to those who nostalgically looked back to the noble and simple lyre of a happier, braver and more virtuous generation.

In Hellenistic and Roman times the lyre seems to have been used far less than the kithara. The latter broadly fulfilled the functions of both and the two were not opposed again. Yet there remained a vaguely discernible air of privilege about the lyre. In contrast to the kithara, it had been the instrument of the amateur in ancient Greece; and at the synagogue of Dura-Europus 3rd-century wall-paintings show David with a lyre and trumpeters in Solomon's temple. This phenomenon appeared again in the Middle Ages when the lyre was associated with King David, as patron of music and figure of Christ. Eventually its shape came to serve as a universal symbol of music in Western civilization: thus it might appear on the cover of 17th-century evangelical hymnals, on the pedal supports of a 19th-century grand piano or as the outline of a glockenspiel in a 20th-century marching band.

The following lyres are entered in this dictionary: 'arṭaba; baku; bangia; barbiton; beganna; brimbiri; chemonget; chepkesem; chepkongo; crwth; edungu; endongo; giga; ginger; goala; gue; hiiukannel; indongoli; jouhikko; kaithros; ketuba; kibugandet; kinnārāt; kipokan; kinnor; kirān; kissar; kithara; krar; kudu (i); lidungu; litungu; lyra Barberina; lyre guitar; masonquo; mi'zaf; mizhar; muwattar; ndongo; nevel; ntongoli; nyatiti; obokana; odi (i); phorminx; psantria; qambūs; qinīn; rabāb; rababa; rapapa; rootsikannel; rotte (ii); shangar; simsimīyya; stråkharpa; tallharpa; ṭambira; ṭanbūra; testudo; thum; timpán; tripous; tum (i); ṭunbūr; tympanum (ii).

BIBLIOGRAPHY

LaurentyC; WachsmannTCU
C. Sachs: *Die Musikinstrumente des alten Ägyptens* (Berlin, 1921)
O. Andersson: *The Bowed-harp* (London, 1930)
C. Sachs: *The History of Musical Instruments* (New York, 1940)
H. Hickmann: *Catalogue général des antiquités égyptiennes du Musée du Caire* (Cairo, 1949)

R. P. Winnington-Ingram: 'The Pentatonic Tuning of the Greek Lyre: a Theory Examined', *Classical Quarterly*, new ser., vi (1956), 169

H. G. Farmer: 'The Music of Islam', *NOHM*, i (1957), 421–77

I. Henderson: 'Ancient Greek Music', *NOHM*, i (1957), 336–403

H. Steger: *David rex et propheta* (Nuremberg, 1961)

E. Winternitz: 'The Survival of the Kithara and the Evolution of the Cittern: a Study in Morphology', *Music, Libraries and Instruments*, ed. U. Sherrington and G. Oldham (London, 1961), 209ff, incl. illustration

H. Owuor: 'Luo Songs', *Black Orpheus*, x (1962), 51

O. Anyumba: 'The Making of a Lyre Musician', *MILA: a Biannual Newsletter of Cultural Research*, i/2 (1970), 28

D. Wulston: 'The Earliest Musical Notation', *ML*, lii (1971), 365

M. Maas: 'On the Shape of the Ancient Greek Lyre', *GSJ*, xxvii (1974), 113

S. Marcuse: *A Survey of Musical Instruments* (London, 1975)

A. A. Moorefield: 'James Bruce: Ethnomusicologist or Abyssinian Lyre?', *JAMS*, xxviii (1975), 493

R. D. Anderson: *Catalogue of Egyptian Antiquities in the British Museum*, iii (London, 1976)

G. A. Plumley: *El tanbur* (Cambridge, 1976)

E. Winternitz: 'Further Evidence of Open Strings in Classical Greek Music, 5th and 4th Centuries, B.C.', *RIdIM Newsletter*, ii/1 (1976), 5

C. Ziegler: *Les instruments de musique égyptiens au musée du Louvre* (Paris, 1979)

For further bibliography *see* ROTTE (ii).
KLAUS WACHSMANN, ROBERT ANDERSON (1),
JAMES W. Mc KINNON (2)

Lyre guitar. A hybrid plucked chordophone, basically a lyre with a fingerboard. Long-necked lutes with lyre-like 'wings' projecting from the soundbox have been discovered in Libyan mosaics, and are pictured in the Utrecht and Canterbury psalters (*c*850 and *c*1250). Renaissance paintings by Lorenzo Costa and del Garbo show lyre guitars held upright, but these may be interpretations of incised strings in classical bas-reliefs. The lyre guitar as a performing instrument appears to have been heralded in about 1780 by a pamphlet, *Plagiat dénoncé aux musiciens et aux amateurs des lyres nouvelles* (in *B-Bc*) by N. Maréchal of Paris.

Parisian instruments by Maréchal, Lacôte, Michelot, Pleyel and Pons were quickly imitated in Caen (Thibout), Mirecourt (Breton, Mousset, Roudhlof), Marseilles (Charles), Naples (Fabricatore) and Berlin (Thielemann). Most extant instruments date from between 1805–10; the earliest reliable date is 1785 (Charles), and the latest 1817 (Fabricatore). These continental forms measured about 80 × 40 × 15 cm, and were usually decorated around the soundhole and soundboard edge. English instruments were sold from 1811 as the six-string Apollo lyre of Edward Light and the 12-string 'Imperyal Lyre' of Angelo Benedetto Ventura.

Continental lyre guitars were tuned like the six-string guitar, and indeed it may be that competition from lyre guitars persuaded other guitar makers more regularly to fit a sixth string. Playing instructions for the lyre guitar appeared as an appendix to some standard guitar manuals, and for a time many French and English song accompaniments were indicated as 'for guitar or lyre'.

The lateral arms which had made it unpopular with professional musicians (with the exception of Schubert's friend Vogl and the French tenor Fabry-Garat) gradually encouraged its amateur and mainly female market to adopt the ordinary guitar or the piano as an accompanying instrument.

BIBLIOGRAPHY

Anon.: 'Einige Worte über die neue französische Lyre (Lyre-Guitarre)', *AMZ*, iii (1801), 786 [Eng. trans. in Bonner, 1972]

R. B. Armstrong: *Musical Instruments*, ii (Edinburgh, 1908)

D. Fryklund: 'Studier över lyragitarren', *STMf*, ix (1927), 117–48

E. Winternitz: *Musical Instruments and their Symbolism in Western Art* (London, 1967)

S. Bonner: *Angelo Benedetto Ventura* (Harlow, 1971)

——: *The Classic Image* (Harlow, 1972)

STEPHEN BONNER

Lyre organisée. A lyre guitar with a keyboard and 15 strings patented by Led'huy of Coucy-les-Châteaux in 1806. Its tone was softer than that of the piano.

Lyre piano. A type of UPRIGHT PIANOFORTE.

Lyrichord. A bowed keyboard instrument invented by the harpsichord maker Roger Plenius and patented in London in 1741. Its gut and metal strings were tuned with lead weights and bowed with clockwork wheels which rotated at different speeds. One section of the lid, controlled by a pedal, could be opened or closed to increase or decrease volume; vibrato was also possible. In 1745 Plenius introduced a harp stop into the instrument, which gave a pizzicato effect. *See also* SOSTENENTE PIANO, §1.

Lyricon. An electronic wind instrument that controls a SYNTHESIZER; it was developed by Bill Bernardi and Roger Noble and manufactured from around 1975 by Computone Inc. (now a subsidiary of Ampeg) in Hanover, Massachusetts, and later in nearby Norwell. It is a solid-bodied metal instrument, resembling an oversized flute though it is much heavier and is played vertically like a clarinet. It produces no acoustic sound but converts

Lyre guitar: detail from 'The Coppenrath Family in a Boating Party' (1807) by Johann Christoph Ruicklake (private collection)

the traditional skills of breath control, embouchure and fingering into electronic signals that control a synthesizer housed in a separate unit (into which the instrument also fits for transporting). The Lyricon is played with a modified tenor saxophone mouthpiece, using a fibrecane reed. The mouthpiece contains a transducer sensitive to pressure on the reed, which makes contact with a flexible rod; this allows the small variations of pitch used in lip vibrato and glissando effects to be reproduced. Another transducer, linked to a level control, is sensitive to breath pressure and permits the effects of soft and hard blowing and various types of attack to be applied to the synthesized sounds. There are 15 keys, laid out in a similar (though simpler) pattern to those of a saxophone or flute; they make an electrical contact when depressed. An unusual feature is a second octave key (played by the thumb), which gives a three-octave range; this can be transposed within a total compass from B' to d'''. The keywork allows fast and fluid playing with exhilarating changes of register.

The tone and register, and certain other effects (including automatic transposition into any of several common keys) can be set on the synthesizer. This consists basically of oscillators and filters (no shaping or pitch controls being necessary). The original version of the Lyricon was designed to synthesize the sounds of a wide range of orchestral and other instruments, and has a bank of filters which select or emphasize the relevant overtones. Lyricon II (1978) is simpler, cheaper and more robust, and was intended chiefly for rock and jazz musicians. It has two oscillators, each offering a square or sawtooth wave; range and tuning controls; a pulse-width control; and controls for the degree of modulation by lip or breath pressure. It also has various filters (lowpass, band-pass and high-pass) and tuning-lock controls, though the oscillators may be tuned apart for certain special effects.

The Lyricon has been used in rock music and jazz, mostly by saxophone players: the session player Tom Scott in Los Angeles and Wayne Shorter of the group Weather Report have featured it, and it can be heard played by Andy Mackay on Paul McCartney's album *Tug of War*. The Swiss composer Bruno Spoerri won first prize at the Ars Electronica festival in Linz in 1979 for his performance on the Lyricon.

BIBLIOGRAPHY

G. Alderman and M. Soboil: 'The Lyricon: the Musician's View'; 'The Lyricon: the Manufacturer's View', *Musician's Guide* (April 1978)

A. Strange: *Electronic Music: Systems, Techniques, and Controls* (Dubuque, Iowa, 2/1983), 57

ANDY MACKAY

Lyro-harpe. A guitar with 19 strings on two necks invented in Berlin in 1837; its range was over four octaves and its powerful tone like that of a harp.

Lyrone. *See* LIRONE.

Lyrophone. A family of DUPLEX instruments, made by Sediva of Odessa in 1887.

Lyro-pianoforte. A hybrid keyboard instrument combining the hammer action of the piano with the jacks of the harpsichord (*see* HARPSICHORD-PIANO). It was invented by Robert Thomas Worton and patented in London in 1861. Each hammer carried a plucking device and the instrument could function either as a piano or as a harpsichord. Worton combined the lyro-pianoforte with his bowed keyboard instrument, the vis-pianoforte, to produce the lyro-vis-pianoforte (*see* SOSTENENTE PIANO, §1).

Lyro viol. *See* LYRA VIOL.

Lyro-vis-pianoforte. A hybrid instrument invented by Robert Worton; it was a combination of his bowed keyboard instrument, the vis-pianoforte, and the LYROPIANOFORTE. *See also* SOSTENENTE PIANO, §1.

Lysarden. Presumably the name given in England to the bass member of the CORNETT family before the SERPENT came into use in the 17th century. Lizards do, after all, resemble snakes, even though they come from different families. A 'lyserden' is listed in the waits' band of Exeter in 1575, according to L. G. Langwill: 'The Waits', *HMYB*, vii (1952), p.176; the Norwich waits owned a 'lyzardyne' in 1585, according to W. L. Woodfill: *Musicians in English Society from Elizabeth I to Charles I* (Princeton, NJ, 1953/R1969), p.85; and a 'lysarden' appears in the inventory made in 1602–3 of the instruments at Hengrave Hall, Suffolk, that belonged to Thomas Kytson, according to F. W. Galpin: *Old English Instruments of Music* (London, 4/1965), p.204.

M

Maass, Nikolaus (*d* Copenhagen, 1615). German organ builder. He was active in central and northern Germany and in Denmark from 1584 to 1615, and came perhaps from Saxony; the supposition that he was from Brabant is not borne out either by Praetorius, who is a major source of information about him, or by the style of his work. Maass worked in 1584 and 1598 on the organ of St Marien, Prenzlau, built by F. Petersen in 1567, and from 1599 to 1603 on another of Petersen's organs, that of St Nikolai, Greifswald (1575). He was granted citizenship in Stralsund in 1592, where in 1592–4 he built a large organ (three manuals, 43 stops). He built another in the region, in the Stadtkirche at Barth, in 1597, and he worked in Grimma, Saxony, at some time before 1598. Maass settled in Copenhagen in autumn 1603 as organ builder to the royal Danish court. He built a large organ in St Nikolai, Flensburg, 1604–9 (three manuals, 38 stops; the case by H. Ringerinck survives). In 1611 he supervised the rebuilding of the Roskilde Cathedral organ, built in 1555 by H. R. Rodensteen. His last large organ, 1613–15, in the Frederiksborg Schlosskirche at Hillerød, was completed after his death by his colleague Johann Lorentz from Saxony, who succeeded him as court organ builder. In important characteristics Maass's organs are in the style of the large central German Baroque organs; his principal model seems to have been David Beck. He equipped the *Hauptwerk*, *Rückpositiv* and Pedal each with a complete Principal chorus and a comprehensive group of foundation stops and, especially in the *Rückpositiv* and Pedal, a colourful series of reed stops. Maass's larger organs have, in addition, a separate *Brustwerk* with its own keyboard, which was also provided with three comprehensive groups of stops – at least that is true of the Stralsund organ; it was a rarity in north German organs of that date. Maass built slider wind-chests; his keyboards range from *C*, *D*, *E* to *g″*, *a″* or *C*, *D*, *E* to *d′* (St Nikolai, Flensburg).

BIBLIOGRAPHY

M. Praetorius: *Syntagma musicum*, ii (Wolfenbüttel, 1618, 2/1619/*R*1958 and 1980)

W. Gurlitt: 'Zum Schülerkreis von Gottfried Fritzsche', *Musik und Kirche*, x (1938), 160

N. Friis: *Orgelbygning i Danmark: renaissance, barok og rokoko* (Copenhagen, 1949)

P. G. Andersen: *Orgelbogen: klangteknik, arkitektur og historie* (Copenhagen, 1956; Eng. trans., 1969)

M. A. Vente: *Die Brabanter Orgel* (Amsterdam, 1958, 2/1963)

——: 'Maass', *MGG*

H. P. Detlefsen: *Musikgeschichte der Stadt Flensburg bis zum Jahre 1850* (Kassel, 1961)

HANS KLOTZ

Ma'āzif. Plural form of MI'ZAF.

Mabu. (1) Wooden trumpet of Buka, Solomon Islands, with a half coconut shell as a mouthpiece. It is played by men and older boys at ceremonial and secular dances in association with panpipes (*ka'ur*). See B. Blackwood: *Both Sides of Buka Passage* (Oxford, 1935), 411; C. Barrett: *Isles of the Sun* (London, 1954), 98.

(2) Bamboo JEW'S HARP of Nissan, Solomon Islands. See F. Krause: 'Zur Ethnographie der Insel Nissan', *Jahrbuch des Stadtischen Museums für Völkerkunde zu Leipzig*, i (1906), 144.

Mabumbumbu. Single-headed footed cylindrical drum of the Nika/Giryama people of Malindi district, Kenya. The membrane is pegged on. The drum is open-ended and is played with the hands.

Maccaferri, Mario (*b* Cento, nr. Bologna, 1900). Italian designer of guitars. His interest in the technical aspects of the guitar developed out of his successful career in early life as a classical guitarist. He had already built a number of other instruments when in the early 1930s he designed a series of guitars for the French company Selmer. Some of these had distinctive D-shaped sound-holes, but the most unconventional feature of their construction was an additional sound chamber contained within the guitar body, the purpose of which was to achieve greater volume than was possible with the normal acoustic guitar. This, as well as the thin woods used, gave the Maccaferri guitars a piercing, treble-dominated sound, much exploited by Django Reinhardt, the most celebrated player of the time to have used them.

After a dispute with Selmer, Maccaferri moved to the USA later in the 1930s. There he experimented with other guitar designs, including a range of plastic models. In the late 1970s Maccaferri authorized the manufacture by a Japanese maker of guitars to his original Selmer design of the 1930s.

BIBLIOGRAPHY

M. Summerfield: *The Jazz Guitar* (Gateshead, 1978)

TONY BACON

MacGregor [Macgregor, McGregor], **Malcolm** (*fl* London, early 19th century). English flute maker. He is known to have worked in London at Bell Yard, Carey Street (1810), and was a partner with Charles Wigley in the firm of Wigley & McGregor, active from 1811 to 1825 in the Strand and in Regent Street. He worked on improvements to the flute. The flute for which he claimed superior tuning (described in his article in the *Transactions of the Society of Arts, Manufactures and*

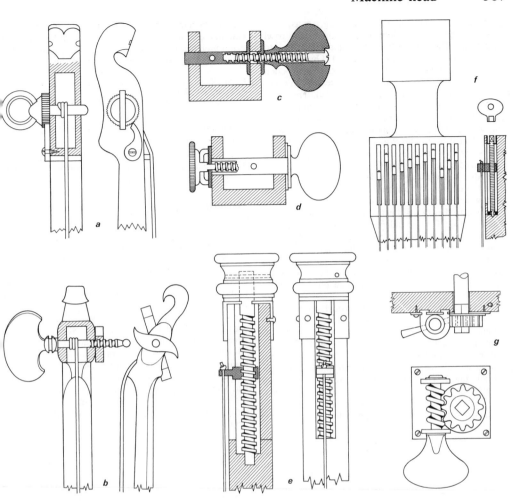

1. Examples of machine heads

Commerce, 1813) gained a silver medal at the exhibition of the Society of Arts in London (1813). MacGregor favoured adjustable slides at a number of points on the instrument. His alto and tenor flutes sometimes had a large hole at the side near the C♯ hole, covered with a thin skin in order to give a reedy tone. These instruments were often built with a turned-back head joint. Between 1812 and 1816 he built a bass flute (patented in 1810) of one solid oval piece of boxwood with the bore doubling back; it had six finger-holes and eight brass keys and overcame the problem of finger-stretching by using obliquely bored finger-holes. The tuning in the second and third octaves was poor. He was awarded a prize in Edinburgh for a bagpipe chanter (1810).

BIBLIOGRAPHY
J. G. Dalyell: *Musical Memoirs of Scotland* (Edinburgh, 1849)
C. Welch: *History of the Boehm Flute* (London, 1883, 2/ 1896/R1961)
R. S. Rockstro: *A Treatise on . . . the Flute* (London, 1890, 2/ 1928/R1967)
H. M. Fitzgibbon: *The Story of the Flute* (London, 1914, 2/1929)
D. C. Miller: *Catalogue of Books and Literary Material relating to the Flute* (Cleveland, 1935)
P. Bate: *The Flute* (London, 1969, 2/1979)
                                    NIALL O'LOUGHLIN

Machada. *See* MACHETE.

Machado e Cerveira, António. *See* CERVEIRA, ANTÓNIO MACHADO E.

Machell, Thomas. Inventor of the dulcitone, one of the TUNING-FORK INSTRUMENTS.

Machete [machada]. Plucked lute of Portugal, the Azores and Brazil, with four, five or six strings. Portuguese sailors supposedly introduced the instrument into the Hawaiian islands, where it was transformed (through such variant forms as the *machête da braça*) into the UKULELE. It is also called a CAVAQUINHO.

Machine drum. A kettledrum whose tuning screws are operated simultaneously, by a pedal, a single master screw or by rotation; *see* TIMPANI, §1.

Machine head. A tuning device that uses mechanical advantage to tune or maintain the pitch of a string. By definition only those devices which increase the leverage on the string, including the direct screw device and the worm-gear mechanism, should be considered machine heads, but by tradition mechanized string-holding devices, such as the ratchet and pawl, lock nuts and patent pegs, are also included.

A ratchet and pawl, or 'wheel and dog', consists of a notched wheel or gear kept in position by the pawl (see fig.1a). The pawl, often spring-loaded, falls into the notches of the wheel as it is turned. On a number of 17th- and 18th-century trumpets marine a wooden lock nut is attached to the end of a threaded peg in order to keep the string from slipping (see fig.1b). The many forms of the patent peg, which use mechanical pressure against the cheeks of the pegbox to maintain the tension, were a 19th-century improvement. Various designs were patented by Joseph Wallis (see fig.1c) and M. H. Collins (fig.1d), and a modern version of the patent peg is produced under the name Caspari.

The direct or vertical screw device (also employed to adjust the tension of bow hairs) consists of a threaded nut to which the string is attached. The nut then slides in the grooved neck of the instrument as the screw is turned (see fig.1e). An adaptation of this principle is found in the watch-key tuning mechanism of J. N. Preston of London, who applied it to the English guitar in the mid-18th century (see fig.1f). The most efficient and enduring of the machine heads is the worm-gear device now used on double basses and plucked string instruments (fig.1g).

Both the ratchet and pawl and vertical screw heads were in use by the end of the 16th century. The latter first appeared on some trumpets marine that are thought to date from the last third of the century. In 1619 Praetorius complained that the coarseness of the teeth on the iron ratchets of the violone did not allow the string to be finely tuned. Worm-gear heads were in evidence in the early 18th century, with some fine examples appearing on Cristofori double basses about 1715.

Although true machine heads appear to have been first used on heavy gut strings, they are particularly appropriate for metal strings because they allow the induction and maintenance of great tension with little effort and no slippage; since the 18th century this has been their primary application. Modern practice has extended the use of the machine head in the form of the fine tuners used on bowed instruments fitted with steel strings.

CECIL ADKINS

Machine stop. (1) A device applied to English harpsichords in the second half of the 18th century by means of which a single PEDAL could be made to control two or more separate registers, overriding their individual handstops. On single-manual harpsichords, when the pedal was depressed the 4' register and the front 8' register were withdrawn, and when the pedal was released both registers were re-engaged. Moreover, when the pedal was depressed slowly, the 4' register was withdrawn before the 8', and when the pedal was released slowly, the 8' register was re-engaged before the 4', thereby permitting the harpsichordist to produce fairly smooth diminuendos and crescendos. On two-manual harpsichords, the machine stop had an identical effect on the registers available on the lower manual but, in addition, when the pedal was depressed, the close-plucking lute stop was engaged in place of the front ('dogleg') 8' register on the upper manual. Both the single-manual and double-manual machine stops could be disengaged when desired, returning the harpsichord to normal handstop operation. See also REGISTRATION, §II, 3.

(2) A device with a similar purpose applied to chamber organs. An extra slider could cancel out the higher-pitched stops when a pedal was depressed, even though their knobs remained drawn. The machine stop was quite common on English chamber organs from the mid-18th century onwards, and was used in echo passages and in pieces having short soft sections or interludes.

BIBLIOGRAPHY
E. M. Ripin: 'Expressive Devices Applied to the Eighteenth-Century Harpsichord', *Organ Yearbook*, i (1970), 64

EDWIN M. RIPIN (1), BARBARA OWEN (2)

Machinga. Metal JEW'S HARP of the Sunwar people of Nepal. See MURCANG.

Macho [machu] **(i).** Double-rank PANPIPES of the Bolivian Alti Plano; it is played in the JULA-JULA ensemble.

Macho (ii). Type of Colombian FRAME DRUM. See BOMBO (ii).

Mackay [Mackey]. American family of merchants, noted for its financial backing of Boston keyboard instrument makers. During the first half of the 19th century members of the family financially supported various Boston instrument makers, including Alpheus Babcock, Thomas Appleton and Jonas Chickering. The most active member was John Mackay (d at sea, 1841), master mariner and Boston merchant, who is also credited with an American patent (first issued 14 August 1822; reissued 23 April 1839) for fitting metal into leather-covered hammerheads to produce a fuller tone.

The *New-England Magazine* (January 1834) claims that Mackay supported the builders Babcock, Appleton and William Goodrich at 6 Milk Street, Boston, from the dissolution of the partnership of Hayts, Babcock and Appleton on 26 May 1815 until 1820. By 1823 Mackay's nephew George D. Mackay (d at sea, 15 Dec 1824) had set up a piano making factory at 7 Parkman's Market with Alpheus Babcock as his superintendent. The inventory of George's factory made by Babcock and Appleton on 24 January 1825 lists nine workbenches, nine finished and nine unfinished square pianos and one unfinished grand as well as tools and supplies. Another inventory (17 October 1825) indicates that the factory was financed by John's mother, Ruth Mackay (b 1743; d Weston, Mass., 10 April 1833), who continued to support John's business with Babcock until 1829. During this time pianos produced by Babcock, marked 'Babcock for G. D. Mackay' or 'Babcock for R. Mackay', included the earliest square pianos to have cast-iron frames in one piece.

From 1830 until his death John Mackay was in business with Jonas CHICKERING. During this period the firm operated from 416 Washington Street and by 1838 from a new factory at no.334. In 1838 the firm's official name was Jonas Chickering & Co. (John Mackay); from 1839 to 1841 it was Chickering & Mackays (John and son William H.) and in 1842 Chickering & Mackay (William H.). After 1842 Chickering bought the Mackay interest. Among those working for Chickering & Mackays was Alpheus Babcock, who assigned his patent (no.1389) on actions to the firm (31 October 1839). Throughout his association with keyboard makers, John Mackay provided capital and business acumen, found new buyers in North and South America and brought back exotic woods and other raw materials.

BIBLIOGRAPHY
'Biographical Memoir of William Goodrich, Organ Builder', *New-England Magazine* (Jan 1834)

℟. C. Parker: *A Tribute to the Life and Character of Jonas Chickering by One who Knew him Well* (Boston, 1854)
℟. M. Ayars: *Contributions to the Art of Music by the Music Industries of Boston 1640 to 1936* (New York, 1937), 106ff
℟. G. Grafing: *Alpheus Babcock: American Pianoforte Maker (1785–1842), his Life, Instruments, and Patents* (diss., U. of Missouri, Kansas City, 1972)

CYNTHIA ADAMS HOOVER

MacKenzie, I(cabod) A(ngus) (*b* Kansas state, *c*1880; *d* Angel's Camp, Calif., 1969). American composer and sound sculptor. He studied music in the San Francisco Bay area, but in the 1920s he abandoned composition, burning all his scores. From that time his interests slowly turned to sound sculpture and for over 30 years he constructed wind-, water-, fire- and gravity-powered works at Angel's Camp in the California mountains. His earliest piece, which used wind chimes, was built in 1934; wind-powered elements that appeared later included bell-chimes, tubular chimes, piano strings and drums struck by beaters, whistle holes and a slide pipe consisting of two concentric tubes. He constructed a total of 53 aeolian instruments. He first used water in a sound sculpture in 1947 and his only work to involve fire was built in 1955. Since his death his sculptures have been dispersed to remote locations; this was done in accordance with his will, which is also the cause of the almost complete lack of information about his work, since it directed that many documents be destroyed or suppressed.

BIBLIOGRAPHY
D. Cope: 'Chronicles of a Cause: I. A. MacKenzie', *Composer*, i/1 (Hamilton, Ohio, 1969), 35
——: *New Directions in Music* (Dubuque, Iowa, 2/1976), 211

HUGH DAVIES

Mackey. *See* MACKAY family.

McLaren, Norman (*b* Stirling, 11 April 1914). Canadian film maker, animator and exponent of DRAWN SOUND, of Scottish birth. He studied at the Glasgow School of Art (1932–6) and then worked as an animator at the GPO Film Unit in London; the unit rejected his first hand-drawn soundtrack, for his film *Book Bargain* (1937), which was consequently released with only a spoken commentary. In 1939 he moved to New York, where he produced several short films, including three with drawn sound (*Allegro*, *Dots* and *Loops*; *see* DRAWN SOUND, fig.1) and a soundtrack without visual images (*Rumba*). He joined the National Film Board of Canada (NFBC) at Ottawa in 1941 and moved with them to Montreal in 1956.

McLaren has specialized in making short animated films in which he has pioneered a wide variety of techniques, especially that of drawing directly onto the film, thus bypassing the use of the camera. He has exploited similar techniques in exploring the possibilities of drawn sound, of which he rapidly became the best-known exponent. He has also investigated the relationship of music to image in films that have used works ranging from Bach and Albinoni to jazz and French–Canadian folksong.

In his early work McLaren drew his music directly onto the narrow optical soundtrack section of the filmstock (this strip has a maximum width of 2·5 mm). But by 1947, pursuing a technique devised by Rudolf Pfenninger, he had built up a library of cards measuring 30·5 × 2·5 cm, on each of which a sound-wave pattern is drawn between one and 120 times to produce every semitone in a range of five octaves. These are then photographed, using masks to modify volume and envelope shape (which governs attack and contour); different exposure times, in combination with the masks and wave patterns, give precise control over pitch (to $\frac{1}{10}$ of a tone), duration (to $\frac{1}{50}$ of a second), rhythm and timbre.

McLaren's films with drawn soundtracks include *Now is the Time* (1951), a stereoscopic and stereophonic 3-D film; *Two Bagatelles* (1952); *Neighbours* (1952), which was awarded an Oscar; *Blinkety Blank* (1955), which features percussive effects scratched onto the black film emulsion; *Mosaic* (1965); and *Synchromy* (1971), in which the drawn patterns used to create the soundtrack form the visual element as well. They are characterized by their inventiveness and wit, and an astonishing degree of interaction between sound and image.

BIBLIOGRAPHY
R. Lewis and N. McLaren: 'Synthetic Sound on Film', *Journal of the Society of Motion Picture Engineers*, l (1948), 233
A. Phillips: 'The Inspired Doodles of Norman McLaren', *Maclean's Magazine* lxv/24 (1952), 22
W. E. Jordan: 'Norman McLaren: his Career and Techniques', *Quarterly of Film, Radio and Television*, viii (1953), 1
N. McLaren: 'Notes on Animated Sound', *Quarterly of Film, Radio and Television*, vii (1953), 223; in R. Manvell and J. Huntley: *The Technique of Film Music* (London, 1957), 169
M. Collins: *Norman McLaren* (Ottawa, 1976), 17, 73
McLaren (Montreal, 1980) [NFBC monograph]

HUGH DAVIES

McTammany, John (*b* Worcester, Mass., 26 June 1845; *d* 26 March 1915). American instrument maker and inventor. In 1868 he developed a player-mechanism for reed organs, using a roll of heavy perforated paper and activated by treadles. A device allowing the player-mechanism to be contained inside the case of the instrument rather than acting on the keys from outside was patented in 1876. The McTammany Organette Co. was founded in Worcester shortly afterwards, probably the first company to deal exclusively in the manufacture of self-playing reed organs. McTammany's improvements to the development of pneumatically operated player-mechanisms led directly to their application to the player piano, but other manufacturers with greater financial resources soon outstripped him.

BIBLIOGRAPHY
A. Dolge: *Pianos and their Makers* (Covina, Calif., 1911/*R*1972)
A. W. J. G. Ord-Hume: *Barrel Organ: the Story of the Mechanical Organ and its Repair* (London, 1978)

BARBARA OWEN

Macuṅga. Metal JEW'S HARP of the Rai people of Nepal. *See* MURCANG.

Madaku. LAMELLAPHONE of the Dongo and Zande peoples of Zaïre. It has wooden keys and a triangular wooden resonator attached to a flat soundboard (*LaurentyS*, 193).

Mādal [mãdal, madal]. Double-headed drum of eastern India and Nepal. Although primarily a tribal instrument, the *mādal* is used to accompany song and dance by Hindu villagers in border areas, such as in the *chau* dance of Purulia district, West Bengal, and in the *dalkhai* and *rasarkali* songs of Sambalpur, Orissa. The name derives from the medieval Sanskrit *mardala*. In Nepal the instrument is of variable size, held horizontally and struck with the hands. It is used to accompany secular song and dance. *See also* KHĪM; MĀDAR; MṚDAṄGA, §2(i).

BIBLIOGRAPHY
T. O. Ballinger and P. H. Bajracharya: 'Nepalese Musical Instruments', *Southwestern Journal of Anthropology*, xvi/4 (1960), 398
S. Ray: *Music of Eastern India* (Calcutta, 1973)
F. Hoerburger: *Studien zur Musik in Nepal* (Regensburg, 1975)
S. Wiehler-Schneider and H. Wiehler: 'A Classification of the Traditional Musical Instruments of the Nevars', *Journal of the Nepal Research Centre*, iv (1980), 67–132
ALASTAIR DICK, MIREILLE HELFFER

Mādalā [mathala]. A cylindrical double-headed drum of south and central India. It was played with the fingers and was similar to the drum *ḍholak* of the north (*see* DHOLAK, §1). It is now obsolescent but was used in the *bajānā* ensemble. *See also* MARDALA.

Mādar [mādal, mandar, mandal, mardal, mādal, madal]. Double-headed drum, with baked clay body and laced skin heads, found among Austro-Asiatic and Dravidian tribal groups as well as non-tribal folk musicians throughout the tribal belt of east-central India, including the states of Orissa, southern Bihar, Madhya Pradesh, West Bengal and eastern Uttar Pradesh.

The size and shape of the *mādar* vary depending on the group and geographic area. The two most common shapes may be generalized as barrel-shaped and conical (straight or slightly waisted). In both the right-hand head is smaller, and higher in pitch, than the left.

The hollow shell of the *mādar* is a thin wall of baked clay whitewashed with white clay or slaked lime. For added strength decorative cowhide lacings about 2 mm wide are pasted around the shell in close parallel bands. Monkey hide is preferred for the right head, but has become scarce so that goatskin may be substituted for it. The left head is usually made of calfhide. The skins are held in place by plaited straw hoops and a strip of skin about 1 cm wide overlapping the outer edge of each head. The skins and hoops are tied in a close network of lacings which runs the length of the drum. Additional thongs of cowhide running from one head to the other hold the skins permanently at the required tension. The right head is usually treated to within 3 or 4 cm of its edge with many layers of a permanent paste of clay and grain, typically rice. Each layer is rubbed well with a stone and allowed to dry. The centre of the left head is covered to roughly 1 to 4 cm from its edge with several, more temporary, layers of the same paste, applied with the hand, without rubbing, and allowed to dry. The left head is decorated with painted geometric designs, and the entire drum is often swathed in a colourful cloth.

Although the *mādar* is primarily associated with tribal groups, its shell is made by non-tribals of the Kumhār (potter) caste and its heads made and attached by members of one of the area's leather-working castes (such as the Mūcī, Ghāsī Mahali, Turi or Goṛāit). The player, usually a man, holds the drum horizontally before him, slung around his neck by a leather or cotton cord. For many tribal groups the drum's presence is essential in the village dancing-ground. *Mādar* players, even more than other drummers, dance as they play, swinging the drum in front of them, turning with it, and bending forward to lower it nearly to the ground. In Orissa and some parts of West Bengal the drum is also part of the percussion ensemble which accompanies the *chau* (*cho*) dance drama and the *nacini* dance. *Mādar* rhythmic patterns and strokes are vocalized in syllables which vary

from village to village and even from drummer to drummer.

The *jaspuria mādar* is the principal drum of many communities of tribal and non-tribal folk musicians of southern Bihar. Its barrel-shaped, or cylindro-barrel shaped, shell can range from 60 to 118 cm in length (on average about 70 cm). Half the instrument, from the right head to the centre, is roughly cylindrical or slightly conical, but from the centre the shell widens to a bulge at approximately three-quarters the distance from the right head, and then narrows slightly towards the left head. Unlike the straight or waisted conical *mādar*, both heads of the *jaspuria mādar* are flush with the outer rims of their hoops. Typically, both heads are left undecorated.

The *jaspuria mādar* is traditionally associated with the Ghāsī caste of leather-workers, who play it, make it and even claim to have invented it. In the past they reserved the drum for accompanying *janāni jhuma* ('women's *jhumar*') – group singing and dancing during the monsoon season – using other drums such as the *ḍholkī* (*see* DHOLAK, §2) in other seasons. In the last 20 or 30 years the *mādar* has been taken up by players of high-status castes and has become the principal drum throughout the year to accompany staged solo singing and most genres of dancing.

The straight or slightly waisted conical types of *mādar* are more common throughout the east-central tribal belt than are the barrel-shaped. Approximately half the drum, from the right head to the centre, is cylindrical or even narrows slightly to a shallow waist. From the centre the shell expands conically towards the left head. Because of its shape, the outer lacings do not touch the drum's body, giving it the illusion of a strict conical shape. The rim around the right head is built up with bamboo strips, so that the head is recessed by 2 or 3 cm from the drum's outer edge.

In southern Bihar this type, of variable size, is associated with different tribal groups who know it by native names of which the most widespread are the *khel* and the *dumang*. The Uraon *khel* is the largest of these drums in southern Bihar, ranging from 60 to 85 cm in length (usually about 60 cm); the right head is 25 cm in diameter, the left 35 cm. It is the most popular drum among the Uraon people, who use it for group singing and in *jadur*, *karam* and *jātra* communal dances.

The Muṇḍā people of southern Bihar use two *mādar*-type drums of different sizes, both called *dumang* in Muṇḍāri; one is about 35 cm long, and the other, perhaps more common, about 50 to 66 cm. Local non-tribal folk musicians refer to the smaller as *jhāldā mādar* and the larger as *mūcī mādar*. The heads are attached and treated in the same manner as those of the *jaspuria mādar*, but the paste covers a larger area of the right head. During the first few decades of the 20th century, and perhaps long before, the *dumang* was the most important drum in the percussion ensemble that accompanied Muṇḍāri processions and communal dancing and singing in the village dancing-ground. The full ensemble consisted of *dumang* players (the lead drummers), with the instruments *nagara* (kettledrum), *rabaga* (double-headed drum), perhaps some *ḍulki* (double-headed drum) and *cuā* or *manjīrā* (cup cymbals). Within the last few generations the *ḍulki* has gradually replaced the *dumang* as the lead drum in the dancing-ground. The *dumang*, however, has still a great deal of symbolic and ceremonial significance for the Muṇḍā people and holds a position of honour in tribal processions, rituals, festivals and in song texts, where it is often paired with the *ḍulki* and sometimes with the *rabaga*.

See also MĀDAL; MANDARI; MRDAṄGA, §2; RŪNJ; TUMDAK'.

BIBLIOGRAPHY
S. C. Roy: *The Orāons of Chōtā Nāgpur* (Calcutta, 1915), 181, 284, 288f
J. Hoffmann and A. van Emelen: *Encyclopaedia mundarica* (Patna, 1938–50), v/1–13, 1110f
K. S. Kothari: *Indian Folk Musical Instruments* (New Delhi, 1968), 41f
O. Prasad: *Munda: Music and Dance* (diss., Ranchi U., 1971), 70
L. Miśra: *Bhāratīya sangīt vādya* (New Delhi, 1973), 175
B. C. Deva: *Musical Instruments of India: their History and Development* (Calcutta, 1978), 95f
CAROL M. BABIRACKI

Maddaḷam [maddale]. A tuned barrel drum of Kerala and Karnataka, south-western India, also known to the Tamil as *mattaḷam*. It is made of wood and has composite heads interlaced by straps and tuned with blocks; tuning paste of the *mṛdaṅga* type is used. It is played with the fingers of the right hand in plaster thimbles. The instrument is important in religious and ceremonial music (*pañcavādyam*), and in theatrical music such as *Kathakali* and *Kutiyattam*, where it leads the orchestra. In Tamil the term 'maddaḷam' may denote the classical *mṛdaṅgam* (*see* MRDAṄGA, §3(ii)). For a similar instrument in Sri Lanka, *see* DEMALA-BERĒ.

For illustration *see* PAÑCAVĀDYAM.

Made. Dance sticks of the Marshall Islands of Micronesia. They are long wooden staffs or spears, some with decorative plaiting, and are used during men's standing dances.

Madedoku. LAMELLAPHONE of the Kilima people of Zaïre (*LaurentyS*, 197).

Madhukarī [madhukaḷī, madhurī]. Names found in medieval Sanskrit texts for an Indian oboe. *See* MAHVARĪ.

Madimba (i). Calabash-resonated XYLOPHONE of the Kanyok, Shongo, Binji, Yeke and Luluwa peoples of Zaïre. Related terms are the Luba *dimba* or *djimba*, Lunda *jimba*, Salampasu *mdimba* and Chokwe NDJIMBA. The frame consists of two wooden planks, narrow side upward, placed within a semicircular wooden bow. In the sides of the planks are a number of holes; through these pass sticks on which the calabashes, each with a vibrating membrane, are suspended. The keys are strung together and separated from the frame by a layer of fibre padding. The number of keys varies according to the type of instrument; the Luba *madimba makata*, as leading or solo xylophone, has nine or ten keys, while the *madimba matshetshe*, the supporting instrument, has seven or eight. The *madimba* is usually associated with a chief and played at his request, for example, to accompany dances at his installation or during festivities of the group. The term *madimba* is also used for the large 17-key 'bow' type xylophone of the Pende people.

BIBLIOGRAPHY
BooneX
F. J. de Hen: *Beitrag zur Kenntnis der Musikinstrumente aus Belgisch Kongo und Ruanda-Urundi* (Tervuren, 1960)
G. Knosp: *Enquête sur la vie musicale au Congo Belge 1934–1935* (Tervuren, 1968)
J. Gansemans: *La musique et son rôle dans la vie sociale et rituelle Luba* (Tervuren, 1978)
——: *Les instruments de musique Luba* (Tervuren, 1980)
K. A. GOURLAY

Madimba (ii). LAMELLAPHONE of the Luishia region of Zaïre (*LaurentyS*, 196).

Madinda. *See* AMADINDA.

Maditsi. Third largest of the DIKOMANA drums of the Gananwa people of southern Africa.

Madobi. Pair of stopped end-blown single-note flutes of the Sena/Tonga people of Zimbabwe. They are played, with others, in a STOPPED FLUTE ENSEMBLE. *See* KATERO.

Madoku. Wooden-keyed LAMELLAPHONE of the Ngbele, Bangba Adoi, Balese and Andekori peoples of northern Zaïre (*LaurentyS*, 197).

Madúbu. Large BULLROARER of the Kiwai people, Western Province, Papua New Guinea. It is used during initiations, for inaugurating new canoes and for garden magic.

BIBLIOGRAPHY
G. Landtman: *Ethnographical Collection from the Kiwai District of British New Guinea in the National Museum of Finland* (Helsinki, 1933), 73
J. Baal: 'The Cult of the Bullroarer in Australia and Southern New Guinea', *Bijdragen tot de taal-, land- en volkenkunde*, cxix (1963), 204

Madudu. X̱YLOPHONE of south-eastern Africa. *See* VALIMBA.

Madvarī. *See* MAHVARĪ.

Maegubuk. Small Korean drum. *See* SOGO (i).

Maelzel, Johann Nepomuk (*b* Regensburg, 15 Aug 1772; *d* at sea, 21 July 1838). German inventor. The son of an organ builder, he settled in Vienna in 1792 and devoted himself to teaching music and to constructing an automatic instrument of flutes, trumpets, drums, cymbals, triangle and strings struck by hammers, which played music by Haydn, Mozart and Crescentini and was sold for 3000 florins. His next machine was the Panharmonicon (exhibited in Vienna in 1804), similar to the first, but with clarinets, violins and cellos added; it was worked by weights acting on cylinders. Maelzel next bought Kempelen's Chessplayer and took it with the Panharmonicon to Paris; later he sold the Chessplayer to Eugene Beauharnais. He then constructed a Trumpeter, which played the Austrian and French cavalry marches and signals, and marches and allegros by Weigl, Dussek and Pleyel. In 1808 he was appointed court mechanician in Vienna, and about that time made some ear trumpets, one of which Beethoven used for years. In 1812 he opened his Kunstkabinett, which had among its attractions the Trumpeter and a new and enlarged Panharmonicon; soon afterwards he made public a musical chronometer, an improvement of a machine by Stöckel, for which he obtained certificates from Beethoven and other leading musicians. The word 'metronome' is first found on his patent of 1815; and although there is a long history of musical time-keepers before him (indeed there remains considerable dispute about his exact contribution to the invention) the familiar wooden-boxed metronome remains to this day almost exactly like his last models of around 1830 (*see* MET-RONOME, figs.3 and 4).

Maelzel and Beethoven were at this time on friendly terms. They had arranged to visit London together, and Maelzel had eased Beethoven's financial straits by urging on him a loan of 50 ducats in gold. In order to add to the attractions of the Panharmonicon, which they proposed to take with them, Maelzel sketched plans for the adaptation of a piece commemorating the battle of Vittoria (21 June 1813) that Beethoven composed for the instrument. Maelzel further induced Beethoven to score the piece for orchestra, with a view to obtaining funds for the journey; thus scored, it was performed at a concert on 8 December 1813, in a programme including Beethoven's Symphony no.7, the marches of Dussek and Pleyel (by the automaton) and the battle-piece. The concert was repeated on 12 December, and the two yielded a profit of over 4000 florins. But Beethoven took offence at Maelzel's having announced the battle-piece as his property, broke completely with him, rejected the Trumpeter and its marches, and held a third concert (2 January 1814) for his sole benefit. Maelzel departed to Munich with his Panharmonicon, including the battle-piece, as arranged on its barrel, and also with a full orchestral score of it, which he had obtained without Beethoven's concurrence. When Maelzel had the orchestral piece performed at Munich Beethoven entered an action against him in the Vienna courts (it is his memorandum of the grounds of this action, as prepared for his advocate, which is usually entitled his 'deposition'). Beethoven also addressed a statement to the musicians of London, entreating them not to support Maelzel.

The action came to nothing, but Maelzel did go to London. On the way there he stopped at Amsterdam demonstrating various mechanical instruments, among them the chronometer that he had been making for a few years. In Amsterdam he met the mechanic Winkel, who seems to have suggested a few refinements to the chronometer. Within a few months Maelzel had patented a new machine, apparently incorporating Winkel's refinements, given it the new name 'metronome' and begun to manufacture it in London and Paris. Wishing to repurchase Kempelen's Chessplayer and to promote his metronome, he returned to Munich and Vienna in 1817. Beethoven's lawsuit was abandoned and the costs divided equally – his own good word was of more consequence than the statements of others, and it seemed prudent to avoid further entanglement with the clever Maelzel. After this Maelzel travelled much, eventually to the USA, where he passed the rest of his life (except for a voyage or two to the West Indies), exhibiting the Chessplayer, the Conflagration of Moscow and his other curious inventions. He was found dead in his berth on board the American brig *Otis*.

Maelzel was evidently a shrewd and energetic businessman. He certainly built on the ideas of others, but he succeeded where they had failed for three reasons: he had a genius and an inexhaustible energy for publicity; he had a sound business sense; and, as concerns the metronome in particular, he continued refining and developing what had already been successful so that his final model had a long-lasting perfection.

BIBLIOGRAPHY

A. W. Thayer: *Beethoven*, iii (Berlin, 1879, rev. 2/1911; Eng. trans., 1921), 382ff

M. Reinitz: *Beethoven im Kampf mit dem Schicksal* (Vienna, 1924)

T. von Frimmel: *Beethoven-Handbuch*, i (Leipzig, 1926), 378ff

G. Haupt: 'J. N. Mälzels Briefe an Breitkopf & Härtel', *Der Bär: Jb von Breitkopf & Härtel 1927*, 122

P. Stadlen: 'Beethoven and the Metronome', *ML*, xlviii (1967), 330

M. S. Selden: 'Henri Berton as Critic', *JAMS*, xxiv (1971), 291

S. Howell: 'Beethoven's Maelzel Canon: another Schindler Forgery?', *MT*, cxx (1979), 987

For further bibliography *see* METRONOME.

ALEXANDER WHEELOCK THAYER/DAVID FALLOWS

Maendler–Schramm. German firm of harpsichord and piano makers. Karl Maendler (*b* Munich, 22 March 1872; *d* Munich, 2 Aug 1958) began as a piano maker. He married Susanne Schramm, daughter of M. J. Schramm, and in due course became head of his father-in-law's piano firm in Munich. It is probable that the firm had already produced harpsichords (one labelled 'M. J. Schramm' is known to exist), but Maendler built up this side of the business, producing his first harpsichord in about 1907, and continuing to make harpsichords, clavichords and pianos until he went blind in 1956. The business then passed to Ernst Zucker. Maendler's main output was of heavily built, mass-produced instruments; he was one of the first to build to the so-called 'Bach disposition' (lower: 16′, 8′; upper: 8′, 4′ – now generally regarded as unauthentic); he also used metal framing. On the other hand, the Händel-Haus at Halle has a Maendler–Schramm harpsichord of 1939 which, except for the typical German pedal mechanism, appears to be a careful copy of a Shudi of 1770.

See also ORFF, CARL.

BIBLIOGRAPHY

J. Wörsching: *Die historischen Saitenklaviere und der moderne Clavichord- und Cembalo-Bau* (Mainz, 1946)

K. Sasse: *Katalog zu den Sammlungen des Händel-Hauses in Halle: Musikinstrumentensammlung: besaitete Tasteninstrumente* (Halle, 1966)

W. J. Zuckermann: *The Modern Harpsichord* (London, 1969)

MARGARET CRANMER

Maestoso (It.: 'majestic'). A term used alone as an indication of mood or as a tempo designation. It also appears as a modification of some other tempo mark. J. G. Walther (1732) described it as 'ansehnlich und langsam, iedoch mit einer lebhaften Expression' ('stately and slow, but with a lively expression'). H. C. Koch (1802) indicated that, like *con gravità*, *maestoso* implied the use of over-dotting (*see* GRAVE). The spelling *majestoso* is also found, particularly in German scores.

For bibliography *see* TEMPO AND EXPRESSION MARKS.

DAVID FALLOWS

Mafili. BOARD ZITHER of the Kumu people of Zaïre. *See* MALIGBANGA.

Mafowa. Ankle rattles of the Tsonga people of southeastern Africa. *See* FOWA.

Magadis. One of several terms for the Greco-Roman angular harp (*see* TRIGŌNON). The extreme difficulty of assigning these terms to specific variations of the general type is illustrated by a passage from Athenaeus's *Deipnosophistai*: 'At this point Aemilianus said: "Look now, Masurius, my friend, I as a lover of music have often considered whether what is called the magadis is a kind of aulos or kithara" '. It is clear that one cannot decide what type of harp the magadis may have been if ancient writers destroy the supposedly firm distinction between harp and kithara and go as far as suggesting that the magadis was a wind instrument.

Nevertheless the overall view created by ancient literature is that the magadis is after all a harp. Moreover it seems to be virtually identical with another harp type, the PĒKTIS, though the term 'magadis' contains the additional suggestion that the instrument could somehow play in octaves. The term 'magadize' (*magadizein*), to sing or play in octaves, occurs several times in later Greek theoretical writings such as that of Pseudo-Aristotle. The instrument may have accomplished this by the device of paired strings tuned in octaves; this idea is suggested by a reference to it as 'dichordos' (two-stringed or double-stringed). This can hardly have meant that the instrument had only two strings since it was elsewhere consistently described and depicted as an instrument with many strings; indeed 20 strings seems a typical number.

The verb magadize seems to have been derived from magadis rather than vice versa because the noun is much older. And, incidentally, the confusion noted above between magadis and aulos seems to have stemmed from the playing of the aulos in octaves by overblowing, perhaps in imitation of the magadis. As to the derivation of the word magadis itself, it is safe to say only that it is a foreign word. The hypothesis that it derives from *magas* ('bridge') is not entirely implausible. This, however, implies that a bridge bisected the strings, and this is not at all borne out by surviving iconography.

BIBLIOGRAPHY

C. Sachs: *Real-Lexikon der Musikinstrumente* (Berlin, 1913/*R*1962, 2/1964)
F. Behn: *Musikleben im Altertum und frühen Mittelalter* (Stuttgart, 1954)

JAMES W. Mc KINNON

Magakhĭṃ. Barrel drum of the Newari people of Nepal. *See* KHĪṂ.

Magbomboyo. LAMELLAPHONE of the Bwa people of northern Zaïre (*LaurentyS*, 192). *See* AGBOMBOYA.

Magbua. LAMELLAPHONE of the Bali people of northeastern Zaïre (*LaurentyS*, 196).

Mager, Jörg (Georg Adam) (*b* Eichstätt, 6 Nov 1880; *d* Aschaffenburg, 7 April 1939). German organist, schoolteacher and instrument inventor. His early interest in microtonal music led him to construct a quarter-tone harmonium in 1911 and then, after World War I, to study electronics in Berlin. He constructed a series of electronic instruments, mostly with keyboards, in Berlin during the 1920s and, from 1929, in Darmstadt, but his hopes for the commercial manufacture of one of them remained unfulfilled. His idealistic and mystical approach led to his eclipse in the mid-1930s with the rise to power of the Nazi party. He died in isolation shortly before the outbreak of World War II, during which all his instruments disappeared or were destroyed. Mager's pioneering efforts to develop a viable electronic instrument (the Omnitonium), capable of 'all sounds and tunings', may have partly inspired J. M. Becker's novel *Syrinx* published in the mid-1920s. His son Siegfried also works in electronic instrument design, and developed, among other things, the hybrid Multimonica made by Hohner and the Mannborg organ.

After moving to Berlin around 1919, Mager worked part-time for the electronics firm Lorenz, in order to learn what was required to produce sounds electronically. He received assistance from Lorenz with his first instrument, the Elektrophon (1921), which was based on a beat-frequency oscillator; like the theremin, ondes martenot and most other instruments of the 1920s it was inspired by the circuitry of a radio receiver. Mager continued to develop the instrument up to 1930 (*see* SPHÄROPHON); in 1928 he replaced the beat-frequency oscillator by an audio oscillator, and the original frequency-control handle by two monophonic manuals, with short keys so that both could be played with one hand. It was still possible to play microtonal music on this Klaviatursphärophon. The circuits of all Mager's electronic instruments appear to have been very simple but ingenious; the electrical amplifier and loudspeaker were not introduced until the mid-1920s, and Mager's early loudspeakers were made from telephone earpieces and a variety of materials that produced different timbres – up to 1930 he patented at least ten such designs (*see* ELECTRONIC INSTRUMENTS, §I, 5(ii)). In his instruments with three and four monophonic manuals and pedal-board each voice could be given a different timbre.

In 1927 Mager demonstrated the Kaleidophon or Kaleidosphon. It had a monophonic keyboard tuned in semitones, but the tuning could be adjusted (as, much later, in some synthesizers) by means of a mechanism that expanded or contracted the basic intervals. Descriptions of its capabilities are not completely clear, but apparently it could produce the equivalent of chords by building up mixtures of overtones, which may have been controlled by a touch-sensitive facility on the keyboard. Glissandos, vibrato and 'timbre trills' were also possible.

In 1929 the city of Darmstadt offered Mager the use of the Prinz-Emil-Schlösschen, where he set up a laboratory and founded the Studiengesellschaft für Elektroakustische Musik. With the assistance of Dr Janovsky he developed the two models of the PARTITUROPHON, and probably the three-manual Klaviatursphärophon, in all of which the manuals were monophonic. Mager's electronic keyboard instruments began to attract more interest in the musical world than had the original Elektrophon, and this led to his being invited to produce sound effects and music for the theatre: in 1931, using Javanese gongs struck by an electromagnetic mechanism and possibly amplified, he provided the bells for performances of *Parsifal* under Toscanini at Bayreuth; he created sound effects, such as thunder, on the Partiturophon for three of the operas in the *Ring* cycle also given at Bayreuth in 1931; and he composed incidental music, including microtonal passages (probably on the Klaviatursphärophon), for 30 performances of Goethe's *Faust* in Darmstadt and Frankfurt in 1932. Hopes for the commercial manufacture of the Partiturophon, which Mager regarded as an instrument suitable for the home, were unfulfilled, and Hitler's coming to power in 1933 heralded a change in Mager's fortunes. In 1935 he had to leave both the castle and his electroacoustic music society, and the last 'official' invitation he received was to contribute music to a film, *Stärker als Paragraphen*, in 1936. Mager composed several short works for his instruments, many of which (together with performances by him of earlier music) were broadcast. They included the Romantic *Weihnachts-Wiegenlied* (1933) for four-manual Partiturophon, and *Seraphicum*, *Dahlienschau-Walzer* and *Ich und Du* (all 1935, the last with alto voice).

BIBLIOGRAPHY

J. Mager: *Vierteltonmusik* (Aschaffenburg, 1915)
——: *Eine neue Epoche der Musik durch Radio* (Berlin, 1924)
——: 'Wie steht es um die Vierteltonmusik?', *Kunstwart* (Aug 1924)
A. Huth: 'Elektrische Tonerzeugung: zu den Erfindungen von Jörg Mager und Leo Theremin', *Die Musik*, xx (1927–8), 42
E. Schenk: *Jörg Mager* (Darmstadt, 1952)
A. Moles: 'Jörg Mager: un pionnier de la musique électronique', *Revue du son*, no.25 (1955), suppl. p.vi; rev. as *Les musiques expérimentales: revue d'une tendance importante de la musique contemporaine* (Paris, 1960), 25
F. K. Prieberg: *Musica ex machina* (Berlin and Frankfurt am Main, 1960), 210
T. L. Rhea: *The Evolution of Electronic Musical Instruments in the United States* (diss., George Peabody College, Nashville, Tenn., 1972), 37; section rev. as 'Joerg Mager: Multi-Keyboardist of the 1930s', *Contemporary Keyboard*, iv/8 (1978), 62
W. D. Kühnelt: 'Elektroakustische Musikinstrumente', in *Für Augen und Ohren* (Berlin, 1980), 52 [exhibition catalogue]

HUGH DAVIES

Maggini, Gio(vanni) Paolo (*b c*1581; *d c*1632). Italian violin maker. The best-known maker of the Brescian School, he was a pupil of Gasparo da Salò. Whereas Gasparo is chiefly noted for his tenor violas, Maggini's output reflected the increased popularity of the violin. His instruments influenced the work of many later makers (including at times Stradivari and Guarneri), though they are now less appreciated than formerly. Maggini's first instruments closely resemble those of Gasparo, not surprisingly as the two had probably worked side by side for a decade or more before Gasparo's death in 1609. There is controversy as to which of the two was the originator of the contralto viola, a landmark in the history of instrument making. Three examples are believed to exist (41·5 cm in length of body) which apparently predate the sole small viola made by Antonio and Girolamo Amati (i) in 1615. Maggini may also have been the first to make a cello smaller in size than the vast instruments commonly in use until the last quarter of the 17th century: the two known survivors, broad in proportion to their length, foreshadow the dimensions favoured by the celebrated Venetian makers a century and more later.

In comparison with those of his Cremonese contemporaries the Amatis, Maggini's violins appear compact in outline: in general the waist of his design is less pronounced than on an Amati instrument with its more rounded, more elegant curves. In addition the arching of back and table are left fuller towards the edge. The violins are of two patterns, the bodies being either rather less than 35·5 cm long or, more usually, about 37 cm. It was the deep, rich sonority of the larger model that encouraged Stradivari to seek a combination of the virtues of Cremona and Brescia with his 'long pattern' violins dated between 1690 and 1699. In general, however, by increasing the volume of air in the body of a violin, the maker runs the risk of losing the essential soprano quality of violin tone, particularly on the lower strings. What Guarneri – more than a century later – sought to do, and achieved with unsurpassed success, was to adapt the compactness of Maggini's form to Cremonese principles of construction, at the same time limiting his dimensions strictly to preserve a much smaller volume of air than the normal Maggini. Maggini's achievement, however, was the creation of a violin with a big, broad tone, darker in colour but with more depth of response

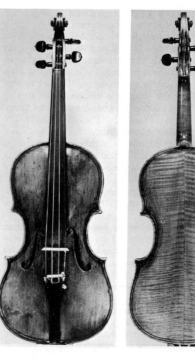

Violin by Gio: Paolo Maggini, Brescia (private collection)

than the Amati. That the later Cremonese makers reacted as they did to his work shows that the tonal characteristics of the Maggini were well appreciated by players of the 17th century, as they were again in the 19th, when innumerable copies were made in the best workshops of Paris as well as Mirecourt, and in the German factories. The copies mostly have more normal dimensions, but are complete with the characteristic double row of purfling, soundholes with small lobes and small wings and other features. Needless to say they lack the rich, glowing red-brown or golden orange varnish, usually quite equal to that of the Amatis, though sometimes with a rather drier appearance. In addition to violins, violas and cellos, Maggini made basses and instruments of the viol family (*see* DOUBLE BASS, fig.2*a*), and also the Brescian cittern.

It is impossible to indicate with conviction the different stages of Maggini's development, as his labels (on which his name appeared as Gio: Paolo Maggini) were never dated. All that is known for certain is that he was still alive in 1626, when he made a tax return, but that he had died by 1632, the year the great plague struck Brescia.

See also FORGERY, §2.

BIBLIOGRAPHY

M. L. Huggins: *Gio: Paolo Maggini: his Life and Work* (London, 1892)

CHARLES BEARE

Magneton. An ELECTRONIC ORGAN developed by Rudolf Stelzhammer with W. Lenk in Vienna in 1932–3. It had two 56-note manuals and a 30-note pedal-board. The sounds were generated by sets of rotating toothed electromagnetic tone-wheels (one set per note) with different profiles to produce a wide range of timbres. The speed of the mechanism could be adjusted to transpose the pitch of the whole instrument within a total range of a 5th. Four switches permitted the connection of loudspeakers that provided different frequency characteristics, and a foot-operated lever added vibrato. The instrument was regarded as particularly appropriate for church use. It won the Gold Medal at the 1935 International Inventions Exhibition in London. Stelzhammer's piano factory also constructed the Superpiano.

BIBLIOGRAPHY
V. Goller: 'Das Magneton', *ZI*, liv (1933), 103
F. Scheminzky: *Die Welt des Schalles* (Graz, 1935), 687
HUGH DAVIES

Magnusson. Swedish family of organ builders. Johannes Magnusson (1852–1923) went to Gothenburg [now Göteborg] in 1874 as a pupil of Salomon Molander (*see* LINDEGRENS ORGELBYGGERI); he worked under Molander for 14 years before opening his own workshop in 1888. His son Anders Magnusson (1882–1956) trained in Zurich and joined the firm in 1910 as his father's assistant and partner. During his directorship the business became a limited company under the name of A. Magnussons Orgelbyggeri. His son Stig Magnusson (*b* 21 April 1920) finished his practical training in 1947 and became a partner in the firm; he took over the directorship on his father's death. He has aimed at limiting the use of electronics as much as possible and improving design within the framework of classical methods of action. His inventions include a mechanical combination system and specially designed valves. His designs, which are also used by other organ builders, have been published in the international specialist press. The firm has built about 400 organs, mainly in the west and south of Sweden. Larger instruments include those in Göteborg Cathedral (1962; 46 stops); Stora Tuna (1969; 43 stops); St Kristine's Church, Göteborg (1970; 50 stops); Karlstad Cathedral (1971; 66 stops); and the Kloster Church, Eskilstuna (1972; 50 stops). Restorations include Anders Jonsson's organ at Konungsund and the organ built by Johan Niclas Cahman in the castle church at Drottningholm.

based on *Sohlmans musiklexikon* (iv, 415–6) by permission of Sohlmans Förlag
BENGT KYHLBERG/ANNA KYHLBERG

Magnusson, Johannes (*b* 11 Nov 1804; *d* 25 March 1875). Swedish organ builder. A self-taught builder, he was gifted and versatile. He built about 20 organs within the Växsjö district, eight of which are still in existence, including the one-manual instrument at Bäckebo (1848) and the two-manual examples at Skirö (1857) and Korsberga (1865). His instruments are remarkable for their classical sound.

BIBLIOGRAPHY
E. Erici: *Inventarium över bevarade äldre kyrkorglar i Sverige* (Stockholm, 1965)
based on *Sohlmans musiklexikon* (iv, 416) by permission of Sohlmans Förlag
BENGT KYHLBERG

Magogo. Single-headed footed drum of the Valley Tonga people of Gwembe district, Zambia. It is open-ended and the membrane is pegged on. It is played with sticks, together with the *masunta* and *mpati* drums.

Magogodo. Gourd-resonated XYLOPHONE of the Nyanja/Manganja people of Malawi.

Magrephah [magrepha] (Heb.: 'shovel', 'rake'). An ancient Jewish musical instrument, probably of the early Christian era, said to have been used in the Second Temple (completed in 516). One Babylonian source distinguished between the hydraulis (*hirdolin*) and the magrephah, which seems to have been shaped somewhat like the ancient symbolic shovel of the Herodian temple. Such shovels (*magrephoth*) were cast down daily, with a loud percussive noise, as a sign of divine vengeance on sinners. The musical instrument may have had a handle-like duct from a wind-raising apparatus (perhaps a forge bellows), and at the end of the handle a small pipe-chest (shaped like the shovel-pan) which held, according to some sources, 100 pipes. Presumably these were short and of random pitch, sounding shrill and loud with the effect of a piercing signal. Such 'instruments' are reported to have been made by 'craftsmen from Alexandria', who were perhaps connected with the pre-Christian Alexandrian craftsmen known for their hydraulic organs, automata and other wind instruments.

BIBLIOGRAPHY
E. Gerson-Kiwi: 'Musique', *Dictionnaire de la Bible* (Paris, 1950)
J. Yasser: 'The Magrepha of the Herodian Temple: a Five-fold Hypothesis', *JAMS*, xiii (1960), 24
PETER WILLIAMS

Magruna. (1) Double idioglot clarinet of Libya. The two tubes are of equal length, made from reed or sometimes metal, tied in parallel so that corresponding holes can be closed simultaneously to make the tubes sound in unison. The bells are made from horn and the reeds are tongues cut from small reedpipes inserted in the principal tubes. *Magruna* musicians, exclusively men, produce an uninterrupted sound from the instrument by a circular breathing technique. Originally used by shepherds to assemble their flocks, the *magruna* is nowadays very popular at festivals, particularly marriages, where it is often played by paid specialists and accompanied by percussion.

(2) Single clarinet of the Arab and Kanembu peoples of north-west Chad. It is copied from the Libyan instrument.

MONIQUE BRANDILY

Ma:gu. DIDJERIDU (aboriginal wooden trumpet) of the Gunwinggu people of northern Australia.

Maguḍi. See MAKUṬĪ.

Magul-berē. Name given to the DAULA, GÄTA-BERĒ or YAK-BERĒ drums of Sri Lanka when they play *magulbera* (characteristic solo drum patterns used to inaugurate any festival or auspicious occasion). Strictly speaking, the *gäta-berē* is used in the Kandyan tradition and the *yak-berē* in the low-country, but in practice the *daula* is often substituted. The term denotes a function and not a particular type of drum, as is sometimes supposed.
NATALIE M. WEBBER

Magwala (i). Side-blown trumpet of the Soga people of Kamodi district, Uganda. They are made from gourds, and eight are played in an ensemble with drums (*kigoma*). See *TraceyCSA*, ii, 321.

Magwala (ii). Cylindrical stopped wooden flute of the Bati people of northern Zaïre (*LaurentyA*, 181).

Mahatī vīnā. A term sometimes applied to the large fretted STICK ZITHER *bīn* of Hindustani or north Indian classical music; *see* VĪNĀ, §7.

Mahillon. Belgian family of wind instrument makers.

(1) **Charles(-Borromée) Mahillon** (*b* Brussels, 4 Nov 1813; *d* Molenbeek-St-Jean, 4 Sept 1887). Having learnt his trade in England he founded the family business in Brussels in 1836 and became celebrated for the excellence of his clarinets. In 1844 he opened a London branch which continued until 1922. Four of his sons devoted themselves either to instrument making or to music publishing.

(2) **Victor-Charles Mahillon** (*b* Brussels, 10 March 1841; *d* St Jean Cap Ferrat, 17 June 1924). Son of (1) Charles Mahillon. Although he succeeded his father in the business, he is best remembered as a learned acoustician and writer, and curator of the Brussels Conservatory Instrumental Museum, to which his own large collection was added (for a discussion of his catalogue of 1888, *see* CLASSIFICATION, appx). He was associated with his younger brother, Joseph, who was also a contributor to the conservatory collection.

See also VALVE (i).

WRITINGS
Les éléments d'acoustique musicale et instrumentale (Brussels, 1874)
Catalogue descriptif et analytique du Musée instrumental du Conservatoire royal de musique de Bruxelles (Ghent, 1880–1922; i, 2/1893; ii, 2/1909)
Hints on Fingering the Boehm Flute (London, c1884) [trans. of ?unpubd orig.]
General Pitch Regulations: V.-C. Mahillon's Table (London, c1884) [trans. of ?unpubd orig.]
How to Tune Piston Instruments (London, c1884) [trans. of ?unpubd orig.]
Le matériel sonore des orchestres de symphonie, d'harmonie et de fanfares, ou vade mecum du compositeur (Brussels, 1897, 5/1920)
Experimental Studies on the Resonance of Conical, Tronco-conical, and Cylindrical Air Columns (London, 1901) [trans. by F. A. Mahon of ?unpubd orig.]
Instruments à vent [trombone, horn, trumpet] (Brussels, 1906–7)
Notes théoriques et practiques sur la résonance des colonnes d'air dans les tuyaux de la facture instrumentale (St Jean Cap Ferrat, 1921)

(3) **Fernand Mahillon** (*b* Brussels, 3 March 1866; *d* Brussels, 6 March 1948). Son of (1) Charles Mahillon. For over 30 years, and until its closure, he managed the London branch which had many army and other government contracts. When he returned to Brussels, Fernand took over the management of the firm on the death of (2) Victor-Charles Mahillon. In 1936 or 1937 the firm became the property of J. A. Smits, who had been with it for many years. Thereafter Mahillon & Cie continued as a limited liability company, but their woodwind-making activities ceased in 1935. Charles Mahillon's fourth son, Adolphe, confined himself exclusively to music publishing in Brussels.

(4) **Fernand-Charles** [Fernand-Victor] **Mahillon** (*d* Brussels, 6 March 1922). Son of (2) Victor-Charles Mahillon. He was associate curator of the Brussels Conservatory collection, and published a *Catalogue abrégé* for the collection in 1911. He died before his father, and his widow and daughters were the proprietors of the firm at the time of its sale.

A trumpet from c1835 at Brussels bears the mark 'B. Mahillon jeune, Brussels'. It is possibly the work of Barthélemy, the younger brother of (1) Charles Mahillon, though his only recorded occupation is as a gunsmith.

PHILIP BATE

Mahlirihliri [moqakhatsana]. A generic term for rattles among the Southern Sotho people of southern Africa. *See* MORUTLHOANA.

Mahoon, Joseph (*fl* 1729–71). ?English spinet and harpsichord maker. He worked in Golden Square, London. In 1729 he was appointed 'harpsichord maker to His Majesty'. Nearly all his surviving instruments are spinets.

A Mahoon harpsichord can be seen in plate 2 of Hogarth's *Rake's Progress* (1735). Of two surviving harpsichords, the single harpsichord of 1742 has a rounded tail, and the large harpsichord of 1738 has various antique features, such as its plain walnut case. Its compass of F', G' to f''' was standard, as was the 8', 8', lute, 4' specification. Less standard was that the lute stop plucked the strings on the lower manual, so that if it was left in contact with the string when the lower 8' was being played, it damped it and gave a kind of buff effect (as directed by notes written in a contemporary hand), a 'not very satisfactory' expedient (Hubbard).

BIBLIOGRAPHY
F. Hubbard: *Three Centuries of Harpsichord Making* (Cambridge, Mass., 1965)
DONALD HOWARD BOALCH, PETER WILLIAMS

Mahōra thuk. BRONZE DRUM of Thailand and Laos. On average the body is 60 cm in diameter and 53 cm high, and the metal head 65 cm in diameter. The sides of the body are slightly concave. The head is made from an alloy of copper, lead and tin in carefully determined proportions, and around the edge of the head are fixed four small metal frogs, at equidistant intervals. Sometimes a raised star pattern, with a varying number of points, can be seen in the centre of the head. The drum is beaten with two padded sticks.

The *mahōra thuk* was held in great respect by the people of northern Thailand, especially the Karen tribe, who also called it the *klǫng kop* ('frog drum') or *klǫng khīat* ('tadpole drum'). Possession of a drum of this type greatly increased the status and prestige of the owner. The drum was formerly used for rain-making ceremonies and at official royal ceremonies, and in certain temples, where it was played with the *sang* (conch-shell trumpet) to summon the monks for daily recitations of the Buddhist scriptures. Drums of this type are also found in Burma and Kampuchea.

See also HPÀ-SI.

BIBLIOGRAPHY
D. Yupho: *Khrŷang dontri Thai* [Thai musical instruments] (Bangkok, 1957, 2/1967; Eng. trans., 1960, 2/1971)
D. Morton: *The Traditional Music of Thailand* (Berkeley, 1976)
DAVID MORTON

Mahōrī. Instrumental ensemble of Thailand, combining melodic and rhythmic percussion and string and wind instruments (see illustration). The term *mahōrī* originally referred only to a string ensemble consisting of a *krajappī* (plucked lute), a *sǫ sām sāi* (spike fiddle), a *thōn* (goblet drum) and a singer who kept time with the *krap phuang* (clappers). Originally played by men, this group of instruments began to be played by women when the ensemble became popular in large households, and this tradition lasted until after the middle of the 19th century. When the women's *mahōrī* fell into disuse, string instruments were added to a small drum, gong and oboe ensemble called the *klǫng khāek*, and this became known

Mahōrī (instrumental ensemble) of Thailand: back row (left to right), ching (cymbals), two sǫ duang (fiddles), khǫng wong yai (gong-chime), thōn and rammanā (goblet and frame drums), khǫng wong lek (gong-chime), two sǫ ū (fiddles), čhāp lek (cymbals); centre, khlui phīang ǫ and khlui ū (duct flutes); centre row, čhakhē (tube zithers, extreme left and right), ranāt ēk and ranāt thum (xylophones); front row, two sǫ sām sāi (spike fiddles)

as the 'string *mahōrī*'. More instruments were added from time to time to form the three standard groups we find today: a small ensemble comprising a *sǫ sām sāi*, a *sǫ duang*, and a *sǫ ū* (bowed string instruments), a *čhakhē* (tube zither), a *khlui phīang ǫ* (duct flute), a *thōn*, a *rammanā* (frame drum), a pair of *ching* (cymbals), a *ranāt ēk* (xylophone) and a *khǫng wong* (gong-chime); a medium-size or double ensemble, which adds to the above an extra *sǫ sām sāi*, *sǫ duang*, *sǫ ū* and *čhakhē* and also a *khlui līp* (duct flute), a pair of *čhāp lek* (cymbals), a *ranāt thum* (xylophone), and a *khǫng wong* (*lek* or *yai*) or a *khǫng klāng* (gong-chimes); and a large ensemble which is the same as the medium-size ensemble but adds a *khlui ū* (duct flute), a *ranāt ēk lek* and a *ranāt thum lek* (xylophones), a pair of *čhāp yai* (cymbals) and a *mōng* (bossed gong). Additional instruments to accommodate a large number of players may be added at informal gatherings.

BIBLIOGRAPHY
D. Yupho: *Khrÿang dontri Thai* [Thai musical instruments] (Bangkok, 1957, 2/1967; Eng. trans., 1960, 2/1971)
D. Morton: *The Traditional Music of Thailand* (Berkeley, 1976)
DAVID MORTON

Māh tāh. Small bronze gong of Patan, Nepal. *See* TAIM NĀIM.

Mahudi. *See* MAKUŢĪ.

Mahuge. Single-headed closed conical drum of the Nyamwezi people of Tabora district, Tanzania. The membrane is laced on and the drum is played with sticks. *See also* NDANDALE.

Mahurī. Oboe of Bengal and Orissa, east India. It is usually a short slender pipe, about 35 cm long, with externally conical wooden body and a small, bulbous bell; the bell is often of metal (cast bronze), and in Orissa has a decorative relief of serpents. There are seven finger-holes. The *mahurī* is used in folk music and dance,

including the *chau* dance-dramas of Purulia district, west Bengal (where these oboes are often called ŚAHNĀĪ), and in Orissa in temple ceremonial. The MOHORĪ is a different, tribal oboe of Orissa and Assam. *See also* MAHVARĪ.

BIBLIOGRAPHY
K. S. Kothari: *Indian Folk Musical Instruments* (New Delhi, 1968)
D. Reck: 'The Music of Matha Chau', *Asian Music*, iii/2 (1972), 8ff
S. Ray: *Music of Eastern India* (Calcutta, 1973)
ALASTAIR DICK

Mahuvar. DOUBLE CLARINET, with gourd wind cap, of Gujarat, west India. *See* PŪNGĪ.

Mahvarī [madvarī, mahuarī, muhurī, madhurī, madhukalī, madhukarī]. The name of an oboe mentioned or described in medieval Sanskrit texts of India. Both the 12th-century *Mānasollāsa* (*muhurī*) and the 13th-century *Saṅgītaratnākara* (*madhukarī*) describe it as being 28 Hindu inches (perhaps 21 English inches, about 53 cm) long, made of wood or horn (which probably means all of wood, or with a horn bell) and similar in shape to the *kāhalā* metal trumpet, with a similar bore (about 3·75 cm at the lower end and almost certainly conical; *see* ŚṚNGA). The mouthpiece is clearly described: it consisted of a copper staple about 7·5 cm long carrying a lip-disc of shell or ivory, and had a reed of *devanala* reed (or possibly *kāśa* grass), previously softened by boiling in milk, and tied round the end. There were seven finger-holes, and a thumb-hole was positioned midway between the end and the first of these, on the underside. The 'sweet tone' is attributed to the staple. A passage later attributed to an earlier writer, Mataṅga (perhaps 10th-century), somewhat garbled but possibly authentic, describes the instrument (*madvarī, mahvarī, madhukalī*) as three-quarters the length of that in the *Saṅgītaratnākara*, and may specify a conical bore.

The most likely derivation of the name is the Arabic term MIZMĀR; the Arabs had conquered Sind in 712 AD, and other Sanskrit texts describe Arabo-Persian military instruments that had been disseminated in India, such as the *tumbakī* (i.e. *dombak*: kettledrum) and the *bukkā* (trumpets). The Sanskrit forms *madhukarī* etc are false re-Sanskritizations. After the Turkish conquest of north India from 1192, the oboe-names *sūrnāī* and ŚAHNĀĪ (related to the Perso-Turkish *surnāy* and ZŪRNĀ) were used, and in late medieval and early modern vernacular literature the two are often mentioned together (as in the 'Persian and Indian types' recorded by Abu'l Fazl *c*1590). The pipe of the Indian type was probably wider and longer than that of the Persian (for illustration *see* NAQ-QĀRAKHĀNA), and may have had a deeper tone.

Versions of the name (though not necessarily denoting the same instrument) are still found, especially in eastern and central India. They include *mahurī* (Bengal and Orissa), *mohorī* (Orissa and Assam), *mohurī* (Madhya Pradesh), *mvāhlī* (Nepal), *morī* (Karnataka), *kā tang-muri* (Meghalay state, formerly Assam) and *mauri dizau* (Nagaland). Elsewhere – as *mahuḍī* (Tamil Nadu) and *mahuvar* (Gujarat) – the term can denote a double clarinet (*see* PŪNGĪ).

See also NĀGASVARAM and MUKHAVĪNĀ.

BIBLIOGRAPHY
Śārṅgadeva: *Saṅgītaratnākara* (13th century), ed. S. Subrahmanya Sastri, iii (Madras, 1951)
N. A. Jairazbhoy: 'A Preliminary Survey of the Oboe in India', *EM*, xiv (1970), 375
B. C. Deva: *Musical Instruments of India* (Calcutta, 1978)
R. Flora: *Double-reed Aerophones in India to AD 1400* (diss., U. of California, Los Angeles, 1983)
A. Dick: 'The Earlier History of the Shawm in India', *GSJ*, xxxvii (1984), 80

ALASTAIR DICK

Maillard, Paul (*fl c*1610–36). French organ builder. He built an organ for the monastery of Feuillants in the rue St Honoré in Paris (*c*1610) and began work on one for the parish church of St Nicolas-des-Champs (1613). In Paris he also worked on the instruments of Ste Opportune (1605–6), Ste Catherine du Val des Écoliers (1606), the Carmelite Friary of Billettes (1607), St Paul (1613–14) and St Pierre des Arcis (1614). In the provinces he supplied new organs for St Firmin du Castillon, Amiens (1614), St Pierre and St Michel du Tertre, Angers (1622; 1624), the Franciscan monastery, Rennes (1628–31), Notre Dame, Lamballe (1630–31), and Notre Dame, Vitré (1636). He also restored instruments in the cathedrals at Vannes, St Malo and Rennes and the abbey of St Aubin and St Laud, Angers.

BIBLIOGRAPHY
J. Martinod: *Répertoire des travaux des facteurs d'orgues*, ii (Paris, 1976)

Mailloche double (Fr.). TAMPON.

Maire, Nicolas (*b* Mirecourt, 20 Dec 1800; *d* Paris, 17 July 1878). French bow maker. His family had included violin makers. Like many of the town's more ambitious young men, he left for Paris to train as a bow maker in the establishment of Jacques Lafleur. There he is thought to have worked alongside Louis Simon Pajeot, who was ten years his senior: some of Maire's bows closely resemble those of Pajeot. On Lafleur's death in 1833 Maire succeeded as head of the shop, and continued to make bows there. He sometimes branded his name on the handle or under the lapping of his bows. Maire ranks among the best of the mid-19th-century Parisian bow makers, and his work varies considerably in style, as he was influenced first by one and then another of the great French craftsmen. Sometimes he made massive octagonal sticks with severe upright heads, at others a smoother, more delicate approach to bow making is noticeable. His bows are responsive and draw a fine sound, making them popular among players.

BIBLIOGRAPHY
R. Vannes: *Essai d'un dictionnaire universel des luthiers* (Paris, 1932, 2/1951/R 1972 as *Dictionnaire universel des luthiers* and R1981 incl. suppl. 1959)
J. Roda: *Bows for Musical Instruments of the Violin Family* (Chicago, 1959)
E. Vatelot: *Les archets français* (Nancy, 1976)
J. Liivoja: 'The Bows of Lafleur, Maire and Pajeot', *The Strad*, xcii (1981–2), 646

CHARLES BEARE

Maizu [maiso]. Single-rank PANPIPES of the Chipaya people of the Department of Oruro, highland Bolivia, known also in the village of Ayparavi as *chirihuana*. The *maizu* ensemble comprises four panpipes, one with three stopped tubes and three with two stopped tubes. The three-pipe instrument (*lutaqa* or IRA (i)) is considered masculine and the two-pipe one (*mataqa* or *arca*) feminine. They are played in hocketing pairs (typical for panpipes on the Peruvian and Bolivian Alti Plano) which incorporate a clay vessel flute (WAUQU) played by the *lutaqa* player. The three two-pipe instruments are played in unison, each by a different performer. Pitches have been recorded as $eb''-g''$ (*arca*) and $c''-eb''-f\#''$ (*ira*), with variations of up to 20 cents higher or lower.

BIBLIOGRAPHY
M. P. Baumann: 'Music, Dance, and Song of the Chipayas (Bolivia)', *Latin American Music Review*, ii (1981), 171–222

JOHN M. SCHECHTER

Majestoso. *See* MAESTOSO.

Makembe (i). Large single clapperless bell of the Ngbaka people of the Central African Republic. It is made from welded iron, and has a protruding handle and divided V-shaped mouth. The bell is held upright by a seated player with its mouth resting on his leg above the knee and its handle in his left hand. He lifts the bell clear of contact to strike it with a curved beater in his right hand. The instrument is played with drums to accompany singing, for example warriors' or hunting songs. See P. Collaer: 'Musics of the Central African Republic', BM 30 L 2310 [disc notes].

K. A. GOURLAY

Makembe (ii). Plural of LIKEMBE. *See* LAMELLAPHONE, §2(iii).

Makhana. RAFT ZITHER of the Luhya people of Kenya.

Mākhīm. Barrel drum of the Newari people of Nepal. *See* KHĪM.

Makhonine violin. An electric violin invented in France around 1933, presumably by Ivan Makhonin (*b* Russia, *c*1886). He emigrated from the USSR in 1920 and in the early 1930s designed an aeroplane with telescopic wings.

Makhweyane [makhoyane, sikhweyane]. Braced gourd-resonated musical bow of the Swazi people of southern Africa. It is similar in construction and performing practice to the Zulu UMAKHWEYANA. *See* MUSICAL BOW, §4, ex.3*b*, fig.2*b*.

Makhwindi [makwindi]. Stringed wind instrument of the Swazi people of southern Africa. *See* GORA.

Makilingu. Cylindrical SLIT-DRUM of the Ngbandi people of Zaïre. Like the Luba KYONDO it appears in three sizes, giving a range of low, medium and high notes. The large 'male' *to-makilingu* is 130 cm in length by 50 cm in diameter, the medium-sized 'female' *ta-makilingu* is 90 cm by 35 cm, and the small 'child' *nyini makilingu* is 50 cm by 20 cm.

Makin organ. An ELECTRONIC ORGAN manufactured in Rochdale, Lancashire, since 1970 by Compton-Makin, which became J. & J. Makin Organs Ltd in 1973. In 1970 the company acquired part of Compton Organs Ltd, including the electrostatic tone-wheel system of sound generation (one wheel per note) of the Compton ELEC-TRONE, which is still in use in combination with micro-processor technology. Additional electronic circuitry provides a more realistic pipe organ sound quality, such as attack and decay characteristics (including the 'chiff' attack found in flute stops), and soft beats for certain stops produced by a 'chorus generator' that adds slightly out-of-tune frequencies. The organs are all custom-built versions of the basic Westmorland model, and mostly have two or three manuals and pedals. They are designed for churches, and one, a four-manual instrument, is in Ripon Cathedral.

BIBLIOGRAPHY
B. Hesford: 'Makin Organs', *MO*, cii (1978–9), 447

HUGH DAVIES

Makkow. Leg rattles of the Tswana people of southern Africa. The modern spelling is MATLHO.

Makondera [makondere]. Side-blown trumpet of eastern Africa. It is composite, made from a horn and gourds. The *makondera* is attributed to Shangungu district, Rwanda, and the *makondere* to the Nyoro people of Bunyoro district, Uganda, and the Nyoro/Haya people of Bukoba district, Tanzania. The instruments are played in ensembles, together with drums, to accompany dancing and at functions connected with royalty. See *TraceyCSA*, ii, 105, 300, 322.
See also AMAKONDERE.

Makpo. Small cylindrical SLIT-DRUM of the Yogo/Bozo people of northern Zaïre. Two of these are played to accompany dancing together with other percussion instruments, such as the *nengangbu* and *ngbemakpo* slit-drums, *nengangbu* bell and *nggabi* drum. See *TraceyCSA*, ii, 265.

Makuta. Term for an Afro-Cuban drum of the Congo people; also a dance and rhythm associated with it. The instrument is tall, barrel-shaped or tubular, single-headed and open, with the head made taut with nails or screws and nuts; apparently the head was originally tensioned with wall-wedges. The *makuta* rhythm requires two *makuta* drums, the larger one barrel-shaped, the other tubular; both are played by a standing player, always with bare hands, the drums resting vertically on the ground. See *OrtizIMA*, iii, 430, 435ff.

JOHN M. SCHECHTER

Makutī [magudi, mahudi]. A name of Tamil Nadu, south India, for the DOUBLE CLARINET with gourd wind cap (*see* PŪNGĪ). It is also known as *pambatti kuḷal*.

Makwindi. *See* MAKHWINDI.

Makyong. *See* ALAT-ALAT MAKYONG.

Mala (i). A term used for several types of aerophone in Latin America.
(1) PANPIPES in the JULA-JULA and LAKITA ensembles of Bolivia.
(2) NOTCHED FLUTE of Bolivia. *See* PACEÑO.
(3) DUCT FLUTE in ensembles of the Bolivian Alti Plano. *See* PINCULLO and TARKA.

Mala (ii). Composite cone whistle of the Madi people of Uganda, constructed on the same principle as the NSEGU. The taper of the cone is more noticeable.

Malaba [maloba]. GROUND HARP of the Gishu people of Uganda. *See* SEKITULEGE.

Malanzi. Transverse flute of the Gogo people of Dodoma district, Tanzania. It is closed at both ends and has two finger-holes.

Malaza. Leg rattles of the Ngoni people of Petanke district, Zambia. They are made from the hard shell of a fruit filled with small seeds or stones, threaded on to sticks in four rows, and strapped to the legs of dancers. See *TraceyCSA*, ii, 71.

Malenge. End-blown single-note flute of the Konjo people of Toro district, Uganda, used in the ILENGA flute ensemble.

Malepe. Bunch of small hand-held bells of the Kamba people of Machakos district, Kenya. They are used in dance-songs.

Maler [Maller, Moller, Muller]. German lute makers. In 1530 Laux [Luca, Lucas] Maler (d ?Bologna, 5 June 1552) formed an association for the making of lutes with his son Sigismond Maler (? d Bologna, before 1552) and a German apprentice, Marcus Sarto. The first reference to Laux Maler in Bologna, where he and his son worked, is dated 1518; by 1523 his work was highly esteemed. Sigismond Maler (whom Vannes mistakenly believed to be the senior of the two) is not known before the 1530 arrangement, and since he is not mentioned in his father's final will, made in 1552, is presumed to have predeceased his father. This final will (an earlier will was made in 1530) shows Laux Maler to have owned four houses and three shops, and to have had on his premises 998 completed lutes (127 further instruments were unfinished, and over 1000 soundboards, most with their roses already carved, are also mentioned). On the basis of these and other figures Prynne (1963) estimated the total output of the Maler workshop to have been around 4000 lutes.

The 1566 Fugger inventory (see Stockbauer, 1874, and Smith, 1980) includes as no.79 'Eine alter gute Lauten von Laux Muller'. By 1648 the excellence of Maler lutes was almost legendary. In that year Jacques Gautier, in correspondence with Huygens (who was anxious to buy a Maler lute), wrote that Maler was the best maker of nine-ribbed Bologna lutes, that probably fewer than 50 still survived, and that certainly fewer than six were known to him in London. Gautier had bought one for Charles I for £100, a considerable sum for those times, and Thomas Mace, writing in 1676, said he had seen this lute and two others: '(pittiful, Old battered cracked things), valued at 100 l [£] a piece'. Gautier also told Huygens that Sigismond Maler had made many 11-ribbed lutes. Sigismond Maler was apparently famous for his varnish: he promised to give the Duke of Ferrara the recipe, but all that is now known is that he used two varieties, compounded by his apprentices.

Baron (1727) called Laux Maler 'without doubt one of the oldest and best masters', and wrote of his lutes that 'it is a source of wonder that he already built them after the modern fashion, namely with the body long in proportion, flat and broad-ribbed'. The rather unexpected reference to 'the modern fashion' is explained by the fact that J. C. Hoffman was then reviving the classic Bologna shape in Leipzig.

Five lutes by Laux Maler, probably all authentic, though all greatly altered, are in collections: one in London (Victoria and Albert Museum), two in Prague (Národní Múzeum), one in Nuremberg (Germanisches Nationalmuseum) and one in Vienna (Kunsthistorisches Museum). None of Sigismond Maler's work is known to survive.

BIBLIOGRAPHY
E. G. Baron: *Historisch-theoretische und practische Untersuchung des Instruments der Lauten* (Nuremberg, 1727/R1965)
J. Stockbauer: *Die Kunstbestrebungen am bayerischen Hofe* (Vienna, 1874)
W. J. A. Jonckbloet and J. P. N. Land, eds.: *Correspondance et oeuvres musicales de Constantin Huygens* (Leiden, 1882)
L. Frati: 'Liutisti e liutai a Bologna', *RMI*, xxvi (1919), 94
R. Vannes: *Essai d'un dictionnaire universel des luthiers* (Paris, 1932, 2/1951/R1972 as *Dictionnaire universel des luthiers*, and R1981 incl. suppl. 1959)
M. W. Prynne: 'The Old Bologna Lute-makers', *LSJ*, v (1963), 18
L. Cervelli: 'Brevi noti sui liutai tedeschi attivi in Italia dal secolo XVI° al XVIII°', *AnMc*, no.5 (1968), 299–337
E. Pohlmann: *Laute, Theorbe, Chitarrone* (Bremen, 1968, rev., enlarged 4/1976)
R. Bletschacher: *Die Lauten- und Geigenmacher des Füssener Landes* (Hofheim am Taunus, 1978)
A. Layer: *Die Allgäuer Lauten- und Geigenmacher* (Augsburg, 1978)
D. A. Smith: 'The Musical Instrument Inventory of Raymond Fugger', *GSJ*, xxxiii (1980), 36

IAN HARWOOD

Mali. PANPIPES in a JULA-JULA ensemble of the Bolivian Alti Plano.

Maliami. (1) Set of cylindrical stopped flutes, threaded on to cord or wire, of the Bwa people of northern Zaïre (*LaurentyA*, 187f).

(2) Wooden VESSEL FLUTE of the Bati people of northern Zaïre (*LaurentyA*, 220).

Maliche. DUCT FLUTE of the Quechua people of Andean Bolivia, similar to the CH'UTU of the Chipayas.

Maligbanga. Large BOARD ZITHER of the Bali Lombi people of north-eastern Zaïre. It is about 70 cm long, 20 cm wide, and has 17 strings of vegetable fibre. Each string passes over a bridge at either end of the board, and in addition across a cylindrical upright piece of wood wedged between the board and the string at different distances to produce different vibrating lengths. The corresponding instrument of the Bali Avakubi people, which measures 60 cm by 25 cm and has 18 strings, is known as *sikwi*. Other board zithers constructed in this way are the two Kumu instruments, the *mafili* with 16

strings and *bafiri* with 12 to 20 strings. The *bafiri* is 70 to 100 cm long and 20 to 40 cm wide; the *mafili* uses tuning wedges of bamboo. *See also* IKIDI and GOMBI (i).

BIBLIOGRAPHY
LaurentyC
F. J. de Hen: *Beitrag zur Kenntnis der Musikinstrumente aus Belgisch Kongo und Ruanda-Urundi* (Tervuren, 1960)
G. Knosp: *Enquête sur la vie musicale au Congo belge 1934–1935* (Tervuren, 1968)

K. A. GOURLAY

Malimba. A variant spelling for MARIMBA. The term is used in wide areas of eastern and south-eastern Africa for a lamellaphone (*see* LAMELLAPHONE, §2 (i)) and a XYLOPHONE (*see also* PANDINGBWA). It is also attributed to the Gogo people of Dodoma district, Tanzania, as the name for a TROUGH ZITHER.

Malinconico (It.: 'sad', 'melancholy'). As a tempo or expression mark it was probably not used much before Boccherini, though Bernardino Bottazzi (1614) wrote of making 'canti fermi melanconici' sound 'allegri'. Beethoven entitled the final *adagio* of his Quartet op.18 no.6 'La malinconia'.

Maline, Guillaume (*b* Mirecourt, 1793; *d* ?c1850–60). French bow maker. Almost nothing is known of his career except that he worked for J.-B. Vuillaume in Paris; there is also evidence of his having produced unbranded sticks for other bow makers in Paris. His heads are quite striking in their individuality and are patterned after Dominique Peccatte but with a more rounded back and wider chamfers. Much of his output is mounted with 'Vuillaume-type' frogs and buttons. The rounded ferrule on these frogs usually has an extended plate which is longer than the arch. Although the circumstances are not known, Maline seems to have been the only 19th-century bow maker to be honoured by the Légion d'honneur, whose cross occasionally follows his brand.

BIBLIOGRAPHY
R. Vannes: *Essai d'un dictionnaire universel des luthiers* (Paris, 1932, 2/1951/R1972 as *Dictionnaire universel des luthiers* and R1981 incl. suppl. 1959)
J. Roda: *Bows for Musical Instruments of the Violin Family* (Chicago, 1959)
E. Doring: *Jean Baptiste Vuillaume of Paris* (Chicago, 1961)
R. Millant: *J.B. Vuillaume: sa vie et son oeuvre* (London, 1972)
E. Vatelot: *Les archets français* (Nancy, 1976)

JAAK LIIVOJA-LORIUS

Maling. Small bell with internal clapper of the Han Chinese. *See* LING.

Malingumu. Side-blown animal-horn trumpet of the Bangubangu people of central-eastern Zaïre (*LaurentyA*, 323, 327).

Malipenga (sing. *lipenga*). Kazoo ensemble of the Tonga, Tumbuka, Chewa and other peoples of southeastern Africa. The instruments are made from gourds, with a buzzing mirliton attached. By singing into them, the effect of a European military band is simulated. *Malipenga* dances, accompanied by the *lipenga* and drums, are said to have originated in military drill music in Tanzania and Malawi during the early 20th century, and they are in the nature of burlesques on British army parades.

BIBLIOGRAPHY
TraceyCSA, ii, 70, 203, 437

Lipenga (kazoo) players performing the malipenga dance, northern Malawi

G. Kubik (and others): *Ostafrika*, Musikgeschichte in Bildern, i/10 (Leipzig, 1982), 192

ANDREW TRACEY, DAVID K. RYCROFT

Maller. *See* MALER family.

Mallta. DUCT FLUTE in an ensemble of the Bolivian Alti Plano. *See* PINCULLO.

Maloba. *See* MALABA.

Malobia. LAMELLAPHONE of the Warega people of Shabunda, Zaïre (*LaurentyS*, 197).

Malongu. BOARD ZITHER of the Balese people of Zaïre (*LaurentyC*, 116).

Malta. (1) A term used in Bolivia for various types of flute. *See* KENA and TARKA.
(2) PANPIPES in SIKU ensembles of the Bolivian Alti Plano.

Maltona. A term used for a particular size of PANPIPES on the island of Taquile, Lake Titicaca, Peru. *See* SIKURI.

Malua [malungg]. Double clapperless bell of the Boma [Mbala] people of Zaïre. *See* GONGA (i).

Maluk. DIDJERIDU (aboriginal wooden trumpet) of the Murinbata people of northern Australia.

Malungu. Cylindrical wooden SLIT-DRUM of the Kakongo people of Zaïre. It has a carved anthropomorphic extension (*LaurentyTF*, 136).

Mama. Term used in the Bolivian Alti Plano for a particular size of instrument in an ensemble. *See* PINCULLO and SIKURI.

Mambabores. Single-string bamboo idiochord TUBE ZITHER of the Teluk Cenderawasih Islands, north-west Irian Jaya (West New Guinea). See J. Kunst: *Music in New Guinea* (The Hague, 1967), 130.

Mambamboli. LAMELLAPHONE of the Andide, Andozi and Anderimba peoples of Zaïre (*LaurentyS*, 197).

Mambira. XYLOPHONE of south-eastern Africa. *See* VALIMBA.

Mambirira. Log XYLOPHONE of the Lomwe people of Malawi. It usually has seven keys and a hexatonic tuning. The *mambirira* is played by a pair of musicians who sit opposite and at a slightly oblique angle to each other. Their playing is interlocking and uses cross-rhythms.

Mambisa. Afro-Cuban single-headed open drum, with nailed head. Its nearly cylindrical body is about a metre tall. In Havana Province, it is hung from the neck and played with two sticks. See *OrtizIMA*, iii, 445.

Mambongwe. Side-blown animal-horn trumpet of the Bangba people of north-eastern Zaïre. It has one stop in the tip (*LaurentyA*, 326).

Mamedaiko. Small Japanese barrel drum (*mame*: 'bean (-sized)'; *daiko/taiko*: generic term for drums). It has a shallow body to which the heads are tacked, rather than laced (*see* TAIKO). Two or three *mamedaiko* are suspended horizontally for use in *geza* music, especially for scenes involving children; their diameters are in the range of 20 to 30 cm.

DAVID W. HUGHES

Mampembe. *See* UMAMPEMBE.

Mampongui-nguembo. Largest of the anthropomorphic wooden trumpets of the Bembe people of the

Republic of the Congo. It is always played as part of an ensemble which includes three other trumpets of the same type. These are differentiated according to size by names derived from family relationships. The *mampon-gui-nguenbo* as the largest is the father, the *nsoni-bungu* the mother, the *lembe-nsoni* the daughter and the *mpandi-nsoni* the son. Each instrument is carved from a single piece of wood, with the air column in the part representing the body and the mouthpiece at the back between the arms of the carved figure. The trumpet is held by gripping the forearms of the figure from the rear and holding it upright in front of the player so that the carved head stands out above the head of the player. This applies to the three largest trumpets; the fourth is held horizontally. The ensemble is completed by two transverse trumpets of different sizes made from the roots of the wild coral tree. The larger is known as *mpolo-mono*, the other as *kinku*. The instruments play in hocket for *Bwete* music; the meaning of this term is unclear as are the circumstances under which the ensemble originally performed, though it was probably in connection with ancestral or funeral rites.

BIBLIOGRAPHY
C. Duvelle: 'Musique Kongo', OCR 35 [disc notes]
K. A. GOURLAY

Mana. Transverse flute of the Senufo people of the Ivory coast. It has three finger-holes and is played in pairs with hourglass drums. Formerly it was part of a court orchestra for paramount chiefs.

Mana embudzi. LAMELLAPHONE of the Sena/Tonga, Nyungwe and Sena peoples of the lower Zambezi valley. It has about 26 keys, with deep notes to the player's left, and is played inside a large calabash resonator.

Mancando (It., from *mancare*: 'to lose', 'to lack'). A performance instruction meaning almost the same as DIMINUENDO; *see also* TEMPO AND EXPRESSION MARKS.

Manche (Fr.). NECK.

Manda. Side-blown animal-horn trumpet of the Fuliru people of eastern Zaïre (*LaurentyA*, 324).

Mandal. *See* MĀDAR.

Mandalone. A large, wire-strung mandolin; *see* MAN-DOLIN, §4.

Mandan. Flute of the Tuburi people of Chad. *See* PARWAYE.

Mandar. *See* MĀDAR.

Mandar bahār. Larger, bass version of the ESRĀJ (long-necked fiddle of Bengal).

Mandari. Double-headed drum of Madhya Pradesh (Bastar district), central India. The truncated conical body, usually of baked clay, is nearly 60 cm long and the heads, of different diameters, are covered with cowhide. They are linked by leather thongs laced in a regular W pattern. The drum is held horizontally, hung by a strap around the neck of the player who strikes each head with one hand. This type of drum is found in the tribal belt covering western Bengal, Orissa, Bihar, eastern Madhya Pradesh and the south of Rajasthan. The names *mādar* and *mādal* represent variants of the Sanskrit word *mardala* (*see* MRDAṄGA, §2).

BIBLIOGRAPHY
W. Kaufmann: 'The Songs of the Hill Maria, Jhoria and Bastar Muria Gond Tribes', *EM*, iv (1960), 115
——: 'The Musical Instruments of the Hill Maria, Jhoria and Bastar Muria Gond Tribes', *EM*, v (1961), 1
B. C. Deva: *Musical Instruments of India: their History and Development* (Calcutta, 1978)
GENEVIÈVE DOURNON

Mander, Noel (Percy) (*b* Crouch, Kent, 19 May 1912). English organ builder and restorer. From 1929 he worked with the firm Rest Cartwright (under the direction of Ivor Davis) and occasionally for Henry Speechly & Sons. In 1936 he opened his own firm, N. P. Mander Ltd, in King's Cross, London, which moved to St Peter's Close in east London in 1945. In 1950 Mander incorporated Henry Speechly & Sons (established 1860), and in 1963 he purchased Thomas Harrison & Sons (established 1830). In 1975 John Pike Mander (*b* London, 1949) joined his father as a partner after serving an apprenticeship with Rudolph von Beckerath in Hamburg.

Mander employs about 30 craftsmen principally building new church organs as well as portatives, positives and regal organs; he prefers to build mechanical action instruments. The firm also restores and rebuilds older instruments, notable examples being the organs in Adlington Hall (built by Smith *c*1690, and restored from a completely derelict state in 1959), and St Mary, Rotherhithe (John Byfield, 1764). New and rebuilt organs include St Paul's Cathedral (1972–7; *see* ORGAN, fig.49); Canterbury Cathedral (1978–9); St Vedast, Foster Lane, London (1962); Corpus Christi College, Cambridge (1969); Merchant Taylor's Hall, London (1966); St Giles Cripplegate, London (1968–9); St James, Clerkenwell, London (1979); and Pembroke College, Cambridge (in the style of Smith, 1980). Mander instruments combine traditional English methods of organ-building (frequently including pipes or casework from older organs) with some neo-classical elements. In addition to his work in Great Britain, Mander has installed instruments in the USA, Bermuda, Oman, Sierra Leone, Nigeria, Iceland and Japan.

WILLIAM J. CONNER/R

Mandidakkā. A large version of the ḌAKKĀ, a medieval Indian variable tension HOURGLASS DRUM.

Mandīrā. Pair of small cup-shaped cymbals of Orissa and Bengal (east India and Bangladesh), of the same type as the *manjīrā* of north India. They are used to accompany dance and song, such as the Baul song (*see* DOTĀRĀ) of Bengal and the narrative *Pālā* and *Dāskāṭhia* forms of Orissa. *See also* TĀL.

BIBLIOGRAPHY
K. S. Kothari: *Indian Folk Musical Instruments* (New Delhi, 1968)
S. Ray: *Music of Eastern India* (Calcutta, 1973)
ALASTAIR DICK

Mandja [mandjanga]. XYLOPHONE of Zaïre. *See* MANZA.

Mandoër (Ger.). MANDORE.

Mandoku. LAMELLAPHONE of the Ndo and Logo peoples of north-eastern Zaïre (*LaurentyS*, 197).

Mandola (It.). MANDORE.

Mandolin (Fr. *mandoline*; Ger. *Mandoline*; It. *mandolino*; Port. *bandolim, bandolino*; Sp. *bandolín, banjolín, mandolina*). A plucked chordophone with a fingerboard and a rounded body, which is either carved from a solid piece of wood, merging smoothly into the neck and sickle-shaped pegbox like a medieval gittern or rebec, or is built up in a lute-like construction; the latter type became universal in the 17th century. Sometimes a lute-type pegbox was fitted, but a curved pegbox surmounted by a carved head, shield or rectangular finial was more characteristic. The name 'mandolin' derives from the Italian 'mandolino' (diminutive of 'mandola'), which is found in sources from the late 17th century onwards. The names 'mandore' and 'mandola' appear in earlier sources, but only after 1570 (a fact pointed out by Karl Geiringer in 1924 but ignored until recently) and were generally retained for the larger, *luthée* instrument that developed in Germany and Italy (see §2). But there seems to have been little standardization of nomenclature, and the above terms (*see also* MANDORE) may refer to instruments in the broad class described above.

1. Structure. 2. Early history. 3. The Neapolitan mandolin. 4. Other types. 5. Repertory.

1. STRUCTURE. The body, neck and pegbox of early mandores were carved to shape and hollowed out from a single solid block of wood (fig.1*a*). Woods known to have been used include sycamore, cypress, cedar and pear. The soundboard, of fir, was glued in place, as was the hardwood fingerboard which lay flush with the soundboard. How the soundboard was barred is not known, but three or four principal transverse bars seem probable. The rose was either cut in the soundboard or was a separate, inset structure of wood or wood and parchment. The classic Arab patterns used in nearly all lutes are not found in mandores of any variety.

Built-up instruments (except the flat-backed types: see §3 below) were constructed in the same way as the lute (fig.1*b*; *see* LUTE, §3). An inventory of a Parisian maker, dated 1606, includes 'two moulds for mandores, with their false tables', the latter being soundboard-shaped templates which preserve the outline of the body at certain stages of its construction. Various deciduous woods such as sycamore, maple, plane, ash, fruit-woods or yew were used for the ribs, and palisander may be found in later instruments. Contrasting coloured woods, or ebony and ivory, were often used for alternate ribs. The neck could be of pine covered with a veneer, or of beech or maple; lime and poplar, often used on contemporary lutes for their lightness, may also have been used on mandores. The hardwood fingerboard was often decorated with inlays and was flush with the soundboard in all *luthée* instruments. The soundboard was of fir or pine, with four or five transverse bars in small instruments and seven in the large German ones. Some small 18th-century French and Italian instruments have three to five short fan-bars below the bridge, and two surviving large German ones have six fan-bars, like a late German lute or theorbo.

The back of the Neapolitan mandolin (see §3) is made up of 11 to 35 ribs, all narrow except the pair next to the soundboard, which are very deep, giving the instrument a U-shaped cross-section (see fig.6 below). From the 19th century onwards it was made with a raised fingerboard extending on to the soundboard. Throughout its history it has had a simple, open soundhole and 14 to 17 metal, ebony or ivory frets, the neck and body

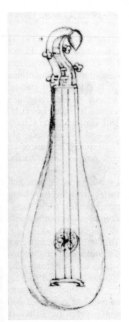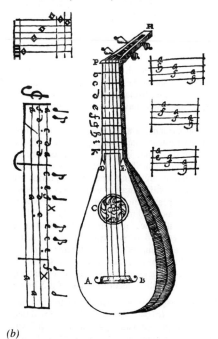

(a)   *(b)*

1. Four-course mandores, including indications of tuning: (a) details from Jacques Cellier's copy (1583–7) of an MS by François Merlin (F–Pn fonds fr.9152, f.166) showing mandore carved from a solid piece of wood; (b) woodcut from Mersenne's 'Harmonie universelle' (1636–7) showing built-up mandore

DELICIÆ MUSICÆ:

BEING, A

Collection of the neweſt and beſt SONGS,

With the Dialogues in the laſt New Play call'd
(*Love's a Jeſt*) Sett by Mr. *John Eccles*. Sung at
His *Majeſties Theatres*. Moſt of the Songs
within the Compaſs of the *Flute*.

WITH

A Thorow-Baſs, for the *Theorbo-Lute*,
Baſs-Viol, Harpſichord, or *Organ*.

Compoſed by ſeveral of the Beſt Maſters.

The Second Book of the Second Volume.·

L O N D O N,

Printed by *J. Heptinſtall*, for *Henry Playford* at his Shop in the *Temple-Change, Fleetſtreet*, where the firſt Volume is to be had; alſo a New Book for the *Flute*, being the Beſt and Eaſieſt Inſtructions yet Publiſh'd. And Sold at *Oxford* by *Francis Dollife* Book-binder, who Sells all other Muſick-Books. 1696.

2. Six-course mandore with nine strings: title-page of 'Deliciae Musicae' published by Henry Playford in 1696

joint coming at the tenth fret. A protective plate is usually inlaid just above the bridge to prevent damage from the plectrum. Flat-backed Neapolitan mandolins have also been made and have been particularly popular in recent years.

Pictorial evidence shows that some 17th- and 18th-century instruments had flat pegboards with the pegs inserted from behind, instead of the usual recurved or lute-like designs. Fanciful variants with bodies made from shells or gourds are mentioned in inventories and survive in museums. Decoration with inlays of ebony, ivory, mother-of-pearl, tortoise-shell and exotic woods seem to have been more common from the later 17th century onwards (but it is these instruments that tend anyway to have been preserved as objects of artistic interest). Plain but attractive examples of mainstream, large German and Neapolitan instruments survive; it seems that the large German ones were always built like contemporary lutes, without applied decoration (see fig.5 below).

2. EARLY HISTORY. In his manuscript treatise on musical instruments (c1640) Pierre Trichet claimed that there was no Latin proper name for 'this modern instrument which one calls mandore'. Trichet is the only source to mention a lost tutor for the mandore published by Adrian Le Roy in 1585 which attributes the origin of the

instrument to the villagers and shepherds of Navarre and Biscay, who played an instrument without frets. The earliest extant references to this type of instrument are in Bermudo's treatise (1555), under the name *bandurria comun*, which was a three-string plucked instrument of the rebec type. It was apparently tuned in 5ths, a 5th and 4th, or a 4th and 5th, the latter being 'the oldest tuning, and the most commonly used today'. Bermudo mentioned that some players did not use frets, while others had up to six or seven, placed sometimes diatonically and sometimes chromatically 'as on a vihuela'. Music for this instrument could be written in tablature, and 'four strings or more' could be fitted if the neck was wide enough. An inventory of instruments in the royal palace in Madrid, dating from 1602, records two 'bandurrias of four courses', and the *Diccionario de autoridades* (Madrid, 1726) describes the bandurria as an instrument 'like a small rebec with three strings . . . hollowed out of one piece of wood . . . or made in the manner of the bandola or lute'.

Inventories of Paris instrument makers first mention mandores in 1587. Both carved and built-up instruments (*mandores a costes*), small and large, are mentioned, and they were made in great numbers. An inventory of 1596 includes 'deux grandes mandores a costes', and one of 1636 seven 'mandorres à quatre cordes', one mandore with 'neuf cordes' (six courses; see below) and three 'mandorres luthées'. Four-course mandores could have four single strings or three pairs and a single top string. Five-course instruments could have single strings, but the Skine Mandore Manuscript (c1630) and the Talbot Manuscript (c1690) both reveal that the bottom course could be doubled, and octaved. The six-course instrument documented by Talbot had the lower three doubled and the rest single. So, in the 17th century, four or seven pegs indicate four courses, six pegs indicate five courses and nine pegs indicate six courses (fig.2). Instruments with paired and octaved courses were known as *mandores luthées*.

Small mandores had a string length of about 30 to 34 cm. The six-course instrument mentioned in the Talbot Manuscript had a string length of 43 cm. Stradivari left data that cover several small mandolas and mandolinos with four, five and six courses, a 'mandolino piu grande' and a 'mandola granda' with a body 46 cm long; this last would probably have had a string length of over 60 cm. In Germany after the mid-18th century, larger, lute-like instruments with six, seven and sometimes eight courses were developed, often with string lengths of 70 to 72 cm. These were *mandores luthées* taken to the limit (see below).

The French instrument used the tunings of 5ths and 4ths in the 16th and 17th centuries, and the top string was lowered two or three semitones for some keys. Contemporary examples of such tunings which agree with the surviving music for the instrument are $c'-g'-c''-g''$ and $c-f-c'-f'-c''$. The music of the Skine Manuscript is mostly for the latter tuning (without specifying pitch), but it contains instructions 'to tune the mandur to the old tune of the lutt' and there is music for that tuning; the Talbot Manuscript gives the five-course tuning as $c-f-a-d'-g'$, which is the common lute tuning of 200 years earlier. The six-course tuning given by Talbot is $c/c'-f/f'-b\flat/b\flat-d'-g'-c''$, which again is the common Renaissance tuning for a high-pitch treble lute and is compatible with the string length of the instrument that Talbot measured. However, the pitch of the five-

3. Back of a five-course mandore with six strings: detail from 'Still Life with Chessboard' (c1630) by Lubin Baugin (Musée du Louvre, Paris)

course tuning does not accord with the size of such instruments as the one so beautifully painted by Baugin (c1630; see fig.3), and it is best to take all these tunings as nominal until there is more firm evidence about the sizes of typical instruments.

In Italy the small instrument with a string length of about 30 cm persisted, with four, five and eventually six paired courses and the curved type of pegbox ending in a square finial (see fig.4). It was usually called a mandola or mandolino, the diminutive becoming standard in the 18th century. (The name 'Milanese mandolin' was not a contemporary term for this type of instrument, and the name 'pandurina', though used by Praetorius (2/1619) did not enjoy wide currency.) It was tuned in a series of 4ths, one documented mid-17th-century four-course tuning being $e'-a'-d''-g''$; this tuning (though not at this pitch) was used for the gittern in the 14th century (see Page, 1980) and goes back to the Arab 'ūd. Five-course instruments were tuned $b-e'-a'-d''-g''$ and six-course ones $g-b-e'-a'-d''-g''$. Six-course instruments were still being played in the late 19th century, sometimes fitted with single strings.

Larger mandolas with a string length of about 55 to 65 cm were also made in Italy, and these were probably tuned in 4ths with a 3rd between the middle courses or the second and third courses. Although there are many examples of such instruments in museums, there is little information available about them. The large German mandores of the 18th century, with a bent-back, lute-like pegbox and a treble rider for the single top string, have also survived in large numbers as compared with lutes of the period (fig.5, p.606). Their necks are usually long enough for nine or ten frets, and their usual

tuning was $D(\text{or } F)-G-c-f-a-d'$, reminiscent of the early bandora. Minor variants are found in some of the many music sources, all of which are in manuscript; the repertory includes solos, duets, songs and music for a variety of chamber ensembles. The Horemans paintings of Bavarian court musicians and instruments (1772) include two six-course mandores of this type and one 13-course lute. It is not clear what the differences between such instruments as these and the gallichone or colachon (see COLASCIONE) may have been at this period. One manuscript of 1735 has a title that begins *Gegenwärtiges Gallishon, oder Mandor Buch*; where the pitch can be determined, the surviving gallichone music is for the d'-pitch tuning used for the mandore. The modern German *Laute* (often known in England as the 'lute-guitar') derives from such instruments, although curiously the Italian type of pegbox, adapted to the fitting of machine heads, is used, and the internal barring is guitar-like.

All the instruments discussed above were usually strung with gut, but Talbot (c1690) and Fouchetti (c1770–80) said that wires were sometimes used. The strings were plucked with fingers or a quill plectrum, or sometimes with a quill tied to the forefinger. The later large German instruments were played with a fully developed finger-plucking technique.

Mandores with two necks and long, open bass strings were an inevitable development; Talbot measured one with string lengths of 48·2 and 104·4 cm and a tuning $C-D-E-F-G-A-B\flat-c/c'-f/f-b\flat/b\flat-d'/d'-g'/g'-c''$. He wrote down another version of this tuning with the fifth course also octaved and with single first and second strings, and he made a note to query which was

4. Six-course mandola ('Milanese mandolin') by Francisco and Giuseppe Presbler, Milan, 1778 (Royal College of Music, London)

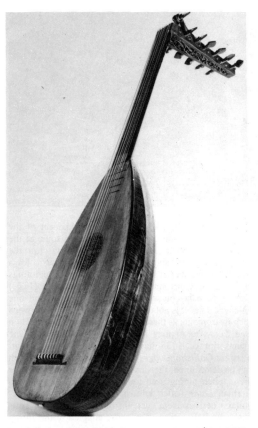

5. *Large mandore by G. F. Wenger, Augsburg, 1742 (Germanisches Nationalmuseum, Nuremberg)*

correct. The first agrees with the details of the instrument he measured, which he called an 'arch-mandore'. It was, in effect, a high-pitch archlute, just as all mandores and mandolins – except the Neapolitan mandolin (see §3 below) and the German mandore-gallichone – were, in effect, high-pitch treble lutes, and were so regarded by contemporary commentators.

3. THE NEAPOLITAN MANDOLIN. The four-course instrument now called 'mandolin' or 'Neapolitan mandolin' can be traced back to the mid-18th century, and it existed alongside the six-course instrument until the latter fell into disuse in the late 19th century. It shares many

characteristics with the *chitarra battente*, but unlike that instrument it has remained in use to the present day. These common characteristics include a very deep body, angled soundboard, end-fixed strings, flat pegboard with sagittal pegs, and a tendency to rather brash and florid decoration (see fig.6). It is tuned to the same pitch and intervals as the violin, $g–d'–a'–e''$, and in its earlier history it was strung with various combinations of gut, brass, silk and steel. Fouchetti (c1770–80) used brass harpsichord strings for the e'' and a' courses, gut ('chanterelles de pardessus de viole') for the d' course and overwound gut or silk for the g course; the last was usually octaved. Baines (1966) gives another method of stringing, using fine gut for the treble course, steel for the second, brass for the third and overwound silk for the fourth. All-steel stringing probably became customary when a fingerboard extending on to the soundboard replaced the earlier type that was flush with the soundboard; this change, together with the introduction of worm-and-pinion tuning-machines, came about in the second quarter of the 19th century. The instrument is always played with a plectrum.

In the later 19th century a tenor 'mandola', tuned an octave below the common instrument, and a 'double bass mandolin' were developed for use in the mandolin orchestras and societies that became popular at that time. Curiously, the earliest surviving Neapolitan mandolins, dating from the 1740s, are of the large tenor type; the earliest surviving common treble instruments date from the 1760s.

4. OTHER TYPES. Many regional variants and hybrids of the mandolin were developed in Italy during the 19th century, and Sachs (1920) and other writers have attempted to classify them. They were vernacular instruments of local importance only. Some had triple courses, some four single or five pairs of strings and some six single strings. Other variations are found in the length of the neck relative to the body, the width of the neck, and the width and depth of the body (see fig.4). Their main interest is that some of them were tuned to the same intervals as the five-course guitar and others matched the tuning of the Renaissance five- and six-course lute. One large, wire-strung type of mandolin, 90 to 100 cm in total length, had the bass courses lying off the fingerboard and running to nuts on the flat peghead. It had six or seven paired courses (except for the treble) tuned $F–(G)–A–d–g–b–e'–a'$, and was referred to variously as a *mandalone*, *arcimandola*, *mandalone da concerto*, *liuto romano* or even *chitarrone*. Another more modern variant is the American flat-backed man-

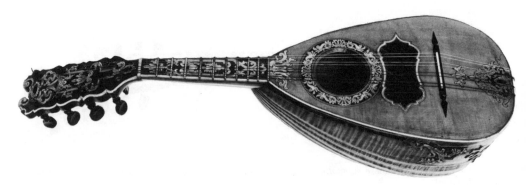

6. *Neapolitan mandolin by Antonio Vinaccia, Naples, 1772 (Victoria and Albert Museum, London)*

dolin, with f-holes and domed soundboard, which may carry electric amplification.

5. REPERTORY. The earliest known publications for the mandore, Pierre Brunet's *Tablature de mandorre* (Paris, 1578) and Adrian Le Roy's *L'instruction pour la mandorre* (Paris, 1585), are both lost. There is however a considerable quantity of manuscript and printed music in French tablature for the four- and five-course mandore in the tuning of 5ths and 4ths, dating from about 1626 onwards, and a smaller amount of manuscript music in Italian tablature for the four-course mandola tuned *e'–a'–d"–g"*, dating from the mid-17th century. One 17th-century manuscript contains a table of chords for playing the instrument from guitar *alfabeto* (*see* GUITAR, §4). After the third quarter of the 17th century the surviving music is in staff notation in the treble clef, and parts for the five- or six-course instrument began to appear in concerted music and opera. Early examples of dramatic works in which the mandolin appears include Antonio Maria Bononcini's *La conquista delle Spagne di Scipione Africano il giovane* (1707), where it joins muted strings in the accompaniment of an aria, Vivaldi's *Juditha triumphans* (1716), Francesco Gasparini's *Lucio Vero* (1719) and Handel's *Alexander Balus* (1748), where it is used with a harp, two flutes and a string orchestra to represent a mythical 'golden lyre'. Vivaldi's concertos for one and two mandolins and chamber ensemble, thought to have been written about 1736, use a range of *g* to *e'''*, which would have been appropriate to the six-course instrument in use at that time.

A substantial body of manuscript music in French tablature still exists for the large German mandore or gallichone; this is for an instrument tuned *D*(or *F*)–*G–c–f–a–d'*, with occasional variants in some sources. Composers named within this repertory include J. G. Albrechtsberger, G. A. Brescianello and Telemann, and there are solo pieces and partitas, duets with treble and bass accompaniment (presumably for violin and cello), duets for mandore (or gallichone) and violin, flute or cello with bass, and evidence of the mandore's use as a CONTINUO instrument (e.g. in instrumental music and in church cantatas by Telemann). A large collection of music in Vienna for mandolin and other instruments, dating from the late 18th century and the early 19th, include chords of five and six notes, which indicates that it was intended for the six-course mandolin; tutors for this instrument were being published in Italy as late as 1913. However, 'Neapolitan' mandolins were made in centres such as Dresden and Prague as well as in France in the last quarter of the 18th century, and it seems probable that this type of instrument, strung with a mixture of wire and gut or silk strings, would have been intended by Mozart for the accompaniment of the serenade in *Don Giovanni* (1787), its associations being southern if not particularly Spanish.

The earliest known tutor for the four-course violin-tuned mandolin, Gabriele Leone's *Methode raisonée pour passer du violon à la mandoline* (Paris, 1770), suggests a reason for the development, or at least the popularity, of the four-course instrument tuned in 5ths. Michel Corrette also published a tutor for 'mandoline a 4 rangs de cordes' in Paris in 1772 and Fouchetti a *Méthode pour apprendre facilement à jouer de la mandoline à 4, et à 6 cordes* (Paris, c1770–80), which makes the point that the ranges of the four- and six-course mandolin were identical, but the six-course instrument was easier to play as the higher positions on the fingerboard could be avoided. Internal evidence suggests that the instrument

that Hummel and Beethoven wrote for was the four-course one, tuned like the violin, but the only certain indicator in music of this period is the presence of five- or six-note chords, which necessarily exclude the four-course instrument.

After something of a lull during the first three quarters of the 19th century, the mandolin regained its popularity and has now achieved the status of a Western 'folk' instrument. Parallel to its revival in Europe, it became popular in many countries outside Europe, notably the USA, Latin America (*see* BANDOLIM and BANDOLÍN) and Japan; the Portuguese are thought to have imported the instrument to Ceylon [now Sri Lanka] (*see* BANDERINHA). It has also been increasingly used in art music of the late 19th and early 20th centuries for colourful effects, for example by Verdi (*Otello*, 1887; *Falstaff*, 1893), Pfitzner (*Palestrina*, 1912–15), Mahler (Seventh and Eighth Symphonies, 1904–5, 1906, and *Das Lied von der Erde*, 1908–9), Schoenberg (*Variations for Orchestra*, 1926–8; *Serenade*, 1920–23) and Stravinsky (*Agon*, 1953–7). Fuller details of the extensive repertory for mandore, mandola and mandolin are given in Tyler (1981, pp.22, 438).

BIBLIOGRAPHY
J. Bermudo: *El libro llamado Declaración de instrumentos musicales* (Osuna, 1555/*R*1957)
M. Praetorius: *Syntagma musicum*, ii (Wolfenbüttel, 1618, 2/1619/*R*1958 and 1980)
J. Skine: Mandore Manuscript (Edinburgh, Advocates Library, ADV.MS.5.2.15)
M. Mersenne: *Harmonie universelle* (Paris, 1636–7/*R*1963; Eng. trans., 1957)
P. Trichet: *Traité des instruments de musique* (F-*Psg* 1070); ed. F. Lesure (Neuilly-sur-Seine, 1957)
Talbot Manuscript (*GB-Och*, Music MS 1187)
Fouchetti: *Méthode pour apprendre facilement à jouer de la mandoline à 4, et à 6 cordes* (Paris, c1770–80)
C. Sachs: *Handbuch der Musikinstrumentenkunde* (Leipzig, 1920, 2/1930), 213f
K. Boss: *Die Mandolinenmusik vor und nach dem Kriege im In- und Auslande* (Nuremberg, 1924)
K. Geiringer: 'Der Instrumenten "Quinterne" und die mittelalterlichen Bezeichnungen der Gitarre, Mandola und das Colascione', *AMw*, vi (1924), 105
K. Wölki: *Die Geschichte der Mandoline* (Berlin, 1939, rev. 2/1974)
F. Lesure: 'La facture instrumentale à Paris au seizième siècle', *GSJ*, vii (1954), 11–52; x (1957), 88
R. Luck: *Ein Beitrag zur Geschichte des Colascione und seiner suddeutschen Tondenkmäler im 18. Jahrhundert* (diss., U. of Erlangen, 1954)
F. Lesure: 'Le traité des instruments de musique de Pierre Trichet', *AnnM*, iii (1955), 283–387; iv (1956), 175–248
M. W. Prynne: 'James Talbot's Manuscript: the Lute Family', *GSJ*, xiv (1961), 52
S. Marcuse: *Musical Instruments: a Comprehensive Dictionary* (New York, 1964)
A. C. Baines: *European and American Musical Instruments* (London, 1966)
E. Pohlmann: *Laute, Theorbe, Chitarrone* (Bremen, 1968, rev., enlarged 4/1976)
K. Coates: 'The Mandoline, an Unsung Serenader', *Early Music*, v (1977), 75
S. Hambly: *Mandolins in the United States since 1880: an Industrial and Sociocultural History of Form* (diss., U. of Pennsylvania, 1977)
L. Wright: 'The Medieval Gittern and Citole: a Case of Mistaken Identity', *GSJ*, xxx (1977), 8–42
M. Hodgson: 'The Identity of 18th century "Lutes"', *FoMRHI Quarterly*, no.14 (1979), 175
——: 'The Development of the Callachon', *FoMRHI Quarterly*, no.15 (1979), 194
C. Page: 'Fourteenth-century Instruments and Tunings: a Treatise by Jean Vailant? (Berkeley, MS 744)', *GSJ*, xxxiii (1980), 17
D. Gill: 'Mandores and Colachons', *GSJ*, xxxiv (1981), 130
J. Tyler: 'The Mandore in the 16th and 17th Centuries', *Early Music*, ix (1981), 22
——: 'The Italian Mandolin and Mandola 1589–1800', *Early Music*, ix (1981), 438

DONALD GILL (1, 2, 5),
RICHARD CAMPBELL/DONALD GILL (3, 4)

Māndolīn. South Asian plucked BOARD ZITHER with mechanized keyboard. *See* BULBULTARANG.

Mandolin harp. A chord zither with melody strings arranged in pairs rather than singly; it is also known as 'mandolin zither'.

Mandolin-lute. A plucked chordophone in the shape of a lute but played like a mandolin. It was invented by ANGELO BENEDETTO VENTURA of London before 1851.

Mandora (It.). MANDORE.

Mandore (Ger. *Mandoër, Mandürichen, Bandürichen*; It. *mandola, mandora, pandora*; Sp. *bandurria, bandola, vandola*). A name used from the 16th century onwards for a family of small plucked string instruments. These are characterized by a fingerboard and a rounded body, either carved from a solid piece of wood merging smoothly into the neck and sickle-shaped peg-box like a medieval gittern or rebec, or built up in a lute-like construction. Praetorius (*Syntagma musicum*, ii, 2/1619) used the term 'pandurina' for this type of instrument, but it did not gain wide currency. As larger instruments of this family were developed in Germany and Italy in the later 17th and early 18th century the name 'mandore' or 'mandola' was applied to them, and the smaller instruments came to be called 'mandolin' or 'mandolino'. This diminutive has survived as the name of an offshoot of the family, the 'Neapolitan' mandolin. For a discussion of the history and repertory of mandore-type instruments, *see* MANDOLIN, §§1, 2 and 4 (with illustrations).

DONALD GILL

Mandoura. Idioglot clarinet of Greece, played mainly in Crete. It is made of a single piece of cane cut so as to leave the top end closed. The reed is made by cutting a tongue in the cane near the sealed end. The *mandoura* has four or five, rarely six finger-holes. It is played mainly by shepherds.

R. CONWAY MORRIS

Mandron. A single-headed cylindrical drum of the rural and urban blacks of Surinam, used in religious rituals.

Mandu. Double-headed cylindrical drum of the Kota people of Gabon. Two *mandu* drums are used with a percussion beam and an antelope-horn trumpet to accompany dances of the *ongala* secret society.

Mandürichen (Ger.). MANDORE.

Mandurria. *See* BANDURRIA.

Mandzika [moudzika]. Cylindrical stopped wooden flute of the Uele people of Zaïre (*LaurentyA*, 174).

Manfúla. Cuban single-headed FRICTION DRUM with internal friction stick or cord. *See* KINFUÍTI.

Mangala. Metal bell of the Hehe people of Iringa district, Tanzania. A set of these is worn on each leg by dancers.

Mangele. Flat-board LAMELLAPHONE of the Lombi people of north-eastern Zaïre. It has metal keys (*LaurentyS*, 195).

Mangenengene. Cluster of metal bells attached to chest strap or harness and forming part of the dancing costumes of the Southern Sotho people of southern Africa. An alternative term, *lifaha*, refers more to decorative bells than musical bells.

Manggasieng. BULLROARER of Minangkabau, West Sumatra. It consists of part of a human skull with a long piece of string threaded through two small holes in the middle. It is used in shamanist rites, and also as a means of magically abducting the soul of a woman. See M. J. Kartomi: 'Tiger-Capturing Music in Minangkabau', *Sumatra Research Bulletin*, ii/1 (1972), 32.

MARGARET J. KARTOMI

Mangkuk. Small white porcelain bowl used as a high-pitched gong in the Batak Karo area of the province of North Sumatra. It is beaten with a metal stick or spoon at regular intervals (every two or four beats, or on every beat). It is part of the *gendang keteng-keteng* ensemble.

MARGARET J. KARTOMI

Mangla. Ankle rattles of some Sara peoples of southern Chad. *See* GODJE.

Mangolongondo. Heptatonic log XYLOPHONE of the Yao people of Malawi. It is similar in construction and playing technique to the Lomwe MAMBIRIRA.

Mangu. Conical drum of the Zimba and Binja peoples of Zaïre (*BooneT*, 31, 58f). *See* DINDO.

Manguaré. A pair of wooden drums of Peru. The Bora Indians of the tropical forest region play them to announce the arrival of visitors and to accompany dancing.

Mangwanda. Iron bell of the Tumbuka/Henga people of Kasungu district, Malawi. They are worn on the legs by dancers.

Mangwilo. XYLOPHONE of the Shirima people of south-eastern Africa; the same instrument is called *dimbila* by the Makonde people. The *mangwilo* is a hexatonic free-key log instrument with six to eight keys resting on two banana trunks, or on a pair of logs padded with grass. It is always played by two players sitting opposite each other. In contrast to the lower Zambezi xylophone tradition (*see* VALIMBA), the keys are struck not at the centre but at the ends, with plain wooden sticks. As in other African log xylophone traditions (in Uganda, Zaïre, Cameroon etc) the playing technique requires the interlocking of the two parts at high speed.

ANDREW TRACEY

Maṇi. Metal bell, with clapper, of Tamil Nadu, India. *See* GHAṆṬĀ.

Manibola. A Malagasy TUBE ZITHER. *See* VALIHA.

Manico (It.). NECK.

Manicorde (Fr.; It. *manicordo*). CLAVICHORD.

Manieren (Ger.: 'manners'). Embellishment, including both free ornamentation and specific ORNAMENTS, but perhaps more characteristically the latter. However, F. W. Marpurg appears to have had largely the former in mind when distinguishing in his *Anleitung zum Clavierspielen* (Berlin, 1755) between *Setz-Manieren*, notated by the composer, and *Spiel-Manieren*, improvised by the performer.

ROBERT DONINGTON

Maṇihorka. Bowed monochord of Latvia. *See* GĪGAS.

Manikarka. Bowed monochord of Lithuania. It consists of a narrow wooden rectangular box up to 100 cm long with a string stretched along the full length of the box; at one end it is fixed to a button, at the other it is wound round a peg. A fretted fingerboard under the string covers a chromatic two-octave range. Letter-names of the notes are often written next to the fingerboard. The soundholes and bridge are below the fingerboard. The *manikarka* is placed on a table and bowed with the player's right hand (usually with a violin bow) and fingered with the left. The instrument produces a soft, muted sound. It was known in Lithuania from the 19th to the early 20th century, and was made locally or imported from neighbouring countries. The name 'manikarka' or 'manakarka' may be a popular distortion of the word 'monochord'. It was used to accompany chorale-singing in the Protestant church; related instruments are the Estonian *mollpill*, the Latvian *gīgas*, the Karelian *versikannel* and the Swedish PSALMODIKON.

ARVYDAS KARAŠKA

Manimba. A term for the Haitian MARIMBA.

Maning gula. Small gong of Indonesia. *See* AGUNG.

Manivelle. A type of MUSICAL BOX.

Manjīrā. Small paired cup cymbals of northern and western India and Pakistan. They are of gun-metal, an alloy of brass with a high proportion of tin, zinc etc, and are generally connected by a long string. They are struck principally edge against edge to produce a bright, shimmering tone, and they are used mainly in accompaniment to the Hindu devotional singing *bhajan*. In Kathiawar, Gujarat, cymbal-playing has, in the words of Bake (1957), 'been raised to an independent art'. The Gujarati *manjīrā* are about 6 cm in diameter and 2 mm thick. The main cup, about 1·5 cm deep, is surmounted by a boss about 7 mm high, often octagonal on the side. The string is knotted inside a hole in the centre of the boss. One cymbal is held firmly in the left hand, with the string wrapped round the crooked first two fingers; the other, hanging on the longer length of the string, is swung to strike the other, and also round the head, shoulders etc in a virtuoso display of striking rhythms. In the *terātālī* dance of Rajasthan women tie up to 20 pairs of *manjīrā* to their legs, back and elbows and strike them with a pair held in the hands. In Sanskrit and Bengali *mañjīrā* denotes pellet bells (*see* GHUṄGRŪ and NŪPUR).

See also CYMBALS, esp. fig.4; MANDĪRĀ; TĀL.

BIBLIOGRAPHY
A. A. Bake: 'The Music of India', *NOHM*, i (1957), 195–225
K. S. Kothari: *Indian Folk Musical Instruments* (New Delhi, 1968)

ALASTAIR DICK

Manjūr. A shaken idiophone used by blacks in the Arabian Gulf area. It consists of sheep or goat hooves sewn with gut or nylon string on to a piece of material in the shape of a skirt, open at the back. It is used only by men, particularly novices, and the hooves are shaken together by movements of the pelvis while the rest of the body remains still. The *manjūr* is included with the *ṭanbūra* (lyre) and four *kuenda* (kettledrums) in the ritual *nūbān* ensemble to accompany singing and dancing. See S. Qassim Hassan: *Les instruments de musique en Irak et leur rôle dans la société traditionelle* (Paris, 1980).

SCHEHERAZADE QASSIM HASSAN

Manman. The largest of three single-headed drums of the *vodun* cult in Haiti. The others are the *seconde* and the *bula* (or *bébé*; see illustration, p.610). All three are made from a hollowed-out log, with the head held in place and tuned by means of pegs tied fast about the drumhead with cord. The bases of all the drums display a remarkable diversity of decorative carvings. The *manman*, 90 to 120 cm high, takes the most important ritual and musical role of the three and is capable of producing a variety of timbres. One hand strikes either the drumhead or its wooden side with a crooked stick, the *baguette*, while the other uses the base of the hand or fingers. The pitch can be altered; strokes near the centre of the drumhead produce low notes and strokes near the rim high notes. The *manman* player also acts as the leader. The *vodun* drums pass through several ceremonies before being used; in one they are clothed as human beings and 'baptized' with names to please the different *loa* (deities). The three drums, with rattles and *ogán* (bell), provide the metro-rhythmic patterns designed to suit the different *loa* and their dances.

MIECZYSLAW KOLINSKI/JOHN M. SCHECHTER

Mannello, Angelo (*b* Morcone, 11 Sept 1858; *d* New York, 4 July 1922). American mandolin maker of Italian birth. Son of a carpenter, he was apprenticed to a Neapolitan woodworker before emigrating in 1885 to New York, where he opened a prosperous workshop. In 1887 he married Filomena Buccini and had begun to employ helpers from his native village. Before 1900 his workshop occupied several quarters in 'Little Italy', and by 1903 he was operating a manufactory in the Bronx, where up to 75 workers, including family members, produced mandolins, guitars and banjos; many of these were sold wholesale to C. Bruno & Son (a major New York musical instrument distributor) for retailing under Bruno's name. Around 1917 Mannello founded the Società Morconese, a fellowship that later became a lodge of the Sons of Italy. In 1918 his factory was destroyed by arson and business declined thereafter.

Mannello was highly regarded for his mandolins, which are of ordinary proportions but ornately inlaid with expensive materials. These gained awards at the World's Columbian Exposition (Chicago, 1893), Tennessee Centennial Exposition (1897), Exposition Universelle Internationale (Paris, 1900), San Francisco Midwinter International Exposition (1900), Pan-American Exposition (Buffalo, 1901) and Louisiana Purchase Exposition (St Louis, 1904). He supplied instruments for

Manman (centre) with seconde (left) and bula (right): single-headed drums of the vodun cult, Haiti

professional bands, including Perara's in Minneapolis, and was represented in Chicago by a sales agent, Cesare Valisi. He presented a fine mandolin to the soprano Adelina Patti. Of Mannello's seven children, three sons worked in the shop but none was adequately trained to carry on the business which failed in the Depression. Two of his mandolins were presented by his descendants to the Metropolitan Museum of Art, New York.

BIBLIOGRAPHY

L. Libin: *American Musical Instruments in the Metropolitan Museum of Art* (New York, 1981) [unpubd catalogue]

LAURENCE LIBIN

Manopan. A trade name used by Euphonika of Leipzig for a small self-playing REED ORGAN operated by an endless card belt; *see* MECHANICAL INSTRUMENT, esp. fig.4.

Mansa. DRUM-CHIME ensemble of the Gwere people of Uganda, consisting of seven Uganda drums and one single-headed drum.

Mantegazza. Italian family of violin makers and restorers. The best-known violin maker of the family was Pietro Giovanni Mantegazza (*fl c*1757–*c*1800); evidently a pupil of Carlo Ferdinando Landolfi, he made a good number of violins of comparable quality in the 1760s and 1770s. He was in business with his brother Domenico, and there was a long family association with the collector Count Cozio di Salabue, beginning in 1776.

Towards 1790 the Mantegazzas began a series of fine contralto violas, modelled in the Amati style and more classical in appearance than the earlier instruments. Although usually bearing the label of Pietro, they may have been made with the help of other members of the family. Francesco and Carlo Mantegazza were probably the second generation, and were well known for their repairs and adjustments.

BIBLIOGRAPHY

R. Vannes: *Essai d'un dictionnaire universel des luthiers* (Paris, 1932, 2/1951/*R*1972 as *Dictionnaire universel des luthiers* and *R*1981 incl. suppl. 1959)

CHARLES BEARE

Mantsakota. Ribbon-reed instrument of the Lovedu and Kwebo (Northern Sotho) peoples of southern Africa resembling the SITLANJANI.

Mantshomane. FRAME DRUM of the Tsonga people of south-eastern Africa. It is usually played by women, to accompany dancing, and also in rites of exorcism.

Mäntyhuilu. DUCT FLUTE of Finland. The player's tongue forms the duct. It has finger-holes. Similar instruments are known among the Finno-Ugrian tribes, the Russians and Siberian peoples.

Manual. A KEYBOARD played by the hands (in contrast to one played by the feet; *see* PEDAL, (5)).

Manualiter. A quasi-Latin term derived from *manualis* ('hand keyboard') to indicate that a piece of organ music so labelled is played on manuals only, as distinct from PEDALITER. As a term it may be older than *pedaliter* (Schlick, *Spiegel der Orgelmacher und Organisten*, 1511), but it was chiefly used by German composers (and copyists) in the 17th and 18th centuries to help organists, otherwise accustomed to playing pedals, where the musical notation was ambiguous; for example, when it was written on two staves (as in most organ music except strict trios until the 1730s) or in tablature (as in the sources of Buxtehude's music, etc). Scheidt (*Tablatura nova*, 1624), however, implied that in organ chorales the pedal could be used to bring out the theme whether or not it was specified, much as some organists today play with a pedal cantus firmus the indicated *manualiter* preludes in the third section of Bach's *Clavier-Übung*.

PETER WILLIAMS

Manza [mandja, mandjanga]. A term for XYLOPHONE in central Africa. (1) Calabash-resonated xylophone of the Mbanja, Sere, Zande and Bwa peoples of Zaïre. It may be differentiated by the addition of a second term, for example the Bwa *manza baigana* and the Zande *manza balanga* and *manza dongese*. Most instruments have nine or ten keys, except that of the Bwa, which has five. In general these xylophones resemble the *madimba* (*see* MADIMBA (i)) in that they have a large 'bow' frame, but differ in that the calabash resonators are fixed in position by being inserted into holes in a board which fits beneath the keys. In some instruments the calabashes are replaced by closed hollow bamboo tubes. The instrument is approximately 85 cm long and may be played standing, the 'bow' resting on the chest of the player, who strikes the keys with two beaters in each hand. The *manza* of the Gandu people of the Central African Republic is also calabash-resonated.

(2) Ten-key frame xylophone. The keys are strung together with fibre and rest on a wooden frame comprising two parallel planks joined at each end by cross-pieces. A bar of fibre and vegetable matter stretches along each side of the frame to separate the keys from the wood. The instrument is known as *manza* and *mandja* by the Ngbandi people and as *mandjanga* by the Mbanja people, who also apply the term to other xylophones. The Yaka xylophone, *itanda*, has 10 or 11 keys. The instruments are beaten with a pair of rubber- or fibre-tipped beaters.

(3) Trough xylophone with 10, 11 or 13 keys. The keys are strung together with fibre, and are separated from the open sides of the barge-shaped wooden trough on which they rest by means of a layer of woven fibre which stretches the full length of each side. The instrument is played with rubber-tipped beaters, a pair for a player on each side. It is reputedly special to the Mbanja people who call it *mandjanga*. Traditionally used for sacred music, it is now restricted to dance rhythms. The Ngombe and Sango peoples use the terms *mandja*, *mandjanga* and *manza* for this and other types of xylophone. The Ngbaka 10- or 12-key xylophone of this type is known as *bandjanga* and the Ngbandi eight-key instrument as *gombi*.

(4) Log xylophone of the Ngbandi and Sango peoples of Zaïre. *See* PANDINGBWA.

BIBLIOGRAPHY

BooneX
F.J. de Hen: *Beitrag zur Kenntnis der Musikinstrumente aus Belgisch Kongo und Ruanda-Urundi* (Tervuren, 1960)
G. Knosp: *Enquête sur la vie musicale au Congo belge 1934–1935* (Tervuren, 1968)

K. A. GOURLAY

Manzisi. Trumpet of the Bongo people of Sudan. It is made from a tree trunk, hollowed out and carved on the outside into the shape of a limbless man. The player produces low staccato sounds by blowing into a square mouth-hole.

Mapengo. (1) Set of cylindrical stopped flutes threaded on to cord or wire of the Bwa people of northern Zaïre (*LaurentyA*, 188f). Other names reported are *gude* and *moleno*.

(2) Wooden cylindrical flute with stops of the Makere people of Zaïre (*LaurentyA*, 173).

Mapindil [nulanting]. Gong in the *kwintangan* gong-chime ensemble of the Yakan people of the southern Philippines. *See also* KULINTANG.

Mapuíp. JEW'S HARP of the forest-dwelling Moré Indians of eastern Bolivia, consisting of a small tongue of palm fibre between 15 and 20 cm long. One end is put into the mouth and supported by the teeth; the other end is supported by one hand. The other hand rubs a small twig (20 cm long), moistened with saliva, on the two strings of the taut fibre. The instrument accompanies lovers' songs.

Maqrūna. DOUBLE CLARINET of the Arab world; *see* MAGRUNA and MIJWIZ.

Maqwāmiyā [mukwamya]. Prayer stick of Ethiopia. It is a wooden stick about 1·5 metres in length, with a handle and a T-shaped tang-cross of silver or brass. It is waved in the air or banged on the floor during the liturgy of the Ethiopian rite.

Maracas. A pair of gourd rattles, most commonly oval. The gourd contains the naturally dried seeds of the fruit.

1. Two pairs of maracas

2. Maracas and harp players, Miranda state, Venezuela

Imitations in wood, wickerwork, bakelite or metal contain beads, small shot, or similar rattling pieces. The name maraca is thought to be of pre-Columbian Araucanian origin. It is applied universally to gourd rattles of the above description. Like all seed-pods and similar rattles the instrument is widespread and of ancient origin. A Guinea legend tells of a goddess forming a maraca by enclosing some white stones in a calabash.

Maracas form an integral part of the rhythm section of Latin American orchestras and are widespread particularly in Colombia, Venezuela and Brazil. In Colombia, they appear in the *conjunto de cumbia* and *conjunto de gaitas* ensembles; smaller maracas known as *gapachos*, as the seeds used are those of the *gapacho* plant, are played in the *chirimía* ensemble of the Andean region. The *clavellinas*, played in the Llanos region of Colombia, are similar to the *gapachos*. Maracas provide the basic rhythmic accompaniment in many ensembles in Venezuela, where they are usually played by the singers. A variety of rattles of the maraca type is used by the Amerindian peoples of Brazil. The pre-Columbian Indian maraca (*mbaracá*) is made of a calabash filled with dry seeds. The Paraguayan maraca is made from a *porrongo* or other type of gourd in which seeds or pebbles are placed; it is played only by men.

Maracas have been adopted by Western rhythm bands and percussion ensembles and are also important instruments in primary school education. Modern composers to score for maracas include Varèse (*Ionisation*, 1934), Prokofiev (*Romeo and Juliet*, 1935) and Malcolm Arnold (Fourth Symphony, 1960). Occasionally maracas are used as 'drumsticks'. This effect is requested in Leonard Bernstein's *Jeremiah Symphony* (1942), Harold Farbermann's Concerto for Timpani and Orchestra (1962) and Marius Constant's ballet *Paradis perdu* (1967).

BIBLIOGRAPHY
IzikowitzMISAI
G. Chase: *A Guide to Latin American Music* (Washington, DC, 1945, 2/1962)
J. Blades: *Percussion Instruments and their History* (London, 1970, rev. 3/1984)
N. Del Mar: *Anatomy of the Orchestra* (London, 1981)
JAMES BLADES, JOHN M. SCHECHTER

Marako. Large conical bark trumpet of the Nanai people of Siberia, used as an elk lure. Strengthened by wooden planks, it is moistened before use.

Marao. Large wooden trumpet of the Siuai people, south-west Bougainville, Solomon Islands, used with panpipes to accompany men's dancing. It is played either through a hole in the end or with a mouthpiece made from a half coconut shell.

BIBLIOGRAPHY
E. W. Chinnery: 'Notes on the Natives of South Bougainville and Mortlock (Tahu)', *Territory of New Guinea Anthropological Report*, no.5 (1931), 103
D. L. Oliver: *A Solomon Island Society* (Cambridge, 1955), 36, 371

Marapo. CLAPPERS of the Tswana people of southern Africa. Like the Zulu AMATHAMBO, these comprise a pair of rib-bones, used for rhythmic song-accompaniment (as in American Christy Minstrel performances). See *KirbyMISA*, 10f, pl.5.

Marbab. SPIKE FIDDLE of Sumatra. *See* ARBAB.

Marcatissimo. *See* MARCATO.

Marcato (It.: 'marked', 'stressed', 'accented'). A performance instruction which seems to have been rare before the 19th century: it is not specifically mentioned in Koch's *Musikalisches Lexikon* (1802) though J. G. Walther did include an entry 'Marqué' in his *Musicalisches Lexicon* of 1732. Its principal use is to draw the attention to the melody or subject when it is in such a position that it might be overlooked, as, for instance, *il basso ben marcato* in Chopin's Krakowiak op.14; or when there are two subjects both of which are to be brought prominently forward, as in the finale of Beethoven's Ninth Symphony, where the two subjects come together in 6/4 time with the words 'Freude, schöner Götterfunken' and 'Seid umschlungen'. In his *Etudes symphoniques* no.2 Schumann has *marcato il canto* below the top line and *marcato il tema* below the bass. In the slow movement of his Quartet op.18 no.6 Beethoven used *queste note ben marcate*. *Marcato* and *ben marcato* are predictably common in Stravinsky, who also used *p ma ben articulato* (Symphonies of Wind Instruments).

The superlative form *marcatissimo* is rarely used but is found, for instance, at the end of Chopin's Etude op.25 no.11 and in the finale of Schumann's F♯ minor sonata. Bartók used it in his Second and Sixth Quartets. Schumann used *sempre marcatissimo* for no.8 of his *Etudes symphoniques*.

For bibliography *see* TEMPO AND EXPRESSION MARKS.
J. A. FULLER MAITLAND/DAVID FALLOWS

Marchi, Giovanni Antonio (*b* 1727 or 1728; *d* ?Milan, 1810). Italian violin maker. There has been considerable confusion about his dates, though it is known that he was active in Bologna, and it has been suggested that he spent his last years in Milan. Several writers follow Lütgendorff in dating him 1660–1726, but de Wit illustrates two labels of 1760 and 1778, causing some to assume that there were two makers of the same name, possibly father and son. However, the discovery of an autograph letter from Marchi to Count Cozio di Salabue, dated 13 May 1805 and stating that he was 78, establishes his date of birth as 1727 or 1728.

Marchi's violins are loosely patterned after the model of Alessandro Gagliano; the similarities are mostly evident in the outline, but Marchi's archings are usually fuller, the soundholes narrower (reminiscent of Stainer) and the purflings and scrolls more carefully finished. The varnish is also richer in texture than that of the average Neapolitan instrument and is generally a golden brown. Because his work is so little known, many otherwise unattributed instruments have been found to bear copies of his labels.

BIBLIOGRAPHY

P. de Wit: *Geigenzettel alter Meister vom 16. bis zur Mitte des 19. Jahrhunderts* (Leipzig, 1902–10/*R*1978)

W. L. von Lütgendorff: *Die Geigen- und Lautenmacher vom Mittelalter bis zur Gegenwart* (Frankfurt am Main, 1904, rev. 6/1922/*R*1968)

R. Vannes: *Essai d'un dictionnaire universel des luthiers* (Paris, 1932, 2/1951/*R*1972 as *Dictionnaire universel des luthiers* and *R*1981 incl. suppl. 1959)

JAAK LIIVOJA-LORIUS

Marconcini, Luigi (*fl* Ferrara and Bologna, *c*1760–91). Italian violin maker. According to some of his labels, he was born in Ferrara. He is reputed to have been a pupil of Omobono Stradivari but if this was so, the influence was not particularly strong. Nevertheless, Marconcini's instruments are built on a Stradivarian outline and with rather full archings. The soundholes are neatly carved and the varnish, usually a golden to orange brown, is of good texture. He seems to have devoted his best efforts to his cellos, most of which are built on a fairly large pattern. An attractive theorbo bearing his label, 'Aloysius Marconcini/Ferrariensis Fecit Ferrarie, Anno 1778', is in the Cologne Museum.

Giuseppe Marconcini (1772–1841), one of Luigi's two sons, studied with Lorenzo Storioni and established himself in Ferrara. His instruments are generally considered superior to those of his father, especially in choice of wood. He worked in the style of Storioni, and his best instruments match his master's in craftsmanship. His varnish is equal to his father's but has more of a red tint. Besides being an able maker, Giuseppe appears also to have been a good violinist and acquaintance of Nicolò Paganini.

BIBLIOGRAPHY

W. L. von Lütgendorff: *Die Geigen- und Lautenmacher vom Mittelalter bis zur Gegenwart* (Frankfurt am Main, 1904, rev. 6/1922/*R*1968)

JAAK LIIVOJA-LORIUS

Marcussen. Danish firm of organ builders. It was founded in 1806 by Jürgen Marcussen (1781–1860); it operated under the name of Marcussen & Reuter from 1826 to 1848, when it became Marcussen & Søn. Johannes Lassen Zachariassen (1864–1922), a great grandson of the founder, was managing director from 1902 to 1922, and his son Sybrand (1900–60) from 1922 to 1960; Sybrand's son Sybrand Jürgen (*b* Flensburg, 22 Oct 1931) became director in 1960. The firm is based in Apenrade, Nord Slesvig, and has been active chiefly in Denmark, but it has also built in northern Germany,

Sweden, Finland and the Netherlands. Among its important works are the organs in Christiansborg Castle, Copenhagen (1829; three manuals, 38 stops; extant); St Nikolai, Kiel (1842; three manuals, 47 stops); Odense Cathedral (1862; three manuals, 40 stops); Lund Cathedral (1863 and 1876; three manuals, 61 stops); St Nicholas, Copenhagen (1930; three manuals, 44 stops); St Oscar, Stockholm (1949; five manuals, 72 stops); Sibbo (1951; three manuals, 38 stops); St Nicholas, Utrecht (1957; three manuals, 33 stops); St Bavo, Haarlem (restoration of the Christian Müller organ in the Grote Kerk, 1959–61; three manuals, 60 stops); Grundtvig Church, Copenhagen (1965; four manuals, 55 stops); Viborg Cathedral (1966; four manuals, 64 stops); the New Cathedral, Linz (1968; four manuals, 70 stops); Lübeck Cathedral (1970; three manuals, 47 stops); St Laurence, Rotterdam (1973; four manuals, 85 stops); St Jacob, Stockholm (1977; five manuals, 84 stops); St Nicholas, Kolding (1977; four manuals, 57 stops); the church in Vestervig (1978; four manuals, 52 stops); and the Nieuwe Kerk, Amsterdam (restoration, 1981). The firm was one of the first, following the 1925 organ conference in Hamburg and Lübeck, to recognize the superiority of the sonic, structural and technical principles of the Baroque organ, and to return to them in its work.

BIBLIOGRAPHY

L. J. Cirsovius: *Lebensbild der Orgelbaumeister Marcussen & Sohn* (Kiel, 1891)

P. Hamburger: *Marcussen & Søn: 1806–1931* (Copenhagen, 1931)

N. Friis: *Marcussen & Søn: 1806–1956* (Apenrade, 1956)

——: 'Marcussen & Sohn', *MGG*

HANS KLOTZ

Mardala. A medieval Sanskrit name for the Indian double-headed drum. *See* MṚDAṄGA, §1; MĀDAR; MADDAḼAM; TAṆṆUMAI.

Mare. Side-blown trumpet of the Lugbara people of Uganda. It consists of a wooden cylinder of wide diameter inserted into a spherical gourd of slightly larger diameter. A circular hole, usually less than 3 cm in diameter, in the side of the cylinder serves as a mouthpiece. The instrument is played with the cheeks fully extended and the mouth pressed against the hole, while the open end is turned downwards or kept under the left arm. Two trumpets of different pitch are used to underline the beat of the drums. See *WachsmannTCU*.

Mariachi. Mexican ensemble of 20th-century popular music. It traditionally consisted of two violins, a vihuela and *jarana* (a small and larger guitar) and a harp or bass guitar. Two trumpets were added during the 1930s.

Mariani, Antonio (*fl* Pesaro, *c*1635–85). Italian violin maker. He is reputed to have been a pupil of G. P. Maggini but his model, although clearly of Brescian descent, is strongly original and in a reactionary way recalls the earlier school of Gasparo da Salò. This has contributed to the fact that many Mariani labels have been applied to instruments of sufficiently primitive appearance (though Mariani's craftsmanship, while not elegant, is not primitive itself). His instruments follow an elongated, fully arched model of standard length. The corners are rather pointed and stiff and the soundholes tend to be longish with narrow or even pointed wings. The scrolls vary in design and size but are stylistically in keeping with the rest of the instrument. The purfling is often inlaid in double rows and additional inlays of cross-hatched patterns are frequently set along the centre joint of the back as well as the flanks of the back and table. Mariani produced the full range of the violin family, including alto and tenor violas and both large and small cellos. The tenor violas have often been cut down in size, an operation which leaves the soundholes looking disproportionately long. His varnish varies from a golden yellow-brown to deep brown and is of very good quality. Unlike the earlier makers of the Brescian school, Mariani always dated his labels.

Luigi Mariani (*fl* Pesaro, *c*1690–1702), son and pupil of Antonio, also worked entirely in Pesaro. His instruments, which are scarce, follow his father's style but are somewhat less elongated in appearance. The corners are less protruding, the scrolls less erratic and the arching considerably flatter. However, the soundholes still follow the earlier Brescian models and the overall outline of the instruments remains faithful to the da Salò school. He also seems to have been much less inclined to use doubled or ornamental purfling. The varnish is similar to his father's but usually of a lighter shade. His labels, which are seldom seen in his instruments, are dated and give his first name as 'Ludovico'.

JAAK LIIVOJA-LORIUS

Marien Trompet (Ger.). TRUMPET MARINE.

Marikumu [epand]. Side-blown ivory trumpet of the Budu people of north-eastern Zaïre. It has a carved mouthpiece and one stop in the tip (*LaurentyA*, 393).

Marimba. Term for a group of idiophones, some of which are plucked (lamellaphones) and some of which are struck (xylophones). In parts of eastern and southern Africa it may denote either type of instrument. In Latin America it is mostly used for the calabash-resonated xylophone introduced from Africa, but in 19th-century Brazil it also applied to calabash-resonated lamellaphones of African origin, and in Colombia it is used generically to denote any melodic instruments other than aerophones (see List, 1968). The name is now almost universally applied to the commercially manufactured, fully resonated orchestral xylophone developed from Latin American models. For full classification details, *see* IDIOPHONE; for marimba lamellaphones, see LAMELLAPHONE, §2(i). *See also* XYLOPHONE, §§3 and 6.

1. Africa and Latin America. 2. The modern orchestral marimba. 3. Partch's marimbas.

1. AFRICA AND LATIN AMERICA. In some Bantu languages the term 'rimba' (or 'limba') (for example, among the Manganja and Lomwe of Malawi and Mozambique) means a single-note xylophone. *Rimba* (or *limba*) generally suggests a 'flattish object sticking out' (Nurse, 1970, p.35), such as a note or key of either a xylophone or a lamellaphone. 'Marimba' (or 'malimba') is derived from the addition of the Bantu cumulative prefix *ma* to the stem *rimba* (or *limba*, *r* and *l* being the same phoneme in many Bantu languages). 'Marimba' is, therefore, the full instrument, consisting of many *rimba* (notes). Among the many different Bantu ethnic groups who use such instruments the prefixes can vary according to the nature of noun classes in the languages concerned. Hence the Lozi of Zambia call their xylophones *silimba*, the Sena of Malawi call theirs *valimba* or *ulimba*, and the Luvale of north-eastern Angola call their two-key instruments *jinjimba*. Nurse (p.34) maintained

that the stem *rimba* must be closely related to the stem *mbira* (or *mbila*) which is also widely used, though only in southern and south-eastern Africa, for both xylophones and lamellaphones, and he suggested metathesis as the reason for this.

The marimba of the Shangana-Ndau people of Mozambique is an example of the calabash-resonated instruments of this area. The calabashes are individually tuned to the pitch of each key and, like many other African instruments, are fitted with a mirliton to modify the timbre: these mirlitons can be made from various types of natural membrane. Tracey (1948) provided a full description of the similar but larger *timbila* xylophones of the Chopi, neighbours of the Shangana-Ndau. An illustration in Merolla da Sorrarto (1692) shows a portable xylophone with calabash resonators from the kingdom of Congo (in northern Angola) called 'marimba'. He wrote that 'mostly four marimbas are played together'. This practice was exported a little later to the north; such groups of four instruments are still played in southern Cameroon, but there the name 'marimba' has become obsolete, giving way to the name 'mendzan' or 'mendzang' (Ngumu, 1976). On the east African coast the instruments associated with the name 'marimba' are quite different from the varieties already described. On the islands of Zanzibar and Pemba and among the Zaramo people of the Tanzanian coast a marimba is a box-resonated xylophone, and in inland Tanzania it is a lamellaphone.

1. *Marimbas (timbila) of the Chopi people, Inhambane district, Mozambique*

2. Marimba de tecomates player, Chichicastenango, Guatemala

African terminology conflicts with the use of the word 'marimba' by Western musicologists during the first half of the 20th century (see Nadel, 1931, Husmann, 1936, and others). Western musicologists developed a 'marimba stereotype' with a tendency to call any African xylophone 'marimba' (but especially those with a portable frame slung around the player's neck) and any lamellaphone 'sanza'.

The calabash-resonated xylophone may have been introduced to Latin America in pre-Columbian times (*IzikowitzMISAI*) or by African slaves in later centuries. It was once known in Peru and is still played in Brazil, Ecuador, Nicaragua, Cuba, Mexico (the *zapotecano*) and Guatemala, where it holds the status of national instrument (*see* XYLOPHONE, §6). Here the instrument was modified by the addition of a second keyboard to give a fully chromatic range. The first of this type were built by Sebastian Hurtado in 1894 and popularized by the famous Hurtado Brothers' Royal Marimba Band of Guatemala.

2. THE MODERN ORCHESTRAL MARIMBA. The manufacture of the modern marimba (fig.3) as used in the orchestra began in the USA in 1910, the earliest experiments being made by J. C. Deagan and U. G. Leedy. Stopped metal tubes graduated in length served as resonators which for very deep notes were made U-shaped. The vibrating membrane feature was used in certain models (the *nadimba*, recently revived). Later experiments included the *octarimba* (obsolete) in which two narrow bars an octave apart in pitch were arranged side by side, the octaves being struck simultaneously by fork beaters. The marimba became a popular instrument in vaudeville and light ensembles. It was considerably enhanced by Clair Omar Musser, virtuoso and composer, who gave a memorable concert with his 100-piece marimba band in 1935 at Carnegie Hall in New York.

With the exception of Percy Grainger, who scored for the marimba and *nadimba* before 1914 (the suite *In a Nutshell*), serious composers neglected the marimba until after World War II. Milhaud's Concerto for marimba and vibraphone (1947), in which the technique of four-hammer playing was exploited, was one of the first postwar compositions to make extensive use of the marimba. The instrument is being increasingly used in the large orchestra. It occurs in Richard Rodney Bennett's First Symphony, Hartmann's Eighth Symphony (which includes cadenzas for two marimbas), Messiaen's *Chronochromie* and Carl Orff's *Antigonae*. Concertos for marimba and orchestra have been written by several composers, including Robert Kurka, James Basta and Paul Creston.

The compass of the orchestral marimba varies. In general the instrument commences at c and ascends three or more octaves. Bass marimbas reach two octaves below c'. An instrument with an extended compass has been termed XYLORIMBA, xylo-marimba and marimba-xylophone; the so-called 'steel marimba' manufactured in 1916 by the Leedy Drum Co. is in fact a VIBRAPHONE. Hard beaters are rarely used on the marimba, as they would damage the slender bars and rob the instrument of its characteristic mellow sound. Music for the instrument is written (usually at actual pitch) in either the treble or bass clef, or at times on a double staff.

3. PARTCH'S MARIMBA. HARRY PARTCH constructed five tuned idiophones, four of which form a family based on the traditional marimba principle of rectangular blocks mounted over resonators and struck with mallets. The Diamond Marimba (1946) consists of 36 blocks of various sizes mounted on closed-ended bamboo resonators; the blocks are arranged in 11 terraced rows in a diamond configuration, the smallest block (sounding the highest note) being furthest from the player and physically the highest (104 cm from the ground). The range of the instrument is nearly three octaves from just above c', and the tuning is based on Partch's 'tonality diamond' (see his *Genesis of a Music*, p.159). The Quadrangularis Reversum was built in 1965 as a companion to the Diamond Marimba, of which its central section is a reversed and inverted version, the block of highest pitch being physically the lowest (86 cm from the ground)

3. Modern four-octave orchestral marimba by J. C. Deagan, Chicago

and the nearest to the player; the playing motion (from back to front) thus produces downward sweeps in the Diamond Marimba and upward ones in the Quadrangularis Reversum. Two 'alto flanks', each consisting of two ranks of longer wooden bars, together with a longer central bar, give an additional range of 21 notes between approximately *c* and *b*.

The Bass Marimba (1950) has 11 wooden blocks, the longest (135 cm) tuned approximately to *C* and the shortest (69 cm) to *b♭*; they are mounted over square, closed-ended resonators, originally made of redwood, but replaced in 1960 by the lower parts of organ pipes with plungers at the closed ends. Since the bars are 152 cm from the ground, a riser is provided on which the player stands. Mallets of different sizes and with heads of different materials are used, and the instrument can also be played with the fingers. Two versions were made of the Marimba Eroica, in 1951 and 1954. The first had three blocks mounted vertically in front of long square pipe resonators held horizontally in a massive frame. The second, improved version is in four separate, free-standing parts, each consisting of a horizontal block mounted over a box-like resonator of slightly greater width and length; the largest block is 230 cm long and 25 cm wide and its resonator stands 122 cm high (again a riser is required by the player). The blocks are tuned to approximately *F″*, *C′*, *E′* and *A′*.

BIBLIOGRAPHY

BooneX; IzikowitzMISAI; KirbyMISA

J. Dos Santos: *Ethiopia oriental e varia historia de consas notaveis do oriente* (Evora, 1609, 2/1891)

G. Merolla da Sorrarto: *Breve e succinta relatione del viaggio nel regno di Congo* (Naples, 1692)

G. M. Theal: *Records of South East Africa* (Cape Town, 1901)

E. G. Richardson: *The Acoustics of Orchestral Instruments and of the Organ* (London, 1929)

S. F. Nadel: *Marimba Musik* (Vienna, 1931)

H. Husmann: 'Marimba und Sansa der Sambesikultur', *Zeitschrift für Ethnologie*, lxviii (1936), 197

H. Tracey: *Chopi Musicians, their Music, Poetry and Instruments* (Oxford, 1948)

A. M. Jones: *Africa and Indonesia: the Evidence of the Xylophone and Other Musical and Cultural Factors* (Leiden, 1964, 2/1970)

G. List: 'The *Mbira* in Cartagena', *JIFMC*, xx (1968), 54

F. Maccallum: *The Book of the Marimba* (New York, 1968)

M. A. Lara: *Origin de la marimba, su desenvolvimiento y otros instrumentos musicos* (Guatemala City, 1970)

A. A. Mensah: 'Principles Governing the Construction of the Silimba – a Xylophone Type found among the Lozi of Zambia', *Review of Ethnology*, iii/3 (1970)

G. T. Nurse: 'Cewa Concepts of Musical Instruments', *African Music*, iv/4 (1970), 34

C. V. Mutwa: *My People: the Incredible Writings of Credo Vusa'mazulu Mutwa* (Harmondsworth, 1971)

F. Ortiz: 'La afro-americana marimba', *Guatemala indigena*, vi/4 (1971), 9

P.-C. Ngumu: 'Les mendzang des Ewondo du Cameroun', *African Music*, v/4 (1975–6)

——: *Les mendzang des chanteurs de Yaoundé* (Vienna, 1976)

G. Kubik: *Angolan Traits in Black Music, Games and Dances of Brazil* (Lisbon, 1979)

GERHARD KUBIK (1), JAMES BLADES (2)
ROSEMARY ROBERTS (3)

Marimba gongs. A METALLOPHONE consisting of a series of plates fitted with resonators. It is similar in sound to a glockenspiel but gentler.

Marimbaphone. An obsolete METALLOPHONE in the form of a steel MARIMBA introduced about 1920 by J. C. Deagan of Chicago. The term remains in use to signify a marimba. Deagan's instrument comprised a series of shallow metal bars arranged chromatically and individually tube-resonated. The tone of the instrument resembled that of the CELESTA (marimba gongs are similarly constructed). The marimbaphone was used primarily in marimba bands and as a solo instrument by stage artists. Percy Grainger was one of the few composers to score for it.

JAMES BLADES

Marimba-xylophone. See XYLORIMBA.

Marimbe. LAMELLAPHONE of Nyoro/Zinza people of Tanzania. It has a box-type body and 18 keys.

Marímbula. A large LAMELLAPHONE of Latin America, belonging to the African *mbira* (thumb piano) family.

It was formerly used as the bass in popular ensembles of the Colombian Atlantic coastal region, and it serves that function today in Puerto Rico. A large wooden box formed the resonating chamber; seven or more metal keys made from old gramophone springs were inserted between metal bridges and tuned by moving their secured end further in or out of the bridges. The player sat on the box with the keys between his legs and plucked them with his thumb and fingers. The *marímbula* was also known on the Pacific coast of Colombia. There its keys were made of *suncho* (metal strips used in crating boxes or cartons). In Cuba the wooden box is usually 60 cm or more in height. Small *marímbulas* similar in size to the African *mbira* are occasionally seen in the outskirts of Havana and in Matanzas Province. The corresponding Haitian instrument is the *marimba* (*manimba*, *malimba*).

GEORGE LIST/JOHN M. SCHECHTER

Marín. Spanish family of organ builders. Gaspar Marín (*b* c1540; *d* early 1600s) established a business at Logroño, Rioja; he built an organ at Huesca Cathedral (1588–9) and maintained the instruments in Oviedo Cathedral. Manuel Marín (*b* c1575; *d* Valladolid, after 1630), probably Gaspar's son, was active in the Valladolid region from 1588 to 1630. He built new organs at S Miguel, Medina del Campo (1591); S María, Torrelobatón (1592); S María, Medina de Rioseco (1608); and several in Valladolid (la Compagnie de Jésus [now S Miguel], 1620; S Lorenzo, 1625; and the convent of S Pablo). He also worked at Horcajo (1588); S María de Pozaldez (1590); S Juan de Mojados (1603); Villabáñez (1608 and 1628) and Valladolid Cathedral. He was one of the most remarkable Castilian organ builders of this period.

BIBLIOGRAPHY
J. A. de La Lama: *El órgano en Valladolid y su provincia: catalogación y estudio* (Valladolid, 1982)

GUY BOURLIGUEUX

Maringa (i). Arched harp of the Bajanje people of Zaïre (*LaurentyC*, 119). See KUNDI (i).

Maringa (ii). LAMELLAPHONE of the Bajanje people of Zaïre. See AGBOMBOYA.

Maringisa. Braced MUSICAL BOW with gourd resonator, of the Tsonga people of Tzaneen district, Transvaal, South Africa.

Marionetta. According to Tinctoris (*De inventione et usu musicae*, c1487), an alternative name for the REBEC.

Marius, Jean (*fl* 1700–16). French harpsichord maker and inventor. He became known for his invention in 1700 of the *clavecin brisé*, a harpsichord made in three sections hinged together so as to fold up into a box; it was designed for travelling. When he presented this invention to the Académie des Sciences he was awarded a royal privilege (equivalent to a patent) for 20 years. Marius also sought to make a keyboard instrument capable of gradations from loud to soft. In 1716 he submitted four different actions for *clavecins à maillets* to the Académie (they are reproduced with translations in Rimbault, 1860, and summarized in Harding, 1933); he received a 20-year royal privilege for them on 4 July 1716. In the first design the hammers, thicker in the

bass than in the treble, were glued directly to the key-levers; there were no dampers. This instrument, which was triple strung, resembled the clavichord in that the hammer acted directly against the string like the tangent of a clavichord; it could, because of its weight, fall away quickly when released (presumably the player was to use a staccato touch). The second design had hammers separate from the key-levers, but there were neither dampers nor escapement, the hammers falling back under their own weight; the action could be built to strike (by means of counterweights) downwards as well as upwards. Marius's third design was for an upright instrument in which a peg attached to a jack struck the strings from behind (the mechanism being similar to that of a clavicytherium), with a piece of cloth around the peg to damp the sound. The fourth design was a harpsichord with a register of quilled jacks and a register of hammers, which could be used together or singly. It seems that imperfections prevented the *clavecins à maillets* from becoming more than a curiosity; examples of the *clavecin brisé* survive (in *D-Bhm* and *F-Pc* collections).

BIBLIOGRAPHY
Machines approuvées par l'Académie royale des sciences, i (Paris, 1735), 193f; iii (Paris, 1777), 83ff
E. F. Rimbault: *The Pianoforte, its Origin, Progress and Construction* (London, 1860)
P. James: *Early Keyboard Instruments* (London, 1930/R1967)
R. E. M. Harding: *The Piano-forte: its History Traced to the Great Exhibition of 1851* (Cambridge, 1933, rev. 2/1978)
G. Juramie: *Histoire du piano* (Paris, 1948)
G. Thibault, J. Jenkins and J. Bran-Ricci: *Eighteenth Century Musical Instruments: France and Britain* (London, 1973)
H. K. H. Lange: 'Das Clavecin brisé von Jean Marius in der Berliner Sammlung und die Schlick-Stimmung', *Mf*, xxxi (1978), 57

MARGARET CRANMER

Markiert (Ger.: 'marked'). See MARCATO.

Markig (Ger.: 'vigorous'). A direction found particularly on long violin lines by Bruckner: *markig*, *lang gezogen* ('energetic, with long bows') appears in the Adagio of his Sixth Symphony, and *sehr markig* in the finale of his Eighth.

Marklove, John Gale (*b* 1827; *d* Utica, NY, 1891). American organ builder of English birth. He studied at the University of Oxford and emigrated to the USA around 1852, entering the organ-building firm of Alvinza Andrews in Utica, New York, in 1853. In 1857 or 1858 he began his own firm, which built a number of distinguished instruments, largely in central New York, although some were sent as far west as Minnesota and South Dakota, and a fairly large organ was built for St John's Church, Montgomery, Alabama. The three-manual organ for Christ Church, Utica (1883), was possibly one of his larger instruments. After his death the firm was continued by his son Clifford in partnership with Clarence E. Morey and Al Barnes, but soon became known as Morey & Barnes, and was continued by Morey from 1897 to 1935.

BIBLIOGRAPHY
R. J. Reich: 'John G. Marklove', *The Tracker*, ii/2 (1957), 3

BARBARA OWEN

Marmara. A medieval Indian folk name for small metal pellet bells. See GHAṆṬĀ and GHUṄGRŪ.

Marombe. LAMELLAPHONE of the Ngbele people of northeastern Zaïre (*LaurentyS*, 192). See AGBOMBOYA.

Marovany. Term used by the Sakalava of Madagascar for the VALIHA, a TUBE ZITHER. It also denotes a BOX ZITHER.

Marqué (Fr.: 'marked'). *See* MARCATO.

Martelé (Fr.). A type of bowstroke; *see* BOW, §II, 1 and 3 (iv, vii).

Martellement (Fr.). A type of mordent; *see* ORNAMENTS, §III, 8–9.

Martenot, Maurice L. E. (*b* Paris, 14 Oct 1898; *d* 8 Oct 1980). French musician and inventor of the ONDES MARTENOT, an early electronic instrument.

Martin (i). French firm of woodwind instrument makers. It was established by 1827 by Jean-François Martin at Ivry-la-Bataille. Some of Martin's instruments were exhibited at the 1834 Paris Exhibition, with bronze medals awarded for flutes and clarinets. The firm became Martin Frères about 1840, possibly on Jean-François' death, and was run by the brothers Jean-Baptiste and Félix Martin in Paris. Instruments from this firm won medals in Paris in 1855, 1867, 1878 and 1889. The firm became known as J.-B. Martin from about 1900. Although various flutes, flageolets and musettes by Martin survive, mostly made by Martin Frères, the business is particularly noteworthy for its clarinets. These were normally built of boxwood, with ivory rings and 13 pillar-mounted keys, using Louis Muller's system.

BIBLIOGRAPHY
C. Pierre: *Les facteurs d'instruments de musique* (Paris, 1893/*R*1971)
L. G. Langwill: *An Index of Musical Wind-instrument Makers* (Edinburgh, 1960, rev., enlarged 6/1980)

NIALL O'LOUGHLIN

Martin (ii). American company of guitar manufacturers. It was founded in New York by Christian Friedrich Martin (*b* Markneukirchen, 31 Jan 1796; *d* Nazareth, Penn., 15 Feb 1873), a German émigré. Martin and his father, Johann Georg Martin, were members of the cabinet makers' guild in Markneukirchen, and were described as guitar makers during a legal dispute with the violin makers' guild over the right to make guitars. Martin is mentioned as having made guitars since before 1826 and as having been foreman in the factory of the Viennese maker of guitars and violins, Johann Georg Stauffer. In autumn 1833 Martin left Germany for New York, setting up a shop and workshop at 196 Hudson Street. A fellow guitar maker from Markneukirchen, Heinrich Schatz, bought land near Nazareth, Pennsylvania, in 1835, and by 1837 was making guitars and selling them through Martin's New York shop, some guitars bearing the label 'Martin and Schatz'. In 1839 Martin moved to the Nazareth area and sold his New York agency to Ludecus & Wolter. Towards the end of this period, Martin also had an association with Charles Bruno, founder of the musical merchandise house, C. Bruno & Son, some guitars being labelled 'Martin and Bruno'. By 1850 Martin had a New York sales outlet at 385 Broadway, and some guitars of this period are labelled 'Martin and Coupa'. In about 1850 the Martin factory was enlarged and in 1859 was moved to Main and North Street, Nazareth.

The business has always been headed by members of the Martin family: Christian Frederick jr (1825–88),

Frank Henry (1866–1948), Christian Frederick III (*b* 1894) and Frank Herbert (*b* 1933); Christian Frederick IV (*b* 1955) is the youngest member of the family now involved in the company. In 1867 the founder and his son went into partnership with the elder Christian Frederick's nephew C. F. Hartmann, under the name C. F. Martin & Co.; in 1921 the company changed its name (and status) to C. F. Martin & Co. Inc. A new workshop and factory were built in 1963 close to the original family home.

Martin's earliest guitars were influenced by the German maker Stauffer, but as the 19th century progressed the Martin brand came to be associated with more distinctive instruments. One of the best and most popular is the Dreadnought flat-top acoustic guitar (introduced in 1931), the many models of which are identified by numbers with the prefix 'D'. Based on instruments designed and built by Martin for the Ditson music store in New York from 1916 or 1917, the Dreadnought is a large guitar with a distinctive wide-waisted shape that has been much copied by other makers. Martin guitars are given model numbers based on a complex system of coding that can indicate size, shape and other design features; besides the 'D' prefix, 'O', 'M' and other prefixes appear.

Martin have also, at various times, produced electric guitars, carved-top guitars, mandolins, ukuleles and tiples, but the principal part of their production is devoted to flat-top guitars, in which they are unequalled. Since 1970 guitars based on Martin designs have been built in Japan and marketed under the name Sigma; they have made available instruments of a comparable quality with those manufactured by Martin in the USA but at a lower price.

BIBLIOGRAPHY
M. Longworth: *Martin Guitars: a History* (Cedar Knolls, NJ, 1975, 2/1980)

JAY SCOTT ODELL, TONY BACON

Martin, Constant. French engineer and designer of electronic instruments. In 1932 he began the research that culminated in 1943 with his first electronic organ, exploring nearly ten methods of sound production. In 1936, in collaboration with the harmonium manufacturer P. Petitqueux, he developed the Mutatone, an electroacoustic harmonium that used electrostatic pickups to amplify the vibrations of the free reeds. In 1937 he produced an electric carillon.

After World War II a range of small one- and two-manual electronic organs was manufactured under licence from Martin as 'Orgues Constant Martin' (1945–9), including the popular Organium which has a single splittable manual (the point at which the split occurs can be varied by a selector switch within the range of a minor 3rd). As with all of Martin's instruments, the sounds are generated by an oscillator for each note. Around 1948 the first of several models of the MILLER ORGAN, based on Martin's designs, was marketed in Britain; the Miller range included two- and three-manual models and the one-manual Martinette. In 1957 an improved range of one- and two-manual instruments was introduced by Nouvelles Orgues Constant Martin in Versailles, and licensed to the Indapel company in San Sebastián, Spain.

In 1947 Martin produced his best-known instrument, the CLAVIOLINE, a monophonic piano attachment which was manufactured in France and licensed to companies in Britain, Germany and the USA, who mostly added their own modifications. In the early 1940s he also produced the *fil chantant*, a three-octave electronic fingerboard instrument, which was used in the circus and existed in two versions: the player either moved a spiral cursor along a string or created an electrical contact between three strings with a metal bar or finger cover. Martin also continued to develop his carillon; an electronic version, using bell-shaped horn attachments on swinging loudspeakers to simulate the movement of bells, was constructed by the Miller company around 1949. One of his carillons was installed in the French pavilion at the 1958 Brussels World Fair.

BIBLIOGRAPHY
J. Castellan: 'Les grandes orgues et l'électricité', *Science et vie*, lxxi (1947), 119
C. Martin: 'L'apport de l'électronique à l'expression musicale', *Science et vie*, lxxviii (1950), 161
——: *La musique électronique: de l'instrument de musique le plus simple aux orgues électroniques* (Paris, 1950)
——: 'The Recent Progress of Electronic Music', *The Organ*, xxx (1951), 198 [see also xxxi (1951), 44, 88]
——: 'Instruments de musique électronique', *Revue du son*, no.25 (1955), 117
——: 'Orgues électroniques d'hier et de demain', *3e congrès international de musique sacrée: Paris 1957*, 412
——: 'Petites et grandes orgues électroniques', *Revue du son*, no.56 (1957), 327

HUGH DAVIES

Martinique. Drum of Haiti and Jamaica. *See* JUBA.

Marúga. A small gourd rattle containing seeds and fitted with a wooden handle, used in Matanzas Province, Cuba, by the chief singer (male or female) in religious music of the Afro-Cuban Lucumí and Arará cults. In the vicinity of Havana the instrument is called a *maraca*, but it is never used in pairs. *See also* MARACAS.

JOHN M. SCHECHTER

Marwas (i). Small double-headed high-pitched drum used in *gambusan* ensembles in Riau province, Bangka island, South Sumatra, the east and south coasts of Sumatra, Lampung province, the north coast of Java and other strongly Muslim areas of Indonesia. There are four sizes. Two skins, with a diameter of about 16 to 20 cm, are laced with leather or plastic to a jackfruit-wood cylindrical body about 8 to 10 cm in height. Formerly black monkey skin was used but today goatskin is normal. At least two and usually four *marwas* are played together on both ends in interlocking fashion, together with a *gambus* (plucked lute) and an optional vocal part. The *marwas* is replaced by frame drums in most *gambusan* ensembles outside Riau. *See also* KETIPUNG and ORKES.

MARGARET J. KARTOMI

Marwas (ii). Bass drum played by Arab men in Malindi district, Kenya. It is played by hand. *See also* HAYIR and ṬĀSA.

Maryna. Bass fiddle of the Wielkopolska region of Poland, with a trapeziform resonator. Nearly 2 metres long, it has three strings tuned in 4ths; three or more jingling discs are attached to the top of the neck. These tinkle when the player strikes the base of the instrument against the floor to emphasize the rhythmic accents of the music. The *maryna* is played in bands with the fiddle and clarinet. *See also* BASY.

Maśak [masak, mashak, mashq]. The name of the traditional BAGPIPE in the Indian subcontinent. In the northern areas the bagpipe has single-reed pipes, usually twinned, one serving for the melody and the other as a drone. The name (Pers.: 'leather bag') suggests a Mid-

dle Eastern origin, though it is found also further south under different names (*śruti upaṅga*, *bajānā śruti*, *titti*), and there appears to be a stylistic relationship in its playing with the indigenous PŪNGĪ (double clarinet with gourd wind cap). In several areas – notably North-West Frontier Province (Pakistan), where it is called also *bīn bājā*, and Rajasthan and Madhya Pradesh (India) – it appears in the folk *naubat* (*see* NAQQĀRAKHĀNA) or ceremonial band, replacing or supporting the *śahnāī* (oboe), though it may also be found in accompaniments to dance (Frontier Province) or popular lyrical music (Madhya Pradesh). In many cases it has been supplanted by the Scottish highland bagpipe, introduced by British regiments, with single-reed drones and double-reed chanter.

In many areas of Rajasthan, notably the south-east, the air reservoir consists of a whole goatskin with the neck and front feet cut off. In the openings in the skin are fixed both the blowing-tube and the two playing-pipes, which are glued together and are 24 cm long, each with six finger-holes. The upper part of each is fitted with a single beating reed, and the melody is played on one, the other serving as a drone. Around Alwar the *masak* is the traditional instrument of the *bhopā* (bard-priests of the divinized hero Bhairoon). In Khairad it is also played, with two or more other instruments, at the time of various ceremonies and celebrations, notably marriages. However, in its traditional form it is becoming rare; as in the north, bagpipes of Scottish construction are frequently preferred.

BIBLIOGRAPHY
C. Sachs: *Die Musikinstrumente Indiens und Indonesiens* (Berlin and Leipzig, 1914, 2/1923), 160f
J. Levy: 'Music from the Shrines of Ajmer and Mundra', Tangent TGM 105 [disc notes]
K. Kothari: *Folk Musical Instruments of Rajasthan* (Borunda, 1977)
B. C. Deva: *Musical Instruments of India* (Calcutta, 1978), 117
R. Qureshi: 'Pakistan', *Grove 6*

ALASTAIR DICK, GENEVIÈVE DOURNON

Maseke. Footed cylindrical drum of the Mbanja people of Zaïre. *See* MOKITA.

Masenqo [masinko, masinqo, massaneqo]. Ethiopian single-string SPIKE FIDDLE with tuning-peg, bridge, and parchment-covered diamond-shaped box resonator. It was known as early as the 18th century and is depicted in an Ethiopian manuscript (*GB–Lbm* Oriental 533; see illustration) and the traveller, James Bruce, noted it in 1774, remarking '[It] is sometimes seen in the hands of the Mahometans, but they have brought it with them

Masenqo (spike fiddle, centre) and an early form of krar (bowl lyre): miniature from an Ethiopian MS, Revelation of St John, early 18th century (GB-Lbm Oriental 533, f.61r)

from Arabia'. The *masenqo* is the characteristic instrument of minstrels, being played only by men, and may be used solo, to accompany the voice, in ensembles with pipes and drums, or in ensembles of up to 20 at important religious festivals. Minstrels use it to provide an ostinato to their chanting of the news and for song accompaniment. It is typically played with a rapid bowing action and with much melodic ornamentation.

RONALD LAH

Mashak [mashq]. *See* MAŚAK.

Mashūra. DOUBLE CLARINET of the Arab world, with unequal tubes, the longer serving as a drone. *See* ARGHŪL.

Masłowski, Leon (*fl* 1800). Polish musical instrument maker. He worked at Poznan, and about 1800 invented the 'harmonic clavichord' (a kind of string instrument with a keyboard). It was introduced in Berlin, where it was renamed 'celizon' in 1805.

CZESŁAW R. HALSKI

Mason & Hamlin. American firm of piano and reed organ makers. It was founded in Boston in 1854 by Henry Mason (1831–90), son of the composer Lowell Mason, and Emmons Hamlin (1821–85). Hamlin had previously been employed by the George A. Prince melodeon factory as superintendent of tuning, in which capacity he had developed the art of voicing free reeds to produce imitative effects. The firm's first instruments were of the traditional melodeon type; it soon began making larger models with a greater variety of stops, and in 1861 changed the name of these products to 'cabinet organ' (sometimes referred to as the 'flat top' melodeon). By 1867, when it was awarded a first prize at the Paris Exposition, the firm was manufacturing about a quarter of America's reed organs. In the 1890s the models for these ranged from the tiny 'Baby' organ (introduced 1881), popular for Sunday schools and summer cottages, to the two-manual-and-pedal 'Church' organ, complete with a superstructure of dummy organ pipes. Mason's son Henry Lowell (*b* 1864) entered the firm in 1888 and became its president in 1906; he also wrote several books on music, including a history of the cabinet organ, published in 1901. At about the turn of the century the firm produced a few pipe organs.

In 1883 Mason & Hamlin began making pianos. Like Brinsmead they developed a machine-screw threaded into a flange on the frame instead of using the usual wrest plank and tuning-pins, in order to eradicate loose pins. This costly process was discontinued in 1905. Richard Gertz, who joined the firm in 1895, developed the 'tension resonator' and the 'duplex scale'. The tension resonator, patented in 1900, consists of radial arms of rigid steel joined under the soundboard and fixed to the inner rim of grands and the frame of uprights. It safeguards the vital $\frac{1}{8}''$ per foot crown that the soundboard needs for full resonance and can, if necessary, be adjusted to restore this curvature. The duplex scale is a system of ALIQUOT scaling to provide sympathetic resonance to enrich the treble of the piano. From about the turn of the century to the 1920s Mason & Hamlin was one of the important American firms, producing a relatively small number of high quality grands and uprights. An unusual feature of the firm's grand pianos is that their spines are angled slightly to the left to permit a larger soundboard. In 1911 the reed organ business was sold to the Aeolian Co. The piano business passed to other companies and in 1932 the Boston plant was moved to East Rochester, New York. The firm subsequently became part of the Aeolian American Corporation in East Rochester, but it has continued to make pianos under its own name.

See also METZLER.

BIBLIOGRAPHY
H. Greeley, L. Case and others: *The Great Industries of the United States* (Hartford, Chicago and Cincinnati, 1872), 109
A. Dolge: *Pianos and their Makers* (Covina, Calif., 1911/*R*1972)
R. F. Gellerman: *The American Reed Organ* (New York, 1973)
MARGARET CRANMER, BARBARA OWEN

Masonquo [masonqo]. Six-string bowl lyre of Eritrea, Ethiopia. It has been reported among the Bija people as *masonqo* (*see* RABABA). See H. Courlander: 'Notes from an Abyssinian Diary', *MQ*, xxx (1944), 345.

Massaneqo. *See* MASENQO.

Mässig (Ger.: 'moderate'). As a tempo indication it is the equivalent of the Italian MODERATO, used either alone or as a qualification of some other term such as BEWEGT. In his C major Fantasia op.17 Schumann translated *mässig, durchaus energisch* as *moderato con energia*. Elsewhere he used *im mässigen Tempo* and *sehr mässig*.

Mastersonic [Goodell and Swedien organ]. An ELECTRONIC ORGAN developed up to 1949 by John D. Goodell of Minnesota Electronics in St Paul, Minnesota, and Ellsworth Swedien of Mastersonics in Minneapolis; it was manufactured in limited numbers (about 50 were constructed). Most of the instruments have five-octave manuals and pedal-board. The sounds are generated by rotating electromagnetic toothed tone-wheels, one for each note, mounted on 12 shafts. Timbres are created from the natural overtone series by the different profiles of the electromagnetic pickups situated around each tone-wheel; an additional set of 12 tone-wheel shafts with only two pickups is used for Flute and Celeste stops that are tuned slightly sharp.

BIBLIOGRAPHY
J. D. Goodell and E. Swedien: 'Design of a Pipeless Organ', *Electronics*, xxii/8 (1949), 92
A. Douglas: *The Electrical Production of Music* (London, 1957), 97
HUGH DAVIES

Masuda, Kan (*b* Nara, 8 March 1950). Japanese sculptor. He began to make sound sculptures in 1974. He went to Spain in 1975, settling in Granada in 1976 and Barcelona in 1980. Practised in working with wood, he continued to use that material in his earliest sound sculptures. From 1977 his works have often been rounded, self-contained shapes (as in the series *Trencall de so*, 'Breaking of sound'), inside which a metal tube with a small hammer or several strings is positioned; in some instances these pieces show the influence on Masuda of a study of the guitar which he carried out in 1976. In 1981–2 a new phase began in which Masuda constructed several wind-operated open-air sound sculptures and a series called *Paisatge del so* ('Landscape of sound'). In works in the latter group one to nine metal 'tuning tubes' hang over large suspended square or rectangular white panels from which obtrude mound shapes with open tops that act as resonators; the tubes are struck by rubber-headed hammers which are activated when the panel is gently touched.

BIBLIOGRAPHY
Kan Masuda: Paisatge del so (escultura sonora) (Barcelona, 1982)
[exhibition catalogue]
HUGH DAVIES

Māṣūl. DUCT FLUTE of the Near East. The term was formerly a generic name for all wind instruments but is now used only for duct flutes, sometimes known loosely as *nāy*, *shamshāl* or *shabbāba*. The *māṣūl* may vary in length from 10 to 55 cm, and may be made from baked clay, wood or reed. The baked clay flute (in Arabic *māṣūla* and in Syriac *ṣfūrta*) is sometimes replaced by a plastic instrument about 10 cm long, with three fingerholes; it is used only by children. The wooden flute from Mandali in north-east Iraq is known by the Kurds as a *blūr* (or *bluir*), *dudak* or *pīk*. It is made from walnut or apricot wood, about 55 cm long, and has six fingerholes and one thumb-hole. It is played by Arabs, Kurds and Turkmens, both young and old, for private entertainment, to accompany songs, and at religious festivals. In Syria the instrument is made from wood or reed and is sometimes known as the *qaṣaba*, *pīk* or even *shabbāba*.

In the Mosul region of northern Iraq a flute made from 'Persian reed' is found. It is 2·5 cm wide and about 30 cm long, and is always cut so that one of the nodes of the reed is present. There are seven holes at the front and one at the rear. It is played by amateurs at family gatherings and by shepherds, and is also used with the *ṭabl* (cylindrical drum) for dancing at festivals.

BIBLIOGRAPHY
S. Qassim Hassan: *Les instruments de musique en Irak et leur rôle dans la société traditionelle* (Paris, 1980)
SCHEHERAZADE QASSIM HASSAN

Māṣūla. A term used in the Near East for various types of whistle, known also as *ṣāfira* or *ṣūṣāya* by the Arabs, *ṣfūrta*, *sharaqta* or *zumbarta* in Syriac and *fīt fīta*, *fiqna* or *pīk* by the Kurds. The most common are those made from a strip of metal, or an apricot or almond stone, smoothed down and hollowed out; many are zoomorphic and modelled in clay (with a whistle mouthpiece) or bulbous and made of pottery.
SCHEHERAZADE QASSIM HASSAN

Masunta. Single-headed footed drum of the Valley Tonga people of Gwembe district, Zambia. It is open-ended and the membrane is pegged on. It is played with the hands, together with the *magogo* and *mpati* drums, to accompany dancing. See *TraceyCSA*, ii, 85.

Māt. Ancient Egyptian term for the NĀY.

Māṭā. Pair of pottery drums of Rajasthan, north India. The instrument consists of two spherical terracotta pots, 42 cm and 44 cm in diameter, whose openings, 30 cm in diameter, are covered with goatskin. The two drums are tuned differently: the deeper is thought of as the male (*nar*) and the higher as the female (*mādā*). Two seated musicians each have one drum before them on the ground and beat the membranes with their hands (for illustration *see* GHAṬA). The ancestral appellation of the drums, *Pābūjī ke nisān* ('the emblem of Pabuji') or *Pābūjī ke māṭe* ('the pots of Pabuji'), bears witness to the function of the instrument: to accompany the epic of a legendary hero, the shepherd–knight Pabu, which is narrated and sung by the bards of the Nayak caste in the regions of Jodhpur and Bikaner (western Rajasthan).

Duct flute of the māṣūl type, Marrakesh, Morocco

BIBLIOGRAPHY
K. S. Kothari: *Indian Folk Musical Instruments* (New Delhi, 1968), 37
K. Kothari: *Folk Musical Instruments of Rajasthan* (Borunda, 1977)
GENEVIÈVE DOURNON

Māṭakī. *See* MĀṬKI.

Matali. Single-headed circular FRAME DRUM of Uganda. The head is of goatskin or sheep hide. It is of Arabic origin, and is used by Muslims to accompany religious poetry.

Mataqa. PANPIPES in the MAIZU ensemble of the Bolivian Alti Plano.

Matari. Circular FRAME DRUM of Kenya. *See* ṬĀR.

Matepe. *See* HERA.

Mathala. *See* MĀDALĀ.

Mathlao. Rattles of the Tswana/Hurutshe people of Zeerust district, Transvaal, South Africa. They are made from a variety of wasps' nests resembling cocoons, and are attached to the legs of dancers (*TraceyCSA*, ii, 255). *See also* MATLHO.

Mathlo. *See* MATLHO.

Mathotse. Hand-held vessel rattle of the Pedi (Northern Sotho) people of southern Africa. It is similar to the Tsonga NDJELE.

Mati gu. Small double-headed barrel drum of the Han Chinese, found especially in Cantonese music (*mati*: 'horse hoof' (a suggestion of shape); Gu: generic term for drums). The drumheads are struck with a slender bamboo beater. As an instrument used in accompanying Cantonese narrative song and opera the *mati gu* is falling from favour, being replaced by the more popular medium-sized woodblock *ban*.

ALAN R. THRASHER

Mātki [mātakī]. Percussion vessel of Rajasthan, India. This domestic clay pitcher is used in many parts of India as a rhythmic percussion instrument. The player places it on his lap or on the ground and strikes one hand against the body and the other hand on the open mouth of the pot. *See also* GHAṬA, §1.

Matlho [mathlo, makkow]. Leg rattles of the Tswana people of southern Africa. They comprise long strings of cocoons containing small stones. These are wound round the legs of male dancers. The DICHELA of the Pedi (Northern Sotho) and the Zulu AMAFOHLWANE are somewhat similar. See *KirbyMISA*, 4, and pll.1*b*, 2*b*.

DAVID K. RYCROFT

Matou qin. Chinese name for a two-string fiddle of the Mongolian people of north China (*matou*: 'horse-head'; *qin*: 'string instrument'). *See* KHUUR.

Matraca [matraka]. A term used in Spain and the New World for various types of CLAPPERS, castanets or rattles on a handle or axle. In Spain it generally denotes a cog rattle (*see* RATCHET). This has been widely used in Spanish and Portuguese churches to summon worshippers, and it is still so used in Mexico. There is a *matraca* above the nine great bells of Toledo Cathedral which is sounded for 48 hours before the Gloria on the Saturday preceding Easter. In the Philippines the *matraca* is used to frighten locusts from the fields, and in Brazil and Chile (see illustration) it accompanies songs and dances. In the Basque region the *matraka* (or *tilitranko*) is a beam held upright in front of the player. At its ends are other, separate pieces of wood which are struck when the beam

Matraca (cog rattle) played at the Fiesta de Las Peñas, Livílcar, Chile

is shaken at its midpoint. It is possible with this *matraka* to play rhythmically – something not possible with the Basque *karraka* (cog rattle). See S. Marcuse: *A Survey of Musical Instruments* (London and Newton Abbot, 1975).

JOHN M. SCHECHTER

Mats, rolled. Idiophone of Fiji and western Polynesia, used to accompany singing and dancing. They occur in Samoa (*see* FALA (i)), Tonga (*see* TAFUA) and in Futuna, Pukapuka, Tokelau, Tuvalu and Uvea. In some places they are beaten with sticks and in others hand-beaten.

Matstsyanka. BAGPIPE of Belorussia. *See* DUDY.

Matsumushi. Pair of tiny Japanese horizontal gongs used in GEZA, the off-stage music of the kabuki theatre. The two gongs are of slightly different pitches; they are struck with two round-ended sticks and are thought to sound like the insect called *matsumushi*. They are used with the *orugōru* (set of bells) in passages related to insects, and may also accompany the forging of a sword by two smiths. Originally one such gong was used to accompany Buddhist folk-hymns (*goeika*). *See also* KANE.

DAVID W. HUGHES

Matsuri-bayashi. Japanese instrumental ensemble used in festivals. *See* HAYASHI.

Matsuridaiko. Japanese drum used in festivals (*matsuri*: 'festival'; *daiko*: generic term for drums). It is usually a long-bodied ŌDAIKO.

Mattakokilā. A Sanskrit name found in medieval Indian literature denoting a 21-string chordophone. *See* SURMAṆḌAL and VĪṆĀ, §4.

Mattaḷam. South Indian Tamil name for a tuned barrel drum. *See* MADDAḶAM.

Mattauphone. A set of musical glasses built by Joseph Mattau of Brussels and shown at the Paris Exposition of 1855. A box 128 cm long and 62·5 cm wide on four legs and standing 94 cm high had 38 glasses with a range from c' to c''''. They were played with the fingers.

Mattox, Charles (*b* Bronson, Kansas, 1910). American sculptor. Many of the kinetic sculptures he has constructed since 1964 in Albuquerque, New Mexico, include sound. These are often based on curved geometrical shapes (usually around 1 metre high but occasionally up to 3 or 4 metres), whose internal cavities are carefully designed to have particular resonant properties; the structures are slowly rotated by a motor or rocked on a curved base by the exhibition visitor, causing sounds to be made by, for example, stainless steel rods (Yellow Rotating Form, 1964), vibrating strings (Musical String Series, from 1966) and hard rubber balls dropping on drum heads (Rotating Drums, *c*1967). Theremin Piece (1969) incorporates the pitch and volume antennae of the theremin as well as chiming rods. His recent work contains more sophisticated electronic devices.

BIBLIOGRAPHY
C. Mattox: 'The Evolution of my Audio-kinetic Sculptures', *Leon-*

ardo, ii (1969), 355; repr. in *Kinetic Art: Theory and Practice*, ed. F. Malina (New York, 1974), 99

HUGH DAVIES

Maucotel. French firm of violin and bow makers and dealers. Charles Maucotel (*b* Mirecourt, 1 Nov 1807; *d* after 1860) served his apprenticeship with Blaise Mast in Mirecourt and later worked for Gand in Paris (from 1834) and for William Davis in London (from 1844). In 1850 he established his own workshop in London, which he operated until his retirement to France in 1860. As far as is known all his mature work bears a brief latinized printed label dated from London. His younger brother, Charles Adolphe Maucotel (*b* Mirecourt, 1820; *d* Paris, 6 Feb 1858), also served his apprenticeship in Mirecourt. Between 1839 and 1845 he had his own workshop in Paris which moved from the rue Croix des Petits Champs to the rue Princesse. It is believed that he committed suicide. Both Charles and Charles Adolphe produced clean work which essentially followed the Mirecourt school and concentrated on the Stradivari and Guarneri patterns.

Ernest Maucotel (*b* Mirecourt, 20 July 1867), grand-nephew of Charles Adolphe, served his apprenticeship with Paul Bailly and completed his training with his uncle Ernest André Salzard in Moscow. On his return to France he became the chief workman for Hippolyte Chrétien Silvestre in Paris and on 1 April 1900 became his partner. The firm produced good violins and bows under the name Silvestre & Maucotel; the bows were made for them by various French and German bow makers including Bazin, Lamy, L. Thomassin and Pfretzschner (*see also* SILVESTRE).

In 1913, after the death of H. C. Silvestre, Paul Deschamp, a connoisseur but not a maker, joined the business. As Maucotel & Deschamp the firm established a fine reputation as one of the leading Parisian dealers.

BIBLIOGRAPHY
R. Vannes: *Essai d'un dictionnaire universel des luthiers* (Paris, 1932, 2/1951/R1972 as *Dictionnaire universel des luthiers* and *R*1981 incl. suppl. 1959)
E. Vatelot: *Les archets français* (Nancy, 1976)
JAAK LIIVOJA-LORIUS

Maultrommel (Ger.). JEW'S HARP.

Maùng. Bossed gong of Burma. A single *maùng* is often used in the HSÀING-WÀING ensemble to mark important structural points in the rhythmic cycle.

Maùng-zaìng. Burmese GONG-CHIME of the HSÀING-WÀING ensemble. It consists of 18 or 19 small horizontally struck knobbed gongs mounted in five rows on straight wooden frames. These knobbed gongs are flatter and generally larger than those of the KYÌ-WÀING. The rows, starting from the one closest to the musician, usually contain three, three, four, three and five or six gongs. The frames are laid flat on the ground except for the largest, deepest-sounding set which is usually propped up against the *kyì-waìng*. This instrument is said to be a recent development, perhaps dating from the 1920s or 1930s.

JUDITH BECKER

Mauracher. Austrian family of organ builders. It included Andreas (*b* 1758; *d* 1824); Andreas's son Karl (*b* Kapfing, 24 Oct 1789; *d* Kapfing, 24 May 1844); Matthias (i) (*b* 1788; *d* 1857); his son Matthias (ii) (also known as Matthäus the elder; *b* Zell-am-Ziller, 20 July

1818; *d* Salzburg, 7 Aug 1884); the sons of Matthias (ii) Josef (*b* Zell, 2 Feb 1845; *d* St Florian, 5 Feb 1907), Hans (*d* 1900) and Matthäus (i) (*b* 1859; *d* 1939); Josef's sons Matthäus (ii) (*b* 1885; *d* 1954) and Anton (*b* 1896; *d* 1962); Albert (*fl* c1870–1910) and Franz (who referred to himself as 'Hans' Erben', i.e. 'Hans's heir'). Matthäus (ii) and Anton worked in Linz as 'Gebrüder Mauracher'. Josef had success as an inventor of special types of chest and key action. The firm was dissolved in 1955.

Various members of the family built organs for: the Sebastianskirche, Salzburg (Karl, 1829; one manual, 12 stops); the Kollegienkirche, Salzburg (Matthias (ii), 1862; three manuals, 34 stops); the monastery, St Florian (Matthias (ii), 1873; four manuals, 78 stops; an enlargement of the organ built by F. X. Chrismann in 1770–72); the monastery, Kremsmünster (Matthias (ii), 1877; four manuals, 60 stops); Ebbs (Albert, 1908; two manuals, 24 stops); the Breitenfelderkirche, Vienna (Josef, 1898; three manuals, 40 stops); the town parish church, Graz (Matthäus (i); three manuals, 38 stops); and St Andreas, Salzburg (Franz, 1903; two manuals, 37 stops). Organs in the following places are attributable to the Gebrüder Mauracher: Klagenfurt Cathedral (1927; three manuals, 43 stops); Familienkirche, Linz (1929; three manuals, 46 stops); the monastery, St Florian (1930; three manuals, 44 stops; an enlargement of the chancel organ); Herz Jesu Kirche, Wels (1930–31; three manuals, 60 stops).

BIBLIOGRAPHY
O. Eberstaller: 'Neue Orgeln in Österreich', *Musik und Kirche*, iv (1932), 30
——: *Orgeln und Orgelbauer in Österreich* (Graz and Cologne, 1955)
R. Federhofer-Königs: 'Mauracher', *MGG*
HANS KLOTZ

Mauri dizau. Oboe of the Dimacha Kachari people of Nagaland, north-east India. It has an externally conical wooden pipe, a large flaring bell and a lip disc on the staple and is played for folkdances together with the cylindrical drum *kharan dizau*. See D. Bhattacharya: 'Music from the Himalayas', Argo RG 530 [disc notes]. *See also* MAHVARĪ.

ALASTAIR DICK

Maussiell, Leonhard (*b* Nuremberg, 9 Jan 1685; *d* after 1765). German violin maker. He probably served his apprenticeship in Augsburg with his grandfather, Matthias Maussiell, though it is also possible that some further study was undertaken during travels in the Tyrol and Italy. Certainly, his best instruments step beyond the usual confines of the German school. His earliest surviving instrument is a *pochette* dated Nuremberg 1708, and his latest a violin of 1766. Maussiell's instruments follow the Stainer and Tecchler models but are too individual to be considered copies. The archings on the smaller instruments are high, while those on his (rarer) large ones vary from broad to medium. Instead of the standard scroll, Maussiell often carved a lion's or woman's head, and he also frequently used fishbone for purfling. His printed labels, which can be large, are in either latinized or germanic type; occasionally he used a much smaller, handwritten label. The varnish is of good quality and usually ranges between a yellow-brown and red-brown. Tonally his larger, flatly arched instruments are best although all his violins tend towards an alto timbre.

BIBLIOGRAPHY
W. L. von Lütgendorff: *Die Geigen- und Lautenmacher von Mittelalter bis zur Gegenwart* (Frankfurt am Main, 1904, rev. 6/1922/R1968)

R. Vannes: *Essai d'un dictionnaire universel des luthiers* (Paris, 1932, 2/1951/R1972 as *Dictionnaire universel des luthiers* and R1981 incl. suppl. 1959)

JAAK LIIVOJA-LORIUS

Ma'wo [mawu, mawuwi]. MUSICAL BOW of the Indians of California, including the Yokuts (*ma'wo*), Maidu (*mawu, mawuwî*), Pomo, Karok, Miwok, Yurok and Diegueno. Musical bows were also found among the Tlingit of Alaska and the Carrier of north-west Canada. Apart from the Apache fiddle (*see* KÍZH KÍZH DÍHÍ), it was the only native string instrument north of Mexico. Various forms existed, ranging from the hunting bow used as a musical instrument by the Yurok to specially-made bows consisting of a thin strip of wood with a string or sinew stretched between the two ends. More elaborate versions, with a central bridge, were used by the Maidu and the Tlingit; the bows of the Yokuts had a tuning peg. The length varied from 90 cm to 2 metres.

The method of playing was similar for all types. The bow was held in the left hand with most of the instrument projecting over the player's left shoulder. The wooden part of the lower end, or sometimes the string, was held between the teeth or in front of the open mouth; the string was either plucked with the fingers of the right hand, or was struck lightly with the fingernails or a twig or a bone. The mouth cavity was used as a resonating chamber and different notes could be produced by varying its size and shape.

The instrument had a barely audible sound and was commonly played for self-entertainment, as a restful diversion. The Yokuts also played it in mourning for a deceased friend or relative; among the Maidu, it was a shaman's instrument.

BIBLIOGRAPHY
H. Besseler and M. Schneider, eds.: *Amerika*, Musikgeschichte in Bildern, i/2 (Leipzig, 1968; Eng. trans., 1973 as *Music of the Americas: an Illustrated Music Anthology of the Eskimo and American Indian Peoples*), 70f
W. Wallace: 'Music and Musical Instruments', *Handbook of North American Indians*, viii: *California*, ed. R. F. Heizer (Washington, DC, 1978), 642

MARY RIEMER-WELLER

Má'xe onéhavo'e (Cheyenne: 'bass drum'). Large double-headed bass drum of the Cheyenne Indians of the northern Plains of the USA.

The 'big drum', a common name used to distinguish the bass drum from the smaller hand-held FRAME DRUM, is found over a wide area of North America, from the western Great Lakes to the northern and southern Plains. It may be of recent origin, influenced by the European bass drum or snare drum. It is generally broad and shallow, about 60 cm in diameter and 20 to 23 cm deep, and was traditionally made from part of a hollowed-out tree trunk. The heads were of untanned hide and were laced together in criss-cross fashion round the frame. Although a European bass drum is now commonly used, the calfskin or plastic heads may be replaced with deer-hide (as among the Flathead of Montana) or buffalo skin (as among the Dakota Indians for use in their sun dance). The padded beaters are 35 to 45 cm long and may be of wood or of fibreglass, a material favoured for its flexibility. Drums made by the Ojibwa of the western Great Lakes have painted heads and are elaborately decorated with cloth and beadwork; they are suspended from four stakes driven into the ground.

The bass drum is usually played by at least four men

Large bass drum of the má'xe onéhavo'e type played by Shawnee Indians of Oklahoma

sitting, kneeling or standing round the instrument. Each man holds a beater in his right hand and sings and drums simultaneously with the others of the group. The drum is used for both sacred and secular occasions; with the rise of pan-Indianism it has become the central instrument of the inter-tribal powwow.

MARY RIEMER-WELLER

May-horn. *See* WHITHORN.

Mayohuacán. A wooden SLIT-DRUM used in Cuba and especially in Santo Domingo at the time of the conquest. It was made from a hollowed tree-trunk, with a large 'H' cut in the side. From this two small tongues protruded, on which the beat was struck.

Ma'yong [makyong]. *See* ALAT-ALAT MAKYONG.

Mayrhofer. German family of musician–instrument makers active in Passau during the 18th century. Its members are generally held to be the collective inventors of the basset-horn and possibly of the bass clarinet. Anton Mayrhofer (i) (*b* ?Austria, ?1706; *d* Passau, 6 July 1774) was an oboist, second violinist, and court trumpeter in Passau, and was among the first clarinettists in that town. A son, Anton Mayrhofer (ii) (*b* Passau, ?1738; *d* Passau, 14 Jan 1794), became a court trumpeter with officer's rank at the age of 22, and was later made director of the court orchestra. He supplemented that income by making violins of 'only average' quality, according to Lütgendorff. Michael Mayrhofer (*b* Passau-Ilzstadt, ?26 June 1707; *d* Passau, 14 Oct 1778), possibly a distant relative, held the post of organist at the Nikolaikirche for some time. Saam (1971) has conjectured that all three contributed to the invention of the basset-horn: Anton (i) as an actual clarinettist, Anton (ii) as a violin maker able to execute the woodcarving required for the curved, 'sickle-form' tube, and Michael with the organist's skill in joining sections of pipe with leather binding. Three Mayrhofer basset-horns (Nuremberg, Passau (*see* BASSET-HORN, fig.1a) and Bonn) and a similarly constructed bass clarinet (Munich) are known, each with the identical stamp in its leather binding, 'ANT et MICH/MAYRHOFER/INVEN. & ELABOR./PASSAVII' within a rococo cartouche. The bass clarinet is distinguished by a full 360° coil of wood tube covered with leather, instead of the characteristic kasten. Whether the Mayr-hofers can be credited with the 'invention' of either type is open to debate and depends on the attribution of several anonymous, 'plank'-form bass clarinets, and the rectangular basset-horn by JOHANN GEORG EISENMENGER.

BIBLIOGRAPHY
W. L. von Lütgendorff: *Die Geigen- und Lautenmacher vom Mittelalter bis zur Gegenwart* (Frankfurt am Main, 1904, rev. 6/1922/R1968)
J. Saam: *Das Bassetthorn* (Mainz, 1971)
P. T. Young: 'A Bass Clarinet by the Mayrhofers of Passau', *JAMIS*, vii (1981), 36
——: *2500 Historical Woodwind Instruments: an Inventory of the Major Collections* (New York, 1982)

PHILLIP T. YOUNG

Mayūrī. A north Indian name for the long-necked fretted fiddle DILRUBĀ.

Maza. Ten-key XYLOPHONE of the Patri people of the Central African Republic. Two *maza* are used with the slit-drum, *ngungu*, and two metal rattles to accompany dance-songs for funeral rites.

Mazāmīr. Plural of MIZMĀR.

Mazanki. Small fiddle of the kit type, played in the Wielkopolska region of Poland (see illustration). About 50 cm long, it has three strings; a typical tuning is a'–e''–b''. The *mazanki* is carved out of one piece of wood (apart from the soundboard), though there are examples made like a violin, and has a bridge constructed so that one foot rests on the soundboard and the other extends through a specially made hole to rest on the back of the instrument.

The *mazanki* was played with the *koziol czarny* (see KOZA) and *dudy wielkopolskie* (bagpipes; see DUDY), but began to be replaced at the turn of the 20th century by a violin with an artificial fret designed to facilitate playing in the first position but in a higher register (see VIOLIN, §IV, 1).

JAN STĘSZEWSKI

Mazhar. Large circular FRAME DRUM (40 to 60 cm wide, otherwise more) with one membrane, found in Egypt, Syria and Turkey. There has been some confusion between MIZHAR and *mazhar*. The former, a chordophone of early Islamic times, is copiously discussed in written sources, while the second is known chiefly through oral transmission and is rarely mentioned in the texts. The two words share the same plural, *mazāhir*. An early literary reference to the *mizhar* or *mazhar* as percussion comes from al-Ṣafadī (13th-century Syria), the historian of Turkmen origins: '*mazhar* is a little *duff*' (see Taymūr, 1963, p.160). Although *mizhar* was called a membranophone by a 16th-century writer (see Shiloah, 1979, p.326), the transfer of *mizhar* (strings) to *mazhar* (percussion), though difficult to date, can be explained philologically.

There are contradictions in the sources, Arab as well as Turkish and Western, on the question of whether the *mazhar* has jingles on the circumference of the frame, as in the DUFF (see also ṬĀR). '*Duff* is a [frame drum] without rings [*jalājil*] inside, but if they are present the instrument is called *mazhar*' (Ṣuyūṭī, *Sunan al-Nasā'ī* [commentary] (Cairo, n.d.), iii, p.195). The definition of *jalājil* was by a 16th-century Egyptian jurist: 'iron rings arranged like a chain inside the *ṭār* (Al-Haythamī:

Kaff al-ra'ā' (Cairo, 1937), p.76). In present-day Egypt, as in Turkey, opinion is divided: 'Among the *dufūf* there exists a large model, *bendīr* or *mazhar*, which has no little cymbals' (Al Hifnī, 1971, p.176); '*mazhar*, kind of *deff* which differs by the absence of cymbals' (Yekta Bey, 1922, v, 3023); '*mazhar*: drum without bells which was never used in secular music (Turkish), but was reserved for the Mevlevi and other religious orders' (Reinhard, 1969, p.101). But other field research agrees with Ṣuyūṭī: '*mazhar* differs from *bendīr* . . . instead of little round plaques of steel hung in holes which have pierced splints, there are little rings that hold these in place' (Villoteau: *Description . . . des instruments de musique* [Egypt], i (Paris, 1809), 988); '*mazhar*, sort of tambourine with bells from Egypt' (Hickmann, 1949, p.481); '*mazhar* or *mizhar* . . . the frame is fitted on its inner side and about halfway up, with little iron rings linked together' (Touma, 1975, p.121).

In resolving these contradictions, it should be noted that the rings are not of Arab origin (see DUFF) but were introduced under Islam and probably came from Iran (see DAIRE). The circular frame drum which in the 18th century carried to Aleppo (Syria) the double name of *duff* or *daira* (with small cymbals; P. Russell: *The Natural History of Aleppo* (London, 1794), i, 152) has since been called *mazhar* by the natives who are unaware of and reject the term *daira*. In Aleppo the tradition of rings inside the frame is upheld, but they have tended to disappear in recent specimens at Damascus.

The *mazhar* has religious significance, though in Syria its usage extends to secular music. It is called on in places of worship, where about a dozen may be assembled. Anyone may play, but usually they are entrusted to those with fine voices. The beating of the *mazhar*

Mazanki (fiddle) from Grodzisk, Poznań province (Państwowe Muzeum Etnograficzne, Warsaw)

creates a deafening noise which heightens tension during ceremonies, most of all in the initiation ordeals of the neophytes. It is played with the right hand at the far side of the frame, striking the edge and the centre; the left hand holds the instrument still and gently inclined outwards to facilitate the swinging of the jingles. The player–singer may hide his face behind the membrane, modifying the timbre of the voice, or move the instrument away and allow the voice to be heard naturally; or he may combine these techniques. The beat of the right hand and the fingers of the left, holding the lower part, cause the jingles to sound and prolong with continuous crackling the effect of the impact. The qualitative duration of a good *mazhar*, with taut, dry skin and therefore with a shrill timbre, is reckoned at not more than 20 minutes; after that the effect of the playing makes the skin relax and the instrument becomes heavier. That is why, on such occasions, a sacristan is charged with reviving it by warming it on a fire.

BIBLIOGRAPHY

GENERAL

V. Mahillon: *Catalogue descriptif du musée instrumental* (Ghent, 1893) [no.110]
H. G. Farmer: 'The Music of Islam', *NOHM*, i (1957/R1975), 421–78
A. Taymūr: *Al-mūsīqā wa'l-ghinā' 'ind al-'arab* [The music and song of the Arabs] (Cairo, 1963)
H. G. Farmer: 'Duff', *EI*
'Tamburello', *Dizionario della musica popolare europea*, ed. R. Leydi and S. Mantovani (Milan, 1970)
H. H. Touma: *Die Musik der Araber* (Wilhelmshaven, 1975; Fr. trans., 1977)
E. R. Perkhun: *Die Theorien zum arabischen Einfluss auf die europäische Musik des Mittelalters* (Walldorf-Essen, 1976)
A. Shiloah: *The Theory of Music in Arabic Writings* (Munich, 1979)
L. Ibsen al-Faruqi: *An Annotated Glossary of Arabic Musical Terms* (Westport, Conn., 1981)

ARAB COUNTRIES

A. Ubarī: *Faṣl asqī al-'iṭāsh* [Letter, quenching the thirsty] (Aleppo, 1929)
H. Hickmann: 'Cymbales et crotales dans l'Egypte ancienne', *Annales du service des antiquités de l'Egypte* (1949), 451–545
——: *Catalogue d'enregistrements de musique folklorique égyptienne* (Baden-Baden, 1958/R1979)
A. ibn Dhurayl: *Al mūsīqā fi Sūriyya* [Music in Syria] (Damascus, 1969)
H. Nixdorff: 'Die Herstellung der syrischen Rahmentrommeln', *Beiträge der Völkerkunde*, xlii (1969), 101–31
A. al-Ḥifnī: *'Ilm al-alāt al-mūsīqiyya* [Studies of musical instruments] (Cairo, 1971)
C. Poché: 'Zikr and Musicology', *The World of Music* (Berlin, 1978) i, 59
P. Lama: *La musique populaire palestinienne* (Paris, 1982)

TURKEY

R. Yekta Bey: 'La musique turque', *EMDC*, I/v (1922), 2945–3064
B. Mauguin: 'Musique de mosquée et musique de confréries', in J. Porte: *Encyclopédie des musiques sacrées* (Paris, 1968), i, 422
K. and U. Reinhard: *Turquie* (Paris, 1969)
M. D. al-Khatīb: *Kashf al-qinā'u' al-masdūl fī ḥikm al-samā' al-māqbūl* [Developing freedom with approval of the exercise of the *samā*'] (n.p., 1973)
N. Uzel: 'Music', *Whirling Dervishes*, ed. I. Friedlander (London, 1975)

CHRISTIAN POCHÉ

Mbabi. Drum of the Bangba people of north-eastern Zaïre (*BooneT*, 69).

Mbaire. XYLOPHONE of the Soga people of Uganda. It has 16 notes and is played by four performers.

Mbala [mbaa]. End-blown wooden trumpet of the Yogo people of northern and the Budu people of north-eastern Zaïre (*LaurentyA*, 337). Seven are played in an ensemble, with other instruments.

M'balah. Ritual bell of the Fali people of Cameroon. It is a double clapperless metal bell which is beaten with an animal horn and used at initiation and funeral ceremonies.

Mbalatt. KETTLEDRUM of the Wolof people of Senegal and the Gambia. *See* GORONG.

Mbala'u. Flute of the Kilba people of north-eastern Nigeria.

Mbalo. End-blown bamboo flute of the Bale and Hima peoples of Rwanda and eastern Zaïre. The flute is 30 to 40 cm long with a diameter of 1·5 to 2·5 cm at the mouthpiece. It has six finger-holes which are grouped in two sets of three, one set near the mouthpiece, the other near the extremity. The flute is played in the evening after work or during the daytime by herders. A smaller bamboo flute, the *rega*, is 20 to 25 cm long and has three finger-holes; it is played with other flutes of the same type at harvest celebrations or the birth of twins.

BIBLIOGRAPHY

F. J. de Hen: *Beitrag zur Kenntnis der Musikinstrumente aus Belgisch Kongo und Ruanda-Urundi* (Tervuren, 1960)
G. Knosp: *Enquête sur la vie musicale au Congo belge 1934–1935* (Tervuren, 1968)

K. A. GOURLAY

Mbalwe. Single-headed open-ended GOBLET DRUM of the Nyanja/Chewa people of Lilongwe district, Malawi. See *TraceyCSA*, ii, 438.

Mbanana. Side-blown animal-horn trumpet of the Mangutu people of north-eastern Zaïre. It has one stop in the tip (*LaurentyA*, 319, 324).

Mbanda. Cylindrical drum of the Konda people of Zaïre. *See* BONDA (i).

Mbangak. Double-headed cylindrical drum of the Angas people of Nigeria. It resembles the GANGA, (1) in construction and method of performance but has sharply differentiated religious and secular functions. When it is to be used by priests, rituals are performed during manufacture to appease the tree and animal spirits, and women and children are forbidden to be present; the priests use it to signal to women and children to conceal themselves while they emerge. Manufacture of the drum for secular use, however, may be watched by anyone. It is stored by the leader of the social organization and played by young specialists alone or in pairs, or with a conical drum and rattles, to accompany dance and song.

K. A. GOURLAY

Mbaraca. The Guaraní (Paraguay) term for MARACAS, reported in Brazil as *mbaracá*.

Mbaya. Side-blown animal-horn trumpet of the Day people of Zaïre. It has one stop in the tip (*LaurentyA*, 327).

Mbebe. Single-string bowed lute (or fiddle) of the Kamba people of Machakos district, Kenya.

Mbe'i. SACRED FLUTES of the Manam Island, Madang Province, Papua New Guinea. There are two in each village, one 'male' and the other 'female', blown on such occasions as the initiation or death of a village chief (*tanepua*), with whom they are closely associated. Women are forbidden to see them, and in the 1930s *mbe'i* were still held in fear and reverence by men and children as well.

BIBLIOGRAPHY
C. Wedgwood: 'Report on Research in Manam Island', *Oceania*, iv (1933), 400
——: 'Women in Manam', *Oceania*, vii–viii (1937), 187

Mbejn. Drum of the Fang people of Gabon. Slightly conical in shape, it is played vertically, and used in pairs with the large *nkul* slit-drum to provide rhythmic accompaniment to large group dances.

Mbeka. Fiddle of Flores, Indonesia. *See* ROBEKA.

Mbenza. Stopped wooden flute with slender conical or cylindrical bore of the Boa (Bwa) people of northern Zaïre (*LaurentyA*, 159, 181).

Mbeta. MOUTH BOW of the Ngbaka people of central Africa.

Mbia. End-blown wooden trumpet of the Mono people of north-western Zaïre. It is made from a hollow root or branch. The term may also refer to a side-blown animal-horn trumpet of the Mono (*LaurentyA*, 323).

Mbike. Single-string fiddle of the Guaycurú people of Resistencia, Chaco Province, Argentina.

Mbila. A term widely used throughout southern and south-eastern Africa for various types of LAMELLAPHONE and XYLOPHONE; its equivalent in some languages of the area is *mbira*. It may come, by a process of metathesis, from the Bantu verb stem 'imba' ('sing'). Among the Venda of southern Africa, the *mbila dza madeza* is a heptatonic lamellaphone with about 26 keys (closely related to the Shona *mbira dza vadzimu*), the *mbila tshipai* a pentatonic or hexatonic lamellaphone with 11 to 18 keys, and the MBILA MTONDO a xylophone of 21 to 24 keys; for further examples and general discussion *see* LAMELLAPHONE, §§1, 2(ii) and MARIMBA, §1. The *mbila* discussed below is the xylophone of the Chopi people of southern Mozambique: one of the most powerful African melodic instruments, it is made in several pitch ranges and played in orchestras whose music represents one of the peaks of African musical creativity. In the singular the Chopi word means one xylophone, while the plural form *timbila* means xylophones and also the music or art of the xylophones. Among the Venda and Shona, who share the term *mbila/mbira*, the singular means one note or key, and the (unvarying) plural means one instrument; another term is therefore used for 'instruments', the Shona, for example, using *mateze* (calabash resonators).

1. Construction and tuning. 2. Orchestra. 3. Performing practice.

1. CONSTRUCTION AND TUNING. The Chopi xylophone is equiheptatonic and has up to 19 fixed keys with individual gourd resonators. The keys are made of sneezewood, a hard, heavy, resinous wood which is fire-tempered to improve its resonance. The frame (see

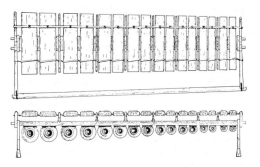

(a)

(b)

1. (a) Plan and side views of sanje mbila (gourd-resonated xylophone) of the Chopi; (b) cross-section showing gourd resonator and buzzer

fig.1*a*), unlike most other African xylophones, consists of a single longitudinal piece of wood with holes along its length, to the underside of which are tied, and then sealed with wax, a row of gourds in graded size, ranging from about 4 cm in diameter for the highest note of the highest pitched *mbila* to about 15 cm for the lowest note of the lowest. A wax nipple is raised up around a hole on the side of each gourd, and over this is stretched a fine membrane from the peritoneum of a cow; this adds a buzzing tone when the air vibrating inside the gourd causes it to move. A cylinder cut from the neck of a small gourd or calabash is attached with wax on to the resonator gourd around the buzzer, with the function of both rounding the tone of the buzzer and protecting it from damage (see fig.1*b*). Several factors contribute to give the *mbila* its powerful tone: the keys are securely but flexibly held, with careful attention paid to the correct nodal points of support; the resonator gourds are firmly attached (not loosely as is the case with the majority of African gourd-resonated xylophones); the resonators are very accurately tuned in unison with the keys above them, and they and their buzzers function highly efficiently. Tuning of the gourds is effected by using wax to open or constrict the hole in the frame and that of the keys by thinning the centre or the ends.

The *mbila* has a short carved leg at each end. It is likely that as recently as last century the majority of *timbila* did not stand on legs, but the gourds rested directly on the ground. Holding the legs in place are the end pieces, usually made of one long piece of wood, curved around in front of the instrument on the player's side to double as a rest for the *mbila* when it is not in use and as a means of controlling it in performance. There are variations by individual makers, as shown in fig.1*a* where the arc is jointed, not curved. The *mbila* is not carried by the arc but by a carrying strap on the side away from the player.

The end pieces are tightly pulled together by two thongs of twisted cowhide, positioned accurately so that they lie exactly under the nodes of the keys. The keys rest on these thongs, and are tied onto them with a leather lace, the lacing passing through the single hole in the keys on the side away from the player, and around the keys on the near side. Another unique feature of the *mbila* is the spacers, narrow slats of wood situated between every two keys whose function is to support the thongs along their length and prevent excessive movement (a disadvantage of some related xylophones such as the Venda *mbila mtondo*). The spacer is tied onto the frame and the thongs pass through two holes in it. The upper edges of the spacers and of the end pieces are decorated with incised carving.

Timbila keys are tuned with a high degree of accuracy to an equi-spaced heptatonic scale at a fixed pitch. Many Chopi instrument makers have absolute pitch in terms of their scale, which is set on the note called *dawumbila* ('the note which gives the quality of the *mbila*'). Most makers use around 252 Hz for this note. Some orchestras have a slightly higher or lower pitch. The first measurement of this pitch was made by Hugh Tracey in 1940, since when it has remained constant. The claim for the Chopi makers' perfect pitch has been supported many times when they have tuned *timbila* far from home, for instance while on a migrant labour contract, and out of touch with any home instrument.

2. ORCHESTRA. *Timbila* are made in several pitch ranges. The *chikonje*, a small nine-key hexatonic *mbila*, is extremely rare and is said by some Chopi to be their original form of the *mbila*. It is notable for the one low note found out of order at the right-hand (top) end of the instrument. The *chilanzane* (or *tshilandzana*) is the highest-pitched and probably the original orchestral *mbila*. It is about 120 cm long and has 14 or 15 keys, the lowest being *dawumbila*. Ancient examples often have only 10 or 12 keys. The *sanje* is similar in every way to the *chilanzane*, but has an addition of up to four keys below *dawumbila* and is up to 180 cm long. The *timbila* orchestra consists largely of this instrument. The *dole* or *mbingwe* is a middle-pitched instrument with 9 to 16 keys which is used more for ritual music, for example boys' initiation, than with the orchestra. It is rare. The *dibhinda* is a low-pitched instrument which starts one octave below *dawumbila* and has 9 to 12 keys and is about 135 cm long. The *chinzumana* (*chikulu, cikulu* or *tshikhulu*) is about 150 cm long, has four keys (each about 90 cm long), is resonated with large calabashes (up to 38 cm in diameter) and is played standing up. It is sometimes not included under the term 'mbila', as its technique is quite different, merely providing a continuous deep drone or 'presence' to underlie the sound of the other instruments.

Before Mozambique's independence in 1975 and the abolition of chiefship, every major and minor chief had his own *timbila* orchestra. The orchestra served as a focal point for a chiefdom's status, and rivalry was often expressed through gatherings where several orchestras would play. Normally today, however, an orchestra meets once a week, at the weekend, and plays for a local audience. Since independence the new patrons are the local party officials, and performances are now held at their residences, confirming that *timbila* are associated by the Chopi with political power. This is also evident from the words of the songs, many of which are concerned with political personages and events. The *timbila* dance is now acknowledged as one of the national dances of Mozambique and is performed on state occasions.

The size of an orchestra varies according to circumstances. Most musicians would say, however, that between 10 and 20 *timbila* would be good. Any less, and they do not give enough power to the dancers, more, and they are hard to coordinate. An average line-up is about ten *sanje*, sometimes one or two *chilanzane*, two *dibhinda*, two *chinzumana* and, very occasionally, a *dole*. The orchestra sits in three rows, leader at centre front, low-pitched instruments at the back (see fig.2). In addition, an orchestra of average size has about four rattle players standing in front, whose main function is to provide a coordinating reference beat, and from 12 to 40 singer-dancers, who stand in a row facing the orchestra.

3. PERFORMING PRACTICE. The performance consists of a series of some 10 or 12 tightly organized movements of differing character, lasting the better part of an hour. It starts with introductory movements from the orchestra (and rattles). Then follow the dance movements, such as the entry, the standing, the call, the shield, the great

2. *Small Chopi orchestra of timbila (gourd-resonated xylophones) of Quissico, Mozambique: front row, chilanzane (left) and two sanje; centre, dibhinda (left) and sanje; back, chinzumana*

song (the climax of the dance) and the councillors' movements. It ends with a restatement of one of the introductory movements. A drum may be used, but in one or two movements only. The orchestra leader, who is normally also the composer, controls the performance from his instrument with aural and visual signals which indicate what is to happen. (See H. T. Tracey; also illustrative are the films *Mgodo wa Mbanguzi*, *Mgodo wa Mkandeni* and *The Chopi Timbila Dance*, made by G. Zantzinger and A. Tracey, available from Pennsylvania State University, USA.)

Although the music has elements in common with several neighbouring musical cultures, it is of singular character and complexity. Individual technique on the *mbila* involves polyphonic and polymetric playing between the two hands with a degree of freedom from fixed patterns in either hand that is unusual in African xylophone playing. The attack is intense, serious, continuous, powerfully rather than playfully rhythmic, rapid and virtuoso. The top players invariably started young.

Harmony, a strong feature of the music, is based primarily on two notes a 4th (or 5th) apart, but unlike most other musics of south-eastern Africa a third note is usually added giving a strong triadic flavour. All intervals in the seven-note equi-spaced scale are used, even, though less often, the 2nd, 7th and 9th. Harmonic movement proceeds both in parallel and contrary motion. All seven triads are used. Harmonic structure normally displays the south-east African preference for the alternation of chords one tone apart. Rhythmic subdivision of the rattle beat is mostly into a pulse of three, four or two; again, unlike most African music, a consistent pulse system is not a necessary basis of the rhythm. The constant is the rattle beat which may be subdivided by the players ad lib. The music is cyclic; eight and 12 rattle beats (and their multiples) per cycle are the most common, but by no means the only number.

One condition of playing is that where there is a song, its key phrases should be audible inside the played patterns. The two hands, which are not often more than an octave apart, share equally in rhythmic and melodic interest, and in providing the notes which contribute to the perceived inherent patterns of the song melody. Yet every player plays in his own style. Except at moments when the orchestra must play in unison, uniformity is not expected. In fact a player tries to choose a style that will contrast with his neighbours, resulting in a dense web of sound from the whole orchestra, which draws strongly on the listener's ability to perceive pattern.

On a personal and aesthetic level the *timbila* and its dance elicit dedicated, all-engrossing artistic involvement, perhaps even more than other similarly well-organized and rehearsed African music/dance forms. The degree of satisfaction and fulfilment which it gives the people is attested by the importance which the Chopi attach to the *timbila* music, the time they devote to it and the large proportion of musicians in the society.

The presence on the south-east coast of Africa of such a developed and isolated xylophone orchestral tradition has intrigued music historians. One prominent theory that has been advanced for its origin, and that of other African xylophone traditions, is that the instrument and its orchestral use were introduced during the 1st millennium AD from Indonesia, a strong xylophone-playing region. The evidence focusses on the structure of the instrument and its tuning system.

See also DIDIMBADIMBA; for further illustration *see* MARIMBA, fig.1.

BIBLIOGRAPHY
H. T. Tracey: *Chopi Musicians: their Music, Poetry and Instruments* (London, 1948/R1970)
A. Tracey: 'Mozambique', *Grove* 6
Sound of Africa, TR 1,2,5,6,11, 197–210 [disc notes]
ANDREW TRACEY

Mbila mtondo [mbila mutondo]. XYLOPHONE of the Venda people of southern Africa. It has between 21 and 24 keys, tuned to the same scale as the MUTAVHA stopped flute ensemble. Calabash resonators, graded in size, are mounted below the keys. A membrane, of cobweb, covers the mouth of each resonator. It requires two players, usually men, squatting side by side, using five rubber-tipped beaters. See *KirbyMISA*, 47ff and pll.16–18.
DAVID K. RYCROFT

Mbili. Metal bell of the Yogo people of northern Zaïre. It is worn on the wrist, while dancing.

Mbinga [mbinga konde]. Small ivory VESSEL FLUTE of the Pende people of south-western Zaïre (*LaurentyA*, 251).

Mbingwe [mbingwi]. XYLOPHONE of Mozambique. *See* MBILA.

Mbio. End-blown NOTCHED FLUTE of the Ngbandi people of north-western Zaïre (*LaurentyA*, 278).

Mbira. A term used, sometimes in the generic sense, for several types of African lamellaphone or for the keys of such instruments; *see* LAMELLAPHONE, §2(ii). The *mbira dza vadzimu* is a large lamellaphone of the Shona-speaking peoples in southern Africa; the *mbira dza vaNdau* is the lamellaphone of the Ndau people of south-eastern Africa; and the *mbira huru* is the obsolescent lamellaphone of the Manyika people of the Zambezi basin, south-eastern Africa, essentially the same as the *mbira dza vadzimu*.

Mbirii. Small finger-bell of the Tende people of Kenya. It is worn by the player of the NTONO (braced musical bow).

Mbirimbiri. BULLROARER of the Bangba and Mayogo peoples of Zaïre. *See* ATUAMBA.

Mbiriwiri. Drum of the Nyanja/Chewa people of Kasungu district, Malawi.

Mbiya. Trumpet ensemble of the Dakpa people of the Central African Republic. Each of the 13 instruments is made from a hollow tree branch and produces one note. The trumpets are of different sizes, the smallest being 26 cm long, the longest 1·7 metres. The ensemble uses hocket technique and plays on such occasions as the return to the village of young initiates. See S. Arom: 'Centre Afrique: danses de la forêt', HM 733 [disc notes].

Mbizi. Wooden CLAPPERS of the Zaramo people of East Africa.

Mboat [m'boat]. Free-reed mouth organ of Vietnam and north-east Kampuchea. *See* MBUAT and BLAY.

Mbonda. Drum of Zaïre. (1) Cylindro-conical drum, with two laced membranes, of the Ngbandi people, also known as *ta ngo*.

(2) A generic name for drums among the Ngombe, Linga and Njolo peoples (*BooneT*, 27, 62, 68).

Mbo nggo [mbo tong]. LAMELLAPHONE, with 12 to 18 keys, of the Tikar people of central Cameroon. The lamellae are made from the hard surface of a raffia stem and are mounted on a box resonator; often the resonator is made from two or three hollowed-out raffia branches. Both the *mbo nggo* and the *mbo tong* are played with the thumb and index fingers of both hands. Another lamellaphone, the *mbo menjang* with an oval box resonator, is used in the cult for dead chiefs and played in their shrine in groups of three or four accompanied by drums. See G. Kubik: 'Cameroon', *Grove 6*.

M'bono. STOPPED FLUTE ENSEMBLE of the Fali people of Cameroon. *See* HUELE.

Mbóu-lóulo. NOTCHED FLUTE of Aoba, Vanuatu, made from thin bamboo about 60 cm long, plugged at the bottom. There are two finger-holes on the top and a thumb-hole at the bottom. See H. Nevermann: 'Völkerkundliches von Aoba', *Ethnologica*, ii (1960), 216.

Mbóu-mbálambála. PANPIPES of Aoba, Vanuatu, with seven graduated bamboo tubes from 10 to 20 cm long. See H. Nevermann: 'Völkerkundliches von Aoba', *Ethnologica*, ii (1960), 216. *See also* BUE BALABALA HANGAVULU.

Mbuat [m'boat]. Free-reed mouth organ, with six pipes, of the Mnong people of central Vietnam. The pipes are divided into two groups (four and two) and are supplied with air by a gourd wind-chest; the pipes have the same names as the gongs in the CING ensemble. The bamboo free reed is fixed against the part of the pipe inside the gourd. Each pipe has a finger-hole on the side and the pipe sounds when this is stopped. The same type of mouth organ appears among other populations in central Vietnam, such as the Jörai (*dding nam*) and the Köho (*komboat*, *rökel*), and among the tribal peoples of north-east Kampuchea.

TRÂN QUANG HAI

Mbugi. Ankle rattle worn by male dancers among the Shambala people of Tanzania. It consists of iron pellet bells on a strip of goat leather.

Mbulumbumba. Braced gourd-resonated MUSICAL BOW of south-western Angola. *See* BURUMBUMBA.

Mbuma. Large SLIT-DRUM of the Mayombe people of Zaïre (*LaurentyTF*, 135).

Mbuwa. Bass PANPIPES played in the MISHIBA panpipes ensemble of the Luba/Songe people of southern Zaïre.

Mchirima. Double-headed cylindro-conical drum of the Digo people of Kenya. The heads are fixed by securing rings and lacing. Several *mchirima* are played with the *chapuo* (double-headed cylindrical drum) and the *gandu* (footed cylindrical drum). All are tuned and are played as part of an ensemble that includes the *chivoti* (transverse flute), the *kayamba* (raft rattle) and the *ukaya* (gong).

Mdimba. Calabash-resonated XYLOPHONE of the Salampasu people of Zaïre. *See* MADIMBA (i).

Meacham. American family of wind instrument and piano makers. John Meacham jr (*b* Enfield, Conn., 2 May 1785; *d* Albany, NY, 8 Dec 1844) and Horace Meacham (*b* Enfield, Conn., 19 July 1789; *d* ?Albany, NY, ?1861) were brothers, and were among the first American wind instrument makers. Their known predecessors include only Gottlieb Wolhaupter (*fl* New York, 1761), Jacob Anthony (*fl* Philadelphia, 1764–1804), John B. Dash (*fl* New York, 1765–83), William Callender (*fl* Boston, ?1790), and George Catlin (*fl* Hartford, 1799–1814, and Philadelphia, 1814–?1852). Both Meacham brothers may have served an apprenticeship under Catlin. The only Meacham instruments known to have been made in Hartford are a boxwood 'straight' model two-key oboe with ivory mounts stamped 'J.Meacham jr/Hartford', the earliest known American oboe, and a handsome four-key bassoon, similarly stamped, which is one of the earliest American bassoons (for illustrations, see Eliason, 1979–80). In either 1810 or 1811 John moved to Albany, and was soon followed by Horace; in 1814 they bought a store and workshop for $7000, a considerable sum at that time for two young men. They used a number of different stamps, of which three are clearly from the period 1811–27: Meacham, J. Meacham, and J. & H. Meacham. When Sylvanus Pond was taken on as a partner the firm became known as Meacham & Pond (1828–33), and after his departure it became Meacham & Co. (1833–*c*1850). The Meachams eventually began also to make pianos, apparently under the influence of Horace's son Roswell. It is doubtful if any instruments were made after *c*1850, although Roswell maintained a 'music and military store' until *c*1860. 31 Meacham instruments survive (see Young, 1982). These are mainly boxwood flutes and clarinets, but there is also a drum, a piccolo, a copper key bugle, the oboe and bassoon mentioned above, and another four-key bassoon stamped 'Meacham/Albany'. It is significant that of seven known American bassoons made before 1860 four were made by Catlin and two by his probable protégés, the Meachams. Another interesting Meacham instrument is the four-key flute once owned by Henry David Thoreau and now in the Concord (Mass.) Antiquarian Society, on which the writer carved his name and '1845'.

BIBLIOGRAPHY

R. E. Eliason: 'Oboes, Bassoons, and Bass Clarinets, made by Hartford, Connecticut, Makers before 1815', *GSJ*, xxx (1977), 43

——: 'The Meachams, Musical Instrument Makers of Hartford and Albany', *JAMIS*, v–vi (1979–80), 54

P. T. Young: *2500 Historical Woodwind Instruments: an Inventory of the Major Collections* (New York, 1982)

PHILLIP T. YOUNG

Me'a ifi lou niu ('the blown thing made from a coconut leaf'). LEAF OBOE of Tonga, used by children. See R. Moyle: 'Tongan Musical Instruments', *GSJ*, xxix (1976), 80.

Mean [meane, mene] (from Old Fr. *moien*, or *meien*: 'middle'). English term referring originally to the middle part of a three-voice polyphonic texture. John Playford (*A Breefe Introduction*, 1654) referred to the second and third strings of the viol as the small and great mean.

Mean-tone. A system of temperament or a tuning of the scale, particularly on instruments lacking any capacity for flexibility of intonation during performance, which differs from the equal-tempered system normally used on such instruments today. In its most restricted sense the term refers, like its German equivalent *mitteltönige Temperatur*, to a tuning with pure major 3rds (frequency ratio 5:4) divided into two equal whole tones (whereas in JUST INTONATION there are two sizes of whole tone corresponding to the ratios 9:8 and 10:9); to achieve this the tuner must temper the 5ths and 4ths, making the 5ths smaller and the 4ths larger than pure by a quarter of the syntonic comma, hence the label '$\frac{1}{4}$-comma mean-tone', a more specific name for the same kind of tuning.

A broader and equally legitimate use of the term (dating back to such 18th-century writers as Sauveur and Estève) includes any Renaissance or Baroque keyboard tuning in which a major 3rd slightly smaller or, more often, slightly larger than pure is divided into two equal whole tones (see Table 1). In $\frac{2}{7}$-comma mean-tone temperament, for example, the major 3rds are $\frac{1}{7}$-comma smaller than pure, whereas in $\frac{2}{9}$-comma mean-tone they are $\frac{1}{9}$-comma larger and in $\frac{1}{6}$-comma mean-tone they are $\frac{1}{3}$-comma larger. In each case the major 6th (or minor 3rd) is perforce tempered the sum of the amounts by which the major 3rd and 4th are rendered larger than pure; and the 12-note scale will include one sour 'wolf 5th' considerably larger than pure because the other 11 are tempered more than enough to make a 'circle' of identical 5ths as in equal temperament. Hence the tuner about to set a mean-tone temperament must choose not only a particular shade of mean-tone (e.g. $\frac{1}{4}$- or $\frac{1}{5}$-comma) but also a particular disposition (e.g. with the wolf 5th at C#–Ab, G#–Eb or D#–Bb).

TABLE 1: Tempering of triadic concords, measured in cents

A negative number means that the interval is smaller than pure. For comparison the equivalent figures are included for equal temperament and Pythagorean intonation.

	4ths	major 3rds	major 6ths	wolf 5th
1/3-comma mean-tone	7	− 7	0	56
2/7-comma mean-tone	6	− 3	3	44
1/4-comma mean-tone	$5\frac{1}{2}$	0	$5\frac{1}{2}$	36
2/9-comma mean-tone	5	2	7	29
1/5-comma mean-tone	$4\frac{1}{2}$	$4\frac{1}{2}$	9	24
1/6-comma mean-tone	4	6	10	$19\frac{1}{2}$
equal temperament	2	14	16	no wolf
Pythagorean intonation	0	$21\frac{1}{2}$	$21\frac{1}{2}$	− $23\frac{1}{2}$

In all mean-tone temperaments the diatonic semitone is larger than the chromatic semitone, so that Eb is higher than D#, Ab higher than G# and so forth; and a diminished 7th (e.g. G#–F) is larger than a major 6th (Ab–F), a diminished 4th (G#–C) larger than a major 3rd (Ab–C), etc. Triads generally sound more resonant in a mean-tone temperament than in equal temperament,

though in varying degrees depending on the musical style, the instrument, the acoustical circumstances and the precise shade of mean-tone used. The most resonant shades are generally those in which the major and minor 3rds are tempered least; but these ($\frac{2}{7}$- or $\frac{1}{4}$-comma mean-tone) also have the largest diatonic semitones and hence the lowest leading notes. Although some 17th-century musicians considered the large diatonic semitone of $\frac{1}{4}$-comma mean-tone to be, as Mersenne (1636–7) put it, one of the greatest sources of beauty and variety in music, most musicians today would be likely to prefer the smaller diatonic semitones of equal temperament or Pythagorean intonation; a modern connoisseur might therefore find in $\frac{1}{5}$- or $\frac{1}{6}$-comma mean-tone a nice compromise between the relative virtues of $\frac{1}{4}$-comma mean-tone and equal temperament. For the history of mean-tone temperaments in performing practice, *see* TEMPERAMENTS, §§2 and 5; see also Padgham, Collins and Parker (1979).

Various shadings of regular mean-tone temperament correspond closely to certain divisions of the octave into more than 12 equal parts. A number of 18th-century theorists aware of these manifold possibilities sought to show that some particular division of the octave (corresponding to some shade of mean-tone) was better than all the others. In the 16th and early 17th centuries Salinas, Costeley and Titelouze had used the 19-tone division (equivalent to $\frac{1}{3}$-comma mean-tone), and in 1691 Christiaan Huygens had advocated the 31-part division (corresponding to $\frac{1}{4}$-comma mean-tone), which Vicentino may have used in the 1550s (see Lindley, 1982). Sauveur (1701) preferred the 43-part division (corresponding to $\frac{1}{5}$-comma mean-tone); Henfling (1710) and Smith (1749) the 50-part division (corresponding to $\frac{5}{18}$-comma mean-tone); Telemann (1743) and Romieu (1758) the 55-part division (corresponding to $\frac{1}{6}$-comma mean-tone); and Riccati (1762) the 74-tone division (corresponding to $\frac{3}{14}$-comma mean-tone). Estève (1755) said that the most perfect system was 'between that of 31 and that of 43', by which he meant some shade of mean-tone between $\frac{1}{4}$- and $\frac{1}{5}$-comma.

The term 'mean-tone temperament' and its Italian equivalent *systema participato* have sometimes been used to refer to certain schemes in which only the seven naturals of the keyboard (and perhaps not even all of them) conform to any of the regular mean-tone patterns discussed above; the characteristics of such irregular tunings are described in TEMPERAMENTS, §§3 and 6, and in WELL-TEMPERED CLAVIER.

For bibliography *see* TEMPERAMENTS.

MARK LINDLEY

Mears & Stainbank. Firm of bell founders, since 1968 called the WHITECHAPEL BELL FOUNDRY.

Meccanica (It.). ACTION.

Mechanical instrument. A musical instrument in which the sound is produced automatically or mechanically, usually without a performer, although some instruments involve a degree of human participation.

1. Types of musical movement.   2. History.

1. TYPES OF MUSICAL MOVEMENT. The most important part of a mechanical instrument or automatophone is the device for regulating the musical sounds, that is, a cylinder, punched cardboard strip, metal disc or similar mechanism. Of these, the cylinder is by far the oldest.

Various sorts of cylinder are illustrated in figs.1, 2, 7, 9.

The cylinder functions as follows: as it revolves slowly, the pegs on its circumference, placed at right angles to its axis, perform certain mechanical actions which can be transmitted over a considerable distance by means of simple levers. When the levers are brought into contact with the valves of the pipes, the pipes sound for as long as the pegs touch the levers. The length of the notes depends on the width of the pegs; the wider the pegs, the longer the valves remain open and the longer the pipe sounds; the narrower the pegs the shorter the notes. This sort of mechanism is illustrated in fig.1.

To sound pipes of varying pitch, the pegs are placed diagonally on the cylinder. Several pegs sound at once if the pegs are placed in a line along the cylinder axis. The placing of a number of pegs of varying width on the cylinder in order to produce a certain melody or harmony forms the chief principle of automatophonic instruments. It then remains to ensure that the cylinder revolves regularly, to maintain an even tempo. The faithful reproduction of the music thus depends primarily on the correct placing of the pegs on the circumference of the cylinder, that is on the correct transferring of the melody to the cylinder circumference with the aid of the pegs; the correct placing of the pegs is the greatest problem in the construction of these instruments.

The cylinder is made of pieces of well-seasoned wood, usually oak, glued firmly together to prevent distortion. The shape of the pegs, at first of hard wood and later invariably of metal, has varied at different periods. From the 18th century wire bridges were used to produce long notes in place of the simple nails employed earlier. The cylinders used in carillons and chiming clocks (fig.2) were constructed to play only one melody and had a large number of holes into which the relevant pegs were fitted (for instance, the cylinder of the Delft carillon in Belgium had 7240 holes, that in Salzburg 7964, and that

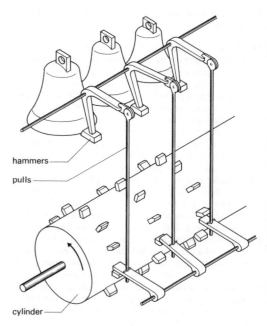

2. *Cylinder mechanism used in carillons and chiming clocks*

in Malmédy as many as 8979). The large number of holes permits the later repinning of the cylinder and thus the changing of the tune. In practice this is not done for carillons more frequently than once a month, since the repinning of the cylinder is difficult and requires much skill and patience. Apart from this, the carillon cylinder's diameter is fairly large, often over a metre, so it can play quite a long tune in one revolution (*see also* CARILLON).

The technique of transferring musical compositions to the cylinder was described in detail by M. D. J. Engramelle. He too considered the greatest problem in constructing automatophonic instruments to be the determination of the exact place where the pegs were to be hammered in (or pressed in with pliers), so as to open the pipe valves correctly and at the proper moment, and suggested various methods for the drawing up of what he called 'situation plans' which were to be traced on the cylinder to facilitate this work. The operation was then called 'annotating' the cylinder. Not only did Engramelle describe how this was done, but he invented a special set of symbols for the purpose and drew up plans for various compositions. The plans were then used to make so-called workshop charts in the form of a flattened-out cylinder, i.e. a rectangle, the width of the cylinder and the length of its circumference. Horizontal lines were to be drawn on this paper, corresponding to the bars of the composition, and vertical lines representing the notes (for illustration, *see* ENGRAMELLE, MARIE DOMINIQUE JOSEPH). The positions of the pegs were then marked in by means of dots and strokes. The finished plan was to be traced on to the cylinder and the pegs driven in. The pegs set out on the surface of the cylinder often made it possible to read an otherwise unknown composition. Experts have reconstructed many historically valuable pieces from cylinders now no longer capable of playing, or from cylinders of instruments no longer available.

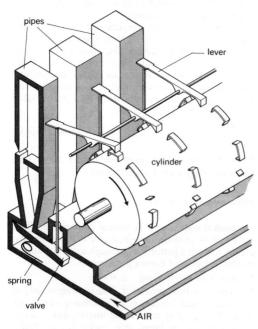

1. *Cylinder mechanism used in mechanical organs*

The disadvantage of cylinders, in spite of the improvements made on them, was that they could record at the most eight compositions, and only a few instruments with interchangeable cylinders were produced.

The French instrument maker Alexandre François Debain invented an ingenious mechanism described in 1846 in his treatise *Antiphonel-harmonium suppléant de l'organiste*. The antiphonel was to replace the organist, and not just any organist, but – to quote the inventor – 'a faultless player who never plays a false note or a false chord'. According to many experts, including Auber, Berlioz, Halévy and Thomas, the antiphonel was remarkable for the ease with which it could be used with any keyboard instrument, for the precision of its performance and for the simplicity of its mechanism. It was an oblong box with a metal lid through which keys resembling those on a keyboard passed. These keys, however, acted in the opposite direction and were operated by jacks with tempered steel hooks at the end; the hooks passed through a comb about 3 cm wide. The five octaves of the keyboard were thus squeezed into the relatively narrow space occupied by the comb.

The composition was not transferred to the cylinder, but to a wooden desk called the planchette, with special iron pegs which replaced the player's fingers. As the planchette moved across the lid of the box, by means of a lever or crank, the iron pegs engaged with the jacks, which acted on the keyboard of the instrument. When used with the harmonium, this mechanism produced dynamic shades by means of different peg heights.

The ideal of Engramelle, who envisaged automatophonic instruments that would permit faithful reproduction of the music, was brought closer to realization by the invention of Martin Corteuile, who in 1852 took out a patent for a perforated cardboard strip, on which the holes engaged with the jacks of the antiphonel; the holes represented the musical score.

Then came the perforated card invented by the Nantes instrument maker J. A. Testé (fig.3). In this there were levers to control the valves which vibrated the free metal reeds. At the other end of the levers jacks were placed in a row as long as the box and protruding slightly above the lid. In this position the valves were open, and when the pedals were pressed all the reeds vibrated simultaneously. Above the jacks was a round metal ledge whose edge almost touched the lid of the instrument. This piece of metal contained the same number of grooves as jacks, and the latter rose through the holes to open the valves. If a cardboard strip was passed between the metal ledge and the lid, all the jacks went down, closed the valves, and rose only when a hole in the cardboard allowed them to do so. Testé called his instrument the cartonium. When played, the cardboard strip on which the holes were arranged according to the music moved regularly across the jacks. Smooth movement was ensured by means of rubber rollers, turned by a crank, which kept the cardboard in position.

Testé's cartonium system was used in practically all the automatophonic instruments with free metal reeds: intonas, aristons, manopans (fig.4) etc. The metal jacks which engaged with the valves of the individual reeds were pressed down by a perforated disc or strip. The mechanism was so simple and so easy to handle that this type of automatophonic instrument was still in use after pneumatic devices were used in other instruments.

A way to use a perforated tin disc with musical boxes was devised in the 1880s (fig.5). Paul Lochmann's mechanism made use of little wheels with hooks, arranged in the shape of a star, which engaged with the teeth of a steel comb. The hooks plucked the teeth of the comb when they came into contact as the disc revolved. Most instruments had two combs, some had as many as four, one above the other. This 'tandem' arrangement required two sets of wheels to pluck the combs. Paul Riessner and Gustav Brachhausen further improved this system by having only one set of wheels pluck the two combs. Since they placed the combs tooth against tooth, one of them had to be plucked in a downward direction, which required special mufflers for the bottom comb (*see* Musical box).

New patents were continually being granted for the construction of the disc mechanism. In 1882 Miguel Boom invented a universal disc, on which the projections could be changed freely, thus varying the music. Ellis Parr constructed an apparatus for reperforating used discs. Ferdinand Schaub perfected the disc projections. Only one thing was now lacking: a means of changing the discs easily, preferably without human assistance. This was finally achieved by the Regina Company of Rahway, NJ, which made polyphons with an automatic device for changing the discs.

The equally ingenious pneumatic system was invented about the same time. It represented an important turning-point in the efforts to achieve a more faithful reproduction of music. In 1842 a Lyons mechanic named

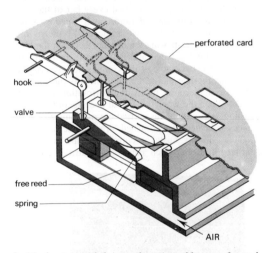

hook
valve
perforated card
free reed
spring
AIR

3. Mechanism with free reeds activated by a perforated card

Charles Félix Seytre patented an instrument called the autophone which – as stated in the patent – played 'all kinds of melodies with the aid of perforated cards, similar to the jacquart, with square or oblong holes according to the length of the notes to be played'. The holes were linked with pipes which conducted compressed air from the pedal bellows to the small cylinders attached to each of the keys of the instrument. In each of the cylinders there was a small air-driven piston which moved a jack, which in turn made the hammer strike the string from below. A similar instrument, worked by sucked-in air, was described by the French organ maker Napoléon Fourneaux. A pneumatic piano was made in New York by Merritt Gally, who patented his invention in 1881.

4. Manopan with perforated card after Testé's model (Národní Muzeum, Prague)

Patents for pneumatic pianos were granted to Bishop & Down four years later.

The last improvement in this field was the invention of the pianola by the American engineer E. S. Votey; it was patented in 1897. Seven years later the firm of M. Welte & Söhne began the manufacture of phonolas in Freiburg. These were in fact the same kind of instrument under two names. The name 'pianola' was used as a trademark by the Anglo-American Aeolian Company and later came to denote any automatophonic piano with a pneumatic system (*see* PLAYER PIANO).

Perforated strips for the pianola were made in two ways. In the metronome method every bar of the composition was of the same duration, as if timed by a metronome. In practice this was achieved by means of a prepared scheme showing the distance between the holes on the perforated ledge and the same distance for the note lengths. Each note of the composition was marked at the appropriate place; the duration was indicated by a stroke at the point where the perforation was to be made. When the whole piece had been recorded in this fashion, perforation was carried out mechanically at the places indicated. The finished strip was tested on the pianola and any mistakes corrected. This produced a master-roll from which cardboard matrices could be

5. Double-disc musical box (the 'Symphonium'), German, late 19th century (private collection)

made, thus permitting the simultaneous perforation of a large number of rolls. The second, and better, method was entirely mechanical. The perforated strips were produced by means of an electrical recording made during the musician's performance. As he played the piano, every key he touched switched on the current, which activated the requisite electromagnet; this, in turn, activated a mechanism recording the strength of each stroke. Slight errors in the pianist's performance could be corrected, and the recording thus obtained was used to produce perforated strips for reproduction.

As there were perforated strips for the pianola, so perforated cards were made for other automatophonic instruments, in particular for orchestrions (*see* ORCHESTRION, (2)); examples include Charles Dawson's autophon, exhibited at the Great Exhibition, Crystal Palace, London (1851). The manufacture of these cards called for considerable skill and precision. The 'orchestrator' (the person who transferred the music to the strip) had first to study the composition in question, particularly if it happened to be an orchestral piece. The prepared pattern was printed on strips of cardboard glued together in the shape of a book. After the card had been perforated it was tested on the instrument for which it was intended, so that any errors made during the transfer of the composition or during the perforation could be corrected. This mastercard served mass reproduction in the same way as the master-roll did for the pianola. Additional perforated cards were frequently used with organs and harmoniums to control the registers.

The slightest error on the cylinder or in the perforated strip resulted in faulty reproduction, easily discernible by the ear, so great care was required in constructing the instruments; every detail had to be calculated with an accuracy of at least a fiftieth of a second. This meant that some of the pegs on the cylinder or the perforations in the strips had to be placed with a precision of up to half a millimetre. Atmospheric conditions or wear could lead to changes in the mechanism which were slight, but sufficient to cause audible faults in the reproduction, especially in the rhythm. There was no way to correct these changes, and when heard repeatedly they became offensive. However, as long as such variations remained within certain limits, they combined with the agogic variations due to the irregular movement of the cylinder or the perforated strip to create a substantial part of the specific charm of mechanical musical reproduction.

2. HISTORY. The endeavour to create sound by mechanical means, without the assistance and intervention of man, can be traced to the remote past. At first, these efforts had practical reasons (signalling) as well as being for cult purposes (to create voices as of the dead). On the Indonesian paddy fields water currents in the irrigation channels still set in motion tuned bamboo tubes, which strike rhythmically against stones and produce repeating musical phrases.

The effects of air currents on string instruments are known from ancient times. Examples include the Indian *karkarí*, whose strings sound in the wind, and several kinds of Aeolian harp in ancient China. The Malay people thrust into the earth a long bamboo tube with holes into which air is driven; the pitch of the resulting notes changes according to the velocity and direction of the air current.

However, all these sound-producing devices lack the most important part of automatophones – the mechanical 'brain'. This was invented only when technology and music were combined. The first attempts in this field were made by the ancient peoples of Asia and Egypt; their automatic statues inspired Hero of Alexandria to devise a mechanically struck instrument (see HYDRAULIS). The Alexandrian tradition was kept alive in Byzantium after the fall of the Roman Empire, and science and technology later reached the Arabs and Persians. From 813 to 833 three brothers, Muhammad, Ahamad and Hasan, called Banū Mūsā, then outstanding organizers of Arab science in Baghdad, constructed the first historically documented automatophone, whose 'brain' was a revolving cylinder with pegs.

In Europe, Leo the Philosopher devised automata with artificial trees and singing birds in the first half of the 9th century for Theophilus Ikonomachus, Emperor of Byzantium. Konrad von Würzburg (c1250) mentioned an artificial tree with birds perched on it, moving their wings and singing (see BIRD INSTRUMENTS). Mechanical instruments – a spinet and two drums with a cylinder – were also constructed by Leonardo da Vinci in the late 15th century.

The creation and performance of music by mechanical means reached a sophisticated stage of development when watchmaking replaced sand-glasses with complicated and artistically executed clockwork mechanism. Clock towers were often equipped with carillons which played a melody by means of a cylinder with pins (see fig.2 above). Fétis said that the first manufacturer of carillons was a 15th-century Dutchman named Koecke. In the course of the 16th and 17th centuries carillons were made in the Low Countries, the greatest being in Amsterdam, Breda, Goes, Middelburg and Delft. They were played by the so-called 'carilloneurs' by means of a keyboard.

In the late Renaissance, artistic cabinets also contained organ automatophones, or mechanical organs. The most famous one, the so-called Pomeranian art cabinet, had a mechanical organ made by A. Langenbucher and M. Genser; it was destroyed in World War II. Mechanical spinets were made especially in Augsburg (Samuel Bidermann, Eisenburger), but the Nuremberg artists Werner, Bullman, Hell, Farfler, Hautsch and others, who built various mechanical instruments, are also mentioned. With the end of the Renaissance came the end of interest in art cabinets, and automatophones found less elegant homes. They became larger, and interchangeable cylinders allowed a larger repertory. Smaller organs were incorporated in clocks (flute-playing clocks), while larger mechanisms were placed in secretaires, mirrors and other furniture.

From the second half of the 18th century and during the whole Biedermeier period, flute-playing clocks with beautifully executed cases were extremely popular. A number of composers, including Mozart, Haydn and C. P. E. Bach, wrote music for these instruments. In the second half of the 18th century their centres of manufacture included London (C. Higginson, J. Cox, E. Norton, W. Carpenter, Marriott) and Berlin (C. Möllinger, C. E. Kleemeyer, K. Ehrbar, J. Elfroth), and later Vienna (Gurck, J. A. Hoyer, Maelzel brothers) and Prague (J. H. D. Sander, P. Heinrich, V. Vencl, B. Biswanger). Mechanical clocks were sometimes combined with stringed automatophones (harp clocks) or carillons. Cheap clocks with glass carillons were manufactured by farmers in the Black Forest (see MUSICAL CLOCK).

The first barrel organs appeared in the 18th century. The smallest, the so-called 'bird organs', were intended to teach birds to sing. The mechanism was simple: a horizontal wooden barrel fitted with pegs was turned by a crank handle in a wooden case; the pegs engaged with valves on several small pipes, and the air chamber was supplied by bellows worked by the same crank handle (see BARREL ORGAN and BIRD INSTRUMENTS). Larger barrel organs were used by beggars, but also found their way to some smaller and poorer churches, where they replaced the organ. The English firm of Flight & Robson manufactured a large number of barrel organs for the church; they played psalms, preludes and hymns, as well as church songs. There are still some in churches in Shelland (Suffolk) and Barnston (Essex). Gavioli, an Italian who lived in Paris at the beginning of the 19th century, was an outstanding maker of barrel organs. Factory manufacture of the instruments was later concentrated in France, Germany and the Austro-Hungarian monarchy. In larger barrel organs the case was divided into two parts: in the upper part were the barrel, the tracture and the bellows, and in the lower part three registers of pipes were placed transversely. The bass pipes were covered, while the other registers, always an octave higher, had double labial pipes. The accommodation of so many pipes in so small a space called for much ingenuity and led to the development at the beginning of the 1860s of barrel organs with upright pipes, using labial as well as reed pipes. This type of barrel organ was known as the 'Wiener Werkl', as Vienna was then the only place manufacturing them.

The construction of barrel organs was considerably influenced by the introduction of free reeds and at the close of the 19th century barrel organs with pipes gave place to cheaper and smaller ones with free reeds. The reeds were often sounded by an interchangeable piece of perforated cardboard (fig.3), or by a folded strip of cardboard instead of by the barrel. This was the basic principle of many automatophones manufactured under different names, such as intona, ariston, manopan, mignon etc. Three fundamental types of automatophone with free reeds were manufactured: the first was based on the barrel or cylinder (barrel organs), the second on the perforated cardboard, and the third on the pneumatic system. All three types survived until the 1920s.

Attempts to imitate the sound of the orchestra resulted in the invention of orchestrions, or mechanical organs (see fig.6), which were often combined with percussion instruments, such as drums, cymbals or triangles, or with a piano. Cherubini and Beethoven composed for J. N. Maelzel's PANHARMONICON. The most ingenious and interesting orchestrion was constructed in 1821 by the Dutchman Dietrich Nikolaus Winkel, who named his new instrument the COMPONIUM (now in the Museum of Musical Instruments in Brussels). The componium consists of an orchestrion proper and a special mechanism which plays variations on a given composition of 80 bars. The bars are interchanged by a lengthwise gearing of two cylinders, thus creating endless variations.

Remarkable for the size and volume of sound are the APOLLONICON (not to be confused with J. H. Völler's APOLLONION), built in 1817 by the English makers Flight & Robson, and the orchestrions of the Kaufmann family, whose automatophones (symphonium, salpingion, aulodion, 'trumpeter') were displayed for a number of years in their own 'acoustic cabinet' in Dresden (see also BELLONION and CHORDAULODION). Very good orchestrions were manufactured by J. H. Heller in Berne, J. Deutschmann in Vienna, Mamert Hock in Saarlouis, James and John Blessing in the Black Forest, and by

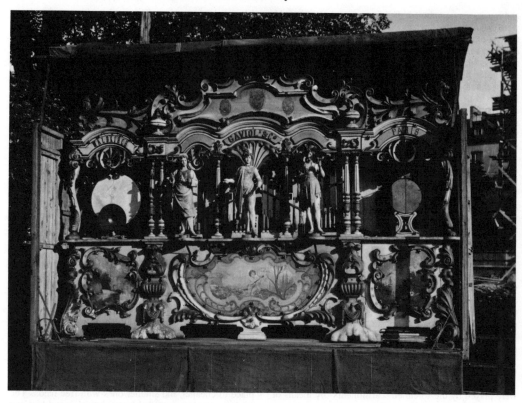

6. *Mechanical organ by Gavioli & Cie, Waldkirch and Paris*

the Riemer brothers in Chrastava in Bohemia. Most of these musical instruments were used in amusement enterprises, in circuses and with merry-go-rounds (*see* FAIRGROUND ORGAN). It was impossible to separate the individual strands of the composition, and the mechanical playing of the violin part did not help to create the impression of an orchestra. Strength of tone was the most important aspect of orchestrions and much less attention was paid to the quality of the music. Because of this orchestrions never rose above the level of the barrel organ.

Good tone, small size and reasonable price contributed to the development and wide distribution of musical boxes in the 19th century. These instruments are based on a metal comb with teeth of different lengths. The first musical boxes were called *carillons à musique* and were sounded by a disc with steel pins. Their manufacture was particularly concentrated in Switzerland, where miniature mechanisms with 15 to 25 teeth were built into various luxury articles, such as watches, seals, walking-sticks, small boxes, candy boxes, jewel caskets and tobacco boxes. At the close of the 18th century David Lecoultre replaced the disc by a pinned cylinder parallel to the comb (fig.7). The teeth of the comb were no longer mounted separately, but in groups of three, four or five, and each group set in a metal plate. In about 1820 the teeth were cut from sheet steel, and several years later dampers were added.

Other improvements of musical boxes included the introduction of resonators, or small lead weights, which were fixed to the underside of the steel bass teeth. The most important of the Geneva manufacturers were the Nicole brothers, who constructed in about 1840 the first musical box of the fortepiano type, containing two combs

of different lengths. Increasing interest and demand on the foreign markets were satisfied by newly-established factories. One of the most important manufacturers was E. Paillard, who founded his factory in St Croix in 1875. The interchangeability of standardized cylinders was a major innovation. But despite these improvements musical boxes could not play more compositions than could cylinder-based mechanisms, and instruments with interchangeable cylinders were extremely expensive. This problem was solved by the German Paul Lochmann, who used a steel disc with protrusions in place of the cylinder (see fig.5 above). In combination with a special mechanism the disc plucked the teeth of the comb the moment the protrusions touched them. These so-called polyphons were characterized by clear, strong tone, and at the beginning of the 20th century an automatic disc-changing device was also introduced.

Their quiet sound and the difficulty of keeping them constantly tuned are the main reasons why more intensive mechanization of stringed musical instruments did not take place until the 19th century. In addition to barrel organs, 'crank-handle pianos', also known as 'piano organs', appeared at that time in Italy and England. In south Italy these musical instruments still provide music for puppet plays. They are more sturdily built than ordinary pianos, in order to withstand frequent use and the effects of the weather. Their felt hammers are covered with leather and the strings are quadrupled. This gives them a sharp sound rather like a xylophone. The mechanism is very simple: the pins on the cylinder press a lever which engages with the hammer (fig.8). There are no dampers, except on some lower notes, and the pins on the cylinder are not adapted to achieve dynamic effects. A similar construction was used for the so-called 'piano orchestrions', which were equipped with additional instruments including the xylophone, drums, cymbal and triangle.

An important change came with the introduction of the pneumatic mechanism, an impulse to which was given by the perforated strip. Patent rights for the use of a pneumatic mechanism for the piano were issued in the USA as early as 1860, but in practice it was only used 20 years later, when Jean Carpentier constructed his 'mélographe' for the registration of compositions, and the 'mélotrope' for re-playing these compositions with the aid of a perforated strip of paper.

At first the pneumatic mechanism was separate from the piano proper, but later it was built in the piano in such a manner that the piano could also be played without it. These 'pianolas' or 'phonolas' were operated by pedals. Electrically operated instruments were introduced later. To replace the performer's ten fingers the pianola was equipped with 88 mechanical 'fingers', which could be used freely with the perforated strip. It was possible, for example, to play bass tunes without the sustaining pedal, or to play arpeggios and accurate trills without fear that the mechanical 'fingers' would be cramped. The pianola made possible rhythmical extravagance and harmonizations never previously attempted by composers, regardless of the requirements of the fingering. In addition, it was possible to control the tempo and muting of the composition, thus giving the 'musician' handling the instrument an illusion that the performance was his own. A prerequisite for perfect operation of the pianola was the ability to handle the pedals rhythmically for the phrasing of the composition. Thus, the technique of operating the pianola had to be as instinctive as that of singing or speaking. (For illustrations, *see* PLAYER PIANO.)

Four types of pneumatic piano reached a high degree

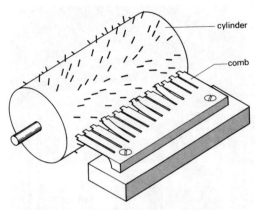

7. Metal comb and cylinder of a musical box

of perfection in the last phase of their development. These were pianolas of the Duo-Art type made by Aeolian; the Welte-Mignon type made by Welte & Söhne; the phonola made by Hupfeld; and the pianola constructed by the Ampico Corporation. Music from the Ampico piano rolls, when issued on LP records in 1966, surprised the public by its technical perfection. The phonola required someone to regulate the tempo, phrasing and volume during the performance, while the Duo-Art, Welte-Mignon and Ampico pianolas could not deviate from an exact and authentic reproduction of the original performance with all its fine distinctions of attack, use of pedal, and choice of tempo and volume.

The pianola was for a long time considered a mere mechanical piano, to play only compositions written for the piano proper. Not until other musical machines (e.g. the gramophone and the radio) were overtaking it in popularity did the pianola enjoy a reputation as an

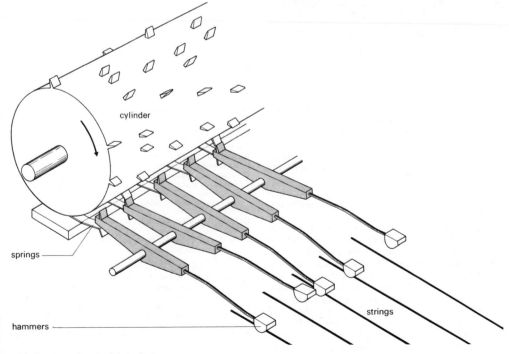

8. Mechanism of a mechanical piano

9. Mechanical violin: Hupfeld's 'Phonoliszt-Violina', Leipzig, c1912 (British Piano Museum Charitable Trust, Brentford)

instrument in its own right, requiring special music and even new compositions (Hindemith and Stravinsky, among others, composed for the pianola). The Aeolian Company in East Rochester, USA, made an attempt to resume the manufacture of pianolas after World War II, but production was stopped again in 1951, apparently for lack of interest.

The complicated system by which bowed instruments are played prevented any attempts at their mechanization for a long time. Frequent attempts had previously been made to replace the bow with some other mechanism, but always without success. It was evident that the usual bow was of no use, and that an endless rotating bow must be introduced. This problem was not solved until 1908, when the first mechanical violin, the 'virtuosa', was constructed in the USA. This was an ordinary violin placed in an instrument containing a number of levers and mechanical 'fingers'; a disc replaced the bow. In 1911 the 'violina' was constructed in Vienna; it consisted of three violins grouped around a common axis and pressed at a given moment against a rotating bow (see fig.9); the pressure was automatically regu-

lated. The 'violinista', made in 1920, was a violin pendant to the pianola. An ordinary violin was placed in a mobile cradle and the individual strings of the instrument were played by rotating it. The bow moved at the required speed according to the desired performance. It was also possible to change the pressure of the bow on the strings at any moment, thereby allowing the use of various techniques such as martelé, spiccato and staccato.

This was the last stage in the development of automatophones; the advance of musical machines eliminated them so quickly that in the 1930s they virtually ceased to exist (though a series of instruments was developed between 1945 and 1961 at White Plains, New York; *see* CROSS–GRAINGER FREE MUSIC MACHINE). Attempts to replace the musical performer with a machine are now represented by modern electronic and cybernetic music-making machines. Automatophones are the only musical instruments that have kept past musical practice alive for later generations. Their cylinders and perforated strips fulfil the same function as modern sound recordings; they provide valuable information about the tuning of musical instruments, performing practice (notably as a source for the study of NOTES INÉGALES) and the tempo of compositions in the past.

BIBLIOGRAPHY

S. de Caus: *Les raisons des forces mouvantes* (Frankfurt am Main, 1615, rev. 2/1624)
R. de Fluctibus: *De naturae simia* (Oppenheim, 1618)
A. Kircher: *Musurgia universalis* (Rome, 1650/R1970)
C. Schott: *Technica curiosa* (Nuremberg, 1664)
A. Kircher: *Phonurgia nova* (Kempten, 1673/R1966)
C. Schott: *Magia universalis naturae et artis* (Bamberg, 1674)
J. Vaucanson: *Le mécanisme du fluteur automate* (Paris, 1738)
M. D. J. Engramelle: *La tonotechnie ou l'art de noter les cylindres* (Paris, 1775)
E. T. A. Hoffmann: *Die Automate* (Berlin, 1819)
J. H. M. Pope: *Geschichte aller Erfindungen und Entdeckungen* (Stuttgart, 1837)
L. Hupfeld: *DEA-Violina* (Leipzig, 1909)
Welte & Söhne: *List of Music for the Welte-Mignon Autograph-piano* (New York, 1912)
H. L. Atta: *The Piano-player* (New York, 1914)
W. B. White: *The Player-piano Up to Date* (New York, 1914)
F. M. Feldhaus: *Die Technik der Vorzeit* (Leipzig, 1914)
E. Newman: *The Piano-player and its Music* (London, 1920)
S. Grew: *The Art of the Player-piano* (London, 1922)
A. Chapuis and E. Gelis: *Le monde des automates* (Paris, 1928)
A. Chapuis: *Automates, machines automatiques et méchanisme* (Lausanne, 1928)
A. Protz: *Mechanische Musikinstrumente* (Kassel, 1939)
A. Chapuis: *Les automates dans les oeuvres d'imagination* (Neuchâtel, 1950)
A. Chapuis and E. Droz: *Les automates* (Neuchâtel, 1950)
A. Chapuis: *Histoire de la boîte à musique et de la musique mécanique* (Lausanne, 1955)
A. Buchner: *Hudební automaty* (Prague, 1959; Eng. trans., 1959)
F. K. Frieberg: *Musica ex machina* (Berlin, 1960)
E. Simon: *Mechanische Musikinstrumente früherer Zeiten und ihre Musik* (Wiesbaden, 1960)
L. G. Langwill and N. Boston: *Church and Chamber Barrel-organs, their Origin, Makers, Music and Location: a Chapter in English Church Music* (Edinburgh, 1967, rev. and enlarged 2/1970)
Q. D. Bowers: *A Guidebook of Automatic Musical Instruments* (New York, 1967–8)
A. W. J. G. Ord-Hume: *Player Piano* (London, 1970)
Q. D. Bowers: *Encyclopedia of Automatic Musical Instruments* (New York, 1972)
A. W. J. G. Ord-Hume: *Clockwork Music: an Illustrated Musical History of Mechanical Musical Instruments* (London, 1973)
The History of Music Machines (New York, 1975) [exhibition catalogue]
H. Weiss-Stauffacher: *Musikautomaten und mechanischen Musikinstrumente* (Zurich, Tokyo and New York, 1976; Eng. trans., 1976)
A. W. J. G. Ord-Hume: *Joseph Haydn and the Mechanical Organ* (Cardiff, 1982)
Early Music, xi (1983) [automatic instruments issue]

ALEXANDR BUCHNER

Mechanik [Mechanismus] (Ger; Fr. *méchanique*). ACTION.

Medesimo tempo (It.: 'the same pace'). A direction to maintain a tempo in spite of apparent disturbances, particularly changes of time signature or note value; *l'istesso tempo* was also used. By the later 19th century these directions were increasingly replaced by equivalence equations.

Médiator (Fr.). PLECTRUM.

Medzang m'biang. A log XYLOPHONE of the Fang/Pahuin peoples of southern Cameroon and northern Gabon. Its keys rest on two banana trunks. The instruments are used exclusively for the Melane ancestor cult and are played in pairs with 15 and 8 keys respectively. *See also* MENDZAN.

Meguguning. Large bronze gong of Alor, Indonesia, used in the SARAFEO ensemble.

Mehter [mehterhane]. Turkish military band, originating in the 14th century. By the 17th century the *mehter* usually consisted of *boru* (trumpets), *nakkare* (small kettledrums), *zil* (cymbals), *çağana* (Turkish crescent), *davul* (cylindrical drums), *zurna* (oboes) and *kös* (large kettledrums). Such instruments were introduced into European military ('Janissary') music and later adopted by orchestras; *see* BAND (i), §II, 2 (i), esp. fig.4.

Meifred, Pierre-Joseph Emile (*b* Colmar, 13 Nov 1791; *d* Paris, 28 Aug 1867). French horn player and designer. He entered Dauprat's horn class at the Paris Conservatoire in 1815 (*premier prix*, 1818) and played in the orchestras of the Théâtre-Italien (from 1819) and Opéra (1820–50). Largely responsible for the founding of the Gymnase Militaire (1836), a school for army musicians, he was bandmaster of the National Guard and was awarded the cross of the Légion d'honneur in 1848. He was a founder-member, and for some years secretary, of the Société des Concerts du Conservatoire, which owed much of its success to his organizing talent.
Mechanically and progressively minded, Meifred devoted himself to the development of the valve horn, then recently introduced from Germany, and at the first Conservatoire concert (9 March 1828) he played a solo of his own composition on this instrument – its first public appearance in France. Together with the Paris instrument maker Labbaye, he greatly improved the German model, adding tuning-slides to the valves and thus making it possible to use crooks in different pitches. In 1834, with Deshayes, Meifred patented a valve with movable shutters within the actual windway (French patent no.4002), though this proved too expensive to market commercially; no specimens are known to have survived. (A somewhat similar arrangement of shutters in the windway is found on a trumpet of 1825 made by Nathan Adams of Lowell, Massachusetts.) It is almost certain that Halary (Jules-Léon Antoine), while designing a system of horn valves in which the third valve raised the pitch of the instrument instead of lowering it, called Meifred into consultation. The latter adopted this arrangement for his own use, an example still followed by many horn players in France. In 1832 a valve horn class was inaugurated at the Conservatoire, with Meifred

as professor, but this was discontinued after his retirement in 1864 and not resumed until 1903 under Brémond.

WRITINGS
De l'étendue, de l'emploi et des ressources du cor (Paris, 1829)
Méthode de cor chromatique ou à pistons (Paris, 1840, rev. 2/1849)
'Notice sur la fabrication des instruments de musique en cuivre', *Annuaire de la Société des anciens élèves des écoles nationales des arts-et-métiers, année 1851* (Paris, 1851)

BIBLIOGRAPHY
R. Morley-Pegge: *The French Horn* (London, 1960, rev. 2/1973)
R. Eliason: 'Early American Valves for Brass Instruments', *GSJ*, xxiii (1970), 86

REGINALD MORLEY-PEGGE/PHILIP BATE

Meinl [formerly Meinl & Lauber]. German firm of brass instrument makers. It was founded in 1956 when Franz Meinl (*b* Graslitz [now Kraslice], 20 May 1910) and his son Ewald (*b* Schönlind, 10 Oct 1937), who had established a bell-making shop the previous year, were joined by Johann Lauber (*b* Plauen, 10 Nov 1919). In 1981 Ewald took over on his own, the firm assuming his name. Franz Meinl was trained by Ignaz Hamm in Rothau, and worked for Gebrüder Stowasser and Bohland & Fuchs (Graslitz). After 1947 he worked on his own in Lenggries and from 1951 in Geretsried (both in Bavaria) making brass instrument bells for other firms. Johann Lauber was trained with Gebrüder Stowasser (1934–7); from 1950 to 1957 he was employed by Böhm & [Andreas] Meinl (Geretsried). Ewald Meinl trained from 1951 to 1955 with his great-uncle, Wenzel Meinl.
Besides being bell makers, they have gained an international reputation for reproductions of historical brass instruments (from 1967 Baroque trumpets, developed with Edward Tarr, from 1968 trombones with Thomas Cramer, from 1970 horns with Horace Fitzpatrick). In 1972 they produced a piccolo Bb/A trumpet with two detachable bells, with Rolf Quinque (of Munich).

EDWARD H. TARR

Mejoranera [mejorana]. A small, short-necked five-string guitar of Panama. It is normally made of cedar, with gut or nylon strings tuned either e'–b–a–a'–d' ('by 25') or e'–b–g–g'–d' ('by 6'). In the 1970s it was replacing the similarly shaped BOCONA to accompany the *mejorana, cumbia* and *punto* (dance and song forms).

JOHN M. SCHECHTER

Melegari, Enrico Clodoveo (*fl* Turin, *c*1860–88). Italian violin maker. His labels indicate that he was originally from Parma and that his address in Turin was via Belfiori, no.20. He worked in association with his brothers Michele and Pietro, who probably served primarily as assistants. Instruments bearing the Melegari label but dating between 1888 and 1893 were probably unfinished works which were completed by the younger brothers after Enrico's death. Melegari's work followed a well-rounded model of classical proportions which was essentially original. The soundholes are also quite individual with rather broad wings and open circles. The scroll is well designed and has a rather prominent eye and rounded throat. Besides the usual printed label his instruments are normally branded MELEGARI on the inside and back rib. Two types of printed label were used, headed either jointly 'Fratelli Melegari' or 'Enrico Melegari Clodoveo'.

BIBLIOGRAPHY
U. Azzolina: *Liuteria italiana dell'ottocento e del novecento* (Milan, 1964)

JAAK LIIVOJA-LORIUS

Melkharmonica (Ger.). A type of NAIL VIOLIN, with wooden rods played with rosined gloves.

Mellophone. A valved brass instrument of circular form in E♭, or F (below the cornet), common in the USA, corresponding to the English TENOR COR and similarly intended to replace the horn in boys' marching bands etc. In the 1950s C. G. Conn brought out a new model, the mellophonium, with a bell of full orchestral horn width but projecting forwards to suit stage performances by bands. It has also been used by jazz soloists.

ANTHONY C. BAINES

Mellotron. An electromechanical keyboard instrument developed by Leslie, Norman and Frank Bradley in Streetly, Birmingham, during 1962–3 and manufactured by Mellotron Manufacturing (later Streetly Electronics) since 1964. A complex sequence of company take-overs in the 1970s led to the company's losing the right to use the name 'Mellotron' (which is formed from the words 'melody electronics'); at the end of 1977 the instrument was renamed the 'Novatron', though the original name continues to be used widely. The Mellotron has been employed chiefly in pop and rock music, including the Beatles' *Strawberry Fields Forever* (1967) and *Days of Future Passed* (1967) by the Moody Blues, one of whose members originally worked for the company.

From 1920 until the 1950s attempts were made with all existing types of recording system (magnetized disc and wire, gramophone record and optical film soundtrack) to create a keyboard instrument that could play back any pre-recorded sounds; until the advent of magnetic tape none of these was successful.

In 1962 the firm of Bradmatic (owned by the three Bradley brothers), which specialized in the manufacture of tape heads, was asked to supply a set of 70 matched playback heads for the prototype of the CHAMBERLIN; the Mellotron is a considerably improved version of the same idea, in which the sounds are produced from a series of pre-recorded magnetic tapes that are individually activated by keys on the keyboard. The first Mellotron (Mark I) was produced in 1964. Mark II (1965) has two 35-note manuals placed side by side; the right-hand one is used for the melody, and the left-hand one is split into two sections which respectively activate 18 rhythms and 17 chords. Smaller, one-manual models followed; Model 300 with a 52-note keyboard in 1968 and Model 400 with 35 notes in 1970. Since 1978 the company has produced, under the name 'Novatron', Model 400 SM, and a two-manual Mark 5 which resembles the Mark II.

The principle of the Mellotron is that each key operates a tape-playback system. When the key is depressed a pinch wheel brings the tape into contact with a rotating spindle (like the capstan on a tape recorder) and draws the tape past a replay head at $7\frac{1}{2}''$ (19 cm) per second. When the key is released a spring returns the tape to its starting point. The maximum duration for any note is eight seconds (ten seconds on the Mark II). The tape is 0·95 cm wide and subdivided into three parallel tracks; in the earlier models each tape was 12·8 metres long and subdivided into six separate sections, individually accessible by means of a forward and rewind control. The track-selection control can be set to intermediate positions to combine the timbres recorded on two adjacent tracks. The most popular version of the Mellotron/Novatron, the Model 400, has a smaller selection of recordings on tapes 1·83 metres long and in a single section; a pitch control can vary the tape speed by plus or minus 20%. A large library of pre-recorded sounds, instrumental and vocal, single notes and brief passages of music, is available on replaceable tape frames; blank tape frames may also be obtained so that the user can record his own sounds. The instrument can be converted to use standard $\frac{1}{4}''$ (6 mm) tape with two tracks (this type of tape was, in fact, used in the Model 300). Many film and broadcasting companies have taken advantage of the adaptability of the Mellotron and have used it with sound-effects recordings.

BIBLIOGRAPHY
A. Douglas: *The Electronic Musical Instrument Manual: a Guide to Theory and Design* (London, 5/1968), 306
B. Harrigan: 'Mellotron's got it Taped!', *Melody Maker* (10 July 1976), 30
D. Crombie: 'The Mellotron/Novatron Story', *Sound International*, no.19 (1979); rev. in *Rock Hardware: the Instruments, Equipment and Technology of Rock*, ed. T. Bacon (Poole, Dorset, 1981), 91

HUGH DAVIES

Melochord. A monophonic electronic keyboard instrument developed by HARALD BODE in Neubeuern, near Munich, and constructed by him and later by the Häberlein company in Munich. Bode made several versions of the instrument, some with one and others with two manuals, during the years 1947–54. It was partly based on his earlier MELODIUM (1938), and included a similar range of filter and vibrato controls; it also introduced a new solution to the problem of obtaining two timbres on a single manual, which Bode had tackled in his Warbo Formant-Orgel (1937).

The Melochord had a five-octave, touch-sensitive keyboard, which could be split into two parts (two octaves in the bass and three in the treble) to control two independent oscillators. The sections could be independently transposed (by octave units) so that the two voices would overlap, and both sections had a volume pedal. Bode frequently performed on the Melochord for Bayerischer Rundfunk in Munich between 1948 and 1951 in light music and music for plays, sometimes as a soloist with orchestra.

Today the Melochord is best known for its rather brief contribution to the early history of taped electronic music in Germany. Around 1951 Dr Werner Meyer-Eppler obtained a Melochord for the Institut für Phonetik und Kommunikationsforschung of the University of Bonn, where he produced sound materials that were used in the early tape compositions of Herbert Eimert and Robert Beyer. Eimert and Beyer were working in Cologne at a studio that was re-equipped in 1953 as the electronic music studio of Nordwestdeutscher Rundfunk. In the same year Bode constructed for NWDR a special studio model of the Melochord to complement the *elektronische Monochord* that was commissioned at the same time, and to connect with other items of studio equipment. It had two three-octave manuals. On the second manual the normal function of pitch control could be disconnected and the associated pitch-following filter operated from the keyboard to modify the timbre of notes played on the first manual. The instrument could be linked to external devices such as a white-noise generator, a reverberation unit, tape loops and a ring modulator, which could supplement the built-in vibrato and filters. These features make the studio model a precursor of the modular synthesizers introduced in the mid-1960s, a partial prototype of which Bode himself constructed in 1959–60. A slightly later version (1954) was a further step towards the modular synthesizer, for it incorporated devices such as the ring modulator. The Cologne Melochord was, in fact, little used in the studio, because the chief interests of the young composers, such as Stockhausen, who worked there lay in a more analytical approach to sound and in tuning systems that the equal-tempered Melochord could not produce.

BIBLIOGRAPHY

H. Bode: 'Das Melochord des Studios für elektronische Musik im Funkhaus Köln', *Technische Hausmitteilungen des Nordwestdeutschen Rundfunks*, vi/1–2 (1954), 27

T. Rhea: 'Bode's Melodium and Melochord', *Contemporary Keyboard*, vi/1 (1980), 68

HUGH DAVIES

Melodeon. (1) A term extensively used in the USA during the first half of the 19th century to designate a small reed organ with a single keyboard and one or two sets of reeds. The 'rocking melodeon' (also known as the lap or elbow organ) is an instrument of this type played on the lap or on a table; its bellows are activated by a rocking motion of the elbow or the heel of the hand. *See* REED ORGAN, §1.

(2) A button ACCORDION: a rectangular, bellows-operated, free-reed instrument with buttons on the right-hand end of the bellows and buttons or keys on the left-hand side. The instrument is single action in that different notes are produced by each button by the press and draw of the bellows. The right-hand buttons are arranged in one or more rows of ten or eleven, each row producing the pitches of two-and-a-half octaves of a major scale. The left-hand buttons can provide tonic and dominant chords to the keys of the rows, and some additional chords (their use is limited by the bellows direction with which each is associated).

An instrument of this type was first patented by Cyril Demian of Vienna in 1829. Melodeons have been mass-produced and widely exported, largely by German firms, since the mid-19th century, and have been widely used in non-Western societies.

BARBARA OWEN (1), GRAEME SMITH (2)

Melodi. Highest-pitched XYLOPHONE in the KOLINTANG orchestra of Minahasa, North Sulawesi. It has two keyboards of 23 keys each, with notes of the standard major scale on the lower keyboard and the accidentals on the upper keyboard, covering a range of over three octaves. The largest key is about 35 cm long, and the lowest note approximately *B*. The instrument is normally played with two sticks about 10 cm long. It produces the main upper melodic line, often in octaves or 3rds, with frequent glissandos.

MARGARET J. KARTOMI

Melodia. An ORGAN STOP.

Melodica. A keyboard HARMONICA manufactured in soprano and alto versions by Hohner in Trossingen from around 1959. The instrument is rectangular and is held vertically, the diatonic keys being played by the right hand and the chromatic ones by the left; it can produce many chords and clusters that are impossible on the harmonica, but whereas in the latter some reeds sound when sucked and others when blown, the Melodica reeds sound only when they are blown. Because it is made of plastic (apart from the reeds, which are metal), the Melodica can be mass-produced at low cost; this and the ease with which learners can master the keyboard and mouthpiece

(a narrow slit that opens out into the reed chamber) have made it very popular in schools as an alternative to the recorder. The alto Melodica has been called for by composers such as David Bedford, Alison Bauld, Anthony Braxton and Rudolf Komorous, and played by Bedford, Bauld and Graham Hearn in improvisations.

Two types of Melodica are manufactured, each in several models of different ranges: the simpler type has a keyboard (normally of two-octave range) that consists of short rectangular buttons; the other has a conventional keyboard of up to three octaves and can be played on a flat surface like a normal keyboard instrument, with the mouthpiece at the end of an extension tube; Jean Tinguely used a Melodica of the latter type in one of his Méta-harmonie sound sculptures. (A similar instrument, the Pianica, marketed by Yamaha, is based on this version of the Melodica.) In 1967 Hohner produced a three-octave monophonic Electra-Melodica (the range of which can be transposed within nine octaves) in which the pressure of the air blown through a tube mouthpiece is used to control the loudness of an electronic oscillator.

HUGH DAVIES

Mélodiflute. A type of small REED ORGAN produced by the the firm of ALEXANDRE in the late 19th century.

Melodika. (1) Name given by JOHANN ANDREAS STEIN to his invention (1772) of a small pipe organ on which a melody could be played, and in which the wind pressure (and thus the volume) was affected by pressure on the key, while the accompaniment was played on the keyboard instrument on which it was placed.

(2) A free-reed keyboard instrument, a type of aeolina, invented by Wilhelm Vollmer & Sohn of Berlin in 1820.

Melodikon. A type of SOSTENENTE PIANO invented by Pierre Riffelsen of Copenhagen in 1800. The sound was produced by tuning-forks coming into contact with a rotating steel cylinder. The lowest note was *c*. *See also* KLAVIZYLINDER.

Melodina. A type of REED ORGAN patented in 1855 by J. L. N. Fourneaux, son of J. B. NAPOLÉON FOURNEAUX.

Mélodion. A square piano designed in 1805 by JOHANN CHRISTIAN DIETZ (i). The mechanism resembled that of Chladni's KLAVIZYLINDER.

Melodium. A monophonic electronic keyboard instrument developed by HARALD BODE with the assistance of OSKAR VIERLING in Berlin in 1938. The circuitry was largely based on that of Bode's Warbo Formant-Orgel (1937). The four-octave keyboard was touch-sensitive. A dozen knobs and switches on the console (which was the size of an upright piano) operated complex filters, a tuning–transposition control, and controls providing octave doubling and mixtures by means of frequency multiplication and division. A pedal was used to produce vibrato by applying frequency modulation of about 6–8 Hz. For a short period Bode appeared as a performer on the Melodium in music for radio, theatre and films and as a soloist with the Berlin Philharmonic, but in 1941 the instrument was cannibalized during the early stages of the work that led to the construction of the MELOCHORD.

BIBLIOGRAPHY
H. Bode: 'Grundsätzliches zum Selbstbau eines Melodiums', *Funk* (1940), 197
——: 'Bekannte und neue Klänge durch elektrische Musikinstrumente', *Funktechnische Monatshefte* (1940), no.5, p.70; simultaneously pubd in *Funk* (1940), nos.9–10
T. Rhea: 'Bode's Melodium and Melochord', *Contemporary Keyboard*, vi/1 (1980), 68

HUGH DAVIES

Mélodore. An alto clarinet made by Coste of Paris in 1847. It was made of wood and had an upturned brass bell like that of an english horn.

Meloli. Plural of MOLOLI.

Mélophone. A portable free-reed instrument shaped like a guitar, harp or cello with a keyboard and bellows (see illustration). It is 80 to 130 cm high and 32 to 65 cm wide, and is played resting on the right thigh; the right hand works the handle (*archet*) of the bellows, which can produce a vibrato effect on all notes and a trumpet-like tone in certain registers. The left hand works the 40 to 84 keys, some with octave couplings, controlling a range of three to five octaves. The mélophone was invented in 1837 by a Parisian watchmaker, Leclerc,

Mélophone, French, after 1842 (Museum of Fine Arts, Boston)

whose instruments were made in Paris by A. Brown. In 1842 C. A. Pellerin and François Durbain obtained licences to manufacture it; Durbain subsequently developed the harmonium, which eventually superseded the mélophone. According to Galpin (*Grove 5*) the mélophone was 'introduced by Halévy into one of his operas'. Examples of the instrument are in the Instruments Museum of the Brussels Conservatory and the Boston Museum of Fine Arts.

STEPHEN BONNER

Mélophonorgue. An accordion patented by J.-B. Leterme of Paris in 1854 and shown at the Paris Exposition of 1855. Two ranks of reeds tuned approximately a quarter-tone apart produced a tremolo effect.

Melophon-zither. A free-reed instrument in the form of a zither, invented by Burger of Budapest and exhibited at the Paris Exposition of 1900.

Melopiano. A device for use with a piano to enable sustained sounds to be produced; see SOSTENENTE PIANO, §4.

Mélotétraphone. An instrument invented by De Vlaminck and Limonier in 1892 which applied a keyboard of three and a half octaves to the fingerboard of a cello. A smaller model using a viola was also built; this was 80 cm long, 25 cm wide and 28 cm high, and had a compass of two and a half octaves. Similar instruments were later built by Egide Dausaert and Victor Mazel of Brussels.

Membranophone. General term for musical instruments that produce their sound from tightly stretched membranes. Membranophones form one of the four main classes of instruments (along with idiophones, chordophones and aerophones – to which a fifth, electronophones, has recently been added) in the system of CLASSIFICATION devised by E. M. von Hornbostel and C. Sachs and published by them in *Zeitschrift für Ethnologie* in 1914 (Eng. trans. in *GSJ*, xiv, 1961, p.3). Their system, the one most commonly used today, is based on Victor Mahillon's division of instruments according to the nature of their vibrating bodies, which he devised for his catalogue of the instruments in the Royal Conservatory in Brussels. Membranophones are subdivided according to whether they are struck drums, plucked drums, friction drums or singing membranes. Struck drums can be struck directly (as with timpani, side drums, tambourines and so on), or indirectly (as with rattle drums). 'Plucked drums' have a string knotted below the centre of the membrane; when the string is plucked its vibrations are transmitted to the membrane (as with the *gopīyantra* and *ānandalaharī* of India). Recent research has shown these to be, in fact, frequency-doubling chordophones; see VARIABLE TENSION CHORDOPHONE. Friction drums are made to vibrate either by means of a stick (*rommelpot*), a cord or the hand. Singing membranes are those which are made to vibrate by speaking or singing into them, as with the kazoo. Each category may be further subdivided according to the more detailed characteristics of an instrument. To each category, Hornbostel and Sachs gave a number derived from the Dewey decimal library classification system; their classification (from the *GSJ* translation, with minor alterations) follows as an appendix to this article.

HOWARD MAYER BROWN

APPENDIX

2 *Membranophones*: the sound is excited by tightly stretched membranes
21 *Struck drums*: the membranes are struck
211 *Drums struck directly*: the player himself executes the movement of striking; this includes striking by any intermediate devices, such as beaters, keyboards etc; drums that are shaken are excluded
211.1 *Kettledrums* (timpani): the body is bowl- or dish-shaped
211.11 *(Separate) kettledrums* (European timpani)
211.12 *Sets of kettledrums* (West Asian permanently joined pairs of kettledrums)
211.2 *Tubular drums*: the body is tubular
211.21 *Cylindrical drums*: the diameter is the same at the middle and the ends; whether or not the ends taper or have projecting discs is immaterial
211.211 *Single-skin cylindrical drums*: the drum has only one usable membrane. In some African drums a second skin forms part of the lacing device and is not used for beating, and hence does not count as a membrane in the present sense
211.211.1 *Open cylindrical drums*: the end opposite from the membrane is open – found in Malacca [now West Malaysia]

211.211.2 *Closed cylindrical drums*: the end opposite from the membrane is closed – found in the West Indies
211.212 *Double-skin cylindrical drums*: the drum has two usable membranes
211.212.1 *(Individual) cylindrical drums* – found in Europe (side drum)
211.212.2 *Sets of cylindrical drums*
211.22* *Barrel-shaped drums*: the diameter is larger at the middle than at the ends; the body is curvilinear – found in Asia, Africa and ancient Mexico
211.23 *Double-conical drums*: the diameter is larger at the middle than at the ends; the body is rectilinear with angular profile – found in India (*mṛdaṅga*)
211.24* *Hourglass-shaped drums*: the diameter is smaller at the middle than at the ends – found in Asia, Melanesia and East Africa
211.25* *Conical drums*: the diameters at the ends differ considerably (minor departures from conicity, inevitably met, are disregarded here) – found in India
211.26* *Goblet-shaped drums*: the body consists of a main section which is either cup-shaped or cylindrical, and a slender stem; borderline cases of this basic design, like those occurring notably in Indonesia, do not affect the identification, so long as a cylindrical form is not in fact reached (*darabukka*)
211.3 *Frame drums*: the depth of the body does not exceed the radius of the membrane; NB the European side drum, even in its most shallow form, is a development from the long cylindrical drum and hence is not included among frame drums
211.31 *Frame drums (without handle)*
211.311 *Single-skin frame drums* (tambourine)
211.312 *Double-skin frame drums* – found in North Africa
211.32 *Frame drum with handle*: a stick is attached to the frame in line with its diameter
211.321 *Single-skin frame drums with handle* (Inuit)
211.322 *Double-skin frame drums with handle* – found in Tibet
212 *Rattle drums* (sub-divisions as for drums struck directly, 211): the drum is shaken; percussion is by impact of pendent or enclosed pellets, or similar objects – found in India and Tibet
22 *Plucked drums*: a string is knotted below the centre of the membrane; when the string is plucked, its vibrations are transmitted to the membrane – found in India (*gopīyantra, ānandalaharī*)
23 *Friction drums*: the membrane is made to vibrate by friction
231 *Friction drums with stick*: a stick is in contact with the membrane is either itself rubbed, or is employed to rub the membrane
231.1 *With inserted stick*: the stick passes through a hole in the membrane
231.11 *Friction drums with fixed stick*: the stick cannot be moved; the stick alone is subjected to friction by rubbing – found in Africa
231.12 *Friction drums with semi-fixed stick*: the stick is movable to a sufficient extent to rub the membrane when it is itself rubbed by the hand – found in Africa
231.13 *Friction drums with free stick*: the stick can be moved freely; it is not itself rubbed, but is employed to rub the membrane – found in Venezuela
231.2 *With tied stick*: the stick is tied to the membrane in an upright position – found in Europe
232 *Friction drum with cord*: a cord, attached to the membrane, is rubbed
232.1 *Stationary friction drum with cord*: the drum is held stationary – found in Europe and Africa
232.11 *Single-skin stationary drums with friction cord*
232.12 *Double-skin stationary drums with friction cord*
232.2 *Friction drum with whirling stick*: the drum is whirled on a cord which rubs on a [resined] notch in the holding stick (*Waldteufel* [cardboard buzzer]) – found in Europe, India and East Africa
233 *Hand friction drums*: the membrane is rubbed by the hand
24 *Singing membranes* (kazoos): the membrane is made to vibrate by speaking or singing into it; the membrane does not yield a note of its own but merely modifies the voice – found in Europe and West Africa
241 *Free kazoos*: the membrane is incited directly, without the wind first passing through a chamber (comb-and-paper)
242 *Tube or vessel-kazoos*: the membrane is placed inside a tube or box – found in Africa (while also East Asian flutes with a lateral hole sealed by a membrane exhibit an adulteration of the principle of the tube kazoo)

Suffixes for use with any division of this class:

6 with membrane glued to drum
7 with membrane nailed to drum
8 with membrane laced to drum
81 *Cord- (ribbon-) bracing*: the cords are stretched from membrane to membrane or arranged in the form of a net, without employing any of the devices described below

811 *without special devices for stretching* – found everywhere
812 *with tension ligature*: cross ribbons or cords are tied round the middle of the lacing to increase its tension – found in Sri Lanka
813 *with tension loops*: the cords are laced in a zig-zag; every pair of strings is caught together with a small ring or loop – found in India
814 *with wedge bracing*: wedges are inserted between the wall of the drum and the cords of the lacing; by adjusting the position of the wedges it is possible to control the tension – found in India, Indonesia and Africa
82 *Cord-and-hide bracing*: the cords are laced at the lower end to a non-sonorous piece of hide – found in Africa
83 *Cord-and-board bracing*: the cords are laced to an auxiliary board at the lower end – found in Sumatra
84 *Cord-and-flange bracing*: the cords are laced at the lower end to a flange carved from the solid – found in Africa
85 *Cord-and-belt bracing*: the cords are laced at the lower end to a belt of different material – found in India
86 *Cord-and-peg bracing*: the cords are laced at the lower end to pegs stuck into the wall of the drum – found in Africa
NB 82 to 86 are sub-divided as 81 above
9 *with membrane lapped on*: a ring is slipped over the edge of the membrane
91 *with membrane lapped on by ring of cord* – found in Africa
92 with membrane lapped on by a hoop
921 without mechanism (European drum)
922 with mechanism
9221 without pedal (machine timpani)
9222 with pedals (pedal timpani)
*To be sub-divided like 211.21
Appendix reprinted from Hornbostel and Sachs, 1914 (by permission of Limbach Verlag, Berlin); Eng. trans., 1961

Mendoza, Domingo de (*b* Lerín, *c*1670; *d* Madrid, 1734). Spanish organ builder. He was a pupil of Juan de Andueza. On the recommendation of the organist Andrés Lorente he built two new organs at Cuenca Cathedral (1692–5). In Madrid he made instruments for the convent of S Felipe el Real (1694) and S María de la Almudena (1696). Charles II of Spain named him maker to his court in 1695 and deputy builder to the royal chapel in 1697. He built new organs at the cathedrals of Sigüenza (1699–1701) and Ávila (1700–01), and maintained the instruments at the primatial church at Toledo and the collegiate church at Pastrana. He was one of the best Spanish organ builders of his time.

GUY BOURLIGUEUX

Mendzan [mendzang, medzang, mendjan, menjyang]. XYLOPHONE of the Beti people at Yaoundé in Cameroon and of the Fang/Pahuin peoples in southern Cameroon and northern Gabon. The term is applied both generically for all xylophones and specifically for a portable xylophone whose strung keys are suspended over a frame of light wood with a gourd resonator under each key. Each resonator has a small hole in the side covered with a fine membrane to form a mirliton. The xylophone is slung by a strap round the player's neck and beaten with either two softwood sticks or two rubber-padded beaters; an arched hoop, resting on the player's thighs, keeps the instrument away from his body. Xylophones are played in ensembles, each instrument having its own name according to its function and number of keys. At Yaoundé, for example, the *omvek* has eleven keys, the *akuda-omvek* ten, the *nyia-mendzang* eight and the *endum*, which has large, solid keys and is used solely for rhythmic purposes, has just four; the ensemble can include the *mvet* (stick zither), clapperless bells and a wicker rattle.

BIBLIOGRAPHY
P.-C. Ngumu: *Les mendzan des chanteurs de Yaoundé* (Vienna, 1978)
K. A. GOURLAY

Mengeris. Single-headed drum of Sarawak, Malaysia.

Meno (It.: 'less'). A word used both adjectivally and adverbially as an adjustment to a tempo or expression mark. *Meno mosso*, normally found in the middle of a movement, indicates a change to a slower tempo. Occasionally it comes at the beginning: the most famous case is Schoenberg's Second String Quartet which opens with the instruction *etwas langsamer anfangend* ('beginning a little more slowly').

Mensur (Ger.). SCALING.

Mentoniera (It.; Fr. *mentonnière*). CHIN REST.

Menza gwe [kalangwa]. Calabash-resonated XYLOPHONE of the Ngbandi people of Zaïre. *See* KALANGBA, (1).

Meporo. Set of four end-blown single-note stopped flutes of the Tswana/Lete people of Botswana. These are the tenor flutes in the DITLHAKA stopped flute ensemble; the set of four bass flutes is called *meporo e metelele*. The other sets are *dinokwana* (alto) and *metenyane* (treble). They were originally made from reeds, but latterly from metal tubing. See *TraceyCSA*, ii, 263.

Mercator [Krämer], Sir **Michael** (*b* Venlo, 1491; *d* 1544). Dutch or German harpsichord maker. He was a maker of virginals to Floris, Count of Egmont. In 1526 he was in England and was included in a list of the musical establishment of Henry VIII and between 1529 and 1532 made 'virginals' for both Henry VIII and Cardinal Wolsey. In 1539 a medal was struck in his honour (perhaps by Hagenauer); an example is in the Department of Coins and Medals at the British Museum.

BIBLIOGRAPHY
A. J. Hipkins: *Musical Instruments, Historic, Rare, and Unique* (Edinburgh, 1887, 2/1921/R1945), v [illustration of the medal]
GUY OLDHAM

Merklin, Joseph (*b* Oberhausen, 17 Jan 1819; *d* Nancy, 10 June 1905). German organ builder. He studied under his father, an organ builder in Freiburg, and under Walcker and Korfmacher. He set up a firm in Brussels in 1843, and in 1853 formed Merklin, Schütze & Cie. Two years later he bought the Ducroquet firm in Paris (*see* DAUBLAINE & CALLINET) and enlarged the organization, with its main office in Lyons from about 1870 (he sold the Lyons firm to Kuhn in 1894, as Michel, Merklin & Kuhn, which after Kuhn's death in 1925 continued as a limited company: *see* KUHN, THEODOR). Merklin was a prolific builder, and a rival to Cavaillé-Coll; but his organs were designed to suit current taste, and many have since been rebuilt. Notable instruments include at Paris St Eugène (1855, 33 stops) and St Eustache (1879, 72), and several at French cathedrals (Bourges, 1860; Arras, 1862; Clermont-Ferrand, 1878; Strasbourg, choir organ, 1878) as well as others abroad. He wrote *Notice sur l'électricité aux grandes orgues* (1887).

Merlin, John Joseph (*b* Huy, nr. Liège, 1735; *d* Paddington, London, 1803). Flemish instrument maker and inventor. He came to England in 1760, and in 1774 patented a 'compound harpsichord' which included a piano action. He also made pianos, besides various inventions

including an invalid chair (which is still used today). A 'compound harpsichord' dated 1780 is in the Deutsches Museum, Munich.

The patent of 1774 claimed that the piano action could be applied to 'an harpsichord of the common kind already made', but the instrument now in Munich is anything but 'common'. From its single manual are played four sets of strings (16', 8', 8' and 4') carried on three bridges; the harpsichord can activate 16', 8' and 4' strings, and the piano (with its action above the strings) 16', 8' and 8'. One row of 8' strings can be undamped; a 'Welsh harp' buffs the 16'; two pedals affect the 16' and pedal action respectively. In addition, the instrument carries a recording device: a clockwork-activated roll of paper may be pricked by the 4' jacks.

Merlin's extravagance of invention should not detract from his positive contribution to the more important basic elements of piano making. The six-octave (*C'* to *c''''*) piano ordered from him by Burney in 1777 shows that he had a realistic idea of the instrument's future requirements; if only for this reason he should not be considered purely as a dynamic-obsessed inventor.

See also HARPSICHORD-PIANO.

BIBLIOGRAPHY
R. E. M. Harding: *The Piano-forte: its History Traced to the Great Exhibition of 1851* (Cambridge, 1933, rev. 2/1978)
R. Russell: *The Harpsichord and Clavichord* (London, 1959, rev. 2/1973)
F. Hubbard: *Three Centuries of Harpsichord Making* (Cambridge, Mass., 1965)
DONALD HOWARD BOALCH, PETER WILLIAMS

Merline (Fr.). A type of bird organ; *see* BIRD INSTRUMENTS.

Meropa. Plural of MOROPA.

Messa di voce (It.: 'placing of the voice'). The singing or playing of a long note so that it begins quietly, swells to full volume, and then diminishes to the original quiet tone. The *messa di voce* was at first looked upon as an ornament. Although originally part of vocal technique the *messa di voce* has also been used in instrumental music. Several treatises, including those for trumpet by Fantini (1638), for flute by Quantz (1752) and for violin by North (1728), Geminiani (1751) and L'Abbé *le fils* (1761), contain descriptions of the *messa di voce*, often (though not always) using the actual term.

Mesto (It.: 'sad', 'sorrowful', 'dejected'). A tempo or mood designation used primarily in the 19th century. The word itself was used in musical contexts by Zarlino (1558) and by Bernardino Bottazzi (1614), as well as by Monteverdi in a celebrated direction in *Il ritorno d'Ulisse*: 'Finita sinfonia in *tempo allegro*, si incomincia la seguente *mesta*, alla bassa sin che Penelope sarà gionta in scena per dar principio al canto'. But this did not bring the word into current musical vocabulary. The most famous uses are probably by Beethoven, who marked the slow movement of his Piano Sonata op.10 no.3 *largo e mesto* and that of his String Quartet op.59 no.1 *adagio molto e mesto*. Bartók's Sixth Quartet opens *mesto*.

For bibliography *see* TEMPO AND EXPRESSION MARKS.
DAVID FALLOWS

Mesuré (Fr.: 'measured'). In time. Couperin (1716) described it as an instruction to play regularly, not freely, and thus as the equivalent of *tempo giusto*. For Rousseau (1768), however, it was the French equivalent of *a tempo* or *a battuta*, an indication to return to the correct tempo after a deviation or specifically at the end of a recitative. Both uses are found in French music of the 18th century.

For bibliography *see* TEMPO AND EXPRESSION MARKS.

DAVID FALLOWS

Méta-harmonie. The generic name of a series of three large sound sculptures incorporating musical instruments and sonorous scrap objects, constructed in 1977–80 by JEAN TINGUELY. Méta-harmonie II (1979; 3·8 × 6·9 × 1·6 metres) runs by means of pulleys and drive belts, powered by several electric motors, and resembles a highly individual combination of the sort of machinery used in a water-mill and an orchestrion (for illustration *see* SOUND SCULPTURE, fig.1). Its sounds are those of an idiosyncratic percussion ensemble, though some are sustained and almost electronic in character; these are produced by two keyboard reed instruments, a Melodica and a toy reed organ, each with a range of just over two octaves, whose notes are played by wheels that move slowly to and fro across the keyboards (only the black keys of the organ are played). The other musical instruments used are side drums, bongos, woodblocks, cymbals, cowbells and other bells, tam-tams and an old upright piano ('played' by two toy figures and a clog); these are supplemented by glass bowls, metal shapes, saucepans and a large tin can.

HUGH DAVIES

Métallicorde à archet. A large, bowed guitar-shaped instrument with metal strings patented by Aloysio of Paris in 1873. It had the resonance of a violin.

Metallophone. A generic term for percussion instruments that consist of a series of tuned metal bars arranged in a single or double row (for details of the Hornbostel–Sachs classification *see* IDIOPHONE). Instruments made of metal slabs were known in China by AD 700. An instrument of Turkish origin consisting of 16 slabs of metal suspended in an upright frame is said to have been introduced into China in the 7th century. Bronze slabs came two centuries later in the form of the Javanese SARON. This bronze metallophone differs from the earliest instruments in that the slabs are suspended horizontally over a cradle of wood similar to the trough xylophone. The *saron* and a similar instrument, the GENDER, have distinctive roles in the GAMELAN ensemble. In the *gender* the tone of each bar is enriched by means of bamboo tubes which are placed in the framework in a vertical position under the slabs. Each bar is tuned by adjusting its length to sound in unison with its corresponding slab.

The Far Eastern metallophones have influenced certain Western orchestral percussion instruments such as the GLOCKENSPIEL and VIBRAPHONE. In modern compositions the term 'metallophone' is applied to a series of alloy bars suspended over a resonance box. The bars are arranged in a single row or in keyboard fashion. A damping mechanism is incorporated in certain models. In some cases the sustaining power is controlled by a magnetized strip of metal which is moved towards or away from the nodal points.

Carl Orff scored for metallophones in a number of his compositions, and in a simple form metallophones are included in 'school percussion'.

The following metallophones are entered in this dictionary: adiaphonon; aiuton; analapos; bell-lyra; bisak beton; celesta; cempres; ch'ŏrhyang; dulcitone; fanxiang; gambang gangsa; gangsa (ii); gender; giying; glockenspiel; handchime; harpophone; jegogan; jublag; kane; kecer; kei; kenyir; klavizylinder; marimba gongs; marimbaphone; panghyang; panmelodikon; penyacah; ranāṭ; rincik (i); saron; saron gantung; selundeng; slenṭem; slenṭo; thālī; tubaphone; vibraphone.

JAMES BLADES

Metallstabharfe (Ger. 'metal rod harp'). A type of NAIL VIOLIN, with metal rods played with rosined gloves.

Métaphone. An accessory stop on French reed organs, patented by Charles Mustel (son of VICTOR MUSTEL) in 1878. It mutes the tone of the instrument by partly closing the reed cell apertures with a strip of soft leather. *See also* REED ORGAN, §2.

Metenyane. Set of four end-blown single-note stopped flutes of the Tswana/Lete people of Botswana. These are the treble flutes in the DITLHAKA stopped flute ensemble. For other sets *see* MEPORO.

Metronome (from Gk. *metron*: 'measure' and *nomos*: 'law'; Fr. *métronome*; Ger. *Metronom, Taktmesser*; It. *metronomo*). An apparatus for establishing musical tempo; more specifically the clockwork-driven double-pendulum device perhaps invented about 1812 by DIETRICH NIKOLAUS WINKEL but refined and patented by JOHANN NEPOMUK MAELZEL in 1815. The name seems to have entered the English and French languages specifically on Maelzel's patents filed in London and Paris; and there is no apparent evidence of its earlier use in any European language.

1. Uses. 2. The 'chronomètre' and other pendulum time-keepers. 3. The metronome and other clockwork devices. 4. Electric and electronic devices.

1. USES. Traditionally the metronome has had two main purposes which should be considered quite separately.

(*a*) To establish an appropriate tempo. Nearly all the main developments have been driven by the need for composers and editors to fix the tempo they considered appropriate for a particular work (but *see* TEMPO AND EXPRESSION MARKS, §4). This began to seem necessary for the first time in the late 17th century when the music of different nationalities evolved markedly different styles and performance conventions but was internationally available. Thus Etienne Loulié (1696) justified his *chronomètre* – the earliest calibrated pendulum for music – by stating with heavy sarcasm that it was of no use to those who knew both French and foreign music intimately, to those who considered only music in the style of Lully to be worth performing, or to those who felt that it did not matter at what speed a work was performed; and he asserted that a composer had managed to send works to Italy with considerable success by attaching such arithmetical tempo indications to them. The need was felt even more strongly at the end of the 18th century when music moved away from the TEMPO GIUSTO that had hitherto governed most music in any particular tradition. The years around 1700 and shortly after 1800 therefore produced the main advances in the history of musical time-keepers. But it may well be true that the metronome would never have become ubiquitous without Beethoven's brief flirtation with it, resulting from his relatively short friendship with Maelzel; this is so even though Beethoven's markings for his own works have normally been ignored or assumed to be wrong. Many would still subscribe to Rousseau's view (1768) that the best metronome for these purposes is a sufficiently sensitive musician who has studied the music carefully.

(*b*) To establish consistency of tempo through a work or an exercise. On this practice there have been marked trends of approval and disapproval, with many fine teachers asserting that it is antimusical and promotes only wooden performance. The earliest writer to suggest such a device was Thomas Mace (1676) who proposed a bullet 'or any *Round Piece*, or what *weighty thing you please*, to the weight of *half a Pound*, or a *Pound*, (more or less)' suspended from the ceiling. He pointed out that the shorter string will have a quicker motion and that 'therefore a *Long String* is *Best* to *Practice* with, *at first*'. Mace was particularly concerned with the habit of changing speed as the music became more complex, as in a set of variations, something that can still be heard in the performances of many first-rate musicians. Related to this use is the practice of taking a technically difficult piece, or more particularly an exercise, at various tempos as regulated by a metronome. Czerny has exercises to be taken at crotchet = 60 and then by gradual increments up to crotchet = 120; and several teachers have advocated practising a work at speeds faster and slower than seems musically correct (and therefore necessarily requiring a metronome to keep them steady) in order to produce more relaxed and controlled playing at a musical tempo. In 1804 J. F. Reichardt observed that even the finest musicians had been unable to play more than a few bars against the clockwork time-keeper devised by J.-A.-C. Charles (see §3); and other writers (among them Mersenne, 1636–7) had similarly implied a preference for flexible tempo.

In the 20th century two further uses have brought with them the need for more sophisticated and adaptable mechanisms.

(*c*) Synchronization. Film composers must almost invariably calculate their music to a fully edited film. Advertising jingles must be judged to a specific 'slot' measured in seconds. In both cases absolute precision is clearly essential, even though the advent of digital recording makes it easy to adjust the length of recorded material. The recording of a commercial lyric in several superimposed layers is best done against a metronomic pulse (normally transferred to the conductor through earphones) rather than against a recording of the previously recorded track or tracks: obviously, if the first recorded track is in any way metrically irregular the synchronization of further tracks will be extremely difficult. Stockhausen's *Gruppen* (1955–7), for three orchestras, calls for 12 different tempos more or less evenly distributed between crotchet = 60 and crotchet = 120: only three of his 12 tempos appear on the traditional metronome. Examples of this kind of use could be multiplied.

(*d*) Comparison of recorded performances. A precise documentation of tempos can help define the style or characteristics of a particular performer or conductor. This use has not yet been exploited with any great rigour, if only because it is rarely possible to define any single movement with a single metronome mark.

(*e*) Finally, the metronome considered largely as an *objet trouvé* (with a heavy inbuilt symbolism) appears as a musical instrument in its own right. Examples include the opening of Ravel's *L'heure espagnole* (1907–9), the third movement ('Cloche-pied au flic') of Villa-Lobos's *Suite suggestive* (1929) and Ligeti's *Poème symphonique* (1962) for 100 metronomes.

2. THE 'CHRONOMÈTRE' AND OTHER PENDULUM TIME-KEEPERS. At the ends of the long multi-section works in his *Polyhymnia caduceatrix* (1619) and his *Puericinium* (1621) Michael Praetorius gave their length in *tempora*; and in his *Syntagma musicum* (iii, 88) he stated that 160 *tempora* would last a quarter of an hour. This tempo (minim = 43) seems improbably slow; but evidently for him and his contemporaries the *tempus* was at least thought not to vary significantly. Similarly Johannes Vetulus de Anagnia 250 years earlier could say that the *brevis* in a trecento *novenaria* lasted $2\frac{1}{2}$ seconds (if Gullo, 1964, has interpreted him correctly). So it is perhaps not surprising that Galileo Galilei's investigations into the workings of a pendulum had no immediate impact on music, whereas they were quickly used in medicine for calculating pulse, following a technique attributed to Santorio Santorio (1561–1636). Mersenne (1636–7) gave an elaborate description of the workings of a pendulum, establishing $3\frac{1}{2}$ feet (1·06 metres) as the length that would beat once a second (*Mouvement des corps*, ii, §§14–16; *De la composition*, v, §11); and he even suggested that a composer wishing to send his music to Constantinople, Persia or China might like to indicate its tempo by means of pendulum lengths (*Des instruments a cordes*, iii, §18). But his scattered and repetitive discussion had no apparent influence in a world that felt little need to communicate music to China; and he implied that the current flexibility of performance tempos would require several different pendulums in the course of a single piece. Mace, though applying the pendulum to music, used it merely to establish stability of tempo (see §1 (b)); the writings of Robert Boyle (1627–91) refer to a 'skilled musician of my acquaintance' doing the same (see Kassler, 1979).

Loulié's famous *chronomètre* was the first device for defining tempo, made necessary simply by the difference between French and Italian music in his time (see fig.1). It was a pendulum mounted on a frame 72 *pouces* (approximately inches) high. The frame was calibrated, and a peg on the fixed end of the cord could be plugged in at various points on the frame, thereby adjusting the length of the hanging part of the cord which formed the pendulum. Its main disadvantage was that the calibrations on the frame were in *pouces* without any intrinsic musical significance and were therefore meaningless to anybody who did not possess a *chronomètre* of Loulié's design. There is no further evidence of its use, though it was to be mentioned and described by many subsequent writers as the first attempt at a musical time-keeper.

Joseph Sauveur (1701) refined Loulié's idea by devising for his *chronomètre* a calibration that made more general sense: the length of each beat was calculated in units of a *tierce* ($\frac{1}{60}$ of a second). His system of *tierces* became standard in the 18th century, and was first used for printed music by L'Affilard soon afterwards in the fifth edition (1705) of his *Principes* where many songs are given such tempo marks – with the added refinement of signs to indicate how many such beats appear in each bar. (It should be mentioned here that Sauveur's *échomètre* was not a time-keeping device at all but a comparative scale that related Loulié's figures to his own *chronomètre* figures as well as to the vibrations of particular pitches.)

If Sauveur had improved the conceptual basis of Loulié's invention, D'Onsembray (1732) improved on it mechanically. By means of a highly sophisticated set of pulleys and a dial, his *métromètre* could measure Sauveur's *tierces* with considerable precision, giving beats from 30 to 68 *tierces* in length, divided into 76 steps each of a half-*tierce*; and a click identified the beginning of each swing. (An example of D'Onsembray's *métromètre* survives in the Conservatoire des Arts et Métiers, Paris, Inv. 1396.)

Further inventions followed, though the exact nature of their novelty is often no longer clear. Fougeau de Moralec attempted to perfect a device that established tempo by means of dripping water (Hellouin, 1900). Godefroi de Viltaneuse produced a *métromètre* in 1779 (mentioned in Grétry, 1797). The composer Jean-Baptiste Davaux devised a *chronomètre* that was manufactured for him by Bréguet; and he included its numbers for his symphonies op.11 of 1784. Almost simultaneously another system was launched, the *plexi-chronomètre* of Renaudin, which had the blessing of the Ecole Royale de Chant. This (like that of D'Onsembray) included an audible click, and seems from his own description to have worked like a small musical box, its main virtue being its small size ($4\frac{1}{2} \times 3\frac{1}{2} \times 3\frac{1}{2}$ *pouces*). A vitriolic correspondence on the relative merits of the two new machines followed in the *Journal de France* (ed. in Brook, 1962, i, 502ff). The firm of Renaudin also marketed a simple pendulum at a much lower price (see Jefferson, 1786).

The *rhythmomètre* of Dubos (given in *FétisB* – perhaps following Weber, 1830 – as 'Duclos' and with the date 1782 for 1787) was rejected by the Académie Royale des Sciences on 30 March 1787 (see Cohen, 1981,

70) but presented to the king and queen on 13 January and eagerly accepted by the Ecole Royale de Chant headed by Gossec (see Brook, 1962, i, 314) for its accuracy and flexibility; no details of its construction seem to survive.

Meanwhile, however, the pendulum was also being used for infinitely simpler devices. William Tans'ur (1746) devoted six pages to the subject, but in terms of specific advice to the musician he found it sufficient to mention that a pendulum 39·2 inches (99·6 cm) long would beat once a second. Similarly Robert Bremner (1756) proposed that a pendulum 8' 8" (2·64 metres) long should be 'hung at the End of all Schools where Church music is taught'. And on a slightly more refined level Henry-Louis Choquel (1759, 2/1762) even applied tempo marks by giving the length of the pendulum needed for each piece, for example (p.176): 'on en aura le mouvement en donnant 18 pouces de longueur au cordon'. (Evidently this was an original idea, for in the preface to the second edition (1762) he stated, in a different context, that he had only just come across Loulié's *Elements*.)

Gabory (1770) had found a simple pendulum sufficient, and Mason (1801) described one in some detail. Thomas Wright used a highly ingenious system in his keyboard concerto of *c*1795, defining in a preface the length of the pendulum as 'the breadth of [a certain number of] Harpsichord and Piano Forte keys, in preference to inches, the former being always at hand, and the difference in Instruments in this respect, so trifling, as to occasion little or no alteration'. Wright seems also to have marketed a simple pendulum working in this way (*see* WRIGHT, THOMAS). Other such devices in England include James Peck's Pendulum or Pocket Metrometer of *c*1803, as well as Rudolph Ackermann's Regulator (a calibrated cord with a weight) and Balance Regulator (the same on a 28 cm frame) of *c*1812 (see Kassler, 1979).

Indeed even after the invention of Maelzel's metronome had quickly made most other systems obsolete, Gottfried Weber continued to recommend the simplicity of the ordinary hand-held pendulum, with its length as the information that should be carried in musical scores: several works by Spohr survive with such measurements in Rhenish inches. Zmeskall followed this by suggesting that the pendulum be calibrated with Maelzel's numbers. It is difficult to say how soon his advice was followed; but such devices are available to this day in the form of suitably calibrated tape-measures with the tape-container serving as the weight.

In the later 19th century other gravity metronomes were devised, among them those of Ihlenburg, Chiappani, Mahagoni (according to Barbacci, 1969) and particularly the highly successful device patented by A. Pinfold of Bradford (fig.2), a balanced weight over a horizontal bar: its mechanics owed much to the Maelzel/Winkel invention (see §3), but its devastating simplicity coupled with its considerable elegance ensured wide sales.

Concerning the more elaborate and sophisticated pendulum devices, various disadvantages seemed important in the years around 1800. First, their size, that of Thiémé (1801) being some 9' (2·75 metres) tall; second, their silence, since it was difficult to perceive the precise moment of change by eye (and several later developments boasted their audibility as an advantage); and third, the lack of a calibration that made musical sense. All

1. 'Chronomètre':
engraving from Loulié's
'Elements ou principes
de musique' (1696)

2. Gravity metronome by A. Pinfold, Bradford, c1890 (Metropolitan Museum of Art, New York)

these disadvantages were rectified in one or other of the 18th-century inventions: Renaudin's was small, as were several of the simple pendulums; D'Onsembray and Renaudin had audible clicks; and Thiémé even mentioned calculations of tempo in beats per minute (as did Thomas Jefferson, 1786), though his actual machine evidently used Sauveur's system of *tierces*. But Guthmann (1806–7) defined all these ideals as being necessary for his 'New time machine which, however, is yet to be invented'. And it seems that one of the major factors in Maelzel's success was his system of counting tempo in terms of beats per minute.

3. THE METRONOME AND OTHER CLOCKWORK DEVICES. Zacconi (1592, f.20v) had associated the movements of a clock with musical movement, though purely as a way of illustrating how various note values move at their own speeds (just as do the differently sized wheels in a clock). But clocks had been common in Europe from the 13th century, with their invention reputedly going back to the 10th century. Apparently the first writer to suggest setting tempos in terms of a clock was William Turner (1724) who described the speed of crotchets in reversed ₵ mensuration as 'counted as fast as the regular Motions of a *Watch*'. Similarly Robert Bremner in the second (1763) edition of his *Rudiments* lamented that his earlier (1756) suggestion of a ubiquitous pendulum (see §2) had not been well received, so he now proposed the use of a clock 'and count the *seconds*, or motions of the pendulum in fours'. Tans'ur (1746) seems to be suggesting the same device.

The theory that Christoph Semmler of Halle (1669–1740) invented a metronome in the 1720s seems to derive only from a statement in Kandler (1817) in an article

that is otherwise largely taken straight from Maelzel's publicity leaflet. As already mentioned, Renaudin's *plexichronomètre* of 1784 apparently worked like a musical box. In 1786 the French physician Jacques-Alexandre-César Charles devised a clockwork *chronomètre musical* some two metres high and he apparently continued to modify it until 1802 when it was seen in action by J. F. Reichardt (1804). In 1798 Anthony George Eckhardt patented in London a clockwork time-keeper calibrated in 'moments' (ten per second) in degrees from five to 100 moments: a barrel drove three interlocking toothed wheels that operated hammers to beat at the required interval of moments. There is no trace of this actually having been manufactured. In 1800 G. E. Stöckel invited subscriptions for his 'Chronometer', built like a large wall-clock with a 2′ (61 cm) pendulum and clearly audible hammers and bells. In spite of written support from J. F. Reichardt, Stöckel had little success; at least, in 1803 he advertised a smaller 'improved model', again inviting subscriptions but this time being more cautious about the terms under which he would actually manufacture the *Zeitmesser*. This time too he had a longer list of famous supporters, including Reichardt, Türk and Rochlitz, but there is again no evidence that the device was ever manufactured.

Among several other new machines of those years, most of which are known only from a brief reference or description, are: a time-keeper by John Chancellor (Coggins, c1822); a chronometer by Henry Smart, brother of Sir George Smart (Coggins, illustrated in Harding, 1938, pl.18), built after the manner of a barrel organ and probably deriving from Eckhardt's machine; a machine in the shape of a pocket-watch made by Sparrevogn of Copenhagen (1817); a new pendulum by Despréaux (described by Fétis as representing no advance on Loulié's original invention of 125 years earlier); a machine for beating time by Charles Claggett (c1793), the Timonicon (c1825) of Mr Galbreath and a 'musical timekeeper' (c1829) by J. B. Barnard (all documented in Kassler, 1979); and other devices by Siegmund Neukomm (1815) and perhaps by Charles Neate in London (mentioned in Lichtenthal, 1826, as 'Neath', though this may refer simply to Neate's description of the Wright pendulum).

This quantity of new machines and of literature describing them was to some extent symptomatic of a general feeling that the time was ripe for a machine that would gain universal acceptance. But it also had two direct consequences. It stimulated considerable interest, so that many leading musicians were concerned with the question of precise tempo even if (or perhaps because) they were dissatisfied with the chronometers that were by then available. And it brought with it a substantial body of expertise and experiment. In short it prepared the ground for Maelzel, a man with relatively little technical or scientific knowledge but considerable musical skill, mechanical experience and business sense.

None of the earlier attempts had achieved any wide or lasting success. Maelzel came to the chronometer about 1808, having spent some years making and demonstrating mechanical instruments of various kinds, both musical and non-musical; and he then devoted over 15 years to refining and promoting his device. The result was a metronome of such perfection that modern metronomes (in the strict sense) differ little from his final model.

To judge from descriptions, his prototype (first mentioned in *AMZ*, 1 Dec 1813) was an ungainly pendulum machine somewhat like that of Stöckel; and its only significant characteristic was that it calculated tempo in terms of beats per minute. It had a range from 48 beats per minute to 160. The story of Beethoven's having composed his canon in honour of Maelzel, *Ta ta ta*, in 1813 must now be discarded as a fiction of Schindler's (if only because it includes the word 'Metronom', not known before 1815), but the *AMZ* report of 1813 states that both Beethoven and Salieri were interested in the new machine. And that is a clue to Maelzel's flair for publicity, one of the qualities without which he would probably have had no more success than the many other makers and inventors mentioned in this article.

On a promotional journey in 1815 Maelzel demonstrated his prototype to Winkel in Amsterdam. Winkel had created something similar, though the small scale of his operation and his general lack of promotion meant that he would never have achieved international success (an example of his 1814 machine is in the Gemeentemuseum, The Hague; reproduced in Kolneder, 1980). On the other hand, Winkel had the clue to reducing the size of the machine, namely a double-ended pendulum which effectively quartered the necessary length of the stem. (This in turn probably owed much to the investigations of the English scientist Henry Kater (1777–1835), who is famous for having brought the understanding of the pendulum to such a point that it could be used to define the exact length of a foot.)

There can be little doubt that Maelzel treated Winkel unscrupulously. According to a later inquiry (reported in de Vos Willems, 1829), Maelzel offered to buy the invention from Winkel. When his offer was refused he simply went to London and Paris, patenting in both cities a new machine – for which he devised the name 'metronome' – incorporating Winkel's crucial insight.

Kolneder (1980) has shown that Maelzel had in fact planned to set up the London factory some years previously, as noted in the *AMZ* article of 1813; and when he met Winkel he was on his way to London with his financial support organized, so Winkel's contribution may have been only a refinement. But Maelzel must nevertheless have worked quickly. The patents were ratified on 1 June 1815 in London and on 14 September 1815 in Paris. By the end of 1816 he had issued a short guide to its use in French (1816); and his letters to Breitkopf & Härtel state that he had also published a *Metronomic Tutor* in English. Further to that, he sent metronomes to 200 composers all over Europe (see Haupt, 1927, p.130, letter of 8 April 1817) – a further example of his commercial initiative. On 18 July 1816 the Leipzig *AMZ* was able to announce that the new metronome was being manufactured in London and in Paris, to regret that Maelzel had not seen fit to entrust his work to German manufacturers, and to state that metronomes from Paris were already on sale at Breitkopf & Härtel's shop.

This new 1815–16 metronome – the one on which all the surviving Beethoven markings were made – was a metal box some 31 cm high; and although the pendulum worked like the later one its calibrations were only from 50 to 160 – in twos from 50 to 60, in threes from 60 to 72, in fours from 72 to 120, in sixes from 120 to 144 and in eights from 144 to 160. (Examples survive in the Gesellschaft der Musikfreunde, Vienna (see fig.3); the private collection of Paul Badura-Skoda, Vienna; and at the Brussels Conservatory.) Within a few years several major composers had issued Maelzel Metronome

(MM) numbers for works by themselves and others. And even though many composers soon concluded that the supposed accuracy of metronome indications was musically speaking a pure chimera, Beethoven's acceptance of it was in itself enough to ensure survival for Maelzel's system.

Considerable research still needs to be done on the developments over the following years during which Maelzel continued to change and refine his metronomes. Already in 1817 he was making silent gravity-driven metronomes which he abandoned in 1821 as being unpopular. From 1821 he started making all his metronomes in mahogany rather than metal (fig.4). In 1828 a clock maker in Amiens named Bienaimé-Fournier had evolved a machine (an example is in The Conservatoire des Arts et Métiers, Paris) with three 'improvements' on Maelzel: ability to remain regular even when not on a horizontal surface; the possibility of changing tempo without stopping the machine; and the addition of a device to strike every two, three, four or six beats. Fétis enthusiastically endorsed this as the successor to Maelzel's machine. But Maelzel, with a characteristic sense for the difference between important and unimportant matters, incorporated only the striking device into his subsequent metronomes. At some stage in the 1820s he also reduced the height to 20 cm; and, perhaps later, expanded the calibrations: they now ran from 40 to 208, in twos from 40 to 50 and in eights from 160 to 208,

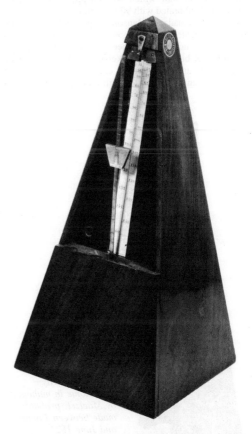

3. Prototype of the modern metronome, made by Maelzel in 1815 (Gesellschaft der Musikfreunde, Vienna)

otherwise precisely as on the earlier metronome. These numbers and these limits have become standard for nearly all musical time-measurers since then, to such an extent that a figure such as crotchet = 130 has been described as 'irrational' simply because it does not appear on Maelzel's system.

Since then the clockwork metronome had remained practically unchanged. Slightly smaller models in a plastic case have been developed; but they usually retain many of the original Maelzel features: a double-ended clockwork-driven pendulum; a stem with ridges for positioning the upper weight which is trapezium-shaped and has a small spring to hold it in position; calibrations written on a scale mounted behind the stem; relatively nonsensical tempo-words added to the calibrations; a bell arrangement for downbeats activated by a little slider at the side; and a triangular (or obelisk-like) shape with a cover on the front that must be taken off before the metronome is operated.

Attempted refinements have been few and mostly short-lived. Hellouin (1900) mentioned French patents by Fayermann (1853, no.17880), Lesfauris (1854, no.20531), Janniard (1859, no.43290), Carden (1865, no.69207) and Metzger (1868, no.80809) as well as what may have been the earliest electric device by Gaiffe (1892); there were certainly many more in other countries. In response to Saint-Saëns's complaints that most metronomes were inaccurate Léon Roques devised a *métronome normal* which was cheap, easy to make, silent, and calibrated with 90 gradations from 30 to 236. In 1893 J. Treadway Hanson proposed (but probably did not execute) an extension that could actually beat time. More successful has been the Swiss-made pocket metronome: built like a pocket-watch, it has one hand that swings and clicks at the correct pace and another hand that can be moved through all degrees from 40 to 200.

4. Silent gravity metronome in mahogany by Maelzel, probably made between January and June 1821 (Metropolitan Museum of Art, New York)

4. ELECTRIC AND ELECTRONIC DEVICES. Such is the range of techniques made available by electronic technology that it may never be possible (or interesting) to detail the various 'metronomes' that have been developed along these lines. The number of new devices far exceeds that known from the years 1780–1830, but few have aroused much interest; and the advent of the synthesizer perhaps makes most of them all but obsolete.

For most mid-20th-century teaching purposes an electric box is used with a light on top that flashes the beats but can be supported by an audible click (such as the model by Franz); again the tempo numbers tend to follow Maelzel's last system. More recently smaller versions have been made, often equipped with an earphone (such as the model by Seiko). More elaborate devices have been made to cope with complex cross-rhythms, 'irrational' tempos and gradual change (see Henck, 1979 and 1980), as demanded by avant-garde scores. There have also been machines that can calculate the tempo of a received signal.

But it may well be true that the metronome still to some extent carries with it the stigma of being meaningless and unmusical in its aims (as in uses (*a*) and (*b*) outlined in §1 above); and this could hamper the success of new inventions to cope with uses (*c*) and (*d*).

BIBLIOGRAPHY

L. Zacconi: *Prattica di musica*, i (Venice, 1592/*R*1967), f.20*v*

M. Mersenne: *Harmonie universelle* (Paris, 1636–7/*R*1963; Eng. trans., 1957)

T. Mace: *Musick's Monument* (London, 1676/*R*1958), 80

E. Loulié: *Elements ou principes de musique* (Paris, 1696/*R*1977, 2/1698; Eng. trans., 1965/*R*1971)

J. Sauveur: *Principes d'acoustique et de musique, ou système general des intervalles des sons* (Paris, 1701/*R*1973); also in *Histoire de l'Académie royale des sciences, année 1701* (Paris, 1704), Mémoires, iv, 315

M. L'Affilard: *Principes très-faciles pour bien apprendre la musique* (Paris, 5/1705/*R*1979)

A. Malcolm: *A Treatise of Musick* (Edinburgh, 1721/*R*1970), 407

W. Turner: *Sound Anatomiz'd* (London, 1724), 20

L.-L. Pajot [Comte d'Onsembray]: 'Description et usage d'un métromètre ou machine pour battre les mesures et les temps de toutes sortes d'airs', *Histoire de l'Académie royale des sciences, année 1732* (Paris, 1735), Mémoires, 182

J.-A. de La Chapelle: *Suite de Vrais principes de la musique* (Paris, 1737)

W. Tans'ur: *A New Musical Grammar: or the Harmonical Spectator* (London, 1746), 41

R. Bremner: *The Rudiments of Music* (Edinburgh, 1756, 2/1763)

H.-L. Choquel: *La musique rendue sensible par la méchanique, ou Nouveau système pour apprendre facilement la musique soi-même* (Paris, 1759, 2/1762)

J.-J. Rousseau: 'Chronomètre', *Dictionnaire de musique* (Paris, 1768/*R*1969)

Gabory: *Manuel utile et curieux sur la mesure du temps* (Angers, 1770)

J. Harrison: *A Description Concerning such a Mechanism as will Afford a Nice or True Mensuration of Time* (London, 1775)

F. Pelletier: *Hommages aux amateurs des arts, ou Mémoire* (St Germain-en-Laye, 1782)

J.-B. Davaux: 'Lettre sur un instrument ou pendule nouveau', *Journal encyclopédique ou universel*, iv/3 (1784), 534

J.-B. Davaux and Renaudin: correspondence in *Journal de Paris*, May–June 1784 [ed. in Brook (1962), i, 502ff]

T. Jefferson: letter of 3 Jan 1786 to Francis Hopkinson, in J. P. Boyd, ed.: *The Papers of Thomas Jefferson*, ix (Princeton, 1954), 146

J.-B. Dubos: 'Chronomètre ou machine pour battre la mésure', MS presented to Académie royale des sciences, 30 March 1787, but not accepted [see Cohen (1981), 70]

F.-J. Gossec: report on Dubos' *rhythmomètre* (Paris, 1787) [lost, cited in *FétisB* ('Duclos'); on date and identification see Brook (1962), i, 314]

J. G. Weiske: *Zwölf geistliche prosaische Gesänge, mit . . . Beschreibung eines Tactmessers* (Leipzig, 1789)

A. Burja: *Beschreibung eines musikalischen Zeitmessers* (Berlin, 1790)

N.-E. Framery: 'Chronomètre', *Encyclopédie méthodique: musique*, i, ed. N.-E. Framery and P.-L. Ginguené (Paris, 1791), 280

T. Wright: preface to *A Concerto for the Harpsichord or Piano Forte* (London, *c*1795)

A. Grétry: *Mémoires, ou essais sur la musique* (Paris, 1797), i, 315

A. G. Eckhardt: *A Certain Instrument to Serve as a General Standard for Regulating the Proper Time of Musical Performance* (English Patent no.2267, 1798)

A. H. Wenk: *Beschreibung eines Chronometers oder musikalischen Taktmessers* (Magdeburg, 1798)

G. E. Stöckel: 'Über die Wichtigkeit der richtigen Zeitbewegung eines Tonstücks, nebst einer Beschreibung meines musikalischen Chronometers', *AMZ*, ii (1799–1800), 657, 673

C. Mason: *Rules on the Times, Metres, Phrases & Accents of Composition* (London, 1801)

F. Thiémé: *Nouvelle théorie sur les différens mouvemens des airs . . . avec le projet d'un nouveau chronomètre* (Paris, 1801/*R*1972)

G. E. Stöckel: 'Noch ein Wort über den musikalischen Zeitmesser', *AMZ*, vi (1803–4), 49

J. F. Reichardt: *Vertraute Briefe aus Paris* (Hamburg, 1804), iii, 311

F. Guthmann: 'Ein neuer Taktmesser, welcher aber erst erfunden werden soll', *AMZ*, ix (1806–7), 117

W. Crotch: *Specimens of Various Styles of Music* (London, *c*1807)

J.-L. Despréaux: *Nouveau chronomètre musical, établi sur des bases astronomiques* (Paris, 1813)

Anon.: suggestion that composers note the performed length of their works, *AMZ*, xv (1813), 305

Anon.: announcement of Maelzel's chronometer, endorsed by Beethoven, Salieri, Weigel, etc, and shortly to be manufactured, *AMZ*, xv (1813), 784

G. Weber: 'Noch einmal ein Wort über den musikalischen Chronometer oder Taktmesser', *AMZ*, xv (1813), 441

A.-L. Bréguet: *Horlogerie pour l'usage civil, chronomètres portatifs* (Paris, *c*1815)

J. Maelzel: *An Instrument or Instruments, Machine or Machines, for the Improvement of all Musical Performance, which I denominate a Metronome or Musical Timekeeper* (English Patent no.3966, 1815)

——: *Pour une espèce de chronomètre appelé métronome en usage dans la musique* (French Patent no.696, 1815)

Anon.: *Notice sur le métronome de J. Maelzel* (Paris, 1816, 2/1822)

Anon.: 'Mälzels Metronom', *AMZ*, xix (1817), 417

Gld. [of Copenhagen]: 'Andreas Christian Sparrevogns Taktuhr', *AMZ*, xix (1817), 233

F. S. Kandler: 'Rückblicke auf die Chronometer und Herrn Mälzels neueste Chronometerfabrik in London', *Wiener AMZ*, i (1817), 33, 41, 49, 57

I. F. Mosel: 'Herrn Johann Mälzels Metronom', *Wiener AMZ*, i (1817), 405

J. G. Weber: *Über chronometrische Tempobezeichnung, welche ohne Chronometermaschine überall sogleich verstanden u. angewendet werden kann* (Mainz, 1817)

Anon.: 'Zur Geschichte des musikal. Metronomen', *AMZ*, xx (1818), 468 [with affidavit from Winkel claiming for himself the invention of Maelzel's machine]

Anon.: 'Maelzel's Metronome', *Quarterly Musical Magazine and Review*, iii (1821), 302

J. Coggins: *The Musical Assistant* (London, *c*1822)

P. Lichtenthal: 'Metronomo', *Dizionario e bibliografia della musica*, i (Milan, 1826)

[Bienaimé-Fournier]: *Notice du métronome perfectionné de Bienaimé* (Amiens, 1828)

F.-J. Fétis: 'Métronome perfectionné de M. Bienaimé', *Revue musicale*, ii (1828), 534

——: 'Sur le métronome de Maelzel', *Revue musicale*, ii (1828), 361

J. N. Hummel: *Ausführliche theoretisch-praktische Anweisung zum Piano-forte-Spiel* (Vienna, 1828), 439

J. de Vos Willems: 'Correspondance', *Revue musicale*, vi (1829), 56

J. G. Weber: 'Chronometer', *Allgemeine Encyclopädie der Wissenschaften und Künste*, ed. J. S. Ersch and J. G. Gruber, xxi (Leipzig, 1830), 204

G. Nottebohm: 'Metronomische Bezeichnungen', *Beethoveniana* (Leipzig, 1872/*R*1970), 126

——: 'Metronomische Bezeichnung der ersten elf Streichquartette', *Zweite Beethoveniana* (Leipzig, 1887/*R*1970), 519

W. S. Rockstro: 'Metronome', *Grove 1*

J. T. Hanson: 'A New Metronome', *PMA*, xx (1893–4), 23

Baudot: 'Utilité d'un appareil enregistreur des mouvements des oeuvres musicales', *Congrès international de musique: Paris 1900*, 38

Canat de Chizy: 'Régularisation des indications et appareils métronomiques', *Congrès international de musique: Paris 1900*, 31

Frémond: 'Régularisation des indications métronomiques', *Congrès international de musique: Paris 1900*, 34

F. Hellouin [Hélouin]: 'Histoire du métronome en France', *Congrès international d'histoire de la musique: Paris 1900*, ed. F. Combarieu, 264; expanded in F. Hellouin: *Feuillets d'histoire musicale française*, i (Paris, 1903), 15

O. Urbach: 'Metronom-Bezeichnungen klassischer Werke', *Neue Musik-Zeitung*, xxxii (1911), 40, 369

O. Baensch: 'Zur neunten Symphonie', *Neues Beethoven-Jb*, ii (1925), 137

P. Rougnon: 'Métronome', *EMDC*, II/i (1925), 323

C. R. Blum: *Das Musik-Chronometer* (Leipzig, 1926)

Z. Drechsel: 'Geschichte des Taktmessers', *ZI*, xlvi (1926), 948

G. Haupt: 'J. N. Mälzels Briefe an Breitkopf & Härtel', *Der Bär 1927*, 122

E. Borrel: 'Les indications métronomiques laissées par les auteurs français du XVIIIe siècle', *RdM*, ix (1928), 149

R. E. M. Harding: 'The Metronome and its Precursors', *Origins of Musical Time and Expression* (London, 1938), 1–35; repr. as *The Metronome and it's Precursors* (Henley, 1983)

R. Kirkpatrick: 'Eighteenth-century Metronomic Indications', *PAMS 1938*, 30

R. Kolisch: 'Tempo and Character in Beethoven's Music', *MQ*, xxix (1943), 169, 291

F. Goebels: 'Metronom', *MGG*

F. Rothschild: 'The Metronome in Beethoven's Time', *Musical Performance in the Times of Mozart and Beethoven* (London, 1961)

B. S. Brook: *La symphonie française dans la seconde moitié du XVIIIe siècle* (Paris, 1962), i, 313, 502

S. Gullo: *Das Tempo in der Musik des XIII. und XIV. Jahrhunderts* (Berne, 1964)

D. Kämper: 'Zur Frage der Metronombezeichnungen Robert Schumanns', *AMw*, xxi (1964), 141

Thayer's Life of Beethoven, ed. E. Forbes (Princeton, 1964), ii, 686

B. S. Brook: 'Le tempo dans l'exécution de la musique instrumentale à la fin du XVIII siècle', *FAM*, xii (1965), 196

P. Stadlen: 'Beethoven and the Metronome – I', *ML*, xlviii (1967), 330

A. Lemke: *Jacob Gottfried Weber: Leben und Werk: ein Beitrag zur Musikgeschichte des mittelrheinischen Raumes* (Mainz, 1968)

R. Barbacci: *El tiempo musical: el metrónomo y sus antecedentes* (Lima, 1969)

R. Angermüller: 'Aus der Frühgeschichte des Metronoms: die Beziehungen zwischen Mälzel und Salieri', *ÖMz*, xxvi (1971), 134

L. Talbot: 'A Note on Beethoven's Metronome', *Journal of Sound and Vibration*, xvii (1971), 323

B. Schlotel: 'Schumann and the Metronome', *Robert Schumann: the Man and his Music*, ed. A. Walker (London, 1972), 109

H. C. Wolff: 'Das Metronom des Louis-Léon Pajot 1735', *Festskrift Jens Peter Larsen* (Copenhagen, 1972), 205

H. Tünker: *Musikelektronik* (Munich, 1973, 2/1974)

E. Schwandt: 'L'Affilard on the French Court Dances', *MQ*, lx (1974), 389

C. Wagner: 'Experimentelle Untersuchungen über das Tempo', *ÖMz*, xxix (1974), 589

H. K. H. Lange: 'Das Fadenpendel-Metronom', *ÖMz*, xxxi (1976), 153

R. E. Maxham: *A Study of Joseph Sauveur's Contributions to Acoustics* (diss., Eastman School of Music, 1976), 25

Beethoven-Kolloquium: Vienna 1977

H. Henck: 'Metronomwerte aus dem Sekundenschlag', *SMz*, cxix (1979), 140

S. Howell: 'Beethoven's Maelzel Canon: Another Schindler Forgery?', *MT*, cxx (1979), 987

J. C. Kassler: *The Science of Music in Britain, 1714–1830: a Catalogue of Writings, Lectures and Inventions* (New York, 1979)

H.-K. Metzger, ed.: *Beethoven: das Problem der Interpretation* (Munich, 1979), Musik-Konzepte, viii

H. Henck: 'Zur Berechnung und Darstellung irrationale Zeitwerte', *SMz*, cxx (1980), 26, 89

W. Kolneder: 'Zur Geschichte des Metronoms', *Hifi-Stereophonie*, xix (1980), 152

W. Rosenberg: 'Das verteufelte Metronom', *Hifi-Stereophonie*, xix (1980), 167

E. Schwandt: 'L'Affilard', *Grove 6*

E. Schwandt and J. O'Donnell: 'The Principles of L'Affilard', *Early Music*, viii (1980), 77

A. Cohen: *Music in the French Royal Academy of Sciences* (Princeton, 1981), 68

P. Stadlen: 'Beethoven and the Metronome [II]', *Soundings*, ix (1982), 38; Ger. version [with severely reduced tables] in Metzger (1979), 12, and in *Beethoven-Kolloquium: Vienna 1977*, 57

For further bibliography *see* TEMPO AND EXPRESSION MARKS.

DAVID FALLOWS

Metziltayim [tziltzelim]. Instruments referred to frequently in the Bible. Because the name almost invariably appears in the dual, indicating that they were used in pairs, and because similar words in other languages in the same geographical area mean cymbal today (e.g. Turkish *zil*), almost all translators of the Bible have agreed that these were cymbals. In the Middle Ages, however, *cymbala*, the term used in the Vulgate, were taken to be small bells, usually provided with internal clappers but nevertheless struck with hand-held hammers (*see* CYMBALUM, illustration). Previous to this, from the 8th century to the 10th or 11th, a frequent interpretation was tong-cymbals, and it is possible that these had been used in ancient Israel; cymbals mounted on tongs were common in ancient Egypt and cymbals of similar size to the Egyptian have been found archaeologically in the ancient Israelite area. Larger, hand-held cymbals have also been found, varying from 8 cm to 13 cm in diameter (Bayer, 1963, group A.II). These are normally made of bronze and, since they are much thicker than our modern cymbals, must have produced notes of definite pitch, a ringing sound rather than a clash. The adjectives used in Psalm cl indicate that they were loud and even raucous in sound.

BIBLIOGRAPHY
B. Bayer: *The Material Relics of Music in Ancient Palestine and its Environs: an Archaeological Inventory* (Tel-Aviv, 1963, 2/1964)
JEREMY MONTAGU

Metzler. English firm of instrument makers, dealers and publishers. It was founded by Valentin Metzler (*d* ?London, *c*1833), originally from Bingen am Rhein, who established the business in London in 1788. He sold flutes, probably of his own manufacture, and repaired brass instruments. His son George Richard Metzler (1797–1867) joined the firm, probably in 1816, as it then became known as Metzler & Son. That year it also started to publish music. In 1833 it was renamed G. Metzler & Co., presumably on the death of Valentin Metzler, and operated from numerous premises in central London. G. R. Metzler retired in 1866 and was succeeded by his son George Thomas Metzler (1835–79). The latter formed a partnership in 1867 with Frank Chappell, who established a connection with the American firm of Mason & Hamlin in Boston. The firm became a limited company in 1893 and was taken over by J. B. Cramer in 1931.

There are many surviving Metzler instruments, covering the full range of woodwind and brass. Besides keyless fifes, the firm produced flutes with one, four (*see* FLUTE, fig.13b), six or eight keys, as well as walking-stick models. Clarinets exist with six or 13 keys and bassoons with six, eight or ten keys. Metzler trumpets and cornets usually had two or three Stölzel valves (often with crooks and tuning-slide); the firm also made slide-trumpets, serpents and ophicleides (*see also* KEYED BUGLE, fig.1). Metzler was known in 1838 to be selling 'improved seraphines', precursors of the reed organ. In 1858 George Richard Metzler built and patented the *sonorophone*, a type of helicon.

For details of the firm's publishing activities, see *Grove 6*.

BIBLIOGRAPHY
Metzler & Son's Clarinet Preceptor (London, *c*1830)
L. A. de Pontécoulant: *Douze jours à Londres* (Paris, 1862)
A. Rose: *Talks with Bandsmen* (London, *c*1894)
L. G. Langwill: *An Index of Musical Wind-instrument Makers* (Edinburgh, 1960, rev., enlarged 6/1980)
NIALL O'LOUGHLIN

Metzler Orgelbau. Swiss firm of organ builders, formerly Metzler & Söhne. It was founded in 1890 in Graubünden by Jakob Metzler. In 1930 his son Oscar moved the company to Dietikon (Zurich). In 1968 the direction was taken over jointly by his sons, Oskar and Hansueli. Although always craftsmanlike, the work of the firm was without special distinction until the mid-1950s when, on the insistence of the family's younger generation, it became more closely allied with the European organ reform movement. It did not achieve outstanding success, however, until its instruments in Schaffhausen and the Grossmünster, Zurich, were built in consultation with the distinguished Danish organ builder and designer Poul Gerhard Andersen. An enlightened tonal design and 'reformed' voicing techniques joined with the firm's traditional precision of workmanship to produce a general excellence which established it as Switzerland's most important builder. A new organ in 1965 for the Cathedral of St Pierre in Geneva (also in collaboration with Andersen) reinforced the firm's position of leadership and its international reputation dates from the completion of that instrument. The first Metzler organ in England was installed at Trinity College, Cambridge, in 1975–6. The firm now specializes in the construction of organs in a severe, neo-classical style more reminiscent of the north German style than is generally typical of Swiss builders. The stop action, as well as the key action, is mechanical (Geneva's St Pierre organ being the last with electric stop action), and all casework is designed on strictly Baroque lines. Unlike most modern builders, Metzler does not use any electric or electronic playing aids, such as combination pistons or crescendo pedal. The instruments are noted for their traditional stop-lists, cohesive and well-balanced ensembles, responsive key action and perfection of construction. Fine examples are those at Netstal, Frauenfeld (Stadtkirche) and Brugg (Evangelische Kirche). Metzler is also known for its meticulous restoration and reconstruction of historical instruments, as at Muri (Aargau), where the two choir organs dating from 1743–4 were restored and the 1628 organ rebuilt; the reconstruction of the Silbermann organ at Basle (Predigerkirche) was completed in 1978. Also noteworthy are the organ of St Pölten Cathedral, Lower Austria, in the old Egedacher case (1973), that of the Augustiner Chorherren Kirche in Reichersberg, Upper Austria, in the rococo case (1981), and that for the Jesuit church in Lucerne, also in the old case but with a new *Rückpositiv* (1982).

GILLIAN WEIR

Meuschel. *See* NEUSCHEL family.

Mey [nay]. Cylindrical oboe of Turkey. Its bore is sometimes slightly tapering and it has seven finger-holes and one thumb-hole. The pipe is made of wood with a large double reed inserted. There are three sizes of *mey*: large (*ana*: 'mother'), medium (*orta*: 'middle') and small (*cura*). Being less strident than the *zurna* (oboe), the *mey* is more suitable for playing indoors (where it is often accompanied by the *dümbelek*), but it is also played

outdoors with the *davul*. See L. Picken: *Folk Musical Instruments of Turkey* (London, 1975).
See also BĀLABĀN, (1) and DUDUK (i).

R. CONWAY MORRIS

Meydan sazı. Turkish long-necked lute. The *meydan sazı* ('public square *saz*') is the largest type of SAZ. It has four or more double courses of strings and is constructed and played like the BAĞLAMA.

Meyer, Conrad (*b* Marburg; *d* Philadelphia, 1881). American piano maker of German origin. He emigrated to Baltimore in 1819, subsequently working for the piano maker Joseph Hisky. In 1829 he settled in Philadelphia where he started his own firm, and in 1833 exhibited one piano with 'shifting or transposing action' and another with an iron frame at the Franklin Institute. He later claimed that this square was made in 1832 and was unique in the USA for its single cast-iron frame. He did not patent it, and was in fact preceded by ALPHEUS BABCOCK, who patented a similar frame in 1825. But Meyer was often credited with this clever design, which permitted greater string tension and consequently a more resonant tone. Spillane (1890) wrote that Meyer made excellent pianos and that on Meyer's death the firm passed to his sons. The firm continued into at least the 1890s.

BIBLIOGRAPHY
D. Spillane: *History of the American Pianoforte* (New York, 1890/*R*1969)
The Crosby Brown Collection of Musical Instruments of all Nations: Catalogue of Keyboard Instruments (New York, 1903)

MARGARET CRANMER

Mezzadri, Alessandro (*fl* Ferrara, *c*1690–1732). Italian violin maker. It has been said that he was a capable performer; a conflict between two careers would certainly explain his meagre output as a maker. There is little doubt that his best instruments have suffered from being relabelled with more famous names. His violins are essentially patterned after the Amati school but there appears to have been no obvious attempt at mere copying. While they tend to be small they invariably give the impression of being larger. The design of the soundholes usually derives from the Amati school, but those cut for his violas often lean towards Brescian models. The few surviving cut-down violas indicate, by the unusual length of their soundholes, that they originally must have measured close to 480 mm (or more) in body length. The quality of varnish can be exceptionally good and varies from a vivid orange-red to a golden brown.

BIBLIOGRAPHY
W. L. von Lütgendorff: *Die Geigen- und Lautenmacher vom Mittelalter bis zur Gegenwart* (Frankfurt am Main, 1904, rev. 6/1922/*R*1968)

JAAK LIIVOJA-LORIUS

Mezzo, mezza (It.: 'half', 'medium'). A word used in several different musical contexts, one of the commonest of which is the mezzo-soprano voice. In current Italian *mezza manica* means the half-position in string playing, *mezza cadenza* a half-cadence or half-close and *mezzotono* a semitone. In addition the following universally used technical meanings appear.

(1) *Mezza voce, mezzavoce* ('half-voice'). A direction in both vocal and instrumental music to produce a quiet, restrained tone, found as early as Tosi's *Opinioni* (1723,

pp.20f), where it is recommended that ascending appoggiaturas, especially those involving chromatic intervals, be performed *mezza voce*. This very specific direction is most often found in operatic scores of the 19th century: in the second act of Verdi's *Otello*, for example, Iago's narration of Cassio's dream ('Era la notte, Cassio dormiva') is marked *mezza voce*; and the opening scene of *Simon Boccanegra* is marked 'tutta questa scena a mezzavoce'. It appears also in instrumental music, for example in the slow movements of Beethoven's opp.106, 109, 125 and 131; in very similar circumstances he also used *sotto voce* (*see* SOTTO). The French equivalent in the 18th century, *à demi* or *à demi voix*, also applied to both vocal and instrumental music. *Mezza voce* is entirely different from MESSA DI VOCE.

(2) *Mezzo-forte, mezzo-piano* (*mf, mp*). Dynamic indications implying moderation. Thus *mezzo-forte* is less loud than *forte*; and *mezzo-piano* is less soft, therefore louder, than *piano*. See also TEMPO AND EXPRESSION MARKS.

(3) *Mezzo-legato, mezzo-staccato* (and *legato-staccato*). Articulations normally designated by a slur with staccato dots beneath it; *see* ARTICULATION.

mf. *Mezzo-forte* (It.: 'moderately loud'); *see* MEZZO, MEZZA, (2).

Mfuhlulu ('ululation'). *See* TSHIHOHO.

Mfunga. Side-blown trumpet of the Nguli people of Zaïre. It is the smallest of the *funga* trumpets made from hollowed-out roots or branches (*LaurentyA*, 332).

Mgba. DRUM-CHIME of the Igbo people of Nigeria.

Mgung. Double clapperless bell of the Mbun people of Zaïre. *See* GONGA (i).

Mhiyém. Wooden cone flute, with one or two fingerholes, of the Shongo people of Zaïre (*LaurentyA*, 149).

Michaelis, Zanetto de. *See* ZANETTO DI MONTICHIARO.

Microchordon. A name used by COLLARD & COLLARD for a small upright piano.

Microtonal instruments. Instruments adapted or specially constructed for performing music in microtonal tuning systems or to give accurate tuning in temperaments other than the 'standard' 12-note equal temperament. (There is considerable overlap between these two functions in some microtonal instruments.) This article deals only with Western instruments; instruments constructed in other parts of the world for the performance of music in systems of intonation other than 12-note equal temperament are dealt with under their own headings.

Three main periods can be distinguished in the development of Western microtonal instruments: the work of theorists in the 16th and 17th centuries, acoustic research in the second half of the 19th century, and the explorations of composers, performers and researchers throughout the 20th century. Until the end of the 19th century there was little interest in microtonal composition based on more than 12 equal divisions of the octave; but this has been the main preoccupation in the 20th century in this area, and many composers who are not primarily concerned with microtonal systems have nonetheless included microtonal inflections in their works at some time, whether for traditional instruments or in electronic music.

In this article instruments are described as having a certain number of notes to the octave; 'equal' and 'unequal' temperaments are respectively those in which the octave is divided into equal or unequal intervals by the notes; 'just' indicates just intonation, and 'mean' mean-tone temperament (both of which are unequal). On some ENHARMONIC KEYBOARD instruments and some instruments constructed since the 19th century certain pitches have duplicate keys for ease of fingering, so that there are more keys than notes to the octave. In other cases a single standard keyboard with 12 keys to the octave is used, together with switches, each of which assigns a specific intonation system to the keyboard.

1. To 1750. 2. 1750–1900. 3. 1900–30. 4. After 1930.

1. To 1750. Before the establishment of equal temperament in the course of the 18th century, a number of investigations were carried out into intonation and tuning systems, in many instances inspired by a renewal of interest in ancient Greece and the three genera (diatonic, chromatic and enharmonic) of the Greek modes. Those principally active in this area in the 16th century were the theorists Francisco de Salinas, who proposed the use of 19 notes to the octave and probably perfected meantone temperament, and Gioseffo Zarlino, who investigated systems of 17 and 19 notes to the octave and contributed significantly to the development of 12-note equal temperament. In the 17th century Nicolaus Mercator

suggested 53 equal divisions of the octave and Marin Mersenne and Christiaan Huygens 31; both systems result virtually in just intonation.

A few microtonal instruments with enharmonic keyboards were constructed during this period for the performance of music in specific intonations. In Venice in 1548 Domenico Pesarese built for Zarlino an enharmonic harpsichord with 19 notes to the octave. Nicola Vicentino made instruments which he called the *arcicembalo* (1555) and *arciorgano* (1561); both had 31 notes to the octave with two manuals each having three terraces of keys, and they were designed to play in mean-tone systems. Around 1590 Elsasz built a *clavicymbalum universale* (19 notes, mean). Over the next 100 years several other enharmonic harpsichords were constructed, principally in Italy, including those of Vito Trasuntino, Fabio Colonna, Giovanni Pietro Polizzino, Francesco Nigetti, Galeazzo Sabbatini, Nicolaus Ramarinus and Giovanni Battista Doni.

2. 1750–1900. During the decades when 12-note equal temperament was first in use other intonation systems persisted, especially in solo performances on keyboard instruments; unaccompanied voices and strings continued (and still continue) to adjust their intonation according to context. By the time the majority of musicians and manufacturers had adopted equal temperament, in some cases as late as the middle of the 19th century, it was the turn of the practitioners of the new science of acoustics to explore different tuning systems. A number of pipe and reed organs were built or modified for this purpose, beginning with Henry Liston's 56-note pipe organ of c1812. Some of them are described in Table 1. Instruments from this period that did not have a keyboard include Thomas Perronet Thompson's enharmon-

TABLE 1

Instrument	Date	Specification	Inventor, builder
'euharmonic organ'	c1850	12 keys, assigned, just	Henry Ward Poole (Boston, Mass.), with Joseph Abbey
'enharmonic organ'	c1851	3 manuals, 44 keys, 40 notes, just, and 12 notes, equal	Thomas Perronet Thompson (London), built by Robson
'justly intoned harmonium'	c1862	2 manuals, 12 keys, 31 notes, just, and 12 notes, equal	Hermann von Helmholtz (Heidelberg), built by J. & P. Schiedmayer
organ (unfinished?)	1867–?	100 keys, 100 notes, just	Henry Ward Poole
2 'mathematical harmoniums'	c1868	36 and 53 notes, just	George Appunn (Hanau)
'just English concertina'	c1870	14 keys, 14 notes, just	Alexander J. Ellis (London)
'enharmonic harmonium'	1872–3	84 keys, 53 notes, equal (= just)	Robert H. M. Bosanquet (Oxford), built by T. A. Jennings
'enharmonic organ'	1875	84 keys, 48 notes, 'Helmholtz temperament' and 36 notes, mean	
'harmonical' / 'just harmonium'	c1874	12 keys, 12 notes, just	Alexander J. Ellis
'voice harmonium'	1875	45 keys, 45 notes, just	Colin Brown (Glasgow)
3 'harmon' harmoniums	1877–87	56 keys, 53 notes, equal (= just)	James Paul White (Springfield, Mass.)
'mathematical harmonium'	c1880	36 notes, just	Gustav Engel (Berlin)
Reinharmonium	c1888	36 notes, just	Carl Andreas Eitz (Eisleben), built by J. & P. Schiedmayer
Reinharmonium	c1888	104 notes, just	
Enharmonium	1889	20 keys, 20 notes, just	Shôhei Tanaka (Berlin), built by Johann Kewitsch
harmonium	1891	45 notes, just	Joachim Steiner (Germany)
'syntonisch reingestimmte Orgel'	1893	20 keys, 36 notes, just	Shôhei Tanaka, built by Walcker

ic guitar (?1829; for illustration *see* JUST INTONATION, fig.5), the 31-note 'githárfa' (Ger. 'Guitharfe') built by the Hungarian physicist József Petzval in Vienna in 1862, and a quarter-tone trumpet (1893, now in the Odessa Conservatory). In 1864 a piano tuned in just intonation was built for the Russian Prince Odoevsky.

3. 1900–30. Around 1890 Carl Andreas Eitz extended his experiments to quarter-tones; similar interests were soon pursued by others, especially in Germany, and inaugurated a new phase in microtonal music. This was characterized by the appearance not only of a considerable number of compositions in various tuning systems, but also of a great variety of specially constructed instruments.

Much of the quarter-tone music written in this period involves retuning or different fingering of existing instruments. The earliest composition to use quarter-tones appears to have been Halévy's *Prométhée enchaîné* (1849), in the string parts; in 1898 the British composer John Foulds wrote a string quartet (now lost) that used quarter-tones, and from 1905 he included microtones for bowed strings in other works. The first important quarter-tone composition, and perhaps the first fully microtonal work, was Charles Ives's *Chorale* for strings; this was variously dated 1903–14 and 1913–14 by the composer, and was probably based on experiments carried out with two pianos tuned a quarter-tone apart around 1900–01. The *Chorale* is also lost, but it was arranged for two pianos by Ives as the last of his *Three Quarter-Tone Pieces for Two Pianos* (1923–4), from which Alan Stout has reconstructed the original.

Other quarter-tone practitioners before 1930 included Julián Carrillo, who evolved the theory of 'the 13th sound' (*el sonido trece*) in 1895, but wrote no microtonal music until 1922; Arthur Lourié, who between 1908 and around 1913 wrote a number of works, including a string quartet (1910); several Soviet composers in the mid-1920s, including Georgy Rimsky-Korsakov, who founded the Petrograd society for quarter-tone music (1923) and directed its ensemble (1925–32), and who wrote parts in his works for quarter-tone harmonium and Emiriton, Arseny Avraamov (who also devised an $\frac{1}{8}$-tone 'universal tonal system'), Nikolay Malakhovsky and Aleksandr Kenel'; and a number of musicians who developed or commissioned special instruments (see below). During this period quarter-tones were also briefly exploited in single works by Vittorio Gnecchi, Ernest Bloch and Alban Berg.

Before the 1890s only a few quarter-tone instruments were constructed; they included one built around 1850 by Alexandre-Joseph Vincent and Bottée de Toulmon, who were inspired by the Greek modes, and a set of tuned glasses and an instrument with about 24 strings made around 1885 by George Ives (the composer's father). From 1890 a considerable number of quarter-tone pianos and harmoniums were built (see Table 2), as well as a few in other tunings. Some of these instruments have two manuals tuned a quarter-tone apart; others have three manuals, the third duplicating the first to allow alternative fingerings (the length of the keys diminishes on each manual, so that on the one furthest from the player the white keys are the same size as the black ones). Those instruments with a single manual, including the harmoniums by Max F. Meyer and von Moellendorf, have unconventional keyboard lay-outs (*see also* KEYBOARD, §3).

TABLE 2

Instrument	Date	Inventor, builder
'achromatisches Klavier' (2 manuals)	1892	G. A. Behrens-Senegalden (Berlin)
harmonium (1 manual)	1902	Max F. Meyer (USA)
harmonium	c1906	Josef Anton Gruss (Franzensbad, Bohemia, now Františkovy Lázně)
harmonium (2 manuals)	1911	Jörg Mager (Aschaffenburg), built by Steinmeyer
piano (unfinished)	c1913–14	Arthur Lourié (St Petersburg), built by Maison Diederichs
'bichromatisches Harmonium' (1 manual)	1915	Willi von Moellendorf (Berlin), built by Otto Pappe
'enharmonium'	1921	Silvestro Baglioni (Rome)
piano (unfinished) (2 manuals)	1922	Ivan Vïshnegradsky (Paris), built by Pleyel
piano (2 manuals)	1924	Moritz Stoehr (New York)
piano (3 manuals)	1924	Alois Hába (Berlin), Ivan Vïshnegradsky (Prague), built by Grotrian-Steinweg
piano (2 manuals)	1924	Alois Hába (Prague), built by Förster
piano (3 manuals)	1925	Alois Hába (Prague), built by Förster
piano (3 manuals)	1928	Ivan Vïshnegradsky (Paris), built by Förster
piano (2 manuals)	1928	Hans Barth (New York), built by George L. Weitz of Baldwin
2 pianinos	1931	Alois Hába, built by Förster
harmonium (3 manuals)	1931	Alois Hába (Prague), built by Förster

Harmoniums using other microtonal tunings were also constructed at about this time. Ferruccio Busoni, inspired in 1907 by reports of the second model of Thaddeus Cahill's TELHARMONIUM (which had 36 notes to the octave in just intonation), experimented in New York (probably in 1910 or 1911) with a rebuilt three-manual harmonium tuned in $\frac{1}{3}$-tones; a two-manual $\frac{1}{6}$-tone instrument constructed for him by J. & P. Schiedmayer was completed only in 1925, several months after his death. In Cambridge Wilfrid Perrett built a harmonium in just intonation with 19 notes to the octave (c1925) which he called the 'olympion'. An electric harmonium designed by Lev Termen around 1926 (but not completed) was tunable in subdivisions of up to $\frac{1}{100}$-tones. Alois Hába commissioned a $\frac{1}{6}$-tone harmonium from August Förster in 1927. In 1932 Shōhei Tanaka, working in Tokyo, produced an instrument with 21 keys per octave (assignable to 46 notes) in just intonation. Around the same time the Polytone, a 60-key, 53-note harmonium with a special keyboard, consisting of ten differently coloured rows of keys, was constructed for the composer Arthur Fickénsher at the University of Virginia. From the early 1930s several 43-note harmoniums were constructed by Harry Partch under the names Ptolemy and CHROMELODEON.

Microtonal instruments other than keyboards from the first half of the 20th century include the quarter-tone clarinet (c1906) of Richard H. Stein; Luigi Russolo's INTONARUMORI (1913–), in all of which divisions of at least $\frac{1}{8}$-tone were possible; a string instrument (1920) that combined features of the violin and balalaika, devised by Mikhail Matyushin (who had published a quarter-tone violin tutor in 1912); Carrillo's $\frac{1}{8}$-tone *octavina* (which resembled a bass guitar), the $\frac{1}{16}$-tone *arpa citera* or 'harmony harp' (c1922), 14 other instruments in the same family tuned to subdivisions between $\frac{1}{4}$- and $\frac{1}{16}$-tones, and a quarter-tone trumpet and horn, all built during the 1920s; the six-string violins that formed part of a microtonal ensemble directed by Paul Specht in the mid-1920s; and the quarter-tone instruments built for Hába (clarinets, 1924 and 1931, by F. W. Kohlert; trumpets with a fourth valve, 1931, by F. A. Haeckel; guitar, 1943). A $\frac{1}{12}$-tone version of the ondes martenot was made in 1938 at the request of the Indian poet and composer Rabindranath Tagore for performing ragas, and in the same year Messiaen composed two quarter-tone *Monodies* for solo ondes martenot. In 1930 Carrillo established the microtonal Orquesta Sonido Trece, which toured in Mexico during the next decade.

4. AFTER 1930.

(i) Harry Partch and the California group. The first substantial range of less conventional microtonal instruments was constructed by the American composer HARRY PARTCH from 1930; they employ a 43-note scale in just intonation. Besides inspiring a considerable number of instrumental inventions, including many later instruments in specific microtonal tunings, Partch's work has shown composers and performers that musicians who are reasonably skilful with tools can themselves create instruments appropriate to their ideas without much expense or assistance.

From the late 1940s Partch spent most of his time in California, where, as a result of his presence and ideas, a group of instrument makers concentrating on microtonal inventions has grown up. Ivor Darreg began to build and compose for new instruments in the mid-1930s (though initially he was probably unaware of Partch's work); he has explored many equal and just systems. He has refretted guitars in 17-, 19-, 22-, 24- and 31-note tunings and has made several versions of three types of steel guitar with two or four separate sets of strings in different tunings (Kosmolyra, Hobnailed Newel Post and the bass Megalyra). The electrically amplified keyboard Megapsalterion (1971), which has 158 strings tuned to an overtone series, was based on his 'amplifying clavichord' (1940).

Ervin Wilson, working in West Hollywood from the early 1960s, has devised many lay-outs for keyboard and keyed percussion instruments in microtonal tunings, refretted guitars and developed several Tubulongs; the latter are tubular metallophones, usually tuned to give 31 equal divisions of the octave but sometimes in other equal or just tunings, and they include the 31-note Chromaphone and the 22-note Transcelest (1967), which has three rows of keys made from square brass tubing. The 19-note Hackleman–Wilson clavichord (1975) was built by Scott Hackleman to Wilson's keyboard design. Another 19-note clavichord was constructed at around the same time by Craig Hundley, a former student of Wilson's. Hundley's instruments also include a Tubulon (a large array of suspended aluminium tubes tuned in 53 equal divisions; fig.1) and the Blaster Beam; this is a water-filled aluminium beam 6 metres in length, along which 24 strings are stretched and amplified by means of movable magnetic and crystal pickups.

Another influential Californian is the composer Lou Harrison, who has constructed many instruments in 12-note equal and other equal and just tunings since around 1940, including his 'tack piano', clavichords and copies of oriental instruments. Later he collaborated with William Colvig, and together they constructed in the early 1970s what was probably the first American gamelan (see §(iii) below).

A younger group, who, unlike Partch, do not restrict their work to a single tuning system, is centred on Jonathan Glasier and the Interval Foundation at San Diego (the Foundation has published a quarterly journal since 1978). In 1977 Glasier built a Harmonic Canon (modelled on that of Partch), which is tunable to any system; other instruments by him are an adaptation of a commercial Hawaiian guitar to create the microtonal 'Fender four-neck steel', and the Godzilla, which consists of tuned metal rods welded to a sawn-off oil drum. Glasier and others are also involved in improvisation, often with inventors of non-specifically tuned instruments, such as Prent Rodgers (who also builds instruments that use 31-note equal or just intonation).

Cris Forster, the curator of the instruments at the Harry Partch Foundation in San Diego, has made several instruments in 56-note just tuning: two of them, the Harmonic/Melodic Canon and Diamond Marimba, were inspired by Partch; a third, Chrysalis (fig.2), consists of

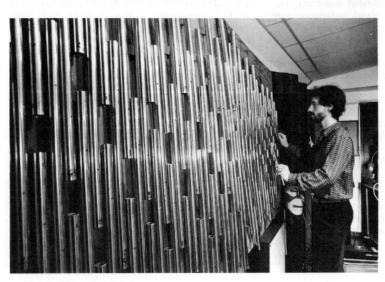

1. Craig Hundley playing a model of his Tubulon (1980)

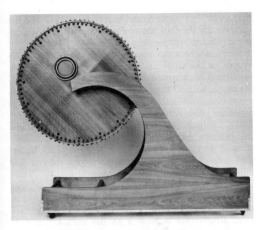

2. Chrysalis (1976) by Cris Forster

a disc mounted vertically on a stand with 82 strings on each face, which radiate out from an off-centre circular bridge. The composer DAVID COPE has constructed several percussion instruments tuned to 33-note just intonation. Other inventions to come out of California include Tillman H. Schafer's Undevigintivox, a 19-note metallophone (early 1960s), and a more recent 53-note metallophone built for L. E. Hanson. Schafer (now based in Boston), Warren F. Kimball and others have refretted guitars. Kimball and Skip La Plante in New York have built microtonal 'harmonic canons' inspired by Partch.

In California there has also been some use of microtones in jazz. In the mid-1960s the Hindustani Jazz Sextet explored both microtones and complex time signatures (from 5/4 to 33/16). The Sextet included two musicians who went on to form their own bands in the late 1960s: the trumpeter Don Ellis, who commissioned from Frank Holton & Co. quarter-tone trumpets with a fourth valve for the whole of his trumpet section; and the percussionist Emil Richards, whose Microtonal Blues Band consisted of several electroacoustic instruments and a wide range of percussion from many cultures, tuned microtonally to give, for instance, 22, 24, 31, 33 and 43 subdivisions of the octave.

(ii) Electronic instruments. Since World War II electronics have been widely applied to microtonal keyboard instruments, and electronic instruments have been used to perform microtonal music. In the late 1940s Percy Grainger, searching for means of producing 'gliding tones', managed to simulate them by using $\frac{1}{6}$- and $\frac{1}{8}$-tone tunings respectively in the first two models of the CROSS-GRAINGER FREE MUSIC MACHINE. Between 1950 and 1957 Evgeny Murzin developed the ANS, a photoelectric composition machine tuned to 72 equal octave divisions. In the mid-1960s Robert A. Moog constructed three microtonal electronic keyboard instruments: one with 43 notes to the octave over a range of four octaves; one with 31 notes to the octave and a total of 479 keys for a range of seven octaves; and one with 137 keys. At about the same time a microtonal version of the ONDIOLINE was produced for the composer Jean-Etienne Marie by Georges Jenny; this could be tuned in a variety of systems (e.g. divisions of the tone into between three and seven). On the basis of principles proposed by Alain Daniélou, Stephan Kudelski designed a 53-note unequally tempered keyboard instrument in the early 1960s

in collaboration with the harpsichord builders Wayland Dobson and Jean Eicher; this was followed in the late 1970s by the S52, built by Claude Cellier and André Kudelski and tuned to 52 notes per octave, with a touch-sensitive keyboard the compass of which can be transposed within a total range of eight octaves. The 31-note Arcifoon was manufactured in Holland from 1971 (see §(iv) below). In the early 1970s George Secor developed the SCALATRON (fig.3), in which each note is independently tunable; Kenneth Macfadyen's 'detunable organ' (1968–9, constructed by A. E. Davies & Son) is similarly conceived, though its tuning (including meantone) can be reset instantly while that of the Scalatron must be fixed one note at a time. An electronic organ constructed by Ivor Darreg in 1962 retunes itself automatically to any of several different systems. The *ekmelische Orgel* of Franz Richter Herf (1973–4), built with the assistance of Rolf Maedel, has three 84-note manuals tuned to 72 divisions of the octave.

Some synthesizer keyboards, which can be adjusted not only in range but also in compass, have been used to create any number of equal divisions of the octave. The American composer Easley Blackwood has used Moog and Polyfusion synthesizers and the Scalatron in this way, and John Eaton has performed on the SYNKET in a number of his microtonal compositions; La Monte Young has used a Moog synthesizer and Terry Riley a Yamaha electronic organ to play music in just intonation. The digital EGG synthesizer adds a manual with three rows of keys tuned in $\frac{1}{4}$-tones (197 keys in all) to an 85-note standard equal-tempered manual. In the early 1950s composers working in the electronic music studio at the Nordwestdeutscher Rundfunk in Cologne used various equal subdivisions of the octave or larger intervals in order to avoid 12-note equal temperament: in Stockhausen's *Studie II* (1954) 28 semitones ($2\frac{1}{4}$ octaves) are divided into 25 equal intervals so that there are no octave relationships, and *Gesang der Jünglinge* (1955–6) uses up to 60 divisions of the octave with vocal material and 42 with electronic sounds.

(iii) American gamelan. In Europe several groups of musicians (often including composers) have been formed, for example in Amsterdam, Basle and London, to perform on genuine Javanese or Balinese gamelans. As well as similar groups, there are in the USA around 25 specially constructed Western gamelans. Many of these were inspired by the gamelan Si Darius (named after the composer Milhaud, who taught at Mills College between 1940 and 1971), which was built in the early 1970s by

3. Second version of the Motorola Scalatron (1979–81), an electronic microtonal keyboard instrument; the 294 colour-coded keys give up to 56 individually tunable notes to the octave and the instrument has a memory that can store up to 17 tuning systems

Harrison and Colvig and for which Harrison has composed several works; this and most of those built on the West Coast are tuned in just intonation. More recently, Harrison and Colvig have produced the gamelan Si Betty (named after a local patroness, Betty Freeman). Three others are well known. Gamelan Son of Lion was constructed in New Jersey in 1974 by the composer and ethnomusicologist Barbara Benary, using designs by Dennis Murphy derived from traditional Javanese instruments; it consists of 21 iron metallophones with tin-can resonators and gongs made from hubcaps and oil drums. Benary, Philip Corner and Daniel Goode are among the composers who have written for and perform in the ensemble, which also plays central Javanese court music. In 1975, David Doty's Other Music gamelan, tuned to 14 unequal divisions of the octave, was built in San Francisco. In Berkeley, California, the composer Daniel Schmidt constructed the similar Western Gamelan in 1976 with Paul Dresher, using aluminium metallophones (some with tin-can resonators). More recently Schmidt has added new timbres, from tuned rod resonators for example; he is also the composer of much of the ensemble's repertory.

(iv) Other developments. Microtonal keyboards have preoccupied inventors rather less in the period since World War II. The 31-NOTE ORGAN of Adriaan Fokker (1950) and its later electronic version the Arcifoon (1971) have a 31-note, equally divided octave, based on Christiaan Huygens's theories; they have a keyboard like that introduced by Bosanquet (see Table 1) with keys in three colours – blue, black and white. A number of composers, including Hába and Vïshnegradsky, have written works for the 31-note organ. In Oslo the composer Eivind Groven built a non-tempered 36-note harmonium (1936), a small pipe organ (1954) and a 43-note electronic organ (1965), all in just intonation; around 1970 a similar complete pipe organ was constructed for him by Walcker. All four instruments use conventional keyboards with assignment facilities. In the 1940s A. R. McClure advocated tuning pianos and organs in mean-tone tuning, and an 'extended meantone organ' with 19 pipes to the octave was built to his specification in 1950; several mean-tone organs have recently been installed in the USA. Arnold Dreyblatt's portable pipe organ in just intonation dates from around 1980.

A series of *pianos metamorfoseadores* (microtonal upright pianos with conventional keyboards), each in a different tuning from $\frac{1}{3}$- to $\frac{1}{16}$-tones, was planned by Car-

4. The manuals of Fokker's 31-note pipe organ, 1945–50 (Teyler Museum, Haarlem); each manual has 143 black, white and blue keys, giving a 31-note octave tuned in equally tempered $\frac{1}{5}$-tones

rillo in 1927; a $\frac{1}{5}$-tone grand was built in 1947 and the uprights (by the Carl Sauter Pianofortefabrik in Spaichingen, Baden-Württemberg) in 1957–8. The range of these pianos becomes smaller as the number of subdivisions of the octave is increased, so that the $\frac{1}{16}$-tone instrument has a compass of a single octave, in the middle range, with 97 keys. Many of Carrillo's instruments are to be housed in the Carrillo Museum in Mexico City. Since the 1930s Augusto Novaro, a former pupil of Carrillo's, has built a number of Novares – pianos that sound less percussive than normal and are tuned in such divisions of the octave as 14, 15, 19, 22, 31 and 53; he has also constructed asymmetrical microtonal bowed and plucked string instruments.

Activities in building microtonal instruments without keyboards have been largely concentrated in California; elsewhere developments have been sporadic. Since 1977 Dean Drummond in New York has built a family of Zoomoozophones – aluminium tube metallophones in 31-note just intonation. In Toronto the composer Gayle Young produced Columbine in 1977–8, a 61-note steel tube metallophone covering nearly three octaves in a 23-note unequal temperament based on frequency ratios; she followed it in 1980 with Amaranth, a koto-like instrument with 24 strings and movable bridges, which is tuned in various systems and can be plucked, struck and bowed. Another recent instrument is the Si-Xen, constructed for Xenakis's *Pléïades* (1976), written for Les Percussions de Strasbourg; this is a set of six 19-note metallophones, each of which has different pitches in an unequal scale of 21 notes to the octave, consisting of alternate $\frac{1}{4}$- and $\frac{1}{3}$-tones. John Grayson in Vancouver has employed non-equal tunings in some of his instruments, such as the Pyrex Marimba (1967) which has 24 notes in a compass of about one and a half octaves. Since Carrillo's death in 1965 the *arpa citera* has been redesigned in Cuernavaca by Oscar Vargas Leal and the composer David Espejo Avilés; several large *arpas armónicas* with 400 notes to the octave have been built, as well as smaller models, including a three-octave version with 100 notes in equal temperament played by Pepe Aton Estevane since the late 1970s. Péter Eötvös has performed on a '55-chord', a specially built Hungarian *citera* tuned in intervals based on the golden section, which results in a logarithmic scale lacking any integral frequency ratios or interval steps of identical size.

Many of the new acoustic and electronic instruments produced by musicians and sound sculptors use non-tempered tunings that are microtonal but do not adhere to any specific system. Examples include some of the work of Mario Bertoncini and the Sonambient series of Harry Bertoia, which produce constellations of microtonal intervals. Microtonal systems are equally feasible with the techniques of DRAWN SOUND, as in the work of Arseny Avraamov.

Most contemporary composers and performers prefer to use conventional instruments that are retuned or specially fingered. Ben Johnston's Sonata (1963) requires a piano tuned in a just system in which only seven pairs of keys, mostly several octaves apart, give octave relationships. Just intonation is also used in La Monte Young's *Well-Tuned Piano* (1964), which has been revived effectively since 1974 with a Bösendorfer piano. Serge Cordier has specialized in tuning pianos to equal temperament with justly tuned 5ths. Bjørn Fongaard has written several works since the mid-1960s involving quarter-tone guitars, and the guitarist John Schneider performs in mean-tone, just and Pythagorean tunings. Since the 1950s Maurice Ohana has used zithers tuned in $\frac{1}{4}$- and $\frac{1}{3}$-tones in several works. Henri Pousseur adopted a 19-note tuning in his solo cello piece *Racine 19* (1975), and quarter-tones have been used, primarily but not exclusively with bowed string instruments, in works by Boulez, Ligeti, Penderecki and Xenakis, and younger composers such as Alain Bancquart. Jean-Etienne Marie has composed for some of Carrillo's instruments (several of which are in her possession), for the microtonal Ondioline and for synthesizers such as an Oberheim. Pavel Blatný wrote a study for quarter-tone trumpet and jazz orchestra in 1964. Microtonal inflections and beats are featured in works by Giacinto Scelsi and Phill Niblock.

In New York a variety of conventional instruments have been played microtonally, especially in the series of concerts given since 1981 under the title American Festival of Microtonal Music; these are organized by a leading participant, the bassoonist Johnny Reinhard. Refretted guitars and the Scalatron have also appeared in these concerts. Tui St George Tucker has specialized in quarter-tones since the 1950s, especially in her compositions for members of the recorder family. A number of microtonal ensembles have been active in the USA, including the Interval Players, The NewBand, Sonora and John Catler's 31-note rock group, J. C. and the Microtones.

BIBLIOGRAPHY

N. Vicentino: *L'antica musica ridotta alla moderna prattica* (Rome, 1555/*R*1959, 2/1557)

G. Zarlino: *Le istitutioni harmoniche* (Venice, 1558/*R*1965, rev. 3/1573/*R*1966)

N. Vicentino: *Descrizione dell'arciorgano* (Venice, 1561; Eng. trans. in Kaufmann, *JMT*, v (1961), 32

F. de Salinas: *De musica libri septem* (Salamanca, 1577)

M. Mersenne: *Harmonie universelle* (Paris, 1636-7/*R*1963), iii; Eng. trans. (1957)

C. Huygens: *Novus cyclus harmonicus*, 1661; in *Opera varia* (Leiden, 1724), 747; ed. in *Oeuvres complètes*, xx (The Hague, 1940)

H. W. Poole: 'An Essay on Perfect Intonation in the Organ', *American Journal of Sciences and the Arts*, 2nd ser., ix (1850), 68, 199

H L. F. von Helmholtz: 'Über musikalische Temperatur', *Natur-historische-Medizinischer Verein Heidelberg* (23 Nov 1860); rev. in *Die Lehre von den Tonempfindungen als physiologische Grundlage für die Theorie der Musik* (Brunswick, 1863, 5/1896), 501, 664, 669; Eng. trans. by A. J. Ellis as *On the Sensations of Tone as a Physiological Basis for the Theory of Music* (London, rev. 2/1885/*R*1954), 310, 422, 429, 466

T. P. Thompson: *On the Principles and Practice of Just Intonation* (London, 9/1866)

H. W. Poole: 'On Perfect Harmony in Music', *American Journal of Science and the Arts*, 2nd ser., xliv (1867), 1

A. J. Ellis: 'On the Temperament of Instruments with Fixed Tones', *Proceedings of the Royal Society*, xiii (1874), 404

R. H. M. Bosanquet: *An Elementary Treatise on Musical Instruments and Temperament* (London, 1876)

G. Engel: *Das mathematische Harmonium: ein Hilfsmittel zur Veranschaulichung der reinen Tonverhältnisse* (Berlin, 1881)

C. Brown: *Music in Common Things* (London, 1885)

S. Tanaka: 'Studien im Gebiete der reinen Stimmung', *VMw*, vi (1890), 1–90

C. A. Eitz: *Das mathematisch-reine Tonsystem* (Leipzig, 1891)

G. A. Behrens-Senegalden: *Die Vierteltöne in der Musik* (Berlin, 1892)

F. Busoni: *Entwurf einer neuen Ästhetik der Tonkunst* (Trieste, 1907, 2/1910/*R*1954); Eng. trans. as *Sketch of a New Esthetic of Music* (New York, 1911/*R*1962)

J. Mager: *Vierteltonmusik* (Aschaffenburg, 1915)

W. von Moellendorf: *Musik mit Vierteltönen* (Leipzig, 1917)

A. Avraamov: 'Jenseits von Temperierung und Tonalität', *Melos*, i (1920), no.6, p.131; no.7, p.160; no.8, p.184

F. Busoni: 'Dritteltonmusik', *Melos*, iii (1922), 198

R. H. Stein: 'Vierteltonmusik', *Die Musik*, xv (1922–3), 510

J. Mager: *Eine neue Epoche der Musik durch Radio* (Berlin, 1924)

E. H. Pierce: 'A Colossal Experiment in "Just Intonation"', *MQ*, x (1924), 326

S. Baglioni: *Udito e voce: elementi fisiologici della parola e della musica* (Rome, 1925)

C. Ives: 'Some "Quarter-tone" Impressions', *Franco-American Music Society Bulletin*, xxv/3 (1925); repr. in *Essays Before a Sonata and Other Writings*, ed. H. Boatwright (New York, 2/1962), 105

G. M. Rimsky-Korsakov: 'Obosnovaniye chetvyortitonovoy muzïkal'noy sistemï' [The basis of the musical quarter-tone system], *De musica*, i (Leningrad, 1925)

L. Kallenbach-Greller: 'Die historischen Grundlagen der Vierteltöne', *AMw*, viii (1926), 473

W. Perrett: *Some Questions of Musical Theory* (Cambridge, 1926)

G. Overmyer: 'Quarter-Tones – and Less', *American Mercury*, xii (1927), 207

G. Rimsky-Korsakov: 'Theorie und Praxis der Reintonsysteme', *Melos*, vii (1928), 15

M. F. Meyer: *The Musician's Arithmetic*, University of Missouri Studies, iv/1 (Columbia, 1929)

J. Yasser: *A Theory of Evolving Tonality* (New York, 1932)

J. Foulds: *Music Today: its Heritage from the Past, and Legacy to the Future* (London, 1934), 59

W. Dupont: *Geschichte der musikalischen Temperatur* (Kassel, 1935)

A. Fickénsher: 'The "Polytone" and the Potentialities of a Purer Intonation', *MQ*, xxvii (1941), 356

E. W. Tipple and R. M. Frye: *A Graphic Introduction to the Harmon* (Boston, 1942)

J. Carrillo: *'Sonido 13': fundamento científico e histórico* (Mexico City, 1948); Eng. trans. in *Soundings*, no. 5 (1973), 64

E. Groven: *Temperering og renstemning* (Oslo, 1948; Eng. trans., 1970)

A. D. Fokker: *Just Intonation and the Combination of Harmonic Diatonic Melodic Groups* (The Hague, 1949), 195–319

H. Partch: *Genesis of a Music* (Madison, Wisc., 1949, rev. 2/1974), 361–457

J. M. Barbour: *Tuning and Temperament: a Historical Survey* (East Lansing, Mich., 1951/*R*1972)

A. R. McClure: 'An Extended Meantone Organ', *The Organ*, xxx (1950–51), 139

H. W. Kaufmann: 'Vicentino's Arciorgano: an Annotated Translation', *JMT*, v (1961), 32

J. Mandelbaum: *Multiple Division of the Octave and the Tonal Resources of the 19-Tone Temperament* (diss., Indiana U., 1961)

Ll. S. Lloyd and H. Boyle: *Intervals, Scales and Temperament* (London, 1963/*R*1978)

A. D. Fokker: *Neue Musik mit 31 Tönen* (Düsseldorf, 1966; Eng. trans. 1975)

H. W. Kaufmann: *The Life and Works of Nicola Vicentino*, MSD, xi (1966), 163

L. Gerdine, P. Yates, B. Johnston, L. A. Hiller, J. Mandelbaum and C. Gamer: 'Microtonal Music in America', *Proceedings of the American Society of University Composers*, ii (1967), 77 [forum]

E. Groven: *Renstemningsautomaten* (Oslo, 1968)

K. A. Macfadyen and D. Greer: 'A Detunable Organ', *MT*, cx (1969), 612

A. Hába: *Mein Weg zur Viertel- und Sechsteltonmusik* (Düsseldorf, 1971)

W. Colvig: 'A Western Gamelan', *Sound Sculpture: A Collection of Essays by Artists*, ed. J. Grayson (Vancouver, 1975), 70

D. Ellis: *Quartertones: a Text with Musical Examples, Exercises and Etudes* (Plainview, NY, 1975)

F. R. Herf: *Die ekmelische Orgel: eine elektronische Feinstufenorgel mit 72 Tonstufen in der Oktave* (Salzburg, 1975)

S. Schneider: *Mikrotöne in der Musik des 20. Jahrhunderts* (Bad Godesberg, 1975)

J.-E. Marie: *L'homme musical* (Paris, 1976), 25–94

Interval – Exploring the Sonic Spectrum (1978–)

K. Terry: 'La Monte Young: Avant-Garde Visionary Composer and Pianist', *Contemporary Keyboard*, vi/8 (1980), 12

E. Blackwood: 'Discovering the Microtonal Resources of the Synthesizer', *Keyboard*, viii/5 (1982), 26

'Microtonal Music', *Ear Magazine East*, vii/5 (1982–3) [special issue]

HUGH DAVIES

Micundo. Plural of MUCUNDO, drum of Angola.

Micupela. Plural of MUCUPELA, drum of Angola.

Midgley–Walker organ. An ELECTRONIC ORGAN developed from the mid-1920s by A. H. Midgley and completed with A. M. Midgley in 1937; a few instruments were made by the organ builders J. W. Walker & Sons in Ruislip, Middlesex, in 1939, but manufacture ceased when war broke out. The Midgley–Walker was a standard organ with full pedal-board. The sounds were generated by 12 rotating electrostatic tone-wheels, in each of which a dielectric disc rotated between two stators. Two sets each of nine dials controlled the addition of selected overtones required for two mutation stops. A. H. Midgley was technical adviser to the John Compton Organ Co. from 1923 and a director from 1933 to 1937; the Compton Electrone, designed by Leslie Bourn, was based on Midgley's ideas, which he had patented in 1931.

BIBLIOGRAPHY
G. Winch and A. M. Midgley: 'Electronic Musical Instruments and the Development of the Pipeless Organ', *Journal of the Institution of Electrical Engineers*, lxxxvi (1940), 517

HUGH DAVIES

Midjwiz. *See* MIJWIZ.

Midmer-Losh. American firm of organ builders. It was founded by Reuben Midmer (1824–95), originally from Sussex, England, who emigrated to New York at the age of 16 and was apprenticed to Thomas Hall. Later he was employed by Ferris & Stuart, but in 1860 he left to form his own company in Brooklyn. At his death his son Reed Midmer became head of the firm, and in 1906 it moved to larger quarters in Merrick, Long Island. By this time over 100 organs had been built for Brooklyn alone. In the 1920s C. Siebert Losh joined the firm, which became known as the Midmer-Losh Organ Co. He was an experimenter, and among the ideas which he promoted was the seven-octave organ keyboard, first used in 1925 in an organ for the Central Christian Church, Miami, Florida. The firm's most notable organ was the enormous instrument completed for the Atlantic City Convention Hall in 1932. This proved to be disastrous financially, however, and the firm closed a few years later.

BIBLIOGRAPHY
W. H. Barnes and E. B. Gammons: *Two Centuries of American Organ Building* (Glen Rock, NJ, 1970)
O. Ochse: *The History of the Organ in the United States* (Bloomington, Ind., 1975)

BARBARA OWEN

Midwinterhorn [midwinterhoorn]. Wooden trumpet of the Low Countries played in east Holland.

Miessner, Benjamin F(ranklin) (*b* ?Huntingdon, Ind., 1890; *d* Miami, Florida, 25 March 1976). American inventor and designer of electroacoustic instruments. Miessner's first inventions included some connected with early radio research (from 1909) and (somewhat later) electric gramophones. In 1921 he developed a 'vibrato pickup' for pianos, and in 1928 Amperite manufactured an electric pickup designed by him for guitars. With his brother Otto (who was head of the music department at the University of Kansas) he invented several musical devices, including the Rhythmicon, an instrument for producing complex rhythmic patterns, similar in conception to Lev Termen's instrument of the same name developed in 1931. After selling his radio patents to RCA for a very large sum of money, Miessner set up a laboratory (Miessner inventions) in Millburn, New Jersey in 1930 to explore further the possibilities of electrifying musical instruments.

Miessner's first goal was to develop a cheap and portable piano for educational purposes. After experiment-

ing with different sound-producing elements and pickups he returned to strings, but removed the piano's soundboard; this formed the basis for his Electronic Piano (*see* ELECTRONIC PIANO, (2)). One aspect of the electric pianos of this type that were developed in the 1930s and 1940s, the innovatory long sustain time made possible by omitting the soundboard, was a principal contributor to their ultimate lack of success, for such an instrument was unsuitable for most of the standard repertory. In 1954 Miessner produced a new 'stringless' electric piano based on struck tuned reeds, which was marketed by the Wurlitzer Co. until the early 1960s. A more advanced design for an electric piano from the early 1970s was turned down by another manufacturer.

Other instruments designed by Miessner during the 1930s included harmoniums with up to four reeds for each note and two electrostatic pickups for each reed, to produce a range of timbres (the Everett Orgatron, later taken over by Wurlitzer, was based on Miessner's patents in this area), and amplified instruments such as guitar, zither, mouth organ, violin, cello, saxophone and clarinet. Around 1939 Tom Adrian Cracraft's All Electronic Orchestra consisted of a Novachord and several amplified string instruments designed by Miessner (*see* ELECTRONIC INSTRUMENTS, fig.1): four violins, cello, double bass, Hawaiian and Spanish guitars, a piano based on Miessner's patents (probably the Electone) and the 'chromatic electronic timpani'. The last consisted of 13 short bass strings, tuned to a chromatic octave and mounted inside a rectangular frame, which were played with timpani sticks, the vibrations being converted by electrostatic pickups into voltage variations and made audible over a loudspeaker; as with the Rhythmicon, Termen produced a similar but electronic instrument at around the same time.

BIBLIOGRAPHY
B. F. Miessner: 'Electronic Music and Instruments', *Proceedings of the Institute of Radio Engineers*, xxiv (1936), 1427
——: 'Electronic Musical Instruments', *Journal of the Acoustical Society of America*, xix (1947), 996
T. L. Rhea: *The Evolution of Electronic Musical Instruments in the United States* (diss., George Peabody College, Nashville, Tenn., 1972), 107, 117; section rev. as 'B. F. Miessner's Electronic Piano', *Contemporary Keyboard*, iv/2 (1978), and 'B. F. Miessner's "Stringless Piano"', *Contemporary Keyboard*, iv/4 (1978), 62

HUGH DAVIES

Mignon. A trade name used by Helbig of Berlin (*c*1903) for a self-playing REED ORGAN operated by a circular card and by WELTE of Freiburg (from 1904) for their reproducing PLAYER PIANO; *see also* MECHANICAL INSTRUMENT.

Miguel, Mariano Tafall y. *See* TAFALL Y MIGUEL, MARIANO.

Mí-gyaùng (Burmese: 'crocodile-zither'). BOX ZITHER of Burma, carved in the shape of a crocodile's head and tail. It has three metal strings which pass over eight to ten raised movable frets on the flat belly of the instrument. This Burmese zither is related to similar instruments distributed widely in South-east Asia. While the crocodile shape is not always found elsewhere, the reptilian name remains in variants such as the Thai ČHAKHĒ ('alligator', wooden tube zither) and the Indonesian and Philippine *kacapi* (box zither; *see* KACAPI (i)). In Burma the *mí-gyaùng* is associated with the Mon, an ethnic group in southern Burma linguistically related to the Mon-Khmer peoples of Thailand and Kampuchea.

Mihbash. *See* JĀWAN.

Mih diple. *See* DIPLE.

Mihiṅgu-berē. *See* DEMALA-BERĒ.

Mijwiz [midjwiz, miǧwiz, mizwidj; mizwij]. Reed instrument, normally a DOUBLE CLARINET, of the Near East, with two parallel pipes of the same length. It is a folk instrument of the MIZMĀR type (*mijwiz* is the vernacular term for 'pair') but the relationship is not always acknowledged. Each reedpipe, about 30 cm long, consists of two sections which fit together and are fastened by string and tar (which at the same time join the two pipes). The small, upper part (about 7 cm) is the actual idioglot single reed (there are two, one for each tube); the tongue is 2 cm long and is down-cut (i.e. it sticks up in the direction of the tube). The tops of the tubes are closed so that the breath must pass through the tongue, and the entire section must be placed deep in the mouth to produce the sound. The two playing pipes generally have six holes and a thumb-hole at the back. The placing of the hands varies according to the players, the relationship of left hand to lower notes and right to higher changing from one village to the next. The range of

Mijwiz (double clarinet) player, Baalbek, Lebanon

the instrument is more than an octave but the player usually hovers around a wide 4th (between a 4th and a 5th). Playing requires circular breathing. Despite this and the parallel tubes, the *mijwiz* is never played with one of the tubes providing a drone; two melodies are played simultaneously, in unison. As one of the tubes is usually tuned slightly higher than the other, beats are produced between the two, which is a desired characteristic.

The *mijwiz* is mainly found on a north–south Mediterranean axis from Iskenderun in Turkey (where the instrument is called *argun* or *argul*, with drone) to Gaza; it dies out towards the east, finishing at Mossul, Iraq (where it is called *mizwij*). The playing style along the Mediterranean coast is florid, with fiorituras, arabesques and features of free improvisation in a nervous, rapid tempo; this contrasts with the more accented, heavier and less ethereal style used in the hinterland. The nasal quality is found everywhere. The instrument is generally played alone, but it may accompany a singer, when it is supported by a *darbukka* (goblet drum). Its repertory is drawn from song tradition, which it dec-

orates in its own way. Particular pieces are not known, except for the *dabka* dance. A pastoral function has often been accorded to the *mijwiz*, and that would be consistent with its social status. Its initial role may have been to lead funeral processions, a custom that persists in Lebanon though it may be replaced by Western-type brass instruments.

BIBLIOGRAPHY
S. Jargy: *La musique arabe* (Paris, 1971)
H. H. Touma: *Die Musik der Araber* (Wilhelmshaven, 1975; Fr. trans., 1977)
S. Qassim Hassan: *Les instruments de musique en Irak et leur rôle dans la société traditionelle* (Paris, 1980)
A. J. Racy: 'Druze Music', *Grove 6*
L. Hage: 'Lebanon', *Grove 6*
A. Shiloah: 'Arab Music', §II, *Grove 6*
                                                    CHRISTIAN POCHÉ

Mikwati wenyere. PANPIPES of the Karanga/Duma people of Zaka district, Zimbabwe. It is the traditional instrument for honouring guardian spirits, the *Songano Mashawi*, and is accompanied by the *hosho* rattle. See *TraceyCSA*, ii, 391.

Miḷāvu [mizhāvu]. Pot-shaped drum of Kerala, south India. Usually made of copper, the drum has a rounded body and a short neck; it can be of different dimensions. The small mouth is covered with a skin which is beaten with the bare hands. The *miḷāvu* is played by members of the Nambiyar community, and accompanies two performances given in temples: in *Cākkiyar kūthu* it is played only with a pair of cymbals, while in *Kuṭṭiyāttam* two *miḷāvu*, of different sizes, are played with an *iḍakka* (variable tension hourglass drum) and a pair of cymbals; according to Rajagopalan, a *kuḷal* (oboe) is also present. See L. S. Rajagopalan: 'Thayambaka (Laya Vinyasa) on the Chenda (Drum)', *Journal of the Music Academy Madras*, xxxviii (1967), 90, 101.

See also MUḶAVU.

                                                    PRIBISLAV PITOËFF

Milenge. Transverse flute of the Sankuru region of Zaïre. Specimens described by Laurenty are unusual in having finger-holes at one side, not in line with the mouth-hole (*LaurentyA*, 285).

Milengi. Cylindrical stopped wooden flute of the Batemba people of Zaïre (*LaurentyA*, 177f).

Milhouse [Millhouse]. English family of woodwind makers. Richard Millhouse (*b* Newark, *c*1725; *d* Newark, 29 Nov 1775) married in Fledborough in 1753, when he was described as a turner. The few surviving instruments stamped 'Millhouse Newark', including a fine bassoon dated 1763 (in the Sheffield Museum), may confidently be ascribed to him. Those stamped 'Milhouse Newark' are presumably by his elder son Richard Milhouse (*b* Newark, 10 Aug 1759; *d* West Retford, Aug 1845). Little is known of his career; his father's will of 1775 instructed his executors to find him a partner to help him run the business until he came of age. He seems to have worked intermittently in Newark and London (Holden's Directory of 1805 lists him in Soho); he was back in Newark in 1822–36.

The most important member of the family was his younger brother William Milhouse (*b* Newark, 14 Aug 1761), who married in Newark in 1786. He moved to London and had opened a shop at 100 Wardour Street by mid-1787, moving at the end of 1797 to 337 Oxford

Street. For nearly 50 years he enjoyed the highest reputation as a maker of woodwind instruments. His trade cards describe him as 'Manufacturer to their Royal Highnesses the Dukes of Kent & Cumberland'; he stamped his instruments 'W. Milhouse London'. An article in *The Harmonicon* (1830) states that 'Great improvements have been made on this instrument [the oboe] by Millhouse, the only maker in England of any celebrity'. He is especially noted for his excellent bassoons, which have survived in comparatively large numbers; he also published some music. In 1822 he was joined by his son Richard Milhouse, who ran the business alone from 1834 to 1840. (For Milhouse instruments *see* OBOE, figs.6*b* and 13*b*.)

R. Milhouse & Sons are mentioned in directories of 1788 and 1794 as instrument makers at Pratt Street, Lambeth, London. None of their instruments has survived and their relationship to the above is not known.

BIBLIOGRAPHY
'On the Oboe and Bassoon', *The Harmonicon*, viii (1830), 192
L. G. Langwill: *An Index of Musical Wind-instrument Makers* (Edinburgh, 1960, rev. 6/1980)

WILLIAM WATERHOUSE

Militär Glockenspiel (Ger.). BELL-LYRA.

Militärkapell (Ger.). Military band; *see* BAND (i), §II, 1(i), 2(i) and §III, 2.

Militärtrommel (Ger.). Side drum; *see* DRUM. §3.

Military band (Fr. *harmonie*; Ger. *Militärkapell*, *Musikkorps*; It. *banda, corpo di musica*). A term dating from the late 18th century used of a regimental band of woodwind, brass and percussion instruments. It is also applied to an ensemble of any sort that plays military music, including signals and military calls; *see* BAND (i), §II, 1(i), 2(i) and §III, 2. In British usage it refers (misleadingly) to mixed wind bands of all types; *see* BAND (i), §III.

Millant. French family of violin and bow makers. The brothers Roger (*b* 1901) and Max (*b* 1903) began their apprenticeship with their grandfather, Sebastian Auguste Deroux, and then worked for Dykes & Son in London. In 1923 they opened their own business at 51 rue de Rome, Paris. They succeeded in establishing a fine reputation and gained first prizes at international exhibitions in The Hague (1949) and Liège (1954). Their violins and cellos are patterned after an original model that combines characteristics of Stradivari and Guarneri, while their violas slightly recall the Tertis model. Their instruments show excellent craftsmanship and choice of wood; the varnish is usually a transparent orange-red. Besides being labelled, their instruments are marked with the letters RMM enclosed in a triangle of purfling below the button. Bows branded R & M MILLANT and R & M.M. were made for the Millant workshop by various Mirecourt bow makers. The brothers collaborated on a *Manuel pratique de lutherie* (Paris, 1952) and Roger Millant published a study of J.-B. Vuillaume (London, 1972); they retired as makers in 1969.

Roger Millant's son Jean-Jacques (*b* 1928) began his apprenticeship with the Morizot brothers at Mirecourt and returned to Paris in 1950 to enter the family workshop. A year later he set up independently in Paris. In 1971 he was named 'Meilleur Ouvrier de France'. His bows, which follow the Peccatte school, are elegantly made and enjoy a fine international reputation; many of them are mounted with either ivory or tortoiseshell frogs. They are branded J.J. MILLANT À PARIS.

Bernard Millant (*b* 1929), son of Max Millant, served his apprenticeship in violin making in 1946-8 with Amédée Dieudonné and later in bow making with the Morizot brothers. After a time in the family workshop he spent a further year of study in the USA (1949). In 1950 he set up independently in Paris. He has achieved distinction in both violin and bow making. The bows follow the Peccatte school and are similar to his cousin's except that the heads are a little more squared. The frogs are almost always mounted in a recessed track carved into the lower three facets of the butt. His bows are branded either BERNARD MILLANT À PARIS or BERNARD MILLANT PARIS and have the year of manufacture stamped in very small digits on the bottom facet of the butt.

BIBLIOGRAPHY
R. Vannes: *Essai d'un dictionnaire universel des luthiers* (Paris, 1932, 2/1951/R1972 as *Dictionnaire universel des luthiers* and R1981 incl. suppl. 1959)
E. Vatelot: *Les archets français* (Nancy, 1976)

JAAK LIIVOJA-LORIUS

Mille, Auguste (*b* Lille, 3 April 1838; *d* ?Paris, *c*1898). French maker of brass instruments. He gained awards for instruments as early as the Paris exhibition of 1855. By 1880 he had become the foreman at the factory of Courtois, which he took over in that year. The new firm took the name of Courtois & Mille. Mille was succeeded in 1898 by E. Delfaux.

Mille was particularly notable for changing the mounting of the pistons and tubing on the cornet from the left-hand side of the instrument to the right. He devised a slide mechanism to avoid the considerable problems on the trombone of playing from B♭ to B♮ or vice versa. Pierre described a collection of 36 instruments displayed, including numerous cavalry trumpets in different keys.

BIBLIOGRAPHY
C. Pierre: *La facture instrumentale à l'Exposition universelle de 1889* (Paris, 1890)

NIALL O'LOUGHLIN

Miller, George (*fl* London, *c*1765-99; *d* after 1814). English woodwind instrument maker, possibly of German origin. His earliest known address is 3 Dacre Street, Westminster. He was the ratepayer there from 1777 to 1784 (followed by Frederick Wolfe in 1784-90 and JOHN CRAMER in 1790-98) though he continued to live there until at least 1788, when he is recorded as having given this address at the Westminster election. It is possible that he was of German extraction and that he attracted other German immigrants to work with him, indeed that he was the maker with whom George Astor first worked on his arrival in England; a clarinet by Miller (in the Glasgow University Collection) bears the address 26 Wych Street, where Astor worked in 1782-97 (Langwill's statement that Miller was the ratepayer at 79 Cornhill in 1775-99, premises subsequently occupied by Astor, is incorrect).

Miller made the earliest surviving English clarinets shown in Zoffany's painting of the Sharpe family on their barge at Fulham (1779; private collection); these instruments, described by Halfpenny (1965), may be dated stylistically to the 1760s. They bear no address and have as a maker's mark a rose on a stem. All his other instruments have a unicorn's head as a maker's mark; this was also used by makers who worked with him, i.e. Cramer, Astor and their successors Bilton, Gerock, Key, Robert Wolfe and Figg.

Miller may be the grantee of British Patent no.3383 of 1 October 1810 for fifes made out of brass; a trade card associated with this (in *GB-Lbm*) reads 'G Miller & Co, 3 Panton St, Haymarket, musical instrument makers to their Majesties'. George Miller was the rate-payer at 3 Panton Street from 1810 to 1814.

BIBLIOGRAPHY

L. G. Langwill: *An Index of Musical Wind-instrument Makers* (Edinburgh, 1960, rev., enlarged 6/1980)
E. Halfpenny: 'Early English Clarinets', *GSJ*, xviii (1965), 42
M. A. Byrne: 'George Miller and John Cramer', *GSJ*, xix (1966), 134

MAURICE BYRNE

Millereau, François (*b* Grosbois, Côte-d'or; *d* ?Paris, ?c1898). French maker of wind instruments. After having worked for G. A. Besson, he established his own business in Paris in 1861. In 1878 he took over the firm of Labbaye, who had himself acquired the firm of Raoux. Millereau gained medals for his instruments at the Paris exhibitions of 1867, 1878 and 1889. In 1898 he was succeeded by his son-in-law Herman Schoenaers, who continued the business until his death in 1931, when it was acquired by Selmer. Like Besson, Millereau specialized in brass but also made some woodwind instruments, his saxophones, oboes and clarinets being highly esteemed. In 1887 he made important modifications to the keywork of the saxophone, extending the range to *b*♭ by means of a flat key played with the right thumb. His brass instruments (trumpets, *cornets à pistons* and saxhorns) gained medals as early as 1867. Millereau also built unusual instruments for other designers, for example a complicated trombone for Bordier in 1881, and an elaborate compensation mechanism for Garigue.

BIBLIOGRAPHY

C. Pierre: *La facture instrumentale à l'Exposition universelle de 1889* (Paris, 1890)
——: *Les facteurs d'instruments de musique* (Paris, 1893/R1971)
L. G. Langwill: *An Index of Musical Wind-instrument Makers* (Edinburgh, 1960, rev., enlarged 6/1980)

NIALL O'LOUGHLIN

Miller organ. An ELECTRONIC ORGAN, several models of which were manufactured by the Miller Organ Co. (founded by Stanley L. Miller) in Norwich, Norfolk, between around 1948 and 1974. All models except the smallest ones were designed for use in churches. The first models, including the one-manual Martinette (without pedals), were designed by CONSTANT MARTIN. The sounds are generated by an oscillator for each note, a principle strongly favoured by Martin; the largest model has about 850. The company also constructed Martin's electronic carillon (c1949). Around 1974 Miller went into receivership, and in 1975 its current models were revived as the NORWICH ORGAN.

BIBLIOGRAPHY

R. H. Dorf: *Electronic Musical Instruments* (New York, 2/1958), 181

HUGH DAVIES

Millhouse. *See* MILHOUSE family.

Milupa. Collective term for single-headed conical open-ended drums of the Lozi and Valley Tonga peoples of Zambia. They are played by hand in conjunction with other instruments. The drums are of three sizes, named *kajakiri*, *sikumwa* and *omutuwa* (or *omutuna* among the Lozi). See *TraceyCSA*, ii, 86, 97.

Mimby chué. End-blown NOTCHED FLUTE of the KENA type, used by the Guaraní Indians of Paraguay. It is made of wood, with five finger-holes and one thumb-hole.

Mimiha. Obsolete irregular PANPIPES of Tonga, with between five and twelve tubes. The term is now applied to the mouth organ. See R. Moyle: 'Tongan Musical Instruments', *GSJ*, xxix (1976), 79.

Mina. A large single-headed cylindrical drum of Vene-zuela, made from a hollowed log. It is supported by two sticks in the form of an 'X' and is played with beaters, while a second player strikes the body of the drum with two small sticks called *laures*. This African-derived drum combines with the *curbata*, a smaller, footed drum, also struck with beaters, to accompany the Afro-Venezuelan *golpe de tambor grande*, a song form performed by blacks at religious festivals.

JOHN M. SCHECHTER

Mingongi. Concussion sticks of eastern Angola. They are used as secret instruments in *mukanda* circumcision schools.

Minimoog. A monophonic SYNTHESIZER designed by ROBERT A. MOOG with James Scott, William Hemsath and Chad Hunt in 1970 and manufactured by the R. A. Moog Co. in Trumansburg, New York (later Moog Music in Buffalo, New York), between 1970 and 1981. The Minimoog has probably been the most popular small synthesizer, especially in the field of rock music, where the distinctive outline of its sloping hinged front panel is still often to be seen; some 13,000 were produced. In 1981 the Minimoog was chosen as one of the 12 most innovative inventions of the last 200 years (together with the telephone, zip fastener, safety razor and ice-cream cone) for the Eureka exhibit at the Smithsonian Institution in Washington DC.

Based partly on the original Moog modular studio synthesizer, the Minimoog introduced the concept of the portable synthesizer (it weighs 13 kg) with integral keyboard; all patching is eliminated by a combination of hard-wired predetermined signal routing and switches on the front panel. The 44-note keyboard is monophonic (the lowest of any group of keys depressed at any one time has preference – the type of 'assignment' system known as 'low-note priority') and has a portamento control. The synthesizer may, alternatively, be controlled by the Ludwig 'Moog' drum or by a fingerboard (or ribbon controller). The sound sources are three oscillators with a choice of six waveforms, a white-noise generator, another sine-wave generator obtainable by tuning the filter, and provision for an external input. In addition to the filter, an envelope shaper and a mixer, several other elements are voltage-controlled. An unusual feature, which was pioneered on the Minimoog and continues to be popular on other synthesizers and electronic keyboard instruments, is the pair of 'performance wheels' situated at the left side of the keyboard for controlling pitch-bend and modulation; a central 'detent' on the pitch wheel permits a rapid return to the normal zero setting.

BIBLIOGRAPHY

D. T. Horn: *Electronic Music Synthesizers* (Blue Ridge Summit, Penn., 1980), 46

HUGH DAVIES

Miningo karipi-karipi. Single-headed open-ended conical drum of the Sena/Tonga people of Mtoko district, Zimbabwe. It is played with sticks and used with a flute ensemble, together with other drums. *See* MUTUMBA (ii).

Minipiano. A seven-octave upright ELECTRIC PIANO manufactured by Hardman, Peck & Co. of New York for a few years from about 1935. Based on the patent for Benjamin F. Miessner's Electronic Piano (*see* ELECTRONIC PIANO, (2)), it had no soundboard, the vibrations of the strings being converted by electrostatic pickups into voltage variations and made audible over a loudspeaker.

HUGH DAVIES

Minjayrah. End-blown flute of the Druze people of Lebanon.

Minnim. A biblical term (*see* BIBLICAL INSTRUMENTS) thought to mean strings and thus string instruments in general.

Minshall organ. An ELECTRONIC ORGAN, several models of which were designed by George Hadden and others and manufactured from around 1950 to the mid-1960s by Minshall Organ of Brattleboro, Vermont; initially the organs were produced in collaboration with the Estey Organ Co. (for promotional purposes) under the name 'Minshall–Estey', but this was changed to 'Minshall' alone around 1953, when Estey were beginning to make their own organs. The Minshall range consists of smaller one and two-manual instruments, including a chord organ. In most of them the sounds are generated by 12 oscillators using frequency division, but at least one early model uses tuned reeds the vibrations of which are converted by electrostatic pickups into voltage variations and made audible over a loudspeaker. Around 1955 several former Minshall designers were involved in the development of the Kinsman organ.

BIBLIOGRAPHY
R. L. Eby: *Electronic Organs* (Wheaton, Ill., 1953), 143
R. H. Dorf: 'The New Minshall Organ', *Audio*, xxxix (1955), no.9, p.25; no.10, p.54; rev. in *Electronic Musical Instruments* (New York, 2/1958), 70

HUGH DAVIES

Minshingaku. The modern Japanese term for the styles of Chinese secular music popularized in Japan during China's Ming and Qing dynasties (*Min*: 'Ming'; *shin*: 'Qing'; *gaku*: 'music'). This music entered Japan in two principal waves: around 1630 and during the early 19th century. The two styles were originally distinct (and can be referred to separately as *mingaku* and *shingaku*), but soon merged. The Sino-Japanese War (1894–5) cast things Chinese out of favour, rapidly diminishing the popularity of this music, and today it is rarely heard outside Nagasaki, its original port of importation. Traditional Japanese popular music and *minshingaku* have, however, interacted to a certain degree.

Most of the instruments which were imported with this music have remained unassimilated in Japan. The main ones together with their Chinese equivalents are: *unra/yunluo* (set of bronze gongs); *mokkin/muqin* (xylophone); *yōkin/yangqin* (box zither); *kokin/huqin* (two-string fiddle; *see* JINGHU); *genkan/ruan* (long-necked lute); *gekkin/yueqin* (short-necked lute); *hakuhan/pai-ban* (clappers); *sanai/suona* (oboe); *shō/sheng* (mouth organ); *biwa/pipa* (pear-shaped lute); *dōshō/dongxiao* (notched flute; *see* XIAO); *teikin/tiqin* (two-string fiddle; *see* BANHU). *See also* MINTEKI. Note, however, that the word *gekkin* in Ming-derived music referred rather to a long-necked lute with octagonal body which is otherwise called *genkan*; this accorded with the usage in China at the time. (A corresponding confusion of names occurs with the Korean *wŏlgŭm*.)

BIBLIOGRAPHY
F. Piggott: *The Music and Musical Instruments of Japan* (London, 1893, 2/1909/R1971), 135
W. P. Malm: 'Chinese Music in the Edo and Meiji Periods in Japan', *Asian Music*, vi/1–2 (1975), 147
Han Kuo-Hang: 'The Modern Chinese Orchestra', *Asian Music*, xi/1 (1979), 1–40
'Gekkin', 'Genkan', *Ongaku daijiten* [Encyclopedia of music] (Tokyo, 1981)

DAVID W. HUGHES

Minteki. Japanese term for transverse flutes of the *di* type (*see* DI (i)), imported from China since the early 17th century for use in *minshingaku* music (*Min*: 'Ming'; *teki*: 'flute'). A similar flute has taken root in Okinawa, probably imported directly from China several centuries earlier; it is used in both classical and folk music. The Okinawans, however, cover the membrane-hole with 'Cellophane' tape, so the *di*'s buzzing effect is lost. In Okinawa this flute is called by such names as *hansō*, *fue*, *fuye*, *fukii* and *pii*. See F. Koizumi, Y. Tokumaru and O. Yamaguchi, eds.: *Asian Musics in an Asian Perspective* (Tokyo, 1977), 151.

DAVID W. HUGHES

Minungu. LAMELLAPHONE of the Chokwe people of southern Zaïre; it is also known as KAKOLONDONDO (*LaurentyS*, 195).

Miphene ya kimbinga. Set of cylindrical stopped flutes made from bamboo or cane of the Pende people of southwestern Zaïre (*LaurentyA*, 208).

Mirdang. *See* MṚDAṄGA, §3.

Miremont, Claude-Augustin (*b* Mirecourt, 1827; *d* Pontorson, 1887). French violin maker. He was a pupil of his father Sebastien, a little-known and unexceptional craftsman who worked at Mirecourt all his life. After working for Claude Collin he moved to Paris in 1844 and was employed by Lafleur and Bernardel *père*. In 1852 he moved to New York, where he worked for nine years before returning to Paris to establish his own shop at 20 rue Faubourg-Poissonnière. There his intimate contact with the work of Stradivari and Guarneri 'del Gesù' inspired him to make instruments that at times rival those of his great competitor J.-B. Vuillaume. The workmanship is refined and delicate, the varnish often of good substance and attractive appearance. The tone of his instruments is remarkably fine, his best-known advocate being the cellist Pierre Fournier, who used his Miremont in preference to Italian instruments for most of his career.

BIBLIOGRAPHY
R. Vannes: *Essai d'un dictionnaire universel des luthiers* (Paris, 1932, 2/1951/R1972 as *Dictionnaire universel des luthiers* and R1981 incl. suppl. 1959)

CHARLES BEARE

Miren. A SLIT-DRUM of Atchin Island, north-east Malekula, Vanuatu. *See* NA-MBWE.

Mīriṣtus. *See* MURISTUS.

Mirliton. A group of acoustic devices that modify the tonal characteristics of vocal or instrumental sounds fed into them. They are not musical instruments in the strictest sense as they do not actually generate sounds. Marcuse (1964), following Galpin (1937), adopted the word 'mirliton', of French origin, as a generic term to cover all such musical auxiliaries whose behaviour depends on the forced vibration of a thin membrane. This membrane may be free, as in the 'comb-and-paper', or may form part of the wall of a tube or vessel containing an air column; its general effect is to add a buzzing or nasal quality. In certain simple mirlitons the membrane may be derived from the wall of a vegetable stem by scraping a thin area, as in a form of *trombetta di cana* mentioned by Bonanni in 1722, but commonly it is made of parchment, treated paper or silk, spider's-egg membrane or even onion skin (whence the name 'onion flute').

Although associated mainly with toy instruments such as the kazoo and bigophone, the mirliton principle is of considerable antiquity. In the Middle Ages the onion flute or *flûte-eunuque* (*see* EUNUCH-FLUTE) was evidently well esteemed, and Mersenne (1636–7) wrote of performances in four- or five-part harmony. A few examples of the eunuch-flute survive and show that it was sometimes made to look like a true musical instrument, even to the provision of (non-functional) finger-holes. The principle can also be used indirectly as in the Indian *nyastaranga*, a brass trumpet closed near the narrow end by a membrane and applied to the side of the larynx while the musician hums or vocalizes. Many African harps and xylophones, for example the Chopi *mbila* and the *madimba* of Zaïre, have a mirliton glued over openings in the gourd resonators, to add a buzzing quality and prolong the sounding note.

Other musical instruments to incorporate the vibrating membrane include the classical Chinese flute *ti-tzu* (*see* DI (i)), the *flauto di voce* of Wigley and McGregor (*c*1810), and the SUDROPHONE.

BIBLIOGRAPHY
M. Mersenne: *Harmonie universelle* (Paris, 1636–7/*R*1963; Eng. trans., 1957)
F. Bonanni: *Gabinetto armonico* (Rome, 1722/*R*1964)
T. S. Wotton: *A Dictionary of Foreign Musical Terms* (Leipzig, 1907)
F. W. Galpin: *Textbook of European Musical Instruments* (London, 1937, 2/1944)
C. Sachs: *The History of Musical Instruments* (New York, 1940)
N. Bessaraboff: *Ancient European Musical Instruments* (New York, 1941, 2/1964)
S. Marcuse: *Musical Instruments: a Comprehensive Dictionary* (New York, 1964)
A. C. Baines: *European and American Musical Instruments* (London, 1966)
                                           PHILIP BATE

Miruli. Log XYLOPHONE of the Gwere people of Uganda. *See* ENTAALA.

Mirumba [mirumbu]. Plural of MURUMBA.

Mirwaḥa. A FLABELLUM used in oriental, Syrian and Orthodox churches.

Mirwās. Double-headed drum of southern Iraq, Kuwait and the Arabian Gulf area. It has a wooden cylindrical body, 13 to 15 cm in depth and 11 to 14 cm in diameter. The heads, usually of sheepskin, are attached by two thin hoops which encircle the skin; thongs are fixed at irregular intervals for reinforcement. The instrument is held vertically on the knee, or in the left hand with the lower membrane resting on the palm so that the middle and ring fingers can strike the *tik* (clear or light) beats. The open right hand strikes the *dum* (dull or heavy) beats on the upper membrane.

In Az Zubayr, southern Iraq, the musicians accompany their songs with the *mirwās*. Throughout the Gulf region the *mirwās* accompanies the *fann al-ṣawt* ('art of the voice'), a traditional vocal type which probably originated in the Arabian Peninsula and the Yemen. A few *mirwās* with two other drums and three *jāhele* (earthen pot idiophones) accompany the *fijirī* and *ḥaddādī* songs of the Gulf pearl-divers. The complex rhythms of Gulf music explain the need for several *mirwās*. One of them takes the lead, altering the rhythmic formulae and improvising; the others accompany.

BIBLIOGRAPHY
S. Qassim Hassan: *Les instruments de musique en Irak et leur rôle dans la société traditionelle* (Paris, 1980)
P. Rovsing Olsen: 'Arabian Gulf', *Grove 6*
T. Kerbage: *The Rhythms of Pearl Diver Music in Qatar* (Doha, Qatar, 1982)
                    SCHEHERAZADE QASSIM HASSAN

Mise en bouche (Fr.). EMBOUCHURE.

Misengo. PANPIPES of the Salampasu people of Zaïre (*LaurentyA*, 214f). *See* MISHIBA.

Misengu. Conical flute of the Yaka people of southwestern Zaïre. It is fashioned from antelope horn with one stop near the tip (*LaurentyA*, 229).

Misewe. Tin-can rattle of the Lala people of Zambia. It is played with the *chirarira* and other drums.

Mishiba (sing. *mushiba*). Raft PANPIPES of the Luba people of Zaïre. It consists of a number of closed bamboo tubes of different lengths bound together with a liana stem so that the longest tube is on the player's left, the shortest on the right. The pipes are held in the left hand and played in sets for the group dance *lushya lwa mishiba*. Among the Luba people of Mutombo-Mukulu an ensemble may consist of ten instruments: a soloist with a seven-pipe instrument, three players of seven-pipe instruments of a different size, and the remainder with sets of four, three and two pipes. The smallest two sets play only an octave ostinato. Knosp's reports from southeastern Zaïre (1934–5) mention four-pipe instruments, the longest being 16 cm, which were used for dancing. They also mention the *misjiba* as a set of five to eight pipes, 5 to 15 cm long, played by one man to accompany dancing at the girls' puberty ceremony. De Hen (1960) gives *mishiba* as the name of the Sampwe people for four-pipe instruments; his list also includes the Kanyok *tshitebb* (five or eight pipes), Mbala *kibalamba* (four to six), Salampasu *misengo* (six or seven) and Sundi *ziphiolo* (three).

BIBLIOGRAPHY
TraceyCSA, ii, 47
F. J. de Hen: *Beitrag zur Kenntnis der Musikinstrumente aus Belgisch Kongo und Ruanda-Urundi* (Tervuren, 1960)
G. Knosp: *Enquête sur la vie musicale au Congo belge 1934–1935* (Tervuren, 1968)
J. Gansemans: *Les instruments de musique Luba* (Tervuren, 1980)
                    J. GANSEMANS, K. A. GOURLAY

Mišnice. BAGPIPE found in Istria, the Kvarner Bay area, Dalmatia and Bosnia and Hercegovina (Yugoslavia). It consists of a skin bag and double chanter with single reeds, and has no drone pipe. It is also known as *diple na meh* (*see* DIPLE).

Missenharter, Carl (*b* Ulm, 17 Sept 1829; *d* New York, after 1887). German brass instrument maker. He received his early training with his father, the instrument maker Johann Anton Missenharter, in Ulm. In 1861 he moved to Stuttgart. At the International Industrial Exhibition in London in 1862 he received a medal for the manufacture of brass instruments. His company, Missenharter & Cie., was granted on 19 June 1869 a French patent for a *cornet d'appel*. A copper tenor-bass trombone in B♭ made about 1861 in the Missenharter factory in Stuttgart with the Württemburg coat-of-arms was lost during World War II.

NIALL O'LOUGHLIN

Misura (It.: 'measure', 'time', 'bar'). A word found in music primarily in the direction *senza misura*: 'without barring' (in the case of recitative sections with only declamatory rhythm), or 'freely', 'without strict regard for the metre'. Where *misura* is used in this last sense (as particularly often by Liszt, for example) the return to strict time is marked by *a tempo*, or simply *giusto*. Within the Italian language *misura binaria* means 'duple time', *misura composta* 'compound time', etc.

Misura vuota. *See* VUOTA.

Miṭbaj. DOUBLE CLARINET of Iraq and the Kurdish people, with two equal tubes. *See also* MIJWIZ.

Miti'gwakik. Tall WATER-DRUM of the Ojibwa Indians of the western Great Lakes region of North America. It is made from a bass-wood log, traditionally hollowed out by burning and scraping. It is about 42 cm deep, with a diameter of about 25 cm at the base decreasing to about 22 cm at the top. A bung-hole is cut in the wall of the drum. The outside is decorated with four heads and an oblong symbol representing a bag containing yarrow, which signifies life. The drumhead is of untanned deer-hide which is held in place by a cloth-wound hoop. In preparation for use the drum is partially filled with water and the head is alternately made wet and heated, and stretched tightly until the proper tone quality is achieved. The drum is beaten with a padded wooden stick which is about 30 cm long and curved to a right angle near the end. The drum is very resonant and can be heard over long distances. It is used during ceremonies of the *mide'wiwin* (grand medicine society).

MARY RIEMER-WELLER

Mitteltönige Temperatur (Ger.). MEAN-TONE temperament.

Mitumbwe. Single-headed closed GOBLET DRUM of the Luba/Sanga people of Zaïre. The membrane is pinned on and weighted. It is beaten by hand and used for dance music together with the *ditumba* and *kayanda* drums.

Mixture stop. An ORGAN STOP composed of several ranks of pipes at various pitches, most often octaves and 5ths. The term is both generic, referring to compound stops in general, and specific, in that Mixture (*Mixtur, mixtuur, mixtura*) is also the name used in some areas and periods for the chief mixture of the Diapason chorus or

pleno (*lleno, plein jeu, ripieno*). The history of mixture stops is the history of the organ itself, from the big *pleno* at Winchester (10th century) through the medieval *Blockwerke* and Renaissance Mixtura (Barcelona, 1480), Locatio (A. Schlick: *Spiegel der Orgelmacher und Organisten*, 1511), Hintersatz, Zimbel and Fourniture to the 19th-century Compensation mixture, Progressio Harmonica, etc. The chief Baroque additions to the chorus mixtures are the wider-scaled solo or colour mixtures, often with a Tierce rank included, such as Cornet, Hörnli, Sesquialtera, Terzian and Carillonmixtur. Some mixtures, such as Rauschpfeife, were chorus stops at one period, solo at another. The term 'mixture' appeared late in England (Father Smith's Temple organ, 1688); James Talbot in his MS of *c*1695 (*GB-Och* Music 1187) used it to include solo mixtures. The contents, planning, voicing and scaling of the various mixture stops distinguish national organ schools and test the skill of both ancient and modern builders more than any solo reed or Principal stop.

PETER WILLIAMS

Mixtur-Trautonium. A monophonic electronic instrument based on the TRAUTONIUM, developed in 1949–52 in Berlin by Oskar Sala (*b* Greiz, Thuringia, 18 July 1910). As a student Sala was involved in the construction of the original Trautonium, was one of the first to play it in 1930 and shortly afterwards became its sole virtuoso. He assisted in the development of the 1932 version of the instrument manufactured by Telefunken, and himself constructed the radio (1935) and concert (1938) versions. The last two both had two fingerboards and featured the use of subharmonic timbres (mirror-image 'overtone' spectra below the fundamental), which Trautwein had proposed in 1930.

Around 1950 Sala improved and extended the subharmonic principle to create a substantially different and more flexible instrument. The Mixtur-Trautonium has a console that resembles a small writing desk, with two touch-sensitive monophonic fingerboards and two pedal controls, which, together with many knobs and switches, make available a sophisticated system of subharmonic mixtures; up to four subharmonic pitches can be added to the note played on each manual, producing a sound that is more like a chord than a special timbre. In 1953–4 Sala added other features which he called 'electronic percussion': white noise, reverberation and a circuit breaker ('electric metronome'); with these devices and, especially when it was combined with electronic and tape (Springer machine) transposition systems in the studio, the instrument came close to being a special type of synthesizer.

The Mixtur-Trautonium was originally used in works by Carl Orff, Hans Werner Henze, Paul Dessau, Sala and others, including a concerto by Harald Genzmer (1952). In the 1950s Sala's own compositions were chiefly tape works produced with the Mixtur-Trautonium for concerts, plays and films. In 1958 he established a permanent electronic music studio centred on the only existing model, where more than 400 scores (over half for films, including Alfred Hitchcock's *The Birds*) have been produced, most of them by Sala.

BIBLIOGRAPHY

O. Sala: 'Das Mixtur-Trautonium', *Melos*, xvii (1950), 247

——: 'Das Mixtur-Trautonium', *Physikalische Blätter*, vi (1950), 390

——: 'Das neue Mixtur-Trautonium', *Musikleben*, vi (1953), 346

——: 'Elektronische Klanggestaltung mit dem Mixtur-Trautonium', *Musik–Raumgestaltung–Elektroakustik*, ed. W. Meyer-Eppler (Mainz, 1955), 78

——: 'Subharmonische elektrische Klangsynthesen', *Klangstruktur der Musik*, ed. F. Winckel (Berlin, 1955), 89
——: 'Mixtur-Trautonium und Studio-Technik', *Gravesaner Blätter*, nos.23–4 (1962), 42 [with Eng. trans., p.53]
T. Rhea: 'Sala & the Mixtur-Trautonium', *Contemporary Keyboard*, v/5 (1979), 70
O. Sala: '50 Jahre Trautonium', *Für Augen und Ohren* (Berlin, 1980), 78 [festival programme book]

HUGH DAVIES

Miyadaiko. Japanese barrel drum. *See* ŌDAIKO.

Mi'zaf (pl. *ma'āzif*). Lyre of pre-Islamic Arabia at the beginning of the Muslim epoch. Archaeological research in Saudi Arabia has brought to light cave drawings showing that there were lyres in the Arabian peninsula between the 3rd and 2nd millennia (E. Anati: *Rock-art in Central Arabia* (Louvain, 1968), 105). These superimpose an ensemble of three lyres, showing them to have a contour akin to the current Ethiopian *begenna*. There is a rectangular soundbox, parallel arms and a transverse yoke to which 14 strings are fastened. It is not known whether this implies the existence of heptatonic scales, especially as nomad Arab music is basically tetrachordal (there were however heptatonic systems at Sa'dah, North Yemen). There are also lyres in South Arabia called *ṭanbūra* and *simsimīyya*, and also the *qambūs*, a six-string lyre (A. Jahn: *Die Mehri sprache* (Vienna, 1902), 273). Like the identification of the *qanbūs* with the lute, the eternal question of the relationship of lyre and lute is little clarified by the 18th-century documentation: *'mi'zaf*, a kind of *ṭunbūr* found among the Yemeni people and in my view now called *qabūs*' (Al-Zabīdī (*d* 1971): *Tāj al 'Arūs*, Beirut, 1888/*R*1965, ''azafa'). Later authors substantiate this continuity: 'Al-Mutarrizi (12th century) specifies the *mi'zaf* as a sort of *ṭunbūr* made by the people of the Yemen' (Farmer, 1931, p.8). These writings after the 10th century are not susceptible of organological analysis but merely confirm the presence of an instrument called the *mi'zaf*. The evidence for the *mi'zaf* as a sort of *ṭunbūr* is corroborated in the 13th century by the earliest Arab encyclopedia – 'when *mi'zaf* is in the singular it refers to a kind of *ṭunbūr* among the Yemeni people' (Ibn Manẓūr: *Lisān al-'Arab*, ''azafa'). Comparative analysis, linked to historical continuity, makes it clear that the *mi'zaf* is a lyre; the only earlier author to come close to stating this is al-Laith ibn Nasr (8th century): 'the *mi'zaf* and/or *mi'zafa* has many strings' (though in this case he may mean the harp: Farmer, ibid).

The three instruments *mi'zaf*, *duff* and *mizmār* constitute, with subsidiary drums, the only ones in pre-Islamic Arabia. The *mi'zaf* is defined by a double psychomotor function: the power to appease and the capacity to excite. The instrument, hardly innovatory in this, conforms to a conception widely spread in the Near East. The function of the *mi'zaf* on the battlefield focusses on death, as in a poem collected by Iṣfahānī: 'Each time the death knell sounds, the *ma'āzif* waken' (*Kitāb al-aghānī al-kabīr*); non-canonical sayings (*ḥadīth*) add: 'When we heard the voice of the *ma'āzif* we were sure that it foretold destruction' (*Lisān al-'Arab*, *Tāj al-'Arūs*, ''azafa'). This helps clarify the reasons for regarding the *ma'āzif* as the herald of the end of time. Canonical *ḥadīth* predict these events 'when wine is drunk, when clothing is in silk, when singing-girls and *ma'āzif* are courted' and that the signs of the end of time will come when 'among my people [Mohammed's remark] there will be those who will exploit the luxury, silk, drink and the *ma'āzif*'.

At the time of al-Fārābī (9th century), the *ma'āzif* no longer had much significance. The theologian Ghazālī (*Ihyā' 'ulūm al-dīn*) replaced the term by *awtār* (the strings). From this stems authors' confusion: *ma'āzif* became a generic term denoting all instruments with voices, then strings alone, then 'open strings' (lyre, harp etc) as opposed to lutes. Thus it is not possible to set up a precise chronology.

BIBLIOGRAPHY
H. G. Farmer: 'Mi'zaf', *EI*
——: *Studies in Oriental Musical Instruments* (London, 1931–9/*R*1978)
J. Robson: 'Kitāb al-Malāhī of Abu Ṭālib al-Mufaḍḍal ibn Salama', *Journal of the Royal Asiatic Society* (1938), 231
——: *Tracts on Listening to Music being Dhamm al-malāhī by Ibn abi'l-Dunyā* (London, 1938)
A. 'Azzāwī: 'Kitāb al-Malāhī by Mufaḍḍal ibn Salama', *Al-Mūsīqā al-'Irāqiyya fī 'ahd al-Mughūl wal Turkumān* [Iraqi music under the Mongols and Turkmen] (Baghdad, 1951)
H. G. Farmer: 'Mi'zaf', *Grove 5*
A. J. Wensinck and J. P. Mensing: *Concordance et indices de la tradition musulmane* (Leiden, 1962) ['azazla; tunbūr; zamara]
A. Shiloah: *The Theory of Music in Arabic Writings* (Munich, 1979)
L. Ibsen al-Faruqi: *An Annotated Glossary of Arabic Musical Terms* (Westport, Conn., 1981)
C. Poché: 'David et l'ambiguité du *mizmār*', *The World of Music* (Berlin, 1983) ii, 58

CHRISTIAN POCHÉ

Mi'zafa. Arab harp of the 9th and 10th centuries. The name is one of two singular forms (with *mi'zaf*) of the earlier plural, *ma'āzif*. Two contemporary documents provide information on the instrument. 'The *mi'zafa* was a many-string instrument of the people of Iraq' (al-Khwārizmī: *Mafātīh al-'ulūm*; see Farmer, 1959, p.3). And in Iṣfahānī's *Kitāb al-aghānī al-kabīr*, the 9th-century musician Muhammad al-Hārith ibn Buskhunr, of southern Iraq, had begun on the *mi'zafa*, but was mocked by those who compared his instrument to a mousetrap, and rejected the instrument in favour of the *'ūd*; this allowed him to abandon the third category of musicians confined to the *maāzif* in the hierarchy instituted by the Sassanid kings and taken up by the Khalifs, and to seek admission to the first. This geographical correspondence is an extension of the great musical vitality of the short-lived 6th-century kingdom of Hira; there the poet Al-A'shā had contact with the Sassanid world, whose musical terminology he arabized (*see also* WANJ).

The identification of the *mi'zafa* with the harp or psaltery is supported by the 10th-century Andalusian anthology of Ibn 'Abd Rabbihi which depicts King David playing the *mi'zafa* while reciting psalms (*'Iqd al-farīd*; Eng. trans. in Farmer, 1942, and 1943–4). The word *mi'zafa* may have fallen into disuse because of confusion with *mi'zaf*. Only a quatrain of the poet Kashājim (*d* 961) speaks in its favour, reckoning it superior to the *mizhar* (lute); the poem describes the instrument as having a soundbox covered with white gazelle skin, with nine strings which 'like an army is instructed to hunt the hearts' (al-Mahdi, 1979, p.158).

BIBLIOGRAPHY
J. Ribera: *Music in Ancient Arabia and Spain* (Stanford, 1929/*R*1970)
H. G. Farmer: *Music: the Priceless Jewel* (Bearsden, 1942)
——: 'The Minstrels of the Golden Age of Islam', *Islamic Culture*, xvii (1943), 273; xviii (1944), 53
——: *The Science of Music in the Mafātīh al-'Ulūm* (London, 1959)
A. Shiloah: *Al-Hassan ibn 'Ali al-Kātib: la perfection des connaissances musicales* (Paris, 1972)
Ṣ. al-Mahdi: *Al-Mūsīqā al-'Arabīyya tārīkhhā wa adabha* [Arab music: history and literature] (Tunis, 1979)

CHRISTIAN POCHÉ

Mizhar. Ancient string instrument of Arabia, possibly a lyre, harp or lute; the term is now used for a FRAME

DRUM. The word 'mizhar' is prominent in poetical works, where in the pre-Islamic period (before 622) it often occurs in close proximity to 'kirān' and seems to indicate a lyre rather than a lute. All that can be said with certainty, however, is that the *mizhar* belonged to the string family. It is not mentioned in poetical sources as a percussion instrument, but a Latin–Arabic glossary of the 11th century translates *mizhar*, or MAZHAR, as 'tinfanum' (tympanum). When the 'ŪD became established as the most important Arabian instrument the term 'mizhar' disappeared from the vocabulary of poetry and entered prose writings as one of several synonyms for the newer instrument (*see also* 'ARṬABA, BARBAṬ, KIRĀN and MUWATTAR). Gradually it took on a quite different connotation, that of a frame drum, and this has persisted in oral tradition to the present day. The string instrument was associated with women, the drum more with men.

An incorrect interpretation of a line by the 6th-century poet Imru'al-Qays has resulted in speculation that the *mizhar* was tuned in 5ths. Later scholars have described it as having two or four strings, a resonator covered with skin (distinguishing it from the '*ūd*) and a neck a third of the length of the instrument. This view of the *mizhar* as a kind of proto-lute is not confirmed in early poetical writings, on which all investigations into the nature of the instrument must depend. The term 'mizhar' ('that which shines') was associated etymologically by scholars with the white skin of the instrument. In fact it seems to be related to terms for fire or a spark, the instrument probably being used to evoke an association with the invisible world (as are the RABABA and ṬANBŪRA).

BIBLIOGRAPHY

H. G. Farmer: 'A Maghribi Work on Musical Instruments', *Journal of the Royal Asiatic Society* (1935), 339

J. Robson: '*Kitāb al-malāhī* of Abū Ṭālib al-Muffaḍḍal Ibn Salam', *Journal of the Royal Asiatic Society* (1938), 231

N. al-Dīn Asad: *al-Qiyān wal Ghinā' 'aṣr al-Jāhilī* [Singing-girls and music in pre-Islamic Arabia] (Beirut, 1960/R1968)

C. Pellat: 'Les esclaves-chanteuses de Ǧahiz', *Arabica*, x (1963), 121

M. S. Ḥāfiẓ: *Tārīkh al-Mūsīqā wa'l ghinā' al-'Arabī* [History of Arabian music and singing] (Cairo, n.d.)

M. Guettat: *La musique classique au Maghreb* (Paris, 1980)
CHRISTIAN POCHÉ

Mizhāvu. See MIḺĀVU.

Mizmār. Generic term from the Arab world for various kinds of wind instrument with single or double reed; in the past it applied to all wind instruments. The term was part of the pre-Islamic Arab inheritance, much discussed and fiercely condemned, but escaped elimination (unlike the *mi'zaf*). It is difficult to disentangle the written and the spoken terminologies. In written texts, the *mijwiz* is a *mizmār*; this applies equally to the *zūrnā*, the double-reed counterpart of the single-reed *mijwiz*. Further, in Arab texts the *mizmār* is associated with another generic name, *zammāra* (from *zamaro*: 'blowing'). This linguistic usage survives in Iraq and Egypt (*zammāra*, double clarinet), Albania (*zumare*) and in Sudan (*zumbara*, long obliquely-held flute). In Aramean countries the pre-Islamic *mizmār* was referred to as *abuba* (double pipe), a term that remains synonymous with *mizmār* in Syriac dialects. The *mizmār* of the Yemen, fixed round the player's mouth by a muzzle, is reminiscent of certain early Phrygian or Greek models, for instance, the *aulos*.

In early Islamic literature, *mizmār* could mean either

Priestesses playing abuba (double pipe) and drum: terracotta statuette, Syrian, Roman period (Musée du Louvre, Paris)

a beautiful voice or a wind instrument; this relationship explains features that survive today. A single or a double flute, when the interpreter plays and sings at the same time, may be called a *mizmār*; this technique, probably lost in the Arab world, survives in Iran (among the Bakhtyari nomads), Pakistan and Rajasthan (India: *nar*). The term *mizmār* also covers any wind instrument (e.g. the *tazamar* of the Algerian Sahara) where the interpreter blows and growls (as in some *mijwiz* techniques) or where he plays and exhales loudly, punctuating his playing with psalmody, as in the *fodhin* (obliquely-held flute) playing of the Afar shepherds of Djibouti who play to the camels – possibly an Arab survival from pre-Islamic antiquity. Any instrument that meets one of the following three criteria may be called *mizmār*: a single-reed instrument with two tubes of equal or different lengths; one with one tube and a single or double reed (*zūrnā*, *ghayṭa*); one that uses circular breathing.

Nowadays, the *mizmār* exists in three main areas: Iraq, with an extension towards the Emirates; Egypt; Tunisia and Morocco. Isolated examples are found in Yemen. In Iraq, the *zummāra* can be a simple clarinet with one tube and six holes (see Qassim Hassan, 1980, pp.55f), also a double clarinet with identical tubes similar to the *mijwiz*. It is played solo and favoured by shepherds. In popular celebrations, it is supplemented with a drum, often a goblet drum (*khashaba*), and required to lead the dances. Of limited compass (a 4th or a 5th), it does not have a drone. The combination of the clarinet and a goatskin bag gave rise to the *jirba* bagpipes in the Gulf States.

In Egypt, the generic terms *zammāra* and *mizmār* denote distinct families: single-reed or clarinet (*zum-*

māra) and double-reed or oboe (*mizmār*). The former, a DOUBLE CLARINET, has two parallel tubes of the same length, 30 to 35 cm. At the head of each tube is a reed (*balūs*) which fits into the body. The tubes are bound together with string dipped in tar and wax. The melodic or principal tube (*rayyīs*: 'the master') has four to six holes which determine its name (*sittawīyya*, six; *rab'awīyya*, four). The adjacent tube (*nawti*), sometimes with no holes, serves as the drone. Some examples are bored similarly in both tubes and possess no drone. In practice, the compass is no more than a 4th. The instrument is played solo but at public celebrations it follows the rhythm of the *darbukka* (goblet drum).

The *mizmār* family is based on a group of three oboes, to which drums (*ṭabl*) are added. These instruments, common in Egypt, correspond to the *zūrnā* or *ghayṭa* type, with a detachable double reed, a pirouette and a flared body carved from apricot wood. In less than a century the oboes have discarded their original Turkish names. The first and most important of the group, the smallest and thus the most shrill, was called *goura* (from the Turkish *cura*: 'small, shrill'), and is now called *sibs*; the second, *zamr*, has become *shalabiyya* or *mizmār sa'īdi*; and the third and largest, in Turkish *kaba* ('big'), has become *telt* ('third'). By contrast with the double clarinets of the Near East and Upper Egypt, the *mizmār* ensemble has its own strictly instrumental repertory, alternating between free, improvised sections and rhythmically strict, melodic ones which are specific dances. The ability to leap an octave and shift the tonic in the process is another Turkish procedure since assimilated by the Egyptian *mizmār*.

In Morocco and Tunisia, the *zamr* is akin to the *zummāra* of Iraq or Egypt, extended by a bell-shaped single or double horn, bearing witness to the links between these countries and the Balkans (the Albanian *zumare* is a product of the same process). The Moroccan instrument is described in detail by Chottin (1938, p.38): it has six parallel holes in both tubes, a restricted compass and no drone. It is apparently not very widespread. The Moroccan *mizmār* or *zamr rīfi* can also be a large double HORNPIPE, over 1 metre long, terminating in two bulls' horns. It comprises three sections: two parallel pipes of reed about 35 cm long, with six finger-holes; these are fitted into two slightly divergent metal pipes, with no holes, about 40 cm in length; these in turn are inserted into two separate horns about 30 cm long. The pipes are held together by metal wire, and the instrument is highly decorated.

From these various considerations, a general conclusion may be drawn. The authentic *mizmār* or *zummāra* is constructed by joining two parallel tubes; there is rarely a drone; and the compass is narrow. Widely found on the Mediterranean coast, the type must have spread long before the rise of Islam. While in the official Islamic texts (*ḥadīth*) *mi'zaf* appears exclusively in the plural (*ma'āzif*) and *duff* in both plural (*dufūf*) and singular, the third instrument of this pre-Islamic trio, the *mizmār*, appears in the singular and only rarely in the plural (*mazāmīr*). This may reflect a musical reality, created by the need for balance between strings and wind. In a bas-relief in the British Museum, a procession of Elamite musicians from the court of Ashurbanipal is shown with seven vertical harps and a psaltery which balance the presence of two wind instruments of the *mizmār* type. In the Umayyad era, the *mizmār* was paired with the lute, an association continued through the Abbasids:

'Zalzal played [the *'ūd*], Barsum blew in the *mizmār* and Ibrahim sang' (Isfahānī: *Kitāb al-aghānī al-kabīr*). This pairing seems to have disappeared from the Arab world; the only echoes are found in south-east Iran, in Baluchistan, where a three-string lute (*tanbur*) is played with a double flute (*donelī*).

BIBLIOGRAPHY

GENERAL

H. G. Farmer: 'Mizmār', *EI*
A. Shiloah: *The Theory of Music in Arabic Writings* (Munich, 1979)
C. Poché: 'David et l'ambiguité du *mizmār*', *The World of Music* (Berlin, 1983), ii, 58

IRAQ AND THE GULF STATES

P. Rovsing Olsen: 'Enregistrements faits à Kuwait et à Bahrain', *Ethnomusicologie III: Wégimont V 1960*, 137–70
S. Qassim Hassan: *Les instruments de musique en Iraq* (Paris, 1980)

EGYPT

T. Alexandru and E. A. Wahba: 'Al-Aghānī wa'l-Mūsīqā š-Ša'abīga'l-Maṣrīya' [The folk music of Egypt], UAR Ministry of Culture EST 52–3 [disc notes]
M. A. Hifnī: *'Ilm al-ālāt al-mūsīqiyya* [Study of musical instruments] (Cairo, 1971)
A. Weber: 'Egypte, les musiciens du Nil', ii, Ocora (1979) [disc notes]
J. Pacholczyk: 'Egypt', §II, *Grove 6*

MOROCCO AND TUNISIA

A. Chottin: *Tableau de la musique marocaine* (Paris, 1938)
J. Jenkins and P. Rovsing Olsen: *Music and Musical Instruments in the World of Islam* (London, 1976)
Ṣ. al-Sharqī: *Adwā 'ala al-mūsīqā al-maghribīyya* [Studies in Moroccan music] (Rabat, 1977)

CHRISTIAN POCHÉ

Mizmār baladī. Egyptian oboe, also called *abā*. See also MIZMĀR.

Mizwid. BAGPIPE of North Africa. See also MIJWIZ.

Mizwij [mizwidj]. See MIJWIZ.

Mjolo. Bracelet or ankle rattle of the Shambala people of Tanzania. It consists of crescent-shaped pellet bells of iron or copper.

Mkhar-rnga ['khar-rnga]. Tibetan gong. See also RNGA.

Mkinda. Double-headed wooden cylindrical drum of the Shambala people of Tanzania.

Mlanzi. Transverse flute of the Gogo people of central Tanzania. It is part of the ensemble for the *chiganda* dance.

Mlele. NOTCHED FLUTE with four finger-holes of the Tachoni people of Kenya. It is made from bamboo, and the notch is U- or V-shaped. The instrument is about 47 cm long, and is used for solo performance. For illustration *see* FLUTE, figs.1*d* and 2*c*.

MM. *Metronom Maelzel* (Ger.). See METRONOME; MAELZEL, JOHANN NEPOMUK; TEMPO AND EXPRESSION MARKS.

Mmaa. Concussion stick CLAPPERS of the Ashanti people of Ghana.

Mmanga. Long bell of the Shambala people of Tanzania, made from one piece of bent metal. It has a single clapper.

Mngoli [kaligo]. Single-string fiddle of south-eastern Africa.

Mõ. Vietnamese SLIT-DRUM. It is made of hollowed-out wood or pieces of bamboo and is used in ceremonial music.

Moana-ngoma. Cylindrical drum of the Ladi (Lari) people of the Republic of the Congo, with a single nailed skin and part-open base. The drum is played in a horizontal position, the drummer sitting astride it and beating it with his hands. It is used with the *tshidukulu*, a closed cylindrical drum with a nailed head, which is beaten with a strip of rubber. The base is extended in the form of a thick stem which forms a handle. In addition to these two drums a metal vessel rattle, *bitsatsa*, made from a tin can, is also used, together with the *mukuiti*, a friction drum. The friction drum player also wears on his wrist an *nsakala* spherical rattle made from fruit husks containing seeds. The whole ensemble is used as rhythmic accompaniment for dancing.

BIBLIOGRAPHY
C. Duvelle: 'Musique Kongo', OCR 35 [disc notes]

K. A. GOURLAY

Mobeke. Whistle of the pygmies of the Central African Republic.

Mock trumpet. A term which seems to have been used about 1700 for an undeveloped CHALUMEAU. The mock trumpet has been confused with the trumpet marine, with which it has no connection. Dart (*GSJ*, vi, 1953, 35) described a book of instructions for playing the mock trumpet, as well as a 'Variety of new Trumpet Tunes Aires Marches and Minuets' for the instrument. This was clearly the chalumeau before its improvement by Denner; it carried three finger-holes for each hand, one thumb-hole, and had no keys. Such an instrument is illustrated as no.221 in the *Catalogue of the Royal Military Exhibition* (ed. C. R. Day, London, 1890), where its length is said to be $8\frac{1}{4}$ inches (*c*23 cm). Its range was g' to g'' and its tone may be assumed to have been strident. The copy described by Dart seems to have been printed in about 1707, but he showed that an earlier edition was printed in 1698. No other music for the chalumeau before its improvement is known.

NICHOLAS SHACKLETON

Modeku. LAMELLAPHONE of the Zande people of northeastern Zaïre. Two types have been reported by de Hen and Laurenty respectively. The first is a wooden-keyed lamellaphone with box-shaped bark resonator; it is also known as *abongwa* (*see* AGBOMBOYA). The second is a wooden-keyed lamellaphone with boat-shaped wooden resonator.

BIBLIOGRAPHY
LaurentyS, 192
F. J. de Hen: *Beitrag zur Kenntnis der Musikinstrumente aus Belgisch Kongo und Ruanda-Urundi* (Tervuren, 1960)

Moderato (It.: 'moderate', 'restrained'). A direction used either alone as a tempo designation or as a qualification to some other direction. It is sometimes abbreviated to *mod.to*. Because verbal directions appeared in 17th-century music only to tell the musician something that his sense of tradition would not tell him, *moderato* did not appear until the very end of the century, when certain composers began marking everything they wrote. Thus François Couperin, who marked everything but his sacred pieces, made considerable use of the French adverbial form *modérément*, and his contemporaries in France also used the adjectival form *modéré*, which has remained in common usage ever since. *Moderato* itself was included in Brossard's *Dictionaire* (1703) as meaning 'with moderation, discretion, wisdom, etc, neither too loud, nor too soft, nor too fast, nor too slowly, etc' – a definition which is in itself a sign of a new generation in tempo and expression marks, one in which for the first time even the ordinary had to be explained. Rousseau (1768) gave *modéré* as the equivalent of the Italian *adagio*, the second of his five main degrees of movement in music. Since the early 19th century, *moderato* has most often appeared either alone or in the compounds *allegro moderato* (a little slower than *allegro*) and *andante moderato* (a little faster than *andante*). For a curious usage in J. S. Bach *see* LENTO.

For bibliography *see* TEMPO AND EXPRESSION MARKS.

DAVID FALLOWS

Moderator pedal [muffler pedal, celeste]. A pedal that introduces a strip of cloth between the hammers and strings of a piano to produce a muted effect. It is still occasionally provided as a middle pedal on upright pianos. The same device, sometimes operated by a knee lever instead of a pedal, was commonly found on German and Austrian grand pianos of the late 18th century and the early 19th, sometimes apparently as a substitute for a true UNA CORDA but more frequently to provide special tone-colour in addition to that provided by the normal 'loud' and 'soft' pedals. Some instruments by Conrad Graf of Vienna have the added refinement of two moderator pedals, one of which inserts the muting cloth farther than the other.

EDWIN M. RIPIN

Modéré (Fr.). *See* MODERATO.

Modifications and new techniques. The instrumentarium of Western music throughout its history has been in a state of continuous change, and every type and period of music has given rise to its own modifications of existing instruments and playing techniques. The desire for instruments capable of greater range, volume and dynamic control has led not only to the use of new materials and improvements in design but also to the invention of new instruments, many of which have achieved small success and are now regarded as little more than curiosities. These developments, naturally, form the matter of many articles in this dictionary, in which the evolution of individual instruments to their present state is fully described. The 20th century has seen an unprecedented expansion in the instrumentarium and a host of new approaches by composers and musicians to the use of existing instruments; because these experiments have often taken place outside the mainstream of musical life it seems appropriate to discuss them as a group.

1. Introduction. 2. Keyboard instruments. 3. Strings. 4. Wind. 5. Percussion.

1. INTRODUCTION. Since 1950 only a small proportion of Western music for ensembles in any style or area, including symphony orchestra, jazz and dance band, rock and folk group, has been played entirely on instruments that existed in, for example, 1900. Considerably more than half of the total output of three of the leading avant-garde composers who first came to prominence in the 1950s, JOHN CAGE, MAURICIO KAGEL and Karlheinz

Stockhausen, includes new resources, ranging from unusual percussion, Renaissance, folk and non-Western instruments to newly invented acoustic, electroacoustic and electronic instruments, as well as Toy INSTRUMENTS, MUSICAL COSTUMES, SOUND EFFECTS, environmental sounds, live electronics and electronic music on tape. Contemporary rock music relies heavily on instruments that were unknown before the 1930s, such as the electric guitar, electronic organ, electric piano and synthesizer. This flood of new instruments has been supplemented by many modifications, both temporary and permanent, of standard instruments in ways that go far beyond the intentions of the manufacturer or original designer; a number of composers have also called for extended performance techniques on traditional instruments.

2. KEYBOARD INSTRUMENTS.

(i) The piano. The instrument that has been modified in the greatest variety of ways is the piano. A comparative newcomer, it was still in the early stages of its evolution in the 19th century, and many versions of both upright and grand forms were constructed. An early modification, which survives today in pianos manufactured by Steinway and many American companies, is the third or 'sostenuto' pedal, first introduced in 1844 by Boisselot in Marseilles, but not established until the American branch of Steinway adopted it in 1874. Bösendorfer grand pianos have an extension of a minor 6th to the normal range in the bass for reinforcing the left hand with octaves; a hinged flap covers these keys when they are not required to prevent confusion in the player's visual orientation. Several modifications to the shape and lay-out of the keyboard, intended to simplify fingering, were tried out between the 1840s and the early 20th century (see also EMANUEL MOÓR PIANOFORTE; JANKO, PAUL VON; KEYBOARD, §3), and from the same period inventors have built microtonal pianos (see MICROTONAL INSTRUMENTS, §2).

In the 20th century many temporary modifications have been made to the piano and new playing techniques applied to it. Isolated effects were required by Schoenberg in the Three Piano Pieces op.11 (1909), in which certain keys are silently depressed to raise the dampers and allow the strings to vibrate sympathetically, and Charles Ives, who in the 'Hawthorne' movement (1911) of his 'Concord' Sonata called for the use of a piece of wood 14¾″ long for the playing of diatonic clusters; string glissandos, played by the fingers, are specified in Rued Langgaard's Sfaerernes musik (1918).

The first composer systematically to explore the possibilities of modifying the piano was Henry Cowell. His innovations included the playing of chromatic and diatonic clusters (in Adventures in Harmony, ?1911, and The Tides of Manaunaun, ?1912) and glissandos across several strings or along single strings, executed with the fingers while the dampers are raised (The Banshee, 1925), plucking the strings (Aeolian Harp, 1923, and Pièce pour piano avec cordes, 1924), damping the strings with the fingers and small mutes, and playing them with hammers and plectra, to create what he termed the 'percussion piano' (The Leprechaun, c1925) and stopping the strings to alter the pitch or produce harmonics (Sinister Resonance, 1925). Sheets of paper are inserted between the strings in Satie's Le piège de Méduse (1914) and an upright piano modified in the same way is proposed as an alternative to the 'luthéal' specified by Ravel in his Tzigane (1924) and L'enfant et les sortilèges (1920–24).

A similar system, in which thin brass tongues folded round strips of felt are placed between the hammers and the strings, was devised by Pleyel to make the sound of the piano resemble that of a harpsichord; it was used in a ballet (1926) by Gabriel Pierné and in Reynaldo Hahn's opera Mozart (1927). In the early 1930s in works for percussion ensemble William Russell specified simple preparations such as a cluster board, string glissandos, and strings plucked and struck by beaters.

The best-known of all piano modifications is John Cage's PREPARED PIANO, devised in 1940 (not, as generally stated, 1938), in which a variety of objects are inserted between the strings, changing both timbre and pitch, to create a one-man percussion ensemble; a range of different, more muted sounds is heard when the soft pedal is depressed (fig.1). The prepared piano was the culmination of Cage's explorations of some of Cowell's ideas – the muting of strings both manually (Imaginary Landscape no.1, 1939) and with metal cylinders (Second Construction, 1940), and sweeping them with a stick

1. John Cage's prepared piano, 1940

(First Construction in Metal, 1939). Up to 1954 he wrote over 20, mostly solo works for the prepared piano, some of them for dance performances. Simple preparations are also used in his works for 'string piano' of the early 1940s. (More recently a number of other composers, including several from Japan, Hungary, Czechoslovakia and Poland, have written for the prepared piano, mainly in ensembles.) Closely associated with Cage around 1940 was LOU HARRISON, who devised the 'tack piano', in which thumb tacks or drawing pins are inserted into the hammers to create a metallic sound quality. This idea (known in German as the 'Reissnagelklavier' or the 'Reisszweckenklavier') was arrived at independently and applied mainly to upright pianos by other musicians, including the composers Henry Brant, Paul Dessau, Kagel, Wilhelm Killmayer and György Ráyki, as well as the honky-tonk pianist Winifred Atwell; old and out-of-tune pianos, which produce a similar effect, have been called for (usually in theatrical contexts in connection with 1920s jazz or other popular musics), notably by Alban Berg, Max Brand, Peter Maxwell Davies, Karl Aage Rasmussen and Irwin Bazelon. The 'percussion piano' of Cowell was further developed by LUCIA DLU-

GOSZEWSKI as the 'timbre piano' (1951), while ANNEA LOCKWOOD and HANS-KARSTEN RAECKE have developed their own, somewhat different approaches to preparing pianos.

The piano has been the subject of many modifications besides that of preparation, and considerable use has been made of different methods of playing the strings, frame and case, both with fingers and various implements, in works by Kagel, Cage, Orff, Lukas Foss, Ben Johnston and others. Pianos with the action removed so that they must be played like a cimbalom have been specified by Peter Maxwell Davies and Denis Aplvor, and the strings are struck with T-shaped 'cluster-sticks' in works by David Bedford and Davide Mosconi. Foss, Bedford, George Crumb, Xenakis and others have called for undamped piano strings which vibrate sympathetically when other instruments are played nearby.

The most radical of all the modifications applied to the piano – electrification – was introduced in the 1920s and 1930s. Instruments such as the ELEKTROCHORD and the NEO-BECHSTEIN-FLÜGEL were adapted versions of the normal piano, electrically amplified to give variations in timbre and volume and a far longer sustain time than normal. These early examples had no soundboards and since the 1930s the sound-generating systems of electric pianos have increasingly used reeds, rods or electronic oscillators instead of strings, while at the same time the outward appearance of the instruments has come to bear less and less resemblance to the acoustic original. The PLAYER PIANO has provided a further means of surpassing the capabilities of the standard piano, and many composers, including Stravinsky, Hindemith, Grainger, Casella, Malipiero, Milhaud, Antheil and Toch have written works for it, culminating in the series of astonishing virtuoso compositions by Conlon Nancarrow, which far exceed in speed and rhythmic complexity anything that a human pianist could play.

(ii) Others. A limited amount of modification has been carried out on other keyboard instruments. Clusters and plucking or striking the strings of the harpsichord have been incorporated into some new repertory for the instrument, in particular works written for Elisabeth Chojnacka. The harpsichord has also been amplified, as in the THIENHAUS-CEMBALO and the electric harpsichord manufactured by Baldwin. As with the piano, a large number of experimental microtonal harmoniums and organs were built, chiefly between the mid-19th century and the 1930s, though a few, notably the 31-NOTE ORGAN of Adriaan Fokker and several electronic instruments, were devised later. The pipe organ has been modified for works commissioned by the organists Karl-Erik Welin and Gerd Zacher, who had built for him an organ with a touch-sensitive Great manual to his own specifications. Glissandos and timbre changes, produced by altering the wind pressure, have been obtained by switching the organ off during a sustained sound, and Zsigmond Szathmáry has removed individual pipes for controlled reduction in wind pressure. The electronic organ, unlike the electric piano, is not (with very rare exceptions) an electronically amplified pipe organ, though a number of hybrid pipe and electronic instruments, which may be regarded as modified pipe organs, have been built.

3. STRINGS.

(i) The guitar. After the piano the instrument that has probably undergone most modification is the guitar, especially in the form of its 20th-century offshoot, the ELECTRIC GUITAR, itself a modification of the existing acoustic instrument. Other long-established commercially manufactured versions of the guitar include the DOBRO, or resonator guitar, which has a metal disc mounted under the bridge to give increased volume, and the HAWAIIAN GUITAR, which evolved from the technique of laying a guitar across the lap and playing it with a slide. Since the 1960s when the electric guitar first enjoyed great popularity a number of new electroacoustic and electronic variants have been devised. The Stick, developed by Emmett Chapman and sold by Stick Enterprises in Los Angeles since 1973, consists of a long, wide, fretted neck with two sets of five strings; the left hand plays the treble ones (tuned in 4ths) and the right the bass ones (in 5ths), hammering them against the frets to set them vibrating. A guitar-like synthesizer controller, the Kaleidophon (*see* KALEIDOPHON (ii)), which also frees the right hand from its normal function, is only one of a number of such instruments developed since the late 1970s. Two devices intended to sustain the notes of the acoustic guitar are the Gizmotron and the Bass Gizmotron, devised by the rock musicians Kevin Godley and Lol Creme and improved by John McConnell around 1971; they each consist of a set of small revolving wheels that activate the strings. The E-bow ('energy bow'), which has a similar purpose, electromagnetically activates only one string at a time. A considerable range of electronic modification devices that process the signal produced by an electric guitar have been manufactured and have become part of the standard equipment used by pop and rock musicians.

Instrument inventors have made further and more unusual experiments with the guitar. Harry Partch refretted guitars in 1934 and 1945 to adapt them for the playing of music in his 43-note system, and many others have made similar adaptations to facilitate playing in various microtonal tunings. Hans Reichel has extended the frets on an acoustic guitar right up to the bridge, and has constructed a bodyless electric guitar which consists of two necks joined together at their lower ends to form a single straight length with pickups attached. Instruments based on the electric guitar have been made by Fred Frith, including an eight-string fretless version with a pickup at each end of the instrument; Glenn Branca has done similar work. Strings about 6 metres long connect a string on each of two acoustic guitars to a low piano string for added resonance in Kagel's *Tactil* (1970).

Particularly in popular music, where the guitar has been most extensively adopted, new and often extravagant performing techniques have been evolved. Some country music performers on the electric Hawaiian guitar use models with four necks, one of which is prepared and reserved for sound effects such as train noises, much as guitarists in Hawaii previously specialized in producing animal and bird sounds. Jimi Hendrix's performances included passages in which he played the instrument with his teeth, without interrupting the flow of the music. Temporary adaptations of the guitar, similar to those found in the prepared piano, have been devised, notably the attachment to the strings of small 'crocodile' clips and the insertion between them of threads of cotton or thin lamellae, and the use of bows and electric motors with the guitar laid on its back; among the exponents of the guitar prepared in such ways are the composer and guitarist William Hellermann, and the improvisers Keith Rowe, David Toop, Frith, Peter Cusack, Gerry Fitzgerald, Eugene Chadbourne (who also plays a modified dobro) and Henry Kaiser. Other new playing techniques involve additional microphones, movable bridges and slides (including the country music 'bottleneck'), scordatura of one or more strings, percussive playing on the body (as in flamenco) and acoustic feedback (pioneered by Hendrix and the improviser Derek Bailey in the late 1960s).

(ii) Others. Bowed strings are probably the group of instruments to which modifications were applied earliest, but paradoxically they have received less attention in the 20th century. Adaptations to the instruments themselves, such as scordatura tunings and the use of the mute, and non-standard performance techniques – for example, playing *col legno*, making percussive effects on the body and producing harmonics – have long since been accepted. Luigi Russolo's ARCO ENARMONICO was a new form of bow designed to eliminate the need for fingering. Electrical amplification of bowed strings was introduced and quite extensively explored in the 1920s and 1930s and, especially since efficient contact pickups have become available (including some that are built into special bridges), has become widespread in all types of music. A number of electric bowed string instruments have been devised with soundboards (bodies) of reduced size, or no soundboards at all (*see also* ELECTRONIC INSTRUMENTS, §I, 2 (i, *c*)); the similar STROH VIOLIN, though itself not electrified, was designed for use in the recording studio.

Other experiments in the adaptation of instruments of the violin family have included the mechanically operated modified string instruments (including two six-string violins with flat bridges for ease of executing triple stopping) constructed by Erich Doerlmann for Herbert Eimert's ballet score *Der weisse Schwan* (1926), and Harry Partch's Adapted Viola (1928–30) with a cello fingerboard, designed for playing microtonal music. New instruments have been constructed with different compasses and size–compass relationships: shortly before 1920 Léo Sir built six such instruments to complement the standard four (they were used in Honegger's *Hymne pour dixtuor à cordes*, 1920); and Carleen Maley Hutchins and Frederick A. Saunders of the Catgut Acoustical Society of America have devised a set of eight instruments (*see* NEW VIOLIN FAMILY) which have had some success (Henry Brant wrote for them in *Consort for True Violins*, 1965); single instruments designed to extend the compass of the normal violin are the VIOLINO GRANDE and Gunnar Schonbeck's treble violin (tuned a 4th higher). Ken Parker has constructed a ten-string double electric violin for the Indian violinist Shankar, in which two separate bodies with five strings each are mounted on a convex support; the strings can be tuned to cover a range from that of the double bass up to the violin. Jon Rose has made and modified a number of bowed strings: his instruments, which have additional strings (including sympathetic strings), bridges and fingerboards, include a ten-string 'double violin' whose two bodies are placed end to end on an extended neck, and a violin and cello with 19 strings. Violins have been made from metal, transparent or coloured perspex (for rock musicians), experimental lopsided instruments have been built, and violins, mandolins and guitars have been constructed from two-ply sheets of wood that are assembled from used matchsticks (some 10,000–12,000 per instrument) with the burnt heads retained for decoration.

Around 1920 Carlos Salzedo devised many new techniques for the harp, including glissandos and the use of a selection of plectra; Anne LeBaron prepares her harp with paper and crocodile clips.

4. WIND.

(i) Brass. Modifications to brass instruments in the 20th century largely fall into three categories: the use of newly invented mutes; the use of 'wrong' mouthpieces; and alterations to the structure of an instrument. A number of new types of mute were introduced in jazz and dance bands in the early years of the 20th century, including a tin-can mute for a cornet (1917), various homemade mutes (used, notably, by the Original Dixieland Jazz Band), the 'wa-wa', aluminium 'hat' (modelled on the Derby bowler hat worn by musicians) and the 'plunger' (which in its original form was a rubber sink plunger without the handle); the last gives a very vocal quality to the sound and was pioneered in the 1920s by, among others, the trumpeter 'Bubber' Miley. John Silber has explored a variety of new mutes for the trombone, including flat discs, found objects and several that incorporate tuned organ reeds. Reeds have also been incorporated into mouthpieces: Silber has used many types of single-reed mouthpiece and another trombonist, Vinko Globokar, has played on different reeds and other mouthpieces; a bassoon reed has been fitted to the French horn by Gordon Mumma and in the Tromboon devised for 'P. D. Q. Bach' by Peter Schickele.

Modification of an instrument by rearranging the tubing or removing or adding sections has been explored by several virtuoso brass players. In *Tubassoon* (1979) Melvyn Poore features quadrophonic amplification of four open sections of the tuba, controlled by the valves and played with a bassoon reed. The tuba player Zdzisław Piernik has created an instrument with multiple bells, which somewhat resembles the experimental trombone, having seven tubes with individual bells, and six valves, invented by Adolphe Sax in the mid-19th century. The improviser George Lewis has treated his trombone by removing sections while playing. In *Bolos* (1962) by Jan Bark and Folke Rabe special effects are produced by hitting the mouthpiece of a trombone with the palm of one hand, blowing through a separate mouthpiece and removing the slide so as to produce a 'vacuum smack'. The distinctive uptilted bell of 'Dizzy' Gillespie's trumpet (originally the result of an accident) was adopted by the trumpet section of his orchestra to compensate for the downwards angle of the instrument when the player was reading from a score.

(ii) Woodwind. Woodwind instruments have been less often subjected to dismantling and rearrangement than brass, though Vinko Globokar's *Discours IV* (1974) calls for three performers playing a single clarinet body with three mouthpieces, and Evan Parker devised a similar Communal Blown Instrument in which a selection of wind mouthpieces are fitted to a single large tube with a horn. Special effects are obtained by using mouthpieces separated from their instruments, such as a double reed or the top joint of a single-reed instrument, and wind instruments with the mouthpiece, reed or top joint removed have been played somewhat in the manner of brass instruments (the first occurrence of the latter technique is probably in the part for sarrusophone in Ravel's opera *L'heure espagnole*, 1907).

The saxophone has been made the basis of several new instruments of an experimental nature: the jazz saxophonist Roland Kirk specialized in playing two unusual variants – the Manzello (a curved soprano, similar to the Saxello) and the Stritch (a straight alto)

– simultaneously with a normal instrument; slide saxophones were briefly popular in the 1920s and 1930s and several modern versions have been made, including Paul Lytton's Lyttonophone; and Jim Sauter and Don Dietrich create a composite saxophone by playing on two instruments with the rims of the bells touching. New designs for woodwind instruments, intended to simplify or extend their playing techniques, include the LOGICAL BASSOON with electric action, the slide VERMEULEN FLUTE, several new systems of keywork devised by Robert Dick, wind instruments that control small synthesizers, such as the LYRICON, ELECTRONIC VALVE INSTRUMENT and VARIOPHON, and the fanciful variants, one of which (fig.2) can be assembled in different ways, invented by HANS-KARSTEN RAECKE. Flutes and pipes have been made of materials such as plastic and (increasingly) bamboo, and David Toop devised a combination of the MIRLITON and a duct flute, in which a live wasp, imprisoned in an enclosed compartment, provides a drone. Devices added to woodwind instruments to modify their sound include the occasional improvised mute, and electronic devices which process the signal the instrument produces (such devices are widely used with other instruments, particularly the electric guitar, but octave multiplier and divider circuits are primarily intended for use with wind instruments).

Extended performance techniques have been thoroughly explored by woodwind players. Flutter-tonguing has become common, and other techniques, such as multiphonics, split notes, circular breathing, and humming, singing or growling while playing, are becoming increasingly so. Key noise is specified in a number of

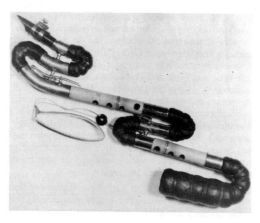

(a)

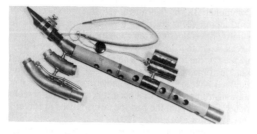

(b)

2. Hans-Karsten Raecke's Multi-variables Steckbambuphon (1977): (a) bass version; (b) soprano version

works, the earliest of which was probably Varèse's *Density 21.5* (1936).

5. PERCUSSION. During the 20th century the greatest expansion of resources has been in the area of percussion; many of the instruments and performance techniques that are now standard in the symphony orchestra were first introduced up to the 1930s in jazz, variety performances, the music hall, accompaniments to 'silent' films and so on. This expansion can be divided into several areas: in addition to the modifications to be considered here, there are the enormous range of noise makers and 'found' instruments required in some experimental works (for examples of which *see* SOUND EFFECTS), the adoption and integration into the orchestra of many non-Western instruments (a process that has gone on for several centuries), the development of new instruments such as the FLEXATONE, MUSICAL SAW and VIBRAPHONE, and the recent evolution of ELECTRONIC PERCUSSION used primarily in rock music.

Familiar instruments have been used in many contexts as the source of new sounds, ranging from the 'rimshot' on drums, which first became popular in the 1920s, and the 'water gong' devised in 1937 by JOHN CAGE, to bowed cymbals and vibraphone keys, cymbals placed on drum skins and the great variety of sounds obtained from a large tam-tam (160 cm diameter) activated by a battery of different objects in Karlheinz Stockhausen's *Mikrophonie I* (1964) (the sounds are also modified electronically and amplified). Substantial amplification of smaller percussion was employed in several works performed by the solo percussionist Max Neuhaus in the mid-1960s.

New variants of existing percussion instruments may be considered in corresponding groups. Several new drums have been devised, such as the Geophone, a rotating drum containing sand, used by Messiaen and others; the BOOBAMS developed by William Loughborough for which Henze has written parts; and the ROTOTOMS invented by Michael Colgrass in the 1960s, which offer the resources of a set of tuned drums and have been employed by Peter Maxwell Davies and other composers, as well as rock musicians. The SIZZLE CYMBAL and HI-HAT, found chiefly in popular music and jazz, have been supplemented in improvisational contexts by cymbals made of scrap and found materials; Paul Burwell has cut small cymbals to square, elliptical and flower-like shapes, altering the ratio between the circumference and the size and therefore modifying the overtones they produce. Chimes and gongs have been made of unusual materials such as marble (Robert Erickson and Gunnar Schonbeck), stone (Carl Orff), glass (ANNEA LOCKWOOD and the members of the GLASS ORCHESTRA), and bamboo, aluminium and steel (David Sawyer's HANDCHIME). Modern versions of the MUSICAL GLASSES, as well as the struck Bouteillophone, are required in a number of 20th-century scores. Early in the century John Taylor of Loughborough constructed a set of cup bells (two and a half octaves) for the Dutch composer Daniël Ruyneman: Ruyneman's own Electrophone electric bells date from around the mid-1930s. Keyed percussion instruments are well represented in the work of Harry Partch and other makers of microtonal instruments; in addition Ron George has built extended vibraphones, Schonbeck has made marimbas out of marble, and Christopher Charles Banta has specialized in building bass and contrabass marimbas with individual resonators. Various types of LAMELLAPHONE have been adopted or constructed, including the MARÍMBULA specified by Cage in *Imaginary Landscape no.3* (1943) and more recently in works by Hans Werner Henze.

Whole families of percussion instruments have been devised and used by LUCIA DLUGOSZEWSKI (fig.3) and large numbers individually by MAURICIO KAGEL for his theatrical works. Several new ergonomically efficient systems for mounting percussion kits have been constructed, including the LOOPS CONSOLE of Ron George. Electrically operated beaters are used to play the group of percussion instruments in a composition by Michael Fahres.

The enormously expanded battery of instruments with which contemporary percussionists are often surrounded is accompanied by an equally large selection of beaters and sticks, and this has often led to the 'wrong' sticks being used, either from choice or because there is no time for the player to change to the appropriate ones. Two types of stick devised in the 20th century are the jazz 'wire brush' of the 1920s (adapted from an outdoor fly swatter) and the 'superball mallet' (based on the eponymous ultra-resilient rubber toy ball) originally constructed in the early 1970s, which is ideal for unusual friction effects. Multi-stick techniques, the player using two or more sticks in each hand, have become quite common; a similar approach is adopted in the part for the tapered kidney-shaped Deri drum in Stockhausen's *Momente*, where a fast tremolo is executed by two sticks held in one hand and pivoting round a third stick which is drawn across the skin of the drum to create a glissando.

BIBLIOGRAPHY

A. Coeuroy: *Panorama de la musique contemporaine* (Paris, 1928), 150

L.-E. Gratia: 'Les instruments de musique du xxe siècle', *Le ménestrel*, xc (1928), 489

H. Cowell: *New Musical Resources* (New York, 1930/*R*1969), 3, 111

'Piano Music by Henry Cowell', Folkways FM 3349 [disc notes]

'Look What's Happening to the Products', *Bandwagon*, xiii/5 (1965), 18

B. Bartolozzi: *New Sounds for Woodwind* (London, 1967, 2/1981)

J. Blades: *Percussion Instruments and their History* (London, 1970, 2/1975, rev.3/1984), 392, 412

R. Smith Brindle: *Contemporary Percussion* (London, 1970)

D. Cope: *New Directions in Music* (Dubuque, Iowa, 1971, 2/1976), 49

E. Richards: *Emil Richards' World of Percussion: a Catalog of 300 Standard, Ethnic and Special Musical Instruments and Effects* (Sherman Oaks, Calif., 1972)

W. Brooks: 'Instrumental and Vocal Resources', *Dictionary of Contemporary Music*, ed. J. Vinton (New York, 1974), 339

P. Burwell, A. Nicholson and S. Beresford: 'A Conversation about Pianos', *Musics*, no.8 (1976), 4

C. Hamm: 'Sound Forms for Piano', New World Records NW 203 [disc notes]

D. L. Harrel: *New Techniques in Twentieth-Century Solo Piano Music: an Expansion of Pianistic Resources from Cowell to the Present* (diss., U. of Texas, Austin, 1976)

J. Blades: *Drum Roll: a Professional Adventure from the Circus to the Concert Hall* (London, 1977)

J. Hol: *Some Saxophone History: its Origin and Early Use* (London, 1982)

S. Papadimitriou: *To "allo" piano* [The other piano] (Thessaloniki, 1983)

HUGH DAVIES

Modjoko. Cylindrical drum of the Ngombe people of Zaïre. *See* BONDA (i).

Moduka. Side-blown animal-horn trumpet of the Ngbele people of north-eastern Zaïre. It has one stop in the tip; it is also known as *nembongo* or *namoduduka* (*LaurentyA*, 321).

3. Some of Lucia Dlugoszewski's ladder harps and tangent rattles (constructed by Ralph Dorazio, 1958–60)

Modulation. In telecommunications usage, and hence in electronic music, the superimposition of characteristics of one signal ('programme') upon another ('carrier'). Many characteristics of signals may be modulated. In frequency modulation the frequency of the carrier is made to conform to the waveshape of the programme: for example, if the programme is a sine wave of frequency 6 Hz and low amplitude, the audible result of modulation will resemble the carrier in all respects except that a vibrato (small variation of pitch) will be superimposed upon it. Alterations in the waveform, frequency or amplitude of the programme will produce results more complex and less easily described; in particular, as its frequency enters the audio range (approximately 18 Hz–22 kHz), distinct new 'sideband' frequencies will be produced. In amplitude modulation it is the amplitude of the carrier that is made to conform to the waveshape of the programme: here the same sine wave of 6 Hz as programme will have the effect of superimposing a tremolo (small variation of dynamic) upon the carrier. Again, more complex results may be produced by changing the programme.

In contrast to these two types of modulation, the distinction between programme and carrier is of less significance for ring modulation, the effect of which is symmetrical. The output from a RING MODULATOR consists of the sum and difference of the frequencies of the inputs: for example, the result of ring modulating two sine waves of 400 Hz and 500 Hz will be two sine waves of 100 Hz and 900 Hz. However, if either or both of the input signals is more complex than a sine wave, as is likely to be the case in a musical context, then the output will be even more complicated since each partial of the one input will be added to and subtracted from each partial of the other. (This is necessarily a simplified description as the amplitudes of each partial also affect the result.)

Frequency, amplitude and ring modulation are the oldest and most familiar modulation processes used in electronic music. However, with the development of VOLTAGE CONTROL systems the number of devices based on the programme–carrier principle has proliferated: all of these perform operations that may legitimately be described as modulations. Pulse modulation, for example, is the modification by control voltage of the length of individual pulses from a pulse generator. Phase modulation is produced by the superimposition of a signal upon itself after an extremely short but continually changing time delay regulated by a control voltage; with a slow rate of change in the time delay the effect upon a complex signal will be of a band of noise sweeping through the signal.

This extension of applications has encouraged a looser use of the term. For instance, location modulation is a variation in the apparent spatial location of a sound (pitch and timbre may also be affected); this may or may not be governed by a control voltage. The term has even been extended beyond the boundaries of electronic music to describe any continuous change in timbre, rhythm or other parameters.

DAVID ROBERTS

Moeck. German firm of music publishers and instrument makers. Founded by Hermann Moeck (i) (*b* Elbing, 9 July 1896; *d* Celle, 9 Oct 1982) in 1925 at Celle, it soon devoted itself to promoting recorders and their music in particular. The journal *Der Blockflötenspiegel* (1931–4, partly in conjunction with Nagels Musikverlag) contributed much to the revival of recorder playing by the clarification and discussion of technical questions. (For further details of the firm's publishing activities see *Grove 6*.)

In 1948 Hermann Moeck (ii) (*b* Lüneburg, 16 Sept 1922), son of the founder, became a partner in charge of the publishing; on his father's retirement in 1960 he also took over the instrument making. In the early 1970s 180 employees were making some 350,000 instruments annually. The aim is to combine the craftsman's skill with the techniques of precision engineering to produce a flow of high-quality early instruments of almost every kind. The firm is known for viols and the Krefeld *Quintfidel*; the tradition of promoting recorders has also been maintained, from 1967 partly in cooperation with FRIEDRICH VON HUENE. In 1964 OTTO STEINKOPF, whose contribution to the revival of many early wind instruments has been unique, joined the firm and the production of those instruments has been rapidly extended. The firm maintains its own instrument museum (founded 1930) as well as a programme of systematic research; it also runs instruction courses on early instruments.

CHRISTOPHER MONK

Moennig. American family of violin dealers and makers. William Heinrich Moennig (*b* Markneukirchen, Saxony, 29 June 1883; *d* Philadelphia, 1962) trained as a violin maker with an uncle in Budapest before going to work with his brother-in-law Julius Guetter in Philadelphia at the beginning of the 20th century. (The family firm, now specializing in the repair and sale of all bowed musical instruments, was founded in 1909.) William Heinrich's son, William Herrman Moennig jr (*b* Philadelphia, 21 July 1905), grew up in an atmosphere of violins and music (the Moennig home was above the business). He became a pupil of his father, who then sent him to study in Markneukirchen and Mittenwald. He qualified as a master violin maker under the auspices of the German Guild.

After World War II William Moennig jr built up a business with a fine reputation among musicians and teachers all over the USA for fair dealing in old instruments. He is one of the leading experts on fine old violins and was the first American member of the International Society of Violin and Bow Makers. His son William Harry Moennig (*b* Philadelphia, 28 Aug 1930) is an excellent craftsman. He trained with Dieudonné in Mirecourt, France, and at the violin making school in Mittenwald under Leo Aschauer, before studying repairing in Philadelphia. In 1975 he took over the running of the business from his father.

CHARLES BEARE

Moer, de. *See* MOORS family.

Moezelzak (i). Idioglot clarinet of Belgium, made of cornstalk. The stalk is cut off so that the upper end is closed and the lower is open. Several deep, oblique incisions are made so that the stalk can be bent in a curve; a tongue is cut in the upper end. By folding and unfolding the stalk different pitches can be produced.

F. J. DE HEN

Moezelzak (ii). BAGPIPE of Belgium. It is known in several forms: with a single drone (13th–16th centuries); without drone, fairly small (15th–19th centuries); with two drones, the bigger resting on the shoulder and the smaller parallel with the chanter (played up to the 20th century); with two parallel drones either tied directly in the bag or placed in a common stock (represented by Pieter Brueghel, among others); and with three drones in a common stock, as pictured in Hendrik Terbrugghen's *The Bagpipe Player* (Ashmolean Museum, Oxford), which may be exceptional.

F. J. DE HEN

Mofferriz [Moferriz, Moferrez, Mufferriz]. Spanish family of organ and instrument makers of Moorish origin. Mahoma Mofferriz (i), called Juan after his conversion to Christianity, died around 1545, probably in Saragossa, where he was in business; he was known as 'the Moor of Saragossa'. He built organs, harpsichords and the earliest claviorgans to be found on the Iberian peninsula, including one for King Manoel I of Portugal (1511). His son Mahoma Mofferriz (ii), who died young (before 1524), built organs in Saragossa; another son, Calema (Miguel after his conversion), and his two sons Miguel (*d* 1545) and Gabriel (i) (*d* 1573), were also organ builders, as was Gabriel's son Juan; Gabriel's son Gabriel (ii) was a maker of string instruments. Brahem (*d c*1513), a maker of organs and other instruments in Saragossa, probably belonged to the same family.

BIBLIOGRAPHY
P. Calahorra Martínez: *La música en Zaragoza en los siglos XVI y XVII*, i (Saragossa, 1977)

GUY BOURLIGUEUX

Mofongo [liba]. Side-blown animal-horn trumpet of the Ngombe and Furu peoples of north-western Zaïre. It has a globular gourd bell and one stop in the tip (*LaurentyA*, 330).

Mō gia trì. Fish-shaped SLIT-DRUM of Vietnam. It is akin to the Chinese woodblock MUYU and is used in Buddhist religious ceremonies.

Mogolo [moglo]. Three-string lute of the Dagomba people of northern Ghana.

Mohali. See MVĀHLĪ.

Mohoceño [asu, bordón, burdón, contrabajo, jatun aymara, jatun tukana]. Name used on the Bolivian Alti Plano for an unbeaked transverse DUCT FLUTE. The word is probably derived from the place-name, Mohoza. The lowest-pitched *mohoceño* is 1·2 to 2·2 metres long, with six finger-holes, and is constructed like the Slovakian *fujara*. At the closed end of the pipe, where the mouthpiece is situated, a second, narrower pipe is attached, which runs alongside the principal pipe for about a third of its length, so that the player can more easily reach the finger-holes. Occasionally some of the holes are filled in. *Mohoceños* are played in ensembles along with other

Mohoceño (transverse duct flute) played by an Aymara Indian, Lake Titicaca, Bolivia

standard duct flutes of various sizes; the same melody is played by all instruments in parallel octaves, 5ths and 4ths, or in parallel tritones. They are often accompanied by a *tambor* (drum). According to M. P. Baumann ('Music of the Indios in Bolivia's Andean Highlands (Survey)', *The World of Music*, xxv/2 (1982), 90) it was the Spaniards who disseminated the *fujara*-type instrument in the New World. See also M. P. Baumann: 'Musica andina de Bolivia', LPLI/S-062 [disc notes].

JOHN M. SCHECHTER

Mohorī. Tribal oboe of Orissa and Assam, east India. It has a stepped pipe of three successively larger, naturally cylindrical segments of bamboo, fitted into each other and perhaps creating an equivalent of a conical bore. Whether they are related to, or are independent *abgefallene* versions of, the east Indian *mahurī* is not known. See N. A. Jairazbhoy: 'A Preliminary Survey of the Oboe in India', *EM*, xiv (1970), 375.
See also MAHVARĪ.

ALASTAIR DICK

Mohurī. Small oboe of Madhya Pradesh, central India. It has a cylindrical, natural bamboo tube and an engraved metal bell. It is about 19 cm long and has seven finger-holes. See K. S. Kothari: *Indian Folk Musical Instruments* (New Delhi, 1968). *See also* MAHVARĪ.

ALASTAIR DICK

Mokena. Obsolete bamboo JEW'S HARP of Tonga.

Mokita. Footed cylindrical drum of the Doko and Ngombe peoples of Zaïre. It is about 60 cm high. The membrane, which is of lizard skin or elephant's ear, has a tuning patch and is nailed to the body. The three or four feet are carved from the same piece of wood and continue the line of the outer casing. Some other drums of this type have feet formed by cutting away triangular crenellations. Local names given by Boone (1951) and de Hen (1960) include the Lesa and Sekata *monkita*, Mbuja *engboma*, Mbanja *maseke*, Loi *empila*, Kutu *itsina*, Saka and Yela *ngomo* and Mbole *ngomba*. The Saka drum (155 cm) is more than double the size of any of the others. The Doko *mokita* is traditionally a chief's drum, played only by the chief, or on his authority, and formerly used for signalling a call to war.

BIBLIOGRAPHY
BooneT, 7, 61, 63f, 68
F.J. de Hen: *Beitrag zur Kenntnis der Musikinstrumente aus Belgisch Kongo und Ruanda-Urundi* (Tervuren, 1960)
G. Knosp: *Enquête sur la vie musicale au Congo belge 1934–1935* (Tervuren, 1968)

K. A. GOURLAY

Mokkin. Japanese term for the Chinese *muqin*, a XYLOPHONE with 16 or 17 keys resembling the Thai *ranāt ēk* but with thicker keys and a flat keyboard. Imported in the late 19th century as part of *minshingaku* music, it is now heard on rare occasions in *geza* (off-stage music of the kabuki theatre) in association with Chinese settings or blind characters. As with some other *geza* instruments, such as the *orugōru* (bells) and the *charumera* (oboe), the *mokkin* does not play a melodic role but simply contributes to the mood of a scene by its presence. One late 19th-century drawing shows the *mokkin* being played with crooked sticks, like those used for African talking drums; more commonly, round-headed wooden sticks resembling those of the Western xylophone are used.

BIBLIOGRAPHY
F. Piggott: *The Music and Musical Instruments of Japan* (London, 1893, 2/1909/R1971), 179
W. P. Malm: *Japanese Music and Musical Instruments* (Rutland, Vermont, 1959), 226
Tōyō Ongaku Gakkai [Society for Asian Music]: *Kabuki ongaku* [Kabuki music] (Tokyo, 1980), pll.37, 22

DAVID W. HUGHES

Mokko. BRONZE DRUM of Bali.

Mokoreie. End-blown flute of the Tswana people of southern Africa. It is similar to the southern Sotho LEKOLILO and the Zulu UMTSHINGO.

Mokoto. (1) Very large cylindrical SLIT-DRUM of the Mbuja people of northern Zaïre; it is also known as *mongungu* (*LaurentyTF*, 133).
   (2) Large SLIT-DRUM of the Ngombe people of northwestern Zaïre; it is carved in a zoomorphic form (*LaurentyTF*, 139).

Mokt'ak. Hand-held SLIT-DRUM of Korea (*mok*: 'wood'; *t'ak*: 'bell'). It is shaped like a somewhat flattened hollow egg, with a handle at the apex and a slit around the other end extending about halfway up either side. There is no standard size and the sound is not precisely pitched. The player strikes near the slit with a wooden mallet. The *mokt'ak* is used only in Buddhist chant, to accompany and punctuate sutra chanting (*yŏmbul*).

The history of the *mokt'ak* in Korea is virtually unknown, since most writings on music stem from the Confucian tradition and fail to mention either Buddhism or most folk practices. Comparable instruments are the Chinese MUYU and Japanese MOKUGYO.

BIBLIOGRAPHY
Byong Won Lee: *An Analytical Study of Sacred Buddhist Chant of Korea* (diss., U. of Washington, Seattle, 1974), 42
ROBERT C. PROVINE

Mokugyo ('wooden fish'). Japanese term for the Chinese woodblock MUYU, classified as a SLIT-DRUM. (It also sometimes refers to the *gyoban*; *see* HAN.) It entered Japan, together with Zen Buddhism, after the 13th century and is paired with the bowl-shaped *kin* bell to provide accompaniment for sutra reading in almost all Buddhist sects (see illustration). It is also used in the kabuki theatre as *geza* (off-stage) music during temple and comic scenes, and has also been played by certain genres of itinerant 'priest'-beggars. During the 20th century the *mokugyo* found its way into Western jazz bands, usually in pairs or sets and often losing the fish symbolism. Another related instrument is the Korean MOKT'AK.

DAVID W. HUGHES

Mokushō. Small spherical woodblock or SLIT-DRUM, used in some Japanese Buddhist ceremonies and also used in the kabuki theatre in *geza* (off-stage) music (*moku*: 'wooden'; *shō*: 'gong'). It is hollow and is set upon three little feet; in shape it resembles a *matsumushi* or a small *hitotsugane* gong. In *geza* music it is used, like the *mokugyo*, in comic scenes as well as in temple settings. See Tōyō Ongaku Gakkai [Society for Asian Music]: *Kabuki ongaku* [Kabuki music] (Tokyo, 1980), pl.26.

DAVID W. HUGHES

Mō làng. Vietnamese wooden SLIT-DRUM. The drum is hollowed out from a tree trunk and closed at both ends with a wooden circle, presenting a long slit; it is struck with a large wooden mallet. In southern Vietnam it is used in villages during the sacrifice of the Heaven and the Earth ceremony and in the Protective Deities cult ceremony, or to sound the alarm for a fire, a bandit attack etc.

TRÂN QUANG HAI

Molea. Cylindrical stopped wooden flute of Zaïre. The *molea* is played in the Stanley Falls region; the *molenge* by the So people (*LaurentyA*, 178f).

Moleno. Set of flutes of the Boa (Bwa) people of northern Zaïre (*LaurentyA*, 188). *See* MAPENGO.

Molero, Fernando. Spanish organ builder of the late 18th century, son-in-law of JULIÁN DE LA ORDEN.

Molimo. Wooden trumpet of the Mbuti pygmies of Zaïre, used for signalling.

Mokugyo (woodblock; right) accompanied by (left) kin (large bowl-shaped bell with hammer) and (centre) two inkin (clapperless bells) at a Zen Buddhist ceremony, Japan

Molinukas (pl. *molinukai*). Clay VESSEL FLUTE of Lithuania, made in a variety of sizes and forms. The most common shapes are those of domestic birds and animals, wild animals or horses with riders (see illustration). The *molinukas* can be from 3 to 20 cm long and 1·5 to 15 cm high. It may have no finger-holes, one or two (one on each side), more rarely up to four. One type of *molinukas*, also known as the 'nightingale', has no finger-holes, but a small soundhole in the upper part of the body. The vessel is filled with water and blown to produce various trilling, glissando and other effects. Until recently, the instrument was known throughout Lithuania, and was made by children or folk craftsmen-potters.

ARVYDAS KARAŠKA

Mollenhauer. German family of woodwind instrument makers. The Mollenhauers were a well-known family active in Hesse from the early 19th century. Johannes Andreas Mollenhauer (*b* Fulda, 31 Aug 1798; *d* Fulda, 30 Aug 1871), who probably learnt instrument making in Vienna, set up his business in 1822. His elder son Gustav (*b* Fulda, 7 Feb 1837; *d* Kassel, 18 Dec 1914), after working for his father, founded in 1864 an apparently independent firm at Kassel, which passed in turn to his two sons, Thomas (ii) (*b* Kassel, 21 Feb 1867; *d* Kassel, 10 July 1938) and Johannes (*b* Kassel, 20 April 1875; *d* Kassel, 22 Feb 1952). The firm's title was Gustav Mollenhauer, Kassel, and in 1900 it became G. Mollenhauer & Söhne; in 1958 the proprietorship passed to Karl Schaub.

Thomas Mollenhauer (i), younger son of Johannes Andreas (*b* Fulda, 22 Feb 1840; *d* Fulda, 1 July 1914), is recorded as having worked for Boehm and Mendler from 1862 to 1864; correspondence dated 1865 suggests that Boehm tried to persuade Mollenhauer to build piccolos on his system, as he did not wish to undertake further experimental work at his advanced age. A letter dated 1878 mentions both alto flutes in F and piccolos on the Boehm system but examples from this period seem to be rare. Between 1865 and 1866 Thomas (i) also worked for Ottensteiner of Munich. His elder son Josef Nikolaus (*b* Fulda, 20 July 1875; *d* Friesenhausen, 12 Oct 1964) worked with Heckel and was later head of the firm J. Mollenhauer & Söhne, Fulda. The younger son Conrad (*b* Fulda, 10 Sept 1876; *d* Friesenhausen, 12 Oct 1943) worked with Rittershausen of Berlin and then Adler of Markneukirchen and established his own business in 1912. His son was Thomas (iii) (*b* Fulda, 17 July 1908; *d* Fulda, 8 Feb 1953), after whose death the firm continued as Conrad Mollenhauer, Fulda, under the direction of his widow.

The Mollenhauers produced a full range of woodwind instruments, together with certain specialities. C. Mollenhauer, Fulda, embarked on a revival of the recorder and in 1954 introduced the Jugendoboe or Choroboe, a simplified oboe conceived by Arnold Klaes for group playing particularly in schools.

BIBLIOGRAPHY

G. Antoni and E. Stein, eds.: *Die Stadt Fulda*, Monographien Deutscher Städte, xxxiv (Berlin, 1930)
A. Klaes: 'Mollenhauer', *MGG*

PHILIP BATE

Moller. See MALER family.

Möller. American firm of organ builders. It was found-

Molinukai (vessel flutes) of Lithuania

ed at Warren, Pennsylvania, in 1875 by Mathias Peter Möller (*b* Denmark; 1854–1937). After training as a mechanic Möller emigrated to the USA in 1872 and worked for Derrick & Felgemaker, organ builders, of Erie, Pennsylvania, developing there an improved windchest. In 1880 he moved his business to Hagerstown, Maryland, where it has remained, becoming the largest manufacturer of organs in the USA. During the 1930s Richard Whitelegg, a noted voicer, was Möller's tonal director. On Möller's death, his son, M. P. Möller jr, became president of the firm, and on the latter's death in 1961, his brother-in-law, W. Riley Daniels, became president; later Daniels's son, Peter Möller Daniels, also became active in the direction of the firm.

The first Möller organs had mechanical action, but Möller soon developed a reliable pneumatic action which was used until electro-pneumatic action was adopted. Although Möller was responsible for some of the largest organ installations in the USA, the firm is also known for its pioneering work in the development of small self-contained organs, sold originally under the name of 'Möller Artiste' but now known as 'Series 70' after revision along more classic lines. Their important installations include those in St George's Church, New York City (1958), the Cathedral of Mary Our Queen, Baltimore (1959), the National Shrine of the Immaculate Conception, Washington (1965), and Heinz Chapel at the University of Pittsburgh (1970).

BIBLIOGRAPHY

W. H. Barnes: *The Contemporary American Organ* (Glen Rock, NJ, 8/1964)
O. Ochse: *The History of the Organ in the United States* (Bloomington, Ind., 1975)

BARBARA OWEN

Möller [Müller], Johann Patroklus (*b* Soest, Westphalia, 1697 or 1698; *d* Lippstadt, 24 July 1772). German organ builder. His father, Martin, was a cabinet maker in Soest. Johann Patroklus was possibly taught by P. H. Varenholt; he settled in Lippstadt in 1720 and became one of the leading organ builders of the region, supplying instruments in the southern part of the Münster district, the northern part of the Sauerland, and in the Detmold district. He was concurrently organist of the

Grosse Marienkirche in Lippstadt. His organs included that for St Thomae, Soest (1720; two manuals, 26 stops); the rebuilding (1734) of the organ at the Grosse Marienkirche, Lippstadt; and organs for Marienmünster Abbey (1736–8; three manuals, 34 stops; still extant); Böddeken Abbey (1744; three manuals, 43 stops; now in Büren); Münster Cathedral (1752–5; three manuals, 55 stops); and Paderborn Cathedral (1754–6; three manuals, 42 stops). The organ built about 1735 for Dahlheim Abbey (three manuals, 45 stops; now in Borgentreich) is also attributed to Möller. He developed the characteristics of the typical 17th-century Westphalian organ, with its rich tone-colour, in an apt and logical manner. In all his organs each manual was provided with a complete Principal chorus (including $5\frac{1}{3}'$, $3\frac{1}{5}'$, Sesquialtera, Mixtur and Zimbel in the Hauptwerk; and in the Positiv $2\frac{2}{3}'$ as well as Sesquialtera and Mixtur or $1\frac{1}{3}'$ and Mixtur) and a respectable group of foundation stops (including Quintaden, Gemshorn, Salicional, Transverse flute and Viola da gamba), in addition to reeds (Trumpet 8' and 4', Fagott and Rankett 16' and Krummhorn and Vox humana 8') and flute upperwork ($2\frac{2}{3}'$, 2', $1\frac{1}{3}'$, 1' and Kornett III). His pedalboards usually had 16' and 8' foundation stops, a 2' or 1' flute, and reeds (Posaune 16', Trumpet 8', Schalmei 4' and Kornett 2'). The synthesis of the styles of NIEHOFF and BECK, already vigorously pioneered by the Bader family, was perfected by Möller in accordance with the needs of his age. Like his predecessors in Westphalia he remained partial to the spring-chest, continuing to incorporate it in his new organs. Möller may be regarded as one of the leading masters of the classical German organ.

BIBLIOGRAPHY
G. Schwake: *Forschungen zur Geschichte der Orgelbaukunst in Nordwestdeutschland* (Münster, 1923)
H. Linssen: 'Die Domorgel zu Münster in Westfalen', *Die Kirchenmusik*, ii (1939), 5, 28
H. Böhringer: *Untersuchungen zum Orgelbau im Hochstift Paderborn* (Cologne, 1949)
R. Reuter: 'Johann Patroklus Müller, Westfalens bedeutendster Orgelbauer im 18. Jahrhundert', *Westfalen*, xxxvii (Münster, 1959)
——: 'Müller', *MGG*
——: *Orgeln in Westfalen* (Kassel, 1965)
U. Wulfhorst: *Der westfälische Orgelbauer Johann Patroklus Möller 1698–1772* (Kassel, 1967)
HANS KLOTZ

Mollpill. Bowed monochord of Estonia, introduced in the 19th century from Sweden (*see* PSALMODIKON). It was used for the accompaniment of spiritual songs, mostly in chapels and schools, in west and north Estonia. It is analogous to the Lithuanian *manikarka* and the Latvian *gīgas*.

Molo. (1) Single-string plucked lute of the Tukulor people of north-eastern Senegal. The soundbox is hemispherical and the cylindrical neck emerges through the cowhide soundtable and acts as the string bearer.

(2) Three-string plucked lute of the Songhay people of Niger and of the Hausa people of Niger and northern Nigeria. It has a wooden boat-shaped soundbox covered with duiker-skin or goatskin. The shortest string acts as a drone. Formerly the *molo* accompanied songs glorifying famous warriors and then later it became associated with the *bori* spirit possession cult. Today it is played mainly for entertainment or to accompany praise-singing.

(3) A term used loosely throughout Hausa-speaking areas of Nigeria to refer to any plucked string instrument, for example the *molo na kara*.

BIBLIOGRAPHY
Ames–KingGHM
E. von Boetticher: 'Spielleute und Märchenzäler Innerafrikas', *Westermans Monatshefte*, lviii (1913–14), 573
K. Krieger: 'Musikinstrumente der Hausa', *Baessler-Archiv*, new ser., xvi (1968), 373
K. A. Gourlay: 'Letter to the Editor', *EM*, xx (1976), 327
B. Surugue: 'Songhay music', *Grove 6*
LUCY DURÁN (1), K. A. GOURLAY (2,3)

Mololi (pl. *meloli*). Generic term for a flute, whistle, or bird sound among the Southern Sotho of southern Africa. *See also* PHALA.

Molo na kara. Six- to nine-string idiochord RAFT ZITHER of the Hausa people of the Zamfara region of Nigeria. The strings, narrow strips of the outer layer of the raft, are adjusted by one or two strong dried grass-blades, inserted underneath. The instrument is played as rhythmic accompaniment by moving a dried grass-blade over the strings. See K. Krieger: 'Musikinstrumente der Hausa', *Baessler-Archiv*, new ser., xvi (1968), 373–430.

Molto (It.: 'much', 'very'). A word used to qualify tempo and expression marks in music: *molto piano, molto grazioso, molto andante* (*see* ANDANTE), etc. It is also found in such contexts as *allegro di molto* (given by Koch, 1802, as the equivalent of *allegro assai*).
For bibliography *see* TEMPO AND EXPRESSION MARKS.

Molu. Double clapperless bell of the Taneka people of Benin. It is used with horns and drums for masked, sacrificial dances after the harvest.

Molumba. Very large cylindrical SLIT-DRUM of the Mbuja people of northern Zaïre (*LaurentyTF*, 133).

Mombili. Side-blown ivory trumpet of the Busu-Libundu people of Zaïre (*LaurentyA*, 375).

Momo. End-blown open bamboo resonating tubes of Damaindeh-Bau village, Finisterre Range, Madang Province, Papua New Guinea. They are 1·8 to 2·4 metres long. The players produce 'spirit cries' by yodelling into the open ends.

Momong. Suspended bronze gong in the *canang* ensemble of the Gayo people in the Takengon area of Central Aceh, Sumatra. Its diameter is about 43 cm, its depth about 10 cm and its boss about 10 cm wide. Pitches are variable; a *momong* used by government officials in Takengon is pitched approximately at D''.
MARGARET J. KARTOMI

Momongan [kolintang besi]. Metal bossed gong of Sumatra and Sulawesi. In the Mandailing area of North Sumatra it is made of bronze and normally played in sets of two to six in the *gondang*, *gordang lima* and *gordang sembilan* ensembles. In Minahasa, North Sulawesi, the *momongan* is about 45 cm in diameter and is played in the *orkes papurungan*.
MARGARET J. KARTOMI

Mompate. A term used by the Ngombe, Mongo, Kota and Mbole peoples of western and northern Zaïre for an ivory trumpet; the Lendo call this instrument *mompati*, the Ngando *mompato* and the Basankusa and Lalia *mompale.* These terms are presumably related to the Mongo, Nkundo and Saka *bompate*, Oli and Ngando *bopate*, Kela *bopati* and Yela *bopatsi*. All terms refer to ivory trumpets, though the Mbole, Lendo and Ngando also use them for trumpets of antelope horn. The trumpets vary in length; they are usually from 40 to 80 cm, though the Mongo reputedly had trumpets 125 cm long. Apart from the Kota instrument, which is end-blown, all are side-blown with a mouthpiece measuring 2 to 4 cm; the Ngombe and Mongo trumpets have a wooden bell, and the mouthpiece is in the shape of an elongated lozenge. Most are single-note, though the Ngando *mompato* has a thumb-hole at the tip, thus enabling the musician to produce two notes; the end-blown Mongo *bompate* allegedly can produce three or four notes. All are signalling instruments, used (at least formerly) for hunting and warfare, except for the Yela *bopatsi* which is blown during dancing. It is unusual for instruments of this type to be known by related terms over such a wide area. Some idea of the variety of names for both ivory and antelope trumpets in Zaïre can be obtained by consulting the sources below. *See also* KIMPUNGIDI and MOTUTU.

BIBLIOGRAPHY
LaurentyA, 388, 399
F.J. de Hen: *Beitrag zur Kenntnis der Musikinstrumente aus Belgisch Kongo und Ruanda-Urundi* (Tervuren, 1960)
G. Knosp: *Enquête sur la vie musicale au Congo belge 1934–1935* (Tervuren, 1968)
K. A. GOURLAY

Monacordio (Sp.). CLAVICHORD.

Monaulos (Gk.). An ancient reed instrument. *See* KALAMOS.

Mönch & Prachtel. German firm of organ builders. The business was founded in Überlingen in 1875 by Xaver Mönch (*d* 1907); when his sons Otto and Franz joined the firm it became known as Xaver Mönch Söhne. From 1907 Otto Mönch (*d* 1954) directed the business on his own, but was later joined by his son Karl-Otto. In the period between the two world wars the firm produced around 100 new organs. In 1967 the workshop was enlarged and modernized and in 1972 Horst-Friedrich Prachtel (*b* Hessen, 23 Jan 1934) joined the firm, which then became known as Mönch & Prachtel. Prachtel, who graduated from the Handwerkskammer, Stuttgart, in 1968, has become a specialist in tone quality. In 1975 Karl-Otto Mönch retired and was succeeded by his son Peter-Otto (*b* Überlingen, 26 Dec 1952), who was trained by Gerhard Schmid in Kaufbeuren and graduated from Stuttgart in 1978; he concentrates on the technical and architectural aspects of organ building. At present the firm has 14 workers and six apprentices (Otto Heuss of Lich and Werner Bosch of Kassel were trained by Mönch).

Between 1952 and 1983 the firm built over 120 new slider-chest organs, almost all with tracker action, mainly in Baden-Württemberg and in Switzerland. They include the organs at St Johannes, Donaueschingen (1963; three manuals, 41 stops); St Konrad, Karlsruhe (1963; three manuals, 36 stops); St Bonifatius, Heidelberg (1964; three manuals, 41 stops); Überlingen Minster (1968; three manuals, 52 stops); Herz-Jesu-Kirche, Winterthur (1969; two manuals, 26 stops); St Elisabeth, Freiburg im Breisgau (1976; two manuals, 20 stops); the Lutheran Church, Tuttlingen (1978; three manuals, 46 stops); the Catholic Church, Aulendorf (1981; three manuals, 37 stops);

Heilig-Geist-Kirche, Offenburg (1982; two manuals, 20 stops); and the Catholic church, Schluchsee (1983; two manuals, 30 stops). Among the firm's restorations are the organs at Heidenhofen (1733/1969; slider-chest organ by Conrad Speissegger; one manual, eight stops); Gutmadingen (1885/1977; cone-chest organ by Xaver Mönch; two manuals, 18 stops); and Owingen (1881/1980; cone-chest organ by Wilhelm Schwarz; two manuals, 15 stops).

HANS KLOTZ

Monda. Cylindrical SLIT-DRUM of the Yaka people of south-western Zaïre. *See* MONDO.

Mondjo. Side-blown ivory trumpet of the Busira region of north-western Zaïre. It has a carved mouthpiece (*LaurentyA*, 404, 424).

Mondo. Term for a medium-sized cylindrical SLIT-DRUM of the Bas-Congo, San Salvador and south-western regions of Zaïre. Amongst the Yaka Nkanu of south-western Zaïre, the instrument (*môndo*) is said to have political power. Amongst the Suku people the narrow slit is widened at each end to make square or circular openings. Other names reported for this type in the south-western regions are *moondo* and *monda* (*LaurentyTF*, 133ff).
See also KYONDO.

Moneke. Wooden flute, with slender conical bore, of the Mamvu people of north-eastern Zaïre (*LaurentyA*, 157).

Mong [mōng, mọng]. Gong of South-east Asia. In the *nobat* ensemble in Sumatra the *mong* is a small bronze bossed gong about 20 cm in diameter; it is played in pairs. The *mōng* (*khọ̄ng mōng*) of Thailand is a wide-flanged bossed gong with a diameter of 30 to 45 cm; the lip flange is 5 cm deep. The instrument is usually hung on a tripod or metal stand and played with a padded beater. In Laos the *mọng* is a large metal gong. The term *mong* may also refer to the six-instrument GONG-CHIME of Shan state, Burma, and the small gong MUNG of Kelantan, Malaysia. *See also* KHỌ̄NG.

Monganze. Large zoomorphic SLIT-DRUM of the Lobala people of Zaïre (*LaurentyTF*, 139).

Mongele. STICK ZITHER of the Saka people of Zaïre (*LaurentyC*, 115). *See* ZEZE (i).

Mongenda. Double drum of the Saka people of Zaïre. The two shells are bound together or carved from a single block (*BooneT*, 63).

Mong-mong. GONG-CHIME of Sumatra and West Malaysia, used in the *biola mendu* ensemble.

Mongmongan. Gong of North Sumatra. *See* GONRANG SIPITUPITU.

Mongom. Side-blown trumpet of Chad. *See* BETENE.

Mongu. Very large cylindrical SLIT-DRUM of the Bango people of northern-central Zaïre; it is also known as *basoko* (*LaurentyTF*, 133).

Mongungu (i). SLIT-DRUM of the Genya people of Zaïre. Its length is about 1·5 metres. A smaller variety is called *mongungu ngole*. The term 'mongungu' also refers to a large cylindrical slit-drum of the Mbuja and Kumu peoples of north and east Zaïre, where it is also known as *mokoto* (*LaurentyTF*, 133).

Mongungu (ii). Long cylindrical drum of the Kumu people of Zaïre (*BooneT*, 4, 64). See LILENGA.

Monk, Christopher (William) (*b* Delhi, 28 Dec 1921). English cornett maker. He studied history at Lincoln College, Oxford, from 1940 to 1944; from 1942 to 1945 he studied the trumpet with George Eskdale. He then became a full-time maker and player of the cornett, sackbut and serpent. His first cornett was completed in March 1955, and his first cornettino in 1956; he first broadcast as cornett player (with Brian Baker) on 25 April 1958. In 1968, with Len Ward, he devised an inexpensive system of manufacturing resin cornetts; thousands of them have since gone to all parts of the world, doing much to stimulate the modern revival of this difficult instrument. He contributed a chapter, 'The Older Brass Instruments: Cornett, Trombone, and Trumpet', to the book edited by Anthony Baines, *Musical Instruments through the Ages* (Harmondsworth, 1961, 2/1966/R1976).

EDWARD H. TARR

Monke, Josef (*b* Elberfeld, 18 March 1882; *d* Cologne, 17 Nov 1965). German brass instrument maker. From 1896 to 1900 he studied instrument making with Mitsching, and trumpet playing with Liebe, in Elberfeld. He then began a series of visits destined to make him one of the best-informed makers of his time: to Knoth (not Kuth) in Danzig (1900), Moritz in Berlin (1901–2), Enders in Mainz (1902), where he worked on the Alschausky trombone (in B♭, with F valve), and to Markneukirchen (1903). In 1904 he became first assistant to Leopold August Schmidt in Cologne (successor to his father, F. A. Schmidt, who had succeeded a certain Schröder in 1848). In 1922, the year following Schmidt's death, Monke opened his own shop, later employing up to 16 workers. Although the firm now makes all brass instruments, their trumpets in particular represent the culmination of the development of the so-called 'Cologne' models, with a wider bore and larger bell than those of Heckel, their chief rivals.

Among Monke's innovations, starting while he was working for Schmidt, were the double-cone mouthpipe (it had formerly been cylindrical); the expanded bore of the valve slides (formerly cylindrical), the slight expansion at the bends allowing a freer air-flow; the refinement of the former Cologne rotary valve mechanism from a single to a double joint system, with open spiral springs instead of the former enclosed 'drum' springs; and the shortening of the third valve slide (*c*1926–7) – a trigger mechanism was added in 1950. In addition he made two important contributions to brass-mouthpiece making by introducing standard tools, which guarantee uniformity, and (in 1908) by inventing the screw-rim mouthpiece. (P. Bate, *The Trumpet and Trombone* (London, 1966), erroneously attributed this innovation to Vincent Bach.)

Since Monke's death, the firm has been directed by his daughter Liselotte (*b* Cologne, 9 June 1923). Wilhelm Monke (*b* Cologne, 27 Nov 1913), Josef's son, studied instrument making with his father from 1928 and, simultaneously, trumpet playing with Ludwig Werle; he passed his *Meisterprüfung* with distinction in 1937. He continued to work for his father until 1945. After that, he not only continued to make brass instruments, but also expanded his business to include sales and service of all other types of musical instrument. He has filled various posts in professional organizations.

Wilhelm's son Friedrich Wilhelm Monke (*b* Cologne, 19 Feb 1943) received his training with his grandfather from 1957 to 1960; his journeyman's examination piece received local and national prizes (1960–61) and he became a master in 1966. Today he is the director of the wind instrument department of his father's firm.

BIBLIOGRAPHY
K. Körner: 'Monke, Josef', and 'Monke, Wilhelm', *Rheinische Musiker*, v, ed. K. G. Fellerer (Cologne, 1967), 110
W. Monke and H. Riedel, eds.: *Lehrbuch des Musikalienhandels* (Bonn, 1971)

EDWARD H. TARR

Monkita [monkela]. Single-headed footed drum of the Lesa and Sakata peoples of equatorial Zaïre, owned exclusively by the chiefs (*BooneT*, 61). See MOKITA.

Monochord [canon harmonicus]. An ancient singlestring instrument first mentioned in Greece in the 5th century BC, and said to have been an invention of Pythagoras. The monochord remained a viable musical device, used mainly for teaching, tuning and experimentation, until the advent of more accurate instruments in the late 19th century.

In its earliest form the monochord's single string was stretched across two fixed bridges which were erected on a plank or table. A movable bridge was then placed underneath the string, dividing it into two sections. The marks indicating the position of the fixed bridge were inscribed on the table beneath the string. The resonating box, seen in drawings after the 12th century, was a late medieval addition which increased the portability in addition to enhancing the tone of the monochord. After 1500 one of the end bridges was replaced with a nut, the attendant lowering of the string enabling the user to press it directly on the belly of the instrument. Although simple to use, this modified monochord was considerably less accurate. The name monochord was usually retained for multi-string instruments when the strings were tuned in unison or when the instrument was used for the same purposes as a monochord. The medieval instrument varied from about 90 to 122 cm in length. During the Middle Ages the selection of a monochord's basic pitch was influenced by its size and by the voice range of the user rather than by any existing standards.

1. Acoustical systems. 2. System of string lengths. 3. Division of the chromatic scale. 4. Uses.

1. ACOUSTICAL SYSTEMS. The divisions of the monochord are usually presented in terms of proportions, string lengths or cents. A fourth method, that of expressing string lengths by means of logarithms, was often used in the 18th century, but this system, like the cents system derived from it, is not proportional and cannot be used on the instrument without further calculation. The first two can be directly applied and are the only kinds of division to have attained any practical significance before the 20th century; this kind of division is designated a manual division.

The Pythagorean concept of division by proportions is based on the relationship of the harmonic and arithmetic means as they are represented by the numbers 6, 8, 9 and 12. The ratio 12:6 produces the octave; 9:6 and 12:8, the 5th; 8:6 and 12:9, the 4th; and 9:8, the major 2nd. Reduced to their lowest terms these ratios are dupla (2:1), sesquialtera (3:2), sesquitertia (4:3) and sesquioctava (9:8). They can be applied to a string in two ways. For example, in fig.1*a*, one whole tone (D down to C) can be produced by dividing half the string length (AY) into eight parts (DY) and then adding an equal ninth portion (sesquioctava) to form the second pitch (CY). Conversely (fig.1*b*) a subsesquioctava proportion (8:9) can be used if the string length AY is divided into nine parts and the second is sounded with only eight of them (BY).

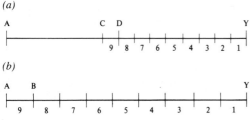

1. Diagrams showing divisions of the monochord

In fig.1*a* the monochord is divided in a descending manner, i.e. from the higher pitches to the lower. The second division (1*b*), moving from the lower to the higher pitches, is an ascending division. It is of course possible to use both techniques alternately in one division. The more complex ratio, like that of the Pythagorean semitone (256:243), can be determined by calculation with simple intervals, e.g. the sum of two whole tones (9/8 × 9/8 = 81/64) is subtracted from the fourth (4/3 − 81/64 = 256/243) – an extremely simple manoeuvre when done on the instrument.

The completion of either of the above divisions in the manner of the Middle Ages would give a two-octave scale in the Pythagorean tuning whose lowest note would be given by the entire length of the string. In general it may be said that the Greek writers up to AD 500 utilized the descending division and subsequently adopted the ascending division. The technique of the latter, originally attempted by Boethius, was first successfully described by Odo of St Maur (Cluny) in *c*1000. Writers of the Renaissance and the post-Renaissance eras preferred the ascending division.

The selection of the technique to be used in working out a specific division was often dependent on its intended usage. Although all medieval divisions achieve the same end and utilize the same four proportions the method of division selected depended on whether it was for a speculative (descending division) or a practical (ascending) treatise. The popularity of the ascending division parallels the rise of the practical treatise in the late Middle Ages.

2. SYSTEM OF STRING LENGTHS. The cumbersome nature of the proportional system together with the difficulty of using a compass to divide the string caused some investigators to adopt the system of string lengths, an accurate and simple method of proportional pitch representation. The only problem with the string lengths lies in the number of units encountered. For example Johann Neidhardt in 1706 specified a string length of 1781·82 units for the second step of his scale. Other advocates, like Marpurg, suggested the use of only three digits to represent the total length of the string; however, this was a compromise rarely admitted by the users of the technique.

3. DIVISION OF THE CHROMATIC SCALE. Semitones can be determined on the monochord by three methods: by extending the superparticular divisions, arithmetically dividing the tone, or by mean-proportional division. In superparticular divisions two complete and different (different even for notes which are enharmonically equivalent) sets of chromatic notes are available. These may be obtained by the successive application of the sesquialtera proportion (beginning with the note F) or of the subsesquialtera proportion (beginning with B). The former will produce a series of perfect 5ths in descending order (called 'flat semitones'), and the latter a set of ascending perfect 5ths ('sharp semitones'). Arithmetical semitones are determined by an equal division of the difference between the string lengths of two pitches a step apart. This method was frequently used in post-medieval times even though the semitones are of unequal size. The mean proportional string lengths necessary for single equal semitones are usually determined by means of the Euclidean construction (a perpendicular erected at the juncture of two string lengths which are used as the diameter of a semicircle will equal the proportional length). To determine two or more mean-proportionals, a mechanical device like the mesolabium (a series of overlapping square frames) can be used to substitute for the mathematical function of the cube root; multiple mean-proportionals can also be formed by means of the sort of geometrical figures used by Lemme Rossi in the 17th century.

4. USES. In addition to its value as an experimental

2. Monochord from 'De musica' by Boethius, Canterbury, 1150 (GB-Cu Ii.3.12, f.61v)

device, the monochord served throughout the Middle Ages as a teaching instrument. Monochord-based diagrams and sets of directions for determining the consonances abound in both speculative and practical treatises of this era. Until the adoption of sight-singing methods based upon the hexachord system, the monochord was used to produce pitches for rote singing; from then until the 13th century it was used mainly to check correct reproduction of intervals. The decline of its pedagogical use after this time is probably due to the introduction of keyboard instruments. The use of the monochord by teachers in the Renaissance was restricted to those few who rigidly maintained the Pythagorean scale as the basis of their musical instruction.

Because so much of the early use of the monochord was didactic, its users attempted to make the division as efficient and accurate as possible. The efficiency of a monochord division depends on the relation between the number of separate measurements and the number of notes produced. The results of these efforts are particularly noticeable after 1450 because after this date each new division often produced a new variation of a given tuning. Often the musician wished to change the tuning but not infrequently he was only seeking a simpler method of division. It would seem that the appearance of an altered tuning bothered the Renaissance musician little, for because of the monochord's inaccuracy, a variation of a few cents (in some cases as much as 22 cents) was a small sacrifice to pay for a more efficient division. A case in point is the division of Ramos de Pareia whose monochord tuning varied widely from the accepted Pythagorean standard. Ramos, however, was apparently not bothered by the pitch deviation as long as he was able to simplify the division. To this end he stated: 'So therefore we have made all of our division very easy, because the fractions are common and not difficult'. In many cases this desire is not stated expressly, as it was by Ramos, but it may be suspected that it served as an underlying cause of many tuning variations in the Renaissance and later eras.

The other areas in which the influence of the monochord is evident are in its instrumental applications and its use as a symbolic device. In the former instance the use of the monochord in ensembles is cited in both Greek and medieval writings. In later times, however, the descendants of the monochord, the clavichord, hurdy-gurdy and trumpet marine, were more frequently used. Throughout the late Middle Ages and the Renaissance the monochord is often mentioned as a basic tool in the design or measurement of bells and organ pipes. Finally, until about 1700, the monochord was commonly used to show the unity existing between man and the universe. It is represented as a divided string whose pitches may represent the solar system (*musica mundana*), the muses, the zodiac, or even bodily functions; often this is being tuned by the hand of God.

BIBLIOGRAPHY

S. Wanlztoeben: *Das Monochord als Instrument und als System* (Halle, 1911)

J. M. Barbour: *Tuning and Temperament* (East Lansing, 1951)

L. W. Gümpel: 'Das Tasten-Monochord Conrads von Zabern', *AMw*, xii (1955), 143

C. Adkins: *The Theory and Practice of the Monochord* (diss., U of Iowa, 1963)

——: 'The Technique of the Monochord', *AcM*, xxxix (1967), 34

T. J. Mathiesen: 'An Annotated Translation of Euclid's Division of a Monochord', *JMT*, xix (1975), 236

CECIL ADKINS

Monochordia. A term used by many 15th- and 16th-century writers for the clavichord; *see* CLAVICHORD, §2.

Monocorde à clavier (Fr.; Ger. *Tastenmonochord*). A keyed monochord invented in 1883 by J. Pousset of Pierre, Meurte-et-Moselle, and first built in 1886. Its body was oval and rested on a table-like stand. The keyboard, with 29 keys (in decreasing size), was set on the neck and gave a compass from *f* to *a″*. The string was of horse hair.

Monocordo (It.; Fr. *monocorde*). An instruction to a string player to execute a passage or piece on one string. The effect was first used by Paganini in his *Sonata Napoleone* (1807).

Monpanana. Side-blown ivory trumpet of the Mangbetu people of north-eastern Zaïre. It has a carved mouthpiece and one stop in the tip (*LaurentyA*, 420).

Montagnana, Domenico (*b* Lendinara, *c*1687; *d* Venice, 7 March 1750). Italian string instrument maker. He went to Venice about 1699 and probably in due course became the pupil and assistant of Matteo Goffriller; in about 1711 he opened his own shop, though at this time he may also have been associated with Francesco Gobetti. Surviving instruments seldom date from earlier than about 1720, but from then on his reputation grew fast and his output was considerable.

Montagnana's violins were made on a number of different patterns. The standard sized flat models make first-rate solo instruments, but others are now less suitable because of their small dimensions or a tendency towards the higher build favoured by Stainer, whose instruments were popular in Venice as elsewhere in Italy. Only one viola has been attributed to Montagnana: the instrument used for many years by Tertis. Its shape, though altered from the instrument's original form, was the inspiration for the 'Tertis' model adopted by many modern makers.

Montagnana is especially famed for his cellos. Encouraged by the cello's particular popularity in Venice, and perhaps commissioned by the four music conservatories, he produced cellos that are regarded by many of today's soloists as ideal. Bold, sometimes massive in appearance, they have much of the quality of sound of the great Cremonese instruments and a greater volume when forcefully played. The novelist Charles Reade dubbed Montagnana 'the mighty Venetian', and all familiar with his work acknowledge its power.

BIBLIOGRAPHY

C. Reade: *Cremona: Violins and Varnish* (Gloucester, 1873/R) [orig. pubd in *Pall Mall Gazette* (Aug 1872)]

C. Beare: *The Venetian Violin Makers* (in preparation)

CHARLES BEARE

Montichiaro, Zanetto di. See ZANETTO DI MONTICHIARO.

Montre (Fr.). An ORGAN STOP.

Mon vang. Bamboo XYLOPHONE of the Shan people of Thailand and Burma.

Monzani, Tebaldo (*b* Modena, 1762; *d* Margate, Kent, 14 June 1839). Italian flute maker, flautist and publisher. He took up residence in London about 1786, establishing his business in 1787 and operating from various premises in the next few years. From 1800 to 1803 he was in partnership with Giambattista Cimadoro as Monzani & Cimador, and from 1805 to 1808 as

Cello by Domenico Montagnana,
Venice, 1710 (private collection)

Monzani & Co. His partnership with the maker HENRY
HILL lasted from 1808 until 1829, when Hill took over
the business on his own, renaming it Hill, late Monzani
& Co. In 1845 the firm's stock was sold at auction.

Monzani played a one-keyed flute when he arrived
from Italy but quickly gained a reputation for introducing numerous improvements. As a maker he used silver
extensively, both for the keys and for the French-style
pin-and-socket joints that he patented in 1812. This used
silver for the lining and a cork covering (rather than
lapping) for the pin. Monzani favoured the extra middle
joints introduced by Tromlitz, as well as a number of
extra keys which did not always improve the tuning as
intended. His flutes almost invariably included integral
C foot-joints and always used small tone-holes instead
of the large ones favoured by the Nicholsons. Monzani's flute tutor *Instructions for the German Flute* (1801,
3/1813) had a wide circulation.

BIBLIOGRAPHY
R. S. Rockstro: *A Treatise on . . . the Flute* (London, 1890, 2/
1928/R1967)
C. Humphries and W. C. Smith: *Music Publishing in the British
Isles* (London, 1954, 2/1970)
L. G. Langwill: *An Index of Musical Wind-instrument Makers*
(Edinburgh, 1960, rev., enlarged 6/1980)
P. Bate: *The Flute* (London, 1969, 2/1979)
NIALL O'LOUGHLIN

Monzo. Trumpet of the Eso people of Zaïre. *See*
MOTUTU.

Moog. A range of synthesizers manufactured by the
R. A. Moog Co. (founded by ROBERT A. MOOG) in Trumansburg, New York; the company later became Moog

Music of Buffalo, New York, and since 1973 it has been
a division of Norlin Industries. In 1964 Moog developed his first voltage-controlled synthesizer modules and
at the end of the year marketed the world's first commercial synthesizer, a modular system intended primarily for studio work, which, with some additions and
improvements, is still produced. It introduced many
features that later became standard in the synthesizer,
including a level of voltage control of one volt per octave.
Synthesizers were first brought to the attention of the
general public by Walter Carlos's best-selling record
Switched-on Bach, released in November 1968, which
was created on the Moog system. Other performers to
have used Moog synthesizers include Richard Teitel-
baum, Keith Emerson and Sun Ra. The 'fat' sound of
Moog instruments is at least partly due to the filters, the
only aspect that Moog was originally able to patent.

In 1970, faced with competition from newer synthesizer companies, Moog and others developed the MINI-
MOOG, a fully portable monophonic instrument designed
for rock music performance. Following the Minimoog
over a dozen models were developed, most now discontinued. They included the small monophonic Sonic
Six and Satellite (c1972) and the monophonic Micro-
moog (marketed 1973–5 – the last one in which Moog
himself made some design contribution). The Poly-
moog, one of the first polyphonic synthesizers (1976–
80; *see* SYNTHESIZER, fig.4), was designed by David Luce,
and the monophonic Prodigy (1979–81) by Richard
Walborn and Tony Marchese. Other Moog instruments
introduced in the late 1970s and early 1980s were the
Opus 3 (a string synthesizer with organ and brass sections), the Liberation (held like a guitar), the Rogue

synthesizer and the Taurus (a bass pedal-board synthesizer controller). Ray Caster's Source, the first of two new hybrid synthesizers controlled by microprocessors, was produced in 1981; it is a monophonic instrument in which almost all the controls, apart from the ever-popular pair of pitch and modulation tone-wheels (first used in the Minimoog), are operated from a large touch panel. The Source was followed in 1982 by the polyphonic Memorymoog designed by Walborn and Caster.

See also SYNTHESIZER.

BIBLIOGRAPHY

R. A. Moog: 'Voltage-controlled Electronic Music Modules', Journal of the Audio Engineering Society, xiii (1965), 200
P. Beaver and B. L. Krause: 'The Nonesuch Guide to Electronic Music', Nonesuch HC-73018 [disc notes]
R. Pellegrino: An Electronic Studio Manual (Columbus, Ohio, 1969)
D. Crombie: 'The Moog Story', Sound International, no.6 (1978), 66
D. T. Horn: Electronic Music Synthesizers (Blue Ridge Summit, Penn., 1980), 34, 46
T. Rhea: 'The Moog Synthesizer', Contemporary Keyboard, vii/3 (1981), 58
J. Lee: 'Interview: Robert Moog', Polyphony (Jan–Feb 1982)

HUGH DAVIES

Moog, Robert A(rthur) (*b* Flushing, NY, 23 May 1934). American designer of electronic instruments, best known for the pioneering MOOG synthesizers; in some circles the name 'Moog' has even been used, loosely, to mean any type of synthesizer. In 1954 Moog formed the R. A. Moog Co. in New York City, under which name he built theremins (five models up to 1962) to finance his studies at Queens College and later at Columbia University. In 1957 he moved to Ithaca, New York, where he gained a doctorate in engineering physics at Cornell University in 1965. At nearby Trumansburg in the spring and summer of 1964 he began to develop his first synthesizer modules in collaboration with the composer Herbert Deutsch; they were demonstrated that autumn at the Audio Engineering Society convention in New York. At the end of 1964 Moog's company marketed the first commercial modular synthesizer. Between 1966 and 1969 he sponsored the Independent Electronic Music Center at the R. A. Moog Co., which published the *Electronic Music Review* and ran an open-access electronic music studio.

During the next decade Moog's work was bound up with the development of the company, which in 1971 became Moog Music and moved to Buffalo, New York; it became a division of Norlin Industries in 1973. His role there as a designer of the synthesizers bearing his name ended around 1973 and he became involved mainly in promotional and managerial duties. At the end of 1977 he left Norlin and in the following year started a new company, Big Briar, in Leicester, North Carolina, which manufactures a range of devices (with keyboards, theremin-type fingerboards or touch-sensitive plates) for precision control of analogue and digital synthesizers.

Moog has also developed circuitry for a wide range of applications: guitar amplifiers, effects boxes, mixers, multi-track tape recorders and variable-speed controllers for tape recorders. He has worked closely with prominent musicians in both the classical and rock fields, designing and equipping complete electronic music studios, and developing custom-built synthesizer systems for Walter Carlos and the rock keyboard player Keith Emerson, and for the electronic music studio at the State University of New York at Albany. He has created specialized electronic instruments and systems for a number of composers, among which are the dancer-responsive

antennae used to activate tape recorders in *Variations V* (1965) by John Cage with the Merce Cunningham Dance Company, and several MICROTONAL INSTRUMENTS, including a four-octave 43-note electronic keyboard instrument for Donald Erb's *Reconnaissance* (1967).

BIBLIOGRAPHY

R. A. Moog: 'The Theremin', Radio and Television News (Jan 1954), 37
——: 'A Transistorized Theremin', Electronics World, lxxi/1 (1961)
——: 'Voltage-controlled Electronic Music Modules', Journal of the Audio Engineering Society, xiii (1965), 200
——: 'Introduction to Programmed Control', Electronic Music Review, no.1 (1967), 23
——: 'Electronic Music – its Composition and Performance', Electronics World, lxxvii/2 (1967), 42
——: 'Electronic Music', Journal of the Audio Engineering Society, xxv (1977), 855
D. Crombie: 'The Moog Story', Sound International, no.6 (1978), 66
T. Rhea: 'The Moog Synthesizer', Contemporary Keyboard, vii/3 (1981), 58
J. Lee: 'Interview: Robert Moog', Polyphony (Jan–Feb 1982)

HUGH DAVIES

Moolo. Three-string plucked lute of the Songhay people of West Africa. *See* MOLO.

Moondo. Cylindrical SLIT-DRUM of the Pende people of south-western Zaïre (*LaurentyTF*, 133). *See* MONDO.

Moor, de. *See* MOORS family.

Moór, Emanuel (*b* Kecskemét, 19 Feb 1863; *d* Chardonne, 20 Oct 1931). Hungarian composer, pianist and inventor of the EMANUEL MOÓR PIANOFORTE.

Moore, A. David (*b* Hanover, New Hampshire, 8 Feb 1946). American organ builder. After graduating from the University of Vermont, he was apprenticed to C. B. Fisk and made two study trips to Europe. He began his own business in North Pomfret, Vermont, completing his first organ, a small one-manual, in 1972. His later work includes a large two-manual instrument for Grace Church, Washington, DC (1981), and a number of restorations. Moore's organs are strongly influenced by the French classical design. All parts of his instruments, including the pipes, are made in his workshop, and locally grown lumber, particularly butternut, is used extensively.

BIBLIOGRAPHY

L. Waters: 'An Interview with A. David Moore', American Organist, xvii (1983), 58

BARBARA OWEN

Moors [Mors, Morss, de Moer, de Moor]. South Netherlands family of organists, organ builders and instrument makers. The Lier branch of the family included Mark (i) (*d* Lier, 1525), who built a 'manucordium' in 1508 for the future Emperor Charles V; Hendrik, who built a small organ for Charles in 1517; Mark (ii) (*d* after 1535), who was a member of Charles's chapel; and several organists of the church of St Gommaar: Bernhard (i), Bernhard (ii) (*d* 1558; son of Mark (i)), and Bernhard (iii) (*d* 1597; possibly the son of Bernhard (ii)).

The Antwerp line was founded by Anton (i) (*d* Antwerp, 1539), who was organist of the abbey of St Michiel in the city, as well as a maker of organs and other instruments. He built small organs for the royal chapels in Brussels (1514) and The Hague (1515), and a clavichord for Eleonore of Habsburg, Charles V's sister, in

1516; in 1529 he was working for Margaret of Austria. Of the sons of Anton (i), the organ builder Cornelis (*b* Antwerp, *c*1500; *d* Antwerp, 1557) remained in his home town, but the organ builder Anton (ii) (*b* Antwerp, *c*1500; *d* before August 1562) and the organists Jakob (*b* Antwerp, *c*1515; *d* ?Berlin, between 1585 and 1602) and Hieronymus (*b* Antwerp, 1521; *d* Schwerin, 16 Dec 1598) went to northern Germany. Cornelis built organs for St Michiel, Ghent (before 1542), St Walburga, Oudenaarde (1542–3), St Katharina, Mechlin (before 1543) and elsewhere. Hieronymus was court organist to Duke Albrecht of Mecklenburg by 1538, and also organist of Schwerin Cathedral from 1552. Hieronymus's son Anton (iii), (*b* Schwerin, *c*1555; *d* Rostock, 1619) was organist of St Jakobi, Rostock from 1573 to 1613, as well as a court musician at Güstrow from time to time. Jakob entered the service of the court at Mecklenburg about 1548, became court organist to Elector August of Saxony in Dresden (1554), and moved to Berlin in 1557 to be organist at the court of Elector Joachim II Hector of Brandenburg. Jakob's son Joachim (*b* ?Berlin, *c*1560; *d* after 1605) was court organist, first in Dresden, 1579–81, and subsequently in Berlin. Anton (ii)'s major work was a large new organ for Onze Lieve Vrouw, in Dendermonde. He worked also for Duke Albrecht of Mecklenburg, from 1555 to 1557, in Schwerin Cathedral (major repairs and enlargement) and Güstrow Cathedral in 1558, and for Elector Joachim II Hector in Berlin from 1559 to 1560. The specification of the 'Mary Organ' in Berlin suggests that it also is the work of Anton (ii). On the evidence of the Schwerin contract of 1555, Anton (ii) was among those leading Brabantine organ builders who had improved on the indigenous type of instrument by grafting on to it the 'new and strange voices' brought to the Low Countries by the Rhenish masters Hans Suys (*see* SUISSE) and PETER BREISIGER.

BIBLIOGRAPHY
A. Werckmeister: *Organum Gruningense redivivum* (Quedlinburg and Aschersleben, 1705, 2/1932)
O. Kade: 'Die Organistenfamilie Mors im 16. Jahrhundert', *MMg*, xxix (1897), 43
W. Haacke: *Die Entwicklungsgeschichte des Orgelbaus im Lande Mecklenburg-Schwerin* (Wolfenbüttel and Berlin, 1935)
H. H. Steves: 'Der Orgelbauer Joachim Wagner', *AMf*, iv (1939), 321; v (1940), 17, 230
J.-A. Stellfeld: 'Bronnen tot de geschiedenis der Antwerpse clavecymbel- en orgelbouwers in de XVIe en XVIIe eeuwen', *Vlaams jaarboek voor muziekgeschiedenis*, iv (1942), 1–110
B. de Keyser: 'Figuren utt vlaanderens orgelhistorie', *De schalmei*, iii (1948), 78
M. A. Vente: *Die brabanter Orgel* (Amsterdam, 1958, 2/1963)
——: 'Mors', *MGG*

HANS KLOTZ

Mooser, (Jean Pierre Joseph) Aloys (*b* Fribourg, baptized 27 June 1770; *d* Fribourg, 19 Dec 1839). Swiss organ builder and piano maker. He was the son of the organ builder Joseph Anton Moser (1731–92), of Niederhelfenschwil, St Gall, who had settled in Fribourg in the 1760s. He studied with his father, who himself had been schooled in the south German organ-building tradition under Johann Michael Bihler of Konstanz, and was thus not a pupil of Silbermann as is sometimes erroneously recorded. Working in Fribourg, he became the best-known Swiss organ builder of the first half of the 19th century. His organs reflect a south German and early Romantic style. The source of his reputation is the large organ in St Nicolas's Cathedral in Fribourg (1824–34), whose Vox humana, with Swell mechanism, aroused special enthusiasm. Its fame, in fact, rests not only on its quality as an instrument, but above all on a pastoral

fantasia, the 'Gewitter', by the cathedral organist Jacques Vogt (1810–69), which has remained on cathedral recital programmes.

Mooser was also well known as a piano maker; the Parisian piano maker Erard attempted to interest him in a collaboration. He had sons who were organ and piano makers, including Joseph, Alexander and Moritz, but their reputations waned after their father's death.

BIBLIOGRAPHY
R. A. Mooser: 'Aloys Mooser, facteur d'orgues à Fribourg', *Nouvelles étrennes fribourgeoises*, lxviii (1935), 119

FRIEDRICH JAKOB

Moppan. Percussion idiophone of Japan. *See* HAN.

Moputu. Side-blown animal-horn trumpet of the So people of Zaïre. It has one stop in the tip (*LaurentyA*, 317).

Moqakana. MOUTH BOW of the Southern Sotho people of southern Africa. *See* LEKOPE.

Moqakhatsana [mahlirihliri]. A generic term for rattles among the Southern Sotho people of southern Africa. *See* MORUTLHOANA.

Moradu. Largest of the DIKOMANA drums of the Gananwa people of southern Africa.

Morao. PANPIPES of the forest-dwelling Moré Indians of eastern Bolivia, consisting of ten hollow reeds. It is used to announce the arrival of young people at the festival.

Morcang [morchang]. *See* MURCANG.

Mordent. A type of ornament which, in its standard form, consists of the very rapid alternation of the main note with a subsidiary note a step below. *See* ORNAMENTS, §III, 8–9.

Moreau, Jacobus Franciscus [Jacob François] (*b* ?Flanders, *c*1684; *d* Rotterdam, 9 Oct 1751). Netherlands organ builder. His parents probably moved to The Hague after his birth. On 7 September 1724, as 'Organ builder Jacob François Moreau of The Hague', he married Isabella Philippa de la Haye (daughter of the organ builder Louis de la Haye the elder of Ghent, who had settled in Antwerp). Later Moreau moved to Rotterdam. He is known to have worked in Brielle (1722), Rotterdam (Oosterkerk and Grote Kerk, 1722–6); Steenbergen (1729); Gouda (Grote Kerk St Jan, 1732–6, three manuals, 52 stops; still extant); Goes (Grote Kerk, 1738); again Rotterdam (Oude Kerk, 1744); and in Baarland and Oosterhout (both extant).

Moreau's specifications followed the style developed by north German masters who had settled in the north Netherlands. His style of voicing however was individual: G. J. Vogler compared Müller's organ in Haarlem and Moreau's instrument in Gouda with two women, one 'belle, superbe, fière', the other (which he preferred) 'douce, aimable, traitable'. The simple frontage of the Gouda instrument follows the style of Walloon organ cases. Moreau's work was continued by his son Johannes Jacobus (*d* *c*1762) and his nephew Louis de la Haye the younger.

BIBLIOGRAPHY

J. Hess: *Beschrijving van het groot en uitmuntend orgel in de St. Jans Kerk te Gouda* (Gouda, 1764)

——: *Dispositien der merkwaardigste Kerk-orgelen, welken in de zeven Vereenigde Provincien als mede in Duytsland en elders aangetroffen worden* (Gouda, 1774)

N. A. Knock: *Dispositien der merkwaardigste Kerk-orgelen welken in de Provincie Friesland, Groningen en Elders aangetroffen worden* (Groningen, 1788, repr. 1959)

J. Hess: *Dispositien van kerk-orgelen, welke in Nederland worden aangetroffen, vervolg* (Amsterdam, 1907)

A. Bouman: *Orgels in Nederland* (Amsterdam, 1943, rev., enlarged 3/1964 as *Nederland . . . orgelland*)

F. Peeters and M. A. Vente: *De orgelkunst in de Nederlanden van de 15e tot de 18e eeuw* (Antwerp, 1971; Eng. trans., 1971)

HANS KLOTZ

Morendo (It.: 'dying'; gerund of *morire*). A word used in musical scores as an instruction to die away gradually, characteristically found at the end of a section, as for instance at the end of the slow movement in Beethoven's String Quartet op.74. It is particularly common in Verdi's work. *Smorzando* has a similar meaning but is less strongly confined to the ends of sections; *diluendo* and CALANDO also appear. Koch (*Musikalisches Lexikon*, 1802) gave an entry under 'Moriente' (the present participle of *morire*).

For bibliography *see* TEMPO AND EXPRESSION MARKS.

DAVID FALLOWS

Morey & Barnes. American firm of organ builders, successors to JOHN GALE MARKLOVE.

Morī. Oboe of Karnataka state, south India. It is about 59 cm long and has a wooden pipe of conical bore, a metal bell, eight finger-holes and four tuning-holes on the side. See K. S. Kothari: *Indian Folk Musical Instruments* (New Delhi, 1968).

See also MAHVARĪ.

ALASTAIR DICK

Morin khuur. Mongolian fiddle. *See* KHUUR.

Moritz. German family of brass and woodwind instrument makers. Its most important members were Johann Gottfried Moritz (*b* 1777; *d* Berlin, 30 July 1840) and his son Carl [Karl] Wilhelm Moritz (*b* Berlin, 7 Dec 1811; *d* Berlin, 18 Oct 1855). J. G. Moritz founded the family business in 1799 in Leipzig, moving to Dresden in 1805, and to Berlin in 1808. On 1 December 1819 he became instrument maker to the Berlin court. C. W. Moritz carried on the business after his father's death, expanding the work to include a range of woodwind instruments. Like his father he became court instrument maker, on 24 October 1840. After his death his work was continued by his sons Wilhelm Moritz (1837–72) and Johann Carl Albert Moritz (1837–97) and succeeding members of the family until 1955.

Although J. G. Moritz built trumpets, keyed bugles and valve horns, he is best known for his work on the valve and on the bass tuba. He invented, jointly with the Berlin maker WILHELM WIEPRECHT, the 'Berliner-Pumpe' valve in 1835. In the same year, he used five of these valves for the bass tuba which he and Wieprecht built (Prussian patent no. 9121 of 1835). Soon afterwards they designed and built a wider-bored version with three or four valves, which they called the bombardon. C. W. Moritz also built many of these instruments, as well as oboes and bassoons with elaborate keywork and the *Klaviatur-Kontrafagott* (patent

1856), a double bassoon with a piano-accordion-type keyboard.

See also TUBA (i) and VALVE (i).

BIBLIOGRAPHY

H. Mendel and A. Reissmann, eds.: *Musikalisches Conversations-Lexikon* (Berlin, 1870–79, 2/1880–83 with suppl., 3/1890–91/*R*1969), vii, p. 173

Zur Hundertjahrfeier der Musikinstrumentenfabrik C. W. Moritz (Berlin, 1908)

C. Sachs: *Handbuch der Musikinstrumentenkunde* (Leipzig, 1920, 2/1930/*R*1970)

A. Carse: *Musical Wind Instruments* (London, 1939/*R*1965)

L. G. Langwill: *An Index of Musical Wind-instrument Makers* (Edinburgh, 1960, rev., enlarged 6/1980)

F. Ernst: 'Die Blasinstrumentenbauer-Familie Moritz in Berlin', *Glareana*, xvii/3–4 (1968), 2

A. Baines: *Brass Instruments* (London, 1976/*R*1980)

C. Bevan: *The Tuba Family* (London, 1978)

NIALL O'LOUGHLIN

Moropa (pl. *meropa*). Women's drum of the Sotho and Tswana peoples of southern Africa. Among the Tswana and Northern Sotho it is a long, conical single-headed drum, carved from a block of wood, and has an integral jug-like handle. The head is pegged into position, and the bottom is open. The *murumba* of the Venda people is similar. The *moropa* is struck with the hands, to accompany girls' initiation songs and dancing. Among the Southern Sotho of Lesotho the name may be applied to various instruments made of animal skin (including the LEKOKO and MORUTLHOANA), generically to membranophones (*see* SEKUPU) and as a specific term for three types of drum. The first is a single-headed globular clay pot drum, which has a projecting base with a large slit or hole through the bottom. It is 30 to 35 cm in diameter and 50 to 60 cm high. The head, made from goatskin or sheepskin, is laced on with leather thongs. This

Moropa of the Pedi people (Northern Sotho), southern Africa

instrument is associated with girls' initiation ceremonies. The second is a tubular or slightly conical single-headed drum of approximately the same size as the above, with the head stretched from leather thongs attached to pegs. Finally, any metal wash tub may be used to accompany women's dances. All three types of instrument are played with either a plucking action of the fingers or by beating with a small blunt stick. The instrument is occasionally misspelt 'morupa'.

BIBLIOGRAPHY
KirbyMISA, 30, pl.11–12.
FELICIA M. MUNDELL, DAVID K. RYCROFT,
CHARLES R. ADAMS

Morothloane. *See* MORUTLHOANA.

Mors [Morss]. *See* MOORS family.

Morton, Alfred (*b* 1827; *d* London, 2 Jan 1898). English wind instrument maker. He began his career as an apprentice to J. T. Uhlmann of Vienna, completing his indentures in 1847. Thereafter he seems for a time to have abandoned the instrument trade, and there is reason to believe that he was engaged in some form of metal working. Towards the last quarter of the century Morton resumed instrument making in London and soon became the leading English maker of his time. Despite his Viennese background, he did not produce instruments of the Austrian/German type; his oboes and bassoons, though somewhat original in style of keywork, were in essence of French proportions. A considerable number of these were made for the British army. Morton was also specially noted for his contrabassoons built respectively for the Grenadier, Coldstream and Scots Guards. A demi contrabassoon in F is reputed to have been built for Sullivan but there is no record that such was ever used in the Savoy operas. From 1872 Morton's sons became his partners and worthily maintained the reputation of the firm. With the adoption in England of the New Philharmonic pitch the Mortons' activities seem to have declined, and few of their instruments in the 'low pitch' survive.

PHILIP BATE

Morupa. *See* MOROPA.

Morutlhoana [leshoao, morothloane]. Ankle-rattles of the Southern Sotho people of southern Africa. They comprise small goatskin bags containing stones, secured to leather bands and tied round the ankles of male dancers. See *KirbyMISA*, 6, pl.3*b*. *See also* MOROPA.

Mosconi, Davide (*b* Milan, 31 July 1941). Italian composer, pianist and designer of instruments. Working in Milan, since the mid-1970s he has composed theatrical concert works in which traditional instruments and their performance techniques have been reassessed, and has devised several large-scale sound environments. In *Quartet* (*c*1975) a harpist with harp is encased in a one-piece fitted, knitted, costume-like covering, a performer on free-reed instruments (mouth organ, accordion and foot-operated table bandoneon) is gradually incapacitated by being mummified in sticky tape, and a violinist and pianist have their fields of operation restricted by specially constructed containers for parts of their instruments. In another work a harp is played by metal mesh gloves to which around 50 nails are attached. Mosconi's

sound environments include *Bell Concert* for the bells of several churches and *Triton* (1976–77), in which many foghorns and related signalling sounds, mostly operated by compressed air, are played in and around a harbour and from boats; in one presentation, in Marseilles in 1981, a large diaphone was played inside a road tunnel beneath part of the harbour, providing a huge 'horn' to project the sound.

Since around 1980 Mosconi has been a member of a multidisciplinary group Giocare con i Suoni, which also includes Giovanni Belgrano and the sculptor Bruno Munari. They have developed a new range of modular instruments designed to educate children between the ages of three and seven years about the nature of instruments and the parameters of sound (as opposed to music alone, which is the basis of, for example, Carl Orff's approach). At the time of writing a kit is being produced by the toy manufacturer Danese in Milan. The instruments demonstrate the basic principles found in each family: a curved slide tube (like that of the swanee whistle) can be fitted with five different mouthpieces, a drum has five interchangeable heads, there is a range of 25 idiophones based on rectangular wooden blocks of identical size, and even a simple synthesizer.

HUGH DAVIES

Moser, Joseph Anton. Swiss organ builder, father of ALOYS MOOSER.

Moshupiane. Globular wooden FRICTION DRUM of the Pedi (Northern Sotho) people of southern Africa. It is sounded by rubbing the head with wetted millet stalks, and used in connection with girls' initiation ceremonies. *See also* MOROPA.

Mōsōbiwa. Japanese lute. *See* BIWA, §3.

Mosso (It.: 'agitated'; past participle of *muovere*, to move). A word that appears by itself as a tempo designation but is more often found in such contexts as *più mosso* (faster) and *meno mosso* (slower). *Allegro assai mosso* was normally the fastest tempo mark for Verdi. Tchaikovsky's Sixth Symphony (first movement) includes eloquent examples of *moderato mosso* and *adagio mosso*. *See also* TEMPO AND EXPRESSION MARKS.

DAVID FALLOWS

Mosu-gitarra. A Basque term for the BIRIMBAO.

Mosumba. Drum of the Tsogo people of Gabon. *See* NDUGU.

Mosu-musika. A Basque term for the BIRIMBAO.

Mõ sừng trâu. Hollowed buffalo-horn, used as a SLIT-DRUM, of southern Vietnam. It is used in the 'five-sound' ensemble NHẠC NGŨ ÂM for ceremonial music and in the ĐẠI NHẠC ensemble for court music.

Motaba. STOPPED FLUTE ENSEMBLE of the Lovedu (Northern Sotho) people of southern Africa, resembling the Venda MUTAVHA.

Motlhatsa. Conical flute of the Tswana people of southern Africa resembling the Pedi *naka ya phatola*.

Moto (It.: 'movement', 'motion'). A word found within the tempo designation *con moto* (with movement) but particularly common as a qualification of another tempo mark: *allegro con moto* was often used by Haydn and Beethoven. *Moto perpetuo* (perpetual motion) is found more often as a description or title of a piece comprising an uninterrupted succession of quick notes than as an instruction of any kind. *Moto* is also applied in Italian writings to contrapuntal contexts: *moto contrario* is 'contrary motion'; *moto obliquo* is 'oblique motion'; and *moto retto* is 'similar motion'.

See also TEMPO AND EXPRESSION MARKS.

DAVID FALLOWS

Motoling. Idiochord TUBE ZITHER of various sizes used in the Motoling area of Minahasa, North Sulawesi, Indonesia. Its three bamboo strings, prised out of the surface, are raised on bridges at both ends and stretched over a small sound-hole. They are beaten with a pair of thin sticks.

MARGARET J. KARTOMI

Motutu. Side-blown trumpet of the Bwaka people of Zaïre. It is made from the horn of a waterbuck, and is traditionally blown only on the death of a notable. Similar trumpets for the Nkundi and Logo are known respectively as *ekungu* and *irili*, and Laurenty attributes a *moturu* to the Ngbaka. Large trumpets were traditionally single-note instruments used for war or funerals. Smaller trumpets, used for sub-chiefs and signalling, had a pierced end; in performance, the extremity was opened or closed with the hand, thus enabling up to four notes to be produced. These animal-horn trumpets have a square or lozenge-shaped mouthpiece and may also have a wooden bell. The Eso *monzo*, made from buffalo horn, was used in warfare. *See also* MOMPATE.

BIBLIOGRAPHY
LaurentyA, 329
S. Chauvet: *Musique nègre* (Paris, 1929)
J.-N. Maquet: *Note sur les instruments de musique congolais* (Brussels, 1956)
H. Burssens: *Les peuplades de l'entre Congo-Ubangi* (London, 1958)
K. A. GOURLAY

Moudzika [mandzika]. Cylindrical stopped wooden flute of the Uele people of Zaïre (*LaurentyA*, 174).

Mount, William Sidney (*b* Setauket, NY, 26 Nov 1807; *d* Setauket, NY, 18 Nov 1868). American painter and violinist, notable for his 'improved' model of the violin, patented in 1852. The patent model, a $\frac{7}{8}$ instrument (Smithsonian Institution, Washington, DC), was patterned after a design which required fewer constituent parts than usual; it incorporated a boutless, almond-shaped body, a 'hollow' (i.e. concave) back, a 'spring-beam' bass-bar and rectangular soundholes. In its final form, as exemplified by a full-sized violin of 1857 (Museums at Stony Brook, NY), it possessed a boutless, guitar-shaped body, the same 'hollow' back, a conventional bass-bar and ordinary soundholes in reversed position. Under the trade name 'The Cradle of Harmony' various models were displayed at the Crystal Palace, New York, during the 1853 Exhibition of Industry of All Nations. Later that year favourable testimonials on behalf of the design were obtained from Uri C. Hill and other professional musicians. In spite of these efforts, which were renewed after the Civil War, investors willing to underwrite the cost of its mass production could not be found.

BIBLIOGRAPHY
A. Frankenstein: *William Sidney Mount* (New York, 1975) [with disc]
A. Buechner: 'William Sidney Mount's "Cradle of Harmony": a Unique 19th Century American Violin', *Journal of the Violin Society of America*, iii/2 (1977), 35–71
ALAN BUECHNER

Mountain dulcimer. *See* APPALACHIAN DULCIMER.

Mouth bow (Fr. *arc musical à bouche*; Ger. *Mundbogen*). A type of MUSICAL BOW which is held against the player's mouth. Classified as a bar zither (*see* CHORDOPHONE), it is widely distributed in Africa, Central and South America, and Oceania (except western Polynesia and Micronesia). As with the jew's harp, harmonic partials are selectively resonated by varying the volume of the mouth cavity, and used melodically. Most mouth bows are heterochord (with a tied-on string) rather than idiochord (with a raised strip) instruments. Most have a single string, though some (for example, in the Highlands of Papua New Guinea, the Bismarck Archipelago, the central Solomon Islands and the Philippines) have two, and the *tingle apho* of the Kara people in southern Ethiopia is made from a forked branch with three prongs, each bearing a string. The stave of the bow may be of round, semicircular or flat section, and often tapers towards the ends. It is usually made from a single length of wood or cane, but some examples, such as the Zulu ISITHONTOLO, have two or three sections (see fig.1). Some bows allow the full length of the string to vibrate as a whole; on others it is divided into two unequal segments by means of a brace (also called a tension noose or tuning noose) which encircles stave and string. Bushmen of south-western Africa often adapt hunting bows for musical use by adding a brace.

There are two main ways of applying the bow to the mouth (see figs.1 and 2). The most common technique is for the back of the bow-stave or one end of it to rest against the player's cheek, slightly parted lips, or side of the mouth (or teeth, though some reports of this may be wrong), with the string (or strings) facing outwards (fig.1). With some single-string bows, the string is allowed to vibrate freely between the player's parted lips; this style is common throughout West Africa, in southeastern Africa (the XIZAMBI), and is also found in Colombia (fig.2). The EKITULENGE of the Konjo people,

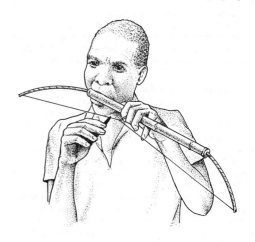

1. Isithontolo (mouth bow) of the Zulu people, southern Africa

Uganda (fig.3), is exceptional in that a small half gourd attached centrally at the back of the stave covers the player's mouth and chin (see *WachsmannTCU*, 382); with the GORA and LESIBA of South Africa a piece of quill which connects one end of the string to the stave passes between the lips and is blown upon to set the string in vibration. Most mouth bows are sounded by plucking the string (or strings) with a fingertip or plectrum, by tapping with a light stick, or by stroking with a friction stick or subsidiary bow. The 'scraped bow' (Ger.: *Schrapbogen*), however, has serrations on the stave which are scraped with a stick or rattle-stick (for example, the *kawayawaya* of the Handa and Humbi in Angola, and the *xizambi* of the Shangana-Tsonga).

Besides the fundamental note yielded by an open string, or by each segment of the string on a braced mouth bow, additional fundamentals (usually only one, but sometimes two) can be obtained by stopping the string with a finger or stick. Since a number of different harmonic partials can be orally resonated above each one, only a very limited number of fundamentals (often just

2. *Unbraced mouth bow (marimba) of the Atlantic coastal region, Palenque, Colombia*

two) is employed; these are usually a whole tone, but sometimes a semitone, a minor or major 3rd, or a 4th apart. Compared with the resonated upper partials, the fundamentals are generally very soft. The effective compass of mouth resonance is from about f' to e''', and the harmonic partials which come within this range are dependent upon the tuning of the fundamentals (see ex.1). (For an example of music played on a South African friction mouth bow see MUSICAL BOW, ex.1.) Since the mouth bow produces a very soft tone, it is played mainly as a solo instrument. Singers sometimes participate, particularly in Africa, where the melodies often imply a text, whether or not this is verbally expressed. Mouth bows are mainly played for entertainment, but ritual uses have been cited; in certain areas they are played only by men, in others (for example in Oceania) only by women, and age restrictions sometimes apply.

The following mouth bows are entered in this dictionary: andobu; badingba; bailol; baka (i); balu; bandingba; barikendikendi; bawa;

3. *Ekitulenge (mouth bow) of the Konjo people, Uganda*

Ex.1 Mouth bow harmonics: *(a)* on the *guma* (braced mouth bow) of the Kung (Bushman) (Westphal, 1978, p.13); *(b)* typical range of unbraced mouth bows such as the Zulu *umqangala*, Sotho *lekope*, Xhosa *inkinge* and *umrhubhe*; *(c)* of the *marimba* (unbraced mouth bow), Colombia (List, 1966, p.37)

(a)

(b)

(c)

o unstopped
● stopped

beng; benta; bogenda; bombo (iv); bongengee; bongo-bongo; bongoga; chibvelani; chigwana; chimazambi; chipendani; chisambi; chizambi; dimbwa; dingba (i); dumba (ii); ekitulenge; gabamboli; gabus; gahakan; gbong-kpala; gedo; godye; gom-gom; gongqin; gora; goukhas; goura; guma; guru; gwaningba; ha; igonga; igwali; ikoka; ingonga; inkinge; inkoko (ii); ipiano; isithontolo; itumbolongonda; kabarome; kalove; kandiri kandiri; kangan; kankarma; kashane; kawayawaya; kawombo; kedondolo; kilibongo; koala; ko'e; kpwokolo; kū; kudungba; kulongkoing; kwadi; kwadili; lekope; lengope; lingongo; lipombo; lonkoko; lugube; lukungu; lusuba; mbeta; moqakana; mouth zither; mqangala; mtangala; mtyángala; ngangan; ninga; nxoronxoro; ohonji; outa; pagolo; papai; penda; picking bow; pingoru; sagaya; setolotolo; t'ha; tingle apho; titapu; tolo-tolo; tsayantur; tshihwana; tshipendani; tshivhana; tshizambi; tumank; ugwala; 'ukēkē; umhubhe; umqangala; umrhubhe; undemoü; une; utete; utiyane; vuhudendung; xizambi.

BIBLIOGRAPHY

*Izikowitz*MISAI; *Kirby*MISA; *Wachsmann*TCU, 311–415
H. Balfour: *The Natural History of the Musical Bow* (Oxford, 1899)
E. M. von Hornbostel: 'The Ethnology of African Sound Instruments', *Africa*, vi (1933), 129, 277–311
J. Kunst: *De toonkunst van Java* (The Hague, 1934; Eng. trans., rev. 2/1949, enlarged 3/1973 as *Music in Java*)
C. M. Camp and B. Nettl: 'The Musical Bow in Southern Africa', *Anthropos*, i (1955), 65
G. List: 'The Musical Bow at Palenque', *JIFMC*, xviii (1966), 36
D. K. Rycroft: 'Friction Chordophones in South Eastern Africa', *GSJ*, xix (1966), 84
G. Kubik: *Mehrstimmigkeit und Tonsysteme in Zentral- und Ostafrika* (Vienna, 1968), 50
D. Taylor: 'The Music of some Indian Tribes in Colombia', *Recorded Sound*, xxix–xxx (1968), suppl.
D. K. Rycroft: *Zulu, Swazi and Xhosa Instrumental and Vocal Music* (Tervuren, 1969) [with disc]
G. Kubik: *Musica tradicional e aculturada dos !Kung' de Angola* (Lisbon, 1970), 30
T. Johnston: 'Xizambi Friction-bow Music of the Shangana-Tsonga', *African Music*, iv/4 (1970), 81
G. Kubik: 'Musical Bows in South Western Angola, 1965', *African Music*, v/4 (1975–6), 98
E. O. J. Westphal and D. K. Rycroft: 'Some Observations on Current Bushman and Hottentot Musical Practices', *Review of Ethnology*, v/2–3 (1978), 9
I. Strecker: *Musik der Hamar, Südäthiopien* (Berlin, 1979) [with disc]
T. Johnston: 'The Mqangala and Xipendana Musical Bows of the Shangana-Tsonga', *Afrika und Übersee*, lxiii (1980), 257
D. K. Rycroft: 'The Musical Bow in Southern Africa', *Papers presented at the Second Symposium on Ethnomusicology* (Grahamstown, 1981), 70

DAVID K. RYCROFT

Mouth harp. *See* MOUTH ORGAN.

Mouth organ [mouth harp] (Ger. *Mundharmonika*). A term applied to several types of free-reed wind instrument (for classification details *see* AEROPHONE). In the West it is generally applied to the HARMONICA (i) and by extension to many mouth-blown instruments of Southeast Asia and the Far East, for example the Chinese SHENG, the Japanese SHŌ (i) and Lao KHAĒN. The following mouth organs are entered in this dictionary: aura; bbare; blay; dding; engkerurai; harmonica (i); he; hnyin; hulu sheng; hwa; kāēng; keledi; khāēn; khim; khung; komboat; lu sheng; mboat; mbuat; mimiha; naw; nung teeree; paisheng; raj; rökel; saenghwang; samputan; sheng; shō (i); sumpotan; töliö; u (i); u (ii); yu (ii).

Mouthpiece (Fr. *embouchure* [of clarinets and saxophones, *bec*]; Ger. *Mundstück* [occasionally *Ansatz*]; It. *bocchino*). That part of a wind instrument which is placed in or against a player's mouth, and which, together with the lips or a cane REED, forms the tone generator.

In brass instruments (including obsolete side-hole types) it is roughly bell-shaped but is much modified by external ornament. Internally it has three important elements: the cup (Fr. *bassin*); the throat (Fr. *grain*) (or orifice at the base of the cup); and the backbore (Fr. *queue*) (or

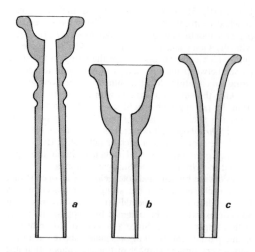

Mouthpieces of (a) a trumpet; (b) a trombone; (c) a horn

expansion) which leads to the main tubing. All three have much influence on the characteristic tone and behaviour of the instrument. The cup varies from shallow hemispherical to deeply conical. The throat may be relatively large, small, sharp-edged, rounded off, or, in such as the horn, virtually non-existent. (This applies also to the backbore.) The rim applied to the lips varies according to individual convenience.

In clarinets and the like the mouthpiece is roughly conical externally for some $\frac{2}{3}$ of its length, after which it is obliquely chamfered off to a chisel-shaped tip (*see* CLARINET, fig.2). Opposite the chamfer is a flat table tangential to the surface, and against this the flat reed is placed. The table is slightly curved towards the tip and this 'lay' allows the reed to vibrate under the influence of the breath and control of the lips. In the upper part of the table is a rectangular or keystone-shaped slot through to the interior. The internal 'tone chamber' may be a simple extension of the main bore of the instrument or it may be enlarged in various ways which have much influence on its internal tuning and general behaviour. Such mouthpieces are today made of wood and various synthetics, others of metal and (more rarely) glass. *See also* ACOUSTICS, §III.

PHILIP BATE

Mouth zither. Term used for a MOUTH BOW with a stick flat enough to require insertion of bridges between the stick and the strings.

Moxos. Bassoon of the Ignatian Indians of Bolivia, probably of post-Conquest origin.

Mozungu. Log XYLOPHONE of the Makere people of Zaïre. *See* PANDINGBWA.

mp. *Mezzo-piano* (It.: 'moderately soft'); *see* MEZZO, MEZZA, (2).

Mpako. End-blown trumpet of central Africa. *See* NYELE.

Mpalampala. *See* IMPALAMPALA.

Mpandi-nsoni. Wooden trumpet of the Bembe people of the Republic of the Congo. *See* MAMPONGUI-NGUEMBO.

Mpanje. Single-headed GOBLET DRUM of the Nyanja/Chewa and Tumbuka/Henga peoples of Malawi. It is open-ended. Two are used to accompany dancing.

Mpati. Single-headed footed drum of the Valley Tonga people of Gwembe district, Zambia. It is open-ended and the membrane is pegged on. It is played with the hands, together with the *magogo* and *masunta* drums.

Mpatsibihugu. Drum of the Tutsi people of Rwanda. *See* INGABE.

Mpero. Conical drum of the Nyoro/Haya people of Tanzania. It is the smallest in the ENKOITO drum set.

Mpetshanga. Conical drum of the Mbun people of Zaïre. *See* MUSHITS.

Mpingi. Cylindrical stopped wooden flute of the Kusu people of Zaïre (*LaurentyA*, 169f).

Mpintintoa. Calabash drum of the Akan people of Ghana. It is nearly spherical, with its body measuring 125 cm in diameter and a top striking surface (duiker or sheephide) measuring 25 cm or more across. The membrane is attached by about seven strings to a circular base ring about 13 cm in diameter and 6 mm thick. The drum is suspended by a pair of shoulder braces to lie just below the player's chest and is beaten with the hands. It is used with the hourglass and cylindrical drums in *mpintin* state drumming. Recently the drum has also begun to be played by boys, in a group that also includes whistle flutes, for entertainment.

BIBLIOGRAPHY
J. H. K. Nketia: *Drumming in Akan Communities of Ghana* (London, 1963)
——: *Our Drums and Drummers* (Accra, 1968)

Mpolomono. Wooden trumpet of the Bembe people of the Republic of the Congo. *See* MAMPONGUI-NGUEMBO.

Mponge [mpongi, m'pugni]. Side-blown trumpet of Zaïre, with one stop in the tip. The *mponge* is reported as an ivory trumpet of the Lia people, believed to be blown on the death of a chief; the *mpongi* as an animal-horn trumpet of the Nkundo, also known as *boonzu*, and as an ivory trumpet of the Jonga (*LaurentyA*, 316, 399, 406); and as a signalling instrument of the Luluwa, made from antelope horn, ivory or a calabash. *See also* KIM-PUNGIDI, (2).

Mpungi. Tubular MIRLITON of the Sanga people of Zaïre (*LaurentyA*, 34).

Mpunguí. Afro-Cuban aerophone formerly used by the Congo people; it was of somewhat uncertain character, possibly a flute or whistle, or a type of panpipe. See *OrtizIMA*, v, 298.

Mqangala. MOUTH BOW of southern Africa. *See* UMQANGALA.

Mṛdaṅga [mṛdaṅgam, mṛdang, mirdang]. An Indian name, in use for over two millennia, for tuned, finger-played, double-headed drums, primarily elongated barrel drums, which give the principal accompaniment to indigenous art-music styles of the Indian high tradition. In the earlier period they were used in theatre music, and since that time they have been employed in concert forms and more elaborate styles of temple and devotional music.

The name occurs from epic and classical times and has long been thought to mean 'having a body [aṅga] of mud or clay [mṛd]'; this explanation is given by the earliest detailed source, the *Nātyaśāstra* (early centuries AD, but see below §1 (i)), and comparison has been made with the modern eastern Indian mṛdaṅga, or KHOL, of clay. Most drums of the mṛdaṅga type, however, are of wood, and Powers has proposed the interesting alternative that the name means 'having a part of earth', referring to the tuning-paste applied to the skins, long an important characteristic of this type, for which earth or mud is prescribed in early sources. The traditional etymology of Indian lexicographers is very different: mṛdam-ga, 'going about while being beaten' (see also *mardala*, §2 (i), below).

Like the even more ancient and historically comprehensive chordophone name *vīṇā*, mṛdaṅga indicates a certain musical status in Indian tradition as much as it does particular types of drum. The earliest known drums of this name are a set of two or three tuned barrel drums used in the ancient theatre. The medieval *mardala*, equated with the names mṛdaṅga or *muraja* in the 13th-century *Saṅgītaratnākara*, was not a barrel drum, being slightly waisted and conical, but had the tuned heads, paste and finger-playing technique of the mṛdaṅga tradition. The tuned barrel drum of the modern southern, or Karnataka, art-music tradition preserves the name (in southern form) as mṛdaṅgam; that of the older-style northern, or Hindustani, music, while often called mṛdaṅg or mirdang, may also be found as *pakhāvaj*, but is treated here as the modern northern representative of the tradition. The mṛdaṅga or khol of the east (Bengal, Orissa, Assam; see fig.1c below) and its relative the *pung* of Manipur should also be discussed here, for although they are found in the villages, they are not folk instruments but accompany primarily the complex devotional music *kīrtan* in the high Hindu tradition of raga and tala music; this tradition of music and drumming was once widespread with regional variation throughout the subcontinent, but is now obscured by the comparatively recent blanket permeation of the modern northern and southern schools. *See also* PACHIMĀ and MADDAĻAM.

The medieval text *Saṅgītaratnākara*, discussing the functions of the four classes of instrument, states that while the strings and wind create melody and idiophones such as the cymbals give metre, the role of the drums is to give 'colour', or texture, to the music, a role still played by the modern mṛdaṅga drums.

In the northern style the mṛdaṅga or pakhāvaj has held its own as an essential accompaniment to the older song forms *dhrupad* and *dhamār*, and to the instruments *bīn* and *rabāb*; however, the drum has until recently been much overshadowed by the much more common Indo-Muslim style – *khayāl* song, and the music of the sitar and *sarod*, among other instruments – with accompaniment provided by the drum *tablā*. This style, developed in India over the last two centuries or more from foreign models, has introduced into the high tradition elements of drumming and metre, as well as concepts qualitatively different from those of indigenous traditions. Nonetheless, it is interesting that the *tablā* borrowed its composite heads and elements of metre and concept from the *mṛdaṅga*, a fact that places it partly in that instrument's tradition.

1. Ancient period: (i) Structure and tuning (ii) Drumming. 2. Medieval period: (i) Structure (ii) Drumming. 3. Modern period: (i) Northern *mṛdang* or *pakhāvaj* (ii) Southern *mṛdaṅgam*.

1. ANCIENT PERIOD. The only detailed textual source for the early *mṛdaṅga* is the dramaturgic treatise *Nāṭyaśāstra*, attributed to the sage Bharata, a composite didactic work, incorporating both verse canon and prose commentary and drawn up cumulatively, probably in the early part of the 1st millennium (but very possibly containing some older material). This does give some details of a composite barrel-drum set called *mṛdaṅga* in the chapter on membranophones. These scattered references partly reflect the cumulative development of the text, but partly also the conception of the set as an element of a higher ensemble, the three *puṣkara* ('rain-clouds'), comprising, as well as the multiple *mṛdaṅga*, the waisted drum *paṇava* and the pot-drum *dardura*. Their origin is ascribed to the sage Svāti (the Pole-star), who made them with the aid of the divine smith Viśvakarman in imitation of the drums of the gods after meditating on the effect of rain on lotus-leaves during the monsoon season.

Marcel-Dubois's authoritative study (1941) of depictions of instruments in ancient Indian sculpture draws attention to a pair of barrel drums frequently seen in the sculpture of the 2nd century BC: one is placed vertically before the seated player, the other rests horizontally, or leans diagonally against the player's left hip, to give three playing heads in all. A few centuries later we find a three-drum set, with two drums standing vertically, giving four heads. This change is implied in the *mṛdaṅga* material of the *Nāṭyaśāstra*.

Among the complex descriptions of the different drums of the set and of their heads (including several alternatives and an apparent synonym), that for the earlier (two-drum) set provides a basic terminology. The vertical drum is often called *mṛdaṅga*, or sometimes *muraja* or *ūrdhvaka* ('uppermost'); the latter term also denotes its head. The horizontal drum is called *āṅkika* ('held over the hip' – just as it was seen in earlier sculpture), and its two faces are quite logically distinguished as *vāmaka* ('left') and *dakṣina* ('right'). The three systems of tuning the heads (*mārjanā*: 'wiping') given later relate primarily to these three. When the third drum was added it was placed vertically to the left of the *ūrdhvaka* and called *ālingya* ('embraced'), not because it was so held but because it was flanked by the *ūrdhvaka* and *vāmaka*; its single head is sometimes referred to as *madhyaka* ('in the middle') or *savyaka* (also 'left', but to be distinguished from *vāmaka*, which becomes 'leftmost').

(i) *Structure and tuning.* These drums were probably of clay. Their size, shape and elements are given in a section near the end of the chapter mentioned above, which (significantly for its date, perhaps) resembles more the detailed physical descriptions of medieval texts than those of earlier, memory-based texts. The right, upright drum *ūrdhvaka* is called 'barley-seed-shaped', because it tapers at the ends, and is said to be four *tāla* (probably a hand-span) long, and 14 fingers in diameter at the head. The horizontal drum *āṅkīka* is three and a half *tāla* long, and its head (or heads) 12 fingers wide; it is

'myrobalan-seed-shaped'. The left vertical drum (*ālingya*) is described as 'cow's-tail' (i.e. truncated-conical) shaped, and is said to be three *tāla* long, with a face eight fingers across. These descriptions do not always tally with ancient depictions. The skins (*candraka*: 'little moon') are of cowhide, white and unblemished, and soaked in cold water overnight before being scoured with mild cow-dung. They are single, not three-layered as has been stated, but wrapped in a threefold arrangement around the hoops (*kakṣā*) with a criss-cross lacing (*svastika*). Marcel-Dubois (1941) gave a development of the main lacing of these drums from an X pattern with a central band, to one in a W, to a complex X network.

The greatest interest attaches to the 'wiping' (*mārjanā*), or tuning, of the heads. This is done preferably with black earth from a river bank, which is smooth when squeezed free of water, and is neither too heavy or solid nor permeated or containing impurities. A dough of wheat or barley flour, or a mixture of these, can be used as an alternative, but this is said to give a monotonous sound. In the absence of further data, we may think of these as wet tuning-loads, like the dough on the left face of the modern *mṛdaṅga*, which lowered the pitch of the skin rather than giving it a pitch rich in harmonics like that of the hard pastes for right-hand faces of the modern drums.

Various origins have been put forward for the tuning-pastes of Indian drums, such as the sacrificial smearing of the blood of an enemy conquered in battle (Sachs, 1914), or the attaching of flour-based pastes as an agrarian rite (Marcel-Dubois). Drums have certainly been worshipped in India (for example the *muracu*, *khol* and *tumdak'*), and the *Nāṭyaśāstra* itself contains a section on the rites attending the installation of theatre drums and the offerings such as honey, rice-pudding, blood and flowers made to (but not on) them. More functionally, however, the pastes may derive from the need, which arises because of the interlacing of the two heads, to adjust the pitch of the second head after the first has been tuned. Thus, paste is prescribed in the *Nāṭyaśāstra* only for the left head of the *āṅkika* (the only drum of the set played on both heads).

There are three tunings, which relate to the top, right and left heads of the older two-piece *mṛdaṅga*: *mayūrī* ('peacock'), consisting of 4th, tonic and 3rd on the top, right and left heads, respectively; *ardhamayūrī* ('half-peacock'), with 6th, 2nd and 1st; and *karmāravī* – an obscure word, perhaps meaning 'the roar of work' but denoting also a melodic mode-species (*jāti*) – with 5th, 1st and 2nd. These are referred to the three ancient parent-scales, the *madhyama-*, *ṣadja-* and *gāndhāra-grāma*, respectively. It will be noticed that the top head takes the 4th, 5th or 6th of the scale: octave registers are not given, and it may be that, since they apply to the largest drum with the widest head, these degrees should be understood as being below the 1st of the scale. The right head takes the 1st or 2nd degree, and the left the 1st, 2nd or 3rd, generally above the right (it is not inconceivable that for *ardhamayūrī* the *āṅkīka* could be turned round). Earth is not applied to the right head; much later in the chapter a stray verse states that an application (*rohaṇa*) of sesamum-paste, cow-butter and oil may be applied only to the *āṅkīka* (see §2 (i) below). The head of the third drum, *ālingya*, is said, apparently as an afterthought and perhaps some centuries later, to be tuned to the 7th (the only note not covered in the three tunings).

(ii) Drumming. The *mṛdaṅga* was mostly played with different hand-stroke qualities (rather than with the fingers) in sequential patterns from head to head. They were called *mārga* ('way'), and there were four: *aḍḍita*, top and *āliṅgya*; *ālipta*, left and top; *vitasta*, top and right; and *gomukha*, the different heads mixed mostly with *āliṅgya*. They are classified into three 'progressions' (*pracāra*): 'regular' (*sama*) when the left is used on top, left or *āliṅgya*, and right on right; 'irregular' (*viṣama*) when the right is used on top or *āliṅgya*; and regular-irregular when the striking is cross-handed. *See also* TANNUMAI.

Two characteristic aspects of Indian drumming are already strikingly evident in the *Nāṭyaśāstra* material. Firstly the canonical series of drum syllables is based in large part on guttural, retroflex, flap and dental consonants, as it still is. Secondly the rather large variety of tonal colours implied by so many drum syllables is produced with the same techniques that are still used. The five basic strokes (*pāṇi-prahata*) are full hand, half hand, quarter hand, side of the hand and forefinger. The five strokes can be made with three degrees of *prahāra* (damping): fully damped, half-damped or undamped. Each individual combination of stroke and damping corresponds with one or more ways of hitting the drumhead; for instance, in one reading *da* is used for the half-hand half-damped stroke but also for the side-hand fully damped stroke; at the same time, the half-hand half-damped stroke is represented not only by *da* but also by *ga* and *dha*. The state of the sources and the nature of the material render any accurate listing impossible, but already the modern pattern of different syllables sometimes representing the same stroke and different strokes sometimes having the same syllable is evident. Indeed, the most modern drum tradition, that of the *tablā*, is also the most consistent in the matter of stroke–syllable correspondence, and may be taken as close to an idealized paradigm.

In the *Nāṭyaśāstra* the manners of playing the *mṛdaṅgam* for different musico-dramatic purposes are carefully prescribed. For instance, when the sentiments of *śṛṅgāra-rasa* (love) or *hāsya-rasa* (humour) are being evoked, generally only the *aṅkīka* (horizontal) drum should be used; conversely, for *bhayānaka* (fear) and *bībhatsa* (disgust) all three drums are needed, one of which is prescribed for these sentiments alone.

More specifically, the drums had two functions: accompanying *dhruva* (interpolated songs) and accompanying the actions and gestures of the actors. For songs of varying dramatic purpose or expression different manners of accompaniment were suitable: *tattva* (matching the song rhythm), *anugata* (filling in the pauses) or *ogha* (fast and independent patterns). More precise ways in which there could be *sāmya* ('conformities') of drum and song are also listed, among them conformities with poetic metre, formal divisions, beats of the controlling tala (time cycle), beginnings and cadences, and so on; by implication, nonconformity in any or all such domains was an alternative in at least the *ogha* accompanying style. Particular drum formulae were associated with the movements of different characters of a drama, such as kings, servants and very low characters.

2. MEDIEVAL PERIOD: MARDALA OR MṚDAṄGA. The medieval inheritor of the *mṛdaṅga* tradition, as represented in important sources such as the *Saṅgītaratnākara* (13th century), is termed *mardala*, though this is equated with the older *mṛdaṅga* or *muraja*. The root for this word and *mṛdaṅga* is the same. The *mardala* body differs somewhat from that of the older *mṛdaṅga* barrel drums, and it has become a single double-headed drum (the old drum-sets becoming rare from around the 8th century); it enters into this tradition by virtue of its paste-tuned heads.

(i) Structure. The *Saṅgītaratnākara* describes the *mardala* as made of citrus (*bīja*) wood, 21 fingers (about 42 cm) long, with a wall a half-finger thick (about 1 cm). The right face is about 26 cm in diameter, the left about 28 cm. Other authors maintain that the body is of acacia or red sandalwood, the wall about 2 cm thick, the length about 60 cm, and the left and right heads 24 cm and 23 cm in diameter. In all cases the modern tradition of a smaller, treble, right head appears to have been reached. The description of the body's shape has been interpreted as a barrel drum by both medieval and modern commentators only by ignoring the grammar of the sentence involved. This reads *mānaṃ yasya manāñ madhyaḥ pṛthur* ('the middle whose measurement is less is wide/extensive'). To interpret this as saying that the middle is wider, or slightly wider, leaves no sense to the construction, and the commentator Siṃhabhūpāla who takes it thus ignores in his comment the word 'less'. The sentence is best taken as meaning that the middle, which extends the whole length of the drum, is slightly less in size (i.e. gently waisted) than the heads. This *mardala* would thus relate very closely to the *mādal*, *mādar*, *mandari* and *tumdak'* of the present-day east-central tribal peoples in shape, rather than to the barrel-shaped *maddaḷam* of the south; like the former it has a truncated-conical (*gopuccha*) appearance (compare the *āliṅgya*, §1 (i) above), but it is in fact slightly waisted under the dense lacing.

The skins are single and are prescribed as thick and round, one finger (about 2 cm) larger than their drumheads; no hoops are attached, but they are pierced all round with 40 holes, and laced together by a leather strap (*vadhra*). This shows now its upper, now its lower side in a pattern called *vignikā* ('recoiling, zigzag'?) by Śārṅgadeva and *karpara* by Siṃhabhūpāla (late 14th century). Two plaited leather rings are tightened over the skins near the head, and to them is attached a doubled holding-band (*kacchā*) with a decorative border of silk threads which is worn around the hips, like that of the contemporary barrel drum *paṭaha*.

A thick tuning-paste made by mixing a glue of boiled rice with ash and pounding them together was applied to both heads; thus the drum 'would sound like thunderclouds'. The paste is called *bohaṇa*, a non-Sanskritic word, by Śārṅgadeva; it is possible that it should be read *rohaṇa* ('application') as mentioned in the *Nāṭyaśāstra* (§1 (i) above), but there is no guarantee of this since the *Saṅgītaratnākara* is in general a well-preserved text, and many ancient drum-terms are of a non-Sanskritic colour. Whether this paste was re-applied wet and fresh, or was hardened and permanent like the modern black pastes of the tuned drums, is not stated. It is of interest that the two important elements of the modern heads, the paste and the composite skins, are found separately in this period on the two most important drums, the *mardala* and the *deśī paṭaha*, respectively.

(ii) Drumming. Familiar principles of drum technique and function may be seen in *Nāṭyaśāstra*, but from *Saṅgītaratnākara* in the 13th century descend some very

specific patterns on which both modern canonical barrel drum traditions are based. By far the most extensive descriptive material and exemplification of drum syllable patterns in *Saṅgītaratnākara* are for the *paṭaha*, which according to *Saṅgītaratnākara* is the same as *mṛdaṅga*, and which is also discussed at some length, and it is the *mardala* patterns which are still so much in evidence in the modern *mṛdaṅga* traditions.

There were and are two originally and fundamentally different kinds of drumstrokes and patterns: a primordial set of four, and a certain number used for filling in between them. *Saṅgītaratnākara* gives *ta dhi thoṃ ṭem* for the primal set, called *śrama-vāhanī* ('carrying the burden'); this is even now the basis for the first sequence learnt in both Hindustani and Carnatic *mṛdaṅga* traditions. It also gives the sequence in repeating pairs, triplets and quadruplets – *ta-ta dhi-dhi . . . ta-ta-ta dhi-dhi-dhi . . .* etc – as they are still given in the first lessons. The last syllable now is usually *nam* (another of seven basic *mardala* strokes in *Saṅgītaratnākara*), but may also be *jhem* or *jhom* in the Carnatic traditions. Although the actual strokes differ not only from north to south but also to some extent within individual traditions, they reveal their antiquity by the fact that the correlation of strokes and syllables for this first pattern *ta dhi tom nam* is in every tradition deviant in one way or another from what are otherwise normal and more recent stroke–syllable correlations.

The second class of strokes in *Saṅgītaratnākara* is called *eka-sara-ṭākanī* ('single-flowing-ṭākanī'), exemplified by combinations of *taka* and *dhikaṭa* said to amount to eight, which are meant to 'break' the sequences of *ta dhi thoṃ ṭem* and provide a 'flow' of drumming. Many examples of the elaboration of the *ta dhi tom nam* succession by means of secondary 'flowing' formulae combined with repetition and recurrence of the four main strokes are given in the 14th-century *Saṅgītôpaniṣat-sārôddhāra* (Sudhākalaśa). Very interesting historically is the association of each variant with a tala, as though for a *ṭhekā* of Hindustani music. Although they are mostly not absolutely identical with existing traditional patterns, some of these patterns are very close, and all are playable. The first quoted below is for *ādī* tala: 'tad dhi thau draim'. Others are 'tattaki/ tat-ta/dhi-dhik-ki/dhid-dhi'; 'tat-ta/dhid-dhi/thau-thau/ dhi draim'; 'karagaḍa naragaḍa/tad-dhi-dhik kaḍa-daragaḍa dhid-dhi kat-thau/dhik-kat-thau draim'.

A longer specimen of *ta dhi thau draim* plus the filler formula *daragaḍa*, unconnected with a specific tala, is given in the chapter on instruments, as an instance of combination for the *mardala*: 'tak-kaḍa daragaḍa/dhik-kaḍa daragaḍa tā-dhik-kaḍa/dā-dhik-kaḍa/daragaḍa dhid-dhik-kaḍa/tā-tak-kaḍa/daragaḍa tak-kaḍa/dā-dhik-kaḍa/daragaḍa dhik-kaḍa daragaḍa daragaḍa tā dhit thau draim'.

Comparing these patterns with the first lessons in south Indian *mṛdaṅgam* traditions shows the continuity in the principle of combining the main strokes with 'flowing' filler patterns, for example *tā–kiṭataka dhī–kiṭataka tom– kiṭataka nam–kiṭataka/tā tā kiṭa dhī dhī kiṭa tom tom kiṭa nam nam kiṭa*. Other and longer formulae of filler syllables are combined with *kiṭataka*, such as *tarikiṭa, takadina, takadimi, jaṇutaka* and so on: *tak-kiṭa kiṭataka takatarikiṭataka/dhik-kiṭa kiṭataka takatarikiṭataka* etc. There is no one-for-one correspondence of single strokes with single syllables, not even in the sets of two, four, six or more, and in each tra-

dition the verbal formulae are played slightly differently. The bulk of the filler, however, is always made with strings of a fully damped three-stroke sequence comprising (a) left hand flat, (b) annular and middle fingers of right hand on black spot, (c) and forefinger likewise, then back to (a) left hand flat, and so on as necessary, the whole laced with other single strokes both damped and more resonant.

Other single strokes or short groups can take the places of *ta dhi tom nam: tak-kum kiṭataka . . . talāngutom kiṭataka . . .* and so on. In due course any anomalous ancient survivals in the fingering of *ta dhi tom nam* themselves are replaced by more appropriate strokes, such as the replacement of ancient damped *dhi* on the black spot with a half-hand undamped *dhi*.

The first lessons for the Hindustani *mṛdaṅg–pakhāvaj* are the ones descended from *Saṅgītaratnākara: tā dīn thūn nā*, and patterns with filler strokes based on them. In this there is a resemblance with the south Indian *mṛdaṅgam* traditions. Beyond these first, obviously anciently embedded, stages the traditions diverge.

3. MODERN PERIOD.

(i) Northern mṛdang or pakhāvaj. The *mṛdang* of Aryan-speaking north and central India (also spelt or pronounced *mirdang*) is frequently called *pakhāvaj*, a name of medieval type. This name is not recorded in the 13th-century *Saṅgītaratnākara*, though other drums are given there with 'folk' variant names consisting partly of *āvaja* or *āvaj*. This term derives from the Sanskrit *ātodya* through the Prakrit *āojja* rather than from *vādya*, as has been stated. The element *pakh-* is indeed the Sanskrit *pakṣa*, but denoted originally a drum played to the side of the body (there would have been nothing remarkable about a double-headed drum played on its sides in terms of older Indian drums; the vertical playing position of the *tablā* became the norm in north India only comparatively recently).

The name *pakhāvaj* would have have been established in the later medieval (Delhi Sultanate) period, for it is recorded in the late 16th-century Mughal *Ā'īn-ī-akbarī*, which states that it was 'held under one arm'. This is confirmed by earlier Mughal painting, which shows the drum being held on a shoulder-strap under the left arm of a standing player and played obliquely. The *Ā'īn* records it as 'lemon-shaped but with flattened ends', that is, a bulging barrel drum similar to the *mṛdaṅga* or *khol* of the east (like the latter, it may at this time have been made of clay, in view of the weight). The text does not record the use of the *mṛdang-pakhāvaj* to accompany the song type *dhrupad*, to which in modern times it is mainly attached; this was accompanied either by the variable tension hourglass drum, the *huruk* or *āvaj* in the case of the *hurukīyā* singers, or (in the case of the Panjabi woman singers *dafjan*) by the frame drum *daph* or the *ḍholak*. The use of the *pakhāvaj* is here recorded either for the Krishna devotees, the *kīrtanya* (Brahmin precentors) and the *bhagatīyā*, or for the dancing-masters *naṭvā* and the lower class of entertainers *kanjarī* (these are all said to be of the Malva-Gujarat region). Two *pakhāvaj* are the drums in the aristocratic house-music (*akhāṛā*) of this period (for illustration *see* AKHĀṚĀ).

The modern *pakhāvaj* tradition has two main contexts: the temple and the concert platform, formerly in the courts and more recently the public hall. These would connect with the earlier traditions of use in *kīrtan* devo-

(a)

(b)

(c)

1. *Mṛdaṅga (double-headed drums) of India: (a)
mṛdang or pakhāvaj of the north; (b) mṛdaṅgam of the
south; (c) mṛdaṅga or khol of the east, accompanied by
kartāl (cymbals)*

cm (R. Stewart: *The Tabla in Perspective*, diss., U. of
California, Los Angeles, 1974).

The skins of the *pakhāvaj* drumhead (*puṙī*) are mostly of goat, previously cleaned by soaking in lime and
water. The main right skin is thinner than the left. Over
both is stretched a thinner skin (compare the *uddalī* of
the medieval *deśī paṭaha*), and the two are bound together
to a four-ply plaited leather hoop (*gajṙī*). The latter is
somewhat larger than the drumhead and when tensioned
is a little lower than the rim; one or two thick skin rings
are stitched under the main skins on to the hoop to protect the drumhead from the edge of the barrel. The greater
part (between two-thirds and three-quarters) of the thin
upper skin is cut away, leaving an outer ring extending
a little from the drum-rim over the cavity on each head.
This is called *cāṇti* (*cāṭi*: ?'slap'; compare *thāp*, below)
or *kinār* ('edge'). To the greater, exposed area of the
lower, main skin on the right head is applied a round,
black tuning-paste in several, progressively smaller,
layers. The essential element in this is iron oxide (Śarmā,
2/1963; Murphy, 1965), mixed in a glue of boiled rice,
and according to Śarmā, blue vitriol (copper sulphate,
nīlathothā) is also present, while other sources specify
a mangosteen tar (*gāb*). Many sources state that the paste
contains metal filings; Murphy has pointed out that this
would be highly abrasive, and that it would not adhere.
This composition of the paste would also apply for the
southern *mṛdaṅgam* and the *tablā*. The area of the main
skin below the paste is first scraped with a blade; the
paste is then applied layer by layer, each rubbed smooth
with a stone when almost dry and dried before application of the next (there are commonly five layers).
Murphy states that the progressively smaller diameter
of each layer is merely aesthetic, but anything else would
increase the load on the drumhead and lower it further
as well as creating a wall at the edge of the paste.

There are thus three areas on the right face, the edge
(*cāṇti*), the middle (*lav*: 'bit'; *sur*: 'pitch') and the black

tional music and the court *akhāṙā*. The former tradition
(*havelī saṅgit*) is associated especially with the most holy
temple towns of the north, such as Benares, Brindaban
(both in Uttar Pradesh), Nathadvara (Rajasthan) and
Poona and Pandharpur (Maharashtra). These provided a
haven for older musical styles and instruments when, in
the last two centuries or so, the taste of the courts turned
increasingly to the newer Indo-Muslim styles, and the
families in service to these temples have often provided
players for more secular contexts. In recent years, the
establishment of *dhrupad mela* festivals in India has seen
a revival of the older styles and their principal accompaniment, the *mṛdang-pakhāvaj*.

Little is known of the development of the composite
drumheads, such as are seen on all three modern regional *mṛdaṅga* of north, south and east with only small
differences of detail (see fig.1). It would seem, however, that it combines the principle of the tuning-paste
of the older *mṛdaṅga–mardala* drums with that of the
double skin recorded for the *deśī* or local *paṭaha* barrel
drum of medieval times.

The modern *pakhāvaj* is of wood. Many shapes and
sizes (chosen or made, as with most Indian instruments,
to fit the player) are found. Modern sources still refer
to the three shapes defined for the ancient *mṛdaṅga* (see
§1 (i), above); however, the most common shape is perhaps rather an asymmetrical biconical barrel (though a
symmetrical bulging barrel is also found). The shell tapers
to the ends from a ridge near to the left-hand head
(fig.1a). The range of dimensions has been given as:
length, 66 to 76 cm; diameter of right head, 16·5 to 19
cm; of left head, 25·5 to 28 cm; and of ridge 20 to 30

(siyāhi, syāhi). The first two occupy about a quarter each of the head, the black about half. Because whole-hand and whole-head strokes predominate on the pakhāvaj, and also because one head when struck makes the other vibrate, these are less specific in pitch and timbre difference than on the finger-played tablā, and all areas of the head may be played both resonant ('open') or non-resonant ('closed'). The main right open pitch is tuned to the singer's or melody instrument's tonic.

The left head has no permanent paste, but a pancake of wheat-dough is applied for each performance, lowering the pitch to an octave below that of the right head. This paste thus performs the adjusting role posited above for the ancient mṛdaṅga, as well as making the head vibrate with great resonance.

The two heads are interlaced by a leather strap (tasmā) laced in a V through 16 holes in either hoop. The skins are tensioned by eight large wooden cylinders (gaṭṭā), one under each V, to the left side of the drum between the ridge and the head. The right head is fine-tuned by means of a small hammer struck on the hoop.

The modern pakhāvaj is usually placed horizontally on the floor before the seated player with the right end resting on a folded cloth (see fig.1a). The principal strokes on either side are whole-hand strokes. Strokes are called bol, denoting (like the ancient vāṣkaraṇa, pāṭa and varṇa) both the action and its notational syllable. These vary according to context, the real notational group being the phrase. Śarmā would classify the right-hand strokes as basically five, the left as two; of these, only two (left-hand gha, right-hand ṭa – the vowel quality varies) are regarded as invariable (acal) in notation and position. The two main resonant, or 'open' (khulā), strokes on the right are tā (a 'slap' – also called thāp), given by the upper (lateral) edge of the hand on the top half of the drum-face, pivoting on the lower (medial) side of the palm to damp the sound slightly; and dī, a forceful tap, immediately rebounding, with four or three fingers on the central black of the head. These two strokes give two different timbres of the system tonic. Also resonant is nā, a strong tap with the top of the right index (or other finger) on the edge of the head. The right two-stroke roll kiṭī (kiṭa, ṭīṭī, tira) is made with the second and third fingers plus the thumb on the centre of the black; these are held down and are 'closed' (band), that is, non-resonant. A similarly made, but resonant double or triple stroke on the edge, is called nanāna or tarāna.

Of the two main left-hand strokes, ghā (resonant) is a strong tap, immediately rebounding, on the whole head (partly on the dough) with the top of the hand, while closed kat is a flat-hand, held-down stroke on the whole head. Ghā played simultaneously with a right-hand stroke (e.g. tā or tiṭa) changes the notation to dh-, thus dhā or dhiṭa. Head-to-head rolls or compound phrases are common, such as kata, taka, kira, krāna (ka-tā-na), the common variational formula ghina-naka, and the ubiquitous cadential formula tiṭa kata gadi gina.

The basic technique of pakhāvaj may be summarized as a series of rolls varying with, and leading to, resonant held strokes both on- and off-beat. The rhythmic values of the notes reflect the changing tensions of the different hand positions and symmetry between the two hands; the main final is usually on dhā, a symmetrical and resonant base-position for both hands. It is said that the great 19th-century pakhavājī Kudau Sinh of Rampur court, by control and balance, could make the drum rise from the floor while playing, a story quite credible to those who have seen the dexterity and beauty of Indian drumming. Since the 18th century, the mrdang-pakhāvaj has been associated in terms of concert music primarily with the dhrupad song form, as well as other vocal forms (notably dhamār) that have come into its orbit.

The vocal and instrumental forms of the older north Indian style accompanied by pakhāvaj are rhythmically organized in a system of metres, tāla (Sanskrit) or tāl (the modern languages). In a piece in one mode or raga throughout, the drum is silent in the first movement (ālāp), which is metrically free. With the commencement of the vocal or instrumental composition initiating the second movement, which is in strict metre, the drum begins to play. The general style of pakhāvaj accompaniment is characterized as 'simultaneous-variational' (sāth saṅgat), which distinguishes it from the alternating variation of the tablā in the newer Indo-Muslim style.

The dhrupad tala system has been characterized as additive, in that the common metres are made up mostly of sub-bars of different lengths, thus: cautāl (cārtāl, dhrupadtāl), 12 beats (4+4+2+2); sūltāl, 10 beats (4+2+4); tīvrātāl, 7 beats (3+2+2); dhamār, 14 beats (5+2+3+4); āṙā ('crooked') cautāl, 14 beats (2+4+4+4). The tala itself has the function of a time signature – a conceptual framework between the musicians. The pakhāvaj, unlike the tablā, does not make much use of a base-rhythm pattern in performance. However, it does have illustrative patterns. These are sometimes called thapiyā ('mark, signature'), or thekā ('support'), following the tablā terminology. The divisive principle common to moric prosody is taught in early lessons through the ancient formula tā dī thun nā, traced from the Middle Ages by Powers (see above, §2(ii)).

The most important aspect of pakhāvaj (as of the vocal) variations is tempo manipulation, for which the general term is bāṇṭ ('division'). In general, these 'mask' rather than 'mark' the tala structure, driving at their conclusion towards the main, first beat of the metre (sam) to coincide with the singer. Sharma (1969) discusses the structure of a typical pakhāvaj dhrupad accompaniment principally in terms of tempo (lay): in the first verse (sthāyī) the drum plays tukṙā prastār or peśkār variations in base-tempo, usually medium; in the second (antarā) it plays double-tempo prastār and tukṙā; in sancārī it plays triple- and in ābhog, quadruple-tempo variations; in subsequent returns to the sthāyī, more complex tempos develop – five or seven against four, for example. This format applies to solo playing, but more adventurous tempos (three-quarters, one-and-a-quarter etc) also occur. Sharma talks of 32 tempo patterns in all. The doubling of tempo within a piece is called dupallī ('two-fold'), and successive doublings tīnpallī, caupallī etc.

Within this are several different types of variational structure organized by tone-colour, repetition and recurrence, and so on. Ṭukṙā ('piece') is a short variation from a few beats to two or three cycles in length, usually with varying strokes and rhythms, and with or without a closing tihāī or triple cadential formula. The term paran (for pūraṇ: 'filler'?; though it has also a more general connotation) is usually reserved for longer structures with manipulation of strokes (bol), tempo and timbre. This often takes the form of theme and tihāī, the latter usually a compound one (cakradār: 'three times three'). An additional and important principle of variation is that of additive extension (prastār), where a particular *bol*-phrase is taken (*ghinanaka* is a favourite one for this) and increasingly varied and complex *bol* are added before it (e.g. *dhā-kiṭa ghinanaka, dhumakiṭa ghinanaka, dhā-kiṭa dhumakiṭa ghinanaka ghinanaka, dhā-kiṭa dhumakiṭa takadhuma ghinanaka*). A piece that further emphasizes the permutation of *bol* (as in *dhumakiṭa takadhuma* above) is called *peśkār* (this has more in common with the *qāidā* than the *peśkār* of the *tablā*). The *relā* ('torrent') of the *pakhāvaj* may derive from imitation of the *tārparan* and *jhālā* patterns of such string instruments as the *bīṇ* and *rabāb* (which the *pakhāvaj* used to accompany) and are fast streams of predominantly closed, rolling *bol*, given in quadruple groupings which are mostly in 12-beat *cautāl* and 16-beat *tritāl* (the favourite instrumental talas). The *parār* is a longer *relā* (around six cycles in length) with a closing *tihāī*. Patterns in one *tāl* may here be fitted into another.

The *pakhāvaj* also plays with *kathak* dance, where in addition to the rhythmic procedures sketched above its *bol* can include lexical words or syllables; this occurs also in religious formulae (*stuti*), where the *bol* correspond prosodically to, and also symbolize, the words of the text.

(ii) Southern mṛdaṅgam. This version of the double-headed barrel drum is used mainly in the performance of *saṅgīta*, a cultivated art music tradition found in the four southern states of India (Tamil Nadu, Andhra Pradesh, Kerala and Karnataka; fig.1*b*). The technique, repertory and individual improvisational performing style are aurally transmitted from master to disciple during long apprenticeships; famous schools evolved in the courts and temples of the rajas and continued to flourish under British rule. The *mṛdaṅgam* is also used to accompany the *bharata nāṭyam* style of dance-mime.

The wooden body of the drum varies between 50 and 70 cm in length depending on the range of pitches desired. It is cylindrical, tapering for approximately half its length; the diameters of the two heads are about 18 and 21 cm. On both heads the wooden rim slopes inward, the angle being shallower on the smaller of the two. Each has a membrane of monkey skin: on the smaller, this membrane is covered with another of calfskin with a circular hole (7 to 8 cm in diameter) at the centre; on the larger is a similar but double membrane of calfskin with a hole of 11 to 12 cm. These extra membranes (*mīṭṭu*) are attached to the stretching mechanism by means of a circle of holes located just beyond the edge of the rim. Through these holes pass strips of bullock hide which are tightly woven into a ring approximately 1·5 cm thick.

At 16 equidistant points on each rim a gap is forced in the weave, allowing a single thong of bullock hide, approximately 20 metres long, to pass through and connect the two rims at each end of the drum. The monkey-skin membranes on each face are laced to the *mīṭṭu* so that, by tightening the thong of bullock hide, the membranes are stretched over each head. As the thong slackens through use, up to 16 cylindrical wooden pegs are inserted between the thong and the wooden body of the drum to sustain the tension.

On the smaller head, nearly all the exposed area of monkey skin is covered by a circular patch of black tuning-paste made from a mixture of powdered waste-iron and rice; the patch is nearly $\frac{1}{2}$ cm thick, tapering towards the edges. Two dozen or so split reeds are inserted between the *mīṭṭu* and the membrane beneath; these add a characteristic 'buzz' to the timbre of the smaller head. No split reeds are used on the larger head, on which the drum rests when not in use. *Mṛdaṅgam* players often make a temporary tuning-paste from a lump of wet *soji* (a type of flour) to apply to the larger head before a performance.

The absolute pitch (*śruti*) of the drum varies according to the preference of the principal performer within the *saṅgīta* ensemble (usually a vocalist, or a melody instrumentalist). Absolute pitch is reckoned in semitones ascending from middle C of the equal-tempered harmonium. The absolute pitch of a *mṛdaṅgam* may be altered by up to two-and-a-half semitones by striking the tightly-woven rings with a hammer and wooden peg to alter the head tension. Most players possess two instruments, enabling an absolute pitch range from *śruti* 2 to 7 (D♭ to F♯). Some male vocalists require *śruti* 1 (C) and a few players possess instruments capable of this pitch.

The *mṛdaṅgam* player is usually seated cross-legged on a mat with the drum resting on its side in front; the right hand strikes the smaller head and the left hand the larger. The drum rests against the right shin, the right foot forming a cradle for the larger head, and the left knee rests on the drum, holding it in position. Sometimes a rolled-up piece of cloth is inserted beneath the drum near the right-hand head in order to tilt it upwards.

Seven basic strokes are recognized. The left head (with the right head damped) may be struck in the centre of the membrane with four fingers together (the pitch may be altered through an octave by varying the striking position); it may also be struck on the *mīṭṭu* (on the side nearest the player), again with four fingers together but with the first joints of the fingers. For the right head (with the left head damped), the player may strike the *mīṭṭu* near the rim (on the side nearest the player) with the first joint of the forefinger, or the exposed membrane between the *mīṭṭu* and the tuning-paste with the first joint of the forefinger. The tuning-paste itself may be struck with the middle and ring fingers together (using the first joints of the fingers), with the first joint of the forefinger, or with the end of the little finger (this is executed with a quick flick of the wrist and produces a characteristically resonant sound).

Each stroke produces a distinct timbre. In the second and fifth types of stroke the pitches produced are indeterminate; the other five strokes produce more determinate pitches and pitch relationships. The lowest pitch produced in the first type is an octave below *shadja* (the system tonic); the third type produces *shadja*, and the fourth a (less determinate) semitone above, the sixth a (barely determinate) 5th above and the seventh *shadja* with a prominent second harmonic. The first and fifth strokes combined produce an indeterminate but very low pitch; this is reckoned as a separate stroke. The *mīṭṭu* strokes require a great deal of force, causing permanent calluses on the finger joints. The different strokes are described and transcribed by means of syllables (such as *tā, dhī, tom, nam*), some of which differ from region to region, and the player learns the instrument in terms of patterned combinations of strokes (*jati*).

In their early training *mṛdaṅgam* students learn to play different *jati* sequences in relation to different talas (metres). There are no fixed relationships between particular *jati* or *jati* sequences and particular talas. The player's rhythmic sense and motor skills are developed through increasingly varied and complex relations between the two: for example, *jati* comprising odd numbers of strokes played in talas comprising even numbers of beats (and vice versa); doubling, halving and trebling the tempos of the *jati* while the tala remains constant; and starting the *jati* sequences on different beats of the tala.

Playing *mṛdaṅgam* in terms of improvising *jati* sequences in relation to a fixed tala is called *konugolu*. This is contrasted with the *tathākāra* approach used when accompanying melody instruments. The *mṛdaṅgam* accompanies only when a tala operates. In compositions, a line of song text occupying a fixed number of measures of the tala may be repeated many times over with progressive melodic elaboration, or the melody instrument may imitate this procedure, dynamically accenting the beats on which the consonants of the song text repeatedly fall. The *mṛdaṅgam* supplies a rhythmic counterpoint to the repeated pattern of accents provided by the melody instrument or voice, along with rolls and flourishes.

During the *kalpana svara* passages which follow improvised *pallavi* (and may follow fixed compositions, called *kṛti*), the melody instrument improvises increasingly long and rhythmically complex sequences, each terminating on the same strong accent of a refrain passage. In *kalpana svara* the melody instrument usually 'challenges' the *mṛdaṅgam* player to repeat immediately the complex rhythmic sequence just played. During such 'contests', the *mṛdaṅgam* player may occasionally replicate a melodic sequence by skilful left-hand strokes.

The solo performance recital traditionally occupies anything from 15 minutes to an hour or more towards the end of a concert by the *saṅgīta* ensemble, following the main raga of the concert. This is the longest item, comprising *ālāpana*, *tānam*, *pallavi* improvisation (or, increasingly nowadays, a *kṛti*) and improvised *kalpana svara*. These last two sections are set to a single tala of fixed tempo. Immediately after *kalpana svara* the *mṛdaṅgam* continues alone into the solo recital, improvising with as many different *jati* and *jati* sequences as possible within the framework of the fixed tala. The player does not mark the strong beats of the tala with regular drumstrokes; throughout the *mṛdaṅgam* solo the principal performer of the ensemble marks the strong beats with movements of the right hand. In this way the complex and varying relationships between the rhythmic accents of the *jati* sequences and the strong beats of the tala are made accessible to the spectators. Towards the end of the solo rhythmic density increases to herald the approach of the climax, which lasts for a minute or two and in which relationships between rhythm and metre display maximum complexity and variability. The solo concludes with three repeats of a pre-arranged terminal *jati*, which concludes precisely on the starting note of the *pallavi* refrain played once by the whole ensemble to terminate the musical item.

Of the talas used in *saṅgīta*, *ādi* (4+2+2) is the most common. However, other talas such as *rūpaka* (2+4), *triputa* (3+2+2), *eka* (4), *khaṇḍa chāpu* (2+3) and *miśra chāpu* (3+4) are frequently heard, and many popular compositions are set to these talas. Occasionally, compositions in *dhruva* (4+2+4+4), *maṭhya* (4+2+4), *jhampa* (7+1+2) and *aṭa* (5+5+2+2) are found – usually in the context of improvised *pallavi*. With the exception of these rarely heard, longer talas, the duration of a single, complete measure of a tala ranges between 2 and 12 seconds. *Ādi tāla* has three tempos – arrived at by doubling and quadrupling the number of beats in the measure. The other talas have a single tempo (though this is variable within limits). *Rūpaka*,

triputa and *khaṇḍa chāpu* are fast tempo talas; *eka* and *miśra chāpu* are medium tempo; *dhruva*, *maṭhya*, *jhampa* and *aṭa* are slow. The slow tempo talas are associated with older compositions.

Other talas are referred to in musical texts (indeed, theoretical systems expounding and naming all the logical variations of tala exist and occupy the attention of many indigenous scholars). *Mṛdaṅgam* players often experiment with theoretically-derived talas, but these experiments tend very rarely to result in public performances.

BIBLIOGRAPHY

Bharatamuni: *Nāṭyaśāstra* (early centuries AD), trans. M. Ghosh (Calcutta, 1961)
Śārṅgadeva: *Saṅgītaratnākara* (13th century), ed. S. Subrahmanya Sastri, iii (Madras, 1951)
S. M. Tagore: *Mṛdanga-mañjari* (Calcutta, 1875)
C. R. Day: *The Music and Musical Instruments of Southern India and the Deccan* (Delhi, 1891/R1977)
A. S. Fox Strangways: *The Music of Hindostan* (Oxford, 1914/R1965)
C. Sachs: *Die Musikinstrumente Indiens und Indonesiens* (Berlin, 1914, 2/1921)
C. Raman and S. Kumar: 'Musical Drums with Harmonic Overtones', *Nature*, civ (1920), 500
C. Marcel-Dubois: *Les instruments de musique de l'Inde ancienne* (Paris, 1941)
P. Sambamoorthy: *A Dictionary of South Indian Music and Musicians* (Madras, 1952–71)
V. Raghavan: 'Why is the Mridanga so called?', *Journal of the Music Academy Madras*, xxvi (1955), 148
Bh. Ś. Śarmā: *Tāl Prakāś* (Hathras, 2/1963)
R. E. Brown: *The Mṛdaṅga: a Study of Drumming in South India* (diss., U. of California, Los Angeles, 1965)
D. Murphy: 'The Structure, Repair and Acoustical Properties of the Classical Drums of India with Specific Reference to the Mṛdaṅga and Tablā', *Journal of the Music Academy Madras*, xxxvi (1965), 223
P. Sambamoorthy: *South Indian Music*, i (Madras, 7/1966, 8/1972); ii (6/1960); iii (6/1964, 7/1973); iv (3/1963); v (2/1963); vi (1969)
T. R. H. Sharma: *The Art of Mridhangam* (Madras, 1969)

ALASTAIR DICK (1(i), 2(i), 3(i)),
HAROLD S. POWERS (1(ii), 2(ii)),
GORDON GEEKIE (3(ii))

Mriqq. FRAME DRUM of Libya; *see* RIQQ.

Mrwaho [mrwahto]. Syriac term for a FLABELLUM used in oriental, Syrian and Orthodox churches.

Msengele. Transverse flute of the Tsonga people of southern Africa, resembling the Venda TSHITIRINGO.

Msōndo. Single-headed vertical drum used by black musicians in southern Iraq, Kuwait and the Gulf region. (The name is from the Bambassi language, of African origin.) It is made from a hollowed palm trunk, or from Java wood or walnut, in the shape of a truncated cone. In recent times metal has also been used. The length varies between 65 and 106 cm; the membrane of cowhide, goatskin or sheepskin is from 17 to 27 cm wide. It is folded over the rim and fixed with wooden pegs and a leather thong which encircles the instrument. The player, standing up, places the drum at an angle between his open legs and strikes it with the palms of both hands. *Msōndo* are used with other instruments in at least three instrumental ensembles: the *al haywa*, the *al wāya* and the *jatānka*.

For illustration *see* ṢRNĀJ.

BIBLIOGRAPHY

S. Qassim Hassan: *Les instruments de musique en Irak et leur rôle dans la société traditionelle* (Paris, 1980)

SCHEHERAZADE QASSIM HASSAN

Mtangala. Mouth bow of the Ngoni people of Zambia resembling the Zulu Umqangala.

Mtiwiso. Single-headed Goblet drum of the Nyanja/Chewa people of Lilongwe district, Malawi. It is open-ended. *See also* Mbalwe.

Mtorilo. *See* Mululi.

Mtot. Single-headed drum of the Lunda people of Zaïre. *See* Ditumba.

Mtyángala. Mouth bow of the Pangwa people of southern Zambia played exclusively by young women.

Muanza. Friction drum of the Nika (Mijikenda) people of Kenya. It is made from a hollowed log about 180 cm long and has a friction cord.

Mubáanga. Wooden cone flute, with one or two finger-holes, of the Pende people of south-western Zaïre (*LaurentyA*, 125).

Mubango. Percussion beam of the Ganda people of Uganda. About 175 to 200 cm long, the beam is placed on the ground and beaten near the ends by two young men in order to induce edible ants to leave the soil.

Mucang [mucanga]. *See* Murcang.

Much'a. Duct flute in an ensemble of the Bolivian Alti Plano. *See* Pincullo.

Muchinga. Drum of the Chopi people of Zavala district, Mozambique.

Muchongoyo. Drum ensemble of the Ndau people of Mozambique. It consists of three double-headed drums beaten by one or two players with sticks.

Mūcī mådar. Double-headed drum of the Muṇḍā people of east India. *See* Mådar.

Mucundo (pl. *micundo*). Open-ended, footed drum of the Chokwe people of Lóvua/Lunda district, Angola. The weighted head is pegged on and the body has small integral carved handles near the top. It is held between the knees and hand-played in conjunction with the *txinguvo, mucupela* and *cassúmbi* drums, to accompany dancing. See Museo do Dundo: *Folclore musical de Angola,* i (1961), 29 and figs.49, 52.
DAVID K. RYCROFT

Mucupela [mucuazo] (pl. *micupela*). Double-headed cylindrical drum of the Chokwe people of Lóvua/Lunda district, Angola. The pegged heads are weighted centrally with a mixture of ash and castor oil. The body has two integral carved handles and a mirliton is inserted in one side. It is laid across the knees and hand-played in conjunction with the *txinguvo, mucundo* and *cassúmbi* drums, to accompany dancing. See Museo do Dundo: *Folclore musical de Angola,* i (1961), 28f and figs.49, 51, 55, 56. *See also* Mukupiela.
DAVID K. RYCROFT

Mudewa. Single-headed cylindrical drum of the Nyanja/Chewa people of Malawi. It is open-ended, with three feet, and has a rectangular hole cut in one side.

Mudidi. Single-headed drum of the Luluwa people of Zaïre. *See* Ditumba.

Mudimba. Trapezoidal Slit-drum of the Sanga people of Zaïre (*LaurentyTF,* 137).

Mudoku. Lamellaphone of the Atalo, Amanga and Andekuju peoples of Zaïre (*LaurentyS,* 197).

Muemvo [mwémvo]. Cylindrical stopped wooden flute of the Mayombe people of Zaïre (*LaurentyA,* 175, 179).

Mufferriz. *See* Mofferriz.

Muffler pedal. *See* Moderator pedal.

Mugabe. Single-headed Goblet drum of the Soga people of Kiguru district, Uganda. It is open-ended and the membrane is pinned on. It is played with the hands.

Muganda. Drum of the Tonga people of Chinteche district, Malawi. It is used with the Malipenga 'singing horn' ensemble.

Muggurmán. Large upright drum, played with the hands for vocal and dance accompaniment by the Shidi, a community of African origin settled in Sind, Pakistan. See N. A. Baloch: *Musical Instruments of the Lower Indus Valley of Sind* (Hyderabad, 1966).

Mugo. Korean court dance, or occasionally the drum played by the dancers in the course of their dance. *See* Kyobanggo.

Mugole. Spike fiddle of the Chewa people of Mozambique.

Mugungu. Cylindrical Slit-drum of the Bali people of north-eastern Zaïre. It is 50 to 150 cm long and 30 to 100 cm in diameter (*LaurentyTF,* 134). *See* Gugu, (1).

Muhambi. Xylophone of the Tswa people of Mozambique. Very similar to the Mbila of the neighbouring Chopi, the *muhambi* is an equi-heptatonic fixed-key instrument with individual gourd resonators and membrane buzzers. It has lighter keys and beaters than Chopi counterparts, resulting in a different tone quality. The *muhambi* is played by adults, mostly in groups of three instruments of different pitch, accompanied by dancers, singers and three drums of different size in the *ndzumba* dance, a suite of three or four contrasting movements, which often include elements of drama or mime. The style is related to that of the Chopi but is freer in form, and includes more improvisation and use of parallel octave part movement. This simpler type of performance may well be the original from which the Chopi developed their complex orchestral style; it is comparable with the Chopi boys' *ngalanga* dance. Xylophones made by the Tswa are bought and played by neighbouring peoples, the Tsonga and the Ndau-Shanga, who adapt their own musical styles to it.

ANDREW TRACEY

Muhonyu. JEW'S HARP of the Orok people of Siberia. It is played mainly by women, often to imitate natural sounds such as animal cries and the sound of wind and rain, or as a courting instrument.

Muhurī. A medieval Indian name for oboes. *See* MAHVARĪ.

Mujemba. LAMELLAPHONE of the Dilolo region of Zaïre (*LaurentyS*, 195). *See* KAKOLONDONDO.

Mujinji. Single-headed GOBLET DRUM of the Valley Tonga people of Zambia. *See* NGOMA.

Mujwiz. Term occasionally applied to a DOUBLE CLARINET of the Arab world. *See also* MIJWIZ.

Mukáada ya mukáanda. Side-blown animal-horn trumpet of the Soka people of western Zaïre (*LaurentyA*, 328).

Mukanda [butanda]. Drum used at initiation dances of the Luba-Shankadi people of Zaïre (*BooneT*, 57).

Mukassi [mukazzi]. NOTCHED FLUTE of the Masaba (Gisu) people of eastern Uganda. *See* KHUMULELE.

Mukelo [mukazu]. *See* MUKUPIELA.

Mukhavīnā. Short oboe of southern India. Currently, *mukhavīnā* carries both a general and a more specific meaning: Deva (1966) has used it to identify the large family of double-reed aerophones found in the subcontinent, of which the Karnatic (south Indian) NĀGASVARAM, the Hindustani (north Indian) ŚAHNĀĪ and the *sanāī* and *sundrī* from Maharashtra, together with various folk instruments, are examples. *Mukhavīnā* also identifies a diminutive *nāgasvaram*, a short conical double-reed aerophone of approximately 35 cm found in south India.

According to Sambamoorthy (1955), a bagpipe known as *śruti upaṅga* provides the drone for the south Indian *mukhavīnā*. It is accompanied by the *mṛdaṅgam* (double-headed drum) or by the *ḍhankī* (a type of kettledrum), and its sound is evidently more subdued than that of many other double-reed aerophones.

The *mukhavīnā* was once used to accompany dance (*see* CINNA MEḺAM): traditional gifts would be presented to the *mukhavīnā* musicians when they visited and played at the homes of various patrons during special festivals such as Dīpāvali and Pongal. Apparently quite rare today, the *mukhavīnā* is reputedly also associated with Vaiṣṇava temples, and with a large ensemble of instruments known as *sarvavādyam*, which, together with dancers and vocalists, performs an elaborate religious ceremony.

The term appears in written sources from the 12th or 13th century AD onwards. Because of its broad connotation it is difficult to know which aerophone is being indicated unless a description is included.

See also MAHVARĪ.

BIBLIOGRAPHY
P. Sambamoorthy: *Catalogue of Musical Instruments Exhibited in the Government Museum, Madras* (Madras, 2/1955), 19f
——: *South Indian Music*, v (2/1963), 215f
B. C. Deva: 'Mukhavina', *Indian Music Journal*, vi (Oct–Nov 1966), 41f

REIS FLORA

Mukkuri [mukkuna]. Idioglot JEW'S HARP of the Ainu people of northern Japan. It is about 15 cm long, 1 to 1·5 cm wide and 2 to 5 mm thick. It is usually made from a single piece of bamboo. The tongue has a short length of string attached through a hole at its base and tied at the other end to a short stick which the player jerks with the right hand. The *mukkuri* was once played by both sexes for courting and dancing, but today it is chiefly played by women. The repertory consists mostly of short improvised pieces of a programmatic nature ('Rain', 'Mother crying for her lost child'). *Mukkuri* is the Hokkaido Ainu name; the Sakhalin Ainu called it *mukkuna*, and their neighbours the Orok had a jew's harp named *muhonyu*.

BIBLIOGRAPHY
Nihon Hōsō Kyōkai [Japan Broadcasting Corporation], ed.: *Ainu dentō ongaku* [Traditional Ainu music] (Tokyo, 1965)
F. Koizumi, Y. Tokumaru and O. Yamaguchi, eds.: *Asian Musics in an Asian Perspective* (Tokyo, 1977), 201

DAVID W. HUGHES

Mukoko. General name for a small wooden SLIT-DRUM, with carved anthropomorphic extension, of the Yaka, Suku, Pende, Ngongo and Mbala peoples of the Bas-Zaïre and Kwango areas of Zaïre. The drum belongs to local doctors and diviners who attempt to contact spirits with it and request answers to the questions of their clients. As a two-toned instrument, the aspect of 'talking' and 'giving a message' is predominant. The slit-drum usually consists of a cylindrical soundbox with a sculpted head as the handle; this head symbolizes the spirit. Other names reported by Laurenty (*LaurentyTF*, 136) for this type of instrument among other peoples of Zaïre are: *mukok*, *mukokk* or *kokk* (Holo), *mukoko dia ngombó* (Pende), and *mukokok* (Suku).

J. GANSEMANS

Mukonzi. Small crescent-shaped wooden SLIT-DRUM of the Bembe people of Zaïre. It is played in pairs and is associated with religious and magical practices. One drum of the pair is called *mukonzi ma lembe*, the other *mukonzi wa banganga* (*LaurentyTF*, 136f).

Mukuiti. FRICTION DRUM of the Lari people of the Republic of the Congo. It consists of an open wooden cylinder with one skin; a wooden stick is firmly attached to the centre of the skin. It is played by moistening the right hand, which is then drawn along the stick, tension being adjusted by pressure on the skin with the left hand. The sound is said to resemble the roaring of an animal. The friction drum player also wears on his wrist an *nsakala* spherical rattle, made from fruit husks containing seeds. *See also* MOANA-NGOMA.

Mukundu. Single-headed open-ended conical drum of the Luvale/Chokwe people of Vila Luzo district, Angola. *See also* IYASHINA.

Mukupiela [mukupela, mukazu, mukelo, mukupel, mukupila]. Short, squat double-headed drum of the Chokwe and other peoples of Zaïre. It has a modified hourglass shape, in which the waist is almost as broad as the ends and the parts of the body above and below it curve outward, then inward, to the skins, which are nailed in place. Most drums are 40 to 50 cm long. Among the Chokwe, the drum, known as *mukupiela*, is played in a horizontal position, and is beaten with the hands to provide additional rhythm to ensembles in which the lead is taken by the *tshingufu* slit-drum. Among the Bakwa, Songo, Mbala, Suku and Yaka peoples this instrument is known as *mukupela* or *mukupila*, while the Sandoa call it *dikubila*, the Sampwe *mukelo* and the Luluwa *kadia m'buji*; the Mbala drum was traditionally used to announce the arrival of a chief. Among the Lunda, the drum, known as *mukupel*, is part of the court orchestra of the emperor; one of the skins has a rubber tuning patch. For the Chokwe drum in Angola *see* MUCUPELA.

BIBLIOGRAPHY
BooneT, 17, 55f, 88f
F.J. de Hen: *Beitrag zur Kenntnis der Musikinstrumente aus Belgisch Kongo und Ruanda-Urundi* (Tervuren, 1960)
B. Schmidt-Wrenger: *Muziek van de Tshokwe uit Zaïre* (Tervuren, 1975)
K. A. GOURLAY

Mukwamya. *See* MAQWĀMIYĀ.

Mukwanga. SCRAPER of the Suku people of Zaïre. *See* BOYEKE.

Mukwéku. Wooden cone flute, with one or two stops, of the Kete people of Zaïre (*LaurentyA*, 132).

Múla. A drum used to accompany the *djuka* (war dance) of the Afro-Cubans. It has cowhide heads, permanently fastened with nails, and is about 1·8 metres long. It is played in a horizontal position, with the player seated astride the instrument. Three drums accompany the war dance. Sometimes all three are referred to as 'múla', but other commentators use three different names: *cachímbo*, *múla* and *akadjá*. See H. Courlander: 'Musical Instruments of Cuba', *MQ*, xxviii (1942), 227.

Mulai. Double basket rattle of the Lozi and Valley Tonga peoples of Zambia.

Mulanji. Transverse flute of the Ndau people of Sipungabera district, Mozambique. It is closed at both ends and has two finger-holes.

Mulapamu. Loosely strung iron rattles of the Jola people of Senegal and the Gambia. They are used as rhythmic accompaniment to women's songs.

Mulavu. The old south Indian Tamil name for a clay pot drum, with a narrow neck covered with skin, found in texts of the 1st millennium AD. It was sounded as a ceremonial instrument together with the *cankam* (conch) and *kombu* (trumpet), and presented as a prize by the king to warriors; it also appeared in the dance orchestra. *See also* MILĀVU.

BIBLIOGRAPHY
S. Ramanathan: *Music in Cilapatikaaram* (diss., Wesleyan U., Middletown, Conn., 1974)
ALASTAIR DICK

Mulele. NOTCHED FLUTE of Kenya.

Mulemba [quinjengue]. An African drum used with other instruments to accompany the Brazilian *batuque* dance. It has a funnel shape and a relatively high pitch.

Mulere. NOTCHED FLUTE of Uganda. *See* NDERE (i).

Muli. *See* MURALĪ.

Mulimba. Trapezoidal drum of the Holoholo people of Zaïre (*LaurentyTF*, 139).

Mulita. Term for a small fretted lute of Argentina. *See* CHARANGO.

Mulizi. Short NOTCHED FLUTE with two finger-holes, of the Shi people of Zaïre, played primarily by cattle-herders.

Mullaikulal. Ancient transverse flute of India. *See* KULAL.

Muller. *See* MALER family.

Müller, Carl August (*b* Adorf, 11 Jan 1804; *d* Mainz, 27 Jan 1870). German brass instrument maker. He founded his firm in Mainz, probably in 1824, producing instruments until at least 1859. He also made instruments for the firm of B. Schott of Mainz from 1830. Müller was in the forefront of the development of the early 19th-century brass instrument mechanisms. His keyed G trumpets (five or six keys) were finely crafted, but he was also very active in producing valved horns, cornets and trumpets (*see* TRUMPET, fig.7g). These instruments were normally fitted with double piston valves following Stölzel, but rotary valves are also found on some instruments. He fitted three valves instead of the then more normal two.

BIBLIOGRAPHY
L. G. Langwill: *An Index of Musical Wind-instrument Makers* (Edinburgh, 1960, rev., enlarged 6/1980)
H. Heyde: *Trompeten Posaunen Tuben* (Leipzig, 1980)
NIALL O'LOUGHLIN

Müller, Christian [Christiaan] (*b* Andreasberg, Harz, Feb 1690; buried Amsterdam, 8 March 1763). German organ builder. He was active in Holland and West Frisia, and is best known for his large organ in the Grote Kerk (St Bavo) in Haarlem (1735–8; three manuals, 60 stops; *see* ORGAN, fig.44; restored 1959–61), which G. J. Vogler compared with the instrument in Gouda by JACOBUS FRANCISCUS MOREAU. Müller also built organs in Alkmaar, Amsterdam, Beverwijk, Leeuwarden and elsewhere. The materials and workmanship of Müller organs are of high quality, but their scalings are relatively unimaginative (all the diapasons in Alkmaar, Beverwijk and Haarlem have exactly the same proportions). Müller's production was carried on by his pupil Johann Heinrich Hartmann Bätz (1709–70), from Frankenroda in Thuringia; Bätz's most important work is in Zierikzee (1770).

BIBLIOGRAPHY
H. L. Oussoren: 'De orgelbouwer Christiaan Müller en zijn werk', *Prospectus van het Haarlemmer orgelconcours in 1959*, 8
——: 'Het Christian Müller-orgel in de Grote St. Bavokerk te Haarlem', *Nederlandse orgelpracht*, ed. J. F. Obermayr and others (Haarlem, 1961), 38–85
HANS KLOTZ

Müller, Iwan (*b* Reval [now Tallinn], Estonia, 3 Dec 1786; *d* Bückeburg, 4 Feb 1854). German inventor, clarinettist and basset-horn player. In 1808 he produced an 18-key basset-horn, and in 1809 a prototype clarinet of the class now known as 'simple system'. The clarinet had 13 keys, seven of which were new, and gave much better intonation through more carefully placed holes. Müller was the first to use stuffed pads over countersunk tone-holes, and in 1817 invented the metal ligature. Early in his career he added three keys to the bassoon, which he played at that time, and later claimed the invention of the alto clarinet. Müller was no less energetic as a performer; his 'carrière agitée', as Fétis called it, took him to all major European cities. Wherever he went he advertised his new clarinet, and his success as an artist inspired composers to write specifically for it.

BIBLIOGRAPHY
FétisB
W. Tenney: 'Ivan Mueller and his New Clarinet', Woodwind Magazine, iii (1951)
F. G. Rendall: The Clarinet (London, 1954, 3/1971)
A. Baines: Woodwind Instruments and their History (London, 1957, 3/1967)
O. Kroll: Die Klarinette (Kassel, 1965; Eng. trans., enlarged, 1968)
P. Weston: Clarinet Virtuosi of the Past (London, 1971)
PAMELA WESTON

Müller, Johann Patroklus. See MÖLLER, JOHANN PATROKLUS.

Muller, Louis (b c1835; d ?Lyons, 1867). French wind instrument maker. He worked in Lyons with his uncle François Sautermeister, and succeeded him in 1830. In 1835 he produced a three-piston cornet (unusual for the time) with an enlarged bore and in 1838 made a horn with two valves operated by small knobs. He also made a bass clarinet (1846) with two parallel tubes like a bassoon, which it was intended to replace as it could descend to C, and a clarinet with 14 keys and four rings. He gained an honourable mention at the Great Exhibition in London in 1851 and a second class medal at the Paris Exhibition of 1855. In the same year he invented the 'Mullerphone', a double-bass clarinet which had parallel tubes (part conical, part cylindrical), a brass bell and unusual key layout. On his death the business was sold to Jean Léon Cousin. Surviving instruments include oboe, clarinets, bass clarinet, bass-horn, cornet, horn and ophicleide.

BIBLIOGRAPHY
L. A. de Pontécoulant: Organographie (Paris, 1861/R1973)
C. Pierre: Les facteurs d'instruments de musique (Paris, 1893/R1971)
L. G. Langwill: An Index of Musical Wind-instrument Makers (Edinburgh, 1960, rev., enlarged 6/1980)
NIALL O'LOUGHLIN

Müller, Matthias (b Wernborn or Frankfurt, 24 Feb 1769; d Vienna, 26 Dec 1844). German piano maker. He is best remembered as an inventor of the UPRIGHT PIANOFORTE. He brought out his model under the name 'Ditanaklasis' in Vienna in 1800, the same year that JOHN ISAAC HAWKINS independently patented his version in Philadelphia and London. Müller's Ditanaklasis was a mere 107 cm high with a compass of F' to C'''' and knee-levers for raising the dampers and softening the tone. The action is an ingenious adaptation of the Viennese grand action and foreshadows the tape-check principle invented by Herman Lichtenthal in 1832 and patented by Robert Wornum in 1842; this mechanism is still in use in modern upright piano actions. In addition to producing improved versions of his Ditanaklasis upright instrument, Müller, an inventive and innovatory piano maker in ultra-conservative Vienna, brought out a 'Gabel-Harmon-Pianoforte', patented in 1827; this was single-strung but made use of hoop-like tuning-forks tuned to

the proper pitch of the strings. This was designed to give them additional resonance and facilitated tuning the strings. In 1829 he was awarded a patent for an iron frame connected with the wrest-pin block by a suspension bar of iron.

BIBLIOGRAPHY
R. E. M. Harding: The Piano-forte: its History Traced to the Great Exhibition of 1851 (Cambridge, 1933, rev. 2/1978)
F. J. Hirt: Meisterwerke des Klavierbaus (Olten, 1955; Eng. trans., 1968, 2/1981)
HOWARD SCHOTT

Mullerphone. A double-bass clarinet invented by LOUIS MULLER in 1855.

Mulodi. Transverse flute with three finger-holes (positioned close to the distal end), of the Lamba people of Zaïre (LaurentyA, 286).

Multiflûte. A metal flute patented by Ullmann of Paris in 1896 and made there by Atlas. It had three interchangeable mouthpieces which allowed it to be played as recorder, transverse flute or flageolet.

Multimonica. A hybrid two-manual organ which is a combination of a reed organ and a piano attachment; it was developed by Siegfried Mager in 1948 and manufactured by Hohner in Trossingen from 1951 (now discontinued). It has two 41-note manuals (in Multimonica II the range is F to a'', in Multimonica III C to e''); the upper, electronic one is monophonic; the lower, reed organ manual has an electrically operated wind supply. The volume of each manual is controlled by an independent knee-lever. Early models incorporated a radio receiver.

HUGH DAVIES

Multiple flute. Term for a DUCT FLUTE with more than one pipe blown simultaneously. The pairing or grouping of duct flutes goes back to antiquity. Earthenware double pipes have been found in Mexico, the two pipes not necessarily being of equal length, and normally having differently placed finger-holes. Triple and quadruple flutes go back to the Teotihuacán culture of Mexico (about AD 500) and quintuple bamboo flutes are still in use among the Caingua Indians of Paraguay (where they are played by women). Some such instruments, for example the Tibetan gling-bu, show the finger-holes identically placed on each pipe; others show considerable divergence, including the Baluchistani doneli, where the melodic flute, on the right, has seven holes and the drone flute, on the left, has eight. The dvojnice of Hercevogina (which takes various names in other parts of Yugoslavia) is made of two divergent pipes, from the same piece of wood, and has different numbers of finger-holes on the tubes. The Indian satārā was also a melody-cum-drone instrument, but it and its successor the algōjā are both played melodically. Clay pipes are found as well as wooden ones, mostly from ancient Mexico.
See also FLAGEOLET.

Multiple stopping. Whereas a single stopped string on any string instrument produces one note, fingers can be pressed down on two, three or four strings to produce double, triple or quadruple stops, that is, multiple stops. The technique of multiple stopping was well known among viol players, as can be seen in such treatises as Ganassi's Regola rubertina (1535), Christopher Simpson's Division Viol (1659) and Mersenne's Harmonie *universelle* (1636). Three- and four-note chords were, however, arpeggiated, the curvature of the early bow making difficult the playing of three or four notes simultaneously except possibly in the case of the LIRONE, whose bridge was low and flat. Double-stop techniques were well developed.

The music of the violin family was very simple until virtuoso technique was demanded by Biagio Marini in his sonatas for violin, op.8 (1626–9). In the fourth sonata, 'per sonar con due corde', double stops occur in a complex contrapuntal section. The second sonata uses 'scordatura' for the first time in violin music; this technique was later developed by Biber (1644–1704), who added more difficult and even some impossible multiple stops, playable only by the employment of scordatura. Open strings are often used. The peak of artistic perfection in the use of multiple stops was reached by Bach in his suites for solo cello and in the sonatas and partitas for solo violin.

In general, the Germans and Bohemians of the late 17th and early 18th centuries were more fascinated by multiple stops than virtuosos of other countries, but the sonatas of J.-M. Leclair (1697–1764), who worked primarily in Paris, are full of octaves and 10ths as well as the more usual 3rds and 6ths. As for Italy, Corelli's sonatas op.5 employ multiple stops as a normal part of violin technique, and in the next generation Paganini achieved a brilliance in their performance probably unsurpassed to this day.

Many difficulties arise in the reading of multiple stops in 17th- and 18th-century violin literature: what is written by the composer is often musically neither possible nor even desirable to play; it is therefore to be assumed that what is written is not what the composer expected to hear. For example, parts often indicate sustained three- and four-note chords: it is left to the performer's discretion to interpret the notation according to the performing practice of the time, and to sustain what is feasible both technically and musically. In Baroque music the word 'arpeggio' appears frequently; in other cases the performer must arpeggiate even without instruction, as in the Chaconne of Bach's second Partita for solo violin. In most cases the strings are stopped as for simultaneously sounding multiple stops, although the notes sound contiguously. Geminiani, in *The Art of Playing on the Violin* (1751), gave 18 ways of arpeggiating a chord progression.

Around 1780 the Tourte bow revolutionized the technique of the violin family by allowing a larger and more sustained tone and stronger accents; three-note chords could more easily and naturally be played simultaneously. The cello method of Louis Duport (Paris, *c*1810) set the technical norm for modern cello playing, specifically treating the subject of double stops which had been largely neglected in methods until then. In 1834 *L'art du violon* by Pierre Baillot standardized the practice of double-stop scales for the violin.

In the 20th century the methods of Auer, Flesch, Dotzauer and Piatti are standard texts for string players wishing to practise double stops. In the music of the present century difficult multiple stops are common. Bartók, for example, wrote minor 9ths just as Paganini used octaves, and Schoenberg delighted in combinations of false and natural harmonics.

See also Bow, §II, 2(x) and 3(xii).

BIBLIOGRAPHY

F. Geminiani: *The Art of Playing on the Violin* (London, 1751/ *R*1952 with introduction by D. Boyden)

T.-J. Tarade: *Traité du violon* (Paris, 1774/*R*1972)
J. L. Duport: *Essai sur le doigté du violoncelle, et sur la conduite de l'archet* (Paris, *c*1810)
P. Baillot: *L'art du violin* (Paris, 1834)
D. Boyden: *The History of Violin Playing from its Origins to 1761* (London, 1965)
——: 'Violinspiel', *MGG*

SONYA MONOSOFF

Mululi [mtorilo]. Flute of the Shambala people of Tanzania. The term refers both to an open tube improvised from plant stalk by cattle herders and to an ornamented transverse flute, usually of bamboo.

Mulumba musseli. Single-headed tubular drum of the Bakwiri people of Cameroon. *See* LITEMBE.

Mulundu chigabana. End-blown trumpet of central Africa. *See* NYELE.

Mumamba. LAMELLAPHONE of the Bemba people of Zambia.

Mumbiki wa ngoma. Single-headed drum of the Pende people of Zaïre. *See* DITUMBA.

Mumboma [tambor mumboma]. Afro-Cuban SLIT-DRUM formerly used by the Congo Mumboma people, of Havana. It consisted of a straight cedar pole, some 25 cm in diameter and some 150 cm tall, placed vertically on the ground. Running nearly its full length was a split about 5 cm wide and the centre was hollowed out. A small figure, said to be a personification of the spirit of the drum, was sculpted at the top of the pole. The body of the drum was struck with two sticks and it was played in ensemble with two other headed drums. The *mumboma* disappeared from Havana at the end of the 19th century. See *OrtizIMA*, iii, 38, 143ff.

JOHN M. SCHECHTER

Muncang [munchang]. *See* MURCANG.

Mundam. Small FRAME DRUM of the Payakumbuh area of Minangkabau, West Sumatra. Its diameter is about 17 cm. It is used in the *talipuak layu* dance.

Mundharmonika (Ger.). HARMONICA (i); *see also* MOUTH ORGAN.

Mundóndòlò. Wooden cone flute, with one or two stops, of the Pende people of south-western Zaïre (*LaurentyA*, 153).

Mundstück (Ger.). MOUTHPIECE.

Mundzika. (1) Spindle-shaped stopped flute of the Uele people of Zaïre (*LaurentyA*, 183).

(2) Wooden VESSEL FLUTE of the Binja people of Zaïre (*LaurentyA*, 220).

Mung [mong]. Small gong of Kelantan, West Malaysia. It is of indefinite pitch, has a central boss and sloping sides and is made of bronze or an alloy of copper, tin and iron. Its diameter is about 18 cm and its depth about 13 cm. It is played suspended horizontally, boss upwards, in a low wooden frame by cords threaded through four holes (two in each side); sometimes it is simply placed on the ground. It may be played singly, in twos or in fours (in which case the gongs are often arranged in a square). The small wooden beater – *paluan mung* (*mong*) – has a head bound with several thicknesses of rubber. The *mung* is a member of the instrumental ensembles used to accompany the *wayang kulit* (shadow-puppet theatre) and folkdances.

JACK PERCIVAL BAKER DOBBS

Mungiri. Metal bell of the Gishu people of Mbale district, Uganda. The bells are attached to the legs of dancers. *See also* KENGELE.

Mungongo. Common term for the mouth-resonated MUSICAL BOW among the Sangu and other peoples of Gabon. The player strikes the string with a stick in one hand, while varying the vibrating length with a stick in the other.

Mungubire. Large double-headed cylindrical drum of the Vira people of Zaïre (*BooneT*, 64f).

Mungungi. Single-headed drum used for dancing by the Mbala and Suku peoples of Zaïre (*BooneT*, 50).

Mungungu. SLIT-DRUM of the Lengola people of Zaïre. *See* GUGU, (1).

Mungwin. Conical drum of the Mbun people of Zaïre. *See* MUSHITS.

Munjeīra. Syrian term for an oblique rim-blown flute. *See* NĀY.

Munsenkele [musenkele]. Footed drum of the Sanga people of Zaïre (*BooneT*, 14, 60). *See* DITUMBA.

Munter (Ger.: 'merry', 'cheerful', 'brisk', 'vigorous'). Perhaps the nearest German equivalent of the Italian ALLEGRO. Schumann used it twice in *Album für die Jugend* op.68: the 'Soldatenmarsch' is marked *munter und straff* with the translation *gaio e deciso*, and 'Fröhlicher Landmann' has *frisch und munter*, translated *animato e grazioso*. It is otherwise relatively rare. *See also* TEMPO AND EXPRESSION MARKS.

Muntshintshi. Large footed drum of the Tsonga people of south-eastern Africa resembling the Venda *ngoma*. It was formerly used for signalling and in the *nkino* dance, when it was accompanied by the smaller *shikolombane* drum and the *bunanga* trumpet ensemble. See *KirbyMISA*, 40f.

Muntundu. Single-headed GOBLET DRUM of the Valley Tonga people of Zambia. *See also* NGOMA.

Munugi. Small HOURGLASS DRUM of the Nupe people of Nigeria. *See* KALANGU.

Munyanga. Rattle of the Luba people of Zaïre. It is made from a stick to which are attached one or more dried fruits, *kisangu*, filled with seeds. This instrument is closely associated with the magical practices of doctors and diviners who use it to call upon their protecting spirits or to drive away evil spirits from the sick.

BIBLIOGRAPHY

F. J. de Hen: *Beitrag zur Kenntnis der Musikinstrumente aus Belgisch Kongo und Ruanda-Urundi* (Tervuren, 1960)

G. Knosp: *Enquête sur la vie musicale au Congo belge 1934–1935* (Tervuren, 1968)

J. Gansemans: *Les instruments de musique Luba* (Tervuren, 1980)

J. GANSEMANS

Muồng. Metal spoons of southern Vietnam. The player holds the handles of two stainless steel spoons in the palm of one hand; he squeezes his forefinger between the two handles to act as a lever, separating the two concave surfaces of the spoons by about 2 mm. Several techniques exist: hitting the knee; scraping along two, three, four or five fingers of the left hand; and running the spoons along the left arm, the bony parts of the hand, the two knees, against the chin or on the mouth (in this case the mouth serving as a resonator, allowing pitch variation by adjustments of the mouth cavity).

TRẦN QUANG HẢI

Mupimpi. Single-headed drum of the Songola people of Zaïre (*BooneT*, 64).

Muqin. Chinese XYLOPHONE. *See* MOKKIN.

Muracu. The old south Indian Tamil name for a large cylindrical drum of state, sacred to kings, in texts of the 1st millennium AD. It was kept in the palace on its own cot and carried out on an elephant to announce proclamations, battle and the dawn. Its sound is compared to thunder. The Sanskrit *muraja* derived from the name.

BIBLIOGRAPHY

S. Ramanathan: *Music in Cilapatikaaram* (diss., Wesleyan U., Middletown, Conn., 1974)

ALASTAIR DICK

Muraja. A medieval Sanskrit name for a drum derived from MURACU. *See also* MṚDANGA, esp. introduction and §1(i).

Muralī [murlā, murlī, muli]. Term for various aerophones of India. (1) Transverse flute. The historical *muralī*, referred to since the times of classical Sanskrit literature (from the early centuries AD), appears to be a synonym of VAṂŚA, denoting a side-blown flute with finger-holes, generally of bamboo. Medieval sources, however, describe it as very large, two *hasta* (cubits) or more in length (i.e. more than 90 cm), and with four finger-holes. The name is important as denoting the flute as one of the main iconographic attributes of the great god Krishna, who is often called *muralīdhara* ('he who holds the flute'; for illustration *see* AKHĀṚĀ), and in this sense appears in many poetic and song texts up to modern times (including the diminutive *muraliyā* in Hindi). In common north Indian usage, however, the name is now rarely used, and does not denote a particular type.

(2) The *muralī* played by the Rawat shepherds of Raipur district, Madhya Pradesh, central India, is a side-blown double DUCT FLUTE. A bamboo pipe, 95 cm long, is divided into two equal parts by two interior plugs inserted on either side of the central bi-partite mouthhole; each part has an air duct (see fig.1). These plug-and-duct devices are similar to those on the Rawat flutes BĀSI and BĀSURI. The melody pipe has five finger-holes; it is blown simultaneously with the drone pipe, the instrument being held transversely.

1. Muralī (side-blown double duct flute) of Raipur district, Madhya Pradesh: detail showing central bi-partite mouth-hole and the two air duct devices

2. Muralī (double clarinet) of the Suraniya Langa, west Rajasthan

(3) The term 'murlī' is used by the Muṇḍāri and Nāgpuri people of southern Bihar to denote an end-blown NOTCHED FLUTE of thick bamboo about 20 to 30 cm long, with five to seven finger-holes and an optional thumb-hole. It is played by both tribal and non-tribal musicians. The word may vary slightly among other communities; among the Uraon tribe, for instance, it is known as muli.

(4) In the folk culture of the north-western areas of the subcontinent – Pakistan, Gujarat, Rajasthan – the term muralī or murlā denotes a DOUBLE CLARINET with wind cap. The Rajasthani muralī, around 62 cm long, comprises three parts: a wooden blowing-tube; an oblong reservoir, of wood or gourd; and two pipes of cylindrical bore, glued together, whose upper ends are fitted with a single beating reed and inserted inside the wind cap (see fig.2). The melody pipe has six holes and the drone three. The technique of continuous breathing (nāksãsī) permits an uninterrupted sound.

This clarinet is one of the instruments peculiar to the Suraniya Langa, a caste of professional musicians living in the desert regions of west Rajasthan, who play it solo, with rare virtuosity, accompanied by the sārindā (fiddle). It resembles the PŪNGĪ (the snake-charmers' instrument), but differences in construction give it a greater range, of over two octaves. The two types of instrument are designated in Rajasthan by different names: pūngī and muralī refer to the shape and size of the wind cap; and agore, mansuri and tanki to the register of the instrument. It is also called bīṇ, which lends it greater significance.

BIBLIOGRAPHY

Śārṅgadeva: Saṅgītaratnākara (13th century), ed. S. Subrahmanya Sastri, iii (Madras, 1951)
C. Sachs: Die Musikinstrumente Indiens und Indonesiens (Berlin and Leipzig, 1914, 2/1923), 158
C. Marcel-Dubois: Les instruments de musique de l'Inde ancienne (Paris, 1941)
K. S. Kothari: Indian Folk Musical Instruments (New Delhi, 1968), 63f
G. Dournon-Taurelle: 'Inde, Rajasthan: musiciens professionels populaires', OCR 81 [disc notes]
K. Kothari: Folk Musical Instruments of Rajasthan (Borunda, 1977)
B. C. Deva: Musical Instruments of India (Calcutta, 1978), 115f
ALASTAIR DICK (1), GENEVIÈVE DOURNON (2, 4), CAROL M. BABIRACKI (3)

Muranzi. Transverse flute of the Ndau (Shona) people of south-eastern Africa, resembling the Venda TSHITI-RINGO.

Murcang [murchang, morcang, mucang, muncang, mursing etc]. A South Asian term for the JEW'S HARP, usually metal and heteroglot. In north-western areas, such as Sind (Pakistan), it is usually called simply cang, this name (and perhaps the instrument) deriving from the chang of adjacent West and Central Asia, and meaning originally 'harp'. The common names of north India – morcang, murcang (Gujarat and Rajasthan), muncang (Kashmir) etc – appear to be compounded from this and the northern words muṅh ('mouth') and mũr ('head'). Further south (e.g. Tamil Nadu) the form mursing is found, perhaps understood as 'mouth-horn' (see ŚRṄGA). The names would thus suggest a southwards diffusion of the instrument from the north-west. It does not derive from a 'Sanskrit mucanga', as stated by Sachs (1914) and others, as this is not recorded in the ancient or medieval periods. In Nepal the variants murcuṅgā, machinga (among the Sunwar people), macuṅga (among the Rai), murjanga (among the Tamang) and kha-wang (among the Thakali) are found. The name can also be applied, however, to idioglot bamboo jew's harps, which are more often (and sometimes also the metal type) given local names (*see* GHORĀLIYAU and TENDOR). This type is common in the north-east (e.g. the GAGANĀ of the Garo people of Assam and the Khasi KĀ-MIEN), presumably related to the widespread South-east Asian types. Thus, as noted by Sachs, India lies at the boundary between the West Asian metal heteroglot type and the East Asian types, mainly idioglot. The Indian bamboo types, now rather rare, may have been the link.

The *murcang* type is common in folk music of many regions. In the south the *mursing* is also found in the rhythm ensemble *tālavādyakaccerī*.

BIBLIOGRAPHY

C. Sachs: *Die Musikinstrumente Indiens und Indonesiens* (Berlin and Leipzig, 1914, 2/1923)
G. Dournon-Taurelle and J. Wright: *Les guimbardes du Musée de l'Homme* (Paris, 1978)

ALASTAIR DICK

Muristus [Mūristus, Mīristus, Mūrtus]. Inventor of organ-like instruments. His name appears only in medieval Arabic sources and he has been inconclusively identified with CTESIBIUS of Alexandria (Farmer, 1931) and with various Greek writers. Two devices were attributed to him. One had 12 pipes, their valves operated in an unspecified fashion, and supplied with wind by the lung power of four men; the other was a primitive quasi-siren, with a hydraulic wind apparatus similar to that of the hydraulis, and therefore looked upon by some as its forerunner.

BIBLIOGRAPHY

H. G. Farmer: *The Organ of the Ancients: from Eastern Sources, Hebrew, Syriac and Arabic* (London, 1931), 16ff, 60ff, 127ff
J. Perrot: *L'orgue de ses origines hellénistiques à la fin du XIIIe siècle* (Paris, 1965; Eng. trans., adapted, 1971), 189ff

JAMES W. MC KINNON

Murjanga [mursing]. South Asian terms for the JEW'S HARP. *See* MURCANG.

Murlā [murlī]. *See* MURALĪ.

Mūrtus. *See* MURISTUS.

Muruas. Term occasionally applied to the MIRWĀS (double-headed drum) of the Arabian Gulf area.

Murumba (pl. *mirumba, mirumbu*). Long conical single-headed alto drum of the Venda people of southern Africa. It is carved from a single block of wood, and has an integral jug-like handle on one side. The head is pegged on, and the bottom is open. In performance, the drum is gripped between the thighs and is played with the hands; in music of the possession cult (*ngoma dza midzimu*) it is beaten with a stick. Players are always female. These drums are used, usually together with the larger *ngoma* and *thungwa* drums, to accompany dancing on occasions such as the *domba* girls' initiation ceremony (see illustration), and the sacred *tshikona* flute dance. The Tswana and Northern Sotho have a similar drum, known as MOROPA. See *KirbyMISA*, passim, esp. pll.10 and 13.

JOHN BLACKING, DAVID K. RYCROFT

Murumbi. Bowl drum of the Sena/Tonga people of Mtoko district, Zimbabwe.

Murup. SACRED FLUTES of the Monumbo people, Madang Province, Papua New Guinea. They are played on the completion of a chief's house, at initiation and after burial of men. See A. C. Haddon: 'Migration of Cultures in British New Guinea', *Journal of the Anthropological Institute of Great Britain and Ireland*, 1 (1920), 254.

Musasa. Wooden flute of the Teke pygmy people of Zaïre. It has a slender conical bore and is bound in animal skin (*LaurentyA*, 165).

Muscal. Old Romanian term, of Oriental origin, for the panpipes. *See* NAI (i).

Muse-au-sac. Bagpipe of Hainaut and east Flanders. *See* BAGPIPE, §6.

Domba initiation dance with mirumba (alto drums, left), ngoma (bass drum, centre) and thungwa (tenor drum, right) of the Venda people, southern Africa

Musebela. Double-headed drum played by royal musicians of the Bemba people of Zambia. It is struck by hand while suspended from the player's neck.

Muselar. A term used by Claas Douwes (*Grondig ondersoek van de toonen der musijk*, Franeker, 1699) and revived by modern writers to designate Flemish virginals which, having their keyboards placed off-centre to the right, consequently have strings that are centrally plucked for most of the instrument's range. This gives the muselar a distinctive flute-like tone of great beauty, quite unlike that produced by any of the registers of a harpsichord or by a virginal of any other design, and since the late 1960s several makers have constructed replicas of the 17th-century originals.

BIBLIOGRAPHY
G. Leonhardt: 'In Praise of Flemish Virginals of the Seventeenth Century', *Keyboard Instruments*, ed. E. M. Ripin (Edinburgh, 1971, 2/1977)

EDWIN M. RIPIN

Musémbu [musémb, muséng]. Wooden flute of Zaïre. Laurenty described the *musémbu* as a flute with slender conical bore of the Dinga and Mbagani peoples, and as a flute with one or two finger-holes of the Dinga. The *musémb* is listed as a flute with one or two finger-holes of the Mbala and *muséng* as a cone flute with one or two finger-holes of the Suku and Salampusu peoples of south-western Zaïre. The latter term may also refer to a cylindrical stopped wooden flute of the Suku people. See *LaurentyA*, passim.

Musengere. KAZOO of the Tonga/Hlanganu people of Bileni district, Mozambique. It is used, with European instruments, to imitate town dance music.

Musenkele. See MUNSENKELE.

Muserule. Cone whistle, made from animal horn, of Lango, Uganda. It is traditionally believed to have been worn by the founder of the Babito dynasty when he received messengers offering him the throne of Nyoro, and the instrument was kept in the throne-room of the *omukama* (ruler) of Nyoro. See *WachsmannTCU*.

Musesegeto. Reed-box rattle of the Konjo people of Uganda. See ENSEGU.

Musette (Fr.; It. *musetta*). (1) A small bagpipe, especially one of aristocratic design which achieved popularity in France in the 17th and early 18th centuries. Courtly ladies and gentlemen would perform in pastoral costume, and treatises were written describing the instrument, with instructions on how to play it and pieces in a special musette tablature (e.g. Borjon de Scellery's *Traité de la musette*, Lyons, 1672, and Jacques Hotteterre's *Méthode pour la musette*, Paris, 1737). Many compositions were written for the musette in the 1720s and 1730s. J. B. Boismortier's works include numerous pieces for one and two musettes, for musette combined with other instruments, and a collection of songs accompanied by musette. Other pieces are in works by J.-B. Anet, Jacques Hotteterre (op.8), J. P. Rameau, Montéclair, and in Henry Expert's edited collection *Amusements des musiciens français du XVIIIᵉ siècle*

Musette played by Gaspard de Gueidan: portrait (1737) by Hyacinthe Rigaud (Musée Granet, Aix-en-Provence)

(Paris, n.d.). For further details *see* BAGPIPE, §6.

(2) The 'musette de Poitou' of the 17th century was a simple bagpipe, and like the *biniou* of Brittany was accompanied by an 'hautbois de Poitou' (a bagless chanter played by another man), or by a consort of such instruments including a bass. The consort was described and illustrated by Mersenne (in *Harmonicorum libri XII*, 1648, 2/1652/R1972, bk5, §34) and is repeatedly mentioned in documents relating to musicians of the Grande Ecurie du Roi at Versailles, who included a group called Les Musettes et Hautbois de Poitou; among its members were Jean Hotteterre and later the flautist Michel de La Barre: see M. Benoit, *Musiques de cour* (Paris, 1971). The 'hautbois de Poitou' had a wooden reed-cap, shown in the frontispiece of C. E. Borjon's *Traité de la musette* (Lyons, 1672).

Woodwind instrument makers in Paris began in the 1830s to produce the small oboe without reed-cap which has since been called 'musette'. It supplied rural colour to the urban *bal musette* and was further popularized at concerts like those of L. A. Jullien, who himself performed on it in England in imitation of the Scottish bagpipe. Pitched a 5th above the oboe and 31 to 36 cm in length, it is made in two joints and has seven finger-holes, a thumb-hole and two vents in the bell. The reed is shaped like that of an oboe, but is a little smaller. Later a simple keywork was added, and such models, usually made of blackwood, were still offered for sale in the 1930s for domestic amusement, along with similarly constructed flageolets. Another type with a wider bore, modelled on the Breton bombarde, was introduced about the middle of the 19th century by Frédéric Triébert: it was named in advertisements 'hautbois pastorale', and subsequently even fitted with a keywork of the Boehm system.

(3) The BASSE DE MUSETTE, an obsolete basset oboe, was probably of Swiss 18th-century origin.

(4) An ORGAN STOP.

BIBLIOGRAPHY

J. G. Sulzer: *Allgemeine Theorie der schönen Künste*, iii (Leipzig, 1793), 780

E. de Bricqueville: *Les musettes* (Paris, 1894)

F. B. Lindemann: *Pastoral Instruments in French Baroque Music: Musette and Vielle* (diss., Columbia U., 1978)

ANTHONY C. BAINES

Musetten-Bass (Ger.). *See* BASSE DE MUSETTE.

Musezza. NOTCHED FLUTE of the Masaba (Gisu) people of eastern Uganda. *See* KHUMULELE.

Mushiba (pl. *mishiba*). PANPIPES of Zaïre.

Mushits. Drum of the Mbun people of Zaïre. Like other Mbun drums (*mungwin*, *mpetshanga* and *gwanbal*), it is distinctive in having a membrane fastened by a cord network to a leather securing ring which is itself nailed in place a little below the top of the casing. The drums have curving sides but are approximately conical in shape and taper to a narrow, elongated base. Most Mbun drums are between 109 and 119 cm high; the *mungwin*, however, is smaller (74 cm). Drums with a similar method of fixing the membrane are attributed to the Mbala and Pindi peoples as *ngomm* and to the Pende as *ngoma*.

BIBLIOGRAPHY

BooneT, 46

F.J. de Hen: *Beitrag zur Kenntnis der Musikinstrumente aus Belgisch Kongo und Ruanda-Urundi* (Tervuren, 1960)

K. A. GOURLAY

Mushondo. Single-headed conical drum of the Nika/Giryama people of Malindi district, Kenya. It is open-ended and the membrane is pinned on. It is played with the hands.

Mushtaq. Persian (Sassanid) panpipes. *See* PANPIPES, §1.

Mushyémm. Wooden cone flute, with one or two stops, of the Teke people of Zaïre (*LaurentyA*, 144).

Musica ficta (Lat.: 'false' or 'feigned music'). The term used loosely to describe accidentals added to sources of early music, by either the performer or the modern editor. More correctly it is used for notes that lie outside the predominantly diatonic theoretical gamut of medieval plainchant, whether written into the source or not. Although the term 'musica ficta' died out during the 16th century, the principle of adding accidentals in performance prevailed well into the following century.

1. Before *c*1500: (i) Introduction and early references (ii) Notation (iii) Theorists' rules (iv) Signatures (v) Tinctoris. 2. *c*1500 to *c*1600: (i) Notation (ii) Performing practice (iii) Contemporary theory and 'rules'. 3. After 1600.

1. BEFORE *c*1500.

(i) Introduction and early references. The terms 'musica ficta' and the synonymous 'musica falsa' (more common in the 13th century) were used by music theorists from the mid-13th century to denote chromatic notes alien to the hexachords that had formed the basis for musical instruction since they were first established by Guido of Arezzo in 1025–6. The hexachords built on *G*, *c* and *f* (and their upper octaves, *g*, *c'*, *f'*, *g'*) comprised the 'white' notes of the modern diatonic scale from *G* to *e''* with the addition of *b♭* and *b♭'*: these were defined as the hexachords of *musica vera* or *recta* (La Fage, Anonymous I) and the constituent pitches similarly as those of *musica vera* or *recta*. The internal arrangement in each hexachord was identical (tone–tone–semitone–tone–tone, identified by the syllables *ut–re–mi–fa–sol–la*), the main purpose of the system being to contain and demonstrate the position of the semitone. The singer moved up and down the overlapping hexachords as the music required, making transitions (known as mutations or *coniuncte*) on notes common to two hexachords, though never between the notes bounding the semitone step *mi–fa*. The application of *musica ficta* was considered part of the performer's art; this is why the terminology of singing teaching rather than that of speculative theory is used for most contemporary statements on the subject: some references also occur in vernacular writings of a non-technical nature. But as with so many other lost traditions of performance, the modern editor lacks sufficient evidence to enable him to make with confidence the decisions taken by medieval singers, especially when more than one solution may be possible in a given situation.

The system of solmization was originally designed for plainchant (which made little or no use of notes extraneous to the hexachords) and had to be extended to cope with the growing demands of polyphony. It was by transposing *recta* hexachords to alien pitches that semitone steps other than B–C, E–F, A–B♭ could take their place within the solmization system. The range of available *ficta* hexachords was increased and rationalized until, in the 1430s, Ugolino of Orvieto recognized a complete system of *ficta* hexachords whose sole purpose was to accommodate chromatic notes. Before it was adulterated by the extra demands of polyphony, the *recta* system as applied to plainchant was not incompatible with the modes, but the introduction of *ficta* notes led theorists from the 13th century onwards (e.g. Johannes de Grocheo) to repudiate the application of modes to polyphony; indeed, it was not until the late 15th and early 16th centuries (Tinctoris, Glarean) that serious attempts were made to assign polyphonic compositions to specific modes.

Even before Guido's hexachords were introduced, B♭ was recognized as part of the regular (*recta*) system of available notes. In addition, earlier theorists made allowance for chromatic alteration other than the alternative inflections of B, although the terms *musica ficta* or *falsa* were not used. The Enchiriadis treatises of about 900 give the earliest explicit and extensive theoretical account of chromatic alteration. The anonymous author of the *Scolica enchiriadis* defined *absonia* (elsewhere *dissonantia*) as the lowering or raising of a note from its normal pitch. The word *vitium* is used in this context and seems to imply no more than a disturbance of the normal scale, the force being very similar to that of the later *falsa* (the term *falsus sonus* in fact appears in this treatise; *GS*, i, 177). The *absonia* arises from faulty intonation (a 'vice' of the human voice to which instruments are less subject) or, more importantly, from the nature of the music, where it has the effect of transplanting or restoring the mode.

Using Daseian signs the author set up tetrachords (disjunctly, with a central semitone flanked by two tones) yielding the remarkable scale G–A–Bb–c–d–e–f–g–a–b♮–c'–d'–e'–f♯'–g'–a'–b♮'–c♯" (Spitta, Jacobsthal, Spiess). This is proposed in addition to the more normal scale, and is specially suited to organum at the 5th: the early use of such extreme chromatic notes seems to be connected with polyphony. For plainchant the author was more conservative but no less ingenious. He evolved a system of pentachords involving *recta* forms as well as the *absonia*. The pitches of eb and f♯ are introduced by changing the Daseian name on one note – in effect a mutation. By extending the tetrachord system to cover the legitimate transpositions of the pentachords with *absonie*, Jacobsthal further advanced the possibility that the Enchiriadis treatises also allow for c♯, g♯, d♯ and Ab.

Odo (10th century) also referred to the 'vice' of additional semitones outside the 'prefixed rule' (*GS*, i, 272) and cited chants in which bb, eb, c♯ and f♯ are required. The derivation of chromatic notes by modal transposition is clearly specified by some 11th-century theorists. Berno of Reichenau recognized transposition of modes up a 5th to make f and f♯ available, or up a 4th to produce e and eb in both cases transposing from b, for which both natural and flat forms are available (*GS*, ii, 75). Johannes Afflighemensis gave more detail but accepted transpositions only up a 5th and only for those modes (1–3) that would not thereby lose their identity (*GS*, ii, 248; ed. J. Smits van Waesberghe, p.101). He also provided for a process of 'emendation' in a few places where the notes can neither be sung at original pitch nor transposed. Odo allowed 'emendation' where necessary, that is, where the piece could not be sung in another mode. Such prescriptions already anticipate later warnings against using *ficta* when the situation could be corrected by other means. The usual reason given for melodic alterations to chant is the avoidance of the tritone. The development of a system of modal transpositions coincided with the rise of a clearer notation of fixed pitches which, however, had very little capacity as yet to cope with chromatic notes.

The first uses of the terms *falsa* or *ficta* are by the 13th-century theorists Johannes de Garlandia and Magister Lambertus. Johannes defined *musica falsa* as 'when we make a tone into a semitone and vice versa' (*CS*, i, 166), a definition later used by Philippe de Vitry (*CS*, iii, 26; see Reaney, Gilles and Maillard, p.22). Lambertus already showed dissatisfaction with the designation *falsa*, 'for it is necessary for achieving good consonance' (*CS*, i, 258); 'it is not so much false as unusual'. Jerome of Moravia equated it with the *synemmenon* (synonymous with *coniuncta*) and based his exposition not on hexachords but on tetrachords. Most other definitions of the 13th and 14th centuries repeat or only slightly vary these. Walter Odington wrote of 'movable solmization names' (*CS*, i, 216), Coussemaker's Anonymous II of 'false mutation, or *falsa musica*' (*CS*, i, 310). An anonymous treatise of 1375 (Crocker, 1967) rejects the terms *falsa* and *ficta*, preferring *coniuncta*, and defines the problem in terms of 'imaginary transposition' of hexachords.

Theorists were divided in opinion about the use of *ficta* in plainchant but those who declared themselves on the subject recognized the need for it in polyphony. Jacques de Liège asserted its importance in plainchant (*CS*, ii, 293ff); Jerome of Moravia, however, allowed it in polyphony but excluded it from plainchant (*CS*, i,

86). Johannes de Garlandia, in his treatise on plainchant and measured music, specified its use in polyphony ('organis'; *CS*, i, 166). Vitry also affirmed its role in polyphony as not false but true and necessary, because, he said, no motet or rondellus could be sung without it (*CS*, iii, 18; Reaney, Gilles and Maillard, p.23). The anonymous Paris theorist of the Berkeley Manuscript (who explicitly dealt with plainchant and specific categories of polyphony) exemplified the *coniuncta* from chant, contrary to 13th-century principles. The early 15th-century Anonymous XI (*CS*, iii, 429) said that *coniuncte* were necessary in both plainchant and polyphony.

(ii) Notation. The 13th-century theorists already mentioned also defined the signs for notating *musica ficta*. Johannes de Garlandia said each tone is divisible into two semitones, and these can be notated (*CS*, i, 166). Lambertus prescribed b and ♮ for the points at which mutations are to be made (*CS*, i, 258). Theorists up to and including Prosdocimus and Ugolino (first half of the 15th century) admitted only these two signs, to distinguish the soft and hard forms of B. The single exception is Marchetto (*c*1318), who used an obliquely written ♯ to distinguish the enharmonic semitone step (e.g. F–F♯) from the smaller semitone (e.g. F♯–G) which corresponds to *mi–fa* in solmization. Although scribes used either ♯ or ♮ for the 'hard' B, the distinction does not seem to have been meaningful. Not until Hothby (*d* 1487) are three possible positions, b, ♮ and ♯, distinguished for each degree of the scale. Nowhere in the period up to 1450 is there any direct theoretical admission that b lowers or that ♮ raises a note: ♮ simply denotes *mi* and b *fa* (that is, they indicate where the semitone lies in relation to the accidental). *Mi–fa* is always a minor semitone, a minor semitone always *mi–fa*. Consequently, in rare cases (Ugolino's treatise and some practical examples), one or other sign may be used to bring the adjoining note to within a semitone of the signed note and not vice versa. In other words, b placed on G may not affect the pitch of G but indicate that, since G is to be sung *fa*, *mi* should be a semitone below it on F♯. The presence of a b on F would not in any case lower its pitch. Occasionally the letters 'F', 'C' and 'G' are used instead of the b sign to indicate the 'soft' forms of those pitches.

Although a means of notation existed it was, for the reasons given above, neither complete nor watertight. There was no need to notate every occurrence of *mi* and *fa*, and in practice this meant that many notes that required chromatic inflection lack the sign – an accidental – that signals this inflection to the modern musician. In practice only a small proportion of the accidentals required in performance were actually notated, though the number indicated (and required) shows a steady increase during the period up to about 1400. The polyphonic and secular monophonic sources of the 13th century add F♯, C♯ and Eb to make distinctions parallel to that between Bb and B♮ found in plainchant sources. Theorists were reticent about omissions until the late 14th century, when the Paris treatise (now in *US-BE*) states that in practice one very rarely found the signs for *fa* and *mi* marked. Prosdocimus de Beldemandis, writing in his counterpoint treatise (*c*1410), addressed to composers rather than to singers, inveighed against the use of too much *musica ficta*. However, it is clear from his exposition and his examples that he envisaged many inflections, and it seems most likely that he was enjoining composers to leave the application of *musica ficta* to the singers, and perhaps also to avoid situations in which too much would be required. The 14th century saw a spectacular increase in marked accidentals until, around 1400, D♯, D♭, G♯, A♭ and G♭ are specifically notated and intended in certain sophisticated repertories such as those of the Chantilly and Old Hall Manuscripts. These were exceptional: some sources remained very sparing in their indications, and there is a general decline in the number indicated from about 1400 onwards.

The main reason for the incomplete provision of accidentals is, as explained above, that the signs were used to indicate solmization and only incidentally did they also indicate inflection. An important secondary reason is the medieval musician's reluctance to admit in theory or to notate in practice something that lay outside the regular, respectable system, although all theorists who discussed the matter acknowledged that it was necessary to good results. For both these reasons, the responsibility for providing the appropriate inflections rested with the performer and, today, rests with the modern editor, who acts on the medieval performer's behalf.

The cross-section of required accidentals that found its way on to the pages of medieval manuscripts includes pitches that fall within the system of *musica recta* as well as many that lie outside it. Additional accidentals required in performance similarly include both *recta* and *ficta* notes. It is therefore not possible to equate *musica ficta* simply with added accidentals. (In modern editions it is usual to distinguish editorial accidentals from those of the source by placing the former above the note, or in brackets, or in small type; with regard to the placing of editorial accidentals, see especially Anglès, 1954; Hewitt, 1942; Jeppesen, 1927; and Lowinsky, 1964 and 1967.)

The placing of accidentals in the sources is not without ambiguities. Some scribes placed the accidental near, above or below the affected note, without regard for the correct placing on the staff: this is particularly common in some late 14th- and early 15th-century Italian and south German sources. Other scribes placed the accidental well in advance of – or even after – the note to which it applied. In view of the close connection between the 'signs' of *musica ficta* and the practice of solmization, it may be that such pre-placing serves as a deliberate advance warning of mutation. Thus the progression *fa–mi* (between which no mutation can take place) is very often preceded, rather than divided, by the ♮ sign indicating *mi*. A consequence of this (solmization) function of an accidental sign is that it does not necessarily apply to more notes than the one to which it most directly refers. In some situations a larger context will be affected, but an accidental, written or not, may easily be overruled (for the sake of contrapuntal propriety) on subsequent appearances of the note.

(iii) Theorists' rules. This evidence of the musical sources, some at least of which were used by performers, is one of the twin foundations on which the performer's art of applying *musica ficta* can partly be reconstructed. For the performers will have applied certain principles which can partly be recovered from theorists, though oral tradition surely accounts for much that is now not known. The other foundation is the theoretical evidence. Since this is drawn largely from counterpoint treatises and takes the view of the composer rather than that of the performer, one of its main values is the light it casts on how the performers should

adjust to each other: many of the theoretical rules are given in terms of harmonic progressions in two parts (appropriate to the compositional principle of superimposed duets then current) rather than for isolated melodic lines. It is also worth noting that some of the most important clues occur not in separate chapters devoted to *musica ficta* but in general discussions of counterpoint.

Since rules for *ficta* are necessarily related to changes in musical style, it is particularly important not to project rules backwards to a period earlier than that in which they were formulated. Even in the writings of 13th-century theorists, both harmonic and melodic reasons for applying *musica ficta* are given. Johannes de Garlandia gave principally melodic rules, requiring 'leading notes' to be a semitone from their destination (*CS*, i, 115). Although the Enchiriadis treatises and other early writings forbid the melodic tritone, this prohibition no longer figures among 13th-century rules. Lambertus stated that the main purpose of *musica ficta* was to achieve perfect vertical consonances on 5ths, octaves and other perfect intervals (*CS*, i, 258): this clearly applies only to polyphony.

These principles are incorporated in the more fully developed expositions of the 14th century, of which that by Jehan des Murs is the fullest and clearest. His rules (*CS*, iii, 71–3) state that, for melodic progressions, lower returning notes (e.g. in the progression G–F–G) should be raised (G–F♯–G); and that leading notes approached by any other means (e.g. by leap) should be raised (e.g. D–F♯–G; this is also implied by the author of the *Quatuor principalia*, *CS*, iv, 250). His harmonic rules state that the sounding of *mi* against *fa* is forbidden in vertical perfect intervals (i.e. 5ths and octaves are to be perfect; this rule is ubiquitous in treatises); and that a perfect interval should be approached by the nearest imperfect interval – a major 3rd will expand to a 5th, a major 6th to an octave, a minor 3rd will contract to a unison, and so on; where one of the parts proceeds by step, this step will, in practice, be a semitone (see ex.1*a*; if both proceed by step, only one will be a semitone). Several theorists gave the important qualification to these rules that they should be effected where possible without resort to *musica ficta*: if the interval or progression can be corrected within the system of *musica recta*, this should be done (see Prosdocimus de Beldemandis, c1410, *CS*, iii, 196–9; Ugolino of Orvieto, c1435, *Declaratio*, ii, 45).

Ex.1

Whereas Jehan des Murs' examples invariably sharpen a leading note in the upper part, using *musica ficta*, one progression may be corrected within the *recta* system by flattening the lower note instead of sharpening the upper, thus placing the semitone step in the lower part (ex.1*b*). A further consequence of the second harmonic rule, applicable to most music up to 1450, is the 'double leading note cadence' in which ex.2*a* results from the superimposition of the legitimate two-part progressions exx.2*b* and 2*c*. (The 'correctness' of this progression has nothing to do with perfecting the vertical 4th, which was not at this period considered a perfect interval for purposes of counterpoint, despite its acoustical status.)

Theorists of the 13th to 15th centuries said surprisingly little about the melodic interval of the tritone. Prosdocimus's music examples make it clear that the leading note principle is to be observed even when the interval preceding the leading note step is forced thereby to be a tritone. An anonymous 15th-century theoretical fragment from Seville (Gallo, 1968) does state explicitly that melodic tritones should be avoided when they return within their own confines, that is, when they are not ancillary to a leading note. True chromatic progressions (e.g. F–F♯–G) are both allowed in theory (Marchetto, *GS*, iii, 82–3) and prescribed in manuscript sources.

In addition to giving rules in specific terms, theorists also expressed the reasons for using *ficta* in more metaphysical terms: for acquiring greater perfection, so that imperfect intervals may acquire some perfection by closer adhesion to perfect ones; for the 'colouring' of dissonances or imperfect intervals; and for the sake of sweeter harmony. From the earliest references in the 13th century onwards, the reasons are also classed as *causa necessitatis* ('by reason of necessity', which aligns with the perfection of vertical consonances) and *causa pulchritudinis* ('by reason of beauty', which corresponds to melodic reasons for chromatic alteration). (See also §2, iii below.)

(iv) Signatures. The phenomenon of 'key' signatures during this period is not illuminated by any of the theorists: at the same time it has proved to be one of the most provoking and controversial issues and has served as the starting-point for many of the most important recent discussions of early *ficta*. The signatures in question are almost always of flats, and the problem is that the number of flats indicated at the beginning of the staves very often differs between different voice-parts of the same piece, the lower part or parts having, usually, one flat more than the upper. From the top downwards, a three-part piece might have parts with signatures of –, –, B♭; –, B♭, B♭; B♭, B♭, B♭ and E♭; B♭, B♭ and E♭, B♭ and E♭. Apel claimed that these 'partial' signatures implied bitonality, the signatures having the modern significance of inflecting all notes written at that pitch level. Lowinsky on the other hand maintained that the basis of 'conflicting' signatures was mainly practical, the signature being omitted when no note of that pitch was required. Hoppin proposed, since the difference in signatures tends to represent pitch levels about a 5th apart, that modal transposition was involved. All these views assume that the signatures have a significance approximately equivalent to that of a modern key signature, affecting all notes at the written pitch of the accidental, perhaps also of its octave transpositions. The possibility remains, however, that they denote the transposition of hexachord systems, especially since hexachords rather than modes form the basis of medieval discussions of *ficta* in polyphony. If the hexachords on G, C and F are transposed one degree flatwards, in the case of a single flat in the signature the hexachords for that part will be on C, F and B♭, leaving two hexachords common to both a signatured and an unsignatured part, and thus a considerable range of *recta* notes, including B♭, which a simultaneous unsignatured part is perfectly free to use. Both parts are also free to add *ficta* where necessary, the naturalizing of B in a part with a flat signature being

no more serious than the sharpening of F in an unsignatured part. Such transpositions of the entire hexachord system seem to have been counted as transposed *recta*, transposition of isolated hexachords as *ficta*. Where there is a signature, the *recta* priorities are established for the duration of the signature, and the singer is free to use the normal hexachord relationships, applying rules and priorities within them. The distinction between applying chromatic alteration by means of transposition and by means of individual emendation does, after all, go back to the 11th-century theorists.

Many changes can be traced from the last quarter of the 15th century onwards. These are due to gradual changes in compositional technique and the approach to dissonance on the one hand, and on the other to attempts (coinciding with the effects of humanism on music theory) to change the theoretical basis of music, restoring the status of the modes (Tinctoris, Glarean) and superseding the old hexachord system by the octave (Ramos), together with fixed designations for ♭, ♮ and ♯ degrees (Hothby).

(v) Tinctoris. Important observations on accidentals are found in the writings of Tinctoris, though modern quotations of his remarks on this subject often fail to take account of the context in which he made them. In the 12 treatises that constitute his *summa* on the music of his time, written between about 1472 and about 1485, Tinctoris's highly systematic exposition of the concepts of gamut, hexachord system, mode and counterpoint are so ordered as to give only brief mention to those deviations occasioned by the needs of musical practice or by *ficta* elements outside the system. In his *Diffinitorium* (1472) Tinctoris gave a classic definition of *musica ficta* as being 'cantus praeter [not propter] regularem manus traditionem editus' ('a way of singing apart from the regular ordering of the [Guidonian] hand'); that the authentic reading is 'praeter' not 'propter' is explicitly clear from at least one authoritative manuscript source and was pointed out by Ambros (*Geschichte der Musik*, ii, 171).

The longest passage by Tinctoris on accidentals occurs in his treatise on the formation of the 'modes', or 'tones' as he called them, *Liber de natura et proprietate tonorum* (chap.8). He presented the modes as being the diverse linear products of the collocation of the several diatonic species of the perfect 4th and 5th. In this chapter, dealing with the 6th mode (the plagal form of the F mode), Tinctoris made clear that in practice the 5th and 6th modes use B♭ not B♮. He added some general comments on the use of the flat, both in linear and in two-part contrapuntal writing. First, the necessity for the flat is twofold – to create perfect consonances in polyphony and to avoid the linear or vertical tritone. Second, the 'signature flat' (or, as he put it, the flat at the beginning of the staff) affects the whole segment (whether of music or of staff is not clear) for which it is given, while the 'accidental' flat lasts as long as the hexachord segment (the *deductio*) before which it is placed. Third, the formation of these two modes with B♭, to avoid the tritone, is well known, so much so that the flat need not always be written down, and if it is, it may be considered an 'ass's mark' – not that all explicit accidentals may be so regarded, but specifically or primarily the flat needed for the 5th and 6th modes (the example illustrating this remark is monophonic). Fourth, linear tritones should also be avoided in other modes, but in polyphony they are sometimes unavoidable, because of inadmissible vertical intervals that may otherwise result, and in such cases the sign ♮ should be used; this passage significantly indicates that for Tinctoris, in two-part polyphony at least, when vertical tritone problems clash with linear tritones the former should take precedence, and it also indicates a rational basis for the use of the natural sign, namely to prevent a *ficta* flat which the singer, following his own part, would normally adopt. Fifth, what is true of the tritone in regular modes is also true of irregular ones in *musica ficta* (i.e. the system of *musica recta* as transposed). Finally, the linear tritone is less difficult to sing when approached by step than by leap.

2. *c*1500 TO *c*1600. Throughout this period the concepts embodied in and entailed by the medieval term *musica ficta* continued to play a role in the interpretation of polyphonic music, and the term itself remained in use by theorists. So long as the traditional gamut and hexachord system stood as the basis of musical structure, the distinction between *musica recta* and *musica ficta* (Bent, 1972) must have influenced both composition and performance, and those accidentals that were *extra manum* (outside the Guidonian hand) were considered variable units within a basically diatonic system. Broad developments in musical practice during the period 1450–1600 rendered the interpretation of unspecified accidentals even more problematic than in the past. These developments include the gradual increase in the number of voices normally used for vocal polyphony, the multiplication of variant versions of works as a result of the invention of music printing, and the rise of experimental chromatic and enharmonic tone systems (such as that of Vicentino) along with the freer exploitation of chromatic degree-inflection by composers outside the ranks of theorists. The period as a whole evidently witnessed a gradual evolution from a prevailing view that the addition of unspecified accidentals by performers was, no doubt in varying degrees, a normal practice, to a prevailing view that such additions were no longer generally regarded as necessary and that composers, copyists and printers alike were becoming accustomed to the specification of many more of the necessary accidentals. Although this latter view apparently took hold by degrees rather than at once, it became more widely held after 1600 than previously. Changes of musical style in the early Baroque period did cause another phase of fluidity in the use of accidentals (see §3), yet the much stronger effect of the inclination to notate accidentals coincided with changing developments in notation and performing practice after about 1600. Thus one can assert with confidence that from about 1450 to about 1600 such a development took place; but it is by no means clear how to derive from it specific standards of interpretation for accidentals in pieces from particular periods, regions, repertories or sources. Thus the basic problems of *musica ficta* remain as controversial throughout the 16th century, and a wide variety of views have been expressed on the subject by modern scholars.

Not only has no single formula been devised that seems readily applicable to all types of *musica ficta* problems, but it seems likely that an attitude of intelligent and well-informed relativism on the matter is historically more realistic than an apocalyptic vision of a universal solution for all cases. In broad terms the problem rests on two parallel inequalities: one lies in the divergence of readings in contemporary musical sources, the other in the relationship of the notation in these sources to the pertinent theoretical literature. The latter ought ideally to provide a set of procedures that would govern the treatment of accidentals, but the treatises are often abstract and elliptical in their discussion of the subject.

(i) Notation. In mensural notation from about 1450 to about 1540 flat signs were in normal and regular use, as accidentals and as signatures, and there is ordinarily no doubt about their meaning. Sharp signs, on the other hand, are extremely scarce in sources of vocal polyphony of the late 15th century and early 16th, whether manuscript or, after 1501, printed. The sharp is used only as an accidental in this entire period, with one or two very particular exceptions in which it appears as a signature (e.g. to express the relationship of a canon at the 5th above, in Willaert's *Musica nova* of 1559). From 1540 on, especially in Italian prints, the sharp sign becomes more frequent, but its placing is still free; it may appear below or before or, sometimes, even after the note affected. When it appears between and below two notes of the same apparent pitch there can be substantial doubt as to whether it refers to both notes (which should therefore have the same pitch) or whether it signals a chromatic inflection from the first note to the second. (For conflicting views on some relevant cases in printed sources of Italian madrigals see Kroyer, 1902, and Ficker, 1914.) The normal sign for the sharp in this period is ✗, but variants of this sign appear. The sign ♮, which had been the traditional sign for *b quadratum* in contradistinction to *b rotundum*, returned around 1540 as a distinctive symbol and attained its modern meaning; Einstein (*The Italian Madrigal*, i, 412) noted its use in a Vicentino madrigal collection of 1542.

A controversy has arisen (see Harrán, 1976 and 1978, and Godt, 1978 and 1979) over the interpretation of the sharp as a 'cautionary sign' in a group of printed collections of madrigals of the 1540s, issued chiefly by Gardane and Scotto in Venice. Harrán presents a sizeable number of cases in which a sharp sign is used 'in situations where *musica ficta* may be applied, but where on harmonic or melodic grounds its application must forcibly be prevented' (1976, p.79). His view is that in these instances the sharp cannot have its normal meaning as a sign to raise the notated pitch a semitone, but rather must be taken as a warning to the singer not to alter the pitch. Though this in part revives a thesis first stated by Kroyer (1902) it goes far beyond Kroyer in scope of evidence and argument. Godt, however, argues that such deviations from the normal experience of performers are wholly implausible on historical and logical grounds, and that the notion of a 'sharp that flats' is not likely to have been either intelligible or familiar to singers. He also notes that there is no evidence for such interpretations apart from these printed collections of music. The matter can scarcely be regarded as resolved, and it is possible that the typographical limitations of the period and the slow evolution of standardized meanings for the signs of the sharp and natural were to a large extent responsible for its origins. If printers were unable to make a typographical distinction between the sharp sign and the newly developing natural sign, they could simply have resorted to the former for all cases in which either sign would have been needed; in this they might even have been following the practices of composers and copyists of the time. Virtually all the cases cited by

Harrán could be resolved reasonably by interpreting the 'cautionary sign' as a sharp used instead of the natural sign.

It should be noted that in lute and other instrumental tablatures of the period accidentals are always specified in full, and some scholars (e.g. Apel) take these sources as being vitally important for the practices of the time. On the other hand, there is no reason to assume that the practices followed by instrumentalists were carried over into the vocal literature, where the tradition of solmization and *musica ficta* particularly applies. There is however much evidence of the increasingly explicit use of accidentals in vocal music itself (see Kroyer) and there can be no doubt that this is closely related to the move towards greater use of chromatic degree-inflection as a tonal device – the two are inseparably linked. Chromaticism is particularly visible in the madrigal from about mid-century, and was greatly developed later by Marenzio and Gesualdo. This type of degree-inflecting chromaticism is actually a tendency away from the medieval tradition of *musica ficta*, with its hexachord basis for the singing of unspecified accidentals. The two patterns co-existed during the 16th century.

Stemming from the concept of *musica ficta* and significantly extending it are works that explore chromatic notes by transposing hexachords to positions other than their traditional ones. Significant works in this tradition are Josquin's *Fortuna d'un gran tempo*, Willaert's puzzle duo (originally conceived as a quartet) *Quid non ebrietas* (Lowinsky, 1943 and 1956) and Greiter's *Passibus ambiguis* (Lowinsky, 1956–7). All of these use hexachord transposition through the circle of 5ths; this is also applied in those examples of motets of the mid-16th century with unspecified chromaticism discovered and described by Lowinsky (1946). The 'secret chromatic art' involved here is in each case a considerable extension of traditional *musica ficta*, in which an entire passage and not merely a single note or a cadence is open to a chromatic interpretation. While the thesis advanced by Lowinsky is still controversial, he brought strong evidence in its favour. Similarly originating in *musica ficta* is a type of chromaticism based on transposition using flat signatures.

Less indebted to the tradition of *musica ficta* than to the more 'progressive' and experimental wing of 16th-century theory are pieces based on chromatic and enharmonic experimentation in imitation of the ancient genera, as well as those originating in a fresh use of chordal chromaticism of a colouristic type. Combining in varying degrees all of these tendencies is an extraordinary chromatic chanson by Guillaume Costeley, *Seigneur Dieu* (see Levy, 1955), which is one of the most remarkable experiments of the century. It should be noted that wherever hexachord chromaticism is used the traditional notational function of the flat is the same (an instruction to sing 'fa') and thus implies the continuity of the solmization traditions, while in degree-inflected chromaticism an increasing departure from notational traditions is evident.

(ii) Performing practice. On this crucial aspect of the problem little can be said, but one must be wary of the facile assumption that singers of the period were universally cognisant of the 'right' approach to the problem and solved it uniformly. On the contrary, there is persuasive evidence that 16th-century musicians found it difficult to know how to apply those rules of *musica*

ficta that were espoused by theorists of their own times. As early as 1524 Giovanni Spataro wrote to Pietro Aaron (in a passage later used verbatim by Aaron in the supplement to his *Toscanello in musica* of 1529, but without credit to Spataro; trans. from Lockwood, 1968):

thus the musician or composer is obliged to indicate his intention, in order that the singer may not chance to do something that was never intended by the composer . . . the singer is not to be expected, on first reading, to sing the proper notes in the places where this sign [♭] may occur, inasmuch as it may belong there, or may not belong there.

In the 1550s the Roman singer and writer Ghiselin Danckerts in an unpublished treatise illustrated the problem from the performer's point of view by means of an anecdote concerning a dispute between two singers of the church of S Lorenzo in Damaso, Rome, which must have occurred between 1538 and 1544 (Lockwood, 1965). The dispute was over the proper way to add accidentals to a composition by the papal singer Juan Escribano. According to Danckerts, he himself was eventually asked to judge the matter, and he explained his decision in substantial detail. Since concrete evidence of actual choices of accidentals made in performance is virtually non-existent, one can only surmise that practices must indeed have differed from place to place and time to time, and that it would probably be a severe historical misjudgment to assume any prevailing uniformity of practice. On the other hand, much can be learnt about the prevailing theoretical assumptions on which judgments and choices could have been made by knowledgeable singers.

(iii) Contemporary theory and 'rules'. In a thorough exposition of the rules of *musica ficta* that were propagated throughout this period, Lowinsky (1964) summed up the prevailing rules under the headings of *causa necessitatis* ('by reason of necessity') and *causa pulchritudinis* ('by reason of beauty'). The former heading includes: first, the rule prohibiting the simultaneous sounding of *mi* against *fa*, that is, diminished octaves and 5ths between two simultaneously sounding voices; second, the rule known from a schoolboy jingle as 'una nota super la, semper est canendum fa' ('a note above *la* is always sung *fa*'), to prevent a linear tritone when a line ascends above the syllable *la* (Pietro Aaron in his *Lucidarium*, 1545, showed this was by no means a universally applicable doctrine); and third, the prohibition of false relations.

Under the heading *causa pulchritudinis* Lowinsky included: first, the rule governing the *subsemitonium modi*, that is, the raising of the leading note at cadential formulae; second, the rule of propinquity, that is, approaching a perfect consonance in two voices by the nearest imperfect consonance; and third, the rule of ending on a complete triad (according to Lowinsky this was known only in the 16th century).

These rules undoubtedly constituted a set of guidelines, inherited from earlier periods (e.g. see §1, iii, above), which 16th-century musicians could recognize as being broadly applicable; Aaron specifically referred to 'ordinary and special rules devised by musicians', and Danckerts referred to reasons for the insertion of accidentals which are directly equivalent to the first three rules cited above. Among the many problems still unsolved is that of how to apply the rules when one contradicts the other or when more than one is applicable. This was illustrated in the period itself by Aaron, in the supplement to his *Toscanello in musica*, where he quoted a passage from the bass part of the third Agnus Dei of Josquin's *Missa 'L'homme armé' super voces musicales* (see ex.3). As Aaron explained, the tritone *f–b* cannot be changed to *f–b♭* since that in turn would cause a diminished 5th *b♭–e*: 'thus the singer will be obliged to sing the harsh tritone for the sake of that interval [a 5th] or rather that syllable which occurs in the position of *hypate meson*, called *E la mi*, because in order to accommodate the interval in the most convenient way, he is forced to break the rule'.

Ex.3

Similar problems inevitably arise in the music of the period. Yet it would be erroneous to assume, as some have done, that because *musica ficta* cannot be applied with absolute consistency and rigour, it ought not to be applied at all in vocal music. There is ample testimony by reliable writers showing that despite the problems inherent in the tradition, it continued to have meaning throughout the 16th century. It has been suggested (Lockwood, 1968) that one useful approach may consist in analysing individual pieces with regard to the definition of classes of linear, harmonic and contrapuntal movement that may require unspecified accidentals, together with exhaustive study of the relevant sources for each work. In this way one may study the problem as consisting of the relationship between those accidentals that are specified and those that are required by the known rules. Since for each of these categories both positive and negative possibilities exist, there will be four potential categories for each situation. By examining these in relation to one another and to the composition as a whole, more and less plausible solutions may emerge.

3. AFTER 1600. Accidentals in the Baroque period, like many other features of notation and performance, went through a long and intermittent transition from the greater fluidity of earlier periods towards the greater fixity of later periods. In early Baroque music accidentals were still a responsibility shared by the composer and the performer and open to a choice of solutions; hence modern editors and performers are concerned primarily with deciding which accidentals are most satisfactory within the original boundaries of the style. By 1700, much of the responsibility for deciding on accidentals and inflections had passed to the composer or printer, but even in late Baroque music the performer will sometimes still have to add or interpret accidentals.

Several principles seem to apply to much Baroque music, probably throughout the period, though with numerous exceptions. Most derive directly from earlier practice. Perhaps the most important general point is that accidentals in Baroque music still serve to inflect a note, giving it a new relative position compared with what in its context it would otherwise have had. This is different from the modern absolute effect of a notated accidental. Thus Christopher Simpson wrote in his *Principles of Practical Musick* (1665): 'That ♭ takes away a *Semitone* from the Sound of the Note before which it is set, to make it more *grave* or *flat*: This ♯ doth add a semitone to the Note to make it more *acute* or sharp'. Hence written C♭ after C♯ may (by inflecting the note a semitone down) mean a modern C♮; and written B♯

after B♭ may mean a modern B♮. This principle was still expressed, with reservations, by Francesco Geminiani (*The Art of Playing on the Violin*, London, 1751, p.3):

A Sharp (♯) raises the Note to which it is prefixed, a Semitone higher . . . A Flat (♭) on the contrary renders the Note to which it is prefixed, a Semitone lower . . . This Rule concerning the Flats and Sharps is not absolutely exact; but it is the easiest and best Rule that can be given to a Learner. This Mark (♮) takes away the Force of both the Sharp and the Flat and restores the Note before which it is placed to its natural Quality.

The natural sign was rare (and strictly applicable only to B) through much of the Baroque period, but came into common though far from exclusive use (applicable to any note) in later Baroque music.

By Baroque convention, a flat or a sharp 'serves only for that particular Note before which it is placed' (Christopher Simpson). Although this was always the theoretical understanding, in practice inconsistencies are numerous, and more or less regular exceptions were to some extent recognized. Notes immediately repeated, or with only one or two other notes intervening, usually (though not invariably) retain the force of an accidental applied to the first of them. This tendency is somewhat weakened if there is a change of harmony and greatly weakened if there is an intervening rest, or the start of a new phrase (see ex.4); still more so if more than one of these circumstances coincide (e.g. if both a rest and the start of a new phrase interrupt the series of repeated notes).

Ex.4 Monteverdi: *Orfeo*, Act 2

It was only in the Classical period that the convention of an accidental ceasing to apply after a bar-line received explicit recognition. D. G. Türk (*Clavierschule*, 1789, p.46) wrote that accidentals 'are valid only through one bar; yet one must not wish to observe this rule too strictly, for such a modifying sign often remains valid through several bars, or indeed so long, until it is cancelled by a ♮'. Ex.4 shows an early Baroque example in Monteverdi's *Orfeo*; the upper voice has the precautionary cancellation of the sharp at the start of the new phrase. The same effect should be understood in the lower voice.

An extension of this understanding of the duration of an accidental, which is clearly derived from earlier practice, is still found widely in early Baroque music, but less so thereafter: while a part remains within the compass of the same hexachord (i.e. without the need for mental mutation into a different hexachord for solmization), there is a strong tendency for the force of an accidental to persist. On any theoretical basis, this should have applied only to flats, but by analogy (or by transposition), it actually applied to sharps as well. In performance, this possibility should on no account be overlooked (at least in all music of the 17th century).

Whereas the force of a modern accidental can only extend forwards, that of a Baroque accidental could, and frequently did, also extend backwards – a principle of great importance in early Baroque music. This is not merely a matter of the admittedly careless placing in printed music, and still more in manuscripts, of the actual signs for accidentals (so much so that it sometimes seems that anywhere would do within reasonable distance around the note meant to be affected, and where there might happen to be room on the paper); but it is also a matter of definite convention, the existence of which was brilliantly noticed, though not followed up, by Jeppesen (1923). An accidental of which the force extends backwards (as well as forwards) may be called 'retrospective'. The plainest cases are those in which a dissonant suspension on a dominant 5-4 resolves ornamentally on to the leading note in a dominant 5-3. Here it was still extremely common in early Baroque music, and not uncommon later, to place the necessary sharp on the main note of resolution but not on the preceding ornamental note or notes (where it is nevertheless ordinarily required; see ex.5, where the sharpened third figured in the continuo confirms that the first C in Cantus I is meant to be retrospectively sharp).

Ex.5

The use of retrospective accidentals in sources of 17th-century music evidently goes far beyond anything that the appearance of the original printed volumes and manuscripts implies (the trouble being precisely that retrospective accidentals look no different from normal ones). There are, of course, many passages that on first thoughts might well appear to need retrospective accidentals, but that prove on careful consideration not to need and sometimes not to tolerate such a solution. But passages where a retrospective accidental provides the most musicianly solution seem to be extremely numerous before and during the early Baroque period, and to a lesser but not inconsiderable extent thereafter.

Many interpretations of accidentals may be suggested by both the melody and the harmony. Baroque melody has some tendency to ascend with sharps and naturals and descend with naturals and flats; to flatten the peak note of a phrase when that note immediately falls again; to sharpen the trough note of a phrase when that note immediately rises again (thus serving as a leading note); to sharpen the 6th of the scale when the 7th is sharpened (to serve as leading note); and generally (though not invariably) to avoid augmented 2nds. Baroque harmony has some tendency to change with a new phrase; to end a minor passage in the major (Picardy 3rd); and to insist on regular (sharp or sharpened) cadential leading notes in dominant to tonic progressions or interrupted cadences. But melodic considerations may prevail over harmonic ones to produce, for example, a diminished- or augmented-octave clash (ex.6).

Ex.6 Coprario: Fantasia *Chi pue mirarvi*

There are ways in which the notation can be actively misleading as to the presence of certain accidentals. Whereas figured basses may use the usual methods of notating accidentals, they carry some particular patterns of error, such as ♭ wrongly written for 6 or 6 for ♭.

Tablature does not notate accidentals separately, but simply shows the fingerings that will produce them so that no ambiguity should arise; but, of course, mistakes can occur. When tablature doubles staff notation, one helps to check the other, but it cannot be assumed (in cases of discrepancy) that the tablature is necessarily right. When tablature stands alone, it may be somewhat more reliable than staff notation, but it is by no means sacrosanct, for tablature not infrequently shows a wrong fingering.

Precautionary accidentals occur often, but very inconsistently, in places where Baroque conventions require them in order to prevent excessive ambiguity. Nevertheless, ambiguities abound for the modern musician as, undoubtedly, they did for the Baroque musician. In practice it is much more important to work out for each passage a suitable scheme of accidentals, reasonably consistent within itself but not rigorously so, than it is to seek an unattainable certainty. It would have been somewhat contrary to the spirit of Baroque music, and especially of early Baroque music, for the composer to assume or for the performer to attempt any such consistent and predictable pattern.

BIBLIOGRAPHY

M. Gerbert, ed.: *Scriptores ecclesiastici de musica sacra* (St Blasien, 1784/*R*1963, 2/1905, 3/1931)

C.-E.-H. de Coussemaker: *Histoire de l'harmonie au moyen-âge* (Paris, 1852), 295–349

——: *Scriptorum de musica medii aevi nova series* (Paris, 1864–76/*R*1963)

A. de La Fage: *Essais de dipthérographie musicale* (Paris, 1864)

G. von Tücher: 'Zur Musikpraxis und Theorie des 16. Jahrhunderts, v: Accidentien und Musica Ficta', *AMZ*, viii (1873)

R. Schlecht: 'Über den Gebrauch des Diesis im 13. u. 15. Jahrhundert', *MMg*, ix (1877), 79, 99

R. Hirschfeld: 'Notizen zur mittelalterlichen Musikgeschichte (Instrumentalmusik und Musica Ficta)', *MMg*, xvii (1885), 61

P. Spitta: 'Die Musica Enchiriadis und ihre Zeitalter', *VMw*, v (1889), 443–82

G. Jacobsthal: *Die chromatische Alteration im liturgischen Gesang der abendländischen Kirche* (Berlin, 1897/*R*1970)

W. Schmidt: *Die Calliopea legale des Johannes Hothby* (Leipzig, 1897)

H. Riemann: *Geschichte der Musiktheorie im IX.–XIX. Jahrhundert* (Leipzig, 1898, 2/1921; Eng. trans., 1962/*R*1974)

T. Kroyer: *Die Anfänge der Chromatik im italienischen Madrigal des XVI. Jahrhunderts* (Leipzig, 1902/*R*1968)

J. Wolf: *Geschichte der Mensuralnotation* (Leipzig, 1904/*R*1965), i, 109ff

A. Einstein: 'Claudio Merulos Ausgabe der Madrigale des Verdelot', *SIMG*, viii (1906–7), 220–54, 516

H. Riemann: 'Verloren gegangene Selbstverständlichkeiten in der Musik des 15.–16. Jahrhunderts', *Musikalisches Magazin*, xvii (Langensalza, 1907)

E. Wilfort: 'Glareans Erwiderung', *ZIMG*, x (1908–9), 337

IMusSCR, iii *Vienna 1909* [articles by Bernoulli, Chilesotti, Kroyer, Schwartz, Wolf]

R. von Ficker: 'Beiträge zur Chromatik des 14. bis 16. Jahrhunderts', *SMw*, ii (1914), 5

K. Dèzes: *Prinzipielle Fragen auf dem Gebiet der fingierten Musik* (diss., Humboldt U., Berlin, 1922)

K. Jeppesen: *Palestrinastil med soerligt henblik paa dissonansbehandlingen* (Copenhagen, 1923; Eng. trans., 1927, 2/1946/ R1970)

E. Frerichs: 'Die Accidentien in Orgeltabulaturen', *ZMw*, vii (1924–5), 99

K. Jeppesen: *Der Kopenhagener Chansonnier* (Copenhagen, 1927)

W. Apel: *Accidentien und Tonalität in den Musikdenkmälern des 15. und 16. Jahrhunderts* (Strasbourg, 1937/R1972)

——: 'Accidentals and the Modes in 15th- and 16th-century Sources', *BAMS*, ii (1937), 289

——: 'The Partial Signatures in the Sources up to 1450', *AcM*, x (1938), 1

J. Levitan: 'Adrian Willaert's Famous Duo *Quidnam ebreitas*', *TVNM*, xv/3 (1938), 166f; xv/4 (1939), 193–233

W. Apel: 'A Postscript to "The Partial Signatures in the Sources up to 1450"', *AcM*, xi (1939), 40

C. Fox: 'Accidentals in Vihuela Tablatures', *BAMS*, iv (1940), 22

W. Apel: *The Notation of Polyphonic Music, 900–1600* (Cambridge, Mass., 1942, rev. 5/1961), 104ff, 120

H. Hewitt: *Harmonice Musices Odhecaton A* (Cambridge, Mass., 1942/R1978), 16

L. Hibberd: '*Musica ficta* and Instrumental Music, c1250–c1350', *MQ*, xxviii (1942), 216

E. E. Lowinsky: 'The Goddess Fortuna in Music, with a Special Study of Josquin's *Fortuna d'un gran tempo*', *MQ*, xxix (1943), 45–77

W. Apel: 'Musica ficta', *Harvard Dictionary of Music* (Cambridge, Mass., 1944, rev. 2/1969)

E. E. Lowinsky: 'The Function of Conflicting Signatures in Early Polyphonic Music', *MQ*, xxxi (1945), 227–60

M. van Crevel: 'Secret Chromatic Art in the Netherlands Motet?', *TVNM*, xvi/4 (1946), 253–304

E. E. Lowinsky: *Secret Chromatic Art in the Netherlands Motet* (New York, 1946/R1967)

L. Schrade: 'A Secret Chromatic Art', *JRBM*, i (1946), 159

M. Johnson: 'A Study of Conflicting Key-signatures in Francesco Landini's Music', *Hamline Studies in Musicology*, ii (1947), 27

J. Smits van Waesberghe, ed.: *Johannes Afflighemensis (Cotto): De musica cum tonario*, CSM, i (1950)

R. Hoppin: 'Partial Signatures and Musica Ficta in some Early 15th-Century Sources', *JAMS*, vi (1953), 197

H. Anglès, ed.: *C. de Morales: Opera omnia*, MME, xv (1954); xx (1959)

E. E. Lowinsky: 'Conflicting Views on Conflicting Signatures', *JAMS*, vii (1954), 181

S. Clercx: 'Les accidents sous-entendus et la transcription en notation moderne', *L'Ars Nova: Wégimont II 1955*, 167

K. Levy: 'Costeley's Chromatic Chanson', *AnnM*, iii (1955), 213–63

G. Reaney: 'Musica Ficta in the Works of Guillaume de Machaut', *L'Ars Nova: Wégimont II 1955*, 196

R. Hoppin: 'Conflicting Signatures Reviewed', *JAMS*, ix (1956), 97

E. E. Lowinsky: 'Adrian Willaert's Chromatic Duo Re-examined', *TVNM*, xviii/1 (1956), 1–36

——: 'Matthaeus Greiter's *Fortuna*: an Experiment in Chromaticism and in Musical Iconography', *MQ*, xlii (1956), 500; xliii (1957), 68

L. Spiess: 'The Diatonic "Chromaticism" of the *Enchiriadis* Treatises', *JAMS*, xii (1959), 1

A. Seay, ed.: *Ugolino of Orvieto: Declaratio musicae disciplinae*, CSM, vii (1959–62)

E. E. Lowinsky: *Tonality and Atonality in Sixteenth-century Music* (Berkeley, 1961, rev. 2/1962)

G. Haydon: 'The Case of the Troublesome Accidental', *Natalicia musicologica Knud Jeppesen* (Copenhagen, 1962), 125

N. Pirrotta, ed.: *The Music of Fourteenth-century Italy*, CMM, viii/3 (1962)

C. Dahlhaus: 'Zu Costeleys chromatischer Chanson', *Mf*, xvi (1963), 253

E. E. Lowinsky: Introduction to *Musica nova*, ed. C. Slim, MRM, i (1964), pp.ix, xiii–xxi

G. Massera: 'Musica inspettiva e accordatura strumentale', *Quadrivium*, vi (1964), 85

G. Reaney, A. Gilles and J. Maillard, eds.: *Philippe de Vitry: Ars nova*, CSM, viii (1964)

L. Lockwood: 'A Dispute on Accidentals in Sixteenth-century Rome', *AnMc*, no.2 (1965), 24

H. Kaufmann: 'A "Diatonic" and a "Chromatic" Madrigal by Giulio Fiesco', *Aspects of Medieval and Renaissance Music: a Birthday Offering to Gustave Reese* (New York, 1966), 474

A. Seay: 'The 15th Century Coniuncta: a Preliminary Study', *Aspects of Medieval and Renaissance Music: a Birthday Offering to Gustave Reese* (New York, 1966), 723

R. Crocker: 'A New Source for Medieval Music Theory', *AcM*, xxxix (1967), 161

E. E. Lowinsky: Introduction to *O. Petrucci: Canti B*, ed. H. Hewitt, MRM, ii (1967), pp.ix–xiv

A. Seay, ed.: *Concerning Music – De musica; Johannes de Grocheo* (Colorado Springs, 1967, 2/1974)

C. Dahlhaus: 'Zur Akzidentiensetzung in den Motetten Josquins des Prez', *Musik und Verlag: Karl Vötterle zum 65. Geburtstag* (Kassel, 1968), 206

F. A. Gallo: 'Alcune fonte poco note di musica teorica e pratica', *L'ars nova italiana del trecento: convegni di studi 1961–1967* (Certaldo, 1968), 49

C. Jacobs: 'Spanish Renaissance Discussion of Musica Ficta', *Proceedings of the American Philosophical Society*, cxii (1968), 277

E. Kottick: 'Flats, Modality and Musica Ficta in some Early Renaissance Chansons', *JMT*, xii (1968), 264

L. Lockwood: 'A Sample Problem of *Musica Ficta*: Willaert's *Pater noster*', *Studies in Music History: Essays for Oliver Strunk* (Princeton, 1968), 161

E. E. Lowinsky: 'Echoes of Adrian Willaert's Chromatic "Duo" in Sixteenth- and Seventeenth-century Compositions', *Studies in Music History: Essays for Oliver Strunk* (Princeton, 1968), 183–238

C. Dahlhaus: 'Tonsystem und Kontrapunkt um 1500', *Jb des Staatlichen Instituts für Musikforschung* (1969), 7

A. Hughes: 'Ugolino: the Monochord and Musica Ficta', *MD*, xxiii (1969), 21

K. P. Bernet Kempers: 'Accidenties', *Renaissance-muziek 1400–1600: donum natalicium René Bernard Lenaerts* (Louvain, 1969), 51

M. L. Martinez-Göllner: 'Marchettus of Padua and Chromaticism', *L'ars nova italiana del trecento II: Certaldo 1969*, 187

G. Reaney: 'Accidentals in Early Fifteenth-century Music', *Renaissance-muziek 1400–1600: donum natalicium René Bernard Lenaerts* (Louvain, 1969), 223

A. Seay: 'The Beginnings of the Coniuncta and Lorenzo Masini's "L'Antefana"', *L'ars nova italiana del trecento II: Certaldo 1969*, 51

D. Crawford: 'Performance and the Laborde Chansonnier: Authenticity of Multiplicities: Musica ficta', *College Music Symposium*, x (1970), 107

R. Bray: 'The Interpretation of Musica Ficta in English Music, c1490–c1580', *PRMA*, xcvii (1970–71), 29

H. M. Brown: 'Accidentals and Ornamentation in Sixteenth-century Intabulations of Josquin's Motets', *Josquin des Prez: New York 1971*, 475–522

G. G. Allaire: *The Theory of Hexachords, Solmization and the Modal System*, MSD, xxiv (1972)

P. Doe: 'Another View of Musica Ficta in Tudor Music', *PRMA*, xcviii (1971–2), 113

M. Bent: 'Musica Recta and Musica Ficta', *MD*, xxvi (1972), 73

A. Hughes: *Manuscript Accidentals: Ficta in Focus, 1350–1450*, MSD, xxvii (1972)

E. E. Lowinsky: 'Secret Chromatic Art Re-examined', *Perspectives in Musicology*, ed. B. S. Brook, E. O. D. Downes and S. van Solkema (New York, 1972), 91–135.

H. Tischler: '"Musica Ficta" in the Thirteenth Century', *ML*, liv (1973), 38; also pubd in *IMSCR*, xi *Copenhagen 1972*, 695

D. Harrán: 'New Evidence for Musica Ficta: the Cautionary Sign', *JAMS*, xxix (1976), 77

J. Haar: 'False Relations and Chromaticism in 16th-century Music', *JAMS*, xxx (1977), 391

R. Bray: 'Sixteenth-century *Musica Ficta*: the Importance of the Scribe', *Journal of the Plainsong and Mediaeval Music Society*, i (1978), 57

I. Godt and D. Harran: 'Comments and Issues', *JAMS*, xxxi (1978), 385

D. Harrán: 'More Evidence for Cautionary Signs', *JAMS*, xxxi (1978), 490

R. Samuel: *Modality, Tonality and Musica ficta in the Sixteenth-century Chanson* (diss., Washington U., 1978)

I. Godt: 'Comments and Issues', *JAMS*, xxxii (1979), 364

G. Reaney: 'Transposition and "Key" Signatures in Late Medieval Music', *MD*, xxxiii (1979), 27

J. van Benthem: 'Fortuna in Focus: Concerning 'Conflicting' Progressions in Josquin's *Fortuna d'un gran tempo*', *TVNM*, xxx (1980), 1–50

W. Apel: 'Punto intenso contra remisso', *Music East and West: Essays in Honor of Walter Kaufmann* (New York, 1981), 175

R. Donington: *Baroque Music: Style and Performance* (London, 1982)

G. Massera: 'Suggestioni teoriche nel *Lucidarium* di Marchetto da

Padova: dai "Generi" alla "Musica colorata", *A Festschrift for Albert Seay: Essays by his Friends and Colleagues* (Colorado Springs, 1982), 1
T. Noblitt: 'Chromatic Cross-relations and Editorial Musica Ficta in Masses of Obrecht', *TVNM*, xxxii (1982), 30
MARGARET BENT (1 (i–iv)), LEWIS LOCKWOOD (1 (v), 2), ROBERT DONINGTON (3), STANLEY BOORMAN (bibliography)

Musical bottles. *See* BOUTEILLOPHONE.

Musical bow [harp bow] (Fr. *arc musical, arc sonore*; Ger. *Musikbogen*; It. *arco sonore*; Sp. *arco musical*). A bow-shaped chordophone consisting solely of a flexible stave, curved by the tension of a string (or strings) stretched between its ends, any associated resonator being either unattached, or detachable without destroying the sound-producing apparatus (see figs.1 and 2, and MOUTH BOW, figs.1–3). Hornbostel and Sachs classified both the musical bow and the 'stick zither' (which has a rigid stave) as types of bar zither (*see* CHORDOPHONE).

1. History. 2. Structure. 3. Resonators. 4. Technique.

1. HISTORY. The musical bow, in various forms, is widely distributed in Africa, America, Oceania, parts of Asia and formerly to a small extent in Europe (East Prussia, the Netherlands, Italy, Latvia and Lithuania). It is frequently played recreationally as a solo instrument or (with a resonator) for song accompaniment, and in some areas is important in magic or religion. In the cave Les Trois Frères in south-western France a rock painting from *c*15,000 BC shows musical use of a bow in a religious ceremony.

Whether the archer's bow or the musical bow came first has long provoked conjecture and contention. Apollo was both an archer and the god of music; Homer and Euripides refer to the musical note emitted by the archer's bowstring and the delight it gave to the ear. Legend in north India names the simple *pināka* musical bow as the prototype of all string instruments and ascribes its invention to the god Shiva. In Japan legend traces the origin of the koto (fretted long zither) to the god Ameno Kamato who placed six archers' longbows close together with their strings uppermost. A southern African San (Bushman) rock painting reported by G. W. Stow depicts similar use of seven shooting bows (see frontispiece in *KirbyMISA*).

The notion that all string instruments evolved from the musical bow was dismissed by Balfour in the late 19th century, but he firmly believed that the musical bow had evolved from the shooting bow. Montandon (1919), however, asserted that the weapon evolved from the musical bow, after the musical bow had changed from an original idiochord form (in which the string is a partially detached strip from the same piece of cane as the stave, lifted on bridges) to heterochord form (with a tied-on string). Hornbostel (1933, p.135) objected that the shooting bow was already known in the earliest cultures. He favoured Sachs's claim that weapon and instrument originated independently but had later become similar in shape.

According to Sachs the earliest musical bow had a separate resonator (the stick being pressed against a vessel placed on the ground) and this had developed via an intermediate form (the ground zither) from the percussion beam (a pole suspended in two nooses above a pit, and struck with two sticks). Sachs (1940, p.56) held that 'those forms of bow which we have good reason to

1. Khoikhoi (Hottentot) woman playing a musical bow (khas): drawing (1834) by Charles Bell (Africana Museum, Johannesburg)

believe are the oldest have nothing to do with a hunters' bow' (being generally too long for shooting, and some of them idiochord, with bridges) and that they were not associated with hunters' beliefs and ceremonies: in many cases only women play them, and they may serve variously to induce meditation, invoke the spirits or accompany initiation.

Some peoples who play musical bows hunt without bows and arrows (as was true of the Zulu in former times), while others (such as the Dan of the Ivory Coast) use a different form of bow for their hunting. The Dan ascribe their musical bow to a genie who used to play it to warn animals of approaching hunters; absentmindedly he once left it on an ant heap, and a hunter appropriated it. On the other hand, there is clear evidence that the San (Bushmen) of southern Africa have long played tunes on their hunting bows, and continue this practice in modern times. In this instance at least, elaborate origin theories have seemed superfluous to some scholars: Kirby in his extensive Bushman studies chose to adopt Balfour's practical view that 'the idea of adapting the shooting bow to musical purposes . . . might well arise in more than one centre, since it involves little more than the appreciation of the musical qualities in the twang of the bow-string, a thing which is almost forced upon the attention of the archer' (Balfour, p.86). The only native string instrument of the North American Indians (apart from the Apache fiddle) was the MA'WO, a musical bow of the Californian tribes. This was often a hunting bow adapted as a musical instrument, though quite elaborate bows were also made specifically for music.

Musical bows are usually played singly, but a few instances of multiple use are known. The pluriarc (which is really a bow lute) resembles a series of bows with a

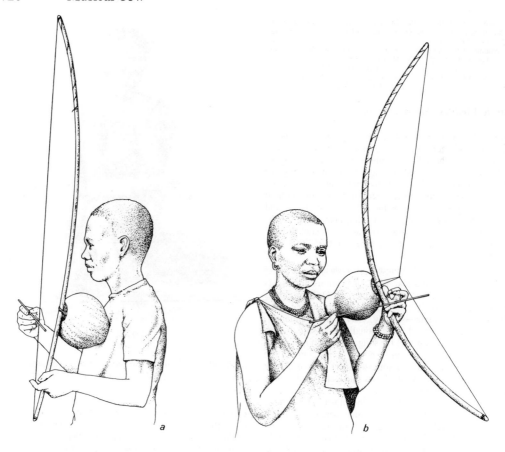

2. *Gourd-resonated musical bows of the Zulu people, southern Africa: (a) ugubhu; (b) umakhweyana*

common resonator. The terms 'ground bow' or 'earth bow' are misnomers (*see* GROUND HARP). The arched harp of Sumeria (depicted on a vase from *c*3000 BC) has some bow-like features and is regarded by Sachs (1940, p.80) as a descendant of the musical bow, hence the occasional use of the term BOW HARP. Similar arched harps survive in many parts of Africa north of the equator (*see* HARP, §6).

2. STRUCTURE. The stave varies from about 50 cm to 3 metres in length with different varieties. It may be of round, semicircular or flat section, and often tapers towards the ends. The dividing line between musical bows and stick zithers (with a rigid stave) is often uncertain, especially with idiochord varieties. Bow staves are usually made from a single length of wood or cane, but a few types have two or three sections (Xhosa UMRHUBHE; Sotho SETOLOTOLO). 'Scraped bows' (Ger. *Schrapbogen*), found in India, central and southern Africa and South America, have serrations along one side of the stave (the instrument being sounded by scraping across these with a stick or rattle-stick). With other types of bow, the string may be set in vibration by plucking it with fingertip or plectrum, by tapping it with a small stick or grass stalk, by stroking it with a friction stick (in Colombia, South Africa, Loango and Marquesas) or with a subsidiary bow (in Patagonia), which, among the

Araucano and Chaco in South America, is interlinked with the main bow.

The blacks and the Indians of the Atlantic coastal region of Colombia play a type of mouth-resonated musical bow known as the *marimba* (*see* MOUTH BOW, fig.2). The bow used by the blacks is stopped by a short wooden rod held in the left hand, thus producing two fundamentals, and the cord is struck near the mouth with a thin piece of bamboo. The Motilón and Guajiro Indians obtain several fundamentals by stopping the cord with the fingers of the left hand; a thin piece of bamboo, moistened by the mouth to create the required friction, is used somewhat like a violin bow to produce the tone. Both types of bow are now rare.

The Aeolian bow, sounded by the force of wind or breath, is exemplified by the tiny 'whizzing bow' swung round like a bullroarer (and thus qualifying as a 'free aerophone') which is found sporadically in West Africa (Liberia), China, Indonesia and eastern Brazil. It is also used, attached to large kites, in Indonesia and eastern Asia (Java: *sundari*; Laos: *tamoo*). Bows sounded with the breath are confined to the South African GORA and its derivatives.

Both idiochord and heterochord musical bows may have one or more strings. The string of the heterochord bow may be made from rattan, vegetable fibre, sinew, twisted animal hairs or wire. It may either vibrate as a whole, or be divided into unequal segments (usually two) by a bridge (*see* MVET) or by a 'brace' (also called 'tuning noose' or 'tension noose') – a loop, passing round both stave and string, which keeps the string pulled inwards, towards the stave. Some braced bows, such as the EGOBOLI of Uganda, have an additional smaller noose near each end for making finer adjustments of the string tension. In rare cases a single bowstring may be laced more than once across the curved frame of the stave, as in the *adungu* of the Acholi in Uganda (*see* ADUNGU (i)). The breath-sounded *gora* is exceptional in that a piece of quill connects the string with the stave at one end.

3. RESONATORS. As far as supplementary resonance is concerned, bows may be subdivided into two broad categories: those without and those with an attached resonator. The first of these may be further divided between bows played entirely without a resonator and others played with a separate resonator. The first of these two types is rare, the north Indian *pināka* being a reported example (Balfour, p.54). Whizzing bows perhaps qualify but are usually considered aerophones. The bow shown in fig.1 appears to have no resonator, but apparently that instrument was often pressed against a wooden dish, dry skin bag or some other vessel which could serve as a temporary independent resonator (*see* KHAS). Similar use of a calabash, bowl, pot, basket, tin can etc, has been widely reported in India, America and Borneo as well as in Africa. Bows with a separate resonator also include the mouth bow, in which the player's mouth cavity supplies resonance: this type is widespread in Africa, South America and Oceania. The stave may be held against the player's mouth, or the string may vibrate freely between the lips (*see* MOUTH BOW, fig.2).

Bows with an attached resonator usually have an open-ended gourd attached in some way to the stave on the opposite side to the string; these, known as gourd bows, are common in equatorial and southern Africa and among Afro-Americans in South America. The bow is usually held vertically, with the opening in the gourd facing the player's chest (fig.2). The BELEMBAUTUYAN of the Chamorro people of the Mariana Islands, Micronesia, is played by a seated or reclining player, the gourd against his stomach. The Indian *ṭuila* and instruments like the *nenjenje* of the Meje in central Africa have similar features but, having rigid flat bars, are really stick zithers. In southern Africa two typical mono-heterochord gourd bows are the Zulu UGUBHU (unbraced, with resonator near the bottom of the stave) and UMAKHWEYANA (braced, with the resonator near the centre, attached to the brace; see fig.2). The opening in the gourd resonators of the Zulu instruments is mostly between 5 and 7 cm in diameter, but in those of most other ethnic groups the hole is larger, or a hemispherical half gourd may be used. In some areas supplementary rattles, bells or jingles are attached to the stave, or used with the beater, and the *kalumbu* of the Valley Tonga (Zambia) may have a mirliton attached to the gourd. In the case of another smaller variety of mono-heterochord gourd bow found in east, central and west Africa, the half-gourd resonator is placed over the player's mouth (e.g. the EKITULENGE of the Konjo in Uganda; *see* MOUTH BOW, fig.3). A polyheterochord U-shaped gourd bow with five to seven strings (known as the forked harp and sometimes nicknamed the belly-harp) is used in the savannah region of West Africa.

4. TECHNIQUE. The fundamental pitch of a musical bow is often varied by the performer. In bows with a bridge

or brace the two unequal segments of the string yield different pitches. Additional pitches may be produced on braced and unbraced bows by stopping the string at one or more points with a finger, thimble, small stick or (as on the Brazilian BERIMBAU) the edge of a coin; harmonics are also often played. On some varieties with an unattached resonator harmonics are produced by touching the string at a nodal point with a finger or with the chin. With many other types the resonance frequency of the resonator is continually altered while playing to amplify one or other of the higher harmonics. The fundamental then serves only as a drone (or provides a simple ground bass if its pitch is varied) while selectively resonated upper partials are used for the melody. With mouth bows the volume of the player's mouth cavity is varied, as in the case of the jew's harp (*see* MOUTH BOW), to produce music as in ex.1.

Ex.1 Music played on the *umrhubhe* (friction mouth bow) of the Mpondo (Xhosa), South Africa, sounded by stroking the string with a friction stick (Rycroft, 1966)

o unstopped
● stopped with left thumb

Pitch on mono-heterochord gourd bows is varied by finger-stopping (as with the unbraced Zulu *ugubhu*), and also, in the case of braced bows like the *umakhweyana*, through striking alternate segments of the string. Harmonic partials above each fundamental may be selectively amplified through covering the opening of the gourd to a varying extent, thereby altering its resonance frequency, as in ex.2. This is achieved by moving it closer to, or further from, the chest while playing. The musical purpose of such movements was misunderstood by earlier investigators, including Kirby (p.198) and Sachs (1940, p.57). A few instances have been reported of players expanding and contracting their stomach muscles instead of moving the instrument. A !Kung Bushman was observed by England doing this with a tin can (in lieu of a gourd) held against his shooting bow to serve as an unattached resonator; it seems likely, however, that he was imitating the gourd-bow technique of some neighbouring peoples. Gourd bows are generally used for self-accompaniment while singing and, certainly among the Nguni, the instrumental ostinato serves as a substitute chorus part, against which the performer takes the antiphonal role of the leading singer.

The classical Nguni instruments are the Zulu *ugubhu*

Ex.2 Song accompaniment played on the Zulu *ugubhu* (unbraced gourd bow), sounded by striking the string with a piece of thatching grass, as in fig.2a (Rycroft, 1975–6)

○ unstopped
● stopped (pinched between left thumb-nail and forefinger)

(fig.2a), Swazi LIGUBHU and Xhosa UHADI. These are large musical bows, about 1·5 metres long, with a gourd-resonator attached near the lower end, and a single un-divided string struck with a piece of thatching grass. The instrument is held vertically in front of the player, so that the circular hole in the gourd faces his left breast or shoulder and can be moved closer or farther away for the selective resonation of harmonics, usually 2nd to 5th partials. Besides the fundamental note yielded by the open string, a second note is obtained by pinching the string near its lower end between the left thumbnail and forefinger as shown in fig.2a, the remaining three fin-gers gripping the stave. The interval between the open and stopped notes produced by Xhosa players is usually roughly a whole tone; the outstanding Zulu musician, Princess Constance Magogo kaDinuzulu, uses a semi-tone varying from 90 to 150 cents on different occa-sions; both sizes of interval have been noted among Swazi players. Selectively resonated harmonics from the two fundamentals, though relatively faint, are used melo-dically as a vocal accompaniment (see ex.2). The resul-

Ex.3 Selectively resonated harmonics on Nguni unbraced gourd bows (see Rycroft, 1969)

(a) Whole-tone stopping on the Xhosa *uhadi*

(b) Semitone stopping on the Zulu *ugubhu*

tant hexatonic scales obtained from whole-tone and semitone stopping are shown in ex.3; though the open-string fundamental is shown as *C*, the tuning is often as much as a 5th lower, and the entire series is transposed accordingly.

A second type of gourd bow, the Zulu *umakhweyana* and the Swazi *makhweyane*, reputedly borrowed from the Tsonga people of Mozambique early in the 19th cen-tury, largely displaced the Zulu *ugubhu* and the Swazi *ligubhu* but was not adopted by the Xhosa. This instru-ment, shown in fig.2b, differs from the earlier type in that the gourd-resonator is slightly smaller and mounted near the centre of the stave instead of at the bottom. In addition the string is tied back by a wire loop or brace attached to the resonator, so that two open notes are obtainable, one from each segment of the string. These notes are tuned anything from a whole tone to a minor 3rd apart, and a third fundamental, usually a semitone higher, can be produced by stopping with a knuckle the lower segment of the string below the restraining loop. This stopped note has a duller sound however and is not always used. Selectively resonated harmonics are used melodically in the same way as on unbraced gourd bows. The notes available from the braced gourd bow, when the two segments of the string are tuned a whole tone apart, are shown in ex.4. Some players may transpose the entire series as much as a minor 3rd higher.

Ex.4 Notes obtainable on the braced gourd bow: the Zulu *umakhweyana* and the Swazi *makhweyane*

The largest collection of recordings of African musi-cal bows is housed at the International Library of Afri-can Music, Rhodes University, Grahamstown, South Africa.

The following musical bows are entered in this dictionary: adingili; adungu (i); akaheto; andobu; arpa-ché; azusayumi; badingba; bailol; baka(i); balu; bandingba; barikendikendi; basoi; bawa; bayi; belem-bautuyan; bendukuku; beng; benta; berimbau; berimbau de barriga; bikife; bogenda; bombo (iv); bongengee; bongo-bongo; bongoga; burumbumba; caramba; cayuave; chibvelani; chigwana; chimazam-bi; chimwanikoda; chipendani; chisambi; chitende; chizambi; chun-ga; cilimbwi; cora; dende; dienguela; dikupu; dimbwa; dingba (i); dumba (ii); egoboli; egobore; ekidongo (i); ekinongo; ekitulenge; elingingile; endono; fusili; gabamboli; gabus; gahakan; gamakhas; gambili; ganza; gárgara; gbong-kpala; gedo; ginyeli; gobo (ii); god-ye; gom-gom; gongqin; gora; goukhas; gourd bow; gowra; gual-ambo; gubo; gulimed; gulutindi; guma; guru; guyrapa-í; gwale; gwaningba; ha; hade; hungo; igonga; igwali; ikoka; indono; ingon-ga; inkinge; inkohlisa; inkoko (ii); ipiano; isiqwemqwemana; isi-thontolo; itumbolongonda; jejo; jinjeram; kabarome; kakulumbumba; kalove; kalumbu; kambili; kandiri kandiri; kangan; kankarma; kar-karí; kashane; kawayawaya; kawombo; kedondolo; khas; kidrigo; kilibongo; kilikingila; kilingbindiri; kitingbi; koala; ko'e; koningei; kon-kón; korongoe; kpwokolo; kū; kubu; kudungba; kulongkoing; kumbili; künkülkawe; kwadi; kwadili; kwendibe; lalango; lekope; lengope; lesiba; ligubhu; lingongo; lipombo; lonkoko; lugube; lukungu; lungungu (i); lusuba; makhweyane; maringisa; ma'wo; mbeta; mbulumbumba; moqakana; mouth bow; mouth zither; mqan-gala; mtangala; mtyángala; mungongo; narimba-ché; ndaludali; ndimga; ndono; ngangan; ngorodo; ngumbo; ngwosto; ninga; nko-ka; nqangala; ntono; nxoronxoro; ohonji; omugoboli; onavillu; outa; pagolo; papai; paruntsi; penda; picking bow; pināk; pingoru; piom pirintzi; pūsliné; quijongo; sagaya; sambi (iii); sanū; segwana; sek-gapa; sekhankula; sekokwane; setolotolo; shitende; sikhweyane;

smuigas; spēles; t'ha; thomo; thongoana; tiepore; tingle apho; titapu; tolo-tolo; tomo; tontórentzi; tsayantur; tshihwana; tshipendani; tshi-tendole; tshivhana; tshizambi; tumank; uele; ugubhu; ugwala; uhadi; 'ukēkē; ukubu; umakhweyana; umhubhe; umqangala; umrhubhe; umuduri; undemoü; une; unkoka; urucungu; utete; utiyane; villu; vīṇā; vuhudendung; xitende; xizambi; zambumbia; zegari.

BIBLIOGRAPHY

IzikowitzMISAI; *KirbyMISA*; *LaurentyC*; *OrtizIMA*; *Wachsmann-TCU*, 311–415

G. Fritsch: *Die Eingeborenen Süd-Afrikas* (Breslau, 1872), 20, 132f, 190f, 225, 327f, 427, 439f

O. T. Mason: 'Geographical Distribution of the Musical Bow', *American Anthropologist*, x (1897), 377

H. ten Kate: 'Geographical Distribution of the Musical Bow', *American Anthropologist*, xi (1898), 93

H. Balfour: *The Natural History of the Musical Bow* (Oxford, 1899)

B. Ankermann: 'Die afrikanischen Musikinstrumente', *Ethnologisches Notizblatt*, iii/1 (1901), 1–134

L. Frobenius: 'Die Saiteninstrumente der Naturvölker', *Prometheus*, xii (1901), 625, 648

G. Montandon: 'La généalogie des instruments de musique et les cycles de civilisation', *Archives suisses d'anthropologie générale*, iii (1919), 1–71

C. Sachs: *Geist und Werden der Musikinstrumente* (Berlin, 1929)

E. M. von Hornbostel: 'The Ethnology of African Sound-instruments', *Africa*, vi (1933), 129, 277–311

J. Kunst: *De toonkunst van Java* (The Hague, 1934; Eng. trans., rev. 2/1949, enlarged 3/1973), 232f

T. Norlind, ed.: *Systematik der Saiteninstrumente* (Stockholm, 1936)

C. Sachs: *The History of Musical Instruments* (New York, 1940)

G.-J. Duchemin: 'Autour d'un arc musical du Saloum oriental', *Première conférence internationale des africanistes de l'ouest: Dakar 1945*, 248

D. K. Rycroft: 'Tribal Style and Free Expression', *African Music*, i/1 (1954), 16

H.-H. Wängler: 'Über südwestafrikanische Bogenlieder', *Afrika und Übersee*, xxxix (1954–5), 49; xl (1955–6), 163

C. M. Camp and B. Nettl: 'The Musical Bow in Southern Africa', *Anthropos*, 1 (1955), 65

H. Fischer: *Schallgeräte in Ozeanien* (Strasbourg, 1958)

S. Marcuse: 'Musical Bow', *Musical Instruments: a Comprehensive Dictionary* (New York, 1964)

G. List: 'The Musical Bow at Palenque', *JIFMC*, xviii (1966), 36

D. K. Rycroft: 'Friction Chordophones in South Eastern Africa', *GSJ*, xix (1966), 84

N. M. England: 'Bushman Counterpoint', *JIFMC*, xix (1967), 58

G. Kubik: *Mehrstimmigkeit und Tonsysteme in Zentral- und Ostafrika* (Vienna, 1968), 50ff, pl.2

D. Taylor: 'The Music of Some Indian Tribes in Colombia', *Recorded Sound*, xxix–xxx (1968), suppl.

D. K. Rycroft: *Zulu, Swazi and Xhosa Instrumental and Vocal Music* (Tervuren, 1969) [with disc]

G. Kubik: *Musica tradicional e aculturada dos !Kung' de Angola* (Lisbon, 1970), 30ff

T. Johnston: 'Xizambi Friction-bow Music of the Shangana-Tsonga', *African Music*, iv/4 (1970), 81

H. Zemp: *Musique Dan* (Paris, 1971)

H. Tracey: *Catalogue: the Sound of Africa Series* (Roodepoort, 1973)

M. Davidson: 'Some Patterns of Rhythm and Harmony in *Kalumbu* Music', *African Music*, v/3 (1973–4), 70

G. Kubik: 'Musical Bows in South-Western Angola, 1965', *African Music*, v/4 (1975–6), 98

D. K. Rycroft: 'The Zulu Bow-songs of Princess Magogo', *African Music*, v/4 (1975–6), 41

——: 'The Musical Bow in Southern Africa', *Papers presented at the Second Symposium on Ethnomusicology* (Grahamstown, 1981), 70

DAVID K. RYCROFT

Musical box. A MECHANICAL INSTRUMENT in which tuned steel prongs are made to vibrate by contact with moving parts driven by a clockwork mechanism. In 1796 Antoine Favre of Geneva is known to have produced music from steel prongs sounded by pins set in a disc or drum. Originally small musical adjuncts to watches, these evolved into larger brass cylinders with steel pins playing a line of tuned teeth (*see* MECHANICAL INSTRUMENT, fig.7), and in turn gave rise to the one-piece tuned steel comb with the essential refinement of steel dampers. Small musical movements were first made in quantity for snuffboxes (Fr. *tabatières*) and were known by the French term. Similarly, large movements, known as *cartels*, took their name from the wall and bracket clocks for which they were first made. These two descriptive names replaced the early term *carillons à musique*.

By about 1825 the musical box was well established in its standard form, with combs having as many as 250 teeth covering a range of about six octaves, and generally tuned to an unequal temperament. Cylinder sizes ranged from those designed for snuff-box miniatures through the common type with diameters of 54 mm, playing one minute per tune, to 100 mm and sometimes even larger, giving playing times of three minutes per tune. Cylinder lengths were up to about 500 mm; a typical good quality box playing eight airs of one minute each with a comb of 96 teeth would have a cylinder of 330 mm. Those with larger diameters were often pinned to play operatic overtures; the tune arrangers became very accomplished, and most effects in an orchestral score were skilfully imitated.

Musical box manufacture grew up mainly in Switzerland (particularly in the Geneva to St Croix region), long famous for precision horology; makers who soon became renowned include Capt, Falconnet, Henriot, Junod, Langdorff, Lecoultre, Mermod, Nicole and Paillard. Those working elsewhere included such makers as Řebíček in Prague, Olbrich in Vienna and L'Epée near Montbéliard in France. L'Epée also produced the 'manivelle', a small hand-cranked musical box for children, generally with tinplate body and playing only one tune.

The combined technical and musical skills of these makers led to various refinements and additions. These included the Mandolin, in which the comb had groups of up to eight teeth tuned to the same pitch and capable of being sounded in rapid succession like a mandolin or for sustained note effect; the Piccolo, in which the comb had additional treble teeth to decorate the melody; and the Forte-piano, which had a second, shorter comb to permit better dynamic contrast. In 1874 Paillard patented the Sublime Harmonie, which had two or more combs with teeth tuned to within about 4 Hz of the same pitch and thus offering both a beat effect and different harmonics which together enhance the performance. The harp-like accompaniment of the Harp Eolienne was effected by a short second comb with a tissue-paper 'zither' below (such tissue rolls could also be applied above the comb). Tuned bells (three to 12), drum (with vellum or brass head, normally with eight strikers) and castanet (hollow wooden block with six or eight strikers) were occasionally added, generally with separate provision to disconnect them. These were operated from untuned teeth on additional combs, which meant longer cylinders or fewer tunes or fewer notes. In the organ attachment, paired reeds (12 to 30) were fitted, tuned to differ in frequency by about 8 Hz, giving the beat effect described as 'Flûte voix célestes'. Only the bells and organ were generally regarded as attractive additions.

Most manufacturers produced most of these varieties under numerous descriptive names (e.g. Flutina, Harpe-harmonique, Expression Extra, Symphonie) that appeared on the tune sheets. But of the thousands of cylinder musical boxes (Nicole Frères alone made about 50,000), the vast majority were of the unadorned single-comb type, unique in being the only musical instrument with tuned steel teeth and in being too delicate for playing by hand. Besides sacred and popular music, arias and overtures from most operas popular between 1830 and 1890 were faithfully reproduced.

Orchestral cylinder musical box by Paillard Vaucher Fils, Swiss, c1888 (private collection)

The small, plain cases of early musical boxes gave way about 1840 to cases of high quality, the lid and front embellished with fine marquetry and sometimes metal and mother-of-pearl inlays. Larger cases also improved the radiation efficiency of the bass notes. Lever winding displaced the separate winding keys about 1860. Longer playing time for one winding was provided on some boxes by double and occasionally quadruple springs. Longer compositions were usually handled by allowing them two or more turns of the cylinder; other devices invented for continuous long-playing were too complex for commercial success.

The basic shortcoming of the cylinder musical box was its limitation to the tunes on its one cylinder. The introduction of interchangeable cylinders left two remaining problems: vulnerability of the comb teeth during the change, and storage of spare cylinders. The latter was sometimes solved by building the box into a piece of furniture with storage drawers. Continued experiments to replace the cylinder by a simple steel disc with projections or slots to play one tune succeeded in about 1889 when Paul Lochmann set up his Symphonion factory in Leipzig. Soon two of his staff left and set up the rival Polyphon factory (*see* POLYPHON (i)), also in Leipzig, and in 1892 they started production in New Jersey, USA, under the name Regina. Mermod and other Swiss manufacturers joined in, and by about 1900 disc machines were available in tremendous numbers and varieties, with discs up to 850 mm in diameter and including such effects as Sublime Harmonie and bells. Slot machines were made for use in public places, some fitted with automatic disc change. The disc machines were mostly mass-produced; their almost unlimited tune variety resulted in their soon eclipsing the cylinder musical box, being themselves duly eclipsed by the gramophone.

Manufacture of musical boxes survived to a limited degree in Switzerland and has started in several countries due to a strong revival of interest.

For further illustration, *see* MECHANICAL INSTRUMENT, fig.5; *see also* BIRD INSTRUMENTS, §2.

BIBLIOGRAPHY

M. M. Curtis: *Story of Snuff and Snuffboxes* (New York, 1935)
R. and M. Norton: *A History of Gold Snuff Boxes* (London, 1938)
J. E. T. Clark: *Musical Boxes: a History and an Appreciation* (Birmingham, 1948, 3/1961)
R. Mosoriak: *The Curious History of Music Boxes* (Chicago, 1953)
A. Buchner: *Hudební automaty* (Prague, 1959; Eng. trans., 1959)
A. W. J. G. Ord-Hume: *Collecting Musical Boxes* (London, 1967)
G. Webb: *The Cylinder Musical Box Handbook* (London, 1968)
F. Baud and others: *Au temps des boîtes à musique* (Lausanne, 1970)
G. Webb: *The Disc Musical Box Handbook* (London, 1971)
D. Tallis: *Musical Boxes* (London, 1971)
A. W. J. G. Ord-Hume: *Musical Box* (London, 1980)
——: *Restoring Musical Boxes* (London, 1980)
G. Webb: *The Musical Box Handbook* (New York, 1984)

H. A. V. BULLEID

Musical clock. A clock combined with a MECHANICAL INSTRUMENT which played music at regular time intervals (every quarter of an hour, half-hour, or hour) or at will. In the Middle Ages astronomical clocks were equipped with carillons (the earliest account from 1352 mentions a carillon in Strasbourg), and in the 16th and 17th centuries there was a great upsurge in the construction of carillons in Flanders and Holland, whence they spread into a number of other countries, especially France and Germany. When spring mechanisms were invented, small carillons were built in portable clocks. These clocks were extremely expensive, but later on cheaper wooden musical clocks with glass carillons were made in the Black Forest region. In these musical clocks eight to sixteen glass bells played short folksongs by means of a cylinder. As early as the 16th century watches were equipped with miniature carillons, and from the 18th century these watches were combined with miniature musical instruments based on the comb mechanism. In the first half of the 19th century the metal bells of the carillon were replaced either by chromatically tuned metal rods, arranged in the manner of the xylophone, or (more frequently) with comb mechanisms, as in the MUSICAL BOX.

In the 18th century the manufacture of musical clocks was concentrated in London. There these instruments were made by outstanding clockmakers, including Barbot, William Carpenter, James Cox, R. Fleetwood, Fox & Sons, Fromanteel & Clark, Henderson, George Higginson, Thomas Larrymore, Marriott, Eardley Norton, Robert Philip, Robert Sellers, Tomlin, and Williamson; musical clocks built by all these clockmakers are now in the largest collection of musical clocks, in the Imperial Palace Museum in Peking. In the 1760s Frederick the Great invited watchmakers from Switzerland to establish the manufacture of musical clocks in Berlin. Among well-known Berlin manufacturers are Konrad Ehrbar, Christian Möllinger, Johann Elfroth and the court watchmaker Pohlmann; the cylinders were pinned by the musician Kummer. While the London manufacturers for the most part made musical clocks with carillons, the Berlin makers concentrated upon flute-playing clocks. Later, the manufacture of musical clocks spread to Paris, Dresden and Prague, but mainly to Vienna, where clocks were made by J. A. Hoyer and J. Janisch. Large flute-playing clocks (Ger. *Flötenuhr*), in fact orchestrions combined with clocks, were made by the Maelzel brothers in Vienna.

Flute-playing clocks played arrangements of music (overtures, arias, parts of flute concertos and sonatas, marches and dance music), but also compositions written exclusively for them. Gerber (*Lexicon*, 1790–92/ R1976) mentioned a flute-playing clock constructed by Primitivus Němec, Prince Esterházy's librarian, whose cylinder played music written by Mozart and Haydn for this instrument. 32 compositions by Haydn for flute-playing clock were published by Nagel in Hanover in

1931 and by Bärenreiter in Kassel in 1954. There are also 28 compositions by C. P. E. Bach, three compositions by Mozart and three by Beethoven.

As well as flute-playing clocks, harp-playing clocks were made, equipped with a stringed automatophone. In Cöthen Castle there was a harp-playing clock made by Johannes Zacharias Fischer from Halle; it was destroyed during World War II. On the cylinders of that instrument were original compositions and arrangements by W. F. Bach (attributed to J. S. Bach when they were published by A. Klughardt in 1897). At the beginning of the 19th century musical boxes almost completely replaced flute-playing and harp-playing clocks.

BIBLIOGRAPHY

G. Kinsky: 'Beethoven und die Flötenuhr', *Beethoven-Almanach*, ed. G. Bosse (Regensburg, 1927)
E. F. Schmid: 'Joseph Haydn und die Flötenuhr', *ZMw*, xiv (1931–2), 193
S. Harcourt-Smith: *A Catalogue of Various Clocks* (Peiping, 1933)
A. Chapuis: *Le Grand Frédéric et ses horlogers* (Lausanne, 1938)
A. Orel: 'Andante für eine Walze: sekundäre Quellen zu Mozarts KV.616', *Acta Mozartiana*, iii/4 (1956), 3
A. Buchner: *Hudební automaty* (Prague, 1959; Eng. trans., 1959)
K. Bormann: *Orgel- und Spieluhrenbau* (Zurich, 1968)
Q. D. Bowers: *Encyclopedia of Automatic Musical Instruments* (New York, 1972)
A. W. J. G. Ord-Hume: *Clockwork Music* (London and New York, 1973)

ALEXANDR BUCHNER

Musical glasses [armonica, harmonica, glass harmonica] (Fr. *verrillon*). Bell-type instruments made of glass or other brittle material that if rubbed in a certain fashion will respond like the strings of a bowed instrument, though with less capacity for nuance. They may also be struck, with moderate force, for quasi-plucking and melodic tremolo effects as on a xylophone, a method that prevails in Asia.

While it is not always possible to distinguish various types of bell or gong-chime among descriptions of ancient instruments, musical glasses in the West were evidently derived from Asian antecedents, particularly in Persia from the 11th century onwards. The earliest known European allusion to musical glasses occurs in Gaffurius's *Theorica musicae* (Milan, 1492), which contains a woodcut showing the musical use of vessels in a 'Pythagorean experiment' (see fig.1). An inventory made in 1596 of the Ambras collection (now in the Kunsthistorisches Museum, Vienna) describes 'Ain Instrument von Glaswerck', three and a third octaves in compass (see Primisser, 1819). These and similar phenomena, such as 'making a cheerful wine-music', described by Harsdörffer, may well have grown up independently of oriental influences, which seem however to have been fairly strong. Diderot referred to the use of musical glasses in ancient Persia; such musical practices had doubtless become known to western Europe through reports of early travellers.

It was apparently during the early 18th century that the glasses came into serious musical use, having been previously regarded in Europe as only a quasi-scientific toy or novel amusement for social gatherings. The sound was produced by striking the sides of the glasses with a stick, which was sometimes muffled. In England the more refined technique of stroking the rims with the fingertips seems to have been first used in 1744 by an Irishman, Richard Pockrich, whose glasses were graded by size and tuned by the addition of water where required to raise their natural pitch. In a concert at the Haymar-ket Theatre, London (23 April 1746; reported in the *General Advertiser*), Gluck played a concerto on 26 glasses; he gave another in Copenhagen in 1749. In London, newspaper announcements testify to the growing popularity of musical glasses in the 1750s. One particularly notable performer was Ann Ford, who married Philip Thicknesse, Gainsborough's friend and biographer. She published the first known method for the instrument in 1761 (unique copy now in *US-CA*) and gave explicit instructions for the use of the moistened pads of the fingers – with precise application of varying degrees of pressure – on the sides and rims of the glass.

Meanwhile, in spring 1761 Benjamin Franklin, then on a visit to England, heard Edmund Delaval, a fellow of Pembroke Hall, Cambridge, play on the glasses. Franklin was so impressed with the instrument that he decided to improve it. He took the bowls of the glasses and fitted them concentrically (the largest on the left) on a horizontal rod, which was actuated by a crank attached to a pedal (see fig.2, p.726). Careful gradation of size ensured a more consistently accurate scale than was possible with water tuning, while the close proximity of the rims (which would be well moistened before use) enabled the player to produce chords and runs with far greater ease than had been possible when each glass stood separate on its base. In a letter (see Sparks) to an Italian scientist named Beccaria, Franklin proposed to call his instrument the 'armonica', as a compliment to the musical Italian language. (The intrusive 'h', of German origin, has no original authority, and only serves to confuse this instrument with the modern harmonica

1. Musical glasses used in a 'Pythagorean experiment': woodcut from Gaffurius's 'Theorica musicae' (1492)

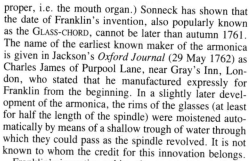

2. *Benjamin Franklin playing the armonica: portrait by Alan Foster (b 1892) (private collection)*

3. *Bruno Hoffmann playing the glass harp, 1971*

proper, i.e. the mouth organ.) Sonneck has shown that the date of Franklin's invention, also popularly known as the GLASS-CHORD, cannot be later than autumn 1761. The name of the earliest known maker of the armonica is given in Jackson's *Oxford Journal* (29 May 1762) as Charles James of Purpool Lane, near Gray's Inn, London, who stated that he manufactured expressly for Franklin from the beginning. In a slightly later development of the armonica, the rims of the glasses (at least for half the length of the spindle) were moistened automatically by means of a shallow trough of water through which they could pass as the spindle revolved. It is not known to whom the credit for this innovation belongs.

Franklin's invention achieved a certain popularity in America, but exercised far more influence in Europe, where it seems to have been introduced by Marianne Davies, a virtuoso who is thought to have received her own armonica from Franklin. She began to tour Europe in 1768, moving in the highest society. In 1773 she became known to the Mozart family, and caused Leopold Mozart to express an interest in owning an armonica himself. She also met Anton Mesmer, the originator of 'magnetism', who developed an enduring devotion to the instrument and used it to induce a receptive state in his hypnotic subjects. As on the glasses (i.e. the instrument in its original form), some of the finest armonica players were women, for instance Marianne Kirchgessner, the remarkable blind performer who became famous throughout Europe between 1790 and her death in 1808; Mozart composed his exquisite Quintet K617 for armonica, flute, oboe, viola and cello for her in 1791.

There is ample testimony that the practice of eliciting sounds from the revolving bowls of the glasses was apt to have a deranging effect on the nerves of the player. Sachs attributed this to 'the irritating permanence of extremely high partials and the continuous contact of

the sensitive fingers with the vibrating bowls'. In some German towns the armonica was banned by the police. Various improvements were attempted, aiming to eliminate the fingers as the means of contact: several types of keyboard were devised, by Hessel at St Petersburg (1782), by H. Klein at Pressburg, by Röllig and by D. J. Nicolai at Görlitz (all 1784), and by Francis Hopkinson in America in 1787; P. J. Frick, a virtuoso armonica player, had introduced pads as early as 1769; and in 1779 Mazzucchi applied a form of violin bow to the instrument. But direct hand contact could not be rivalled for natural tone quality, whatever the gain might otherwise be in facility and speed of execution.

The heyday of the armonica in Europe lasted until about 1830. Its distinctive tone of vibrant, piercing sweetness caught the imagination of various French and German Romantic writers; Goethe, for instance, wrote that in the sustained chords of this music he could detect 'Die Herzblut der Welt'. Even while the armonica was at the height of its popularity, the earlier form never quite lost its appeal; Ann Ford, for instance, was still playing the musical glasses in 1790. After the armonica had become a museum piece, the glasses lingered, at least in Britain, throughout the 19th century, and were often heard in music halls and sometimes at evangelical meetings. In the 20th century they have been revived by the German virtuoso Bruno Hoffmann (see fig.3) under the name 'glass harp'; his playing of the Mozart quintet has been recorded.

BIBLIOGRAPHY

G. P. Harsdörffer: *Deliciae physico-mathematicae* (Nuremberg, 1677), 147

A. Ford: *Instructions for the Playing of the Musical Glasses* (London, 1761)

D. Diderot, ed.: 'Verres, musique des', *Encyclopédie*, xvii (Paris, 1765)

K. L. Röllig: *Ueber die Harmonika* (Berlin, 1787)

J. C. Muller: *Anleitung zum Selbstunterricht an der Harmonika* (Leipzig, 1788)

F. C. Bartl: *Nachrichten von der Harmonika* (Prague, 1796)

G. von Graubenfeld: *Aestetische Gedänken über Bartl's Tasten-harmonika* (Vienna, 1798)

R. Rochlitz: 'Ueber die vermeintliche Schädlichkeit des Harmonika-spiels', *AMZ*, i (1798), 97

A. Primisser: *Die Kaiserlich-Königliche Ambraser-Sammlung* (Vienna, 1819), 219

J. Sparks, ed.: *The Works of Benjamin Franklin*, vi (Boston, 1840), 245

C. F. Pohl: *Zur Geschichte der Glasharmonika* (Vienna, 1862; Eng. trans., 1862)

D. J. O'Donoghue: *An Irish Musical Genius: Richard Pockrich the Inventor of the Musical Glasses* (Dublin, 1899)

O. G. T. Sonneck: 'Benjamin Franklin's Musical Side', *Suum cuique* (New York, 1916)

W. Lüthge: 'Die Glasharmonika, das Instrument der Wertherzeit', *Der Bär* (1925), 98

C. Sachs: *History of Musical Instruments* (New York, 1940), 404

A. H. King: 'The Musical Glasses and Glass Harmonica', *PRMA*, lxxii (1945–6), 97

B. Hoffmann: 'Glasharmonika und Glasharfe', *Musica*, iv (1950), 327

——: 'Glasharmonika', *MGG* [incl. list of music for the armonica]

A. H. King: 'Some Notes on the Armonica', *MMR*, lxxxvi (1956), 61

B. Matthews: 'The Davies Sisters, J. C. Bach and the Glass Harmonica', *ML*, lvi (1975), 150

B. Hoffmann: *Ein Leben für die Glasharfe* (Backnang, 1983)

ALEC HYATT KING

Musical saw. See SAW, MUSICAL.

Musical telegraph. An electromagnetic keyboard instrument developed in Chicago between 1874 and 1877 by Elisha Gray (*b* Barnesville, Ohio, 2 Aug 1835; *d* Newtonville, Mass., 21 Jan 1901), an inventor in the field of telegraphy. Gray's aim was not primarily musical; the two versions of his instrument were intended to help him solve the major communications problem of the time, that of multiplexed telegraphy – the simultaneous transmission over a single telegraph wire of several Morse code messages, each at a different pitch. The 1877 model of the 'musical telegraph' demonstrated that independent messages could be separated out at the receiving end simply on the basis of their pitch content. (Alexander Graham Bell's telephone rapidly diminished the importance of Gray's inventions, though recently multiplexing techniques have in turn expanded the capabilities of telephone systems.)

Starting with one- and two-note transmitters and receivers, by the summer of 1874 Gray had built a first 'musical telegraph' (or 'telephone') with a range of one diatonic octave; in 1876 he demonstrated an improved model (called the 'electromusical' or 'electroharmonic piano' in later sources) with two diatonic octaves. The sound was produced by steel reeds caused to vibrate by electromagnets, which were switched on and off by a keyboard that could be some distance from them. In the original model the sounds were heard over receivers made from a violin, a paper drum and a washbasin: in the first two a metal strip (instead of an electromagnetic coil) was placed on the violin bridge and the drum skin; in the third an electromagnet was mounted close to the centre of a metal washbasin suspended from a stand (this was probably the first use of an electrical 'loudspeaker' in connection with a musical instrument). Between the reeds, with their associated electromagnets, and the receiver, the connecting wire could be of any length, depending on the strength of the batteries at the transmission end and on weather conditions; Gray demonstrated transmission and reception over a distance of 2400 miles in 1874.

During the next two years Gray pursued various ideas for multiplexed telegraphy and, less seriously, speech transmission (in which his experiments were overtaken in 1876 by Bell's telephone). In the improved model of the 'musical telegraph' electromagnetically vibrated reeds were incorporated in the receiver as well as the transmitter; to give them greater resonance they were mounted inside a row of square-sectioned wooden resonators, resembling organ pipes, which were placed on top of a grand piano. In April 1877 Gray staged a week of concert demonstrations of the improved model in New York, Brooklyn and Washington. The music was played by Frederick Boscovitz in Philadelphia (mainly with only one hand), and heard by audiences at the other end of a specially installed telephone line; the programme included *Home, Sweet Home*, an aria from Flotow's *Martha*, and *Yankee Doodle* as an encore.

For illustration *see* ELECTRONIC INSTRUMENTS, fig.3.

BIBLIOGRAPHY

'Music By Telegraph', *New York Times* (10 July 1874), 2

E. Gray: 'On the Transmission of Musical Tones Telegraphically', *Scientific American Supplement*, i (1876), 92

'Music By Telegraph: Prof. Gray's Telephone Concert', *New York Times* (3 April 1877), 5

'Professor Gray's Telephone', *Scientific American*, xxxvi (1877), 263

E. Gray: *Experimental Researches in Electro-Harmonic Telegraphy and Telephony, 1876–1878* (New York, 1878); repr. in *The Telephone: an Historical Anthology*, ed. G. Shiers (New York, 1977)

E. Gray: *Nature's Miracles* (New York, 1900)

R. V. Bruce: *Bell: Alexander Graham Bell and the Conquest of Solitude* (Boston and London, 1973), 113

D. A. Hounshell: 'Elisha Gray and the Telephone: On the Disadvantages of being an Expert', *Technology and Culture*, xvi/2 (1975), 133

H. C. Schonberg: 'When Music was Broadcast by Telephone', *New York Times* (11 May 1975), §D, p.17

HUGH DAVIES

Music box. See MUSICAL BOX.

Music Easel. A SYNTHESIZER manufactured in a number of models by BUCHLA.

Musik bambu. See ORKES.

Musikbogen (Ger.). MUSICAL BOW.

Musikkorps (Ger.). Military band; *see* BAND (i), §II, 1(i), 2(i) and §III, 2.

Musikmaskin I (Swed.: 'Music Machine I'). A sound sculpture constructed in Stockholm in 1961 by Knut Wiggen and Per-Olof Strömberg, with Öyvind Fahlström. This automated electronic sound machine produced randomized musical structures over 20 loudspeaker channels. It was designed as a prototype for Musikmaskin II, which was the initial, conceptual stage in the development of the Elektronmusikstudion in Stockholm (*see* EMS (ii)).

BIBLIOGRAPHY

'Wiggens Musikmaskin', *Nutida musik*, v/2 (1961–2), 19

HUGH DAVIES

Musokolome. GROUND HARP of the Soga people of Uganda. See SEKITULEGE.

Musompola. Drum of the Luba people of Zaïre. See DITUMBA.

Mustel, Victor (*b* Le Havre, 13 June 1815; *d* Paris, 26 Jan 1890). French manufacturer of harmoniums. His several inventions resulted in the instrument known as the Mustel organ. Orphaned at the age of 12, he was apprenticed to a shipbuilder and in 1838 set up in business for himself in that trade in Sanvic. Endowed from youth with a peculiarly constructive genius, he first attempted to make musical instruments by devoting himself to the improvement of an accordion which he had bought at Le Havre. Elated with his success, he disposed of his workshop in May 1844 and set out for Paris with his wife and two children. For the next nine years he worked in several different workshops, but never obtained high wages. In 1853 he determined to start in business for himself as a harmonium maker, and in 1855 he exhibited his harmonium with 'Double Expression' and a new stop (Harpe éolienne), for which he gained a medal of the first class. For the first year after this Mustel (now assisted by his two sons) did fairly well, but business rapidly declined, and he would perhaps have been obliged to give up but for the sale of a little land which he had inherited from his father. Even in 1866 his receipts did little more than cover costs, but from that date the firm of Victor Mustel & ses Fils gained a reputation as noteworthy in England as in France. The present name of the firm is Mustel & Cie.

The inventions due to the Mustels are the 'double expression' (patented in 1854), whereby the natural preponderance of the bass notes over those of the treble is, with complete power of increase and decrease in either half, brought under direct control of the player by means of knee pedals (*genouillères*) that control the energy and pressure of the wind; the 'Forte expressif', a divided swell governed by pneumatic action; and the 'Harpe éolienne', a tremolo register of two ranks of vibrators, 2′ pitch, which offer a gently beating variation to the unison by being slightly higher and lower than the normal pitch of the instrument, the impression of which remains unimpaired. Later Mustel inventions were the Typophone and Métaphone. The first of these is a keyboard percussion instrument made of tuning-forks in resonance boxes of the proper acoustic capacity; it probably influenced Mustel's son Auguste in his invention of the celesta (1886), based on similar principles. The Métaphone (patented 1878) was devised by his other son Charles to soften the strident tones of the harmonium. This softening effect is produced by a sliding shutter of leather to each compartment and governed by draw-stops, as with other modifications of tone and power.

See also REED ORGAN, §§1–2, esp. Table 1 and fig.3, and VIBRAPHONE.

BIBLIOGRAPHY
A. Mustel: *L'orgue-expressif ou Harmonium* (Paris, 1903)
L. Hartmann: *Das Harmonium* (Leipzig, 1913)
E. Mallin: *The Orchestral Organist & the Mustel Organ* (Paris, 1921)

A. J. HIPKINS/R

Musuntu. Single-headed cylindrical drum of the Valley Tonga people of Zambia. It is similar to the GAYANDA drum.

Muswai. Gourd vessel rattle of the Luba people of Zaïre. It has internal strikers of sorghum seeds; the shell is often perforated and small straw plugs inserted so that the seeds hit them when the rattle is shaken. The contemporary *muswai* is woven from reeds in the same shape as the traditional instrument, and is used during religious ceremonies by both Catholics and Protestants to provide rhythmic accompaniment to songs. The Luba assign a magical power to this instrument, which is often inserted in the straw roof of a hut in order to keep away evil spirits. See J. Gansemans: *Les instruments de musique Luba* (Tervuren, 1980).

J. GANSEMANS

Muta (It.: 'change'). A performing instruction: 'Muta in La' would mean change to an instrument in A, or change the tuning-crook of a wind instrument to put it in A.

Mutanda. Conical drum of the Ndau people of Chipinga district, Zimbabwe. It is made from wood of the mutanda tree.

Mutation stop. In modern organ usage, mutations are those single-rank stops, usually of wide or fairly wide-scaled pipes with a high lead content, pitched at the 5th, 3rd, 7th, 9th, etc, of an upper octave; hence their other names: 'overtone stops', *Aliquotstimmen*, etc. Common examples are the Nasard, Larigot and Tierce; sometimes the stop has two ranks (e.g. Terzian), in which case it really belongs to the mixtures; sometimes the stop is scaled, voiced and constructed of a metal suitable for a Principal rank (e.g. Twelfth), in which case it is not a Flute mutation. Historically, the picture is not simple. *Mutationen* could mean any stops, a synonym for *Stimmen* (J. B. Samber, *Continuatio ad manuductionem organicam*, 1707); in late medieval contracts, *mutaciones* denoted much the same as *jeux* or *jochs*, i.e. registrations or, simply, different sounds (Minorites' church, Barcelona, 1480); in classical French usage, mutation stops include any rank (such as 2′ flutes or even solo reeds) which are of wide scale or drawn outside the *plein jeu* chorus (Paris, 1647). The term does not refer to the 'changing' of the fundamental tone to an overtone, as often stated in English sources, but to the varieties of tone or *mutaciones* such stops afford.

PETER WILLIAMS

Mutavha. In southern Africa, the Venda term for a complete set of stopped flutes (*see* NANGA (i) and STOPPED FLUTE ENSEMBLE) and also for a row of keys on a xylophone or *mbila* (lamellaphone).

Mutbej [muṭbiq, muṭabbiq]. Terms occasionally applied to a DOUBLE CLARINET of the Arab world. *See also* MIJWIZ.

Mute (Fr. *sourdine*; Ger. *Dämpfer*; It. *sordino*). A mechanical device used on musical instruments to muffle the tone, i.e. to alter the timbre, in the process the volume is usually somewhat decreased.

Two debated points about the meaning of 'with the mute' may be settled here. First, in works that consist of several movements the instruction *con sordino* ('with mute') applies only to the movement concerned. Thus, in Mozart's String Quintet in G minor (K516), the term *con sordino* over all parts at the beginning of the third movement applies only to that movement. Second, the claim that *con sordino* is synonymous with 'soft' is dis-

(a)   (b)

1. Mutes for instruments of the violin family: (a) a conventional three-pronged mute; (b) a Roth (or Roth-Sihon) mute

proved by the specified variety of dynamic markings in the movement just mentioned, including *piano*, *forte*, *crescendo* and *sforzando*.

1. Strings. 2. Wind. 3. Other.

1. STRINGS. In instruments of the violin family the typical mute takes the form of a three-pronged clamp (sometimes two- or five-pronged), made of such materials as metal (particularly steel and aluminium), ivory, bakelite or wood (especially ebony and boxwood) (see fig.1). Attached to the bridge, the mute absorbs some of the vibrations and makes the sound relatively veiled and a bit nasal; the degree of muting and the difference of tone-colour depend on the material used for the mute, its mass and the firmness with which it is attached to the bridge (*see* ACOUSTICS, §I, 3). Originally a separate accessory, the mute is sometimes installed on the instrument between bridge and tailpiece, to be pushed up against the bridge for muting as needed. 'Practice' mutes are exceptionally heavy, and are used to decrease the volume to a fraction of the normal sound for convenience when practising (their use in concert performance is occasionally requested by experimental composers). A 'wolf mute' is sometimes used to correct the WOLF effect at the major 6th or 7th above the open G string of the cello.

The mute has been used on bowed string instruments since at least the 17th century, and was described by Mersenne (1636–7). Mutes are specified in all five string parts in several passages in Act 2 (scenes iii and iv) of Lully's *Armide* (1686), among them the famous air 'Plus j'observe' (scene iii). Similarly Purcell specified mutes for the violins in the air 'See, even night herself is here' from *The Fairy Queen* (1692).

2. WIND.

(i) Woodwind. The flute is virtually never muted, but the loud high notes of the piccolo have been moderated by the covering of the middle and foot joints with a tube which has cloth-covered holes. In the 18th century the oboe was occasionally muted by the insertion of cottonwool, paper or pear-shaped pieces of hardwood into the bell. Some 18th-century specimens of the wooden oboe mute have survived; they impart a veiled quality throughout the range, most evident in the notes that issue through the lower holes. Muting is now generally accomplished by stuffing a cloth or handkerchief into the bell, a method also used by saxophonists and bassoonists; it is sometimes applied to low notes in order to make them more akin in tone quality to those in other

registers. German bassoonists sometimes use a mute made of a brass cylinder around which some soft material is wound. Bassoonists and clarinettists have also used mutes made of a sound-absorbent material, for example in the form of a disc of a size that fits just inside the bell (it may have a central hole to enable the player to insert or remove it easily). A type of clarinet mute is known to have existed in the 18th century, although nothing precise is known about it: in 1785 the firm of instrument makers named Tuerlinckx, in Mechelen, listed an order for '23 clarinets with A-joints and *sourdine*' for sale to a military band (see *Bulletin du Cercle archéologique, littéraire & artistique de Malines*, xxiv, 1914, p.176). Berlioz muted the clarinet by wrapping the bell in a bag made of cloth or leather, an example that evidently had no imitators, although around 1930 dance-band clarinettists occasionally used a type of cardboard megaphone for the purpose. It should be borne in mind that a mute applied to the bell of a woodwind instrument is likely to be unevenly effective, as compared with one applied to a brass instrument, as the proportion of the sound issuing from the bell is not constant.

(ii) Brass. Mutes are applied to brass instruments as much for modifying the tone colour as for softening the tone. The earliest known mute for the trumpet is that illustrated by Mersenne in 1636–7 (see fig.2). His description makes it clear that this, like some types of modern mute, raised the pitch of the instrument by a tone. The Dresden horn player Anton Hampel established the basis of a non-transposing mute about 1760; experimenting with a cotton mute, he also developed the technique of playing chromatically on the natural horn and instituted the somewhat veiled quality of tone that results from positioning the hand in the instrument's bell. (For a fuller discussion of pitch changes caused by muting *see* HORN, §2; see also Gregory, 49ff.) Altenburg (1795) gave five reasons for muting the (nat-

2. Trumpet and mute (top right): engraving from Mersenne's 'Harmonie universelle' (1636–7)

(a)   *(b)*

3. Horn mutes: (a) all-purpose mutes made of fibre-board and wood, with cork strips which prevent the conical portion actually closing the bell and raising the pitch (the interior shape is a hollow cylinder, the lower half of which serves as a resonance chamber); (b) mute made of brass and cork, producing a brassier tone than (a) and raising the pitch by a semitone (the interior shape follows the outline of the exterior)

ural) trumpet: secret military retreat; use at funerals; embouchure development; prevention of 'screeching'; and improving intonation.

A mute acts on the principle of the Helmholtz resonator, changing the instrument's timbre by reducing the intensity of certain partials and amplifying others. Additional effects of muting may include, besides changes in pitch, attenuation of volume and increased directivity. The player almost always has to adjust, when he mutes his instrument, to some alteration in its response.

During the 20th century, largely because of the work of jazz orchestrators, a considerable range of mutes has been developed. Mutes may be constructed from aluminium, brass, copper, wood, papier-mâché, cardboard, fibre, composition, polystyrene and rubber. Few types of mute are equally effective in all registers, and there are particular problems in muting the lower notes of a brass instrument without affecting its tuning. To a large extent such problems, although they have been the subject of research, are solved empirically. Final adjustments are often left to the player who may file the corks that support the mute to achieve the best effect with the minimum disturbance to the instrument's normal blowing characteristics.

The trumpet in particular, and to a lesser extent the trombone, is played with a large variety of mutes; these are listed and described below. The 19th-century 'echo cornet' had an integral mute controlled by a fourth valve. Until the 20th century the only mute used regularly in the symphony orchestra was the straight mute (it has been used on the tenor and bass tubas since Strauss's *Don Quixote*, 1897). On the horn, muting may be done by hand, indicated by the term 'stopped' (Fr. *sons bouchés*, Ger. *gestopft*, It. *chiuso*), or with a mute that is pear-shaped or in the form of a truncated cone (see fig.3); some mechanical mutes affect pitch, and may

contain a tuning-screw regulator to adjust intonation, while some horns incorporate a stopping valve to compensate for the change in pitch caused by muting. A special effect on the horn is the use of 'brassy' or *cuivré* (Fr.) notes (Ger. *schmetternd* or *blechern*): this is produced by fully stopping the horn and blowing hard, which raises the pitch as well as producing a harsh and metallic effect. The most famous instance of the use of muted horns is in the music for the bleating sheep in Strauss's *Don Quixote*, where flutter-tongue effects are used at dynamic levels from *pp* to *ff*.

Of the types of mute listed below, (a) to (c) are in standard use, most notably on the trumpet and trombone; (d) to (h) are less common, some of them being modifications of the standard types; and (i) to (o) outline other devices used in muting.

(a) Straight mute. Its shape is conical (though when made of metal often pear-shaped), with the wider end closed. Longitudinal strips of cork hold it in position, allowing some air to pass between the walls of the instrument and the mute. It is usually made of aluminium, fibre, cardboard or polystyrene, often plaster- or stone-lined. The sound is pure: incisive when blown hard. Straight mutes are available for all brass instruments and instructions to use a mute generally refer to this type.

(b) Cup mute. This is essentially a straight mute with the wide end bearing a cup which more or less covers the bell. The cup is often adjustable to provide a greater or lesser degree of muting and usually contains a lining of felt. The sound is attenuated and lacks edge yet has a certain roundness. Cup mutes are normally used only for the trumpet and trombone.

(c) Harmon mute (wah-wah). A metal mute held in the bell of the instrument by a cork collar so that all the air is directed through the mute. An adjustable (often removable) tube allows different amounts of air to enter the mute chamber. The sound is distant, with an edge which varies in presence according to the position of the tube. The outer face of the mute carries a bowl-shaped indentation; a 'wah-wah' effect can be produced by covering and uncovering this with the palm of the hand while playing. The mute is available for trumpet and trombone.

(d) Bucket mute (velvetone). A parallel-sided bucket is filled with absorbent material and usually clipped on to the trumpet or trombone bell by means of spring steel strips which hold it at a fixed distance from the instrument. The sound is quiet and dull.

(e) Practice mute. A type of straight mute with a heavy cork collar that drastically reduces the sound output. It is available for trumpet, trombone, horn and tuba.

(f) Mica mute. A variety of cup mute with a rubber edge around the cup. The sound is similar but much quieter and slightly more edgy. It is normally played close to a microphone.

(g) Whispa mute. A microphone is also necessary for this mute as its tone is otherwise inaudible. All the sound goes into a chamber filled with sound-absorbent material and it can escape only through small holes.

(h) Solo tone mute (mega, double or clear tone). A double straight mute which has a nasal yet resonant timbre. It is rarely required and is used only by the trumpet (e.g. in Bartók's Violin Concerto, 1937–8, where the instruction '*doppio sordino*' appears).

(i) Plunger. This rubber or metal cup is like a drain-clearing device but lacks a handle. By skilful manipulation the natural sound can be distorted in such a way that the trumpet or trombone seems almost to speak and sing.

(j) Hat (derby). This mute is a metal bowler hat, usually stone-lined, which is normally held by the left hand over the trumpet or trombone bell. In the 1920s and 1930s, however, it was sometimes fixed to the top of the mute stand so that players could quickly blow into or out of it. When the instrument is blown 'in hat' the basic tone is retained but with reduced intensity. (In *An American in Paris*, 1928, Gershwin calls for trumpeters to play 'in felt crown'; Stravinsky requests 'hat over bell' for trumpet and trombone in *Ebony Concerto*, 1945.)

(k) Handkerchief (cloth). A modified version of 'hat over bell' can be achieved by the use of a handkerchief or cloth. The technique is usually restricted to the trumpet (in, for example, Ives's *The Unanswered Question*, 1906).

(l) Conner–Gossick mute. An improved mute was designed by Rex Conner and Ben Gossick of the University of Kentucky during the 1970s. It resembles a large harmon mute held tightly against the bell and incorporates an outlet duct; interchangeable ducts provide other possibilities of timbre. The mute is said to assist uniform tone over the entire range and assist articulation of the lower notes, but because of its size it has so far been made only for use in the vertical bell of the tuba.

(m) Hand over bell. The effect of 'hand over bell' is slightly to diminish the sound of the trumpet or trombone. It was characteristic of the Glenn Miller band in the 1930s and 1940s, where the brass could produce a subtle 'wah' in complete rhythmic accord by this method.

(n) Hand in bell. A technique very occasionally required of trumpeters. The tone becomes increasingly muffled and the pitch of the note progressively lower as the hand is inserted further into the bell.

(o) In stand. Playing a trumpet or trombone into the music on the stand (from a distance of about 10 cm seems the most effective) may be seen as the reverse of the *Schalltrichter in die Höhe* (raised bell) technique found particularly in Mahler. Since orchestral brass players tend anyway to blow into the music to some extent it is not markedly successful. If the bell is held too close to the music intonation and pitch are affected.

3. OTHER. Kettledrums are muted by placing a cloth or handkerchief on the drumhead, opposite the striking point (*see* TIMPANI, §2).

On the harp, a species of muted tone may be produced by a method of plucking that stops the string as soon as the note is produced (*sons étouffés*). This sound resembles a short, dry, string pizzicato, quite different from the usual warm, vibrant tone of the harp as normally plucked (*laissez vibrer*).

A mute effect is also possible on the harpsichord and piano. On the former, a device called a BUFF STOP presses felts or leathers against a whole set of strings, thereby muting the tone and shortening its period of resonance, the resulting sound being almost like pizzicato. The piano has both dampers and mutes. The damper, which is made of felt, is used not to dampen (i.e. to lessen or muffle) the sound but to extinguish it. When

the damper pedal is depressed, all the dampers are raised from the strings, allowing them to ring freely, also inducing sympathetic vibrations from other strings. If the damper pedal is not used, the strings are automatically dampened and cease to sound the moment the finger releases the key. The 'soft' pedal is the modern version of a mute on the piano (see UNA CORDA). It reduces the volume of sound by shifting the whole row of hammers a short distance to the right (Ger. *Verschiebung*, 'shifting') so that (in the modern grand piano) they hit only two of the three strings for each note (or, in the lower register, one of two). In Beethoven's time, the row of hammers could be moved to strike either one string (called *una corda*) or two strings (*due corde*) of the normal three. In his Hammerklavier Sonata op.106 (third movement), Beethoven called for *una corda*, then 'gradually two, then three strings', an effect no longer possible on the modern piano.

Some early pianos had true mute stops – strips of leather, cloth or other material interposed between hammers and strings to mute and change the timbre. In 1783 Broadwood of London patented (under the name 'sourdin') a mute stop in which a long strip of leather was applied against the strings by the action of a pedal. Several of Beethoven's pianos (e.g. his Erard of 1803) were equipped with mute stops. Some modern upright pianos still use a strip of felt to achieve this muting effect.

The term 'sordino', however, has caused some confusion, as it is also the normal term for a damper. The direction *senza sordini* evidently requires the damper pedal to be depressed to raise the dampers. The first edition of Beethoven's Piano Sonata op.27 no.2 gives the direction, 'One should play this whole piece very delicately and *senza sordino*'; and above the bass staff, 'always pianissimo and *senza sordino*'. Interpreted literally, this seems to mean that the damper pedal should be kept down continuously from the beginning to the end of the movement. The result is a confusion of blurred harmony, less so perhaps in the weak-toned Viennese pianos of Beethoven's time than on modern instruments. No really satisfactory explanation of this direction has yet been offered, despite the suggestion that Beethoven's *senza sordino* meant 'without a mute stop' (see D. Arnold and N. Fortune, eds.: *The Beethoven Companion*, London, 1971, pp.50ff).

BIBLIOGRAPHY
M. Mersenne: *Harmonie universelle* (Paris, 1636–7/*R*1963; Eng. trans., 1957)
J. E. Altenburg: *Versuch einer Anleitung zur heroisch-musikalischen Trompeter- und Pauker-Kunst* (Halle, 1795/*R*; Eng. trans., 1974)
C. Forsyth: *Orchestration* (London, 1914, 2/1935, repr. 1948)
W. Piston: *Orchestration* (New York, 1955)
A. Baines: *Woodwind Instruments and their History* (London, 1957, 3/1967)
R. Russell: *The Harpsichord and Clavichord* (London, 1959, rev. 2/1973)
M. J. Kurka: *A Study of the Acoustical Effects of Mutes on Wind Instruments* (Chicago, 1961)
D. D. Boyden: *The History of Violin Playing from its Origins to 1761* (London, 1965)
R. B. Gregory: *The Horn* (London, 2/1969)
W. S. Newman: 'Beethoven's Pianos versus his Piano Ideals', *JAMS*, xxiii (1970), 484
R. B. Gregory: *The Trombone* (London, 1973)
C. J. Bevan: *The Tuba Family* (London, 1978)
A. Blatter: *Instrumentation/Orchestration* (New York, 1980)
N. Del Mar: *Anatomy of the Orchestra* (London, 1981)
            DAVID D. BOYDEN (1, 3), CLIFFORD BEVAN (2)

Mutengesa. Royal drum of the Nyoro people of Uganda. See NTIMBO, (1).

Mutenyane (pl. *metenyane*). End-blown single-note flute of the Tswana/Lete people of Botswana. This is the leading flute, of highest pitch, in their DITLHAKA (stopped flute ensemble).

Mutetere. Transverse flute of the Valley Tonga people of Gwembe district, Zambia. It may be made from a section of an old bicycle pump.

Mutetule usibgwa. Transverse flute of the Valley Tonga people of Gwembe district, Zambia. It is open at the far end and has three finger-holes. This flute is played in the fields when the maize ripens.

Mutiiti. Cylindro-conical drum of the Manyisi people of Kenya. *See* ISUGUTI.

Mutin, Charles. French organ builder, pupil and successor of ARISTIDE CAVAILLÉ-COLL.

Mutisánguisi. Afro-Cuban FRICTION DRUM formerly used by the Congo people; it comprised a soundbox formed of a rectangular section of horsehide. See *OrtizIMA*, v, 201.

Mutoto. Single-headed footed drum of the Lunda people of south-western Zaïre (*BooneT*, 14).

Mutshahats. LAMELLAPHONE of the Akwa-Songo people of Zaïre. It has metal keys and a box resonator hollowed out at the end nearest the player (*LaurentyS*, 195).

Mutshakatha [thuzo]. Leg rattles of the Venda people of southern Africa, used by dancers. They comprise a number of hollow globular fruit shells containing small stones, threaded on parallel sticks (like an abacus) and tied to the legs. *KirbyMISA*, 5, pl. 3*c*.

DAVID K. RYCROFT

Mutshapata. LAMELLAPHONE of the Chokwe people of Zaïre. *See* TSHISAJI.

Mutta. Small oboe of the northern Sind and Multan (lower Panjab) areas, Pakistan. *See* SHARNAI.

Mutumba (i). SLIT-DRUM of the Lunda people of south-ern Zaïre. The name also means 'canoe'. It is played in conjunction with xylophones.

Mutumba (ii). Single-headed open-ended conical drum of the Sena/Tonga people of Mtoko district, Zimbabwe. A single player beats it by hand, together with the *jenje* drum. These and two other drums, *miningo karipi-karipi* and *usindi*, accompany an ensemble of four flute sets (*see* KATERO) for *gororambe* dances. See *TraceyCSA*, ii, 175f.

DAVID K. RYCROFT

Mutumbwe [mutumbi]. Single-headed drum of the Luba and Sanga peoples of Zaïre. *See* DITUMBA.

Muvungu. Obsolete name for the KYAA (stamping tube) of the Kamba people of Kenya.

Muwannaj. A term sometimes used for the WANJ (Arab harp).

Muwattar. Arabian lyre, harp or lute. The name is derived from *watar* ('string') and was introduced into pre-Islamic poetry by Labīd (*c*570–660) in the line: 'A singing-girl with a *muwattar* which she plays with her thumb'. The mention of the thumb suggests a lyre or harp rather than a lute, but this remains conjectural. Although rare, the term 'muwattar' is used again in the 10th and 11th centuries by Abbasid chroniclers and those of Moorish Spain, who define the instrument as a lute. Some 20th-century scholars have compared the instrument to the *mizhar* as a proto-lute, but one played with the thumb (referring to Labīd); according to other theories, without any historical basis, the early *muwattar* was a monochord. *See also* 'ŪD.

BIBLIOGRAPHY
H. G. Farmer: *A History of Arabian Music to the Thirteenth Century* (London, 1929/*R*1973)
J. Robson: 'Kitāb al-malāhī of Abū Ṭālib al-Muffaḍḍal Ibn Salama', *Journal of the Royal Asiatic Society* (1938), 231
N. al-Dīn Asad: al-Qiyān wal Ghinā' 'aṣr al-Jāhilī [Singing-girls and music in pre-Islamic Arabia] (Beirut, 1960/*R*1968)
M. Guettat: *La musique classique du Maghreb* (Paris, 1980)
L. I. al Faruqi: *An Annotated Glossary of Arabic Musical Terms* (Westport, Conn., 1981)

CHRISTIAN POCHÉ

Muwere. End-blown trumpet of central Africa. *See* NYELE.

Muxukitarra. JEW'S HARP of the Basque region.

Muyang. Spherical bronze pellet bells of Madhya Pradesh (Bastar district), central India. One or more rows of *muyang*, 3 to 4 cm in diameter, are attached, together with *irna* bells, to the small of the back of Muria and Maria boys for their tribal dances (for illustration *see* GHANṬĀ). See G. Dournon: 'Inde, musique tribale du Bastar', LDX 74736 [disc notes].

GENEVIÈVE DOURNON

Muyemba [muyembba]. LAMELLAPHONE of the Akwa-Sonde and Pende peoples of Zaïre (*LaurentyS*, 195). See KAKOLONDONDO.

Muyu ('wooden fish'). Woodblock or SLIT-DRUM of the Han Chinese, used especially to accompany Buddhist

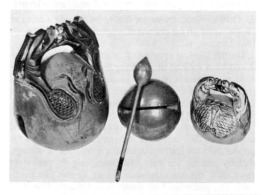

Muyu (slit-drums) with hammer from China; the central one is turned over to show the slit (private collection)

chant. Carved from a block of camphor wood, the instrument appears in the abstract shape of a fish – squat and wedge-shaped – with carved iconic representations of a tail, scales and eyes. Its hollowed-out interior section and frontal slit (extending 180° around the instrument) form the mouth (see illustration). The instrument is either lacquered red or left unlacquered, may measure between about 5 cm and 60 cm in diameter and is struck with a padded or unpadded beater. Small *muyu* may be carried in one hand (with the beater in the other), while larger instruments usually rest on round cushions set on special tables. According to Buddhist legend and present-day belief, a sense of watchfulness is encouraged by striking a wooden representation of a fish, since it is thought that fish remain awake both day and night. In a religious context the *muyu* is used primarily in Buddhist temples, struck with regular beats to accompany the prayer-chanting of monks and nuns. The instrument is also used in the percussion section of Cantonese ensembles to accompany vocal and instrumental music. The Japanese *mokugyo* and Korean *mokt'ak* are related instruments. Other Chinese woodblocks include the *ban*.

ALAN R. THRASHER

Muzika-barškalas. Shepherd's fiddle of Lithuania. It consists of a wooden board (of fir, pine or aspen) 30 cm long and 15 cm wide, with a narrow central 'neck' 5 cm wide. The board carries a wooden bridge (*pastauka*). Two to six, most often four, horsehair strings run the length of the board and are fixed at either end with wooden nails. The bow is made from a willow branch 1·5 cm thick and 30 cm long, with a length of horsehair fixed in notches at either end. The instrument has no regular tuning; it is played like the violin but is of limited musical scope. The *muzika-barškalas* was used mostly by shepherds until the early 20th century to play simple songs and dance-tunes or improvisations.

ARVYDAS KARAŠKA

Muziki. Single-headed closed conical drum of the Nyamwezi people of Tabora district, Tanzania. The membrane is pegged on and the drum is beaten with the hands. *See also* NDANDALE.

Muzungu [mzungu]. STAMPING TUBE of the Pare people of Tanzania. It is made of a piece of bamboo with a cylindrical wooden resonator, and played in pairs.

mv. *Mezza voce. See* MEZZO, MEZZA, (1).

Mvāhlī [mohali]. A term used by the Newari people of Nepal for various kinds of oboe. Two types – straight and curved – are used in the Kathmandu valley, each made up of a wooden tube, with seven holes at the front and one at the back, and a metal bell. The mouthpiece consists of a metal tube whose base is set into a metal disc, fitted with a reed made from a *kayosim* leaf folded in four. There are several sizes of straight oboe, and the curved type is called *desīmvāhlī*, seeming to indicate an Indian origin. The *mvāhlī* is generally used with the *dholak* (drum) and the *babu* (cymbals), and plays an important role in various instrumental ensembles. *See also* MAHVARĪ and SAHANAI.

BIBLIOGRAPHY
T. O. Ballinger and P. H. Bajracharya: 'Nepalese Musical Instruments', *Southwestern Journal of Anthropology*, xvi/4 (1960), 398
F. Hoerburger: *Studien zur Musik in Nepal* (Regensburg, 1975)
S. Wiehler-Schneider and H. Wiehler: 'A Classification of the Traditional Musical Instruments of the Nevars', *Journal of the Nepal Research Centre*, iv (1980), 67–132

MIREILLE HELFFER

Mvet. An idiochord STICK ZITHER with a notched bridge. It is unique to an area of western central Africa which includes southern Cameroon, Gabon, equatorial Guinea, northern areas of the Republic of the Congo and the south-west of the Central African Republic. Unlike other stick zithers it has a central notched bridge which supports its five strings in a plane at right angles to that of the string-bearer. Its invention is attributed to the people of the Pahuin group (known variously as the Fang, Fan, Fanwe, Mfang, Mpangwe, Pangwe) and, according to tradition, its first player was Efandene Mvie. First described by Hornbostel as a 'Pangwe' instrument, it is thought to be a development of the monochord stick zither of the Fang and other peoples.

The traditional Pahuin *mvet* is made from a raffia branch about 1·5 metres long. Five idiochord strings are raised from the hard surface of the branch and are supported at their centre by a notched bridge. Small rings of fibre are wound round the ends of the strings and the branch; the *mvet* is tuned by adjusting these rings to shorten or lengthen the strings. One to six gourd resonators are attached to the back of the string-bearer. The player holds the *mvet* horizontally with the central half-calabash against his chest and plucks the strings with the fingers of both hands (see illustration).

Pahuin mvet (stick zither), Ngambe, central Cameroon, 1964

Contemporary instruments tend to have metal strings and only four of them are used, thus producing eight notes of different pitch. One modern instrument of the Bamum people of southern Cameroon is known to have eight strings on a rounded bar base with a large central calabash flanked by two smaller ones.

The term 'mvet' applies not only to the instrument but to a whole associated complex of music, mime, dance and oral tradition; the name denotes all that is spoken to the accompaniment of the instrument. Three kinds of performance are recognized: *mvet bibon* (lyrical), *mvet engubi* (stories, recent legends, chronicles and genealogies) and *mvet ekang* (epic). In performance an epic poem begins with a recital of the genealogies of *mvet* players and is often accompanied by a chorus led by the *mvet* player's wife. At moments of heightened emotion, the player may hand the instrument to his wife and dance, imitating the gestures, voice and character of the human or superhuman creatures of his narrative.

The *mvet* players occupy a unique social position. They are semi-professionals who are initiated into their craft under contract to a master, as a part of which in the past the pupil had to offer his sister in marriage to the teacher. The players undergo physical, mental and intellectual tests which culminate with a faultless recital of the complex and lengthy genealogies required in performance.

BIBLIOGRAPHY

E. M. von Hornbostel: 'Die Musik der Pangwe', *Die Pangwe*, ed. G. Tessman (Berlin, 1913)

Eno-Belinga: *Littérature et musique populaire en Afrique noire* (Toulouse, 1965)

S. Awona: 'Bikud-Si et mvet', *Les danses du Cameroun/Cameroonian Dances*, i (Yaoundé, 1967), 87

F. Bebey: *Musique de l'Afrique* (Paris, 1969)

Eno-Belinga: 'Musique traditionelle et musique moderne au Cameroun', *Bulletin of the International Committee on Urgent Anthropological and Ethnological Research*, xi (1969), 83

———: *Découverte des chantefables beti-bulu-fang du Cameroun* (Paris, 1970)

H. Pepper: 'Un mvet de Zwè Nguéma', *Classiques africains*, ix, ed. P. and P. de Wolf (Paris, 1972) [with discs]

P. Alexandre: 'Introduction to a Fang Oral Art Genre: Gabon and Cameroon Mvet', *Bulletin of the School of Oriental and African Studies*, xxxvii (1974), 1

J. H. K. Nketia: *The Music of Africa* (New York, 1974)

G. Kubik: 'Cameroon', *Grove 6*

P. Sallée: 'Gabon', *Grove 6*

M. Vuylsteke: 'Musiques du Gabon', OCR 41 [disc notes]

GERHARD KUBIK/K.A. GOURLAY

Mveul. Four-string PLURIARC of the Fang (Pahuin) people of Gabon. It is played with xylophones and drums in funeral dances, marriage ceremonies and social dances.

Mvuli [mvudi]. Side-blown animal-horn trumpet of the KaKongo people of Zaïre (*LaurentyA*, 322).

Mwaka. Small SLIT-DRUM of the Bas-Congo region of south-western Zaïre; it is played in pairs (*LaurentyTF*, 135).

Mwana nzambi. Side-blown gourd trumpet of the Holo people of western and central Zaïre (*LaurentyA*, 310).

Mwanzi. Wooden cone flute, with one or two stops, of the Zande people of north-eastern Zaïre (*LaurentyA*, 119).

Mwari. Side-blown trumpet of the Gwari people of Nigeria. It is made from either cow or antelope horn and is used, according to locality, by hunters for signalling, to encourage communal farming, or at the funeral of an important person.

Mwarutu. Small VESSEL FLUTE of the Digo people of south-eastern Kenya with a mouth-hole and two finger-holes. It is made from a dried fruit.

Mweembo. Side-blown funeral horn of the Ila people of Zambia.

Mwémfu. Cylindrical stopped wooden flute of the Sundi people of Zaïre (*LaurentyA*, 178).

Mwemo [mwemvu]. Wooden cone flute, with one or two stops, of the Suku people of south-western Zaïre (*LaurentyA*, 134ff).

Mwémvo [muemvo]. Cylindrical stopped wooden flute of the Mayombe people of Zaïre (*LaurentyA*, 175, 179).

Mwimbi. Long cylindro-conical drum of the Bembe people of Zaïre. *See* KIMBANDU.

Mwironge. *See* UMWILENGE.

Myel bul. DRUM-CHIME ensemble of the Langi people of Uganda. It consists of six Uganda drums and one single-headed drum.

Myōhachi. Large Japanese hand-cymbals. *See* DŌBATSU.

Mzungu. *See* MUZUNGU.

N

Na (i). Large flat bronze gong of Korea. *See* CHING (i).

Na (ii). Korean CONCH-SHELL TRUMPET. *See* NAGAK.

Naas. Copper KETTLEDRUM of the Zaghawa people of the Ouaddai region of north-eastern Chad. It is often over 50 cm in diameter. *Naas* drums, which are normally played in pairs with two straight sticks, are insignia of the power of the sultans and seizing them is equivalent to seizing power. This tradition is supposed to have begun with a wooden *dinger* drum; later among most groups the *naas* replaced the *dinger*. In a special ritual procession the drums are suspended from camel saddles. A drummer sitting in the saddle beats one on each side, while a second drummer, his back to the first, plays a third drum hanging over the camel's tail; either jujube-tree sticks or ostrich-feather fans are used to beat the drums.

See also NIHASS.

BIBLIOGRAPHY
M.-J. Tubiana: *Survivances préislamiques en pays Zaghawa* (Paris, 1964)

MONIQUE BRANDILY, K. A. GOURLAY

Naas (copper kettledrums) of the Zaghawa sultans, north-eastern Chad

Nabal. Long brass trumpet of Korea. It is also pronounced *nap'al*. The only surviving metal wind instrument in Korea, it is constructed in three collapsible sections. Its current use is limited to the military processional music *Taech'wit'a*, in which it is required to produce only a single pitch, alternating long-sustained notes with the conch-shell trumpet *nagak*.

The *nabal* bears some resemblance to the *taegak* ('large trumpet') described in the treatise *Akhak kwebŏm* (1493), but otherwise there is little documentary evidence of its history in Korea. A similar instrument is the Chinese LABA (i).

BIBLIOGRAPHY
Sŏng Hyŏn, ed.: *Akhak kwebŏm* [Guide to the study of music] (Seoul, 1493/*R*1975), 8.8*b*
Chang Sa-hun: *Han'guk akki taegwan* [Korean musical instruments] (Seoul, 1969), 56

ROBERT C. PROVINE

Nabita [bita]. Drum of central Africa. (1) Long, slightly conical double-headed drum of the Mamvu, Ngbele, Makere and Bati peoples of Zaïre. The two skins are laced together by a comparatively small number of parallel cords, and are struck with a wooden beater. The *nabita* varies in length from 86 to 100 cm, the majority being 86 to 90 cm. Other drums of this type played in Zaïre include the *tchembe* of the above three groups, the Zande and Barambo *ndima* and *gaza*, Mangbetu *lari*, Bangba *bongwabi* (*bongwadi*, *bongwaki*) and Bwa *elembe* and *esembe*. *See also* DINDO.

(2) Single-headed closed conical drum of the Meje people of Zaïre. Four are played in conjunction with the *emandru*, *nedundu* and *nekbokbo* drums.

BIBLIOGRAPHY
BooneT, 25f, 69f
F. J. de Hen: *Beitrag zur Kenntnis der Musikinstrumente aus Belgisch Kongo und Ruanda-Urundi* (Tervuren, 1960)
G. Knosp: *Enquête sur la vie musicale au Congo belge 1934–1935* (Tervuren, 1968)

K. A. GOURLAY

Nabla. *See* NEVEL.

Nāc [nautch]. Instrumental ensemble of south India. *See* CINNA MELAM.

Nacaires (Fr.; Sp. *nacara*). NAKERS.

Nacchera [naccheroni] (It.). NAKERS. The plural form, *nacchere*, means CASTANETS; *see also* RATTLE.

Nacchini [Nachini, Nanchini], **Pietro** [Nakić, Petar] (baptized Podgrebaća, Bulić, Dalmatia, Feb 1694; *d* Conegliano, Treviso, 1765). Italian organ builder. His place of birth was then part of the Venetian Republic. He studied philosophy at Sebenico, theology in Venice (he became a Franciscan monk) and organ building under Giovanni Battista Piaggio (Piaggia, Piazza), also in Venice. By his industry and excellent workmanship he established himself as the principal organ builder of his time in Venice, Dalmatia and the surrounding area. For a short period in 1729 he worked with Pierantoni and Pescetti.

The development of the Italian organ under Nacchini may be seen in the specifications of two fine organs surviving in Venice. The first, op.160, for S Maria dei Derelitti (S Maria del Riposo or Chiesa dell'Ospedaletto) (1751, restored by Ruffatti, 1960), had one manual, *C* (short) to *c‴*, 45 notes; nine separate ranks of chorus stops from Principale (8′) and Ottava (both divided) to Trigesimasesta, Voce umana, Flauto in ottava (4′ divided), Flauto in XII, Ottavino soprani, Tromboncini (8′ divided), Pedal (*C* to *a*, 18 notes), Contrabassi 16′, Ottava 8′, Tremolo, Timballi. The second, in 1759 for Chiesa della Pietà (S Maria della Visitazione), had one manual, *C* (short) to *f‴*, 50 notes. The specification was the same as the S Maria dei Derelitti, with an added Flauto reale soprani 8′ (showing the same trend as the French organ of the time, both forerunners of Bishop's Clarabella) but without the Pedal Ottava or the two accessories. The Ottavino, a 2′ flute, is generally considered to have been introduced by Callido's sons, so this stop in both these organs, as well as those below, was almost certainly originally a treble Cornetto (a single-rank tierce).

Other organs in Venice and the immediate surroundings which survive, at least in part, include: S Francesco della Vigna (1733; enlarged to two manuals in 1909 with tubular pneumatic action); op.80, S Cassiano, Sestiere di Santa Croce (1742; two manuals; probably reconstructed by the sons of Gaetano Callido after 1813); S Rocco (Sestiere di S Polo) (1743; one manual, *C* short to *c‴*, 45 notes, 18 pedals, a small organ restored by Tamburini in 1959 and in practically original condition); op.98, S Servilio (Sestiere de Dorsoduro) (1745; one manual, *C* short to *c‴*, 45 notes, nearly original condition, Swell shutters); op.133, S Giovanni Elemosinario (Sestiere di S Polo) (1749; altered at the end of the 19th century but still with tracker action); S Stefano (Sestiere di S Marco) (1752; rebuilt 1910, two manuals, tubular pneumatic action); op.276, S Pietro di Castello (1754; rebuilt 1898, five octaves from *F′*, tracker action); Isola di S Giorgio Maggiore (mid-18th century; renovated 1887, compass enlarged, Cornetta converted to Ottavino soprano, Trombe in place of Violoncello which was itself almost certainly an earlier addition); S Giustina, Padua (1735; rebuilding of double organ by Casparini); Basilica del Santo (1741; two of the four organs).

Nacchini built about 500 organs. He invented the *tira-tutti*, a stop-knob which brings on the whole of the ripieno ranks, and a forerunner of composition pedals. His pupils included Francesco Dacci (Dazzi), Gaetano Callido (at some time between 1748 and 1763), who may be considered his successor, and Franz Xaver Chrismann, who incorporated many features of Nacchini's Italian style into a new and particular type of Austrian organ.

BIBLIOGRAPHY

S. dalla Libera: *L'arte degli organi a Venezia* (Venice, 1962)

L. Šaban: 'Graditelj orgulja Petar Nakić i Šibenik' [The organ builder Petar Nakić and Šibenik], *Radovi Instituta Jogoslavenske adademije znanosti i umjetnosti*, xiii–xiv (Zadar, 1967), 401

——: 'Contributo alla biografia di don Pietro Nakić', *L'organo*, ix (1972), 1

I. Faulend-Heferer: 'Nakićeva orgulje iz 1762 u samostanskoj crkvi sv Frane u Šibeniku' [Nakić's 1762 organ in St Francis's Church in Šibenik], *Arti musices*, iv (1973), 47–99

L. Šaban: 'Umjetnost i djela graditelja orgulja Petra Nakića u Dalmaciji i Istri' [The art and works of the organ builder Petar Nakić in Dalmatia and Istria], *Arti musices*, iv (1973), 5–45

GUY OLDHAM

Nachschlag (Ger.). A term used to denote particular ornaments. *See* ORNAMENTS, §VIII, where its uses are indexed.

Nachthorn (Ger.). An ORGAN STOP.

Nachtigaal (Dutch; Fr. rossignol à eau). Earthenware whistle of the Low Countries. The 'nightingale' is filled with water, and when the player blows he may, by varying the pressure, produce trills and other effects recalling the song of the nightingale and the blackbird.

Nachtigall (Ger.). A bird-imitating ORGAN STOP (*Vogelgesang*).

Nād. End-blown animal-horn trumpet of Sind, Pakistan. *See* NAFĪL.

Nādagam-berē. Small barrel drum of Sri Lanka. *See* DEMALA-BERĒ.

Nadd [naddu]. *See* NAŘ.

Na den. Arched harp of Burma. A descendant of the Mesopotamian harp (*see* HARP, §§2 and 7), it is made by the Karen and Mon hill peoples of Lower Burma and has five to seven strings, tuned by pegs; the only other surviving arched harp in Burma is the classical *saùng-gauk*. See T. and A. Stern: '"I Pluck my Harp": Musical Acculturation among the Karen of Western Thailand', *EM*, xv (1971), 186–219.

Nachtigaal (private collection)

Naderman. French family of musicians, publishers and instrument makers.

(1) Jean-Henri Naderman (*b* Fribourg, 1735; *d* Paris, 4 Feb 1799). Publisher and instrument maker. In 1774 he became 'maître juré de la corporation', later styling himself 'Editeur, Luthier, Facteur des Harpes et autres instruments de musique'. (As a publisher, he produced much chamber music for the harp, and numerous works were either composed or arranged by his elder son (2) François-Joseph.) Naderman's importance as a harp maker should not be underestimated. He worked from premises in the rue d'Argenteuil where he made many harps of the single-action type. He was appointed harp maker to Marie-Antoinette in 1778; at least two of the authenticated harps he made for her are to be found in public collections (Kunsthistorisches Museum, Vienna, and Conservatoire de Musique, Paris; see illustration). His harps are highly ornate – carved, gilded and decorated in the Vernis Martin style; from the mechanical and constructional points of view they were considered the most superior instruments of their time. They were given due credit in the Report on Sébastien Erard's new harp made by the Académie des Sciences et des Beaux-Arts, signed by Méhul, Gossec, Charles and Prony on 17 April 1815. Naderman continued to use the pedal-operated hook mechanism rather than the improved *béquilles* system invented by the Cousineaus in 1782; he also continued to use the staved construction for the bodies of his harps. The defects attendant on the employment of both mechanical and constructional methods are outlined by Pierre Erard in *The Harp in its present Improved State* (1821).

Working with the harpist J. B. Krumpholtz, Naderman made several improvements to his harp. In 1783 he placed a damping mechanism along the length of the centre strip of the soundboard which was operated by an eighth pedal placed to the player's left (*harpe à sourdine*). In 1785 he produced a short-lived instrument (*harpe augmentée*, further developed the same year into the *harpe à renforcement*) which was intended to improve the resonance of the harp's enclosed box; five pedal-operated shutters were placed in the central back panel of the harp between the pedals operated by the left (D, C, B) and right (E, F, G, A) feet. The improved harp was played by Madame Krumpholtz before the Académie des Sciences on 21 November 1787, when the programme included Krumpholtz's 6th Sonata (specially written to illustrate the capabilities of the new instrument) and where the harp received approval. The only new element to be permanently retained was that of the shutters in the back of the harp; this idea was also incorporated into Erard's harps, the first of which was made in 1786 (*see* ERARD). Jacques-Georges Cousineau became harp maker to Marie-Antoinette in 1788, and after this time the firm of Naderman appears to have concentrated its activities more on the publishing side, though it continued to make harps in a rather less ornate and exaggerated style. After Naderman's death his widow and sons continued both publishing and harp-making activities at the rue de Richelieu premises to which the firm had moved in 1787. In 1835 the publishing house either went out of business or was taken over by G.-J. Sieber.

(2) (Jean-) François-Joseph Naderman (*b* Paris, 1781; *d* Paris, 3 April 1835). Harpist and composer, son of (1) Jean-Henri Naderman, and the most celebrated

Harp by Jean-Henri Naderman, Paris, 1780 (Conservatoire de Musique, Paris)

member of the family. It has been suggested that he was a harp student of Krumpholtz, but though the latter was closely associated with his father it is unlikely that the young Naderman studied with him at anything but a superficial level since Krumpholtz committed suicide in 1790 after some years of accruing mental stress; moreover, even in his mature compositions Naderman shows none of the influence of Krumpholtz, either in his handling of the limited resources of the single-action harp or in his writing for the instrument. After the Restoration (1815) he was appointed harpist to the royal chapel and finally, in 1825, was made the first professor of harp at the Conservatoire, his brother (3) Henri acting as his deputy. The harp adopted by the Naderman brothers for use at the Conservatoire was the single-action model made by the family firm rather than the double-action Erard harp which was favoured by Prony.

As court composer and leading harpist to the king, François-Joseph Naderman wrote much music for the harp. His solo harp music was intended to display technical brilliance, and lacks any depth, though his studies and in particular his *7 Sonates progressives* are still used as teaching material. Considered to be old-fashioned even in his own day in his approach both to music and technique, there is no doubt that he was hidebound by the limitations of the single-action harp to which he was entirely committed and to which he would admit no superior, despite the acceptance and continuing success of Erard's double-action harps since their introduction to England (1811) and France (1812). Though he held on to his teaching post at the Conservatoire he stubbornly refused to consider the greater scope offered by Erard's instrument, and it was left to his successor, Antoine Prumier (1794–1868) to introduce the double-action harp.

(3) **Henri Naderman** (*b* Paris, *c*1780; *d* Paris, after 1835). Instrument maker, son of (1) Jean-Henri Naderman. His early training was directed towards harp making and the business side of the family firm, but he also took enough harp lessons from his brother to enable him to be appointed his official deputy both at the royal chapel and at the Conservatoire. By 1825, when his brother was appointed to the newly created professorship of harp at the Conservatoire, the Nadermans were the only firm left in Paris making single-action harps. Despite Prony's submission (1815) that the double-action harp should be the one adopted by the Conservatoire, the Nadermans made certain that only the single-action harp made by their firm should be used. In November 1827 Fétis published an article in the *Revue musicale* drawing public attention to the superiority of the Erard double-action harp over the kind adopted by the Conservatoire; this sparked off an acrimonious public correspondence between Henri Naderman and Fétis. Motivated by self-justification, misguided self-interest, pride, arrogance and jealous protection of the Nadermans' business interests, Henri's retrograde arguments appear pathetic and slightly ridiculous, especially in view of the fact that after the expiry of Erard's 1802 French patent for a new fork mechanism the Nadermans introduced this mechanism to their own instruments, thus tacitly admitting its superiority over their own hook mechanism.

WRITINGS
Observations sur la harpe à double mouvement, ou Réponse à la note de M. Prony (Paris, 1815)
Réfutation de ce qui a été dit en faveur des différents mécanismes de la harpe à double mouvement (Paris, 1828)
Supplément à la Réfutation (Paris, 1828)

BIBLIOGRAPHY
FétisB; *GerberNL*
J. B. Krumpholtz: 'Explanations and Engravings of Improvements to the Harp as Effected by J. H. Naderman to Plans by Krumpholtz', *Deux derniers sonates de la collection de pièces de différent genres* op.14 (Paris, *c*1788)
P. Erard: *The Harp in its Present Improved State Compared with the Original Pedal Harp* (London, 1821/*R*1980)
F. J. Fétis: *Revue musicale*, no.59 (1827)
——: *Lettre à M. Henri Naderman au sujet de sa réfutation de la Revue musicale sur la harpe à double mouvement de M. Sébastien Erard* (Paris, 1828)
F.-J. Naderman: *Ecole ou méthode raisonnée pour la harpe, adopté par le Conservatoire: avant-propos* op.91 (Paris, *c*1832)
Review of *Ecole ou méthode raisonnée pour la harpe, AMZ*, xxxv (1833), 577
Rapport fait le 17 Avril 1815 sur la harpe à double mouvement de l'invention de Sébastien Erard (Paris, 1834/*R*1980)
T. aus dem Winkel: 'Einige Worte über die Harfe mit doppelter Bewegung', *AMZ*, xxxvi (1834), 65
de Prony: *Note sur les avantages du nouvel établissement d'un professorat de harpe a l'Ecole Royale de Musique et de Declamation* (Paris, 1834/*R*1980)
W. von Metzsch-Schilbach: *Briefwechsel eines deutschen Fürsten mit einer jungen Künstlerin* (Berlin, 1893)
H. J. Zingel: *Harfe und Harfenspiel* (Halle, 1932)
C. Hopkinson: *A Dictionary of Parisian Music Publishers 1700–1950* (London, 1954)
C. Johansson: *French Music Publishers' Catalogues of the Second Half of the Eighteenth Century* (Stockholm, 1955), 106
A. Devriès and F. Lesure: *Dictionnaire des éditeurs de musique français*, i (Geneva, 1979), 122f
ANN GRIFFITHS

Nadi [nadjiangbwa]. Wooden flute, with slender conical bore, of the Barambo people of Zaïre (*LaurentyA*, 158, 167).

Nādī [nālī]. An ancient Sanskrit term meaning 'pipe' and probably denoting a flute. *See* VAMŚA, §1.

Nadimba. Marimba with a vibrating membrane, used in the Western orchestra; *see* MARIMBA, §2.

Nadjolea. Long rim-blown flute of the Mangbetu people of northern Zaïre (*LaurentyA*, 295).

Nadjotoro. Cylindro-conical drum, with two laced membranes, of the Makere people of Zaïre (*BooneT*, 32).

Nádsíp. Clarinet of Hungary. It has six to eight finger-holes and is used as a melody instrument by shepherds (see illustration).

Nádsíp (clarinet) player, Great Hungarian Plain, 1969

Nafa. (1) SLIT-DRUM of Western Polynesia. It was present in Tonga in pre-contact times, and in 1784 Captain Cook reported it as between 90 and 120 cm long, twice as thick as a man and hollowed out entirely with an 8 cm slit running its full length. It was beaten to accompany dance with two sticks about 30 cm long and 'as thick as the wrist'. It produced a powerful sound and different notes were obtained by beating the drum in the middle or near the end. The *nafa* is now used only to accompany the *me'etu'upaki* dance; for other purposes it has been displaced by the LALI. In Samoa it was rare by 1897 and is now obsolete; it is thought to have been a medium-sized drum played with two sticks like the Tongan *nafa*. In other places the *nafa* resembles those of Tonga and Samoa. In Tikopia it is a short trough of carved wood, beaten as a sounding board to mark the

Slit-drum (nafa) of Tonga, Western Polynesia, as illustrated in J. S. C. Dumont d' Urville's 'Voyage de la corvette L'Astrolabe' (1830–35)

rhythm of the dance. In Tuvalu it is a rectangular slit-drum about 120 cm long with a narrow slot. It is beaten, like the smaller PĀTĒ, with two sticks (*kauta*) to accompany dance. In Niue it is described as small and canoe-shaped with a narrow slit. In Uvea it is equated with the *lali*.

(2) A double-headed skin drum of Tonga, made from a 44-gallon metal drum covered at each end with cowhide and beaten with two soft-headed drumsticks. It is used to accompany the acculturated *mā'ulu'ulu* dance.

See also NAWA.

BIBLIOGRAPHY
E. Loeb: *History and Traditions of Niue* (Honolulu, 1926), 94
E. G. Burrows: *Ethnology of Uvea* (Honolulu, 1937), 145
R. Firth: *The Work of the Gods in Tikopia* (London, 1940), 215
G. Koch: *Die Materielle Kultur der Ellice-Inseln* (Berlin, 1961), 174
R. Moyle: 'Samoan Musical Instruments', *EM*, xviii (1974), 63
——: 'Tongan Musical Instruments', *GSJ*, xxx (1977), 86f, 101ff
MERVYN McLEAN

Nafīl. End-blown trumpet of Sind, Pakistan. It is made of the horn of the ibex (*sarah*), cut at both ends. Formerly two sizes, small (*singrī*) and large (*nād* or *nafīl*), were found. See N. A. Baloch: *Musical Instruments of the Lower Indus Valley of Sind* (Hyderabad, 1966).

Nafīr [nfīr, karnā]. An Arabic and Persian name (from the 11th century) for a straight, end-blown, metal trumpet of limited range (usually no more than two notes) used in the Islamic world. It can be seen in Turkish, Persian and Mughal miniatures of battle scenes, and was carried to Europe by soldiers returning from the crusades. *Nafīr* are often played with double-reed instruments and kettledrums, primarily for military and ceremonial music. In the Maghrib the *nafīr* is used to signal the Islamic month of Ramadan. The Moors brought it to Spain and Portugal where it is known as *añafil* and *anafir* respectively; it also spread to India where it is known as the *karnā* and *karnay*. A long silver trumpet, the *nafiri*, is used in Malaysia in the Kedah, Perak, Selangor and Trengganu *nobat* (court ensembles). *See also* NAQQĀRAKHĀNA.

BIBLIOGRAPHY
S. Marcuse: *A Survey of Musical Instruments* (Newton Abbot and London, 1975), 819
J. Jenkins and P. Rovsing Olsen: *Music and Musical Instruments in the World of Islam* (London, 1976), 55
WILLIAM J. CONNER, MILFIE HOWELL

Nafiri. (1) Oboe of Sumatra and Malaysia. In the Bengkalis–Siak area of Riau province, Sumatra, it is made of copper or wood. It has a double reed of coconut leaf or rattan fitting through a square plate on to a tube with seven front finger-holes and one thumb-hole, with a flare at the bottom. It is used in the *nobat* ensemble in Riau and the Malay peninsula. With a *gendang* (drum) and a gong it accompanies the 'red fingernail dance' in Pulau Tujuh, Riau.

(2) Malaysian trumpet. *See* NAFĪR.

MARGARET J. KARTOMI

Nagak. CONCH-SHELL TRUMPET of Korea (*na*: 'conch'; *gak*: 'horn'). It is also called *na* or *sora*. Since the *nagak* is made from a natural shell there is no standard size or pitch. Construction consists merely of fashioning a smooth mouthpiece at the narrow end of the conch shell. The instrument produces a single deep pitch (*B* in the case of the instrument at the National Classical Music Institute in Seoul) and the timbre is warm and hornlike, but not brassy.

The *nagak* was played during royal processions in Korea as early as the Koryŏ dynasty (918–1392) and was used during the Chosŏn period (1392–1910) primarily in the military processional band. The treatise *Akhak kwebŏm* (1493) describes the instrument as part of the dance paraphernalia in performances of the Sacrifice to Royal Ancestors (*Chongmyo*).

At present the *nagak* is used only in the ensemble for *Taech'wit'a* (military processional music), in which it alternates long-held notes with the *nabal* trumpet.

See also FALUO and HÕRAGAI.

BIBLIOGRAPHY
Sŏng Hyŏn, ed.: *Akhak kwebŏm* [Guide to the study of music] (Seoul, 1493/R1975), 8.9a
Chang Sa-hun: *Han'guk akki taegwan* [Korean musical instruments] (Seoul, 1969), 54f
ROBERT C. PROVINE

Nagara. Term for a number of double-headed drums of Azerbaijan (USSR). All have wooden frames, sometimes with small soundholes. The heads are tightened with crossed lacing and are played with the bare hands or with wooden mallets with spherical or hooked ends. The drums have different names according to size. The *kyos* (great *nagara*) is 50 to 60 cm in diameter and was formerly made in villages from a tree-trunk. Wider distribution of the drum encouraged skilled craftsmen to produce more refined instruments. During performance the *kyos* is suspended from the shoulder on a leather strap and struck with a beater on one side, rarely on both.

The *bala nagara* or *chure nagara* (medium *nagara*) is 35 to 40 cm in diameter and is primarily an ensemble instrument. Held under the left arm, it may be beaten on one membrane with bare hands or with one hand and a beater. Occasionally both membranes are played; the rim of the drum is played with the fingers, the centre with the palms. The *kichik nagara* (small *nagara*) is also played in ensembles and orchestras. The *nagara* is used with other instruments in the performance of folk music: an ensemble of two *kyos* and two *zurnas* (folk oboes) perform at open-air dances, marches and demonstrations. *Nagaras* were formerly played during the hunt.

JOHANNA SPECTOR

Nagārā [nagārā, nagaṙa, naqqāra, naghārā etc]. South Asian names for a KETTLEDRUM of the Middle Eastern

Court nagārā (kettledrums) player, Kishangarh, Rajasthan

NAQQĀRA type; the Arabic spelling is retained only in Urdu. Often, but not always, played in pairs, kettledrums have been the leading instrument of military bands and of the ceremonial band *naubat*, *naubatkhāna* or *naqqārakhāna* of courts, shrines and temples in South Asia since the Middle Ages. They are also widespread in this area as folk and tribal instruments, to accompany dancing, hunting etc; both folk and court *nagārā* are closely associated with oboes and horns. In Nepal the *nagārā*, a large kettledrum with metal body, is found mainly in temples and princely palaces. Very large pairs are still to be seen at the ancient palaces of Kathmandu and Bhatgaon but they are now used only rarely. The Newari people of Nepal called the instrument *jornagārā* or *dohranagārā*.

1. Military and court usage. 2. Tribal and folk instruments.

1. MILITARY AND COURT USAGE. Kettledrums are first clearly described in South Asia, in medieval Sanskrit texts. Two sizes are mentioned: the larger *nihsāna* and the smaller *tumbakī*. Both were of metal, had interior jingling metal cups and were beaten with leather straps. They were often paired, and are described as terrifying war instruments. They probably reached India after the Arab conquest of Sind, in AD 712, together with the other Arab military instruments, the oboe and trumpet (*see* MAHVARĪ and BUKKĀ), also described in contemporary Sanskrit texts. The name *tumbakī*, at least, derives from the Arabic *tumbak*; it probably still survives in Indian regional names such as *timki*, *tāmāk* and *tamukku*. The derivation of *nihsāna* is less clear: it may be from *nihsvāna* ('sounding out', as in *nissān* (Orissa) and *pābūjī ke nisān* (Rajasthan); *see* MĀTĀ). The ancient drum name *dundubhi* has often been mistranslated as 'kettledrum'.

With the establishment of Muslim Turko-Afghan rule under the Delhi Sultanate from 1192, the name *naqqāra* was adopted in India, often in an Indo-Aryan form as *nagārā*, *nagārā* etc. While it continued to function as an important military drum throughout the Muslim period, the *nagārā* soon became important also as a leading instrument of the palace ceremonial band NAQQĀRAKHĀNA, or NAUBAT. Like the *nihsāna-tumbakī* before it, the *naqqāra/nagārā* was here played in pairs of a treble and bass drum. Although the term may in South Asia be generic for such paired kettledrums, it is clear that in the late medieval and early Mughal periods, as indi-

cated by the *Ā'īn-i-ākbarī*, it denoted higher-pitched pairs of such drums, played alongside lower-pitched or tenor pairs known as *kuvargah* or *damāmā*, and with the large, single, bass kettledrums (*see* TABAL, BHER) depicted in Mughal painting. In these sources one leading drum-pair is often depicted in the centre of the band, frequently placed on a richly embroidered cushion.

In the late Mughal and early modern periods the *nagārā* may be seen depicted in other court music scenes also, accompanying female dancers. The *nagārā* survives in modern times in a few, much reduced *naubat* bands found mainly at Muslim shrines (*dargāh*) such as those at Ajmer in Rajasthan and Mundra in Cutch.

The court *nagārā* as it survives today consists of two hemispherical metal bowls (somewhat pointed at the base) – the smaller on the right (*jil*, *jhil*, from the Arabo-Persian *zir*), and the larger on the left (*dhāma*). The single skins are braced with X-lacing, divided by cross-lacing in the centre. Tuning is variously effected by heat, the pouring in of water through a small hole in the base, and, in the case of the bass left-hand drum, by an interior resinous tuning-load stuck under the skin. The drums are either placed on their sides, with the two heads facing inwards, or with the right almost horizontal; they are struck with two sticks, short and thick with tapering heads (see illustration). Though precise pitch is neither possible nor desired, the relationship between the drumheads appears to be of a 4th or 5th (the left at the dominant or subdominant below the right). The timbre difference is very noticeable, the right having a tight, metallic tone and the left a dark, dull thud (*see also* TABLĀ). The structural parameters of the different strokes are given by Stewart (1974) as: pitch – the categories of high and low between the two heads (corresponding to the important Middle Eastern concept *zir-bam*); resonance, relating to the checking or releasing of the drumhead with the stick; timbre, relating to position (rim to centre of head); and force of stroke. The two sticks may be used on the same head. In much of this the *nagārā* has contributed to the evolution of the *tablā*. In modern times its metric framework is similar to that of the *tablā* (*tāl* such as *tīntāl*, *dādrā*, *jhap*, *dīpcandī* etc), with the form *thekā* (basic pattern) plus variations, playing together with the *śahnāī* (oboe).

See also ṬĀSA and ḌUGGĪ.

2. TRIBAL AND FOLK INSTRUMENTS. In southern Bihar the large single-headed kettledrum is found among tribal groups (*nagara*) and folk musicians of certain scheduled castes (*nāgara*, *nakāra*, *nagārā*, *nagera*). The drums range in size from small, with a head diameter and height of about 40 cm, to extremely large, with a head diameter of about 114 cm and a height of about 110 cm. The smallest, traditionally associated with the Santāl tribe, is also used by other communities in staged dance performances, while Christian converts of the tribes of southern Bihar use some of the largest. The *nagara* of the Muṇḍā people, one of the largest tribal groups in the area, commonly has a head diameter of about 60 to 70 cm and may range in height from 50 to 60 cm.

In the early decades of this century the frames were made of either clay or iron. Nowadays, they are formed from thin bands of sheet iron nailed together horizontally. The inner surface of the hollow frame is coated with a mixture of tree resin and vermilion. An ox or buffalo hide is stretched over the open top of the bowl-shaped body, overlapping the rim; it is secured by an elaborate zig-zag network of laces of twisted cowhide which runs through one or two rows of eyelets in the skin and continues down the outside of the entire frame. Every 8 to 10 cm the laces are woven around horizontal belts of flat cowhide, from two to seven in all, which encircle the frame, and finally around a small straw or rope ring at the bottom of the bowl. Additional horizontal bands of twisted cowhide are woven into the laces close to the rim for reinforcement. The frame has a small plugged hole in the bottom through which water or oil, preferably mustard or *karanj* oil, is poured to preserve the skin and control its tension. In the centre of the head's outer surface is a patch, which may extend only a few cm from the centre or may nearly cover the head, covered with a temporary paste of tree resin and/or burnt oil residue.

Although *nagaṛa* are most commonly associated with all tribal groups, their frames are made by the Lohār community of blacksmiths, and the heads made and attached by the Ghāsī community of leatherworkers, who also play the *nagaṛa*, together with other drums.

The *nagaṛa* is played with a pair of sticks, each about 30 to 40 cm long and slightly curved at the playing end. When used in the percussion ensemble which accompanies communal dancing the drum is slung from the player's neck by a leather or cloth strap; the drummer dances as he plays. Less often, the *nagaṛa* accompanies small-group singing, in which case it is placed on the ground in front of the seated drummer.

Among tribal groups, such as the Muṇḍā, Santāl, Ho and Uraon, the *nagaṛa* is associated primarily with outdoor communal dancing and processions. Because of its thunderous sound it is also used to call people to gatherings such as the hunt. In the typical percussion ensemble which accompanies Muṇḍāri dancing, several *nagaṛa* players join men playing the drums *ḍulki* and *rabaga* (and occasionally a *dumaṅg*) and small cymbals and bells. Muṇḍāri *nagaṛa* are often owned jointly by an individual and an entire village or neighbourhood, which contributes to its maintenance.

Among folk musicians of the Nāgpuri tradition, such as the Ghāsī, the *nagaṛa* is most properly played with *ḍholkī*, *ḍhāk* and *karah* drums and the *śahnāī* oboe to accompany *mardana jhumar* ('men's *jhumar*') and *domkac* (marriage season) dancing and singing; today in some areas it may be used in *janāni jhumar* dancing and singing as well. Ghāsī musicians are also hired to play the *nagaṛa* with the *śahnāī* (oboe), *narsīgā* and *bheṛ* (trumpets) and *ḍhāk* (drum) at tribal and non-tribal weddings, for Śaiva worship and for *paīki* (sword-dances) and with *ḍholkī* (drum) and *śahnāī* for the *chau* (*cho*) dance drama in southern Bihar and bordering areas of western Bengal and Orissa. In both tribal and non-tribal percussion ensembles the *nagaṛa* drummer is musically dependent on the lead drummer, playing either a *ḍholkī*, *ḍhāk* or *mādar*, with the same patterns, though slightly out of phase, as those of the lead drum's left head. *Nagaṛa* drum patterns are most often vocalized as part of lead drum patterns.

Large, metal- or clay-bodied kettledrums similar to the *nagaṛa* are found throughout the tribal belt of central India under different names. Examples include the tribal *dhol* of West Bengal and Madhya Pradesh; the *damua* of the Uraon people of southern Bihar; and the *dhamsā* of tribal groups in Orissa.

BIBLIOGRAPHY

Abu'l Faẓl: *Ā'īn-i-ākbarī* (c1590), trans. H. Blochmann in *The Imperial Musicians* (Calcutta, 1873, 2/1927), 680ff; trans. H. S. Jarrett, rev. Sarkar in *Saṅgīt*, Bibliotheca Indica, cclxx (Calcutta, 1948), 260ff

N. A. Willard: *A Treatise on the Music of Hindustan* [1834]; repr. in S. M. Tagore, *Hindu Music from Various Authors* (Calcutta, 1875, enlarged 2/1882/R1965)

S. C. Roy: *The Orāons of Chōtā Nāgpur* (Calcutta, 1915), 181f

J. Hoffmann and A. van Emelen: *Encyclopaedia mundarica*, v/1–13 (Patna, 1938–50), 2369f, 2908ff

S. Marcuse: *Musical Instruments: a Comprehensive Dictionary* (Garden City, NY, 1964/R1975), 141, 161, 357

K. S. Kothari: *Indian Folk Musical Instruments* (New Delhi, 1968), 38f

M. Helffer: 'Fanfares villageoises au Népal', *Objets et mondes*, ix/1 (1969), 51

J. Levy: *Music from the Shrines of Ajmer and Mundra*, Tangent TGM 105 [disc notes]

O. Prasad: *Munda: Music and Dance* (diss., Ranchi U., 1971), 71f

R. Stewart: *The Tabla in Perspective* (diss., U. of California, Los Angeles, 1974)

B. C. Deva: *Musical Instruments* (New Delhi, 1977), 45f

——: *Musical Instruments of India: their History and Development* (Calcutta, 1978), 78ff

A. Dick: 'The Earlier History of the Shawm in India', *GSJ*, xxxvii (1984), 80

ALASTAIR DICK (1), CAROL M. BABIRACKI (2)

Nagarit. KETTLEDRUM of Ethiopia, always played in pairs. They are often used in processions and public festivals, a pair being slung one on each side of a horse. The *nagarit* is a traditional symbol of power; processions of the emperor included 44 *nagarit* pairs, and those of princes included 22 pairs. The Emperor Haile Selassie had an ensemble of 400 *nagarit*.

See also NAQQĀRA.

RONALD LAH

Nāgasvaram [nāgasuram, nāyanam]. Conical oboe of south India. It is approximately 95 cm long, and its large double reed, of cane, is fashioned similarly to that of the ŚAHNĀĪ. The reed is mounted on a short, stubby conical staple, which is inserted into a conical wooden pipe containing seven equidistant finger-holes, and no thumb-hole; five additional holes are bored near the distal end of the pipe, two on each side and one on top. These holes, which may or may not be completely or partially filled with wax, assist in tuning the instrument. A widely flared wooden bell is attached to the distal end of the pipe. Additional reeds, staples and supporting paraphernalia are strung and kept together, to be readily accessible during performance. Although the instrument exists in longer (*bārī*) and shorter (*ṭimirī*) examples, with several gradations between, the longer variety has become more popular during this century. A metal bell is usually associated with the shorter *nāgasvaram*.

Three fingers are used in the proximal position and four in the distal position (either hand can be proximal or distal). Skilful lip command of the pliable double reed, which facilitates a wide variation of pitch and dynamic, is the principal feature of *nāgasvaram* technique. The range of the instrument is two octaves.

Historically, the term is mentioned in a religious text dating from the middle of the 1st millennium AD, but this reference may be to the markedly different snake charmer's pipe. It has been reported that an instrument resembling a *nāgasvaram* is depicted on an 11th-century sculpture of the Vīrabhadra temple in Asandi, Karnataka, and the term appears again in written sources from the 14th century onwards. Some scholars consider the *nāgasvaram* to be derived from the *śahnāī*. The common modern Tamil name is *nāyanam*. Intriguing as various clues may be, without new evidence a definitive history of the instrument will remain impossible (*see also* MAHVARĪ).

The exceedingly vibrant, penetrating sound of the *nāgasvaram*, valued as auspicious, endears it to nearly

Periya melam (temple instrumental ensemble), with (left to right) tavil (barrel drum), nāgasvaram (oboe) and ottu (drone oboe), Ambalapuzha, Kerala, south India

everyone. It is the leading instrument of the ensemble played with the drum *tavil* and the drone oboe *ottu* (see illustration) mainly in Hindu temples, generally at the time of morning and evening *pūjā* (worship), and during temple processions and festivals. In addition it appears on the concert stage, is in great demand for wedding celebrations and also contributes music for dancing and dramas in folk traditions.

Part of the repertory of the *nāgasvaram* is derived from the Karnatic (south Indian) art music tradition, which is based on vocal music. The *ālāpana* exposition of a raga is followed by a particular vocal composition, parts of which are subjected to variations. Additionally, a body of instrumental compositions without any text (*mallārī*) is performed solely on the *nāgasvaram*. A composition in slow tempo is varied through performance at double, quadruple and octuple tempos. Skelton (1971) reported that different tempos may be mixed together, and that a composition may be performed in triplet patterns as well. These pieces are performed only when the deity is believed to be present.

In Andhra *nāgasvaram* can also denote the PŪNGĪ (double clarinet with gourd wind cap).

BIBLIOGRAPHY

T. V. Pillai: 'Nagasvaram', *Journal of the Music Academy Madras*, xx (1949), 110 [in Tamil]

V. Raghavan: 'Nagasvara', *Journal of the Music Academy Madras*, xx (1949), 155; xxvi (1955), 149

W. Skelton: 'The Nagaswaram and the South Indian Hindu Festival', *Asian Music*, ii/1 (1971), 18

REIS FLORA

Nagauta. Genre of Japanese dance music, performed both in the kabuki theatre and to accompany dance recitals in a non-kabuki context (*naga*: 'long'; *uta*: 'song'). Since the late 19th century it has also come to be performed without dance – the so-called 'concert *nagauta*'.

Nagauta developed during the 17th century out of certain popular song and dance traditions as well as from the nō dance-drama. By the end of the century it was regularly accompanied by the instrumental ensemble found today: SHAMISEN (lute), SHINOBUE (transverse flute) and the four instruments used in nō: NŌKAN (transverse flute), KOTSUZUMI and ŌTSUZUMI (hourglass drums) and SHIMEDAIKO (barrel drum). The instruments, excluding the shamisen, are often referred to collectively as the *hayashi* or *narimono*. There may be as many as eight shamisen (as a rule the number of shamisen and singers must agree), four *kotsuzumi* and two *shimedaiko*, but never more than one *ōtsuzumi* and flute. In the kabuki theatre a *nagauta* performance may be accompanied further by instruments in the off-stage *geza* music.

BIBLIOGRAPHY

W. P. Malm: *Japanese Music and Musical Instruments* (Rutland, Vermont, 1959), 213ff

——: *Nagauta: the Heart of Kabuki Music* (Tokyo, 1963/*R*1973)

——: '"Four Seasons of the Old Mountain Woman": an Example of Japanese *Nagauta* Text Setting', *JAMS*, xxxi (1978), 83–117

DAVID W. HUGHES

Nāgbīn. A north Indian name for the PŪNGĪ (double clarinet with gourd wind cap).

Nägel (Ger.). BRAY.

Nagelclavier (Ger.: 'nail piano'). A variant of the NAIL VIOLIN, in which nails mounted on an oblong block of wood are bowed by a continuous rosined band, controlled from a keyboard.

Nagelgeige [Nagelharmonika] (Ger.). NAIL VIOLIN.

Nāgeśvar. A name used in Orissa, east India, for the PŪNGĪ (double clarinet with gourd wind cap).

Naghara. *See* NAQQĀRA.

Naghārā. Pair of clay drums, of the KETTLEDRUM type, of Sind, Pakistan. The instrument and its name derive from the Arabic *naqqāra* and the South Asian *nagārā*, important members of the ceremonial band *naubat* or NAQQĀRAKHĀNA. In Sind the *naghārā* is played to accompany *mātam* (mourning-songs) during the Shī'ite lamentation of Muharram. See N. A. Baloch: *Musical Instruments of the Lower Indus Valley of Sind* (Hyderabad, 1966).

ALASTAIR DICK

Naghora. *See* NAQQĀRA.

Nagiambwa. Set of cylindrical stopped flutes, threaded on to cord or wire, of the Barambo people of Zaïre (*LaurentyA*, 189).

Nagphani. Serpentine trumpet of Rajasthan. *See also* BĀNKIĀ.

Nagydob. Hungarian term for the bass drum, used in country brass bands.

Nahābat [nahabet]. *See* NAUBAT.

Nahara. *See* NEGARA.

Nahashch'id 'aghááł. Rattle used by the Navajo Indians of the south-western USA for ceremonial purposes concerning badger power.

Nai (i). PANPIPES of Romania. The earliest evidence for its existence in Romania is from archaeological sources; the earliest documentary sources date from the 16th and 17th centuries. From the second half of the 18th century

Nai (panpipes) played by Fănică Luca, Romania

the *nai* appeared frequently in the *taraf* ensembles of the *lăutari* (professional folk musicians) in Romanian principalities. The oldest native names for the instrument are *fluierar, fluierici, fluierător, şuieraş* etc; in addition the term 'muscal' is found, like the *nai*, of oriental origin. These terms, and the fact that both early and contemporary pipes are made of bamboo stems, have led to the hypothesis that a fusion occurred between an ancient, rural instrument and an oriental professional one, the older type giving way to the new.

The 'classical' Romanian *nai* consists of a concave row of 20 pipes, of different lengths and diameters, in order of size. The pipes are open at the upper end and glued together; they rest on a slightly curved stick or, more recently, are set into a curved pipe. The lower ends of the pipes are stopped with cork and filled with beeswax; the tuning is regulated by the quantity of wax. The *nai* produces a diatonic scale from *b′* to *g⁗*, with F♯s. Intermediate notes can be obtained by slightly modifying the angle of the instrument during performance. This leads to the characteristic portamento effects in slow melodies. The *nai* is played by *lăutari*, who have recently introduced additional pipes. Such modified instruments may have 25, 28 or 30 pipes, expanding the lower register.

Between the two World Wars the *nai* almost disappeared but was successfully revived, largely owing to the work of Fănică Luca (1894–1968), who trained many successful young *nai* players.

TIBERIU ALEXANDRU

Nai [nāī] **(ii).** *See* NĀY.

Nail piano. *See* NAGELCLAVIER.

Nail violin (Fr. *violon de fer*; Ger. *Nagelgeige, Nagelharmonika, Eisenvioline*; It. *violino di ferro*). A friction IDIOPHONE (not a violin) consisting of metal, glass or wooden rods (which are in some cases bowed, in others struck) fastened at one end to a sounding-board. The earliest instrument to employ this method of sound production was invented in 1740 by Johann Wilde, a German violinist in St Petersburg. The suggestion for its construction originated in Wilde's accidentally scraping the hair of his bow across the metal peg upon which he was about to hang it, and in so doing producing a musical sound of distinctive quality. The flat wooden sounding-board is usually in a half-moon shape and the metal nails are firmly fastened perpendicularly around the edge of the curved side. As these nails diminish in height the notes rise in pitch, and the chromatic nails are distinguished by being slightly bent; the nails sound an octave lower than would rods of the same length fastened at both ends or suspended (the principle is similar to the one at work in stopped pipes). The instrument was held in the left hand by a hole underneath, and the sound was produced by rubbing a strong, well-rosined, black-haired bow across the nails. In 1780 it was improved by the addition of sympathetic strings. Senal, a Viennese artist, excelled upon it. In 1791 a new oblong arrangement of it, the *Nagelclavier*, was produced by Träger of Bernberg (Saxony). It was played by a treadle-operated band coated with rosin, and controlled from a keyboard. In the 19th century a type in which wooden rods were played with rosined gloves was known as the *Stockspiel* or *Melkharmonica* (probably because of its resemblance to an inverted milking-stool). Mid-19th-century variants of the nail violin, which are struck rather than bowed, are the TOY PIANO and the chimes in some household clocks.

Most writers assume that the nail violin disappeared in the second half of the 19th century, but in recent years the principle has been revived in several instruments and sound sculptures, usually in a circular form resembling the *Stockspiel*; the 'nails' are bowed or struck or both. Between the wars a *Metallstabharfe*, in which vertical metal rods, fixed halfway along their length in a horizontal frame, are rubbed with rosined gloves, was used in variety performances in Germany. Some electric carillons are based on struck rods, and amplified struck rods produce the sounds in the electric pianos of HAROLD RHODES. MAURICIO KAGEL has constructed large instruments with metal and wooden rods, Daniel Schmidt has built percussion in which tuned wooden rods are both struck and used as resonators, and DAVID COPE has incorporated the components of the nail violin into a hybrid instrument called the Logsprinoka; in Richard Waters's WATERPHONE upright rods mounted on a water-filled resonator are played with a stick, the hand or a bow (for illustration *see* SOUND SCULPTURE, fig.2). One of the Baschet brothers' STRUCTURES SONORES (many of which use the nail violin principle) has a resonating base on which a hard ball rolls about, striking stainless-steel rods. A similar idea is used in a toy instrument that consists

Nail violin, early 19th century (Royal College of Music, London)

of a container with a suspended beater inside, which hits a circle of nails when the container is rocked; Hugh Davies's Macro-Process Organ incorporates a motorized version of the same mechanism. Much longer flexible metal rods are used in the SONAMBIENT sound sculptures of Harry Bertoia, instruments made by DAVID SAWYER and ROBERT RUTMAN, and amplified instruments played by electric motors (made by MAX EASTLEY) and by compressed air (MARIO BERTONCINI); in these the 'unbalanced' relationship between the diameter and length of the rods produces a rich and resonant spectrum.

BIBLIOGRAPHY
C. Sachs: *Handbuch der Musikinstrumentenkunde* (Leipzig, 2/1930), 66

E. HERON-ALLEN/HUGH DAVIES

Nainala. DOUBLE CLARINET, with free reeds, of Sri Lanka. Two slender reedpipes, approximately 15 cm long, are fitted into a gourd, which acts as a wind cap. At the top of the pipes, and therefore enclosed in the gourd, are two thin reed tubes, with idioglot reeds cut from them. The right pipe has six finger-holes and the left two tuning-holes on the underside. A simpler version of the pipe, without the gourd wind cap, is widely used. As its name ('cobra pipe') suggests, the instrument is used exclusively for snake-charming.

NATALIE M. WEBBER

Najr. *See* JĀWAN.

Naka. Term for flute, especially stopped flutes (*see* STOPPED FLUTE ENSEMBLE) among certain peoples of southern Africa. (1) Stopped conical flute of the Tswana people. It is made from the lower leg-bone of the secretary bird, covered with lizard skin, and is used for divining and to ward off lightning. The TSULA of the Pedi is similar.

(2) Stopped flute of the Lovedu (Northern Sotho) people, used in the *motaba* stopped flute ensemble.

(3) Stopped flute ensemble of the Ndebele people of the Transvaal, South Africa.

(4) Generic name for flute among the Pedi (Northern Sotho) people. The name *naka ya lehlaka* covers either a transverse flute, similar to the Venda TSHITIRINGO, or an end-blown stopped pipe, of reed, without finger-holes. The latter yields one note, other notes being interspersed through whistling as the breath is drawn in. It is played by herdboys. The *naka ya phatola* (or *naka ya makoditsane*) is a conical flute made from wood, covered with buckskin and woven wirework, and treated with medicinal charms. It is placed against the hollowed tongue for sounding. With the lower end either open or closed by a finger, two notes can be produced, plus several overblown harmonic partials of these. It was used by warriors, as a signal instrument. The *naka ya sefako* is a conical flute made from horn. The wide end serves as the mouthpiece and there is a small finger-hole near the tip. It was formerly sounded by medicine men to ward off hailstorms. Its construction and playing technique are similar to those of the Southern Sotho *lekhitlane* (*see* LEKHITLANE, (1)).

BIBLIOGRAPHY
KirbyMISA, 90, 97ff and pll.37a–b, 43b

DAVID K. RYCROFT

Nakamunsale. Side-blown trumpet of the Ganda people of Uganda. *See* AMAKONDERE.

1. Nakers (naqqāra) from Tunisia

Nakers (from Arabic *naqqāra*; Fr. *nacaires*; It. *nacchera*, *naccheroni*; Sp. *nacara*). Small kettledrums of medieval Europe, of Arab or Saracen origin. The instruments are now represented in North Africa, Turkey, Egypt and Syria by small drums with bowl-shaped bodies of wood, metal or clay, and covered on their open top with animal skin (see fig.1). As early as the 13th century the French were using the term *nacaires* and the Italians *naccheroni*. 'Nakers' (or its equivalent) is recorded in English literature from the latter half of the 14th century. In an old Cornish drama, *Ordinale de origine mundi*, written at the end of the 14th century, 'nakrys' are mentioned together with 'psalmus' (shawms). Chaucer coupled 'nakeres' with pipes, trombes and clariounes in his *Knight's Tale*.

From the numerous representations of the instruments of this period it is clear that nakers were like small kettledrums, more or less hemispherical in shape, from 15 to 25 cm in diameter, and with a common feature in the single skin. The heads were attached in various ways:

2. Pair of nakers from the Luttrell Psalter, English, early 14th century (GB-Lbm Add.42130, f.176r)

nailed, braced with cords or neck-laced. The bowls, which seem to vary little in diameter, were of wood or metal, or in some cases of clay. Nakers are frequently illustrated with snares, a feature observed both in England and on the Continent. With isolated exceptions these small drums were played in pairs and were suspended in front of the player by means of a strap round the waist or the shoulder, or placed on the ground. In most cases they were played with two drumsticks. These were invariably of wood, though in Hans Holbein's woodcut 'Die Fürstin' from *Totentanz* (1538) the nakerer (a skeleton playing on a single drum suspended from his waist) plays with a pair of thigh bones.

Literary references confirm the use of small kettledrums in Europe from the middle of the 13th century onwards. Jean Sire de Joinville in a description of the crusade of Louis IX (1248–54) wrote of tabors called *nacaires*: 'Lor il fist sonner les tabours que l'on appelle nacaires'. Nakers first appeared in England in the early 14th century. In 1304 Edward I's musicians included a nakerer ('Janino le Nakerer') and in 1349 *nacaires* helped to celebrate the entry of Edward III into Calais. Excellent examples of the nakerer at work are found in the Luttrell Psalter (early 14th century, now in *GB-Lbm* Add.42130). One illustration (see fig.2) shows the player with a pair of small drums at his waist and a stick in each hand. In another illustration a pair of larger drums are placed on the ground. In this case the performer uses two curved drumsticks in the form of a crook, similar to the crozier sticks illustrated in an early 13th-century Arabic manuscript and in an 18th-century Ethiopian manuscript of the *Revelation of St John the Divine* (*Lbm* Oriental 533, f.34r). A carving on the choir seats of Worcester Cathedral (late 14th century) portraying a tournament scene shows a nakerer and a performer on the 'clarion', an early association of trumpet and kettledrum. The nakers are portrayed with snares, and the two short drumsticks have bulbous heads.

Until the 17th century there is widespread evidence, pictorial and otherwise, of small kettledrums. Their purpose was twofold: played by men they were used mainly for martial purposes (as in the tournament scene referred to above and also in Chaucer's *Knight's Tale*: 'bloody sownes of bataille'); played by angels and women, as they are frequently portrayed in illuminations and sculptures, nakers appear as delicate instruments associated with soft-toned instruments and chamber music. They were also used in dance and processional music, and probably for accompanying songs, particularly where the song was in a dance rhythm. More elaborate rhythms may have been used on the nakers than on the small tabor played with the pipe, partly because two sticks were used, and partly because with two contrasting sounds possible the player would not be restricted to using different note values to mark the strong beats.

See also NAQQĀRA and TIMPANI, §3.

BIBLIOGRAPHY
F. W. Galpin: *Old English Instruments of Music* (London, 1910, rev. 4/1965 by T. Dart)
J. Montagu: *The World of Medieval and Renaissance Musical Instruments* (London, 1976)
——: *Making Early Percussion Instruments* (London, 1976)
D. Munrow: *Instruments of the Middle Ages and Renaissance* (London, 1976)

JAMES BLADES

Naki. Obsolete upright SLIT-DRUM of Malekula, Vanuatu, formed from a hollow log with a narrow slit along

its length and a human face carved on top. They were up to 3·6 metres high and were erected in groups around the village dancing-ground to provide music for dances. They were also used for signalling news of events such as murders, fighting, births, deaths and the arrival of strangers. The signals could reportedly be heard for 6 to 8 km. See T. W. Leggatt: 'Musical Instruments of Malekula', *Science of Man*, vi (1903), 135.

MERVYN McLEAN

Nakić, Petar. *See* NACCHINI, PIETRO.

Nakkare. *See* NAQQĀRA.

Nakpéa. Obsolete upright SLIT-DRUM of Nguna Island, Efate, Vanuatu. A *nakpéa* was set up for each deceased chief. It was formed from a log about 3·7 to 4·3 metres long, set upright in the ground. Above the slit a human face was carved and then painted. Orchestras of *nakpéa* played at rituals, the most important of which were pig-killing ceremonies associated with the men's graded society. Destruction of *nakpéa* began at the behest of missionaries in 1879, the last one finally rotting away at Mēre village in the 1930s.

BIBLIOGRAPHY
A. Don: *Peter Milne (1834–1924), Missionary to Nguna* (Dunedin, 1927), 31, 204
K. Huffman: 'Slitdrums', *Nabanga*, no.77 (1978), 20

MERVYN McLEAN

Nakpéa of Vanuatu, now obsolete: watercolour (1875), attributed to Adam B. Messer (Alexander Turnbull Library, Wellington, New Zealand)

Naku. Single-headed closed conical drum of the Ganda people of Buganda district, Uganda. The membrane is laced on. It is played with the hands. *See also* NTAMIVU.

Nakulā. A medieval Indian term for a two-string STICK ZITHER; *see* VĪṆĀ, §4.

Nal [lal]. End-blown stopped bamboo flute of the Sara people of southern Chad; it is played in consort using hocket technique (*see* STOPPED FLUTE ENSEMBLE). The Sara-Madjingaye group use 12 *nal* pipes of different lengths; the Sara-Kaba, who term the pipe *lal*, use eight. The players move in a circle around an ensemble, usually of drums although the Sara-Kaba group include a xylophone and animal horn as part of the ensemble.

BIBLIOGRAPHY
C. Duvelle and M. Vuylstèke: 'Anthologie de la musique du Tchad', OCR 36–8 [disc notes]

Nāl. Double-headed drum of the Ḍholak type used in Gujarat and Maharashtra, west India. The wooden body tapers towards the right head, the two goatskin membranes being held by hoops which are tightened by ropes. The slightly smaller, and higher-pitched, right head may be pasted with a mixture of iron filings for added resonance. The instrument is used for accompanying many kinds of dance and song and may be played sitting or standing. The length of the body is around 60 cm. The *nāl* is now used also in north India, where it often has metal screw tuning-rods.

BIBLIOGRAPHY
L. Miśra: *Bhāratīya Saṅgīta-vādya* (New Delhi, 1973), 175
B. C. Deva: *Musical Instruments of India: their History and Development* (Calcutta, 1978), 84

JONATHAN KATZ

Nala-mālē. Obsolete Panpipes of Sri Lanka. It was used by the Vedda (the aboriginals of Sri Lanka) as part of a New Year ritual which took the form of a religious game: two teams, one representing the gods, competed in a competition involving the throwing and catching of pots. The winners celebrated their victory by beating drums and blowing *nala-mālē*. See O. Pertold: *Ceremonial Dances of the Sinhalese* (Dehiwala, 1973), 36.
NATALIE M. WEBBER

Nālī. *See* Nāḍī.

Nālikaipparai. An ancient south Indian Tamil name for a circular drum. *See* Parai.

Nallari. Conical wooden oboe of Korea. *See* T'aep'yŏngso.

Nama. Sacred flutes of the Gahuku-Gama people, Central Highlands, Papua New Guinea. They are made of bamboo about 75 cm long with a mouth-hole 8 to 10 cm from one end. When they are played the end nearest the mouth-hole is closed with a handful of mud. They are held in the left hand while the palm of the right alternately opens and closes the far end to produce different notes. As elsewhere in New Guinea they are played in pairs of unequal size, referred to as age-mates (*ahuru*). See K. E. Read: 'Nama Cult of the Central Highlands, New Guinea', *Oceania*, xxiii (1952), 5.
MERVYN McLEAN

Namaddu. A set of tuned drums of the Gwere people of Uganda. *See* Uganda drum.

Namalwa. Single-headed cylindrical Friction drum of the Mbunda and Valley Tonga peoples of Zambia.

Namarin. Small Japanese bell found on household Buddhist altars. *See* Kin (ii).

Nambimbaye. Set of stopped flutes, threaded together, of the Makere people of Zaïre (*LaurentyA*, 200).

Nambimbo. Wooden flute of the Makere people of Zaïre (*LaurentyA*, 158f, 179f, 188, 200). *See* Ambimbo.

Nambongo. Side-blown ivory trumpet of the Mayogo people of north-eastern Zaïre. It has a carved mouthpiece (*LaurentyA*, 373).

Na-mbwe. General term for the vertical Slit-drum of Atchin Island, north-east Malekula, Vanuatu, used in sets of three or more standing upright, with the lower end buried in the ground. The largest or 'mother' drum (*miren*) is up to 3 metres high and is played by the leader, an older man, who strikes it with a softwood stick about 40 cm long, held in both hands. Flanking the *miren* are two or more secondary upright drums (*pwe-tur*), 2 to 2·7 metres high, played by middle-aged married men with a single stick held in the right hand. All are surmounted by carved faces with the slit as the mouth. Portable slit-drums (*tsoron*) are placed horizontally on the ground in front of the upright drums and played with two sticks by younger, mostly unmarried, men. With few exceptions the drums are used for accompanying dancing and for summoning members of other villages to dance in rituals involving boar sacrifice.
MERVYN McLEAN

Namoduduka. Side-blown animal-horn trumpet of the Ngbele people of north-eastern Zaïre. It has one stop in the tip. It is also known as *nembongo* and *moduka* (*LaurentyA*, 319).

Namombwele. Lamellaphone of Zaïre. It has wooden keys and a boat-shaped wooden resonator (*LaurentyS*, 192).

Nanchini, Pietro. *See* Nacchini, Pietro.

Nandomo. Arched harp of the Mangbetu people of Zaïre. *See* Kundi (i).

Nanduni [nanduruni, nantuni]. Double-chested plucked lute of Kerala, south India. The neck and soundbox, of roughly equal length, are carved from a single piece of wood. The soundbox is in two sections: the smaller, upper chest is round, and the larger, lower one roughly ovoid in shape, both with vertical sides and a flat back. The sections are separated by a narrow waist. Near the lower end of the wooden soundtable is a deep wooden bridge, either flat, rectangular or a truncated pyramid, and, below this, a frontal string holder. The slender neck, of round section, terminates in a pegbox, open from front to back, with one lateral peg on either side; both pegs and a projection above the box are in a bulb design. There are two fibre or gut strings. The frets (from 5 to 14 have been recorded) are high wooden blocks fixed at the bottom of the neck and the top of the soundbox. The *nanduni* is played with a horn or hollowed wooden plectrum worn on the finger, for drone or rhythmic accompaniment.

The origin and affinities of this lute are not certain: from the fact that the pitch from open string to first fret is a 5th and from other data Sachs (1914) regarded it as descended from the pear-shaped short lute of the Ancient Indian period (*see* Vīṇā, §3), like the Chinese *pipa* (see Pipa (i), §1). It is played by the Maṇṇān (washermen) and other castes of central Kerala to accompany religious songs.

BIBLIOGRAPHY
C. Sachs: *Die Musikinstrumente Indiens und Indonesiens* (Berlin and Leipzig, 1914, 2/1923)

P. Sambamoorthy: *Catalogue of Musical Instruments Exhibited in the Government Museum, Madras* (Madras, 3/1962)

C. Choondal: 'Nantuṇi', *Journal of the Music Academy Madras*, xlvi (1975)

B. C. Deva: *Musical Instruments of India* (Calcutta, 1978)

ALASTAIR DICK

Nanga (i). Stopped flute of the Venda people of southern Africa. A *mutavha* (set) of these reed flutes can be tuned to a heptatonic scale ranging over three octaves; they are used for the sacred music of *tshikona* dance. Each player blows one flute and the various notes are combined in hocket fashion (*see* STOPPED FLUTE ENSEMBLE). A different kind of river-reed was used to make a pentatonic set for the play-dances *givha*, *visa*, or *tshikanganga*. *Nanga* can also refer to single, unrelated stopped flutes, made of animal horn, for example the *nanga ya ntsa*. Made from the horn of a duiker, it is used for calling dogs. It resembles the Bushman *garras*. The *nanga ya danga* is another small stopped flute of the Venda. It is made from the wing bone of a vulture and resembles the Pedi *tsula*. It was formerly made by doctors, who compelled sorcerers to blow the flutes to warn people to keep away (*KirbyMISA*, 101). The *nanga ya davhi* is a Venda conical flute, similar in construction and use to the *naka ya phatola* of the Pedi.

JOHN BLACKING, DAVID K. RYCROFT

Nanga (ii). Seven-string TROUGH ZITHER of the Bembe people of Zaïre and the Nyoro/Haya people of Tanzania. *See* INANGA.

Nanga (iii). Side-blown animal-horn trumpet of the Oshwe people of north-western Zaïre. It has one stop in the tip (*LaurentyA*, 321).

Nangara. Double-headed drum of the Teda and Daza peoples of northern Chad. It is approximately 50 cm high and the diameter of the struck head is between 30 and 45 cm. It is often used with a second drum, the *kwelli*, which resembles the *nangara* but is half its size. Both drums have two membranes which are laced to an ovoid wooden body. Only adult males may play the drums. They are struck with straight sticks, by two men if only the *nangara* is used, or by three if both instruments are played together. The *nangara* is sometimes used to punctuate proclamations, and in this case it is struck with only one stick. The *kwelli* is also used alone and struck with only one stick both for signalling and to punctuate proclamations. *See also* NUGARA.

BIBLIOGRAPHY
M. Brandily: *Instruments de musique et musiciens instrumentistes chez les Teda du Tibesti (Tchad)*, Annales sciences humaines (Tervuren, 1974)

MONIQUE BRANDILY

Nango. Horizontal eight-string harp of the Ganda people of Jinja district, Uganda.

Nanhu. Chinese two-string fiddle. *See* ERHU.

Naniwóa. Side-blown CONCH-SHELL TRUMPET of Wuvulu Island, Bismarck Archipelago. See P. Hambruch: *Wuvulu und Aua (Maty- und Durour-Inseln)* (Hamburg, 1908), 125.

Nanteressi. Long transverse flute of the Dompago people of Benin. It is played in pairs, or as a group of three with clapper bells, to encourage boys before circumcision.

Nantuni. *See* NANDUNI.

Nao. Ancient Chinese bell. *See* ZHONG.

Não bạt. Small cymbals of Vietnam.

Naobo. Bronze cymbals of the Han Chinese. *See* BO (i).

Nap'al. Long brass trumpet of Korea. *See* NABAL.

Naqqāra [naghara, naghora, nakkare]. KETTLEDRUM of the Islamic world, the Caucasus and Central Asia. It is widely used in military music as well as in religious and ceremonial music (*see* NAQQĀRAKHĀNA); it is often a symbol of royalty and is sometimes played with trumpets. *Naqqāra* are usually played in pairs and tuned to different pitches, exceptions being the large types from India and the USSR. They are made of silver, copper, brass, wood or pottery. *Naqqāra* have been played in Turkey, Syria and Egypt since the Middle Ages. Carried on horseback or on camels, they are beaten with a stick, the higher-pitched of the two on the player's right.

In Turkey the *nakkare* is an instrument of the Ottoman *mehter* (military or janissary band), made of copper with a skin membrane. It is played singly, held in the left hand or hung from the neck, and in pairs. In 20th-century Iran and Morocco they are usually made of pottery and the Moroccan types consist of a large and a small kettledrum laced together with gut. The *naghara* of Armenia is made of clay with a skin membrane and

Naqqāra (kettledrum) player, Iraq

Naqqārakhāna ensemble led by one pair of tenor kettledrums (centre), with two oboes of the Persian type (to the leader's right and left) and one oboe of the Indian type (behind); (front, from left) one bass drum and five pairs of treble kettledrums; (behind, from left) cymbals, one curved and four straight trumpets: detail from a painting (17th century) depicting the surrender of Kandahar (private collection)

is played in *sazandar* and *ashugh* ensembles. The drums are warmed before playing so that the membrane is tightened in order to give a good sound. In the 1920s and 1930s, V. Buni's 'Erevan Oriental Symphony Orchestra' used *naghara* with a screw tuning mechanism which enabled the instruments to be tuned in 4ths. The *naghara* is also known as the *tmbla*; in Georgia it is called the *diplipito*. *Naghora* were formerly used for military and state music by the Uzbek, Uighur and Tajik peoples of Central Asia.

Local variant names and uses of the *naqqāra* include the *nuqairat* of the north African Berbers and Syrians and the *nagarit* which is widely used in Ethiopian military and religious music. Large kettledrums spread to India where (known as *nagārā*) they are used in temples for ceremonial music. In Pakistan the *naqqāra* is widely used for outdoor music-making. *Naqqārā* are played in Surinam. The *naqqāra* is also the instrument from which the European KETTLEDRUM and NAKERS developed.

For further illustration *see* NAKERS, fig.1.

BIBLIOGRAPHY
J. Blades: *Percussion Instruments and their History* (London, 1970, 2/1974, rev. 3/1984)
S. Marcuse: *A Survey of Musical Instruments* (Newton Abbot and London, 1975), 160ff
J. Jenkins and P. Rovsing Olsen: *Music and Musical Instruments in the World of Islam* (London, 1976), 75
WILLIAM J. CONNER, MILFIE HOWELL,
ROBERT AT'AYAN

Naqqārakhāna [naqqārakhāna, tablkhāna]. An outdoor band of West and Central Asia, the Indian subcontinent, Malayasia and Sumatra, used for royal, ceremonial, civic or military music. Its typical instrumentation includes oboes, horns or trumpets, and drums, and sometimes cymbals. *Naqqārakhāna* means '*naqqāra* house', the large kettledrum (*naqqāra*) being often housed in a pavilion at the gateway of palaces, Muslim

shrines or Hindu temples. Its origins appear to lie in Persia and Central Asia, and its specific role is to play at sunrise, sunset and certain other times of day, a tradition which may point to an early connection with Zoroastrianism. In South Asia it is often called *naubat* (a Persian word denoting watches or stages of the day) or *naubatkhāna*. For the South-east Asian ensemble, *see* NOBAT.

At Sanchi, in central India, what appears to be a representation of a *naqqārakhāna* band was sculpted at about the time of Christ. It consists of a pair of conical pipes, two S-shaped trumpets and two drums. The players' costumes suggest that they were probably Scythians (*Śaka*) or Parthians. Oboes, trumpets and drums of Arabo-Persian origin are recorded in India from the late 1st millennium (*see* MAHVARĪ), but the *naubat* orchestra is first mentioned in South Asia in the early period of Turko-Iranian rule, the Delhi Sultanate (1193–1526), for example the *nāobatikā* of the Maithili work *Varṇaratnākara* (*c*1325), and during this period the band's instruments were frequently mentioned (*see* ŚAHNĀĪ, NAGĀRĀ, §1, and NĀGASVARAM). In South Asia the *naubat* appears to have replaced the earlier Hindu–Buddhist royal band, the *pañcamahāśabda* (which was similar but with conch-shell trumpets (*see* ŚAŃKH) instead of oboes), and spread throughout the subcontinent, functioning at state, religious and military occasions and as folk and tribal dance bands, processional bands for weddings etc.

During the Delhi Sultanate and the succeeding Mughal period (1526–1858) the *naubat* was part of the insignia of feudal rank in India, its use granted and its size determined by the Emperor. The Emperor's own *naqqārakhāna* was naturally the largest of all; that of the great Mughal ruler, Akbar, described by his chronicler Abu'l Faẓl (*c*1590), contained 18 pairs of *kuwar-gāh*, or *damāma* (bass drums), about 20 pairs of *naqqāra* (treble and bass kettledrums), four *duhul* (cylindrical drums), several *karnā* (long trumpets) of gold, silver and brass, nine *surnā* (oboes), *nafīr* (trumpets), *sīng* (brass curved trumpets) and three pairs of *sanj* (cymbals). Faẓl also gave an important account of the melodies and scoring of the Mughal *naqqārakhāna*, and of Akbar's performing ability, especially on *naqqāra*.

With the abolition of monarchies in the area *naqqārakhāna* bands have been reduced in number, but a few small ones still exist, such as the one at the shrine of Imam Reza at Mashad, Iran, and that at the shrine (*dargāh*) of Mu'inuddin Chishti at Ajmer, India. In South Asia the highland war pipe, brought by Scottish regiments during the British raj, has largely replaced the oboe in the folk *naubat*.

BIBLIOGRAPHY
Abu'l Faẓl: *Ā'īn-i-ākbarī* (c1590), trans. H. Blochmann in *The Imperial Musicians* (Calcutta, 1873, 2/1927), 53
N. A. Jairazbhoy: 'A Preliminary Survey of the Oboe in India', *EM*, xiv (1970), 375
J. Levy: 'Music from the Shrines of Ajmer and Mundra', TGM 105 [disc notes]
J. Baily: 'A Description of the Naqqarakhana of Herat', *Asian Music*, ii/2 (1980), 1
A. Dick: 'The Earlier History of the Shawm in India', *GSJ*, xxxvii (1984), 80

JOHN BAILY, ALASTAIR DICK

Naṙ [narh, nadd, naddu]. Obliquely held end-blown flute of Sind, Pakistan, and Rajasthan, India. The name means simply 'cane', and the flute is similar to the NĀY of West and Central Asia and the Baluchi *nel*, of which it forms an eastward extension. The flute is made of the desert reed *sacco kangor*; it is hollow for its whole length, which may be from about 60 to 100 cm. A smaller and thinner variety, the *kani*, about 30 to 46 cm long, is also found in Sind. The mouthpiece is the end of the pipe, conically bevelled or fitted with a similar cap of tin. There are four equidistant finger-holes towards the lower end. The flute is held obliquely and the breath directed towards the edge of the mouthpiece (see illustration).

In spite of its simple construction the *naṙ* has a complex playing technique, with cross-fingerings, blowing control and partial opening; the performer may also hum a drone while playing. In Sind the *naṙ* has a rich repertory (in Rajasthan the instrument is confined to some desert peoples of pastoral origin in the west, bordering on Sind); it is divided into two categories: *gur* – instrumental pieces defined as 'lyrical expression of love' and played on the *kani*; and *phuk* – pieces based on brief poetic texts symbolizing 'the lover's call to the beloved', played on large *naṙ*. A system of seven key-fingerings

Naṙ (obliquely held end-blown flute) played by a shepherd, Jaisalmer district, Rajasthan

for the main sub-categories was reached in the 19th century. In upper Sind, under Baluchi influence, the *naṙ* also accompanies *bait* (long ballad poems), which are sometimes sung by the flautist himself.
See also BĀS.

BIBLIOGRAPHY
N. A. Baloch: *Musical Instruments of the Lower Indus Valley of Sind* (Hyderabad, 1966)
K. S. Kothari: *Indian Folk Musical Instruments* (New Delhi, 1968)
G. Dournon: 'Flutes du Rajasthan', LDX 76645 [disc notes]

ALASTAIR DICK

Narakuṇḍa. A composite pot-drum of Andhra Pradesh, south-eastern India. *See* TANTIPĀNAI.

Narampupāṇai [narambupāṇai]. A composite pot-drum of Tamil Nadu, south-eastern India. *See* TANTIPĀNAI.

Nārelī. SPIKE FIDDLE of Rajasthan, north-west India. *See* RĀVAṆHATTHĀ.

Nar hunkarnio. FRICTION DRUM of the Bhil people of Rajasthan, north India. The body is made from an earthenware pot; a peacock quill passes through the body and the skin and is rubbed with the hand. The instrument is used as a bird- and animal-scarer.

Nārī hambān. BAGPIPE of northern Iraq. *See* QIRBA.

Narimba-ché. Term for a MUSICAL BOW about 2 metres long reported in the late 19th century among the Kekchi Indians of Guatemala. *See* CARAMBA.

Narimono. Japanese term for the *hayashi* ensemble of drums (*kotsuzumi*, *ōtsuzumi* and *shimedaiko*) and flutes (*nōkan* and *shinobue*) in the kabuki and bunraku theatres, and for similar ensembles in some other contexts.

Narme ney. Early name for the BĀLABĀN.

Narsīgā [narsīghā, narsiṅga, narsinghā]. Metal trumpet of Nepal, and Himachal Pradesh and southern Bihar, India. In Bihar and Himachal Pradesh the instrument is S-shaped and made of copper or brass. Folk musicians of the Ghāsi, Ḍom and other similar communities play the *narsīgā* in ensemble with the *śahnāī*, *ḍhāk*, *ḍholkī*, *bhēr* and *nagaṙa* at weddings and for the *paīki* sword dance. Although nowadays the *narsīgā* is associated primarily with non-tribal musicians, in the early 20th century it was also found among tribal groups, particularly the Uraōns, who called it BĀK. In southern Bihar the *narsīgā* is also known as KURUDUTU and *turhī*. According to Deva (1978), the S-shaped trumpet is found throughout India, made of brass, copper or silver, measuring 115 cm long and more.

The Nepalese *narsiṅga*, which is curved, is played by the *damāi* tailor–musicians, singly, in pairs or as a member of a larger group such as the *damāi bāja*.

BIBLIOGRAPHY
S. C. Roy: *The Mundas and their Country* (Calcutta, 1912/R1970), 217
——: *The Oraōns of Chōtā Nāgpur* (Calcutta, 1915), 183
M. Helffer: 'Fanfares villageoises au Nepal', *Objets et mondes*, ix/1 (1969), 51
B. C. Deva: *Musical Instruments of India: their History and Development* (Calcutta, 1978), 112f

CAROL M. BABIRACKI, MIREILLE HELFFER

Nasale (Fr.; Ger. *Nasal-Register*, *Nasalzug*). LUTE STOP.

Nasard (?Fr.; Ger. *Nasat*). An ORGAN STOP (also a harpsichord stop). There may have been an early French woodwind instrument of this name.

Nasardos (Sp.). An ORGAN STOP.

Naseré. A flattened globular VESSEL FLUTE of the Pilagá and other Indians of Chaco, Argentina, made from hardwood with two lateral holes. It is used for signalling or for recreation.

Nasis [nasisi]. Rattle of the Cuna Indians of the San Blas Islands of Panama. It consists of a dried gourd into which small seeds have been inserted, and has handles of deer bone wrapped with waxed braided cord.

Nason. An ORGAN STOP.

Nassarre, José (*fl* Mexico, 1730–36). Spanish organ builder. It is possible that he was related to the famous theorist and organist Pablo Nassarre, whose *Escuela música* (Saragossa, 1723–4) contains a chapter on organ building. He is first heard of in Mexico in 1730, when he built a large organ for Guadalajara Cathedral; now lost, possibly through damage to the cathedral in an earthquake of 1818, the organ was described as having 2226 pipes and two façades, a typical feature of Spanish cathedral organs.

Nassarre's next known work is another large instrument, built for Valladolid (now Morelia) Cathedral in 1732, and doubtless similar to the Guadalajara organ, as its cost was the same: 20,000 pesos. Nassarre's assistant for this was José Cacela, who also helped him with the later Mexico City cathedral organs. Of the Valladolid organ, only one façade of the original case remains, removed to the west gallery and incorporated into a modern instrument.

Two instruments by Nassarre survive in the Metropolitan Cathedral in Mexico City. In 1734 he was employed to improve the organ built by Jorge de SESMA and installed by TIBURCIO SANS in 1695, and to add a *Cadereta* (Positive) to it; he was engaged to build a new organ in 1735, facing the old one in the choir of the cathedral. In 1736 he totally rebuilt and enlarged the Sesma organ so that it matched in size and appearance the new organ of 1735. Both of these instruments were restored under the supervision of the Dutch organ builder D. A. Flentrop, who made the final inspection of the work in 1978.

The quality of Nassarre's work is that of a master builder, and these two organs are among the most monumental in the Spanish classical style to be found anywhere. Facing each other on either side of the choir, they have façades on both choir and ambulatory sides, with batteries of horizontal reed stops mounted in each of the four façades. The Gospel organ has 84 half-registers (including 15 façade reed registers) and six pedal registers; the Epistle organ has 79 half-registers (including 15 façade reed registers) and six pedal registers. It is likely that Nassarre built other Mexican instruments, possibly in the basilica of Guadaloupe and elsewhere, although evidence has not yet been found to confirm such speculation.

BIBLIOGRAPHY
Gazeta de México, no.37 (1730) [on Guadalajara Cathedral organ]; no.60 (1734) [Valladolid/Morelia]; no.93 (1735), nos.105,107 (1736) [Metropolitan Cathedral, Mexico City]
G. Saldivar: *Historia de la música en México: epocas precortesiana y colonial* (Mexico City, 1934)
J. Estrada: *Músic y músicos de la epoca virreinal* (Mexico City, 1973)
J. Fesperman: *Organs in Mexico* (Raleigh, North Carolina, 1981)
S. C. W. Platt: 'Organs of the Vice-regal Period in Four Mexican Cathedrals', *Organ Yearbook*, xii (1981), 55
D. A. Flentrop: *The Organs of Mexico Cathedral* (Washington, DC, 1983)

JOHN FESPERMAN

Natmat woywoy. SCRAPER of Motalava in the Banks Islands of Melanesia. It consists of a stone which is scraped with a leaf-stalk. The loud rasping sound it produces formerly represented the voice of the spirit 'natmat woywoy'. Although this is no longer believed, the performers still remain inside a leaf enclosure while playing and only men are allowed to see the instrument.

Naṭṭuva tālam. Cymbals of south India. *See* TĀLAM.

Naturale (It.). A direction found in Western music indicating the cancellation of a special effect (generally the use of mutes, or, in vocal music, of falsetto).

Natural notes. The notes of the harmonic series of a brass instrument, particularly of a 'natural' instrument, i.e. one not provided with valves, slide or keys in order to change the tube length while playing, and therefore confined to one series of harmonics or to such other series that are made available by changes of crook. The French expression 'sons naturels' is also used in music for horn to countermand 'sons bouchés' ('stopped notes') and in music for violin, harp, etc, to countermand playing in harmonics.

Naturhorn (Ger.). Hand horn; *see* HORN.

Natwarischpfiffe. Swiss transverse flute, made of wood, with six finger-holes and a thumb-hole, used particularly in the Canton Valais.

Naubat [naubatkhāna, nahābat, nahabet]. South Asian terms denoting the military and court and temple ceremonial band NAQQĀRAKHĀNA, of Persian and Central Asian origin. The term *naubat* means literally 'the stages [of the court or temple day]', marked by the band; it can also denote the kettledrums used in it.

Nautch. *See* NĀC.

Navajo violin. *See* KÍZH KÍZH DÍHÍ.

Näverlur. Wooden trumpet of Scandinavia. *See* LUR, (2).

Naw. Free-reed mouth organ of the Lahu people of northern Thailand, Laos and Burma. It has five bamboo tubes of varying lengths which fit into a gourd windchest.

Nawa. A term once applied in Pukapuka to the small

SLIT-DRUM and to the double-headed skin drum of European design. See E. and P. Beaglehole: *Ethnology of Pukapuka* (Honolulu, 1938), 216. *See also* NAFA.

Nay. Alternative name for the Turkish MEY and Armenian *duduk* (*see* DUDUK (i)).

Nāy [nai, nāī, nay, ney]. Oblique rim-blown flute of the Middle East, Iran and Central Asia. The term derives from the old Persian for 'reed' and by extension 'reed flute'. The instrument has been known in the Near East since antiquity; iconographic and written documents attest its use by the ancient Egyptians in the 3rd millennium BC. A particularly striking example of its use occurs on a ceremonial slate palette (*c*3000 BC, now in the Ashmolean Museum, Oxford), on which a fox plays the instrument for a dancing giraffe and ibex; a Sumerian silver flute dating from 2450 BC has been found in the royal cemetery of Ur in Southern Mesopotamia. The term 'nāy' is the generic Arabic name for several folk flutes (*see also* MĀṢŪL) as well as the specific term for the reed flute used in Arab art music; the name was formerly used in Near Eastern countries but today has replaced such Maghribi terms as *qaṣaba*.

The classical Arab *nāy* consists of an open-ended segment of 'Persian reed' (*Arundo donax*) with six fingerholes in front and one at the back; the edge of the tube at the top is lightly bevelled. It may vary in length from 32 to 81 cm and generally contains eight nodes and nine antinodes. The reedpipe from which the instrument is made should be not less than three years old and the tube must be hard, smooth and compact; the distance between the nodes is taken into consideration. Several instruments can sometimes be made from one long reed stem.

In Arab countries the classical *nāy* is made in several lengths. Each instrument is designated by the name of its fundamental note (given by opening the first hole): *nāy māhūr* (C), *nāy dūkāh* (D), *nāy buselik* (E), *nāy chargāh* (F), *nāy nawā* (G), *nāy ḥusaynī* (A), *nāy 'ajam* (B♭), *nāy kardān* (c), and so on. Theoretically, it is possible to have a *nāy* for each semitone of a chromatic scale, and for some quarter-tones; in practice each maker has a restricted number of models to suit the requirements of the music played in his area. Apart from making the *nāy* according to the musician's individual requirements, there are three methods of placing the fingerholes: this may be done by measuring (*al baḥr*), calculation (*al ḥisāb*) or analogy (*al muqābala*). The *nāy* is a difficult instrument to play because the bevelled mouth-hole remains completely open, only partly resting on the lower lip. Musicians often use different sizes of *nāy* during a concert, but a virtuoso can play the three-octave range on one instrument by altering the position of his fingers on the holes, by movements of the lips and head, and by breath control.

The *nāy* is an urban instrument and the only wind instrument used in Arab art music. As part of the *al-takht al-sharqī* ('oriental') ensemble found in large Arab towns, it appears alongside the *'ūd* (lute), the *qānūn* (box zither) and two membranophones: the *daff* (frame drum) and the single-headed *dunbuk*. As a solo instrument it is used for improvising passages (*taqsīm*) and accompanying religious songs. It is the main instrument of the *dhikr* ceremony of the Mawlawiyya Sufis (for illustration of the Iraqi *nāy, see* FLUTE, fig.2a).

Player of the popular nāy (rim-blown flute), Fez, Morocco

The popular Arab *nāy* may be made of wood, reed or metal, and has many local names: *shabbāba*, *blūr* and *bluīr* in Iraq; *shabbāba*, *shāqūla*, *pīk* and *munjeīra* in Syria and Lebanon; *ṣuffāra*, *salāmiyya*, *gaṣba* or *qawwāl* in Egypt; *zumbara* in the Sudan; *qaṣba* in Yemen; and *qoṣba*, *qaṣaba*, *qaṣṣāba*, *juwāk* or *fhal* in North Africa. It does not conform to the rigorous norms of the classical instrument. The reedpipe *nāy* varies in length from 20 to 80 cm and is not always completely straight. It can be made from one segment of reed which may include three or four nodes and whose diameter may vary between 1·5 and 2·5 cm. The number of holes varies from three to ten; they are distributed in several different ways but usually begin at the second antinode from the bottom. The upper opening may be bevelled, or it may be capped with a conical metal mouthpiece (as in the *shāqūla* of Deir ez Zōr, eastern Syria). The metal *nāy* (*shamshal*, *bluīr*, *qaṣba*) is 30 to 40 cm long, and sometimes has a bevelled mouth-hole. Near Eastern models have six finger-holes and one thumb-hole, while the North African *qaṣaba* has seven finger-holes and one thumb-hole. The metal *nāy* is held and played in the same way as those of reed or wood. (For the wooden *nāy, see* SHABBĀBA.)

The *ney* of Iran is primarily a classical instrument; it is made of reed with seven nodes, 40 to 80 cm long, and has five finger-holes and one thumb-hole producing the basic pitches *c'–d'–e'–f'–f♯'–g'–a'* (the e and a are a quarter-tone flat). Other notes can be obtained by varying the breath pressure, and the range can thus be extended to two and a half octaves. As the bevelled edge of the mouth-hole is sharp on the inside, it is often covered by a metal band to prevent damage to the instrument. The joints are sometimes made at the nodes of the tube, and can be decorated with engraving.

Players of the *ney* in Iran place the rim between their teeth, which produces a warmer and more powerful tone; this more difficult technique is a 19th-century development, apparently inspired by the Turkmen *ney*. The *ney* is the only wind instrument in the classical Persian orchestra, but its melodic and rhythmic resources fit it equally for solo performance. The great *ney* tradition is preserved at Isfahan, where its repertory (*radif*) includes pieces reserved exclusively for it.

Various popular forms of the instrument are known, made of wood, reed or metal and with various vernacular names, for example the Baluchi *nel*, Turkmen *düdük* and Kurdish *shimshal*.

The *ney* of Azerbaijan is 60 to 70 cm long, and also made of wood, reed, brass or copper, with three to six finger-holes. The player holds the instrument obliquely, with its head in the corner of his mouth. It is now rare; once it was common, particularly as a shepherd's instrument.

The Turkish *ney* is played in classical *fasıl* (art music) and is an important member of the ensembles that play at the ceremonies of the Mevlevî (whirling dervishes). It is similar to the Arab *nāy* in construction but has a wooden cap to facilitate blowing and tone-production.

The instrument is also played by the Karakalpak, Uighur, Uzbek and Tajik peoples of Central Asia, where it can be made of a variety of materials which are often described by a prefix, for example *agach-nai* ('wooden nai').

BIBLIOGRAPHY

G. A. Villoteau: 'Description historique, technique et littéraire des instrumens de musique des orientaux', *Description de l'Egypte* (Paris, 1826)

M. K. al-Khula'ī: *Kitāb al-mūsīqā al-sharqiyya* [The book of oriental music] (Cairo, 1904)

E. Zonis: *Classical Persian Music* (New York, 1973), 162ff

J. Jenkins and P. Rovsing Olsen: *Music and Musical Instruments in the World of Islam* (London, 1976), 53f

H. H. Touma: *La musique arabe* (Paris, 1977)

M. Guettat: *La musique classique du Maghreb* (Paris, 1980)

S. Q. Hassan: *Les instruments de musique en Irak et leur rôle dans la société traditionnelle* (Paris, 1980)

J. During: *La musique iranienne: tradition et évolution* (in preparation)

A. Ibrāhīm: *Şinā'at al-nāy fī Baghdād* [The manufacture of the nāy in Baghdād] (in preparation)

SCHÉHÉRAZADE Q. HASSAN, JEAN DURING

Nāyanam. *See* NĀGASVARAM.

Nayi maùng. Large gong of Burma; it was beaten in the palace to signal the time of day.

Nāykhĭm. Small double-headed barrel drum of the Newari people of Nepal. It owes its name to its executants, people of the butchers' caste (*nāy*). The drum is small and is carried by means of a leather strap slung around the player's neck. The right head is struck with a wooden stick and the left one with the hand. It is used with *chusyāḥ* (cymbals) and *kāhāḥ* (long trumpets) during funerals. It is similar to the *dhāḥ*, but smaller. *See also* KHĬM.

BIBLIOGRAPHY

T. O. Ballinger and P. H. Bajracharya: 'Nepalese Musical Instruments', *Southwestern Journal of Anthropology*, xvi/4 (1960), 398

F. Hoerburger: *Studien zur Musik in Nepal* (Regensburg, 1975)

S. Wiehler-Schneider and H. Wiehler: 'A Classification of the Traditional Musical Instruments of the Nevars', *Journal of the Nepal Research Centre*, iv (1980), 67–132

MIREILLE HELFFER

Nbogoi. Small Cuban woodblock or SLIT-DRUM. *See* CAJITA CHINA.

Nchomane. FRAME DRUM of the Tsonga, Hlengwe and Ndau peoples of south-eastern Africa. It is played with the right hand or with a stick while the left hand varies the tone by pressing the underside of the skin. It is used in religious, especially divination, ceremonies.

ANDREW TRACEY

Nchuko. Drum of the Chopi people of Zavala district, Mozambique. It is the second largest in a set of three, used with xylophones. The other drums are the *nkulu* and *nzomana*. See *TraceyCSA*, ii, 21.

Ncwa. Cone whistle of the Nyoro people of Uganda. *See* NSEGU.

Ndall. Side-blown trumpet of the Yanzi people of Zaïre. It is made from a hollowed-out root or branch (*LaurentyA*, 332).

Ndaludali. Gourd-resonated MUSICAL bow of the Zaramo people of Tanzania.

Ndamba. SCRAPER of the Luvale people of southern Africa.

Ndamula. Single-headed open-ended HOURGLASS DRUM of the Hehe people of Iringa district, Tanzania. The membrane is pegged on.

Ndandale. Single-headed closed conical drum of the Nyamwezi people of Tabora district, Tanzania. The membrane is laced on and the drum is played with sticks. Together with the *mahuge*, *ndondo* and *muziki* drums, it has ritual functions connected with the chief. See *TraceyCSA*, ii, 336. *See also* LUGAYA.

Ndandi. LAMELLAPHONE of the Lala people of Zambia. *See* NDIMBA.

Ndanya. Drum of the Luba people of Zaïre. *See* DITUMBA.

Ndara (i). African XYLOPHONE. (1) Eight-key pit xylophone of the Alur people of Uganda. The wooden keys are loosely placed across two grass bundles which are pegged to the ground. Pegs serve as separating sticks. The instrument is mounted over a pit and played by one player. The style of performance and the tuning are distinct from those of other xylophones of Uganda. Traditionally the instrument was used for entertainment of the sultan of Alur. See *WachsmannTCU*.

(2) Xylophone of the Dhola people of Uganda. It has 13 slabs, laid across two banana stalks, and is played by two men.

(3) Log xylophone of the Ndo and Nande peoples of Zaïre. *See* PANDINGBWA.

Ndara (ii). BOARD ZITHER of the Andekobe people of Zaïre (*LaurentyC*, 116).

Ndavui. *See* DAVUI.

Ndele. End-blown NOTCHED FLUTE of the Soga people of Uganda. *See* NDERE (i).

Ndémbb [ndeémlebu, ndémbo]. Wooden cone flute, with one or two finger-holes, of the Holo and Pende peoples of south-western Zaïre (*LaurentyA*, 129, 135, 151f).

Ndembe-ndembe [ndémbandèmb]. VESSEL FLUTE and wooden cone flute of the Mbala people of northern Zaïre (*LaurentyA*, 81f, 146).

Ndeng-ndeng. 15-string RAFT ZITHER of the Angas people of Nigeria, with the strings arranged in five groups of three. In construction the instrument resembles the Birom YOMKWO but is played differently: the *ndeng-ndeng* is held with the strings on the side away from the player; the strings are plucked with the fingers of both hands, never with the thumbs.

Ndere [mulere, ndele] (pl. *endere*) (**i**). NOTCHED FLUTE, with four finger-holes, of the Ganda and Soga peoples of southern Uganda. Among the Ganda the swamp-reed *Phragmites mauretanicus* is the preferred material, but other materials including aluminium are also used. Copper or brass wire, rubber bands, beads and goat-hair tassels may be used for decoration. The finger-holes are positioned to give a pentatonic scale of large tones, which varies from flute to flute but which is compatible with the pitch systems of the Ganda and Soga songs from which the flute repertories are derived. The length is commonly around 40 to 46 cm, but the former palace ensembles of the king of Buganda included a band of flutes and drums known as the *abalere gwa kabaka* ('the king's flautists') which used *endere* of six different sizes in ensemble. The longest flute (*c*70 cm) was called *enkologi* and was twice as long as the shortest, *entemyo*. Other names in ascending order of size were *ntabitabi*, *nsaasi*, *entengezzi* and *ekiwuuwe* (the local name for *Phragmites*, also related to the verb *okufuuwe*, 'to blow').

The *ndere* has no precisely defined usage, being a popular domestic instrument. It is used during herding but is also played solo or in small ensembles with drums and other instruments to accompany singing and dancing at weddings and beer parties. Among the Ganda it also features prominently in the musical ensembles that accompany rival teams at wrestling matches.

Similar four-holed flutes are common elsewhere in Uganda. In the south-west, in Nkore and Kigezi, the instrument is called *omukuri*, while the Nyoro and Tooro call it *nyamulere* or *omuceewe*. Variants of the name are given to similar wider-bored bamboo flutes by the Nilotic and other peoples of northern Uganda, such as *olere* (Acholi), *oleta* (Lango), *aulero* (Teso) and *olera* (Madi). Rather different Ugandan notched flutes are the KHUMULELE of the Masaba (Gisu) people and the NYAMULERE of the Konzo.

BIBLIOGRAPHY
WachsmannTCU
P. R. Cooke: *The Ganda Ndere* (diss., U. of Wales, Cardiff, 1970)

Ensemble of endere (notched flutes) accompanied by (right) three Uganda drums and (left) engalabi (single-headed drum)

P. R. Cooke and M. Doornbos: 'Rwenzururu Protest Songs', *Africa*, lii/1 (1982), 50

PETER COOKE

Ndere (ii). Five-string plucked lute of Senegal and the Gambia. It has a boat-shaped soundbox and resembles the KHALAM.

Nderua. *See* DERUA.

Ndilkal 'agháář. Navajo Indian name for the PEYOTE RATTLE.

Ndima [dima]. Drum of central Africa. (1) Long drum, with two laced membranes, of the Zande and Barambo peoples of Zaïre. *See* NABITA, (1).

   (2) Conical drum, with two laced membranes, of the Zande people of Zaïre. *See* DINDO.

   (3) Closed conical drum of the Abangba and Ngala peoples of Zaïre; the membrane is laced on.

K. A. GOURLAY, DAVID K. RYCROFT

Ndimba. A small LAMELLAPHONE of the Nsenga people of the Zambezi basin of south-eastern Africa. The same instrument is called *ndandi* by the Lala, *kangombio* by the Lozi and *kathandi* or *sithandi* by the Mbunda and the peoples as far west as northern Namibia. It has 13 or 14 keys arranged with the largest on the left (unlike most other lamellaphones in south-eastern Africa, which have them in the centre); in the west, the keys are fine-tuned with wax under the tips. There is a membrane buzzer in the middle of the soundboard. The *ndimba* is a professional musician's instrument and is played over a small gourd resonator with the thumbs.

ANDREW TRACEY

Ndimga. Type of MUSICAL BOW in south-eastern Africa. *See also* CHITENDE.

Ndimo [ndimu]. Drum of the Bandiya (Zande) people of Zaïre. *See* DINDO.

Ndjanga. Box-resonated LAMELLAPHONE of the Yans

people of Zaïre. It has metal keys (*LaurentyS*, 194). *See* KISAANJ.

Ndjele. Hand-held vessel rattle of the Tsonga people of southern Africa. It is made from a perforated oval calabash containing small stones, and has a stick handle. It is used, together with the *mantshomane* drum, for exorcism. *See KirbyMISA*, 8, pl.4*a*.

Ndjimba. Large curved calabash-resonated XYLOPHONE of the Chokwe people of Zaïre. The keys are strung together by a bark cord and suspended within a frame made from three branches. There are two types: a larger instrument with 17 keys, which can be played solo, and a smaller one with 11 keys, which is always played with the larger. Each player uses two wooden stick beaters, the ends of which are thickened with rubber or bark. The player of the larger instrument may also hold two *lusangu* gourd rattles in his right hand. Every *ndjimba* player has a short personal melody of his own composition with which he will usually conclude the performance.

BIBLIOGRAPHY

B. Schmidt-Wrenger: *Muziek van de Tshokwe uit Zaïre* (Tervuren, 1975)

J. GANSEMANS, K. A. GOURLAY

Ndoje. Side-blown ivory trumpet of the Mangutu people of Zaïre. It has a carved mouthpiece and one stop in the tip. The term may also refer to a side-blown wooden trumpet of the Mangutu (*LaurentyA*, 338, 371).

Ndoko. LAMELLAPHONE of the Ngombe people of Zaïre. *See* EKEMBI.

Ndond [ndondd]. Wooden cone flute, with one or two finger-holes, of the Lele people of south-western Zaïre (*LaurentyA*, 139, 153).

Ndondo. Single-headed closed conical drum of the Nyamwezi people of Tabora district, Tanzania. The membrane is laced on and the drum is played with sticks. *See also* NDANDALE.

Ndjimba (calabash-resonated xylophone) of the Chokwe people, Zaïre

2. Ndongo (bowl lyre) with two endingidi (spike fiddles), two notched flutes and Uganda drum of the Ganda people, Uganda

1. Bowl lyre of the ndongo type: the coloured striping is typical of the Soga people, Uganda

Ndongo [endongo]. Eight-string bowl lyre of the Ganda people of Uganda. It is one of a number of Ugandan bowl lyres (see fig.1), such as the *ntongoli* of the Soga people, the Samia *edungu*, the Luo lyre (all with eight strings), the Logoli *litungu* and the Gwe lyre (seven strings), and the Madi and Lugbara *odi* (five strings). The bowl lyre was imported into the region by Nilotic groups and travelled from east to west in the southern part of the country. Major differences exist between instruments of Bantu groups, such as the *ndongo*, and those of the Nilotes. Among the Bantu the bowl is shallow and either trough or food-bowl shaped; among the Nilotes it is deep with a spherical knob at the back. The Madi *odi* uses a tortoise-shell. In the *ndongo* and other Bantu instruments the two arms carrying the yoke enter the bowl to rest below the rim at the tailpiece, leaving hardly any bulge in the surface of the skin; in Nilotic instruments they are prominent above the rim and cause bulges in the surface of the skin. In Bantu lyres the arms tend to form a V; in Nilotic to be parallel.

The number of strings varies according to ethnic group. They are attached at one end to a string holder (in the *ndongo* by means of pieces of gut-string tied with a slip-knot) and at the other to the yoke by a few turns round a strip of cloth, bark-cloth or banana fibre which is wrapped round the yoke; the turning of this 'bulge' adjusts the tension and so enables the instrument to be tuned. Ganda and Soga lyres have no bridges, but the Samia, Jopadhola and other peoples under Luo influence fit a raft of four hollow reeds to the skin by two lumps of wax beneath the strings. The Gwe and Gishu use bridges of thin, rectangular lamellae with notches to guide the strings; the Madi bridge is a carved piece of wood with two feet, which stands on the skin. As strings are of similar length, they are tuned in an order to suit the convenience of the player. In performance the left arm of the lyre rests in the left hand so that the thumb, middle and ring fingers are able to pluck the three nearest strings; the little finger of the right hand is hooked round the right arm of the lyre to enable the right hand to pluck the remaining strings. The lyre is used both as a solo instrument and in small ensembles. Among the Ganda

it is played with *endingidi* (spike fiddles), notched flutes and an accompanying drum (see fig.2); Soga music includes one or two bowl lyres of different sizes, two tube fiddles and a Uganda drum. See *WachsmannTCU*.
K. A. GOURLAY

Ndono. Braced gourd-resonated MUSICAL BOW of the Nyamwezi/Sukuma people of Tanzania.

Ndualala. Small bells of the Gogo people in the central region of Tanzania.

Ndugu. Large drum of the Tsogo people of Gabon. It has a laced membrane and is played vertically as part of an ensemble accompanying masked dances. The ensemble includes the *mosumba*, a drum with a nailed membrane which is played vertically.

Nduisi. Single-headed open-ended conical drum of the Nyanja/Manganja people of southern Malawi. The membrane is pegged on and weighted. This is one of the nine tuned drums in the LIKHUBA set.

Ndulele. Side-blown animal-horn trumpet of the Gogo people of central Tanzania. It is one of the instruments used in the *nindo* dance.

Nduma. Double-headed conical drum of the Langbase and Gbanziri peoples of Zaïre. *See* DINDO.

Ndumbu (pl. *vandumbu*). End-blown wooden trumpet of the Mbwela and Nkangala peoples of south-eastern Angola. It has a conical bore, hollowed out by burning, and is covered in plant leaves secured by vegetable fibres. The instruments are kept in a river concealed from women and blown only at night for secret ceremonies by men and boys. They are of two sizes. The larger is from 300 to 500 cm long; it is apparently not lip-sounded but used somewhat like a megaphone. The smaller is from 100 to 130 cm long and has a detachable mouthpiece; whether this reflects early European influence is uncertain. A number of harmonics are elicited from it, sometimes reaching the 7th, 8th or 9th partials. See G. Kubik: 'Angola: Mukanda na Makisi', MC11 [disc notes].
GERHARD KUBIK, DAVID K. RYCROFT

Ndundu [ndumba] **(i).** Cylindro-conical drum of the Ngombe and Poto peoples of Zaïre, also known as *totoro* by the Ngombe (*BooneT*, 31, 68f). *See* DINDO.

Ndundu (ii). Semicircular SLIT-DRUM of the Mbuti pygmies of Ituri Forest, Zaïre.

Ndung. End-blown stopped bamboo pipe of the Bamileke-Banjun people of Cameroon. It is played in a consort of nine pipes of different sizes with drums and tubular bamboo rattles for social dancing. *See also* STOPPED FLUTE ENSEMBLE.

Ndungo. Afro-Cuban drum, now obsolete. *See* DUNGO.

Ndungu. Cylindro-conical drum of the Konda and Yembe peoples of Zaïre; *see* BOKENZA. The name is also used for drums of the lower Congo region and as an alternative to *lokilo* among the Lia (Bolia) further to the north-east (*BooneT*, 34, 48, 61).

Nduntsi. Single-headed HOURGLASS DRUM of the Hehe people of Iringa district, Tanzania. It is open-ended, and the membrane is pegged on.

Nduvu. *See* DUVU.

Ndwala. Metal bell of the Gogo people of Dodoma district, Tanzania. It is worn on the legs of singers and dancers.

Ndwi [n'dweie]. Alarm drum of the Lesa and Sakata peoples of equatorial Zaïre (*BooneT*, 61).

Ndyele. *See* BANGWE.

Ndzumba. Sacred, communally owned drum of the Tsonga people of Mozambique and South Africa.

Ne [neo]. Slit percussion tube of the Mandinka people of Senegal and the Gambia. It is made of iron and struck with both ends of an iron rod (*loyo*). It is played exclusively by women professional singers as rhythmic accompaniment to the *kora* (harp-lute; *see* KORA (i)) and other instruments of the *jali* caste.

LUCY DURÁN

Nê. Wooden flute of the Bati, Boa (Bwa) and Sere peoples of north and north-eastern Zaïre. The same name is applied by the Sere to sets of stopped flutes threaded on to a wire or cord (*LaurentyA*, 87, 118, 163ff, 176, 179, 190f).

Nebel. *See* NEVEL.

Nebuguwu. Drum of the Lele people of south-western Zaïre, used to accompany the chief's journeys (*BooneT*, 69).

Neck (Fr. *manche*; Ger. *Hals*; It. *manico*). As applied to such string instruments as those of the violin, viol, lute and guitar families, essentially the projecting handle to which part of the fingerboard is fastened. The player holds the instrument by the neck (handle) with one hand, and with the other plucks or bows the strings that run over the fingerboard. The neck is most often a separate piece (as on the violin), joined to the body by nailing or gluing (or both). Sometimes the neck is an integral part of the body, as in a rebec. The size and shape of the neck depend on its function and the number of strings involved. The violin neck, for example, is relatively thin since it carries only four strings; it is relatively short because it needs to be only long enough to accommodate the player's hand comfortably in the space between the body proper and the pegbox (*see* VIOLIN, fig.2). The necks of viols generally carry six strings and have, as a consequence, to be broader than those of violins. Similarly lutes have broad necks to carry their numerous strings (from six to 14). The chitarrone must have a long neck to accommodate its long strings. A large viola d'amore, with seven playing strings above the fingerboard and seven or more (up to 14) sympathetic strings below it, must have a broad neck strong enough to bear the tension of its strings.

Sometimes the size, shape or other factors change in the course of an instrument's history as playing conditions change. Before about 1800, for instance, the neck of the violin was (compared with the modern instrument) relatively short and thick, and it emerged straight from the body. After about 1800 the violin neck was thrown back so that the line of the neck (viewed from the side) was tilted upwards from pegbox to body in order to meet a higher bridge and to permit the use of the higher tensions essential to the increased volume demanded by larger concert halls and orchestras.

See also FINGERBOARD, (1), and PEGBOX.

DAVID D. BOYDEN

Nedomu [neduma]. Arched harp of the Mangbetu and Meje peoples of Zaïre (*LaurentyC*, 119). *See* KUNDI (i).

Neduku [nedima]. *See* NENDIMA.

Nedundu. Large bell-shaped SLIT-DRUM of the Meje people of Zaïre. It is played in conjunction with other drums. *See also* NABITA, (2).

Nedun kuḷal [nedun kuzhal]. Double DUCT FLUTE, with central blowing-hole, of Tamil Nadu, south India. It consists of a long, thick bamboo tube with three interior internodes. Above each node a hole is made connecting the neighbouring internodes; these are covered with thin metal sheets to create the ducts. A reed blowing-tube is inserted into the central internode (the instrument is held vertically) and the breath is channelled through the two ducts. The lowermost internode, where the melody is played, has eight holes, and the uppermost gives a drone. The 'nedunguzhal' illustrated by Sambamoorthy (1962) seems to be a *buguri*. *See also* DOBANDĪ BĀSĪ and PĀVA.

BIBLIOGRAPHY
P. Sambamoorthy: *Catalogue of Musical Instruments Exhibited in the Government Museum, Madras* (Madras, 3/1962)
B.C. Deva: *Musical Instruments of India* (Calcutta, 1978)
ALASTAIR DICK

Neffāra. Transverse flute of the Moors of Mauritania.

Nefir [nüfür]. Long trumpet of Turkey and Azerbaijan,

without finger-holes; probably analogous to the Arab NAFĪR. The *nefir* is reputed to have been used as a signal instrument by the dervish orders, but is no longer in use. See L. Picken: *Folk Musical Instruments of Turkey* (London, 1975).

Negara [nahara]. Hemispherical KETTLEDRUM of the *nobat* court ensemble in Kedah, West Malaysia. Related instruments include the *nenggara* of Trengganu and the *nengkara* of Perak. The *negara* is made of metal and its head is laced with cords. It is placed on the ground, inclined slightly towards the player. The *nenggara* is a large single-headed footed drum about 38 cm high and is heavily encased in silver and decorated with delicate foliated designs. The head is made of goatskin and is tuned with 15 silver tuning keys, 18 cm below the rim. The drum is held tilted slightly forward by one player and struck with strips of rattan by another. The *nengkara* is made of wood and has a head diameter of 39 cm, slightly longer than the height of the drum. According to Linehan (1951) the *nengkara* was traditionally made from a special kind of wood. *See also* NAGĀRĀ.

BIBLIOGRAPHY
W. Linehan: 'The Nobat and the Orang Kalau of Perak', *Journal of the Malayan Branch of the Royal Asiatic Society*, xxiv/3 (1951), 60
JACK PERCIVAL BAKER DOBBS

Neguru. Small zoomorphic SLIT-DRUM of the Ngbele (Mangbele) people of south-western Zaïre (*LaurentyTF*, 140). *See* GUGU, (1).

Nehémb [ntshémb, tshyémb]. Wooden cone flute, with one or two finger-holes, of the Lele people of south-western Zaïre (*LaurentyA*, 122ff, 148).

Neischl. *See* NEUSCHEL family.

Nekamu. Cylindrical stopped wooden flute of the Barambo people of Zaïre (*LaurentyA*, 175).

Nekbokbo. Small wooden SLIT-DRUM of the Meje people of Zaïre. Two are played in conjunction with other drums. *See also* NABITA, (2) and NKUMVI.

Nekere. Set of cylindrical stopped flutes, threaded on to cord or wire, of the Angba people of northern Zaïre (*LaurentyA*, 189).

Nekira [nekire]. Cylindrical stopped wooden flute of the Meje and Mamvu peoples of north-eastern Zaïre (*LaurentyA*, 177f).

Nekpopo. SLIT-DRUM of the Bangba people of Zaïre. *See* NKUMVI.

Neku. Small buffalo-horn trumpet of Nepal. It is blown directly or using a bamboo tube. In the Kathmandu valley *neku* are often played in pairs: one is called *bā-neku* ('father horn'), the other *mā-neku* ('mother horn'). Their main use is in the numerous religious festivals of the summer, during the month of Shravan.
MIREILLE HELFFER

Nel. Baluchi term for the NĀY.

Nembongo. Side-blown animal-horn trumpet of north-eastern Zaïre. Among the Ngbele people it has one stop in the tip and is also known as *namoduduka* and *moduka* (*LaurentyA*, 319). The term (and *nembongaye*) denotes an ivory trumpet with carved mouthpiece among the Barambo, Makere, Mayogo and Meje peoples (*LaurentyA*, 360ff, 415).

Nemessányi, Samuel Felix (*b* Liptószentmiklós, 1 Dec 1837; *d* Budapest, 5 March 1881). Hungarian violin maker. He received his training from Johann Baptist Schweitzer and Thomas Zach in Pest and Anton Sitt in Prague. He established himself in Pest in 1863 and can be regarded as the best Hungarian maker of his time. His preference was the Guarneri 'del Gesù' model although he occasionally copied Stradivari, Maggini and other masters. In his endeavour to produce cleanly crafted instruments based on the great Italian models, his approach to violin making was essentially similar to that of J.-B. Vuillaume. Lütgendorff's claim that Nemessányi's 'del Gesù' copies could hardly be distinguished from the originals, though far-fetched at the time, was prophetic in that the additional years have succeeded in imparting a genuine look of age. However, his violins are not truly Italianate in appearance or tone. Nemessányi often used one-piece tables and worked out a comparatively successful system of varnishing; although alcohol-based, the varnish possesses a softness which quite belies this. His violins have a strongly aggressive tone, lacking a little in flexibility; his violas, mostly of smaller size, are quite scarce and his cellos, very fine instruments normally based on the Stradivari model, are greatly sought after. Nemessányi's rather dissolute life brought him to an untimely death so that his output is not at all large.

BIBLIOGRAPHY
Remenyi archives, private collection, Toronto
W. L. von Lütgendorff: *Die Geigen- und Lautenmacher vom Mittelalter bis zur Gegenwart* (Frankfurt am Main, 1904, rev. 6/1922/R1968)
JAAK LIIVOJA-LORIUS

Nemva. Wooden flute of the Sere people of north-eastern Zaïre. It has a slender conical bore and is bound in animal skin (*LaurentyA*, 164).

Nenbongbo. Struck double bell of the Meje people of Zaïre. It is played in conjunction with the *nabita* and other drums.

Nendima [nedima, nendime, neduku]. Cylindro-conical drum, with two laced membranes, of the Barambo people of north-eastern Zaïre (*BooneT*, 29). *See* DINDO.

Nengangbu. Pod-shaped SLIT-DRUM of the Yogo/Bozo people of northern Zaïre. *See* MAKPO.

Nengbombo. Metal double bell of the Yogo/Bozo people of northern Zaïre. *See* MAKPO.

Nengbwanga. Wooden flute, with slender conical bore, of the Meje people of Zaïre; it is decorated with metallic binding. The term may also refer to a cylindrical stopped flute of the Meze (*LaurentyA*, 162, 180).

Nenggara [nengkara]. Drums of West Malaysia. *See* NEGARA.

Nengnong. Idiochord TUBE ZITHER of the Batak Toba area of the province of North Sumatra, Indonesia. It is found also in the Mandailing area under the name of GONDANG BULUH or *nungneng*.

Nengombi [nengonibi]. BOARD ZITHER of Zaïre. *See* GOMBI (i).

Nenjenje. Two-string STICK ZITHER of the Meje people of north-eastern Zaïre. Stopping is done on one string while the other provides a drone. A piece of quill at the far end adds a buzzing sound. It is used for song accompaniment. See *TraceyCSA*, ii, 272.

Neo-Bechstein-Flügel (Ger.: 'Neo-Bechstein grand piano') [Bechstein-Nernst-Siemens-Flügel]. An ELECTRIC PIANO designed around 1928–30 by the German physicist (Hermann) Walther Nernst (1864–1941), with the assistance of OSKAR VIERLING, S. Francó and H. Driescher; it was manufactured in limited numbers from 1931 to the end of the decade by Bechstein in Berlin, in collaboration with the electrical company Siemens & Halske. This 88-note grand piano cost slightly less than the cheapest conventional piano made by Bechstein.

The strings of the Neo-Bechstein are struck by lightweight 'microhammers' operated by an adaptation of the normal mechanism, so that while the action is gentler the touch is identical with that of a conventional piano. There is a single string for each note in the treble and bass ranges, and two strings each for the middle-range of notes from e♭ to f♯'''. The microhammers produce less than normal energy in the strings, which are shorter, thinner and less highly tensioned than conventional piano strings. The sound quality is purer, and the strings are damped less quickly, because there is no soundboard to absorb their vibrations. Each group of five single or double strings is amplified by means of an electromagnetic pickup. With the amplification system switched off the instrument produces a harpsichord- or spinet-like quality – the 40 notes with double strings in fact match the compass of the spinet. Volume is controlled by the left pedal, which can produce a crescendo or maintain tones at a constant level of loudness, giving a sound somewhat like that of an organ. The sustaining pedal operates in the normal way by lifting the dampers from the strings, but the notes resonate for about three times as long as normal; a special left-hand lever brings into operation an additional set of dampers which reduce resonance to that of a conventional piano. Most models of the Neo-Bechstein had a built-in radio and could be connected to a record turntable. The instrument was used in several film scores during the 1930s and was found to be suitable for both early and contemporary music; but it failed to achieve lasting success, perhaps because it was less appropriate for the Romantic repertory from Chopin to Debussy.

For illustration *see* ELECTRIC PIANO, fig.1.

BIBLIOGRAPHY
F. W. Winckel: 'Das Radio-Klavier von Bechstein-Siemens-Nernst', *Die Umschau*, xxxv (1931), 840
J. B. Collins: 'Der Bechstein-Nernst-Siemens-Flügel', *Die Musik*, xxiv (1931–2), 73
R. Raven-Hart: 'Keyboard and Loud Speaker: how the "Neo-Bechstein" Piano Works', *Wireless World*, xxxii (1933), 67
T. Rhea: 'The Neo-Bechstein Electric Piano', *Contemporary Keyboard*, iv/1 (1978), 54

HUGH DAVIES

Nepoko. Tulip-shaped SLIT-DRUM of the Angba people of northern Zaïre (*LaurentyTF*, 139).

Nerube. Small, zoomorphic SLIT-DRUM of the Barambo and Ngbele (Mangbele) peoples of Zaïre (*LaurentyTF*, 139). *See* GUGU, (1).

Nerumbwen. A SLIT-DRUM in the ensemble of Seniang, Malekula, Vanuatu. *See* HINEN NIMBWILEI.

Neuhaus, Max (*b* Beaumont, Texas, 9 Aug 1939). American percussionist and sound sculptor. He studied at the Manhattan School of Music. In the course of his career as a soloist working with an avant-garde repertory, Neuhaus began in 1964 to amplify certain instruments. In 1965 he started to use acoustic feedback, and in 1966 he produced a special electronic circuit to be connected to a home hi-fi system; this was manufactured as Max-Feed by Mass Art in New York. In the same year he presented *Public Supply*, in which he mixed and modified sounds phoned in to a local radio station over ten lines by members of the public. The concept of *Public Supply* was expanded to a national scale in *Radio Net* (1977).

Neuhaus's first semi-permanent sound installation, Drive-In Music, ran for six months (1967–8) in Buffalo, New York; it consisted of 20 low-powered radio transmitters, spaced out along a mile of straight road, which broadcast electronic sounds that changed according to weather conditions and were audible only over car radios. In 1969 Neuhaus gave up his career as a percussionist to concentrate on building sound sculptures. Since 1971 a series of his pieces has explored underwater sounds, starting with Water Whistle in which small whistles, connected to flexible plastic tubing, placed under water in a swimming pool, are operated by jets of water at pressure; this, together with the movements of swimmers, causes the whistles to change direction, affecting the total sound complex. His other environments have featured electronic sounds: in the permanent installation below a ventilation grille on a traffic island in Times Square, New York (1977), a large loudspeaker emits a rich low sound, the timbre of which is affected by temperature and wind; this is in marked contrast to the delicate clicks heard from loudspeakers distributed throughout a building in Walkthrough (Brooklyn, 1973), and installed high up in a large tree in a wooded park at the Documenta 6 exhibition (Kassel, 1977). In each context the sounds are only minimally obtrusive, are well matched to the environment, and make an illuminating statement about it. In 1978–80 Neuhaus developed a 'multi-synthesizer' to assist in the design of more complex sound structures; it makes use of a light-pen to operate a microcomputer system by remote control.

BIBLIOGRAPHY
M. Neuhaus: 'A Max Sampler', *Source*, no.5 (1969), 48
——: 'Water Whistle', *Source*, no.11 (1972), 48
D. Feldman: 'Max Neuhaus Interview', *Ear Magazine*, v/5 (1980), 8

HUGH DAVIES

Neuhoff. *See* NIEHOFF family.

Neupert. German firm of piano and harpsichord makers. Founded by Johann Christoph Neupert (1848–1921) in 1868 as piano builders, it was among the first German firms to add harpsichords, clavichords and fortepianos to its production, in 1907–8. The company had begun to assemble a collection of historical stringed keyboard instruments even earlier, in 1895. Eventually this grew to number more than 250 specimens when it was donated to the Germanisches National Museum in Nuremberg in 1968 (a number of instruments from the collection considered to duplicate other examples had been transferred to the Händel-Haus Museum in Halle in 1939).

Hanns Neupert (*b* Bamberg, 22 Feb 1902; *d* Bamberg, 9 Nov 1980) joined the firm as technical director in 1928, after a three-year apprenticeship in piano building and studies in musicology and physics at the universities of Erlangen and Munich. He wrote a number of works dealing with historical stringed keyboard instruments and their revival in the 20th century; among them are *Das Cembalo* (Kassel, 1933; Eng. trans., 1960) and *Das Klavichord* (Kassel, 1949; Eng. trans., 1965). (See obituary in *English Harpsichord Magazine*, ii (1981), 200.)

The firm's harpsichord production has generally been typical of the pre-1939 modern German school: heavily constructed, open at the bottom, a very long treble scale, with a 16' register in the larger instruments, registration pedals and, from about 1930, adherence to the so-called 'Bach disposition', now held to be unauthentic. Neupert clavichords and fortepianos are more closely modelled on 18th-century prototypes. Reproduction instruments were occasionally produced before 1970, but it is only since then that a number of models of harpsichords in more traditional styles have been added to the established line of modern instruments.

For illustration of a Neupert instrument *see* HARPSICHORD, fig.19.

HOWARD SCHOTT

Neuschel [Neuschl, Neischl, Neyschl, Meuschel]. German family of brass instrument makers. The oldest Nuremberg dynasty of brass instrument makers, it was founded by Hans Neuschel the elder (*d* Nuremberg, 1503 or 1504). He became a coppersmith in 1479 and is recorded that same year as having made slides (*Ziehstücke*) for either trumpets or trombones. In addition to making brass instruments, he was a Stadtpfeifer from 1491 until his death.

Hans Neuschel the younger (*d* Nuremberg, 1533), who was a son of Hans the elder and became a coppersmith in 1493, was the most famous member of the family, both as an instrument maker and a trombonist – the Meuschelstrasse in Nuremberg is named after him. Like his father, he was also a Stadtpfeifer. He is said to have improved the art of trombone making in 1498. His instruments carried the hallmark of a crown. By order of Emperor Maximilian I, in 1512, his likeness was included in one of Hans Burgkmair's woodcuts for the series 'The Triumph of Maximilian'. The command to the artist was: 'On the same chariot there shall be five shawms, trombones and crumhorns; and Neyschl shall be the master'. Pope Leo X ordered silver trombones from him, which he delivered personally. His brother Lienhard (*d* Nuremberg, 1515) worked with him in his shop.

According to Nickel (1971), Georg [Jörg] Stengel (*d* Nuremberg, 1557), 'genannt Neuschel' – he assumed the family name in 1537 – was the adopted son of Hans the younger, from whom he learnt his trade. He later took over the Neuschel workshop, and his privilege of carrying Hans's hallmark was renewed by Emperor Charles V in 1551. Besides making brass instruments, he was also a dealer in woodwind and percussion instruments. He sold 12 'deutsche' and 12 'welsche' trumpets and two military kettledrums to the King of Poland for 200 guilders, and other complete sets of trumpets for similar prices to courts in Berlin, Dresden and Munich. An order placed in 1541 by Duke Albrecht of Prussia, however, was apparently never delivered because that monarch refused to pay more than 60 guilders. A tenor trombone made by Georg in 1557 is part of the Vienna collection (formerly in the Clemencic, Baines and Galpin collections). Nickel has shown that the Neuschels may have been related to the other great family of brass instrument makers, the Schnitzers, as Georg's wife Anna was apparently the widow of the Munich Stadtpfeifer Anton SCHNITZER. Anton's and Anna's presumed son, Anton Schnitzer the elder, learnt brass instrument making from his stepfather, on whose death he took over the Neuschel workshop.

BIBLIOGRAPHY

R. Eitner: 'Briefe von Jorg Neuschel in Nürnberg nebst einigen anderen', *MMg*, ix (1877), 149

F. Jahn: 'Die Nürnberger Trompeten- und Posaunenmacher im 16. Jahrhundert', *AMw*, vii (1925), 23

W. Wörthmüller: 'Die Nürnberger Trompeten- und Posaunenmacher des 17. und 18. Jahrhunderts', *Mitteilungen des Vereins für Geschichte der Stadt Nürnberg*, xlv (1954), 208; xlvi (1955), 372

E. Nickel: *Der Holzblasinstrumentenbau in der freien Reichsstadt Nürnberg* (Munich, 1971)

EDWARD H. TARR

Nevel [nebel] (Heb.; pl. *nevalim*; Syriac *nabla*). One of the BIBLICAL INSTRUMENTS. Judging from the number of references to this instrument in the Bible, it was second in importance only to the KINNOR. It is usually translated into English as psaltery and, while there is little doubt that this is incorrect, there is much doubt and debate as to what it really was. Scholars remain divided between a lyre, presumably of different type from the *kinnor*, and a harp. The name is sometimes coupled with *'asor*, suggesting that the instrument had ten strings, but in Psalm xcii.3 the two terms are contrasted. It is possible that *nevalim* existed in several sizes, so that this reference might be to both bass and normal varieties. *See also* PSALTERY, §1 and HARP, §2.

JEREMY MONTAGU

Newphonion. A valved brass instrument invented by Henry Distin about 1863. The *Revue musicale* of that year described its sound as harsh and lacking in refinement.

New Violin Family [Violin Octet]. A consort of eight acoustically balanced instruments in graduated sizes and tunings, ranging from the contrabass violin (tuned like the double bass) to the treble violin (an octave above the normal violin). This family of instruments developed out of the violin research by the physicist Frederick A. Saunders of Harvard, who began work in 1933. Tests made on excellent violins established some of the acoustical characteristics found in violins of desirable tone quality. These characteristics were projected, by the application of scaling theory, into seven other tone ranges, and gave rise to a new family of violins embodying the results of theoretical and practical

TABLE 1: Measurements and scaling factors for the New Violin Family

| Instrument name | Tuning | Hz | Length in centimetres | | | Relative scaling factors* | | |
			Overall	Body	String	Body length	Resonance placement	String tuning
Treble	$g'-d''-a''-e'''$	392 587·4 880 1318·5	c48	28·6	26	·75	·50	·50
Soprano	$c'-g'-d''-a''$	261·6 392 587·4 880	54–5	31·2	30	·89	·67	·67
Mezzo	$g-d'-a'-e''$	196 293·7 440 659·2	62–3	38·2	32·7	1·07	1·00	1·00
Violin	$g-d'-a'-e''$	196 293·7 440 659·2	59–60	35·5	32·7	1·00	1·00	1·00
Viola	$c-g-d'-a'$	131·8 196 293·7 440	70–71	c43	37–8	1·17	1·33	1·50
Alto	$c-g-d'-a'$	131·8 196 293·7 440	82–3	50·8	42·5	1·44	1·50	1·50
Tenor	$G-d-a-e'$	98 146·8 220 329·6	c107	65·4	60·8	1·82	2·00	2·00
Cello	$C-G-d-a$	65·4 98 146·8 220	c124	75–6	68–9	2·13	2·67	3·00
Baritone	$C-G-d-a$	65·4 98 146·8 220	c142	86·4	72	2·42	3·00	3·00
Small bass	$A'-D-G-c$	55 73·4 98 131·8	c171	104·2	92	2·92	4·00	4·00
Double bass	$E'-A'-D-G$	41·2 55 73·4 98	178–98	109–22	104–17	3·09–3·43	4·00	6·00
Contrabass	$E'-A'-D-G$	41·2 55 73·4 98	213–14	130	110	3·60	6·00	6·00

*Scaling based on the violin as 1·00

experiments (see Table 1). This research was coordinated by members of the Catgut Acoustical Society (founded by Saunders in 1963), and the first set of the new instruments had been prepared by 1965. The instruments are designed to possess a homogeneity of tone which distinguishes them from the existing family of strings (in which the acoustical characteristics and tonal qualities of the viola, cello and double bass contrast with the violin and each other; *see* ACOUSTICS, §I). It is intended that the instruments be used in ensembles of up to eight; as solo instruments with distinctive characteristics; to blend and contrast with other instruments (particularly wind) or the human voice; to augment the strings in the symphony orchestra; and in combination with electronic sounds (where their clarity and distinctiveness have been found most effective). Michael Prae-

torius, in his *Syntagma musicum* (2/1619), listed a family of eight *Geigen* with practically the same tonal ranges and tunings.

The treble violin or sopranino, tuned $g'-d''-a''-e'''$, is the smallest and highest member of the octet; its dimensions are approximately those of a quarter-size violin, and it can be played either under the chin or, rebec style, on the arm. It has very thick top and back plates, extra-large f-holes, and small holes strategically placed in its shallow ribs so that its main resonances occur at the desired frequencies. The extremely strong and thin E string (tuned to 1320 Hz) is made from carbon rocket wire, which has a tensile strength nearly twice that of normal E-string wire. The short strings of the treble violin make it possible to play a tremolo in intervals of up to an octave and double stops of up to a 12th. The soprano

Instruments of the New Violin Family developed by the Catgut Acoustical Society: front row (left to right), baritone violin, small bass violin, contrabass violin, mezzo violin, soprano violin, treble violin; behind, tenor violin (left) and alto violin (right)

violin or descant is tuned an octave above the normal viola (*c'–g'–d"–a"*); it is comparable to a three-quarter violin in size and string length, though it is somewhat broader in outline and has shallower ribs. The mezzo violin is an enlarged version of the normal (35·5 cm) instrument, with a body length of 38·2 cm, though its ribs are about half the usual height; it maintains the standard string length. It has large top and back plates and is thus more powerful, particularly on the lower strings, than the normal violin. The alto violin, tuned *c–g–d'–a'*, is essentially an enlarged viola but has additional clarity and power. Its body length (50·8 cm) makes it difficult to play under the chin, so it is often played like the cello, but on a longer peg; the strings have been shortened to 42·5 cm to facilitate viola fingering.

The tenor violin, tuned *G–d–a–e'*, is similar in size to a three-quarter cello, but has thicker top and back plates, and shallower ribs that give it more the appearance of an enlarged violin. The baritone violin is tuned *C–G–d–a* like the cello, and has a nearly comparable string length but larger body dimensions. Since its resonances are lower than those of the cello, the tones on the C and G strings are unusually clear and powerful; its A-string resonances are not stronger than its lower tones, however, as is the case with the normal cello. The small bass violin is tuned *A'–D–G–c*, a 4th above the double bass; it is about the size of a three-quarter bass and has a similar string length, but rounded shoulders and an arched back like the violin. The contrabass

violin, tuned *E'–A'–D–G*, has a body length of 130 cm but a string length of only 110 cm. Its size, comparatively light construction and the tuning of its plates cause the lower notes to produce organ-type sonorities.

BIBLIOGRAPHY

M. Praetorius: *Syntagma musicum*, ii (Wolfenbüttel, 1618, 2/1619/*R*1958 and 1980)

C. M. Hutchins: 'The Physics of Violins', *Scientific American* (1962), Nov, 78

——: 'Founding a Family of Fiddles', *Physics Today*, xx (1967), 23

C. A. Taylor: 'The New Violin Family and its Scientific Background', *Soundings*, vii (1978), 110

CARLEEN M. HUTCHINS

Ne'xegaku (Omaha: *ne'xe*, 'water vessel'; *gaku*, 'to beat'). WATER-DRUM of the Omaha Indians of the central Plains area of the USA. It was made from part of a hollowed-out tree trunk; the head was of buffalo skin. As with the Ojibwa drum, MITI'GWAKIK, much care was taken to achieve a resonant tone.

Ney. *See* NĀY.

Neya. Drum of the Makonde people of Mozambique.

Ney-e anbān. Single-reed BAGPIPE with double chanter, found in south-west Iran and certain villages of Azerbaijan. Similar bagpipes are played in Armenia (*parkapzuk*), Georgia (*gudastviri*) and the countries of the Persian Gulf.

Neyschl. *See* NEUSCHEL family.

Nezeza. Basket rattle of the Meje people of Zaïre. It is played in conjunction with the *nabita* and other drums.

Nfīr. *See* NAFĪR.

Ngaba. Drum of Angola, reported in the Kongo/Mbundu region between 1683 and 1688. See G. Merolla: *Breve e succinta relatione del viaggio nel regno di Congo nell'Africa Meridionale* (Naples, 1692).

Ngabi. Single-headed conical closed drum of the Abangba people of north-eastern Zaïre. The membrane is laced on.

Ngal. Reed external DUCT FLUTE of the Yap Islands of Micronesia. It is similar to the *ngaok* flute of Palau. See R. Born: 'Einige Bemerkungen über Musik, Dichtkunst und Tanz der Yapleute', *Zeitschrift für Ethnologie*, xxxv (1903), 134.

Ngambi. XYLOPHONE of south-eastern Africa. *See* VALIMBA.

Ngangan. MOUTH BOW of the Ngbaka people of the Central African Republic. It consists of a wooden stick with a liana string, which is placed between the lips without touching them, while the player strikes the string with a stick in his right hand and modulates it with a second stick (or the back of a penknife) in his left. The instrument is used to accompany the performance of chronicles, fables and complaints.

BIBLIOGRAPHY
S. Arom: 'Centre Afrique: danses de la forêt', HM 733 [disc notes]
K. A. GOURLAY

Ngaok. Reed external DUCT FLUTE of the Palau Islands of Micronesia. It has four finger-holes and is played either solo or to accompany song. *See also* NGAL.

Ngao-ngao. Bamboo clarinet of Flores, Indonesia. *See* ORUPI.

Ngarabi. Single-headed drum about 150 cm long of the Ziba people of Tanzania. It is made from a hollowed log and lizardskin, and is beaten with the hands.

Ngato. LAMELLAPHONE of the Ngombe people of north-western Zaïre. It has a carved wooden resonator fitted under an ovoid soundtable and seven to ten wooden keys (*LaurentyS*, 192).

Ngbandje. BOARD ZITHER of the Mbuja people of Zaïre (*LaurentyC*, 116). *See* GOMBI (i).

Ngbemakpo. Large cylindrical SLIT-DRUM of the Yogo/Bozo people of northern Zaïre. It is played, with other percussion instruments, for dancing. *See* MAKPO.

Ngbengbe. Wooden concussion CLAPPERS of the Mbuti pygmies of Zaïre.

Ngbereia. Wooden flute, with slender conical bore, of the Mbuti pygmies of Zaïre (*LaurentyA*, 156).

Ngcongolo. End-blown flute of the Bomvana (Xhosa) people of southern Africa, resembling the Zulu UMTSHINGO.

Ngedegwu. XYLOPHONE of the Igbo people of Nigeria. (1) A two-key instrument with the keys attached to the top of an open clay pot by a peg at each end, but separated from the pot by a woven grass collar. Xylophones of this type are also known as *ekere-iko* or *okobolo*. Sometimes a bucket is used instead of a pot.
(2) A log xylophone with up to 13 wooden keys laid across two banana stems. The keys are either strung together or else pegged to prevent slipping. The instrument is known as *igo* in the Udi area, as *ngelenge* in Owerri, and elsewhere as *ikwembgo*. Up to eight instruments may be played at one time. If used singly, two players perform on one instrument. The xylophone is used at festivals and funerals, during wrestling and for the imitation of tonal speech patterns in story-telling.

BIBLIOGRAPHY
W.W.C. Echezona: 'Igbo Music', *Grove 6*
A.N.G. Okasa: 'Ibo Musical Instruments', *Nigeria Magazine*, lxxv (1962), 4

Ngelenge. XYLOPHONE of the Igbo people of Nigeria. (1) A log xylophone, known also as *ngedegwu* and *odome*.
(2) A term in some areas for a wooden trough xylophone with eight keys.

Ngenge. SPIKE FIDDLE of the Fula people of Sierra Leone.

Ngetundo. Term meaning 'lion' used by the Nandi people of western Kenya for a FRICTION DRUM with a goatskin membrane and for an ovoid wooden BULL-ROARER with a goatskin string. Both instruments are used at circumcision rites.

Nggabi. Single-headed closed conical drum of the Yogo/Bozo people of northern Zaïre. The membrane is laced on. It is played, with other percussion instruments, to accompany dancing. *See* MAKPO.

Nggo. GONG-CHIME of Flores, Indonesia. The bronze bossed gongs (*go*) are held vertically by rope passing through two small holes in their deep rims, and suspended from either a wooden frame or the player's left hand. They are beaten with a stick held in the right hand. They consist of a *nggo ria*, which is the largest (about 40 cm in diameter with a boss about 12 cm in diameter), two pairs of *nggo loo* (about 17·5 cm in diameter with a boss of about 7·5 cm) and a *nggo diri* (about 12 cm in diameter with a boss of about 5 cm). If suspended from a wooden frame, one of each pair of *nggo loo* is hung underneath the other. They are played with a goblet drum in the *nggo lamba* and a cylindrical drum in the *nggo laba* ensembles on festive or solemn occasions.
MARGARET J. KARTOMI

Nggoec. Bamboo or metal JEW'S HARP of the Mnong people of central Vietnam.

Nggor [ngor]. Double-headed barrel drum of the Mnong people of central Vietnam. The drum is hollowed out from a tree trunk and closed at both ends with a stretched buffalo skin; it is beaten by two drummers, each with two wooden mallets, and is a favourite festival instrument. It is often accompanied by the *nung* (free-reed buffalo horn).

TRÂN QUANG HAI

Nghomba. Single-headed drum of the Tumbwe people of eastern Zaïre (*BooneT*, 16, 60). *See also* NGOMA.

Ngime. Fiddle of the Mandinka and Soninke peoples of West Africa; it is similar to the *kundye* of the Susu.

Ngizing. Open drum of the Angas people of Nigeria. It is slightly conical, approximately 100 to 130 cm long, with a mahogany body and membrane of cowhide or bush-animal skin. The membrane is lapped with small loops and adjusted by means of evenly spaced, thick wooden pegs. The player sits astride the *ngizing* and beats it with his hands. Formerly restricted to use for hunting, communal labour and circumcision dances, it is now in general use.

Ngkul [nkul]. Large SLIT-DRUM of the Fang people of southern Cameroon and northern Gabon. The drum is used both to signal messages and to accompany dances; during the dances the drummer controls dance movements through the use of different pitches and rhythms.

Ngo [ta ngo, nyi ngo]. Cylindro-conical drum of the Ngbandi people of Zaïre (*BooneT*, 27ff, 78). *See* DINDO.

Ngoli. Long NOTCHED FLUTE of the Ngbandi people of north-western Zaïre. It is made from the dried flower-spike of the giant Lobelia plant or similar plant stems and has two finger-holes. Its narrow bore allows the player to sound the 2nd to 4th harmonics with ease (*LaurentyA*, 283). *See also* EKINIMBA.

Ngoma [engoma, goma, gomo, ingoma, iñgoma, ng'oma, ngomba, ngomm, ngomo etc]. A common term (with many variants) used generically for many kinds of drum among the numerous Bantu-speaking peoples of central, eastern-central and southern Africa. However, 'ngoma' often has a wider meaning, at its widest standing for music and dancing (and the associated feasting), and for ceremonies in which drumming occurs. Because of its use as a general name for drum it often appears in the catalogues of instrument collections (e.g. *BooneT*). It has, for example, been reported in Kenya as a cylindrical drum (Marach people; *see* INDONYI), in Tanzania as a conical drum (Nyoro/Haya), and in Zaïre among numerous peoples as a cylindrical, conical or cylindro-conical drum (see below and *see* BONDA (i), DINDO, DITUMBA, KIMBANDU, MOKITA, MUSHITS). It has also been applied to a GOBLET DRUM (see below), HOUR-GLASS DRUM (Gogo of Tanzania; *see* NYANYÚLUA), UGANDA DRUM (see below) and FRICTION DRUM (in Angola; *see* KWITA).

Among different peoples *ngoma* can variously denote a dance, a drum ensemble, the most important drum of an ensemble, or individual drums. Use of the name is sometimes indicative that drums have special sacred or magical properties. *Ngoma dza midzimu* ('drums of the ancestor spirits') is the term used by the Venda of the Transvaal for spirit possession dances; the bass drum in the accompanying ensemble, a large hemispherical drum with a single head, resembling the two drums with which it is played (*see* MURUMBA), is itself called *ngoma*. Common nomenclature also includes *ngoma* in compound forms. In Zaïre, for example, *ngoma ya shina*, *ngoma ya mukondo*, *ngoma ya ditumba*, *ngoma ka tumba* and *ngoma ka loponde* are names given by various peoples for a cylindrical or goblet drum of a type known to the Luba, Sanga, Sampwe and Zela as DITUMBA; *ngomo yeka* is a cylindrical drum of the Kusu (*see* BONDA (i)). Goblet drums of the Valley Tonga people of Zambia, which are played with the *nyele* trumpet ensemble to accompany the *ngoma* dance, are known by the term *ngoma* but also have specific names (from smallest to largest): *gogogo, kingaridi, chamutanda, mujinji, pininga* and *pati*.

Ngoma drums may also be associated with royal power, as was frequently the case, for example, among the kingdom states of central Africa. Among the drum

1. Iñgoma ensemble of double-headed drums, Rwanda, 1927

2. *Drums of the iñgoma ensemble of Burundi*

ensembles of Rwanda, those usually cited as *iñgoma* (fig.1) were formerly played only for the rulers (Tutsi). They consisted of sets of up to nine laced drums of the Uganda drum type beaten with drumsticks, struck with awesome power and precision to the accompaniment of praise verses. Each drum in the ensemble had its own pitch and special name: the leading drum was known as *ishakwe* or *ishako* while others were commonly known as *indahura*, *indamutsa* and *igihumulizo*. In Burundi (fig.2) the ensemble was even larger, up to 25 drums (with single pegged heads) being used in a single set. This ensemble formerly performed only at the court at the behest of the king but like the Rwanda set is now played generally at festive occasions. In performance the drums are placed in a semicircle and each drummer is called into position by the leader, who beats the central drum while dancing. The master-drummer declaims in praise of the person in authority present and the performance usually continues until each drummer has had an opportunity to appear as soloist.

BIBLIOGRAPHY
BooneT; KirbyMISA, 34, 41, 56, 85, 156, 262 and pl. 13; TraceyCSA, ii
F. J. de Hen: *Beitrag zur Kenntnis der Musikinstrumente aus Belgisch Kongo und Ruanda-Urundi* (Tervuren, 1960)
J. Gansemans: 'Rwanda', *Grove 6*
M. Vuylstèke: 'Musique du Burundi', OCR 40 [disc notes]

Ngombi (i). Arched harp of Cameroon, the Central African Republic and Gabon. It has eight or ten strings, tuning-pegs and a skin-covered, rectangular wooden soundbox. The strings pass through holes in the soundtable; the handle is sometimes decorated with dry seeds which rattle during performance. Some examples are decorated with intricate carvings (see illustration). The player is seated and holds the instrument upright between his legs with the base resting on the ground and the handle pointing away from him so that the strings are on the side furthest from him. He plucks the strings with fingers and thumbs of both hands. The ten-string harp of the Ngbaka of the Central African Republic may be used by itself to accompany sung narratives, which open with a harp solo designed to set the mood, or it may be played with the double clapperless iron bell, *kpolo*, as accompaniment to love songs, for example, or cursing songs. The ten strings enable a double pentatonic scale to be produced.

In Cameroon and Gabon the eight-string *ngombi* of the Fang, Tsogo, Miene and related peoples is a sacred harp used in Bwete and related cults. The instrument is believed to be the same as the *ombi* or *wombi*, reported

Ngombi (ten-string arched harp) of the Central African Republic

by early authorities as accompanying healing songs among the Fang people, and the *gonfi* or *ngonfi*, which is used in the Bwete cult by the Sangu and pygmies.

See also HARP, §6, esp. fig.29d.

BIBLIOGRAPHY
S. Chauvet: *Musique nègre* (Paris, 1929)
J-N. Maquet: *Note sur les instruments de musique congolais* (Brussels, 1956)
S. Arom: 'Centre Afrique: danses de la forêt', HM 733 [disc notes]
S. Arom and G. Dournon-Taurelle: 'République Centre-Africaine: musiques d'initiation', HM 934 [disc notes]
P. Collaer: 'Musics of the Central African Republic', BM30 L2310 [disc notes]
M. Vuylstèke: 'Musiques du Gabon', OCR 41 [disc notes]
K. A. GOURLAY

Ngombi (ii). LAMELLAPHONE of the Mbuja people of northern Zaïre. It has a carved wooden resonator fitted under an ovoid soundtable and seven to ten wooden keys (*LaurentyS*, 192).

Ngombo. Cylindrical wooden SLIT-DRUM of the Chokwe people of southern Zaïre. It has a carved anthropomorphic extension which represents a divine spirit (*LaurentyTF*, 136).

Ngomi. PLURIARC of the Soyo people of Zaïre (*LaurentyC*, 118). *See* LUKOMBE (i).

Ngomo [ngomm] **(i).** Generic term for drum in central, eastern-central and southern Africa. *See* NGOMA.

Ngomo (ii). SLIT-DRUM of the Kusu people of Zaïre (*LaurentyTF*, 141).

Ngonfi (i). Five-string plucked lute of the Bembe people of the Republic of the Congo. It has metal strings that are tuned with large upright tuning pegs fitted with metal jingles. The semi-cylindrical body is placed between the legs of the player, who is seated on the ground. The strings are plucked with the thumb and forefinger of each hand. The instrument is used mainly to accompany singing. See C. Duvelle: 'Musique Kongo', OCR 35 [disc notes].

Ngonfi (ii). Eight-string arched harp of the Masango people of Gabon. *See* NGOMBI (i).

Ngonge. (1) War drum of the Tetela people of Zaïre, also known as *ngomo ka ahuka*. It is struck with one stick (*BooneT*, 52).
(2) Double clapperless bell of Zaïre, also reported as *ngongi*. *See* GONGA (i).

Ngoni. *See* NKONI.

Ngọp ngāēp. SCRAPER of Laos. It consists of two sticks of wood, of unequal length, joined by a string; each has coins on a nail at one end. The notches carved on one of the sticks are scraped with a piece of wood.

Ngorodo. MUSICAL BOW of the Bambara people of Mali, played by children. It has a horsehair string and is placed on top of a half-calabash. The player's left hand presses on the string with a small stick, while his right hand taps it with another stick. See C. Béart: 'Jeux et jouets de l'ouest africain', *Mémoires de l'Institut français d'Afrique noire* (Dakar, 1955).

Ngororombe. PANPIPES ensemble of the Shona people of southern Africa.

Ngosa. BULLROARER of the Kai people of Morobe Province, Papua New Guinea. It was used during the *balum* circumcision ceremony to represent the monster Ngosa. See A. C. Haddon: 'Migration of Cultures in British New Guinea', *Journal of the Anthropological Institute of Great Britain and Ireland*, 1 (1920), 253.

Ngū'. Vietnamese SCRAPER derived from the Chinese YU (i). It is in the form of a wooden tiger, with 27 notches along the serrated backbone, crouching on a square wooden base. At the end of a piece of music the tiger is struck three times on the head, and then a brush of split bamboo is run once along its back. It is used in Confucian temple music. *See also* Ŏ.
TRÂN QUANG HAI

Ngubi. Side-blown ivory or wooden trumpet of the Mvuba people of north-eastern Zaïre (*LaurentyA*, 334, 397).

Ngudi [nguri]. Large SLIT-DRUM of south-western Zaïre. It is played in pairs; the smaller of the pair is called *mwaka* (*LaurentyTF*, 135).

Ngulang. SPIKE LUTE of the Bana people of northern Cameroon. It has a bowl-shaped gourd resonator, and is one of many similarly shaped lutes distributed over a wide area of West Africa. See R. Blench: 'The Morphology and Distribution of Sub-Saharan Musical Instruments', *Musica asiatica*, iv (1984), 170.

Ngule. Cruciform clay whistle of the Angas people of Nigeria. It has a finger-hole in each side and is used by herdboys for signalling or to accompany singing and dancing groups.

Ngulo. Large double-headed drum of the Kotoko people of the Logone river in central Chad. It is usually made of palmyra wood in the shape of a truncated cone, about a metre high, with cowhide membranes laced together by thongs. In each village there is one *ngulo*, which is replaced when age makes it unusable; the old one is thrown in the river. Although entrusted to one person, for whom it serves as a symbol of authority, the *ngulo* always remains the collective property of the village inhabitants. It has a very powerful sound which travels far and it is struck to signal announcements and during the fishing season to summon the widely scattered villagers. Among the Kotoko people on the lower course of the Chari river the drum is called *kongguli* but has the same functions.
MONIQUE BRANDILY

Ngulu. Small zoomorphic SLIT-DRUM of the Mangutu people of Zaïre (*LaurentyTF*, 139).

Ngumbi. BOARD ZITHER of the Zande people of Zaïre (*LaurentyC*, 116). *See* GOMBI (i).

Ngumbo. MUSICAL BOW of southern Africa. *See* UGUB-HU.

Ngungu. SLIT-DRUM of the Patri people of the Central African Republic (*see* MAZA) and the Mayombe people of Zaïre (*LaurentyTF*, 136).

Ngunte. Conical drum of the Nyanja/Manganja people of Malawi. It is the largest of nine in the LIKHUBA drum set.

Nguri. *See* NGUDI.

Nguru. End-blown flute of the Maori people of New Zealand. It is 8 to 10 cm long and is made of wood, clay, stone or whale's tooth. One end is open as in the KOOAUAU and the other finishes with a small hole in the centre of a tapered, upturned snout. The prototypal shape seems to have been either the whale tooth or the stem of a gourd. Early reports describe it as a whistle, worn

Nguru (end-blown flute) of the Maori people, New Zealand, from Oruarangi Pa, Matatoki (Auckland Institute and Museum)

about the neck and yielding a shrill sound. It was possibly used for signalling, as some writers have suggested, but its primary use was as a flute. It was blown at the wide end with the mouth in the same manner as the *kooauau*. This method of blowing produces normal *kooauau* scales except for an extension downwards – usually by a major 2nd or minor 3rd – of one or two extra notes in the case of instruments with extra fingerholes underneath the snout. The *nguru* was therefore simply a variety of *kooauau*, though its shape was different.

MERVYN McLEAN

Ngū tuyệt. String ensemble of central Vietnam. It consists of the five 'perfect' instruments: a ĐÀN TRANH (16-string board zither); a ĐÀN NHỊ (two-string fiddle); a ĐÀN NGUYỆT (moon-shaped lute); a ĐÀN TỲ BÀ (pear-shaped lute); and a ĐÀN TAM (three-string lute) or *đàn độc huyền* (single-string box zither; *see* ĐÀN BÀU). The ensemble is used in the chamber music *ca huế*.

TRÂN QUANG HAI

Ngwánana. Wooden flute of the Mayombe people of Zaïre (*LaurentyA*, 163).

Ngwomi [ngwim, ngwen]. PLURIARC of the Teke (Tegue) people of Zaïre and Gabon, and the Hum and Yans people of Zaïre. *Ngwim* is the Hum term, *ngwen* the Yans (*see also* LUKOMBE (i)). The Teke term *ngwomi* denotes a large five-string instrument whose string-bearer and strings are almost perpendicular to its soundbox, which is rectangular. A buzzing effect is produced by metal

jingles on the string-bearers. The name *ngwomi* is related to *ngombi*, a term for arched harp among more northerly peoples. See *LaurentyC*, 117; P. Sallée: 'Gabon', *Grove 6*.

Ngwosto. Braced MUSICAL BOW with gourd resonator of the Mbun people of Zaïre (*LaurentyC*, 113). *See* KAKULUMBUMBA

Ngyela. BOARD ZITHER of the Luba people of Zaïre. *See* IKIDI.

Nhạc. Vietnamese pellet bell; also a term meaning 'music'.

Nhạc huyền. Vietnamese court orchestra, now obsolete.

Nhạc ngũ âm. Ceremonial folk ensemble of southern Vietnam (*ngũ*: 'five'; *âm*: 'sounds'). It comprises two groups: the civilian *phe văn* and the military *phe võ*. The civilian group is composed of four different two-string fiddles and one kind of drum: the principal fiddle *đàn cò chánh*; a small fiddle *đàn cò chỉ*; a bamboo sound-box fiddle *đàn cò gáo tre*; a coconut-shell soundbox fiddle *đàn cò gáo dừa* (*see* ĐÀN CÒ); and a pair of *trống nhạc* (shallow barrel drums), a *trống bát cấu* (small single-headed barrel drum) or a *trống cơm* (barrel-shaped 'rice drum'; *see* TRỐNG), depending on the musical context. One of the fiddles may be replaced by a transverse flute. The military group uses the following instruments: a *trống nhạc*; a *cái bồng* (single-headed hourglass drum); a *mõ sừng trâu* (hollowed buffalo-horn used as a slit-drum); a ĐÂÙ (small flat gong); a pair of *chập bạt* (small cym-

Ngwomi (pluriarc) of the Teke people of Gabon

bals; *see* CHÁP); and a *kèn trung* (medium-pitched oboe; *see* KÈN BÀU).

TRÂN QUANG HAI

Nhã [tiểu] **nhạc** (*nhã*: 'elegant'; *tiểu*: 'small'; *nhạc*: 'music']. Vietnamese ensemble of 14 instruments. It is the equivalent of the Chinese *yayue*, the Korean *aak* and the Japanese *gagaku*. The ensemble comprises four *ống địch* (transverse flutes); two ĐÀN NHỊ (two-string fiddles); two ĐÀN NGUYỆT (moon-shaped lutes); two ĐÀN TAM (three-string lutes); a ĐÀN TỲ BÀ (pear-shaped lute); a ĐÀN DIỆN CỔ (small single-headed drum); a *tam âm la* (set of three small gongs); and SINH TIỀN (coin clappers). Sometimes the ensemble is reduced to nine instruments by halving the number of *ống địch* and string instruments (retaining one *đàn tỳ bà*). *See also* ĐẠI NHẠC.

TRÂN QUANG HAI

Nhị huyền. Two-string fiddle of Vietnam. The name is a translation of the Chinese 'erxian' ('two strings'; *see* ERHU), but is used only rarely.

Nī 'au kani (*nī'au*: 'coconut leaflet midrib'; *kani*: 'to sound'). Obsolete JEW'S HARP of Hawaii, presumably made from coconut leaf midrib. N. Emerson (*Unwritten Literature of Hawaii* (Washington, DC, 1909, p.147) glosses it as 'singing splinter' and describes it as made by holding a reed of thin bamboo against a slit cut out in a larger piece of bamboo which was applied to the mouth. It seems probable that both forms of instrument were used. The sole specimen in the Bernice P. Bishop Museum, Honolulu, made out of wood, is of doubtful authenticity. See P. Buck: *Arts and Crafts of Hawaii* (Honolulu, 1935), 395.

MERVYN McLEAN

Nicholson. English firm of organ builders. It was established in Rochdale about 1816 and later run by Richard Nicholson, whose brothers established workshops in Walsall, Worcester and Newcastle upon Tyne. Nicholson of Walsall became Nicholson & Lord and worked mostly in Staffordshire; their largest organ was in Walsall Town Hall. The Worcester branch, founded in 1841, is still in business and absorbed the Walsall firm in 1955. An unspoilt organ which dates from 1844 survives in the Countess of Huntingdon's chapel in Worcester, and the organ built for Manchester Cathedral in 1861 was transferred to Holy Trinity Church, Bolton. A large organ was constructed for Worcester Music Hall in 1854 but was destroyed in a storm; it was replaced in 1879, but the hall burnt down two years later. Nicholson provided the new hall with a third organ (now dismantled) in 1884.

BIBLIOGRAPHY
L. Elvin: *The Harrison Story* (Lincoln, 1973)
D. C. Wickens: 'A Remarkable Worcester Organ', *The Organ*, liii (1973–4), 5

MICHAEL SAYER

Nicolas, Didier (*b* Mirecourt, 23 Jan 1757; *d* Mirecourt, 1833). French violin maker. Nicknamed 'le Sourd', he served his apprenticeship in Mirecourt, where he established his shop, 'A la Ville de Cremonne'; this title appears in the shape of a triangular brand in the

label area of his instruments. He used the Stradivari model as a starting-point but his own is altogether more full and heavy. The distance between the soundholes usually exceeds that of almost any other maker. In his later years he employed extra craftsmen to make violins to his specifications so that the quality of instruments bearing the Nicolas brand can vary considerably. The triangular brand was eventually purchased by Honoré Derazey and later by Paul Mougenot; it has also appeared in instruments produced by the Mirecourt firm of M. Laberte & Magnie. Instruments made by Nicolas himself usually bear the inscription 'D. Nicolas aîné Mirecourt', in ink by the soundpost.

BIBLIOGRAPHY
R. Vannes: *Essai d'un dictionnaire universel des luthiers* (Paris, 1932, 2/1951/R1972 as *Dictionnaire universel des luthiers* and R1981 incl. suppl. 1959)

JAAK LIIVOJA-LORIUS

Niçude (Omaha: 'whistle'). Bone whistle of the Omaha Indians of the central Plains of the USA. It is made from the wing bone of an eagle and is about 15 cm long. It has a whistle flue opening but no finger-holes. It produces only one shrill note which, when played repeatedly, was said to be in imitation of an eagle's call. The whistle was played only during parts of the *wa'wan* ceremony.

MARY RIEMER-WELLER

Niçude tunga (Omaha: *niçude*, 'whistle'; *tunga*, 'big'). COURTING FLUTE of the Omaha Indians of the Plains area of the USA.

Nidaiko. Barrel drum of Japan. *See* NINAIDAIKO.

Niehoff [Nyhoff; Nyeuwenhoff or Nyeuwenhuys in the Low Countries; Niegehoff in Lower Saxony; and Neuhoff in Franconia]. Family of organ builders active in the Low Countries, the Rhineland, Hessen and Franconia. They include the brothers Heinrich (*b* c1495; *d* 's-Hertogenbosch, Dec 1560) and Hermann (*b* c1495; *d* after 1546), Heinrich's son Nikolaus (*b* Amsterdam, c1525; *d* 's-Hertogenbosch, c1604) and Nikolaus's son Jakob (*b* 's-Hertogenbosch, c1565; *d* ?Cologne, 1626). The family originated in Münster; in 1540 Heinrich was called 'Hendrik van Munster' in 's-Hertogenbosch, and the authentic form of the name, Niehoff, is even now more common in Münster than anywhere else.

About 1520 Heinrich went to work for Johann Kavelens (*d* Amsterdam, 1532), whose workshop was in Amsterdam though the type of organs he built suggests that he originally came from the Rhine valley north of Cologne (the assertion that his surname was Franckens and that he came from Koblenz is erroneous). Heinrich won the master's approval and took over the business in 1533. He moved to 's-Hertogenbosch in 1538. In 1537 or 1538, on the instructions of the church of St Jan in 's-Hertogenbosch, he visited Maastricht and Liège to study the new type of organ being introduced to the Low Countries by PETER BREISIGER, who was working in Maastricht, and Hans Suys (*see* SUISSE), who was probably at Liège. He returned to 's-Hertogenbosch accompanied by Suys as his business partner. After Suys's death, at the latest in 1544, he took Jasper Johannsen [Brouckmann] (*d* 1558) of Münster as his associate. In 1561 Nikolaus Niehoff took over the business, which he conducted in partnership with Arnold Lampeler until 1573; he was eventually succeeded by his son Jakob.

Together with Suys, Heinrich Niehoff built the organ in the Oude Kerk, Amsterdam (1539–45; three manuals, 25 stops), which was later played by Sweelinck. Instruments built with Johannsen include those at Zierikzee (1547–9; two manuals, c18 stops), St Petri, Hamburg (1548–51; three manuals, c35 stops), St Johannis, Lüneburg (1551–3; three manuals, 26 stops; the case and several stops survive), and St Jan, Gouda (1556–8; two manuals, 18 stops; the case is preserved at Abcoude). Nikolaus worked in Cologne Cathedral (1569–73; three manuals, 25 stops), in Mainz Cathedral (1584–5) and elsewhere, and perhaps built the organ of St Johannis in Hamburg (1567) which, rebuilt by Arp Schnitger, is now in Cappel, Wursten. Jakob built organs in the abbey at Steinfeld, Eifel (c1600; 13 stops extant), St Johann Baptist, Cologne (1613–15), and Würzburg Cathedral (1615–18; two manuals, 20 stops).

Heinrich Niehoff adopted the type of organ developed by Johann Kavelens, the first builder deliberately to incorporate a group of wide-scale pipes to contrast with the Principal chorus. Johann had taken up the store of new, 'alien' stops imported by Suys and had added these, together with the spring-chest principle, to the basic scheme of the north Rhineland organ. He divided the *Hauptwerk* into Principal (with Diapason, Principal, full Mixture and sharp Mixture) and *Oberwerk* (comprising the remainder of the flues – including the flute upperwork – and the reeds). There were, in addition, a *Rückpositiv* (with the same three groups of stops) and Pedal (with Trumpet 8′ and Flute 2′). The keyboard ranges were F′ to a″, C to a″, F to a″ and F to d′; and there were couplers from *Oberwerk* to *Rückpositiv* and from Principal to Pedal. This was the model also followed by two other Brabantine families of organ builders: the Lampelers of Mill (the brothers Arnold, Reinhard and Dietrich), who built instruments at St Lambertus, Münster (1573–9; three manuals, 25 stops), and Münster Cathedral (1585–8; three manuals, 26 stops), and the Hocque(t)s of Grave (Florenz and the brothers Nikolaus and Florenz), who built instruments at Cleves Abbey (1575), Trier Cathedral (1590–93; three manuals, 25 stops), Echternach Abbey (1605), and St Jan, 's-Hertogenbosch (1618–34; the case and some ranks of pipes survive). Heinrich Niehoff exercised a powerful influence on organ building in Hamburg.

BIBLIOGRAPHY
M. Praetorius: *Syntagma musicum*, ii (Wolfenbüttel, 1618, 2/1619/R1958 and 1980)
W. Lootens: *Beschrijving van het oude en het nieuwe orgel in de Groote of Lievensmonsterkerk der stadt Zierikzee* (Zierikzee, 1771/R1966)
H. Klotz: *Über die Orgelkunst der Gotik, der Renaissance und des Barock* (Kassel, 1934, 2/1975), 93ff, 174f
G. Fock: 'Hamburgs Anteil am Orgelbau im niederdeutschen Kulturgebiet', *Zeitschrift des Vereins für Hamburgische Geschichte*, xxxviii (1939), 289
H. Klotz: 'Die Kölner Domorgel von 1569/73', *Musik und Kirche*, xiii (1941), 105
M. A. Vente: *Bouwstoffen tot de geschiedenis van het Nederlandse orgel in de 16e eeuw* (Amsterdam, 1942)
H. Klotz: 'Niederländische Orgelbaumeister am Trierer Dom', *Mf*, ii (1949), 36
B. Bijtelaar: 'De orgels van Sweelinck', *Het orgel*, xlix (1953), 137, 151, 165; l (1954), 2
M. A. Vente: *Proeve van een repertorium van de archivalia betrekking hebbende op het Nederlandse orgel en zijn makers tot omstreeks 1630* (Brussels, 1956)
——: *Die Brabanter Orgel* (Amsterdam, 1958, 2/1963)
——: 'Niehoff', *MGG*
——: 'Orgel', §V, 1, *MGG*
R. Reuter: *Orgeln in Westfalen* (Kassel, 1965)

HANS KLOTZ

Nigen-kin. Generic term for two-string long zithers of Japan (*nigen*: 'two-string'; *kin*: a zither). (1) The *yakumo-goto* (or *izumo-goto*) was invented by Nakayama Kinshu in 1820 under 'divine inspiration', to provide offertory music at the Izumo Taisha, one of Japan's main Shintō shrines, near Yakumo. He is said to have made the first instrument from a half-tube of bamboo – thus fortuitously recapturing the shape from which Asian long zithers are thought to have developed. Subsequent *yakumo-goto* are of Japanese cedar or Paulownia, but three bamboo nodes are etched on the soundboard to recall the original instrument.

The *yakumo-goto* is approximately the same size and shape as the early hollow-body *ichigen-kin* (single-string zither), from which it presumably derives; since the *yakumo-goto*'s two silk strings are tuned in unison, the playing technique is also quite similar (on occasion, however, only one string is 'fingered', the other serving as a drone). The plectrum and left-hand tube are sometimes identical to those for the *ichigen-kin*, but more often the left-hand tube is a perfect cylinder, not truncated diagonally as in the *ichigen-kin*; the plectrum is of bone or horn and much smaller than for the single-string instrument. The *yakumo-goto* has 31 inlaid position markers and the *ichigen-kin* 12. Unlike the *ichigen-kin*, the strings of the *yakumo-goto* pass over a nut and through a common hole in the soundboard before attaching to the tuning pegs. The *yakumo-goto* tradition spread rapidly, both as sacred and secular music. A large repertory survives but it is now almost never performed.

(2) The *azuma-ryū* ('eastern-style') *nigen-kin* was evolved from the *yakumo-goto* by the kabuki drummer Tōsha Rosen during the 1870s. It has been used as a solo instrument (to perform Rosen's compositions), as an instrument of *geza* music in the kabuki theatre, and in ensemble with the shamisen and other instruments. It differs from the *yakumo-goto* mainly in having larger bridges, only two decorative tassels, and no backboard. The *azuma-ryū nigen-kin* tradition has fared much better than that of the *yakumo-goto*.

BIBLIOGRAPHY
K. Hirano: 'Azuma-ryū nigen-kin', Tokyo: King Records, 1975 [disc notes]
F. Koizumi, Y. Tokumaru and O. Yamaguchi, eds.: *Asian Musics in an Asian Perspective* (Tokyo, 1977), 250
K. Hirano: 'Nigen-kin', *Ongaku daijiten* [Encyclopedia of music] (Tokyo, 1981)

DAVID W. HUGHES

Niggell, Sympert (*b* Schwangau, 14 April 1710; *d* Füssen, 17 July 1785). German violin maker. He can be regarded as the foremost 18th-century violin maker at Füssen. His work is of graceful proportions, reminiscent of the models of Albani and Stainer. The choice of wood is invariably good but the varnish, which varies from yellow-brown and light red to red-brown, is usually of brittle texture. Although still comparatively little known, his violins can be exceptionally fine examples of Stainer-based work. Besides his usual printed label, Niggell occasionally branded his work with his initials. The death register contains the following entry: 'Sympertus Niggl viduus obiit 17 VII 1785 chelificum facile celeberrimus, vir sancte simplex et rectus'. See W. L. von Lütgendorff: *Die Geigen- und Lautenmacher vom Mittelalter bis zur Gegenwart* (Frankfurt am Main, 1904, rev. 6/1922/R1968).

JAAK LIIVOJA-LORIUS

Nihass. Large Sudanese copper KETTLEDRUM with a cowhide membrane. It is used in the northern, central and western Sudan (for illustration *see* DRUM, fig.1*b*), and is played in time of war, or to announce a great calamity or the death of a chief. In tribal wars in the past the victors immediately took possession of the opponents' *nihass*. These drums are now owned only by ruling families; some of them date back hundreds of years. In Chad the drum has been documented as *naas*.

Niḥsāṇa. Large KETTLEDRUM mentioned in medieval Sanskrit texts. *See* NAGĀRĀ, §1.

Nijūgen [nijūgen-sō]. Japanese long zither (*nijūgen*: '20-string'; *sō*: a zither). It is one of the few modifications of the standard KOTO which seem likely to endure. Devised in 1969 by the composer Miki Minoru and performer Nosaka Keiko, its extra strings fill the 'gaps' in the traditional pentatonic tunings rather than extend the range. Several composers have written for the instrument and it has attracted well over 100 students. Despite its name it has 21 strings, the extra one being the result of a later addition.

DAVID W. HUGHES

Nike mela. MIRLITON of the Gbande people of Liberia. It is made from a small wooden tube with windows in the sides across which are glued pieces of spider's web. The instrument is used for the simulation of spirit voices in the *poro* cult.

Ninaidaiko [nidaiko]. Japanese barrel drum, resembling a small DADAIKO, used when gagaku (court music) is performed in procession (*ninai*: 'carried'; *daiko/taiko*: generic term for drums). The head diameter is about 75 cm. Two people carry the drum, which hangs from a horizontal pole, while the performer walks beside it. Its use survives mainly at the Shitennōji Temple, Osaka. *See* F. Piggott: *The Music and Musical Instruments of Japan* (London, 1893, 2/1909/R1971), 164.

DAVID W. HUGHES

Ninaishōko [nishoko]. Japanese gong used in processions. *See* SHŌKO.

Nineteenth. An ORGAN STOP.

Ninga. MOUTH BOW of the Zande people of Zaïre; it is also known as *gwaningba* (*LaurentyC*, 113). *See* LUSUBA.

Nini. Single-string fiddle of northern Chad. *See* FININI.

Ni-no-tsuzumi. HOURGLASS DRUM of Japan. *See* TSUZUMI.

Niojiao hao. End-blown animal-horn trumpet of southeast China and Taiwan. *See* JIAO (i).

Nishōko. *See* NINAISHŌKO.

Nissān. KETTLEDRUM of Orissa, eastern India, used in tribal dances. *See* NAGĀRĀ, §1.

Nitrowski. Polish family of organ builders. Jerzy

Nitrowski (*b c*1605; *d* after 1673) worked on the organ at St Andrew's, Olkusz, from 1631 to 1633. In 1632 he finished the organ (still extant) in St James's, Lewocza, begun between 1625 and 1628 by Hans Hummel of Nuremberg or Coburg; between 1638 and 1641 he built an organ in St Mary's, Kraków (also attributed to Jozef Nitrowski). In 1662 (as 'Jerzy of Danzig') he built the organ in Gniezno Cathedral and in 1672–3 he and his son Andrzej (*b c*1640; *d* 1697) built an organ in St Mary's, Danzig (now Gdańsk), for 7500 florins.

Andrzej Nitrowski worked on a large organ in St Mary's, Sandomierz (now the cathedral), between 1694 and 1697; this instrument, completed in 1698 by Mateusz Brandt from Torún, had three manuals, pedals and 51 stops, and was well known outside Poland. His brother Daniel Nitrowski (*b c*1635; *d* after 1683) built the organ in Pelplin Cathedral between 1674 and 1680 (with assistance from JAN WULF of Malbork), worked in Danzig around 1683, and in that year built a new organ in Frombork Cathedral. The Nitrowski family built instruments in the northern Polish style, using mutations and reeds alongside an appropriate number of diapason chorus and foundation stops.

BIBLIOGRAPHY
J. Mattheson: *Niedtens musikalischer Handleitung anderer Theil . . . mit . . . einem Anhang von mehr als 60 Orgel-Wercken versehen* (Hamburg, 1721)
J. Hess: *Dispositien der merkwaardigste kerk-orgelen, welke in de zeven Vereenigde Provincien als mede in Duytsland en Elders aangetroffen worden* (Gouda, 1774/R1945)
M. Gliński, ed.: *Instrumenty muzyczne* (Warsaw, 1929)
H. Rauschning: *Geschichte der Musik und Musikpflege in Danzig* (Danzig, 1931)
W. Kreth: *Die Kemper-Orgeln im Dom zu Frauenburg* (Reinfeld, 1935)
A. Chybiński: *Slownik muzyków dawnej Polski* [Dictionary of early Polish musicians] (Kraków, 1949)
J. Gołos: *Zarys historii budowy organów w Polsce* [Outline of the history of Polish organ building] (Bydgoszcz, 1966)
——: 'Polskie organy i muzyka organowa', in J. Gołos and E. Smulikowska: *Prospekty organowe w Polsce jako dziela sztuki* (Warsaw, 1972)
HANS KLOTZ

Niu. Bronze bell of the Han Chinese. *See* ZHONG.

Nivi-grotu. A trumpet made from a bull's horn, used by the Guaymi Indians of the central provinces of Panama.

Nja. Leg rattles worn by dancers of the Igbo people of Nigeria.

Njagba-ogene. Double clapperless iron bell of the Igbo people of Nigeria. It is about 60 cm long.

Njanju. End-blown single-note flute of the Konjo people of Toro district, Uganda, used in the ILENGA flute ensemble.

Njari. A lamellaphone of the *mbira* type (*see* LAMELLAPHONE, §2(ii)) especially associated with the Nyungwe people of Mozambique and the Karanga and Zezuru peoples of Zimbabwe. It is a large instrument with from 18 to more than 30 keys and is played inside a large shell-decorated calabash resonator with the thumbs and index fingers. It is used for both religious and secular purposes. A larger version (*njari huru*) is played by the Chikunda people of the Zambezi basin.

ANDREW TRACEY

N'jarka. Single-string fiddle of Mali.

Njele. Hand-held rattle of the Chopi people of Zavala district, Mozambique. Several of these are used together to accompany xylophones.

Njongo. Single-headed closed conical drum of the Ganda people of Buganda district, Uganda. The membrane is laced on. It is played with sticks. *See also* NTAMIVU.

Njung. Log XYLOPHONE with eight to ten keys of the Bafut people of Cameroon. The keys are placed on banana logs and the instrument is used with horn, drum and scraper to accompany social songs.

Nkak. Large single-headed cylindrical drum of the Bamileke and Bamileke-Bangulap peoples of Cameroon. It is closed, with a carved-out base. In performance one player strikes the shell with two sticks, while a second beats the membrane with his hands. Among the Bamileke-Bamengum people the drum is known as *nket*. The drum may be used with a large slit-drum and tubular bamboo rattles to provide rhythmic accompaniment to a women's mourning lament, or with an open single-headed tubular drum, known to the Bamileke as *ntem* and to the Bamileke-Bamengum as *nto*. The Bamileke use the two drums with tubular bamboo rattles and nine different-sized bamboo flutes to accompany social dancing on happy occasions; the Bamileke-Bamengum use them with four clapperless bells and three metal rattles for the *lali* secret war dance, which is danced by a secret society with the musicians concealed.

BIBLIOGRAPHY
T. Nikiprowetzky: 'Musiques du Cameroun', OCR 25 [disc notes]
K. A. GOURLAY

Nkanika. Cast, flanged and shouldered clapper bell of the Ibibio and Efik peoples of Nigeria. Among the Ibibio it is tied, together with a tiny *nyoro* bell, to the waists of ceremonial masked dancers to sound their approach.

Nket. Drum of Cameroon. *See* NKAK.

Nkhombo. 'Singing horn' or kazoo of the Tumbuka/Henga people of Karonga district, Malawi. It is similar to the *lipenga* (*see* MALIPENGA) of the Nyanja/Chewa people.

Nkisansi. Box-resonated LAMELLAPHONE of the Bwalayulu people of Zaïre. It has metal keys (*LaurentyS*, 194). *See* KISAANJ.

Nkn nkwa. Stick rattle of the Igbo people of Imo State, Nigeria. Pieces of gourd or light wood are strung on a long stick which is held at each end. It is shaken as accompaniment to dancing or to signal to musicians to change rhythm.

Nkoka. Braced gourd-resonated MUSICAL BOW of the Tsonga people of south-eastern Africa. *See* CHITENDE.

Nkoko. (1) General term in Zaïre for a small SLIT-DRUM carved from a wooden stick, also known as *nkonko* or *khoko*. The name is often associated with specific peoples and functions. For example, *nkonko za nkimba* or *nkonko a lemba* indicates a drum used for the secret cults of the Nkimba or Lemba respectively.

(2) Wooden, cylindrical slit-drum, with carved anthropomorphic extension, of the Suku and Holo peoples of south-western Zaïre (*LaurentyTF*, 136).

Nkola [tamatama]. Large LAMELLAPHONE, with a wooden box resonator, of the Fang people of Gabon.

Nkonénu. Wooden cone flute, with one or two fingerholes, of the Kuba (Ngend) people of south-western Zaïre (*LaurentyA*, 151).

Nkonga. Mouth-resonated simple chordophone of the Twa people of Zaïre (*LaurentyC*, 110). *See* EMANA.

Nkoni [ngoni]. Plucked lute of the Manding peoples of West Africa. Ibn Baṭṭūṭa, who visited the Mali Empire in 1353, described the *nkoni* (see Gibb, 1929) and it was also written about by Mungo Park in the late 18th century. After the decline of the Mali Empire in the 15th century the Manding moved westwards into Guinea, Senegal and the Gambia, and the distribution of the instrument in its various names (*nkoni, koni, konimesin* and *konting*) reflects this migration. Among the Bamana (Bambara) people of Mali today the *nkoni* is a three- to five-string plucked lute, although three strings are most common. In construction it is almost identical to the KONTING and KHALAM although larger than them. Like both these instruments the *nkoni* is played exclusively by men from the professional musicians' caste. One of the main melody instruments of the Bamana, it is used to accompany praise singing and historical narrative. As the *subaga-nkoni* ('sorcerer's *nkoni*') it has a wooden soundbox carved to form the back of a standing figure, its master, and the musicians are reputed to make the instrument play from a distance.

BIBLIOGRAPHY
M. Park: *Travels in the Interior Districts of Africa* (London, 1799)
H. A. R. Gibb, trans.: *Ibn Baṭṭūṭa: Travels in Asia and Africa, 1325–1354* (London, 1929)
C. Nourrit and B. Pruitt, eds.: *Musique traditionelle de l'Afrique noire, discographie Mali 1978* (Paris, 1978)
W. Dalby: 'Mali', *Grove 6*
LUCY DURÁN

Nkonko. Small SLIT-DRUM of the lower Congo region of Zaïre (*LaurentyTF*, 136); *see* NKOKO. The name can also denote a membranophone; *see* DITUMBA.

Nkonkonto. Struck stick idiophone of the Lala people of Zambia. It accompanies drums such as the CHIRARIRA.

Nkonzi. Small, crescent-shaped SLIT-DRUM of the Woyo and Kongo peoples of the lower Congo region of Zaïre. The *nkonzi* is played during the Lemba ritual and belongs to secret societies, who use it to accompany their dances. Medicine men use it to cure sick persons, and it also plays an important role in the *nkisi* cult. These drums are never used for signalling (*LaurentyTF*, 139).
J. GANSEMANS

Nkpane. Large clapperless iron bell of the Kabre people of northern Togo. It is played by initiates during funeral processions together with drums and the smaller double clapperless bell *elolom*.

Nkporo. Large hollow wooden percussion block of the Ibibio people of Nigeria. *See* NTAKOROK.

Nkuanzi. Crescent-shaped SLIT-DRUM of the Mayombe people of Zaïre (*LaurentyTF*, 139).

Nkul. See NGKUL.

Nkulu. Drum of the Chopi people of Zavala district, Mozambique. It is the largest in a set of three drums, used with xylophones. The other drums are *nchuko* and *nzomana*.

Nkumvi. SLIT-DRUM of the Luba people of Zaïre. It is made from a single piece of wood in the shape of a small-based trapezoid, 110 cm in overall length, 70 cm high, with a slit about 3 cm wide. The two lateral sides have different thicknesses and produce four tones, two on each side. The instrument belongs to the chief and is used both for sending messages in connection with court life and to accompany dances performed during initiation rites. The range of the drum is about 20 to 30 km. It is usually played in the evening or very early in the morning. The list of names given by Knosp (1968) and de Hen (1960) for trapeziform slit-drums suggests a close linguistic relationship. Cognate with the *nkumvi* are the Ankoro and Sampwe *kiumvi* and Kabongo *kiumvu*, while *lukumbi* is attributed to the Ombo, Bangubangu, Songola, Lega and Kusu, *lukombi* to the Nkutshu and Tetela, *lukombe* to the Kusu, and *lokole* and *lokombe* to northern and north-western peoples such as the Mongo, Doko, Nkundu, Kota, Mbole and Yela. The Eso, however, call the drum *bosuli*, the Bangba *nekpopo*, the Meje *nekbokbo* and the Mamvu and Mangutu *kpwokpwo*. Drums vary in length from 50 to 150 cm on the longer, upper side and from 40 to 50 cm on the base, with corresponding heights of 50 to 100 cm. Almost all drums are played with two beaters, most of them with latex heads. Use of the drum as a signalling instrument is more common than as accompaniment for dancing, which occurs more in the south and east than in the north-west. *See also* TSHINGUFU.

BIBLIOGRAPHY
LaurentyTF
F. J. de Hen: *Beitrag zur Kenntnis der Musikinstrumente aus Belgisch Kongo und Ruanda-Urundi* (Tervuren, 1960)
G. Knosp: *Enquête sur la vie musicale au Congo belge 1934–1935* (Tervuren, 1968)
J. Gansemans: *Les instruments de musique Luba* (Tervuren, 1980)
                  J. GANSEMANS, K. A. GOURLAY

Nkundi. Arched harp of the Zande, Bondo and Bari peoples of Zaïre (*LaurentyC*, 119). *See* KUNDI (i).

Nkuti kubidi. GROUND HARP of the Luba people of Zaïre (*LaurentyC*, 111). *See* BABAKUNGU.

Nkwa. Open conical drum of the Igbo people of Owerri, Nigeria. *See* IGBA (i).

Nkwagasho. Obsolete SCRAPER of the Shambala people of Tanzania. It consisted of two thin notched sticks attached to a board.

Nkwit. FRICTION DRUM of the Mbun people of Zaïre. *See* KWITA.

Nkwong. Conical flanged and welded clapperless bell of the Ibibio people of Nigeria. It is large compared to the *akankan*, another Ibibio bell. Clapperless bells of this type are very prominent in the music of secret societies, where they are used solo to announce the appearance of a mask, or in sets with drums for dancing. See S. E. Akpabot: *Ibibio Music in Nigerian Culture* (East Lansing, Mich., 1975).

Nnawuta. Double clapperless iron bell of the Ashanti people of Ghana. *See also* DAWURO.

Nnkul. Cylindrical SLIT-DRUM of the Mbun people of south-western Zaïre (*LaurentyTF*, 133).

Nnonka. Variable tension HOURGLASS DRUM of Ghana. *See* DONNO.

Nō [noh]. Term for a genre of Japanese musical dance-drama, literally translated as 'accomplishment' or 'skill'. It developed from folk antecedents such as *sarugaku* and *dengaku* and had reached a first approximation of its present form by the early 15th century. Between the 17th and the late 19th centuries the main guilds of nō in Edo (Tokyo) were under the patronage of the military government, and it was then that the music arrived at its modern form. Nō plays are accompanied by four instruments: the NŌKAN (transverse flute), KOTSUZUMI and ŌTSUZUMI (hourglass drums) and SHIMEDAIKO (barrel drum), termed collectively the *hayashi*, or sometimes *shibyōshi* ('four rhythm instruments'). As a rule one of each instrument is used, but in many plays the *shimedaiko* is not used at all, and multiple *kotsuzumi* are very occasionally called for. The music has both tutti and solo instrumental passages. In addition to full-scale nō there are also various types of performance which omit the *hayashi*. The genre of farce known as *kyōgen*, closely related to nō, sometimes uses the full *hayashi*, or just the *kotsuzumi*.

BIBLIOGRAPHY
S. Kishibe: 'Japan', §III, 2, *Grove 6*
A. Tamba: *The Musical Structure of Noh* (Tokyo, 1981)
                  DAVID W. HUGHES

Noack, Fritz (*b* Wolgast, Germany, 25 Sept 1935). American organ builder. He was apprenticed to Rudolph von Beckerath (1954–8) and worked later as a journeyman with Klaus Becker and Ahrend & Brunzema. He went to the USA in 1959, working first for Estey, then for Charles Fisk, opening his own workshop in Lawrence, Massachusetts, in 1960. He then moved to Andover, Massachusetts, and in 1970 (as Noack Organ Co. Inc.) to Georgetown, Massachusetts. Noack's work has been almost exclusively with mechanical-action organs, and although his background is German, he has also assimilated aspects of the American tradition in his work. Influenced initially by *Bauhaus* ideas, his case designs tend to be simple, balanced, and musically functional in accordance with the *Werkprinzip*. His more important organs include those in Unity Church, St Paul, Minnesota (1965), Brandeis University (1967), Trinity Lutheran Church, Worcester, Massachusetts (1967), the Emma Willard School (1970), Ardmore Methodist Church, Winston-Salem, North Carolina (1978), and the Presbyterian Church, Beckley, West Virginia (1979). He has also built positive organs, regals and compact practice organs.

BIBLIOGRAPHY
G. Bozeman: 'The Noack Organ Co. of Georgetown, Mass.', *Art of the Organ*, i/2 (1971), 19
U. Pape: *The Tracker Organ Revival in America* (Berlin, 1978)
                  BARBARA OWEN

Nobat. Court orchestra of West Malaysia and Indonesia. Each of the royal courts of Kedah, Perak, Selangor and Trengganu has its own *nobat* band – a mark of the ruler's sovereignty and an essential part of his regalia. The band plays at his installation and at weddings or funerals of the royal family, and marks specific times such as the breaking of the Muslim fast. In function and composition it is related to the NAQQĀRAKHĀNA of the Middle East: both these ensembles have the same basic instruments and in both a drum is accorded special respect. The ruler of Malacca is thought to have adopted the tradition of possessing a drum of sovereignty in the early 15th century. The first mention of the *nobat* on the peninsula, in the *Sejarah Melayu* ('Malay annals'), indicates that it was used in Malacca during the reign of Sultan Muhammed Shah (1424–41). The rulers who did homage to his successors and asked for the drum of sovereignty included the Rajah of Kedah. The Kedah *nobat*, which is the oldest in West Malaysia and is always used on royal occasions, now has six instruments: a *negara* or *nahara* (a metal kettledrum), two *gendang* (double-headed drums), one *nafiri* (a long silver trumpet), one *serunai* (oboe) and one suspended gong. After the Portuguese capture of Malacca its ruler Raja Muzaffar migrated to Perak, taking a *nobat* with him for his installation. The Perak *nobat* now comprises one *nengkara* (*negara*), one *gendang nobat*, one *gendang kecil* (small *gendang*), one *nafiri* and one *serunai*. In Kedah and Perak only *orang kalur* ('hereditary families') may play the instruments; spirits are said to inhabit them and illnesses have been reported when they were maltreated. In both states the instrumental pieces are called *man*. Selangor acquired its *nobat* when its first ruler travelled to Perak to seek recognition and to be installed to the sound of its *nobat*. The Selangor *nobat* instruments are one *lengkara* (kettledrum), two *gendang besar*, two *gendang kecil*, one *nafiri* and one *serunai*. When Sultan Abdul Rahman Muazam Shah II abdicated from Riau-Lingga in 1911 he gave his *nobat* to Trengganu. The Trengganu *nobat* now consists of one *nenggara* (kettledrum) and two *gendang nobat* (all three are encased in silver), one *nafiri*, one *serunai* and a pair of *kopok-kopok* (small cymbals, also of silver). The delicately decorated *gendang* drums have 15 tuning keys each.

A *nobat* ensemble from the one-time Kingdom of Daik in the Riau archipelago, Indonesia, is still to be found in the Museum Kandil Riau, Tanjung Pinang. It consists of two *gendang panjang* (double-headed drums), two *gendang penganak* (small copper drums), two *kencane* (frame drums), two *mong* (small hand-held gongs), three *gong*, one *tawak* (small suspended gong), one *nafiri* (oboe) and two *serunai* (oboes). As there is no longer a sovereign in Indonesia, the *nobat* in Riau is never played today. It was last played in 1911 when the last Sultan fled. It is kept in the Museum Kandil Riau, and the owner burns incense every week in front of it. The *nobat* in the Sri Indrapura palace at Siak, Riau province, is similar to that from Daik.

BIBLIOGRAPHY

R. O. Winstedt: 'The Perak Royal Musical Instruments', *Journal of the Malayan Branch of the Royal Asiatic Society*, xii (1929), 451

W. Linehan: 'The Nobat and the Orang Kalau of Perak', *Journal of the Malayan Branch of the Royal Asiatic Society*, xxiv/3 (1951), 60

M. Sheppard: *Taman Indera, a Royal Pleasure Ground* (Kuala Lumpur, 1972)

JACK PERCIVAL BAKER DOBBS,
MARGARET J. KARTOMI

Nobilmente (It.: 'nobly', 'majestically'; adverb from *nobile*, noble). A direction used both as a tempo designation and as a mark of expression in the works of Elgar but few other composers. It appears on a sketch (at the Elgar Birthplace) for 'Nimrod' in the *Enigma* variations and on the published score (1899) of Elgar's piano transcription of the work, but not in the orchestral full score published some months later. Its first appearance on one of his printed orchestral scores is in his *Cockaigne* overture (1901), and he used it often after that. Vaughan Williams used it in his score for *Coastal Command* (1942), almost certainly with the Elgarian style in mind. Nobility in music is an ideal that has been favoured only by particular composers at particular times, so the history of the word is otherwise scattered. An early example is in François Couperin, who several times gave the direction *noblement sans lenteur* (nobly without being slow). *See also* TEMPO AND EXPRESSION MARKS.

DAVID FALLOWS, MICHAEL KENNEDY

Noblet. French firm of woodwind instrument makers. It was founded in 1750 at La Couture Boussey by Clair Noblet (*b* 11 Nov 1728; *d* March 1800). It is not known who was his immediate successor, though this may have been the Denis Noblet sometimes said to have been the founder. At various unrecorded dates in the 19th century the firm came under the control of Nicolas Denis Noblet (*b* June 1797; *d* 10 Oct 1874), Nicolas Prudent Noblet (*b* Aug 1818; *d* 10 April 1871) and Denis Toussaint Noblet (*b* 18 March 1850; *d* 28 Aug 1919). In 1904 the Noblet business was sold to Georges LEBLANC. Noblet is now run as an associated subsidiary company of Leblanc in Paris.

During the time of its independent existence Noblet produced fifes, flutes without keys (or with a few keys) and clarinets fitted with six to 16 keys. A four-key flute marked 'D. Noblet ainé' in Oxford (Bate Collection), fitted with metal-mounted tenons and screwed-in pillars, probably dates from the second quarter of the 19th century. The present company specializes in clarinets, pitched in E♭, C, B♭ and A, and alto and bass clarinets. It also produces flutes, piccolos and oboes.

NIALL O'LOUGHLIN

Nōdaiko. Japanese barrel drum used in the nō dance-drama. *See* SHIMEDAIKO.

Nogo [nodo, noedo, noego, to, yŏngdo, yŏnggo]. Barrel drums of Korea. Seven types, of related construction and function, are discussed here: *nogo* ('road drum'), *noego* ('thunder drum'), and *yŏnggo* ('spirit drum'), all mounted in a wooden two-pillar stand; and *nodo*, *noedo*, *yŏngdo* and *to* (*to* or *do* referring to shaken drums), all mounted on a pole and played by twirling and shaking. The chief differences between these various instruments are in the number of barrels and in their colour and function in sacrificial rites.

The *nogo* and *nodo* each have two red barrels and are used in sacrifices to human spirits (e.g. the Sacrifice to Confucius; see illustration). The obsolete *noego* and *noedo* each had three black barrels and were used in sacrifices to heavenly spirits (e.g. the Sacrifice to Wind, Clouds, Thunder and Rain). The obsolete *yŏnggo* and *yŏngdo* each had four yellow barrels and were used in sacrifices to earthly spirits (e.g. the Sacrifice to Earth and Grain). The long obsolete *to* had a single barrel and was used in court banquets in the early 15th century.

The *nogo*, *noego* and *yŏnggo* were all suspended in two-pillar decorated wooden frames. At the top ends of the frame were two wooden dragons with long tassels

Nodo (double barrel drum) of the hŏn'ga (courtyard ensemble) at the twice-yearly Sacrifice to Confucius, Seoul, Korea

hanging from their mouths; in the top centre was a fire symbol. The pillars were mounted on two wooden stands, each consisting of four sitting tigers. In performance the drums were struck with a mallet.

The small *nodo*, *noedo*, *yŏngdo* and *to* each were pierced by a wooden shaft and had knotted leather thongs hanging from the sides of the drum bodies. When the shaft was twirled backwards and forwards the thongs would strike the heads from centrifugal force, making a rustling sound.

All these drums were considered Chinese and were used only in *hŏn'ga* (courtyard ensembles) of ritual music (*aak*) for sacrificial rites. They were constructed in Korea in the 15th century, based on descriptions in Chinese theoretical sources. The treatise *Akhak kwebŏm* (1493) contains detailed descriptions and drawings of these drums.

The *nogo*, *noego* and *yŏnggo* were played, together with the large drum *chin'go*, as part of the starting and stopping signals for the *hŏn'ga* and as punctuation after every four notes of the slow melody. The *nodo*, *noedo* and *yŏngdo* were played only as part of starting signals for the *hŏn'ga*.

All Korean court sacrificial rites, except for two involving human spirits (Confucius and Royal Ancestors), were abolished at the beginning of the 20th century, and as a result only the *nogo* and *nodo* survive in current use. Historical examples of the *noego*, *noedo*, *yŏnggo* and *yŏngdo* survived until their destruction during the Korean War (1950–53); current models in museums are reconstructions.

The Japanese FURITSUZUMI and Chinese TAOGU are related to the *nogo*.

BIBLIOGRAPHY
Sŏng Hyŏn, ed.: *Akhak kwebŏm* [Guide to the study of music] (Seoul, 1493/R1975), 6.7b–9b
Chang Sa-hun: *Han'guk akki taegwan* [Korean musical instruments] (Seoul, 1969), 139ff

ROBERT C. PROVINE

Noh. *See* NŌ.

Nōkan. Transverse bamboo flute, with seven finger-holes, of the Japanese nō theatre. It is also used in dance music (*nagauta*), off-stage music of the kabuki theatre (*geza*) and some folk musics. The *nōkan* resembles the RYŪTEKI in many ways (the internal metal weight, the bark wrapping, the lacquered bore etc), and it is assumed that it developed from the *ryūteki*, although this development cannot be charted historically. But the *nōkan* is of a much more complex construction. It is about 40 cm long and is fashioned not from a single tube of bamboo but from three to six short lengths joined together. In addition, some older flutes were made from lengths of bamboo which had been split lengthwise into several segments and then reassembled – possibly to adjust the bore, but the reason is not known for certain. There is no evidence to support the frequently encountered claim that such segments were reassembled inside-out to give a harder surface to the bore. This would have been rendered unnecessary in any case by the advent, apparently in the late 19th century, of the practice of lacquering the bore. The hard outer skin of the bamboo is, however, shaved off – in order, some say, to give the appearance of having been turned inside-out. The type of bamboo used is *medake* (*Nipponocalamus simonii*). The *nōkan*'s most distinctive feature (of unknown origin) is the *nodo* ('throat'), a short tube inserted in the bore between the mouth-hole and the nearest finger-hole; it causes the overblown octave to be sharp at the lower end and flat at the top. On a typical flute the internal diameter is approximately 11 mm at the *nodo* and 16 mm near the closest finger-hole, tapering again to 11 mm at the lower end.

Since the *nōkan* does not share a melody with another instrument or with the voice there is less need for a pitch standard than there is with the *ryūteki*, and individual flutes may vary somewhat both in basic pitch and in interval structure. This variation is not, however, related to the differences in schools of performers. A typical range is about *b–f♯'''*. Visually the most obvious distinctions between these two types of flute are that the red lacquer of the *nōkan*'s bore extends to the surface through the finger-holes, and that the ornament (*kashiragane*) embedded in the left end is generally of metal in the case of the *nōkan* but is embroidered on a red ground in the *ryūteki*.

Nōkan technique features many cross-fingerings (unlike the *ryūteki*), constant delicate ornamentation and pitch gliding; the execution of these features varies both between schools and among individuals within each school. The repertory consists of several dozen named pieces with specific uses, as well as some less fully structured pieces; much of it falls into stock phrases of one or more eight-beat bars. In *nagauta* and *geza* music one flautist is in charge of both the *nōkan* and another transverse flute, the *shinobue*. Nō pieces are used especially in plays and dances derived from nō plays but also, for example, to set an elevated mood; the pieces are of necessity greatly truncated. In certain local festival musics several less well-made (i.e. cheaper) *nōkan* may be used together to play simple melodies.

For illustration *see* SHINOBUE.

BIBLIOGRAPHY
W. P. Malm: *Japanese Music and Musical Instruments* (Rutland, Vermont, 1959), 119ff
D. Berger: 'The Nō-kan: its Construction and Music', *EM*, ix (1965), 221

R. Emmert and Y. Minegishi, eds.: *Musical Voices of Asia* (Tokyo, 1980), 243
A. Tamba: *The Musical Structure of Noh* (Tokyo, 1981), 147
'Fue', *Ongaku daijiten* [Encyclopedia of music] (Tokyo, 1981)

DAVID W. HUGHES

Nokukwane. See SEKOKWANE.

Nondji m'dom. Sacred drum of the Fali people of Cameroon. See TONDJI M'DOM.

Nonga. Long cylindrical, footed drum, with nailed membrane, of the Nkutu and Yaelima peoples of Zaïre. The sides of the cylinder are straight for most of their length but are conical just above a short base which is almost as wide as the drumhead. Drums vary in height from 110 to 120 cm and are often decorated with geometrical or zoomorphic patterns.

BIBLIOGRAPHY
BooneT, 43
F.J. de Hen: *Beitrag zur Kenntnis der Musikinstrumente aus Belgisch Kongo und Ruanda-Urundi* (Tervuren, 1960)

K. A. GOURLAY

Nong nôt. GONG-CHIME of the Mon people of Burma and Thailand. See PAT KÔN CHOH.

Nonnengeige (Ger.). TRUMPET MARINE.

Nontow. Side-blown trumpet of the Kabre people of northern Togo. It is made from an antelope horn and played with side-blown bamboo trumpets for dancing of the senior age-group.

Noone guddalavani burra. Drone chordophone ('plucked drum') of Andhra, south India. It is similar to the *tuntune* of Maharashtra: the body is a hollow, tapering cylinder (often metal) whose lower end is covered with a skin; a steel string passes up through the body from the centre of the skin and is secured to a tuning-peg inserted through the top of a neck fixed to the side of the body. The instrument is plucked by the finger to accompany vocal music, and its name indicates its use by soothsayers. See K. S. Kothari: *Indian Folk Musical Instruments* (New Delhi, 1968). *See also* ĀNANDALAHARĪ.

ALASTAIR DICK

Noopur. See NŪPUR.

Noordsche balk (Dutch: 'Nordic beam'). The Dutch name for the various zithers of the Low Countries, either made of, or having the appearance of, the lengths of Scandinavian deal known as 'Nordic beams'. See H. Boone: 'De hommel in de Lage Landen', *Brussels Museum of Musical Instruments Bulletin*, v (1975) [special issue, incl. Eng. and Fr. summaries].

Noot. See NUT (ii).

Nordström, Sven (*b* 4 Feb 1801; *d* 16 Feb 1887). Swedish organ builder. Having retired for reasons of health from service as a master-gunner with the Jönköping regiment, he began in 1834 to build small-scale organs at Norra Solberga in Jönköping province. He built altogether about 38 organs, including those at Hult Church (1841; 11 stops), Söderköping (1845; two manuals, 21 stops), Väster Eneby (1850; two manuals), Malilla (1850), Flisby (1856; two manuals), Ledberg (1852), Normlösa (1854) and Kuddby (1882). His masterpiece was the 26-stop organ in St Olai, Norrköping (1871). A number of his instruments (including those listed above, except that at Hult) survive, many of them unaltered; they show a high standard of artistry and craftsmanship, and their sound clearly derives from the classic 18th-century Swedish organ-building tradition. During the 1850s Sven's younger brother Eric Nordström began to assist in the workshop, gradually taking over a larger share of responsibility. In 1853 the brothers moved to Flisby and at the end of the 1870s to Eksjö.

BIBLIOGRAPHY
E. Erici: *Orglar och orgelbyggare i Linköpings stift i ord och bild* (1949)
——: *Inventarium över bevarade äldre kyrokorglar i Sverige* (Stockholm, 1965)
based on *Sohlmans musiklexikon* (iv, 742–3) by permission of Sohlmans Förlag

BENGT KYHLBERG

Norman, Barak (*b* c1670; *d* London, c1740). English string instrument maker. He was the most important of the early English makers and is especially noted for his viols and lutes, but he also made violins and is said to have been one of the earliest English makers of cellos. Norman's bass viols are particularly sought after, and several have been altered to cellos. Because his early instruments closely resemble the Stainerish models of Thomas Urquhart, it is possible that Norman was his pupil. However, Haweis maintained that Richard Meares was Norman's teacher, probably because Meares was a follower of the Brescian school, whose style Norman adopted in his later instruments. According to Hawkins, Norman lived first in Bishopsgate and then in St Paul's Churchyard, where he had his workshop. Norman's work is characterized by beautiful modelling, good wood (the backs usually cut on the slab) and a very dark brown varnish. The tone is strong and rich. Early specimens are highly arched like those of the early German school, but his later work closely resembles that of Maggini, with medium arching and elaborate double purfling, including floral designs on the back and belly. Most of Norman's instruments carry his monogram (see Vannes, no.3197) inlaid in purfling in the centre of the back and on the belly under the wide portion of the fingerboard. His soundholes are serpentine or c-holes or f-holes. His scrolls are exquisitely cut (some of the open Gothic variety), but carved heads and conventional scrolls are also usual. A viol bearing the label 'Barak Norman, at the Bass Viol in St. Pauls Alley London, Fecit 1690' is the earliest recorded, but other types of label by him are also known (see Vannes and Lütgendorff). By 1715 Norman had formed a partnership with Nathaniel Cross, and certain instruments were made by them jointly. Two such examples, a viol and a cello, are mentioned in the list (quoted by Hawkins) of instruments left by Thomas Britton, a famous small-coal merchant. Instruments by Norman are in collections of the Royal College of Music, London (see illustration); the Paris Conservatoire; the Smithsonian Institution, Washington, DC; the Musikinstrumenten-Sammlung (Staatliches Institut für Musikforschung), Berlin; and the Victoria and Albert Museum, London, as well as in the possession of several private owners and collectors.

BIBLIOGRAPHY
HawkinsH
C. Stainer: *A Dictionary of Violin Makers* (London, 1896/R1973)

Division viol by Barak Norman, London, 1692 (Royal College of Music, London)

W. L. von Lütgendorff: *Die Geigen- und Lautenmacher vom Mittelalter bis zur Gegenwart* (Frankfurt am Main, 1904, rev. 6/1922/R1968)

H. R. Haweis: *Old Violins and Violin Lore* (London, 1906), 125

R. Vannes: *Essai d'un dictionnaire universel des luthiers* (Paris, 1932, 2/1951/R1972 as *Dictionnaire universel des luthiers*, and R1981 incl. suppl. 1959)

W. Henley: *Universal Dictionary of Violin and Bow Makers* (Brighton, 1959)

MURRAY LEFKOWITZ

Norman & Beard. English firm of organ builders. It was founded by William Norman, one of a Norwich family trading as a cabinet maker in Marylebone, London. He occasionally made organ cases for the nearby firm of J. W. Walker, whose staff he later joined, going on to work for T. C. Lewis; he retired to Diss, Norfolk,

about 1872. William's son Ernest William Norman (1852–1927) began his apprenticeship with Walker but left about 1868 to set up as an organ builder in Diss, where he was joined by his brother Herbert John (1861–1936) and an apprentice George Wales Beard, the firm becoming known as Norman Bros. & Beard. Beard ran a retail music shop in Beccles and in 1896, when he was formally taken into partnership, it was renamed Norman & Beard.

By the late 1870s the firm had acquired a workshop in Norwich and a tuning contract for the cathedral organ there. A new purpose-built factory was opened in 1898, the largest and most advanced of its time. By 1916 the firm had built over 1400 new organs, but loss of their younger men to the army led to amalgamation with Hill & Son (*see* HILL (i)) in London and, after completing the organ for Johannesburg Town Hall, the Norwich factory was closed. The firm survives as HILL, NORMAN & BEARD.

Norman & Beard's organs were solid and durable, their exhaust-pneumatic action mechanisms outlasting all other non-mechanical systems. The firm was briefly influenced by the methods of Robert Hope-Jones, for whom Norman & Beard made consoles and subcontracted complete organs. In addition to organs, vast numbers of piano pedal-boards were made and supplied to organists for practising. The firm's business and technical records of 1879–1916 (with those of Hill for 1838–c1960) are in the English Organ Archive, Keele University.

MICHAEL SAYER

Northumbrian pipes. Term applied to various types of bagpipe of northern England; *see* BAGPIPE, §5.

Norwich organ. An ELECTRONIC ORGAN, several models of which have been manufactured by Norwich Organ Manufacturers in Norwich since 1975. The organs are designed for use in churches, and are based on the defunct MILLER ORGAN with extensive technological improvements; the names of the individual models (such as Sprowston, Norfolk and Classic) are taken from the Miller range. The original Miller system of an oscillator for each note has been combined in the Norwich organ with one in which the sound is produced by 12 oscillators using frequency division. A special feature is the electronic simulation of the 'chiff' transient attack found in flute stops on pipe organs.

HUGH DAVIES

Nose flute. Any kind of flute, tubular or vessel, side- or end-blown, which is sounded by nasal breath. Such flutes have a very wide distribution, but are particularly common in the Pacific Islands and South-east Asia. Sachs suggested that the origin of nose flutes lies in the association of nasal breath with magic and religious rites. In Oceania the nose flute is pre-eminently an instrument of Polynesia and Micronesia. It is only rarely reported for mainland New Guinea but is present in the offshore D'Entrecasteaux group to the south-west and in the Bismarck Archipelago to the north-west. Southwards in Melanesia it is prominent only in areas adjacent to western Polynesia as in New Caledonia and the Loyalty Islands (*see* THITH) and in Fiji (*see* DULALI, DUVU TAVU). In Micronesia it was formerly widespread in the Caroline Islands where it was present in Palau, Yap, Truk (*see* ANIN), Satowal (*see* JANIL), Nomoi, Ponape (*see* KĀŠ) and Mokil. In Polynesia it was present almost everywhere except New Zealand (see FANGUFANGU, KO'E, KOFE, 'OHE HANO IHU, PU IHU, PU KO'E, VIVO (i)).

For illustration see FLUTE, fig.2h.

The following nose flutes are entered in this dictionary: aangyn; aduteli; angun; anin; bali-ing; bangsi; bidi; bitu ceguvi; bolukuluku; bukanga; dibolo; dulali; duvu tavu; enongol; fangufangu; ifonge na ndzulu; ipu hōkiokio; janil; kabili; kaleleng; kāš; ko'e; kofe; 'ohe hano ihu; pensol; pu ihu; pu ko'e; sangui; selengut; sigu; thith; tongali; turali; vivo (i).

BIBLIOGRAPHY
C. Sachs: *The History of Musical Instruments* (New York, 1940), 46
S. Wolf: *Zum Problem der Nasenflöte* (Leipzig, 1941)
                                                    MERVYN McLEAN

Notched flute. An end-blown flute (open or stopped) with a V- or U-shaped notch cut or burned into its upper rim to facilitate tone production. No clear line can be usefully drawn between rim-blown flutes (for example, many used in panpipes) having gently cupped rims and 'notched' flutes with shallow U-shaped notches. An enormous variety of notched flutes used solo and as ensemble instruments are found widely distributed across Africa, the Far East, the Pacific Islands and Central and South America. Notched flutes of bone, with three equidistant finger-holes, were used in the Chavín culture of Peru (900–200 BC). The coastal Chancay culture of Peru (1300–1438), noted for its white-on-black pottery, produced cane or clay notched flutes with four to eight finger-holes. The Chiriguano of Argentina and the Tucano of the Colombian Amazon region use notched flutes, which are also found in Venezuela. The modern Chinese *xiao*, of bamboo, has its notch cut into a natural node forming the upper end of the flute, the node serving, like the player's lower lip in other varieties, to seal off the upper end of the flute. Thus the *xiao* is intermediate between notched and duct flutes.

For illustrations see FLUTE, figs.1d and 2c.

The following notched flutes are entered in this dictionary: alele; amakondele; arote; chōk; dilitili; dōshō; ekinimba; ekiwuuwe; elele; embilta; emibanda; enkologi; entemyo; entengezzi; falĕndag; flautilla; fornke; foro; hitoyogiri; igemfe; imbande; kaur; kena; khumulele; kimsa ppía; kotake; lengwane; lichiwayu; liku; loti; mala (ii); mbio; mbóu-lóulo; mimby chué; mlele; mukassi; mulele; mulere; mulizi; muralī; musezza; ndele; ndere (i); ngoli; ntabitabi; nyamulere; odurugya; olera; ompa; omubanda; omukuri; paceño; paldong; palĕndag; paqi; parundag; parwaye; pensol; putu (ii); shakuhachi; taikapusiphia; tanso; tanteki; tifigim; tokoro; t'ongso; t'ungae; t'ungso; ulele; umpa; umwilenge; whistle; xiao; yak; yue; yuping xiao.

PETER COOKE, JOHN M. SCHECHTER

Notes inégales (Fr.: 'unequal notes'). A rhythmic convention according to which certain divisions of the beat move in alternately long and short values, even if they are written equal.

1. Definition. 2. French practice. 3. Theoretical and mechanical evidence. 4. Application outside France. 5. Jazz.

1. DEFINITION. As it existed in France from the mid-16th century to the late 18th the convention of *notes inégales* was first of all a way of gracing or enlivening passage-work, especially improvised diminutions. As styles changed and the figurations born of diminution entered the essential melodic vocabulary, inequality permeated the musical language. Its application was regulated by metre and note values; it always operated within the beat, never distorting the beat itself. The degree of inequality (i.e. the ratio between the lengths of the long and short notes of each pair) could vary from the barely perceptible to the equivalent of double dotting, according to the character of the piece and the taste of the performer. Inequality was considered one of the chief

resources of expression, and it varied according to expressive needs within the same piece or even within the same passage; where it was felt to be inappropriate it could be abandoned altogether unless explicitly demanded.

Inequality is usually defined as the uneven performance of evenly written values. Although the practical problem is certainly that of deciding when to alter what appears on the page, the rhythmic convention itself is independent of questions of notation. French composers frequently wrote out inequality with dotted figures, sometimes to resolve doubt, sometimes to ensure a sharply dotted effect, and sometimes for no apparent reason. Outside France, where performers could not be counted on to alter the rhythm in given situations, a composer who particularly wanted inequality had to indicate it. To insist that *notes inégales* are, by definition, always written equal is to mask a great deal of evidence that can help in mapping the geographical extent of the convention, and in deciding whether or not it affected only music in French styles.

2. FRENCH PRACTICE. The evidence for *notes inégales* in French music is found first of all in instruction manuals in connection with *mesure*, i.e. time beating and metre. They tell in varying detail what note values are normally unequal and under what conditions. The number, distribution and consistency of these accounts show beyond any possible doubt that inequality was a normal component of musical education in France in the 17th and 18th centuries. Further explanations and examples exist in dictionaries, treatises and *avertissements* to editions. The note-by-note treatment of whole pieces can be studied on barrel organs and in instructions for making them. The scores themselves supply examples of notated inequality and written directions for the treatment of particular pieces. Finally, dotted and undotted versions of the same passages may be taken as evidence that the undotted versions were dotted in performance, even though other explanations cannot be ruled out.

The code that emerges from the many dozens of French instruction books that appeared between about 1660 and the Revolution shows a remarkable uniformity; it is admirably rational and even 'scientific'. These books, however, were addressed to children, amateurs and teachers; they are rarely concerned with the analysis and description of professional performance, and they answer only the easy questions, leaving the hard ones to the instructor or to that imaginary oracle, *le bon goût*. For the only French attempt at true analysis one must turn to M. D. J. Engramelle and his works on mechanical instruments written in the 1770s; but, as the author himself is careful to point out, his analysis is of a style of execution which would 'disgust' Lully, Corelli, Couperin 'and even Rameau', so much had fashions changed. The books usually concentrate on the question of which note values are to be made unequal in the different metres. Occasional disagreements arise from the fact that the metrical system was in a state of transition from the proportions and *tactus* of the Renaissance to modern metres and beats.

In the 17th century the time signature '3' could mean any simple triple metre. In the 18th it usually meant only 3/4 and implied the French style; the signature '3/4' was associated at first with Italian style, but it gradually lost this connotation. Triple metre could be taken (as today) in one or three beats, depending on the tempo, or in two unequal beats. ¢ was taken in two fairly slow beats or four faster ones; 4/8 was taken in two. Although barring in the 17th century did not always correspond to modern usage, it did not affect inequality. In the first decades of the 18th century a code governing the relationship of inequality to metre crystallized. In simple metres with two or four beats to the bar, notes of the value of a quarter of a beat or less were unequal. Thus quavers were unequal in 2 (= 2/2) and ¢ (when taken in two beats), and semiquavers were unequal in C, ¢ (when taken in four beats) and 4/8. Semiquavers were also unequal in 2/4 according to most writers, though Loulié (1696) specified unequal quavers. Crotchets were unequal in 3/2 and quavers in 3, 6/4, 9/4 and 12/4. Opinion was divided about 3/4, some writers treating it like 3, some placing inequality on the semiquavers, and some implying that its Italian connotations cancelled inequality altogether. In all metres with 8 as a denominator semiquavers were unequal. 'Croches blanches' (whitened quavers and semiquavers) had no special rhythmic significance, as far as can be determined (for three pieces in this notation see *Les folies françoises* in François Couperin's *Troisième livre*, 1722). Underlying all these rules was the assumption that the principal unit of melodic movement in a piece corresponded to the theoretically unequal one for that metre. (In courantes in 3/2, crotchets were equal and quavers unequal.) Inequality did not, however, move up to values larger than the theoretically unequal ones. A useful table summarizing the unequal values for each metre in a selection of sources throughout the period of these manuals is given by Neumann (1965, p.322).

It is extremely difficult to evaluate the roles of theory and practice in all of this. To some extent writers were trying to describe usage in a number of well-defined rhythmic styles, each associated with a certain metre and genre. The rules themselves must have influenced practice to some extent among the musicians who grew up with them. But there are many references to how hard it was to give general principles (e.g. Bailleux, 1770) and to the fact that style and taste were the final arbiters. Occasionally an author spelt out exceptions, as did Démoz de La Salle (1728, p.166):

In the expression of declamatory *airs*, in recitatives, or in solos [*récits*] measured *in two or three simple beats*, theoretically unequal quavers are very often performed equal according to the expression of the words and the style of the melody. And in recitatives, bass solos, or other [pieces] measured *in four simple beats*, quavers which are naturally equal in their motion are, on the contrary, often sung unequal, also according to the style of the melody, and according to how regularly these kinds of *airs* are written and how well they express the text.

What is certain is that inequality suffused French thinking about performance, in which it constituted one of the most important and difficult questions. Borin (1722, p.26) summed it up: 'Expression . . . consists principally in knowing what notes are equal or unequal'.

The careful composer who wished to ensure inequality or equality in doubtful situations used symbols or written directions. The dot of addition was the usual sign for inequality; very occasionally there was no compensatory shortening of the second note of the pair (Nivers, 1665; Perrine, c1680). The reasoning of Bacilly (1668) with regard to dots is worth noting: they were normally left unwritten in order to avoid tempting the player to jerkiness. He explained written dots in a particular example, however, as a warning 'not to omit them in singing, which would [otherwise] lack all grace'

(p.233). The symbol for equality was dots or strokes over the notes (the dots simply meant equal; the strokes meant equal and staccato). In ex.1 the distinction between equal and unequal notes is very carefully made. The

Ex.1 F. Couperin: *Pièces de clavecin, troisième livre* (1722), 'Les vieux galans et les Trésorieres surannées'

simplest written directions were 'notes égales' or 'croches égales' to cancel inequality, and 'pointé' (sometimes qualified) to ensure it. Most other terms are themselves ambiguous. 'Piqué' meant either sharply dotted or equal and staccato. 'Louré' meant slightly unequal to Loulié but legato and in the style of a loure (the dance or bagpipes) to others. 'Mesuré', 'marqué' and 'martelé' had meanings of their own which might or might not imply equality in a given situation. 'Gracieusement' probably implied inequality where metre and note values permitted.

Certain features of the music itself were generally understood to impose equality. Corrette (1741) and one or two others cited specific instances in chaconnes and passacailles where typical upbeat patterns throw an accent on normally unequal quavers, thus equalizing them. It is probably of such rhythms that certain writers were thinking when they forbade inequality in situations where normally unequal values were mixed with smaller ones (see ex.2). When the inequality descended to the smaller values, a question arose as to the treatment of the

Ex.2 Lully: *Armide*, passacaille, Act 5 scene ii

theoretically unequal ones. Common sense and several sources indicate that they would become equal, but some (e.g. Démoz de La Salle, 1728) seem to imply that they remained unequal. They do not comment on the odd rhythms that would result from simultaneous inequality at two or three levels.

Certain theorists associated inequality with conjunct motion and equality with disjunct, saying that normally unequal notes became equal when the melody moved by leap (see ex.3). The reasons probably had something

Ex.3 Montéclair: *Nouvelle méthode* (Paris, 1709), p.15

to do with the individual emphasis that each note receives in this kind of line, and also with the resemblance of such lines to those of Italian allegros, which were typically combined with smaller running values in such a way as to make inequality impossible. *Batteries* (i.e. arpeggios and broken-chord figures such as those in Couperin's *Le tic-toc-choc* from the *Troisième livre*) are also to be played equally. Inequality in disjunct melodies certainly existed, but it was usually written out and possibly sharper than the usual kind (see, for example,

Couperin's *Les guirlandes* in the *Quatrième livre*). Shifts between conjunct and disjunct motion within the same piece may or may not signal corresponding shifts between inequality and equality. A piece such as the courante from Rameau's *Nouvelles suites* (c1728), in which overdotting of the principal motif is established by inequality in the accompanying part at the beginning and then cast into doubt by strongly disjunct contexts later on, raises questions which each player must answer for himself (see ex.4).

Ex.4 Rameau: *Nouvelles suites de pièces de clavecin* (Paris, c1728), Courante p.4

Reprise

Modern discussions of inequality often list additional contra-indications which are either based on a single, usually dubious source or are outright fabrications: the presence of syncopated notes (Lacassagne, 1766, as reported in Borrel, 1934); the presence of rests of the same value as the notes in question (Borrel); the fact that the notes are in an accompanying part (Emy de L'Ilette, c1810, as reported in Borrel); allemandes (Dolmetsch's misreading of the sources, 1915); repeated notes, slurs over more than two notes, and motion that is too fast (Quantz, 1752, as reported by Borrel and others); motion that is too slow (Saint-Lambert, 1702, as reported by Donington, 3/1974). None of these has the force of a rule and most are refuted by the sources. Only the long slur seems at times to be intended to cancel pairing and to suggest to the player that only the first note should be emphasized.

Reverse inequality (i.e. short–long alteration) had a shadowy existence in France. It was mentioned as an afterthought by Loulié (1696, p.71) that in 3 the first halves of beats may be made shorter than the second halves; most theorists are silent on the subject. François Couperin's sign for it was a dot over the second of two slurred quavers (*Premier livre*). There was no special term; 'couler', which Donington and others have taken for one, simply refers to the slur and has no rhythmic significance. Couperin's example and explanation were copied by Pierre-Claude Foucquet (*Les caractères de la Paix*, 1749), while Dupuits (1741) used a slur with the dot over the first note. Both signs are extremely rare.

Alteration of ternary groups was generally discouraged, most writers who discussed them at all expressly excluding it from triplets or the quavers in 6/8 etc. But Mercadier de Belesta (1776) and a few others allowed the first note to be lengthened at the expense of the second, producing the rhythm of a French gigue. A topic which is often improperly included in discussions of *notes inégales* is the assimilation of duple to triple rhythm (*see* DOTTED RHYTHMS). That this was a widespread habit in all countries in the Baroque period cannot be disputed.

But there is a fundamental difference between this kind of alteration and *notes inégales* as defined in this article. The long–short pairing that results cannot vary with the requirements of embellishment or expression, since it must be synchronized with a rhythm that already exists elsewhere in the texture; it does not add a fresh nuance; and its origin and purpose are different (see Collins, 1966). The performance of gigues in 4/4 time or other duple metres raises problems of rhythmic alteration which are again not those of *notes inégales*. Such gigues are found in considerable numbers in England, France and Germany; the best known are those in Bach's First French Suite and Sixth Partita for harpsichord. Although it is virtually certain that radical rhythmic alteration was sometimes demanded by this notation, in the 17th century the purpose and results were something other than embellishment or expression. Except for McIntyre's study (1965) this topic remains largely unexplored.

The classification of notes into metrically strong and weak ones was a feature of music theory in all countries throughout the 17th and 18th centuries and has occasioned enormous difficulties for those who argue about *notes inégales*. Notes on first beats, first parts of any beat, or first parts of parts were strong in relation to a succeeding note of similar value. Thus notes whose value was half that of the next larger metrical unit (this would exclude, for example, quavers in 6/8) proceeded in strong–weak pairs beginning at the bar-line. At first glance the system appears to have much in common with the convention of inequality, but the differences are fundamental. The strong–weak classification applied to notes of any value in any style, and it was an analytical distinction independent of performance. The terminology varied: the French said 'first' and 'second' or 'strong' and 'weak'; the Italians 'good' and 'bad'; the Germans any of these and also 'intrinsically long' and 'intrinsically short'. Walther's explanation ('Quantitas notarum', *Musicalisches Lexicon*, 1732) of these last invites misunderstanding: 'according to [its extrinsic quantity], each note is equal in length to similar ones in performance; according to [its intrinsic quantity], however, [the notes are] of unequal length' – i.e. they are defined metrically as long and short even though they are played equal (for the opposite interpretation see Collins, 1967, p.483). French writers made it clear that inequality and the strong–weak distinction were two different things. The former was restricted in application, decorative or expressive, and easily heard; the second was universal, structural, and need not be heard at all, though attention to it enhanced performance.

The relation between *notes inégales* and what may be called, after Quantz, the 'splendid style' (used to represent 'das Prächtige'), whose most familiar manifestation is the first half of the French overture, has never been adequately discussed. Whereas *notes inégales* were a way of enlivening the ornamental passages of a musical core, the splendid style was a characteristic of the core itself (*see* DOTTED RHYTHMS). The dotting was not confined to small note values but operated at higher metrical levels, including the beat, and it was always smartly articulated, never subtle. Neither was the splendid style necessarily French (although the convention of *notes inégales* allowed the French to leave the smaller values undotted, as in the Offertory from François Couperin's *Messe des paroisses*); examples may be found in Lorenzo Allegri's *Primo libro delle musiche* (1618; see Beck, 1964). At the higher metrical levels the dotting had to be written out in France as elsewhere, and the contrast between long and short notes was exaggerated to give an effect of great energy.

The unequal melismas of the Renaissance were adopted by the early Baroque concertato, which itself engendered a new instrumental dotted style involving repeated notes (see Monteverdi's six-part *Magnificat* for examples of the first, and his *Sonata sopra Sancta Maria* for the second). From these two elements a 'dotted manner' appears to have developed along a separate path from *notes inégales* or the 'splendid style', resulting in a long line of sometimes obsessively dotted pieces as diverse as the second partita from Biber's *Harmonia artificiosa-ariosa*, Contrapunctus II from Bach's *Art of Fugue*, sonatas by Benedetto Marcello and even the second movement of Schumann's *Phantasie* op.17. The chief characteristic of this style is a relentless nervous energy quite unlike the grace or piquancy which is the normal effect of *notes inégales*; nevertheless there must have been some interaction between the two styles in the 17th century and it is not now possible to draw a clean line between them. Bach's Contrapunctus VI is marked 'Im Stile francese', but since the underlying contrapuntal tissue is as unlike as possible what a French composer would have written, the persistent dotting at the level of the quaver sounds far more Germanic or Italian than French; only the *tirades* and other appurtenances of the 'splendid style' at a higher metrical level carry out the promise of the superscription. The semiquaver motion, which begins to dominate about halfway through, would have been unequal in a French piece; if what Bach intended for it were known, an understanding of his attitude towards *notes inégales* would be clearer.

3. THEORETICAL AND MECHANICAL EVIDENCE. Although the history of *notes inégales* may stretch back to the modal rhythms of the Middle Ages, the first explicit description was by Loys Bourgeois (1550), who explained it in its essential features as an embellishment of diminutions, linked to metre. Similar though less detailed references are to be found in Spanish treatises by Tomás de Santa Maria (1565) and Cerone (1613), and there are examples of dotted diminutions in Ortiz (1553), Ganassi dal Fontego (1535), Conforti (1593) and other manuals. Chailley's thesis (1960) that inequality arose from French declamation cannot be sustained, since it was typically applied not to succession of syllables but to decorative prolongations of single syllables. Furthermore the Spaniards, whose language was spoken very differently from French, wrote of it in the same terms. There are sporadic references to both long–short and short–long inequality in Italian sources of the first half of the 17th century (Caccini, 1601/2; Frescobaldi, 1615; Puliaschi, 1618) and brief mentions of the normal kind by Bernhard (1657) and Burwell (c1660–70). If the momentum of unequal diminution established in the 16th century continued in the art of performers, it was largely undocumented by theorists. But shortly after the mid-17th century the French descriptions began, to continue without interruption almost until the Revolution. These were supplemented by strong evidence for the practice in England and the Low Countries, and by much less clear evidence for Italy and Germany. The Italians in particular seemed inclined as much towards reverse inequality as towards the usual kind, in the mid-18th century as well as in the early 17th. Scheibe attributed its invention to Tartini (*Compendium musices*, MS, 1728–36; see

Benary, 1960); it became a cliché of the *galant* style and Burney complained of it.

Except for scattered echoes, *notes inégales* disappeared from French theory and pedagogy towards the end of the 18th century; they had never been a regular feature of theory or pedagogy elsewhere. The practice of inequality was far broader, however, and it persisted in various ways well into the 19th century.

4. APPLICATION OUTSIDE FRANCE. Whether the conventions of *notes inégales* should be applied to the music of non-French composers, particularly J. S. Bach, is a question which has engaged the attention of scholars and performers ever since Dolmetsch (1915) recommended it for parts of Handel's *Messiah* and Bach's *St Matthew Passion*. After World War II a number of writers (Babitz, Donington, Dürr, Geoffroy-Dechaume, Sachs and others) took up and enlarged on Dolmetsch's views, analysing early fingering, bowing and tonguing, amassing instances of passages in both dotted and undotted versions, and combing the theorists in order to show that inequality was a normal resource of Baroque music in all countries (though not in all styles), and therefore that one might, should or must – depending on the recklessness of the argument – sometimes alter evenly written notes in non-French music. Then Frederick Neumann (1965) dismantled the entire structure of post-Dolmetsch research on inequality, piece by piece. This unleashed a controversy lasting several years during which the 'left', represented chiefly by Donington, Collins and Babitz (in order of increasingly vehement advocacy of a broad application of *notes inégales*), were stimulated to uncover a great deal of new evidence in their favour, while Neumann on the 'right' resolutely defended Germany and Bach against the alien taint by discrediting their authorities and refuting their evidence. The entire controversy, though distorted by arbitrary assumptions on both sides (especially the assumption that *notes inégales* are by definition written equal) and weighted down by futile struggles over isolated authorities such as Quantz, is indispensable reading for anyone wishing to pursue the subject.

The real issue was not whether Bach and other non-French composers used *notes inégales* – countless scores show that they did. Although never clearly stated, the issue was rather whether they ever failed to write them out when they wanted them. The evidence is different for different countries. Purcell's normal treatment of running quavers in 3/4 time was to dot them (examples include 'Thou tun'st this world' and 'The Airy Violin' from the *Saint Cecilia Ode*, 1692). English harpsichord music from Locke onwards is full of written inequality, most commonly in preludes and allemandes (Alcock, Clarke, Croft, Felton, Gunn, Richard Jones, Moss, Nares, Roseingrave [Introduction to Scarlatti's sonatas], J. C. Smith, Symonds); pieces by G. B. Draghi and Handel (e.g. the opening movements of the sixth, seventh and eighth 'great' suites) are in this tradition. But unwritten inequality too is suggested by multiple versions of pieces from Jenkins to Handel (Johnson, 1967, found that the most frequent discrepancy in mid-17th-century English ensemble manuscripts involved even quaver figures in one source appearing as dotted figures in another), and dotting was explicitly recommended by Burwell in her instruction book for the lute (MS, c1660–70; see Dart, 1958) and by North – 'tho' not express'd', to give 'a life and spirit to the stroke' (see Wilson, 1959). Whether these references are to isolated pairs or continuous inequality is not certain; but Corrette (1735), who had been to England, clearly meant the latter when he stipulated that quavers were to be dotted in English 'vaudevilles and contredances' in 6/4, such as *Bartholomew Fair, Hunt the Squirrel, Lilliburlero* and *Hoopt Pettycoat*. Versions of pieces by Handel for automatic instruments also show some added inequality, both in the scores (Squire, 1919) and on the instruments themselves, for instance the last movement of op.4 no.2 on a late 18th-century barrel organ (Fuller, 1974 and 1980). In 1771 Anselm Bayly advised unequal quavers as possible in an anthem by Greene (see Pont, 1966).

The French influence was strong in Belgium and the Netherlands, not only in French-speaking regions but among the Dutch as well, as can be seen from the correspondence of Constantijn Huygens from the mid-17th century and the activity of the Amsterdam presses later on. A treatise in Dutch by Frischmuth (1758) specified unequal semiquavers for allemandes and unequal quavers for courantes.

French dance music had become thoroughly naturalized in Italy by the 1660s, as specific labels and styles of pieces by Uccellini, Giuseppe Columbi, G. M. Bononcini (i) and G. B. Vitali show – the aria and allemande especially being frequently dotted (Klenz, 1962). The recommendations of Frescobaldi and others and the Italian propensity for short–long patterns have been noted. Lorenzoni (1779), who cited Loulié, Rousseau and Quantz, recommended normal inequality to enhance the distinction between 'good' and 'bad' notes, and many more clues to rhythmic alteration have been collected by Collins, Pont, Donington and others. But none of this adds up to an expected norm of inequality, and certain typical italianisms expressly demanded that at least the quavers should be even, as in 'walking' basses and vigorous allegros. French authors disagreed with each other and sometimes with themselves about Italian music. In *L'école d'Orphée* (1738) Corrette said of the metre ¢ that it was 'much in use in Italian music. . . . The quavers are played equal and second semiquavers are hurried'. A similar rule (i.e. specifying unequal semiquavers) was given for 3/8 time, and Handel, Giovanni Bononcini, Pepusch, Alessandro Scarlatti and Porpora were cited for examples. At the same time the French 3 with unequal quavers was distinguished from the Italian 3/4 with unequal semiquavers. In Corrette's flute tutor (c1742) the wording was much the same, except that 'semiquavers are also sometimes played equally in the allegros and prestos of sonatas and concertos'. In his cello method (1741) the reference to unequal semiquavers in 3/4 was dropped, and the courante from Corelli's op.5 no.7 was cited as a piece in 3/4 where the quavers must be equal – not a contradiction but a shift of emphasis.

François Couperin (1716) said firmly that the Italians wrote their music as they intended it to sound, while the French dotted conjunct quavers in performance; yet he wrote a 'courante a l'italiéne' in conjunct quavers and marked it 'pointé-coulé' (*Concerts royaux*, 1722). Loulié (1696), Brossard (1703) and Rousseau (1768) excluded inequality from Italian music; others besides Corrette seem to admit it (Mussard, 1779; Rollet, 1760). Azaïs (1776) wrote that foreigners in France played unequal quavers in 3/4. The uncertainty about foreign music must have reflected a diversity of practice among musicians in Paris. There are so many imponderables – not least

the possibility that some visiting Italians may have tried to please French audiences by adopting their style of playing – that it is advisable to keep an open mind on the subject. In French music composed under Italian influence the situation was still more complicated, as there were real efforts at stylistic synthesis from Lully onwards. What Couperin expected from his players in *Les goûts réunis*, and what Mondonville meant when he wrote that in his pieces for harpsichord with voice (1747) one must 'distinguish the phrases which are in French style from those which require the Italian style', are among the problems posed.

French dancing-masters, musicians and their music spread over Germany from the early 17th century, and knowledge of French performing style kept pace. In 1664 Johann Caspar Horn published five ballets 'to be played in French style', and much later Marpurg (1749) remarked on how Quantz, Benda and Graun played 'in a very French manner'. Georg Muffat (1698) explained *notes inégales* clearly and authoritatively to the Germans, and direct French influence on Froberger, Buxtehude, Kusser, J. C. F. Fischer, J. S. Bach and a legion of others is documented. The French overture became an obsession; Telemann is estimated to have composed some 1000 overture-suites. Yet although Printz (1678) recommended inequality as a device to keep the tempo under control, and C. P. E. Bach (1753–62) as a way to treat two semiquavers following a quaver in the accompaniment of an adagio, only one German writer besides Muffat treated the convention in terms approaching those of the French, that is, as a normal way of playing a substantial amount of music; this was Quantz (1752). As he did not say that his remarks applied only to French music – indeed they include no mention of French music at all – his passage has acquired a kind of scriptural status for those who wish to alter even rhythms in Bach, and it has become a principal target of attack by the right. But even the most subtle exegesis cannot make Quantz say that Bach wished his rhythms to be altered in performance; the most that can be concluded is that Quantz himself might have played Bach that way, and perhaps that the trio sonata from *The Musical Offering* was subjected to inequality when (or if) it was played at Potsdam. On the other hand the best efforts of a Frederick Neumann can produce nothing but silence to prove that Bach did not want alteration.

For the modern performer the best advice on playing Bach is to keep in mind the details of the music: the shape of the motifs and the 'inner length' of the 'good' and 'bad' notes. If the result of these attentions is inequality, then no-one can say it is wrong. Even in French music, however, where inequality is mandatory, it should never be rigid; Cossart-Cotte (1974) found only one example of consistent inequality in 500 samples taken from mechanical instruments (see also Fuller, 1974). *Notes inégales* are decorative, expressive and spontaneous.

Modern discussions of inequality in Baroque music often conclude with an appeal to 'good taste' as the final arbiter in good performance. The idea comes directly from innumerable similar appeals by 18th-century French writers, and is dangerously misleading. It is indeed taste that decides, but the taste of the period when the music was written. Alien taste is laboriously acquired, and never completely so except by imitation; one need only imagine with what degree of authenticity some future musician might succeed in reproducing the 'taste' of a Charlie

Parker from written documents alone. Taste is the most inconstant of values, and it was a conflict of taste far more than of objective findings which lay at the root of the inequality controversy of the 1960s and fuelled its partisan zeal.

5. JAZZ. *Notes inégales* may have lived on in France after the 18th century in the semi-popular styles of *opéra comique*; in any case they reappear in a context far removed from the elegance of the *ancien régime* (though not nearly so far from the French opera of New Orleans) – in American jazz. Here they permeate a living tradition of improvised diminution whose rhythmic conventions are remarkably reminiscent of the old French code. Jazz is organized rhythmically in layers corresponding to chord changes at each half-bar or larger unit, a crotchet beat, and a melodic line in mostly smaller values. Inequality operates only at the last level, but there it is virtually omnipresent on duple subdivisions of the beat, even when the motion is extremely rapid. The characteristic syncopation of jazz is the result of a rhythmic shift of the syncopated note corresponding to the displacement of metrically weak values caused by the inequality. As with the old code, the degree of inequality is freely variable (there was a tendency in earlier jazz for the inequality to be more pronounced; this also varied with the tempo – the faster, the milder). But with the exception of triplets, quintuplets etc, which are played evenly, strict equality must be expressly demanded in a written part by some direction like 'straight eighths' – an exact American equivalent for 'croches égales'. On wind instruments passage-work is generally legato, and it is a highly characteristic feature of jazz that second notes of pairs are softer than first ones unless deliberately accented. Although 'solos' are improvised, they are often transcribed from recordings for purposes of study and teaching; such transcriptions rarely show the inequality, and yet no musicians would think of playing the notes in their exact values. To do so would be to negate the style of the music.

BIBLIOGRAPHY

WaltherML

S. di Ganassi dal Fontego: *Opera intitulata Fontegara* (Venice, 1535/R1934 and 1970; Eng. trans., 1959)
L. Bourgeois: *Le droict chemin de musique* (Geneva, 1550/R1954)
D. Ortiz: *Trattado de glosas* (Rome, 1553); ed. M. Schneider (Berlin, 1913, 2/1936/R1961)
T. de Santa Maria: *Libro llamado Arte de tañer fantasia* (Valladolid, 1565/R1972)
G. L. Conforti: *Breve e facile maniera d'essercitarsi . . . a far passaggi* (Rome, ?1593/R1922)
G. Diruta: *Il Transilvano* (Venice, 1593–1609/R1969)
G. B. Bovicelli: *Regole, passaggi di musica* (Venice, 1594/R1957)
G. Caccini: *Le nuove musiche* (Florence, 1601/2/R1973); ed. H. W. Hitchcock (Madison, 1970)
P. Cerone: *El melopeo y maestro* (Naples, 1613/R1969)
G. Frescobaldi: *Toccate e partite d'intavolatura di cimbalo* (Rome, 1615); prefaces in *SartoriB*; Eng. trans. in A. Dolmetsch: *The Interpretation of the Music of the Seventeenth and Eighteenth Centuries* (London, 1915, 2/1944/R1969)
G. D. Puliaschi: *Musiche varie a una voce* (Rome, 1618)
C. Bernhard: *Tractatus compositionis augmentatus* (MS, 1657); pr. in J. Müller-Blattau: *Die Kompositionslehre Heinrich Schützens* (Leipzig, 1926, 2/1963)
G.-G. Nivers: *Livre d'orgue* (Paris, 1665)
B. de Bacilly: *Remarques curieuses sur l'art de bien chanter* (Paris, 1668, 3/1679/R1971, 4/1681; Eng. trans., 1968)
W. Printz: *Musica modulatoria vocalis* (Schweidnitz, 1678)
Perrine: *Pieces de luth en musique* (Paris, 1680)
N. Gigault: *Livre de musique* (Paris, 1683)
J. Rousseau: *Traité de la viole* (Paris, 1687/R1975)
A. Raison: *Livre d'orgue* (Paris, 1688)
G. Jullien: *Premier livre d'orgue* (Paris, 1690)

Anon.: *Manière de toucher lorgue* (MS, F-Pa 3042, ff.100–19, c1690); pr. in W. Pruitt: 'Un traité d'interprétation du XVIIe siècle', *L'orgue* (1974), no.152, p.99
M. L'Affilard: *Principes très-faciles pour bien apprendre la musique* (Paris, 1694, 5/1705/R1971, 11/1747)
G. Muffat: *Florilegium primum* (Augsburg, 1695)
E. Loulié: *Eléments ou principes de musique* (Paris, 1696, 2/1698/R1971; Eng. trans., 1965)
G. Muffat: *Florilegium secundum* (Passau, 1698)
M. Marais: *Pièces de violes* [2e livre] (Paris, 1701/R1972)
M. de Saint-Lambert: *Les principes du clavecin* (Paris, 1702/R1972)
S. de Brossard: *Dictionaire de musique* (Paris, 1703/R1964)
J. Hotteterre: *Principes de la flûte traversière* (Paris, 1707, 7/1741; Eng. trans., 1968)
M. P. de Montéclair: *Nouvelle méthode pour aprendre la musique* (Paris, 1709)
——: *Méthode facile pour aprendre à jouer du violon* (1711–12)
F. Couperin: *L'art de toucher le clavecin* (Paris, 1716, 2/1717/R1969; Eng. trans., 1974)
H. B. Dupont: *Principes de musique par demandes et par réponces* (Paris, 1718)
J. Hotteterre: *L'art de préluder* (Paris, 1719)
Borin: *La musique théorique et pratique* (Paris, 1722)
Démoz de La Salle: *Méthode de musique selon un nouveau système* (Paris, 1728)
M. Corrette: *Méthode pour apprendre aisément à jouer de la flûte traversière* (Paris, 1735; Eng. trans. in C. Farrar: *Michel Corrette and Flute Playing in the Eighteenth Century*, Brooklyn, 1970)
Vague: *L'art d'apprendre la musique* (Paris, 1733)
A. de Villeneuve: *Nouvelle méthode . . . pour apprendre la musique et les agréments du chant* (Paris, 1733, 2/1756)
M. P. de Montéclair: *Petite méthode pour apprendre la musique aux enfans* (Paris, c1735)
——: *Principes de musique* (Paris, 1736/R1972)
J. A. de La Chapelle: *Les vrais principes de la musique* (Paris, 1736–52)
F. David: *Méthode nouvelle ou Principes généraux pour apprendre facilement la musique* (Paris, 1737)
J. Hotteterre: *Méthode pour la musette* (Paris, 1737/R1977)
M. Corrette: *L'école d'Orphée* (Paris, 1738/R1973)
——: *Méthode théorique et pratique pour apprendre en peu de tems le violoncelle* (Paris, 1741/R1972)
J.-B. Dupuits: *Principes pour toucher de la vièle* (Paris, 1741)
P. Duval: *Méthode agréable et utile pour apprendre facilement à chanter juste avec goût et précision* (Paris, 1741, ?2/1775/R1972)
F. C. X. Vyon: *La musique pratique et théorique* (Paris, 1742, 2/1744)
P. Denis: *Nouveau système de musique pratique* (Paris, 1747)
M. Corrette: *Méthode pour apprendre facilement à jouer du pardessus de viole* (Paris, 1748)
F. W. Marpurg: *Der critische Musicus an der Spree* (Berlin, 15 April 1749/R1970)
C. Buterne: *Méthode pour apprendre la musique vocale et instrumentale* (Rouen, 1752)
J. J. Quantz: *Versuch einer Anweisung die Flöte traversiere zu spielen* (Berlin, 1752, 3/1789/R1953; Eng. trans., 1966)
C. P. E. Bach: *Versuch über die wahre Art das Clavier zu spielen* (Berlin, 1753–62, 2/1787–97/R1957; Eng. trans., 1949)
A. J. Dumas: *L'art de la musique* (Paris, 1753)
T. Bordet: *Méthode raisonnée pour apprendre la musique* (Paris, 1755)
L. Mozart: *Versuch einer gründlichen Violinschule* (Augsburg, 1756/R1956, 3/1787/R1968; Eng. trans., 1948, 2/1951)
P. Denis: *Nouvelle méthode pour apprendre en peu de tems la musique et l'art de chanter* (Paris, 1757)
M. Corrette: *Le parfait maître à chanter* (Paris, 1758, 2/1782)
L. Frischmuth: *Gedagten over de beginselen en onder wyzingen des clavecimbaals* (Amsterdam, 1758)
H. L. Choquel: *La musique rendue sensible par la méchanique* (Paris, 1759, 2/1762/R1972)
Anon.: *Nouvelle méthode pour apprendre à jouer du violon* (n.p., c1760)
L. C. Bordier: *Nouvelle méthode de musique* (Paris, 1760)
Morel de Lescer: *Science de la musique vocale* (Paris, c1760)
Rollet: *Méthode pour apprendre la musique sans transposition* (Paris, 1760)
Boüin: *La vielleuse habile* (Paris, 1761)
Anon.: *Elémens de musique* (MS, F-V, after 1761)
C. R. Brijon: *Réflexions sur la musique et la vraie manière de l'exécuter sur le violon* (Paris, 1763/R1972)
P. Duval: *Principes de la musique pratique par demandes et par réponses* (Paris, 1764)
J. Lacassagne: *Traité général des élémens du chant* (Paris, 1766/R1972)
J.-J. Rousseau: *Dictionnaire de musique* (Paris and Amsterdam, 1768/R1969; Eng. trans., c1775)

Dard: *Nouveaux principes de musique* (Paris, 1769)

P.-J. Roussier: *Méthode de musique sur un nouveau plan* (Paris, 1769)

A. Bailleux: *Méthode pour apprendre facilement la musique vocale et instrumentale* (Paris, 1770)

A. Bayly: *A Practical Treatise on Singing and Playing* (London, 1771)

A.-F. Cajon: *Elémens de musique avec des leçons à une et 2 voix* (Paris, 1772)

Raparlier: *Principes de musique, les agréments du chant* (Lille, 1772/R1972)

T. J. Tarade: *Traité du violon* (Paris, c1774, 2/?1777–9/R1972)

Anon.: *Principes de musique* (Paris, 1775) [unique copy in *US-NH*]

M. D. J. Engramelle: *La tonotechnie ou l'art de noter les cylindres* (Paris, 1775/R1971)

C. F. A. Pollet: *Méthode pour apprendre à pincer du cistre ou guittare allemande* (Paris, c1775)

F. Roussel: *Le guide musical* (Paris, 1775)

Torlez: *Méthode de musique* (Paris, c1775)

H. Azaïs: *Méthode de musique sur un nouveau plan* (Sorèze, 1776)

J.-B. Mercadier de Belesta: *Nouveau système de musique théorique et pratique* (Paris, 1776)

F. Bédos de Celles: *L'art du facteur d'orgues*, iv (Paris, 1778/R1966)

A. Lorenzoni: *Saggio per ben sonare il flauto traverso* (Vicenza, 1779/R1969)

Mussard: *Nouveau principes pour apprendre à jouer de la flutte traversière* (Paris, 1779)

C. R. Brijon: *L'Apollon moderne* (Lyons, 1780)

M. Corette: *L'art de se perfectionner dans le violon . . . suite de L'école d'Orphée* (Paris, 1782/R1973)

P. Marcou: *Elémens théoriques et pratiques de musique* (London and Paris, 1782)

M. Corrette: *La belle vielleuse* (Paris, 1783/R1977)

Cleret fils: *Principes de musique vocale*; *Principes de musique* (MSS, *F-Pn*, 1786)

Anon.: *Méthode de harpe* (Paris, c1787)

A. F. Emy de L'Ilette: *Théorie musicale* (Paris, c1810)

E. Borrel: *Contribution à l'interprétation de la musique française au XVIIIe siècle* (Paris, 1914)

A. Dolmetsch: *The Interpretation of the Music of the Seventeenth and Eighteenth Centuries* (London, 1915, 2/1944/R1969)

W. B. Squire: 'Handel's Clock Music', *MQ*, v (1919), 538

J. Arger: *Les agréments et le rhythme* (Paris, 1921)

B. Bruck: *Wandlungen des Begriffs Tempo rubato* (diss., U. of Erlangen, 1928)

E. Borrel: 'Les notes inégales dans l'ancienne musique française', *RdM*, xii (1931), 278

——: *L'interprétation de la musique française de Lully à la Révolution* (Paris, 1934)

S. Babitz: 'A Problem of Rhythm in Baroque Music', *MQ*, xxxviii (1952), 533–65

C. Sachs: *Rhythm and Tempo* (New York, 1953)

H.-P. Schmitz: *Die Tontechnik des Père Engramelle* (Kassel, 1953)

T. Dart: *The Interpretation of Music* (London, 1954, 4/1967)

A. Dürr: *J. S. Bach: Magnificat*, Neue Ausgabe sämtlicher Werke, II/3, *Kritischer Bericht* (Kassel, 1955), 46

E. Borrel: 'A propos des "Nottes inégales"', *RdM*, xli (1958), 87

T. Dart: 'Miss Mary Burwell's Instruction Book for the Lute', *GSJ*, xi (1958), 3–62

N. Powell: *Rhythmic Freedom in the Performance of French Music from 1650 to 1735* (diss., Stanford U., 1958)

B. Seagrave: *The French Style of Violin Bowing and Phrasing from Lully to Jacques Aubert (1650–1730)* (diss., Stanford U., 1958)

E. Harich-Schneider: 'Über die Angleichung nachschlagender Sechzehntel an Triolen', *Mf*, xii (1959), 35

J. Wilson, ed.: *Roger North on Music* (London, 1959)

P. Benary: *Die deutsche Kompositionslehre des 18. Jahrhunderts* (Leipzig, 1960)

E. Bodky: *The Interpretation of Bach's Keyboard Works* (Cambridge, Mass., 1960)

J. Chailley: 'A propos des notes inégales', *RdM*, xlv (1960), 89

R. Donington: *Tempo and Rhythm in Bach's Organ Music* (London, 1960)

E. Jacob: 'Über die Angleichung nachschlagender Sechszehntel an Triolen', *Mf*, xiii (1960), 268

S. Babitz: 'On Using J. S. Bach's Keyboard Fingerings', *ML*, xliii (1962), 123

W. Klenz: *Giovanni Maria Bononcini of Modena* (Durham, North Carolina, 1962)

R. Donington: *The Interpretation of Early Music* (London, 1963, rev. 3/1974)

M.-C. Alain: 'Appunti sulla maniera francese', *L'organo*, v (1964–7), 6

H. Beck: *Die Suite*, Mw, xxvi (1964; Eng. trans., 1966)

A. Geoffroy-Dechaume: *Les 'secrets' de la musique ancienne* (Paris, 1964)

T. E. Warner: *Indications of Performance Practice in Woodwind Instruction Books of the 17th and 18th Centuries* (diss., New York U., 1964)

D. Boyden: *The History of Violin Playing from its Origins to 1761* (London, 1965)

R. McIntyre: 'On the Interpretation of Bach's Gigues', *MQ*, li (1965), 478

F. Neumann: 'La note pointée et le soi-disant "manière française"', *RdM*, li (1965), 66

——: 'The French *Inégales*, Quantz, and Bach', *JAMS*, xviii (1965), 313–58

M. Collins: 'The Performance of Triplets in the 17th and 18th Centuries', *JAMS*, xix (1966), 281–328 [see also R. Donington, F. Neumann, G. Pont, ibid, 112, 435, 437]

F. Neumann: 'External Evidence and Uneven Notes', *MQ*, lii (1966), 448

S. Babitz: 'Concerning the Length of Time that Every Note must be Held', *MR*, xxviii (1967), 21

S. Babitz, J. Byrt and M. Collins: 'Three Further Views on Notes Inégales', *JAMS*, xx (1967), 473

R. Donington: 'A Problem of Inequality', *MQ*, liii (1967), 503

J. T. Johnson: 'How to "Humour" John Jenkins' Three-part Dances', *JAMS*, xx (1967), 197

F. Neumann: 'The Use of Baroque Treatises on Musical Performance', *ML*, xlviii (1967), 315

T. E. Warner: *An Annotated Bibliography of Woodwind Instruction Books, 1600–1830* (Detroit, 1967)

S. Babitz: 'Restoring Baroque Inequality', *American Recorder*, ix (1968), 7

S. Babitz and G. Pont: 'Early Music Laboratory Discussion Letter', *Discussion Letters*, i (1969)

S. Babitz: 'On Using Early Keyboard Fingering', *The Diapason*, lx (1969), no.3, p.15; no.4, p.21; no.5, p.21 [see also P. le Huray, ibid, no.7, p.10; no.8, p.14; no.9, p.10]

M. Collins: 'A Reconsideration of French Overdotting', *ML*, l (1969), 111

J. Fesperman: 'Rhythmic Alteration in Eighteenth-century French Keyboard Music', *Organ Institute Quarterly*, ix (1969)

E. Shay: *Notes inégales and François Couperin's Messe à l'usage des paroisses* (diss., U. of Cincinnati, 1969)

S. Babitz: *The Great Baroque Hoax* (Los Angeles, 1970)

W. Kolneder: *Georg Muffat zur Aufführungspraxis* (Strasbourg, 1970)

H. Schott: *Playing the Harpsichord* (New York, 1971)

J. C. Casell: *Rhythmic Inequality and Tempo in French Music between 1650 and 1740* (diss., U. of Minnesota, 1973)

B. B. Mather: *Interpretation of French Music from 1675 to 1775* (New York, 1973)

F. Cossart-Cotte: ' "Documents sonores" de la fin du XVIIIe siècle: leurs enseignements pour l'interprétation', *L'interprétation de la musique française aux XVIIe et XVIIIe siècles*, ed. E. Weber (Paris, 1974), 139

D. Fuller: 'Mechanical Musical Instruments as a Source for the Study of *Notes inégales*', *Bulletin of the Musical Box Society (International)*, xx (1974), 281

W. Pruitt: 'Un traité d'interprétation du XVIIe siècle', *L'orgue* (1974), no.152, p.99

J. Saint-Arroman: 'Les inégalités', *L'interprétation de la musique française aux XVIIe et XVIIIe siècles*, ed. E. Weber (Paris, 1974), 67

D. Fuller: 'Dotting, the "French Style" and Frederick Neumann's Counter-reformation', *Early Music*, v (1977), 517

F. Neumann: *Ornamentation in Baroque and Post-Baroque Music, with Special Emphasis on J.S. Bach* (Princeton, 1978)

D. Fuller: *Mechanical Musical Instruments as a Source for the Study of Notes Inégales* (Cleveland, 1979)

D. Fuller, ed.: *G. F. Handel: Two Ornamental Organ Concertos as Played by an Early Barrel Organ* (Hackensack, NJ, 1980)

D. Fuller: 'Analyzing the Performance of a Barrel Organ', *Organ Yearbook*, xi (1980), 104

W. Malloch: 'The Earl of Bute's Machine Organ: a Touchstone of Taste', *Early Music*, xi (1983), 172

D. Fuller: 'The "Dotted Style" in Bach, Handel and Scarlatti', *Bach, Handel and Scarlatti*, ed. P. Williams (Cambridge, 1985)

DAVID FULLER

Notstok. Colloquial Scandinavian term for the PSALMODIKON.

Novachord. A keyboard instrument resembling an ELECTRONIC ORGAN, developed by Laurens Hammond and C. N. Williams and manufactured by the Hammond Organ Co. in Chicago from 1939; it was discontinued during World War II. Designed to follow up the success of the company's electronic organ, the Novachord has a six-octave console resembling that of a square piano. The sounds are generated by 12 oscillators using frequency division – the Novachord was probably the first commercial instrument to adopt such a system, which has since been used in many types of electronic organ. Like the Hammond Solovox, the Novachord uses vibrating reeds to produce two different speeds of vibrato by modulating the frequency of each oscillator. 14 controls, mounted on a vertical panel above the keyboard, affect timbre, attack (which ranges from 'percussion' to 'singing'), decay and vibrato. Three pedals control volume and sustain; a fourth pedal permits the operation of the sustain by either foot.

The Novachord was sometimes known as an 'electrical orchestra' because of its ability to imitate the sounds of most orchestral instruments, as well as the harpsichord and piano; it was also capable of producing a range of new sounds. In May 1939 Ferde Grofé presented a Novachord orchestra (four Novachords and one Hammond organ) at the New York World Fair, and a Novachord was included in Tom Adrian Cracraft's All Electronic Orchestra. The Novachord was used in film scores and (together with an electric piano) in Hanns Eisler's *Kammersinfonie* (1940, originally written as the soundtrack for the film *Eis/White Flood*, which did not appear until 1943). Its initial popularity was not sustained, partly owing to the instability of its approximately 160 valves.

BIBLIOGRAPHY
F. D. Merrill jr: 'The Novachord', *Electronics*, xii/11 (1939), 16
S. K. Lewer: *Electronic Musical Instruments* (London, 1948), 36
A. Douglas: *The Electronic Musical Instrument Manual: a Guide to Theory and Design* (London, 5/1968), 213
T. L. Rhea: *The Evolution of Electronic Musical Instruments in the United States* (diss., George Peabody College, Nashville, Tenn., 1972), 163; section rev. as 'The Novachord', *Contemporary Keyboard*, v/1 (1979), 62
HUGH DAVIES

Novatron. *See* MELLOTRON.

Nqangala. Unbraced mouth-resonated MUSICAL BOW of the Ngoni people of south-eastern Africa. It is played only by women. *See also* UMQANGALA.

Nruas tuag [nruas dab]. Single-headed cylindrical wooden drum of the Hmong people of northern Vietnam, Laos, north-eastern Thailand and southern China. Covered at one end with cow- or roedeer-skin which is pegged and laced, this drum, called 'death drum' or 'funeral drum', is played at funerals and at the ceremony of the cow sacrifice to the *dab* deities; after the ceremony it is destroyed.
TRÂN QUANG HAI

Nruas yug. Double-headed cylindrical wooden drum of the Hmong people of northern Vietnam, Laos, north-eastern Thailand and southern China. The body is hollowed out from a tree trunk and covered at both ends with cowhide which is pegged and laced; it is beaten with two wooden mallets at funerals or at the ancestors' cult ceremonies. After a ceremony the drum is kept at the chief's house.
TRÂN QUANG HAI

Nsaasi. Flat tin rattle of the Soga people of Kigulu district, Uganda.

Nsak. Wicker vessel rattle of the Ibibio people of Nigeria. The instruments have stones inside and can have one or two chambers with a wood or gourd base. Their chief use is by women as part of an instrumental ensemble on ceremonial occasions.

Nsakala. Rattle of the Lari people of the Republic of the Congo. *See* MUKUITI.

Nsambi (i). Three-string fiddle of the Lari people of the Republic of the Congo. Metal strings are used and tuning is effected by means of pegs which pass through a flat portion at the end of the neck. A stone is used for a bridge, and the strings are tautened by means of a nut. The wooden soundbox is rectangular with shoulders cut diagonally across near the neck. The instrument is used to accompany the player while singing. See C. Duvelle: 'Musique Kongo', OCR 35 (1967) [disc notes].
K. A. GOURLAY

Nsambi (ii). Five-string PLURIARC of Gabon (Punu people) and western Angola; it is known as far south as the Kalahari desert in Botswana. *Nsambi* was the name reported in 1692 by Merolla (*Breve e succinta relatione del viaggio nel Regno di Congo nell'Africa Meridionale*) for a five-string pluriarc in the Kongo/Kimbundu region of Angola. Among the Humbi and Handa in southwestern Angola it usually has eight strings and is played by one musician, with the string-bearers away from his body, while another musician sings. The Punu instrument, whose strings are made of plant fibre, is used with the *obaka* percussion beam to accompany men singing. The *nsambi kizonzolo* is a five-string pluriarc of the Lari people of the Republic of the Congo. It has raffia strings and a rectangular wooden soundbox and soundtable. The bows are fixed to the base of the soundbox. The player plucks the strings with both hands, and uses the instrument to accompany his singing.
See also TSAMBI (i).

BIBLIOGRAPHY
C. Duvelle: 'Musique Kongo', OCR 35 (1967) [disc notes]
G. Kubik: 'Angola', *Grove 6*

Nsansi. Term for the LAMELLAPHONE in the Zambezi basin of south-eastern Africa. *See* KASANDJI.

Nsegu. Composite wooden cone flute of western Uganda. It is made from two wooden troughs, each a half-tube, which are held together by the trachea of a cow or the skin of a lizard, leaving enough space between them for the slightly cone-shaped cavity of the instrument (see illustration, p.784). It often has a finger-hole at the bottom. Flutes of this type either serve as an instrument of the court jester, as with the *ncwa* in Nyoro, or form sets of up to twenty which combine in hocket to perform melodies. A Nyoro legend recounts how an *nsegu* flute once saved the life of the heir to the throne during the absence of King Chwa I on a war expedition. In Toro the *nsegu* formerly awakened the *omukama* (ruler) at night and in the morning, while in Nkole it formed part of the regalia of the *omugabe*. See *WachsmannTCU*.
K. A. GOURLAY

Nsengu. Wooden cone whistle made in various sizes of the Amba people of Uganda. It has a cut-away

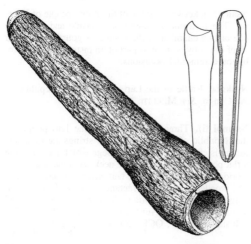

Nsegu (cone flute) of Uganda

mouthpiece and a very small hole at the sharp tip which is cut off at an angle. *Nsengu* are carried on hunting expeditions where they are used for signalling.

Nsense. *See* ZEZE (i).

Nshyemb [nshemm, nshyém, nshiyem]. Wooden cone flute of the Kuba and Ngend peoples of Zaïre. Among the Kuba the term can also denote an ivory cone flute or a VESSEL FLUTE (*LaurentyA*, 56, 139, 149, 265).

Nsoni-bungu. Trumpet of the Bembe people of the Republic of the Congo. *See* MAMPONGUI-NGUEMBO.

Ntabitabi. NOTCHED FLUTE of Buganda district, Uganda. *See* NDERE (i).

Ntahera. Set of five or seven ivory trumpets of the Ashanti and other peoples of southern Ghana. They are played at the court of paramount chiefs.

Ntakorok. Small hollow percussion block of the Ibibio people of Nigeria. Resembling a SLIT-DRUM in shape, it is used with a large hollow wooden block, the *nkporo*, in instrumental groups for women's *ebre* music. The blocks provide continuous rhythm while a clapperless bell is used for improvisation.

Ntamivu [entamiivu]. Single-headed closed conical drum of the Ganda people of Buganda district, Uganda. The membrane is laced on, and it is struck with beaters. This is the largest in a set of five drums formerly played at the Kabaka's palace, in conjunction with a xylophone. The *naku* and *njongo* are two of the smaller drums in the set. See *TraceyCSA*, ii, 309.

Ntanda. DRUM-CHIME of south-eastern Africa. *See* LIKHUBA.

Ntara. XYLOPHONE of the Nyoro people of Uganda. It has 16 keys, lying on two banana stalks, and is played by four men.

Ntem. Single-headed open tubular drum of the Bamileke people of Cameroon. *See* NKAK.

Ntendo. Treble PANPIPES of the MISHIBA panpipes ensemble of the Luba/Songe people of southern Zaïre.

Ntenga. Single-headed conical laced drum of the Ganda people of Buganda district, Uganda.

Nterero. Single-headed closed conical drum of the Rwanda people of Rwanda. It is the second drum in a set of 15 drums; the largest is the *chihumurizo*.

Ntewe. Conical drum of the Nyanja/Manganja people of Malawi. It is one of nine in the LIKHUBA drum set.

Nthikwi. Single-headed barrel drum of the Nyanja/Manganja people of Malawi. It is open-ended.

Ntimbo. (1) Open GOBLET DRUM of the Nyoro and Toro areas of Uganda (for illustration *see* DRUM, fig.3c). The cup of the drum is about 27 cm high and the stem 24 cm. The skin is that of a water lizard. The drum is carried under the arm on a leather belt slung from the left shoulder, and is beaten with both hands. The drums were traditionally used as royal instruments; in Nyoro a set of *ntimbo* was used at the coronation, the leading drum, *mutengesa*, being part of the royal insignia. In Toro the *ntimbo* were sounded whenever the *omukama* (ruler) was in residence, and for the induction of a lay person as priest of the *embandwa* cult, which was associated with the Bacwezi dynasty. See *WachsmannTCU*.
(2) Conical drum of the Nyoro/Haya people of Tanzania. It is the 'starting drum' in the ENKOITO drum set, and keeps the basic rhythm. See *TraceyCSA*, ii, 299, 328.

Nting. Tall, thin open conical drum of the Ibibio people of Nigeria. It is laced and secured in the same manner as the IBID drum.

Nto. Single-headed open tubular drum of the Bamileke-Bamengum people of Cameroon. *See* NKAK.

Ntongoli. Bowl lyre of the Ganda and Soga peoples of Uganda. *See* NDONGO.

Ntongoni. Six-string horizontal harp of the Soga/Gwere people of Mbale district, Uganda.

Ntono. Braced MUSICAL BOW of the Tende people of the Kenya–Tanzania border area. It has a half-calabash resonator opposite the brace, which is placed off-centre. There is an additional small brace about 10 cm from the top of the bow. The bow is held in the left hand and stopped by a gourd 'finger-stall' on the middle finger, while the string is tapped by a stick held in the right hand. A small peapod-shaped bell, *mbirii*, is worn on the little finger of the right hand. The *ntono* is used to accompany the player's own singing. See G. Hyslop: *Musical Instruments of East Africa*, i: *Kenya* (Nairobi, 1975).

Ntsambi. PLURIARC of the Sundi people of Zaïre (*LaurentyC*, 118). *See also* LUKOMBE (i) and NSAMBI (ii).

Ntshémb. *See* NEHÉMB.

Ntshinda. *See* TSINDA.

Ntu. Large SLIT-DRUM of the Bamileke people of Cameroon. It is beaten with two sticks as part of a rhythmic ensemble accompanying song and dance.

Ntum. Single-headed HOURGLASS DRUM of the Bamileke-Bafussam people of Cameroon. Very large with a ring carved round its waist, it is used as part of an instrumental ensemble to accompany dancing. The player holds the drum between his legs and plays it with his hands.

Nuanarit. A term for drum in the special shamanic language used at Ammassalik in eastern Greenland. *See also* AJA (ii).

Núdi. Clarinet of the Mordvin people (USSR), possibly related to the Russian *zhaleyka*. It has a double pipe (very rarely single) with three finger-holes in each pipe, and is made of cane or bird-bone. Some instruments have three or four pipes, of equal or unequal length.

Nüfür. *See* NEFIR.

Nugara. Large double-headed laced drum of the Tundjer people of central Chad. It has an ovoid wooden body with two cowhide membranes. In all respects, including usage, it is almost identical to the NANGARA of the Teda and Daza peoples.

Nulanting. Gong of the Philippines. *See* MAPINDIL.

Numena. Small oboe of Flores, Indonesia. It consists of a bamboo leaf doubled up and jammed between a piece of split bamboo or flat piece of wood. See J. Kunst: *Music in Flores* (Leiden, 1942), 156.

Nung. Free-reed aerophone of the Mnong people of central Vietnam. It is made from a buffalo horn which is side-blown.

Nungneng. TUBE ZITHER of Sumatra. *See* GONDANG BULUH.

Nunib [≠nunib]. Small stopped flute of the Bergdama people of south-western Africa. It is made from the top of a springbok horn, and was formerly used for signalling during hunting. It resembles the Bushman *garras*.

Nunns & Clark. American firm of piano manufacturers, active in New York from 1836 to 1860. The brothers Robert and William Nunns arrived in New York from London around 1821 (William on 21 November 1821) and worked for Kearsing & Sons, piano makers, until starting their own firm, R. & W. Nunns, in 1823. They are reputed to have introduced a French-style 'rocker' action to American pianos and manufactured some instruments for sale under other makers' names (e.g.

Dubois & Stodart). In 1833 the English immigrant John Clark joined the firm, which became Nunns, Clark & Co. until William withdrew in 1839; the business, thereafter known as (R.) Nunns & Clark, continued until 1860, though Clark is not listed in city directories after 1858. William operated separate piano concerns from 1836 until 1853, sometimes in conjunction with Augustus Brumley (1836) or John and Charles Fischer (1843–48). William Steinway is reputed to have worked for W. Nunns at the time of the latter's bankruptcy in 1853, ironically the same year that Nunns & Clark exhibited to general acclaim at the Crystal Palace, New York. An extraordinarily ornate Nunns & Clark square piano, dated 1853 (now in the Metropolitan Museum of Art), shows the heavily carved rosewood casework for which the firm was renowned; though highly decorative, the piano is of standard design internally. In 1855 the firm employed 83 men and boys and produced 300 pianos worth $150,000 at a factory at Setauket, Long Island. Robert continued to be listed in New York directories as late as 1868. William Nunns jr, Robert Nunns jr, and John Francis Nunns were also active in the trade into the 1860s.

BIBLIOGRAPHY
L. Libin: *American Musical Instruments in the Metropolitan Museum of Art* (New York, 1981) [unpubd catalogue]
N. Groce: *Musical Instrument Making in New York City during the Eighteenth and Nineteenth Centuries* (diss., U. of Michigan, 1982)
LAURENCE LIBIN

Nunuha. A SLIT-DRUM in the PARA NI 'O'O ensemble of the 'Are'are people, Malaita, Solomon Islands.

Nunut. *See* LAUNUT.

Nūpur [nūpura, noopur]. A South Asian name for various jingles, either hollow rings with metal pellets or strings with attached small spherical bells containing pellets. They are worn on different parts of the body – ankles, waist, wrist or finger – in song or dance accompaniments (as well as serving as a ladies' ornament). The term has been in use since classical times (for roughly two millennia). The hollow anklet with pellets is especially common in rural music and dance: it is used, for example, by the Baul musicians of Bengal (east India and Bangladesh). It is known by other names in different regions, including *silampu* (Tamil Nadu), *gaggara* (Mysore) and *painjan* (north India). The type with metal pellet bells threaded on a string is generally used by dancers of the various classical styles (*see* GHUṄGRŪ). The *kiṅkiṇī jāla* is a waistband garlanded with small pellet bells.

BIBLIOGRAPHY
B. C. Deva: *Musical Instruments of India* (Calcutta, 1978)
ALASTAIR DICK

Nuqairat. Kettledrums of the north African Berbers. *See* NAQQĀRA.

Nuren [feko, glekor, klekor, sunding]. Bamboo ring flute of Flores, Indonesia. The upper end is closed by a node, but most of this is cut away, leaving a thin disc and a small semi-oval opening. A flat bamboo or rattan ring, placed round the node, conducts the player's breath through the slit formed by the node and the ring against the sharp bottom edge of the opening. The instrument is called *nuren* or *feko* in the Larantuka area, *klekor* in the Riangwulu area, *glekor* in the Sikka area, *feko* in the Lio area and *sunding* in the Manggarai area. In the east and central parts of Flores the flutes measure between 30 and 49 cm in length, and there are usually five or six finger-holes; the western type is between 64 and 71 cm long and has four, six or three finger-holes. To the latter type a sound funnel is sometimes added, made of coconut leaf wound into a spiral.

The name 'nuren' is used also in the extreme east and west of Flores for a bamboo ring flute (known also as *feko* or *welo*) which has an external duct and a complete ring of bamboo leaf. It is about 40 cm long and has six finger-holes.

BIBLIOGRAPHY
J. Kunst: *Music in Flores* (Leiden, 1942)

MARGARET J. KARTOMI

Nürnberger, (Franz) Albert (*b* Markneukirchen, 24 April 1854; *d* Markneukirchen, 1931). German bow maker. His father, Franz Albert Nürnberger the elder, was also a bow maker and they founded their business in 1880. Made from the finest materials, Albert Nürnberger bows are strong and generally well balanced, and are sometimes preferred by players to those of his French and English contemporaries. Expert knowledge is required to distinguish his work, as his brand ALBERT NÜRNBERGER was also used by his son Karl Albert (*b* 1906), another fine craftsman, and by his successors who now control the business in East Germany. The modern bows do not compare in quality with those of the early decades of the 20th century.

BIBLIOGRAPHY
W. L. von Lütgendorff: *Die Geigen- und Lautenmacher vom Mittelalter bis zur Gegenwart* (Frankfurt am Main, 1904, 6/1922/R1968)
J. Roda: *Bows for Musical Instruments of the Violin Family* (Chicago, Ill., 1959)

CHARLES BEARE

Nut (Fr. *sillet*; Ger. *Sattel*, *Obersattel*; It. *capo tasto*) (i). In string instruments, the thin ridge inserted between the pegbox and fingerboard, and at a right angle to them (*see* VIOLIN, fig.5). It is generally of ebony or other hardwood, though sometimes of ivory (especially in early instruments). The strings, secured at the lower end of the instrument, run over the bridge and then over the nut to the pegs or other tightening devices. The nut serves several purposes: it raises the strings sufficiently above the fingerboard to allow the open strings to sound freely in a given length from nut to bridge; like the bridge, the nut holds the strings at fixed distances apart by means of grooves cut in its top; and the nut adds a frictional resistance that helps the pegs in holding the strings, especially where the pegbox (or pegboard) is bent back appreciably, as often happens in lutes.

For the meaning of 'nut' when speaking of a bow *see* FROG.

DAVID D. BOYDEN

Nut [noot] (ii). Percussion vessel of Kashmir, South Asia. A large clay waterpot is placed on a cushion-ring before the seated player and beaten with the hands. The *nut* is widely used in Kashmiri folk music. The *garā* of Kashmir is similar, but has *ghungrū* (jingles) attached. *See also* GHAṬA, §1.

Nutting, William (*b* Randolph, Vermont, 28 March 1815; *d* Bellows Falls, Vermont, 21 Oct 1869).

American organ builder. Largely self-taught, he built his first instrument, a small chamber organ, in 1838. For several years he worked in conjunction with his younger brother Rufus, a maker of reed organs who in 1848 patented a type of reed organ which he called the Aeolodeon, said to have a sweeter and less nasal tone than other small reed organs of the melodeon kind. William Nutting soon became the leading organ builder of northern New England, moving to a larger workshop in Bellows Falls in 1853. From that year until his death he was organist of Immanuel Church, playing an organ of his own manufacture. He is known to have built at least 30 church organs, most of them for Vermont, as well as an undetermined number of chamber organs.

BIBLIOGRAPHY
B. Owen: *The Organ in New England* (Raleigh, North Carolina, 1979)

BARBARA OWEN

Nuung teeree. Mouth organ, with three holes and a single pipe, of the Mnong people of central Vietnam.

Nuzha. Turkish and Arab BOX ZITHER or psaltery of the Seljuk and Ottoman periods (*c*1300–*c*1700). It is rectangular in shape but has strings of varying lengths. Those running the full length of the instrument are paired and mounted parallel along the soundbox, fixed to pegs on the left; between them are further strings, of variable length, fixed to pegs on the surface of the soundbox, forming a particular design (in some cases in the form of an X). It seems likely that some of the strings would resonate sympathetically. The number of strings could vary, at the maker's whim, from 32 to 108; so could the disposition of the shorter set of strings. The instrument had two bridges. It was probably held horizontally and the strings plucked.

The invention of the *nuzha* is attributed to Ṣafī al-Dīn (?1224–94). His writings apart, only two documents are at present known that attest its existence: the anonymous 14th-century Persian treatise *Kanz al-tuhaf* drawn up for a Turkish prince (see illustration) and the musical commentaries of the Turk Ahmet Oğlu Şükrullah (1388-*c*1470). *Nuzha* (Turkish: *nuzhe*) literally means

Nuzha (box zither), with sympathetic strings forming an X: drawing from 'Kanz al-tuḥaf' (author unknown), a 14th-century Persian treatise (GB-Lbm Oriental 2361, f.264r)

that which delights; the instrument was considered the most pleasing after the *jank*. *Nuzha* and *qānūn* are often cited together but should not be presumed to share an ancestry – although the Persian treatise already cited refers to the *nuzha* as having double the surface area of the *qānūn*. The term *nuzha* disappeared after the 15th century, and the instrument's real life was no more than two centuries long, but the rectangular shape (which had been known previously) survived; it is illustrated in a well-known engraving, by G. Scotin, of the early 18th century, of a girl playing the canon (reproduced in Bonanni's *Gabinetto armonico* of 1722, where it is called *salterio turchesco*).

BIBLIOGRAPHY

C. Huart: 'Musique persane', *EMDC*, I/v (1922), 3072
R. Yekta Bey: 'La musique turque', *EMDC*, I/v (1922), 3013
H. G. Farmer: 'The canon and eschaquiel of the Arabs', *Journal of the Royal Asiatic Society* (1926), 239 [repr. in *Studies in Oriental Music*, 1931/R1978]
F. Harrison and J. Rimmer: *Filippo Bonanni: Antique Musical Instruments and their Players* (New York, 1964)
H. G. Farmer: *Islam*, Musikgeschichte in Bildern, iii/2 (Leipzig, 1966, 2/1976)
S. A. Rashid: *Al-Ālāt al-mūsīqīyya fi al-'usūr al-Islāmīyya* [The musical instruments of Islam] (Baghdad, 1975), 213ff

CHRISTIAN POCHÉ

Nwakpo. Bamboo flute with five finger-holes of the Igbo people of Nigeria.

Nxoronxoro. MOUTH BOW of the Kung Bushman people of south-western Africa, resembling the Tsonga XIZAMBI.

Nyaanyooru. Single-string fiddle of the Fula people of the Gambia. *See* GOGE.

Nyahura. Single-headed closed conical drum of the Rwanda people of Rwanda. It is the first drum in a set of 15 drums; the largest is the *chihumurizo*.

Nyalebe. Royal drum of the Nyoro and Toro peoples of Uganda. *See* UGANDA DRUM.

Nyamarra. Side-blown animal-horn trumpet of the Nyoro people of Uganda. *See* AMAKONDERE.

Nyaminyeko. Conical drum of the Nyoro/Haya people of Tanzania. It is the bass drum in the ENKOITO drum set, upon which syncopations are played.

Nyamulere. Tall NOTCHED FLUTE of the Konjo people of western Uganda. Usually made of bamboo, it is 60 to 68 cm long and has a wide bore. Four finger-holes near the base give a roughly diatonic scale with a step of approximately a semitone between the two lowest notes. The flute is played by men, at beer parties and other social occasions, with drum accompaniment. The repertory is based on songs, many of which during the period of Konjo rebellion (1962–8) were strongly political in content. The name has also been used for smaller flutes of the neighbouring Nyoro and flutes of the Nande people of north-eastern Zaïre (*see* NDERE (i)).

BIBLIOGRAPHY

WachsmannTCU, 339f
P. R. Cooke and M. Doornbos: 'Rwenzururu Protest Songs', *Africa*, lii/1 (1982), 50

PETER COOKE

Nyang. Iron ankle rattle of the Birom people of Nigeria, constructed and used in the same way as the Hausa AKAYAU.

Nyanga (i). Ensemble of PANPIPES used to accompany the *nyanga* circle dance of the Nyungwe people of south-eastern Africa. The dance is performed by 20 to 30 men, each with a two-, three-, or four-note instrument making in all a heptatonic compass of three and a half octaves. The men dance irregularly phrased steps as they play,

Part of a nyanga (panpipes) ensemble of the Nyungwe people at Nsava, near Tete, Mozambique

interspersing sung notes with blown notes, and each interlocking his part with that of the others so that there is a continuous sound of both blown and sung notes, to which the voices of women singers are added.
See also STOPPED FLUTE ENSEMBLE.

ANDREW TRACEY

Nyanga (ii). Side-blown trumpet of the Shona people of southern Africa. Made from an antelope horn, it was used as a signal instrument. *See also* PARAPANDA.

Nyanyúlua. Single-headed open hourglass drums (see HOURGLASS DRUM) of the Gogo people of central Tanzania. They are played exclusively by women and used in the *ngoma* dance with one large drum, raft rattles and whistles. The large drum is known as *ngoma fúmbwa* and is about 55 to 60 cm high, single-headed and open-ended.

Nyastaranga. MIRLITON of India and Bangladesh. It consists of a small brass trumpet closed by a membrane at the narrow end; a pair of these is applied to the larynx as the performer hums and sings.

Nyatiti. Lyre of the Luo people of Kenya.

Nyckelharpa [nyckelgiga] (Swed.; Ger. *Schlüssel-fidel*). A keyed fiddle. It was used throughout Scandinavia and in north Germany for popular dance and festive music.

15th-century frescos from Uppland (the last region in which the *nyckelharpa* survived) show instruments with about seven and 12 keys. The *Schlüsselfidel* imperfectly depicted by Agricola (*Musica instrumentalis deudsch*, 1529) had six strings, that shown by Praetorius (*Syntagma musicum*, 2/1619) four strings and 14 keys, and an obsolete Swedish form three bowed strings and several sympathetic strings. The oldest extant *nyckelharpan*, from the 16th and 17th centuries, represent two different types: one with an elongated body in the shape of a figure of 8 with a flat bottom and a flat belly, separately made; the other with either a pear- or a boat-shaped body, made in a single piece with the neck, and with a slightly vaulted belly. The boat shape became normal from the late 17th century, with marked middle bouts, a high border and a strongly vaulted belly with two oval soundholes. More recently the body has come to resemble that of the violin family, with a slightly vaulted belly and two f-holes. The bottom and the belly are now often made separately and the wooden tuning-pegs are supplemented or even replaced by a guitar-like tuning mechanism. Ancient *nyckelharpan* had one melody string and strings for mixtures and drones, and up to 12 wooden keys, each with from one to three tangents, set in a frame along the neck and part of the body. The compass has gradually been increased by the addition of more keys. In the late 18th century the *kontra-basharpa* was developed, with two melody strings tuned to *a'* and *d'* placed on either side of one or two bass drone strings tuned to *g* and *c*; a number of sympathetic strings were added, some passing over the flat or slightly curved bridge and some alongside it. The *silverbas-harpa* has two adjacent melody strings (*a'* and *c'*) and bass strings (*g* and *c*, the latter silver-wound) and two rows of keys. The *kontrabasharpa med dubbellek* (*dub-*

Man playing a keyed fiddle (nyckelharpa): watercolour by Per Nordquist, early 19th century (Nordiska Museet, Stockholm)

bellek: 'double rows of keys') supplements this with a third melody string (*d'*) on the other side of the bass and sympathetic strings. In the 1920s the development of the fully chromatic *nyckelharpa* began with three rows of keys for the melody strings (*a'*, *c'* and *g*; sometimes with a fourth key row for an additional one, *e''*) and with sympathetic strings representing a full chromatic scale. The *nyckelharpa* plays an important role in the folk music movement in Sweden and many people study its construction and playing technique.

The instrument has also been found in Norway, where it is known as the *lökkelje*.

BIBLIOGRAPHY
K. P. Leffler: *Om nyckelharpospelet på Skansen* (Stockholm, 1899)
O. Andersson: *Stråkharpan* (Stockholm, 1923)
J. Ling: *Nyckelharpan* (diss., U. of Uppsala, 1967; Stockholm, 1967)
M. Müller: 'Der himmlische Lobgesang in Rynkeby: eine dänische iknographische Quelle des 16 Jahrhunderts', *Studia instrumentorum musicae popularis*, iv (Stockholm, 1976), 70
G. Ahlbäck: *Nyckelharpfolket: om nyckelharprörelsen, en 1970-talsföreteelse* (Stockholm, 1980)
JOAN RIMMER, BIRGIT KJELLSTRÖM

Nyefe. Stopped end-blown flute used in the ceremonial rain-dance of the Kabre people of north Togo. The flutes are used in conjunction with wooden and pot drums. Before the performance a small quantity of water is inserted in each flute and the players, who are women, sing rather than blow into the instruments. The higher, or male, flute is held in the right hand, the lower, or female, in the left. See R. Verdier: 'Musique Kabré du Nord-Togo', OCR 16 [disc notes].

Nyele. End-blown trumpet of the Valley Tonga people of Zambia. Sets of *nyele* are made from antelope horns of different lengths; they form an ensemble of about 17, played in hocket style, with a set of NGOMA drums. Names of the instruments, from smallest to largest, are *kampeko, simulya sikiri, senseku, jingainga, pindakati, muwere, siamupa, mpako, fulwa, saina, mulundu chigabana, gapalikwa, fumbira momba, tiabutiabu, tandamubbgwa, tandawanyoko* and *tukirauso*. See *TraceyCSA*, ii, 84.

DAVID K. RYCROFT

Nyere. End-blown stopped flute of the Shona/Zezuru people of Zimbabwe. It is used in an ensemble; each player blows two or three, in turn, as required. *See* STOPPED FLUTE ENSEMBLE.

Nyeri. Transverse flute of the Karanga/Mhari people of Zimbabwe. It is closed at both ends and has two finger-holes.

Nyeuwenhuys [Nyhoff]. *See* NIEHOFF family.

Nyia-mendzang. XYLOPHONE of the Beti people of Yaounde, Cameroon. *See* MENDZAN.

Nyikirizo. Drum of the Nyoro/Haya people of Bukoba district, Tanzania.

Nyima' lwakwĭt. Drum beater made from willow sticks; it was used with the basket drum (KWĔNXO') of the Yuman Indians of the south-western USA. It was also used as a rattle.

Nyimba (i). Hand-held gourd rattle of the Nyoro/Haya people of Bukoba district, Tanzania.

Nyimba (ii). Drum of the Toro people of Uganda. *See* UGANDA DRUM.

Nyi ngo. *See* NGO.

Nyini makilingu. SLIT-DRUM of the Ngbandi people of Zaïre. *See* MAKILINGU.

Nyo. Vessel rattle of the Igbo people of Nigeria. It is made from a gourd strung with beads or beans.

Nyō (i). Japanese vessel rattle used in Buddhist music. It is about 20 to 30 cm long with a spherical head (*see* SUZU) and a metal handle, and is generally cast in one piece of copper. The Chinese *nao* (*see* ZHONG) is a related instrument.

Nyō (ii). Japanese thin-walled hanging gong, used with the cymbals *dōbatsu* in esoteric Buddhist services. *See* DORA.

Nyōhachi. Large Japanese cymbals. *See* DŌBATSU.

Nyonganyonga. A large LAMELLAPHONE of the Barwe, Gorongozi and Sena peoples of the Zambezi basin, south-eastern Africa. It has 26 or 27 keys and is played inside a large shell-decorated calabash resonator with the thumbs and index fingers.

Nyoro. Bell of the Ibibio people of Nigeria. *See* NKANIKA.

Nza. Generic term for flute in north-western Zaïre and Uganda. In Zaïre the *nza beka, nza liza* and the *nza ngu* of the Mbanja people are sets of stopped flutes threaded onto cord or wire; the *nza bugni* of the Mbanja is a cylindrical stopped wooden flute; and the *nza pipwa* of the Sango a wooden flute with a slender conical bore (*LaurentyA*, 155, 178, 189f). The *nzakubela* is an end-blown single-note flute of the Konjo people of Toro district, Uganda, used in the ILENGA flute ensemble.

Nzenze. Flat-board LAMELLAPHONE of the Kumu and Luba peoples of eastern and south-eastern Zaïre. It has wooden keys, sometimes fitted over a resonating vessel (*LaurentyS*, 193). The term can also denote the *zeze* or *nzeze* stick zither.

Nzeze [nsense, nzenze, oda] **(i).** STICK ZITHER of the Bali people of north-eastern Zaïre (*LaurentyC*, 115). *See* ZEZE (i).

Nzeze (ii). Two-string fiddle of the Gogo people of Tanzania. *See* CHIZEZE.

Nzisi. Bell rattle of the Nyakyusa people of Tukuyu district, Tanzania.

Nzomana. Drum of the Chopi people of Zavala district, Mozambique. It is the smallest in a set of three drums, used with xylophones. The other drums are *nchuko* and *nkulu*.

Nzoro. Metal bells of the Zande people of the Central African Republic, used on feast days with xylophone and drums to accompany the *gbainlain* dance.

Nzuga. Pellet bells of the Digo people of Kenya. A string of up to 60 bells may be worn by drummers to provide additional rhythm while drumming.

Nzumari [zumari]. Oboe of the Digo people of Kenya. The Arabic origin of the instrument is evident from the name (derived from *zamaro*: 'to blow'; *see* MIZMĀR). It resembles North or West African oboes (*see* ALGAITA) but is made of different materials. The reed is made from local reed grass, the lip shield from a section of fine coconut shell, and the main tube from bamboo (15 cm long). The bell is carved from wood and fastened by a plaited ring of string. There are six finger-holes in the bamboo section. Among the Duruma people the instrument is known as *bung'o* and is tuned differently. The oboe is played solo with percussion accompaniment on the *kayamba* (raft rattle). See G. Hyslop: *Musical Instruments of East Africa, i: Kenya* (Nairobi, 1975).

K. A. GOURLAY

O

Ŏ. Wooden SCRAPER of Korea in the form of a sitting tiger with a serrated backbone. It preserves one historical type of the Chinese YU (i). The carved wooden tiger, about 100 cm long and 40 cm high, sits on a rectangular wooden platform about 40 cm high. There should be 27 notches along the serrated backbone. It is played with a split bamboo whisk: the head is struck three times and then the whisk is dragged down the backbone (see illustration). This pattern is given three times as part of the signal for the music to halt. The sound comes, in fact, from the bamboo whisk and not from the *ŏ* itself.

Two *ŏ* were received from China in 1116, and the instrument has been used in ritual music (*aak*) ever since. It now appears only in the ensembles performing at the twice-yearly Sacrifice to Confucius and the annual Sacrifice to Royal Ancestors (*Chongmyo*) in Seoul. The *ŏ* in the *tŭngga* (terrace ensemble) has the special name *kal*. The only musical function of the *ŏ* is to give the stopping signal, and it is always paired with the *ch'uk*, which gives part of the starting signal.

BIBLIOGRAPHY
Sŏng Hyŏn, ed.: *Akhak kwebŏm* [Guide to the study of music] (Seoul, 1493/*R*1975), 6.11*b*–12*a*
Chang Sa-hun: *Han'guk akki taegwan* [Korean musical instruments] (Seoul, 1969), 125f

ROBERT C. PROVINE

Obadan. Small cylindrical drum of the Yoruba people of Nigeria. *See* GBEDU.

Obaka. Small wooden percussion beam of the Punu people of Gabon. It rests on the ground and is struck with rods by several men as rhythmic accompaniment to the *nsambi* (pluriarc) and male singing.

Obati [tilboro, tilliko, tillikoro]. Idioglot transverse clarinet of the Hausa people of Nigeria. *See* CLARINET, TRANSVERSE.

Obbligato (It.: 'necessary'). An adjective or noun referring to an independent part in concerted music, ranking in importance just below the principal melody and not to be omitted. Obbligato is the opposite of AD LIBITUM when the latter qualifies the mention of a part in a title. Used in connection with a keyboard part in the 18th century, obbligato (and its synonym in this case, 'concertato') designated a fully written-out part instead of a figured bass. Sometimes obbligato means simply independent, as in C. P. E. Bach's *Orchester Sinfonien*

mit zwölf obligaten Stimmen (1780). The archetype of the obbligato part is the instrumental solo which, with a basso continuo, constitutes the accompaniment of vast numbers of late Baroque arias. The roots of the instrumental obbligato to vocal music could be said to reach as far back as medieval polyphony, but the direct antecedents of the late Baroque phenomenon are to be found in the *concertato* style of the early 17th century. Schütz's *Benedicam Dominum in omni tempore* (*Symphoniae sacrae*, i, 1629) for soprano, tenor, bass, and continuo, with obbligato 'cornetto, o violino' is an early example, and the trumpet arias in later 17th-century opera carry on the development. A pinnacle is reached with the violin solo in the Benedictus of Beethoven's Mass in D. Leopold Mozart's sinfonia, *Jagd Parthia*, has a cuckoo obbligato.

DAVID FULLER

Oberheim. A range of synthesizers designed by Tom Oberheim and, since the late 1970s, by a team, and

Ŏ (scraper) of Korea

790

manufactured since 1974 by Oberheim Electronics, at first in Santa Monica, California, then (from *c*1980) in Los Angeles. While working as an electronics engineer for a small computer company in the late 1960s Oberheim built amplification equipment for musicians in his spare time. He was asked to construct a ring modulator, and the success of the original device led to requests for others. In 1971 the Maestro company marketed both Oberheim's ring modulator and his phase shifter; Oberheim Electronics was set up in connection with their production. In 1973, when he was working as an agent for ARP synthesizers, Oberheim devised a digital sequencer and the following year he and Jim Cooper developed the 'Synthesizer Expander Module', which is, in fact, a small monophonic synthesizer with two oscillators. In 1974–5 Oberheim marketed the first polyphonic synthesizers, the three-octave Oberheim 2-Voice and four-octave 4-Voice; these were based on the expander module (one module for each voice) combined with a keyboard developed by the newly formed E-mu Systems. The 8-Voice (one or two manuals) and less popular 6-Voice followed soon afterwards. Their semi-modular design permits the addition of an output mixer, and an optional sequencer, or a 16-channel polyphonic memory, or both.

In 1976 the OB-1 lead synthesizer, a fully programmable monophonic synthesizer, was produced, followed in 1979 by the programmable polyphonic OB-X. The latter was updated at the end of 1980 as the OB-Xa, a five-octave four-, six- or eight-voice, microprocessor-controlled system with 120 (originally 32) programs; the OB-Xa combines the various elements pioneered by Oberheim in earlier synthesizers, but loses some of its flexibility in the areas of microtonal tuning and external computer control. A model of somewhat reduced capabilities, the four-octave, four-, five-, or six-voice OB-SX with 56 programs, was derived from the OB-Xa, and the OB-Xpander (1982) is a four-voice synthesizer expander module with 120 programs. In 1981 a polyphonic digital sequencer, the 16-voice DSX, was introduced, and in the same year Oberheim produced an electronic percussion unit, the DMX, in which up to 100 rhythmic sequences can be stored, using digitized recordings of 24 percussion instruments (it was followed in 1983 by the expanded DX model). Since 1976 all Oberheim instruments (apart from the OB-SX) have included a cassette interface for the storage of 'patches' on a standard cassette tape recorder.

See also SYNTHESIZER.

BIBLIOGRAPHY

D. Heckman: 'Tom Oberheim's Magical Music Machines', *High Fidelity* (April 1977), 127
D. Milano: 'Tom Oberheim: Designer of Synthesizers', *Contemporary Keyboard*, iii/5 (1977), 20
D. T. Horn: *Electronic Music Synthesizers* (Blue Ridge Summit, Penn., 1980), 73

HUGH DAVIES

Oberlender. German family of woodwind instrument makers. The most important members of the family, active in Nuremberg, are Johann Wilhelm Oberlender (i) (*b* Nuremberg, 1681; *d* Nuremberg, 1763) and his son Johann Wilhelm Oberlender (ii) (*b* Nuremberg, 1712; *d* Nuremberg, 1779). The elder Oberlender gained recognition as a master craftsman in 1705, while his son joined the workshop of Jacob Denner in 1735. Surviving instruments include recorders, flutes, *flûtes d'amour* and clarinets. Among these are a treble recorder in box-

wood with superbly carved ornamentation by the elder Oberlender, and a fine ivory flute with one silver key by the son (both in the Karl-Marx-Universität, Leipzig). *Flûtes d'amour*, possibly by the younger Oberlender, have one key and A and E finger-holes obliquely bored to avoid stretching. They are pitched in A. An interesting clarinet in D in Berlin uses two keys for *a'*, either operating also as a speaker key and both together producing *b♮'*. As a similar mechanism exists on some Jacob Denner instruments, this was probably the work of the younger Oberlender.

A piccolo and clarinet stamped F. Oberländer [sic] (in the Nordiska Museet, Stockholm) are probably by another member of the family.

BIBLIOGRAPHY

R. S. Rockstro: *A Treatise on . . . the Flute* (London, 1890, 2/1928/*R*1967)
H. Fitzgibbon: *The Story of the Flute* (London, 1914, 2/1929)
L. G. Langwill: *An Index of Musical Wind-instrument Makers* (Edinburgh, 1960, rev., enlarged 6/1980)
H. Heyde: *Flöten* (Leipzig, 1978)
P. T. Young: *Twenty-five Hundred Historical Woodwind Instruments* (New York, 1982)

NIALL O'LOUGHLIN

Obermayer, Joseph (*b* Starnberg, nr. Munich, 17 Oct 1878; *d* Starnberg, 13 July 1966). German harp maker. He established his harp making concern in Munich in 1928, and produced his first instruments in the 1930s. His factory was bombed during World War II, but he re-established himself in 1944 in Kufstein, Austria. In 1952 Obermayer moved his factory to his home town, and he was joined there by his chief assistant from Kufstein, Maximilian Horngacher. After the sudden death of Obermayer's son in 1960, Horngacher was gradually trained to take over the business; this he did on Obermayer's death in 1966.

Obermayer produced three styles of harp. Shortly before his death he developed and built a fourth type in a more modern style, without the traditional gilding. Horngacher has continued to produce all four models; in 1970 he was awarded a gold medal for exceptional craftsmanship by the state of Bavaria. Individually hand-built, the Obermayer–Horngacher harps are particularly notable for their reliability, their stability of pitch, the meticulous precision of their mechanism and their brilliant sound. This latter property may be attributable to the tuned cast-metal ribs, rather than the usual wooden ones, which are used in the construction of the harp's soundbox.

ANN GRIFFITHS

Obersattel (Ger.). NUT (i).

Oberwerk (Ger.: 'upper department'). The upper chest and manual of a German organ, often (since *c*1840) provided with SWELL shutters, able by its position to take larger pipes than the BRUSTWERK and other minor chests of a WERKPRINZIP organ. In many sources (e.g. the autograph registrations in Bach's Concerto BWV596) *Oberwerk* denotes HAUPTWERK, i.e. the main chest above the player, as opposed to the CHAIR ORGAN.

Praetorius (*Syntagma musicum*, 2/1619) used other phrases such as 'Oben in der Brust' or 'oberste Positiff' if he wished to refer to the *Oberwerk*. Schlick (*Spiegel der Orgelmacher und Organisten*, 1511) disparagingly mentioned small subsidiary chests placed within the main case, but the *Oberwerk* found on such organs as Kampen (1523) was a major department. That called *boven int werck* at Amsterdam Oude Kerk in 1543 had two chests and took all the colour stops away from the *Hauptwerk*, which was thereby kept to a size convenient for builder and bellows-blower. Such a department was very useful when it had its own keyboard and became highly developed, those in the big four-manual organs of Schnitger (*c*1690) still full of flutes, full-length reeds and other colours giving variety. The *Unterwerke, Seitenwerke, Echowerke* and *Kronwerke* ('under, side, echo, crowning, departments') found in later Baroque and Romantic organs are of much less musical significance.

PETER WILLIAMS

Obia. Double-headed portable cylindrical drum of the Igbo people of Nigeria.

Oblicus calamus. *See* KALAMOS.

Obligato. *See* OBBLIGATO.

Obliquus calamus. *See* KALAMOS.

Obodom. Wooden SLIT-DRUM of the Ibibio and Efik peoples of Nigeria. It is made from a hollow log and has a single slit running between two rectangular openings. The *obodom* is used solo for summoning an assembly, or in groups of two or three to accompany dancing, when its function is primarily rhythmic though sometimes it is used to signal to the dancers. See S. E. Akpabot: *Ibibio Music in Nigerian Culture* (East Lansing, Mich., 1975).

Oboe (Fr. *hautbois*; Ger. *Hoboe, Oboe*; It. *oboe*). The principal soprano double-reed woodwind instrument in Western music. The term is also used in the classification by Hornbostel and Sachs (*see* AEROPHONE) for any double-reed instrument (though 'shawm' is favoured by some organologists); the Western oboe, however, is distinguished by specific features of bore, reed, fingering etc. A list of non-Western oboes entered in this dictionary follows at the end of this entry.

See also ORGAN STOP (*Hautbois*).

1. General. 2. Acoustics. 3. Early history and construction. 4. The 18th century. 5. The 19th century and after. 6. Larger oboes. 7. Technique and capabilities. 8. Performers and teachers. 9. Repertory and its history.

1. GENERAL. At present, it is both unwise and ungracious to regard one orchestral instrument as more important than, or superior to, another, but since musical history shows that it was around the oboe that the woodwind section of the orchestra as we know it was built up, it may perhaps be given pride of place. As made today, the oboe consists of a slender tube of hardwood (occasionally of ebonite, plastic or metal and, in earlier years, of rosewood, boxwood or some fruit-tree woods) some 59 cm long, in three sections united by tenon-and-socket joints. The bore, which is narrow and conoidal, expands fairly regularly for about five-sixths of its length and then opens out more rapidly to form a moderate bell (see fig.1). This expansion takes the shape of a smooth curve or a succession of cones, according to the formulae adopted by different makers and worked out experimentally by them. The effective length of the

tube is made variable by means of 16 to 20 side-holes, six of them directly under the player's fingers and the rest controlled by mechanism which is sometimes most ingenious and complicated. Today, there are at least four systems of KEYWORK applied to the oboe.

The instrument is sounded by means of a reed formed

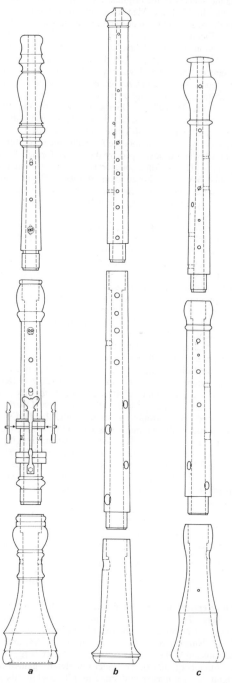

1. *Diagrams comparing the bores and placement of holes on three oboes: (a) 18th-century two-keyed; (b) modern French; (c) modern Viennese*

of two hollowed-out blades of thin 'cane', actually the semi-tropical grass *Arundo donax* or *Arundo sativa* (see figs.8 and 12 below). These are bound face to face with thread to a narrow tapered metal tube, slightly flattened at the tip, termed a 'staple'. This forms an extension to the bore but does not necessarily match it in diameter, a point of considerable acoustic significance. At their free ends, the blades are scraped down to a feather edge. When placed between the lips and blown through, the blades of the reed vibrate together, alternately opening and closing the elliptical chink between them and thus transmitting bursts of energy to the air column in the body tube. The proper management of this very delicate apparatus is probably the most difficult part of oboe technique for the learner to acquire or for the teacher to impart. In recent years, certain American makers have produced tiny single-reed mouthpieces of clarinet type for the oboe and bassoon but these do not seem to be used greatly except in special circumstances.

The compass of the modern oboe extends from $b\flat$ to a''' – in all, 36 notes, of which the first 16 are fundamental tones, each sounded by its appropriate length of tube. Acoustically, the remainder are harmonics of the notes actually fingered and are produced by changes of 'lip' on the reed, assisted by the use of certain speaker or octave keys. There are alternative fingerings for the notes above d''', which are valuable at times to the advanced player for their special tonal characteristics, although they are not equally available on all types of instrument.

In addition to the treble or soprano oboe in C, the family includes the following deeper-toned members (see fig.2): the oboe d'amore, in A, usually regarded as the alto but sometimes as a mezzo-soprano member; the english horn (or cor anglais) in F, the tenor of the group though sometimes called alto; and the baritone oboe, also in C but an octave below the soprano. At one time there was a military soprano in B♭ and examples, made chiefly in France, are still occasionally to be found. The larger oboes are today built with a pear-shaped bell with a constricted opening (Ger. *Liebesfuss*) but models with a normal bell are not unknown. On the basis of this, some scholars have felt it necessary to postulate a subgroup within the main family and this may be justified in terms of the most strict classification. The peculiar properties of the bulb bell are discussed briefly in §2.

2. ACOUSTICS. Research has shown that the acoustics of the oboe, in common with other woodwind, are complex and involve many factors which go beyond the simple assumptions of classical physics. Briefly, the conoidal bore of the oboe has properties analogous with those of a cylindrical pipe open at both ends. It readily sounds its 1st harmonic (i.e. overblows at the octave), thus providing a second register with the fingering of the first repeated, and its tones are highly complex, containing both even- and odd-numbered partials. Tonal analysis has shown that the harmonic content varies considerably from note to note and the resultant changes in timbre are quite evident to a sensitive ear. In the first octave the harmonics are very prominent but the relative power of the fundamental increases as the scale ascends. This variation can be attributed in a large measure to departures in the bore from an ideal geometrical form, such as the cavities formed by closed tone holes, and to the size and depth of these when open. All wind

instruments are 'coupled acoustic systems', comprising a generator (in this case the reed) and what is commonly, though somewhat inaccurately, called the RESONATOR, in this case the air column. It is an oversimplification to consider these elements separately. There is interaction between the vibrations of the reed blades and those natural to the air column and these affect each other

(a)   (b)   (c)   (d)

2. *The modern oboe family: (a) soprano in C; (b) oboe d'amore in A; (c) english horn (cor anglais) in F; (d) baritone in C*

3. Double-reed instrument with a bulb bell, and clappers: miniature from the 'Cantigas de Santa María', Spanish, late 13th century (E-E b.I.2, f.295v)

mutually, with results that are now partly understood and which can be expressed by mathematical formulae. Here, however, it is probably sufficient to regard the reed as a sort of valve, which transforms a steady stream of wind supplied by the player into a pulsating body. This energizes the air column in the tube of the instrument, the frequency of the pulsations being near to one natural to the air column and dictated mainly by its dimensions. (For further discussion of the oboe, *see* ACOUSTICS, §III, 3 and 5.)

The bulb bell, which is so conspicuous a feature of the larger oboes, is of ancient origin and is depicted in the late 13th-century *Cantigas de Santa María* (E-E b.I.2; see fig.3). For many years, it has been considered to be the source of the very characteristic timbre of the deeper members of the family but its form and dimensions vary a great deal with different instrument makers. Recent experiments suggest that it exerts little influence that the unaided ear can detect beyond the first three or four notes of the scale. Considered apart from the rest of the body tube, its chief property is that of cavity resonance at certain frequencies, and it may be that its effect is to emphasize those frequencies and their multiples when they occur in the harmonic make-up.

3. EARLY HISTORY AND CONSTRUCTION. The French word 'hautbois' (high-, strong-, loud-, or principal-wood) in its various spellings was applied to the smaller members of the SHAWM family, both in France and England, long before the emergence of the special type that now bears the name; these instruments had an important place in the 'loud music' of the Middle Ages. Indeed, the double-reed principle can be traced back almost as far as can any record of Man as a music maker. By the 16th century, both Germany and Italy had their own names for the shawm but, when the oboe proper came into being, both these areas adopted for it a phonetic version of the French name. This seems to indicate that the new instrument reached them by way of France and that it must have penetrated to most important musical centres in Europe comparatively quickly. In England, where a form

of the word (hoboy, hoyboye, howboie) was already a common alternative to wayght or wayte for the watchman's outdoor reedpipe, the new instrument was differentiated as the 'French hautboy' or 'French hoboy'. With the decline of the shawms in England and the acceptance of the oboe into art music, the distinction of 'French' was dropped gradually and 'hoboy' became common usage. This persisted until about 1770, when the swing of fashion dictated the adoption of the Italian form 'oboe'.

The somewhat fanciful names which have been applied to the tenor oboe have not, so far, been explained satisfactorily. The French 'haute-contre de hautbois' and 'taille' are self-explanatory, but how 'cor anglais' and its German translation 'englisches Horn' originated remains a mystery. The suggestion that the name is a corruption of 'cor anglé' derived from an 18th-century form with an obtuse-angled tube can hardly be sustained on etymological grounds. The Italian term 'oboe da caccia' (reserved by such organologists as Sachs and Bessaraboff for a curved, open-bell form of the tenor with a relatively wide bore) may perhaps stem from the use of such an instrument in formal music associated with the chase, although later research tends to discount this idea (*see* OBOE DA CACCIA). Otherwise there is a lack of positive evidence. Bach, however, wrote only 'oboe da caccia' or 'taille' on his scores, whatever tenor instrument he may have had in mind, while the translation 'corno inglese' was used by Jommelli as early as 1741.

The suffix 'd'amour' or 'd'amore' seems at different times to have been applied somewhat indiscriminately to woodwind in general when pitched a minor 3rd below the standard instrument and, in the case of reed instruments, it has come to be associated particularly with the bulb bell. This may have been because of the tone-mellowing effect, more fancied than real, that was formerly attributed to this device. Hence the terms 'd'amore bell' and 'Liebesfuss' are now used, whatever the actual pitch of the instrument referred to.

It is now generally accepted that the true oboe, with its characteristic three-joint structure, originated in the hands of that remarkable group of players and instrument makers – including the Philidors, the Chédevilles and the Hotteterres – who flourished at the French court in the early and mid-17th century, and it has been argued with some force that Jean Hotteterre (i) deserves credit as the actual creator of the instrument. All these men, as members of the Grande Ecurie du Roi, were of course well acquainted with the outdoor and military shawms and no doubt these formed the basis of their experiments. But the creation of the new oboe was not merely a matter of improvement. Between the two instruments there is a distinction of form, construction and musical purpose and, for some long time, the two existed side by side, each fulfilling its own social function.

The musical superiority of the true oboe was achieved by the abolition of the pirouette (*see* SHAWM), thus allowing a more delicate control of the reed between the lips and thus a greater compass, by some redesign of the bore and by an alteration to the size and disposition of the finger-holes which would allow a fully chromatic system of 'fork' or 'cross' fingerings through two octaves. At the same time, the relative intonation of the two registers was improved. Such work called for fine adjustment of internal dimensions, the undercutting of tone holes, etc, and it seems likely that the jointed construction was adopted to facilitate this. It would have been a task already familiar to men skilled in making the refined musettes – delicate little bagpipes – then fashionable in court circles and, indeed, the elegance of this work is clearly reflected in some of the earliest surviving examples of the oboe. These were often elaborately decorated and mounted, a sure sign that they were highly prized and of aristocratic status. In the new instruments, the considerable length of the tube below the finger-holes, a characteristic of the shawms, was much reduced, only a short cylindrical section at the root of the bell being retained and vented by two open holes, which determined the effective length of the whole air column (fig.5, p.796). As in most contemporary woodwind, there were six primary holes, set in two more or less evenly spaced groups of three, with a larger space occupied by the middle socket between them. At the lower end a further hole, controlled by an articulated open-standing key, extended the compass by a whole tone, and above this a closed hole with a key (at first duplicated on the right and left) gave the chromatic semitone $d\sharp'$. Although the nominal primary scale was that of D major, the six finger-holes were usually somewhat ambiguous in their tuning, leaving great latitude to the player in the matter of intonation and inflection. Further chromatic possibilities were commonly provided by making the third and fourth holes small and in pairs instead of single. The opening of one or both together provided an alternative fingering for certain semitones. The missing $c\sharp'$ was at first obtainable only by the rather uncertain expedient of partly closing the 'great' key, or by sharpening the c' by sheer strength of lip. Many early instruction books omit any reference at all to this note. Two final features are the sharp increase in diameter or 'step' in the bore often found at the middle and bell joints, and the thick inturned bell rim. The former probably began as a deliberate acoustic structure concerned with the system of tuning adopted, but the latter was until recently commonly explained as an attempt to strengthen the instrument at its most vulnerable point. It has been suggested that the undercutting at the lip of the bell was intended to limit the 'running' of possible splits; in the mid-1970s, however, it was demonstrated that the degree of undercutting is vitally concerned with internal tuning and the mutual regulation of the components of the tonal spectrum. Both are prominent features of the modern Vienna-style oboe, and are also found in many French instruments as late as the mid-19th century.

The distinguishing features of the emergent oboe were as follows: three sections united by tenon-and-socket joints; a primary six-hole scale from d', extended downwards by the 'great' key to c'; a two-octave compass; one or two 'less' keys, providing $d\sharp'$; a bell vented by two open holes; and a reed mounted on a staple clear of the body and with no pirouette. It was in this form that, by the beginning of the 18th century, the oboe had become known in all the most important musical centres of Europe (see fig.5b).

France and England provide the fullest early documentation of the new 'hautbois'. Cambert's *Pomone* (Paris, 1671) is usually cited as its first public appearance, although there is some evidence that Lully had already introduced it in *L'amour malade* (1657). Fortunately, English sources are remarkably helpful for the period up to the end of the 17th century and enable its rising vogue to be traced in some detail. The oboe appears to have reached England, again under Cambert's influence, for the masque of *Calisto*, organized by John Crowne and Nicholas Staggins in 1674. For this production, extra musicians were brought over from France, among them the reed and recorder players Paisible, de Bresmes, Guiton and Boutet. This certainly suggests that the new instrument had some special virtues, for, at the time, English shawms were readily available, several members of the Staggins family alone being waits. Like Cambert, Paisible remained in England and entered the king's service, and contemporary evidence suggests very strongly that he was the first in England to use the true oboe professionally. Evidently the musical climate of Restoration England was favourable both to visiting musicians and to the instruments they brought with them (as can be learnt from Pepys's diary, among other sources). Two years after the performance of *Calisto*, Etherege referred to the 'French hautboys' in *The Man of Mode*; in 1678 the Horse Grenadiers adopted the instrument, and three years later it made its first appearance in one of Purcell's scores, *Swifter, Isis, swifter flow*. An English drawing in Randle Holme's *Academy of*

4. The Douze Grands Hautbois from the Grande Ecurie du Roi at the coronation of Louis XV at Rheims in 1715: detail from an anonymous contemporary engraving

5. (a) Treble shawm, ?Spanish, 16th century (Conservatoire Royal de Musique, Brussels); (b) oboe by C. Rijkel, Amsterdam, c1695 (Gemeentemuseum, The Hague)

(a)   (b)

bois', with detailed measurements and a tablature or fingering chart (see Baines, 1948). From the same period, too, come three English instruction books for the instrument: *Plaine and Easie Directions*, *The Sprightly Companion*, both of 1695, and *Military Musick, or The Art of Playing on the Hautbois* (1697). In addition, Walsh published a tablature for 'hautboy' in his *Second Book of Theatre Musick* (1699).

With fairly abundant information about the form and use of the early oboe, it is a pity that so much less is known about the reed used, though this is inevitable considering the delicacy of its structure and the perishable nature of its material. The most that can be gathered from somewhat crude illustrations is that early reeds were, by modern standards, rather broad relative to their length, and wedge-shaped. Talbot's measurements suggest that they were little different from those used with the shawms. There is no contemporary suggestion that the new oboe was essentially a softer-toned instrument than the shawm, but its flexibility and dynamic range were commented upon both by Talbot and by the author of *The Sprightly Companion* (probably the younger John Banister), who wrote in his preface that it was 'not much Inferior to the Trumpet' and that 'with a good reed and skilful hand it sounds as easy and soft as the flute'. No doubt it was these two characteristics which commended the true oboe to musicians in general and led to its wide and rapid adoption.

4. THE 18TH CENTURY. The 100 years from 1690 cover what can be called the 'three- and two-key' phase of oboe evolution. It was during this period that the instrument was fully accepted into the developing mixed orchestra, first doubling the strings but very soon as a most expressive solo voice in its own right. In chamber combinations, too, it soon proved its value and stimulated some of the finest wind writing of all time. The early 1700s saw the appearance of the first important continental instruction books – those of Freillon Poncein (1700), J. M. Hotteterre (1707), Eisel (Erfurt, 1737) and Minguet y Yrol (Madrid, 1754) – as well as the reprinting of several English books.

The first part of the 18th century was a period of consolidation, and the years before 1750 saw both a desire for technical amelioration and also the first signs of emerging national characteristics. The duplicate $d\sharp'$ key on the left was provided less often, and it would seem that by then players in general had settled for 'left hand above right', as is standard today. The double touchpiece of the 'great' key, however, persisted for many years as an ornamental feature. Thereafter a remarkable variation in the external appearance of the instrument is noticeable and, among surviving specimens, four distinct types can be recognized: the earliest and most highly ornamented form, which today is often referred to as the Baroque oboe, in which the finial at the top is distinctly reminiscent of the shawm's pirouette (fig.5b); a mid-century type, mainly French, in which ornamental turning is reduced to a mere bulb near the top and somewhat swollen sockets (fig.6a); an exclusively English type, with a completely straight profile and minimal expansion at the sockets (fig.6b); a reversion late in the century to ornamental turning, though in a less elegant form and with a more nearly conical bell (fig.6c). In this last form, there is a tendency towards a more strict tuning of the finger-holes. By the last decade of the century, some players on the transverse flute were regularly

Armoury (1688) is well known, although in it only the 'great' key is shown. From 1690 until his death, Purcell used the instrument in all his larger works and wrote at least three obbligato parts for solo oboe which, by their recognition of the essential character of the instrument – its lyricism and rustic sprightliness in *Come ye Sons of Art* (1694), its capacity for romantic meditation – far outstrip anything by his contemporaries.

Just after Purcell's death, James Talbot of Trinity College, Cambridge, recorded among his personal notes 'the present Hautbois not 40 years old and an improvement of the great French hautbois which is like our Weights' (shawms) – the only contemporary reference to the age and genesis of the instrument. Talbot, who was in direct touch with Paisible and other musicians of his time, also left a full description of the 'French haut-

using three semitone keys in addition to the essential $d\sharp'$ on the foot joint. Their equivalents were not added to the oboe for some time, probably because in its original form it was the more amenable of the two to satisfactory fork fingering. Nevertheless, certain oboes produced by the Dresden makers Grundmann and Grenser at the end of the century show what appear to be experiments in that direction.

From the second half of the 18th century there is the first positive, though scanty, evidence of the reeds used. In a few museums, there are staples of rolled-up sheet metal with remnants of the cane attached, which can be dated $c1770$ (see fig.12a below). These fragments, together with one or two compartmented reed cases of about the same date, give a clue to the dimensions of the blades when complete – approximately 9 mm wide at the tip and still proportionately short. However, it is an error – often repeated – to assume that the tone from such reeds was necessarily coarse. The oboe illustration in Diderot's *Encyclopédie* (1751–65) shows a very peculiar reed, long, constructed without a staple and lapped apparently for insertion directly into the top of the instrument. As, however, this illustration bears no specific caption, and a very similar but larger one appears properly captioned on the bassoon plate in the same volume, it must be regarded with some suspicion.

5. THE 19TH CENTURY AND AFTER. Although the two-key oboe remained in use, and was probably still being made as late as $c1820$ (and here it must be noted that, after the initial stages, English practice lagged behind that of the Continent), the 19th century was the period of oboe mechanization. Between 1800 and 1825 eight keys appeared, at first as alternatives to accepted fingerings, or to improve intonation, but later as primary facilities. It is almost impossible to date the advent of these individually but their order of arrival seems likely to have been: (i) the 'speaker' or octave key, which is frequently found as an obvious addition to cherished two-key instruments; (ii) a closed G$\sharp$ key for the left little finger, supplementing but not necessarily replacing the twinned third holes; (iii) a vent key between holes 4 and 5 to improve the F$\sharp$. This was opened by the right little finger and, though awkward, survived until about 1840, when it gave place to the open-standing ring or 'spectacle' device borrowed from Boehm's reformed flute and applied to both oboe and clarinet; (iv) a closed key, which eliminated the uncertain fingering for $c\sharp'$; (v) a closed F key, as on the contemporary flute, set crosswise between holes 5 and 6; (vi) a closed B$\flat$ key on the upper joint; (vii) a closed C$\sharp$ key, also on the upper joint; (viii) a long-shanked open key, covering one of the vent-holes in the bell and extending the compass down to b. With this, the second hole in the bell was often, but not always, omitted. The placing of the touchpieces of keys (iv), (vi), (vii) and (viii) above remained variable for some years before becoming standardized. On the upper joint, the B$\flat$ was given to either the left thumb or the right forefinger, sometimes both; the C to the right forefinger or left ring finger and the bell key to either the left little finger or the left thumb. Of all these additions, however, it is the low $c\sharp'$, usually given to the right little finger, that shows most variety. Since the key covered a small hole placed below that for the c' key, some device was needed to enable a single pressure to close the one and open the other simultaneously to sound $c\sharp'$, as well as to allow the c' to be closed independently for

the bell note. A simple crossing of the touchpieces served at first but this necessitated a sliding movement of the fingertip in some passages. To ease or obviate this, many mechanical arrangements, from simple rollers to ingenious leverages, have been devised and today there is little difficulty. On some mid-century German instruments, however, the $c\sharp'$ was allocated to the left little finger, with an interposed lever to close the c', and on later examples both touches were provided.

Thus a fully-equipped oboe such as Beethoven might have known in his last years would have had 14 tone holes and one speaker key, and would have been fully chromatic from b upwards without recourse to fork fingering. By this time, also, advanced players had, by

(a)   *(b)*   *(c)*

6. *Three 18th-century oboes: (a) by Thomas Lot, Paris, c1775; (b) by W. Milhouse, Newark, c1765 (Bate Collection, University of Oxford); (c) by Goulding, London, c1800*

special fingerings and lip technique, extended their range upwards to *f'''* or, exceptionally, to *a'''*. By 1825, Josef Sellner of the Viennese court orchestra had added some duplicate touchpieces and thus created his so-called '13-key oboe', the most advanced of its time (see fig.11*a* below). This still remains the basis of the Vienna-style instrument as used today. At this stage, too, there is evidence of concern with variable pitch standards: German and Austrian makers began to provide their best instruments with either a small telescopic tuning-slide at the top, or alternative upper joints on the *pièce de rechange* principle. In fact, *pièces de rechange* for oboes are recorded as early as 1798 (see fig.7) but they seem to have been quite exceptional at that time.

In spite of an apparent ascendancy of the Viennese oboe in the third decade of the 19th century, the mechanized French instrument then began an independent existence. There is reason to think that divergences between French- and German-speaking ideals of reed

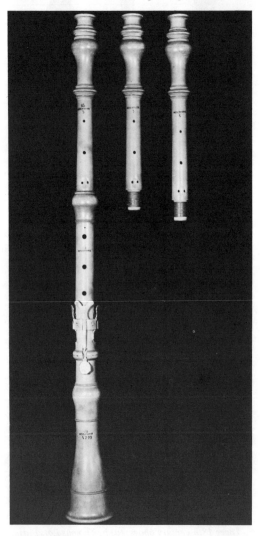

7. *Oboe in C (with two pièces de rechange) by Johann Gottfried Liebel Adorf, Germany, 1798 (Dayton C. Miller Flute Collection, Library of Congress, Washington, DC)*

tone were already evident before 1800, the former tending to sensitivity and refinement, the latter favouring warmth and robustness. The first two professors at the Paris Conservatoire, Sallantin (who taught from 1794 to after 1816) and Vogt (1813–58), adhered to the old simple instrument, but many of their younger pupils had different ideas. First, perhaps, among them was Henri Brod, who in 1839 began to manufacture oboes whose delicacy of construction combined with practicality has never been surpassed. He adopted the new keys and made several mechanical improvements, including a 'see-saw' arrangement for the *c'* and *c♯'* touchpieces, and a device to make positive the uncertain but essential half-closing of the top finger-hole (fig.10*b*). Since his time, some form of apparatus for this has been included in the key-work of even the simplest oboes. Contemporary with Brod were the first of the celebrated TRIÉBERT family, in whose hands the French instrument progressed to its finest form. Their work included a complete redesigning of the bore, tending always to greater tonal refinement, as well as progressive improvements to the key mechanism. In all, this firm produced six *systèmes* (with variations), the principal features of which are illustrated in fig.10. Their most important innovations were the *système 5*, the so-called 'thumb-plate' model, and the *système 6* or 'Conservatoire' oboe of the mid-1870s (fig.10*c* and *d*), both of which have certain special virtues and are in extensive use today. In the thumb-plate model, the holes for B♭ and C on the upper joint have keys lightly sprung to stand open while their tails overlap, the C on top of the B♭. Attached to the C key is a ring surrounding the B hole and to the B♭ a touchpiece for the right forefinger. Both key-tails engage with a rather strong spring carried by a pivoted thumb-plate at the back of the joint. The effect is that, when the oboe is held in the normal manner, the pressure of the left thumb closes the two keys against the bias of their own springs but a pressure of the right forefinger sufficient to overcome the plate spring allows one or both to fly open, depending on whether or not the left middle finger is holding down its ring. Thus the notes *b♭'* and *c''* can be made either by the orthodox fingering or by a simple release of the left thumb in passages where the right hand is not readily available.

On its introduction, the *système 5* method did not appeal to some players, who mistrusted a mechanism that depended on the mutual opposition of springs of different strength. Frederick Triébert, therefore, set himself to the task of finding some other arrangement. He abolished the thumb-plate entirely and transferred its function of closing the B♭ and C holes to a ring for the right forefinger (fig.10*d*). This constituted the basic *système 6*, but work did not stop there. After Triébert's death in 1878, the elder Lorée, for many years foreman to the firm, continued the experiments and soon produced the *système A6* in which any of the first three fingers of the right hand could operate the B♭–C mechanism. The eminent Georges Gillet had much influence on Lorée's work and, in 1882, he secured the adoption of *A6* in his class at the Conservatoire – hence the use of the title for this type of French oboe. Today both these models are produced with great perfection by many fine makers, although some have made yet further adjustments to the bore (and the reed). In many parts of the world today, there is a preference for a 'darker' and more compact tone than that of the later Lorée examples. In addition, the Triéberts produced a very

8. 'The Oboe Player': portrait (c1770) attributed to Johann Zoffany with detail of reed (Smith College Museum of Art, Northampton, Massachusetts)

tional bore, and such oboes find some employment today, particularly among 'double-handed' musicians. An extreme case is the 'saxophone-fingered' oboe, whose designation is self-explanatory. Recently some English music teachers have recommended the modified-bore Boehm oboe for use in schools, because of its marginally simpler fingering.

While the French-style instrument is undoubtedly predominant today, there remain a few centres where, under Austrian or Italian influence, an improved version of the Sellner oboe is preferred. The principal stronghold of the Viennese instrument is Vienna itself but even there by 1954 manufacture had greatly declined, and the successors to the great name of Zuleger, for example, produce mainly oboes and clarinets on the French pattern. During the 19th century German makers developed a somewhat extreme version of the Viennese oboe, with an enlarged upper bore, and sometimes, as with HECKEL instruments, a third octave key. These instruments are known to have persisted in Russia until about 1960, when a large government order from Paris seemed to indicate a change of taste or, perhaps, a desire to 'come into line', at a time when Russian musicians were becoming internationally prominent.

A fair number of datable French reeds survive from about the middle of the 19th century (see fig.12*b*), and these show a progressive refinement similar to that of the oboe itself. By the end of the Triébert period the modern form, with almost parallel sides, was fully established in France, and the blades had reached their narrowest width: something under 6·5 mm (see fig.12*c*). Today most players favour a rather wider reed of the same shape but the size, strength and 'scrape' of an oboe reed are still extremely personal matters (*see* REED). The same applies also to the use of a turn of fine, stiff wire

advanced oboe following the ideas of A. M.-R. Barret, who was highly influential in England in the 1860s. It combined the facilities of both the thumb-plate and right-hand rings to release the Bb and C keys and seems to have anticipated the true 'Conservatoire' action (figs.10*e* and 11*b*). It incorporated other modifications as well. By this time the second octave key, introduced before 1850, had become accepted as essential; on Barret's oboe the choice of key at any given time was made automatic. Some players today use 'automatics' on other models and some an independent third octave key, but, on the whole, they seem to be in a minority. More common is the so-called 'plateau' model with all holes covered, as produced by Lorée under the direction of the greatly respected Fernand Gillet.

The radical reforms applied to the flute by Boehm about 1830, once they had gained a measure of acceptance, were almost bound to have repercussions on other woodwind. In 1844 L.-A. Buffet of Paris patented an oboe designed on Boehm's acoustic principles, with a system of ring-keys to correspond (fig.11*c*). Boehm himself was actually concerned with the production of this instrument. Oboes of this type found some welcome in military circles, but the powerful and somewhat 'open' tone, due to the large bore and tone holes, failed to appeal to the majority of French oboists. In England, however, the celebrated Lavigne adopted the Boehm-type instrument and had a number of versions constructed to his own ideas. The Triéberts and other French makers attempted to apply Boehm keywork to a more conven-

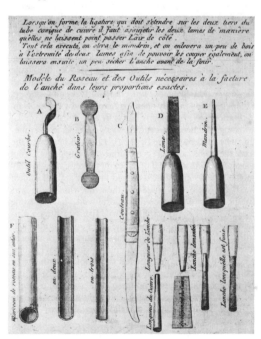

9. Oboe reeds (before and after binding) and reed-making tools: engraving from F. Garnier's 'Méthode raisonnée pour le hautbois' (c1800)

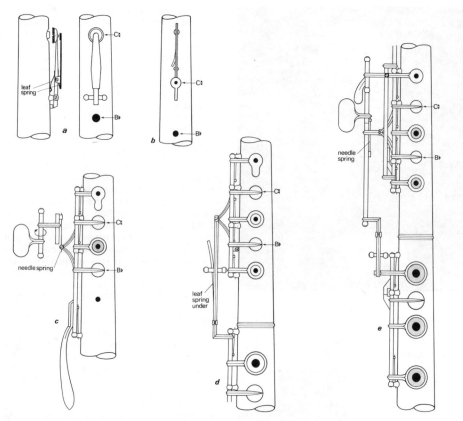

10. Details of oboe keywork: (a) half-hole plate found on some early Triébert oboes; (b) Brod's half-hole plate, c1839; (c) Triébert's thumb-plate action; (d) Triébert's 'Conservatoire' action for B♭ and C♮, including the half-hole plate; (e) combined 'Conservatoire' and thumb-plate actions, known as the 'full Barret'

about the blades, its ends being twisted together. This arrangement provides a minute adjustment to the shape of the blade opening and is regarded as essential in all the larger double reeds, but comparatively few players except perhaps in Italy seem to favour it for the soprano instrument. With modern German and Austrian reeds, a vestige of the 18th-century wedge shape may sometimes be discerned (see fig.12d). Like the blades of the reed, the staple, too, has been refined progressively. From a simple rolled-up piece of sheet metal kept airtight only by the thread lapping it, it passed through several stages. First, the seam was soldered, then the whole tube was solid-drawn on a tapered mandrel and, lately, some makers have been producing it to a fine finish by a process of electro-deposition. Sometimes a tiny collar was fitted to hold the root of the blades, but this seems now to be rather out of favour. The oldest surviving Triébert reeds show the lapping carried the whole length of the staple and expanded at the foot into a cigar-shaped plug. By the mid-19th century, however, this had been replaced by a layer of thin cork sheet, which ensured an accurate fit in a cylindrical recess – usually metal-lined – at the top of the bore.

6. LARGER OBOES. The history of the deeper-toned oboes in the main parallels that of the soprano instrument, though not quite consistently.

The OBOE D'AMORE has played the smallest part in European music of any of the oboes and, but for its employment by Bach and one or two later composers, might be regarded as of little significance. Its origin is obscure, but it has been suggested that pitched in A it may at first have been used simply as a lower alternative to the C instrument. From the two-key stage onwards, the oboe has always been regarded as fully chromatic, but in its earlier days it was by no means easy to handle fluently in the more extreme keys. The various pitch standards observed in the early 18th century must also have presented serious problems. But beyond the considerations of playing convenience, Bach seems to have scored for various instruments simply for their colour and emotional appeal. It is almost certain that it was in these terms that Strauss thought of the oboe d'amore in his *Symphonia domestica* (1904). After the 18th century, the instrument passed into oblivion for many years until it was revived in 1884 by Charles Mahillon of Brussels for 'authentic' Bach performances. This recreation took the form of an enlarged normal oboe of its time with an open bell and a short curved crook to carry the reed. Today, as a result of further work by Lorée, the instrument is regularly supplied with the *Liebesfuss* (see fig.2b above). It is built to all recognized systems of keywork but the compass does not usually descend below (written) *b*.

The tenor oboe (ENGLISH HORN), built a 4th or more commonly a 5th below the treble, was certainly known before the end of the 17th century and Talbot wrote that in his time its structure was no different. The first recorded orchestral use was in Purcell's *Dioclesian* (1691) but for a time thereafter a number of respectable authorities seem not to have known of it. In the first years of the 18th century, it appears to have been used mainly in a military context and parts for *taille* or *haute-contre de hautbois* are found in many of the marches of the Philidor Collection (sold in 1978; now in *F-Pn* and elsewhere; printed in G. Kastner, *Manuel géneral de musique militaire*, 1848). Undoubtedly it also had its place among the Douze Grands Hautbois du Roi at the 1715 coronation (fig.4 above). Then, the shape of the continental tenor seems to have been curiously unstable and examples are known varying from the gently curved to completely straight or with an obtuse angle between the joints. English makers, however, appear to have remained faithful to the older form and about 1750 produced a curious bell-less variety which they termed *vox humana* and which is quite unknown elsewhere. The reason for bending the body of the tenor oboe has not been fully explained and there are several theories. The consensus is that the bending represents an attempt to make a long instrument less unwieldy for outdoor and, particularly, military use. For a brief discussion of the bulb bell, today an essential feature of the instrument, and its special nomenclature, see §§2 and 3 above.

Shortly before 1839, Brod produced his *cor anglais moderne*, the first completely straight continental tenor of modern type, and he dealt with its inconvenient length by using a curved brass crook to carry the reed. Thereafter, the modern history of the instrument is the same as that of the soprano, except that, for some years, a curved upper joint alone persisted in France. For a long time, the construction of these curved joints, almost invariably concealed by a covering of polished and tooled leather, was a subject of controversy among organologists. Curved tubes, of course, could be made in two halves hollowed out of plank wood glued together face to face, as they are in cornetts, and this seems to have been the method of choice for the oboes da caccia, but there is no evidence of such a technology with the more sophisticated bulb-bell instruments. It has been argued that these joints must have been formed by hot-bending with the aid of steam, but this theory can be challenged on the grounds of proven instability. There is some evidence, however, that since the 18th century wood-turners have known of a chemical process to render wood to a degree flexible. If joints so prepared moved a little from time to time, it would presumably have been of little significance in the case of two-key instruments. Recently it has been discovered that joints sufficiently stable to bear pillar-mounted keywork without danger of binding were actually produced by turning and boring in the usual way: narrow wedges were cut out almost, but not completely, across the tube, which could then be bent in a series of obtuse angles and caulked with waterproof cement. The joins were retained in apposition, either by a wooden or metal splint applied along the inner curvature or by wooden keys let in and pegged across the junctions. The Triéberts produced particularly fine examples but in their very latest curved joints introduced a more advanced technique. In them, the sections were completely separate and were united by small independent tenons, the resulting bore approaching more nearly to a perfect curve than that produced by the older method.

Unlike the oboe d'amore, the BARITONE OBOE, an octave below the soprano, is of considerable importance in its own right. Its early history is obscure and, in the 17th century, its possible function in the wind ensemble was, in fact, taken over by the jointed bassoon, which in France was known as *basse de hautbois*. The earliest undoubted baritone oboe at present known is one made by Charles Bizet probably before 1750, now in the Paris Conservatoire collection. In this example the obvious problem of excessive length was overcome by doubling the bore on itself by means of a sort of bassoon 'boot'. A bassoon-style crook carried the reed and the awkward distance between adjacent finger-holes was reduced by boring

(a)   *(b)*   *(c)*

11. *Three 19th-century oboes: (a) by Stephen Koch, Vienna, c1825 (Sellner's 13-key model); (b) by Triébert, Paris (Barret's model of 1860); (c) by L.-A. Buffet, Paris (Boehm system as patented by Buffet in 1844) (Bate Collection, University of Oxford)*

(a)   (b)   (c)   (d)   (e)

12. *Oboe reeds from the late 18th century to the 20th:
(a) late 18th century (Bate Collection, University of
Oxford); (b) by Triébert, c1850; (c) modern French; (d)
modern Viennese; (e) modern American (normal scrape)*

these obliquely through thickenings in the tube wall. No
doubt the tone was somewhat modified by these features
and the paucity of surviving examples suggests that, at
this period, the instrument did not get far beyond the
experimental stage. In the 19th century most of the difficulties were smoothed out with the development of
modern keywork but it is notable that the Triéberts persisted with the old reflected tube (see fig.14c).

Brod commended this Triébert model in the second
volume of his *Méthode* (1835), so it is particularly interesting that a completely straight baritone oboe by Brod
– a simple enlargement of his 'cor anglais moderne'
– exists. This instrument is probably unique but does
seem to have anticipated the work of Lorée, who, in
1839, revised the baritone oboe completely on the most
modern lines, leaving it as efficient as any other member of the family (see fig.2d above). Today, the HECKEL-
PHONE frequently replaces the true baritone oboe, in some
opinions not always to advantage. Delius, although he
often designated parts 'bass oboe', intended them to be
played by the heckelphone, as German editions of his
scores show.

Outside the orchestral family, which is the main concern here, there remain a few exceptional instruments,
both large and small, which must be classified as oboes.
Oboes in high D or E♭ are comparatively well known,
and they have been constructed in all the recognized key
systems, including the Boehm. They are mainly continental military instruments, used to impart brilliance to
brass and reed ensembles. Others appear to be no more
than instrument makers' improvements on the bucolic
'musette', some retaining even the characteristic musette
fingering, complete with a hole at the back for the left
thumb. These would appear to have been intended only
for rustic music but others have attained higher status
and are true oboes by definition. For example, a small

instrument illustrated in a tutor for the Boehm system
oboe bears the title 'pastoral oboe' and was evidently
intended for serious music. At the other extreme, a contrabass or 'great bass' oboe was designed by the celebrated maker Delusse in the 18th century. This
instrument, now in the Paris Conservatoire collection,
is recorded in a music almanac for 1784 as played for
some time by the Opéra bassoonist Lemarchand. Constant Pierre (*La facture instrumentale à L'Exposition
universelle*, 1890) wrote that Lorée, having introduced
his new oboe d'amore and baritone oboe the previous
year, was proposing to complete the family with a
contrabass. No further account is known of this proposed monster, which might have carried the true oboe
timbre down as far as that of the contemporary bassoon.

Finally, the ingenious, though abortive, oboe of Giorgi
and Schaffner is worth mentioning. Patented in France
in 1889, this instrument was based on the theory that
every semitone in the octave should be sounded by its
own appropriate length of tube. This was achieved by
providing a series of rectangular holes, each large enough
virtually to terminate the air column and render negli-
gible the mass of air below, and was further effected by
making all the cover-plates stand open at rest and linking them by an arrangement of bell-cranks and connecting rods. The mechanism provided for a logical
system of sequential fingering. The inventors applied
their principle to the flute and clarinet as well but the
idea seems to have been defeated by the extreme com-
plication of the keywork. It seems likely that the Giorgi–
Schaffner oboe would have been open to the same tonal
objections as the first Boehm-system instrument but it
is difficult to judge from the few examples, which now
survive only as collectors' pieces.

7. TECHNIQUE AND CAPABILITIES. While never regarded
as an easy instrument to learn, the oboe, by reason of
its expressiveness, variety of tone and great dynamic
range, is probably one of the most rewarding. It is
undoubtedly at its best in a medium compass, around *f'*
to *b''*, and in this range its tone is sweetest, neither too
reedy (as it sometimes tends to be lower down) nor thin
(as in the acute register). Within these rather narrow
limits of an octave and a 4th the widest dynamics from
a full singing *forte* to the faintest *pianissimo* are readily
available, and within them most composers from the time
of Gluck onwards have written their most satisfying
orchestral solos. The symphonies of Beethoven and
Schubert are full of perfect examples. In more modern
works oboe solos are at times carried up to the extreme
notes with great effect, and here the vocal quality of the
middle register is replaced by a unique and valuable
incisiveness. The oboe is capable of great agility, and
scale and arpeggio passages, diatonic and chromatic, are
readily played both staccato and legato. Double and triple
tonguing are both employed, though 'flutter-tonguing'
as sometimes demanded by an inconsiderate composer
can be performed by only a few players and to a limited
degree. Wide skips, grace notes and many shakes are
also possible, though with the last there are a few notable difficulties in spite of the facilities offered by modern keywork. With his instrument of 1860–62, Barret
claimed to have achieved perfect shakes on every note,
but most players today seem to distrust so much automatic mechanism. The reason for this is not difficult to
find. Consider, for example, fork fingering, which is
still the most convenient way of producing certain notes

in certain combinations. In the 18th century these notes could be sounded in no other way, and there is no doubt that the placing and dimensions of some of the holes were conditioned by this. Forked notes had, if possible, to be as good as any others, and if an overall consistency could be obtained by some slight sacrifice in the others, the compromise was often worth making. With the freedom in placing holes made possible by keywork, a curious anomaly sometimes appeared. A player wishing as a convenience to 'fork' a note could find that the hole involved, though now ideal for its primary function, was out of tune for anything else. The solution then was to provide yet more mechanism which would operate automatically whenever the fork was used. As a consequence of such problems there is a tendency for the instrument maker to offer the player a multiplicity of devices many of which may be used only very occasionally. On the whole, it seems best to follow the example of many leading players who choose and master a limited number of additions to the basic keywork which prove most useful most of the time. The choice is of course an individual one and may well depend on the player's natural dexterity.

The extension of the lower compass of the oboe to *b♭* by means of keywork has given the advanced player another additional facility in what are commonly called the harmonics. Properly speaking all notes from *c♯″* upwards where the primary fingering repeats itself with the addition of the 'half-hole' or a speaker key are harmonics, but the oboist makes no distinction about these in his mind and regards them as normal. The extra harmonics are obtained by fingering the first four notes of the scale together with the first speaker key, and the second four together with the second speaker. Thus *b♭*, *b♮*, *c′*, *c♯′* with the first speaker become *f″*, *f♯″*, *g″*, *g♯″*, and *d′*, *d♯′*, *e′*, *f′* with the second speaker become *a″*, *a♯″*, *b″*, *c‴* (i.e. a 12th higher). These notes are a useful addition to the oboist's resources particularly in solo work and have a very individual tone-colour although they require care and cannot be attacked *forte*. Unfortunately they are not available on oboes with some types of automatic octave action, unless these are provided with a cancelling device, as on the full Barret model. Certain of the highest notes of the normal compass can also be sounded as 12ths or as superoctaves according to a variety of possible fingerings; again, a slight and useful difference in timbre is noticeable.

The first essential in oboe playing, as in singing (some of the greatest oboe players have also been singers), is of course a controlled and unlaboured breathing, regardless of the style of embouchure used. Surprisingly little positive information about this is to be found in even the most esteemed instruction books, and no doubt it is a matter that teachers have found easier to impart by example than by description. Rothwell's *Oboe Technique* (1953), however, has much sound advice on breathing. The oboist's difficulty is that the narrow opening of the reed will allow only a small quantity of air to pass in a given time, but it requires that quantity to be at a fairly high pressure. This calls for a considerable volume of air in reserve, which must be discharged when possible. It is difficult to clear the lungs of stale, oxygenless air before the whole volume has passed through the instrument. Most oboists agree that deep and unhurried abdominal breathing through the mouth best meets the case, advantage being taken of every opportunity to breathe offered by the music. A

device of jewellers and other users of the old mouth blowpipe is to employ the cheeks as an air reservoir while refilling the lungs through the nose. Certain oboists have by these means achieved unbroken phrases of phenomenal length, but many regard this as no more than a meretricious trick. A development of the mouth-reservoir principle is found in the use of the aerophore, a small foot-operated bellows attached to a tiny delivery tube which the player can keep in the corner of his mouth while still controlling his reed. However, once welcomed as the solution to all breathing problems, this apparatus is now little encountered.

The question of vibrato in wind playing has aroused the most violent feeling. With the exception of numerous players who practise period techniques on Baroque or Classical instruments, some degree of vibrato is now-

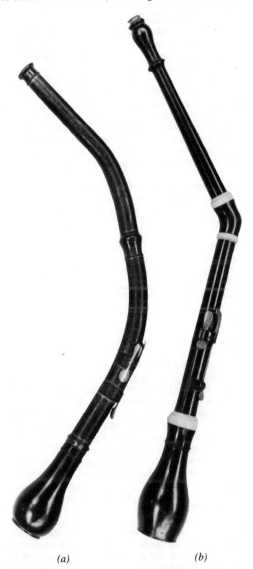

(a)   *(b)*

13. Two late 18th-century english horns: (a) by Bimboni, Florence; (b) by Milhouse, London (private collections)

adays regarded as a legitimate part of oboe technique; in the USA it is the subject of considerable study. As an embellishment, its use should always be governed by considerations of good taste and musical fitness in prevailing circumstances.

Even though not often called for today, muting can be applied to the oboe as long as one or two of the lowest holes are kept open. With the two-key 18th-century instrument there is evidence that a ball of cotton or lamb's wool was frequently placed in the bell, and pear-shaped wooden plugs for the same purpose survive. These seem to have acted mainly as tone modifiers which brought the quality of the bell note more into line with the higher sounds. With modern instruments this seems hardly necessary and probably the muting specified in, for example, the last few bars of *Petrushka* was intended to secure the softest possible *pianissimo*.

Since the 1960s woodwind technique has included the production of chords. Some players have, by means of special fingerings and a very sensitive control of the generator (be it reed or air-jet), found a method of reinforcing some partials simultaneously to an abnormal extent. Some are able to sustain one of these frequencies while trilling on another. Further, some partials are known to be dissonant with respect to their fundamental, and dissonance is characteristic of some of these chords. Other frequencies present seem to be quite unrelated to the fundamental in any way so far recognized. Bartolozzi's *New Sounds for Woodwind* (1967) and Singer's *Metodo per oboe* (1969) describe these techniques.

8. PERFORMERS AND TEACHERS. The development of the oboe has been influenced by players and player–teachers as well as makers. Among the earliest professional players were the Philidors, a highly esteemed family who served in the French court from the mid-17th century onwards. They were versatile, most of them playing the trumpet marine, fife and crumhorn as well as the hautbois; thus they formed a link between the old reed instruments and the new. The Hotteterre and Chédeville families also flourished at the French court; Jacques Hotteterre, who played the *basse de hautbois*, published *Principes de la flûte traversière . . . et du haut-bois* (1707) and wrote a considerable quantity of music with important oboe parts.

Giuseppe Sammartini (1695–1750) was an oboist and composer from Milan, whose works, together with those of his brother Giovanni Battista, were much esteemed in England during the first half of the 18th century. He played in the opera orchestra at the King's Theatre in London, and according to Burney his playing was notable for its rare refinement of tone. One of Sammartini's pupils was Thomas Vincent (c1720–1783), whose method of playing (according to *BurneyH*) raised the oboe to eminence as a solo instrument, though William Thomas Parke, for one, was critical of his tone. In England the virtuosity of the Besozzi family was much admired, and there is little doubt that their playing influenced English taste. The first two generations of the family, to which the outstanding players belonged, could have known only the two-keyed oboe; their performances and compositions are better documented than most, and are therefore valuable as evidence of the instrument's capabilities in the hands of experts. Johann Christian Fischer (1733–1800) was probably the most influential oboist of the 18th century, although opinions differed as to his tone and style and his powers are known to have declined in his later years. Parke, though often

an acid critic, evinced considerable admiration for his 'soft and sweet tone and expressive style'. Parke was himself a performer of repute; according to his own account, his ability to play in the highest register of the oboe attracted much admiration.

Another 18th-century virtuoso, Ludwig August Lebrun (1746–90), played in the court orchestra of his native Mannheim and that of Munich; his extensive tours brought him great fame as one of the leading oboists of his day. Johann Friedrich Alexander Griesbach is known to have been first oboist with the Philharmonic Society in London from 1813 to 1831. It is generally thought that he was the last notable player in England to use the old-fashioned broad reed, and according to a critic in the *Harmonicon* for 1830 his tone was clear and powerful. The same writer goes on to mention Griesbach's successor, H. A. Grattan-Cooke, whose reed was smaller and finer. W. E. Davies was of the opinion that Grattan-Cooke, and possibly his contemporary Crozier, were the last important English players to stand out against the influx of French instruments in the mid-19th century.

Pierre-Joachim-Raymond Soler (1810–50), a Spaniard who completed his musical education in Paris, won a *premier prix* at the Conservatoire in 1836. His proficiency on the Boehm-system oboe was much praised by the distinguished performer and teacher Enrique Marzo. Another *premier prix* winner at the Conservatoire was Antoine Joseph Lavigne (1816–86), principal oboist at the Théâtre Italien for several years. He gained his greatest fame in England, however, where he appeared mainly as a soloist, though a member of the Hallé Orchestra from 1861. His loud, unyielding tone was sometimes criticized, but Lavigne was regarded as a player with remarkable gifts of execution and phrasing. Perhaps the finest oboist of the late 19th century in Britain was Desiré Alfred Lalande (1866–1904), who played in leading orchestras in England and Scotland. The delicacy and refinement of his performances did much to foster appreciation of the French school of oboe playing in England at a period when German artists were predominant.

Notable oboe professors at the Paris Conservatoire include Antoine Sallantin (1754–1816), August-Gustave Vogt (1781–1870), Stanislas Verroust (1814–63), Charles-Louis Triébert (1810–67), Félix Charles Berthélemy (1829–68), Charles Joseph Colin (1832–81) and Georges Gillet (1854–1934). Among influential players who held professorships at English colleges were Apollon Marie-Rose Barret (1804–79), whose magnificent technique was internationally recognized, and William Malsch (1855–1924), widely regarded as both the best player in London and the most influential teacher of his time. Malsch's assistant at Trinity College, London, was A. J. B. Dubrucq, whose tone was described by a contemporary as 'simply heavenly', and his technique as equally beyond reproach. Other players of remarkable technical ability were Charles Reynolds (1843–1916) and particularly Leon Goossens (*b* 1897), whose sweet tone and exceptionally refined, expressive playing set new standards; many composers have been induced by his artistry into writing concertos and other oboe works.

Probably the most influential player and teacher in the USA was Marcel Tabuteau (1887–1966). Among distinguished oboists who were at different times his pupils were Harold Gomberg (long principal oboist of the New York PO) and his brother Ralph (of the Boston

SO), Robert Bloom (teacher at Yale and in New York), John Mack (Cleveland Orchestra) and Marc Lifschey (San Francisco SO). Other leading American players include Roy Still (Chicago SO) and John Delany (formerly Philadelphia Orchestra). The most prominent French figure is Pierre Pierlot (*b* 1921), a professor at the Conservatoire since 1949 and a refined solo and ensemble player; among German oboists a leading figure is the distinguished Berlin PO principal, Lothar Koch, a player of unusual tonal sweetness. The revival of the Baroque oboe has attracted several accomplished players, outstanding among them being the Swiss Michel Piguet (*b* 1932), who has worked with the Schola Cantorum Basiliensis. Modern oboe playing has been influenced by the ability of some players to sound chords, double trills and glissandos. A leading exponent of such effects is the Swiss oboist Heinz Holliger (*b* 1939), whose normal tone tends towards the French ideal (he was a Pierlot pupil) in its lightness and brilliance; he has also experimented with sounds produced by a microphone placed within the bore of the instrument.

9. REPERTORY AND ITS HISTORY.

(i) Up to 1750. Following the advent of the oboe around 1660 in the Grande Ecurie of Louis XIV, music which actually specified the instrument began to appear. One of the first works in which it was required was Cambert's opera *Pomone* (1671). It also appears in music by Purcell before 1700, notably *Come ye Sons of Art* (1694), in which it is assigned a florid obbligato part in the aria 'Bid the Virtues'. During the 18th century the use of the oboe greatly increased. The instrument became reliable in the hands of skilled players, and the volume of the music written for it strongly reflects this. In France, Germany, Italy and England it became established in numerous roles. Not only was it allowed solo passages in dramatic or large-scale vocal and choral works, but it also came to take a leading part in much orchestral and instrumental music. As a solo instrument with continuo, it was often an alternative to the flute or violin, and one or both of the solo melody instruments in the trio sonata. It was frequently used both in solo concertos and in concerti grossi, and featured regularly in chamber concertos by such composers as Vivaldi. By the end of the Baroque period there existed a wide repertory by numerous composers. In the Classical period it became one of the most frequently used wind instruments in the orchestra, where strings with two oboes and two horns was a standard ensemble, used by virtually every court orchestra and required by most early symphony composers. The oboe also appeared in various chamber combinations with other wind instruments and with solo strings, as well as being treated as a solo instrument.

Composers who had witnessed the early years of the oboe began to use it regularly in the early 18th century. This can be seen in the two *Livres de pièces* of 1712 and 1714 by Anne Danican Philidor and in the numerous pieces, sonatas, suites and treatises by Jacques-Martin Hotteterre. By composing a great deal of music for the instrument, Hotteterre did much to popularize it at this stage. At this time, too, composers such as François Couperin wrote much music which, while not specifically designed for the oboe, was appropriate to it; indeed it was often mentioned as an alternative to the more usual violin. Once the instrument was fully established in France, it soon came to be used by leading composers in Germany, Italy and England.

In Italy, Albinoni was one of the first composers to

(a)   *(b)*   *(c)*

14. (a) Oboe d'amore by P. Wolraupier, 18th century (Conservatoire Royal de Musique, Brussels); (b) tenor oboe by M. Lot, Paris, c1775 (Royal College of Music, London); (c) baritone oboe by Triébert, Paris, c1860 (Bate Collection, University of Oxford)

exploit the oboe's potential. His 24 concertos (op.7, 1715, and op.9, 1722) represent a large body of fine works for one or two instruments, and show that the oboe was capable of negotiating complex and demanding music. Vivaldi's use of solo instruments is also justly famous. Two concertos from his op.7 (RV464 and 465) are for oboe and two of his op.8 set (RV449 and 454) were additionally arranged for solo oboe; all these date from before 1725. There are two concertos for oboe and violin (RV543 and 548) and numerous concerti grossi where it is used in a concertino group. In the chamber concertos the oboe features prominently. Sonatas with continuo for solo oboe (RV53) and two oboes (RV81) survive. The parts in these works vary from the fairly straightforward to the extremely taxing, and testify to the high standard of playing of contemporary oboists.

The use of the oboe by Bach and Handel was also extensive. In two of Bach's Brandenburg Concertos it is used as part of a concertino group. Three are used in no.1, with the leading player involved in a florid dialogue with the solo *violino piccolo* in the slow movement; in no.2 it is used on equal terms with the trumpet, recorder and violin. Bach's use of the oboe as an obbligato instrument in the large-scale choral works and cantatas is particularly notable, for example the aria 'Ich will bei meinem Jesu wachen' from the *St Matthew Passion*; he also made extensive use of the oboe d'amore and the oboe da caccia in these works. His Harpsichord Concerto in A may originally have been composed for oboe d'amore. The oboe seems to have been Handel's most favoured orchestral wind instrument. It appears prominently in the op.3 concerti grossi (traditionally if misleadingly called the 'Hautboy Concertos'), most of the organ concertos, the *concerti a due cori* and the suites and overtures. Further, Handel's autograph of the op.6 concertos contains oboe parts in four works (nos.1, 2, 5 and 6) though these were not included in the published texts. One should also mention the three early solo concertos with strings and continuo, and numerous trio sonatas; the authenticity of the six 'Halle' sonatas for two oboes (or oboe and violin) and continuo must however at best be doubted, in spite of his assertion that he wrote 'like the devil' for the instrument in his youth.

The same variety is displayed in the works of most other composers of the first half of the 18th century. Important additions were made by C. P. E. Bach, Besozzi, Jean-Baptiste Loeillet, John Loeillet of London, Alessandro Marcello, Molter, Pepusch, Quantz, Telemann and Zelenka. Solo sonatas are the most common form, with a particularly large contribution from Telemann. The combination of instruments in the trio sonata was not always specified, and oboes were an accepted option along with recorders, flutes and violins, as available. Some composers specified the oboe: Jean-Baptiste Loeillet, for example, identified certain of his trio sonatas from op.1 (nos.1, 3 and 5) and from op.2 (nos.2, 4 and 6) as intended for recorder, oboe and continuo. There is an especially fine set of six sonatas for two oboes, bassoon and continuo by Jan Dismas Zelenka, possibly dating from as early as 1715.

(ii) Classical period. The second half of the 18th century saw the virtual disappearance of the solo sonata for oboe. Orchestral use of the instrument continued to be strong as it was frequently employed in pairs together with pairs of horns, for example in the earlier symphonies of Haydn and Mozart. With the increasing use of larger wind sections in the orchestra, the flute assumed equal status with the oboe; towards the end of the century the oboe had to share honours with the clarinet, and was sometimes even replaced by it, as in some works by Mozart. In his operas, piano concertos and symphonies especially, Mozart's writing for the oboe, as for other wind instruments, shows particular sympathy and understanding of its capabilities.

The developments at Mannheim, particularly under Johann and Carl Stamitz, helped encourage the composition of numerous solo concertos and concertos for solo groups, usually under the title sinfonia concertante. Examples are by Carl Stamitz, J. C. Bach (T286/4 for oboe, violin, viola and cello, and T287/2 for oboe and cello), Haydn (op.84, for oboe, bassoon, violin and cello), Pleyel (Ben 114 and 115), Salieri (one with flute, one with violin and cello) and possibly Mozart (K297b, for oboe, clarinet, bassoon and horn, is of doubtful authenticity). The most famous solo concerto of the Classical period is that in C by Mozart (K314), for long known only in its D major transcription for flute. Two concertos by J. C. Bach are worthy of mention, as is a concerto attributed to Haydn. Less well known is a group of concertos by the oboist Ludwig August Lebrun, which date from the last quarter of the 18th century. Solo wind instruments were also featured with a string group, usually a trio consisting of violin, viola and cello. Numerous quartets for oboe and string trio were composed by members of the Mannheim school, for example Christian Cannabich and Carl Stamitz, as well as later composers such as Abel, J. C. Bach and Vanhal. Mozart followed with his fine quartet in F (K370/368b, 1781), the touchstone of such writing, and a work which combines effortless virtuosity with the composer's sense of what the instrument could be made to do.

While the wind ensemble was used frequently in the early 18th century, it was generally employed only for music of no great depth. The development of Harmoniemusik (music for wind ensemble) towards the end of the century was a phenomenon that left the oboe and the clarinet as joint leaders. Mozart's two octet serenades (K375 and K388/384a), especially the latter, brought this type of music to a new maturity and depth; this was largely achieved by Mozart's superb handling of the oboe parts. Other examples of the genre include numerous arrangements of items from Mozart's operas; here the oboe is often treated as a solo instrument, especially when it takes over a vocal line. Although they strictly belong to the 19th century, the wind ensemble works of Krommer (who also composed an oboe concerto) are similar in spirit and style to works of the later 18th century, as well as in their use of the oboe as a leading melody instrument. The development of the clarinet, and its clear superiority over the oboe in volume and as a marching instrument, led to its largely replacing the oboe in band and ensemble music in the later decades of the century.

(iii) 19th century. The requirements of the oboe as an orchestral instrument were considerably increased in the 19th century. The symphonies of Beethoven, Schubert, Brahms, Bruckner and Mahler, for example, each use the instrument in a highly effective but often demanding way, as do the operas by such composers as Weber, Berlioz, Verdi and Wagner. The oboe as a solo instrument in its own right was not so highly appreciated, perhaps because it did not aspire to the 'heroic' status

of the piano or violin that so dominated 19th-century concerto writing. Examples of works for oboe and orchestra are relatively few, and generally not of the first rank: they include works by Bellini, Donizetti, Hummel, d'Indy and Krommer. The most important development in chamber music was the establishment of the wind quintet in the hands of Danzi (nine works; opp.56, 67 and 68) and Reicha (24 works; opp.88, 91, 99 and 100). Here the melodic interest was naturally shared between the flute, to some extent the clarinet, and the oboe. As in the later 18th century, the combination of oboe and piano was limited in its use, and is found mostly in minor works by composers such as Franck, Reger, Spohr and Saint-Saëns as well as Schumann (*Romanzen* op.94).

(iv) 20th century. While the 19th century was a fallow period in the development of the oboe repertory, the 20th century has amply compensated with an enormous burst of activity among composers of all styles. The main achievement has been the revival of the oboe as a solo instrument in the hands of such fine players as Leon Goossens and Heinz Holliger, and a huge expansion of the chamber music repertory. There has also been a considerable increase in the demands made on the wind section of the orchestra, a process which has affected the oboe as much as other wind instruments. The 20th-century oboe repertory is considerably more varied in style and technique than that of previous centuries. Some composers have been content to imitate 18th-century methods, combinations and forms, but since the 1950s others have included many new techniques. It is now no longer unusual for a player to be required to produce a wide range of multiple sonorities, microtones and many other special effects.

This development can be noted in the concertos written for the oboe. That by Richard Strauss (1945) is quite clearly an imitation of classical models, and the concerto by Vaughan Williams is a work in the English 'pastoral' style, as are to a greater or lesser extent the concertos by Rawsthorne, Geoffrey Bush, Malcolm Arnold, Holst (Fugal Concerto for flute and oboe) and Kenneth Leighton (*Veris gratia* for oboe, cello and strings). The broadly neo-classical middle ground has been covered in concertos by Lennox Berkeley (Sinfonia Concertante), Françaix, Genzmer, Ibert, Honegger (Concerto da camera for flute and english horn), Frank Martin (Concerto for seven instruments) and Martinů, as well as the American Benjamin Lees and the Yugoslav Bruno Bjelinski. 12-note methods are used in the Concertino by Skalkottas, the Concerto Grosso for oboe and harp by Elisabeth Lutyens, and the single-movement *Aulodie* by Wolfgang Fortner.

More recent works for oboe and orchestra have tended not to fall into the traditional concerto form, although that by Bernd Alois Zimmermann, three by Bruno Maderna and Ligeti's Double Concerto for flute and oboe (1972) are still called concertos, as is Henze's freely developing work for oboe and harp (1966). In the Ligeti work there is considerable use of microtones and textural manipulation but relatively little virtuosity. Gordon Crosse's beautiful *Ariadne* (1972) is an elegant concerto for oboe and a dozen other players, which is in part rhythmically free and in part strictly measured. The elaboration of freely articulated melodic lines against changing orchestral textures is taken further in Penderecki's *Capriccio* (1966), *Contemplation* (1966) by Mil-

an Stibilj, *Episodes lyriques* (1974) by Ivo Petrić and Berio's *Chemins IV* (1975). The first two works are accompanied by strings; textures are created in the first by freely coordinated ostinatos and in the second by complex but exactly synchronized cross-rhythms. *Episodes lyriques* has passages of free rhythm in spatial notation, with frequent points of coordination. *Chemins IV* is an orchestral elaboration of the solo piece *Sequenza VII*. One of the major compositions of the composer-oboist Heinz Holliger is *Siebengesang* (1966–7), a study in varying orchestral and vocal textures which complement the elaborate oboe part. Mention should also be made of Globokar's *Ausstrahlungen* (1972), which, although written for oboe, clarinet, saxophone or bassoon, is a good example of an avant-garde concerto for a woodwind instrument; some of the instructions are given in graphic notation.

The large wind ensemble has enjoyed some popularity in the 20th century. Richard Strauss, following the example of Mozart, featured the oboe prominently in such works as the early Serenade op.7 (1881), the Suite op.4 (1884) and in the large-scale sonatinas of 1943–5. The oboe has important parts in Stravinsky's *Symphonies of Wind Instruments* (1920) and Varèse's *Octandre* (1923), but has otherwise played less important a role in this genre than the clarinet. This is even more noticeable in wind bands, where oboes are heavily outnumbered by clarinets.

Of more importance is the vast repertory for the wind quintet of flute, oboe, clarinet, bassoon and horn. While the oboe no longer dominates the group, as it did in the works of Danzi and Reicha, it still plays a very important part. This is as clear in the charming quintet by Carl Nielsen (1922), which emphasizes the instrumental character of each instrument, as in the massive and somewhat austere Quintet (op.26) by Schoenberg, which suppresses these characters. A large group of light-hearted French wind quintets shows a great fondness for bright and incisive oboe tone. Particularly notable are works by Bozza, Françaix, Ibert, Jolivet, Milhaud, and the Sextet (wind quintet with piano) by Poulenc. The same fondness for the oboe is found in serially based quintets by Gerhard, Lutyens, Seiber and Henze, and the French-influenced works of Elliott Carter and Walter Piston, but rather less in the Germanic quintets of Hindemith and Reizenstein. More recent quintets have moved away from the light style; these include the pointillist *Zeitmasze* (english horn replaces horn) and *Adieu* by Stockhausen, the pithy Ten Pieces by Ligeti, and the severely metrical Woodwind Quintet by the American Donald Martino. The woodwind quartet (without horn), though less popular, has produced good works by Babbitt, Villa-Lobos and Wellesz.

Chamber music combining oboe with strings has made a reappearance in the 20th century, especially in England (provoked by Goossens's artistry). The combination of oboe and string quartet is found in works by Bax (1922) and Bliss (1927), and the quartet of oboe, violin, viola and cello is used to great effect in Britten's Phantasy Quartet (1932), Nicola LeFanu's delicate, spidery Variations and Oliver Knussen's tense and fertile Cantata (1977). Smaller groupings that include the oboe have proliferated in European and American music. Solo works that have established their classic status are few, but include Britten's *Six Metamorphoses* (1951), Berio's *Sequenza VII* (1969) and Globokar's demanding *Atemstudie* (1972). Two of Stockhausen's solo works, *Solo*

(1966) and *Spiral* (1969), though not specifically for the oboe, have been successfully tackled by Holliger. Composers have produced many sonatas for oboe and piano, many of which are of an undemanding, recreational nature. The more durable works include those by Berkeley, Hindemith, Kelemen, Krenek, Malipiero, Piston, Poulenc and Reizenstein. Of the small number of pieces for mixed ensembles the most noteworthy are quartets for flute, oboe, cello and harpsichord by Elliott Carter (Sonata, 1952) and by David Gow, trios for oboe, viola and harp by Holliger and for flute, oboe and piano by Thea Musgrave, and the Terzetto (1925) for flute, oboe and viola by Gustav Holst.

The following oboes are entered in this dictionary: abā; agida (i); aizai; algaita; alita; alto fagotto; anjomara; bajoncillo; bālabān; baritone oboe; bassanello; basse de musette; Basset:Nicolo; bass oboe; basson d'amour; bassonore; bassoon; bili (ii); bolingozo; bombarde; bramevac; bulo surik; bung'o; būq; calandrone; caledonica; charamel; charumera; chirimía; cléron pastoral; contrabassophon; contrebasse à anche; cornamusa; courtaut; crumhorn; curtal; dachui; dai-hichiriki; desīmvāhlī; Deutsche Schalmey; dīrgha horanǎva; dolzaina; donsaina; duduk (i); dulcian; dulzaina (i); english horn; fadno; fifi; gaita; ghayṭa; ghazzi; gralla; guan; haidi; ha-rib; harmonie-bass; hautbois de Poitou; heckelphone; hichiriki; hnè; Hochquintfagott; hoḍügi; hojŏk; horanava; hujia; hyang-p'iri; jina; jinkojiao; kabiry; karamouza; karnā (ii); kā tang-muri; kèn bàu; klaviaturkontrafagott; kŏl; kortholt; kungkurak; madhukarī; mahurī; mahvarī; mauri dizau; mey; mizmar; mizmār baladī; mohorī; mohurī; morī; moxos; muhurī; mutta; mvāhlī; nafiri; nāgasvaram; nallari; numena; nzumari; oboe da caccia; oboe d'amore; ottu; pereṇed; pereret; phǎn ty; pī; piffaro; pile; pī ọ̄; pipāṇī; pipiza; p'iri; pŏdŭl p'iri; pommer; pumhart; qarnāṭa; Quartfaggot; Quintfaggot; racket; Rackettenfagott; raita; rgya-gling; rhaita; sagwan; sahanai; śahnāi; saleot; sanai; saronen; sarrusophone; sarunai; Schreyerpfeife; Schryari; selompret; se-p'iri; serunai kayu; seurune kaleë; shalabiyya; sharnai; shawm; sibs; sompret; sona; ṣ; sopila; sordun; sorna; sraļai; ṣṛnāj; still shawm; strack; sundrī; suona; surlă; surle; sur-na; surnai; surnāī; svirale; swaenap; tae-p'iri; t'aep'yŏngso; tang-p'iri; tárogató; tarompet; tartŏld; telt; tenoroon; tetepret; tŏjin-bue; tola waghe; tontarde; Tristan Schalmei; tritonikon; trompe de charivari; trompetica china; truba od kore; trubka; tulila; whithorn; xyu; zamr; zournas; zumali; zumari; zurla; zūrnā.

BIBLIOGRAPHY

INSTRUCTION BOOKS

?J. Banister: *The Sprightly Companion* (London, 1695)
J. P. Freillon Poncein: *La véritable manière d'apprendre à jouer en perfection du hautbois* (Paris, 1700)
J. M. Hotteterre: *Principes de la flûte traversière . . . et du hautbois* (Paris, 1707, 7/1741; Eng. trans., 1968)
Anon.: *Complete Tutor to the Hautboy* (London, c1715)
P. Prelleur: *The Modern Musick-master* (London, 1731/R1965) [oboe section derived from previous item]
?J. C. Fischer: *New and Complete Instructions for the Oboe or Hoboy* (London, c1772, 4/1802)
F. J. Garnier: *Méthode raisonnée pour le hautbois* (Paris, c1800)
G. Vogt: *Méthode de hautbois* (MS, *F-Pn*, after 1813)
J. Sellner: *Theoretisch-praktische Oboeschule* (Vienna, 1825, rev. 2/1901; It. trans., c1827)
H. Brod: *Méthode* (Paris, 1835)
A. M.-R. Barret: *Complete Method* (London, 2/1862)
L. Bas: *Méthode nouvelle de hautbois* (Paris, n.d.)

OTHER STUDIES

D. Diderot and J. d'Alembert: *Encyclopédie, ou Dictionnaire raisonné des sciences, arts et métiers* (Lausanne and Berne, 1751–65; suppls., Paris, 1776–7, 1780)
W. T. Parke: *Musical Memoirs* (London, 1830)
H. Lavoix: *Histoire de l'instrumentation* (Paris, 1878)
C. Sachs: *Real-Lexikon der Musikinstrumente* (Berlin, 1913/R1962)
L. Bechler and B. Rahm: *Die Oboe* (Leipzig, 1914/R1972)
C. Sachs: *Handbuch der Musikinstrumentenkunde* (Leipzig, 1920, 2/1930)
A. Carse: *The History of Orchestration* (London, 1925/R1964)
——: *Musical Wind Instruments* (London, 1939/R1965)
A. Baines: 'James Talbot's Manuscript, I: Wind Instruments', *GSJ*, i (1948), 9
E. Halfpenny: 'The English Debut of the French Hautboy', *MMR*, lxxix (1949), 149
——: 'The English 2- and 3-keyed Hautboy', *GSJ*, ii (1949), 10
——: 'A 17th-century Tutor for the Hautboy', *ML*, xxx (1949), 355
J. Marx: 'The Tone of the Baroque Oboe', *GSJ*, iv (1951), 3
E. Halfpenny: 'The "Tenner Hoboy"', *GSJ*, v (1952), 17

L. G. Langwill: 'The Waits', *HMYB*, vii (1952), 178
E. Halfpenny: 'The French Hautboy: a Technical Survey', *GSJ*, vi (1953), 23; viii (1955), 50
E. Rothwell: *Oboe Technique* (London, 1953)
P. A. T. Bate: *The Oboe* (London, 1956, rev. 2/1962, 3/1975)
A. C. Baines: *Woodwind Instruments and their History* (London, 1957, 3/1967)
L. G. Langwill: *An Index of Musical Wind-instrument Makers* (Edinburgh, 1960, rev., enlarged 6/1980)
J. Eppelsheim: *Das Orchester in den Werken Jean-Baptiste Lullys* (Tutzing, 1961)
M. Piguet: 'The Baroque Oboe', *Recorder and Music Magazine*, ii (1967), 171
T. E. Warner: *Annotated Bibliography of Woodwind Instruction Books, 1600–1830* (Detroit, 1967)
J. C. Heiss: 'Some Multiple-sonorities for Flute, Oboe, Clarinet, and Bassoon', *PNM*, vii/1 (1968), 136
H. O. Koch: *Die Spezialtypen der Blasinstrumente in der 1. Hälfte des 18. Jahrhunderts im deutschen Sprachraum* (Mannheim, 1969)
K. Ventzke: *Boehm-Oboen und die neueren französischen Oboen-Systeme* (Frankfurt am Main, 1969)
E. Nichel: *Holzblasinstrumentenbau in Nürnberg* (Munich, 1971)
D. L. Busch: *A Technical Comparison of an 1802, a 1916 and a 1968 Oboe and Related Reed-making and Performance Problems* (diss., Louisiana State U., 1972)
U. Sirker: 'Methoden der Klangfarbenforschung, dargestellt an quasi-stationären Klängen von Doppelrohrblattinstrumenten', *Musicae scientiae collectanea: Festschrift Karl Gustav Fellerer* (Cologne, 1973), 561
S. Marcuse: *A Survey of Musical Instruments* (Newton Abbot and London, 1975)
B. Haynes: 'Oboe Fingering Charts 1695–1816', *GSJ*, xxxi (1978), 68
D. Jones: 'A Three-keyed Oboe by Thomas Collier', *GSJ*, xxxi (1978), 36
B. Haynes: 'Tonality and the Baroque Oboe', *Early Music*, vii (1979), 355
D. A. Ledet: *Oboe Reed Styles* (Bloomington, Ind., 1981)
F. Fleurot: *Le hautbois dans la musique française, 1650–1800* (Paris, 1984)

PHILIP BATE (1–8), NIALL O'LOUGHLIN (9)

Oboe da caccia (It.: 'oboe of the chase'; Ger. *Jagd-Hautbois*). This term has been applied to the tenor OBOE (english horn) in general, although both Curt Sachs and Bessaraboff preferred to reserve it specifically for a mid-18th-century tenor oboe with a large open bell, of which a few examples survive. According to Sachs's interpretation of an entry in Zedler's *Universal-Lexikon* (Halle, 1732–54) such instruments were at that period used in formal music associated with the hunt. In 1973, however, Dahlqvist published the results of a re-examination of Zedler and other contemporary material and concluded that the term 'Jagd-Hautbois' signified not an instrument but a hunt-servant musician. There is an analogy in the word 'Regimentshautbois', also used by Zedler, and signifying simply a military bandsman. Beyond this there is little firm evidence about the origin of its name.

BIBLIOGRAPHY
R. Dahlqvist: 'Taille, Oboe da Caccia, and Corno Inglese', *GSJ*, xxvi (1973), 58

PHILIP BATE

Oboe d'amore (It.: 'oboe of love'; Fr. *hautbois d'amour*; Ger. *Liebes-Oboe*; It. also *oboe luongo*). The alto of the OBOE family, a transposing instrument pitched a minor 3rd below the oboe. It now has keywork appropriate to all the accepted fingering systems, though its compass is not commonly extended below (written) *b*. Though characteristically supplied with the pear-shaped bell of all the deeper-toned oboes, modern oboes d'amore occasionally have normal open bells.

PHILIP BATE

Oboezug (Ger.). LUTE STOP.

Obokana. Bowl lyre of the Gusii people of Kenya. It is 106 cm long and has a resonating bowl of about 45 cm long, 43 cm wide and 23 cm deep. In construction and method of performance the instrument resembles the Litungu, though the pitch level is much lower.

Obonu. Drum ensemble used for royal music by the Ga people of southern Ghana.

Oboro ekpa. Set of four or more idiochord stick zithers of the Igbo people of Nigeria.

Obterre. *See* Hotteterre family.

Obukhov, Nikolay [Nicolas Obouhow]. Russian composer and inventor of the Croix sonore.

Obukondere bwa baswezi. Mirliton of Uganda. It is made from a hollow stalk of pawpaw or thin bamboo, covered with the membrane from spider's egg capsules. It is used by women members of the *baswezi* cult at the funeral of a fellow member.

Obulere. Raft Panpipes of the Soga people of Uganda. It consists of a single row of eight to 13 pipes made usually from elephant grass, bound together by two lines of horizontal lacing (for illustration *see* Flute, fig.2*b*). Modern instruments may be made from other materials, for example, the plastic from old bicycle pumps. The open end is blown across while the nodes which block the other ends form a line of regular steps diagonally across the raft. The pipes are played in ensemble, grouped in three pairs, usually to the accompaniment of two drums (see illustration, below). *See* WachsmannTCU.

K. A. GOURLAY

Oburengo. Ritual gourd rattle of Nkole, Uganda. It is played for the *emandwa* spirit cult by the leader of the ceremony. *See also* Enyimba.

Obute. Side-blown trumpet of the Acholi people of Uganda. It is made from an animal horn with a plain, oval blow-hole in the side. The hole is made in the middle of the horn if the tip is left solid, nearer the tip when

Obulere (panpipes) ensemble of the Soga people, Uganda, 1965

the tip is pierced to provide a stop. Traditionally the horn was blown as an alarm signal, to call people on special occasions such as the death of an important person, and in warfare. *See* WachsmannTCU.

Ocarina (It.: 'little goose'). A Vessel flute in the shape of a large, elongated egg, hollow, and usually made of terracotta. In its side is a flattened tube with a hole at its base; the player blows down the tube, and so across the hole, setting the mass of air in the instrument in vibration. The standard Western ocarina is said to have been invented by Giuseppe Donati of Budrio, Italy, c1860. It has eight finger-holes in front and two thumb-holes at tne back. Because it behaves as a simple resonator, the pitch rises by the same amount each time a finger-hole of a particular size is opened, irrespective of the position of the hole. The rate of vibration is determined by the total internal volume of the instrument and the sizes of the holes uncovered. The ocarina is extremely popular as a child's instrument, in the USA and in Europe. Varieties of it are extensively used in folk music.

Ocarina, Meissen, 19th century (Horniman Museum, London)

In Latin America, ocarinas are popular in Costa Rica (the collection in the Museo Nacional includes an example with six holes capable of playing 18 scalar chromatic pitches), in Colombia, where they occasionally augment the *chirimía* ensemble, in Guatemala, where pre-Columbian ocarinas and whistles unearthed by Maya agriculturalists are regarded as sacred, in Panama, where they are played by Guaymi Indians, and in Peru, where the Iawa and Bora Indians of the tropical forests play ocarinas of beeswax (*roekua*) or clay. They are also popular in eastern Europe, where ovoid or carrot-shaped instruments with ten finger-holes are made as well as zoomorphic figurines with one or two.

Occhio (It.: 'eye'). *See* Soundhole.

Octarimba. Experimental marimba of the 20th century; *see* Marimba, §2.

Octava (Sp.). (1) Octave.
(2) An Organ stop (*Octave*).

Octave (Fr. *octave*; Ger. *Oktave*; It. *ottava*; Gk. *diapasōn*). (1) The interval between any two notes that are seven diatonic scale degrees apart (e.g. or *c–c'*, *d–d'*). It is the interval by which any scale – diatonic, chromatic, pentatonic or otherwise – is normally identified. Because of its acoustical properties it plays a significant role in the construction and playing of instruments, particularly keyboard and woodwind instruments (e.g. those that have 'octave keys'), and is of fundamental importance to the concept of register, both in a theoretical sense and as it concerns instruments (for fuller discussion see *Grove 6*).

(2) An ORGAN STOP.

Octave courte (Fr.). SHORT OCTAVE.

Octavin (Ger. *Oktavin*) **(i).** A single-reed woodwind instrument, conical in bore. Its invention is usually attributed to JULIUS JEHRING (1824–1905), a bassoon maker; in fact, Oskar Adler, a maker in Markneukirchen, and Hermann Jordan of the same town were granted the German patents (on 27 September and 11 October 1893) and a British patent (31 October 1893). The instrument, 40 cm high, is made of rosewood (palisander), resembling the butt-joint of a bassoon. To the wider bore is fitted a small metal bell, turned outwards at a right-angle; to the narrower, an ebonite joint is added, terminating in a clarinet-type beak mouthpiece. 14 keys and three rings are fingered, much as a simple-system oboe. It was originally made in C and B♭ with compass from *a* to *f'''* (or *g* to *e♭'''*); there is also a straight, single-tube model, and a bass, descending to *G*, is mentioned by W. Altenburg (*Die Klarinette*, 1904). The octavin, which attained no popularity, has a tone somewhat like that of the soprano saxophone but less pleasant. The instrument is illustrated in A. Carse, *Musical Wind Instruments* (London, 1939/R1965), pl.IX E.

LYNDESAY G. LANGWILL

Octavin (Fr.) **(ii).** An ORGAN STOP.

Octavina. A plucked string instrument invented by Julián Carrillo around 1922; it resembled a bass guitar and was tuned in ⅛-tones; *see* MICROTONAL INSTRUMENTS, §3.

Octobass. A large, three-string DOUBLE BASS.

Octochord. An eight-string device for calculating interval ratios, invented by G. J. Vogler (1749–1814).

Oda. STICK ZITHER of the Bali people of north-eastern Zaïre; it is also known as *nzenze* and *nzeze* (*LaurentyC*, 115). *See* ZEZE (i).

Odab. Drum of the *taganing* drum-chime of North Sumatra. *See* TAGANING.

Ōdaiko. A general term for large, heavy-bodied Japanese barrel drums (*ō*: 'large'; *daiko/taiko*: generic term for drums; *ōdaiko* is written with the same characters as DADAIKO and the two are distinguished only by context). Most have a body length longer than their diameter, although a shallow-bodied HIRADAIKO may also be called *ōdaiko* when paired with a smaller drum. Every *ōdaiko* has two membranes which are tacked on (*see also* TAIKO). The *ōdaiko* is used in different contexts. In the kabuki theatre in *geza* (off-stage) music an *ōdaiko* with a diameter of nearly 100 cm plays a leading role in setting atmosphere, through a large number of stereotyped

patterns; the many different drumsticks can create a surprising variety of effects. An *ōdaiko* is the essential instrument in most *bon* (ancestral festival) dances; it is often placed on a tower in the centre of the circle of dancers. In Buddhist music the drum is most prominent at Zen temples, where it may be called *hokku* ('(Buddhist) law drum'); it plays a similar part to the Korean PŎPKO. At other festivals an *ōdaiko* may be wheeled around on a stand or wagon in procession. The drum once served as a battle signal.

In all but a few cases the *ōdaiko* is positioned with the heads vertical and played on one head only; occasionally each head is struck by a different performer. It is often struck on the rim for special effect; this is rare for drums with the heads laced on. Several more specific names designate the *ōdaiko* used in particular contexts (even though the drums may be identical), such as *miyadaiko*, *matsuridaiko*, *yaguradaiko* and *jindaiko*.

BIBLIOGRAPHY
W. P. Malm: *Japanese Music and Musical Instruments* (Rutland, Vermont, 1959)

DAVID W. HUGHES

Oddone, Carlo Giuseppe (*b* Turin, 1866; *d* Rivaldoro, nr. Turin, *c*1936). Italian violin maker. After studying with Gioffredo Rinaldi in Turin, he worked for F. W. Chanot in London (1898–1901). In 1901 he returned to Turin, where he established a fine reputation. His work is mostly patterned after Stradivari and Guarneri although he also occasionally copied other masters. The craftsmanship is careful and the wood well chosen, with good quality varnish, usually of a middle yellow to plum red colour; the scrolls are normally edged in black. Oddone's instruments are beginning to mellow in tone and are stepping out of the orchestral category previously assigned them. His output exceeded 300 and all instruments are numbered on the label. He also used the brand ODDONE-TORINO in the interior of the instrument.

BIBLIOGRAPHY
R. Vannes: *Essai d'un dictionnaire universel des luthiers* (Paris, 1932, 2/1951/R1972 as *Dictionnaire universel des luthiers* and R1981 incl. suppl. 1959)

JAAK LIIVOJA-LORIUS

Odell. American firm of organ builders. It was founded (as J. H. & C. S. Odell) in 1859 by John Henry Odell (1830–99) and Caleb Sherwood Odell (1827–93) in New York. Before starting their own company, the Odell brothers had worked for Ferris & Stuart, and for William Robjohn, whom they succeeded. Although the firm's output was never great and was largely confined to the New York area, the Odells are credited with several important inventions, mostly patented during the 1860s and 1870s, including a reversible coupler action, an early combination action and a crescendo pedal. They were also early experimenters with tubular-pneumatic action. Among their more notable instruments were those built for the Fort Street Presbyterian Church, Detroit (1876), and Fifth Avenue Presbyterian Church, New York (1893). After the deaths of the founders, the scope of the company's work gradually narrowed to small organs, rebuilding and maintenance. The firm was run by William and J. F. Odell in the 1970s.

BIBLIOGRAPHY
O. Ochse: *The History of the Organ in the United States* (Bloomington, Ind., 1975)
J. Ogasapian: *Organ Building in New York City, 1700–1900* (Braintree, Mass., 1977)

BARBARA OWEN

Odéophone. An improved version of the KLAVIZYLIN-DER, invented in London by Vanderburg of Vienna about 1818.

Odi (i). Five-string bowl lyre of the Madi, Lugbara and Kakwa peoples of Uganda. *See* NDONGO.

Odi [idi] **(ii).** Double-headed HOURGLASS DRUM of the Igbo people of Nigeria.

Odima [oduma]. Large clapperless bell of the Igbo people of Nigeria. *See* ALO.

Oding. Transverse flute of the Eton people of southern Cameroon; it is played by women.

Odo. Ivory trumpet of the Igbo people of Nigeria.

Odoardi, Giuseppe (*b* Poggio di Bretta, 6 April 1746; *d* ?Ascoli, after 1786). Italian violin maker. Nicknamed 'Il Vilano d'Ascoli', he was self-taught and produced around 200 instruments in his short lifespan. He did not restrict himself to any one model and his style is thus difficult to categorize. He appears to have patterned his model after Stradivari but was also influenced by the Montagnana and Mariani styles. The scroll usually has a fine sweep with the inner turns rather on the small side. The black stripes of the purfling are often much thinner than the middle white stripe. Tonally his instruments are well above average for the time and occasionally even superior. The Antonio Odoardi mentioned in some sources as having possibly been his father appears now more likely to have been his nephew.

BIBLIOGRAPHY
R. Vannes: *Essai d'un dictionnaire universel des luthiers* (Paris, 1932, 2/1951/R1972 as *Dictionnaire universel des luthiers* and R1981 incl. suppl. 1959)
JAAK LIIVOJA-LORIUS

Odol. Log drum of the Tiboli people of Mindanao, southern Philippines. *See also* TUNGTUNG.

Odome. Large 12-key log XYLOPHONE of the Igbo people of Nigeria, originally named *ngelenge*.

Odu. Side-blown ivory trumpet of the Igbo people of Nigeria. It is 30 to 120 cm in length, and is used for speech imitation. Its use is normally the prerogative of men of high rank.

Oduk [akua oduk]. Side-blown trumpet of the Ibibio people of Nigeria, usually made from antelope horn. It is played only by master musicians, who can produce up to four tones, and is used as obbligato to an instrumental ensemble or solo to punctuate statements by the lead singer of a chief. If made from ivory, the horn is known as *akua oduk* and a set of seven of different sizes are played in hocket (*see also* UTA). See S. E. Akpabot: *Ibibio Music in Nigerian Culture* (East Lansing, Mich., 1975).

Oduma. *See* ODIMA.

Odurugya. Long NOTCHED FLUTE of Ghana. It is made from a husk of cane and played at the court of the head of the traditional Ashanti political union.

Odyssey. A monophonic SYNTHESIZER manufactured by the ARP Instruments division of Tonus Inc. in Newton Highlands, near Boston, Massachusetts (later in nearby Newton and Lexington), from 1971 until the company's demise in 1981. Designed as a rival to the Minimoog, the Odyssey is partly based on the ARP 2600 model. Like the Minimoog, it has an integral keyboard and all patching is eliminated by a combination of hard-wired predetermined signal routing and several selector switches on the front panel. The range of the three-octave keyboard can be transposed within a total of seven octaves; the keyboard includes a portamento control. The soundsources are two oscillators with a choice of four waveforms, a white-noise generator and a further sine-wave generator obtainable by tuning the filter. In addition to the filter the sound-processing devices include two envelope shapers, a ring modulator, a sample-and-hold random note generator and a mixer; these involve several elements of voltage control. Towards the end of the 1970s the original pitch-bend knob was replaced by two left-hand pressure-sensitive rubber touch-pads (in addition to one for depth of modulation). ARP's Avatar guitar synthesizer is partly based on the Odyssey.

BIBLIOGRAPHY
D. Friend, A. R. Pearlman and T. D. Piggott: *Learning Music with Synthesizers* (Milwaukee, 1974)
HUGH DAVIES

Oeku. Turtle-shell rattle of the San Juan Pueblo Indians of New Mexico. It consists of a hollowed-out turtle shell to which 'jingles' made of deer hoofs or pig knuckles are attached by leather thongs drawn through holes in the upper shell. The rattle is tied just below a dancer's right knee with a leather thong which passes through holes in the plastron. It is worn by all dancers in the *okushare* (turtle dance), part of a winter ceremony at San Juan Pueblo.
MARY RIEMER-WELLER

Oeoe. Obsolete Hawaiian BULLROARER. It was used as a toy. See S. Culin: 'Hawaiian Games', *American Anthropologist*, i, (1899), 220.

'Ofe. Bamboo STAMPING TUBE of Samoa, now obsolete. See R. Moyle: 'Samoan Musical Instruments', *EM*, xviii (1974), 64. *See also* KOFE.

Oficleide (It.). OPHICLEIDE.

Ogán [ogā]. Iron bell used in various drum ensembles of Afro-Cuban and Haitian *vodun* cults. In the *hun* ensemble of the Afro-Cuban Arará cult, it is a single inverted bell like the BANKÁ, with an external beater. A double *ogán* (two bells joined by an iron loop) serves for mourning music in Matanzas Province. Instead of the loop handle some double *ogán* have straight handles forged together. The *ogán* is now obsolescent and is being replaced by various metal objects, including blades from agricultural tools and chain links; these also are called *ogán*. See H. Courlander: 'Musical Instruments of Cuba', *MQ*, xxviii (1942), 227.
JOHN M. SCHECHTER

Oganga. Double-headed cylindrical drum of the Janji, Kurama and Piti peoples of Nigeria. *See* GANGA, (1).

Ogege. Clapperless bell of the Igala people of Nigeria. *See* AGOGO.

Ogene [ogele, ugele, ogenni] **(i).** Clapperless iron bell of the Igbo people of Nigeria. It is about 30 cm high and is beaten with a piece of hardwood, which may have soft padding at the end. Bells are single, double (*ogene mkpi nabo*) or triple (*ogene mkpi ito*). They are used for signalling (e.g. announcing the appearance of a mask), with slit-drums and rattles in divination, and as rhythm instruments during dancing. *See also* ALO and AREKWA.

BIBLIOGRAPHY
A. N. G. Okasa: 'Ibo Musical Instruments', *Nigeria Magazine*, lxxv (1962), 4
W. W. C. Echezona: 'Ibo Music', *Nigeria Magazine*, lxxxiv (1965), 45
——: 'Igbo Music', *Grove 6*

Ogene (ii). VESSEL FLUTE of the Igbo people of Nigeria. *See* UGENE.

Ogia. Wooden flute with slender conical bore of the Mamvu people of north-eastern Zaïre (*LaurentyA*, 157).

Ogirigboh. SLIT-DRUM of the Igede people of Nigeria. It consists of a hollow log of wood with a single slit running between two rectangular openings. A smaller version, constructed on the same pattern, is known as the *ogirigboh ochichehi*. Both slit-drums have been used for as long as can be remembered to send signals, and as part of an instrumental ensemble to provide rhythmic background for dancing. See B. Ranung: 'Music of Dawn and Day: Music and Dance Associations of the Igede of Nigeria', LXLP 513–4 [disc notes].

Ogudú. Afro-Cuban drum dedicated by the Yorubas to the deity Ochosi. It is single-headed, open and shaped like a slightly truncated cone with its two ends of slightly different diameter; it measures about 40 to 50 cm in height and about 25 to 30 cm in diameter at the top. The head is made taut with hooked pegs (spikes), cord and hoop, like the ARARÁ drums. It carries a string of pellet bells round its body. See *OrtizIMA*, iv, 87f.

JOHN M. SCHECHTER

Oguk. *See* UKÚK.

Ogumh. LAMELLAPHONE of the Igede people of Nigeria. Its eight metal keys are mounted on a wooden box resonator and plucked with the thumbs. The instrument is used either solo or to accompany songs either for entertainment or for private musical meditation.

Ogumogu. LAMELLAPHONE of the Idoma and Ijo peoples of Nigeria. Its metal keys are mounted on a board fixed into a half-calabash resonator. Holes in the board permit insertion of the fingers of both hands while the thumbs pluck the keys. The Idoma use the *ogumogu* as a 'talking' instrument.

BIBLIOGRAPHY
R. G. Armstrong: 'Talking Drums in the Benue-Cross Rivers Region of Nigeria', *Phylon*, xv (1954), 355
E. J. Alagoa: 'Ijo Origins and Migrations', *Nigeria Magazine*, xci (1966), 279

Ogung. Gong of North Sumatra, Indonesia. In the Pakpak Dairi area the name is used for a bossed gong or for a set of four gongs in the *genderang* and *gendang* ceremonial orchestra, and in the *gerantung* ensemble.

They are made of bronze or iron and may measure 40 cm in diameter. They are known individually as *pong-pong*, *poi*, *tapudep* and *panggora*.

In Mandailing the *ogung* is a deep-rimmed iron or bronze gong suspended from the ceiling of a traditional house (*sopo godang*) or from a separate wooden frame. There it is played in pairs, the slightly larger 'female' gong (*ogung induk* or *ogung dadaboru*) being about 48 cm in diameter and the 'male' (*ogung jantan* or *ogung pangiring*) about 43 cm in diameter. Both are played on the boss with a padded wooden beater. The *ogung* is used in the three main Mandailing orchestras, the *gordang sembilan*, *gordang lima* and *gondang*.

BIBLIOGRAPHY
M. J. Kartomi: 'Ceremonial Music of the Mandailing *Raja* Tradition', *Asian Music*, xii/2 (1981), 74–108
L. Moore: 'An Introduction to the Music of the Pakpak Dairi of North Sumatra', *Indonesia Circle* (1981), no.24, p.39
MARGARET J. KARTOMI

'Ohe hano ihu. Hawaiian NOSE FLUTE. It consists of a length of bamboo with a nose-hole cut at an angle above the closed node end and two or three finger-holes along the tube towards the open end (see illustration).

'Ohe hano ihu (bamboo nose flute) of Hawaii

'Ohe ka'eke. Hawaiian STAMPING TUBE. *See* KĀ'EKE'EKE.

Ohgiwe ka'nohko'wah. WATER-DRUM of the Iroquois Indians of the north-eastern USA. It is played only by men and used only during the *ohgiwe*, an all-night feast of the dead. It is about 18 cm in diameter and has a thicker drumhead and produces a lower sound than the KA'NOHKO'WAH, which is used in the majority of Iroquois social dances and in many rituals.

Ohiva. Trumpet of the Herero people of south-western Africa. It was made from the horn of a gemsbok and used as a signal instrument. It is reported as being end-blown, but this seems unlikely; neighbouring peoples have side-blown instruments (*see* LEPAPATA). See *KirbyMISA*, 84.

Ohonji [onkhonji]. Braced MOUTH BOW of south-western Angola. The string-bearer is held in the mouth against the right inner cheek.

Ohyŏn. Korean plucked lute. *See* PIPA (i), §2.

Oja (i). Flute of the Igbo people of Nigeria. It is wooden, with two opposed finger-holes. The end-blown *oja osisi* is cruciform and often decorated with incised designs; it is used either in solo performance of melodies or for signalling. The *oja ufele* is a globular VESSEL FLUTE; *see* UGENE.

Oja (ii). Wooden CLAPPERS of the Igbo people of Nigeria.

Okanga. Double-headed portable cylindrical drum of the Igbo people of Nigeria.

Ōkawa. Japanese HOURGLASS DRUM. *See* ŌTSUZUMI.

Okbe. Gourd trumpet of Nigeria. *See* EGBE.

Okedō. Japanese cylindrical drum with heads laced to the body. The name *okedō* ('bucket-body') refers to the drum's shape; typically it is 28 cm in diameter and 42 cm long. The drum is mostly used today in the kabuki theatre as an instrument of *geza* (off-stage) music, although identical or similar drums occur in conjunction with some folk Buddhist group singing and with certain *shishi* (lion, deer) dances of east Japan. The distinctive feature of these drums is that the heads are laced directly to the body, rather than first being lapped on to an iron ring, a more common method in Japan (*see* TAIKO). Relatively loose lacing results in a short, flat sound compared with most other Japanese drums. See W. P. Malm: *Japanese Music and Musical Instruments* (Rutland, Vermont, 1959), 227.

DAVID W. HUGHES

Okike. Large ivory side-blown trumpet of the Igbo people of Nigeria, approximately 90 to 120 cm long. Only *ozo* initiates are entitled to own the trumpets, which are used for sending messages with sounds of differing lengths.

Okobolo. Two-key XYLOPHONE of the Igbo people of Nigeria. *See* NGEDEGWU, (1).

Okoco. Tortoise-shell dance rattle of the Acholi people of Uganda. The shell is fixed to the arm above the elbow by a plaited leather bracelet. A row of short iron chains are attached to the lower part of the shell; they beat against each other, the shell acting as a resonator.

Okónkole. A drum of the Afro-Cuban Lucumí cult. *See* BATÁ.

Okoroko. Leg rattles worn by dancers among the Igbo people of Nigeria.

Okpai [okpe]. Gourd trumpet of Nigeria. *See* EGBE.

Okpelé [okuelé]. Yoruba term for a rare Afro-Cuban shaken wooden idiophone, shaped like a bell without a clapper. Pieces of bullhide, attached by knots to two sides of the quadrilateral instrument, strike the outer walls when the instrument is shaken by its handle. It is used by the Iyesá blacks to evoke the dead. In Cuba, the term *okuelé* is used. See *OrtizIMA*, ii, 29f.

JOHN M. SCHECHTER

Okpirih. Small open conical drum of the Igede people of Nigeria. *See* EGBONG.

Okpokolo. SLIT-DRUM of the Igbo people of Nigeria. It is made from an internode of bamboo, and has a single slit. The Igbo *okpokolo mbe* (or *opokolo mbekwu*) is a struck tortoise-shell used only in sacred ceremonies. It is credited with magical powers and divine properties and must not be handled by 'unclean' people. *See also* EKWE, (1).

Okporo [kokpworo]. Cylindro-conical drum of the Mono people of Zaïre (*BooneT*, 27f, 66). *See* DINDO.

Oktave (Ger.). (1) OCTAVE.
(2) An ORGAN STOP (*Octave*).

Oktavflöte (Ger.). PICCOLO; *see* FLUTE, §3.

Oktavhorn. *See* PRIMHORN.

Oktavin (Ger.). OCTAVIN.

Oktávka. Folk fiddle of Czechoslovakia. *See* VIOLIN, §IV, 1.

Okuelé. (1) Cuban term for a shaken wooden idiophone. It is bell-shaped but lacks a clapper, using instead pieces of bullhide attached to the external walls. *See* OKPELÉ.
(2) Afro-Cuban family of three different-sized drums. They are all single-headed, open and goblet-shaped, like certain of the ARARÁ drums, and with the 'foot' typical of the *ararás*. Unlike them, however, their heads are not made taut by spikes, cords and hoops, but with nails. The two smaller *okuelé* drums are played with sticks, the largest with the bare hands; they are accompanied by *ágbe* (rattle) and *agogo* (struck idiophone). See *OrtizIMA*, ii, 29; iv, 88f.

JOHN M. SCHECHTER

Okuma. Open conical drum of the people of Brass, Nigeria. *See* IGBA (i).

Ōkurauro. End-blown metal flute of Japan. It was invented in the late 1920s by Ōkura Kishichirō, and combines a *shakuhachi*-style mouthpiece with a Boehm-system flute body. The name is a contraction of 'Ōkura aulos'. The *ōkurauro* did not find favour with the musical public, and was short-lived.

BIBLIOGRAPHY
W. P. Malm: *Japanese Music and Musical Instruments* (Rutland, Vermont, 1959), 159
——: 'Ōkurauro', *Ongaku daijiten* [Encyclopedia of music] (Tokyo, 1981)

DAVID W. HUGHES

Okwah. Idioglot transverse clarinet of the Duka people of Nigeria. *See* CLARINET, TRANSVERSE.

Okwo. A generic term for SLIT-DRUM among the Igbo people of Nigeria. It covers, for example, the *okwo-agida*, which is 90 cm long and has a single slit, and the *okwo-mata*, which is 45 cm long with a single slit. *See also* EKWE.

Okworo [okworro]. Cylindro-conical drum of the Gobu, Ngombe and Togbo peoples of Zaïre (*BooneT*, 27, 66). *See* DINDO.

Olat. JEW'S HARP of the northern Philippines. *See* AFIW.

Olbrichklaviatur. A keyboard invented by the Berlin pianist Emil Olbrich in 1890 on which the black keys were less than the standard height by 3 to 4 mm.

Oldalfuvós furulya. Transverse flute of Hungary. *See* HARÁNTFURULYA.

Oldovini, Paschaly Caetanus (*fl* 1758–77). Portuguese organ builder. An inscription on the organ built for Évora Cathedral in 1758 confirms that he was of Italian origin. His work in Portugal, displaying a mixture of both Portuguese and Italian traditions, is of a high quality and not much influenced by the then prevailing Baroque style. He apparently worked in Évora for a number of years on projects at the cathedral, where he restored the Renaissance organ (built by Heitor Lobo), and constructed two other organs, one in 1758 and a smaller Positiv of *c*1760. A small organ built for Crato parish church is dated 1769, and an impressive instrument, similar in design to the 1758 organ for Évora Cathedral, was installed in Elvas Cathedral in 1777. There is considerable evidence to suggest that the historic organ in Faro Cathedral was repaired by Oldovini, who, at the same time, may have installed its unusual *Brustwerk*. Faro Cathedral contains another small organ built by him, and an instrument in the chapel of Senhor dos Passos, S Matriz, Viana do Castelo, is also strongly suggestive of his work.

W. D. JORDAN

Ole-ole [puyu-puyu barang nyemei]. Idioglot clarinet of the Mandailing, Angkola and Batak Toba areas of North Sumatra, Indonesia. It has a rice-stalk reed with

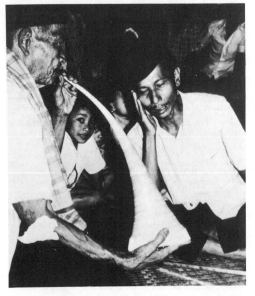

Idioglot clarinet (pupuik gadang) of the ole-ole type, West Sumatra, 1976

Oliphant, known to have been the property of the Polish King Jan Sobieski in 1683 (Národni Muzeum, Prague)

slits which expand when blown and produce a small range of pitches when the player's lip pressure is varied. The reed, about 9 cm long, is fitted into the narrow opening at the top of the cone-shaped body so that one-third of its length protrudes for the player to blow. The body itself is made of bamboo or of strips of fresh coconut leaf, wound to overlap each other. These last only a month or so and the rice-stalk reed is usable only once. The *ole-ole* may serve as the leading melodic instrument in a *gondang* ensemble. A similar instrument in Minangkabau, West Sumatra, is called *pupuik gadang* (or *pupuik batang padi*; see illustration). *See also* IYUP-IYUP.

MARGARET J. KARTOMI

Olera [olere, oleta]. NOTCHED FLUTE of Uganda. *See* NDERE (i).

Oli. JEW'S HARP of Minahasa, North Sulawesi, Indonesia. It is made of the stem of the sugar-palm leaf or from bamboo, in a long rectangular shape with string attached. The tongue is about 2 to 4 mm thick at one end and about 4 to 8 mm at the other. It varies in length between about 110 and 80 mm and in width between about 14 and 8 mm. Two *oli* are played with other instruments in the *orkes oli* (*see* ORKES).

MARGARET J. KARTOMI

Oliko [gbere]. Cone whistle of the Madi people of Uganda. It is made from the end of a gourd, and has a straight rim mouthpiece and a fine hole at the tip. The instrument is used by boys at play. The Acholi have a similar instrument, but with a cupped mouthpiece.

Olimong. DUCT FLUTE of the north Philippines. *See* ONGIYONG.

Olingo. Side-blown ivory trumpet of the Bira people of Zaïre. It has a carved mouthpiece and one stop in the tip (*LaurentyA*, 398).

Oliphant (from Old Fr. *olifant*: 'elephant', properly *cor d'olifant*). Medieval end-blown ivory horn, finely carved and prized by the wealthy classes mainly as a token of land tenure, or by churches as a reliquary, rather than as a musical instrument. Oliphants were made from the 10th century and particularly in the 11th, largely by Muslim craftsmen in south Italy and Sicily. There is no proof that either Roland or Charlemagne possessed an oliphant and sounded it in battle, despite a mention in the *Chanson de Roland*, though among the surviving examples some have traditionally been attributed to these heroes. Unlike earlier specimens the 11th-century oliphants were left smooth in two places to accommodate metal bands which took a slinging chain. Some 60 of this type are known, including the 'horn of Ulph' in York Minster. Other examples of ivory horns, which continued to be made until the 18th century, are fewer and more variable in appearance.

BIBLIOGRAPHY
F. Crane: *Extant Medieval Musical Instruments: a Provisional Catalogue by Types* (Iowa City, 1972)

ANTHONY C. BAINES

Ombgwe (end-blown flute) of the Karanga people, Zimbabwe

Olkipilli. Pipe of Finland, similar to the RUOKOPILLI but made of straw.

Oloan. Gong in a *gondang* ensemble of North Sumatra, Indonesia. *See* GONDANG, (3).

Olobendo. Transverse flute with eight finger-holes from the Benguela region of Angola (*LaurentyA*, 286).

Olodero. PERCUSSION BEAM of the Alur people of Uganda. It is approximately 175 to 200 cm long and is placed on the ground and beaten near the ends by two young men. It is played with the *adungu* arched harp to accompany dancing.

Ologion. Rattle of the Edo-speaking peoples, Nigeria.

Olson–Belar Sound Synthesizer. *See* RCA ELECTRONIC MUSIC SYNTHESIZER.

Olubeye. Stick rattle of Uganda. Among the Nyole people it is approximately 100 cm long and threaded with 20 or more oncoba fruits. Among the Alur, Acholi, Nyoro, Toro and Nkole peoples several short sticks, each with three or four fruit shells, are held parallel by thongs attached at each end; the rattle is wound round the calf of a dancer. See *WachsmannTCU*.

Oluika. (1) Side-blown trumpet of the Tachoni people of Kenya. It is made from an animal horn with a hole cut in the side. The instrument produces only one note and supplies a drone to singing.
(2) Side-blown trumpet of the Bukhayo people of Kenya. It is made from the horn of a species of buck, to which is added a cow-horn bell, the two parts being wrapped round by a hide strap at the joint. The player is able to produce a number of notes by placing his left hand over the open end and overblowing. It is played to accompany songs. See G. Hyslop: *Musical Instruments of East Africa*, i: *Kenya* (Nairobi, 1975).

Olwet. End-blown trumpet of the Acholi people of Uganda. It has a narrow cylindrical bore, and the mouthpiece is a straight rim into which a funnel-shaped mouthpiece is inserted. The bell is made from a piece of gourd which opens out but is bent back to face the player. Similar instruments are found in Ganda and Toro, but have an obliquely cut mouthpiece. The Ganda and Toro instruments are considered imitations of European bugles, whereas the Acholi instrument is regarded as indigenous. The *icombi* trumpet of the Buluceke area of Gishu is similar; it has an obliquely cut mouthpiece, but is distinguished in that the bell is made from an elongated spherical gourd fixed to the tube by its narrow end and a small hole is cut in the apex. See *WachsmannTCU*.
See also ASUKUSUK.

Ombgwe. End-blown flute, with spherical mouthpiece, of the Karanga (Shona) people of Zimbabwe. It consists of a stopped pipe, of reed, with two finger-holes. The top is inserted into the shell of a monkey orange (*Strychnos spinosa*) with a mouth-hole at the end. It is played by boys. The performer sings at the same time as blowing his flute. The Venda KHUMBGWE is similar. See *KirbyMISA*, 129f, pl.45.

DAVID K. RYCROFT

Ombi. Eight-string arched harp of the Fang/Pahuin people of northern Gabon. *See* NGOMBI (i).

Omele [oumalay]. Drum of Nigeria (*omele*) and the West Indies (*oumalay*). *See* BATA; BATÁ; BATA KOTO.

Omichicahuaztli [omitzicahuastli]. SCRAPER of the Aztec people of Mexico, used especially for funeral music. It consisted of a long serrated stick or bone scraped with a smaller stick.

Omnichord. An electronic instrument manufactured by Suzuki in Hamamatsu, Japan, from 1981. It resembles a zither or autoharp, both visually and in playing technique. The instrument offers 27 chords, selected by push-buttons, which are 'strummed' in arpeggiated form on a touch-plate. It also incorporates 'walking bass' and electronic percussion units. In 1983 Suzuki developed the Tronichord, based on the Omnichord, in which the push-buttons are replaced by touch-plate sensors.

HUGH DAVIES

Omniton. A contrabass OPHICLEIDE with keys mounted on rod axles with needle springs. It was exhibited by Jean-Louis Antoine (*see* HALARY) in 1849, probably privately as it is not documented in L. A. de Pontécoulant's *Organographie* (Paris, 1861), which chronicles all the Parisian Expositions de l'Industrie at that time. It may be inferred from its name that the omniton could play in all keys, and therefore that it had at least 11 keys. Its pitch is unknown, and no examples appear to have survived. See C. Pierre: *Les facteurs d'instruments de musique* (Paris, 1893).

STEPHEN WESTON

Omnitonium. The name given by JÖRG MAGER to an electronic instrument which he tried to develop during the 1920s.

Om-om. Idioglot clarinet of the S'adan and north-west Toraja areas of central Sulawesi. *See* IYUP-IYUP.

Ompa [umpa]. NOTCHED FLUTE of the Bali people of Zaïre made from the stem of a plant of the same name. It has three finger-holes and is 40 to 50 cm long with a diameter of 3 cm at the mouthpiece and 4 cm at the far end. The mouthpiece is partly closed with resin and a V-shaped notch is made in the side. The flute is used for solo performance.

BIBLIOGRAPHY
F.J. de Hen: *Beitrag zur Kenntnis der Musikinstrumente aus Belgisch Kongo und Ruanda-Urundi* (Tervuren, 1960)
G. Knosp: *Enquête sur la vie musicale au Congo belge 1934–1935* (Tervuren, 1968)

K. A. GOURLAY

Omubanda [omuceewe] (pl. *emibanda*). NOTCHED FLUTE of the Nyoro (Nkole) people of Ankole district, Uganda. It is open-ended with four finger-holes, and is used for duet playing, with percussion accompaniment, to provide dance music (*TraceyCSA*, ii, 304). *See also* NDERE (i).

Omugoboli. Braced MUSICAL BOW with gourd resonator of Uganda, known in Rwanda as *omudage*. *See* EGO-BOLI.

Omujariko. A term used by the Iru people of Nkole in Uganda for the SEKITULEGE (ground harp).

Omukuri [omukuli]. NOTCHED FLUTE of Uganda. *See* NDERE (i).

Omutuna. Drum of the Lozi people of Mongu district, Zambia. *See* MILUPA.

Omutuwa. Single-headed conical drum of the Valley Tonga people of Gwembe district, Zambia. It is one of their three MILUPA drums.

Omvek. XYLOPHONE of the Beti people at Yaoundé, Cameroon. *See* MENDZAN.

Omwomba. Side-blown wooden trumpet of the Kerebe people on the island of Bukerebe in Lake Victoria, Tanzania. It was made from a hollowed-out branch, 4 to 6 cm in diameter, and one end was closed.

Onat. JEW'S HARP of the northern Philippines. *See* AFIW.

Onavillu. Struck MUSICAL BOW of Kerala, south India. *See* VILLU.

Onça. FRICTION DRUM of northern Brazil. *See* KWITA.

Ondeggiando (It.). *See* ONDULÉ.

Ondende. Set of stopped flutes of the Makere people of Zaïre (*LaurentyA*, 200).

Ondes martenot (Fr. 'martenot waves'). A monophonic electronic instrument invented by Maurice Martenot (*b* Paris, 14 Oct 1898; *d* 8 Oct 1980), whose original name for it was 'ondes musicales'. Martenot, who had studied piano, cello and composition at the Paris Conservatoire, first presented his instrument on 20 April 1928 as the soloist in Levidis's *Poème symphonique*, conducted by Rhené-Baton. Martenot was very active in promoting and developing the instrument, on which his sister Ginette became a leading performer, and it found favour with a number of composers including Milhaud, Jolivet, Koechlin, Schmitt, Ibert and Honegger, who were among the first to write works for or incorporating it. Varèse first used it as a substitute for the sirens in a performance of *Amériques* (30 May 1929, Paris) and later wrote for two ondes martenot in the revised version of *Ecuatorial*. Messiaen wrote for six ondes martenot in *Fêtes des belles eaux* (1937) and, more importantly, gave a prominent part to the instrument in the *Trois petites liturgies de la présence divine* (1944) and the *Turangalîla-symphonie* (1948), where the unmistakable association of the instrument with the human voice creates the impression of a goddess-like figure, without the human limitations of range or power. In 1947 Martenot was able to establish classes in the ondes martenot at the Paris Conservatoire. A year later Jolivet wrote a concerto for the instrument, and during the same period Boulez briefly became known as a performer on it and wrote an ondes martenot quartet (1945–6, withdrawn). The instrument is still frequently used in works by younger French composers. Apart from concert works and much film music (a total of perhaps 1000 works), it has also been employed in French theatres, including the Comédie-Française and the Folies-Bergère.

Some of the enthusiasm which composers felt for the instrument is conveyed by Honegger. In *Je suis com-*

positeur (Paris, 1951) he compared it with the double bassoon, writing 'The device known as ondes martenot could replace it with advantage. This instrument has power, a speed of utterance, which is not to be compared with those gloomy stove-pipes looming up in orchestras'. The ondes martenot is not specifically a bass instrument, however, for its range extends upwards beyond that of the piano.

The earliest version of the ondes martenot (1928) consisted of two units, in front of which the performer stood: the principal one had a 'pull-wire' operated with the right hand, and the other had controls manipulated by the left. In a later version the pull-wire was replaced by a horizontal ribbon controller (*ruban*), with a dummy keyboard behind it for pitch orientation, and in the early 1930s a functioning keyboard was added to the ribbon controller. The ondes martenot can produce only one note at a time (if more than one is played, the lowest is selected). The keyboard directly controls the frequency of a variable oscillator; the signal is then amplified and radiated as sound from a loudspeaker. Of striking design, the speaker cabinets stand free from the main body of the instrument (see illustration). The right hand plays the keyboard, of which each key is capable of slight lateral movement, microtonally shifting the pitch and enabling the performer to create a vibrato. Wide glissando sweeps and expressive portamentos are available by means of a finger-ring attached to a ribbon; the sliding of the ribbon, by means of the ring, controls the frequency. Here a heterodyne principle is used, similar to that of the ring modulator. A fixed oscillator with a frequency of 80 kHz is heterodyned, or modulated with a variable oscillator that is lower than the fixed oscillator by the frequency desired. Thus, to produce concert *a'* with a frequency of 440 Hz, the frequency of the variable oscillator is 79,560 Hz (80 kHz − 440 Hz). The resulting frequency difference, comparable to a difference tone in acoustical systems, is then amplified and heard through the loudspeaker in the normal way. The left hand is used to control potentiometers governing filters, which change the harmonic spectrum and thus the timbre, and also the degree of amplification, which varies the dynamic.

The instrument has been manufactured since 1929, at first by Gaveau in Paris and later by Martenot's own company, La Lutherie Electronique at Neuilly-sur-Seine, near Paris. Various improvements have been made over the years, including the addition of two special loudspeakers, the *palme* and the *diffuseur métallique* (patented in 1947). The ondes martenot may be said to be

Concert model of the ondes martenot by Maurice Martenot: two loudspeakers are shown, a conventional one and the 'palme' (with 12 sympathetic strings on each face); a third, the 'diffuseur métallique', is not shown

one of the most successful electronic instruments developed before the synthesizer.

BIBLIOGRAPHY
Ct. Hourst: 'Les instruments musicaux électriques: le Martenot', *L'ingénieur-constructeur*, xxviii (1929), 268
M. Martenot: *Méthode pour l'enseignement des ondes musicales* (Paris, 1931)
B. Disertori: 'Le onde Martenot: lo strumento nuovo d'una nuova èra', *RMI*, xliii (1939), 383
M. Martenot: 'Lutherie électronique', *Cahiers Renaud-Barrault*, nos.2–3 (1954), 69; repr. in *La musique et ses problèmes contemporains: 1953–1963* (Paris, 1963), 77
——: 'Künstlerische und technische Merkmale des elektronischen Musikinstruments: Zukunftsperspektiven', *Musik–Raumgestaltung–Elektroakustik*, ed. W. Meyer-Eppler (Mainz, 1955), 72
F. K. Prieberg: *Musik des technischen Zeitalters* (Zurich, 1956), 49
——: *Musica ex machina* (Berlin and Frankfurt am Main, 1960), 203, 214
J.-E. Marie: 'Lutherie électronique: le Martenot', *Histoire de la musique*, ii: *Du XVIIIe siècle à nos jours*, ed. Roland-Manuel (Paris, 1963), 1425
J. Laurendeau: 'Un instrument au son électronique: l'onde martenot', *Vie musicale* (1967), nos.5–6, p.11
T. L. Rhea: *The Evolution of Electronic Musical Instruments in the United States* (diss., George Peabody College, Nashville, Tenn., 1972), 62; section rev. as 'Martenot's Musical Waves', *Contemporary Keyboard*, iv/10 (1978), 62

RICHARD ORTON

Ondioline. A monophonic, three-octave PIANO ATTACHMENT developed by Georges Jenny around 1938–40 and manufactured by Les Ondes Georges Jenny (later known as La Musique Electronique) in Paris from 1941 until about 1976 (when Jenny died). The instruments were individually built by Jenny himself; during the early 1950s they were also available in kit form. The sound is generated by a single oscillator. The range of the touch-sensitive keyboard can be set within a total compass of eight octaves by means of an octave transposition switch, and octave doubling is possible. Complex waveforms are produced with up to 50 overtones. Volume is controlled by a knee-lever, and percussive attacks can be produced by means of a finger-wire. Sideways movement of the finger moves the keyboard itself and produces a vibrato similar to that obtainable from the ondes martenot. The Ondioline has been much used in film and theatre music, light music and cabaret, often as a solo instrument. It was played, with piano accompaniment, at the top of the Atomium building at the Brussels World Fair in 1958. Its principal exponent in serious music has been the composer Jean-Etienne Marie, for whom Jenny constructed a special four-octave model which could be tuned in a variety of microtonal systems ($\frac{1}{3}$-, $\frac{1}{4}$-, $\frac{1}{5}$-, $\frac{1}{6}$-, or $\frac{1}{7}$-tones). During the 1950s and early 1960s a version of the Ondioline, known as the Pianoline, was manufactured in West Germany by Lipp & Sohn; and in Holland the Orcheline, a combination of the Ondioline with a harmonium, was produced.

BIBLIOGRAPHY
J.-E. Marie: *Musique vivante* (Paris, 1953), 178
G. Jenny: 'Initiation à la lutherie électronique', *Toute la radio* (1955), 289, 397, 455; (1956), 23, 67
——: *L'Ondioline* (Paris, ?1957)
J.-E. Marie: 'Lutherie électronique: ondioline', *Histoire de la musique*, ii: *Du XVIIIe siècle à nos jours*, ed. Roland-Manuel (Paris, 1963), 1431

HUGH DAVIES

Ondium Péchadre. A monophonic electronic instrument developed by H. C. R. Péchadre in France in 1930. It was roughly heart-shaped and was light and easily portable. In performance the base rested on the knees of the seated player and the instrument was supported against the edge of a table. The sound was generated by a beat-frequency oscillator, the pitch of which was controlled by the right hand by means of a pointer moved round a calibrated semicircular dial; the range was about six octaves. Sound was heard only when a push-button was depressed by a finger of the left hand; the amount of pressure affected the volume. Another left-hand control produced sharp attacks like those of plucked string instruments; the timbre could also be modified.

BIBLIOGRAPHY
E. Weiss: 'Un appareil de musique radioélectrique: l'Ondium Péchadre', *La nature*, lviii (1930), 64

HUGH DAVIES

Ondulé (Fr.; It. *ondeggiando*). In string playing, a 'wavy' motion executed by moving the bow back and forth across two or more adjacent strings. The player achieves this with an up-and-down motion of the wrist. *See* BOW, §II, 2 (vii).

DAVID D. BOYDEN

Ongiyong. DUCT FLUTE of the Ifugao people of the northern Philippines; among the Kalinga people it is known as *olimong*, and among the Ibaloi as *kulasing*. In the southern Philippines the Hanunoo people know it as *pituh*.

Ongo. End-blown long wooden trumpet of the Broto people of the Central African Republic. It is 120 to 150 cm long. Eight *ongo* of different sizes, one so heavy that it is played with the end resting on the ground, are blown with four short end-blown trumpets of horn, using hocket technique, for initiation ceremonies. See C. Duvelle: 'Musique centrafricaine', OCR 12 [disc notes].

K. A. GOURLAY

Ongoma. Double-headed cylindrical drum of the Herero people of south-western Africa. The body is carved from wood. The heads are made from calfskin and are either lapped on, with thongs, or laced on, as with a European side-drum, from which the instrument was possibly copied (*see* ISIGUBHU). It is played by men, but has no ritual use. The drum is beaten on one head only, with two knobbed sticks. See *KirbyMISA*, 46.

Ông sáo. Transverse flute of Vietnam, used in the HÁT CẢI LƯƠNG ensemble. *See also* SÁO.

Onguna na bagada. Percussion instrument, literally 'the talking branch', of Nzakara women of the Central African Republic. The instrument consists of a large earthenware pot into which a woman, who is seated on the ground, thrusts her forearms in such a way that she can bring the pot backwards and forwards to her bare breast, thus opening or closing the mouth of the pot. A slanting branch is placed under the pot to support it; the other end of the branch rests against a tree, where it is kept steady by a second woman. A third woman squats on the ground and strikes the branch at its mid-point with two sticks. The vibrations produced are passed to the pot which amplifies them, while, by opening and closing the mouth of the pot, the woman is able to produce changes in pitch, including rapidly ascending glissandos. The instrument is used as rhythmic accompaniment to women singing.

BIBLIOGRAPHY
P. Collaer: 'Musics of the Central African Republic', BM30 L2310 [disc notes]

K. A. GOURLAY

Ongungu. Cylindrical SLIT-DRUM of the Mbole and Opala peoples of Zaïre (*LaurentyTF*, 134). *See* GUGU, (1).

Onion flute. A MIRLITON whose membrane is made of onion skin. *See also* EUNUCH-FLUTE.

Onkhonji. *See* OHONJI.

Òn-mok-tayàw. SPIKE FIDDLE of Burma. It has a coconut-shell resonator; the bow is threaded between the two strings.

Onó'kah kastaweh'shae'. Animal-horn vessel rattle of the Iroquois Indians of north-eastern North America. It is made from a piece of cow horn about 6 to 8 cm long with a diameter of about 3 cm at one end increasing to 6 cm. A wooden handle is passed through the length of the horn so that it projects slightly at the narrow end, where it is wedged in place. About a dozen small shot pellets or steel bearings are inserted into the horn and it is closed with a wooden plug. The handle may be carved or inscribed with a name or date. The total length of the instrument is from about 20 to 30 cm.

The rattle is normally held in the right hand and struck against the left palm or, if seated, against the left thigh. The beat is usually a simple duple, punctuated at specific places in a song by a steady roll produced by holding the rattle upright and moving it in a small circle. It is used to accompany social dance and ceremonial songs, either alone or with the water-drum KA'NOHKO'WAH. The drum is played by the leader while all other singers in the ensemble shake rattles.

The cow-horn rattle is a recent adoption and seems to have come from the west. It has replaced the cylindrical bark rattle of the Iroquois and the gourd and cylindrical bark rattles of the neighbouring Wabanaki (who make a simpler horn rattle). The Iroquois still use other bark and gourd rattles, such as the *osnóh' kastaweh'shae'* and *onyohsa' kastaweh'shae'*.

BIBLIOGRAPHY

H. C. Conklin and W. C. Sturtevant: 'Seneca Indian Singing Tools at Coldspring Longhouse: Musical Instruments of the Modern Iroquois', *Proceedings of the American Philosophical Society*, xcvii (1953), 262–90

MARY RIEMER-WELLER

Onyohsa' kastaweh'shae' (Seneca: 'gourd rattle'). Vessel rattle of the Iroquois Indians of north-eastern North America. It is also called *íi'tostha' kastaweh'shae'*, after *íi'tos*, the society of mystic animals for which it is used. It is made from a dried squash or pumpkin gourd 10 to 20 cm long and 15 to 20 cm in diameter; it contains small shot pellets and has a stick handle. The overall length is around 30 cm.

One of the *íi'tos* ceremonies, the Eagle Dance, employs a smaller version of the rattle, for which a small cowhorn rattle, *onó'kah kastaweh'shae'*, may be substituted.

MARY RIEMER-WELLER

'O'o. SLIT-DRUM of the 'Are'are people of Malaita, Solomon Islands. It is beaten singly with two sticks to transmit messages such as the announcement of a death, the proclamation of a feast or the upbraiding of a pig thief; see H. Zemp: 'Instruments de musique de Malaita', *Journal de la Société des Océanistes*, xxvii/30

(1971), 43f. For the use of the instrument in ensemble *see* PARA NI 'O'O.

Opačica. DUCT FLUTE of Bosnia and Hercegovina (Yugoslavia). *See* SVIRALA.

Opanda. LAMELLAPHONE of the Igbo people of Nigeria with up to ten metal keys and a wooden box resonator.

Ope. Side-blown ivory trumpet of the Edo/Bini people of Nigeria, also known as *akohen*. The *ope*, together with special drums, form part of the paraphernalia of royal office.

Open harp. Term used in the Hornbostel–Sachs classification for a harp with no forepillar, further subdivided into 'arched' and 'angular' harps. *See* HARP, esp. §1.

Open notes. On valved brass instruments, the notes of the harmonic series produced without lowering any valve. In brass parts, however, 'open' (Fr. *ouvert*, etc) countermands 'muted' or 'stopped'.

Open string. In string instruments, a string played at its full sounding-length without 'stopping' (that is, without touching the string or pressing it down with the finger). In unfretted string instruments there is a difference between the sound of an open string and the sound of a stopped string sounding the same pitch. Open E string on the violin, for instance, has a different timbre from a note of the same pitch produced by stopping the A string a 5th above. Because of this difference, open strings are generally avoided, and the notes in question normally played 'stopped' unless a small 'o' is placed over the note to indicate that it is to be played 'open'. In fretted instruments, such as viols and lutes, there is also a difference between stopped and open strings, but this difference is considerably less than in unfretted instruments because a string stopped by pressing down on a fret has a more 'open' quality than a string stopped on the unfretted fingerboard; in this way all notes on the fretted instruments approach the sound of the open string. In French lute and viol tablature open strings are indicated by 'a', in Italian by 'o', and in German tablatures by a different letter for each string.

DAVID D. BOYDEN

Opere. Cylindrical drum of the Yoruba people of Nigeria. *See* GBEDU.

Operenten [apentemma]. Hand drum of Ghana.

Ophibariton (Fr.). RUSSIAN BASSOON.

Ophicleide (Fr. *ophicléide, basse d'harmonie, contrebasse d'harmonie*; Ger. *Ophikleide*; It. *oficleide*). An obsolete lip-energized brass wind instrument belonging to the keyed bugle family, to which it forms the natural bass. It was patented by the French maker Halary (Jean Hilaire Asté) in 1821. The word 'ophicleide' (in the original French 'ophicléide') was compounded from the Greek 'ophis' (a serpent) and 'kleis' (a cover or stopper), and therefore might reasonably be translated as 'keyed serpent' (except for quite basic principles, however, the instrument does not have much in common with the SERPENT, not even with those late types in which direct fingering was abandoned and all note-holes were controlled by keys). 'Ophicléide', though intended as the specific name for the largest of the homologous set of instruments covered by Halary's 1821 patent, soon became generic for all sizes. The name was later extended to other instruments of like pitch and use, and some early bass tubas or bombardons were known as 'ophicléide à piston' or 'valve ophicleide' (*see* TUBA (i)). The tone of the instrument when well played is full and resonant; the derogatory comments of some musical historians seem little justified, as does the unkind nickname 'chromatic bullock' which so amused some Victorian reporters. Today in Britain there is a revival of interest in the ophicleide, as there is in the keyed bugle in the USA, and a number of professional brass players are giving attention to its technique. Composers such as Mendelssohn, Schumann, Verdi and Wagner wrote important parts for it; its characteristic tone is not always well replaced in their works by the orchestral tuba.

See also ORGAN STOP.

1. Description. 2. History.

1. DESCRIPTION. The bore of the ophicleide, except for a moderate bell flare, is strictly conical, and has a large mean diameter relative to its length – proportions typical of the bugle. The main tube, which in the C bass instrument is about 2·44 metres long, is bent in the form of a narrow U, the limbs being only about 1·25 cm apart. The narrower limb terminates about 30 cm short of the bell rim with a cylindrical socket into which the crook fits. The crook, usually either circular or folded into an ellipse, completes the bore and carries at its narrow end the mouthpiece, which stands approximately at right angles to the main tubing. The elliptical form of crook, typical of later ophicleides, often incorporates a U-shaped tuning-slide. The mouthpiece was usually similar to that of a bass trombone, though as with all brasses individual preference often called for other types. In rare instances ophicleides were built with the main body of wood, either covered with leather like serpents or highly polished (*see* §2). The ophicleide has been built in a number of sizes. A celebrated instruction book, the *Méthode complète d'ophicléide* (Paris, n.d.) of Caussinus and F. Berr, mentions no fewer than six: altos in F or Eb, basses in C or Bb and contrabasses in F or Eb. A contralto in Ab is also known to have existed (an example is in the Paris Conservatoire Museum), though in general the smaller instruments seem to have been less satisfactory than the bass and contrabass.

Ophicleides have been built with nine to 12 keys, 11 being by far the commonest number. The lowest, placed near the bell, stands open at rest; all the others stand closed. (A screw to hold the bell-key closed functions only to insure against damage when the instrument is laid aside.) The touchpieces controlling the keys are in two groups, arranged to be played with the left hand above the right, as with the bassoon. In early ophicleides the key-heads were simple flat discs, faced with leather, which closed down on collars surrounding the holes. With these, fairly heavy springing was needed to ensure airtight closure; later instruments had cupped key-heads with stuffed pads. At first sight the sizing and disposition of the holes may seem somewhat haphazard, and indeed there are minor differences between instruments of the same nominal pitch by different makers.

With all the keys at rest, the bass ophicleide in C is capable of sounding the first eight or so notes of the harmonic series whose fundamental is 8' C, that is C, c, g, c', e', g', bb', c'' (here the terms 'fundamental' and 'harmonic' are used in the broad sense common among playing musicians). Closing the lowest key lowers the series by a semitone; on an 11-key instrument the keys, used singly or in combination, provide the player with 12 effective tube lengths whose fundamental notes are a semitone apart. By appropriate choice of fundamentals and harmonics the player can command a chromatic range of three octaves or so. Moreover, for some notes duplicate fingerings are possible since their frequencies occur among the harmonics of more than one series. The choice of fingering cannot always have been an easy one, and this may to some extent account for the discrepancies found among different instruction books, of which a considerable number had appeared before the mid-19th century. Ex.1 indicates the commonest fingerings and alternatives – a fingering chart from A. Héral's *Méthode pour neuf, dix et onze clés* (Paris, n.d.).

Ex.1

Alto ophicleides were made in Eb and F, a 4th above the bass ophicleides. Halary originally called them 'quinticlaves'. They were used only in military and brass bands, where they reinforced the horns and bassoons and filled out the middle of the harmony. Extant instruments are mostly in Eb, with a compass of D to eb''. Berlioz was critical of the alto ophicleide, which seems to have been an unreliable instrument. It was soon replaced by the valved clavicor, patented in 1838. Contrabass ophicleides (known also as 'monster ophicleides') were pitched an octave below the alto ophicleide, the F instrument having a compass of E' to ab'. The earliest use of the instrument in England was at the Birmingham Festival in 1834, when it was played by William Ponder. After Ponder's death in 1841 the Frenchman

Prospère took over as 'monster ophicleidist' for the English festivals. A contrabass in the Brussels conservatory collection (no.1248) is a military instrument, with a gaping serpent's head in place of the normal bell and a crook coiled round the throat. In 1858 Tollot designed a contrabass ophicleide in which the first key was replaced by a valve. The instrument is in the Paris Conservatoire Museum (no.655 in Chouquet's catalogue).

While the ophicleide undoubtedly surpassed the upright serpent and the bass horn in power and clarity, it did have serious defects. As with all 'cup-mouthpiece with side-hole' instruments, notes requiring holes remote from the bell are as a rule poorer and weaker than others. As ex.1 shows, for certain notes two or three adjacent keys must be kept open at the same time, and indeed some advanced instruments had overlapping touchpieces to provide for this. Sometimes choice of available harmonics helped, but finally the matter rested with the player and his ability to play with an even tone quality over a wide range. In addition, although the fundamental tones were doubtless 'built in' to be in tune with each other, the unavoidable deviation from a theoretically perfect cone that was imposed by the presence of side-hole collars and other features led to inaccurate intervals between some of the harmonics. Furthermore, naturally spaced harmonics do not always coincide with the notes of the equal-tempered scale. To play the ophicleide well required an acute ear and a strong lip. That the instrument proliferated as it did and gained such esteem speaks highly for some of its players.

2. HISTORY. It has often been said that the ophicleide owes its origin to some upright form of serpent imported into France during the Napoleonic Wars. A more plausible, though still unsubstantiated, story is that while reviewing allied troops after Waterloo the Grand Duke Konstantin of Russia was so impressed by the playing of John Distin, solo keyed bugle in the Grenadier Guards Band, that he requested a copy of Distin's instrument. Distin complied by taking his bugle to Halary in Paris to be copied. In 1817 Halary submitted to the Institut de France, the Académie Royale des Beaux Arts and the Athénée des Arts three instruments which he called, respectively: 'clavitube' (a normal keyed bugle despite his description of it as 'trompette à clef'); 'quinticlave' (an alto built in upright form); and 'ophicléide' (the bass instrument known today). These were patented in 1821, with a supplementary coverage for three additional keys on the ophicleide in 1822. The nine-key ophicleide of 1821, however, seems to have been the basis of future work. In 1825 Halary retired from business; his successor Jean-Louis Antoine, who also adopted the name Halary, devoted himself to improving the piston valve, then newly imported from Germany. In 1822 Labbaye *fils* secured a patent for a ten-key ophicleide made in four demountable sections which could be packed inside each other for easy transport (certainly an attractive feature, for the instrument's thin-walled body was easily dented and put out of alignment). Yet another version, in which six of the 11 keys were open-standing, was patented in 1827, by Sautermeister of Lyons. This design may have had acoustical advantages, but it failed to catch on. Protagonists of the serpent, meanwhile, sought to modernize the older instrument to meet the challenge of the evidently superior ophicleide. Between 1820 and 1830 a number of variants, mostly in upright form, appeared under such names as 'basson russe' (*see* RUSSIAN BAS-

Bass ophicleide in C by P. L. Gautrot, Paris, c1850 (Royal College of Music, London)

SOON) 'bassoon serpent' or 'ophibaryton', OPHIMONO-CLEIDE and 'serpent Forveille'. These attained a passing vogue on the Continent, while in England Frichot's BASS-HORN was popular. A wooden soprano ophicleide by Dupré of Tournai, known as a TUBA-DUPRÉ, was shown at the Haarlem Exhibition in 1825, and in 1849 Halary exhibited his OMNITON, a contrabass ophicleide.

How and when the ophicleide was introduced into England is not known, but a surviving instrument marked 'Ophicleide or Quint-tube Halary Inventor Made by P. Turton 5 Wormwood Gate Dublin 1829' may suggest that the ophicleide came from Ireland as did the parent keyed bugle. From contemporary press notices and concert programmes it is known that in 1834, at the Handel Commemoration in Westminster Abbey and at Birmingham, both bass and contrabass ophicleides were played, and at York in the following year there were no fewer than three ophicleides, four serpents and a HIBERNICON. Wooden-bodied models appear in English makers' lists about this time under the title of SERPENTCLEIDE.

In an attempt to adapt valves to the ophicleide tube Guichard of Paris patented (1832) a valved ophicleide, virtually a primitive tuba. Such instruments had little success, however, partly because of the mechanical and acoustical inefficiency of early valves, and partly because of the intonation problems inherent in the additive three-valve system before the development of compensation (see VALVE (i)). Between about 1830 and 1850 the Halary type of ophicleide became the most popular, and advances were made mostly in performing standards rather than in technical improvements. In 1833 the Berlin firm of Griessling & Schlott brought out an improved bass ophicleide (see HARMONIEKONTRABASS). A contrabass instrument in F, called a serpent-bombardon, was designed about 1840 by the Bohemian V. F. Červený, and another was made by Andreas Barth of Munich (see KONTRASTBOMBARDON). By about 1850, however, valves in general had been much improved and the ophicleide in its turn was obsolescent, despite the patenting of a number of new types. In 1852 Couturier of Lyons produced an instrument with only six keys, the others being replaced in some unexplained manner by a single valve. Gautrot aîné, an inveterate experimenter, also proposed two very complicated instruments, neither of which succeeded (if indeed they ever got beyond the drawing-board). In 1858 the second Halary listed a normal ophicleide with improved keys on rod axles. Two English patents have also come to light, that of Robinson in 1851 and one granted to Macfarlane, Newton & Carte in 1860. An unpatented improvement was the 12th key on the extant instruments of the English virtuoso, Samuel Hughes (1825–91). This gave alternative fingerings for G♯ in the bottom octave and eliminated the slurring problems on some 11-keyed ophicleides.

As late as 1916 the catalogue of Couesnon (Paris) offered ophicleides, but the four instruments listed were stock models, the last of which was made in 1850. A single ophicleide is listed as in the Paris Opéra orchestra in 1915, but as this follows three trombones and there is no tuba, a valved bass may be implied.

BIBLIOGRAPHY

F. Gevaert: Traité général d'instrumentation (Ghent, 1863)
G. Chouquet: Le Musée du Conservatoire national de musique (Paris, 1875)
C. Pierre: Les facteurs d'instruments de musique (Paris, 1893)
A. Carse: Musical Wind Instruments (London, 1939/R1965)
——: The Orchestra from Beethoven to Berlioz (Cambridge, 1948)
A. Baines: Brass Instruments, their History and Development (London, 1976/R1980)
C. Bevan: The Tuba Family (London, 1978)

S. J. Weston: 'Improvements to the Nine-keyed Ophicleide', GSJ, xxxvi (1983), 109
For a list of ophicleide tutors, see Grove 5.

REGINALD MORLEY-PEGGE/PHILIP BATE, STEPHEN WESTON

Ophimonocleide. An upright SERPENT, shaped like an OPHICLEIDE, with six finger-holes and a single open-standing key. It was patented by Jean-Baptiste Coëffet of Chaumont-en-Vexin, Oise, on 2 May 1828 (French patent no.2338). It has a brass bell section and crook, joined by a wooden section into which the finger-holes are bored, and a wooden bow. Between the two sets of finger-holes is a pompe – a double slide which enables the pitch to be altered by about three-quarters of a tone from opera to cathedral pitch. The open-standing key, like the first key of the ophicleide, stands near the bell and lowers the pitch by a semitone when all the finger-holes are closed.

In other respects the ophimonocleide may be regarded as an upright keyless serpent in D, its fundamental being D. The key is used for all C♯s and G♯s, F and B in the third octave and E♭ and F in the highest register. Coëffet described the third-octave B as 'parfaitement bon', unlike that of the ordinary serpent, and likened the tone of that octave to the sound of a horn. It is possible that the low C♯ can be lipped down several semitones, as on other serpents. The crook incorporates a boule-à-vis – a brass sphere which can be unscrewed to drain the condensation; the device was first used on Sautermeister's 'nouvel ophicléide' of 1827.

The only ophimonocleide known to Morley-Pegge in 1954 is now in the Bate Collection, University of Oxford. Among others which have come to light since then is one in the Royal College of Music, London, and an incomplete specimen in the City Museum, Sheffield. Each of these is inscribed 'Coëffet'.

BIBLIOGRAPHY

H. Lavoix: Histoire de l'instrumentation (Paris, 1878)
A. Jacquot: Guide de l'art instrumental: dictionnaire pratique et raisonné des instruments de musique (Paris, 1886)
C. Sachs: Real-Lexikon der Musikinstrumente (Berlin, 1913/R1962)
R. Morley-Pegge: 'Serpent Forveille', Grove 5
L. G. Langwill: An Index of Musical Wind-instrument Makers (Edinburgh, 1960, rev., enlarged 6/1980)
A. Baines: The Bate Collection of Historical Wind Instruments (Oxford, 1976)

STEPHEN WESTON

Opi. Side-blown animal-horn trumpet of Nigeria. Among the Igede people it is used only on special occasions; it 'speaks' in the Izi language at the funeral of a member of the inner circle of warriors. The Igede opikeh is a small side-blown antelope-horn trumpet which is used to make short statements in aitah war music. The Igbo opi is made from the horn of a cow or other animal, and is used during dances and for signalling. Among the Igbo the prefix opi can also denote a flute: opi-nta is a bamboo flute; opi-ukwu a wooden flute with cupped mouthpiece.

Opo. Side-blown trumpet of the Idoma people of Nigeria. It is made from the horn of either a cow or an antelope and produces five or six notes. The opo is used by dance societies or in hunting.

Opokolo mbekwu. SLIT-DRUM of the Igbo people of Nigeria. See OKPOKOLO.

Opon. Small KETTLEDRUM of the Yoruba people of Nigeria. See GUDU-GUDU.

Opop. Flat gong in a TOPAYYA ensemble of the Kalinga people of the northern Philippines.

Oporo. Side-blown animal-horn trumpet of Kenya.

Opporo [okworro]. Cylindro-conical drum of the Gobu and Togbo peoples of Zaïre (*BooneT*, 27, 66). *See* DINDO.

Oprekelj. BOX ZITHER (dulcimer) of Slovenia (Yugoslavia).

Opuk agoya. Arched harp of the Acholi people of Uganda. *See* ENNANGA.

Orage (Fr.). A pedal on French organs of the Romantic period built by Cavaillé-Coll and others from *c*1856 onwards. It played several of the lowest pedal pipes at once, producing an effect like thunder. *See* ORGAN, §VI, 3.

Oramics. A photoelectric composition machine developed by Daphne Oram (*b* Devizes, Wilts., 31 Dec 1925) at Fairseat, Kent, in 1962–5. Oram worked as a music balancer for the BBC and in 1958 she was the cofounder of the BBC Radiophonic Workshop, of which she became director. In 1959 she left to pursue her interest in synthesized music, which dated back to 1944, and began in 1962 to build the Oramics system on which she had been experimenting for eight years.

Oramics is intended for studio use rather than live performance. It uses a synchronized set of ten parallel tracks of sprocketed transparent 35 mm film, on which details of each component of the sound are drawn in erasable ink (*see* DRAWN SOUND). Three tracks are required for the digitally notated pitches, up to six for the analogue notation of envelopes, rhythm and duration, dynamics, vibrato, reverberation and timbre mixes, and one track for control signals. Timbre is originated by waveshape outlines drawn on glass slides; these control the scanning process of four cathode-ray tubes. The film tracks can be wound backwards and forwards manually for immediate verification of notated sounds; when the score is complete they are transported through the photoelectric sound-generating system by a motor at 10 cm per second. Oramics is considerably cheaper than comparable computerized systems, and requires no technical knowledge on the part of the composer. Many subtle adjustments, including timbre–amplitude–vibrato interaction, microtonal tuning and reverberation, are simple to make. Only one model of the system exists (in Oram's own small electronic music studio); its development continues.

For illustration *see* DRAWN SOUND, fig.2.

BIBLIOGRAPHY
D. Oram: *An Individual Note of Music, Sound and Electronics* (London, 1972), 97
A. Douglas: *Electronic Music Production* (London, 1973), 92
HUGH DAVIES

Orchestra (from Gk. *orchēstra*: 'a dancing place'; Fr. *orchestre*; Ger. *Orchester*; It. *orchestra*). In the Greek theatre it denoted the more or less semicircular space in front of the stage where the chorus not only sang but danced. In the Roman theatre this space, bearing the same name, was reserved for the seats of senators. Later

the word was applied to the stage itself and was so defined by Isidore of Seville (*Etymologiarium*, xviii.44) about the beginning of the 7th century. The term was revived in France in the late 17th century and was borrowed by Mattheson for the title of his book *Das neu-eröffnete Orchestre* (Hamburg, 1713), a general introduction to music for the educated public: he admitted that the word was not very common and called it a 'galante Expression', defining it as the place in front of the stage where the instrumentalists and their director sat. Though still not common in Germany, by the early 18th century the word had become applied in France to the players themselves and soon acquired general currency. Roger North in 1728 (see Wilson, 1959), objecting to the misuse of a classical term, wrote of 'the orchestre, as it is (improperly) called'. The term 'chapel' and its cognates (*cappella, chapelle, Kapelle* etc) was widely applied to court, ecclesiastical and private musical establishments in the 17th and 18th centuries, and often signified what is now meant by 'orchestra'.

Modern writers sometimes use the term 'orchestra' for a wide variety of instrumental ensembles, from the world of non-Western societies to the Renaissance courts. It seems simpler to define it as an organized body of bowed strings with more than one player to a part, to which may be added any number of wind and percussion instruments. An ensemble consisting wholly of wind instruments, whether woodwind and brass or brass alone, is normally described as a band (*see* BAND (i)). For a summary of the changes in the typical composition of orchestras from the early 17th century to the 20th see Table 1 below (p.834).

The origins of the orchestra can be seen in the 16th century in two configurations: the separate consorts of instruments in the major courts; and the special assemblies of various instruments for important ceremonies, especially the weddings and funerals of royalty. The royal houses of London, Paris, Florence and Munich were of particular importance in these practices.

In the 17th century the composition of the ensemble

1. The Dresden Hofkapelle in the Zwinger opera house during a performance of Lotti's 'Teofane' in 1719: detail of a pen and ink drawing with wash by an unknown artist (Kupferstichkabinett, Dresden)

2. Torchlight concert by the Jena Collegium Musicum: watercolour (1744) by an unknown German artist (Museum für Kunst und Gewerbe, Hamburg); the collegium musicum (around a three-manual harpsichord) is presenting a professor with a festive musical greeting, while a congratulatory poem is borne in on a cushion (centre)

varied from place to place both in number and in type of instrument. The string ensemble was fostered in Italy, particularly in Rome, and in the English and French courts the specialized timbre of its constituent instruments was developed. Brass ensembles, an outgrowth of the *Stadtpfeifer* tradition, were employed in Germany in the performance of suites. The most important developments in the 17th century resulted from the introduction of the violin in Germany and the fusion of brass and woodwind instruments with strings in northern Italy, particularly in Venice. The instrumental ensemble at St Mark's, Venice, was initially chartered as a predominantly brass group in the later 16th century, but Monteverdi succeeded in introducing additional strings into the orchestra of 16 that he enlisted in 1614. This basic group was augmented by as many as four organs and up to 12 extra players on special occasions. With the decline of polychoral music, and of the cornett as a principal treble instrument, the orchestra became a predominantly string one. However, in this context the doubling of the continuo line by a violone lacking an obbligato part can be inferred only from the second half of the 17th century onwards. Elsewhere in Italy practices continued to vary locally, from institution to institution within one place, and from occasion to occasion within one institution. Private performances in Roman

palaces appear to have involved more performers, for example, than music in the Roman churches. In Bologna the bass register seems to have been emphasized on paramount feasts (as is evident from the distribution of performers added in 1692) but not on ordinary feasts.

The development of the court orchestra in Vienna during the century preceding the advent of Haydn forms an especially interesting chapter in the orchestra's history. In contrast to the Italian churches, the Viennese court encouraged music of a secular character in the 17th century and, to judge by surviving repertory, this influenced the composition of the group. Between 1700 and 1730 the number of players in the Viennese orchestra increased from about 40 to over 60 and the proportions were redesigned to provide greater emphasis on woodwind and low string instruments. Caldara's tastes, formed earlier in Venice and Rome, would seem to have governed an important measure of this change. During the next half century there was continued refinement of the woodwind section and a gradual decrease in the use of brass and percussion instruments which, combined with a reduction to a little over 30 players, produced the final outlines of the classical symphony orchestra.

Early examples of doubled strings include the *Balet comique de la Royne* (1581) and Monteverdi's *Orfeo* (1607); but these occasional ensembles can hardly be described as orchestras. The permanent French and English court ensembles grew out of Italian viol consorts which had been established in Paris and London by the middle of the 16th century. By the beginning of the reign of James I the royal ensemble had a regular membership of nine or ten 'violins' (violins, violas and cellos), but for masques and other special occasions they were augmented to as many as 25 or 30 (e.g. for Ben Jonson's *Pleasure Reconciled to Virtue*, 1618). In Paris Louis XIII reorganized his players as the 24 Violons du Roi in 1626. The composition of this five-part ensemble was given by Mersenne (*Harmonie universelle*, 1636–7) as six *dessus*, six *basses*, four *haute-contres*, four *tailles* and four *quintes*. The *dessus* were violins, the *basses* cellos. Mersenne's treatise is a little vague about the other three instruments, beyond saying that they were all larger than the *dessus*, they were of different sizes and they were tuned in unison. This seems to imply that they were all violas of different sizes. This constitution seems to have been continued throughout the 17th century. The double bass was gradually integrated into both the court and Opéra orchestras in Paris in the first quarter of the 18th century. Before that it had been used at the Opéra only for scenes involving violent storms, earthquakes and invocations. In England a list of the king's violins in 1631 details three trebles, two contra-tenors, three tenors, two low tenors and four basses – which may imply the same organization as the 24 Violons du Roi. Whether the 24 violins established by Charles II originally followed the French model cannot be determined. In fact most 17th-century orchestral music in England (in odes, theatre music and anthems) was in four parts, not five, with two violins as the two upper parts. In Italy too, where a five-part string ensemble was common in Venetian opera, two violins were preferred for the upper parts. According to Roger North (see Wilson, 1959), the double bass was first used in London theatre orchestras in the 1690s as the result of attempts there to produce Italian opera.

A major reform of the wind instruments was effected in Paris in the 1670s and 1680s by members of the Hotteterre and Chédeville families, working under the influence of Lully. Such men created the so-called 'Baroque' flute, recorder, oboe and bassoon by redesigning Renaissance instruments. By the mid-18th century these new wind instruments had been adopted by orchestras throughout western Europe. During the latter part of the 17th century and the first part of the 18th a number of German and Austrian courts maintained ensembles closely modelled on the court orchestras at Versailles. The basic ensemble consisted of strings, two oboes, bassoon and continuo. Additional wind instruments usually formed a separate category: they were normally part of a court military establishment (this applies particularly to trumpets and timpani) or drawn from local guilds. Recorders, and sometimes transverse flutes (*flûtes d'Allemagne*), were used in French and Venetian opera, and trumpets and timpani were introduced for music of a festal or military character. All these instruments were also employed in England and Germany as occasion demanded.

One factor that offsets the implications of reports of fixed numbers of instruments for ensembles in the 16th, 17th and early 18th centuries is the widespread practice of employing twice the number of players normally used and requiring them to alternate in identically formed groups. The German courts were exceptional in that most seem to have retained on a regular basis only a small ensemble that could not have allowed for such rotations.

Another practice that existed in the 17th century but was more conspicuous in the early 18th was that of employing soloists for occasions of special importance; their addition could change the character and balance of the orchestra. Thus statistics such as those shown in Table 1 may not exactly match the requirement of specific contemporary works (if the statistics are derived from orchestra documents) or the normal composition of the orchestra (if they are derived from scores). The entries for Bologna in 1694 illustrate the divergence possible within one group. A final factor that makes statistics require careful interpretation is the practice of employing a single player to perform on various instruments (e.g. horn and trumpet in the 18th century or the common doubling of flute and piccolo).

In the early years of the 18th century, the four-part string ensemble became widely accepted as normal

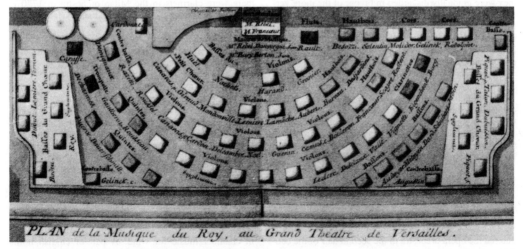

3. *Disposition of the orchestra at the Grand Théâtre de Versailles in 1773, giving the name of each player: detail of a watercolour by François Metoyen (Bibliothèque de Versailles); the orchestra is in semicircles centred on the 'batteur de mesure', who beats time facing the stage*

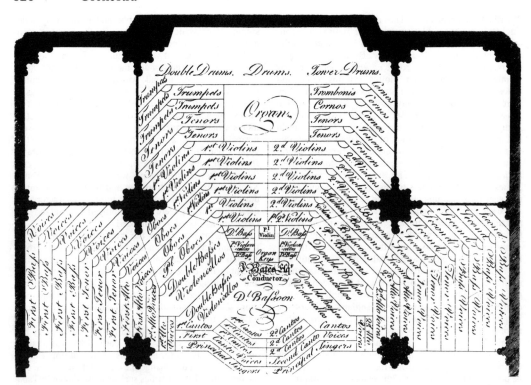

4. Plan of the orchestra and chorus for the Handel Commemoration at Westminster Abbey in 1784: engraving from Burney's 'An Account of the Musical Performances in Westminster Abbey . . . in Commemoration of Handel' (1785)

(except in France), and it is possible to see something like a standard pattern in the court orchestras of Germany and Austria. To oboes and bassoons were added flutes, and a pair of horns rapidly became accepted as essential. Trumpets and timpani were available as required. Flutes and oboes were often played by the same performers. Recorders were still used, but their tone was found to be too weak for an orchestral ensemble and they were gradually discarded in favour of the more versatile flute. Trombones (as well as cornetts) were reserved for church music, as they had been in the past, and formed no part of a normal orchestra. Handel's use of trombones in *Saul* and *Israel in Egypt* (both 1738) was exceptional.

Outside court circles it was impossible in the early 18th century to depend on a standard complement of wind, and composers had to make do with whatever was available. When Bach wrote for three horns (BWV143) or four trumpets (BWV63, 119) or two oboes d'amore and two oboes da caccia (*Christmas Oratorio*), it was presumably because the necessary players happened to be on hand. Keiser was exceptionally fortunate at Hamburg in being able to write for five bassoons. Similarly it may be supposed that Handel was able to write independent parts for harp in *Esther*, *Giulio Cesare* and *Alexander Balus* because he could call on the services of a particularly accomplished player: elsewhere the harp was normally treated as a continuo instrument until it entered the opera orchestra in the second half of the century.

Vivaldi included clarinets in three of his concertos, but his use of instruments was hardly representative of

current practice. Clarinets were admitted to the opera orchestra in Paris about the middle of the century and in due course found their way into orchestras in Germany and Austria (Mannheim, Munich, Vienna). J. C. Bach used them in the London opera orchestra in the early 1760s. They do not appear to have formed part of the opera orchestra in Milan or Naples until the end of the century; the statement made by some writers that there were clarinets in the Milan orchestra in 1770 is due to a misreading of Leopold Mozart's letter of 15 December, which refers to clarini (trumpets), not clarinetti (there are no clarinets in Mozart's *Mitridate*). Mozart is however thought to have composed a divertimento (K113) with clarinets in Milan in 1771. Haydn did not write for clarinets in a symphony until 1793.

Extensions to the woodwind families had a somewhat chequered history. The tenor oboe (*taille des hautbois* or simply *taille*) was introduced into French military music in the 17th century and was also known in England (Purcell, *Dioclesian*, 1690), although it was not a normal constituent of the orchestra. With the alternative name of oboe da caccia (allegedly derived from its use at hunting parties) it was used in Germany from about 1720: it could be associated with the oboes to form a reed trio, or alternatively two oboes da caccia could replace the oboes. In a modified form, now known as english horn or cor anglais, it appeared sporadically in opera and oratorio between about 1740 and 1780, and in chamber music for wind. A pair of english horns actually replaces oboes in Haydn's Symphony no.22 (1764), though the instrument was clearly not generally available, since the parts were rewritten for performances other than those at Eisenstadt. The oboe d'amore, an alto oboe, did not survive the early 18th century. The basset-horn, designed as a tenor clarinet, dates from 1760. Two basset-horns were occasionally used to replace clarinets but, like english horns, they were not always available. Attempts to produce a bass oboe were not conspicuously successful, but a double bassoon was used at the Handel Commemoration at Westminster Abbey in 1784 (see fig.4) and sporadically thereafter.

Throughout the 17th century and the first half of the 18th, harmonic support to the orchestra was invariably provided by harpsichord, theorbo, harp or (in church) the organ (*see* CONTINUO). Of these the harpsichord became the standard instrument for concerts and opera, although for Italian opera it was common practice to employ two harpsichords as well as one or more lutes, theorbos or harps. Handel's opera orchestra in London had two harpsichords and a lute. The practice of writing figured basses declined, except for church music, after the middle of the century, but as late as the first decade of the 19th century some orchestras still used a keyboard instrument to hold the ensemble together or to supply the implied harmony. The scores of Mozart's piano concertos show that the pianist was expected to play in the tuttis as well as in the solo passages. This convention was maintained well into the 19th century by Hummel in his piano concertos. As the role of the keyboard continuo declined, violinist-conductors came into prominence. In Italian opera, the composer was expected to preside over the first three performances from the first harpsichord, after which the principal first violinist was in charge. In concerts, the keyboard player was customarily subordinate to the principal first violin. Exceptions seem to have been made only in the case of distinguished composers. Handel directed his oratorios from the harpsichord or organ – sometimes from an ingenious combination of the two. Haydn 'presided at the pianoforte' when his symphonies were performed in London (see fig.7, p.829). Conducting was considered necessary only in choral music, particularly if the performers were widely dispersed. The Paris Opéra was exceptional in having a conductor to beat time.

By the end of the 18th century the standard large orchestra consisted of two flutes, two oboes, two clarinets, two bassoons, two or four horns, two trumpets, timpani and strings. The number of each string instrument varied according to the resources available or the building in which performances were given. Heinrich Koch stated (*Musikalisches Lexikon*, 1802) that for church or theatre music one could make do with four or five violins, four or five seconds, two or three violas, two or three cellos and two double basses, but that for symphonies (where, Koch said, there are more wind instruments) a string section of 6.6.4.4.3 represents the smallest number permitting correct balance. The large opera houses in Italy – Milan and Naples – had considerably larger string sections than was normal elsewhere. Leopold Mozart, in the letter referred to above, gave the numbers at Milan in 1770 as 14 first violins, 14 second violins, six violas, two cellos and six double basses – a rather odd proportion to modern ears, but one which was duplicated at the Turin and Naples operas. In the same year, according to Burney (*The Present State of Music in France and Italy*, 1771, p.353), the orchestra at Naples had 18 first violins, 18 second violins, two

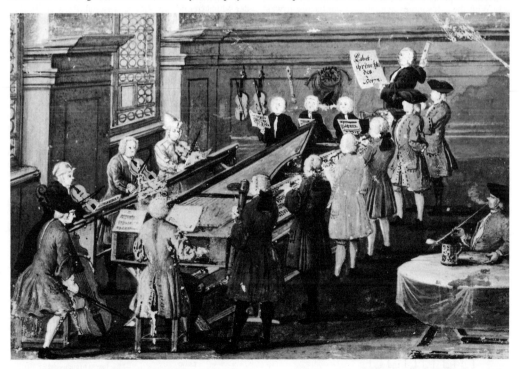

5. *Rehearsal by a collegium musicum for the performance of a cantata 'Lobet ihr Knechte des Herrn': painting (c1775) from a family album (Germanisches Nationalmuseum, Nuremberg); the disposition of the musicians around the harpsichord illustrates the late Baroque placement*

cellos (on which Burney commented adversely) and five double basses: he did not give the number of violas. Elsewhere, apart from exceptionally small groups, the total number of violins ranged roughly from eight to 28.

The number of wind players to a part varied. Quantz (*Versuch*, 1752, p.185) recommended that with an orchestra of 12 violins, three violas, four cellos and two double basses there should be four flutes, four oboes, three bassoons (with two horns if needed), in addition to two harpsichords and a theorbo (see fig.6). These proportions, however, were not generally observed. Three or even four bassoons were by no means uncommon, but duplication of flutes and oboes was less frequent, and a number of orchestras (including the Milan opera) had only two of each woodwind even when they had four horns. Rousseau (*Dictionnaire de musique*, 1768) maintained that in 1754 the orchestra which had the best distribution was the Elector of Saxony's at Dresden: it included eight first violins, seven second violins, four violas, three cellos, three double basses, two flutes, five oboes, five bassoons, two horns and two harpsichords (see fig.10, p.831). According to Galeazzi (*Elementi*, 1791) the best arranged orchestra around 1790 was the opera orchestra of Turin, which consisted of 23 violins, seven violas, five cellos, seven double basses, five flutes and oboes, two clarinets, three bassoons, four horns, two trumpets, timpani and two harpsichords (see fig.10). In the latter half of the century the demands of opera north of the Alps sometimes required the addition of piccolo, trombones, harp and percussion to the standard organization in the theatre – piccolo and percussion for exotic or 'Turkish' music and trombones for scenes of a solemn, supernatural or particularly dramatic character. With these resources available in the theatre it was only natural that Haydn should have taken advantage of them to include trombones in *The Creation* (1798) and *The Seasons* (1801): both works also employ the double bassoon (as does Mozart's *Maurerische Trauermusik* K477); and in *The Seasons* there are instructions to introduce a triangle and tambourine at the end of the drinking chorus, although no parts are provided for them.

A second major reform in instrument construction occurred in the mid-19th century. The string instruments were rebuilt to allow for higher string tension which permitted a more brilliant timbre, greater volume and higher standard pitch. The Tourte bow pattern, first championed by Viotti, gradually became standard. The flute, oboe and clarinet were completely redesigned on principles established by Theobald Boehm. (The Boehm bassoon was never accepted.) The trumpets and horns acquired valves. These new instruments were accepted only very slowly and long co-existed with a large variety of more or less successful alternative and hybrid forms. The new wind instruments facilitated legato playing and the performance of chromatic music, and they had a more powerful tone.

Efforts to define the exact composition of the orchestra of the early 19th century meet with a number of obstacles which in themselves are illuminating. The size of the orchestra came to vary considerably according to its situation and function. A chamber orchestra of about 35 served for festivities, including dances and serenades, in the private palaces of Austria. At the other end of the spectrum those orchestras whose chief responsibility was to accompany choruses, especially in the performance of oratorios, became quite large, often exceeding 80. The cultish popularity of Handel's *Messiah* around the turn of the century can be seen to have been involved in this development, but the resources remained stable as the repertory changed. The standard symphony orchestra was intermediate in size between these two, numbering in the case of Beethoven (excluding the choral Ninth) about 55. A Beethoven letter of 1813 requesting an orchestra of only half that size has been postulated by Biba (1977, p.88) to represent the minimum requirements for reading through orchestral scores, not those for actual performance.

The string section underwent continual expansion as the century progressed. By 1842 the number of string instruments in concerts sponsored by the Gesellschaft der Musikfreunde in Vienna was stabilized at 70. The orchestras of Bruckner and Mahler came to be known for their huge size. Mahler differentiated first, second and third cellos as well as first, second and third double basses in, for example, his First Symphony (Budapest, 1889).

The number and variety of wind instruments in use became highly variable, as the briefest examination of scores will show. By the early part of the 19th century trombones had been accepted as normal members of the symphony orchestra. The need to reinforce them with another bass instrument was supplied by introducing the serpent (Mendelssohn, *St Paul*, 1836), long known in French churches and military music, or the ophicleide

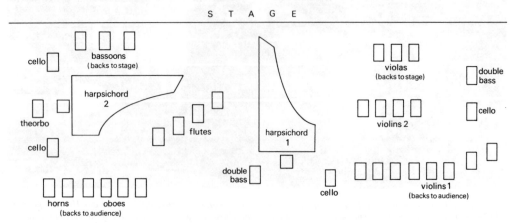

STAGE

6. Theatre orchestra seating plan based on Quantz's suggestions in his 'Versuch' (1752)

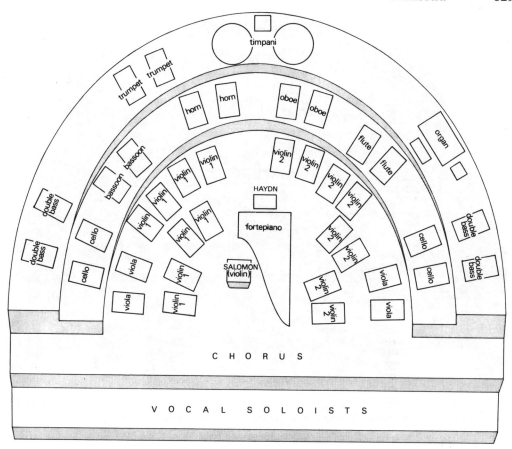

7. Hypothetical reconstruction (by Neal Zaslaw, after contemporary sources) of the amphitheatre arrangement of the orchestra introduced to London by Haydn for the Salomon concerts of 1791–3: positions are indicated for the organ, chorus and soloists (although oratorios were not given at these concerts)

(Mendelssohn, overture to *A Midsummer Night's Dream*, 1826). The invention of the bass tuba in the 1830s gradually made these instruments obsolete, though as late as 1874 Verdi was writing for the ophicleide in his Requiem. Valves were responsible for an addition to the brass family – the cornet. It was sometimes used as a substitute for the trumpet, but two cornets in addition to trumpets became standard in French orchestras, which also maintained four bassoons, used more often to double two parts than in four-part harmony. The english horn re-entered the orchestra, usually singly though examples occur of a pair of instruments being used (Halévy, *La juive*, 1835). The E♭ clarinet, a military band instrument, was introduced into the orchestra by Berlioz (*Symphonie fantastique*, 1830) but was not accepted as a normal member until the latter part of the century. The bass clarinet made its first appearance in opera (Meyerbeer, *Les Huguenots*, 1836). The saxophone family, invented in the 1840s, made an impression on composers of the time, who wrote for a quartet of saxophones, or, more frequently, used a single instrument as a soloist. But its career in the orchestra was comparatively brief, and although it has occasionally been used by later composers it has remained on the fringe of the standard orchestral ensemble. A new keyboard instrument, the celesta, which was first used

in an orchestral work in Tchaikovsky's *Nutcracker* (1892), proved a strong attraction later to impressionist composers.

The uses made of more conventional and better established instruments were equally noteworthy. Berlioz's *Symphonie fantastique* was robustly orchestrated for an ensemble of 85 including three cornets, two tubas, a bass drum and six pianos. The emphasis on brass instruments in Bruckner's symphonies and in Verdi's operas was, to judge by their imitators, as important as the invention of new instruments. Overall, the textural image remained a potent force in the 19th-century exploration of orchestral colour. This is shown in works such as Mahler's *Lieder eines fahrenden Gesellen* (orchestral version, 1897) for soprano, strings, harp, triangle, and a fluctuating complement of woodwind and horns.

The most far-reaching changes in the constitution of the 19th-century orchestra were made by Wagner. Unlike earlier composers, most of whom had been content to write for the instrumental forces that were available, he made his own decisions and expected to see his intentions realized. In this he was not always successful. *Lohengrin* calls for an orchestra of three flutes, three oboes (one doubling english horn), three clarinets (one doubling bass clarinet), three bassoons, four horns, three trumpets, three trombones, tuba, timpani, percussion,

8. *Rehearsal in the Bayreuth Festspielhaus conducted by Hermann Levi: drawing (1882) by Josef Grief (Richard Wagner Gedenkstätte, Bayreuth); Wagner is reaching through the hole at the top of the pit*

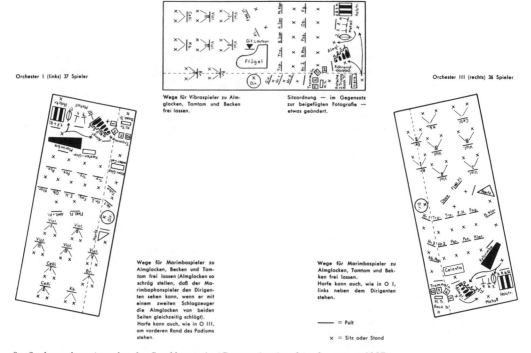

9. *Orchestral seating plan for Stockhausen's 'Gruppen' printed in the score (1957)*

Diſtribuzione dell' Orcheſtra del R. Teatro di Dreſda.

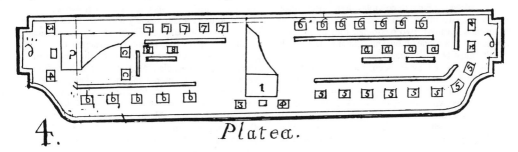

4.   *Platea.*

Spiegazione delle Cifre.

1. Primo Cembalo	4. Controbaſſi	
2. Secondo Cembalo	5. Primi Violini	
3. Violoncelli	6. Secondi Violini , col	
	dorſo rivolto verſo il	
	Palco .	
7. Oboe	b. Fagotti	
8. Viole	c. Corni da Caccia	
a. Viole	d. Una tribuna da ciaſche-	
	dun lato , per le Trom-	
	be, ed i Timpani .	

Diſtribuzione dell' Orcheſtra del R. Teatro di Torino

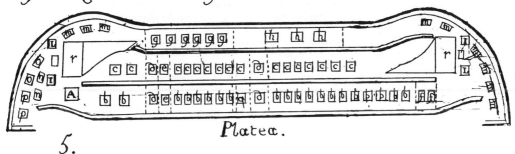

5.   *Platea.*

Spiegazione delle lettere.

A Sito del Direttore dell' orcheſtra più elevato degli al-tri ——— Num. 1.	L Controbaſſi primi 2	
	m Baſſi ; cioè Vio-loncelli , e Con-trobaſſi ——— 9.	
b Violini Primi --- 20.	n Altri Corni da Cac-cia ——— 2.	
c Violini Secondi -- 16.		
d Oboe ——— --- 4.	o Timpano ——— 1.	
e Clarinetti -- ——— 2.	p Trombe ——— --- 2.	
f Corni da Caccia - 2.	q Primo Violino de' Balli ——— 1.	
g Viole ——— --- 6.		
h Fagotti ——— ——— 3.	r Cembali ——— 2.	
I Violoncelli primi - 2.		
	Totale ——— 75.	

10. *Distribution of the theatre orchestras of Dresden (under Hasse, 1754, top) and of Turin (c1790): engraving from Galeazzi's 'Elementi' (1791–6; the Dresden plan was taken from Rousseau's 'Dictionnaire de musique', 1768). 'Platea' indicates the position of the audience; note that in the Dresden plan 'd' indicates a platform on each side for trumpets and timpani, and the second violins, oboes and violas sit with their backs to the stage*

harp and strings, in addition to an ensemble on the stage. But when Liszt gave its first performance at Weimar in 1850 he had to make do with an orchestra of five first violins, six second violins, three violas, four cellos, three double basses, two flutes, two oboes, two clarinets (one doubling bass clarinet), two bassoons, four horns, two trumpets, one trombone, tuba and timpani. The result can hardly have been adequate.

Wagner seems to have been more fortunate in Munich, where *Tristan und Isolde* was first performed in 1865. The demands of *Die Meistersinger* (Munich, 1868) conformed with the normal resources of an opera orchestra of the time. But *Der Ring des Nibelungen* extended the orchestra considerably beyond the normal limits. Wagner not only specified the exact number of strings required: 16 first violins, 16 second violins, 12 violas, 12 cellos and eight double basses, but also increased the woodwind section to three flutes and piccolo, three oboes and english horn, three clarinets and bass clarinet, with three bassoons as in *Lohengrin*. New instruments had to be made for the brass section: a bass trumpet in addition to three ordinary trumpets, a double-bass trombone in addition to three tenor trombones and one bass. There were now six harps and eight horns; four of the horn players had to be prepared to play a new set of specially designed tubas. The purpose of this apparent extravagance was not to increase the volume of sound (though it undoubtedly does this at moments of climax) but to provide a wider variety of tone colour.

The conception of a large department of wind players remained constant, and the numbers were enlarged still further; the enormous orchestras employed in Strauss's *Elektra* (1908) and Schoenberg's *Gurrelieder* (completed in 1911), however, do not represent normal 20th-century practice. Modern versions of old instruments like the oboe d'amore and the basset-horn, which were in any case necessary for authentic performances of works by Bach and Mozart, were introduced into the 20th-century orchestra. The problem of providing an adequate bass to the oboes and english horn was solved by the invention of the heckelphone in 1904, and the clarinet family was extended still further by the introduction of a contrabass instrument. The attempt to replace the double bassoon by the double-bass sarrusophone, a military band instrument, had only limited success.

The most notable development in the 20th century was the enormous increase in the number of percussion instruments, including many of eastern or exotic origin. Among the better known examples of exotic instrumentation are Stravinsky's *Petrushka* (Paris, 1911), which involves bass drum, long drum, snare drum, cymbals, gong, triangle, tambourine, xylophone, glockenspiel and celesta, as well as two harps. Another is Bartók's Concerto for Orchestra (Boston, 1944), which requires side drum, bass drum, tam-tam, cymbals, triangle and two harps.

Conventional 20th-century orchestras, like their predecessors, vary in size, generally for economic reasons. Published statistics are not always a reliable guide, since they do not always make clear how many of the players listed are regularly employed. There is, however, a standard proportion between the various sections of the string body: thus an orchestra with 16 first violins will on average have 12 violas, ten cellos and eight double basses. It is not unusual to have a few more first than second violins. The minimum number of wind instruments is three flutes (one player doubling piccolo), three oboes (one doubling english horn), three clarinets (one doubling bass clarinet), three bassoons (one doubling double bassoon), four horns, three trumpets, three trombones and tuba; but since many modern works call for more than these it is frequently necessary to engage extra players for particular performances. Most orchestras regularly employ five horns, the function of the fifth player being to save the energies of the first horn for solo passages. A single timpanist is generally sufficient, but two are often required and the number of other percussion players will vary from one occasion to another. Two harps are necessary for many modern works, although often they do little more than double each other at the unison or the octave. Piano and celesta are often played by members of the orchestra normally engaged in other duties.

The seating of an orchestra is a matter on which there has never been complete agreement. Quantz (1752) suggested two different seating plans for the orchestra of his time – one for the theatre (see fig.6), the other for the concert room. In both arrangements the harpsichord is in the centre; but in the theatre the player faces the stage, while in the concert room he faces the audience. A second harpsichord in the theatre is set at right angles to the first; the disposition of the other instruments being as in fig.6. In the concert room the cello and double bass are behind the harpsichord and the flutes are in front. The remaining strings are to the left, with none on the right. The arrangement in the Dresden opera about the same time was roughly similar to Quantz's plan, except that the oboes were at the back and the bassoons in front. The Dresden plan (fig.10), with the wind on one side and the strings on the other, was, according to Galeazzi (1791–6), excellent for aiding good ensemble, but if a well-blended sound were the objective, then the plan of the Turin orchestra about 1790 was preferable (fig.10). The opera orchestra of Naples observed a plan similar to that used at Turin.

In concert orchestras it was common practice to place the first and second violins on opposite sides of the platform. Haydn introduced to London an amphitheatre arrangement for Salomon's orchestra which was employed in England well into the 19th century (fig.7). Since World War II many orchestras on both sides of the Atlantic have adopted what is sometimes called the 'American seating plan', after its use in the 1920s and 1930s by Leopold Stokowski with the Philadelphia Orchestra, though in fact it had earlier been used in England by such conductors as Beecham and Wood. Here the first and second violins are grouped together at the conductor's left, the cellos on his right with the violas behind them, and the double basses in a semicircle behind the cellos and violas (fig.12). Few orchestras still maintain the traditional separation of the two violin sections. Strong arguments have been advanced in favour of both these dispositions. In the theatre a different arrangement is sometimes found, with most of the strings on the left and the wind on the right. The festival theatre at Bayreuth has its own arrangement, at least as intended by Wagner. Here the orchestra is seated on a series of descending tiers, with the strings in front and the wind behind (fig.8).

As orchestras increased in size in the course of the 19th century the problem of accommodation in the theatre pit became acute, particularly in the case of Wagner's operas. Wagner originally intended the first performance of *Tristan* to be given in the Residenz-

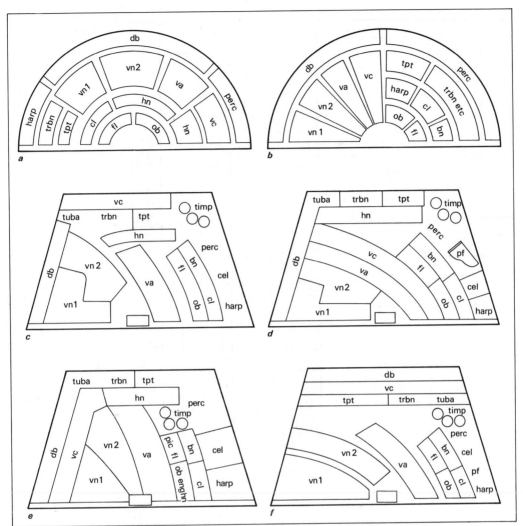

11. *Some of Leopold Stokowski's orchestral seating plans: (a) was used for the Philadelphia Orchestra in 1932 and (e) was used for the American Symphony Orchestra at Carnegie Hall (1971–2)*

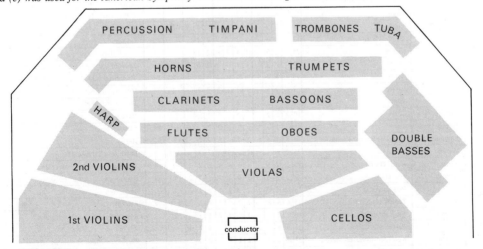

12. *A standard disposition of a modern symphony orchestra*

TABLE 1

Date	City	Institution	Violins	Violas	Cellos	Double Basses	Viols	Flutes	Oboes	Clarinets	Bassoons	Horns	Trumpets/Cornet(t)s	Trombones/Tubas	Timpani/other	Keyboard	Plucked strings	Repertory
1589	Florence	court					9	1					1	4			13	Wedding intermedio, no. 1
1603	Venice	St Mark's church	2										3	5		(2)		Gabrieli canzonas
1607	Mantua	Gonzaga Palace, theatre	4	4	2	2	3	2					4/2	4		6	6	Monteverdi *Orfeo*
1634	London	King's Violins	4	7	4													William Lawes, Ives (masques)
1663	Bologna	S Petronio	2	2	2	1								2		2	1	Cazzati
1665	Venice	Teatro SS Giovanni e Paolo	2	2		1										3	2	Cavalli
1670s–80s	Paris	24 Violons du Roi, Opéra	6	12	6			2	2		1		2		1	1		Lully operas
1680	Vienna	court	10								1		5	3		3	1	Schmelzer, Draghi
1685	Venice	St Mark's	8	11	2	3			1				2	3		(2)	4	Sacred vocal works; Legrenzi etc
1689	Rome	Palazzo Pamphili	39	10	17	10							2				1	Corelli sinfonia, Lulier
1692	Rome	S Lorenzo	17	4	7	4							2				3	Corelli
1694	Bologna	S Petronio	3	2	1	1								2		2	1	Colonna, Torelli
1694	Bologna	S Petronio, feast day	10	8	3	6							4	10		4	5	Colonna, Torelli
1700	Vienna	court	16	1							1		9	4		5	4	Fux, G. Bononcini
1702	Versailles	chapel	4	1	2	3		2	1		1						1	'Solemn music'
1707	Milan	theatre	18	8	3	3			6		2	1				2		operas
1707	Venice	Ospedale della Pietà	7	2	6	1			1							4	2	Gasparini, Vivaldi
1708	Mühlhausen	church	2	1	1	1		2	2		1		3		1	1		Bach Cantata no. 71
1708	Rome	Palazzo Bonelli, oratorio	6	2	1	1										1		A. Scarlatti *Annunziata*
1708	Rome	Palazzo Bonelli, oratorio	23	4	6	6	1		4				2	1		1		Handel *La resurrezione*
1708	Venice	St Mark's church	10	3	1	1			1				2	2		(2)	3	Biffi, Lotti, Pollarolo
1710	Rome	Palazzo Ruspoli	11	4	2	2			3							?		Caldara *S Francesco*
1714–15	Weimar	Hofkapelle	3						1		1		6		1	1		Italian concertos
1717	Cöthen	court	3		1		1	2	1		1		2		1	1		Bach concertos, cantatas
1722	Cöthen	court	2	1	1	1		1	3		1		3	1		1		Bach suites
1728	London	King's Theatre	22	2	3	2		2	2		3	2				2	1	Handel operas
1730	Leipzig	Thomaskirche	6	4	2	1			3		2		3		1	2		Bach cantatas
1730	Vienna	court	26		7	3	2		5		4	2	14	4	2	8	1	Caldara
1734	Dresden	court	12	4	5	2		3	3		2	2	2			2		Pisendel, Hasse, Vivaldi
c1740	Venice	Ospedaletto	8	4	4	3										1		Porpora
1740s–50s	Naples	Teatro San Carlo	28	5	2	4			4		2		4		1	2		Porpora, Feo, Leo, Jommelli
1751	Paris	Opéra	16	6	7	5		2	3		4		1		1	1		Rameau
1754	Dresden	court	15	4	3	3		2	5		5	2				2		Pisendel, Hasse
1754	London	Foundling Hospital Chapel	14	5	3	2			4		4					1		Handel *Messiah*
1754	Berlin	court	12	4	4	2	1	4	3		4	2	2		1	2	1	C.P.E. Bach, Graun, Quantz
1756	Vienna	court	9		2	2			3		1		4	5	2	6		Wagenseil
1766	Venice	St Mark's church	12	6	4	5		2	2				2	2		2		Galuppi
1770s	Paris	Opéra	24	5	12	5		4	4	2	8	2	2		1	1		Gluck, Piccinni
1770s	Salzburg	court	18	2	2	1		1	2		3	2	2	3	1	1		Leopold and Wolfgang Mozart, Michael Haydn
1770s	Mannheim	court	20	4	4	4		3	3	3	4	4	2		1	1		Mannheim school, Stamitz, Mozart
1778	Paris	Concert Spirituel	22	6	9	6		2	2	2	2	2	2		1			Gossec, J.C. Bach, Mozart, Haydn, Paisiello
1782	Vienna	court	12	4	3	3		2	2		2					2		Mozart, Salieri etc
1783	Eszterháza	court	10	2	2	2			2		2	2				1		Haydn
1791	Vienna	court	15		2	2			2	2	2	2			1	2		Salieri, Mozart
1791–3	London	Hanover Square Rooms	16	4	4	4		2	2		2	2	2		1	1		Haydn
1807–8	Vienna	university	25	7	6	4		(2)	(2)	(2)	(2)	(2)	(2)		(1/1)			Beethoven Symphonies 1–4
1811	Berlin	Court Opera	25	5	10	5		4	5	4	4	8	2	3		?1		Spontini *La vestale*, Weber *Abu Hassan*
1813	Vienna	concert	8	2	2	2		2	2	2	2	2	2	2	1			Beethoven
1814	Vienna	Redoutensaal	36	14	12	17		2	2	2	2	2	2	2	1			Beethoven
1814	Milan	Teatro alla Scala	25	6	4	8		2	2	2	2	4	2	1	1/1			Rossini
1817	Vienna	Tonkünstler-Soziatät	40	8	7	7		2	1	2	1	1				2		Beethoven and Haydn oratorios
1818	Naples	Teatro San Carlo	24	6	6	7		2	2	2	2	4	2	3	1/1			Rossini
1824	Vienna	Kärntnertortheater· concert	24	10	6	6		2	2	2	2	2	2	2	1			Beethoven Ninth Symphony
1825	Dresden	Court Opera	10	2	2	2		3	2	2	2	4	2	3		?1		Weber *Der Freischütz, Euryanthe*
1828	Paris	Société des Concerts	30	7	12	8		4	3	4	4	4	2	4	1			Cherubini

Date	City	Institution	Violins	Violas	Cellos	Double Basses	Viols	Flutes	Oboes	Clarinets	Bassoons	Horns	Trumpets/Cornet(t)s	Trombones/Tubas	Timpani/other	Keyboard	Plucked strings	Repertory
			STRINGS					WOODWIND				BRASS			PERC.			
1839	Leipzig	Gewandhaus	17	5	5	4		2	2	2	2	2	2		1			Mendelssohn, Schumann
1839	Paris	Opéra	24	8	10	8		3	3	2	4	4	4	3	1/1			Meyerbeer, Halévy, Berlioz
1839	Paris	Opéra-Comique	16	5	6	6		3	3	3	3	6	3	4	?1/?		2	Auber, Boieldieu, Hérold, Adam, Donizetti La fille du régiment
1844	Berlin	Court Opera	16	6	10	5		4	2	4	4	4	4	3/1	?1/?		2	Wagner Der fliegende Holländer
1845	Turin	Teatro Regio	21	4	4	6		3	2	2	2	4	2	3		1	1	Donizetti, Verdi
1851	Weimar	Court Opera	11	3	4	3		2	2	2	2	4	2	1	?1			Liszt Les préludes, piano concertos
1855	Paris	Opéra	22	8	10	8		3	3	3	4	5	4	3/1	?1/?		2	Meyerbeer, Gounod, Verdi Les vêpres siciliennes
1865	Leipzig	Gewandhaus	30	8	9	5		2	2	2	2	4	2	3	1			Mendelssohn, Schumann etc
1867	Vienna	court	13		2	2		1	3	2	3	2		2	3			
1876	Bayreuth	Festspielhaus	32	12	12	8		4	4	4	3	8	4	5	?/?		6	Wagner Ring
1876	Karlsruhe	court	18	4	4	4		2	2	2	3	4	2	3	1			Brahms First Symphony
1900	Vienna	Philharmonic Orchestra	33	11	10	10		4	4	4	4	8	4	5/1	2/3		1	Mahler, Strauss etc
1905	Turin	Teatro Regio	25	7	7	7		3	3	3	3	4	4	3/1	1/2		2	Puccini, Wagner
1929	Dresden	State Opera	33	11	11	11		6	6	6	6	10	6	6/1	2/4			Strauss
1934	London	Boyd Neel Orchestra	11	3	3	2			2				2			1	1	Respighi, Holst, Elgar, Vaughan Williams
1968	Leipzig	Gewandhaus	55	21	19	14		7	7	7	7	11	7	9	7		3	Shostakovich Symphony no. 12
1974	New York	New York Philharmonic	34	12	12	9		4	4	5	4	6	4	4/1	2/3	2	1	Boulez, Carter

Note: This chart attempts to show the typical composition of orchestras for which works in the present-day repertory were originally written. The figures have been drawn from standard reference works and from specialized studies listed in the bibliography. They must be taken as indicative in only a general sense, as forces varied from piece to piece, from occasion to occasion, and from year to year, as well as from place to place. To facilitate reference and comparison, instruments of the same families are grouped together without indication. Hence violins of all sizes appear in one column, as do: flutes, piccolos, alto flutes and recorders; oboes, english horns and tenor oboes; clarinets of all sizes; bassoons and double bassoons; trumpets and cornet(t)s; horns and Wagner tubas; trombones of all sizes and tubas, serpents and ophicleides. Figures in brackets denote forces inferred from the orchestration.

theater in Munich; but though it was ideal for the singers, it was unsuitable for the orchestra, since the pit was 60 cm too high and the lights on the players' desks were on a level with the knees of the characters on the stage. Even in the court theatre, where the work was eventually performed, the orchestra pit was too small. The problem of acoustics, with which Quantz had been concerned, was now acute. As early as 1797, Grétry (*Mémoires, ou Essais sur la musique*, iii, 32) had proposed the construction of a theatre in which the orchestra pit would be screened from the sight of the audience and separated from them by a stone wall. It was left to Wagner to put this idea into practice in his theatre at Bayreuth, where the orchestra pit is not only deep but is also made invisible to the audience by the intervention of a convex screen.

Although the conventional symphony orchestra is still constituted according to the formulas of the late 19th century, there are three other substantial lines of orchestral development: the chamber orchestra; the modified orchestra of avant-garde works; and the orchestra of period instruments.

In the decades between the two world wars, a number of chamber orchestras were founded, the best known of which was perhaps the Basle Chamber Orchestra conducted by Paul Sacher. The groups arose out of a reaction against the overblown post-romantic orchestra of such composer-conductors as Mahler and Strauss, and out of the financial stringencies of the period. Such ensembles were ideal for the new, leaner style of orchestration found in works of the period by Hindemith, Bartók, Stravinsky and others. Later 20th-century repertory for chamber orchestra has favoured ensembles that involve a large number of percussion instruments, although the precise selection varies from work to work. In many works of the 1960s and 1970s these instruments are played serially rather than in ensemble. In other works a single representative of one timbre family (e.g. oboe to represent woodwinds) is contrasted with remnants of a conventional orchestra (string, brass, or percussion ensemble). The harp has enjoyed a notable degree of popularity in the chamber setting.

The idea of timbre has dominated much of the multi-media repertory of avant-garde composers, but here, although the motivation may be said to be 'orchestral', the execution may involve material synthesized electronically. The synthesis of processed vocal and instrumental sounds with live performance by orchestra and/or voice(s) was particularly exploited in the 1960s and resulted in such works as Berio's *Sinfonia* (New York, 1968). Other multi-media composers whose experiments with contrasted sonorities have drawn considerable attention have been Nono and Boulez. An extension of the symphonic idea is also manifest in multi-sensory works that require the perception of visual motion, such as filmed material in the case of Maderna or moving objects in that of Riley, coordinated with musical motion. The current frontiers of multi-media composition are still absorbed in questions of timbre, such as the artificial creation of sounds considered characteristic of orchestral instruments and electronic transformation by gradual degrees of one timbre into another. (*See also* ELECTRONIC INSTRUMENTS.)

The creation of orchestras with instruments appropriate to repertories of earlier centuries has been a feature of the 1970s and 1980s. Renaissance ensembles have become commonplace and professional Baroque chamber orchestras thrive in Europe and North America. The application of authentic performance standards to the classical repertory is a major task of the present. The first recording of all the Mozart symphonies according to such standards was completed in 1982 by the Academy of Ancient Music under the direction of Jaap Schroeder and Christopher Hogwood. The 19th-century orchestral repertory still needs scholarly investigation to facilitate authenticity in performance.

The economic position of orchestras has never been completely stable. Court orchestras in the 18th century, often established as much for prestige as for musical reasons, were subject to the whims or the financial resources of their employers. An orchestra could be dismissed without notice, as happened at Grosswardein in 1769 after the bishop had been accused of permitting stage performances during Lent and sanctioning other irregularities. With the gradual disappearance of many court establishments during the 19th century, opera houses were for a time the principal sources of employment. When both Germany and Austria became republics in the 20th century the existing court operas and orchestras were taken over by states and municipalities. Independent orchestras, for example those in England and the USA, relied for a long time on high prices for admission and the generosity of private patrons. It was not until the establishment of the Arts Council of Great Britain after World War II that orchestras in England were able to receive support from the state. In the USA orchestras continued to be given financial help by local associations of individual supporters, later supplemented by monies from non-profit foundations, from municipal and state governments and by the National Endowment for the Arts. The establishment all over the world of orchestras formed specifically for broadcasting provided a new source of maintenance. Orchestras not directly employed by a state, a municipality or a public organization are either self-governing or controlled by an independent board of directors. The concentration of orchestras in large cities undoubtedly favours those who live there; but the widespread practice of touring extends the opportunity of hearing orchestral music, which is limited only by the lack of suitable halls in smaller centres. The frequent visits paid by orchestras to other countries, combined with the striking increase in the quality and availability of orchestral recordings, encourage comparison and help to maintain standards.

BIBLIOGRAPHY

J. J. Quantz: *Versuch einer Anweisung die Flöte traversiere zu spielen* (Berlin, 1752, 3/1789/R1953; Eng. trans., 1966)
F. Galeazzi: *Elementi teorico-practici di musica con un saggio sopra l'arte di suonare il violino analizzata, ed a dimostrabili principi ridotta* (Rome, 1791–6)
Agenda musical pour l'année 1836 (Paris, 1836/R1981)
A. Elwart: *Histoire de la Société des Concerts du Conservatoire Impérial de Musique* (Paris, 2/1864), 71–109
L. von Köchel: *Die kaiserliche Hof-Musikkapelle in Wien von 1543 bis 1867* (Vienna, 1869/R1976)
A. Sandberger: *Beiträge zur Geschichte der bayerischen Hofkapelle unter Orlando di Lasso* (Leipzig, 1894–5)
W. Kleefeld: 'Das Orchester der Hamburger Oper, 1678–1738', *SIMG*, i (1899–1900), 219–89
H. Goldschmidt: *Studien zur Geschichte der italienischen Oper im 17. Jahrhundert*, i (Leipzig, 1901/R1967)

L. Schiedermair: 'Die Blütezeit der Öttingen-Wallerstein'schen Hofkapelle', *SIMG*, ix (1907–8), 83
R. Haas: 'Zur Frage der Orchesterbesetzungen in der zweiten Hälfte des 18. Jahrhunderts', *IMusSCR, iii Vienna 1909* [Haydn Zentenarfeier], 159
H. C. de Lafontaine: *The King's Musick: a Transcript of Records relating to Music and Musicians* (London, 1909/R1973)
F. Volbach: *Das moderne Orchester in seiner Entwicklung* (Leipzig, 1910, 2/1919)
G. Cucuel: *Etudes sur un orchestre au XVIII* siècle* (Paris, 1913)
——: *La Pouplinière et la musique de chambre au XVIII* siècle* (Paris, 1913/R1971)
A. Dandelot: *La Société des Concerts du Conservatoire de 1828 à 1923* (Paris, 1923)
Y. Lacroix: 'L'orchestre des électeurs de Trèves au XVIII* siècle', *ReM*, ix (1927–8), 38, 130
K. Stephenson: *Hundert Jahre Philharmonische Gesellschaft in Hamburg* (Hamburg, 1928)
E. Creuzburg: *Die Gewandhaus-Konzerte zu Leipzig, 1781–1931* (Leipzig, 1931)
R. Haas: *Aufführungspraxis der Musik* (Potsdam, 1931/R1949)
C. S. Terry: *Bach's Orchestra* (London, 1932, 2/1958)
F. Klein: *Geschichte des Orchestervereins der Gesellschaft der Musikfreunde von 1859–1934* (Vienna, 1934)
P. Bekker: *The Story of the Orchestra* (New York, 1936)
H. von Kralik: *Die Wiener Philharmoniker: Monographie eines Orchesters* (Vienna, 1938, 2/1957 as *Das grosse Orchester*)
O. Schreiber: *Orchester und Orchester-Praxis in Deutschland zwischen 1780 und 1850* (Berlin, 1938)
A. Carse: *The Orchestra in the XVIIIth Century* (Cambridge, 1940/R1969)
J. Erskine: *The Philharmonic-Symphony Society of New York: its First Hundred Years* (New York, 1942)
W. Jerger: *Die Wiener Philharmoniker: Erbe und Sendung* (Vienna, 1942, 2/1943)
T. Russell: *Philharmonic* (London, 1942)
R. Nettel: *The Orchestra in England: a Social History* (London, 1946, 3/1956)
R. Elkin: *Royal Philharmonic: the Annals of the Royal Philharmonic Society* (London, 1947)
M. Pincherle: *L'orchestre de chambre* (Paris, 1948)
A. Carse: *The Orchestra from Beethoven to Berlioz* (Cambridge, 1948)
J. H. Mueller: *The American Symphony Orchestra: a Social History of Musical Taste* (Bloomington, Ind., 1951)
H. Foss and N. Goodwin: *London Symphony: Portrait of an Orchestra* (London, 1954)
S. T. Worsthorne: *Venetian Opera in the Seventeenth Century* (Oxford, 1954/R1968)
E. Borrel: 'L'orchestre du Concert Spirituel et celui de l'Opéra de Paris, de 1751 à 1800, d'après les spectacles de Paris', *Mélanges d'histoire et d'esthétique musicales offerts à Paul-Marie Masson* (Paris, 1955), ii, 9
J. Wilson, ed.: *Roger North on Music* (London, 1959)
N. Broder: 'The Beginnings of the Orchestra', *JAMS*, xiii (1960), 175
H. von Kralik: *Die Wiener Philharmoniker und ihre Dirigenten* (Vienna, 1960).
J. Eppelsheim: *Das Orchester in den Werken Jean-Baptiste Lullys* (Tutzing, 1961)
R. L. Weaver: 'Sixteenth Century Instrumentation', *MQ*, xlvii (1961), 363
B. S. Brook: *La symphonie française dans la seconde moitié du XVIII* siècle* (Paris, 1962)
H. Becker: 'Orchester', §B, *MGG*
A. Cavicchi: 'Una sinfonia inedita di Arcangelo Corelli nello stile del concerto grosso venticinque anni prima dell'opera VI', *Le celebrazioni del 1963 e alcune nuove indagini sulla musica italiana del XVIII e XIX secolo*, Chigiana, xx (1963), 43
D. D. Boyden: *The History of Violin Playing from its Origins to 1761* (London, 1965)
D. Arnold: 'Orchestras in 18th-century Venice', *GSJ*, xix (1966), 3
S. H. Hansell: 'Orchestral Practice at the Court of Cardinal Pietro Ottoboni', *JAMS*, xix (1966), 398
U. Kirkendale: *Antonio Caldara: sein Leben und seine venezianisch-römischen Oratorien* (Graz and Cologne, 1966)
C. H. Mahling: 'Mozart und die Orchesterpraxis seiner Zeit', *MJb 1967*, 229
O. Jander: 'Concerto Grosso Instrumentation in Rome in the 1660's and 1670's', *JAMS*, xxi (1968), 168
A. Schnoebelen: 'Performance Practices at San Petronio in the Baroque', *AcM*, xii (1969), 37
M. Benoit: *Musique de cour: chapelle, chambre, écurie* (Paris, 1971)
J. Harich: 'Das Haydn-Orchester im Jahre 1780', *Haydn Yearbook*, viii (1971), 5
C. H. Mahling: 'Herkunft und Sozialstatus des höfischen Orches-

termusikers im 18. und frühen 19. Jahrhundert in Deutschland', *Der Sozialstatus des Berufsmusikers vom 17. bis 19. Jahrhundert*, ed. W. Salmen (Kassel, 1971; Eng. trans., 1983), 103

——: *Orchester und Orchestermusiker in Deutschland von 1700 bis 1850* (Habilitationsschrift, U of Saarbrücken, 1971)

J. Sehnal: 'Obsazení v chrámové hudbě 17. a 18. století na Moravě' [Musical forces used in performances of church music in Moravia in the 17th and 18th centuries], *HV*, viii (1971), 236

J. Anthony: *French Baroque Music from Beaujoyeulx to Rameau* (London, 1973, rev. 2/1978)

S. Davis: 'The Orchestra under Clemens Wenzeslaus: Music at a Late-eighteenth-century Court', *JAMIS*, i (1974), 86

W. Dean: 'A French Traveller's View of Handel's Operas', *ML*, lv (1974), 172

R. Donington: 'Choirs and Orchestras', *The Interpretation of Early Music* (London, rev. 3/1974), 583ff

C. Dahlhaus: 'Was ist ein Orchester?', *Melos/NZM*, i (1975), 374

H. Rösing: 'Zum Begriff "Orchester", in europäischer und aussereuropäischer Musik', *AcM*, xlvii (1975), 134

E. Selfridge-Field: *Venetian Instrumental Music from Gabrieli to Vivaldi* (Oxford, 1975)

H. Shanet: *Philharmonic: A History of New York's Orchestra* (New York, 1975)

D. Charlton: 'Orchestra and Image in the Later Eighteenth Century', *PRMA*, cii (1975–6), 1

S. Gerlach: 'Haydns Orchestermusiker von 1761 bis 1774', *Haydn-Studien*, iv/1 (1976), 35

N. Zaslaw: 'Toward the Revival of the Classical Orchestra', *PRMA*, ciii (1976–7), 158

O. Biba: 'Concert Life in Vienna', *Beethoven, Performers, and Critics: Detroit 1977*, 77

G. Ellero and others: *Arte e musica all'Ospedaletto: scheda d'archivio sull'attività musicale degli Ospedali dei derelitti e dei mendicanti di Venezia (sec. XVI–XVIII)* (Venice, 1978)

G. Rostirolla: 'Il periodo veneziano di Francesco Gasparini', *Francesco Gasparini (1661–1727): atti del 1° convegno internazionale: Camaiore 1978*, 85

A. Basso: *Frau Musika: la vita e le opere di J. S. Bach*, i: *1685–1723* (Turin, 1979)

N. Zaslaw: 'The Compleat Orchestral Musician', *Early Music*, vii (1979), 46; viii (1980), 71

G. Sadler: 'The Role of the Keyboard Continuo in French Opera', *Early Music*, viii (1980), 148

N. Del Mar: *Anatomy of the Orchestra* (London, 1981)

M. Cyr: 'Basses and basse continue in the Orchestra of the Paris Opéra 1700–1764', *Early Music*, x (1982), 155

P. Muck: *Einhundert Jahre Berliner Philharmonisches Orchester* (Tutzing, 1982)

G. Sadler: 'Rameau's Singers and Players at the Paris Opéra', *Early Music*, xi (1983), 453

E. Bernard: 'A Glance at the Archives of some Parisian Orchestral Societies', *19th Century Music*, vii (1983–4), 104

D. K. Holoman: 'Orchestral Material from the Library of the Société des Concerts', *19th Century Music*, vii (1983–4), 106

JACK WESTRUP (with NEAL ZASLAW
and ELEANOR SELFRIDGE-FIELD)

Orchestral chimes. *See* TUBULAR BELLS.

Orchestrelle. The trade name of a full-sized player REED ORGAN made by the Aeolian Co. of New York in the early 20th century.

Orchestrion. (1) The name given by Georg Joseph Vogler to a large, and, for its time, somewhat revolutionary organ with which he toured England and the Continent in 1789 and 1790. The organ, embodying the principles of his SIMPLIFICATION SYSTEM, had four manuals, pedals and 63 stops, all fitted into a case 9' square. Many of the stops in this organ were free reeds, and these were under variable wind pressure. This, combined with the fact that the entire instrument was enclosed in a swell-box, gave the organ an unusually wide range of expression, possibly its most notable feature.

(2) A term, originally of German origin, widely used in the 19th and 20th centuries to denote a complex MECHANICAL INSTRUMENT played by pinned barrels or perforated cards or paper rolls. Orchestrions are differentiated from the related street and fairground organs by the fact that they were intended only for indoor use, and for the performance of classical music and dances from the orchestral repertory. They were thus more sophisticated in their voicing, capabilities and design than their outdoor counterparts, and required lower wind pressures.

An early prototype of the orchestrion was Maelzel's PANHARMONICON; another instrument of the orchestrion type was Winkel's COMPONIUM. Martin Blessing (1774–1847), a maker of barrel organs in the Black Forest, is said to have been the father of the orchestrion industry in Germany. Among those trained in his workshop were Michael Welte (1807–80) of Freiburg, perhaps the most notable manufacturer of orchestrions, and the pair that went on to found their own business as Imhof & Mukle in 1850. Other makers included the Kaufmann family of Dresden, who toured England with their instruments in 1851, and such makers of barrel, street and fair-ground organs as Gavioli and Limonaire in Paris, Bruder and Ruth in Germany, Mortier in the Netherlands and Chiappa in London.

Orchestrions became increasingly popular in the late 19th and early 20th century as domestic entertainment for the wealthy, and as a substitute for salon orchestras in hotels, restaurants and dance halls. The application of water or electrical power increased their practicality in the 1880s and 1890s, and Emil Welte's invention of pneumatic action in 1887 made possible greater mechanical complexity and a wider variety of effects. In addition to various types of imitative organ pipes and percussion devices, some large models also contained piano actions or chimes. Early orchestrions were operated by pinned barrels (*see* BARREL ORGAN, esp. fig.1), but by the end of the 19th century virtually all makers were using punched cards, which were hinged together and transferred from one folded stack to another as they passed through the playing mechanism; this resulted in easier changing, the playing of longer works and economy of space.

At the height of its popularity and development, the orchestrion was capable of producing convincing performances of orchestral music, as proved by surviving examples in such collections as 'Van Speeldoos tot Pierement' in Utrecht. In the early 20th century smaller instruments gave way to less costly player pianos, which developed out of the same technology; the invention of electro-pneumatic organ action made possible full-scale self-playing residence organs which could reach considerable size. The orchestrion could not compete with these, and after the effects of World War I on the German musical instrument industry (particularly Welte) orchestrions were no longer made.

See also KUNZ, THOMAS ANTON.

BIBLIOGRAPHY

K. Bormann: *Orgel- und Spieluhrenbau* (Zurich, 1968)

Q. D. Bowers: *Encyclopedia of Automatic Musical Instruments* (Vestal, NY, 1972)

A. W. J. G. Ord-Hume: *Clockwork Music* (London and New York, 1973)

BARBARA OWEN

Orden, Julián de la (*b* Barchín del Hoyo, *c*1730; *d* Málaga, 21 Jan 1794). Spanish organ builder. Son of the organ builder Pedro de la Orden, he succeeded Juan Ruiz Fresneda as official builder to Cuenca Cathedral in 1762, for which he supplied two fine instruments in 1768 and 1770. He then built two magnificent organs for Málaga Cathedral (1778 and 1782). He also worked at Sacedón (1778), at the church of Santiago, Málaga, the church at Cómpeta and the cathedral at Burgo del Osma (1766). His daughter Catalina married Fernando Molero, official builder at Cuenca Cathedral in 1785–9 and among those who worked on the organs at Murcia Cathedral in 1799.

BIBLIOGRAPHY

Relación de lo que contienen los órganos de la Santa Iglesia Catedral de Málaga (Málaga, 1783)

A. Llordén: 'Notas de los maestros organeros que trabajaron en Málaga', *AnM*, xiii (1958), 167

R. González de Amezua y Noriega: *Perspectivas para la historia del órgano español* (Madrid, 1970)

GUY BOURLIGUEUX

Ore. Arched harp of the Madi people of Uganda. *See* ENNANGA.

Orff, Carl (*b* Munich, 10 July 1895; *d* Munich, 29 March 1982). German composer and educationist. In 1924 he joined Dorothee Günther in founding a school in Munich for the coordinated teaching of music, gymnastics and dance. His experience there led him to devise means of allowing students to improvise their own instrumental accompaniments. To enable them to do so without first acquiring advanced keyboard fluency he introduced a great variety of percussion instruments. Some of these were already used in the orchestra and in jazz ensembles, but others were modelled on the melodic and heterophonic bar-instruments of the Indonesian gamelan. To ensure that the instruments, while simple to play, should also be of sound workmanship and satisfying musical quality, Orff enlisted the services of Karl Maendler, a maker of high-grade pianos and harpsichords. Each type of instrument was constructed in two or three sizes, all with interchangeable bars or keys to produce any required scale or mode. To a nucleus of tuned instruments could be added drums, cymbals, claves and other percussion, as well as recorders and string instruments based on medieval, Renaissance or Baroque originals.

After World War II Orff's educational work was sponsored by the West German radio and education authorities. A new workshop, Studio 49, was set up in Munich in 1949 under the leadership of Klaus Becker-Ehmck (a former pupil of Maendler) in order to meet the widespread demand for the Orff instruments. All the instruments produced by the firm are of the highest quality. The resonance boxes of bar instruments are made of sprucewood; xylophone bars are of Brazilian rosewood, those for glockenspiels of nickel-plated steel and those for metallophones of a specially produced aluminium alloy. Triangles are made of very expensive, specially alloyed steel; castanets, woodblocks and claves are of rosewood. Cymbals are made from silver-bronze rather than brass. The Orff system of graded musical education (*Orff-Schulwerk*) and its instruments have spread throughout the world, raising standards far beyond the limited scope of the previous 'percussion band'.

BIBLIOGRAPHY

W. Twittenhoff: *Orff-Schulwerk: Einführung* (Mainz, 1930)

S. Boehm: *Spiele mit dem Orff-Schulwerk: elementare Musik und Bewegung für Kinder* (Stuttgart, 1975)

J. Horton: 'Carl Orff', *Some Great Music Educators*, ed. K. Simpson (London, 1976)

JOHN HORTON

Organ (Fr. *orgue, orgues*; Dutch, Ger. *Orgel*; It., Sp. *organo*; Dan. *Orglet*; from Gk. *organon* via Lat. *organum*). A wind instrument consisting of one or more scale-like rows of individual pipes which are made to sound by air under pressure directed from a wind-raising device and admitted to the pipes by means of valves operated from a keyboard. Although this definition could include such instruments as the REGALS, PORTATIVE, POSITIVE and CLAVIORGAN, this article is concerned with the larger organ proper. 'Organ', 'orgue' and 'organo' are also used in the sense of *Werk* to denote each manual or pedal department of the whole instrument. Before about 1675 such terms applied only to departments built into separate organ cases; in England, Echoes and Swells were not usually called 'Swell Organ' before about 1800, although by about 1850 all departments of an organ were so distinguished ('Solo Organ', 'Pedal Organ' etc).

The organ is, together with the clock, the most complex of all mechanical instruments developed before the Industrial Revolution. Among musical instruments its history is the most involved and wide-ranging, and its extant repertory the oldest and largest (*see* KEYBOARD MUSIC, §§I–II; *see also* CONTINUO). Despite its essentially indirect and therefore relatively inflexible production of sound, no other instrument has inspired such avowed respect as the organ, 'that great triumph of human skill . . . the most perfect musical instrument' (*Grove I*), 'in my eyes and ears . . . the king of instruments' (Mozart, letter to his father, 17–18 October 1777).

I. Word origin. II. Construction. III. Pipework. IV. The classical and medieval organ. V. The organ 1450–1800. VI. Some developments 1800–1930. VII. The Organ Revival. VIII. Recent research and areas for study.

I. Word origin. Plato (*Laws*) and Aristotle (*Politics*) both used the term 'organon' to denote a tool or instrument in a general sense: something with which to do a job of work (*ergon*, from root *uerğ*-; cf *Werk*, 'work'). Plato (*Republic*) and later authors also used it to denote any kind or all kinds of musical instrument or contrivance. No Greek author used it to mean 'pipe organ', and even Hero of Alexandria's term 'hydraulic organ' (1st century AD) uses 'organ' in the sense of tool, so that the whole term properly indicates 'an aulos-like device or instrument, operated by water'. (In this context, moreover, 'aulos' may indicate not the musical wind instrument of that name but 'pipe', 'conduit' etc; i.e. 'hydraulic' refers to the water and air conduits.) Classical and patristic Latin shows a fairly clear evolution of the terms 'organum', 'organa', 'organis' from a general to a specific sense, and a musical connection is often clear from the context, more consistently so than in Greek. 9th- and 10th-century Arabic had its own versions of the Greek, for example *hedhrula* ('hydraulis') and *urghanon* ('organon'). The use of 'organum' to denote a kind of polyphony is of course post-classical.

In his commentary on Psalm cl St Augustine correctly explained the Vulgate word 'organum' as derived from 'a Greek term', and thought it unlikely to be correct in this psalm. He defined it as follows (the English translation is by John of Trevisa, 1398): 'Organum is a generall name of all Instrumentes of Musyk: and is nethelesse specyaly aproprryte to the Instrument that is made of many pipes; and blowen wyth belowes'. In one sentence St Augustine used the singular *organum* and the plural *organa* for the same object, thus foreshadowing late medieval usage of the plural in English and in Old High German (Notker Labeo's *diu organâ* and *orglun*) and present-day usage in Slav (*varhany*, *orgány*: plural). The English derivatives of 'organ' ('organic', 'organize') are mostly post-medieval terms, and are sometimes found first in the musical sense (i.e. 'organic': 'like organs'), sometimes first in the non-musical sense: 'organize', 'to give an orderly structure to', appears in the 17th century, while 'organize', 'to supply one or more sets of organ pipes to a harpsichord or piano', appears in the 18th century, probably from French usage. The plural 'organs' denoting a single object (e.g. *orgues/ogres*, *Orgenen/Orgeln* in 12th-century French and German verse) belongs to the musical use of the term. In some languages, notably French, the singular *orgue* seems much the later term, but documents are inconsistent (e.g. 'money paied to the organe maker for the orgonis', 14th century). A 'pair of organs' was a phrase used in 17th-century England generally to denote an organ of two manuals, or more exactly of two cases (Great and Choir organ; *see* DOUBLE ORGAN); during the 16th century, particularly in documents prepared by non-musicians, a 'pair of organs or virginals' may perhaps have indicated an instrument with longer than average compass, but more probably meant merely an 'instrument of many pipes or strings' (cf a 'pair of stairs' in 15th-century French and English). Biblical use of 'organ' in English translations is unreliable. Septuagint Greek uses *organon* most often in its general sense of 'tool'; Old Testament Hebrew uses *ûgab* on four occasions, apparently to indicate some kind of wind instrument, perhaps a vertical flute; Vulgate Latin uses *organum* indiscriminately for both.

II. Construction.

There are three main parts to the construction of an organ: the wind-raising device, the chest with its pipes, and the (keyboard and valve) mechanism admitting wind to the pipes. These three parts are common to any pipe organ; it is in their precise nature that essential differences lie – from the small hydraulic organ of the 3rd century BC to the monster electric organ of the 1920s. At different points in history builders have tended to develop different parts of the instrument, while at other times (*c*1400 and *c*1850) all parts saw intense development.

1. Hydraulic organ. 2. A medieval chest. 3. A medieval bellows. 4. A chamber organ action. 5. Details of medieval and Renaissance chests. 6. Mechanical action. 7. Key-mechanism of a single-manual organ. 8. Wedge-bellows. 9. A German-Dutch organ. 10. Barker-lever action. 11. Cone-chest. 12. Reservoir and feeder-bellows. 13. Tubular-pneumatic action. 14. An electric action.

1. HYDRAULIC ORGAN. Fig.1*a* outlines the blowing mechanism described by Hero of Alexandria (?1st century AD): on its upward stroke, a piston pump (operated by the oblique-lying lever) pushes air to close the inlet valve on the right and to pass through the conduit to the *pnigeus*, a hemispherical chamber containing and surrounded by water in a cistern. The air forces the water out through the opening at the bottom of the *pnigeus*, raising the water level in the cistern; the weight of the displaced water gives pressure to the air thus forced along the exhaust conduit to the pipe-chest. Evidently a valve (not shown by Hero) prevented air from escaping along the first conduit back to the piston chamber. Once the pressurized air has reached the chest, its access to the speaking pipes is controlled by the mechanism shown in fig.1*b*: when the key is depressed, a perforated slip running between the top of the wind-chest and the pipe-foot moves into position, and the air under pressure passes through to the pipe-foot; when the hand releases the key, a strong spring pulls the slider back to its first position, and the wind is cut off. Other hydraulic organs differed significantly. Vitruvius (early 1st century) provided wind for his pipes from two cylinders operating in alternation, thus (unless otherwise contrived) requiring two blowers, as is clear from many late Roman depictions. Since Hero's sketch is merely diagrammatic, it is possible that the Greek hydraulis also normally had two blowers. Vitruvius recorded another advance in organ design: his ranks of pipes were 'separable', i.e. each rank of pipes had a valve which could be closed and the wind thereby prevented from reaching the pipes of that rank. In the hydraulis the water cistern is in effect a reservoir of air under pressure; the wind itself could be raised by means other than piston and cylinder.

2. A MEDIEVAL CHEST. Fig.2 (p.840) shows how in Theophilus's organ (11th century) the wind, raised by two or more bellows operated by the blowers' body-weight, is admitted to the several ranks of pipes when a perforated hand-slider is pulled out until its hole is aligned with the vertical channel between the wind-chest and the pipe-foot; to obtain a 'clean' sound, the slider must be operated as quickly as possible. To stop the

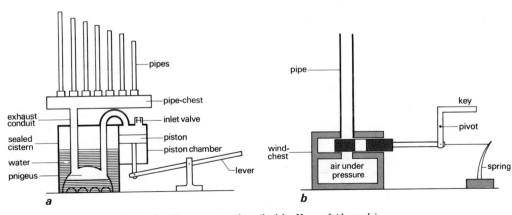

1. Blowing mechanism of the hydraulic organ, as described by Hero of Alexandria

sound, the slider is pushed back. The whole chest could be made of wood or moulded metal.

Other medieval chests differed significantly. According to the description in the Berne Codex (11th century), the wind did not pass to the two ranks of pipes from one duct but each pipe had its own duct from the wind-chamber below; thus the hand-slider required as many holes to be aligned as there were ranks. Also the 'key' was (like Hero's) a pivoted square which, when depressed, would push the slider into sounding position, while a spring pulled it back afterwards to its blocking position. Early medieval positives and portatives probably worked by one or other of such systems, which do not of themselves presuppose any particular size.

3. A MEDIEVAL BELLOWS. In fig.3, also derived from Theophilus's organ, air is fed in turn by three 'feeder-bellows' through channels meeting inside the *conflatorium* to make one central duct (the inner construction is shown with dotted lines); before the channels meet, the

wind passes through a copper valve which flaps open as the bellows send out air and flaps closed as soon as they are emptied. The collected wind is then directed along a trunk curving up to the pipe-chest. There may be more than one *conflatorium*, and the bellows can be in pairs or larger sets.

4. A CHAMBER ORGAN ACTION. In the 'pin action' portrayed in fig.4, wind accumulated in the lower chamber or pallet box is admitted to each upper chamber or groove when the corresponding key depresses the hinged pallet. The new, crucial device in this system is the pallet and its groove, both of unknown origin. The effectiveness and versatility of the resulting chest construction promoted the development of the Renaissance organ. In theory and (many organists believe) in practice, the grooved or 'barred' chest facilitates tonal blend between the several pipes belonging to each key. Later medieval positives probably had a similar action, in most cases to fewer (and often sliderless) ranks of pipes; later medi-

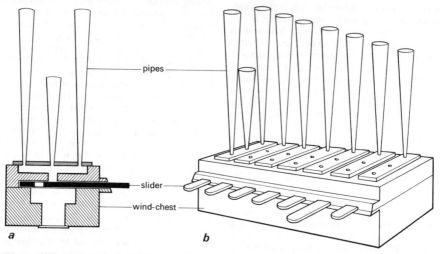

2. The chest of Theophilus's organ: (a) cross-section; (b) perspective view

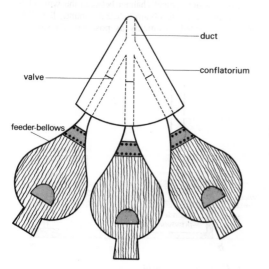

3. Bellows of Theophilus's organ

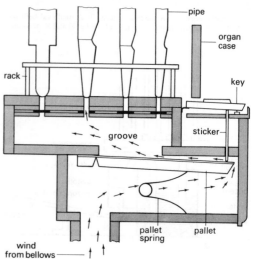

4. Pin action in a Renaissance chamber organ

eval portatives also probably worked from a similar (though simpler and more compact) pin action, whatever the shape and size of the keys.

5. DETAILS OF MEDIEVAL AND RENAISSANCE CHESTS. Fig.5a shows a medieval block-chest: the opened pallet admits wind to all the pipes on one groove (i.e. all those belonging to one key) and the player is unable to separate the ranks of pipes. To obtain variety of sound some organs had grooves divided into two parts, each with its own pallet; each resulting 'half-chest' could have its wind blocked off with a valve somewhere between bellows and pallet box, though in practice the front half-chest (whose pipes were those of the case front or Open and perhaps Stopped Diapasons) played all the time. Each key in such a double chest operated two pallets and two pallet-springs. The reliability and wind-saving virtues of this system gave it some popularity in the Netherlands during the 15th century.

In the slider-chest (? late 15th century) shown in fig.5b, the opened pallet admits wind to each single or multirank 'stop' by means of a perforated slip of wood ('slider') running longitudinally in the board between the pipe-foot and the groove on the upper level of the chest. The slider can be aligned either to allow wind to pass through ('stop drawn') or to prevent it passing through ('stop pushed in'). By means of rods, trundles and levers, the sliders can also be operated by a 'stop-knob' near the player (below and in front of the chest itself). Sliders were known first in small organs, perhaps from about 1400, but were not much used in larger ones (or the larger departments of two-manual organs) until the 16th century.

Fig.5c shows a spring-chest (early 16th century) in which the opened pallet admits wind to each single or multi-rank stop by means of a secondary pallet or 'groovevalve' for each, which is operated by the stop-lever bar. The spring acting on the secondary pallet also causes the bar to spring back to the 'off' position unless prevented (i.e. unless the player notches the stop-lever at the keyboard into the 'on' position).

Other spring-chests differed significantly. Many Italian ones from the late 15th century onwards had their secondary pallets placed vertically rather than horizontally, with the result that the bar moved horizontally. Because brass springs lose their flexibility in time, some builders in 16th-century Italy and 17th-century Germany designed the chest so that all the secondary pallets belonging to one groove could on occasion be pulled out in one strip (looking like a long, narrow drawer) and the faulty spring replaced without dismantling the pallet box.

The spring-chest is troublesome to make, as 17th-century theorists like Mersenne and Werckmeister noted; it also takes up more room than a slider-chest. But it is said that spring-chests last longer, and (though no results of controlled experiments have been published) cause the pipes to speak better. Since there can be no loss of wind through shrinking or warping of sliders, spring-chests probably contribute to greater stability of tuning, although their complexity is also likely to make them more sensitive to the extremes of humidity and dryness found in modern, centrally-heated churches. While the spaciousness of the chests dictated by the spatial requirements of the 'groove-valves' makes pipes and action more accessible for tuning and repair, it also causes the main key pallets to be made larger, making the touch

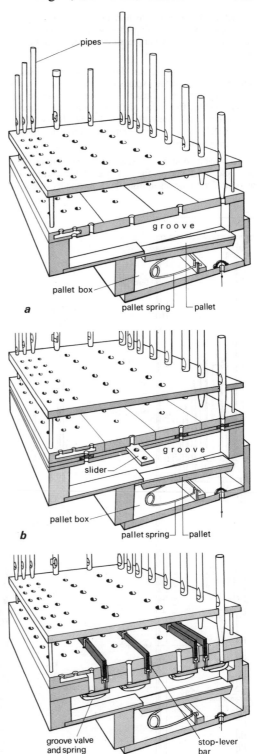

5. Medieval and Renaissance chests: (a) medieval block-chest; (b) ?late 15th-century slider-chest; (c) early 16th-century spring-chest

heavier and less sensitive than that of slider-chest organs. This may be why the spring-chest was abandoned in the north, where higher wind pressures complicated this situation.

6. MECHANICAL ACTION. In Fig.6*b* the mechanisms illustrated in fig.6*a* are expanded and augmented by the device of the roller, which, by displacing leverage laterally, enables the width of the keyboard to be much less than that of a rank of pipes. Fig.6*b* shows all the mechanical devices in a theoretically complete 'tracker action mechanism'.

7. KEY-MECHANISM OF A SINGLE-MANUAL ORGAN. The principle illustrated in fig.7 is one of the commonest associated with the organ from the 17th century onwards.

Even older (used from at least the 15th century) is the so-called 'suspended' action, found in early organs such as that in Oosthuizen (*c*1530) and used by the French into the early 19th century, although superseded by the later version in England and Germany. In a suspended action (Fr. *traction suspendu*) the fulcrum of the key is at the far end, the tracker being attached to the middle of the key and thence to a rollerboard and to the chest (fig.8, p.844). As there is no transfer of motion in this type of action, it tends to be lighter and more sensitive, even in fairly large organs such as the late 18th-century Cliquot organ at Poitiers Cathedral (1787–90). In later periods subsidiary chests might be added (e.g. a *Brustwerk* above the music desk, a Pedal section behind the main chest); the case might lose its simple shallow design

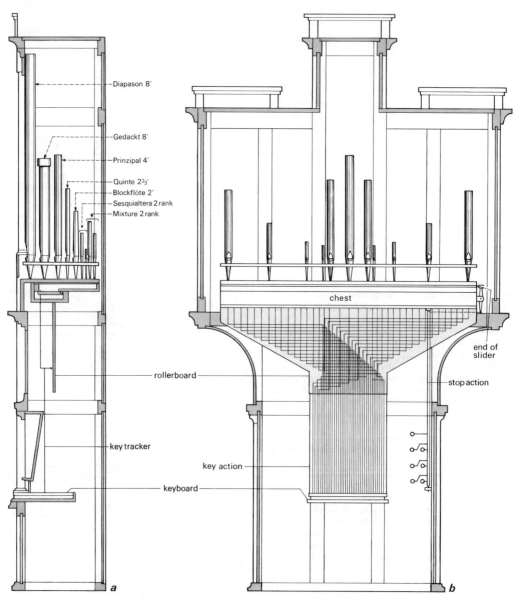

6. Tracker action mechanism

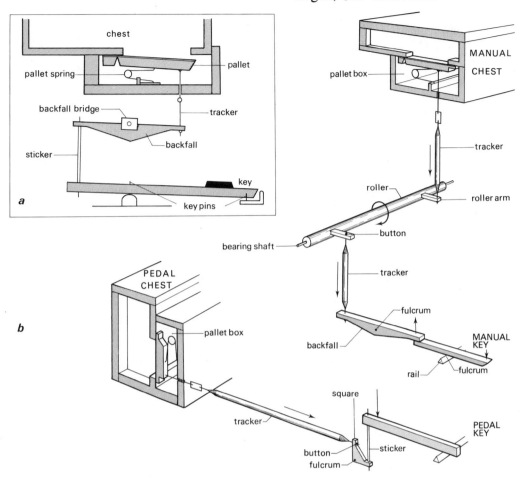

7. *Key-mechanism of a single-manual organ with balanced action*

and altar-like facial curves; the action might have splayed trackers or backfalls instead of a rollerboard, etc (see also §VIII, 2, below).

8. WEDGE-BELLOWS (late medieval *Spanbalg*). 'Span' denotes a 'board'; wedge-bellows (whether single as in fig.9*a*, or multifold as in fig.9*b*, p.845) are constructed of hinged wooden boards, ribs, and strips of leather. Both kinds can be small and simple, worked directly by hand or by the body-weight of the bellows blower; larger versions with operating levers are depicted here. The multifold design shows the principle of alternation between two bellows, the use of a lead or stone weight to increase the weight of the upper board whose fall expels air under pressure from the cocked bellows, and the wind canal going directly from bellows to pipes, without collection or stabilization other than that resulting from the cushioning of air in the wind-trunk.

Wind pressure has varied over the centuries, one purpose of the hydraulis system being to supply air on a higher and steadier pressure than ordinary forge-bellows. Such *Spanbälge* as these were made to supply an average pressure of 75–100 mm; i.e. the wind was sufficient to displace by 75–100 mm the level of water in an open glass U-tube.

Two other types of feeder-bellows were of particular

significance, though neither necessarily supposed a reservoir between bellows and chest. The square, lantern-shaped bellows (Fr. *soufflets à lanterne*) were known by at least about 1625; the top was raised by a pulley and the inflated bellows slowly collapsed, expelling wind through the trunk below. The box-bellows (Ger. *Kastenbalg*) worked on the principle of a pulley-raised box falling slowly within a second, slightly larger open-topped box and expelling wind through a trunk below; such bellows, which did not have perishable leather hinges, were known from the 17th century though only perfected by about 1825.

All of these types of bellows sucked in air through apertures opened by an intake valve which closed as soon as the full bellows began to expel wind; all had a further valve in the trunk which allowed wind to pass along from the bellows but checked it from rushing back when the bellows were reinflated.

9. A GERMAN-DUTCH ORGAN. Fig.10*a* (p.846) shows a four-manual instrument in cross-section; only a selection of pipe-ranks is indicated. In this design, the pedal-chests may be to the left and right of the main case or (with less immediacy of sound) behind it. The space between stool and Chair Organ was often enlarged in Roman Catholic countries to accommodate a choir and

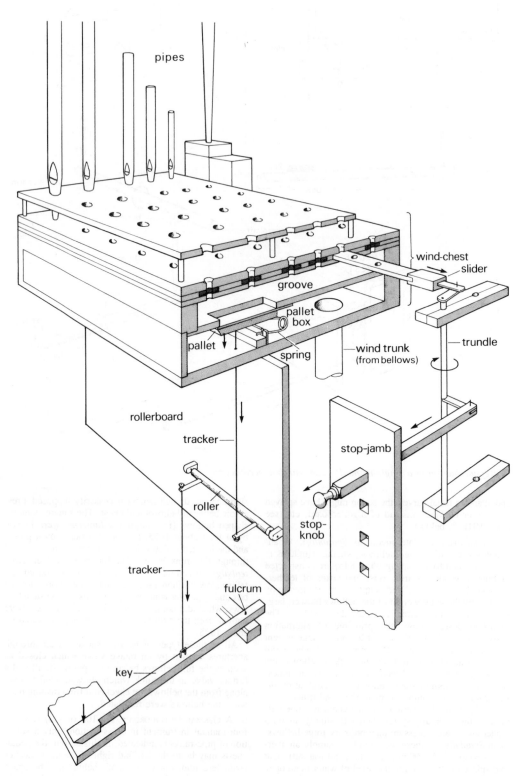

8. Key- and stop-mechanism of a single-manual organ with suspended action

orchestra; special stops (French Cornet), chests (German echo chests), and toy stops (all countries) could be conducted off the main wind-trunks, as could whole additional divisions (Spain, Portugal); one or more departments could be enclosed in a Swell box; Tremulants could be fixed in the main trunk, a subsidiary department trunk, or the trunk of an isolated stop (fig.10*b* and *c*).

10. BARKER-LEVER ACTION. Fig.11*a* (p.847) illustrates the principles of a 19th- and 20th-century mechanism constantly redesigned and patented by countless builders. When a key is depressed, air under pressure from the main bellows is admitted through a pallet-like valve to inflate small bellows (one for each key) which in moving travel sufficiently to pull a tracker connected with the pipe-chest pallet. On release the exhaust valve at the top allows the small bellows to deflate immediately. In this way, average light finger pressure on the key brings into play a wind-power sufficient to operate pallets at some distance from the player, especially those of large-scale pipes, perhaps on chests working under high wind pressure (e.g. Solo Organs). The pneumatic unit, or 'Barker lever', is placed near the keyboard, at a point where the tracker rises vertically from the keys. Perhaps one of its most important applications is to inter-manual couplers, allowing additional manuals to be coupled to the main manual without increasing key resistance. (*See also* BARKER, CHARLES SPACKMAN.)

11. CONE-CHEST (*Kegellade*). The cone-chest, or ventil-chest with cone-shaped valves, is found particularly in 19th-century German organs (fig.11*b* shows a mid-century example) and was one of several chests developed between 1775 and 1875 in the interests of mechanical reliability. Though bulky, the cone-chest avoided the faults to which a working slider-chest was subject; it also required less refined and skilled construction. In the cone-chest all the pipes belonging to a rank are mounted on one channel running the length of the chest; to the whole of this channel wind is admitted when the stop-knob is drawn. There are no lateral channels or grooves in such 'barless chests'. Each key activates a series of cone-shaped valves, one for each stop; thus although only one stop may be required by the organist, all the other valves move, producing an 'accompaniment'. The valves need not be cone-shaped; they may even be replaced by little discs operated by small bellows-like pneumatic motors ('bellows-chest').

The membrane-chest, associated with simple pneumatic or electric actions, also has longitudinal channels and is thus another 'barless or stop-channel chest' (*Registerkanzellenlade*). It works on an abundance of wind and may be explained without a diagram; air pressure from below the channel pushes a membrane up against the mouth of a conduit leading to each pipe-foot, thus preventing wind held inside the channel from reaching the mouth of the conduit and hence the pipe; the depressed key releases the pressure from below the channel, so that the membrane is pushed down from the end of the conduit by the wind destined for the pipe-foot itself. German and American builders of the later 19th century devoted much energy and ingenuity to devising such ventil wind-chests, often in clear rivalry to each other.

12. RESERVOIR AND FEEDER-BELLOWS. Feeder-bellows (cocked and compressed in *Spanbalg* fashion) expel air under pressure to a receiver or reservoir, shown in the top of fig.12 (p.848), which then delivers the wind to the trunks at a constant pressure. The reservoir or main bellows has 'inverted ribs' (lower ribs closing inwards and upper ribs closing outwards) for stability of exhaust pressure. In England this system dates from about 1762; the inverted rib construction was not adopted in the USA until the mid-19th century and was seldom used on the Continent. Some reservoirs were merely a second diagonal single-fold bellows into which the first sent wind (Snetzler, *c*1740), but by 1825 or so, horizontal bellows of the type shown were usual. During the 19th century, various means were employed to supply energy sufficient to raise the feeder-bellows, for example by mains water under pressure actuating cylinders moving the feeder-arms, or electric motors driving the feeders. Later, devices delivering wind directly to the reservoirs were used, notably the electric rotating-fan motor (from about 1890); most organs old and new are now fed with wind by this method. Moreover, within the airtight chamber of the blower more than one fan can rotate along the same spindle, each successive fan increasing the pressure as it receives and passes on the wind. The wind can be tapped off at any stage and conducted to the appropriate reservoir at the pressure required.

13. TUBULAR-PNEUMATIC ACTION. When a key is depressed, air under pressure in the touch-box above the key is admitted along the lead tubing to the pneumatic motor operating the pipe-chest pallet. To compensate for loss of force in the wind as it passes along the tub-

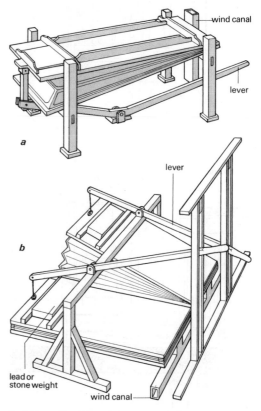

9. *Late medieval Spanbalg (wedge-bellows): (a) single; (b) multifold*

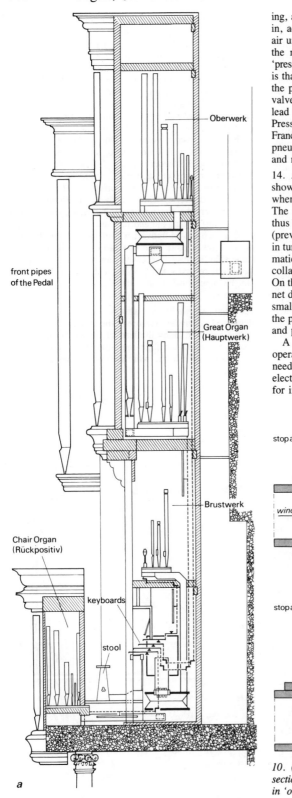

front pipes
of the Pedal

Oberwerk

Great Organ
(Hauptwerk)

Brustwerk

Chair Organ
(Rückpositiv)

keyboards

stool

a

ing, a secondary or 'relay' pneumatic motor may be built in, adjacent to the pallet box. Such a system works by air under pressure near the key being admitted towards the mechanism operating the pallet, hence the name 'pressure-pneumatic action'. 'Exhaust-pneumatic action' is that in which the air under pressure is contained near the pipe-chest pallet, pushing it closed when at rest; a valve near the key allows this wind to escape along the lead tubing away from the pallet, thus pulling it open. Pressure-pneumatic action never became popular in France, and in England many builders preferred exhaust-pneumatic, believing it to be more prompt, more silent and more durable (see fig.13a and b, p.848).

14. AN ELECTRIC ACTION. In the 'electro-pneumatic action' shown in fig.14 (p.849), an electro-magnet is activated when the key is depressed and its curcuit completed. The armature acts as a valve, rising to the magnet and thus allowing the wind to escape from a pneumatic relay (previously filled with wind from the pallet box) which in turn collapses, opening the port below the main pneumatic motor and thus allowing its wind to escape. On collapsing, the pneumatic motor pulls down the pallet. On the release of the key, the circuit is broken, the magnet drops the armature-valve and wind is restored to the small pneumatic motor, while the external spring closes the port under the main pneumatic motor which inflates and pushes up the pallet.

A 'direct electric action' is one in which a magnet operates the pallet itself, pulling it open; such pallets need to be small, however, and the consumption of electric current is high. The system is suitable chiefly for individual pipes (e.g. those of the unit-chest organ

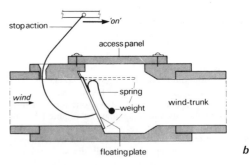

stop action

'on'

access panel

wind

spring

weight

wind-trunk

floating plate

b

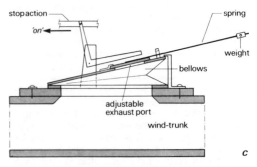

stop action

'on'

spring

weight

bellows

adjustable
exhaust port

wind-trunk

c

10. (a) Four-manual German-Dutch organ in cross-section; (b) Tremblant doux, and (c) Tremblant fort shown in 'on' position (arrows show movement of stop action)

discussed below in §VI, 4) and has never been highly favoured for important organs outside the USA. The electric magnet, generally quicker than the electric motor, may be applied to other moving parts of the organ, particularly the stop-action (sliders etc) and couplers. Electric actions allow the keyboards to be placed as far from the pipes as required; unfortunately they also deprive the organist of control over pipe-speech, and in practice they satisfy only those builders whose tonal ideals, like their instruments, are virtually outside the realm of true organs.

III. Pipework. There are several classes of organ pipes, the two oldest and most integral to the development of the organ being flue pipes and reed pipes. More common by far, though not necessarily more varied, are flue pipes. Both types operate on the coupled-air system of sound production common to flutes, recorders, oboes, clarinets etc.

1. Flue pipes. 2. Reed pipes. 3. Free reeds. 4. Diaphones (valvular reeds).

1. FLUE PIPES. Air under pressure from the chest passes through the foot-hole (bore) at the bass of the pipe-foot (fig.15, p.849) and so through the flue or windway, to issue in a flat sheet of wind striking the edge of the upper lip; the refracted wind causes eddies to form at the mouth, first on one side of the upper lip, then on the other. The pipe's natural frequency is coupled to the note of the 'edge tones' produced at the upper lip and gives to the eddies a rate of production that becomes the frequency of the note produced. Thus the effective length of the pipe is the principal factor in the pitch of the note.

Pitch and timbre are affected by several other factors, few of which, however, are variable outside narrow limits. A narrow pipe, to produce a certain pitch, must be longer than a wide one; a conical one must likewise be longer if it narrows towards the top, but shorter if it tapers outwards. Such variations in shape, however, are generally more important for their effect on a pipe's timbre than on its pitch. A cylindrical pipe stopped at the end will sound approximately an octave lower than if it were open, for a conical pipe the difference is not quite so great. A half-stopped cylindrical pipe (i.e. with its cap pierced and perhaps a tube passing through the hole) speaks somewhat higher than a stopped pipe.

The narrower the mouth or the smaller the flue, then the smaller the volume of air (at any given pressure) striking the upper lip and the softer the sound; the higher the mouth in relation to its width (i.e. the greater the 'cut-up'), then the rounder, duller or more flute-like the tone; the narrower the pipe as a whole, the richer the harmonic spectrum and the more string-like the tone. It has been said that the harder the metal, the richer the harmonic spectrum; or the more lead contained in the pipe-alloy, the 'duller' the sound. But recent work (Backus and Hundley, 1966) has established from theoretical and experimental evidence that 'the steady tone of a pipe does not depend on the material of the pipe-wall. The belief that the use of tin in constructing pipes gives a better tone appears to be a myth unsupported by the evidence'. Experienced voicers, however, will aver that the composition of pipe metal does affect tone quality, and that it is impossible to match exactly the tone quality of two otherwise identical pipes made of very different alloys. More to the point, perhaps, is that tin-lead alloys are easy to work and shape, thus allowing

the builder a high degree of adjustment at the parts of the pipe crucial to voicing processes (see also §VIII, 3, below).

Most of these factors can be used only to a certain degree: a point is soon reached when a pipe will not speak at all, even when other factors are altered, e.g. increasing or decreasing the wind pressure. Consequently the various interrelated factors require pragmatic expertise in their manipulation.

In addition to its more general usage, the term 'scale' refers to a pipe's diameter in relation to a norm ('wide' or 'narrow' scale), and the relationship or ratio between one pipe's diameter and that of its octave below in the same rank (3:5 etc). One well-known norm is the *Normprinzipal* suggested at the German Organ Reform conferences in the 1920s; this norm is 'one pipe larger'

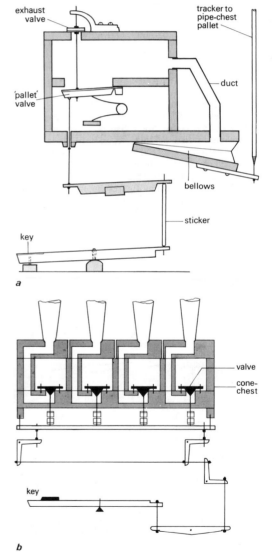

11. (a) Barker-lever action; (b) mid-19th-century cone-chest

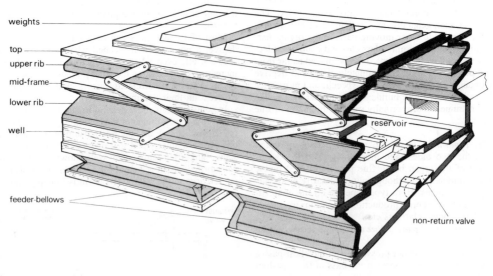

12. Reservoir and feeder-bellows

than that promulgated by J. G. Töpfer about 1845 (thus the diameter of Töpfer's *C* pipe is that of the *Normprinzipal C♯*). G. A. Sorge had been the first to use logarithms to find constant scalings for organ pipes (1758), calculating pipe diameter, pipe length, mouth width and mouth height by this method. Other 17th- and 18th-century theorists (such as Mersenne and Bédos de Celles) suggested scaling-figures by means of tables culled from practical experience and from the empiricism of organ builders themselves. Only two generations after Sorge did Töpfer develop the idea of arithmetical calculation for pipes (with immense influence on builders of his time); he calculated the cross-

sectional area of a pipe an octave higher than the given pipe by applying the ratio 1 : √8. Thus a pipe with half the diameter of a given pipe is not an octave (12 pipes) above but 16 or 17 pipes above. Such a factor as 1 : √8 was itself reasonable, and many older builders had worked more or less to it, though empirically and not rigidly; indeed, Töpfer's formula can be deplored for the encouragement it gave to 19th-century 'organ-factory builders' who applied a constant scale irrespective of the acoustics of the church or indeed any other variable of importance to organ tone.

Fig.16 (p.850) shows some flue-pipe shapes and is scaled to indicate the relative sizes of different types all

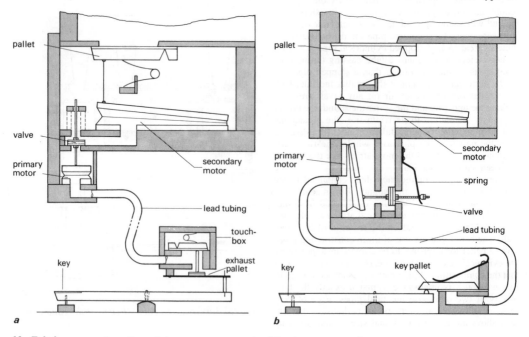

13. Tubular-pneumatic actions: (a) pressure-pneumatic; (b) exhaust-pneumatic

producing the same *C*. (The *Normprinzipal* diameter of the *C* pipe at a pitch standard of *a'* = 435 is 155·5 mm; at a pitch standard of *a'* = 440, the diameter for *C* would be reduced to 154·17 mm – a fine point of difference since variations in temperature will change the pitch this much). Most historic types of English Open Diapason, French Montre and Venetian Principale have been wider in scale than the *Normprinzipal*, and for many builders it remains merely one of the possible norms. It must also be remembered that the diagram does not refer to factors other than scaling, such as wind pressure. Mouth widths are usually expressed as proportions of the circumference, and those ordinarily used range from 2 : 7 down to 1 : 6, though further extremes have been used for special effects. The cut-up is expressed as a fraction of the mouth width, 'quarter cut-up' indicating that the mouth is a quarter as high as it is wide.

Wooden pipes are either stopped (most commonly 8', then 16' and 4') or open (16', 8', 4', 2'); sometimes half-stopped wooden pipes (i.e. with a pierced stopper) of the Rohrflöte or Spillflöte type are found, especially in small organs. Metal or wood conical pipes narrowing towards the top have been found in the largest Dutch, German and Spanish organs since about 1540. Metal pipes with 'pavilions' (inverted conical caps) were made especially by French and English builders for about a century from about 1840, both on the flute and string side of tone-colour. Overblowing pipes have also been popular in large organs and in special instruments made for colourful secular use; the most common during the period *c*1600–1800 was the narrow-scaled, narrow-mouthed open cylindrical pipe, overblowing to the 2nd partial or 'at the octave' above. Such pipes require to be twice as long as the pitch length (8' for 4' pitch). Stopped pipes overblow to the 3rd partial or 'at the 12th' above, and require to be three times as long as the normal stopped length (6' for 4' pitch). Overblowing flute pipes (Flûte harmonique etc) became widely used after the middle of the 19th century, having been developed to a high degree in France. Such pipes are of double length but of the scale of a normal-length open flute, and are pierced at the node (approximately halfway up from the mouth) with one or two small holes. Given full wind, such pipes will overblow, giving a strong, sweet and rather fundamental tone not unlike that of the modern orchestral flute. Alternatively, to prevent overblowing in narrow-scaled string-toned pipes, or to aid tuning at the mouth of stopped pipes, 'ears' or 'beards' are often added: short metal plates or rods of metal soldered or held to the sides of (and sometimes below) the mouth, protruding from it and helping to direct the vortices of wind on to the edge of the upper lip.

2. REED PIPES. Air under pressure from the chest passes through the bore into the boot and so through the opening in the shallot (fig.17, p.851); in so doing the wind sets the thin, flexible brass reed-tongue into vibration; this in turn sets the air column in the pipe or resonator into vibration, producing a coupled system. The frequency of the note produced is determined by the length of the air column in the resonator and by the length, mass and stiffness of the reed-tongue.

The pitch and tone of the pipe are affected by many factors; if all the factors are constant, then the longer the reed-tongue, the lower the pitch. To produce a required pitch in reed pipes with either cylindrical or conical resonators, the resonator must be shorter the

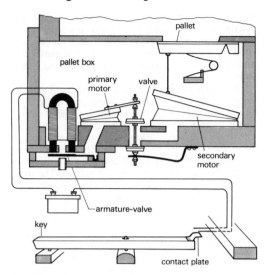

14. Electro-pneumatic action

longer the tongue. But in practice this property is used within only a small margin, as the tone is more immediately and strikingly affected by a change in the relationship between tongue length and resonator length. Natural 'full-length' cylindrical resonators correspond roughly to the length of stopped pipes of the same pitch, natural 'full-length' conical resonators to somewhat less than open pipes; such 'resonance length' for conical reeds is as little as three-quarters of the pitch length, i.e. 6' or 7' length for an 8' Trumpet. A reed pipe will speak without its resonator, whose purpose is therefore to

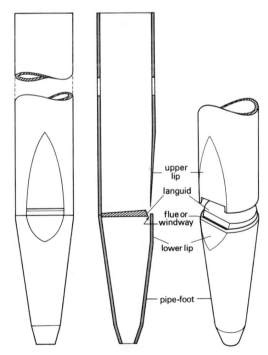

15. Foot of a flue pipe from the front, in cross-section and in perspective

reinforce certain partials, to 'give tone' to the pipe. But in a reed with a resonator a point is soon reached, if the reed-resonator relationship is altered, when the pipe will either overblow or not speak at all. This is particularly true of double-cone reeds such as Oboes and Schalmeys.

The thinner the tongue, the richer the harmonics in the tone it produces. Wider resonators produce stronger tone; conical resonators produce a 'thicker' partial-content than cylindrical. The resonator gives its air column its own natural frequency; when this is greater than that of the tongue (i.e. when the pipe is shorter than the tongue requires for both to respond naturally to the same pitch) the tone becomes brighter, richer in partials. The more open the shallot, the louder and richer the tone; to obtain brilliance from partly closed shallots, higher wind pressure is required; to obtain a rounder, more horn-like tone, 19th-century builders opened their shallots higher up the reed, the curved tongue thus closing the opening before its travel was complete. As in the case of flue pipes, it has been established recently that the hardness of the resonator material (brass, tin, lead, wood, in that order) is unlikely to influence the tone, tradition and hearsay notwithstanding. However, the hardness of the tongue material is a definite factor in tone quality. The commonest material used by modern builders is what is known

as 'half-hard' brass, but soft brass, hard brass and even the very hard phosphor bronze are also used in certain instances. The thickness of the tongue likewise has an effect on tone.

Reeds with very short resonators (whatever their shape), and usually small scale, are called regal stops and were known from at least about 1475. In practice, most regals are either predominantly conical in shape or predominantly cylindrical; they also exhibit an inconstant scale (i.e. relative to the reed-tongues, the resonators in the treble are progressively longer than in the bass). Reed stops with resonators twice or even four times natural length were sometimes made in the later 19th century, especially by French and English builders, and became equivalent to overblowing flue pipes. 19th-century builders, particularly in those two countries, very often placed their reeds on higher wind pressure than the flue stops (18 cm upwards); the desire to supply 'carrying power' by such means, particularly in the treble, had grown in France from about the second third of the 18th century onwards.

Fig.18 (p.852) shows models of some of the more popular reeds of the early 17th century (Praetorius, 2/ 1619; fig.18a) and the late 19th (Audsley, 1905; fig.18b). A great deal depends on the use of various shapes and proportions of shallots or 'reeds', and these, like the

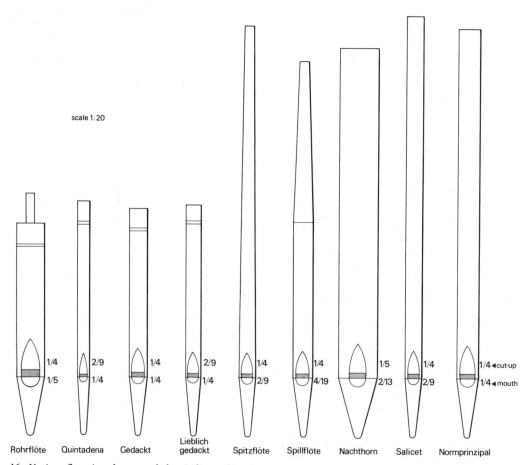

scale 1:20

| | Rohrflöte | Quintadena | Gedackt | Lieblich gedackt | Spitzflöte | Spillflöte | Nachthorn | Salicet | Normprinzipal |

16. *Various flue-pipe shapes scaled to indicate the relative sizes of different pipes all producing the same C*

tube, block and boot, may be made of wood (though this is more often a feature of low-pitched pedal reeds than a general alternative).

3. FREE REEDS. Free reeds were developed in Europe (probably after the Chinese *sheng*) towards the end of the 18th century in several areas around the Baltic, and offered the first radically different type of organ pipe since flues and reeds had been perfected. Instead of a shallot (an orifice in the reed) against which the tongue beats when wind excites it, a thick oblong plate of brass (smaller than the corresponding reed of a reed pipe) is perforated with a narrow opening through which vibrates the close-fitting brass tongue (fig.19, p.853). It swings freely, hence 'free reed'. The boot needs to be larger than that of a corresponding reed stop to allow copious winding. When made by German builders about 1825 or French builders about 1850, free reeds had resonators of various types and tone-colour, thus being legitimate ranks of organ pipes. Some stops, however, such as the Physharmonika had instead of individual pipe-resonators one resonating chamber common to all notes of the rank, thus taking less room on the chest and less time at the factory. It was such pipeless free reeds that led to the various kinds of harmonium or REED ORGAN of the 19th century. Free reeds could be mass-produced more easily than the so-called beating-reed stops, although in itself the workmanship was not inferior. The best builders by no means regarded them as easy alternatives to beating reeds.

Though less incisive in articulation and weaker in volume than beating reeds, the free reed had a quality highly favoured by its period: it could be made 'expressive'. On admitting more wind to a free reed, the amplitude, but not the frequency, of the swinging tongue is increased; it can thus produce a louder tone without rising in pitch, like a more or less excited tuning-fork but unlike a beating reed. When it was a separate stop in a large organ, however, such a property of the free reed could not easily be exploited. Rarely outside the period 1810–1910, and then most often only in parts of northern France, central Germany and northern Italy, did the free reed and its meagre tone achieve much popularity.

4. DIAPHONES (VALVULAR REEDS). In 1894 Robert Hope-Jones took out a patent for a 'pipe' making use of the age-old observation that any device allowing puffs of compressed air to be projected into a tube or resonating box (i.e. into a chamber holding a column of non-pressurized air) will create a sound if the frequency becomes audible (fig.20, p.853). On activation from the keyboard, air under pressure is admitted through the bore and sets the thin 'vibrator' into motion, whereupon the pallet-like disc attached to its free end admits a rapid and regular succession of puffs of air into the resonator (i.e. the pipe standing above). Like the free reed, it increases in volume but not in frequency as the wind pressure is increased; but unlike the free reed, much power can be achieved by such means. The tone itself is always 'unblending' and useful only in organs conceived on ideals current in a few areas of Europe and the USA between 1900 and 1940.

IV. The classical and medieval organ. Since the 3rd century BC it has been possible to regard the organ as an instrument composed of four elements: (i) a wind-raising device operated by lever, pulley or other mechanism, directing air under pressure to (ii) a 'chest' in

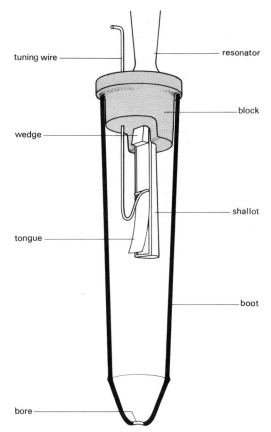

17. Foot of a reed pipe

which the wind is stored until admitted by (iii) a mechanism operated by some kind of keyboard to (iv) one or more rows of pipes (*see* RANK). The absence of any one of these elements prevents an instrument from being properly considered an organ, however well it is fashioned. But other instruments could well have presented models or given ideas to early organ makers, particularly those in east Mediterranean countries. It is unlikely that at any single period the hydraulic organ was so firmly established that builders were indifferent to the influence of such wind instruments as the SYRINX, the MAGREPHAH or the BAGPIPE.

The most comprehensive recent surveys of archaeological and documentary evidence relating to classical and medieval organs are the books of Jean Perrot (1965) and K.-J. Sachs (1970).

1. Greek and Roman antiquity. 2. The Byzantine organ. 3. The organ of the Arabs. 4. Early church organs. 5. Medieval organ theorists. 6. The church organ 1100–1450. 7. The 15th-century positive and portative.

1. GREEK AND ROMAN ANTIQUITY. No evidence, literary, iconographical, archaeological or even mythological, suggests that the pipe organ existed before the Hellenistic period or originated in any other than the Hellenistic sphere of influence. Later texts such as Athenaeus's *Deipnosophistae* (AD *c*200) and Vitruvius's *De architectura* (? early 1st century AD) accredit it to one man, Ctesibius, an Alexandrian engineer and practical theoretician of the 3rd century BC. For him, the HYDRAULIS

was more a demonstration of the principles of hydraulics (i.e. the science of water channelled for power) than a musical instrument as such. Thus Pliny the elder's reference to Ctesibius's 'hydraulicis organis' should be understood to mean 'hydraulic machines or contrivances'. Curt Sachs's assessment of Ctesibius's achievement as uniting a mechanically raised and constant wind supply to a set of panpipes is not a totally unreasonable conjecture; but the surviving accounts of his work (written after his time) make it clear that he had also incorporated a wind-chest and even some kind of keyboard. Thus the hydraulis has the essential features of an organ. That Ctesibius was also said by Vitruvius to have invented a water clock offers an interesting parallel to the makers of organs and clocks in the medieval cathedrals of western Europe: such makers were, in effect, specialists in complex machinery. (*See also* WATER ORGAN.)

The principle of the water-pump is shown in fig.1. But forge bellows were known much earlier, and their power potential had already been described in the *Iliad*.

Bellows could have provided wind either directly to a regulator-chest under a row of pipes, or indirectly via the cistern of a water organ. But there is no evidence that either of these was done before the 2nd century AD, and it is possible that the organ was indeed born as a kind of engineering model, demonstrating the efficiency of Ctesibius's wind-raising and wind-stabilizing equipment. Hero's account gives no details of the pipes (whether flue or reed, open or stopped) or what the material, size, compass, tuning, pitch or voicing were. Certainly the term 'hydraulic' does not of itself imply an *aulos*-like sound (see §I). The attributions of tonal power to the larger outdoor organs of the late Roman Empire can be interpreted in several ways; they might, for instance, refer to the putative high Mixture of the *magrephah*.

Vitruvius's musical interests are more obvious than Hero's. The ranks of his organ were made to play separately (though for what reason is not known) by means of a specially constructed chest in which a channel ran

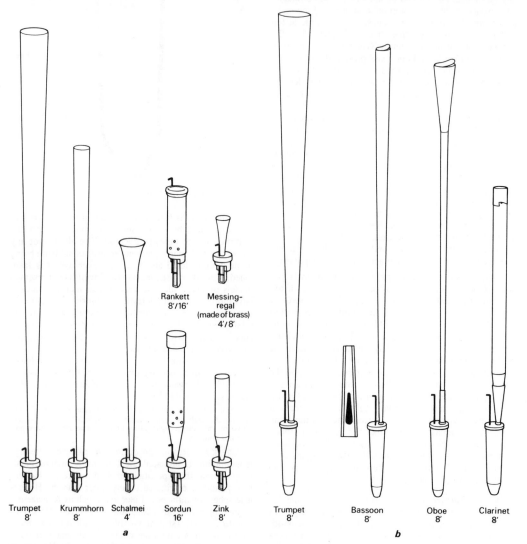

Trumpet 8′   Krummhorn 8′   Schalmei 4′   Rankett 8′/16′   Sordun 16′   Messing-regal (made of brass) 4′/8′   Zink 8′

a

Trumpet 8′   Bassoon 8′   Oboe 8′   Clarinet 8′

b

18. *Reed pipes: (a) after Praetorius, 2/1619; (b) after Audsley, 1905*

lengthways under each row of pipes, wind being admitted to the channel through a valve operated by an iron handle. The keys are returned to position by an iron spring, unlike Hero's piece of horn. As the key was set immediately under its pipes, either the close-set pipes or (more likely) the keys may have been unequally spaced; in either event organ playing would be rather awkward.

The oldest reference to organ playing is a century and a half after Ctesibius: the 'Delphic inscription' (90 BC), full of implication about the organ's fame. Cicero, Lucretius, Petronius and other authors wrote of its powers, presumably not all from hearsay, and at least one emperor (Nero) let himself be known as an inordinate organ player. By the 2nd century AD the Roman organ was heard in some of the more important theatres, games, amphitheatres, circuses, banquets and perhaps processions; a 3rd-century source (a Greek inscription at Rhodes) even suggests that it was played in Dionysian festivals. But the cylinder-pump water organ had so many disadvantages – requiring precision engineering and good metal, yet difficult to maintain, move and keep from corrosion – that it is easy to imagine bellows being applied over the years. Eventually, they replaced both pump and cistern, but it is not known when, where and how. Sources of the 2nd century (Julius Pollux) and 4th century (Porfyrius Optatianus) may refer to bellows replacing either pump or cistern. Even in the later Roman Empire, however, organs were to be heard, and such poets as Claudian (c400) show organ playing to have been a major contribution to the celebrations attending accessions to a consulate, weddings and banquets during a period when 'the singer has thrust out the philosopher' (Ammianus Marcellinus, c350). Inscriptions found in several provinces far from Rome (Arles, Colchester, Budapest, Asia Minor) make it clear that organ playing was well known in gladiator contests (see fig.21, p.854).

The few 5th- and 6th-century references include one or two by early Church Fathers, particularly those on the south and east coasts of the Mediterranean. But whether it was from personal experience that such writers as Boethius wrote of hydraulic organs, or Cassiodorus of a bellows-organ with wooden keys, is not certain; nor has 20th-century research shown what music the organ played, much less whether it played polyphony. Much can be tentatively conjectured from the iconographical evidence. The Nennig mosaic, for example (see HYDRAULIS, fig.1), shows an organ rather over two metres high and one metre wide, with its player poised during a gladiator fight to play at a suitable moment – perhaps as a death signal, or to rouse the spectators, or to 'illustrate' the action. The player is seated or standing in an elevated position, watching the combat over his 27 or 28 pipes. These pipes decrease in length very little over the compass, but it is not known whether this is due to an enharmonic tuning or to pictorial licence. A modern reconstruction of a hydraulis such as classical authors have described is shown in fig.22 (p.855).

Parts of two Roman organs are said still to exist: fragments from Pompeii (now in the Museo Nazionale, Naples) and major remnants of a small organ found in Aquincum, Hungary (now in the Aquincum Museum, Budapest; fig.23, p.856). But the Pompeii fragments, which seem to belong to two different instruments, are not certainly parts of an organ, although their pipes are cast, like an organ. The Aquincum organ was more

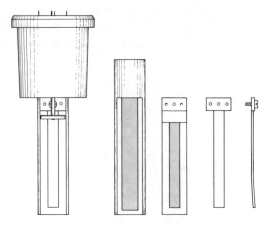

19. Free reed of an organ pipe

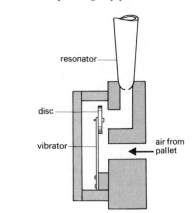

20. Diaphone or valvular reed

complete, and was so 'reconstructed' in 1959 that its parts are not now open to more enlightened interpretation. Its dedicatory plaque has the date 228. It has four rows of 13 bronze flue pipes, one row open and three stopped with oak stoppers; all pipes are cast. The windchest was made of wood, lined inside and out with thin bronze sheets. The whole organ is very small, about 60 cm high, 38 cm wide and 25 cm deep. Inside the chest below each row of pipes runs a channel to which wind is admitted by slotted metal sliders pierced with one central hole; the wooden keys operate further sliders and are pressed down by the player. The pipes show a complex structure at the mouth, whereby the airstream is directed by the shape of the pipe-foot itself on to the upper lip; the open and stopped pipes differ in detail but not in principle.

Two crucial questions remain about the Aquincum organ. First, how did the organ receive its wind? No trace of this part of the mechanism exists, and until recently it was not known whether the organ was a small Vitruvian hydraulis (as the inscription 'hydra' on it suggests) or a cisternless bellows-organ of the later medieval type, with wood and leather bellows of a kind liable to perish easily or be later misunderstood by inexperienced archaeologists. It has recently been shown, however, that the organ was not bellows-blown but was a water organ or hydraulis (see §VIII, 4). Second, were

21. *Hydraulic organ, with tuba and two cornua, at a gladiator contest: Roman mosaic (1st century AD) from a villa at Dar Buk Ammera, near Zliten, Libya (Archaeological Museum, Tripoli)*

the four ranks designed to be played together at choice or do the non-proportional variations in length between one rank and another – which can be modified by the stoppers or, in the case of the open pipes, by bronze tuning-slides – indicate that each rank played 13 notes of one particular mode? The latter has been plausibly suggested by Walcker-Mayer (1970), who gave the open rank a Pythagorean diatonic scale and the three stopped ranks sections of the Hyperiastian, Lydian and Phrygian *tonoi*. The little organ would then have been able to make a single-rank, portative-like contribution of treble flute sounds to music in four different *tonoi*, the make-up and character of which exercised theorists over many centuries (see also §VIII, 4, below). Some late sources suggest that different wind and string instruments had different *tonoi*. While iconographic remains are usually untrustworthy or vague (certainly it is over-optimistic to see the 'Carthage terracotta' shown in fig.24, p.857, as representing a three-rank, quarter-tone organ), it is possible that rows of pipes were tuned, if not 'microtonally' (too modern a concept), at least so that several modal scales were possible.

Reconstructions of the water organ suggest that it might have had a wind pressure anywhere between 7·5 cm and 30 cm; also unknown is whether the pipework was always flue and, if so, whether the diameters were constant. While written sources give no firm evidence, iconography seems to suggest that: the pipes were usually flue; their diameter was constant; the tuning (in the more complete examples) was not diatonic, chromatic or enharmonic but multiple, providing a choice of modes for rather less than an octave; and multi-rank chests may have provided different timbres with or without octave- and 5th-sounding ranks. But none of these conclusions is reliable. The Aquincum organ supports the case for flue pipes, contradicts the suggestion that the diameter

was constant, and leaves the tuning and timbre uncertain.

2. THE BYZANTINE ORGAN. By the end of the 5th century the new Roman Empire of the east, with its base at Constantinople, had achieved a character of its own, intellectually conservative and favouring a world of abstract thought far removed from the practical technology of ancient Alexandria and Rome. Although the old Greek treatises were preserved in Byzantine copies and hence known to the Arabs, engineering projects like organ making remained undeveloped for a millennium. But by the 8th century western Europe itself no longer knew such masterpieces of Roman engineering as the Vitruvian hydraulis. All the sources suggest that the European 9th- and 10th-century 'organ revival' came about because the instrument was reintroduced from Byzantium.

Despite some hints in the sources, the organ was certainly not used in the Byzantine Church itself (and indeed is still not). But at least two facts seem to be clear: that most references relate to bellows-organs, and that the instrument continued to be part of the secular, courtly pomp in the capital city. In the first connection, a 10th-century Arabic source suggests that three (or two) bellows fed air into a large reservoir below the pipe-chest; in the second, it was no doubt because of their use at banquets, chariot races, weddings, processions and the like that organs were decked out in gold and costly decoration. Both the 'blue' and 'green' factions at court had an organ, but the instrument otherwise naturally remained a rarity. At his palace the emperor had both automata (the famous 'golden tree' with moving, whistling birds activated by wind under water pressure; see fig.25, p.858) and true organs, in which at least one emperor (Theophilus, 9th century) took an interest. Nothing is known of the pipework, sound, compass, precise function or repertory of the organ in the Great Reception Room, or indeed anywhere else, though one 9th-century source does refer to '60 copper pipes' in what appears to have been a large table-organ.

Organs became objects of visual and aural show, eliciting wonder and respect as diplomatic gifts or signs of royal power. In 757 a famous diplomatic instrument was sent to Pepin, King of the Franks at Compiègne; many sources of the period lay great store by this gift to Pepin. Later a monk of St Gall (? Notker Balbulus) reported that the 'King of Constantinople' also sent an organ to Charlemagne in 812, with bronze pipes, 'bellows of bull leather' and three sound-effects (rumbling thunder, trembling lyre, tinkling *cymbala*) possibly indicating *pleno*, flutes and little bells; but the source is doubtful, the language hyperbolic (or possibly psalmodic), and the whole reference perhaps merely a gloss on the Pepin episode. In any case such instruments were not church organs but extravagant gifts, like the 13th-century organ of 90 pipes sent from one Arab court to the Emperor of China.

An event of evident importance in the 9th-century chronicles was the arrival at Aachen in 826 of Georgius, a Venetian priest who undertook to construct a hydraulis. According to a poem glorifying Charlemagne's son Louis, Georgius's organ was a kind of royal or national symbol of power: 'The organ, not seen in France before, a subject of pride for the Greeks, the only reason the people of Constantinople felt themselves your master: even the organ is now represented in Aachen'. Its intricate technology must have been the justification for such respect. The Aachen organ was used for occasions of pomp, not for chapel services; the Utrecht Psalter (compiled in France, perhaps near Rheims) depicts, with little understanding, a hydraulis taking part in an ensemble illustrating Psalm cxlix (see fig.26, p.859); this too has little to do with church services.

3. THE ORGAN OF THE ARABS. The high level of Arabic and Islamic culture from the 8th century to the 10th gave theorists and craftsmen the opportunity to work on bellows-organs; theorists in particular knew of such 'instruments' but seem rarely, if ever, to have seen one. A famous source, the Epistle to (or from) Muristus, describes two organs, one of which is a kind of siren or signal-organ; the sources containing Muristus's writings are also interesting in that two of them (in Beirut and in the British Museum) show particularly clearly how a diagrammatic plan can become, under the scribe's hand, an unintelligible pattern of abstract design.

Nothing is known of Muristus, and the graphic similarity of his name in Arabic to Qatasibiyus (Ctesibius) was pointed out in 1931 by Farmer; Muristus appears to have been a Greek (or Byzantine), and in any case derived his instruments directly from Ctesibius's *Commentaries*. But neither of them is a true organ. The first contains a chest of 12 pipes fed with wind from the lungs of four men blowing gently through tubes into a regulator; the weight of the pipes compresses the wind; the pipes themselves appear to be reeds, all of the same length but of varying diameter and requiring different volumes of wind; the wind is admitted to each pipe through a valve, presumably one worked by some kind of key. This seems to be the instrument of 'formidable power' referred to in the 'Letter to Dardanus' once attributed to St Jerome. The second or 'Great organ' is

a signal-organ not perhaps unlike the (smaller) *magrephah* and containing a siren pipe or pipes blown at great pressure, used in battle by the Greeks, according to Muristus, or for similar purposes by other Middle Eastern peoples. The siren worked on the same principle as the hydraulis, four pumps or cylindrical bellows providing wind pressurized by water in a cistern.

There is no evidence that the organ became known again in western Europe through the cultural activities of the Arab caliphate of Córdoba in Spain. But the possibility that this might have been the case adds further importance to any work undertaken on this period in Iberian musical history, for links may perhaps be discovered between Spanish–Arab instrument making and 9th-century Benedictine musical life. In the eastern caliphates organs seem to have developed into mere ingenious automata; but even in that state the Eastern organ seems not to have survived the fall of Constantinople in 1453.

4. EARLY CHURCH ORGANS. The famous gift to King Pepin in 757 was a Byzantine organ, called 'organum' in the chronicles and still perhaps regarded as an 'engineering contrivance' rather than a musical instrument. The supposed gift to Charlemagne in 812 was also Byzantine. The fanciful clock given to the emperor in 807 by an envoy of the Persian king was Arabic; the priest Georgius, sent to Aachen in 826, was Venetian, but possibly trained in Byzantium. Several Western writers from the 8th century to the 13th knew of the Greek-Roman organ but in most cases from vague written sources from which even the more astute authors got the impression that the pipes were made to sound by water – an idea sustained by the Jesuit amateur physicists of a later century. The

22. *Reconstruction in diagram form of the hydraulis described in Greek and Latin sources*

(a)

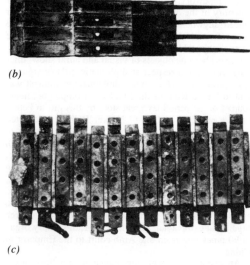

(b)

(c)

23. Remains of a Roman organ (AD 228) found at Aquincum (Aquincum Museum, Budapest): (a) pipes; (b) sliders; (c) sliders in position

well-known picture in the Utrecht Psalter (see fig.26) of a hydraulic organ with two players and four alternating pump blowers is also based on a misunderstanding of the Mediterranean water organ. Many of the early church writers refer to organs in such hyperbolic or apparently unreal terms that their sources of 'information' must have been in most cases literary. It is even possible that such references to organs with 100 pipes, like that of St Aldhelm, were mistaken allusions to *hydra*, the 100-headed monster whose name is the same as a documented abbreviation for the hydraulis. All ecclesiastical references to organs before the 10th century are to be treated with caution, and even scepticism.

All these organs were secular. One of the great unsolved puzzles of music history is how and why the organ came to be almost exclusively a church instrument in western Europe from about 900 to about 1200. The early church was subject to two particular influences against any instrument in church, and especially in the liturgy: the liturgy's origins in the Jewish synagogue, and Patristic resistance to anything of profane or luxurious association. By the 9th century, however, the intellectual and liturgical style of the church had changed. Like sung organum, the instrument owed a great deal to Benedictine cultural centres, not only in their literacy and scholarship but also in the opportunities which their large churches gave to the advancement of music. The monastic revival in the late 10th century must itself have been a factor in the appearance of organs, which had become ingenious objects for the use of the clergy, not the people. The organ was never officially approved or even acknowledged in any known papal or pontifical document despite the traditional legend that Pope Vitalian (657–72) introduced it. Nor, for one reason or another, are any of the references to organs placed or used in church before the 9th century at all reliable.

Organs, like tower bells later, were one of the irrelevances complained of by the new reformed order of the

Cistercians, judging by remarks made by St Aelred, abbot of Rievaulx in 1166; his reference to the sound of the bellows, the tinkling of bells and the harmony of organ pipes is highly reminiscent of older reports. St Aelred also referred to the crowd of people watching this display as if in a theatre, 'not a place of worship', which suggests that organs were placed inside buildings, perhaps for example a large Benedictine church. But all this does not necessarily indicate that an organ was used during the service, nor even before or after the service. Perhaps it was rather an object of curiosity, like a cathedral almanac clock. Other 12th-century sources imply more clearly that an organ was used in some way during the services, perhaps for signalling purposes, like bells at the Elevation.

Whether organs were used liturgically is not clear from the many 9th- and 10th-century references to them. The notice describing the consecration in 972 of the Benedictine abbey of Bages, Spain, for example, makes it clear that an organ played near the entrance, 'praising and blessing the Lord'; but to surmise more is conjecture. Much the same could be said for the archiepiscopal coronation at Cologne Cathedral in 950. Pope John VIII (872–82) wrote of an organ required 'for the purpose of teaching the science of music', for which it remained useful to scribes writing about and teaching musical proportions, for example at Benedictine centres such as Fleury and St Gall. The practical function of organs set up by, or in memory of, great abbots or landowners is unknown; reference to organs used on feast days (e.g. in the Life of St Oswald, 925–92) suggests if anything that they were extra-liturgical, a kind of church carnival object. The Benedictine abbot Gerbert (Archbishop of Rheims, 991–5) was said by William of Malmesbury to have had a hydraulic organ put into the cathedral: an object of mechanical ingenuity, once again coupled with a clock in the written account. Gerbert may have learnt the principles of the water organ from the Arabs in

Córdoba, where he lived for a time, since Benedictine manuscripts of the period do not suggest any practical familiarity with the writings of Hero or Vitruvius. Nothing is known of other 10th-century organs, such as that set up in Halberstadt Cathedral under its Benedictine bishop Hildeward; nor are contemporary references such as those of Notker Balbulus (*d*912) helpful towards an understanding of the nature and purpose of organs. So many of these writers, often interpreted literally, were merely indulging in metaphor.

One detail of the Bages consecration of 972 was that the organ music 'could be heard from afar', which may or may not imply that the organ was outside the church. But a large number of references, second-hand or glossed though many must be, suggest that the organ was a loud instrument by standards of the day. Is it possible to see the famous late 10th-century organ in one of the adjacent cathedrals of Winchester as a signal-organ, used on feast days to summon the congregation or overawe them (perhaps before or after services)? This does not preclude its having keys and some musical potential; 'signal-organ' describes its tone, something obviously more sophisticated than Muristus's war-siren. If the Winchester organ was placed near the west or south door (stone screens were not known until the next century, and at Winchester only the nave may have been capacious enough) its use could hardly have been liturgical. Nor is it easy to see how an organ could have been liturgical in a much partitioned church of the type known to the later Cistercians.

The Winchester organ was built by about 990, some decades after the Benedictines were fully established there and later than modern commentators have said. Details of it appear in a fanciful verse letter written shortly afterwards by the monk Wulfstan. Much quoted, much translated and much misunderstood, the poem speaks of 26 bellows and 400 pipes in ten ranks, with the 40 notes arranged as two sets of 20 keys played by 'two brethren of concordant spirit'. Each key was a perforated slider pushed in and probably pulled out – hence the need for two or more players. Clearly some kind of organ did exist; but there are good reasons for distrusting Wulfstan's account: despite the fanciful references by St Aldhelm to what appear to be 100- and 1000-pipe organs, there are no other firm details extant of such large organs, at Winchester or anywhere else; the numbers given for bellows, blowers (70), pipes, ranks and keys are not plausible, whatever the diameter of the pipes and however the wind was raised (even the number of players smacks of literary tradition or at least of the poorly drawn hydraulis in the Utrecht Psalter, perhaps known to Wulfstan personally); the general style and character of Wulfstan's poem are those of an impressionable layman not concerned with technical accuracy (for further details see McKinnon, 1974).

Theophilus's organ (see fig.2) could be placed within the wall, presumably at gallery level, with only its chest and pipes visible from the church and these indeed covered by a cloth 'tent' when not in use. Later 13th-century screen organs would have been equally well placed, in some cases better placed, when they came to serve as *alternatim* instruments in the liturgy. Many details of Theophilus's organ are unclear, not least its function in the church. Theophilus was a monk, probably German, working in the first half of the 11th century on a large encyclopedia describing techniques used in making church objects – glass blowing, painting, gilding, metal forg-

ing, bell casting, organ making. The sources of his treatise leave its authenticity uncertain, the last part of it probably being a later compilation. A second 11th-century treatise is the anonymous Berne Codex, a manuscript possibly originating at the Benedictine abbey of Fleury; a third is a note by Aribo on pipe making. These three sources are rather more practical than many later medieval manuscripts (see §5 below).

Theophilus first advised his reader or builder to equip himself with a treatise on pipe measurement ('lectio mensurae'); this 'lectio' would presumably contain a table of concrete values or actual pipe-scales, rather than mere Pythagorean ratios. The pipe copper was to be beaten very thin and shaped on a gently conical mandrel (i.e. the foot and the resonator would be of one conical piece), a statement not easily credible. Information in the Berne Codex seems to suggest the familiar pipe-foot. Theophilus's pipes are equal in diameter, which may not be unreasonable in an organ of less than two octaves. The Berne Codex gives 'almost 4''' as the longest pipe but does not indicate the length of the foot unit. It is not certain that actual pipes could be made to the given scales since no allowance is made for end correction, and the compass and arrangement correspond rather to the 'theoretical' texts then in circulation. The pipes are soldered, and their mouths probably resemble the pressed-

24. *Terracotta lamp in the form of a hydraulic organ (? 2nd century AD) found at Carthage (Musée National, Carthage)*

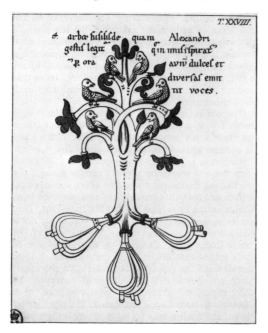

T: XXVIII.

25. Byzantine automaton, with whistling birds activated by wind kept under water pressure: drawing after a 12th-century MS from St Blasien, published by Gerbert in his 'De cantu' (1774)

in apertures familiar from late Roman iconography. Theophilus also referred to voicing of the pipes carried out at the mouth, whereby the tone could be made 'more rotund' ('grossam') or 'thinner' ('graciliorem'). No chest is known to have had sliders or separate stops, and the organ supplied a strong sound rather than the Vitruvian–Aquincum variety of softer organ-colour.

In his section on forging Theophilus described bellows, and from other sources of the period it seems that such bellows were large, capacious, and planned to compensate for leaks between feeder and pipe. The feeders direct wind into a *conflatorium* or receiver, shown in some 11th- or 12th-century miniatures such as the Harding Bible (see fig.27, p.860) and Cambridge Psalter. In the Berne Codex the valve preventing the return of wind when the bellows are refilled is placed in the collector, while Theophilus's valve is in the head of each bellows. The main duct can be curved or straight (? not mitred) and is usually shown as generously proportioned. The keys of the Berne Codex organ closely resemble Hero's, consisting of a 'square' depressed at one end, pushing in a perforated slider (to which it is attached) at the other, and pulled back by a horn-spring to which it is tied. By the 13th century, according to a miniature in the Belvoir Castle Psalter (see fig.28, p.861), organists were using their fingers separately (and rather elegantly) to depress the keys, which in this miniature were broader and more substantial than some reproductions of it suggest.

5. MEDIEVAL ORGAN THEORISTS. In the absence of any known organ remains between the 3rd-century organ of Aquincum and the (?) late 14th-century positives of Sweden (see §6 below), historians must turn to the body of 'medieval organ pipe theory', readings of which have led to some misleading ideas about medieval organs.

The many sources have been seen as 'treatises on organ building' (Frotscher, Mahrenholz, Fellerer) or 'treatises on pipe measurement' (Perrot, 1965); but after 1966 researches into the now completely collated texts (see K.-J. Sachs, 1970) have led to a new assessment of their purposes.

The texts, in some cases only a few sentences in clerical Latin, fall into three main categories. The largest group (about 30 texts in 155 sources from the 10th century onwards) are those concerned with the length of organ pipes calculated by ratios from an 'initial' pipe, itself of no specified length; most of the length measurements take account of end correction which, in the case of a row of pipes of the same width and mouth shape, is constant. A smaller group of texts (11, in 11 sources) is concerned with the width or diameter of organ pipes, ignoring end correction in calculating the length; some of these discuss the relationship of mouth width, cut-up and foot-hole to the pipe diameter; none dates from before the 14th century. Neither of these two groups covers the whole subject, since in fact variable pipe-widths and quasi-Pythagorean demonstration of end correction are mutually exclusive. The third group of texts (three only, all 11th-century) deals with technical pipe making. These texts are Theophilus's *De diversis artibus* (bk 3, pp.81ff), *Cuprum purissimum* (the Berne Codex), and the section 'Sicut fistulae' on pipe making from Aribo's *Musica*. Some aspects of the organs described in this last group of sources have received attention in §4 above.

The 'pipe-length treatises' rarely offer concrete usable measurements, nor do they outline any pattern of values in which practical experience may have had a hand. Instead, the scalings concern proportional value corresponding to the Pythagorean ratios known from monochord theory. On the one hand, it is obviously possible to make an organ without determining the acoustical phenomenon of pipes; on the other, no careful measuring of pipes leads to usable pitches without proper tuning. Many treatises so resemble the numerous scaling texts for the monochord and *cymbala* that the significance of their pipe-scalings should not be interpreted in isolation; for pipes, strings and bells might have been cited primarily as examples of Pythagorean ratios according to which a pipe approximately half as long as another will sound the octave above, one approximately two-thirds as long the 5th above, and so on. Comprehensive instruction treatises covering such matters include the works of Notker Labeo, Aribo, Engelbert of Admont, Jerome of Moravia, Walter Odington and Georgius Anselmi; an important branch in the tradition was the widely known *Scolia enchiriadis* of the late 9th century. In no way were such sources recipes for making instruments; rather, they outlined the kind of number theory which theorists since Boethius had applied to music.

Both Theophilus and the writer of the Berne Codex were dependent on ancient accounts, namely those of Vitruvius and Hero. Aribo's account probably refers back to a manuscript tradition around the uncertain figure of Wilhelm of Hirsau, who seems indeed to have been concerned with actual pipe measurement. Most of the copies of a text ascribed to him are provided with drawings showing the scale of the first pipe (not unlike the measure line in Schlick's *Spiegel*, 1511). But in other writers, end correction, the very factor 'disturbing' the neat theory of Pythagorean ratios, was itself determined proportionally, calculated as a fraction of the diameter. For such calculation the diameter was assumed to be constant; hence the frequently repeated conclusion that the medieval organ builder made a rank of pipes all to the same diameter. Optimistically interpreted iconography has been seen to support this idea. But it should be remembered that the general medieval approach to making things (i.e. before print technology brought craftsmen gradually to depend on visual models) weighs against the practical significance of written-down treatises. Only two of the texts cover organ building as such, and they are partly derived or even (in the case of Theophilus) the result of a compilation. Moreover, practical details such as the remark in the Berne Codex that pipes follow the modern diatonic genus ('si . . . sit diatonicum genus quo maxime decurrent moderne cantilene') do not necessarily indicate an actual organ used in liturgical music. The Sélestat manuscript (11th century) and the Berne Codex describe pipe-chests of seven notes, and the former seems to make it clear that its three ranks are unison, octave, unison; at the same time, an 11th- or 12th-century miniature, in the Harding Bible, shows a keyboard of C, D, E, F, G, A, B♭, B♮, a set of keys showing one each of the known notes (see fig.27). But it is not known whether these treatises and miniatures reflect more than certain literate, second-hand and even non-empirical traditions passed on, perhaps indirectly, to their scribal 'authors'.

6. THE CHURCH ORGAN 1100–1450. Rarely in music history is conjecture taken more confidently as fact than in this area. Despite bold and apparently plausible modern assertions that playing in 4ths and 5ths was known by 9th-century clerical organists, that *alternatim* chants were known in the Mass during the 11th century, or that large organs played the *puncti organici* (and even the quicker upper parts or *voces organales*) in the Île-de-France organa of the 13th century, there is no irrefutable evidence to support them. It may be reasonable to assume that in the larger Benedictine abbeys (St Gall, Metz, Benevento) polyphony, organ playing and troping of plainchant were all linked; but it is not known during which century the more cosmopolitan of the abbeys may have begun to use the organ more integrally during Mass than they were ever to use their other expensive mechanical equipment such as bells or clocks. Nor are

technical matters concerning the structure of organs any more certain. There is no evidence that, between the 10th and 12th centuries, octave- and 5th-speaking ranks were used in abundance, or that reed and stopped pipes were also known, as more than one modern writer has claimed. Much later still, basic assumptions are unreliable. Iconography by no means establishes that organists had to use all of each hand to thump the keys, at this or any point in organ history. Nor are archives less equivocal; church accounts do not prove that the 'little organs' sometimes mentioned from about 1390 onwards were second manuals of large organs or that, if so, such manuals were placed together or had the same pitch. Possibly the second keyboard, up until at least the time of the Innsbruck Hofkirche organ (1550; the oldest extant two-manual organ), should be seen rather as an extension to the compass of the first. Organ research from about 1960 has been directed towards a circumspect interpretation of the evidence, and a new period of doubt about the evolution of the organ is inevitable.

Certainly the period 1100–1450 was one of great activity. During the 11th century more organs are known to have been in monastic churches throughout western Europe; they were played at ceremonies (probably outside the liturgy) and succumbed to the fires that frequently swept medieval cathedrals (Canterbury 1114, Freising 1158, Merseburg, 1199) – which suggests perhaps that they were fixed in place. Some literary sources imply that the organ was played during Mass, for instance the *Roman de brut* (c1155, Normandy):

> Quant li messe fu commensie . . .
> Mout oissiés orgues sonner
> Et clercs chanter et orguener

– but such references are vague and merely image-evoking; poets' sources were usually other poets. More authentic sources of the 9th and 10th centuries suggest, however, that sequences as well as the *Te Deum* were the most open to polyphonic vocal treatment, just as later they were the movements most closely associated with the organ. A small portative and psaltery are shown in a 12th-century miniature but no ecclesiastical function is implied, any more than for the portatives illustrating psalms in earlier psalters (e.g. the organa hanging

26. *Hydraulic organ (centre) with horns, cymbals, lyres, a psaltery and lute: drawing illustrating Psalm cxlix from the Utrecht Psalter (9th or 10th century, possibly after a model from 5th- or 6th-century Alexandria or Byzantium) (NL-Uu 32, f.83r)*

27. *Organ with sliders and a conflatorium: drawing from the Harding Bible, French, 11th or 12th century (F-Dm 14, f.13v)*

on willow trees at Psalm cxxxvii in the Stuttgart Psalter, 10th century). But by the 13th century all instruments other than the organ were excluded from various churches in Spain, Italy and France. The phrase 'great organs' is found in church documents (e.g. Erfurt Peterskirche, 1291) and by 1296 one French bishop referred to the organ sounding five times in connection with the Sanctus – perhaps as a signal rather than for music as such. There is no evidence that it played the tenor in Sanctus movements or in any motet following at that point during Mass. But by the end of the 13th century secular cathedrals from Exeter to Prague, Barcelona to Lübeck, were as likely to have organs as the larger abbey churches. Whether erected on screens (as in England) or hanging on an upper wall of nave or quire, the organs were usually located near the *cantores*, i.e. no longer near the west or south entrances nor specifically near the main altar. It is not known, however, when large organs were fixed in Theophilus's manner, and illustrations for psalm texts usually show much smaller organs in ensemble. The phenomenon of the smaller fixed organ attached to, associated with, and in some cases paid for by specially bequeathed chapels belongs to the 15th rather than the 13th century.

The large organ seems to have been an exclusively ecclesiastical instrument from the 9th-century Western Church to 17th-century Italy. Probably by the late 13th century the cathedral or abbey organ was occasionally used in *alternatim* music with the *cantores*, though presumably not with the congregation itself. Jovannes de Florentia referred (c1350) to rendition 'partim organo partim modulatis per concentum vocibus'. Early 15th-century keyboard repertory extant in the Faenza Codex

(*I-FZc* 117) complements such explicit references as the mid-15th-century Castilian rubric 'los organos tañían un verso et los clerigos cantavan otre'. 14th-century documents usually suggest that whatever the organ played, it did so on traditional church or local feast days, for example at Halberstadt Cathedral on Christmas Day, for Easter Week, Sunday after Easter, *Kreuzerfindung*, Reliques of St Stephen, Ascension, SS Peter and Paul, Dispersal of the Apostles, Mary Magdalene, SS Stephen and Sixtus, Assumption, Patron, Nativity of Mary, St Michael, St Gall, All Saints and 12 other feast days including Trinity and Annunciation. For three centuries organs were used only on feast days. But by the end of the 13th century some churches had decreed against other instruments (Milan, 1287); by the 14th, *alternatim* performances took place, especially in the Office; by the early 15th, many areas, such as the Upper Rhineland, north-central Germany, some English and Italian cities, and the stretch from Rouen to Utrecht, had organs in most of their larger churches, and the future of the instrument was completely assured.

It is impossible to trace this history step by step, despite a certain amount of archival, musical and iconographical evidence. But certain general points can be made about the 14th and early 15th centuries. Organs became known in cathedrals less as an exception and more as a norm; by 1425 the large positive (with front pipes arranged from left to right) was usually distinct from the fixed church organ (with front pipes in mitre form with a set of larger pipes to each side, thus requiring a rollerboard). All the evidence suggests that only open metal flue pipes were known, though some commentators have seen such references as 'plom . . . per las horguenas' (Eglise des Cordeliers, Avignon, 1372) as evidence that lead pipes were used for distinctive tone-colour. Larger organs in certain areas (Normandy and later the Netherlands) occasionally had Trompes during the period 1390–1450 (i.e. a set of ten or so large open metal Bourdon pipes, possibly played by a separate manual or pedal keyboard and placed to one side, or both sides, of the main organ). Presumably they also had a BLOCKWERK, although apart from the number of pipes in a few famous examples (e.g. 2000 at Amiens in 1429) little is known in this regard before 1450. Presumably the pitch of their compass, whether from (apparent) *B* or any other note, was roughly equivalent to men's voices, the total compass perhaps divided up and distributed over more than one keyboard. However, so many unknowns of paramount importance are raised by such summaries that describing the church organ before its clearly defined types of 1450 is mostly a matter of citing facts about individual instruments.

The organ at Sion, Switzerland, is usually dated about 1380 and has been much rebuilt. Despite opinions expressed on its tone, and although some of the original pipework seems to be incorporated in the present organ, nothing is certain of its original sound, disposition, compass, pitch, voicing, pressure, bellows, position, purpose or provenance. Nevertheless, its case (fig.29, p.862) shows interesting elements: it has the typical shape for such instruments, with the central mitre lines (like Arnaut de Zwolle's organ at Salins); the castellated 'towers' to left and right overhang the sides; and the wings (painted and perhaps made about 1434–7) enclose the pipes completely. At Bartenstein in East Prussia parts of the organ dated about 1395 existed before World War

II. The organ had a large chest for 27 keys (?*FGA–a′*) with three divisions for large chorus of nine (bass) to 21 (treble) ranks, case-pipes of 16′, and Principals 8′ + 4′. An ingenious reconstruction of the chest was sketched by Karl Bormann in 1966 but little is certain, particularly the stop-mechanism whereby wind was admitted to chorus and principals at will; perhaps the device was made not in 1395 but one or two centuries later (see §V, 3 below). The organ at Norrlanda (*c*1380), now pipeless and in the Stockholm Museum, is a large positive with a putative *Blockwerk* of three to six ranks. A set of 12 rollers conveys not only both pedal and manual key-travel to the larger pipes held in small side towers but also the action of certain pairs of keys (*C*♯/*c*♯, *D*♯/*d*♯, *F*♯/*f*♯, *G*♯/*g*♯) to a single pallet. This is so sophisticated an arrangement, not least in its resulting chromatic keyboard of nearly two octaves (*C–a* or *c–a′*; fig.30, p.863), that doubts must also arise about the age of the organ – which is in any case constructed out of panels from some older choir stalls.

Extant 12th- and 13th-century church accounts merely record the presence of an organ; about many areas of Europe, curiously little is known. Only during the 15th century were the great Gothic churches of some areas constructed (e.g. in the Netherlands), but many were immediately provided with an organ as part of the regular furniture. The first real details of church organs occur in such documents as builders' contracts from about 1390 onwards, when for reference purposes the anonymous scribe would distinguish the 'opus maius' from the 'parvum opus organum' (Utrecht Cathedral, perhaps suggesting an organ with *Rückpositiv*) or the 'principaulx' pipes from the Bourdons (Rouen Cathedral, suggesting Trompes and other major Fourniture ranks), or even by 1420 'cinch tirants', suggesting separate stops in a large positive (Aragonese royal chapel). Otherwise it was enough for an organ to be entrusted to the craftsman concerned, who had merely to see that it was 'decent, good and to the honour' of the church (S Giovanni Evangelista, Venice, 1430).

Henri Arnaut de Zwolle, writing in the 1440s, described several organs he knew, including those at Salins (*c*1400, *Blockwerk* of 6–15 ranks) and Dijon (*c*1350, 8–24 ranks); an account of his treatise is given below (§V, 1). The most famous 14th-century organ is that of Halberstadt Cathedral (*c*1361, rebuilt 1495), described in some detail by Praetorius (2/1619). The four keyboards were as follows: I, called *Diskant* by Praetorius, playing the plenum (case pipes + Hintersatz Mixture), *B–c′* (14 keys); II, also called *Diskant*, playing case pipes (Prinzipal) only, same compass; III, called *Bassklavier*, *B–a* (12 keys, long protruding levers perhaps worked by the knee, playing the 12 large bass pipes); IV, pedal keyboard, same compass as III, used with (perhaps pulling down the keys of) the top manual. The largest rank of pipes was at the equivalent of 32′ pitch, the total number about 1192, from 16 ranks at pedal *B* to 56 at top manual *a′*. (These pitch names are by Praetorius; it should be remembered that in this or any other account of a keyboard instrument before about 1500, to express the compass of pitches in terms of *c–a* or *b–c′* etc is anachronistic and hence misleading).

Praetorius by no means understood the historical nature of such old organs, nor is it clear from his report what in the organ dated from 1361, what from 1495. But it is probable from his account that the *Blockwerk* had multiple ranks of octaves and 5ths such that the manual disposition was approximately as follows:

B–e $16.16.8.8.8.5\frac{1}{3}.5\frac{1}{3}.5\frac{1}{3}.5\frac{1}{3}.4.4.4.4.4.2\frac{2}{3}.2\frac{2}{3}.2\frac{2}{3}.2\frac{2}{3}.2\frac{2}{3}.2\frac{2}{3}$
$2.2.2.2.2.2.1.1.1.1.1.1$

f–c′ $16.16.8.8.8.8.5\frac{1}{3}.5\frac{1}{3}.5\frac{1}{3}.5\frac{1}{3}.5\frac{1}{3}.4.4.4.4.4.4.2\frac{2}{3}.2\frac{2}{3}.2\frac{2}{3}.2\frac{2}{3}.$
$2\frac{2}{3}.2\frac{2}{3}.2\frac{2}{3}.2.2.2.2.2.2.2.2.1.1.1.1.1.1.1.1.1$

d′–a′ $16.16.8.8.8.8.8.5\frac{1}{3}.5\frac{1}{3}.5\frac{1}{3}.5\frac{1}{3}.5\frac{1}{3}.5\frac{1}{3}.4.4.4.4.4.4.4.2\frac{2}{3}.2\frac{2}{3}.$
$2\frac{2}{3}.2\frac{2}{3}.2\frac{2}{3}.2\frac{2}{3}.2\frac{2}{3}.2\frac{2}{3}.2\frac{2}{3}.2.2.2.2.2.2.2.2.2.2.$
$2.1.1.1.1.1.1.1.1.1.1.1.1.1$

From the details given, the pitch level seems to have been *a′* = *c*505. Praetorius also described the sound of this *Blockwerk* (*see* BLOCKWERK). 20 bellows supplied the wind, all presumably needing to be operated for the plenum, though his drawing shows only two men.

Praetorius gave other details about organs he described as old, and his suggestions could be the starting-point for organ historians. For example, he guessed that semitones appeared in keyboard compass from about 1200 and pedals from about 1220, that by 1450 only open pipes were known, but that spring-chests had been built by about 1400 and separate stops by about 1250. The first date is late by two centuries if it is a question of B♭ only, perhaps a reasonable guess if intended to refer to the first *ficta* semitone (i.e. other than B♭), but early by at least one century if all five semitones were meant. The date for pedals must be about a century too early. The date for open pipes is probably correct, and that for spring-chests could be correct but is probably a little early. The date for separate stops seems early by at least two centuries if it refers to a full-sized church *Orgelwerk*. Other details given by Praetorius are more certain, for example that some keys were as broad as about 60 mm, that some keyboards had a compass of *B–f′* or *c–a′* (diatonic only) and the curious-seeming statement that some early pedals played only the bass notes. Obvious though the last may appear, the large Bourdons or 'teneurs' (Notre Dame, Rouen, 1382) may in fact

28. King David playing a positive organ (apparently depressing the keys with separate fingers), with a symphonia (hurdy-gurdy) and cymbalum: miniature from the Rutland (Belvoir) Psalter (f.97v), English, c1270 (private collection)

29. *Organ (c1380, pedal pipes 1718), perhaps from Abondance Abbey (Savoy), now on the west wall of the Cathedral of Notre Dame de Valère, Sion*

often have been operated by a keyboard played in the hands or even by the knees. The term 'teneur' is evocative, but what it signifies is uncertain; perhaps the keys played the long notes of a vocal composition or an *Intavolierung*; perhaps 'teneurs' meant merely large pipes as distinct from small ('menus' at Rouen, 1382, 'Diskant' in Praetorius). Certainly the playing of a cantus firmus *en taille* on the pedals is a later speciality of the 16th century. But whatever 'teneurs' was meant to imply, builders of the period knew well how to fashion pipes of various sizes and scale, according to Praetorius.

At the end of the 14th century, then, a large organ within the area Rouen–Utrecht–Madgeburg–Orvieto–Rouen might be presumed to have had a *Blockwerk* of anything up to 80 or more ranks with open cylindrical pipes of metal, played by a broad-keyed manual of 16 to 22 notes, possibly with a further keyboard playing Trompes with or without their own chorus mixture, and exceptionally with a second smaller organ in some way connected with the first. Smaller but independent organs may have had, by custom, a longer compass, smaller keys, and a *Blockwerk* of fewer ranks. Not enough is yet known for generalizations to be made about the organ of about 1390 outside the region specified above.

7. THE 15TH-CENTURY POSITIVE AND PORTATIVE. Although the POSITIVE and the PORTATIVE each form virtually separate subjects, they offer a useful gloss on organ history at this point because each demonstrates a striking uniformity unknown to the larger fixed organ, and each demonstrates the limitations of iconographical evidence. Portatives were small portable organs blown by a pair of bellows operated by one of the player's hands (usually the left), and played by his other hand on a keyboard of up to two octaves, composed most often of touch-buttons; the instrument would have one rank of pipes arranged in one or two (very rarely three) apparent rows. Such are the highly detailed and prettily finished portatives depicted by such painters as Memling (three examples, that at Bruges is the clearest: for illustration *see* PORTATIVE) and the Master of St Barthélémy (two examples). Positives were blown by a pair of larger bellows operated by a second person (fig.31, p.864), and were played by both of the organist's hands on a more or less chromatic keyboard exceeding two octaves (usually beginning at *B*) and composed of short finger-keys; two rows of pipes would form one complete rank, often with Bourdon pipes pitched in the bass, perhaps an octave below. Some portatives also had (shorter) Bourdon pipes. In all known cases the pipes were open and of metal; the scaling is progressive and the diameters diminish, at least in the better depictions; cut-ups often appear low and the scale narrow; unless chords of more than two notes were played, the wind supplied by the hand bellows must have been quite adequate, though presumably low in pressure.

That paintings always leave problems of interpretation may be demonstrated by one of the best known of all organ paintings, the Van Eyck altarpiece at Ghent (1432). Despite the beauty and apparent precision of the picture, the pertinent section of which is reproduced in fig.32 (p.865), there are several puzzles. The front pipes, though painted well, are not placed naturally; the tips of the feet rest right at the front of the chest top-board, while each pipe corpus, whatever its diameter, passes behind the supporting brace, itself, however, of constant thickness. The feet of the inner row of pipes are placed almost without depth of perspective, all exactly in the middle of those of the first row – despite the latter's perspective. Unless the keyboard ran no higher than appears (blocked by the player's hand and arm) the two rows of pipes must produce only one rank; yet if the keyboard continued up symmetrically (as far to the right as the bass goes to the left) the organ would have at least 35 keys, implying a unique pipework of two non-chromatic ranks. The line made by the pipe-tops corresponds neither quite to a diatonic nor to a chromatic tuning, and the pipes in the bass are unnaturally narrow in scale. Apart from these problems of depiction, the painting gives no information at all on certain points, such as the purpose of the latch-key on the lower left; if it is for a Tremulant, one might expect other evidence of the period for such stops; if it is a stop mechanism operating a valve to the rear chest, one must assume that there are other pipes not seen but making up the second rank; if it is a key to operate Bourdon or drone pipes, the pipes should be in evidence. Such questions can be answered plausibly enough, but only by means of simple conjecture, for comparisons with other instruments are too distant to be useful.

V. The organ 1450–1800. While much research

remains to be done for the beginning of this period, especially on developments in German organs of the area Mainz–Nuremberg–Innsbruck–Basle–Mainz, a provisional historical sketch can be derived from Henri Arnaut's treatise and from certain documents concerning organs about 1450 that contain details necessary to those drawing up church contracts (such was the growing complexity and variety of the organ).

1. The treatise of Henri Arnaut de Zwolle. 2. Developments 1450–1500. 3. Arnolt Schlick's 'Spiegel der Orgelmacher'. 4. The new potential of the 16th century. 5. Structural developments about 1600. 6. The Werkprinzip organ. 7. The French classical organ. 8. The English organ. 9. The Spanish Baroque organ. 10. The 18th-century Italian organ. 11. The organ of J. S. Bach. 12. Splendours of northern Europe, 1650–1800. 13. Organs in the Americas.

1. THE TREATISE OF HENRI ARNAUT DE ZWOLLE. Although concerned primarily with small organs, Arnaut's treatise (*F-Pn* lat.7295; ed. and facs. in Le Cerf and Labande, 1932) throws much light on the potential which organs were seen to have by 1450. The treatise was written in Dijon between 1436 and 1454, partly by Arnaut, a Dutch polymath at the Burgundian court of Philip the Good, and partly by two other authors or scribes. It reflects a lively cultural exchange between Burgundy, Paris and the Low Countries, which, however, is sometimes overestimated in the absence of primary source material for other major 'organ schools' of the period. Arnaut's remarks are more practical than those of any treatise since the 11th century. His description of an organ pipe is empirical and systematic; details suggest a widely tapered scale, i.e. with some ten semitones narrower than *Normalmensur* at bass *B* but some seven semitones wider than *Normalmensur* at a hypothetical treble *b″*. The mouth width is about a quarter of the circumference ($\frac{2}{7}$ for bigger-toned pipes), the cut-up a quarter of the mouth width; the foot-hole diameter of a quarter of the pipe width was large, though easily reducible. From the measurements it is unclear whether Arnaut was working from two pitches of $a' = c395$ and $a' = c435$ or from a mean *tonus cori* of $a' = c415$. Two portative or positive chests ('ciste portivorum') are drawn and described. In one, a single rank of pipes for the compass $b-g'''\ a'''$ is arranged 'ad modum mitre episcopalis' (i.e. as a mitre, tallest pipes in the middle); in the other, a rank for the compass $b-f'''$ is arranged in the more usual chromatic manner, tallest to left, shortest to right ('ciste communis' or 'the usual chest'). Arnaut also drew the front of a standard larger organ of the Sion type, probably the instrument at Salins (Salin, formerly in Burgundy), whose 4′ *Blockwerk* he later specified as *B* (6 ranks)–*f″* (21 ranks).

On f.127 of Arnaut's manuscript occurs the first incontrovertible reference in organ building to reed stops. On a page of scarcely 20 words (and ten figures) apropos the 'diapason . . . calamorum dei custodientium' ('scales . . . of the pipes in the church of the Dei custodientes') occurs the phrase 'l'anche de F', which apparently refers to the reed and block of a reed pipe. Arnaut seems to be saying that a rank of such pipes from *B* to *b′* needs eight different sizes of block. Why he gave no other details is unknown.

Of the organ of about 1350 in Notre Dame, Dijon, Arnaut noted that the pipes (*B–a″*) are already old and corroded ('antiqui et pulverosi'); the pipe mouths were generally about half an octave too narrow, in his opinion. The Fourniture is mentioned, apparently the only separable part of the plenum. The total number of pipes in the organ was 768; the leather bellows (?*c*1350,

?*c*1440) had three folds and measured *c*160 cm by *c*70 cm. Arnaut also gave in tabular form the disposition of four different *Blockwerke*, one of *F* (8 ranks)–*e‴* (21 ranks), two of *B′–f″* (6–21, 6–15 ranks) and one of *B′* (10 ranks)–*a′b′* (26 ranks). The first has three categories (Principal, Cymbale, Fourniture), suggesting 'stops' made to play separately by two manuals or perhaps by some mechanical device (possibly a divided chest operated by a *Sperrventil*). The Principal 8′ has at the top four ranks and the Fourniture 14 (making 8.8.8.5$\frac{1}{3}$.5$\frac{1}{3}$.4.4.4.4.4.4.4.4.4); the Cymbale is nothing less than a three-rank *Terzzimbel*, indeed the first documented mixture containing a Tierce rank. The Cymbale repeats, 29.31.33 at *B*, 8.10.15 at *e‴*.

One of the other three organs was apparently that at Salins, which had a long-compass 4′ *Blockwerk* of:

B′–E	8.8.15.15.19.22
F–B♭	8.8.15.15.19.19.22.22
B–e	8.8.12.12.15.15.19.19.22.22
f–b♭	8.8.12.12.15.15.19.19.19.22.22.22
b–e′	8.8.12.12.15.15.15.19.19.19.22.22.22
f′–b♭′	8.8.8.12.12.15.15.15.19.19.19.22.22.22.22
b′–f″	8.8.8.12.12.15.15.15.19.19.19.22.22.22.22

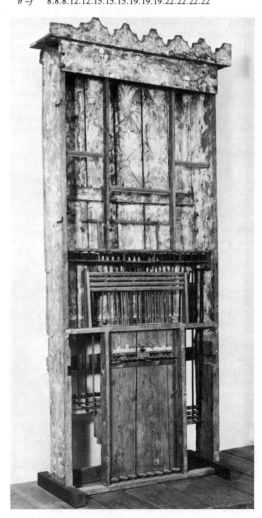

30. *Positive organ (c1380, now pipeless) from Norrlanda (Musikmuseet, Stockholm)*

Even more important, perhaps, is that Arnaut's Fourniture is not an accumulative *Blockwerk* but a Mixture that breaks back in the upper octaves.

Arnaut referred also to the 12 'fistulas tenoris' at St Cyr (probably Nevers Cathedral), i.e. 12 Trompes or bass pipes, half as long again as the lowest ranks of the chorus. These pipes had no Fourniture ranks of their own, and were thus presumably played from a separate keyboard. At the church of the Cordeliers (?Dijon), the ten 'subdupla tenoris' pipes had a separate keyboard which could couple with that of the chorus, thus affording three effects: the usual chorus, the chorus + *tenor* or Bourdon pipes, or *tenor* pipes played by the left hand while the right hand played the chorus or *discantus*. It is unclear whether 'double Principal' ('duplicia principalia') meant that the 8′ Diapason had two open pipes or one open and one stopped; nor is it clear from later accounts (e.g. the contract at All Hallows, Barking, 1519) what exactly 'double principals' meant, despite assertions made by some modern writers. The 'simplicia principalia' of the Dijon court chapel organ was described by Arnaut as 'in duo divisa', which may mean either one halved rank (with treble and bass stops) or the usual paired Principals separated off, perhaps by a slider. Two quints and an octave gave the organ a total of 'quinque registra' ('five registers'), possibly with five push-pull slider-ends.

Further light is thrown on Chair organs ('tergali positivo'). Arnaut described one with 195 pipes, *FG–f″* at 4′ pitch and a four- to seven-rank *Blockwerk* of octave ranks only. The front pipes were of tin, the others of lead, the measurements of neither the mouths nor the foot-holes were systematic or regular in the particular

31. Positive organ: engraving of an organist and his wife by Israel van Meckenem (d 1503)

Chair organ Arnaut was referring to, and he was puzzled as to why it nevertheless sounded well.

Though never completed, Arnaut's draft treatise stands as something unique in organ building, not least in its description of certain *Blockwerk* or *plein jeu* choruses, the most characteristic of all organ sounds. During the whole of the next century no source was to describe in such detail how an organ builder could plan his chorus. Contemporary documents, like modern histories, prefer to dwell on the new colour stops and other, essentially secondary effects.

2. DEVELOPMENTS 1450–1500. Not only do Arnaut's remarks give a partial picture of the organ at this period, but contracts and other documents from other areas of Europe give corroborating details. Thus the organ at St Sebald, Nuremberg (by H. Traxdorf, 1439–41) had Principal, Fourniture and Cymbale, perhaps of the type described by Arnaut. Such a division of the chorus became a kind of norm, not only at Nuremberg but also at St Florian, Koblenz (1467), St George, Hagenau (1491), Weimar (1492), St Peter, Basle (1496), Louvain (1522) and in organs farther west. Yet it seems that the instrument of 1474–83 in S Petronio, Bologna, already had a large-scale, 50-note complement of nine single-rank stops (smaller in all respects than the organ as it now is), thus presenting a quite different tradition of organ building.

Clearly the crucial questions are: how were stops separated, giving the organ different colours or effects, and why did builders of some areas give an organ several manuals while those in others concentrated on one manual? As to the second question, it can only be conjectured that southern builders learnt earlier than northern – perhaps their materials made it more feasible – how variety could be given by one keyboard with separate ranks and a long, versatile compass (e.g. the 53 or 54 notes at S Martino, Lucca, in 1473); and that northern builders, requiring only a few different effects (Diapasons alone, or the plenum) found that two or even three shorter or unequal keyboards with one or two registrations each were more useful and probably more powerful. Division of an organ into several chests was practical from the point of view of wind supply. As to the first question of how stops were separated, the situation is clearer. Several documents from the middle of the 15th century onwards refer to the varieties of sound achieved by a particular organ: Arnaut used 'registra'; references in church archives include, 'registros' (Treviso, 1436), 'tirans' (Aragon, 1420; Barcelona, 1480), 'division de veus' (St Mathieu, Perpignan, 1516), 'dreen gelueden' ('three sounds', Grote Kerk, Zwolle, 1447) and even 'a la moderna cum registri sei' ('with six stops in the modern manner', Cattaro, 1488). How were these varieties achieved? 'Registers' and 'tirants' (even five 'registres sive tirans' at Avignon in 1539) certainly suggest slider-chests (see fig.5b). After all, the Roman organ of Aquincum had latitudinal sliders, and its keys admitted wind to the pipes by these means. Longitudinal sliders running the whole length of a rank of pipes were different only in application, not in principle. However, when and where stop-sliders were first made is not known; no doubt they first appeared on small organs. A further system, the spring-chest (see fig.5c), was reinvented in the Netherlands about 1520 to give greater reliability in larger organs, but was already known in Italy during the previous century: Orvieto Cathedral is said to have had an organ in 1480 with two spring-stops and two slider-stops. The most common 15th-century arrangement, particularly in the area from Rouen to Zwolle, was the 'double chest', useful especially for Chair organs. In such a chest the channels were divided into two parts, front (case pipes) and back (Mixture or Hintersatz), each with its wind box, the back one of which was provided with a shut-off valve allowing the Mixture to be taken off. Evidence for such chests is fairly clear from several Dutch contracts of the period (Zwolle, 1447; The Hague, 1487).

Much less clear is the origin of stopped pipes, although it is usual to suppose that the 'double Principal' of late 15th-century organs implied an inner rank of stopped pipes sounding with the open case pipes. 'Coppel' was a name used at first probably for case pipes (Limburg, 1471), later for stopped Diapason pipes (Bienne, Switzerland, 1517). Much the same may be said about the term 'Flotwerck' (Bassevelde, 1481). The 'lead pipes' for inner ranks referred to in contracts of many languages and areas have also often been assumed to be stopped pipes, but the documentary evidence is unclear. The Quintadena is a stopped rank referred to and often called *Schallpfeifen* early in the next century; it is possible that the emphasis on new organ colours at this later period was responsible for stopped pipes in general. Thus the stopped Holpyp is authenticated from about 1500, but hardly before. Schlick (1511) was still ambiguous about stopped pipes; even Flute stops at that period (e.g. St Michel, Bordeaux, 1510) were open, as indeed they remained in Italian organs of a later century.

To sum up, in 1500 the average organ in northern Italy or southern France could be expected to have a chorus of ten or so separate stops, probably achieved with a spring-chest if the organ were somewhat large, with sliders if smaller; the upper ranks may have been duplicated here and there. Spain, at least in cities influenced by Flemish or 'German' builders (Barcelona, Valencia), followed more the transalpine organ. The bigger instruments of the Netherlands and Rhineland had two or even three manual departments, in most cases each with its own keyboard but all at the same (or octave) pitch. The English organ, judging by the All Hallows document of 1519 (see §8 below), was of the smaller Dutch kind, though it is possible that at least in secular or aristocratic circles Italian organs were known.

Some examples of organ schemes at their best before the turn of the century are shown in Tables 1–3 (p.866). That such schemes were distinctly regional can be seen in a 1000-pipe instrument built by the German Bernhard Dilmano at Milan in 1464–6, probably a large northern organ of Principal, Mixture, Zimbel etc. The instrument was updated in 1487 but still had only eight separate stop-levers in 1508. However, it is not known how many ranks of a native Italian organ of 1475 would be separate (as in later Italian organs). As to the sound of such organs, only conjectures can be made, even when much of the original material still exists, as it does at S Petronio, Bologna. Although some contracts make it clear that specific sweetness or strength of tone was often required, much – perhaps too much – can be read into the use of words like 'lieblich' or 'süss' in early documentation.

See also §VIII, 5, below.

3. ARNOLT SCHLICK'S 'SPIEGEL DER ORGELMACHER'. Against the background of the special effects demanded

32. *Angel musicians with positive organ, harp and fiddle: panel from a polyptych, 'The Adoration of the Lamb' (1432), by Jan Van Eyck, in the cathedral of St Bavon, Ghent*

of new organs and promised to their clients by the builders, for example the Schwiegel, Waldhorn, Quintadena (Scheelpipen), Trumpets, Shawms, Zinks, Rauschpipe, Drums and 'other unusual stops' promised by Hans Suys at Antwerp Cathedral in 1509, Arnolt Schlick wrote a splendid, forthright little book on organs, publishing it in 1511 under imperial auspices and indeed apparently intending it as a kind of standard code of practice for organ builders in Maximilian's empire. Schlick lived in the central Palatinate court town of Heidelberg, and no doubt his influence was wide. The organ described in his *Spiegel* contained about 15 stops, 'not too many of the same type', as shown in Table 4. Schlick said that in addition, the *Hauptwerk* might contain a Krummhorn ('Kromphörner') and the pedal a Klein octaff and Zymmel, but that the latter two do not belong there. All stops should be playable separately so that the pedal if required could take the cantus firmus. The Hintersatz should not contain the very low ranks of the 'large Mixture' (? i.e. old *Blockwerk*), nor the 'low-pitched 3rds and 5ths' sometimes met with. There is little point in making separate $5\frac{1}{3}'$ stops, while the addition of various little chests such as *Brustwerke* merely increases cost and produces 'much sauce for little fish'. Reeds are not unreliable if properly made, and Schlick thought a competent organist could soon learn how to make the necessary minor adjustments to them. Stop-levers (preferably not push-pull) should be conveniently placed, not too long or too heavy to work from the keyboards.

Thus Schlick knew an organ of Principals, Mixtures and reeds; two manuals and pedal; probably a manual coupler; different open metal scalings (circumference to length 1 : 5, 1 : 6 or 1 : 7); and conical metal pipes, but not, evidently, stopped pipes or wooden ones. He recommended a compass of *F–a″* and a pitch level about a tone lower than that of today (his $a' = 374$–92, depending on the diameter of the pipe). The pipe metal was pure (or mostly pure) tin and the Principal was doubled (two open metal ranks of different scale). While recommending an irregular tuning with an A♭ that could also serve (if ornamented) as G♯ in a cadence on A, Schlick recognized that some preferred a regular meantone temperament (with major 3rds slightly larger than pure).

Some of Schlick's general attitudes to organs are informative. He felt that eight or nine stops in the Great were all that were needed; they should be clearly different in tone; and the second manual was to be regarded as a kind of small positive, in no sense a match for the Great. The organ (or a quire organ version of it) was used in connection with the liturgy, he observed; the priest at the altar was given notes for most Mass movements from the Gloria onwards. And since the organ had a particular part to play in such music as sequences, it was placed near the choir for convenience. The pedal may have been transmitted from the Great; certainly it should have stops of the same pitch as the main manual. The pedal must have separable stops like the Great; it should not be made up only of suboctave stops, as it then inverts the harmony. (This must presumably be a double reference to organs with extra large pedal pipes always sounded by the pedal keyboard, and to the practice, then probably rather new, of using the pedals to play inner tenor or cantus firmus lines.) Reed stops can be made well (some are mentioned that sounded new though nine years old). As to Mixtures, neither those consisting of 5ths and octaves nor those of 3rds and 5ths should contain low ranks. The full chorus should be able to play chords, i.e. the 5th ranks in Mixtures should not produce too dissonant a sound when the 5th C–G or the 3rd C–E is played; at the same time, the precise number of ranks in a Mixture depends on the size of the church. Manual keys should not be too long or short, too wide or narrow, nor spaced too far or too near; the given measurements suggest relatively stubby keys with an octave span about the same as on modern instruments.

Some of Schlick's own music in *Tablatur etlicher Lobgesang* (1512) is contrapuntal in a way that closely anticipates later organ chorales which use the theme

---

TABLE 1

Netherlands (Oude Kerk, Delft)

Adriaan Pieterszoon, 1458 (rebuild)

Grote werk: Blockwerk of 38 keys (*FG A–g″ a″*), 16′, ranks from about 6 to 32 (total *c*750 pipes)

Rugpositief: Double chest of 28 keys (*f–g″a″*), with two 'sounds', *een doef* (2-rank Principal 4′ or 8′) and *positief* (Mixture)

TABLE 2

Rhineland (St George, Hagenau)
F. Krebs, 1491

Manual
'driifach fleiten' (3-rank Principal 8′, 8′, ?4′)
'das werk' (Mixture)
'ein zymmet' (Zimbel)

Positif
'zwifach' (2-rank Principal or perhaps 'chest with two stops')

Pedal
'fleiten' (Principal)
'klein tenor' (? Principal octave above)
'zymmet' (Zymbel)

TABLE 3

Italy (S Giustina, Padua)
Leonhard of Salzburg, 1493

One manual of 38 keys (*FG A–g″a″*)

Tenori	8	Decimanona	$1\frac{1}{3}$
Ottava	4	Vigesimaseconda	1
Decimaquinta	2	Flauto	8

TABLE 4

Organ described by A. Schlick (1511)

Hauptwerk
'die Principaln' (2- or more rank Principal)
'ein Oktaff einer langen mess' ('long Octave', or *doppel* if a large organ was required)
'Gemsserhörner . . . kurtz weit moss' ('wide Gemshorn', an octave above the Principals)
'ein Zymmel' (Zimbel)
'Hindersatz' (large chorus mixture)
'die rauss Pfeifen' (Rauschpfeife imitating a shawm, ?i.e. a reed stop)
'hültze Glechter' (an unusual stop 'whose sound resembles that of small boys hitting a pot with a spoon', ?i.e. Quintadena)
'der Zinck' (Zink or Cornett, either a reed or a Tierce-holding flue Mixture)
'Schwiegeln' (Flageolet, ? of 2′)
'Register . . . gleich ein Positiff ein Regall oder ein Superregral' (another stop . . . 'like a Positive, Regal or Octave-regal', ? i.e. a Regal stop)

Rückpositiv
'die Principaln' (Principal, 'either of wood or of tin voiced like wood')
'Gemsslein' (small Gemshorn)
'Hindersetzlein' (small Mixture)
'guts rheins Zymmelein' ('good clean Zimbel', ? i.e. without Tierce)

Pedal
'Principaln ym Pedal' (Principal, ? transmitted from the *Hauptwerk*)
'Octaff'
'Hindersats' (Octave and Mixture, ? also transmitted)
'Trommetten oder Busaun' (Trompete or Posaune)

---

imitatively in three or four parts; in such pieces the pedal took the tune when it appeared in the bass. Schlick also knew pedal playing in two, three and even four parts, as well as pedal runs; for none of these functions would the old Trompes have been useful. The inner-voice cantus firmus technique, however, apparently requiring pedals for music from the Buxheim Organbook onwards, should not necessarily be taken at face value: such organ 'scores' must often have been open to various interpretations or playing methods.

The largest chapters of the *Spiegel* are concerned with tuning (*see* TEMPERAMENTS, §3), the making of chests, and the bellows. Schlick's advice is always very practical; for example, the wind must be generous (presumably for homophonic textures on full organ), the organ constantly played (even during Advent and Lent), and only the best and most experienced builders trusted. The little book thus surveys the whole field of organ activity – building, playing, composing – and even the long chapters on chests and tuning are full of good, pithy advice. For its size and single purpose, the *Spiegel* has never been bettered.

4. THE NEW POTENTIAL OF THE 16TH CENTURY. Soon after 1500 organs could produce a greater variety of colour and tonal effects than ever before because they had separate stops or several keyboards, or both. Many new stops (above all Flutes and reeds) were invented, and one or two extant documents of the period indicate how they were used. About 1510 in both the Rhineland (Worms) and southern France (Bordeaux), such documents contained advice (perhaps from the builder) about registration (*see* REGISTRATION, §I). Plena were mentioned, of course, but more interesting in view of Baroque registration were the two- or three-stop combinations; the list in Table 5 can be inferred from the Bordeaux 'instruction pour le jeu d'orgue'. The Bordeaux organ

TABLE 5

16 + 8	16 + 8 + 4 + 1⅓
16 + 1⅓	8 + 4 + 2⅔ + 2 + 1⅓ + 1
16 + 8 + 4	etc

was an Italianate instrument of nine separate single-rank stops, and within a small spectrum such ranks would yield many combinations. More instructive still are the German registrations (St Andreas, Worms; see Table 6), since they concern an organ with pedal and multi-rank stops. Schlick too wanted stops drawn in different combinations, and registrations changed.

TABLE 6

Germany (St Andreas, Worms)
*c*1510

Principals 4' or 2' alone
Hohlflöte 8' + Principal 4' or Hohlflöte 4'
Principals 4' + 2'
Principal 4' + Hohlflöte 4'
Hohlflöten 8' + 4' + Quinte 1⅓'
Regal 8' + Hohlflöte 8' + Quinte 1⅓' make an imitation Zink
Regal 8' + Hohlflöte 8' make an imitation Krummhorn
Zimbel best with the two Hohlflöten
Manual and Pedal mixtures only in the plenum
Drum stop bad outside the key of C
Tremulant not to be used with the Regal
Posaune not to be used alone 'on account of the force of the wind'

Particularly important in the documents concerning such new organs as that of Daniel van der Distelen for one of the guild-chapels in Antwerp Cathedral (1505) was the implied distribution of sounds into distinct groups: Principals, Flutes, Reeds and Mixtures. From then on, such families were to be paramount. Mutations, whether scaled as Principals or Flutes, belonged to more southern organs at that period; but at Antwerp there were at least four reeds, all for specific colour imitations

(Cornett, Bagpipe-Regal, Trumpet and Krummhorn/Dulzian). Such imitations became so important during the 16th century that both reed pipes and compound flue stops were used to give the desired effects; often it is not clear from a document which of the two a certain Zink, Cornet, Nachthorn or Rauschpipe was. Trumpets and Krummhorns, however, were always imitated by reed stops. It is also unclear from the documents of about 1510 whether the many kinds of Flute mentioned were open or stopped. In most cases it could well be that they were open and that stopped pipes were reserved for special colour stops like the Quintadena or perhaps for the inseparable second ranks backing the Open Diapasons of the case front. In 1518 Sager promised in his contract with St Mary Magdalene, Basle, that 'the stopped pipes shall be bold and sweet [*tapferer und liblich*] so that they are not too puerile [*nit zu kindlich*] but audible throughout the church'.

During the period from 1500 to 1550 Flemish, north German, north French and Spanish organs had much in common. The Dutch in particular developed a mature organ of archaic features, described in Vente's *Die brabanter Orgel* (1958). In 1510, however, the organ of the Upper Rhineland may have been the most advanced in Europe, having (in addition to Principal and Mixture stops) wide Flutes, narrow stopped pipes, several reeds and smaller *Brustwerk* chests as at Bozen, (1495). As so often, very little real connection between this type of organ and the music supposedly written for it can be demonstrated; it is even difficult to understand the relation between Schlick's own music and the organ he prescribed. The connections seen by many modern writers between a south German organ of about 1520 and the group of south German tablature sources of the same period are only speculative. In fact there was in about 1510 so much international activity between builders that national types are difficult to distinguish.

The early 16th century organ was full of colour: manual reeds, regals in the Postive departments (*Rückpositiv*, *Brustwerk*), pedal reeds; Gedackt, Quintadena, Rohrflöte stops (Alkmaar, St Laurents, small organ, 1511); Gemshorn and Hohlflöte; Sifflöte, Schwegel 1⅓' and other Flute mutations. The last are very significant, often uncertain in documents but usually associated with some special colour effect and even special etymology ('Nasard', 'Larigot'). Tremulants, toy stops and moving statuary were known by the end of the 15th century. The structural developments were very important, particularly the Netherlands builders' division of the Great organ into two departments (each often with its own manual): Principal chorus and trumpets on the HAUPTWERK, and Flutes, Gedackts and mutations on the upper chest or OBERWERK. This separation ensured good wind supply, greater freedom of registration, safer chest construction and better acoustical dispersal from shallower cases. The *Oberwerk* was to influence, even create, the special potential of the north German WERKPRINZIP organ of the next century. Some examples typifying the schemes of about 1550 at their best, organs to which the previous developments were leading, are given in Tables 7–10 (pp.868–9).

In the Iberian Peninsula, organs were generally built by Italians (e.g. Évora Cathedral, 1562) or Netherlanders (El Escorial, *c*1580); there were scarcely distinct Iberian characteristics. Yet Évora had more Mixtures than an Italian organ, and El Escorial had its secondary manual in the form of an internal *Positive* rather than a

Dutch-Flemish *Rückpositiv*. In England organs appear to have remained single-manual instruments until the late 16th or early 17th century, although some of these, particularly in large monastic foundations, may have reached a fairly good size before the Reformation. While early 17th-century English organs had the Italianate characteristic of single, individually available ranks at unison and quint pitches, early 16th-century organs were more Flemish in style and appear to have had the partially divided *blockwerk* scheme of north-west continental organs of c1500. Wooden pipes, and even organs with only wooden pipes, were known in the 16th century, but there is no evidence of reed pipes having been incorporated into large church organs until the late 17th century, although small REGALS containing both reed (short-length) and flue pipes were much in evidence and are described in some detail in an inventory of Henry VIII's household furnishings. Early in the 16th century the English organ acquired a slightly larger key compass than the organs of northern Europe, an advantage it held into the 18th century. The DOUBLE ORGAN with Great and Chair (*Rückpositiv*) division appeared very early in the 17th century, and inspired the writing of a type of voluntary in which solo passages were played by the left hand on the Great against an accompaniment on the Chair, both hands usually going to the Great in the final section.

As both the Innsbruck and Brescia organs still exist, various subjective descriptions of their tone have been made. At Brescia (see Table 9) the average to narrow scalings (apparently untransposed) and the low pressure give a mild tone, round, rich and singing. Low pressure may also explain the absence of reed stops in such organs, or vice versa. The downward compass of Italian organs varied with the size of the church: the larger the church, the lower the compass. The top note was almost always *a″*, the bottom *c*, *G* or *F* (positives), *C*, *G′*, *F′*, or even *C′* (full-sized organs). The organ at S Petronio, Bologna, went to *A′* or *G′* at 16′ pitch (i.e. into the 32′ octave). When pedal-boards were added later to such organs, they were thought of as mechanical conveniences for pulling down the bass keys. As for the pipe-work, only open metal pipes were included. The ranks of the separated high stops break back no higher than the pipe sounding *c♯″″″*; i.e. the top treble of the compass has an accumulation of ranks usually no higher than Principale 2′, resulting in a kind of circumscribed *Blockwerk*. The lower ranks are often divided between *b* and *c′*. Musically, such organs had a distinct function and character. Costanzo Antegnati's rules for registration (1608) show timbre, musical style and liturgical function to have been effectively combined; for example, the ripieno or tutti for sustained music of the *durezze e ligature* styles was applied to such pieces as toccatas at the end of the 'Deo gratias'. Flute stops of all pitches were 'da concerto' (i.e. 'for solo use'), not for accompanying motets or filling out the ripieno. The undulating Fiffaro was drawn with the Principale alone and played slow music 'as smoothly and legato as possible', often with melodic snatches in the right hand (cf Frescobaldi's toccatas). Some useful combinations were those shown in Table 11. At the same time, as Diruta showed, some keys (i.e. ecclesiastical tones) were associated with particular moods and hence particular registrations. He recommended 16′ with Flauto 8′ for the mournfulness of E minor (Phrygian); but for D minor (Dorian, full and grave) he added

as alternative suggestions 16.8 and 16.16. For F major (Lydian, moderately gay) he recommended 8.4 with Flauto 4; but for G major (Mixolydian, mild and lively), 8.4.2. Equally important is that three is the largest number of stops drawn in many such lists of registrations, apart from the various big ripieni used only once or twice in a service. It is never certain how far or wide such rules apply, but much Italian music of about 1620 can be seen in terms of the older Antegnati organ, more modest though the organs of Rome, Naples and else-

---

TABLE 7

The Netherlands (Oude Kerk, Amsterdam)
Hendrik and Herman Niehoff, with Hans Suys 'von Köln', 1539–42

Das Prinzipal (Hauptwerk)		*Oberwerk*	
Probably *FG A–g″a″*		*C–a″* (? no g♯″)	
Prinzipal	16	Two chests	
Oktave	8 + 4	Prinzipal	8
Mixtur		Holpijp	8
Scharf		Offenflöte	4
		Quintadena	8 or 4
Rückpositiv		Gemshorn	2
F–a″ (? no g♯″)		Sifflöte	1 or 1⅓
Two chests		Terzzimbel (?)	
Prinzipal	8	Trompete	8
Oktave	4	Zinck	(? 8 treble)
Mixtur			
Scharf		*Pedal*	
(these four to make		*F–d′* could be coupled to	
the Prinzipal)		*F′* of the *Hauptwerk*	
Quintadena	8	*C–d′* for own stops	
Holpijp	4	Nachthorn	2
Krummhorn (?)	8	Trompete	8
Regal	8		
Baarpijp (regal)	8		
Schalmei	4		

Pedal stops placed on *Hauptwerk* chest
Keyboards not aligned: *Oberwerk* above *Rückpositiv*, *Hauptwerk* probably a 4th to the left or 5th to the right
Six bellows (probably single-fold)
Wind pressure: c90 mm
Couplers: ? *Rückpositiv* to *Hauptwerk*; *Rückpositiv* to *Oberwerk*
Tremulant (? in the main trunk)
All chests probably spring-chests
Alterations in 1544: *Hauptwerk* made 'stronger'; *Oberwerk* Quintadena replaced by a Nasard; *Rückpositiv* Krummhorn replaced by Sifflöte 1⅓
Holpijp stops were probably Chimney Flutes

TABLE 8

Central Europe (Hofkirche, Innsbruck)
G. Ebert, 1555–61

Hauptwerk		*Rückpositiv*	
CDEFGA–g″a″		*FGA–g″a″*	
Prinzipal	8	Prinzipal	4
Gedackt	8	Gedackt	4
Oktave	4	Mixtur	
Quinte	2⅔	Hörnlein	
Superoktave	2	Zimbel	
Hörnlein	II	Tremulant	
Hintersatz	X		
Zimbel	II		
Trompete	8		
Regal			

Pedal
(activating second row of pallets in *Hauptwerk* chest; ? 16th century)

Seven or eight bellows in original organ
Pitch: *a′* = 445
Rückpositiv chest under organ stool
Suspended action (keys hanging from trackers)
Tremulant undulations decrease as larger pipes played (*tremblant doux*)
Rückpositiv rollerboard original (*Hauptwerk* new)

TABLE 9

Italy (S Giuseppe, Brescia)
Graziadio Antegnati, 1581

One manual ($C'D'F'G'A'–g''a''$, 53 notes)

Principale	8 (halved) (16' from C)
Ottava	4 (8' from C)
Quintadecima	2 (etc)
Decimanona	$1\frac{1}{3}$
Vigesimaseconda	1
Vigesimasesta	$\frac{2}{3}$
Vigesimanona	$\frac{1}{2}$
Trigesimaterza	$\frac{1}{3}$
Trigesimasesta	$\frac{1}{4}$
Flauto in ottava	4
Flauto in duodecima	$2\frac{2}{3}$
Flauto in quintadecima	2
Fiffaro	8 (treble)

Pedal pulldowns, original compass uncertain
Originally spring-chest
Wind pressure: $c42$ mm
Pitch: about one semitone above $a' = 440$

TABLE 10

France (St Gervais and St Protais, Gisors)
N. Barbier, 1580

Grand orgue		*Positif*	
Montre (tin)*	16	Bourdon (lowest)	8
Montre (lead)*	8	octave of wood	
Bourdon (lead)*	8	?Prestant (lead)	4
Prestant (tin)*	4	?Doublette (lead)	2
Flûte (lead)*	4	Petite Quinte (tin)	$1\frac{1}{3}$
Nasard (lead)*	II	Cymbale (tin)	II
Doublette (tin)*	2	Cromorne	8
Sifflet (lead)			
Fourniture (tin)*	IV	*Pèdale*	
Cymbale (tin)*	III	Jeu de pédale (wood)	8
Quinte-flûte (lead)	?$1\frac{1}{3}$	Sacquebouttes (tin)**	8 (from F')
Cornet (from c')	V		
Trompette	8		
Clairon	4		
Voix humaine			

Compass $C–c'''$ (48 notes)
Positif inside main case (the 4' rank may have been a stopped 4' Bourdon)
Tremulant (? in main trunk)
Coupler: *Positif* to *Grand orgue*
Pedal reed on two chests either side of the *Grand orgue*
Grand orgue spring-chest
Four bellows (5' × 2', Flemish foot)
Grand orgue Quinte-flûte *à biberon*, i.e. Chimney Flute with domed cap
1618: Chair organ added by C. Carlier
Principals and reeds, tin bodies with lead feet

*servant pour le Plein jeu
**possibly 16'

TABLE 11

Ottava 8' + Flauto 8', good for quick passages and canzonas
Principale + Flauto in duodecima, good for quick passages and canzonas
Principale + Flauto in quintadecima, good for quick passages
Pedal pipes, good for occasional long note in a toccata
Ripieno: $16.8.4.2\frac{2}{3}.2.1\frac{1}{3}.1.\frac{2}{3}$

Mezzo ripieno: $8.4.1.\frac{2}{3}$ with Flauto in ottava
 or 8.4 with Flauto in ottava
 or 8.4 with Flauto in duodecima
Use half-stops 'per far dialoghi'

where seem to have been. The greatest developments in Italian organ building between 1475 and 1575 were rather in the design of the cases (Gothic to Renaissance; see fig.33, p.870) than in the technical or musical sphere, where there is an unusual conformity.

The Innsbruck organ (see Table 8, and fig.34, p.872) is very strong in tone, neither manual proving useful for accompanying a choir. The cases are shallow (*Rückpositiv* less than 50 cm), the chests spacious, the organs contained in resonant wooden boxes. Since all the Chair organ stops have close equivalents in the Great organ, yet at only 4' pitch (as so often during the 16th century and late 15th), the two manuals can be regarded partly as extensions of each other in different directions. Indeed, the Innsbruck organ puts in a new light the perennial question of the purpose of second manuals (a question rarely admitting of any obvious answer, despite common assumptions). The stopped pipes at Innsbruck are very strong in tone, with a big mouth and a tone-colour ranging from wide, vague flute sound in the bass to strong, breathy treble colour. The two Hörnli stops are very keen, repeating Terzzimbeln. Throughout the organ there is a distinct change of tone from bass to treble, enabling the *Hauptwerk* bass keys to produce a different quality of sound from right-hand solo lines in the treble.

The Amsterdam organ (see Table 7) was that known to Sweelinck and shows the 'Brabant organ' at its most characteristic: big Principal chorus, large flute stops on an *Oberwerk* chest, smaller stops but yet greater variety in the Chair organ, and the pedals playing the *Hauptwerk* chorus for plenum registrations, and also a pair of high-pitched, strong-toned solo stops for (presumably) cantus firmus music. The sheer variety in the manuals alone would have encouraged variations on psalm tunes and folk melodies over the next century or so, even had there been no tradition of weekday organ recitals occasioned by the prohibition of the use of the organ in the Reformed liturgy until early in the 17th century. From surviving examples of Niehoff pipework, it seems that the inner parts were of thick, hammered lead of good quality; the Principals were narrow in the bass, round in the treble; and the whole had a mild-voiced, singing quality quite different from the Baroque organ. Flutes were wide to very wide; reeds penetrating, particularly in the bass. The spring-chests were considered an advance on the slider-chests already known for smaller organs (Alkmaar small organ, extant slider-chest of 1511) or for the Chair organs of larger instruments; and in some areas (north Italy, Westphalia) spring-chests of different types remained popular for well-spaced, large-scaled organs. The Amsterdam organ was evidently of a very high class, and its concept and musical repertory were known in Brabant, the Netherlands, Cologne, Würzburg, Lüneburg and much farther east. Some examples had big pedals, resulting during the period 1575–1600 in an organ type known from Groningen to Danzig, Frederiksborg to Prague, and passed on by a group of composers directly or indirectly under Sweelinck's influence.

The musical position of the organ at Gisors (see Table 10) is less certain, as indeed is that of all French organs before about 1660. The French organ of 1520–75 often had a wide array of colour, whether of the Bordeaux–Italian type in the south, or the southern Flemish variety of reeds and compound stops in the north. Reeds of 16', 8' and 4' could be expected in a larger organ of about 1575; so could one or more Quint mutations; 8', 4' and

33. Ss Annunziata, Florence, showing the southern organ of a pair built in 1523 and facing each other across the east end of the nave

possibly 16' ranks of stopped (often wooden) pipes; a few 'obsolescent' stops like the 1' Principal; and even a mounted Cornet, often called 'Flemish horn' (see 'Cornet' in ORGAN STOP). In many respects the Gisors organ was Flemish: the *Positiv* construction (in French instruments the Chair organ had become temporarily uncommon), the spring-chests, the *CD–c'''* compass, the Quint flutes of 1⅓', the 8' pedal stops, and the *grand ravalement* for the pedal reed. In sound, no doubt the instrument was nearer to the Netherlands organs of Niehoff than to the late classical French organs of F.-H. Clicquot.

5. STRUCTURAL DEVELOPMENTS ABOUT 1600. From the many enormous and apparently amorphous organ specifications given by Praetorius it could be reasonably thought that many central German builders of the late 16th century did not have clear control of the organs that their technology enabled them to build. The number of stops and stop types listed by Praetorius is evidence of his attempt to give order to a somewhat embarrassing luxury of choice. The number of 4' solo Flutes alone, for instance – narrow, wide, open, stopped, chimney, spindle, narrow-stopped, narrow-conical and overblowing–narrow-stopped – contrasts strongly with the systematized French classical organ of average size, where there was probably only one plain Stopped Diapason 4', and that with a very specific function. Some

of the biggest organs, such as those in Prague and Danzig, are scarcely credible: Prague Týn Church appears to have had a four-manual, 70-stop organ built between 1556 and 1588, but it is likely that it was a conglomerate instrument, finished in part, no doubt, but never all playable or ready at once.

More important was the potential opened up by new mechanical skill in disposing multiple chests–giving the Pedal, for example, a pair of back or side chests for the large pipes, using front chests for middle Principals and a *Brustwerk* chest or two for smaller-scaled solo stops. Each pedal key then connected with two or even three pallets. The first such 'multiple action' may have been built earlier in the century in the central Netherlands (Antwerp Cathedral, 1505; St Zwysen, Diest, 1523), but the evidence is inconclusive. Certainly by the end of the century extravagant court chapel organs were built with some of the richest mechanical layouts ever known before pneumatic action, allowing an immense array of stop combinations. If the simple organ of 1563 for the Dresden court chapel allowed 77 manual combinations with its 13 stops and Tremulant, as stated in a contemporary document, then hundreds were no doubt possible on the famous Groningen court chapel organ of 1592–6 (see Table 12). Whether there was enough fish for all this sauce might have been doubted by Schlick.

Clearly the Groningen organ offered many colourful effects, particularly those of two or three stops only;

indeed, the number of stops normally drawn at once by organists of that time cannot be assumed from modern practices. With the exception of three Principal choruses of four or five stops, the registrations at Dresden (referred to above) were all of three stops or less. Quite apart from what this fact might imply about the state of contemporary wind-raising techniques, it suggests that organs of the period were geared towards subtle colour and musical variety, at least in smaller churches or those with good vocal or instrumental traditions. As to the 'multiple chests' themselves, a very plausible attempt to describe their complex action, double pallets, transmission and extension system has been made by Bunjes (1966). The most useful arrangement was the most traditional and long-lived, namely the multiple pedal division in which the biggest bass pipes would take one or two chests, and the cantus firmus and other high stops another chest. Wind could be prevented by a *Sperrventil* from entering any chest not immediately needed; and a low pressure could be the better sustained if no chest was above a certain size.

A circumspect reading of Praetorius reveals three main types of complex layout, two of them multiple-action: (i) the double action enabling two or more chests to be played by one keyboard (e.g. *Brustwerk* and *Oberwerk* from *Oberwerk* keys only); (ii) the transmission chest (with two pallets), enabling one or more ranks of pipes to be played by two keyboards (usually the bigger stops of the *Oberwerk* played by pedal keys); (iii) octave and even quint transmission or 'extension', i.e. a chest construction enabling a rank of pipes to be played at unison, quint or octave pitches. The third was very rare, but important in view of later developments. Since couplers were also much to the fore in organs using complex action, and since the *Sperrventil* increased the registration possibilities (by making drawn stops inoperative until required), it can be seen that an important musical aim was maximum variety for a given number of ranks. But such aids had the potentially bad effect of overemphasizing the main *Oberwerk* chest to the detriment of true secondary manuals, weakening the independence of the pedal, and encouraging the cultivation of intricate workmanship as an end in itself. But the Chair organ remained an independent department in the major organs, and as such helped to provide the right conditions for most idiomatic organ music of 17th-century Germany, as it also did in France, the Netherlands, Scandinavia and England.

6. THE WERKPRINZIP ORGAN. The Chair organ was indeed the manual that supplied the true balanced chorus to the Great; but in areas or periods in which second manuals were required for simple echo effects or soft background colours (Spain and Italy during the whole period, France during the 16th century, England after 1700) or in smaller churches where expense had to be avoided, the Chair organ was dispensed with and smaller chests were incorporated in the main case.

The visual characteristics of the WERKPRINZIP organ (the term is a modern one, coined by the 20th-century reformers) – the single main case, the Chair organ, the separate pedal towers – were all known by the end of the 14th century. But by the time of Praetorius, owing to the range of available organ colour and the widespread mechanical skill in making good actions, builders were able to develop a type of instrument using such features put to new, unified purpose. Scheidt's remarks

in his *Tabulatura nova* (1624) imply a sophisticated and codified practice for organs and their music, and show the instrument to have developed well along the lines laid down by Schlick and beyond recognition of those laid down by Arnaut. Indeed, it is a mistake to relate the *Werkprinzip* Chair organ and (even more so) its pedal towers to the organ of Arnaut's period. It is often very uncertain whether in about 1450 the Chair organ of a large instrument had the same pitch as the Great or its keys aligned with it; nor was two-manual playing necessarily known outside Schlick's area and period. Similarly, although side towers or Trompes held bass pipes, they were not necessarily played by pedal keys; in any case, a vital function of *Werkprinzip* pedal towers is that they contain cantus firmus solo stops near to the Protestant congregation situated in or below the gallery. No doubt the larger instruments of about 1550 might have had pedal towers combining both characteristics; but the *Werkprinzip* organ flourished many hundreds of kilometres north-east of the areas knowing the old Trompes.

One of the attractions of the *Werkprinzip* was that an organ could be altered and its potential enlarged simply by adding a new department to the old. While the famous Totentanz organ of Lübeck (destroyed in 1942) is much less understood than modern references to it suggest, it is certain that its four departments expressed the ideals of four quite different periods: the Great organ, the late

TABLE 12

Groningen court chapel organ
Details from M. Praetorius: *Syntagma musicum*, ii (Wolfenbüttel, 1618, 2/1619/R1958 and 1980), 188f
Case extant (since 1770 in Halberstadt Martinskirche)
David Beck, 1592–6

Im Oberwerck Manual		*Im Rückpositiff*	
Principal	8	Principal	4
Zimbeldoppelt		Gemsshorn	4
Gross Querflöit	8	Quintadehn	8
Mixtur	(?)8	Spitzflöite	2
Nachthorn	4	Gedact	4
Holflöiten	8	Octava	2
Klein Querflöite	4	Quinta	1⅓
Quinta	5⅓	Subflöite	1
Octava	4	Mixtur	(?)4
Grobgedact	8	Zimbel	2⅔
Gemsshorn	8	Sordunen	16
Gross Quintadehna	16	Trommet	8
		Krumbhorn	8
Im Pedal auff der Oberlade		Klein Regal	4
(Pedal stops on upper chest)			
Untersatz	16	*In den beyden Seit Thörmen zum*	
Octaven Bass	8	*Pedal*	
Quintadeen Bass	16	(Pedal stops in the large side	
Klein Octaven Bass	4	towers)	
Klein Quintaden Bass	4	Gross Principal Bass	16
Rauschquinten Bass		Gross Gemsshorn	
Holflöiten Bass	2	Bass	16
Holquinten Bass		Gross Querflöiten	
Nachthorn Bass	4	Bass	8
Mixtur		Gemsshorn Bass	8
		Kleingedact Bass	4
Fornen in der Brust		Quintflöiten Bass	5⅓
zum Manual		Sordunen Bass	16
(*Brustwerk* keyboard)		Posaunen Bass	16
Klein Gedact	2	Trommeten Bass	8
Klein Octava	1	Schallmeyen Bass	4
Klein Mixtur	2		
Zimbeldoppelt		*In der Brust auff beyden Seiten zum*	
Rancket	8	*Pedal*	
Regal	8	(Pedal stops on small *Brustwerk*	
Zimbel Regal	2	side chests	
		Quintflöiten Bass	10⅔ (sic)
		Bawrflöiten Bass	4
		Zimbel Bass	2⅔
		Rancket Bass	8
		Krumbhorn Bass	8
		Klein Regal Bass	4

15th century; the Chair organ, the mid-16th century; the *Brustwerk*, the early 17th; and the completed pedal organ, the mid-18th. Many famous organs of this type in northern Europe (e.g. Jakobikirche, Lübeck; Johanniskirche, Lüneburg) are in fact composite instruments (quite apart from modern rebuilds), accumulations of *Werke* constantly altered in compass, specification, tuning and no doubt voicing by builder after builder. The big organs of the Neihoffs, the Scherers, and the Compenius and Fritzsche families were like living organisms; except for the large chamber organ in the chapel of Frederiksborg Castle, Denmark, none remains in anything like its original state.

Organ historians are often tempted to trace the organ's evolution in terms of the best-known builders. Frequently, however, contributions are attributed to a builder on the basis of mere conjecture or even fable. Probably not a single item in the list of innovations commonly attributed to Gottfried Fritzsche, for instance, is specifically his: inclusion of a fourth manual; more systematic use of 32' and 16' reeds to written *C*; introduction to north Germany of rare stops, both flue (Viol, Schwiegel, imitative flutes) and reed (Sordun, Ranket); contrast between narrow 'male' and wide 'female' stops (e.g. Nasat $2\frac{2}{3}$' and Quinte $2\frac{2}{3}$' on the same manual); reduction of the big Brabant Scharf Mixture to a high repeating two-rank Zimbel; greater use of tin in the pipe metal, and also of wooden pipes (reeds, flues, stopped, open); and systematic adherence to *C* compass, often with split

keys (*d♯/e♭* etc). But they certainly belong to his period. Such a list, taken with the provincialisms running through Praetorius's *Syntagma musicum* (2/1619), does lead to a distinct kind of organ. The chief musical characteristics of the *Werkprinzip* thus emerging in a purer form in the north were: the contrast between a full, round *Hauptwerk* and a thin, piercing, more variable *Rückpositiv*; the versatile pedal; and the clarity of the whole in average parish churches of little reverberation. In most cases it was the *Rückpositiv* that was understood to be the 'solo manual'. The idiom was clearly defined for organists, who seem to have been in little need of registration hints either from composers or from builders. (Balanced contrast could easily be achieved between two manuals if the same number of stops was drawn in each.) Explicit and firm registration rules have been formulated only in areas and at periods in which organs were more uniform (e.g. in northern Italy *c*1600, France *c*1700 and England *c*1800).

The Hamburg *Werkprinzip* organ reached maturity and indeed satiation in the work of Arp Schnitger, famous in his day far and wide, the possessor of many privileges, and, with Gottfried Silbermann, the inspiration for the German Organ Reform (*Orgelbewegung*) of the 1920s. Despite work in progress, surprisingly little is certain about Schnitger – how responsible he was for his instruments (his workshop was large and active), what his scaling policy was (scales vary hugely, depending on the church, the pitch, the value of the old pipework

34. *Organ by Jörg Ebert (1551–61) in the Hofkirche, Innsbruck; the Annunciation scene on the shutters was typical of 16th-century Venetian organs, while the flat Rückpositiv, designed as a small version of the main case, was unfamiliar outside southern Germany*

he re-used, etc), what his pitch and temperature were, why he usually changed small multifold bellows to large single-fold bellows in his rebuilds, why he dropped the *Rückpositiv* in his late work around Berlin, and who designed his cases (see fig.35, p.875). Research has established that his wind pressures varied between 94 mm or higher (the large organs in Hamburg) and 67 mm, an average being about 85 mm (Nikolaikirche, Flensburg). Table 13 gives the stop list of his first four-manual organ (destroyed in 1842). Such very large organs give a kind of highest common factor of instruments known to such composers as Buxtehude, Lübeck and Bruhns and on which toccatas and chorales of the older composers (Scheidemann, Weckmann, Tunder and others) were still played. In some areas of the Netherlands, north Germany and Scandinavia, such an organ remained the model until 1850 or so, and the *Werkprinzip* can be recognized behind later organs very different in sound and appearance from the Hamburg Nikolaikirche.

7. THE FRENCH CLASSICAL ORGAN. In northern Italy the 'classical Brescian organ' of the late 16th century remained a norm to which the occasional 17th-century two-manual organ was an exception (and probably built by a foreign builder); it was only in the mid-17th century that the French organ achieved its classical form, intimately bound up with music of a distinct and well-characterized idiom. The very number of *Livres d'orgue* published suggests a remarkably unified 'organ school'. Every stop in a French organ of about 1700 came to have an appointed purpose, and the *livres* from Nivers (1665) to Marchand (*c*1715) and beyond give the impression that late 17th-century Paris had shaken off outside influences past and present.

But Flemish influence had originally been paramount in northern France as Italian had been in parts of southern France. Titelouze's plenum was much the same as that of a Dutch composer. Even the Cornet was Netherlands, from the time of the organ in Antwerp (1565) onwards. Yet while many details in Mersenne's *Harmonie universelle* may point to northern influences like Praetorius, important moves towards the organ of the *livres d'orgue* were made at this period, above all in Paris. Narrow- and wide-scaled Tierces soon became common (narrow at St Nicolas-des-Champs, 1618; wide at St Jacques-de-la-Boucherie, 1631) and with them a general change towards mutation colour (e.g. more $1\frac{3}{5}$' ranks, fewer 1'). Mersenne knew Tierces as ranks used both in the *plein jeu* and for solo combinations. More important still were the new short-compass keyboards of solo or quasi-solo character: the 25-note Cornet manual (i.e. a *Récit*) at St Séverin, Paris (1610), set a new fashion, though intended at first only as a little keyboard giving the raised Cornet chest a second row of keys. Were the little extra chest to be placed below the *Grand orgue* it would be called *Echo* and probably have a shorter keyboard and more ranks. By 1660 a large organ could be expected to have four manuals (two plus two halves) supplying classical Great–Chair organ contrast and also right-hand solo manuals for music influenced by the monodic *récit dramatique* of the *ballet de cour*.

The organ played by Nicolas Lebègue (see Table 14), one of the organists to Louis XIV, shows the French scheme of the period at its best. Rarely can an organ have been so closely related to the music of its period as such an instrument to the works of Lebègue, Raison, de Grigny, Couperin and others (for fuller discussion see E. Higginbottom: 'Organ mass', *Grove 6*). Stand-

TABLE 13

Nikolaikirche, Hamburg
Arp Schnitger, 1682–7

Hauptwerk		*Oberwerk*	
Prinzipal	16 (case)	Weitpfeife	8
Quintadena	16	Hohlflöte	8
Rohrflöte	16	Rohrflöte	8
Oktave	8	Quintatön	8
Spitzflöte	8	Oktave	4
Salizional	8	Spitzflöte	4
Quinte (? open)	$5\frac{1}{3}$	Nasat	$2\frac{2}{3}$
Oktave	4	Gemshorn	2
Oktave	2	Scharf	VI–IX
Flachflöte	2	Zimbel	III
Rauschpfeife	III	Trompete	8
Mixtur	VI–X	Krummhorn	8
Scharf	III	Vox humana	8
Trompete	16	Trompete	4

Rückpositiv		*Brustwerk*	
Bourdon	16	Blockflöte	8
Prinzipal	8 (case)	Prinzipal	4
Gedackt	8	Rohrflöte	4
Quintatön	8	Quinte	$2\frac{2}{3}$
Oktave	4	Waldflöte	2
Blockflöte	4	Nasat	$1\frac{1}{3}$
Querflöte	2	Terzian	II
Sifflöte	$1\frac{1}{3}$	Scharf	IV–VI
Sesquialtera	II	Dulzian	8
Scharf	VI–IX	Bärpfeife	8
Dulzian	16		
Trichterregal	8	*Pedal*	
Schalmei	4	Prinzipal	32 (case)
		Oktave	16
Compass: ? CD–d'–c'''		Sub-bass	16
Three Tremulants		Oktave	8
Ventil to each chest		Quinte	$5\frac{1}{3}$
Wind pressure: c71 mm		Oktave	4
Pitch: about $\frac{3}{4}$ tone above		Nachthorn	4
a' = 440		Rauschpfeife	III
Couplers unknown		Mixtur	X
		Posaune	32
		Posaune	16
		Dulzian	16
		Trompete	8
		Krummhorn	8
		Trompete	4
		Cornett	2

TABLE 14

St Louis-des-Invalides, Paris
Alexandre Thierry, 1679–87

Grand orgue		*Positif*	
CD–c'''		CD–c'''	
Montre	16	Montre	8
Bourdon	16	Bourdon	8
Montre	8	Prestant	4
Bourdon	8	Flûte	4
Prestant	4	Nasard	$2\frac{2}{3}$
Flûte	4	Doublette	2
Grosse Tierce	$3\frac{1}{5}$	Tierce	$1\frac{3}{5}$
Nasard	$2\frac{2}{3}$	Larigot	$1\frac{1}{3}$
Doublette	2	Fourniture	III
Quarte de Nasard	2	Cymbale	II
Tierce	$1\frac{3}{5}$	Cromorne	8
Fourniture	V	Voix humaine	8
Cymbale	IV		
Cornet	V	*Pédale*	
Trompette	8	A'–f (20 notes)	
Clairon	4	Flûte	8
Voix humaine	8	Trompette	8

Echo		*Récit*	
c–c'''		c'–c'''	
Bourdon	8	Cornet	V
Flûte	4	Trompette	8
Nasard	$2\frac{2}{3}$		
Quarte	2	Tremulants	
Tierce	$1\frac{3}{5}$	Coupler: *Positif* to	
Cymbale	II	*Grand orgue*	
Cromorne	8		

ardization was one of the chief aims. To obtain the PLEIN
JEU for those movements in the Mass that required it,
for example, the organist drew the Principals 16′, 8′,
4′, 2′, then added the Fourniture, whose composition
was almost certainly something like:

C–e	15.19.22.26.29
f–e′	8.12.15.19.22
f′–c‴	1.5.8.12.15

and then finally the Cymbale:

C–B	29.33.36
c–e	26.29.33
f–b	22.26.29
c′–e′	19.22.26
f′–b′	15.19.22
c″–e″	12.15.19
f″–c‴	8.12.15

which, if it was a large four-rank Cymbale, included
the 26th as well. Such schemes were formulated by Bédos
de Celles at the end of the great period but can be taken
as typical; thus, for instance, his specification of 1766
(for the case design, see fig.36) is almost indistinguishable from that of the 1674 organ at Le Petit Andely.
Important points about the French chorus, which also
influenced Silbermann in Saxony, are that the Cymbale
broke back more often than the Fourniture but generally
duplicated the Fourniture in the treble; no rank is higher
than 2′ at c‴ (i.e. 28 mm long); and ranks were not
duplicated in either Mixture. The *plein jeu* was rarely
brilliant, never shrill; it was rather a further 'colour' of
the organ.

Pitch, at least from about 1680, was a semitone below
a′ = 440. Pipe metal was hammered, including the lead
pipes for flute stops. The keyboards were always pivoted at the end, and the mechanism suspended from the
chests above, trackers passing straight to the pallet box
ranged vertically above the keys (fig.37, p.877). The
Positif stickers connect with a lever which raises the
pallet placed above the channel-end. Such systems were
simple, logical and very easy for the player.

To obtain the GRAND JEU, the organist drew a varying
combination of reeds, Cornet, Prestant 4′ and Tierces.
The reeds supplied volume and brilliance; the Cornet
boosted the thin reed trebles; the Tierces encouraged the
overtone level that gave prominence; and the Prestants
strengthened the basic tone without taking too much wind
or adding obtrusive 8′ flue sound. Fugues were often
played on such registrations, and other fugal colours,
such as Tierce combinations with Tremulant, give an
impression quite different from that of Italian or German fugues of the period 1650–1750. On larger organs,
a pair of Trompettes on the *Grand orgue* after about
1750 gave a timbre peculiar to the bass depth and brilliance of French reeds. Late in the period a Trompette
was also put on the *Positif*, and after Notre Dame, Paris
(organ by Thierry, 1733), Bombarde manuals were also
occasionally included – keyboards coupled to the *Grand
orgue* and playing the large-scaled Bombarde 16′, perhaps with other large reeds. The chief purpose of this
was to give the ranks their own chest and wind supply,
which was often experimentally high by the end of the
classical period. Similarly, it was the treble 'boosting'
supplied by the Cornet that led eventually to higher
pressures and double-length harmonic resonators during
the next century. The reed basses, however, remained
the chief glory, encouraging composers to write special
'basse de trompette' music from about 1650 onwards.
'De grosse taille' ('of large scale') is a phrase often
applied in 17th-century contracts to the Trompette.

Even in *plein jeu* registrations, the French organ was
not overdrawn. Only a handful of stops was involved
in any of the characteristic French registrations, and all
the codified ingenuity – native to the organ of this country, as to so much else – was geared towards clearly
marked colours. Thus the texture of a piece marked
'Tierce en taille', one of the most beautiful effects known
to organists, would consist of the following elements:
(i) left hand on *Postif*, Bourdon 8′ + Prestant 4′ +
Doublette 2′ + Nasard + Tierce (perhaps + Larigot),
playing a free melody in the middle of the texture, gamba-
like; (ii) right hand on *Grand orgue*, Bourdons 16′ +
8′ + 4′ ('jeux doux'), playing accompaniment above or
around the melody; and (iii) pedal playing the bass line
on a Flûte 8′ (or perhaps coupled to *Grand orgue* Bourdon 16′). There was some variety in such registrations:
Bédos de Celles, for instance, did not like 16′ manual
stops in accompaniments. On the other hand, the Tierces
were so characteristic of French organs that many combinations were possible: a right-hand Cornet line on the
Grand orgue, for instance, could be accompanied in
dialogue by a left hand *Jeu de tierce* registration on the
Positif. From D'Anglebert (1689) onwards, Quatuors and
Trios had been played using three different colours
including pedal; indeed, the chief purpose of the pedal
was 'pour pouvoir jouer les trios' (according to Joyeuse's contract at Auch in 1688) and to play 8′ and 16′
cantus firmus in pieces built on a plainsong. The biggest
drain on wind supply and narrow channels must have
been the slower, sustained music written for *concert de
flûtes* and *fonds d'orgue* registrations, comprising all
available Montres, Prestants, open Flûtes and Bourdons. Such sounds became fashionable about 1750; but
whatever the combination, no organist in the provinces
need have been in doubt about how the Parisian composers expected their pieces to sound.

The splendid French organ at the eve of the Revolution (1789) may well have been far superior to the
music written for it, as were the Dutch organ of 1700
and the English organ of 1850; but it is the very decadence of the music that best draws out the extravagant
contrasts, brilliant reeds, round flutes, echoes, big choruses and immense colour potential available on such
extant late instruments as those at St Maximin-en-Var
(J.-E. Isnard, 1773) and Poitiers Cathedral (F.-H. Clicquot, 1787–90). The French organ received a serious
setback when the Revolution disrupted life in the cities.
It was ripe for development at the very moment when
Clicquot's sons became soldiers; but not until St Denis
in 1841 did Poitiers have a worthy successor.

8. THE ENGLISH ORGAN. Rimbault thought that the John
Roose at work on the organ of York Minster in 1457
was the 'first English organ builder of whom we have
any authentic account'. But Roose was almost certainly
not English, for a builder of the name lived in Utrecht
during the 16th century and built the organ in the Was-
serkirche, Münster, in 1572. The name appears to be
High or Low Dutch and pinpoints the likely influences
on English organs at the beginning of the period. The
Flemish organ taken to Louth in about 1500 is a rare
example of such explicit influence, but the unique document concerning the organ at All Hallows, Barking, in
1519 (quoted by Rimbault in 1855 and copied unveri-
fied ever since) also seems to suggest a Flemish organ:
the pryncipale to conteyn the length of v foote, so following wt Bassys called Diapason to the same, conteyning length of x foot or

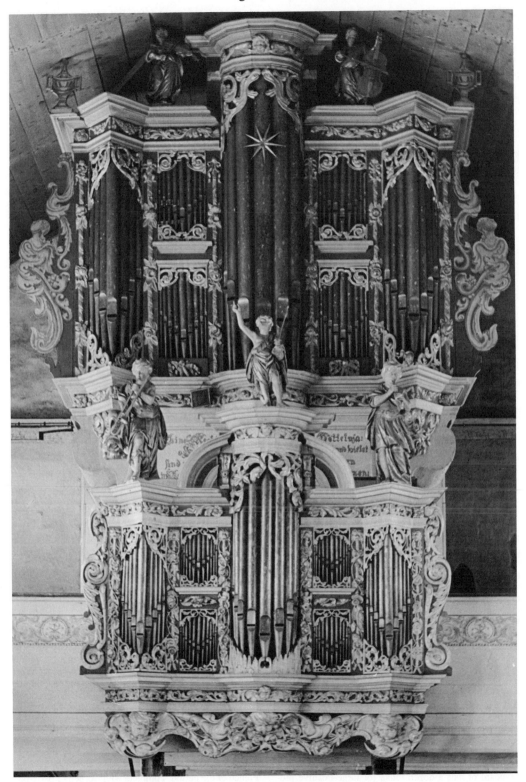

35. *Organ by Arp Schnitger (1695), originally in the Johanniskirche, Hamburg, now in the west-end gallery of the village church at Cappel*

36. *Design for a grand organ case: engraving from 'L'art du facteur d'orgues' (1766–78) by Bédos de Celles*

more: And to be dowble pryncipalls thoroweout the seid instrument. This probably means:

the Chorus [a kind of divided *Blockwerk*, like the Dutch *Principael*] to have several ranks from 5' C upwards [compass *CDEFGA–g"a"*, perhaps at low pitch, the scribe's foot-stand being now unknown], those inside the organ being of [almost] as good metal as those in the casefront; with a suboctave of wooden pipes [or, with a set of incorporated bass pipes].

It is interesting that Arnaut too wrote of 'double Principals', a phrase in other organ documents of about 1500 taken to mean a pair of open and stopped Diapason ranks; his use of the term 'diapason' was more in the common tradition of Greek terminology but possibly suggested to English builders a useful term for the basic rank 'running through all' the compass. The 1519 'Bassys' may have been Trompes-like bass pipes of the kind often pictured in small portable organs of the period. Either way, the English terms 'Diapason' and 'stop' were already in use.

It is not known if any English organs before 1600 had separate quint ranks, but the inventories of Henry VIII's instruments mention more than one Cymbale stop of two ranks, presumably including a quint. Whether they were English-built instruments is also unknown, however. By 1550 extreme miserliness already characterized the commissions given for English organs (as it continued to do for the next three centuries), and an English organ of 1600 would most likely have had no more than one keyboard of half a dozen ranks (of large-Positive proportions). It is thus possible that Italian rather than Dutch influences are reflected in the English organ between about 1525 and about 1600. But no known documents give any definite detail of a single organ before 1606 (accounts of King's College, Cambridge), and it is therefore very tempting to make much of the 'small regals' mentioned at St Martin-in-the-Fields in 1561, the putative stop list of the clock-organ sent to the Sultan of Turkey in 1599, the compass of '27 plain keys' at Coventry in 1526, the 'cimbale' and regals mentioned in the inventories of Henry VIII's instruments (1547), or the French–Flemish elements in extant late 16th-century cases at Tewkesbury, Gloucester and Framlingham.

For Worcester Cathedral in 1613 Thomas Dallam made what was or became a standard English Double organ (see Table 15). At York in 1632 a similar instrument by Dallam had a compass of 51 notes, three bellows and 'drawinge stoppes' (a term analogous to the French *tirants* and lending credence to the supposition, drawn from earlier references, that stops in the previous century were commonly controlled by levers rather than draw-knobs). It is not known whether the 51 notes gave a compass of $CD–d'''e'''$ or $G'A'B\flat'B'CDE–c'''$, or some similar long compass, though the latter is the more likely. Though small, this type of organ led to a genre of organ music (the double voluntary) and gave good service to choirs placed below (near the screen over which the Chair organ hung); it was quite independent of organs abroad. The nomenclature (Fifteenth, Two & Twentieth etc) and compass, however, were distinctly Italianate. Likewise the use of wooden pipes, sometimes to the exclusion of metal ones (just as in the Italian 'organi de legno' and small quire organs of central Europe). The relationship of the two manuals was also comparable to that found in the occasional two-manual Italian organ (e.g. S Maria in Aracoeli, Rome, 1585–7) and in no way resembled that of the Dutch or German *Hauptwerk* and *Rückpositiv*.

TABLE 15

Worcester Cathedral
Thomas Dallam, 1613

Great organ		*Chair organ*	
Open Diapason	8	Diapason of wood	8
Open Diapason	8	(probably open)	
Principal	4	Principal	4
Principal	4	Flute of wood	4
Small Principal	2	Small Principal	2
Small Principal	2	Two & Twentieth	1
Recorder (stopped)	?4		
(perhaps 8)			

Pitch: Open Diapason *C* to be 'of 10 foot long' (i.e. probably sounding A♭ at *a'* = 440; but foot-standard uncertain)
Pitch names of stops not specified

Larger secular organs like those at Chirk Castle (1631) and Adlington Hall (possibly but not certainly as early as c1650) would have second manuals contained within the main case and even held on the same chest. More important is the tonal scheme that emerged. Mutations began to appear, and the Adlington Hall Great organ has what seems to be an original specification of $8.8.4.2\frac{2}{3}.2.2.1\frac{3}{5}.1\frac{1}{3}.1.8.8.$ All its ranks were single, as at Great Packington 80 years later; it is still far from the scheme prepared by Robert Dallam in 1654 for a Great organ at the Priory of Lesneven, Brittany: $8.V.8.4.4.2\frac{2}{3}.2.2.1\frac{3}{5}.1\frac{1}{3}.1.III.II.8.8.8.4,$ which is pure French of the period, complete with Cornet V, two Mixtures, reeds, regals and mutations. By then, Dallam was at work in France, and the Civil War (1642–9) and subsequent Restoration (1660) were to give a change of direction to the English organ.

Though exaggerated by English 18th-century historians, the French influences on the English organ, through Renatus Harris, were very important. Harris was the son of Thomas Dallam's daughter and Thomas Harris (Harrison). In 1686 he replanned (in the new style) his father's organ of 1638 at Magdalen College, Oxford, doing away with the paired ranks of stops which, he pointed out, were difficult to keep in tune and gave little return in increased sound. Therefore the 1638 Great organ of 8.8.4.4.2.2.1.1 (all open) would be better replanned (1686) as Open 8.Stopped 8.4.2⅔.2.1⅗.II–III. Soon after 1661 Robert Dallam had put in a scheme for New College, Oxford, that was of particular importance as an indication of new tastes: it was a complete French organ of two manuals and 24 stops, showing a Fourniture breaking back once each octave and a Simbale breaking back twice each octave (see §7 above). But other English builders continued the styles of 1640 after 1660, and the picture is much less clear and detailed than is suggested by most modern writers. It does indeed seem that it was Harris and Father Smith (who built several organs in Hoorn, Holland, had previously worked in Bremen and was probably a north German by birth) who gave impetus to the new directions.

Smith's Chapel Royal organ in Whitehall, described in Table 16, was made between 1662 and 1672. Any north European influences that were felt through Smith's work seem to have been dominated by Harris's French innovations, although Smith obtained the two best-known commissions (the Temple Church, 1683–7, and St Paul's Cathedral, 1694–9). But terminology itself is a poor

guide; the Great organ Sesquialtera, for example, may have been originally called something else, a Tierce Mixture of the later Harris type, an English Bass Cornet, or a Dutch or German Mixture of octaves and quints. Certainly the Echo Cornet was, despite its name, a Dutch Sesquialtera; and the first known Mixture by a completely native builder (Thamar for Winchester Cathedral, 1665) was called 'Fourniture'. The picture is therefore confusing, although it is very significant that the first English treatise to deal with the organ (by James

TABLE 16

Chapel Royal, Whitehall
'Father' Smith, 1662–72

Great organ		*Choir organ*	
G'A'–c'''		*G'A'–c'''*	
Open Diapason	8	Stopped Diapason	8
Stopped Diapason	8	Principal	4
Principal	4	Flute (wood, from *c♯'*)	
Block Flute (metal, from (*c♯'*)		Vox humana	8
Twelfth	2⅔	Cremona	8
Fifteenth	2		
Sesquialtera	III	*Echo*	
Cornet (from *c♯'*)	III	*ga–c'''*	
Trumpet	8	Open Diapason	8
		Principal	4
		Cornet	II
		Trumpet	8

Account in Leffler's MS (*c*1810), where it is noted that 'the Echo is placed immediately over the Keys – behind the Music Desk – and not as usual enclosed in a box'
Pitch length of the flute stops uncertain (? both 8')
Cornett II '12th & Tierce' = Sesquialtera 12.17
Great organ listed with a wooden Flute, perhaps this should be a 2' Flute for the Choir organ
Compass as given by Leffler
? Tremulant

37. *Cross-section through an 18th-century French organ, showing among other details the multifold bellows, narrow wind-trunk, trackers and rollerboard, pallets for the Grand orgue side-chest for pedals, and Positif (behind the player): engraving from 'L'art du facteur d'orgues' (1766–78) by Bédos de Celles*

Talbot, c1687) was French-influenced, by Mersenne's writings and Harris's organs.

Yet curiously little is clear about the Smith–Harris organs; it is not known whether the Choir organ chests were placed in the upper or lower part of the organ; whether the Whitehall Echo was a kind of *Brustwerk*; whether they were French in conception; whether the early Sesquialteras had a Tierce rank; whether the Trumpets were French or Dutch; or whether the Diapason scalings, voicing, key-action, chest construction, metals and wind pressure were traditional English (i.e. Italian-influenced) or French. The absence of real technical information and of properly assembled documents dealing with the English organ at two of its most crucial periods, 1660–90 and 1820–50, means that no adequate history of the English organ can yet be written. The three or four original attempts made since 1850 have necessarily been selective and conjectural.

38. *Organ by Richard Bridge (1730) in Christ Church, Spitalfields, London*

Some general points are fairly certain, however. Harris was probably born in England, though brought up in Brittany, and Smith was almost certainly of continental birth and lineage; both at any rate had considerable European training. By at least the 1680s even Smith was making French-influenced organs, despite the Holflute, Spitts flute, Cimball, Quinta Dena and Gedackt at the Temple and St Paul's; old-English–Italian influences were still strong enough for builders to dispense with pedals (though perhaps not always pulldowns which, like Tremulants and Couplers, were often not specified in contracts); builders kept to a longer compass than in France and the Netherlands (F′ at the Temple, C′ intended at St Paul's); and the largest organ was under 30 stops. Indeed, although Harris enlarged the organ of Salisbury Cathedral by adding a French battery of Mixtures and mutations (on the Great organ a Tierce, Cornet V, Fourniture III, and Cymbale II; on the Positif a Larigot) and noted that the Tierce 'is a Stop of much variety', the instrument was nevertheless still unable to produce the full Parisian effect of *Tierce en taille*; neither were comparable organs in Brittany and Flanders. Much evidence, particularly the extant examples from organs of the later Harris school (c1720–50), suggests that the reeds which now could be expected in an average-sized English organ were of French quality, but there seems to have been a general opinion among musicians that both reeds and Mixtures were unnecessary. Of reeds, Roger North wrote in about 1720: 'the basses will always snore, and that defect cannot be conquered, so that in Organs they are rather an incumbrance than useful'; and of Mixtures and mutations, J. Blewitt wrote in about 1790 that they are 'put in by Organ-Builders, merely to make a show of Stops to draw, at a small expense . . . they only encumber an organ'. As for pedals, Harris himself recommended them in his 1712 scheme for St Paul's on the two grounds that the organist would then 'be able to do as much as if he had four hands . . . and therefore Pedals are used in all the great Organs beyond the seas', but no English pedal pipes are known for certain to have existed before the 'six large Trumpet Pipes down to 16 foot tone to be used with a pedal or without' at St Paul's in 1720–21; and then it is clear that they could be played from the Great organ. (The first separate pedal pipes seem to be those of St Catherine-by-the-Tower, 1778.) From 1712, what occupied much more attention was the expressive use made of the box enclosing the little Echo chests in a three- or (as at St Magnus, London Bridge, 1712) four-manual organ. Abraham Jordan, the builder at St Magnus, claimed this SWELL organ as an original invention, though similar devices had been applied to solo stops in Spanish organs over the previous half-century or so, and Harris claimed to have tried it out in the Salisbury organ. By 1730 every average new organ had a Swell; by 1825 it was ousting the Choir organ as the chief second manual.

In view of these appallingly limited views on what organs were for, it is surprising that the Harris school was allowed to build an organ so effective as that at St Mary Redcliffe, Bristol, seems to have been (see Table 17). Its pedal pulldowns seem (from the circular published by Harris & Byfield) to have been able to draw the octave above on the Great, i.e. both from 16′ (or C′) and from 8′ (or C); the builders also betrayed an attitude of the period in adding that although pedals had been supplied 'not withstanding the Touch is as good as need be desired'. Clearly the Harris school was com-

TABLE 17

St Mary Redcliffe, Bristol
Harris & Byfield, 1726

Great organ		Chair organ	
C′–d‴ (63 notes)		G′–d‴ (56 notes)	
Open Diapason	8	Stopped Diapason	8
Open Diapason	8	Principal	4
Stopped Diapason	8	Flute almain	4 (? or 8′, half-
Principal	4		compass)
Twelfth (G′–d‴	2⅔	Flute	2 (? or 4′)
only)		Sesquialtera	III
Fifteenth (G′–d‴	2	Bassoon	8
only)			
Tierce (G′–d‴	1⅗	Swell	
only)		G′–d‴ (44 notes)	
Sesquialtera	V	Open Diapason	8
Cornet (from c′)	V	Stopped Diapason	8
Trumpet	8	Principal	4
Clarion	4	Flute	4
		Sesquialtera	III
Pedal		Trumpet	8
1 octave pulldown		Hautboy	8
		Cremona	8
		French Horn	8

Four bellows
Couplers: Great organ to Pedal; Great organ octave to Pedal

petent on the technical side, for in 1725 at St Dionis Backchurch, London, it had even attempted regulation of the wind by fitting springs to the four bellows.

The strength of British insular traditions is also clear in the work of John Snetzler, a German Swiss who worked with the Egedacher firm of Passau and, like many other keyboard makers, went to London early in the 1740s. Certain of Snetzler's techniques, particularly the voicing and actions, may derive from the Egedachers, but again despite the popular accounts remarkably little of importance is known about Snetzler, or even why so many extant chamber organs are ascribed to him. Nevertheless, the English nature of his specifications is clear from written evidence, and only his earliest major organs like that at King's Lynn (1754) show obvious foreign influence (e.g. the manual 16′ Bourdon). There is evidence that Snetzler attempted to introduce other up-to-date central European colour stops, such as Viola da Gamba, Salicional, overblowing German Flute, or overblowing Dulciana; but only the easiest of these, the narrow-scaled, open cylindrical Dulciana, caught the taste of English organists. Such Dulcianas soon became necessary on all organs containing more than four stops. Its held-in tone seems indeed to have coloured English organ building in general; at least Snetzler's contemporary Samual Green was recognized in the best circles of his day as the builder of large organs little superior in tone to chamber organs. That he might lead fashion by enclosing whole organs in Venetian swells such as used by some English harpsichord makers is further condemnation of his ideas.

Snetzler's organ of 1757 in the Savoy Chapel had several foreign features: manual coupler (rare), Tremulant (fairly rare), pedal pulldowns (rare in organs of this size). But these devices remained without much influence. The German Chapel in the Savoy, however, was interesting in one respect: it was a foreign church and as such points to an interesting factor in English organ building over the whole period 1750–1875, namely the 'advanced' ideas put into practice in organs built not for Anglican or established churches but for the chapels of embassies, and later for Methodist churches and those of other evangelical movements. From 1800 to 1875 it was the concert hall and eventually (after about 1835) the town hall that commissioned organs incorporating the most advanced techniques of building or the most cosmopolitan German-inspired stop lists. Such influences were already fairly strong in the late 18th century, partly through the émigré builders like Snetzler, partly through travellers like Burney, partly through touring virtuosos like Abbé Vogler, and not least through the inactivity in the established church itself. The virtues (such as they were) of English organ music in the form of solo-stop voluntaries by John Stanley and his contemporaries were also fast disappearing by 1790. Both the instrument and its repertory were ripe for German and other continental influences early in the next century.

See also §VIII, 5, below.

9. THE SPANISH BAROQUE ORGAN. The organ of the Iberian peninsula has many special characteristics. Yet Baroque organs of Spain and Portugal differ in detail from area to area, and while the visual parts of such instruments were indigenous and individual, their musical characteristics are founded more securely in common European traditions. In 1500 Spanish organs stood at much the same point as those of northern France, the Netherlands and northern Germany. The influences were Dutch rather than Italian – a Pedro Flamench ('Peter the Fleming') was at work in Barcelona in 1540 – and even the term 'Fleutes' for Principals (a later term was Flautado) was Netherlands. Principals and Mixtures (Mixtura, Forniment, Simbalet) were the stop changes or mutaciones available on the new big organs of 1550, although positives were already showing an array of slider-stops, including regals, reeds and wooden flutes. Evidently Dutch builders brought Chimney Flutes and Quintadenas with them, and by the 1550s new large organs of spendid proportions could be expected to have large-scaled reed stops. Often these reeds had colourful names: Trompetas naturals a la tudesca ('German or Dutch trumpet stops with natural-length resonators'), Clarins de mar ('trumpets of the sea', as used for naval signals) or Clarins de galera, molt sonoroses ('gallery trumpets, very sonorous') at Lérida in 1554. Although none of these was horizontal, the terms are evocative and probably played their part in the evolution of the remarkable Iberian reed stops.

Just as Flemish singers were called to Philip II's court chapel in Madrid, so Flemish organ builders were commissioned (notably the Brebos family), putting into practice their up-to-date ideas at El Escorial. The Brebos organ had a large Hoofdwerk of two chests and big flue and reed choruses, as well as flute mutations; the pedal was similarly a large modern department. But the only other manual was a Brustwerk (though one of 12 stops), and indeed Chair organs were never to become important in Spanish organ building. Barcelona seems to have been a centre for German builders, but registrations left at S Juan de las Abadesas, Barcelona, in 1613 show the stops to have been used in a traditional or old-fashioned way, and during the 17th century emphasis shifted south and west.

Nobody knows when the first reeds were placed EN CHAMADE. The term is French and refers to trumpet calls when parleys are summoned (Lat. clamare); but placing regals and (a little later) reeds horizontally in the case front was convenient for sound (penetrating in big churches where the organ did not face the congregation), accessibility (for quick tuning), reliability (gathering little dust), economy (replacing cathedral trumpeters) and appearance (see fig.39). They may date from about 1620, perhaps at first in the south. But the documents rarely specify whether reeds were horizontal or not, just as documents before the end of the 18th century rarely specify whether or not 'Eco' chests or interior Trumpets and Cornets were placed in a Swell box. The fine organ at Alcalá de Henares, for instance, had some specially described reed stops which may well have been horizontal (Juan de Echevarría, c1680): Trompetas reales, 'of which there can be three kinds'; Dulzainas; Orlos, resembling 'the guitar and harpsichord' (*zitara y clavicordio*); Trompeta mayor, 'a stop found in few other organs'; Bajoncillos, 'also newly invented'; Voz humanas; and Angeles o Serafines, angel statues blowing trumpets. By 1750 a large organ would have a huge battery of reeds, vertical and horizontal, many kinds of chorus, large Swell departments and even a pedal rank or two. The well-known organ of Granada (fig.40, p.xxx) can be taken as an example and its stop list is given in Table 18. No large Spanish organ can be called fully 'typical'. As in Italy during the next century, the larger the organ, the greater the variety of solo stops; the large organ of Toledo (1796), however, shows no advance on the concept of smaller organs built nearly a century earlier.

The only known registration guide of the Spanish Baroque organ, made at Segovia Cathedral in about 1770,

TABLE 18

Granada Cathedral			
Organ on Epistle side, case dated 1747			
Organo grande			
(left-hand stops)		(right-hand stops)	
Flautado	16	Flautado	16
Flautado	8	Flautado	8
Flautado	8	Flautdao	8
Flautado violón	8	Flautado violón	8
'Quintatön'	8	'Quintatön'	8
Octava	4	Flauta traversa	8
Lleno		Octavo	4
Nasardos	IV	Lleno	
Bombardos	16	Corneta	V
Trompeta	8	Bombardos	16
Trompeta*	8	Trompeta	8
Orlos*	8	Trompeta*	8
Viola* (regal)	8 (wood)	Orlos*	8
Clarin*	4	Oboe*	8
Clarin*	4	Regalia*	8
Clarin de atras*	4	Clarin de atras*	8 (? 16)
(facing side-aisle)		Clarin*	4
Violeta* (regal)	2	Trompeta	16
		magna*	
Cadireta (Chair organ)			
(left-hand stops)		(right-hand stops)	
Flautado violón	8	Flautado violón	8
Octava	4	Octava	4
Tapadillo	4	Tapadillo	4
Nasardo	$2\frac{2}{3}$	Flauta	4
Nasardo	2	Lleno	III
Nasardo	$1\frac{1}{3}$	Corneta	III
Lleno	III	Trompeta magna	8
Trompeta recordata	8	(full-length)	
(short)		Viejos	8
		Clarin (en	8
Organo expresivo (Swell)		chamade)	
Flautado violón	8		
Flauta armonica	8	*Pedal*	
Trompeta	8	Flautado	16
Oboe	8	Flautado	8
Voz humana	8		

Compass: now C'–b–c''', complete
Some Swell stops and stop names of doubtful origin
* = horizontal

suggests the few staple requirements organists made of these extravagant creations. They comprise French *dialogues* (two-part pieces with mutation stops or reeds in each hand), regal solos (e.g. Dulzaina in either hand), half-stops for each hand on the same manual, echo effects and manual contrasts for two- or three-part music, flutes contrasted with reeds (? in homophonic music), inner vertical reeds with outer horizontal trumpets, cornets and reeds 8', 4' or 8', 2' combined. Because of the halved stops ('medio registro'), the right hand could produce a line lower than that of the left hand, or one very much higher. The 'Swell' is also mentioned, not for swelling but to soften the effect of certain registrations. Pedals are ignored.

Over the whole period, the bellows of the Iberian organ were usually multifold and generally operated by hand. Wind pressure was low (c50–60 mm), though up to 90 mm on larger instruments. The chests were always slider-chests, usually divided into bass and treble (i.e. not C and C♯ chests as elsewhere). The division was between b and c' in Catalonia, between c' and c♯' elsewhere. As in French organs, the pallets are ranged vertically above the keys. The chest layout is often very complicated, each group of stops set on quasi-separate chests at different heights, easy to tune and reach, and often some way removed from the pallet. Neither bellows nor trunks and channels allow the families of stops to be combined, but the rigidity of registration enabled builders to include helpful accessories like 'shifting movements' to aid stop-changes. Subsidiary chests like Echo organs are placed on the floor of the main case ('cadireta interior') and operated by a sticker action; if there is a Chair organ, the pallets are below and directly in line with the lower keyboard, and the channels pass below the close-spaced organist's seat. A middle manual may operate pallets of a pair of chests placed in the rear case front of the organ, facing the side aisle. There are no manual couplers. Pedal keys are short, sometimes mushroom-shaped, usually encompassing only a few notes; there may be a rank of eight to ten wooden pipes but most pedals are pulldowns, presumably for *points d'orgue* and cadences. The hinged lid of the Swell box – known for Cornet chests by about 1675 but including reeds by about 1710 – was raised by a pulley and rope operated by a pedal-lever that needed to be kept down if the lid was to remain open.

The scaling of the Principal is often narrow, the tone restrained; Flutes are gentle, and the Cornets expansive but thinner than the French. The quiet Flutes contrast greatly with the reeds, which were designed to fill the spaces of a large Spanish church outside the immediate intimacy of the quire or *coro* over which the organ looms. Horizontal reeds and regals encouraged solo music, and Correa de Arauxo's 1626 publication shows a matured technique of left- or right-hand solos, a technique not very different in effect from other 17th-century dialogue music such as the English double voluntary. The reeds also played chords, not only for the celebrated *batallas* (battle-pieces) but also for imposing intradas on feast days.

At Saragossa (extant case dated 1443; see fig.41, p.884) Spanish *coro* organs were already placed between pillars. It was probably this position that encouraged large flat façades bearing little resemblance to the inner construction of the organ itself, indeed often giving it the appearance of having more chest levels than it has. Certainly the amount of empty space within a Spanish organ absorbs strong partials in the plenum and helps to produce the mild quality of the flue choruses.

10. THE 18TH-CENTURY ITALIAN ORGAN. The essentials of the Brescian classical organ were established by 1575 at the latest: large, shallow cases (somewhat altar-like in shape, open-spaced above the pipes), with one chest at the level of the case pipes (spring-chest, mortised with well-spaced channels often of equal size), and multifold bellows and low wind pressure. The compass would rise to *a″* or *c‴*, with all but case pipes of leaded metal (thick-walled, Principals relatively narrow in the bass, Flutes wider with smaller mouths) and completely separate ranks (the upper of which break back an octave at regular intervals). The tuning would be some form of meantone temperament, but the general pitch level would vary from organ to organ ('come si vuole', as Antegnati remarked), sometimes with an octave or so of pedal pulldowns (short keys sloping up like a reading-desk or 'pedali a leggio'), and occasionally after about 1600 with wooden Pedal Principals. Registration was standardized, and each combination suggested to the player a certain modal style to be played at a certain moment of the Mass (e.g. 'Voce umana' for the Elevation) and vice versa.

Italian builders and organists remained faithful to these ideas, modifying them gradually but leaving them recognizable even in the large organs of 1850. Yet it could be that historians have overemphasized the Brescian organ, for each city or region had its own version of the general plan. Certainly a Flemish builder Vicenzo Fulgenzi had already introduced stopped pipes (Flute $2\frac{2}{3}'$), Chimney Flute (2'), conical flute ($1\frac{2}{3}'$), reeds (Tromboni 8') and regals (Voce umana 4') at Orvieto Cathedral by 1600, as well as a Tremulant and an aviary of toy stops. Less than a century later, another German (the Silesian Johann Caspar, or Eugen Casparini) was introducing Mixtures and even Cornets in organs of the Tyrol, as well as confirming the trend towards the German–French *C–c‴* compass. But indirect Italian influences appear to have been strong elsewhere early in the 17th century, notably Provence, England (college chapels) and Jesuit Poland (conventual churches). Second manuals remained the exception, and the one made by the Dalmatian builder Petar Nakic (Pietro Nacchini) for S Antonio, Padua, in 1743–9 presented a character little different from that of S Maria in Aracoeli, Rome, in 1587: I Ripieno, Voce umana, two flutes, Tierce, regal; II Ripieno, Voce umana, one flute, Tierce, regal; Pedal 16'. As builders began collecting the upper Ripieno ranks on to one slider, a Mixture resulted that was not so different from a French *Fourniture cymbalisée*. A particular taste grew during the 18th century for Tierce or (as they were called) Cornetto ranks, but these had already been included in some two-manual registrations written down in Rome in 1666. Moreover, during the 18th century large, experimental organs were built on special commission, spreading new ideas from Bergamo to Sicily. But although rivalry with the fine organs 'at Marseilles, Trent and Hamburg' may have been the motive behind the five-manual organ at S Stefano dei Cavalieri, Pisa (Azzolino Bernardino della Ciaia, 1733–7), and elsewhere, the result was peculiarly unlike any of them. The 1730s may have seen a parting of the ways when builders throughout Europe were developing techniques beyond musical requirements; but the five-manual, three-console, 55-stop organ at Catania, Sicily (Duomo

39. Organ with reeds en chamade in the convent of S Maria, Arouca, Portugal

del Piano, 1755), though admired and even copied in the next century, was little more than an accumulation of several classical Italian organs, collected together. The effect of Spanish rule on the Kingdom of Naples has yet to be explored from the point of view of organ building, but it seems doubtful whether Spanish influences ever went further east than the Balearics.

A characteristic and influential organ of the later 18th century was the Venetian, brought to fruition by Nacchini and his pupil and successor Gaetano Callido. The Callido firm built hundreds of single-manual organs and many with two manuals (the pipes of the second being enclosed in a Swell box from about 1785), summing up many of the 17th- and 18th-century trends, discarding the more extravagant elements, giving their organs a velvety tone far removed from Antegnati; indeed in their wide-scaled Principals they influenced many a so-called *Italienisch Prinzipal* in modern German organs. The stop list of an instrument by Callido is given in Table 19 (p.883); for ease of tuning, the regal stops were placed in front, standing vertically before the Principale. Registrations provided by Callido elsewhere show orchestral imitations to have been important to organists of the period; there is no subtle play of two manuals, and in general Swell shutters seem to have been used either quite open or quite closed, rather than expressively.

See also §VIII, 5, below.

11. THE ORGAN OF J. S. BACH. In many ways the organs of Bach's main area of activity, Thuringia, Weimar and

40. *Organ (1745–7) at Granada Cathedral, showing the rear façade of the Epistle organ, with tiers of dummy pipes or flats, and a single rank of reeds en chamade (8' treble, 4' bass); note the low cut-up of the mouths of the large pipes to right and left*

Leipzig, showed the same kind of influences as his music: a basic German traditionalism tempered with French colour and Italian fluency. Neither the organ nor the music was as local in origin or as independent of other regional ideas as was usually the case elsewhere, even in the mid-18th century. Bach himself is known to have been intimately acquainted with organ music of many countries and periods, as were such contemporaries as J. G. Walther; later colleagues, however, seem in some respects to have had less wide knowledge. C. P. E. Bach's remark that his father registered stops 'in his own manner', 'astounding' other organists, might conceivably refer to either a French or a 17th-century north German approach to stop-combinations, neither of which may have been familiar to players of the younger generation, who thought that 'the art died with him'. On the other hand, J. S. Bach is said to have complained that Gottfried Silbermann's Mixtures were 'over-weak', with 'not enough sharp penetration', as if he did not appreciate that Silbermann's French *plein jeu* was different in function from a north German *organo pleno*, being one of the many colours rather than a total chorus. Moreover, the period in which Bach worked was one of a changing aesthetic for organs, when the large west-end organ became increasingly associated with congregational hymn singing, requiring big chests, large bellows capacity, many 8' stops, a powerful 16' pedal tone and a range of sound characterized more by extremes of loud and soft than by a full array of equal, piquant colours.

Apart from the qualities of his music, then, the position of Bach in organ history is important, and can serve to show some of the currents affecting the flow of German organ music. In the course of two centuries, the area between Hanover and Breslau produced great builders (the Fritzsche and Compenius families, Casparini, Silbermann, Joachim Wagner, Engler, Hildebrandt and Schulze) and some even more influential theorists (Praetorius, Werckmeister, Adlung, Agricola, Knecht, Seidel and Töpfer). Its composers included many who travelled to hear and see great organ traditions elsewhere (for example Bach, who went to Lübeck to hear Buxtehude and to Hamburg to prove his ability on a Schnitger organ) or who settled down in another part of Germany and formed schools of keyboard playing around them (Froberger, Pachelbel, C. P. E. Bach). Many details of the stop lists of J. S. Bach's organs at Arnstadt (1703–7), Mühlhausen (1707–8) and Weimar (1708–17) will forever remain unclear, as will larger matters of registration and tonal effect; but the Arnstadt organ (see Table 20) can be taken as typical, one known by the Pachelbel school as well as Bach's family. The particular lack of second manual on this instrument, the pedal department, and the range of 8' manual colours had long been traditional in this part of Germany, and in style the Weimar court chapel organ followed much the same patterns.

Larger church organs began to allow for new attitudes towards the plenum. When Bach lived in Lüneburg in 1700 or visited Lübeck in 1706 organists there would not have 'mixed the families' of organ stops by drawing more than one rank of any given pitch even on the larger organs. The *Werkprinzip* organist played in a more discreet, regulated manner. As Werckmeister had written in 1698, organists should not draw two stops of the same pitch because wind supply and tuning problems would prevent them from being fully in tune together, but by

1721, shortly after Bach's visit to Hamburg, Mattheson was suggesting an *organo pleno* of all stops except reeds – Principals, Bourdons, Salicionals, Flutes, Quintatöne, Octaves, Fifths, Mixtures, Tierce, Sesquialteras etc. The significance of any remark made by Mattheson, or its precise meaning, is often a matter of conjecture, but a little later Adlung and Agricola both seem to have supported the idea of mixed stops. Adlung thought that good modern bellows ought to allow an organist to draw Manual Prinzipal 8' + Gedackt 8' + Gemshorn 8' + Rohrflöte 8' with Pedal Contrabass 32' + Posaune 32' + Sub-bass 16' + Violon 16' + Posaune 16' + Oktave 8' + Gedackt 8'; and composers such as Gronau drew Prinzipal 8' + Flute 8' + Oktave 4' + Flute 4' + Salicet 4' + Trompete 8' + Oboe 8' to bring out the melody of an organ chorale. Thus, during Bach's lifetime, ideas about what constituted Full organ were in the process

TABLE 19

S Maria Assunta, Candide
Gaetano Callido, 1797–9 (opus 367)

Organo grande F'–f'''		*Organo piccolo* F'–f'''	
Principale	8 (halved)	Principale	8 (halved)
Ottava	4	Ottava	4 (halved)
Decimaquinta	2	Decimaquinta	2
Decimanona	$1\frac{1}{3}$	Decimanona	$1\frac{1}{3}$
Vigesimaseconda	1	Vigesimaseconda	1
Vigesimasesta	$\frac{2}{3}$	Voce umana	8 (treble)
Vigesimanona	$\frac{1}{3}$	Flauto	4
Trigesimaterza	$\frac{1}{3}$ (to f only)	Flauto	$2\frac{2}{3}$
Trigesimasesta	$\frac{1}{4}$ (to f only)	Flauto	$1\frac{3}{5}$ (treble)
Voce umana	8 (treble)	Tromboncini	8 (halved)
Flauto in ottava	4 (halved)	Violoncello	8 (halved)
Flauto in duodecima	$2\frac{2}{3}$ (halved)	*Pedal*	
Cornetto	$1\frac{3}{5}$ (treble)	CDEFGA–b♭	
Violetta	4 (treble)	Contrabassi	16
Tromboncini	8 (halved)	Ottava	8
		Ottava	4
Tamburo (drum stop)		Tromboni (reed)	?8

Halved stops divided at a/b♭
Second manual chest to left of keyboards

TABLE 20

Bonifaciuskirche, Arnstadt
J. F. Wender, 1703

Hauptwerk (Oberwerk)		*Brustwerk*	
Quintadena*	?16	Stillgedackt	8
Prinzipal	8	Hohlflöte** (g–d''')	8
Viola da gamba	8	Prinzipal	4
Gemshorn*	8	Nachthorn	4
Grobgedackt	8	Quinte	$2\frac{2}{3}$
Quinte* (open)	$5\frac{1}{3}$	Spitzflöte	2
Oktave	4	Sesquialtera	?II
Oktave	2	Mixtur	IV
Mixtur	IV		
Zimbel	III	*Pedal*	
Trompete	· 8	Sub-bass	16
		Violon Bass	16
		Prinzipal Bass	8
		Posaune	16

Compass: *CDE–d'–d'''*
Couplers: *Hauptwerk* to Pedal: (? *Brustwerk* to Pedal, *Brustwerk* to *Hauptwerk*); (? *Hauptwerk* to Pedal coupler stop later addition)
Two tuned Zimbelsterne (*Glockenaccord*, ?1703)
Tremulant (*Hauptwerk*)

*pitch length uncertain
**compass and manual uncertain

41. Organ (1443) at Saragossa Cathedral; the reeds en chamade were added possibly in the 18th century

of changing, as were ideas about the number and kind of solo stops.

In Lüneburg, Lübeck and Hamburg Bach would have heard organs with *Rückpositiven*, but after about 1710 Chair organs were rare in new instruments of his own area; some cities had not known them since about 1650. The *Rückpositiv* at Mühlhausen already had a stop list (8.8.4.4.2.2.1⅓.?.II.III) quite different from the bright, colourful manual of Dutch and French organs, and, where gallery space was sufficient, builders preferred to hold such second-manual chests within the Great case, usually above the Great. The resulting 'Oberwerk' was thus different in origin from the Niehoff–Schnitger *Oberwerk*. At the same time French influences appeared; pedals became increasingly less able to provide solo colour for cantus firmus music, itself a dying genre; and organs took on a stereotyped character that varied only if the builder was sensitive to different voicing and scalings demanded by different church acoustics.

The privileged organ builder to the court of Saxony was Gottfried Silbermann, a native of Saxony who had learnt in France and Alsace and returned to make the friendship of such composers as Kuhnau and Bach. Silbermann's early and largely extant organ in Freiberg Cathedral (1710–14) already demonstrated many of these developments (see fig.42 and Table 21). Here was not a mass of clumsy auxiliary stops, but a unique blend of

Saxon and Parisian elements, full of well-thought-out balance between the three manuals, and implying a mode of registration needing to be learnt carefully by the organist. Silbermann's voicing is strong, particularly of the Principals; his smaller village organs have great power and energy. Wind pressure (as in Joachim Wagner's organs) was *c*94 mm (manuals) and *c*104 mm (pedals) in later organs, about 10 mm higher than that of good large organs of about 1700.

There is little direct connection between any of Bach's organ music and such instruments as that at Freiberg; but were the Trio Sonatas, for instance, known to the organist of such a church, he may well have drawn for lively movements the combination of stops noted by the local priest as having been recommended at Silbermann's Fraureuth organ (1739–42) for *jeu de tierce en dialogue* (called *Tertien-Zug zweystimmig*): right hand Prinzipal 8′ + Rohrflöte 8′ + Oktave 4′ + Quinte 2⅔′ + Prinzipal 2′ + Tierce 1⅗′; left hand Gedackt 8′ + Rohrflöte 4′ + Nasard 2⅔′ + Oktave 2′ + Quinte 1⅓′ + Sifflöte 1′; and Pedal Sub-bass 16′ + Posaune 16′. Given a free choice, as he may have been in the design for Hildebrandt's large organ at St Wenzel, Naumburg (1743–6), Bach might well have chosen to combine the features of several organ types: three manuals including Chair organ, 53 stops including Cornet and solo pedal stops, and each manual designed as an entity with its

TABLE 21

Freiberg Cathedral
Gottfried Silbermann, 1710–14

Hauptwerk		*Oberwerk*	
Bourdon (lead)	16	Quintadena (tin)	16
Prinzipal (tin)	8	Prinzipal (tin)	8
Rohrflöte (lead)	8	Gedackt (lead)	8
Viola da gamba (tin)	8	Quintadena (tin)	8
		Oktave (tin)	4
Oktave (tin)	4	Spitzflöte (tin)	4
Quinte (tin)	2⅔	Superoktave (tin)	2
Superoktave (tin)	2	Flachflöte (tin)	
Tierce (lead)	1⅗	Mixtur (tin)	III
Mixtur (tin)	IV	Zimbel (tin)	II
Zimbel (tin)	III	Cornet (lead)	V
Cornet (lead) (mounted)	V	(boxed)	
		Krummhorn (tin)	8
Trompete	8	Vox humana (tin)	8
Clarin	4		
		Pedal	
Brustwerk		Untersatz (same slider as Oktave)	32 (stopped wood)
Gedackt (lead)	8		
Prinzipal (tin)	4		
Rohrflöte (lead)	4	Prinzipal	16
Nasat (lead)	2⅔	Oktave	16 (wood)
Oktave (tin)	2	(same slider as Untersatz)	
Tierce (lead)	1⅗		
Quinte (tin)	1⅓	Sub-bass	16 (stopped wood)
Sifflöte (tin)	1	Oktave (tin)	8
Mixtur	III	Oktave (tin)	4
		Mixtur (tin)	VI
		Posaune (lead)	16
		Trompete (lead)	8
		Clarin (lead)	4

Lead = metal with high lead content (Gedackts, wooden pipes in bass)
Tremulant *fort* to three manuals together
Tremulant *doux* for Vox humana
Sperrventile to each department
Couplers: *Oberwerk* to *Hauptwerk*; *Brustwerk* to *Hauptwerk*; (original *Hauptwerk* to Pedal uncertain)
Pitch: about ⅞ tone higher than *a*′ = 440
Wind pressure: *c*85 mm (manual), *c*94 mm (pedal)
Compass: CD–*c*′–*c*‴
Zimbel ranks duplicate smaller pipes of mixtures
Cornets: 1.8.12.15.17

own auxiliary stops (Viola, Fugara, Unda maris, Weitpfeife, Spillflöte etc). As in all organs frequently played by Bach, Naumburg had several string-toned stops, either narrow cylindrical or conical. Tierce ranks, alone or as constituents of the Sesquialtera–Cornet, were indispensable for solo melodic lines in an organ chorale. Manual reeds were never numerous (even at Naumburg, they accounted for less than 10% of the manual stops) and were, except Vox humana and Krummhorn, for chorus purposes. The Mixtures at Naumburg were more in the bright German tradition than Silbermann's *pleins jeux*, and the pedal reeds (32′, 16′, 8′, 4′) no doubt had little of Silbermann's élan. A contemporary critic of one of Hildebrandt's organs in Dresden thought its tone dull and heavy, owing to increased wind pressure, higher cut-ups, and new voicing methods in general which spoilt the Praetorian 'Lieblichkeit der Harmonie'. But such factors were characteristic of the new mode of the 1730s and 1740s in general.

In view of the cross-currents in German organ design from 1700 to 1750, it is not surprising that Bach should have left only a few registrations, and those only of a general nature. The published Schübler preludes (c1746) make it clear whether the pedal is a 16′ quasi-continuo bass line or a 4′ cantus firmus melody line, but they do not specify colour. The manual Prinzipal 8′ and pedal Trompete 8′ registered in the autograph manuscript of the *Orgelbüchlein* prelude BWV600 are there as much to indicate that the canonic voices are to sound an octave apart as to suggest actual stops to be drawn. For a concerto or a prelude and fugue it is rarely clear on whose authority the manuals (and particularly the manual changes) have been specified in the manuscript copies. The subject is thus open to many solutions and suggestions. But on no single organ that Bach is known to have played would all his organ music have sounded at its best or been given a registration suitable to its carefully conceived style and genre.

See also §VIII, 5, below.

12. SPLENDOURS OF NORTHERN EUROPE, 1650–1800. Between 1725 and 1750 a large number of important organs were built: the great organs of Haarlem, Gouda, Weingarten, Herzogenburg, Naumburg, Dresden, Breslau, Potsdam, Uppsala, Catania, Pisa, Tours, Paris (Notre Dame), Granada and Braga. All these and many other organs of their type were designed both to fill their churches with big sound and to tickle the ear with delicate effects. Neither purpose was known to the 16th-century builder. The very tendency to build organs exclusively at the west end of the church pinpoints this move towards extremes of sound, for apart from the large conventual churches and larger French parish churches, the new west-end organ was the only instrument in the building, especially in Protestant countries, where the need for a smaller auxiliary organ in the liturgy had largely disappeared. The generation of builders who produced the even bigger, later organs of the 18th century (Toledo, St Maximin, Hamburg Michaeliskirche, Rostock Marienkirche, Arnhem, Nijmegen, Amorbach, St Florian and Oliwa) or theorists who planned yet bigger ones (Vogt, 1719 and Bédos de Celles, 1766–78) were mostly seeking to exploit the same extremes.

Earlier, however, characteristic national developments had frequently resulted in organs which, though conceived within classical limits and not, as it were, stepping outside idiomatic, traditional usage, nonethe-

less had greater potential than their composers seem to have been aware of. Thus the problem with organs of 1650 to 1750 is to know for certain what they were meant to play and how they were meant to sound, whereas the problem with organs of 1750 to 1850 is that the music for which they were built, often with great ingenuity and unsurpassed technical skill, may be difficult to admire.

Two good examples of the northern organ in about 1650 are at Klosterneuburg and Alkmaar; both retain many features of their originals in spite of extensive rebuilding. Much is still unknown, however, of the detail of the originals, and it is necessary to rely on the stop lists, given in Table 22 (p.886). At Klosterneuburg neither the *Brustwerk* nor even the *Rückpositiv* competes with the main chest (*Hauptwerk* and Pedal), either in sound or appearance. The *Hauptwerk* dominates the ensemble, in the true 16th-century tradition of central Europe; perhaps it, not the pedal, was originally meant to take the 16′ pipes in the case. The instrument should be seen not so much as a three-manual organ but as a group of three independent organs: *Hauptwerk* for postludes etc, *Rückpositiv* for interludes and major accompaniments, *Brustwerk* for continuo. It is uncertain whether the organ originally had manual reeds, other than the Regal; but mutations are also few, and colours were obtained by a variety of 8′ and 4′ ranks. 8′ colour stops were becoming very popular throughout the area Vienna–Ulm–Prague–Vienna, and on paper the main chests of such organs often appear misleadingly large. 14 out of 28 stops at the Prague Týn Church (J. H. Mundt, 1671–3) were on the *Hauptwerk*, 16.8.8.8.8.8.4.4.2⅔.2.1⅓.1. VI.IV, but four of the 8′ stops were colour changes, not chorus ranks. Salicional 8′, Viola 8′ and similar stops

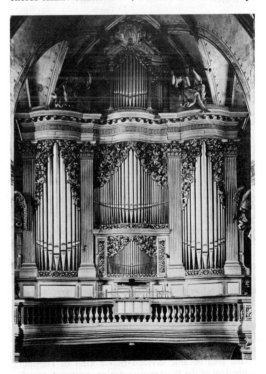

42. *Organ by Gottfried Silbermann (1710–14; case by E. Lindner) in Freiberg Cathedral*

TABLE 22

Augustinerchorherrenstift, Klosterneuburg
J. Scherer, *c*1550, J. G. Freundt, 1636–42

Hauptwerk
CDEFGA–*c‴*

Prinzipal	8
Prinzipalflöte	8 (wide)
Coppel	8 (wide)
Quintadena	8
Oktave	4
Offenflöte	4 (wide)
Dulcian (Tolkaan)	4
Oktavcoppel	4 (wide)
Quinte	2⅔
Superoktave	2
Mixtur	XII–XIV (4')
Zimbel	II (½')
Posaune (1950)	16
Posaune (1950)	8

Brustwerk

Coppel	4
Prinzipal	2
Spitzflöte	2
Regal	8

Pedal

Portunprinzipal	16 (case)
Sub-bass	16
Oktave	8
Choralflöte (open)	8 (wide)
Superoktave	4
Mixtur	VI–VIII (4')
Rauschwerk	III (2')
Posaune	16
Posaune	8

Rückpositiv

Nachthorngedackt	8 (wide)
Prinzipal	4
Spitzflöte	4
Kleincoppel	4
Oktave	2
Superoktave	1
Zimbel	II
Krummhorn	8

All metal pipes
Pedal and *Hauptwerk* ranks all
  placed on the same chest
Some stop names conjectural
Coupler: *Rückpositiv* to
  Hauptwerk
Wind pressure 55–65 mm

St Laurents (Groote Kerk), Alkmaar
L. Eckmans, Galtus & Germer Hagerbeer, 1639–45

Hauptwerk (manual III)
F'–*d‴* (short, for first 2 stops)
C–*d‴* (short)

Praestant	16
Praestant	8
Oktave	4
Grosser Scharf	
Kleiner Scharf	
Terzian	
Trompete	8

Rückpositiv (I)
C–*d‴* (short)

Praestant	8
Quintadena	8
Oktave	4
Flöte	4
Superoktave	2
Tierce	1⅗ (?1685)
Nasard	1⅓
Quintanus	1⅓
Sifflöte	1
Mixtur	III–IV
Scharf	IV
Sesquialtera	(?1685)
(treble)	
Trompete	8

Unterwerk (II)
C–*d‴* (short)

Bourdon	16
Praestant	8
Holpijp	8
Oktave	4
Quintadena	8
Offenflöte	4
Echo Holpijp	4
Superoktave	2
Tierce	1⅗ (?1685)
Nasard	1⅓
Gemshorn	1⅓
Sifflöte	1
Sesquialtera	II
Trompete	8
Vox humana	4

Pedal
F'–*f'* (at present) coupled to
  Hauptwerk
C–*f'* (at present) for pedal
  stops

Prinzipal	8
Oktave	4
Trompete	8

Couplers etc unknown
Rebuilt 1685 (J. Duyschot),
1723–6 (F. C. Schnitger)

43. Organ by L. Eckmans, Galtus & Germer Hagerbeer (1639–45; case by Jacob van Campen) in the Groote Kerk, Alkmaar

were characteristic of late 17th-century Habsburg Europe; Salicet 4', Fugara 4' and Dulciana 4' were common by the early 18th century; and reeds, except a pedal rank or two, gradually disappeared. Theorists like the Cistercian writer Vogt (1719) emphasized 8' colour stops; and for such registration rules as those given by J. B. Samber (1704), the conical Viola 8' was useful in many varied combinations: continuo playing, Viola 8'; fantasias, Viola 8' + Flöte 4'; fugues, Viola 8' + Mixtur III; versets, Viola 8' + Zimbel II.

Soon after the organ at Klosterneuburg, organ cases in the area became divided into a kind of Habsburg equivalent of the *Werkprinzip* design, with one case for the *Hauptwerk*, one for the Pedal and one for an Echo chest (Waldhausen, 1677). Such division led over the years to a rigorously applied design followed by most Austrian organs of the mid-18th century, with a half-case to one side of the west-end gallery (*Hauptwerk*), a second half-case to the other (Pedal) and a *Rückpositiv* in front, the total gallery being spacious enough to accommodate a considerable choir and orchestra for the Mass on feast days. By 1740 or so, the keyboards would be placed (in the form of a 'detached console') in a commanding position on the gallery floor, and the various parts of the case strewn around the west-end windows. In theory such an arrangement would encourage idiomatic, two-chorus organ music of the north German type, but in practice it did not.

Little is known about the music played on the great series of Dutch organs built between the death of Sweelinck (1621) and the vogue for Bach's music two centuries later. But the array of mutations and flute and reed colours on the St Laurents instrument at Alkmaar would have made possible an immense variety in the settings of, and variations on, psalm tunes. In the 1685 rebuild the *Hauptwerk* chest had to be lowered (see fig.43), perhaps because by then the organist wished to be able to accompany the congregation during hymns (but such accompaniment was then still new). It is clear how the Alkmaar organ developed from the Brabant organ of Niehoff with its limited pedal, big *Hauptwerk* chorus, 8' *Rückpositiv* used for solo effects, and a quasi-

Oberwerk (here placed below the main chest, however) with stops found on the main manual of other European organs. According to John Evelyn's diary, such Dutch organs were used 'only for show and to recreate the people before and after their Devotions, while the Burgomasters were walking and conferring about their affairs'. By association, then, the organs were secular, often indeed owned by the town council, who saw such magnificent creations as objects of rivalry. Hence the building of the organ at St Bavo, Haarlem by Christian Müller (1735–8) is to be seen as a sign of competition with Zwolle (Grote Kerk; new organ by Schnitger's sons, 1718–21), Alkmaar (rebuilt 1723–6), Amsterdam (Oude Kerk; Christian Vater, 1724–6), Gouda (St Jan; Jean Moreau, 1733–6) and elsewhere. Moreau was from the south; but Müller, Vater and F. C. Schnitger were German, and from then the Dutch organ was dominated by German builders who imported new ideas (big pedals from Hamburg, heavy voicing from Westphalia), added them to Dutch features, and produced large, powerful instruments, but unfortunately often without either German brilliance (which Marcussen mistakenly tried to 'correct' at Haarlem in 1961 with new pedal Mixtures and a new Great Mixture which unsuccessfully attempts to convert the 16′ chorus to an 8′ chorus) or French

éclat (thin reed trebles and a Cornet designed to outline the psalm-tune melody rather than to function in a *grand jeu*). Although such tonal matters are subjective, the cases themselves can be more clearly seen to have lost their native Dutch characteristics, particularly the well-featured, classical, almost clock-like designs of the 17th century, and to have begun to sprawl. It is true that at Haarlem, Müller and his architect kept the traditional vertical emphasis and other essential details in the arrangement of towers and flats; but even there the classical pediment surmounting the best old Dutch cases gave way to an unstructural, Baroque coat-of-arms (see fig.44, p.888).

Although the condition of the organs at Weingarten and Haarlem is not anything like as authentic as their fame leads admirers to assume, they do serve on paper (see Table 23) as useful examples of their 'schools', being at once both traditional and exceptional, both formative and unapproachably 'ideal'. The details of the Weingarten organ – the bells, the cherrywood stops, the ivory pipes, the doubled ranks, the undulating colours, the big Mixtures, the complex action – require a book to themselves, and it could be that a first-rate restoration of the instrument would fill out its tone. Nevertheless, the principles behind its dispensing of organ colours can

TABLE 23

St Baaf, Haarlem Christian Müller, 1735–8				Benediktinerabtei, Weingarten Joseph Gabler, 1737–50			
Hauptwerk		*Oberwerk*		*Hauptwerk*		*Rückpositiv* (south case,	
Praestant	16	Quintadena	16	Prinzipal	16	manual keys)	
Bourdon	16	Praestant (doubled	8	Prinzipal (narrow)	8	Prinzipal doux	8
Oktave (doubled	8	rank from *g*)		Rohrflöte (narrow)	8	Flûte douce	8
rank from *g*)		Quintadena	8	Oktave*	4	Quintatön	8
Rohrflöte	8	Baarpijp (conical)	8	Superoktave*	2	Violoncello	8
Viola de gamba*	8	Oktave	4	Hohlflöte*	2	Rohrflöte	4
Rohrquinte	5⅓	Flachflöte	4	Piffaro	V–VII	Querflöte (wood)	4
Oktave	4	Nasard	2⅔	Sesquialtera	IX–VIII	Flauto traverso*	4
Gemshorn	4	Nachthorn	2	Mixtur	XXI–XX	Flageolet	2
Quintpraestant	2⅔	Flageolet	1⅓	Zimbel	XII	Piffaro	VI–V
Waldflöte	2	Sesquialtera	II	Trompete	8	Cornet (narrow)	XI–VIII
Terzian	II	Mixtur*	IV–VI			Vox humana	8
Mixtur	IV–X	Zimbel*	III	*Oberwerk*		Hautboy	4
Trompete	16	Schalmei	8	Bourdon (part	16	Carillon (32 bells,	
Trompete	8	Dulzian	8	wood)*		*f*–*c‴*)	
Hautboy	8	Vox humana	8	Prinzipal	8		
Trompete	4			Coppel	8	*Pedal*	
		Pedal		Violoncello*	8	(*a*) main case	
Rückpositiv		Praestant	32	Salizional	8	Contrabass (open)*	32
Praestant (doubled	8	Praestant	16	Hohlflöte (wood)	8	Sub-bass	32
rank from *g*)		Sub-bass*	16	Unda maris (wood)	8	Oktave (wood)	16
Quintadena*	8	Rohrquinte	10⅔	Mixtur	IX–XII	Violon*	16
Holpijp	8	Oktave	8	*Kronpositiv* (high		Mixtur	V–VI
Oktave	4	Holpijp	8	chest played from		Bombarde	16
Flûte douce	4	Quintpraestant	5⅓	*Oberwerk* keys)		Posaune (wood)	16
Spitzflöte	2⅔	Oktave	4	Oktave douce (bass)	4	Carillon (20 bells at 2′)	
Superoktave	2	Holpijp	2	(treble)	8	(*b*) north *Rückpositiv* case	
Sesquialtera	II–IV	Rauschquinte	III	Viola douce*	8	Quintatön	16
(doubled		Posaune	32	Nasat	2⅔	Superoktave	8
rank from *c′*)		Posaune	16	Zimbel	II	Flûte douce	8
Cornet (from *c′*)	V	Trompete	8			Violoncello	28
Mixtur	VI–VIII	Trompete	4	*Unterwerk*		Hohlflöte	4
Zimbel*	III	Zink	2	Bourdon (wood)	16	Cornet	XI–X
Fagott	16			Prinzipal (part wood)		Sesquialtera	VII–VI
Trompete	8	Two Tremulants		Quintatön	8	Trompete	8
Trichterregal*	8	Couplers: *Oberwerk* to		Flöte (wood,	8	Fagott	8
		Hauptwerk: *Rückpositiv* to		conical)			
*replaced in 1961		*Hauptwerk*; (Pedal couplers		Viola douce	8		
		1961)		Oktave (conical)	4	*La Force*, pedal 'stop', playing	
		Wind pressure *c*75 mm		Hohlflköte*	4	48 pipes of C major triad (4′)	
		Pitch: *a′* = *c*440		Piffaro douce	II	Compass: *C*–*g*–*c‴*, complete	
		All pipes of metal		Superoktave		Stops marked * have doubled	
		Compass: *C*–*d′*–*d‴*, complete		(conical)	2	ranks for all or part of the	
		(contract gave *c‴*; pedal		Mixtur	V–VI	compass	
		now to *f′*)		Cornet (narrow)	VI–V	Wind pressure now 70 mm	
				Hautboy	8	Modern pitch	
				Tremulant			

be seen, and Gabler's little quire organ in the same church contained an even clearer indication of his passion for 8' and 4' colour stops. Some writers have described the west-end organ as a 'Rococo–Gothic conception', but it is more like a southern European grotto organ. Three echo divisions (*Oberwerk, Unterwerk, Kronpositiv*) are bound to lead to a mocking of true organ tone, however logical an extension it may have been of current ideas in south Germany as a whole. Only the two *Rückpositiven* offer well-balanced effects in the idiomatic north-German manner; yet to an 18th-century organist visiting Weingarten after Salzburg Cathedral (organ by J. C. Egedacher, 1703–6), such *Rückpositiven* must have seemed conservative and slightly puzzling. The original mechanical action must have been very troublesome to make, since even in this sprawling and unique case (see fig.45) only eight of all the case pipes do not speak; clearly the detached console was the only practical arrangement. The influence of the whole instrument was wide and long-lasting; theory books (e.g. Hawkins, 1776; Bédos de Celles, 1766–78) gave it notoriety, and it held a significant position between the colourful Renaissance organ of south Germany and the large factory organs of the 1830s.

Swabia also saw a remarkably good compromise organ during the 1760s: the larger instrument at Ottobeuren,

44. *Organ by Christian Müller (1735–8; case probably by J. van Logteren) in the Groote Kerk, Haarlem*

TABLE 24

Michaeliskirche, Hamburg
J. G. Hildebrandt, 1762–7

Hauptwerk			*Oberwerk*	
Prinzipal (tin)	16		Bourdon (metal)	16
Quintadena (metal)	16		Prinzipal*	8
Oktave* (tin)	8		Spitzflöte (metal)	8
Gedackt (metal)	8		Quintatön (metal)	8
Gemshorn (tin)	8		Unda maris (tin)	8 (treble)
Viola da gamba (tin)	8		Oktave (tin)	4
Quinte (tin)	$5\frac{1}{3}$		Spitzflöte (metal)	4
Oktave (tin)	4		Quinte (tin)	$2\frac{2}{3}$
Gemshorn (metal)	4		Oktave (tin)	2
Nasat (metal)	$2\frac{2}{3}$		Rauschpfeife (tin)	II
Oktave (tin)	2		Zimbel (tin)	V
Sesquialtera (tin)	II		Echo Cornet (tin)	V (treble)
Mixtur (tin)	VIII		Trompete* (tin)	8
Scharf (tin)	V		Vox humana (tin)	8
Cornet (tin)	V			
	(treble)		*Pedal*	
Trompete (tin)	16		Prinzipal (tin)	32
Trompete (tin)	8		Sub-bass (stopped)	32
			Prinzipal (tin)	16
Brustwerk			Sub-bass (stopped)	16
Rohrflöte (metal)	16		Rohrquinte (metal)	$10\frac{2}{3}$
Prinzipal* (tin)	8		Oktave (tin)	8
Flauto traverso	8		Quinte (tin)	$5\frac{1}{3}$
(metal)			Oktave (tin)	4
Gedackt (metal)	8		Mixtur (tin)	X
Rohrflöte (metal)	8		Posaune (tin)	32
Oktave (tin)	4		Posaune (tin)	16
Rohrflöte (metal)	4		Fagott (tin)	16
Nasat (metal)	$2\frac{2}{3}$		Trompete (tin)	8
Oktave (tin)	2		Trompete (tin)	4
Tierce (tin)	$1\frac{2}{3}$			
Quinte (tin)	$1\frac{1}{3}$			
Sifflöte (tin)	1			
Rauschpfeife (tin)	II–III			
Zimbel (tin)	V			
Chalumeau (tin)	8			

Compass: *C–d'–f'''*, complete
Zimbelstern
Tremulant (*Hauptwerk*), i.e. *tremblant fort*
Schwebung (*Oberwerk*), i.e., *tremblant doux*
Couplers: *Haputwerk* to Pedal; (? *Oberwerk* to *Hauptwerk*)
Swell for three stops (? last three of *Oberwerk*)
Stops marked * have doubled ranks for part of the compass

built by K. J. Riepp (1761–8), incorporated French elements (learnt by its builder in Burgundy) and German ones (learnt in the vicinity of Lake Constance). Most major organs in both parish and conventual churches in Switzerland, Württemberg, and Bavaria had such a mingling of organ cultures as to create distinct styles of their own; but the one at Ottobeuren was a simple amalgam. All the classical French registrations were possible on it, but so were German pedal music and hymn variations, from the evidence of its stop list.

Such composite schemes were curiously rare in the 18th century. It was more characteristic of organ building in general that even adjacent areas (e.g. Carinthia and Veneto, or Saxony and Bohemia) had totally different organs, as if builders of one area or religious denomination were thoroughly opposed to the ideals of their neighbours. Some of the major religious orders, particularly the Cistercian and Augustinian, had something of an international style crossing political frontiers, but even this kind of uniformity was not conspicuous. It was regional style that carried the day, giving the organ at Klosterneuburg, for example, great influence over the one built nearby a century later by a foreign builder well versed in other organ types (Augustinerstift, Herzogenburg; J. Henke, 1747–52). It may well have been such provincialism, however, that helped

45. *Organ by Joseph Gabler (1737–50) in the west end of the church of Weingarten Abbey, showing the two Rückpositiven (manual and pedal)*

to produce the good, conservative designs (Amorbach; Rot an der Rot), the late flowers of Baroque organ art that were able to resist the emaciating extremes of fashion.

The large organs of the late 18th century were individually distinctive, keeping regional characteristics despite the availability to organists of many printed sources of music from other countries. The Michaeliskirche in Hamburg had a 70-stop, three-manual organ by J. G. Hildebrandt (son of Silbermann's pupil Zacharias Hildebrandt); although he took with him many Saxon colours (Cornet, Unda maris, Chalumeau etc) and followed contemporary ideas common to many regions (no *Rückpositiv*, thickening Quints etc), the instrument remained a Hamburg organ, more complete and comprehensive than an organ could have been anywhere else. The massive case (for which Burney did not care) has an unmistakable 19th-century look about it; the stop list (Table 24) is typical of a large organ, but many writers who heard the instrument commented on its 'noble power', described by Burney as 'more striking by its force and the richness of the harmony than by a clear and distinct melody'. Yet the organ was no mere sacrifice to fashion, which was then rather geared to imitations of orchestral families, of wind concertos, and the like. Theorists like Hess and Knecht encouraged particular imitations of string stops and in general helped to deceive organists into thinking they could duplicate orchestral effects. So did Abbé Georg Joseph Vogler, who typifies the less reputable side of late 18th-century organ playing, and whose bizarre organ-concert programmes sometimes proved irresistible to popular audiences in large cities from London to Vienna. Vogler's SIMPLIFICATION SYSTEM, however, has received more attention than it merits historically, for the development of the organ would have been little different without him. More important was the impasse brought about at the end of the century by the technical perfection of the late Baroque organ. Quite apart from the Napoleonic holocaust, the organ historian must feel that the multiplied colour stops of St Florian and Oliwa monastic churches (1770s), the reeds of St Maximin, Poitiers and Toledo, and the choruses of Hamburg and Rostock parish churches, all pushed the classical organ as far as it would go. A total rethinking was necessary early in the next century.

13. ORGANS IN THE AMERICAS. The Spanish conqueror Cortez arrived in Central America in 1519; Franciscan and Dominican missionaries arrived soon after, and by 1530 a small organ is recorded in use at the newly founded Mexico City Cathedral. By the end of the 16th century music had been published in Mexico, and the use of organs and other instruments in churches was fairly widespread. During the 17th century the use of organs spread to Peru and other areas south of Mexico, as well as to northern missions; in 1630 17 small organs are recorded in what is now the state of New Mexico. Organs were both imported from Spain and built by immigrant builders and by Indians taught by them, and surviving cases indicate that some were fairly large, although more were of positive size.

In 1667 the new cathedral of Mexico City was dedicated, and a large Spanish organ was ordered in 1688 and first used in 1695. A number of other large cathedral organs followed, in places such as Puebla and Guadalajara, and a second organ for Mexico City Cathedral, facing the first, was completed by José Nassarre in 1735. Meanwhile organs had been introduced by the French colonists in Canada as early as 1657 (Quebec City), and between 1698 and 1705 a two-manual organ was imported for the church of Notre Dame in Montreal.

In the English colonies on the eastern seaboard of America, the first recorded use of an organ in church was at a Lutheran ordination in Philadelphia in 1703. This was a small positive borrowed from some German settlers who had arrived in 1694. In 1713 a four-stop chamber organ, possibly the work of Smith, was placed in King's Chapel, Boston. Previously in a residence, it is known to have existed as early as 1708 and it may have been imported before 1700.

Although English organs began to be imported in increasing numbers during the remainder of the 18th century, with significant examples of the work of Jordan, Bridge, England and Snetzler reaching American shores, the first to build organs in the colonies was J. G. Klemm, a Saxon who emigrated in 1733. While most of Klemm's instruments were small, he built one of three manuals for Trinity Church, New York, in 1741. His work was carried on by David Tannenberg, who built over 40 organs between 1758 and 1804, mostly

for a small area of Pennsylvania. Tannenberg's work reflects the influence of the Silbermann school, and he was familiar with the writings of Sorge.

Because of Puritan (Calvinist) objections to the use of instruments in worship, nearly all colonial organs until the end of the 18th century were located in Anglican, Lutheran or Moravian churches, and chamber organs were as popular as in England. The first organ builder in Boston was a multi-faceted craftsman, Thomas Johnston, but it was not until the first decades of the 19th century that one could pursue the trade of organ building full-time in the English colonies. English organs by builders such as Gray and Elliot were occasionally imported as late as the 1830s, but by this time, although the Pennsylvania German school had virtually died out, a vigorous native school, encouraged by an increasing demand for church organs, was established in Boston and New York. The founder of the Boston group was William Goodrich, self-taught and exceptionally gifted, in whose workshop were trained Thomas Appleton, George Stevens, and Elias and George G. Hook, who were to make Boston a major centre of organ building by the middle of the 19th century. Thomas Hall was the first New York builder of importance, but he was eclipsed by his pupil Henry Erben, who in turn trained many later builders.

The work of the early 19th-century builders was rooted in the English tradition, both visually and tonally, although it had many unique characteristics of its own. Stop lists reflected English conventions, voicing was mild but lively and casework was often exceptionally handsome. The long (G or sometimes even F) compass was used until the middle of the century, as were various forms of mean-tone tuning. Pipe metal was usually about 25% tin, zinc for basses not coming into use until almost 1850, and stopped diapasons were almost invariably of wood, along with 4′ Flute stops. Casework was of either mahogany veneer or pine, the latter always painted, sometimes to resemble hardwood. Few of the larger organs of this period remain intact, but in 1982 a fine 1830 Appleton organ was restored by the Metropolitan Museum in New York.

VI. Some developments 1800–1930

1. General influences about 1800. 2. 19th-century technical advances. 3. Some influential organs. 4. Electricity and the organ. 5. The nature of organs about 1900.

1. GENERAL INFLUENCES ABOUT 1800. A total rethinking did not manifest itself until well into the 19th century. In some countries, notably Italy, England, the Netherlands and Scandinavia, there was little perceptible change in direction until the second third of the century; the chief difference between an average organ of 1790 and 1840 in these countries was that the latter was bigger, and the builder had probably explored further the simple colour stops, Swell boxes and pedal departments. But colour stops were by nature foreign to Scandinavian organs, pedals to English and Swell boxes to Dutch. In other countries, notably France, Spain, Austria, central and southern Germany and their neighbours (Bohemia, Poland etc), events outside music not only caused organ building to receive less attention and money from churches but gave to the revival of organs in the 1830s an impetus towards new techniques.

In Austria the reforms of church music undertaken by Joseph II during the 1780s encouraged simple organs in parish churches – instruments contrasting hugely with the large monastic creations of St Florian (1770) and Heiligenkreuz (1802). In countries occupied by the French in the wake of the Revolution, such as the Netherlands, Spain, south Germany, Austria, Prussia, Poland and Moravia, services were often suspended. Only here and there were organs destroyed; more physical damage was done in France itself, where it was followed by a scarcity of funds and then, after 1815, an equally harmful overreaction: from 1792 a church may have been closed to Christian use but its organ was just as useful for 'awakening and inspiring a holy love of the Fatherland', as the new département administrators knew. But in Germany and Austria it was the dissolution of the monasteries (particularly after 1803) that changed organ tradition. In Spain and Portugal the organ suffered an eclipse, only partial in some areas but severely evident in others, taken in the wake of Wellington's and Napoleon's armies and by the reappropriation (*desamortización*) of church funds in 1830. Farther north, Denmark kept its organ traditions largely undisturbed, but Sweden produced some advanced ideas in the 1820s, not least as a result of cultural ties with Saxony and central Germany.

Some of the important influences on organs and their music at the end of the 18th century were more directly musical. One was the theory of difference tones, quite familiar to theorists since Tartini. Vogler's ideas were based in part on the observation that the exploitation of harmonics might enable builders to dispense with large pipes, the combination of 16′, $10\frac{2}{3}$′ and $6\frac{2}{5}$′, for instance, producing a 32′ effect. But the idea is too naive for serious consideration, and Vogler must have had other assets to justify the respect with which he was held in Sweden and Salzburg. $10\frac{2}{3}$′ ranks had been known in Silesia and Bohemia during the late 17th century, and a flat 7th appeared in one Berlin organ of 1776.

A second major influence, or a symptom of the new emphases, was the idea propounded by J. H. Knecht (1795) and others that the organ was a kind of one-man orchestra, its three manuals having an orchestral spectrum of strings, brass and woodwind. To this end, Vogler's specially made organ, the Orchestrion, was hawked all over Europe during the 1790s. There was of course nothing new either in stops imitating string instruments or in regarding the organ as a 'compendium of all instruments whatsoever' (Mersenne, 1636–7); nor were organ transcriptions new, being as old as written-down organ music itself. But by 1800 the orchestra itself was heavier, more stratified and conventionalized than it was in 1600, and imitations of it would therefore be farther removed from the organ's own nature.

A third factor was the general assumption that the hundreds of new parish church organs of average size required in about 1820 were to be built chiefly for the sake of accompanying the congregation, for which 8′ stops were the most useful. This was partly because mutations were less carefully made in a period of quickly built organs, partly because intelligent theorists like Wilke despised Voglerian claims about harmonic stops, and partly because Mixtures were difficult to justify in theory. Some of the ill-repute of Mixtures in the period must have been due to their all too common Tierce rank (particularly ill-suited to equal temperament, which was coming into use in this period in all countries save England and the USA, where it was not accepted until the 1850s), and such compromise all-purpose Mixtures as those of Snetzler and countless other builders

throughout Europe were neither good chorus Mixtures nor good solo Cornets. Such an organ as that at Karlskrona, Sweden (P. Z. Strand, 1827), must have got its characteristic 'decadent' specification, whatever its voicing, in reaction to poorly made mutations and Mixtures too often met with at the time:

I	16.16.8.8.8.4.4.2.8
II	8.8.8.4.4.8
Pedal	16.8.8.4.16

A further influence on the design of organs soon after 1820 was the international scope of the repertory available to an average organist. In England, for example, such firms as Boosey imported an immense amount of German organ music of all kinds during the first few decades of the century. These imports reached their culmination in the international Bach revival. Bach sonatas and other major works ('Grand Preludes and Fugues') were available from 1800 and shortly after; for his sake alone, countless old English and French organs, and some Italian and Spanish, were being altered by 1840: pedals added, short manuals completed, second choruses added. The result, however, was not that national organ types lost their identity but that they kept it in a less overt and certainly less charming manner, so that the Bach revival rarely led in any country to well-balanced classical organs of the Silbermann type. No doubt this situation was in part due to the 'organ ethos' of the period: a general anti-Baroque view of organs as sombre, solemn, ecclesiastical and ecclesiological objects whose music (as can be seen from Vincent Novello's travel diaries) was expected to be more 'elevated' than the *galanteries* of the previous generation. But it prompted organists of different national schools to suppose that their organ alone was the best for Bach; countless English organists, for example, have resisted the idea that Bach did not write for the Swell pedal.

Apart from the details produced by such factors, several general observations can be made. There were strangely few magnificent organs built anywhere between 1800 and 1825, and the new big instruments of 1825–50 show a bigger break with the past than those of any other period in organ history. Casework as well underwent extreme changes in design and ornamental detail. While it is probably true that in 1830 churches spent less on their organs than they did in 1730, the later organs were in fact larger. In proportion to material bulk a Walcker organ must have cost only a fifth of the price of a Silbermann. The sounds the new organs were expected to produce accorded with the sobriety and gloom of the post-Revolution church, although the organist had a more variegated repertory to choose from than at any previous period. Few great organ builders stand out between 1800 and 1825, and major practical and theoretical developments were left to the next generation. Some areas, however, kept their traditions: the *Brustwerk* of 1898 at St Anders, Copenhagen, must be regarded as a survival rather than a revival.

In the USA, particularly in Boston and New York, a native school of builders was rapidly developing in the early 19th century to meet the needs of the many new churches in the expanding cities and prospering rural areas. These builders, notably Goodrich and Appleton in Boston, and Erben and Hall in New York, worked in the refined style inherited from 18th-century England and may be said to have brought it to its final fruition. By the 1850s the effect of continental developments, both tonal and mechanical, was being felt, and large factories (such as that of E. & G. G. Hook in Boston) were replacing the small workshops.

2. 19TH-CENTURY TECHNICAL ADVANCES. Audsley's monument to the Romantic organ, *The Art of Organbuilding* (1905), shows that the organ builder of about 1900 had a vast array of pipework to choose from; he also had many types of chest, action, bellows, gadgets and case designs at his disposal. On the whole Audsley was describing a high-quality instrument, but the profusion of elements he described affected the smallest and cheapest builder. Similarly, the organist's repertory was in theory immense. It was towards these two positions of technical and musical profusion, of embarrassing choice for both builder and player, that the organ gradually moved during the 19th century.

Although the period is now poorly documented and ill-understood in detail, the general outlines are clear. Different areas of Europe exercised major influence at different periods, and often an individual builder advanced concepts or techniques without which the overall development would have been different. Publicity for a new idea became increasingly easy (particularly from such concourses as the Great Exhibition in London, 1851); builders travelled far (like Cavaillé-Coll) to view developments, published papers or became associated with well-known theorists, and took commissions much farther from home than they had been used to doing (early examples were central German builders at work in the Netherlands or Scandinavia about 1760). New and rare stops were introduced into such foreign organs, perhaps sometimes for ostentation (e.g. Schulze's three-sided and wooden cylindrical pipes at Doncaster, 1862). An advanced organ of 1825 anywhere in Europe would at any rate have features gathered from various sources: from changing taste (several string stops), theory book notions of harmonics, quick factory methods, foreign influences (e.g. English Swells) and new visual ideas. 40 years later the amalgam was yet richer, and huge organs produced in the factories of Walcker, Sauer, Willis and Cavaillé-Coll were taken all over the world.

Thus the developments about 1825 in central Germany had an influence throughout Europe, not least because English and French organs of the period were particularly susceptible to new ideas. The theorists Wolfram (1815), Seidel (1843) and above all Töpfer (1833, 1843, 1855) were better known in Hamburg, Paris and London than Praetorius had been and had even crossed the ocean to America. Töpfer's new scientific description of the techniques of building (with tables and technical details for pipe-scales, wind-chambers, pallets, bellows, action etc) were immensely useful to every new builder. His ratio for pipe-scales (the so-called Normal Scale or Diapason Norm) was a theoretical model, not honed to the particular conditions of any church or local tradition; but it was adopted by builders of cheaper, commercial organs, and indeed forms part of the definition of the 'cheap, commercial organ'. J. F. Schulze also found it useful, and in itself it is not far removed from what had been customary in central Germany.

Töpfer's calculation was that the area of the cross-section of a Principal pipe was $\sqrt{8}$ times the area of the cross-section of a pipe an octave higher. Scaling therefore halved at the 17th inclusive pipe (i.e. eight whole tones above). So it had for many an organ before Töpfer. (But he seems to have thought that if pipes retained their proportions the ratio would be $\sqrt{16} : 1$, while constant

diameter would be $\sqrt{1} : 1$ and a mean thus $\sqrt{8} : 1$.) Such a simple constant was convenient at the workbench. So were Töpfer's other formulae for calculating the wind consumption and the height of the pipe mouth. Meanwhile the improved bellows and reservoirs of his period not only allowed copious wind and constant pressure but encouraged builders to experiment with higher pressure for the pipes or with pipes scaled to either extreme. Organists now demanded to be able to play with heavier registrations; these were at least as important as constant scalings, and Töpfer has perhaps been unjustly maligned for his $\sqrt{8} : 1$ formula.

Many of the experiments were short-lived. Free reeds were popular in central Germany from about 1780 to 1850 but not often elsewhere, although Gray and Davidson used 32' free reeds at the Crystal Palace (1857) and Leeds Town Hall (1859), and they were sporadically used as a novelty stop in large American organs as late as the 1870s. New materials, such as the cast-iron case and zinc pipes at Hohenofen (1818), became associated with poorer instruments once the novelty had worn off. Double pedal-boards and solo manuals were reserved for the largest instruments, though octave couplers and detached consoles never lost popularity once they had gained it soon after 1830. In England, Swell boxes were constantly 'improved', most often with a view to reducing the closed box to a true *pp* (Hodges of Bristol, 1824). In Germany, J. Wilke wrote major articles during the 1820s in the *Allgemeine musikalische Zeitung* listing devices for producing Swell effects such as triple touch, operating couplers or bringing on more stops as the key was depressed; increased wind admitted to the free reed stops (Grenié, Paris); lowered wind pressure brought about by a net curtain in the wind-trunk (Vogler); 'roof swells', devices for raising the lid of Swell boxes; and 'Door swells' or 'jalousie swells', the English systems of (horizontal) Venetian shutters, perhaps encasing a complete organ. For most of the century, the Swell box mechanism remained simple, as indeed the idea itself is extremely primitive: horizontal shutters were controlled by a wooden or metal foot-lever hanging to the right of the pedal keys, which had to be notched into position if the box was to remain open. With such pedals, constant see-sawing and swelling of sound were not very practical. Only occasionally were other systems tried, such as Bryceson's hydraulic system of about 1865 in which water was communicated along a lead pipe from the pedal to the Swell mechanism.

The resulting organ of about 1840 was usually a compromise between old and new. At Halberstadt Cathedral, for example, J. F. Schulze built a four-manual organ in which three manuals and pedal were of the large, standard classical type familiar in the later 18th century, and couplers and accessories were conventional, even to a Zimbelstern; but the fourth manual, its purpose very unclassical, played new stops in a high echo chest:

Lieblich Gedackt	16	(wood)
Lieblich Gedackt	8	(wood)
Terpodion	8	(tin)
Flauto traverso	8	(turned wood)
Harmonika	8	(wood)
Prinzipal	4	
Flauto traverso	4	(turned wood)
Physharmonika	8	(zinc) (free reed)

Such echo organs were a luxury, like apse organs in a few English cathedrals a century later. More popular in the advanced organ of 1850 were the SOLO ORGAN and the full Swell organ with its characteristic 16' reed and bright Mixture (Henry Willis, 1855). In Germany, Swells of the distant *Echowerk* type remained popular and still colour German organ design.

It was E. F. Walcker who is said to have invented (or improved) the cone-chest (*Kegellade*, see fig.11*b*), which he patented in 1842. Cavaillé-Coll, Willis and other great builders rejected it, as did American builders after a brief experimental attempt by the avant-garde Boston builder Simmons in his organ for Harvard University (1859). In America, cone-chests were briefly attempted a decade later (again unsuccessfully, due to the adverse effects of the climate) by the immigrant Moritz Baumgarten, who had trained with Walcker. But Walcker's output was immense, and certainly the boom in north European organ building meant that the more systematic a builder's concepts (and hence his workshop), the bigger part he could play in providing organs for the hundreds of new parish churches of that period. Metal-planing machines, for example, were drawn by Töpfer and manufactured by Walcker; such machine tools provided pipe metal of great precision and uniformity, obviating all capricious and 'imperfect' elements in pipe manufacture. The Walcker firm moved to Ludwigsburg in 1820 and was able from there to command a vast area of central Europe. Its organ for the Paulskirche, Frankfurt (1827–33), was highly influential, with its 74 stops on three manuals and two pedal-boards; but it too was a compromise. The 14-stop Swell was a large Echo organ, with free reeds and Dulcianas; the action was mechanical, the chests slider-chests, the couplers standard. However, the Swell mechanism was balanced (as a contemporary English account said, 'the pedals for expression are placed on an axis'); and once the free reeds were replaced by long-resonator reed stops, the specification became standard. Indeed, the whole Walcker style had great influence, from the Rhine to the Black Sea. But in 1849 (Ulm Minster) and 1863 (Music Hall, Boston, USA), Walcker monster organs still had not outgrown compromise; more thoroughly modern designs were achieved by builders less set in their ways, such as A. W. Gottschalg whose large organ for Cologne Cathedral was influenced by Cavaillé-Coll. The influence of the Walcker instrument in Boston on American organ building, already well established in its own conventions, has been much overrated. The cone-chest had already been tried and rejected, Americans continued to develop their own scaling and voicing systems (although influenced by Töpfer and other theorists and by general European trends), and the only real novelty, the free reed stops, enjoyed but limited vogue. The importation of the Walcker organ was, in truth, an aberration, for in the period in which it was built the major American builders could and did produce large, well-engineered and tonally sophisticated Romantic organs for large churches, cathedrals and concert halls.

In France much important work was done during the 1820s and 1830s before Cavaillé-Coll began to dominate the scene. The Englishman John Abbey went to France (at the instigation of Erard) to work in the Restoration period, taking with him the improved English bellows-with-magazine, Venetian Swell and refined voicing, and rebuilding organs from Rheims to Caen. His Swell at Amiens in 1833, for example, was a typical English Echo organ of 1750: 8.8.4.V.8.8. Farther east, Daublaine & Callinet came under the Walcker influence with their free reeds, double pedal-boards and general specifications in a few large organs, but essentially Cal-

linet and his fellow Alsatian Stiehr remained conservative. Their small and average-sized church organs retained the basic classical physical and tonal layout in the mid-19th century, but with some suppression of upperwork and introduction of Gambas and Harmonic Flutes, and with the use of free reeds with resonators. By 1841 Cavaillé-Coll was making overblowing stops, both flue and reed. His new scheme that year for the organ of St Denis is discussed in §3 below.

High pressure was applied to reeds in England by the late 1830s, the first well-known example being Hill's Tuba mirabilis at Birmingham Town Hall (1840). But although by 1855 Hopkins could write that 'stops of this kind are now made by nearly all the English organbuilders', no real technical details are known of these early stops. On the analogy of wood and brass wind instrument playing in general, treble pipes in the reed ranks were also put on higher pressure ('increased the weight in the treble by an inch' is Hopkins's phrase) from the organ of St Denis onwards. This of itself was a major advance, as can be readily seen by comparing a Trumpet at St Sulpice with one at Haarlem. For centuries French builders had appreciated that reed trebles needed 'boosting' if the splendid bass was not to peter out above g' or so: hence one of the functions of the mounted Cornet. Cavaillé-Coll's overblowing doublelength flue and reed pipes were thus new not in principle but in character. A Flûte harmonique or Trompette harmonique is so made for bigger, rounder tone and, unlike the narrow-scaled overblowing flutes of the 17th century, always requires strong, copious wind. The formation of nodes in overblowing flue pipes is helped by a small hole piercing the pipe rather less than halfway along from the mouth, the exact position affecting the overtone content of the pipe. In reeds, the hole is not necessary. The tone of neither flue nor reed harmonic pipes blends idiomatically with the Principal chorus; 17thcentury builders therefore reserved such flutes for solo colour, but the larger 19th-century organs contained small choruses of harmonic stops. Reed and flue harmonic stops show the desire felt in the 1840s for smooth reeds that stay in tune, and precisely voiced flue stops with no subsidiary 'chiff' (a puff of wind articulating the start of each note). Full- or double-length resonators gave smoothness to the reeds, while in flue pipes the chiff was eliminated by a mouth paraphernalia of nicked languids, 'ears and beard' and rollerboards aiding prompt, smooth speech.

Further technical advances made between 1825 and 1845 concern the action. Many 19th-century builders were ingenious with mechanisms composed of wooden levers, rods, battens etc for such accessories as double Venetian swells (H. Willis, Gloucester Cathedral, 1847), stop-combinations (Ladegast, Sauer, Roosevelt), crescendo pedals (Haas) and various couplers. Improved bellows-with-reservoir, greater application of two or even more wind pressures in an organ, improved slider-chests (and eventually cone-chests) were all at the skilled builder's disposal by 1845 at the latest. So was the 'Barker lever' or mechanical-pneumatic action (see fig.11*a*). By 1833, Booth in England and Hamilton in Scotland had constructed such actions. C. S. Barker worked on power pneumatics and compressed air, offering an apparatus to York Minster (1833), Birmingham Town Hall (1834–5) and, in France, to Cavaillé-Coll (1837). The pneumatic principle could also be applied to sliders and to such accessories as 'thumb-pistons' (H. Willis,

46. Organ by Daublaine & Callinet (1854) at St Eustache, Paris

1851). Barker's French patent was taken out in 1839 (his own notes, quoted by Hopkins and others, sketched the development as he saw it), and he applied his action to the organ under construction at St Denis by Cavaillé-Coll, whose high-pressure stops were indeed said to have been unplayable without this key-action. It was probably also in France that the first fully pneumatic action was made, in which all the tracker's backfalls, squares, rollers etc were replaced by one pneumatic tube from key to pallet. The system is accredited to P.-A. Moitessier (1845), and was later modified with a partly mechanical action and adopted by such major builders as Willis (St Paul's Cathedral, 1872). Although Walcker applied this so-called tubular pneumatic action to his cone-chests in 1889, on the whole the action gained only a minor success outside England (and, to some extent, the USA) because the action was sluggish when the keys were too far removed from the chests. As for the chests themselves, English and French builders preferred improved slider-chests to barless chests, often modify-

ing the larger pallets with secondary mechanism allowing them to be opened without undue key-pressure (Willis patent dated 1861, etc). Audsley was witness to much American activity in designing 'pneumatic chests' in the late 19th century. Around the turn of the century, American builders such as Steere and Estey developed a reliable tubular-pneumatic action using ventil-chests which they employed quite extensively, as did Möller and some of the midwestern builders, but other builders, such as Hook & Hastings, Hutchings and, in Canada, Casavant, went almost directly from Barker-machine mechanical to electro-pneumatic actions.

Electric actions were devised during the same period in England (Wilkinson 1826, Gauntlett 1852, Goundry 1863) and France (Du Moncel, Barker, Stein & fils). Electro-pneumatic action (see fig.14) overcomes the difficulty of directly opening a pallet by electro-magnets in that the magnet opens instead the smaller valve of a pneumatic motor which then opens the pallet. One such system is usually accredited to Péchard (c1860), who

took out a joint patent with Barker in 1868, and who in turn licensed Bryceson to build such an action in the Theatre Royal, Drury Lane (1868). According to Hopkins, an electrification for the organ at Gloucester Cathedral for the Three Choirs Festival of 1868 allowed the keyboards to be placed nearer the conductor, far from the pipes, an obvious and updated version of the 'long movements' of the tracker-action organ used in the 1784 Commemoration of Handel in Westminster Abbey. A decade or more before the end of the century Walcker in Germany, Merklin in France, Roosevelt in the USA, and Willis in England were all producing reliable electric actions and could thus build detached consoles some way away from the organs high up at the west end or in a triforium gallery of the quire. The stop mechanism could also be operated electrically (Bryceson patent, 1868). Particularly in the USA, where church or cathedral organs were less bound by tradition than in England, many electric actions were patented and improved during the 1890s, becoming a norm shortly after 1900, some 25 years before the Willis firm, for example, turned exclusively to electro-pneumatic action. During the 20th century, particularly before the Organ Revival made itself felt, most important organ builders throughout the world devised one or other type of electro-pneumatic action (see Whitworth, 1930). Clearly electric systems could serve the accessories such as stop-combinations ('free combinations', 'adjustable combinations') whereby a button or switch of some kind could bring on preselected stops, or Swell pedals operating variously worked shutters around part or all of the pipework. Most of the ingenuity exercised on such accessories belongs to the early 20th century rather than the 19th.
See also §VIII, 5, below.

3. SOME INFLUENTIAL ORGANS. Reference has already been made to Walcker's organ for the Paulskirche, Frankfurt, and Schulze's for Halberstadt Cathedral. Walcker's habitual style is close to such later 18th-century organs as that at St Michael, Hamburg, with a large, heavy Great organ (often 32') and a pedal booming and powerful yet removed from true chorus purposes. Other German firms such as Schulze and Ladegast seem often to have made a brighter sound, with large-scale Mixtures and a tonal chorus brash yet recognizably in a tradition. Schulze's influence in England was great, as his large Diapasons caught the taste of the time and indeed governed it for some decades after the Great Exhibition of 1851. Even his little colour stop, the narrow-scaled Lieblich Gedackt, became standard in English organs for the next 100 years. Such builders had a high standard of workmanship and the mass of 'good solid pipework' of foundational pitches in an influential organ like Sauer's for the Thomaskirche, Leipzig, was seen as a great advance on the little Baroque ranks of a Silbermann or Schnitger. The craftsmanship and materials in a major Cavaillé-Coll organ are immensely impressive, as are the spaciousness and complicated actions (allowing pipes 'room to speak') and the careful planning of several chest levels. The drawings of the various elevations, tiers and cross-sections of the St Sulpice organ, for example, are witness to one of the great engineering masterpieces of the 19th century.

Although the St Denis organ has a well-known position in organ history, few technical details have been published and only its restoration will make its real character clearer. The casework had already been

designed when several builders tendered for the work, and Cavaillé-Coll's two plans of 1833 and 1841 show the great changes in organ building during that crucial decade. Flutes and mutations were reduced, overblowing stops were introduced, string stops gave a new stridency, Barker's action allowed new arrangements of the chests, and the wind supply was increased and improved. Despite its ancestry in Bédos de Celles' scheme for a large 32' organ, the instrument at St Denis (see Table 25) was a great step along the 19th-century path. The Bombarde and Pedal departments became an ideal for hundreds of French or French-inspired organs over the next century or so; the scaling throughout became wider than classical French, and the voicing, as well as the wind pressure, stronger. It is not always clear how Cavaillé-Coll intended his organs to be registered, but since such stops as the Flûte harmonique are simply new versions of the auxiliary 8' ranks drawn in old *fonds d'orgue* combinations, it is likely that he expected them to be used in choruses. Much the same could be said

TABLE 25

St Denis Abbey (now Cathedral), Paris
Aristide Cavaillé-Coll, 1833–41

Grand orgue (II)		*Positif* (I)	
Montre	32	Bourdon	16
Montre	16	Bourdon	8
Bourdon	16	Salicional	8
Montre	8	Flûte (open)	8
Bourdon	8	Prestant	4
Viole	8	Flûte*	4
Flûte traverse*	8	Nasard ou quinte	2⅔
Flûte traverse*	4	Doublette	2
Prestant	4	Flageolet	2
Nasard ou quinte	2⅔	Tierce	1⅗
Doublette	2	Fourniture	IV
Grande Fourniture	IV	Cymbale	IV
Petite Fourniture	IV	Trompette*	8
Grande Cymbale	IV	Cor d'harmonie	8 (? bass)
Petite Cymbale	IV	Hautbois	8
Cornet (mounted)	V		(? treble)
Trompette*	8		
Trompette*	8	Cromorne	8
Basson	8 (? bass)	Clairon*	4
Cor anglais	8	Tremblant	
	(? treble)		
Clairon*	4		
		Bombarde (III)	
		Grand Cornet	VII
Récit (IV)		Bourdon	16
Bourdon	8	Bourdon	8
Flûte*	8	Flûte	8
Flûte*	4	Prestant	4
Quinte	2⅔	Nasard ou quinte	2⅔
Octavin*	2	Doublette	2
Trompette*	8	Bombarde	16
Voix humaine*	8	Trompette*	8
Clairon*	4	Trompette*	8
		Clairon*	4
		Clairon*	4

Pédal			
Flûte ouverte	32	Compass: *C–f–f'''* (pedal reeds *F'–*	
Flûte ouverte	16	*f*)	
Flûte ouverte	8	Harmonic and reed stops on heav-	
Gros Nasard	5⅓	ier wind	
ou quinte		Combination pedals (swell, cou-	
Flûte ouverte	4	plers IV/II, III/II, II/II, I/II,	
Basse-contre	16 (24)	high-pressure basses, high-	
Bombarde	16 (24)	pressure trebles, sub-octave	
Basson	8 (12)	coupler to all manuals, pedal	
Trompette	8 (12)	couplers to all manuals)	
Trompette	8 (12)	*Grand orgue* did not play until II/	
Clairon	4 (6)	II pedal operated	
Clairon	4 (6)	Stops marked* are double-length	
		harmonic stops	

for the string stops (complete with tuning-slots at the top of the pipe) and the thick stopped Bourdons. Nicking of languids was generally severe, at least in later organs of this builder; this, added to the slots cut into even the smallest Mixture pipes, aided smooth, constant tone. Conical and narrow-scaled stopped pipes were not conspicuous, and Cavaillé-Coll's spectrum of pipe forms was not particularly great. The foundation stops (*jeux de fonds*) of one manual were placed on one wind chest, the reeds and (sometimes) flute mutations (*jeux de combinaison*) were placed on another. Each chest could have its own wind pressure and each could be controlled by a valve that admitted wind only when required, thus allowing a registration to be 'prepared'. The *Grand orgue* was never underbuilt in relation to the Swell, as it often was in England. Feeder and reservoir bellows were generous, and the pneumatic action somewhat cumbersome in the space it took. As with Schulze organs, soundboards were ample in size for the boldly treated pipework. But neither electric actions nor general crescendo gadgets were found on Cavaillé-Coll's organs.

In Italy, Serassi, like his French and English colleagues, 'extended' local traditions and made many quite large organs of a curious Venetian compromise. The main manual would control 20 or more stops, including 16' or even 32' Principale and flutes and violas of 8' and 4'; most chorus stops were divided; the highest ranks were collected into Mixtures; and solo and chorus reeds were strong in tone. One or two subsidiary manuals, of six to ten halved stops often in a Swell box, provided echo effects but no true chorus. The compass was long (frequently from *C'*); the pedal organ had six to eight bass stops; and there were many accessories, both sounding (bells, thunder, drum) and mechanical (composition pedals, couplers, including octave and sub-octave).

In Spain, organ building came to something of a standstill, while the farther cities of eastern Europe were completely conquered by central German and Bohemian organ building, organ repertory and organ players, as once they might have been by Austrian. The outposts of German organ art in east Prussia and Silesia had long known large instruments (both Protestant and Roman Catholic) and the new techniques led to wide dissemination of ideas. Occasionally a builder would try something new, such as Buchholz's solo organ: 16.8.8.8.8.8.4, in Kronstadt Cathedral (1839); but on the whole builders were more anxious to improve action, accessories, bellows and chests of the more conventional organs.

In many ways the country best able to develop its organ was England, where a new awareness of foreign designs and repertory coincided with favourable economic conditions. While much work remains to be done on the position of the organ in France and Italy during the period 1830–50, the general picture of the English organ is clear enough. During the 1820s, the Choir organ was superseded by the Swell; pedals came to be regarded as normal (though only with a rank or two of large-scaled wooden pipes); the compass generally remained no lower than *G'*; and organists did as well as they could with the newly favoured music of J. S. Bach – *Das wohltemperirte Clavier* being as much played as the true organ music. Much of the newness of the British organ before Henry Willis's influential instrument for the 1851 Exhibition has been accredited to the friendship between H. J. Gauntlett, the composer and organist, and William

Hill, organ builder and former partner in the firm of Elliot. About 1833 Gauntlett visited Haarlem, apparently on the advice of Samuel Wesley (who presumably knew of it from Burney's account in his *Travels*), and there are various hints throughout Gauntlett's career as *Orgelsachverständiger* ('expert adviser on organs') that such instruments were in his mind. His personal library too shows him to have been a good example of the outward-looking early Victorian musician. Of the dozen or so organs built by Hill under Gauntlett's influence, certainly the one at Great George Street Chapel, Liverpool (1841), was the most indicative of things to come. Like Hopkins, Gauntlett knew enough German organ music to see the *C* compass as most useful for manuals, while S. S. Wesley favoured *G'* compass even on the new Willis masterpiece of St George's Hall, Liverpool. Much the same reason lay behind Gauntlett's scheme for the pedal departments of larger organs, for example the one at Christ Church, Newgate Street (1838); such a scheme (see Table 26) presupposed 'continental scaling' and not the large open-wood pedal scales described by Hopkins as over twice too large.

TABLE 26

Open Diapason	16
Open Diapason	16
Montre	16
Bourdon	16
Principal	8
Fifteenth	4
Tierce Mixture	V
Larigot Mixture	V
Contra Posaune	16
Posaune	8

Cavaillé-Coll visited Hill's workshops in 1844, as he did others at that period, and the influence they had on each other deserves closer study. The French, German and Italian stop names of many Hill–Gauntlett organs suggest at least paper knowledge of and interest in foreign organs; as late as 1871, Willis's new organ for the Albert Hall can be related closely to Cavaillé-Coll's for St Sulpice. Hill's Liverpool organ was a compromise between traditional English and new continental styles, with a 16-stop Swell (including 16' reed), a small Choir organ of flutes, a high-pressure Tuba played from the Swell, six couplers, five composition pedals, and a complete compass of *C–d'f'''*. Hill also designed a new kind of pallet that slid open and admitted high-pressure wind without increasing the touch-resistance. Neither he nor Gauntlett felt obliged to give up the long-established tradition of combining many international features: their organ at St Olave, Southwark (1846), for instance, was almost Serassian in its big Great and its solo Swell. It was left to Willis's organ for St George's Hall, Liverpool (1855), to establish fully the 'first modern British organ' (see Table 27), which remained an ideal throughout the British Empire at its apogee. Less opulent instruments by Willis and the builders he influenced would merely have had fewer choices of 8' and 4' colour. Large though such organs were, their priority was not music and its needs; rather they encouraged even further the age-old regard for large organs *per se*, useful for transcriptions of orchestral and vocal music but nonetheless basically engineering projects with fashionable paraphernalia – in this case, inclined stop-jambs, pneumatic thumb-pistons, concave and radiating pedal-board (perfected by Willis soon after 1851), Barker levers to each

TABLE 27

St George's Hall, Liverpool
Reconstructed 1867, under supervision of W. T. Best

Choir organ: 16.8.8.8.8.8.8.4.4.4.$2\frac{2}{3}$.2.2.IV.8.8.8.4
Great organ: 16.8.8.8.8.8.8.$5\frac{1}{3}$.4.4.4.4.$3\frac{1}{5}$.$2\frac{2}{3}$.2.2.II.V.IV.16.8.8.8.4.4
Swell organ: 16.8.8.8.8.8.4.4.4.$2\frac{2}{3}$.2.2.2.II.V.16.16.8.8.8.8.8.8.4.4
Solo organ: 16.8.8.4.2.16.8.8.8.8.4.8.8.8.4 (last four on heavy wind, 380 mm to 500 mm)
Pedal: 32.32.16.16.16.16.8.8.$5\frac{1}{3}$.4.V.IV.32.16.16.8.4

Compass: *G′–a‴*; pedal *C–f′*
Ten couplers (including Suboctave Swell to Great, Superoctave Swell to Great)
42 pneumatic pistons
Two bellows blown by a steam engine (8 horsepower)
Wind pressure: from 90 mm to 510 mm
Pneumatic lever (doubled for pedals)

department, varied wind pressures, new wind-raising devices, pneumatic couplers and a Swell pedal. The Swell alone was a good example of the general attitude. Of the 'double Venetian front' at Gloucester Cathedral (1847), Willis himself observed that 'the pianissimo was simply astounding' but gave no reason why he thought this a desirable aim.

The old-fashioned unequal temperament at Liverpool, applied on the advice of S. S. Wesley, was changed in 1867 (though the old *G′* compass was not changed to *C* until 1898). The wind pressure of the solo reeds was raised to 48·5 cm in the bass and 62 cm in the treble. Along with greater power went the demand for apparatus to control it. In 1857 Willis had patented a crescendo pedal – a foot-lever rotating a cylinder that activated pneumatic motors at the ends of the sliders. There were many other devices. In later organs, Willis took his schemes to a logical end by ousting the Choir organ for a Solo organ in certain three-manual instruments (e.g. Sheldonian Theatre, Oxford, 1877); already at Gloucester (1847) the Swell had been made nearly three times as large as the Choir. Thus the fitful English secondary chorus, first documented in the early 17th-century Chair organs, became 'obsolete'.

It is clear from the lists of specifications given by Hopkins and Rimbault, as it is in earlier lists by Seidel, Hamilton and others, that each major firm about 1850 had its hallmarks. Each introduced into many organs a characteristic stop (e.g. Hill's Octave Clarion 2′) or principle of construction or occasional foible (e.g. Cavaillé-Coll's Septime ranks); each had its own patented action, chest and wind-raising device, and each had a known attitude towards some major development like harmonic reeds, exploiting them or rejecting them as the case might be. Major German organs built about 1860 were in general either less inventive or more traditional than in England and France, and this difference was reflected in those organs of the USA and the British Empire that followed the foreign models favoured by their respective builders. St George's Hall, Liverpool, had the ideal town-hall organ, a distinct type anticipated by such concert organs as Elliot's in the Hanover Square Rooms, London (1804, 12 stops). It was the secular organ (Exeter Hall, London, and Birmingham Town Hall, both 1849) that first saw the application of the pneumatic lever to key action, and one of Hill's secular organs in London (The Panopticon, 1853) that first had pneumatically operated sliders, as well as higher pressure for treble pipes and a reversible crescendo pedal pushing out the organ stops one by one. The Solo organ or fourth manual, whether enclosed (Leeds, 1859) or not, also had its origins in the town-hall organ. The emphasis behind such contemporary designs as, say, Willis's organ for St Paul's Cathedral and Hill's for Melbourne Town Hall, Australia, reflects their ecclesiastical and secular natures: one would expect the latter to have bigger Solo manuals, smaller Choir manuals, perhaps a bigger compass, and certainly a larger array of unusual tone-effects.

It was the crescendo and diminuendo of a British town-hall organ (Glasgow; T. C. Lewis, 1877) that led Hans von Bülow to write to the local newspaper and claim never to have 'met with an organ so good in Germany'. Indeed, by comparison the German organ may well have seemed a dreary instrument, with little ability to blend or offer the organist much delight in its tone, touch or musical potential. It can hardly be assumed, however, that the tone of new German organs did not occasionally delight; organists may well have liked the sounds produced by Schulze's highly differentiated voicing in a small two-manual like that at Etzelbach (1869). Such an organ (see Table 28) was utterly typical in its day, though in some ways Schulze was old-fashioned (e.g. with his diagonal bellows at Doncaster, 1862).

TABLE 28

Manual I		*Manual II*	
Bordun	16	Lieblich Gedackt	8
Prinzipal	8	Salizional	8
Hohlflöte	8	Dolce	8
Gamba	8	Gedacktflöte	4
Oktave	4		
Mixture	III	*Pedal*	
		Sub-bass	16
		Violonbass	16
Couplers: Manual I to II; Manual I to Pedal		Gedacktbass	8

Much German music of the late 19th century was written for a large, somewhat sombre-voiced instrument which depended for effect more on weight and extremes of loudness and softness than on the sort of colour provided by, for instance, Cavaillé-Coll's Bombarde manual or Willis's Swell. Indeed, the very size and gravity of such instruments is their chief musical attribute, and Liszt, Reubke, Reger and others capitalized impressively on these qualities. Specifications were often much more classical in appearance than their voicing and general tone justify. Extremes of timbre in the form of harmonic reed choruses were not much favoured, and it is not always easy to see exactly why a German organ, even in its various neo-classical guises, needed a third or fourth manual. The large instrument in Magdeburg Cathedral (see Table 29), built by the firm of Reubke, expresses the potential sought by such composers as its scion Julius Reubke (1834–58). Walcker's organ of 1886 for St Stephen's Cathedral, Vienna, was even less systematic, with an ordinary Pedal but a huge Great organ manual of 35 stops strewn over the west end, and two

TABLE 29

Magdeburg Cathedral
Reubke, 1856–61

I: 16.16.8.8.8.$5\frac{1}{3}$.4.4.4.$2\frac{2}{3}$.2.IV.IV.IV.16.8
II: 16.8.8.8.8.8.4.4.2.II.V.III.8
III: 16.8.8.8.8.8.4.4.4.$2\frac{2}{3}$.2.V.16
IV: 16.8.8.8.8.8.4.4.4.$2\frac{2}{3}$.2.IV.8.8
V: 8.8.8.4.$2\frac{2}{3}$.2.II–III (Echo played from III)
Pedal I: 32.32.16.16.16.$10\frac{2}{3}$.8.8.8.$5\frac{1}{3}$.4.2.V.IV.32.16.8.4
Pedal II: 16.8.8.$5\frac{1}{3}$.4.2.16

further manuals; only one stop was in a Swell box. Similarly, not until 1857 at Ulm did Walcker use the Barker lever and not until 1890 a fully pneumatic action. A lack of inventiveness was also evident in the stop lists themselves: Sauer's two organs in Leipzig, both with about 60 stops (the Petrikirche, 1885, and the Thomaskirche, 1889), had almost identical specifications, both full of heavy 8' stops. Such were the instruments played by Reger and Straube, and for which registrations were fairly standardized. Thus 8' ranks were mixed freely, according to choice, but a 4' stop aided their blend, particularly a wide 4' above a narrow 8'. An organ that cannot provide an accompaniment of Gedackt 8' + Voix céleste 8' + Spitzflöte 4' voiced on late 19th-century principles cannot provide the sounds intended by Reger.

For such music it is also vital to be able to change stops quickly. Accessories became a priority, and by 1900 a German organ of 12 speaking stops could have as many as 12 'aids'. This was in addition to the Swell, which by then usually took the form of a cylinder rolled by the foot (Walze) and operating horizontal shutters. Other aids were the manual coupler, pedal coupler, octave and suboctave couplers, several pre-set combinations (labelled p, mf, pp etc), one or more free combinations (set as required), General Crescendo (likewise operated by a foot cylinder or Rollschweller) and so on. But it is a mistake to assume that such composers as Reger necessarily required a General Crescendo or fixed combinations. The free combination, which requires good precision work on the builder's part, is more useful, whether mechanical or pneumatic. Thus a large proportion of any organ's cost in about 1900 must have been allocated to the accessories, particularly in the untraditional and large organs of the USA (Roosevelt) and Canada (Casavant Frères). Similarly, the high-pressure reeds and large-mouth flues (called Seraphon) made by Weigle between 1890 and 1940 needed careful engineering, 'hard' though the tone undeniably sounded even at the time (as is shown by Schweitzer's opinion of the Stuttgart Liederhalle organ built in 1894–5).

Although all 19th-century organs may now deserve the status of historical monuments, little musical sense can be made of such mature Romantic organs as Weigle's at Lauterbach (1906), of which the stop list is given in Table 30. Such organs were not so much 'Romantic'

TABLE 30

Lauterbach
Weigle, 1906

Manual I		Manual II	
Bourdon	16	Geigenprinzipal*	8
Prinzipal	8	Flöte*	8
Gedackt*	8	Viola	8
Flûte octaviante	8	Quintatön	8
Gamba*	8	Salizional	8
Dulziana	8	Aeoline	8
Oktave	4	Voix céleste	8
Rohrflöte	4	Fugara	4
Oktave	2	Traversflöte	4
Mixtur	IV–V	Kornett	III–IV
Trompete	8	Oboe (flue)	8
Tuba mirabilis	8		
		Stops marked * were	
		Seraphon stops	
Pedal			
Kontrabass	16		
Violonbass	16		
Sub-bass	16		
Quintatön	16		
Violoncello	8		
Posaune	16		

as perversions of a legitimate ideal current from Gabler to Walcker; it is hard to see them being fashionable again. Yet even Weigle's Stuttgart organ was criticized by Audsley in 1905 for making 'absolutely no attempt to place at the disposal of the virtuoso the ready means of producing complicated orchestral effects or of massing special tone-colours'. Why Audsley and his contemporaries found such aims important is puzzling.

As an example of a true Romantic organ close to the music of a lively, century-long tradition, Ladegast's organ for Merseburg Cathedral (built 1859–62 in a classical case by Thayssner), for which Liszt wrote his Prelude and Fugue on B–A–C–H, would serve, although it is of interest that this large organ possesses no enclosed divisions, nor playing aids beyond a few couplers and Sperrventils; so would Cavaillé-Coll's for Ste Clotilde, Paris, where César Franck was organist from 1859 to 1890:

Grand orgue	16.16.8.8.8.8.4.4.2⅔.2.V.16.8.4
Positif	16.8.8.8.8.8.4.4.2⅔.2.8.8.4
Récit	8.8.8.8.4.2.8.8.4
Pédale	32.16.8.4.16.16.8.4

The superiority of Cavaillé-Coll's voicing, particularly of the reeds, would have given Franck a more musical instrument than Weigle's at Lauterbach. The several 8' stops are there for variety, and registrations followed traditional ideas of plein jeu, grand jeu, fonds d'orgue etc, for which the pédales de combinaison were essential. In general the principles behind the specification at Ste Clotilde were quite different from those of Weigle, though it cannot be assumed that the French repertory from Franck to Messiaen necessarily requires the edgy tone and reed brilliance of French organs. Certainly, however, French builders remained faithful to slider-chests both in practice and theory (cf J. Guédon: Nouveau manuel, 1903).

As an example of fin de siècle development beyond the demands of organ music, the Great organ manual of Walcker's Paulskirche organ, Frankfurt (1827), can be compared with its rebuild by the same firm 72 years later. The stop list alone makes clear the change of taste and the manner in which the over-confident revision destroyed the early 19th-century monument:

(1827) 32.16.16.16.8.8.8.8.5⅓.4.4.4.3⅕.2⅔.2.2.1⅗.2.2.1⅗.1.
        Cornet.V.IV.16.8 mechanical action, slider-chest
(1899) 16.16.8.8.8.8.8.8.8.4.4.4.2.2.Cornet.VI.16.8.8.4
        pneumatic action, cone-chest

4. ELECTRICITY AND THE ORGAN. Apart from electronic 'organs', the instruments of Robert Hope-Jones and his lesser imitators are considered the worst in organ design. Unfortunately not a single Hope-Jones organ survives in authentic form, so severe has been the rejection and so untrustworthy the working parts of his instruments. In specification they extend the principles behind such organs as that at Lauterbach by omitting all ranks above a wide flute 2', resulting in such schemes as the following for the Great organ manual at Worcester Cathedral (1896): 16.8.8.8.8.8.4.4.2.16.8 plus ten couplers to Great and seven composition keys. The tone was characterized by a corresponding smoothing out of acoustic 'interest' and a princely indifference to traditional chorus-blending. Ignored by French and German organ historians, Hope-Jones built few instruments himself and had only limited business success in Britain and the USA; but his influence was great and typifies the trend against which the Organ Revival reacted.

During the 25 years from 1889 to 1914 Hope-Jones

made two major contributions: to key-action (electric, with stop-switches for registration, 'double touch' for keys and accessories), and to pipework and specification (large harmonic Trombas, very narrow Trumpets, heavy-pressure Diapasons with leathered lips to reduce brightness, very narrow string stops and wide-scaled Clarabellas). His diaphone pipe of 1893 was itself a new departure (see fig.20), many examples of which can still be heard in the English-speaking world. Though no doubt more effective as a foghorn (an earlier version was accepted as such by the Canadian government, and diaphones were used as lighthouse fog-signals as late as the 1960s by the US Coast Guard), diaphone is a good guide to the tone required by some musicians about 1900. Hope-Jones's actions were too finely designed for organs (they were more effective in telephone exchanges), but the period was one of experiment in electrical technology and his contributions are important. So many devices or facilities, such as those enabling the organist to 'prepare' stops which remained silent until required, or to open Swell shutters one by one, were made much easier with electricity; so was 'borrowing' stops, still disapproved of by Audsley in 1905 but in principle leading to 'unit-chests', 'extension organs' and other systems using one rank of pipes for several purposes. Hope-Jones thus typifies a movement that led to such extraordinary achievements for their time as the stadium organ in Chicago (Bartola, 1929) where 44 ranks of pipes and various percussion effects produced an organ of six manuals (hanging in lofts above an auditorium of 25,000 seats) controlled by a movable console of 884 stop-knobs and accessories, and blown by pressures of 40 to 140 cm, the latter for the diaphones. The extension organ of 1938 in the Civic Hall, Wolverhampton, was more modest and typical (see Table 31).

Electricity has been used to replace key-pallet action (see fig.14), operate stop-mechanisms and accessories (couplers, combinations, tremulant, Swell shutters etc), drive a motor for raising the wind and replace older chest types. The design of circuits requires great skill and was perfected only during the 20th century. Certain sophisticated gadgets like Willis's 'infinite speed and gradation Swell' (where the amount by which the pedal is pushed forward is a measure of the speed at which the shutters open) date from the 1930s. In 1905 Audsley was still justifying the 'incomplete' nature of his discussion of electro-pneumatic actions by 'the tentative state of that branch of organ construction at this time'. By then, however, knowledge of such actions was advanced enough for E. M. Skinner's system to be applied at St Bartholomew, New York, to a console playing two organs, one at each end of the church. Skinner was perhaps America's most innovatory designer of actions; his 'pitman-chest', still widely used in the USA, was first developed during his employment with Hutchings in the 1890s and was a radical departure from other systems then in use which were, with the exception of Austin's equally original 'Universal Air Chest', largely electrified adaptations of the older slider-, ventil-, or cone-chests.

Perhaps the most radical application of electricity to organ building was that enabling any key to be connected to any pipe; each pipe can be given its own little chest or 'unit' to stand on, and such unit-chests can be used for one or more ranks of an organ. A 2' pipe could be c' of a nominal 8' rank, c of a 4' rank, F of a $2\frac{2}{3}'$ rank, etc, and the row of pipes 'extended' to allow com-

plete compass at all levels. The principle of 'extension' was known to Praetorius for a little table positive, and Marcussen applied it to six of his *Hauptwerk* stops at Siseby in 1819; an 'extension organ' is merely one taking the idea of such 'duplexed ranks' to a logical conclusion. Clearly electric actions made such systems much easier, either by unit-chests or by electric couplers. That the idea is basically inimical to true organ tone, since no consistently scaled rank will serve two purposes, did not escape the attention of the better builders. At Wolverhampton, for example, the principle is applied very discreetly. But extended ranks cannot provide as much power and variety as their stop-knobs promise, and

TABLE 31

Civic Hall, Wolverhampton
John Compton Organ Co., 1938

Chamber I	Pitch	Pipes	Pedal	Choir	Great
Sub-bass	32	62	32.16.8.4		
Contrabass	16	56	16.8.4		
Bombarde	16	56	16.8.4		
Contra Salicional	16	109	16.8	16.8.4.$2\frac{2}{3}$.2.$1\frac{1}{3}$.1	
Gemshorn	8	61		8	
Vox angelica	4	49		8 (from c)	
Lieblich Gedackt	16	97	16	16.8.4.2	
Claribel Flute	8	61		8	
Flauto traverso	4	61		4	
Nazard	$2\frac{2}{3}$	61		$2\frac{2}{3}$	
Tierce	$1\frac{3}{5}$	61		$1\frac{3}{5}$	
Double Open Diapason	16	97	16.$10\frac{2}{3}$.$5\frac{1}{3}$	8	16.8.4.2
First Diapason	8	61			8
Second Diapason	8	61			8
Stopped Diapason	8	61			8
Octave	4	61			4
Twelfth	$2\frac{2}{3}$	61			$2\frac{2}{3}$
Superoctave	2	61			2
Furniture IV	$1\frac{1}{3}$	244			IV
Harmonics V	$6\frac{2}{3}$	364	V at 16', V at 8'		V
Contra Posaune	16	85	16.8	8	16.4
Tromba	8	61			8
Horn	8	61		8	8
Chamber II				**Swell**	**Solo**
Contra Viola	16	85	16	16.8.4	
Geigen	8	61		8	
Voix célestes	4	49		8 (from c)	
Rohrflute	8	61		8	
Geigen Octave	4	61		4	
Fifteenth	2	61		2	
Mixture IV	$1\frac{1}{3}$	244		IV	
Double Trumpet	16	85	16	16.4	8
Trumpet	8	61		8	8
Hautboy	8	61		8	
Violoncello	8	61			8
Viole céleste	8	61			8
Harmonic Flute	8	61			8
Harmonic Flute	4	61			4
Clarinet	8	61			8
Orchestral Oboe	8	61		Choir	8
Tuba	8	73		8	8.4

Contained in two Swell boxes in the roof of the hall, without case or case front, the sound escaping between plaster roof-sections
50 ranks of pipes
Electric action for keys, stops and accessories
26 double-touch pistons to manuals and pedal
20 toe-pistons
11 other pistons, 3 Tremulants and 2 'Sustainers' (Choir, Solo)
15 couplers
Electronic section for Solo Organ (flute and reed effects, chimes)

builders therefore compensated by coarsening yet further the tonal quality of the pipes concerned: the pressure was raised, languids sharp-angled, upper lips 'leathered' (i.e. thin leather glued round the edge of the lip), scaling enlarged or narrowed excessively, perhaps with a double languid (drawing in air from outside) or double mouth (two sides of a square pipe provided with a mouth), reed-tongues 'weighted' to encourage stronger foundational tone, cheaper metal used, and often (in the pedals) a diaphone-type resorted to (with cylindrical resonator-tubes of large diameter). Many of the orchestral colours imitated by builders and recommended by influential writers were themselves ephemeral (e.g. the euphonium). New chests, particularly the pitman-chest (as designed by E. M. Skinner) were devised in which the key and drawstop had equal access to the pallet valve below the pipe, only sounding it when both were activated.

Builders of the period 1840–1940 often disagreed with one another's taste in details. Hope-Jone's diaphones were not made by most builders or Cavaillé-Coll's slotted pipes by others, or English leathered Diapasons outside a certain period, or the unit-chest by most builders of church organs. The origin of many voicing techniques, such as weighting reed-tongues with brass or lead, is obscure; so many had their origins in much earlier periods that only the extremes of various kinds (high pressure, diaphone pipes, electro-pneumatic action etc) can be dated from the 19th century. It was these extremes that led to the cinema organ about 1925. A large-looking Wurlitzer organ of this highly idiosyncratic period contained only a few ranks of pipes voiced to either extreme and 'extended' to provide many stops available at every pitch on every manual: a *reductio ad absurdum* of the principle of 'floating' chests. With its percussion traps and effects, its high-pressure pipework enclosed in one or two grille-fronted chambers, its movable console operating electric actions and sound-modifiers, the cinema organ can be seen not only following on from the 'serious' organs of Hope-Jones, Pendlebury, Franklin Lloyd and others, but as an updated version of Vogler's orchestrion. Again it was not the church organ but the secular that demonstrated an idea taken to its logical end.

5. THE NATURE OF ORGANS ABOUT 1900. To most musicians outside the organ world, and to an increasing number within it, the mature post-Romantic organ of about 1900 produces an unsatisfactory sound even when playing music written at the time. Whether the builder at the turn of the century was more indifferent to the musical purposes of organs, or whether the music itself was less suited to the organ idiom, than had been the case about 1700 is impossible to say. It is assumed too readily that the Romantic organ was in this respect different from and inferior to its predecessor. But in its ingenious mechanism and sophisticated technology, the organ of 1900 had much in common with the Greek hydraulis: technical ingenuity merely outstripped musical application or at least pushed it into second place.

The real difference between an average organ of 1900 and of 1700 is at once more elusive and more obvious: it sounds different. Builder and player had consciously rejected the sound of old organs, but the reason for it has to be defined and refined by each interpreter of organ history. It was not the desire for intense tone as such; 16th-century voicing must often have been taken 'to the limit', though naturally on lower pressure. It was not the newly invented pipe forms themselves; every period invented colourful stops that were by nature peripheral to the basic Diapason chorus, though less numerous. It was not pneumatic and electric actions which, though invariable and therefore requiring less 'lively' voicing, were invented only for practical convenience. It was not the imitation of orchestral sound as such, despite the orchestra's increased intensity. It was not the sombre setting in the 19th-century church that forced organ builders to avoid Baroque brilliance (nor in any case were church organs as 'advanced' as secular). It was not that organists became more out of touch with general musical taste; on the contrary, a parish church organist of 1900 knew much more of the contemporary situation in orchestral music than did one of 1700. It was not that organ building became merely a technical end in itself; the moving statuary of a late medieval organ bewitched the impressionable observer even more than Willis's Tubas. Nor is it easy to define the interaction of organs and music. On one hand an organ may appear to be ahead of its music: it was the 'orchestral counterpoint' of Cavaillé-Coll's organs (melody–accompaniment–bass) that suggested the texture of so much of Franck's music, not vice versa. On the other hand, the music often seems ahead of the organ: Liszt's Prelude and Fugue on B–A–C–H was written for the classical organ of Merseburg which, as can still be heard, aimed at a contrapuntal clarity quite different from the atmospherics demanded by Liszt.

It is difficult to be certain of basic facts. Fewer scaling figures of the organs by Cavaillé-Coll, for example, have been published than of those by Clicquot or Silbermann, while virtually no such details of English organs are known outside a few builders' workshops. The sheer size, number and variety of the period's large organs overwhelm the historian, as they did contemporary writers. Some of the qualities admired during their day, such as reliability, were traditional; but others, particularly the appearance of solid workmanship, may have had a bad influence. For instance, small pipes in mutations and Mixtures were often said by theorists of about 1820 to be old builders' means of deceiving clients. The sound produced by the new arrays of 8' foundational stops need not have been 'solid' and indeed was too frequently either aggressive or puny; the *Hauptwerk* built by Gabler for the quire organ of Weingarten Abbey in 1739 had a specification as much dominated by 8' stops as any of 1900: 8.8.8.8.8.8.8.4.4.2.XII, but (quite apart from the Mixture) the sound is unlikely to have been anything like Hope-Jones's in Worcester Cathedral. The first might be considered to lead directly to the second, but it was more the indefinable factors, the 'spirit of the times', that were manifest in the tone itself.

Characteristics tend to run together in organ building: electric action (slow, remote, invariable) from a detached console (gadget-ridden, distracting) to chests of pipes crude in tone (planned, manufactured, spaced and voiced untraditionally) and placed behind a pseudo-front (not an integrated resonating case), the whole catering for music written either for another kind of instrument (voices, orchestra) or for another culture. It is hardly surprising that in sum the organist's art became a kind of guesswork, isolated, insular and often chauvinistic.

VII. The Organ Revival

'Organ Revival' is a term used increasingly often as an

English equivalent to *Orgelbewegung* (coined about 1930 as a simplified form of Gurlitt's phrase *Orgel-Erneuerungsbewegung* of 1926). The movement is concerned with 'reviving' some of the 'historic principles' of the organ, because it was thought in German musicological circles of the 1920s that the 'true purpose and nature' of the organ had 'declined' and required 'regeneration'. Although such words are still much used in Germany, it is probably fair to say that most of the best results have been achieved by organ builders of other countries, notably the Netherlands, Denmark and Switzerland.

During the 1920s, not least in the light of current political movements, many aspects of German cultural life were re-examined, and before 1933 there were more or less formulated movements in folk music, youth music, church music, and the music of particular composers (e.g. the *Schützbewegung*). These movements had certain aims or assumptions in common, for their followers:

(i) reacted to a previous period. In the *Orgelbewegung*, a protest against the thick, loud sonorities of the orchestral organ, the factory organ, the 'expressive' or symphonic organ, the organ as an engineered machine rather than an apparatus or 'tool of music'. As such, reacting against late 19th-century organ ideals is equivalent to reacting against late 19th-century music, and insufficient explanation has been given for why an organ of Sauer is less worthy of revival than, say, Wagner's *Parsifal*.

(ii) assumed that criteria could be determined. In 1906 Schweitzer's test for an organ, 'the best and sole' standard, was its fitness for playing J. S. Bach's music. Unfortunately, that ideal in the 1820s had already deflected the French and English organs from the better features of their native paths; and it is not *per se* a reliable criterion, since not only do opinions differ as to the 'nature of Bach's organ' but the composer himself played organs of quite opposing aims. The 'Bach organ' was more a generic term merely signifying instruments built and voiced 'in the Baroque manner'. Schweitzer's rallying-cry was perhaps not to be taken too literally, though several builders in Alsace and south Germany met under its banner and adopted stop lists (if nothing else) conducive to Bach registration. The resulting 'Alsatian Organ Reform' has been seen as the precursor of the Organ Revival.

(iii) attempted in general to lead to standardization. Schweitzer's views expressed at the Vienna Congress of the International Musicological Society in 1909 and at the 3rd Organ Conference at Freiberg in 1927 aimed at a general return to old ideals. Although in 1909 it may have been reasonable to equate *tonschön* with *alt*, a blanket equation of the two leads to over-uniformity and a kind of lazy norm often to be heard as simple anonymity in the tone of hundreds of neo-Baroque organs built in Germany since the mid-1930s.

1. Early indications. 2. German developments in the 1920s. 3. Old organs. 4. Scandinavian and Dutch organs. 5. The Organ Revival in the USA. 6. England, France and Italy. 7. Some German developments since World War II. 8. The present situation.

1. EARLY INDICATIONS. Schweitzer's book *J. S. Bach, le musicien-poète* (1905) and the pamphlet *Deutsche und französische Orgelbaukunst* (1906) were highly formative, and still govern German attitudes to the 20th-century organ. A precursor in the workings of the Alsatian Organ

Reform has been seen in Emil Rupp, for whom Walcker built a 'reformed organ' at St Paul, Strasbourg, in 1907. But equally indicative of the inevitable change in direction were works of more general musical scholarship. For example, Guilmant's series of old French organ music (begun in 1901 under the title 'Archives des maîtres de l'orgue') was much in advance of Karl Straube's 'editions' of old German composers (1904). Also important was the pioneering work in the interpretation of old music published by Arnold Dolmetsch and others. Dolmetsch no doubt owed much to a favourable musical climate in England where Charles Salaman, Carl Engel and A. J. Hipkins had already reintroduced the harpsichord to public music-making. But as in France and Germany, renewed interest in harpsichords did not necessarily lead to enlightenment with regard to organs. Nevertheless what Dolmetsch wrote in 1915 reflected his views over the past decades and summed up the situation admirably for anyone wishing to heed them:

Church organs had that power based on sweetness which constitutes majesty. The change came on, and for the sake of louder tone, pressure of wind was doubled and trebled. The same pressure acting on the valves which let the wind into the pipes made them too heavy for the fingers to move through the keys. A machine was then invented which did the work at second hand [and] the music of the organ dragged on after the player's fingers as best it could. Personal touch, which did so much for phrasing and expression, was destroyed.

Then fashion decreed that the organ should be an imitation of the orchestra. . . . The organist, if he is clever, can give a chromolithograph of the *Meistersinger* Prelude; but he has not the right tone with which to play a chorale, if his organ is up-to-date. Modern compositions are intended for this machine, and all is well with them; but it is a revelation to hear Handel's or Bach's music on a well-preserved old organ.

There is nothing here about 'the Baroque organ', and the word was only later taken over from art historians to evoke an organ type more imaginary than real.

In England practice did not reflect enlightened theory. The ideas of organ advisers like Thomas Casson (1842–1910) and George Dixon (1870–1950) kept early 20th-century organs from being any worse; but they were still only insular compromises. As with so many English writers of the period 1875–1975, their emphasis on stop lists and imaginary 'ideal organs' was not basic enough to lead to radical rethinking. Factions in organ building are common, and in France any modern organ has one of two totally opposed characters depending on what the builder and his adviser favour. But in England, almost all organists have still only a compromise instrument of mixed and dubious lineage going back to William Hill and taking in a few non-establishment influences from Hope-Jones on one hand and D. A. Flentrop on the other. *Grove 5* ('Organ') gives the specifications of several such organs, often well built and at great expense.

2. GERMAN DEVELOPMENTS IN THE 1920s. A practical step was taken in 1921 when Oscar Walcker, with the collaboration of Wilibald Gurlitt, designed and built the Freiburg Praetorius-Orgel, inaugurated by Karl Straube. This was the first attempt at reconstructing the tonal character of a so-called Baroque organ according to some of the details given by Praetorius in his *De organographia* (*Syntagma musicum*, ii). Compromises were evident: suitable casework was not made, the stop list was modified, the pipes were placed not on a sliderchest but a 'stop-channel chest', and the action was electro-pneumatic. But the organ was very significant, not least in the publicity it gained during the organ conference held at Freiburg in 1926 before 600 members. After the instrument was destroyed in 1944, a second,

less compromising one was made in 1954–5. The change in approach indicates clearly how German organ thinking had developed over 30 or so years: Gurlitt was still the adviser, but the organ was built by Walcker-Mayer with the collaboration of acoustic and technical experts (Lottermoser, E. K. Rössler) and closely modelled on the first specification in Praetorius's *De organographia*, with data taken from extant pipework by Praetorius's friend Esaias Compenius, and with mean-tone tuning, a slider-chest, mechanical action and a thorough *Werkprinzip* structure; the stop list is given in Table 32. Were

TABLE 32

Freiburg University, 'Praetorius' organ II
W. Walcker-Mayer, 1954–5

Oberwerk		*Rückpositiv*	
Principal	8	Principal	4
Gedackt	8	Quintadena	8
Oktave	4	Hohlflöte	4
Gemshorn	4	Nachthorn (wood)	4
Gedackt (wood)	4	Blockflöte	2
Nasat	$2\frac{2}{3}$	Oktave	2
Scharfquinta	$4 (?1\frac{1}{3})$	Quinta	$1\frac{1}{3}$
Superoktave	2	Zimbel	
Mixtur III	2	Schalmei	8
Brustpositiv		*Pedal*	
Krummhorn (wood)	8	Untersatz (open	
Quintetz	$1\frac{1}{3} (?4)$	wood)	16
Zimbel	II	Posaune (Sordun)	16
Sifflöte	1	Dolcan	8
		Bauerflötlein	1
		Singend Cornet	2

Zimbelstern
Tremulants *(Oberwerk, Rückpositiv)*
Couplers: *Rückpositiv* to *Oberwerk*; *Oberwerk* to *Pedal*; *Rückpositiv* to *Pedal*

a third Praetorius organ to be built, one could expect that all compromises away from his specification would be dropped and an early 17th-century casework incorporated, being an integral part of the total sound-production. In 1969 Walcker-Mayer showed the firm's continuing activity in experimental old organs by producing a further reconstruction-copy of the Roman organ of Aquincum.

Although both Schweitzer's and Gurlitt's views were directed towards certain music – that of J. S. Bach on the one hand and that of Scheidt and Schütz on the other – results were only gradually seen in organ building. After Rupp and Walcker visited Mutin, Cavaillé-Coll's successor, one or two organs were built with the express purpose of combining the musical potential of the German and French organs. One such instrument was at St Reinold, Dortmund, inaugurated in 1909 by Schweitzer and attracting the attention of Reger, for whom a festival was held at Dortmund in 1910. The dual polyphonic–homophonic nature of Reger's mature style would in theory gain much from the character of an Alsatian Reform organ. The eclecticism aimed at in such organs was elusive and may well be illusory; but it led to giant organs such as that at Passau Cathedral (Steinmeyer, 1930; 208 stops) in which one section serves as a 'German Romantic organ', another has a 'French character' (reeds, Cornet), and yet another provides a 'Baroque department'. While in north Germany such firms as Ott and Kemper remained closer to orderly tradition, the influence of Steinmeyer was wide, and only gradually has eclecticism begun to lose its lustre.

Yet returning to full *Werkprinzip* design was also only gradual. Like the 1921 Praetorius-Orgel, the influential organ of St Mary, Göttingen (Furtwängler & Hammer,

1925), was a compromise with pneumatic action, but in its specification and scalings, prepared by Christhard Mahrenholz, it pointed the way to future development:

Hauptwerk	16.8.8.8.4.4.2.V.V.8
Rückpositiv	8.8.8.4.4.2.2.III.II.16.8
Oberwerk	8.8.8.4.4.2$\frac{2}{3}$.2.1.III.16.8.4
Pedal	16.16.10$\frac{2}{3}$.8.8.8.4.2.IV.32.16.2.16.8.4

The 'Hindemith organ' – that thought ideal for the performance of his sonatas – was itself a mean between extremes: but important work was begun on technical aspects of organ building, and a climate of opinion was being created with regard to acoustics (*Akustische Zeitschrift*, 1936; *AMf*, 1939), slider-chests and their influence on tone (H. H. Jahnn: *Der Einfluss der Schleiflade*, 1931), pallets (*ZI*, 1933), casework (W. Supper: *Architekt und Orgelbau*, 1934) and scaling (Mahrenholz, 1938). In Italy questions concerning old organs had been discussed for many years (e.g. *Musica sacra*, 1901–3), and even large electric organs like that in the Pontificio Istituto di Musica Sacra (Rome, 1933) had never shaken off traditional features. But in France technical achievement lagged behind historical research: the documents and archives published by Raugel and Dufourcq led to the discovery of many old organs, as a result of which almost all were rebuilt over the next few decades, and many altered beyond recognition.

3. OLD ORGANS. The position of surviving old organs in the Organ Reform was a difficult one. Important though the Schnitger organ in Hamburg's Jakobikirche or the Lübeck Totentanzorgel were to a writer like H. H. Jahnn (*Kongressbericht: Leipzig 1925*), or the Silbermann in Freiberg to E. Flade (*3. Tagung für deutsche Orgelkunst: Freiberg in Sachsen 1927*), in practice they were, obviously, not suitable for all the organ repertory. They would not allow, for instance, the gradual crescendo demanded by Reger and obtained on one manual by piling up three or four 8′ stops before the first 4′ was added. Oversimplified claims were often made – for instance, that 'stop-channel chests' are by nature 'bad'. It is probably true that, compass apart, an organ of 1700 is more versatile than one of 1900; but no valid doctrine can be formed on the basis of such a generalization.

Nevertheless, the beauty of the Freiberg Cathedral organ was not questioned, and publication in facsimile of treatises by Werckmeister, Praetorius, Bédos de Celles, Mattheson, Adlung and Schlick heightened interest in the few extant remains of organs they described. One result, however, was that much-altered instruments were over-respected, and an organ like that at Amorbach (1774–82) or the Totentanzorgel gave, over the years, many misleading impressions. In this respect, progress since the 1920s has been slow, however well the music itself has been understood. Enlightened opinion may no longer claim that 'it is the large Schnitger organ that best corresponds to the demands made by J. S. Bach's music' (Klotz, 1934), but it is still almost impossible to be sure what kind of sound Schnitger was aiming at.

As examples of ill-conceived restorations, many organs in England, Ireland, France, Spain and Germany could be described, and as much damage has been done during the last 30 years as at any other period. The organ of Herzogenburg Abbey, Austria, can serve as an example. By 1964 most of its original character had either survived or was fairly easily ascertainable; but the 'restoration' of that year resulted in major changes based upon unauthentic concepts. The main chests were enlarged to give a modern compass of *C–f'–g'''*, thus discarding the original short octaves, the incomplete (but characteristic) pedals and most of the original chests; the action was discarded and newly made; manual and pedal Mixtures were changed in content; new ranks and stops of a kind unsuitable to an Austrian organ of 1749 were made; the instrument was revoiced throughout; and the original detached console was discarded and replaced by a new oak console. This organ would need a radical rebuild if it were ever again to give an organist a true impression of the instruments known to Mozart.

By 1971, however, certain builders were attempting closer authenticity in their restorations, as is shown in a second Austrian organ, that of the Hofkirche, Innsbruck (see Table 8 and fig.34). Here the original wind-trunk was preserved, the wind pressure ascertained and voicing recovered; the original short *C–a"* compass was restored (though the keys perhaps date from the 18th century); the original pitch level (*a'* = 445), case, chests etc were restored; and the instrument was tuned in an unequal temperament. Were the modern bellows to supply wind with fluctuations characteristic of the period, the organ would represent well the contemporary ideals of restoration.

4. SCANDINAVIAN AND DUTCH ORGANS. An especially more radical rethinking of the organ appears to have been achieved in Scandinavia, but it is more likely that national organ types had been less extremely developed there during the crucial period 1870–1910. It is less a question of revival than of survival of old organ design. On the whole the Swedish organ had become more 'decadent' than the Danish, but interest in, for instance, mutations survived here and there. Naturally, German stop-channel chests were found in Scandinavia, and Theodor Frobenius, a German-born builder who settled in Copenhagen, made the first Danish electric action. But the ideas aired by the Alsatian Organ Reform soon became respected in Denmark.

Simpler than the organ at St Mary, Göttingen, yet put in a very imposing case by builders alert to correct acoustical placing, was the quire organ of the extraordinary Grundtvigskirke, Copenhagen (1940), built by Marcussen. In 1920 the head of this firm was Sybrand Zachariassen, who was joined a little later by P. G. Andersen; by the late 1930s the firm was producing almost nothing but mechanical action and doing good formative work in restoration (Sorø Cathedral, 1942). The Grundtvigskirke organ was quite uneclectic (see Table 33).

In the same year (1940) a *Rückpositiv* was added by Frobenius to the early 16th-century *Hauptwerk* from St Petri, Malmö, now in Malmö Museum, showing that builders were aware of the practical convenience of *Werkprinzip* elements. By 1944 the new organ of Jae-

TABLE 33

Grundtvigskirke, Copenhagen
Marcussen, 1940

Hoofdwerk		*Rugwerk*		*Pedal*	
Principal*	8	Principal*	4	Sub-bass	16
Nachthorn	8	Gedakt	8	Bordun	8
Octav	4	Rørfløtje	4	(transmitted)	
Quint	2⅔	Quintatøn	2	Octav	4
Octav	2	Scharf	II	(transmitted)	
Mixtur	IV	Krumhorn	8	Dulcian	16

The *Hoofdwerk* and Pedal pipes are on the same chest
* = case pipes

gersborg, near Copenhagen, had three uncompromising *Werkprinzip* manuals complete with a Trumpet *en chamade*, so made for power rather than for imitations of Spanish tone. (This has remained true of *Orgelbewegung* reeds *en chamade*.) Important too were the smaller organs made by the new builders after the war. Flentrop's eight-stop organ at Schoondijke (1951) was in its way even more influential than his perfect *Werkprinzip* organ at Doetinchem (1952), which soon became a model for the design of *Hauptwerk* + *Rückpositiv* + Pedal towers. (The stop lists of both are given in Table 34.)

TABLE 34

Schoondijke
Flentrop, 1951

One manual, *C–e'''*

Prestant	4
Holpijp	8 (halved)
Quintadeen	8
Spitsfluit	4 (halved)
Octaaf	2
Scherp	IV
Sesquialter	II (treble)
Ranket	16 (halved)

Doetinchem
Flentrop, 1952

Hoofdwerk		*Rugwerk*	
Prestant	8	Prestant	4
Quintadeen	16	Holpijp	8
Roerfluit	8	Quintadeen	8
Octaaf	4	Roerfluit	4
Ged. Fluit	4	Octaaf	2
Nasard	2⅔	Quint	1⅓
Octaaf	2	Scherp (1')	IV
Mixtur (1⅓')	V–VI	Sesquialter	II (treble)
Trompet	8	Dulciaan	8

Borstwerk		*Pedaal*	
Prestant	2	Prestant	16
Fluit (wood)	8	Octaaf	16
Fluit	4	Octaaf	4
Gemshoorn	2	Nachthoorn	2
Octaaf	1	Mixtur (2')	IV
Cymbel (1⅓')	II	Bazuin	16
Regaal	4	Schalmei	4

Couplers: *Rugwerk* to *Hoofdwerk*; *Borstwerk* to *Hoofdwerk*; *Hoofdwerk* to *Pedaal*; *Rugwerk* to *Pedaal*

Open-toe voicing, mechanical action and encased departments were by now standard among the younger builders. Such instruments went far beyond the theories of the *Orgelbewegung*, and it is a mistake to regard them as mere 17th- or 18th-century pastiche. Frequently they serve as practical demonstrations of intricate theory and knowledge. Frobenius's paper on end correction, for example (Copenhagen, 1947), is the most important work by an organ builder in this field since Cavaillé-Coll.

5. THE ORGAN REVIVAL IN THE USA. The main builders of the early revival in USA were Holtkamp of Cleveland and G. D. Harrison, an Englishman working for the Skinner Organ Co. In 1933 Holtkamp had contracted for a *Rückpositiv* in the large organ of the Cleveland Museum of Art, but the slider-chest had a multiple-valve system doomed to be dropped in the purer atmosphere after the war. Harrison's influence on tone was more important than his structural reforms, for he had applied low pressure to a fairly large organ contracted for at Groton in 1935. This organ, like the slightly smaller but more coherent instrument built a year earlier for the Church of the Advent in Boston, was one of the first

47. *Organ by the Holtkamp Organ Co. (inaugurated 1967) at the University of New Mexico, Albuquerque*

attempts in the USA at a large, classically designed instrument, although its voicing hardly follows classical principles and its general effect lacks articulation. More successful, and certainly more influential, was the small, unencased, two-manual organ built in 1937 for the Germanic (now Busch–Reisinger) Museum at Harvard University, which was heard by a vast audience through the broadcasts and recordings of E. Power Biggs, an early champion of the Reform movement. These and other isolated instruments of the period testify to a growing

interest in historic European principles among some American organists and builders, Cavaillé-Coll and Silbermann being especially admired. Such organs, for all their drawbacks of voicing and electric action, possessed greater clarity than had been heard from American organs for some decades, and they made their point musically. Partly due to Holtkamp's efforts, most of these organs were free-standing rather than in the all-too-common chambers, but the musical importance of casework was as yet unrealized, and only low wind pressures and gentle voicing curbed a tendency of 'pipes-in-the-open' to sound raw and unblending.

But soon after World War II growing awareness changed the mainstream. Academic and musicological writers leant heavily on 17th-century German literature and indeed tried to create a more rational language of organ terms (Bunjes, 1966), while organists and organ students became much influenced by the various restored organs of West Germany. The relative inaccessibility of East German organs, notably those of Silbermann, has affected American–European organ design. European builders exported small but important organs to the USA (Rieger about 1952, Flentrop in 1954) and Beckerath consolidated the trend by taking a 44-stop four-manual organ to Cleveland in 1957. Large firms like Schlicker were bound to be influenced by such instruments, and while Beckerath went on to build several equally important organs in Canada, other builders like Charles Fisk of Methuen (later Gloucester), who very early showed an inclination toward French classical elements as opposed to the more popular German Baroque, and Casavant Frères of Quebec soon produced their own versions of the new styles. Casavant's organ of 1963 in Acadia University (see Table 35) is a typical small organ of the kind inspired by such builders as Beckerath. From the point of view of the Organ Revival, such instruments were far in advance of the huge unencased organs made by the larger firms (e.g. Möller's paired organs in the church of the Immaculate Conception, Washington, DC, 1970), although it is fair to point out that inventive and contemporary visual effects can often be achieved with unencased chests.

TABLE 35

Acadia University
Casavant Frères, 1963

Hauptwerk		Brustwerk		Pedal	
Quintaden	16	Gedackt	8	Sub-bass	16
Prinzipal	8	Spitzflöte	4	Prinzipal	8
Rohrflöte	8	Prinzipal	2	Choralbass	4
Oktav	4	Quinte	$1\frac{1}{3}$	Mixtur (2')	IV
Waldflöte	4	Sesquialtera	II	Fagott	16
Flachflöte	2	Zimbel ($\frac{1}{4}$')	II		
Mixtur (1')	IV	Holzregal	8		
Trompete	8				

Couplers: *Hauptwerk* to Pedal; *Brustwerk* to Pedal; *Brustwerk* to *Hauptwerk*

Mechanical action

Many North American builders are willing to consult advisers who have practical or theoretical knowledge of historic organ types of Europe; at its best the collaboration is highly successful. Flentrop's organ of 1958 for the Busch–Reisinger Museum at Harvard reflects a further element: the strength of taste developed by players (in this instance E. Power Biggs) experienced in European organs. In North America, Flentrop, Metzler, Ahrend & Brunzema and others have gone on to build important instruments of great beauty, and recently other influences have become evident, such as the French elements in the stop list and voicing at St Thomas, New York (G. F. Adams, 1969), or the Italian elements in the large electric organ of the First Congregational Church, Los Angeles (Schlicker, 1969). It is true that neither instrument demonstrates a thorough understanding of its quasi-models, but such attempts are important stepping-stones towards stricter historical copies – a trend also followed by American harpsichord makers over

recent years and one leading to less compromising organs (see §8 below). The specific influence of the German-orientated *Orgelbewegung* may well be waning in the USA and Canada; like the new organ terminology sometimes attempted, it was too artificial a graft to bear much fruit.

6. ENGLAND, FRANCE AND ITALY. It seems to be true that the Organ Revival in England 'really took root only with the opening of the organ for the Royal Festival Hall, London, in 1954' (Clutton and Niland, 1963; see fig.48, p.906). Despite careful planning by the adviser (Ralph Downes) and meticulous workmanship by the builders (Harrison & Harrison), the composite nature of the organ made it little more than a quickly dated compromise. Its 103 stops give the impression of immense adaptability, and the German flutes, Anglo-German chorus and French reeds allow many types of organ music to be given reasonable performance; but the very size (quite apart from the semi-unencased construction and the electropneumatic action) make true sympathy with most musical styles impossible. Although much admired by players in both England and the USA, the instrument has had curiously few successors: new designs have not appeared, despite an awareness of continental organs (e.g. the Organ Club's visit to Frobenius in 1958) and the obvious qualities of tracker action (St Vedast, London, rebuilt by Noel Mander, using an 18th-century case and much antique pipework). J. W. Walker's organ of 1959 in the Italian Church, London, showed a rather confused scheme, but it helped to open the path to 'Baroque' influences;

Great organ	16.8.8.4.4.$2\frac{2}{3}$.2.II.IV.8
Choir organ	8.4.4.2.2.1$\frac{1}{3}$.II.III.8
Swell organ	8.8.8.8.4.4.$2\frac{2}{3}$.2.IV.16.8.8
Pedal	32.16.16.16.8.8.8.5$\frac{1}{3}$.4.4.IV.16.16.8.4

The French organ has developed on rather similar lines, 'neo-classical' indicating a frenchified composite organ designed with both de Grigny and Bach, both Franck and Messiaen in mind. Most major French churches have such organs, many made by Gonzalez with the advice of Norbert Dufourcq, a collaboration which also unfortunately engineered the rebuilding of many intact classical and Romantic organs in a hybrid quasi-Germanic mould, with the stated aim of making them more fit for the playing of Bach. Closer imitations of old French styles have been attempted more recently, for example the partial copy of a Bédos de Celles organ (complete with low pitch) by J.-G. Koenig at Sarre-Union (1968). In particular, the importance of the traditional French classic form of 'suspended' action has been recognized, and such actions, notable for their sensitivity, have since successfully been made by American, Dutch and German builders as well as the French. In both England and France, 'restoration' of old organs has been almost universally disastrous. French builders and advisers have not by any means abandoned the ideals which caused the 1693/1832 pedal department (Flutes 8' and 4' (C–e), Trompette 8' and Clairon 4' (*ravalement F'–e*)) at Auch Cathedral to be altered in 1959 (Principal 16', Sub-bass 16', Bourdon 8', Flûte 8', Flûte 4', Bombarde 16', Trompette 8', Clairon 4'). Few builders in England or France have shown enlightened attitudes towards the subtler historical problems of pitch and voicing, although in France the journal *Connaissance de l'orgue* has helped propagate better ideas, as has the *Organ Yearbook* in England and the Organ Historical Society in the USA.

In Italy the late 1960s saw a movement towards a kind of modified *Werkprinzip* organ but with characteristic Italian choruses and even at times Italian reeds. The organ at S Maria Assunta (B. Formentelli, 1967–8) has a *grand'organo* of $8.4.2.1\frac{1}{3}.1.\frac{2}{3}.\frac{1}{2}.\frac{1}{3}$ + $\frac{1}{4}.8.4.2\frac{2}{3}.2.1\frac{3}{5}.8.4$, the last of them reeds. Large three-manual organs such as that at the Chiesa dei Servi, Bologna (Tamburini), united an Italian chorus, German mutations, Spanish Trumpet, Italian compass, mechanical action and general *Werkprinzip* relationships between the manuals. Smaller organs too have attempted comprehensiveness; the instrument at S Severino, Bologna (G. Zanin & Figlio, 1968), has the following scheme:

Grand'organo	$8.4.2.1\frac{1}{3}$.1.IV.8.2.II.8.8
Positivo	$8.4.2.1\frac{1}{3}.1.8.2\frac{2}{3}.8$
Pedale	16.8.8.4.16

7. Some German developments since World War II. An important factor in postwar Germany was the prominence and high standard of many new and small firms, while the older and larger ones faded into the background. The appointment of organ advisers for each of the districts of Germany encouraged smaller builders as it also encouraged local variety and enterprise. From the early 1950s Beckerath of Hamburg and the two Schuke firms of Berlin (East and West) produced organs of strong character, often influenced by old instruments they had rebuilt (Schnitger organs rebuilt by Beckerath, Joachim Wagner organs by Alexander Schuke); as noted above, Beckerath also took instruments to the USA and, in 1970, a smaller example to Britain (Clare College, Cambridge). Ahrend and his former partner Brunzema (pupils of Paul Ott) continued the trend towards strong-toned organs, omitting mutations and relying on highly coloured flue and reed stops (usually made of hammered metal); old instruments restored by the firm (e.g. at Westerhusen) have a natural, unforced but startlingly powerful, breathy tone. The organ at Westerhusen, like Metzler's restoration at Nieuw Scheemda, Führer's at Hohenkirchen and Ahrend's in Stade, is a revelation of the musical colour open to a 17th-century organist of Friesland and Groningen. The stop lists seem nondescript; an example by Ahrend & Brunzema (Bremen-Oberneuland, 1966) is:

Hauptwerk	16.8.8.4.4.2.Mixtur.8
Rückpositiv	$8.4.4.2.1\frac{1}{3}$.II.Scharf.8
Pedal	16.8.4.16.8.2

But the sound is far from nondescript, and the idiosyncratic tone of such instruments is well removed from the neo-Baroque anonymity typical of so many organs of the 1950s.

Before 1973 German builders rarely developed good designs for organ cases, relying on simple geometric shapes that are pleasing but repetitive and often careless. Some imagination has been shown here and there in designing a sinuous front with 'modern' motifs (Marktkirche, Hanover; by Beckerath, 1954, see fig.50) and the square or rectangular box sometimes conforms with its surroundings (Gedächtniskirche, Berlin; by Schuke, 1962). Non-German builders more often tend to look at old models, as witness the influence of the Perpignan organ on that at Linz Cathedral (Marcussen–

48. Organ by Harrison & Harrison (inaugurated 1954) in the Royal Festival Hall, London

49. Console of the organ at St Paul's Cathedral, London, rebuilt (1972–7) by N. P. Mander

Andersen, 1968). Swells, either as enclosed *Oberwerk* or enclosed *Brustwerk*, are still popular in Germany, and it is often not possible to see them as anything more than ambiguous in nature and limited in conviction. On the other hand, standard German practice in making mechanical action has done little but good, and German builders are correct to point out that 'Recent organ music (such as Ligeti's *Volumina*) with its note-clusters, requires mechanical action. . . . The cluster technique shows complex flutter beats; the foreign nature of untempered, non-harmonic sound-elements can be produced only by mechanical action and its associated voicing' (*ISO Information*, viii, 1972, p.45).

8. THE PRESENT SITUATION. While it must be assumed that compromise organs and eclectic organs, will continue to be built over the next few decades, in three respects knowledge has increased beyond the level anticipated by the Organ Reformers of 1920. These are: understanding the true nature of each particular organ type; deducing the requirements of each particular composer; and restoring old organs without compromise. Naturally, the three trends are closely related but only in the widest sense are they historically committed: they do not favour any one period and they recognize that even the eclectic organ is a historical phenomenon. At the same time it is possible to imagine organs of a new type, wild developments beyond the dreams of Hope-Jones in which new pipe forms or electronic sound-producers are operated by whatever means contemporary technology suggests, 'organs' for which some schools of composition have already found appropriate musical language.

The lines of development in Europe are evident in the work of a few builders whose specialized and conscientious restoration of old organs (of whatever period) is matched by a pronounced notion, in their new organs, of what constitutes tonal beauty. A good example is Metzler & Söhne of Dietikon, Switzerland. They have restored several Baroque Swiss organs to their intended tone, in some cases surprisingly strong; meanwhile a certain line of development can be discerned in their new organs. The one at Grossmünster, Zurich (1959), has a *Werkprinzip* case of modern geometric design and

a huge stop list composite in its make-up (Swell, reeds *en chamade*, harmonic Trumpet, Septime etc) though without a full palette of string and Romantic flute stops. At Frauenfeld (1969) they made fewer compromises: the third manual is a truer *Brustwerk*, the stop list is thoroughly classical and the large, shallow, solid oak case is more truly fitting in its context. The importance of this case to the sound cannot be overemphasized; the whole organ shows (in the words of the builder) 'a logical arrangement deplored by adversaries as being merely historical yet [which] is modern in design and technologically advanced'. Such builders have a wide spectrum of historic colour at their disposal, including rarer stops like Dolkan, Suavial, doubled case-pipes (joined at the feet) and French reeds. The enthusiasm aroused by Metzler's organ in St Pierre, Geneva (1965), assures the firm of a place in organ history, not least for its attempt to pay tribute to classical French colours.

The tendency towards strict and specific stylistic imitation is becoming increasingly marked. A builder may introduce 'flexible' wind supply to a restored organ (Évora Cathedral, 1562; restored by Flentrop, 1969), imitating the wind and voicing conditions of the original instrument; or a completely new organ in old style may be built, attempting to imitate the qualities of sound due to the old manner of wind supply, voicing, scaling, pipe material, chests, mechanism, casework and stop lists of the model copied. Such an instrument was completed in 1972 at the Ashland Avenue Baptist Church, Toledo, Ohio (John Brombaugh & Co.; fig.51, p.909), its 19 stops following models by the 16th-century Dutch master Hendrik Niehoff. Whether the original compass, pitch-level, key-shapes and other factors crucial to the musical repertory of a particular old organ are also copied must depend on the purpose of the modern counterpart. An exhibition or museum organ may be built to suit the purist; a church is usually assumed to be subject to what are called 'liturgical demands' – Swell boxes for Anglican chant, a large compass for modern organ music, standard pitch for accompaniment, etc. It is probable that the gap between the two kinds of organ, secular and ecclesiastical, will grow, and the secular will remain the more advanced, even though this may mean strict fidelity to what had been thought to be obsolete ideals. One particular avenue opened to exploration in the late 1970s has to do with temperament. Interest in pre-19th-century music and its authentic performance has sparked a growing interest in various historical unequal temperaments. Werckmeister and Kirnberger tunings are gaining acceptance in church organs and are extensively used by some builders along with their own 'shop' temperaments; builders such as Fisk, Noack, Brombaugh, Taylor, Mander, Ahrend, Garnier, Führer, Flentrop, Riel, Koenig and Kern are now routinely tuning even large instruments in unequal temperaments. A four-manual Flentrop at Duke University, Durham, North Carolina, (1976) is tuned in Chaumont, and Fisk's large (1978) four-manual at House of Hope Church in St Paul,

Minnesota, is tuned to a special shop temperament. Split-key mean-tone instruments have been built by Brombaugh (Oberlin College, Ohio, 1981) and Fisk (Wellesley College, Massachusetts, 1981; see fig.53, p.914). Metzler's church organ at Frauenfeld has an unequal temperament, and its low pressure (manuals 75 mm, pedal 85 mm) combines with the voicing techniques to suggest, in the words of the builders, 'a choir's breathing. The over-perfected and explosive speech of the neo-Baroque organ of the fifties has completely disappeared. One can once again experience with this instrument that an organ is a large wind instrument'. See also §VIII, 7.

VIII. Recent research and areas for study

Although those periods in the history of the organ or those aspects of its construction that are still imperfectly understood may appear to be matters for the scholar or theorist, in practice all such knowledge affects at least the better informed organ builders and players of today. For them, to understand the function and functioning of an organ or organ type of the past is a living part of their thought and work today. This is a distinctly new phenomenon in the history of all instrument making and reflects a fuller and more complete understanding of the past than was previously possible or even thought desirable. Conversely, it has only gradually become clear how inadequate are certain older ideas on the history of organs because those engaged today in the practical issues of performance and construction have found them to be so. Thus in the following outline of the areas still imperfectly understood there are many practical lessons for performer and builder.

1. Word origin. 2. Construction. 3. Pipework. 4. The classical and medieval organ. 5. The organ 1450–1800. 6. Some developments 1800–1930. 7. The Organ Revival.

1. WORD ORIGIN. Though it might be thought a rarefied aspect of organ study, the understanding of how words were used at particular moments in the history of the instrument is often important for an understanding in general of how the instrument evolved. For example, it has become clear that at a crucial point in the development of Western music, during and around the 9th century, 'organum' in original sources can mean not an instrument at all but an 'organ of learning', such as a book; there are other examples of this ambiguous usage, such as 'psalterium' (a psalter or a psaltery) and even, later on, 'manual' (a handbook or a keyboard). Thus every single reference in Christian sources to organs before the church contracts of the high Middle Ages needs to be scanned anew and tested against this possibility. Later terms are of course less open to such ambiguity, but a wider reading outside musical sources can shed new light on difficult words. One example can be found in 16th-century Portugal, where church accounts speak of choir stalls as the 'cadeira'; this suggests that the 'cadeireta' or 'Chair organ' is so called not because it is behind the organist's chair but because it was part of (hanging over or built into the superstructure of) the choir stalls. Perhaps then one is also to infer that at first it was seen not as a 'second manual' to the large organ but as a more or less independent (if small) instrument: the large organ for special occasions (i.e. a kind of signal-organ), the small for the choir work (i.e. a musical participant). Some such situation was the case in Durham Cathedral where, according to a report made in 1672, there was or had been in the previous century a large

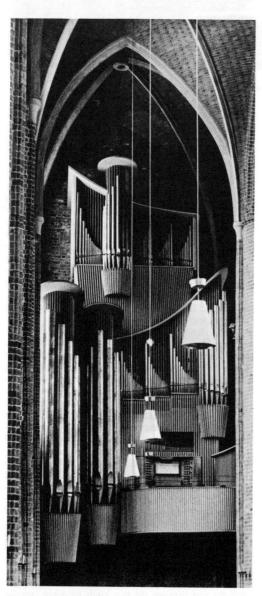

50. Organ by Rudolph von Beckerath (1954) in the Marktkirche, Hanover

51. Organ by John Brombaugh & Co. (1972) in the Ashland Avenue Baptist Church, Toledo, Ohio

organ called the Cryers (*Schreier*? – a *Blockwerk*?) used on special occasions and placed on the north of the quire, and an organ of wooden pipes 'over the quire door'.

Another example of the need to be alerted to word-implications is the use in 18th-century Germany of the word 'Brustwerk': some references (e.g. Walther's *Lexicon* of 1732, under 'Brust') say it can be placed above the Great, still (in a sense) 'within the breast' of the organ but obviously bigger, more diffuse and no longer geared towards bass continuo work at the level of the gallery floor near the singers. In such cases, 'Brustwerk' means the same as 'Oberwerk'.

2. CONSTRUCTION. The work of the better builders of today, prompted in particular by the increasing number of players aware of the characteristics of touch and the nature of historic organ types, has become more and more directed towards the simplest kind of keyboard mechanism, the 'suspended action'. This is the system shown in fig.8. Here the keys hang from their trackers, and their 'feel' is an incomparable combination of the light and the crisp. Not only the *Haupt* or *Brustwerk* manuals can be so made, but such builders as Joachim Wagner, working in Prussia during the Bach period, designed a suspended action for both his *Haupt* and *Oberwerk* manuals that could serve as a model for any builder today who wished to take the 'tracker revival' one step further.

A similar point can be made about the two kinds of Tremulant, known now from their codification in French sources as Tremblant fort and Tremblant doux but at one time more widespread than those terms suggest. The Tremblant doux, or internal tremulant, achieves its effect by disturbing the flow of wind in the wind-trunk by means of a floating plate which, when released by the stop action, oscillates up and down with the aid of a weighted spring. The Tremblant fort, as its name implies, gives a stronger undulation to the wind flow by the oscillation of a small bellows which emits small puffs of air through a small exhaust port. When not in use, the plate of the Tremblant doux is pushed up against the side of the wind-trunk, and the bellows of the Tremblant fort is fixed in a closed position (see fig.10*b* and *c*). Not only modern 'copies' (Basle, Leonhardskirche, T. Kuhn, 1969; Montreal, McGill University, H. Wolff, 1981) but new instruments are likely to have both types of Tremulant. From an understanding of historical tastes, witnessed by both written sources and a few extant examples, has come an awareness that most Tremulants of the last 200 years beat too fast for earlier music, and that organ Tremulant effects were attempted by composers in certain 'affecting' music (e.g. Scheidt, Kuhnau, J. S. Bach's *Erbarm dich mein* BWV721).

A further kind of historic awareness, though of a different ethos, is the respect paid to the experiments of the great 19th-century engineer-builders, in particular the sensitive and durable electric actions (such as Willis's for Canterbury Cathedral in 1886) and the ingenious systems of the innovators. Though apparently irrelevant to the revival of early music as now understood, the achievements of the inventive years around 1900 earn their own respect. Of the many publications from that period, one example – the report of Robert Hope-Jones's organ in the McEwan Hall, University of Edinburgh – can be taken to show the obvious awe and delight in such skill (quoted from T. Elliston: *Organs and Tuning*, London, 1898):

It may be interesting to learn. . .that the action of all the key-boards together requires no more electricity than is needed for the common household electric bells, and this current is supplied by a few dry

52. Organ by Jürgen Ahrend (1981) in the Church of the Augustins, Toulouse

cells. This may be more easily comprehended when it is understood that all the current is required to do is to energise a very small electro-magnet, which has to attract a minute armature (in shape of a circular metal disc as light as a pin) away from the valve-seat on which it rests. This disc only moves one-sixty-fourth part of an inch, but in so doing it opens up a way of escape for compressed air, which immediately causes the sudden collapse of a small motor, and at the same moment pulls down the pallet and allows the wind to rush into the pipe.

3. PIPEWORK. Amongst the many areas of constant experimentation and discovery for an organ builder are the ways in which a pipe behaves, particularly in two respects: its winding (what kind of wind it receives and the way it treats it or is treated by it) and its material (the nature of its metal or wood, whether or not the metal is hammered or beaten, how hard the wood is). In the absence of data provided by controlled experiments, builders and those attempting to understand the art can only agree with Bédos de Celles (*L'art du facteur d'orgues*, 1766–8, Pt ii) on the need to hammer pipe metal (especially that for the case-pipes), on the desirability of hardening with alloys the metal used for pipefeet but not for the pipe-bodies, and on the visual effect of lacquering the pipes. How far the current trends amongst thinking organ builders for varnishing all pipes and 'thus improving their tone' (as distinct from their looks) can actually be supported by proper evidence has not yet been tested, but if it were a valid point it is strange that Bédos of all people did not say so. Either way, the wider use of Bédos's treatise in recent English, German and French editions continues to keep alive the basic issues. Much work still needs to be done on the way pipes are actually made to speak by wind passing through them – work done not so much from the point of view of the physicist as by the builder; Charles Fisk's essay (in Pape, 1978) deserves follow-up studies by those properly qualified, especially in its suggestion that organ counterpoint, in its mixing of sustained and moving lines, is by nature an essay 'in the handling of organ wind – when to disturb the wind deliberately [by moving from one note to another, causing movement of the pallet and thus changes in the status of the wind] and when not'. That in the earliest periods of organ history the method and quality of wind supply was a preoccupation of the more literate and scientifically trained minds is clear from Greek, Latin and Arabic authors, all of whom described the making of organs entirely in terms of their windraising and its application; pipe-making and practical tuning were not subjects for philosophers, but windraising was.

4. THE CLASSICAL AND MEDIEVAL ORGAN. Werner Walcker-Mayer's suggestion that the four ranks of the Roman organ of Aquincum were made according to four particular modes or *tonoi* (see §IV, 1) has not been proved or disproved during the last decade or so, but it has been material to the continual attempt to understand the evolution of the octave-scale and the keyboard.

```
1 (open):     g   a  bb c'  d' eb' e'  f'  g' a'  bb c'' d''
2 (stopped):  e  f♯ g   a   b  c' c♯' d' e' f♯' g'  a' b'
3 (stopped):  d   e  f   g   a bb b   c'  d' e'  f'  g' a'
4 (stopped):  c   d  eb  f   g ab a   bb c' d' eb' f' g'
```

Thus, if the Aquincum organ did have the above notes supplied by its four registers (as suggested by Walcker-Mayer), it did not support J. P. Kirnberger's observation that in the strict modal system the pitch of notes differed depending on their position: a Pythagorean E calculated as a 3rd from C would not be the same note calculated as a 2nd from D; and C–D, D–E would be two different kinds of 2nd (*Die Kunst des reinen Satzes in der Musik*, i, 1771, pp.4ff). Whether or not Kirnberger was right to claim that the different 'moods' attributed by ancient writers to the different modes came from this difference in tuning is likewise uncertain (ii, 1776, pp.49–50), but he was probably right to claim that the 'moods' were as much a question of the kind of music sung as of the nature of the modes themselves; of course, the two ideas are not contradictory.

If the four registers of the Aquincum organ produced different C's etc depending on modal context, the medieval keyboard scales appear even more of a compromise than they must have done to the generations of theorists from the later 15th century onwards who discussed organ tuning and temperaments, precisely perhaps because the 'rise of the triad', as it is usually called (e.g. Lindley, 1980), required new thinking about the major 3rd. Also, perhaps the well-known medieval compass from B arose because in theory its first four notes (B–C–D–E) would correspond to the Greek diatonic tetrachord (semitone–tone–tone); so would E–F–G–A, and the note between the two (Bb) would be the first semitone to be added (not necessarily higher than the others in the actual keyboard: see fig.27), and would be desirable as the octave-scale produced notes sung in the common repertory. But if each key played only one tone, without the variability at each step that strict modal accuracy would have required and which the Aquincum organ may have provided, the medieval keyboard was from the start so inaccurate that it could well have forced music into adopting simpler scale-types, i.e. the medieval modes. 'Music' in this sense has to be understood as literate music of the Western kind, distinct from music of other cultures and from the vocal 'folk-music' of Western culture. This whole area – the evolution of the keyboard, the relationship of fixed and non-variable tones to the development of modes and thus diatonic scales, and the effect of these developments on the tuning of the 12 notes of the octave – has often received attention in the past but deserves a total rethinking in the coming years, now that sources are so much better understood.

It has also been recently shown, very convincingly, that the Aquincum organ was a WATER ORGAN or HYDRAULIS, rather than a bellows-blown organ (E. L. Szonntagh, *Scientific Honeyweller*, ii, 1981, pp.54–60), but in the case of the oldest Christian drawing of an organ (the Utrecht Psalter; see fig.26) the doubts have always been about other details: the two players, what they are doing with their hands, why there are only twice four pipes and what the significance is of the apparent pipe-lengths (ratio of 1 : 2 : 3 : 4). One recent examination (Hardouin, 1966) has suggested that the instrument looks like a siren organ of the kind described by Muristus (see §IV, 3), even as far as the pipe-proportions; the four sounds might even correspond to those of the four bells used for signalling in the liturgy (*quadrillon = carillon*). However, as with so much medieval 'evidence', there may well be other elements in the representation disguising, even destroying, the technical information we are hoping to see there. For example, if a vertical line is drawn down from the central figure at the top (a central figure of some importance, of course), each half of the drawing closely mirrors the other, including the angels, the winds, the two ranks of instrumentalists, the hydraulis-pumpers, the organists and (though not in mirror image) the pipes. Nevertheless, whether or not the sets of four pipes symbolize the four winds (i.e. artefacts activated by wind), it cannot be assumed, as it often is, that the organist's hands as drawn are placed without any knowledge or understanding: the mechanism of Arab 'organs' took the form of some kind of lever somewhere near the foot of the pipe. Of course, whether or not the drawing reflects Byzantine influence, it could certainly be the product of someone who had never seen any such instrument and was relying on written sources (a verbal description, diagram etc).

That the Utrecht Psalter drawing might have been of some kind of signal-organ raises the question of how organs came to be used in the Western church and what they were used for. Recent work (Williams, 1980) suggests that truly musical use of organs is unlikely to date back earlier than the 12th century, especially the *alternatim* use with the choir. Even then, it was a question of special occasions in the most important monastic or secular churches. The earliest appearance of the organ in church, perhaps in the 9th century and certainly in the 10th and 11th centuries, probably related more to noise than to music, i.e. it was used for signalling purposes (perhaps as a kind of bell-substitute), not for music in the liturgy. In Constantinople, the *organon* was used on particular days during processions and receptions in the area around the emperor's palace – when the people cried 'Agios' ('Holy') in the courtyard outside to mark the close when the celebrant signalled, after the people had acclaimed the emperor, after a processional song and in the hall as the emperor was enthroned. Not only a Carolingian king but a powerful Benedictine abbot or bishop may well have received the same kind of treatment in his palace or cathedral. This is almost certainly the origin of organs in the service of the only provincial Christian church to have had them, i.e. Charlemagne's western European church under allegiance to Rome.

Two further ancient and famous organs known about from written sources continue to attract attention: Winchester and Grado. After attempts to reduce the exaggerated language of the 10th-century poem describing the first and to place it as a signal-organ in the westwork of the Saxon Cathedral of Winchester, a recent interpretation has seen it as an organ of 40 (not 400) pipes, ten keys playing four pipes each (1.8.12.15, perhaps like the Utrecht Psalter organ) and twice 13 bellows (Hardouin, 1981). But much still remains to be conjectured about the early organ – why it was an attribute only of the western European church (Carolingian-Benedictine), what ranks it had, how the keyboard evolved, where it was placed in church, whether it played any bigger part in the abbey than, for example, the clock, and what it had to do with early polyphony. At least one important experiment was made during the 1980s: in the Netherlands, Louis Huivenaar and Jan de Briujn reconstructed conical pipes of the kind described by Theophilus (see §IV, 5) and placed them on a chest made, after imaginative reconstruction-work, according to Zarlino's description of the (?)11th-century chest from Grado, Venice (*Sopplimenti musicali*, iii, 1558, pp.290–91). Though a crude block made presumably from a rough copy by somebody unacquainted with organs, Zarlino's drawing does show some salient points: there were 15 notes (probably push-pull sliders activated by spade-shaped 'keys' not entirely unlike those in fig.27), two ranks of pipes (Zarlino himself said that there was no way of telling whether they were of metal or wood, at unison or octave pitch), and, at the rear of the chest, round sockets into which the bellows had fitted (perhaps

a pair, or three as in Virdung: see Meyer, ed. and trans., p.32), 'such as one sees them placed in modern regals'. Huivenaar and Briujn's experiments suggest that the conical pipes had a very strong and complex overtone content, producing a quite extraordinary vocal quality, sustaining the pitch and serving for playing a chant-melody with a constancy totally unavailable on any other instrument of the time, much less the human voice. A not dissimilar breathy, ringing quality of tone can still be heard in the three very old ranks of the famous organ at Sion, Switzerland (see §IV, 6).

5. THE ORGAN 1450–1800. Recent work has been directed towards the historical position of Henri Arnaut's manuscript treatise (Sachs, 1980), towards an understanding of the 15th-century keyboard (Meeùs, 1971; Lindley, 1980; de Graaf, 1982) and, in one very notable case, towards a circumspect restoration of an extant old organ (S Petronio, Bologna, reopened 1982). For its theoretical discussion of pipe-scales, Arnaut's treatise now seems more indebted to earlier writings than was previously thought; on its more practical side, it is clear on the one hand that the two forms of pipe-mouth were accurate enough for them still to be found in the 17th century, on the other that the celebrated reference to reed stops cannot be dated to the 15th century with total certainty. Also uncertain in date, though confidently ascribed to 1380 in the century after A. G. Hill so dated it in his book of drawings (1883–91), is the extant Gothic case in Salamanca, now thought by de Graaf (1982) to belong to about 1500. Its compass seems to have been C/E-c''' (45 keys), not as a unicum but as one of the then long compasses known to Italian and Spanish builders who built according to the space or money available. It had a half-stop (from f), probably a pitch approximately a major 3rd above a' = 440, pipe-rack above the mouths not below, and at least one kind of *subsemitonium* (divided sharp, as in some Italian long-compass organs of the 15th century).

More certain is the Bologna organ. It had ten stops of 51 notes ($F'G'A'$-a'', ranks at 16[=24]. $8.4.2\frac{2}{3}.2.1\frac{1}{3}.1.\frac{2}{3}.\frac{1}{2}$.Flute 4), a pedal probably of 17 notes (corresponding to the three larger pipe-flats in the façade) and a pitch of a' = $c521$. As for the early 16th-century organ in general, facsimile editions with translations of Schlick and Virdung make more accessible the salient characteristics, particularly those of the all-important Rhineland organ of $c1500$ which Schlick described with a forthrightness still worth heeding – for instance, when he described the essential uselessness of split sharps as a method of dealing with temperament problems. It is also clear that the thick slider positioned above the slider-chest and directing the wind through curling ducts between pallet and pipe (described by Schlick as the 'four-finger-thick slider') is not only to be seen as yet another attempt by late medieval builders to make firmly constructed, fault-free chests (see §II, 5) but must also have resulted in a controlled wind-attack for the speech of each pipe.

The speech of pipes, their winding and their tuning, become more and more the concern of both historically minded players and carefully reasoning builder-restorers. The newly restored Gothic organ of Lübeck (the small organ in the Jakobikirche), though now predominantly in the form given it by Friedrich Stellwagen in 1636, has a partly complete Principal chorus of the late 15th century, built up of pipes of 97% (or more) of lead. The characteristics of Stellwagen's flues and reeds raise all the questions of how such pipes spoke and what kind of sound they were meant to produce – in particular, what kind of vocal quality they were imitating, as all organs must. The evolution of singing tone in 16th-century Europe is itself a major question for historians – though one would not think so from reading standard histories of music – and for the moment one can suggest only generalities: for example, just as voices were beginning to produce the smooth characteristics of 'bel canto' (was the production of sweet, lyrical tone still one of the 'new' elements in Caccini's *Le nuove musiche* of 1601?), so organs were expected to smooth out some of the rougher characteristics of earlier tone. Thus, somewhere during the 16th century (perhaps in Hamburg, about 1550), builders began to make reed-shallots in such a way as to thicken the tone, i.e. thin out the overtone content: shapes were changed (narrowed), and edges were leaded and even leathered (so that the tongue came into contact with lead or leather, not brass). It seems as if those countries where church music progressed in purer form by remaining more exclusively vocal and polyphonic (Italy, Spain, England) preferred to do without reeds. During the 1980s there may well be spectacular restorations of the north European organs with massive choruses and quieter colour-stops (Hagerbeer's organ in the Nieuwe Kerk, Amsterdam; Schnitger's in the Maartenskerk, Groningen); but from the point of view of music's evolution as a whole there is no doubt that more thought must be given to the singing, vocal traditions of Italian organs.

In general terms, it cannot be doubted that over the centuries the changing ideas of what constituted 'good singing' were reflected in contemporary organ building, not only in tone but in tuning. A crucial characteristic of the north European organ during the 17th century must be the mean-tone tunings long preferred by builders but constantly modified by composers whose assumptions – like that of other craftsmen in the western European traditions – had been that their duty was to develop and to achieve new things in new ways. It is certainly no coincidence that the most startling things done in harmony in the period around 1600 were in those areas in which solo or choral singing, and vocal counterpoint, were paramount (Italy and England). In France, the organ by 1675 had developed voicing and colouring which (whether or not they can be likened to the newly standardized French nasal vowel-sounds) were essentially unsuitable for vocal music but which could serve very well as interludes to it, consciously different from it in tone and thus making excellent *alternatim* idioms for the Mass and Offices. For the Parisian, the organ was no longer seen as a voice-substitute; the Principals became rounder, the reeds yet more *éclatant*, and the liturgists found it necessary to specify certain sounds at certain moments lest the wide-ranging palette of colours become chaotic or anarchic (for liturgical use see Van Wye, 1980). For the German organ, a useful starting-point for those in coming years anxious to understand the general lines of development for organ tone might well be to assume that the Reformation brought with it a change of emphasis away from properly trained singers towards the fuller and coarser sound of congregations, and thus away from discreet vocal tone in organs towards the leaded reeds and thicker *organo pleno* of a later age.

In J. S. Bach's Thuringia and Saxony, the organ's primary purpose in most churches – to accompany or at least to introduce the chorales for the congregation, perhaps from time to time performing 'recital music' – may well have made it seem best to builders to remove the (by then) heavy pedal to the back of the organ, to deepen the casework generally, to remove the immediacy of pipe-sounds and to add string stops. The effect was gradually to 'round out' the tone, both in its colours and in its acoustical properties (the two have tended to go together in organ history) – and this on behalf of the congregation who were positioned in several galleries around the flat-ceilinged churches. In the case of the 'Italian Baroque organ', a well-restored instrument such as that of Gaetano Callido in Calceranica (near Trent) is witness to a vocal ideal still by no means spent at the end of the 18th century: both Principale 8′ and Voce umana speak with an age-old breathy tone that has a variable edge to it (variable because of its sensitivity to keyboard-touch). This is perennially useful for Italian vocal (but not German instrumental) counterpoint. The very excellence of workmanship in a Callido organ, including that of the screw-adjusted regals, shows that the Italian efforts up to 1800 and beyond were always geared to this vocal quality, eschewing the hard plena, the reeds, the auxiliary chests, the versatile pedals and all the other clever gadgets of the organ north of the Alps.

In the case of the English organ, the tastes and priorities of the old builders are only gradually becoming clearer, and no documentary history of the English organ has yet been made. A new transcription of the All Hallows, Barking, document of 1519 (see §V, 8, and Blewitt and Thompson, 1977) has not clarified the issues except to establish how uncertain the scribe was of the technical details he was being asked to write down. His specification for the inner pipes, that they 'shalle be as fyne metalle and stuff as the utter partes that ys to say of pure Tyne', has muddled the information he was given: one can guess that the case-pipes were to be of tin, the inner of metal (stuff, *étoffe*) but in their way as good in quality as the case-pipes. This suggests that the vocal quality of the organ's basic sound, i.e. the case-principals or Diapasons, was richer than it would be if they were made of the lead then becoming popular in northern Europe (cf. Lübeck above) but less so in Italy. The scribe's following phrase, 'of pure Tyne wythe as fewe stoppes as may be conuenient', can now be seen as meaning not 'with as few separated ranks and stop-knobs as convenient' (whatever that could mean) but 'with as few stopped pipes as its position on the screen makes desirable' (i.e. for the sight-lines not to be harmed by pipes protruding from the top).

Putting English organs more in their general European background can certainly lead to interesting possibilities in some instances, as in the idea, for example, that the larger pipes at All Hallows, Barking, like some at Coventry and later in Exeter Cathedral, were rather in the manner of the continental Trompes (see §IV, 6, and Owen, 1980) – though the modest size of at least the All Hallows and Coventry organs would make it impossible for such bass pipes to serve as they did at Rouen, Haarlem etc. As for the organ of the Restoration period, it is clear that Smith's and Harris's organs had much the same purpose as those in Thuringia and Saxony summarized above, though parsimony made pedals so rare as to be virtually unknown. Also, the Breton influences on Harris, and via him on Smith, resulted in an array of frenchified colours more suitable for French

Mass-interludes of the kind familiar in several areas removed from Paris (e.g. Walloon Flanders, now Belgium). As the Breton influences on the Dallams and on Harris gradually become clearer (see Bicknell, 1981), so do the Frisian on Smith (Rowntree, 1978; Thistlethwaite, 1978); it is not quite accurate to refer to 'French' or 'Dutch' in these contexts. From the stop lists alone one might think that the English organ tone was, at any rate before the Smith–Harris generation, closely related to the Italian organ in its two vocal ideals, i.e. for the main manual to sing as a voice and for the subsidiary manual to accompany the voice:

Dallam Organ at Durham Cathedral (1620? before 1661?)

Great 8.8.4.4.2⅔.2.1.'Furnetura'

Choir 8.4.2.1.Flute

In coming years, comparisons with the other organ cultures of Europe may well shed further light on the aims of the several historic English organ types. A good example is the fact that Joachim Hess, in his Dutch treatise of 1774, was surprised by the effect of a Swell on an English organ imported to Curaçao in 1770. It seems astonishing that he needed news from across the Atlantic to tell him that Swell boxes produced a realistic crescendo – until one appreciates that only the closed-toe English voicing (in its keeping the wind back from the languid and lip) made such Swells useful in the way they would not be with more forthright voicing. Unless he travelled away from northern Europe, an author had no conception of such organ tone (Hess, 1774, p.99), and to this day northern builders seem not to have grasped the fact that a true Swell needs very particular voicing methods.

6. SOME DEVELOPMENTS 1800–1930. That at least at times the Dutch builders kept to older notions well into the 19th century is clear from recently published gazetteers (*Langs Nederlandse Orgels*, 1977–9). *Rückpositiv* departments were added to new organs soon after they were made (at Genemuiden in 1824–9, at Oldemarkt in 1828–49), even sometimes only as case-fronts (at Enschede in 1892). In comparison, France in the 1840s was full of experimentation, not only in the celebrated work of Cavaillé-Coll at St Denis (Hardouin, 1980) but in the new actions and construction of countless builders, such as the *orgue à piston* (a 'barless chest') announced in 1845 by Claude Frères and reported on by Guédon in 1903. Guédon's book describes many a device of the period (such as Moitessier's pneumatic action of 1745: see §VI, 3) and served as a kind of French equivalent to Audsley's treatise (1905). Less clear are the reasons for the recent marked increase in interest (particularly in Germany and those parts of the organ world concerned with French organ music since c1850) shown in the works and theories of Aristide Cavaillé-Coll (Douglass, 1980; Huybens, 1979; Sabatier, 1979; Salies, 1979). The amount of detail released by such studies probably amounts to more than that for any other organ builder who ever lived, and the admiration frequently expressed for the few relatively untouched Cavaillé-Coll organs (e.g. St Sernin, Toulouse, 1887) suggests that especially for those players in the USA and Germany who went through the less pleasant phases of the *Orgelbewegung* (see §VII), the warm Romantic tone and sheer craftsmanship of such organs serve as a fine antidote. This is so perhaps precisely because Cavaillé-Coll organs have an orchestral palette, pneumatic actions and a voicing style totally opposed to the

vocal/mean-tone immediacy of organ tone in c1600. One might think such French organs have a very circumscribed musical quality and usefulness. But that orchestral palette is richer and better-blending than much of the neo-Baroque tone of 1950; and those actions are not more unpleasant than the actions (often of metal, with many squares etc) made in the same period. One author (Sabatier, 1979) asks whether the recent admiration for Cavaillé-Coll does not 'invite one to pursue one's own ideal for the exploitation of resources offered by modern technology and further creation of a new instrument in the dimension of our time'. But it could be thought that there lurk here too many begged questions concerning an instrument that is by nature a 15th-century achievement, if not invention.

In the interests of a nostalgic searching for heavier organ tone than Baroque revivals have provided, a certain interest in Robert Hope-Jones is also being revived in English-speaking circles (e.g. essays in *The Organ*, 1981, 1982). That his actions often failed is accounted for by a too low amperage, not unexpected in days before the universal availability of electricity; their principles of construction are now much admired for the degree of technological inventiveness they exhibit. Besides, as Fanselau has shown (1973), understanding the Hope-Jones organ is still important for grasping the aims of a major school of composition and one that is by no means extinct. The claims made for Hope-Jones's organ in Edinburgh were quoted above (§VIII, 2) and, as a reaction to the propaganda for the (often poor) tracker actions over the last quarter-century, the revived interest in them is understandable. Similarly, that the extension organ born of Hope-Jones's work is not entirely without virtues (i.e. organ-building logic) is now often pointed out; the sheer workmanship is admired (as indeed it is admirable) and the stop lists themselves, such as that for the Civic Hall, Wolverhampton (see §VI, 4), are often claimed to leave unencumbered a full Diapason chorus irrespective of the auxiliary ranks that are so extended. It can be assumed, however, that even in the interests of 'giving each period its own praise', the organ world is not yet ready for a Hope-Jones copy or for a revival of the Wolverhampton voicing.

7. THE ORGAN REVIVAL. The over-simplification of the issues involved in organ building put about by the Organ Revival, especially its German form the *Orgelbewegung*, have become increasingly clear to both good builders and careful scholars. The history of the Revival itself can also now be seen as more complex than those many German authors who were chiefly indebted to other German authors have interpreted it. For example, an enlightened Swiss attitude was already clear from Jacques Handschin's paper ('Die Orgelbewegung in der Schweiz') given at the *Freiberger Tagung* of 1927 and from Kuhn's *Rückpositiv* at Berne Münster in 1930 (a more French than German department in this instance). The revised edition of P. H. Kriek's *Organum novum* (1981) has traced in more detail the priorities of the Dutch builders during the 20th century. In Germany itself there were some marked contradictions between one kind of activity and another, between the advanced (i.e. historically aware) ideas and the conventional. At one of the worst periods, a *Werkprinzip* organ could receive sympathetic consideration (e.g. the pedal-towers added at Stendal Marienkirche between 1940 and 1944) or a church could find itself guided by its repertory towards old ideas (e.g.

53. *Organ by C. B. Fisk (1981) at Wellesley College,
Massachusetts*

the little choir organ built for the Thomaskirche, Leipzig,
in 1932 with pipes made to some kind of Schnitger scale).
On the other hand, while in 1932–3 the Hildebrandt organ
at St Wenzel, Naumburg (§V, 11), was remade according to its stop list of 1746, it was given at the same time
a new electric console in a different gallery! Historicism
took the form of so electrifying the pallets that the old
trackers and old keyboards were left.

These and similar incidents become clearer as more
and more archival and other material is published;
although there is still no full history of the German organ
or separation of the main issues appearing in the many
gazetteer-like books, journals and articles in German,
the organ student is in a better position as each year
passes. Such organs as Charles Fisk's Fritzsche-
influenced instrument in Wellesley College, Massachusetts (1981), with its traditional wedge-shaped bellows
worked by the blower's body-weight and old elements
such as the case, keys, voicing and split-sharp tuning,
raise and interpret these issues as perhaps no other
endeavour can.

BIBLIOGRAPHY

HawkinsH

A. Schlick: *Spiegel der Orgelmacher und Organisten* (Speyer,
1511/*R*1959; ed. and Eng. trans. E. B. Barber, Buren, 1980)
S. Virdung: *Musica getutscht* (Basle, 1511; ed. and Eng. trans. C.
Meyer, 1980)
C. Antegnati: *L'arte organica* (Brescia, 1608/*R*1958)
M. Praetorius: *Syntagma musicum*, ii (Wolfenbüttel, 1618, 2/
1619/*R*1958 and 1980)
M. Mersenne: *Harmonie universelle* (Paris, 1636–7/*R*1963; Eng.
trans., 1957)
A. Werckmeister: *Orgelprobe* (Frankfurt am Main, 1681, enlarged
2/1698/*R*1970, ?5/1783)
J. P. Bendeler: *Organopoeia* (Frankfurt am Main, 1690/*R*1972,
2/1739)
J. B. Samber: *Manuductio ad organum* (Salzburg, 1704–7)
A. Werckmeister: *Organum gruningense redivivum* (Quedlinburg,
1705)
P. M. Vogt: *Conclave thesauri magnae artis musicae* (Prague, 1719)
F. E. Niedt: *Musicalische Handleitung*, iii, ed. J. Mattheson (Ham-
burg, 1721)
J. H. Biermann: *Organographia hildesiensis specialis* (Hildesheim,
1738)
C. G. Meyer: *Sammlung einiger Nachrichten von berühmten Orgel-
werken in Teutschland* (Breslau, 1757)
G. A. Sorge: *Die geheim gehaltene Kunst von Mensuration von
Orgel-Pfeiffen* (MS, c1760; ed. and Eng. trans. C. O. Bleyle,
Buren, 1978)
F. Bédos de Celles: *L'art du facteur d'orgues* (Paris, 1766–78/*R*1965)
J. Adlung: *Musica mechanica organoedi* (Berlin, 1768/*R*1961)

A. A. Hülphers: *Historisk afhandling om musik och instrumenter*
(Westerås, 1773/*R*1971)
J. Hess: *Dispositien der merkwaardigste kerk-orgelen, welke in de
zeven Veréenigde Provincien als mede in Duytsland en elders
aangehoffen worden* (Gouda, 1774/*R*1945)
N. A. Knock: *Dispositien der merckwaardigste kerk-orgelen welke
in de Provincie Friesland, Groningen en elders aangehoffen wor-
den* (Groningen, 1788/*R*1971)
J. H. Knecht: *Vollständige Orgelschule* (Leipzig, 1795)
G. C. F. Schlimmbach: *Ueber die Structur, Erhaltung, Stimmung,
Prüfung etc. der Orgel* (Leipzig, 1801/*R*1966)
J. Hess: *Dispositien van kerk-orgelen . . . in Nederland* (Gouda,
1815)
J. C. Wolfram: *Anleitung zur Kenntniss, Beurtheilung und Erhal-
tung der Orgeln* (Gotha, 1815/*R*1962)
G. Serassi: *Sugli organi, lettere a G. S. Mayr, P. Bonfichi e C.
Bigatti* (Bergamo, 1816; ed. O. Mischiati, Bologna, 1973)
J. G. Töpfer: *Die Orgelbaukunst* (Weimar, 1833)
J. A. Hamilton: *Catechism of the Organ* (London, 1842, enlarged
3/1865)
J. J. Seidel: *Die Orgel und ihr Bau* (Breslau, 1843/*R*1962)
J. Sutton: *A Short Account of Organs* (London, 1847)
P. M. Hamel: *Nouveau manual complet du facteur d'orgues* (Paris,
1849)
E. J. Hopkins and E. F. Rimbault: *The Organ: its History and Con-
struction* (London, 1855, enlarged 3/1877/*R*1972)
J. G. Töpfer: *Die Theorie und Praxis des Orgelbaues* (Weimar,
1855, enlarged 2/1888/*R*1972)
A. de Pontécoulant: *Organographie* (Paris, 1861/*R*1973)
E. F. Rimbault: *The Early English Organ-builders and their Works*
(London, 1865/*R*1978)
A. G. Hill: *The Organ-cases and Organs of the Middle Ages and
Renaissance* (London, 1883–91/*R*1966)
M. H. van 't Kruijs: *Verzameling van disposities der verschillende
orgels in Nederland* (Rotterdam, 1885/*R*1962)
J. W. Warman: *The Organ: Writings and other Utterances on its
Structure, History, Procural, Capabilities, etc.* (London, 1898–
?1904)
J. Guédon: *Nouveau manuel complet du facteur d'orgues* (Paris,
1903)
G. A. Audsley: *The Art of Organ-building* (New York, 1905/*R*1965)
L. Burgemeister: *Der Orgelbau in Schlesien* (Strasbourg, 1925)
E. Flade: *Der Orgelbauer Gottfried Silbermann* (Leipzig, 1926/
*R*1953)
A. Freeman: *Father Smith* (London, 1926; ed. J. Rowntree, Oxford,
1977)
W. Gurlitt, ed.: *Freiberger Tagung für Deutsche Orgelkunst: Frei-
berg 1926* (Augsburg, 1926)
G. Frotscher: *Die Orgel* (Leipzig, 1927)
F. Raugel: *Les grandes orgues des églises de Paris et du département
de la Seine* (Paris, 1927)
K. G. Fellerer: *Orgel und Orgelmusik: ihre Geschichte* (Augsburg
1929)
E. Rupp: *Die Entwicklungsgeschichte der Orgelbaukunst* (Ein-
siedeln, 1929)
C. Mahrenholz: *Die Orgelregister* (Kassel, 1930, 2/1942/*R*1968)
R. Whitworth: *The Electric Organ* (London, 1930, 3/1948)
H. G. Farmer: *The Organ of the Ancients from Eastern Sources*
(London, 1931)
P. Smets: *Orgeldispositionen: eine Handschrift aus dem XVIII.
Jahrhundert* (Kassel, 1931)
R. Weber: *Die Orgeln von Joseph Gabler und Johannes Nepomuk
Holzhay* (Weilheim-Teck, 1931)
G. Le Cerf and E.-R. Labande: *Instruments de musique du XVᵉ
siècle: les traités d'Henri-Arnaut de Zwolle et de divers anonymes*
(Paris, 1932/*R*1972)
N. Dufourcq: *Documents inédits relatifs à l'orgue français* (Paris,
1934, enlarged 2/1971)
H. Klotz: *Über die Orgelkunst der Gotik der Renaissance und des
Barock* (Kassel, 1934, rev. 2/1975)
N. Dufourcq: *Esquisse d'une histoire de l'orgue en France* (Paris,
1935)
W. Haacke: *Die Entwicklungsgeschichte des Orgelbaus im Lande
Mecklenburg-Schwerin* (Wolfenbüttel, 1935)
F. Blume: *Michael Praetorius und Esaias Compenius Orgeln Ver-
dingnis* (Wolfenbüttel, 1936)
H. Hickmann: *Das Portativ* (Kassel, 1936/*R*1972)
B. Wester: *Gotisk resning i svenska orglar* (Stockholm, 1936)
P. Smets: *Die Orgelregister: ihr Klang und Gebrauch* (Mainz, 1937)
C. Mahrenholz: *Die Berechnung der Orgelpfeifenmensuren* (Kas-
sel, 1938/*R*1968)
H. Meyer: *Karl Joseph Reipp, der Orgelbauer von Ottobeuren*
(Kassel, 1938)
I. Rücker: *Die deutsche Orgel am Oberrhein um 1500* (Freiburg,
1940)
J. Wörsching: *Die Orgelbauerfamilie Silbermann in Strassburg im
Elsass* (Mainz, 1941, 2/1960)

M. A. Vente: *Bouwstoffen tot de geschiedenis van het Nederlandse orgel in de 16e eeuw* (Amsterdam, 1942)

V. Němec: *Pražské varhany* [Prague organs] (Prague, 1944)

N. Frobenius and F. Ingerslev: *Some Measurements of the End-corrections and Acoustic Spectra of Cylindrical Open Flue Organ Pipes* (Copenhagen, 1947)

N. Friis: *Orgelbygning i Danmark* (Copenhagen, 1949, 2/1971)

W. David: *Joh. Seb. Bachs Orgeln* (Berlin, 1951)

W. L. Sumner: *The Organ: its Evolution, Principles of Construction and Use* (London, 1952, rev., enlarged 4/1973)

U. Dähnert: *Die Orgeln Gottfried Silbermanns in Mitteldeutschland* (Leipzig, 1953/R1971)

M. A. Vente and W. Kok: 'Organs in Spain & Portugal', *The Organ*, xxxiv (1954–5), 193; xxxv (1955–6), 136; xxxvi (1956–7), 155, 203; xxxvii (1957–8), 37

O. Eberstaller: *Orgeln und Orgelbauer in Oesterreich* (Graz, 1955)

P. G. Andersen: *Orgelbogen* (Copenhagen, 1956; Eng. trans., 1969)

R. Lunelli: *Der Orgelbau in Italien in seinen Meisterwerken* (Mainz, 1956)

T. Peine: *Der Orgelbau in Frankfurt-am-Main* (Frankfurt, 1956)

M. A. Vente: *Proeve van een repertorium van de archivalia betrekking hebbende op het Nederlandse orgel* (Brussels, 1956)

G. A. C. de Graaf: *Literatuur over het orgel* (Amsterdam, 1957)

R. Lunelli: *L'arte organaria del rinascimento in Roma* (Florence, 1958)

M. A. Vente: *Die brabanter Orgel* (Amsterdam, 1958, 2/1963)

F. Bösken: *Die Orgelbauerfamilie Stumm aus Rhaunen-Sulzbach und ihr Werk* (Mainz, 1960)

L. I. Royzman: *Organnaya kul'tura Estonii* [The organ culture of Estonia] (Moscow, 1960)

U. Dähnert: *Der Orgel- und Instrumentenbauer Zacharias Hildebrandt* (Leipzig, 1962)

J. Fellot: *L'orgue classique français* (Paris, 1962)

W. Kaufmann: *Die Orgeln des alten Herzogtums Oldenburg* (Oldenburg, 1962)

S. dalla Libera: *L'arte degli organi a Venezia* (Venice, 1962)

C. Clutton and A. Niland: *The British Organ* (London, 1963, 2/1982)

E. Erici: *Inventarium över bevarade äldre kyrkorglar i Sverige* (Stockholm, 1965)

F. Jakob: *Der Orgelbau im Kanton Zürich* (Zurich, 1965)

P. Meyer-Siat: *Les Callinet: facteurs d'orgues à Rouffach* (Paris, 1965)

J. Perrot: *L'orgue de ses origines hellénistiques à la fin du XIIIe siècle* (Paris, 1965; Eng. trans., abridged, 1971)

R. Reuter: *Orgeln in Westfalen* (Kassel, 1965)

J. Backus and T. C. Hundley: 'Wall Vibrations in Flue Organ Pipes and their Effect on Tone', *Journal of the Acoustical Society of America*, xxxix (1966), 936

K. Bormann: 'Die gotische Orgel von Bartenstein', *Ars organi*, xxix (1966), 989

——: *Die gotische Orgel zu Halberstadt* (Berlin, 1966)

P. Bunjes: *The Praetorius Organ* (St Louis, 1966)

S. dalla Libera: *L'arte degli organi nel Veneto: la diocesi di Céneda* (Venice, 1966)

P. Hardouin: 'De l'orgue de Pépin à l'orgue médiéval', *RdM*, lii (1966), 21–54

W. Lottermoser and J. Meyer: *Orgel-Akustik in Einzeldarstellungen* (Frankfurt am Main, 1966)

R. Quoika: *Der Orgelbau in Böhmen und Mähren* (Mainz, 1966)

P. Williams: *The European Organ 1450–1850* (London, 1966/R1978)

W. H. Armstrong: *Organs for America* (Philadelphia, 1967)

F. Bösken: *Quellen und Forschungen zur Orgelgeschichte des Mittelrheins*, i (Mainz, 1967)

H. H. Eggebrecht: *Die Orgelbewegung* (Stuttgart, 1967)

G. Frotscher: *Orgeln* (Karlsruhe, 1968)

W. Kaufmann: *Die Orgeln Ostfrieslands* (Zurich, 1968)

P. Schuberth: *Kaiserliche Liturgie* (Göttingen, 1968)

W. Müller: *Auf den Spuren von Gottfried Silbermann* (Kassel, 1968, 2/1982)

F. Douglass: *The Language of the Classical French Organ* (New Haven, 1969)

N. Dufourcq: *Le livre de l'orgue français 1589–1789*, ii: *Le buffet* (Paris, 1969)

P. Hardouin, P. Williams and H. Klotz: 'Pour une histoire du plein-jeu', *Renaissance de l'orgue* (1968), no.1, p.21; (1969), no.2, p.6; no.3, p.3; no.4, p.6; (1970), nos.5–6, p.31; no.7, p.9; no.8, p.17; *Connaissance de l'orgue* (1971), no.1, p.4; nos.2–3, p.6; no.4, p.8

E. N. Matthews: *Colonial Organs and Organbuilders* (Melbourne, 1969)

G. Radole: *L'arte organaria in Istria* (Bologna, 1969)

K. Schütz: *Der Wiener Orgelbau in der zweiten Hälfte des 18. Jahrhunderts* (Vienna, 1969)

F. Jakob: *Der Orgelbau im Kanton Zürich von seine Anfängen bis zur Mitte des 19. Jahrhunderts* (Berne and Stuttgart, 1969–71)

Organ Yearbook (1970–)

R. G. de Amezua y Noriega: *Perspectivas para la historia del órgano español* (Madrid, 1970)

J. Jongepier: *Frieslands orgelpracht* (Sneek, 1970)

J. R. Sharp: *Tonal Design of the American Organ: 1910–1969* (diss., Michigan State U., 1970)

J. Martinod: *Répertoire des travaux des facteurs d'orgues* (Paris, 1970–76)

K. J. Sachs: *Mensura fistularum: die Mensurierung der Orgelpfeifen im Mittelalter*, i (Stuttgart, 1970)

W. Walcker-Meyer: *Die römische Orgel von Aquincum* (Stuttgart, 1970; Eng. trans., 1972)

N. Meeùs: *La naissance de l'octave courte et ses différentes formes au 16e siècle* (diss., U. of Louvain, 1971)

F. Peeters and M. A. Vente: *De orgelkunst in de Nederlanden* (Antwerp, 1971; Eng. trans., 1971)

W. Adelung: *Orgeln der Gegenwart* (Kassel, 1972)

C. de Azevedo: *Baroque Organ-cases of Portugal* (Amsterdam, 1972)

J. Golos: *Polskie organy i muzyka organowa* (Warsaw, 1972)

H. Haselböck: *Barocker Orgelschatz in Niederösterreich* (Vienna, 1972)

E. Schäfer: *Laudatio organi: eine Orgelfahrt* (Leipzig, 1972)

J. H. Kluiver: *Historische orgels in Zeeland* (Sneek, 1972–6)

S. L. Carlsson: *Sveriges kyrkorglar* (Lund, 1973)

R. Fanselau: *Die Orgel im Werk Edward Elgars* (Göttingen and Kassel, 1973)

A. Forer: *Orgeln in Österreich* (Vienna and Munich, 1973)

R. Menger: *Das Regal* (Tutzing, 1973)

O. Mischiati and L. F. Tagliavini: 'Un anonimo trattato francese d'arte organaria del XVIII secolo', *L'organo*, xi (1973), 3–94

O. Schumann: *Orgelbau im Herzogtum Schleswig vor 1800* (Munich, 1973)

J. Uhlworm: *Chorgestühl und Orgelprospekt in England* (Berlin, 1973)

J. A. Villard: *L'oeuvre de François-Henri Clicquot, facteur d'orgues du roy* (Poitiers, 1973)

G. Fock: *Arp Schnitger und seine Schule* (Kassel, 1974)

P. Hardouin: 'Twelve Well-known Positive Organs', *Organ Yearbook*, v (1974), 20

J. McKinnon: 'The 10th-century Organ at Winchester', *Organ Yearbook*, v (1974), 4

L. A. E. Pereira: 'A organaria portuguesa no secolo XVIII', *Bracara Augusta*, xxviii (1974), 492

U. Pineschi: 'L'uso dei registri dell'organo pistoiese nei secoli XVIII e XIX', *L'organo*, xii (1974), 3

L. F. Tagliavini: 'Considerazioni sulle vicende storiche del "coriste"', *L'organo*, xii (1974), 119

J. Fesperman: *Two Essays on Organ Design* (Raleigh, North Carolina, 1975)

J. Goebel: *Theorie und Praxis des Orgelpfeiffenklanges* (Frankfurt am Main, 1975)

P. Hardouin: *Le grand orgue de Saint Gervais à Paris* (Paris, rev. 3/1975)

O. Ochse: *The History of the Organ in the United States* (Bloomington, Ind., and London, 1975)

G. Radole: *L'arte organaria a Trieste* (Bologna, 1975)

J. P. Rowntree and J. F. Brennan: *The Classical Organ in Britain* (Oxford, 1975–9)

W. Schlepphorst: *Der Orgelbau im westlichen Niedersachsen* (Kassel, 1975)

R. Skupnik: *Der hannoversche Orgelbauer Christian Vater, 1679–1756* (Kassel, 1976)

N. Thistlethwaite: *'E pur si muove*: English Organ-building 1820–1851', *Organ Yearbook*, vii (1976), 101

B. Billeter: 'Albert Schweitzer und sein Orgelbauer', *Acta organologica*, xi (1977), 173–225

P. R. W. Blewitt and H. C. Thompson: *The Duddyngton Manuscripts at All Hallows-by-the-Tower* (London, 1977)

A. J. Gierveld: *Het nederlandse huisorgel in de 17de en 18de eeuw* (Utrecht, 1977)

L'orgue français (Paris, 1977) [*ReM* special no.]

J. Ogasapian: *Organ Building in New York City: 1700–1900* (Braintree, Mass., 1977)

U. Pape: *Frühromantischer Orgelbau in Niedersachsen* (Berlin, 1977)

L. Souberbielle, ed.: *Le plein-jeu de l'orgue français à l'époque classique (1660–1740)*, i (Montoire-sur-Loire, 1977)

K. Szigeti: 'Az orgonaépités története Magyarországon Budavár elestéig, 1541–ig' [The history of organ building in Hungary up to 1541], *Magyar zenetörténeti tanulmányok Zoltán Kodály*, ed. F. Bónis (Budapest, 1977), 263

L. F. Tagliavini: 'L'organo in Giappone', *L'organo*, xv (1977), 127

W. Salmen, ed.: *Orgel und Orgelspiel im 16. Jahrhundert* (Innsbruck, 1977)

H. Winter and C. Edskes: *Orgelstudien*, ii: *Cappel* (Hamburg, 1977); i: *Stade* (Hamburg, 1979)

Langs nederlandse orgels (Baarn, 1977–9)

H. Grugger: *Die bernischen Orgeln* (Berne, 1978)

J. Guillou: *L'orgue, souvenir et avenir* (Paris, 1978)

U. Pape: *The Tracker Organ Revival in America* (Berlin, 1978)
J. Rowntree: 'Bernard Smith (c1629–1708) Organist and Organ-builder, his Origins', *JBIOS*, ii (1978), 10
N. Thistlethwaite: 'Organo pneumatico', *JBIOS*, ii (1978), 31–62
P. P. Donati: 'Regesto documentario', in *Arte nell'Aretino* (Florence, 1979) [index of terms used in contracts etc]
J. A. Ferguson: *Walter Holtkamp, American Organ Builder* (Kent, Ohio, 1979)
G. Huybens, ed.: *Complete Theoretical Works of A. Cavaillé-Coll* (Buren, 1979) [facs.]
R. Lüttman: *Das Orgelregister und sein instrumentales Vorbild in Frankreich und Spanien vor 1800* (Kassel, 1979)
B. Owen: *The Organ in New England* (Raleigh, North Carolina, 1979)
L. Roizman: *Organ* (Moscow, 1979)
F. Sabatier: 'La palette sonore de Cavaillé-Coll', *Jeunesses et orgue*, x (1979) [special no.]
P. Salies and others, eds.: *L'orgue de l'Insigne Basilique Saint-Sernin Toulouse* (Toulouse, 1979)
U. Dähnert: *Historische Orgeln in Sachsen* (Leipzig, 1980)
F. Douglass: *Cavaillé-Coll and the Musicians* (Raleigh, North Carolina, 1980)
J. Fesperman: *Organs in Mexico* (Raleigh, North Carolina, 1980)
P. Hardouin: 'Les grandes orgues de la Basilique de Saint Denis en France', *Connaissance de l'orgue* (1979–80) [special no.]
M. Lindley: 'Pythagorean Intonation and the Rise of the Triad', *RMARC*, xvi (1980), 4–61
W. Kluge: 'Die statische Festigkeit von Orgelpfeifen', *Acta organologica*, xiv (1980), 251
O. Mischiati: *L'organo di Santa Maria di Campagna a Piacenza* (Piacenza, 1980)
B. Owen: 'The Evidence for Trompes in the 16th-century English Organ', *Visitatio organorum*, ed. A. Dunning (Utrecht, 1980), 489ff
K.-J. Sachs: *Mensura fistularum*, ii (Murrhardt, 1980)
B. van Wye: 'Ritual Use of the Organ in France', *JAMS*, xxxiii (1980), 287–325
P. Williams: *A New History of the Organ: from the Greeks to the Present Day* (London, 1980)
——: 'How did the Organ become a Church Instrument?', *Visitatio organorum*, ed. A. Dunning (Utrecht, 1980), 603ff
S. Bicknell: 'English Organ-building 1642–1685', *JBIOS*, v (1981), 5
F. Brouwer: *Orgelbewegung und Orgelgegenbewegung* (Utrecht, 1981)
J. Ferrard: *Orgues du Brabant Wallon* (Brussels, 1981)
W. Hüttel: 'Zwei Meisterwerke der sächsisch-thüringischen Orgelbaukunst im 18. Jahrhundert', *Acta organologica*, xv (1981), 76
P. Hardouin: 'Encore Winchester', *Connaissance de l'orgue*, xxxix–xl (1981), 20
P. H. Kriek: *Organum novum redivivum* (Buren, 1981) [rev. edn of P. H. Kriek and H. S. J. Zandt: *Organum novum* (Sneek, 1964)]
H. Wohnfurter: *Die Orgelbauerfamilie Bader 1600–1742* (Kassel, 1981)
G. A. C. de Graaf: 'The Gothic Organ in the Chapel of St Bartholomew in Salamanca', *ISO Information*, xxii (1982), 9

PETER WILLIAMS (with BARBARA OWEN, §§II, V, VI and VII)

Organetto (It.) (1) A term for a small organ, notably the 14th- and 15th-century instrument generally known as PORTATIVE.

(2) A term occasionally applied to a street organ or a street piano. An *organetto a manovella* (It.) is a BARREL ORGAN.

(3) Small diatonic accordion of Italy. Since the 19th century it has largely replaced the bagpipe in Italy and is found in a wide area from Romagna to southern Italy and Sardinia. The *organetto* repertory is largely that of the bagpipe; it is often paired with the tambourine, castanets or triangle.

Organina. A name applied to various types of automatic REED ORGAN. In the late 19th century it was adopted as a trade name for related instruments by the Massachusetts Organ Co. and the Automatic Organ Co. of Boston. The French maker Jérôme Thibouville, best known for his brass and woodwind instruments, used the name for a small automatic reed organ he made in 1905.

Organino (It.) A term for a small organ, notably the 14th- and 15th-century instrument generally known as PORTATIVE.

Organisirte Trompete (Ger.) A type of KEYED TRUMPET developed in the 1790s by Anton Weidinger.

Organistrum. *See* HURDY-GURDY.

Organized hurdy-gurdy. *See* LIRA ORGANIZZATA.

Organo. A five-octave, keyless ELECTRONIC ORGAN developed by James A. Koehl and manufactured by the F. C. Lowrey Co. of Chicago in 1949; it was the first of a series of electronic organs made by the company (*see* LOWREY ORGAN). A long flat panel, placed along the back of the piano keyboard, contains mechanisms that are operated when the piano is played; a small control panel is clamped to the front of the keyboard. The sound is generated by 12 oscillators using frequency division. Timbre, vibrato and register controls can be applied to the complete keyboard or to either of the two sections (the two lower and three upper octaves) into which it can be split. The Organo was so successful that for a while it was incorporated into pianos sold by other companies (Janssen, Kimball, Story & Clark, and others).

BIBLIOGRAPHY
'Converts Piano to Organ', *Electronics*, xxii/8 (1949), 116
R. H. Dorf: 'The Lowrey Organo', *Electronic Musical Instruments* (New York, 2/1958), 108

HUGH DAVIES

Organochordium [organochordon]. A type of CLAVIORGAN built in 1782–9 by the Danish organ builder Kirschnigk and developed by Georg Joseph Vogler, with Rackwitz of Stockholm; *see also* REED ORGAN, §1.

Organology (Ger. *Instrumentenkunde*). The descriptive and analytical study of musical instruments. The term was introduced by Bessaraboff to distinguish the 'scientific and engineering aspects' of instruments from the broader study of music. An essential part of organology is the analytical classification of instruments from different epochs and cultures (*see* CLASSIFICATION); their historical development and musical uses are also widely considered to fall under the heading of organology, though not necessarily the development of genres associated with them nor the details of their repertory. An organologist might also describe certain aspects of playing technique that particularly affect musical style. Organology has become prominent in ethnomusicological research, as an instrument from an exotic culture can be described in some detail even before other aspects of its music are understood; but a later trend is to integrate the study of instruments 'with descriptions of musical culture and musical style' (see Nettl, 1964). The term 'organology' has occasionally been applied to the study of pipe organs, but its standard meaning is derived from the Greek *organon* ('tool' or 'instrument') and from Praetorius's title *De organographia* (1618, the second volume of his treatise *Syntagma musicum*).

BIBLIOGRAPHY
N. Bessaraboff: *Ancient European Musical Instruments* (Cambridge, Mass., 1941), p.xxvi
B. Nettl: *Theory and Method in Ethnomusicology* (New York, 1964), 215
W. M. Oler: 'Definition of Organology', *GSJ*, xxiii (1970), 170
Archiv für Musikorganologie (1976–)

Organophone. A harmonium invented by A. F. Debain of Paris, in which the reeds or vibrators were raised within instead of being beneath the channels.

Organo-piano. A combination of a piano and an *orgue expressif* with two manuals, built by Achille Müller and shown at the Paris Exposition of 1834, where it was awarded the bronze medal.

Organo pleno [pieno] (It.: 'full organ'). A term for an organ REGISTRATION using the major choruses of the instrument. It has rarely, if ever, denoted that the composer has required the organist to draw every stop; since *c*1850 most composers other than French have left it to the organist's discretion and the organ-bellows' capacity.

Before that, both the term itself and the registration it indicated varied according to period and area. The 15th-century BLOCKWERK was itself the *plenum* of larger organs, from Spain to the Baltic, from Italy to the North Sea; if it were referred to in a document such as a contract, it would be called 'Principal'. When or where this Diapason chorus was separated into several single or multiple ranks, a term such as *grand jeu* would indicate the total or full organ (St Michel, Bordeaux, 1510), perhaps without flutes, like the 'compimento de l'organo' at S Martino, Bologna (1556). (*See* GRAND JEU.)

Plenum and the German terms *volles Werk* and *zum gantzen Werck* are chiefly 17th-century terms, referring to the Diapason chorus codified in many 16th-century sources; the last phrase, however, often means that a stop runs 'through the whole compass', not that it joins 'the total chorus'. In Italy *ripieno* was based on single ranks excluding Flutes (Antegnati, 1608), but later examples are known to have included a Tierce rank (Trent Cathedral, 1687), as sometimes happened with the PLEIN JEU in France (*c*1620). In Spain, *plé* (16th century) indicated the chorus in general, *lleno* (17th century) the main Mixture.

From *das Werck* at Hagenau in 1491, which was the total chorus Mixture excluding Diapason and Zimbel, to Mattheson's treatises of 1721, the German organ progressed towards heavier and thicker *plena*, including all stops except reeds, and used not so much for particular colour, like the French *grands* and *pleins jeux*, as for massive effects in preludes, toccatas, etc. Some writers, like Praetorius and Werckmeister, insisted that 'families' of stops should not be mixed. It is unlikely that J. S. Bach had a specific combination in mind when he asked for *organum plenum*, whether in 1715 or 1745; however, a contemporary organ builder, Gottfried Silbermann, directed organists to use the manual coupler but no manual reeds or Tierces in the *plenum* (Fraureuth, 1739).

See also FULL ORGAN and GRAND CHOEUR.   PETER WILLIAMS

Organo tedesco (It.). BARREL ORGAN.

Organ point. An ambiguous term in English, owing its existence to the fact that it is the literal equivalent of the Latin *punctus organi* or *organicus punctus*, the German *Orgelpunkt*, and the French *point d'orgue*. Although listed in all musical dictionaries, the English term is usually avoided in practical situations in favour of the more precise 'pedal' or PEDAL POINT and PAUSE or FERMATA. *Organicus punctus* is found as early as Franco of

Cologne (*Ars cantus mensurabilis*, *c*1260), who used it for the penultimate note of a tenor at which the regular measure is suspended. Tinctoris (*Terminorum musicae diffinitorium*, *c*1472–3) applied it to the sign of the corona, which by that time was used in various situations where it was necessary for one part to pay attention to the other parts instead of to the beat: on final notes which must be prolonged and released together, in canons, where one part might have to prolong a final note until the other parts caught up, and in passages of block chords where each note was to be prolonged for effect (e.g. Dufay's *Supremum est mortalibus*).

In French, *point d'orgue* was applied in the 17th century to both the corona and the harmonic pedal. The latter meaning, though rare, is found in Furetière's *Dictionnaire universel*, which was published in 1690 (though the reference is to the usage of the mid-17th century): 'Le point d'orgue est proprement une tenuë en Musique, et est en usage en plusieurs parties quand on veut que l'une continuë long-tems sur un même ton, tandis que les autres font differents accords'.

In the 18th century, the term began to take on the additional meaning of the ornamental cadenza often demanded by the *point d'orgue*, whereas the meaning of harmonic pedal gradually dropped way. Cohen (*JAMS*, xxiv, 1971, p.76) cited Etienne Loulié's use of the curious term *ostinatione* for pedal point in a manuscript composition treatise (before 1718). In 1854, the Escudier brothers (*Dictionnaire de musique théorique et historique*) defined *point d'orgue* simply as 'passage brillant que fait la partie principale dans un solo', while 19th-century treatises on fugue (Cherubini, Fétis) introduced the term *pédale*, which they had doubtless imported from Italy, where it is found with its modern meaning as early as 1802 (Sabbatini). 20th-century French dictionaries distinguish sharply between *point d'orgue* and *pédale*; the former never means the latter.

Orgelpunkt seems to have entered German terminology by way of French usage rather than of Latin. Early German usage prefers 'Pausa generalis' or 'Corona' for the fermata, and it is under 'Corona' that Walther (*Musicalisches Lexicon*, 1732) gave his main definition – adding, however, that 'die Franzosen nennen es *point d'orgue*'. The other meaning of the French term crops up in Heinichen's explanation of a prolonged *tasto solo* note in figured bass (*Der General-Bass*, 1728), where he wrote that the French called it *point d'orgue* because one could hold a note with the pedals and play all sorts of 'variations and foreign syncopations' with both hands. By the mid-18th century, the corona had come to be called *Fermate* (C. P. E. Bach and Quantz), and Marpurg was using *point d'orgue* for the pedal near the end of a fugue. By the end of the century *point d'orgue* had been taken over as *Orgelpunkt*, in which form it was defined by Sulzer (*Allgemeine Theorie*, 1771–4) and Koch (*Musikalisches Lexikon*, 1802) as a harmonic pedal, with no mention of the sign of the corona. Unfortunately, however, Koch gave *point d'orgue* as the French equivalent for *Orgelpunkt* – just when the French themselves had managed to differentiate it clearly from *pédale*. Thus began the confusion, which was compounded by English writers seizing upon the cognate without specifying which meaning they attached to it.

Modern French and German usage is clear: French *point d'orgue* means German *Fermate*; German *Orgelpunkt* means French *pédale*. English usage avoids 'organ point'; 'pause', 'fermata' and 'pedal' are preferred.
                                                DAVID FULLER

Organ stop. Just as the term 'stop' is of uncertain origin and meaning, so the many stop names have a complex history and usage. Thus, for example, Spitzflöte may be said to be 'a stop consisting of open metal pipes made of an alloy with high or fairly high tin content and shaped conically, so that the pipe is tapered from the mouth upwards, giving a tone rather flute-like in character but richer in formants, and serving as a solo or chorus colour halfway between the flute and the diapason ranks'. But all stop names leave many factors unclear, and 'Spitzflöte' cannot be thought of as indicating more than an approximate sound or pipe construction in organs of certain kinds, since (a) the name signifies different sounds (timbre, volume) in different organs, from one builder, area or period to another, such details as mouth size, wind pressure, scaling and metal alloy being varied; (b) the name would arise at first only in a large organ of c1580 when a builder wished to distinguish in his contract between one open metal stop and another; (c) the name would be used only in northern Europe, but the pipe form elsewhere; (d) although some builders elsewhere had an equivalent in their own language for the name (Flauto a cuspido, Flûte à fuseau, etc), few used it, preferring either to leave such ranks without names that indicated pipe construction or to give them a more fanciful name indicating tone-colour – especially in the 19th century; (e) conical pipes might be used for a rank (or part of a rank) already given another name indicating some other factor in its nature or function (e.g. 'Nasard'); (f) occasionally, especially during the 19th century, a builder might use the name for a rank imitating the tone-quality it is associated with though constructed differently, perhaps of wooden pipes or open cylindrical metal pipes. *See also* REGISTRATION, §I.

The evolution of stop names naturally reflects the evolution of the organ as a complex instrument. During the 15th century in northern France, the Netherlands and the Rhineland, such terms as 'Principal' were used to indicate the basic sound of the organ, the *pleno* chorus; and the case pipes (Prestant, Montre, Doif, etc) were increasingly specified in sources, they being the first ranks to be separated off from the chorus in a big church organ. In most cases large secular organs, which had a longer tradition for separate and sometimes highly colourful ranks, have no associated verbal descriptions that specify names. By 1500, builders were making many kinds of ranks and almost without exception giving them the names of instruments or sounds which the ranks were thought to imitate (Trumpet, Horn, Nine-holed Flute), sometimes picturesquely so (Old Women's Voice, Nightingale), even when we now scarcely recognize them as orchestral instruments (Gemshorn, Swiss flute, etc). It is quite misleading to assume that the 19th-century liking for orchestral effects was in itself a sign of decadence in organ building. The exceptions to these instrumental names were important, since they usually indicated the construction of pipes concerned and were thus intrinsic to the organ as an independent instrument (Gedackt, Hohlflöte, Spitzflöte, etc). The origin of some stop names is particularly difficult to understand, including those that appear to be words taken from other contexts – musical (Diapason, Regal), architectural (Trompes), theoretical (Sesquialtera) or even onomatopoeic (Bourdon). In some cases, notably Trompes and Bourdons, it is not clear whether the use of the term in the organ context precedes any other. By the end of the 16th century, names in all countries and languages had become regular and reliable as indications of a stop's purpose, if not always of its tone; whether such names remained in the builder's contracts or were actually written on stop labels at the organ is less clear. Labels were hardly necessary, for instance, on Italian and English organs, and remained uncommon on chamber organs until the late 18th century.

The great organ theorists and those giving lists of specifications, such as Praetorius, Mattheson, Bédos de Celles and Hopkins (for bibliographical details *see* ORGAN), gave a somewhat misleading impression of the uniformity and reliability of stop names. Readers of Praetorius, for instance, are led to believe not only that the names of the many Regal stops were neatly codified but also that such stops were more important – i.e. common over a wider area and for a longer time – than was indeed the case. Certainly written reports must always have increased the interest of organists and builders in new or foreign stops, particularly perhaps in those cases where writers expressed doubt as to the success of a certain builder in imitating such sounds as the human voice, sea waves, orchestral horn and so on. Remarkably few stops in name, sound or construction originated during the 18th century, and many of those so popular in the 19th (overblowing stops, string-scale flues) originated in the early 17th. The cheap workmanship of so many 19th-century organs meant an abuse of many stop names, but the mid-20th-century revival has led to a return to traditional practices.

The definitions or descriptions that follow have been compiled with certain points in mind: (a) transliterations of stop names (e.g. Kwinta for Quinte) are not given, nor nordic variants of German names (e.g. Spetsfloït for Spitzflöte) unless they indicate a different kind of stop (e.g. Baarpijp and Bärpfeife); (b) a short phrase indicates the family of stops which a name indicates, flue or reed, open, closed or semi-closed, metal or wood; two stops of the same name can have a different combination of such factors, as they can also serve quite different purposes from organ to organ (chorus/solo; Principal/Flute/mutation); (c) examples are taken from typical instruments, and no attempt has been made to list every maker's fanciful name or wayward invention; (d) examples may refer to a stop whose pipes are constructed in the manner normally associated with the name even when the builder's own term is unknown; (e) only few names are included of those families of stops invented at different periods for purposes of little relevance to idiomatic organ music, particularly Renaissance and Baroque toy stops (birds, tinkling bells, etc), late 18th-century free reeds of the harmonium type, late 19th-century high-pressure flue or valvular reed stops; (f) stop types with names in several languages (e.g. Querflöte, Flauto traverso) are entered under the most commonly used name unless a difference in construction is implied (e.g. Nachthorn, Cor de nuit). For further details see Williams (1966).

Cross-references within this article are indicated in the form 'See under *Cornett*'; cross-references to other articles are in the usual form '*See* CORNETT'.

Aeolina. (1) A narrow metal flue stop of soft tone first found in Germany c1820.

(2) A free reed of gentle tone, invented c1815 (?by Eschenbach) and popular in central Germany (Schulze etc).

(3) With free reeds with derived names: 'Claveoline' 8' or 16', sometimes with wooden resonators (by Beyer, c1820), 'Aeolodicon' 16' (Walcker, c1840).

Baarpijp (Dutch). (1) Barem was a soft Gedackt stop during Praetorius's period (c1620).

(2) 'Baarpyp' at Haarlem (1735–8) and other Dutch

organs of that period was a soft stop of tapered pipes. In earlier sources (from the late 16th century), often the same as Quintadena. The name may come from *baar* (Middle Dutch: 'bright') or *barem* ('to scream'), or from the German *Baar* ('pole' or 'rod'). But see under *Bärpfeife*.

Bajete, Bajón (Sp.). Late 17th-century Spanish reeds: a 4′ Bajete was gentle in tone, often a bass-half stop only, sometimes *en chamade*; Bajón was an 8′ Bassoon stop (the 4′ version called 'Bajoncillo'), stronger in tone, usually with flaring metal resonators. 'Bajoncillo y Clarín' was a single 4′ rank in two halves.

Bärpfeife (?Ger., ?Dutch). A reed stop of the mid-16th century (name first used by Niehoff ?*c*1540), the predecessor of Regal stops with fanciful resonators, strong in tone. 'Schreyer' (Praetorius, 2/1619) or 'Kryther' (St Eusebius, Arnhem, 1506) seem to be alternative names. The term has nothing to do with growling bears, however coarse the tone.

Bassflute. A 19th-century 8′ pedal stop, usually of stopped wood (like the 16′ Bourdon), sometimes open; 'Flötenbass' is an older German equivalent, of various constructions.

Basson (Fr). See under *Fagotto*.

Bassoon. (1) An English reed stop of quiet tone, once found frequently from *c*1680 onwards (R. Harris), particularly on the CHAIR ORGAN; most examples probably had small-scaled flaring resonators.
(2) An English 19th-century reed stop, usually called Fagotto, of the same construction but at 16′ pitch on the Swell organ.
(3) A French 18th- and 19th-century reed stop, serving as the bass half to a treble Hautbois.
(4) On 19th-century English and American organs, the separately drawing bass octave of an Oboe or Hautboy.

Bauernflöte (Ger.: 'peasant's fife'). A penetrating 2′ or 1′ flue stop, open wide scale, sometimes stopped or as a Chimney Flute, found especially in (*a*) the Brabant organ of *c*1550, (*b*) the Fritzsche–Compenius organ of *c*1620 and (*c*) organs of Saxony *c*1690; popular as a 1′ solo pedal stop for cantus firmus music.

Bazuin, Buzain (Dutch). See under *Posaune*.

Bell-diapason (Fr. *flûte à pavillon*). French stop from the 1840s, containing cylindrical pipes with a flaring cone soldered at the top; a loud Flute.

Bell Gamba. A tapered flue stop of 16′ or 8′ pitch with a short, conical section at the top of the pipes, found on 19th-century continental and American organs.

Bifara, Biffaro. (1) A double Flute whose pipes have two mouths at different heights, producing a soft tremulant sound and popular in south Germany and Austria from *c*1660.
(2) In Walcker's organs (*c*1830) a double rank of 8′ stopped and 4′ open, producing a soft, string-like tone.

Blockflöte (Ger.). A wide conical metal flue stop imitating the recorder; it can be open, closed or overblowing (*c*1620), sometimes made of oak (late 17th-century Friesland and England), usually at 4′ pitch.

Blockwerk (Ger; Dutch *blokwerk*). Not strictly a stop name, it denotes the undivided chest of the medieval organ based on a 'double Principal' without other 'stops' separated off. *See* BLOCKWERK.

Bocktremulant (Ger.). See under *Tremulant*.

Bombardon (Fr. *bombarde*; Ger. *Bomhard*, *Pommer*). (1) In France, the basic manual or pedal 16′ reed, from at least 1587 (Arras), of great importance to the French classical organ, with strong tone, metal or wood resonators and sometimes its own keyboard (Notre Dame, Paris, 1733).
(2) 'Pombarda', according to Praetorius, was a 16′ or 8′ reed of strong tone and two-thirds length resonators.
(3) 'Bombarda' signified long pedal reeds on the enlarged Italian organ of *c*1820 (Serassi).
(4) 'Bombardon' was the name given to a rather mild-toned English Bombarde of *c*1850.

Bourdon (Fr.). (1) The earliest 'Barduni' were low-compass bass pipes played not by manual keys but 'latched' on (Arnaut de Zwolle, *c*1450) (see under *Trompes*).
(2) Occasionally, 'Perduyn' or 'Pardoenen' indicated case-front pipes (*c*1550), more often inside pipes an octave below the case pipes.
(3) The most important use of the term was for the stopped pipes an octave below the main Diapason rank in the French organ. The scaling was narrow – stopped wood for lower octaves, stopped or Rohrflöte metal for the upper – and the musical application larger than for any other stop.
(4) A medium- to large-scale 16′ pedal stop of stopped wood, often found in English and American organs from *c*1820 onwards.

Campanello (It.). (1) See under *Carillon*.
(2) A high repeating wide-scaled mutation, giving a bell-like effect on organs that needed it (England, Germany, *c*1850).

Carillon. Various stops achieving bell-like effects. (1) Real bells of 4′ or 2′ pitch, played by hands or feet, on many organs from Weingarten (1737–50) onwards; there were trackers to small striking hammers.
(2) A common Italian stop of the same type, popular in the early 19th century.
(3) An important Dutch Tierce Mixture found *c*1750–1850 as a kind of Echo Cornet.

Celeste. See under *Unda maris*, *Voix céleste*.

Celestina. A soft 4′ open wood Flute, sometimes found in English organs *c*1860.

Cembalo (It., Cz.). See under *Zimbel*.

Chalumeau (Fr.). (1) The same as Schalmei in some German sources of the 18th century.
(2) A small-scaled flaring reed stop in central Germany *c*1750, sometimes cylindrical.

Cheio (Port.). A chorus Mixture of the same type as Compuestas de Lleno (Sp.).

Chimney Flute. See under *Rohrflöte*.

Chirimía (Sp.). A kind of 4′ or 2′ Schalmei, imitating the shawm in 17th- and 18th-century organs, sometimes *en chamade*.

Choralbass, Choralflöte (Ger.). An open metal or wood 4′ Flute found on the pedals of 17th- and 18th-century German organs for playing cantus firmus melodies; in some cases an open manual 8′ Flute.

Cimbala (Sp.). See under *Zimbel*.

Clairon (Fr.). See under *Clarion*.

Clarabella. The early 19th-century English and American name for an open wood Flute of pretty tone (used by Bishop, *c*1825), often in the treble only, originally replacing an 18th-century mounted Cornet and useful for solos.

Claribel flute. A mid-19th-century name for a fairly strong Great organ 4′ Flute (Willis, *c*1860), sometimes harmonic for the top octave.

Clarin (Sp.). Spanish Trumpets of various kinds, originating mostly in the later 17th century. (1) An 8′ Clarin was a standard Trumpet vertical inside the organ or horizontal at the case front. 'Real' Trumpets (Clarines, Trompetas) were usually vertical (not horizontal), the name indicating 'real' in the sense of 'full-length resonators'; but by *c*1750 'trompeta real' often meant 'royal trumpet'.

(2) 'Clarin de eco' was a smaller-scaled Trumpet in an Echo or Swell box.

(3) 'Clarín fuerte [suave]': a strong [soft] Trumpet, both with flaring tin resonators.

(4) Clarines usually indicates a 2′ reed of soft Trumpet tone, sometimes a bass-half stop only.

(5) 'Clarín de batalla', 'Clarín de compaña': military-like Trumpet stops *en chamade*.

Clarinet. A reed stop of many different types and purposes. (1) Clarinette was a Spanish Regal, sometimes *en chamade* ('little Clarín'), found in the heyday of Iberian organs (*c*1750).

(2) Clarinetto: an Italian Regal (18th century); or a German pedal Clarin 2′ stop (*c*1830) or 4′ (*c*1775).

(3) Clarinetto was occasionally a clarinet-imitating reed stop in *c*1790 (south Germany). As 'Clarinet', 'Clarionet' or 'Cremona' it is frequently found in English and American Choir organs from the early 19th century onwards; its cylindrical resonators show its ancestry in the Cromorne [Krummhorn].

Clarino (It.). See under *Clarion*.

Clarion (Ger., Fr. *clairon*; It. *clarino*). Reed stops. (1) A 4′ Clairon is the main French chorus Trumpet, supplementary to the Trompette 8′, common on the main manual from at least *c*1580, and as such found elsewhere both in frenchified organs (England, Alsace) and those quite independent (central Germany).

(2) Clarino: a rare Italian Trumpet, of metal or wood; Trombetta and Clarone were other Italian terms used here and there from *c*1600.

Claron (Sp.). A Nasardos or Tierce Mixture.

Compensationsmixtur. See under *Mixture*.

Compuestas (Sp.). A mixture or Lleno, like the Fourniture but more varied in content.

Contra (Lat.) Used with the meaning 'an octave below'; found especially in the latinized stop lists of *c*1800. (1) Contrebasses were 19th-century French strong-toned pedal stops imitating the double bass (Cavaillé-Coll).

(2) Contrabass more generally indicates a (pedal) stop an octave below the open Principal.

(3) Contras are Spanish pedal ranks of open or stopped pipes, often without their own stop-knob; thus Contras en Bombardas denotes the 16′ pedal Bombarde.

Coppel, Koppel (Ger.; Lat. *copula*). (1) A coupler.

(2) A stopped 16′, 8′ or 4′ rank in Habsburg Europe, sometimes called 'Koppelflöte'. In many organs, the equivalent of the Gedackt, and made of metal or wood.

(3) Coppel elsewhere sometimes indicates a Gemshorn, Spillflöte or even Principal (*c*1540), probably so called because it was coupled to or drawn with Principals, Flutes or reeds.

Cor anglais (Fr.; It. *corno inglese*). 19th-century reeds with narrow resonators shaped like the orchestral instrument (*c*1850); in Italy the stop is older (used by Serassi, *c*1820) and its tone is coarser, with wide cylindrical resonators.

Cor de nuit (Fr.). An open or stopped flue rank of wide scale, at 8′, 4′ or 2′, found in French organs *c*1850 and those in England and the USA which they influenced.

Cornamusa (It.). A Regal toy stop once common (*c*1600) and producing the drone sound of two held reed pipes, thus leaving the hands free to play 'zampogna' or 'musette' music.

Cornet (Fr.; It. *cornetto, corneta*; Sp. *corneta*). Various stops imitating the CORNETT. (1) A very important French solo Mixture stop, one to three examples of which were found on every classical organ from 1650 to 1850; treble only, from *c*′, with five wide-scaled ranks (1.8.12.15.17) often placed on their own small chests ('mounted Cornet') from *c*1640. Examples during the second half of the 16th century were often given a distinguishing name, such as 'Cornetz à boucquin', 'Nachthorn', 'Cornet d'Allemagne', or stop 'imitating the zink'. The term is not to be confused with the organ stop, Cornett, though sources are often unclear on this point.

(2) Cornetto and Corneta were Italian Flute mutation ranks, from *c*1680 – primo might be the Tierce, secondo the Nasard, terzo the Quarte de nasard, etc.

(3) Spanish Cornet stops ('Corneta clara', 'reale', 'tolosana', i.e. 'from Toulouse') were also common but not so stereotyped in pipe content.

(4) Cornets often had fewer ranks in the 19th century (two-rank Cornettin in Sweden), or were built up of Geigen pipes (France) and Dulciana pipes ('Dulciana Cornet' in England).

Cornett, Kornett (Ger.). A reed stop imitating the Zink or CORNETT, usually in the pedals, of 4′ or 2′ pitch, and found throughout central and northern Germany from 1600 to 1800. Praetorius noted that the flaring resonators are only just longer than those of the 'Trichterregal'. 'Singende Kornette' were so called partly because of the smooth tone, partly because such stops were used for melodic cantus firmus lines.

Corno (It.). A name found fairly frequently for various stops. (1) Italian Cornetto, a reed stop in old sources.

(2) Corno dolce is either a soft reed stop (built by Serassi, *c*1810) probably developed from Venetian Regals, or a wide Flute stop in Italy (*c*1750–1900), sometimes inverted conical.

(3) Corno di bassetto, like the Corno inglese, is an imitative reed stop of the 19th century, with cylindrical resonators (used by Willis).

Cornopean. An English reed stop (Hill, Willis) imitating the *cornet à pistons*, of rather thin tone, 8′ pitch and chiefly of use on the mid-19th-century Swell organ.

Cromorne (Fr.; Ger. *Krummhorn*). Reed stops imitating the crumhorn; later versions of the name (Cormorne, Cremona) are corrupt. (1) German Krummhorn stops were of varied construction (Praetorius, 2/1619) – with metal or wood resonators, open or stopped, short or half-length, cylindrical, double-cone-shaped, etc.

(2) French Cromornes appeared somewhat later, i.e. late in the 16th century, becoming the standard *Positiv* reed in the classical organ, usually of narrow, cylindrical, half-length, metal resonators. The tone was modified as builders in *c*1800 began to make it resemble the clarinet.

(3) English Cremona stops date from c1680 and presumably copied French models, keeping the same design until they began to disappear in c1900.

Cymbale (Fr.). See under *Zimbel*.

Decem, Decima (It.: 'tenth'). A mutation rank sounding the 10th or 17th; largely a theorist's term (Samber, 1704–7; Adlung, 1768).

Diapason (?Gk.). (1) Octave stops, sounding an octave above the case pipes, according to theorists (Werckmeister, 1705; Hess, 1774); found in organs with grecized stop names c1790.

(2) In England, the term may have denoted Trompes in c1500, but by 1613 it had its present meaning of Open Diapason (main Principal rank, usually 8') and Stopped Diapason (Gedackt). As a term, 'Diapason' may be derived from Dutch Doif (c1450) and only later taking on a quasi-Greek form that is scarcely relevant; as a registration direction, 'Diapasons' is an indication to use the Stopped Diapason, whose mild but harmonically rich tone has a strong emphasis on the quint, to colour the Open Diapason. English builders seem to have prided themselves on their Diapason tone, Renatus Harris's examples (c1690) being already richer than those of his French models; as such, it helped to hinder the development of the English organ, its very name giving the stop a mystique absent from more traditional terms like Montre and Principal.

Diaphone. One of Hope-Jones's valvular reeds, useful in cinemas. *See* ORGAN, §III, 4 and fig.20.

Diez (Sp.: 'ten'). Hence 'Diez y novena' is the 19th or Larigot $1\frac{1}{3}'$ (sometimes chorus Quint).

Doef, Doif, Doff, Doof (Dutch). Terms denoting the Principal stop in those early sources that used the word 'Prinzipal' to mean 'plenum' or main chorus, from c1450; e.g. 'le prestant ou doeuf' at Namur, 1598. Spellings are sometimes confusing, e.g. Praetorius's 'Doiflöte' is a Doppelflöte, not a Doef.

Dolcan (Ger.). See under *Tolkaan*.

Dolce (It.; Fr. *douce*). The verbal coincidence of Dolce, Dolcan, Dulciana and Dulzian has led to much confusion; probably all terms derive from Dulcis, a stop with 'sweet' tone. Dolce or Flauto dolce was common for any soft stop from c1600 to 1800, whether wood or metal, narrow cylindrical or conical. Adlung gave other spellings and versions: Dulzfloit, Dolzflöte, Dulceflöt, Süssflöte.

Doppelflöte (Ger.). See under *Bifara*. From c1600 to c1900 makers experimented with pipes with two mouths, either for soft undulating effects or for greater volume (c1830). Late 19th-century German and American examples are of stopped wooden pipes with a powerful fundamental tone; the stoppers are occasionally bored.

Double. A prefix indicating pitch an octave lower than usual (Double Trumpet, Double Diapason).

Doublette (Fr.). The 2' Principal rank of the French classical organ. The name was often used in the larger organs of the more cosmopolitan English builders of c1860, under the influence of Cavaillé-Coll's large 2' ranks.

Douce (Fr.) See under *Dolce*.

Dulcian, Dulciana. Gentle flue stops of various form, found in the non-Latin countries of Europe from at least c1640, and in name deriving presumably from *dulcis*

('sweet'). Early examples in Austria and hence, through Snetzler, in England, were as likely to have been small-scaled inverted conical Dolcan stops as the narrow, small-mouthed, miniature Diapason ranks familiar in most 19th-century organs, either as single ranks or in Mixtures. The earlier examples, especially c1725, seem mostly to have been at 4', not 8'; by 1820, 16' stops were also common in larger English organs, particularly on the Choir manual.

Dulzian (Ger.; Dutch *dulciaan*; Sp. *dulcayna*; Cz. *dulceon*). A reed stop of fairly gentle tone, with cylindrical resonators incorporating a conical foot, of 16' (pedal, manual) or 8' (secondary manuals), found in the Netherlands and north Germany. Early forms of the name were Touzyn, Toussein, Douseynen (c1510), showing a different origin from Dolcan–Tolkaan, despite Praetorius's confusion. Some Dulzians had fanciful resonators, some were similar to Cromornes. Iberian Dulcaynas were short conical reeds (c1740), often *en chamade* below the Trompetas, closer as an imitation of the medieval instrument DULZAINA than the northern types.

Echo. (1) A small-scaled Cornet in many 18th-century German organs.

(2) A prefix indicating a soft colour-stop (Echo Flute, Echo Gamba, etc) in 18th- and 19th-century organs throughout northern Europe.

English Horn. An imitative, double-belled reed stop, developed in the 1920s by the American builder Skinner; it is smoother in tone than the older Cor Anglais, and different in construction.

Erzähler (Ger.: 'narrator'). A narrow, tapered flue stop of soft tone, developed by Skinner in the early 20th century and still popular with American organ builders; it is often accompanied by a Celeste rank.

Espigueta (Sp.). See under *Rohrflöte*.

Euphone. One of the free reeds invented c1820 and found on French and Italian organs, often with no resonators.

Faberton (?Ger.). Probably a corruption of 'faburden', but apparently a stop producing a high, tinkling, bell-like tone, perhaps a Mixture (c1490), or a high Principal rank (c1550) or a high, wide mutation stop (c1700).

Fagotto (Fr. *basson*; Ger., Dutch *Fagott*). (1) The German 16' or 8' Fagotto was a fairly soft-toned reed with long narrow resonators, from c1575 onwards; it could be open, stopped (Niedt, 1721), or fanciful in shape (Praetorius, 2/1619).

(2) 'Basson' by Bédos de Celles' period (c1775) was a French reed with short conical pipes, sometimes capped with a double cone.

(3) In Italy, a rare wooden Regal (c1675); in Spain, a short reed with half-length resonators, sometimes *en chamade*; in England, the name occurs only in the bigger organs c1860 for a narrow conical 16' Swell reed.

Feldpfeife, Feldtrompete (Ger.). 'Feld' here means 'field' in the military sense. (1) A narrow open flue stop of assertive Flute tone, usually at 2' or 1', found occasionally in 17th-century German organs.

(2) The German imitative trumpet, not *en chamade* as in Spain but often held in the case vertically; others were interior trumpets, all of a thin, strong tone.

Fernflöte (Ger.: 'far-away flute'). Found in a few English and American Echo organs, in imitation of the *Kronwerk* flutes of south Germany c1750 or (more directly) their successors in the large organs of *c*1840.

Fiffaro (It.). See under *Bifara* and *Piffaro*.

Fifteenth. The Principal 2′ rank on English organs (any manual), so called from at least *c*1610, although early contracts qualify it as 'small principal'. *See also* SUPER-OCTAVE.

Flachflöte (Ger.). Probably a corruption of 'flageolet–flute' rather than 'flat-flute' (i.e. one made of wide, shallow, wooden pipes). The name was used for several pipe forms. (1) 8′, 4′ or 2′ conical pipes (Praetorius, 2/1619), perhaps like a Spillflöte (Zang, 1829), with strong, round tone.

(2) French Flageolets of the early 17th century were usually 1′ or 1⅓′ ranks of open cylindrical pipes (see under *Larigot*).

Flageolet (Fr.). See under *Flachflöte*. Also a name very common in 19th-century England (used by Willis) for a round, wide, rather discreet rank of metal 2′ pipes.

Flautado (Sp.). The Principal or Diapason pipes, 32′, 16′ or 8′ (52, 26 and 13 *palmos*) in the organs of Spain, Roussillon, etc, from *c*1475. The name probably originated in Flauto, etc, but later became more specific: 'Flautado de violon', the Spanish Gedackt rank (usually of wood) in the 17th and 18th centuries; 'Flautadito', the 4′ Principal or Octave stop.

Flautino (It.). 19th-century name in Germany, England, etc, for a soft 2′ or 4′ open Flute.

Flauto (It.; Eng. *flute*; Ger. *Flöte*; Fr. *flûte*). Originally, the generic term for organ pipes other than the Mixtures when the *Blockwerk* was divided into 'stops'; later a word applied throughout Europe either to stopped pipes of 8′ or 4′ (as in 18th-century England) or to colour-stops with prefixes denoting shape (Spitzflöte, etc), sound (Sifflöte, etc) or function (Flûte majeur, etc). Thus 'driifach fleiten' at Hagenau in 1491 indicated the three-rank Principal (? 8′ 8′ 4′); 'verdeckt floutwerk' indicated the Gedackts at Einsiedeln, Stiftskirche in 1558; 'flauto coperto' indicated a stopped Flute rank (a Nasard 2⅔′) at Orvieto Cathedral in 1591 and 'flauto reale', an open Flute rank in Venetian organs *c*1800. Other terms would indicate department ('flûte de pédale' was the 8′ or 4′ stopped wooden rank in the French classical organ), construction ('flûte à fusée' was a Spitzflöte at Bordeaux, 1627), imitation ('flûte à neuf trous', the 16th-century French Recorder stop), compass ('dessus de flûte', a treble open imitative Flute stop of French organs *c*1740), etc. In addition, there were many attempts at imitating the recorder or transverse flute, usually specified in the name, e.g. 'Flauto allemano' or 'travesiera' in Spain, 'Querflöte' or 'flauto traverso' in Germany, 'flûte d'amour' in exceptional organs anywhere; on the other hand, 'Flet' was the usual Habsburg name for stopped ranks of ordinary 4′ or 8′ Gedackt type. Some of the flute imitations were highly ingenious, involving overblowing (central Germany, *c*1610; France and England, *c*1850), fanciful construction or exotic woods (south Germany, *c*1725; southern Italy, *c*1725; Netherlands, *c*1775), and in some cases with conduits leading the air under pressure to strike a flute-like lip in the pipe mouth (Westphalia and Spain, *c*1775).

Flute. See under *Flauto*.

Flûte à cheminée (Fr.). See under *Rohrflöte*.

Flûte à pavillon (Fr.). Used *c*1850 for a large-scale metal

8′ flue stop, whose cylindrical pipes are capped by inverted conical *pavillons*; common in large organs *c*1875–1925.

Flûte d'amour (Fr.). A mild 4′ Flute of wood, sometimes stopped, often found in American organs from the late 19th century onwards.

Flûte harmonique (Fr.). The term was first used by Cavaillé-Coll, and hence his disciples in England and the USA, to describe the large-scale open metal Flute rank incorporating the 17th-century technique of over-blowing, aided by each pipe having a small hole bored halfway along the pipe cylinder. The resulting 1st harmonic tone is strong.

Fourniture (Fr.). French classical Mixture 'furnishing' the *pleno* with the ranks separated off from the Montres in early 16th-century organs; see also under *Mixture*. In the stereotyped 18th-century organ, the Fourniture broke only once in each octave, the Cymbale twice. The term was also to be found in England in the organs of the French influenced Renatus Harris (*c*1680 onwards), where however they frequently contained a Tierce rank, particularly by *c*1740.

French Horn. An imitative reed stop, made in England and the USA *c*1875–1950, often of high-pressure reeds with thick tongues; also occasionally found in 18th-century England, where the pipes probably took the form of a large-scale wide-flaring Hautbois.

Fugara. A term derived from Slav words for a shepherd's pipe (e.g. Polish *fujara*) and denoting a soft, rather slow-speaking string-toned stop of 8′ or 4′; first known in 17th-century Silesia, soon after in Bohemia, Austria, Switzerland, Swabia, etc. The pipes were usually long, narrow, metal, cylindrical, but slightly tapered forms were also known – both types reminiscent of the German Viola da gamba stop.

Gaitas (Sp.). A regal with short resonators, imitating the bagpipe with its thin, nasal but quiet tone, known in Spain from *c*1600.

Gamba. See under *Viola da gamba* and *Geigen*.

Gedackt (Ger.). A rank of 'stopped' pipes, more specifically the Stopped Diapason of German organs, in Austria called Coppel, in France Bourdon, etc. In England the term was first used *c*1850 in connection with the narrow-scaled Lieblich Gedackt.

Geigen (Ger.). A 'string-toned' or narrow-scaled stop, usually of open metal pipes, found in central Germany *c*1620 and becoming indispensable in all national types of 19th-century organ. 'String-toned' is only a comparative or analogous term.

Gemshorn (Ger.). A sharply tapering, wide metal Flute stop, with a tone between that of flute and string (more towards the former) and known from at least 1500 in the Rhinelands, where it imitated the GEMSHORN. The shape and tone were more widely known than the name, and many mutation stops in France and Spain have pipes of this kind. 19th-century organs have narrower, more string-toned Gemshorn stops than the classic ranks of 16′, 8′, 4′, 2′, 5⅓′, 2⅔′ and 1⅓′ noted by Praetorius.

Glockenspiel (Ger.). Usually a row of steel, copper or bronze bars hit by hammers activated by pedals or the keys of a secondary manual; in organs of 1720 (Swabia, Silesia, Saxony) of soprano or bass compass only, in organs of 1920 often complete. See under *Carillon*. Some

Glockenspiels were called 'Stahlspiel' ('steel instrument').

Gravissima (Lat.). A 64' 'Acoustic Bass' stop whose tone was produced by a 32' pipe sounding with a softer pipe of $21\frac{1}{3}'$; made by several 19th-century builders (Schulze, Willis, Walcker).

Gross. A prefix generally indicating a stop of large scale (Grossflöte, Gross Gamba), but also applied to a mutation stop pitched an octave lower than usual (Gross Tierce).

Haemiol, Hemiol. A term derived from Slav words for 'delicate' (e.g. Czech *jemny*) and used in central Europe during the 17th and 18th centuries for a soft, narrow-scaled, small-mouthed flue stop.

Harfe, Harfa, Harp, etc. A Regal toy stop found on some 16th-century organs, probably giving a kind of bagpipe drone effect. Some complete Regal ranks of 16' or 8' were also so called, in Central Germany (Harfen-regal) *c*1620, Spain *c*1750.

Harmonic (Fr. *harmonique*). A prefix (suffix) generally used to denote pipes of double length (Harmonic Flute, Trompette harmonique).

Harmonia, Harmonika. Although these terms occasionally appear in early contracts, they were chiefly used by certain 19th-century builders for soft stops of various kinds: Harmonia aetheria, a soft Echo Mixture as in Schulze's instruments; Harmonika, a soft open flue stop of indeterminate tone (Walcker) or a free reed stop (*c*1830).

Hautbois, Hautboy, Oboe. Like Cornet, Hautbois has indicated stops of several kinds over the centuries, all presumably imitating the instrument which itself changed and inspired builders in various ways. (1) In early 16th-century French organs, Hautbois was probably a registration (i.e. Flutes and mutations), not a stop; by *c*1600 the stop called Hautboy-Cornet was probably a strong-toned reed stop.
(2) The French classical Hautbois originated as a soft *récit* Trompette, with small-scaled flaring metal resonators; called 'French Schalmei' by Mattheson, and found on most French organs and those they influenced elsewhere, notably England (Harris).
(3) In Germany, stops of this name had various constructions, from fanciful Regals to small-scaled Schalmeien, none very important.
(4) 19th-century attempts to imitate the tone varied from free reeds (*c*1840, France, central Germany) to the ubiquitous, ultimately French-inspired English Swell Oboe.

Hintersatz (Ger.). The ranks of pipes 'placed behind' the case pipes in the late medieval organ, thus the Mixture of the *Blockwerk* remaining when the Prestants were separated off. Schlick (1511) assumed that it would contain at least 16–18 ranks. To some extent, the name remained as an occasional alternative for 'Mixtur'.

Hohlflöte, Hohlpfeife (Ger.; Dutch *holpijp*). (1) Rather wide, open cylindrical metal pipes between Principal and Nachthorn in scale, found in organs of central and north Germany from *c*1500. The name is probably derived not from *hohl* ('hollow') but from *Holunder* ('elder tree', see under *Salicet*). Many German contracts of the 18th century confuse *Hol*, *Hohl* and *Holz* (wood) as stop-name prefixes, and the popular 19th-century stop can usually be assumed to be of wooden pipes.

(2) During the 16th century, the name in its various forms often indicated a stopped rank of wide scale (Rhineland, south Germany). In Holland, it might be a Gedackt, Rohrflöte or even Quintatön, many 18th-century examples being simple stopped Flutes.

Horn, Hörnli (Ger.). (1) Several kinds of imitative reed stop (see under *French Horn*).
(2) Suffix for a group of stop names (Gemshorn, Nachthorn), like the related term 'Cornet' popular with 16th-century builders expanding organ colours.
(3) More specifically, the Hörnli a 16th-century stop found in the upper and lower Rhineland composed of the same ranks as stops elsewhere called Cornet and Sesquialtera, i.e. a solo (or solo and chorus) Tierce Mixture.
(4) Horn Diapason was a late 19th-century stop whose Diapason-scale pipes had a vertical slot cut at the top and back, the tone apparently hardened in the process.

Jubal, Tubal. A rare open Flute found in some German organs *c*1690–1740 to imitate the imagined sounds produced by Jubal, the 'Inventor of Music'.

Jula, Iula. A rare stop name with different meanings in different German organs: a Quint (J. Samber, 1707), a Spitzflöte (Zang, 1829), a soft, narrow mutation (Praetorius).

Kalkant (Ger.). An accessory stop-lever found in Germany over the centuries, which when pulled caused a bell to ring and communicated with the bellows-blower.

Keraulophon. A quasi-Greek term invented by Gray in *c*1820 to denote a stop type long known by other builders, i.e. a quiet, reedy-toned 8' Flute stop. The pipes usually have a hole near the top.

Kinura. A keen-toned reed stop with very narrow cylindrical resonators, often used in cinema organs.

Koppel (Ger.). See under *Coppel*.

Kornett (Ger.). See under *Cornett*.

Krummhorn. See under *Cromorne*.

Kuckuck (Ger.). See under *Vogelgesang*.

Kützialflöte (Ger.). An open Flute of 4', 2' or sometimes 1' pitch, occasionally found on German organs from Praetorius onwards, evidently imitating a Slav instrument (*cewzial*: 'flute').

Larigot (Fr.). A term probably derived from 'l'arigot' ('flageolet' – cf *haricot*) and used in the 16th century (and hence the later French classical organ in general) to denote the $1\frac{1}{3}'$ wide mutation rank found in large and small organs and used for both chorus and solo registrations. Outside France, other terms like Superquinte, Quintanus and Flageolet were used.

Lieblich Gedackt (Ger.). (1) The 'pleasant stopped rank' known from at least Praetorius onwards to refer to the Stopped Diapason used for continuo playing or for soft (often echo) effects.
(2) More specifically, the pretty-toned Gedackt made popular by the influential 19th-century builders (Walcker, Schulze), of metal or wood, with a high cut-up and characteristic tone.

Lleno. See under *Compuestas*; see also ORGANO PLENO.

Major, Minor. Terms denoting the size (rather than function) of a stop. Flöte major [minor] were common in 18th-century Habsburg Europe for 8' and 4' Gedackts; 'Majorbass' was fairly common in Germany between

1650 and 1900 for the 16' or 32' open or stopped pedal rank.

Melodia. A medium- to wide-scaled open wood Flute stop of 8' pitch; the pipes usually have reversed mouths and sometimes sunken blocks. It was widely used in England and the USA from the middle of the 19th century.

Mixture (Fr. *fourniture*; Ger. *Mixtur*). Names for the collected ranks of the *Blockwerk* when the Principals and Flutes had been separated off, the contents, planning, voicing, making and scaling of which distinguish national organ schools as much as any other stop. 'Mixture' was normally used to denote the Principal-scaled chorus Mixture as distinct from the high Zimbeln or the solo Cornets. The 'true Mixture' is often said to contain Octave and Quint ranks only, but Tierces have been found in many national types of Mixture (17th century Spain, 18th century England), some of which were highly influential during the 19th century. Early names for the stop (presumably activated by levers) were 'Position', 'Locatio', 'Starkwerk', all known before 1520; late types were the 'Compensationsmixtur' and 'Progressio harmonica' (both *c*1820), the former of which decreased in number of ranks, strength and volume as it ascended, the latter of which increased.

Montre (Fr.). The case pipes of the French organ, corresponding to the English Open Diapason, the German Prestant and the Italian Principale. Early alternative names included 'le principal de devant', and 'devanture en monstre' (Reims Cathedral 1570). The tone of the classical French Montre was somewhat more foundational or fluty than the various English Open Diapason types.

Nachthorn (Ger.). A term probably derived from *Nachhorn* or *Nachsatz*, i.e. a rank of pipes distinguished from the *Hintersatz*, and nothing to do with Cor de nuit in origin. (1) Nachthornen were frequently the same as Cornets in the 16th century, more particularly in northern France and the Netherlands, cf the Spanish term Nasardos.
(2) By Praetorius's time, the name denoted a rank of very wide-scale 4' or 2' pipes, stopped like the Quintatön and more horn-like than the Hohlflöte, owing to its Quint partial. The familiar 17th-century Nachthorn useful in the north German repertory was a very wide metal open Flute, used for cantus firmus in manual or pedal.

Nachtigall (Ger.). See under *Vogelgesang*.

Nasard (?Fr.; Ger. *Nasat*). Terms probably derived from *Nachsatz*, i.e. the rank or ranks between the Principals and the *Hintersatz* of a separated *Blockwerk*. Early usages of the name refer to a registration or effect rather than a single rank of pipes (*c*1530, France), and *nazard* meant the rank helping to produce the characteristic sound, i.e. $2\frac{2}{3}'$ or $1\frac{1}{3}'$ Flutes. The form could be open or stopped, Chimney Flute or tapered. The French classical Nasard was usually a stopped rank of $2\frac{2}{3}'$, often a Rohrflöte for some or all its compass, that on the *Grand orgue* usually different in type from that of the *Positiv* manual. In Germany, there was frequently no distinction drawn in stop lists between Quinte and Nasard, nor were the differences in form, volume, tone and function between the two so clear-cut as in France.

Nasardos (Sp.). A term probably derived from 16th-century French and Flemish usage to denote either the single mutation ranks (Octave, Quint or Tierce) making up the Corneta or, more importantly, the chorus/solo Mixture; a kind of bass version of the treble Corneta and found over the centuries on most Iberian organs.

Nason (?Eng.). A stopped Flute introduced to England at the end of the 17th century by Smith and copied by many builders for two centuries. Very often of oak, with a characteristic sweet tone, the Nason is only a Gedacktflöte and the origins of its name are unclear.

Night Horn. See under *Nachthorn*.

Nineteenth. The English term is meant to indicate the Principal-scaled $1\frac{1}{3}'$ rank, something more like the Italian Decimanona than the classical French Larigot.

Octave (Fr. *prestant*; Ger. *Oktave*; It. *ottava*; Sp. *octava*). (1) The 4' Principal of an organ based on an 8' Open Diapason, or 8' of one based on a 16' Diapason, etc. In England, 'Octave 4'' implies a strong Principal 4' rank, such special meaning originating *c*1850.
(2) A prefix indicating pitch an octave higher than usual (Octave Flute).

Octavin (Fr.; It. *ottavina*). Open metal Flutes made by Venetian builders *c*1790 and Cavaillé-Coll *c*1860.

Open Diapason. See under *Diapason*, *Principal*.

Ophicleide. Strong reed stop supposedly imitating the OPHICLEIDE and popular as a pedal rank in Willis organs.

Orchestral. A prefix denoting a stop of particularly imitative tone (Orchestral Oboe, Orchestral Flute), found in many early 20th-century organs.

Orlos (Sp.). An 8' Regal with short cylindrical resonators, sometimes *en chamade* and common in Iberian organs by *c*1730.

Pauke, Trommel (Ger.; It. *timballo*; Sp. *tambor*). Drum stops were popular in the larger organs of all European countries until the early 19th century, and the percussion varieties in theatre organs *c*1920 were only revivals. Sometimes real timpani were provided, tunable and played by *putti* activated by pedal levers (Berlin, *c*1730), but more usually the many drum-effects were produced by two or more large-scaled wooden pipes out of tune with each other. Frequently the quasi-pitches produced were A and D, allowing realistic 'trumpet-and-drums' music: 'with trumpet, shawm or fife' according to the Trier Cathedral contract of 1537 (P. Briesger).

Piccolo. A 19th-century 2' or 1' Flute stop made by English builders to a design labelled Octavin, Flöte, Flageolet, etc, by other builders; pipes are sometimes of harmonic (double) length.

Pifano (Sp.). Open or stopped Flute 4' or 2'; the name was used over the centuries and was probably a corruption of Pfeife, etc.

Piffaro, Fiffaro (It.). Although in other musical contexts Fiffaro often denoted a reed instrument, organ stops of this name fall into two different classes. (1) An open Flute found in Rhineland organs of the 16th century, high-pitched and later overblowing or double-mouthed, producing a tone imitative of the cross-blown fife.
(2) An important Italian stop of the 16th century onwards; of treble compass Principal-scaled pipes mistuned with the Principale 8' and thus producing an undulating effect (Schwebung), more singing and less reedy than 19th-century *céleste* stops.

Pommer (Ger.). See under *Bombardon*.

Portunal (*flöte*) (Ger.). A term, probably a corruption of Bourdon, denoting in 17th- and 18th-century German organs a rank of 8′ or 4′ open wood or metal pipes (sometimes inverted conical), producing a modified Open Flute colour.

Posaune (Ger.; Dutch *bazuin, buzain*). A common name for 16′ or 32′ pedal reed stops of varied construction in certain areas and periods. Resonators two-thirds long were generally considered desirable, but they could be wood or metal. The 'stille Posaune' seems, from Praetorius, to have been a stopped reed, but many builders used 'Posaune' in general for their big reed other than the Bombarde, from at least *c*1580 onwards.

Praestant (Lat.; Fr., Ger. *Prestant*). Pipes 'standing in the front' of the organ case. (1) In Holland, since 'Principal' denoted the main chorus as a whole in *c*1525, 'Praestant' was used to refer to the case pipes or Open Diapason itself. German builders *c*1550–1800 used Praestant and Principal as synonyms, depending on local custom.

(2) In France, 'Prestant' soon came to denote the 4′ Principal rank distinct from the Montre 8′, as 'Principal' in England has always indicated the 4′ Principal rank distinct from the Open Diapason 8′; both French and English usage was established by 1600.

Principal (Ger. *Prinzipal*). See also under *Praestant*. The term first arose soon after 1500 in the Netherlands (and hence probably in England) to denote not a single rank of pipes but the Diapason chorus as a whole, i.e. the undivided Mixture or *pleno*; in English and American organs from the 18th century onwards, however, it usually denotes a 4′ stop. By Praetorius's time, the 'stop formerly called Praestant or Doeff' was called Prinzipal in Germany. In the 20th century, Prinzipal has become useful as a term denoting the relatively colourless German basic 8′ rank as opposed to the various English Diapason tones.

Quartane. See under *Rauschpfeife*.

Quarte de nasard (Fr.). The stop a 4th above the Nasard on the French classical organ, i.e. a 2′ Flute mutation rank rather than the chorus Doublette. Usually open, the bass octave was sometimes a Chimney Flute.

Querflöte (Ger.). The transverse flute has been imitated in various ways. The organ stop so called is properly an open cylindrical metal or wood stop, usually 4′, overblowing to the 1st or 2nd overtone because of the narrow scale and small mouth; a small hole halfway along the pipe facilitates the overblowing (cf Cavaillé-Coll's Flûte harmonique). Such overblowing Schweizerpfeifen seem to have been known in late 15th-century south Germany. The effect is gentle. Construction can vary: stopped and wide scaled (Praetorius, 2/1619); long, narrow pipes overblowing at the 12th (built by Compenius, Fritzsche); conical (Snetzler); 'blown from the side' (Wagner); simple stopped 2′ Flutes (*c*1600); fanciful large-scale pipes (*c*1840), perhaps of turned hardwood (*c*1730).

Quint. Like Nineteenth, Fifteenth, etc, Quint has usually since *c*1550 indicted chorus ranks (not Flute mutations) sounding $10\frac{2}{3}′$, $5\frac{1}{3}′$, $2\frac{2}{3}′$, and $1\frac{1}{3}′$. *See also* QUINT, §(3).

Quintadecima (It.). The Fifteenth or 2′ Principal chorus rank, sometimes perhaps doubled or paired in Italian organs before *c*1500.

Quintadena, Quintatön (Ger.). An important stop of narrow-scaled, stopped metal pipes, preferably of a high tin content, blown on generous wind and producing a quiet tone with a marked 5th (i.e. 2nd overtone) in it; the pipes are near overblowing. Like other basic organ-pipe shapes, it was known by 1500 and more commonly used throughout Europe than the name itself. The origin of the term is uncertain, all the variants (e.g. Quintade, Quintaden, Quintiten) suggesting the '5th-tone' nature of the sound. Schällenpfeifen ('bell-pipes', referring to the tone) was an early 16th-century alternative name; a Gedacktpommer was a strong-voiced 4′ Quintatön in the 17th century. Many types of Stopped Diapason before *c*1775 have much of the tonal quality of a Quintadena.

Rankett, Rackett (Ger.). A 16′ Regal with short resonators and gentle tone, found fairly often from the end of the 16th century in northern Europe, particularly in small organs and the secondary manuals of large ones. Shape and materials varied, but the pipes were always short. Such Regals were entirely out of fashion from 1710 to 1930.

Rauschpfeife, Rauschquint, Rauschwerk (Ger.). Words of doubtful origin – probably unconnected with *rauschen* ('to murmur') – properly denoting three distinct kinds of chorus Mixture in the various German organ types from *c*1575. (1) Rauschpfeife of two ranks (15.19 or 2′ + $1\frac{1}{3}′$); other additional ranks would be the 12th and 22nd.

(2) Rauschquinte of two ranks (12.15 or $2\frac{2}{3}′$ + 2′), otherwise called Quartane. Neither term was used reliably by builders until recently.

(3) Rauschwerk is frequently used to replace one or other term; but for early sources (e.g. A. Schlick, 1511), 'Rauschwerk' was a term denoting either a semi-Flute solo compound stop imitating a reed instrument, or a reed stop itself, probably of more refined tone than the Trompete. 'Rauschende Zimbel' (Russzimbel, etc) was an early term for, it seems, high Mixtures, perhaps with Tierce ranks.

Recorder. In England, the term appears in a few 17th-century contracts to refer to an unspecified Flute stop: perhaps 4′ stopped pipes.

Regal. A term of uncertain origin (*see* REGALS) denoting a family of organ stops probably descending from the late medieval instrument; the small or very small resonators made such ranks useful in the subsidiary chests of larger organs. Early 16th-century names were frequently specific, at other times more cumbersome, such as 'Regal to make the human voice' (Vox humana). Fanciful names and pipe forms were found chiefly in northern Germany from *c*1575 to *c*1700 and should not be overestimated: Apfelregal (short resonators with a little round perforated ball at the end), Geigenregal (delicate 4′ Regal, treble sounding as a violin when drawn with a Quintatön, according to Praetorius), Harfenregal, Jungfernregal (thin tone 'like a girl's voice'), Knopfregal and Kopfregal ('knob-' and 'head-shaped Regal'), Messingregal (short brass pipes), Singendregal ('singing Regal' of light tone, useful for cantus firmus melodies), Trichterregal (important type with 'funnel-shaped' or conical resonators like small trumpets). In other countries, Regals usually had freer names, e.g. Orlos, Tromboncini, Vox humana.

Resultant. A pedal stop, usually of 32′ pitch, made up of 16′ and $10\frac{2}{3}′$ ranks of pipes sounding simultaneously.

Ripieno (It.). (1) The full chorus, i.e. either a registration of drawn stops or the *Blockwerk* itself.

(2) The classical Italian chorus Mixture, known when single ranks became less the norm on the Italian organ than they had once been (*c*1800).

Rohrflöte (Ger.; Eng. *Chimney Flute*; Fr. *flûte à cheminée*; It. *Flauto a camino*; Sp. *Espigueta*). The name of an important pipe form known throughout Europe but so called only north of a line from Breslau to Antwerp. The pipes are 'half stopped', the metal canisters or stoppers pierced to allow a narrow tube to pass through. The length and width of the tube has varied from builder to builder, some tubes held entirely within the pipe and not protruding. The resultant tone is very charming, the stopped Flute sound modified by several faint overtones. 19th-century Chimney Flutes are basically the same in construction, but the name was often given to plain Flute stops. The pipe form probably originated in the Rhineland at the end of the 15th century; some early Dutch examples were called 'Hohlflöte' in the sources. Praetorius noted that such stops could be at 16', 8', 4', 2' and even 1'; Adlung (1768) added the mutations: $10\frac{2}{3}'$, $5\frac{1}{3}'$, $2\frac{2}{3}'$ and $1\frac{1}{3}'$. In France and Spain, certain pipes (e.g. the lower octaves) in a Flute rank might be Chimney Flutes, as could a complete rank in Cornets; Mersenne (1636–7) noted that the length of tube affected the sound. Some early 20th-century builders, especially in the USA, made use of internal, inverted chimneys, thought to be more stable.

Rossignol (Fr.). See under *Vogelgesang*.

Sackbut. A term occasionally used *c*1550 or *c*1850 (both periods notable for ingenious inventors) for big reed stops, bigger than Posaunen.

Salicet, Salicional. A term derived from Latin *salix* ('willow tree') during the later 16th century to denote a rank of open cylindrical pipes of narrow (sometimes conical) scale giving a fairly delicate, almost string-like tone by way of auxiliary 8' or 4' colour extra to the Flutes and Principals. The most common pitch may have been 4', as it was for the early Dulciana. The stop was a speciality of Habsburg Europe until itinerant builders took it elsewhere (e.g. Snetzler to England, where it became very popular in the 19th century at both 8' and 4' (Salicet) pitches). The small mouths made side ears advisable. In central Germany *c*1725, 'Sollicinal' was a two-rank Sesquialtera.

Schalmei (Ger.). (1) From *c*1550, a reed stop with narrow flaring resonators giving it a tone closer to a smooth trumpet than a real shawm. The tone must have varied over the centuries, but the stop seems to have been particularly associated with cantus firmus playing. Rare from 1750 to 1930.

(2) In some central European sources of *c*1775, Schalmei seems to have been an auxiliary 8' flue stop.

Scharf (Ger.; Dutch *scherp*). Narrow-scale chorus Mixture of 'sharp' penetrating tone, found throughout northern Europe from *c*1500 onwards. (1) Early Dutch and German Scharf Mixtures were high-pitched like the Zimbel, and properly distinct from the Terzzimbel.

(2) The basic Mixture of subsidiary manuals was often called Scharf whether or not it was Zimbel-like. Those of the mid-19th century frequently contained a high Tierce rank.

Schnarrwerk (Ger.). 17th-century term for the 'rattling stops' or Regals.

Schwebung (Ger.). See under *Tremulant* and *Piffaro*.

Schwegel, Schweigel (Ger.). A term derived from High German *suegela* ('flute') to denote a delicate Flute stop of fairly narrow scale, common in south and central Germany from 1550 to 1850, chiefly on subsidiary manuals. Some 'Schwegli' were $1\frac{1}{3}'$, others 4', 2' and even 8' (the last especially *c*1750); some open wide pipes, others conical, yet others double conical or overblowing. 19th-century Schwegels are usually bland, wide, high Flutes.

Schweizerpfeife (Ger.). To play a flute 'in the Swiss manner' in early 16th-century sources meant to play it cross-blown, like a fife. (1) Organ imitations of the period took various forms (see under *Querflöte* and *Flauto*).

(2) In the 18th century, the name often denoted an 8' or 4' rank, inverted conical or narrow cylindrical, either way resembling the so-called Viola da gamba in tone.

Sedecima (?It.). A term found in Habsburg Europe of the 17th and 18th centuries to denote a $1\frac{1}{3}'$ Sifflöte.

Septième (Fr.). Cavaillé-Coll's name (hence that used by English builders) for the 'Seventh' or $4\frac{4}{7}'$, $2\frac{2}{7}'$ and $1\frac{1}{7}'$ mutation series, first known as an idea in Prussia *c*1780 but coming into prominence as (*a*) an extra colour in a large organ of *c*1860, (*b*) a sharply colourful rank in the *Oberwerk* of a neo-Baroque organ of *c*1950, particularly in Germany.

Seraphon. Weigle's name for a group of high-pressure flue and reed stops popular in Germany during the early 20th century.

Sesquialtera. A term perhaps derived from the Latin sesquialtera ('one and a half') and used to denote a two-rank solo/chorus mutation stop containing the 12th and 17th ($2\frac{2}{3}'$ + $1\frac{3}{5}'$), written carelessly as 'Quinte 3' + Terz 2' = 3:2 = $1\frac{1}{2}'$. Other forms of the name suggest clever etymologies: 'Sexquialter' (England, late 18th century) apparently referring to the 6th contained between the $2\frac{2}{3}'$ and $1\frac{3}{5}'$ pipe. 'Sex quintaltra' and 'Sexquintalter' (ditto), 'Flautt in 6ta' (Italy, late 17th century), etc. F. Hocque's phrase 'Sesquialtera called by some Vox humana or Nasard', for what was in fact a Cornet stop (Trier Cathedral, 1590), shows the interdependence of names at that period. (1) The classic two-rank Sesquialtera was a flute-like semi-Cornet solo stop, often treble only, found in north-west German organs of *c*1630–1790.

(2) The English Sesquialtera was, during the late 17th century, a bass complement to the treble Cornet stop; during the 18th century a complete chorus Mixture including a narrow-scaled Tierce rank; and during the 19th century often the only Mixture (still with a Tierce) in the whole organ.

Seventeenth. See under *Tierce*.

Sifflöte (Ger.). A term probably derived from *siffler*, 'to whistle', although many German spellings suggest a wider derivation: cyvelet (Amsterdam, Oude Kerk, 1539 – cf zuffolo: 'shepherd's fife'), Sufflet (Dresden, 1563), Schufflet (Münster, 1579), Suff Flöte (by C. Donat (i), 1683), Suiflöt/Duiflot and Subflöte (Praetorius, 2/1619). (1) A high-pitched Flute stop, narrow, wide or conical; good examples have a characteristic sibilant tone.

(2) Throughout its period of popularity, the stop could be either 1' or $1\frac{1}{3}'$, some builders (e.g. G. Silbermann) preferring the first, others (e.g. Schnitger) the second.

Much the same was true of the Sedecima, the Sifflöte of Habsburg countries.

Sordun. A very short stopped Regal imitating a woodwind instrument, soft (cf sordino) and somewhat thin in tone, popular during the 17th century in north central Germany.

Soubasse (Fr.). See under *Sub-Bass.*

Sperrventil (Ger.). The 'blocking valve' for preventing wind reaching a chest, saving it for other chests or keeping it from sounding a ciphering note. Such valves were the first means of dividing the *Blockwerk* in some instances; they remained a common accessory in northern Europe until *c*1850. During the 19th century, the valve's potential as a registration aid was exploited by such builders as Cavaillé-Coll who (like certain 17th-century builders) made several chests for each department or manual, each of which could have prepared stops that would sound only when the valve was activated.

Spillflöte (Ger.). Probably a corruption of 'spindle-flute', a rank of open, wide cylindrical pipes which suddenly taper towards the top. The pipe form could be used for an 8', 4' or 2' stop (north Germany, 17th century) or for part of a mutation rank (various countries) of discreet tone.

Spitzflöte (Ger.). The 'pointed flute' stop whose pipe form – gently tapering or conical from mouth to top – was more common than the occurrences of its name suggest, especially outside Germany, Holland and Scandinavia. The taper is more pronounced than that of the Gemshorn, and the tone is that of a reedy or breathy flute, good for blending either at 8' pitch or as a mutation. Such pipe forms are known from the late 15th century (8' at Lübeck Totentanzorgel, 1492) and frequently had a part in a French mutation rank, a Spanish Corneta, an Italian Flauto; the name itself appears to be late 16th century. 19th-century examples in Germany and England tend to be too string-like in tone.

Stentorphone. One of Weigle's late 19th-century open flue stops of very loud, nondescript tone, popular in larger German and American organs *c*1890–1920.

Stopped Diapason. See under *Diapason, Gedackt.*

Suavial, Suabe Flöte (?Ger.). A term probably derived from *suavis* ('sweet'; not from Swabia, 'schwäbisch') and used to denote a narrow-scaled 8' or 4' metal stop popular in southern Germany, Switzerland and the Habsburg countries from *c*1710 to the early 19th century. Burney described one in Frankfurt as 'meant for that sweet stop in Mr. Snetzler's organs which he calls the Dulciana'.

Sub-Bass (Ger.; Fr. *soubasse*). An unspecific term that usually denoted a stopped wooden rank of 16' pedal pipes of average scale. During the 19th century, some German and French builders used it for the 32' Bourdon rank.

Superoctave. See under *Fifteenth; see also* SUPER-OCTAVE.

Tambor. See under *Pauke.*

Tapada, Tapadillo (Sp.; It. *tappato*). Prefix denoting 'stopped' pipes. Tapadillo was the 17th–18th-century Spanish Flute 4', usually stopped but on occasion open, conical or a Rohrflöte.

Tenori (It.). An occasional 16th-century name for the Principal 8'.

Tenoroon (?Eng.). The name applied in some early 19th-century sources to describe a flue or reed stop of short compass, often going no lower than Tenor C in the bass.

Terpodion. A quasi-Greek name for delicate stops of 'delightful' tone in early 19th-century German organs.
(1) A free reed (*c*1830).
(2) Small-scaled open metal flue (used by Schulze).

Tertian, Terzian (Ger.). Properly a two-rank solo and chorus Tierce Mixture found more especially in northern Europe during the 17th and 18th centuries and consisting of the ranks 17.19 (1⅗' + 1⅓') as opposed to the 12.17 of the Sesquialtera. Theorists have pointed out that it could contain 15.17 ranks (Werckmeister, 1705) or 10.12 (Adlung, 1768), and many examples did break back an octave around *c'*. As with all mutations, the scaling was somewhat wider than Principal.

Terza mano (It.). The 'third hand' or octave coupler found on late 18th-century and 19th-century Italian organs, feasible in view of the often long compass of the main manuals.

Terzzimbel. See under *Zimbel.*

Theorbe (Ger.; Sp. *tiorba*). (1) German reed stop of the 17th–18th centuries, rare but of a distinct type, i.e. gentle 16' tone imitating, in some way, the theorbo.
(2) More familiar Spanish reed with short resonators, often *en chamade, c*1750.

Tibia (Lat.). General name for 'pipe', used in the Latinate contracts of the late 18th century and by the technician-inventors of the late 19th century. Thus Tibia angusta is a narrow Flute, Tibia clausa a Gedackt, 'cuspida' a Spitzflöte, 'sylvestris' a Waldflöte, etc.

Tierce (Fr.; Ger. *Terz, Tertia*). The 1⅗' Flute mutation rank, more particularly of the French classical organ. Such third-sounding ranks were contained in Arnaut de Zwolle's Cymbale of *c*1450, but evidently their scaling widened over the centuries, achieving a characteristic horn tone by 1750. Some Parisian organs *c*1630 had two such ranks, one wide the other narrow, the latter thus used in one or other *pleno*. The Double Tierce 3⅕' (Grosse Tierce) was first known *c*1660 and contributed to the array of melodic colours in French organ music. Outside France, the stop was found as a single mutation rank only in organ types influenced by the French, e.g. those of the Rhineland or Saxony. Besides French terms, 18th-century names were Ditonus, Decima, Sixtil (all in various northern European countries) and Corneta (Italy).

Tiratutti (It.). A mechanical device known in Italian organs from *c*1700 whereby the organist could 'draw all the pleno ranks' at once.

Tolkaan (Dutch; Ger. *Dolcan*). A term of uncertain origin denoting a rank of open inverted conical metal or wood pipes, often confused with Dulzian, Dulciana, etc. As in other instances, the pipe form was known in more versions and over greater areas than the name itself. The Tolkaan was a speciality of large Dutch and Hanseatic organs of *c*1580, as was the Trichterflöte ('funnel-shaped flute') early in the next century. The pipe form was also found in the case of Spanish flutes, Austrian Dulcianas, Neapolitan Voci umani (all of *c*1750) and many soft or fairly soft colour-stops in German organs *c*1825.

Tremulant (Fr. *tremblant*; It. *tremolo, temblor*). An important accessory stop contained in most larger European organs from *c*1500 to the present day, although not always specified in the contract. Two chief types were known to 17th- and 18th-century builders, the French usually incorporating an example of each: (1) Tremblant fort (Bocktremulant) was also called 'Tremblant à vent perdu', i.e. a sprung valve, balanced and adjustable, which would allow wind to escape intermittently from the trunk, the remaining wind admitted in uneven pulses to the pipe chests.

(2) Tremblant doux did not allow wind to escape but acted as a sprung gate in the trunk, momentarily blocking the flow when activated. The latter was especially suitable for a single chest or even isolated stop, serving as a Schwebung, e.g. for the Vox humana. It is clear from some musical imitations of the Tremulant c1600 that the pulse or rate of trembling then normal was slower than the various familiar 19th-century Tremulants.

Trichterregal. See under *Regal.*

Trombone. See under *Posaune.*

Tromboni, Tromboncini (It.). (1) A 'small-large trumpet' reed stop introduced now and then into Italy by various Flemish or German builders.

(2) Tromboni were long and strong-toned 16' or 8' reed stops on many national types of organ c1820.

(3) Tromboncini were an important type of Regal on Venetian organs of the late 18th century, with very small-scale square-sectioned metal resonators standing in front of the case pipes.

Trommel (Ger.). See under *Pauke.*

Trommet, Trompete, Trompette, Trumpet, etc (Ger.). A very familiar imitative reed stop with long, flaring or inverted-conical resonators, metal or wood, found in most organ types since c1500 and taking various forms. (Organs without a Trumpet were the classical Italian organ of c1600, the English pre-Restoration organ, and the mature Habsburg organ of the 18th century.) The resonators should be about two-thirds long (6' for 8' C). German and English Trumpets 1650–1950 varied from builder to builder; 17th-century German Trumpets were often short, especially if the flaring was marked and the pipes placed vertically in the case front. 18th-century French Trumpets developed great power and attack, especially in the bass, often using higher pressures, wider tongues and bigger resonators. Spanish Trumpets also followed certain conventions: the Trompeta real was a full-size vertical reed within the organ; Trompeta bastarda had shorter resonators, often *en chamade*; Trompeta magna/de batalla/imperial were horizontal Trumpets, often of suboctave pitches (16', even 32', in the treble). During the late 19th century, exceptional organs in any city of Europe might have had highly imitative Trumpet stops, with higher pressures, perhaps brass resonators, arranged as a fan or *en chamade*.

Trompes (Fr.). The large open bass pipes placed apart from, and on either side of, the *Grand orgue* of many large French and Dutch organs of the later 15th century. A set of ten was fairly common. Other names (e.g. *turres* at Angers Cathedral in 1416) were sometimes found; 'trompe' may signify the 'pendentive' or carved wooden semicircular console on which the pipes were placed.

Trumpet. See under *Trommet.*

Tuba. Except in the Latinate contracts of c1800, 'Tuba' as a stop name is found almost entirely in the 19th and 20th centuries, and denotes a louder and smoother reed stop than the usual Trumpet, taking whatever form the builder found useful for increasing volume.

Twelfth. The rank of $2\frac{2}{3}'$ open metal pipes forming part of the Diapason chorus. Some early Twelfths, however, were more Nasard-like, especially in England c1725.

Twenty-second. A Principal stop of 1' pitch.

Uccelli (It.). See under *Vogelgesang.*

Unda maris (Lat.). A term applied in south Germany during the 18th century – and hence through Walcker (c1830) to most major builders of the 19th century – to denote a rank of narrow, open 8' metal pipes, tuned slightly sharp or flat (either to a second rank standing with it or to the organ as a whole) and so producing an undulating effect. The effect was known more widely than the name, being mentioned by Mersenne (1636–7), found in the classical Italian organ as Piffaro, and impressing the many 18th- and early 19th-century builders looking for colourful Flute and String stop varieties.

Untersatz (Ger.). The term for pipes placed on a chest below (and at the back of) the main chest of organs in north and central Germany c1575–1825, i.e. pipes of the larger pedal stops. In practice, the term thus denotes various 16' or 32' pedal stops, particularly stopped wood 32' ranks.

Usignuolo (It.). See under *Vogelgesang.*

Viejas (Sp.). The 'old women's voice', or thin Vox humana of Spanish organs c1750, often *en chamade*. Other fanciful names for particularly thin Vox humana stops were Viejos (Spain, c1750), Jungfernregal (Germany, c1625) and Vox pueri/tauri (Italy, c1600).

Viola da gamba. The name for a large number of stop-types whose only common characteristic is their claiming to imitate the string instrument. (1) In c1620, often a Tolkaan.

(2) During the 17th century in central Europe as a whole, many narrow cylindrical stops bore the name Viola da gamba or Viol d'amour as well as Salicional, Dulciana, etc.

(3) Many Gamba stops contained conical pipes, like narrow Spitzflöten – Saxony c1725, England and south Germany c1850, northern Italy c1880.

(4) Many Gamba stops of the 18th century are either very flute-like (south Germany) or soft, discreet stops of sweet, breathy Diapason tone (as those of G. Silbermann).

(5) In Italy and Spain from c1750, 'Viola' often denoted a regal stop of one or other kind.

Viola pomposa. A broad and fairly strong string-toned stop, developed by G. D. Harrison in the 1930s, and used since in large American organs.

Viole d'orchestre. A very narrow-scaled, keen-sounding string stop, found mostly in organs built in the first half of the 20th century.

Violetta (It.; Sp. *violeta*). (1) Regal stops, with very small open conical resonators of 4' or 2', made in the late 18th century.

(2) Miscellaneous string-toned flue stops, 8', 4' or 2', on various of the later 19th-century organ types.

Violina. A medium-scaled 4' stop of string tone, frequently found in the Swell division of 19th-century English and American organs.

Violón (Sp.; Ger. *Violon*). (1) In Spain, an important term for the Stopped Diapason on the Baroque organ, manual or pedal. Thus 'Flautado violón' was the Bourdon.

(2) A common German open pedal stop of medium volume and nondescript tone, found during the 18th and 19th centuries. Often a substitute for the Prinzipal 16'.

Violoncello (It.). (1) A Venetian regal stop at 8', with small rectangular cross-section resonators of boxwood or pine, placed vertically in front of the case pipes, and in use from c1750 onwards.

(2) Narrow flue stops of various periods and areas in Germany, c1700–1900.

(3) An 8' pedal stop frequently found in 19th- and 20th-century English and American organs.

Vogelgesang, Kuckuck, Nachtigall, rossignol, uccelli, usignuolo. National names for the bird-imitating toy stops popular from at least 1450 to 1800 and again in theatre organs c1925. Each builder had his own way of planning such quasi-automata; if the tiny pipes were suspended in water, the twittering was thought to resemble a nightingale; if two were involved and stood a 3rd apart, a cuckoo resulted; if air supply allowed it (and often so much air was taken that no other stops could be drawn), moving statuary might complete the picture; and so on. An important example was the 'Vogelgesang durchs ganze pedal' (Praetorius) which was not a toy stop so much as either a tiny high Mixture of indeterminate pitch adding a soft glitter, or a regular high Flute stop.

Voix céleste (Fr.). A term apparently dating from the 1840s to denote a long-familiar effect achieved in the same way as Unda maris and Piffaro. The narrow-scaled pipes usual for such stops c1840–1940 gave a sharp heterodyne effect, less voice-like than that intended by classic Italian builders of c1600.

Vox angelica (Lat.) (1) Small reed stops of 2' found in the organs of some German builders c1750 (Stumm).

(2) Soft small-scaled flue stops on various 19th-century organ-types, including Italian.

(3) A free-reed stop used by Walcker and other 19th-century German builders.

Vox humana (Lat.; It. *voce umana*; Fr. *voix humaine*; Sp. *voz humana*). The name of numerous stops whose common characteristic is the claim to imitate the human voice, particularly its thin, undulating quality, and always at 8'. (1) The Renaissance Voce umana was the same as Piffaro.

(2) Some 16th-century builders used the term for a registration (e.g. Regal + Nasard + Larigot) or for the Regal 'helping to make the Vox humana effect'.

(3) Many Regal types during the 17th and 18th centuries were invented for the purpose, with resonators open, closed; of brass, hardwood; short, half-stopped, cylindrical, capped and pierced, double conical, bulbous, etc. Some had their own Schwebung (see the definition of Tremulant). During the late 19th and early 20th centuries, some builders (e.g. Willis) made Vox humanas in the traditional manner of Regals, often the only timbre in the whole organ that could be regarded as traditional.

Waldflöte (Ger.). A 'forest flute' stop. (1) A wide-scaled conical metal Flute of 2' (sometimes $2\frac{2}{3}$' or $1\frac{1}{3}$') in 17th-century German organs; Praetorius referred to open pipes, though instruments in the Habsburg countries have stopped ones, most were wide-scaled.

(2) Open Flutes of 8' or 4' pitch in English, German and American organs of the 19th century, sometimes metal but usually wood.

Zimbel (Ger.; Eng. *Cimball, Cymbal*; Fr. *cymbale*; It.,

Cz. *cembalo*; Sp. *cimbala, zimbala*; Port. *resimbala*). The important high chorus Mixture separated from the basic Mixture as the *Blockwerk* became divided; in many cases the same as Scharf. (1) Some early Zimbeln contained a Tierce (Terzzimbel), c1450–1550 or later, Praetorius recommending such high Mixtures (15.17.19).

(2) The classical French Cymbale was a high Mixture of octaves and 5ths, the ranks breaking twice per octave (cymbalisée).

(3) The 'repeating Zimbel' was a single-rank or compound stop repeating at every octave, c1600–1750 in Germany, perhaps in reference to the medieval cymbala or small tuned bells.

Zimbelstern (Ger.). A very common toy stop, found mostly in northern Europe c1490–1790 but occasionally elsewhere, and consisting of a revolving star placed towards the top of an organ case to whose wind-blown driving-wheel behind the case is attached a set of bells, tuned or (before c1700) untuned. Mattheson (1713) thought the effect good for feast days.

Zink (Ger.). Like Cornet, Zink denotes an imitative stop achieving a cornett-like tone either with reed pipes or as a compound flue stop. (1) A Tierce Mixture of the latter type in some early 16th-century contracts.

(2) A reed or Regal stop in others of the same period; later, 'Zinken oder Cornett' was normally a reed stop of the Schalmei kind, particularly a pedal 2' reed stop useful for cantus firmus melodies in Lutheran Germany.

BIBLIOGRAPHY

J. I. Wedgwood: *A Comprehensive Dictionary of Organ Stops* (London, 1905)
N. A. Bonavia-Hunt: *Modern Organ Stops* (London, 1923)
C. Mahrenholz: *Die Orgelregister: ihre Geschichte und ihr Bau* (Kassel, 1930, enlarged 2/1942/R1968)
G. A. Audsley: *Organ-stops and their Artistic Registration* (New York, 1949)
W. L. Sumner: *The Organ* (London, 1952, 4/1973)
T. Schneider: *Die Namen der Orgelregister* (Kassel, 1958)
P. Smets: *Die Orgelregister, ihr Klang und Gebrauch* (Mainz, 1958)
P. Hardouin: 'Essai d'une sémantique des jeux de l'orgue', *AcM*, xxxiv (1962), 29
S. Irwin: *Dictionary of Pipe Organ Stops* (New York, 1962)
P. Williams: *The European Organ 1450–1850* (London, 1966/R1978)
Mahrenholz, Sumner and Williams include further bibliography.

PETER WILLIAMS, BARBARA OWEN

Organum hydraulicum (Lat.). WATER ORGAN.

Orgatron. An ELECTRONIC ORGAN developed by Frederick Albert Hoschke and manufactured by the Everett Piano Co. in South Haven, Michigan, between 1934 and 1940. The Orgatron was taken over in 1946 by Wurlitzer, who used an improved and modified version of the principle in their electronic organs until the mid-1960s. The Orgatron was designed for use in churches and was the first electronic organ to be manufactured on a large scale. Several one- and two-manual models were produced; the STM-1, for example, offered the resources of a small standard church organ with two five-octave manuals, a 32-note pedal-board and five stops; it also included tubular chimes. The sounds were generated by reeds installed in a soundproof chamber and operated by suction; the vibrations of the reeds were converted by electrostatic pickups into voltage variations and made audible over a loudspeaker (this sound-generating system was based on a patent by BENJAMIN F. MIESSNER). Tremolo was produced by means of a motorized paddle that rotated in front of the loudspeaker.

HUGH DAVIES

Orgelbau Bautzen. German firm of organ builders; *see* EULE.

Orgelbewegung (Ger.). A term sometimes used to refer to the organ revival of the early 20th century; *see* ORGAN, §VII.

Orgelklavier (Ger.). CLAVIORGAN.

Orgelleier (Ger.). LIRA ORGANIZZATA.

Orglice. PANPIPES of Slovenia (Yugoslavia). The instrument is symmetrical in form, with the longest pipes in the middle.

Orgue à manivelle [de Barbarie] (Fr.). BARREL ORGAN.

Orgue de chambre [orgue de salon] (Fr.). CHAMBER ORGAN.

Orgue des ondes (Fr.: 'organ of the waves'). *See* COUPLEUX–GIVELET ORGAN.

Orgue expressif (Fr.; Ger. *Expressionsorgel*). An organ containing free-reed pipes with resonators, a precursor of the REED ORGAN. It was exhibited in Paris by Gabriel-Joseph Grenié in 1810. Its double bellows and reservoir system permitted dynamic variation through control of wind pressure by the player's feet on blowing treadles. The term 'orgue expressif' was later applied to any French harmonium having this kind of expression capability.

Orgue hydraulique (Fr.). WATER ORGAN.

Orgue radiosynthétique (Fr.: 'radiosynthetic organ'). A four-manual electroacoustic pipe organ, designed by Abbé Pujet in France in 1934 and constructed by Cavaillé-Coll, with electrical work by the firm of Thompson-Houston. The pipes were enclosed in three chambers and the sounds from each chamber were amplified by means of a microphone and loudspeaker. Some of the lowest notes were produced as difference tones, and timbres were synthesized by mixtures of pipes with 'neutral' timbres; the total number of pipes for 51 stops was thereby reduced from the more than 4000 needed in a conventional organ of this size to only 1200, none of which had to be more than 2·5 metres long. The shortcomings of the instrument included the quality of the amplification system and the picking up by the microphones of incidental mechanical noises. At least one organ constructed to Pujet's design was installed in a church – the Maronite Church of Notre Dame du Liban in Paris.

BIBLIOGRAPHY
J. Castellan: 'Les grandes orgues et l'électricité', *Science et vie*, lxxi (1947), 115

HUGH DAVIES

Orgue trompette. *See* SALPING ORGANUM.

Orguinette. Trade name of a small automatic REED ORGAN made by the Mechanical Orguinette Co. of New York (founded in 1878 and later absorbed by the Aeolian Co.).

Ori. End-blown composite trumpet of the Bari people of north-eastern Zaïre. It is made from strips of bamboo held together by coiled lengths of bark (*LaurentyA*, 343).

Oribao. JEW'S HARP of the northern Philippines. *See* AFIW.

Oribe. Four-tube PANPIPES of the Ocaina Indians of the Peruvian tropical forest region.

Oriri. Single-headed drum of the Igbo people of Nigeria.

Oriwa. End-blown gourd trumpet of the Logo people of north-eastern Zaïre; it is also known as *kangamva* (*LaurentyA*, 308).

Orkes. A term (from the Dutch *orkest*: 'orchestra') used throughout Indonesia and parts of Malaysia for a variety of relatively recent instrumental groups. It is most common in Minahasa, North Sulawesi, where it refers to any kind of instrumental ensemble. The *orkes bambu melalu* or *orkes bambu suling* comprises about 12 to 20 *suling* (bamboo flutes) and trumpets. It has become known as a national Indonesian ensemble under the name 'Musik bambu'. The flutes play mainly diatonic melodies accompanied by harmonies on the *overtoon* and other bamboo trumpets of various pitches. Similar ensembles are called *pompang* in Ambon, Maluku, and *bas-suling* in the Toraja area of central Sulawesi. A similar ensemble, the *orkes bambu seng*, consists of about 20 bamboo and zinc flutes and trumpets. Other ensembles found in Minahasa include the *orkes bia*, an ensemble of about 20 conch-shell trumpets of various sizes, which have holes pierced in the shells to control pitch and volume; *orkes kolintang*, an orchestra of xylophones (*see* KOLINTANG); *orkes oli*, comprising two *oli* (jew's harps), one *arababu* (fiddle), two *sasahaeng* (bamboo idiophone–aerophones) and two *bansi* (duct flutes); and the *orkes papurungan*, an ensemble consisting of *bia*, *rebana* (frame drum) or *gendang* (double-headed cylindrical drum), *kolintang*, *bansi* and *momongan* (gong).

In the Ngada area of eastern Flores and on Lembata island, the *orkes suling* consists of at least 40 bamboo ring flutes and two drums. The flutes are of six sizes, all with six finger-holes, a hole covered in leaf below a cork stopper or node in the bamboo, and a hole below the node for blowing. The holes are burnt into the tube with a hotspike. The *suling bas* (bass flute) is about 70 cm long and 3 cm in diameter, the *suling bariton* about 60 cm long and 3 cm wide, the two *suling alto* and the *suling sopran* about 45 cm long and 1·5 cm wide, and the *suling pikolo* about 8 cm long and 1 cm wide. An orchestra may consist of one or two *suling pikolo*, six to eight *suling bas* and seven or eight *suling alto*, placed from left to right in front; 15 to 20 *suling sopran* four rows of players) and seven or eight *suling bariton* in the middle; and a large and small drum at the back. The players face a conductor standing in front. The orchestra plays at church celebrations and weddings, and formerly played many Dutch marches.

Ensembles are often used on specific occasions such as accompanying theatre performances, festive occasions and weddings. Theatre ensembles include the *orkes*

Abdul Muluk which accompanies Abdul Muluk theatre shows on the South Sumatra and Jambi coasts. In Jambi province it comprises one or more *biola* (violin), a *jidur* (drum) and a *ketawak-tawakan* (gong). In the Palembang area it comprises three *biola*, a *jidur* and a *ketawak* (gong). The *orkes lenong* accompanies all-night *lenong* theatre performances in Jakarta, Java. It often comprises two large and one small *gendang* (double-headed cylindrical drums), a *kecrek* (pair of metal bars beaten rhythmically together), a *gambang* (xylophone), a *bonang* (gong-chime), a pair of *goöng* (gongs), a *suling* and a *rebab* (spike fiddle).

The *orkes penggual* of the Karo area of North Sumatra is used to accompany festive outdoor occasions, such as Independence Day celebrations. It consists of one large *sarune* (oboe) or *biola*, two *gung* (gongs), of which one is a *gung penganak* (small gong), two *gendang Melayu* (double-headed Malay drums) and a singer. It plays mostly popular Karo or Malay songs, often to accompany the Karo version of the Malay *ronggeng* dance as it is practised on the east coast of North Sumatra. The vocal melodies are often harmonically generated but are accompanied in non-harmonic Karo fashion by the drums and gongs. The *orkes gambus* is found in Muslim areas of Malaysia and Indonesia, including the northern coast of Java and the coast of West Sumatra. It consists of several *gambus* (lutes), *biola* and vocalists. The repertory consists of religious and love songs which show Middle Eastern influence. The *orkes Lampung* of Lampung province, Sumatra, comprises a *biola*, *gambus*, *suling*, *gendang* and two *ketipung* or *marwas* (small double-headed drums).

Recently developed ensembles include the *orkes Melayu* and the *orkes talempong*. The *orkes Melayu*, a Malay orchestra, plays harmonic music developed in the past few centuries in Malay-speaking coastal areas of Indonesia and Malaysia. It is also often referred to as *dung-det* after the most common sound pattern of one of its drums. It is especially popular in the Minangkabau coastal area of West Sumatra, where many items in its repertory have developed, and reflects the history of trading contacts with the Middle East and Europe. Indian film music has influenced its style recently. The ensemble may include *tambur* (tambourines), bongo drums, *dombak* (single-headed goblet-shaped drum), *dholak* (an Indian drum), a *śruti-box* (Indian style harmonium), accordeon, *biola*, guitars and even organ, piano and band percussion. The *orkes talempong* of Padang Panjang, West Sumatra, a large modern orchestra mainly of bronze instruments, was specially created for the academy and conservatory there. It comprises *aguang* (suspended bossed gongs), four sets of four *canang* (horizontal bossed gongs), six to eight sets of four *talempong* (horizontal gongs), a *gandang* (drum), a *sadam* (duct flute) and a *saluang* (end-blown flute). The horizontal gongs are arranged in carved wooden frames with legs so that the players, who beat them with soft wooden hammers, play standing. The instruments are traditional but their combination in this orchestra, their playing positions and their repertory are modern.

MARGARET J. KARTOMI

Orlo (Sp.). A word used of a wind instrument, perhaps the CRUMHORN.

Orlos (Sp.). An ORGAN STOP.

Ornaments. Those more or less brief and conventional formulae of embellishment which have always been liable to occur within traditions of free ornamentation (*see* IMPROVISATION), and which proliferated in European music of the Baroque period. (*See also* CADENZA.)

I. Introduction. II. The appoggiatura family. III. The shake family. IV. The division family. V. Compound ornaments. VI. The English virginalists' strokes. VII. The ornaments summarized by function. VIII. Index to ornaments and table of signs.

I. Introduction. Throughout much of the history of western European music, performers have been inclined to embellish the notes provided them by the composer. Even in the Middle Ages and the Renaissance, it is convenient to make a distinction between two kinds of embellishment. On the one hand, the technique of applying improvised or semi-improvised running figuration patterns to a given melody, so-called divisions or *passaggi*, creates melodic variation. Graces, on the other hand, are conventional melodic ornaments applied to single notes; by the Baroque era graces were indicated by a variety of stylized signs, most of which had, at least by intention, a particular meaning.

Signs indicating ornaments appear even in chant notation. SIGNIFICATIVE LETTERS added beside neumes in some Western chant notations, for example, affect the rhythm, pitch or manner of execution of the notes, and the so-called liquescent neumes (such as the quilisma and the shape later called the plica) appear to indicate some special kind of voice production, perhaps the constricting of a note in order to help articulation. Some medieval writers on chant and on polyphony describe ornamentation, as Edward Roesner (1979) among others, has pointed out. But the earliest stylized signs indicating precisely where unwritten graces were to be added would seem to be those used in some manuscripts of keyboard music in the 14th and 15th centuries. The Robertsbridge manuscript, dating from the first half of the 14th century, includes small circles above some notes, which may or may not indicate ornaments. Special symbols, normally a (second) downward stem attached to a note, to which a triangular loop has been added, certainly indicate ornaments in all the German manuscripts of keyboard music written during the 15th century, not only the Buxheim Organbook but also the smaller tablatures (published by Willi Apel). There is little doubt that these signs instruct the player to add an ornament, but no source makes clear precisely which is intended, or even whether the signs indicate a particular kind of decoration or merely signal the place where any appropriate ornament could (or should) have been added.

The distinction between divisions and graces was made, or at least implied, by a number of writers in the 16th century. For example, Martin Agricola in his *Musica instrumentalis deudsch* (1529, 5/1545) states that all instrumentalists should learn how to decorate their performances the way organists did, with 'Coloriren' or 'Coloratur', that is, *passaggi* as well as 'Mordanten' (i.e. graces). And although Silvestro di Ganassi devoted almost all his recorder treatise, *Fontegara* (1535), to *passaggi*, near the end he wrote that the easiest ornaments of all are *tremoli*, by which he meant the graces now called trill and mordent. Diego Ortiz, in his viol treatise, *Trattado de glosas sobre clausulas* (1553), also seems to have distinguished between graces and divisions when he advised viol players to mix some 'quiebros amortiguados' (muted trills) among their 'passos' or *passaggi*. And with varying degrees of clarity and detail authors throughout the rest of the century continued to divide ornaments into these two separate but related categories.

Attempts to indicate particular ornaments were not by any means clear or consistent in the 16th century. Musicians evidently experimented with various kinds of signs to indicate graces and these appeared chiefly in tablatures for plucked instruments and for keyboards, 'playing scores' that indicate details of performance more explicitly than other kinds of source. A number of anthologies of lute music from the 16th century, for example, include idiosyncratic signs for various kinds of ornaments. Thus Vicenzo Capirola in his manuscript anthology of about 1517 used dotted red numbers to identify the upper auxiliary of a mordent and two dots above the number of the fret for the grace he called 'tremolo d'un tasto solo' (a tremolo on one fret), by which he meant a mordent, usually alternating between the first fret and the open string. And in the 1548 Milanese edition of Pietro Paolo Borrono's music, the anonymous editor inserted parentheses to isolate the two notes of a mordent. Diana Poulton (1975) describes and explains other kinds of grace that appear in English lutebooks of the 16th and early 17th centuries; Howard Mayer Brown in his book on embellishing 16th-century music (1976) included a table of 16th-century graces, derived from Italian and Spanish treatises, that consist mostly of so-called *tremoli* (i.e. mordents) and *groppi* (trills), with a handful of more specialized signs found only in one or two sources and thus apparently not widely used during the period. English virginalists also indicated graces by adding diagonal strokes to the stems of some notes. The precise meaning of the strokes is not clear; for further details see §VI below.

In short, the 15th and 16th centuries appear to have been a time of experimentation with graces and ways of indicating them. By the second half of the 16th century, the mordent and the trill were clearly differentiated even if separate unambiguous signs for them were not yet in common use. It may be no exaggeration to suggest that instrumentalists in the 16th century had already begun to add a trill or some similar ornament to the penultimate note at most cadences (there is even evidence to suggest that some of the trills were unmeasured).

The Baroque tendency to favour specific ornaments received particular impetus from French lutenists of the 17th century, imitated directly by soloists on the bass viol and the harpsichord. No other national school elaborated so extensive and complex a series of signs for indicating ornaments, but the French signs and usages were imported and adapted with increasing thoroughness in some German schools during and after the lifetime of J. S. Bach, whose harpsichord music is so much indebted to the French; C. P. E. Bach amplified and modified the French ornaments to form a group that remained in standard use until the generation of Beethoven and never altogether lost its influence.

The proliferation of ornaments and the proliferation of their signs were not entirely the same. In some national schools, for instance in Italy, ornaments were often left unnotated or vaguely notated. Certainly the French harpsichordists, who used the most numerous and elaborate signs, also used the most numerous and elaborate ornaments: but ornaments not appearing in notation were habitually used elsewhere more than in France.

The signs for ornaments were often used casually, inconsistently and uncertainly. This is just as true of J. S. Bach as of most others; for whereas he was untypical in notating most of the figuration which others would have left to be supplied as free ornamentation, he was quite typical in using the signs for specific ornaments inconsistently. Insofar as he had definite intentions they must be gleaned rather from the music than from the notation, by recovering the Baroque understanding of what makes good ornaments in what contexts. And indeed in general, apart from French music for the lute, bass viol or harpsichord, it is more often the context than the signs which must lead to an interpretation of the ornaments required. No single rendering should be taken as definitive; the typical Baroque preference was to leave the ornaments, like so many other elements in the interpretation, to the spontaneous invention of the performer guided by common conventions of which some were permissive though others (particularly for cadential trills and for appoggiaturas in recitative) were almost as specific as if they had been part of the notation. It is crucial however that the performer's option be exercised within the boundaries of the style. There are the outer boundaries of that general Baroque style which, however diversified, retains nevertheless something distinctive in comparison with earlier and later periods (to mention the most rudimentary case, a Baroque trill normally begins on the beat and on the upper note). There are also the local and temporal boundaries of the many Baroque styles individually, which set their own distinctive limitations and their own requirements.

The musical illustrations in Baroque tables of ornaments provide valuable approximations of the actual rhythms and stresses in performance. No table however can show exactly how an ornament will sound; the nuances are as important as the notes and are very hard to learn except by hearing good demonstrations. An understanding of what the table intends has to be built up from seasoned experience of how the commonest ornaments shape up in actual sound. Of course the tables are particularly useful in those rather special situations, of which French harpsichord music is the leading example, where a multiplicity of signs must be minutely understood and scrupulously interpreted. But not even in the case of François Couperin, who complained of performers who failed to render his ornaments as specified, is there any artistic (still less any moral) obligation to perform every ornament as it is notated. On the contrary, the performer retains the usual Baroque liberty to make the interpretation ultimately his own affair, and should therefore change an ornament if he cannot bring it off stylishly as it stands. Nonetheless, since Couperin expressly asked for (but evidently did not always get) a definitive rendering of his notated ornaments, the performer will certainly want to follow his recommendations in the main, and will find this greatly to the advantage of the music. The care taken by Couperin and a number of other French composers, together with their German imitators, merits the performer's care in return.

Since one ornament may be given different signs and different names, and one sign or name may be given to different ornaments, the ornaments must be understood by their substance rather than by their appearance in notation or their appellation in treatises. The most common ornaments (and the most necessary in ordinary circumstances) are not complicated; they fall into a few serviceable types, of which long appoggiaturas, upper-note trills, accented slides, turns and quick mordents provide most of the later Baroque requirements. In circumstances (usually French or derived from French) where the performer must execute complicated deviations from these basic ornaments, it is often very difficult to provide a definitive interpretation of their signs, because most areas in which serious disagreement obtains among modern scholarly interpreters were almost certainly open to as much disagreement among Baroque performers themselves. The evidence is most consistent for the most basic ornaments, especially the long appoggiatura (e.g. in recitative) and the cadential trill; the least basic ornaments, on the other hand, offer the most scope for individuality.

In order to help to cut through the confusion of Baroque signs and names to an understanding of their substance, this article will consider both the historical development and the artistic function of the chief families of Baroque ornaments. This was not systematically attempted by contemporary writers; but there is a hint in C. P. E. Bach's suggestive reflections in part i of his *Versuch über die wahre Art das Clavier zu spielen* (1753). This valuable source is mostly though not invariably reliable for late Baroque procedures, including those of his father, from whom he claimed to have learnt the larger part of what he knew (for a contrary view, however, see Neumann, 1978).

'No-one at all doubts the necessity of ornaments', wrote C. P. E. Bach (p.51); they are 'indispensable':

[They] connect notes; they enliven them; they give them where necessary a special emphasis and weight; they make them agreeable and arouse as a consequence a special attention; they help to make the content clear; whether this is sad or joyful or otherwise constituted as it may be, in such manner they always contribute to it their own [share]; they afford a considerable part of the occasion and the material for true performance.

This description suggests various musical functions which for practical purposes will be distinguished in §VII under the headings of melody (for those ornaments that, in C. P. E. Bach's phrase, 'connect notes'), rhythm (for those that give 'emphasis and weight'), harmony (for many of those that contribute to a disposition 'sad or joyful or otherwise'), and coloration. In §§II–VI however the ornaments will be surveyed historically by family. (For ornaments used in continuo accompaniment *see* Continuo, §5.)

II. The appoggiatura family. In principle, this group comprises those ornamental notes that 'lean' (the Italian verb is *appoggiare*) on the following, so-called 'main' note, which is written in normal notation. In the appoggiatura proper, formerly called forefall, backfall, halffall, beat, prepare or lead (Fr. *appoggiature, port de voix, chute, accent, appuy, coulé*; Ger. *Vorschlag, Accent*; It. *appoggiatura, portamento*), the main note is postponed by a single conjunct or disjunct accessory note. Disjunct appoggiaturas are comparatively rare, but when they do occur their rhythmic interpretation is the same as that of a conjunct appoggiatura. If the accessory note is a tone or semitone above its main note it is called a descending or superior appoggiatura (backfall; Fr. *coulé, chute*, etc, *en descendant*; Ger. *Accent fallend*). If it is a tone or semitone below the main note it is called an ascending or inferior appoggiatura (forefall; Fr. *coulé, chute*, etc, *en montant*; Ger. *Accent steigend*). The old English term 'half-fall' refers to an appoggiatura ascending by a semitone.

Quantz stated (1752, p.77) that an appoggiatura,

being a retardation from the note before, may be taken from above or below, according to the note which precedes it. When the note before is one or two steps higher than that which bears an appoggiatura, this must be taken from above. When the note before is lower, it must be taken from below.

His rule is useful, but not invariable. C. P. E. Bach (1753, p.62) said merely that 'an appoggiatura may be a repetition of the note before or otherwise' (and added that 'the following [i.e. main] note can go [by step] upwards and downwards and can leap'). Where the appoggiatura is a repetition of the note before, it may be accurately described as a note of retardation, on the analogy of its opposite, the note of anticipation. An appoggiatura which proceeds by leap is, in fact, ordinarily a note of retardation, as shown in ex.1 (C. P. E. Bach, Table III, fig.1). The appoggiatura proper may

Ex.1

vary greatly in length, depending on its musical and historical context. Moreover, while it would be desirable to limit the meaning of the word to this particular type of ornament, the leading authorities have not done so. This article therefore surveys the history and interpretation of the appoggiatura itself under five headings, and then discusses four types of ornament that belong to the same family even though they are not examples of the appoggiatura proper.

1. The indeterminate appoggiatura. 2. The long appoggiatura. 3. The short appoggiatura. 4. Unwritten appoggiaturas. 5. Post-Baroque appoggiaturas. 6. The double appoggiatura. 7. The slide. 8. The simultaneous appoggiatura. 9. The passing appoggiatura.

1. THE INDETERMINATE APPOGGIATURA. Appoggiaturas shown by early Baroque authorities tend to be moderately short and to fulfil a melodic rather than a harmonic function. But as the appoggiatura gradually acquired, during the Baroque period, a predominantly harmonic function, the long appoggiatura came to be distinguished with growing explicitness from the short. C. P. E. Bach made this distinction the foundation of his treatment: he called long appoggiaturas 'variable' because of the diversity of rules governing their duration in different contexts, and short appoggiaturas 'invariable' (which does not however, rule out some leeway for nuance). This basis of classification has been the source of considerable subsequent confusion, because it seems to imply that a 'variable' appoggiatura may be arbitrarily shortened; but such is not the case. Appoggiaturas of moderate length occurred with striking effect in the Celtic tradition of vertical harmony recalled by the Jacobean harp manuscript *GB-Lbm* Add.14905, which Dolmetsch transcribed in 1937. Ex.2 is from his table of ornaments.

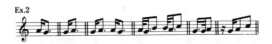

Ex.2

In the central medieval tradition of horizontal harmony, melodic steps equivalent to appoggiaturas abound; there is no reason to doubt that the ornament was also introduced impromptu. To some extent, however, movement by appoggiatura was supplanted during the

Renaissance by suspensions. The Baroque age restored to the appoggiatura an importance which it has never since lost. During the 19th century it ceased to be regarded as an ornament and became incorporated in the written melody. In this form the Romantics relied on it extensively; it is ubiquitous in Wagner and Mahler, both short and long, but particularly long.

Praetorius showed appoggiaturas (2/1619, p.233) among a large number of alternative connecting figures under the general heading of *accenti*. His appoggiaturas ascend by a tone or semitone and take a third from the time of their succeeding main note; he attached no special prominence to them, and the contexts in which he showed them are typical only of the early Baroque styles, as can be seen in ex.3. Frescobaldi and other early Baroque composers used written-out appoggiaturas fairly frequently. Those in ex.4 (from Frescobaldi's *Partite sopra l'aria della Romanesca* and from the second *Toccata avanti il ricercare* in his *Fiori musicali*) are short and on the beat, and include a preparation by leap as well as by step.

Ex.3

Ex.4

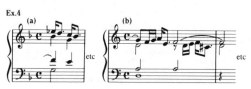

Conjunct appoggiaturas are shown by a number of other 17th-century authorities from Mersenne (1636–7) onwards, under a variety of names, and in a majority of cases short. The ascending appoggiatura is called a beat by Simpson (1659) and Playford (1660 and later edns.), a forefall by Locke (1673) and Purcell (1699) and a half-fall ('ever from a Half-note beneath') by Mace (1676). Their sign is an ascending stroke, and the explanations shown in exx.5a (Playford) and 5b (Purcell) are typical.

Ex.5

(a) A beat   (b) A forefall

These 17th-century writers call the descending appoggiatura a backfall. Their sign is either a stroke like that of the forefall but descending (Purcell, as in ex.6, and Locke) or a comma above or to the left of the main note (Playford – as in ex.7 – Simpson and Mace). Grassi-

Ex.6

(a) A backfall   (b) A plain note and shake

Ex.7   A backfall

neau's signs (1740, p.102) are the same; his terms, by then perhaps standard in English, are forefall and backfall. Prelleur (1731) concurred, and T.B.'s *Compleat Musick-master* (3/1722, p. 27) used these terms but gave different signs for the viol.

2. THE LONG APPOGGIATURA. In late 17th-century France, and elsewhere during the 18th century, the fairly short appoggiatura yielded in popularity to the long one. Ex.8a shows how D'Anglebert (1689) illustrated the 'Cheute ou port de voix en montant' and 'en descendant'; ex.8b is from Dieupart (c1720). The flautist Jacques Hotteterre, like Dieupart and others, restricted the term 'port de voix' to ascending appoggiaturas, but used 'coulement' (from *couler*: 'to slur') for the descending appoggiatura (1707, p.28):

> The Port-de-voix is a stroke of the tongue anticipated by a step, beneath the Note on which one wishes to make it. The Coulement is taken a step above, and hardly ever occurs except in descending intervals of a Third . . . often one links mordents with Ports-de-voix.

His illustrations are shown in ex.9.

Ex.8
(a)

Cheute ou port de voix en montant   en descendant

(b)

Port de voix   Cheute
Forefall up   Backfall

Ex.9

(a) Ports-de-voix

(b) Coulements

Ex.10 is from J. S. Bach's *Clavier-Büchlein vor Wilhelm Friedemann Bach* (1720). There are no sufficient grounds in any contemporary evidence for doubting that the great majority of J. S. Bach's appoggiaturas are long, however notated, and that this example, so far as it goes, is characteristic of his music. Gottlieb Muffat's *Componimenti* (c1739) shows a similar execution; his signs are a quaver printed small (as so often later) and the inclined strokes of the English notation.

In his books of 1749 and 1751 Geminiani demon-

Ex.10

Accent   Accent
steigend   fallend

strated the descending appoggiatura as in ex.11, and stated:

> The Superior Apogiatura is supposed to express Love, Affection, Pleasure, etc. It should be made pretty long, giving it more than half the length or time of the Note it belongs to, observing to swell the Sound by Degrees. . . . If it be made short, it will lose much of the aforesaid qualities; but will always have a pleasing effect, and it may be added to any note you will. . . .
>
> The Inferior Apogiatura has the same qualities with the preceding, except that it is much more confin'd, as it can only be made when the Melody rises the Interval of a second or third, observing to make a Beat on the following Note.

Ex.11

By 'making a beat' Geminiani meant adding a mordent on the main note. So common was this combination that several English expositors used the term 'beat' for the combined ornament, or even for the appoggiatura itself (as has been mentioned); Mace used 'beat' for a plain mordent. The combination of appoggiatura and mordent is the normal Baroque interpretation of the French *port de voix*, the *pincé* (mordent) on its resolution being taken for granted.

Swelling the sound in all possible contexts was an obsession of Geminiani's. In this context it can seldom amount to more than a mild *sforzando* introduced (as the true *sforzando* should be) just after the attack. It is not very often desirable; what really matters is to die away on the main note, which forms the resolution. Witness Galliard, in a footnote to his translation (1742) of Tosi's *Opinioni*: 'you lean on the first to arrive at the note intended; and you dwell longer on the Preparation than on the Note for which the preparation is made'; Couperin (1716, p.22): 'strike [appoggiaturas] with the harmony, that is to say in the time which would be given to the succeeding note'; Quantz (p.77, writing for flute players, but giving generally applicable principles): 'The tongue should mildly stress the appoggiaturas, swell them, if there is time, and slur the ensuing note somewhat more softly. This sort of grace is called Abzug and is derived from the Italians'; and C. P. E. Bach (1753, p.64): 'all appoggiaturas are played louder than the succeeding note, including any ornaments which it may carry, and are slurred with it, whether slurs are written or not'.

These last two rules are of paramount importance, especially for long appoggiaturas. The appoggiatura itself takes the beat and thus (usually with emphasis) the accent which would otherwise have been taken by the main note. Only the main note of course is delayed; the rest of the chord is struck on the beat, simultaneously with the appoggiatura. By far the commonest and most typical appoggiaturas form discords (or at least 4ths); the main note is then to be regarded as literally the resolution of the appoggiatura and, like all Renaissance, Baroque and Classical notes of resolution, must sound more softly than the discordant note that it resolves. To slur a discord into its resolution is generally appropriate, and in the case of appoggiaturas this instruction must be regarded as invariable. These points are confirmed by Quantz (p.77):

> Appoggiaturas . . . are not only ornaments but actual necessities . . . if a melody is to have a refined appearance, it must always have more concords than discords. But when there are several consonances in succession, and after some quick notes there comes a long consonance, the ear can easily get tired of it. Dissonances are sometimes needed then to stimulate and awaken it. This is where

appoggiaturas can make a great contribution; for they turn into dissonances, as 4ths and 7ths, when they are before the [main note] third or sixth . . . resolved by the following [main] note.

and by C. P. E. Bach (p.75):

> Appoggiaturas . . . improve the melody as well as the harmony . . . they smooth connections between notes, shorten notes which might seem too long, and please the ear by a repetition of the sound before . . . they bring variety to the harmony, which in their absence might seem too simple.

These passages draw attention to melodic as well as harmonic functions; when appoggiaturas are long, however, it is their harmonic function which is most significant and characteristic.

Ex.12 is from Quantz's Table VI, illustrating some of his rules (pp.79f) for deciding the length of appoggiaturas:

> Hold the appoggiatura half the length of the main note. [But] if the appoggiatura has to ornament a dotted note, that note is divided into three parts, of which the appoggiatura takes two, and the main note one only: that is to say, the length of the dot. . . . When in 6/4 or 6/8 time two notes are tied, and the first is dotted . . . hold the appoggiatura the complete length of the first note including its dot. . . . When an appoggiatura is attached to a note which is followed by a rest, give the whole length of the main note to the appoggiatura, and give the length of the rest to the main note.

Ex.12

C. P. E. Bach (pp.65ff) gave similar instructions but mentioned important exceptions:

> The general rule for the length of appoggiaturas is to take from the succeeding note, if duple, half its length, . . . and if triple . . . two-thirds of its length . . . there are cases in which [the appoggiatura] must be prolonged beyond its normal length for the sake of the expressive feeling conveyed. Hence it may take more than half the length of the succeeding [duple] note. Sometimes the length is determined by the harmony.

These last suggestions are particularly to be observed. The length of an appoggiatura must finally depend not on rule but on musicianship. When confronted with an 18th-century appoggiatura the performer may wisely start from the presumption that it is long (unless the context is one of those, described below, in which the true short appoggiatura is implied). If this presumption proves justified in practice he should attack the appoggiatura with conviction and hold it for the full duration indicated by its context in accordance with the rules already cited from Quantz and C. P. E. Bach. If circumstances warrant and the harmony permits he may even prolong it beyond the requirements of the rule for further expressiveness. Where an appoggiatura of extreme or even of standard length would weaken rather than strengthen the harmony, however, it must be curtailed in order to minimize the disadvantage. For example, an ornamental appoggiatura may occasionally be found superimposed on what is in effect an appoggiatura already written into the melody. Where the latter has already changed a concord into a discord, the superimposition is likely to restore the original situation by reverting to concord; and in such a case (rare, since fortunately even the Baroque imagination faltered at quite so self-negating a reduplication) Baroque authorities instruct the performer to make the superimposed appoggiatura as short as possible. There are other situations in which what is written as a discord becomes changed to concord by an appoggiatura, and here too the appoggiatura must be shortened. It would be hard to find clearer confirmation of the essentially harmonic value with which Baroque composers invested this ornament. Ex.13a and b (taken from Quantz's Table VI and discussed by him on p.79) should therefore be performed as in ex.13c and d respectively.

Ex.13

C. P. E. Bach (p.68) warned against introducing bad musical grammar by adding an appoggiatura where it will cause consecutive 5ths or octaves, and said that even the shortest appoggiatura is to be avoided in that event. But a majority of Baroque authorities added that incorrect progressions at the speed of most ornaments do not actually offend the ear and therefore such ornaments may be freely tolerated. Moreover consecutive 5ths or octaves are not incorrect when taken as accented passing notes, which most appoggiaturas are; such progressions are by no means to be avoided (ex.14, from the finale of C. P. E. Bach's first 'Prussian' Sonata, shows that he was capable of composing such progressions with written-out appoggiaturas). C. P. E. Bach pointed out

Ex.14

that a long appoggiatura forming an octave with the bass will make a weak effect even in the absence of forbidden consecutives, and his advice was to make such an appoggiatura short; the example from his Table IV cited on p.66 is in fact an ornamental appoggiatura superimposed on one already written into the melody (though he did not so describe it), and it is not easy to envisage this inherently weak situation arising elsewhere. He then added ex.15a, an appoggiatura forming a diminished octave, which he required to be taken long because of its particularly discordant character, presumably as in ex.15b.

In a few instances a composer may himself have carelessly misjudged the effect of introducing an appoggiatura, and where this is very evident the ornament should either be omitted or taken as short as possible. But ordinarily the solution intended can be found by a consideration of the harmony and will prove satisfactory provided that a correct length is given to the appoggiatura. In most cases the standard rules will determine the length, but where the consequence of applying them is musically weak or inconsistent, they must be brought to bear in the spirit but not in the letter. As regards consistency it should be remembered that imitative phrases require the same embellishment. Where the length of an appoggiatura seems doubtful at its first entry, subsequent imitation may occur in a context that decides the question unequivocally. The solution imposed by that context can then safely be transferred to other appearances, except in the very rare circumstance where, because the same solution is plainly impossible, consistency must be sacrificed to musical sense.

Dolmetsch (1915), in his excellent discussion of appoggiaturas, cited ex.16, from book 2 of the '48'.

Ex.16

According to Quantz's rule translated above in connection with ex.12, the first pair of these appoggiaturas should be played as crotchets, resolving on to the main notes where the ensuing rest appears; but the result would be nonsensical harmony. Moreover the second pair is not followed by a rest; it must (by a rule previously cited from Quantz) be played as quavers. The latter solution should therefore be applied to both pairs alike, and subsequently throughout the piece. This choice is confirmed by the fact that in bars 44–5 of the same prelude Bach indicated similar balancing phrases and wrote the quaver length in full ordinary notation instead of using ornamental appoggiaturas.

Where the main note is exceptionally long the appoggiatura may be resolved a little earlier than the strict rule would otherwise permit; but modern performers are more likely to make it too short than too long.

Where an appoggiatura is prefixed to a dotted note in duple time, the treatment of the note following the dot requires some elucidation. Fundamentally the situation is governed by a rule of very general application in Baroque music. C. P. E. Bach (p.127) stated it thus: 'The short notes following dots are always taken shorter than their written length'. Quantz added (p.270) that 'the dotted note must be stressed and the bow stopped' (i.e. a silence of articulation interpolated during the dot), which gives the interpretation shown in ex.17. The English translation (c1775) of Quantz's chapters on ornamentation illuminates the application of this rule to appoggiaturas (p.18).

Pointed [i.e. dotted] Semiquavers in slow Time, especially if Concords, as 3ds, 5ths, 6ths and 8ths found rather too languid with-

Ex.15

out they are intermix'd with Discords, as a 2d 4th 7th or 9th from which chiefly the Apogiatura takes its rise, which sometimes end by mezzo Trillos or Beats. . . . The short Note after the Point is always to be play'd very quick. An Apogiatura prefix'd to a pointed Note, must be play'd exactly to the time of the larger or principal Note, and the latter to the time of the Point, and be play'd softer than the former.

Ex.17

Taken in conjunction, these rules account for ex.18, from C. P. E. Bach (Table III, fig.6; cf p.65). He did not show a silence of articulation; presumably this was left as usual to the performer's option.

Ex.18

3. THE SHORT APPOGGIATURA. The short appoggiatura proper, which corresponds to what in 19th- and 20th-century music may be called a grace note or (incorrectly) an acciaccatura, is sometimes written in modern editions as a small quaver with a cross-stroke, but this notation did not become customary until the 19th century. In Baroque music the length of an appoggiatura must always be determined by context, rule and musicianship, and never by appearance. A small minority of late Baroque musicians attempted to indicate the length by their notation, but this practice remained exceptional. In Haydn, Mozart and even Beethoven the rules of Quantz and C. P. E. Bach still apply in almost all respects, and the appoggiaturas shown by these composers must be interpreted almost entirely in the light of the Baroque conventions, rather than by their literal appearance.

The main rules given by C. P. E. Bach for recognizing the short appoggiatura are as follows (1753, pp.65f):

It is only natural that the invariable short appoggiatura should most often appear before short notes. It is written [unfortunately only by C. P. E. Bach himself and a few others] with one, two, three or more tails, and is played so fast that the ensuing note loses scarcely any of its length. It also appears before long notes [especially] when a note is repeated . . . [or] with syncopations.
(14). When the appoggiaturas fill in leaps of a third, they are also short. But in an Adagio the sentiment is more expressive if they are taken as if the first quavers of triplets and not as semi-quavers. . . . The appoggiaturas before [actual] triplets are taken short to avoid obscuring the rhythm. . . . When the appoggiatura forms an octave with the bass other than a diminished octave it is taken short. . . . If a note rises a second and at once returns . . . a short appoggiatura will occur on the middle note.

From the numerous examples that C. P. E. Bach appended, those in ex.19 illustrate most of the contexts in which he required a short appoggiatura.

Ex.19

The attempt to establish an exact notation for appoggiaturas, avoiding uncertainty as to the length intended, seems to have originated in Marpurg's *Die Kunst das Clavier zu spielen* (1750). Marpurg showed the older

symbols such as a slanting cross, an inverted comma or a slanting line. And when he used the familiar 'grace notes' printed small he partly followed the normal fashion of leaving their length to convention, so that a long appoggiatura may be indicated by a 'grace note' of apparently short duration. Ex.20 illustrates however his partial attempt (Table III) to indicate their approximate duration. Quantz (p.77) merely stated that appoggiaturas

are written with little added notes, so that they shall not be mistaken for normal notes, and they take their value from the notes before which they are set. It scarcely matters whether they have more than one tail, or whether they have none. But it is customary to write them with only one tail. And those with two tails are only made use of before notes from which none [sic] of their value can be taken: as before one or more long notes, such as crotchets or minims, of the same pitch. These little notes with double tail are executed very briefly, whether taken from above or below, and they are taken on the beat of the main note.

This last statement confirms that even short appoggiaturas are played on the beat and not before it. They take its natural accent and may be further emphasized if desired. The convention of distinguishing short from long appoggiaturas by their notation was carried considerably further by C. P. E. Bach, who claimed general acceptance for it, though there is little evidence of this either in his day or later. The modern performer cannot be too strongly warned against ignore the apparent duration of the 'grace note' in music earlier than the second quarter of the 19th century – and even thereafter to view it with circumspection.

Ex.20

It should be remembered that the same length of appoggiatura will sound short in a slow passage but long in a fast passage; that the length of any appoggiatura must therefore be judged in relation to its main note; and that even the short appoggiatura is not in reality invariable but must be adapted to the harmony and other circumstances, though the latitude available to it is less than that of the long or 'variable' appoggiatura.

4. UNWRITTEN APPOGGIATURAS. Often the performer may or indeed should add an appoggiatura of appropriate duration even when there is no indication or sign in the written text. Both Quantz and C. P. E. Bach gave hints for recognizing such situations, and both stressed the absolute necessity for adding an appoggiatura in certain instances. C. P. E. Bach's rules are detailed, lengthy and informative but not easily summarized, and they should be consulted directly. Quantz wrote (p.77):

It does not suffice to know how to perform the appoggiaturas according to their character and difference, where they are indicated; you have also to know how to apply them suitably where they are not. Here is a rule which can be used for understanding them. When, after one or more short notes on the down or the up beat of the bar, there follows a long note which remains in consonant harmony, you must take an appoggiatura before the long note . . . the previous note will decide whether the appoggiatura should be taken from above or from below . . . appoggiaturas are mostly used before notes preceded or succeeded by faster notes . . . most trills demand an appoggiatura [as preparation].

There is one special case in which a convention of notation used throughout the 18th century necessitates an appoggiatura that is very far from obvious in the written text: in Baroque recitative many cadences, whether passing or final, appear to end on two repeated notes (so written to indicate to the accompanist the fundamental harmony) that are actually intended to be executed as an appoggiatura and its resolution, as in the second part of ex.21 (J. A. Scheibe in Marpurg's *Kritische Briefe*, 1760–64, p.352) and as suggested for ex.22 (from the Dublin manuscript of *Messiah*). So fond were Baroque musicians of this kind of appoggiatura that in what Tosi called a *cadenza tronca* ('truncated' or 'broken cadence') they preferred the second rendering shown in ex.23 (J. F. Agricola, 1757, p.154) even though it involves an appoggiatura that is dissonant as well as disjunct. Hansell ('The Cadence in 18th-century Recitative', *MQ*, liv (1968), p.228) hazarded that in such cases the appoggiatura was doubled by an acciaccatura in the accompanist's chord. Heinichen (1728, p.624) said that, while the best way to render recitative cadences was as in ex.24a, the rendering shown in ex.24b was among those sanctioned by long use in theatrical music and should therefore be tolerated as an exception to the general rules of harmonic logic. Whether the accompanist makes an acciaccatura or, perhaps more likely, a quick 4–3 suspension, the Baroque acceptance of an appoggiatura in this awkward situation indicates how unstylish it would be for a modern performer to omit it in exx.21, 22 or 24a. (See also Dean, 1977.)

Ex.21

Ex.22

Thou shalt break them　　with a rod of i - ron,

Thou shalt dash them to pieces　　like a potter's ves-sel.

Ex.23

e non a-mo-re.　　e non a-mo-re.

Ex.24

5. Post-Baroque appoggiaturas. A generation after C. P. E. Bach, Türk's *Clavierschule* of 1789 gave nine somewhat controversial rules for the use of appoggiaturas. Türk discussed both short and long appoggiaturas, including one of remarkable length, shown in ex.25;

Ex.25

Adagio　　taken

and he reiterated the normal rule that 'every long appoggiatura is to be played with more emphasis than the ensuing note'. There followed a period of some confusion, in which many ornaments underwent gradual transition, the appoggiatura among them. The transition may be traced through Cramer's *Instructions for the Pianoforte* (1812), Hummel's *Anweisung* (1828) and other works to Spohr's distinct but brief rules for both long and short appoggiaturas in his *Violinschule* of 1832:

> If the appoggiatura stands before a note which can be divided into equal parts, it obtains the half of its value. . . . . Before a note with a dot it obtains the value of the note, which then begins only at the dot. . . . . Where there are two dots the appoggiatura obtains the value of the note and this then begins with the first dot.

The first of these rules remains unchanged from the Baroque period. The second is also stated in the normal Baroque form, but without any reference to the complementary Baroque rule regarding tied notes in 6/4 or 6/8 time (i.e. that the appoggiatura should be held the complete length of the first note including its dot). This omission results in an ambiguity which may be illustrated from bars 12–16 in the slow movement of Beethoven's String Quartet op.127 (see ex.26). The Flonzaley Quartet, which generally retained a great deal of the 'Classical' tradition in its playing, took the appoggiaturas here as short semiquavers before the beat, thereby confirming the degradation of tradition in this particular respect, since neither musically nor musicologically is such a solution tenable. It is more usual and more nearly justifiable to take them as accented quavers on the beat. But Spohr's second rule would make them crotchets, and in this form they sound better still. Quantz's and C. P. E. Bach's rule for compound duple (in this instance quadruple) time would make them dotted crotchets, a solution perfectly feasible and, when its unfamiliarity has worn off, preferable in the musical context of this work.

Ex.26 Beethoven: String Quartet op.127, 2nd movt
Adagio, ma non troppo e molto cantabile

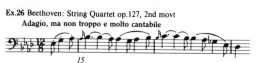

Like Türk, Spohr still confirmed the Baroque rule for timing and accentuation: 'As the appoggiatura always falls on the accented part of the bar, mark it more strongly than the note before, and always in one bowing'. This applies to both long and short appoggiaturas. Of the latter he merely wrote: 'The short appoggiatura, distinguished from the long appoggiatura by a cross-cut, lessens the note before which it stands by very little of its value. It is quickly and lightly united with this in one bowing'. This short value is thus still to be taken from the following note (i.e. on the beat) and not from the previous one.

The transition in the treatment of the appoggiatura came

near to completion by about the mid-19th century: long appoggiaturas were increasingly written into the melody as ordinary notes while short ones frequently continued to appear as ornaments. As Spohr already indicated, the short could be distinguished by a stroke across their tails; but this potentially valuable innovation, like so many others, failed to gain regular acceptance. In Baroque music it was not a regular convention, and in most cases today merely indicates the modern editor's opinion that the appoggiatura thus shown is to be taken short. In 19th- and 20th-century music this notation may be original, perhaps indicating a minimum length and a maximum sharpness; that is, it may distinguish the very short from the moderately short appoggiatura. But not even this distinction is to be relied upon, the stroked and the unstroked forms being still very inconsistently employed.

It has become customary, on no very good authority, to regard the majority of short appoggiaturas in 19th- and 20th-century music as intended to be brought before the beat (borrowing time from the previous instead of the ensuing note) and to be unaccented. There are a few uncertain instances where such treatment appears to have some sanction in the 19th-century tradition, and a still smaller number in which there is no uncertainty, notably Schumann's appoggiaturas, which are placed before the bar-line as an admirably clear indication that they are to be taken before the beat. The complaints of C. P. E. Bach and others show that a small minority either favoured or had unintentionally fallen into the same interpretation even in the Baroque period. Nevertheless the rule of playing short appoggiaturas on the beat must be regarded as the standard at all periods. The long appoggiatura is capable only of being taken on the beat unless of course it is misinterpreted as a short appoggiatura.

One of the most extreme exponents of the appoggiatura in the 20th century was Mahler. Long appoggiaturas incorporated in ordinary notation are so characteristic of both his melody and his harmony that they could not well be developed further. In many cases they are resolved only indirectly or not at all. They are very expressive and they afford an admirable instance of an ornament at first improvised, later prescribed and finally absorbed as an integral rather than an ornamental ingredient of style. Mahler also used the short appoggiatura, which his disciple Bruno Walter always took accented on the beat and with a slightly lingering timing, and which would fall far short of its intended effect if misplaced before the beat and unaccented.

6. THE DOUBLE APPOGGIATURA (Fr. *port de voix double*; Ger. *Anschlag*). This ornament consists of two preparatory notes, the second conjunct with and (usually) higher than the main note. Normally the first accessory note is also conjunct with the main note or is a repetition of the last note sounded. Marpurg (1756) illustrated both types (see ex.27a and b) and included an example with the first accessory note a step above the main note (ex.27c). This variant, though untypical of the orna-

ment, often appears written into the melody and was certainly not excluded altogether from improvised embellishment. Marpurg also showed a double appoggiatura in which the first accessory note was dotted – with curious effect in the interpretation of the ornament (ex.27d).

Quantz stated (p.134) that the double appoggiatura 'must be joined very quickly, but softly, to the [main] note. The [main] note must be slightly louder than the accessory notes'. He thus in effect distinguished the behaviour of the double appoggiatura from that of the appoggiatura proper. In his illustrations the first accessory note is a step below the main note (ex.28).

Ex.28

 etc

C. P. E. Bach however illustrated (pp.85ff) double appoggiaturas in which 'the preceding note is repeated and followed by the note above the main note' as well as those with 'the note below and then the note above' the main note. He added that in the latter type the first accessory note may be dotted, though not in rapid passages. He gave three rules: the accessory notes 'are played more softly than the main note'; nevertheless 'the [main] note yields as much of its length as the ornament requires' (in other words the ornament, though soft and unaccented, takes the beat); and 'all three notes', two accessory and one main, 'are slurred'.

Dolmetsch cited (p.258) ex.29 from J. S. Bach, a form of double appoggiatura in which the first accessory note does not fit the specifications recognized by theory. Its

Ex.29

treatment in performance is evidently identical with that of the regular forms. From the point of view of its function the double appoggiatura is not very well named; moreover, confusion can arise because the term is used with two other meanings. It may mean, quite naturally, a normal initial appoggiatura on two notes of the same chord simultaneously (as in ex.16), just as a triple or quadruple appoggiatura means three or four appoggiaturas so taken; it may also mean the ornament described in §7 under its admirable English name 'slide'. When found in Chopin and the 19th-century Romantics, the double appoggiatura should be treated in exact accordance with the rules of Quantz and C. P. E. Bach.

7. THE SLIDE (Fr. *coulé*; *flatté*; Ger. *Schleifer*). This ornament, also known as the elevation, whole-fall, slur or double backfall, consists of a little conjunct run of two accessory notes leading to its main note. Both ascending and descending forms are common, but the ascending is more typical. It may be dotted or undotted; again both forms are common, but the undotted form is more typical. It appears among the Celtic harp ornaments transcribed by Dolmetsch in 1937 (see ex.30). Caccini (1601/2, preface; translated by Playford, p.42)

Ex.27

Ex.30

confirmed that the slide was familiar in his day as an improvised connecting figure:

> There are some therefore that in the *Tuning* of the first *Note*, Tune it a *Third* under . . . it agrees not in many Cords, although in such places as it may be used, it is now become so ordinary, that instead of being a Grace (because some stay too long in the third Note under, whereas it should be but lightly touched) it is rather tedious to the Ear.

Bovicelli (1594) and Praetorius (2/1619, p.233) also showed the ascending slide, particularly in the dotted or more-than-dotted form disliked by Caccini. Ex.31a is from Playford's 'Table of graces proper to the viol or violin' (1660 and later edns., p.116), showing the descending slide as a 'double backfall' and indicating it with two commas (his sign for the descending appoggiatura or 'backfall' being the single comma shown in ex.7). Ex.31b shows his use of an upright cross to indicate an ascending slide or 'elevation'. Both slides are of the even, undotted form which may be taken as typical for the 17th century.

Ex.31

(a) A double backfall

(b) Elevation

Simpson (1659, p.12) concurred, and Mace (1676, p.105), though he called the ascending slide a 'wholefall', gave the same sign as Playford. Purcell (1699; see ex.32) called it a 'slur', a translation of the French *coulé*; his notation suggests the harmonic context in which an ascending slide may most freely be used (other circumstances permitting). This may be compared with Chambonnières' notation in his *Pièces de clavessin* (1670; see ex.33), where he showed the bottom note held in the manner that every harpsichordist of his day would instinctively favour in keeping with the normal technique of holding down notes of the same harmony for maximum resonance. This form of execution (the French term is 'coulé sur une tierce') may therefore be taken as correct and normal for keyboard instruments.

Ex.32

A slur is marked thus

Ex.33

Coulé

Ex.34, from D'Anglebert, clearly differentiates slides on a harmonic 3rd from those on a melodic 3rd, showing the lower note held only in the former case. Whether a keyboard player would nevertheless hold it in the latter depends chiefly on the harmonic movement. Saint-Lambert stated that D'Anglebert's three *coulés* on successive notes are intended for use only in *pièces graves* (that is why they are given in white notation); in organ music, which is implied, the lower note would not be held. Gottlieb Muffat (c1739) showed three dots under the normal slanting stroke when he wished the lower

note to be taken off short, thus suggesting that it would be normal to hold it. On other than keyboard instruments this refinement of course is not feasible.

Ex.34

sur 2 notes de suite   autre   autre

The dotted slide, somewhat neglected in the 17th century, returned to favour in the 18th, though without displacing the undotted slide. At this date it became somewhat mannered in execution and in this form is less generally applicable, being chiefly characteristic of the Berlin school of Quantz and C. P. E. Bach. Quantz (p.197) regarded the dotted version as standard: 'When, in a slow movement, one finds added small quavers, the first of which is dotted, they take the time of the succeeding main note, and the main note takes only the time of the dot. They must be played caressingly'. The undotted slide 'belongs to the French style rather than the Italian' and 'must not be played so slowly' but 'with rapidity'. Exx.35 and 36, from Marpurg (1756) and C. P. E. Bach (1753, p.107), cover the main varieties.

Ex.35

(a)

(b)

Ex.36

Walther (1708) is among a small minority showing the slide as a melodic ornament leading up to the beat (i.e. as unaccented passing notes) instead of in its basic function as a harmonic ornament on the beat. The great majority of authorities show the slide taken from the time of the succeeding note (i.e. accented and on the beat). Ex.37 (C. P. E. Bach, Table VI) is an extreme example. C. P. E. Bach also showed three-note slides which are in fact, as he himself stated, inverted turns.

The slides that open the first subject of Beethoven's String Quartet op.135 are best taken, throughout the movement, according to the normal Baroque and post-Baroque rules: accented and on the beat; modern custom misinterprets them in both respects. Similar examples are not at all uncommon in the 19th century. During the same period it became customary in keyboard music to write a tie across the ornament when the first note is meant to be held down.

Ex.37

8. THE SIMULTANEOUS APPOGGIATURA (Fr. *pincé étouffé*; Ger. *Zusammenschlag*; It. *acciaccatura*). This ornament consists of an accessory note a semitone below its main note; both are struck simultaneously, but the accessory note is no sooner struck than released, as shown in ex.38. In practice the ornament is confined to keyboard instruments. Though in construction it resembles an appoggiatura, in effect and function it more nearly approaches the mordent. Its Italian name means 'crushed stroke', its German name 'together-stroke', and its French name 'smothered mordent'.

Ex.38

Geminiani (1749, p.4) described the acciaccatura as 'perform'd by touching the key lightly, and quitting it with such a Spring as if it were Fire'. Marpurg and C. P. E. Bach both discussed it as a form of mordent; C. P. E. Bach wrote (1753, p.80) that 'it can only be taken suddenly, that is to say unslurred to the note before', which implies a silence of articulation before the ornament. There is no Baroque sign for it; but it will be found written as an extraneous note into the chord in a number of Baroque passages whose interpretation will not make sense until it is detected and treated correctly in the manner suggested by Geminiani. Except when it occurs in the middle of an arpeggiated chord, it takes the beat, and it is always more or less sharply accented.

Since the Italian name 'acciaccatura' has been familiarly but incorrectly anglicized to denote a rapid initial appoggiatura of the ordinary kind, the term 'simultaneous appoggiatura' is to be preferred. This term is an approximate translation of *Zusammenschlag*, which is comparable to the German names for the initial appoggiatura (*Vorschlag*: 'fore-stroke'), the passing appoggiatura next to be described (*Nachschlag*: 'afterstroke') and the double appoggiatura (*Doppelvorschlag*: 'double-forestroke').

There is also a species of non-harmonic passing note used in broken chords, which can be called 'passing acciaccatura' (see §IV, 4).

9. THE PASSING APPOGGIATURA (Ger. *Nachschlag, durchgehender Vorschlag*). This ornament consists of a passing note interpolated between two main notes a 3rd apart and descending (or, exceptionally, ascending). It was described by German authorities of the second half of the 18th century as an appoggiatura that flouts normal expectation by preceding the beat to which it is attached. They substantiated this view by showing it as slurred, not in the manner of a passing note to the note before, but in the manner of an appoggiatura to the note after. Nevertheless it is in substance not an appoggiatura (since it does not 'lean'), but a passing note unusually phrased. Its use (especially French) is quite important; only its

misclassification (as an appoggiatura instead of a passing note) is unfortunate, but too well established to be ignored here. Although taken between the beats, the passing appoggiatura may be accented, thus departing still further from the behaviour of a normal passing note. Quantz (p.78) stated distinctly that 'one must lengthen the dots, and accent the first of each two slurred notes'. Ex.39 is from his Table VI (his reference to Table IV is a misprint); he stated that ex.39a should be performed as in ex.39b and not as in ex.39d (which is actually one of the ways of playing ex.39c). Leopold Mozart (1756, pp.199f) suggested the same timing as did Marpurg (1750), who included ascending examples and turned to the left the tails of the small notes that indicated passing appoggiaturas. Türk (1789, p.231) referred to this useful distinction as already obsolete; unfortunately it was always exceptional.

Ex.39

It is by no means easy to recognize the passing appoggiatura where, as is often the case, its notation is identical with that of the appoggiatura proper. Quantz (p.78) provided this clue: 'There are two varieties of appoggiatura. Some are taken like accented notes on the accented beat'. These are the normal appoggiaturas. 'The others are taken like passing notes on the unaccented beats.' These are the passing appoggiaturas. At first sight Quantz, in calling them 'passing', appears to have been contradicting his own assertion, just quoted, that they must be accented; but he was no doubt speaking relatively: an unaccented beat readily submits to being preceded by a passing appoggiatura slightly more accented than itself. Ex.40 shows Dolmetsch's suggested interpretation (p.152) of what he considered passing appoggiaturas in J. S. Bach's 23rd prelude from book 2 of the '48'. Considerations both of melody and of harmony

Ex.40

should be taken into account when detecting passing appoggiaturas. As the symbols are usually identical, it is an excellent plan to give first priority to the normal long appoggiatura; if that is unsuitable, to try the normal short appoggiatura; and finally to attempt a passing appoggiatura. It is in this order that the Baroque appoggiaturas would almost certainly appear if numerically reckoned.

III. The shake family

1. The tremolo. 2. The vibrato. 3. Varieties of the trill. 4. Renaissance and early Baroque trills. 5. The Baroque trill. 6. Half-trills. 7. Later trills. 8. Varieties of the mordent. 9. Historical survey of mordents.

1. THE TREMOLO (Fr. *balancement*; Ger. *Bebung*; It. *tremolo, tremoletto, trillo, mordente fresco*). This ornament, also known as the organ shake or trill, consists of pulsations in the volume of a note. In modern usage the term describes a reiteration more distinct than was necessarily implied in the 17th and 18th centuries. The tremolo and the vibrato serve comparable functions and are sufficiently alike to have become occasionally confused. In the *Bebung*, an effect feasible only on the clavichord, the two are in fact not sharply distinguishable, since the mechanical action which produces a vibrato (or fluctuation in pitch) necessarily induces some degree of tremolo. Tremolos in the Celtic harp music transcribed by Dolmetsch in 1937 are illustrated in ex.41.

Ex.41

Under the name 'trillo' Praetorius (2/1619, p.237) gave several varieties of tremolo. Ex.42a shows the ornament in its purest form; ex.42b and c show it combined with its relative the *ribattuta*, a rhythmic variant of the modern trill or shake (see §3). As Praetorius

Ex.42

observed, 'these ornaments occur in Claudio Monteverdi', and they were in fact freely improvised by singers in a variety of contexts. Caccini gave examples in his *Nuove musiche* (1601/2) and Playford's translation (1664 and later edns.) gave additional instructions including the following:

The *Trill* . . . is by a beating in the Throat on the Vowel (*a'h*) . . . rather the shaking of the Uvula or Pallate on the Throat, in one sound, upon a Note . . . I have heard of some that have attained it by this manner, in singing a plain song, of 6 Notes up and 6 down, they have in the midst of every Note beat or shaked with their finger upon their Throat, which by often practice came to do the same Notes exactly without. . . . The *Trill*, or *Shake* of the Voice, being the most usual Grace, is made in *Closes, Cadences*, and other places, where by a long Note an *Exclamation* or *Passion* is expressed, the Trill is made in the latter part of any such Note; but most usually upon binding Notes in *Cadences* and *Closes*, and on that Note that precedes the closing Note. Those who once attain to the perfect use of the Trill, other Graces will become easie.

The vocal tremolo here described – almost certainly a medieval heritage – passes readily not only into the vibrato with which it is so commonly confused, but also

into a still wider fluctuation of pitch, namely a trill in the later sense of that word. It is possible that Playford had these extensions in mind also when describing the contexts to which his 'trill' is suitable.

In a pipe organ, stops can be devised to simulate mechanically the vocal tremolo. Other instruments may imitate it in two ways: by reiterating the note after the manner of a modern tremolo or by reiterating adjacent notes after the manner of a modern trill or shake. The modern tremolo in its measured form is peculiarly adapted to bowed instruments, for which it was early indicated by Monteverdi in his *Combattimento di Tancredi e Clorinda* (1624). Simpson described the unmeasured form in 1659 (p.10): 'Some also affect a Shake or Tremble with the Bow, like the Shaking-Stop of an Organ, but the frequent use thereof is not (in my opinion) much commendable'. Mace (1676, p.103) described two methods of performing a tremolo on the lute, under the name of 'shake' (hard or soft). L'Affilard in 1694 and Brossard in 1703 correctly demonstrated the old vocal tremolo. Brossard said of the sign 'tr' that 'it is very often, in Italian music, the sign that one must beat several times on the same note, at first somewhat slowly, then ending with as much lightness and rapidity as the throat can make'. In 1723 Tosi denounced the old Italian tremolo under the name of 'mordente fresco'. His illustration shows rapidly reiterated notes of constant duration. Earlier authorities however described or illustrated the vocal tremolo as beginning slowly and accelerating in a wayward fashion impossible to notate exactly, and to be learnt only by imitating a good master. It is this acceleration that chiefly differentiates the early vocal tremolo from its later and from its instrumental counterparts.

Modern performers of the early vocal tremolo tend to make the pulsations too distinct. Only the lightest of reiterated impulses that do not distinctly interrupt the sound are what this difficult but once favoured ornament requires. Anything more prominent becomes distracting and unmusical. In early 17th-century Italian music the abbreviations *t*, *tr* or *tri* for *trillo* may indicate the vocal tremolo of Caccini, Monteverdi and their contemporaries. Subsequently, although the ornament survived and even spread to other countries, the symbols and the name 'trillo' must usually be interpreted as bearing their later connotation of 'shake'.

The tremolo characteristic of the clavichord results from an exaggeration of that even rocking of the key (as C. P. E. Bach described it) which produces its vibrato. The German word 'Bebung' (tremor) was used of both effects, which contemporary performers seldom distinguished in theory. But C. P. E. Bach (pp.8 and 126) used two terms, 'Bebung' and 'Tragen der Töne', of which the first signifies the vibrato (a regular feature of the instrument) and the second 'an added pressure after a note', which, like the vocal tremolo, almost but not wholly amounts to its reiteration. The latter was described by Türk (1789, p.293) under the names 'Bebung', 'balancement' (Fr.) and 'tremolo' (It.) as useful only on long notes and in music of a sorrowful nature; he also said: 'One holds down the finger for the duration of the note, and tries to reinforce the tone by gentle reiterated pressure . . . one must avoid the detestable exaggeration resulting from excessive pressure'. (For its notation, *see* BEBUNG ex.1.)

For a discussion of the notation and technique of modern instrumental varieties of tremolo *see* TREMOLO.

2. THE VIBRATO (Fr. *plainte, flattement, langueur, aspiration, tremblement mineure, tremblement sans appuyer, pincé, battement*; Ger. *Bebung, Schwebung*; It. *vibrato*). This embellishment, also called the close shake or sting, consists of a more or less noticeable fluctuation of pitch through all or part of the duration of a note. Vibrato was mentioned by Ganassi (1542), Martin Agricola (1545, pp.42f) and Mersenne (1636–7).

On string instruments two techniques for vibrato were recommended by later Baroque authorities. The first, that of rocking a single finger, produces the normal modern vibrato, which may vary in rapidity or intensity from a scarcely perceptible enlivening of the tone to a distressing exaggeration. The other Baroque technique, that of rocking one finger while allowing a second finger to beat lightly upon the string as nearby as possible, usually produces a prominent effect and is capable of still more extreme exaggeration. Simpson (1659, p.11) described the two-finger vibrato under the name 'close-shake': 'We shake the Finger as close and near the sounding Note as possible may be, touching the String with the Shaking finger so softly and nicely that it make no variation of Tone. This may be used where no other Grace is concerned'. Under the heading 'Shaked Graces' Playford (1660 and later edns.) included in his 'Table of Graces proper to the Viol or Violin' a graphic depiction of the vibrato as a series of demisemiquavers on the same note but alternatively a little higher and lower within their space. His sign is a dot placed above the note; his term 'a close shake'. This may be interpreted as a vibrato of either variety; it is not clear how far the two were distinguished either in name or in practice.

Mace (1676, p.109) described the modern single-finger vibrato under the name of 'sting'. De Machy stated (1685): 'The *Aspiration*, also called *Plainte*, is done by varying the finger on the fret . . . the *Tremblement sans appuyer* is done by two fingers held close together, and pressing very lightly on the string'. Marais (*Pieces de violes*, 1696) gave 'Pincé ou flattement' for the two-finger vibrato and 'Plainte' for the one-finger vibrato. In his music the former is frequently indicated by a thin, horizontal wavy line and the latter by a vertical wavy line; but the player may of course also use his own initiative. Jean Rousseau (1687, pp.101–2) used 'plainte' for a portamento and 'langueur' and 'batement' for both the one- and two-finger vibrato; he recommended the latter to excess:

The *Batement* is made when two fingers being pressed one against the other, the one is held on the string, and the next strikes it very lightly . . . imitates a certain sweet agitation of the Voice . . . is used in all contexts where the length of the Note permits, and should last as long as the note.
The *Langueur* is made by varying the finger on the Fret. It is ordinarily used when it is necessary to take a Note with the little finger, and time permits; it should last as long as the Note. This ornament is to replace the Batement unavailable when the little finger is held down.

Geminiani's sign for the 'close shake' (1751, p.8) is a thin jagged horizontal line easily confused with that which often denotes a trill or a long mordent elsewhere; he wrote:

you must press the Finger strongly upon the String of the Instrument, and move the Wrist in and out slowly and equally [on long notes for expression, but] on short Notes, it only contributes to make their Sound more agreable and for this Reason it should be made use of as often as possible.

This is the modern vibrato, and the modern fashion of using it continually; but in that respect tastes have often differed. Leopold Mozart (1756) called the vibrato 'tremolo', but explained it as Geminiani had: 'the finger pressed strongly down on the string . . . a small movement with the whole hand . . . forwards and backwards'. Unlike Geminiani however he denounced players who 'tremble on each note as if they had the palsy'. He distinguished three rates of vibrato: slow (shown by UUUU), accelerating (UUuu) and fast (uuuuuuu). Hotteterre (1707, pp.30–33) gave instructions for making a vibrato on the flute under the names 'Flattement' and 'Tremblement mineur'.

The *Bebung* of the clavichord, when not carried to the extent of a tremolo, is a normal vibrato. C. P. E. Bach (p.126) gave it the same rare sign (a row of dots surmounted by a slur) as he gave for his *Tragen der Töne*, which on different notes amounts to a portato but on a single note to a tremolo. He stated that 'the finger depressing and holding the key is gently rocked'. The portato and the tremolo are special effects; but the vibrato is as regular a resource of the clavichord as it is of the violin.

3. VARIETIES OF THE TRILL (Fr. *cadence, tremblement, trille, pincé renversé*; Ger. *Triller*; It. *trillo, tremoletto, groppo*). The trill, or shake, consists of a more or less rapid alternation of the main note with the one a tone or semitone above it. Trills may conveniently be distinguished according to how they begin, how long they last, and how they end. The manner in which they begin depends on whether their function is primarily melodic or harmonic. The Renaissance trill serves mainly a melodic purpose, breaking up and intensifying its note, and therefore might as well begin on its main note as on the auxiliary a tone or semitone above. Whereas the early Baroque trill has both melodic and harmonic uses, the later one performs primarily a harmonic and only secondarily a melodic function: with rare special exceptions it begins on the upper, auxiliary note, which is accented and (usually) prolonged. But the post-Baroque trill gradually lost its harmonic function until in late Classical and modern times it became once again a primarily melodic ornament; the necessity for beginning it with the accented upper auxiliary disappeared, and in practice the modern trill, unless otherwise written, is begun on its main note.

Baroque writers often distinguished between trills with a strongly accented and more or less prolonged initial upper auxiliary and those with a less strongly accented, unprolonged initial upper auxiliary; the former were regarded as prepared, the latter as unprepared. Today it is more important to distinguish between trills with an initial upper auxiliary (of whatever length and emphasis) and trills that begin on the main note; in this article, the former will be referred to as upper-note trills and the latter lower-note.

In an upper-note trill the initial auxiliary note is more prominent than the main note. When such a trill embellishes a normal cadence it gives the dominant triad the effect of 5-4–5-3 or 6-3–5-3; a double trill will give the effect of 6-4–5-3. Innumerable Baroque cadences are transformed from triteness to interest by the accented discord and ornamental resolution thus introduced where there is no sign for the trill in the written text. Hence Tosi's remark (1723, p.25) that 'he who has a very fine Trill, even if he were deprived of all other ornaments, always enjoys the advantage of coming without difficulty to the cadences, where it is most essential'. Tosi was not referring to the modern, lower-note trill, which is useless as a cadential formula in Baroque music because it fails to introduce the accented discord, which should be its chief purpose.

Very short trills lose the character of the ornament. A trill consisting of a single reiteration of three notes is in fact an inverted (upper) mordent or *Schneller*; when it has two reiterations of five notes it is a double inverted mordent. In slow time three reiterations may still resemble a mordent, but on a short or rapid note they will almost certainly be felt as a trill. In an upper-note trill a double reiteration of four notes, especially if the first note were tied to the previous main one, would produce that special form of prepared inverted mordent prevalent in the 18th century under the name of *Pralltriller* ('compact' trill; see §6); and on very short notes this would sound like a trill. In effect the difference between an inverted mordent and a trill is sometimes merely one of degree (hence one French term for trill: *pincé renversé* – inverted mordent). When enough reiterations occur to preclude the effect of a mordent, but not enough to fill the complete or virtually complete duration of the ornamented note, the ornament may be called a half-trill.

Apart from their preparation or duration, trills may be distinguished by the manner in which they end. Half-trills merge into their main note simply by prolonging its last reiteration to complete the duration required. A full-length trill may likewise end with the last sounding of its main note, very slightly longer than the preceding soundings so that the listener, hearing it thus emphasized, may perceive it as the main note. Any trill that ends in this way may be described as without termination. Although the modern practice is to take trills generally without termination, in the vast majority of Baroque and in much post-Baroque music this treatment, when applied to complete trills, is historically incorrect and musically damaging (though perhaps less damaging than the omission of a harmonically essential upper-note preparation).

Apart from the *Pralltriller* and the half-trill (which is normally upper-note but unterminated) the chief exception to the Baroque rule of supplying both preparation and termination to a trill, whether so written or not, is as follows: certain very long notes on the harpsichord or clavichord are given trills to avoid an excessive diminution of tone, and to add to the intensity and interest of the melodic line; by analogy similar trills of exceptional duration may be used on other instruments. Unlike the vast majority of Baroque trills these very prolonged trills have no harmonic function, being used solely for the purposes of melodic continuity, coloration and intensification. They therefore require no upper-note preparation and are often best without one; they may be begun on their main note and the accent kept there throughout, leaving the written harmony undisturbed. Nor do they require a termination, though one may be permitted in many instances. If the note following the ornamented one falls on a relatively weak beat, the normal execution of an unterminated trill (i.e. with a slight dwelling on the last sounding of the main note) may be preferable; but if the note following the ornamented one falls on an accented beat it is generally preferable to finish with a turn.

For Baroque trills in general the standard forms of termination are the turn and the note of anticipation. Irregular terminations of greater complexity are relatively uncommon and never essential, since they can

without incorrectness be replaced by a standard termination. If possible they should of course be used when called for by signs, but they are not part of the indispensable equipment for interpreting Baroque music. Trills end with a turn by merely substituting for the last appearance of the upper auxiliary a lower auxiliary lying a tone or semitone below the main note. The last note of the ornament is still the main note, but in this context it will not be dwelt on individually; rather, the speed of reiteration will normally remain constant to the end. This rule is not without qualification, however: (*a*) if the entire trill is taken fairly slowly the last two notes may be dwelt on slightly for a particularly lingering effect – this method is easily capable of abuse and should be used seldom and with discretion; (*b*) the entire trill may start slowly and accelerate as it proceeds – this technique will decrease the brilliance but increase the expressiveness of the ornament, and should be confined to suitable examples; and (*c*) after the completion of the ornament, and immediately before the next note, a very brief silence of articulation may in a few rare cases be desirable – the slightest exaggeration of this effect however will ruin the melodic flow. These qualifications are matters of finesse; the crude but safe rule is a constant speed of reiteration throughout the trill, except of course for its upper-note preparation.

This rule applies regardless of how the termination is notated (if it is notated at all). The two notes constituting the termination may be shown as quavers, semiquavers or demisemiquavers; they may appear either as part of the notated time-value or (printed small) outside it; or they may be suggested by one of the signs listed in §VIII. They may also very often be introduced by the performer where there is nothing in the notation to suggest them. In each case their duration is determined by the speed and expression of the trill itself, not by appearances. They are often described as the 'turn' of the trill, though strictly it is not the last two but the last four notes of the ornament thus terminated that, if taken in isolation, would constitute a turn. There are cases where a rapid turn may be allowed to substitute for a trill on short and quick notes, especially very low notes, where the tolerance for speed of reiteration is considerably less than in a higher register. In yet more extreme cases where a trill is indicated on a particularly short note the trill may actually be reduced to a single appoggiatura (several Baroque authorities analysed the trill as a series of reiterated upper appoggiaturas alternating with its main note). In normal cases (i.e. where trills are given enough time to develop fully) the effect of a 'turned' termination may be described as that of merging a trill imperceptibly into a turn.

Trills ending with a note of anticipation cease from reiteration somewhat before they otherwise would, and dwell slightly on the last sounding of the main note. In this respect they resemble unterminated trills, but the lingering may be a little earlier and may include a discreet silence of articulation; at the last moment before the ensuing note is due a note of anticipation follows, at the pitch of the ensuing note. As with turned trills, the simplest rule is to maintain a constant speed of reiteration. The device of gradually accelerating is less suited to a trill ending with a note of anticipation than to one ending in a turn, except in certain very expressive passages. In general the silence of articulation before the note of anticipation may be a little longer in brilliant contexts and a little shorter in expressive ones, but if it disappears entirely the note of anticipation will in effect be slurred to its preceding ornament; this is permissible in cantabile passages or at considerable speed in brilliant passages, but must otherwise be regarded as exceptional. If the entire trill is taken fairly slowly the note of anticipation may be slightly emphasized; but under no circumstances should it be heavy or long for, regardless of how it might appear in notation, it is governed by the general rule for dotted figures in Baroque music: it must be late in appearing, short in duration, and only lightly emphasized. Ex.43b suggests approximately how ex.43a should be rendered with a trill (one does not of course measure the re-soundings shown as demisemiquavers).

Ex.43

When no termination is shown, it is necessary in music earlier than the mid-19th century to introduce one of the two standard terminations unless there is a positive reason for making an exception. The choice of termination is determined by the context, the turn inclining to expressiveness and the note of anticipation to brilliance. In post-Baroque music the first termination is the more likely where none is written, since the second, if intended, will almost certainly appear in the text.

Trills are normally diatonic unless chromatic alterations are shown by accidentals above the sign (to affect the upper subsidiary) or below (to affect the lower subsidiary if there is a turn). Chopin had a characteristic liking for chromatically raised turns at the end of trills.

One other kind of trill should be mentioned here: the *ribattuta* (Ger. *Zurückschlag*), a modification of the old vocal tremolo where instead of a reiteration of the same note, an alternation of two adjacent notes is produced with a similar technique, described by Caccini (1601/2) as a 'beating of the throat'. The *ribattuta* begins on the main note and its rhythm is uneven but it accelerates until the ornament passes insensibly into a trill, either in the old Italian sense of tremolo as in ex.42c or in the modern sense as in ex.44, from Caccini's *Euridice* (1600). Ex.45 gives an approximate, generalized model

Ex.44

Ex.45

of the combined *ribattuta* and standard trill. The *ribattuta* occurs in Leopold Mozart's *Violinschule* (1756, p.219) and is still found occasionally in the 19th century. C. P. E. Bach showed it (1753, Table IV) as an instrumental ornament leading to a compound ascending trill (ex.46; see also §V, 2).

Ex.46

4. RENAISSANCE AND EARLY BAROQUE TRILLS. Notes approximating to written-out trills occur among the numerous divisions given in the 16th-century treatises as examples of the art of impromptu ornamentation. They are usually found as the concluding portion of a comparatively long and elaborate division, from which they are distinguished by no particular attention or nomenclature. In such circumstances the notes in question are probably intended at their face value rather than at the indeterminate rate of reiteration that would characterize true trills. Thus ex.47a and b (Ganassi, 1535) should probably be executed as written. Nevertheless it is also possible that the written-out form was, as early as 1500, merely a conventional indication for the true trill; and it seems virtually certain that such is the case with late 16th-century examples like ex.49 (Diruta, 1593, p.18) and ex.50 (Conforti, 1593, p.25). Ex.48 is from Ortiz (1553; modern edn., p.12). While some of these formulae are ornamental versions of standard cadences and have harmonic significance, others provide exclusively melodic embellishment.

Ex.47 Ganassi, trill formulae

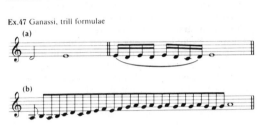

Ex.48 Ortiz, trill formula

Ex.49 Diruta, trill formula

Ex.50 Conforti, groppi

di sopra

di sotto

Conforti used the term 'groppo' for figures some (but not all) of which approximate closely to trills. Diruta used 'groppo' for a variety of divisions, some of which terminate in trill-like figures, 'tremolo' for lower-note, unterminated trills and 'tremoletto' for half-trills and inverted mordents. In Italian keyboard music of this period the abbreviations *g* for *groppo* or *gruppo* and *t* for *tremolo* are not uncommon: a trill is intended, and the first appearance of the ornament is generally written out in the conventional approximation. Sometimes it is thus written out throughout, as in ex.51, a typical instance from the *Tabulatur Buch* (1607) of Bernhard Schmid. From the late 16th century onwards a true trill (the reit-

Ex.51

erations being not literally measured but indeterminate) is likely to have been intended by such conventional formulae of notation wherever they appear. The evidence for this is of several kinds. Frescobaldi, who wrote out many of his trills, in the preface to his *Toccate e partite* (1615) said 'you must not divide the trill exactly note for note, but merely try to make it rapid'. In general the same passage is often found in one manuscript with a sign for a trill and in another with a written-out trill; or the number of reiterations shown written out is sometimes twice as many, or half as many again, in one manuscript as in another. No such difference in execution can be intended. Finally, the number of reiterations shown sometimes does not add up to any strict subdivision of the time occupied (e.g. Diruta, 1593, p.20). From these various clues we may infer that the written-out figure had become a mere arbitrary convention, not (as a rule) to be performed literally but with the unmeasured freedom proper to the trill itself.

In ex.52, from Caccini's *Euridice* (1600), the last seven 'semiquavers' indicate an unprepared trill with turned termination. Later in the same opera a normal Baroque trill on the dotted quaver is required (ex.53). In ex.54, from Act 3 of Monteverdi's *Orfeo* (1607), the demisemiquavers probably represent a trill, upper-note and terminated, though if taken strictly their effect is almost identical, since here the convention and the notation are not far apart. Shortly afterwards the figure shown in ex.55 occurs; it is probably best taken as a trill begun very slowly but steadily accelerating up to and including its termination.

Ex.52

Ex.53

Ex.54

Ex.55

In English keyboard music of the late 16th and early 17th centuries written-out figures of this kind must almost invariably be regarded as ordinary trills. The same is true of the school of Sweelinck and others on whom the influence of the great English school was so considerable. Although in the 17th century there are isolated instances where legitimate doubt may be felt whether to interpret the figure strictly or conventionally, in all normal cases no such doubt can survive the preponderance of evidence that the interpretation should not be metrically regimented. Mace in *Musick's Monument* (1676, pp.103–4) described both lower- and upper-note trills, calling the latter a 'back-fall shaked'. Playford showed none starting on the main note but illustrated the upper-note trill as in ex.56 (1660, p.79, and later edns.). Chambonnières gave it as in ex.57.

Ex.56

A backfall shaked

Ex.57

Cadence   Exécution

5. THE BAROQUE TRILL. Purcell gave no lower-note trill in his posthumously published *Lessons* (1699), but ex.58 shows a trill with the initial upper note both prolonged and unprolonged. Jean Rousseau's *Traité de la viole* (1687, p.76) makes the common Baroque distinction between trills prepared (*avec appuy*) and unprepared (*sans appuy*) in the Baroque sense (i.e. trills begun with the upper note prolonged as opposed to those begun on an unprolonged upper note). This usage was confirmed by D'Anglebert in his *Pièces de clavecin* (1689), from which ex.59 is taken. This clarification of the term 'appuyer'

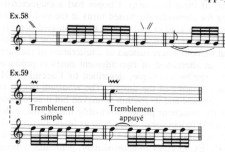

Ex.58

Ex.59

Tremblement simple   Tremblement appuyé

shows that all standard Baroque cadential trills start on the upper note although only in some of them is it prolonged. The interpretation given here has been disputed by Neumann. It is however explicitly confirmed by Loulié, who wrote (*Eléments*, 1696, p.70) that 'when the voice remains appreciably' (*demeure sensiblement*) on the upper-note start, 'this is called preparing the trill' (*appuyer le tremblement*) for a time 'longer or shorter in proportion to the duration of the note trilled'; but that 'when the voice does not remain appreciably' on the upper-note start 'the trill is called "unprepared trill" [*non appuyé*] or without preparation' (*sans appuy*). Loulié's term for the upper-note start is 'an appoggiatura' (*coulé*), which he described as reiterated 'from a little sound [*petit son*] to an ordinary note, one degree lower'.

Hotteterre (1707, p.11) gave a clear explanation of

the fully prepared trill in terms of transverse-flute fingering. It is to be begun on 'the sound above' and slurred 'without taking breath or giving further strokes of the tongue'. This slurring of the preparation to its ensuing trill falls under the general rule by which appoggiaturas are normally slurred to their resolutions. Hotteterre continued: 'the trilling finger should remain on its hole to conclude the trill', with the effect of ending the trill on its main note and, it is perhaps implied, of slightly prolonging it. This prolongation of the main note at the end of a trill, intended only in unterminated trills or in trills terminated by a note of anticipation, is confirmed by other authorities, such as T.B. in his *Compleat Musickmaster* (3/1722, p.41): 'always let the Proper Note be distinctly hear'd at last'. The ear can thus sense which is the main note; in the case of trills terminating in a turn the same effect is produced by the turn itself, which passes below the main note to the other side and lends it slight prominence by, as it were, drawing a mental circle round it.

Another important point made by Hotteterre is that

The number of reiterations is governed solely by the duration of the note. Above all, attention must be paid to not being in a hurry to attack the trill, but on the contrary to hold it up [by its preparation] to more than half the duration of the [main] note, especially in grave movements.

This is very long preparation indeed but it is common in the French school, where it is sometimes even written out, usually in a manner that indicates clearly whether the note preceding the trill is an appoggiatura slurred to it or a main note divided from it (as seems to be the case in ex.56). Where the notation is ambiguous circumstances must guide the performer. If the preceding note is actually an appoggiatura separate from the trill, the initial upper note of the trill itself will be unprolonged (as in ex.56) or only slightly prolonged, and must certainly be slurred to the rest of the trill. Outside France it was by no means rare for a trill to have a long preparation, but it was less characteristic, particularly when taken to an extreme. Hotteterre also added that 'the least number of reiterations possible on short trills is three finger-strokes', making six notes in all. And he warned more than once and with considerable emphasis that necessary ornaments are not generally marked except in pieces 'which the Masters write for their pupils'.

Couperin's *L'art de toucher le clavecin* (1716, p.23) makes clear that 'whatever the note on which the trill is shown, it must invariably be begun on the tone or semitone above'. He further gave as a general rule what was certainly a frequent recourse, though not suitable in every case: 'although the trills are marked as regular in the table of ornaments in my first book, they are nevertheless to begin more slowly than they finish; but the gradation must be imperceptible'. This sentence confirms that the interpretative notations in Couperin's table (1713) are far from literally exact. It is apparent from this table that he took some degree of preparation so entirely for granted that the considerable preparation in exx.63 and 64 was deemed no more than an obvious and minimum ingredient of the trill itself; the term 'appuyé' (prepared; literally 'leant on') is reserved for the much longer preparation in ex.60a. Meanwhile, in exx.61a and 62a Couperin made a curious distinction between 'open' and 'closed' trills solely on the basis of the direction taken by the subsequent main note. Since his notation is ambiguous an approximate interpretation is given at exx.60b, 61b and c, 62b and c, 63b and 64b.

Ex.60
(a) Tremblement appuyé et lié
(b)

Ex.61
(a) Tremblement ouvert
(b)
(c)

Ex.62
(a) Tremblement fermé
(b)
(c)

Ex.63
(a)   (b) Tremblement lié sans être appuyé

Ex.64
(a)   (b) Tremblement détaché

Tosi, the best authority for the Italian vocal taste of his period, took a view slightly less extreme than Couperin and close in line with English practice (1742, p.28): 'The trill for its beauty wants to be prepared; nevertheless, its preparation is not always required, since neither time nor taste will always permit it; it is [however] called for in all final cadences'. By 'preparation' Tosi meant (like the French *appuy*) the prolonging of the initial note of the trill, and he was right to insist on its indispensability in cadential trills, where the resulting modification of the harmony is particularly essential. Tosi gave no music example; but his English translator Galliard in 1742 and his German translator J. F. Agricola in 1757 both did so independently, and both showed only the upper-note start.

The same instruction is found in the German authorities. C. P. E. Bach stated (p.65) that 'the [long] appoggiatura . . . is found before cadential trills' (*Schluss-Trillern*); and his illustration further serves to decide an important point of disagreement among recent scholars. It has been maintained, with apparent plausibility, that Baroque trills should begin on their main note where to begin them on their upper auxiliary would result in the immediate repetition of the preceding main note. Since C. P. E. Bach (1753, p.65 and Table III, fig.IV*a*) gave only one illustration of the prolonging of the initial upper auxiliary to form an accented appoggiatura preparing the cadential trill, and showed that initial upper note as the immediate repetition of the preceding note without any comment to suggest that the case is in any way unusual, it must be concluded that the supposed exception to the rule had no existence, at any rate in the crucial case of the cadential trill. In the case of non-cadential trills there was during the main Baroque period some latitude to prolong the preceding main note into a tied appoggiatura. C. P. E. Bach's illustration (Table III) is shown at ex.65*a*, Donington's interpretation at ex.65*b*, and the effect of tying the preceding note to the trill at ex.65*c* (cf exx.60–64).

Ex.65

Quantz (p.86) gave the alternative of a moderate prolongation or a substantial one, adding that 'this appoggiatura, whether long or [relatively] short, must always be accented'. Only in exceptional circumstances may it be 'as quick as the other notes of the trill; for example, when a new phrase begins with a trill after a rest' (a cadential trill is, of course, the reverse of exceptional and is necessarily excluded from this exemption). Quantz stated categorically (p.85) that whether appearing in the written notation or not 'both the appoggiatura [preparation] and the termination are implied'.

Marpurg (*Principes du clavecin*, 1756, p.66), discussing, like C. P. E. Bach, harpsichord methods (Loulié and Tosi had the voice in mind), repeated that the trill 'starts on the accessory note', adding (p.68) that 'the leant-on or prepared trill [occurs] when one remains a little time on the accessory note before making the beating, or when one starts with a slow beating and increases the speed by a kind of gradation'. Leopold Mozart (*Violinschule*, 1756, p.219) told violinists that the trill can either start at once from the upper note, unprolonged, or 'be prepared by a descending appoggiatura which is suspended rather longer'; his music examples for each begin clearly on the upper note.

Examples of the two standard terminations (by turn and by note of anticipation) have already been given, as well as of unterminated trills (standard only for half trills and for full trills in certain limited circumstances). Some examples from Playford's *Introduction* (1660, p.79, and later edns.) have exceptional preparations which will be discussed later, but their terminations are standard. Ex.66 ends in a turn (the appoggiatura *e″* which follows

is not, of course, part of the trill). Ex.67 ends in a note of anticipation, to be interpreted as at ex.67*b*, according to the usual Baroque rule for such dotted figures. Various authenticated rhythms are shown in exx.68–73.

Ex.66

Elevation

Ex.67

(a) Cadent

(b)

Ex.68 Purcell: *Lessons* (1696), shake turn'd

Ex.69 Tosi: *Opinioni* (1723)

Ex.70 Muffat: *Componimenti* (*c*1739)

Ex.71 Rameau: *Pièces de clavecin* (1731)

Cadence   Cadence appuyée   Double Cadence

Ex.72 Marpurg: *Anleitung zum Clavierspielen* (2/1765)

Ex.73 Leopold Mozart: *Violinschule* (1756)

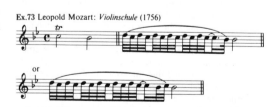

or

C. P. E. Bach (1753, p.76) merely gave the standard rule that 'the termination must be played at the same speed as the trill'. This agrees with Quantz (p.85): 'The end of each trill consists of two little notes, which follow the note of the trill and are made at the same speed'. C. P. E. Bach, again in agreement with Quantz, said that all trills on notes of fair length need a termination (by which he meant a turn) unless followed by quick notes which serve the purpose (in which he included the note of anticipation to be shortened and preceded by a silence of articulation in the standard manner). The trill and its turn must, said Quantz, be slurred.

Leopold Mozart (p.220) and Marpurg (1756, p.66) mentioned, like Couperin (1716, p.23), a gradual increase in the speed of reiteration, though unlike Couperin they regarded this only as an option; the turn would then take its speed from the end of the acceleration, merely continuing the rhythmic development of the trill, unless it were to fall into one of the exceptional rhythms shown above. But as Tartini justly remarked in a letter of 1760 (published with a translation by Burney in 1771, pp.7f), trills of different speeds must by practised, 'for the same shake will not serve with equal propriety for a slow movement as for a quick one'. The possibility of acceleration does not apply to quick and brilliant trills; nor does the licence by which the turn at the end of slow trills may as a rare exception be taken at slightly slower speed than the trill itself. While the degree of acceleration generally varies with speed and context it should, if present at all, be inconspicuous. Leopold Mozart, who allotted the slow trill to sad, slow pieces, the medium to lively yet moderate pieces and the rapid to very lively pieces, suggested that 'the accelerating trill is used mostly in cadenzas' and recommended increasing the volume in proportion to the speed (pp.220f). He warned never to trill too rapidly (especially on low notes); the result was known as a 'goat's trill'. This seems a clear reminiscence of Quantz (pp.84f), who advised a speed 'even but moderate', more rapid on high than on low notes but avoiding both 'the very slow trill' and 'the very rapid trill, which the French call goaty' (chevroté); while 'in a sad piece the trill should be slow, but in a gay one more rapid'.

6. HALF-TRILLS. One appropriate place for these is on short, rapid notes where the necessary telescoping may reduce an unterminated trill to a *Pralltriller* or even an inverted mordent (or may reduce a terminated trill to a four- or five-note turn). C. P. E. Bach (1753, pp.81f) stated that 'the half- or compact trill [*halber oder Prall-Triller*] . . . may be used on rapid notes, but must be taken at such speed that one will not be aware of the ornamented note as having been deprived of any of its time-value'. This requirement cannot be literally fulfilled, but the hearer can be deceived into feeling that it has if the execution is sufficiently brilliant. Even when a half-trill appears at the beginning of a longer note, it must still itself be 'snapped' with the utmost rapidity. C. P. E. Bach added (p.84) that it is virtually impossible to execute this ornament crisply enough on the piano – an observation which applies *a fortiori* to the heavier touch of the modern instrument. Partly for this reason and partly from ignorance modern pianists render the ornament incorrectly as an inverted mordent (*Schneller*) by leaving out its first (upper) note. Ex.74*a* shows Bach's illustration of a typical situation in which the half-trill stands on a short or rapid note: ex.74*b* shows the incorrect modern rendering and ex.74*c* the correct Baroque

one. Exceptions occur only when the speed of the passage makes too difficult or clumsy the repetition of the preceding note as illustrated in ex.74*c*; in that event the trill is necessarily shorn of its upper-note start and becomes identical with the inverted (upper) mordent or *Schneller* (see §8). The speed at which the transition should occur is a matter of taste and style, musical context, the touch of the instrument and the player's skill; a pianist should resort to a mordent more readily than a harpsichordist, this being one respect in which the newer instrument, with all its excellence, cannot match the older. C. P. E. Bach (p.83) allowed the *Pralltriller* only on intervals of a descending 2nd (the first note of this interval might however be an unwritten but improvisatorily introduced appoggiatura). Ex.75, from the table of ornaments in the preface of J. C. F. Bach's *Musikalische Nebenstunden* (1787), recalls an example given by C. P. E. Bach (Table IV) that is identical except for the (presumably accidental) omission of the first tie. This form of the *Pralltriller*, with its initial upper note tied to the previous main note or appoggiatura, seems eventually to have caused it to be confused with an upper mordent (see §7).

Ex.75

C. P. E. Bach called the *Pralltriller* (p.82) 'the most indispensable, the most attractive, and yet the most difficult of ornaments'. This is an exaggeration; the cadential trill is more necessary. Nevertheless the half-trill is frequent and valuable and was particularly cultivated by violinists, to whom its execution presents no technical difficulties. C. P. E. Bach also noted that when the ornament with an appoggiatura is executed on the final note of a phrase and carries (or implies) a phrase sign 'the appoggiatura is held decidedly long and the [half-]trill is quickly snapped as the fingers leave the keys'. Part of his illustration is shown in ex.76*a*, and the interpretation which his words imply at ex.76*b*. His preference was for the shortest version possible (the 'halber oder Prall-Triller'); but longer half-trills as illustrated in ex.76*c* also exist. The lower-note half-trill resulted, like the lower-note trill, from the influence of Hummel (*Anweisung*, 1828) and of Spohr, from whose *Violinschule* (1832, p.160) ex.77 is taken.

Ex.76

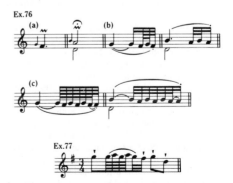

Ex.77

7. LATER TRILLS. The rules governing trills in the Baroque period were largely carried over into the period of the Viennese Classics. Clementi's *Introduction to . . . the*

Ex.74

Pianoforte (1801) gives all trills an unprolonged upper-note start except after a rest (as in Baroque rules), after a quick scale, when marked *sf*, or on the middle note of a chord. Pollini's *Metodo*, adopted by the Milan Conservatory in 1811, and Cramer's *Instructions* (1812) give all trills starting on the upper note, as did Rode, Kreutzer and Baillot in their *Méthode de violon* for the Paris Conservatoire (1803). But a move had already been made in the direction of the modern trill beginning not on its upper but on its lower (i.e. main) note. Manfredini's *Regole armoniche* (1775) gives the lower-note trills shown in ex.78, and Adam Père's *Méthode* (1798)

Ex.78

includes some lower- as well as upper-note examples. Hummel in his *Anweisung zum Piano-forte Spiel* (1828, p.386) stated that his predecessors always used the initial upper note; he advanced the novel counter-argument that the main note ought to be more emphatically impressed on the ear than the subsidiary note and that piano technique makes it easier for the fingers to start on the main note, hence trills should start there unless otherwise shown. Spohr in his *Violinschule* (1832, p.154) extended this argument to the violin and stated that Hummel was its first promulgator. The real reason for the change of fashion represented by these writers and their followers is that the need to stress an initial upper note for harmonic purposes had lessened. The typical Baroque cadence by dominant discord and resolution had become outmoded, and with its decline the harmonic function of the cadential trill was vanishing in favour of a return to the merely decorative and melodic function. Nevertheless there is evidence that the initial upper note continued to be used by many performers and intended by many composers of the 19th century. Garcia's *Hints on Singing* (London, 1894), perhaps the last full expression of the great bel canto tradition, with characteristic singer's conservatism shows all trills with upper-note starts, on the beat, in perfectly normal late Baroque fashion.

The standard termination by a turn remained in use and was generally intended in the absence of a written alternative such as the note of anticipation. Hummel labelled the trill terminated by a turn 'perfect' and the unterminated trill 'imperfect'. Spohr (1832, p.155) wrote that 'generally the Turn (at least in modern compositions) is written with small notes; where this is not the case, the Scholar has to supply them' except where the shake is too short to admit it or the context prevents it. He repeated the usual Baroque advice on the speed of trills, adding: 'a shake must never begin quick and terminate slow'. The rules governing both terminations remained basically unchanged, except that where no termination was written the Baroque option to play a note of anticipation instead of a turn scarcely persisted. Hummel stated in his *Klavierschule* (1828, p.387) that 'every true trill must have a termination [*Nachschlag*], even if it is not marked', and he showed the turned ending with the word 'Nachschlag' attached to it. With rare exceptions he required it to be played at the same speed as the trill. For bringing in the orchestra after a cadenza

however he allowed it to be slower than the trill and further showed a note of anticipation.

It is particularly interesting that this note of anticipation was still shown, even by Hummel, in the standard Baroque rhythm, delayed and preceded by a rest and shortened to a demisemiquaver. Even in the music of Beethoven's time, then, there is no excuse for taking the note of anticipation at its heavy literal length; still less in that of J. S. Bach and Handel. Neither is it any more correct (though certainly less damaging) to apply the modern trill to Beethoven than to J. S. Bach. It is from Clementi's influence rather than from Hummel's that one may gauge the general practice of Beethoven's time. Beethoven, like Bach, was inconsistent in the notation of ornaments, implicitly assuming that the performer's training would lead him to the correct interpretation. Hence Beethoven's trills should begin with the upper note, in most cases not prolonged but nevertheless convincingly accented; and there can be no doubt that the majority of them, in the absence of a written termination, should end in the standard turn. Thus the trill in bar 7 of the Adagio in his String Quartet op.127 should receive a brief initial appoggiatura from above and end in a turn at the same speed as the trill, though neither is written or at present customary in performance. The trill which opens the Violin Sonata op.96 is an interesting case: under one Baroque rule, trills that begin a phrase lack the usual initial upper note; this one might therefore begin on its main note but end in a turn though none is written. The Scherzo of the String Quartet op.127 abounds in trills, some with written terminal turns, others without; all require them. A few additional trills should be supplied to match those written (e.g. violin II, bar 10, cf bar 281; viola, bar 20, cf bar 291). As if to emphasize the transitional and inconsistent state of Beethoven's ornamentation a brief appoggiatura to the trill is actually marked (for no obvious reason, among many trills not so marked) in bar 56 of the Adagio of this quartet. Yet Chopin still expected the initial appoggiatura, and clearly marked any exception with grace notes; ex.79b and *d* show how ex.79a and *c*, from his op.19, should therefore be interpreted.

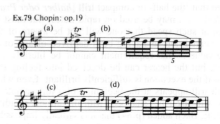

Ex.79 Chopin: op.19

The inference is that down to and including Beethoven the initial upper note was the norm, the initial lower note the exceptional innovation; but by Chopin's time this innovation was sufficiently established to require some indication (as in ex.79c) if it was to be excluded. Thereafter the modern trill appears to have become predominantly though not exclusively established. The modern trill, which is lower-note and unterminated unless otherwise shown in the text, is neither a harmonic ornament nor scarcely a melodic one, but rather an ornament of emphasis or a coloration of the texture. Such trills, like the modern orchestral or pianistic two-note tremolos (which differ from them only in covering an interval larger than a semitone or whole tone), are an ingredient less of ornamentation than of scoring.

8. VARIETIES OF THE MORDENT (Fr. *mordant, pincé, pincement, battement, martellement;* Ger. *Mordent, Mordant, Beisser;* It. *mordente).* The mordent, known earlier as the open shake or beat, in its standard form consists in the very rapid alternation of the main note with a subsidiary note a step below. In this form it is also known as a lower mordent. Its variant the inverted mordent, also known as an upper mordent, consists in the alternation of the main note with a subsidiary note a step above. There has been considerable confusion between the two, perhaps originated and certainly encouraged by Hummel and his admirers (such as Spohr in the second quarter of the 19th century), who confounded their names, signs and functions. Consequently those modern performers who are unaware that the upper mordent passed out of fashion during the mid-Baroque often use it in inappropriate contexts. Historically it has some Renaissance justification, and after its mid-Baroque eclipse by the lower mordent it returned to favour gradually from the time of C. P. E. Bach until about 1830.

Although trills and mordents are closely related (see §3), it is important to remember that the reiterations of a trill invariably lie between the main note and the note a step above, while those of a standard mordent lie between the main note and the note a step below (often chromatically altered to a semitone). In exceptional circumstances such as discussed in connection with ex.74*b* a quick half-trill that has lost its upper-note preparation will behave like an upper mordent; in such cases either name or sign would be appropriate. In less rapid passages, however, this confusion can be avoided by remembering that although a trill may still be telescoped it need not (and in Baroque music should not) be deprived of its characteristic upper-note preparation.

C. P. E. Bach applied the name 'Schneller' (from *schnellen:* 'to jerk') to the single upper mordent (i.e. main note, upper subsidiary, main note). Since he separated his treatment of it from his treatment of the standard mordent by two other ornaments, it seems likely that he regarded the connection between them as more theoretical than practical. At any rate his designation, and his description of the *Schneller* as a 'brief inverted mordent' (echoing the French term 'pincé renversé' or 'reversé') were unfortunately not standardized. Marpurg regarded the *Schneller* as a form of *Pralltriller,* overlooking the essential difference that the latter has an upper-note preparation. This confusion is readily explained. The *Pralltriller* occurs most characteristically in passages descending by step. The preparation is often tied to the preceding note (a step above), as in ex.80*a* and *b,* from Türk's *Clavierschule* (1789, p.272). The resulting syncopation is likely to atrophy, with it the distinction between the *Pralltriller* and *Schneller.* Thus Türk included ex.80*c* even though he had earlier (p.251), like C. P. E. Bach, regarded it as a *Schneller.* The confusion of the 18th-century authorities has since increased, so that today a standard German term for an inverted mordent is *Pralltriller.* It is however preferable to adhere to C. P. E. Bach's terminology, in which the *Schneller* is an unprepared single upper mordent, while what might be called a prepared upper mordent should rather be regarded as a brief upper-note half-trill, the *Pralltriller.*

There are two closely related forms of prepared lower

Ex.30

mordent. A number of 17th- and 18th-century authorities illustrated a lower appoggiatura passing into a lower mordent on its note of resolution (an upper appoggiatura was not permitted to do so, though it might well pass into a half-trill). Playford (1660 and later edns.) for example gave it as 'shak'd beat'; Jean Rousseau exaggerated to the point of stating that every (lower) appoggiatura ends in a (lower) mordent. Technically this is not a single but a compound ornament (though no more so than a normal trill prepared by a prolonged upper note). And just as the first note of an upper-note trill, though always accented, need not be prolonged, so the first lower note of a prepared lower mordent need not be prolonged into a lower appoggiatura. In that event there is no temptation to regard the ornament as a compound one; and this is the second of the two forms referred to above in which the preparation of a lower mordent can appear. Where the initial lower note is long it has always been regarded as a lower appoggiatura leading to a mordent; where it is short it has (if illustrated at all) been shown as part of the mordent of which it forms the preparation.

Unlike upper mordents, lower mordents have to be considered in a variety of lengths. The shortest, the unprepared single lower mordent (main, lower, main note), is the most characteristic and ubiquitous. In Baroque usage it is invariably taken on the beat of its main note and given either the accent proper to that beat (whether strong or weak) or an accent in excess of that proper to that beat (if strong, and in certain cases, such as syncopations, even if weak). Since it never falls before the beat, it always takes its time from its ensuing main note and never from the note that precedes it; but because it is without exception taken quickly and brilliantly (and almost always as quickly and brilliantly as possible) the time stolen from its main note is scarcely appreciable. These rules need to be applied all the more conscientiously for having fallen into neglect in modern times, when the habit of bringing in most ornaments before the beat, before the accent and at a slow speed, though never countenanced by teachers like Tovey, has taken a widespread hold.

An unprepared double lower mordent (two reiterations totalling five notes: main, subsidiary, main, subsidiary, main) obeys the same rules, except that its speed and accentuation are less likely to be extreme and it is less likely to appear on weak beats. On notes of sufficient length or slowness more than two repercussions may occur. The more prolonged the mordent, the more it assumes the character best described as a species of 'inverted trill'; thus long mordents may if desired be taken more slowly than short ones, though it would be a mistake to accelerate a mordent as some trills may be accelerated; and it must be remembered that all mordents end on their main note, without termination, and must at the very least let the main note sound after them long enough to be apprehended clearly.

Where a lower mordent is prepared by an appoggiatura from below, the appoggiatura may vary from moderately short to decidedly long. In this context both the mordent and its main note are to be regarded as the resolution of the appoggiatura, with a resulting reversal of the rules governing other mordents. Neither the mordent nor its main note must receive an accent, in accordance with the overriding rule that the resolution of an appoggiatura must be softer and less emphatic than the appoggiatura. The speed of the mordent must not be excessive and may at times be slower than would otherwise be permissible. The mordent itself may be single, double or even, in exceptionally languishing or weighty contexts, of still more reiterations. Mordent and main note must be slurred to their preceding appoggiatura, and the main note must not be held on but lightened and if necessary shortened. All the expression and most of the attention must, as usual, be focussed on the appoggiatura. But the time value of the mordent is still to be robbed from its ensuing main note. Where the note of preparation is short enough to be regarded not as an appoggiatura but as merely the start of a prepared mordent, it will still behave in the same way, taking the accent and falling under the same slur as the rest of the mordent. The rules for the execution of the single upper mordent before about 1830 are identical with those for the single lower mordent.

There are very few restrictions on the positions in which mordents may appear. Long mordents are of course appropriate only to reasonably long or slow notes. In ascending scale passages the lower mordent is proper, in descending scale passages the upper (when not anachronistic). Both these rules were strongly stated by C. P. E. Bach, but he did not give the reason for them; an upper mordent in an ascending scale would anticipate the next note of the scale, as would a lower mordent in a descending scale; the result would sound weak and unmusical. It is less easy to decide whether to use an (unprepared) upper mordent or a brief (prepared) half-trill (*Pralltriller*) in a descending scale passage; as a rough guide, in music before about 1830 the half-trill is usually preferable if there is time for it, but in later music the upper mordent may be more freely introduced.

The subsidiary note of a mordent should on the whole be diatonic unless an accidental is written above or below or to one side of the sign. In many circumstances the subsidiary note of a lower mordent may however be chromatically sharpened, even in the absence of a written indication, if the result is musically justified; but it must not be assumed that this unwritten sharpening is ever obligatory. It is likely to be inadvisable on the third or the seventh degree of the scale, or on a note preceded or followed by the note a tone below. The main varieties of mordent are therefore: (*a*) The unprepared lower mordent (the standard variety); single, double or longer. (*b*) The prepared lower mordent (prepared by a more or less lengthy lower appoggiatura); single, double or longer. (*c*) The unprepared upper (inverted) mordent or *Schneller*; single only (longer ones being best viewed as unprepared half-trills). (*d*) The prepared upper (inverted) mordent or *Pralltriller*; single only (longer ones being

best viewed as prepared half-trills, and even the single being often viewed as such). The rare and somewhat dubiously named 'slow mordent' of C. P. E. Bach (1753, p.103, misnumbered 85) is discussed in §9.

9. HISTORICAL SURVEY OF MORDENTS. In the Buxheim Organbook and later sources of German Renaissance keyboard music mordents are indicated by an ornamental sign consisting of a slash or hook as shown in ex.81. H. Buchner in his *Fundamentum* (*c*1520) wrote that they are executed by holding the main note while making (presumably one or two) reiterations of the auxiliary. Ammerbach in his *Orgel oder Instrument Tabulatur* (1571) illustrated mordents with ex.82 and specified that if the main note is ascending then the lower auxiliary should be used for the mordent, and vice versa. Written-out figures resembling mordents appear in several 16th-century treatises, but as fragments of melody rather than the sharp little ornament that constitutes a proper mordent. Ex.83*b* shows a prolonged lower-note mordent labeled *tremulus descendens* by Praetorius in 1619 (p.235) and defined as 'the shaking of the voice over a note'; he preferred however the *tremulus ascendens* (ex.83*a*).

Ex.81

Ex.82

Ex.83

(a)   (b)

Mace in *Musick's Monument* (1676, p.105) described a prolonged lower mordent in terms of lute technique. The repercussions are to be 'in quick motion' and 'always into a *Half Note beneath*'. This would suggest either that Mace intended an invariable chromatic sharpening of the subsidiary note whenever this, if diatonic, would stand at a whole tone below, or that he confined the ornament to notes diatonically a semitone distant from the note below. The latter seems more probable, but neither can be applied literally to the music of his period in general. T. B.'s *Compleat Musick-master* (3/1722, p.27) states that on viols 'a Beat . . . is always from the half Note below', but that on the violin, which of course is not fretted, 'a Beat . . . proceeds from the Note, or half Note next below' (p.41). This may leave room for a degree of choice according to personal preference. C. P. E. Bach remarked that the 'brilliance [of the mordent] is often increased by raising [chromatically] the lower note', but Leopold Mozart (1756, p.245) insisted that one should take 'the prolonged mordent from below [i.e. prepared], and invariably from the semitone', while his illustrations not only show this prepared and prolonged mordent confined to the semitone both diatonic and chromatic, but actually give only two cases of shorter, unprepared mordents, each chromatically sharpened (pp.242 and 245; see ex.84). He called his prolonged prepared mordent by the different name of 'battement', and revealed its affinities by adding that 'this *battement* is used in lively movements instead of the appoggiatura and mordent' (i.e. where there is no time for a longer preparation by appoggiatura).

Ex.84

To revert to chronological order: Simpson in 1659 (p.12) and Playford in his *Introduction* (1660, p.79, and later edns.) gave 'a shaked beat' amounting to a prepared and prolonged lower mordent. The interval (see ex.85) is diatonically a semitone. Chambonnières in his *Pièces* (1670) gave a single unprepared lower mordent (ex.86) under the name of 'pincement'. An amusing

Ex.85

Ex.86

explanation of the mordent given under the name of *martellement* by de Machy in his *Pièces de viole* (1685) makes it abundantly plain how rapidly this ornament is to be executed: 'lift the finger from the note as soon as sounded, and replace it at the same time'. He said that the 'double martellement' should be performed in the same manner. Jean Rousseau in his *Traité de la viole* (1687, p.87) said that 'the finger stopping a Note first makes two or three little repercussions more brilliantly and rapidly than a trill, and then remains on the Fret'. He added that 'the Mordent is always inseparable from the Appoggiatura, for the Appoggiatura must always be terminated by a Mordent'. In other words, he recognized only what is in effect a well-prepared lower mordent; but it has been seen that this limitation cannot be taken quite literally. Rousseau further said that 'the Mordent is ordinarily made on the second Note of an ascending Semitone . . . especially when ascending from a short one to a long'. His remaining rules are valuable but less generally applicable. He permitted mordents of a whole tone as well as of a semitone.

Georg Muffat in the preface to his *Apparatus* (1690) used the letter *t* to designate a normal trill, with its upper subsidiary, and the stroked *t* for 'a half-trill, commonly called a mordent . . . with the lower subsidiary, which is often (if the ear does not forbid it) a whole tone below'. To call a lower mordent a half-trill is incorrect and confusing; but that Muffat should have done so confirms the close affinity between trills and mordents to which attention has already been drawn. By implication, both diatonic and chromatic mordents are allowed.

Couperin (1716) explained that 'every mordent must be set on the note over which it is placed. . . . The repercussions and the note held at the end must all be included within the time-value of the main note'. This confirms what his notation leaves ambiguous, that the little notes in ex.87, from his first book of *Pièces de clavecin* (1713), were meant to be taken, in the usual Baroque fashion, accented and on (not before) the beat.

Gottlieb Muffat included a comprehensive range of lower mordents in his *Componimenti* (c1739; see ex.88, from p.107). Rameau, Dieupart, Mondonville, Mattheson, Quantz and others concurred. In the music of J. S. Bach mordents should be applied similarly; his brief examples in the *Clavier-Büchlein* (1720) are in line with those of Gottlieb Muffat. But it must be remembered that Bach's signs for the mordent, as for other ornaments, are very casual and variable.

Ex.87

Pincé simple   Pincé double

Ex.88

Ex.89 is taken from C. P. E. Bach, who called the mordent (pp.98ff, misnumbered 80ff)

an essential ornament for connecting notes, filling them out and rendering them brilliant. It may be either long or short . . . [and] is particularly valuable in an ascending step or leap. It seldom occurs on descending leaps and never on descending steps . . . when it follows an appoggiatura the mordent is taken lightly in accordance with the rule governing the performance of appoggiaturas [i.e. their resolutions]. . . . In the case of long mordents one must not hinder the beauty of the resonance. As with the others, he should not use them on every long note, nor continue them too long. In all filling out by mordents, there must always remain still a little space of time over unembellished, and the best-used mordent becomes offensive when carried like a trill rapidly into the succeeding note. Mordents, expecially short mordents, lend brilliance to leaping, detached notes. . . . Of all ornaments, mordents are most commonly introduced by the performer into the bass, especially at the peak of a phrase reached by step or leap. . . . In the use of accidentals this ornament adapts itself to its context, in the same way as does the trill. Its brilliance is often heightened by sharpening the lower note [in illustrating this point C. P. E. Bach set an accidental above the mordent sign, though the note to be sharpened is of course the one below the main note]. . . . The mordent and the half-trill are opposite ornaments. This latter may be used only in one way, namely over a step when it descends, which is just where a mordent never stands.

Ex.89d is not a true mordent, but is described as a 'slow mordent' by C. P. E. Bach (p.103, misnumbered 85) on the unconvincing ground that its notes are the same. Interestingly enough, he also regarded the acciaccatura as a species of condensed mordent rather than a condensed appoggiatura.

Ex.89

(a)   (b)   (c)♯   (d)

The generations of Haydn, Mozart and Beethoven, relying as they did on C. P. E. Bach's monumental treatise, made little change in their treatment of mordents. Leopold Mozart (1756, pp.242ff) had slightly confused the matter by including as mordents two fairly unrelated ornaments (a 'double appoggiatura' in C. P. E. Bach's sense, and a species of trill); but the true mordents which he showed are of the classical pattern. Türk in his *Clavierschule* (1789, p.272) made the very natural but unfortunate confusion already mentioned between the true (unprepared) *Schneller* or upper mordent and the true (prepared) *Pralltriller* or half-trill; otherwise he concurred with the preceding authorities and provided a good and clear selection of lower mordents. He included both prepared and unprepared specimens, calling the latter 'mordents' (p.275) and the former 'battements' (p.281), which he described as 'closely resembling the mordent'. He illustrated them with ex.90.

Ex.90

Clementi in his *Introduction to . . . the Pianoforte* (1801), having given the normal trill begun on its upper note, added a 'short shake beginning by the note itself' and 'transient of passing shakes', each of which is identical to the single unprepared upper mordent (*Schneller*). But he also gave, under the name of 'beat', lower mordents both prepared and unprepared. His rule for chromatic alteration, which reflects a change from the Baroque usage, is on an ascending step to equate the subsidiary of the mordent with the preceding note, but on leaps or first notes of passages invariably to use a semitone. Hummel in his *Anweisung* (1828, p.387) described the 'mordente' as an abbreviated form of the unterminated trill, beginning with its main note, touching the note above and returning to its main note; in other words, he described as mordent the unprepared upper (inverted) mordent or *Schneller*. This error was substantially augmented by Spohr in his *Violinschule* (1832), where the *Schneller* is called a *Pralltriller* (p.160) and given the sign proper to a lower mordent in the text (though its own normal sign in the music), while the name 'mordente' (p.168) is appropriated to the turn (but Leopold Mozart had initiated this second confusion).

Later in the 19th century passages occur in which an upper mordent is written out in small notes before a main note bearing a sign of accentuation. In the more recent of such examples it appears that this notation is meant literally, and that the mordent is to precede the beat. But in the Romantics this method of execution can only be regarded as exceptional, and it has no place in the Classics, being alien to the natural character of the ornament.

IV. The division family. This heading includes a number of ornaments closely related to the art of melodic variation. The general name 'division' with its equivalents in other languages (It. *passaggio, minuta*; Sp. *glosa, diferencia*; etc) was applied from the 16th century to the 18th, and indicates the subdividing of long notes into briefer ones. The ornaments in this family are often less crystallized in form and nomenclature than those of the appoggiatura or shake families discussed above.

1. Passing notes. 2. Changing notes. 3. Varieties of the turn. 4. Historical survey of turns. 5. Varieties of broken chord. 6. Historical survey of broken chords. 7. Broken notes.

1. PASSING NOTES. These connect disjunct main notes, and include one form of the so-called 'passing appoggiatura' (a single passing note) and two forms of *tirata* (a succession of passing notes). Some mid-18th-century writers, including C. P. E. Bach, described a 'passing appoggiatura' taken, unlike any true appoggiatura, before the ensuing beat, but nonetheless accented more strongly than the beat. This last point differentiates it from an ordinary passing note (which in this metrical position would normally be unaccented). The name 'passing appoggiatura' however was used by other writers of the same period (e.g. Leopold Mozart, 1756, p.206) for a normal passing note, taken not only before the beat but also unaccented. Leopold Mozart wrote, in connection with ex.91:

These appoggiaturas do not belong to the time of the principal note to which they descend but must be played in the time of the preceding note [i.e. before the beat]. . . . It is customary to use these passing appoggiaturas in a series of notes lying a third apart. . . . The semiquaver is taken quite smoothly and quietly, the accent always falling on the quaver.

Ex.91

Without embellishment   Thus it could be written

But they are played thus and are better written so

The run, under its Italian name 'tirata' (Fr. *tirade, coulade*), was applied to a series of two or more passing notes connecting consecutive main notes separated by an interval larger than a 3rd. Where the passing notes fill the entire interval stepwise (either diatonically or, on occasion, chromatically), they are of the ordinary 'strict' variety recognized in harmony textbooks. But where there is a melodic leap between the first main note and the beginning of the series of passing notes, the latter are called 'free' by some writers on harmony. Further refinements of description found in some early authorities (e.g. 'cascata doppia' and 'cascata per raccore il fiato' in Caccini's *Nuove musiche* of 1601/2) need no further discussion. The name 'tirata' however does not seem to have referred to an elaborate series of notes changing direction in the middle. Exx.92 and 93, based on examples in Leopold Mozart's *Violinschule* (1756, pp.250ff), illustrate the free *tirata* as well as the strict, the chromatic as well as the diatonic.

Ex.92

Adagio   Adagio   Adagio

Ex.93

Molto allegro

Adagio

[sic]

2. CHANGING NOTES.

2. CHANGING NOTES. These ornaments consist most often of notes interpolated between main notes that are identical or conjunct with each other. Figures referred to in various modern textbooks as *cambiata*, *échapée*, auxiliary note, returning note, alternating note, etc, may be included in this category; also the note of anticipation ('cadent') when added ornamentally to the written text. The most general late Renaissance and Baroque term is *groppo* (*gruppo*, *gruppetto*), though some 18th-century writers (e.g. Leopold Mozart) narrowed the meaning of that term to certain restricted instances. Baroque authorities included the turn under the same heading; but that ornament is so important as to merit separate discussion below.

Some German writers viewed as a single type of ornament the note of anticipation, the springer, and any similar note slipped in at the end of one main note and just before the beginning of the next. Their name for it (among other uses of that word) was *Nachschlag*. The cadent (note of anticipation) was sometimes regarded as an ornament and can often be introduced impromptu. It is shown as in ex.94*a* by Simpson (1659, p.12) and Playford (1660, p.74, and later edns.) but should as a rule be made rhythmically more pungent in keeping with the usual convention affecting dotted notes in appropriate circumstances before the acceptance of the double dot in the mid-18th century; thus ex.94*a* should actually be rendered approximately as in ex.94*b*. Ex.95 is from Marpurg (1756, Table IV).

Ex.94

(a) A cadent   (b)

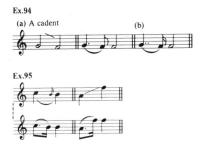

Ex.95

The springer, acute or sigh (Fr. *accent*, *aspiration*, *plainte*; Ger. *Nachschlag*) was illustrated by Playford as in ex.96. The simplest of changing notes, it is rhythmically akin to an unaccented 'passing appoggiatura'.

Ex.96

C. P. E. Bach treated it as if it were an appoggiatura that had flouted the rules; but really it is in no sense akin to an appoggiatura, being always gracefully unaccented, slurred to the previous note, and played or sung before the beat of the ensuing note. It is among the varied group of relatives included by Praetorius in 1619 (p.233) in his category of *accenti*; Simpson (1659, p.12) as well as Playford called it a springer; Mace's term (1676) was 'spinger'. Jean Rousseau (1687), Georg Muffat (1695), Loulié (1696), Saint-Lambert (1707), François Couperin (1713) and Marpurg (1756) are among the Baroque authorities who depicted it as an ornament; ex.97 is from Marpurg. In subsequent periods however it was always embodied in the written text, in ordinary notation.

Early examples of *groppo* include embryonic forms

Ex.97

of the ordinary Baroque trill mingled inextricably with ornaments which fall under the heading of changing notes (see exx.47–9). Later examples are more circumscribed, as in ex.98, from Leopold Mozart (1756, p.247).

Ex.98

3. VARIETIES OF THE TURN (Fr. *doublé, cadence, double-cadence, brisé, tour de gosier*; Ger. *Doppelschlag, Halbzirkel*; It. *groppo, gruppetto, circolo mezzo*). In a turn, or single relish, the main note alternates with its two auxiliaries a step above and below. As a type of *groppo* it was given the name 'circolo mezzo', which evokes nicely the encircling of the main note by its auxiliaries. The uses of the turn have not substantially changed, though methods of notating it have; for modern performers it is one of the least troublesome of Baroque ornaments, the traditions guiding its proper application not having been broken or seriously distorted.

There are two main varieties of turn: those falling at the beginning of their main note and thus bearing (or sometimes even emphasizing) its accent, and those introduced after the beginning of the main note and thus unaccented. There are few restrictions on the places appropriate to a turn except that there must be sufficient time to fit one in and a general suitability to its rather expressive character. C. P. E. Bach wrote that it is 'so to speak too obliging. It fits almost everywhere and is in consequence much abused'.

The chief difficulties in its use concern its timing and rhythm. Fashions have varied in different schools and periods, and even among individual composers. The choice of accented or unaccented turn may or may not be indicated by the location of the sign (when one is used); placed directly above a note the sign properly implies an accented turn on that note; placed above but slightly to the right of a note it properly implies an unaccented turn in greater or lesser degree subsequent to the beginning of that note. In both accented and unaccented turns the standard number of notes required is four, and their standard order is: upper subsidiary, main note, lower subsidiary, main note. This order may, though much less frequently, be reversed to produce an 'inverted' turn: lower subsidiary, main note, upper subsidiary, main note. As in the case of mordents, a still clearer nomenclature would be 'upper turn' for the standard form and 'lower turn' for the inverted.

When the number of notes in an accented turn is the standard four, the main note is necessarily preceded by its first subsidiary, and the musical effect is somewhat comparable to a short appoggiatura (usually from above), which having resolved on to its main note overshoots its mark, thus touching the opposite subsidiary and rebounding once more on to the main note. But when the number of notes in an unaccented turn is the standard four, the main note is heard and part of its length already compassed before the first subsidiary of the ornament itself occurs. The impression may (especially at high speed) be gained that an ornament of five notes instead of four has been heard. And there are indeed turns genuinely comprising five instead of four notes. When an accented turn has the exceptional five notes, the main note is struck first but lasts no longer than the subsequent first auxiliary, the musical effect being somewhat comparable to that of a lower-note trill. When an unaccented turn has the exceptional five notes, the main note, which has already been sounded before the ornament begins, is reiterated as part of the ornament.

An accidental above the sign for a turn properly indicates that the upper auxiliary should be chromatically altered; if below, the lower auxiliary. In Baroque music an accidental may sometimes be placed to the left of the sign when the first subsidiary note is to be affected, or to the right when the second is to be affected (C. P. E. Bach). But the placing of all such indications is unreliable, and chromatic alteration may be introduced in the absence of written indication under circumstances similar to those governing the chromatic alteration of mordents, but less freely. When both subsidiary notes would be diatonically a whole tone apart from their main note a Baroque musician might raise the lower one chromatically as indicated, for example, in a little table of ornaments by Edward Bevin included in a 17th-century hand in a manuscript of virginal music (see ex.149). This option later became the common though not invariable rule; and the so-called 'chromatic turn, in which both subsidiary notes stand at a semitone's distance (thus reducing the total compass to a diminished 3rd), found considerable favour in Chopin as an ornament and in Sibelius as an element of written figuration.

The main categories of turn are therefore the upper or standard turn as opposed to the lower or inverted turn; the accented as opposed to the unaccented turn; and the four-note as opposed to the five-note turn.

4. HISTORICAL SURVEY OF TURNS. 16th-century treatises on division, for instance Ortiz's *Trattado* of 1553 (from which ex.99 is taken), include a variety of figures, closely related to the Baroque turn, which did not survive as specific ornaments although as elements of written figuration they remained common enough. But ex.100, an exceptional instance from the table of ornaments in

Ex.99
(a)

(b) (no clef)

(c) (no clef)

Ex.100

Ex.101 Purcell: *Lessons* (1696), accented five-note turn

Ex.102 Loulié: *Eléments* (1696), accented turn

Ex.103 Couperin: *Pièces* (1713), accented turn
Doublé

Ex.104 J. S. Bach: *Clavier-Büchlein* (1720), accented turn

Ex.105 Marpurg: *Principes* (1756)

Ex.106 C. P. E. Bach, accented turns

Chambonnières' *Pièces de clavessin* (1670), suggests that some of these freer variants underwent almost the same crystallization as the turn in its strictest sense. Exx.101–6 are in the main self-explanatory. The uneven rhythm of ex.102 is probably a hint not meant literally; that in ex.105 is for slower passages in particular. As usual in written-out explanations of ornaments, the notation gives only an approximation of the rhythm, which requires a certain flexibility in performance.

C. P. E. Bach's instructions for the turn are full and elaborate. He laid considerable emphasis on its 'brilliant' character and said 'it is nearly always taken rapidly' (see ex.106). He continued:

[The turn] is used in slow as well as quick movements. It is not satisfactory on a very short note, since the time needed to perform its several notes may obscure the melody. . . . A broad understanding of its proper use may be acquired by regarding the turn as an ordinary terminated trill in telescoped form . . . it should not be substituted for an ordinary trill on a long note [since it] would leave part of the length unfilled. . . . It follows from its resemblance to the terminated trill that the turn is better suited by an ensuing note which ascends than by one which descends. . . . In spite of the musical value of this ornament, its sign is hardly familiar except on the keyboard. It is often shown by the signs for the trill or even for the mordent, which last two are also much confused. [Where a trill sign is shown] the speed of a passage may make it [the trill] impossible . . . here the performer should take

Ex.107 C. P. E. Bach, unaccented turns on dotted notes

Ex.108 C. P. E. Bach, accented five-note turns

Ex.109 C. P. E. Bach, unaccented four-note turn

a turn. . . . Similar as the turn and the trill are, they are unlike in two respects. First: because the last notes of a turn are not quickly connected with the following notes, there is always a small space between these and the following notes [not to be taken too literally]. Second: the turn may sometimes in slow, expressive movements replace its brilliance by a deliberately broad rendering. . . . The turn may stand between a note . . . and the following note [i.e. the unaccented turn] . . . [A]fter a dotted note . . . two notes acquire dots and the turn falls between them . . . often used when the time is so slow that [the dotted note] would sound sluggish if unornamented [see ex.107].

When a turn stands on detached notes it gains in brilliance when preceded by a note of the same pitch as the main note [i.e. the genuine five-note turn; see ex.108 and cf. ex.109].

His preference for an uneven rhythm in accented turns except where the speed precludes it was not without precedent, but for music down to and including that of J. S. Bach an even performance must be regarded as standard; in later music an uneven performance is frequently appropriate. As for unaccented turns, C. P. E. Bach's rule, according to which the last note of the turn itself acquires a dot as in ex.107, continued to be valid in subsequent periods; the main note following the turn is shortened just as it would be if the note bearing the unaccented turn were instead double-dotted as in ex.110. Without expressly stating it C. P. E. Bach hinted that this double-dotting of the main note, like other rhythmic modifications in connection with the turn, is applicable only at slow and moderate, not at rapid tempos. Later authorities appear not to have accorded specific recognition to the expressive, 'double-dotted' rendering, and though it may have remained while the direct influence of C. P. E. Bach's treatise persisted (into the generation of Beethoven and a little beyond), it need not subsequently be taken into account. It should certainly be borne in mind for the slow movements of Mozart or Beethoven. In most other respects C. P. E. Bach is, even today, a reliable guide for the turn.

Exx.111–21, from *Grove 3*, give Tovey's interpretation of a number of passages and may be found enlightening. In ex.111 the appoggiatura persists just beyond the beat (exactly as it does when preparing a trill); the same occurs if a note serving the function of an appoggiatura appears as part of the written text. Ex.115 might be rendered as in ex.110; but since the third dotted figure bears no turn it was probably meant – at that

Ex.110 Correct rhythm of unaccented turn on dotted (equivalent to double-dotted) note

Ex.111 W. F. Bach, five-note unaccented turn preceded by appoggiatura

Ex.112 Haydn, unaccented turn misleadingly notated

Ex.113 Mozart, accented turn (played on the second main *f"*) misleadingly notated

Ex.114 Mozart, unaccented turn, ambiguously notated

Ex.115 Mozart, unaccented turns misleadingly notated

Ex.116 Mozart, accented turn, uneven to fill a long note

Ex.117 Mozart, accented turn, even to fit into a short note

Ex.118 Beethoven, unaccented turn, soon and slow in expressive adagio

Ex.119 Beethoven, unaccented turn, late and quick in brilliant prestissimo

Ex.120 Beethoven, unaccented turn on a dotted note leading to a pair

Ex.121 Beethoven, accented five-note turn (*cf.* ex.119, unaccented four-note turn)

date – to be taken literally, without double-dotting; hence in the interpretation favoured by Tovey the three figures match rhythmically. In the course of the 19th century the turn showed the usual tendency to merge into the ordinarily notated figuration and to lose its ornamental character. Wagner, for example, used the turn sign in his early music but later wrote it out (as in Brünnhilde's main theme in the *Ring*). Mahler made it almost as much a feature of his idiom as the long appoggiatura (e.g. in the last movement of his Ninth Symphony).

5. VARIETIES OF BROKEN CHORD (Fr. *arpégé, harpégé, arpègement, harpègement, batterie*; Ger. *Brechung, Harpeggio*; It. *arpeggio, harpeggiato, battimento*). In music of the 19th and 20th centuries the term 'arpeggio' and its symbols imply the progressive retarding of each but the first note of the arpeggiated chord in ascending order, beginning with the bass note and ending with the treble. The degree of retardation is at the performer's discretion, being ordinarily greater in slow and expressive passages than in fast and brilliant ones. The effect is natural to plucked instruments such as the harp and stringed keyboard instruments such as the piano, but figuration derived from it is commonly found implied or fully written out for other instruments as well.

In music of the Baroque period the normal modern arpeggio was to a greater or lesser degree the normal treatment of full or moderately full chords on most instruments. On the lute or the guitar simultaneous chords of up to four notes are possible but do not ordinarily sound as satisfactory as chords more or less spread or broken. On the clavichord and harpsichord completely full simultaneous chords are possible and easy, but they are satisfactory on the clavichord only as a special effect and are extremely unpleasant on the harpsichord, where a slight spreading is (or should be) invariably used for all chords of three notes, and considerable spreading is usual for the fuller chords. A harpsichordist or clavichordist might also arpeggiate with both hands simultaneously rather than in succession, or arpeggiate with one hand though playing unarpeggiated the chord notes assigned to the other. The Baroque violin was often fitted with a bridge less steeply arched than the modern one, allowing three-part chords to be held more purely; similar considerations apply to the viol; but the standard treatment of chords was then as now slightly *arpeggiando*.

Only those forms of arpeggio elaborate enough to be fully written out in ordinary notation now were normally regarded as ornaments worthy of mention in the Baroque period. Though not kept very distinct from one another by the early authorities, they include various ways of breaking the chord; downwards instead of upwards (with the treble note taking the beat); once completely up and down again; more than once completely up and down; the same but ending at the top instead of at the bottom; and once completely up and partly down again (especially so as to end on the note from which the melody continues if the melody is in an inner part rather than in the treble or bass). For these varieties of broken chord there are three important rules. The first is to start the arpeggio not before but on the beat. The second, given by most Baroque treatises on accompaniment but generally valid in other circumstances too, is to use the arpeggio to fill in (with suitable diversity) notes which because of their length would otherwise tend to drag or even (e.g. on the lute or the

harpsichord) fade away before their time. The third rule, given particularly clearly by Rameau in the preface to his *Pièces de clavecin en concerts* (1741), is to respect the part-writing by ending the chord on the note from which the melody continues. There are also broken chords more elaborate than would for the most part be recognized now as arpeggios at all, but which were nevertheless regarded by the Baroque authorities as extensions of the same principle. It is here that one can see most clearly the part played by the arpeggio as a species of division and, like other forms of division, a branch of improvised figuration.

Arpeggiated passages of any variety may sometimes be further complicated by the insertion of additional notes not present in the chords and even harmonically foreign to them. The added note is best regarded as an ornament, and can usually be accounted for as an acciaccatura; 'passing acciaccatura' would be an appropriate term. Several may be written into the same chord, which then presents an appearance of extreme thickness and dissonance. Alternatively the added notes may be indicated by signs or left entirely to discretion. The name 'figured arpeggio' has been suggested for such chords.

Apart from the organ it is the rule in every variety of broken chord to hold as many of the notes as possible, except that any foreign notes are to be released as soon as sounded. On the clavichord and harpsichord in general this is normal technique in figured passages wherever the harmony makes it desirable and the fingers can compass it; on the piano the technique is normally replaced by the use of the sustaining pedal. On plucked instruments such as the lute and bowed instruments such as the viol similar instructions are given to keep the fingers of the left hand firmly on their notes even after the right hand or bow has passed to another string, in order that the resonance of the whole chord may be sustained; and this, too, is part of the normal technique of these instruments, especially of the lute, while in Baroque music the instruments of the violin family require the same technique.

The main varieties of broken chord are therefore chords broken in strict succession from bass to treble, or up and down again, or repeatedly so, or partly so; chords broken as two coinciding units, one in each hand, or broken in one hand only; chords broken not in strict succession, but in a variety of patterns; and chords broken in any of the above ways but with the momentary interpolation of foreign notes not intended to be sustained with the others.

6. HISTORICAL SURVEY OF BROKEN CHORDS. As a mere embellishment of the texture with little or no melodic significance, the main source of broken chords lies in the technique of such instruments as the lute, harp and harpsichord. But as melodic figuration of chord sequences their main source is the Renaissance and Baroque art of division and of improvisation generally.

The *arpeggiando* ('harp-style') figuration of chord sequences was a feature of the toccata in its original 16th-century sense of a 'touch piece' in which lutenists and others tried their touch, loosened their fingers and checked their tuning before embarking on a more formal passage. Even after such touch-piece preludings had crystallized into more or less formal compositions, many traces of their improvisatory origins remained for a time, among others the presence in the notation of plain chords intended to be figured extempore (as in the first prelude of J. S. Bach's '48'). Frescobaldi in the preface to his *Toccate* (1615–16) wrote:

the openings of the toccatas are to be taken *adagio* and *arpeggiando*; and likewise with suspensions or indeed discords, even in the middle of the works one breaks them together so as not to leave the instrument empty: which breaking [*battimento*] is to be executed at the discretion of the performer.

In his *Capricci* (1624) he added 'It is well to linger *arpeggiando* on certain discords so as to attack with more spirit the following passage'. Ex.122 shows the first two bars of a solution propounded by Dolmetsch (1915, p.216) for the opening of Frescobaldi's *Toccata otava* published in 1637.

Ex.122

Mace in 1676 (p.101) described the lutenist's 'Raking play', where the bass and treble notes sound together and lead to a downward arpeggio ending on the bass reiterated ('the *General* way of Playing all . . . Full, or Fuller stops'); later he gave (p.249) the normal upward arpeggio for full chords on the bass viol, insisting that the bass note, sounded first, be given 'a good full share of your Bow, (Singly, by It self, before you slide it upon the Rest) and Leave it likewise with a little Eminence of Smartness, by swelling the Bow a little, when you part with that String'. His illustrations of broken chords on the big accompanying lute include some very free and inventive figuration (see ex.123; transcribed by Dolmetsch, p.264).

Purcell's name for the broken chord was 'battery', but his explanation is obscure (*Lessons*, 1699). D'Anglebert (1689) put the name 'cheute' (appoggiatura, i.e. 'passing acciaccatura') and the sign for it before two of his examples of arpeggio, apparently considering that an appoggiatura in such a position implies an arpeggio on the chord (which is by no means necessarily the case); where there is no appoggiatura, he wrote 'arpégé' and

Ex.123

Ex.124 D'Anglebert, broken chords, figured and unfigured

Ex.125

used one of the commoner French signs for the arpeggio, shown in ex.124. Couperin's explanation of the signs (1713) is less clear than Chambonnières', shown in ex.125.

Marais in his *Pieces de viole* (1717) used the name 'harpègement' and the same sign as D'Anglebert, but mentioned only upward breaking. Dieupart in his Suites (1720) also followed D'Anglebert. Rameau (1724) placed a vertical wavy line after chords to specify arpeggiation with acciaccaturas. Geminiani in his *Treatise of Good Taste* (1749) used a word of his own, 'tatto', to describe such acciaccaturas; his musical illustration is shown in ex.126. C. P. E. Bach's examples are shown in ex.127. J. C. F. Rellstab in his explanatory *C. P. E. Bachs Anfangsgründe* (1790) gave an interpretation of plain chords marked 'Arpeggio' (in a fantasia by C. P. E. Bach) breathtaking in its range and boldness, one even changing the bass. But here arpeggios cease to be ornaments and become passage-work.

Ingenuity is sometimes required to apply the rule (specified by Rameau but very pertinent to J. S. Bach) that an arpeggiated chord should end with the note from

Ex.126 Geminiani, figured broken chords

Ex.127 C. P. E. Bach, broken chords, plain and figured

Ex.128 J. S. Bach – Dolmetsch, broken chords with inner melody

which the melody continues. Dolmetsch (p.274) gave the solution shown in ex.128 to a vexed passage in the 21st prelude from the '48'; a modicum of élan, some freedom of rhythm and perhaps a little stolen time is often necessary to bring out the sense.

7. BROKEN NOTES. The expressive truncation of a note at its beginning, as shown in exx.129 (Couperin, 1717) and 130 (Rameau, 1731), was an ornament of the French school, though possibly known and taken for granted elsewhere. Couperin, describing it in his treatise of 1717, wrote that 'as for the *suspension*, it is virtually confined to slow and expressive movements' and that the length of the delay would be determined by the performer's taste. The remainder of the harmony normally appears in its expected position on the beat. The term 'demi-soupir', as well as 'suspension', was sometimes applied to this ornament, and the fact that Brossard in his dictionary (1703) defined the Italian cognate *mezzo-sospiro* as a figure (identical with the modern quaver rest) which 'marks that one is silent for the eighth part of a bar' suggests that the ornament may originally have been a vocal device.

The expressive delay of melodic notes, but without an articulative silence, had been viewed both as a branch of expression (as it normally is today) and as a branch of ornamentation. Ex.131, from the preface to Caccini's *Nuove musiche*, is one of several examples there that are probably typical of much early 17th-century practice, at least among singers. Türk in his *Clavierschule* (1789, p.374) showed similar instances (see ex.132). The actual nuance of such rubatos can of course be rendered only very approximately in notation.

Exx.133 (D'Anglebert, 1689) and 130 (Rameau) show staccato treated as an ornament. But since mordents and normal Baroque trills take an accent, and since the Baroque accent is not a *sforzando* but a crisp attack requiring for its effect a preceding silence, nearly every Baroque performer would have rendered the staccato specified in D'Anglebert's examples. The liberal use of staccato in general was taken for granted, as the late 18th-century evidence supplied by Engramelle so unmistakably indicates. When staccato was specified in the notation, however, a dash above the note, not a dot (which had other meanings), was the standard sign. Gottlieb Muffat in c1739 and Geminiani in 1749 showed it as reducing the length by half; in 1751 Geminiani in his *Art of . . . the Violin* showed a reduction by three-quarters. Couperin, showing a reduction by a quarter, had explained in 1717 that 'the note marked is to be detached, but less so in expressive than in light and rapid movements'.

V. Compound ornaments. Certain Baroque ornaments were so customarily combined in pairs as to give rise to compound ornaments best considered in their own right. Though not involving new principles or new material, they were sometimes given their own signs and described individually in treatises of the Baroque

Ex.129 Couperin, suspension

Ex.130 Rameau

Son coupé   Suspension

Ex.131 Caccini, *tempo rubato* (old sense)

Ex.132 Türk, *tempo rubato* (old sense)

(a)   (b)   (c)

Ex.133 D'Anglebert: *Pièces* (1689), expressive silences

Détaché avant un tremblement   Détaché avant un pincé

period. The compounds discussed below gained a more or less established position.

1. Appoggiatura with mordent, trill or turn. 2. Turn with trill. 3. Double cadence and double relish.

1. APPOGGIATURA WITH MORDENT, TRILL OR TURN. A mordent on the note of resolution following an appoggiatura is so natural that Jean Rousseau in his *Traité de la viole* (1687) regarded the two, by a pardonable exaggeration, as inseparable. Matheson (1739) said that 'In singing, there is hardly an ascending appoggiatura without a mordent'. Hotteterre in his *Principes de la flûte* (1707) took a more moderate view: 'One often links mordents with appoggiaturas'. Playford (1660, p.74, and later edns.) and Simpson (1659, p.12) had illustrated such a combination, which they called a 'shaked Beat', as in ex.85; Purcell (1699) gave it as a single ornament as in

Ex.134 Purcell, appoggiatura and mordent

ex.134 under the usual English name 'beat' for an appoggiatura alone. D'Anglebert (1689), Dandrieu (c1710) and Couperin (1713) each used a compound sign. D'Anglebert used the name 'cheute et pincé', Dandrieu 'port de voix et pincé', and Couperin 'port de voix simple' (where the mordent is single) or 'port de voix double' (where it is double).

When the first note of an upper-note trill is prolonged, it may be regarded as an appoggiatura; accordingly the ornament was sometimes written with an appoggiatura or with a special sign (see §VIII). In this guise the *cadence appuyée* can be described as a compound ornament in deference to those Baroque authorities who regarded it as such. When an appoggiatura is prefixed to a trill or mordent it should normally resolve, not exactly on a beat or subdivision of a beat, but just after, almost with the effect of an unmeasured prolongation.

An appoggiatura-like small note appearing before a main note with a turn sign was C. P. E. Bach's indication for his five-note turns (see ex.108). However his *prallender Doppelschlag* ('trilled turn') illustrated in ex.135a and *Doppelschlag von unten* illustrated in ex.135b actually represent more feasibly the application of an appoggiatura to a turn.

Ex.135 C. P. E. Bach
(a) trilled turn

(b) ascending turn

2. TURN WITH TRILL (Fr. *tremblement coulé*; Ger. *doppelt Cadence*). One form, beginning with an inverted turn, was the 'ascending trill' (Fr. *tremblement coulé en montant*; Ger. *Triller von unten*) as illustrated in exx.136a and c and 137. Playford showed it as a variant of both his 'elevation' and his 'cadent' (see exx.66 and 67) and it was almost certainly intended by Locke's reference to 'Forefall and Shake' in his *Melothesia* (1673). The compound of a normal turn leading into a trill, as illustrated by exx.136b and d and 138, is called a 'descending trill' (Fr. *tremblement coulé en descendant*; Ger. *Triller von oben*). The English authors do not seem to have recognized it; but it was given by D'Anglebert (1689) and C. P. E. Bach as well as J. S. Bach and Marpurg.

3. DOUBLE CADENCE AND DOUBLE RELISH. L'Affilard (1694) used the term 'double cadence couplée' for the combination of an unaccented turn leading to an upper-note trill, as in ex.139. Georg Muffat illustrated the same compound in 1695 (see ex.140), and in the first half of the 18th century it became a frequent and characteristic cadential formula. Ex.141 shows three possible rhythms for its execution (ex.141a being derived specifically from ex.140). The term 'double cadence' was used by D'Anglebert (1689) and Dieupart (c1720) for the compounds

Ex.136 J. S. Bach, ascending and descending trills

Ex.137 Marpurg, descending trills

Ex.138 Marpurg, ascending trills

Ex.139 L'Affilard, 'double cadence couplée'

Ex.140 Georg Muffat: *Florilegium* (1695), double cadence

Ex.141
(a)

(b)

(c)

Ex.142 D'Anglebert, double cadence

Ex.143 Dieupart, double cadence

shown in exx.142 and 143 respectively; and J. S. Bach used the German cognate for his ascending and descending trills (see ex.136).

In 17th-century English sources a compound ornament called a double relish seems to have been cast in a role analogous to that of the later double cadence shown in ex.141 (which however certainly arrived in England with Handel, if it had not already become familiar). The most typical and beautiful form of double relish, shown in ex.144, was given by Playford, Simpson (1659, p.12)

Ex.144

double relish

Ex.145

and Mace (1676, p.107). Although the first note of the trill is ostensibly of the same duration as the others, Mace seems to have implied a slight, appoggiatura-like prolongation when he said that the 'backfall' of a 'single relish' (i.e. the initial upper note of a trill) 'would always be performed very strongly, and smartly'. A second form of double relish, shown in ex.145, was given in substantially the same form by Playford and Simpson. The concluding appoggiatura in such a compound might of course be embellished with a lower mordent on resolving, as discussed in §1.

VI. The English virginalists' strokes. These do not represent a family in any structural sense, and in substance they probably include nothing that has not already been described. They are given separate treatment here because as ornament signs they present special problems of interpretation, possibly because the late 16th century is a relatively early period for ornament signs in such profusion. There is no known contemporary table of ornaments explaining them, and the tables that begin to show them in the latter half of the 17th century indicate a diversity of meanings. Meanwhile they occur quite inconsistently in different manuscripts of the same piece, and where their appearance in one manuscript is replaced by written-out notation in another, this notation is not itself always consistent.

Ex.146

Although the two signs employed – the single and double stroke as shown in ex.146 – appear sometimes to have had distinct meanings, it is by no means clear that they were always discriminated. Passages such as those in exx.147 and 148 have prompted the suggestion that the single stroke might indicate an ornament to be played before the main note while a double stroke might indicate one to be executed on the pulse of the main note. This suggestion is ingenious but lacking in documentary support. Neither sign can bear a single

Ex.147

Ex.148

meaning consistently because solutions which are probable in one context are impossible (e.g. from shortage of time) in another. Like the subsequently frequent '+' and '×', the virginalists' strokes (which were also used by English organists) may perhaps best be regarded as hints generally for some ornament rather than specifically for any one kind of ornament. Presumably the double stroke might have implied in many instances a more elaborate ornament than the single stroke, but even that assumption should not be relied on. In certain cases a single or double stroke may well have been intended as a visual aid to 'score-reading' rather than an ornament sign; one suspects this when every note of a cantus firmus is identically garnished in such fashion. In manuscripts similar strokes also occasionally appear, naturally enough, as erasure signs.

1. The single stroke. 2. The double stroke.

1. THE SINGLE STROKE. According to Playford (1660), Simpson (1659) and Mace (1676) – all of whom really postdate the age of virginal music – a single stroke indicates a lower appoggiatura if it appears before the note (or the lutenists' letter) or a springer if it appears over the note (or letter). But in virginal music the stroke is never found before its note, and appears over it only when there is no tail for it to cross; moreover neither an appoggiatura nor a springer seems musically appropriate in a majority of its contexts in virginal music. D'Anglebert (1689; see ex.124) and later composers for the harpsichord often used a (rising) stroke crossing the tail to mean an upward arpeggio. It seems musically impossible for this to have any connection with the virginalists' ornament; it is clearly borrowed from the French lutenists' sign as shown, for example, in Denis Gaultier's *Rhétorique* (c1650–60). A more likely source of the virginalists' stroke is the 15th-century mordent sign shown in ex.81.

A brief table of 'graces in play', signed by or attributed to a certain Edward Bevin in an English manuscript (*GB-Lbm* Add.31403) of perhaps as late as c1700 but containing keyboard music composed at the beginning of the 17th century, includes what certainly appears to be the virginalists' single rising stroke across the tail, and explains it (without naming it) as in ex.149. Evidently the stroke here indicates a slide in the dotted form popular (though not to the exclusion of the undotted form) at the beginning of the 17th century. The first slide in ex.149 is a simple ornament; the second is compounded with an upper grace note of sorts; and the third leads into a double relish. The indications of fingering are from the source. The evidence of this table should be taken seriously, since a slide – dotted or undotted – is musically satisfactory in many, though not all, contexts.

Ex.149 Edward Bevin, single stroke for slides

It is true that Playford, Simpson and Mace used the sign '+' for a slide. But Chambonnières (1670), Purcell (1699) and later authorities showed a rising stroke between the heads of notes to be joined by a slide, the same sign also having been used for the 'passing acciaccaturas' inserted (with an effect very like that of a slide) between the harmonic notes of figured arpeggios.

2. THE DOUBLE STROKE. In Playford, Simpson and Mace the double stroke is not found at all. Locke (1673), Purcell (1699) and T.B. (3/1722, p.41) called it a shake; and Purcell and Prelleur (1731) showed it as a trill and as a half-trill. Geminiani (1751) called it a 'beat' in the text and a 'mord[en]te' in the illustrations, using it as a mordent short or long. Though not entirely confined to England, the double stroke appears to have been mainly an English and Dutch ornament of the 16th and 17th centuries. It displays to the historian a significant though not uninterrupted continuity from the early virginalists onwards and may often be taken as a fairly explicit indication of what most English 17th-century authorities meant by 'shaking': a short or long trill or lower mordent. The trill would be prepared as usual; the mordent might be prepared by a lower appoggiatura, but not necessarily. This interpretation accords with such clues as can be found in parallel manuscript versions, where a double stroke in one copy is often replaced by a written-out trill in another, or cases like the Mulliner Book, in which the sign tends to appear where space is cramped but the written-out convention where space allows. The number of reiterations shown does not always add up correctly from a metrical point of view, or may vary where different copies of the same passage have the same trill written out – an indication that the embellishments are in fact merely trills conventionally written out rather than divisions meant to be played literally. Such evidence suggests that even figures as unassuming as ex.150a and c can stand for a trill. But in some contexts only a mordent or unterminated half-trill is musically satisfactory as a rendering of the double stroke.

In ex.151, the opening of John Bull's splendid Queen Elizabeth's Pavan, no difference of speed appears to have been intended between the reiterations shown as quavers and those shown as semiquavers. The second half of bars 1, 3 and 4, and the second quarter of bar 2, are all meant as normal trills at the same speed, their first notes well accented and if desired a little prolonged, their turns at the same speed as their main reiterations. The double stroke in bar 1 may be a lower single or double mordent; the single stroke in bar 4 may also be a lower mordent, probably best single. Since various manuscripts of the same piece of virginal music are often garnished differently with ornamental strokes, it need not be regard-

ed as obligatory to insert all the ornaments indicated in any one version; and ornaments not shown may at times be desirable or even necessary, especially at cadences.

English lute manuscripts of the Elizabethan age contain a similar proliferation of ornaments in which no two sources show precise agreement; but the very frequency of the ornaments indicates a rich tradition of embellishment. There are however some descriptions of their meanings, particularly in Thomas Robinson's *Schoole of Musicke* (London, 1603); and there is a list of signs in the Margaret Board Lutebook (R. Spencer's private collection) on f.32 (see Poulton, 1975). These all belong marginally to a larger continental tradition of lute ornaments described by Mersenne (1636–7), exemplified in Besard and Vallet, and growing out of a history including the circle (meaning a falling appoggiatura) in the Milano–Borrono publications of 1548 and 1550 as well as the elaborately, if ambiguously, described ornaments in the 'Capirola' Manuscript (c1517; *US-Cn*). See LUTE, §6.

VII. The ornaments summarized by function.
When C. P. E. Bach, affirming (in the passage quoted at the end of §I) the importance of well-rendered ornaments, said that their functions include connecting notes, enlivening them, giving them weight and emphasis, and contributing to a disposition 'sad or joyful or otherwise', he implicitly suggested a basis for a more systematic consideration of functions – melodic, colouristic, rhythmic and harmonic – such as might promote good style and assurance in the performance of ornaments by present-day students of Baroque music.

To 'connect' notes is a melodic function. An ornament whose function is primarily melodic requires some (though not necessarily much) length but little accentuation. On the beat, it will take the natural accent without necessarily increasing it. Off the beat, it will slip smoothly into place and sound more decorative than prominent. A clear example of a melodic ornament in this sense is the unaccented turn (see exx.107–20). Several other ornaments of the division family are also primarily melodic, including the *tirata* (ex.92–3) and other forms of *groppo* as well as all but the most rhythmically incisive types of passing note and changing note. Broken chords often represent a melodic enrichment of harmonic progressions, though a steady flow of arpeggiation is colouristic in function. Some trills are more significant for their effect on the melodic line (e.g. where they

Ex.150

Ex.151 Bull, 'shaked' ornaments

have the feel of a 'passing ornament') than on the harmonic progression (e.g. creating the effect of a 4–3 appoggiatura and resolution in Baroque cadences). Primarily melodic trills do not demand preparation by their upper note, though from Byrd to Beethoven they usually expect it; they normally require a termination, and if this happens to be specified in the notation its rhythm should be interpreted conventionally and not literally. Compound ornaments involving a trill or turn are often predominantly melodic in function (see exx.135, 136c, 138, 142–3, 145). Modern trills may be primarily colouristic rather than melodic; in either case they are lower-note (i.e. they start with their main note, which should not be prolonged unless so marked though it may be accented at discretion), and no termination should be applied if none is shown.

Coloration of the texture is a subsidiary function which may be served by a Baroque ornament or by an element classified by some Baroque authorities (though not by present-day theorists) as an ornament. The very long trills most characteristically found on the harpsichord, for example, do not function primarily as melody, rhythm or harmony. Instead they partly sustain the sound (which on the harpsichord would otherwise die down too soon) and partly colour it with a lively glitter and pulsation, a function which they may also serve by analogy on instruments capable of sustaining the sound indefinitely. The prominent form of Baroque vibrato also colours the sound so conspicuously that it was commonly treated by Baroque authorities as an ornament related to the trill. The kind of early Baroque vocal tremolo shown in ex.42a may also be counted here. One might call such ornaments, which 'enliven' notes in one of the ways that C. P. E. Bach as a harpsichordist may have had in mind, 'colouring ornaments'. Not all forms of Renaissance and Baroque vibrato however were sufficiently pronounced to be regarded by contemporary theorists as an ornament; and testimony from Ganassi onwards confirms that the technique of an unprominent vibrato was employed on bowed strings and some woodwind instruments as well as vocally.

To give 'emphasis and weight' is a rhythmic function. An ornament whose function is primarily rhythmic requires little length but decided accentuation. On the beat, it will not only take the natural accent but increase it, resulting in a reinforcement of the natural rhythm. Off the beat, it will take an accent contrary to the metre, resulting in a displacement of the natural rhythm comparable to syncopation. A typical representative of ornaments creating rhythmic accentuation is the mordent as shown in exx.86–8 (Leopold Mozart wrote (p.244) that 'the mordent must be used only when it is desired to give special emphasis to a note'). The shorter the mordent, the greater its rhythmic accentuation, longer mordents tending to be more or less melodic in function. The genuine short appoggiatura (see ex.19), taken crisply and brilliantly, also serves a primarily rhythmic function; likewise the acciaccatura, the sort of double appoggiatura shown in exx.27–9 and the quick, undotted slide when it functions as a conjunct double appoggiatura (i.e. taken on the beat as in exx.30–35a; the long slide, often uneven in rhythm, tends towards the melodic function, as do those slides that occasionally occur before the beat, i.e. functioning as a pair of passing notes). Broken notes (see exx.129–32) are rhythmic ornaments in a different sense: they expressively disturb the rhythm of a melody rather than accentuating any particular main note.

To contribute to a disposition 'sad or joyful or otherwise' is an expressive activity which may characterize the melodic function, and to a lesser degree the rhythmic function, but is perhaps most often a harmonic function. An ornament whose function is primarily harmonic requires substantial length and accentuation. Epitomizing harmonic ornaments in this sense are some of the most characteristic of all Baroque ornaments: the cadential trill (as in exx.60, 62, 65), the long appoggiatura (as in exx.12, 15) and their compounds. On the beat they increase the natural accent – producing however not so much a reinforcement of a natural rhythm as an alteration of the notated harmony: the notated main note, far from being brought into melodic or rhythmic prominence, will be delayed and subordinated by the ornament, which 'usurps' the stress. Since the main note is usually consonant but the accessory note ornamenting it is usually dissonant, an expressive intensification or even exacerbation of the harmony is gained. Off the beat, no functional alteration of the harmony would result; such an ornament could thus occur off the beat only in the sense of being prepared before but suspended over the pulse, on which a modification of the harmony (usually from consonance to dissonance) may then occur as a contrapuntal suspension. The discord is still stressed on the beat and resolved with appropriate suavity by the delayed main note. Except when tied over in this way, all long appoggiaturas, and the initial note of a cadential trill, should be executed firmly on the beat and slurred to their main note.

It is possible for a simple ornament and quite usual for a compound ornament to serve more than one of these functions at the same time. Thus an ornament whose primary function is to place rhythmic emphasis on the main note may, if prolonged, fill it out melodically as well, though the more it fills out the less it will emphasize. For such reasons it is sometimes uncertain into which category an ornament should be placed; but its interpretation can always be arrived at by allowing due weight to each function which it appears to serve: for the melodic function, smoothness; for the rhythmic function, sharpness; for the harmonic function, expressiveness.

VIII. Index to ornaments and table of signs

Abzug (appoggiatura), II, 1–3
Accent: (springer), IV, 2; (appoggiatura), II, 1–3
Acciaccatura: (simultaneous appoggiatura), II, 8; (in broken chords), IV, 5–6; (misnomer for short appoggiatura), II, 3
Acute (springer), IV, 2
Alternating note (as ornament), IV, 2
Anschlag (double appoggiatura), II, 6
Anticipation, note of (as ornament), IV, 2
Appuy (appoggiatura), II, 1–3; III, 5; V, 1
Arpeggio (as ornament), IV, 5–6
Ascending trill, V, 2
Aspiration: (vibrato), III, 2; (springer), IV, 2; (curtailed note), IV, 7
Auxiliary note (as ornament), IV, 2
Backfall: (upper appoggiatura), II, 1–3; backfall shaked, III, 4; double backfall (slide), II, 7
Balancement: (tremolo), III, 1; (vibrato), III, 2
Battement: (vibrato), III, 2; (mordent), III, 8–9; (long trill), III, 3
Battery, batterie (broken chord), IV, 5–6
Battimento (broken chord), IV, 5–6
Bearing (slide), II, 7
Beat: (appoggiatura), II, 1–3; (mordent), III, 8–9; (mordent after appoggiatura), V, 1; shaked beat, III, 8–9
Bebung, III, 1–2
Beisser (mordent), III, 8–9
Brechung (broken chord), IV, 5–6
Brisé (turn), IV, 3–4
Broken chords, IV, 5–6
Cadence: (trill), III, 3–5; (turn), IV, 3–4; (ascending or descending trill), V, 2
Cadence appuyée, III, 5; V, 1

TABLE OF ORNAMENT SIGNS

Sign	Ornament	Guide to use or source	Section
•	Vibrato, tremolo	17th-century Fr. and Eng.	III, 1, 2
⁝	Curtailed note	Mace	IV, 7
••	Single relish (virtually brief trill with turned ending)	Mace; also 17th-century Eng. repeat sign	III, 4; V, 3
⟋ ⁚	Prepared long mordent	17th century Eng.	III, 9; V, 1
•⁚• or ⁚•\\ ∴	Double relish	17th-century Eng.	V, 3

Sign	Ornament	Guide to use or source	Section
	Ascending trill with or without turned ending	17th-century Eng.	V, 2
	(a) Curtailed note (b) More generally staccato	(a) Couperin, Rameau (b) 18th century	IV, 7
⌐ or ∟	Quaver rest sign over note or inverted quaver rest sign under note: curtailed note	D'Anglebert	IV, 7
	(a) Above note: mordent (b) After note: *Nachschlag*	(a) Mace (b) Loulié	(a) III, 9 (b) IV, 2
	Rising stroke through stem if there is one: (a) Mordent (b) Half-shake (c) ?Trill (d) Ascending slide	Late 16th- to early 17th-century Eng. and 17th-century Dutch virginalists (use not entirely certain)	VI; VI, 1 (a) III, 4, 8, 9 (b) III, 4 (c) III, 4 (d) II, 7
	Ascending slide	Gottlieb Muffat	II, 7
	Through stem if there is one: ascending slide	Bevin	II, 7
	Through stem if there is one: ascending slide leading to trill	Bevin	VI, 1
etc	(a) Acciaccatura (b) Short appoggiatura	(a) Marpurg onwards (b) 19th century (Spohr, Czerny and others)	(a) II, 8 (b) II, 5
or	Acciaccatura	C. P. E. Bach, Marpurg and others	II, 8
	(a) Through stem or (b) Before stem: both arpeggio (usually ascending) (c) Between staves or note-heads	(a) Chiefly Fr., 17th century and later (b) Marais (c) D'Anglebert	IV, 6
	Between and above notes: springer; accent	17th-century Eng., and 18th-century Fr.	IV, 2
	Before note: (a) Lower appoggiatura (b) Ascending slide (c) Rising note of anticipation or similar *Nachschlag*	(a) Widely used 17th- to mid-18th-century Eng., Ger. and It. (b) Chiefly Fr., same dates; also given by Türk (c) Later 18th-century Ger., esp. Türk	(a) II, 1 (b) II, 7 (c) IV, 2
	Variant of (b) above	Gottlieb Muffat	II, 7
	Between heads of notes: (a) Ascending slide (b) Slide-like acciaccatura in chord or arpeggio	(a) 17th- and 18th-century Eng., Fr. and Ger. (b) 18th-century Ger., incl. J. S. Bach	(a) II, 7 (b) IV, 6; II, 7
	Variant of above, but ? confined to (slide-like) acciaccatura in chord or arpeggio	Late 18th and early 19th centuries (Türk, Clementi, L. Adam *père*)	IV, 6; II, 8
	Falling stroke across stem: descending arpeggio	D'Anglebert, Gottlieb Muffat, Marpurg and others	IV, 6
	Before note: (a) Falling note of anticipation (cadent) (b) Upper appoggiatura (c) Descending slide	(a) 17th-century Eng., incl. Purcell; also Türk (b) Walther, Gottlieb Muffat (c) Türk	(a) IV, 2 (b) II, 1 (c) II, 7
	Between heads of notes: descending slide	Couperin	II, 7
	Double rising stroke through stem if there is one: (a) Trill (b) Half-shake (c) Mordent	Late 16th- to early 17th-century Eng. and 17th-century Dutch virginalists (use not entirely certain)	VI; VI, 2 (a) III, 4 (b) III, 4 (c) III, 9
	The same above or below the stem; probably variant of above	Eng. and Dutch, 2nd half of 17th century; Geminiani, Kuhnau	III, 5

Sign	Ornament	Guide to use or source	Section
⟍⟍	Probably further variant of above	Some Italians (Pasquali, Pollini), James Hook, Clementi	III, 5, 7
‖	(a) Probably further variant of above (b) *Nachschlag*	Marpurg and others	(a) III, 5 (b) IV, 2
⟍⟋	Probably further variant of above	Pollini, Clementi and others	III, 7
⟍⟮	Appoggiatura-prepared trill	Late 17th-century Eng.	III, 5; VI; VI, 2
⟱⟮	Trill with turned ending	Bevin	III, 5; VI; VI, 2
⟰⟮	? Variant of above: trill with turned ending	Purcell	III, 5; VI; VI, 2
c	Letter *c* above note: ascending slide	Murschhauser	II, 7
9	*Groppo*: often in form of trill	Early 17th-century It.	IV, 2; III, 4
⟋⟍⟍	Mordent	Murschhauser	III, 9
t	(a) *Trillo* = tremolo (b) Trill (c) Tremolo = trill	(a) Late 16th- to 17th-century It. (b) Widespread (c) Late 16th- to 17th-century It.	(a) III, 1 (b) III, 3–7 (c) III, 4
ṭ	Appoggiatura-prepared trill	Gottlieb Muffat	III, 5
t⟋⟍⟍	Trill full length of note	Georg Muffat	III, 5
t or tↄ	Trill with turned ending	Georg and Gottlieb Muffat	III, 5
tr ∾	Trill with turned ending	Occasionally found	III, 3–7; V
t̸	Mordent	Georg Muffat	III, 9
tr (early form sometimes **tri**)	(a) *Trillo* = tremolo (b) Trill (any length or variety)	(a) Late 16th- to 17th-century It. (b) Very common and widespread	(a) III, 4 (b) III, 3–7
tr⟋⟍⟍	Continuous trill	Couperin; Tartini; subsequently well established	III, 5, 7
+ (cf below; the two are largely interchangeable)	(a) Ascending slide (b) Lower appoggiatura (c) Trill (d) Unspecified hint to ornament	(a) 17th-century Eng.; 18th-century Fr. and Ger. (b) Chambonnières (c) Very common, esp. on vn and fl: the main usage (d) Not uncommon	(a) II, 7 (b) II, 1 (c) III, 4, 5
× (cf above; the two are largely interchangeable)	(a) Ascending slide (b) Upper appoggiatura (c) Trill (d) Mordent (e) Unspecified hint to ornament	(a) Heinichen (b) Marpurg (c) Lully, Mondonville; not uncommon (d) 18th-century Fr. and Ger.: the main usage (e) Not uncommon	(a) II, 7 (b) II, 3 (c) III, 5 (d) III, 9
⊕	Appoggiatura-prepared trill	L'Affilard	III, 5
⌃	(a) Springer (b) Upper appoggiatura (*coulement*)	(a) 18th-century Ger. (b) Hotteterre	(a) IV, 2 (b) II, 2
>	Upper appoggiatura (very like accentuation sign)	Murschhauser	II, 1–3
⌄	(a) Mordent (prepared or unprepared) (b) Inverted springer (c) Lower appoggiatura	(a) L'Affilard, Loulié (b) Walther, Türk (c) Murschhauser	(a) III, 9 (b) IV, 2 (c) II, 1–3
∿	(a) Trill (b) *Pralltriller* (half-shake) (c) *Schneller* (inverted, i.e. upper, mordent)	(a) Ubiquitous Fr. and Ger. from 17th century: the correct usage (b) Türk (c) Türk, Spohr, Czerny (a misappropriation)	(a) III, 4 (b) III, 3, 6 (c) III, 3, 9
∿∿	(a) Trill (variant of above, sometimes implying more reiterations, giving longer duration) (b) Double mordent (c) Appoggiatura-prepared lower mordent (d) Prepared trill (e) Ascending trill (f) Vibrato (g) Tremolo	(a) Ubiquitous Fr. and Ger. from 17th century: the correct usage (b) Loulié (c) ?Locke, Purcell (d) L'Affilard (e) Gottlieb Muffat (f) Mace (g) L'Affilard	(a) III, 4 (b) III, 9 (c) III, 9 (d) III, 5 (e) V, 2 (f) III, 2 (g) III, 1

Sign	Ornament	Guide to use or source	Section
	(a) Long trill (b) Long mordent (c) Vibrato in general (d) Special form of vibrato (e) Measured or unmeasured tremolo	(a) Later 18th-century Ger. onwards (b) Couperin (c) A few violinists down to Spohr and others (d) Marais (e) Mainly 17th-century It.	(a) III, 7 (b) III, 9 (c) III, 2 (d) III, 2 (e) III, 1
	Trills on one main note separated by recurrence of main note plain	Geminiani	—
	Appoggiatura-prepared trill	17th- and 18th-century Fr. and Ger.	III, 4, 5
	Appoggiatura-prepared trill with turned ending	Marpurg	III, 5; V, 2
	Variant of above	Marpurg	III, 5; V, 2
	Trill with turned ending	18th-century Ger., incl. J. S. Bach	III, 5; V, 2
	Variant of above	D'Anglebert	III, 5
	Variant of above	18th-century Fr.	III, 5; V, 2
	Further variant of above	Rameau, Marpurg (Fr. trans.), Türk	III, 5; V, 2
	(a) Trill with turned ending (b) Special telescoped form of (a): 'trilled turn' (prallender or getrillerter Doppelschlag) (c) 5-note turn	(a) Couperin, J. S. Bach; common 18th century to early 19th (b) C. P. E. Bach, Türk (c) Ger. down to Beethoven	(a) III, 5 (b) V, 1 (c) IV, 4
	Variant of above	J. F. Agricola	III, 5; V, 1
	Ascending trill with turned ending	Marpurg	III, 5; V, 2
	Ascending trill	Gottlieb Muffat	V, 2
	Ascending trill with turned ending	Gottlieb Muffat	V, 2
	(a) Ascending trill (b) Appoggiatura-prepared trill	(a) 17th- to 18th-century Fr. and Ger., incl. J. S. Bach (b) Marpurg	(a) V, 2 (b) III, 5
	(a) Ascending trill with turned ending (b) Appoggiatura-prepared lower mordent	(a) 18th-century Ger., incl. J. S. Bach (b) Dandrieu	(a) V, 2 (b) III, 8, 9
	Variant of above	Marpurg	V, 2
	Ascending trill with turned ending	Marpurg	V, 2
	Descending trill	17th- to 18th-century Fr. and Ger., incl. J. S. Bach	V, 2
	Descending trill with turned ending	18th-century Ger., incl. J. S. Bach	V, 2
	Descending trill with turned ending	Marpurg	V, 2
	Variant of above	Marpurg	V, 2
	Variant of above	Marpurg	V, 2
	(a) Mordent (b) Inverted (i.e. upper) mordent (Schneller)	(a) Ubiquitous later 17th- and 18th-century Fr. and Ger.: the correct usage (b) Hummel	(a) III, 8, 9 (b) III, 8, 9
	Mordent: variant of (a) above	Couperin	III, 8, 9
	(a) Mordent (further variation of (a) above, sometimes implying more reiterations, giving longer duration) (b) Inverted (i.e. upper) mordent (Schneller; but under misnomer Pralltriller)	(a) Ubiquitous Fr., from 17th century, and Ger., from early 18th, incl. J. S. Bach: the correct usage (b) Preface to Spohr's Violinschule	(a) III, 8, 9 (b) III, 8, 9
	Mordent: variant of (a) above	Chambonnières	III, 8, 9
	Continuous mordent	Couperin	III, 8, 9
	'Triple mordent'	Loulié	III, 8, 9

Sign	Ornament	Guide to use or source	Section
∿	Slide (sometimes implying ascending); also the 'direct' showing at end of line which note next line starts with	18th-century Ger., incl. J. S. Bach	II, 7
ℳ	Inverted variant of above, occasionally used for descending slide	Walther	II, 7
∾	(a) Turn (b) Inverted turn	(a) D'Anglebert; ubiquitous sign from 17th century to present: the correct usage (b) Hummel, Spohr (as 'mordent')	IV, 4
⌇	Inverted variant of above: (a) Inverted turn (b) Standard turn	(a) Marpurg, C. P. E. Bach, Clementi and others: the correct usage (b) C. P. E. Bach, Türk; also Hummel, Spohr (as 'mordent')	IV, 4
∽	(a) Turn (b) Inverted turn	(a) L'Affilard, Türk, Czerny (b) Clementi, Hummel	IV, 4
S	Inverted turn	Marpurg	IV, 4
⌖	Trill with turned ending	Geminiani	III, 5
♪∾	5-note turn	C. P. E. Bach, Türk, Hummel	IV, 4
♫∾	Ascending turn	C. P. E. Bach	V, 1
⸲	Comma over note or above, but to left: (a) Upper appoggiatura ('backfall') (b) Trill (viewed as 'backfall shaked')	(a) 17th-century Eng. (b) 17th- to early 18th-century Eng. and Fr.	(a) II, 1 (b) III, 5
⸲	Comma after note: (a) Trill (b) Lower appoggiatura (c) Mordent	(a) 17th- and 18th-century Fr.: the main usage (b) 17th-century Fr. lutenists (c) 17th- and 18th-century Fr.	(a) III, 5 (b) II, 1 (c) III, 9
⸲⸲	Double comma: descending slide	17th-century Eng.	II, 7
⸲	Inverted comma between notes: springer	L'Affilard	IV, 2
(	Inverted comma before note: appoggiatura	17th- to 18th-century Fr.; also Walther	II, 2
)	Inverted comma after note: mordent	D'Anglebert	III, 9
↳	Comma-like curve before note: lower appoggiatura	Early 18th-century Ger., incl. J. S. Bach	II, 2
↰	Comma-like curve before and above note: upper appoggiatura	Early 18th-century Ger., incl. J. S. Bach	II, 2
◡♩	Double comma-like curve rising to note: lower appoggiatura	Early 18th-century Ger., incl. J. S. Bach	II, 2
◠♩	Double comma-like curve falling to note: upper appoggiatura	Early 18th-century Ger., incl. J. S. Bach	II, 2
(	Small bracket-like curve to left of notes: (a) Ascending slide (b) Appoggiatura (c) Mordent (d) Indicates the (slide-like) figuring of an arpeggio between the notes bracketed	(a) 17th- to 18th-century Fr. (b) D'Anglebert (c) Marpurg (d) D'Anglebert; fairly common: the most important usage	(a) II, 7 (b) II, 2 (c) III, 9 (d) IV, 6; II, 7
((	Double bracket-like curve before arpeggio: doubly figured (see (d) above)	Marpurg	IV, 6
)	Small bracket-like curve to right of notes: descending slide	D'Anglebert	II, 7
(⸲) or ⸲⸲	Small bracket-like curves or commas on either side of note: prepared mordent	D'Anglebert	III, 9
⁘ or ⁘	(a) Tremolo (b) Bebung (on clvd)	18th-century Ger., incl. J. S. Bach	(a) III, 2 (b) III, 1

Sign	Ornament	Guide to use or source	Section
	Truncated note	Couperin, Rameau	IV, 7
	Appoggiatura-prepared trill (misuse of above)	Mondonville	III, 5
	Pause mark, often implying cadenza	Explained by 18th-century authorities	–
	Large bracket-like curve before chord: arpeggio	Purcell, Dieupart, Cranmer	IV, 6
(see also below)	(a) Before chord: arpeggio (b) Before note: vibrato	(a) late 17th-century Eng. (Purcell) and Fr. (Lebègue); became common in 18th century and the established sign in 19th (b) Marais	(a) IV, 6 (b) III, 2
(see also above)	After chord with rising or falling stroke across stem to indicate arpeggio: arpeggio to be figured	Rameau	IV, 6
	Before chord: ascending arpeggio	17th-century Fr.; common in 18th century and into 19th	IV, 6
	Hooked zigzag to left of chord, slur sign to right: variant of above	17th-century Fr.	IV, 6
	Before chord: descending arpeggio	Couperin, Türk	IV, 6
	Hooked zigzag to left of chord, slur sign to right: variant of above	17th-century Fr.	IV, 6
	Before chord: arpeggio	Türk	IV, 6
	Before chord: ascending arpeggio	18th-century Ger.	IV, 6
	Before chord: descending arpeggio	18th-century Ger.	IV, 6
	Between staves: notes so joined to be played simultaneously	Dandrieu in unmeasured preludes	–
	Between staves: notes so joined are unison	Couperin	–
	Between melodic notes: *tirata*	Occasionally found in 17th and 18th centuries, various localities	IV, 1

BIBLIOGRAPHY

WaltherML

P. Aaron: *Thoscanello de la musica* (Venice, 1523/*R*1969; Eng. trans., 1970)

M. Agricola: *Musica instrumentalis deudsch* (Wittenberg, 1529/*R*1969 incl. *Musica figuralis deudsch*, enlarged 5/1545)

S. di Ganassi: *Opera intitulata Fontegara* (Venice, 1535, repr. 1934; Ger. trans., 1956; Eng. trans., 1959)

——: *Regola rubertina* (Venice, 1542/*R*1970)

D. Ortiz: *Trattado de glosas sobre clausulas y otros generos de puntos en la musica de violones* (Rome, 1553; Ger. trans., 1936 and 1961)

E. N. Ammerbach: *Orgel oder Instrument Tabulatur* (Leipzig, 1571/*R*)

G. dalla Casa: *Il vero modo di diminuir* (Venice, 1584/*R*1970)

G. Bassano: *Ricercate passaggi et cadentie, per potersi essercitar nel diminuir* (Venice, 1585)

——: *Motetti, madrigali et canzoni francese . . . diminuti per sonar con ogni sorte di stromenti* (Venice, 1591/*R*)

R. Rogoni Taeggio: *Passaggi per potersi essercitare nel diminuire* (Venice, 1592)

G. L. Conforti: *Breve et facile maniera d'essercitarsi . . . a far passaggi* (Rome, 1593, ?2/1603)

G. Diruta: *Il transilvano* (Venice, 1593–1609/*R*1978)

G. B. Bovicelli: *Regole, passaggi di musica, madrigali, e motetti passeggiati* (Venice, 1594/*R*1957)

G. Caccini: *Le nuove musiche* (Florence, 1601/2, repr. 1930, 1934 and 1973; Eng. trans., 1970)

A. Agazzari: *Del sonare sopra 'l basso con tutti li stromenti e dell'uso loro nel conserto* (Siena, 1607, repr. 1933 and 1969; Eng. trans. in Strunk, 1950)

G. L. Conforti: *Passaggi sopra tutti li salmi* (Venice, 1607)

G. G. [J. H.] Kapsberger: *Libro primo di arie passeggiate* (Rome, 1612)

——: *Libro primo de mottetti passeggiati* (Rome, 1612)

G. Frescobaldi: *Toccate e partite . . . libro primo* (Rome, 1615, 2/1615–16; Eng. trans. of preface in Dolmetsch, 1915, pp.4ff; both prefaces in *SartoriB*, pp.207, 219)

M. Praetorius: *Syntagma musicum*, iii (Wolfenbüttel, 1618, 2/1619/*R*1958 and 1976)

F. Rognoni Taeggio: *Selva de varii passaggi* (Milan, 1620/*R*1970)

G. Frescobaldi: *Fiori musicali* (Venice, 1635)

M. Mersenne: *Harmonie universelle* (Paris, 1636–7/*R*1963; partial Eng. trans., 1957)

J. Denis: *Traité de l'accord de l'espinette* (Paris, 1650/*R*1969)

J. Playford: *A Briefe Introduction to the Skill of Musick for Song and Violl* (London, 1654, 7/1674/*R*1966, 12/1694/*R*1972) [edns. from 1660 incl. table of ornaments; edns. from 1664 incl. preface by Caccini]

C. Simpson: *The Division-violist: or, An Introduction to the Playing upon a Ground* (London, 1659, rev., enlarged 2/1665/*R*1955 as *Chelys: minuritionum artificio exornata . . . The Division-viol*)

J. Millet: *La belle méthode: ou, L'art de bien chanter* (Lyons, 1666/*R*1973)

B. de Bacilly: *Remarques curieuses sur l'art de bien chanter* (Paris, 1668, 3/1679/*R*1971; Eng. trans., 1968)

[J. C.] de la Barre: *Airs à deux parties avec les seconds couplets en diminution* (Paris, 1669)

J. C. de Chambonnières: *Les pièces de clavessin* (Paris, 1670/*R*1967)

M. Locke: *Melothesia: or, Certain General Rules for Playing upon a Continued-bass* (London, 1673)

T. Mace: *Musick's Monument* (London, 1676/*R*1958 and 1966) [incl. transcr. of music]

J. Rousseau: *Méthode claire, certaine et facile, pour apprendre à chanter la musique* (Paris, 1678)

De Machy: *Pièces de viole* (Paris, 1685/*R*1973)

M. Marais: Prefaces to *Pieces [de viole]* (Paris, 1686–1725/*R*)

J. Rousseau: *Traité de la viole* (Paris, 1687/*R*1965)

J.-H. D'Anglebert: *Pièces de clavecin* (Paris, 1689)

G. Muffat: *Apparatus musico-organisticus* (Salzburg, 1690) [see also Kolneder, 1970]

M. L'Affilard: *Principes très-faciles pour bien apprendre la musique* (Paris, 1694, 5/1705/R1971)

E. Loulié: *Eléments ou principes de musique* (Paris, 1696/R; Eng. trans., 1965/R1971)

H. Purcell: *A Choice Collection of Lessons for the Harpsichord or Spinet* (London, 1696, 3/1699)

G. Muffat: *Suavioris harmoniae instrumentalis hyporchematicae Florilegium* (Augsburg and Passau, 1695–8; partial Eng. trans. in Strunk, 1950; remainder in K. Cooper and J. Zsako: 'Georg Muffat's Observations on the Lully Style of Performance', *MQ*, liii (1967), 220) [see also Kolneder, 1970]

S. de Brossard: *Dictionnaire des termes* (Paris, 1701, enlarged 2/1703/R1964 as *Dictionaire de musique*)

M. de Saint-Lambert: *Les principes du clavecin, contenant une explication exacte de tout ce qui concerne la tablature et le clavier* (Paris, 1702/R1974)

T. B. [? Thomas Brown]: *The Compleat Musick-master* (London, 1704, 3/1722)

J. M. Hotteterre: *Principes de la flûte traversière* (Paris, 1707, 2/1728, repr. 1941; Eng. trans., 1968)

M. de Saint-Lambert: *Nouveau traité de l'accompagnement du clavecin, de l'orgue et des autres instruments* (Paris, 1707/R1974)

J. G. Walther: *Praecepta der musicalischen Composition* (MS, D-WRtl, 1708); ed. P. Benary (Leipzig, 1960)

F. Couperin: *Pièces de clavecin*, i (Paris, 1713/R) [incl. table of ornaments]

A. Corelli: *Sonate . . . opera quinta, parte prima: troisième édition où l'on a joint les agréemens* (Amsterdam, ?1715)

F. Couperin: *L'art de toucher le clavecin* (Paris, 1716, enlarged 2/1717/R1969)

J. S. Bach: *Clavier-Büchlein vor Wilhelm Friedemann Bach* (1720/R1959); ed. W. Plath, Neue Ausgabe sämtlicher Werke, 5th ser., v (Kassel, 1962) [incl. table of ornaments]

C. Dieupart: *Six suittes de clavessin* (Amsterdam, c1720)

P. F. Tosi: *Opinioni de' cantori antichi e moderni* (Bologna, 1723/R1966; Eng. trans., 1742, 2/1743/R1969 as *Observations on the Florid Song*)

J. P. Rameau: *Pièces de clavecin*, ii (Paris, 1724/R1967, rev. 2/1731 [with table of ornaments])

W. Babell: *XII Solos . . . with Proper Graces adapted to Each Adagio, by the Author* (London, c1725)

J. D. Heinichen: *Der General-Bass in der Composition, oder: Neue und gründliche Anweisung* (Dresden, 1728)

[P. Prelleur:] *The Modern Musick-master* (London, 1731/R1965)

J. A. Scheibe: *Der critische Musikus* (Hamburg, 1738–40, enlarged 2/1745/R1970)

J. Mattheson: *Der vollkommene Capellmeister* (Hamburg, 1739/R1954)

G. Muffat: *Componimenti musicali per il cembalo* (Augsburg, c1739/R; repr. in F. Chrysander: *Supplement to the Complete Works of Händel*, v (Leipzig, 1896)

J. Grassineau: *A Musical Dictionary* (London, 1740)

F. Geminiani: *A Treatise of Good Taste in the Art of Musick* (London, 1749/R1969)

F. W. Marpurg: *Die Kunst das Clavier zu spielen*, i (Berlin, 1750, rev., enlarged 4/1762/R1969; Fr. trans., Berlin, 1756 as *Principes du clavecin*)

F. Geminiani: *The Art of Playing on the Violin* (London, 1751/R1952)

J. le Rond d'Alembert: *Elémens de musique théorique et pratique* (Paris, 1752/R1957)

J. J. Quantz: *Versuch einer Anweisung die Flöte traversiere zu spielen* (Berlin, 1752, 3/1789/R1953; Eng. trans., 1966)

C. P. E. Bach: *Versuch über die wahre Art das Clavier zu spielen*, i (Berlin, 1753); ii (Berlin, 1762/R1957); (Eng. trans., rev., 1949)

J. (or J.-A.) B. Bérard [?J. Blanchet]: *L'art du chant* (Paris, 1755/R1967; Eng. trans., 1969)

F. W. Marpurg: *Anleitung zum Clavierspielen* (Berlin, 1755, 2/1765/R1969)

L. Mozart: *Versuch einer gründlichen Violinschule* (Augsburg, 1756/R1922, 3/1787/R1956; Eng. trans., 1948)

J. F. Agricola: *Anleitung zur Singkunst* (Berlin, 1757/R1966)

[H. L. Choquel]: *La musique rendue sensible* (Paris, 1759, 2/1762/R1972)

N. Pasquali: *The Art of Fingering the Harpsichord* (Edinburgh, ?1760)

C. Zaccari: *The True Method of Playing an Adagio made Easy by Twelve Examples* (London, c1765)

J.-J. Rousseau: *Dictionnaire de musique* (Paris, 1768/R1969)

G. Tartini: *Traité des agréments de la musique* (Paris, 1771) [trans. of *Regole per arrivare a ben saper suonar il violino*, MS, *I-Vc*, before 1756]

D. G. Türk: *Clavierschule, oder Anweisung zum Clavierspielen für Lehrer und Lernende* (Leipzig and Halle, 1789/R1967)

J.-B. Cartier: *L'art du violon* (Paris, 1798, enlarged 3/c1801/R1973)

P. M. Baillot, R. Kreutzer and P. Rode: *Méthode de violon* (Paris, 1803)

J. A. Amon: *Recueil de vingt-six cadences ou points d'orgue faciles pour la flûte* (Offenbach, 1806)

J. N. Hummel: *Ausführlich theoretisch-practische Anweisung zum Piano-forte Spiel* (Vienna, 1828/R; Eng. trans., London, 1829)

L. Spohr: *Violinschule* (Vienna, 1832/R1960; Eng. trans., c1880)

E. Dannreuther: *Musical Ornamentation* (London, 1893–5)

B. Garcia: *Hints on Singing* (London and New York, 1894/R1970) [trans. of M. Garcia: *Traité complet de l'art du chant*, Paris, 1840]

M. Kuhn: *Die Verzierungs-Kunst in der Gesangs-Musik des 16.–17. Jahrhunderts (1535–1650)* (Leipzig, 1902)

A. Schering: 'Zur instrumentalen Verzierungskunst im 18. Jahrhundert', *SIMG*, vii (1905–6), 365

M. Seiffert: 'Die Verzierung der Sologesänge in Händel's "Messias"', *SIMG*, viii (1906–7), 581

H. Goldschmidt: *Die Lehre von der vokalen Ornamentik* (Charlottenburg, 1907)

A. Beyschlag: *Die Ornamentik der Musik* (Leipzig, 1908/R1953)

A. Dolmetsch: *The Interpretation of the Music of the XVIIth and XVIIIth Centuries Revealed by Contemporary Evidence* (London, 1915, 2/1946/R1969)

F. Haböck: *Die Gesangskunst der Kastraten* (Vienna, 1923)

——: *Die Kastraten und ihre Gesangskunst* (Stuttgart, Berlin and Leipzig, 1927)

C. G. Hamilton: *Ornaments in Classical and Modern Music* (Boston, 1930/R1976)

R. M. Haas: *Aufführungspraxis der Musik* (Wildpark-Potsdam, 1931)

A. Schering: *Aufführungspraxis alter Musik* (Leipzig, 1931)

E. T. Ferand: *Die Improvisation in der Musik* (Zurich, 1938)

P. C. Aldrich: *The Principal Agréments of the Seventeenth and Eighteenth Centuries* (diss., Harvard U., 1942)

P. C. Aldrich: 'Bach's Technique of Transcription and Improvised Ornamentation', *MQ*, xxxv (1949), 28

——: *Ornamentation in J. S. Bach's Organ Works* (New York, 1950)

O. Strunk, ed. and trans.: *Source Readings in Music History* (New York, 1950, 2/1965)

I. Horsley: 'Improvised Embellishment in the Performance of Renaissance Polyphonic Music', *JAMS*, iv (1951), 3

W. Emery: *Bach's Ornaments* (London, 1953)

R. T. Dart: *The Interpretation of Music* (London, 1954, 4/1967)

H. Engel: 'Diminution', *MGG*

H.-P. Schmitz: *Die Kunst der Verzierung im 18. Jahrhundert* (Kassel, 1955, 3/1973)

E. T. Ferand: *Die Improvisation in Beispielen*, Mw, xii (1956, rev. 2/1961; Eng. trans., 1961)

E. and P. Badura-Skoda: *Mozart-Interpretation* (Vienna, 1957; Eng. trans., 1962)

V. Duckles: 'Florid Embellishment in English Song of the Late 16th and Early 17th Centuries', *AnnM*, v (1957), 329

W. H. Rubsamen: 'The Justiniane or Viniziane of the 15th Century', *AcM*, xxix (1957), 172

I. Horsley: 'The Solo Ricercar in Diminution Manuals: New Light on Early Wind and String Techniques', *AcM*, xxxiii (1961), 29

J. A. Westrup: 'The Cadence in Baroque Recitative', *Natalicia musicologica Knud Jeppesen* (Copenhagen, 1962), 243

P. C. Aldrich: 'On the Interpretation of Bach's Trills', *MQ*, xlix (1963), 289

W. Apel, ed.: *Keyboard Music of the Fourteenth and Fifteenth Centuries*, CEKM, i (1963)

R. Donington: *The Interpretation of Early Music* (London, 1963, rev. 3/1974) [incl. extensive bibliography]

G. Rose: 'Agazzari and the Improvising Orchestra', *JAMS*, xviii (1965), 382

K. Wichmann: *Vom Vortrag des Recitativs und seiner Erscheinungsformen: ein Beitrag zur Gesangspädagogik* (Leipzig, 1965)

G. von Dadelsen: 'Verzierungen', *MGG* [incl. extensive bibliography]

E. T. Ferand: 'Didactic Embellishment Literature in the Late Renaissance: a Survey of Sources', *Aspects of Medieval and Renaissance Music: a Birthday Offering to Gustave Reese* (New York, 1966), 154

K. Wichmann: *Der Ziergesang und die Ausführung der Appoggiatura: ein Beitrag zur Gesangspädagogic* (Leipzig, 1966)

E. P. Schwandt: *The Ornamented Clausula Diminuta in the Fitzwilliam Virginal Book* (diss., Stanford U., 1967)

P. Williams: 'The Harpsichord Acciaccatura: Theory and Practice in Harmony, 1650–1750', *MQ*, liv (1968), 503

A. Curtis: *Sweelinck's Keyboard Music: a Study of English Elements in Seventeenth-century Dutch Composition* (Leiden and London, 1969, 2/1972)

F. Neumann: 'Couperin and the Downbeat Doctrine for Appoggiaturas', *AcM*, xli (1969), 71; for replies see *AcM*, xlii (1970), 252, and xliii (1971), 106

M. Vinquist and others, eds.: 'Bibliography of Performance Practices', *CMc* (1969), no.8; suppl.i (1970), no.10; suppl.ii (1971), no.12; repr. with suppl.i as *Performance Practice: a Bibliography*, ed. M. Vinquist and N. Zaslaw (New York, 1971)

W. Kolneder: *Georg Muffat zur Aufführungspraxis* (Strasbourg and Baden-Baden, 1970) [repr. and discussion of all prefaces, music exx. etc bearing on interpretation]

J. A. Westrup: *Musical Interpretation* (London, 1971)

R. Donington: *A Performer's Guide to Baroque Music* (London, 1973)

D. Poulton: 'Graces of Play in Renaissance Lute Music', *Early Music*, iii (1975), 107

H. M. Brown: *Embellishing Sixteenth-century Music* (London, 1976)

B. B. Mather and D. Lasocki: *Free Ornamentation in Woodwind Music, 1700–1775* (New York, 1976)

H. Schenker: 'A Contribution to the Study of Ornamentation', *Music Forum*, iv (1976), 1–140

W. Dean: 'The Performance of Recitative in Late Baroque Opera', *ML*, lviii (1977), 389

C. Johnson: 'Spanish Keyboard Ornamentation, 1535–1626', *The Diapason*, lxix/1 (1978), 1

F. Neumann: *Ornamentation in Baroque and Post-Baroque Music, with Special Emphasis on J. S. Bach* (Princeton, 1978)

J. E. Smiles: 'Directions for Improvised Ornamentation in Italian Method Books of the Late Eighteenth Century', *JAMS*, xxxi (1978), 495

E. Roesner: 'The Performance of Parisian Organum', *Early Music*, vii (1979), 174

D. Fuller: 'An Unknown French Ornament Table from 1699', *Early Music*, ix (1981), 55

ROBERT DONINGTON

Oro. Wooden BULLROARER of the Yoruba people of Nigeria and Benin. The term applies equally to the stick which is used for whirling the flat, thin, tongue-shaped

1. Three views of the orpharion by Francis Palmer, English, 1617 (Musikhistorisk Museum, Copenhagen)

2. Front and back views of
an orpharion, maker unknown
(Historisches Museum,
Frankfurt am Main)

bullroarer and to the secret society responsible for its use. Formerly the society, through the 'voice' of the bullroarer, was concerned with the administration of justice, including the pursuit and execution of wrong-doers. The *oro* is believed to be 'male' and is always accompanied by one very small and two large drums and by a female singer (his 'wife') who uses a spider's web mirliton as a voice modifier. For certain rituals bullroarers of different pitches are used in consort.

BIBLIOGRAPHY
C. A. Moloney: 'On the Melodies of the Volof, Mandingo, Ewe, Yoruba and Houssa People of West Africa', *Journal of the Manchester Geographical Society*, v (1889), 277
G. Rouget: 'Benin', *Grove 6*

Orodo. Arched harp of the Madi people (of Moyo), Uganda. *See* ENNANGA.

Orpharion. A wire-strung plucked instrument of the BANDORA family, of similar scalloped shape but smaller and tuned like the lute. It appeared slightly later than the bandora, the first literary reference to it being in a poem (1590) by Michael Drayton. Thereafter it was mentioned with increasing familiarity and was listed in household inventories so frequently that it must have been played almost as widely as the lute. By the end of

the 17th century it had fallen into disuse, along with many other plucked instruments. The curious name of the instrument was also used for the title of a book, *Greenes Orpharion* (1599), which the author derives from 'Orpheus and Arion, two, famous in their time for their instruments'. It would seem that, like the bandora, the orpharion was redolent of classical symbolism (see Wells, 1982).

Of the surviving instruments hitherto thought to be orpharions, the earliest, made by John Rose in 1580, may well be a high-pitch bandora (*see* BANDORA for fur-ther discussion). Another, by Francis Palmer and dated 1617, is housed in the Claudius Collection at Copen-hagen (see fig.1). It has nine double courses and is exactly the shape depicted in contemporary illustrations. Although it is a little smaller than the scale drawing of Praetorius (2/1619), all its dimensions are within a centimetre of those recorded around 1690 by Talbot (see Gill, *GSJ*, 1960). The bridge and frets are slanted to give a pro-gressive increase in string length from treble (53·5 cm) to bass (60·5 cm). The pegbox, topped with a carved head in typical English style, is of 'viol' type with lat-eral pegs. The instrument's ribs do not taper in depth, but the neck is cut away on the bass side as on a cittern. Until very recently this instrument was the only exam-ple of its type known to have survived, though certain features and marks on the pegbox and head suggest that

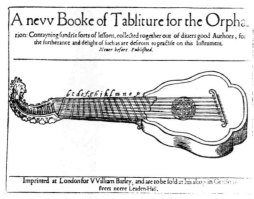

3. Title-page, with woodcut of an orpharion, from William Barley's 'A New Booke of Tabliture for the Orpharion' (1596)

it is not quite in its original state (see Segerman and Abbott, 1976).

In 1982, however, attention was drawn to another orpharion in the Historisches Museum, Frankfurt am Main (see Segerman, 1982; fig. 2). This anonymous, undated eight-course instrument is much smaller than the one in Copenhagen and has string lengths of only 42·5 cm (treble) and 48 cm (bass). To judge from photographs, there are again features here that may not be original, including the pegbox, metal tuning pins, bridge position and possibly the bridge itself, which may date from a restoration carried out in 1957. Nevertheless the instrument is of great interest. A larger example, with nine courses, was reported in 1983 at the Städtisches Museum, Brunswick.

The earliest collection of orpharion music is found in William Barley's *New Booke of Tabliture*, published in three parts for Lute, Orpharion and Bandora in 1596. This also contains the first full description and illustration of the instrument, described as 'the Stately Orpharion'. Barley continues:

. . . the Orpharion is strong with more stringes than the Lute, and also hath more frets or stops, and whereas the Lute is strong with gut stringes, the Orpharion is strong with wire stringes, by reason of which manner of stringing, the Orpharion doth necessarilie require a more gentle and drawing stroke than the Lute, I mean the fingers of the right hand must be easilie drawen over the stringes, and not suddenly griped, or sharpelie stroken as the Lute is: for if yee should doo so, then the wire stringes would clash or jarre together the one against the other; which would be a cause that the sounde would bee harsh and unpleasant.

Barley's reference to the number of strings is explained by the fact that his lute has only six courses, whereas his orpharion has seven, as can be seen in his illustration (fig.3) and in the music itself. The lowest course is tuned a tone below the sixth, giving the intervals 2–4–4–3–4–4. It has been suggested that this setting for the seventh course distinguishes orpharion music from that for the lute, but in fact there is a considerable repertory, both English and continental, for a seven-course lute tuned the same way. The woodcut also shows the sloping bridge and frets, which had great importance as far as the open string range was concerned; indeed, it was this increase in range that made the orpharion possible.

Whereas the bandora was never extended beyond seven courses, the development of the orpharion was roughly the same as that of the lute. Praetorius (2/1619) illustrated a seven-course instrument, but gave tunings for

eight courses ($D–F–G–c–f–a–d'–g'$, and a tone higher). The undated instrument in Frankfurt has eight courses; the Palmer at Copenhagen and the Brunswick example have nine. Ten courses are required for the orpharion pavan in Pilkington's second set of madrigals (1624). When Talbot noted the dimensions of an orpharion (c1690), he added:

'Tis a kind of tenor to the Cittern carrying 9 double ranks sometimes 7. Fretts 15. Some like the English Theorbo carrie 5 double 8ve ranks of open Basses on 5 Nutts on long head besides those 7 on the plate'.

Because of the identity of tuning, there is nothing to distinguish music for orpharion from that for lute; indeed, the two instruments were largely regarded as interchangeable, as is made clear by the title-pages of many of the English books of 'lute' songs published between 1597 and 1622. Two of the Cambridge consort books (*GB-Cu* Dd. 5.20 f.10^v and Dd. 5.21 f.11) contain pieces designated as 'for 3 Orph' and 'for iij Wiers', including a bass instrument, which Praetorius called PENORCON, pitched a 4th below the others and tuned like a bass lute.

BIBLIOGRAPHY

W. Barley: *A New Booke of Tabliture for the Bandora* (London, 1596)
——: *A New Booke of Tabliture for the Orpharion* (London, 1596)
M. Praetorius: *Syntagma musicum*, ii (Wolfenbüttel, 1618, 2/1619/R1958 and 1980)
D. Gill: 'An Orpharion by John Rose', *LSJ*, ii (1960), 33
——: 'The Orpharion and Bandora', *GSJ*, xiii (1960), 14
——: 'James Talbot's Manuscript: the Wire-strung Fretted Instruments and the Guitar', *GSJ*, xv (1962), 60
J. Godwin: 'Instruments in Robert Fludd's *Utriusque cosmi . . . historia'*, *GSJ*, xxvi (1973), 2
——: 'Robert Fludd on the Lute and Pandora', *LSJ*, xv (1973), 11
R. Hadaway: 'An Instrument-maker's Report on the Repair and Restoration of an Orpharion', *GSJ*, xxviii (1975), 37
E. Segerman and D. Abbott: 'On the Palmer Orpharion', *FoMRHI Quarterly*, iii (1976), 48
D. Gill: 'Wire-strung Plucked Instruments Contemporary with the Lute', *Lute Society Booklets*, iii (1977)
——: 'Bandora, Orpharion and Guitar', *GSJ*, xxxi (1978), 144
I. Harwood: 'A Case of Double Standards? Instrumental Pitch in England *c*.1600', *Early Music*, ix (1981), 470
E. Segerman: 'Orpharion News', *FoMRHI Quarterly*, xxvii (1982), 25
R. H. Wells: 'The Orpharion: Symbol of a Humanist Ideal', *Early Music*, x (1982), 427

IAN HARWOOD

Orphica. A portable piano, designed for outdoor use, which could be played either while resting in the performer's lap or while supported by a strap round his neck, like a guitar (see illustration). Invented by Karl Leopold Röllig about 1795, it has a small soundbox containing a two- to four-octave keyboard that activates a simple Viennese action; the strings run transversely across the soundbox from a harp-shaped open frame at the performer's left to tuning-pins set at the right.

BIBLIOGRAPHY

K. L. Röllig: *Orphica: ein musikalisches Instrument* (Vienna, 1795)
'Saitenklaviere', *Kunsthistorisches Museum: Katalog der Sammlung alter Musikinstrumenten*, i (Vienna, 1966), 80

EDWIN M. RIPIN

Orqo. PANPIPES of the CHIRIHUANO ensemble of Bolivia.

Orugōru. Japanese idiophone used in the kabuki theatre in GEZA (off-stage) music. The *orugōru* consists of three or four tiny thick-walled hemispherical bells attached to a wooden rack with their mouths towards the player, who strikes them lightly with round-ended wooden sticks. The resulting tinkling sound was apparently thought similar to the Dutch music box known as the *orgel* (Jap. *orugōru*). The bells are graduated in size, but they are not tuned according to any system.

In *geza* music the *orugōru* is used in light-hearted scenes, or to accompany butterflies in flight etc. See S. Kishibe: *The Traditional Music of Japan* (Tokyo, 1966, 2/1981), pl.64.

DAVID W. HUGHES

Orunsa. Set of frame drums of the Yoruba people of West Africa. *See* SAKARA.

Orupi [hu'a-ha'u, ngao-ngao]. Heteroglot bamboo clarinet in central and mid-western Flores, Indonesia. It consists of an open bamboo tube about 7 to 12 cm long, with no finger-holes. See J. Kunst: *Music in Flores* (Leiden, 1942), 155f.

Orutu. Single-string fiddle of the Luo people of Kenya. *See* SIIRIRI.

Osa. Set of wooden bells of the Igbo people of Nigeria. They are mounted round the rim of a wooden wheel and used at the *onyima* festival.

Osborne [Osborn], **John** (*b* New England, *c*1792; *d* New York, 27 May 1835). American piano manufacturer. He was one of several outstanding apprentices who learnt his craft under Benjamin Crehore of Milton, Massachusetts, often called the founder of the New England piano industry. According to Oliver (1878), he served this apprenticeship during the years (*c*1808–14) when Crehore was associated with the Boston shop of Lewis and

Lady playing an orphica: engraving from K. L. Röllig's 'Orphica: ein musikalisches Instrument' (1795)

Alpheus Babcock and Thomas Appleton. By 1815 Osborne set up his own firm in Newbury Street, Boston, moving by 1819 to Orange Street, where he trained such apprentices as Jonas Chickering (1819–23), Lemanuel and Timothy Gilbert and John Dwight.

Advertising himself as a builder of upright, grand, square and cabinet pianos, Osborne soon became known for his fine craftsmanship. After his short partnership in 1822 with James Stewart, he remained in Boston until 1829, when he moved to Albany to work first for Meacham & Pond and then in partnership with Peter King (1831–3). In 1833 he moved to New York; his pianos won several awards, including the first premium at the American Institute. According to Spillane, in October 1834 Osborne moved into a large factory which he had built in Third Avenue at 14th Street. The firm of Stodart, Worcester & Dunham occupied the building by 1836, followed by a succession of piano manufacturers until 1880.

Osborne pianos can be seen in American museums and private collections. His square instruments are similar to those of his contemporaries, with mahogany veneer, fretted nameboard, and a range of *F'* to *c''''*. An Osborne upright at the Smithsonian Institution represents one of the earliest extant uprights built in New England. Dating from about 1820, it has a range of *F'* to *f''''*, two pedals (damper and una corda) and a handsome case that includes a radially pleated drapery drawn together at the centre with a brass medallion.

BIBLIOGRAPHY
R. Parker: *A Tribute to the Life and Character of Jonas Chickering* (Boston, Mass., 1854), 40ff
H. K. Oliver: *Reports and Awards of the International Exhibition, 1876* (Philadelphia, 1878), 28f
D. Spillane: *History of the American Pianoforte* (New York, 1890/*R*1969), 54ff, 87ff, 139, 156f

CYNTHIA ADAMS HOOVER

Oscillator. An electronic device that generates a single periodic waveform; *see* SYNTHESIZER, §I, 3. For the independent use of oscillators as musical instruments, *see* ELECTRONIC INSTRUMENTS, §IV, 6(iii).

Oscillion. A monophonic electronic instrument developed at the Franklin Institute in Philadelphia in 1937 by William E. Danforth for William F. G. Swann; it was designed to replace missing instruments in the amateur Swarthmore Symphony Orchestra (conducted by Swann). It consisted of a wooden box about 30 cm long, which was held on the left arm; a resistance strip fingerboard, played by the right hand, controlled the frequency of an oscillator, while the left hand operated a lever controlling the volume and buttons that altered the pitch range within a total compass of over four octaves. At least two instruments were constructed.

BIBLIOGRAPHY
T. L. Rhea: *The Evolution of Electronic Musical Instruments in the United States* (diss., George Peabody College, Nashville, Tenn., 1972), 80

HUGH DAVIES

Oseke. STOPPED FLUTE ENSEMBLE of the Alur people of Uganda consisting of several end-blown stopped flutes of different lengths.

Osha. Leg rattles worn by dancers among the Igbo people of Nigeria.

Osnóh' kastaweh'shae' (Seneca: 'bark rattle'). Vessel rattle of the Iroquois Indians of north-eastern North America. It is also called *osnóh' ká'nowa'* ('bark turtle'). It is made of hickory bark and is constructed only in late spring or early summer, when bark is easily stripped from the tree. A strip of unblemished bark, about 60 cm long, is removed in one piece from a sapling 8 to 10 cm in diameter. The bark is folded in half from top to bottom; the two ends are allowed to curl and fit into each other to form a handle. The resulting container is long and triangular. Chokecherry pips or pebbles are inserted through the end and the small hole is closed with a plug, 8 to 10 cm long, whittled from the sapling. A hole is drilled through the handle, which is threaded with string or cord for hanging. The rattle may be varnished and the maker's initials carved near the top; other decoration is rare. Rattles may be from 20 to 35 cm long and 8 to 22 cm wide at the top; they are narrow from front to back, measuring 4 to 7 cm.

The bark rattle may be used as a substitute for the great turtle rattle, KANYÁHTE' KÁ'NOWA', that is carried by the False Faces at the mid-winter ceremony; hence its other name.   MARY RIEMER-WELLER

Ossia (It.: 'alternatively'; originally *o sia*: 'or be it'). A word used in musical scores – as also, more rarely, *oppure* (particularly in Verdi), *overo* or *ovvero* (literally 'or rather') – to mark an alternative to a passage. This occurs in several different circumstances: (*i*) simplified readings, particularly in 19th-century piano music; (*ii*) embellished versions, particularly in bel canto vocal music; (*iii*) in scholarly texts, readings from other sources or alternative interpretations of the same source; (*iv*) changes made to accommodate the music to an instrument with a slightly shorter range, whether a piano with a smaller keyboard or an oboe, for instance, playing violin music; (*v*) alternative orchestration for an orchestra smaller or larger than that originally intended.
                                   DAVID FALLOWS

Ósun. Afro-Cuban rattle of the Lucumí cult. At the top of a vertical iron bar, fixed to a base or nailed into the ground, are four small cones, soldered at their vertices and containing seeds, bones or pebbles. Their bases support a thin metal plate, set horizontally and with the figure of a standing bird at its centre. The instrument symbolizes a mythical being to whom offerings are made; it 'calls' the being by being shaken, the objects within the cones creating the sound. If the *ósun* has an upward-facing cup at the top, into which a figure of a rooster has been soldered, the sound is made instead by small hanging pellet-bells. See *OrtizIMA*, ii, 325ff.
                                   JOHN M. SCHECHTER

Osur. Transverse flute of the Maria aborigines of Madhya Pradesh (Bastar district), central India. *Osur* is a Gondi word and denotes one of the rare melodic instruments used by the tribal populations of Bastar, a bamboo flute about 70 cm long with four finger-holes. *See* VAMŚA.

                                   GENEVIÈVE DOURNON

Otchissage. Term for a LAMELLAPHONE in 19th-century Brazil. The instrument, now obsolete in Brazil, was of the African KISAANJ type, transplanted with the slave trade.

Ōteki. Japanese term which once designated any transverse flute but now refers to the RYŪTEKI. The same characters can be pronounced *yokobue*, denoting other transverse flutes. The Chinese pronunciation of *ōteki* is *hengdi* (*see* DI (i)).

Otongoli. Arched harp of the Gwere people of Uganda. *See* ENNANGA.

Ōtsuzumi. Japanese HOURGLASS DRUM, with the heads laced to the body (*ō*: 'large'; *tsuzumi*: generic term for hourglass drums). It is frequently paired with the smaller but similar KOTSUZUMI, and the pair is given the covering term *daishō* ('large–small'); its other names are *ōkawa* ('large skin') and *dai* ('large'). Its structure is similar to that of the *kotsuzumi*, but the heads are thicker and the body usually less ornate. The body is about 12 cm in diameter and 29 cm long; the head diameter is about 23 cm. As with the *kotsuzumi* the front head is slightly thicker than the rear one. The *ōtsuzumi* is held horizontally on the left thigh by the left hand; the right hand strikes the head. There is less tonal variety than in the *kotsuzumi*, and to produce the high, crisp, ringing tone the heads must be subjected to a dry heat before each performance and strung very tightly; as a result they have a short life. The instrument is used in the same genres as the *kotsuzumi*. In folk music it is often struck with a stick rather than the hand.

BIBLIOGRAPHY
W. P. Malm: *Japanese Music and Musical Instruments* (Rutland, Vermont, 1959), 122ff
R. Emmert and Y. Minegishi, eds.: *Musical Voices of Asia* (Tokyo, 1980), 246
A. Tamba: *The Musical Structure of Nō* (Tokyo, 1981), 161
                                   DAVID W. HUGHES

Ott, Paul (*b* Oberteuringen, 23 Aug 1903). German organ builder. At first his ideas were concerned with organ action, but in 1930, encouraged by Karl Vötterle and Christhard Mahrenholz, he began to build a positive organ (one manual, 5½ stops). In 1932 he established his own business in Göttingen, where it is still active. By World War II Ott had built over 50 instruments, mostly positives and other small organs. The most notable is the house organ built with his brother-in-law, Erich Thienhaus, and Helmut Bornefeld, for the organist and composer Hugo Distler in Stuttgart (1938–9; two manuals, 15 stops) and now in St Jakobi, Lübeck. Examples of his extensive restoration work include organs at St Wilhadi, Stade (1937–8), Cappel (1937–9; 1950), Norden (1947–8; 1956–60), Lemgo (1947–50), St Cosmae, Stade (1948–9), Fröndenberg (1951–3) and Borgentreich (1951–3). After 1945 Ott's business became one of the most important firms of organ builders in Germany. New organs were constructed for Wolfsburg (1951), Leer (1951–5), Bremen (1952–3), Hanover (1954–6), Göttingen (1955) and Bonn (1956); instruments made by the firm are exported as far as Norway, Japan and the USA. In 1956 Ott was joined by his son Dieter (*b* 1934).

                                   UWE PAPE

Ottava (It.). (1) OCTAVE.
(2) An ORGAN STOP (*Octave*).

Ottava alta, bassa, sopra, sotta. *See* ALL'OTTAVA.

Ottava stesa (It.: 'extended octave'). A term found in 17th-century inventories, applied to several types of (unaltered) bass octave in the compass of certain keyboard instruments; *see* HARPSICHORD, §4 (iii).

Ottavino (It.). (1) PICCOLO; *see* FLUTE, §3.

(2) The octave SPINET, a plucked string keyboard instrument that plays at a 4' pitch, also called *spinettino* or *spinetta ottavina*.

(3) An ORGAN STOP (*Octavin*).

Ottoni (It.). BRASS INSTRUMENTS.

Ottu. Oboe of south India. It is similar to the NĀGASVARAM, which it accompanies, but is slightly longer (about 80 cm). Since it is used as a drone instrument, it has no finger-holes; there are often four or five holes at the rear, however, which may be blocked with wax to adjust the key note.

Otule. Set of cone flutes of the Lango people of Uganda. They are made from animal horn, the tips of which are left solid; three finger-holes are made along the inside curvature. The flutes are 20 to 55 cm long, and are divided into groups according to size; in one terminology these are *min bilo* ('mother flute', low pitch), *adadang* or *adange* (medium) and *atin bilo* ('child', high). Clay imitations are made if no horns are available, the clay being built up in coils around a core which is later removed. See *WachsmannTCU*.

Ouchard. French family of bow makers. Emile François Ouchard (1872–1951) was apprenticed to Eugene Cuniot-Hury from 1884; after 1912 he continued running this shop with his master's widow, assuming complete management in 1926. His bows, while not elegantly finished, are well made and show ample evidence of a clearly developed style, though remaining fairly conservative throughout his career. Their box-like heads have rather straight chamfers, while the frogs are fairly low, with rounded heels. The buttons are either silver-capped or banded. They are branded EMILE OUCHARD, though some of his work doubtless appears under Cuniot-Hury's brand.

Emile François' son, Emile A. Ouchard (1900–1969), who became the most important member of the family, appears to have learnt the craft from his father in Mirecourt. He went to Paris in 1941 and soon afterwards emigrated to the USA, working in New York and later in Chicago. In the mid-1950s he returned to France and set up shop in the provinces. His bows, while similar in appearance to those of the Voirin–Lamy school, have quite different playing qualities; many players find his sticks rather stiff. The frogs, of conventional design, are usually mounted in a recessed track which is carved into the three lower facets of the butt. The buttons are either capped or banded and are often threaded to the screw-shaft. He used various forms of his name as his brand; some bows of the 1940s are also stamped with the year of manufacture under the frog.

Bernard Ouchard (*b* 1925), son and pupil of E. A. Ouchard, accompanied his father to Paris in 1941. During World War II he enlisted with the French army and in 1949 joined the workshop of Pierre Vidoudez in Geneva. He remained there as a bow maker until 1971, when he was appointed professor of bow making at the Mirecourt school. His bows, whose sticks are mostly octagonal, are of elegant proportions and are apparently based on a kind of Peccatte model. They are branded with his surname only, although much of his work bears the Vidoudez brand.

BIBLIOGRAPHY
J. Roda: *Bows for Musical Instruments of the Violin Family* (Chicago, 1959)
E. Vatelot: *Les archets français* (Nancy, 1976)
                                    JAAK LIIVOJA-LORIUS

Ougdyé. African harp. *See* HARP, §6 (ii).

Ouïe (Fr.). SOUNDHOLE.

Oumalay. *See* OMELE.

Oupa. BULLROARER of the Nyali people of Zaïre. *See* ATUAMBA.

Outa. Braced MOUTH BOW of the Herero and Damara (Nama) peoples of south-western Africa. It is often adapted from a hunting bow (which bears the same name). The stave is held against the player's slightly parted lips while the string is struck with a thin stick. Mouth-resonated harmonics are used melodically. Among the Damara it is also known as *goukhas*. See *Kirby-MISA*, 226f, pl.64(i).

                                    DAVID K. RYCROFT

Outi. Greek name for the 'ŪD played in Thrace and by Greek refugees from Turkey. It was formerly one of the principal melodic instruments of the *café-aman* (a kind of oriental *café-chantant*) and was commonly played throughout Greece in communities of refugees from Asia Minor, but is now becoming rare.

Ovation. American company of guitar manufacturers. It was founded in Bloomfield, Connecticut, in the 1960s by Charles Huron Kaman (*b* 1919) as a subsidiary of the Kaman Corp., which makes aerospace products. Kaman became interested in guitars and guitar production, and began to test for this purpose materials that the company had developed in experiments on the vibrational and acoustical properties of helicopter rotor blades. The result was the first series of Ovation acoustic guitars, introduced in 1966 and 1967, which included the Balladeer six-string and the Pacemaker 12-string models. Both had Ovation's now famous rounded back, made from a synthetic material resembling fibreglass (patented by Ovation as 'Lyrachord'), which enhances reflection, and thereby projection, of the sound.

Three years later Kaman unveiled another innovation in the form of a pickup built into the bridge saddles of the instrument; this senses vibrations in both the strings and the top of the guitar, and is connected to a small pre-amplifier inside the body, which is controlled by a volume potentiometer mounted on the heel of the instrument. This device effectively creates a hybrid 'electric-acoustic' guitar, which has become the first choice of many pop guitarists who want to achieve the sound quality of a good acoustic instrument at relatively high amplification levels on stage. Ovation has also produced some less successful solid-bodied electric guitars, including the Breadwinner (1972), and the UK II (1979) the body of which is made of another plastic developed by Ovation (patented as 'Urelite') over an aluminum frame.

The most expensive and distinguished of Ovation's guitars are the Adamas models, launched in the mid-1970s. The top is made from a sandwich of ultra-stiff graphite fibre and wood, and has multiple soundholes, positioned at the upper end, for extra projection.

BIBLIOGRAPHY
T. Bacon, ed.: *Rock Hardware: the Instruments, Equipment and Technology of Rock* (Poole, Dorset, 1981)
T. Wheeler: *American Guitars: an Illustrated History* (New York, 1982)

TONY BACON

Ovcharska svirka (Bulg.: 'shepherds' flute'). *See* SVIRKA.

Ove. SLIT-DRUM of Mangaia in the Cook Islands.

Overblowing. Under certain physical conditions an air column can break up into aliquot parts each of which will vibrate at a frequency that is in direct proportion to the fundamental frequency. Thus it is sometimes possible for a tube of a given length to sound not only its fundamental but also the octave, 12th, etc, of its lowest note as 'harmonics' in a manner somewhat analogous to the behaviour of a lightly stopped violin string. In woodwind instruments this phenomenon provides the basis of their second and higher registers. The 'harmonic' behaves virtually as a new fundamental at twice, thrice, etc, the frequency of the original. 'Overblowing' is the term applied to the process by which the player brings about the conditions necessary for these higher modes of vibration in his air column. With the flute it includes an increase in blowing pressure, modification of the shape of the jet of air issuing from the lips, and the angle at which this strikes the far edge of the mouth-hole. In reed-playing it involves, as well as increased wind pressure, the adjustment of the pressure and position of the lips on the reed blade. Modern reed instruments have certain very small 'speaker' holes in the body tube which assist the process. The muscular adjustments required are extremely small and subtle, and are learnt only by long and assiduous practice. Once acquired, however, they become quite automatic to the player.

PHILIP BATE

Overdotting. *See* DOTTED RHYTHMS; NOTES INÉGALES; PERFORMING PRACTICE, §5.

Overspun string. String with a core of gut or metal that is wound round along its length with a coil or coils of a (relatively thin) ductile wire to increase its mass without increasing stiffness. In non-keyboard string instruments gut cores are generally overspun with aluminium or silver. The steel bass strings of the piano are covered with copper.

FRANK HUBBARD

Overstrung. A term applied to a piano in which the strings are arranged in two nearly parallel planes, with the bass strings passing diagonally over those in the middle range. Both groups may thus fan out over the soundboard and make more effective use of its entire area. Because of the fanning out of the long bass strings and their diagonal orientation, an overstrung grand piano has a characteristically wide tail compared with that of a straight-strung instrument, in which the strings do not fan out and the bass strings run entirely to the left of the treble strings (*see* PIANOFORTE, figs.27, 28, 29*b* and 30). The term should not be confused with CROSS-STRUNG.

EDWIN M. RIPIN

Overtoon. Bamboo trumpet played in the *orkes bambu melalu* of Minahasa, North Sulawesi. It consists of two vertical and one adjoining pieces of bamboo, and resembles the BAS (i) of the Toraja area of central Sulawesi.

Ower-ower. BULLROARER of Central Java. *See* JATA.

Oyara. Double clapperless bell, made of wood, of the Igbo people of Nigeria.

Oyo. Rattle of the Igbo people of Nigeria. (1) The most common term for the Igbo's flattened conical wicker vessel rattle which has a calabash or wooden base and integral handles. The rattles are usually played in pairs by a single performer holding one in each hand.

(2) Gourd vessel rattle with a network of external strikers (seeds, stones, pieces of iron).

Ozi. Single-headed funeral drum of the Igbo people of Nigeria.

Ò-zi. Burmese GOBLET DRUM. It is about 3 metres long; the drum is suspended by a sash passing over the player's shoulder and chest so as to present the drumhead at an angle to his hands. It is played on festive occasions such as rice transplanting, processions with gifts to the monastery, mobile movie advertisements etc, in an ensemble with the *palwei* (flute) or *hnè* (oboe), *walek-hkok* (bamboo clappers) and *yagwìn* (cymbals).

Ozohahi. Ankle rattles of the Herero people of south-western Africa. They comprise cocoons containing small stones, strung on leather strips and worn round the ankles of women dancers. The Zulu *amafohlwane* are somewhat similar. See *KirbyMISA*, 3.

DAVID K. RYCROFT

Ožragis. Lithuanian trumpet or reedpipe made of goat horn. It is from 25 to 50 cm long; the upper end is 2 to 3 cm wide, the lower end 5 to 12 cm wide. The *ožragis* has two to six finger-holes which can produce a range of up to one octave, or it may have no finger-holes. The trumpet *ožragis* has a mouthpiece, a small rounded cavity, in the upper end. Another type of *ožragis*, similar to the BIRBYNĖ, has a single reed inserted in the upper end, or attached to a clarinet-like mouthpiece. The *ožragis* was used as a pastoral signalling instrument throughout Lithuania until the first half of the 20th century. It could be played solo or in duet to perform song, dance and march tunes, and in ensemble with the accordion and *būgnelis* (small frame drum) to play for weddings and festivals. Instruments resembling the *ožragis* could be made of other animal horns, by shepherds, hunters and foresters. The traditional and a modified *ožragis* are nowadays used in folk music groups.

ARVYDAS KARAŠKA

Illustration Acknowledgments

We are grateful to those listed below for permission to reproduce copyright illustrative material, and those contributors who supplied or helped us obtain it. Every effort has been made to contact copyright holders; we apologize to anyone who may have been omitted. Brian and Constance Dear prepared the maps and technical diagrams, and Oxford Illustrators the typographic diagrams (except where otherwise stated). Photographs acknowledged to the following sources are Crown copyright: Her Majesty the Queen, the Science Museum and the National Monuments Record. The following forms of acknowledgment are used where the copyright of an illustration is held by a contributor:

photo John Smith – John Smith is contributor and photographer
John Smith – John Smith is contributor and copyright holder
photo John Smith, London – John Smith is a contributor (not of the article concerned) and photographer
John Smith, London – John Smith is a contributor (not of the article concerned) and copyright holder.

Where illustrations are taken from books out of copyright, the full title and place and date of publication are given, unless in the caption. Some illustrations are reprinted from *The New Grove Dictionary of Music and Musicians*.

Gaasay photo Bernard Surugue, Bondy
Gadulka photo Vergilii Atanassov
Gagaku photo Robert Garfias, Irvine, California
Gagliano W. E. Hill & Sons, Great Missenden / photo Desmond Hill
Gaita Fundação Calouste Gulbenkian, Lisbon
Gajde *1a* Musée de l'Homme, Paris; *1b* photo Vergilii Atanassov
Gambang *1* Department of Information, Jakarta; *2* Yale University Press, New Haven, Connecticut: from C. McPhee, *Music in Bali* (1966)
Gambus Margaret J. Kartomi / photo H. Kartomi, Clayton, Victoria
Gamelan *1* after E. Heins; *2* Department of Information, Jakarta; *3* photo Benedict R. Anderson, Ithaca, New York; *4, 5* Etnomusicologisch Centrum 'Jaap Kunst', Amsterdam / photo Jaap Kunst
Ganga *1* photo Anthony King; *2* Monique Brandily / photo Max-Yves Brandily, Paris
Gangsa (i) CICM Missionaries, Manila, Philippines / photo Francisco Billiet
Gangsa (ii) photo Ernst Heins, Amsterdam
Garamut Museum für Völkerkunde und Schweizerisches Museum für Völkskunde, Basle / photo René Gardi
Gardon photo Bálint Sárosi, Budapest
Gashi Monique Brandily / photo Max-Yves Brandily, Paris
Gäṭa-berē photo Natalie M. Webber
Gemshorn (i) Horace Fitzpatrick
Gender Department of Information, Jakarta
Ghaṇṭā photo Geneviève Dournon, Paris
Ghaṭa photo Geneviève Dournon, Paris
Ghayṭa photo Jean Jenkins, London
Ghichak Society for Cultural Relations with the USSR, London
Ghorāliyau photo Geneviève Dournon
Ghuṅgrū photo Publications Division of India, Ministry of Education and Broadcasting, New Delhi
Gintang photo Deben Bhattacharya, Paris
Gittern *1, 2* photo Laurence Wright; *3* Mansell Collection, London, and Alinari, Florence; *4* Patrimonio Nacional, Madrid
Goffriller, Matteo W. E. Hill & Sons, Great Missenden / photo Desmond Hill
Goge photo Gérard Payen, Abidjan
Gondang Etnomusicologisch Centrum 'Jaap Kunst', Amsterdam
Gong *1* Horniman Museum, London; *3a* photo Robert Garfias, Irvine, California; *3b* Popperfoto, London; *3c–d* International Institute for Comparative Music Studies and Documentation, Berlin / photo Joachim Wenzel; *5* Bibliothèque Nationale, Paris
Gong-chime after E. Heins
Gongophone photo Gerhard Kubik

Goong lu Musée de l'Homme, Paris / photo J. Oster
Gopīyantra photo Deben Bhattacharya, Paris
Gora *1* photo Faculty of Music, University of Cape Town, Rondebosch
Ground harp photo Hugo Zemp, Paris
Gshang Trustees of the British Museum, London
Guadagnini W. E. Hill & Sons, Great Missenden / photo Desmond Hill
Guarneri *1* W. E. Hill & Sons, Great Missenden / photo Desmond Hill
Guitar *2* State Hermitage Museum, Leningrad; *3* Bibliothèque Nationale, Paris; *4* Stadtbibliothek, St Gall; *5a–c* Royal College of Music, London; *5d* Harvey Turnbull; *6, 9* Ashmolean Museum, Oxford; *7* Christie, Manson & Woods Ltd, London; *8, 14* Victoria and Albert Museum, London; *11, 13* British Library, London; *12* Jack and Dorinda Schuman, Cleveland, Ohio; *15* Spanish Guitar Centre, Bristol; *16* photo Erich Auerbach, London; *17* Country Music Hall of Fame and Museum, Nashville, Tennessee; *18* photo Michel Hetier, Paris
Guntang Yale University Press, New Haven, Connecticut: from C. McPhee, *Music in Bali* (1966)
Gusle Vlatko Dabac, Zagreb / photo Tošo Dabac
Gusli Society for Cultural Relations with the USSR, London

Haegŭm Dabo Korea, Seoul
Handbell *1* Anglia Television Ltd, Norwich; *2b–d, f* American Guild of English Handbell Ringers Inc., Dayton, Ohio: after P. Price, 'Handbells from Earliest Times', *Overtones*, xix/3 (May–June 1973); *3* Bodleian Library, Oxford
Hardanger fiddle *1a* Mittet Foto, Oslo; *1b* Historisk Museum, Bergen
Harmonica (i) *2* M. Hohner Ltd, London
Harp *1, 29* after Donn Carter, Malibu, California; *2, 5* Trustees of the British Museum, London; *3* Egyptian Museum, Cairo; *6, 17* photo Musées Nationaux, Paris; *7* after J. Rimmer; *8* University of Glasgow Library (Hunterian Collection); *9, 12, 19* Victoria and Albert Museum, London; *10* Germanisches Nationalmuseum, Nuremberg; *11* Board of Trinity College, Dublin; *14* Galleria e Museo Estense, Modena; *15, 16* Conservatoire Royal de Musique, Brussels / photo Nicolas Meeùs; *18, 22, 23* British Library, London; *20, 27* Joan Rimmer / photo Frank Harrison, Canterbury; *21* Metropolitan Museum of Art (Crosby Brown Collection, 1889), New York; *24* after Wilfred Smith, London; *26* photo IFOT, Grenoble; *28a* photo John M. Schechter; *28b* photo Isabel Aretz, Caracas; *30* Alice Lawson Aber, Walnut Creek, California
Harp-lute (i) after R. Knight

979

Harp-lute (ii) *1*, *2a* British Library, London; *2b* Victoria and Albert Museum, London

Harpsichord *2*, *11* Bibliothèque Nationale, Paris; *3*, *7*, *9* Victoria and Albert Museum, London; *4* photo Grant O'Brien; *5* Yale University Collection of Musical Instruments, New Haven, Connecticut / photo Thomas A. Brown; *6* Trustees of the National Gallery, London; *10* Russell Collection of Harpsichords and Clavichords, University of Edinburgh; *13* Warwickshire Museum Service, Warwick; *14* Gesellschaft der Musikfreunde, Vienna / photo Kunsthistorisches Museum; *15* Museum für Kunst und Gewerbe, Hamburg; *16* Library of Congress, Washington, DC; *18* Société Pleyel SA, Paris; *19* J. C. Neupert, Bamberg and Nuremberg; *20* Frank Hubbard Harpsichord Kits Inc., Waltham, Massachusetts

Hatzotzerah Egyptian Museum, Cairo

Hawaiian guitar CBS Musical Instruments, Fullerton, California

Heckelphone photo Sotheby Parke Bernet & Co., London

Helicon Germanisches Nationalmuseum (Rück Collection), Nuremberg

Hĕvisi Deben Bhattacharya, Paris / photo Wevrukannala

Hibernicon Bate Collection of Historical Instruments, Faculty of Music, University of Oxford

Hichiriki photo Tadashi Kimura, Tokyo

Hiohkat National Anthropological Archives, Smithsonian Institution, Washington, DC

Hnè Arts of Asia, Hong Kong / photo Stephen Markbreiter

Hoddu photo Jim Rosellini, Venice, California

Hommel Musikmuseet, Stockholm

Horn *1a*, *11* Paxman of Covent Garden, London; *1b* Boosey & Hawkes Ltd, London; *2* Universitätsbibliothek, Heidelberg; *3a* Staatliche Kunstsammlungen, Dresden; *3b* Horniman Museum, London; *3c* City Museum and Art Gallery, Gloucester; *4*, *6* Giraudon, Paris; *5* Museo Civico, Turin; *7* photo Bibliothèque Nationale, Paris; *8a–b*, *9* Conservatoire National Supérieur de Musique, Paris; *8c* Germanisches Nationalmuseum (Rück Collection), Nuremberg; *10* Bate Collection of Historical Instruments, Faculty of Music, University of Oxford

Hornpipe *1* National Monuments Record, London; *2* Pitt Rivers Museum, University of Oxford

Hosszú furulya photo Bálint Sárosi, Budapest

Hourglass drum photo Cootje van Oven, Freetown, Sierra Leone

Hudko photo Mireille Helffer

Huehuetl Museo de Arqueología, Toluca

Hun (i) photo Robert C. Provine

Hurdy-gurdy *1* photo MAS, Barcelona; *2* British Library, London; *3* Metropolitan Museum of Art (Crosby Brown Collection, 1889), New York; *4* photo Musées Nationaux, Paris; *5* Archiv für Kunst und Geschichte, Berlin

Husla Musikhistorisk Museum, Copenhagen

Hydraulis *1* photo Rheinisches Landesmuseum, Trier

Iconography of music *1* Master and Fellows of Corpus Christi College, Cambridge; *2* British Library, London; *3* Uitgeverij Frits Knuf BV, Buren: from C. Burney, *An Account of the Musical Performances in Westminster Abbey and the Pantheon, May 26th, 27th, 29th; and June the 3rd and 5th 1784* (facs., 1964); *4* Giraudon, Paris

Idakka photo Pribislav Pitoëff, Paris

Igemfe Witwatersrand University Press and Mrs N. Parnell, Johannesburg, and Faculty of Music, University of Cape Town, Rondebosch: from P. R. Kirby, *The Musical Instruments of the Native Races of South Africa* (1934) / photo W. P. Paff

Ikoro Meki Nzewi, Nsukka, Nigeria

Improvisation Bärenreiter-Verlag, Kassel: from H.-P. Schmitz, *Die Kunst der Verzierung im 18. Jahrhundert* (1955)

Imzad Tolia Nikiprowetzky, Paris / photo Hassan Yacouba, Ministère de l'Information de la République du Niger

Inanga photo Jos Gansemans, Tervuren

Ingqongqo Witwatersrand University Press and Mrs N. Parnell, Johannesburg, and Faculty of Music, University of Cape Town, Rondebosch: from P. R. Kirby, *The Musical Instruments of the Native Races of South Africa* (1934) / photo P. R. Kirby

Ipu hula photo Bernice P. Bishop Museum, Honolulu

Irish harp National Museum of Ireland, Dublin

Janko, Paul von Smithsonian Institution, Washington, DC

Jantar photo Geneviève Dournon

Jāwan photo Deben Bhattacharya, Paris

Jew's harp *1a*, *2b* Conservatoire Royal de Musique, Brussels: after J. Wright, 'Another Look into the Organology of the Jew's Harp', *Brussels Museum of Musical Instruments Bulletin*, ii (1972); *1b* photo Elisabeth Agate, Burford, Oxfordshire; *2a* photo Axel Poignant, London

Jinghu photo Hedda Morrison, Canberra

Jouhikko National Museum of Finland, Helsinki

Joze International Institute for Comparative Music Studies and Documentation, Berlin / photo H. H. Touma

Juru photo Hugo Zemp, Paris

Just intonation *4a*, *5* British Library, London; *7* Uitgeverij Frits Knuf BV, Buren

Ka'ara President and Fellows of Harvard College, Peabody Museum, Harvard University, Cambridge, Massachusetts / photo Hillel Burger

Kagel, Mauricio *1* photo Fritz Peyer, Hamburg; *2* photo Zoltan Nagy, Stuttgart

Kakaki *1* Anthony King; *2* photo Gerhard Kubik, Vienna

Kakko Japan Information Centre, London

Kalali Monique Brandily / photo Max-Yves Brandily, Paris

Kalapácsos kereplő after B. Sárosi

Kamãícã photo Geneviève Dournon, Paris

Kamãnche *1* Iranian Embassy, London; *2* Freer Gallery of Art, Smithsonian Institution, Washington, DC

Kamu-purui photo Roque Cordero

Kantele *2* National Museum of Finland, Helsinki

Karna (i) Popperfoto, London

Kateobak Margaret J. Kartomi / photo H. Kartomi, Clayton, Victoria

Kaval photo Vergilii Atanassov

Kaw law photo Terry E. Miller, Kent, Ohio

Kayagŭm photo Byong Won Lee, Honolulu

Kazoo Horniman Museum, London

Keledi Museum Nasional, Jakarta

Kelei photo Cootje van Oven, Freetown, Sierra Leone

Kemençe Ursula Reinhard, Berlin

Kena South American Pictures, Woodbridge / photo Tony Morrison

Kertok kelapa photo Jack Percival Baker Dobbs

Keyboard *1* Antikvarisk-Topografiska Arkivet, Stockholm; *2* British Library, London; *3* Smithsonian Institution, Washington, DC

Keyed bugle *1* Horniman Museum, London; *2* Music Division, Library of Congress, Washington, DC

Khāen photo Terry E. Miller

Khais Africana Museum, Johannesburg

Khuur Věra Jislová, Prague

Kilaut Arktisk Institut, Charlottenlund, Denmark

Kinnor Department of Antiquities and Museums, Jerusalem

Kirckman *1* Victoria and Albert Museum, London

Kit *1* Bildarchiv Preussischer Kulturbesitz, Berlin; *2a*, *2d* Victoria and Albert Museum, London; *2b–c* Royal College of Music, London; *3* Conservatoire National Supérieur de Musique, Paris

Kithara Museum of Fine Arts (J. M. Rodocanachi Fund), Boston

Kízh kízh díhí *1a* National Anthropological Archives, Smithsonian Institution, Washington, DC; *1b* Museum of the American Indian, Heye Foundation, New York

Kkwaenggwari Dabo Korea, Seoul

Kokle Alexandr Buchner, Prague

Kokyū Japan Foundation, Tokyo

Kŏmun'go *1* photo Byong Won Lee, Honolulu; *2* photo Robert C. Provine

Kondingi photo Cootje van Oven, Freetown, Sierra Leone

Konghou photo Robert C. Provine

Kongoma photo Cootje van Oven, Freetown, Sierra Leone

Kŏni Musée de l'Homme, Paris / photo J. Dournes

Kooauau Auckland Institute and Museum

Kora *1* photo Anthony King; *2* photo Gilbert Rouget, Paris; *3* after A. King

Koto *1*, *2* W. Adriaansz

Kotsuzumi Japan Information Centre, London

Koturka photo Geneviève Dournon

Kulintang *1* after J. Maceda; *2* photo Robert Garfias, Irvine, California

Kultrún Musée de l'Homme, Paris / photo C. Joseph

Kundu (i) photo Axel Poignant, London

Kundung photo Anthony King, Zaria, Nigeria

Kuu Monique Brandily / photo Max-Yves Brandily, Paris

Kyì-waìng Arts of Asia, Hong Kong / photo Stephen Markbreiter

Lali Ministry of Information, Suva

Lamellaphone *1*, *2* Gerhard Kubik / (*1*) photo M. Djenda; *4* African Music Society, Grahamstown: from A. Tracey, 'The Original African Mbira?', *African Music*, v/2 (1972); *5* from G. Kubik, 'Carl Mauch's Mbira Musical Transcriptions of 1872', *Review of Ethnology*, iii (1971)

Langeleik Norsk Folkemuseum, Oslo

Langspil National Museum of Iceland, Reykjavik

Laouto photo Lucy Durán, London

Larchemi Grigol Chkhikvadze, Tbilisi

Launeddas Horniman Museum, London

Launut Auckland Institute and Museum

Leonardo da Vinci Bibliothèque de l'Institut de France / photo J. Colomb-Gérard

Lesiba *1*, *2* photo Charles R. Adams

Lira da braccio *1* Museo del Prado, Madrid; *2* Kunsthistorisches Museum, Vienna; *4* Mansell Collection, London, and Alinari, Florence; *5* Österreichische Nationalbibliothek, Vienna

Lirone Staatliche Kunstsammlungen, Dresden / Deutsche Fotothek Dresden

Lithophone *1* photo ACL, Brussels; *2* Fitz Park Museum, Keswick

Litungu R. D. Wambugu, Ministry of Education Inspectorate, Nairobi / photo Kenya Information Services

Lituus Mansell Collection, London, and Alinari, Florence

Logier, Johann Bernhard British Library, London

Logo photo Richard M. Moyle, Auckland

Lozhky photo ACL, Brussels

Łppumin Museum of the American Indian, Heye Foundation, New York / photo William Wildschut

Luc huyền cầm International Institute for Comparative Music Studies and Documentation, Berlin / photo Nguyên Huu Ba

Lur Nationalmuseet, Copenhagen

Lute *3* Editions Payot, Paris: from A. Schaeffner, *Origine des instruments de musique* (1936); *4a* Trustees of the British Museum, London; *4b* British Library, London; *4c*, *15* photo Musées Nationaux, Paris; *6* Patrimonio Nacional, Madrid; *7* Wallraf-Richartz-Museum, Cologne / photo Rheinisches Bildarchiv; *8* Bibliothèque Nationale, Paris; *9a* Musei Comunali, Florence; *9b–f*, *12* Kunsthistorisches Museum, Vienna; *9g* Germanisches Nationalmuseum, Nuremberg; *10* Rijksmuseum, Amsterdam; *11* Kunsthalle, Hamburg; *13*, *14* Trustees of the National Gallery, London

Lyra photo Lucy Durán, London

Lyra viol *1* International Repertory of Musical Iconography (RIdIM), New York; *2* Ashmolean Museum, Oxford

Lyre *1a* from *A Picture Book of Uganda* (Uganda Department of Information, n.d.); *1b* Klaus Wachsmann; *1c* R. D. Wambugu, Ministry of Education Inspectorate, Nairobi / photo Kenya Information Services; *2* Bibliothèque Nationale, Paris; *3* Pontificia Commissione di Archeologia Sacra, Rome; *4* Trustees of the British Museum, London; *5* Staatliche Antikensammlungen und Glyptothek, Munich

Lyre guitar photo Westfälisches Landesmuseum für Kunst und Kulturgeschichte, Münster

Maggini, Gio(vanni) Paolo W. E. Hill & Sons, Great Missenden / photo Desmond Hill

Mahōrī Department of Fine Arts, Bangkok

Malipenga Gerhard Kubik, Vienna / photo M. Djenda

Mandolin *1a* Bibliothèque Nationale, Paris; *1b* British Library, London; *3* photo Musées Nationaux, Paris; *4* Royal College of Music, London; *5* Germanisches Nationalmuseum (Rück Collection), Nuremberg; *6* Victoria and Albert Museum, London

Manman photo G. E. Simpson, Oberlin College, Ohio

Maracas *2* photo Robert Garfias, Irvine, California

Marimba *1* International Library of African Music, Grahamstown / photo Hugh Tracey; *2* photo Robert Garfias, Irvine, California; *3* J. C. Deagan, Chicago

Masenqo British Library, London

Māṣūl Popperfoto, London

Matraca photo María Ester Grebe, Santiago, Chile

Má'xe onéhavo'e photo National Film Board of Canada, Montreal

Mazanki Państwowe Muzeum Etnograficzne, Warsaw / photo Lech Trojanowski

Mbila *1* Andrew Tracey: from H. Tracey, *Chopi Musicians: their Music, Poetry and Instruments* (1948); *2* International Library of African Music, Grahamstown / photo Lynn Acutt

Mechanical instrument *1–3*, *7*, *8* after A. Buchner; *4*, *6* Alexandr Buchner; *5* Sotheby Parke Bernet & Co., London; *9* British Piano Museum Charitable Trust, Brentford / photo Times Newspapers Ltd

Mélophone Museum of Fine Arts, Boston

Metronome *2*, *4* Metropolitan Museum of Art, New York; *3* Gesellschaft der Musikfreunde, Vienna

Microtonal instruments *1* Craig Hundley, Beverly Hills / photo Victoria Mihich, Los Angeles; *2* Cris Forster, Chrysalis Foundation, San Diego / photo Will Gullette; *3* McMaster University, Hamilton, Ontario / photo Audio-Visual Services; *4* Stichting Huygens-Fokker, Haarlem / photo C. de Boer

Mijwiz International Institute for Comparative Music Studies and Documentation, Berlin / photo Joachim Wenzel

Mizmār photo Musées Nationaux, Paris

Modifications and new techniques *1* Performing Artservices Inc., New York; *2* Hans-Karsten Raecke, Lüneburg; *3* Center for Integrative Education, New Rochelle, New York: from *Main Currents*

in Modern Thought, xxx/1 (Sept–Oct 1973)

Mohoceño South American Pictures, Woodbridge / photo Tony Morrison

Mokugyo National Research Institute of Cultural Properties, Tokyo / photo Michiko Satô

Molinukas photo Arvydas Karaška

Monochord *2* Syndics of Cambridge University Library

Montagnana, Domenico W. E. Hill & Sons, Great Missenden / photo Desmond Hill

Moropa Witwatersrand University Press and Mrs N. Parnell, Johannesburg: from P. R. Kirby, *The Musical Instruments of the Native Races of South Africa* (1934) / photo W. P. Paff

Mouth bow *2* photo George List, Bloomington, Indiana; *3* photo Klaus Wachsmann

Mrdanga *1a–b* photo Robert Garfias, Irvine, California; *1c* International Institute for Comparative Music Studies and Documentation, Berlin / photo Alain Daniélou

Muralī *1*, *2* photo Geneviève Dournon

Murumba photo John Blacking

Musette Design and Artists Copyright Society Ltd, London / photo Caisse Nationale des Monuments Historiques et des Sites

Musical bow *1* Africana Museum, Johannesburg

Musical box photo Sotheby Parke Bernet & Co., London

Musical glasses *1* British Library, London; *2*, *3* Bruno Hoffmann, Stuttgart / (*3*) photo Alan Clifton

Mute *1a*, *3* David D. Boyden; *1b* photo Mick Baines, London

Mvet photo Gerhard Kubik

Naas Musée de l'Homme, Paris / photo Tubiana

Naderman Conservatoire National Supérieur de Musique, Paris

Nádsíp photo Bálint Sárosi, Budapest

Nafa photo University of Auckland

Nagārā photo Deben Bhattacharya, Paris

Nāgasvaram photo Deben Bhattacharya, Paris

Nai (i) Institutul de Cercetări Etnologice și Dialectologice, Bucharest

Nail violin Royal College of Music, London

Nakers *1* Musée de l'Homme, Paris / photo D. Champault; *2* British Library, London

Nakpéa Alexander Turnbull Library, National Library of New Zealand, Wellington

Naqqāra International Institute for Comparative Music Studies and Documentation, Berlin / photo H. H. Touma

Naqqārakhāna from A. H. Fox Strangways, *The Music of Hindostan* (Oxford, 1914)

Nar photo Geneviève Dournon, Paris

Nāy photo Jean Jenkins, London

Ndere (i) photo Klaus Wachsmann

Ndjimba Musée Royal de l'Afrique Centrale, Tervuren

Ndongo *1*, *2* photo Klaus Wachsmann

New Violin Family Catgut Acoustical Society Inc., Montclair / photo John Castronovo

Ngoma *1* photo Jos Gansemans, Tervuren; *2* Ocora Radio France, Paris: from record sleeve, *Musique de Burundi* (1968) / photo Michel Vuylsteke

Ngombi (i) photo Simha Arom, Paris

Nguru Auckland Institute and Museum / photo C. A. Schollum

Ngwomi photo Pierre Sallée, Paris

Nogo photo Robert C. Provine

Norman, Barak Royal College of Music, London

Nuzha British Library, London

Nyanga (i) International Library of African Music, Grahamstown / photo Andrew Tracey

Nyckelharpa Nordiska Museet, Stockholm

Ŏ photo Robert C. Provine

Oboe *2*, *12b–e*, *13* Philip Bate; *3* Patrimonio Nacional, Madrid; *4*, *9* Bibliothèque Nationale, Paris; *5a*, *14a* Conservatoire Royal de Musique, Brussels; *5b* Gemeentemuseum, The Hague; *6a–b*, *11*, *12a*, *14c* Bate Collection of Historical Instruments, Faculty of Music, University of Oxford; *7* Music Division, Library of Congress, Washington, DC; *8* Smith College Museum of Art (Gift of Mr and Mrs Allan D. Emil, 1956), Northampton, Massachusetts; *14b* Royal College of Music, London

Obulere photo Peter Cooke, Edinburgh

Ocarina Horniman Museum, London

'Ohe hano ihu photo Bernice P. Bishop Museum, Honolulu

Ole-ole Margaret J. Kartomi / photo H. Kartomi, Clayton, Victoria

Oliphant Alexandr Buchner, Prague

Ombgwe photo Faculty of Music, University of Cape Town, Rondebosch

Ondes martenot Librairie Larousse, Paris

Ophicleide Royal College of Music, London

Orchestra *1* Staatliche Kunstsammlungen, Dresden / Deutsche Fotothek Dresden; *2* Museum für Kunst und Gewerbe, Hamburg; *3* Bibliothèque Municipale, Versailles; *5* Germanisches National-museum, Nuremberg; *8* Richard-Wagner-Gedenkstätte, Bayreuth; *9* Universal Edition (London) Ltd; *10* Royal College of Music, London

Organ *1–3* Oxford University Press: after J. Perrot, *The Organ from its Invention in the Hellenistic Period to the End of the 13th Century* (Eng. trans., 1971); *4* Faculty of Music, University of Edinburgh: after S. Newman and P. Williams, *The Russell Collection of Early Keyboard Instruments* (Edinburgh, 1968); *5, 6, 9, 10a* Fonds Mercator SA, Antwerp: after D. A. Flentrop, from F. Peeters and M. A. Vente, *The Organ and its Music in the Netherlands* (Eng. trans., 1971); *7a, 11a, 13* Macdonald & Co., London: after W. L. Sumner, *The Organ: Its Evolution, Principles of Construction and Use* (4/1973); *7b, 16, 18a* Paul G. Bunjes, Melrose Park, Illinois: after P. G. Bunjes, *The Praetorius Organ* (1966); *11b* George Allen & Unwin Ltd, London, and Oxford University Press Inc., New York: after P. G. Andersen, *Organ Building and Design* (1969); *12, 17, 18b, 19* after G. A. Audsley, *The Art of Organ-building* (repr. 1965); *21* Museum of Classical Archaeology, Tripoli; *22, 23, 25* Jean Perrot, Sainte Geneviève (*22, 23* from L. Nagy, *Az Aquincumi orgona/Die Orgel von Aquincum*, 1933); *24* Musée National, Carthage; *26* Bibliotheek der Rijksuniversiteit, Utrecht; *27* Bibliothèque Publique, Dijon; *28* The Duke of Rutland and the Roxburghe Club: from facs., ed. E. G. Millar (Oxford, 1937); *29* Orgelbau Th. Kuhn AG, Männedorf / photo Maurice Wenger, Sion; *30* Antikvarisk-Topografiska Arkivet, Stockholm / photo Nils Lagergren; *32* Giraudon, Paris; *33* photo Gino Barsotti, Florence; *34* Hofkirche, Innsbruck; *35* photo Viktor Rihsé, Stade; *38* National Monuments Record, London; *39* Carlós de Azeredo, Lisbon; *40, 41* photo MAS, Barcelona; *42* Bavaria-Verlag, Gauting bei Munich; *43* Rijksdienst voor de Monumentenzorg, Zeist; *44* Kerkelijk Bureau de Hervormde Gemeente, Haarlem; *45* Bildarchiv Foto Marburg / photo Lala Aufsberg; *46* photo J. L. Coignet, Châteauneuf, Val-de-Bargis; *47* University of New Mexico Photo Service, Albuquerque; *48* Greater London Council; *49* N. P. Mander Ltd, London / photo Sydney W. Newbery; *50* photo Heinrich Weber, Hanover; *51* John Brombaugh & Co., Middletown, Ohio; *52* Jürgen Ahrend, Leer; *53* C. B. Fisk Inc., Gloucester, Massachusetts / photo Robert Cornell

Orpharion *1* Musikhistorisk Museum, Copenhagen; *2* Historisches Museum, Frankfurt am Main; *3* British Library, London

Orphica Gesellschaft der Musikfreunde, Vienna